Global Development Finance

Country Tables

Global Development Finance

Country Tables

2000

THE WORLD BANK

First printing May 2000

Global Development Finance was formerly published under the title *World Debt Tables*.

This publication has been compiled by the staff of the Financial Data Team of the World Bank's Development Economics Vice Presidency. The World Bank does not accept responsibility for the accuracy or completeness of this publication. Any judgments expressed are those of World Bank staff or consultants and do not necessarily reflect the views of the Board of Executive Directors or the governments they represent.

ISBN 0-8213-4544-3
ISSN 1020-5454

Table of Contents

Preface

Global Development Finance consists of two volumes: *Analysis and Summary Tables* and *Country Tables. Analysis and Summary Tables* contains analysis and commentary on recent developments in international finance for developing countries, together with summary statistical tables for selected regional and analytical groups comprising 149 developing countries.

Country Tables contains statistical tables on the external debt of the 137 countries that report public and publicly guaranteed debt under the Debtor Reporting System (DRS). Also included are tables of selected debt and resource flow statistics for individual reporting countries as well as summary tables for regional and income groups.

Earlier this year, country tables and summary statistics were also made available on CD-ROM through an advance release edition.

For the convenience of readers, charts on pages xx to xxii summarize graphically the relation between debt stock and its components; the computation of net flows, aggregate net resource flows, and aggregate net transfers; and the relation between net resource flows and the balance of payments. Exact definitions of these and other terms used in *Global Development Finance* are found in the Sources and Definitions section.

The economic aggregates presented in the tables are prepared for the convenience of users. Although debt indicators can give useful information about developments in debt-servicing capacity, conclusions drawn from them will not be valid unless accompanied by careful economic evaluation. The macroeconomic information provided is from standard sources, but many of them are subject to considerable margins of error, and the usual care must be taken in interpreting the indicators. This is particularly the case for the most recent year or two, when figures are preliminary and subject to revision.

This volume was prepared by the Financial Data Team of the Development Data Group, led by Punam Chuhan and comprising Nanasamudd Chhim, Mahyar Eshragh-Tabary, Nevin Fahmy, Shelley Fu, Ibrahim Levent, Mohey Ragab, Gloria Reyes, and Alagiri Venkatesan. The team was assisted by Sheku Bengura, Kabinah Fofanah, Demet Kaya, Alexandra Merlino, Stephane Ritz, Haiyan Shi, and Lisa Simms. Soong Sup Lee provided the macroeconomic data. Many others inside the World Bank provided helpful input, especially the staff of the Development Prospects Group, and the country economists who reviewed the data. The principal editor was Meta de Coquereaumont and the volume was laid out by Wendy Guyette with Communications Development Incorporated. The work was carried out under the direction of Shaida Badiee.

Acronyms and Abbreviations

BIS	Bank for International Settlements
CRS	Creditor Reporting System (of the OECD)
DAC	Development Assistance Committee (of the OECD)
DDSR	Debt and debt service reduction
DRS	Debtor Reporting System (of the World Bank)
GNP	Gross national product
IBRD	International Bank for Reconstruction and Development/World Bank
IDA	International Development Association (of the World Bank)
IMF	International Monetary Fund
LIBOR	London interbank offer rate
MYRA	Multiyear rescheduling agreement
OECD	Organisation for Economic Co-operation and Development
OPEC	Organization of Petroleum Exporting Countries
RXD	Revised external debt
SDR	Special drawing right (of the IMF)
WBXD	World Bank External Debt System

Note for World Wide Web users

Recent, high-frequency debt statistics for 176 developing and transition economies are now available on a multiagency Web site. The data include key debt indicators such as bank loans, debt securities issued abroad, Brady bonds, and multilateral claims, with emphasis on debt due within a year. The tables on this site can be accessed in both page-image and spreadsheet format. Go to

http://www.worldbank.org/data/jointdebt.html

Methodology

The World Bank is the sole repository for statistics on the external debt of developing countries on a loan-by-loan basis. The Debtor Reporting System (DRS), set up in 1951 to monitor these statistics, is maintained by the staff of the Financial Data Team (FIN), part of the Development Data Group of Development Economics.

Methodology for aggregating data

Using the DRS data, in combination with information obtained from creditors through the debt data collection systems of other agencies such as the Bank for International Settlements (BIS) and the Organisation for Economic Co-operation and Development (OECD), the staff of the Financial Data Team estimate the total external indebtedness of developing countries. The data are also supplemented by estimates made by country economists of the World Bank and desk officers of the International Monetary Fund (IMF).

Converting to a common currency

Since debt data are normally reported to the World Bank in the currency of repayment, they have to be converted into a common currency (usually U.S. dollars) to produce summary tables. Stock figures (such as the amount of debt outstanding) are converted using end-period exchange rates, as published in the IMF's *International Financial Statistics* (line ae). Flow figures are converted at annual average exchange rates (line rf). Projected debt service is converted using end-period exchange rates. Debt repayable in multiple currencies, goods, or services and debt with a provision for maintenance of value of the currency of repayment are shown at book value. Because flow data are converted at annual average exchange rates and stock data at year-end exchange rates, year-to-year changes in debt outstanding and disbursed are sometimes not equal to net flows (disbursements less principal repayments); similarly, changes in debt outstanding including undisbursed debt differ from commitments less repayments. Discrepancies are particularly significant when exchange rates have moved sharply during the year; cancellations and reschedulings of other liabilities into long-term public debt also contribute to the differences.

Public and publicly guaranteed debt

All data related to public and publicly guaranteed debt are from debtors except for lending by some multilateral agencies, in which case data are taken from the creditors' records. These creditors include the African Development Bank, the Asian Development Bank, the Central Bank for Economic Integration, the IMF, the Inter-American Development Bank, and the International Bank for Reconstruction and Development (IBRD) and the International Development Association (IDA). (The IBRD and IDA are components of the World Bank.)

Starting with the 1988–89 edition of *World Debt Tables* (as this book was previously titled), all data pertaining to World Bank loans from 1985 onward are recorded at their current market value. Starting with the 1991–92 edition, all data pertaining to Asian Development Bank loans from 1989 onward are recorded at their current market value. Starting with the 1998 edition, all data pertaining to African Development Bank and African Development Fund loans from 1997 onward are recorded at their current market value as well.

Private nonguaranteed debt

The DRS was expanded in 1970 to incorporate private nonguaranteed long-term debt. Reports, submitted annually, contain aggregate data for disbursed and outstanding debt, disbursements, principal repayments, interest payments, principal and interest rescheduled for the reporting year, and projected payments of principal and interest. Data are usually presented in dollars and currency conversion is not necessary. A few reporting countries choose to provide data on their private nonguaranteed debt in the loan-by-loan format used for reporting public and publicly guaranteed debt. In those cases the currency conversion and projection methodology just described is used.

Although the reporting countries fully recognize the importance of collecting data on private nonguaranteed debt when it constitutes a significant portion of total external debt, detailed data are available only in countries that have registration requirements covering private debt, most commonly in connection with exchange controls. Where formal registration of foreign borrowing is not mandatory, compilers must rely on balance of payments data and financial surveys.

Thirty-four countries report their private nonguaranteed debt to the DRS. Estimates are made for 43 others that do not report but for which this type of debt is known to be significant.

For private nonguaranteed debt that is not reported, the standard estimation approach starts from a calculation of the stock of debt outstanding, using data available from creditors. Figures on guaranteed export credits, obtained from the OECD's Creditor Reporting System (CRS), are supplemented by loan-by-loan information on official lending to private borrowers and by information on noninsured commercial bank lending to the private sector.

Disbursements and debt service payments for private nonguaranteed debt are more difficult to estimate. Amortization is estimated by making an assumption regarding the proportion of debt repaid each year and then applying these ratios to generate a first approximation of annual principal repayments. Disbursements are then estimated as a residual between net flows (equal to the change in the stock of debt) and estimated amortization. Interest payments are estimated by applying an assumed average interest rate to the stock of debt outstanding.

Data on the balance of payments flows provide useful guidelines in the process of building a time series because private nonguaranteed debt can be treated as a residual between total net long-term borrowing and net long-term borrowing recorded in the DRS for public and publicly guaranteed debt.

Short-term debt

The World Bank regards the individual reporting country as the authoritative source of information on its own external liabilities. But for short-term debt, defined as debt with an original maturity of one year or less, accurate information is not widely available from debtors. By its nature, short-term debt is difficult to monitor; loan-by-loan registration is normally impractical, and most reporting arrangements involve periodic returns to a country's central bank from its banking sector. Since 1982 the quality of such reporting has improved, but only a few developing countries have figures available for short-term debt.

Where information from debtors is not available, data from creditors can indicate the magnitude of a country's short-term debt. The most important source is the BIS's semiannual series showing the maturity distribution of commercial banks' claims on developing countries. Those data are reported residually. However, an estimate of short-term liabilities by original maturity can be calculated by deducting from claims due in one year those that had a maturity of between one and two years twelve months earlier.

There are several problems with this method. Valuation adjustments caused by exchange rate movements will affect the calculations, as will prepayment and refinancing of long-term maturities falling due. Moreover, not all countries' commercial banks report in a way that allows the full maturity distribution to be determined, and the BIS data include liabilities only to banks within the reporting area. Nevertheless, combining these estimates with data on officially guaranteed short-term suppliers' credits compiled by the OECD gives what may be thought of as a lower-bound estimate of a country's short-term debt. Even on this basis, however, the results need to be interpreted with caution. Where short-term debt has been rescheduled, the effect of lags in reporting and differences in the treatment of the rescheduled debt by debtors and creditors may result in double counting if short-term debt derived from creditor sources is added to long-term debt reported by the country to obtain total external liabilities.

Some of the short-term debt estimates published are drawn from debtor and creditor sources, but most are from creditor sources. Only for a few countries can the data be regarded as authoritative, but they offer a guide to the size of a country's short-term (and, hence, its total) external debt. The quality of these data is likely to improve.

Use of IMF credit

Data related to the operations of the IMF come from the IMF Treasurer's Department and are converted from special drawing rights (SDRs) into dollars using end-of-period exchange rates for stocks and average over the period exchange rates for converting flows, as described earlier. IMF trust fund loans and operations under the structural adjustment and enhanced structural adjustment facilities are presented together with all of the Fund's special facilities (the buffer stock, compensatory financing, extended fund, and oil facilities).

Treatment of arrears

The DRS collects information on arrears in both principal and interest. Principal in arrears is included and identified in the amount of long-term debt outstanding. Interest in arrears of long-term debt and the use of IMF credit is included and identified in the amount of short-term debt outstanding. If and when interest in arrears is capitalized under a debt reorganization agreement, the amount of interest capitalized will be added to the amount of long-term debt outstanding and the corresponding deduction made from the amount of short-term debt outstanding.

Treatment of debt restructurings

The DRS attempts to capture accurately the effects of the different kinds of restructurings on both debt stocks and debt flows, consistent with the circumstances under which the restructuring takes place. Whether a flow has taken place is sometimes difficult to determine.

In compiling and presenting the debt data, a distinction is made between cash flows and imputed flows. Based on this criterion, rescheduled service payments and the shift in liabilities from one financial instrument to another as a result of rescheduling are considered to be imputed flows.

The imputed flows are recorded separately in the Revised External Debt (RXD) system and the new World Bank External Debt System (WBXD), but these debt restructuring transactions are not evident in the main body of the debt data—only the resulting effect of these transactions is reflected.

Changes in creditor and debtor status that can result from debt restructuring are also reflected. For example, when insured commercial credits are rescheduled, the creditor classification shifts from private sources to official sources (bilateral). This reflects the assumption of the assets by the official credit insurance agencies of the creditor countries. The debts to the original creditors are reduced by the amounts rescheduled, and a new obligation to the official creditor agencies is created. This shift also applies to private nonguaranteed debt that is reduced by the amounts rescheduled, which in turn are included in the public and publicly guaranteed debt owed to official creditors. On the debtor side, when a government accepts responsibility for the payment of rescheduled debt previously owed by private enterprises, the DRS registers a change in debtor categories in the DRS. Similarly, when short-term debt is included in a restructuring agreement, the rescheduled amount is shifted from short-term to long-term debt.

Methodology for projecting data

An important feature of the WBXD and the RXD system of the DRS is its ability to project future disbursements of unutilized commitments and future debt service payments.

Undisbursed debt

Projections of disbursements help underpin future capital requirements in the implementation of externally financed projects. In addition, they help determine the interest portion of projected debt service. Future interest payments are based on projected debt outstanding that is itself determined by projected disbursements and repayments. The underlying assumptions of these projections are that loan commitments will be fully utilized and that the debtor country will repay all sums due. Future disbursements and debt service refer only to existing debt and do not reflect any assumptions on future borrowing.

Disbursement projections use two methods:

- *Specific schedules.* Debtor countries are requested to submit a calendar of future disbursements, if available, at the time individual loans are first reported. Country authorities are in a better position to provide estimated disbursement schedules when there is a solid public sector investment program in place.

- *Standard schedules.* In the absence of specific schedules, the RXD and WBXD system projects disbursements by applying a set of profiles to the last actual undisbursed balance of individual loans. The profiles are derived under the assumption that specific sources of funds have some common characteristics that cause them to disburse, in the aggregate, in some observable pattern. Accordingly, some thirty profiles have been derived that roughly correspond to creditor type. Profiles exist for concessional and nonconcessional loans from official creditors. For bilateral lending, profiles have been developed for the Development Assistance Committee, the Organization of Petroleum-Exporting Countries (OPEC), and other creditor groupings. For multilateral lending, specific profiles are available for major international organizations. An estimating equation for each profile is derived by applying regression analysis techniques to a body of data that contains actual disbursement information for more than 100,000 loans. Although these standard profiles are reestimated from time to time, under the best scenario they can only approximate the disbursement pattern of any single loan.

Future debt service payments

Most projections of future debt service payments generated by the RXD and WBXD system are based on the repayment terms of the loans. Principal repayments (amortization) are based on the amount of loan commitments, and the amortization profile of most loans follows a set pattern. Using the first and final payment dates and the frequency of the payments, the system calculates the stream of principal payments due. If future payments are irregular, the RXD and WBXD system requires a schedule.

Projected future interest payments are calculated similarly. Interest is based on the amount of debt disbursed and outstanding at the beginning of the period. Again, using the first and final interest payment dates and the frequency of payments, the system calculates the stream of interest payments due. If interest payments are irregular, the RXD and WBXD system requires a schedule.

The published figures for projected debt service obligations are converted into U.S. dollars using the end-December 1998 exchange rates. Likewise the projection routine for variable interest rate debt, such as commercial bank debt based on the London interbank offer rate (LIBOR), assumes that the rate prevailing at the end of December 1998 will be effective throughout.

Sources and definitions

This edition of *Global Development Finance* presents reported or estimated data on the total external debt of all low- and middle-income countries.

Format

The *Country Tables* volume of *Global Development Finance* has been expanded to include summary tables along with the standard country tables for the 137 individual countries that report to the World Bank's Debtor Reporting System (DRS). Summary tables present selected debt and resource flow statistics for the individual reporting countries and external debt data for regional and income groups. Regional and income group totals in the summary tables include estimates for the twelve low- and middle-income countries that do not report to the DRS. Because these estimates are not shown separately in the tables, most group totals are larger than the sum of the DRS figures shown. The format of the regional and income group tables draws on the individual country table format and includes graphic presentations.

For the 137 individual countries that report to the World Bank's DRS, tables are presented in a four-page layout containing ten sections.

SECTION 1 summarizes the external debt of the country.

Total debt stocks (EDT) consist of public and publicly guaranteed long-term debt, private nonguaranteed long-term debt (whether reported or estimated by the staff of the World Bank), the use of IMF credit, and estimated short-term debt. Interest in arrears on long-term debt and the use of IMF credit are added to the short-term debt estimates and shown as separate lines. Arrears of principal and of interest have been disaggregated to show the arrears owed to official creditors and those owed to private creditors. Export credits and principal in arrears on long-term debt are shown as memorandum items.

Total debt flows are consolidated data on disbursements, principal repayments, and interest payments for total long-term debt and transactions with the IMF.

Net flows on debt are disbursements on long-term debt and IMF purchases minus principal repayments on long-term debt and IMF repurchases up to 1984. Beginning in 1985 this line includes the change in stock of short-term debt (including interest arrears for long-term debt). Thus if the change in stock is positive, a disbursement is assumed to have taken place; if negative, a repayment is assumed to have taken place.

Total debt service (TDS) shows the debt service payments on total long-term debt (public and publicly guaranteed and private nonguaranteed), use of IMF credit, and interest on short-term debt.

SECTION 2 provides data series for aggregate net resource flows and net transfers (long term).

Net resource flows (long term) are the sum of net resource flows on long-term debt (excluding IMF) plus net foreign direct investment, portfolio equity flows, and official grants (excluding technical cooperation). Grants for technical cooperation are shown as a memorandum item. Also shown as memorandum items are official net resource flows and private net resource flows. Official net resource flows are the sum of net flows on long-term debt to official creditors (excluding the IMF) plus official grants (excluding technical cooperation). Private net resource flows are the sum of net flows on debt to private creditors plus net foreign direct investment and portfolio equity flows. Official net transfers and private net transfers are shown as memorandum items as well.

Net transfers (long term) are equal to net long-term resource flows minus interest payments on long-term loans and foreign direct investment profits.

SECTION 3 provides data series for major economic aggregates. The gross national product (GNP) series uses yearly average exchange rates in converting GNP from local currency into U.S. dollars. The economic aggregates are prepared for the convenience of users; the usual caution should be exercised in using them for economic analysis.

SECTION 4 provides debt indicators: ratios of debt and debt service to some of the economic aggregates.

SECTION 5 provides detailed information on stocks and flows of long-term debt and its various components. Data on bonds issued by private entities without public guarantee, compiled for major borrowers, are included in private nonguaranteed debt. IBRD loans and IDA credits are shown as memorandum items.

SECTION 6 provides information on the currency composition of long-term debt. The six major currencies in which the external debt of low- and middle-income countries is contracted are separately identified, as is debt denominated in special drawing rights and debt repayable in multiple currencies.

SECTION 7 provides information on restructurings of long-term debt starting in 1985. It shows both the stock and flows rescheduled each year. In addition, the amount of debt forgiven (interest forgiven is shown as a memorandum item) and the amount of debt stock reduction (including debt buyback) are also shown separately. (See the Methodology section for a detailed explanation of restructuring data.)

SECTION 8 reconciles the stock and flow data on total external debt for each year, beginning with 1989. This section is designed to illustrate the changes in stock that have taken place due to five factors: the net flow on debt, the net change in interest arrears, the capitalization of interest, the reduction in debt resulting from debt forgiveness or other debt reduction mechanisms, and the cross-currency valuation effects. The residual difference —the change in stock not explained by any of the factors identified above—is also presented. The residual is calculated as the sum of identified accounts minus the change in stock. Where the residual is large it can, in some cases, serve as an illustration of the inconsistencies in the reported data. More often, however, it can be explained by specific borrowing phenomena in individual countries. These are explained in the Country Notes section.

SECTION 9 provides information on the average terms of new commitments on public and publicly guaranteed debt and information on the level of commitments from official and private sources.

SECTION 10 provides anticipated disbursements and contractual obligations on long-term debt contracted up to December 1998.

Sources

The principal sources of information for the tables in these two volumes are reports to the World Bank through the DRS from member countries that have received either IBRD loans or IDA credits. Additional information has been drawn from the files of the World Bank and the IMF.

Reporting countries submit detailed (loan-by-loan) reports through the DRS on the annual status, transactions, and terms of the long-term external debt of public agencies and that of private ones guaranteed by a public agency in the debtor country. This information forms the basis for the tables in these volumes.

Aggregate data on private debt without public guarantee are compiled and published as reliable reported and estimated information becomes available. This edition includes data on private nonguaranteed debt reported by 34 developing countries and complete or partial estimates for an additional 43 countries.

The short-term debt data are as reported by the debtor countries or are estimates derived from creditor sources. The principal creditor sources are the semiannual series of commercial banks' claims on developing countries, published by the Bank for International Settlements (BIS), and data on officially guaranteed suppliers' credits compiled by the Organisation for Economic Co-operation and Development (OECD). For some countries, estimates were prepared by pooling creditor and debtor information.

Interest in arrears on long-term debt and the use of IMF credit are added to the short-term debt estimates and shown as separate lines in section 1. Arrears of interest and of principal owed to official and to private creditors are identified separately.

Export credits are shown as a memorandum item in section 1. They include official export credits, and suppliers' credits and bank credits officially guaranteed or insured by an export credit agency. Both long-term and short-term export credits are included. The source for this information is the Creditor Reporting System (CRS) of the OECD.

Data on long-term debt reported by member countries are checked against, and supplemented by, data from several other sources. Among these are the statements and reports of several regional development banks and government lending agencies, as well as the reports received by the World Bank under the CRS from the members of the Development Assistance Committee (DAC) of the OECD.

Every effort has been made to ensure the accuracy and completeness of the debt statistics. Nevertheless, quality and coverage vary among debtors and may also vary for the same debtor from year to year. Coverage has been improved through the efforts of the reporting agencies and the work of World Bank missions, which visit member countries to gather data and to provide technical assistance on debt issues.

Definitions

For all regional, income, and individual country tables, data definitions are presented below or footnoted where appropriate. Data definitions for other summary tables are, likewise, consistent with those below.

Summary debt data

TOTAL DEBT STOCKS are defined as the sum of public and publicly guaranteed long-term debt, private nonguaranteed long-term debt, the use of IMF credit, and short-term debt. The relation between total debt stock and its components is illustrated on page xx.

Long-term external debt is defined as debt that has an original or extended maturity of more than one year and that is owed to nonresidents and repayable in foreign currency, goods, or services. Long-term debt has three components:

- *Public debt*, which is an external obligation of a public debtor, including the national government, a political subdivision (or an agency of either), and autonomous public bodies
- *Publicly guaranteed debt*, which is an external obligation of a private debtor that is guaranteed for repayment by a public entity
- *Private nonguaranteed external debt*, which is an external obligation of a private debtor that is not guaranteed for repayment by a public entity.

In the tables, public and publicly guaranteed long-term debt are aggregated.

Short-term external debt is defined as debt that has an original maturity of one year or less. Available data permit no distinction between public and private nonguaranteed short-term debt.

Interest in arrears on long-term debt is defined as interest payment due but not paid, on a cumulative basis.

Principal in arrears on long-term debt is defined as principal repayment due but not paid, on a cumulative basis.

The memorandum item *export credits* includes official export credits, suppliers' credits, and bank credits officially guaranteed or insured by an export credit agency. Both long-term and short-term credits are included here.

Use of IMF credit denotes repurchase obligations to the IMF with respect to all uses of IMF resources (excluding those resulting from drawings in the reserve tranche) shown for the end of the year specified. Use of IMF credit comprises purchases outstanding under the credit tranches, including enlarged access resources and all special facilities (the buffer stock, compensatory financing, extended fund, and oil facilities), trust fund loans, and operations under the structural adjustment and enhanced structural adjustment facilities. Data are from the Treasurer's Department of the IMF.

- *IMF purchases* are total drawings on the general resources account of the IMF during the year specified, excluding drawings in the reserve tranche.
- *IMF repurchases* are total repayments of outstanding drawings from the general resources account during the year specified, excluding repayments due in the reserve tranche.

To maintain comparability between data on transactions with the IMF and data on long-term debt, use of IMF credit outstanding at year end (stock) is converted to dollars at the SDR exchange rate in effect at the end of the year. Purchases and repurchases (flows) are converted at the average SDR exchange rate for the year in which transactions take place.

Net purchases will usually not reconcile changes in the use of IMF credit from year to year. Valuation effects from the use of different exchange rates frequently explain much of the difference, but not all. Other factors are increases in quotas (which expand a country's reserve tranche and can thereby lower the use of IMF credit as defined here), approved purchases of a country's currency by another member country drawing on the general resources account, and various administrative uses of a country's currency by the IMF.

TOTAL DEBT FLOWS include disbursements, principal repayments, net flows and transfers on debt, and interest payments.

Disbursements are drawings on loan commitments during the year specified.

Principal repayments are the amounts of principal (amortization) paid in foreign currency, goods, or services in the year specified.

Net flows on debts (or net lending or net disbursements) are disbursements minus principal repayments.

Interest payments are the amounts of interest paid in foreign currency, goods, or services in the year specified.

Net transfers on debt are net flows minus interest payments (or disbursements minus total debt service payments).

The concepts of net flows on debt, net transfers on debt, and aggregate net flows and net transfers are illustrated on pages xxi and xxii.

Total debt service paid (TDS) is debt service payments on total long-term debt (public and publicly guaranteed and private nonguaranteed), use of IMF credit, and interest on short-term debt.

Aggregate net resource flows and transfers

NET RESOURCE FLOWS (LONG-TERM) are the sum of net resource flows on long-term debt (excluding IMF) plus non-debt-creating flows.

NON-DEBT-CREATING FLOWS are net foreign direct investment, portfolio equity flows, and official grants (excluding technical cooperation). Net foreign direct investment and portfolio equity flows are treated as private source flows. Grants for technical cooperation are shown as a memorandum item.

Foreign direct investment (FDI) is defined as investment that is made to acquire a lasting management interest (usually 10 percent of voting stock) in an enterprise operating in a country other than that of the investor (defined according to residency), the investor's purpose being an effective voice in the management of the enterprise. It is the sum of equity capital, reinvestment of earnings, other long-term capital, and short-term capital as shown in the balance of payments.

Portfolio equity flows are the sum of country funds, depository receipts (American or global), and direct purchases of shares by foreign investors.

Grants are defined as legally binding commitments that obligate a specific value of funds available for disbursement for which there is no repayment requirement.

The memo item *technical cooperation grants* includes free-standing technical cooperation grants, which are intended to finance the transfer of technical and managerial skills or of technology for the purpose of building up general national capacity without reference to any specific investment projects; and investment-related technical cooperation grants, which are provided to strengthen the capacity to execute specific investment projects.

Profit remittances on foreign direct investment are the sum of reinvested earnings on direct investment and other direct investment income and are part of net transfers.

Major economic aggregates

Five economic aggregates are provided for the reporting economies.

Gross national product (GNP) is the measure of the total domestic and foreign output claimed by residents of an economy, less the domestic output claimed by nonresidents. GNP does not include deductions for depreciation. Data on GNP are from the Macroeconomic Data Team of the Development Economics Development Data Group of the World Bank.

Exports of goods and services (XGS) are the total value of goods and services exported as well as income and worker remittances received.

Imports of goods and services (MGS) are the total value of goods and services imported and income paid.

International reserves (RES) are the sum of a country's monetary authority's holdings of special drawing rights (SDRs), its reserve position in the IMF, its holdings of foreign exchange, and its holdings of gold (valued at year-end London prices).

Current account balance is the sum of the credits less the debits arising from international transactions in goods, services, income, and current transfers. It represents the transactions that add to or subtract from an economy's stock of foreign financial items.

Data on exports and imports (on a balance of payments basis), international reserves, and current account balances are drawn mainly from the files of the IMF, complemented by World Bank staff estimates. Balance of payments data are presented according to the fifth edition of the IMF's *Balance of Payments Manual,* which made several adjustments to its presentation of trade statistics. Coverage of goods was expanded to include in imports the value of goods received for processing and repair (on a gross basis). Their subsequent re-export is recorded in exports (also on a gross basis). This approach will cause a country's imports and exports to increase without affecting the balance of goods. In addition, all capital transfers, which were included with current transfers in the fourth edition of the *Balance of Payments Manual,* are now shown in a separate capital (as opposed to financial) account, and so do not contribute to the current account balance.

Debt indicators

The macroeconomic aggregates and debt data provided in the tables are used to generate ratios that analysts use to assess the external situations of developing countries. Different analysts give different weights to these indicators, but no single indicator or set of indicators can substitute for a thorough analysis of the overall situation of an economy. The advantage of the indicators in *Global Development Finance* is that they are calculated from standardized data series that are compiled on a consistent basis by the World Bank and the IMF. The ratios offer various measures of the cost of, or capacity for, servicing debt in terms of the foreign exchange or output forgone. The following ratios are provided based on total external debt:

EDT/XGS is total external debt to exports of goods and services (including workers' remittances).

EDT/GNP is total external debt to gross national product.

TDS/XGS, also called the debt service ratio, is total debt service to exports of goods and services (including workers' remittances).

INT/XGS, also called the interest service ratio, is total interest payments to exports of goods and services (including workers' remittances).

INT/GNP is total interest payments to gross national product.

RES/EDT is international reserves to total external debt.

RES/MGS is international reserves to imports of goods and services.

Short-term/EDT is short-term debt to total external debt.

Concessional/EDT is concessional debt to total external debt.

Multilateral/EDT is multilateral debt to total external debt.

Long-term debt

Data on long-term debt include eight main elements:

DEBT OUTSTANDING AND DISBURSED is the total outstanding debt at year end.

DISBURSEMENTS are drawings on loan commitments by the borrower during the year.

PRINCIPAL REPAYMENTS are amounts paid by the borrower during the year.

NET FLOWS received by the borrower during the year are disbursements minus principal repayments.

INTEREST PAYMENTS are amounts paid by the borrower during the year.

NET TRANSFERS are net flows minus interest payments during the year; negative transfers show net transfers made by the borrower to the creditor during the year.

DEBT SERVICE (LTDS) is the sum of principal repayments and interest payments actually made.

UNDISBURSED DEBT is total debt undrawn at year end; data for private nonguaranteed debt are not available.

Data from individual reporters are aggregated by type of creditor. *Official creditors* includes multilateral and bilateral debt.

- *Loans from multilateral organizations* are loans and credits from the World Bank, regional development banks, and other multilateral and intergovernmental agencies. Excluded are loans from funds administered by an international organization on behalf of a single donor government; these are classified as loans from governments.
- *Bilateral loans* are loans from governments and their agencies (including central banks), loans from autonomous bodies, and direct loans from official export credit agencies.

Private creditors include bonds, commercial banks, and other private creditors. Commercial banks and other private creditors comprise bank and trade-related lending.

- *Bonds* include publicly issued or privately placed bonds.
- *Commercial banks* are loans from private banks and other private financial institutions.
- *Other private* includes credits from manufacturers, exporters, and other suppliers of goods, and bank credits covered by a guarantee of an export credit agency.

Four characteristics of a country's debt are given as memorandum items for long-term debt outstanding and disbursed (LDOD).

Concessional LDOD conveys information about the borrower's receipt of aid from official lenders at concessional terms as defined by the DAC, that is, loans with an original grant element of 25 percent or more. Loans from major regional development banks—African Development Bank, Asian Development Bank, and the Inter-American Development Bank—and from the World Bank are classified as concessional according to each institution's classification and not according to the DAC definition, as was the practice in earlier reports.

Variable interest rate LDOD is long-term debt with interest rates that float with movements in a key market rate such as the London interbank offer rate (LIBOR) or the U.S. prime rate. This item conveys information about the borrower's exposure to changes in international interest rates.

Public sector LDOD and private sector LDOD convey information about the distribution of long-term debt for DRS countries by type of debtor (central government, state and local government, central bank; private bank, private debt).

Currency composition of long-term debt

The six major currencies in which the external debt of low- and middle-income countries is contracted are separately identified, as is debt denominated in special drawing rights and debt repayable in multiple currencies.

Debt restructurings

Debt restructurings include restructurings in the context of the Paris Club, commercial banks, debt-equity swaps, buybacks, and bond exchanges. Debt restructuring data capture the noncash or inferred flows associated with rescheduling and restructuring. These are presented to complement the cash-basis transactions recorded in the main body of the data.

Debt stock rescheduled is the amount of debt outstanding rescheduled in any given year.

Principal rescheduled is the amount of principal due or in arrears that was rescheduled in any given year.

Interest rescheduled is the amount of interest due or in arrears that was rescheduled in any given year.

Debt forgiven is the amount of principal due or in arrears that was written off or forgiven in any given year.

Interest forgiven is the amount of interest due or in arrears that was written off or forgiven in any given year.

Debt stock reduction is the amount that has been netted out of the stock of debt using debt conversion schemes such as buybacks and equity swaps or the discounted value of long-term bonds that were issued in exchange for outstanding debt.

Debt stock-flow reconciliation

Stock and flow data on total external debt are reconciled for each year, beginning with 1989. The data show the changes in stock that have taken place due to the net flow on debt, the net change in interest arrears, the capitalization of interest, the reduction in debt resulting from debt forgiveness or other debt reduction mechanisms, and the cross-currency valuation effects. The residual difference—the change in stock not explained by any of these factors—is also presented, calculated as the sum of identified accounts minus the change in stock.

Average terms of new commitments

The average terms of borrowing on public and publicly guaranteed debt are given for all new loans contracted during the year and separately for loans from official and private creditors. To obtain averages, the interest rates, maturities, and grace periods in each category have been weighted by the amounts of the loans. The grant equivalent of a loan is its commitment (present) value, less the discounted present value of its contractual debt service; conventionally, future service payments are discounted at 10 percent. The grant element of a loan is the grant equivalent expressed as a percentage of the amount committed. It is used as a measure of the overall cost of borrowing. Loans with an original grant element of 25 percent or more are defined as concessional. The average grant element has been weighted by the amounts of the loans.

Commitments cover the total amount of loans for which contracts were signed in the year specified; data for private nonguaranteed debt are not available.

Projections on existing pipeline

Projected *debt service* payments are estimates of payments due on existing debt outstanding, including undisbursed. They do not include service payments that may become due as a result of new loans contracted in subsequent years. Nor do they allow for effects on service payments of changes in repayment patterns owing to prepayment of loans or to rescheduling or refinancing, including repayment of outstanding arrears, that occurred after the last year of reported data.

Projected *disbursements* are estimates of drawings of unutilized balances. The projections do not take into account future borrowing by the debtor country. See Methodology section for a detailed explanation of how undisbursed balances are projected.

Exchange rates

Data received by the World Bank from its members are expressed in the currencies in which the debts are repayable or in which the transactions took place. For aggregation, the Bank converts these amounts to U.S. dollars using the IMF par values or central rates, or the current market rates where appropriate. Service payments, commitments, and disbursements (flows) are converted to U.S. dollars at the average rate for the year. Debt outstanding and disbursed at the end of a given year (a stock) is converted at the rate in effect at the end of that year. Projected debt service, however, is converted to U.S. dollars at rates in effect at end-December 1998. Debt repayable in multiple currencies, goods, or services and debt with a provision for maintenance of value of the currency of repayment are shown at book value.

Adjustments

Year-to-year changes in debt outstanding and disbursed are sometimes not equal to net flows; similarly, changes in debt outstanding, including undisbursed, differ from commitments less repayments. The reasons for these differences are cancellations, adjustments caused by the use of different exchange rates, and the rescheduling of other liabilities into long-term public debt.

Domestic debt

Domestic debt is defined as debt issued by central governments in local fixed-income markets. A database has been created targeting 15 countries, and the coverage is likely to expand. The database begins in 1997. Data are captured at a disaggregated, monthly issue level, providing the transparency needed in such a high-frequency market. Data are collected from government sources—such as central banks and national treasuries—and market sources.

Symbols

The following symbols have been used throughout:

- 0.0 indicates that a datum exists, but is negligible, or is a true zero.
- .. indicates that a datum is not available.
- Dollars are current U.S. dollars unless otherwise specified.

Debt stock and its components

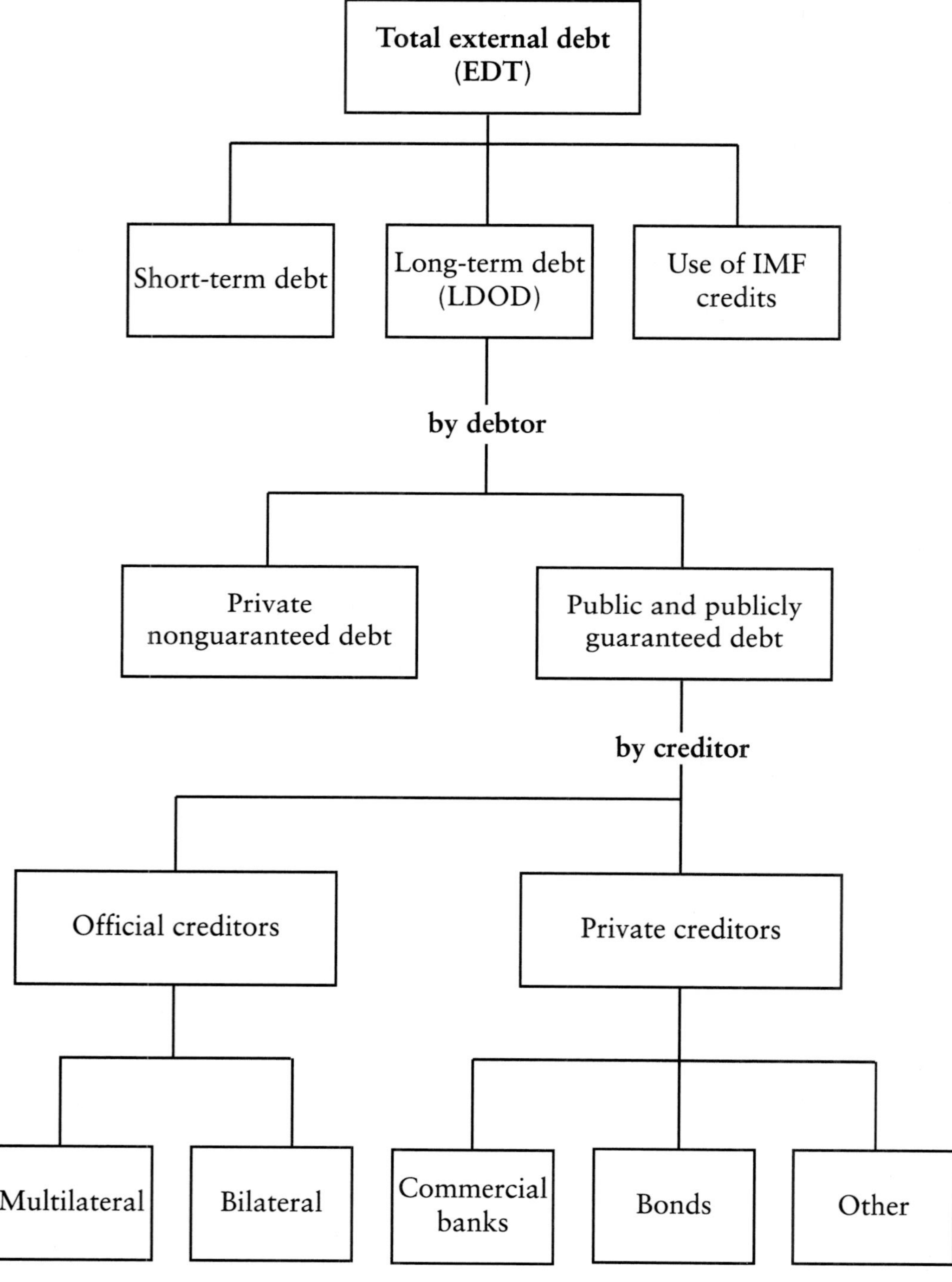

Aggregate net resource flows and net transfers (long-term) to developing countries

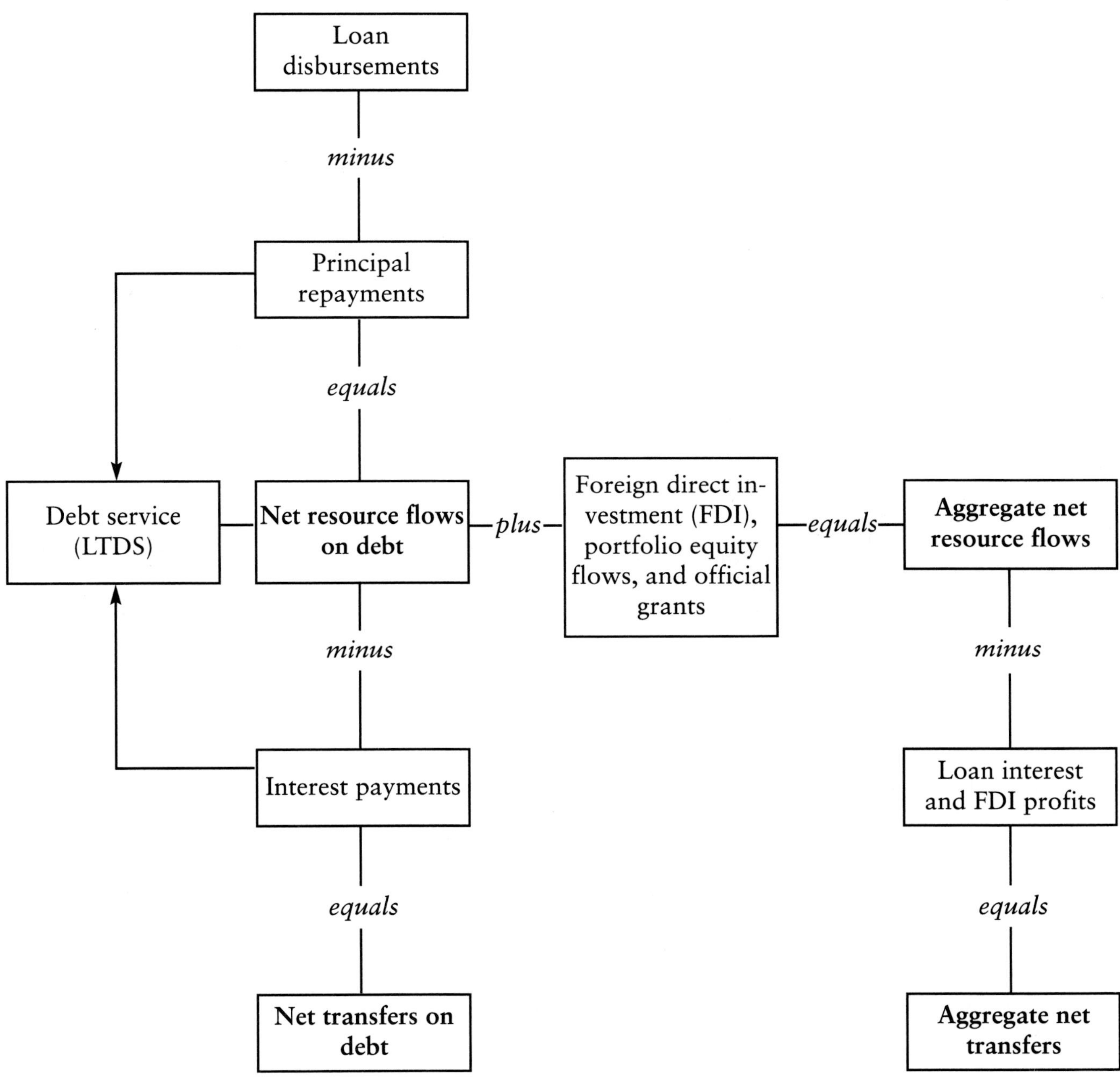

Aggregate net resource flows (long-term) and the balance of payments

	Credits	*Debits*
Current account	• Exports of goods and services • Income received • Current transfers Including workers' remittances and private grants	• Imports of goods and services • Income paid • Current transfers
	• Official unrequited transfers (by foreign governments)	• Official unrequited transfers (by national government)
Capital and financial account	• Official unrequited transfers (by foreign governments) • Foreign direct investment (by nonresidents) (disinvestment shown as negative)	• Official unrequited transfers (by national government) • Foreign direct investment (by residents) (disinvestment shown as negative)
	• Portfolio investment (by nonresidents) (amortizations shown as negative) • Other long-term capital inflows (by nonresidents) (amortizations shown as negative)	• Portfolio investment (abroad by residents) (amortizations shown as negative) • Other long-term capital outflow (by residents) (amortizations shown as negative)
	• Short-term capital inflow	• Short-term capital outflow
Reserve account	Net changes in reserves	

Aggregate net resource flows

Net resource flows on debt (long-term)

Country groups

Regional groups

East Asia and the Pacific

Cambodia (A)
China (P)
Fiji (A)
Indonesia (P)
Korea, Rep. (E)
Lao PDR (P)
Malaysia (P)
Mongolia (P)
Myanmar (A)
Papua New Guinea (A)
Philippines (A)
Samoa (A)
Solomon Islands (A)
Thailand (P)
Tonga (E)
Vanuatu (E)
Vietnam (E)
Kiribati
Korea, Dem. Rep.

Europe and Central Asia

Albania (A)
Armenia (A)
Azerbaijan (A)
Belarus (A)
Bosnia and Herzegovina[a] (E)
Bulgaria (P)
Croatia (A)
Czech Republic (P)
Estonia (A)
Georgia (A)
Hungary (A)
Kazakhstan (A)
Kyrgyz Republic (A)
Latvia (A)
Lithuania (P)
Macedonia, FYR (A)
Moldova (A)
Poland (A)
Romania (A)
Russian Federation[b] (E)
Slovak Republic (A)
Tajikistan (A)
Turkey (A)
Turkmenistan (A)
Ukraine (A)
Uzbekistan (A)
Yugoslavia, FR (Serbia and Montenegro)[a] (E)
Gibraltar

Latin America and the Caribbean

Argentina (A)
Barbados (A)
Belize (A)
Bolivia (A)
Brazil (P)
Chile (A)
Colombia (E)
Costa Rica (A)
Dominica (A)
Dominican Republic (A)
Ecuador (E)
El Salvador (A)
Grenada (A)
Guatemala (A)
Guyana (A)
Haiti (P)
Honduras (A)
Jamaica (E)
Mexico (A)
Nicaragua (A)
Panama (A)
Paraguay (A)
Peru (A)
St. Kitts and Nevis (A)
St. Lucia (A)
St.Vincent and the Grenadines (A)
Trinidad and Tobago (E)
Uruguay (A)
Venezuela, R.B. de (E)
Antigua and Barbuda
Cuba
Suriname

Middle East and North Africa

Algeria (A)
Djibouti (E)
Egypt, Arab Rep. (A)
Iran, Islamic Rep. (A)
Jordan (A)
Lebanon (A)
Morocco (A)
Oman (A)
Syrian Arab Republic (E)
Tunisia (E)
Yemen, Rep. (E)
Bahrain
Iraq
Libya
Saudi Arabia

South Asia

Bangladesh (A)
Bhutan (A)
India (E)
Maldives (A)
Nepal (A)
Pakistan (A)
Sri Lanka (A)
Afghanistan

Sub-Saharan Africa

Angola (A)
Benin (A)
Botswana (A)
Burkina Faso (A)
Burundi (A)
Cameroon (P)
Cape Verde (A)
Central African Republic (A)
Chad (E)
Comoros (E)
Congo, Dem. Rep. (E)
Congo, Rep. (E)
Côte d'Ivoire (E)
Equatorial Guinea (E)
Eritrea (A)
Ethiopia (A)
Gabon (A)
Gambia, The (A)
Ghana (A)
Guinea (E)
Guinea-Bissau (P)
Kenya (A)
Lesotho (A)
Liberia (E)
Madagascar (A)
Malawi (P)
Mali (A)
Mauritania (A)
Mauritius (A)
Mozambique (A)
Niger (A)
Nigeria (E)
Rwanda (A)
São Tomé and Principe (A)
Senegal (P)
Seychelles (A)
Sierra Leone (A)
Somalia (E)
South Africa (E)
Sudan (E)
Swaziland (E)
Tanzania (A)
Togo (A)
Uganda (A)
Zambia (A)
Zimbabwe (A)
Namibia

Note: Countries printed in normal type are reporters to the Debtor Reporting System (DRS); those printed in italics do not report to the DRS but are included in aggregate tables. Letters in parenthesis indicate DRS reporters' status: (A) as reported, (P) preliminary, and (E) estimated. The status "as reported" indicates that the country was fully current in its reporting under the DRS and that World Bank staff are satisfied that the reported data give an adequate and fair representation of the country's total public debt. "Preliminary" data are based on reported or collected information but, because of incompleteness or other reasons, include an element of staff estimation. "Estimated" data indicate that countries are not current in their reporting and that a significant element of staff estimation has been necessary in producing the data tables.

a. For Bosnia and Herzegovina total debt, excluding IBRD and IMF obligations and short-term debt, is included under Yugoslavia, FR (Serbia and Montenegro).

b. Includes the debt of the former Soviet Union on the assumption that 100 percent of all outstanding external debt as of December 1991 has become a liability of the Russian Federation.

Income groups

Low-income countries

Angola
Armenia
Azerbaijan
Bangladesh
Benin
Bhutan
Burkina Faso
Burundi
Cambodia
Cameroon
Central African Republic
Chad
China
Comoros
Congo, Dem. Rep.
Congo, Rep.
Côte d'Ivoire
Eritrea
Ethiopia
Gambia, The
Ghana
Guinea
Guinea-Bissau
Haiti
Honduras
India
Indonesia
Kenya
Kyrgyz Republic
Lao PDR
Lesotho
Liberia
Madagascar
Malawi
Mali
Mauritania
Moldova
Mongolia
Mozambique
Myanmar
Nepal
Nicaragua
Niger
Nigeria
Pakistan
Rwanda
São Tomé and Principe
Senegal
Sierra Leone
Solomon Islands
Somalia
Sudan
Tajikistan
Tanzania
Togo
Turkmenistan
Uganda
Vietnam
Yemen, Rep.
Zambia
Zimbabwe
Afghanistan
Korea, Dem. Rep.

Middle-income countries

Albania
Algeria
Argentina
Barbados
Belarus
Belize
Bolivia
Bosnia and Herzegovina
Botswana
Brazil
Bulgaria
Cape Verde
Chile
Colombia
Costa Rica
Croatia
Czech Republic
Djibouti
Dominica
Dominican Republic
Ecuador
Egypt, Arab Rep.
El Salvador
Equatorial Guinea
Estonia
Fiji
Gabon
Georgia
Grenada
Guatemala
Guyana
Hungary
Iran, Islamic Rep.
Jamaica
Jordan
Kazakhstan
Korea, Rep.
Latvia
Lebanon
Lithuania
Macedonia, FYR
Malaysia
Maldives
Mauritius
Mexico
Morocco
Oman
Panama
Papua New Guinea
Paraguay
Peru
Philippines
Poland
Romania
Russian Federation
Samoa
Seychelles
Slovak Republic
South Africa
Sri Lanka
St. Kitts and Nevis
St. Lucia
St. Vincent and the Grenadines
Swaziland
Syrian Arab Republic
Thailand
Tonga
Trinidad and Tobago
Tunisia
Turkey
Ukraine
Uruguay
Uzbekistan
Vanuatu
Venezuela, R.B. de
Yugoslavia, FR (Serbia and Montenegro)
Antigua and Barbuda
Bahrain
Cuba
Gibraltar
Iraq
Kiribati
Libya
Namibia
Saudi Arabia
Suriname

Note: Countries printed in normal type are reporters to the Debtor Reporting System (DRS); those printed in italics do not report to the DRS but are included in aggregate tables. Low-income countries are those in which 1998 GNP per capita (calculated using the *World Bank Atlas* method) was no more than $760; middle-income countries are those in which GNP per capita was between $761 and $9,360.

Debt tables

Note to users

Long-term public and publicly guaranteed debt data are as reported for 92 countries; for 45 other countries the data are preliminary (that is, substantially based on reported data) or estimated by World Bank staff (the status of each country is given in the Country Groups section).

For 23 of the 24 countries reporting private nonguaranteed debt, data for 1998 are as reported. Data for the one other country are preliminary or estimates by World Bank staff.

Data for exports, imports, and international reserves are standard series drawn from the International Monetary Fund (IMF) and maintained in the data files of the World Bank. Data for gross national product denominated in U.S. dollars are drawn directly from the files of the Macroeconomic Data Team of the Development Data Group of the World Bank. Data for direct foreign investment are drawn from the IMF, and data for grants are drawn from the OECD and supplemented by estimates by World Bank staff. The charts on pages xx to xxii are intended to help the reader interpret the debt stocks and flows reported in the tables.

For the period 1991–98 all ruble debt owed to the former Soviet Union is converted at a rate of $1 = 0.6 ruble, except in cases where a bilateral agreement specifying a different conversion rate is in place. This valuation method does not constitute an endorsement by World Bank staff of the appropriateness or validity of this method or the exchange rate used. The appropriate valuation is a matter to be resolved bilaterally between the Russian Federation and its debtor countries.

The following abbreviations are used in the principal ratios and indicator charts:

EDT	Total external debt, including short-term and use of IMF credit
LDOD	Total long-term debt outstanding and disbursed
INT	Total interest payments on long-term and short-term debt, including IMF charges
TDS	Total debt service on long-term debt and short-term (interest only), including IMF credits
FDI	Foreign direct investment
GNP	Gross national product
XGS	Exports of goods and services
MGS	Imports of goods and services
RES	International reserves

EXTERNAL DEBT

(US$ million, unless otherwise indicated)

	Total debt stock		Total debt / GNP (%)		Long-term debt / total debt (%)		Distribution of long-term debt (%)					
							Multilateral		Bilateral		Private	
	1993	1998	1993	1998	1993	1998	1993	1998	1993	1998	1993	1998
Albania	773	821	64	26	21	88	17	34	69	29	14	38
Algeria	26,020	30,665	54	68	95	93	12	15	14	53	75	32
Angola	10,574	12,173	326	297	82	87	1	3	21	28	78	70
Argentina	65,325	144,050	28	49	81	75	15	12	18	7	67	81
Armenia	134	800	7	42	100	71	45	76	55	24	0	0
Azerbaijan	36	693	1	18	100	53	0	54	100	28	0	18
Bangladesh	14,650	16,376	43	37	94	97	59	67	39	32	2	1
Barbados	571	608	35	..	61	64	47	65	10	4	43	31
Belarus	969	1,120	4	5	89	68	13	37	56	27	32	36
Belize	199	338	39	52	90	84	35	42	45	35	20	23
Benin	1,447	1,647	70	72	95	89	50	64	50	36	0	0
Bhutan	97	120	46	32	98	100	58	68	30	32	12	0
Bolivia	4,307	6,078	78	73	90	75	52	59	42	34	7	6
Botswana	660	548	15	12	99	93	73	73	20	22	7	5
Brazil	143,836	232,004	34	31	78	87	8	8	18	6	73	85
Bulgaria	12,202	9,907	115	83	80	84	5	15	17	14	78	70
Burkina Faso	1,117	1,399	55	54	95	88	74	89	25	11	0	0
Burundi	1,061	1,119	110	128	94	96	82	85	18	15	0	0
Cambodia	1,829	2,210	91	78	92	95	0	13	100	87	0	0
Cameroon	7,456	9,829	67	119	87	84	22	18	55	74	23	8
Cape Verde	148	244	41	50	95	97	73	76	25	20	2	5
Central African Republic	875	921	68	89	88	90	69	75	28	24	3	1
Chad	768	1,091	53	65	93	92	78	81	21	17	1	2
Chile	20,637	36,302	47	48	78	79	27	5	5	2	68	93
China	85,928	154,599	20	16	82	82	15	18	19	18	66	64
Colombia	18,942	33,263	24	33	81	81	37	17	12	5	51	78
Comoros	185	203	70	103	92	93	76	85	24	15	0	0
Congo, Dem. Rep.	11,270	12,929	135	208	78	69	25	25	65	65	10	9
Congo, Rep.	5,081	5,119	308	307	81	83	13	15	57	66	30	19
Costa Rica	3,863	3,971	53	39	88	83	36	42	37	24	27	34
Cote d'Ivoire	19,071	14,852	211	145	72	85	26	28	37	38	37	34
Croatia	1,614	8,297	15	38	92	83	20	8	14	14	66	77
Czech Republic	9,294	25,301	27	45	67	61	13	4	6	2	80	93
Djibouti	264	288	56	..	87	92	50	55	50	45	0	0
Dominica	96	109	50	47	96	83	67	67	33	33	0	0
Dominican Republic	4,860	4,451	54	30	79	79	23	29	51	53	26	18
Ecuador	14,150	15,140	103	82	72	85	23	25	22	16	55	59
Egypt, Arab Rep.	30,509	31,964	67	37	93	87	13	15	77	81	10	3
El Salvador	2,033	3,633	29	31	95	77	56	63	34	22	10	15
Equatorial Guinea	264	306	176	76	81	71	41	45	52	48	7	7
Eritrea	..	149	..	19	..	97	..	53	..	47	..	0
Estonia	154	782	4	15	62	57	47	31	15	8	38	61
Ethiopia	9,703	10,352	158	160	96	93	20	27	73	69	8	4
Fiji	330	193	21	13	86	89	58	71	11	11	31	19
Gabon	3,861	4,425	100	91	76	87	14	14	66	82	20	3
Gambia, The	426	477	118	117	82	95	78	79	21	21	1	0
Georgia	559	1,674	17	32	100	79	17	33	70	66	12	1
Ghana	4,888	6,884	84	92	75	85	66	61	25	25	9	14
Grenada	136	183	56	56	68	62	45	44	45	50	11	6
Guatemala	3,190	4,565	28	24	84	69	33	38	39	35	28	27
Guinea	2,848	3,546	90	102	93	88	42	54	54	45	4	1

EXTERNAL DEBT

(US$ million, unless otherwise indicated)

	Total debt stock		Total debt / GNP (%)		Long-term debt / total debt (%)		Distribution of long-term debt (%)					
							Multilateral		Bilateral		Private	
	1993	1998	1993	1998	1993	1998	1993	1998	1993	1998	1993	1998
Guinea-Bissau	787	964	355	504	91	91	46	47	51	53	3	0
Guyana	1,954	1,653	533	249	89	83	33	51	63	45	4	4
Haiti	803	1,048	44	27	81	94	80	85	10	15	10	0
Honduras	4,077	5,002	120	97	92	87	52	55	35	32	13	13
Hungary	24,364	28,580	65	62	87	83	16	6	3	3	81	90
India	94,342	98,232	34	23	91	95	32	33	33	25	35	42
Indonesia	89,172	150,875	59	176	80	81	25	15	37	25	38	60
Iran, Islamic Rep.	23,502	14,391	29	13	25	58	4	6	49	53	48	41
Jamaica	4,102	3,995	108	63	85	82	33	31	55	41	12	28
Jordan	7,609	8,485	142	147	89	87	14	22	49	59	37	19
Kazakhstan	1,728	5,714	7	26	94	81	2	27	86	18	12	56
Kenya	7,111	7,010	156	62	82	85	45	50	26	35	29	15
Korea, Rep.	47,202	139,097	14	44	74	68	9	12	18	1	73	86
Kyrgyz Republic	290	1,148	7	69	79	82	21	58	79	38	0	4
Lao PDR	1,985	2,437	150	199	98	97	23	40	77	60	0	0
Latvia	236	756	4	12	52	66	54	58	33	16	13	26
Lebanon	1,345	6,725	17	41	27	71	22	10	57	7	21	83
Lesotho	541	692	49	65	93	95	72	75	24	16	4	8
Liberia	1,957	2,103	..	..	56	52	39	38	43	44	18	18
Lithuania	328	1,950	5	19	61	68	50	26	18	18	32	56
Macedonia, FYR	1,042	2,392	43	97	88	89	25	22	32	44	43	35
Madagascar	3,805	4,394	118	119	87	93	44	43	53	56	3	1
Malawi	1,826	2,444	82	137	95	95	84	86	13	13	3	1
Malaysia	26,149	44,773	43	65	73	81	8	4	15	8	77	88
Maldives	112	180	65	58	97	94	55	67	38	20	7	13
Mali	2,902	3,202	109	120	96	88	40	56	60	44	0	0
Mauritania	2,141	2,589	245	273	89	86	39	45	60	54	1	1
Mauritius	1,008	2,482	32	60	89	77	31	14	39	17	31	70
Mexico	131,734	159,959	34	42	69	78	18	14	11	5	71	81
Moldova	278	1,035	6	63	69	79	30	42	71	23	0	35
Mongolia	384	739	74	75	88	86	21	57	48	39	31	4
Morocco	21,459	20,687	83	60	97	99	28	31	47	38	26	31
Mozambique	5,212	8,208	271	223	93	93	16	25	80	49	3	26
Myanmar	5,757	5,680	..	..	94	89	25	24	70	66	5	11
Nepal	2,010	2,646	52	54	97	98	82	86	14	12	4	1
Nicaragua	11,409	5,968	821	336	83	87	12	34	66	58	22	8
Niger	1,542	1,659	97	82	90	92	54	63	33	32	13	5
Nigeria	30,699	30,315	162	79	87	78	16	17	52	57	32	26
Oman	2,657	3,629	28	..	87	61	7	9	18	20	75	72
Pakistan	24,527	32,229	49	53	87	89	46	46	43	37	11	17
Panama	6,958	6,689	100	78	55	86	16	17	18	6	66	77
Papua New Guinea	3,269	2,692	69	77	91	92	29	35	15	19	56	47
Paraguay	1,596	2,305	23	27	82	71	53	60	33	33	14	7
Peru	23,573	32,397	60	53	72	74	16	19	58	48	26	33
Philippines	35,936	47,817	65	70	83	82	26	20	45	31	29	48
Poland	45,176	47,708	53	30	93	87	4	5	74	60	22	35
Romania	4,239	9,513	16	25	55	82	42	30	26	22	32	48
Russian Federation	111,731	183,601	29	69	90	79	1	5	52	42	46	53
Rwanda	909	1,226	47	61	92	91	82	86	18	14	0	0
Samoa	194	180	125	102	72	86	89	94	10	6	0	0
Sao Tome and Principe	209	246	497	684	87	95	65	69	35	31	1	0

EXTERNAL DEBT

(US$ million, unless otherwise indicated)

	Total debt stock		Total debt / GNP (%)		Long-term debt / total debt (%)		Distribution of long-term debt (%) Multilateral		Bilateral		Private	
	1993	1998	1993	1998	1993	1998	1993	1998	1993	1998	1993	1998
Senegal	3,803	3,861	73	83	81	85	54	59	41	40	5	1
Seychelles	157	187	34	36	84	78	36	40	37	39	27	21
Sierra Leone	1,396	1,243	194	198	55	76	36	55	60	44	3	1
Slovak Republic	3,393	9,893	28	49	63	78	14	9	8	6	79	86
Solomon Islands	151	152	59	52	96	98	46	61	12	9	41	30
Somalia	2,501	2,635	..	..	76	72	39	39	59	59	2	2
South Africa	..	24,712	..	19	..	54	..	0	..	0	..	100
Sri Lanka	6,854	8,526	67	55	89	91	39	42	51	49	10	10
St. Kitts and Nevis	54	115	29	43	93	97	51	36	41	49	9	15
St. Lucia	99	184	22	32	96	69	68	68	32	26	0	6
St. Vincent and the Grenadines	97	420	42	139	76	24	69	64	31	34	0	1
Sudan	15,837	16,843	226	183	60	58	21	21	59	58	21	21
Swaziland	208	251	20	19	96	89	54	67	45	33	1	0
Syrian Arab Republic	19,976	22,435	149	138	81	73	5	4	88	89	7	7
Tajikistan	385	1,070	13	49	100	77	0	13	82	65	18	21
Tanzania	6,781	7,603	156	94	86	85	41	49	52	47	7	4
Thailand	52,717	86,172	43	76	57	69	10	8	22	23	68	69
Togo	1,278	1,448	106	97	87	90	56	61	40	39	4	0
Tonga	44	65	30	37	99	99	62	74	38	17	0	9
Trinidad and Tobago	2,240	2,193	53	36	87	74	15	38	26	9	59	53
Tunisia	8,692	11,078	63	58	88	89	41	35	41	38	18	27
Turkey	68,608	102,074	38	50	73	73	19	9	15	11	66	80
Turkmenistan	276	2,266	5	88	100	77	9	2	44	14	47	84
Uganda	3,029	3,935	96	58	86	86	66	72	29	26	4	2
Ukraine	3,855	12,718	6	30	96	74	4	21	75	29	21	50
Uruguay	4,851	7,600	38	37	71	71	32	27	7	7	61	65
Uzbekistan	1,032	3,162	5	16	91	88	0	10	84	39	16	51
Vanuatu	42	63	23	28	93	86	68	82	30	18	2	0
Venezuela, R.B. de	37,539	37,003	64	40	80	90	10	9	3	5	88	86
Vietnam	24,168	22,359	188	82	89	88	0	6	95	71	4	22
Yemen, Rep.	5,923	4,138	133	105	90	87	21	42	47	53	32	5
Yugoslavia, FR (Serbia/Montenegro)	12,709	13,742	..	..	86	81	11	11	27	27	63	62
Zambia	6,485	6,865	215	217	68	78	38	42	54	55	8	3
Zimbabwe	4,299	4,716	68	80	79	75	38	48	31	34	31	18
All developing countries	1,777,529	2,536,046	38	42	79	80	18	16	36	26	46	58
East Asia & Pacific	383,106	667,522	32	40	78	77	16	14	35	22	49	65
Europe & Central Asia	308,939	480,539	31	49	84	78	8	8	41	30	51	62
Latin America & Caribbean	548,994	786,019	40	41	77	81	16	13	25	14	60	73
Middle East & North Africa	193,661	208,059	43	36	72	79	14	15	53	52	34	33
South Asia	148,012	163,775	39	29	91	94	37	39	38	32	25	29
Sub-Saharan Africa	194,817	230,132	71	72	81	78	29	32	47	45	24	24
Severely indebted low income	295,169	361,702	104	139	82	82	23	22	53	43	24	35
Severely indebted middle income	353,542	531,233	45	43	78	82	10	10	37	22	52	67
Moderately indebted low income	171,399	191,556	41	32	89	92	39	42	36	30	25	28
Moderately indebted middle income	479,760	700,047	41	57	80	79	14	11	28	24	57	65
Other developing countries	477,658	751,508	24	28	74	75	14	15	33	20	53	65
Low income	563,685	721,592	49	39	84	85	27	27	43	34	30	39
Middle income	1,213,844	1,814,454	34	43	77	78	13	11	33	22	54	66
Special Program of Assistance	103,619	113,678	126	114	83	87	38	43	48	46	14	11
Heavily indebted poor countries	205,512	213,960	142	115	82	83	28	34	56	50	17	16

Note: Individual country data are shown for Debtor Reporting System countries only. Data for Bosnia and Herzegovina are not shown separately. Totals include estimates for countries not part of the DRS.

EXTERNAL DEBT

Short-term debt contracted in 1998, so that its share in total external debt fell to 16 percent, down from 20 percent in 1997. With reserves higher as well, the ratio of short-term debt to reserves also fell.

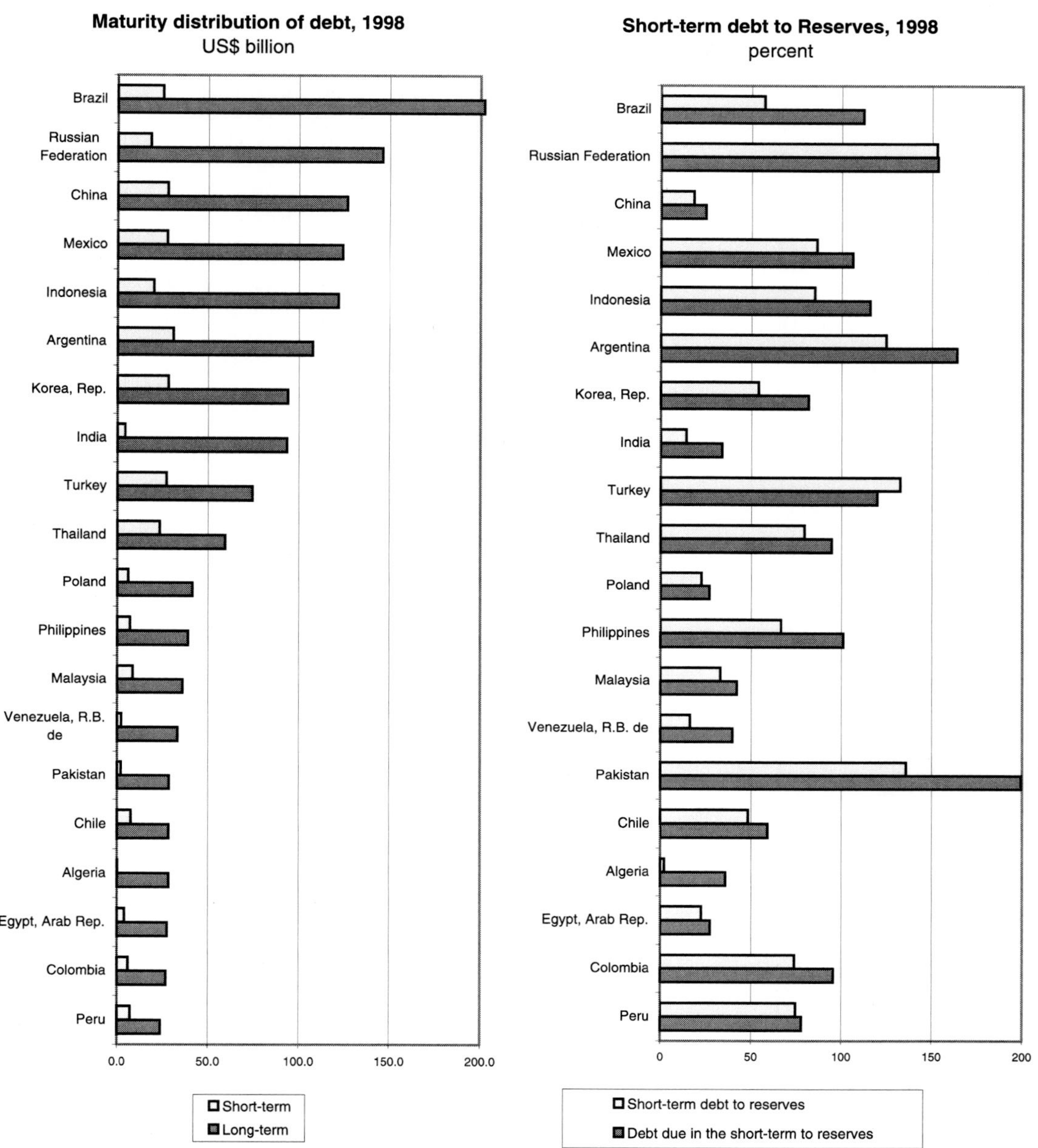

Note: Country selection is based on size of external debt at end-1998. Short-term debt is debt with an original maturity of one year or less (and includes interest arrears). Debt due in the short term is debt due within a year and is comprised of liabilities to banks, debt securities issued abroad, and non-bank credits. Debt due in the short term is larger than short-term debt but when these data are derived from different sources this may not hold. Reserves are the sum of a country's monetary authority's holdings of special drawing rights, its reserve position in the IMF, its holding of foreign exchange, and its holdings of gold (valued at year-end London prices)

Source: Debtor Reporting System and Joint BIS-IMF-OECD-World Bank statistics on external debt (also available on the World Bank website: http://www.worldbank.org/data).

AGGREGATE NET RESOURCE FLOWS (long-term)

(US$ million, unless otherwise indicated)

	Aggregate net resource flows (excl. IMF)		Private flows: Foreign direct investment		Portfolio equity		Bonds		Bank and trade-related lending		Official flows (including grants)	
	1993-97	1998	1993-97	1998	1993-97	1998	1993-97	1998	1993-97	1998	1993-97	1998
Albania	224	240	64	45	0	0	0	0	1	-3	159	198
Algeria	689	-1,427	10	5	4	2	-277	0	298	-1,328	654	-106
Angola	899	249	251	360	0	0	0	0	354	-320	293	209
Argentina	15,302	19,553	5,216	6,150	2,009	50	6,139	9,037	986	3,662	952	654
Armenia	198	321	18	232	0	0	0	0	0	0	180	89
Azerbaijan	526	1,178	419	1,023	0	0	0	0	2	58	106	97
Bangladesh	1,149	1,303	36	308	24	3	0	0	-38	-23	1,126	1,015
Barbados	79	34	12	15	67	0	4	-23	-15	0	11	42
Belarus	309	216	64	149	0	0	0	0	58	-27	187	94
Belize	38	63	15	20	0	0	0	0	2	6	20	37
Benin	209	186	16	34	0	0	0	0	0	0	194	152
Bhutan	43	28	0	0	0	0	0	0	-2	-2	45	30
Bolivia	951	1,194	374	872	0	0	-1	0	63	-12	514	334
Botswana	13	107	-12	95	0	0	0	0	2	-4	23	16
Brazil	22,689	59,393	8,015	31,913	4,562	542	3,409	1,409	7,992	20,521	-1,288	5,008
Bulgaria	477	673	173	401	286	66	-96	-57	-81	88	195	175
Burkina Faso	303	268	0	0	0	0	0	0	0	0	303	268
Burundi	170	70	1	1	0	0	0	0	-1	1	170	68
Cambodia	406	343	154	121	0	0	0	0	1	-3	251	225
Cameroon	293	238	17	50	0	0	0	0	-34	-49	311	237
Cape Verde	84	107	8	14	0	0	0	0	2	-1	74	94
Central African Republic	127	101	2	5	0	0	0	0	0	0	126	96
Chad	198	128	18	16	0	0	0	0	0	0	180	112
Chile	5,358	9,190	3,288	4,638	427	87	689	702	1,542	3,825	-587	-62
China	52,859	45,230	36,313	43,751	4,493	1,273	1,990	1,587	4,912	-3,936	5,151	2,554
Colombia	5,115	3,798	2,440	3,038	205	26	990	1,752	1,760	-1,187	-280	168
Comoros	25	25	2	2	0	0	0	0	0	0	23	23
Congo, Dem. Rep.	151	97	1	1	0	0	0	0	0	0	150	97
Congo, Rep.	216	50	6	4	0	0	0	0	31	0	179	46
Costa Rica	340	796	370	559	1	0	4	184	-25	57	-10	-5
Cote d'Ivoire	737	729	198	435	11	6	0	-23	-81	-237	608	548
Croatia	911	1,763	266	873	22	205	110	89	475	499	37	97
Czech Republic	3,240	3,197	1,364	2,554	83	129	184	837	1,508	-188	101	-135
Djibouti	64	56	3	6	0	0	0	0	0	0	61	50
Dominica	35	44	20	21	0	0	0	0	0	0	16	23
Dominican Republic	240	807	266	691	0	74	0	-4	-39	10	14	36
Ecuador	837	838	531	831	1	0	-29	-10	178	-238	156	254
Egypt, Arab Rep.	2,309	2,458	775	1,076	611	494	0	0	-307	-186	1,229	1,073
El Salvador	389	428	12	12	0	0	0	0	-5	230	382	186
Equatorial Guinea	130	37	112	24	0	0	0	0	0	0	18	13
Eritrea	110	139	0	0	0	0	0	0	0	0	110	139
Estonia	287	781	199	581	5	53	24	17	-6	63	65	67
Ethiopia	639	500	6	4	0	0	0	0	-59	2	692	494
Fiji	40	72	49	75	0	0	0	0	-9	-9	0	6
Gabon	5	-64	-99	-50	0	0	0	0	-33	-7	137	-8
Gambia, The	53	46	10	13	0	0	0	0	-2	0	44	33
Georgia	216	207	21	50	0	0	0	0	-1	7	197	150
Ghana	972	579	134	56	199	15	50	0	58	-29	532	537
Grenada	31	23	21	21	0	0	0	0	-1	0	11	2
Guatemala	256	897	89	673	0	0	36	-31	-22	-21	154	276
Guinea	302	227	6	1	0	0	0	0	-5	-10	301	237

AGGREGATE NET RESOURCE FLOWS (long-term)

(US$ million, unless otherwise indicated)

	Aggregate net resource flows (excl. IMF)		Private flows: Foreign direct investment		Private flows: Portfolio equity		Private flows: Bonds		Private flows: Bank and trade-related lending		Official flows (including grants)	
	1993-97	1998	1993-97	1998	1993-97	1998	1993-97	1998	1993-97	1998	1993-97	1998
Guinea-Bissau	70	61	1	1	0	0	0	0	0	0	69	60
Guyana	165	205	84	95	0	0	0	0	-5	-4	86	114
Haiti	346	225	3	11	0	0	0	0	0	0	344	214
Honduras	358	375	65	84	0	0	19	-32	33	141	242	182
Hungary	3,888	3,815	2,415	1,936	730	259	1,062	688	-261	1,801	-57	-869
India	6,959	7,604	1,934	2,635	2,920	342	480	4,120	776	-946	848	1,453
Indonesia	10,655	-808	3,866	-356	2,879	250	1,923	-141	803	-3,512	1,183	2,951
Iran, Islamic Rep.	-2,130	-325	20	24	0	0	0	0	275	564	-2,424	-914
Jamaica	165	534	148	369	0	0	67	250	-10	-33	-40	-52
Jordan	443	633	72	310	21	11	20	-10	-146	-104	476	425
Kazakhstan	1,465	2,337	752	1,158	10	0	110	100	211	725	382	353
Kenya	220	149	14	11	11	4	0	0	-151	-72	346	206
Korea, Rep.	15,126	13,201	1,668	5,415	3,414	4,096	8,701	1,220	820	-3,087	523	5,558
Kyrgyz Republic	228	293	55	109	0	0	0	0	0	-2	173	185
Lao PDR	293	242	87	46	0	0	0	0	0	0	205	196
Latvia	376	530	268	357	5	4	8	0	9	5	86	164
Lebanon	757	1,941	56	200	49	147	386	1,350	103	43	164	201
Lesotho	214	325	122	265	0	0	0	0	4	16	88	43
Liberia	105	76	19	16	0	0	0	0	0	0	85	60
Lithuania	384	1,183	128	926	5	0	40	0	84	57	127	200
Macedonia, FYR	80	545	13	118	0	0	0	0	-4	72	71	356
Madagascar	374	414	11	16	0	0	0	0	-5	-1	367	399
Malawi	328	359	1	1	0	24	0	0	-9	-1	335	335
Malaysia	10,256	8,529	4,733	5,000	2,237	592	1,659	-314	1,759	3,017	-131	235
Maldives	37	41	8	11	0	0	0	0	2	7	27	23
Mali	327	268	32	17	0	0	0	0	0	0	295	251
Mauritania	224	129	7	5	0	0	0	0	5	-2	212	126
Mauritius	279	-70	29	12	18	8	150	0	76	-99	6	9
Mexico	20,128	22,428	9,381	10,238	5,062	730	6,439	2,428	-325	9,792	-428	-760
Moldova	180	100	26	85	0	0	15	0	46	-23	92	39
Mongolia	131	134	13	19	0	0	0	0	-15	-12	134	127
Morocco	657	936	514	322	136	174	59	0	-46	470	-5	-29
Mozambique	844	1,081	50	213	0	0	0	0	3	-4	791	872
Myanmar	229	272	107	70	11	0	0	0	40	83	72	119
Nepal	304	253	13	12	0	0	0	0	-8	-13	298	253
Nicaragua	503	703	85	184	0	0	-2	0	-21	-13	440	531
Niger	213	208	-9	1	0	0	0	0	-22	-24	243	230
Nigeria	1,085	598	1,503	1,051	6	2	0	0	-360	-25	-64	-430
Oman	169	-248	78	106	19	10	45	0	-33	-330	60	-34
Pakistan	3,010	1,871	636	500	640	0	144	0	395	306	1,195	1,066
Panama	590	1,600	504	1,206	28	0	106	218	-24	34	-25	141
Papua New Guinea	352	418	143	110	127	0	-8	0	-146	120	237	188
Paraguay	261	305	198	256	0	0	0	0	-23	-20	86	69
Peru	4,393	3,024	2,153	1,930	1,449	174	-148	0	266	620	673	300
Philippines	4,521	2,764	1,409	1,713	1,244	454	1,589	151	-73	269	352	178
Poland	5,896	9,716	3,331	6,365	598	969	361	1,202	-72	1,117	1,677	63
Romania	1,944	1,825	466	2,031	3	42	290	0	398	-247	787	-1
Russian Federation	7,225	20,142	2,275	2,764	1,325	296	927	11,538	214	4,748	2,483	796
Rwanda	415	285	3	7	0	0	0	0	0	0	412	278
Samoa	29	15	4	3	0	0	0	0	0	0	26	12
Sao Tome and Principe	31	15	0	0	0	0	0	0	0	0	31	15

AGGREGATE NET RESOURCE FLOWS (long-term)

(US$ million, unless otherwise indicated)

	Aggregate net resource flows (excl. IMF)		Private flows: Foreign direct investment		Private flows: Portfolio equity		Private flows: Bonds		Private flows: Bank and trade-related lending		Official flows (including grants)	
	1993-97	1998	1993-97	1998	1993-97	1998	1993-97	1998	1993-97	1998	1993-97	1998
Senegal	461	341	56	40	0	0	0	0	-7	-16	411	317
Seychelles	43	69	34	52	0	0	0	0	-1	5	11	12
Sierra Leone	135	97	0	5	0	0	0	0	-6	0	140	92
Slovak Republic	993	1,691	246	562	21	0	170	-570	350	1,488	205	211
Solomon Islands	33	47	17	23	0	0	0	0	-2	0	18	24
Somalia	315	68	1	0	0	0	0	0	0	0	315	68
South Africa	4,240	1,029	1,489	550	1,986	619	918	303	-313	-689	161	246
Sri Lanka	701	818	193	193	68	6	10	65	-25	61	454	493
St. Kitts and Nevis	31	36	18	24	0	0	0	0	3	-2	10	14
St. Lucia	65	67	37	46	0	0	0	0	0	7	28	14
St. Vincent and the Grenadines	53	66	34	40	0	0	0	0	1	0	18	26
Sudan	256	558	20	371	0	0	0	0	0	0	237	187
Swaziland	67	99	48	80	0	0	0	0	-1	0	20	19
Syrian Arab Republic	256	143	139	80	0	0	0	0	-20	-4	137	67
Tajikistan	127	70	12	18	0	0	0	0	14	-21	101	72
Tanzania	763	939	100	172	0	0	0	0	3	-16	660	783
Thailand	9,511	8,987	2,264	6,941	1,195	2,341	2,652	-632	1,752	-826	1,647	1,162
Togo	109	112	0	0	0	0	0	0	-1	0	110	112
Tonga	18	9	2	2	0	0	0	0	0	-2	17	9
Trinidad and Tobago	434	733	510	730	0	0	17	0	-109	31	17	-28
Tunisia	898	619	367	650	0	40	263	0	-16	4	284	-76
Turkey	5,896	1,585	731	940	720	880	1,646	-535	3,188	357	-389	-57
Turkmenistan	291	601	43	130	0	0	0	0	209	343	39	128
Uganda	650	744	112	200	0	0	0	0	-10	-2	548	546
Ukraine	921	2,438	314	743	0	0	-56	1,076	310	267	353	351
Uruguay	518	696	135	164	7	0	201	336	48	-5	127	201
Uzbekistan	500	733	110	200	0	0	0	0	184	392	207	140
Vanuatu	44	46	30	27	0	0	0	0	0	0	14	19
Venezuela, R.B. de	2,739	8,008	1,978	4,435	546	64	56	1,408	106	959	53	1,142
Vietnam	1,910	2,150	1,193	1,200	164	0	0	0	159	-368	394	1,318
Yemen, Rep.	277	6	98	-210	0	0	0	0	1	0	178	216
Yugoslavia, FR (Serbia/Montenegro)	800	182	5	0	0	0	0	0	0	0	795	182
Zambia	505	281	61	72	0	0	0	0	-27	-32	472	241
Zimbabwe	395	68	47	76	19	3	-30	-30	-25	-266	384	285
All developing countries	269,348	318,325	112,185	170,942	40,319	15,567	43,390	39,658	30,016	41,534	43,438	48,804
East Asia & Pacific	106,875	82,838	52,058	64,162	15,763	9,007	18,506	1,870	9,938	-7,790	10,610	15,531
Europe & Central Asia	39,393	59,562	13,779	24,350	3,813	2,904	4,795	14,385	6,720	11,704	10,286	4,946
Latin America & Caribbean	83,063	136,972	36,020	69,323	14,366	1,748	17,995	17,627	12,347	38,156	2,336	9,909
Middle East & North Africa	7,470	11,472	3,287	5,054	840	879	556	1,340	453	1,950	2,334	2,260
South Asia	12,852	12,586	2,820	3,659	3,653	351	634	4,185	1,104	-615	4,641	4,987
Sub-Saharan Africa	19,694	14,895	4,222	4,394	1,884	679	904	250	-546	-1,872	13,230	11,173
Low income	98,013	77,859	48,014	53,517	11,377	1,921	4,590	5,482	6,900	-8,556	27,132	25,496
Middle income	172,701	240,465	64,171	117,425	28,942	13,646	38,800	34,175	23,116	50,090	17,672	25,130
Heavily indebted poor countries	16,376	15,900	3,336	4,479	396	48	67	-54	307	-984	12,269	11,226

Note: Individual country data are shown for Debtor Reporting System countries only. Data for Bosnia and Herzegovina are not shown separately. Totals include estimates for countries not part of the DRS. Data for 1993-97 represent average annual flows.

AGGREGATE NET RESOURCE FLOWS (long-term)

Long-term private capital flows were lower in 1998, pulled down by declining debt and portfolio equity flows. By contrast, foreign direct investment was more resilient in the face of financial crisis.

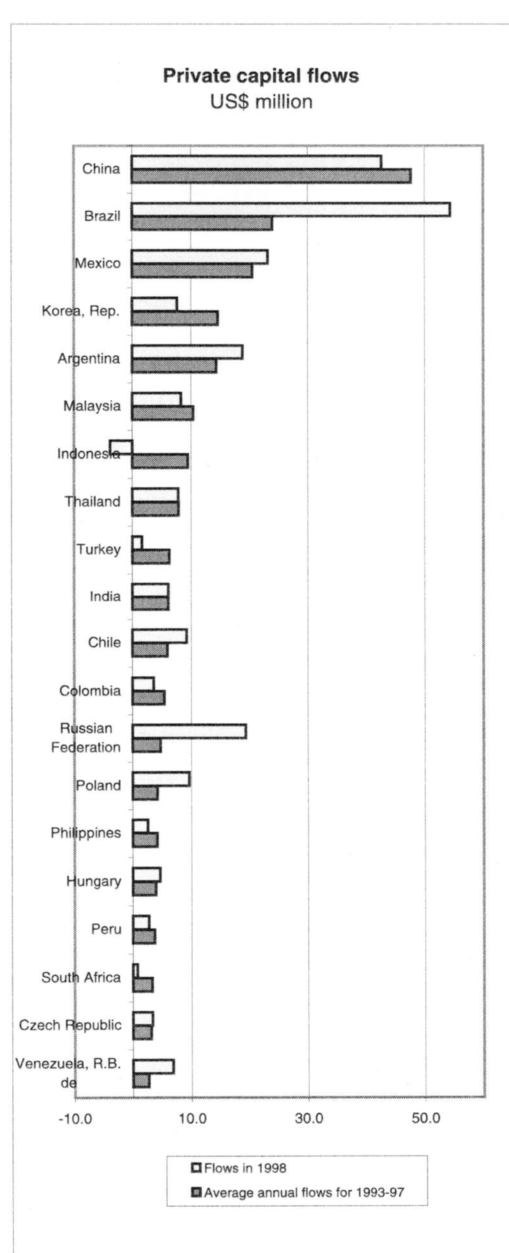

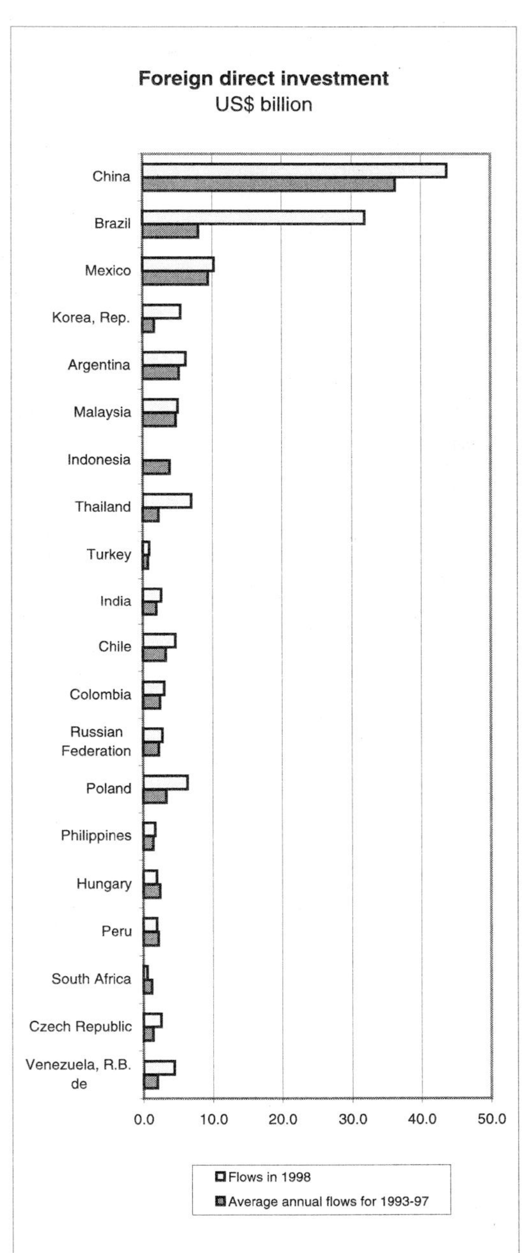

Note: Country selection is based on average annual capital flows during 1993-97, and shows the largest recipients.

NET FLOWS AND TRANSFERS ON DEBT

(US$ million, unless otherwise indicated)

	Net flows on debt		Net transfers on debt		Net flows on debt / GNP (%)		Net flows on long-term debt: Total		Official (excl. IMF)		Private	
	1993-97	1998	1993-97	1998	1993-97	1998	1993-97	1998	1993-97	1998	1993-97	1998
Albania	46	70	34	45	3	2	58	76	57	79	1	-3
Algeria	747	-1,609	-1,112	-3,601	2	-4	605	-1,541	584	-213	21	-1,328
Angola	265	-147	48	-587	8	-4	385	-327	30	-7	354	-320
Argentina	13,933	11,633	8,684	2,657	5	4	8,049	13,322	925	623	7,124	12,699
Armenia	122	114	114	94	6	6	91	40	91	40	0	0
Azerbaijan	108	165	100	144	3	4	50	126	48	68	2	58
Bangladesh	356	342	163	162	1	1	440	335	478	359	-38	-23
Barbados	-7	31	-48	-10	-1	..	-6	15	5	38	-11	-23
Belarus	258	-83	208	-148	1	0	156	64	97	91	58	-27
Belize	48	-120	37	-141	8	-18	13	12	11	5	2	6
Benin	104	-23	84	-49	5	-1	66	32	66	32	0	0
Bhutan	8	-3	5	-5	3	-1	8	-1	10	2	-2	-2
Bolivia	336	928	163	737	5	11	283	90	220	102	63	-12
Botswana	-5	-33	-45	-59	0	-1	-12	-33	-14	-29	2	-5
Brazil	12,627	21,179	3,613	8,715	2	3	10,044	26,841	-1,357	4,911	11,401	21,930
Bulgaria	105	-81	-301	-606	1	-1	-63	105	114	74	-177	32
Burkina Faso	100	62	82	44	5	2	79	54	79	54	0	0
Burundi	21	10	10	1	2	1	29	18	30	17	-1	1
Cambodia	60	56	53	48	2	2	50	52	49	55	1	-3
Cameroon	197	65	-18	-171	2	1	72	-89	106	-40	-34	-49
Cape Verde	15	31	11	27	3	6	15	31	13	32	2	-1
Central African Republic	24	-11	18	-19	2	-1	28	-6	28	-6	0	0
Chad	74	24	65	12	5	1	66	28	66	28	0	0
Chile	2,771	2,274	1,396	138	5	3	1,586	4,439	-645	-87	2,231	4,527
China	15,311	-3,593	9,983	-10,818	2	0	11,772	-61	4,870	2,288	6,902	-2,349
Colombia	3,041	1,146	1,236	-803	3	1	2,397	673	-353	107	2,750	566
Comoros	7	-5	6	-6	3	-3	6	-1	6	-1	0	0
Congo, Dem. Rep.	14	-13	-2	-32	0	0	12	0	12	0	0	0
Congo, Rep.	40	-66	-91	-90	3	-4	36	-7	5	-7	31	0
Costa Rica	-41	365	-261	150	-1	4	-63	212	-42	-29	-21	241
Cote d'Ivoire	638	-1,064	153	-1,778	6	-10	98	-225	179	35	-81	-260
Croatia	734	1,251	576	922	4	6	585	651	-1	64	586	588
Czech Republic	2,853	1,823	2,092	304	6	3	1,724	459	32	-189	1,692	648
Djibouti	14	3	11	1	3	..	13	2	13	2	0	0
Dominica	3	4	0	1	1	2	2	-1	2	-1	0	0
Dominican Republic	-37	134	-223	-59	0	1	-71	-19	-31	-25	-40	6
Ecuador	618	76	6	-790	4	0	254	-59	106	188	149	-247
Egypt, Arab Rep.	-84	818	-1,296	-83	0	1	-135	-453	171	-268	-307	-186
El Salvador	325	337	198	163	4	3	181	297	186	67	-5	230
Equatorial Guinea	8	12	7	10	4	3	3	0	3	0	0	0
Eritrea	19	71	18	67	2	9	19	65	19	65	0	0
Estonia	125	64	110	25	3	1	54	89	36	9	18	80
Ethiopia	158	93	110	43	3	1	150	78	209	75	-59	2
Fiji	-23	-44	-40	-55	-1	-3	-26	-17	-18	-8	-9	-9
Gabon	38	-172	-159	-344	1	-4	18	-66	50	-60	-33	-7
Gambia, The	9	12	3	5	2	3	16	9	18	9	-2	0
Georgia	154	163	136	118	5	3	99	103	100	96	-1	7
Ghana	407	283	277	93	6	4	428	269	321	297	108	-29
Grenada	4	54	2	50	2	16	4	-2	5	-2	-1	0
Guatemala	207	314	63	114	1	2	58	72	44	124	14	-52
Guinea	184	-43	137	-99	5	-1	128	54	133	64	-5	-10

NET FLOWS AND TRANSFERS ON DEBT

(US$ million, unless otherwise indicated)

	Net flows on debt		Net transfers on debt		Net flows on debt / GNP (%)		Net flows on long-term debt					
							Total		Official (excl. IMF)		Private	
	1993-97	1998	1993-97	1998	1993-97	1998	1993-97	1998	1993-97	1998	1993-97	1998
Guinea-Bissau	23	11	19	6	10	6	22	12	22	12	0	0
Guyana	12	27	-28	-36	3	4	12	6	17	10	-5	-4
Haiti	55	-3	42	-22	2	0	50	80	50	80	0	0
Honduras	246	233	63	25	7	5	199	128	147	18	52	109
Hungary	642	2,829	-1,130	1,335	2	6	654	1,567	-147	-921	801	2,488
India	431	3,044	-4,160	-2,074	0	1	1,547	4,151	291	977	1,256	3,174
Indonesia	7,263	-4,935	1,291	-12,060	4	-6	3,696	-957	969	2,696	2,726	-3,653
Iran, Islamic Rep.	-676	2,351	-1,938	1,550	0	2	-2,198	-379	-2,472	-943	275	564
Jamaica	-41	1	-259	-208	-1	0	-78	73	-135	-144	57	217
Jordan	210	-87	-111	-568	4	-2	138	39	264	153	-126	-114
Kazakhstan	854	1,307	749	1,024	4	6	676	1,164	355	339	321	825
Kenya	-46	-118	-324	-283	0	-1	-53	-63	98	9	-151	-72
Korea, Rep.	20,673	7,190	15,532	-1,022	4	2	10,042	3,687	521	5,554	9,520	-1,867
Kyrgyz Republic	159	137	143	110	7	8	117	139	117	140	0	-2
Lao PDR	101	66	95	58	6	5	92	78	92	78	0	0
Latvia	96	207	76	175	2	3	72	100	56	95	17	5
Lebanon	644	1,653	479	1,294	5	10	582	1,487	93	94	488	1,393
Lesotho	41	22	27	1	3	2	41	26	36	10	4	16
Liberia	-3	3	-5	3	..	..	1	0	1	0	0	0
Lithuania	301	361	265	293	4	3	217	175	93	119	124	57
Macedonia, FYR	79	407	46	306	3	16	35	399	40	327	-4	72
Madagascar	83	100	45	46	2	3	103	44	108	45	-5	-1
Malawi	123	112	90	87	7	6	125	121	134	122	-9	-1
Malaysia	5,522	-3,361	3,664	-5,830	7	-5	3,263	2,922	-156	219	3,418	2,703
Maldives	14	20	11	16	7	6	14	16	12	9	2	7
Mali	159	-36	121	-62	7	-1	90	50	90	50	0	0
Mauritania	102	-84	61	-126	10	-9	65	-7	60	-5	5	-2
Mauritius	294	-25	212	-179	7	-1	216	-102	-9	-3	226	-99
Mexico	7,296	9,363	-2,958	-3,226	2	2	5,647	11,427	-467	-793	6,114	12,220
Moldova	192	-55	167	-99	8	-3	138	3	77	26	61	-23
Mongolia	60	89	50	80	7	9	61	61	76	74	-15	-12
Morocco	-381	-26	-1,686	-1,050	-1	0	-255	92	-268	-377	13	470
Mozambique	204	203	142	162	8	6	194	194	191	199	3	-4
Myanmar	17	230	-46	216	..	..	10	135	-30	52	40	83
Nepal	140	120	109	92	3	2	137	124	145	137	-8	-13
Nicaragua	62	-20	-35	-184	5	-1	92	174	114	187	-22	-13
Niger	32	33	15	21	2	2	28	49	50	73	-22	-24
Nigeria	-549	-269	-1,473	-826	-2	-1	-461	-487	-101	-463	-360	-25
Oman	147	1	-36	-217	1	..	44	-366	32	-36	12	-330
Pakistan	1,199	821	104	-128	2	1	1,543	1,197	1,004	891	539	306
Panama	-92	411	-350	25	-1	5	35	383	-47	131	82	253
Papua New Guinea	-191	99	-321	35	-4	3	-138	100	17	-20	-154	120
Paraguay	97	182	-7	76	1	2	40	28	62	48	-23	-20
Peru	1,543	1,100	440	-456	3	2	552	681	434	61	118	620
Philippines	2,865	-3,544	691	-5,830	4	-5	1,614	413	98	-6	1,516	419
Poland	769	4,210	-659	2,586	1	3	443	1,832	153	-487	290	2,319
Romania	1,337	-325	990	-873	4	-1	1,383	-379	695	-132	688	-247
Russian Federation	4,874	21,824	2,102	16,036	1	8	2,649	16,997	1,508	711	1,141	16,286
Rwanda	51	79	44	69	3	4	46	79	46	79	0	0
Samoa	9	18	7	16	6	10	8	0	8	0	0	0
Sao Tome and Principe	9	5	8	4	23	14	11	4	11	4	0	0

NET FLOWS AND TRANSFERS ON DEBT

(US$ million, unless otherwise indicated)

	Net flows on debt		Net transfers on debt		Net flows on debt / GNP (%)		Net flows on long-term debt: Total		Official (excl. IMF)		Private	
	1993-97	1998	1993-97	1998	1993-97	1998	1993-97	1998	1993-97	1998	1993-97	1998
Senegal	48	97	-37	-9	1	2	60	49	67	65	-7	-16
Seychelles	-2	33	-8	25	0	6	2	9	3	4	-1	5
Sierra Leone	36	46	12	36	5	7	49	22	55	22	-6	0
Slovak Republic	958	829	582	248	6	4	687	1,077	167	159	520	918
Solomon Islands	0	14	-3	12	0	5	0	13	1	14	-2	0
Somalia	-1	5	-2	5	..	..	0	0	0	0	0	0
South Africa	3,231	-287	1,948	-1,816	2	0	605	-386	0	0	605	-386
Sri Lanka	304	357	152	207	2	2	282	505	297	379	-15	126
St. Kitts and Nevis	13	8	11	3	5	3	13	6	10	8	3	-2
St. Lucia	12	30	6	22	2	5	7	6	7	-1	0	7
St. Vincent and the Grenadines	38	161	31	145	15	53	4	14	3	15	1	0
Sudan	-35	-13	-46	-16	0	0	32	-1	32	-1	0	0
Swaziland	32	-127	23	-136	2	-9	1	3	2	3	-1	0
Syrian Arab Republic	137	1,285	-69	1,042	1	8	48	-32	68	-28	-20	-4
Tajikistan	80	135	78	112	4	6	67	-5	53	16	14	-21
Tanzania	147	140	65	28	3	2	131	120	128	135	3	-15
Thailand	10,473	-10,998	6,491	-16,440	7	-10	5,955	-364	1,551	1,094	4,404	-1,458
Togo	22	49	7	37	2	3	33	48	34	48	-1	0
Tonga	2	1	2	0	1	1	2	2	3	3	0	-2
Trinidad and Tobago	-66	-12	-230	-137	-1	0	-83	-6	9	-37	-92	31
Tunisia	543	-681	10	-1,233	3	-4	427	-133	180	-137	247	4
Turkey	6,263	4,082	1,941	-788	3	2	4,138	-297	-696	-118	4,834	-179
Turkmenistan	345	449	313	357	10	17	241	466	32	123	209	343
Uganda [a]	219	102	179	68	5	2	207	111	216	113	-10	-2
Ukraine	1,175	1,255	819	686	2	3	461	1,597	207	253	254	1,344
Uruguay	464	787	111	340	3	4	364	524	115	193	249	332
Uzbekistan	507	245	419	97	2	1	374	520	190	128	184	392
Vanuatu	2	12	1	10	1	5	0	12	1	12	0	0
Venezuela, R.B. de	-269	1,042	-2,495	-1,376	-1	1	203	3,487	42	1,119	161	2,367
Vietnam	412	338	240	-86	2	1	269	719	110	1,087	159	-368
Yemen, Rep.	-51	183	-89	131	-1	5	73	91	73	91	1	0
Yugoslavia, FR (Serbia/Montenegro)	200	-1,767	158	-1,823	..	..	-2	0	-2	0	0	0
Zambia	127	25	-83	-45	4	1	101	-49	128	-17	-27	-32
Zimbabwe	209	-368	-22	-587	3	-6	117	-164	173	132	-56	-296
All developing countries	138,964	76,329	45,528	-43,753	2.5	1.3	88,664	104,708	15,257	23,517	73,406	81,191
East Asia & Pacific	62,492	-18,424	37,359	-52,143	3.7	-1.1	36,624	7,271	8,180	13,190	28,444	-5,919
Europe & Central Asia	22,946	39,939	9,491	20,810	2.2	4.0	15,029	27,356	3,514	1,268	11,515	26,089
Latin America & Caribbean	43,085	50,681	8,593	4,347	2.6	2.6	29,782	62,700	-560	6,917	30,342	55,783
Middle East & North Africa	1,552	684	-7,764	-8,238	0.4	0.1	-77	1,488	-1,086	-1,802	1,010	3,290
South Asia	2,481	4,691	-3,673	-2,046	0.5	0.8	4,011	6,318	2,273	2,747	1,738	3,571
Sub-Saharan Africa	6,409	-1,241	1,522	-6,483	2.2	-0.4	3,294	-424	2,937	1,198	358	-1,621
Low income	29,901	-2,758	8,129	-28,573	1.9	-0.2	23,292	7,667	11,803	10,740	11,490	-3,073
Middle income	109,063	79,087	37,400	-15,180	2.7	1.9	65,371	97,042	3,455	12,777	61,917	84,265
Heavily indebted poor countries	4,670	1,922	1,551	-1,729	2.9	1.0	3,853	2,085	3,479	3,123	375	-1,038

Note: Individual country data are shown for Debtor Reporting System countries only. Data for Bosnia and Herzegovina are not shown separately. Totals include estimates for countries not part of the DRS. Data for 1993-97 represent average annual flows. \a Debt service payments to IDA and IMF repurchases and charges include payments from the HIPC Trust Fund, IDA Grants, and IMF Trust Fund, under the HIPC initiative.

NET FLOWS AND TRANSFERS ON DEBT

Net private debt flows fell nearly seventy-five percent in 1998, led by a sharp reversal in short-term debt.

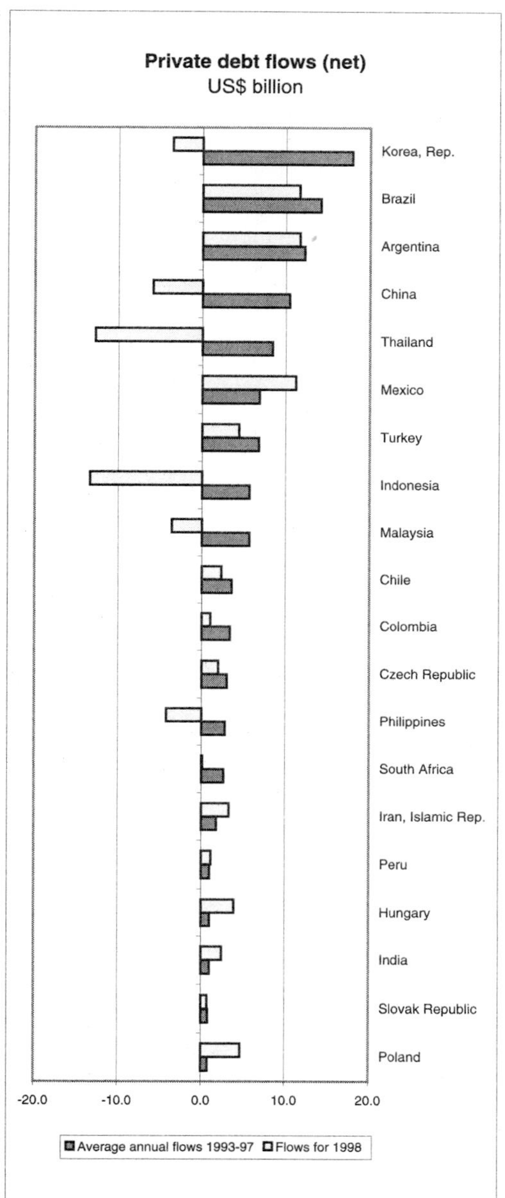

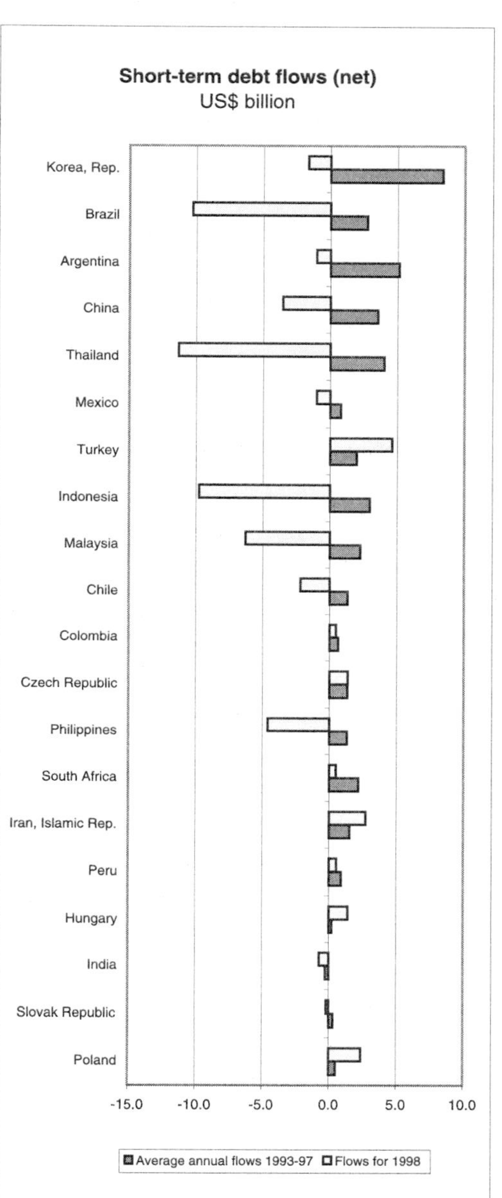

Note: Country selection is based on average annual private debt flows during 1993-97, and shows the largest recipients.

NET FINANCIAL FLOWS FROM MULTILATERAL INSTITUTIONS, 1998*

(US $ millions, unless otherwise indicated)

		Public and publicly guaranteed									
		World Bank		IMF		Reg. Dev. Banks		Others	EBRD	IFC
	Total	IBRD	IDA	conc.	non-conc.	conc.	non-conc.			
Albania	75.4	0.0	62.8	8.0	-1.2	0.0	0.0	5.7	-1.1	1.2
Algeria	89.5	-152.0	0.0	0.0	-91.6	0.0	42.7	291.7	0.0	-1.3
Angola	36.5	0.0	35.8	0.0	0.0	0.0	0.7	0.0	0.0	0.0
Argentina	1,097.7	1,678.4	0.0	0.0	-656.9	-1.9	66.9	0.0	0.0	11.3
Armenia	98.7	-0.2	42.9	51.3	-0.6	0.0	0.0	5.3	0.0	0.0
Azerbaijan	209.7	0.0	20.6	19.8	21.4	0.0	0.0	21.7	60.5	65.7
Bangladesh	526.1	-4.4	290.4	-102.3	134.5	181.4	1.5	25.4	0.0	-0.3
Barbados	36.1	4.5	0.0	0.0	0.0	-1.6	12.1	26.4	0.0	-5.3
Belarus	-10.5	3.6	0.0	0.0	-24.3	0.0	0.0	9.8	0.4	0.0
Belize	16.0	1.3	0.0	0.0	0.0	0.0	0.7	10.9	0.0	3.1
Benin	21.5	0.0	15.6	-5.3	0.0	5.0	0.0	6.5	0.0	-0.3
Bhutan	4.6	0.0	0.5	0.0	0.0	3.8	0.0	0.3	0.0	0.0
Bolivia	52.6	-12.8	81.9	5.0	0.0	85.8	-62.3	-34.8	0.0	-10.3
Botswana	-22.8	-12.9	-0.5	0.0	0.0	2.8	-8.9	-3.3	0.0	-0.1
Brazil	10,465.4	245.0	0.0	0.0	4,617.8	0.0	1,318.3	4,150.0	0.0	134.4
Bulgaria	320.7	176.4	0.0	0.0	127.9	0.0	0.0	5.5	9.0	2.0
Burkina Faso	71.8	0.0	52.5	15.1	0.0	12.0	-1.9	-6.0	0.0	0.0
Burundi	9.1	0.0	18.5	-8.7	0.0	3.8	-4.1	-0.4	0.0	0.0
Cambodia	45.9	0.0	19.2	-1.4	0.0	28.0	0.0	0.1	0.0	0.0
Cameroon	32.3	-65.3	73.7	73.3	-16.3	12.5	-13.6	-25.7	0.0	-6.3
Cape Verde	23.1	0.0	22.5	0.0	0.0	1.9	-0.9	0.0	0.0	-0.4
Central African Republic	-7.8	0.0	-3.4	5.8	-7.6	-0.5	-1.7	-0.3	0.0	0.0
Chad	29.2	0.0	14.7	7.1	-7.0	18.6	0.0	-4.1	0.0	0.0
Chile	-107.8	-34.5	-0.7	0.0	0.0	-1.0	-42.8	0.6	0.0	-29.3
China	2,312.2	1,078.0	553.8	0.0	0.0	0.0	622.0	1.5	0.0	56.9
Colombia	280.8	-47.7	-0.7	0.0	0.0	-12.2	149.8	210.6	0.0	-19.0
Comoros	1.5	0.0	2.8	-0.2	0.0	0.0	0.0	-1.1	0.0	0.0
Congo, Dem. Rep.	-0.7	0.0	0.0	-0.2	-0.5	0.1	0.0	0.0	0.0	0.0
Congo, Rep.	-2.4	-3.3	-0.4	0.0	-0.8	0.0	-3.6	0.0	0.0	5.7
Costa Rica	-8.0	-20.6	-0.2	0.0	0.0	-11.1	9.9	16.9	0.0	-2.8
Cote d'Ivoire	207.8	-139.5	189.7	168.1	0.0	55.5	-38.1	-23.9	0.0	-4.0
Croatia	200.8	91.5	0.0	0.0	-8.9	0.0	0.0	53.3	47.0	17.9
Czech Republic	-122.7	-20.8	0.0	0.0	0.0	0.0	0.0	-130.0	-29.1	57.2
Djibouti	6.2	0.0	1.7	0.0	3.2	1.7	0.0	-0.4	0.0	0.0
Dominica	-0.5	0.4	1.5	-0.2	0.0	0.0	0.0	-2.2	0.0	0.0
Dominican Republic	54.0	-6.3	-0.7	0.0	25.2	11.5	13.9	5.7	0.0	4.7
Ecuador	171.9	5.9	-1.1	0.0	-67.1	-3.8	88.0	154.3	0.0	-4.4
Egypt, Arab Rep.	10.9	-66.9	39.3	0.0	0.0	13.4	-63.1	67.3	0.0	20.9
El Salvador	89.8	6.7	-0.8	0.0	0.0	-7.0	84.5	-10.8	0.0	17.3
Equatorial Guinea	-2.6	0.0	-0.1	-2.9	0.0	0.7	-0.3	0.0	0.0	0.0
Eritrea	31.7	0.0	6.3	0.0	0.0	6.4	0.0	18.6	0.0	0.4
Estonia	49.1	10.3	0.0	0.0	-25.4	0.0	0.0	-0.6	63.8	0.9
Ethiopia	98.1	0.0	51.4	16.2	0.0	27.7	-1.6	4.3	0.0	0.0
Fiji	-5.2	-0.5	0.0	0.0	0.0	0.0	-1.7	-2.9	0.0	-0.1
Gabon	-23.6	-2.7	0.0	0.0	-22.6	0.2	2.5	-1.0	0.0	0.0
Gambia, The	13.3	0.0	1.7	-0.2	0.0	4.4	-1.1	8.7	0.0	-0.2
Georgia	102.7	0.0	52.9	37.7	-0.9	0.0	0.0	6.0	6.7	0.4
Ghana	208.9	-4.1	244.8	6.1	-33.3	13.2	-15.0	1.0	0.0	-3.8
Grenada	-0.1	0.0	0.9	0.0	0.0	0.0	0.0	-1.0	0.0	0.0
Guatemala	159.8	13.8	0.0	0.0	0.0	-1.8	100.0	15.9	0.0	31.9
Guinea	97.7	0.0	61.1	22.6	0.0	17.8	-32.7	27.7	0.0	1.2

NET FINANCIAL FLOWS FROM MULTILATERAL INSTITUTIONS, 1998*

(US $ millions, unless otherwise indicated)

		Public and publicly guaranteed								
		World Bank		IMF		Reg. Dev. Banks		Others	EBRD	IFC
	Total	IBRD	IDA	conc.	non-conc.	conc.	non-conc.			
Guinea-Bissau	14.6	0.0	4.8	2.6	0.0	8.5	-0.4	-0.8	0.0	-0.1
Guyana	8.5	-4.7	8.6	-7.6	-1.8	16.7	-8.7	6.0	0.0	0.0
Haiti	124.2	0.0	34.0	0.0	-5.3	47.1	0.0	-0.5	0.0	0.0
Honduras	97.5	-48.2	62.0	-1.8	64.4	31.6	-0.6	-24.1	0.0	14.3
Hungary	-1,184.8	-802.3	0.0	0.0	-161.1	0.0	0.0	-178.2	-41.4	-1.8
India	657.7	-307.4	578.5	390.2	0.0	0.0	400.5	-14.9	0.0	-88.2
Indonesia	7,119.3	479.1	-21.1	0.0	5,772.2	-1.3	873.9	49.5	0.0	-33.1
Iran, Islamic Rep.	-58.0	-22.0	0.0	0.0	0.0	0.0	0.0	-36.7	0.0	0.0
Jamaica	-45.2	-40.6	0.0	-16.9	0.0	-4.7	22.5	-3.2	0.0	-2.3
Jordan	213.2	-27.4	-2.4	0.0	22.8	0.0	0.0	181.5	0.0	38.7
Kazakhstan	570.0	210.8	0.0	0.0	114.9	20.8	114.5	18.1	56.0	35.0
Kenya	-32.9	-65.9	108.2	-62.5	0.0	7.0	-16.3	-15.2	0.0	11.7
Korea, Rep.	9,725.6	2,875.0	-3.5	0.0	5,155.8	0.0	1,678.3	0.0	0.0	20.0
Kyrgyz Republic	117.4	0.0	65.5	14.6	-11.6	43.3	0.0	9.3	-1.1	-2.5
Lao PDR	85.0	0.0	23.7	-6.4	0.0	61.7	0.0	4.8	0.0	1.2
Latvia	77.6	78.2	0.0	0.0	-24.8	0.0	0.0	16.8	7.8	-0.4
Lebanon	126.8	38.4	0.0	0.0	0.0	0.0	0.0	51.8	0.0	36.6
Lesotho	7.9	-1.1	12.5	0.0	-4.9	3.1	-2.5	0.8	0.0	0.0
Liberia	0.0	0.0	0.0	0.0	0.0	0.0	0.0	0.0	0.0	0.0
Lithuania	86.5	57.1	0.0	0.0	-28.0	0.0	0.0	27.3	30.2	-0.2
Macedonia, FYR	74.1	39.2	28.9	12.3	-2.3	0.0	0.0	-5.3	1.1	0.0
Madagascar	46.7	-1.5	64.5	-13.9	0.0	7.7	-6.5	-2.8	0.0	-0.7
Malawi	118.3	-9.7	119.7	0.7	-8.6	14.6	4.7	-3.2	0.0	0.2
Malaysia	204.0	208.4	0.0	0.0	0.0	0.0	1.0	-5.3	0.0	0.0
Maldives	12.8	0.0	3.6	0.0	0.0	0.2	0.0	9.6	0.0	-0.6
Mali	66.9	0.0	39.0	3.0	0.0	16.7	0.0	3.4	0.0	4.9
Mauritania	9.1	-1.8	21.1	-6.9	0.0	6.3	-5.6	-8.1	0.0	4.0
Mauritius	2.6	-6.1	-0.6	0.0	0.0	-0.4	-2.1	12.2	0.0	-0.4
Mexico	-779.4	25.9	0.0	0.0	-1,063.3	-2.8	290.3	0.0	0.0	-29.6
Moldova	-31.6	25.6	2.3	0.0	-64.0	0.0	0.0	2.3	2.2	0.0
Mongolia	49.4	0.0	16.7	-1.3	0.0	31.9	0.0	2.0	0.0	0.0
Morocco	202.1	-7.6	-1.4	0.0	0.0	4.4	53.5	154.5	0.0	-1.3
Mozambique	206.9	0.0	127.8	9.7	0.0	64.2	-5.8	9.7	0.0	1.3
Myanmar	-24.3	0.0	0.0	0.0	0.0	-19.4	-0.8	-4.1	0.0	0.0
Nepal	154.0	0.0	51.9	-6.6	0.0	87.7	0.0	2.3	0.0	18.7
Nicaragua	208.6	-8.9	103.5	22.8	0.0	95.4	-6.2	0.0	0.0	2.0
Niger	75.9	0.0	42.8	19.8	-7.5	15.7	0.0	5.1	0.0	0.0
Nigeria	-158.7	-226.8	133.8	0.0	0.0	10.0	-60.3	0.0	0.0	-15.4
Oman	-10.0	-4.0	0.0	0.0	0.0	0.0	0.0	-4.1	0.0	-1.9
Pakistan	542.6	-66.8	172.0	51.1	-28.5	236.1	96.0	96.3	0.0	-13.5
Panama	211.2	65.1	0.0	0.0	27.3	-6.5	110.4	1.3	0.0	13.6
Papua New Guinea	-8.7	-15.2	-2.4	0.0	-4.1	2.8	8.5	1.8	0.0	-0.1
Paraguay	71.7	14.7	-1.5	0.0	0.0	16.7	43.1	-1.3	0.0	0.0
Peru	202.0	207.1	0.0	0.0	-145.3	-6.6	170.0	-38.1	0.0	15.0
Philippines	735.3	-94.8	6.5	0.0	651.4	21.3	152.5	0.4	0.0	-2.0
Poland	-13.8	-22.6	0.0	0.0	0.0	0.0	0.0	0.0	13.4	-4.7
Romania	-32.0	84.3	0.0	0.0	-125.2	0.0	0.0	-38.1	0.0	47.1
Russian Federation	6,884.8	1,160.3	0.0	0.0	5,326.8	0.0	0.0	4.1	383.0	10.6
Rwanda	94.6	0.0	61.6	13.8	0.0	14.3	0.0	4.7	0.0	0.3
Samoa	0.7	0.0	2.2	0.0	0.0	-0.9	0.0	-0.6	0.0	0.0
Sao Tome and Principe	4.5	0.0	1.7	-0.2	0.0	3.0	0.0	0.0	0.0	0.0

NET FINANCIAL FLOWS FROM MULTILATERAL INSTITUTIONS, 1998*

(US $ millions, unless otherwise indicated)

		Public and publicly guaranteed							EBRD	IFC
		World Bank		IMF		Reg. Dev. Banks		Others		
	Total	IBRD	IDA	conc.	non-conc.	conc.	non-conc.			
Senegal	71.8	-5.5	73.8	9.1	-21.0	19.0	-15.6	7.3	0.0	4.6
Seychelles	2.0	-0.3	0.0	0.0	0.0	0.2	1.4	0.5	0.0	0.3
Sierra Leone	28.8	-0.8	18.6	0.0	15.7	4.3	0.0	-3.6	0.0	-5.4
Slovak Republic	-4.4	-1.7	0.0	0.0	-67.5	0.0	0.0	88.2	-25.8	2.4
Solomon Islands	14.6	0.0	1.7	0.0	0.0	14.0	0.0	-1.1	0.0	0.0
Somalia	0.0	0.0	0.0	0.0	0.0	0.0	0.0	0.0	0.0	0.0
South Africa	0.4	0.0	0.0	-416.8	0.0	0.0	0.0	0.0	0.0	0.4
Sri Lanka	105.9	-5.8	83.6	-81.9	0.0	105.8	0.0	-0.8	0.0	4.9
St. Kitts and Nevis	6.0	0.1	0.0	0.0	2.2	0.0	0.0	3.7	0.0	0.0
St. Lucia	0.5	1.3	1.2	0.0	0.0	0.0	0.0	-2.0	0.0	0.0
St. Vincent and the Grenadines	8.4	-0.1	0.1	0.0	0.0	0.0	0.0	8.4	0.0	0.0
Sudan	0.0	0.0	0.0	0.0	-57.2	0.0	-1.3	0.0	0.0	0.0
Swaziland	7.8	-0.1	-0.3	0.0	0.0	2.3	5.9	1.0	0.0	-1.1
Syrian Arab Republic	-22.0	-21.6	-1.5	0.0	0.0	0.0	0.0	1.1	0.0	0.0
Tajikistan	122.7	0.0	37.9	54.7	10.2	0.0	0.0	17.4	0.0	2.5
Tanzania	132.7	-12.1	84.7	10.7	0.0	53.4	-2.5	-0.2	0.0	-1.3
Thailand	1,565.2	319.2	-2.3	0.0	678.4	-1.6	493.2	70.3	0.0	8.0
Togo	57.5	0.0	39.3	3.3	0.0	3.6	-0.1	11.4	0.0	0.0
Tonga	4.4	0.0	0.0	0.0	0.0	4.6	0.0	-0.2	0.0	0.0
Trinidad and Tobago	12.4	7.1	0.0	0.0	-4.2	-0.1	12.3	-2.7	0.0	0.0
Tunisia	-109.8	-36.5	-2.1	0.0	-49.7	0.0	-14.4	-6.5	0.0	-0.6
Turkey	-658.2	-365.8	-5.9	0.0	-223.4	0.0	0.0	-142.9	0.0	79.8
Turkmenistan	14.5	2.4	0.0	0.0	0.0	0.0	0.0	15.5	-3.4	0.0
Uganda [a]	126.3	0.0	104.6	-12.2	0.0	47.0	-8.0	-14.7	0.0	9.5
Ukraine	729.7	384.7	0.0	0.0	277.4	0.0	0.0	42.9	24.6	0.0
Uruguay	316.6	65.3	0.0	0.0	154.9	-1.7	99.2	1.2	0.0	-2.3
Uzbekistan	76.0	13.0	0.0	0.0	0.0	0.5	1.4	51.0	6.7	3.4
Vanuatu	11.5	0.0	0.6	0.0	0.0	11.2	0.0	0.0	0.0	-0.3
Venezuela, R.B. de	158.9	8.0	0.0	0.0	-445.7	-1.3	440.3	109.8	0.0	47.8
Vietnam	313.7	0.0	253.1	0.0	-77.9	117.7	0.0	16.7	0.0	4.1
Yemen, Rep.	166.6	0.0	110.7	59.7	12.2	0.0	0.0	-19.8	0.0	3.8
Yugoslavia, FR (Serbia/Montenegro)	0.0	0.0	0.0	0.0	0.0	0.0	0.0	0.0	0.0	0.0
Zambia	7.9	-21.1	39.4	0.0	0.0	11.4	-15.5	-8.0	0.0	1.7
Zimbabwe	26.3	-3.3	28.2	-19.0	23.9	4.6	-17.7	18.3	0.0	-8.8
All developing countries	46,874.1	6,831.8	4,815.7	-25.7	19,258.7	1,708.5	7,193.0	5,457.6	614.2	582.1
East Asia & Pacific	22,148.5	4,849.2	848.2	-9.0	12,175.8	269.9	3,826.8	132.9	0.0	54.7
Europe & Central Asia	7,932.9	1,124.0	442.8	198.4	5,142.5	64.5	116.0	-93.4	614.2	323.9
Latin America & Caribbean	12,913.9	2,126.2	288.0	1.3	2,502.0	241.0	2,912.0	4,600.8	0.0	190.0
Middle East & North Africa	615.1	-299.3	144.3	59.7	-103.0	19.4	18.7	680.3	0.0	94.9
South Asia	2,003.7	-384.4	1,180.5	-530.0	106.0	615.0	588.0	118.0	0.0	-79.1
Sub-Saharan Africa	1,264.0	-583.9	1,911.9	253.9	-564.6	498.6	-268.5	18.9	0.0	-2.3
Low income	7,990.7	587.4	4,310.7	-282.9	-40.4	1,609.4	1,499.0	216.2	60.5	30.8
Middle income	39,532.1	6,244.4	505.0	-54.5	19,297.2	271.2	6,878.3	5,285.4	553.7	551.3
Heavily indebted poor countries	2,678.0	-405.2	2,349.0	345.2	-147.3	852.5	-263.3	-91.2	0.0	38.4

* Data includes only debt flows. \a Debt service payments to IDA and IMF repurchases and charges include payments from the HIPC Trust Fund, IDA Grants, and IMF Trust Fund, under the HIPC initiative.

Note: Loans from major regional developments banks, the IMF, and the World Bank are classified as concessional according to each institutions's classification. Otherwise, concessionality of flows are as defined by DAC. EBRD and IFC data are for loans to the private sector without government guarantees.

NET FINANCIAL FLOWS FROM MULTILATERAL INSTITUTIONS, 1998*

International rescue packages to help countries effected by the financial crises that began in Asia in 1997 and spread more widely in 1998 boosted net flows from multilaterals. However, these increased flows only partially offset the decline in private source financing to low- and middle-income countries.

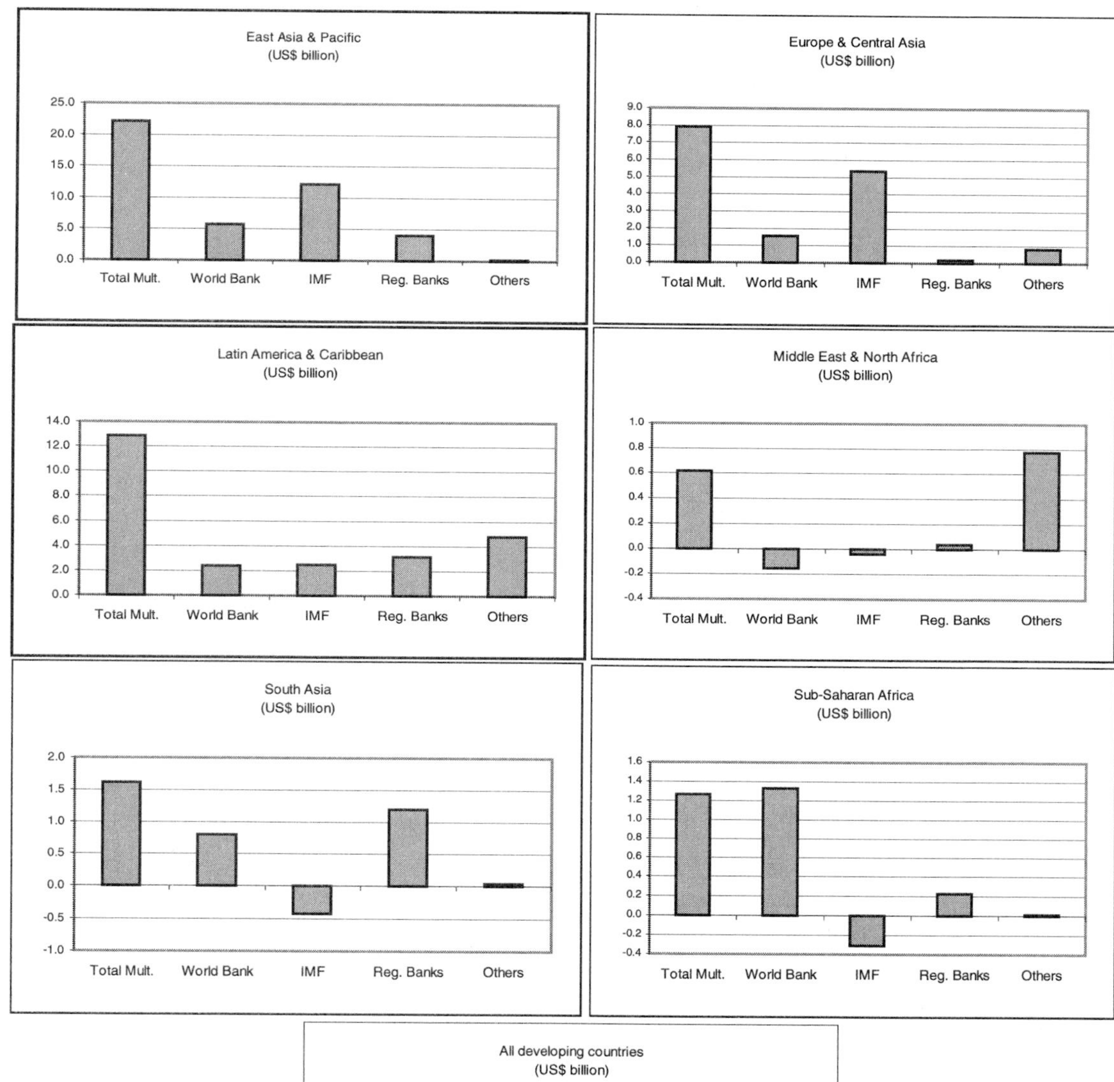

All developing countries
(US$ billion)

50.0
45.0
40.0
35.0
30.0
25.0
20.0
15.0
10.0
5.0
0.0

Total Mult. World Bank IMF Reg. Banks Others

INTERNATIONAL BOND ISSUES AND OUTSTANDINGS

(US $ million, unless otherwise indicated)

	Outstandings						New Issues						Repayments	
	1997			1998			1997			1998				
	PPG Bonds	Brady Bonds	PNG Bonds	PPG Bonds	Brady Bonds	PNG Bonds	Total	PPG Bonds	PNG Bonds	Total	PPG Bonds	PNG Bonds	1997	1998
Albania	225	..	..	225	..	..	..	..	..	..	..	..	..	
Argentina	26,746	20,817	10,311	37,747	17,949	11,873	13,011	9,927	3,084	15,743	11,768	3,976	6,206	6,706
Barbados	63	..	..	40	..	..	..	..	..	..	..	..	4	23
Bolivia	9	..	..	9	..	..	..	..	..	..	..	..	3	
Brazil	16,224	35,512	14,820	16,132	35,672	16,779	10,012	4,262	5,750	6,423	2,935	3,489	8,791	5,014
Bulgaria	94	4,977	..	42	4,977	..	..	..	..	..	..	..	62	57
Chile	0	..	3,764	0	..	4,466	1,050	0	1,050	863	..	863	11	161
China	12,616	..	2,412	13,941	..	1,198	4,623	3,105	1,518	1,794	1,325	469	1,294	207
Colombia	4,366	..	809	6,200	..	821	1,144	1,144	..	2,132	2,132	..	76	380
Congo, Dem. Rep.	4	..	..	4	..	..	..	..	..	..	..	..	..	
Costa Rica	48	556	..	241	548	..	50	50	..	200	200	..	10	16
Cote d'Ivoire	..	2,457	..	0	2,434	..	..	..	..	..	..	..	..	23
Croatia	534	..	..	644	..	..	531	531	..	101	101	..	46	11
Czech Republic	672	..	457	1,376	..	671	264	264	..	837	637	200	59	
Dominican Republic	0	518	..	0	514	..	..	..	..	..	..	..	2	4
Ecuador	0	5,834	..	0	5,825	..	..	..	..	..	..	..	136	10
Estonia	34	..	81	54	..	87	81	..	81	17	17	..	..	
Ghana	..	..	250	..	..	250	..	..	..	..	..	..	..	
Guatemala	337	..	..	307	..	..	150	150	..	..	..	..	44	31
Honduras	62	..	..	..	..	..	..	..	..	..	..	..	30	32
Hungary	10,565	..	..	12,010	..	90	436	436	..	2,334	2,248	85	1,648	1,646
India	1,948	..	3,802	6,002	..	3,647	2,021	650	1,371	4,534	4,234	300	152	413
Indonesia	1,191	..	9,661	1,191	..	9,596	3,428	50	3,378	500	..	500	309	641
Jamaica	278	..	55	528	..	55	200	200	..	250	250	..	..	
Jordan	886	..	..	875	..	..	100	100	..	..	..	..	10	10
Kazakhstan	550	..	..	550	..	100	350	350	..	100	..	100	..	
Korea, Rep.	21,086	..	18,555	24,454	..	20,106	14,456	8,214	6,242	6,396	5,656	739	4,002	5,176
Latvia	..	..	30	..	..	30	30	..	30	..	..	..	33	
Lebanon	1,040	..	885	2,499	..	785	1,119	644	475	1,450	1,450	..	400	100
Lithuania	200	..	..	200	..	..	200	200	..	..	..	..	110	
Malaysia	8,265	..	3,752	8,338	..	3,785	2,590	746	1,844	..	..	..	86	314
Mauritius	150	..	600	150	..	600	600	..	600	..	..	..	..	
Mexico	28,644	23,795	15,810	29,903	24,082	16,546	16,485	12,795	3,690	12,692	7,694	4,998	16,012	10,264
Moldova	75	..	..	75	..	..	75	75	..	..	..	..	..	
Morocco	251	..	..	267	..	..	..	..	..	..	..	..	..	
Nigeria	0	2,051	..	0	2,051	..	..	..	..	..	..	..	..	
Oman	225	..	..	225	..	..	225	225	..	..	..	..	..	
Pakistan	675	..	45	675	..	45	375	375	..	..	..	..	..	
Panama	1,221	2,107	321	1,572	2,027	246	1,446	1,200	246	352	352	..	987	134
Peru	0	4,130	..	0	4,130	150	..	..	..	..	..	..	802	
Philippines	3,999	2,229	5,274	4,188	2,170	5,366	2,659	866	1,793	590	500	90	28	439
Poland	927	6,037	850	2,076	5,289	1,678	1,203	400	803	1,950	1,138	812	..	748
Romania	1,241	..	75	1,343	..	75	422	347	75	..	..	..	..	
Russian Federation	4,585	..	1,905	15,981	..	2,190	5,460	3,555	1,905	11,607	11,329	278	..	69
Slovak Republic	850	..	100	280	..	100	..	..	..	..	..	..	10	570
South Africa	3,631	..	395	3,649	..	786	1,323	1,278	45	373	..	373	253	70
Sri Lanka	50	..	..	115	..	..	50	50	..	65	65	..	..	
Thailand	2,766	..	11,411	3,035	..	10,627	2,319	1,055	1,264	300	300	..	593	932
Trinidad and Tobago	425	..	..	425	..	..	..	..	..	..	..	..	150	
Tunisia	1,112	..	..	1,200	..	..	586	586	..	..	..	..	..	
Turkey	15,075	..	124	14,632	..	794	3,711	3,711	..	2,667	1,997	670	1,736	3,201
Uganda	4	..	..	4	..	..	..	..	..	..	..	..	..	
Ukraine	1,120	..	..	2,318	..	..	..	..	..	1,111	1,111	..	..	35
Uruguay	1,701	730	196	2,033	692	260	571	471	100	794	694	100	122	458
Venezuela, R.B. de	7,371	12,189	319	7,291	11,428	2,694	4,715	4,515	200	2,950	500	2,450	4,888	1,542
Vietnam	..	560	..	..	560	..	..	..	..	..	..	..	..	
Zimbabwe	60	..	..	30	..	..	..	..	..	..	..	..	30	30

INTERNATIONAL BOND ISSUES AND OUTSTANDINGS

(US $ million, unless otherwise indicated)

	Outstandings							New Issues						Repayments	
	1997			1998				1997			1998				
	PPG Bonds	Brady Bonds	PNG Bonds	PPG Bonds	Brady Bonds	PNG Bonds	Total	PPG Bonds	PNG Bonds	Total	PPG Bonds	PNG Bonds		1997	1998
All developing countries	184,199	124,499	107,068	225,077	120,346	116,493	98,070	62,526	35,544	79,123	58,631	20,492		49,133	39,466
East Asia & Pacific	49,923	2,788	51,064	55,147	2,729	50,677	30,075	14,036	16,039	9,580	7,781	1,798		6,312	7,709
Europe & Central Asia	36,747	11,014	3,622	51,807	10,266	5,815	12,762	9,868	2,894	20,723	18,577	2,146		3,703	6,338
Latin America & Caribbean	87,494	106,189	46,404	102,428	102,866	53,889	48,834	34,715	14,120	42,399	26,524	15,875		38,273	24,772
Middle East & North Africa	3,513	0	885	5,067	0	785	2,031	1,556	475	..	1,450	..		410	110
South Asia	2,673	0	3,847	6,792	0	3,692	2,446	1,075	1,371	4,599	4,299	300		152	413
Sub-Saharan Africa	3,849	4,508	1,245	3,837	4,485	1,636	1,923	1,278	645	..	..	373		283	123
Low income	16,635	5,067	16,170	21,922	5,045	14,735	10,523	4,255	6,267	6,828	5,559	1,269		1,815	1,345
Middle income	167,564	119,432	90,898	203,155	115,302	101,758	87,547	58,271	29,276	72,296	53,072	19,223		47,318	38,120
Heavily indebted poor countries	79	3,017	250	17	2,994	250	..	..	..	..	..	..		33	54

Note: PPG bonds exclude Brady bonds. PPG stands for public and publicly guaranteed. PNG stands for private non-guaranteed.

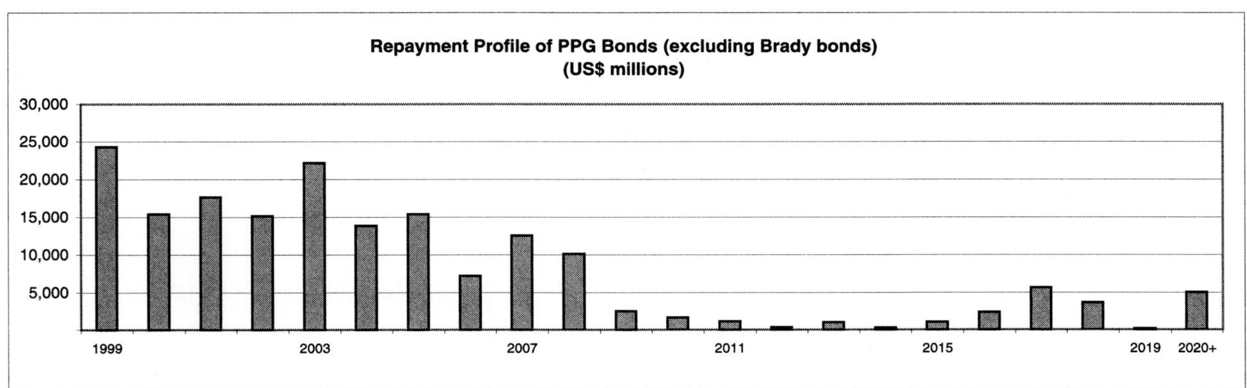

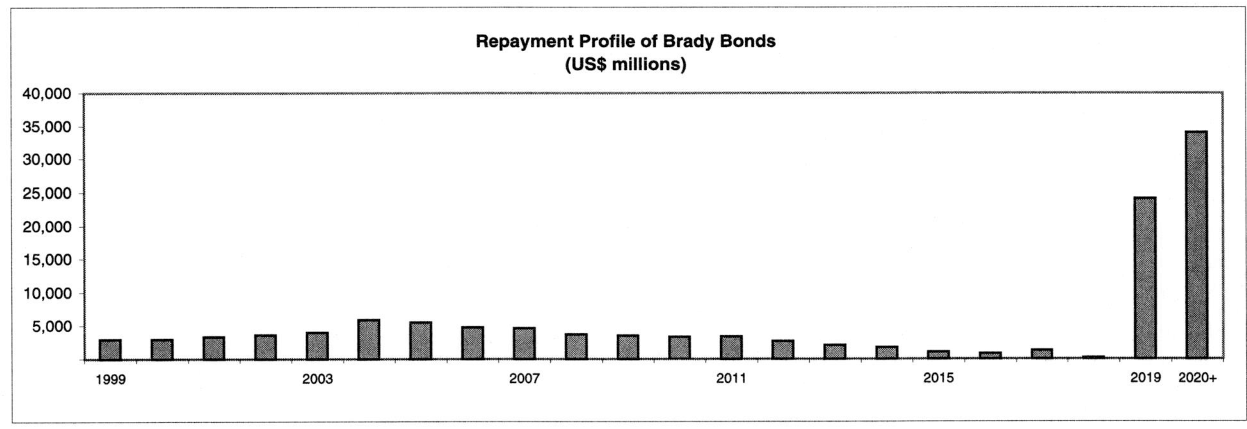

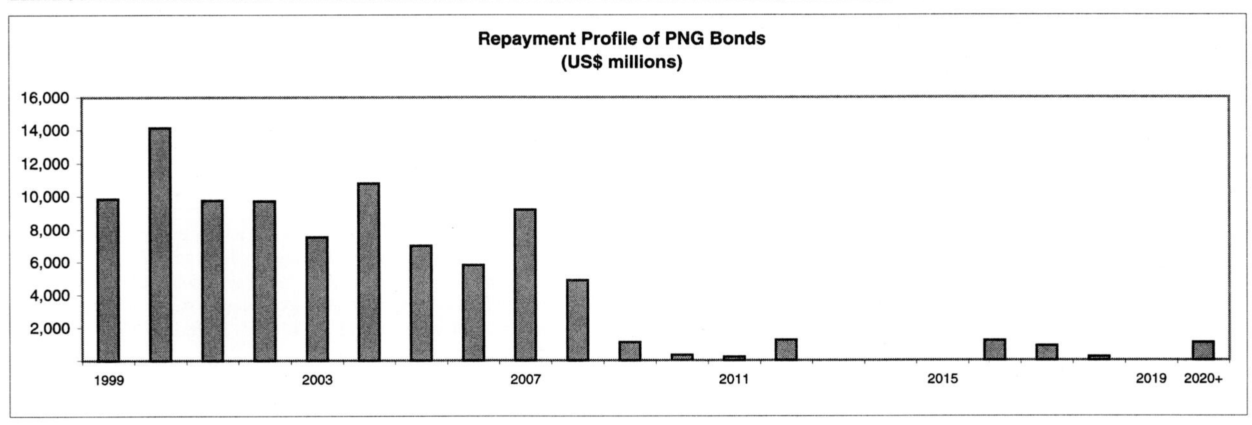

Domestic Debt

Why focus on local-currency debt? Local currency securities in emerging markets have grown rapidly in number of issues and trading volumes over the past five years. The impetus for their growth has come in part from a desire of national authorities to develop money markets, so as to improve instruments of monetary control and as a prelude to deepening bond markets; from fiscal pressures; and from foreign investor demand. The expansion of local currency debt markets, the importance of local currency securities for global investors, and the realization that total liabilities matter—not just external debt—are but some of the reasons for introducing domestic debt in this year's *Global Development Finance*.

The pronounced growth of local currency debt markets represents an important new financing trend in emerging market economies. Much of this debt is central government obligations (the government fixed-income sector is usually the most liquid segment of the local currency debt market), with the remainder largely commercial bank CDs, commercial paper, and other money market instruments. Local currency fixed-income instruments provide opportunities to global investors seeking to invest in emerging markets or diversify their exposure. Through these instruments investors can gain exposure to local interest rate and foreign exchange risk. Typically, yields are attractive to investors and the instruments are of short duration; often the investments are funded through "carry trade", short-term borrowing in a major currency such as U.S. dollars or Japanese yen.

Financial crises in the 1990s have shown that both local currency and foreign currency debt are relevant for country analysis. The composition of debt—currency structure, maturity, and indexation features—matters in analyzing the vulnerability of the fiscal position or balance sheet to shocks. For example, the larger the unhedged foreign currency composition of the debt or the foreign currency-indexed component of debt, the larger will be the cost of servicing the debt in the event of an adverse exchange rate shock. Again, the greater the inflation-indexed component of debt, the larger is the impact of an adverse supply shock (higher cost of borrowing and revaluation of the principal). Also, the shorter the maturity structure of debt, the greater the vulnerability to liquid shocks.

About the data. The data draw on a pilot database on debt securities issued by central governments in domestic or local fixed-income markets. The database includes treasury bills and government notes and bonds denominated in local and foreign currency (the bulk of issues are local currency, however). The stock of government domestic debt is narrowly defined to include only central government direct obligations. It does not include state and local borrowings, central bank debt instruments, or explicit guarantees by the central government. Central government domestic securities outstanding are measured at face or book values rather than current market values. Thus the stock figures represent the amount that would need to be paid at the time the obligations are due. The exceptions are inflation-indexed or exchange rate-indexed securities, whose amounts due will be affected by the movement of the index or rate to which the value of the security is linked. However, the data do not reflect these movements.

The maturity composition of government domestic debt is based on original repayment terms on securities outstanding (see chart on page 31).

The security-level data are collected from both government and market sources. Stocks are converted into a common currency (U.S. dollars) using end-of-period exchange rates. In the table and charts that follow, stocks are converted into U.S. dollars using end-1998 exchange rates.

Government debt outstanding as a percentage of GNP, 1998

	Total debt	Domestic debt
Argentina	37.2	12.3
Brazil	23.6	14.1
China	11.8	8.0
Colombia	17.9	7.2
Czech Rep.	12.2	11.5
Hungary	28.5	25.9
India	30.3	16.0
Korea	10.2	4.9
Mexico	22.2	8.6
Philippines	42.6	13.5
Poland	29.7	8.9
South Africa	44.4	36.5
Thailand	13.7	6.2
Turkey	43.2	27.9
Ukraine	23.4	5.2

Note: Total government debt is the aggregate of domestic and external debt of the central government. Domestic debt comprises securities issued in local fixed-income markets and external debt comprises direct government borrowings—loans and debt securities—issued overseas in foreign currency. It does not include central bank debt, including IMF credits and central bank instruments.

Source: National authorities, Bloomberg, and World Bank Debtor Reporting System.

Domestic Debt

Governments in a number of emerging market economies can now raise substantial funds in their own local markets, generally reflecting markets of increasing depth and financial sophistication. But in many countries, markets still do not afford significant maturity transformation, so average maturities of local borrowing are short term.

Central Government Debt, 1998
US $ billion

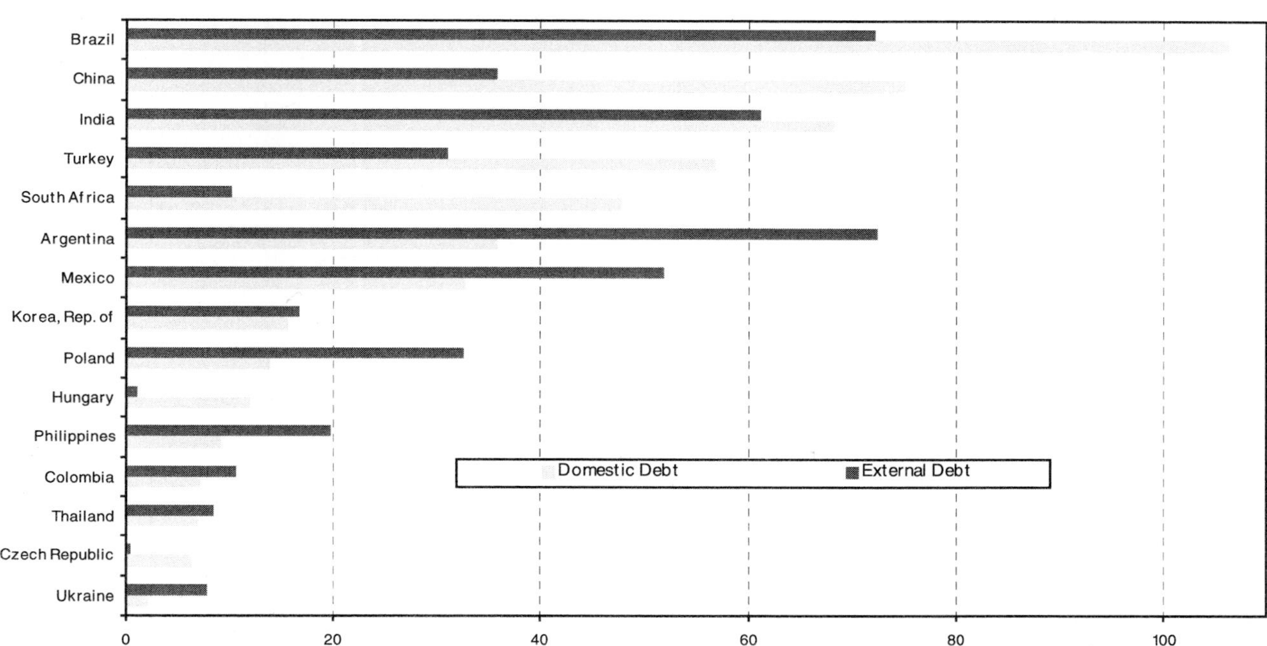

Maturity composition of government debt outstanding, 1998
percent

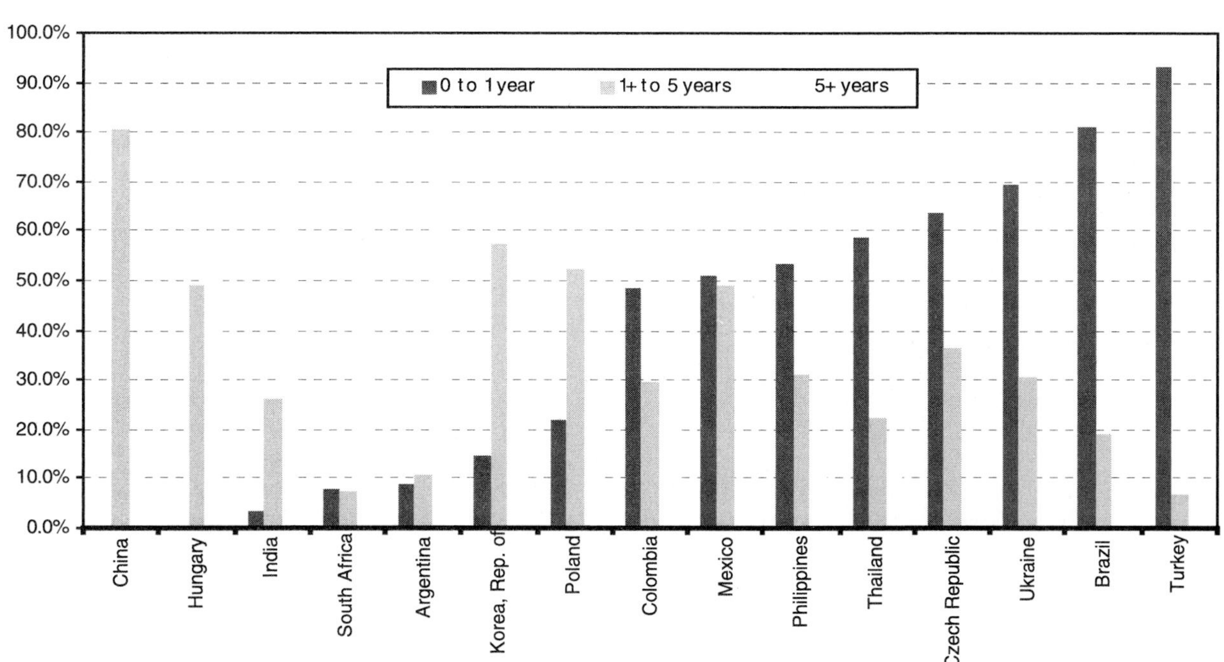

Summary tables

ALL DEVELOPING COUNTRIES

(US$ million, unless otherwise indicated)

	1970	*1980*	*1990*	*1993*	*1994*	*1995*	*1996*	*1997*	*1998*	*1999*
1. SUMMARY DEBT DATA										
TOTAL DEBT STOCKS (EDT)	..	**609,403**	**1,460,343**	**1,777,529**	**1,969,044**	**2,139,456**	**2,229,400**	**2,326,457**	**2,536,046**	**2,553,988**
Long-term debt (LDOD)	**61,145**	**451,524**	**1,181,110**	**1,411,180**	**1,564,437**	**1,653,951**	**1,708,480**	**1,786,391**	**2,030,343**	**2,070,720**
Public and publicly guaranteed	45,768	380,953	1,115,596	1,283,185	1,375,599	1,432,451	1,424,201	1,411,963	1,529,249	1,580,107
Private nonguaranteed	15,377	70,571	65,513	127,995	188,838	221,500	284,279	374,428	501,094	490,613
Use of IMF credit	**756**	**12,246**	**34,652**	**39,885**	**44,144**	**61,101**	**60,106**	**70,797**	**93,839**	**81,002**
Short-term debt	..	**145,633**	**244,581**	**326,463**	**360,462**	**424,404**	**460,814**	**469,269**	**411,865**	**402,266**
of which interest arrears on LDOD	..	2,475	52,700	46,016	43,013	43,644	38,926	30,269	36,193	40,743
Official creditors	..	2,027	19,631	20,302	22,955	25,452	25,193	23,420	27,199	..
Private creditors	..	447	33,068	25,714	20,058	18,191	13,733	6,848	8,994	..
Memo: principal arrears on LDOD	..	2,507	59,560	81,534	92,717	107,988	104,231	79,607	91,841	98,387
Official creditors	..	1,244	27,273	39,278	48,565	59,879	61,506	59,505	65,426	..
Private creditors	..	1,262	32,287	42,256	44,151	48,109	42,725	20,102	26,415	..
Memo: export credits	..	7,728	301,045	352,364	380,327	371,350	359,354	364,271	386,573	..
TOTAL DEBT FLOWS										
Disbursements	**13,251**	**113,657**	**137,218**	**182,235**	**184,810**	**239,674**	**277,505**	**331,584**	**319,972**	**245,979**
Long-term debt	12,920	107,641	128,974	175,234	176,408	211,760	268,847	308,387	290,842	231,054
IMF purchases	331	6,016	8,244	7,001	8,401	27,914	8,659	23,197	29,129	14,925
Principal repayments	**6,742**	**44,473**	**93,720**	**106,760**	**119,598**	**139,416**	**171,342**	**199,621**	**196,031**	**214,094**
Long-term debt	6,000	42,472	85,531	101,423	112,775	128,326	163,715	191,078	186,134	186,332
IMF repurchases	743	2,002	8,189	5,338	6,823	11,090	7,627	8,544	9,896	27,762
Net flows on debt	**15,847**	**111,038**	**60,045**	**112,050**	**113,570**	**167,735**	**149,097**	**152,368**	**76,329**	**20,659**
of which short-term debt	..	41,854	16,548	36,576	48,358	67,477	42,933	20,405	-47,612	-11,226
Interest payments (INT)	..	**48,859**	**70,487**	**68,655**	**78,208**	**100,940**	**106,533**	**112,838**	**120,083**	**135,266**
Long-term debt	2,355	32,790	54,703	52,298	60,765	77,135	80,957	87,074	94,868	111,378
IMF charges	0	471	2,504	2,346	1,807	2,791	2,310	2,207	3,406	4,821
Short-term debt	..	15,597	13,280	14,010	15,636	21,014	23,267	23,557	21,807	19,067
Net transfers on debt	..	**62,179**	**-10,442**	**43,393**	**35,361**	**66,795**	**42,563**	**39,529**	**-43,753**	**-114,607**
Total debt service paid (TDS)	..	**93,331**	**164,208**	**175,416**	**197,807**	**240,356**	**277,877**	**312,460**	**316,113**	**349,360**
Long-term debt	8,353	75,261	140,234	153,723	173,541	205,461	244,672	278,153	281,003	297,710
IMF repurchases and charges	743	2,473	10,694	7,684	8,630	13,881	9,938	10,750	13,303	32,583
Short-term debt (interest only)	..	15,597	13,280	14,010	15,636	21,014	23,267	23,557	21,807	19,067
2. AGGREGATE NET RESOURCE FLOWS AND NET TRANSFERS (LONG-TERM)										
NET RESOURCE FLOWS	**11,074**	**82,692**	**98,529**	**219,169**	**220,356**	**257,172**	**313,143**	**343,726**	**318,325**	**290,699**
Net flow of long-term debt (ex. IMF)	6,921	65,169	43,442	73,810	63,634	83,433	105,133	117,310	104,708	44,722
Foreign direct investment (net)	2,207	4,400	24,130	65,992	88,841	104,989	130,845	170,258	170,942	191,991
Portfolio equity flows	0	0	2,757	51,016	35,161	36,057	49,170	30,191	15,567	27,587
Grants (excluding technical coop.)	1,947	13,123	28,198	28,351	32,720	32,693	27,996	25,968	27,108	26,399
Memo: technical coop. grants	1,754	6,356	14,306	18,200	16,858	20,051	18,637	15,505	16,052	15,875
official net resource flows	5,369	34,854	55,922	53,363	45,912	53,904	31,003	39,833	50,625	51,961
private net resource flows	5,705	47,838	42,606	165,806	174,445	203,268	282,140	303,894	267,700	238,738
NET TRANSFERS	**2,256**	**26,195**	**26,274**	**143,992**	**134,699**	**153,536**	**202,202**	**224,884**	**188,227**	**137,724**
Interest on long-term debt	2,355	32,790	54,703	52,298	60,765	77,135	80,957	87,074	94,868	111,378
Profit remittances on FDI	6,464	23,708	17,553	22,878	24,892	26,503	29,985	31,768	35,230	41,597
Memo: official net transfers	4,503	28,730	35,737	29,586	20,285	23,385	11	11,099	22,604	20,155
private net transfers	-2,247	-2,535	-9,464	114,407	114,413	130,151	202,192	213,785	165,623	117,569
3. MAJOR ECONOMIC AGGREGATES										
Gross national product (GNP)	698,173	3,006,505	4,271,676	4,677,874	4,995,290	5,693,402	6,241,332	6,457,678	6,017,872	6,156,074
Exports of goods & services (XGS)	..	689,112	898,946	1,080,007	1,244,848	1,524,860	1,688,314	1,822,068	1,715,333	1,869,660
of which workers remittances	..	14,359	25,207	34,332	38,084	42,494	48,827	54,614	47,503	49,442
Imports of goods & services (MGS)	..	676,215	928,822	1,217,603	1,343,025	1,647,043	1,815,967	1,938,905	1,801,217	1,833,479
International reserves (RES)	..	212,177	222,924	364,073	428,716	538,198	620,109	649,234	699,746	757,526
Current account balance	..	-6,134	-22,992	-127,044	-90,036	-111,893	-116,373	-109,979	-74,102	-25,800
4. DEBT INDICATORS										
EDT / XGS (%)	..	88.4	162.5	164.6	158.2	140.3	132.1	127.7	147.9	136.6
EDT / GNP (%)	..	20.3	34.2	38.0	39.4	37.6	35.7	36.0	42.1	41.5
TDS / XGS (%)	..	13.5	18.3	16.2	15.9	15.8	16.5	17.2	18.4	18.7
INT / XGS (%)	..	7.1	7.8	6.4	6.3	6.6	6.3	6.2	7.0	7.2
INT / GNP (%)	..	1.6	1.7	1.5	1.6	1.8	1.7	1.8	2.0	2.2
RES / EDT (%)	..	34.8	15.3	20.5	21.8	25.2	27.8	27.9	27.6	29.7
RES / MGS (months)	..	3.8	2.9	3.6	3.8	3.9	4.1	4.0	4.7	5.0
Short-term / EDT (%)	..	23.9	16.8	18.4	18.3	19.8	20.7	20.2	16.2	15.8
Concessional / EDT (%)	..	18.2	21.5	21.1	20.4	19.4	18.2	16.1	14.9	18.6
Multilateral / EDT (%)	..	8.0	14.3	14.0	14.0	13.6	12.9	12.5	12.9	13.5

ALL DEVELOPING COUNTRIES

(US$ million, unless otherwise indicated)

5. LONG-TERM DEBT

	1970	1980	1990	1993	1994	1995	1996	1997	1998	1999
DEBT OUTSTANDING (LDOD)	**61,145**	**451,524**	**1,181,110**	**1,411,180**	**1,564,437**	**1,653,951**	**1,708,480**	**1,786,391**	**2,030,343**	**2,070,720**
Public and publicly guaranteed	**45,768**	**380,953**	**1,115,596**	**1,283,185**	**1,375,599**	**1,432,451**	**1,424,201**	**1,411,963**	**1,529,249**	**1,580,107**
Official creditors	32,258	178,102	605,134	761,027	832,031	864,278	832,237	794,444	852,901	875,471
Multilateral	7,323	48,850	208,245	249,091	275,060	290,759	286,550	289,598	326,307	345,741
Concessional	2,072	18,291	68,877	87,572	99,198	106,844	111,256	113,778	124,076	147,377
Bilateral	24,934	129,251	396,889	511,937	556,971	573,519	545,688	504,845	526,594	529,730
Concessional	21,441	92,315	244,878	287,105	303,332	307,994	294,661	260,417	253,850	328,753
Private creditors	13,510	202,851	510,464	522,158	543,569	568,174	591,963	617,519	676,349	704,636
Bonds	1,804	13,103	107,429	161,518	234,722	257,369	293,379	308,698	345,423	369,934
Commercial banks	3,649	127,483	257,692	221,162	168,869	173,937	174,024	207,868	236,757	235,301
Other private	8,057	62,266	145,342	139,478	139,979	136,868	124,561	100,953	94,169	99,401
Private nonguaranteed	**15,377**	**70,571**	**65,513**	**127,995**	**188,838**	**221,500**	**284,279**	**374,428**	**501,094**	**490,613**
Bonds	0	0	837	31,800	56,874	61,557	85,031	107,068	116,493	116,777
Commercial banks	15,377	70,571	64,677	96,195	131,965	159,943	199,248	267,360	384,601	373,836
Memo:										
IBRD	4,387	22,155	95,573	102,691	110,108	113,869	107,160	106,036	115,927	120,458
IDA	1,832	11,888	45,103	58,310	66,505	71,630	75,219	77,474	84,159	88,919
DISBURSEMENTS	**12,920**	**107,641**	**128,974**	**175,234**	**176,408**	**211,760**	**268,847**	**308,387**	**290,842**	**231,054**
Public and publicly guaranteed	**8,763**	**86,187**	**110,120**	**126,263**	**115,726**	**143,262**	**164,473**	**178,944**	**174,531**	**174,863**
Official creditors	4,922	28,941	53,292	54,023	49,816	66,135	56,535	65,352	67,149	71,026
Multilateral	1,206	9,353	27,798	31,319	29,289	32,269	33,536	40,642	44,773	39,686
Concessional	256	2,878	6,874	7,757	9,167	8,812	9,981	9,186	8,890	9,178
Bilateral	3,718	19,589	25,494	22,704	20,528	33,866	22,999	24,710	22,375	31,340
Concessional	2,948	11,041	15,411	12,338	12,755	14,283	12,222	10,549	13,853	13,013
Private creditors	3,840	57,245	56,828	72,241	65,910	77,127	107,939	113,593	107,382	103,837
Bonds	146	1,698	6,158	26,023	24,143	29,902	58,610	62,526	58,631	56,544
Commercial banks	1,313	34,047	17,993	17,968	17,773	26,614	29,653	32,054	34,766	25,465
Other private	2,381	21,501	32,677	28,250	23,995	20,611	19,676	19,013	13,986	21,828
Private nonguaranteed	**4,158**	**21,454**	**18,854**	**48,971**	**60,682**	**68,497**	**104,373**	**129,443**	**116,312**	**56,191**
Bonds	0	0	701	19,856	24,174	19,124	32,623	35,544	20,492	13,693
Commercial banks	4,158	21,454	18,153	29,115	36,508	49,373	71,750	93,900	95,820	42,498
Memo:										
IBRD	679	4,478	13,587	13,143	11,580	13,237	13,358	17,660	17,560	14,581
IDA	173	1,587	4,378	4,862	6,065	5,474	6,313	5,933	5,558	5,647
PRINCIPAL REPAYMENTS	**6,000**	**42,472**	**85,531**	**101,423**	**112,775**	**128,326**	**163,715**	**191,078**	**186,134**	**186,332**
Public and publicly guaranteed	**3,545**	**30,721**	**76,158**	**75,175**	**83,449**	**97,243**	**120,069**	**128,863**	**112,579**	**119,661**
Official creditors	1,500	7,210	25,568	29,010	36,625	44,924	53,529	51,487	43,631	45,464
Multilateral	385	1,660	12,552	16,448	19,211	21,350	21,059	19,834	18,787	19,734
Concessional	30	104	906	1,257	1,404	1,584	1,759	1,803	1,941	1,916
Bilateral	1,116	5,550	13,017	12,563	17,413	23,576	32,470	31,653	24,844	25,730
Concessional	617	2,518	5,841	5,630	7,010	8,989	8,987	10,383	10,599	7,301
Private creditors	2,045	23,510	50,591	46,165	46,824	52,319	66,540	77,376	68,947	74,197
Bonds	143	514	5,681	8,943	7,167	12,879	21,801	36,783	26,588	31,945
Commercial banks	675	13,762	23,527	17,654	19,167	19,807	27,297	24,533	25,266	25,935
Other private	1,226	9,235	21,383	19,568	20,491	19,632	17,442	16,060	17,094	16,317
Private nonguaranteed	**2,454**	**11,751**	**9,373**	**26,249**	**29,326**	**31,084**	**43,646**	**62,215**	**73,556**	**66,671**
Bonds	0	0	0	289	2,997	5,332	7,034	12,349	12,878	13,249
Commercial banks	2,454	11,751	9,373	25,959	26,330	25,752	36,612	49,865	60,677	53,422
Memo:										
IBRD	248	1,062	8,488	10,383	11,887	12,134	11,998	10,934	10,729	10,053
IDA	0	31	251	398	458	546	593	649	743	856
NET FLOWS ON DEBT	**6,921**	**65,169**	**43,442**	**73,810**	**63,634**	**83,433**	**105,133**	**117,310**	**104,708**	**44,722**
Public and publicly guaranteed	**5,218**	**55,466**	**33,960**	**51,089**	**32,278**	**46,019**	**44,406**	**50,081**	**61,951**	**55,202**
Official creditors	3,422	21,731	27,724	25,013	13,192	21,211	3,007	13,865	23,517	25,562
Multilateral	821	7,693	15,246	14,871	10,078	10,920	12,478	20,808	25,986	19,952
Concessional	226	2,774	5,967	6,500	7,764	7,228	8,222	7,383	6,949	7,262
Bilateral	2,602	14,039	12,477	10,142	3,114	10,291	-9,471	-6,943	-2,468	5,610
Concessional	2,331	8,525	9,570	6,708	5,745	5,295	3,235	167	3,254	5,712
Private creditors	1,795	33,736	6,237	26,076	19,086	24,809	41,399	36,216	38,435	29,640
Bonds	3	1,184	477	17,080	16,976	17,023	36,808	25,743	32,043	24,599
Commercial banks	638	20,286	-5,534	314	-1,395	6,807	2,357	7,521	9,500	-470
Other private	1,154	12,266	11,294	8,681	3,504	979	2,235	2,953	-3,108	5,511
Private nonguaranteed	**1,703**	**9,703**	**9,482**	**22,722**	**31,356**	**37,414**	**60,727**	**67,228**	**42,756**	**-10,480**
Bonds	0	0	701	19,566	21,178	13,792	25,589	23,194	7,615	444
Commercial banks	1,703	9,703	8,781	3,156	10,179	23,621	35,138	44,034	35,142	-10,924
Memo:										
IBRD	431	3,415	5,100	2,759	-306	1,104	1,360	6,727	6,831	4,528
IDA	173	1,556	4,127	4,465	5,607	4,928	5,721	5,284	4,816	4,791

ALL DEVELOPING COUNTRIES

(US$ million, unless otherwise indicated)

	1970	1980	1990	1993	1994	1995	1996	1997	1998	1999
INTEREST PAYMENTS (LINT)	**2,355**	**32,790**	**54,703**	**52,298**	**60,765**	**77,135**	**80,957**	**87,074**	**94,868**	**111,378**
Public and publicly guaranteed	**1,597**	**25,762**	**49,615**	**45,356**	**51,285**	**63,895**	**65,022**	**66,054**	**68,758**	**76,466**
Official creditors	866	6,125	20,185	23,778	25,627	30,519	30,992	28,733	28,020	31,806
Multilateral	308	2,552	10,863	13,000	13,634	14,031	13,790	12,870	13,244	15,425
Concessional	19	167	633	831	925	1,010	1,065	1,090	1,133	1,227
Bilateral	558	3,573	9,323	10,777	11,993	16,488	17,202	15,863	14,777	16,381
Concessional	389	1,836	4,324	5,660	5,714	6,164	6,031	5,564	5,538	5,631
Private creditors	730	19,636	29,430	21,578	25,659	33,376	34,029	37,321	40,738	44,660
Bonds	97	950	4,599	8,524	11,168	16,899	16,783	19,732	22,393	25,012
Commercial banks	252	14,430	17,838	7,657	7,704	9,382	10,662	11,699	13,020	15,297
Other private	381	4,257	6,994	5,397	6,786	7,093	6,585	5,890	5,325	4,351
Private nonguaranteed	**758**	**7,029**	**5,087**	**6,943**	**9,480**	**13,239**	**15,935**	**21,020**	**26,110**	**34,912**
Bonds	0	0	8	1,048	2,923	4,438	5,464	7,431	8,516	9,340
Commercial banks	758	7,029	5,079	5,896	6,558	8,801	10,471	13,589	17,594	25,572
Memo:										
IBRD	243	1,814	7,130	8,004	8,002	8,139	7,807	6,893	7,029	7,885
IDA	12	79	303	395	433	504	512	531	554	597
NET TRANSFERS ON DEBT	**4,566**	**32,380**	**-11,260**	**21,511**	**2,868**	**6,298**	**24,176**	**30,235**	**9,840**	**-66,656**
Public and publicly guaranteed	**3,621**	**29,706**	**-15,654**	**5,732**	**-19,008**	**-17,876**	**-20,616**	**-15,974**	**-6,807**	**-21,264**
Official creditors	2,556	15,606	7,538	1,235	-12,435	-9,308	-27,986	-14,869	-4,503	-6,244
Multilateral	513	5,141	4,385	1,871	-3,556	-3,112	-1,312	7,938	12,742	4,527
Concessional	207	2,607	5,334	5,668	6,839	6,218	7,157	6,293	5,816	6,035
Bilateral	2,044	10,466	3,154	-636	-8,879	-6,197	-26,674	-22,806	-17,246	-10,771
Concessional	1,942	6,688	5,247	1,049	32	-868	-2,797	-5,398	-2,283	81
Private creditors	1,064	14,099	-23,192	4,498	-6,574	-8,567	7,369	-1,105	-2,303	-15,020
Bonds	-95	234	-4,122	8,556	5,807	124	20,026	6,011	9,651	-413
Commercial banks	386	5,856	-23,371	-7,343	-9,099	-2,576	-8,305	-4,179	-3,521	-15,767
Other private	774	8,009	4,300	3,284	-3,282	-6,115	-4,351	-2,938	-8,432	1,160
Private nonguaranteed	**945**	**2,674**	**4,395**	**15,779**	**21,877**	**24,175**	**44,793**	**46,209**	**16,646**	**-45,392**
Bonds	0	0	693	18,519	18,255	9,354	20,126	15,763	-901	-8,896
Commercial banks	945	2,674	3,702	-2,740	3,621	14,821	24,668	30,446	17,548	-36,496
Memo:										
IBRD	188	1,601	-2,031	-5,246	-8,309	-7,036	-6,448	-166	-198	-3,357
IDA	162	1,476	3,825	4,069	5,175	4,425	5,209	4,753	4,262	4,194
DEBT SERVICE (LTDS)	**8,353**	**75,261**	**140,234**	**153,723**	**173,541**	**205,461**	**244,672**	**278,153**	**281,003**	**297,710**
Public and publicly guaranteed	**5,141**	**56,481**	**125,774**	**120,531**	**134,735**	**161,138**	**185,091**	**194,918**	**181,337**	**196,127**
Official creditors	2,366	13,335	45,753	52,788	62,252	75,444	84,522	80,220	71,651	77,270
Multilateral	693	4,212	23,414	29,448	32,845	35,380	34,849	32,704	32,031	35,159
Concessional	49	271	1,540	2,089	2,328	2,594	2,825	2,893	3,073	3,143
Bilateral	1,674	9,123	22,340	23,340	29,406	40,063	49,673	47,516	39,621	42,111
Concessional	1,006	4,353	10,165	11,291	12,723	15,152	15,019	15,948	16,136	12,932
Private creditors	2,776	43,147	80,021	67,743	72,484	85,695	100,570	114,697	109,685	118,857
Bonds	241	1,463	10,280	17,467	18,336	29,779	38,584	56,515	48,980	56,957
Commercial banks	927	28,191	41,365	25,311	26,871	29,190	37,959	36,232	38,286	41,232
Other private	1,608	13,492	28,377	24,965	27,276	26,726	24,027	21,951	22,418	20,668
Private nonguaranteed	**3,212**	**18,780**	**14,460**	**33,192**	**38,806**	**44,323**	**59,581**	**83,234**	**99,665**	**101,583**
Bonds	0	0	8	1,337	5,919	9,770	12,497	19,781	21,394	22,589
Commercial banks	3,212	18,780	14,452	31,855	32,887	34,553	47,083	63,454	78,272	78,994
Memo:										
IBRD	491	2,877	15,619	18,389	19,889	20,273	19,806	17,826	17,757	17,938
IDA	12	110	553	792	891	1,050	1,105	1,180	1,296	1,453
UNDISBURSED DEBT	**17,055**	**141,726**	**215,433**	**253,245**	**256,887**	**258,895**	**245,187**	**231,506**	**237,009**	**..**
Official creditors	13,195	90,987	162,768	190,129	200,371	204,133	189,985	180,588	186,431	..
Private creditors	3,859	50,739	52,665	63,117	56,516	54,762	55,202	50,918	50,578	..
Memorandum items										
Concessional LDOD	23,514	110,606	313,755	374,676	402,529	414,838	405,916	374,195	377,925	476,130
Variable rate LDOD	16,160	191,475	441,999	549,985	628,346	688,670	741,553	846,341	1,005,313	..
Public sector LDOD	43,501	340,613	1,049,845	1,209,457	1,304,373	1,360,452	1,350,951	1,337,582	1,371,406	..
Private sector LDOD	17,648	84,369	74,201	136,572	194,350	227,464	291,157	377,184	577,793	..
6. CURRENCY COMPOSITION OF LONG-TERM DEBT (PERCENT)										
Deutsche mark	8.6	6.6	8.6	7.7	7.8	8.2	8.3	7.5	7.7	..
French franc	5.2	5.5	5.7	4.5	4.5	4.7	4.4	3.7	3.6	..
Japanese yen	2.3	6.9	10.5	12.1	12.9	12.6	11.6	10.4	10.8	..
Pound sterling	11.2	3.4	2.3	1.6	1.5	1.3	1.4	1.4	1.3	..
Swiss franc	1.1	1.6	1.9	1.2	1.0	1.0	0.8	0.6	0.5	..
U.S.dollars	47.1	49.8	41.2	44.5	44.4	44.9	47.3	52.4	51.7	..
Multiple currency	11.6	10.9	14.7	14.5	14.5	14.2	13.4	12.0	8.3	..
Special drawing rights	0.0	0.0	0.2	0.2	0.3	0.3	0.3	0.3	0.3	..
All other currencies	13.0	8.4	9.9	8.7	8.4	8.3	8.0	6.8	7.4	..

ALL DEVELOPING COUNTRIES

(US$ million, unless otherwise indicated)

	1970	1980	1990	1993	1994	1995	1996	1997	1998	1999
7. DEBT RESTRUCTURINGS										
Total amount rescheduled	117	3,325	79,335	64,371	91,324	31,838	32,412	48,808	38,633	..
Debt stock rescheduled	0	1	61,910	23,796	54,025	6,897	6,896	1,607	31,613	..
Principal rescheduled	0	393	10,307	18,003	15,677	15,295	15,971	35,357	6,339	..
Official	0	137	5,829	6,789	4,475	6,914	6,379	6,846	4,407	..
Private	0	257	4,478	11,214	11,202	8,382	9,592	28,511	1,933	..
Interest rescheduled	..	..	5,844	16,010	16,600	5,221	7,314	9,040	1,583	..
Official	0	38	4,617	3,784	3,332	2,270	2,065	2,461	1,200	..
Private	0	33	1,227	12,225	13,268	2,951	5,250	6,579	382	..
Debt forgiven	10	269	12,620	2,494	7,705	2,297	5,967	3,364	680	..
Memo: interest forgiven	0	0	2,889	306	698	1,001	1,871	625	608	..
Debt stock reduction	0	0	25,196	6,602	13,266	4,224	9,892	18,817	3,050	..
of which debt buyback	0	0	4,360	542	1,709	162	3,665	10,050	2,117	..
8. DEBT STOCK-FLOW RECONCILIATION										
Total change in debt stocks	..	..	104,506	156,014	191,516	170,413	89,944	97,058	209,591	..
Net flows on debt	15,847	111,038	60,045	112,050	113,570	167,735	149,097	152,368	76,329	20,659
Net change in interest arrears	..	..	15,539	-1,271	-3,003	631	-4,718	-8,656	5,923	..
Interest capitalized	..	..	5,844	16,010	16,600	5,221	7,314	9,040	1,583	..
Debt forgiveness or reduction	..	..	-33,457	-8,554	-19,262	-6,359	-12,194	-12,131	-1,613	..
Cross-currency valuation	..	..	52,278	975	54,953	11,260	-49,878	-55,587	41,511	..
Residual	..	..	4,255	36,805	28,656	-8,074	324	12,024	85,857	..
9. AVERAGE TERMS OF NEW COMMITMENTS										
ALL CREDITORS										
Interest (%)	5.0	9.2	7.0	5.6	5.6	6.1	6.4	6.6	6.8	..
Maturity (years)	20.9	15.8	18.1	14.6	15.7	13.6	12.9	13.8	12.6	..
Grace period (years)	6.4	4.8	5.6	4.9	5.2	4.6	5.4	6.5	5.9	..
Grant element (%)	29.6	7.0	18.3	22.3	24.4	20.2	17.2	17.0	16.7	..
Official creditors										
Interest (%)	3.6	5.5	5.5	4.8	4.9	5.8	4.8	5.4	5.2	..
Maturity (years)	28.2	24.0	22.2	21.4	22.1	19.2	21.2	20.1	18.5	..
Grace period (years)	9.0	6.3	6.6	6.1	6.3	5.4	6.0	5.7	5.3	..
Grant element (%)	41.1	28.2	29.4	32.5	33.3	26.9	31.8	27.9	30.5	..
Private creditors										
Interest (%)	7.2	12.0	8.5	6.3	6.3	6.4	7.3	7.3	7.9	..
Maturity (years)	9.8	9.8	13.9	9.4	8.9	7.4	8.3	10.0	8.8	..
Grace period (years)	2.6	3.7	4.5	4.0	4.0	3.9	5.1	7.0	6.4	..
Grant element (%)	12.0	-8.5	6.5	14.2	14.8	13.0	9.2	10.3	7.7	..
Memorandum items										
Commitments	11,958	98,279	124,356	143,189	119,600	153,069	171,836	182,474	174,224	..
Official creditors	7,213	41,519	63,903	62,918	61,628	79,787	60,874	69,263	69,247	..
Private creditors	4,745	56,759	60,454	80,270	57,971	73,282	110,962	113,212	104,977	..

10. GRAPH OF AGGREGATE NET RESOURCE FLOWS

(current prices, US$ million)

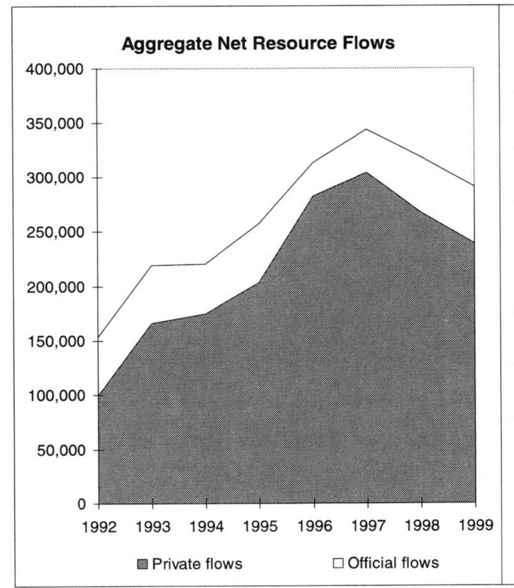

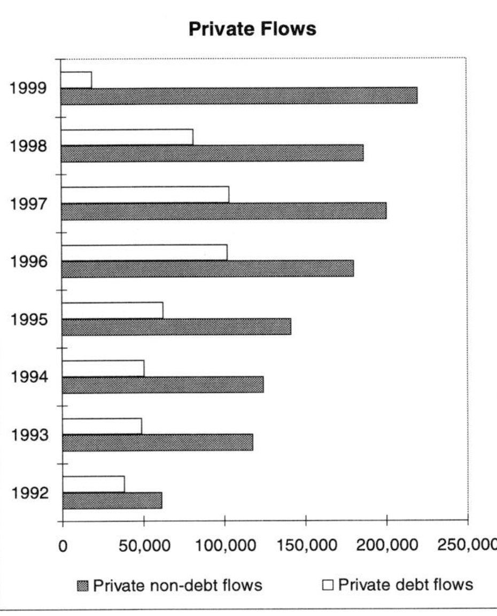

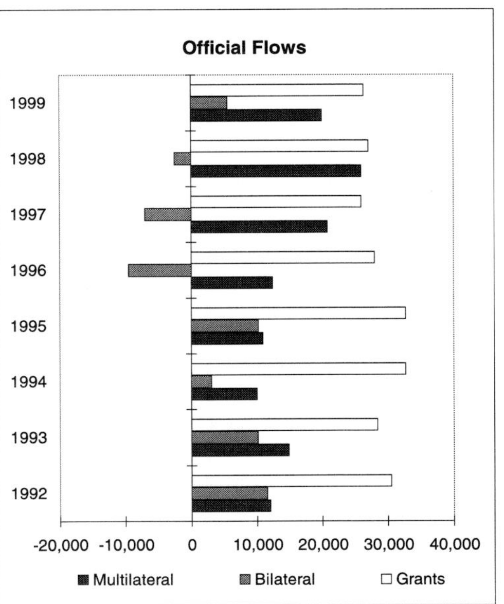

EAST ASIA AND PACIFIC

(US$ million, unless otherwise indicated)

	1970	1980	1990	1993	1994	1995	1996	1997	1998	1999
1. SUMMARY DEBT DATA										
TOTAL DEBT STOCKS (EDT)	..	94,080	274,071	383,106	463,076	530,546	591,348	648,931	667,522	659,389
Long-term debt (LDOD)	7,987	66,674	222,811	297,212	347,379	375,527	403,845	447,245	517,051	530,541
Public and publicly guaranteed	5,808	55,620	195,775	247,459	267,168	283,719	287,186	304,499	337,690	364,954
Private nonguaranteed	2,179	11,054	27,035	49,753	80,212	91,809	116,659	142,746	179,361	165,587
Use of IMF credit	224	2,234	2,085	1,430	1,494	1,337	1,175	17,997	31,407	22,772
Short-term debt	..	25,172	49,176	84,465	114,203	153,682	186,328	183,689	119,064	106,076
of which interest arrears on LDOD	..	2	1,889	2,325	2,702	2,869	3,116	1,792	2,031	2,030
Official creditors	..	1	1,139	1,776	2,140	2,292	2,551	1,733	1,970	..
Private creditors	..	1	751	549	562	577	565	59	61	..
Memo: principal arrears on LDOD	..	5	2,965	6,835	9,229	10,877	12,579	9,551	15,076	15,077
Official creditors	..	1	1,790	6,272	8,626	10,149	11,858	9,305	10,305	..
Private creditors	..	4	1,175	563	604	729	721	246	4,771	..
Memo: export credits	..	330	35,572	52,066	68,011	75,124	74,882	85,558	93,229	..
TOTAL DEBT FLOWS										
Disbursements	2,058	17,400	35,514	54,322	64,261	72,728	92,592	114,695	70,472	65,384
Long-term debt	1,993	16,251	35,455	54,014	63,985	72,525	92,397	97,189	55,353	62,827
IMF purchases	66	1,149	58	308	275	203	195	17,506	15,118	2,557
Principal repayments	834	5,857	24,516	33,715	34,380	38,169	46,754	45,446	51,034	67,801
Long-term debt	816	5,619	23,230	33,521	34,079	37,779	46,439	45,170	48,083	56,609
IMF repurchases	18	238	1,286	194	301	390	314	276	2,951	11,192
Net flows on debt	3,072	18,320	20,041	33,174	59,242	73,872	78,238	67,934	-18,424	-15,404
of which short-term debt	..	6,777	9,044	12,567	29,361	39,312	32,399	-1,315	-37,862	-12,987
Interest payments (INT)	..	7,677	15,251	17,610	20,132	26,819	29,031	32,071	33,719	35,683
Long-term debt	238	4,636	11,938	13,834	15,503	18,650	19,347	22,221	24,583	28,411
IMF charges	0	77	245	127	72	69	41	51	1,265	2,208
Short-term debt	..	2,964	3,068	3,649	4,556	8,100	9,644	9,799	7,870	5,064
Net transfers on debt	..	10,643	4,790	15,563	39,110	47,053	49,206	35,863	-52,143	-51,087
Total debt service paid (TDS)	..	13,534	39,767	51,326	54,512	64,988	75,785	77,517	84,752	103,484
Long-term debt	1,053	10,256	35,168	47,356	49,583	56,428	65,786	67,391	72,666	85,020
IMF repurchases and charges	18	314	1,531	321	373	459	355	327	4,216	13,400
Short-term debt (interest only)	..	2,964	3,068	3,649	4,556	8,100	9,644	9,799	7,870	5,064
2. AGGREGATE NET RESOURCE FLOWS AND NET TRANSFERS (LONG-TERM)										
NET RESOURCE FLOWS	2,148	13,102	27,026	82,353	90,398	108,095	126,254	127,685	82,838	89,216
Net flow of long-term debt (ex. IMF)	1,177	10,632	12,225	20,493	29,906	34,747	45,958	52,019	7,271	6,218
Foreign direct investment (net)	267	1,318	11,135	39,124	45,149	52,003	59,878	64,137	64,162	61,532
Portfolio equity flows	0	0	1,571	20,648	12,613	18,274	18,089	9,193	9,007	18,966
Grants (excluding technical coop.)	703	1,152	2,095	2,088	2,729	3,072	2,329	2,337	2,398	2,500
Memo: technical coop. grants	402	1,045	2,558	3,219	3,130	3,441	3,230	2,819	2,860	2,700
official net resource flows	1,317	4,186	8,306	10,086	7,771	11,782	5,578	18,241	15,589	15,269
private net resource flows	831	8,916	18,720	72,267	82,627	96,313	120,677	109,444	67,249	73,947
NET TRANSFERS	1,557	3,493	9,978	61,351	66,975	80,277	96,367	94,354	46,344	46,600
Interest on long-term debt	238	4,636	11,938	13,834	15,503	18,650	19,347	22,221	24,583	28,411
Profit remittances on FDI	354	4,973	5,110	7,168	7,919	9,168	10,541	11,111	11,911	14,205
Memo: official net transfers	1,241	3,107	4,004	4,275	1,430	4,978	-621	12,048	8,744	7,497
private net transfers	316	386	5,973	57,075	65,546	75,300	96,988	82,306	37,600	39,103
3. MAJOR ECONOMIC AGGREGATES										
Gross national product (GNP)	133,684	443,994	919,508	1,213,245	1,444,044	1,757,971	1,974,312	1,971,227	1,662,278	1,892,543
Exports of goods & services (XGS)	..	..	252,826	365,024	450,976	568,587	625,604	691,257	636,185	698,665
of which workers remittances	..	310	1,116	1,143	1,587	1,780	3,272	6,389	1,318	856
Imports of goods & services (MGS)	..	..	261,293	396,330	473,031	612,339	679,185	693,599	548,493	645,593
International reserves (RES)	..	..	86,264	121,246	162,785	200,582	247,433	245,307	297,969	342,978
Current account balance	..	..	-5,610	-26,287	-17,103	-39,670	-49,953	1,467	87,134	61,053
4. DEBT INDICATORS										
EDT / XGS (%)	..	..	108.4	105.0	102.7	93.3	94.5	93.9	104.9	94.4
EDT / GNP (%)	..	21.2	29.8	31.6	32.1	30.2	30.0	32.9	40.2	34.8
TDS / XGS (%)	..	..	15.7	14.1	12.1	11.4	12.1	11.2	13.3	14.8
INT / XGS (%)	..	..	6.0	4.8	4.5	4.7	4.6	4.6	5.3	5.1
INT / GNP (%)	..	1.7	1.7	1.5	1.4	1.5	1.5	1.6	2.0	1.9
RES / EDT (%)	..	..	31.5	31.7	35.2	37.8	41.8	37.8	44.6	52.0
RES / MGS (months)	..	..	4.0	3.7	4.1	3.9	4.4	4.2	6.5	6.4
Short-term / EDT (%)	..	26.8	17.9	22.1	24.7	29.0	31.5	28.3	17.8	16.1
Concessional / EDT (%)	..	18.4	28.1	24.4	21.7	19.4	16.8	12.0	13.7	27.9
Multilateral / EDT (%)	..	8.3	14.2	12.3	11.4	10.6	9.1	9.0	10.7	11.7

EAST ASIA AND PACIFIC

(US$ million, unless otherwise indicated)

	1970	1980	1990	1993	1994	1995	1996	1997	1998	1999
5. LONG-TERM DEBT										
DEBT OUTSTANDING (LDOD)	**7,987**	**66,674**	**222,811**	**297,212**	**347,379**	**375,527**	**403,845**	**447,245**	**517,051**	**530,541**
Public and publicly guaranteed	**5,808**	**55,620**	**195,775**	**247,459**	**267,168**	**283,719**	**287,186**	**304,499**	**337,690**	**364,954**
Official creditors	3,719	27,349	117,606	150,801	163,387	170,492	162,774	160,007	182,553	199,059
Multilateral	497	7,818	38,789	47,278	52,808	56,464	53,812	58,366	71,197	77,244
Concessional	36	1,308	7,453	10,645	12,289	13,523	14,323	14,803	16,751	34,327
Bilateral	3,221	19,531	78,817	103,523	110,579	114,028	108,962	101,641	111,356	121,815
Concessional	2,803	16,002	69,464	82,817	88,222	89,173	84,734	63,233	74,390	149,812
Private creditors	2,090	28,271	78,169	96,658	103,781	113,227	124,412	144,492	155,138	165,895
Bonds	125	1,946	14,377	25,073	29,035	34,443	42,562	52,711	57,876	65,472
Commercial banks	329	13,889	38,073	39,713	40,688	44,311	43,646	54,814	69,937	67,473
Other private	1,636	12,437	25,719	31,873	34,059	34,473	38,203	36,966	27,325	32,950
Private nonguaranteed	**2,179**	**11,054**	**27,035**	**49,753**	**80,212**	**91,809**	**116,659**	**142,746**	**179,361**	**165,587**
Bonds	0	0	650	8,648	25,227	26,074	39,709	51,064	50,677	48,599
Commercial banks	2,179	11,054	26,386	41,105	54,985	65,734	76,950	91,682	128,684	116,988
Memo:										
IBRD	444	4,952	23,416	26,267	28,397	30,075	28,079	29,699	35,490	38,185
IDA	33	961	5,228	7,571	8,767	9,774	10,545	10,983	12,203	12,814
DISBURSEMENTS	**1,993**	**16,251**	**35,455**	**54,014**	**63,985**	**72,525**	**92,397**	**97,189**	**55,353**	**62,827**
Public and publicly guaranteed	**1,197**	**12,789**	**24,085**	**39,620**	**36,740**	**43,184**	**46,293**	**60,251**	**42,683**	**53,066**
Official creditors	699	3,958	11,701	15,021	13,874	17,869	14,064	25,468	21,576	22,050
Multilateral	81	1,575	4,944	6,135	6,242	6,284	6,427	12,222	12,897	8,712
Concessional	8	151	1,027	1,244	1,177	1,336	1,536	1,448	1,311	1,348
Bilateral	619	2,383	6,757	8,887	7,632	11,585	7,638	13,246	8,679	13,338
Concessional	546	1,380	5,892	4,598	5,312	6,052	5,446	4,313	7,061	7,072
Private creditors	498	8,831	12,384	24,599	22,866	25,315	32,229	34,783	21,108	31,016
Bonds	0	280	1,834	7,668	8,290	8,903	13,901	14,036	7,781	11,177
Commercial banks	114	4,288	4,680	8,611	6,136	9,230	9,040	10,613	8,863	9,030
Other private	384	4,263	5,870	8,320	8,440	7,182	9,289	10,134	4,463	10,809
Private nonguaranteed	**796**	**3,462**	**11,370**	**14,394**	**27,246**	**29,342**	**46,104**	**36,938**	**12,670**	**9,761**
Bonds	0	0	530	4,419	13,729	10,721	18,428	16,039	1,798	2,640
Commercial banks	796	3,462	10,840	9,975	13,517	18,621	27,676	20,899	10,872	7,121
Memo:										
IBRD	64	1,047	2,677	3,451	3,444	3,312	3,095	6,465	6,964	4,892
IDA	5	92	604	922	904	934	1,135	1,013	920	705
PRINCIPAL REPAYMENTS	**816**	**5,619**	**23,230**	**33,521**	**34,079**	**37,779**	**46,439**	**45,170**	**48,083**	**56,609**
Public and publicly guaranteed	**425**	**3,674**	**18,572**	**24,173**	**22,742**	**24,643**	**30,092**	**25,745**	**21,491**	**33,075**
Official creditors	86	924	5,490	7,024	8,832	9,159	10,816	9,564	8,386	9,281
Multilateral	22	268	2,684	3,290	4,284	3,601	5,100	3,783	2,950	3,251
Concessional	0	7	80	132	147	132	142	137	142	188
Bilateral	64	656	2,806	3,735	4,548	5,558	5,716	5,781	5,436	6,030
Concessional	38	340	1,491	2,162	2,795	3,352	3,708	3,209	3,772	2,675
Private creditors	339	2,750	13,082	17,150	13,909	15,485	19,276	16,181	13,105	23,794
Bonds	32	41	3,148	3,534	2,384	2,759	4,030	2,678	2,775	4,872
Commercial banks	40	795	6,014	7,628	5,763	6,253	10,320	8,802	6,706	13,002
Other private	268	1,913	3,921	5,988	5,763	6,472	4,926	4,701	3,624	5,920
Private nonguaranteed	**391**	**1,945**	**4,658**	**9,348**	**11,338**	**13,135**	**16,347**	**19,426**	**26,592**	**23,534**
Bonds	0	0	0	0	1,000	1,410	2,176	3,634	4,934	4,718
Commercial banks	391	1,945	4,658	9,348	10,338	11,725	14,171	15,792	21,658	18,816
Memo:										
IBRD	22	184	2,009	2,208	3,137	2,612	2,957	2,617	2,114	2,199
IDA	0	2	21	35	47	54	61	64	72	94
NET FLOWS ON DEBT	**1,177**	**10,632**	**12,225**	**20,493**	**29,906**	**34,747**	**45,958**	**52,019**	**7,271**	**6,218**
Public and publicly guaranteed	**772**	**9,115**	**5,513**	**15,447**	**13,998**	**18,540**	**16,201**	**34,506**	**21,193**	**19,991**
Official creditors	614	3,034	6,211	7,997	5,042	8,710	3,249	15,904	13,190	12,769
Multilateral	59	1,307	2,260	2,845	1,958	2,683	1,327	8,439	9,947	5,461
Concessional	8	144	947	1,112	1,030	1,204	1,395	1,312	1,170	1,160
Bilateral	555	1,727	3,951	5,152	3,084	6,026	1,921	7,466	3,243	7,308
Concessional	508	1,040	4,401	2,436	2,517	2,700	1,737	1,104	3,289	4,397
Private creditors	158	6,081	-698	7,449	8,956	9,830	12,953	18,602	8,003	7,222
Bonds	-32	238	-1,314	4,134	5,906	6,143	9,871	11,358	5,006	6,305
Commercial banks	74	3,493	-1,333	983	372	2,977	-1,281	1,811	2,157	-3,972
Other private	116	2,350	1,950	2,332	2,677	710	4,363	5,433	839	4,889
Private nonguaranteed	**405**	**1,517**	**6,712**	**5,046**	**15,908**	**16,206**	**29,757**	**17,512**	**-13,922**	**-13,773**
Bonds	0	0	530	4,419	12,729	9,311	16,252	12,405	-3,136	-2,078
Commercial banks	405	1,517	6,182	627	3,179	6,896	13,505	5,107	-10,786	-11,695
Memo:										
IBRD	42	862	668	1,243	307	700	138	3,847	4,849	2,693
IDA	5	89	583	888	857	880	1,073	949	848	611

EAST ASIA AND PACIFIC

(US$ million, unless otherwise indicated)

	1970	1980	1990	1993	1994	1995	1996	1997	1998	1999
INTEREST PAYMENTS (LINT)	**238**	**4,636**	**11,938**	**13,834**	**15,503**	**18,650**	**19,347**	**22,221**	**24,583**	**28,411**
Public and publicly guaranteed	**164**	**3,417**	**10,141**	**10,997**	**11,735**	**13,519**	**13,165**	**14,309**	**15,488**	**17,119**
Official creditors	76	1,079	4,302	5,810	6,341	6,804	6,199	6,194	6,845	7,772
Multilateral	26	548	2,450	2,871	3,089	3,271	3,024	2,781	3,288	4,005
Concessional	0	12	64	100	111	126	132	129	127	146
Bilateral	50	531	1,852	2,940	3,253	3,533	3,175	3,412	3,557	3,767
Concessional	40	295	1,217	1,943	2,018	2,191	1,899	1,762	1,604	1,887
Private creditors	88	2,338	5,840	5,187	5,394	6,716	6,966	8,115	8,644	9,347
Bonds	9	103	1,108	1,274	1,270	1,724	1,948	3,029	3,550	3,898
Commercial banks	12	1,340	3,017	2,132	1,992	2,759	2,811	2,753	3,079	3,928
Other private	67	895	1,715	1,781	2,132	2,233	2,208	2,334	2,015	1,521
Private nonguaranteed	**73**	**1,219**	**1,797**	**2,837**	**3,768**	**5,130**	**6,182**	**7,911**	**9,095**	**11,292**
Bonds	0	0	6	188	912	1,770	2,347	3,395	3,584	3,557
Commercial banks	73	1,219	1,791	2,650	2,857	3,360	3,834	4,517	5,511	7,735
Memo:										
IBRD	25	406	1,783	1,945	2,075	2,168	2,033	1,866	2,142	2,466
IDA	0	7	35	49	60	70	73	76	77	86
NET TRANSFERS ON DEBT	**939**	**5,996**	**287**	**6,658**	**14,403**	**16,097**	**26,611**	**29,798**	**-17,312**	**-22,193**
Public and publicly guaranteed	**608**	**5,698**	**-4,628**	**4,450**	**2,263**	**5,021**	**3,036**	**20,197**	**5,705**	**2,872**
Official creditors	538	1,955	1,910	2,187	-1,300	1,906	-2,951	9,711	6,346	4,997
Multilateral	33	759	-190	-26	-1,131	-588	-1,697	5,657	6,659	1,456
Concessional	8	132	883	1,013	920	1,078	1,263	1,183	1,042	1,014
Bilateral	505	1,196	2,099	2,213	-169	2,494	-1,254	4,053	-314	3,541
Concessional	468	746	3,184	493	499	509	-162	-658	1,685	2,510
Private creditors	70	3,743	-6,537	2,263	3,562	3,115	5,987	10,486	-641	-2,125
Bonds	-41	135	-2,422	2,861	4,636	4,419	7,923	8,329	1,457	2,407
Commercial banks	61	2,153	-4,350	-1,148	-1,620	218	-4,091	-941	-921	-7,900
Other private	50	1,454	234	551	546	-1,522	2,155	3,099	-1,177	3,368
Private nonguaranteed	**332**	**298**	**4,915**	**2,209**	**12,140**	**11,076**	**23,575**	**9,601**	**-23,017**	**-25,065**
Bonds	0	0	524	4,232	11,817	7,541	13,905	9,010	-6,720	-5,635
Commercial banks	332	298	4,391	-2,023	323	3,536	9,670	590	-16,297	-19,430
Memo:										
IBRD	17	457	-1,115	-702	-1,768	-1,469	-1,895	1,982	2,707	227
IDA	5	82	548	839	797	811	1,000	873	771	525
DEBT SERVICE (LTDS)	**1,053**	**10,256**	**35,168**	**47,356**	**49,583**	**56,428**	**65,786**	**67,391**	**72,666**	**85,020**
Public and publicly guaranteed	**589**	**7,091**	**28,713**	**35,171**	**34,477**	**38,163**	**43,257**	**40,054**	**36,979**	**50,194**
Official creditors	162	2,003	9,791	12,834	15,174	15,963	17,015	15,757	15,230	17,053
Multilateral	48	816	5,134	6,161	7,372	6,872	8,124	6,564	6,237	7,256
Concessional	0	20	144	232	257	257	274	265	269	334
Bilateral	114	1,187	4,658	6,674	7,801	9,091	8,891	9,193	8,993	9,797
Concessional	78	634	2,708	4,105	4,812	5,543	5,608	4,971	5,376	4,562
Private creditors	427	5,088	18,922	22,336	19,303	22,200	26,243	24,296	21,749	33,141
Bonds	41	144	4,256	4,808	3,654	4,484	5,978	5,707	6,325	8,770
Commercial banks	52	2,135	9,031	9,759	7,755	9,012	13,131	11,554	9,784	16,930
Other private	334	2,809	5,636	7,769	7,894	8,704	7,134	7,035	5,640	7,441
Private nonguaranteed	**464**	**3,165**	**6,455**	**12,185**	**15,106**	**18,266**	**22,529**	**27,337**	**35,687**	**34,826**
Bonds	0	0	6	188	1,912	3,180	4,523	7,029	8,518	8,275
Commercial banks	464	3,165	6,449	11,997	13,194	15,085	18,006	20,309	27,169	26,551
Memo:										
IBRD	46	590	3,792	4,153	5,212	4,780	4,990	4,483	4,256	4,665
IDA	0	9	56	84	107	124	135	140	149	180
UNDISBURSED DEBT	**2,096**	**29,817**	**46,995**	**59,731**	**65,473**	**70,833**	**68,445**	**67,280**	**67,790**	..
Official creditors	1,481	21,001	34,874	44,249	51,181	54,916	52,162	53,038	61,320	..
Private creditors	615	8,815	12,121	15,482	14,293	15,917	16,282	14,242	6,470	..
Memorandum items										
Concessional LDOD	2,839	17,310	76,918	93,462	100,511	102,695	99,056	78,037	91,141	184,139
Variable rate LDOD	2,205	25,278	82,156	107,962	143,740	162,280	187,797	235,213	294,674	..
Public sector LDOD	4,788	46,077	188,759	236,289	258,638	274,602	277,110	296,226	261,576	..
Private sector LDOD	3,199	17,240	30,137	54,078	82,238	94,386	120,103	144,160	247,999	..

6. CURRENCY COMPOSITION OF LONG-TERM DEBT (PERCENT)

	1970	1980	1990	1993	1994	1995	1996	1997	1998	1999
Deutsche mark	7.1	5.0	3.7	2.4	2.8	2.8	2.5	2.3	2.4	..
French franc	2.6	3.2	2.3	1.6	1.6	1.6	1.5	1.2	1.8	..
Japanese yen	7.3	18.0	28.8	29.1	30.3	28.4	24.9	21.7	23.4	..
Pound sterling	4.7	1.7	0.9	0.6	0.5	0.4	0.5	0.7	0.6	..
Swiss franc	0.8	1.0	0.9	0.6	0.6	0.5	0.4	0.3	0.2	..
U.S.dollars	50.4	40.8	24.0	32.1	31.9	36.0	41.9	51.5	40.7	..
Multiple currency	8.0	16.6	22.0	19.4	18.9	18.0	16.3	13.3	7.3	..
Special drawing rights	0.0	0.0	0.1	0.1	0.1	0.1	0.1	0.1	0.2	..
All other currencies	19.1	7.6	15.3	11.4	10.7	9.9	9.8	6.8	6.0	..

EAST ASIA AND PACIFIC

(US$ million, unless otherwise indicated)

	1970	1980	1990	1993	1994	1995	1996	1997	1998	1999
7. DEBT RESTRUCTURINGS										
Total amount rescheduled	0	0	1,478	934	0	329	179	747	25,283	..
Debt stock rescheduled	0	0	0	69	0	0	0	0	27,002	..
Principal rescheduled	0	0	848	531	0	170	115	410	496	..
Official	0	0	172	272	0	156	115	15	307	..
Private	0	0	676	259	0	14	0	395	189	..
Interest rescheduled	..	..	186	204	0	104	4	305	5	..
Official	0	0	107	112	0	104	4	2	5	..
Private	0	0	80	92	0	0	0	303	0	..
Debt forgiven	0	45	0	30	0	44	9	1	6	..
Memo: interest forgiven	0	0	0	20	0	7	0	0	0	..
Debt stock reduction	0	0	1,803	0	0	0	0	249	0	..
of which debt buyback	0	0	721	0	0	0	0	31	0	..
8. DEBT STOCK-FLOW RECONCILIATION										
Total change in debt stocks	..	..	32,848	38,561	79,970	67,470	60,802	57,583	18,592	..
Net flows on debt	3,072	18,320	20,041	33,174	59,242	73,872	78,238	67,934	-18,424	-15,404
Net change in interest arrears	..	..	521	-96	378	167	247	-1,324	239	..
Interest capitalized	..	..	186	204	0	104	4	305	5	..
Debt forgiveness or reduction	..	..	-1,082	-30	0	-44	-9	-219	-6	..
Cross-currency valuation	..	..	10,426	7,931	15,246	-909	-14,673	-15,017	15,184	..
Residual	..	..	2,755	-2,621	5,105	-5,720	-3,004	5,903	21,595	..
9. AVERAGE TERMS OF NEW COMMITMENTS										
ALL CREDITORS										
Interest (%)	5.0	9.7	6.7	5.3	5.3	5.7	5.9	6.0	5.9	..
Maturity (years)	22.9	16.2	19.1	15.3	16.5	14.7	14.3	12.7	14.0	..
Grace period (years)	6.3	4.8	5.4	4.6	5.6	5.1	5.6	5.2	5.1	..
Grant element (%)	35.4	6.6	22.6	25.3	27.7	23.8	22.0	20.1	23.1	..
Official creditors										
Interest (%)	4.1	6.0	5.0	4.8	4.8	5.3	4.7	5.8	4.8	..
Maturity (years)	28.5	22.7	24.5	21.6	22.7	21.9	23.6	18.8	19.0	..
Grace period (years)	7.4	6.8	7.1	5.9	6.3	5.6	6.2	5.7	5.6	..
Grant element (%)	45.6	29.1	37.5	36.1	36.8	32.5	38.3	26.8	32.1	..
Private creditors										
Interest (%)	6.8	13.0	8.4	5.6	5.7	6.0	6.5	6.2	7.4	..
Maturity (years)	12.2	10.3	13.6	11.1	11.3	8.7	10.0	7.8	7.0	..
Grace period (years)	4.4	2.9	3.6	3.8	4.9	4.7	5.2	4.7	4.4	..
Grant element (%)	15.8	-13.8	7.3	18.2	20.1	16.5	14.6	14.7	10.5	..
Memorandum items										
Commitments	1,729	19,472	26,928	50,029	42,160	51,553	49,302	59,384	40,916	..
Official creditors	1,138	9,239	13,644	19,736	19,316	23,360	15,441	26,428	23,755	..
Private creditors	591	10,232	13,284	30,293	22,845	28,193	33,861	32,957	17,161	..

10. GRAPH OF AGGREGATE NET RESOURCE FLOWS

(current prices, US$ million)

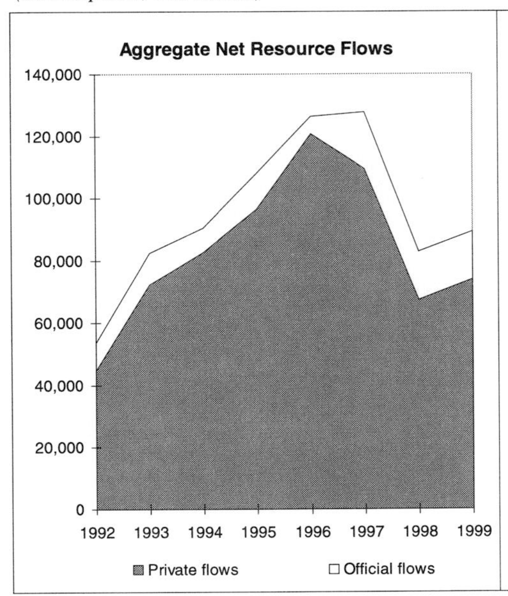

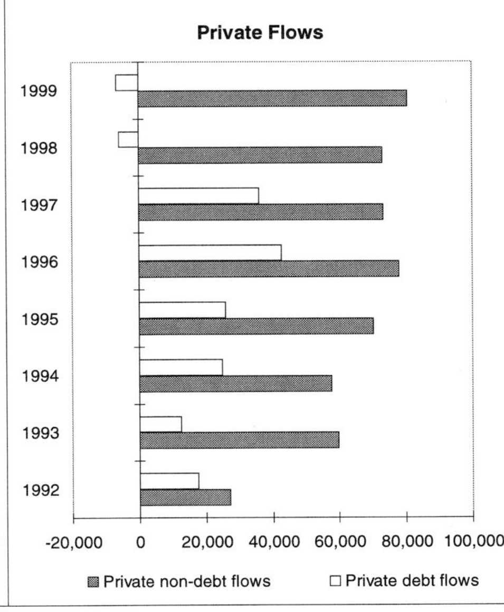

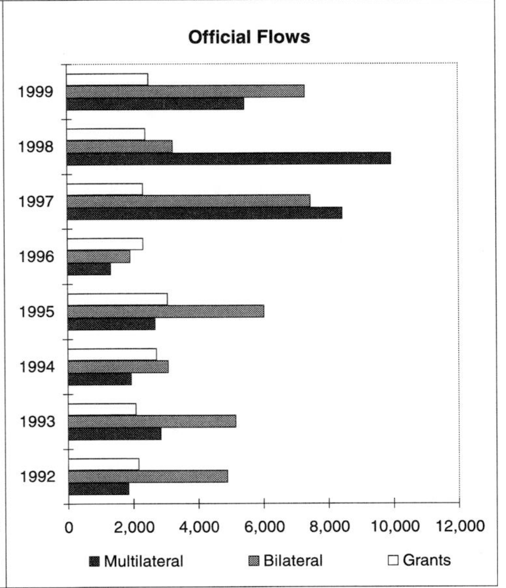

EUROPE AND CENTRAL ASIA

(US$ million, unless otherwise indicated)

	1970	1980	1990	1993	1994	1995	1996	1997	1998	1999
1. SUMMARY DEBT DATA										
TOTAL DEBT STOCKS (EDT)	..	**75,394**	**220,428**	**308,939**	**326,029**	**352,457**	**369,566**	**390,507**	**480,539**	**485,916**
Long-term debt (LDOD)	**3,965**	**56,196**	**178,266**	**258,196**	**277,201**	**289,905**	**296,342**	**311,176**	**374,244**	**382,773**
Public and publicly guaranteed	3,069	44,656	173,345	246,092	262,578	270,877	268,976	269,127	293,468	296,571
Private nonguaranteed	896	11,540	4,921	12,103	14,624	19,028	27,366	42,050	80,775	86,202
Use of IMF credit	**74**	**2,143**	**1,305**	**8,449**	**11,725**	**16,942**	**20,052**	**21,195**	**27,661**	**24,523**
Short-term debt	..	**17,055**	**40,857**	**42,294**	**37,103**	**45,610**	**53,172**	**58,136**	**78,635**	**78,620**
of which interest arrears on LDOD	..	312	13,041	7,057	7,079	8,345	9,832	5,320	7,666	12,029
Official creditors	..	13	6,573	1,065	1,872	2,328	2,542	2,657	4,155	..
Private creditors	..	299	6,468	5,992	5,207	6,018	7,290	2,663	3,511	..
Memo: principal arrears on LDOD	..	56	6,326	16,386	20,670	30,493	32,828	14,463	15,257	20,256
Official creditors	..	21	4,584	2,644	4,439	8,204	8,188	8,312	8,557	..
Private creditors	..	35	1,742	13,743	16,231	22,289	24,640	6,151	6,701	..
Memo: export credits	..	10	66,608	85,217	84,532	88,987	88,389	83,272	92,902	..
TOTAL DEBT FLOWS										
Disbursements	**1,082**	**21,007**	**30,164**	**30,893**	**26,193**	**36,046**	**45,267**	**54,037**	**66,444**	**39,566**
Long-term debt	1,007	19,768	29,417	28,605	21,607	27,892	40,050	50,665	59,037	36,716
IMF purchases	75	1,238	748	2,288	4,586	8,154	5,217	3,372	7,407	2,850
Principal repayments	**584**	**7,131**	**19,817**	**11,989**	**18,686**	**22,822**	**23,293**	**24,511**	**33,747**	**29,252**
Long-term debt	512	6,802	19,085	11,770	16,794	19,774	21,773	23,566	31,681	23,264
IMF repurchases	72	329	732	219	1,893	3,047	1,520	945	2,066	5,988
Net flows on debt	**1,486**	**22,062**	**3,223**	**23,916**	**2,493**	**21,267**	**28,050**	**39,002**	**39,939**	**8,858**
of which short-term debt	..	8,186	-7,125	5,012	-5,013	8,042	6,076	9,475	7,242	-1,456
Interest payments (INT)	..	**5,396**	**12,333**	**8,979**	**10,075**	**14,570**	**16,049**	**17,599**	**19,129**	**24,487**
Long-term debt	148	3,409	9,650	7,065	8,066	11,950	12,979	14,176	15,238	19,301
IMF charges	0	103	128	416	500	711	783	909	1,059	1,381
Short-term debt	..	1,884	2,555	1,498	1,510	1,909	2,288	2,514	2,832	3,805
Net transfers on debt	..	**16,666**	**-9,110**	**14,936**	**-7,582**	**6,697**	**12,001**	**21,403**	**20,810**	**-15,629**
Total debt service paid (TDS)	..	**12,527**	**32,149**	**20,969**	**28,762**	**37,391**	**39,342**	**42,110**	**52,876**	**53,739**
Long-term debt	660	10,211	28,735	18,835	24,860	31,724	34,752	37,742	46,919	42,565
IMF repurchases and charges	72	432	860	636	2,392	3,758	2,302	1,854	3,124	7,369
Short-term debt (interest only)	..	1,884	2,555	1,498	1,510	1,909	2,288	2,514	2,832	3,805
2. AGGREGATE NET RESOURCE FLOWS AND NET TRANSFERS (LONG-TERM)										
NET RESOURCE FLOWS	**608**	**13,277**	**12,591**	**32,281**	**22,710**	**36,914**	**48,454**	**59,849**	**59,562**	**45,063**
Net flow of long-term debt (ex. IMF)	495	12,966	10,332	16,836	4,814	8,118	18,277	27,099	27,356	13,452
Foreign direct investment (net)	58	28	1,051	6,335	7,014	16,885	15,825	22,838	24,350	24,020
Portfolio equity flows	0	0	185	984	2,200	2,729	8,345	4,808	2,904	2,841
Grants (excluding technical coop.)	56	283	1,023	8,126	8,682	9,183	6,007	5,105	4,953	4,750
Memo: technical coop. grants	47	156	415	2,803	2,781	4,653	4,082	2,804	4,204	3,500
official net resource flows	346	3,405	4,942	11,693	11,813	10,706	11,244	9,217	6,220	6,939
private net resource flows	262	9,872	7,649	20,587	10,897	26,208	37,210	50,633	53,342	38,124
NET TRANSFERS	**426**	**9,837**	**2,723**	**24,427**	**13,785**	**24,046**	**34,241**	**44,232**	**42,563**	**23,466**
Interest on long-term debt	148	3,409	9,650	7,065	8,066	11,950	12,979	14,176	15,238	19,301
Profit remittances on FDI	34	31	218	788	858	918	1,235	1,441	1,761	2,296
Memo: official net transfers	272	2,636	2,704	9,133	8,953	5,931	5,961	3,437	1,528	1,957
private net transfers	154	7,201	18	15,294	4,832	18,116	28,279	40,796	41,035	21,509
3. MAJOR ECONOMIC AGGREGATES										
Gross national product (GNP)	..	..	1,187,761	987,671	861,162	971,626	1,100,870	1,125,495	988,917	1,152,533
Exports of goods & services (XGS)	..	..	..	209,427	242,082	306,456	343,232	364,968	359,206	363,478
of which workers remittances	..	..	..	..	..	4,974	5,495	5,950	7,411	7,568
Imports of goods & services (MGS)	..	..	..	238,234	245,507	322,180	369,644	401,506	396,269	364,256
International reserves (RES)	..	..	..	40,388	47,968	89,944	93,350	99,524	103,066	107,921
Current account balance	..	..	..	-17,319	4,605	-5,238	-15,131	-24,588	-24,278	-15,337
4. DEBT INDICATORS										
EDT / XGS (%)	..	..	..	147.5	134.7	115.0	107.7	107.0	133.8	133.7
EDT / GNP (%)	..	..	18.6	31.3	37.9	36.3	33.6	34.7	48.6	42.2
TDS / XGS (%)	..	..	..	10.0	11.9	12.2	11.5	11.5	14.7	14.8
INT / XGS (%)	..	..	..	4.3	4.2	4.8	4.7	4.8	5.3	6.7
INT / GNP (%)	..	..	1.0	0.9	1.2	1.5	1.5	1.6	1.9	2.1
RES / EDT (%)	..	..	..	13.1	14.7	25.5	25.3	25.5	21.5	22.2
RES / MGS (months)	..	..	..	2.0	2.3	3.4	3.0	3.0	3.1	3.6
Short-term / EDT (%)	..	22.6	18.5	13.7	11.4	12.9	14.4	14.9	16.4	16.2
Concessional / EDT (%)	..	9.0	5.7	7.7	7.2	7.2	6.8	5.6	5.0	5.0
Multilateral / EDT (%)	..	5.8	7.6	6.8	7.3	7.5	7.3	7.4	6.6	7.0

EUROPE AND CENTRAL ASIA

(US$ million, unless otherwise indicated)

	1970	1980	1990	1993	1994	1995	1996	1997	1998	1999
5. LONG-TERM DEBT										
DEBT OUTSTANDING (LDOD)	**3,965**	**56,196**	**178,266**	**258,196**	**277,201**	**289,905**	**296,342**	**311,176**	**374,244**	**382,773**
Public and publicly guaranteed	**3,069**	**44,656**	**173,345**	**246,092**	**262,578**	**270,877**	**268,976**	**269,127**	**293,468**	**296,571**
Official creditors	2,647	18,377	64,506	126,380	138,795	139,113	140,343	135,049	143,639	142,391
Multilateral	635	4,363	16,728	20,851	23,632	26,315	26,942	29,029	31,748	34,152
Concessional	113	242	920	1,249	1,406	1,815	2,018	2,326	2,900	3,582
Bilateral	2,013	14,015	47,779	105,530	115,163	112,798	113,402	106,020	111,891	108,239
Concessional	1,739	6,516	11,731	22,499	22,045	23,714	23,016	19,532	21,187	20,698
Private creditors	422	26,279	108,839	119,712	123,782	131,764	128,633	134,078	149,830	154,180
Bonds	41	200	11,902	25,107	42,948	46,942	45,898	47,761	62,073	67,969
Commercial banks	10	16,727	66,609	57,067	44,727	48,900	51,661	68,109	70,925	69,824
Other private	371	9,352	30,328	37,538	36,108	35,923	31,075	18,209	16,832	16,387
Private nonguaranteed	**896**	**11,540**	**4,921**	**12,103**	**14,624**	**19,028**	**27,366**	**42,050**	**80,775**	**86,202**
Bonds	0	0	16	50	149	188	851	3,622	5,815	8,741
Commercial banks	896	11,540	4,905	12,053	14,474	18,840	26,515	38,428	74,961	77,461
Memo:										
IBRD	297	3,323	10,272	11,764	14,078	16,057	16,798	19,187	20,952	22,319
IDA	83	189	157	192	310	669	1,117	1,483	1,991	2,482
DISBURSEMENTS	**1,007**	**19,768**	**29,417**	**28,605**	**21,607**	**27,892**	**40,050**	**50,665**	**59,037**	**36,716**
Public and publicly guaranteed	**540**	**16,470**	**27,656**	**23,884**	**17,778**	**21,294**	**28,366**	**30,977**	**37,346**	**27,419**
Official creditors	480	4,768	7,063	6,471	6,410	6,538	11,055	9,272	8,846	8,591
Multilateral	163	1,023	2,380	4,308	3,660	4,409	5,212	6,549	5,363	5,190
Concessional	7	10	14	158	174	439	525	597	581	724
Bilateral	317	3,745	4,683	2,163	2,750	2,130	5,843	2,723	3,482	3,401
Concessional	271	1,642	941	675	880	1,073	1,133	933	1,225	798
Private creditors	61	11,702	20,593	17,414	11,368	14,756	17,311	21,706	28,500	18,828
Bonds	0	80	1,959	8,531	4,152	5,791	6,376	9,868	18,577	11,319
Commercial banks	0	5,064	4,350	2,538	3,091	5,222	7,477	8,592	6,911	4,723
Other private	61	6,559	14,284	6,344	4,125	3,743	3,457	3,247	3,012	2,786
Private nonguaranteed	**466**	**3,298**	**1,761**	**4,721**	**3,830**	**6,598**	**11,684**	**19,688**	**21,691**	**9,297**
Bonds	0	0	0	0	99	36	671	2,894	2,146	2,927
Commercial banks	466	3,298	1,761	4,721	3,730	6,562	11,013	16,794	19,546	6,370
Memo:										
IBRD	55	833	1,218	1,709	2,619	2,696	3,326	4,677	3,357	2,624
IDA	7	0	0	49	117	370	477	433	449	497
PRINCIPAL REPAYMENTS	**512**	**6,802**	**19,085**	**11,770**	**16,794**	**19,774**	**21,773**	**23,566**	**31,681**	**23,264**
Public and publicly guaranteed	**305**	**4,761**	**17,588**	**10,528**	**14,326**	**16,879**	**18,243**	**17,231**	**24,478**	**19,394**
Official creditors	189	1,646	3,144	2,903	3,279	5,015	5,819	5,160	7,578	6,402
Multilateral	81	154	1,455	1,832	2,072	3,033	3,060	2,435	3,709	2,519
Concessional	23	2	23	27	46	66	197	140	131	11
Bilateral	108	1,492	1,690	1,071	1,207	1,982	2,759	2,725	3,868	3,883
Concessional	47	477	433	545	493	524	522	690	836	709
Private creditors	116	3,115	14,443	7,625	11,046	11,864	12,424	12,071	16,900	12,992
Bonds	2	15	66	722	1,564	3,791	4,647	3,618	6,338	6,402
Commercial banks	2	1,367	8,785	4,235	5,970	4,306	4,737	5,601	6,679	3,827
Other private	112	1,733	5,593	2,669	3,512	3,767	3,040	2,852	3,883	2,763
Private nonguaranteed	**208**	**2,041**	**1,497**	**1,242**	**2,468**	**2,895**	**3,530**	**6,335**	**7,203**	**3,870**
Bonds	0	0	0	16	0	0	0	86	0	0
Commercial banks	208	2,041	1,497	1,226	2,468	2,895	3,530	6,250	7,203	3,870
Memo:										
IBRD	13	133	1,133	943	1,129	1,191	1,605	1,187	2,233	1,258
IDA	0	1	4	6	6	6	6	6	6	6
NET FLOWS ON DEBT	**495**	**12,966**	**10,332**	**16,836**	**4,814**	**8,118**	**18,277**	**27,099**	**27,356**	**13,452**
Public and publicly guaranteed	**236**	**11,710**	**10,068**	**13,356**	**3,452**	**4,415**	**10,123**	**13,747**	**12,868**	**8,025**
Official creditors	291	3,122	3,919	3,568	3,131	1,523	5,237	4,111	1,268	2,189
Multilateral	82	869	925	2,476	1,588	1,376	2,152	4,114	1,654	2,671
Concessional	-15	9	-10	131	128	373	327	457	450	713
Bilateral	209	2,253	2,994	1,092	1,543	147	3,085	-3	-386	-482
Concessional	224	1,165	507	129	388	548	611	243	389	89
Private creditors	-55	8,588	6,149	9,789	322	2,892	4,886	9,635	11,601	5,836
Bonds	-2	65	1,893	7,810	2,589	2,000	1,729	6,250	12,239	4,917
Commercial banks	-2	3,698	-4,435	-1,696	-2,880	916	2,740	2,991	233	896
Other private	-51	4,825	8,691	3,676	613	-24	418	395	-871	23
Private nonguaranteed	**259**	**1,257**	**264**	**3,480**	**1,361**	**3,703**	**8,154**	**13,353**	**14,488**	**5,427**
Bonds	0	0	0	-16	99	36	671	2,808	2,146	2,927
Commercial banks	259	1,257	264	3,496	1,262	3,667	7,483	10,544	12,342	2,500
Memo:										
IBRD	42	700	85	766	1,490	1,505	1,722	3,490	1,124	1,366
IDA	7	-1	-4	43	111	364	471	427	443	491

EUROPE AND CENTRAL ASIA

(US$ million, unless otherwise indicated)

	1970	1980	1990	1993	1994	1995	1996	1997	1998	1999
INTEREST PAYMENTS (LINT)	**148**	**3,409**	**9,650**	**7,065**	**8,066**	**11,950**	**12,979**	**14,176**	**15,238**	**19,301**
Public and publicly guaranteed	**115**	**2,561**	**9,209**	**6,756**	**7,583**	**11,263**	**12,104**	**13,106**	**12,414**	**13,877**
Official creditors	74	769	2,238	2,561	2,860	4,775	5,283	5,780	4,692	4,982
Multilateral	24	298	1,207	1,283	1,451	1,552	1,767	1,607	1,753	1,871
Concessional	2	4	39	45	53	51	45	37	38	43
Bilateral	50	471	1,031	1,277	1,409	3,224	3,515	4,173	2,939	3,111
Concessional	35	153	246	648	577	804	806	841	793	859
Private creditors	40	1,792	6,971	4,195	4,724	6,487	6,821	7,326	7,722	8,895
Bonds	1	36	739	1,487	2,105	3,301	3,109	3,069	3,664	4,762
Commercial banks	1	1,176	4,743	2,050	1,514	1,917	2,592	3,338	3,207	3,340
Other private	38	580	1,489	658	1,105	1,269	1,120	920	851	793
Private nonguaranteed	**34**	**849**	**442**	**310**	**483**	**687**	**874**	**1,070**	**2,825**	**5,424**
Bonds	0	0	1	2	2	13	16	54	259	416
Commercial banks	34	849	440	308	481	674	858	1,016	2,566	5,008
Memo:										
IBRD	16	257	809	731	844	938	1,181	1,032	1,136	1,220
IDA	1	1	1	1	2	3	5	8	11	14
NET TRANSFERS ON DEBT	**346**	**9,557**	**682**	**9,770**	**-3,253**	**-3,832**	**5,298**	**12,923**	**12,118**	**-5,849**
Public and publicly guaranteed	**121**	**9,149**	**860**	**6,601**	**-4,131**	**-6,848**	**-1,981**	**640**	**455**	**-5,852**
Official creditors	217	2,353	1,681	1,007	272	-3,252	-46	-1,669	-3,425	-2,793
Multilateral	58	571	-281	1,192	137	-176	384	2,508	-100	800
Concessional	-17	5	-48	86	75	322	282	420	411	670
Bilateral	159	1,782	1,963	-185	134	-3,077	-430	-4,176	-3,325	-3,593
Concessional	189	1,013	261	-519	-189	-255	-195	-597	-403	-770
Private creditors	-95	6,796	-822	5,594	-4,402	-3,595	-1,935	2,309	3,880	-3,059
Bonds	-4	30	1,154	6,323	484	-1,301	-1,380	3,181	8,576	155
Commercial banks	-3	2,522	-9,178	-3,746	-4,394	-1,002	148	-347	-2,975	-2,444
Other private	-89	4,245	7,202	3,017	-493	-1,293	-703	-525	-1,722	-770
Private nonguaranteed	**225**	**408**	**-178**	**3,169**	**879**	**3,016**	**7,280**	**12,283**	**11,663**	**3**
Bonds	0	0	-1	-18	98	23	655	2,755	1,887	2,511
Commercial banks	225	408	-176	3,188	781	2,993	6,625	9,528	9,776	-2,508
Memo:										
IBRD	26	443	-724	35	646	566	541	2,459	-12	146
IDA	7	-2	-5	42	110	362	466	419	431	477
DEBT SERVICE (LTDS)	**660**	**10,211**	**28,735**	**18,835**	**24,860**	**31,724**	**34,752**	**37,742**	**46,919**	**42,565**
Public and publicly guaranteed	**419**	**7,321**	**26,797**	**17,283**	**21,908**	**28,142**	**30,347**	**30,337**	**36,891**	**33,271**
Official creditors	263	2,415	5,382	5,464	6,139	9,791	11,102	10,940	12,270	11,384
Multilateral	105	452	2,662	3,116	3,523	4,585	4,828	4,041	5,463	4,390
Concessional	25	6	62	72	99	117	243	177	169	54
Bilateral	158	1,963	2,720	2,348	2,616	5,206	6,274	6,899	6,807	6,994
Concessional	82	629	680	1,193	1,069	1,328	1,328	1,530	1,628	1,568
Private creditors	156	4,906	21,414	11,820	15,770	18,352	19,246	19,397	24,621	21,887
Bonds	4	50	804	2,208	3,668	7,092	7,757	6,687	10,001	11,164
Commercial banks	3	2,542	13,528	6,285	7,484	6,223	7,329	8,939	9,886	7,167
Other private	150	2,314	7,083	3,327	4,617	5,036	4,160	3,772	4,734	3,556
Private nonguaranteed	**241**	**2,890**	**1,939**	**1,552**	**2,951**	**3,582**	**4,405**	**7,405**	**10,028**	**9,294**
Bonds	0	0	1	18	2	13	16	139	259	416
Commercial banks	241	2,890	1,937	1,533	2,949	3,569	4,389	7,266	9,770	8,878
Memo:										
IBRD	29	389	1,943	1,674	1,973	2,130	2,785	2,218	3,369	2,478
IDA	1	3	5	7	7	9	11	14	17	20
UNDISBURSED DEBT	**1,835**	**13,650**	**17,081**	**30,684**	**30,359**	**32,538**	**34,093**	**30,412**	**30,169**	..
Official creditors	1,613	6,155	9,330	18,502	19,402	21,126	22,570	21,170	21,297	..
Private creditors	222	7,496	7,750	12,182	10,957	11,412	11,523	9,242	8,872	..
Memorandum items										
Concessional LDOD	1,851	6,758	12,652	23,748	23,451	25,529	25,034	21,859	24,087	24,280
Variable rate LDOD	952	25,866	89,476	135,506	135,839	144,551	150,717	179,092	222,106	..
Public sector LDOD	2,843	43,792	171,643	244,515	260,825	268,514	266,001	266,051	289,986	..
Private sector LDOD	1,122	12,379	5,982	13,201	15,803	20,954	29,523	43,137	84,720	..
6. CURRENCY COMPOSITION OF LONG-TERM DEBT (PERCENT)										
Deutsche mark	16.0	11.1	25.0	21.0	20.6	22.2	22.9	20.5	21.7	..
French franc	2.7	9.3	5.0	3.3	3.1	3.3	3.4	2.6	2.5	..
Japanese yen	0.1	2.4	7.5	8.6	9.2	9.6	9.3	7.3	6.5	..
Pound sterling	5.0	2.6	1.8	1.2	0.9	0.8	0.9	0.7	0.7	..
Swiss franc	1.4	4.6	6.5	3.1	2.0	2.1	1.7	0.7	0.5	..
U.S.dollars	44.7	42.0	32.1	44.6	45.4	42.8	44.4	53.9	53.4	..
Multiple currency	15.2	21.6	10.5	8.0	9.1	9.8	9.9	8.6	8.0	..
Special drawing rights	0.0	0.0	0.0	0.0	0.0	0.0	0.0	0.0	0.0	..
All other currencies	14.9	6.3	11.3	10.1	9.6	9.2	7.2	5.4	5.2	..

EUROPE AND CENTRAL ASIA

(US$ million, unless otherwise indicated)

	1970	1980	1990	1993	1994	1995	1996	1997	1998	1999
7. DEBT RESTRUCTURINGS										
Total amount rescheduled	0	1,757	3,559	28,061	22,520	11,594	10,442	36,108	5,529	..
Debt stock rescheduled	0	0	0	2,259	6,903	225	1,735	1,235	151	..
Principal rescheduled	0	20	1,391	13,085	6,394	7,461	6,288	29,068	3,966	..
Official	0	17	746	3,708	495	4,029	2,988	3,753	2,875	..
Private	0	3	645	9,377	5,898	3,432	3,300	25,315	1,091	..
Interest rescheduled	..	..	2,168	6,380	5,709	1,381	1,151	5,356	530	..
Official	0	7	1,998	2,341	762	777	525	587	373	..
Private	0	1	170	4,039	4,947	604	626	4,769	158	..
Debt forgiven	0	0	233	664	3,800	3	580	56	99	..
Memo: interest forgiven	0	0	61	0	0	0	15	3	13	..
Debt stock reduction	0	0	1,779	1,674	7,680	146	17	1,819	0	..
of which debt buyback	0	0	883	0	1,379	30	0	0	0	..
8. DEBT STOCK-FLOW RECONCILIATION										
Total change in debt stocks	..	..	21,722	55,741	17,091	26,428	17,109	20,940	90,034	..
Net flows on debt	1,486	22,062	3,223	23,916	2,493	21,267	28,050	39,002	39,939	8,858
Net change in interest arrears	..	..	5,211	-2,253	23	1,266	1,486	-4,512	2,346	..
Interest capitalized	..	..	2,168	6,380	5,709	1,381	1,151	5,356	530	..
Debt forgiveness or reduction	..	..	-1,130	-2,338	-10,101	-119	-597	-1,875	-99	..
Cross-currency valuation	..	..	13,095	-5,867	10,467	6,760	-11,515	-12,903	8,238	..
Residual	..	..	-846	35,901	8,499	-4,128	-1,466	-4,127	39,079	..
9. AVERAGE TERMS OF NEW COMMITMENTS										
ALL CREDITORS										
Interest (%)	4.2	10.3	8.4	6.0	6.7	6.3	6.5	6.9	7.5	..
Maturity (years)	19.2	12.4	16.6	10.0	12.0	11.7	11.2	10.3	11.9	..
Grace period (years)	6.8	4.3	5.5	4.8	4.7	4.8	4.1	4.8	8.0	..
Grant element (%)	37.3	1.7	8.3	17.0	16.2	17.9	16.0	14.8	10.6	..
Official creditors										
Interest (%)	3.8	7.6	7.9	5.3	6.3	5.7	5.4	5.6	5.4	..
Maturity (years)	20.1	16.7	13.5	14.9	15.4	16.6	14.8	17.0	16.8	..
Grace period (years)	7.3	5.2	5.9	4.9	4.9	5.1	4.9	5.4	5.5	..
Grant element (%)	40.3	18.7	11.8	25.8	21.1	25.8	25.4	27.1	28.5	..
Private creditors										
Interest (%)	6.3	11.2	8.6	6.3	7.0	6.7	7.5	7.4	8.2	..
Maturity (years)	13.3	10.9	18.0	7.8	9.2	8.3	8.1	7.1	10.3	..
Grace period (years)	3.6	4.1	5.3	4.8	4.6	4.6	3.5	4.6	8.8	..
Grant element (%)	18.2	-4.4	6.6	13.0	12.1	12.7	8.2	8.9	4.8	..
Memorandum items										
Commitments	759	12,607	30,568	28,431	18,588	23,220	33,651	31,625	37,261	..
Official creditors	654	3,332	9,598	8,872	8,433	9,318	15,370	10,232	9,135	..
Private creditors	105	9,275	20,970	19,559	10,156	13,902	18,281	21,394	28,126	..

10. GRAPH OF AGGREGATE NET RESOURCE FLOWS

(current prices, US$ million)

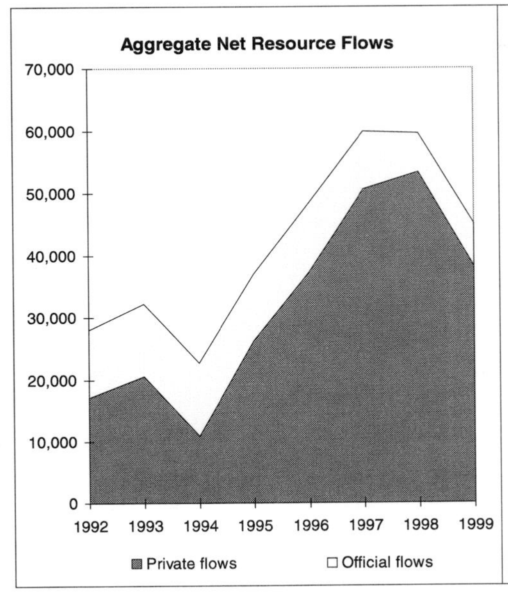

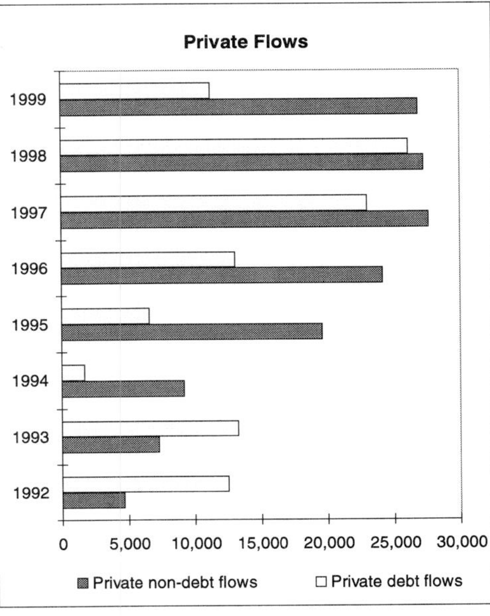

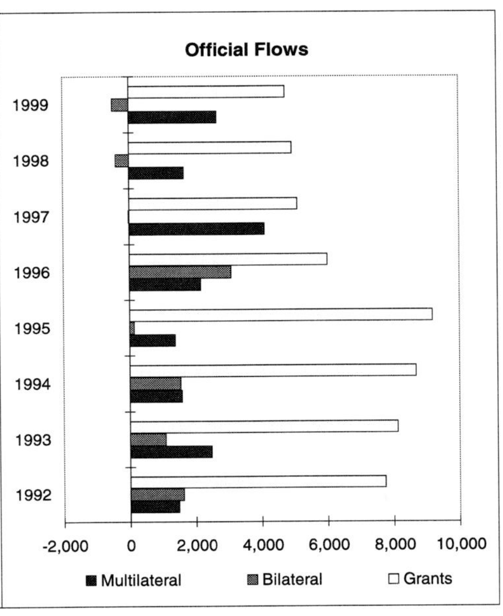

LATIN AMERICA AND THE CARIBBEAN

(US$ million, unless otherwise indicated)

	1970	1980	1990	1993	1994	1995	1996	1997	1998	1999
1. SUMMARY DEBT DATA										
TOTAL DEBT STOCKS (EDT)	..	**257,259**	**475,867**	**548,994**	**588,279**	**652,539**	**676,287**	**714,256**	**786,019**	**792,652**
Long-term debt (LDOD)	**27,631**	**187,249**	**380,169**	**423,956**	**456,485**	**495,135**	**527,145**	**558,694**	**640,533**	**649,000**
Public and publicly guaranteed	15,758	144,791	355,117	366,703	384,221	407,799	410,301	394,726	424,246	440,630
Private nonguaranteed	11,873	42,458	25,051	57,253	72,265	87,336	116,844	163,967	216,287	208,370
Use of IMF credit	**128**	**1,413**	**18,298**	**14,255**	**13,849**	**26,719**	**23,892**	**18,563**	**21,969**	**21,020**
Short-term debt	..	**68,597**	**77,400**	**110,783**	**117,945**	**130,685**	**125,250**	**137,000**	**123,518**	**122,632**
of which interest arrears on LDOD	..	60	25,566	18,019	12,702	9,538	3,219	2,603	3,636	3,631
Official creditors	..	16	3,852	3,129	2,998	2,809	1,523	1,468	1,547	..
Private creditors	..	44	21,713	14,890	9,704	6,728	1,696	1,135	2,090	..
Memo: principal arrears on LDOD	..	606	24,553	20,679	20,381	16,529	8,053	8,010	8,289	8,291
Official creditors	..	78	7,370	5,564	6,570	6,054	3,319	3,222	3,286	..
Private creditors	..	528	17,183	15,115	13,811	10,474	4,734	4,788	5,003	..
Memo: export credits	..	554	72,068	91,842	95,693	79,014	73,753	68,108	71,733	..
TOTAL DEBT FLOWS										
Disbursements	**6,493**	**44,779**	**34,238**	**57,678**	**52,322**	**90,950**	**103,247**	**123,538**	**144,195**	**97,412**
Long-term debt	6,368	44,364	29,402	55,008	51,155	75,178	101,792	122,761	139,159	89,546
IMF purchases	124	415	4,836	2,671	1,166	15,772	1,455	777	5,036	7,866
Principal repayments	**3,734**	**21,694**	**22,791**	**36,711**	**36,105**	**43,458**	**66,244**	**91,496**	**78,992**	**87,114**
Long-term debt	3,436	21,202	19,137	33,158	33,662	40,563	62,816	86,788	76,460	78,299
IMF repurchases	298	492	3,655	3,553	2,442	2,894	3,428	4,709	2,532	8,815
Net flows on debt	**7,545**	**46,074**	**20,564**	**41,036**	**28,696**	**63,396**	**37,886**	**44,409**	**50,681**	**9,417**
of which short-term debt	..	22,989	9,118	20,069	12,479	15,904	884	12,366	-14,522	-881
Interest payments (INT)	..	**24,601**	**22,813**	**24,340**	**28,547**	**37,503**	**39,713**	**42,353**	**46,335**	**53,469**
Long-term debt	1,393	17,567	18,815	18,397	21,966	29,603	30,954	34,399	38,196	45,968
IMF charges	0	95	1,459	1,241	722	1,107	1,106	928	828	980
Short-term debt	..	6,939	2,538	4,702	5,858	6,792	7,653	7,026	7,310	6,521
Net transfers on debt	..	**21,473**	**-2,249**	**16,695**	**149**	**25,894**	**-1,826**	**2,055**	**4,347**	**-44,052**
Total debt service paid (TDS)	..	**46,295**	**45,605**	**61,052**	**64,652**	**80,960**	**105,957**	**133,849**	**125,327**	**140,583**
Long-term debt	4,828	38,769	37,952	51,555	55,629	70,166	93,770	121,187	114,656	124,267
IMF repurchases and charges	298	588	5,114	4,794	3,165	4,001	4,534	5,636	3,361	9,795
Short-term debt (interest only)	..	6,939	2,538	4,702	5,858	6,792	7,653	7,026	7,310	6,521
2. AGGREGATE NET RESOURCE FLOWS AND NET TRANSFERS (LONG-TERM)										
NET RESOURCE FLOWS	**4,177**	**29,897**	**21,699**	**65,691**	**61,689**	**75,418**	**99,460**	**113,362**	**136,972**	**107,209**
Net flow of long-term debt (ex. IMF)	2,932	23,162	10,265	21,850	17,494	34,614	38,976	35,974	62,700	11,247
Foreign direct investment (net)	1,091	6,148	8,188	13,747	28,392	29,827	43,408	64,725	69,323	89,375
Portfolio equity flows	0	0	896	27,185	13,160	7,643	13,893	9,947	1,748	3,588
Grants (excluding technical coop.)	154	587	2,350	2,909	2,645	3,333	3,183	2,716	3,201	2,999
Memo: technical coop. grants	259	776	2,041	2,466	2,414	2,758	2,521	2,392	2,193	2,250
official net resource flows	988	5,284	9,288	5,569	1,274	12,605	-5,086	-2,376	10,118	9,311
private net resource flows	3,189	24,614	12,411	60,123	60,415	62,814	104,546	115,738	126,854	97,898
NET TRANSFERS	**756**	**7,454**	**-3,474**	**38,305**	**29,816**	**35,233**	**56,095**	**65,412**	**83,259**	**43,025**
Interest on long-term debt	1,393	17,567	18,815	18,397	21,966	29,603	30,954	34,399	38,196	45,968
Profit remittances on FDI	2,029	4,876	6,358	8,989	9,907	10,583	12,411	13,550	15,517	18,216
Memo: official net transfers	687	3,305	3,120	-2,408	-7,023	3,059	-14,229	-10,273	2,409	-624
private net transfers	69	4,149	-6,593	40,712	36,840	32,174	70,324	75,686	80,850	43,649
3. MAJOR ECONOMIC AGGREGATES										
Gross national product (GNP)	162,753	754,716	1,072,872	1,383,699	1,555,133	1,706,546	1,800,949	1,916,117	1,925,227	1,717,342
Exports of goods & services (XGS)	..	127,980	186,130	220,308	255,643	305,949	336,437	372,544	373,495	407,388
of which workers remittances	..	1,187	4,730	7,366	9,450	11,104	11,090	11,661	12,964	14,131
Imports of goods & services (MGS)	..	160,470	194,845	271,729	312,608	350,551	382,146	445,628	471,669	443,766
International reserves (RES)	5,481	57,381	58,341	117,829	113,793	139,044	164,588	174,814	165,274	164,142
Current account balance	..	-30,194	-1,578	-44,810	-50,361	-37,072	-38,385	-65,221	-89,650	-58,349
4. DEBT INDICATORS										
EDT / XGS (%)	..	201.0	255.7	249.2	230.1	213.3	201.0	191.7	210.5	194.6
EDT / GNP (%)	..	34.1	44.4	39.7	37.8	38.2	37.6	37.3	40.8	46.2
TDS / XGS (%)	..	36.2	24.5	27.7	25.3	26.5	31.5	35.9	33.6	34.5
INT / XGS (%)	..	19.2	12.3	11.1	11.2	12.3	11.8	11.4	12.4	13.1
INT / GNP (%)	..	3.3	2.1	1.8	1.8	2.2	2.2	2.2	2.4	3.1
RES / EDT (%)	..	22.3	12.3	21.5	19.3	21.3	24.3	24.5	21.0	20.7
RES / MGS (months)	..	4.3	3.6	5.2	4.4	4.8	5.2	4.7	4.2	4.4
Short-term / EDT (%)	..	26.7	16.3	20.2	20.1	20.0	18.5	19.2	15.7	15.5
Concessional / EDT (%)	..	9.3	10.2	10.1	9.9	9.1	8.5	7.9	3.9	4.0
Multilateral / EDT (%)	..	5.5	12.7	12.0	11.8	11.2	10.5	9.9	10.5	11.3

LATIN AMERICA AND THE CARIBBEAN

(US$ million, unless otherwise indicated)

	1970	1980	1990	1993	1994	1995	1996	1997	1998	1999
5. LONG-TERM DEBT										
DEBT OUTSTANDING (LDOD)	**27,631**	**187,249**	**380,169**	**423,956**	**456,485**	**495,135**	**527,145**	**558,694**	**640,533**	**649,000**
Public and publicly guaranteed	**15,758**	**144,791**	**355,117**	**366,703**	**384,221**	**407,799**	**410,301**	**394,726**	**424,246**	**440,630**
Official creditors	8,118	44,942	146,563	170,705	177,821	191,494	172,190	159,262	170,513	176,352
Multilateral	2,945	14,120	60,510	65,853	69,396	73,318	71,193	70,668	82,650	89,553
Concessional	305	2,359	5,919	6,874	7,329	7,924	8,482	9,239	9,736	10,441
Bilateral	5,173	30,821	86,053	104,853	108,424	118,176	100,997	88,594	87,864	86,799
Concessional	3,920	21,551	42,453	48,699	50,722	51,746	48,782	47,179	21,068	21,112
Private creditors	7,640	99,850	208,555	195,998	206,400	216,305	238,111	235,464	253,733	264,278
Bonds	1,234	9,599	75,976	103,043	152,822	165,758	195,721	193,683	205,294	213,243
Commercial banks	3,071	77,085	103,602	76,190	38,527	36,459	30,191	30,510	38,603	41,685
Other private	3,334	13,166	28,977	16,766	15,051	14,088	12,200	11,271	9,836	9,350
Private nonguaranteed	**11,873**	**42,458**	**25,051**	**57,253**	**72,265**	**87,336**	**116,844**	**163,967**	**216,287**	**208,370**
Bonds	0	0	171	22,308	30,295	33,829	40,983	46,404	53,889	53,378
Commercial banks	11,873	42,458	24,880	34,946	41,970	53,507	75,861	117,563	162,398	154,992
Memo:										
IBRD	2,067	7,706	34,760	34,558	35,419	36,391	33,989	31,806	34,518	35,631
IDA	112	427	1,117	1,646	1,900	2,186	2,411	2,621	2,989	3,462
DISBURSEMENTS	**6,368**	**44,364**	**29,402**	**55,008**	**51,155**	**75,178**	**101,792**	**122,761**	**139,159**	**89,546**
Public and publicly guaranteed	**3,608**	**31,403**	**24,700**	**27,255**	**25,223**	**46,556**	**58,406**	**56,023**	**60,297**	**61,107**
Official creditors	1,339	6,817	13,919	12,567	10,095	23,734	12,682	12,899	20,688	21,410
Multilateral	581	2,957	9,089	9,086	6,692	10,011	9,617	10,868	16,385	14,296
Concessional	76	492	452	603	650	812	919	819	828	978
Bilateral	757	3,861	4,831	3,481	3,403	13,724	3,065	2,031	4,303	7,114
Concessional	434	1,118	2,532	1,570	1,212	1,556	1,217	985	908	1,089
Private creditors	2,270	24,586	10,781	14,688	15,128	22,822	45,724	43,124	39,609	39,697
Bonds	129	1,219	1,938	9,809	9,369	13,694	36,744	34,715	26,524	30,382
Commercial banks	1,150	19,937	5,715	3,076	3,869	7,326	7,251	7,061	12,470	7,307
Other private	992	3,430	3,127	1,804	1,890	1,802	1,729	1,348	615	2,008
Private nonguaranteed	**2,760**	**12,960**	**4,702**	**27,753**	**25,932**	**28,622**	**43,386**	**66,739**	**78,863**	**28,439**
Bonds	0	0	171	14,642	9,934	7,412	12,129	14,120	15,875	7,771
Commercial banks	2,760	12,960	4,531	13,111	15,999	21,210	31,257	52,619	62,987	20,668
Memo:										
IBRD	354	1,586	6,139	4,803	3,052	4,642	4,421	4,393	5,768	4,946
IDA	9	60	119	167	208	277	304	343	309	498
PRINCIPAL REPAYMENTS	**3,436**	**21,202**	**19,137**	**33,158**	**33,662**	**40,563**	**62,816**	**86,788**	**76,460**	**78,299**
Public and publicly guaranteed	**1,665**	**14,241**	**16,921**	**18,839**	**20,214**	**27,474**	**41,692**	**54,922**	**39,726**	**41,943**
Official creditors	505	2,121	6,981	9,908	11,467	14,463	20,951	17,991	13,772	15,098
Multilateral	169	703	4,738	6,649	7,202	8,368	7,084	6,933	6,219	7,218
Concessional	7	36	147	244	250	281	251	270	272	249
Bilateral	336	1,418	2,243	3,259	4,264	6,095	13,867	11,058	7,553	7,880
Concessional	119	368	727	432	660	938	955	1,114	1,142	972
Private creditors	1,160	12,120	9,940	8,931	8,747	13,011	20,741	36,931	25,954	26,845
Bonds	77	401	2,008	3,656	2,335	5,699	11,581	29,792	17,078	20,294
Commercial banks	609	9,371	5,223	1,888	2,212	4,335	6,325	4,838	6,045	4,088
Other private	475	2,348	2,709	3,387	4,200	2,978	2,835	2,302	2,832	2,463
Private nonguaranteed	**1,771**	**6,960**	**2,216**	**14,319**	**13,449**	**13,090**	**21,124**	**31,865**	**36,734**	**36,356**
Bonds	0	0	0	273	1,997	3,922	4,858	8,480	7,694	8,282
Commercial banks	1,771	6,960	2,216	14,046	11,452	9,168	16,267	23,385	29,039	28,074
Memo:										
IBRD	105	394	3,310	4,496	4,531	4,984	4,339	3,962	3,642	3,833
IDA	0	2	9	10	11	21	16	18	21	24
NET FLOWS ON DEBT	**2,932**	**23,162**	**10,265**	**21,850**	**17,494**	**34,614**	**38,976**	**35,974**	**62,700**	**11,247**
Public and publicly guaranteed	**1,944**	**17,162**	**7,779**	**8,416**	**5,010**	**19,082**	**16,715**	**1,100**	**20,571**	**19,164**
Official creditors	834	4,696	6,938	2,660	-1,371	9,272	-8,269	-5,092	6,917	6,312
Multilateral	412	2,254	4,351	2,438	-510	1,643	2,533	3,934	10,166	7,078
Concessional	69	457	305	359	400	530	668	549	556	729
Bilateral	422	2,442	2,588	222	-861	7,628	-10,802	-9,027	-3,249	-766
Concessional	316	750	1,805	1,138	553	619	262	-129	-234	117
Private creditors	1,109	12,466	841	5,757	6,381	9,811	24,983	6,192	13,654	12,852
Bonds	52	819	-70	6,152	7,034	7,995	25,163	4,922	9,446	10,088
Commercial banks	541	10,565	492	1,188	1,657	2,992	927	2,224	6,426	3,219
Other private	517	1,082	419	-1,584	-2,310	-1,176	-1,106	-954	-2,218	-455
Private nonguaranteed	**989**	**6,000**	**2,486**	**13,434**	**12,483**	**15,532**	**22,262**	**34,874**	**42,129**	**-7,917**
Bonds	0	0	171	14,369	7,937	3,491	7,271	5,639	8,181	-511
Commercial banks	989	6,000	2,315	-935	4,546	12,042	14,990	29,234	33,948	-7,406
Memo:										
IBRD	249	1,192	2,829	307	-1,479	-342	82	431	2,126	1,113
IDA	9	59	110	157	198	256	288	325	288	474

LATIN AMERICA AND THE CARIBBEAN

(US$ million, unless otherwise indicated)

	1970	1980	1990	1993	1994	1995	1996	1997	1998	1999
INTEREST PAYMENTS (LINT)	**1,393**	**17,567**	**18,815**	**18,397**	**21,966**	**29,603**	**30,954**	**34,399**	**38,196**	**45,968**
Public and publicly guaranteed	**764**	**13,138**	**16,553**	**15,131**	**17,813**	**23,455**	**23,310**	**23,429**	**25,175**	**28,912**
Official creditors	301	1,979	6,168	7,976	8,297	9,546	9,143	7,898	7,708	9,935
Multilateral	157	1,000	4,157	5,066	4,856	4,944	4,739	4,543	4,536	5,628
Concessional	7	48	104	126	135	151	132	141	168	173
Bilateral	144	979	2,011	2,911	3,441	4,601	4,404	3,355	3,172	4,307
Concessional	75	401	773	745	801	721	685	642	693	309
Private creditors	463	11,159	10,385	7,156	9,515	13,909	14,166	15,531	17,467	18,977
Bonds	72	727	2,398	5,315	7,304	11,273	10,656	12,996	14,249	15,103
Commercial banks	227	9,447	6,704	1,042	1,487	1,725	2,798	1,961	2,665	3,372
Other private	164	985	1,282	798	724	911	713	574	553	502
Private nonguaranteed	**628**	**4,429**	**2,262**	**3,266**	**4,154**	**6,148**	**7,644**	**10,970**	**13,021**	**17,056**
Bonds	0	0	0	857	1,988	2,597	2,983	3,690	4,228	4,910
Commercial banks	628	4,429	2,262	2,409	2,166	3,551	4,661	7,280	8,793	12,146
Memo:										
IBRD	114	633	2,538	3,040	2,654	2,657	2,488	2,175	2,116	2,535
IDA	1	3	7	9	10	23	17	18	20	22
NET TRANSFERS ON DEBT	**1,540**	**5,595**	**-8,550**	**3,453**	**-4,473**	**5,012**	**8,023**	**1,574**	**24,504**	**-34,721**
Public and publicly guaranteed	**1,179**	**4,024**	**-8,774**	**-6,716**	**-12,803**	**-4,373**	**-6,595**	**-22,329**	**-4,605**	**-9,748**
Official creditors	533	2,717	769	-5,317	-9,668	-274	-17,412	-12,990	-792	-3,623
Multilateral	256	1,254	194	-2,627	-5,366	-3,301	-2,206	-608	5,630	1,450
Concessional	62	409	201	233	264	379	536	408	387	556
Bilateral	278	1,464	576	-2,689	-4,302	3,027	-15,206	-12,381	-6,422	-5,073
Concessional	241	350	1,031	394	-248	-103	-423	-771	-927	-192
Private creditors	646	1,307	-9,544	-1,399	-3,135	-4,099	10,817	-9,339	-3,813	-6,125
Bonds	-20	92	-2,468	838	-270	-3,278	14,507	-8,074	-4,803	-5,015
Commercial banks	313	1,118	-6,212	146	170	1,266	-1,871	263	3,761	-153
Other private	353	97	-864	-2,382	-3,035	-2,087	-1,819	-1,527	-2,770	-957
Private nonguaranteed	**360**	**1,571**	**224**	**10,168**	**8,330**	**9,385**	**14,618**	**23,903**	**29,108**	**-24,973**
Bonds	0	0	171	13,513	5,949	894	4,288	1,949	3,953	-5,421
Commercial banks	360	1,571	53	-3,344	2,381	8,491	10,329	21,954	25,155	-19,552
Memo:										
IBRD	135	559	291	-2,734	-4,133	-2,999	-2,406	-1,744	11	-1,422
IDA	8	56	102	148	187	234	271	307	268	452
DEBT SERVICE (LTDS)	**4,828**	**38,769**	**37,952**	**51,555**	**55,629**	**70,166**	**93,770**	**121,187**	**114,656**	**124,267**
Public and publicly guaranteed	**2,429**	**27,380**	**33,474**	**33,970**	**38,026**	**50,929**	**65,001**	**78,352**	**64,901**	**70,855**
Official creditors	806	4,100	13,150	17,884	19,764	24,009	30,094	25,889	21,480	25,033
Multilateral	326	1,703	8,895	11,714	12,058	13,312	11,823	11,476	10,755	12,846
Concessional	14	84	251	370	385	432	383	411	441	422
Bilateral	479	2,397	4,255	6,170	7,705	10,696	18,271	14,413	10,725	12,187
Concessional	193	768	1,500	1,177	1,460	1,659	1,641	1,757	1,834	1,281
Private creditors	1,624	23,279	20,324	16,087	18,263	26,920	34,907	52,462	43,422	45,822
Bonds	149	1,128	4,406	8,971	9,639	16,972	22,237	42,788	31,327	35,397
Commercial banks	837	18,818	11,928	2,931	3,699	6,060	9,123	6,799	8,709	7,460
Other private	638	3,333	3,991	4,185	4,925	3,889	3,548	2,875	3,385	2,965
Private nonguaranteed	**2,400**	**11,389**	**4,478**	**17,585**	**17,602**	**19,237**	**28,768**	**42,835**	**49,754**	**53,412**
Bonds	0	0	0	1,130	3,985	6,518	7,841	12,170	11,922	13,192
Commercial banks	2,400	11,389	4,478	16,455	13,618	12,719	20,927	30,665	37,832	40,220
Memo:										
IBRD	219	1,028	5,848	7,536	7,185	7,641	6,827	6,137	5,757	6,368
IDA	1	5	17	19	21	43	33	36	41	46
UNDISBURSED DEBT	**5,052**	**35,100**	**43,502**	**54,719**	**59,092**	**58,420**	**57,029**	**56,388**	**58,140**	..
Official creditors	3,237	20,566	30,616	39,139	43,194	44,296	40,941	41,298	41,780	..
Private creditors	1,815	14,534	12,886	15,580	15,898	14,123	16,087	15,090	16,360	..
Memorandum items										
Concessional LDOD	4,224	23,910	48,373	55,573	58,052	59,670	57,264	56,419	30,804	31,553
Variable rate LDOD	12,501	117,249	196,403	223,732	237,967	266,972	291,480	323,162	381,516	..
Public sector LDOD	15,266	124,655	325,018	332,649	350,796	374,000	376,556	360,899	387,077	..
Private sector LDOD	12,370	48,219	28,399	58,975	74,012	89,257	118,660	165,412	220,702	..

6. CURRENCY COMPOSITION OF LONG-TERM DEBT (PERCENT)

	1970	1980	1990	1993	1994	1995	1996	1997	1998	1999
Deutsche mark	7.8	5.5	5.8	4.5	4.4	5.1	5.9	5.6	5.4	..
French franc	2.3	1.8	3.6	2.6	2.5	2.5	2.1	1.8	1.3	..
Japanese yen	0.1	4.4	5.7	6.2	6.4	7.0	6.7	6.0	5.6	..
Pound sterling	4.6	1.4	1.4	0.9	0.9	0.8	0.8	1.0	0.8	..
Swiss franc	1.9	1.2	0.9	0.5	0.5	0.5	0.4	0.4	0.4	..
U.S.dollars	63.0	63.1	54.9	55.8	56.8	57.3	58.3	59.8	66.3	..
Multiple currency	16.9	9.4	17.5	18.4	18.0	16.8	15.5	14.1	8.4	..
Special drawing rights	0.0	0.0	0.0	0.0	0.0	0.0	0.0	0.0	0.0	..
All other currencies	3.6	3.4	2.5	2.2	2.2	2.1	2.5	3.0	6.0	..

LATIN AMERICA AND THE CARIBBEAN

(US$ million, unless otherwise indicated)

	1970	1980	1990	1993	1994	1995	1996	1997	1998	1999
7. DEBT RESTRUCTURINGS										
Total amount rescheduled	117	1,124	63,742	30,076	46,692	7,922	11,146	2,163	5,022	..
Debt stock rescheduled	0	1	59,087	18,489	36,263	3,350	3,158	370	4,459	..
Principal rescheduled	0	104	3,059	2,747	1,886	1,066	3,337	784	111	..
Official	0	0	1,535	2,282	1,443	865	1,307	689	99	..
Private	0	104	1,524	465	443	200	2,031	95	11	..
Interest rescheduled	..	..	1,507	8,823	8,039	2,505	4,858	943	458	..
Official	0	0	960	1,069	584	658	756	509	308	..
Private	0	0	547	7,754	7,455	1,846	4,103	434	150	..
Debt forgiven	6	28	180	724	86	626	1,294	328	249	..
Memo: interest forgiven	0	0	259	8	185	773	1,691	15	24	..
Debt stock reduction	0	0	21,302	4,660	5,126	3,704	8,487	11,936	2,729	..
of which debt buyback	0	0	2,756	525	323	102	3,363	9,850	2,100	..
8. DEBT STOCK-FLOW RECONCILIATION										
Total change in debt stocks	..	..	22,582	39,196	39,285	64,260	23,748	37,970	71,764	..
Net flows on debt	7,545	46,074	20,564	41,036	28,696	63,396	37,886	44,409	50,681	9,417
Net change in interest arrears	..	..	9,061	-2,901	-5,317	-3,164	-6,319	-616	1,033	..
Interest capitalized	..	..	1,507	8,823	8,039	2,505	4,858	943	458	..
Debt forgiveness or reduction	..	..	-18,726	-4,859	-4,889	-4,228	-6,418	-2,414	-878	..
Cross-currency valuation	..	..	10,506	-310	8,190	2,433	-9,078	-10,886	6,897	..
Residual	..	..	-332	-2,592	4,565	3,317	2,817	6,534	13,572	..
9. AVERAGE TERMS OF NEW COMMITMENTS										
ALL CREDITORS										
Interest (%)	7.0	11.5	7.9	6.8	6.4	7.2	7.6	7.7	7.9	..
Maturity (years)	14.4	11.3	15.0	12.1	12.0	9.8	9.6	14.5	9.7	..
Grace period (years)	3.6	4.2	5.1	4.5	4.3	3.5	5.9	8.9	5.8	..
Grant element (%)	16.6	-5.8	12.2	15.3	17.3	12.5	9.5	10.9	8.8	..
Official creditors										
Interest (%)	6.0	7.8	7.0	6.2	6.1	7.5	6.0	6.6	6.9	..
Maturity (years)	23.4	17.0	18.0	17.8	18.6	14.1	19.7	17.8	12.1	..
Grace period (years)	5.5	4.5	4.9	4.8	5.2	4.0	5.1	4.5	3.4	..
Grant element (%)	27.4	14.6	18.6	22.5	24.4	15.8	25.9	20.1	14.4	..
Private creditors										
Interest (%)	7.7	13.0	9.1	7.2	6.7	6.7	8.0	8.2	8.5	..
Maturity (years)	8.9	9.0	11.1	8.3	5.9	4.1	7.1	13.3	8.4	..
Grace period (years)	2.4	4.1	5.3	4.3	3.4	2.9	6.1	10.5	7.1	..
Grant element (%)	10.1	-14.2	3.6	10.5	10.6	8.1	5.4	7.4	5.7	..
Memorandum items										
Commitments	4,373	33,271	26,283	30,419	30,754	49,598	60,410	62,221	63,721	..
Official creditors	1,645	9,641	15,088	12,148	14,790	28,153	12,057	17,017	22,568	..
Private creditors	2,727	23,630	11,195	18,271	15,964	21,445	48,354	45,204	41,153	..

10. GRAPH OF AGGREGATE NET RESOURCE FLOWS

(current prices, US$ million)

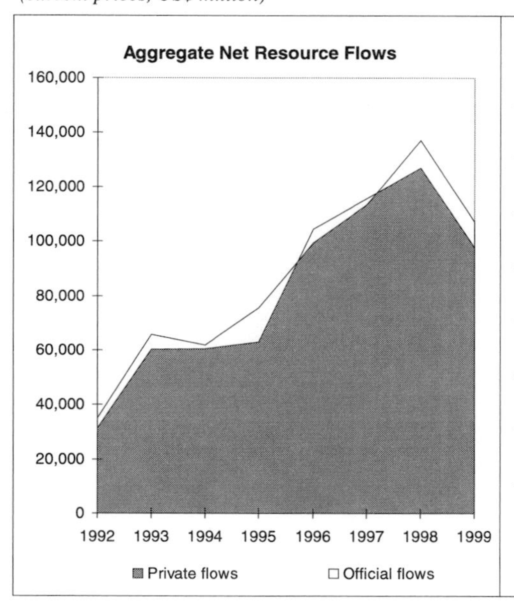

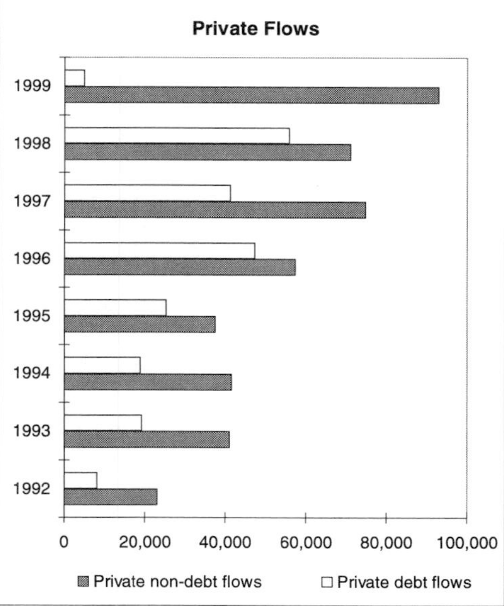

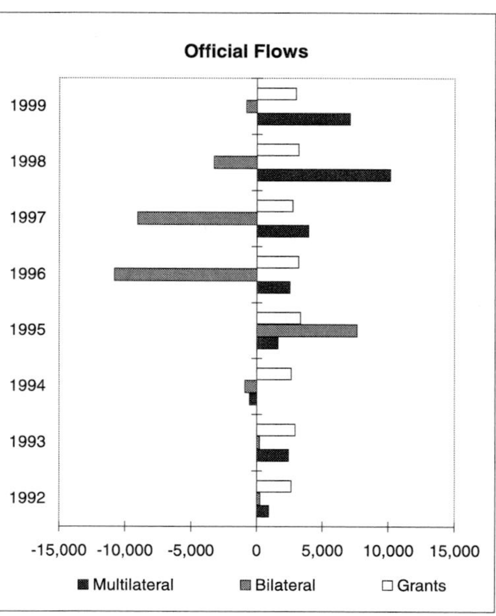

MIDDLE EAST AND NORTH AFRICA

(US$ million, unless otherwise indicated)

	1970	1980	1990	1993	1994	1995	1996	1997	1998	1999
1. SUMMARY DEBT DATA										
TOTAL DEBT STOCKS (EDT)	..	**83,836**	**183,205**	**193,661**	**208,223**	**211,182**	**204,844**	**194,438**	**208,059**	**214,192**
Long-term debt (LDOD)	**4,168**	**61,770**	**137,500**	**138,893**	**158,179**	**164,435**	**159,056**	**150,326**	**164,114**	**169,456**
Public and publicly guaranteed	4,153	61,175	135,998	138,011	155,958	161,121	155,326	145,713	159,644	161,414
Private nonguaranteed	15	595	1,502	882	2,221	3,314	3,729	4,613	4,471	8,042
Use of IMF credit	**100**	**916**	**1,815**	**1,324**	**1,946**	**2,177**	**2,752**	**2,874**	**2,954**	**2,976**
Short-term debt	..	**21,150**	**43,890**	**53,444**	**48,098**	**44,571**	**43,037**	**41,239**	**40,991**	**41,760**
of which interest arrears on LDOD	..	391	2,877	1,715	2,008	2,297	2,541	2,254	2,433	2,430
Official creditors	..	391	1,650	1,460	1,724	1,987	2,231	2,093	2,266	..
Private creditors	..	0	1,228	255	283	310	310	161	167	..
Memo: principal arrears on LDOD	..	114	8,167	5,850	7,195	8,696	9,924	8,731	9,683	9,683
Official creditors	..	108	3,593	4,262	5,371	6,689	7,760	7,533	8,368	..
Private creditors	..	6	4,574	1,588	1,825	2,007	2,164	1,198	1,314	..
Memo: export credits	..	3,668	62,532	61,425	71,753	67,905	64,746	62,948	64,222	..
TOTAL DEBT FLOWS										
Disbursements	**891**	**12,328**	**14,660**	**16,290**	**16,588**	**14,127**	**14,110**	**12,631**	**15,149**	**19,071**
Long-term debt	853	11,978	14,595	16,274	15,653	13,537	13,121	11,893	14,698	18,562
IMF purchases	38	350	65	16	935	590	989	739	451	509
Principal repayments	**413**	**5,062**	**15,694**	**14,031**	**13,874**	**13,932**	**15,211**	**15,923**	**13,705**	**11,743**
Long-term debt	383	4,830	15,297	13,494	13,468	13,542	14,874	15,482	13,211	11,256
IMF repurchases	31	233	397	537	406	390	337	441	494	487
Net flows on debt	**1,030**	**8,664**	**627**	**6,218**	**7,860**	**-444**	**-1,074**	**-4,802**	**684**	**8,101**
of which short-term debt	..	1,397	1,661	3,960	5,146	-638	28	-1,511	-761	773
Interest payments (INT)	..	**6,456**	**8,586**	**8,887**	**8,580**	**10,094**	**9,854**	**9,162**	**8,922**	**9,394**
Long-term debt	100	3,935	5,202	5,610	5,879	7,215	7,481	6,550	6,632	7,123
IMF charges	0	33	181	108	74	112	107	127	127	131
Short-term debt	..	2,488	3,203	3,169	2,627	2,767	2,266	2,486	2,164	2,140
Net transfers on debt	..	**2,208**	**-7,959**	**-2,669**	**-719**	**-10,538**	**-10,928**	**-13,964**	**-8,238**	**-1,293**
Total debt service paid (TDS)	..	**11,518**	**24,280**	**22,919**	**22,454**	**24,026**	**25,065**	**25,085**	**22,627**	**21,137**
Long-term debt	482	8,764	20,499	19,104	19,347	20,757	22,355	22,031	19,843	18,379
IMF repurchases and charges	31	265	578	645	480	502	444	568	621	618
Short-term debt (interest only)	..	2,488	3,203	3,169	2,627	2,767	2,266	2,486	2,164	2,140
2. AGGREGATE NET RESOURCE FLOWS AND NET TRANSFERS (LONG-TERM)										
NET RESOURCE FLOWS	**1,145**	**8,501**	**9,910**	**9,174**	**9,778**	**3,171**	**7,401**	**8,385**	**11,472**	**19,884**
Net flow of long-term debt (ex. IMF)	470	7,149	-703	2,779	2,185	-5	-1,753	-3,589	1,488	7,306
Foreign direct investment (net)	294	-3,313	2,458	3,783	3,351	-199	3,581	5,917	5,054	8,070
Portfolio equity flows	0	0	0	0	106	203	1,632	2,259	879	608
Grants (excluding technical coop.)	381	4,665	8,155	2,611	4,136	3,172	3,941	3,797	4,051	3,900
Memo: technical coop. grants	269	990	2,558	2,717	2,263	2,579	2,389	1,838	1,713	2,100
official net resource flows	573	9,537	9,542	5,521	3,358	1,531	2,273	-456	2,249	3,240
private net resource flows	572	-1,035	369	3,653	6,420	1,640	5,128	8,841	9,223	16,644
NET TRANSFERS	**-1,899**	**-5,284**	**3,425**	**2,276**	**2,631**	**-5,300**	**-1,469**	**401**	**3,331**	**10,955**
Interest on long-term debt	100	3,935	5,202	5,610	5,879	7,215	7,481	6,550	6,632	7,123
Profit remittances on FDI	2,944	9,850	1,284	1,288	1,268	1,256	1,388	1,434	1,509	1,806
Memo: official net transfers	508	8,583	7,089	2,709	186	-2,840	-2,640	-4,565	-1,744	-902
private net transfers	-2,407	-13,866	-3,664	-434	2,445	-2,460	1,172	4,966	5,075	11,857
3. MAJOR ECONOMIC AGGREGATES										
Gross national product (GNP)	41,690	405,482	427,672	448,858	437,740	473,866	534,225	576,251	577,145	484,093
Exports of goods & services (XGS)	..	205,736	160,839	157,000	154,534	175,173	198,284	199,807	161,119	192,376
of which workers remittances	..	5,104	10,507	13,213	11,161	11,978	11,965	12,359	10,072	10,553
Imports of goods & services (MGS)	..	144,421	144,477	162,073	145,151	160,783	171,947	175,057	168,443	151,105
International reserves (RES)	4,477	76,217	39,150	47,916	52,580	56,949	60,516	65,299	65,756	69,550
Current account balance	..	46,988	1,861	-24,632	-11,344	-7,046	2,266	-1,327	-23,448	6,683
4. DEBT INDICATORS										
EDT / XGS (%)	..	40.8	113.9	123.4	134.7	120.6	103.3	97.3	129.1	111.3
EDT / GNP (%)	..	20.7	42.8	43.2	47.6	44.6	38.3	33.7	36.1	44.2
TDS / XGS (%)	..	5.6	15.1	14.6	14.5	13.7	12.6	12.6	14.0	11.0
INT / XGS (%)	..	3.1	5.3	5.7	5.6	5.8	5.0	4.6	5.5	4.9
INT / GNP (%)	..	1.6	2.0	2.0	2.0	2.1	1.8	1.6	1.6	1.9
RES / EDT (%)	..	90.9	21.4	24.7	25.3	27.0	29.5	33.6	31.6	32.5
RES / MGS (months)	..	6.3	3.3	3.6	4.4	4.3	4.2	4.5	4.7	5.5
Short-term / EDT (%)	..	25.2	24.0	27.6	23.1	21.1	21.0	21.2	19.7	19.5
Concessional / EDT (%)	..	21.5	24.1	25.9	25.9	27.1	29.8	29.9	28.8	28.1
Multilateral / EDT (%)	..	6.7	8.6	9.8	10.1	10.8	11.4	11.4	11.4	11.4

MIDDLE EAST AND NORTH AFRICA

(US$ million, unless otherwise indicated)

	1970	1980	1990	1993	1994	1995	1996	1997	1998	1999
5. LONG-TERM DEBT										
DEBT OUTSTANDING (LDOD)	**4,168**	**61,770**	**137,500**	**138,893**	**158,179**	**164,435**	**159,056**	**150,326**	**164,114**	**169,456**
Public and publicly guaranteed	**4,153**	**61,175**	**135,998**	**138,011**	**155,958**	**161,121**	**155,326**	**145,713**	**159,644**	**161,414**
Official creditors	3,045	31,474	80,849	91,919	108,533	116,172	115,087	107,291	109,790	107,868
Multilateral	172	5,606	15,729	18,989	21,083	22,882	23,329	22,081	23,797	24,387
Concessional	32	2,554	3,608	4,167	4,606	5,236	5,852	6,230	6,832	7,375
Bilateral	2,873	25,869	65,121	72,930	87,450	93,290	91,758	85,210	85,994	83,481
Concessional	2,466	15,482	40,598	45,996	49,309	51,896	55,240	51,833	53,133	52,790
Private creditors	1,109	29,701	55,149	46,092	47,424	44,949	40,239	38,422	49,854	53,546
Bonds	38	720	2,234	1,719	1,757	2,036	2,486	3,513	5,067	6,725
Commercial banks	56	10,331	18,130	16,388	17,221	16,852	15,995	19,141	22,069	23,028
Other private	1,014	18,650	34,785	27,984	28,446	26,061	21,758	15,768	22,718	23,793
Private nonguaranteed	**15**	**595**	**1,502**	**882**	**2,221**	**3,314**	**3,729**	**4,613**	**4,471**	**8,042**
Bonds	0	0	0	0	0	50	410	885	785	1,040
Commercial banks	15	595	1,502	882	2,221	3,264	3,319	3,728	3,686	7,002
Memo:										
IBRD	139	2,384	8,301	9,308	9,978	10,671	10,053	8,789	8,823	8,855
IDA	32	669	1,774	1,885	1,985	2,105	2,219	2,360	2,559	2,732
DISBURSEMENTS	**853**	**11,978**	**14,595**	**16,274**	**15,653**	**13,537**	**13,121**	**11,893**	**14,698**	**18,562**
Public and publicly guaranteed	**845**	**11,725**	**14,456**	**16,092**	**14,121**	**12,284**	**12,388**	**10,853**	**13,718**	**14,706**
Official creditors	420	5,781	6,368	6,511	5,295	5,871	6,315	4,991	3,728	5,548
Multilateral	32	705	2,392	2,807	2,821	3,367	3,541	2,857	2,594	3,269
Concessional	8	182	243	485	534	772	932	780	734	863
Bilateral	388	5,076	3,976	3,705	2,474	2,504	2,775	2,133	1,134	2,279
Concessional	255	3,451	1,913	1,796	1,783	2,113	1,755	1,342	859	1,340
Private creditors	425	5,943	8,087	9,581	8,827	6,414	6,073	5,863	9,991	9,158
Bonds	5	66	0	15	672	888	531	1,556	1,450	1,756
Commercial banks	17	1,631	807	1,004	2,178	1,279	2,727	1,894	3,918	3,283
Other private	403	4,246	7,280	8,561	5,977	4,247	2,815	2,413	4,623	4,119
Private nonguaranteed	**8**	**254**	**139**	**183**	**1,532**	**1,253**	**733**	**1,040**	**980**	**3,856**
Bonds	0	0	0	0	0	85	360	475	0	355
Commercial banks	8	254	139	183	1,532	1,168	373	565	980	3,501
Memo:										
IBRD	23	421	1,164	1,099	1,017	1,455	1,231	832	648	978
IDA	8	82	38	69	88	128	179	249	180	213
PRINCIPAL REPAYMENTS	**383**	**4,830**	**15,297**	**13,494**	**13,468**	**13,542**	**14,874**	**15,482**	**13,211**	**11,256**
Public and publicly guaranteed	**380**	**4,716**	**15,120**	**13,269**	**13,237**	**13,321**	**14,530**	**15,283**	**12,151**	**10,971**
Official creditors	228	910	4,982	3,601	6,073	7,512	7,983	9,244	5,530	6,208
Multilateral	16	202	1,314	1,550	1,799	2,094	1,939	2,685	2,065	2,511
Concessional	0	6	147	158	171	199	208	232	265	259
Bilateral	212	708	3,667	2,051	4,274	5,418	6,043	6,559	3,464	3,697
Concessional	137	386	1,621	673	766	705	1,089	1,203	1,313	990
Private creditors	152	3,806	10,139	9,668	7,164	5,809	6,547	6,039	6,621	4,763
Bonds	3	33	148	663	445	278	5	410	10	10
Commercial banks	2	1,465	2,120	2,688	2,199	1,671	2,531	2,239	2,659	2,022
Other private	146	2,309	7,871	6,317	4,521	3,861	4,011	3,390	3,952	2,731
Private nonguaranteed	**3**	**114**	**177**	**226**	**231**	**221**	**344**	**198**	**1,060**	**285**
Bonds	0	0	0	0	0	0	0	0	100	100
Commercial banks	3	114	177	226	231	221	344	198	960	185
Memo:										
IBRD	16	140	761	899	1,008	1,118	1,071	1,298	948	946
IDA	0	1	14	22	25	28	30	42	36	40
NET FLOWS ON DEBT	**470**	**7,149**	**-703**	**2,779**	**2,185**	**-5**	**-1,753**	**-3,589**	**1,488**	**7,306**
Public and publicly guaranteed	**465**	**7,009**	**-665**	**2,823**	**884**	**-1,037**	**-2,142**	**-4,430**	**1,567**	**3,735**
Official creditors	192	4,871	1,387	2,910	-779	-1,641	-1,668	-4,253	-1,802	-660
Multilateral	16	503	1,078	1,256	1,021	1,273	1,602	173	529	758
Concessional	8	175	97	327	363	573	724	549	469	604
Bilateral	176	4,368	309	1,654	-1,800	-2,914	-3,269	-4,426	-2,330	-1,418
Concessional	117	3,065	292	1,123	1,017	1,408	666	139	-454	350
Private creditors	273	2,137	-2,052	-87	1,662	604	-474	-177	3,370	4,395
Bonds	2	34	-148	-648	228	610	526	1,146	1,440	1,746
Commercial banks	15	167	-1,313	-1,683	-22	-392	196	-345	1,260	1,261
Other private	257	1,937	-591	2,244	1,457	386	-1,196	-977	670	1,388
Private nonguaranteed	**5**	**140**	**-38**	**-43**	**1,301**	**1,032**	**389**	**841**	**-80**	**3,571**
Bonds	0	0	0	0	0	85	360	475	-100	255
Commercial banks	5	140	-38	-43	1,301	947	29	366	20	3,316
Memo:										
IBRD	8	281	403	200	9	337	160	-466	-300	32
IDA	8	81	24	47	64	100	149	207	144	173

MIDDLE EAST AND NORTH AFRICA

(US$ million, unless otherwise indicated)

	1970	1980	1990	1993	1994	1995	1996	1997	1998	1999
INTEREST PAYMENTS (LINT)	**100**	**3,935**	**5,202**	**5,610**	**5,879**	**7,215**	**7,481**	**6,550**	**6,632**	**7,123**
Public and publicly guaranteed	**99**	**3,885**	**5,094**	**5,555**	**5,805**	**7,108**	**7,285**	**6,285**	**6,453**	**6,955**
Official creditors	65	954	2,453	2,812	3,172	4,372	4,913	4,109	3,993	4,142
Multilateral	9	239	866	1,137	1,281	1,377	1,377	1,294	1,280	1,430
Concessional	0	19	60	78	93	111	136	156	168	184
Bilateral	56	715	1,588	1,674	1,891	2,995	3,537	2,815	2,714	2,712
Concessional	42	336	453	729	818	988	1,132	981	1,016	1,041
Private creditors	34	2,931	2,641	2,744	2,633	2,737	2,372	2,177	2,460	2,813
Bonds	2	71	159	70	79	88	145	173	249	356
Commercial banks	0	1,488	942	1,107	1,159	1,206	946	763	1,034	1,578
Other private	32	1,372	1,540	1,567	1,395	1,443	1,281	1,241	1,177	879
Private nonguaranteed	**1**	**50**	**108**	**54**	**74**	**107**	**196**	**264**	**179**	**168**
Bonds	0	0	0	0	0	0	2	37	77	68
Commercial banks	1	50	108	54	74	107	194	227	101	100
Memo:										
IBRD	9	198	598	685	756	750	688	625	582	635
IDA	0	5	13	14	14	15	16	20	18	18
NET TRANSFERS ON DEBT	**370**	**3,214**	**-5,905**	**-2,830**	**-3,694**	**-7,220**	**-9,234**	**-10,138**	**-5,144**	**183**
Public and publicly guaranteed	**366**	**3,124**	**-5,758**	**-2,733**	**-4,922**	**-8,145**	**-9,427**	**-10,715**	**-4,886**	**-3,220**
Official creditors	127	3,917	-1,066	98	-3,951	-6,013	-6,581	-8,362	-5,795	-4,802
Multilateral	8	264	213	120	-260	-104	225	-1,121	-751	-672
Concessional	8	156	37	250	270	462	588	393	301	420
Bilateral	120	3,653	-1,279	-21	-3,691	-5,909	-6,806	-7,241	-5,044	-4,130
Concessional	76	2,729	-161	394	199	421	-466	-842	-1,469	-691
Private creditors	239	-794	-4,692	-2,831	-971	-2,133	-2,846	-2,353	910	1,582
Bonds	-1	-38	-307	-718	148	522	382	973	1,191	1,390
Commercial banks	14	-1,321	-2,255	-2,790	-1,181	-1,598	-750	-1,108	226	-317
Other private	225	565	-2,131	677	62	-1,057	-2,477	-2,218	-506	509
Private nonguaranteed	**4**	**90**	**-146**	**-98**	**1,227**	**926**	**193**	**577**	**-259**	**3,403**
Bonds	0	0	0	0	0	85	358	438	-177	187
Commercial banks	4	90	-146	-98	1,227	841	-165	139	-81	3,216
Memo:										
IBRD	-1	83	-195	-485	-746	-413	-528	-1,090	-882	-603
IDA	8	76	11	34	49	86	133	187	127	155
DEBT SERVICE (LTDS)	**482**	**8,764**	**20,499**	**19,104**	**19,347**	**20,757**	**22,355**	**22,031**	**19,843**	**18,379**
Public and publicly guaranteed	**479**	**8,601**	**20,214**	**18,824**	**19,042**	**20,430**	**21,815**	**21,569**	**18,604**	**17,926**
Official creditors	293	1,864	7,435	6,413	9,245	11,883	12,896	13,353	9,523	10,350
Multilateral	24	441	2,180	2,687	3,080	3,471	3,316	3,978	3,346	3,941
Concessional	0	25	207	235	264	310	344	387	433	443
Bilateral	268	1,423	5,255	3,725	6,165	8,413	9,580	9,374	6,178	6,409
Concessional	179	723	2,074	1,402	1,584	1,693	2,221	2,184	2,329	2,031
Private creditors	186	6,737	12,779	12,411	9,798	8,546	8,919	8,216	9,081	7,576
Bonds	6	104	307	733	524	366	150	583	259	366
Commercial banks	3	2,952	3,062	3,794	3,358	2,877	3,477	3,002	3,693	3,600
Other private	178	3,681	9,411	7,884	5,915	5,303	5,292	4,631	5,129	3,610
Private nonguaranteed	**3**	**164**	**285**	**280**	**305**	**328**	**540**	**463**	**1,239**	**453**
Bonds	0	0	0	0	0	0	2	37	177	168
Commercial banks	3	164	285	280	305	328	538	426	1,061	285
Memo:										
IBRD	24	338	1,359	1,584	1,764	1,867	1,759	1,922	1,530	1,581
IDA	0	6	27	36	39	43	45	61	54	58
UNDISBURSED DEBT	**1,916**	**28,066**	**31,780**	**36,439**	**31,377**	**31,718**	**26,245**	**22,699**	**29,816**	..
Official creditors	1,543	15,995	18,912	24,065	22,283	23,322	19,246	16,855	15,710	..
Private creditors	374	12,072	12,869	12,374	9,093	8,396	6,999	5,843	14,106	..
Memorandum items										
Concessional LDOD	2,499	18,036	44,206	50,163	53,915	57,133	61,092	58,063	59,964	60,165
Variable rate LDOD	41	10,209	29,818	33,049	46,559	49,656	46,586	42,461	41,171	..
Public sector LDOD	4,131	53,445	115,211	117,602	135,216	141,181	135,859	123,168	125,653	..
Private sector LDOD	37	741	1,583	1,185	1,588	1,680	1,862	2,286	2,607	..
6. CURRENCY COMPOSITION OF LONG-TERM DEBT (PERCENT)										
Deutsche mark	7.7	6.4	6.6	6.8	7.0	7.1	6.4	5.9	5.4	..
French franc	18.6	9.3	11.1	10.6	10.7	11.5	11.4	10.3	9.6	..
Japanese yen	0.0	5.7	6.3	8.7	8.8	8.7	8.2	7.8	7.6	..
Pound sterling	4.1	1.3	1.5	1.2	1.1	1.0	1.1	1.1	0.9	..
Swiss franc	1.1	1.3	0.9	0.7	0.7	0.8	0.6	0.6	0.6	..
U.S.dollars	33.0	46.4	38.2	37.2	38.5	37.7	38.2	39.4	38.3	..
Multiple currency	3.1	4.7	7.5	8.8	8.6	8.8	8.6	8.1	3.9	..
Special drawing rights	0.0	0.0	0.4	0.2	0.2	0.2	0.2	0.2	0.2	..
All other currencies	32.5	12.4	12.4	11.3	11.4	12.3	13.1	11.5	11.5	..

MIDDLE EAST AND NORTH AFRICA

(US$ million, unless otherwise indicated)

	1970	1980	1990	1993	1994	1995	1996	1997	1998	1999
7. DEBT RESTRUCTURINGS										
Total amount rescheduled	0	0	4,565	4,446	15,786	8,954	6,138	3,355	854	..
Debt stock rescheduled	0	0	2,732	2,979	10,785	3,178	1,805	0	0	..
Principal rescheduled	0	0	1,039	1,116	4,286	4,944	3,731	2,944	760	..
Official	0	0	679	186	718	703	525	602	216	..
Private	0	0	360	930	3,568	4,241	3,207	2,343	545	..
Interest rescheduled	..	..	219	349	655	528	397	250	81	..
Official	0	0	137	56	170	132	96	107	54	..
Private	0	0	82	293	486	397	301	143	27	..
Debt forgiven	0	3	10,614	231	338	358	52	2,264	17	..
Memo: interest forgiven	0	0	2,481	147	84	7	5	340	1	..
Debt stock reduction	0	0	0	97	0	13	9	0	0	..
of which debt buyback	0	0	0	0	0	0	0	0	0	..
8. DEBT STOCK-FLOW RECONCILIATION										
Total change in debt stocks	..	..	-5,727	5,339	14,562	2,960	-6,338	-10,406	13,621	..
Net flows on debt	1,030	8,664	627	6,218	7,860	-444	-1,074	-4,802	684	8,101
Net change in interest arrears	..	..	-1,478	212	292	289	244	-287	179	..
Interest capitalized	..	..	219	349	655	528	397	250	81	..
Debt forgiveness or reduction	..	..	-10,614	-328	-338	-371	-61	-2,264	-17	..
Cross-currency valuation	..	..	6,113	-770	6,470	2,606	-4,941	-6,468	4,016	..
Residual	..	..	-593	-343	-378	351	-903	3,165	8,677	..
9. AVERAGE TERMS OF NEW COMMITMENTS										
ALL CREDITORS										
Interest (%)	4.6	6.4	7.4	5.5	5.5	6.0	5.3	5.5	5.7	..
Maturity (years)	18.6	18.1	13.5	14.7	13.2	14.1	13.3	14.7	12.0	..
Grace period (years)	6.2	4.7	4.0	4.7	4.0	4.5	4.0	6.1	2.5	..
Grant element (%)	33.5	23.7	15.7	23.2	22.5	21.7	24.2	25.9	20.3	..
Official creditors										
Interest (%)	3.7	4.7	5.5	5.4	4.9	5.3	5.1	4.5	3.7	..
Maturity (years)	23.5	24.1	21.4	19.2	19.1	18.0	17.0	17.7	20.5	..
Grace period (years)	8.4	5.9	6.3	5.9	6.0	5.1	5.1	5.2	5.6	..
Grant element (%)	43.6	38.2	32.2	29.4	32.2	28.1	29.8	33.5	42.2	..
Private creditors										
Interest (%)	6.3	8.6	8.8	5.7	6.2	7.0	5.6	6.9	6.2	..
Maturity (years)	9.4	10.7	7.6	8.5	6.7	7.9	8.7	10.5	9.9	..
Grace period (years)	2.0	3.1	2.4	3.0	1.9	3.5	2.7	7.3	1.7	..
Grant element (%)	14.7	5.7	3.4	14.8	11.9	11.7	17.1	15.4	14.8	..
Memorandum items										
Commitments	1,207	11,467	15,347	13,483	8,482	11,708	8,538	6,899	14,707	..
Official creditors	785	6,363	6,573	7,755	4,410	7,201	4,772	3,994	2,978	..
Private creditors	423	5,104	8,774	5,727	4,073	4,507	3,766	2,905	11,729	..

10. GRAPH OF AGGREGATE NET RESOURCE FLOWS

(current prices, US$ million)

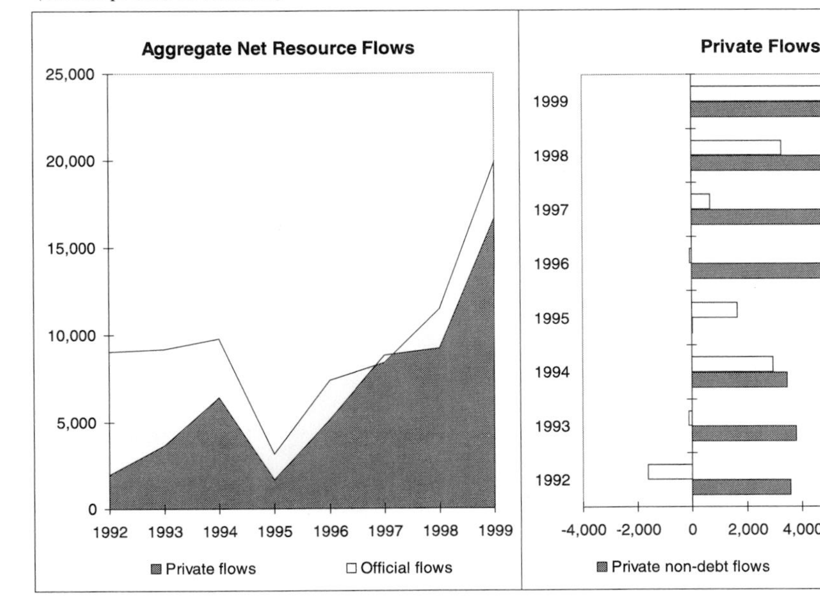

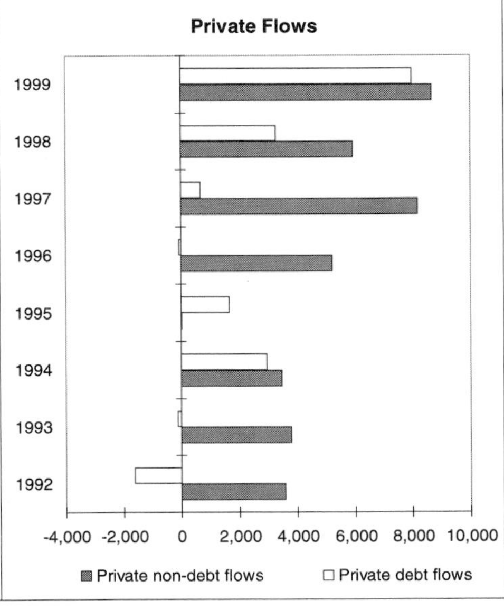

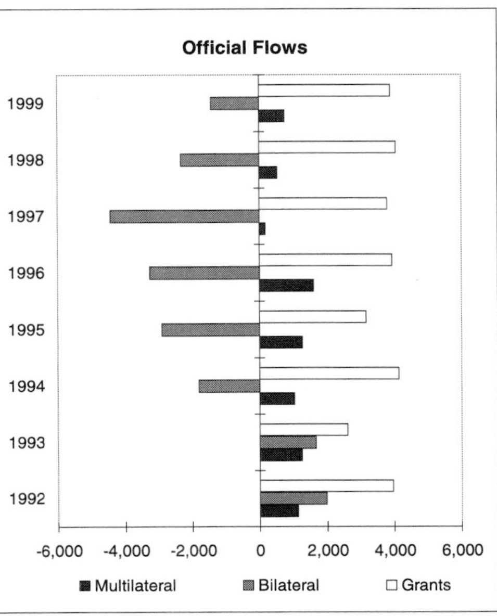

SOUTH ASIA

(US$ million, unless otherwise indicated)

	1970	1980	1990	1993	1994	1995	1996	1997	1998	1999
1. SUMMARY DEBT DATA										
TOTAL DEBT STOCKS (EDT)	..	**38,015**	**129,899**	**148,012**	**162,129**	**157,371**	**155,522**	**155,259**	**163,775**	**170,739**
Long-term debt (LDOD)	**11,327**	**33,053**	**112,991**	**134,547**	**147,907**	**143,031**	**141,395**	**144,255**	**154,151**	**159,848**
Public and publicly guaranteed	11,222	32,696	111,263	131,630	140,221	134,730	131,931	132,624	143,063	147,169
Private nonguaranteed	105	357	1,727	2,917	7,687	8,301	9,465	11,630	11,088	12,679
Use of IMF credit	**124**	**2,508**	**4,537**	**7,410**	**7,211**	**5,252**	**3,795**	**2,781**	**2,461**	**2,401**
Short-term debt	..	**2,454**	**12,371**	**6,056**	**7,011**	**9,087**	**10,331**	**8,223**	**7,163**	**8,490**
of which interest arrears on LDOD	..	0	17	33	47	56	125	119	261	261
Official creditors	..	0	7	8	14	21	22	24	106	..
Private creditors	..	0	11	25	32	35	103	96	156	..
Memo: principal arrears on LDOD	..	0	34	37	52	81	196	213	508	509
Official creditors	..	0	34	27	35	36	58	58	242	..
Private creditors	..	0	1	9	17	45	138	154	267	..
Memo: export credits	..	28	9,370	11,070	13,155	14,591	13,991	14,137	15,044	..
TOTAL DEBT FLOWS										
Disbursements	**1,476**	**6,358**	**12,256**	**13,443**	**13,578**	**11,785**	**12,074**	**13,984**	**15,547**	**13,291**
Long-term debt	1,466	4,711	10,381	12,871	13,058	11,583	11,918	13,704	15,230	12,670
IMF purchases	10	1,647	1,875	572	520	202	155	280	316	621
Principal repayments	**721**	**1,552**	**5,316**	**6,397**	**9,499**	**11,593**	**10,516**	**11,302**	**9,653**	**8,195**
Long-term debt	461	1,226	4,148	6,017	8,185	9,597	9,084	10,194	8,913	7,514
IMF repurchases	260	326	1,168	380	1,314	1,996	1,432	1,109	740	681
Net flows on debt	**1,180**	**5,850**	**8,495**	**1,815**	**5,021**	**2,259**	**2,734**	**579**	**4,691**	**6,423**
of which short-term debt	..	1,045	1,555	-5,232	942	2,067	1,175	-2,102	-1,203	1,327
Interest payments (INT)	..	**1,217**	**6,192**	**5,477**	**6,100**	**6,582**	**6,056**	**6,556**	**6,736**	**7,016**
Long-term debt	282	864	4,734	4,694	5,380	5,723	5,373	5,785	6,204	6,561
IMF charges	0	61	253	316	269	233	150	91	63	56
Short-term debt	..	292	1,204	467	451	627	533	680	469	399
Net transfers on debt	..	**4,633**	**2,303**	**-3,662**	**-1,079**	**-4,323**	**-3,323**	**-5,977**	**-2,046**	**-593**
Total debt service paid (TDS)	..	**2,770**	**11,507**	**11,874**	**15,599**	**18,175**	**16,571**	**17,858**	**16,389**	**15,211**
Long-term debt	743	2,090	8,883	10,711	13,565	15,320	14,457	15,979	15,117	14,075
IMF repurchases and charges	260	387	1,420	695	1,584	2,228	1,582	1,199	804	737
Short-term debt (interest only)	..	292	1,204	467	451	627	533	680	469	399
2. AGGREGATE NET RESOURCE FLOWS AND NET TRANSFERS (LONG-TERM)										
NET RESOURCE FLOWS	**1,329**	**6,470**	**9,221**	**12,235**	**15,254**	**9,798**	**13,878**	**13,229**	**12,586**	**11,817**
Net flow of long-term debt (ex. IMF)	1,005	3,484	6,233	6,854	4,873	1,986	2,835	3,510	6,318	5,156
Foreign direct investment (net)	69	185	464	1,118	1,595	2,953	3,526	4,908	3,659	3,420
Portfolio equity flows	0	0	105	2,025	6,223	2,340	5,198	2,477	351	1,091
Grants (excluding technical coop.)	255	2,800	2,419	2,238	2,563	2,519	2,319	2,335	2,258	2,150
Memo: technical coop. grants	138	690	1,583	1,681	1,513	1,564	1,454	1,243	1,134	1,225
official net resource flows	1,250	5,232	7,047	5,810	6,078	3,005	4,845	3,600	5,005	6,938
private net resource flows	79	1,238	2,174	6,425	9,176	6,793	9,033	9,629	7,581	4,879
NET TRANSFERS	**1,033**	**5,584**	**4,394**	**7,428**	**9,744**	**3,924**	**8,311**	**7,158**	**6,052**	**4,867**
Interest on long-term debt	282	864	4,734	4,694	5,380	5,723	5,373	5,785	6,204	6,561
Profit remittances on FDI	14	22	92	113	129	152	194	286	330	389
Memo: official net transfers	1,014	4,579	4,733	3,141	3,150	-5	2,053	932	2,259	4,043
private net transfers	19	1,005	-339	4,287	6,594	3,928	6,258	6,226	3,793	824
3. MAJOR ECONOMIC AGGREGATES										
Gross national product (GNP)	85,391	237,953	405,725	379,616	433,684	482,663	523,002	548,563	560,450	604,825
Exports of goods & services (XGS)	4,108	23,542	39,674	51,982	61,833	72,821	79,688	85,063	86,616	105,083
of which workers remittances	..	4,913	4,833	7,653	10,846	11,135	15,297	15,613	13,512	14,383
Imports of goods & services (MGS)	5,770	29,615	52,723	59,667	70,756	86,213	94,538	98,187	97,588	106,708
International reserves (RES)	..	15,404	8,893	21,497	34,085	30,704	30,940	34,784	37,375	39,899
Current account balance	..	-4,882	-11,637	-5,535	-6,848	-10,974	-12,811	-10,962	-7,719	-9,586
4. DEBT INDICATORS										
EDT / XGS (%)	..	161.5	327.4	284.7	262.2	216.1	195.2	182.5	189.1	162.5
EDT / GNP (%)	..	16.0	32.0	39.0	37.4	32.6	29.7	28.3	29.2	28.2
TDS / XGS (%)	..	11.8	29.0	22.8	25.2	25.0	20.8	21.0	18.9	14.5
INT / XGS (%)	..	5.2	15.6	10.5	9.9	9.0	7.6	7.7	7.8	6.7
INT / GNP (%)	..	0.5	1.5	1.4	1.4	1.4	1.2	1.2	1.2	1.2
RES / EDT (%)	..	40.5	6.9	14.5	21.0	19.5	19.9	22.4	22.8	23.4
RES / MGS (months)	..	6.2	2.0	4.3	5.8	4.3	3.9	4.3	4.6	4.5
Short-term / EDT (%)	..	6.5	9.5	4.1	4.3	5.8	6.6	5.3	4.4	5.0
Concessional / EDT (%)	..	74.2	56.3	55.5	56.0	56.6	51.9	49.5	50.6	50.2
Multilateral / EDT (%)	..	24.6	29.5	33.8	35.1	36.3	36.4	36.0	36.6	36.5

SOUTH ASIA

(US$ million, unless otherwise indicated)

	1970	1980	1990	1993	1994	1995	1996	1997	1998	1999
5. LONG-TERM DEBT										
DEBT OUTSTANDING (LDOD)	**11,327**	**33,053**	**112,991**	**134,547**	**147,907**	**143,031**	**141,395**	**144,255**	**154,151**	**159,848**
Public and publicly guaranteed	**11,222**	**32,696**	**111,263**	**131,630**	**140,221**	**134,730**	**131,931**	**132,624**	**143,063**	**147,169**
Official creditors	10,542	30,289	86,873	101,326	112,682	109,589	106,484	102,305	108,841	113,905
Multilateral	2,205	9,345	38,287	50,024	56,963	57,097	56,596	55,903	59,895	62,345
Concessional	1,347	7,842	26,975	33,683	38,176	39,468	40,087	40,037	43,009	44,885
Bilateral	8,337	20,944	48,586	51,302	55,719	52,492	49,887	46,402	48,945	51,560
Concessional	7,544	20,379	46,172	48,463	52,572	49,565	40,644	36,856	39,815	40,860
Private creditors	680	2,407	24,390	30,304	27,539	25,142	25,447	30,320	34,222	33,264
Bonds	14	2	2,639	3,832	3,890	3,407	1,664	2,673	6,792	6,678
Commercial banks	54	1,671	16,823	19,906	15,332	14,162	16,716	21,881	22,720	22,327
Other private	612	734	4,929	6,566	8,317	7,573	7,068	5,766	4,710	4,259
Private nonguaranteed	**105**	**357**	**1,727**	**2,917**	**7,687**	**8,301**	**9,465**	**11,630**	**11,088**	**12,679**
Bonds	0	0	0	794	1,203	1,065	2,478	3,847	3,692	3,543
Commercial banks	105	357	1,727	2,123	6,484	7,236	6,987	7,783	7,397	9,136
Memo:										
IBRD	852	1,242	9,646	12,609	14,165	13,035	11,861	11,253	11,191	11,117
IDA	1,347	7,065	21,070	25,583	28,421	29,001	29,433	29,761	31,377	32,638
DISBURSEMENTS	**1,466**	**4,711**	**10,381**	**12,871**	**13,058**	**11,583**	**11,918**	**13,704**	**15,230**	**12,670**
Public and publicly guaranteed	**1,438**	**4,414**	**10,128**	**11,416**	**11,760**	**9,649**	**10,433**	**11,140**	**14,122**	**10,189**
Official creditors	1,317	3,372	7,048	6,954	7,855	6,272	7,161	7,823	8,017	8,757
Multilateral	198	1,416	4,439	4,379	4,863	3,968	4,581	4,090	4,101	4,582
Concessional	84	1,183	2,364	2,144	2,942	2,273	2,703	2,254	2,509	2,481
Bilateral	1,119	1,956	2,608	2,575	2,992	2,304	2,580	3,733	3,916	4,175
Concessional	1,002	1,754	2,044	1,995	2,419	2,004	1,839	2,305	3,213	1,937
Private creditors	121	1,042	3,081	4,462	3,905	3,377	3,272	3,317	6,105	1,432
Bonds	0	0	427	0	150	86	425	1,075	4,299	100
Commercial banks	16	797	2,067	2,118	1,062	1,902	1,798	1,753	1,177	290
Other private	105	245	587	2,344	2,692	1,389	1,049	489	629	1,042
Private nonguaranteed	**28**	**297**	**253**	**1,455**	**1,298**	**1,934**	**1,486**	**2,564**	**1,109**	**2,481**
Bonds	0	0	0	794	412	520	785	1,371	300	0
Commercial banks	28	297	253	661	885	1,414	701	1,193	809	2,481
Memo:										
IBRD	108	190	1,576	1,566	1,055	860	1,056	1,032	664	1,053
IDA	84	928	1,584	1,427	1,860	1,372	1,634	1,500	1,602	1,741
PRINCIPAL REPAYMENTS	**461**	**1,226**	**4,148**	**6,017**	**8,185**	**9,597**	**9,084**	**10,194**	**8,913**	**7,514**
Public and publicly guaranteed	**435**	**1,128**	**3,789**	**5,347**	**7,794**	**9,100**	**8,542**	**9,559**	**8,314**	**6,624**
Official creditors	323	940	2,420	3,381	4,340	5,786	4,635	6,557	5,270	3,969
Multilateral	64	135	1,011	1,534	1,867	2,227	1,875	2,027	1,986	1,998
Concessional	0	24	241	354	395	470	505	566	631	574
Bilateral	259	805	1,409	1,848	2,473	3,559	2,760	4,530	3,284	1,971
Concessional	166	731	1,257	1,399	1,981	3,034	2,289	3,604	2,662	1,218
Private creditors	113	188	1,369	1,965	3,453	3,313	3,907	3,002	3,045	2,655
Bonds	3	0	280	338	404	311	1,242	2	264	267
Commercial banks	12	44	371	829	1,685	1,983	1,695	1,342	984	861
Other private	98	145	718	798	1,365	1,019	970	1,657	1,796	1,527
Private nonguaranteed	**26**	**98**	**359**	**670**	**391**	**498**	**542**	**635**	**599**	**890**
Bonds	0	0	0	0	0	0	0	150	149	149
Commercial banks	26	98	359	670	391	498	542	485	450	741
Memo:										
IBRD	64	99	553	926	1,019	1,173	1,077	1,036	1,049	1,127
IDA	0	19	151	239	269	318	340	366	421	480
NET FLOWS ON DEBT	**1,005**	**3,484**	**6,233**	**6,854**	**4,873**	**1,986**	**2,835**	**3,510**	**6,318**	**5,156**
Public and publicly guaranteed	**1,003**	**3,286**	**6,339**	**6,070**	**3,966**	**549**	**1,891**	**1,581**	**5,807**	**3,565**
Official creditors	995	2,432	4,628	3,573	3,515	486	2,526	1,265	2,747	4,788
Multilateral	134	1,281	3,428	2,845	2,996	1,741	2,706	2,063	2,115	2,584
Concessional	84	1,160	2,123	1,790	2,546	1,802	2,198	1,688	1,878	1,907
Bilateral	861	1,150	1,200	728	519	-1,255	-180	-797	632	2,204
Concessional	836	1,023	787	596	438	-1,030	-449	-1,300	551	719
Private creditors	8	854	1,712	2,497	451	64	-635	315	3,061	-1,223
Bonds	-3	0	147	-338	-254	-226	-817	1,073	4,035	-167
Commercial banks	4	753	1,696	1,289	-622	-81	103	411	193	-571
Other private	8	101	-131	1,546	1,327	370	80	-1,169	-1,167	-485
Private nonguaranteed	**2**	**199**	**-107**	**784**	**906**	**1,436**	**944**	**1,929**	**510**	**1,591**
Bonds	0	0	0	794	412	520	785	1,221	151	-149
Commercial banks	2	199	-107	-10	494	916	159	708	359	1,740
Memo:										
IBRD	44	91	1,023	640	37	-314	-21	-5	-384	-74
IDA	84	909	1,433	1,188	1,591	1,054	1,295	1,133	1,181	1,261

SOUTH ASIA

(US$ million, unless otherwise indicated)

	1970	1980	1990	1993	1994	1995	1996	1997	1998	1999
INTEREST PAYMENTS (LINT)	**282**	**864**	**4,734**	**4,694**	**5,380**	**5,723**	**5,373**	**5,785**	**6,204**	**6,561**
Public and publicly guaranteed	**276**	**832**	**4,587**	**4,489**	**4,897**	**5,060**	**4,823**	**5,465**	**5,586**	**5,971**
Official creditors	236	653	2,314	2,670	2,928	3,009	2,792	2,668	2,747	2,895
Multilateral	58	181	1,072	1,434	1,565	1,645	1,512	1,428	1,362	1,470
Concessional	9	55	206	268	293	318	322	325	329	353
Bilateral	179	472	1,241	1,236	1,363	1,365	1,281	1,240	1,385	1,425
Concessional	137	443	1,073	1,051	1,142	1,102	1,016	901	804	869
Private creditors	40	179	2,273	1,819	1,970	2,050	2,031	2,797	2,839	3,076
Bonds	1	0	182	258	221	192	590	117	139	353
Commercial banks	3	123	1,806	1,246	1,218	1,313	935	2,247	2,340	2,430
Other private	36	56	285	315	530	545	506	433	361	293
Private nonguaranteed	**6**	**32**	**148**	**206**	**483**	**663**	**550**	**321**	**618**	**590**
Bonds	0	0	0	1	21	58	91	156	268	256
Commercial banks	6	32	148	205	462	604	459	165	351	334
Memo:										
IBRD	48	104	753	918	979	995	890	789	723	734
IDA	9	47	150	185	197	215	216	217	225	234
NET TRANSFERS ON DEBT	**723**	**2,620**	**1,498**	**2,160**	**-507**	**-3,737**	**-2,538**	**-2,276**	**113**	**-1,405**
Public and publicly guaranteed	**727**	**2,453**	**1,753**	**1,581**	**-931**	**-4,510**	**-2,932**	**-3,884**	**222**	**-2,406**
Official creditors	759	1,778	2,314	903	588	-2,524	-266	-1,403	0	1,893
Multilateral	77	1,100	2,356	1,411	1,432	96	1,195	634	754	1,114
Concessional	75	1,105	1,918	1,523	2,254	1,484	1,877	1,362	1,548	1,554
Bilateral	682	678	-42	-508	-844	-2,620	-1,461	-2,037	-753	779
Concessional	700	580	-286	-455	-705	-2,132	-1,466	-2,201	-253	-150
Private creditors	-32	675	-561	678	-1,519	-1,987	-2,666	-2,481	221	-4,299
Bonds	-4	0	-35	-596	-475	-418	-1,407	957	3,896	-520
Commercial banks	1	631	-110	43	-1,841	-1,394	-833	-1,836	-2,147	-3,001
Other private	-28	44	-416	1,231	797	-175	-426	-1,602	-1,528	-778
Private nonguaranteed	**-4**	**167**	**-255**	**579**	**424**	**774**	**394**	**1,608**	**-108**	**1,001**
Bonds	0	0	0	793	392	462	694	1,065	-117	-405
Commercial banks	-4	167	-255	-215	32	312	-300	543	9	1,406
Memo:										
IBRD	-4	-13	271	-278	-942	-1,309	-911	-794	-1,107	-808
IDA	75	862	1,282	1,004	1,393	839	1,078	916	956	1,027
DEBT SERVICE (LTDS)	**743**	**2,090**	**8,883**	**10,711**	**13,565**	**15,320**	**14,457**	**15,979**	**15,117**	**14,075**
Public and publicly guaranteed	**711**	**1,960**	**8,376**	**9,835**	**12,691**	**14,159**	**13,365**	**15,023**	**13,900**	**12,595**
Official creditors	559	1,594	4,734	6,051	7,268	8,796	7,427	9,225	8,016	6,864
Multilateral	121	316	2,083	2,968	3,432	3,872	3,387	3,456	3,347	3,468
Concessional	10	78	447	621	688	789	827	892	960	927
Bilateral	438	1,277	2,650	3,083	3,836	4,924	4,041	5,770	4,669	3,396
Concessional	303	1,174	2,330	2,450	3,124	4,136	3,305	4,505	3,466	2,087
Private creditors	152	367	3,642	3,784	5,423	5,363	5,938	5,798	5,884	5,731
Bonds	4	0	462	596	625	503	1,832	119	403	620
Commercial banks	15	166	2,177	2,076	2,903	3,296	2,631	3,589	3,324	3,291
Other private	133	201	1,003	1,113	1,895	1,564	1,476	2,090	2,157	1,820
Private nonguaranteed	**32**	**130**	**507**	**876**	**874**	**1,161**	**1,092**	**956**	**1,217**	**1,480**
Bonds	0	0	0	1	21	58	91	306	417	405
Commercial banks	32	130	507	875	853	1,102	1,001	649	800	1,075
Memo:										
IBRD	112	204	1,306	1,843	1,998	2,169	1,968	1,825	1,771	1,861
IDA	10	66	301	423	466	533	556	584	646	714
UNDISBURSED DEBT	**3,419**	**14,301**	**41,877**	**39,715**	**39,754**	**36,562**	**34,709**	**32,681**	**30,143**	..
Official creditors	3,041	12,954	38,809	35,045	36,358	34,512	32,675	29,325	27,306	..
Private creditors	379	1,347	3,068	4,670	3,396	2,050	2,034	3,356	2,838	..
Memorandum items										
Concessional LDOD	8,891	28,222	73,147	82,147	90,748	89,034	80,731	76,893	82,824	85,745
Variable rate LDOD	105	1,008	14,692	21,506	27,553	27,433	30,003	33,928	34,932	..
Public sector LDOD	10,777	31,006	105,448	125,517	133,895	128,477	125,494	126,460	136,670	..
Private sector LDOD	550	852	2,497	3,649	8,436	8,975	10,307	12,332	12,018	..
6. CURRENCY COMPOSITION OF LONG-TERM DEBT (PERCENT)										
Deutsche mark	9.7	8.3	5.9	5.3	5.9	5.8	5.2	4.6	4.8	..
French franc	1.5	2.3	1.7	1.6	1.9	2.0	1.8	1.7	1.7	..
Japanese yen	5.5	8.8	11.9	15.0	17.3	16.1	14.8	13.6	15.1	..
Pound sterling	22.5	17.7	4.8	3.8	3.4	3.4	3.2	3.0	2.7	..
Swiss franc	0.4	0.3	0.5	0.5	0.6	0.6	0.5	0.4	0.3	..
U.S.dollars	42.0	41.9	51.6	48.4	43.7	44.3	47.1	50.9	50.6	..
Multiple currency	8.5	7.3	13.6	16.9	18.8	19.2	18.7	17.6	17.1	..
Special drawing rights	0.0	0.0	0.8	0.8	1.0	1.1	1.3	1.3	1.4	..
All other currencies	9.9	9.6	4.6	3.6	3.4	3.3	3.2	2.8	2.5	..

SOUTH ASIA

(US$ million, unless otherwise indicated)

	1970	1980	1990	1993	1994	1995	1996	1997	1998	1999
7. DEBT RESTRUCTURINGS										
Total amount rescheduled	0	0	0	0	0	0	1	0	0	..
Debt stock rescheduled	0	0	0	0	0	0	0	0	0	..
Principal rescheduled	0	0	0	0	0	0	0	0	0	..
Official	0	0	0	0	0	0	0	0	0	..
Private	0	0	0	0	0	0	0	0	0	..
Interest rescheduled	..	..	0	0	0	0	0	0	0	..
Official	0	0	0	0	0	0	0	0	0	..
Private	0	0	0	0	0	0	0	0	0	..
Debt forgiven	0	6	0	2	2	7	0	0	0	..
Memo: interest forgiven	0	0	0	0	0	0	0	0	0	..
Debt stock reduction	0	0	0	0	0	0	0	0	0	..
of which debt buyback	0	0	0	0	0	0	0	0	0	..
8. DEBT STOCK-FLOW RECONCILIATION										
Total change in debt stocks	..	..	13,280	5,051	14,117	-4,758	-1,849	-263	8,516	..
Net flows on debt	1,180	5,850	8,495	1,815	5,021	2,259	2,734	579	4,691	6,423
Net change in interest arrears	..	..	5	8	13	10	69	-5	142	..
Interest capitalized	..	..	0	0	0	0	0	0	0	..
Debt forgiveness or reduction	..	..	0	-2	-2	-7	0	0	0	..
Cross-currency valuation	..	..	2,533	2,097	8,112	-3,795	-5,114	-3,376	2,864	..
Residual	..	..	2,247	1,134	974	-3,225	463	2,540	820	..
9. AVERAGE TERMS OF NEW COMMITMENTS										
ALL CREDITORS										
Interest (%)	2.6	4.7	4.6	4.9	3.5	3.8	4.3	4.6	5.7	..
Maturity (years)	32.6	32.5	24.7	20.9	25.9	25.0	21.7	19.8	17.6	..
Grace period (years)	9.8	7.5	7.7	5.8	7.7	7.7	7.0	6.2	6.4	..
Grant element (%)	30.5	21.4	25.3	20.3	31.8	24.7	17.8	20.5	29.7	..
Official creditors										
Interest (%)	2.3	2.2	3.6	3.3	3.0	3.6	4.0	3.6	4.1	..
Maturity (years)	34.9	39.4	28.9	27.2	28.0	26.8	27.0	26.7	27.8	..
Grace period (years)	10.6	8.8	8.1	7.5	8.3	8.1	7.8	7.6	7.7	..
Grant element (%)	32.5	27.4	28.9	28.0	34.9	26.8	23.3	25.9	47.6	..
Private creditors										
Interest (%)	5.9	12.8	6.7	7.5	7.2	5.7	5.2	6.4	7.3	..
Maturity (years)	11.6	10.9	15.2	10.5	8.6	6.1	7.4	7.9	7.2	..
Grace period (years)	2.7	3.6	6.8	3.1	3.4	3.8	4.7	3.8	5.1	..
Grant element (%)	12.1	2.6	17.1	7.7	6.1	2.6	2.8	11.1	11.5	..
Memorandum items										
Commitments	2,002	8,182	13,719	13,193	10,085	7,788	12,085	12,337	11,575	..
Official creditors	1,798	6,227	9,524	8,211	8,996	7,120	8,832	7,787	5,835	..
Private creditors	203	1,956	4,195	4,982	1,088	669	3,253	4,551	5,740	..

10. GRAPH OF AGGREGATE NET RESOURCE FLOWS

(current prices, US$ million)

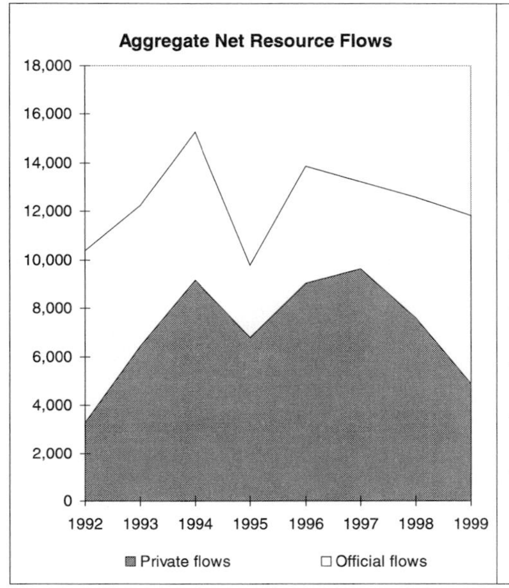

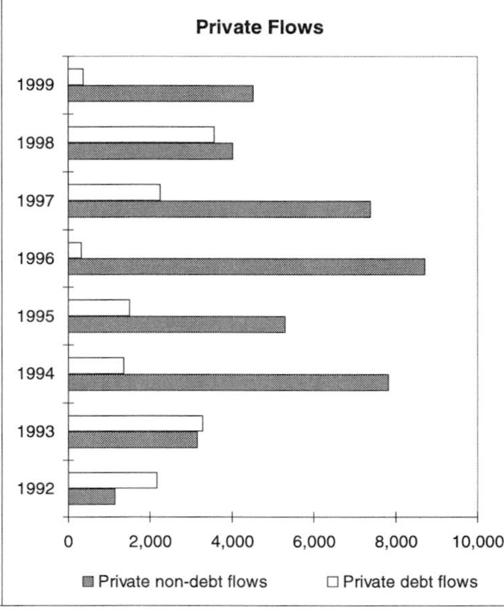

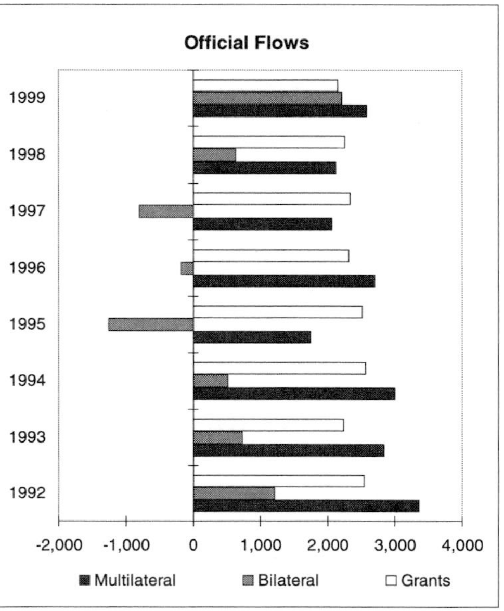

SUB-SAHARAN AFRICA

(US$ million, unless otherwise indicated)

	1970	1980	1990	1993	1994	1995	1996	1997	1998	1999
1. SUMMARY DEBT DATA										
TOTAL DEBT STOCKS (EDT)	**..**	**60,820**	**176,873**	**194,817**	**221,308**	**235,360**	**231,833**	**223,067**	**230,132**	**231,100**
Long-term debt (LDOD)	**6,067**	**46,581**	**149,374**	**158,376**	**177,286**	**185,918**	**180,696**	**174,696**	**180,250**	**179,102**
Public and publicly guaranteed	5,758	42,014	144,098	153,290	165,455	174,206	170,481	165,274	171,138	169,369
Private nonguaranteed	309	4,567	5,276	5,086	11,830	11,713	10,216	9,423	9,112	9,733
Use of IMF credit	**106**	**3,033**	**6,612**	**7,018**	**7,920**	**8,674**	**8,441**	**7,388**	**7,388**	**7,310**
Short-term debt	**..**	**11,206**	**20,887**	**29,423**	**36,102**	**40,769**	**42,696**	**40,983**	**42,494**	**44,688**
of which interest arrears on LDOD	..	1,710	9,308	16,868	18,475	20,538	20,094	18,181	20,166	20,362
Official creditors	..	1,606	6,411	12,864	14,206	16,016	16,325	15,445	17,157	..
Private creditors	..	104	2,897	4,004	4,269	4,522	3,768	2,736	3,009	..
Memo: principal arrears on LDOD	..	1,726	17,514	31,747	35,189	41,313	40,651	38,640	43,027	44,571
Official creditors	..	1,037	9,902	20,509	23,524	28,748	30,322	31,075	34,668	..
Private creditors	..	689	7,613	11,238	11,665	12,566	10,328	7,565	8,360	..
Memo: export credits	..	3,138	54,895	50,744	47,183	45,729	43,593	50,248	49,443	..
TOTAL DEBT FLOWS										
Disbursements	**1,253**	**11,786**	**10,387**	**9,608**	**11,868**	**14,038**	**10,216**	**12,698**	**8,165**	**11,255**
Long-term debt	1,234	10,569	9,725	8,462	10,950	11,044	9,569	12,175	7,364	10,733
IMF purchases	19	1,217	662	1,146	918	2,994	648	523	801	522
Principal repayments	**456**	**3,176**	**5,587**	**3,917**	**7,054**	**9,443**	**9,325**	**10,944**	**8,899**	**9,989**
Long-term debt	393	2,792	4,634	3,463	6,587	7,071	8,728	9,879	7,787	9,390
IMF repurchases	63	384	952	454	467	2,372	596	1,066	1,112	599
Net flows on debt	**1,533**	**10,069**	**7,095**	**5,891**	**10,258**	**7,386**	**3,263**	**5,246**	**-1,241**	**3,264**
of which short-term debt	..	1,459	2,295	201	5,444	2,791	2,372	3,493	-507	1,998
Interest payments (INT)	**..**	**3,512**	**5,313**	**3,361**	**4,774**	**5,373**	**5,831**	**5,097**	**5,242**	**5,217**
Long-term debt	194	2,379	4,363	2,698	3,971	3,995	4,824	3,944	4,015	4,014
IMF charges	0	103	238	138	170	559	123	101	65	65
Short-term debt	..	1,030	712	525	634	819	884	1,052	1,162	1,138
Net transfers on debt	**..**	**6,556**	**1,782**	**2,530**	**5,483**	**2,013**	**-2,568**	**150**	**-6,483**	**-1,953**
Total debt service paid (TDS)	**..**	**6,689**	**10,900**	**7,278**	**11,829**	**14,816**	**15,156**	**16,041**	**14,142**	**15,206**
Long-term debt	586	5,171	8,997	6,161	10,558	11,066	13,552	13,822	11,802	13,404
IMF repurchases and charges	63	487	1,191	593	637	2,931	720	1,166	1,177	664
Short-term debt (interest only)	..	1,030	712	525	634	819	884	1,052	1,162	1,138
2. AGGREGATE NET RESOURCE FLOWS AND NET TRANSFERS (LONG-TERM)										
NET RESOURCE FLOWS	**1,667**	**11,445**	**18,082**	**17,437**	**20,528**	**23,777**	**17,696**	**21,216**	**14,895**	**17,509**
Net flow of long-term debt (ex. IMF)	841	7,776	5,090	4,999	4,363	3,973	840	2,297	-424	1,343
Foreign direct investment (net)	428	33	834	1,885	3,340	3,521	4,627	7,734	4,394	5,574
Portfolio equity flows	0	0	0	174	860	4,868	2,012	1,507	679	492
Grants (excluding technical coop.)	398	3,636	12,157	10,379	11,965	11,414	10,217	9,678	10,246	10,100
Memo: technical coop. grants	639	2,699	5,151	5,314	4,758	5,057	4,962	4,410	3,948	4,100
official net resource flows	895	7,212	16,799	14,685	15,619	14,276	12,149	11,607	11,444	10,264
private net resource flows	772	4,234	1,283	2,752	4,910	9,501	5,548	9,609	3,452	7,245
NET TRANSFERS	**383**	**5,111**	**9,228**	**10,206**	**11,747**	**15,355**	**8,657**	**13,327**	**6,679**	**8,810**
Interest on long-term debt	194	2,379	4,363	2,698	3,971	3,995	4,824	3,944	4,015	4,014
Profit remittances on FDI	1,090	3,956	4,490	4,533	4,811	4,427	4,216	3,946	4,202	4,685
Memo: official net transfers	781	6,521	14,087	12,735	13,590	12,263	9,487	9,522	9,409	8,184
private net transfers	-398	-1,411	-4,859	-2,529	-1,844	3,093	-830	3,805	-2,730	626
3. MAJOR ECONOMIC AGGREGATES										
Gross national product (GNP)	59,687	259,402	280,690	274,443	268,025	303,416	314,041	329,318	318,228	304,738
Exports of goods & services (XGS)	..	92,852	84,374	79,127	81,207	96,898	106,562	108,953	96,322	102,670
of which workers remittances	..	775	776	1,548	1,245	1,522	1,707	2,643	2,227	1,951
Imports of goods & services (MGS)	..	93,307	91,549	92,833	96,107	115,084	118,809	125,331	120,854	122,051
International reserves (RES)	3,085	22,950	15,417	15,198	17,503	20,976	23,283	29,507	30,306	33,036
Current account balance	..	429	-1,766	-8,461	-8,984	-11,894	-2,360	-9,347	-16,142	-10,264
4. DEBT INDICATORS										
EDT / XGS (%)	..	65.5	209.6	246.2	272.5	242.9	217.6	204.7	238.9	225.1
EDT / GNP (%)	..	23.5	63.0	71.0	82.6	77.6	73.8	67.7	72.3	75.8
TDS / XGS (%)	..	7.2	12.9	9.2	14.6	15.3	14.2	14.7	14.7	14.8
INT / XGS (%)	..	3.8	6.3	4.3	5.9	5.5	5.5	4.7	5.4	5.1
INT / GNP (%)	..	1.4	1.9	1.2	1.8	1.8	1.9	1.6	1.7	1.7
RES / EDT (%)	..	37.7	8.7	7.8	7.9	8.9	10.0	13.2	13.2	14.3
RES / MGS (months)	..	3.0	2.0	2.0	2.2	2.2	2.4	2.8	3.0	3.2
Short-term / EDT (%)	..	18.4	11.8	15.1	16.3	17.3	18.4	18.4	18.5	19.3
Concessional / EDT (%)	..	26.9	33.1	35.7	34.3	34.3	35.7	37.2	38.7	39.1
Multilateral / EDT (%)	..	12.5	21.6	23.7	23.1	23.2	23.6	24.0	24.8	25.1

SUB-SAHARAN AFRICA

(US$ million, unless otherwise indicated)

	1970	1980	1990	1993	1994	1995	1996	1997	1998	1999
5. LONG-TERM DEBT										
DEBT OUTSTANDING (LDOD)	**6,067**	**46,581**	**149,374**	**158,376**	**177,286**	**185,918**	**180,696**	**174,696**	**180,250**	**179,102**
Public and publicly guaranteed	**5,758**	**42,014**	**144,098**	**153,290**	**165,455**	**174,206**	**170,481**	**165,274**	**171,138**	**169,369**
Official creditors	4,187	25,671	108,737	119,897	130,813	137,419	135,359	130,530	137,565	135,896
Multilateral	869	7,599	38,203	46,097	51,178	54,684	54,678	53,552	57,021	58,060
Concessional	240	3,986	24,001	30,953	35,391	38,877	40,495	41,142	44,848	46,767
Bilateral	3,318	18,072	70,534	73,800	79,636	82,735	80,681	76,978	80,544	77,836
Concessional	2,970	12,385	34,459	38,631	40,462	41,900	42,245	41,783	44,257	43,481
Private creditors	1,571	16,343	35,361	33,394	34,642	36,787	35,122	34,744	33,573	33,473
Bonds	352	637	301	2,744	4,271	4,784	5,048	8,357	8,322	9,847
Commercial banks	128	7,780	14,455	11,900	12,373	13,254	15,816	13,414	12,502	10,964
Other private	1,090	7,927	20,604	18,750	17,998	18,749	14,258	12,973	12,749	12,662
Private nonguaranteed	**309**	**4,567**	**5,276**	**5,086**	**11,830**	**11,713**	**10,216**	**9,423**	**9,112**	**9,733**
Bonds	0	0	0	0	0	350	600	1,245	1,636	1,476
Commercial banks	309	4,567	5,276	5,086	11,830	11,363	9,616	8,178	7,476	8,257
Memo:										
IBRD	587	2,548	9,178	8,185	8,072	7,641	6,381	5,302	4,953	4,351
IDA	226	2,577	15,756	21,435	25,121	27,895	29,494	30,267	33,040	34,791
DISBURSEMENTS	**1,234**	**10,569**	**9,725**	**8,462**	**10,950**	**11,044**	**9,569**	**12,175**	**7,364**	**10,733**
Public and publicly guaranteed	**1,133**	**9,386**	**9,095**	**7,997**	**10,105**	**10,295**	**8,587**	**9,700**	**6,365**	**8,376**
Official creditors	667	4,244	7,193	6,498	6,287	5,851	5,257	4,900	4,295	4,670
Multilateral	150	1,676	4,554	4,604	5,012	4,231	4,159	4,057	3,433	3,637
Concessional	72	860	2,773	3,123	3,691	3,181	3,366	3,288	2,928	2,784
Bilateral	517	2,568	2,639	1,895	1,276	1,620	1,098	844	861	1,033
Concessional	441	1,697	2,090	1,705	1,149	1,486	832	673	587	777
Private creditors	466	5,142	1,902	1,498	3,818	4,444	3,330	4,801	2,070	3,706
Bonds	12	52	0	0	1,510	541	632	1,278	0	1,810
Commercial banks	16	2,331	374	621	1,437	1,655	1,361	2,140	1,426	832
Other private	437	2,759	1,529	877	871	2,248	1,336	1,383	644	1,064
Private nonguaranteed	**101**	**1,183**	**630**	**466**	**845**	**748**	**981**	**2,475**	**999**	**2,357**
Bonds	0	0	0	0	0	350	250	645	373	0
Commercial banks	101	1,183	630	466	845	398	731	1,830	626	2,357
Memo:										
IBRD	75	400	813	516	392	274	229	263	159	88
IDA	61	425	2,034	2,228	2,888	2,392	2,585	2,396	2,099	1,993
PRINCIPAL REPAYMENTS	**393**	**2,792**	**4,634**	**3,463**	**6,587**	**7,071**	**8,728**	**9,879**	**7,787**	**9,390**
Public and publicly guaranteed	**336**	**2,200**	**4,169**	**3,019**	**5,138**	**5,826**	**6,970**	**6,123**	**6,419**	**7,654**
Official creditors	171	668	2,552	2,193	2,634	2,989	3,326	2,971	3,097	4,506
Multilateral	33	198	1,349	1,593	1,986	2,027	2,001	1,971	1,858	2,237
Concessional	0	30	268	343	394	435	456	459	500	635
Bilateral	137	471	1,202	600	647	962	1,326	1,000	1,239	2,269
Concessional	110	216	311	419	315	436	424	563	874	737
Private creditors	166	1,532	1,618	826	2,504	2,836	3,644	3,152	3,323	3,148
Bonds	27	24	31	30	37	40	296	283	123	100
Commercial banks	10	721	1,015	387	1,337	1,260	1,689	1,711	2,194	2,135
Other private	129	787	572	409	1,130	1,536	1,660	1,158	1,006	913
Private nonguaranteed	**57**	**592**	**465**	**444**	**1,449**	**1,245**	**1,758**	**3,756**	**1,368**	**1,736**
Bonds	0	0	0	0	0	0	0	0	0	0
Commercial banks	57	592	465	444	1,449	1,245	1,758	3,756	1,368	1,736
Memo:										
IBRD	29	111	721	913	1,062	1,056	950	835	743	690
IDA	0	6	51	86	102	120	140	153	187	212
NET FLOWS ON DEBT	**841**	**7,776**	**5,090**	**4,999**	**4,363**	**3,973**	**840**	**2,297**	**-424**	**1,343**
Public and publicly guaranteed	**797**	**7,186**	**4,926**	**4,977**	**4,967**	**4,470**	**1,617**	**3,577**	**-55**	**722**
Official creditors	497	3,576	4,642	4,306	3,654	2,862	1,932	1,929	1,198	164
Multilateral	117	1,478	3,204	3,010	3,025	2,204	2,159	2,085	1,575	1,400
Concessional	72	830	2,506	2,780	3,297	2,746	2,910	2,829	2,427	2,149
Bilateral	380	2,098	1,437	1,295	628	658	-227	-156	-378	-1,236
Concessional	330	1,482	1,779	1,286	834	1,050	408	109	-287	40
Private creditors	300	3,610	285	672	1,314	1,608	-315	1,648	-1,253	558
Bonds	-14	28	-31	-30	1,473	501	337	995	-123	1,710
Commercial banks	6	1,610	-641	234	100	395	-328	429	-769	-1,303
Other private	308	1,972	957	468	-260	711	-323	225	-361	151
Private nonguaranteed	**44**	**590**	**165**	**22**	**-604**	**-496**	**-777**	**-1,281**	**-369**	**621**
Bonds	0	0	0	0	0	350	250	645	373	0
Commercial banks	44	590	165	22	-604	-846	-1,027	-1,926	-742	621
Memo:										
IBRD	45	289	92	-397	-670	-782	-721	-572	-584	-602
IDA	61	419	1,983	2,142	2,787	2,273	2,445	2,243	1,912	1,781

SUB-SAHARAN AFRICA

(US$ million, unless otherwise indicated)

	1970	1980	1990	1993	1994	1995	1996	1997	1998	1999
INTEREST PAYMENTS (LINT)	**194**	**2,379**	**4,363**	**2,698**	**3,971**	**3,995**	**4,824**	**3,944**	**4,015**	**4,014**
Public and publicly guaranteed	**178**	**1,929**	**4,032**	**2,428**	**3,452**	**3,490**	**4,334**	**3,461**	**3,642**	**3,632**
Official creditors	114	691	2,711	1,950	2,029	2,014	2,662	2,086	2,035	2,080
Multilateral	34	286	1,111	1,209	1,393	1,242	1,372	1,217	1,025	1,021
Concessional	1	29	162	215	240	254	298	302	301	328
Bilateral	79	405	1,600	740	636	771	1,291	868	1,010	1,059
Concessional	61	209	562	545	358	358	492	438	629	666
Private creditors	64	1,238	1,321	478	1,423	1,477	1,672	1,375	1,607	1,552
Bonds	11	13	13	121	189	322	336	348	542	540
Commercial banks	8	857	625	80	334	462	579	638	696	649
Other private	45	368	682	277	900	693	757	389	368	363
Private nonguaranteed	**16**	**451**	**331**	**271**	**519**	**505**	**489**	**483**	**373**	**382**
Bonds	0	0	0	0	0	0	25	99	101	133
Commercial banks	16	451	331	271	519	505	465	384	272	249
Memo:										
IBRD	32	216	651	686	695	630	527	407	332	295
IDA	1	16	97	138	149	178	185	192	204	223
NET TRANSFERS ON DEBT	**648**	**5,398**	**728**	**2,301**	**392**	**-22**	**-3,983**	**-1,647**	**-4,439**	**-2,671**
Public and publicly guaranteed	**619**	**5,258**	**894**	**2,549**	**1,515**	**979**	**-2,717**	**116**	**-3,698**	**-2,910**
Official creditors	383	2,885	1,930	2,356	1,625	849	-730	-157	-838	-1,916
Multilateral	83	1,193	2,094	1,801	1,632	962	787	868	550	379
Concessional	71	801	2,344	2,564	3,057	2,492	2,613	2,527	2,126	1,821
Bilateral	301	1,693	-164	555	-7	-113	-1,518	-1,024	-1,388	-2,295
Concessional	269	1,272	1,218	742	475	692	-85	-329	-915	-626
Private creditors	236	2,373	-1,036	194	-110	131	-1,987	273	-2,860	-994
Bonds	-25	15	-44	-151	1,284	179	1	646	-665	1,170
Commercial banks	-2	753	-1,266	153	-234	-66	-908	-209	-1,465	-1,952
Other private	263	1,604	274	191	-1,160	18	-1,080	-164	-730	-212
Private nonguaranteed	**28**	**140**	**-166**	**-249**	**-1,123**	**-1,001**	**-1,266**	**-1,763**	**-741**	**239**
Bonds	0	0	0	0	0	350	226	546	272	-133
Commercial banks	28	140	-166	-249	-1,123	-1,351	-1,492	-2,309	-1,014	372
Memo:										
IBRD	13	72	-559	-1,083	-1,366	-1,412	-1,248	-978	-915	-897
IDA	60	403	1,886	2,003	2,638	2,094	2,260	2,051	1,709	1,558
DEBT SERVICE (LTDS)	**586**	**5,171**	**8,997**	**6,161**	**10,558**	**11,066**	**13,552**	**13,822**	**11,802**	**13,404**
Public and publicly guaranteed	**514**	**4,129**	**8,201**	**5,447**	**8,590**	**9,316**	**11,305**	**9,584**	**10,062**	**11,286**
Official creditors	284	1,359	5,263	4,142	4,663	5,003	5,988	5,057	5,132	6,586
Multilateral	68	484	2,461	2,803	3,379	3,269	3,372	3,189	2,884	3,258
Concessional	1	59	429	559	635	689	754	761	801	963
Bilateral	216	876	2,802	1,340	1,283	1,733	2,616	1,868	2,249	3,328
Concessional	172	425	873	964	674	794	917	1,001	1,503	1,403
Private creditors	230	2,769	2,938	1,304	3,927	4,313	5,317	4,527	4,929	4,700
Bonds	38	37	44	151	226	362	632	631	665	640
Commercial banks	18	1,578	1,640	468	1,671	1,722	2,268	2,349	2,890	2,784
Other private	174	1,155	1,254	686	2,030	2,230	2,417	1,548	1,374	1,276
Private nonguaranteed	**72**	**1,043**	**796**	**714**	**1,968**	**1,750**	**2,248**	**4,238**	**1,740**	**2,118**
Bonds	0	0	0	0	0	0	25	99	101	133
Commercial banks	72	1,043	796	714	1,968	1,750	2,223	4,139	1,640	1,985
Memo:										
IBRD	61	328	1,372	1,599	1,758	1,686	1,477	1,241	1,074	985
IDA	1	22	148	224	250	299	325	345	390	435
UNDISBURSED DEBT	**2,736**	**20,793**	**34,198**	**31,957**	**30,832**	**28,824**	**24,668**	**22,047**	**20,951**	**..**
Official creditors	2,281	14,316	30,227	29,128	27,952	25,960	22,391	18,902	19,019	..
Private creditors	455	6,476	3,971	2,829	2,880	2,864	2,277	3,145	1,933	..
Memorandum items										
Concessional LDOD	3,210	16,371	58,460	69,583	75,852	80,777	82,740	82,925	89,105	90,248
Variable rate LDOD	356	11,865	29,455	28,230	36,688	37,779	34,971	32,485	30,915	..
Public sector LDOD	5,697	41,638	143,767	152,885	165,003	173,678	169,931	164,779	170,445	..
Private sector LDOD	370	4,939	5,603	5,484	12,273	12,212	10,703	9,857	9,747	..
6. CURRENCY COMPOSITION OF LONG-TERM DEBT (PERCENT)										
Deutsche mark	6.6	7.0	6.4	5.2	5.7	5.7	5.0	4.6	4.7	..
French franc	14.4	13.8	14.1	13.1	12.7	12.9	12.3	10.6	10.8	..
Japanese yen	0.1	5.4	4.0	5.1	5.4	5.4	5.0	4.9	5.5	..
Pound sterling	22.5	5.7	5.4	3.9	3.8	3.6	4.0	3.9	3.8	..
Swiss franc	0.3	1.7	2.1	1.8	1.6	1.7	1.5	1.4	1.4	..
U.S.dollars	21.5	35.4	36.5	40.2	40.6	41.0	43.3	47.0	47.2	..
Multiple currency	11.2	8.8	10.4	10.5	10.2	10.0	9.3	8.7	7.6	..
Special drawing rights	0.0	0.0	0.6	0.9	0.9	1.0	1.0	1.0	1.1	..
All other currencies	23.4	22.1	20.5	19.4	18.9	18.7	18.4	17.8	17.9	..

SUB-SAHARAN AFRICA

(US$ million, unless otherwise indicated)

	1970	1980	1990	1993	1994	1995	1996	1997	1998	1999
7. DEBT RESTRUCTURINGS										
Total amount rescheduled	0	444	5,990	854	6,327	3,039	4,506	6,435	1,945	..
Debt stock rescheduled	0	0	91	1	74	144	198	2	0	..
Principal rescheduled	0	269	3,970	524	3,111	1,655	2,500	2,150	1,007	..
Official	0	120	2,696	340	1,819	1,160	1,445	1,787	910	..
Private	0	149	1,274	184	1,292	494	1,055	363	97	..
Interest rescheduled	..	..	1,764	254	2,197	702	904	2,186	508	..
Official	0	31	1,416	207	1,817	599	683	1,257	461	..
Private	0	31	348	47	380	103	221	929	47	..
Debt forgiven	3	187	1,593	842	3,479	1,260	4,032	715	309	..
Memo: interest forgiven	0	0	87	131	429	214	161	267	572	..
Debt stock reduction	0	0	312	172	460	361	1,379	4,813	321	..
of which debt buyback	0	0	0	17	8	29	302	169	17	..
8. DEBT STOCK-FLOW RECONCILIATION										
Total change in debt stocks	..	..	19,802	12,128	26,491	14,053	-3,528	-8,766	7,065	..
Net flows on debt	1,533	10,069	7,095	5,891	10,258	7,386	3,263	5,246	-1,241	3,264
Net change in interest arrears	..	..	2,219	3,759	1,608	2,063	-445	-1,912	1,984	..
Interest capitalized	..	..	1,764	254	2,197	702	904	2,186	508	..
Debt forgiveness or reduction	..	..	-1,905	-996	-3,931	-1,592	-5,110	-5,358	-613	..
Cross-currency valuation	..	..	9,605	-2,107	6,468	4,164	-4,557	-6,937	4,311	..
Residual	..	..	1,025	5,327	9,891	1,331	2,418	-1,991	2,116	..
9. AVERAGE TERMS OF NEW COMMITMENTS										
ALL CREDITORS										
Interest (%)	3.7	7.0	4.3	3.2	4.0	3.8	3.8	4.7	2.2	..
Maturity (years)	23.9	17.3	25.3	27.3	22.1	22.1	22.9	19.4	30.8	..
Grace period (years)	9.7	5.0	6.9	7.7	6.1	5.3	6.2	6.0	7.6	..
Grant element (%)	47.5	21.7	43.5	51.6	42.1	41.9	43.6	33.5	61.4	..
Official creditors										
Interest (%)	2.0	4.1	3.5	2.6	2.4	1.9	1.8	1.6	1.3	..
Maturity (years)	32.0	25.1	28.3	31.8	31.7	32.0	32.9	37.4	35.8	..
Grace period (years)	14.3	6.7	7.8	8.9	8.4	8.7	8.8	9.2	8.9	..
Grant element (%)	67.4	42.7	51.2	60.6	61.4	65.8	66.9	70.8	72.4	..
Private creditors										
Interest (%)	6.6	10.0	8.1	6.0	6.3	5.8	6.4	6.6	6.9	..
Maturity (years)	10.2	9.4	11.7	7.8	7.9	12.1	10.1	8.4	7.7	..
Grace period (years)	1.8	3.3	2.8	2.2	2.8	1.8	2.9	4.1	1.2	..
Grant element (%)	13.3	0.2	7.7	12.6	13.5	17.6	13.9	10.7	10.4	..
Memorandum items										
Commitments	1,890	13,280	11,512	7,634	9,530	9,203	7,849	10,008	6,044	..
Official creditors	1,194	6,718	9,476	6,196	5,684	4,636	4,403	3,806	4,976	..
Private creditors	696	6,562	2,035	1,438	3,846	4,567	3,447	6,202	1,068	..

10. GRAPH OF AGGREGATE NET RESOURCE FLOWS

(current prices, US$ million)

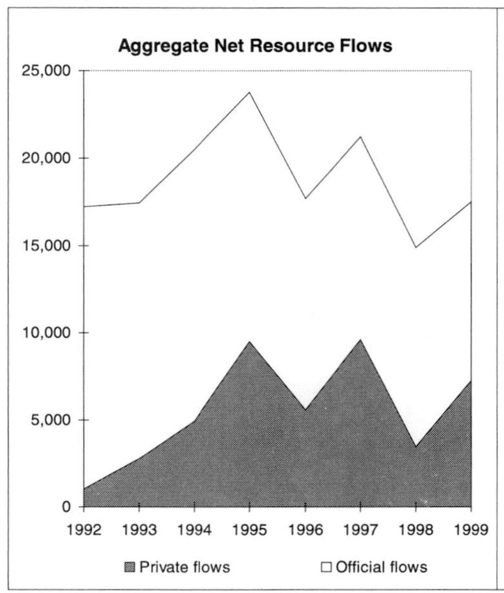

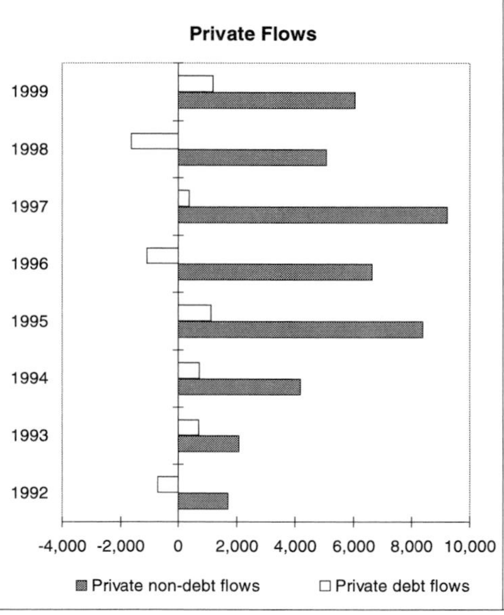

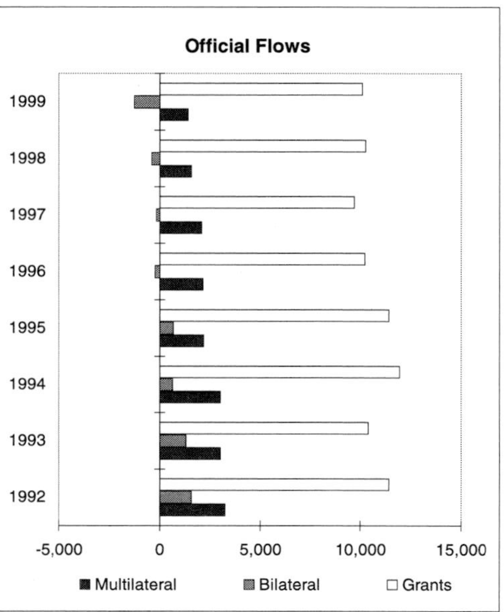

LOW-INCOME COUNTRIES

(US$ million, unless otherwise indicated)

	1970	1980	1990	1993	1994	1995	1996	1997	1998	1999
1. SUMMARY DEBT DATA										
TOTAL DEBT STOCKS (EDT)	..	**131,253**	**477,947**	**563,685**	**624,255**	**662,587**	**669,124**	**680,146**	**721,592**	**730,215**
Long-term debt (LDOD)	**20,286**	**108,649**	**406,677**	**475,928**	**530,979**	**553,875**	**550,663**	**559,310**	**610,973**	**619,084**
Public and publicly guaranteed	19,392	100,419	389,596	453,459	491,857	504,768	497,197	494,235	511,587	526,586
Private nonguaranteed	894	8,230	17,081	22,469	39,122	49,107	53,466	65,075	99,386	92,498
Use of IMF credit	**318**	**5,310**	**11,752**	**13,504**	**14,383**	**13,553**	**12,336**	**13,971**	**20,516**	**22,508**
Short-term debt	..	**17,294**	**59,518**	**74,252**	**78,893**	**95,159**	**106,125**	**106,864**	**90,103**	**88,623**
of which interest arrears on LDOD	..	1,724	12,985	20,797	23,663	25,446	24,218	20,669	23,057	23,253
Official creditors	..	1,611	8,657	15,468	17,970	20,145	19,675	17,796	19,841	..
Private creditors	..	112	4,327	5,329	5,692	5,301	4,543	2,872	3,216	..
Memo: principal arrears on LDOD	..	1,764	23,717	43,579	51,185	58,251	57,045	49,971	58,440	59,990
Official creditors	..	1,046	13,580	30,055	36,757	43,492	44,422	41,627	46,436	..
Private creditors	..	718	10,137	13,523	14,429	14,759	12,622	8,344	12,004	..
Memo: export credits	..	357	78,129	88,112	96,596	102,535	103,111	114,365	119,141	..
TOTAL DEBT FLOWS										
Disbursements	**3,426**	**24,796**	**43,277**	**51,073**	**51,956**	**59,449**	**64,592**	**71,710**	**53,285**	**51,757**
Long-term debt	3,354	21,984	40,776	50,005	50,304	55,843	63,303	67,521	46,063	48,612
IMF purchases	72	2,812	2,502	1,069	1,652	3,606	1,290	4,189	7,221	3,145
Principal repayments	**1,287**	**6,843**	**20,846**	**26,430**	**30,395**	**38,793**	**42,983**	**42,776**	**39,895**	**43,127**
Long-term debt	979	6,139	18,133	25,539	28,632	34,411	40,933	40,999	38,396	41,911
IMF repurchases	308	704	2,713	891	1,764	4,381	2,050	1,778	1,498	1,216
Net flows on debt	**3,641**	**21,585**	**32,213**	**20,153**	**23,707**	**35,325**	**33,805**	**36,514**	**-2,758**	**1,195**
of which short-term debt	..	3,632	9,783	-4,490	2,147	14,669	12,195	7,581	-16,147	-7,435
Interest payments (INT)	..	**6,452**	**18,858**	**17,646**	**20,535**	**23,263**	**22,916**	**24,498**	**25,816**	**27,513**
Long-term debt	517	4,735	15,125	14,436	17,136	18,753	19,259	20,055	21,360	23,844
IMF charges	0	153	585	504	417	775	266	195	323	474
Short-term debt	..	1,565	3,147	2,706	2,981	3,736	3,391	4,249	4,132	3,195
Net transfers on debt	..	**15,133**	**13,355**	**2,506**	**3,172**	**12,062**	**10,889**	**12,016**	**-28,573**	**-26,318**
Total debt service paid (TDS)	..	**13,295**	**39,705**	**44,077**	**50,931**	**62,056**	**65,899**	**67,274**	**65,711**	**70,640**
Long-term debt	1,495	10,873	33,259	39,975	45,769	53,164	60,192	61,054	59,757	65,755
IMF repurchases and charges	308	857	3,299	1,396	2,181	5,156	2,317	1,973	1,822	1,690
Short-term debt (interest only)	..	1,565	3,147	2,706	2,981	3,736	3,391	4,249	4,132	3,195
2. AGGREGATE NET RESOURCE FLOWS AND NET TRANSFERS (LONG-TERM)										
NET RESOURCE FLOWS	**3,662**	**23,264**	**44,282**	**80,971**	**94,960**	**96,269**	**105,536**	**112,317**	**77,859**	**75,569**
Net flow of long-term debt (ex. IMF)	2,375	15,845	22,642	24,466	21,672	21,431	22,370	26,523	7,667	6,701
Foreign direct investment (net)	270	250	5,732	34,307	41,378	47,502	56,047	60,837	53,517	49,526
Portfolio equity flows	0	0	417	8,382	14,640	10,423	12,312	11,128	1,921	5,615
Grants (excluding technical coop.)	1,018	7,170	15,491	13,816	17,270	16,913	14,807	13,830	14,755	13,727
Memo: technical coop. grants	1,039	3,925	8,108	8,445	7,868	8,609	8,405	7,200	6,715	6,667
official net resource flows	2,868	15,032	29,451	28,968	30,105	29,733	23,669	23,173	25,495	26,689
private net resource flows	794	8,232	14,831	52,003	64,855	66,535	81,866	89,144	52,365	48,880
NET TRANSFERS	**2,238**	**12,652**	**25,685**	**62,371**	**73,242**	**72,458**	**79,939**	**85,497**	**49,268**	**42,584**
Interest on long-term debt	517	4,735	15,125	14,436	17,136	18,753	19,259	20,055	21,360	23,844
Profit remittances on FDI	908	5,877	3,472	4,164	4,582	5,060	6,338	6,766	7,231	9,141
Memo: official net transfers	2,504	13,321	22,194	20,974	21,151	20,442	14,339	14,204	16,306	16,723
private net transfers	-266	-669	3,491	41,398	52,091	52,016	65,600	71,294	32,963	25,861
3. MAJOR ECONOMIC AGGREGATES										
Gross national product (GNP)	248,430	742,411	1,106,437	1,156,429	1,325,793	1,573,076	1,780,707	1,888,841	1,838,357	1,958,244
Exports of goods & services (XGS)	..	..	185,363	236,491	286,825	346,745	396,962	445,581	427,189	480,308
of which workers remittances	..	5,603	6,976	10,067	13,326	14,050	19,904	23,895	17,265	16,951
Imports of goods & services (MGS)	..	..	201,333	280,336	312,580	390,740	434,135	459,353	442,572	489,939
International reserves (RES)	..	46,984	60,751	67,937	113,835	138,010	179,247	219,236	234,632	253,513
Current account balance	..	-8,406	-7,516	-32,608	-14,735	-29,537	-19,707	460	4,896	-7,680
4. DEBT INDICATORS										
EDT / XGS (%)	..	..	257.8	238.4	217.6	191.1	168.6	152.6	168.9	152.0
EDT / GNP (%)	..	17.7	43.2	48.7	47.1	42.1	37.6	36.0	39.3	37.3
TDS / XGS (%)	..	..	21.4	18.6	17.8	17.9	16.6	15.1	15.4	14.7
INT / XGS (%)	..	..	10.2	7.5	7.2	6.7	5.8	5.5	6.0	5.7
INT / GNP (%)	..	0.9	1.7	1.5	1.6	1.5	1.3	1.3	1.4	1.4
RES / EDT (%)	..	35.8	12.7	12.1	18.2	20.8	26.8	32.2	32.5	34.7
RES / MGS (months)	..	..	3.6	2.9	4.4	4.2	5.0	5.7	6.4	6.2
Short-term / EDT (%)	..	13.2	12.5	13.2	12.6	14.4	15.9	15.7	12.5	12.1
Concessional / EDT (%)	..	43.7	40.5	39.7	39.4	37.8	36.2	32.3	33.7	38.2
Multilateral / EDT (%)	..	15.1	20.8	22.6	23.2	23.0	22.6	22.1	22.8	23.7

LOW-INCOME COUNTRIES

(US$ million, unless otherwise indicated)

	1970	1980	1990	1993	1994	1995	1996	1997	1998	1999
5. LONG-TERM DEBT										
DEBT OUTSTANDING (LDOD)	**20,286**	**108,649**	**406,677**	**475,928**	**530,979**	**553,875**	**550,663**	**559,310**	**610,973**	**619,084**
Public and publicly guaranteed	**19,392**	**100,419**	**389,596**	**453,459**	**491,857**	**504,768**	**497,197**	**494,235**	**511,587**	**526,586**
Official creditors	16,882	71,387	279,876	331,830	365,013	376,772	366,389	347,803	375,057	388,173
Multilateral	3,127	19,848	99,613	127,623	144,510	152,273	151,155	150,346	164,393	173,369
Concessional	1,623	13,294	57,529	73,690	84,046	90,331	93,936	96,101	104,985	112,507
Bilateral	13,755	51,539	180,264	204,208	220,504	224,499	215,234	197,457	210,663	214,804
Concessional	12,446	44,066	136,125	150,285	161,809	160,092	148,114	123,243	138,113	166,645
Private creditors	2,510	29,032	109,721	121,628	126,844	127,996	130,808	146,432	136,530	138,413
Bonds	340	883	9,061	14,561	17,961	17,636	16,186	21,702	26,967	26,790
Commercial banks	200	13,896	56,354	58,263	54,522	54,988	60,595	76,103	70,876	67,875
Other private	1,970	14,253	44,305	48,805	54,361	55,373	54,027	48,627	38,688	43,748
Private nonguaranteed	**894**	**8,230**	**17,081**	**22,469**	**39,122**	**49,107**	**53,466**	**65,075**	**99,386**	**92,498**
Bonds	0	0	120	2,583	3,535	5,575	10,544	16,170	14,735	13,739
Commercial banks	894	8,230	16,961	19,887	35,586	43,532	42,922	48,905	84,651	78,759
Memo:										
IBRD	1,444	4,922	31,504	36,776	40,369	40,634	37,202	34,956	36,655	37,481
IDA	1,587	10,529	41,705	54,232	62,048	66,655	69,816	71,750	77,766	81,821
DISBURSEMENTS	**3,354**	**21,984**	**40,776**	**50,005**	**50,304**	**55,843**	**63,303**	**67,521**	**46,063**	**48,612**
Public and publicly guaranteed	**3,021**	**19,735**	**34,928**	**46,569**	**43,692**	**45,994**	**47,275**	**49,966**	**40,740**	**44,172**
Official creditors	2,358	9,867	21,670	23,960	24,332	26,366	23,438	24,567	24,558	28,006
Multilateral	376	3,772	11,989	13,378	14,965	13,680	14,345	14,194	13,914	15,349
Concessional	170	2,290	5,805	6,276	7,823	7,116	7,980	7,457	7,219	7,373
Bilateral	1,982	6,095	9,681	10,582	9,367	12,685	9,093	10,374	10,644	12,657
Concessional	1,798	4,624	7,741	6,417	7,022	6,940	6,081	4,918	9,037	6,965
Private creditors	662	9,868	13,258	22,609	19,360	19,629	23,837	25,399	16,182	16,166
Bonds	6	147	704	2,889	3,487	1,914	3,712	4,255	5,559	1,760
Commercial banks	44	4,171	6,144	9,481	4,712	8,835	9,692	10,562	5,398	3,411
Other private	613	5,550	6,410	10,240	11,161	8,879	10,433	10,581	5,225	10,995
Private nonguaranteed	**333**	**2,249**	**5,848**	**3,435**	**6,612**	**9,848**	**16,027**	**17,555**	**5,323**	**4,440**
Bonds	0	0	120	1,611	907	2,827	4,695	6,267	1,269	0
Commercial banks	333	2,249	5,728	1,824	5,704	7,021	11,332	11,288	4,054	4,440
Memo:										
IBRD	194	939	4,024	4,273	4,040	3,681	3,466	3,743	3,516	3,979
IDA	147	1,478	4,125	4,565	5,747	4,956	5,721	5,336	4,984	5,161
PRINCIPAL REPAYMENTS	**979**	**6,139**	**18,133**	**25,539**	**28,632**	**34,411**	**40,933**	**40,999**	**38,396**	**41,911**
Public and publicly guaranteed	**832**	**4,711**	**16,078**	**20,978**	**24,240**	**29,106**	**33,047**	**32,257**	**26,858**	**30,977**
Official creditors	508	2,005	7,710	8,808	11,498	13,545	14,577	15,224	13,818	15,044
Multilateral	98	392	3,335	4,534	6,239	6,184	7,537	6,435	5,522	6,529
Concessional	1	62	575	810	940	1,087	1,115	1,172	1,281	1,473
Bilateral	410	1,613	4,376	4,275	5,259	7,362	7,040	8,790	8,296	8,515
Concessional	293	1,142	2,515	2,795	3,567	5,124	4,352	5,696	6,139	3,541
Private creditors	325	2,707	8,368	12,170	12,742	15,561	18,470	17,032	13,040	15,933
Bonds	26	29	730	1,676	895	1,806	3,082	1,149	348	1,936
Commercial banks	30	967	3,874	6,017	5,201	6,849	9,028	9,246	7,101	7,267
Other private	268	1,711	3,764	4,478	6,647	6,907	6,360	6,637	5,591	6,730
Private nonguaranteed	**147**	**1,427**	**2,055**	**4,561**	**4,392**	**5,305**	**7,886**	**8,742**	**11,539**	**10,934**
Bonds	0	0	0	0	0	120	225	666	997	997
Commercial banks	147	1,427	2,055	4,561	4,392	5,185	7,661	8,076	10,542	9,937
Memo:										
IBRD	92	238	2,072	2,855	3,639	3,537	3,787	3,374	2,929	3,104
IDA	0	26	220	352	410	493	537	579	673	779
NET FLOWS ON DEBT	**2,375**	**15,845**	**22,642**	**24,466**	**21,672**	**21,431**	**22,370**	**26,523**	**7,667**	**6,701**
Public and publicly guaranteed	**2,188**	**15,023**	**18,850**	**25,591**	**19,453**	**16,888**	**14,229**	**17,709**	**13,882**	**13,195**
Official creditors	1,851	7,862	13,960	15,152	12,835	12,821	8,862	9,343	10,740	12,962
Multilateral	278	3,380	8,654	8,844	8,727	7,497	6,808	7,759	8,392	8,820
Concessional	169	2,228	5,229	5,466	6,882	6,029	6,865	6,284	5,938	5,900
Bilateral	1,573	4,483	5,306	6,308	4,108	5,324	2,054	1,584	2,348	4,142
Concessional	1,505	3,482	5,226	3,621	3,454	1,817	1,729	-779	2,898	3,424
Private creditors	337	7,161	4,890	10,440	6,618	4,067	5,367	8,366	3,142	233
Bonds	-20	118	-26	1,213	2,592	109	631	3,107	5,210	-176
Commercial banks	14	3,204	2,270	3,464	-488	1,986	663	1,316	-1,703	-3,856
Other private	344	3,838	2,646	5,762	4,513	1,973	4,073	3,944	-365	4,265
Private nonguaranteed	**187**	**821**	**3,792**	**-1,125**	**2,220**	**4,543**	**8,141**	**8,813**	**-6,216**	**-6,494**
Bonds	0	0	120	1,611	907	2,707	4,470	5,602	272	-997
Commercial banks	187	821	3,672	-2,737	1,312	1,836	3,671	3,212	-6,487	-5,497
Memo:										
IBRD	103	701	1,952	1,418	401	144	-321	370	587	875
IDA	147	1,453	3,906	4,213	5,337	4,463	5,184	4,757	4,311	4,382

LOW-INCOME COUNTRIES

(US$ million, unless otherwise indicated)

	1970	1980	1990	1993	1994	1995	1996	1997	1998	1999
INTEREST PAYMENTS (LINT)	**517**	**4,735**	**15,125**	**14,436**	**17,136**	**18,753**	**19,259**	**20,055**	**21,360**	**23,844**
Public and publicly guaranteed	**473**	**3,872**	**14,049**	**13,074**	**15,462**	**16,650**	**16,928**	**17,518**	**16,942**	**17,180**
Official creditors	365	1,711	7,258	7,995	8,954	9,292	9,331	8,970	9,189	9,966
Multilateral	92	617	3,478	4,360	4,931	5,031	4,854	4,496	4,372	4,906
Concessional	10	106	428	571	647	708	748	759	783	850
Bilateral	272	1,094	3,780	3,634	4,023	4,261	4,477	4,474	4,818	5,060
Concessional	214	787	2,347	2,710	2,736	2,739	2,612	2,434	2,451	2,747
Private creditors	108	2,161	6,791	5,079	6,509	7,358	7,598	8,548	7,753	7,214
Bonds	11	30	625	693	728	933	1,311	957	934	1,161
Commercial banks	13	1,323	4,071	2,623	2,773	3,492	3,332	4,833	4,447	4,142
Other private	84	808	2,095	1,764	3,007	2,933	2,955	2,758	2,373	1,911
Private nonguaranteed	**44**	**862**	**1,077**	**1,362**	**1,674**	**2,103**	**2,331**	**2,537**	**4,418**	**6,664**
Bonds	0	0	0	53	138	231	420	777	1,200	1,094
Commercial banks	44	862	1,077	1,309	1,536	1,872	1,910	1,760	3,218	5,570
Memo:										
IBRD	79	419	2,386	2,773	2,969	3,024	2,770	2,420	2,338	2,539
IDA	10	70	279	366	401	469	476	488	511	551
NET TRANSFERS ON DEBT	**1,858**	**11,111**	**7,517**	**10,030**	**4,536**	**2,679**	**3,111**	**6,467**	**-13,694**	**-17,143**
Public and publicly guaranteed	**1,716**	**11,152**	**4,801**	**12,517**	**3,990**	**238**	**-2,699**	**191**	**-3,060**	**-3,985**
Official creditors	1,486	6,151	6,702	7,157	3,881	3,529	-469	373	1,551	2,996
Multilateral	186	2,762	5,177	4,485	3,795	2,466	1,954	3,262	4,021	3,914
Concessional	159	2,122	4,802	4,894	6,235	5,320	6,118	5,525	5,156	5,050
Bilateral	1,300	3,389	1,526	2,673	85	1,063	-2,422	-2,889	-2,470	-918
Concessional	1,291	2,695	2,881	912	719	-922	-883	-3,213	448	677
Private creditors	229	5,000	-1,900	5,360	109	-3,291	-2,231	-182	-4,610	-6,981
Bonds	-31	89	-650	520	1,864	-824	-680	2,149	4,277	-1,337
Commercial banks	1	1,881	-1,801	841	-3,261	-1,506	-2,669	-3,517	-6,149	-7,998
Other private	260	3,030	551	3,998	1,506	-960	1,118	1,185	-2,738	2,354
Private nonguaranteed	**143**	**-41**	**2,716**	**-2,488**	**546**	**2,441**	**5,810**	**6,277**	**-10,634**	**-13,158**
Bonds	0	0	120	1,558	769	2,476	4,050	4,825	-929	-2,091
Commercial banks	143	-41	2,596	-4,046	-223	-35	1,760	1,452	-9,705	-11,067
Memo:										
IBRD	23	282	-434	-1,355	-2,568	-2,880	-3,091	-2,050	-1,750	-1,664
IDA	137	1,383	3,627	3,847	4,936	3,994	4,709	4,269	3,800	3,831
DEBT SERVICE (LTDS)	**1,495**	**10,873**	**33,259**	**39,975**	**45,769**	**53,164**	**60,192**	**61,054**	**59,757**	**65,755**
Public and publicly guaranteed	**1,305**	**8,583**	**30,126**	**34,052**	**39,703**	**45,756**	**49,975**	**49,775**	**43,800**	**48,157**
Official creditors	872	3,716	14,968	16,803	20,452	22,837	23,908	24,195	23,007	25,010
Multilateral	190	1,009	6,812	8,893	11,170	11,214	12,392	10,931	9,894	11,435
Concessional	11	169	1,003	1,382	1,588	1,795	1,863	1,932	2,063	2,323
Bilateral	682	2,707	8,156	7,910	9,282	11,623	11,517	13,263	13,114	13,575
Concessional	508	1,929	4,861	5,505	6,302	7,862	6,964	8,131	8,590	6,288
Private creditors	433	4,868	15,159	17,249	19,251	22,919	26,068	25,580	20,793	23,147
Bonds	37	58	1,354	2,369	1,623	2,739	4,393	2,106	1,282	3,097
Commercial banks	43	2,290	7,945	8,640	7,974	10,341	12,360	14,078	11,548	11,409
Other private	352	2,520	5,860	6,242	9,654	9,840	9,315	9,396	7,963	8,641
Private nonguaranteed	**190**	**2,290**	**3,132**	**5,923**	**6,066**	**7,407**	**10,217**	**11,278**	**15,957**	**17,598**
Bonds	0	0	0	53	138	351	645	1,443	2,198	2,091
Commercial banks	190	2,290	3,132	5,870	5,928	7,057	9,572	9,836	13,759	15,507
Memo:										
IBRD	171	658	4,458	5,628	6,608	6,561	6,557	5,794	5,266	5,643
IDA	10	95	498	717	811	962	1,012	1,067	1,184	1,330
UNDISBURSED DEBT	**6,715**	**49,727**	**107,482**	**110,502**	**111,560**	**113,291**	**107,287**	**100,044**	**95,924**	..
Official creditors	5,855	37,714	89,951	92,203	97,158	98,203	91,071	85,101	89,947	..
Private creditors	860	12,013	17,532	18,300	14,402	15,088	16,216	14,943	5,977	..
Memorandum items										
Concessional LDOD	14,069	57,361	193,654	223,975	245,854	250,423	242,050	219,344	243,099	279,152
Variable rate LDOD	940	21,612	89,097	102,613	126,396	141,595	147,629	174,997	206,068	..
Public sector LDOD	18,906	94,891	379,468	439,998	478,033	490,489	482,790	480,063	445,969	..
Private sector LDOD	1,379	9,215	18,262	23,719	40,881	51,277	55,815	67,253	152,500	..

6. CURRENCY COMPOSITION OF LONG-TERM DEBT (PERCENT)

	1970	1980	1990	1993	1994	1995	1996	1997	1998	1999
Deutsche mark	8.0	7.2	5.1	4.0	4.4	4.5	4.0	3.6	4.0	..
French franc	5.5	6.7	5.8	5.1	5.0	5.2	4.9	4.2	4.8	..
Japanese yen	4.6	9.1	13.2	14.8	16.4	15.1	13.5	12.1	13.7	..
Pound sterling	19.4	8.2	3.6	2.5	2.4	2.3	2.3	2.3	2.2	..
Swiss franc	0.5	0.9	1.0	0.8	0.8	0.9	0.8	0.7	0.7	..
U.S.dollars	36.1	37.1	36.7	39.9	38.8	40.2	43.7	50.5	41.4	..
Multiple currency	8.3	10.4	15.1	15.4	15.6	15.5	14.6	12.9	9.5	..
Special drawing rights	0.0	0.0	0.5	0.6	0.6	0.7	0.8	0.8	0.9	..
All other currencies	17.8	15.9	16.7	14.2	13.5	13.3	13.0	10.5	10.3	..

LOW-INCOME COUNTRIES

(US$ million, unless otherwise indicated)

	1970	*1980*	*1990*	*1993*	*1994*	*1995*	*1996*	*1997*	*1998*	*1999*
7. DEBT RESTRUCTURINGS										
Total amount rescheduled	0	1,202	6,567	2,263	4,806	3,290	6,045	8,220	5,700	..
Debt stock rescheduled	0	0	91	72	0	144	1,232	467	3,198	..
Principal rescheduled	0	269	4,033	983	2,378	1,908	3,105	3,061	1,509	..
Official	0	120	2,832	504	1,437	1,267	2,000	2,011	1,218	..
Private	0	149	1,201	479	942	642	1,106	1,050	291	..
Interest rescheduled	..	..	1,857	450	1,764	858	1,142	2,547	542	..
Official	0	31	1,497	303	1,452	698	908	1,281	492	..
Private	0	31	360	146	312	159	235	1,267	49	..
Debt forgiven	2	190	1,576	851	3,290	1,813	4,058	3,104	376	..
Memo: interest forgiven	0	0	97	152	429	986	1,087	610	594	..
Debt stock reduction	0	0	353	172	468	1,560	4,445	5,177	321	..
of which debt buyback	0	0	0	17	8	119	302	200	17	..
8. DEBT STOCK-FLOW RECONCILIATION										
Total change in debt stocks	..	..	58,557	28,100	60,570	38,333	6,537	11,022	41,446	..
Net flows on debt	3,641	21,585	32,213	20,153	23,707	35,325	33,805	36,514	-2,758	1,195
Net change in interest arrears	..	..	2,944	3,763	2,866	1,784	-1,228	-3,548	2,388	..
Interest capitalized	..	..	1,857	450	1,764	858	1,142	2,547	542	..
Debt forgiveness or reduction	..	..	-1,929	-1,005	-3,751	-3,254	-8,201	-8,082	-680	..
Cross-currency valuation	..	..	19,050	4,637	24,192	-284	-19,167	-19,900	16,721	..
Residual	..	..	4,423	103	11,792	3,905	187	3,491	25,233	..
9. AVERAGE TERMS OF NEW COMMITMENTS										
ALL CREDITORS										
Interest (%)	3.1	6.8	5.5	4.9	4.5	5.2	5.2	5.3	4.7	..
Maturity (years)	28.8	21.3	22.1	18.5	21.4	18.1	17.1	16.1	20.3	..
Grace period (years)	9.7	5.7	6.2	5.2	6.3	5.0	5.1	4.7	6.2	..
Grant element (%)	41.1	20.1	27.9	27.6	33.9	26.8	24.3	23.5	36.5	..
Official creditors										
Interest (%)	2.2	3.6	4.0	3.8	3.9	4.5	3.9	4.2	3.7	..
Maturity (years)	33.7	29.9	27.0	25.4	26.2	24.4	26.8	26.2	26.6	..
Grace period (years)	11.8	7.7	7.5	7.0	7.4	6.5	7.3	6.7	7.2	..
Grant element (%)	48.7	36.3	38.5	39.1	40.8	35.7	38.6	35.8	47.8	..
Private creditors										
Interest (%)	6.5	11.0	7.9	6.0	5.7	6.4	6.6	6.4	6.9	..
Maturity (years)	10.2	9.6	13.7	11.3	11.2	8.0	7.5	7.0	7.0	..
Grace period (years)	1.9	2.9	4.0	3.2	3.9	2.6	3.0	3.0	4.0	..
Grant element (%)	12.9	-2.0	9.8	15.7	19.1	12.7	10.2	12.3	12.2	..
Memorandum items										
Commitments	4,428	30,558	42,143	55,384	42,697	51,433	51,501	47,744	35,325	..
Official creditors	3,489	17,625	26,667	28,198	29,119	31,520	25,558	22,711	24,056	..
Private creditors	939	12,933	15,476	27,185	13,578	19,913	25,943	25,032	11,268	..

10. GRAPH OF AGGREGATE NET RESOURCE FLOWS

(current prices, US$ million)

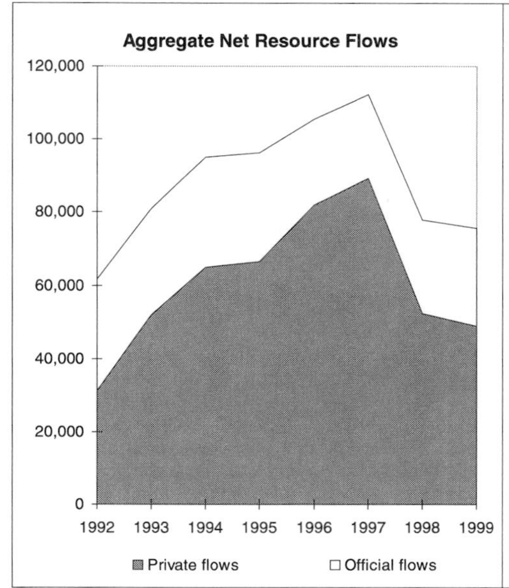

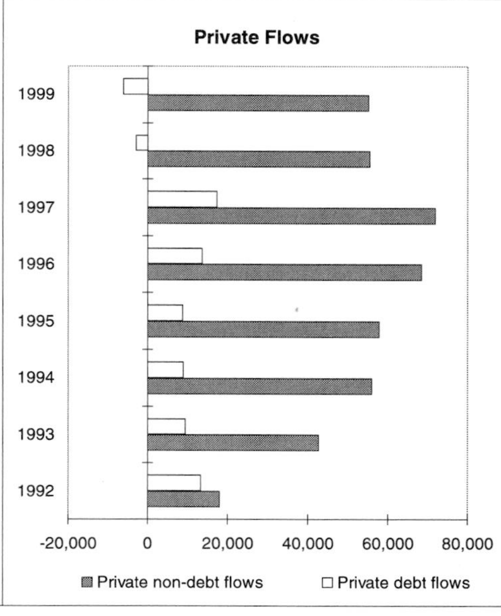

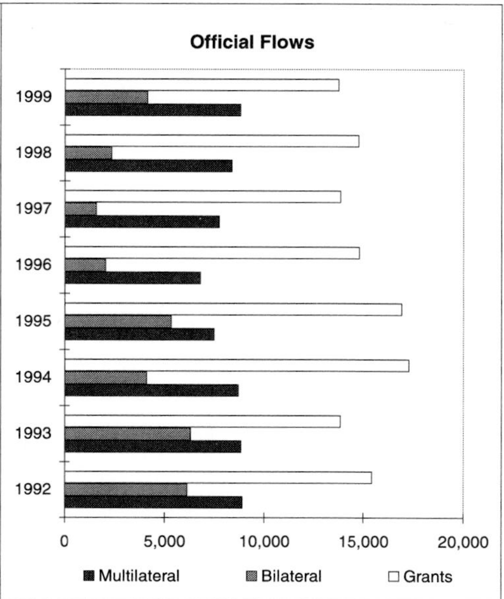

MIDDLE-INCOME COUNTRIES

(US$ million, unless otherwise indicated)

	1970	1980	1990	1993	1994	1995	1996	1997	1998	1999
1. SUMMARY DEBT DATA										
TOTAL DEBT STOCKS (EDT)	..	**478,150**	**982,396**	**1,213,844**	**1,344,789**	**1,476,869**	**1,560,276**	**1,646,311**	**1,814,454**	**1,823,773**
Long-term debt (LDOD)	**40,859**	**342,874**	**774,432**	**935,252**	**1,033,459**	**1,100,076**	**1,157,817**	**1,227,080**	**1,419,370**	**1,451,636**
Public and publicly guaranteed	26,376	280,534	726,000	829,726	883,743	927,683	927,004	917,727	1,017,662	1,053,521
Private nonguaranteed	14,483	62,341	48,432	105,525	149,717	172,393	230,813	309,353	401,708	398,115
Use of IMF credit	**438**	**6,937**	**22,899**	**26,381**	**29,761**	**47,548**	**47,770**	**56,826**	**73,323**	**58,494**
Short-term debt	..	**128,339**	**185,064**	**252,211**	**281,569**	**329,245**	**354,689**	**362,405**	**321,762**	**313,643**
of which interest arrears on LDOD	..	751	39,715	25,219	19,351	18,197	14,708	9,600	13,136	17,490
Official creditors	..	416	10,974	4,834	4,985	5,307	5,518	5,624	7,359	..
Private creditors	..	335	28,741	20,385	14,366	12,890	9,190	3,976	5,778	..
Memo: principal arrears on LDOD	..	743	35,843	37,955	41,532	49,737	47,186	29,636	33,401	38,397
Official creditors	..	198	13,693	9,223	11,809	16,387	17,083	17,878	18,990	..
Private creditors	..	545	22,150	28,733	29,723	33,350	30,103	11,758	14,411	..
Memo: export credits	..	7,371	222,916	264,252	283,731	268,815	256,243	249,906	267,432	..
TOTAL DEBT FLOWS										
Disbursements	**9,826**	**88,861**	**93,941**	**131,162**	**132,854**	**180,226**	**212,914**	**259,874**	**266,687**	**194,222**
Long-term debt	9,567	85,657	88,199	125,229	126,104	155,917	205,544	240,866	244,779	182,442
IMF purchases	259	3,204	5,742	5,933	6,749	24,308	7,369	19,008	21,908	11,780
Principal repayments	**5,455**	**37,630**	**72,874**	**80,330**	**89,202**	**100,624**	**128,359**	**156,845**	**156,135**	**170,967**
Long-term debt	5,021	36,333	67,398	75,884	84,143	93,915	122,782	150,079	147,738	144,421
IMF repurchases	435	1,297	5,476	4,447	5,059	6,708	5,577	6,766	8,398	26,546
Net flows on debt	**12,205**	**89,453**	**27,832**	**91,896**	**89,863**	**132,410**	**115,292**	**115,853**	**79,086**	**19,464**
of which short-term debt	..	38,222	6,766	41,065	46,212	52,808	30,738	12,824	-31,465	-3,791
Interest payments (INT)	..	**42,407**	**51,629**	**51,008**	**57,673**	**77,677**	**83,617**	**88,340**	**94,267**	**107,753**
Long-term debt	1,838	28,056	39,577	37,863	43,629	58,383	61,698	67,019	73,508	87,534
IMF charges	0	319	1,919	1,842	1,390	2,016	2,044	2,012	3,083	4,347
Short-term debt	..	14,032	10,133	11,304	12,654	17,278	19,877	19,308	17,676	15,872
Net transfers on debt	..	**47,046**	**-23,797**	**40,887**	**32,189**	**54,734**	**31,674**	**27,514**	**-15,180**	**-88,289**
Total debt service paid (TDS)	..	**80,036**	**124,503**	**131,339**	**146,876**	**178,300**	**211,978**	**245,185**	**250,402**	**278,720**
Long-term debt	6,858	64,388	106,976	113,747	127,772	152,297	184,480	217,099	221,246	231,955
IMF repurchases and charges	435	1,616	7,395	6,288	6,449	8,725	7,621	8,777	11,481	30,893
Short-term debt (interest only)	..	14,032	10,133	11,304	12,654	17,278	19,877	19,308	17,676	15,872
2. AGGREGATE NET RESOURCE FLOWS AND NET TRANSFERS (LONG-TERM)										
NET RESOURCE FLOWS	**7,412**	**59,429**	**54,246**	**138,198**	**125,397**	**160,904**	**207,607**	**231,409**	**240,465**	**215,130**
Net flow of long-term debt (ex. IMF)	4,546	49,325	20,800	49,345	41,961	62,002	82,763	90,787	97,042	38,021
Foreign direct investment (net)	1,937	4,150	18,398	31,685	47,464	57,488	74,798	109,422	117,425	142,465
Portfolio equity flows	0	0	2,340	42,634	20,521	25,634	36,858	19,063	13,646	21,972
Grants (excluding technical coop.)	929	5,953	12,707	14,535	15,451	15,781	13,189	12,138	12,353	12,672
Memo: technical coop. grants	715	2,431	6,199	9,755	8,990	11,443	10,232	8,306	9,337	9,208
official net resource flows	2,501	19,822	26,471	24,395	15,807	24,171	7,334	16,660	25,130	25,272
private net resource flows	4,911	39,606	27,775	113,803	109,589	136,733	200,274	214,749	215,335	189,858
NET TRANSFERS	**18**	**13,543**	**589**	**81,621**	**61,457**	**81,078**	**122,263**	**139,387**	**138,959**	**95,140**
Interest on long-term debt	1,838	28,056	39,577	37,863	43,629	58,383	61,698	67,019	73,508	87,534
Profit remittances on FDI	5,556	17,831	14,080	18,714	20,310	21,444	23,647	25,002	27,999	32,456
Memo: official net transfers	2,000	15,409	13,544	8,612	-865	2,943	-14,328	-3,104	6,299	3,432
private net transfers	-1,982	-1,866	-12,955	73,009	62,322	78,135	136,591	142,491	132,660	91,708
3. MAJOR ECONOMIC AGGREGATES										
Gross national product (GNP)	419,298	2,275,079	3,163,695	3,521,234	3,669,468	4,120,426	4,460,684	4,568,857	4,179,164	4,197,830
Exports of goods & services (XGS)	..	551,478	715,939	844,141	958,309	1,178,532	1,291,621	1,376,595	1,288,116	1,419,272
of which workers remittances	..	8,756	18,231	24,265	24,758	28,444	28,923	30,719	30,238	29,920
Imports of goods & services (MGS)	..	537,951	728,668	937,419	1,030,516	1,256,300	1,381,804	1,479,556	1,358,351	1,343,540
International reserves (RES)	..	165,192	162,172	296,136	314,880	400,189	440,863	429,998	465,114	510,681
Current account balance	..	2,272	-15,476	-94,436	-75,301	-82,356	-96,666	-110,440	-78,998	-26,353
4. DEBT INDICATORS										
EDT / XGS (%)	..	86.7	137.2	143.8	140.3	125.3	120.8	119.6	140.9	128.5
EDT / GNP (%)	..	21.0	31.1	34.5	36.7	35.8	35.0	36.0	43.4	43.4
TDS / XGS (%)	..	14.5	17.4	15.6	15.3	15.1	16.4	17.8	19.4	19.6
INT / XGS (%)	..	7.7	7.2	6.0	6.0	6.6	6.5	6.4	7.3	7.6
INT / GNP (%)	..	1.9	1.6	1.5	1.6	1.9	1.9	1.9	2.3	2.6
RES / EDT (%)	..	34.6	16.5	24.4	23.4	27.1	28.3	26.1	25.6	28.0
RES / MGS (months)	..	3.7	2.7	3.8	3.7	3.8	3.8	3.5	4.1	4.6
Short-term / EDT (%)	..	26.8	18.8	20.8	20.9	22.3	22.7	22.0	17.7	17.2
Concessional / EDT (%)	..	11.1	12.2	12.4	11.7	11.1	10.5	9.4	7.4	8.5
Multilateral / EDT (%)	..	6.1	11.1	10.0	9.7	9.4	8.7	8.5	8.9	9.5

MIDDLE-INCOME COUNTRIES

(US$ million, unless otherwise indicated)

	1970	1980	1990	1993	1994	1995	1996	1997	1998	1999
5. LONG-TERM DEBT										
DEBT OUTSTANDING (LDOD)	**40,859**	**342,874**	**774,432**	**935,252**	**1,033,459**	**1,100,076**	**1,157,817**	**1,227,080**	**1,419,370**	**1,451,636**
Public and publicly guaranteed	**26,376**	**280,534**	**726,000**	**829,726**	**883,743**	**927,683**	**927,004**	**917,727**	**1,017,662**	**1,053,521**
Official creditors	15,376	106,715	325,258	429,197	467,017	487,506	465,848	446,640	477,844	487,298
Multilateral	4,197	29,002	108,633	121,468	130,550	138,486	135,395	139,252	161,914	172,372
Concessional	449	4,997	11,348	13,882	15,152	16,513	17,319	17,677	19,090	20,857
Bilateral	11,179	77,712	216,625	307,729	336,467	349,020	330,454	307,388	315,930	314,926
Concessional	8,995	48,249	108,753	136,821	141,523	147,902	146,547	137,174	115,737	135,044
Private creditors	11,000	173,819	400,743	400,529	416,725	440,177	461,156	471,087	539,819	566,223
Bonds	1,465	12,219	98,368	146,958	216,761	239,732	277,193	286,996	318,457	343,144
Commercial banks	3,448	113,587	201,338	162,899	114,346	118,950	113,429	131,765	165,881	167,426
Other private	6,087	48,013	101,037	90,673	85,618	81,495	70,534	52,326	55,481	55,653
Private nonguaranteed	**14,483**	**62,341**	**48,432**	**105,525**	**149,717**	**172,393**	**230,813**	**309,353**	**401,708**	**398,115**
Bonds	0	0	717	29,218	53,339	55,982	74,487	90,898	101,758	103,038
Commercial banks	14,483	62,341	47,716	76,308	96,378	116,411	156,326	218,455	299,950	295,077
Memo:										
IBRD	2,943	17,233	64,069	65,915	69,740	73,235	69,958	71,080	79,272	82,977
IDA	246	1,360	3,397	4,079	4,457	4,975	5,402	5,723	6,393	6,532
DISBURSEMENTS	**9,567**	**85,657**	**88,199**	**125,229**	**126,104**	**155,917**	**205,544**	**240,866**	**244,779**	**182,442**
Public and publicly guaranteed	**5,742**	**66,452**	**75,192**	**79,694**	**72,034**	**97,268**	**117,198**	**128,978**	**133,790**	**130,691**
Official creditors	2,564	19,074	31,622	30,063	25,484	39,769	33,096	40,785	42,591	43,020
Multilateral	829	5,581	15,810	17,941	14,324	18,589	19,191	26,449	30,859	24,337
Concessional	86	588	1,069	1,481	1,345	1,696	2,001	1,729	1,671	1,925
Bilateral	1,735	13,493	15,813	12,122	11,161	21,181	13,906	14,336	11,732	18,683
Concessional	1,150	6,418	7,670	5,922	5,733	7,343	6,142	5,632	4,816	6,048
Private creditors	3,178	47,377	43,570	49,631	46,550	57,499	84,102	88,194	91,200	87,671
Bonds	140	1,551	5,454	23,134	20,656	27,988	54,898	58,271	53,072	54,782
Commercial banks	1,269	29,876	11,850	8,488	13,060	17,779	19,961	21,492	29,368	22,056
Other private	1,769	15,951	26,266	18,010	12,834	11,732	9,243	8,432	8,761	10,833
Private nonguaranteed	**3,824**	**19,205**	**13,007**	**45,535**	**54,071**	**58,649**	**88,346**	**111,888**	**110,989**	**51,751**
Bonds	0	0	581	18,244	23,267	16,297	27,928	29,276	19,223	13,693
Commercial banks	3,824	19,205	12,426	27,291	30,804	42,352	60,418	82,612	91,765	38,058
Memo:										
IBRD	484	3,538	9,563	8,870	7,541	9,557	9,892	13,917	14,044	13,349
IDA	26	108	253	297	318	518	593	598	574	397
PRINCIPAL REPAYMENTS	**5,021**	**36,333**	**67,398**	**75,884**	**84,143**	**93,915**	**122,782**	**150,079**	**147,738**	**144,421**
Public and publicly guaranteed	**2,713**	**26,009**	**60,081**	**54,197**	**59,210**	**68,137**	**87,022**	**96,607**	**85,721**	**88,684**
Official creditors	993	5,205	17,858	20,202	25,127	31,379	38,952	36,263	29,813	30,420
Multilateral	287	1,268	9,217	11,915	12,972	15,166	13,522	13,399	13,265	13,205
Concessional	29	42	331	447	463	497	645	631	660	563
Bilateral	706	3,937	8,641	8,288	12,155	16,213	25,430	22,863	16,548	17,215
Concessional	323	1,376	3,326	2,835	3,443	3,866	4,635	4,687	4,460	3,760
Private creditors	1,720	20,804	42,223	33,995	34,082	36,758	48,070	60,344	55,907	58,264
Bonds	117	485	4,952	7,267	6,273	11,073	18,720	35,634	26,239	30,009
Commercial banks	645	12,795	19,653	11,637	13,966	12,959	18,268	15,287	18,165	18,668
Other private	958	7,524	17,619	15,091	13,843	12,726	11,082	9,423	11,503	9,587
Private nonguaranteed	**2,308**	**10,324**	**7,317**	**21,688**	**24,934**	**25,779**	**35,760**	**53,473**	**62,017**	**55,737**
Bonds	0	0	0	289	2,997	5,212	6,809	11,684	11,881	12,252
Commercial banks	2,308	10,324	7,317	21,399	21,938	20,567	28,951	41,789	50,136	43,485
Memo:										
IBRD	156	825	6,416	7,529	8,248	8,597	8,211	7,560	7,800	6,649
IDA	0	5	32	46	48	53	56	70	70	77
NET FLOWS ON DEBT	**4,546**	**49,325**	**20,800**	**49,345**	**41,961**	**62,002**	**82,763**	**90,787**	**97,042**	**38,021**
Public and publicly guaranteed	**3,030**	**40,443**	**15,111**	**25,497**	**12,825**	**29,131**	**30,177**	**32,372**	**48,069**	**42,007**
Official creditors	1,572	13,869	13,764	9,861	357	8,390	-5,856	4,522	12,777	12,600
Multilateral	543	4,313	6,592	6,027	1,351	3,422	5,670	13,049	17,594	11,132
Concessional	57	546	738	1,034	882	1,199	1,357	1,099	1,011	1,362
Bilateral	1,029	9,556	7,172	3,834	-995	4,968	-11,525	-8,527	-4,816	1,468
Concessional	827	5,043	4,344	3,087	2,291	3,478	1,506	945	356	2,288
Private creditors	1,458	26,575	1,347	15,636	12,468	20,741	36,032	27,850	35,293	29,407
Bonds	23	1,066	502	15,867	14,383	16,915	36,178	22,637	26,833	24,773
Commercial banks	624	17,081	-7,803	-3,150	-906	4,821	1,693	6,205	11,203	3,388
Other private	811	8,428	8,648	2,919	-1,009	-994	-1,839	-991	-2,742	1,246
Private nonguaranteed	**1,517**	**8,881**	**5,690**	**23,848**	**29,137**	**32,870**	**52,586**	**58,415**	**48,972**	**-3,986**
Bonds	0	0	581	17,955	20,270	11,085	21,119	17,593	7,343	1,441
Commercial banks	1,517	8,881	5,109	5,893	8,866	21,785	31,467	40,823	41,629	-5,427
Memo:										
IBRD	328	2,714	3,148	1,341	-707	960	1,681	6,357	6,244	6,700
IDA	26	103	221	252	270	465	536	527	505	320

MIDDLE-INCOME COUNTRIES

(US$ million, unless otherwise indicated)

	1970	1980	1990	1993	1994	1995	1996	1997	1998	1999
INTEREST PAYMENTS (LINT)	**1,838**	**28,056**	**39,577**	**37,863**	**43,629**	**58,383**	**61,698**	**67,019**	**73,508**	**87,534**
Public and publicly guaranteed	**1,124**	**21,889**	**35,567**	**32,282**	**35,823**	**47,246**	**48,094**	**48,536**	**51,816**	**59,286**
Official creditors	501	4,414	12,927	15,783	16,673	21,228	21,662	19,764	18,831	21,840
Multilateral	216	1,934	7,385	8,640	8,703	9,000	8,935	8,373	8,872	10,519
Concessional	9	60	205	260	277	302	318	331	350	377
Bilateral	285	2,479	5,543	7,143	7,969	12,227	12,726	11,389	9,959	11,321
Concessional	175	1,049	1,977	2,950	2,978	3,425	3,419	3,130	3,087	2,884
Private creditors	623	17,476	22,639	16,499	19,150	26,018	26,431	28,773	32,985	37,446
Bonds	86	921	3,974	7,831	10,440	15,967	15,472	18,775	21,459	23,851
Commercial banks	239	13,106	13,767	5,034	4,931	5,890	7,330	6,866	8,574	11,155
Other private	297	3,449	4,898	3,633	3,779	4,161	3,630	3,132	2,952	2,440
Private nonguaranteed	**714**	**6,166**	**4,010**	**5,581**	**7,806**	**11,136**	**13,604**	**18,483**	**21,692**	**28,248**
Bonds	0	0	8	994	2,784	4,208	5,044	6,654	7,315	8,246
Commercial banks	714	6,166	4,003	4,587	5,022	6,929	8,560	11,829	14,376	20,002
Memo:										
IBRD	164	1,394	4,744	5,232	5,033	5,115	5,037	4,473	4,692	5,346
IDA	2	10	24	29	31	35	37	43	43	46
NET TRANSFERS ON DEBT	**2,708**	**21,269**	**-18,777**	**11,482**	**-1,668**	**3,619**	**21,065**	**23,768**	**23,533**	**-49,513**
Public and publicly guaranteed	**1,905**	**18,554**	**-20,456**	**-6,785**	**-22,998**	**-18,115**	**-17,917**	**-16,165**	**-3,747**	**-17,279**
Official creditors	1,070	9,455	836	-5,922	-16,315	-12,837	-27,517	-15,242	-6,054	-9,240
Multilateral	328	2,378	-792	-2,614	-7,351	-5,577	-3,266	4,675	8,722	613
Concessional	48	486	532	774	605	897	1,039	768	660	985
Bilateral	743	7,077	1,629	-3,308	-8,964	-7,260	-24,251	-19,917	-14,776	-9,853
Concessional	652	3,994	2,366	137	-687	53	-1,914	-2,185	-2,731	-596
Private creditors	835	9,099	-21,292	-862	-6,683	-5,277	9,600	-923	2,308	-8,039
Bonds	-64	145	-3,472	8,036	3,943	948	20,706	3,862	5,374	922
Commercial banks	385	3,975	-21,570	-8,184	-5,838	-1,070	-5,636	-662	2,629	-7,767
Other private	514	4,979	3,749	-714	-4,789	-5,155	-5,469	-4,123	-5,695	-1,194
Private nonguaranteed	**803**	**2,715**	**1,679**	**18,266**	**21,331**	**21,734**	**38,983**	**39,932**	**27,280**	**-32,234**
Bonds	0	0	573	16,961	17,486	6,878	16,076	10,938	27	-6,805
Commercial banks	803	2,715	1,106	1,305	3,845	14,857	22,907	28,994	27,253	-25,429
Memo:										
IBRD	165	1,319	-1,597	-3,891	-5,741	-4,156	-3,357	1,884	1,552	1,354
IDA	25	93	198	222	238	431	500	484	462	274
DEBT SERVICE (LTDS)	**6,858**	**64,388**	**106,976**	**113,747**	**127,772**	**152,297**	**184,480**	**217,099**	**221,246**	**231,955**
Public and publicly guaranteed	**3,836**	**47,898**	**95,648**	**86,478**	**95,032**	**115,382**	**135,116**	**145,143**	**137,537**	**147,970**
Official creditors	1,494	9,619	30,786	35,985	41,800	52,607	60,614	56,026	48,645	52,260
Multilateral	502	3,203	16,602	20,555	21,675	24,166	22,458	21,773	22,138	23,724
Concessional	38	103	537	707	740	799	962	961	1,010	940
Bilateral	992	6,416	14,184	15,430	20,125	28,441	38,156	34,253	26,507	28,536
Concessional	498	2,424	5,304	5,786	6,421	7,289	8,055	7,817	7,547	6,644
Private creditors	2,343	38,279	64,862	50,493	53,233	62,776	74,502	89,117	88,893	95,710
Bonds	204	1,405	8,926	15,098	16,713	27,040	34,192	54,409	47,698	53,860
Commercial banks	884	25,901	33,419	16,672	18,897	18,849	25,598	22,153	26,739	29,823
Other private	1,255	10,973	22,517	18,723	17,622	16,886	14,712	12,555	14,455	12,027
Private nonguaranteed	**3,022**	**16,490**	**11,328**	**27,269**	**32,740**	**36,915**	**49,364**	**71,956**	**83,709**	**83,985**
Bonds	0	0	8	1,284	5,781	9,419	11,852	18,338	19,196	20,498
Commercial banks	3,022	16,490	11,320	25,985	26,959	27,496	37,512	53,618	64,512	63,487
Memo:										
IBRD	320	2,219	11,161	12,761	13,281	13,712	13,249	12,032	12,491	11,995
IDA	2	15	55	75	80	88	93	113	112	123
UNDISBURSED DEBT	**10,340**	**91,999**	**107,951**	**142,743**	**145,327**	**145,604**	**137,900**	**131,462**	**141,085**	..
Official creditors	7,340	53,273	72,818	97,926	103,213	105,929	98,915	95,487	96,484	..
Private creditors	2,999	38,726	35,133	44,817	42,114	39,675	38,986	35,976	44,602	..
Memorandum items										
Concessional LDOD	9,445	53,246	120,101	150,702	156,675	164,415	163,867	154,852	134,827	155,901
Variable rate LDOD	15,221	169,864	352,902	447,372	501,950	547,075	593,925	671,344	799,246	..
Public sector LDOD	24,595	245,722	670,377	769,459	826,340	869,963	868,161	857,519	925,437	..
Private sector LDOD	16,269	75,154	55,939	112,853	153,469	176,187	235,343	309,930	425,294	..

6. CURRENCY COMPOSITION OF LONG-TERM DEBT (PERCENT)

	1970	1980	1990	1993	1994	1995	1996	1997	1998	1999
Deutsche mark	9.0	6.4	10.5	9.7	9.7	10.3	10.6	9.7	9.6	..
French franc	4.9	5.0	5.6	4.2	4.3	4.4	4.2	3.5	3.0	..
Japanese yen	0.7	6.1	9.1	10.6	10.9	11.2	10.5	9.5	9.3	..
Pound sterling	5.2	1.7	1.6	1.1	0.9	0.8	0.9	0.9	0.8	..
Swiss franc	1.6	1.8	2.3	1.4	1.0	1.1	0.9	0.5	0.4	..
U.S.dollars	55.1	54.4	43.6	46.9	47.6	47.5	49.3	53.5	56.8	..
Multiple currency	14.1	11.1	14.5	14.0	14.0	13.5	12.8	11.5	7.8	..
Special drawing rights	0.0	0.0	0.1	0.0	0.0	0.0	0.1	0.1	0.1	..
All other currencies	9.4	5.7	6.2	5.6	5.6	5.6	5.3	4.9	6.0	..

MIDDLE-INCOME COUNTRIES

(US$ million, unless otherwise indicated)

	1970	1980	1990	1993	1994	1995	1996	1997	1998	1999
7. DEBT RESTRUCTURINGS										
Total amount rescheduled	117	2,123	72,768	62,108	86,518	28,547	26,366	40,588	32,933	..
Debt stock rescheduled	0	1	61,819	23,724	54,025	6,753	5,664	1,140	28,415	..
Principal rescheduled	0	124	6,274	17,020	13,299	13,387	12,866	32,296	4,830	..
Official	0	17	2,996	6,285	3,039	5,647	4,379	4,834	3,188	..
Private	0	107	3,277	10,736	10,260	7,740	8,486	27,461	1,642	..
Interest rescheduled	..	..	3,987	15,560	14,836	4,363	6,171	6,493	1,041	..
Official	0	7	3,121	3,481	1,880	1,572	1,157	1,181	708	..
Private	0	1	867	12,079	12,956	2,792	5,015	5,312	333	..
Debt forgiven	7	79	11,044	1,643	4,414	485	1,909	260	305	..
Memo: interest forgiven	0	0	2,793	154	269	15	784	15	14	..
Debt stock reduction	0	0	24,843	6,431	12,798	2,663	5,448	13,640	2,729	..
of which debt buyback	0	0	4,360	525	1,702	43	3,363	9,850	2,100	..
8. DEBT STOCK-FLOW RECONCILIATION										
Total change in debt stocks	..	..	45,949	127,914	130,946	132,080	83,407	86,036	168,145	..
Net flows on debt	12,205	89,453	27,832	91,896	89,863	132,410	115,292	115,853	79,086	19,464
Net change in interest arrears	..	..	12,595	-5,034	-5,868	-1,154	-3,489	-5,107	3,536	..
Interest capitalized	..	..	3,987	15,560	14,836	4,363	6,171	6,493	1,041	..
Debt forgiveness or reduction	..	..	-31,528	-7,549	-15,510	-3,105	-3,993	-4,049	-934	..
Cross-currency valuation	..	..	33,228	-3,662	30,761	11,544	-30,711	-35,687	24,790	..
Residual	..	..	-168	36,703	16,864	-11,980	137	8,534	60,624	..
9. AVERAGE TERMS OF NEW COMMITMENTS										
ALL CREDITORS										
Interest (%)	6.2	10.3	7.8	6.1	6.2	6.5	6.9	7.0	7.4	..
Maturity (years)	16.3	13.3	16.1	12.2	12.5	11.3	11.1	13.0	10.7	..
Grace period (years)	4.5	4.4	5.2	4.8	4.6	4.5	5.6	7.2	5.9	..
Grant element (%)	22.7	1.1	13.3	18.9	19.1	16.8	14.2	14.7	11.7	..
Official creditors										
Interest (%)	5.0	6.9	6.6	5.6	5.8	6.7	5.6	6.0	6.0	..
Maturity (years)	23.0	19.6	18.8	18.1	18.4	15.8	17.2	17.2	14.2	..
Grace period (years)	6.4	5.3	5.9	5.3	5.4	4.6	5.1	5.2	4.3	..
Grant element (%)	34.0	22.3	22.9	27.2	26.7	21.0	26.9	24.0	21.3	..
Private creditors										
Interest (%)	7.4	12.2	8.8	6.4	6.5	6.4	7.5	7.5	8.0	..
Maturity (years)	9.6	9.8	13.9	8.4	8.1	7.2	8.6	10.8	9.0	..
Grace period (years)	2.7	3.9	4.7	4.4	4.1	4.4	5.8	8.2	6.6	..
Grant element (%)	11.8	-10.4	5.4	13.4	13.5	13.0	9.0	9.8	7.1	..
Memorandum items										
Commitments	7,531	67,720	82,214	87,805	76,903	101,636	120,335	134,730	138,899	..
Official creditors	3,725	23,894	37,236	34,720	32,510	48,267	35,317	46,551	45,191	..
Private creditors	3,806	43,826	44,978	53,085	44,393	53,369	85,018	88,180	93,709	..

10. GRAPH OF AGGREGATE NET RESOURCE FLOWS

(current prices, US$ million)

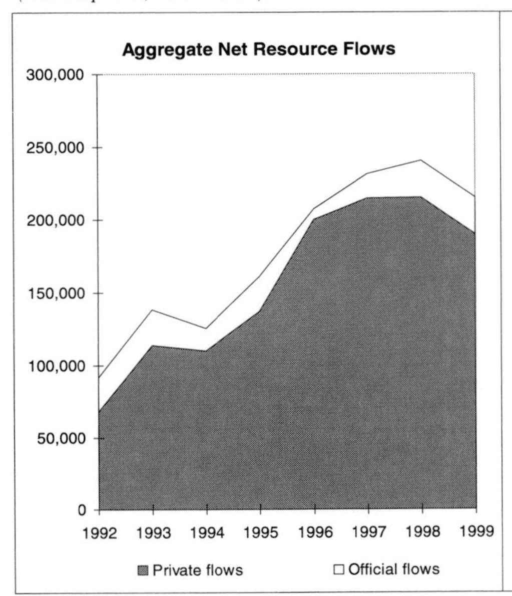

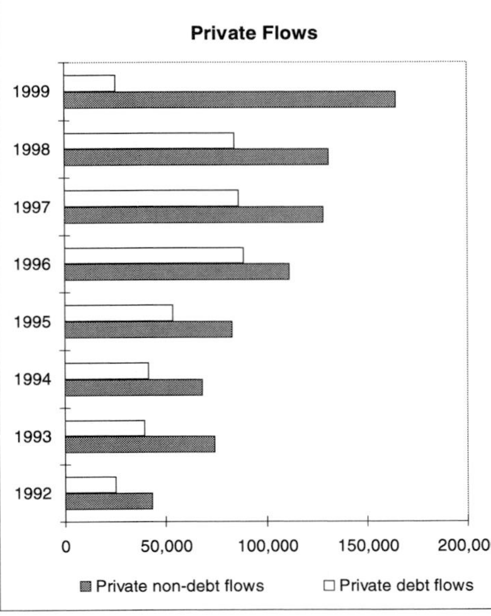

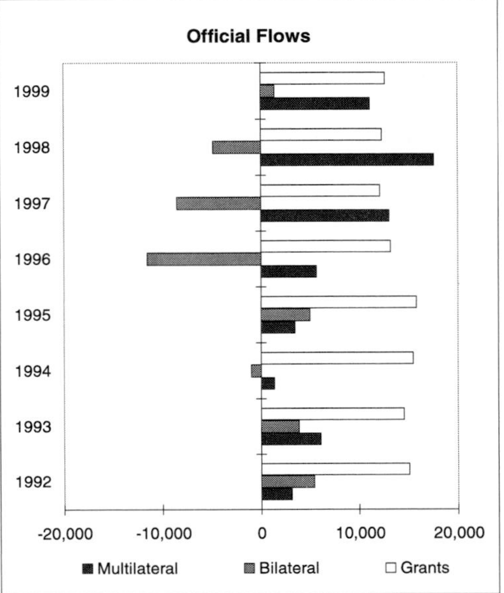

Country tables

ALBANIA

(US$ million, unless otherwise indicated)

	1970	1980	1990	1992	1993	1994	1995	1996	1997	1998
1. SUMMARY DEBT DATA										
TOTAL DEBT STOCKS (EDT)	..	..	**348.6**	**632.6**	**773.0**	**851.1**	**643.6**	**672.1**	**706.0**	**820.6**
Long-term debt (LDOD)	..	..	**35.7**	**126.9**	**166.0**	**215.6**	**516.7**	**586.3**	**603.3**	**721.2**
Public and publicly guaranteed	..	..	35.7	126.9	166.0	215.6	516.7	586.3	603.3	701.3
Private nonguaranteed	..	..	0.0	0.0	0.0	0.0	0.0	0.0	0.0	19.8
Use of IMF credit	**0.0**	**0.0**	**0.0**	**13.3**	**29.7**	**54.2**	**64.5**	**54.2**	**55.0**	**64.4**
Short-term debt	..	..	**312.9**	**492.4**	**577.4**	**581.3**	**62.3**	**31.6**	**47.8**	**34.9**
of which interest arrears on LDOD	..	..	0.0	2.8	0.9	1.6	1.6	1.5	3.8	3.8
Official creditors	..	..	0.0	0.0	0.3	1.3	1.6	1.5	1.0	1.0
Private creditors	..	..	0.0	2.8	0.6	0.3	0.0	0.0	2.8	2.8
Memo: principal arrears on LDOD	..	..	0.0	23.4	15.5	25.7	27.0	33.4	33.4	33.4
Official creditors	..	..	0.0	4.0	5.5	17.7	17.7	17.7	17.7	17.7
Private creditors	..	..	0.0	19.4	10.0	8.0	9.4	15.8	15.8	15.8
Memo: export credits	..	..	16.0	24.0	31.0	29.0	34.0	37.0	30.0	195.0
TOTAL DEBT FLOWS										
Disbursements	..	..	**33.1**	**66.2**	**81.2**	**74.8**	**74.6**	**84.0**	**64.6**	**95.3**
Long-term debt	..	..	33.1	52.6	64.6	52.5	63.9	84.0	52.4	87.3
IMF purchases	0.0	0.0	0.0	13.6	16.6	22.2	10.7	0.0	12.1	8.0
Principal repayments	..	..	**0.0**	**0.0**	**5.0**	**8.1**	**1.6**	**13.6**	**15.9**	**12.7**
Long-term debt	..	..	0.0	0.0	5.0	8.1	0.4	5.3	8.0	11.6
IMF repurchases	0.0	0.0	0.0	0.0	0.0	0.0	1.2	8.3	8.0	1.2
Net flows on debt	..	..	**271.6**	**135.8**	**163.1**	**69.9**	**-105.0**	**39.8**	**62.6**	**69.7**
of which short-term debt	..	..	238.5	69.6	86.9	3.2	-178.0	-30.6	13.9	-12.9
Interest payments (INT)	..	..	**3.1**	**2.0**	**3.0**	**10.2**	**8.8**	**15.1**	**23.4**	**24.5**
Long-term debt	..	..	3.1	1.9	2.1	9.1	4.5	12.8	20.8	21.6
IMF charges	0.0	0.0	0.0	0.1	0.9	1.1	1.3	0.9	0.5	0.8
Short-term debt	..	..	0.0	0.0	0.0	0.0	3.0	1.4	2.0	2.1
Net transfers on debt	..	..	**268.5**	**133.8**	**160.1**	**59.7**	**-113.8**	**24.7**	**39.2**	**45.2**
Total debt service paid (TDS)	..	..	**3.1**	**2.0**	**8.1**	**18.3**	**10.4**	**28.7**	**39.3**	**37.2**
Long-term debt	..	..	3.1	1.9	7.1	17.2	4.9	18.1	28.8	33.2
IMF repurchases and charges	0.0	0.0	0.0	0.1	0.9	1.1	2.5	9.2	8.4	2.0
Short-term debt (interest only)	..	..	0.0	0.0	0.0	0.0	3.0	1.4	2.0	2.1
2. AGGREGATE NET RESOURCE FLOWS AND NET TRANSFERS (LONG-TERM)										
NET RESOURCE FLOWS	..	..	**35.0**	**406.2**	**300.9**	**165.8**	**210.1**	**282.2**	**159.5**	**240.1**
Net flow of long-term debt (ex. IMF)	..	..	33.1	52.6	59.6	44.4	63.5	78.7	44.5	75.8
Foreign direct investment (net)	..	..	0.0	20.0	58.0	53.0	70.0	90.1	48.0	45.0
Portfolio equity flows	..	..	0.0	0.0	0.0	0.0	0.0	0.0	0.0	0.0
Grants (excluding technical coop.)	..	..	1.9	333.6	183.4	68.4	76.6	113.4	67.0	119.3
Memo: technical coop. grants	..	..	9.2	11.5	24.5	27.3	32.3	49.6	28.0	28.3
official net resource flows	..	..	3.8	383.0	231.8	120.9	140.5	187.6	112.6	198.0
private net resource flows	..	..	31.2	23.2	69.1	44.9	69.6	94.6	46.9	42.1
NET TRANSFERS	..	..	**31.9**	**404.3**	**298.8**	**156.6**	**205.6**	**269.4**	**138.7**	**218.4**
Interest on long-term debt	..	..	3.1	1.9	2.1	9.1	4.5	12.8	20.8	21.6
Profit remittances on FDI	..	..	0.0	0.0	0.0	0.0	0.0	0.0	0.0	0.0
Memo: official net transfers	..	..	3.8	382.7	231.3	113.2	136.6	182.7	107.4	192.2
private net transfers	..	..	28.1	21.6	67.5	43.4	69.0	86.7	31.3	26.2
3. MAJOR ECONOMIC AGGREGATES										
Gross national product (GNP)	..	..	2,105.6	674.3	1,207.6	1,988.2	2,480.0	2,753.0	2,335.0	3,112.0
Exports of goods & services (XGS)	..	..	353.6	242.9	528.9	540.2	760.3	956.2	550.7	832.9
of which workers remittances	..	..	0.0	150.0	274.8	264.7	384.6	499.6	266.9	452.3
Imports of goods & services (MGS)	..	..	486.9	667.3	794.4	774.8	864.6	1,123.3	820.6	949.6
International reserves (RES)	..	..	..	..	166.5	223.6	265.3	323.4	342.4	382.2
Current account balance	..	..	-118.3	-50.7	14.9	-157.3	-11.5	-107.3	-272.2	-65.1
4. DEBT INDICATORS										
EDT / XGS (%)	..	..	98.6	260.4	146.2	157.6	84.7	70.3	128.2	98.5
EDT / GNP (%)	..	..	16.6	93.8	64.0	42.8	26.0	24.4	30.2	26.4
TDS / XGS (%)	..	..	0.9	0.8	1.5	3.4	1.4	3.0	7.1	4.5
INT / XGS (%)	..	..	0.9	0.8	0.6	1.9	1.2	1.6	4.3	2.9
INT / GNP (%)	..	..	0.2	0.3	0.3	0.5	0.4	0.6	1.0	0.8
RES / EDT (%)	..	..	..	..	21.5	26.3	41.2	48.1	48.5	46.6
RES / MGS (months)	..	..	..	..	2.5	3.5	3.7	3.5	5.0	4.8
Short-term / EDT (%)	..	..	89.8	77.8	74.7	68.3	9.7	4.7	6.8	4.3
Concessional / EDT (%)	..	..	0.6	7.8	13.3	18.1	34.0	42.1	43.5	50.0
Multilateral / EDT (%)	..	..	0.0	0.3	3.6	7.7	17.8	22.5	23.2	29.5

ALBANIA

(US$ million, unless otherwise indicated)

	1970	1980	1990	1992	1993	1994	1995	1996	1997	1998
5. LONG-TERM DEBT										
DEBT OUTSTANDING (LDOD)	..	..	**35.7**	**126.9**	**166.0**	**215.6**	**516.7**	**586.3**	**603.3**	**721.2**
Public and publicly guaranteed	..	..	**35.7**	**126.9**	**166.0**	**215.6**	**516.7**	**586.3**	**603.3**	**701.3**
Official creditors	..	..	2.0	63.5	142.9	196.4	266.7	332.0	351.0	450.5
Multilateral	..	..	0.0	2.0	27.6	65.7	114.6	151.1	164.0	241.9
Concessional	..	..	0.0	2.0	27.6	65.5	109.8	141.6	154.6	232.1
Bilateral	..	..	2.0	61.5	115.3	130.6	152.1	180.9	187.0	208.5
Concessional	..	..	2.0	47.6	75.2	88.7	109.1	141.4	152.4	178.0
Private creditors	..	..	33.7	63.3	23.1	19.2	250.0	254.2	252.3	250.9
Bonds	..	..	0.0	0.0	0.0	0.0	225.0	225.0	225.0	225.0
Commercial banks	..	..	0.0	0.0	0.0	0.0	0.0	0.0	0.0	0.0
Other private	..	..	33.7	63.3	23.1	19.2	25.0	29.2	27.3	25.9
Private nonguaranteed	..	..	**0.0**	**0.0**	**0.0**	**0.0**	**0.0**	**0.0**	**0.0**	**19.8**
Bonds	..	..	0.0	0.0	0.0	0.0	0.0	0.0	0.0	0.0
Commercial banks	..	..	0.0	0.0	0.0	0.0	0.0	0.0	0.0	19.8
Memo:										
IBRD	0.0	0.0	0.0	0.0	0.0	0.0	0.0	0.0	0.0	0.0
IDA	0.0	0.0	0.0	2.0	27.6	64.7	109.0	137.2	148.2	220.1
DISBURSEMENTS	..	..	**33.1**	**52.6**	**64.6**	**52.5**	**63.9**	**84.0**	**52.4**	**87.3**
Public and publicly guaranteed	..	..	**33.1**	**52.6**	**64.6**	**52.5**	**63.9**	**84.0**	**52.4**	**87.3**
Official creditors	..	..	1.9	49.4	48.4	52.5	63.9	78.4	51.8	87.3
Multilateral	..	..	0.0	2.1	25.8	36.0	48.0	41.4	22.3	69.3
Concessional	..	..	0.0	2.1	25.8	35.8	43.3	35.9	21.5	68.1
Bilateral	..	..	1.9	47.3	22.6	16.5	15.9	37.0	29.5	17.9
Concessional	..	..	1.9	47.3	19.4	15.9	15.9	37.0	29.5	17.9
Private creditors	..	..	31.2	3.2	16.2	0.0	0.0	5.6	0.7	0.0
Bonds	..	..	0.0	0.0	0.0	0.0	0.0	0.0	0.0	0.0
Commercial banks	..	..	0.0	0.0	0.0	0.0	0.0	0.0	0.0	0.0
Other private	..	..	31.2	3.2	16.2	0.0	0.0	5.6	0.7	0.0
Private nonguaranteed	..	..	**0.0**	**0.0**	**0.0**	**0.0**	**0.0**	**0.0**	**0.0**	**0.0**
Bonds	..	..	0.0	0.0	0.0	0.0	0.0	0.0	0.0	0.0
Commercial banks	..	..	0.0	0.0	0.0	0.0	0.0	0.0	0.0	0.0
Memo:										
IBRD	0.0	0.0	0.0	0.0	0.0	0.0	0.0	0.0	0.0	0.0
IDA	0.0	0.0	0.0	2.1	25.8	35.0	43.3	32.3	18.9	62.8
PRINCIPAL REPAYMENTS	..	..	**0.0**	**0.0**	**5.0**	**8.1**	**0.4**	**5.3**	**8.0**	**11.6**
Public and publicly guaranteed	..	..	**0.0**	**0.0**	**5.0**	**8.1**	**0.4**	**5.3**	**8.0**	**10.4**
Official creditors	..	..	0.0	0.0	0.0	0.0	0.0	4.2	6.1	8.6
Multilateral	..	..	0.0	0.0	0.0	0.0	0.0	0.8	1.3	0.8
Concessional	..	..	0.0	0.0	0.0	0.0	0.0	0.0	0.4	0.0
Bilateral	..	..	0.0	0.0	0.0	0.0	0.0	3.3	4.9	7.8
Concessional	..	..	0.0	0.0	0.0	0.0	0.0	0.9	1.4	3.2
Private creditors	..	..	0.0	0.0	5.0	8.1	0.4	1.1	1.8	1.8
Bonds	..	..	0.0	0.0	0.0	0.0	0.0	0.0	0.0	0.0
Commercial banks	..	..	0.0	0.0	0.0	0.0	0.0	0.0	0.0	0.0
Other private	..	..	0.0	0.0	5.0	8.1	0.4	1.1	1.8	1.8
Private nonguaranteed	..	..	**0.0**	**0.0**	**0.0**	**0.0**	**0.0**	**0.0**	**0.0**	**1.1**
Bonds	..	..	0.0	0.0	0.0	0.0	0.0	0.0	0.0	0.0
Commercial banks	..	..	0.0	0.0	0.0	0.0	0.0	0.0	0.0	1.1
Memo:										
IBRD	0.0	0.0	0.0	0.0	0.0	0.0	0.0	0.0	0.0	0.0
IDA	0.0	0.0	0.0	0.0	0.0	0.0	0.0	0.0	0.0	0.0
NET FLOWS ON DEBT	..	..	**33.1**	**52.6**	**59.6**	**44.4**	**63.5**	**78.7**	**44.5**	**75.8**
Public and publicly guaranteed	..	..	**33.1**	**52.6**	**59.6**	**44.4**	**63.5**	**78.7**	**44.5**	**76.9**
Official creditors	..	..	1.9	49.4	48.4	52.5	63.9	74.2	45.6	78.7
Multilateral	..	..	0.0	2.1	25.8	36.0	48.0	40.6	21.0	68.5
Concessional	..	..	0.0	2.1	25.8	35.8	43.3	35.9	21.1	68.1
Bilateral	..	..	1.9	47.3	22.6	16.5	15.9	33.6	24.6	10.2
Concessional	..	..	1.9	47.3	19.4	15.9	15.9	36.1	28.1	14.7
Private creditors	..	..	31.2	3.2	11.1	-8.1	-0.4	4.5	-1.1	-1.8
Bonds	..	..	0.0	0.0	0.0	0.0	0.0	0.0	0.0	0.0
Commercial banks	..	..	0.0	0.0	0.0	0.0	0.0	0.0	0.0	0.0
Other private	..	..	31.2	3.2	11.1	-8.1	-0.4	4.5	-1.1	-1.8
Private nonguaranteed	..	..	**0.0**	**0.0**	**0.0**	**0.0**	**0.0**	**0.0**	**0.0**	**-1.1**
Bonds	..	..	0.0	0.0	0.0	0.0	0.0	0.0	0.0	0.0
Commercial banks	..	..	0.0	0.0	0.0	0.0	0.0	0.0	0.0	-1.1
Memo:										
IBRD	0.0	0.0	0.0	0.0	0.0	0.0	0.0	0.0	0.0	0.0
IDA	0.0	0.0	0.0	2.1	25.8	35.0	43.3	32.3	18.9	62.8

ALBANIA

(US$ million, unless otherwise indicated)

	1970	1980	1990	1992	1993	1994	1995	1996	1997	1998
INTEREST PAYMENTS (LINT)	..	..	**3.1**	**1.9**	**2.1**	**9.1**	**4.5**	**12.8**	**20.8**	**21.6**
Public and publicly guaranteed	..	..	**3.1**	**1.9**	**2.1**	**9.1**	**4.5**	**12.8**	**20.8**	**20.9**
Official creditors	..	..	0.0	0.3	0.5	7.7	3.9	4.9	5.2	5.8
Multilateral	..	..	0.0	0.0	0.0	0.2	0.6	1.4	1.9	2.1
Concessional	..	..	0.0	0.0	0.0	0.2	0.6	0.9	1.1	1.4
Bilateral	..	..	0.0	0.3	0.5	7.4	3.3	3.5	3.3	3.7
Concessional	..	..	0.0	0.1	0.3	3.1	1.8	2.0	2.1	2.7
Private creditors	..	..	3.1	1.6	1.6	1.5	0.6	7.9	15.6	15.1
Bonds	..	..	0.0	0.0	0.0	0.0	0.0	7.5	15.2	14.6
Commercial banks	..	..	0.0	0.0	0.0	0.0	0.0	0.0	0.0	0.0
Other private	..	..	3.1	1.6	1.6	1.5	0.6	0.5	0.5	0.4
Private nonguaranteed	..	..	**0.0**	**0.0**	**0.0**	**0.0**	**0.0**	**0.0**	**0.0**	**0.8**
Bonds	..	..	0.0	0.0	0.0	0.0	0.0	0.0	0.0	0.0
Commercial banks	..	..	0.0	0.0	0.0	0.0	0.0	0.0	0.0	0.8
Memo:										
IBRD	0.0	0.0	0.0	0.0	0.0	0.0	0.0	0.0	0.0	0.0
IDA	0.0	0.0	0.0	0.0	0.0	0.2	0.6	0.9	1.0	1.2
NET TRANSFERS ON DEBT	..	..	**30.0**	**50.6**	**57.5**	**35.3**	**58.9**	**65.9**	**23.6**	**54.1**
Public and publicly guaranteed	..	..	**30.0**	**50.6**	**57.5**	**35.3**	**58.9**	**65.9**	**23.6**	**56.0**
Official creditors	..	..	1.9	49.1	47.9	44.9	60.0	69.3	40.4	72.8
Multilateral	..	..	0.0	2.1	25.8	35.7	47.4	39.2	19.1	66.4
Concessional	..	..	0.0	2.1	25.8	35.6	42.8	35.0	20.0	66.8
Bilateral	..	..	1.9	47.0	22.1	9.1	12.6	30.1	21.3	6.5
Concessional	..	..	1.9	47.2	19.1	12.9	14.1	34.1	26.0	12.0
Private creditors	..	..	28.1	1.6	9.6	-9.5	-1.0	-3.5	-16.8	-16.8
Bonds	..	..	0.0	0.0	0.0	0.0	0.0	-7.5	-15.2	-14.6
Commercial banks	..	..	0.0	0.0	0.0	0.0	0.0	0.0	0.0	0.0
Other private	..	..	28.1	1.6	9.6	-9.5	-1.0	4.0	-1.6	-2.2
Private nonguaranteed	..	..	**0.0**	**0.0**	**0.0**	**0.0**	**0.0**	**0.0**	**0.0**	**-1.9**
Bonds	..	..	0.0	0.0	0.0	0.0	0.0	0.0	0.0	0.0
Commercial banks	..	..	0.0	0.0	0.0	0.0	0.0	0.0	0.0	-1.9
Memo:										
IBRD	0.0	0.0	0.0	0.0	0.0	0.0	0.0	0.0	0.0	0.0
IDA	0.0	0.0	0.0	2.1	25.8	34.8	42.8	31.5	17.9	61.6
DEBT SERVICE (LTDS)	..	..	**3.1**	**1.9**	**7.1**	**17.2**	**4.9**	**18.1**	**28.8**	**33.2**
Public and publicly guaranteed	..	..	**3.1**	**1.9**	**7.1**	**17.2**	**4.9**	**18.1**	**28.8**	**31.3**
Official creditors	..	..	0.0	0.3	0.5	7.7	3.9	9.1	11.4	14.4
Multilateral	..	..	0.0	0.0	0.0	0.2	0.6	2.3	3.2	3.0
Concessional	..	..	0.0	0.0	0.0	0.2	0.6	0.9	1.5	1.4
Bilateral	..	..	0.0	0.3	0.5	7.4	3.3	6.8	8.2	11.5
Concessional	..	..	0.0	0.1	0.3	3.1	1.8	2.9	3.5	5.9
Private creditors	..	..	3.1	1.6	6.6	9.5	1.0	9.1	17.4	16.9
Bonds	..	..	0.0	0.0	0.0	0.0	0.0	7.5	15.2	14.6
Commercial banks	..	..	0.0	0.0	0.0	0.0	0.0	0.0	0.0	0.0
Other private	..	..	3.1	1.6	6.6	9.5	1.0	1.6	2.3	2.2
Private nonguaranteed	..	..	**0.0**	**0.0**	**0.0**	**0.0**	**0.0**	**0.0**	**0.0**	**1.9**
Bonds	..	..	0.0	0.0	0.0	0.0	0.0	0.0	0.0	0.0
Commercial banks	..	..	0.0	0.0	0.0	0.0	0.0	0.0	0.0	1.9
Memo:										
IBRD	0.0	0.0	0.0	0.0	0.0	0.0	0.0	0.0	0.0	0.0
IDA	0.0	0.0	0.0	0.0	0.0	0.2	0.6	0.9	1.0	1.2
UNDISBURSED DEBT	..	..	**20.1**	**104.5**	**133.7**	**209.4**	**312.0**	**378.4**	**328.5**	**358.1**
Official creditors	..	..	0.0	69.9	116.0	190.5	299.0	377.6	328.5	351.4
Private creditors	..	..	20.1	34.6	17.7	19.0	13.1	0.8	0.0	6.8
Memorandum items										
Concessional LDOD	..	..	2.0	49.7	102.8	154.2	218.9	282.9	307.0	410.1
Variable rate LDOD	..	..	33.7	77.2	52.2	49.2	279.2	283.6	279.8	297.1
Public sector LDOD	..	..	35.7	126.9	166.0	215.6	516.7	586.3	603.3	701.3
Private sector LDOD	..	..	0.0	0.0	0.0	0.0	0.0	0.0	0.0	19.8

6. CURRENCY COMPOSITION OF LONG-TERM DEBT (PERCENT)

	1970	1980	1990	1992	1993	1994	1995	1996	1997	1998
Deutsche mark	..	..	100.0	56.4	21.7	19.9	9.2	9.3	9.7	9.3
French franc	..	..	0.0	0.0	0.4	0.3	0.1	0.1	0.1	0.0
Japanese yen	..	..	0.0	0.0	0.0	3.9	1.6	2.7	2.8	2.9
Pound sterling	..	..	0.0	0.0	0.0	0.0	0.0	0.0	0.0	0.0
Swiss franc	..	..	0.0	0.0	0.0	0.0	0.0	0.0	0.0	0.0
U.S.dollars	..	..	0.0	12.9	41.7	49.4	75.1	73.1	72.4	72.3
Multiple currency	..	..	0.0	0.0	0.0	0.0	0.0	0.0	0.0	0.0
Special drawing rights	..	..	0.0	0.0	0.0	0.0	0.0	0.1	0.2	0.5
All other currencies	..	..	0.0	30.7	36.2	26.5	14.0	14.7	14.8	15.0

ALBANIA

(US$ million, unless otherwise indicated)

	1970	1980	1990	1992	1993	1994	1995	1996	1997	1998
7. DEBT RESTRUCTURINGS										
Total amount rescheduled	..	..	0.0	0.0	39.4	0.0	230.9	0.0	0.0	0.0
Debt stock rescheduled	..	..	0.0	0.0	0.0	0.0	225.0	0.0	0.0	0.0
Principal rescheduled	..	..	0.0	0.0	39.3	0.0	0.0	0.0	0.0	0.0
Official	..	..	0.0	0.0	0.0	0.0	0.0	0.0	0.0	0.0
Private	..	..	0.0	0.0	39.3	0.0	0.0	0.0	0.0	0.0
Interest rescheduled	..	..	0.0	0.0	0.0	0.0	0.0	0.0	0.0	0.0
Official	..	..	0.0	0.0	0.0	0.0	0.0	0.0	0.0	0.0
Private	..	..	0.0	0.0	0.0	0.0	0.0	0.0	0.0	0.0
Debt forgiven	..	..	0.0	0.0	0.0	8.4	0.0	0.0	0.0	0.0
Memo: interest forgiven	..	..	0.0	0.0	0.0	0.0	0.0	0.0	0.0	0.0
Debt stock reduction	..	..	0.0	0.0	0.0	0.0	146.0	0.0	0.0	0.0
of which debt buyback	..	..	0.0	0.0	0.0	0.0	30.0	0.0	0.0	0.0
8. DEBT STOCK-FLOW RECONCILIATION										
Total change in debt stocks	..	..	274.2	121.1	140.4	78.1	-207.5	28.5	34.0	114.6
Net flows on debt	..	..	271.6	135.8	163.1	69.9	-105.0	39.8	62.6	69.7
Net change in interest arrears	..	..	0.0	-2.4	-2.0	0.7	0.0	-0.1	2.3	0.0
Interest capitalized	..	..	0.0	0.0	0.0	0.0	0.0	0.0	0.0	0.0
Debt forgiveness or reduction	..	..	0.0	0.0	0.0	-8.4	-116.0	0.0	0.0	0.0
Cross-currency valuation	..	..	4.9	-12.2	-9.3	9.1	6.4	-5.1	-19.4	13.1
Residual	..	..	-2.3	0.0	-11.4	6.8	7.0	-6.1	-11.5	31.7
9. AVERAGE TERMS OF NEW COMMITMENTS										
ALL CREDITORS										
Interest (%)	..	..	10.0	1.8	0.9	1.7	1.9	1.4	0.5	2.2
Maturity (years)	..	..	4.7	31.5	36.0	34.6	25.6	33.3	39.8	31.3
Grace period (years)	..	..	2.8	9.0	9.6	9.2	7.7	10.6	10.3	8.0
Grant element (%)	..	..	-0.4	65.4	76.3	69.5	60.2	72.0	82.6	61.8
Official creditors										
Interest (%)	..	..	0.0	1.6	0.9	1.7	1.9	1.4	0.5	2.0
Maturity (years)	..	..	0.0	32.8	36.0	34.6	25.7	33.3	39.8	33.2
Grace period (years)	..	..	0.0	9.3	9.6	9.2	7.6	10.6	10.3	8.5
Grant element (%)	..	..	0.0	67.9	76.3	69.5	60.4	72.0	82.6	65.5
Private creditors										
Interest (%)	..	..	10.0	5.8	0.0	0.0	3.0	0.0	0.0	5.8
Maturity (years)	..	..	4.7	5.0	0.0	0.0	22.7	0.0	0.0	5.0
Grace period (years)	..	..	2.8	1.5	0.0	0.0	11.7	0.0	0.0	1.5
Grant element (%)	..	..	-0.4	10.8	0.0	0.0	55.9	0.0	0.0	10.8
Memorandum items										
Commitments	..	..	49.8	76.5	96.3	120.3	174.9	176.2	33.8	100.7
Official creditors	..	..	0.0	73.1	96.3	120.3	168.7	176.2	33.8	94.0
Private creditors	..	..	49.8	3.4	0.0	0.0	6.2	0.0	0.0	6.8

10. CONTRACTUAL OBLIGATIONS ON OUTSTANDING LONG-TERM DEBT

	1999	2000	2001	2002	2003	2004	2005	2006	2007	2008
TOTAL										
Disbursements	83.9	101.6	70.5	45.4	25.8	13.6	7.1	2.0	0.3	0.0
Principal	17.5	21.3	16.6	25.2	24.3	23.8	28.0	35.2	29.1	29.6
Interest	22.3	23.4	25.5	25.9	25.8	25.3	24.7	23.7	22.8	22.0
Official creditors										
Disbursements	83.9	101.6	70.5	45.4	25.8	13.6	7.1	2.0	0.3	0.0
Principal	11.6	16.1	12.2	20.7	20.4	23.8	28.0	32.7	29.1	29.5
Interest	6.8	8.2	10.4	11.0	10.9	10.6	10.0	9.1	8.2	7.4
Bilateral creditors										
Disbursements	19.9	17.9	10.8	6.9	3.2	1.7	0.8	0.0	0.0	0.0
Principal	9.1	11.7	2.3	9.9	7.7	8.8	11.0	14.8	10.7	11.3
Interest	3.4	3.3	3.2	3.2	3.1	3.0	2.9	2.6	2.4	2.2
Multilateral creditors										
Disbursements	64.0	83.7	59.7	38.5	22.5	11.9	6.3	2.0	0.3	0.0
Principal	2.5	4.4	9.9	10.8	12.7	15.0	17.1	17.9	18.4	18.1
Interest	3.4	4.8	7.2	7.8	7.9	7.6	7.1	6.5	5.8	5.1
Private creditors										
Disbursements	0.0	0.0	0.0	0.0	0.0	0.0	0.0	0.0	0.0	0.0
Principal	5.9	5.2	4.4	4.4	3.9	0.0	0.0	2.5	0.0	0.2
Interest	15.5	15.3	15.2	14.9	14.9	14.8	14.8	14.6	14.6	14.6
Commercial banks										
Disbursements	0.0	0.0	0.0	0.0	0.0	0.0	0.0	0.0	0.0	0.0
Principal	0.0	0.0	0.0	0.0	0.0	0.0	0.0	0.0	0.0	0.0
Interest	0.0	0.0	0.0	0.0	0.0	0.0	0.0	0.0	0.0	0.0
Other private										
Disbursements	0.0	0.0	0.0	0.0	0.0	0.0	0.0	0.0	0.0	0.0
Principal	5.9	5.2	4.4	4.4	3.9	0.0	0.0	2.5	0.0	0.2
Interest	15.5	15.3	15.2	14.9	14.9	14.8	14.8	14.6	14.6	14.6

ALGERIA

(US$ million, unless otherwise indicated)

	1970	1980	1990	1992	1993	1994	1995	1996	1997	1998
1. SUMMARY DEBT DATA										
TOTAL DEBT STOCKS (EDT)	..	**19,365**	**27,877**	**27,078**	**26,020**	**29,973**	**32,781**	**33,421**	**30,890**	**30,665**
Long-term debt (LDOD)	**940**	**17,040**	**26,416**	**25,489**	**24,847**	**28,178**	**31,042**	**31,062**	**28,710**	**28,469**
Public and publicly guaranteed	940	17,040	26,416	25,489	24,847	28,178	31,042	31,062	28,710	28,469
Private nonguaranteed	0	0	0	0	0	0	0	0	0	0
Use of IMF credit	**0**	**0**	**670**	**795**	**471**	**1,159**	**1,478**	**2,031**	**2,018**	**2,011**
Short-term debt	..	**2,325**	**791**	**794**	**702**	**637**	**261**	**328**	**162**	**186**
of which interest arrears on LDOD	..	0	0	1	2	1	3	0	0	0
Official creditors	..	0	0	0	1	0	0	0	0	0
Private creditors	..	0	0	1	1	1	3	0	0	0
Memo: principal arrears on LDOD	..	2	1	6	9	1	1	0	0	0
Official creditors	..	0	0	1	3	1	0	0	0	0
Private creditors	..	2	0	6	6	1	1	0	0	0
Memo: export credits	..	0	13,220	13,391	14,095	16,814	18,133	18,266	17,081	16,061
TOTAL DEBT FLOWS										
Disbursements	**313**	**3,398**	**6,935**	**7,536**	**6,501**	**5,638**	**4,158**	**3,629**	**2,110**	**1,511**
Long-term debt	313	3,398	6,935	7,536	6,501	4,797	3,684	2,885	1,646	1,167
IMF purchases	0	0	0	0	0	841	475	744	465	344
Principal repayments	**35**	**2,529**	**6,779**	**7,227**	**7,282**	**3,546**	**2,391**	**2,079**	**2,372**	**3,143**
Long-term debt	35	2,529	6,779	7,061	6,953	3,351	2,220	1,943	2,021	2,708
IMF repurchases	0	0	0	166	329	195	171	136	350	435
Net flows on debt	**279**	**1,261**	**-892**	**-138**	**-874**	**2,028**	**1,390**	**1,620**	**-427**	**-1,609**
of which short-term debt	..	392	-1,049	-446	-93	-64	-378	70	-166	24
Interest payments (INT)	..	**1,556**	**2,025**	**2,083**	**1,781**	**1,561**	**1,814**	**2,094**	**2,049**	**1,992**
Long-term debt	10	1,440	1,784	1,814	1,704	1,496	1,723	2,006	1,944	1,879
IMF charges	0	0	62	70	42	31	69	75	93	99
Short-term debt	..	116	179	200	36	33	22	13	13	15
Net transfers on debt	..	**-294**	**-2,917**	**-2,221**	**-2,655**	**467**	**-424**	**-474**	**-2,476**	**-3,601**
Total debt service paid (TDS)	..	**4,084**	**8,803**	**9,310**	**9,063**	**5,107**	**4,204**	**4,173**	**4,420**	**5,136**
Long-term debt	45	3,968	8,562	8,875	8,657	4,847	3,942	3,948	3,965	4,587
IMF repurchases and charges	0	0	62	235	371	226	240	211	443	534
Short-term debt (interest only)	..	116	179	200	36	33	22	13	13	15
2. AGGREGATE NET RESOURCE FLOWS AND NET TRANSFERS (LONG-TERM)										
NET RESOURCE FLOWS	**381**	**1,295**	**202**	**557**	**-344**	**1,536**	**1,540**	**1,040**	**-327**	**-1,427**
Net flow of long-term debt (ex. IMF)	279	869	156	474	-453	1,446	1,464	943	-376	-1,541
Foreign direct investment (net)	47	349	0	12	15	18	5	4	7	5
Portfolio equity flows	0	0	0	0	0	5	1	5	8	2
Grants (excluding technical coop.)	56	77	45	71	93	67	70	88	34	107
Memo: technical coop. grants	44	96	107	109	122	96	101	126	110	106
official net resource flows	88	399	626	310	93	943	1,019	1,020	195	-106
private net resource flows	294	896	-424	247	-438	593	521	20	-523	-1,321
NET TRANSFERS	**221**	**-831**	**-1,734**	**-1,457**	**-2,198**	**-90**	**-328**	**-1,106**	**-2,406**	**-3,421**
Interest on long-term debt	10	1,440	1,784	1,814	1,704	1,496	1,723	2,006	1,944	1,879
Profit remittances on FDI	150	687	152	200	150	130	145	140	135	115
Memo: official net transfers	84	239	314	-61	-272	545	215	-215	-931	-1,302
private net transfers	137	-1,071	-2,047	-1,396	-1,926	-635	-543	-891	-1,475	-2,119
3. MAJOR ECONOMIC AGGREGATES										
Gross national product (GNP)	4,760	41,147	59,812	46,958	48,013	40,343	39,057	44,486	45,649	45,400
Exports of goods & services (XGS)	..	14,906	13,887	12,905	11,772	10,749	12,271	15,108	16,110	12,238
of which workers remittances	..	406	352	829	700	1,115	1,294	1,045	1,075	1,080
Imports of goods & services (MGS)	..	14,552	12,448	11,219	10,232	11,505	12,842	12,282	11,357	11,771
International reserves (RES)	352	7,064	2,703	3,318	3,656	4,813	4,164	6,296	9,667	8,452
Current account balance	..	249	1,420	..	..	..	..	..	..	..
4. DEBT INDICATORS										
EDT / XGS (%)	..	129.9	200.7	209.8	221.0	278.9	267.2	221.2	191.7	250.6
EDT / GNP (%)	..	47.1	46.6	57.7	54.2	74.3	83.9	75.1	67.7	67.5
TDS / XGS (%)	..	27.4	63.4	72.1	77.0	47.5	34.3	27.6	27.4	42.0
INT / XGS (%)	..	10.4	14.6	16.1	15.1	14.5	14.8	13.9	12.7	16.3
INT / GNP (%)	..	3.8	3.4	4.4	3.7	3.9	4.6	4.7	4.5	4.4
RES / EDT (%)	..	36.5	9.7	12.3	14.1	16.1	12.7	18.8	31.3	27.6
RES / MGS (months)	..	5.8	2.6	3.6	4.3	5.0	3.9	6.2	10.2	8.6
Short-term / EDT (%)	..	12.0	2.8	2.9	2.7	2.1	0.8	1.0	0.5	0.6
Concessional / EDT (%)	..	6.6	3.1	3.9	5.1	6.9	9.4	9.8	10.2	10.7
Multilateral / EDT (%)	..	1.5	7.3	10.2	11.2	11.2	11.9	12.2	12.5	14.3

ALGERIA

(US$ million, unless otherwise indicated)

	1970	1980	1990	1992	1993	1994	1995	1996	1997	1998
5. LONG-TERM DEBT										
DEBT OUTSTANDING (LDOD)	**940**	**17,040**	**26,416**	**25,489**	**24,847**	**28,178**	**31,042**	**31,062**	**28,710**	**28,469**
Public and publicly guaranteed	**940**	**17,040**	**26,416**	**25,489**	**24,847**	**28,178**	**31,042**	**31,062**	**28,710**	**28,469**
Official creditors	485	3,495	5,595	6,268	6,259	10,664	15,395	17,938	18,245	19,414
Multilateral	16	284	2,032	2,765	2,900	3,344	3,915	4,085	3,854	4,390
Concessional	0	14	76	100	153	155	292	334	362	385
Bilateral	470	3,211	3,563	3,503	3,359	7,319	11,480	13,853	14,391	15,025
Concessional	470	1,255	784	956	1,160	1,899	2,790	2,951	2,775	2,892
Private creditors	454	13,545	20,822	19,221	18,588	17,514	15,647	13,124	10,465	9,054
Bonds	5	410	1,420	1,281	645	261	0	0	0	0
Commercial banks	20	5,503	6,051	5,319	4,876	4,909	4,916	4,628	4,265	3,952
Other private	430	7,632	13,351	12,622	13,067	12,344	10,732	8,496	6,200	5,102
Private nonguaranteed	**0**	**0**	**0**	**0**	**0**	**0**	**0**	**0**	**0**	**0**
Bonds	0	0	0	0	0	0	0	0	0	0
Commercial banks	0	0	0	0	0	0	0	0	0	0
Memo:										
IBRD	16	253	1,208	1,474	1,512	1,709	2,049	1,939	1,795	1,676
IDA	0	0	0	0	0	0	0	0	0	0
DISBURSEMENTS	**313**	**3,398**	**6,935**	**7,536**	**6,501**	**4,797**	**3,684**	**2,885**	**1,646**	**1,167**
Public and publicly guaranteed	**313**	**3,398**	**6,935**	**7,536**	**6,501**	**4,797**	**3,684**	**2,885**	**1,646**	**1,167**
Official creditors	45	566	1,753	1,418	1,138	1,529	1,592	1,577	1,208	768
Multilateral	0	54	612	548	477	701	932	823	792	594
Concessional	0	1	9	19	58	6	149	64	54	64
Bilateral	45	512	1,141	869	661	828	660	755	415	174
Concessional	45	78	282	203	294	386	502	322	158	69
Private creditors	268	2,832	5,182	6,118	5,363	3,268	2,092	1,308	438	400
Bonds	5	30	0	0	0	0	0	0	0	0
Commercial banks	17	891	406	1,256	458	123	255	141	33	22
Other private	246	1,911	4,776	4,863	4,905	3,145	1,837	1,167	405	378
Private nonguaranteed	**0**	**0**	**0**	**0**	**0**	**0**	**0**	**0**	**0**	**0**
Bonds	0	0	0	0	0	0	0	0	0	0
Commercial banks	0	0	0	0	0	0	0	0	0	0
Memo:										
IBRD	0	39	300	268	176	300	554	286	250	56
IDA	0	0	0	0	0	0	0	0	0	0
PRINCIPAL REPAYMENTS	**35**	**2,529**	**6,779**	**7,061**	**6,953**	**3,351**	**2,220**	**1,943**	**2,021**	**2,708**
Public and publicly guaranteed	**35**	**2,529**	**6,779**	**7,061**	**6,953**	**3,351**	**2,220**	**1,943**	**2,021**	**2,708**
Official creditors	13	244	1,172	1,178	1,138	653	643	646	1,046	981
Multilateral	3	42	312	334	351	450	454	411	698	412
Concessional	0	1	6	8	8	7	11	16	12	31
Bilateral	10	203	861	844	787	203	189	235	348	569
Concessional	10	72	97	78	76	54	43	98	118	148
Private creditors	22	2,284	5,606	5,883	5,816	2,698	1,577	1,297	975	1,728
Bonds	0	15	16	129	663	445	278	0	0	0
Commercial banks	2	918	1,330	938	1,107	382	220	178	132	501
Other private	19	1,352	4,261	4,816	4,046	1,872	1,078	1,119	843	1,227
Private nonguaranteed	**0**	**0**	**0**	**0**	**0**	**0**	**0**	**0**	**0**	**0**
Bonds	0	0	0	0	0	0	0	0	0	0
Commercial banks	0	0	0	0	0	0	0	0	0	0
Memo:										
IBRD	3	13	130	166	170	208	260	252	234	208
IDA	0	0	0	0	0	0	0	0	0	0
NET FLOWS ON DEBT	**279**	**869**	**156**	**474**	**-453**	**1,446**	**1,464**	**943**	**-376**	**-1,541**
Public and publicly guaranteed	**279**	**869**	**156**	**474**	**-453**	**1,446**	**1,464**	**943**	**-376**	**-1,541**
Official creditors	32	322	580	240	0	876	949	932	162	-213
Multilateral	-3	13	300	214	126	252	478	412	94	182
Concessional	0	0	3	11	50	-1	138	49	43	33
Bilateral	35	309	281	25	-126	625	471	520	68	-395
Concessional	35	6	185	125	218	332	460	224	40	-79
Private creditors	247	548	-424	235	-453	570	515	11	-537	-1,328
Bonds	5	15	-16	-129	-663	-445	-278	0	0	0
Commercial banks	15	-27	-924	318	-649	-259	35	-37	-99	-479
Other private	227	559	515	46	859	1,273	759	49	-438	-849
Private nonguaranteed	**0**	**0**	**0**	**0**	**0**	**0**	**0**	**0**	**0**	**0**
Bonds	0	0	0	0	0	0	0	0	0	0
Commercial banks	0	0	0	0	0	0	0	0	0	0
Memo:										
IBRD	-3	26	170	101	6	92	294	34	17	-152
IDA	0	0	0	0	0	0	0	0	0	0

ALGERIA

(US$ million, unless otherwise indicated)

	1970	1980	1990	1992	1993	1994	1995	1996	1997	1998
INTEREST PAYMENTS (LINT)	**10**	**1,440**	**1,784**	**1,814**	**1,704**	**1,496**	**1,723**	**2,006**	**1,944**	**1,879**
Public and publicly guaranteed	**10**	**1,440**	**1,784**	**1,814**	**1,704**	**1,496**	**1,723**	**2,006**	**1,944**	**1,879**
Official creditors	4	159	312	371	365	398	804	1,235	1,126	1,196
Multilateral	1	29	117	196	205	203	251	281	252	279
Concessional	0	1	6	6	5	6	8	15	16	18
Bilateral	3	130	195	175	160	196	553	954	874	917
Concessional	3	35	17	20	21	50	83	129	103	107
Private creditors	6	1,280	1,472	1,443	1,338	1,098	918	771	818	683
Bonds	0	45	105	90	68	49	13	0	0	0
Commercial banks	0	672	526	358	355	343	253	206	259	229
Other private	6	563	841	994	915	707	653	565	559	454
Private nonguaranteed	**0**	**0**	**0**	**0**	**0**	**0**	**0**	**0**	**0**	**0**
Bonds	0	0	0	0	0	0	0	0	0	0
Commercial banks	0	0	0	0	0	0	0	0	0	0
Memo:										
IBRD	1	25	73	112	113	119	137	139	120	124
IDA	0	0	0	0	0	0	0	0	0	0
NET TRANSFERS ON DEBT	**269**	**-570**	**-1,627**	**-1,339**	**-2,156**	**-50**	**-259**	**-1,063**	**-2,319**	**-3,420**
Public and publicly guaranteed	**269**	**-570**	**-1,627**	**-1,339**	**-2,156**	**-50**	**-259**	**-1,063**	**-2,319**	**-3,420**
Official creditors	28	162	268	-131	-365	478	145	-303	-964	-1,409
Multilateral	-4	-17	183	18	-79	49	227	131	-158	-97
Concessional	0	-1	-2	5	45	-7	130	34	27	15
Bilateral	32	179	85	-150	-286	429	-83	-434	-806	-1,312
Concessional	32	-29	168	105	197	282	377	94	-62	-186
Private creditors	240	-732	-1,896	-1,208	-1,791	-528	-403	-760	-1,355	-2,011
Bonds	5	-30	-120	-220	-731	-493	-291	0	0	0
Commercial banks	14	-699	-1,450	-40	-1,004	-601	-218	-243	-358	-708
Other private	221	-4	-326	-948	-56	566	105	-517	-996	-1,303
Private nonguaranteed	**0**	**0**	**0**	**0**	**0**	**0**	**0**	**0**	**0**	**0**
Bonds	0	0	0	0	0	0	0	0	0	0
Commercial banks	0	0	0	0	0	0	0	0	0	0
Memo:										
IBRD	-4	0	97	-11	-107	-27	157	-105	-103	-276
IDA	0	0	0	0	0	0	0	0	0	0
DEBT SERVICE (LTDS)	**45**	**3,968**	**8,562**	**8,875**	**8,657**	**4,847**	**3,942**	**3,948**	**3,965**	**4,587**
Public and publicly guaranteed	**45**	**3,968**	**8,562**	**8,875**	**8,657**	**4,847**	**3,942**	**3,948**	**3,965**	**4,587**
Official creditors	17	404	1,485	1,549	1,503	1,051	1,447	1,881	2,172	2,177
Multilateral	4	71	429	530	556	652	705	692	951	691
Concessional	0	2	12	14	13	13	19	31	28	48
Bilateral	13	333	1,056	1,019	947	399	742	1,189	1,221	1,486
Concessional	13	107	114	98	97	104	125	228	221	255
Private creditors	28	3,564	7,078	7,326	7,154	3,796	2,495	2,068	1,793	2,411
Bonds	0	60	120	220	731	493	291	0	0	0
Commercial banks	3	1,590	1,856	1,296	1,462	725	473	384	391	730
Other private	25	1,915	5,102	5,811	4,961	2,579	1,732	1,684	1,401	1,680
Private nonguaranteed	**0**	**0**	**0**	**0**	**0**	**0**	**0**	**0**	**0**	**0**
Bonds	0	0	0	0	0	0	0	0	0	0
Commercial banks	0	0	0	0	0	0	0	0	0	0
Memo:										
IBRD	4	39	203	278	282	327	397	391	353	332
IDA	0	0	0	0	0	0	0	0	0	0
UNDISBURSED DEBT	**738**	**11,717**	**12,862**	**14,753**	**14,482**	**11,591**	**10,071**	**7,096**	**6,022**	**5,475**
Official creditors	579	4,169	5,164	5,666	6,660	5,966	5,931	4,883	4,356	3,899
Private creditors	159	7,548	7,698	9,086	7,822	5,625	4,140	2,213	1,666	1,576
Memorandum items										
Concessional LDOD	470	1,269	860	1,056	1,313	2,053	3,082	3,285	3,137	3,277
Variable rate LDOD	26	4,265	10,712	11,897	12,509	14,681	16,657	16,723	15,833	15,316
Public sector LDOD	940	17,040	26,336	25,369	24,742	28,083	30,954	30,972	28,593	28,309
Private sector LDOD	0	0	80	120	105	95	89	90	116	160

6. CURRENCY COMPOSITION OF LONG-TERM DEBT (PERCENT)

	1970	1980	1990	1992	1993	1994	1995	1996	1997	1998
Deutsche mark	1.9	9.9	10.5	8.3	6.6	6.3	7.2	6.9	6.6	6.7
French franc	36.0	10.9	16.8	13.1	11.9	13.8	16.2	16.9	15.5	15.1
Japanese yen	0.0	13.4	15.2	15.4	16.0	15.2	13.2	12.2	11.8	12.1
Pound sterling	8.3	2.2	1.5	1.1	0.9	1.0	0.9	1.0	1.1	1.0
Swiss franc	0.2	2.7	0.8	0.6	0.5	0.6	0.7	0.5	0.5	0.4
U.S.dollars	37.0	41.5	33.8	39.8	43.0	40.9	38.3	39.0	41.5	44.8
Multiple currency	1.7	3.4	4.9	6.8	7.4	7.5	8.0	7.7	7.9	1.8
Special drawing rights	0.0	0.0	0.0	0.0	0.0	0.0	0.0	0.0	0.0	0.0
All other currencies	14.9	16.0	16.5	14.9	13.7	14.7	15.5	15.8	15.1	18.1

ALGERIA

(US$ million, unless otherwise indicated)

	1970	1980	1990	1992	1993	1994	1995	1996	1997	1998
7. DEBT RESTRUCTURINGS										
Total amount rescheduled	..	..	0	0	0	4,229	5,096	3,674	2,295	559
Debt stock rescheduled	..	..	0	0	0	0	0	0	0	0
Principal rescheduled	..	..	0	0	0	3,740	4,410	3,250	2,118	545
Official	..	..	0	0	0	541	535	363	224	83
Private	..	..	0	0	0	3,199	3,875	2,887	1,895	462
Interest rescheduled	..	..	0	0	0	457	381	289	89	0
Official	..	..	0	0	0	79	68	46	20	0
Private	..	..	0	0	0	377	312	243	69	0
Debt forgiven	..	..	0	0	0	0	0	4	10	0
Memo: interest forgiven	..	..	0	0	0	0	0	0	0	0
Debt stock reduction	..	..	0	0	0	0	0	0	0	0
of which debt buyback	..	..	0	0	0	0	0	0	0	0
8. DEBT STOCK-FLOW RECONCILIATION										
Total change in debt stocks	..	..	806	-1,126	-1,058	3,953	2,808	640	-2,531	-224
Net flows on debt	279	1,261	-892	-138	-874	2,028	1,390	1,620	-427	-1,609
Net change in interest arrears	..	..	0	1	1	-1	2	-3	0	0
Interest capitalized	..	..	0	0	0	457	381	289	89	0
Debt forgiveness or reduction	..	..	0	0	0	0	0	-4	-10	0
Cross-currency valuation	..	..	1,826	-860	-128	1,537	837	-1,285	-1,829	1,166
Residual	..	..	-127	-129	-57	-67	198	23	-355	218
9. AVERAGE TERMS OF NEW COMMITMENTS										
ALL CREDITORS										
Interest (%)	5.7	8.1	8.4	5.7	5.5	5.5	6.5	5.5	5.6	5.3
Maturity (years)	12.7	12.5	9.0	10.8	10.1	8.9	8.5	9.1	10.6	11.2
Grace period (years)	3.6	3.5	2.5	4.7	4.4	3.0	2.8	2.9	3.2	3.2
Grant element (%)	23.0	8.3	6.9	19.9	18.1	16.5	12.3	17.1	16.6	19.2
Official creditors										
Interest (%)	2.8	7.7	7.0	5.9	5.4	5.0	6.2	5.8	5.5	6.2
Maturity (years)	23.9	17.7	16.8	15.2	13.9	14.1	9.6	10.3	11.1	14.8
Grace period (years)	9.2	5.2	4.0	6.9	6.7	5.8	3.3	3.7	3.6	3.6
Grant element (%)	54.3	13.5	19.5	25.1	25.0	25.7	14.5	17.4	17.1	18.8
Private creditors										
Interest (%)	6.4	8.4	8.9	5.7	5.6	5.7	7.1	4.8	5.8	4.4
Maturity (years)	9.8	9.7	6.4	9.9	8.1	6.2	6.2	6.4	8.7	7.5
Grace period (years)	2.1	2.6	2.0	4.3	3.2	1.5	1.9	1.1	1.7	2.8
Grant element (%)	14.8	5.5	2.8	18.9	14.6	11.6	7.8	16.5	14.7	19.7
Memorandum items										
Commitments	378	3,538	8,059	9,983	6,785	3,438	2,426	2,298	1,562	818
Official creditors	79	1,258	1,987	1,653	2,289	1,201	1,630	1,580	1,239	417
Private creditors	299	2,279	6,072	8,330	4,497	2,237	795	718	322	400

10. CONTRACTUAL OBLIGATIONS ON OUTSTANDING LONG-TERM DEBT

	1999	2000	2001	2002	2003	2004	2005	2006	2007	2008
TOTAL										
Disbursements	2,376	1,330	716	285	95	42	21	8	3	0
Principal	3,490	3,036	2,852	2,548	2,338	2,206	2,223	2,233	2,741	2,807
Interest	1,888	1,795	1,650	1,498	1,341	1,193	1,048	901	753	565
Official creditors										
Disbursements	1,337	1,006	617	261	86	42	21	8	3	0
Principal	1,449	1,503	1,564	1,458	1,418	1,458	1,557	1,686	2,059	2,294
Interest	1,276	1,276	1,221	1,146	1,058	965	867	762	647	505
Bilateral creditors										
Disbursements	545	339	170	61	28	18	9	3	0	0
Principal	752	781	799	777	855	953	1,101	1,295	1,695	1,943
Interest	938	921	883	840	791	737	675	602	517	403
Multilateral creditors										
Disbursements	792	667	447	200	57	24	12	5	3	0
Principal	697	721	765	681	563	505	456	391	364	351
Interest	338	355	337	306	267	229	192	160	130	102
Private creditors										
Disbursements	1,039	324	99	24	9	0	0	0	0	0
Principal	2,041	1,533	1,289	1,090	920	748	666	547	683	513
Interest	612	519	429	352	284	228	181	139	106	60
Commercial banks										
Disbursements	134	3	0	0	0	0	0	0	0	0
Principal	376	435	509	458	445	398	370	319	224	206
Interest	252	231	200	169	140	111	87	63	45	31
Other private										
Disbursements	905	321	99	24	9	0	0	0	0	0
Principal	1,665	1,098	780	632	476	350	296	228	459	307
Interest	359	287	229	183	144	117	94	76	61	29

ANGOLA

(US$ million, unless otherwise indicated)

	1970	1980	1990	1992	1993	1994	1995	1996	1997	1998
1. SUMMARY DEBT DATA										
TOTAL DEBT STOCKS (EDT)	..	..	**8,594**	**10,061**	**10,574**	**11,297**	**11,512**	**11,225**	**11,841**	**12,173**
Long-term debt (LDOD)	..	..	**7,605**	**8,132**	**8,694**	**9,126**	**9,553**	**10,055**	**10,571**	**10,616**
Public and publicly guaranteed	..	..	7,605	8,132	8,694	9,126	9,553	10,055	10,571	10,616
Private nonguaranteed	..	..	0	0	0	0	0	0	0	0
Use of IMF credit	**0**	**0**	**0**	**0**	**0**	**0**	**0**	**0**	**0**	**0**
Short-term debt	..	..	**989**	**1,929**	**1,881**	**2,171**	**1,959**	**1,170**	**1,270**	**1,556**
of which interest arrears on LDOD	..	..	204	609	890	1,138	1,234	495	550	656
Official creditors	..	..	52	147	195	234	276	170	188	216
Private creditors	..	..	152	462	695	905	958	325	362	441
Memo: principal arrears on LDOD	..	..	496	1,954	3,165	3,769	4,200	1,635	1,731	2,048
Official creditors	..	..	86	559	822	895	1,098	381	414	482
Private creditors	..	..	410	1,396	2,343	2,874	3,102	1,254	1,317	1,566
Memo: export credits	..	..	1,639	1,928	2,197	2,084	2,263	2,007	2,303	2,045
TOTAL DEBT FLOWS										
Disbursements	..	..	**862**	**647**	**685**	**417**	**550**	**778**	**1,307**	**586**
Long-term debt	..	..	862	647	685	417	550	778	1,307	586
IMF purchases	0	0	0	0	0	0	0	0	0	0
Principal repayments	..	..	**183**	**144**	**62**	**152**	**331**	**552**	**716**	**914**
Long-term debt	..	..	183	144	62	152	331	552	716	914
IMF repurchases	0	0	0	0	0	0	0	0	0	0
Net flows on debt	..	..	**977**	**907**	**295**	**306**	**-89**	**176**	**636**	**-147**
of which short-term debt	..	..	298	404	-329	42	-308	-50	45	180
Interest payments (INT)	..	..	**143**	**101**	**91**	**106**	**132**	**342**	**414**	**439**
Long-term debt	..	..	100	47	25	51	79	293	367	394
IMF charges	0	0	0	0	0	0	0	0	0	0
Short-term debt	..	..	43	54	66	55	53	49	46	45
Net transfers on debt	..	..	**834**	**805**	**203**	**201**	**-220**	**-166**	**222**	**-587**
Total debt service paid (TDS)	..	..	**326**	**246**	**153**	**258**	**463**	**894**	**1,129**	**1,353**
Long-term debt	..	..	283	191	87	203	410	845	1,083	1,308
IMF repurchases and charges	0	0	0	0	0	0	0	0	0	0
Short-term debt (interest only)	..	..	43	54	66	55	53	49	46	45
2. AGGREGATE NET RESOURCE FLOWS AND NET TRANSFERS (LONG-TERM)										
NET RESOURCE FLOWS	..	..	**536**	**976**	**1,095**	**735**	**797**	**682**	**1,183**	**249**
Net flow of long-term debt (ex. IMF)	..	..	679	503	624	264	219	226	591	-327
Foreign direct investment (net)	..	..	-335	288	302	170	250	181	350	360
Portfolio equity flows	..	..	0	0	0	0	0	0	0	0
Grants (excluding technical coop.)	..	..	192	186	170	301	328	275	242	216
Memo: technical coop. grants	..	..	36	89	69	69	73	114	57	52
official net resource flows	..	..	302	239	182	340	423	297	225	209
private net resource flows	..	..	235	738	913	395	374	385	959	40
NET TRANSFERS	..	..	**122**	**567**	**670**	**275**	**268**	**-11**	**391**	**-596**
Interest on long-term debt	..	..	100	47	25	51	79	293	367	394
Profit remittances on FDI	..	..	314	362	400	410	450	400	425	450
Memo: official net transfers	..	..	283	224	175	330	411	270	203	195
private net transfers	..	..	-161	343	495	-55	-143	-281	188	-790
3. MAJOR ECONOMIC AGGREGATES										
Gross national product (GNP)	..	..	8,227	3,511	3,239	1,943	2,300	4,106	4,282	4,098
Exports of goods & services (XGS)	..	..	4,003	3,991	3,018	3,180	3,852	5,406	5,267	3,930
of which workers remittances	..	..	0	0	0	0	0	0	..	..
Imports of goods & services (MGS)	..	..	4,161	4,828	3,852	3,765	4,302	5,980	6,262	5,914
International reserves (RES)	..	..	..	..	..	..	213	552	396	203
Current account balance	..	..	-236	-735	-668	-340	-295	3,266	-852	-1,776
4. DEBT INDICATORS										
EDT / XGS (%)	..	..	214.7	252.1	350.4	355.3	298.9	207.6	224.8	309.8
EDT / GNP (%)	..	..	104.5	286.6	326.4	581.4	500.5	273.4	276.6	297.1
TDS / XGS (%)	..	..	8.1	6.2	5.1	8.1	12.0	16.5	21.4	34.4
INT / XGS (%)	..	..	3.6	2.5	3.0	3.3	3.4	6.3	7.9	11.2
INT / GNP (%)	..	..	1.7	2.9	2.8	5.4	5.7	8.3	9.7	10.7
RES / EDT (%)	..	..	..	..	..	..	1.9	4.9	3.4	1.7
RES / MGS (months)	..	..	..	..	..	..	0.6	1.1	0.8	0.4
Short-term / EDT (%)	..	..	11.5	19.2	17.8	19.2	17.0	10.4	10.7	12.8
Concessional / EDT (%)	..	..	13.9	12.9	12.4	12.4	12.9	19.3	18.8	21.3
Multilateral / EDT (%)	..	..	0.7	1.1	1.2	1.5	1.7	1.9	2.0	2.3

ANGOLA

(US$ million, unless otherwise indicated)

	1970	1980	1990	1992	1993	1994	1995	1996	1997	1998
5. LONG-TERM DEBT										
DEBT OUTSTANDING (LDOD)	..	..	**7,605**	**8,132**	**8,694**	**9,126**	**9,553**	**10,055**	**10,571**	**10,616**
Public and publicly guaranteed	..	..	**7,605**	**8,132**	**8,694**	**9,126**	**9,553**	**10,055**	**10,571**	**10,616**
Official creditors	..	..	1,839	1,932	1,923	2,093	2,226	2,879	2,888	3,231
Multilateral	..	..	57	112	125	164	192	218	234	279
Concessional	..	..	20	41	51	88	119	151	168	212
Bilateral	..	..	1,782	1,820	1,798	1,929	2,035	2,661	2,655	2,952
Concessional	..	..	1,177	1,261	1,264	1,318	1,371	2,013	2,062	2,385
Private creditors	..	..	5,767	6,200	6,771	7,033	7,326	7,176	7,682	7,386
Bonds	..	..	0	0	0	0	0	0	0	0
Commercial banks	..	..	196	214	229	612	924	4,705	5,405	5,128
Other private	..	..	5,571	5,987	6,542	6,422	6,402	2,471	2,278	2,258
Private nonguaranteed	..	..	**0**	**0**	**0**	**0**	**0**	**0**	**0**	**0**
Bonds	..	..	0	0	0	0	0	0	0	0
Commercial banks	..	..	0	0	0	0	0	0	0	0
Memo:										
IBRD	0	0	0	0	0	0	0	0	0	0
IDA	0	0	0	6	15	50	81	115	136	179
DISBURSEMENTS	..	..	**862**	**647**	**685**	**417**	**550**	**778**	**1,307**	**586**
Public and publicly guaranteed	..	..	**862**	**647**	**685**	**417**	**550**	**778**	**1,307**	**586**
Official creditors	..	..	169	94	36	73	119	55	34	75
Multilateral	..	..	5	21	14	33	30	38	28	36
Concessional	..	..	4	6	10	33	30	38	28	36
Bilateral	..	..	164	73	22	40	89	17	6	38
Concessional	..	..	54	34	21	40	33	5	6	0
Private creditors	..	..	693	553	649	344	431	723	1,273	512
Bonds	..	..	0	0	0	0	0	0	0	0
Commercial banks	..	..	17	9	16	299	396	685	1,219	452
Other private	..	..	676	544	633	45	35	38	54	60
Private nonguaranteed	..	..	**0**	**0**	**0**	**0**	**0**	**0**	**0**	**0**
Bonds	..	..	0	0	0	0	0	0	0	0
Commercial banks	..	..	0	0	0	0	0	0	0	0
Memo:										
IBRD	0	0	0	0	0	0	0	0	0	0
IDA	0	0	0	6	10	33	30	38	28	36
PRINCIPAL REPAYMENTS	..	..	**183**	**144**	**62**	**152**	**331**	**552**	**716**	**914**
Public and publicly guaranteed	..	..	**183**	**144**	**62**	**152**	**331**	**552**	**716**	**914**
Official creditors	..	..	60	41	24	33	24	33	51	82
Multilateral	..	..	4	0	0	0	2	0	1	0
Concessional	..	..	0	0	0	0	0	0	0	0
Bilateral	..	..	56	40	24	33	22	33	50	82
Concessional	..	..	1	3	2	9	3	8	11	13
Private creditors	..	..	123	104	38	119	307	519	665	832
Bonds	..	..	0	0	0	0	0	0	0	0
Commercial banks	..	..	24	5	1	48	108	310	518	729
Other private	..	..	100	98	38	72	199	209	146	103
Private nonguaranteed	..	..	**0**	**0**	**0**	**0**	**0**	**0**	**0**	**0**
Bonds	..	..	0	0	0	0	0	0	0	0
Commercial banks	..	..	0	0	0	0	0	0	0	0
Memo:										
IBRD	0	0	0	0	0	0	0	0	0	0
IDA	0	0	0	0	0	0	0	0	0	0
NET FLOWS ON DEBT	..	..	**679**	**503**	**624**	**264**	**219**	**226**	**591**	**-327**
Public and publicly guaranteed	..	..	**679**	**503**	**624**	**264**	**219**	**226**	**591**	**-327**
Official creditors	..	..	110	53	13	40	95	21	-17	-7
Multilateral	..	..	1	21	14	33	29	38	27	36
Concessional	..	..	4	6	10	33	30	38	28	36
Bilateral	..	..	109	32	-2	7	67	-16	-44	-44
Concessional	..	..	53	31	18	31	30	-2	-5	-13
Private creditors	..	..	570	450	611	225	124	204	609	-320
Bonds	..	..	0	0	0	0	0	0	0	0
Commercial banks	..	..	-7	4	16	252	288	375	701	-278
Other private	..	..	577	446	595	-27	-164	-171	-92	-43
Private nonguaranteed	..	..	**0**	**0**	**0**	**0**	**0**	**0**	**0**	**0**
Bonds	..	..	0	0	0	0	0	0	0	0
Commercial banks	..	..	0	0	0	0	0	0	0	0
Memo:										
IBRD	0	0	0	0	0	0	0	0	0	0
IDA	0	0	0	6	10	33	30	38	28	36

ANGOLA

(US$ million, unless otherwise indicated)

	1970	1980	1990	1992	1993	1994	1995	1996	1997	1998
INTEREST PAYMENTS (LINT)	..	..	**100**	**47**	**25**	**51**	**79**	**293**	**367**	**394**
Public and publicly guaranteed	..	..	**100**	**47**	**25**	**51**	**79**	**293**	**367**	**394**
Official creditors	..	..	19	14	8	10	12	27	22	14
Multilateral	..	..	2	5	0	0	1	1	1	1
Concessional	..	..	0	0	0	0	0	1	1	1
Bilateral	..	..	16	9	8	10	12	26	21	13
Concessional	..	..	1	3	3	7	7	2	6	2
Private creditors	..	..	81	33	18	40	67	266	345	380
Bonds	..	..	0	0	0	0	0	0	0	0
Commercial banks	..	..	8	5	3	11	33	227	306	365
Other private	..	..	74	27	15	30	34	39	39	15
Private nonguaranteed	..	..	**0**	**0**	**0**	**0**	**0**	**0**	**0**	**0**
Bonds	..	..	0	0	0	0	0	0	0	0
Commercial banks	..	..	0	0	0	0	0	0	0	0
Memo:										
IBRD	0	0	0	0	0	0	0	0	0	0
IDA	0	0	0	0	0	0	0	1	1	1
NET TRANSFERS ON DEBT	..	..	**579**	**456**	**598**	**214**	**140**	**-67**	**224**	**-722**
Public and publicly guaranteed	..	..	**579**	**456**	**598**	**214**	**140**	**-67**	**224**	**-722**
Official creditors	..	..	91	39	5	30	83	-5	-39	-21
Multilateral	..	..	-2	16	14	33	28	37	27	35
Concessional	..	..	4	6	10	33	30	37	27	35
Bilateral	..	..	92	23	-9	-3	55	-42	-65	-56
Concessional	..	..	52	29	15	24	23	-5	-11	-15
Private creditors	..	..	488	417	593	184	57	-62	263	-700
Bonds	..	..	0	0	0	0	0	0	0	0
Commercial banks	..	..	-15	-1	13	241	255	148	394	-643
Other private	..	..	503	418	580	-57	-198	-210	-131	-58
Private nonguaranteed	..	..	**0**	**0**	**0**	**0**	**0**	**0**	**0**	**0**
Bonds	..	..	0	0	0	0	0	0	0	0
Commercial banks	..	..	0	0	0	0	0	0	0	0
Memo:										
IBRD	0	0	0	0	0	0	0	0	0	0
IDA	0	0	0	6	10	33	30	37	27	35
DEBT SERVICE (LTDS)	..	..	**283**	**191**	**87**	**203**	**410**	**845**	**1,083**	**1,308**
Public and publicly guaranteed	..	..	**283**	**191**	**87**	**203**	**410**	**845**	**1,083**	**1,308**
Official creditors	..	..	78	55	31	43	36	60	73	96
Multilateral	..	..	6	5	0	1	3	1	1	1
Concessional	..	..	0	0	0	0	0	1	1	1
Bilateral	..	..	72	50	31	43	34	59	71	95
Concessional	..	..	2	5	5	15	10	10	17	15
Private creditors	..	..	205	136	56	160	374	785	1,010	1,212
Bonds	..	..	0	0	0	0	0	0	0	0
Commercial banks	..	..	31	11	3	58	141	538	824	1,094
Other private	..	..	173	126	53	101	233	248	186	118
Private nonguaranteed	..	..	**0**	**0**	**0**	**0**	**0**	**0**	**0**	**0**
Bonds	..	..	0	0	0	0	0	0	0	0
Commercial banks	..	..	0	0	0	0	0	0	0	0
Memo:										
IBRD	0	0	0	0	0	0	0	0	0	0
IDA	0	0	0	0	0	0	0	1	1	1
UNDISBURSED DEBT	..	..	**1,356**	**1,588**	**1,309**	**1,219**	**1,112**	**857**	**904**	**663**
Official creditors	..	..	493	750	688	705	612	344	280	245
Private creditors	..	..	863	838	621	515	500	513	624	418
Memorandum items										
Concessional LDOD	..	..	1,197	1,302	1,315	1,405	1,490	2,164	2,231	2,597
Variable rate LDOD	..	..	450	362	366	548	850	1,345	1,486	1,183
Public sector LDOD	..	..	7,600	8,125	8,687	9,097	9,523	10,030	10,542	10,590
Private sector LDOD	..	..	5	7	7	29	30	25	28	26

6. CURRENCY COMPOSITION OF LONG-TERM DEBT (PERCENT)

	1970	1980	1990	1992	1993	1994	1995	1996	1997	1998
Deutsche mark	..	..	0.3	0.2	0.2	0.2	0.2	0.3	0.2	0.2
French franc	..	..	3.6	3.6	3.5	3.9	4.4	3.9	3.3	3.5
Japanese yen	..	..	0.3	0.3	0.3	0.4	0.3	0.3	0.7	1.1
Pound sterling	..	..	1.4	1.0	0.9	0.9	0.9	0.9	0.9	0.9
Swiss franc	..	..	0.7	0.2	0.1	0.1	0.1	0.3	0.2	0.2
U.S.dollars	..	..	80.7	81.8	82.7	81.9	80.9	87.4	88.9	88.2
Multiple currency	..	..	0.5	1.1	1.0	1.0	1.0	0.8	0.7	0.8
Special drawing rights	..	..	0.0	0.0	0.1	0.3	0.5	0.7	0.7	0.9
All other currencies	..	..	12.5	11.8	11.2	11.3	11.7	5.4	4.4	4.2

ANGOLA

(US$ million, unless otherwise indicated)

	1970	1980	1990	1992	1993	1994	1995	1996	1997	1998
7. DEBT RESTRUCTURINGS										
Total amount rescheduled	..	..	252	0	0	273	437	1,545	94	318
Debt stock rescheduled	..	..	53	0	0	0	0	0	0	0
Principal rescheduled	..	..	160	0	0	205	360	1,216	28	17
Official	..	..	16	0	0	33	0	267	0	0
Private	..	..	143	0	0	172	360	950	28	17
Interest rescheduled	..	..	43	0	0	44	70	235	0	34
Official	..	..	8	0	0	7	0	38	0	0
Private	..	..	35	0	0	37	70	196	0	34
Debt forgiven	..	..	0	0	0	0	0	3,746	0	0
Memo: interest forgiven	..	..	0	0	0	0	0	3	0	0
Debt stock reduction	..	..	0	0	0	0	0	0	0	0
of which debt buyback	..	..	0	0	0	0	0	0	0	0
8. DEBT STOCK-FLOW RECONCILIATION										
Total change in debt stocks	..	..	1,303	1,059	513	723	215	-287	616	332
Net flows on debt	..	..	977	907	295	306	-89	176	636	-147
Net change in interest arrears	..	..	130	227	281	249	96	-739	56	106
Interest capitalized	..	..	43	0	0	44	70	235	0	34
Debt forgiveness or reduction	..	..	0	0	0	0	0	-3,746	0	0
Cross-currency valuation	..	..	181	-73	-56	108	92	-66	-122	71
Residual	..	..	-27	-3	-6	16	46	3,854	47	268
9. AVERAGE TERMS OF NEW COMMITMENTS										
ALL CREDITORS										
Interest (%)	..	..	6.9	5.6	6.5	6.9	8.1	7.3	8.0	7.4
Maturity (years)	..	..	10.1	13.1	6.1	3.8	8.7	4.3	2.9	7.2
Grace period (years)	..	..	2.5	3.2	1.3	0.8	0.4	1.3	0.4	0.7
Grant element (%)	..	..	14.2	23.0	9.6	5.1	5.4	6.2	2.6	10.2
Official creditors										
Interest (%)	..	..	5.7	3.0	0.7	10.2	8.1	2.8	0.0	3.6
Maturity (years)	..	..	14.1	31.6	39.8	7.7	9.9	29.6	0.0	21.3
Grace period (years)	..	..	3.7	7.7	10.3	1.9	0.4	7.1	0.0	1.3
Grant element (%)	..	..	22.0	56.9	80.6	2.3	6.4	57.5	0.0	39.1
Private creditors										
Interest (%)	..	..	7.7	6.8	6.8	6.2	8.1	7.5	8.0	8.4
Maturity (years)	..	..	7.5	4.0	4.6	3.0	8.6	3.1	2.9	3.6
Grace period (years)	..	..	1.8	1.0	0.9	0.6	0.4	1.0	0.4	0.6
Grant element (%)	..	..	9.0	6.3	6.4	5.6	5.4	3.7	2.6	2.8
Memorandum items										
Commitments	..	..	523	851	460	329	420	781	1,215	437
Official creditors	..	..	210	281	20	56	3	36	0	89
Private creditors	..	..	313	571	441	273	417	745	1,215	348

10. CONTRACTUAL OBLIGATIONS ON OUTSTANDING LONG-TERM DEBT

	1999	2000	2001	2002	2003	2004	2005	2006	2007	2008
TOTAL										
Disbursements	265	204	100	17	8	4	3	3	2	1
Principal	1,302	990	625	507	442	417	373	338	327	326
Interest	438	362	419	382	350	322	296	273	252	231
Official creditors										
Disbursements	74	51	29	15	7	4	3	3	2	1
Principal	150	116	214	213	179	169	168	164	154	153
Interest	31	25	135	123	112	102	93	84	75	67
Bilateral creditors										
Disbursements	24	20	14	9	6	4	3	3	2	1
Principal	136	103	200	198	165	159	158	154	147	146
Interest	24	18	130	119	108	99	90	82	73	65
Multilateral creditors										
Disbursements	50	31	15	6	1	0	0	0	0	0
Principal	14	13	13	15	15	10	10	9	7	8
Interest	7	6	6	5	4	3	3	2	2	2
Private creditors										
Disbursements	191	153	71	2	1	0	0	0	0	0
Principal	1,152	874	411	294	263	248	206	175	173	173
Interest	406	337	284	259	238	220	202	189	176	164
Commercial banks										
Disbursements	6	4	2	1	0	0	0	0	0	0
Principal	846	609	247	216	210	208	167	136	136	136
Interest	350	293	253	236	220	205	190	179	168	158
Other private										
Disbursements	185	149	70	1	1	0	0	0	0	0
Principal	306	265	164	78	54	40	38	38	37	37
Interest	56	44	31	23	18	15	13	10	8	6

ARGENTINA

(US$ million, unless otherwise indicated)

	1970	1980	1990	1992	1993	1994	1995	1996	1997	1998
1. SUMMARY DEBT DATA										
TOTAL DEBT STOCKS (EDT)	..	**27,151**	**62,730**	**68,937**	**65,325**	**75,760**	**99,364**	**111,934**	**130,828**	**144,050**
Long-term debt (LDOD)	**5,169**	**16,768**	**49,203**	**50,447**	**53,153**	**64,378**	**71,878**	**82,144**	**92,972**	**107,652**
Public and publicly guaranteed	1,878	10,175	47,403	48,203	46,783	51,255	55,811	63,076	67,562	76,799
Private nonguaranteed	3,291	6,593	1,800	2,244	6,369	13,123	16,066	19,068	25,411	30,853
Use of IMF credit	**0**	**0**	**3,083**	**2,314**	**3,520**	**4,211**	**6,131**	**6,293**	**5,868**	**5,442**
Short-term debt	..	**10,383**	**10,445**	**16,176**	**8,653**	**7,171**	**21,355**	**23,498**	**31,988**	**30,956**
of which interest arrears on LDOD	..	0	7,562	9,076	1	1	0	0	0	0
Official creditors	..	0	132	627	0	0	0	0	0	0
Private creditors	..	0	7,429	8,450	1	1	0	0	0	0
Memo: principal arrears on LDOD	..	0	4,369	5,782	0	0	0	0	0	0
Official creditors	..	0	224	430	0	0	0	0	0	0
Private creditors	..	0	4,145	5,352	0	0	0	0	0	0
Memo: export credits	..	0	8,964	9,749	11,593	12,514	12,262	11,791	10,601	10,951
TOTAL DEBT FLOWS										
Disbursements	**907**	**4,705**	**1,693**	**3,281**	**10,884**	**9,586**	**11,333**	**18,670**	**19,536**	**25,261**
Long-term debt	907	4,705	1,255	2,458	9,272	8,709	8,968	17,874	19,095	25,261
IMF purchases	0	0	437	824	1,613	876	2,365	796	442	0
Principal repayments	**771**	**1,848**	**3,436**	**2,054**	**2,586**	**1,938**	**3,575**	**6,829**	**10,938**	**12,596**
Long-term debt	771	1,848	2,738	1,156	2,202	1,523	3,090	6,398	10,459	11,940
IMF repurchases	0	0	697	898	384	415	484	431	479	657
Net flows on debt	**774**	**6,329**	**-1,743**	**3,406**	**10,484**	**6,166**	**21,943**	**13,984**	**17,089**	**11,633**
of which short-term debt	..	3,472	0	2,179	2,186	-1,482	14,185	2,143	8,491	-1,032
Interest payments (INT)	..	**2,330**	**2,749**	**2,858**	**3,317**	**3,927**	**5,406**	**6,225**	**7,370**	**8,976**
Long-term debt	338	1,338	2,241	2,434	2,543	3,223	4,404	4,721	5,763	7,139
IMF charges	0	0	277	178	206	203	275	270	276	264
Short-term debt	..	992	231	246	568	502	727	1,233	1,332	1,574
Net transfers on debt	..	**3,999**	**-4,492**	**548**	**7,167**	**2,238**	**16,537**	**7,759**	**9,719**	**2,657**
Total debt service paid (TDS)	..	**4,178**	**6,185**	**4,912**	**5,903**	**5,866**	**8,981**	**13,054**	**18,308**	**21,573**
Long-term debt	1,109	3,186	4,980	3,590	4,745	4,746	7,494	11,119	16,222	19,078
IMF repurchases and charges	0	0	975	1,077	590	618	759	701	755	921
Short-term debt (interest only)	..	992	231	246	568	502	727	1,233	1,332	1,574
2. AGGREGATE NET RESOURCE FLOWS AND NET TRANSFERS (LONG-TERM)										
NET RESOURCE FLOWS	**143**	**3,537**	**387**	**6,104**	**15,393**	**11,839**	**11,403**	**18,880**	**18,993**	**19,553**
Net flow of long-term debt (ex. IMF)	135	2,857	-1,483	1,302	7,069	7,186	5,878	11,476	8,635	13,322
Foreign direct investment (net)	11	678	1,836	4,384	2,763	3,432	5,279	6,513	8,094	6,150
Portfolio equity flows	0	0	13	392	5,529	1,205	211	864	2,236	50
Grants (excluding technical coop.)	-3	2	21	27	32	16	36	27	28	31
Memo: technical coop. grants	13	35	84	84	81	80	84	85	77	66
official net resource flows	49	61	590	116	2,705	718	1,440	-15	-86	654
private net resource flows	94	3,476	-203	5,988	12,689	11,121	9,963	18,895	19,079	18,899
NET TRANSFERS	**-268**	**1,594**	**-2,491**	**2,826**	**11,904**	**7,496**	**5,699**	**12,659**	**11,630**	**10,614**
Interest on long-term debt	338	1,338	2,241	2,434	2,543	3,223	4,404	4,721	5,763	7,139
Profit remittances on FDI	73	605	637	845	946	1,120	1,300	1,500	1,600	1,800
Memo: official net transfers	16	-85	102	-638	1,717	-532	-17	-1,389	-1,378	-587
private net transfers	-284	1,679	-2,593	3,464	10,187	8,028	5,716	14,048	13,008	11,201
3. MAJOR ECONOMIC AGGREGATES										
Gross national product (GNP)	30,396	76,287	135,150	224,522	233,818	254,008	253,687	266,859	286,464	291,049
Exports of goods & services (XGS)	..	11,202	16,654	17,806	19,120	23,006	29,518	33,016	36,430	37,051
of which workers remittances	..	0	0	0	42	47	41	41	41	43
Imports of goods & services (MGS)	..	15,999	13,100	24,024	27,567	34,314	34,928	39,859	48,860	52,093
International reserves (RES)	682	9,297	6,222	11,447	15,499	16,003	15,979	19,719	22,425	24,856
Current account balance	..	-4,774	4,552	-5,487	-8,003	-10,949	-4,938	-6,468	-12,035	-14,697
4. DEBT INDICATORS										
EDT / XGS (%)	..	242.4	376.7	387.2	341.7	329.3	336.6	339.0	359.1	388.8
EDT / GNP (%)	..	35.6	46.4	30.7	27.9	29.8	39.2	42.0	45.7	49.5
TDS / XGS (%)	..	37.3	37.1	27.6	30.9	25.5	30.4	39.5	50.3	58.2
INT / XGS (%)	..	20.8	16.5	16.1	17.4	17.1	18.3	18.9	20.2	24.2
INT / GNP (%)	..	3.1	2.0	1.3	1.4	1.6	2.1	2.3	2.6	3.1
RES / EDT (%)	..	34.2	9.9	16.6	23.7	21.1	16.1	17.6	17.1	17.3
RES / MGS (months)	..	7.0	5.7	5.7	6.8	5.6	5.5	5.9	5.5	5.7
Short-term / EDT (%)	..	38.2	16.7	23.5	13.3	9.5	21.5	21.0	24.5	21.5
Concessional / EDT (%)	..	1.3	0.8	1.6	2.9	3.0	2.8	2.2	1.7	1.5
Multilateral / EDT (%)	..	4.0	8.8	8.2	11.8	11.1	10.0	9.2	8.2	8.8

ARGENTINA

(US$ million, unless otherwise indicated)

	1970	1980	1990	1992	1993	1994	1995	1996	1997	1998
5. LONG-TERM DEBT										
DEBT OUTSTANDING (LDOD)	**5,169**	**16,768**	**49,203**	**50,447**	**53,153**	**64,378**	**71,878**	**82,144**	**92,972**	**107,652**
Public and publicly guaranteed	**1,878**	**10,175**	**47,403**	**48,203**	**46,783**	**51,255**	**55,811**	**63,076**	**67,562**	**76,799**
Official creditors	635	1,897	11,723	13,758	17,440	19,451	21,524	20,327	18,783	20,082
Multilateral	279	1,081	5,504	5,628	7,719	8,369	9,935	10,300	10,685	12,682
Concessional	1	36	30	27	12	10	9	7	5	3
Bilateral	356	816	6,219	8,130	9,721	11,082	11,590	10,028	8,098	7,400
Concessional	166	329	498	1,105	1,882	2,251	2,737	2,487	2,270	2,207
Private creditors	1,243	8,278	35,679	34,445	29,343	31,804	34,287	42,748	48,778	56,716
Bonds	386	832	11,514	11,620	28,117	30,430	32,670	41,435	47,563	55,696
Commercial banks	121	6,065	22,661	21,618	804	916	1,207	1,050	1,045	918
Other private	735	1,381	1,504	1,207	422	459	410	264	171	102
Private nonguaranteed	**3,291**	**6,593**	**1,800**	**2,244**	**6,369**	**13,123**	**16,066**	**19,068**	**25,411**	**30,853**
Bonds	0	0	21	1,671	5,225	7,366	7,582	8,760	10,311	11,873
Commercial banks	3,291	6,593	1,779	573	1,144	5,757	8,484	10,308	15,100	18,980
Memo:										
IBRD	181	404	2,609	2,505	3,739	4,109	4,913	5,372	5,495	7,188
IDA	0	0	0	0	0	0	0	0	0	0
DISBURSEMENTS	**907**	**4,705**	**1,255**	**2,458**	**9,272**	**8,709**	**8,968**	**17,874**	**19,095**	**25,261**
Public and publicly guaranteed	**482**	**2,836**	**1,234**	**1,058**	**5,667**	**4,370**	**6,618**	**13,004**	**11,866**	**14,257**
Official creditors	162	273	1,015	754	3,315	1,469	2,803	1,658	1,899	2,478
Multilateral	63	205	842	352	2,540	787	1,936	1,564	1,671	2,459
Concessional	0	6	0	0	0	0	0	0	0	0
Bilateral	98	69	174	402	775	683	867	94	228	19
Concessional	46	13	149	2	575	238	630	34	97	11
Private creditors	321	2,563	219	304	2,351	2,901	3,815	11,346	9,967	11,779
Bonds	119	136	0	250	2,211	2,713	3,630	11,204	9,927	11,768
Commercial banks	53	2,173	183	33	91	110	119	142	40	11
Other private	149	253	36	21	49	77	66	0	0	0
Private nonguaranteed	**424**	**1,869**	**21**	**1,400**	**3,605**	**4,339**	**2,350**	**4,870**	**7,229**	**11,004**
Bonds	0	0	21	1,400	3,605	2,430	834	2,490	3,084	3,976
Commercial banks	424	1,869	0	0	0	1,910	1,516	2,380	4,145	7,029
Memo:										
IBRD	32	71	405	171	1,507	548	941	1,077	797	2,029
IDA	0	0	0	0	0	0	0	0	0	0
PRINCIPAL REPAYMENTS	**771**	**1,848**	**2,738**	**1,156**	**2,202**	**1,523**	**3,090**	**6,398**	**10,459**	**11,940**
Public and publicly guaranteed	**343**	**1,141**	**2,738**	**921**	**2,152**	**1,033**	**1,825**	**3,306**	**6,992**	**6,345**
Official creditors	109	214	446	664	643	767	1,399	1,700	2,013	1,855
Multilateral	16	117	397	594	563	694	545	613	617	719
Concessional	0	4	2	2	2	2	2	2	2	2
Bilateral	94	97	49	71	79	74	854	1,088	1,396	1,136
Concessional	11	34	0	0	13	20	58	103	144	205
Private creditors	234	928	2,293	256	1,510	266	427	1,606	4,979	4,490
Bonds	20	178	878	219	1,409	136	128	1,275	4,738	4,244
Commercial banks	69	481	1,343	14	49	63	173	208	153	175
Other private	145	268	72	24	52	67	125	122	88	70
Private nonguaranteed	**428**	**707**	**0**	**235**	**50**	**490**	**1,265**	**3,092**	**3,468**	**5,595**
Bonds	0	0	0	15	50	290	631	1,311	1,468	2,462
Commercial banks	428	707	0	220	0	200	634	1,781	2,000	3,133
Memo:										
IBRD	5	34	233	383	334	425	259	282	299	350
IDA	0	0	0	0	0	0	0	0	0	0
NET FLOWS ON DEBT	**135**	**2,857**	**-1,483**	**1,302**	**7,069**	**7,186**	**5,878**	**11,476**	**8,635**	**13,322**
Public and publicly guaranteed	**139**	**1,695**	**-1,504**	**137**	**3,514**	**3,337**	**4,793**	**9,698**	**4,875**	**7,912**
Official creditors	52	59	570	90	2,673	702	1,404	-42	-114	623
Multilateral	48	88	445	-242	1,976	93	1,391	951	1,054	1,740
Concessional	0	3	-2	-2	-2	-2	-2	-2	-2	-2
Bilateral	5	-29	125	332	696	609	13	-994	-1,167	-1,117
Concessional	35	-20	149	2	562	219	572	-69	-48	-194
Private creditors	87	1,635	-2,074	47	842	2,635	3,388	9,740	4,989	7,289
Bonds	99	-42	-878	31	803	2,577	3,502	9,930	5,190	7,523
Commercial banks	-16	1,692	-1,160	19	42	48	-54	-67	-113	-164
Other private	4	-16	-36	-3	-3	10	-60	-122	-88	-70
Private nonguaranteed	**-4**	**1,162**	**21**	**1,165**	**3,555**	**3,849**	**1,085**	**1,778**	**3,761**	**5,410**
Bonds	0	0	21	1,385	3,555	2,140	203	1,179	1,616	1,514
Commercial banks	-4	1,162	0	-220	0	1,710	882	599	2,145	3,896
Memo:										
IBRD	27	37	172	-211	1,173	123	682	795	498	1,678
IDA	0	0	0	0	0	0	0	0	0	0

ARGENTINA

(US$ million, unless otherwise indicated)

	1970	*1980*	*1990*	*1992*	*1993*	*1994*	*1995*	*1996*	*1997*	*1998*
INTEREST PAYMENTS (LINT)	**338**	**1,338**	**2,241**	**2,434**	**2,543**	**3,223**	**4,404**	**4,721**	**5,763**	**7,139**
Public and publicly guaranteed	**121**	**842**	**2,097**	**2,308**	**2,326**	**2,662**	**3,519**	**3,779**	**4,532**	**5,469**
Official creditors	33	147	488	754	988	1,250	1,458	1,374	1,292	1,240
Multilateral	17	98	407	489	519	653	675	677	730	761
Concessional	0	1	1	1	1	1	0	0	0	0
Bilateral	16	49	81	265	469	597	782	697	562	479
Concessional	4	15	0	0	43	73	114	114	103	100
Private creditors	88	695	1,609	1,554	1,338	1,412	2,062	2,405	3,241	4,229
Bonds	23	80	973	812	1,282	1,346	1,960	2,290	3,155	4,129
Commercial banks	9	504	623	736	28	42	72	93	71	90
Other private	56	111	14	6	28	25	30	23	15	10
Private nonguaranteed	**217**	**496**	**144**	**126**	**217**	**560**	**885**	**942**	**1,230**	**1,669**
Bonds	0	0	0	38	172	469	641	691	806	907
Commercial banks	217	496	144	89	46	92	244	251	424	763
Memo:										
IBRD	11	37	182	228	233	284	306	326	335	375
IDA	0	0	0	0	0	0	0	0	0	0
NET TRANSFERS ON DEBT	**-203**	**1,519**	**-3,724**	**-1,132**	**4,526**	**3,964**	**1,473**	**6,755**	**2,873**	**6,183**
Public and publicly guaranteed	**19**	**853**	**-3,601**	**-2,171**	**1,189**	**674**	**1,273**	**5,919**	**342**	**2,443**
Official creditors	19	-87	81	-665	1,685	-548	-54	-1,416	-1,406	-617
Multilateral	30	-10	38	-731	1,458	-560	715	274	323	978
Concessional	0	1	-2	-3	-2	-2	-2	-2	-2	-2
Bilateral	-11	-77	44	66	228	12	-769	-1,690	-1,729	-1,596
Concessional	31	-35	149	2	519	145	458	-183	-150	-294
Private creditors	0	940	-3,683	-1,506	-497	1,223	1,327	7,335	1,748	3,060
Bonds	77	-122	-1,851	-781	-479	1,231	1,542	7,640	2,035	3,395
Commercial banks	-25	1,189	-1,782	-718	14	6	-126	-160	-184	-254
Other private	-52	-127	-50	-8	-31	-14	-89	-145	-102	-80
Private nonguaranteed	**-221**	**666**	**-123**	**1,039**	**3,338**	**3,289**	**200**	**835**	**2,531**	**3,740**
Bonds	0	0	21	1,347	3,384	1,671	-438	487	810	607
Commercial banks	-221	666	-144	-309	-46	1,618	638	348	1,721	3,134
Memo:										
IBRD	16	0	-10	-439	940	-161	376	469	162	1,304
IDA	0	0	0	0	0	0	0	0	0	0
DEBT SERVICE (LTDS)	**1,109**	**3,186**	**4,980**	**3,590**	**4,745**	**4,746**	**7,494**	**11,119**	**16,222**	**19,078**
Public and publicly guaranteed	**464**	**1,983**	**4,836**	**3,229**	**4,478**	**3,696**	**5,344**	**7,085**	**11,524**	**11,814**
Official creditors	143	361	934	1,419	1,630	2,017	2,856	3,074	3,305	3,096
Multilateral	33	215	804	1,083	1,082	1,347	1,220	1,289	1,347	1,481
Concessional	0	5	2	3	2	2	2	2	2	2
Bilateral	109	146	130	336	548	671	1,636	1,785	1,957	1,615
Concessional	15	48	0	0	56	93	171	216	247	305
Private creditors	321	1,623	3,902	1,810	2,848	1,678	2,488	4,011	8,219	8,719
Bonds	42	258	1,851	1,031	2,691	1,482	2,088	3,564	7,893	8,373
Commercial banks	78	985	1,966	751	77	105	245	301	224	265
Other private	201	380	86	29	80	92	155	145	102	80
Private nonguaranteed	**646**	**1,203**	**144**	**361**	**267**	**1,050**	**2,150**	**4,035**	**4,698**	**7,264**
Bonds	0	0	0	53	222	759	1,272	2,003	2,274	3,369
Commercial banks	646	1,203	144	309	46	292	878	2,032	2,424	3,895
Memo:										
IBRD	16	71	414	611	567	709	565	608	635	725
IDA	0	0	0	0	0	0	0	0	0	0
UNDISBURSED DEBT	**576**	**2,272**	**2,427**	**3,888**	**3,885**	**4,823**	**6,680**	**6,029**	**6,428**	**8,396**
Official creditors	324	1,218	2,009	3,489	3,456	4,244	6,186	5,679	6,016	8,277
Private creditors	252	1,054	419	399	428	579	494	350	412	119
Memorandum items										
Concessional LDOD	167	365	529	1,132	1,894	2,261	2,745	2,493	2,274	2,210
Variable rate LDOD	3,291	12,417	28,307	27,813	25,781	33,570	36,763	39,502	47,743	56,274
Public sector LDOD	1,780	7,979	45,252	46,161	46,771	51,246	55,792	63,052	67,496	76,755
Private sector LDOD	3,390	8,795	3,969	4,304	6,393	13,139	16,088	19,111	25,492	30,917
6. CURRENCY COMPOSITION OF LONG-TERM DEBT (PERCENT)										
Deutsche mark	15.8	9.5	10.3	8.9	8.0	9.3	11.3	14.8	13.2	14.0
French franc	1.8	1.2	1.5	1.3	1.0	1.0	1.3	1.0	0.7	0.6
Japanese yen	0.2	5.8	6.6	6.5	4.5	6.4	9.3	8.4	6.8	6.2
Pound sterling	2.9	1.6	1.1	0.8	0.2	0.2	0.2	0.4	0.8	0.7
Swiss franc	1.9	3.4	2.1	1.8	1.1	1.2	1.6	1.3	0.9	0.7
U.S.dollars	47.7	64.6	53.9	55.2	67.8	64.2	58.7	57.0	61.3	63.2
Multiple currency	17.7	10.3	20.4	22.1	14.6	14.1	14.0	12.6	11.1	4.6
Special drawing rights	0.0	0.0	0.0	0.0	0.0	0.0	0.0	0.0	0.0	0.0
All other currencies	12.0	3.6	4.1	3.4	2.8	3.6	3.6	4.5	5.2	10.0

ARGENTINA

(US$ million, unless otherwise indicated)

	1970	1980	1990	1992	1993	1994	1995	1996	1997	1998
7. DEBT RESTRUCTURINGS										
Total amount rescheduled	..	..	932	631	26,503	847	248	0	0	0
Debt stock rescheduled	..	..	0	0	18,036	0	0	0	0	0
Principal rescheduled	..	..	512	523	973	844	198	0	0	0
Official	..	..	381	456	963	834	158	0	0	0
Private	..	..	131	67	10	10	40	0	0	0
Interest rescheduled	..	..	420	107	7,495	3	50	0	0	0
Official	..	..	382	88	88	3	22	0	0	0
Private	..	..	38	19	7,407	0	29	0	0	0
Debt forgiven	..	..	0	0	0	0	0	0	0	0
Memo: interest forgiven	..	..	0	0	0	0	0	0	0	0
Debt stock reduction	..	..	7,202	661	3,265	399	863	0	2,700	2,729
of which debt buyback	..	..	1,232	0	0	0	0	0	2,085	2,100
8. DEBT STOCK-FLOW RECONCILIATION										
Total change in debt stocks	..	..	-2,887	2,908	-3,612	10,435	23,603	12,571	18,894	13,222
Net flows on debt	774	6,329	-1,743	3,406	10,484	6,166	21,943	13,984	17,089	11,633
Net change in interest arrears	..	..	1,920	452	-9,076	0	-1	0	0	0
Interest capitalized	..	..	420	107	7,495	3	50	0	0	0
Debt forgiveness or reduction	..	..	-5,970	-661	-3,265	-399	-863	0	-615	-629
Cross-currency valuation	..	..	1,617	-735	-150	1,427	752	-1,893	-2,615	2,362
Residual	..	..	869	339	-9,100	3,238	1,721	480	5,035	-144
9. AVERAGE TERMS OF NEW COMMITMENTS										
ALL CREDITORS										
Interest (%)	7.3	13.7	6.6	8.3	7.1	7.2	6.9	8.4	8.2	8.9
Maturity (years)	11.9	8.6	17.4	16.5	11.7	9.7	11.1	8.3	14.4	13.0
Grace period (years)	2.9	4.5	4.0	5.7	6.0	4.0	4.7	7.2	12.1	10.9
Grant element (%)	12.6	-17.5	18.5	9.6	15.2	12.7	14.1	3.9	8.2	6.0
Official creditors										
Interest (%)	7.5	6.1	6.7	8.3	6.4	5.8	6.5	7.0	7.0	8.4
Maturity (years)	16.6	14.0	18.9	18.0	15.2	16.7	16.2	15.0	16.3	11.3
Grace period (years)	3.5	5.3	4.5	5.8	4.8	4.9	4.7	5.1	4.1	4.2
Grant element (%)	11.4	20.1	19.2	10.0	20.3	25.0	19.6	17.2	16.8	8.8
Private creditors										
Interest (%)	7.3	14.3	6.0	8.1	7.8	8.3	7.4	8.6	8.5	9.1
Maturity (years)	10.6	8.2	8.4	6.5	8.0	4.4	4.7	7.5	14.0	13.8
Grace period (years)	2.7	4.4	1.4	5.0	7.3	3.3	4.6	7.5	13.9	13.8
Grant element (%)	13.0	-20.5	14.1	7.2	9.6	3.3	7.2	2.3	6.1	4.8
Memorandum items										
Commitments	493	3,058	800	2,281	5,256	5,390	8,382	12,489	15,676	16,766
Official creditors	104	221	688	1,977	2,756	2,338	4,668	1,320	2,980	4,992
Private creditors	389	2,837	113	304	2,500	3,053	3,714	11,169	12,696	11,775

10. CONTRACTUAL OBLIGATIONS ON OUTSTANDING LONG-TERM DEBT

	1999	2000	2001	2002	2003	2004	2005	2006	2007	2008
TOTAL										
Disbursements	3,199	1,455	1,217	941	631	372	244	139	107	62
Principal	12,933	10,538	10,168	11,579	12,525	9,146	7,255	4,150	3,943	6,155
Interest	7,785	7,116	6,384	5,853	5,180	4,377	3,762	3,312	2,977	2,501
Official creditors										
Disbursements	3,122	1,426	1,205	941	631	372	244	139	107	62
Principal	2,780	2,514	2,137	3,279	3,196	1,978	1,945	1,889	1,848	1,571
Interest	1,495	1,522	1,429	1,314	1,100	902	786	666	545	426
Bilateral creditors										
Disbursements	397	225	122	59	22	9	5	0	0	0
Principal	1,718	1,437	937	748	603	602	577	521	487	299
Interest	450	357	275	221	182	147	112	79	48	21
Multilateral creditors										
Disbursements	2,725	1,200	1,083	882	609	363	240	139	107	62
Principal	1,062	1,077	1,201	2,531	2,592	1,376	1,368	1,368	1,362	1,272
Interest	1,045	1,165	1,154	1,093	918	754	674	587	497	405
Private creditors										
Disbursements	78	29	12	0	0	0	0	0	0	0
Principal	10,153	8,024	8,031	8,300	9,329	7,169	5,310	2,261	2,095	4,585
Interest	6,289	5,594	4,955	4,539	4,080	3,475	2,976	2,647	2,432	2,075
Commercial banks										
Disbursements	78	29	12	0	0	0	0	0	0	0
Principal	226	205	116	108	72	69	66	62	62	16
Interest	68	56	45	36	28	23	18	13	8	4
Other private										
Disbursements	0	0	0	0	0	0	0	0	0	0
Principal	9,927	7,819	7,916	8,192	9,258	7,099	5,244	2,199	2,033	4,569
Interest	6,222	5,538	4,910	4,503	4,052	3,452	2,958	2,634	2,424	2,071

ARMENIA

(US$ million, unless otherwise indicated)

	1970	1980	1990	1992	1993	1994	1995	1996	1997	1998
1. SUMMARY DEBT DATA										
TOTAL DEBT STOCKS (EDT)	..	..	..	..	**133.9**	**214.3**	**370.7**	**549.9**	**665.5**	**799.7**
Long-term debt (LDOD)	..	..	..	..	**133.9**	**188.6**	**298.3**	**432.0**	**511.4**	**564.0**
Public and publicly guaranteed	..	..	..	..	133.9	188.6	298.3	432.0	511.4	564.0
Private nonguaranteed	..	..	..	..	0.0	0.0	0.0	0.0	0.0	0.0
Use of IMF credit	..	..	..	..	**0.0**	**24.6**	**70.2**	**116.5**	**132.1**	**190.4**
Short-term debt	..	..	..	..	**0.0**	**1.1**	**2.1**	**1.4**	**22.0**	**45.2**
of which interest arrears on LDOD	..	..	..	..	0.0	1.1	1.1	0.0	0.0	0.0
Official creditors	..	..	..	..	0.0	1.1	1.1	0.0	0.0	0.0
Private creditors	..	..	..	..	0.0	0.0	0.0	0.0	0.0	0.0
Memo: principal arrears on LDOD	..	..	..	..	0.0	31.2	75.4	64.0	53.2	56.2
Official creditors	..	..	..	..	0.0	31.2	75.4	64.0	53.2	56.2
Private creditors	..	..	..	..	0.0	0.0	0.0	0.0	0.0	0.0
Memo: export credits	..	..	..	..	0.0	0.0	0.0	2.0	0.0	7.0
TOTAL DEBT FLOWS										
Disbursements	..	..	..	..	**87.3**	**84.7**	**148.5**	**196.1**	**131.7**	**112.9**
Long-term debt	..	..	..	..	87.3	60.5	102.4	147.1	108.5	61.6
IMF purchases	..	..	..	..	0.0	24.2	46.1	49.0	23.2	51.3
Principal repayments	..	..	..	..	**0.6**	**0.0**	**2.8**	**38.5**	**10.4**	**22.5**
Long-term debt	..	..	..	..	0.6	0.0	2.8	38.5	10.4	21.9
IMF repurchases	..	..	..	..	0.0	0.0	0.0	0.0	0.0	0.6
Net flows on debt	..	..	..	..	**79.6**	**84.7**	**146.6**	**158.0**	**141.9**	**113.6**
of which short-term debt	..	..	..	..	-7.2	0.0	1.0	0.4	20.6	23.2
Interest payments (INT)	..	..	..	..	**1.4**	**4.4**	**8.5**	**11.5**	**17.3**	**19.5**
Long-term debt	..	..	..	..	1.4	4.4	6.7	8.3	13.4	14.3
IMF charges	..	..	..	..	0.0	0.0	1.7	3.2	3.3	3.4
Short-term debt	..	..	..	..	0.0	0.0	0.0	0.1	0.6	1.8
Net transfers on debt	..	..	..	..	**78.1**	**80.3**	**138.2**	**146.5**	**124.6**	**94.1**
Total debt service paid (TDS)	..	..	..	..	**2.0**	**4.4**	**11.3**	**50.0**	**27.7**	**42.0**
Long-term debt	..	..	..	..	2.0	4.4	9.6	46.8	23.8	36.2
IMF repurchases and charges	..	..	..	..	0.0	0.0	1.7	3.2	3.3	4.0
Short-term debt (interest only)	..	..	..	..	0.0	0.0	0.0	0.1	0.6	1.8
2. AGGREGATE NET RESOURCE FLOWS AND NET TRANSFERS (LONG-TERM)										
NET RESOURCE FLOWS	..	..	..	..	**183.6**	**239.5**	**204.2**	**179.6**	**182.9**	**321.4**
Net flow of long-term debt (ex. IMF)	..	..	..	..	86.8	60.5	99.5	108.6	98.1	39.7
Foreign direct investment (net)	..	..	..	..	0.0	8.0	14.0	17.6	51.0	232.0
Portfolio equity flows	..	..	..	..	0.0	0.0	0.0	0.0	0.0	0.0
Grants (excluding technical coop.)	..	..	..	..	96.8	171.0	90.7	53.4	33.8	49.7
Memo: technical coop. grants	..	..	..	..	12.7	14.8	38.6	84.8	14.0	24.4
official net resource flows	..	..	..	..	183.6	231.5	190.2	162.0	131.9	89.4
private net resource flows	..	..	..	..	0.0	8.0	14.0	17.6	51.0	232.0
NET TRANSFERS	..	..	..	..	**182.2**	**235.1**	**197.5**	**170.3**	**167.5**	**304.1**
Interest on long-term debt	..	..	..	..	1.4	4.4	6.7	8.3	13.4	14.3
Profit remittances on FDI	..	..	..	..	0.0	0.0	0.0	1.0	2.0	3.0
Memo: official net transfers	..	..	..	..	182.2	227.1	183.5	153.7	118.5	75.1
private net transfers	..	..	..	..	0.0	8.0	14.0	16.6	49.0	229.0
3. MAJOR ECONOMIC AGGREGATES										
Gross national product (GNP)	..	..	..	..	2,014.4	2,358.5	2,883.1	1,599.5	1,641.9	1,901.9
Exports of goods & services (XGS)	..	..	..	..	173.5	229.0	366.5	457.3	477.9	473.6
of which workers remittances	..	..	..	..	..	..	12.4	11.1	8.7	10.1
Imports of goods & services (MGS)	..	..	..	..	295.5	438.4	746.5	921.5	992.9	1,031.2
International reserves (RES)	..	..	..	..	13.6	36.1	111.2	168.2	239.2	327.7
Current account balance	..	..	..	..	-66.8	-103.8	-224.1	-290.7	-306.5	-390.3
4. DEBT INDICATORS										
EDT / XGS (%)	..	..	..	..	77.2	93.6	101.2	120.3	139.3	168.8
EDT / GNP (%)	..	..	..	..	6.7	9.1	12.9	34.4	40.5	42.1
TDS / XGS (%)	..	..	..	..	1.2	1.9	3.1	10.9	5.8	8.9
INT / XGS (%)	..	..	..	..	0.8	1.9	2.3	2.5	3.6	4.1
INT / GNP (%)	..	..	..	..	0.1	0.2	0.3	0.7	1.1	1.0
RES / EDT (%)	..	..	..	..	10.2	16.9	30.0	30.6	36.0	41.0
RES / MGS (months)	..	..	..	..	0.6	1.0	1.8	2.2	2.9	3.8
Short-term / EDT (%)	..	..	..	..	0.0	0.5	0.6	0.3	3.3	5.7
Concessional / EDT (%)	..	..	..	..	12.4	9.7	28.5	36.7	38.9	39.7
Multilateral / EDT (%)	..	..	..	..	45.3	48.6	56.1	56.8	55.6	53.9

ARMENIA

(US$ million, unless otherwise indicated)

	1970	1980	1990	1992	1993	1994	1995	1996	1997	1998
5. LONG-TERM DEBT										
DEBT OUTSTANDING (LDOD)	..	..	..	..	**133.9**	**188.6**	**298.3**	**432.0**	**511.4**	**564.0**
Public and publicly guaranteed	..	..	..	..	**133.9**	**188.6**	**298.3**	**432.0**	**511.4**	**564.0**
Official creditors	..	..	..	..	133.9	188.6	298.3	432.0	511.4	564.0
Multilateral	..	..	..	..	60.7	104.1	208.0	312.1	370.0	431.0
Concessional	..	..	..	..	0.0	5.6	90.9	175.3	242.1	296.7
Bilateral	..	..	..	..	73.2	84.6	90.3	119.9	141.4	133.0
Concessional	..	..	..	..	16.6	15.1	14.9	26.4	16.6	21.1
Private creditors	..	..	..	..	0.0	0.0	0.0	0.0	0.0	0.0
Bonds	..	..	..	..	0.0	0.0	0.0	0.0	0.0	0.0
Commercial banks	..	..	..	..	0.0	0.0	0.0	0.0	0.0	0.0
Other private	..	..	..	..	0.0	0.0	0.0	0.0	0.0	0.0
Private nonguaranteed	..	..	..	..	**0.0**	**0.0**	**0.0**	**0.0**	**0.0**	**0.0**
Bonds	..	..	..	..	0.0	0.0	0.0	0.0	0.0	0.0
Commercial banks	..	..	..	..	0.0	0.0	0.0	0.0	0.0	0.0
Memo:										
IBRD	..	..	..	..	0.5	1.6	4.8	9.8	9.9	9.7
IDA	..	..	..	..	0.0	5.6	90.9	174.0	240.3	292.8
DISBURSEMENTS	..	..	..	..	**87.3**	**60.5**	**102.4**	**147.1**	**108.5**	**61.6**
Public and publicly guaranteed	..	..	..	..	**87.3**	**60.5**	**102.4**	**147.1**	**108.5**	**61.6**
Official creditors	..	..	..	..	87.3	60.5	102.4	147.1	108.5	61.6
Multilateral	..	..	..	..	63.4	37.3	102.4	123.0	81.7	57.1
Concessional	..	..	..	..	0.0	5.5	88.5	88.3	77.1	44.7
Bilateral	..	..	..	..	24.0	23.2	0.0	24.1	26.8	4.5
Concessional	..	..	..	..	2.3	0.0	0.0	15.3	1.2	4.5
Private creditors	..	..	..	..	0.0	0.0	0.0	0.0	0.0	0.0
Bonds	..	..	..	..	0.0	0.0	0.0	0.0	0.0	0.0
Commercial banks	..	..	..	..	0.0	0.0	0.0	0.0	0.0	0.0
Other private	..	..	..	..	0.0	0.0	0.0	0.0	0.0	0.0
Private nonguaranteed	..	..	..	..	**0.0**	**0.0**	**0.0**	**0.0**	**0.0**	**0.0**
Bonds	..	..	..	..	0.0	0.0	0.0	0.0	0.0	0.0
Commercial banks	..	..	..	..	0.0	0.0	0.0	0.0	0.0	0.0
Memo:										
IBRD	..	..	..	..	0.5	1.0	3.4	5.4	0.9	0.0
IDA	..	..	..	..	0.0	5.5	88.5	87.0	76.5	42.9
PRINCIPAL REPAYMENTS	..	..	..	..	**0.6**	**0.0**	**2.8**	**38.5**	**10.4**	**21.9**
Public and publicly guaranteed	..	..	..	..	**0.6**	**0.0**	**2.8**	**38.5**	**10.4**	**21.9**
Official creditors	..	..	..	..	0.6	0.0	2.8	38.5	10.4	21.9
Multilateral	..	..	..	..	0.0	0.0	0.0	10.1	5.3	9.1
Concessional	..	..	..	..	0.0	0.0	0.0	0.0	0.0	0.0
Bilateral	..	..	..	..	0.6	0.0	2.8	28.4	5.1	12.8
Concessional	..	..	..	..	0.0	0.0	0.0	3.7	0.1	0.1
Private creditors	..	..	..	..	0.0	0.0	0.0	0.0	0.0	0.0
Bonds	..	..	..	..	0.0	0.0	0.0	0.0	0.0	0.0
Commercial banks	..	..	..	..	0.0	0.0	0.0	0.0	0.0	0.0
Other private	..	..	..	..	0.0	0.0	0.0	0.0	0.0	0.0
Private nonguaranteed	..	..	..	..	**0.0**	**0.0**	**0.0**	**0.0**	**0.0**	**0.0**
Bonds	..	..	..	..	0.0	0.0	0.0	0.0	0.0	0.0
Commercial banks	..	..	..	..	0.0	0.0	0.0	0.0	0.0	0.0
Memo:										
IBRD	..	..	..	..	0.0	0.0	0.0	0.0	0.0	0.2
IDA	..	..	..	..	0.0	0.0	0.0	0.0	0.0	0.0
NET FLOWS ON DEBT	..	..	..	..	**86.8**	**60.5**	**99.5**	**108.6**	**98.1**	**39.7**
Public and publicly guaranteed	..	..	..	..	**86.8**	**60.5**	**99.5**	**108.6**	**98.1**	**39.7**
Official creditors	..	..	..	..	86.8	60.5	99.5	108.6	98.1	39.7
Multilateral	..	..	..	..	63.4	37.3	102.4	112.9	76.4	48.0
Concessional	..	..	..	..	0.0	5.5	88.5	88.3	77.1	44.7
Bilateral	..	..	..	..	23.4	23.2	-2.8	-4.2	21.7	-8.3
Concessional	..	..	..	..	2.3	0.0	0.0	11.7	1.1	4.4
Private creditors	..	..	..	..	0.0	0.0	0.0	0.0	0.0	0.0
Bonds	..	..	..	..	0.0	0.0	0.0	0.0	0.0	0.0
Commercial banks	..	..	..	..	0.0	0.0	0.0	0.0	0.0	0.0
Other private	..	..	..	..	0.0	0.0	0.0	0.0	0.0	0.0
Private nonguaranteed	..	..	..	..	**0.0**	**0.0**	**0.0**	**0.0**	**0.0**	**0.0**
Bonds	..	..	..	..	0.0	0.0	0.0	0.0	0.0	0.0
Commercial banks	..	..	..	..	0.0	0.0	0.0	0.0	0.0	0.0
Memo:										
IBRD	..	..	..	..	0.5	1.0	3.4	5.4	0.9	-0.2
IDA	..	..	..	..	0.0	5.5	88.5	87.0	76.5	42.9

ARMENIA

(US$ million, unless otherwise indicated)

	1970	1980	1990	1992	1993	1994	1995	1996	1997	1998
INTEREST PAYMENTS (LINT)	..	..	..	..	**1.4**	**4.4**	**6.7**	**8.3**	**13.4**	**14.3**
Public and publicly guaranteed	..	..	..	..	**1.4**	**4.4**	**6.7**	**8.3**	**13.4**	**14.3**
Official creditors	..	..	..	..	1.4	4.4	6.7	8.3	13.4	14.3
Multilateral	..	..	..	..	1.3	4.4	6.7	2.9	9.6	7.3
Concessional	..	..	..	..	0.0	0.0	0.2	0.8	1.2	1.7
Bilateral	..	..	..	..	0.0	0.0	0.1	5.4	3.8	7.0
Concessional	..	..	..	..	0.0	0.0	0.1	0.3	0.4	0.5
Private creditors	..	..	..	..	0.0	0.0	0.0	0.0	0.0	0.0
Bonds	..	..	..	..	0.0	0.0	0.0	0.0	0.0	0.0
Commercial banks	..	..	..	..	0.0	0.0	0.0	0.0	0.0	0.0
Other private	..	..	..	..	0.0	0.0	0.0	0.0	0.0	0.0
Private nonguaranteed	..	..	..	..	**0.0**	**0.0**	**0.0**	**0.0**	**0.0**	**0.0**
Bonds	..	..	..	..	0.0	0.0	0.0	0.0	0.0	0.0
Commercial banks	..	..	..	..	0.0	0.0	0.0	0.0	0.0	0.0
Memo:										
IBRD	..	..	..	..	0.0	0.1	0.2	0.4	0.6	0.6
IDA	..	..	..	..	0.0	0.0	0.2	0.8	1.2	1.7
NET TRANSFERS ON DEBT	..	..	..	..	**85.4**	**56.1**	**92.8**	**100.3**	**84.7**	**25.5**
Public and publicly guaranteed	..	..	..	..	**85.4**	**56.1**	**92.8**	**100.3**	**84.7**	**25.5**
Official creditors	..	..	..	..	85.4	56.1	92.8	100.3	84.7	25.5
Multilateral	..	..	..	..	62.0	32.9	95.7	110.0	66.8	40.7
Concessional	..	..	..	..	0.0	5.5	88.3	87.5	75.9	43.0
Bilateral	..	..	..	..	23.4	23.2	-2.9	-9.6	17.9	-15.3
Concessional	..	..	..	..	2.3	0.0	-0.1	11.4	0.7	4.0
Private creditors	..	..	..	..	0.0	0.0	0.0	0.0	0.0	0.0
Bonds	..	..	..	..	0.0	0.0	0.0	0.0	0.0	0.0
Commercial banks	..	..	..	..	0.0	0.0	0.0	0.0	0.0	0.0
Other private	..	..	..	..	0.0	0.0	0.0	0.0	0.0	0.0
Private nonguaranteed	..	..	..	..	**0.0**	**0.0**	**0.0**	**0.0**	**0.0**	**0.0**
Bonds	..	..	..	..	0.0	0.0	0.0	0.0	0.0	0.0
Commercial banks	..	..	..	..	0.0	0.0	0.0	0.0	0.0	0.0
Memo:										
IBRD	..	..	..	..	0.5	0.9	3.2	5.1	0.3	-0.8
IDA	..	..	..	..	0.0	5.5	88.3	86.2	75.3	41.2
DEBT SERVICE (LTDS)	..	..	..	..	**2.0**	**4.4**	**9.6**	**46.8**	**23.8**	**36.2**
Public and publicly guaranteed	..	..	..	..	**2.0**	**4.4**	**9.6**	**46.8**	**23.8**	**36.2**
Official creditors	..	..	..	..	2.0	4.4	9.6	46.8	23.8	36.2
Multilateral	..	..	..	..	1.3	4.4	6.7	13.0	14.9	16.4
Concessional	..	..	..	..	0.0	0.0	0.2	0.8	1.2	1.7
Bilateral	..	..	..	..	0.6	0.0	2.9	33.8	8.9	19.8
Concessional	..	..	..	..	0.0	0.0	0.1	4.0	0.5	0.6
Private creditors	..	..	..	..	0.0	0.0	0.0	0.0	0.0	0.0
Bonds	..	..	..	..	0.0	0.0	0.0	0.0	0.0	0.0
Commercial banks	..	..	..	..	0.0	0.0	0.0	0.0	0.0	0.0
Other private	..	..	..	..	0.0	0.0	0.0	0.0	0.0	0.0
Private nonguaranteed	..	..	..	..	**0.0**	**0.0**	**0.0**	**0.0**	**0.0**	**0.0**
Bonds	..	..	..	..	0.0	0.0	0.0	0.0	0.0	0.0
Commercial banks	..	..	..	..	0.0	0.0	0.0	0.0	0.0	0.0
Memo:										
IBRD	..	..	..	..	0.0	0.1	0.2	0.4	0.6	0.8
IDA	..	..	..	..	0.0	0.0	0.2	0.8	1.2	1.7
UNDISBURSED DEBT	..	..	..	..	**80.9**	**171.2**	**188.9**	**116.7**	**133.0**	**199.9**
Official creditors	..	..	..	..	80.9	171.2	188.9	116.7	133.0	199.9
Private creditors	..	..	..	..	0.0	0.0	0.0	0.0	0.0	0.0
Memorandum items										
Concessional LDOD	..	..	..	..	16.6	20.7	105.9	201.8	258.7	317.7
Variable rate LDOD	..	..	..	..	113.1	163.8	189.3	228.1	179.0	172.6
Public sector LDOD	..	..	..	..	133.9	188.6	298.3	432.0	511.4	564.0
Private sector LDOD	..	..	..	..	0.0	0.0	0.0	0.0	0.0	0.0
6. CURRENCY COMPOSITION OF LONG-TERM DEBT (PERCENT)										
Deutsche mark	..	..	..	..	0.0	0.0	0.0	0.0	0.0	0.0
French franc	..	..	..	..	0.0	0.0	0.0	0.3	0.5	0.6
Japanese yen	..	..	..	..	0.0	0.0	0.0	0.0	0.0	0.0
Pound sterling	..	..	..	..	0.0	0.0	0.0	0.0	0.0	0.0
Swiss franc	..	..	..	..	0.0	0.0	0.0	0.0	0.0	0.0
U.S.dollars	..	..	..	..	31.9	42.0	62.6	77.4	86.8	87.0
Multiple currency	..	..	..	..	0.4	0.8	1.6	2.3	1.9	1.7
Special drawing rights	..	..	..	..	0.0	0.0	0.0	0.3	0.4	0.7
All other currencies	..	..	..	..	67.7	57.2	35.8	19.7	10.4	10.0

ARMENIA

(US$ million, unless otherwise indicated)

	1970	1980	1990	1992	1993	1994	1995	1996	1997	1998
7. DEBT RESTRUCTURINGS										
Total amount rescheduled	..	..	..	..	45.1	0.0	0.0	34.0	73.7	0.0
Debt stock rescheduled	..	..	..	..	0.0	0.0	0.0	0.0	73.7	0.0
Principal rescheduled	..	..	..	..	30.8	0.0	0.0	0.0	0.0	0.0
Official	..	..	..	..	0.0	0.0	0.0	0.0	0.0	0.0
Private	..	..	..	..	30.8	0.0	0.0	0.0	0.0	0.0
Interest rescheduled	..	..	..	..	0.0	0.0	0.0	0.0	0.0	0.0
Official	..	..	..	..	0.0	0.0	0.0	0.0	0.0	0.0
Private	..	..	..	..	0.0	0.0	0.0	0.0	0.0	0.0
Debt forgiven	..	..	..	..	0.0	0.0	0.0	0.0	0.0	0.0
Memo: interest forgiven	..	..	..	..	0.0	0.0	0.0	0.0	0.0	0.0
Debt stock reduction	..	..	..	..	0.0	0.0	0.0	0.0	0.0	0.0
of which debt buyback	..	..	..	..	0.0	0.0	0.0	0.0	0.0	0.0
8. DEBT STOCK-FLOW RECONCILIATION										
Total change in debt stocks	..	..	..	..	93.0	80.4	156.3	179.2	115.6	134.2
Net flows on debt	..	..	..	..	79.6	84.7	146.6	158.0	141.9	113.6
Net change in interest arrears	..	..	..	..	0.0	1.1	0.1	-1.1	0.0	0.0
Interest capitalized	..	..	..	..	0.0	0.0	0.0	0.0	0.0	0.0
Debt forgiveness or reduction	..	..	..	..	0.0	0.0	0.0	0.0	0.0	0.0
Cross-currency valuation	..	..	..	..	-26.9	-17.2	-1.8	-9.1	-7.6	4.1
Residual	..	..	..	..	40.4	11.8	11.4	31.4	-18.8	16.5
9. AVERAGE TERMS OF NEW COMMITMENTS										
ALL CREDITORS										
Interest (%)	..	..	..	..	4.4	3.2	1.4	1.8	1.8	0.7
Maturity (years)	..	..	..	..	10.9	20.7	32.6	33.7	28.8	34.6
Grace period (years)	..	..	..	..	3.4	6.0	9.2	9.1	8.3	10.1
Grant element (%)	..	..	..	..	23.8	46.7	71.7	68.6	64.8	78.6
Official creditors										
Interest (%)	..	..	..	..	4.4	3.2	1.4	1.8	1.8	0.7
Maturity (years)	..	..	..	..	10.9	20.7	32.6	33.7	28.8	34.6
Grace period (years)	..	..	..	..	3.4	6.0	9.2	9.1	8.3	10.1
Grant element (%)	..	..	..	..	23.8	46.7	71.7	68.6	64.8	78.6
Private creditors										
Interest (%)	..	..	..	..	0.0	0.0	0.0	0.0	0.0	0.0
Maturity (years)	..	..	..	..	0.0	0.0	0.0	0.0	0.0	0.0
Grace period (years)	..	..	..	..	0.0	0.0	0.0	0.0	0.0	0.0
Grant element (%)	..	..	..	..	0.0	0.0	0.0	0.0	0.0	0.0
Memorandum items										
Commitments	..	..	..	..	124.0	172.8	131.1	78.8	132.3	124.5
Official creditors	..	..	..	..	124.0	172.8	131.1	78.8	132.3	124.5
Private creditors	..	..	..	..	0.0	0.0	0.0	0.0	0.0	0.0

10. CONTRACTUAL OBLIGATIONS ON OUTSTANDING LONG-TERM DEBT

	1999	2000	2001	2002	2003	2004	2005	2006	2007	2008
TOTAL										
Disbursements	62.2	54.8	39.0	24.8	13.6	3.5	1.9	0.0	0.0	0.0
Principal	22.4	30.0	32.5	20.3	20.9	21.6	23.8	27.4	21.7	13.3
Interest	14.2	13.7	12.5	11.2	10.2	9.1	8.0	6.8	5.5	4.9
Official creditors										
Disbursements	62.2	54.8	39.0	24.8	13.6	3.5	1.9	0.0	0.0	0.0
Principal	22.4	30.0	32.5	20.3	20.9	21.6	23.8	27.4	21.7	13.3
Interest	14.2	13.7	12.5	11.2	10.2	9.1	8.0	6.8	5.5	4.9
Bilateral creditors										
Disbursements	5.4	3.6	2.2	1.3	0.6	0.1	0.1	0.0	0.0	0.0
Principal	12.8	20.4	22.9	10.7	11.4	11.4	11.4	11.5	6.4	1.3
Interest	6.4	5.9	4.9	4.0	3.5	3.0	2.5	1.9	1.3	1.1
Multilateral creditors										
Disbursements	56.8	51.3	36.8	23.5	13.0	3.4	1.8	0.0	0.0	0.0
Principal	9.6	9.6	9.6	9.6	9.6	10.3	12.5	15.9	15.3	12.0
Interest	7.8	7.8	7.6	7.2	6.7	6.1	5.5	4.9	4.2	3.7
Private creditors										
Disbursements	0.0	0.0	0.0	0.0	0.0	0.0	0.0	0.0	0.0	0.0
Principal	0.0	0.0	0.0	0.0	0.0	0.0	0.0	0.0	0.0	0.0
Interest	0.0	0.0	0.0	0.0	0.0	0.0	0.0	0.0	0.0	0.0
Commercial banks										
Disbursements	0.0	0.0	0.0	0.0	0.0	0.0	0.0	0.0	0.0	0.0
Principal	0.0	0.0	0.0	0.0	0.0	0.0	0.0	0.0	0.0	0.0
Interest	0.0	0.0	0.0	0.0	0.0	0.0	0.0	0.0	0.0	0.0
Other private										
Disbursements	0.0	0.0	0.0	0.0	0.0	0.0	0.0	0.0	0.0	0.0
Principal	0.0	0.0	0.0	0.0	0.0	0.0	0.0	0.0	0.0	0.0
Interest	0.0	0.0	0.0	0.0	0.0	0.0	0.0	0.0	0.0	0.0

AZERBAIJAN

(US$ million, unless otherwise indicated)

	1970	1980	1990	1992	1993	1994	1995	1996	1997	1998
1. SUMMARY DEBT DATA										
TOTAL DEBT STOCKS (EDT)	..	..	..	..	**35.5**	**112.8**	**321.0**	**438.3**	**506.7**	**693.4**
Long-term debt (LDOD)	..	..	..	..	**35.5**	**103.2**	**206.1**	**247.9**	**235.9**	**370.7**
Public and publicly guaranteed	..	..	..	..	35.5	103.2	206.1	247.9	235.9	307.7
Private nonguaranteed	..	..	..	..	0.0	0.0	0.0	0.0	0.0	63.0
Use of IMF credit	..	..	..	..	**0.0**	**0.0**	**100.9**	**175.0**	**266.8**	**321.2**
Short-term debt	..	..	..	..	**0.0**	**9.6**	**14.0**	**15.5**	**4.0**	**1.5**
of which interest arrears on LDOD	..	..	..	..	0.0	3.6	6.0	2.5	0.0	0.0
Official creditors	..	..	..	..	0.0	3.6	6.0	2.5	0.0	0.0
Private creditors	..	..	..	..	0.0	0.0	0.0	0.0	0.0	0.0
Memo: principal arrears on LDOD	..	..	..	..	0.0	20.3	35.5	35.5	0.0	24.8
Official creditors	..	..	..	..	0.0	20.3	35.5	35.5	0.0	24.8
Private creditors	..	..	..	..	0.0	0.0	0.0	0.0	0.0	0.0
Memo: export credits	..	..	..	..	0.0	0.0	0.0	0.0	18.0	73.0
TOTAL DEBT FLOWS										
Disbursements	..	..	..	..	**0.0**	**67.4**	**205.0**	**124.7**	**196.0**	**170.1**
Long-term debt	..	..	..	..	0.0	67.4	102.1	46.6	91.3	128.9
IMF purchases	..	..	..	..	0.0	0.0	103.0	78.1	104.7	41.3
Principal repayments	..	..	..	..	**0.0**	**0.0**	**0.0**	**0.0**	**57.6**	**2.7**
Long-term debt	..	..	..	..	0.0	0.0	0.0	0.0	57.6	2.7
IMF repurchases	..	..	..	..	0.0	0.0	0.0	0.0	0.0	0.0
Net flows on debt	..	..	..	..	**0.0**	**73.4**	**207.0**	**129.7**	**129.4**	**164.9**
of which short-term debt	..	..	..	..	0.0	6.0	2.0	5.0	-9.0	-2.5
Interest payments (INT)	..	..	..	..	**0.0**	**0.3**	**10.1**	**9.8**	**20.3**	**21.2**
Long-term debt	..	..	..	..	0.0	0.0	8.7	4.3	11.6	11.2
IMF charges	..	..	..	..	0.0	0.0	1.1	4.9	8.1	9.8
Short-term debt	..	..	..	..	0.0	0.3	0.3	0.6	0.5	0.1
Net transfers on debt	..	..	..	..	**0.0**	**73.1**	**196.9**	**119.8**	**109.1**	**143.8**
Total debt service paid (TDS)	..	..	..	..	**0.0**	**0.3**	**10.1**	**9.8**	**77.9**	**23.8**
Long-term debt	..	..	..	..	0.0	0.0	8.7	4.3	69.3	13.9
IMF repurchases and charges	..	..	..	..	0.0	0.0	1.1	4.9	8.1	9.8
Short-term debt (interest only)	..	..	..	..	0.0	0.3	0.3	0.6	0.5	0.1
2. AGGREGATE NET RESOURCE FLOWS AND NET TRANSFERS (LONG-TERM)										
NET RESOURCE FLOWS	..	..	..	..	**12.6**	**233.5**	**490.2**	**716.1**	**1,177.5**	**1,178.2**
Net flow of long-term debt (ex. IMF)	..	..	..	..	0.0	67.4	102.1	46.6	33.7	126.2
Foreign direct investment (net)	..	..	..	..	0.0	22.0	330.0	627.0	1,115.0	1,023.0
Portfolio equity flows	..	..	..	..	0.0	0.0	0.0	0.0	0.0	0.0
Grants (excluding technical coop.)	..	..	..	..	12.6	144.1	58.1	42.5	28.7	29.0
Memo: technical coop. grants	..	..	..	..	9.3	3.3	20.8	17.9	15.3	25.4
official net resource flows	..	..	..	..	12.6	211.5	160.2	89.1	54.4	97.4
private net resource flows	..	..	..	..	0.0	22.0	330.0	627.0	1,123.1	1,080.8
NET TRANSFERS	..	..	..	..	**12.6**	**233.5**	**481.5**	**711.8**	**1,165.9**	**1,167.0**
Interest on long-term debt	..	..	..	..	0.0	0.0	8.7	4.3	11.6	11.2
Profit remittances on FDI	..	..	..	..	0.0	0.0	0.0	0.0	0.0	0.0
Memo: official net transfers	..	..	..	..	12.6	211.5	151.5	84.8	42.8	89.6
private net transfers	..	..	..	..	0.0	22.0	330.0	627.0	1,123.1	1,077.4
3. MAJOR ECONOMIC AGGREGATES										
Gross national product (GNP)	..	..	..	..	4,640.0	3,287.8	2,887.1	3,164.4	3,750.9	3,912.9
Exports of goods & services (XGS)	..	..	..	..	697.0	822.0	794.0	805.7	1,172.9	1,047.8
of which workers remittances	..	..	..	..	..	0.0	0.0	0.0	0.0	0.0
Imports of goods & services (MGS)	..	..	..	..	887.0	1,018.1	1,305.4	1,803.3	2,133.4	2,476.3
International reserves (RES)	..	..	..	..	0.6	2.0	120.9	211.3	466.1	447.3
Current account balance	..	..	..	..	-160.0	-121.0	-400.7	-931.2	-915.7	-1,364.5
4. DEBT INDICATORS										
EDT / XGS (%)	..	..	..	..	5.1	13.7	40.4	54.4	43.2	66.2
EDT / GNP (%)	..	..	..	..	0.8	3.4	11.1	13.9	13.5	17.7
TDS / XGS (%)	..	..	..	..	0.0	0.0	1.3	1.2	6.6	2.3
INT / XGS (%)	..	..	..	..	0.0	0.0	1.3	1.2	1.7	2.0
INT / GNP (%)	..	..	..	..	0.0	0.0	0.4	0.3	0.5	0.5
RES / EDT (%)	..	..	..	..	1.7	1.8	37.7	48.2	92.0	64.5
RES / MGS (months)	..	..	..	..	0.0	0.0	1.1	1.4	2.6	2.2
Short-term / EDT (%)	..	..	..	..	0.0	8.5	4.4	3.5	0.8	0.2
Concessional / EDT (%)	..	..	..	..	0.0	52.6	31.8	31.7	37.8	33.6
Multilateral / EDT (%)	..	..	..	..	0.0	7.5	30.8	31.4	30.0	28.8

AZERBAIJAN

(US$ million, unless otherwise indicated)

	1970	1980	1990	1992	1993	1994	1995	1996	1997	1998
5. LONG-TERM DEBT										
DEBT OUTSTANDING (LDOD)	..	..	..	..	**35.5**	**103.2**	**206.1**	**247.9**	**235.9**	**370.7**
Public and publicly guaranteed	..	..	..	..	**35.5**	**103.2**	**206.1**	**247.9**	**235.9**	**307.7**
Official creditors	..	..	..	..	35.5	103.2	206.1	247.9	227.8	302.3
Multilateral	..	..	..	..	0.0	8.4	98.8	137.5	151.9	199.4
Concessional	..	..	..	..	0.0	0.0	30.2	64.3	115.5	144.9
Bilateral	..	..	..	..	35.5	94.8	107.3	110.3	75.9	102.8
Concessional	..	..	..	..	0.0	59.3	71.8	74.8	75.9	88.3
Private creditors	..	..	..	..	0.0	0.0	0.0	0.0	8.1	5.4
Bonds	..	..	..	..	0.0	0.0	0.0	0.0	0.0	0.0
Commercial banks	..	..	..	..	0.0	0.0	0.0	0.0	0.0	0.0
Other private	..	..	..	..	0.0	0.0	0.0	0.0	8.1	5.4
Private nonguaranteed	..	..	..	..	**0.0**	**0.0**	**0.0**	**0.0**	**0.0**	**63.0**
Bonds	..	..	..	..	0.0	0.0	0.0	0.0	0.0	0.0
Commercial banks	..	..	..	..	0.0	0.0	0.0	0.0	0.0	63.0
Memo:										
IBRD	..	..	..	..	0.0	0.0	0.0	0.0	0.0	0.0
IDA	..	..	..	..	0.0	0.0	30.2	64.3	115.5	141.3
DISBURSEMENTS	..	..	..	..	**0.0**	**67.4**	**102.1**	**46.6**	**91.3**	**128.9**
Public and publicly guaranteed	..	..	..	..	**0.0**	**67.4**	**102.1**	**46.6**	**91.3**	**68.4**
Official creditors	..	..	..	..	0.0	67.4	102.1	46.6	83.3	68.4
Multilateral	..	..	..	..	0.0	8.2	89.5	43.5	82.1	42.3
Concessional	..	..	..	..	0.0	0.0	30.2	35.8	55.4	24.1
Bilateral	..	..	..	..	0.0	59.3	12.5	3.0	1.2	26.1
Concessional	..	..	..	..	0.0	59.3	12.5	3.0	1.2	11.6
Private creditors	..	..	..	..	0.0	0.0	0.0	0.0	8.1	0.0
Bonds	..	..	..	..	0.0	0.0	0.0	0.0	0.0	0.0
Commercial banks	..	..	..	..	0.0	0.0	0.0	0.0	0.0	0.0
Other private	..	..	..	..	0.0	0.0	0.0	0.0	8.1	0.0
Private nonguaranteed	..	..	..	..	**0.0**	**0.0**	**0.0**	**0.0**	**0.0**	**60.5**
Bonds	..	..	..	..	0.0	0.0	0.0	0.0	0.0	0.0
Commercial banks	..	..	..	..	0.0	0.0	0.0	0.0	0.0	60.5
Memo:										
IBRD	..	..	..	..	0.0	0.0	0.0	0.0	0.0	0.0
IDA	..	..	..	..	0.0	0.0	30.2	35.8	55.4	20.6
PRINCIPAL REPAYMENTS	..	..	..	..	**0.0**	**0.0**	**0.0**	**0.0**	**57.6**	**2.7**
Public and publicly guaranteed	..	..	..	..	**0.0**	**0.0**	**0.0**	**0.0**	**57.6**	**2.7**
Official creditors	..	..	..	..	0.0	0.0	0.0	0.0	57.6	0.0
Multilateral	..	..	..	..	0.0	0.0	0.0	0.0	57.6	0.0
Concessional	..	..	..	..	0.0	0.0	0.0	0.0	0.0	0.0
Bilateral	..	..	..	..	0.0	0.0	0.0	0.0	0.0	0.0
Concessional	..	..	..	..	0.0	0.0	0.0	0.0	0.0	0.0
Private creditors	..	..	..	..	0.0	0.0	0.0	0.0	0.0	2.7
Bonds	..	..	..	..	0.0	0.0	0.0	0.0	0.0	0.0
Commercial banks	..	..	..	..	0.0	0.0	0.0	0.0	0.0	0.0
Other private	..	..	..	..	0.0	0.0	0.0	0.0	0.0	2.7
Private nonguaranteed	..	..	..	..	**0.0**	**0.0**	**0.0**	**0.0**	**0.0**	**0.0**
Bonds	..	..	..	..	0.0	0.0	0.0	0.0	0.0	0.0
Commercial banks	..	..	..	..	0.0	0.0	0.0	0.0	0.0	0.0
Memo:										
IBRD	..	..	..	..	0.0	0.0	0.0	0.0	0.0	0.0
IDA	..	..	..	..	0.0	0.0	0.0	0.0	0.0	0.0
NET FLOWS ON DEBT	..	..	..	..	**0.0**	**67.4**	**102.1**	**46.6**	**33.7**	**126.2**
Public and publicly guaranteed	..	..	..	..	**0.0**	**67.4**	**102.1**	**46.6**	**33.7**	**65.7**
Official creditors	..	..	..	..	0.0	67.4	102.1	46.6	25.7	68.4
Multilateral	..	..	..	..	0.0	8.2	89.5	43.5	24.5	42.3
Concessional	..	..	..	..	0.0	0.0	30.2	35.8	55.4	24.1
Bilateral	..	..	..	..	0.0	59.3	12.5	3.0	1.2	26.1
Concessional	..	..	..	..	0.0	59.3	12.5	3.0	1.2	11.6
Private creditors	..	..	..	..	0.0	0.0	0.0	0.0	8.1	-2.7
Bonds	..	..	..	..	0.0	0.0	0.0	0.0	0.0	0.0
Commercial banks	..	..	..	..	0.0	0.0	0.0	0.0	0.0	0.0
Other private	..	..	..	..	0.0	0.0	0.0	0.0	8.1	-2.7
Private nonguaranteed	..	..	..	..	**0.0**	**0.0**	**0.0**	**0.0**	**0.0**	**60.5**
Bonds	..	..	..	..	0.0	0.0	0.0	0.0	0.0	0.0
Commercial banks	..	..	..	..	0.0	0.0	0.0	0.0	0.0	60.5
Memo:										
IBRD	..	..	..	..	0.0	0.0	0.0	0.0	0.0	0.0
IDA	..	..	..	..	0.0	0.0	30.2	35.8	55.4	20.6

AZERBAIJAN

(US$ million, unless otherwise indicated)

	1970	1980	1990	1992	1993	1994	1995	1996	1997	1998
INTEREST PAYMENTS (LINT)	..	..	..	..	**0.0**	**0.0**	**8.7**	**4.3**	**11.6**	**11.2**
Public and publicly guaranteed	..	..	..	..	**0.0**	**0.0**	**8.7**	**4.3**	**11.6**	**8.8**
Official creditors	..	..	..	..	0.0	0.0	8.7	4.3	11.6	7.8
Multilateral	..	..	..	..	0.0	0.0	1.9	0.3	2.0	1.5
Concessional	..	..	..	..	0.0	0.0	0.0	0.3	0.5	0.9
Bilateral	..	..	..	..	0.0	0.0	6.8	4.0	9.7	6.3
Concessional	..	..	..	..	0.0	0.0	6.8	4.0	9.7	6.2
Private creditors	..	..	..	..	0.0	0.0	0.0	0.0	0.0	1.0
Bonds	..	..	..	..	0.0	0.0	0.0	0.0	0.0	0.0
Commercial banks	..	..	..	..	0.0	0.0	0.0	0.0	0.0	0.0
Other private	..	..	..	..	0.0	0.0	0.0	0.0	0.0	1.0
Private nonguaranteed	..	..	..	..	**0.0**	**0.0**	**0.0**	**0.0**	**0.0**	**2.4**
Bonds	..	..	..	..	0.0	0.0	0.0	0.0	0.0	0.0
Commercial banks	..	..	..	..	0.0	0.0	0.0	0.0	0.0	2.4
Memo:										
IBRD	..	..	..	..	0.0	0.0	0.0	0.0	0.0	0.0
IDA	..	..	..	..	0.0	0.0	0.0	0.3	0.5	0.9
NET TRANSFERS ON DEBT	..	..	..	..	**0.0**	**67.4**	**93.4**	**42.2**	**22.1**	**115.0**
Public and publicly guaranteed	..	..	..	..	**0.0**	**67.4**	**93.4**	**42.2**	**22.1**	**56.9**
Official creditors	..	..	..	..	0.0	67.4	93.4	42.2	14.0	60.6
Multilateral	..	..	..	..	0.0	8.2	87.6	43.2	22.5	40.8
Concessional	..	..	..	..	0.0	0.0	30.2	35.5	54.9	23.2
Bilateral	..	..	..	..	0.0	59.3	5.7	-1.0	-8.5	19.8
Concessional	..	..	..	..	0.0	59.3	5.7	-1.0	-8.5	5.4
Private creditors	..	..	..	..	0.0	0.0	0.0	0.0	8.1	-3.7
Bonds	..	..	..	..	0.0	0.0	0.0	0.0	0.0	0.0
Commercial banks	..	..	..	..	0.0	0.0	0.0	0.0	0.0	0.0
Other private	..	..	..	..	0.0	0.0	0.0	0.0	8.1	-3.7
Private nonguaranteed	..	..	..	..	**0.0**	**0.0**	**0.0**	**0.0**	**0.0**	**58.1**
Bonds	..	..	..	..	0.0	0.0	0.0	0.0	0.0	0.0
Commercial banks	..	..	..	..	0.0	0.0	0.0	0.0	0.0	58.1
Memo:										
IBRD	..	..	..	..	0.0	0.0	0.0	0.0	0.0	0.0
IDA	..	..	..	..	0.0	0.0	30.2	35.5	54.9	19.7
DEBT SERVICE (LTDS)	..	..	..	..	**0.0**	**0.0**	**8.7**	**4.3**	**69.3**	**13.9**
Public and publicly guaranteed	..	..	..	..	**0.0**	**0.0**	**8.7**	**4.3**	**69.3**	**11.5**
Official creditors	..	..	..	..	0.0	0.0	8.7	4.3	69.3	7.8
Multilateral	..	..	..	..	0.0	0.0	1.9	0.3	59.6	1.5
Concessional	..	..	..	..	0.0	0.0	0.0	0.3	0.5	0.9
Bilateral	..	..	..	..	0.0	0.0	6.8	4.0	9.7	6.3
Concessional	..	..	..	..	0.0	0.0	6.8	4.0	9.7	6.2
Private creditors	..	..	..	..	0.0	0.0	0.0	0.0	0.0	3.7
Bonds	..	..	..	..	0.0	0.0	0.0	0.0	0.0	0.0
Commercial banks	..	..	..	..	0.0	0.0	0.0	0.0	0.0	0.0
Other private	..	..	..	..	0.0	0.0	0.0	0.0	0.0	3.7
Private nonguaranteed	..	..	..	..	**0.0**	**0.0**	**0.0**	**0.0**	**0.0**	**2.4**
Bonds	..	..	..	..	0.0	0.0	0.0	0.0	0.0	0.0
Commercial banks	..	..	..	..	0.0	0.0	0.0	0.0	0.0	2.4
Memo:										
IBRD	..	..	..	..	0.0	0.0	0.0	0.0	0.0	0.0
IDA	..	..	..	..	0.0	0.0	0.0	0.3	0.5	0.9
UNDISBURSED DEBT	..	..	..	..	**250.0**	**329.4**	**413.3**	**226.8**	**295.2**	**578.1**
Official creditors	..	..	..	..	250.0	329.4	413.3	226.8	279.1	477.0
Private creditors	..	..	..	..	0.0	0.0	0.0	0.0	16.1	101.0
Memorandum items										
Concessional LDOD	..	..	..	..	0.0	59.3	102.0	139.1	191.5	233.2
Variable rate LDOD	..	..	..	..	35.5	103.2	175.9	183.6	119.2	212.3
Public sector LDOD	..	..	..	..	35.5	103.2	206.1	247.9	235.9	313.1
Private sector LDOD	..	..	..	..	0.0	0.0	0.0	0.0	0.0	63.0

6. CURRENCY COMPOSITION OF LONG-TERM DEBT (PERCENT)

	1970	1980	1990	1992	1993	1994	1995	1996	1997	1998
Deutsche mark	..	..	..	..	0.0	0.0	0.0	0.0	0.5	3.6
French franc	..	..	..	..	0.0	0.0	0.0	0.0	0.0	0.0
Japanese yen	..	..	..	..	0.0	0.0	0.0	0.0	0.0	2.5
Pound sterling	..	..	..	..	0.0	0.0	0.0	0.0	0.0	0.0
Swiss franc	..	..	..	..	0.0	0.0	0.0	0.0	0.0	0.0
U.S.dollars	..	..	..	..	0.0	57.5	51.4	60.0	99.5	94.5
Multiple currency	..	..	..	..	0.0	0.0	0.0	0.0	0.0	0.0
Special drawing rights	..	..	..	..	0.0	0.0	0.0	0.0	0.0	0.0
All other currencies	..	..	..	..	0.0	42.5	48.6	40.0	0.0	0.0

AZERBAIJAN

(US$ million, unless otherwise indicated)

	1970	1980	1990	1992	1993	1994	1995	1996	1997	1998
7. DEBT RESTRUCTURINGS										
Total amount rescheduled	..	..	..	..	35.5	0.0	0.0	0.0	0.0	0.0
Debt stock rescheduled	..	..	..	..	0.0	0.0	0.0	0.0	0.0	0.0
Principal rescheduled	..	..	..	..	0.0	0.0	0.0	0.0	0.0	0.0
Official	..	..	..	..	0.0	0.0	0.0	0.0	0.0	0.0
Private	..	..	..	..	0.0	0.0	0.0	0.0	0.0	0.0
Interest rescheduled	..	..	..	..	..	0.0	0.0	0.0	0.0	0.0
Official	..	..	..	..	0.0	0.0	0.0	0.0	0.0	0.0
Private	..	..	..	..	0.0	0.0	0.0	0.0	0.0	0.0
Debt forgiven	..	..	..	..	0.0	0.0	0.0	0.0	35.5	0.0
Memo: interest forgiven	..	..	..	..	0.0	0.0	0.0	0.0	2.5	0.0
Debt stock reduction	..	..	..	..	0.0	0.0	0.0	0.0	0.0	0.0
of which debt buyback	..	..	..	..	0.0	0.0	0.0	0.0	0.0	0.0
8. DEBT STOCK-FLOW RECONCILIATION										
Total change in debt stocks	..	..	..	..	..	77.3	208.2	117.3	68.3	186.7
Net flows on debt	..	..	..	..	0.0	73.4	207.0	129.7	129.4	164.9
Net change in interest arrears	..	..	..	..	..	3.6	2.4	-3.6	-2.5	0.0
Interest capitalized	..	..	..	..	..	0.0	0.0	0.0	0.0	0.0
Debt forgiveness or reduction	..	..	..	..	..	0.0	0.0	0.0	-35.5	0.0
Cross-currency valuation	..	..	..	..	..	-22.2	-3.3	-11.4	-0.1	1.9
Residual	..	..	..	..	..	22.4	2.0	2.6	-22.9	19.9
9. AVERAGE TERMS OF NEW COMMITMENTS										
ALL CREDITORS										
Interest (%)	..	..	..	..	3.1	6.3	1.4	2.4	3.5	2.9
Maturity (years)	..	..	..	..	7.7	9.4	32.2	27.9	22.3	29.0
Grace period (years)	..	..	..	..	5.2	3.7	9.4	7.8	6.6	7.8
Grant element (%)	..	..	..	..	31.1	15.3	71.8	59.5	47.9	58.3
Official creditors										
Interest (%)	..	..	..	..	3.1	6.3	1.4	2.4	3.0	1.1
Maturity (years)	..	..	..	..	7.7	9.4	32.2	27.9	24.9	37.0
Grace period (years)	..	..	..	..	5.2	3.7	9.4	7.8	7.4	9.5
Grant element (%)	..	..	..	..	31.1	15.3	71.8	59.5	54.0	76.4
Private creditors										
Interest (%)	..	..	..	..	0.0	0.0	0.0	0.0	7.3	8.5
Maturity (years)	..	..	..	..	0.0	0.0	0.0	0.0	4.8	4.9
Grace period (years)	..	..	..	..	0.0	0.0	0.0	0.0	1.4	2.4
Grant element (%)	..	..	..	..	0.0	0.0	0.0	0.0	6.3	3.6
Memorandum items										
Commitments	..	..	..	..	250.0	144.1	187.8	40.5	189.3	316.9
Official creditors	..	..	..	..	250.0	144.1	187.8	40.5	165.1	237.9
Private creditors	..	..	..	..	0.0	0.0	0.0	0.0	24.2	79.0

10. CONTRACTUAL OBLIGATIONS ON OUTSTANDING LONG-TERM DEBT

	1999	2000	2001	2002	2003	2004	2005	2006	2007	2008
TOTAL										
Disbursements	180.6	178.9	107.0	60.4	28.8	14.4	7.2	0.6	0.2	0.0
Principal	59.8	57.7	69.0	68.2	46.9	20.1	14.2	16.1	18.0	25.9
Interest	13.3	12.2	16.0	15.2	11.6	8.5	7.5	6.8	6.2	5.6
Official creditors										
Disbursements	136.0	144.2	92.2	54.4	28.0	14.4	7.2	0.6	0.2	0.0
Principal	33.7	37.0	24.7	26.2	15.4	15.4	14.2	16.1	18.0	25.9
Interest	10.8	10.5	9.8	10.0	9.1	8.3	7.5	6.8	6.2	5.6
Bilateral creditors										
Disbursements	50.3	67.3	44.9	29.4	16.7	8.3	4.3	0.4	0.0	0.0
Principal	26.8	28.6	4.8	4.8	4.8	4.8	1.1	1.1	1.3	7.8
Interest	4.9	3.6	2.3	2.3	2.1	1.9	1.7	1.7	1.7	1.8
Multilateral creditors										
Disbursements	85.7	76.9	47.3	25.0	11.3	6.1	2.9	0.2	0.2	0.0
Principal	6.9	8.4	19.9	21.4	10.6	10.6	13.1	15.0	16.7	18.1
Interest	5.9	6.8	7.4	7.7	7.0	6.4	5.8	5.2	4.5	3.8
Private creditors										
Disbursements	44.6	34.7	14.8	6.1	0.8	0.0	0.0	0.0	0.0	0.0
Principal	26.1	20.7	44.4	42.0	31.5	4.7	0.0	0.0	0.0	0.0
Interest	2.5	1.7	6.2	5.2	2.5	0.2	0.0	0.0	0.0	0.0
Commercial banks										
Disbursements	27.4	18.8	7.4	3.4	0.0	0.0	0.0	0.0	0.0	0.0
Principal	0.0	0.0	19.0	19.0	19.0	0.0	0.0	0.0	0.0	0.0
Interest	0.0	0.0	4.0	2.7	1.2	0.0	0.0	0.0	0.0	0.0
Other private										
Disbursements	17.2	15.9	7.4	2.6	0.8	0.0	0.0	0.0	0.0	0.0
Principal	26.1	20.7	25.4	23.0	12.5	4.7	0.0	0.0	0.0	0.0
Interest	2.5	1.7	2.2	2.5	1.3	0.2	0.0	0.0	0.0	0.0

BANGLADESH

(US$ million, unless otherwise indicated)

	1970	1980	1990	1992	1993	1994	1995	1996	1997	1998
1. SUMMARY DEBT DATA										
TOTAL DEBT STOCKS (EDT)	..	**4,230**	**12,769**	**13,928**	**14,650**	**16,258**	**16,325**	**16,007**	**15,125**	**16,376**
Long-term debt (LDOD)	..	**3,594**	**11,987**	**12,963**	**13,815**	**15,392**	**15,501**	**15,327**	**14,578**	**15,804**
Public and publicly guaranteed	..	3,594	11,987	12,963	13,815	15,392	15,501	15,327	14,578	15,804
Private nonguaranteed	..	0	0	0	0	0	0	0	0	0
Use of IMF credit	..	**424**	**626**	**732**	**682**	**669**	**622**	**517**	**372**	**422**
Short-term debt	..	**212**	**156**	**233**	**153**	**197**	**203**	**163**	**175**	**150**
of which interest arrears on LDOD	..	0	1	3	5	12	19	0	0	0
Official creditors	..	0	1	3	5	12	19	0	0	0
Private creditors	..	0	0	0	0	0	0	0	0	0
Memo: principal arrears on LDOD	..	0	11	15	19	34	30	18	14	15
Official creditors	..	0	11	14	19	30	30	18	14	15
Private creditors	..	0	0	0	0	4	0	0	0	0
Memo: export credits	..	0	329	744	960	913	466	437	430	512
TOTAL DEBT FLOWS										
Disbursements	..	**970**	**1,368**	**1,082**	**707**	**1,017**	**679**	**1,151**	**704**	**870**
Long-term debt	..	743	1,307	959	667	1,017	679	1,151	704	736
IMF purchases	..	227	61	123	40	0	0	0	0	135
Principal repayments	..	**199**	**573**	**402**	**392**	**406**	**623**	**485**	**519**	**503**
Long-term debt	..	65	362	314	301	350	562	400	405	401
IMF repurchases	..	134	211	88	91	56	61	85	114	102
Net flows on debt	..	**872**	**883**	**693**	**233**	**648**	**55**	**645**	**197**	**342**
of which short-term debt	..	102	88	13	-82	37	-1	-21	12	-25
Interest payments (INT)	..	**79**	**218**	**172**	**176**	**198**	**189**	**213**	**186**	**180**
Long-term debt	..	50	167	153	163	187	176	200	175	170
IMF charges	..	13	42	10	6	4	3	3	2	2
Short-term debt	..	16	9	9	7	7	10	10	9	8
Net transfers on debt	..	**794**	**665**	**521**	**57**	**451**	**-134**	**432**	**11**	**162**
Total debt service paid (TDS)	..	**278**	**791**	**574**	**568**	**603**	**812**	**698**	**705**	**683**
Long-term debt	..	115	529	467	465	537	738	600	580	570
IMF repurchases and charges	..	147	253	99	96	60	64	88	116	104
Short-term debt (interest only)	..	16	9	9	7	7	10	10	9	8
2. AGGREGATE NET RESOURCE FLOWS AND NET TRANSFERS (LONG-TERM)										
NET RESOURCE FLOWS	..	**1,679**	**1,720**	**1,458**	**1,029**	**1,486**	**830**	**1,390**	**1,009**	**1,303**
Net flow of long-term debt (ex. IMF)	..	678	945	646	366	668	117	751	299	335
Foreign direct investment (net)	..	0	3	4	14	11	2	14	141	308
Portfolio equity flows	..	0	0	0	0	48	33	30	11	3
Grants (excluding technical coop.)	..	1,001	772	809	650	760	678	595	558	657
Memo: technical coop. grants	..	159	239	309	291	294	292	277	232	203
official net resource flows	..	1,668	1,650	1,442	1,023	1,456	891	1,377	884	1,015
private net resource flows	..	11	70	17	7	30	-60	13	124	288
NET TRANSFERS	..	**1,629**	**1,553**	**1,306**	**866**	**1,298**	**654**	**1,179**	**809**	**1,103**
Interest on long-term debt	..	50	167	153	163	187	176	200	175	170
Profit remittances on FDI	..	0	0	0	0	0	0	12	25	30
Memo: official net transfers	..	1,621	1,495	1,299	870	1,279	723	1,184	715	850
private net transfers	..	9	59	7	-4	19	-69	-6	94	254
3. MAJOR ECONOMIC AGGREGATES										
Gross national product (GNP)	..	17,641	30,487	32,306	33,967	34,532	38,770	41,514	42,408	44,127
Exports of goods & services (XGS)	..	1,174	2,731	3,406	3,944	4,293	5,490	5,907	6,663	7,495
of which workers remittances	..	197	761	848	944	1,089	1,198	1,217	1,475	1,525
Imports of goods & services (MGS)	..	2,622	4,346	4,112	4,685	4,871	6,652	7,802	7,860	8,240
International reserves (RES)	..	331	660	1,853	2,447	3,175	2,376	1,869	1,611	1,936
Current account balance	..	-844	-1,574	-578	-619	-420	-920	-1,636	-931	-253
4. DEBT INDICATORS										
EDT / XGS (%)	..	360.4	467.5	409.0	371.5	378.7	297.4	271.0	227.0	218.5
EDT / GNP (%)	..	24.0	41.9	43.1	43.1	47.1	42.1	38.6	35.7	37.1
TDS / XGS (%)	..	23.7	29.0	16.9	14.4	14.1	14.8	11.8	10.6	9.1
INT / XGS (%)	..	6.7	8.0	5.1	4.5	4.6	3.4	3.6	2.8	2.4
INT / GNP (%)	..	0.4	0.7	0.5	0.5	0.6	0.5	0.5	0.4	0.4
RES / EDT (%)	..	7.8	5.2	13.3	16.7	19.5	14.6	11.7	10.7	11.8
RES / MGS (months)	..	1.5	1.8	5.4	6.3	7.8	4.3	2.9	2.5	2.8
Short-term / EDT (%)	..	5.0	1.2	1.7	1.0	1.2	1.2	1.0	1.2	0.9
Concessional / EDT (%)	..	81.9	90.2	89.8	91.4	92.3	93.3	94.4	95.2	95.6
Multilateral / EDT (%)	..	30.2	51.1	53.8	55.3	57.1	59.8	61.5	63.5	64.7

BANGLADESH

(US$ million, unless otherwise indicated)

	1970	1980	1990	1992	1993	1994	1995	1996	1997	1998
5. LONG-TERM DEBT										
DEBT OUTSTANDING (LDOD)	..	**3,594**	**11,987**	**12,963**	**13,815**	**15,392**	**15,501**	**15,327**	**14,578**	**15,804**
Public and publicly guaranteed	..	**3,594**	**11,987**	**12,963**	**13,815**	**15,392**	**15,501**	**15,327**	**14,578**	**15,804**
Official creditors	..	3,538	11,725	12,657	13,519	15,123	15,328	15,185	14,464	15,713
Multilateral	..	1,276	6,529	7,495	8,097	9,284	9,766	9,844	9,611	10,596
Concessional	..	1,214	6,432	7,434	8,038	9,226	9,710	9,795	9,563	10,547
Bilateral	..	2,263	5,196	5,162	5,422	5,839	5,562	5,341	4,853	5,118
Concessional	..	2,248	5,086	5,074	5,351	5,782	5,521	5,311	4,831	5,104
Private creditors	..	56	262	305	296	269	173	142	114	91
Bonds	..	0	0	0	0	0	0	0	0	0
Commercial banks	..	0	34	29	26	28	32	26	20	17
Other private	..	56	228	277	271	241	142	117	94	74
Private nonguaranteed	..	**0**	**0**	**0**	**0**	**0**	**0**	**0**	**0**	**0**
Bonds	..	0	0	0	0	0	0	0	0	0
Commercial banks	..	0	0	0	0	0	0	0	0	0
Memo:										
IBRD	..	55	64	60	58	58	55	47	38	36
IDA	..	926	4,095	4,534	4,824	5,378	5,638	5,713	5,701	6,168
DISBURSEMENTS	..	**743**	**1,307**	**959**	**667**	**1,017**	**679**	**1,151**	**704**	**736**
Public and publicly guaranteed	..	**743**	**1,307**	**959**	**667**	**1,017**	**679**	**1,151**	**704**	**736**
Official creditors	..	726	1,205	907	632	996	667	1,144	704	736
Multilateral	..	307	849	661	553	816	492	652	522	629
Concessional	..	306	819	661	553	816	492	649	515	628
Bilateral	..	419	356	246	79	181	175	492	182	107
Concessional	..	419	356	244	78	181	175	492	182	107
Private creditors	..	17	102	52	36	21	12	8	0	0
Bonds	..	0	0	0	0	0	0	0	0	0
Commercial banks	..	0	22	0	0	6	6	0	0	0
Other private	..	17	80	52	36	14	6	8	0	0
Private nonguaranteed	..	**0**	**0**	**0**	**0**	**0**	**0**	**0**	**0**	**0**
Bonds	..	0	0	0	0	0	0	0	0	0
Commercial banks	..	0	0	0	0	0	0	0	0	0
Memo:										
IBRD	..	0	0	0	0	0	0	0	0	0
IDA	..	156	484	327	306	412	197	279	299	352
PRINCIPAL REPAYMENTS	..	**65**	**362**	**314**	**301**	**350**	**562**	**400**	**405**	**401**
Public and publicly guaranteed	..	**65**	**362**	**314**	**301**	**350**	**562**	**400**	**405**	**401**
Official creditors	..	59	327	274	258	300	454	362	378	377
Multilateral	..	1	63	72	72	81	105	114	126	135
Concessional	..	1	45	57	68	77	100	109	121	130
Bilateral	..	58	264	202	187	219	349	248	252	242
Concessional	..	54	251	188	172	204	333	237	244	234
Private creditors	..	6	35	40	43	49	108	39	28	23
Bonds	..	0	0	0	0	0	0	0	0	0
Commercial banks	..	0	2	3	3	4	2	6	6	3
Other private	..	6	33	37	40	45	106	33	22	21
Private nonguaranteed	..	**0**	**0**	**0**	**0**	**0**	**0**	**0**	**0**	**0**
Bonds	..	0	0	0	0	0	0	0	0	0
Commercial banks	..	0	0	0	0	0	0	0	0	0
Memo:										
IBRD	..	0	2	3	4	4	5	5	5	4
IDA	..	0	13	20	28	33	41	50	54	62
NET FLOWS ON DEBT	..	**678**	**945**	**646**	**366**	**668**	**117**	**751**	**299**	**335**
Public and publicly guaranteed	..	**678**	**945**	**646**	**366**	**668**	**117**	**751**	**299**	**335**
Official creditors	..	667	878	633	373	696	212	782	326	359
Multilateral	..	306	786	589	481	735	387	538	396	494
Concessional	..	306	774	604	485	739	392	540	394	497
Bilateral	..	361	92	44	-108	-39	-174	244	-70	-136
Concessional	..	365	105	56	-93	-23	-158	255	-62	-128
Private creditors	..	11	67	13	-7	-29	-96	-31	-28	-23
Bonds	..	0	0	0	0	0	0	0	0	0
Commercial banks	..	0	20	-3	-3	2	4	-6	-6	-3
Other private	..	11	47	16	-5	-31	-99	-25	-22	-21
Private nonguaranteed	..	**0**	**0**	**0**	**0**	**0**	**0**	**0**	**0**	**0**
Bonds	..	0	0	0	0	0	0	0	0	0
Commercial banks	..	0	0	0	0	0	0	0	0	0
Memo:										
IBRD	..	0	-2	-3	-4	-4	-5	-5	-5	-4
IDA	..	156	472	307	278	380	155	229	245	290

BANGLADESH

(US$ million, unless otherwise indicated)

	1970	1980	1990	1992	1993	1994	1995	1996	1997	1998
INTEREST PAYMENTS (LINT)	..	**50**	**167**	**153**	**163**	**187**	**176**	**200**	**175**	**170**
Public and publicly guaranteed	..	**50**	**167**	**153**	**163**	**187**	**176**	**200**	**175**	**170**
Official creditors	..	48	155	143	153	176	168	193	169	166
Multilateral	..	11	53	64	71	78	87	86	84	86
Concessional	..	8	48	60	68	75	84	83	82	84
Bilateral	..	37	102	79	82	98	81	107	85	80
Concessional	..	36	92	71	75	91	76	104	83	78
Private creditors	..	2	11	10	10	11	8	7	6	4
Bonds	..	0	0	0	0	0	0	0	0	0
Commercial banks	..	0	1	1	1	1	0	1	0	1
Other private	..	2	11	9	10	10	8	6	5	3
Private nonguaranteed	..	**0**	**0**	**0**	**0**	**0**	**0**	**0**	**0**	**0**
Bonds	..	0	0	0	0	0	0	0	0	0
Commercial banks	..	0	0	0	0	0	0	0	0	0
Memo:										
IBRD	..	3	4	4	4	4	4	3	3	2
IDA	..	6	28	32	36	39	42	42	42	43
NET TRANSFERS ON DEBT	..	**628**	**779**	**493**	**203**	**480**	**-59**	**551**	**124**	**165**
Public and publicly guaranteed	..	**628**	**779**	**493**	**203**	**480**	**-59**	**551**	**124**	**165**
Official creditors	..	620	723	490	220	520	45	589	157	193
Multilateral	..	295	733	525	410	656	300	452	312	408
Concessional	..	298	726	545	417	664	308	457	312	414
Bilateral	..	325	-10	-36	-190	-137	-255	137	-155	-215
Concessional	..	329	13	-14	-168	-114	-234	151	-144	-206
Private creditors	..	8	56	3	-18	-40	-104	-38	-33	-27
Bonds	..	0	0	0	0	0	0	0	0	0
Commercial banks	..	0	20	-4	-3	2	3	-6	-6	-4
Other private	..	8	36	7	-14	-41	-107	-32	-27	-24
Private nonguaranteed	..	**0**	**0**	**0**	**0**	**0**	**0**	**0**	**0**	**0**
Bonds	..	0	0	0	0	0	0	0	0	0
Commercial banks	..	0	0	0	0	0	0	0	0	0
Memo:										
IBRD	..	-3	-5	-7	-7	-7	-8	-8	-7	-7
IDA	..	150	443	275	242	341	114	187	204	247
DEBT SERVICE (LTDS)	..	**115**	**529**	**467**	**465**	**537**	**738**	**600**	**580**	**570**
Public and publicly guaranteed	..	**115**	**529**	**467**	**465**	**537**	**738**	**600**	**580**	**570**
Official creditors	..	107	482	417	411	476	622	554	547	543
Multilateral	..	12	116	136	143	159	192	199	210	221
Concessional	..	8	93	116	136	152	184	192	203	214
Bilateral	..	94	366	282	268	317	430	355	337	322
Concessional	..	90	343	258	246	294	409	341	326	312
Private creditors	..	8	47	49	53	60	116	46	33	27
Bonds	..	0	0	0	0	0	0	0	0	0
Commercial banks	..	0	2	4	3	5	3	6	6	4
Other private	..	8	44	46	50	56	114	39	27	24
Private nonguaranteed	..	**0**	**0**	**0**	**0**	**0**	**0**	**0**	**0**	**0**
Bonds	..	0	0	0	0	0	0	0	0	0
Commercial banks	..	0	0	0	0	0	0	0	0	0
Memo:										
IBRD	..	3	5	7	7	7	8	8	7	7
IDA	..	6	41	52	64	71	83	92	96	105
UNDISBURSED DEBT	..	**2,113**	**4,153**	**4,132**	**4,084**	**4,192**	**4,096**	**2,864**	**2,585**	**3,178**
Official creditors	..	2,059	4,002	4,040	4,022	4,041	3,957	2,733	2,454	3,088
Private creditors	..	54	151	92	62	151	139	131	131	91
Memorandum items										
Concessional LDOD	..	3,462	11,518	12,508	13,389	15,007	15,231	15,105	14,394	15,651
Variable rate LDOD	..	5	34	62	64	60	53	42	31	22
Public sector LDOD	..	3,592	11,984	12,960	13,814	15,391	15,501	15,327	14,578	15,804
Private sector LDOD	..	2	3	2	1	1	0	0	0	0

6. CURRENCY COMPOSITION OF LONG-TERM DEBT (PERCENT)

	1970	1980	1990	1992	1993	1994	1995	1996	1997	1998
Deutsche mark	..	0.2	0.2	0.1	0.1	0.1	0.1	0.1	0.1	0.1
French franc	..	1.2	1.5	1.2	1.0	1.1	0.7	0.9	1.0	1.0
Japanese yen	..	21.6	24.1	25.5	26.1	26.2	25.2	23.5	21.7	21.9
Pound sterling	..	17.4	5.1	4.4	4.1	3.6	3.5	3.4	3.4	3.1
Swiss franc	..	0.2	0.1	0.0	0.0	0.0	0.0	0.2	0.2	0.2
U.S.dollars	..	42.6	48.6	46.4	45.2	43.1	43.0	43.1	44.1	43.5
Multiple currency	..	7.4	15.0	18.0	19.1	20.9	22.3	22.6	22.6	23.3
Special drawing rights	..	0.2	0.9	1.0	1.6	2.6	3.1	3.8	4.5	4.7
All other currencies	..	9.2	4.5	3.4	2.8	2.4	2.1	2.4	2.4	2.2

BANGLADESH

(US$ million, unless otherwise indicated)

	1970	1980	1990	1992	1993	1994	1995	1996	1997	1998
7. DEBT RESTRUCTURINGS										
Total amount rescheduled	..	..	0	0	0	0	0	0	0	0
Debt stock rescheduled	..	..	0	0	0	0	0	0	0	0
Principal rescheduled	..	..	0	0	0	0	0	0	0	0
Official	..	..	0	0	0	0	0	0	0	0
Private	..	..	0	0	0	0	0	0	0	0
Interest rescheduled	..	..	0	0	0	0	0	0	0	0
Official	..	..	0	0	0	0	0	0	0	0
Private	..	..	0	0	0	0	0	0	0	0
Debt forgiven	..	..	0	0	2	2	0	0	0	0
Memo: interest forgiven	..	..	0	0	0	0	0	0	0	0
Debt stock reduction	..	..	0	0	0	0	0	0	0	0
of which debt buyback	..	..	0	0	0	0	0	0	0	0
8. DEBT STOCK-FLOW RECONCILIATION										
Total change in debt stocks	..	..	1,650	445	723	1,608	67	-318	-882	1,250
Net flows on debt	..	872	883	693	233	648	55	645	197	342
Net change in interest arrears	..	..	1	1	2	7	7	-18	0	0
Interest capitalized	..	..	0	0	0	0	0	0	0	0
Debt forgiveness or reduction	..	..	0	0	-2	-2	0	0	0	0
Cross-currency valuation	..	..	367	-130	388	572	-96	-406	-435	490
Residual	..	..	399	-119	102	382	101	-539	-644	418
9. AVERAGE TERMS OF NEW COMMITMENTS										
ALL CREDITORS										
Interest (%)	..	1.7	1.9	1.1	1.1	1.3	1.9	1.1	1.7	1.5
Maturity (years)	..	36.0	33.6	35.9	35.2	33.3	37.8	32.7	37.7	39.5
Grace period (years)	..	9.0	9.3	9.8	9.7	8.9	10.0	8.7	9.9	10.1
Grant element (%)	..	68.6	67.6	74.7	75.0	70.8	69.0	71.7	70.7	73.6
Official creditors										
Interest (%)	..	1.5	1.3	0.9	1.1	1.0	1.9	1.1	1.7	1.5
Maturity (years)	..	36.8	36.3	37.4	35.2	35.1	37.8	32.7	37.7	39.5
Grace period (years)	..	9.2	10.0	10.1	9.8	9.3	10.0	8.7	9.9	10.1
Grant element (%)	..	70.4	73.8	77.6	75.0	74.6	69.0	71.7	70.7	73.6
Private creditors										
Interest (%)	..	7.5	6.7	4.0	0.8	5.0	0.0	0.0	0.0	0.0
Maturity (years)	..	10.7	11.3	13.8	38.4	12.3	0.0	0.0	0.0	0.0
Grace period (years)	..	2.4	3.1	4.3	8.9	4.3	0.0	0.0	0.0	0.0
Grant element (%)	..	11.3	16.5	33.2	79.0	25.9	0.0	0.0	0.0	0.0
Memorandum items										
Commitments	..	1,036	1,447	1,177	717	1,421	687	257	974	1,033
Official creditors	..	1,004	1,290	1,101	712	1,311	687	257	974	1,033
Private creditors	..	32	157	76	6	109	0	0	0	0

10. CONTRACTUAL OBLIGATIONS ON OUTSTANDING LONG-TERM DEBT

	1999	2000	2001	2002	2003	2004	2005	2006	2007	2008
TOTAL										
Disbursements	923	802	576	411	242	118	69	15	3	0
Principal	493	509	515	537	560	591	606	608	625	657
Interest	186	183	179	173	166	158	150	155	151	145
Official creditors										
Disbursements	871	777	568	407	242	118	69	15	3	0
Principal	457	478	495	517	541	573	588	600	624	657
Interest	180	177	174	169	163	156	148	154	151	144
Bilateral creditors										
Disbursements	88	59	35	24	15	7	5	4	2	0
Principal	299	302	298	304	307	314	305	299	292	286
Interest	83	78	73	68	63	58	53	48	43	39
Multilateral creditors										
Disbursements	783	717	533	383	227	111	64	12	1	0
Principal	158	176	197	214	234	259	283	301	332	370
Interest	97	99	101	101	100	98	96	106	108	106
Private creditors										
Disbursements	52	26	9	4	0	0	0	0	0	0
Principal	37	31	20	20	19	19	19	8	1	1
Interest	6	6	5	4	3	2	2	1	0	0
Commercial banks										
Disbursements	0	0	0	0	0	0	0	0	0	0
Principal	2	2	0	1	1	1	1	1	1	1
Interest	1	1	1	1	1	1	1	1	0	0
Other private										
Disbursements	52	26	9	4	0	0	0	0	0	0
Principal	35	29	19	19	18	18	18	7	0	0
Interest	5	5	4	4	3	2	1	0	0	0

BARBADOS

(US$ million, unless otherwise indicated)

	1970	1980	1990	1992	1993	1994	1995	1996	1997	1998
1. SUMMARY DEBT DATA										
TOTAL DEBT STOCKS (EDT)	**..**	**165.7**	**683.0**	**609.6**	**570.6**	**618.0**	**599.5**	**583.5**	**571.9**	**607.8**
Long-term debt (LDOD)	**12.9**	**97.8**	**504.1**	**400.6**	**348.8**	**374.0**	**372.1**	**383.7**	**367.6**	**387.8**
Public and publicly guaranteed	12.9	97.8	504.1	400.6	348.8	374.0	372.1	383.7	367.6	387.8
Private nonguaranteed	0.0	0.0	0.0	0.0	0.0	0.0	0.0	0.0	0.0	0.0
Use of IMF credit	**0.0**	**2.9**	**0.7**	**50.7**	**50.6**	**53.8**	**37.1**	**9.4**	**0.0**	**0.0**
Short-term debt	**..**	**65.0**	**178.1**	**158.4**	**171.3**	**190.3**	**190.3**	**190.4**	**204.3**	**220.0**
of which interest arrears on LDOD	..	0.0	0.2	0.4	0.3	0.3	0.3	0.3	0.3	0.0
Official creditors	..	0.0	0.2	0.4	0.3	0.3	0.3	0.3	0.3	0.0
Private creditors	..	0.0	0.0	0.0	0.0	0.0	0.0	0.0	0.0	0.0
Memo: principal arrears on LDOD	..	0.0	0.7	1.2	1.0	1.3	1.3	1.1	1.1	0.0
Official creditors	..	0.0	0.7	1.2	1.0	1.3	1.3	1.1	1.1	0.0
Private creditors	..	0.0	0.0	0.0	0.0	0.0	0.0	0.0	0.0	0.0
Memo: export credits	..	0.0	99.0	84.0	71.0	89.0	115.0	106.0	61.0	41.0
TOTAL DEBT FLOWS										
Disbursements	**0.0**	**38.4**	**90.6**	**65.5**	**14.4**	**62.9**	**54.6**	**54.2**	**40.1**	**61.1**
Long-term debt	0.0	38.4	90.6	13.6	14.4	62.9	54.6	54.2	40.1	61.1
IMF purchases	0.0	0.0	0.0	51.9	0.0	0.0	0.0	0.0	0.0	0.0
Principal repayments	**0.0**	**14.2**	**92.2**	**58.9**	**71.3**	**46.5**	**76.9**	**61.7**	**53.2**	**46.4**
Long-term debt	0.0	8.7	88.4	58.9	71.3	46.5	58.8	35.0	44.2	46.4
IMF repurchases	0.0	5.5	3.7	0.0	0.0	0.0	18.0	26.7	9.0	0.0
Net flows on debt	**0.0**	**10.2**	**18.8**	**-4.4**	**-43.9**	**35.4**	**-22.2**	**-7.4**	**0.8**	**30.7**
of which short-term debt	..	-14.0	20.4	-11.0	13.0	19.0	0.0	0.1	13.9	16.0
Interest payments (INT)	**..**	**11.1**	**48.6**	**42.6**	**40.8**	**40.7**	**41.4**	**39.4**	**40.3**	**40.3**
Long-term debt	0.8	5.8	39.3	32.2	28.3	27.1	27.2	26.7	30.2	29.7
IMF charges	0.0	0.3	0.4	2.4	3.0	2.7	2.8	1.2	0.2	0.0
Short-term debt	..	5.0	8.9	8.1	9.5	10.9	11.4	11.6	9.9	10.6
Net transfers on debt	**..**	**-0.9**	**-29.8**	**-47.0**	**-84.8**	**-5.3**	**-63.7**	**-46.8**	**-39.5**	**-9.6**
Total debt service paid (TDS)	**..**	**25.2**	**140.7**	**101.6**	**112.2**	**87.2**	**118.3**	**101.2**	**93.5**	**86.7**
Long-term debt	0.8	14.5	127.7	91.1	99.7	73.6	86.0	61.7	74.5	76.1
IMF repurchases and charges	0.0	5.8	4.1	2.4	3.0	2.7	20.9	27.9	9.1	0.0
Short-term debt (interest only)	..	5.0	8.9	8.1	9.5	10.9	11.4	11.6	9.9	10.6
2. AGGREGATE NET RESOURCE FLOWS AND NET TRANSFERS (LONG-TERM)										
NET RESOURCE FLOWS	**9.4**	**33.2**	**14.4**	**-31.5**	**-28.3**	**31.5**	**9.0**	**274.6**	**109.0**	**34.0**
Net flow of long-term debt (ex. IMF)	0.0	29.7	2.1	-45.3	-56.9	16.4	-4.2	19.3	-4.1	14.7
Foreign direct investment (net)	8.7	2.8	11.0	14.0	9.0	12.9	12.0	13.0	14.0	15.0
Portfolio equity flows	0.0	0.0	0.0	0.0	0.0	0.0	0.0	240.0	96.0	0.0
Grants (excluding technical coop.)	0.7	0.7	1.3	-0.2	19.6	2.2	1.2	2.3	3.1	4.3
Memo: technical coop. grants	0.8	2.7	2.4	3.0	2.3	2.1	1.9	1.8	1.8	1.3
official net resource flows	0.7	14.4	17.4	-8.2	8.9	-8.6	-5.6	35.8	23.2	42.1
private net resource flows	8.7	18.8	-3.0	-23.3	-37.2	40.1	14.6	238.8	85.8	-8.1
NET TRANSFERS	**4.4**	**22.6**	**-34.0**	**-72.7**	**-64.7**	**4.4**	**-22.3**	**243.9**	**73.8**	**-1.6**
Interest on long-term debt	0.8	5.8	39.3	32.2	28.3	27.1	27.2	26.7	30.2	29.7
Profit remittances on FDI	4.2	4.8	9.1	9.0	8.0	0.0	4.0	4.0	5.0	6.0
Memo: official net transfers	0.7	11.8	3.0	-22.3	-4.8	-22.9	-18.0	24.0	9.7	27.2
private net transfers	3.7	10.8	-37.0	-50.4	-59.9	27.3	-4.3	219.9	64.1	-28.8
3. MAJOR ECONOMIC AGGREGATES										
Gross national product (GNP)	180.8	836.9	1,699.9	1,548.3	1,609.9	1,670.7	1,683.2	..	..	..
Exports of goods & services (XGS)	101.7	594.0	928.9	878.5	948.7	1,087.0	1,249.3	1,349.2	1,363.7	1,405.3
of which workers remittances	0.0	..	26.0	32.0	31.5	37.4	42.4	48.3	55.0	61.2
Imports of goods & services (MGS)	148.7	632.2	953.4	743.5	867.8	950.4	1,150.5	1,236.4	1,405.3	1,452.8
International reserves (RES)	16.6	80.6	117.5	140.0	150.5	195.8	219.1	289.7	264.9	253.2
Current account balance	-41.8	-16.8	-7.8	143.4	70.3	134.6	90.1	104.4	-49.3	-56.0
4. DEBT INDICATORS										
EDT / XGS (%)	..	27.9	73.5	69.4	60.2	56.9	48.0	43.3	41.9	43.3
EDT / GNP (%)	..	19.8	40.2	39.4	35.4	37.0	35.6	..	..	..
TDS / XGS (%)	..	4.2	15.2	11.6	11.8	8.0	9.5	7.5	6.9	6.2
INT / XGS (%)	..	1.9	5.2	4.9	4.3	3.7	3.3	2.9	3.0	2.9
INT / GNP (%)	..	1.3	2.9	2.8	2.5	2.4	2.5	..	..	..
RES / EDT (%)	..	48.6	17.2	23.0	26.4	31.7	36.6	49.7	46.3	41.7
RES / MGS (months)	1.3	1.5	1.5	2.3	2.1	2.5	2.3	2.8	2.3	2.1
Short-term / EDT (%)	..	39.2	26.1	26.0	30.0	30.8	31.7	32.6	35.7	36.2
Concessional / EDT (%)	..	22.3	13.3	11.2	11.5	9.7	9.2	11.2	10.8	12.5
Multilateral / EDT (%)	..	20.3	26.5	28.2	28.7	26.0	26.8	32.7	36.1	41.8

BARBADOS

(US$ million, unless otherwise indicated)

	1970	1980	1990	1992	1993	1994	1995	1996	1997	1998
5. LONG-TERM DEBT										
DEBT OUTSTANDING (LDOD)	**12.9**	**97.8**	**504.1**	**400.6**	**348.8**	**374.0**	**372.1**	**383.7**	**367.6**	**387.8**
Public and publicly guaranteed	**12.9**	**97.8**	**504.1**	**400.6**	**348.8**	**374.0**	**372.1**	**383.7**	**367.6**	**387.8**
Official creditors	0.0	60.6	246.0	209.0	199.8	189.9	186.6	212.1	224.5	267.6
Multilateral	0.0	33.7	180.9	171.7	164.0	160.8	160.9	190.6	206.7	253.8
Concessional	0.0	20.8	56.8	54.6	52.2	49.5	46.0	57.4	54.5	70.3
Bilateral	0.0	26.8	65.1	37.3	35.8	29.1	25.8	21.6	17.8	13.8
Concessional	0.0	16.2	33.7	13.9	13.5	10.6	9.3	8.2	7.3	5.4
Private creditors	12.9	37.2	258.2	191.6	149.0	184.1	185.5	171.6	143.1	120.2
Bonds	12.9	16.7	69.2	40.1	44.7	45.1	78.9	70.2	63.1	40.0
Commercial banks	0.0	20.5	163.1	134.8	92.3	131.8	104.2	101.4	80.0	80.2
Other private	0.0	0.1	25.9	16.7	12.0	7.2	2.4	0.0	0.0	0.0
Private nonguaranteed	**0.0**	**0.0**	**0.0**	**0.0**	**0.0**	**0.0**	**0.0**	**0.0**	**0.0**	**0.0**
Bonds	0.0	0.0	0.0	0.0	0.0	0.0	0.0	0.0	0.0	0.0
Commercial banks	0.0	0.0	0.0	0.0	0.0	0.0	0.0	0.0	0.0	0.0
Memo:										
IBRD	0.0	0.9	36.0	26.7	22.0	19.6	19.3	15.6	13.7	18.3
IDA	0.0	0.0	0.0	0.0	0.0	0.0	0.0	0.0	0.0	0.0
DISBURSEMENTS	**0.0**	**38.4**	**90.6**	**13.6**	**14.4**	**62.9**	**54.6**	**54.2**	**40.1**	**61.1**
Public and publicly guaranteed	**0.0**	**38.4**	**90.6**	**13.6**	**14.4**	**62.9**	**54.6**	**54.2**	**40.1**	**61.1**
Official creditors	0.0	16.6	33.9	13.6	13.2	12.9	14.6	54.2	40.1	61.1
Multilateral	0.0	12.3	21.9	12.2	9.1	11.7	12.9	53.5	39.1	60.8
Concessional	0.0	10.4	1.7	1.5	1.1	0.5	0.3	15.2	1.0	19.5
Bilateral	0.0	4.4	12.1	1.4	4.1	1.2	1.7	0.8	1.0	0.2
Concessional	0.0	1.1	2.5	1.1	0.8	0.3	0.4	0.2	0.2	0.2
Private creditors	0.0	21.7	56.6	0.0	1.2	50.0	40.0	0.0	0.0	0.0
Bonds	0.0	16.7	0.0	0.0	0.0	0.0	40.0	0.0	0.0	0.0
Commercial banks	0.0	5.1	56.6	0.0	1.2	50.0	0.0	0.0	0.0	0.0
Other private	0.0	0.0	0.0	0.0	0.0	0.0	0.0	0.0	0.0	0.0
Private nonguaranteed	**0.0**	**0.0**	**0.0**	**0.0**	**0.0**	**0.0**	**0.0**	**0.0**	**0.0**	**0.0**
Bonds	0.0	0.0	0.0	0.0	0.0	0.0	0.0	0.0	0.0	0.0
Commercial banks	0.0	0.0	0.0	0.0	0.0	0.0	0.0	0.0	0.0	0.0
Memo:										
IBRD	0.0	0.8	5.4	2.8	2.4	2.6	3.5	0.9	3.1	8.7
IDA	0.0	0.0	0.0	0.0	0.0	0.0	0.0	0.0	0.0	0.0
PRINCIPAL REPAYMENTS	**0.0**	**8.7**	**88.4**	**58.9**	**71.3**	**46.5**	**58.8**	**35.0**	**44.2**	**46.4**
Public and publicly guaranteed	**0.0**	**8.7**	**88.4**	**58.9**	**71.3**	**46.5**	**58.8**	**35.0**	**44.2**	**46.4**
Official creditors	0.0	3.0	17.8	21.6	24.0	23.7	21.4	20.8	20.0	23.3
Multilateral	0.0	0.6	13.2	16.8	18.6	17.9	16.3	15.8	15.2	19.4
Concessional	0.0	0.1	2.2	3.0	3.4	3.4	3.7	3.7	3.4	3.8
Bilateral	0.0	2.4	4.6	4.8	5.4	5.8	5.1	5.0	4.8	3.9
Concessional	0.0	0.3	0.9	0.9	1.1	1.2	1.7	1.3	1.2	1.8
Private creditors	0.0	5.7	70.6	37.3	47.4	22.8	37.4	14.2	24.2	23.1
Bonds	0.0	0.0	44.1	0.0	0.0	4.9	5.3	4.6	4.1	23.0
Commercial banks	0.0	5.4	20.2	32.5	42.6	13.1	27.2	7.2	20.1	0.1
Other private	0.0	0.3	6.2	4.8	4.8	4.8	4.8	2.4	0.0	0.0
Private nonguaranteed	**0.0**	**0.0**	**0.0**	**0.0**	**0.0**	**0.0**	**0.0**	**0.0**	**0.0**	**0.0**
Bonds	0.0	0.0	0.0	0.0	0.0	0.0	0.0	0.0	0.0	0.0
Commercial banks	0.0	0.0	0.0	0.0	0.0	0.0	0.0	0.0	0.0	0.0
Memo:										
IBRD	0.0	0.0	7.1	7.7	7.9	6.5	4.7	3.3	3.7	4.2
IDA	0.0	0.0	0.0	0.0	0.0	0.0	0.0	0.0	0.0	0.0
NET FLOWS ON DEBT	**0.0**	**29.7**	**2.1**	**-45.3**	**-56.9**	**16.4**	**-4.2**	**19.3**	**-4.1**	**14.7**
Public and publicly guaranteed	**0.0**	**29.7**	**2.1**	**-45.3**	**-56.9**	**16.4**	**-4.2**	**19.3**	**-4.1**	**14.7**
Official creditors	0.0	13.7	16.1	-8.0	-10.7	-10.8	-6.8	33.5	20.1	37.8
Multilateral	0.0	11.7	8.6	-4.6	-9.5	-6.2	-3.4	37.7	23.9	41.5
Concessional	0.0	10.4	-0.5	-1.5	-2.3	-2.9	-3.4	11.5	-2.4	15.7
Bilateral	0.0	2.0	7.5	-3.4	-1.3	-4.6	-3.4	-4.2	-3.8	-3.7
Concessional	0.0	0.8	1.6	0.2	-0.3	-0.8	-1.3	-1.1	-0.9	-1.7
Private creditors	0.0	16.0	-14.0	-37.3	-46.2	27.2	2.6	-14.2	-24.2	-23.1
Bonds	0.0	16.7	-44.1	0.0	0.0	-4.9	34.7	-4.6	-4.1	-23.0
Commercial banks	0.0	-0.4	36.4	-32.5	-41.4	36.9	-27.2	-7.2	-20.1	-0.1
Other private	0.0	-0.3	-6.2	-4.8	-4.8	-4.8	-4.8	-2.4	0.0	0.0
Private nonguaranteed	**0.0**	**0.0**	**0.0**	**0.0**	**0.0**	**0.0**	**0.0**	**0.0**	**0.0**	**0.0**
Bonds	0.0	0.0	0.0	0.0	0.0	0.0	0.0	0.0	0.0	0.0
Commercial banks	0.0	0.0	0.0	0.0	0.0	0.0	0.0	0.0	0.0	0.0
Memo:										
IBRD	0.0	0.8	-1.7	-4.9	-5.5	-3.9	-1.2	-2.4	-0.6	4.5
IDA	0.0	0.0	0.0	0.0	0.0	0.0	0.0	0.0	0.0	0.0

BARBADOS

(US$ million, unless otherwise indicated)

	1970	1980	1990	1992	1993	1994	1995	1996	1997	1998
INTEREST PAYMENTS (LINT)	**0.8**	**5.8**	**39.3**	**32.2**	**28.3**	**27.1**	**27.2**	**26.7**	**30.2**	**29.7**
Public and publicly guaranteed	**0.8**	**5.8**	**39.3**	**32.2**	**28.3**	**27.1**	**27.2**	**26.7**	**30.2**	**29.7**
Official creditors	0.0	2.6	14.4	14.1	13.7	14.3	12.4	11.8	13.5	14.9
Multilateral	0.0	1.6	11.5	11.1	11.3	12.3	10.4	10.2	12.3	13.6
Concessional	0.0	0.5	1.6	1.6	1.5	1.4	1.4	1.4	2.1	2.7
Bilateral	0.0	1.1	2.9	3.0	2.4	2.0	1.9	1.6	1.2	1.3
Concessional	0.0	0.4	0.4	0.3	0.3	0.2	0.2	0.1	0.1	0.3
Private creditors	0.8	3.2	24.9	18.1	14.7	12.8	14.9	14.9	16.7	14.7
Bonds	0.8	0.0	8.1	2.7	3.1	3.2	3.1	6.6	6.0	5.0
Commercial banks	0.0	3.1	15.5	13.9	10.4	8.8	11.3	8.2	10.7	9.7
Other private	0.0	0.1	1.3	1.5	1.2	0.8	0.5	0.1	0.0	0.0
Private nonguaranteed	**0.0**	**0.0**	**0.0**	**0.0**	**0.0**	**0.0**	**0.0**	**0.0**	**0.0**	**0.0**
Bonds	0.0	0.0	0.0	0.0	0.0	0.0	0.0	0.0	0.0	0.0
Commercial banks	0.0	0.0	0.0	0.0	0.0	0.0	0.0	0.0	0.0	0.0
Memo:										
IBRD	0.0	0.2	2.9	2.4	2.1	1.7	1.6	1.3	1.0	0.9
IDA	0.0	0.0	0.0	0.0	0.0	0.0	0.0	0.0	0.0	0.0
NET TRANSFERS ON DEBT	**-0.8**	**23.9**	**-37.2**	**-77.5**	**-85.3**	**-10.7**	**-31.4**	**-7.4**	**-34.4**	**-15.0**
Public and publicly guaranteed	**-0.8**	**23.9**	**-37.2**	**-77.5**	**-85.3**	**-10.7**	**-31.4**	**-7.4**	**-34.4**	**-15.0**
Official creditors	0.0	11.1	1.7	-22.0	-24.4	-25.1	-19.2	21.7	6.6	22.9
Multilateral	0.0	10.2	-2.9	-15.7	-20.8	-18.4	-13.8	27.5	11.6	27.8
Concessional	0.0	9.8	-2.1	-3.2	-3.8	-4.3	-4.8	10.2	-4.5	13.0
Bilateral	0.0	0.9	4.5	-6.3	-3.6	-6.6	-5.3	-5.8	-5.0	-4.9
Concessional	0.0	0.4	1.2	-0.1	-0.6	-1.1	-1.5	-1.3	-1.0	-1.9
Private creditors	-0.8	12.8	-38.8	-55.4	-60.9	14.4	-12.2	-29.1	-40.9	-37.9
Bonds	-0.8	16.7	-52.2	-2.7	-3.1	-8.1	31.6	-11.2	-10.1	-28.0
Commercial banks	0.0	-3.5	20.9	-46.4	-51.8	28.1	-38.6	-15.5	-30.8	-9.8
Other private	0.0	-0.4	-7.5	-6.3	-6.0	-5.6	-5.2	-2.5	0.0	0.0
Private nonguaranteed	**0.0**	**0.0**	**0.0**	**0.0**	**0.0**	**0.0**	**0.0**	**0.0**	**0.0**	**0.0**
Bonds	0.0	0.0	0.0	0.0	0.0	0.0	0.0	0.0	0.0	0.0
Commercial banks	0.0	0.0	0.0	0.0	0.0	0.0	0.0	0.0	0.0	0.0
Memo:										
IBRD	0.0	0.7	-4.7	-7.4	-7.6	-5.6	-2.8	-3.8	-1.6	3.6
IDA	0.0	0.0	0.0	0.0	0.0	0.0	0.0	0.0	0.0	0.0
DEBT SERVICE (LTDS)	**0.8**	**14.5**	**127.7**	**91.1**	**99.7**	**73.6**	**86.0**	**61.7**	**74.5**	**76.1**
Public and publicly guaranteed	**0.8**	**14.5**	**127.7**	**91.1**	**99.7**	**73.6**	**86.0**	**61.7**	**74.5**	**76.1**
Official creditors	0.0	5.6	32.2	35.7	37.6	38.0	33.8	32.5	33.5	38.2
Multilateral	0.0	2.1	24.7	27.9	29.9	30.1	26.7	26.0	27.6	33.0
Concessional	0.0	0.6	3.8	4.6	4.9	4.8	5.1	5.0	5.4	6.4
Bilateral	0.0	3.4	7.5	7.8	7.8	7.8	7.1	6.6	6.0	5.2
Concessional	0.0	0.7	1.3	1.2	1.4	1.4	1.8	1.5	1.2	2.1
Private creditors	0.8	8.9	95.5	55.4	62.0	35.6	52.2	29.1	40.9	37.9
Bonds	0.8	0.0	52.2	2.7	3.1	8.1	8.4	11.2	10.1	28.0
Commercial banks	0.0	8.5	35.8	46.4	53.0	21.9	38.6	15.5	30.8	9.8
Other private	0.0	0.4	7.5	6.3	6.0	5.6	5.2	2.5	0.0	0.0
Private nonguaranteed	**0.0**	**0.0**	**0.0**	**0.0**	**0.0**	**0.0**	**0.0**	**0.0**	**0.0**	**0.0**
Bonds	0.0	0.0	0.0	0.0	0.0	0.0	0.0	0.0	0.0	0.0
Commercial banks	0.0	0.0	0.0	0.0	0.0	0.0	0.0	0.0	0.0	0.0
Memo:										
IBRD	0.0	0.2	10.0	10.1	10.0	8.2	6.3	4.7	4.7	5.1
IDA	0.0	0.0	0.0	0.0	0.0	0.0	0.0	0.0	0.0	0.0
UNDISBURSED DEBT	**2.8**	**78.4**	**110.1**	**49.5**	**130.8**	**139.0**	**128.6**	**197.8**	**160.2**	**221.6**
Official creditors	2.8	70.8	63.6	48.3	130.8	139.0	128.6	197.8	160.2	221.6
Private creditors	0.0	7.6	46.4	1.2	0.0	0.0	0.0	0.0	0.0	0.0
Memorandum items										
Concessional LDOD	0.0	37.0	90.5	68.6	65.7	60.0	55.3	65.6	61.8	75.6
Variable rate LDOD	0.0	15.9	155.8	81.5	57.5	50.0	30.3	54.4	66.7	95.3
Public sector LDOD	12.9	97.8	499.5	398.1	347.4	373.4	371.9	383.7	367.6	387.8
Private sector LDOD	0.0	0.0	4.6	2.6	1.3	0.6	0.2	0.0	0.0	0.0

6. CURRENCY COMPOSITION OF LONG-TERM DEBT (PERCENT)

	1970	1980	1990	1992	1993	1994	1995	1996	1997	1998
Deutsche mark	0.0	0.0	0.6	0.3	0.1	0.0	0.0	0.0	0.0	0.0
French franc	0.0	0.0	0.0	0.0	0.0	0.0	0.0	0.0	0.0	0.0
Japanese yen	0.0	0.0	13.7	10.0	12.8	12.1	10.5	7.9	6.3	0.0
Pound sterling	100.0	6.4	13.6	15.8	14.6	12.6	12.6	13.4	13.6	12.9
Swiss franc	0.0	0.0	0.0	0.0	0.0	0.0	0.0	0.0	0.0	0.0
U.S.dollars	0.0	30.7	35.3	32.9	27.4	34.8	36.9	37.3	38.2	48.0
Multiple currency	0.0	30.5	31.9	38.5	42.6	38.9	38.5	39.9	40.4	37.6
Special drawing rights	0.0	0.0	0.0	0.0	0.0	0.0	0.0	0.0	0.0	0.0
All other currencies	0.0	32.4	4.9	2.5	2.5	1.6	1.5	1.5	1.5	1.5

BARBADOS

(US$ million, unless otherwise indicated)

	1970	1980	1990	1992	1993	1994	1995	1996	1997	1998
7. DEBT RESTRUCTURINGS										
Total amount rescheduled	..	..	0.0	0.0	0.0	0.0	0.0	0.0	0.0	0.0
Debt stock rescheduled	..	..	0.0	0.0	0.0	0.0	0.0	0.0	0.0	0.0
Principal rescheduled	..	..	0.0	0.0	0.0	0.0	0.0	0.0	0.0	0.0
Official	..	..	0.0	0.0	0.0	0.0	0.0	0.0	0.0	0.0
Private	..	..	0.0	0.0	0.0	0.0	0.0	0.0	0.0	0.0
Interest rescheduled	..	..	0.0	0.0	0.0	0.0	0.0	0.0	0.0	0.0
Official	..	..	0.0	0.0	0.0	0.0	0.0	0.0	0.0	0.0
Private	..	..	0.0	0.0	0.0	0.0	0.0	0.0	0.0	0.0
Debt forgiven	..	..	0.0	20.4	0.0	0.0	0.0	0.0	0.0	0.3
Memo: interest forgiven	..	..	0.0	0.0	0.0	0.0	0.0	0.0	0.0	0.0
Debt stock reduction	..	..	0.0	0.0	0.0	0.0	0.0	0.0	0.0	0.0
of which debt buyback	..	..	0.0	0.0	0.0	0.0	0.0	0.0	0.0	0.0
8. DEBT STOCK-FLOW RECONCILIATION										
Total change in debt stocks	..	..	39.4	-42.5	-39.0	47.4	-18.5	-16.0	-11.6	36.0
Net flows on debt	0.0	10.2	18.8	-4.4	-43.9	35.4	-22.2	-7.4	0.8	30.7
Net change in interest arrears	..	..	-1.6	0.0	-0.1	0.0	0.0	0.0	0.0	-0.3
Interest capitalized	..	..	0.0	0.0	0.0	0.0	0.0	0.0	0.0	0.0
Debt forgiveness or reduction	..	..	0.0	-20.4	0.0	0.0	0.0	0.0	0.0	-0.3
Cross-currency valuation	..	..	20.0	-15.7	2.4	6.1	-2.1	-0.5	-5.3	0.5
Residual	..	..	2.2	-2.0	2.6	5.9	5.8	-8.1	-7.1	5.3
9. AVERAGE TERMS OF NEW COMMITMENTS										
ALL CREDITORS										
Interest (%)	3.0	7.1	10.2	7.6	6.9	10.1	10.0	3.8	5.2	6.9
Maturity (years)	29.6	15.5	18.6	14.8	21.8	8.7	10.8	16.7	15.4	23.3
Grace period (years)	7.1	5.9	15.3	5.3	5.7	4.3	6.2	4.5	5.0	6.5
Grant element (%)	54.6	18.3	-5.5	13.5	20.0	1.2	-1.1	37.4	28.2	20.6
Official creditors										
Interest (%)	3.0	6.1	6.5	7.6	6.9	7.2	6.3	3.8	5.2	6.9
Maturity (years)	29.6	19.9	15.4	14.8	21.8	20.3	18.1	16.7	15.4	23.3
Grace period (years)	7.1	5.2	4.9	5.3	5.7	4.4	3.6	4.5	5.0	6.5
Grant element (%)	54.6	26.6	21.7	13.5	20.0	17.3	20.9	37.4	28.2	20.6
Private creditors										
Interest (%)	0.0	8.3	11.7	0.0	0.0	11.2	10.4	0.0	0.0	0.0
Maturity (years)	0.0	10.3	19.8	0.0	0.0	4.2	10.0	0.0	0.0	0.0
Grace period (years)	0.0	6.6	19.3	0.0	0.0	4.2	6.5	0.0	0.0	0.0
Grant element (%)	0.0	8.7	-16.1	0.0	0.0	-5.1	-3.6	0.0	0.0	0.0
Memorandum items										
Commitments	2.5	61.9	102.0	21.2	96.1	69.6	44.4	124.1	5.3	129.5
Official creditors	2.5	33.3	28.5	21.2	96.1	19.6	4.4	124.1	5.3	129.5
Private creditors	0.0	28.6	73.5	0.0	0.0	50.0	40.0	0.0	0.0	0.0

10. CONTRACTUAL OBLIGATIONS ON OUTSTANDING LONG-TERM DEBT

	1999	2000	2001	2002	2003	2004	2005	2006	2007	2008
TOTAL										
Disbursements	51.5	61.2	43.4	28.8	18.7	11.0	5.2	0.6	0.6	0.0
Principal	60.6	30.1	30.0	39.7	37.6	39.4	37.5	28.5	25.3	24.3
Interest	32.4	30.4	30.9	30.4	28.7	26.7	24.4	22.2	20.6	19.2
Official creditors										
Disbursements	51.5	61.2	43.4	28.8	18.7	11.0	5.2	0.6	0.6	0.0
Principal	30.3	30.1	30.0	29.7	27.6	29.4	27.5	28.5	25.3	24.3
Interest	18.5	20.0	20.5	20.3	19.6	18.7	17.4	15.9	14.4	13.0
Bilateral creditors										
Disbursements	1.1	0.7	0.3	0.0	0.0	0.0	0.0	0.0	0.0	0.0
Principal	2.9	2.4	1.5	0.7	0.7	0.7	0.7	0.7	0.7	0.7
Interest	0.9	0.7	0.6	0.5	0.5	0.5	0.4	0.4	0.3	0.3
Multilateral creditors										
Disbursements	50.4	60.5	43.1	28.8	18.7	11.0	5.2	0.6	0.6	0.0
Principal	27.4	27.7	28.5	29.0	26.8	28.7	26.7	27.8	24.5	23.5
Interest	17.6	19.3	19.9	19.7	19.1	18.2	17.0	15.6	14.1	12.7
Private creditors										
Disbursements	0.0	0.0	0.0	0.0	0.0	0.0	0.0	0.0	0.0	0.0
Principal	30.3	0.0	0.0	10.0	10.0	10.0	10.0	0.0	0.0	0.0
Interest	13.9	10.4	10.4	10.1	9.1	8.1	7.0	6.2	6.2	6.2
Commercial banks										
Disbursements	0.0	0.0	0.0	0.0	0.0	0.0	0.0	0.0	0.0	0.0
Principal	30.3	0.0	0.0	0.0	0.0	0.0	0.0	0.0	0.0	0.0
Interest	9.7	6.2	6.2	6.2	6.2	6.2	6.2	6.2	6.2	6.2
Other private										
Disbursements	0.0	0.0	0.0	0.0	0.0	0.0	0.0	0.0	0.0	0.0
Principal	0.0	0.0	0.0	10.0	10.0	10.0	10.0	0.0	0.0	0.0
Interest	4.2	4.2	4.2	3.9	2.9	1.8	0.8	0.0	0.0	0.0

BELARUS

(US$ million, unless otherwise indicated)

	1970	*1980*	*1990*	*1992*	*1993*	*1994*	*1995*	*1996*	*1997*	*1998*
1. SUMMARY DEBT DATA										
TOTAL DEBT STOCKS (EDT)	..	..	..	..	**969**	**1,273**	**1,667**	**1,096**	**1,162**	**1,120**
Long-term debt (LDOD)	..	..	..	..	**866**	**1,100**	**1,275**	**720**	**675**	**766**
Public and publicly guaranteed	..	..	..	..	865	1,100	1,255	690	652	748
Private nonguaranteed	..	..	..	..	1	1	20	30	23	18
Use of IMF credit	..	..	..	..	**96**	**102**	**283**	**274**	**257**	**243**
Short-term debt	..	..	..	..	**7**	**70**	**110**	**102**	**230**	**111**
of which interest arrears on LDOD	..	..	..	..	7	15	18	10	1	5
Official creditors	..	..	..	..	0	0	0	2	1	4
Private creditors	..	..	..	..	7	15	18	8	0	1
Memo: principal arrears on LDOD	..	..	..	..	0	135	140	12	1	9
Official creditors	..	..	..	..	0	0	0	1	1	6
Private creditors	..	..	..	..	0	135	140	11	0	4
Memo: export credits	..	..	..	..	211	379	399	352	279	280
TOTAL DEBT FLOWS										
Disbursements	..	..	..	..	**429**	**329**	**440**	**113**	**87**	**131**
Long-term debt	..	..	..	..	331	329	258	113	87	131
IMF purchases	..	..	..	..	98	0	182	0	0	0
Principal repayments	..	..	..	..	**3**	**88**	**108**	**65**	**75**	**92**
Long-term debt	..	..	..	..	3	88	108	65	75	68
IMF repurchases	..	..	..	..	0	0	0	0	0	24
Net flows on debt	..	..	..	..	**426**	**296**	**369**	**49**	**149**	**-83**
of which short-term debt	..	..	..	..	0	55	36	1	137	-123
Interest payments (INT)	..	..	..	..	**12**	**31**	**72**	**56**	**75**	**65**
Long-term debt	..	..	..	..	11	22	58	39	55	44
IMF charges	..	..	..	..	1	5	10	12	12	12
Short-term debt	..	..	..	..	0	4	4	4	9	9
Net transfers on debt	..	..	..	..	**414**	**265**	**296**	**-7**	**74**	**-148**
Total debt service paid (TDS)	..	..	..	..	**15**	**119**	**180**	**120**	**150**	**157**
Long-term debt	..	..	..	..	13	110	166	104	129	111
IMF repurchases and charges	..	..	..	..	1	5	10	12	12	36
Short-term debt (interest only)	..	..	..	..	0	4	4	4	9	9
2. AGGREGATE NET RESOURCE FLOWS AND NET TRANSFERS (LONG-TERM)										
NET RESOURCE FLOWS	..	..	..	..	**505**	**335**	**307**	**159**	**240**	**216**
Net flow of long-term debt (ex. IMF)	..	..	..	..	328	241	150	48	12	64
Foreign direct investment (net)	..	..	..	..	10	15	20	73	200	149
Portfolio equity flows	..	..	..	..	0	0	0	0	0	0
Grants (excluding technical coop.)	..	..	..	..	167	79	136	38	27	3
Memo: technical coop. grants	..	..	..	..	12	13	27	27	15	24
official net resource flows	..	..	..	..	379	231	183	72	71	94
private net resource flows	..	..	..	..	126	104	123	87	169	122
NET TRANSFERS	..	..	..	..	**494**	**313**	**249**	**120**	**185**	**172**
Interest on long-term debt	..	..	..	..	11	22	58	39	55	44
Profit remittances on FDI	..	..	..	..	0	0	0	0	0	0
Memo: official net transfers	..	..	..	..	373	223	151	54	48	68
private net transfers	..	..	..	..	121	90	98	66	137	104
3. MAJOR ECONOMIC AGGREGATES										
Gross national product (GNP)	..	..	..	..	26,729	20,095	18,192	18,564	20,839	22,537
Exports of goods & services (XGS)	..	..	..	..	3,112	2,912	5,083	6,799	8,379	8,015
of which workers remittances	..	..	..	..	0	0	29	30	48	32
Imports of goods & services (MGS)	..	..	..	..	4,294	3,602	5,386	7,363	9,209	9,068
International reserves (RES)	..	..	..	..	..	101	377	469	394	339
Current account balance	..	..	..	..	-1,113	-641	-253	-503	-798	-945
4. DEBT INDICATORS										
EDT / XGS (%)	..	..	..	..	31.2	43.7	32.8	16.1	13.9	14.0
EDT / GNP (%)	..	..	..	..	3.6	6.3	9.2	5.9	5.6	5.0
TDS / XGS (%)	..	..	..	..	0.5	4.1	3.6	1.8	1.8	2.0
INT / XGS (%)	..	..	..	..	0.4	1.1	1.4	0.8	0.9	0.8
INT / GNP (%)	..	..	..	..	0.0	0.2	0.4	0.3	0.4	0.3
RES / EDT (%)	..	..	..	..	..	7.9	22.6	42.8	33.9	30.3
RES / MGS (months)	..	..	..	..	..	0.3	0.8	0.8	0.5	0.5
Short-term / EDT (%)	..	..	..	..	0.7	5.5	6.6	9.3	19.8	9.9
Concessional / EDT (%)	..	..	..	..	48.1	36.2	28.6	7.8	7.4	7.7
Multilateral / EDT (%)	..	..	..	..	11.5	13.6	11.3	20.0	22.3	25.3

BELARUS

(US$ million, unless otherwise indicated)

	1970	*1980*	*1990*	*1992*	*1993*	*1994*	*1995*	*1996*	*1997*	*1998*
5. LONG-TERM DEBT										
DEBT OUTSTANDING (LDOD)	..	..	..	..	**866**	**1,100**	**1,275**	**720**	**675**	**766**
Public and publicly guaranteed	..	..	..	..	**865**	**1,100**	**1,255**	**690**	**652**	**748**
Official creditors	..	..	..	..	593	718	769	361	384	488
Multilateral	..	..	..	..	112	173	188	219	259	283
Concessional	..	..	..	..	0	0	0	0	0	0
Bilateral	..	..	..	..	481	545	582	142	125	205
Concessional	..	..	..	..	467	461	477	86	86	86
Private creditors	..	..	..	..	272	382	486	329	268	260
Bonds	..	..	..	..	0	0	0	0	0	0
Commercial banks	..	..	..	..	0	0	0	0	2	13
Other private	..	..	..	..	272	382	486	329	267	247
Private nonguaranteed	..	..	..	..	**1**	**1**	**20**	**30**	**23**	**18**
Bonds	..	..	..	..	0	0	0	0	0	0
Commercial banks	..	..	..	..	1	1	20	30	23	18
Memo:										
IBRD	..	..	..	..	0	101	116	121	124	135
IDA	..	..	..	..	0	0	0	0	0	0
DISBURSEMENTS	..	..	..	..	**331**	**329**	**258**	**113**	**87**	**131**
Public and publicly guaranteed	..	..	..	..	**329**	**329**	**238**	**96**	**87**	**131**
Official creditors	..	..	..	..	212	211	131	57	64	111
Multilateral	..	..	..	..	116	111	77	47	64	30
Concessional	..	..	..	..	0	0	0	0	0	0
Bilateral	..	..	..	..	96	100	54	10	0	81
Concessional	..	..	..	..	81	30	20	10	0	0
Private creditors	..	..	..	..	117	117	107	39	23	20
Bonds	..	..	..	..	0	0	0	0	0	0
Commercial banks	..	..	..	..	0	0	0	0	2	11
Other private	..	..	..	..	117	117	107	39	21	9
Private nonguaranteed	..	..	..	..	**2**	**0**	**20**	**17**	**0**	**0**
Bonds	..	..	..	..	0	0	0	0	0	0
Commercial banks	..	..	..	..	2	0	20	17	0	0
Memo:										
IBRD	..	..	..	..	0	100	11	14	13	4
IDA	..	..	..	..	0	0	0	0	0	0
PRINCIPAL REPAYMENTS	..	..	..	..	**3**	**88**	**108**	**65**	**75**	**68**
Public and publicly guaranteed	..	..	..	..	**2**	**87**	**108**	**58**	**68**	**63**
Official creditors	..	..	..	..	0	60	84	23	20	20
Multilateral	..	..	..	..	0	60	70	4	7	16
Concessional	..	..	..	..	0	0	0	0	0	0
Bilateral	..	..	..	..	0	0	15	19	13	4
Concessional	..	..	..	..	0	0	0	0	0	0
Private creditors	..	..	..	..	2	27	24	35	47	43
Bonds	..	..	..	..	0	0	0	0	0	0
Commercial banks	..	..	..	..	0	0	0	0	0	0
Other private	..	..	..	..	2	27	24	35	47	43
Private nonguaranteed	..	..	..	..	**1**	**1**	**0**	**7**	**7**	**5**
Bonds	..	..	..	..	0	0	0	0	0	0
Commercial banks	..	..	..	..	1	1	0	7	7	5
Memo:										
IBRD	..	..	..	..	0	0	0	0	0	0
IDA	..	..	..	..	0	0	0	0	0	0
NET FLOWS ON DEBT	..	..	..	..	**328**	**241**	**150**	**48**	**12**	**64**
Public and publicly guaranteed	..	..	..	..	**327**	**242**	**130**	**38**	**19**	**68**
Official creditors	..	..	..	..	212	152	47	33	43	91
Multilateral	..	..	..	..	116	51	8	43	56	13
Concessional	..	..	..	..	0	0	0	0	0	0
Bilateral	..	..	..	..	96	100	39	-9	-13	77
Concessional	..	..	..	..	81	30	20	10	0	0
Private creditors	..	..	..	..	115	90	83	5	-24	-22
Bonds	..	..	..	..	0	0	0	0	0	0
Commercial banks	..	..	..	..	0	0	0	0	2	11
Other private	..	..	..	..	115	90	83	5	-26	-34
Private nonguaranteed	..	..	..	..	**1**	**-1**	**20**	**10**	**-7**	**-5**
Bonds	..	..	..	..	0	0	0	0	0	0
Commercial banks	..	..	..	..	1	-1	20	10	-7	-5
Memo:										
IBRD	..	..	..	..	0	100	11	14	13	4
IDA	..	..	..	..	0	0	0	0	0	0

BELARUS

(US$ million, unless otherwise indicated)

	1970	1980	1990	1992	1993	1994	1995	1996	1997	1998
INTEREST PAYMENTS (LINT)	..	..	..	..	**11**	**22**	**58**	**39**	**55**	**44**
Public and publicly guaranteed	..	..	..	..	**11**	**22**	**57**	**36**	**51**	**41**
Official creditors	..	..	..	..	5	7	32	17	23	26
Multilateral	..	..	..	..	5	6	23	13	17	19
Concessional	..	..	..	..	0	0	0	0	0	0
Bilateral	..	..	..	..	0	2	10	4	5	7
Concessional	..	..	..	..	0	1	1	2	2	2
Private creditors	..	..	..	..	5	15	25	18	29	15
Bonds	..	..	..	..	0	0	0	0	0	0
Commercial banks	..	..	..	..	0	0	0	0	0	0
Other private	..	..	..	..	5	15	25	18	28	15
Private nonguaranteed	..	..	..	..	**0**	**0**	**0**	**3**	**3**	**3**
Bonds	..	..	..	..	0	0	0	0	0	0
Commercial banks	..	..	..	..	0	0	0	3	3	3
Memo:										
IBRD	..	..	..	..	0	2	8	8	8	8
IDA	..	..	..	..	0	0	0	0	0	0
NET TRANSFERS ON DEBT	..	..	..	..	**317**	**219**	**93**	**9**	**-42**	**20**
Public and publicly guaranteed	..	..	..	..	**316**	**220**	**73**	**2**	**-32**	**27**
Official creditors	..	..	..	..	207	144	15	16	21	65
Multilateral	..	..	..	..	111	46	-15	30	39	-6
Concessional	..	..	..	..	0	0	0	0	0	0
Bilateral	..	..	..	..	96	98	30	-14	-18	70
Concessional	..	..	..	..	81	29	19	8	-2	-2
Private creditors	..	..	..	..	110	75	58	-14	-53	-38
Bonds	..	..	..	..	0	0	0	0	0	0
Commercial banks	..	..	..	..	0	0	0	0	1	11
Other private	..	..	..	..	110	75	58	-14	-54	-49
Private nonguaranteed	..	..	..	..	**1**	**-1**	**20**	**7**	**-10**	**-7**
Bonds	..	..	..	..	0	0	0	0	0	0
Commercial banks	..	..	..	..	1	-1	20	7	-10	-7
Memo:										
IBRD	..	..	..	..	0	98	4	6	6	-4
IDA	..	..	..	..	0	0	0	0	0	0
DEBT SERVICE (LTDS)	..	..	..	..	**13**	**110**	**166**	**104**	**129**	**111**
Public and publicly guaranteed	..	..	..	..	**13**	**109**	**165**	**94**	**119**	**104**
Official creditors	..	..	..	..	5	67	117	41	43	46
Multilateral	..	..	..	..	5	65	92	17	25	35
Concessional	..	..	..	..	0	0	0	0	0	0
Bilateral	..	..	..	..	0	2	24	24	18	11
Concessional	..	..	..	..	0	1	1	2	2	2
Private creditors	..	..	..	..	7	42	49	53	76	58
Bonds	..	..	..	..	0	0	0	0	0	0
Commercial banks	..	..	..	..	0	0	0	0	0	0
Other private	..	..	..	..	7	42	49	53	76	58
Private nonguaranteed	..	..	..	..	**1**	**1**	**0**	**11**	**10**	**8**
Bonds	..	..	..	..	0	0	0	0	0	0
Commercial banks	..	..	..	..	1	1	0	11	10	8
Memo:										
IBRD	..	..	..	..	0	2	8	8	8	8
IDA	..	..	..	..	0	0	0	0	0	0
UNDISBURSED DEBT	..	..	..	..	**498**	**410**	**295**	**242**	**283**	**610**
Official creditors	..	..	..	..	302	280	255	190	203	95
Private creditors	..	..	..	..	195	130	40	52	80	515
Memorandum items										
Concessional LDOD	..	..	..	..	467	461	477	86	86	86
Variable rate LDOD	..	..	..	..	452	578	690	513	458	524
Public sector LDOD	..	..	..	..	865	1,100	1,255	690	652	748
Private sector LDOD	..	..	..	..	1	1	20	30	23	18

6. CURRENCY COMPOSITION OF LONG-TERM DEBT (PERCENT)

	1970	1980	1990	1992	1993	1994	1995	1996	1997	1998
Deutsche mark	..	..	..	..	17.6	23.2	26.4	41.8	34.8	29.6
French franc	..	..	..	..	0.0	0.0	0.0	0.0	0.0	0.0
Japanese yen	..	..	..	..	0.0	2.9	2.4	3.0	2.2	2.3
Pound sterling	..	..	..	..	0.0	0.0	0.0	0.0	0.0	0.0
Swiss franc	..	..	..	..	0.0	0.0	0.7	1.1	0.8	0.6
U.S.dollars	..	..	..	..	63.9	55.5	52.7	27.7	35.3	41.7
Multiple currency	..	..	..	..	0.0	9.4	11.2	17.5	19.0	18.0
Special drawing rights	..	..	..	..	0.0	0.0	0.0	0.0	0.0	0.0
All other currencies	..	..	..	..	18.5	9.0	6.6	8.9	7.9	7.8

BELARUS

(US$ million, unless otherwise indicated)

	1970	1980	1990	1992	1993	1994	1995	1996	1997	1998
7. DEBT RESTRUCTURINGS										
Total amount rescheduled	..	..	..	..	385	0	0	0	0	0
Debt stock rescheduled	..	..	..	..	0	0	0	0	0	0
Principal rescheduled	..	..	..	..	0	0	0	0	0	0
Official	..	..	..	..	0	0	0	0	0	0
Private	..	..	..	..	0	0	0	0	0	0
Interest rescheduled	..	..	..	..	..	0	0	0	0	0
Official	..	..	..	..	0	0	0	0	0	0
Private	..	..	..	..	0	0	0	0	0	0
Debt forgiven	..	..	..	..	0	0	0	553	0	0
Memo: interest forgiven	..	..	..	..	0	0	0	15	0	0
Debt stock reduction	..	..	..	..	0	0	0	0	0	0
of which debt buyback	..	..	..	..	0	0	0	0	0	0
8. DEBT STOCK-FLOW RECONCILIATION										
Total change in debt stocks	..	..	..	..	..	303	395	-572	66	-42
Net flows on debt	..	..	..	..	426	296	369	49	149	-83
Net change in interest arrears	..	..	..	..	..	8	3	-9	-8	3
Interest capitalized	..	..	..	..	..	0	0	0	0	0
Debt forgiveness or reduction	..	..	..	..	..	0	0	-553	0	0
Cross-currency valuation	..	..	..	..	..	29	33	-38	-49	29
Residual	..	..	..	..	..	-30	-10	-20	-26	9
9. AVERAGE TERMS OF NEW COMMITMENTS										
ALL CREDITORS										
Interest (%)	..	..	..	..	7.2	6.7	5.7	6.1	5.7	4.3
Maturity (years)	..	..	..	..	12.4	11.8	14.0	16.9	6.8	7.6
Grace period (years)	..	..	..	..	4.6	3.7	4.8	4.5	1.8	3.1
Grant element (%)	..	..	..	..	4.2	16.3	25.3	22.8	14.0	22.2
Official creditors										
Interest (%)	..	..	..	..	6.9	6.9	5.2	4.5	5.8	5.7
Maturity (years)	..	..	..	..	13.9	13.0	16.0	16.8	8.3	9.7
Grace period (years)	..	..	..	..	5.2	4.0	5.6	6.8	1.6	1.7
Grant element (%)	..	..	..	..	2.2	16.9	29.9	35.6	14.6	16.9
Private creditors										
Interest (%)	..	..	..	..	7.8	5.9	8.1	6.3	5.5	4.2
Maturity (years)	..	..	..	..	9.3	7.4	5.8	16.9	4.4	7.6
Grace period (years)	..	..	..	..	3.4	2.6	1.6	4.2	2.1	3.1
Grant element (%)	..	..	..	..	8.6	14.2	5.9	21.0	13.0	22.2
Memorandum items										
Commitments	..	..	..	..	468	287	145	61	140	455
Official creditors	..	..	..	..	321	226	117	8	85	1
Private creditors	..	..	..	..	147	61	28	53	55	454

10. CONTRACTUAL OBLIGATIONS ON OUTSTANDING LONG-TERM DEBT

	1999	2000	2001	2002	2003	2004	2005	2006	2007	2008
TOTAL										
Disbursements	311	185	73	34	2	2	1	0	0	0
Principal	150	117	205	207	181	169	159	33	29	24
Interest	55	56	52	42	32	23	15	9	7	5
Official creditors										
Disbursements	49	25	10	5	2	2	1	0	0	0
Principal	52	55	64	69	66	61	58	28	25	22
Interest	32	30	26	23	18	14	10	7	5	4
Bilateral creditors										
Disbursements	4	1	0	0	0	0	0	0	0	0
Principal	18	19	20	21	21	16	16	4	4	4
Interest	9	8	7	6	5	4	3	2	2	2
Multilateral creditors										
Disbursements	46	24	10	5	2	2	1	0	0	0
Principal	34	37	44	48	45	45	42	24	21	19
Interest	23	22	20	17	13	10	7	5	3	2
Private creditors										
Disbursements	262	161	63	29	0	0	0	0	0	0
Principal	98	62	141	138	114	108	101	5	4	2
Interest	24	26	25	20	14	9	5	2	1	1
Commercial banks										
Disbursements	226	156	61	28	0	0	0	0	0	0
Principal	3	3	94	95	96	94	94	3	2	0
Interest	10	17	18	15	11	7	3	0	0	0
Other private										
Disbursements	36	5	2	1	0	0	0	0	0	0
Principal	95	59	47	43	19	14	7	2	2	2
Interest	14	9	7	4	3	2	2	1	1	1

BELIZE

(US$ million, unless otherwise indicated)

	1970	1980	1990	1992	1993	1994	1995	1996	1997	1998
1. SUMMARY DEBT DATA										
TOTAL DEBT STOCKS (EDT)	..	**62.9**	**154.2**	**187.6**	**198.7**	**200.7**	**260.5**	**286.9**	**454.8**	**337.6**
Long-term debt (LDOD)	**4.1**	**46.9**	**147.7**	**176.6**	**179.5**	**184.2**	**220.3**	**251.5**	**269.4**	**282.2**
Public and publicly guaranteed	4.1	46.9	136.6	170.2	175.9	182.7	220.3	251.5	269.4	282.2
Private nonguaranteed	0.0	0.0	11.1	6.4	3.6	1.5	0.0	0.0	0.0	0.0
Use of IMF credit	**0.0**	**0.0**	**0.4**	**0.0**	**0.0**	**0.0**	**0.0**	**0.0**	**0.0**	**0.0**
Short-term debt	..	**16.0**	**6.1**	**11.0**	**19.1**	**16.5**	**40.2**	**35.4**	**185.3**	**55.4**
of which interest arrears on LDOD	..	0.0	0.9	0.9	2.1	2.5	5.1	4.9	3.3	4.9
Official creditors	..	0.0	0.4	0.8	1.0	1.3	2.6	3.2	2.1	3.1
Private creditors	..	0.0	0.5	0.1	1.1	1.2	2.4	1.7	1.3	1.8
Memo: principal arrears on LDOD	..	0.0	2.0	2.2	2.8	6.1	11.4	8.1	8.1	8.5
Official creditors	..	0.0	0.8	2.2	2.3	3.9	5.1	4.1	3.8	4.4
Private creditors	..	0.0	1.2	0.1	0.5	2.1	6.4	4.0	4.4	4.0
Memo: export credits	..	0.0	30.0	31.0	34.0	47.0	41.0	38.0	32.0	30.0
TOTAL DEBT FLOWS										
Disbursements	**4.3**	**13.7**	**22.3**	**38.0**	**18.5**	**19.3**	**31.2**	**60.5**	**48.8**	**36.3**
Long-term debt	4.3	13.7	22.3	38.0	18.5	19.3	31.2	60.5	48.8	36.3
IMF purchases	0.0	0.0	0.0	0.0	0.0	0.0	0.0	0.0	0.0	0.0
Principal repayments	**0.0**	**0.6**	**12.9**	**12.8**	**14.3**	**18.8**	**26.2**	**27.3**	**25.4**	**24.7**
Long-term debt	0.0	0.6	9.9	12.8	14.3	18.8	26.2	27.3	25.4	24.7
IMF repurchases	0.0	0.0	3.0	0.0	0.0	0.0	0.0	0.0	0.0	0.0
Net flows on debt	**4.3**	**-8.9**	**10.2**	**25.2**	**11.0**	**-2.5**	**26.2**	**28.5**	**174.8**	**-119.9**
of which short-term debt	..	-22.0	0.8	0.0	6.8	-3.0	21.2	-4.7	151.5	-131.5
Interest payments (INT)	..	**3.1**	**7.2**	**6.5**	**7.0**	**8.3**	**11.3**	**12.7**	**14.1**	**20.9**
Long-term debt	0.0	0.9	6.6	6.1	6.2	7.3	9.9	10.8	9.3	15.1
IMF charges	0.0	0.0	0.2	0.0	0.0	0.0	0.0	0.0	0.0	0.0
Short-term debt	..	2.2	0.4	0.4	0.8	0.9	1.4	1.9	4.9	5.8
Net transfers on debt	..	**-12.0**	**3.0**	**18.7**	**4.0**	**-10.8**	**14.9**	**15.8**	**160.7**	**-140.8**
Total debt service paid (TDS)	..	**3.6**	**20.1**	**19.3**	**21.4**	**27.1**	**37.5**	**40.0**	**39.6**	**45.6**
Long-term debt	0.0	1.5	16.5	18.9	20.5	26.1	36.1	38.1	34.7	39.8
IMF repurchases and charges	0.0	0.0	3.2	0.0	0.0	0.0	0.0	0.0	0.0	0.0
Short-term debt (interest only)	..	2.2	0.4	0.4	0.8	0.9	1.4	1.9	4.9	5.8
2. AGGREGATE NET RESOURCE FLOWS AND NET TRANSFERS (LONG-TERM)										
NET RESOURCE FLOWS	**6.1**	**21.9**	**33.7**	**47.5**	**30.9**	**28.4**	**33.0**	**51.1**	**44.7**	**62.7**
Net flow of long-term debt (ex. IMF)	4.3	13.1	12.4	25.2	4.2	0.5	5.0	33.2	23.3	11.6
Foreign direct investment (net)	0.0	0.0	17.0	16.0	9.0	15.0	21.0	15.0	17.0	20.0
Portfolio equity flows	0.0	0.0	0.0	0.0	0.0	0.0	0.0	0.0	0.0	0.0
Grants (excluding technical coop.)	1.8	8.8	4.4	6.3	17.7	13.0	7.0	2.9	4.4	31.1
Memo: technical coop. grants	1.1	2.4	13.0	13.8	16.1	9.2	11.9	10.7	6.9	3.5
official net resource flows	6.1	16.1	11.1	29.7	20.2	15.9	15.7	29.8	19.3	36.5
private net resource flows	0.0	5.8	22.6	17.8	10.7	12.5	17.3	21.3	25.4	26.2
NET TRANSFERS	**6.1**	**21.0**	**19.7**	**28.9**	**12.3**	**8.3**	**10.1**	**28.3**	**22.4**	**32.6**
Interest on long-term debt	0.0	0.9	6.6	6.1	6.2	7.3	9.9	10.8	9.3	15.1
Profit remittances on FDI	0.0	0.0	7.5	12.4	12.4	12.8	13.0	12.0	13.0	15.0
Memo: official net transfers	6.1	15.2	6.9	25.1	15.0	10.5	8.1	21.4	12.2	26.7
private net transfers	0.0	5.8	12.8	3.8	-2.7	-2.2	2.0	6.9	10.2	5.9
3. MAJOR ECONOMIC AGGREGATES										
Gross national product (GNP)	51.5	192.8	396.0	467.4	507.4	529.6	570.5	607.1	625.9	650.2
Exports of goods & services (XGS)	..	..	268.9	306.1	301.5	293.5	314.1	328.6	356.5	352.8
of which workers remittances	..	..	13.7	16.2	13.1	13.0	13.9	13.2	17.8	19.0
Imports of goods & services (MGS)	..	..	269.2	348.9	366.4	348.0	350.6	353.2	405.4	429.2
International reserves (RES)	..	12.7	69.8	52.9	38.7	34.5	37.6	58.4	59.4	44.1
Current account balance	..	..	15.4	-28.6	-48.5	-40.1	-17.2	-6.6	-31.9	-59.8
4. DEBT INDICATORS										
EDT / XGS (%)	..	..	57.4	61.3	65.9	68.4	82.9	87.3	127.6	95.7
EDT / GNP (%)	..	32.6	38.9	40.1	39.2	37.9	45.7	47.3	72.7	51.9
TDS / XGS (%)	..	..	7.5	6.3	7.1	9.2	11.9	12.2	11.1	12.9
INT / XGS (%)	..	..	2.7	2.1	2.3	2.8	3.6	3.9	4.0	5.9
INT / GNP (%)	..	1.6	1.8	1.4	1.4	1.6	2.0	2.1	2.3	3.2
RES / EDT (%)	..	20.2	45.3	28.2	19.5	17.2	14.4	20.4	13.1	13.1
RES / MGS (months)	..	..	3.1	1.8	1.3	1.2	1.3	2.0	1.8	1.2
Short-term / EDT (%)	..	25.4	4.0	5.9	9.6	8.2	15.4	12.3	40.7	16.4
Concessional / EDT (%)	..	48.8	52.5	46.1	42.0	41.6	35.7	41.0	24.9	32.4
Multilateral / EDT (%)	..	35.8	37.4	34.1	31.7	35.4	34.4	31.4	23.2	35.4

BELIZE

(US$ million, unless otherwise indicated)

	1970	1980	1990	1992	1993	1994	1995	1996	1997	1998
5. LONG-TERM DEBT										
DEBT OUTSTANDING (LDOD)	**4.1**	**46.9**	**147.7**	**176.6**	**179.5**	**184.2**	**220.3**	**251.5**	**269.4**	**282.2**
Public and publicly guaranteed	**4.1**	**46.9**	**136.6**	**170.2**	**175.9**	**182.7**	**220.3**	**251.5**	**269.4**	**282.2**
Official creditors	4.1	39.9	118.3	143.1	144.4	151.4	175.8	200.7	210.2	216.7
Multilateral	0.0	22.5	57.7	63.9	63.0	71.0	89.7	90.0	105.4	119.4
Concessional	0.0	19.6	30.1	34.9	34.1	34.5	43.2	40.8	39.0	38.8
Bilateral	4.1	17.4	60.6	79.2	81.4	80.4	86.1	110.7	104.7	97.4
Concessional	0.0	11.1	50.9	51.5	49.3	48.9	49.9	76.9	74.2	70.5
Private creditors	0.0	7.1	18.2	27.1	31.6	31.3	44.5	50.8	59.2	65.5
Bonds	0.0	0.0	0.0	0.0	0.0	0.0	0.0	0.0	0.0	0.0
Commercial banks	0.0	0.0	16.4	23.4	22.0	24.3	38.7	47.9	47.7	55.3
Other private	0.0	7.1	1.8	3.7	9.6	7.0	5.8	2.9	11.5	10.2
Private nonguaranteed	**0.0**	**0.0**	**11.1**	**6.4**	**3.6**	**1.5**	**0.0**	**0.0**	**0.0**	**0.0**
Bonds	0.0	0.0	0.0	0.0	0.0	0.0	0.0	0.0	0.0	0.0
Commercial banks	0.0	0.0	11.1	6.4	3.6	1.5	0.0	0.0	0.0	0.0
Memo:										
IBRD	0.0	0.0	17.5	19.2	20.1	25.6	29.5	32.5	39.9	41.4
IDA	0.0	0.0	0.0	0.0	0.0	0.0	0.0	0.0	0.0	0.0
DISBURSEMENTS	**4.3**	**13.7**	**22.3**	**38.0**	**18.5**	**19.3**	**31.2**	**60.5**	**48.8**	**36.3**
Public and publicly guaranteed	**4.3**	**13.7**	**18.0**	**38.0**	**18.5**	**19.3**	**31.2**	**60.5**	**48.8**	**36.3**
Official creditors	4.3	7.8	13.3	31.0	11.8	14.7	25.8	45.0	31.7	22.3
Multilateral	0.0	4.6	5.9	8.9	4.2	10.6	12.4	10.0	26.4	19.0
Concessional	0.0	3.2	2.3	5.4	1.9	1.5	3.4	1.0	2.4	1.7
Bilateral	4.3	3.3	7.5	22.1	7.6	4.1	13.4	35.0	5.3	3.3
Concessional	0.0	0.7	4.6	7.0	0.0	0.0	3.5	30.4	1.8	0.8
Private creditors	0.0	5.8	4.6	7.0	6.7	4.6	5.3	15.5	17.0	14.0
Bonds	0.0	0.0	0.0	0.0	0.0	0.0	0.0	0.0	0.0	0.0
Commercial banks	0.0	0.0	4.6	6.3	0.0	4.6	4.8	15.5	7.0	14.0
Other private	0.0	5.8	0.0	0.8	6.7	0.0	0.5	0.0	10.0	0.0
Private nonguaranteed	**0.0**	**0.0**	**4.3**	**0.0**	**0.0**	**0.0**	**0.0**	**0.0**	**0.0**	**0.0**
Bonds	0.0	0.0	0.0	0.0	0.0	0.0	0.0	0.0	0.0	0.0
Commercial banks	0.0	0.0	4.3	0.0	0.0	0.0	0.0	0.0	0.0	0.0
Memo:										
IBRD	0.0	0.0	3.4	2.4	2.1	6.4	5.6	7.5	12.6	4.0
IDA	0.0	0.0	0.0	0.0	0.0	0.0	0.0	0.0	0.0	0.0
PRINCIPAL REPAYMENTS	**0.0**	**0.6**	**9.9**	**12.8**	**14.3**	**18.8**	**26.2**	**27.3**	**25.4**	**24.7**
Public and publicly guaranteed	**0.0**	**0.6**	**9.0**	**10.3**	**11.5**	**16.7**	**24.7**	**27.3**	**25.4**	**24.7**
Official creditors	0.0	0.5	6.6	7.6	9.3	11.8	17.1	18.2	16.8	16.9
Multilateral	0.0	0.4	2.7	4.1	4.7	5.3	7.2	6.8	6.5	6.1
Concessional	0.0	0.3	1.5	2.0	2.1	2.1	3.2	3.0	2.8	2.5
Bilateral	0.0	0.1	3.9	3.5	4.7	6.5	10.0	11.3	10.4	10.9
Concessional	0.0	0.1	1.1	1.6	1.5	1.6	2.6	4.1	3.7	4.8
Private creditors	0.0	0.1	2.4	2.7	2.2	4.9	7.6	9.1	8.6	7.8
Bonds	0.0	0.0	0.0	0.0	0.0	0.0	0.0	0.0	0.0	0.0
Commercial banks	0.0	0.0	2.3	1.8	1.5	2.3	4.7	6.3	7.2	6.4
Other private	0.0	0.1	0.1	0.9	0.7	2.7	2.9	2.9	1.4	1.4
Private nonguaranteed	**0.0**	**0.0**	**0.9**	**2.5**	**2.8**	**2.1**	**1.5**	**0.0**	**0.0**	**0.0**
Bonds	0.0	0.0	0.0	0.0	0.0	0.0	0.0	0.0	0.0	0.0
Commercial banks	0.0	0.0	0.9	2.5	2.8	2.1	1.5	0.0	0.0	0.0
Memo:										
IBRD	0.0	0.0	0.6	1.3	1.6	2.3	2.5	2.3	2.3	2.7
IDA	0.0	0.0	0.0	0.0	0.0	0.0	0.0	0.0	0.0	0.0
NET FLOWS ON DEBT	**4.3**	**13.1**	**12.4**	**25.2**	**4.2**	**0.5**	**5.0**	**33.2**	**23.3**	**11.6**
Public and publicly guaranteed	**4.3**	**13.1**	**8.9**	**27.7**	**7.0**	**2.6**	**6.5**	**33.2**	**23.3**	**11.6**
Official creditors	4.3	7.3	6.7	23.4	2.5	2.9	8.7	26.9	14.9	5.4
Multilateral	0.0	4.2	3.1	4.8	-0.4	5.3	5.2	3.2	20.0	13.0
Concessional	0.0	2.8	0.8	3.5	-0.2	-0.6	0.3	-2.0	-0.5	-0.8
Bilateral	4.3	3.1	3.6	18.6	2.9	-2.4	3.5	23.6	-5.1	-7.6
Concessional	0.0	0.7	3.5	5.4	-1.5	-1.6	0.9	26.2	-1.9	-4.0
Private creditors	0.0	5.8	2.2	4.3	4.5	-0.4	-2.2	6.3	8.4	6.2
Bonds	0.0	0.0	0.0	0.0	0.0	0.0	0.0	0.0	0.0	0.0
Commercial banks	0.0	0.0	2.3	4.5	-1.5	2.3	0.2	9.2	-0.1	7.6
Other private	0.0	5.8	-0.1	-0.2	6.0	-2.7	-2.4	-2.9	8.6	-1.4
Private nonguaranteed	**0.0**	**0.0**	**3.4**	**-2.5**	**-2.8**	**-2.1**	**-1.5**	**0.0**	**0.0**	**0.0**
Bonds	0.0	0.0	0.0	0.0	0.0	0.0	0.0	0.0	0.0	0.0
Commercial banks	0.0	0.0	3.4	-2.5	-2.8	-2.1	-1.5	0.0	0.0	0.0
Memo:										
IBRD	0.0	0.0	2.8	1.1	0.5	4.1	3.1	5.2	10.3	1.3
IDA	0.0	0.0	0.0	0.0	0.0	0.0	0.0	0.0	0.0	0.0

BELIZE

(US$ million, unless otherwise indicated)

	1970	1980	1990	1992	1993	1994	1995	1996	1997	1998
INTEREST PAYMENTS (LINT)	**0.0**	**0.9**	**6.6**	**6.1**	**6.2**	**7.3**	**9.9**	**10.8**	**9.3**	**15.1**
Public and publicly guaranteed	**0.0**	**0.9**	**5.6**	**5.4**	**5.8**	**7.2**	**9.8**	**10.8**	**9.3**	**15.1**
Official creditors	0.0	0.9	4.2	4.6	5.2	5.4	7.6	8.4	7.1	9.8
Multilateral	0.0	0.6	2.7	2.8	2.8	2.8	4.0	4.2	3.8	5.2
Concessional	0.0	0.5	1.0	0.9	0.8	0.8	1.1	1.1	0.8	0.8
Bilateral	0.0	0.3	1.5	1.7	2.5	2.6	3.7	4.2	3.3	4.6
Concessional	0.0	0.0	0.6	0.5	0.6	0.6	0.8	1.5	1.1	2.5
Private creditors	0.0	0.0	1.4	0.9	0.6	1.8	2.2	2.4	2.2	5.3
Bonds	0.0	0.0	0.0	0.0	0.0	0.0	0.0	0.0	0.0	0.0
Commercial banks	0.0	0.0	1.4	0.5	0.3	1.2	1.6	2.1	2.0	4.2
Other private	0.0	0.0	0.0	0.4	0.2	0.6	0.6	0.4	0.2	1.1
Private nonguaranteed	**0.0**	**0.0**	**0.9**	**0.7**	**0.4**	**0.1**	**0.1**	**0.0**	**0.0**	**0.0**
Bonds	0.0	0.0	0.0	0.0	0.0	0.0	0.0	0.0	0.0	0.0
Commercial banks	0.0	0.0	0.9	0.7	0.4	0.1	0.1	0.0	0.0	0.0
Memo:										
IBRD	0.0	0.0	1.1	1.4	1.4	1.5	1.9	2.0	2.1	2.4
IDA	0.0	0.0	0.0	0.0	0.0	0.0	0.0	0.0	0.0	0.0
NET TRANSFERS ON DEBT	**4.3**	**12.2**	**5.8**	**19.1**	**-2.0**	**-6.9**	**-4.9**	**22.4**	**14.1**	**-3.5**
Public and publicly guaranteed	**4.3**	**12.2**	**3.3**	**22.3**	**1.2**	**-4.6**	**-3.4**	**22.4**	**14.1**	**-3.5**
Official creditors	4.3	6.4	2.5	18.8	-2.7	-2.5	1.1	18.5	7.8	-4.4
Multilateral	0.0	3.6	0.4	1.9	-3.2	2.5	1.2	-1.0	16.2	7.7
Concessional	0.0	2.3	-0.3	2.6	-1.0	-1.4	-0.9	-3.1	-1.3	-1.7
Bilateral	4.3	2.9	2.1	16.9	0.4	-5.0	-0.2	19.5	-8.3	-12.2
Concessional	0.0	0.7	3.0	4.8	-2.1	-2.2	0.0	24.7	-3.0	-6.5
Private creditors	0.0	5.8	0.8	3.5	4.0	-2.2	-4.4	3.9	6.2	0.9
Bonds	0.0	0.0	0.0	0.0	0.0	0.0	0.0	0.0	0.0	0.0
Commercial banks	0.0	0.0	1.0	4.0	-1.8	1.1	-1.5	7.1	-2.2	3.3
Other private	0.0	5.8	-0.2	-0.5	5.8	-3.3	-3.0	-3.2	8.4	-2.4
Private nonguaranteed	**0.0**	**0.0**	**2.5**	**-3.2**	**-3.2**	**-2.2**	**-1.6**	**0.0**	**0.0**	**0.0**
Bonds	0.0	0.0	0.0	0.0	0.0	0.0	0.0	0.0	0.0	0.0
Commercial banks	0.0	0.0	2.5	-3.2	-3.2	-2.2	-1.6	0.0	0.0	0.0
Memo:										
IBRD	0.0	0.0	1.7	-0.3	-0.9	2.6	1.2	3.2	8.2	-1.1
IDA	0.0	0.0	0.0	0.0	0.0	0.0	0.0	0.0	0.0	0.0
DEBT SERVICE (LTDS)	**0.0**	**1.5**	**16.5**	**18.9**	**20.5**	**26.1**	**36.1**	**38.1**	**34.7**	**39.8**
Public and publicly guaranteed	**0.0**	**1.5**	**14.7**	**15.7**	**17.3**	**23.9**	**34.5**	**38.1**	**34.7**	**39.8**
Official creditors	0.0	1.4	10.8	12.2	14.6	17.2	24.8	26.5	23.9	26.7
Multilateral	0.0	1.0	5.4	6.9	7.4	8.1	11.2	11.0	10.3	11.3
Concessional	0.0	0.9	2.5	2.9	2.9	2.9	4.3	4.1	3.6	3.4
Bilateral	0.0	0.4	5.4	5.3	7.1	9.1	13.6	15.5	13.6	15.4
Concessional	0.0	0.1	1.6	2.1	2.1	2.2	3.5	5.7	4.8	7.3
Private creditors	0.0	0.1	3.8	3.6	2.7	6.7	9.8	11.6	10.8	13.1
Bonds	0.0	0.0	0.0	0.0	0.0	0.0	0.0	0.0	0.0	0.0
Commercial banks	0.0	0.0	3.7	2.3	1.8	3.4	6.3	8.4	9.2	10.7
Other private	0.0	0.1	0.2	1.3	0.9	3.3	3.5	3.2	1.6	2.4
Private nonguaranteed	**0.0**	**0.0**	**1.8**	**3.2**	**3.2**	**2.2**	**1.6**	**0.0**	**0.0**	**0.0**
Bonds	0.0	0.0	0.0	0.0	0.0	0.0	0.0	0.0	0.0	0.0
Commercial banks	0.0	0.0	1.8	3.2	3.2	2.2	1.6	0.0	0.0	0.0
Memo:										
IBRD	0.0	0.0	1.8	2.7	3.1	3.8	4.4	4.3	4.4	5.1
IDA	0.0	0.0	0.0	0.0	0.0	0.0	0.0	0.0	0.0	0.0
UNDISBURSED DEBT	**0.0**	**22.7**	**61.6**	**53.3**	**99.7**	**93.1**	**97.4**	**78.7**	**73.8**	**97.7**
Official creditors	0.0	17.9	50.5	52.0	74.3	78.1	85.6	70.3	66.7	82.7
Private creditors	0.0	4.8	11.1	1.2	25.4	15.0	11.8	8.3	7.0	15.0
Memorandum items										
Concessional LDOD	0.0	30.7	81.0	86.3	83.4	83.4	93.1	117.7	113.3	109.2
Variable rate LDOD	0.0	0.0	38.6	42.8	39.9	42.8	56.6	57.2	61.4	59.8
Public sector LDOD	4.1	46.9	136.6	170.2	175.9	182.7	220.3	251.5	269.4	282.2
Private sector LDOD	0.0	0.0	11.1	6.4	3.6	1.5	0.0	0.0	0.0	0.0
6. CURRENCY COMPOSITION OF LONG-TERM DEBT (PERCENT)										
Deutsche mark	0.0	0.9	0.7	0.4	0.3	0.3	0.2	0.2	0.1	0.1
French franc	0.0	0.0	0.0	0.0	0.0	0.0	0.0	0.0	0.0	0.0
Japanese yen	0.0	0.0	0.0	0.0	0.0	0.0	0.0	0.0	0.0	0.0
Pound sterling	100.0	15.3	23.6	16.7	14.4	13.0	10.3	7.9	6.4	5.5
Swiss franc	0.0	0.0	0.0	0.0	0.0	0.0	0.0	0.0	0.0	0.0
U.S.dollars	0.0	29.4	45.2	52.4	56.4	55.8	62.4	67.6	68.6	83.6
Multiple currency	0.0	23.4	23.4	19.0	18.3	20.0	17.6	16.0	17.1	2.9
Special drawing rights	0.0	0.0	0.5	0.2	0.7	0.8	0.6	0.5	0.4	0.3
All other currencies	0.0	31.0	6.6	11.3	9.9	10.1	8.9	7.8	7.4	7.6

BELIZE

(US$ million, unless otherwise indicated)

	1970	1980	1990	1992	1993	1994	1995	1996	1997	1998
7. DEBT RESTRUCTURINGS										
Total amount rescheduled	..	..	0.0	7.3	0.0	0.0	0.0	0.0	0.0	0.0
Debt stock rescheduled	..	..	0.0	7.3	0.0	0.0	0.0	0.0	0.0	0.0
Principal rescheduled	..	..	0.0	0.0	0.0	0.0	0.0	0.0	0.0	0.0
Official	..	..	0.0	0.0	0.0	0.0	0.0	0.0	0.0	0.0
Private	..	..	0.0	0.0	0.0	0.0	0.0	0.0	0.0	0.0
Interest rescheduled	..	..	0.0	0.0	0.0	0.0	0.0	0.0	0.0	0.0
Official	..	..	0.0	0.0	0.0	0.0	0.0	0.0	0.0	0.0
Private	..	..	0.0	0.0	0.0	0.0	0.0	0.0	0.0	0.0
Debt forgiven	..	..	9.1	0.0	0.0	0.0	0.0	0.0	0.0	0.0
Memo: interest forgiven	..	..	0.0	0.0	0.0	0.0	0.0	0.0	0.0	0.0
Debt stock reduction	..	..	0.0	0.0	0.0	0.0	0.0	0.0	0.0	0.0
of which debt buyback	..	..	0.0	0.0	0.0	0.0	0.0	0.0	0.0	0.0
8. DEBT STOCK-FLOW RECONCILIATION										
Total change in debt stocks	..	..	9.2	16.8	11.0	2.0	59.8	26.4	167.9	-117.1
Net flows on debt	4.3	-8.9	10.2	25.2	11.0	-2.5	26.2	28.5	174.8	-119.9
Net change in interest arrears	..	..	0.3	0.3	1.3	0.3	2.6	-0.1	-1.6	1.5
Interest capitalized	..	..	0.0	0.0	0.0	0.0	0.0	0.0	0.0	0.0
Debt forgiveness or reduction	..	..	-9.1	0.0	0.0	0.0	0.0	0.0	0.0	0.0
Cross-currency valuation	..	..	8.2	-7.9	-1.5	4.0	1.1	-1.6	-5.5	1.2
Residual	..	..	-0.3	-0.8	0.3	0.2	30.0	-0.4	0.1	0.0
9. AVERAGE TERMS OF NEW COMMITMENTS										
ALL CREDITORS										
Interest (%)	7.0	5.6	5.0	6.2	6.2	5.8	6.0	4.3	6.8	6.5
Maturity (years)	26.0	18.0	10.0	18.3	11.8	14.7	17.6	17.4	15.1	18.2
Grace period (years)	3.0	4.7	2.5	2.7	3.1	4.2	3.9	12.6	4.3	4.4
Grant element (%)	20.7	29.0	21.2	21.5	15.9	22.5	23.0	37.1	20.0	20.8
Official creditors										
Interest (%)	7.0	4.4	5.0	6.2	6.4	5.8	5.9	5.2	5.0	6.3
Maturity (years)	26.0	25.0	10.0	19.0	16.0	17.6	17.9	20.7	17.7	23.2
Grace period (years)	3.0	6.7	2.5	2.8	4.4	5.2	3.9	15.4	5.3	5.2
Grant element (%)	20.7	43.0	21.2	22.3	19.6	26.4	23.3	38.7	31.8	25.2
Private creditors										
Interest (%)	0.0	7.2	0.0	7.1	6.0	5.9	8.6	1.8	10.4	6.9
Maturity (years)	0.0	7.7	0.0	5.9	6.6	5.5	4.8	7.0	10.0	9.6
Grace period (years)	0.0	1.7	0.0	1.4	1.6	1.0	0.3	3.5	2.3	2.9
Grant element (%)	0.0	8.6	0.0	7.9	11.4	10.0	2.7	32.0	-2.6	13.2
Memorandum items										
Commitments	4.3	11.6	5.0	43.8	68.4	23.5	29.2	49.9	46.7	60.1
Official creditors	4.3	6.9	5.0	41.4	37.5	17.8	28.7	37.9	30.7	38.1
Private creditors	0.0	4.7	0.0	2.4	30.9	5.6	0.5	12.0	16.0	22.0

10. CONTRACTUAL OBLIGATIONS ON OUTSTANDING LONG-TERM DEBT

	1999	2000	2001	2002	2003	2004	2005	2006	2007	2008
TOTAL										
Disbursements	31.8	26.6	16.1	9.6	5.8	3.6	2.0	0.9	0.8	0.4
Principal	26.3	29.4	31.2	28.7	28.7	25.4	22.4	21.2	25.3	16.3
Interest	16.2	16.2	15.6	14.5	13.3	12.0	10.5	9.2	8.0	6.4
Official creditors										
Disbursements	21.4	22.7	15.2	9.6	5.8	3.6	2.0	0.9	0.8	0.4
Principal	18.1	19.0	18.0	19.4	19.4	19.1	17.8	16.7	16.6	14.8
Interest	11.7	11.9	11.8	11.4	10.8	9.9	9.0	8.1	7.2	6.3
Bilateral creditors										
Disbursements	3.8	3.5	2.4	1.7	1.2	0.7	0.5	0.5	0.4	0.2
Principal	8.5	8.0	7.5	7.8	7.5	6.8	5.7	5.4	5.4	5.0
Interest	4.2	4.0	3.7	3.5	3.2	3.0	2.7	2.5	2.3	2.1
Multilateral creditors										
Disbursements	17.7	19.3	12.8	8.0	4.6	2.9	1.5	0.4	0.4	0.2
Principal	9.6	11.0	10.5	11.6	11.9	12.3	12.1	11.3	11.3	9.8
Interest	7.5	7.9	8.1	7.9	7.5	7.0	6.3	5.6	4.9	4.2
Private creditors										
Disbursements	10.3	3.8	0.9	0.0	0.0	0.0	0.0	0.0	0.0	0.0
Principal	8.2	10.4	13.1	9.3	9.3	6.3	4.6	4.6	8.7	1.4
Interest	4.5	4.3	3.8	3.1	2.6	2.0	1.5	1.1	0.8	0.1
Commercial banks										
Disbursements	10.3	3.8	0.9	0.0	0.0	0.0	0.0	0.0	0.0	0.0
Principal	8.1	10.4	12.3	8.5	8.5	5.5	3.8	3.8	3.3	1.4
Interest	3.5	3.3	2.8	2.2	1.8	1.3	0.9	0.6	0.3	0.1
Other private										
Disbursements	0.0	0.0	0.0	0.0	0.0	0.0	0.0	0.0	0.0	0.0
Principal	0.1	0.1	0.8	0.8	0.8	0.8	0.8	0.8	5.4	0.0
Interest	1.0	1.0	1.0	0.9	0.8	0.7	0.7	0.6	0.5	0.0

BENIN

(US$ million, unless otherwise indicated)

	1970	1980	1990	1992	1993	1994	1995	1996	1997	1998
1. SUMMARY DEBT DATA										
TOTAL DEBT STOCKS (EDT)	..	**424**	**1,292**	**1,373**	**1,447**	**1,589**	**1,614**	**1,594**	**1,624**	**1,647**
Long-term debt (LDOD)	**41**	**334**	**1,219**	**1,324**	**1,371**	**1,487**	**1,483**	**1,448**	**1,393**	**1,469**
Public and publicly guaranteed	41	334	1,219	1,324	1,371	1,487	1,483	1,448	1,393	1,469
Private nonguaranteed	0	0	0	0	0	0	0	0	0	0
Use of IMF credit	**0**	**16**	**18**	**22**	**43**	**71**	**84**	**99**	**95**	**94**
Short-term debt	..	**73**	**55**	**27**	**33**	**31**	**47**	**47**	**136**	**85**
of which interest arrears on LDOD	..	5	21	9	13	8	8	8	8	7
Official creditors	..	0	19	8	12	7	7	7	7	6
Private creditors	..	5	2	1	1	1	1	1	1	1
Memo: principal arrears on LDOD	..	14	78	68	70	72	71	72	71	73
Official creditors	..	1	69	65	67	68	67	68	68	69
Private creditors	..	13	9	4	4	4	4	4	3	4
Memo: export credits	..	0	303	237	215	144	174	150	125	98
TOTAL DEBT FLOWS										
Disbursements	**2**	**71**	**120**	**81**	**103**	**130**	**115**	**128**	**57**	**62**
Long-term debt	2	62	120	81	81	104	101	109	51	62
IMF purchases	0	10	0	0	22	26	14	20	6	0
Principal repayments	**1**	**6**	**21**	**15**	**18**	**21**	**26**	**28**	**32**	**35**
Long-term debt	1	6	19	15	18	20	24	26	28	29
IMF repurchases	0	0	2	0	0	1	2	2	4	5
Net flows on debt	**1**	**42**	**92**	**39**	**87**	**112**	**105**	**101**	**114**	**-23**
of which short-term debt	..	-24	-8	-27	2	3	16	0	89	-50
Interest payments (INT)	..	**14**	**18**	**13**	**14**	**20**	**24**	**18**	**23**	**26**
Long-term debt	0	3	14	11	12	19	21	16	18	21
IMF charges	0	0	0	0	0	0	0	1	1	1
Short-term debt	..	11	4	2	1	1	2	2	4	5
Net transfers on debt	..	**27**	**74**	**26**	**73**	**92**	**81**	**82**	**91**	**-49**
Total debt service paid (TDS)	..	**20**	**38**	**28**	**32**	**41**	**50**	**46**	**55**	**61**
Long-term debt	2	9	33	26	31	39	46	42	46	50
IMF repurchases and charges	0	0	2	0	0	1	2	3	5	6
Short-term debt (interest only)	..	11	4	2	1	1	2	2	4	5
2. AGGREGATE NET RESOURCE FLOWS AND NET TRANSFERS (LONG-TERM)										
NET RESOURCE FLOWS	**17**	**101**	**213**	**239**	**206**	**197**	**227**	**242**	**175**	**186**
Net flow of long-term debt (ex. IMF)	1	56	102	65	63	84	77	83	23	32
Foreign direct investment (net)	7	4	1	7	10	5	1	36	27	34
Portfolio equity flows	0	0	0	0	0	0	0	0	0	0
Grants (excluding technical coop.)	9	41	110	166	134	108	149	123	126	120
Memo: technical coop. grants	6	26	5	55	56	52	61	67	78	67
official net resource flows	9	97	212	232	196	192	226	206	148	152
private net resource flows	8	4	1	7	10	5	1	36	27	34
NET TRANSFERS	**13**	**96**	**199**	**228**	**194**	**178**	**206**	**226**	**158**	**165**
Interest on long-term debt	0	3	14	11	12	19	21	16	18	21
Profit remittances on FDI	4	3	0	0	0	0	0	0	0	0
Memo: official net transfers	9	95	198	221	184	173	205	190	131	132
private net transfers	4	1	1	7	10	5	1	36	27	34
3. MAJOR ECONOMIC AGGREGATES										
Gross national product (GNP)	330	1,402	1,806	1,579	2,066	1,462	1,965	2,176	2,111	2,280
Exports of goods & services (XGS)	..	318	465	666	681	641	730	772	632	571
of which workers remittances	..	77	89	130	103	82	92	81	67	..
Imports of goods & services (MGS)	..	428	492	774	769	655	926	806	795	814
International reserves (RES)	16	15	69	249	248	262	202	266	256	261
Current account balance	..	-36	24	5	16	85	-83	-41	-154	-157
4. DEBT INDICATORS										
EDT / XGS (%)	..	133.1	277.9	206.2	212.6	247.9	221.0	206.7	256.9	288.6
EDT / GNP (%)	..	30.2	71.5	87.0	70.0	108.7	82.1	73.3	76.9	72.2
TDS / XGS (%)	..	6.4	8.2	4.2	4.7	6.4	6.8	5.9	8.7	10.6
INT / XGS (%)	..	4.5	3.8	1.9	2.1	3.2	3.2	2.4	3.6	4.5
INT / GNP (%)	..	1.0	1.0	0.8	0.7	1.4	1.2	0.8	1.1	1.1
RES / EDT (%)	..	3.5	5.4	18.1	17.2	16.5	12.5	16.7	15.8	15.9
RES / MGS (months)	..	0.4	1.7	3.9	3.9	4.8	2.6	4.0	3.9	3.9
Short-term / EDT (%)	..	17.3	4.3	2.0	2.3	1.9	2.9	2.9	8.4	5.1
Concessional / EDT (%)	..	39.2	78.1	80.5	80.5	79.9	77.7	81.1	77.9	81.0
Multilateral / EDT (%)	..	24.5	41.6	45.9	47.2	49.0	54.0	56.6	53.6	56.6

BENIN

(US$ million, unless otherwise indicated)

	1970	1980	1990	1992	1993	1994	1995	1996	1997	1998
5. LONG-TERM DEBT										
DEBT OUTSTANDING (LDOD)	**41**	**334**	**1,219**	**1,324**	**1,371**	**1,487**	**1,483**	**1,448**	**1,393**	**1,469**
Public and publicly guaranteed	**41**	**334**	**1,219**	**1,324**	**1,371**	**1,487**	**1,483**	**1,448**	**1,393**	**1,469**
Official creditors	29	217	1,202	1,319	1,368	1,483	1,479	1,445	1,390	1,465
Multilateral	0	104	537	630	683	779	871	902	871	933
Concessional	0	84	497	595	653	755	847	878	852	904
Bilateral	29	113	665	689	685	704	608	543	519	533
Concessional	29	82	512	510	512	515	407	415	413	429
Private creditors	11	118	17	5	4	4	4	4	3	4
Bonds	0	0	0	0	0	0	0	0	0	0
Commercial banks	0	0	0	0	0	0	0	0	0	0
Other private	11	118	17	5	4	4	4	4	3	4
Private nonguaranteed	**0**	**0**	**0**	**0**	**0**	**0**	**0**	**0**	**0**	**0**
Bonds	0	0	0	0	0	0	0	0	0	0
Commercial banks	0	0	0	0	0	0	0	0	0	0
Memo:										
IBRD	0	0	0	0	0	0	0	0	0	0
IDA	0	52	326	389	418	464	498	520	510	543
DISBURSEMENTS	**2**	**62**	**120**	**81**	**81**	**104**	**101**	**109**	**51**	**62**
Public and publicly guaranteed	**2**	**62**	**120**	**81**	**81**	**104**	**101**	**109**	**51**	**62**
Official creditors	2	58	120	81	81	104	101	109	51	62
Multilateral	0	24	91	71	71	95	84	81	42	45
Concessional	0	19	82	67	69	91	79	77	41	34
Bilateral	1	35	29	9	10	9	18	27	9	17
Concessional	1	16	29	9	10	9	18	27	9	17
Private creditors	1	4	0	0	0	0	0	0	0	0
Bonds	0	0	0	0	0	0	0	0	0	0
Commercial banks	0	0	0	0	0	0	0	0	0	0
Other private	1	4	0	0	0	0	0	0	0	0
Private nonguaranteed	**0**	**0**	**0**	**0**	**0**	**0**	**0**	**0**	**0**	**0**
Bonds	0	0	0	0	0	0	0	0	0	0
Commercial banks	0	0	0	0	0	0	0	0	0	0
Memo:										
IBRD	0	0	0	0	0	0	0	0	0	0
IDA	0	12	56	33	30	29	31	41	20	20
PRINCIPAL REPAYMENTS	**1**	**6**	**19**	**15**	**18**	**20**	**24**	**26**	**28**	**29**
Public and publicly guaranteed	**1**	**6**	**19**	**15**	**18**	**20**	**24**	**26**	**28**	**29**
Official creditors	1	2	18	15	18	20	24	26	28	29
Multilateral	0	1	18	13	16	13	17	16	18	18
Concessional	0	0	7	6	10	9	12	12	14	15
Bilateral	1	2	0	2	2	7	8	10	10	11
Concessional	1	1	0	2	2	3	3	3	4	5
Private creditors	0	3	0	0	0	0	0	0	0	0
Bonds	0	0	0	0	0	0	0	0	0	0
Commercial banks	0	0	0	0	0	0	0	0	0	0
Other private	0	3	0	0	0	0	0	0	0	0
Private nonguaranteed	**0**	**0**	**0**	**0**	**0**	**0**	**0**	**0**	**0**	**0**
Bonds	0	0	0	0	0	0	0	0	0	0
Commercial banks	0	0	0	0	0	0	0	0	0	0
Memo:										
IBRD	0	0	0	0	0	0	0	0	0	0
IDA	0	0	1	2	2	3	3	3	4	4
NET FLOWS ON DEBT	**1**	**56**	**102**	**65**	**63**	**84**	**77**	**83**	**23**	**32**
Public and publicly guaranteed	**1**	**56**	**102**	**65**	**63**	**84**	**77**	**83**	**23**	**32**
Official creditors	0	56	102	65	63	84	77	83	23	32
Multilateral	0	23	73	58	55	82	67	65	24	27
Concessional	0	19	75	60	59	82	67	65	27	19
Bilateral	0	33	29	7	8	3	10	18	-2	5
Concessional	0	15	29	7	8	7	15	25	4	12
Private creditors	1	0	0	0	0	0	0	0	0	0
Bonds	0	0	0	0	0	0	0	0	0	0
Commercial banks	0	0	0	0	0	0	0	0	0	0
Other private	1	0	0	0	0	0	0	0	0	0
Private nonguaranteed	**0**	**0**	**0**	**0**	**0**	**0**	**0**	**0**	**0**	**0**
Bonds	0	0	0	0	0	0	0	0	0	0
Commercial banks	0	0	0	0	0	0	0	0	0	0
Memo:										
IBRD	0	0	0	0	0	0	0	0	0	0
IDA	0	12	55	31	28	26	28	37	16	16

BENIN

(US$ million, unless otherwise indicated)

	1970	1980	1990	1992	1993	1994	1995	1996	1997	1998
INTEREST PAYMENTS (LINT)	**0**	**3**	**14**	**11**	**12**	**19**	**21**	**16**	**18**	**21**
Public and publicly guaranteed	**0**	**3**	**14**	**11**	**12**	**19**	**21**	**16**	**18**	**21**
Official creditors	0	2	14	11	12	19	21	16	18	21
Multilateral	0	1	13	8	9	8	9	9	10	10
Concessional	0	1	6	5	6	6	7	8	9	8
Bilateral	0	1	1	3	4	11	13	7	8	11
Concessional	0	0	1	2	3	3	4	2	3	4
Private creditors	0	1	0	0	0	0	0	0	0	0
Bonds	0	0	0	0	0	0	0	0	0	0
Commercial banks	0	0	0	0	0	0	0	0	0	0
Other private	0	1	0	0	0	0	0	0	0	0
Private nonguaranteed	**0**	**0**	**0**	**0**	**0**	**0**	**0**	**0**	**0**	**0**
Bonds	0	0	0	0	0	0	0	0	0	0
Commercial banks	0	0	0	0	0	0	0	0	0	0
Memo:										
IBRD	0	0	0	0	0	0	0	0	0	0
IDA	0	0	2	3	3	3	4	4	4	4
NET TRANSFERS ON DEBT	**1**	**53**	**88**	**54**	**50**	**66**	**56**	**67**	**5**	**12**
Public and publicly guaranteed	**1**	**53**	**88**	**54**	**50**	**66**	**56**	**67**	**5**	**12**
Official creditors	0	54	88	55	50	66	56	67	5	12
Multilateral	0	21	60	50	47	74	58	56	14	17
Concessional	0	18	69	55	53	76	60	57	18	11
Bilateral	0	33	28	4	4	-8	-3	11	-9	-5
Concessional	0	15	28	5	5	4	11	23	2	8
Private creditors	1	-1	0	0	0	0	0	0	0	0
Bonds	0	0	0	0	0	0	0	0	0	0
Commercial banks	0	0	0	0	0	0	0	0	0	0
Other private	1	-1	0	0	0	0	0	0	0	0
Private nonguaranteed	**0**	**0**	**0**	**0**	**0**	**0**	**0**	**0**	**0**	**0**
Bonds	0	0	0	0	0	0	0	0	0	0
Commercial banks	0	0	0	0	0	0	0	0	0	0
Memo:										
IBRD	0	0	0	0	0	0	0	0	0	0
IDA	0	12	53	29	25	23	24	34	12	12
DEBT SERVICE (LTDS)	**2**	**9**	**33**	**26**	**31**	**39**	**46**	**42**	**46**	**50**
Public and publicly guaranteed	**2**	**9**	**33**	**26**	**31**	**39**	**46**	**42**	**46**	**50**
Official creditors	2	4	32	26	30	39	46	42	46	50
Multilateral	0	2	31	21	24	21	25	25	28	28
Concessional	0	1	13	11	16	15	18	20	23	23
Bilateral	2	2	1	5	6	18	21	16	18	22
Concessional	2	1	1	4	5	5	6	4	7	9
Private creditors	0	4	0	0	0	0	0	0	0	0
Bonds	0	0	0	0	0	0	0	0	0	0
Commercial banks	0	0	0	0	0	0	0	0	0	0
Other private	0	4	0	0	0	0	0	0	0	0
Private nonguaranteed	**0**	**0**	**0**	**0**	**0**	**0**	**0**	**0**	**0**	**0**
Bonds	0	0	0	0	0	0	0	0	0	0
Commercial banks	0	0	0	0	0	0	0	0	0	0
Memo:										
IBRD	0	0	0	0	0	0	0	0	0	0
IDA	0	0	3	4	5	6	7	7	8	8
UNDISBURSED DEBT	**15**	**532**	**414**	**486**	**409**	**358**	**368**	**356**	**318**	**377**
Official creditors	15	154	414	486	409	358	368	356	318	377
Private creditors	0	379	0	0	0	0	0	0	0	0
Memorandum items										
Concessional LDOD	29	166	1,009	1,105	1,165	1,270	1,253	1,293	1,265	1,333
Variable rate LDOD	0	2	26	104	101	109	120	15	13	14
Public sector LDOD	41	334	1,219	1,324	1,371	1,487	1,483	1,448	1,393	1,469
Private sector LDOD	0	0	0	0	0	0	0	0	0	0
6. CURRENCY COMPOSITION OF LONG-TERM DEBT (PERCENT)										
Deutsche mark	5.2	0.3	0.3	0.2	0.2	0.2	0.3	0.2	0.2	0.2
French franc	16.8	27.2	18.7	21.4	20.4	20.0	13.1	10.1	9.2	8.5
Japanese yen	0.0	0.0	0.0	0.0	0.0	0.0	0.0	1.1	1.0	2.2
Pound sterling	0.0	0.0	0.9	0.4	0.4	0.4	0.4	0.3	0.3	0.3
Swiss franc	0.0	0.1	0.0	0.0	0.0	0.0	0.0	0.0	0.0	0.0
U.S.dollars	6.7	18.9	50.8	49.7	50.0	49.3	51.8	54.1	55.3	54.6
Multiple currency	0.0	6.7	7.3	9.8	10.4	11.0	13.6	14.6	14.5	14.7
Special drawing rights	0.0	0.0	1.9	1.8	1.8	1.9	1.9	2.0	2.0	1.9
All other currencies	71.3	46.8	20.1	16.7	16.8	17.2	18.9	17.6	17.5	17.6

BENIN

(US$ million, unless otherwise indicated)

	1970	1980	1990	1992	1993	1994	1995	1996	1997	1998
7. DEBT RESTRUCTURINGS										
Total amount rescheduled	..	..	12	71	12	6	6	129	0	0
Debt stock rescheduled	..	..	0	0	0	0	0	120	0	0
Principal rescheduled	..	..	9	4	2	2	0	0	0	0
Official	..	..	4	3	2	2	0	0	0	0
Private	..	..	5	1	0	0	0	0	0	0
Interest rescheduled	..	..	1	10	4	4	3	6	0	0
Official	..	..	0	10	4	4	3	6	0	0
Private	..	..	1	0	0	0	0	0	0	0
Debt forgiven	..	..	122	2	1	5	137	0	1	0
Memo: interest forgiven	..	..	3	2	3	2	2	4	0	0
Debt stock reduction	..	..	0	0	0	0	0	80	0	0
of which debt buyback	..	..	0	0	0	0	0	0	0	0
8. DEBT STOCK-FLOW RECONCILIATION										
Total change in debt stocks	..	..	50	49	74	142	25	-20	30	23
Net flows on debt	1	42	92	39	87	112	105	101	114	-23
Net change in interest arrears	..	..	-8	-8	4	-5	0	0	0	-1
Interest capitalized	..	..	1	10	4	4	3	6	0	0
Debt forgiveness or reduction	..	..	-122	-2	-1	-5	-137	-80	-1	0
Cross-currency valuation	..	..	56	-31	-27	28	30	-19	-33	21
Residual	..	..	31	41	9	8	24	-29	-49	26
9. AVERAGE TERMS OF NEW COMMITMENTS										
ALL CREDITORS										
Interest (%)	1.8	8.3	1.3	1.3	0.9	0.8	1.3	1.1	1.8	1.9
Maturity (years)	32.0	11.7	39.2	37.7	26.3	40.5	33.1	35.0	23.9	33.1
Grace period (years)	7.0	3.7	8.4	9.5	9.1	9.9	8.7	9.2	6.8	8.7
Grant element (%)	59.9	8.9	72.0	73.5	70.9	79.7	70.4	74.1	57.3	65.5
Official creditors										
Interest (%)	1.1	4.4	1.3	1.3	0.9	0.8	1.3	1.1	1.8	1.9
Maturity (years)	36.0	26.1	39.2	37.7	26.3	40.5	33.1	35.0	23.9	33.1
Grace period (years)	8.0	5.3	8.4	9.5	9.1	9.9	8.7	9.2	6.8	8.7
Grant element (%)	67.7	40.7	72.0	73.5	70.9	79.7	70.4	74.1	57.3	65.5
Private creditors										
Interest (%)	6.0	8.8	0.0	0.0	0.0	0.0	0.0	0.0	0.0	0.0
Maturity (years)	7.5	9.9	0.0	0.0	0.0	0.0	0.0	0.0	0.0	0.0
Grace period (years)	0.5	3.5	0.0	0.0	0.0	0.0	0.0	0.0	0.0	0.0
Grant element (%)	11.7	4.8	0.0	0.0	0.0	0.0	0.0	0.0	0.0	0.0
Memorandum items										
Commitments	7	448	85	123	25	57	111	120	39	115
Official creditors	6	51	85	123	25	57	111	120	39	115
Private creditors	1	397	0	0	0	0	0	0	0	0

10. CONTRACTUAL OBLIGATIONS ON OUTSTANDING LONG-TERM DEBT

	1999	2000	2001	2002	2003	2004	2005	2006	2007	2008
TOTAL										
Disbursements	86	100	74	51	32	17	11	4	2	0
Principal	42	40	34	40	66	66	68	71	72	74
Interest	21	21	21	21	21	20	19	18	17	16
Official creditors										
Disbursements	86	100	74	51	32	17	11	4	2	0
Principal	42	40	34	40	66	66	68	71	72	74
Interest	21	21	21	21	21	20	19	18	17	16
Bilateral creditors										
Disbursements	5	6	4	3	2	1	1	1	0	0
Principal	17	14	7	8	34	32	32	33	33	34
Interest	10	10	9	9	9	8	8	7	7	6
Multilateral creditors										
Disbursements	82	94	70	48	30	16	10	3	2	0
Principal	25	26	28	31	32	34	36	38	39	40
Interest	10	11	12	12	12	11	11	10	10	9
Private creditors										
Disbursements	0	0	0	0	0	0	0	0	0	0
Principal	0	0	0	0	0	0	0	0	0	0
Interest	0	0	0	0	0	0	0	0	0	0
Commercial banks										
Disbursements	0	0	0	0	0	0	0	0	0	0
Principal	0	0	0	0	0	0	0	0	0	0
Interest	0	0	0	0	0	0	0	0	0	0
Other private										
Disbursements	0	0	0	0	0	0	0	0	0	0
Principal	0	0	0	0	0	0	0	0	0	0
Interest	0	0	0	0	0	0	0	0	0	0

BHUTAN

(US$ million, unless otherwise indicated)

	1970	1980	1990	1992	1993	1994	1995	1996	1997	1998
1. SUMMARY DEBT DATA										
TOTAL DEBT STOCKS (EDT)	..	..	**83.5**	**89.2**	**96.6**	**104.5**	**105.8**	**113.7**	**120.3**	**119.6**
Long-term debt (LDOD)	..	..	**80.3**	**88.3**	**94.9**	**103.8**	**105.2**	**113.6**	**118.3**	**119.6**
Public and publicly guaranteed	..	..	80.3	88.3	94.9	103.8	105.2	113.6	118.3	119.6
Private nonguaranteed	..	..	0.0	0.0	0.0	0.0	0.0	0.0	0.0	0.0
Use of IMF credit	**0.0**	**0.0**	**0.0**	**0.0**	**0.0**	**0.0**	**0.0**	**0.0**	**0.0**	**0.0**
Short-term debt	..	..	**3.3**	**0.9**	**1.7**	**0.7**	**0.6**	**0.1**	**2.0**	**0.0**
of which interest arrears on LDOD	..	..	0.3	0.6	0.7	0.7	0.6	0.0	0.0	0.0
Official creditors	..	..	0.3	0.6	0.7	0.7	0.6	0.0	0.0	0.0
Private creditors	..	..	0.0	0.0	0.0	0.0	0.0	0.0	0.0	0.0
Memo: principal arrears on LDOD	..	..	1.5	2.9	2.1	1.3	0.2	0.0	0.0	0.0
Official creditors	..	..	1.5	2.9	2.1	1.3	0.2	0.0	0.0	0.0
Private creditors	..	..	0.0	0.0	0.0	0.0	0.0	0.0	0.0	0.0
Memo: export credits	..	..	17.0	14.0	20.0	17.0	25.0	23.0	15.0	12.0
TOTAL DEBT FLOWS										
Disbursements	..	..	**8.4**	**10.7**	**11.8**	**10.8**	**9.9**	**15.2**	**16.8**	**6.5**
Long-term debt	..	..	8.4	10.7	11.8	10.8	9.9	15.2	16.8	6.5
IMF purchases	0.0	0.0	0.0	0.0	0.0	0.0	0.0	0.0	0.0	0.0
Principal repayments	..	..	**2.9**	**4.1**	**4.6**	**5.1**	**7.2**	**4.3**	**4.9**	**7.0**
Long-term debt	..	..	2.9	4.1	4.6	5.1	7.2	4.3	4.9	7.0
IMF repurchases	0.0	0.0	0.0	0.0	0.0	0.0	0.0	0.0	0.0	0.0
Net flows on debt	..	..	**6.5**	**5.9**	**7.9**	**4.7**	**2.7**	**11.0**	**13.8**	**-2.5**
of which short-term debt	..	..	1.0	-0.7	0.7	-1.0	0.0	0.1	1.9	-2.0
Interest payments (INT)	..	..	**2.3**	**1.8**	**2.5**	**2.4**	**2.6**	**2.6**	**2.4**	**2.2**
Long-term debt	..	..	2.0	1.8	2.4	2.4	2.6	2.6	2.3	2.2
IMF charges	0.0	0.0	0.0	0.0	0.0	0.0	0.0	0.0	0.0	0.0
Short-term debt	..	..	0.2	0.0	0.1	0.0	0.0	0.0	0.1	0.0
Net transfers on debt	..	..	**4.2**	**4.1**	**5.4**	**2.2**	**0.1**	**8.3**	**11.4**	**-4.7**
Total debt service paid (TDS)	..	..	**5.2**	**5.9**	**7.1**	**7.5**	**9.8**	**6.9**	**7.2**	**9.2**
Long-term debt	..	..	5.0	5.9	7.0	7.5	9.8	6.9	7.1	9.2
IMF repurchases and charges	0.0	0.0	0.0	0.0	0.0	0.0	0.0	0.0	0.0	0.0
Short-term debt (interest only)	..	..	0.2	0.0	0.1	0.0	0.0	0.0	0.1	0.0
2. AGGREGATE NET RESOURCE FLOWS AND NET TRANSFERS (LONG-TERM)										
NET RESOURCE FLOWS	..	..	**22.4**	**38.8**	**42.0**	**48.1**	**42.0**	**37.1**	**44.0**	**27.7**
Net flow of long-term debt (ex. IMF)	..	..	5.5	6.6	7.2	5.7	2.7	10.9	11.9	-0.5
Foreign direct investment (net)	..	..	0.0	0.0	0.0	0.0	0.0	0.0	0.0	0.0
Portfolio equity flows	..	..	0.0	0.0	0.0	0.0	0.0	0.0	0.0	0.0
Grants (excluding technical coop.)	..	..	16.9	32.2	34.9	42.5	39.3	26.3	32.1	28.3
Memo: technical coop. grants	..	..	24.7	20.7	25.7	26.5	27.0	27.6	23.5	19.7
official net resource flows	..	..	25.0	41.2	44.3	50.4	44.3	39.4	46.3	30.0
private net resource flows	..	..	-2.6	-2.4	-2.3	-2.3	-2.3	-2.3	-2.3	-2.3
NET TRANSFERS	..	..	**20.4**	**37.0**	**39.6**	**45.7**	**39.4**	**34.5**	**41.7**	**25.6**
Interest on long-term debt	..	..	2.0	1.8	2.4	2.4	2.6	2.6	2.3	2.2
Profit remittances on FDI	..	..	0.0	0.0	0.0	0.0	0.0	0.0	0.0	0.0
Memo: official net transfers	..	..	24.6	40.6	43.0	48.8	42.3	37.3	44.3	28.0
private net transfers	..	..	-4.2	-3.6	-3.4	-3.1	-2.9	-2.8	-2.6	-2.4
3. MAJOR ECONOMIC AGGREGATES										
Gross national product (GNP)	..	..	266.0	216.1	211.8	250.7	270.2	295.4	367.3	372.6
Exports of goods & services (XGS)	..	..	94.9	85.7	91.6	83.7	90.2	120.8	121.2	145.9
of which workers remittances	..	..	0.0	0.0	0.0	0.0	0.0	0.0	0.0	0.0
Imports of goods & services (MGS)	..	..	122.9	110.4	161.9	130.4	132.3	163.8	183.3	203.0
International reserves (RES)	..	..	86.0	77.9	..	115.2	124.3	184.0	181.2	249.6
Current account balance	..	..	-28.0	-24.7	-70.3	-40.0	-34.1	-37.2	-56.2	-46.6
4. DEBT INDICATORS										
EDT / XGS (%)	..	..	88.0	104.1	105.5	124.9	117.3	94.1	99.3	82.0
EDT / GNP (%)	..	..	31.4	41.3	45.6	41.7	39.2	38.5	32.8	32.1
TDS / XGS (%)	..	..	5.5	6.9	7.8	9.0	10.9	5.7	5.9	6.3
INT / XGS (%)	..	..	2.4	2.1	2.7	2.9	2.9	2.2	2.0	1.5
INT / GNP (%)	..	..	0.9	0.8	1.2	1.0	1.0	0.9	0.7	0.6
RES / EDT (%)	..	..	103.0	87.3	..	110.2	117.5	161.8	150.6	208.7
RES / MGS (months)	..	..	8.4	8.5	..	10.6	11.3	13.5	11.9	14.8
Short-term / EDT (%)	..	..	4.0	1.0	1.8	0.7	0.6	0.1	1.7	0.0
Concessional / EDT (%)	..	..	74.0	83.9	86.5	90.7	93.0	96.0	96.4	100.0
Multilateral / EDT (%)	..	..	50.2	56.6	56.6	59.5	64.5	61.3	61.1	67.9

BHUTAN

(US$ million, unless otherwise indicated)

	1970	1980	1990	1992	1993	1994	1995	1996	1997	1998
5. LONG-TERM DEBT										
DEBT OUTSTANDING (LDOD)	..	..	**80.3**	**88.3**	**94.9**	**103.8**	**105.2**	**113.6**	**118.3**	**119.6**
Public and publicly guaranteed	..	..	**80.3**	**88.3**	**94.9**	**103.8**	**105.2**	**113.6**	**118.3**	**119.6**
Official creditors	..	..	61.8	74.7	83.6	94.8	98.4	109.1	116.0	119.6
Multilateral	..	..	41.9	50.5	54.7	62.2	68.2	69.7	73.5	81.2
Concessional	..	..	41.9	50.5	54.7	62.2	68.2	69.7	73.5	81.2
Bilateral	..	..	19.9	24.3	28.9	32.6	30.2	39.5	42.5	38.4
Concessional	..	..	19.9	24.3	28.9	32.6	30.2	39.5	42.5	38.4
Private creditors	..	..	18.5	13.6	11.3	9.0	6.8	4.5	2.3	0.0
Bonds	..	..	0.0	0.0	0.0	0.0	0.0	0.0	0.0	0.0
Commercial banks	..	..	0.0	0.0	0.0	0.0	0.0	0.0	0.0	0.0
Other private	..	..	18.5	13.6	11.3	9.0	6.8	4.5	2.3	0.0
Private nonguaranteed	..	..	**0.0**	**0.0**	**0.0**	**0.0**	**0.0**	**0.0**	**0.0**	**0.0**
Bonds	..	..	0.0	0.0	0.0	0.0	0.0	0.0	0.0	0.0
Commercial banks	..	..	0.0	0.0	0.0	0.0	0.0	0.0	0.0	0.0
Memo:										
IBRD	0.0	0.0	0.0	0.0	0.0	0.0	0.0	0.0	0.0	0.0
IDA	0.0	0.0	16.1	17.7	18.6	20.9	22.5	22.8	22.5	23.9
DISBURSEMENTS	..	..	**8.4**	**10.7**	**11.8**	**10.8**	**9.9**	**15.2**	**16.8**	**6.5**
Public and publicly guaranteed	..	..	**8.4**	**10.7**	**11.8**	**10.8**	**9.9**	**15.2**	**16.8**	**6.5**
Official creditors	..	..	8.4	10.7	11.8	10.8	9.9	15.2	16.8	6.5
Multilateral	..	..	7.2	4.2	4.0	4.8	5.8	4.8	9.2	5.6
Concessional	..	..	7.2	4.2	4.0	4.8	5.8	4.8	9.2	5.6
Bilateral	..	..	1.2	6.5	7.8	6.0	4.1	10.3	7.5	0.9
Concessional	..	..	1.2	6.5	7.8	6.0	4.1	10.3	7.5	0.9
Private creditors	..	..	0.0	0.0	0.0	0.0	0.0	0.0	0.0	0.0
Bonds	..	..	0.0	0.0	0.0	0.0	0.0	0.0	0.0	0.0
Commercial banks	..	..	0.0	0.0	0.0	0.0	0.0	0.0	0.0	0.0
Other private	..	..	0.0	0.0	0.0	0.0	0.0	0.0	0.0	0.0
Private nonguaranteed	..	..	**0.0**	**0.0**	**0.0**	**0.0**	**0.0**	**0.0**	**0.0**	**0.0**
Bonds	..	..	0.0	0.0	0.0	0.0	0.0	0.0	0.0	0.0
Commercial banks	..	..	0.0	0.0	0.0	0.0	0.0	0.0	0.0	0.0
Memo:										
IBRD	0.0	0.0	0.0	0.0	0.0	0.0	0.0	0.0	0.0	0.0
IDA	0.0	0.0	2.0	0.6	0.9	1.3	1.2	1.4	1.1	0.7
PRINCIPAL REPAYMENTS	..	..	**2.9**	**4.1**	**4.6**	**5.1**	**7.2**	**4.3**	**4.9**	**7.0**
Public and publicly guaranteed	..	..	**2.9**	**4.1**	**4.6**	**5.1**	**7.2**	**4.3**	**4.9**	**7.0**
Official creditors	..	..	0.3	1.7	2.4	2.8	4.9	2.0	2.6	4.8
Multilateral	..	..	0.0	0.1	0.2	0.6	0.6	0.8	0.9	1.0
Concessional	..	..	0.0	0.1	0.2	0.6	0.6	0.8	0.9	1.0
Bilateral	..	..	0.3	1.6	2.2	2.2	4.3	1.2	1.7	3.8
Concessional	..	..	0.3	1.6	2.2	2.2	4.3	1.2	1.7	3.8
Private creditors	..	..	2.6	2.4	2.3	2.3	2.3	2.3	2.3	2.3
Bonds	..	..	0.0	0.0	0.0	0.0	0.0	0.0	0.0	0.0
Commercial banks	..	..	0.0	0.0	0.0	0.0	0.0	0.0	0.0	0.0
Other private	..	..	2.6	2.4	2.3	2.3	2.3	2.3	2.3	2.3
Private nonguaranteed	..	..	**0.0**	**0.0**	**0.0**	**0.0**	**0.0**	**0.0**	**0.0**	**0.0**
Bonds	..	..	0.0	0.0	0.0	0.0	0.0	0.0	0.0	0.0
Commercial banks	..	..	0.0	0.0	0.0	0.0	0.0	0.0	0.0	0.0
Memo:										
IBRD	0.0	0.0	0.0	0.0	0.0	0.0	0.0	0.0	0.0	0.0
IDA	0.0	0.0	0.0	0.0	0.0	0.1	0.1	0.2	0.2	0.2
NET FLOWS ON DEBT	..	..	**5.5**	**6.6**	**7.2**	**5.7**	**2.7**	**10.9**	**11.9**	**-0.5**
Public and publicly guaranteed	..	..	**5.5**	**6.6**	**7.2**	**5.7**	**2.7**	**10.9**	**11.9**	**-0.5**
Official creditors	..	..	8.1	9.0	9.4	7.9	5.0	13.1	14.2	1.7
Multilateral	..	..	7.2	4.1	3.8	4.2	5.3	4.0	8.4	4.6
Concessional	..	..	7.2	4.1	3.8	4.2	5.3	4.0	8.4	4.6
Bilateral	..	..	0.9	4.9	5.6	3.7	-0.3	9.1	5.8	-2.9
Concessional	..	..	0.9	4.9	5.6	3.7	-0.3	9.1	5.8	-2.9
Private creditors	..	..	-2.6	-2.4	-2.3	-2.3	-2.3	-2.3	-2.3	-2.3
Bonds	..	..	0.0	0.0	0.0	0.0	0.0	0.0	0.0	0.0
Commercial banks	..	..	0.0	0.0	0.0	0.0	0.0	0.0	0.0	0.0
Other private	..	..	-2.6	-2.4	-2.3	-2.3	-2.3	-2.3	-2.3	-2.3
Private nonguaranteed	..	..	**0.0**	**0.0**	**0.0**	**0.0**	**0.0**	**0.0**	**0.0**	**0.0**
Bonds	..	..	0.0	0.0	0.0	0.0	0.0	0.0	0.0	0.0
Commercial banks	..	..	0.0	0.0	0.0	0.0	0.0	0.0	0.0	0.0
Memo:										
IBRD	0.0	0.0	0.0	0.0	0.0	0.0	0.0	0.0	0.0	0.0
IDA	0.0	0.0	2.0	0.6	0.9	1.3	1.1	1.2	0.9	0.5

BHUTAN

(US$ million, unless otherwise indicated)

	1970	1980	1990	1992	1993	1994	1995	1996	1997	1998
INTEREST PAYMENTS (LINT)	..	..	**2.0**	**1.8**	**2.4**	**2.4**	**2.6**	**2.6**	**2.3**	**2.2**
Public and publicly guaranteed	..	..	**2.0**	**1.8**	**2.4**	**2.4**	**2.6**	**2.6**	**2.3**	**2.2**
Official creditors	..	..	0.4	0.6	1.3	1.6	2.0	2.1	2.0	2.0
Multilateral	..	..	0.3	0.4	0.5	0.5	0.6	0.7	0.6	0.7
Concessional	..	..	0.3	0.4	0.5	0.5	0.6	0.7	0.6	0.7
Bilateral	..	..	0.1	0.2	0.8	1.1	1.4	1.5	1.3	1.4
Concessional	..	..	0.1	0.2	0.8	1.1	1.4	1.5	1.3	1.4
Private creditors	..	..	1.6	1.2	1.1	0.8	0.6	0.5	0.3	0.1
Bonds	..	..	0.0	0.0	0.0	0.0	0.0	0.0	0.0	0.0
Commercial banks	..	..	0.0	0.0	0.0	0.0	0.0	0.0	0.0	0.0
Other private	..	..	1.6	1.2	1.1	0.8	0.6	0.5	0.3	0.1
Private nonguaranteed	..	..	**0.0**	**0.0**	**0.0**	**0.0**	**0.0**	**0.0**	**0.0**	**0.0**
Bonds	..	..	0.0	0.0	0.0	0.0	0.0	0.0	0.0	0.0
Commercial banks	..	..	0.0	0.0	0.0	0.0	0.0	0.0	0.0	0.0
Memo:										
IBRD	0.0	0.0	0.0	0.0	0.0	0.0	0.0	0.0	0.0	0.0
IDA	0.0	0.0	0.1	0.1	0.1	0.1	0.2	0.2	0.2	0.2
NET TRANSFERS ON DEBT	..	..	**3.5**	**4.9**	**4.8**	**3.2**	**0.1**	**8.3**	**9.6**	**-2.7**
Public and publicly guaranteed	..	..	**3.5**	**4.9**	**4.8**	**3.2**	**0.1**	**8.3**	**9.6**	**-2.7**
Official creditors	..	..	7.7	8.4	8.1	6.3	3.0	11.0	12.2	-0.3
Multilateral	..	..	6.9	3.6	3.3	3.7	4.7	3.4	7.7	4.0
Concessional	..	..	6.9	3.6	3.3	3.7	4.7	3.4	7.7	4.0
Bilateral	..	..	0.8	4.8	4.8	2.6	-1.7	7.6	4.5	-4.3
Concessional	..	..	0.8	4.8	4.8	2.6	-1.7	7.6	4.5	-4.3
Private creditors	..	..	-4.2	-3.5	-3.3	-3.1	-2.9	-2.7	-2.6	-2.4
Bonds	..	..	0.0	0.0	0.0	0.0	0.0	0.0	0.0	0.0
Commercial banks	..	..	0.0	0.0	0.0	0.0	0.0	0.0	0.0	0.0
Other private	..	..	-4.2	-3.5	-3.3	-3.1	-2.9	-2.7	-2.6	-2.4
Private nonguaranteed	..	..	**0.0**	**0.0**	**0.0**	**0.0**	**0.0**	**0.0**	**0.0**	**0.0**
Bonds	..	..	0.0	0.0	0.0	0.0	0.0	0.0	0.0	0.0
Commercial banks	..	..	0.0	0.0	0.0	0.0	0.0	0.0	0.0	0.0
Memo:										
IBRD	0.0	0.0	0.0	0.0	0.0	0.0	0.0	0.0	0.0	0.0
IDA	0.0	0.0	1.9	0.5	0.8	1.1	0.9	1.0	0.8	0.4
DEBT SERVICE (LTDS)	..	..	**5.0**	**5.9**	**7.0**	**7.5**	**9.8**	**6.9**	**7.1**	**9.2**
Public and publicly guaranteed	..	..	**5.0**	**5.9**	**7.0**	**7.5**	**9.8**	**6.9**	**7.1**	**9.2**
Official creditors	..	..	0.7	2.3	3.7	4.5	6.9	4.2	4.6	6.8
Multilateral	..	..	0.3	0.6	0.7	1.1	1.2	1.5	1.5	1.7
Concessional	..	..	0.3	0.6	0.7	1.1	1.2	1.5	1.5	1.7
Bilateral	..	..	0.4	1.7	3.0	3.3	5.7	2.7	3.1	5.1
Concessional	..	..	0.4	1.7	3.0	3.3	5.7	2.7	3.1	5.1
Private creditors	..	..	4.2	3.5	3.3	3.1	2.9	2.7	2.6	2.4
Bonds	..	..	0.0	0.0	0.0	0.0	0.0	0.0	0.0	0.0
Commercial banks	..	..	0.0	0.0	0.0	0.0	0.0	0.0	0.0	0.0
Other private	..	..	4.2	3.5	3.3	3.1	2.9	2.7	2.6	2.4
Private nonguaranteed	..	..	**0.0**	**0.0**	**0.0**	**0.0**	**0.0**	**0.0**	**0.0**	**0.0**
Bonds	..	..	0.0	0.0	0.0	0.0	0.0	0.0	0.0	0.0
Commercial banks	..	..	0.0	0.0	0.0	0.0	0.0	0.0	0.0	0.0
Memo:										
IBRD	0.0	0.0	0.0	0.0	0.0	0.0	0.0	0.0	0.0	0.0
IDA	0.0	0.0	0.1	0.1	0.1	0.2	0.3	0.3	0.3	0.4
UNDISBURSED DEBT	..	..	**48.4**	**64.9**	**49.3**	**44.9**	**57.6**	**40.1**	**20.4**	**41.5**
Official creditors	..	..	48.4	64.9	49.3	44.9	57.6	40.1	20.4	41.5
Private creditors	..	..	0.0	0.0	0.0	0.0	0.0	0.0	0.0	0.0
Memorandum items										
Concessional LDOD	..	..	61.8	74.7	83.6	94.8	98.4	109.1	116.0	119.6
Variable rate LDOD	..	..	0.0	0.0	0.0	0.0	0.0	0.0	0.0	0.0
Public sector LDOD	..	..	80.3	88.3	94.9	103.8	105.2	113.6	118.3	119.6
Private sector LDOD	..	..	0.0	0.0	0.0	0.0	0.0	0.0	0.0	0.0

6. CURRENCY COMPOSITION OF LONG-TERM DEBT (PERCENT)

	1970	1980	1990	1992	1993	1994	1995	1996	1997	1998
Deutsche mark	..	..	0.0	0.0	0.0	0.0	0.0	0.0	0.0	0.0
French franc	..	..	0.0	0.0	0.0	0.0	0.0	0.0	0.0	0.0
Japanese yen	..	..	0.0	0.0	0.0	0.0	0.0	0.0	0.0	0.0
Pound sterling	..	..	0.0	0.0	0.0	0.0	0.0	0.0	0.0	0.0
Swiss franc	..	..	0.0	0.0	0.0	0.0	0.0	0.0	0.0	0.0
U.S.dollars	..	..	43.1	36.2	32.3	29.6	28.5	24.7	21.5	22.5
Multiple currency	..	..	22.8	27.1	27.2	28.7	31.5	30.0	32.5	34.6
Special drawing rights	..	..	9.3	10.2	10.7	11.1	12.1	11.2	10.7	11.4
All other currencies	..	..	24.8	26.5	29.8	30.6	27.9	34.1	35.3	31.5

BHUTAN

(US$ million, unless otherwise indicated)

	1970	1980	1990	1992	1993	1994	1995	1996	1997	1998
7. DEBT RESTRUCTURINGS										
Total amount rescheduled	..	..	0.0	0.0	0.0	0.0	0.0	0.7	0.0	0.0
Debt stock rescheduled	..	..	0.0	0.0	0.0	0.0	0.0	0.0	0.0	0.0
Principal rescheduled	..	..	0.0	0.0	0.0	0.0	0.0	0.0	0.0	0.0
Official	..	..	0.0	0.0	0.0	0.0	0.0	0.0	0.0	0.0
Private	..	..	0.0	0.0	0.0	0.0	0.0	0.0	0.0	0.0
Interest rescheduled	..	..	0.0	0.0	0.0	0.0	0.0	0.3	0.0	0.0
Official	..	..	0.0	0.0	0.0	0.0	0.0	0.3	0.0	0.0
Private	..	..	0.0	0.0	0.0	0.0	0.0	0.0	0.0	0.0
Debt forgiven	..	..	0.0	0.0	0.0	0.0	0.0	0.0	0.0	0.0
Memo: interest forgiven	..	..	0.0	0.0	0.0	0.0	0.0	0.0	0.0	0.0
Debt stock reduction	..	..	0.0	0.0	0.0	0.0	0.0	0.0	0.0	0.0
of which debt buyback	..	..	0.0	0.0	0.0	0.0	0.0	0.0	0.0	0.0
8. DEBT STOCK-FLOW RECONCILIATION										
Total change in debt stocks	..	..	9.7	2.9	7.4	7.9	1.3	8.0	6.6	-0.7
Net flows on debt	..	..	6.5	5.9	7.9	4.7	2.7	11.0	13.8	-2.5
Net change in interest arrears	..	..	0.3	0.1	0.1	0.0	-0.1	-0.6	0.0	0.0
Interest capitalized	..	..	0.0	0.0	0.0	0.0	0.0	0.3	0.0	0.0
Debt forgiveness or reduction	..	..	0.0	0.0	0.0	0.0	0.0	0.0	0.0	0.0
Cross-currency valuation	..	..	0.6	-1.5	-1.7	0.6	-1.7	-1.0	-3.9	-0.4
Residual	..	..	2.3	-1.7	1.2	2.6	0.4	-1.7	-3.3	2.2
9. AVERAGE TERMS OF NEW COMMITMENTS										
ALL CREDITORS										
Interest (%)	..	..	0.0	4.4	0.7	1.0	1.3	0.0	0.0	2.1
Maturity (years)	..	..	0.0	18.4	39.9	39.6	33.4	0.0	0.0	39.6
Grace period (years)	..	..	0.0	5.1	10.4	10.1	11.3	0.0	0.0	10.1
Grant element (%)	..	..	0.0	35.4	80.8	78.2	73.8	0.0	0.0	68.8
Official creditors										
Interest (%)	..	..	0.0	4.4	0.7	1.0	1.3	0.0	0.0	2.1
Maturity (years)	..	..	0.0	18.4	39.9	39.6	33.4	0.0	0.0	39.6
Grace period (years)	..	..	0.0	5.1	10.4	10.1	11.3	0.0	0.0	10.1
Grant element (%)	..	..	0.0	35.4	80.8	78.2	73.8	0.0	0.0	68.8
Private creditors										
Interest (%)	..	..	0.0	0.0	0.0	0.0	0.0	0.0	0.0	0.0
Maturity (years)	..	..	0.0	0.0	0.0	0.0	0.0	0.0	0.0	0.0
Grace period (years)	..	..	0.0	0.0	0.0	0.0	0.0	0.0	0.0	0.0
Grant element (%)	..	..	0.0	0.0	0.0	0.0	0.0	0.0	0.0	0.0
Memorandum items										
Commitments	..	..	0.0	48.0	5.4	5.4	24.0	0.0	0.0	27.9
Official creditors	..	..	0.0	48.0	5.4	5.4	24.0	0.0	0.0	27.9
Private creditors	..	..	0.0	0.0	0.0	0.0	0.0	0.0	0.0	0.0

10. CONTRACTUAL OBLIGATIONS ON OUTSTANDING LONG-TERM DEBT

	1999	2000	2001	2002	2003	2004	2005	2006	2007	2008
TOTAL										
Disbursements	11.1	10.5	7.9	5.3	3.4	2.1	1.2	0.2	0.0	0.0
Principal	5.0	5.0	5.2	5.3	5.3	5.0	4.8	5.7	6.2	4.4
Interest	2.1	2.0	1.9	1.7	1.6	1.4	1.3	1.4	1.4	1.3
Official creditors										
Disbursements	11.1	10.5	7.9	5.3	3.4	2.1	1.2	0.2	0.0	0.0
Principal	5.0	5.0	5.2	5.3	5.3	5.0	4.8	5.7	6.2	4.4
Interest	2.1	2.0	1.9	1.7	1.6	1.4	1.3	1.4	1.4	1.3
Bilateral creditors										
Disbursements	3.6	2.2	1.4	0.6	0.3	0.1	0.0	0.0	0.0	0.0
Principal	3.9	3.9	3.9	3.9	3.9	3.3	2.8	3.2	3.5	1.2
Interest	1.3	1.1	1.0	0.8	0.7	0.5	0.4	0.2	0.1	0.0
Multilateral creditors										
Disbursements	7.5	8.2	6.6	4.7	3.1	1.9	1.2	0.2	0.0	0.0
Principal	1.2	1.2	1.3	1.3	1.4	1.7	2.0	2.5	2.7	3.2
Interest	0.9	0.9	0.9	0.9	0.9	0.9	0.9	1.2	1.2	1.3
Private creditors										
Disbursements	0.0	0.0	0.0	0.0	0.0	0.0	0.0	0.0	0.0	0.0
Principal	0.0	0.0	0.0	0.0	0.0	0.0	0.0	0.0	0.0	0.0
Interest	0.0	0.0	0.0	0.0	0.0	0.0	0.0	0.0	0.0	0.0
Commercial banks										
Disbursements	0.0	0.0	0.0	0.0	0.0	0.0	0.0	0.0	0.0	0.0
Principal	0.0	0.0	0.0	0.0	0.0	0.0	0.0	0.0	0.0	0.0
Interest	0.0	0.0	0.0	0.0	0.0	0.0	0.0	0.0	0.0	0.0
Other private										
Disbursements	0.0	0.0	0.0	0.0	0.0	0.0	0.0	0.0	0.0	0.0
Principal	0.0	0.0	0.0	0.0	0.0	0.0	0.0	0.0	0.0	0.0
Interest	0.0	0.0	0.0	0.0	0.0	0.0	0.0	0.0	0.0	0.0

BOLIVIA

(US$ million, unless otherwise indicated)

	1970	1980	1990	1992	1993	1994	1995	1996	1997	1998
1. SUMMARY DEBT DATA										
TOTAL DEBT STOCKS (EDT)	..	**2,702**	**4,275**	**4,235**	**4,307**	**4,877**	**5,282**	**5,200**	**5,248**	**6,078**
Long-term debt (LDOD)	**491**	**2,274**	**3,864**	**3,810**	**3,879**	**4,313**	**4,707**	**4,550**	**4,570**	**4,551**
Public and publicly guaranteed	480	2,182	3,687	3,669	3,695	4,122	4,468	4,265	4,144	4,307
Private nonguaranteed	11	92	177	140	184	191	239	285	426	245
Use of IMF credit	**6**	**126**	**257**	**249**	**221**	**264**	**268**	**276**	**248**	**264**
Short-term debt	..	**303**	**154**	**176**	**207**	**300**	**307**	**374**	**430**	**1,262**
of which interest arrears on LDOD	..	3	6	11	14	34	20	26	4	3
Official creditors	..	2	2	2	3	21	7	14	4	3
Private creditors	..	1	4	9	11	13	13	12	0	0
Memo: principal arrears on LDOD	..	22	31	18	39	103	40	64	37	37
Official creditors	..	15	9	8	20	82	21	50	18	19
Private creditors	..	7	22	10	19	20	19	14	18	18
Memo: export credits	..	0	794	723	606	602	634	514	488	387
TOTAL DEBT FLOWS										
Disbursements	**58**	**553**	**331**	**445**	**369**	**437**	**519**	**497**	**671**	**372**
Long-term debt	58	457	300	394	369	393	494	448	648	326
IMF purchases	0	96	31	51	0	44	26	49	23	46
Principal repayments	**19**	**145**	**241**	**167**	**195**	**188**	**199**	**230**	**263**	**277**
Long-term debt	19	145	196	130	166	173	173	199	229	236
IMF repurchases	0	0	46	37	29	15	26	32	34	41
Net flows on debt	**130**	**180**	**32**	**313**	**203**	**322**	**341**	**329**	**486**	**928**
of which short-term debt	..	-228	-57	35	28	73	20	62	78	833
Interest payments (INT)	..	**220**	**144**	**121**	**139**	**160**	**173**	**183**	**212**	**192**
Long-term debt	7	173	117	109	127	148	155	163	190	145
IMF charges	0	3	13	4	2	1	1	2	1	1
Short-term debt	..	45	14	7	10	11	17	17	21	46
Net transfers on debt	..	**-40**	**-112**	**192**	**64**	**162**	**168**	**146**	**273**	**737**
Total debt service paid (TDS)	..	**366**	**385**	**288**	**334**	**348**	**372**	**413**	**475**	**468**
Long-term debt	26	319	313	239	293	321	328	362	418	381
IMF repurchases and charges	0	3	59	41	31	16	28	34	36	42
Short-term debt (interest only)	..	45	14	7	10	11	17	17	21	46
2. AGGREGATE NET RESOURCE FLOWS AND NET TRANSFERS (LONG-TERM)										
NET RESOURCE FLOWS	**-34**	**407**	**333**	**621**	**524**	**647**	**1,023**	**1,115**	**1,447**	**1,194**
Net flow of long-term debt (ex. IMF)	39	312	104	264	203	221	321	249	419	90
Foreign direct investment (net)	-76	47	27	93	145	145	374	474	731	872
Portfolio equity flows	0	0	0	0	0	0	0	0	0	0
Grants (excluding technical coop.)	3	48	202	264	175	281	327	392	297	232
Memo: technical coop. grants	9	41	115	174	190	190	217	195	199	184
official net resource flows	39	204	330	536	367	496	608	596	505	334
private net resource flows	-73	203	3	85	157	151	415	519	942	860
NET TRANSFERS	**-59**	**214**	**199**	**492**	**371**	**469**	**835**	**912**	**1,214**	**990**
Interest on long-term debt	7	173	117	109	127	148	155	163	190	145
Profit remittances on FDI	17	19	17	20	26	30	33	40	43	60
Memo: official net transfers	35	161	230	441	258	367	474	448	357	197
private net transfers	-94	53	-30	51	113	102	360	464	858	793
3. MAJOR ECONOMIC AGGREGATES										
Gross national product (GNP)	..	..	4,627	5,315	5,530	5,793	6,495	7,361	7,765	8,343
Exports of goods & services (XGS)	..	1,046	998	792	907	1,201	1,264	1,344	1,516	1,551
of which workers remittances	..	0	2	1	1	1	2	2	2	64
Imports of goods & services (MGS)	..	1,112	1,354	1,567	1,649	1,554	1,809	1,968	2,388	2,490
International reserves (RES)	46	553	511	480	572	793	1,005	1,302	1,359	1,155
Current account balance	..	-6	-199	-534	-506	-90	-303	-380	-551	-673
4. DEBT INDICATORS										
EDT / XGS (%)	..	258.4	428.6	535.0	474.9	406.0	417.9	387.0	346.1	391.9
EDT / GNP (%)	..	..	92.4	79.7	77.9	84.2	81.3	70.7	67.6	72.8
TDS / XGS (%)	..	35.0	38.6	36.4	36.8	28.9	29.4	30.7	31.3	30.2
INT / XGS (%)	..	21.1	14.4	15.3	15.4	13.3	13.7	13.6	14.0	12.4
INT / GNP (%)	..	..	3.1	2.3	2.5	2.8	2.7	2.5	2.7	2.3
RES / EDT (%)	..	20.5	12.0	11.3	13.3	16.3	19.0	25.0	25.9	19.0
RES / MGS (months)	..	6.0	4.5	3.7	4.2	6.1	6.7	7.9	6.8	5.6
Short-term / EDT (%)	..	11.2	3.6	4.2	4.8	6.2	5.8	7.2	8.2	20.8
Concessional / EDT (%)	..	24.6	44.2	44.7	49.9	49.8	51.6	56.4	56.5	52.9
Multilateral / EDT (%)	..	16.6	37.2	43.2	46.4	46.7	48.8	50.7	51.1	44.3

BOLIVIA

(US$ million, unless otherwise indicated)

	1970	1980	1990	1992	1993	1994	1995	1996	1997	1998
5. LONG-TERM DEBT										
DEBT OUTSTANDING (LDOD)	**491**	**2,274**	**3,864**	**3,810**	**3,879**	**4,313**	**4,707**	**4,550**	**4,570**	**4,551**
Public and publicly guaranteed	**480**	**2,182**	**3,687**	**3,669**	**3,695**	**4,122**	**4,468**	**4,265**	**4,144**	**4,307**
Official creditors	275	1,110	3,362	3,393	3,611	4,040	4,396	4,219	4,102	4,260
Multilateral	26	447	1,589	1,828	1,998	2,276	2,579	2,636	2,681	2,692
Concessional	26	178	882	989	1,096	1,231	1,397	1,534	1,685	1,790
Bilateral	249	663	1,773	1,565	1,613	1,764	1,817	1,583	1,421	1,569
Concessional	239	487	1,006	903	1,052	1,197	1,327	1,397	1,280	1,423
Private creditors	205	1,072	325	276	84	83	73	46	42	46
Bonds	67	73	35	35	18	17	17	17	9	9
Commercial banks	2	603	213	190	19	22	19	13	13	18
Other private	136	395	77	51	47	43	37	16	20	19
Private nonguaranteed	**11**	**92**	**177**	**140**	**184**	**191**	**239**	**285**	**426**	**245**
Bonds	0	0	0	0	0	0	0	0	0	0
Commercial banks	11	92	177	140	184	191	239	285	426	245
Memo:										
IBRD	0	175	194	146	129	116	95	61	37	26
IDA	18	64	393	464	547	648	770	843	930	1,045
DISBURSEMENTS	**58**	**457**	**300**	**394**	**369**	**393**	**494**	**448**	**648**	**326**
Public and publicly guaranteed	**55**	**441**	**300**	**391**	**319**	**369**	**427**	**357**	**379**	**316**
Official creditors	45	198	291	388	317	360	427	349	371	309
Multilateral	2	108	204	249	228	301	382	284	356	250
Concessional	2	28	90	80	105	130	174	188	227	193
Bilateral	43	91	86	139	89	59	45	65	14	58
Concessional	33	31	85	110	86	57	45	63	14	55
Private creditors	10	242	9	4	2	8	0	8	8	7
Bonds	0	0	0	0	0	0	0	0	0	0
Commercial banks	0	55	0	1	2	8	0	1	2	6
Other private	10	187	9	2	0	0	0	6	6	1
Private nonguaranteed	**3**	**16**	**0**	**2**	**51**	**25**	**67**	**91**	**269**	**11**
Bonds	0	0	0	0	0	0	0	0	0	0
Commercial banks	3	16	0	2	51	25	67	91	269	11
Memo:										
IBRD	0	73	0	0	0	0	0	0	0	0
IDA	2	2	49	55	66	80	113	100	136	88
PRINCIPAL REPAYMENTS	**19**	**145**	**196**	**130**	**166**	**173**	**173**	**199**	**229**	**236**
Public and publicly guaranteed	**17**	**126**	**172**	**126**	**160**	**154**	**155**	**155**	**168**	**209**
Official creditors	9	43	163	116	125	145	147	145	162	207
Multilateral	2	7	117	87	99	110	120	135	152	193
Concessional	2	1	14	15	17	20	22	24	26	26
Bilateral	7	36	46	29	26	35	27	10	10	14
Concessional	5	15	9	4	3	9	3	2	4	9
Private creditors	8	84	9	10	35	9	8	9	6	3
Bonds	0	1	0	0	0	0	0	0	3	0
Commercial banks	1	49	4	3	30	5	4	6	2	1
Other private	7	33	6	7	5	4	4	3	2	2
Private nonguaranteed	**2**	**19**	**24**	**4**	**7**	**19**	**18**	**44**	**61**	**27**
Bonds	0	0	0	0	0	0	0	0	0	0
Commercial banks	2	19	24	4	7	19	18	44	61	27
Memo:										
IBRD	0	3	21	22	23	24	27	25	19	13
IDA	0	0	2	2	2	2	2	3	4	6
NET FLOWS ON DEBT	**39**	**312**	**104**	**264**	**203**	**221**	**321**	**249**	**419**	**90**
Public and publicly guaranteed	**38**	**315**	**128**	**266**	**159**	**215**	**273**	**203**	**211**	**106**
Official creditors	36	156	128	272	192	215	280	204	209	102
Multilateral	0	101	87	162	129	191	263	149	205	58
Concessional	0	28	77	66	88	110	152	164	201	167
Bilateral	36	55	41	110	63	24	18	55	4	44
Concessional	28	17	76	106	83	48	42	62	11	46
Private creditors	2	159	0	-6	-33	0	-8	-2	2	4
Bonds	0	-1	0	0	0	0	0	0	-3	0
Commercial banks	-1	6	-4	-2	-28	3	-4	-5	1	5
Other private	3	154	3	-4	-5	-4	-4	3	4	-1
Private nonguaranteed	**1**	**-3**	**-24**	**-2**	**44**	**6**	**49**	**47**	**208**	**-16**
Bonds	0	0	0	0	0	0	0	0	0	0
Commercial banks	1	-3	-24	-2	44	6	49	47	208	-16
Memo:										
IBRD	0	70	-21	-22	-23	-24	-27	-25	-19	-13
IDA	2	2	47	54	64	77	111	97	132	82

BOLIVIA

(US$ million, unless otherwise indicated)

	1970	1980	1990	1992	1993	1994	1995	1996	1997	1998
INTEREST PAYMENTS (LINT)	**7**	**173**	**117**	**109**	**127**	**148**	**155**	**163**	**190**	**145**
Public and publicly guaranteed	**7**	**164**	**103**	**98**	**112**	**132**	**137**	**150**	**150**	**138**
Official creditors	4	43	101	95	109	130	133	148	149	137
Multilateral	1	21	69	78	86	90	100	104	100	93
Concessional	1	2	10	13	13	16	17	18	20	22
Bilateral	3	21	32	17	24	40	33	44	49	44
Concessional	3	11	6	9	13	22	24	33	41	37
Private creditors	3	121	2	3	3	3	4	1	1	1
Bonds	1	3	0	0	0	0	0	0	0	0
Commercial banks	0	96	1	1	1	1	1	1	0	0
Other private	2	22	2	2	2	2	3	1	1	1
Private nonguaranteed	**1**	**9**	**14**	**12**	**15**	**16**	**19**	**14**	**40**	**6**
Bonds	0	0	0	0	0	0	0	0	0	0
Commercial banks	1	9	14	12	15	16	19	14	40	6
Memo:										
IBRD	0	10	15	14	12	11	9	7	4	3
IDA	0	1	3	3	4	4	6	5	6	7
NET TRANSFERS ON DEBT	**32**	**138**	**-13**	**155**	**76**	**73**	**166**	**86**	**230**	**-55**
Public and publicly guaranteed	**31**	**151**	**25**	**168**	**47**	**82**	**136**	**53**	**61**	**-32**
Official creditors	33	113	28	177	83	85	147	56	60	-35
Multilateral	0	79	18	85	43	101	163	45	105	-35
Concessional	0	25	66	53	75	94	135	147	181	146
Bilateral	33	34	9	92	39	-16	-16	11	-45	0
Concessional	26	6	71	97	70	26	18	28	-31	9
Private creditors	-1	38	-3	-9	-35	-3	-11	-3	1	3
Bonds	-1	-4	0	0	0	0	0	0	-3	0
Commercial banks	-1	-90	-4	-3	-29	2	-5	-6	1	5
Other private	1	132	2	-6	-7	-6	-7	3	3	-2
Private nonguaranteed	**0**	**-12**	**-38**	**-13**	**29**	**-10**	**30**	**33**	**168**	**-22**
Bonds	0	0	0	0	0	0	0	0	0	0
Commercial banks	0	-12	-38	-13	29	-10	30	33	168	-22
Memo:										
IBRD	0	60	-36	-35	-35	-35	-36	-32	-24	-16
IDA	2	1	45	50	60	73	105	92	126	75
DEBT SERVICE (LTDS)	**26**	**319**	**313**	**239**	**293**	**321**	**328**	**362**	**418**	**381**
Public and publicly guaranteed	**23**	**290**	**275**	**224**	**272**	**286**	**291**	**304**	**318**	**348**
Official creditors	13	85	263	211	234	275	280	293	310	344
Multilateral	3	28	186	165	185	200	220	239	252	286
Concessional	3	3	24	28	30	36	39	41	46	48
Bilateral	10	57	77	46	49	75	60	54	59	58
Concessional	7	25	14	13	16	31	27	35	45	46
Private creditors	11	205	12	13	38	12	11	11	7	4
Bonds	1	4	0	0	0	0	0	0	3	0
Commercial banks	1	145	4	4	31	6	5	7	2	1
Other private	8	56	8	9	7	6	7	4	3	3
Private nonguaranteed	**3**	**28**	**38**	**16**	**22**	**34**	**37**	**58**	**101**	**33**
Bonds	0	0	0	0	0	0	0	0	0	0
Commercial banks	3	28	38	16	22	34	37	58	101	33
Memo:										
IBRD	0	13	36	35	35	35	36	32	24	16
IDA	0	1	4	5	6	7	8	8	10	13
UNDISBURSED DEBT	**72**	**954**	**1,123**	**1,208**	**1,040**	**1,195**	**1,446**	**1,345**	**1,108**	**1,257**
Official creditors	66	804	1,107	1,191	1,026	1,189	1,432	1,330	1,097	1,238
Private creditors	6	150	16	17	14	7	14	14	12	19
Memorandum items										
Concessional LDOD	265	665	1,888	1,891	2,147	2,428	2,724	2,931	2,964	3,212
Variable rate LDOD	11	719	918	810	656	734	850	761	897	690
Public sector LDOD	467	2,166	3,687	3,669	3,695	4,122	4,468	4,265	4,144	4,307
Private sector LDOD	24	107	177	140	184	191	239	285	426	245

6. CURRENCY COMPOSITION OF LONG-TERM DEBT (PERCENT)

	1970	1980	1990	1992	1993	1994	1995	1996	1997	1998
Deutsche mark	2.3	6.8	7.0	8.9	9.2	9.6	10.0	9.6	8.5	9.1
French franc	0.1	0.8	2.2	2.3	2.2	2.2	2.1	1.4	1.3	1.4
Japanese yen	0.0	1.7	10.0	11.8	14.0	14.0	13.1	12.2	11.3	12.1
Pound sterling	0.0	2.0	0.9	0.7	0.7	0.6	0.7	0.5	0.5	0.4
Swiss franc	0.0	0.3	0.7	0.8	0.1	0.1	0.0	0.0	0.0	0.0
U.S.dollars	85.9	65.1	41.3	33.2	30.6	31.0	32.8	35.2	37.3	39.1
Multiple currency	11.7	18.1	29.4	33.4	35.1	34.4	33.6	34.1	34.7	31.2
Special drawing rights	0.0	0.0	0.0	0.0	0.0	0.0	0.1	0.1	0.1	0.2
All other currencies	0.0	5.2	8.5	8.9	8.1	8.1	7.6	6.9	6.3	6.5

BOLIVIA

(US$ million, unless otherwise indicated)

	1970	1980	1990	1992	1993	1994	1995	1996	1997	1998
7. DEBT RESTRUCTURINGS										
Total amount rescheduled	..	..	153	125	115	0	196	433	301	0
Debt stock rescheduled	..	..	0	0	0	0	0	0	0	0
Principal rescheduled	..	..	81	70	71	0	138	427	300	0
Official	..	..	69	62	70	0	137	420	300	0
Private	..	..	12	8	1	0	1	7	0	0
Interest rescheduled	..	..	63	54	40	0	46	4	0	0
Official	..	..	59	52	39	0	46	4	0	0
Private	..	..	4	2	1	0	1	1	0	0
Debt forgiven	..	..	92	60	55	17	74	181	83	15
Memo: interest forgiven	..	..	60	6	1	0	8	0	12	0
Debt stock reduction	..	..	20	20	171	0	0	0	0	0
of which debt buyback	..	..	4	2	27	0	0	0	0	0
8. DEBT STOCK-FLOW RECONCILIATION										
Total change in debt stocks	..	..	143	174	72	570	405	-81	47	830
Net flows on debt	130	180	32	313	203	322	341	329	486	928
Net change in interest arrears	..	..	-44	-4	3	20	-14	5	-22	0
Interest capitalized	..	..	63	54	40	0	46	4	0	0
Debt forgiveness or reduction	..	..	-109	-77	-198	-17	-74	-181	-83	-15
Cross-currency valuation	..	..	135	-62	9	165	48	-132	-149	113
Residual	..	..	65	-50	16	80	57	-107	-185	-197
9. AVERAGE TERMS OF NEW COMMITMENTS										
ALL CREDITORS										
Interest (%)	1.9	8.4	4.2	3.0	3.2	3.4	3.8	1.8	4.8	1.5
Maturity (years)	47.7	15.5	29.1	30.3	25.2	28.2	28.7	31.7	19.3	36.2
Grace period (years)	4.0	4.5	7.9	9.0	7.4	7.3	7.7	8.7	5.4	9.9
Grant element (%)	66.6	13.0	47.8	56.9	51.3	51.2	49.7	63.1	35.2	71.5
Official creditors										
Interest (%)	1.8	8.1	4.1	3.0	3.2	3.4	3.8	1.8	4.8	1.5
Maturity (years)	48.2	21.5	29.4	30.5	25.2	28.2	28.9	32.5	19.8	37.1
Grace period (years)	4.0	5.3	7.9	9.0	7.4	7.3	7.8	9.0	5.5	10.1
Grant element (%)	67.4	20.4	48.3	56.9	51.3	51.2	50.0	64.3	36.0	72.5
Private creditors										
Interest (%)	12.0	8.7	9.4	2.2	0.0	0.0	6.7	0.3	5.5	1.5
Maturity (years)	5.5	10.1	5.8	18.5	0.0	0.0	5.4	6.9	6.0	9.4
Grace period (years)	3.5	3.9	1.5	7.0	0.0	0.0	1.0	0.6	1.3	5.3
Grant element (%)	-6.9	6.4	1.0	52.9	0.0	0.0	8.0	27.7	12.6	43.9
Memorandum items										
Commitments	24	370	549	420	156	501	677	291	190	450
Official creditors	24	176	542	413	156	501	671	281	183	436
Private creditors	0	194	7	7	0	0	6	9	6	15

10. CONTRACTUAL OBLIGATIONS ON OUTSTANDING LONG-TERM DEBT

	1999	2000	2001	2002	2003	2004	2005	2006	2007	2008
TOTAL										
Disbursements	385	346	220	151	89	42	21	2	1	0
Principal	231	241	231	247	249	234	222	212	206	175
Interest	163	159	149	140	127	115	104	96	88	80
Official creditors										
Disbursements	377	339	216	151	89	42	21	2	1	0
Principal	198	207	199	216	219	203	191	181	175	171
Interest	141	141	134	126	117	107	99	93	86	80
Bilateral creditors										
Disbursements	46	34	21	12	6	3	1	0	0	0
Principal	27	35	41	44	50	49	49	49	47	48
Interest	45	47	46	45	45	44	43	41	40	39
Multilateral creditors										
Disbursements	331	305	196	139	83	40	19	2	1	0
Principal	172	172	158	173	169	154	142	132	128	123
Interest	97	94	88	81	72	63	56	52	46	41
Private creditors										
Disbursements	8	7	3	1	0	0	0	0	0	0
Principal	33	34	32	30	30	31	31	31	31	3
Interest	21	18	15	13	10	8	6	3	2	0
Commercial banks										
Disbursements	3	1	0	0	0	0	0	0	0	0
Principal	2	2	2	2	2	1	1	1	1	1
Interest	0	1	0	0	0	0	0	0	0	0
Other private										
Disbursements	5	6	3	1	0	0	0	0	0	0
Principal	32	32	30	28	28	30	30	30	30	3
Interest	21	17	15	13	10	8	6	3	2	0

BOSNIA AND HERZEGOVINA

(US$ million, unless otherwise indicated)

	1970	*1980*	*1990*	*1992*	*1993*	*1994*	*1995*	*1996*	*1997*	*1998*
1. SUMMARY DEBT DATA										
TOTAL DEBT STOCKS (EDT)	..	..	..	..	..	..	..	..	..	..
Long-term debt (LDOD)	..	..	..	..	..	..	..	..	..	..
Public and publicly guaranteed	..	..	..	..	..	..	..	..	..	..
Private nonguaranteed	..	..	..	..	..	..	..	..	..	..
Use of IMF credit	..	..	..	..	**28**	**30**	**48**	**45**	**41**	**77**
Short-term debt	..	..	..	..	**2**	**39**	**31**	**73**	**57**	**81**
of which interest arrears on LDOD	..	..	..	..	..	..	..	..	..	..
Official creditors	..	..	..	..	..	..	..	..	..	..
Private creditors	..	..	..	..	..	..	..	..	..	..
Memo: principal arrears on LDOD	..	..	..	..	..	..	..	..	..	..
Official creditors	..	..	..	..	..	..	..	..	..	..
Private creditors	..	..	..	..	..	..	..	..	..	..
Memo: export credits	..	..	..	..	91	166	144	208	197	259
TOTAL DEBT FLOWS										
Disbursements	..	..	..	..	..	..	..	..	..	..
Long-term debt	..	..	..	..	..	..	..	..	..	..
IMF purchases	..	..	..	..	0	0	46	0	0	33
Principal repayments	..	..	..	..	..	..	..	..	..	..
Long-term debt	..	..	..	..	..	..	..	..	..	..
IMF repurchases	..	..	..	..	0	0	28	2	1	0
Net flows on debt	..	..	..	..	..	..	..	..	..	..
of which short-term debt	..	..	..	..	..	..	..	..	..	..
Interest payments (INT)	..	..	..	..	..	..	..	..	..	..
Long-term debt	..	..	..	..	..	..	..	..	..	..
IMF charges	..	..	..	..	0	0	5	2	2	3
Short-term debt	..	..	..	..	..	..	..	..	..	..
Net transfers on debt	..	..	..	..	..	..	..	..	..	..
Total debt service paid (TDS)	..	..	..	..	..	..	..	..	..	..
Long-term debt	..	..	..	..	..	..	..	..	..	..
IMF repurchases and charges	..	..	..	..	0	0	33	4	3	3
Short-term debt (interest only)	..	..	..	..	..	..	..	..	..	..
2. AGGREGATE NET RESOURCE FLOWS AND NET TRANSFERS (LONG-TERM)										
NET RESOURCE FLOWS	..	..	..	..	..	..	..	..	..	..
Net flow of long-term debt (ex. IMF)	..	..	..	..	..	..	..	..	..	..
Foreign direct investment (net)	..	..	..	..	..	..	..	..	..	..
Portfolio equity flows	..	..	..	..	..	..	..	..	..	..
Grants (excluding technical coop.)	..	..	..	..	32	384	863	635	700	469
Memo: technical coop. grants	..	..	..	..	0	7	61	86	76	239
official net resource flows	..	..	..	..	..	..	..	..	..	..
private net resource flows	..	..	..	..	..	..	..	..	..	..
NET TRANSFERS	..	..	..	..	..	..	..	..	..	..
Interest on long-term debt	..	..	..	..	..	..	..	..	..	..
Profit remittances on FDI	..	..	..	..	..	..	..	..	..	..
Memo: official net transfers	..	..	..	..	..	..	..	..	..	..
private net transfers	..	..	..	..	..	..	..	..	..	..
3. MAJOR ECONOMIC AGGREGATES										
Gross national product (GNP)	..	..	..	..	..	..	..	..	..	..
Exports of goods & services (XGS)	..	..	..	..	..	..	..	..	..	..
of which workers remittances	..	..	..	..	..	..	..	..	..	..
Imports of goods & services (MGS)	..	..	..	..	..	..	..	..	..	..
International reserves (RES)	..	..	..	..	..	..	..	..	..	..
Current account balance	..	..	..	..	..	..	..	..	..	..
4. DEBT INDICATORS										
EDT / XGS (%)	..	..	..	..	..	..	..	..	..	..
EDT / GNP (%)	..	..	..	..	..	..	..	..	..	..
TDS / XGS (%)	..	..	..	..	..	..	..	..	..	..
INT / XGS (%)	..	..	..	..	..	..	..	..	..	..
INT / GNP (%)	..	..	..	..	..	..	..	..	..	..
RES / EDT (%)	..	..	..	..	..	..	..	..	..	..
RES / MGS (months)	..	..	..	..	..	..	..	..	..	..
Short-term / EDT (%)	..	..	..	..	..	..	..	..	..	..
Concessional / EDT (%)	..	..	..	..	..	..	..	..	..	..
Multilateral / EDT (%)	..	..	..	..	..	..	..	..	..	..

BOSNIA AND HERZEGOVINA

(US$ million, unless otherwise indicated)

	1970	1980	1990	1992	1993	1994	1995	1996	1997	1998
5. LONG-TERM DEBT										
DEBT OUTSTANDING (LDOD)	..	..	..	..	..	..	..	..	..	..
Public and publicly guaranteed	..	..	..	..	..	..	..	..	..	..
Official creditors	..	..	..	..	..	..	..	..	..	..
Multilateral	..	..	..	..	..	..	..	..	..	..
Concessional	..	..	..	..	..	..	..	..	..	..
Bilateral	..	..	..	..	..	..	..	..	..	..
Concessional	..	..	..	..	..	..	..	..	..	..
Private creditors	..	..	..	..	..	..	..	..	..	..
Bonds	..	..	..	..	..	..	..	..	..	..
Commercial banks	..	..	..	..	..	..	..	..	..	..
Other private	..	..	..	..	..	..	..	..	..	..
Private nonguaranteed	..	..	..	..	..	..	..	..	..	..
Bonds	..	..	..	..	..	..	..	..	..	..
Commercial banks	..	..	..	..	..	..	..	..	..	..
Memo:										
IBRD	..	..	..	..	424	452	472	589	566	581
IDA	..	..	..	..	0	0	0	109	167	312
DISBURSEMENTS	..	..	..	..	..	..	..	..	..	..
Public and publicly guaranteed	..	..	..	..	..	..	..	..	..	..
Official creditors	..	..	..	..	..	..	..	..	..	..
Multilateral	..	..	..	..	..	..	..	..	..	..
Concessional	..	..	..	..	..	..	..	..	..	..
Bilateral	..	..	..	..	..	..	..	..	..	..
Concessional	..	..	..	..	..	..	..	..	..	..
Private creditors	..	..	..	..	..	..	..	..	..	..
Bonds	..	..	..	..	..	..	..	..	..	..
Commercial banks	..	..	..	..	..	..	..	..	..	..
Other private	..	..	..	..	..	..	..	..	..	..
Private nonguaranteed	..	..	..	..	..	..	..	..	..	..
Bonds	..	..	..	..	..	..	..	..	..	..
Commercial banks	..	..	..	..	..	..	..	..	..	..
Memo:										
IBRD	..	..	..	..	0	0	0	0	0	0
IDA	..	..	..	..	0	0	0	110	65	135
PRINCIPAL REPAYMENTS	..	..	..	..	..	..	..	..	..	..
Public and publicly guaranteed	..	..	..	..	..	..	..	..	..	..
Official creditors	..	..	..	..	..	..	..	..	..	..
Multilateral	..	..	..	..	..	..	..	..	..	..
Concessional	..	..	..	..	..	..	..	..	..	..
Bilateral	..	..	..	..	..	..	..	..	..	..
Concessional	..	..	..	..	..	..	..	..	..	..
Private creditors	..	..	..	..	..	..	..	..	..	..
Bonds	..	..	..	..	..	..	..	..	..	..
Commercial banks	..	..	..	..	..	..	..	..	..	..
Other private	..	..	..	..	..	..	..	..	..	..
Private nonguaranteed	..	..	..	..	..	..	..	..	..	..
Bonds	..	..	..	..	..	..	..	..	..	..
Commercial banks	..	..	..	..	..	..	..	..	..	..
Memo:										
IBRD	..	..	..	..	0	0	0	25	0	0
IDA	..	..	..	..	0	0	0	0	0	0
NET FLOWS ON DEBT	..	..	..	..	..	..	..	..	..	..
Public and publicly guaranteed	..	..	..	..	..	..	..	..	..	..
Official creditors	..	..	..	..	..	..	..	..	..	..
Multilateral	..	..	..	..	..	..	..	..	..	..
Concessional	..	..	..	..	..	..	..	..	..	..
Bilateral	..	..	..	..	..	..	..	..	..	..
Concessional	..	..	..	..	..	..	..	..	..	..
Private creditors	..	..	..	..	..	..	..	..	..	..
Bonds	..	..	..	..	..	..	..	..	..	..
Commercial banks	..	..	..	..	..	..	..	..	..	..
Other private	..	..	..	..	..	..	..	..	..	..
Private nonguaranteed	..	..	..	..	..	..	..	..	..	..
Bonds	..	..	..	..	..	..	..	..	..	..
Commercial banks	..	..	..	..	..	..	..	..	..	..
Memo:										
IBRD	..	..	..	..	0	0	0	-25	0	0
IDA	..	..	..	..	0	0	0	110	65	135

BOSNIA AND HERZEGOVINA

(US$ million, unless otherwise indicated)

	1970	1980	1990	1992	1993	1994	1995	1996	1997	1998
INTEREST PAYMENTS (LINT)	..	..	..	..	..	..	..	..	..	..
Public and publicly guaranteed	..	..	..	..	..	..	..	..	..	..
Official creditors	..	..	..	..	..	..	..	..	..	..
Multilateral	..	..	..	..	..	..	..	..	..	..
Concessional	..	..	..	..	..	..	..	..	..	..
Bilateral	..	..	..	..	..	..	..	..	..	..
Concessional	..	..	..	..	..	..	..	..	..	..
Private creditors	..	..	..	..	..	..	..	..	..	..
Bonds	..	..	..	..	..	..	..	..	..	..
Commercial banks	..	..	..	..	..	..	..	..	..	..
Other private	..	..	..	..	..	..	..	..	..	..
Private nonguaranteed	..	..	..	..	..	..	..	..	..	..
Bonds	..	..	..	..	..	..	..	..	..	..
Commercial banks	..	..	..	..	..	..	..	..	..	..
Memo:										
IBRD	..	..	..	..	0	0	0	180	36	35
IDA	..	..	..	..	0	0	0	0	1	1
NET TRANSFERS ON DEBT	..	..	..	..	..	..	..	..	..	..
Public and publicly guaranteed	..	..	..	..	..	..	..	..	..	..
Official creditors	..	..	..	..	..	..	..	..	..	..
Multilateral	..	..	..	..	..	..	..	..	..	..
Concessional	..	..	..	..	..	..	..	..	..	..
Bilateral	..	..	..	..	..	..	..	..	..	..
Concessional	..	..	..	..	..	..	..	..	..	..
Private creditors	..	..	..	..	..	..	..	..	..	..
Bonds	..	..	..	..	..	..	..	..	..	..
Commercial banks	..	..	..	..	..	..	..	..	..	..
Other private	..	..	..	..	..	..	..	..	..	..
Private nonguaranteed	..	..	..	..	..	..	..	..	..	..
Bonds	..	..	..	..	..	..	..	..	..	..
Commercial banks	..	..	..	..	..	..	..	..	..	..
Memo:										
IBRD	..	..	..	..	0	0	0	-205	-36	-35
IDA	..	..	..	..	0	0	0	110	64	134
DEBT SERVICE (LTDS)	..	..	..	..	..	..	..	..	..	..
Public and publicly guaranteed	..	..	..	..	..	..	..	..	..	..
Official creditors	..	..	..	..	..	..	..	..	..	..
Multilateral	..	..	..	..	..	..	..	..	..	..
Concessional	..	..	..	..	..	..	..	..	..	..
Bilateral	..	..	..	..	..	..	..	..	..	..
Concessional	..	..	..	..	..	..	..	..	..	..
Private creditors	..	..	..	..	..	..	..	..	..	..
Bonds	..	..	..	..	..	..	..	..	..	..
Commercial banks	..	..	..	..	..	..	..	..	..	..
Other private	..	..	..	..	..	..	..	..	..	..
Private nonguaranteed	..	..	..	..	..	..	..	..	..	..
Bonds	..	..	..	..	..	..	..	..	..	..
Commercial banks	..	..	..	..	..	..	..	..	..	..
Memo:										
IBRD	..	..	..	..	0	0	0	205	36	35
IDA	..	..	..	..	0	0	0	0	1	1
UNDISBURSED DEBT	..	..	..	..	..	..	..	..	..	..
Official creditors	..	..	..	..	..	..	..	..	..	..
Private creditors	..	..	..	..	..	..	..	..	..	..
Memorandum items										
Concessional LDOD	..	..	..	..	..	..	..	..	..	..
Variable rate LDOD	..	..	..	..	..	..	..	..	..	..
Public sector LDOD	..	..	..	..	..	..	..	..	..	..
Private sector LDOD	..	..	..	..	..	..	..	..	..	..

6. CURRENCY COMPOSITION OF LONG-TERM DEBT (PERCENT)

	1970	1980	1990	1992	1993	1994	1995	1996	1997	1998
Deutsche mark	..	..	..	..	..	..	..	..	..	..
French franc	..	..	..	..	..	..	..	..	..	..
Japanese yen	..	..	..	..	..	..	..	..	..	..
Pound sterling	..	..	..	..	..	..	..	..	..	..
Swiss franc	..	..	..	..	..	..	..	..	..	..
U.S.dollars	..	..	..	..	..	..	..	..	..	..
Multiple currency	..	..	..	..	..	..	..	..	..	..
Special drawing rights	..	..	..	..	..	..	..	..	..	..
All other currencies	..	..	..	..	..	..	..	..	..	..

BOSNIA AND HERZEGOVINA

(US$ million, unless otherwise indicated)

	1970	1980	1990	1992	1993	1994	1995	1996	1997	1998
7. DEBT RESTRUCTURINGS										
Total amount rescheduled	..	..	..	..	..	..	..	..	..	..
Debt stock rescheduled	..	..	..	..	..	..	..	..	..	..
Principal rescheduled	..	..	..	..	..	..	..	..	..	..
Official	..	..	..	..	..	..	..	..	..	..
Private	..	..	..	..	..	..	..	..	..	..
Interest rescheduled	..	..	..	..	..	..	..	..	..	..
Official	..	..	..	..	..	..	..	..	..	..
Private	..	..	..	..	..	..	..	..	..	..
Debt forgiven	..	..	..	..	..	..	..	..	..	..
Memo: interest forgiven	..	..	..	..	..	..	..	..	..	..
Debt stock reduction	..	..	..	..	..	..	..	..	..	..
of which debt buyback	..	..	..	..	..	..	..	..	..	..
8. DEBT STOCK-FLOW RECONCILIATION										
Total change in debt stocks	..	..	..	..	..	..	..	..	..	..
Net flows on debt	..	..	..	..	..	..	..	..	..	..
Net change in interest arrears	..	..	..	..	..	..	..	..	..	..
Interest capitalized	..	..	..	..	..	..	..	..	..	..
Debt forgiveness or reduction	..	..	..	..	..	..	..	..	..	..
Cross-currency valuation	..	..	..	..	..	..	..	..	..	..
Residual	..	..	..	..	..	..	..	..	..	..
9. AVERAGE TERMS OF NEW COMMITMENTS										
ALL CREDITORS										
Interest (%)	..	..	..	..	..	..	..	..	..	..
Maturity (years)	..	..	..	..	..	..	..	..	..	..
Grace period (years)	..	..	..	..	..	..	..	..	..	..
Grant element (%)	..	..	..	..	..	..	..	..	..	..
Official creditors										
Interest (%)	..	..	..	..	..	..	..	..	..	..
Maturity (years)	..	..	..	..	..	..	..	..	..	..
Grace period (years)	..	..	..	..	..	..	..	..	..	..
Grant element (%)	..	..	..	..	..	..	..	..	..	..
Private creditors										
Interest (%)	..	..	..	..	..	..	..	..	..	..
Maturity (years)	..	..	..	..	..	..	..	..	..	..
Grace period (years)	..	..	..	..	..	..	..	..	..	..
Grant element (%)	..	..	..	..	..	..	..	..	..	..
Memorandum items										
Commitments	..	..	..	..	..	..	..	..	..	..
Official creditors	..	..	..	..	..	..	..	..	..	..
Private creditors	..	..	..	..	..	..	..	..	..	..

10. CONTRACTUAL OBLIGATIONS ON OUTSTANDING LONG-TERM DEBT

	1999	2000	2001	2002	2003	2004	2005	2006	2007	2008
TOTAL										
Disbursements	..	..	..	..	..	..	..	..	..	..
Principal	..	..	..	..	..	..	..	..	..	..
Interest	..	..	..	..	..	..	..	..	..	..
Official creditors										
Disbursements	..	..	..	..	..	..	..	..	..	..
Principal	..	..	..	..	..	..	..	..	..	..
Interest	..	..	..	..	..	..	..	..	..	..
Bilateral creditors										
Disbursements	..	..	..	..	..	..	..	..	..	..
Principal	..	..	..	..	..	..	..	..	..	..
Interest	..	..	..	..	..	..	..	..	..	..
Multilateral creditors										
Disbursements	28	23	14	9	6	3	2	0	0	0
Principal	3	3	8	26	26	26	26	28	33	36
Interest	42	42	41	41	39	37	36	34	32	31
Private creditors										
Disbursements	..	..	..	..	..	..	..	..	..	..
Principal	..	..	..	..	..	..	..	..	..	..
Interest	..	..	..	..	..	..	..	..	..	..
Commercial banks										
Disbursements	..	..	..	..	..	..	..	..	..	..
Principal	..	..	..	..	..	..	..	..	..	..
Interest	..	..	..	..	..	..	..	..	..	..
Other private										
Disbursements	..	..	..	..	..	..	..	..	..	..
Principal	..	..	..	..	..	..	..	..	..	..
Interest	..	..	..	..	..	..	..	..	..	..

BOTSWANA

(US$ million, unless otherwise indicated)

	1970	1980	1990	1992	1993	1994	1995	1996	1997	1998
1. SUMMARY DEBT DATA										
TOTAL DEBT STOCKS (EDT)	..	146.7	563.0	611.8	659.6	688.7	703.4	613.5	562.0	548.2
Long-term debt (LDOD)	17.4	142.7	557.2	605.5	651.8	677.5	693.2	607.5	522.0	508.2
Public and publicly guaranteed	17.4	142.7	557.2	605.5	651.8	677.5	693.2	607.5	522.0	508.2
Private nonguaranteed	0.0	0.0	0.0	0.0	0.0	0.0	0.0	0.0	0.0	0.0
Use of IMF credit	0.0	0.0	0.0	0.0	0.0	0.0	0.0	0.0	0.0	0.0
Short-term debt	..	4.0	5.8	6.3	7.8	11.2	10.2	6.0	40.0	40.0
of which interest arrears on LDOD	..	0.0	2.6	3.1	4.6	7.8	6.2	0.0	0.0	0.0
Official creditors	..	0.0	1.3	1.0	1.6	2.3	0.2	0.0	0.0	0.0
Private creditors	..	0.0	1.3	2.1	3.0	5.5	6.0	0.0	0.0	0.0
Memo: principal arrears on LDOD	..	0.0	2.7	7.7	7.4	12.6	8.9	0.0	0.0	0.0
Official creditors	..	0.0	0.9	6.6	6.2	6.7	2.9	0.0	0.0	0.0
Private creditors	..	0.0	1.8	1.1	1.2	5.9	6.0	0.0	0.0	0.0
Memo: export credits	..	0.0	128.0	115.0	99.0	102.0	85.0	74.0	85.0	78.0
TOTAL DEBT FLOWS										
Disbursements	5.7	27.5	29.7	84.4	101.9	52.0	65.9	28.1	22.0	20.0
Long-term debt	5.7	27.5	29.7	84.4	101.9	52.0	65.9	28.1	22.0	20.0
IMF purchases	0.0	0.0	0.0	0.0	0.0	0.0	0.0	0.0	0.0	0.0
Principal repayments	0.2	6.4	67.0	62.0	56.8	61.9	64.6	73.2	74.5	53.3
Long-term debt	0.2	6.4	67.0	62.0	56.8	61.9	64.6	73.2	74.5	53.3
IMF repurchases	0.0	0.0	0.0	0.0	0.0	0.0	0.0	0.0	0.0	0.0
Net flows on debt	5.6	8.1	-37.2	22.4	45.1	-9.7	1.9	-43.1	-18.4	-33.3
of which short-term debt	..	-13.0	0.1	0.0	0.0	0.2	0.6	2.0	34.0	0.0
Interest payments (INT)	..	9.1	39.4	35.9	33.3	30.9	27.7	78.5	29.2	25.3
Long-term debt	0.4	7.6	39.2	35.7	33.1	30.7	27.5	78.2	27.8	23.0
IMF charges	0.0	0.0	0.0	0.0	0.0	0.0	0.0	0.0	0.0	0.0
Short-term debt	..	1.5	0.2	0.2	0.2	0.2	0.2	0.3	1.4	2.3
Net transfers on debt	..	-1.0	-76.6	-13.5	11.8	-40.6	-25.8	-121.6	-47.7	-58.6
Total debt service paid (TDS)	..	15.4	106.4	97.9	90.1	92.8	92.3	151.7	103.7	78.6
Long-term debt	0.6	13.9	106.2	97.7	89.9	92.6	92.1	151.4	102.3	76.3
IMF repurchases and charges	0.0	0.0	0.0	0.0	0.0	0.0	0.0	0.0	0.0	0.0
Short-term debt (interest only)	..	1.5	0.2	0.2	0.2	0.2	0.2	0.3	1.4	2.3
2. AGGREGATE NET RESOURCE FLOWS AND NET TRANSFERS (LONG-TERM)										
NET RESOURCE FLOWS	14.9	183.3	136.0	73.0	-189.7	9.3	99.9	56.0	88.7	106.9
Net flow of long-term debt (ex. IMF)	5.6	21.1	-37.3	22.4	45.1	-9.9	1.3	-45.1	-52.4	-33.3
Foreign direct investment (net)	0.0	111.6	95.0	-2.0	-287.0	-14.0	70.0	71.0	100.0	95.0
Portfolio equity flows	0.0	0.0	0.0	0.0	0.0	0.1	0.0	0.1	0.0	0.0
Grants (excluding technical coop.)	9.3	50.6	78.4	52.6	52.2	33.1	28.5	30.0	41.2	45.2
Memo: technical coop. grants	2.7	47.5	60.7	57.3	56.7	45.0	51.4	37.0	41.0	31.7
official net resource flows	12.0	68.9	59.5	77.7	68.0	25.2	36.1	-6.5	-6.3	16.4
private net resource flows	2.9	114.4	76.5	-4.7	-257.7	-15.9	63.8	62.5	95.0	90.5
NET TRANSFERS	14.5	68.2	-200.9	-247.7	-472.8	-301.4	-227.6	-332.2	-279.2	-216.0
Interest on long-term debt	0.4	7.6	39.2	35.7	33.1	30.7	27.5	78.2	27.8	23.0
Profit remittances on FDI	0.0	107.5	297.7	285.0	250.0	280.0	300.0	310.0	340.0	300.0
Memo: official net transfers	11.6	62.3	23.3	44.2	36.0	-4.3	11.6	-76.2	-31.8	-5.0
private net transfers	2.9	5.9	-224.2	-291.9	-508.8	-297.1	-239.2	-256.0	-247.4	-211.0
3. MAJOR ECONOMIC AGGREGATES										
Gross national product (GNP)	101.0	1,097.4	3,659.9	4,259.6	4,470.3	4,179.6	4,866.5	4,869.1	4,797.2	4,631.5
Exports of goods & services (XGS)	..	747.5	2,421.1	2,475.3	2,468.0	2,291.2	2,903.8	2,890.5	3,652.1	2,939.0
of which workers remittances	..	0.0	..	..	..	..	..	8.3	0.1	0.4
Imports of goods & services (MGS)	..	953.5	2,508.9	2,346.4	2,041.9	2,141.4	2,565.3	2,566.1	3,132.0	3,008.7
International reserves (RES)	..	343.7	3,385.3	3,844.6	4,153.1	4,462.4	4,764.4	5,097.6	5,740.4	6,025.2
Current account balance	..	-151.1	-19.3	197.7	426.9	211.6	299.7	495.0	721.5	170.1
4. DEBT INDICATORS										
EDT / XGS (%)	..	19.6	23.3	24.7	26.7	30.1	24.2	21.2	15.4	18.7
EDT / GNP (%)	..	13.4	15.4	14.4	14.8	16.5	14.5	12.6	11.7	11.8
TDS / XGS (%)	..	2.1	4.4	4.0	3.7	4.1	3.2	5.3	2.8	2.7
INT / XGS (%)	..	1.2	1.6	1.5	1.4	1.4	1.0	2.7	0.8	0.9
INT / GNP (%)	..	0.8	1.1	0.8	0.7	0.7	0.6	1.6	0.6	0.6
RES / EDT (%)	..	234.3	601.3	628.4	629.6	647.9	677.3	830.9	1,021.4	1,099.1
RES / MGS (months)	..	4.3	16.2	19.7	24.4	25.0	22.3	23.8	22.0	24.0
Short-term / EDT (%)	..	2.7	1.0	1.0	1.2	1.6	1.5	1.0	7.1	7.3
Concessional / EDT (%)	..	40.5	32.8	38.2	40.0	42.6	48.3	52.5	51.6	54.0
Multilateral / EDT (%)	..	57.5	69.6	75.7	72.0	72.2	69.1	70.5	68.1	67.8

BOTSWANA

(US$ million, unless otherwise indicated)

	1970	1980	1990	1992	1993	1994	1995	1996	1997	1998
5. LONG-TERM DEBT										
DEBT OUTSTANDING (LDOD)	**17.4**	**142.7**	**557.2**	**605.5**	**651.8**	**677.5**	**693.2**	**607.5**	**522.0**	**508.2**
Public and publicly guaranteed	**17.4**	**142.7**	**557.2**	**605.5**	**651.8**	**677.5**	**693.2**	**607.5**	**522.0**	**508.2**
Official creditors	14.2	134.9	529.8	584.7	603.9	627.5	646.3	571.6	494.4	484.0
Multilateral	5.2	84.3	391.6	463.2	475.0	497.2	486.0	432.5	382.5	371.5
Concessional	5.2	31.5	112.7	153.1	170.5	194.3	206.1	202.0	192.2	194.0
Bilateral	8.9	50.6	138.2	121.6	128.9	130.2	160.2	139.2	111.8	112.5
Concessional	6.0	27.9	71.9	80.3	93.6	98.8	133.7	120.3	97.6	101.8
Private creditors	3.2	7.8	27.4	20.8	47.9	50.0	47.0	35.9	27.6	24.2
Bonds	2.6	2.5	0.0	0.0	0.0	0.0	0.0	0.0	0.0	0.0
Commercial banks	0.0	0.0	10.5	10.0	38.6	42.0	40.3	33.6	25.8	22.4
Other private	0.6	5.3	16.9	10.8	9.3	8.0	6.7	2.3	1.8	1.8
Private nonguaranteed	**0.0**	**0.0**	**0.0**	**0.0**	**0.0**	**0.0**	**0.0**	**0.0**	**0.0**	**0.0**
Bonds	0.0	0.0	0.0	0.0	0.0	0.0	0.0	0.0	0.0	0.0
Commercial banks	0.0	0.0	0.0	0.0	0.0	0.0	0.0	0.0	0.0	0.0
Memo:										
IBRD	0.0	50.0	155.2	129.3	124.7	113.6	96.3	68.8	47.1	36.2
IDA	5.2	15.6	13.6	12.9	12.4	12.0	11.5	11.0	10.6	10.1
DISBURSEMENTS	**5.7**	**27.5**	**29.7**	**84.4**	**101.9**	**52.0**	**65.9**	**28.1**	**22.0**	**20.0**
Public and publicly guaranteed	**5.7**	**27.5**	**29.7**	**84.4**	**101.9**	**52.0**	**65.9**	**28.1**	**22.0**	**20.0**
Official creditors	2.8	24.7	29.7	84.4	71.5	52.0	65.9	28.1	22.0	20.0
Multilateral	1.6	15.5	23.2	79.3	57.1	45.7	21.9	26.2	20.3	17.9
Concessional	1.6	5.8	14.1	16.4	25.8	26.8	13.0	13.0	11.5	6.7
Bilateral	1.2	9.2	6.5	5.1	14.4	6.3	44.0	1.9	1.7	2.1
Concessional	1.2	2.7	3.9	4.8	14.1	6.1	44.0	1.9	1.7	2.1
Private creditors	2.9	2.8	0.0	0.0	30.4	0.0	0.0	0.0	0.0	0.0
Bonds	2.6	0.0	0.0	0.0	0.0	0.0	0.0	0.0	0.0	0.0
Commercial banks	0.0	0.0	0.0	0.0	30.4	0.0	0.0	0.0	0.0	0.0
Other private	0.3	2.8	0.0	0.0	0.0	0.0	0.0	0.0	0.0	0.0
Private nonguaranteed	**0.0**	**0.0**	**0.0**	**0.0**	**0.0**	**0.0**	**0.0**	**0.0**	**0.0**	**0.0**
Bonds	0.0	0.0	0.0	0.0	0.0	0.0	0.0	0.0	0.0	0.0
Commercial banks	0.0	0.0	0.0	0.0	0.0	0.0	0.0	0.0	0.0	0.0
Memo:										
IBRD	0.0	9.7	7.0	4.8	12.4	1.1	0.6	0.0	0.0	0.0
IDA	1.6	0.0	0.0	0.0	0.0	0.0	0.0	0.0	0.0	0.0
PRINCIPAL REPAYMENTS	**0.2**	**6.4**	**67.0**	**62.0**	**56.8**	**61.9**	**64.6**	**73.2**	**74.5**	**53.3**
Public and publicly guaranteed	**0.2**	**6.4**	**67.0**	**62.0**	**56.8**	**61.9**	**64.6**	**73.2**	**74.5**	**53.3**
Official creditors	0.1	6.4	48.6	59.3	55.7	59.9	58.4	64.6	69.5	48.8
Multilateral	0.0	5.7	36.9	49.1	45.5	50.1	48.7	49.4	46.7	40.7
Concessional	0.0	0.1	2.7	5.4	7.8	9.1	6.3	9.1	10.9	9.4
Bilateral	0.1	0.7	11.7	10.2	10.3	9.9	9.7	15.3	22.8	8.2
Concessional	0.0	0.0	3.4	3.7	4.9	4.5	4.6	6.1	18.8	4.4
Private creditors	0.0	0.0	18.5	2.7	1.1	2.0	6.2	8.6	5.0	4.5
Bonds	0.0	0.0	0.0	0.0	0.0	0.0	0.0	0.0	0.0	0.0
Commercial banks	0.0	0.0	0.2	0.2	0.2	0.2	4.5	4.3	4.5	4.4
Other private	0.0	0.0	18.3	2.5	0.9	1.8	1.7	4.3	0.5	0.0
Private nonguaranteed	**0.0**	**0.0**	**0.0**	**0.0**	**0.0**	**0.0**	**0.0**	**0.0**	**0.0**	**0.0**
Bonds	0.0	0.0	0.0	0.0	0.0	0.0	0.0	0.0	0.0	0.0
Commercial banks	0.0	0.0	0.0	0.0	0.0	0.0	0.0	0.0	0.0	0.0
Memo:										
IBRD	0.0	5.4	19.0	20.6	19.8	21.0	23.7	20.9	16.5	12.9
IDA	0.0	0.1	0.3	0.4	0.4	0.4	0.5	0.5	0.5	0.5
NET FLOWS ON DEBT	**5.6**	**21.1**	**-37.3**	**22.4**	**45.1**	**-9.9**	**1.3**	**-45.1**	**-52.4**	**-33.3**
Public and publicly guaranteed	**5.6**	**21.1**	**-37.3**	**22.4**	**45.1**	**-9.9**	**1.3**	**-45.1**	**-52.4**	**-33.3**
Official creditors	2.7	18.3	-18.9	25.1	15.8	-7.9	7.6	-36.5	-47.5	-28.8
Multilateral	1.6	9.8	-13.7	30.2	11.6	-4.3	-26.8	-23.1	-26.4	-22.7
Concessional	1.6	5.7	11.4	11.0	18.0	17.7	6.7	3.9	0.6	-2.7
Bilateral	1.1	8.5	-5.2	-5.1	4.1	-3.6	34.4	-13.4	-21.1	-6.1
Concessional	1.2	2.7	0.5	1.1	9.3	1.7	39.4	-4.3	-17.1	-2.3
Private creditors	2.9	2.8	-18.5	-2.7	29.3	-2.0	-6.2	-8.6	-5.0	-4.5
Bonds	2.6	0.0	0.0	0.0	0.0	0.0	0.0	0.0	0.0	0.0
Commercial banks	0.0	0.0	-0.2	-0.2	30.2	-0.2	-4.5	-4.3	-4.5	-4.4
Other private	0.3	2.8	-18.3	-2.5	-0.9	-1.8	-1.7	-4.3	-0.5	0.0
Private nonguaranteed	**0.0**	**0.0**	**0.0**	**0.0**	**0.0**	**0.0**	**0.0**	**0.0**	**0.0**	**0.0**
Bonds	0.0	0.0	0.0	0.0	0.0	0.0	0.0	0.0	0.0	0.0
Commercial banks	0.0	0.0	0.0	0.0	0.0	0.0	0.0	0.0	0.0	0.0
Memo:										
IBRD	0.0	4.3	-11.9	-15.8	-7.5	-19.9	-23.1	-20.9	-16.5	-12.9
IDA	1.6	0.0	-0.3	-0.4	-0.4	-0.4	-0.5	-0.5	-0.5	-0.5

BOTSWANA

(US$ million, unless otherwise indicated)

	1970	1980	1990	1992	1993	1994	1995	1996	1997	1998
INTEREST PAYMENTS (LINT)	**0.4**	**7.6**	**39.2**	**35.7**	**33.1**	**30.7**	**27.5**	**78.2**	**27.8**	**23.0**
Public and publicly guaranteed	**0.4**	**7.6**	**39.2**	**35.7**	**33.1**	**30.7**	**27.5**	**78.2**	**27.8**	**23.0**
Official creditors	0.4	6.6	36.2	33.5	32.0	29.5	24.5	69.7	25.5	21.4
Multilateral	0.0	4.7	27.9	25.9	24.8	24.9	21.0	63.0	20.8	17.6
Concessional	0.0	0.2	2.5	2.8	2.6	1.8	1.6	4.1	4.0	3.5
Bilateral	0.4	1.9	8.3	7.6	7.3	4.7	3.5	6.7	4.7	3.8
Concessional	0.2	0.5	1.8	2.4	3.0	1.5	1.0	4.3	3.0	2.5
Private creditors	0.0	1.0	3.0	2.2	1.1	1.2	3.0	8.5	2.4	1.5
Bonds	0.0	0.2	0.0	0.0	0.0	0.0	0.0	0.0	0.0	0.0
Commercial banks	0.0	0.5	0.1	0.9	0.3	0.3	2.7	6.5	2.2	1.4
Other private	0.0	0.3	3.0	1.3	0.7	0.8	0.3	2.0	0.2	0.2
Private nonguaranteed	**0.0**	**0.0**	**0.0**	**0.0**	**0.0**	**0.0**	**0.0**	**0.0**	**0.0**	**0.0**
Bonds	0.0	0.0	0.0	0.0	0.0	0.0	0.0	0.0	0.0	0.0
Commercial banks	0.0	0.0	0.0	0.0	0.0	0.0	0.0	0.0	0.0	0.0
Memo:										
IBRD	0.0	4.4	14.2	11.4	9.9	9.3	8.6	6.2	4.3	2.9
IDA	0.0	0.1	0.1	0.1	0.1	0.1	0.1	0.1	0.1	0.1
NET TRANSFERS ON DEBT	**5.1**	**13.5**	**-76.5**	**-13.3**	**12.0**	**-40.6**	**-26.2**	**-123.3**	**-80.3**	**-56.3**
Public and publicly guaranteed	**5.1**	**13.5**	**-76.5**	**-13.3**	**12.0**	**-40.6**	**-26.2**	**-123.3**	**-80.3**	**-56.3**
Official creditors	2.2	11.7	-55.1	-8.5	-16.3	-37.5	-16.9	-106.2	-72.9	-50.2
Multilateral	1.6	5.1	-41.6	4.3	-13.1	-29.2	-47.8	-86.1	-47.2	-40.4
Concessional	1.6	5.5	8.9	8.3	15.4	15.9	5.1	-0.2	-3.5	-6.2
Bilateral	0.6	6.6	-13.5	-12.7	-3.1	-8.3	30.9	-20.1	-25.7	-9.9
Concessional	1.0	2.1	-1.4	-1.3	6.3	0.2	38.4	-8.6	-20.1	-4.8
Private creditors	2.9	1.9	-21.5	-4.9	28.3	-3.1	-9.3	-17.1	-7.4	-6.0
Bonds	2.6	-0.2	0.0	0.0	0.0	0.0	0.0	0.0	0.0	0.0
Commercial banks	0.0	-0.5	-0.2	-1.1	29.9	-0.5	-7.2	-10.8	-6.7	-5.8
Other private	0.2	2.5	-21.3	-3.8	-1.7	-2.6	-2.0	-6.3	-0.7	-0.2
Private nonguaranteed	**0.0**	**0.0**	**0.0**	**0.0**	**0.0**	**0.0**	**0.0**	**0.0**	**0.0**	**0.0**
Bonds	0.0	0.0	0.0	0.0	0.0	0.0	0.0	0.0	0.0	0.0
Commercial banks	0.0	0.0	0.0	0.0	0.0	0.0	0.0	0.0	0.0	0.0
Memo:										
IBRD	0.0	-0.1	-26.1	-27.2	-17.4	-29.2	-31.7	-27.1	-20.8	-15.8
IDA	1.6	-0.2	-0.4	-0.5	-0.5	-0.5	-0.6	-0.6	-0.6	-0.6
DEBT SERVICE (LTDS)	**0.6**	**13.9**	**106.2**	**97.7**	**89.9**	**92.6**	**92.1**	**151.4**	**102.3**	**76.3**
Public and publicly guaranteed	**0.6**	**13.9**	**106.2**	**97.7**	**89.9**	**92.6**	**92.1**	**151.4**	**102.3**	**76.3**
Official creditors	0.6	13.0	84.7	92.8	87.8	89.5	82.8	134.3	95.0	70.3
Multilateral	0.0	10.4	64.8	75.0	70.2	74.9	69.7	112.4	67.5	58.3
Concessional	0.0	0.3	5.2	8.2	10.4	10.9	8.0	13.1	15.0	12.9
Bilateral	0.5	2.6	20.0	17.9	17.5	14.5	13.1	21.9	27.5	11.9
Concessional	0.2	0.5	5.2	6.2	7.9	5.9	5.6	10.4	21.8	6.8
Private creditors	0.1	1.0	21.5	4.9	2.1	3.1	9.3	17.1	7.4	6.0
Bonds	0.0	0.2	0.0	0.0	0.0	0.0	0.0	0.0	0.0	0.0
Commercial banks	0.0	0.5	0.2	1.1	0.5	0.5	7.2	10.8	6.7	5.8
Other private	0.1	0.3	21.3	3.8	1.7	2.6	2.0	6.3	0.7	0.2
Private nonguaranteed	**0.0**	**0.0**	**0.0**	**0.0**	**0.0**	**0.0**	**0.0**	**0.0**	**0.0**	**0.0**
Bonds	0.0	0.0	0.0	0.0	0.0	0.0	0.0	0.0	0.0	0.0
Commercial banks	0.0	0.0	0.0	0.0	0.0	0.0	0.0	0.0	0.0	0.0
Memo:										
IBRD	0.0	9.7	33.1	32.0	29.8	30.3	32.2	27.1	20.8	15.8
IDA	0.0	0.2	0.4	0.5	0.5	0.5	0.6	0.6	0.6	0.6
UNDISBURSED DEBT	**31.1**	**159.6**	**410.4**	**312.7**	**240.7**	**189.2**	**101.6**	**80.0**	**52.2**	**27.6**
Official creditors	31.1	118.1	373.2	277.8	237.6	185.8	101.6	80.0	52.2	27.6
Private creditors	0.0	41.6	37.2	34.9	3.1	3.4	0.0	0.0	0.0	0.0
Memorandum items										
Concessional LDOD	11.2	59.4	184.7	233.3	264.1	293.1	339.9	322.3	289.7	295.8
Variable rate LDOD	0.0	0.0	73.1	71.4	105.4	110.3	105.8	87.4	67.2	58.0
Public sector LDOD	17.4	142.7	557.2	605.5	622.8	645.2	662.7	583.4	505.2	494.8
Private sector LDOD	0.0	0.0	0.0	0.0	29.0	32.3	30.5	24.1	16.7	13.4
6. CURRENCY COMPOSITION OF LONG-TERM DEBT (PERCENT)										
Deutsche mark	0.0	0.0	0.3	0.2	4.6	4.9	4.5	4.1	3.3	2.7
French franc	0.0	0.0	1.6	1.2	1.0	1.1	1.0	0.6	0.6	0.6
Japanese yen	0.0	0.0	4.3	5.8	6.0	6.5	11.3	11.4	9.6	11.1
Pound sterling	81.8	27.3	10.9	6.9	5.7	5.0	4.3	4.3	4.2	3.5
Swiss franc	0.0	0.0	0.0	0.0	0.0	0.0	0.0	0.0	0.0	0.0
U.S.dollars	0.0	23.8	11.7	10.8	10.5	10.7	11.3	11.7	12.5	12.0
Multiple currency	0.0	44.1	54.4	57.6	53.5	51.5	47.4	45.3	44.5	42.7
Special drawing rights	0.0	0.0	0.0	0.2	0.2	1.4	1.4	1.7	1.9	2.0
All other currencies	18.2	4.8	16.8	17.3	18.5	18.9	18.8	20.9	23.4	25.4

BOTSWANA

(US$ million, unless otherwise indicated)

	1970	1980	1990	1992	1993	1994	1995	1996	1997	1998
7. DEBT RESTRUCTURINGS										
Total amount rescheduled	..	..	0.0	0.0	0.0	0.0	0.0	0.0	0.0	0.0
Debt stock rescheduled	..	..	0.0	0.0	0.0	0.0	0.0	0.0	0.0	0.0
Principal rescheduled	..	..	0.0	0.0	0.0	0.0	0.0	0.0	0.0	0.0
Official	..	..	0.0	0.0	0.0	0.0	0.0	0.0	0.0	0.0
Private	..	..	0.0	0.0	0.0	0.0	0.0	0.0	0.0	0.0
Interest rescheduled	..	..	0.0	0.0	0.0	0.0	0.0	0.0	0.0	0.0
Official	..	..	0.0	0.0	0.0	0.0	0.0	0.0	0.0	0.0
Private	..	..	0.0	0.0	0.0	0.0	0.0	0.0	0.0	0.0
Debt forgiven	..	..	0.0	0.0	0.0	0.0	0.0	0.0	0.0	0.0
Memo: interest forgiven	..	..	0.0	0.0	0.0	0.0	0.0	0.0	0.0	0.0
Debt stock reduction	..	..	0.0	0.0	0.0	0.0	0.0	0.0	0.0	0.0
of which debt buyback	..	..	0.0	0.0	0.0	0.0	0.0	0.0	0.0	0.0
8. DEBT STOCK-FLOW RECONCILIATION										
Total change in debt stocks	..	..	8.2	-8.0	47.8	29.1	14.7	-89.9	-51.5	-13.8
Net flows on debt	5.6	8.1	-37.2	22.4	45.1	-9.7	1.9	-43.1	-18.4	-33.3
Net change in interest arrears	..	..	2.1	-0.3	1.5	3.3	-1.6	-6.2	0.0	0.0
Interest capitalized	..	..	0.0	0.0	0.0	0.0	0.0	0.0	0.0	0.0
Debt forgiveness or reduction	..	..	0.0	0.0	0.0	0.0	0.0	0.0	0.0	0.0
Cross-currency valuation	..	..	29.0	-24.6	-4.0	20.6	1.8	-24.9	-26.7	13.6
Residual	..	..	14.3	-5.5	5.2	15.0	12.6	-15.7	-6.4	5.9
9. AVERAGE TERMS OF NEW COMMITMENTS										
ALL CREDITORS										
Interest (%)	0.6	6.0	6.9	5.3	3.7	3.6	0.0	3.0	0.0	6.9
Maturity (years)	38.9	18.4	14.8	19.3	25.1	11.8	0.0	14.9	0.0	15.2
Grace period (years)	10.0	4.0	4.3	4.7	7.0	4.0	0.0	3.9	0.0	6.0
Grant element (%)	79.7	24.2	17.1	29.4	47.4	32.7	0.0	39.6	0.0	20.9
Official creditors										
Interest (%)	0.1	6.0	5.7	5.4	3.7	3.6	0.0	3.0	0.0	6.9
Maturity (years)	40.7	18.4	16.9	19.2	25.1	11.8	0.0	14.9	0.0	15.2
Grace period (years)	9.4	4.0	4.4	5.0	7.0	4.0	0.0	3.9	0.0	6.0
Grant element (%)	84.9	24.2	25.0	29.0	47.4	32.7	0.0	39.6	0.0	20.9
Private creditors										
Interest (%)	7.3	0.0	8.9	4.1	0.0	0.0	0.0	0.0	0.0	0.0
Maturity (years)	16.9	0.0	11.6	20.6	0.0	0.0	0.0	0.0	0.0	0.0
Grace period (years)	16.3	0.0	4.1	0.6	0.0	0.0	0.0	0.0	0.0	0.0
Grant element (%)	19.6	0.0	4.6	34.6	0.0	0.0	0.0	0.0	0.0	0.0
Memorandum items										
Commitments	37.6	69.3	79.4	79.8	50.0	6.2	0.0	8.4	0.0	1.1
Official creditors	34.7	69.3	48.4	73.8	50.0	6.2	0.0	8.4	0.0	1.1
Private creditors	2.9	0.0	31.0	6.1	0.0	0.0	0.0	0.0	0.0	0.0

10. CONTRACTUAL OBLIGATIONS ON OUTSTANDING LONG-TERM DEBT

	1999	2000	2001	2002	2003	2004	2005	2006	2007	2008
TOTAL										
Disbursements	14.8	9.0	3.1	0.4	0.3	0.0	0.0	0.0	0.0	0.0
Principal	60.6	54.1	47.6	38.3	33.6	29.7	27.1	26.0	25.4	19.6
Interest	20.9	17.9	15.0	12.5	10.5	8.8	7.4	6.2	5.0	3.8
Official creditors										
Disbursements	14.8	9.0	3.1	0.4	0.3	0.0	0.0	0.0	0.0	0.0
Principal	55.3	48.8	42.3	37.4	32.7	28.8	26.2	25.2	24.5	18.8
Interest	19.1	16.5	14.0	11.7	9.7	8.2	6.9	5.7	4.6	3.5
Bilateral creditors										
Disbursements	0.5	0.4	0.0	0.0	0.0	0.0	0.0	0.0	0.0	0.0
Principal	11.8	10.8	9.9	8.1	6.8	6.3	6.3	6.0	5.7	5.4
Interest	3.4	3.0	2.6	2.2	1.9	1.7	1.5	1.4	1.2	1.1
Multilateral creditors										
Disbursements	14.2	8.6	3.1	0.4	0.3	0.0	0.0	0.0	0.0	0.0
Principal	43.5	37.9	32.4	29.4	26.0	22.5	20.0	19.2	18.8	13.4
Interest	15.7	13.5	11.4	9.5	7.8	6.4	5.3	4.3	3.4	2.5
Private creditors										
Disbursements	0.0	0.0	0.0	0.0	0.0	0.0	0.0	0.0	0.0	0.0
Principal	5.3	5.3	5.3	0.9	0.9	0.9	0.9	0.8	0.8	0.8
Interest	1.8	1.4	1.1	0.8	0.7	0.6	0.5	0.5	0.4	0.3
Commercial banks										
Disbursements	0.0	0.0	0.0	0.0	0.0	0.0	0.0	0.0	0.0	0.0
Principal	5.2	5.2	5.2	0.7	0.7	0.7	0.7	0.7	0.7	0.7
Interest	1.6	1.3	1.0	0.7	0.6	0.5	0.5	0.4	0.3	0.3
Other private										
Disbursements	0.0	0.0	0.0	0.0	0.0	0.0	0.0	0.0	0.0	0.0
Principal	0.2	0.2	0.2	0.2	0.2	0.2	0.2	0.2	0.2	0.2
Interest	0.2	0.1	0.1	0.1	0.1	0.1	0.1	0.1	0.0	0.0

BRAZIL

(US$ million, unless otherwise indicated)

	1970	1980	1990	1992	1993	1994	1995	1996	1997	1998
1. SUMMARY DEBT DATA										
TOTAL DEBT STOCKS (EDT)	..	**71,520**	**119,877**	**128,741**	**143,836**	**151,209**	**159,037**	**180,785**	**198,231**	**232,004**
Long-term debt (LDOD)	**5,020**	**57,981**	**94,340**	**103,852**	**112,903**	**119,620**	**128,399**	**145,275**	**163,771**	**202,054**
Public and publicly guaranteed	3,314	41,375	87,669	90,672	91,988	94,919	97,569	96,321	87,963	98,959
Private nonguaranteed	1,706	16,605	6,671	13,180	20,916	24,701	30,830	48,953	75,808	103,095
Use of IMF credit	**0**	**0**	**1,821**	**799**	**304**	**186**	**142**	**68**	**31**	**4,825**
Short-term debt	..	**13,540**	**23,716**	**24,090**	**30,629**	**31,403**	**30,496**	**35,443**	**34,429**	**25,125**
of which interest arrears on LDOD	..	14	8,791	4,292	7,226	1,352	804	1,443	929	1,905
Official creditors	..	0	332	339	1,380	842	428	403	369	378
Private creditors	..	13	8,459	3,953	5,847	510	377	1,040	560	1,527
Memo: principal arrears on LDOD	..	432	3,699	3,961	5,136	3,254	3,885	2,976	3,273	3,479
Official creditors	..	3	789	753	812	834	781	751	749	776
Private creditors	..	429	2,911	3,209	4,324	2,420	3,104	2,224	2,524	2,703
Memo: export credits	..	0	23,906	28,471	26,959	26,389	21,477	20,710	20,096	22,770
TOTAL DEBT FLOWS										
Disbursements	**1,783**	**11,418**	**4,081**	**9,393**	**14,721**	**11,490**	**20,017**	**29,686**	**44,807**	**66,882**
Long-term debt	1,783	11,418	4,081	9,213	14,721	11,490	20,017	29,686	44,807	62,243
IMF purchases	0	0	0	180	0	0	0	0	0	4,639
Principal repayments	**531**	**6,848**	**5,912**	**4,836**	**6,812**	**9,581**	**10,920**	**14,444**	**29,531**	**35,422**
Long-term debt	456	6,848	5,147	4,256	6,309	9,447	10,871	14,374	29,499	35,401
IMF repurchases	75	0	765	579	503	134	49	70	33	21
Net flows on debt	**1,966**	**9,462**	**-1,732**	**8,560**	**11,514**	**8,557**	**8,738**	**19,550**	**14,776**	**21,179**
of which short-term debt	..	4,892	99	4,003	3,605	6,648	-359	4,308	-500	-10,280
Interest payments (INT)	..	**7,909**	**2,256**	**3,830**	**4,431**	**6,631**	**10,761**	**10,635**	**12,614**	**12,465**
Long-term debt	221	6,384	2,026	2,949	3,222	5,115	8,959	8,770	11,228	10,964
IMF charges	0	0	231	90	39	14	10	5	2	1
Short-term debt	..	1,525	0	792	1,170	1,503	1,792	1,860	1,384	1,500
Net transfers on debt	..	**1,552**	**-3,989**	**4,730**	**7,083**	**1,926**	**-2,023**	**8,915**	**2,162**	**8,715**
Total debt service paid (TDS)	..	**14,757**	**8,169**	**8,666**	**11,243**	**16,213**	**21,681**	**25,078**	**42,145**	**47,887**
Long-term debt	677	13,232	7,173	7,205	9,531	14,562	19,830	23,144	40,726	46,365
IMF repurchases and charges	75	0	996	669	542	148	59	75	35	22
Short-term debt (interest only)	..	1,525	0	792	1,170	1,503	1,792	1,860	1,384	1,500
2. AGGREGATE NET RESOURCE FLOWS AND NET TRANSFERS (LONG-TERM)										
NET RESOURCE FLOWS	**1,777**	**6,494**	**-36**	**8,790**	**15,263**	**10,266**	**18,481**	**30,573**	**38,864**	**59,393**
Net flow of long-term debt (ex. IMF)	1,327	4,570	-1,066	4,957	8,412	2,043	9,146	15,312	15,308	26,841
Foreign direct investment (net)	421	1,911	989	2,061	1,292	3,072	4,859	11,200	19,652	31,913
Portfolio equity flows	0	0	0	1,734	5,500	5,082	4,411	3,981	3,835	542
Grants (excluding technical coop.)	28	14	41	38	59	69	65	80	68	97
Memo: technical coop. grants	32	83	157	179	185	196	239	246	230	184
official net resource flows	212	839	-599	-893	-951	-2,065	-1,510	-452	-1,464	5,008
private net resource flows	1,565	5,656	562	9,682	16,214	12,330	19,991	31,025	40,328	54,385
NET TRANSFERS	**1,168**	**-845**	**-3,954**	**5,007**	**9,902**	**2,701**	**6,922**	**18,603**	**24,336**	**44,430**
Interest on long-term debt	221	6,384	2,026	2,949	3,222	5,115	8,959	8,770	11,228	10,964
Profit remittances on FDI	387	955	1,892	834	2,139	2,450	2,600	3,200	3,300	4,000
Memo: official net transfers	161	395	-1,868	-2,031	-2,370	-3,812	-3,321	-2,179	-3,158	3,435
private net transfers	1,008	-1,240	-2,086	7,038	12,272	6,513	10,243	20,782	27,494	40,995
3. MAJOR ECONOMIC AGGREGATES										
Gross national product (GNP)	41,729	227,300	452,628	383,199	427,629	537,368	693,009	762,250	804,140	758,869
Exports of goods & services (XGS)	..	23,331	36,854	42,718	46,026	53,046	58,989	59,722	65,846	64,644
of which workers remittances	..	56	527	1,719	1,123	1,834	2,891	1,866	1,324	963
Imports of goods & services (MGS)	..	36,250	40,949	37,099	46,486	54,788	77,855	83,545	96,827	98,946
International reserves (RES)	1,190	6,875	9,200	23,265	31,747	38,492	51,477	59,685	51,706	43,902
Current account balance	..	-12,831	-3,823	6,089	20	-1,153	-18,136	-23,248	-30,491	-33,829
4. DEBT INDICATORS										
EDT / XGS (%)	..	306.6	325.3	301.4	312.5	285.1	269.6	302.7	301.1	358.9
EDT / GNP (%)	..	31.5	26.5	33.6	33.6	28.1	23.0	23.7	24.7	30.6
TDS / XGS (%)	..	63.3	22.2	20.3	24.4	30.6	36.8	42.0	64.0	74.1
INT / XGS (%)	..	33.9	6.1	9.0	9.6	12.5	18.2	17.8	19.2	19.3
INT / GNP (%)	..	3.5	0.5	1.0	1.0	1.2	1.6	1.4	1.6	1.6
RES / EDT (%)	..	9.6	7.7	18.1	22.1	25.5	32.4	33.0	26.1	18.9
RES / MGS (months)	..	2.3	2.7	7.5	8.2	8.4	7.9	8.6	6.4	5.3
Short-term / EDT (%)	..	18.9	19.8	18.7	21.3	20.8	19.2	19.6	17.4	10.8
Concessional / EDT (%)	..	2.5	2.4	2.0	1.8	1.6	1.5	1.1	0.8	0.7
Multilateral / EDT (%)	..	4.3	9.5	7.8	6.6	6.2	5.9	5.2	5.1	7.0

BRAZIL

(US$ million, unless otherwise indicated)

	1970	*1980*	*1990*	*1992*	*1993*	*1994*	*1995*	*1996*	*1997*	*1998*
5. LONG-TERM DEBT										
DEBT OUTSTANDING (LDOD)	**5,020**	**57,981**	**94,340**	**103,852**	**112,903**	**119,620**	**128,399**	**145,275**	**163,771**	**202,054**
Public and publicly guaranteed	**3,314**	**41,375**	**87,669**	**90,672**	**91,988**	**94,919**	**97,569**	**96,321**	**87,963**	**98,959**
Official creditors	1,779	7,306	29,252	30,277	30,028	29,388	28,444	26,550	23,567	29,298
Multilateral	376	3,092	11,391	10,067	9,479	9,375	9,366	9,404	10,065	16,320
Concessional	7	72	16	6	6	1	1	0	0	0
Bilateral	1,403	4,214	17,861	20,209	20,549	20,013	19,078	17,146	13,502	12,979
Concessional	1,308	1,678	2,867	2,510	2,514	2,467	2,357	1,939	1,541	1,630
Private creditors	1,535	34,069	58,417	60,396	61,960	65,531	69,125	69,771	64,396	69,661
Bonds	0	3,233	2,339	10,766	11,604	53,566	54,615	57,403	51,736	51,804
Commercial banks	748	24,329	47,461	44,480	45,761	7,569	10,804	9,493	10,442	15,924
Other private	787	6,507	8,617	5,150	4,595	4,396	3,706	2,875	2,219	1,934
Private nonguaranteed	**1,706**	**16,605**	**6,671**	**13,180**	**20,916**	**24,701**	**30,830**	**48,953**	**75,808**	**103,095**
Bonds	0	0	0	2,803	7,366	9,391	11,290	14,135	14,820	16,779
Commercial banks	1,706	16,605	6,671	10,377	13,550	15,310	19,541	34,818	60,988	86,317
Memo:										
IBRD	206	2,035	8,427	7,238	6,575	6,311	6,038	5,876	5,743	6,298
IDA	0	0	0	0	0	0	0	0	0	0
DISBURSEMENTS	**1,783**	**11,418**	**4,081**	**9,213**	**14,721**	**11,490**	**20,017**	**29,686**	**44,807**	**62,243**
Public and publicly guaranteed	**883**	**8,226**	**3,206**	**2,266**	**3,693**	**3,122**	**7,921**	**10,182**	**11,470**	**19,865**
Official creditors	260	1,343	1,316	911	877	1,047	2,005	3,149	3,011	9,387
Multilateral	108	535	1,001	883	865	950	1,257	2,263	2,718	6,978
Concessional	0	3	0	0	42	0	0	0	0	0
Bilateral	152	809	315	28	13	98	748	886	293	2,409
Concessional	96	46	80	5	9	3	216	3	4	286
Private creditors	623	6,883	1,890	1,355	2,816	2,074	5,916	7,033	8,459	10,478
Bonds	0	378	200	820	1,320	402	1,661	4,345	4,262	2,935
Commercial banks	333	4,874	864	341	1,385	1,328	4,140	2,525	4,037	7,519
Other private	290	1,631	826	194	111	345	115	162	159	25
Private nonguaranteed	**900**	**3,192**	**875**	**6,947**	**11,028**	**8,368**	**12,096**	**19,504**	**33,337**	**42,378**
Bonds	0	0	0	2,405	4,761	3,516	4,563	5,058	5,750	3,489
Commercial banks	900	3,192	875	4,542	6,267	4,853	7,533	14,446	27,587	38,890
Memo:										
IBRD	61	343	782	581	471	640	838	1,500	1,416	1,240
IDA	0	0	0	0	0	0	0	0	0	0
PRINCIPAL REPAYMENTS	**456**	**6,848**	**5,147**	**4,256**	**6,309**	**9,447**	**10,871**	**14,374**	**29,499**	**35,401**
Public and publicly guaranteed	**256**	**3,878**	**4,139**	**2,928**	**3,103**	**4,924**	**6,391**	**7,084**	**11,191**	**11,693**
Official creditors	76	518	1,955	1,841	1,887	3,181	3,580	3,681	4,544	4,476
Multilateral	32	164	1,518	1,568	1,652	1,674	1,683	1,517	1,335	1,265
Concessional	1	2	6	5	42	1	1	1	0	0
Bilateral	45	354	438	274	235	1,506	1,897	2,164	3,209	3,211
Concessional	40	97	22	21	32	200	357	303	295	276
Private creditors	180	3,360	2,184	1,087	1,216	1,744	2,811	3,403	6,647	7,217
Bonds	0	32	71	302	502	604	919	1,272	3,825	3,423
Commercial banks	137	2,430	1,616	162	129	370	1,050	1,428	2,211	3,377
Other private	43	898	496	623	585	770	842	704	611	418
Private nonguaranteed	**200**	**2,970**	**1,008**	**1,328**	**3,206**	**4,523**	**4,480**	**7,290**	**18,308**	**23,708**
Bonds	0	0	0	0	198	1,507	2,670	2,132	4,967	1,591
Commercial banks	200	2,970	1,008	1,328	3,008	3,016	1,810	5,158	13,341	22,117
Memo:										
IBRD	14	98	1,251	1,266	1,279	1,346	1,377	1,222	1,049	995
IDA	0	0	0	0	0	0	0	0	0	0
NET FLOWS ON DEBT	**1,327**	**4,570**	**-1,066**	**4,957**	**8,412**	**2,043**	**9,146**	**15,312**	**15,308**	**26,841**
Public and publicly guaranteed	**627**	**4,348**	**-933**	**-662**	**590**	**-1,803**	**1,530**	**3,098**	**279**	**8,172**
Official creditors	184	825	-639	-931	-1,010	-2,134	-1,575	-532	-1,533	4,911
Multilateral	76	371	-517	-685	-787	-725	-426	746	1,383	5,713
Concessional	-1	2	-6	-5	0	-1	-1	-1	0	0
Bilateral	108	454	-123	-246	-223	-1,409	-1,149	-1,278	-2,916	-802
Concessional	57	-50	58	-16	-22	-198	-141	-299	-291	9
Private creditors	444	3,523	-294	268	1,600	331	3,105	3,630	1,812	3,261
Bonds	0	346	129	518	817	-202	743	3,074	438	-488
Commercial banks	196	2,444	-753	179	1,256	958	3,090	1,097	1,826	4,142
Other private	247	733	330	-429	-474	-425	-728	-541	-452	-393
Private nonguaranteed	**700**	**222**	**-133**	**5,619**	**7,822**	**3,845**	**7,616**	**12,214**	**15,029**	**18,670**
Bonds	0	0	0	2,405	4,563	2,009	1,894	2,925	783	1,898
Commercial banks	700	222	-133	3,214	3,259	1,836	5,722	9,289	14,246	16,772
Memo:										
IBRD	47	245	-469	-685	-808	-706	-539	278	368	245
IDA	0	0	0	0	0	0	0	0	0	0

BRAZIL

(US$ million, unless otherwise indicated)

	1970	1980	1990	1992	1993	1994	1995	1996	1997	1998
INTEREST PAYMENTS (LINT)	**221**	**6,384**	**2,026**	**2,949**	**3,222**	**5,115**	**8,959**	**8,770**	**11,228**	**10,964**
Public and publicly guaranteed	**132**	**4,253**	**1,566**	**2,398**	**2,172**	**3,966**	**6,864**	**5,715**	**5,670**	**5,149**
Official creditors	51	444	1,270	1,139	1,420	1,748	1,810	1,727	1,694	1,573
Multilateral	21	255	966	887	868	781	750	679	689	738
Concessional	0	3	1	0	17	0	0	0	0	0
Bilateral	30	189	304	252	552	967	1,060	1,048	1,005	836
Concessional	28	48	9	12	11	19	91	61	49	43
Private creditors	81	3,809	296	1,260	753	2,218	5,053	3,988	3,976	3,576
Bonds	0	234	14	125	435	1,735	4,416	3,123	3,205	2,502
Commercial banks	45	3,128	46	888	136	300	373	656	655	952
Other private	36	446	236	247	182	183	265	209	117	122
Private nonguaranteed	**89**	**2,132**	**460**	**551**	**1,050**	**1,149**	**2,095**	**3,055**	**5,558**	**5,814**
Bonds	0	0	0	85	313	656	837	1,028	1,323	1,399
Commercial banks	89	2,132	460	466	737	493	1,258	2,027	4,235	4,415
Memo:										
IBRD	11	177	725	647	579	537	491	416	380	378
IDA	0	0	0	0	0	0	0	0	0	0
NET TRANSFERS ON DEBT	**1,106**	**-1,815**	**-3,092**	**2,008**	**5,190**	**-3,072**	**187**	**6,542**	**4,081**	**15,878**
Public and publicly guaranteed	**495**	**95**	**-2,499**	**-3,061**	**-1,582**	**-5,768**	**-5,333**	**-2,617**	**-5,391**	**3,022**
Official creditors	132	381	-1,909	-2,069	-2,429	-3,881	-3,385	-2,259	-3,226	3,338
Multilateral	55	116	-1,483	-1,572	-1,654	-1,505	-1,176	67	695	4,976
Concessional	-1	-1	-6	-6	-17	-1	-1	-1	0	0
Bilateral	78	265	-427	-498	-775	-2,376	-2,209	-2,326	-3,921	-1,638
Concessional	29	-98	49	-28	-33	-216	-232	-361	-340	-34
Private creditors	363	-286	-590	-991	847	-1,887	-1,948	-358	-2,164	-315
Bonds	0	112	115	393	383	-1,937	-3,673	-49	-2,767	-2,990
Commercial banks	151	-684	-799	-710	1,120	658	2,717	441	1,171	3,190
Other private	212	287	94	-675	-656	-608	-992	-750	-569	-515
Private nonguaranteed	**611**	**-1,910**	**-593**	**5,068**	**6,772**	**2,696**	**5,521**	**9,159**	**9,471**	**12,855**
Bonds	0	0	0	2,320	4,250	1,353	1,057	1,897	-540	499
Commercial banks	611	-1,910	-593	2,748	2,522	1,343	4,464	7,262	10,011	12,357
Memo:										
IBRD	36	68	-1,193	-1,332	-1,387	-1,242	-1,031	-138	-12	-133
IDA	0	0	0	0	0	0	0	0	0	0
DEBT SERVICE (LTDS)	**677**	**13,232**	**7,173**	**7,205**	**9,531**	**14,562**	**19,830**	**23,144**	**40,726**	**46,365**
Public and publicly guaranteed	**388**	**8,131**	**5,705**	**5,326**	**5,275**	**8,890**	**13,254**	**12,799**	**16,861**	**16,842**
Official creditors	127	962	3,225	2,980	3,306	4,928	5,390	5,408	6,238	6,049
Multilateral	53	419	2,484	2,455	2,519	2,455	2,434	2,196	2,024	2,003
Concessional	1	4	6	6	60	1	1	1	0	0
Bilateral	75	543	742	525	787	2,473	2,957	3,212	4,214	4,047
Concessional	68	144	31	33	42	219	448	364	344	320
Private creditors	261	7,169	2,480	2,347	1,969	3,962	7,864	7,391	10,623	10,793
Bonds	0	266	85	427	937	2,339	5,335	4,395	7,029	5,925
Commercial banks	182	5,558	1,663	1,050	264	670	1,423	2,084	2,866	4,329
Other private	79	1,345	733	870	767	953	1,107	912	728	540
Private nonguaranteed	**289**	**5,102**	**1,468**	**1,879**	**4,256**	**5,672**	**6,575**	**10,345**	**23,866**	**29,523**
Bonds	0	0	0	85	511	2,163	3,507	3,160	6,290	2,990
Commercial banks	289	5,102	1,468	1,794	3,745	3,509	3,069	7,185	17,576	26,533
Memo:										
IBRD	25	275	1,975	1,913	1,858	1,883	1,868	1,638	1,428	1,373
IDA	0	0	0	0	0	0	0	0	0	0
UNDISBURSED DEBT	**1,493**	**14,046**	**12,953**	**14,434**	**14,403**	**16,817**	**14,677**	**14,628**	**15,928**	**15,190**
Official creditors	806	6,359	6,864	9,114	9,216	10,608	9,475	9,030	10,707	9,814
Private creditors	688	7,687	6,089	5,320	5,188	6,210	5,202	5,598	5,221	5,376
Memorandum items										
Concessional LDOD	1,315	1,750	2,884	2,517	2,520	2,468	2,358	1,939	1,541	1,630
Variable rate LDOD	2,111	41,557	66,638	76,649	84,570	82,781	89,866	105,036	128,747	156,845
Public sector LDOD	3,206	39,296	87,099	90,227	91,574	94,453	96,725	95,563	87,355	96,860
Private sector LDOD	1,814	18,685	7,241	13,626	21,329	25,167	31,674	49,712	76,415	105,195
6. CURRENCY COMPOSITION OF LONG-TERM DEBT (PERCENT)										
Deutsche mark	7.3	8.1	8.9	6.8	5.8	4.3	5.1	5.6	4.8	3.1
French franc	0.2	2.5	6.6	5.0	4.0	3.3	3.3	2.6	1.9	1.1
Japanese yen	0.0	8.5	7.3	6.1	6.4	5.0	6.3	6.3	5.3	4.3
Pound sterling	7.6	2.5	1.8	1.1	1.2	1.1	0.9	1.2	1.3	0.9
Swiss franc	2.2	1.3	1.0	0.8	0.7	0.3	0.3	0.2	0.3	0.3
U.S.dollars	72.1	67.8	60.4	61.9	63.0	68.5	67.3	66.7	67.6	73.7
Multiple currency	9.6	7.2	12.8	17.3	18.1	17.3	16.6	16.2	16.8	13.6
Special drawing rights	0.0	0.0	0.0	0.0	0.0	0.0	0.0	0.0	0.0	0.0
All other currencies	1.0	2.1	1.2	1.0	0.8	0.2	0.2	1.2	2.0	3.0

BRAZIL

(US$ million, unless otherwise indicated)

	1970	1980	1990	1992	1993	1994	1995	1996	1997	1998
7. DEBT RESTRUCTURINGS										
Total amount rescheduled	..	..	1,316	12,850	1,425	43,451	234	298	288	148
Debt stock rescheduled	..	..	0	0	0	35,758	0	0	0	0
Principal rescheduled	..	..	1,066	4,577	921	76	0	3	0	6
Official	..	..	212	1,991	792	0	0	0	0	0
Private	..	..	854	2,586	128	76	0	3	0	6
Interest rescheduled	..	..	275	8,355	491	7,273	0	298	288	148
Official	..	..	69	972	397	0	0	0	0	0
Private	..	..	205	7,384	94	7,273	0	298	288	148
Debt forgiven	..	..	0	0	0	0	0	0	0	0
Memo: interest forgiven	..	..	0	0	0	0	0	0	0	0
Debt stock reduction	..	..	1,259	257	0	4,104	0	0	3,294	0
of which debt buyback	..	..	776	0	0	204	0	0	2,694	0
8. DEBT STOCK-FLOW RECONCILIATION										
Total change in debt stocks	..	..	5,344	7,817	15,095	7,373	7,828	21,748	17,446	33,773
Net flows on debt	1,966	9,462	-1,732	8,560	11,514	8,557	8,738	19,550	14,776	21,179
Net change in interest arrears	..	..	5,603	-6,227	2,935	-5,874	-548	639	-514	976
Interest capitalized	..	..	275	8,355	491	7,273	0	298	288	148
Debt forgiveness or reduction	..	..	-483	-257	0	-3,900	0	0	-600	0
Cross-currency valuation	..	..	3,102	-1,495	-154	1,582	435	-1,843	-2,150	1,296
Residual	..	..	-1,420	-1,119	310	-264	-798	3,104	5,646	10,175
9. AVERAGE TERMS OF NEW COMMITMENTS										
ALL CREDITORS										
Interest (%)	7.0	12.2	8.2	7.7	8.2	8.0	6.9	8.3	8.0	8.7
Maturity (years)	14.0	10.9	11.6	12.4	8.4	11.5	7.6	7.7	14.4	5.5
Grace period (years)	3.3	4.0	3.7	4.0	4.0	3.7	2.9	3.5	2.8	2.8
Grant element (%)	17.1	-9.8	9.0	11.1	7.7	10.2	10.9	7.0	7.9	3.9
Official creditors										
Interest (%)	5.8	9.5	7.4	7.3	7.1	6.7	5.4	7.1	6.4	6.9
Maturity (years)	24.8	13.8	15.2	17.2	17.7	18.9	19.7	16.4	18.2	6.2
Grace period (years)	5.8	3.7	4.1	4.5	5.0	5.2	4.8	3.4	4.2	1.8
Grant element (%)	29.1	4.2	14.9	15.3	17.6	20.3	27.3	15.2	20.0	7.4
Private creditors										
Interest (%)	7.5	13.0	9.0	8.4	8.6	9.0	7.5	8.8	8.9	10.2
Maturity (years)	9.4	10.0	7.6	4.5	4.5	6.0	3.0	4.3	12.1	5.0
Grace period (years)	2.2	4.1	3.2	3.2	3.6	2.5	2.1	3.6	2.0	3.6
Grant element (%)	12.0	-14.0	2.6	4.2	3.6	2.7	4.6	3.7	0.7	1.0
Memorandum items										
Commitments	1,439	10,066	2,980	4,215	3,972	5,716	7,302	10,708	13,623	19,119
Official creditors	431	2,303	1,552	2,620	1,162	2,430	2,019	3,006	5,099	8,514
Private creditors	1,008	7,762	1,427	1,595	2,810	3,286	5,283	7,702	8,524	10,605

10. CONTRACTUAL OBLIGATIONS ON OUTSTANDING LONG-TERM DEBT

	1999	2000	2001	2002	2003	2004	2005	2006	2007	2008
TOTAL										
Disbursements	4,278	2,561	1,730	1,070	620	333	196	108	72	28
Principal	56,889	28,147	22,939	17,240	15,261	12,232	11,043	7,153	5,982	6,144
Interest	11,275	8,441	6,610	5,721	5,117	4,646	3,845	3,130	2,698	2,143
Official creditors										
Disbursements	2,688	2,137	1,576	1,056	619	333	196	108	72	28
Principal	8,636	4,019	2,541	2,652	2,627	2,644	2,617	2,600	1,343	1,213
Interest	1,971	1,550	1,439	1,338	1,204	1,050	886	718	568	485
Bilateral creditors										
Disbursements	864	572	340	188	93	48	18	0	0	0
Principal	4,774	1,013	1,072	1,133	1,125	1,203	1,271	1,352	195	178
Interest	828	537	492	433	366	295	216	131	62	52
Multilateral creditors										
Disbursements	1,824	1,564	1,236	868	527	285	178	108	72	28
Principal	3,862	3,006	1,469	1,519	1,503	1,441	1,346	1,248	1,148	1,035
Interest	1,143	1,013	947	906	837	755	670	586	507	433
Private creditors										
Disbursements	1,590	424	154	14	0	0	0	0	0	0
Principal	48,252	24,129	20,398	14,587	12,633	9,588	8,426	4,553	4,639	4,931
Interest	9,304	6,891	5,171	4,383	3,913	3,596	2,959	2,412	2,130	1,658
Commercial banks										
Disbursements	1,378	373	134	6	0	0	0	0	0	0
Principal	13,487	984	475	377	349	293	234	223	127	4
Interest	1,080	165	127	100	76	54	35	20	5	0
Other private										
Disbursements	212	51	20	7	0	0	0	0	0	0
Principal	34,765	23,145	19,924	14,211	12,284	9,295	8,192	4,330	4,513	4,927
Interest	8,224	6,726	5,045	4,282	3,837	3,543	2,924	2,392	2,125	1,658

BULGARIA

(US$ million, unless otherwise indicated)

	1970	1980	1990	1992	1993	1994	1995	1996	1997	1998
1. SUMMARY DEBT DATA										
TOTAL DEBT STOCKS (EDT)	..	..	**10,890**	**11,854**	**12,202**	**9,805**	**10,305**	**10,058**	**9,859**	**9,907**
Long-term debt (LDOD)	..	..	**9,834**	**9,670**	**9,717**	**8,421**	**9,068**	**8,573**	**8,145**	**8,331**
Public and publicly guaranteed	..	..	9,834	9,670	9,717	8,421	8,726	8,160	7,721	7,781
Private nonguaranteed	..	..	0	0	0	0	342	413	424	550
Use of IMF credit	**0**	**0**	**0**	**590**	**632**	**941**	**717**	**586**	**942**	**1,116**
Short-term debt	..	..	**1,056**	**1,594**	**1,853**	**443**	**520**	**899**	**772**	**460**
of which interest arrears on LDOD	..	..	226	1,524	1,814	117	82	134	214	216
Official creditors	..	..	5	29	59	16	5	10	9	8
Private creditors	..	..	221	1,495	1,755	102	76	124	205	208
Memo: principal arrears on LDOD	..	..	356	4,962	5,882	303	256	154	409	173
Official creditors	..	..	1	139	237	21	25	25	24	23
Private creditors	..	..	354	4,823	5,645	281	231	129	384	150
Memo: export credits	..	..	4,798	1,230	1,261	1,360	1,492	1,427	1,222	1,317
TOTAL DEBT FLOWS										
Disbursements	..	..	**876**	**559**	**361**	**730**	**235**	**316**	**702**	**1,003**
Long-term debt	..	..	876	276	318	397	235	200	214	692
IMF purchases	0	0	0	282	43	333	0	116	489	311
Principal repayments	..	..	**865**	**223**	**85**	**518**	**569**	**700**	**435**	**770**
Long-term debt	..	..	865	138	85	450	323	476	347	587
IMF repurchases	0	0	0	85	0	69	246	225	89	183
Net flows on debt	..	..	**-14**	**-398**	**245**	**499**	**-221**	**-57**	**59**	**-81**
of which short-term debt	..	..	-24	-733	-32	288	113	327	-208	-314
Interest payments (INT)	..	..	**510**	**227**	**242**	**168**	**575**	**548**	**497**	**525**
Long-term debt	..	..	452	161	186	111	501	485	436	458
IMF charges	0	0	0	36	37	40	50	29	31	45
Short-term debt	..	..	58	30	19	16	24	35	30	22
Net transfers on debt	..	..	**-523**	**-625**	**3**	**331**	**-796**	**-605**	**-438**	**-606**
Total debt service paid (TDS)	..	..	**1,375**	**450**	**327**	**686**	**1,144**	**1,249**	**933**	**1,295**
Long-term debt	..	..	1,317	300	271	561	824	960	783	1,045
IMF repurchases and charges	0	0	0	121	37	109	296	254	120	228
Short-term debt (interest only)	..	..	58	30	19	16	24	35	30	22
2. AGGREGATE NET RESOURCE FLOWS AND NET TRANSFERS (LONG-TERM)										
NET RESOURCE FLOWS	..	..	**19**	**262**	**336**	**556**	**425**	**431**	**639**	**673**
Net flow of long-term debt (ex. IMF)	..	..	11	138	234	-53	-88	-276	-133	105
Foreign direct investment (net)	..	..	4	42	55	105	90	109	505	401
Portfolio equity flows	..	..	0	0	0	400	400	500	130	66
Grants (excluding technical coop.)	..	..	4	81	47	103	22	98	137	102
Memo: technical coop. grants	..	..	0	47	33	43	91	57	42	112
official net resource flows	..	..	61	140	315	452	33	116	62	175
private net resource flows	..	..	-42	121	22	104	392	315	576	498
NET TRANSFERS	..	..	**-433**	**100**	**150**	**443**	**-79**	**-64**	**190**	**202**
Interest on long-term debt	..	..	452	161	186	111	501	485	436	458
Profit remittances on FDI	..	..	0	0	0	2	3	11	12	14
Memo: official net transfers	..	..	47	54	211	381	-146	-57	-84	35
private net transfers	..	..	-480	46	-61	62	67	-7	275	166
3. MAJOR ECONOMIC AGGREGATES										
Gross national product (GNP)	..	..	19,083	10,203	10,641	9,580	12,680	9,441	9,702	11,937
Exports of goods & services (XGS)	..	..	7,070	5,152	4,990	5,277	6,926	6,437	6,488	5,861
of which workers remittances	..	..	0	0	0	..	..	..	..	..
Imports of goods & services (MGS)	..	..	8,905	5,555	6,126	5,475	7,084	6,526	6,298	6,467
International reserves (RES)	..	..	..	1,241	1,052	1,397	1,635	864	2,548	3,127
Current account balance	..	..	-1,710	-360	-1,099	-32	-26	16	427	-376
4. DEBT INDICATORS										
EDT / XGS (%)	..	..	154.0	230.1	244.5	185.8	148.8	156.3	152.0	169.0
EDT / GNP (%)	..	..	57.1	116.2	114.7	102.3	81.3	106.5	101.6	83.0
TDS / XGS (%)	..	..	19.4	8.7	6.6	13.0	16.5	19.4	14.4	22.1
INT / XGS (%)	..	..	7.2	4.4	4.9	3.2	8.3	8.5	7.7	9.0
INT / GNP (%)	..	..	2.7	2.2	2.3	1.8	4.5	5.8	5.1	4.4
RES / EDT (%)	..	..	..	10.5	8.6	14.3	15.9	8.6	25.8	31.6
RES / MGS (months)	..	..	..	2.7	2.1	3.1	2.8	1.6	4.9	5.8
Short-term / EDT (%)	..	..	9.7	13.5	15.2	4.5	5.1	8.9	7.8	4.6
Concessional / EDT (%)	..	..	0.7	0.3	1.2	1.6	1.8	1.8	1.6	1.6
Multilateral / EDT (%)	..	..	2.0	2.4	3.6	8.4	11.9	12.2	10.8	12.7

BULGARIA

(US$ million, unless otherwise indicated)

	1970	1980	1990	1992	1993	1994	1995	1996	1997	1998
5. LONG-TERM DEBT										
DEBT OUTSTANDING (LDOD)	..	..	**9,834**	**9,670**	**9,717**	**8,421**	**9,068**	**8,573**	**8,145**	**8,331**
Public and publicly guaranteed	..	..	**9,834**	**9,670**	**9,717**	**8,421**	**8,726**	**8,160**	**7,721**	**7,781**
Official creditors	..	..	1,669	1,846	2,097	2,344	2,839	2,665	2,319	2,468
Multilateral	..	..	222	284	444	819	1,222	1,224	1,067	1,262
Concessional	..	..	0	0	0	0	0	0	0	0
Bilateral	..	..	1,447	1,562	1,654	1,525	1,617	1,441	1,252	1,206
Concessional	..	..	77	35	142	153	186	179	159	162
Private creditors	..	..	8,165	7,823	7,620	6,077	5,887	5,496	5,402	5,313
Bonds	..	..	327	332	348	5,411	5,412	5,155	5,072	5,019
Commercial banks	..	..	7,084	7,335	7,135	577	394	269	261	256
Other private	..	..	753	156	137	88	81	72	69	38
Private nonguaranteed	..	..	**0**	**0**	**0**	**0**	**342**	**413**	**424**	**550**
Bonds	..	..	0	0	0	0	0	0	0	0
Commercial banks	..	..	0	0	0	0	342	413	424	550
Memo:										
IBRD	0	0	0	152	158	415	444	453	501	697
IDA	0	0	0	0	0	0	0	0	0	0
DISBURSEMENTS	..	..	**876**	**276**	**318**	**397**	**235**	**200**	**214**	**692**
Public and publicly guaranteed	..	..	**876**	**276**	**318**	**397**	**235**	**139**	**189**	**387**
Official creditors	..	..	80	139	318	375	106	139	182	387
Multilateral	..	..	44	103	207	365	15	122	180	386
Concessional	..	..	0	0	0	0	0	0	0	0
Bilateral	..	..	36	36	111	10	92	17	2	0
Concessional	..	..	0	33	111	0	32	15	2	0
Private creditors	..	..	796	137	0	22	129	0	6	0
Bonds	..	..	65	0	0	16	33	0	0	0
Commercial banks	..	..	652	126	0	6	96	0	0	0
Other private	..	..	79	12	0	0	0	0	6	0
Private nonguaranteed	..	..	**0**	**0**	**0**	**0**	**0**	**61**	**25**	**306**
Bonds	..	..	0	0	0	0	0	0	0	0
Commercial banks	..	..	0	0	0	0	0	61	25	306
Memo:										
IBRD	0	0	0	92	3	246	15	53	101	197
IDA	0	0	0	0	0	0	0	0	0	0
PRINCIPAL REPAYMENTS	..	..	**865**	**138**	**85**	**450**	**323**	**476**	**347**	**587**
Public and publicly guaranteed	..	..	**865**	**138**	**85**	**450**	**323**	**452**	**325**	**378**
Official creditors	..	..	23	80	51	27	96	120	257	313
Multilateral	..	..	22	56	43	20	25	23	191	205
Concessional	..	..	0	0	0	0	0	0	0	0
Bilateral	..	..	1	24	8	7	71	98	65	108
Concessional	..	..	0	0	0	0	0	9	8	7
Private creditors	..	..	842	58	34	423	228	332	69	65
Bonds	..	..	0	0	0	223	39	205	62	57
Commercial banks	..	..	241	39	21	200	183	122	3	7
Other private	..	..	601	19	13	0	7	5	5	1
Private nonguaranteed	..	..	**0**	**0**	**0**	**0**	**0**	**23**	**21**	**209**
Bonds	..	..	0	0	0	0	0	0	0	0
Commercial banks	..	..	0	0	0	0	0	23	21	209
Memo:										
IBRD	0	0	0	0	0	0	0	13	16	20
IDA	0	0	0	0	0	0	0	0	0	0
NET FLOWS ON DEBT	..	..	**11**	**138**	**234**	**-53**	**-88**	**-276**	**-133**	**105**
Public and publicly guaranteed	..	..	**11**	**138**	**234**	**-53**	**-88**	**-313**	**-137**	**9**
Official creditors	..	..	57	59	268	348	10	19	-74	74
Multilateral	..	..	21	47	164	345	-11	100	-11	182
Concessional	..	..	0	0	0	0	0	0	0	0
Bilateral	..	..	36	12	103	3	21	-81	-63	-108
Concessional	..	..	0	33	111	0	32	6	-6	-7
Private creditors	..	..	-46	79	-34	-401	-98	-332	-63	-65
Bonds	..	..	65	0	0	-207	-6	-205	-62	-57
Commercial banks	..	..	411	87	-21	-194	-86	-122	-3	-7
Other private	..	..	-522	-7	-13	0	-7	-5	2	-1
Private nonguaranteed	..	..	**0**	**0**	**0**	**0**	**0**	**38**	**4**	**96**
Bonds	..	..	0	0	0	0	0	0	0	0
Commercial banks	..	..	0	0	0	0	0	38	4	96
Memo:										
IBRD	0	0	0	92	3	246	15	40	85	176
IDA	0	0	0	0	0	0	0	0	0	0

BULGARIA

(US$ million, unless otherwise indicated)

	1970	1980	1990	1992	1993	1994	1995	1996	1997	1998
INTEREST PAYMENTS (LINT)	..	..	**452**	**161**	**186**	**111**	**501**	**485**	**436**	**458**
Public and publicly guaranteed	..	..	**452**	**161**	**186**	**111**	**501**	**465**	**423**	**445**
Official creditors	..	..	14	86	104	71	179	173	146	140
Multilateral	..	..	13	15	23	27	62	73	64	62
Concessional	..	..	0	0	0	0	0	0	0	0
Bilateral	..	..	0	71	81	43	117	100	82	78
Concessional	..	..	0	0	0	2	4	9	8	7
Private creditors	..	..	438	75	82	41	323	292	277	305
Bonds	..	..	16	16	24	36	315	279	275	304
Commercial banks	..	..	337	53	55	5	7	12	1	1
Other private	..	..	85	7	3	0	1	1	0	0
Private nonguaranteed	..	..	**0**	**0**	**0**	**0**	**0**	**20**	**13**	**13**
Bonds	..	..	0	0	0	0	0	0	0	0
Commercial banks	..	..	0	0	0	0	0	20	13	13
Memo:										
IBRD	0	0	0	7	12	15	31	30	31	37
IDA	0	0	0	0	0	0	0	0	0	0
NET TRANSFERS ON DEBT	..	..	**-441**	**-23**	**48**	**-164**	**-589**	**-760**	**-569**	**-352**
Public and publicly guaranteed	..	..	**-441**	**-23**	**48**	**-164**	**-589**	**-778**	**-560**	**-436**
Official creditors	..	..	44	-27	164	278	-168	-155	-221	-66
Multilateral	..	..	8	33	141	317	-72	27	-75	120
Concessional	..	..	0	0	0	0	0	0	0	0
Bilateral	..	..	35	-60	23	-40	-96	-181	-145	-186
Concessional	..	..	0	33	111	-2	28	-2	-13	-14
Private creditors	..	..	-484	4	-116	-442	-421	-624	-339	-370
Bonds	..	..	49	-16	-24	-243	-321	-484	-337	-361
Commercial banks	..	..	74	34	-76	-199	-93	-133	-4	-8
Other private	..	..	-608	-14	-17	0	-7	-6	2	-1
Private nonguaranteed	..	..	**0**	**0**	**0**	**0**	**0**	**18**	**-9**	**84**
Bonds	..	..	0	0	0	0	0	0	0	0
Commercial banks	..	..	0	0	0	0	0	18	-9	84
Memo:										
IBRD	0	0	0	85	-9	230	-16	10	54	140
IDA	0	0	0	0	0	0	0	0	0	0
DEBT SERVICE (LTDS)	..	..	**1,317**	**300**	**271**	**561**	**824**	**960**	**783**	**1,045**
Public and publicly guaranteed	..	..	**1,317**	**300**	**271**	**561**	**824**	**917**	**749**	**823**
Official creditors	..	..	37	166	154	97	274	294	403	453
Multilateral	..	..	36	71	66	47	87	96	255	267
Concessional	..	..	0	0	0	0	0	0	0	0
Bilateral	..	..	1	95	89	50	187	198	148	186
Concessional	..	..	0	0	0	2	4	17	16	14
Private creditors	..	..	1,280	133	116	464	550	624	346	370
Bonds	..	..	16	16	24	259	354	484	337	361
Commercial banks	..	..	578	92	76	205	189	133	4	8
Other private	..	..	686	26	17	0	7	6	5	1
Private nonguaranteed	..	..	**0**	**0**	**0**	**0**	**0**	**43**	**34**	**222**
Bonds	..	..	0	0	0	0	0	0	0	0
Commercial banks	..	..	0	0	0	0	0	43	34	222
Memo:										
IBRD	0	0	0	7	12	15	31	43	47	57
IDA	0	0	0	0	0	0	0	0	0	0
UNDISBURSED DEBT	..	..	**271**	**335**	**447**	**382**	**783**	**716**	**710**	**473**
Official creditors	..	..	25	323	439	351	775	709	710	470
Private creditors	..	..	246	12	8	31	8	7	0	3
Memorandum items										
Concessional LDOD	..	..	77	35	142	153	186	179	159	162
Variable rate LDOD	..	..	7,714	7,478	7,394	6,687	7,175	7,081	6,871	7,175
Public sector LDOD	..	..	9,834	9,670	9,717	8,421	8,726	8,160	7,721	7,781
Private sector LDOD	..	..	0	0	0	0	342	413	424	550
6. CURRENCY COMPOSITION OF LONG-TERM DEBT (PERCENT)										
Deutsche mark	..	..	33.9	32.1	29.7	6.4	7.3	5.1	4.6	5.0
French franc	..	..	0.5	0.4	0.4	0.4	0.5	0.5	0.4	0.4
Japanese yen	..	..	6.6	6.7	8.3	8.8	8.1	6.5	5.4	4.8
Pound sterling	..	..	0.3	0.2	0.2	0.2	0.2	0.3	0.3	0.2
Swiss franc	..	..	7.7	6.7	6.5	1.1	1.1	1.0	1.0	0.8
U.S.dollars	..	..	42.1	45.5	45.7	71.8	67.1	70.2	75.2	82.2
Multiple currency	..	..	2.5	1.6	1.6	4.9	5.1	5.6	6.0	1.0
Special drawing rights	..	..	0.0	0.0	0.0	0.0	0.0	0.0	0.0	0.0
All other currencies	..	..	6.4	6.8	7.6	6.4	10.6	10.8	7.1	5.6

BULGARIA

(US$ million, unless otherwise indicated)

	1970	1980	1990	1992	1993	1994	1995	1996	1997	1998
7. DEBT RESTRUCTURINGS										
Total amount rescheduled	..	..	0	271	17	5,306	54	17	0	0
Debt stock rescheduled	..	..	0	0	0	3,395	0	0	0	0
Principal rescheduled	..	..	0	219	16	222	41	0	0	0
Official	..	..	0	219	16	153	36	0	0	0
Private	..	..	0	0	0	69	5	0	0	0
Interest rescheduled	..	..	0	52	1	1,678	10	0	0	0
Official	..	..	0	52	1	57	9	0	0	0
Private	..	..	0	0	0	1,621	1	0	0	0
Debt forgiven	..	..	0	0	0	0	0	21	7	0
Memo: interest forgiven	..	..	0	0	0	0	0	0	0	0
Debt stock reduction	..	..	0	0	0	2,871	0	0	0	0
of which debt buyback	..	..	0	0	0	423	0	0	0	0
8. DEBT STOCK-FLOW RECONCILIATION										
Total change in debt stocks	..	..	753	93	348	-2,397	500	-247	-200	48
Net flows on debt	..	..	-14	-398	245	499	-221	-57	59	-81
Net change in interest arrears	..	..	226	760	290	-1,697	-36	52	81	2
Interest capitalized	..	..	0	52	1	1,678	10	0	0	0
Debt forgiveness or reduction	..	..	0	0	0	-2,448	0	-21	-7	-64
Cross-currency valuation	..	..	728	-279	-154	232	132	-185	-206	124
Residual	..	..	-188	-42	-34	-661	616	-35	-127	68
9. AVERAGE TERMS OF NEW COMMITMENTS										
ALL CREDITORS										
Interest (%)	..	..	9.1	5.5	5.8	6.6	5.5	6.6	6.2	4.0
Maturity (years)	..	..	3.4	12.4	14.7	13.2	15.4	14.8	15.4	19.0
Grace period (years)	..	..	2.3	5.2	4.0	4.9	5.1	5.9	6.3	5.2
Grant element (%)	..	..	2.3	24.8	22.8	16.5	24.4	19.9	22.8	38.7
Official creditors										
Interest (%)	..	..	9.3	4.9	5.8	6.7	6.0	6.6	6.2	4.0
Maturity (years)	..	..	6.1	13.8	14.7	14.7	17.5	14.8	15.4	19.2
Grace period (years)	..	..	3.0	5.8	4.0	5.7	5.4	5.9	6.3	5.3
Grant element (%)	..	..	2.6	29.6	22.8	18.0	25.0	19.9	22.8	39.1
Private creditors										
Interest (%)	..	..	9.1	6.7	0.0	6.1	3.4	0.0	0.0	5.6
Maturity (years)	..	..	3.1	9.5	0.0	4.8	4.7	0.0	0.0	8.9
Grace period (years)	..	..	2.3	3.9	0.0	0.6	3.2	0.0	0.0	0.9
Grant element (%)	..	..	2.3	14.5	0.0	8.2	21.7	0.0	0.0	15.2
Memorandum items										
Commitments	..	..	563	372	443	339	635	131	265	156
Official creditors	..	..	52	252	443	288	530	131	265	154
Private creditors	..	..	511	120	0	51	105	0	0	3

10. CONTRACTUAL OBLIGATIONS ON OUTSTANDING LONG-TERM DEBT

	1999	2000	2001	2002	2003	2004	2005	2006	2007	2008
TOTAL										
Disbursements	126	84	64	48	36	23	16	10	8	5
Principal	587	456	604	459	576	418	397	397	478	470
Interest	446	422	419	406	378	350	325	301	276	247
Official creditors										
Disbursements	124	83	63	47	36	23	16	10	8	5
Principal	330	267	499	287	260	207	153	153	138	130
Interest	161	144	125	96	81	66	54	46	37	29
Bilateral creditors										
Disbursements	26	39	26	17	10	5	3	0	0	0
Principal	269	184	329	195	112	99	14	19	8	8
Interest	76	60	44	24	14	8	4	3	3	3
Multilateral creditors										
Disbursements	99	44	37	30	26	18	14	10	8	5
Principal	60	82	170	93	148	108	139	135	130	122
Interest	86	84	81	72	67	58	51	42	34	26
Private creditors										
Disbursements	1	1	0	0	0	0	0	0	0	0
Principal	257	190	104	171	316	211	244	244	340	340
Interest	284	278	294	310	297	284	270	256	239	219
Commercial banks										
Disbursements	1	1	0	0	0	0	0	0	0	0
Principal	103	19	19	0	0	0	0	0	0	0
Interest	7	3	1	0	0	0	0	0	0	0
Other private										
Disbursements	0	0	0	0	0	0	0	0	0	0
Principal	154	170	85	171	316	211	243	243	340	340
Interest	278	275	293	310	297	284	270	256	239	219

BURKINA FASO

(US$ million, unless otherwise indicated)

	1970	1980	1990	1992	1993	1994	1995	1996	1997	1998
1. SUMMARY DEBT DATA										
TOTAL DEBT STOCKS (EDT)	..	**330**	**834**	**1,040**	**1,117**	**1,129**	**1,267**	**1,294**	**1,297**	**1,399**
Long-term debt (LDOD)	**21**	**281**	**750**	**979**	**1,066**	**1,040**	**1,136**	**1,160**	**1,139**	**1,229**
Public and publicly guaranteed	21	281	750	979	1,066	1,040	1,136	1,160	1,139	1,229
Private nonguaranteed	0	0	0	0	0	0	0	0	0	0
Use of IMF credit	**0**	**15**	**0**	**9**	**21**	**48**	**75**	**81**	**92**	**112**
Short-term debt	..	**35**	**84**	**52**	**30**	**41**	**56**	**53**	**66**	**59**
of which interest arrears on LDOD	..	0	21	12	12	11	12	10	7	7
Official creditors	..	0	14	11	11	10	11	8	5	5
Private creditors	..	0	7	1	1	1	1	2	2	2
Memo: principal arrears on LDOD	..	0	64	28	35	36	37	38	33	37
Official creditors	..	0	34	26	34	34	35	35	30	33
Private creditors	..	0	30	2	1	2	3	3	3	4
Memo: export credits	..	0	200	148	79	65	98	83	86	85
TOTAL DEBT FLOWS										
Disbursements	**2**	**70**	**79**	**143**	**151**	**132**	**139**	**113**	**89**	**104**
Long-term debt	2	65	79	143	138	107	112	103	71	86
IMF purchases	1	4	0	0	12	25	27	10	18	18
Principal repayments	**2**	**11**	**19**	**15**	**20**	**27**	**29**	**31**	**34**	**34**
Long-term debt	2	11	18	15	20	27	29	30	32	32
IMF repurchases	0	0	1	0	0	0	0	1	2	3
Net flows on debt	**1**	**56**	**70**	**105**	**109**	**117**	**124**	**81**	**71**	**62**
of which short-term debt	..	-3	10	-24	-22	12	14	0	15	-7
Interest payments (INT)	..	**12**	**16**	**19**	**18**	**17**	**20**	**17**	**18**	**18**
Long-term debt	0	6	10	14	16	15	17	15	15	15
IMF charges	0	0	0	0	0	0	0	1	0	1
Short-term debt	..	5	6	5	2	2	2	2	3	3
Net transfers on debt	..	**45**	**54**	**86**	**91**	**100**	**104**	**64**	**53**	**44**
Total debt service paid (TDS)	..	**22**	**34**	**33**	**38**	**44**	**49**	**49**	**52**	**53**
Long-term debt	2	17	28	29	36	42	46	45	47	47
IMF repurchases and charges	0	0	1	0	0	0	0	2	2	3
Short-term debt (interest only)	..	5	6	5	2	2	2	2	3	3
2. AGGREGATE NET RESOURCE FLOWS AND NET TRANSFERS (LONG-TERM)										
NET RESOURCE FLOWS	**13**	**142**	**218**	**332**	**345**	**293**	**323**	**307**	**249**	**268**
Net flow of long-term debt (ex. IMF)	0	55	61	128	119	80	83	73	39	54
Foreign direct investment (net)	0	0	0	0	0	1	0	0	0	0
Portfolio equity flows	0	0	0	0	0	0	0	0	0	0
Grants (excluding technical coop.)	13	88	158	204	227	212	240	234	210	214
Memo: technical coop. grants	8	73	117	137	136	111	123	113	95	91
official net resource flows	13	138	219	332	345	292	323	307	249	268
private net resource flows	0	4	0	0	0	1	0	0	0	0
NET TRANSFERS	**11**	**128**	**209**	**318**	**329**	**278**	**305**	**292**	**234**	**253**
Interest on long-term debt	0	6	10	14	16	15	17	15	15	15
Profit remittances on FDI	2	9	0	0	0	0	0	0	0	0
Memo: official net transfers	13	135	209	318	329	277	305	292	234	253
private net transfers	-1	-7	0	0	0	1	0	0	0	0
3. MAJOR ECONOMIC AGGREGATES										
Gross national product (GNP)	421	1,698	2,757	1,988	2,039	1,840	2,343	2,530	2,368	2,569
Exports of goods & services (XGS)	..	376	506	452	429	361	455	441	398	495
of which workers remittances	..	150	140	129	117	80	110	110	88	87
Imports of goods & services (MGS)	..	596	776	686	707	521	691	762	694	811
International reserves (RES)	36	75	305	345	387	241	352	343	348	373
Current account balance	..	-49	-77	-23	-71	15	-81	-232	-237	-225
4. DEBT INDICATORS										
EDT / XGS (%)	..	88.0	164.7	229.9	260.0	312.6	278.3	293.4	326.3	282.8
EDT / GNP (%)	..	19.5	30.3	52.3	54.8	61.3	54.1	51.1	54.8	54.5
TDS / XGS (%)	..	5.9	6.8	7.4	8.9	12.1	10.7	11.0	13.0	10.7
INT / XGS (%)	..	3.1	3.1	4.2	4.2	4.6	4.3	3.9	4.6	3.7
INT / GNP (%)	..	0.7	0.6	1.0	0.9	0.9	0.8	0.7	0.8	0.7
RES / EDT (%)	..	22.6	36.5	33.2	34.6	21.4	27.8	26.5	26.8	26.7
RES / MGS (months)	..	1.5	4.7	6.0	6.6	5.6	6.1	5.4	6.0	5.5
Short-term / EDT (%)	..	10.6	10.1	5.0	2.7	3.6	4.4	4.1	5.1	4.2
Concessional / EDT (%)	..	67.0	71.6	78.9	81.9	80.2	79.0	83.9	83.1	83.7
Multilateral / EDT (%)	..	42.9	67.8	68.5	70.9	78.1	77.7	78.9	77.3	78.2

BURKINA FASO

(US$ million, unless otherwise indicated)

	1970	1980	1990	1992	1993	1994	1995	1996	1997	1998
5. LONG-TERM DEBT										
DEBT OUTSTANDING (LDOD)	**21**	**281**	**750**	**979**	**1,066**	**1,040**	**1,136**	**1,160**	**1,139**	**1,229**
Public and publicly guaranteed	**21**	**281**	**750**	**979**	**1,066**	**1,040**	**1,136**	**1,160**	**1,139**	**1,229**
Official creditors	21	261	712	973	1,062	1,036	1,131	1,155	1,135	1,225
Multilateral	0	142	565	712	792	881	984	1,021	1,003	1,094
Concessional	0	133	460	615	702	810	916	960	953	1,048
Bilateral	21	119	147	262	270	154	147	134	132	130
Concessional	18	89	138	205	213	96	86	125	124	122
Private creditors	0	20	38	5	4	4	5	4	4	4
Bonds	0	0	0	0	0	0	0	0	0	0
Commercial banks	0	1	1	0	0	0	0	0	0	0
Other private	0	19	38	5	4	4	5	4	4	4
Private nonguaranteed	**0**	**0**	**0**	**0**	**0**	**0**	**0**	**0**	**0**	**0**
Bonds	0	0	0	0	0	0	0	0	0	0
Commercial banks	0	0	0	0	0	0	0	0	0	0
Memo:										
IBRD	0	0	0	0	0	0	0	0	0	0
IDA	0	77	282	364	425	518	608	636	636	710
DISBURSEMENTS	**2**	**65**	**79**	**143**	**138**	**107**	**112**	**103**	**71**	**86**
Public and publicly guaranteed	**2**	**65**	**79**	**143**	**138**	**107**	**112**	**103**	**71**	**86**
Official creditors	2	59	79	143	138	107	112	103	71	86
Multilateral	0	26	45	110	118	100	106	90	66	83
Concessional	0	22	34	104	112	98	104	89	65	83
Bilateral	2	33	34	33	21	7	6	13	5	2
Concessional	1	19	34	29	19	7	6	13	5	2
Private creditors	0	6	0	0	0	0	0	0	0	0
Bonds	0	0	0	0	0	0	0	0	0	0
Commercial banks	0	0	0	0	0	0	0	0	0	0
Other private	0	6	0	0	0	0	0	0	0	0
Private nonguaranteed	**0**	**0**	**0**	**0**	**0**	**0**	**0**	**0**	**0**	**0**
Bonds	0	0	0	0	0	0	0	0	0	0
Commercial banks	0	0	0	0	0	0	0	0	0	0
Memo:										
IBRD	0	0	0	0	0	0	0	0	0	0
IDA	0	12	15	50	64	79	85	50	35	58
PRINCIPAL REPAYMENTS	**2**	**11**	**18**	**15**	**20**	**27**	**29**	**30**	**32**	**32**
Public and publicly guaranteed	**2**	**11**	**18**	**15**	**20**	**27**	**29**	**30**	**32**	**32**
Official creditors	2	8	18	15	20	27	29	30	32	32
Multilateral	0	3	13	14	18	25	24	25	27	27
Concessional	0	2	10	8	10	17	16	20	21	22
Bilateral	2	5	4	1	2	2	5	5	5	5
Concessional	1	3	3	1	1	1	4	4	4	5
Private creditors	0	2	0	0	0	0	0	0	0	0
Bonds	0	0	0	0	0	0	0	0	0	0
Commercial banks	0	0	0	0	0	0	0	0	0	0
Other private	0	2	0	0	0	0	0	0	0	0
Private nonguaranteed	**0**	**0**	**0**	**0**	**0**	**0**	**0**	**0**	**0**	**0**
Bonds	0	0	0	0	0	0	0	0	0	0
Commercial banks	0	0	0	0	0	0	0	0	0	0
Memo:										
IBRD	0	0	0	0	0	0	0	0	0	0
IDA	0	0	1	2	3	3	4	4	4	6
NET FLOWS ON DEBT	**0**	**55**	**61**	**128**	**119**	**80**	**83**	**73**	**39**	**54**
Public and publicly guaranteed	**0**	**55**	**61**	**128**	**119**	**80**	**83**	**73**	**39**	**54**
Official creditors	0	51	61	128	119	80	83	73	39	54
Multilateral	0	23	32	96	100	75	82	65	40	57
Concessional	0	21	24	96	102	81	88	70	45	62
Bilateral	0	28	29	32	19	5	1	7	-1	-3
Concessional	1	16	31	29	18	6	2	9	0	-3
Private creditors	0	4	0	0	0	0	0	0	0	0
Bonds	0	0	0	0	0	0	0	0	0	0
Commercial banks	0	0	0	0	0	0	0	0	0	0
Other private	0	4	0	0	0	0	0	0	0	0
Private nonguaranteed	**0**	**0**	**0**	**0**	**0**	**0**	**0**	**0**	**0**	**0**
Bonds	0	0	0	0	0	0	0	0	0	0
Commercial banks	0	0	0	0	0	0	0	0	0	0
Memo:										
IBRD	0	0	0	0	0	0	0	0	0	0
IDA	0	12	14	48	61	76	81	46	30	53

BURKINA FASO

(US$ million, unless otherwise indicated)

	1970	1980	1990	1992	1993	1994	1995	1996	1997	1998
INTEREST PAYMENTS (LINT)	**0**	**6**	**10**	**14**	**16**	**15**	**17**	**15**	**15**	**15**
Public and publicly guaranteed	**0**	**6**	**10**	**14**	**16**	**15**	**17**	**15**	**15**	**15**
Official creditors	0	4	10	14	16	15	17	15	15	15
Multilateral	0	2	7	9	11	11	11	13	12	12
Concessional	0	1	4	5	5	6	7	10	9	9
Bilateral	0	2	3	5	5	4	6	2	4	3
Concessional	0	1	3	1	1	1	1	1	3	3
Private creditors	0	3	0	0	0	0	0	0	0	0
Bonds	0	0	0	0	0	0	0	0	0	0
Commercial banks	0	0	0	0	0	0	0	0	0	0
Other private	0	2	0	0	0	0	0	0	0	0
Private nonguaranteed	**0**	**0**	**0**	**0**	**0**	**0**	**0**	**0**	**0**	**0**
Bonds	0	0	0	0	0	0	0	0	0	0
Commercial banks	0	0	0	0	0	0	0	0	0	0
Memo:										
IBRD	0	0	0	0	0	0	0	0	0	0
IDA	0	1	2	3	3	3	4	5	5	5
NET TRANSFERS ON DEBT	**-1**	**49**	**51**	**114**	**103**	**65**	**65**	**58**	**24**	**39**
Public and publicly guaranteed	**-1**	**49**	**51**	**114**	**103**	**65**	**65**	**58**	**24**	**39**
Official creditors	0	47	51	114	103	65	65	58	24	39
Multilateral	0	22	25	87	88	64	70	52	28	45
Concessional	0	20	20	91	97	75	81	60	35	52
Bilateral	0	26	27	27	14	1	-5	6	-4	-6
Concessional	0	16	28	27	17	5	1	8	-3	-6
Private creditors	0	1	0	0	0	0	0	0	0	0
Bonds	0	0	0	0	0	0	0	0	0	0
Commercial banks	0	0	0	0	0	0	0	0	0	0
Other private	0	2	0	0	0	0	0	0	0	0
Private nonguaranteed	**0**	**0**	**0**	**0**	**0**	**0**	**0**	**0**	**0**	**0**
Bonds	0	0	0	0	0	0	0	0	0	0
Commercial banks	0	0	0	0	0	0	0	0	0	0
Memo:										
IBRD	0	0	0	0	0	0	0	0	0	0
IDA	0	11	12	45	58	73	77	42	26	48
DEBT SERVICE (LTDS)	**2**	**17**	**28**	**29**	**36**	**42**	**46**	**45**	**47**	**47**
Public and publicly guaranteed	**2**	**17**	**28**	**29**	**36**	**42**	**46**	**45**	**47**	**47**
Official creditors	2	12	28	29	36	42	46	45	47	47
Multilateral	0	5	21	23	30	36	36	38	38	38
Concessional	0	3	14	13	16	23	23	29	30	31
Bilateral	2	7	7	6	6	5	11	7	9	8
Concessional	1	3	6	2	2	1	5	5	8	8
Private creditors	0	5	0	0	0	0	0	0	0	0
Bonds	0	0	0	0	0	0	0	0	0	0
Commercial banks	0	0	0	0	0	0	0	0	0	0
Other private	0	5	0	0	0	0	0	0	0	0
Private nonguaranteed	**0**	**0**	**0**	**0**	**0**	**0**	**0**	**0**	**0**	**0**
Bonds	0	0	0	0	0	0	0	0	0	0
Commercial banks	0	0	0	0	0	0	0	0	0	0
Memo:										
IBRD	0	0	0	0	0	0	0	0	0	0
IDA	0	1	3	5	6	6	8	9	9	11
UNDISBURSED DEBT	**10**	**218**	**540**	**582**	**549**	**540**	**463**	**366**	**401**	**434**
Official creditors	9	214	525	568	536	525	448	351	389	420
Private creditors	1	4	15	14	13	14	16	15	13	14
Memorandum items										
Concessional LDOD	18	221	597	820	914	906	1,001	1,085	1,077	1,171
Variable rate LDOD	0	12	2	6	6	6	7	0	0	0
Public sector LDOD	21	276	749	979	1,066	1,040	1,136	1,160	1,139	1,229
Private sector LDOD	0	5	1	0	0	0	0	0	0	0
6. CURRENCY COMPOSITION OF LONG-TERM DEBT (PERCENT)										
Deutsche mark	10.1	12.1	0.0	0.1	0.1	0.1	0.1	0.1	0.1	0.1
French franc	32.7	31.3	16.6	18.3	16.9	7.0	6.5	3.6	3.5	3.2
Japanese yen	0.0	0.0	0.0	0.0	0.0	0.0	0.0	0.0	0.0	0.0
Pound sterling	20.2	0.7	0.5	0.4	0.3	0.4	0.3	0.0	0.0	0.0
Swiss franc	0.0	0.0	0.0	0.0	0.0	0.0	0.0	0.0	0.0	0.0
U.S.dollars	0.0	28.8	39.2	40.0	42.9	52.8	56.0	61.0	62.4	63.8
Multiple currency	0.0	8.9	15.3	16.9	17.4	19.2	18.8	19.2	19.1	19.4
Special drawing rights	0.0	0.0	2.1	2.5	2.3	2.3	2.2	2.1	2.0	1.7
All other currencies	37.0	18.2	26.3	21.8	20.1	18.2	16.1	14.0	12.9	11.8

BURKINA FASO

(US$ million, unless otherwise indicated)

	1970	1980	1990	1992	1993	1994	1995	1996	1997	1998
7. DEBT RESTRUCTURINGS										
Total amount rescheduled	..	..	0	14	6	0	0	44	1	0
Debt stock rescheduled	..	..	0	0	0	0	0	44	0	0
Principal rescheduled	..	..	0	8	3	0	0	0	0	0
Official	..	..	0	7	3	0	0	0	0	0
Private	..	..	0	0	1	0	0	0	0	0
Interest rescheduled	..	..	0	5	2	0	0	0	0	0
Official	..	..	0	5	2	0	0	0	0	0
Private	..	..	0	0	0	0	0	0	0	0
Debt forgiven	..	..	5	0	2	123	15	3	1	1
Memo: interest forgiven	..	..	0	0	2	0	0	0	0	0
Debt stock reduction	..	..	0	0	0	0	0	16	0	0
of which debt buyback	..	..	0	0	0	0	0	0	0	0
8. DEBT STOCK-FLOW RECONCILIATION										
Total change in debt stocks	..	..	117	72	77	12	138	27	3	102
Net flows on debt	1	56	70	105	109	117	124	81	71	62
Net change in interest arrears	..	..	6	0	0	-1	1	-2	-3	0
Interest capitalized	..	..	0	5	2	0	0	0	0	0
Debt forgiveness or reduction	..	..	-5	0	-2	-123	-15	-18	-1	-1
Cross-currency valuation	..	..	37	-23	-20	4	15	-8	-15	8
Residual	..	..	9	-14	-13	15	13	-25	-49	33
9. AVERAGE TERMS OF NEW COMMITMENTS										
ALL CREDITORS										
Interest (%)	2.3	4.3	2.5	0.8	1.2	0.9	0.8	1.2	0.6	3.0
Maturity (years)	36.3	21.5	27.5	41.6	33.0	38.0	39.9	31.6	42.8	22.0
Grace period (years)	8.1	6.5	8.7	10.0	8.0	9.8	10.4	8.5	10.4	6.0
Grant element (%)	61.9	37.8	59.0	80.6	69.4	78.4	80.8	70.3	82.9	47.7
Official creditors										
Interest (%)	1.7	4.0	2.5	0.8	1.2	0.9	0.8	1.2	0.6	3.0
Maturity (years)	40.6	23.0	27.5	41.6	33.0	38.0	39.9	31.6	42.8	22.0
Grace period (years)	8.9	7.0	8.7	10.0	8.0	9.8	10.4	8.5	10.4	6.0
Grant element (%)	69.4	40.9	59.0	80.6	69.4	78.4	80.8	70.3	82.9	47.7
Private creditors										
Interest (%)	6.8	7.3	0.0	0.0	0.0	0.0	0.0	0.0	0.0	0.0
Maturity (years)	7.2	5.6	0.0	0.0	0.0	0.0	0.0	0.0	0.0	0.0
Grace period (years)	2.8	1.1	0.0	0.0	0.0	0.0	0.0	0.0	0.0	0.0
Grant element (%)	11.3	6.6	0.0	0.0	0.0	0.0	0.0	0.0	0.0	0.0
Memorandum items										
Commitments	9	115	90	169	105	100	37	24	132	108
Official creditors	8	104	90	169	105	100	37	24	132	108
Private creditors	1	10	0	0	0	0	0	0	0	0

10. CONTRACTUAL OBLIGATIONS ON OUTSTANDING LONG-TERM DEBT

	1999	2000	2001	2002	2003	2004	2005	2006	2007	2008
TOTAL										
Disbursements	119	118	76	49	28	12	7	4	2	1
Principal	36	38	39	42	45	47	47	47	47	49
Interest	15	15	15	15	15	15	15	14	13	13
Official creditors										
Disbursements	119	118	76	49	28	12	7	4	2	1
Principal	36	38	39	42	45	47	47	47	47	49
Interest	15	15	15	15	15	15	15	14	13	13
Bilateral creditors										
Disbursements	12	16	11	8	5	3	2	2	1	1
Principal	7	7	7	7	8	8	8	9	9	9
Interest	3	3	3	3	3	4	4	3	3	3
Multilateral creditors										
Disbursements	106	102	65	41	23	9	5	2	1	0
Principal	29	31	33	35	37	39	39	38	38	40
Interest	12	12	12	12	12	12	11	11	10	10
Private creditors										
Disbursements	0	0	0	0	0	0	0	0	0	0
Principal	0	0	0	0	0	0	0	0	0	0
Interest	0	0	0	0	0	0	0	0	0	0
Commercial banks										
Disbursements	0	0	0	0	0	0	0	0	0	0
Principal	0	0	0	0	0	0	0	0	0	0
Interest	0	0	0	0	0	0	0	0	0	0
Other private										
Disbursements	0	0	0	0	0	0	0	0	0	0
Principal	0	0	0	0	0	0	0	0	0	0
Interest	0	0	0	0	0	0	0	0	0	0

BURUNDI

(US$ million, unless otherwise indicated)

	1970	1980	1990	1992	1993	1994	1995	1996	1997	1998
1. SUMMARY DEBT DATA										
TOTAL DEBT STOCKS (EDT)	**..**	**166**	**907**	**1,022**	**1,061**	**1,123**	**1,158**	**1,127**	**1,066**	**1,119**
Long-term debt (LDOD)	**7**	**118**	**851**	**947**	**998**	**1,062**	**1,095**	**1,081**	**1,022**	**1,079**
Public and publicly guaranteed	7	118	851	947	998	1,062	1,095	1,081	1,022	1,079
Private nonguaranteed	0	0	0	0	0	0	0	0	0	0
Use of IMF credit	**8**	**36**	**43**	**62**	**58**	**56**	**48**	**38**	**28**	**20**
Short-term debt	**..**	**12**	**13**	**13**	**5**	**6**	**15**	**8**	**16**	**20**
of which interest arrears on LDOD	..	0	0	1	1	1	2	5	9	12
Official creditors	..	0	0	1	1	1	2	5	9	12
Private creditors	..	0	0	0	0	0	0	0	0	0
Memo: principal arrears on LDOD	..	0	0	6	12	12	3	15	27	44
Official creditors	..	0	0	6	12	12	3	15	27	44
Private creditors	..	0	0	0	0	0	0	0	0	0
Memo: export credits	..	0	15	15	5	5	2	0	0	0
TOTAL DEBT FLOWS										
Disbursements	**4**	**45**	**96**	**126**	**77**	**53**	**45**	**35**	**19**	**31**
Long-term debt	1	39	96	107	77	53	45	35	19	31
IMF purchases	3	6	0	18	0	0	0	0	0	0
Principal repayments	**1**	**4**	**28**	**24**	**23**	**28**	**27**	**21**	**20**	**21**
Long-term debt	0	4	28	22	19	22	18	12	12	13
IMF repurchases	0	0	1	2	4	6	9	9	8	9
Net flows on debt	**3**	**40**	**65**	**101**	**45**	**25**	**26**	**4**	**3**	**10**
of which short-term debt	..	-1	-3	-1	-8	1	8	-10	4	1
Interest payments (INT)	**..**	**4**	**14**	**16**	**13**	**13**	**12**	**10**	**9**	**9**
Long-term debt	0	2	12	14	12	12	11	9	9	8
IMF charges	0	1	0	0	0	0	0	0	0	0
Short-term debt	..	2	2	1	1	1	1	0	0	1
Net transfers on debt	**..**	**36**	**51**	**85**	**32**	**12**	**15**	**-5**	**-6**	**1**
Total debt service paid (TDS)	**..**	**9**	**42**	**40**	**36**	**41**	**39**	**31**	**29**	**30**
Long-term debt	1	6	40	36	31	34	29	21	21	21
IMF repurchases and charges	0	1	1	3	5	6	9	9	8	9
Short-term debt (interest only)	..	2	2	1	1	1	1	0	0	1
2. AGGREGATE NET RESOURCE FLOWS AND NET TRANSFERS (LONG-TERM)										
NET RESOURCE FLOWS	**8**	**74**	**205**	**238**	**169**	**274**	**258**	**96**	**54**	**70**
Net flow of long-term debt (ex. IMF)	1	35	69	86	58	31	27	23	7	18
Foreign direct investment (net)	0	0	1	1	0	0	2	1	1	1
Portfolio equity flows	0	0	0	0	0	0	0	0	0	0
Grants (excluding technical coop.)	7	39	135	151	112	243	229	72	46	51
Memo: technical coop. grants	11	45	61	79	57	49	44	3	19	13
official net resource flows	8	76	210	239	171	275	257	96	53	68
private net resource flows	0	-3	-5	-1	-1	-1	1	0	1	2
NET TRANSFERS	**8**	**72**	**189**	**220**	**154**	**259**	**244**	**85**	**44**	**61**
Interest on long-term debt	0	2	12	14	12	12	11	9	9	8
Profit remittances on FDI	0	0	3	4	3	3	3	2	1	1
Memo: official net transfers	8	76	198	225	159	262	246	87	44	60
private net transfers	0	-4	-9	-6	-4	-4	-2	-2	0	1
3. MAJOR ECONOMIC AGGREGATES										
Gross national product (GNP)	235	922	1,117	1,072	965	912	988	886	944	872
Exports of goods & services (XGS)	..	..	98	108	100	104	139	57	100	76
of which workers remittances	..	..	0	0	0	0	0	0	0	..
Imports of goods & services (MGS)	..	..	341	347	310	286	300	159	156	188
International reserves (RES)	15	105	112	180	170	211	216	146	118	70
Current account balance	..	..	-69	-60	-28	-17	-8	-40	4	-103
4. DEBT INDICATORS										
EDT / XGS (%)	..	..	929.1	943.0	1,064.7	1,083.4	830.9	1,973.7	1,062.3	1,481.4
EDT / GNP (%)	..	18.0	81.2	95.4	110.0	123.2	117.2	127.1	112.9	128.3
TDS / XGS (%)	..	..	43.4	36.5	36.2	39.5	27.7	53.6	29.0	40.0
INT / XGS (%)	..	..	14.4	14.5	13.0	12.6	8.5	16.8	9.0	11.7
INT / GNP (%)	..	0.5	1.3	1.5	1.4	1.4	1.2	1.1	1.0	1.0
RES / EDT (%)	..	63.2	12.3	17.6	16.0	18.8	18.7	13.0	11.1	6.3
RES / MGS (months)	..	..	3.9	6.2	6.6	8.9	8.7	11.0	9.1	4.5
Short-term / EDT (%)	..	7.2	1.5	1.3	0.5	0.5	1.3	0.7	1.5	1.8
Concessional / EDT (%)	..	62.6	85.9	87.1	89.2	90.1	90.4	92.3	92.8	93.7
Multilateral / EDT (%)	..	35.7	72.8	74.6	77.0	78.4	80.0	81.8	81.9	82.3

BURUNDI

(US$ million, unless otherwise indicated)

	1970	1980	1990	1992	1993	1994	1995	1996	1997	1998
5. LONG-TERM DEBT										
DEBT OUTSTANDING (LDOD)	**7**	**118**	**851**	**947**	**998**	**1,062**	**1,095**	**1,081**	**1,022**	**1,079**
Public and publicly guaranteed	**7**	**118**	**851**	**947**	**998**	**1,062**	**1,095**	**1,081**	**1,022**	**1,079**
Official creditors	6	110	842	943	995	1,060	1,093	1,080	1,021	1,078
Multilateral	5	59	660	763	817	881	926	921	872	921
Concessional	1	55	598	710	768	833	880	882	840	891
Bilateral	1	51	182	180	179	179	167	159	149	157
Concessional	1	49	182	180	179	179	167	159	149	157
Private creditors	2	8	9	4	3	2	2	1	1	1
Bonds	0	0	0	0	0	0	0	0	0	0
Commercial banks	0	5	1	0	0	0	0	0	0	0
Other private	1	4	8	4	3	2	2	1	1	1
Private nonguaranteed	**0**	**0**	**0**	**0**	**0**	**0**	**0**	**0**	**0**	**0**
Bonds	0	0	0	0	0	0	0	0	0	0
Commercial banks	0	0	0	0	0	0	0	0	0	0
Memo:										
IBRD	3	0	0	0	0	0	0	0	0	0
IDA	1	37	398	473	509	556	591	588	567	603
DISBURSEMENTS	**1**	**39**	**96**	**107**	**77**	**53**	**45**	**35**	**19**	**31**
Public and publicly guaranteed	**1**	**39**	**96**	**107**	**77**	**53**	**45**	**35**	**19**	**31**
Official creditors	1	39	94	107	77	53	45	35	19	30
Multilateral	1	21	64	85	69	48	41	34	16	30
Concessional	0	20	61	82	68	47	40	33	16	30
Bilateral	0	18	30	23	7	5	4	1	3	0
Concessional	0	18	30	23	7	5	4	1	3	0
Private creditors	0	0	2	0	0	0	0	0	0	1
Bonds	0	0	0	0	0	0	0	0	0	0
Commercial banks	0	0	0	0	0	0	0	0	0	0
Other private	0	0	2	0	0	0	0	0	0	1
Private nonguaranteed	**0**	**0**	**0**	**0**	**0**	**0**	**0**	**0**	**0**	**0**
Bonds	0	0	0	0	0	0	0	0	0	0
Commercial banks	0	0	0	0	0	0	0	0	0	0
Memo:										
IBRD	0	0	0	0	0	0	0	0	0	0
IDA	0	12	49	49	36	28	27	17	12	24
PRINCIPAL REPAYMENTS	**0**	**4**	**28**	**22**	**19**	**22**	**18**	**12**	**12**	**13**
Public and publicly guaranteed	**0**	**4**	**28**	**22**	**19**	**22**	**18**	**12**	**12**	**13**
Official creditors	0	1	19	20	18	21	17	12	12	13
Multilateral	0	0	11	13	11	15	12	11	12	12
Concessional	0	0	6	7	8	10	8	5	8	8
Bilateral	0	1	8	6	7	6	5	1	0	0
Concessional	0	1	8	6	7	6	5	1	0	0
Private creditors	0	3	8	2	1	1	1	1	0	0
Bonds	0	0	0	0	0	0	0	0	0	0
Commercial banks	0	2	5	0	0	0	0	0	0	0
Other private	0	1	3	2	1	1	1	1	0	0
Private nonguaranteed	**0**	**0**	**0**	**0**	**0**	**0**	**0**	**0**	**0**	**0**
Bonds	0	0	0	0	0	0	0	0	0	0
Commercial banks	0	0	0	0	0	0	0	0	0	0
Memo:										
IBRD	0	0	0	0	0	0	0	0	0	0
IDA	0	0	1	2	2	2	3	3	4	6
NET FLOWS ON DEBT	**1**	**35**	**69**	**86**	**58**	**31**	**27**	**23**	**7**	**18**
Public and publicly guaranteed	**1**	**35**	**69**	**86**	**58**	**31**	**27**	**23**	**7**	**18**
Official creditors	1	38	75	88	59	32	28	23	7	17
Multilateral	1	20	53	71	58	33	29	23	4	18
Concessional	0	20	55	74	60	37	32	28	8	22
Bilateral	0	17	22	17	1	-1	-1	1	3	0
Concessional	0	17	22	17	1	-1	-1	1	3	0
Private creditors	0	-3	-6	-2	-1	-1	-1	-1	0	1
Bonds	0	0	0	0	0	0	0	0	0	0
Commercial banks	0	-1	-5	0	0	0	0	0	0	0
Other private	0	-1	-1	-2	-1	-1	-1	-1	0	1
Private nonguaranteed	**0**	**0**	**0**	**0**	**0**	**0**	**0**	**0**	**0**	**0**
Bonds	0	0	0	0	0	0	0	0	0	0
Commercial banks	0	0	0	0	0	0	0	0	0	0
Memo:										
IBRD	0	0	0	0	0	0	0	0	0	0
IDA	0	12	48	48	35	26	24	14	7	19

BURUNDI

(US$ million, unless otherwise indicated)

	1970	1980	1990	1992	1993	1994	1995	1996	1997	1998
INTEREST PAYMENTS (LINT)	**0**	**2**	**12**	**14**	**12**	**12**	**11**	**9**	**9**	**8**
Public and publicly guaranteed	**0**	**2**	**12**	**14**	**12**	**12**	**11**	**9**	**9**	**8**
Official creditors	0	1	11	14	12	12	11	9	9	8
Multilateral	0	1	9	11	9	9	9	9	9	7
Concessional	0	0	5	6	6	6	6	6	7	6
Bilateral	0	0	2	3	3	3	2	0	0	1
Concessional	0	0	2	3	3	3	2	0	0	1
Private creditors	0	1	1	0	0	0	0	0	0	0
Bonds	0	0	0	0	0	0	0	0	0	0
Commercial banks	0	1	1	0	0	0	0	0	0	0
Other private	0	0	1	0	0	0	0	0	0	0
Private nonguaranteed	**0**	**0**	**0**	**0**	**0**	**0**	**0**	**0**	**0**	**0**
Bonds	0	0	0	0	0	0	0	0	0	0
Commercial banks	0	0	0	0	0	0	0	0	0	0
Memo:										
IBRD	0	0	0	0	0	0	0	0	0	0
IDA	0	0	3	3	3	4	5	4	5	4
NET TRANSFERS ON DEBT	**1**	**33**	**56**	**72**	**46**	**19**	**16**	**14**	**-2**	**10**
Public and publicly guaranteed	**1**	**33**	**56**	**72**	**46**	**19**	**16**	**14**	**-2**	**10**
Official creditors	1	37	64	74	47	19	17	15	-2	10
Multilateral	1	20	44	61	50	24	20	14	-5	11
Concessional	0	20	51	68	55	31	26	22	1	16
Bilateral	0	17	20	13	-3	-5	-3	1	3	-1
Concessional	0	17	20	13	-3	-5	-3	1	3	-1
Private creditors	0	-4	-7	-2	-1	-1	-1	-1	0	1
Bonds	0	0	0	0	0	0	0	0	0	0
Commercial banks	0	-2	-6	0	0	0	0	0	0	0
Other private	0	-2	-1	-2	-1	-1	-1	-1	0	1
Private nonguaranteed	**0**	**0**	**0**	**0**	**0**	**0**	**0**	**0**	**0**	**0**
Bonds	0	0	0	0	0	0	0	0	0	0
Commercial banks	0	0	0	0	0	0	0	0	0	0
Memo:										
IBRD	0	0	0	0	0	0	0	0	0	0
IDA	0	11	45	44	31	21	20	10	3	15
DEBT SERVICE (LTDS)	**1**	**6**	**40**	**36**	**31**	**34**	**29**	**21**	**21**	**21**
Public and publicly guaranteed	**1**	**6**	**40**	**36**	**31**	**34**	**29**	**21**	**21**	**21**
Official creditors	1	2	30	33	30	33	28	21	21	21
Multilateral	1	1	20	24	20	24	20	20	21	19
Concessional	0	0	10	13	14	16	15	11	15	14
Bilateral	0	1	10	10	10	9	8	1	0	1
Concessional	0	1	10	10	10	9	8	1	0	1
Private creditors	0	4	9	2	1	1	1	1	0	0
Bonds	0	0	0	0	0	0	0	0	0	0
Commercial banks	0	2	6	0	0	0	0	0	0	0
Other private	0	2	4	2	1	1	1	1	0	0
Private nonguaranteed	**0**	**0**	**0**	**0**	**0**	**0**	**0**	**0**	**0**	**0**
Bonds	0	0	0	0	0	0	0	0	0	0
Commercial banks	0	0	0	0	0	0	0	0	0	0
Memo:										
IBRD	0	0	0	0	0	0	0	0	0	0
IDA	0	0	4	5	5	6	8	7	9	10
UNDISBURSED DEBT	**2**	**184**	**459**	**426**	**410**	**369**	**311**	**232**	**145**	**119**
Official creditors	2	184	459	426	410	368	311	232	145	119
Private creditors	0	0	0	0	0	0	0	0	0	0
Memorandum items										
Concessional LDOD	2	104	780	891	946	1,012	1,047	1,041	989	1,048
Variable rate LDOD	0	0	0	0	0	0	0	0	0	0
Public sector LDOD	6	117	850	946	998	1,062	1,095	1,081	1,022	1,079
Private sector LDOD	2	1	2	2	0	0	0	0	0	0

6. CURRENCY COMPOSITION OF LONG-TERM DEBT (PERCENT)

	1970	1980	1990	1992	1993	1994	1995	1996	1997	1998
Deutsche mark	17.8	1.8	0.5	0.2	0.1	0.1	0.1	0.1	0.1	0.1
French franc	0.0	1.1	4.4	5.8	5.5	5.8	6.1	5.8	5.3	5.4
Japanese yen	0.0	0.0	2.0	2.8	3.0	3.1	2.9	2.6	2.5	2.6
Pound sterling	0.0	0.0	0.0	0.0	0.0	0.0	0.0	0.0	0.0	0.0
Swiss franc	0.0	0.0	0.0	0.0	0.0	0.0	0.0	0.0	0.0	0.0
U.S.dollars	15.1	34.4	50.3	52.4	52.9	53.5	54.9	55.3	56.4	56.9
Multiple currency	34.2	16.1	21.6	21.0	21.5	22.0	22.4	22.9	22.2	21.7
Special drawing rights	0.0	0.0	2.8	2.5	2.3	2.3	2.0	1.9	1.8	1.8
All other currencies	32.9	46.6	18.4	15.3	14.7	13.2	11.6	11.4	11.7	11.5

BURUNDI

(US$ million, unless otherwise indicated)

	1970	1980	1990	1992	1993	1994	1995	1996	1997	1998
7. DEBT RESTRUCTURINGS										
Total amount rescheduled	..	..	0	0	0	0	0	0	0	0
Debt stock rescheduled	..	..	0	0	0	0	0	0	0	0
Principal rescheduled	..	..	0	0	0	0	0	0	0	0
Official	..	..	0	0	0	0	0	0	0	0
Private	..	..	0	0	0	0	0	0	0	0
Interest rescheduled	..	..	0	0	0	0	0	0	0	0
Official	..	..	0	0	0	0	0	0	0	0
Private	..	..	0	0	0	0	0	0	0	0
Debt forgiven	..	..	105	5	0	0	16	0	0	0
Memo: interest forgiven	..	..	1	0	0	0	1	0	0	0
Debt stock reduction	..	..	0	0	0	0	0	0	0	0
of which debt buyback	..	..	0	0	0	0	0	0	0	0
8. DEBT STOCK-FLOW RECONCILIATION										
Total change in debt stocks	..	..	19	59	39	62	35	-31	-61	53
Net flows on debt	3	40	65	101	45	25	26	4	3	10
Net change in interest arrears	..	..	-1	1	1	0	1	3	4	4
Interest capitalized	..	..	0	0	0	0	0	0	0	0
Debt forgiveness or reduction	..	..	-105	-5	0	0	-16	0	0	0
Cross-currency valuation	..	..	16	-12	-4	12	11	-11	-18	13
Residual	..	..	43	-26	-3	24	12	-27	-50	27
9. AVERAGE TERMS OF NEW COMMITMENTS										
ALL CREDITORS										
Interest (%)	2.9	1.3	0.9	0.7	1.1	0.8	0.8	0.0	0.0	2.0
Maturity (years)	4.7	41.8	40.1	41.1	45.0	49.8	38.0	0.0	0.0	3.1
Grace period (years)	2.2	8.9	10.3	10.2	10.0	10.3	9.8	0.0	0.0	0.2
Grant element (%)	20.3	73.6	78.7	80.6	78.7	83.3	78.4	0.0	0.0	12.2
Official creditors										
Interest (%)	2.3	1.3	0.9	0.7	1.1	0.8	0.8	0.0	0.0	0.0
Maturity (years)	4.8	41.8	40.1	41.1	45.0	49.8	38.0	0.0	0.0	0.0
Grace period (years)	2.5	8.9	10.3	10.2	10.0	10.3	9.8	0.0	0.0	0.0
Grant element (%)	22.5	73.6	78.7	80.6	78.7	83.3	78.4	0.0	0.0	0.0
Private creditors										
Interest (%)	7.6	0.0	0.0	0.0	0.0	0.0	0.0	0.0	0.0	2.0
Maturity (years)	3.6	0.0	0.0	0.0	0.0	0.0	0.0	0.0	0.0	3.1
Grace period (years)	0.1	0.0	0.0	0.0	0.0	0.0	0.0	0.0	0.0	0.2
Grant element (%)	3.8	0.0	0.0	0.0	0.0	0.0	0.0	0.0	0.0	12.2
Memorandum items										
Commitments	1	102	126	82	71	7	39	0	0	1
Official creditors	1	102	126	82	71	7	39	0	0	0
Private creditors	0	0	0	0	0	0	0	0	0	1

10. CONTRACTUAL OBLIGATIONS ON OUTSTANDING LONG-TERM DEBT

	1999	2000	2001	2002	2003	2004	2005	2006	2007	2008
TOTAL										
Disbursements	47	31	18	12	6	2	1	1	0	0
Principal	41	36	36	34	32	32	31	32	33	33
Interest	11	10	10	9	8	8	8	7	7	7
Official creditors										
Disbursements	47	31	18	12	6	2	1	1	0	0
Principal	40	36	36	34	32	32	31	32	33	33
Interest	11	10	10	9	8	8	8	7	7	7
Bilateral creditors										
Disbursements	10	8	5	2	1	1	1	1	0	0
Principal	16	13	13	12	10	9	8	7	7	7
Interest	2	2	2	2	2	2	1	1	1	1
Multilateral creditors										
Disbursements	37	23	14	9	4	1	0	0	0	0
Principal	24	23	24	23	22	23	23	25	26	26
Interest	8	8	7	7	7	7	6	6	6	6
Private creditors										
Disbursements	0	0	0	0	0	0	0	0	0	0
Principal	1	0	0	0	0	0	0	0	0	0
Interest	0	0	0	0	0	0	0	0	0	0
Commercial banks										
Disbursements	0	0	0	0	0	0	0	0	0	0
Principal	0	0	0	0	0	0	0	0	0	0
Interest	0	0	0	0	0	0	0	0	0	0
Other private										
Disbursements	0	0	0	0	0	0	0	0	0	0
Principal	1	0	0	0	0	0	0	0	0	0
Interest	0	0	0	0	0	0	0	0	0	0

CAMBODIA

(US$ million, unless otherwise indicated)

	1970	1980	1990	1992	1993	1994	1995	1996	1997	1998
1. SUMMARY DEBT DATA										
TOTAL DEBT STOCKS (EDT)	..	..	**1,854**	**1,840**	**1,829**	**1,915**	**2,035**	**2,100**	**2,129**	**2,210**
Long-term debt (LDOD)	..	..	**1,688**	**1,680**	**1,685**	**1,745**	**1,946**	**2,013**	**2,031**	**2,102**
Public and publicly guaranteed	..	..	1,688	1,680	1,685	1,745	1,946	2,013	2,031	2,102
Private nonguaranteed	..	..	0	0	0	0	0	0	0	0
Use of IMF credit	**0**	**0**	**27**	**15**	**9**	**30**	**72**	**69**	**65**	**67**
Short-term debt	..	..	**140**	**145**	**135**	**140**	**17**	**19**	**33**	**42**
of which interest arrears on LDOD	..	..	107	113	104	110	5	5	7	11
Official creditors	..	..	106	113	103	110	5	5	7	11
Private creditors	..	..	0	0	0	0	0	0	0	0
Memo: principal arrears on LDOD	..	..	393	328	447	577	588	708	828	949
Official creditors	..	..	393	328	447	577	588	708	828	949
Private creditors	..	..	0	0	0	0	0	0	0	0
Memo: export credits	..	..	8	8	13	22	17	10	13	10
TOTAL DEBT FLOWS										
Disbursements	..	..	**0**	**0**	**14**	**75**	**128**	**77**	**40**	**56**
Long-term debt	..	..	0	0	5	55	85	77	40	56
IMF purchases	0	0	0	0	9	20	43	0	0	0
Principal repayments	..	..	**0**	**11**	**15**	**0**	**4**	**4**	**4**	**6**
Long-term debt	..	..	0	0	0	0	4	4	4	4
IMF repurchases	0	0	0	11	15	0	0	0	0	1
Net flows on debt	..	..	**15**	**-11**	**-1**	**73**	**106**	**74**	**49**	**56**
of which short-term debt	..	..	15	0	0	-2	-18	1	13	5
Interest payments (INT)	..	..	**30**	**2**	**19**	**2**	**2**	**6**	**6**	**7**
Long-term debt	..	..	29	1	0	0	1	4	5	5
IMF charges	0	0	0	0	18	1	1	1	1	1
Short-term debt	..	..	1	1	1	1	1	1	1	2
Net transfers on debt	..	..	**-15**	**-13**	**-21**	**71**	**103**	**68**	**43**	**48**
Total debt service paid (TDS)	..	..	**30**	**13**	**34**	**2**	**6**	**10**	**10**	**13**
Long-term debt	..	..	29	1	0	0	5	8	9	9
IMF repurchases and charges	0	0	0	11	33	1	1	1	1	2
Short-term debt (interest only)	..	..	1	1	1	1	1	1	1	2
2. AGGREGATE NET RESOURCE FLOWS AND NET TRANSFERS (LONG-TERM)										
NET RESOURCE FLOWS	..	..	**23**	**132**	**235**	**287**	**544**	**560**	**406**	**343**
Net flow of long-term debt (ex. IMF)	..	..	0	0	5	55	81	73	36	52
Foreign direct investment (net)	..	..	0	33	54	69	151	294	203	121
Portfolio equity flows	..	..	0	0	0	0	0	0	0	0
Grants (excluding technical coop.)	..	..	23	99	176	163	312	194	167	170
Memo: technical coop. grants	..	..	19	107	124	116	143	150	123	121
official net resource flows	..	..	23	99	181	218	381	269	206	225
private net resource flows	..	..	0	33	54	69	164	290	200	118
NET TRANSFERS	..	..	**-6**	**132**	**234**	**284**	**541**	**556**	**402**	**338**
Interest on long-term debt	..	..	29	1	0	0	1	4	5	5
Profit remittances on FDI	..	..	0	0	2	2	2	0	0	0
Memo: official net transfers	..	..	-6	99	181	217	380	265	202	220
private net transfers	..	..	0	33	53	67	162	290	200	118
3. MAJOR ECONOMIC AGGREGATES										
Gross national product (GNP)	..	..	1,115	1,980	2,012	2,399	2,907	3,111	3,040	2,845
Exports of goods & services (XGS)	..	..	..	323	357	556	989	829	922	843
of which workers remittances	..	..	..	9	9	10	10	10	10	10
Imports of goods & services (MGS)	..	..	..	528	608	933	1,442	1,385	1,311	1,354
International reserves (RES)	..	..	..	..	24	118	192	266	299	324
Current account balance	..	..	..	-93	-104	-157	-186	-185	-210	-224
4. DEBT INDICATORS										
EDT / XGS (%)	..	..	..	569.3	512.3	344.1	205.8	253.4	230.8	262.1
EDT / GNP (%)	..	..	166.4	92.9	90.9	79.8	70.0	67.5	70.0	77.7
TDS / XGS (%)	..	..	..	4.0	9.6	0.3	0.7	1.2	1.1	1.5
INT / XGS (%)	..	..	..	0.6	5.4	0.3	0.2	0.7	0.6	0.9
INT / GNP (%)	..	..	2.7	0.1	1.0	0.1	0.1	0.2	0.2	0.3
RES / EDT (%)	..	..	..	..	1.3	6.2	9.4	12.7	14.0	14.7
RES / MGS (months)	..	..	..	..	0.5	1.5	1.6	2.3	2.7	2.9
Short-term / EDT (%)	..	..	7.5	7.9	7.4	7.3	0.9	0.9	1.5	1.9
Concessional / EDT (%)	..	..	91.0	91.3	92.1	90.9	93.0	93.6	93.3	93.2
Multilateral / EDT (%)	..	..	0.1	0.0	0.3	3.0	5.8	8.9	10.1	12.5

CAMBODIA

(US$ million, unless otherwise indicated)

	1970	1980	1990	1992	1993	1994	1995	1996	1997	1998
5. LONG-TERM DEBT										
DEBT OUTSTANDING (LDOD)	..	..	**1,688**	**1,680**	**1,685**	**1,745**	**1,946**	**2,013**	**2,031**	**2,102**
Public and publicly guaranteed	..	..	**1,688**	**1,680**	**1,685**	**1,745**	**1,946**	**2,013**	**2,031**	**2,102**
Official creditors	..	..	1,688	1,680	1,685	1,745	1,934	2,003	2,025	2,099
Multilateral	..	..	1	0	5	58	118	188	215	276
Concessional	..	..	1	0	5	58	118	188	215	276
Bilateral	..	..	1,686	1,680	1,680	1,687	1,816	1,815	1,810	1,822
Concessional	..	..	1,686	1,680	1,680	1,683	1,776	1,778	1,771	1,783
Private creditors	..	..	0	0	0	0	13	10	6	3
Bonds	..	..	0	0	0	0	0	0	0	0
Commercial banks	..	..	0	0	0	0	0	0	0	0
Other private	..	..	0	0	0	0	13	10	6	3
Private nonguaranteed	..	..	**0**	**0**	**0**	**0**	**0**	**0**	**0**	**0**
Bonds	..	..	0	0	0	0	0	0	0	0
Commercial banks	..	..	0	0	0	0	0	0	0	0
Memo:										
IBRD	0	0	0	0	0	0	0	0	0	0
IDA	0	0	0	0	0	39	65	108	132	157
DISBURSEMENTS	..	..	**0**	**0**	**5**	**55**	**85**	**77**	**40**	**56**
Public and publicly guaranteed	..	..	**0**	**0**	**5**	**55**	**85**	**77**	**40**	**56**
Official creditors	..	..	0	0	5	55	69	77	40	56
Multilateral	..	..	0	0	5	50	61	77	40	47
Concessional	..	..	0	0	5	50	61	77	40	47
Bilateral	..	..	0	0	0	4	9	0	0	9
Concessional	..	..	0	0	0	0	9	0	0	9
Private creditors	..	..	0	0	0	0	16	0	0	0
Bonds	..	..	0	0	0	0	0	0	0	0
Commercial banks	..	..	0	0	0	0	0	0	0	0
Other private	..	..	0	0	0	0	16	0	0	0
Private nonguaranteed	..	..	**0**	**0**	**0**	**0**	**0**	**0**	**0**	**0**
Bonds	..	..	0	0	0	0	0	0	0	0
Commercial banks	..	..	0	0	0	0	0	0	0	0
Memo:										
IBRD	0	0	0	0	0	0	0	0	0	0
IDA	0	0	0	0	0	38	25	46	30	19
PRINCIPAL REPAYMENTS	..	..	**0**	**0**	**0**	**0**	**4**	**4**	**4**	**4**
Public and publicly guaranteed	..	..	**0**	**0**	**0**	**0**	**4**	**4**	**4**	**4**
Official creditors	..	..	0	0	0	0	1	1	1	1
Multilateral	..	..	0	0	0	0	0	0	0	0
Concessional	..	..	0	0	0	0	0	0	0	0
Bilateral	..	..	0	0	0	0	1	1	1	1
Concessional	..	..	0	0	0	0	0	0	0	0
Private creditors	..	..	0	0	0	0	3	3	3	3
Bonds	..	..	0	0	0	0	0	0	0	0
Commercial banks	..	..	0	0	0	0	0	0	0	0
Other private	..	..	0	0	0	0	3	3	3	3
Private nonguaranteed	..	..	**0**	**0**	**0**	**0**	**0**	**0**	**0**	**0**
Bonds	..	..	0	0	0	0	0	0	0	0
Commercial banks	..	..	0	0	0	0	0	0	0	0
Memo:										
IBRD	0	0	0	0	0	0	0	0	0	0
IDA	0	0	0	0	0	0	0	0	0	0
NET FLOWS ON DEBT	..	..	**0**	**0**	**5**	**55**	**81**	**73**	**36**	**52**
Public and publicly guaranteed	..	..	**0**	**0**	**5**	**55**	**81**	**73**	**36**	**52**
Official creditors	..	..	0	0	5	55	68	76	39	55
Multilateral	..	..	0	0	5	50	61	77	40	47
Concessional	..	..	0	0	5	50	61	77	40	47
Bilateral	..	..	0	0	0	4	8	-1	-1	8
Concessional	..	..	0	0	0	0	9	0	0	9
Private creditors	..	..	0	0	0	0	13	-3	-3	-3
Bonds	..	..	0	0	0	0	0	0	0	0
Commercial banks	..	..	0	0	0	0	0	0	0	0
Other private	..	..	0	0	0	0	13	-3	-3	-3
Private nonguaranteed	..	..	**0**	**0**	**0**	**0**	**0**	**0**	**0**	**0**
Bonds	..	..	0	0	0	0	0	0	0	0
Commercial banks	..	..	0	0	0	0	0	0	0	0
Memo:										
IBRD	0	0	0	0	0	0	0	0	0	0
IDA	0	0	0	0	0	38	25	46	30	19

CAMBODIA

(US$ million, unless otherwise indicated)

	1970	1980	1990	1992	1993	1994	1995	1996	1997	1998
INTEREST PAYMENTS (LINT)	..	..	**29**	**1**	**0**	**0**	**1**	**4**	**5**	**5**
Public and publicly guaranteed	..	..	**29**	**1**	**0**	**0**	**1**	**4**	**5**	**5**
Official creditors	..	..	29	1	0	0	1	4	5	5
Multilateral	..	..	0	1	0	0	1	1	2	2
Concessional	..	..	0	1	0	0	1	1	2	2
Bilateral	..	..	29	0	0	0	0	3	3	3
Concessional	..	..	29	0	0	0	0	1	1	1
Private creditors	..	..	0	0	0	0	0	0	0	0
Bonds	..	..	0	0	0	0	0	0	0	0
Commercial banks	..	..	0	0	0	0	0	0	0	0
Other private	..	..	0	0	0	0	0	0	0	0
Private nonguaranteed	..	..	**0**	**0**	**0**	**0**	**0**	**0**	**0**	**0**
Bonds	..	..	0	0	0	0	0	0	0	0
Commercial banks	..	..	0	0	0	0	0	0	0	0
Memo:										
IBRD	0	0	0	0	0	0	0	0	0	0
IDA	0	0	0	0	0	0	0	1	1	1
NET TRANSFERS ON DEBT	..	..	**-29**	**-1**	**5**	**54**	**80**	**68**	**32**	**47**
Public and publicly guaranteed	..	..	**-29**	**-1**	**5**	**54**	**80**	**68**	**32**	**47**
Official creditors	..	..	-29	-1	5	54	67	72	35	50
Multilateral	..	..	0	-1	5	50	60	76	39	45
Concessional	..	..	0	-1	5	50	60	76	39	45
Bilateral	..	..	-29	0	0	4	8	-4	-4	5
Concessional	..	..	-29	0	0	0	9	-1	-1	8
Private creditors	..	..	0	0	0	0	13	-3	-3	-3
Bonds	..	..	0	0	0	0	0	0	0	0
Commercial banks	..	..	0	0	0	0	0	0	0	0
Other private	..	..	0	0	0	0	13	-3	-3	-3
Private nonguaranteed	..	..	**0**	**0**	**0**	**0**	**0**	**0**	**0**	**0**
Bonds	..	..	0	0	0	0	0	0	0	0
Commercial banks	..	..	0	0	0	0	0	0	0	0
Memo:										
IBRD	0	0	0	0	0	0	0	0	0	0
IDA	0	0	0	0	0	38	24	45	30	18
DEBT SERVICE (LTDS)	..	..	**29**	**1**	**0**	**0**	**5**	**8**	**9**	**9**
Public and publicly guaranteed	..	..	**29**	**1**	**0**	**0**	**5**	**8**	**9**	**9**
Official creditors	..	..	29	1	0	0	2	5	6	6
Multilateral	..	..	0	1	0	0	1	1	2	2
Concessional	..	..	0	1	0	0	1	1	2	2
Bilateral	..	..	29	0	0	0	1	4	4	4
Concessional	..	..	29	0	0	0	0	1	1	1
Private creditors	..	..	0	0	0	0	3	3	3	3
Bonds	..	..	0	0	0	0	0	0	0	0
Commercial banks	..	..	0	0	0	0	0	0	0	0
Other private	..	..	0	0	0	0	3	3	3	3
Private nonguaranteed	..	..	**0**	**0**	**0**	**0**	**0**	**0**	**0**	**0**
Bonds	..	..	0	0	0	0	0	0	0	0
Commercial banks	..	..	0	0	0	0	0	0	0	0
Memo:										
IBRD	0	0	0	0	0	0	0	0	0	0
IDA	0	0	0	0	0	0	0	1	1	1
UNDISBURSED DEBT	..	..	**651**	**7**	**128**	**131**	**201**	**212**	**226**	**209**
Official creditors	..	..	651	7	128	115	201	212	226	209
Private creditors	..	..	0	0	0	16	0	0	0	0
Memorandum items										
Concessional LDOD	..	..	1,688	1,680	1,685	1,741	1,894	1,965	1,985	2,059
Variable rate LDOD	..	..	0	0	0	0	0	0	0	0
Public sector LDOD	..	..	1,688	1,680	1,685	1,745	1,946	2,013	2,031	2,102
Private sector LDOD	..	..	0	0	0	0	0	0	0	0

6. CURRENCY COMPOSITION OF LONG-TERM DEBT (PERCENT)

	1970	1980	1990	1992	1993	1994	1995	1996	1997	1998
Deutsche mark	..	..	0.4	0.0	0.0	0.0	0.3	0.2	0.2	0.2
French franc	..	..	0.5	0.4	0.4	0.4	1.0	0.9	1.1	1.1
Japanese yen	..	..	0.6	0.6	0.7	0.7	1.2	1.1	0.9	1.0
Pound sterling	..	..	0.0	0.0	0.0	0.0	0.0	0.0	0.0	0.0
Swiss franc	..	..	0.0	0.0	0.0	0.0	0.0	0.0	0.0	0.0
U.S.dollars	..	..	12.6	12.6	12.5	14.6	20.2	21.7	22.3	22.6
Multiple currency	..	..	0.0	0.0	0.3	1.1	2.7	4.0	4.1	5.6
Special drawing rights	..	..	0.0	0.0	0.0	0.0	0.0	0.0	0.0	0.0
All other currencies	..	..	85.9	86.4	86.1	83.2	74.6	72.1	71.4	69.5

CAMBODIA

(US$ million, unless otherwise indicated)

	1970	1980	1990	1992	1993	1994	1995	1996	1997	1998
7. DEBT RESTRUCTURINGS										
Total amount rescheduled	..	..	0	0	0	0	240	12	5	0
Debt stock rescheduled	..	..	0	0	0	0	0	0	0	0
Principal rescheduled	..	..	0	0	0	0	109	7	3	0
Official	..	..	0	0	0	0	108	7	3	0
Private	..	..	0	0	0	0	0	0	0	0
Interest rescheduled	..	..	..	0	0	0	103	4	2	0
Official	..	..	0	0	0	0	103	4	2	0
Private	..	..	0	0	0	0	0	0	0	0
Debt forgiven	..	..	0	7	0	0	6	0	0	0
Memo: interest forgiven	..	..	0	4	0	0	7	0	0	0
Debt stock reduction	..	..	0	0	0	0	0	0	0	0
of which debt buyback	..	..	0	0	0	0	0	0	0	0
8. DEBT STOCK-FLOW RECONCILIATION										
Total change in debt stocks	..	..	..	-22	-11	86	120	65	28	81
Net flows on debt	..	..	15	-11	-1	73	106	74	49	56
Net change in interest arrears	..	..	..	-1	-10	7	-105	0	1	4
Interest capitalized	..	..	..	0	0	0	103	4	2	0
Debt forgiveness or reduction	..	..	..	-7	0	0	-6	0	0	0
Cross-currency valuation	..	..	..	-1	1	3	2	-4	-6	5
Residual	..	..	..	-2	0	3	20	-8	-18	17
9. AVERAGE TERMS OF NEW COMMITMENTS										
ALL CREDITORS										
Interest (%)	..	..	0.0	0.0	0.9	0.7	1.8	3.3	1.1	0.5
Maturity (years)	..	..	0.0	0.0	39.9	25.0	37.5	39.7	38.3	39.5
Grace period (years)	..	..	0.0	0.0	10.4	6.7	9.7	10.2	9.7	10.0
Grant element (%)	..	..	0.0	0.0	79.6	58.5	69.8	57.9	76.0	82.5
Official creditors										
Interest (%)	..	..	0.0	0.0	0.9	1.1	1.8	3.3	1.1	0.5
Maturity (years)	..	..	0.0	0.0	39.9	33.6	37.5	39.7	38.3	39.5
Grace period (years)	..	..	0.0	0.0	10.4	9.2	9.7	10.2	9.7	10.0
Grant element (%)	..	..	0.0	0.0	79.6	73.2	69.8	57.9	76.0	82.5
Private creditors										
Interest (%)	..	..	0.0	0.0	0.0	0.0	0.0	0.0	0.0	0.0
Maturity (years)	..	..	0.0	0.0	0.0	5.0	0.0	0.0	0.0	0.0
Grace period (years)	..	..	0.0	0.0	0.0	1.0	0.0	0.0	0.0	0.0
Grant element (%)	..	..	0.0	0.0	0.0	24.3	0.0	0.0	0.0	0.0
Memorandum items										
Commitments	..	..	0	0	127	53	161	94	75	31
Official creditors	..	..	0	0	127	37	161	94	75	31
Private creditors	..	..	0	0	0	16	0	0	0	0

10. CONTRACTUAL OBLIGATIONS ON OUTSTANDING LONG-TERM DEBT

	1999	2000	2001	2002	2003	2004	2005	2006	2007	2008
TOTAL										
Disbursements	58	56	42	29	15	5	3	1	0	0
Principal	133	130	39	41	42	45	47	47	48	49
Interest	10	10	10	10	10	10	10	10	11	10
Official creditors										
Disbursements	58	56	42	29	15	5	3	1	0	0
Principal	130	130	39	41	42	45	47	47	48	49
Interest	10	10	10	10	10	10	10	10	11	10
Bilateral creditors										
Disbursements	1	2	2	1	1	0	0	0	0	0
Principal	130	130	39	40	41	42	42	39	37	37
Interest	6	6	6	5	5	5	4	4	3	3
Multilateral creditors										
Disbursements	57	54	41	28	15	5	3	1	0	0
Principal	0	0	0	0	2	3	5	8	11	12
Interest	3	4	5	5	5	5	6	6	8	8
Private creditors										
Disbursements	0	0	0	0	0	0	0	0	0	0
Principal	3	0	0	0	0	0	0	0	0	0
Interest	0	0	0	0	0	0	0	0	0	0
Commercial banks										
Disbursements	0	0	0	0	0	0	0	0	0	0
Principal	0	0	0	0	0	0	0	0	0	0
Interest	0	0	0	0	0	0	0	0	0	0
Other private										
Disbursements	0	0	0	0	0	0	0	0	0	0
Principal	3	0	0	0	0	0	0	0	0	0
Interest	0	0	0	0	0	0	0	0	0	0

CAMEROON

(US$ million, unless otherwise indicated)

1. SUMMARY DEBT DATA

	1970	1980	1990	1992	1993	1994	1995	1996	1997	1998
TOTAL DEBT STOCKS (EDT)	..	**2,588**	**6,679**	**7,415**	**7,456**	**8,326**	**9,346**	**9,542**	**9,267**	**9,829**
Long-term debt (LDOD)	**145**	**2,251**	**5,598**	**6,523**	**6,505**	**7,537**	**8,259**	**8,210**	**7,860**	**8,274**
Public and publicly guaranteed	136	2,073	5,368	6,269	6,236	7,304	8,062	8,001	7,662	8,096
Private nonguaranteed	9	178	230	254	269	233	197	209	198	179
Use of IMF credit	**0**	**59**	**121**	**63**	**16**	**44**	**51**	**72**	**93**	**156**
Short-term debt	..	**278**	**960**	**830**	**935**	**745**	**1,036**	**1,260**	**1,314**	**1,398**
of which interest arrears on LDOD	..	9	191	296	484	264	395	788	185	172
Official creditors	..	3	87	188	361	134	247	650	78	64
Private creditors	..	6	105	108	123	130	147	138	108	109
Memo: principal arrears on LDOD	..	7	350	448	651	538	620	774	490	529
Official creditors	..	2	103	126	255	198	243	377	170	199
Private creditors	..	5	247	322	396	340	376	398	320	329
Memo: export credits	..	0	2,193	2,228	2,246	2,575	2,797	2,719	2,494	2,603
TOTAL DEBT FLOWS										
Disbursements	**40**	**626**	**718**	**669**	**499**	**478**	**121**	**230**	**296**	**266**
Long-term debt	40	614	718	669	499	447	108	201	259	192
IMF purchases	0	12	0	0	0	31	13	29	37	73
Principal repayments	**6**	**131**	**270**	**203**	**282**	**204**	**217**	**248**	**281**	**297**
Long-term debt	6	114	269	149	235	198	211	242	270	281
IMF repurchases	0	17	1	54	47	6	6	6	11	16
Net flows on debt	**33**	**538**	**685**	**380**	**134**	**305**	**64**	**-188**	**673**	**65**
of which short-term debt	..	43	237	-86	-83	30	160	-169	657	97
Interest payments (INT)	..	**149**	**252**	**191**	**189**	**181**	**214**	**262**	**232**	**236**
Long-term debt	5	119	198	152	156	155	173	235	189	178
IMF charges	0	2	11	8	3	2	2	3	3	3
Short-term debt	..	28	43	31	30	24	39	24	40	55
Net transfers on debt	..	**389**	**433**	**189**	**-55**	**123**	**-150**	**-449**	**440**	**-171**
Total debt service paid (TDS)	..	**280**	**522**	**394**	**471**	**385**	**431**	**510**	**513**	**533**
Long-term debt	11	233	467	300	391	353	384	477	459	459
IMF repurchases and charges	0	19	13	62	50	7	9	9	15	19
Short-term debt (interest only)	..	28	43	31	30	24	39	24	40	55

2. AGGREGATE NET RESOURCE FLOWS AND NET TRANSFERS (LONG-TERM)

	1970	1980	1990	1992	1993	1994	1995	1996	1997	1998
NET RESOURCE FLOWS	**70**	**659**	**649**	**753**	**379**	**573**	**109**	**233**	**174**	**238**
Net flow of long-term debt (ex. IMF)	33	500	449	520	264	249	-103	-41	-11	-89
Foreign direct investment (net)	16	130	-113	29	5	-9	7	35	45	50
Portfolio equity flows	0	0	0	0	0	0	0	0	0	0
Grants (excluding technical coop.)	21	29	313	204	110	333	205	239	139	276
Memo: technical coop. grants	17	85	128	133	121	101	124	117	95	107
official net resource flows	44	250	774	650	368	641	167	221	157	237
private net resource flows	26	409	-125	103	11	-68	-58	12	16	1
NET TRANSFERS	**61**	**425**	**451**	**601**	**223**	**418**	**-65**	**-2**	**-16**	**59**
Interest on long-term debt	5	119	198	152	156	155	173	235	189	178
Profit remittances on FDI	4	115	0	0	0	0	0	0	0	0
Memo: official net transfers	40	208	649	563	238	507	14	0	-16	77
private net transfers	21	216	-198	38	-15	-90	-79	-2	1	-18

3. MAJOR ECONOMIC AGGREGATES

	1970	1980	1990	1992	1993	1994	1995	1996	1997	1998
Gross national product (GNP)	1,025	5,618	10,674	10,751	11,160	7,307	7,437	8,518	8,506	8,232
Exports of goods & services (XGS)	306	1,912	2,320	2,409	2,090	1,767	2,088	2,128	2,384	2,389
of which workers remittances	..	11	61	36	44	23	28	67	60	68
Imports of goods & services (MGS)	329	2,478	2,418	2,764	2,647	2,087	2,188	2,471	2,667	2,660
International reserves (RES)	81	206	37	30	14	14	15	14	10	1
Current account balance	1	-495	-196	-216	-620	-324	-71	-375	-258	-235

4. DEBT INDICATORS

	1970	1980	1990	1992	1993	1994	1995	1996	1997	1998
EDT / XGS (%)	..	135.4	287.9	307.8	356.8	471.2	447.5	448.3	388.8	411.4
EDT / GNP (%)	..	46.1	62.6	69.0	66.8	113.9	125.7	112.0	108.9	119.4
TDS / XGS (%)	..	14.6	22.5	16.3	22.5	21.8	20.7	24.0	21.5	22.3
INT / XGS (%)	..	7.8	10.8	7.9	9.0	10.3	10.3	12.3	9.7	9.9
INT / GNP (%)	..	2.7	2.4	1.8	1.7	2.5	2.9	3.1	2.7	2.9
RES / EDT (%)	..	8.0	0.6	0.4	0.2	0.2	0.2	0.2	0.1	0.0
RES / MGS (months)	3.0	1.0	0.2	0.1	0.1	0.1	0.1	0.1	0.0	0.0
Short-term / EDT (%)	..	10.8	14.4	11.2	12.5	9.0	11.1	13.2	14.2	14.2
Concessional / EDT (%)	..	33.7	27.4	31.6	33.3	42.1	43.9	43.6	44.7	45.5
Multilateral / EDT (%)	..	16.7	19.7	19.7	19.2	20.0	18.0	16.4	15.8	15.1

CAMEROON

(US$ million, unless otherwise indicated)

	1970	1980	1990	1992	1993	1994	1995	1996	1997	1998
5. LONG-TERM DEBT										
DEBT OUTSTANDING (LDOD)	**145**	**2,251**	**5,598**	**6,523**	**6,505**	**7,537**	**8,259**	**8,210**	**7,860**	**8,274**
Public and publicly guaranteed	**136**	**2,073**	**5,368**	**6,269**	**6,236**	**7,304**	**8,062**	**8,001**	**7,662**	**8,096**
Official creditors	124	1,237	3,885	4,998	5,038	6,292	7,112	7,182	7,082	7,615
Multilateral	20	432	1,317	1,458	1,429	1,665	1,678	1,568	1,465	1,487
Concessional	12	210	341	337	335	558	611	670	735	835
Bilateral	104	805	2,568	3,539	3,609	4,627	5,434	5,614	5,618	6,128
Concessional	95	663	1,488	2,002	2,149	2,949	3,494	3,486	3,408	3,635
Private creditors	12	836	1,484	1,271	1,198	1,012	950	819	580	480
Bonds	0	0	0	0	0	0	0	0	0	0
Commercial banks	0	193	503	442	406	415	418	365	310	318
Other private	12	643	981	829	793	597	532	455	269	162
Private nonguaranteed	**9**	**178**	**230**	**254**	**269**	**233**	**197**	**209**	**198**	**179**
Bonds	0	0	0	0	0	0	0	0	0	0
Commercial banks	9	178	230	254	269	233	197	209	198	179
Memo:										
IBRD	3	152	651	723	707	695	639	520	410	350
IDA	9	146	238	232	227	406	443	513	609	701
DISBURSEMENTS	**40**	**614**	**718**	**669**	**499**	**447**	**108**	**201**	**259**	**192**
Public and publicly guaranteed	**29**	**564**	**665**	**542**	**419**	**440**	**108**	**176**	**245**	**182**
Official creditors	27	250	559	528	395	440	108	176	245	182
Multilateral	10	72	200	130	72	280	82	106	147	106
Concessional	6	22	2	14	9	217	38	85	122	92
Bilateral	18	178	359	398	324	159	26	70	98	76
Concessional	15	120	106	366	302	154	26	70	98	75
Private creditors	1	314	107	14	24	0	0	0	0	0
Bonds	0	0	0	0	0	0	0	0	0	0
Commercial banks	0	115	11	0	0	0	0	0	0	0
Other private	1	199	97	14	24	0	0	0	0	0
Private nonguaranteed	**11**	**50**	**53**	**127**	**80**	**7**	**0**	**25**	**14**	**10**
Bonds	0	0	0	0	0	0	0	0	0	0
Commercial banks	11	50	53	127	80	7	0	25	14	10
Memo:										
IBRD	3	28	75	54	59	22	6	6	6	3
IDA	4	19	0	0	0	180	35	84	120	79
PRINCIPAL REPAYMENTS	**6**	**114**	**269**	**149**	**235**	**198**	**211**	**242**	**270**	**281**
Public and publicly guaranteed	**5**	**82**	**139**	**91**	**170**	**155**	**183**	**229**	**244**	**261**
Official creditors	4	29	97	82	137	131	146	194	227	222
Multilateral	0	10	68	60	102	119	130	146	163	124
Concessional	0	2	7	7	8	9	10	10	30	14
Bilateral	4	19	29	21	35	12	16	48	64	98
Concessional	3	12	17	13	29	4	3	4	20	61
Private creditors	0	53	41	10	33	24	36	35	17	39
Bonds	0	0	0	0	0	0	0	0	0	0
Commercial banks	0	18	28	0	16	23	26	29	12	12
Other private	0	35	14	10	17	1	11	7	6	27
Private nonguaranteed	**2**	**32**	**130**	**57**	**65**	**43**	**28**	**13**	**25**	**20**
Bonds	0	0	0	0	0	0	0	0	0	0
Commercial banks	2	32	130	57	65	43	28	13	25	20
Memo:										
IBRD	0	4	42	30	87	82	92	82	76	69
IDA	0	1	3	2	5	4	4	5	5	5
NET FLOWS ON DEBT	**33**	**500**	**449**	**520**	**264**	**249**	**-103**	**-41**	**-11**	**-89**
Public and publicly guaranteed	**24**	**482**	**527**	**451**	**249**	**284**	**-75**	**-53**	**1**	**-79**
Official creditors	23	221	461	447	258	308	-39	-18	18	-40
Multilateral	9	63	131	70	-30	161	-49	-40	-17	-18
Concessional	6	21	-4	7	1	209	28	75	92	78
Bilateral	14	159	330	377	289	147	10	22	35	-22
Concessional	12	109	89	353	273	150	24	67	79	13
Private creditors	1	261	66	4	-9	-24	-36	-35	-17	-39
Bonds	0	0	0	0	0	0	0	0	0	0
Commercial banks	0	97	-17	0	-16	-23	-26	-29	-12	-12
Other private	1	164	83	4	7	-1	-11	-7	-6	-27
Private nonguaranteed	**9**	**18**	**-77**	**69**	**15**	**-35**	**-28**	**12**	**-11**	**-10**
Bonds	0	0	0	0	0	0	0	0	0	0
Commercial banks	9	18	-77	69	15	-35	-28	12	-11	-10
Memo:										
IBRD	3	24	33	24	-28	-60	-85	-76	-70	-65
IDA	4	19	-3	-2	-5	176	31	80	115	74

CAMEROON

(US$ million, unless otherwise indicated)

	1970	1980	1990	1992	1993	1994	1995	1996	1997	1998
INTEREST PAYMENTS (LINT)	**5**	**119**	**198**	**152**	**156**	**155**	**173**	**235**	**189**	**178**
Public and publicly guaranteed	**4**	**104**	**181**	**114**	**136**	**141**	**163**	**230**	**179**	**174**
Official creditors	4	42	125	87	130	134	152	221	174	159
Multilateral	1	18	73	65	96	112	80	100	91	59
Concessional	0	2	4	3	3	4	6	4	10	6
Bilateral	3	24	52	22	34	23	72	121	82	100
Concessional	2	13	28	13	21	15	48	33	51	56
Private creditors	1	62	56	27	6	6	10	9	6	15
Bonds	0	0	0	0	0	0	0	0	0	0
Commercial banks	0	23	40	25	2	6	5	7	2	5
Other private	1	39	16	2	4	1	5	2	4	10
Private nonguaranteed	**1**	**15**	**17**	**38**	**20**	**15**	**11**	**5**	**10**	**4**
Bonds	0	0	0	0	0	0	0	0	0	0
Commercial banks	1	15	17	38	20	15	11	5	10	4
Memo:										
IBRD	0	13	49	33	87	58	56	47	37	28
IDA	0	1	2	1	3	2	3	3	4	5
NET TRANSFERS ON DEBT	**28**	**381**	**252**	**368**	**108**	**93**	**-277**	**-276**	**-200**	**-267**
Public and publicly guaranteed	**19**	**378**	**346**	**337**	**113**	**144**	**-238**	**-283**	**-178**	**-253**
Official creditors	19	180	336	360	128	174	-191	-239	-155	-199
Multilateral	9	45	59	5	-126	49	-129	-140	-108	-77
Concessional	6	19	-8	4	-2	205	23	71	82	72
Bilateral	11	135	277	355	254	125	-62	-99	-47	-122
Concessional	10	96	61	340	252	136	-24	34	28	-42
Private creditors	0	199	10	-23	-15	-31	-47	-44	-23	-54
Bonds	0	0	0	0	0	0	0	0	0	0
Commercial banks	0	73	-57	-25	-17	-29	-31	-36	-13	-17
Other private	0	125	66	2	2	-2	-16	-8	-10	-37
Private nonguaranteed	**9**	**3**	**-94**	**32**	**-5**	**-50**	**-39**	**7**	**-21**	**-14**
Bonds	0	0	0	0	0	0	0	0	0	0
Commercial banks	9	3	-94	32	-5	-50	-39	7	-21	-14
Memo:										
IBRD	3	12	-16	-9	-114	-119	-141	-123	-107	-94
IDA	4	18	-4	-3	-8	174	28	76	110	69
DEBT SERVICE (LTDS)	**11**	**233**	**467**	**300**	**391**	**353**	**384**	**477**	**459**	**459**
Public and publicly guaranteed	**9**	**186**	**320**	**205**	**306**	**296**	**345**	**459**	**423**	**435**
Official creditors	8	71	222	168	267	265	299	415	400	381
Multilateral	1	28	141	126	198	231	211	246	255	183
Concessional	0	4	11	10	11	13	15	14	40	19
Bilateral	7	43	81	43	70	34	88	169	146	198
Concessional	6	25	46	26	50	18	50	36	70	117
Private creditors	1	115	98	37	39	31	47	44	23	54
Bonds	0	0	0	0	0	0	0	0	0	0
Commercial banks	0	42	67	25	17	29	31	36	13	17
Other private	1	74	30	12	21	2	16	8	10	37
Private nonguaranteed	**2**	**47**	**147**	**95**	**85**	**58**	**39**	**18**	**35**	**24**
Bonds	0	0	0	0	0	0	0	0	0	0
Commercial banks	2	47	147	95	85	58	39	18	35	24
Memo:										
IBRD	0	17	91	63	173	140	147	129	113	97
IDA	0	2	4	3	8	6	8	8	10	10
UNDISBURSED DEBT	**104**	**619**	**1,844**	**1,586**	**1,454**	**1,341**	**1,111**	**991**	**816**	**1,064**
Official creditors	103	545	1,526	1,344	1,248	1,125	1,021	987	812	1,060
Private creditors	1	74	318	243	206	216	90	4	4	4
Memorandum items										
Concessional LDOD	107	873	1,829	2,340	2,484	3,507	4,105	4,156	4,142	4,470
Variable rate LDOD	9	499	854	1,216	1,234	1,276	1,290	1,371	1,322	1,279
Public sector LDOD	128	2,006	5,245	6,162	6,139	7,233	7,985	7,929	7,602	8,037
Private sector LDOD	17	245	353	361	366	304	274	281	257	238
6. CURRENCY COMPOSITION OF LONG-TERM DEBT (PERCENT)										
Deutsche mark	10.7	8.6	16.9	16.3	15.7	16.7	17.5	17.7	17.7	17.7
French franc	15.8	36.8	31.4	35.3	37.2	34.1	34.6	35.0	33.9	33.7
Japanese yen	0.0	0.0	0.3	0.3	0.3	0.4	0.3	0.3	0.3	0.3
Pound sterling	2.8	2.0	2.3	1.6	1.6	1.2	1.0	1.0	0.7	0.6
Swiss franc	0.0	0.0	1.1	1.0	1.0	1.1	1.1	1.0	1.0	0.9
U.S.dollars	22.7	19.2	11.0	10.4	10.1	11.9	11.4	12.5	17.0	23.0
Multiple currency	4.9	10.5	16.5	16.6	16.5	14.6	12.5	10.7	9.2	4.2
Special drawing rights	0.0	0.0	0.0	0.0	0.1	0.1	0.2	0.2	0.2	0.2
All other currencies	43.1	22.9	20.5	18.5	17.5	19.9	21.4	21.6	20.0	19.4

CAMEROON

(US$ million, unless otherwise indicated)

	1970	1980	1990	1992	1993	1994	1995	1996	1997	1998
7. DEBT RESTRUCTURINGS										
Total amount rescheduled	..	..	75	988	0	1,298	642	656	982	370
Debt stock rescheduled	..	..	0	0	0	0	0	0	0	0
Principal rescheduled	..	..	26	408	0	493	298	187	416	218
Official	..	..	7	215	0	244	204	147	306	147
Private	..	..	19	193	0	248	94	40	110	71
Interest rescheduled	..	..	22	386	0	475	155	67	566	152
Official	..	..	6	102	0	376	131	59	538	141
Private	..	..	16	283	0	99	25	8	28	11
Debt forgiven	..	..	10	29	0	533	0	1	83	33
Memo: interest forgiven	..	..	0	0	0	13	0	0	92	18
Debt stock reduction	..	..	0	0	0	0	0	0	0	0
of which debt buyback	..	..	0	0	0	0	0	0	0	0
8. DEBT STOCK-FLOW RECONCILIATION										
Total change in debt stocks	..	..	1,239	518	41	870	1,020	196	-275	562
Net flows on debt	33	538	685	380	134	305	64	-188	673	65
Net change in interest arrears	..	..	115	-80	188	-220	131	393	-602	-13
Interest capitalized	..	..	22	386	0	475	155	67	566	152
Debt forgiveness or reduction	..	..	-10	-29	0	-533	0	-1	-83	-33
Cross-currency valuation	..	..	529	-323	-291	568	520	-469	-748	387
Residual	..	..	-103	184	10	275	150	393	-80	4
9. AVERAGE TERMS OF NEW COMMITMENTS										
ALL CREDITORS										
Interest (%)	4.7	6.9	6.6	4.5	4.9	2.3	2.2	1.3	0.5	1.1
Maturity (years)	28.4	23.3	15.1	19.5	18.1	31.9	26.7	35.2	38.8	36.8
Grace period (years)	8.0	5.9	5.3	7.1	10.2	9.4	8.0	8.8	9.3	9.8
Grant element (%)	39.9	25.9	21.2	37.7	36.3	63.7	58.8	71.7	81.6	75.1
Official creditors										
Interest (%)	4.6	6.1	6.6	4.3	4.9	2.3	2.2	1.3	0.5	1.1
Maturity (years)	28.8	24.8	15.2	20.3	18.1	31.9	26.7	35.2	38.8	36.8
Grace period (years)	8.1	6.3	5.3	7.4	10.2	9.4	8.0	8.8	9.3	9.8
Grant element (%)	40.4	30.6	21.3	39.7	36.3	63.7	58.8	71.7	81.6	75.1
Private creditors										
Interest (%)	6.0	14.7	7.0	8.1	0.0	0.0	0.0	0.0	0.0	0.0
Maturity (years)	7.2	8.2	13.2	7.4	0.0	0.0	0.0	0.0	0.0	0.0
Grace period (years)	1.7	2.4	2.7	2.9	0.0	0.0	0.0	0.0	0.0	0.0
Grant element (%)	13.0	-21.2	14.4	6.5	0.0	0.0	0.0	0.0	0.0	0.0
Memorandum items										
Commitments	42	170	479	272	347	403	143	351	25	385
Official creditors	41	155	473	255	347	403	143	351	25	385
Private creditors	1	15	6	16	0	0	0	0	0	0

10. CONTRACTUAL OBLIGATIONS ON OUTSTANDING LONG-TERM DEBT

	1999	2000	2001	2002	2003	2004	2005	2006	2007	2008
TOTAL										
Disbursements	323	291	199	125	70	32	18	5	2	0
Principal	231	326	409	448	481	504	531	490	427	401
Interest	188	280	356	336	313	289	264	230	209	191
Official creditors										
Disbursements	319	291	199	125	70	32	18	5	2	0
Principal	206	289	379	421	466	489	514	486	423	398
Interest	178	269	345	327	304	281	256	229	208	190
Bilateral creditors										
Disbursements	142	110	62	36	19	10	5	2	1	0
Principal	72	161	249	302	362	391	424	405	357	334
Interest	118	213	295	283	267	248	229	207	190	175
Multilateral creditors										
Disbursements	177	180	137	89	51	21	13	3	1	0
Principal	134	128	130	119	105	98	90	81	66	63
Interest	61	56	51	44	38	32	27	22	18	15
Private creditors										
Disbursements	4	0	0	0	0	0	0	0	0	0
Principal	25	37	30	28	15	15	17	4	4	4
Interest	10	11	11	9	9	9	9	1	1	1
Commercial banks										
Disbursements	4	0	0	0	0	0	0	0	0	0
Principal	4	0	0	0	0	0	0	0	0	0
Interest	0	0	0	0	0	0	0	0	0	0
Other private										
Disbursements	0	0	0	0	0	0	0	0	0	0
Principal	21	37	30	28	15	15	17	4	4	4
Interest	10	11	11	9	9	9	9	1	1	1

CAPE VERDE

(US$ million, unless otherwise indicated)

	1970	1980	1990	1992	1993	1994	1995	1996	1997	1998
1. SUMMARY DEBT DATA										
TOTAL DEBT STOCKS (EDT)	..	..	**135.3**	**142.1**	**147.8**	**176.3**	**214.3**	**202.1**	**207.0**	**243.7**
Long-term debt (LDOD)	..	..	**130.6**	**136.1**	**140.8**	**166.4**	**185.0**	**196.0**	**200.1**	**237.3**
Public and publicly guaranteed	..	..	130.6	136.1	140.8	166.4	185.0	196.0	200.1	237.3
Private nonguaranteed	..	..	0.0	0.0	0.0	0.0	0.0	0.0	0.0	0.0
Use of IMF credit	**0.0**	**0.0**	**0.0**	**0.0**	**0.0**	**0.0**	**0.0**	**0.0**	**0.0**	**0.0**
Short-term debt	..	..	**4.7**	**6.0**	**7.0**	**9.9**	**29.3**	**6.1**	**6.9**	**6.4**
of which interest arrears on LDOD	..	..	2.3	2.0	3.0	3.9	4.7	5.0	3.9	3.5
Official creditors	..	..	1.9	1.6	2.6	3.4	4.0	4.2	3.3	3.4
Private creditors	..	..	0.4	0.4	0.4	0.5	0.7	0.8	0.5	0.1
Memo: principal arrears on LDOD	..	..	11.1	10.6	15.0	17.0	20.0	21.4	19.6	20.5
Official creditors	..	..	10.4	9.8	13.9	15.7	18.5	19.6	17.4	18.3
Private creditors	..	..	0.7	0.8	1.1	1.3	1.6	1.8	2.2	2.2
Memo: export credits	..	..	11.0	13.0	13.0	13.0	19.0	27.0	27.0	35.0
TOTAL DEBT FLOWS										
Disbursements	..	..	**12.1**	**18.2**	**10.3**	**28.5**	**21.4**	**23.6**	**21.6**	**46.6**
Long-term debt	..	..	12.1	18.2	10.3	28.5	21.4	23.6	21.6	46.6
IMF purchases	0.0	0.0	0.0	0.0	0.0	0.0	0.0	0.0	0.0	0.0
Principal repayments	..	..	**3.7**	**8.1**	**4.4**	**6.0**	**5.5**	**5.0**	**9.7**	**15.4**
Long-term debt	..	..	3.7	8.1	4.4	6.0	5.5	5.0	9.7	15.4
IMF repurchases	0.0	0.0	0.0	0.0	0.0	0.0	0.0	0.0	0.0	0.0
Net flows on debt	..	..	**10.7**	**11.6**	**5.9**	**24.5**	**34.6**	**-5.0**	**13.9**	**31.0**
of which short-term debt	..	..	2.4	1.6	0.0	2.0	18.7	-23.6	2.0	-0.1
Interest payments (INT)	..	..	**2.0**	**3.1**	**2.1**	**3.2**	**4.1**	**2.8**	**4.2**	**3.7**
Long-term debt	..	..	1.9	2.9	1.9	3.0	3.4	2.6	4.1	3.6
IMF charges	0.0	0.0	0.0	0.0	0.0	0.0	0.0	0.0	0.0	0.0
Short-term debt	..	..	0.1	0.1	0.1	0.2	0.8	0.3	0.1	0.2
Net transfers on debt	..	..	**8.7**	**8.6**	**3.8**	**21.3**	**30.4**	**-7.8**	**9.7**	**27.3**
Total debt service paid (TDS)	..	..	**5.7**	**11.2**	**6.5**	**9.2**	**9.6**	**7.8**	**13.9**	**19.2**
Long-term debt	..	..	5.6	11.1	6.4	9.0	8.9	7.6	13.8	19.0
IMF repurchases and charges	0.0	0.0	0.0	0.0	0.0	0.0	0.0	0.0	0.0	0.0
Short-term debt (interest only)	..	..	0.1	0.1	0.1	0.2	0.8	0.3	0.1	0.2
2. AGGREGATE NET RESOURCE FLOWS AND NET TRANSFERS (LONG-TERM)										
NET RESOURCE FLOWS	..	..	**85.9**	**72.3**	**66.7**	**87.3**	**87.1**	**90.3**	**88.0**	**106.6**
Net flow of long-term debt (ex. IMF)	..	..	8.3	10.0	5.9	22.5	15.9	18.6	11.9	31.1
Foreign direct investment (net)	..	..	0.0	-1.0	3.0	2.0	10.0	12.0	13.0	14.0
Portfolio equity flows	..	..	0.0	0.0	0.0	0.0	0.0	0.0	0.0	0.0
Grants (excluding technical coop.)	..	..	77.5	63.2	57.8	62.8	61.3	59.8	63.0	61.5
Memo: technical coop. grants	..	..	20.4	45.3	42.6	37.6	40.4	37.3	33.8	35.6
official net resource flows	..	..	86.0	73.4	63.7	85.3	72.9	73.0	74.7	93.8
private net resource flows	..	..	-0.1	-1.1	3.0	2.0	14.2	17.3	13.3	12.8
NET TRANSFERS	..	..	**84.0**	**69.3**	**64.8**	**84.3**	**83.7**	**87.8**	**83.8**	**103.0**
Interest on long-term debt	..	..	1.9	2.9	1.9	3.0	3.4	2.6	4.1	3.6
Profit remittances on FDI	..	..	0.0	0.0	0.0	0.0	0.0	0.0	0.0	0.0
Memo: official net transfers	..	..	84.1	70.5	61.8	82.3	69.5	70.8	71.7	90.8
private net transfers	..	..	-0.1	-1.2	3.0	2.0	14.2	17.0	12.1	12.2
3. MAJOR ECONOMIC AGGREGATES										
Gross national product (GNP)	..	..	340.5	394.9	359.5	407.3	487.4	485.3	477.4	489.6
Exports of goods & services (XGS)	..	..	119.3	130.3	127.8	148.5	191.4	203.1	213.7	193.6
of which workers remittances	..	..	56.0	74.0	73.8	83.1	103.9	98.7	74.2	71.9
Imports of goods & services (MGS)	..	..	153.1	198.2	185.2	234.4	300.7	284.9	295.5	317.0
International reserves (RES)	..	..	77.0	75.8	57.7	42.1	57.3	51.8	41.8	37.1
Current account balance	..	..	-3.8	-12.1	-23.9	-45.7	-61.6	-35.0	-29.7	-58.0
4. DEBT INDICATORS										
EDT / XGS (%)	..	..	113.4	109.0	115.7	118.7	112.0	99.5	96.9	125.9
EDT / GNP (%)	..	..	39.7	36.0	41.1	43.3	44.0	41.6	43.4	49.8
TDS / XGS (%)	..	..	4.8	8.6	5.1	6.2	5.0	3.8	6.5	9.9
INT / XGS (%)	..	..	1.7	2.4	1.6	2.2	2.1	1.4	2.0	1.9
INT / GNP (%)	..	..	0.6	0.8	0.6	0.8	0.8	0.6	0.9	0.8
RES / EDT (%)	..	..	56.9	53.3	39.0	23.9	26.8	25.6	20.2	15.2
RES / MGS (months)	..	..	6.0	4.6	3.7	2.2	2.3	2.2	1.7	1.4
Short-term / EDT (%)	..	..	3.5	4.2	4.7	5.6	13.7	3.0	3.3	2.6
Concessional / EDT (%)	..	..	70.5	73.5	72.7	75.6	68.6	76.3	78.4	79.4
Multilateral / EDT (%)	..	..	64.3	68.2	69.6	74.5	67.2	72.7	72.5	73.8

CAPE VERDE

(US$ million, unless otherwise indicated)

	1970	1980	1990	1992	1993	1994	1995	1996	1997	1998
5. LONG-TERM DEBT										
DEBT OUTSTANDING (LDOD)	..	..	**130.6**	**136.1**	**140.8**	**166.4**	**185.0**	**196.0**	**200.1**	**237.3**
Public and publicly guaranteed	..	..	**130.6**	**136.1**	**140.8**	**166.4**	**185.0**	**196.0**	**200.1**	**237.3**
Official creditors	..	..	128.1	133.9	138.7	164.3	178.6	184.3	188.1	226.5
Multilateral	..	..	87.0	96.9	102.9	131.4	143.9	147.0	150.0	179.8
Concessional	..	..	68.4	79.1	82.7	111.0	122.6	127.0	133.7	164.2
Bilateral	..	..	41.2	37.0	35.8	32.9	34.6	37.3	38.1	46.7
Concessional	..	..	27.0	25.4	24.7	22.3	24.5	27.1	28.6	29.4
Private creditors	..	..	2.5	2.2	2.2	2.2	6.4	11.8	12.0	10.8
Bonds	..	..	0.0	0.0	0.0	0.0	0.0	0.0	0.0	0.0
Commercial banks	..	..	0.0	0.0	0.0	0.0	0.0	0.0	0.0	0.0
Other private	..	..	2.5	2.2	2.2	2.2	6.4	11.8	12.0	10.8
Private nonguaranteed	..	..	**0.0**	**0.0**	**0.0**	**0.0**	**0.0**	**0.0**	**0.0**	**0.0**
Bonds	..	..	0.0	0.0	0.0	0.0	0.0	0.0	0.0	0.0
Commercial banks	..	..	0.0	0.0	0.0	0.0	0.0	0.0	0.0	0.0
Memo:										
IBRD	0.0	0.0	0.0	0.0	0.0	0.0	0.0	0.0	0.0	0.0
IDA	0.0	0.0	13.6	17.1	20.6	26.6	33.0	39.3	45.1	70.2
DISBURSEMENTS	..	..	**12.1**	**18.2**	**10.3**	**28.5**	**21.4**	**23.6**	**21.6**	**46.6**
Public and publicly guaranteed	..	..	**12.1**	**18.2**	**10.3**	**28.5**	**21.4**	**23.6**	**21.6**	**46.6**
Official creditors	..	..	12.1	18.2	10.3	28.5	17.1	18.3	20.1	46.6
Multilateral	..	..	6.0	17.0	10.3	28.0	14.9	15.4	19.5	30.3
Concessional	..	..	6.0	13.1	5.6	27.1	13.7	14.5	19.2	30.3
Bilateral	..	..	6.1	1.2	0.0	0.6	2.2	2.9	0.7	16.3
Concessional	..	..	0.7	1.2	0.0	0.6	2.2	2.9	0.7	2.2
Private creditors	..	..	0.0	0.0	0.0	0.0	4.2	5.3	1.5	0.0
Bonds	..	..	0.0	0.0	0.0	0.0	0.0	0.0	0.0	0.0
Commercial banks	..	..	0.0	0.0	0.0	0.0	0.0	0.0	0.0	0.0
Other private	..	..	0.0	0.0	0.0	0.0	4.2	5.3	1.5	0.0
Private nonguaranteed	..	..	**0.0**	**0.0**	**0.0**	**0.0**	**0.0**	**0.0**	**0.0**	**0.0**
Bonds	..	..	0.0	0.0	0.0	0.0	0.0	0.0	0.0	0.0
Commercial banks	..	..	0.0	0.0	0.0	0.0	0.0	0.0	0.0	0.0
Memo:										
IBRD	0.0	0.0	0.0	0.0	0.0	0.0	0.0	0.0	0.0	0.0
IDA	0.0	0.0	2.0	1.2	3.5	5.0	6.0	7.6	8.3	22.7
PRINCIPAL REPAYMENTS	..	..	**3.7**	**8.1**	**4.4**	**6.0**	**5.5**	**5.0**	**9.7**	**15.4**
Public and publicly guaranteed	..	..	**3.7**	**8.1**	**4.4**	**6.0**	**5.5**	**5.0**	**9.7**	**15.4**
Official creditors	..	..	3.6	8.0	4.4	6.0	5.5	5.0	8.5	14.2
Multilateral	..	..	2.5	5.1	3.5	5.3	4.8	4.8	7.0	6.9
Concessional	..	..	1.0	3.9	1.9	3.0	3.5	3.1	5.1	5.3
Bilateral	..	..	1.1	2.9	0.9	0.7	0.7	0.2	1.4	7.4
Concessional	..	..	0.2	1.6	0.5	0.3	0.2	0.2	0.8	1.1
Private creditors	..	..	0.1	0.1	0.0	0.0	0.0	0.0	1.2	1.2
Bonds	..	..	0.0	0.0	0.0	0.0	0.0	0.0	0.0	0.0
Commercial banks	..	..	0.0	0.0	0.0	0.0	0.0	0.0	0.0	0.0
Other private	..	..	0.1	0.1	0.0	0.0	0.0	0.0	1.2	1.2
Private nonguaranteed	..	..	**0.0**	**0.0**	**0.0**	**0.0**	**0.0**	**0.0**	**0.0**	**0.0**
Bonds	..	..	0.0	0.0	0.0	0.0	0.0	0.0	0.0	0.0
Commercial banks	..	..	0.0	0.0	0.0	0.0	0.0	0.0	0.0	0.0
Memo:										
IBRD	0.0	0.0	0.0	0.0	0.0	0.0	0.0	0.0	0.0	0.0
IDA	0.0	0.0	0.0	0.0	0.1	0.1	0.1	0.1	0.1	0.2
NET FLOWS ON DEBT	..	..	**8.3**	**10.0**	**5.9**	**22.5**	**15.9**	**18.6**	**11.9**	**31.1**
Public and publicly guaranteed	..	..	**8.3**	**10.0**	**5.9**	**22.5**	**15.9**	**18.6**	**11.9**	**31.1**
Official creditors	..	..	8.5	10.2	5.9	22.5	11.6	13.2	11.7	32.3
Multilateral	..	..	3.5	11.9	6.8	22.7	10.1	10.6	12.4	23.4
Concessional	..	..	5.1	9.2	3.7	24.1	10.2	11.5	14.1	25.0
Bilateral	..	..	4.9	-1.7	-0.9	-0.2	1.6	2.7	-0.7	8.9
Concessional	..	..	0.6	-0.4	-0.5	0.2	2.0	2.7	-0.1	1.1
Private creditors	..	..	-0.1	-0.1	0.0	0.0	4.2	5.3	0.3	-1.2
Bonds	..	..	0.0	0.0	0.0	0.0	0.0	0.0	0.0	0.0
Commercial banks	..	..	0.0	0.0	0.0	0.0	0.0	0.0	0.0	0.0
Other private	..	..	-0.1	-0.1	0.0	0.0	4.2	5.3	0.3	-1.2
Private nonguaranteed	..	..	**0.0**	**0.0**	**0.0**	**0.0**	**0.0**	**0.0**	**0.0**	**0.0**
Bonds	..	..	0.0	0.0	0.0	0.0	0.0	0.0	0.0	0.0
Commercial banks	..	..	0.0	0.0	0.0	0.0	0.0	0.0	0.0	0.0
Memo:										
IBRD	0.0	0.0	0.0	0.0	0.0	0.0	0.0	0.0	0.0	0.0
IDA	0.0	0.0	2.0	1.2	3.4	4.9	5.9	7.4	8.2	22.5

CAPE VERDE

(US$ million, unless otherwise indicated)

	1970	1980	1990	1992	1993	1994	1995	1996	1997	1998
INTEREST PAYMENTS (LINT)	..	..	**1.9**	**2.9**	**1.9**	**3.0**	**3.4**	**2.6**	**4.1**	**3.6**
Public and publicly guaranteed	..	..	**1.9**	**2.9**	**1.9**	**3.0**	**3.4**	**2.6**	**4.1**	**3.6**
Official creditors	..	..	1.9	2.9	1.9	3.0	3.4	2.2	3.0	3.0
Multilateral	..	..	1.2	1.9	1.7	2.8	3.3	2.0	2.1	2.4
Concessional	..	..	0.5	0.9	0.7	2.0	2.3	1.1	1.4	1.8
Bilateral	..	..	0.7	1.0	0.2	0.2	0.1	0.2	0.8	0.6
Concessional	..	..	0.0	0.1	0.1	0.1	0.1	0.2	0.4	0.5
Private creditors	..	..	0.0	0.1	0.0	0.0	0.0	0.3	1.2	0.6
Bonds	..	..	0.0	0.0	0.0	0.0	0.0	0.0	0.0	0.0
Commercial banks	..	..	0.0	0.0	0.0	0.0	0.0	0.0	0.0	0.0
Other private	..	..	0.0	0.1	0.0	0.0	0.0	0.3	1.2	0.6
Private nonguaranteed	..	..	**0.0**	**0.0**	**0.0**	**0.0**	**0.0**	**0.0**	**0.0**	**0.0**
Bonds	..	..	0.0	0.0	0.0	0.0	0.0	0.0	0.0	0.0
Commercial banks	..	..	0.0	0.0	0.0	0.0	0.0	0.0	0.0	0.0
Memo:										
IBRD	0.0	0.0	0.0	0.0	0.0	0.0	0.0	0.0	0.0	0.0
IDA	0.0	0.0	0.1	0.1	0.1	0.2	0.2	0.2	0.3	0.4
NET TRANSFERS ON DEBT	..	..	**6.5**	**7.1**	**3.9**	**19.5**	**12.5**	**16.0**	**7.8**	**27.6**
Public and publicly guaranteed	..	..	**6.5**	**7.1**	**3.9**	**19.5**	**12.5**	**16.0**	**7.8**	**27.6**
Official creditors	..	..	6.6	7.3	3.9	19.5	8.3	11.0	8.7	29.3
Multilateral	..	..	2.3	10.0	5.0	19.8	6.8	8.5	10.3	21.0
Concessional	..	..	4.6	8.4	3.0	22.2	7.9	10.4	12.7	23.2
Bilateral	..	..	4.3	-2.7	-1.1	-0.3	1.5	2.5	-1.6	8.3
Concessional	..	..	0.6	-0.5	-0.6	0.1	2.0	2.5	-0.5	0.6
Private creditors	..	..	-0.1	-0.2	0.0	0.0	4.2	5.0	-0.9	-1.8
Bonds	..	..	0.0	0.0	0.0	0.0	0.0	0.0	0.0	0.0
Commercial banks	..	..	0.0	0.0	0.0	0.0	0.0	0.0	0.0	0.0
Other private	..	..	-0.1	-0.2	0.0	0.0	4.2	5.0	-0.9	-1.8
Private nonguaranteed	..	..	**0.0**	**0.0**	**0.0**	**0.0**	**0.0**	**0.0**	**0.0**	**0.0**
Bonds	..	..	0.0	0.0	0.0	0.0	0.0	0.0	0.0	0.0
Commercial banks	..	..	0.0	0.0	0.0	0.0	0.0	0.0	0.0	0.0
Memo:										
IBRD	0.0	0.0	0.0	0.0	0.0	0.0	0.0	0.0	0.0	0.0
IDA	0.0	0.0	1.9	1.1	3.3	4.7	5.7	7.2	7.9	22.1
DEBT SERVICE (LTDS)	..	..	**5.6**	**11.1**	**6.4**	**9.0**	**8.9**	**7.6**	**13.8**	**19.0**
Public and publicly guaranteed	..	..	**5.6**	**11.1**	**6.4**	**9.0**	**8.9**	**7.6**	**13.8**	**19.0**
Official creditors	..	..	5.5	10.9	6.4	9.0	8.9	7.3	11.4	17.2
Multilateral	..	..	3.7	7.0	5.3	8.1	8.1	6.9	9.2	9.3
Concessional	..	..	1.4	4.7	2.7	5.0	5.8	4.2	6.5	7.1
Bilateral	..	..	1.8	3.9	1.1	0.9	0.7	0.4	2.3	8.0
Concessional	..	..	0.2	1.7	0.6	0.4	0.3	0.4	1.2	1.7
Private creditors	..	..	0.1	0.2	0.0	0.0	0.0	0.3	2.4	1.8
Bonds	..	..	0.0	0.0	0.0	0.0	0.0	0.0	0.0	0.0
Commercial banks	..	..	0.0	0.0	0.0	0.0	0.0	0.0	0.0	0.0
Other private	..	..	0.1	0.2	0.0	0.0	0.0	0.3	2.4	1.8
Private nonguaranteed	..	..	**0.0**	**0.0**	**0.0**	**0.0**	**0.0**	**0.0**	**0.0**	**0.0**
Bonds	..	..	0.0	0.0	0.0	0.0	0.0	0.0	0.0	0.0
Commercial banks	..	..	0.0	0.0	0.0	0.0	0.0	0.0	0.0	0.0
Memo:										
IBRD	0.0	0.0	0.0	0.0	0.0	0.0	0.0	0.0	0.0	0.0
IDA	0.0	0.0	0.1	0.1	0.2	0.2	0.4	0.4	0.4	0.6
UNDISBURSED DEBT	..	..	**99.9**	**124.2**	**161.3**	**175.8**	**168.7**	**132.9**	**116.4**	**150.9**
Official creditors	..	..	99.9	124.2	161.3	163.8	160.9	130.5	115.5	150.0
Private creditors	..	..	0.0	0.0	0.0	12.0	7.8	2.4	0.9	0.9
Memorandum items										
Concessional LDOD	..	..	95.5	104.4	107.4	133.3	147.1	154.2	162.3	193.6
Variable rate LDOD	..	..	0.0	0.0	0.0	0.0	0.0	0.0	0.0	0.0
Public sector LDOD	..	..	130.6	136.1	140.8	166.4	185.0	196.0	200.1	237.3
Private sector LDOD	..	..	0.0	0.0	0.0	0.0	0.0	0.0	0.0	0.0

6. CURRENCY COMPOSITION OF LONG-TERM DEBT (PERCENT)

	1970	1980	1990	1992	1993	1994	1995	1996	1997	1998
Deutsche mark	..	..	0.0	0.0	0.0	0.0	0.0	0.0	0.0	0.0
French franc	..	..	0.0	0.0	0.0	0.0	0.0	0.0	0.0	0.0
Japanese yen	..	..	0.0	0.0	0.0	0.0	0.0	0.0	0.0	0.0
Pound sterling	..	..	0.0	0.0	0.0	0.0	0.0	0.0	0.0	0.0
Swiss franc	..	..	0.0	0.0	0.0	0.0	0.0	0.0	0.0	0.0
U.S.dollars	..	..	38.1	35.1	35.5	33.2	35.4	39.9	43.6	50.3
Multiple currency	..	..	15.9	12.7	11.4	8.9	7.6	6.2	5.8	5.0
Special drawing rights	..	..	0.1	0.8	1.8	3.4	3.7	3.8	4.1	4.0
All other currencies	..	..	45.9	51.4	51.3	54.5	53.3	50.1	46.5	40.7

CAPE VERDE

(US$ million, unless otherwise indicated)

	1970	1980	1990	1992	1993	1994	1995	1996	1997	1998
7. DEBT RESTRUCTURINGS										
Total amount rescheduled	..	..	0.0	0.0	0.0	0.0	0.0	0.0	2.6	0.0
Debt stock rescheduled	..	..	0.0	0.0	0.0	0.0	0.0	0.0	0.0	0.0
Principal rescheduled	..	..	0.0	0.0	0.0	0.0	0.0	0.0	1.9	0.0
Official	..	..	0.0	0.0	0.0	0.0	0.0	0.0	1.9	0.0
Private	..	..	0.0	0.0	0.0	0.0	0.0	0.0	0.0	0.0
Interest rescheduled	..	..	0.0	0.0	0.0	0.0	0.0	0.0	0.7	0.0
Official	..	..	0.0	0.0	0.0	0.0	0.0	0.0	0.7	0.0
Private	..	..	0.0	0.0	0.0	0.0	0.0	0.0	0.0	0.0
Debt forgiven	..	..	8.2	0.0	0.0	0.0	0.0	0.0	0.0	0.4
Memo: interest forgiven	..	..	0.8	0.0	0.0	0.0	0.0	0.0	0.0	0.0
Debt stock reduction	..	..	0.0	0.0	0.0	0.0	0.0	0.0	0.0	0.0
of which debt buyback	..	..	0.0	0.0	0.0	0.0	0.0	0.0	0.0	0.0
8. DEBT STOCK-FLOW RECONCILIATION										
Total change in debt stocks	..	..	7.6	7.2	5.7	28.5	38.0	-12.2	4.9	36.7
Net flows on debt	..	..	10.7	11.6	5.9	24.5	34.6	-5.0	13.9	31.0
Net change in interest arrears	..	..	-0.2	-0.3	1.0	0.8	0.8	0.3	-1.2	-0.4
Interest capitalized	..	..	0.0	0.0	0.0	0.0	0.0	0.0	0.7	0.0
Debt forgiveness or reduction	..	..	-8.2	0.0	0.0	0.0	0.0	0.0	0.0	-0.4
Cross-currency valuation	..	..	3.9	-2.8	-1.1	4.5	2.4	-3.0	-5.9	4.1
Residual	..	..	1.3	-1.4	0.0	-1.4	0.2	-4.5	-2.7	2.4
9. AVERAGE TERMS OF NEW COMMITMENTS										
ALL CREDITORS										
Interest (%)	..	..	1.5	2.0	2.0	3.2	0.8	0.8	0.7	1.4
Maturity (years)	..	..	42.6	33.1	30.9	21.8	39.8	39.8	50.1	23.4
Grace period (years)	..	..	9.1	7.5	8.0	5.0	10.3	10.3	10.6	5.7
Grant element (%)	..	..	73.0	63.1	62.4	45.2	80.6	80.6	83.5	50.3
Official creditors										
Interest (%)	..	..	1.5	2.0	2.0	2.5	0.8	0.8	0.7	1.4
Maturity (years)	..	..	42.6	33.1	30.9	25.9	39.8	39.8	50.1	23.4
Grace period (years)	..	..	9.1	7.5	8.0	6.1	10.3	10.3	10.6	5.7
Grant element (%)	..	..	73.0	63.1	62.4	54.2	80.6	80.6	83.5	50.3
Private creditors										
Interest (%)	..	..	0.0	0.0	0.0	5.0	0.0	0.0	0.0	0.0
Maturity (years)	..	..	0.0	0.0	0.0	12.0	0.0	0.0	0.0	0.0
Grace period (years)	..	..	0.0	0.0	0.0	2.5	0.0	0.0	0.0	0.0
Grant element (%)	..	..	0.0	0.0	0.0	23.4	0.0	0.0	0.0	0.0
Memorandum items										
Commitments	..	..	35.9	49.0	48.6	41.3	11.5	11.4	10.3	85.5
Official creditors	..	..	35.9	49.0	48.6	29.3	11.5	11.4	10.3	85.5
Private creditors	..	..	0.0	0.0	0.0	12.0	0.0	0.0	0.0	0.0

10. CONTRACTUAL OBLIGATIONS ON OUTSTANDING LONG-TERM DEBT

	1999	2000	2001	2002	2003	2004	2005	2006	2007	2008
TOTAL										
Disbursements	42.4	41.2	26.8	16.7	10.7	6.3	3.8	1.1	0.5	0.1
Principal	22.2	13.4	13.1	11.8	12.9	13.3	13.3	13.5	12.0	12.9
Interest	3.5	3.9	4.1	4.2	4.1	3.9	3.7	3.4	3.1	2.8
Official creditors										
Disbursements	41.7	40.9	26.8	16.7	10.7	6.3	3.8	1.1	0.5	0.1
Principal	21.0	12.2	11.9	10.6	11.7	12.1	12.1	12.3	12.0	12.9
Interest	3.0	3.5	3.8	3.9	3.9	3.7	3.5	3.3	3.1	2.8
Bilateral creditors										
Disbursements	7.3	9.1	6.0	4.0	2.4	1.4	0.9	0.5	0.2	0.1
Principal	13.2	4.0	3.8	2.9	3.6	3.6	3.6	3.6	3.2	3.2
Interest	0.6	0.8	0.9	1.0	1.0	0.9	0.8	0.7	0.6	0.5
Multilateral creditors										
Disbursements	34.4	31.9	20.8	12.8	8.3	4.9	2.9	0.6	0.3	0.0
Principal	7.8	8.2	8.1	7.6	8.1	8.5	8.5	8.7	8.9	9.7
Interest	2.4	2.7	2.8	2.9	2.9	2.8	2.7	2.6	2.4	2.2
Private creditors										
Disbursements	0.7	0.3	0.0	0.0	0.0	0.0	0.0	0.0	0.0	0.0
Principal	1.2	1.2	1.2	1.2	1.2	1.2	1.2	1.2	0.0	0.0
Interest	0.5	0.4	0.3	0.3	0.2	0.2	0.1	0.0	0.0	0.0
Commercial banks										
Disbursements	0.0	0.0	0.0	0.0	0.0	0.0	0.0	0.0	0.0	0.0
Principal	0.0	0.0	0.0	0.0	0.0	0.0	0.0	0.0	0.0	0.0
Interest	0.0	0.0	0.0	0.0	0.0	0.0	0.0	0.0	0.0	0.0
Other private										
Disbursements	0.7	0.3	0.0	0.0	0.0	0.0	0.0	0.0	0.0	0.0
Principal	1.2	1.2	1.2	1.2	1.2	1.2	1.2	1.2	0.0	0.0
Interest	0.5	0.4	0.3	0.3	0.2	0.2	0.1	0.0	0.0	0.0

CENTRAL AFRICAN REPUBLIC

(US$ million, unless otherwise indicated)

	1970	1980	1990	1992	1993	1994	1995	1996	1997	1998
1. SUMMARY DEBT DATA										
TOTAL DEBT STOCKS (EDT)	**..**	**194.7**	**698.5**	**813.9**	**875.1**	**888.0**	**946.0**	**932.8**	**883.0**	**921.3**
Long-term debt (LDOD)	**24.1**	**146.5**	**624.1**	**729.6**	**773.2**	**802.4**	**853.9**	**850.4**	**801.5**	**829.8**
Public and publicly guaranteed	24.1	146.5	624.1	729.6	773.2	802.4	853.9	850.4	801.5	829.8
Private nonguaranteed	0.0	0.0	0.0	0.0	0.0	0.0	0.0	0.0	0.0	0.0
Use of IMF credit	**0.0**	**23.5**	**36.7**	**30.4**	**28.8**	**41.4**	**34.9**	**27.6**	**18.6**	**17.6**
Short-term debt	**..**	**24.6**	**37.7**	**53.9**	**73.1**	**44.3**	**57.2**	**54.8**	**62.9**	**73.9**
of which interest arrears on LDOD	..	10.6	15.0	27.9	39.1	25.3	35.7	38.5	44.9	59.5
Official creditors	..	1.7	13.1	24.6	35.3	23.7	31.7	37.2	43.6	58.6
Private creditors	..	8.8	1.9	3.3	3.7	1.5	4.0	1.3	1.2	0.8
Memo: principal arrears on LDOD	..	43.5	23.2	50.7	70.9	58.1	74.2	85.0	94.9	94.8
Official creditors	..	16.9	19.6	43.4	60.2	51.2	60.6	70.8	81.3	84.2
Private creditors	..	26.7	3.6	7.3	10.7	7.0	13.6	14.2	13.6	10.6
Memo: export credits	..	0.0	63.0	52.0	52.0	43.0	44.0	36.0	26.0	55.0
TOTAL DEBT FLOWS										
Disbursements	**1.7**	**39.8**	**121.1**	**45.9**	**49.7**	**59.3**	**32.6**	**26.9**	**6.4**	**14.6**
Long-term debt	1.7	25.2	112.8	45.9	49.7	44.0	32.6	26.9	6.4	3.4
IMF purchases	0.0	14.7	8.3	0.0	0.0	15.3	0.0	0.0	0.0	11.2
Principal repayments	**2.4**	**6.7**	**17.4**	**6.8**	**3.3**	**12.4**	**10.0**	**8.0**	**11.6**	**22.4**
Long-term debt	2.4	1.0	7.6	5.1	1.7	7.7	2.6	1.8	4.1	9.4
IMF repurchases	0.0	5.7	9.8	1.7	1.6	4.8	7.4	6.2	7.5	13.0
Net flows on debt	**-0.7**	**31.1**	**106.6**	**39.4**	**54.4**	**31.8**	**25.1**	**13.8**	**-3.5**	**-11.3**
of which short-term debt	..	-2.0	2.9	0.3	8.0	-15.0	2.4	-5.1	1.7	-3.5
Interest payments (INT)	**..**	**3.3**	**11.8**	**8.7**	**5.9**	**10.7**	**5.7**	**4.9**	**4.0**	**8.0**
Long-term debt	0.7	0.4	9.0	6.6	3.5	8.1	3.5	3.4	2.4	6.7
IMF charges	0.0	0.8	1.2	0.3	0.2	0.7	1.0	0.8	0.7	0.4
Short-term debt	..	2.1	1.6	1.8	2.2	2.0	1.2	0.7	0.9	0.9
Net transfers on debt	**..**	**27.8**	**94.9**	**30.7**	**48.4**	**21.1**	**19.3**	**8.9**	**-7.5**	**-19.3**
Total debt service paid (TDS)	**..**	**10.0**	**29.1**	**15.5**	**9.2**	**23.2**	**15.7**	**12.9**	**15.6**	**30.4**
Long-term debt	3.1	1.4	16.6	11.7	5.3	15.8	6.1	5.2	6.5	16.1
IMF repurchases and charges	0.0	6.5	11.0	1.9	1.8	5.4	8.4	7.0	8.2	13.4
Short-term debt (interest only)	..	2.1	1.6	1.8	2.2	2.0	1.2	0.7	0.9	0.9
2. AGGREGATE NET RESOURCE FLOWS AND NET TRANSFERS (LONG-TERM)										
NET RESOURCE FLOWS	**6.8**	**85.1**	**192.4**	**121.5**	**128.4**	**137.8**	**139.6**	**149.2**	**81.0**	**101.3**
Net flow of long-term debt (ex. IMF)	-0.7	24.1	105.2	40.8	47.9	36.3	30.0	25.1	2.3	-6.0
Foreign direct investment (net)	1.2	5.3	1.0	-11.0	-10.0	4.0	3.0	5.0	5.5	5.0
Portfolio equity flows	0.0	0.0	0.0	0.0	0.0	0.0	0.0	0.0	0.0	0.0
Grants (excluding technical coop.)	6.4	55.7	86.2	91.7	90.5	97.5	106.6	119.1	73.2	102.3
Memo: technical coop. grants	8.1	34.2	56.9	52.5	51.2	42.7	46.8	41.8	26.1	26.2
official net resource flows	6.8	80.7	192.0	133.1	138.4	134.0	136.6	144.2	75.5	96.3
private net resource flows	0.0	4.4	0.4	-11.6	-10.0	3.8	3.0	5.0	5.5	5.0
NET TRANSFERS	**4.7**	**84.7**	**181.4**	**114.9**	**124.9**	**129.2**	**135.5**	**144.8**	**77.3**	**93.6**
Interest on long-term debt	0.7	0.4	9.0	6.6	3.5	8.1	3.5	3.4	2.4	6.7
Profit remittances on FDI	1.4	0.0	2.1	0.0	0.0	0.5	0.6	1.0	1.3	1.0
Memo: official net transfers	6.5	80.4	183.9	126.5	134.9	126.0	133.1	140.8	73.1	89.6
private net transfers	-1.8	4.3	-2.5	-11.6	-10.0	3.2	2.4	4.0	4.2	4.0
3. MAJOR ECONOMIC AGGREGATES										
Gross national product (GNP)	186.4	799.6	1,465.1	1,418.7	1,280.1	832.2	1,100.9	1,049.0	989.4	1,037.8
Exports of goods & services (XGS)	..	205.4	220.4	167.4	186.2	179.0	200.6	162.9	171.2	145.5
of which workers remittances	..	0.0	0.0	0.0	..	..	..	..	..	..
Imports of goods & services (MGS)	..	329.2	432.5	363.9	313.2	267.1	323.5	240.8	258.1	273.4
International reserves (RES)	1.4	61.7	122.9	103.8	116.3	214.3	237.9	236.3	181.8	145.7
Current account balance	..	-43.1	-89.1	-83.1	-13.0	-24.7	-61.9	-79.4	-94.2	-89.2
4. DEBT INDICATORS										
EDT / XGS (%)	..	94.8	317.0	486.2	470.0	496.0	471.5	572.8	515.9	633.4
EDT / GNP (%)	..	24.4	47.7	57.4	68.4	106.7	85.9	88.9	89.3	88.8
TDS / XGS (%)	..	4.9	13.2	9.3	4.9	13.0	7.8	7.9	9.1	20.9
INT / XGS (%)	..	1.6	5.4	5.2	3.2	6.0	2.8	3.0	2.3	5.5
INT / GNP (%)	..	0.4	0.8	0.6	0.5	1.3	0.5	0.5	0.4	0.8
RES / EDT (%)	..	31.7	17.6	12.8	13.3	24.1	25.2	25.3	20.6	15.8
RES / MGS (months)	..	2.3	3.4	3.4	4.5	9.6	8.8	11.8	8.5	6.4
Short-term / EDT (%)	..	12.6	5.4	6.6	8.4	5.0	6.1	5.9	7.1	8.0
Concessional / EDT (%)	..	30.1	73.1	77.2	77.0	81.4	80.9	82.3	82.0	82.1
Multilateral / EDT (%)	..	27.4	65.2	62.1	61.1	66.8	67.3	69.2	68.5	67.7

CENTRAL AFRICAN REPUBLIC

(US$ million, unless otherwise indicated)

	1970	1980	1990	1992	1993	1994	1995	1996	1997	1998
5. LONG-TERM DEBT										
DEBT OUTSTANDING (LDOD)	**24.1**	**146.5**	**624.1**	**729.6**	**773.2**	**802.4**	**853.9**	**850.4**	**801.5**	**829.8**
Public and publicly guaranteed	**24.1**	**146.5**	**624.1**	**729.6**	**773.2**	**802.4**	**853.9**	**850.4**	**801.5**	**829.8**
Official creditors	17.9	98.3	602.6	709.4	751.9	784.8	835.6	836.2	787.9	819.2
Multilateral	0.2	53.3	455.5	505.4	534.8	593.2	636.2	645.2	604.5	623.3
Concessional	0.2	41.6	429.4	485.6	515.6	580.0	622.3	631.1	590.6	611.0
Bilateral	17.7	44.9	147.0	204.0	217.1	191.6	199.4	191.0	183.4	195.9
Concessional	14.8	17.0	81.5	142.9	158.6	142.6	142.6	136.9	133.5	145.7
Private creditors	6.1	48.3	21.6	20.2	21.3	17.6	18.4	14.2	13.6	10.6
Bonds	0.0	0.0	0.0	0.0	0.0	0.0	0.0	0.0	0.0	0.0
Commercial banks	0.0	0.0	0.0	0.0	0.0	0.0	0.0	0.0	0.0	0.0
Other private	6.1	48.3	21.6	20.2	21.3	17.6	18.4	14.2	13.6	10.6
Private nonguaranteed	**0.0**	**0.0**	**0.0**	**0.0**	**0.0**	**0.0**	**0.0**	**0.0**	**0.0**	**0.0**
Bonds	0.0	0.0	0.0	0.0	0.0	0.0	0.0	0.0	0.0	0.0
Commercial banks	0.0	0.0	0.0	0.0	0.0	0.0	0.0	0.0	0.0	0.0
Memo:										
IBRD	0.0	0.0	0.0	0.0	0.0	0.0	0.0	0.0	0.0	0.0
IDA	0.2	28.8	265.1	299.5	323.2	377.2	414.0	422.0	403.0	413.3
DISBURSEMENTS	**1.7**	**25.2**	**112.8**	**45.9**	**49.7**	**44.0**	**32.6**	**26.9**	**6.4**	**3.4**
Public and publicly guaranteed	**1.7**	**25.2**	**112.8**	**45.9**	**49.7**	**44.0**	**32.6**	**26.9**	**6.4**	**3.4**
Official creditors	1.5	25.2	112.8	45.9	49.7	44.0	32.6	26.9	6.4	3.4
Multilateral	0.2	13.7	95.2	32.6	31.5	44.0	32.6	26.9	6.4	3.4
Concessional	0.2	13.5	93.6	32.1	31.5	44.0	32.0	26.9	5.3	3.4
Bilateral	1.3	11.5	17.6	13.3	18.1	0.0	0.0	0.0	0.0	0.0
Concessional	1.0	5.5	16.1	13.3	18.1	0.0	0.0	0.0	0.0	0.0
Private creditors	0.2	0.0	0.0	0.0	0.0	0.0	0.0	0.0	0.0	0.0
Bonds	0.0	0.0	0.0	0.0	0.0	0.0	0.0	0.0	0.0	0.0
Commercial banks	0.0	0.0	0.0	0.0	0.0	0.0	0.0	0.0	0.0	0.0
Other private	0.2	0.0	0.0	0.0	0.0	0.0	0.0	0.0	0.0	0.0
Private nonguaranteed	**0.0**	**0.0**	**0.0**	**0.0**	**0.0**	**0.0**	**0.0**	**0.0**	**0.0**	**0.0**
Bonds	0.0	0.0	0.0	0.0	0.0	0.0	0.0	0.0	0.0	0.0
Commercial banks	0.0	0.0	0.0	0.0	0.0	0.0	0.0	0.0	0.0	0.0
Memo:										
IBRD	0.0	0.0	0.0	0.0	0.0	0.0	0.0	0.0	0.0	0.0
IDA	0.2	10.3	70.4	20.7	23.7	40.1	29.8	22.9	4.6	0.2
PRINCIPAL REPAYMENTS	**2.4**	**1.0**	**7.6**	**5.1**	**1.7**	**7.7**	**2.6**	**1.8**	**4.1**	**9.4**
Public and publicly guaranteed	**2.4**	**1.0**	**7.6**	**5.1**	**1.7**	**7.7**	**2.6**	**1.8**	**4.1**	**9.4**
Official creditors	1.1	0.1	7.0	4.5	1.7	7.5	2.6	1.8	4.1	9.4
Multilateral	0.0	0.1	3.2	4.3	1.7	6.4	2.6	1.8	4.1	9.4
Concessional	0.0	0.1	1.8	2.1	1.2	4.3	2.2	1.7	4.0	7.2
Bilateral	1.1	0.0	3.8	0.2	0.0	1.0	0.0	0.0	0.0	0.1
Concessional	0.5	0.0	0.9	0.2	0.0	1.0	0.0	0.0	0.0	0.1
Private creditors	1.4	0.9	0.6	0.6	0.0	0.2	0.0	0.0	0.0	0.0
Bonds	0.0	0.0	0.0	0.0	0.0	0.0	0.0	0.0	0.0	0.0
Commercial banks	0.0	0.0	0.0	0.0	0.0	0.0	0.0	0.0	0.0	0.0
Other private	1.4	0.9	0.6	0.6	0.0	0.2	0.0	0.0	0.0	0.0
Private nonguaranteed	**0.0**	**0.0**	**0.0**	**0.0**	**0.0**	**0.0**	**0.0**	**0.0**	**0.0**	**0.0**
Bonds	0.0	0.0	0.0	0.0	0.0	0.0	0.0	0.0	0.0	0.0
Commercial banks	0.0	0.0	0.0	0.0	0.0	0.0	0.0	0.0	0.0	0.0
Memo:										
IBRD	0.0	0.0	0.0	0.0	0.0	0.0	0.0	0.0	0.0	0.0
IDA	0.0	0.1	0.5	0.8	1.0	1.2	1.3	1.4	1.3	3.6
NET FLOWS ON DEBT	**-0.7**	**24.1**	**105.2**	**40.8**	**47.9**	**36.3**	**30.0**	**25.1**	**2.3**	**-6.0**
Public and publicly guaranteed	**-0.7**	**24.1**	**105.2**	**40.8**	**47.9**	**36.3**	**30.0**	**25.1**	**2.3**	**-6.0**
Official creditors	0.4	25.0	105.8	41.4	47.9	36.5	30.0	25.1	2.3	-6.0
Multilateral	0.2	13.6	92.0	28.3	29.8	37.5	30.0	25.1	2.3	-6.0
Concessional	0.2	13.4	91.8	30.0	30.3	39.6	29.8	25.2	1.3	-3.8
Bilateral	0.2	11.4	13.8	13.0	18.1	-1.0	0.0	0.0	0.0	-0.1
Concessional	0.5	5.5	15.2	13.1	18.1	-1.0	0.0	0.0	0.0	-0.1
Private creditors	-1.2	-0.9	-0.6	-0.6	0.0	-0.2	0.0	0.0	0.0	0.0
Bonds	0.0	0.0	0.0	0.0	0.0	0.0	0.0	0.0	0.0	0.0
Commercial banks	0.0	0.0	0.0	0.0	0.0	0.0	0.0	0.0	0.0	0.0
Other private	-1.2	-0.9	-0.6	-0.6	0.0	-0.2	0.0	0.0	0.0	0.0
Private nonguaranteed	**0.0**	**0.0**	**0.0**	**0.0**	**0.0**	**0.0**	**0.0**	**0.0**	**0.0**	**0.0**
Bonds	0.0	0.0	0.0	0.0	0.0	0.0	0.0	0.0	0.0	0.0
Commercial banks	0.0	0.0	0.0	0.0	0.0	0.0	0.0	0.0	0.0	0.0
Memo:										
IBRD	0.0	0.0	0.0	0.0	0.0	0.0	0.0	0.0	0.0	0.0
IDA	0.2	10.2	69.9	19.9	22.7	38.9	28.5	21.5	3.3	-3.4

CENTRAL AFRICAN REPUBLIC

(US$ million, unless otherwise indicated)

	1970	1980	1990	1992	1993	1994	1995	1996	1997	1998
INTEREST PAYMENTS (LINT)	**0.7**	**0.4**	**9.0**	**6.6**	**3.5**	**8.1**	**3.5**	**3.4**	**2.4**	**6.7**
Public and publicly guaranteed	**0.7**	**0.4**	**9.0**	**6.6**	**3.5**	**8.1**	**3.5**	**3.4**	**2.4**	**6.7**
Official creditors	0.3	0.3	8.1	6.6	3.5	8.0	3.5	3.4	2.4	6.7
Multilateral	0.0	0.3	5.1	3.7	3.4	7.8	3.5	3.3	2.4	6.3
Concessional	0.0	0.2	2.8	2.9	2.4	6.3	3.4	3.2	2.4	5.2
Bilateral	0.3	0.0	3.1	2.9	0.1	0.1	0.0	0.1	0.0	0.4
Concessional	0.2	0.0	1.9	2.7	0.0	0.1	0.0	0.0	0.0	0.2
Private creditors	0.4	0.1	0.8	0.0	0.0	0.1	0.0	0.0	0.0	0.0
Bonds	0.0	0.0	0.0	0.0	0.0	0.0	0.0	0.0	0.0	0.0
Commercial banks	0.0	0.0	0.0	0.0	0.0	0.0	0.0	0.0	0.0	0.0
Other private	0.4	0.1	0.8	0.0	0.0	0.1	0.0	0.0	0.0	0.0
Private nonguaranteed	**0.0**	**0.0**	**0.0**	**0.0**	**0.0**	**0.0**	**0.0**	**0.0**	**0.0**	**0.0**
Bonds	0.0	0.0	0.0	0.0	0.0	0.0	0.0	0.0	0.0	0.0
Commercial banks	0.0	0.0	0.0	0.0	0.0	0.0	0.0	0.0	0.0	0.0
Memo:										
IBRD	0.0	0.0	0.0	0.0	0.0	0.0	0.0	0.0	0.0	0.0
IDA	0.0	0.2	1.5	2.1	2.1	2.8	2.9	2.9	1.9	4.1
NET TRANSFERS ON DEBT	**-1.4**	**23.8**	**96.3**	**34.2**	**44.4**	**28.2**	**26.5**	**21.7**	**-0.2**	**-12.7**
Public and publicly guaranteed	**-1.4**	**23.8**	**96.3**	**34.2**	**44.4**	**28.2**	**26.5**	**21.7**	**-0.2**	**-12.7**
Official creditors	0.1	24.7	97.6	34.8	44.4	28.6	26.5	21.7	-0.2	-12.7
Multilateral	0.2	13.3	86.9	24.6	26.4	29.7	26.5	21.8	-0.2	-12.3
Concessional	0.2	13.2	88.9	27.1	27.9	33.3	26.4	22.0	-1.1	-9.0
Bilateral	-0.1	11.4	10.7	10.2	18.0	-1.1	0.0	-0.1	0.0	-0.4
Concessional	0.3	5.5	13.4	10.4	18.1	-1.1	0.0	0.0	0.0	-0.2
Private creditors	-1.6	-0.9	-1.4	-0.6	0.0	-0.4	0.0	0.0	0.0	0.0
Bonds	0.0	0.0	0.0	0.0	0.0	0.0	0.0	0.0	0.0	0.0
Commercial banks	0.0	0.0	0.0	0.0	0.0	0.0	0.0	0.0	0.0	0.0
Other private	-1.6	-0.9	-1.4	-0.6	0.0	-0.4	0.0	0.0	0.0	0.0
Private nonguaranteed	**0.0**	**0.0**	**0.0**	**0.0**	**0.0**	**0.0**	**0.0**	**0.0**	**0.0**	**0.0**
Bonds	0.0	0.0	0.0	0.0	0.0	0.0	0.0	0.0	0.0	0.0
Commercial banks	0.0	0.0	0.0	0.0	0.0	0.0	0.0	0.0	0.0	0.0
Memo:										
IBRD	0.0	0.0	0.0	0.0	0.0	0.0	0.0	0.0	0.0	0.0
IDA	0.2	10.0	68.4	17.8	20.6	36.1	25.6	18.5	1.4	-7.5
DEBT SERVICE (LTDS)	**3.1**	**1.4**	**16.6**	**11.7**	**5.3**	**15.8**	**6.1**	**5.2**	**6.5**	**16.1**
Public and publicly guaranteed	**3.1**	**1.4**	**16.6**	**11.7**	**5.3**	**15.8**	**6.1**	**5.2**	**6.5**	**16.1**
Official creditors	1.4	0.5	15.2	11.2	5.3	15.4	6.1	5.2	6.5	16.1
Multilateral	0.0	0.4	8.3	8.0	5.1	14.3	6.1	5.1	6.5	15.7
Concessional	0.0	0.3	4.6	4.9	3.6	10.6	5.6	4.9	6.4	12.4
Bilateral	1.4	0.1	6.9	3.1	0.1	1.1	0.0	0.1	0.0	0.4
Concessional	0.6	0.0	2.7	2.9	0.0	1.1	0.0	0.0	0.0	0.2
Private creditors	1.8	0.9	1.4	0.6	0.0	0.4	0.0	0.0	0.0	0.0
Bonds	0.0	0.0	0.0	0.0	0.0	0.0	0.0	0.0	0.0	0.0
Commercial banks	0.0	0.0	0.0	0.0	0.0	0.0	0.0	0.0	0.0	0.0
Other private	1.8	0.9	1.4	0.6	0.0	0.4	0.0	0.0	0.0	0.0
Private nonguaranteed	**0.0**	**0.0**	**0.0**	**0.0**	**0.0**	**0.0**	**0.0**	**0.0**	**0.0**	**0.0**
Bonds	0.0	0.0	0.0	0.0	0.0	0.0	0.0	0.0	0.0	0.0
Commercial banks	0.0	0.0	0.0	0.0	0.0	0.0	0.0	0.0	0.0	0.0
Memo:										
IBRD	0.0	0.0	0.0	0.0	0.0	0.0	0.0	0.0	0.0	0.0
IDA	0.0	0.3	2.0	2.9	3.1	4.0	4.2	4.4	3.2	7.7
UNDISBURSED DEBT	**12.6**	**60.7**	**235.8**	**231.3**	**187.0**	**133.3**	**119.1**	**83.0**	**65.5**	**45.7**
Official creditors	10.8	60.7	235.8	231.3	187.0	133.3	119.1	83.0	65.5	45.7
Private creditors	1.7	0.0	0.0	0.0	0.0	0.0	0.0	0.0	0.0	0.0
Memorandum items										
Concessional LDOD	15.1	58.6	510.9	628.5	674.2	722.6	765.0	768.0	724.1	756.7
Variable rate LDOD	0.0	2.8	0.0	0.0	0.0	5.2	6.3	5.8	5.1	5.2
Public sector LDOD	24.1	146.5	624.1	729.1	772.7	802.2	853.7	850.1	800.3	828.5
Private sector LDOD	0.0	0.0	0.0	0.5	0.5	0.2	0.3	0.2	1.2	1.3

6. CURRENCY COMPOSITION OF LONG-TERM DEBT (PERCENT)

	1970	1980	1990	1992	1993	1994	1995	1996	1997	1998
Deutsche mark	19.5	1.2	0.7	0.5	0.5	0.4	0.4	0.3	0.3	0.3
French franc	39.9	16.9	11.0	10.2	10.2	5.5	5.4	5.1	4.8	4.7
Japanese yen	0.0	0.0	0.7	0.7	0.7	0.7	0.7	0.6	0.6	0.6
Pound sterling	0.4	0.8	0.1	0.1	0.1	0.0	0.0	0.0	0.0	0.0
Swiss franc	0.0	7.5	2.6	1.9	1.8	2.6	2.8	2.4	2.4	1.9
U.S.dollars	1.7	35.8	43.6	49.0	50.6	55.3	56.2	57.5	58.7	59.1
Multiple currency	0.0	7.5	21.5	20.0	19.0	19.3	18.5	18.5	17.5	17.7
Special drawing rights	0.0	0.0	7.6	6.8	6.9	7.2	6.9	7.2	7.1	7.4
All other currencies	38.5	30.3	12.2	10.8	10.2	9.0	9.1	8.4	8.6	8.3

CENTRAL AFRICAN REPUBLIC

(US$ million, unless otherwise indicated)

	1970	1980	1990	1992	1993	1994	1995	1996	1997	1998
7. DEBT RESTRUCTURINGS										
Total amount rescheduled	..	..	4.4	0.0	0.0	38.5	7.6	0.0	0.0	15.2
Debt stock rescheduled	..	..	0.0	0.0	0.0	0.0	0.0	0.0	0.0	0.0
Principal rescheduled	..	..	2.6	0.0	0.0	21.5	4.4	0.0	0.0	7.3
Official	..	..	2.6	0.0	0.0	13.1	4.4	0.0	0.0	7.3
Private	..	..	0.0	0.0	0.0	8.4	0.0	0.0	0.0	0.0
Interest rescheduled	..	..	0.3	0.0	0.0	12.9	0.9	0.0	0.0	3.4
Official	..	..	0.3	0.0	0.0	11.5	0.9	0.0	0.0	3.4
Private	..	..	0.0	0.0	0.0	1.5	0.0	0.0	0.0	0.0
Debt forgiven	..	..	153.1	0.0	0.0	49.2	1.1	3.7	0.0	0.7
Memo: interest forgiven	..	..	4.4	0.0	0.0	4.5	0.2	3.5	0.0	1.9
Debt stock reduction	..	..	0.0	0.0	0.0	0.0	0.0	0.0	0.0	0.0
of which debt buyback	..	..	0.0	0.0	0.0	0.0	0.0	0.0	0.0	0.0
8. DEBT STOCK-FLOW RECONCILIATION										
Total change in debt stocks	..	..	5.0	19.7	61.2	12.9	57.9	-13.2	-49.8	38.3
Net flows on debt	-0.7	31.1	106.6	39.4	54.4	31.8	25.1	13.8	-3.5	-11.3
Net change in interest arrears	..	..	-1.9	9.6	11.2	-13.8	10.5	2.7	6.4	14.6
Interest capitalized	..	..	0.3	0.0	0.0	12.9	0.9	0.0	0.0	3.4
Debt forgiveness or reduction	..	..	-153.1	0.0	0.0	-49.2	-1.1	-3.7	0.0	-0.7
Cross-currency valuation	..	..	20.9	-11.8	-7.7	7.6	11.5	-11.4	-14.4	8.3
Residual	..	..	32.2	-17.5	3.4	23.6	11.2	-14.7	-38.3	24.1
9. AVERAGE TERMS OF NEW COMMITMENTS										
ALL CREDITORS										
Interest (%)	2.0	0.6	1.0	1.9	0.7	0.0	0.8	1.0	0.0	0.0
Maturity (years)	35.8	12.5	37.6	37.1	49.6	0.0	39.7	49.8	0.0	0.0
Grace period (years)	7.9	4.3	10.2	9.0	10.5	0.0	10.2	9.2	0.0	0.0
Grant element (%)	62.8	39.0	77.0	68.5	83.2	0.0	80.5	80.2	0.0	0.0
Official creditors										
Interest (%)	1.0	0.6	1.0	1.9	0.7	0.0	0.8	1.0	0.0	0.0
Maturity (years)	47.5	12.5	37.6	37.1	49.6	0.0	39.7	49.8	0.0	0.0
Grace period (years)	9.9	4.3	10.2	9.0	10.5	0.0	10.2	9.2	0.0	0.0
Grant element (%)	79.6	39.0	77.0	68.5	83.2	0.0	80.5	80.2	0.0	0.0
Private creditors										
Interest (%)	4.6	0.0	0.0	0.0	0.0	0.0	0.0	0.0	0.0	0.0
Maturity (years)	8.0	0.0	0.0	0.0	0.0	0.0	0.0	0.0	0.0	0.0
Grace period (years)	3.4	0.0	0.0	0.0	0.0	0.0	0.0	0.0	0.0	0.0
Grant element (%)	23.0	0.0	0.0	0.0	0.0	0.0	0.0	0.0	0.0	0.0
Memorandum items										
Commitments	6.5	38.4	174.9	52.9	13.0	0.0	16.6	4.9	0.0	0.0
Official creditors	4.6	38.4	174.9	52.9	13.0	0.0	16.6	4.9	0.0	0.0
Private creditors	1.9	0.0	0.0	0.0	0.0	0.0	0.0	0.0	0.0	0.0

10. CONTRACTUAL OBLIGATIONS ON OUTSTANDING LONG-TERM DEBT

	1999	2000	2001	2002	2003	2004	2005	2006	2007	2008
TOTAL										
Disbursements	17.7	13.4	8.3	4.2	1.7	0.3	0.1	0.0	0.0	0.0
Principal	21.6	23.4	24.8	25.1	23.0	22.9	22.4	22.9	18.1	19.0
Interest	8.9	8.6	8.5	8.3	7.8	7.3	6.8	6.3	5.9	5.7
Official creditors										
Disbursements	17.7	13.4	8.3	4.2	1.7	0.3	0.1	0.0	0.0	0.0
Principal	21.6	23.4	24.8	25.1	23.0	22.9	22.4	22.9	18.1	19.0
Interest	8.9	8.6	8.5	8.3	7.8	7.3	6.8	6.3	5.9	5.7
Bilateral creditors										
Disbursements	0.0	0.0	0.0	0.0	0.0	0.0	0.0	0.0	0.0	0.0
Principal	10.0	10.3	10.5	11.4	10.4	9.6	8.4	8.6	2.9	2.9
Interest	3.7	3.6	3.7	3.7	3.2	2.8	2.4	2.0	1.7	1.7
Multilateral creditors										
Disbursements	17.7	13.4	8.3	4.2	1.7	0.3	0.1	0.0	0.0	0.0
Principal	11.7	13.1	14.3	13.7	12.5	13.3	14.0	14.3	15.2	16.0
Interest	5.2	5.0	4.8	4.7	4.6	4.5	4.4	4.2	4.1	4.0
Private creditors										
Disbursements	0.0	0.0	0.0	0.0	0.0	0.0	0.0	0.0	0.0	0.0
Principal	0.0	0.0	0.0	0.0	0.0	0.0	0.0	0.0	0.0	0.0
Interest	0.0	0.0	0.0	0.0	0.0	0.0	0.0	0.0	0.0	0.0
Commercial banks										
Disbursements	0.0	0.0	0.0	0.0	0.0	0.0	0.0	0.0	0.0	0.0
Principal	0.0	0.0	0.0	0.0	0.0	0.0	0.0	0.0	0.0	0.0
Interest	0.0	0.0	0.0	0.0	0.0	0.0	0.0	0.0	0.0	0.0
Other private										
Disbursements	0.0	0.0	0.0	0.0	0.0	0.0	0.0	0.0	0.0	0.0
Principal	0.0	0.0	0.0	0.0	0.0	0.0	0.0	0.0	0.0	0.0
Interest	0.0	0.0	0.0	0.0	0.0	0.0	0.0	0.0	0.0	0.0

CHAD

(US$ million, unless otherwise indicated)

	1970	1980	1990	1992	1993	1994	1995	1996	1997	1998
1. SUMMARY DEBT DATA										
TOTAL DEBT STOCKS (EDT)	**..**	**284**	**524**	**723**	**768**	**828**	**902**	**997**	**1,026**	**1,091**
Long-term debt (LDOD)	**33**	**259**	**464**	**671**	**713**	**759**	**833**	**914**	**939**	**1,005**
Public and publicly guaranteed	33	259	464	671	713	759	833	914	939	1,005
Private nonguaranteed	0	0	0	0	0	0	0	0	0	0
Use of IMF credit	**3**	**14**	**31**	**30**	**28**	**43**	**49**	**65**	**61**	**64**
Short-term debt	**..**	**12**	**30**	**22**	**26**	**27**	**20**	**18**	**26**	**23**
of which interest arrears on LDOD	..	7	6	13	16	19	11	8	7	9
Official creditors	..	5	4	11	14	17	11	8	7	8
Private creditors	..	2	2	2	2	2	0	0	0	0
Memo: principal arrears on LDOD	..	31	16	26	27	32	34	35	30	38
Official creditors	..	12	13	22	24	28	34	35	30	36
Private creditors	..	20	3	3	3	3	0	0	0	2
Memo: export credits	..	0	52	51	32	34	63	85	77	78
TOTAL DEBT FLOWS										
Disbursements	**10**	**5**	**112**	**143**	**58**	**83**	**72**	**125**	**92**	**52**
Long-term debt	6	5	104	143	58	69	60	101	80	40
IMF purchases	4	0	8	0	0	15	13	24	11	11
Principal repayments	**3**	**5**	**7**	**4**	**8**	**9**	**10**	**16**	**24**	**23**
Long-term debt	3	3	3	4	6	8	3	10	12	12
IMF repurchases	0	3	4	0	2	2	7	6	11	11
Net flows on debt	**7**	**-8**	**107**	**120**	**51**	**72**	**63**	**110**	**77**	**24**
of which short-term debt	..	-8	2	-20	1	-2	1	2	9	-5
Interest payments (INT)	**..**	**1**	**5**	**7**	**9**	**9**	**6**	**14**	**12**	**12**
Long-term debt	0	0	3	6	8	8	4	13	10	11
IMF charges	0	1	0	0	0	1	1	1	1	1
Short-term debt	..	0	2	1	1	0	1	0	1	1
Net transfers on debt	**..**	**-9**	**102**	**113**	**42**	**63**	**57**	**96**	**65**	**12**
Total debt service paid (TDS)	**..**	**6**	**12**	**11**	**17**	**18**	**16**	**30**	**35**	**36**
Long-term debt	3	3	7	10	14	15	7	23	22	23
IMF repurchases and charges	0	3	4	0	2	2	8	7	12	12
Short-term debt (interest only)	..	0	2	1	1	0	1	0	1	1
2. AGGREGATE NET RESOURCE FLOWS AND NET TRANSFERS (LONG-TERM)										
NET RESOURCE FLOWS	**15**	**24**	**247**	**253**	**173**	**203**	**190**	**233**	**190**	**128**
Net flow of long-term debt (ex. IMF)	3	3	100	139	52	61	56	91	68	28
Foreign direct investment (net)	1	0	0	2	15	27	13	18	15	16
Portfolio equity flows	0	0	0	0	0	0	0	0	0	0
Grants (excluding technical coop.)	12	22	147	112	106	115	121	124	107	83
Memo: technical coop. grants	10	12	61	68	71	49	63	54	46	44
official net resource flows	13	24	248	252	159	176	177	215	175	112
private net resource flows	3	0	-1	2	14	27	13	18	15	16
NET TRANSFERS	**13**	**24**	**244**	**259**	**165**	**195**	**186**	**220**	**179**	**116**
Interest on long-term debt	0	0	3	6	8	8	4	13	10	11
Profit remittances on FDI	2	0	0	-11	0	0	0	0	0	1
Memo: official net transfers	12	24	245	246	151	168	173	202	165	101
private net transfers	1	0	-1	13	14	27	13	18	14	15
3. MAJOR ECONOMIC AGGREGATES										
Gross national product (GNP)	470	1,038	1,730	1,905	1,461	1,152	1,410	1,591	1,492	1,666
Exports of goods & services (XGS)	..	71	274	227	203	196	327	271	293	334
of which workers remittances	..	0	0	0	0	1	..	..	..	..
Imports of goods & services (MGS)	..	83	511	482	466	424	512	535	534	555
International reserves (RES)	2	12	132	84	43	80	147	169	139	120
Current account balance	..	12	-46	-86	-117	-38	-12	-95	-120	-113
4. DEBT INDICATORS										
EDT / XGS (%)	..	398.2	191.1	318.8	377.5	422.8	275.6	368.1	350.5	326.9
EDT / GNP (%)	..	27.4	30.3	38.0	52.5	71.9	64.0	62.7	68.8	65.5
TDS / XGS (%)	..	8.4	4.4	4.8	8.4	9.2	4.8	11.1	12.0	10.6
INT / XGS (%)	..	0.8	1.9	3.0	4.4	4.4	1.7	5.2	4.0	3.7
INT / GNP (%)	..	0.1	0.3	0.4	0.6	0.8	0.4	0.9	0.8	0.7
RES / EDT (%)	..	4.1	25.2	11.7	5.6	9.7	16.3	16.9	13.6	11.0
RES / MGS (months)	..	1.7	3.1	2.1	1.1	2.3	3.4	3.8	3.1	2.6
Short-term / EDT (%)	..	4.1	5.7	3.1	3.4	3.2	2.2	1.8	2.6	2.1
Concessional / EDT (%)	..	60.2	76.8	74.5	77.1	81.4	76.9	76.5	78.6	80.0
Multilateral / EDT (%)	..	26.2	63.4	70.2	72.3	72.8	74.8	73.5	73.2	74.6

CHAD

(US$ million, unless otherwise indicated)

	1970	1980	1990	1992	1993	1994	1995	1996	1997	1998
5. LONG-TERM DEBT										
DEBT OUTSTANDING (LDOD)	**33**	**259**	**464**	**671**	**713**	**759**	**833**	**914**	**939**	**1,005**
Public and publicly guaranteed	**33**	**259**	**464**	**671**	**713**	**759**	**833**	**914**	**939**	**1,005**
Official creditors	25	205	455	664	708	753	831	897	922	987
Multilateral	2	75	332	508	555	603	675	733	751	814
Concessional	2	75	322	426	482	560	625	687	712	778
Bilateral	23	131	123	156	153	150	156	164	171	174
Concessional	23	97	80	112	110	114	69	77	94	95
Private creditors	8	54	9	7	6	6	2	17	17	17
Bonds	0	0	0	0	0	0	0	0	0	0
Commercial banks	1	1	0	0	0	0	0	0	0	0
Other private	7	53	9	7	6	6	2	17	17	17
Private nonguaranteed	**0**	**0**	**0**	**0**	**0**	**0**	**0**	**0**	**0**	**0**
Bonds	0	0	0	0	0	0	0	0	0	0
Commercial banks	0	0	0	0	0	0	0	0	0	0
Memo:										
IBRD	0	0	0	0	0	0	0	0	0	0
IDA	0	36	186	259	284	332	379	433	457	488
DISBURSEMENTS	**6**	**5**	**104**	**143**	**58**	**69**	**60**	**101**	**80**	**40**
Public and publicly guaranteed	**6**	**5**	**104**	**143**	**58**	**69**	**60**	**101**	**80**	**40**
Official creditors	3	5	104	143	58	69	60	101	80	40
Multilateral	0	5	72	130	56	62	60	101	74	40
Concessional	0	5	71	55	55	62	60	99	74	40
Bilateral	3	0	32	13	3	6	0	0	6	0
Concessional	2	0	25	13	3	6	0	0	6	0
Private creditors	3	0	0	0	0	0	0	0	0	0
Bonds	0	0	0	0	0	0	0	0	0	0
Commercial banks	0	0	0	0	0	0	0	0	0	0
Other private	3	0	0	0	0	0	0	0	0	0
Private nonguaranteed	**0**	**0**	**0**	**0**	**0**	**0**	**0**	**0**	**0**	**0**
Bonds	0	0	0	0	0	0	0	0	0	0
Commercial banks	0	0	0	0	0	0	0	0	0	0
Memo:										
IBRD	0	0	0	0	0	0	0	0	0	0
IDA	0	0	48	33	25	38	42	68	49	18
PRINCIPAL REPAYMENTS	**3**	**3**	**3**	**4**	**6**	**8**	**3**	**10**	**12**	**12**
Public and publicly guaranteed	**3**	**3**	**3**	**4**	**6**	**8**	**3**	**10**	**12**	**12**
Official creditors	1	3	3	4	5	7	3	10	12	12
Multilateral	0	2	3	3	5	6	3	8	10	11
Concessional	0	2	2	3	1	6	2	7	6	7
Bilateral	1	1	0	1	1	2	1	2	3	1
Concessional	1	1	0	0	0	0	0	0	0	0
Private creditors	1	0	1	0	1	0	0	0	0	0
Bonds	0	0	0	0	0	0	0	0	0	0
Commercial banks	0	0	0	0	0	0	0	0	0	0
Other private	1	0	1	0	1	0	0	0	0	0
Private nonguaranteed	**0**	**0**	**0**	**0**	**0**	**0**	**0**	**0**	**0**	**0**
Bonds	0	0	0	0	0	0	0	0	0	0
Commercial banks	0	0	0	0	0	0	0	0	0	0
Memo:										
IBRD	0	0	0	0	0	0	0	0	0	0
IDA	0	0	1	1	0	2	1	2	2	3
NET FLOWS ON DEBT	**3**	**3**	**100**	**139**	**52**	**61**	**56**	**91**	**68**	**28**
Public and publicly guaranteed	**3**	**3**	**100**	**139**	**52**	**61**	**56**	**91**	**68**	**28**
Official creditors	1	3	101	140	53	61	57	91	68	28
Multilateral	0	3	69	127	51	56	57	93	64	29
Concessional	0	3	68	53	54	57	57	92	68	34
Bilateral	1	-1	32	13	2	5	-1	-2	4	-1
Concessional	1	-1	25	13	3	6	0	0	6	0
Private creditors	2	0	-1	0	-1	0	0	0	0	0
Bonds	0	0	0	0	0	0	0	0	0	0
Commercial banks	0	0	0	0	0	0	0	0	0	0
Other private	2	0	-1	0	-1	0	0	0	0	0
Private nonguaranteed	**0**	**0**	**0**	**0**	**0**	**0**	**0**	**0**	**0**	**0**
Bonds	0	0	0	0	0	0	0	0	0	0
Commercial banks	0	0	0	0	0	0	0	0	0	0
Memo:										
IBRD	0	0	0	0	0	0	0	0	0	0
IDA	0	0	48	32	24	36	41	67	47	15

CHAD

(US$ million, unless otherwise indicated)

	1970	1980	1990	1992	1993	1994	1995	1996	1997	1998
INTEREST PAYMENTS (LINT)	**0**	**0**	**3**	**6**	**8**	**8**	**4**	**13**	**10**	**11**
Public and publicly guaranteed	**0**	**0**	**3**	**6**	**8**	**8**	**4**	**13**	**10**	**11**
Official creditors	0	0	3	6	8	8	4	13	10	11
Multilateral	0	0	2	4	6	6	4	9	7	8
Concessional	0	0	2	3	3	4	3	7	5	6
Bilateral	0	0	1	2	2	2	0	3	3	3
Concessional	0	0	1	1	2	1	0	0	0	0
Private creditors	0	0	0	0	0	0	0	0	0	0
Bonds	0	0	0	0	0	0	0	0	0	0
Commercial banks	0	0	0	0	0	0	0	0	0	0
Other private	0	0	0	0	0	0	0	0	0	0
Private nonguaranteed	**0**	**0**	**0**	**0**	**0**	**0**	**0**	**0**	**0**	**0**
Bonds	0	0	0	0	0	0	0	0	0	0
Commercial banks	0	0	0	0	0	0	0	0	0	0
Memo:										
IBRD	0	0	0	0	0	0	0	0	0	0
IDA	0	0	1	2	2	3	3	3	3	4
NET TRANSFERS ON DEBT	**3**	**3**	**97**	**134**	**44**	**53**	**52**	**78**	**58**	**17**
Public and publicly guaranteed	**3**	**3**	**97**	**134**	**44**	**53**	**52**	**78**	**58**	**17**
Official creditors	1	3	98	134	45	54	52	78	58	17
Multilateral	0	3	67	123	45	51	53	84	58	21
Concessional	0	3	66	50	51	53	54	85	63	28
Bilateral	1	-1	31	11	0	3	-1	-5	0	-4
Concessional	0	-1	24	12	1	5	0	0	6	0
Private creditors	2	0	-1	-1	-1	0	0	0	0	0
Bonds	0	0	0	0	0	0	0	0	0	0
Commercial banks	0	0	0	0	0	0	0	0	0	0
Other private	2	0	-1	-1	-1	0	0	0	0	0
Private nonguaranteed	**0**	**0**	**0**	**0**	**0**	**0**	**0**	**0**	**0**	**0**
Bonds	0	0	0	0	0	0	0	0	0	0
Commercial banks	0	0	0	0	0	0	0	0	0	0
Memo:										
IBRD	0	0	0	0	0	0	0	0	0	0
IDA	0	0	47	31	22	34	38	64	43	11
DEBT SERVICE (LTDS)	**3**	**3**	**7**	**10**	**14**	**15**	**7**	**23**	**22**	**23**
Public and publicly guaranteed	**3**	**3**	**7**	**10**	**14**	**15**	**7**	**23**	**22**	**23**
Official creditors	2	3	6	9	13	15	7	22	22	23
Multilateral	0	2	5	7	11	12	6	17	16	19
Concessional	0	2	4	6	4	10	6	14	11	12
Bilateral	2	1	1	2	2	3	1	5	6	4
Concessional	2	1	1	1	2	1	0	0	0	0
Private creditors	1	0	1	1	1	0	0	0	0	0
Bonds	0	0	0	0	0	0	0	0	0	0
Commercial banks	0	0	0	0	0	0	0	0	0	0
Other private	1	0	1	1	1	0	0	0	0	0
Private nonguaranteed	**0**	**0**	**0**	**0**	**0**	**0**	**0**	**0**	**0**	**0**
Bonds	0	0	0	0	0	0	0	0	0	0
Commercial banks	0	0	0	0	0	0	0	0	0	0
Memo:										
IBRD	0	0	0	0	0	0	0	0	0	0
IDA	0	0	2	3	2	4	4	5	5	7
UNDISBURSED DEBT	**18**	**94**	**372**	**315**	**317**	**329**	**387**	**318**	**287**	**292**
Official creditors	11	76	372	315	317	329	387	318	287	292
Private creditors	7	18	0	0	0	0	0	0	0	0
Memorandum items										
Concessional LDOD	24	171	402	538	592	674	694	763	807	873
Variable rate LDOD	0	1	0	0	0	0	0	3	1	1
Public sector LDOD	33	259	464	671	713	758	833	914	939	1,005
Private sector LDOD	0	0	0	0	0	0	0	0	0	0

6. CURRENCY COMPOSITION OF LONG-TERM DEBT (PERCENT)

	1970	1980	1990	1992	1993	1994	1995	1996	1997	1998
Deutsche mark	10.8	2.7	1.5	0.8	0.7	0.7	0.1	0.1	0.0	0.0
French franc	35.1	14.5	9.1	8.7	8.0	8.5	7.6	6.4	5.6	5.8
Japanese yen	0.0	0.0	0.0	0.0	0.0	0.0	0.0	0.0	0.0	0.0
Pound sterling	1.2	0.2	0.1	0.0	0.0	0.0	0.0	0.0	0.0	0.0
Swiss franc	0.0	0.0	0.0	0.0	0.0	0.0	0.0	0.0	0.0	0.0
U.S.dollars	4.0	18.9	49.0	45.0	45.5	50.2	51.6	53.4	56.9	55.9
Multiple currency	3.7	9.7	25.7	22.9	24.2	26.6	26.3	25.4	23.2	23.5
Special drawing rights	0.0	0.0	0.0	0.0	0.0	0.1	0.2	0.2	0.2	0.2
All other currencies	45.2	54.0	14.6	22.6	21.6	13.9	14.2	14.5	14.1	14.6

CHAD

(US$ million, unless otherwise indicated)

	1970	1980	1990	1992	1993	1994	1995	1996	1997	1998
7. DEBT RESTRUCTURINGS										
Total amount rescheduled	..	..	8	0	0	0	56	33	10	3
Debt stock rescheduled	..	..	0	0	0	0	0	0	0	0
Principal rescheduled	..	..	3	0	0	0	2	3	7	2
Official	..	..	3	0	0	0	1	3	7	2
Private	..	..	1	0	0	0	1	0	0	0
Interest rescheduled	..	..	1	0	0	0	7	1	1	1
Official	..	..	1	0	0	0	7	1	1	1
Private	..	..	0	0	0	0	1	0	0	0
Debt forgiven	..	..	12	0	0	0	55	11	2	2
Memo: interest forgiven	..	..	0	0	0	0	8	1	1	1
Debt stock reduction	..	..	0	0	0	0	0	0	0	0
of which debt buyback	..	..	0	0	0	0	0	0	0	0
8. DEBT STOCK-FLOW RECONCILIATION										
Total change in debt stocks	..	..	125	94	45	61	74	95	29	65
Net flows on debt	7	-8	107	120	51	72	63	110	77	24
Net change in interest arrears	..	..	-1	3	3	3	-7	-3	-1	1
Interest capitalized	..	..	1	0	0	0	7	1	1	1
Debt forgiveness or reduction	..	..	-12	0	0	0	-55	-11	-2	-2
Cross-currency valuation	..	..	8	-13	-10	-18	12	-7	-15	9
Residual	..	..	21	-16	1	4	55	5	-32	32
9. AVERAGE TERMS OF NEW COMMITMENTS										
ALL CREDITORS										
Interest (%)	5.7	0.0	1.7	4.4	1.0	1.0	0.9	0.9	0.7	0.4
Maturity (years)	8.3	0.0	30.3	27.4	36.8	37.5	39.8	37.4	47.2	39.8
Grace period (years)	1.0	0.0	9.2	6.8	11.8	9.8	9.1	9.7	10.3	7.3
Grant element (%)	14.3	0.0	66.4	39.0	74.8	76.9	77.5	76.3	83.2	80.8
Official creditors										
Interest (%)	3.7	0.0	1.7	4.4	1.0	1.0	0.9	0.9	0.7	0.4
Maturity (years)	10.0	0.0	30.3	27.4	36.8	37.5	39.8	37.4	47.2	39.8
Grace period (years)	1.8	0.0	9.2	6.8	11.8	9.8	9.1	9.7	10.3	7.3
Grant element (%)	25.5	0.0	66.4	39.0	74.8	76.9	77.5	76.3	83.2	80.8
Private creditors										
Interest (%)	6.3	0.0	0.0	0.0	0.0	0.0	0.0	0.0	0.0	0.0
Maturity (years)	7.8	0.0	0.0	0.0	0.0	0.0	0.0	0.0	0.0	0.0
Grace period (years)	0.7	0.0	0.0	0.0	0.0	0.0	0.0	0.0	0.0	0.0
Grant element (%)	11.1	0.0	0.0	0.0	0.0	0.0	0.0	0.0	0.0	0.0
Memorandum items										
Commitments	10	0	85	123	99	62	106	45	75	32
Official creditors	2	0	85	123	99	62	106	45	75	32
Private creditors	8	0	0	0	0	0	0	0	0	0

10. CONTRACTUAL OBLIGATIONS ON OUTSTANDING LONG-TERM DEBT

	1999	2000	2001	2002	2003	2004	2005	2006	2007	2008
TOTAL										
Disbursements	65	83	61	39	22	13	7	1	0	0
Principal	28	30	32	33	35	33	34	34	35	34
Interest	15	14	14	13	13	13	12	12	11	10
Official creditors										
Disbursements	65	83	61	39	22	13	7	1	0	0
Principal	26	28	31	32	34	32	33	32	34	33
Interest	14	14	14	13	13	13	12	11	11	10
Bilateral creditors										
Disbursements	1	1	1	0	0	0	0	0	0	0
Principal	10	11	13	13	13	10	9	8	8	8
Interest	6	5	5	4	4	4	4	4	4	3
Multilateral creditors										
Disbursements	64	82	60	39	22	13	7	1	0	0
Principal	16	18	18	19	21	22	23	24	26	25
Interest	9	9	9	9	9	8	8	8	7	7
Private creditors										
Disbursements	0	0	0	0	0	0	0	0	0	0
Principal	2	2	1	1	1	1	1	1	1	1
Interest	0	0	0	0	0	0	0	0	0	0
Commercial banks										
Disbursements	0	0	0	0	0	0	0	0	0	0
Principal	0	0	0	0	0	0	0	0	0	0
Interest	0	0	0	0	0	0	0	0	0	0
Other private										
Disbursements	0	0	0	0	0	0	0	0	0	0
Principal	2	2	1	1	1	1	1	1	1	1
Interest	0	0	0	0	0	0	0	0	0	0

CHILE

(US$ million, unless otherwise indicated)

	1970	1980	1990	1992	1993	1994	1995	1996	1997	1998
1. SUMMARY DEBT DATA										
TOTAL DEBT STOCKS (EDT)	**..**	**12,081**	**19,227**	**19,134**	**20,637**	**24,728**	**25,562**	**27,404**	**31,443**	**36,302**
Long-term debt (LDOD)	**2,567**	**9,399**	**14,689**	**15,181**	**16,031**	**17,999**	**18,607**	**20,414**	**21,522**	**28,547**
Public and publicly guaranteed	2,066	4,705	10,426	9,578	8,867	8,995	7,178	4,883	4,367	4,986
Private nonguaranteed	501	4,693	4,263	5,603	7,164	9,004	11,429	15,531	17,155	23,560
Use of IMF credit	**2**	**123**	**1,157**	**722**	**476**	**291**	**0**	**0**	**0**	**0**
Short-term debt	**..**	**2,560**	**3,382**	**3,231**	**4,130**	**6,438**	**6,955**	**6,990**	**9,921**	**7,756**
of which interest arrears on LDOD	..	0	0	0	0	0	0	0	0	0
Official creditors	..	0	0	0	0	0	0	0	0	0
Private creditors	..	0	0	0	0	0	0	0	0	0
Memo: principal arrears on LDOD	..	0	0	0	0	0	0	0	0	0
Official creditors	..	0	0	0	0	0	0	0	0	0
Private creditors	..	0	0	0	0	0	0	0	0	0
Memo: export credits	..	0	2,062	2,064	2,242	2,583	2,335	2,049	1,774	2,065
TOTAL DEBT FLOWS										
Disbursements	**655**	**3,551**	**2,253**	**1,736**	**2,182**	**2,922**	**3,821**	**6,644**	**6,217**	**6,784**
Long-term debt	655	3,551	2,253	1,736	2,182	2,922	3,821	6,644	6,217	6,784
IMF purchases	0	0	0	0	0	0	0	0	0	0
Principal repayments	**254**	**1,513**	**980**	**1,353**	**1,721**	**1,692**	**3,671**	**4,677**	**2,857**	**2,345**
Long-term debt	207	1,462	771	1,150	1,472	1,482	3,369	4,677	2,857	2,345
IMF repurchases	47	52	209	203	249	211	303	0	0	0
Net flows on debt	**809**	**2,963**	**1,682**	**1,414**	**1,360**	**3,538**	**667**	**2,001**	**6,291**	**2,274**
of which short-term debt	..	925	409	1,032	899	2,308	517	35	2,932	-2,165
Interest payments (INT)	**..**	**1,193**	**1,792**	**1,340**	**1,121**	**1,268**	**1,462**	**1,464**	**1,561**	**2,136**
Long-term debt	104	918	1,364	1,135	933	929	1,114	1,185	1,070	1,694
IMF charges	0	12	118	70	43	22	13	0	0	0
Short-term debt	..	262	310	136	145	317	335	279	490	442
Net transfers on debt	**..**	**1,771**	**-110**	**74**	**239**	**2,270**	**-795**	**537**	**4,731**	**138**
Total debt service paid (TDS)	**..**	**2,706**	**2,772**	**2,693**	**2,842**	**2,960**	**5,133**	**6,142**	**4,418**	**4,481**
Long-term debt	311	2,380	2,135	2,285	2,405	2,411	4,483	5,863	3,927	4,039
IMF repurchases and charges	47	64	327	273	292	232	316	0	0	0
Short-term debt (interest only)	..	262	310	136	145	317	335	279	490	442
2. AGGREGATE NET RESOURCE FLOWS AND NET TRANSFERS (LONG-TERM)										
NET RESOURCE FLOWS	**381**	**2,312**	**2,465**	**1,902**	**2,233**	**4,958**	**3,759**	**6,741**	**9,100**	**9,190**
Net flow of long-term debt (ex. IMF)	448	2,090	1,481	586	710	1,441	452	1,967	3,360	4,439
Foreign direct investment (net)	-79	213	590	937	1,034	2,583	2,978	4,624	5,219	4,638
Portfolio equity flows	0	0	320	323	405	867	274	103	486	87
Grants (excluding technical coop.)	12	9	73	56	84	67	54	47	35	25
Memo: technical coop. grants	19	37	71	92	90	88	97	89	78	72
official net resource flows	67	-136	367	111	-125	-122	-1,755	-595	-339	-62
private net resource flows	314	2,447	2,098	1,792	2,358	5,080	5,514	7,336	9,439	9,252
NET TRANSFERS	**173**	**1,307**	**766**	**-130**	**502**	**3,078**	**1,645**	**4,455**	**6,630**	**5,845**
Interest on long-term debt	104	918	1,364	1,135	933	929	1,114	1,185	1,070	1,694
Profit remittances on FDI	104	86	335	897	798	950	1,000	1,100	1,400	1,650
Memo: official net transfers	28	-216	-16	-285	-508	-501	-2,143	-869	-500	-181
private net transfers	145	1,523	782	156	1,010	3,580	3,788	5,324	7,129	6,027
3. MAJOR ECONOMIC AGGREGATES										
Gross national product (GNP)	7,987	26,544	28,549	39,915	43,708	47,201	56,810	65,522	67,553	76,232
Exports of goods & services (XGS)	..	6,276	10,705	12,923	12,213	15,000	20,226	19,861	21,858	20,088
of which workers remittances	..	0	..	0	0	0	..	..	..	..
Imports of goods & services (MGS)	..	8,360	11,387	14,259	15,087	16,917	21,883	23,878	26,107	24,690
International reserves (RES)	392	4,128	6,784	9,790	10,369	13,802	14,860	15,520	17,845	16,014
Current account balance	..	-1,971	-485	-958	-2,554	-1,585	-1,350	-3,510	-3,728	-4,139
4. DEBT INDICATORS										
EDT / XGS (%)	..	192.5	179.6	148.1	169.0	164.9	126.4	138.0	143.9	180.7
EDT / GNP (%)	..	45.5	67.4	47.9	47.2	52.4	45.0	41.8	46.6	47.6
TDS / XGS (%)	..	43.1	25.9	20.8	23.3	19.7	25.4	30.9	20.2	22.3
INT / XGS (%)	..	19.0	16.7	10.4	9.2	8.5	7.2	7.4	7.1	10.6
INT / GNP (%)	..	4.5	6.3	3.4	2.6	2.7	2.6	2.2	2.3	2.8
RES / EDT (%)	..	34.2	35.3	51.2	50.2	55.8	58.1	56.6	56.8	44.1
RES / MGS (months)	..	5.9	7.2	8.2	8.3	9.8	8.2	7.8	8.2	7.8
Short-term / EDT (%)	..	21.2	17.6	16.9	20.0	26.0	27.2	25.5	31.6	21.4
Concessional / EDT (%)	..	5.6	1.9	1.5	1.3	1.3	1.3	1.2	1.1	1.1
Multilateral / EDT (%)	..	2.9	21.6	22.6	21.0	17.7	11.2	7.6	5.1	4.2

CHILE

(US$ million, unless otherwise indicated)

	1970	1980	1990	1992	1993	1994	1995	1996	1997	1998
5. LONG-TERM DEBT										
DEBT OUTSTANDING (LDOD)	**2,567**	**9,399**	**14,689**	**15,181**	**16,031**	**17,999**	**18,607**	**20,414**	**21,522**	**28,547**
Public and publicly guaranteed	**2,066**	**4,705**	**10,426**	**9,578**	**8,867**	**8,995**	**7,178**	**4,883**	**4,367**	**4,986**
Official creditors	1,179	1,360	5,182	5,187	5,104	5,156	3,582	2,711	2,163	2,133
Multilateral	176	351	4,143	4,333	4,327	4,374	2,871	2,092	1,587	1,533
Concessional	20	50	33	29	27	25	23	21	19	17
Bilateral	1,003	1,009	1,039	855	777	782	711	619	576	600
Concessional	658	628	334	250	247	285	308	307	331	365
Private creditors	887	3,345	5,244	4,390	3,764	3,839	3,596	2,172	2,205	2,853
Bonds	60	106	39	320	0	0	0	0	0	0
Commercial banks	291	2,420	4,748	3,799	3,553	3,728	3,509	2,152	2,132	2,784
Other private	536	818	457	271	210	111	87	20	73	70
Private nonguaranteed	**501**	**4,693**	**4,263**	**5,603**	**7,164**	**9,004**	**11,429**	**15,531**	**17,155**	**23,560**
Bonds	0	0	0	0	286	377	866	2,725	3,764	4,466
Commercial banks	501	4,693	4,263	5,603	6,878	8,627	10,563	12,806	13,391	19,094
Memo:										
IBRD	111	163	1,860	1,928	1,902	1,919	1,372	1,093	980	945
IDA	19	21	14	13	12	11	11	10	9	9
DISBURSEMENTS	**655**	**3,551**	**2,253**	**1,736**	**2,182**	**2,922**	**3,821**	**6,644**	**6,217**	**6,784**
Public and publicly guaranteed	**407**	**857**	**708**	**670**	**293**	**463**	**342**	**975**	**685**	**1,029**
Official creditors	130	62	650	549	270	351	194	157	167	149
Multilateral	34	46	583	480	247	292	146	126	108	94
Concessional	0	3	0	0	0	0	0	0	0	0
Bilateral	97	15	67	69	24	59	48	31	59	55
Concessional	44	3	0	13	24	59	48	31	59	55
Private creditors	277	796	58	121	23	113	148	818	519	880
Bonds	0	55	0	120	0	0	0	0	0	0
Commercial banks	119	568	37	0	23	113	141	808	458	880
Other private	158	172	21	0	0	0	7	10	60	0
Private nonguaranteed	**247**	**2,694**	**1,545**	**1,066**	**1,889**	**2,459**	**3,479**	**5,669**	**5,532**	**5,755**
Bonds	0	0	0	0	286	91	500	1,870	1,050	863
Commercial banks	247	2,694	1,545	1,066	1,603	2,368	2,979	3,799	4,482	4,892
Memo:										
IBRD	27	14	251	200	107	81	83	75	85	71
IDA	0	0	0	0	0	0	0	0	0	0
PRINCIPAL REPAYMENTS	**207**	**1,462**	**771**	**1,150**	**1,472**	**1,482**	**3,369**	**4,677**	**2,857**	**2,345**
Public and publicly guaranteed	**166**	**891**	**500**	**632**	**880**	**646**	**2,277**	**2,960**	**995**	**441**
Official creditors	75	206	356	495	480	539	2,004	799	541	236
Multilateral	15	15	263	349	353	430	1,884	719	476	173
Concessional	0	0	2	2	2	2	2	2	2	2
Bilateral	61	191	93	146	126	109	119	80	64	63
Concessional	21	69	32	23	24	25	29	28	26	30
Private creditors	90	685	144	137	401	107	273	2,162	454	205
Bonds	5	4	7	0	320	0	0	0	0	0
Commercial banks	32	464	32	61	21	4	240	2,086	447	201
Other private	54	217	105	76	60	104	33	76	7	3
Private nonguaranteed	**41**	**571**	**271**	**518**	**592**	**835**	**1,092**	**1,717**	**1,863**	**1,904**
Bonds	0	0	0	0	0	0	11	11	11	161
Commercial banks	41	571	271	518	592	835	1,081	1,706	1,852	1,743
Memo:										
IBRD	10	9	119	168	172	192	704	263	109	105
IDA	0	0	1	1	1	1	1	1	1	1
NET FLOWS ON DEBT	**448**	**2,090**	**1,481**	**586**	**710**	**1,441**	**452**	**1,967**	**3,360**	**4,439**
Public and publicly guaranteed	**242**	**-34**	**208**	**38**	**-587**	**-183**	**-1,935**	**-1,986**	**-309**	**588**
Official creditors	55	-145	294	54	-209	-189	-1,810	-642	-374	-87
Multilateral	19	31	319	131	-107	-138	-1,739	-593	-369	-79
Concessional	0	3	-2	-2	-2	-2	-2	-2	-2	-2
Bilateral	36	-176	-25	-77	-103	-51	-71	-49	-5	-9
Concessional	23	-66	-32	-10	-1	34	19	4	33	24
Private creditors	187	111	-86	-16	-378	6	-125	-1,344	65	675
Bonds	-5	52	-7	120	-320	0	0	0	0	0
Commercial banks	87	104	5	-60	1	109	-99	-1,278	11	679
Other private	105	-45	-85	-76	-60	-104	-26	-66	54	-3
Private nonguaranteed	**206**	**2,123**	**1,274**	**548**	**1,297**	**1,624**	**2,387**	**3,952**	**3,669**	**3,851**
Bonds	0	0	0	0	286	91	489	1,859	1,039	702
Commercial banks	206	2,123	1,274	548	1,012	1,533	1,898	2,093	2,630	3,149
Memo:										
IBRD	18	5	132	32	-65	-111	-621	-188	-25	-35
IDA	0	0	-1	-1	-1	-1	-1	-1	-1	-1

CHILE

(US$ million, unless otherwise indicated)

	1970	1980	1990	1992	1993	1994	1995	1996	1997	1998
INTEREST PAYMENTS (LINT)	**104**	**918**	**1,364**	**1,135**	**933**	**929**	**1,114**	**1,185**	**1,070**	**1,694**
Public and publicly guaranteed	**78**	**483**	**1,112**	**806**	**652**	**565**	**653**	**535**	**292**	**622**
Official creditors	40	80	384	396	383	379	387	274	161	119
Multilateral	9	26	313	345	341	353	348	190	136	99
Concessional	0	1	1	0	0	0	0	0	0	0
Bilateral	31	54	71	51	43	27	39	84	24	20
Concessional	12	22	9	6	6	6	6	60	6	6
Private creditors	39	403	729	410	269	186	266	261	131	503
Bonds	2	5	2	18	15	0	0	0	0	0
Commercial banks	19	325	688	369	238	175	258	256	130	499
Other private	17	73	39	24	16	11	8	5	1	4
Private nonguaranteed	**26**	**435**	**252**	**329**	**280**	**365**	**461**	**651**	**778**	**1,072**
Bonds	0	0	0	0	4	13	26	59	192	267
Commercial banks	26	435	252	329	277	352	435	591	587	806
Memo:										
IBRD	6	16	130	144	142	140	137	89	68	58
IDA	0	0	0	0	0	0	0	0	0	0
NET TRANSFERS ON DEBT	**343**	**1,171**	**117**	**-549**	**-223**	**511**	**-662**	**781**	**2,290**	**2,745**
Public and publicly guaranteed	**163**	**-517**	**-905**	**-768**	**-1,240**	**-748**	**-2,588**	**-2,521**	**-601**	**-33**
Official creditors	15	-225	-90	-342	-593	-568	-2,197	-916	-535	-206
Multilateral	10	5	7	-214	-447	-490	-2,087	-783	-505	-177
Concessional	0	2	-3	-3	-2	-2	-2	-2	-2	-2
Bilateral	5	-230	-96	-127	-146	-77	-110	-133	-30	-29
Concessional	11	-88	-42	-16	-7	28	13	-57	27	19
Private creditors	148	-292	-815	-427	-647	-180	-391	-1,605	-67	173
Bonds	-7	47	-9	103	-335	0	0	0	0	0
Commercial banks	68	-221	-683	-430	-236	-66	-357	-1,534	-119	180
Other private	87	-118	-123	-99	-76	-114	-34	-71	52	-8
Private nonguaranteed	**180**	**1,688**	**1,022**	**219**	**1,017**	**1,259**	**1,926**	**3,302**	**2,891**	**2,779**
Bonds	0	0	0	0	282	78	463	1,800	847	435
Commercial banks	180	1,688	1,022	219	735	1,181	1,463	1,502	2,044	2,343
Memo:										
IBRD	12	-11	2	-112	-207	-251	-758	-277	-93	-93
IDA	0	0	-1	-1	-1	-1	-1	-1	-1	-1
DEBT SERVICE (LTDS)	**311**	**2,380**	**2,135**	**2,285**	**2,405**	**2,411**	**4,483**	**5,863**	**3,927**	**4,039**
Public and publicly guaranteed	**244**	**1,374**	**1,612**	**1,438**	**1,533**	**1,211**	**2,930**	**3,495**	**1,286**	**1,063**
Official creditors	115	287	740	891	863	918	2,391	1,073	701	355
Multilateral	24	41	576	695	694	782	2,233	908	613	271
Concessional	0	1	3	3	2	2	2	2	2	2
Bilateral	91	245	164	196	169	136	158	164	89	84
Concessional	33	90	42	29	30	30	36	88	32	36
Private creditors	129	1,088	873	547	670	293	539	2,423	585	708
Bonds	7	8	9	18	335	0	0	0	0	0
Commercial banks	51	789	720	430	259	179	498	2,342	578	700
Other private	71	290	144	100	76	114	41	80	8	8
Private nonguaranteed	**67**	**1,006**	**523**	**847**	**872**	**1,200**	**1,553**	**2,368**	**2,641**	**2,976**
Bonds	0	0	0	0	4	13	37	70	203	428
Commercial banks	67	1,006	523	847	868	1,187	1,516	2,297	2,438	2,549
Memo:										
IBRD	16	25	249	312	314	332	841	352	178	163
IDA	0	0	1	1	1	1	1	1	1	1
UNDISBURSED DEBT	**469**	**432**	**1,550**	**1,847**	**1,792**	**1,270**	**1,196**	**952**	**834**	**506**
Official creditors	180	186	1,364	1,758	1,572	1,078	1,101	861	568	214
Private creditors	289	246	186	89	221	192	95	91	266	293
Memorandum items										
Concessional LDOD	678	678	367	279	274	310	331	328	350	382
Variable rate LDOD	501	7,104	11,126	11,894	12,856	14,903	16,461	18,854	20,425	27,471
Public sector LDOD	1,978	4,587	10,422	9,576	8,867	8,995	7,178	4,883	4,367	4,846
Private sector LDOD	589	4,811	4,267	5,605	7,164	9,004	11,429	15,531	17,155	23,700

6. CURRENCY COMPOSITION OF LONG-TERM DEBT (PERCENT)

	1970	1980	1990	1992	1993	1994	1995	1996	1997	1998
Deutsche mark	5.6	5.9	4.7	3.7	3.3	3.7	4.5	3.6	2.0	1.9
French franc	2.1	6.3	1.1	0.7	0.7	0.6	0.7	0.8	0.8	0.6
Japanese yen	0.0	1.8	8.2	8.2	8.4	8.8	9.5	8.6	7.2	7.0
Pound sterling	7.4	1.0	3.4	2.7	2.7	2.8	2.9	0.5	0.4	0.3
Swiss franc	0.9	0.4	0.6	0.5	0.6	0.7	0.9	0.3	0.2	0.2
U.S.dollars	75.1	74.6	40.2	37.7	34.9	34.9	42.3	45.8	54.9	79.2
Multiple currency	6.7	7.0	39.4	44.9	48.1	47.5	38.0	39.8	34.2	10.6
Special drawing rights	0.0	0.0	0.0	0.0	0.0	0.0	0.0	0.0	0.0	0.0
All other currencies	2.2	3.0	2.4	1.6	1.3	1.0	1.2	0.6	0.3	0.2

CHILE

(US$ million, unless otherwise indicated)

	1970	1980	1990	1992	1993	1994	1995	1996	1997	1998
7. DEBT RESTRUCTURINGS										
Total amount rescheduled	..	..	4,173	133	0	0	0	1	0	0
Debt stock rescheduled	..	..	4,170	132	0	0	0	0	0	0
Principal rescheduled	..	..	0	0	0	0	0	0	0	0
Official	..	..	0	0	0	0	0	0	0	0
Private	..	..	0	0	0	0	0	0	0	0
Interest rescheduled	..	..	0	0	0	0	0	0	0	0
Official	..	..	0	0	0	0	0	0	0	0
Private	..	..	0	0	0	0	0	0	0	0
Debt forgiven	..	..	0	15	0	0	0	0	0	0
Memo: interest forgiven	..	..	0	0	0	0	0	0	0	0
Debt stock reduction	..	..	1,101	279	264	32	145	34	0	0
of which debt buyback	..	..	0	0	0	0	0	0	0	0
8. DEBT STOCK-FLOW RECONCILIATION										
Total change in debt stocks	..	..	1,195	1,187	1,503	4,092	834	1,842	4,039	4,859
Net flows on debt	809	2,963	1,682	1,414	1,360	3,538	667	2,001	6,291	2,274
Net change in interest arrears	..	..	0	0	0	0	0	0	0	0
Interest capitalized	..	..	0	0	0	0	0	0	0	0
Debt forgiveness or reduction	..	..	-1,101	-294	-264	-32	-145	-34	0	0
Cross-currency valuation	..	..	337	-186	46	250	-110	-194	-144	61
Residual	..	..	277	253	362	336	422	68	-2,108	2,524
9. AVERAGE TERMS OF NEW COMMITMENTS										
ALL CREDITORS										
Interest (%)	6.8	13.9	7.8	6.8	3.1	7.5	6.2	5.6	6.2	6.0
Maturity (years)	12.4	8.4	17.6	20.1	12.2	13.3	18.0	7.0	6.2	5.0
Grace period (years)	3.5	3.7	4.2	5.6	4.8	6.0	5.4	5.3	3.9	2.6
Grant element (%)	15.6	-18.0	12.0	21.3	34.2	13.9	24.2	19.1	13.8	11.2
Official creditors										
Interest (%)	6.5	8.7	7.7	6.8	1.9	6.3	6.1	4.7	1.0	0.0
Maturity (years)	21.0	15.1	18.4	20.3	15.8	22.1	19.5	20.9	10.0	0.0
Grace period (years)	6.7	3.6	4.3	5.6	3.7	5.0	5.8	8.7	1.5	0.0
Grant element (%)	24.4	6.0	12.8	21.4	43.0	22.6	26.2	38.8	36.4	0.0
Private creditors										
Interest (%)	6.9	14.4	9.3	5.1	4.2	8.3	6.8	5.6	6.3	6.0
Maturity (years)	11.1	7.7	7.6	5.8	8.9	7.7	9.6	5.9	6.1	5.0
Grace period (years)	3.0	3.7	2.3	3.2	5.9	6.7	3.0	5.0	3.9	2.6
Grant element (%)	14.3	-20.4	1.7	16.1	26.2	8.3	13.7	17.5	13.5	11.2
Memorandum items										
Commitments	361	835	1,049	655	317	181	314	885	711	903
Official creditors	46	74	967	646	151	70	265	63	9	0
Private creditors	314	761	82	9	166	111	49	821	702	903

10. CONTRACTUAL OBLIGATIONS ON OUTSTANDING LONG-TERM DEBT

	1999	2000	2001	2002	2003	2004	2005	2006	2007	2008
TOTAL										
Disbursements	231	140	72	32	15	9	6	1	1	1
Principal	2,348	2,596	4,474	3,191	3,240	1,607	2,000	2,628	1,280	1,023
Interest	1,569	1,445	1,333	1,076	863	1,034	604	484	328	242
Official creditors										
Disbursements	68	52	38	24	15	9	5	1	1	1
Principal	295	281	276	274	243	202	169	139	85	80
Interest	133	118	103	88	72	57	44	32	24	19
Bilateral creditors										
Disbursements	31	22	14	8	5	3	2	1	1	0
Principal	120	103	93	93	62	21	12	13	15	15
Interest	17	14	11	9	7	5	5	5	5	4
Multilateral creditors										
Disbursements	37	31	23	16	11	6	4	0	0	0
Principal	175	178	183	181	181	181	157	126	70	65
Interest	116	104	92	79	66	52	39	27	19	14
Private creditors										
Disbursements	163	87	34	8	0	0	0	0	0	0
Principal	2,053	2,315	4,198	2,917	2,997	1,405	1,830	2,489	1,195	942
Interest	1,436	1,327	1,229	989	791	977	560	452	304	224
Commercial banks										
Disbursements	163	87	34	8	0	0	0	0	0	0
Principal	188	475	1,131	625	233	221	120	20	18	14
Interest	170	156	140	72	36	19	11	5	4	3
Other private										
Disbursements	0	0	0	0	0	0	0	0	0	0
Principal	1,865	1,841	3,066	2,292	2,763	1,184	1,711	2,470	1,177	929
Interest	1,266	1,171	1,090	917	755	958	549	447	300	221

CHINA

(US$ million, unless otherwise indicated)

	1970	1980	1990	1992	1993	1994	1995	1996	1997	1998
1. SUMMARY DEBT DATA										
TOTAL DEBT STOCKS (EDT)	..	..	**55,301**	**72,428**	**85,928**	**100,457**	**118,090**	**128,817**	**146,697**	**154,599**
Long-term debt (LDOD)	..	..	**45,515**	**58,663**	**70,632**	**82,974**	**95,764**	**103,410**	**115,233**	**126,667**
Public and publicly guaranteed	..	..	45,515	58,463	70,076	82,391	94,675	102,260	112,821	99,424
Private nonguaranteed	..	..	0	200	556	583	1,090	1,150	2,412	27,243
Use of IMF credit	**0**	**0**	**469**	**0**	**0**	**0**	**0**	**0**	**0**	**0**
Short-term debt	..	..	**9,317**	**13,765**	**15,296**	**17,483**	**22,325**	**25,407**	**31,464**	**27,933**
of which interest arrears on LDOD	..	..	0	0	0	0	0	0	0	0
Official creditors	..	..	0	0	0	0	0	0	0	0
Private creditors	..	..	0	0	0	0	0	0	0	0
Memo: principal arrears on LDOD	..	..	0	0	0	0	0	0	0	0
Official creditors	..	..	0	0	0	0	0	0	0	0
Private creditors	..	..	0	0	0	0	0	0	0	0
Memo: export credits	..	..	8,076	12,790	15,851	23,371	26,520	28,737	31,967	33,164
TOTAL DEBT FLOWS										
Disbursements	..	..	**9,665**	**16,505**	**19,559**	**16,151**	**21,985**	**21,114**	**23,976**	**11,148**
Long-term debt	..	..	9,665	16,505	19,559	16,151	21,985	21,114	23,976	11,148
IMF purchases	0	0	0	0	0	0	0	0	0	0
Principal repayments	..	..	**3,809**	**5,213**	**6,727**	**6,343**	**9,070**	**10,260**	**11,527**	**11,209**
Long-term debt	..	..	3,319	5,213	6,727	6,343	9,070	10,260	11,527	11,209
IMF repurchases	0	0	490	0	0	0	0	0	0	0
Net flows on debt	..	..	**8,267**	**14,277**	**14,363**	**11,995**	**17,758**	**13,936**	**18,506**	**-3,593**
of which short-term debt	..	..	2,410	2,985	1,531	2,187	4,842	3,082	6,057	-3,532
Interest payments (INT)	..	..	**3,248**	**3,405**	**3,439**	**4,792**	**5,996**	**5,496**	**6,918**	**7,226**
Long-term debt	..	..	2,534	2,708	2,630	3,844	4,657	4,685	5,553	5,575
IMF charges	0	0	66	0	0	0	0	0	0	0
Short-term debt	..	..	649	697	809	948	1,340	812	1,365	1,651
Net transfers on debt	..	..	**5,018**	**10,872**	**10,924**	**7,203**	**11,761**	**8,440**	**11,588**	**-10,818**
Total debt service paid (TDS)	..	..	**7,057**	**8,618**	**10,166**	**11,135**	**15,066**	**15,756**	**18,445**	**18,435**
Long-term debt	..	..	5,853	7,921	9,357	10,187	13,726	14,944	17,080	16,784
IMF repurchases and charges	0	0	555	0	0	0	0	0	0	0
Short-term debt (interest only)	..	..	649	697	809	948	1,340	812	1,365	1,651
2. AGGREGATE NET RESOURCE FLOWS AND NET TRANSFERS (LONG-TERM)										
NET RESOURCE FLOWS	..	..	**10,082**	**23,969**	**44,437**	**47,847**	**51,900**	**54,743**	**65,370**	**45,230**
Net flow of long-term debt (ex. IMF)	..	..	6,346	11,292	12,832	9,808	12,915	10,854	12,449	-61
Foreign direct investment (net)	..	..	3,487	11,156	27,515	33,787	35,849	40,180	44,236	43,751
Portfolio equity flows	..	..	0	1,194	3,818	3,915	2,807	3,466	8,457	1,273
Grants (excluding technical coop.)	..	..	249	327	272	337	329	243	227	267
Memo: technical coop. grants	..	..	393	446	486	484	559	534	463	508
official net resource flows	..	..	1,975	2,670	4,887	3,454	8,231	4,643	4,542	2,554
private net resource flows	..	..	8,107	21,299	39,550	44,392	43,669	50,100	60,828	42,676
NET TRANSFERS	..	..	**7,502**	**21,239**	**41,457**	**43,503**	**46,493**	**48,559**	**58,017**	**37,055**
Interest on long-term debt	..	..	2,534	2,708	2,630	3,844	4,657	4,685	5,553	5,575
Profit remittances on FDI	..	..	46	22	350	500	750	1,500	1,800	2,600
Memo: official net transfers	..	..	1,444	1,993	4,060	2,324	6,943	3,333	2,757	742
private net transfers	..	..	6,058	19,246	37,397	41,179	39,550	45,226	55,260	36,314
3. MAJOR ECONOMIC AGGREGATES										
Gross national product (GNP)	..	..	355,609	418,396	430,858	541,496	688,446	804,056	882,321	942,385
Exports of goods & services (XGS)	..	..	60,515	84,640	91,350	125,313	152,781	180,668	214,848	213,414
of which workers remittances	..	..	124	228	108	395	350	1,672	4,423	247
Imports of goods & services (MGS)	..	..	48,668	79,166	104,023	118,345	152,248	173,882	185,851	188,121
International reserves (RES)	..	..	34,476	24,853	27,348	57,781	80,288	111,729	146,448	152,843
Current account balance	..	..	11,997	6,401	-11,609	6,908	1,618	7,243	29,718	29,325
4. DEBT INDICATORS										
EDT / XGS (%)	..	..	91.4	85.6	94.1	80.2	77.3	71.3	68.3	72.4
EDT / GNP (%)	..	..	15.6	17.3	19.9	18.6	17.2	16.0	16.6	16.4
TDS / XGS (%)	..	..	11.7	10.2	11.1	8.9	9.9	8.7	8.6	8.6
INT / XGS (%)	..	..	5.4	4.0	3.8	3.8	3.9	3.0	3.2	3.4
INT / GNP (%)	..	..	0.9	0.8	0.8	0.9	0.9	0.7	0.8	0.8
RES / EDT (%)	..	..	62.3	34.3	31.8	57.5	68.0	86.7	99.8	98.9
RES / MGS (months)	..	..	8.5	3.8	3.2	5.9	6.3	7.7	9.5	9.8
Short-term / EDT (%)	..	..	16.9	19.0	17.8	17.4	18.9	19.7	21.5	18.1
Concessional / EDT (%)	..	..	17.6	15.8	15.7	15.9	15.2	14.5	12.3	17.4
Multilateral / EDT (%)	..	..	11.1	11.9	12.4	13.5	13.8	13.7	12.9	14.4

CHINA

(US$ million, unless otherwise indicated)

	1970	1980	1990	1992	1993	1994	1995	1996	1997	1998
5. LONG-TERM DEBT										
DEBT OUTSTANDING (LDOD)	..	..	**45,515**	**58,663**	**70,632**	**82,974**	**95,764**	**103,410**	**115,233**	**126,667**
Public and publicly guaranteed	..	..	**45,515**	**58,463**	**70,076**	**82,391**	**94,675**	**102,260**	**112,821**	**99,424**
Official creditors	..	..	14,514	19,105	24,339	28,973	36,982	39,433	39,755	45,146
Multilateral	..	..	6,111	8,614	10,690	13,588	16,302	17,695	18,973	22,283
Concessional	..	..	3,119	4,391	5,285	6,231	7,180	7,715	7,954	8,945
Bilateral	..	..	8,403	10,491	13,650	15,385	20,680	21,737	20,782	22,863
Concessional	..	..	6,599	7,041	8,165	9,729	10,792	11,006	10,148	17,892
Private creditors	..	..	31,001	39,358	45,737	53,418	57,693	62,828	73,066	54,278
Bonds	..	..	5,426	5,449	7,715	11,087	10,684	11,106	12,616	13,941
Commercial banks	..	..	14,520	17,913	20,678	21,475	23,869	24,437	34,873	24,400
Other private	..	..	11,055	15,996	17,344	20,856	23,140	27,285	25,577	15,937
Private nonguaranteed	..	..	**0**	**200**	**556**	**583**	**1,090**	**1,150**	**2,412**	**27,243**
Bonds	..	..	0	200	556	583	1,090	1,150	2,412	1,198
Commercial banks	..	..	0	0	0	0	0	0	0	26,045
Memo:										
IBRD	0	0	2,865	3,752	4,549	5,933	7,209	7,616	8,239	9,644
IDA	0	0	3,016	4,286	5,160	6,097	7,038	7,579	7,830	8,693
DISBURSEMENTS	..	..	**9,665**	**16,505**	**19,559**	**16,151**	**21,985**	**21,114**	**23,976**	**11,148**
Public and publicly guaranteed	..	..	**9,665**	**16,308**	**19,227**	**16,151**	**21,441**	**20,985**	**22,458**	**10,679**
Official creditors	..	..	2,578	3,103	5,501	4,200	9,073	5,669	6,214	5,012
Multilateral	..	..	1,158	1,523	2,252	2,559	2,838	2,797	2,939	2,830
Concessional	..	..	511	788	892	686	822	816	715	602
Bilateral	..	..	1,420	1,580	3,249	1,642	6,235	2,872	3,275	2,182
Concessional	..	..	1,022	223	923	1,171	1,533	1,388	248	2,046
Private creditors	..	..	7,088	13,204	13,727	11,951	12,368	15,316	16,244	5,667
Bonds	..	..	277	894	2,737	3,337	1,224	2,777	3,105	1,325
Commercial banks	..	..	3,247	5,062	5,622	2,380	4,977	4,915	5,889	1,537
Other private	..	..	3,564	7,248	5,367	6,234	6,167	7,624	7,249	2,805
Private nonguaranteed	..	..	**0**	**198**	**332**	**0**	**544**	**129**	**1,518**	**469**
Bonds	..	..	0	198	332	0	544	129	1,518	469
Commercial banks	..	..	0	0	0	0	0	0	0	0
Memo:										
IBRD	0	0	591	553	977	1,380	1,457	1,286	1,562	1,474
IDA	0	0	507	778	869	680	812	811	713	592
PRINCIPAL REPAYMENTS	..	..	**3,319**	**5,213**	**6,727**	**6,343**	**9,070**	**10,260**	**11,527**	**11,209**
Public and publicly guaranteed	..	..	**3,319**	**5,213**	**6,727**	**6,343**	**9,070**	**10,260**	**11,320**	**8,182**
Official creditors	..	..	851	760	886	1,083	1,171	1,269	1,899	2,724
Multilateral	..	..	220	215	272	359	420	414	554	575
Concessional	..	..	0	5	7	12	19	27	34	40
Bilateral	..	..	631	545	614	725	751	854	1,345	2,150
Concessional	..	..	145	142	204	276	315	387	385	1,514
Private creditors	..	..	2,468	4,453	5,841	5,260	7,899	8,991	9,421	5,458
Bonds	..	..	325	1,095	831	461	1,451	1,716	1,087	0
Commercial banks	..	..	808	2,046	2,893	1,803	2,645	4,132	5,159	3,018
Other private	..	..	1,335	1,312	2,117	2,997	3,803	3,143	3,175	2,440
Private nonguaranteed	..	..	**0**	**0**	**0**	**0**	**0**	**0**	**207**	**3,027**
Bonds	..	..	0	0	0	0	0	0	207	207
Commercial banks	..	..	0	0	0	0	0	0	0	2,820
Memo:										
IBRD	0	0	216	196	245	315	350	343	351	396
IDA	0	0	0	2	4	9	14	20	26	38
NET FLOWS ON DEBT	..	..	**6,346**	**11,292**	**12,832**	**9,808**	**12,915**	**10,854**	**12,449**	**-61**
Public and publicly guaranteed	..	..	**6,346**	**11,095**	**12,500**	**9,808**	**12,371**	**10,725**	**11,138**	**2,497**
Official creditors	..	..	1,727	2,343	4,615	3,117	7,902	4,401	4,315	2,288
Multilateral	..	..	938	1,308	1,980	2,200	2,418	2,383	2,385	2,255
Concessional	..	..	511	782	885	674	804	789	681	563
Bilateral	..	..	789	1,035	2,635	917	5,484	2,018	1,930	32
Concessional	..	..	877	81	720	895	1,218	1,001	-137	531
Private creditors	..	..	4,620	8,751	7,885	6,691	4,469	6,325	6,823	209
Bonds	..	..	-48	-201	1,906	2,876	-227	1,061	2,019	1,325
Commercial banks	..	..	2,439	3,016	2,729	577	2,332	783	730	-1,481
Other private	..	..	2,229	5,936	3,250	3,237	2,364	4,481	4,075	366
Private nonguaranteed	..	..	**0**	**198**	**332**	**0**	**544**	**129**	**1,311**	**-2,558**
Bonds	..	..	0	198	332	0	544	129	1,311	262
Commercial banks	..	..	0	0	0	0	0	0	0	-2,820
Memo:										
IBRD	0	0	376	357	732	1,066	1,107	943	1,211	1,078
IDA	0	0	507	777	865	671	798	791	687	554

CHINA

(US$ million, unless otherwise indicated)

	1970	1980	1990	1992	1993	1994	1995	1996	1997	1998
INTEREST PAYMENTS (LINT)	..	..	**2,534**	**2,708**	**2,630**	**3,844**	**4,657**	**4,685**	**5,553**	**5,575**
Public and publicly guaranteed	..	..	**2,534**	**2,708**	**2,618**	**3,818**	**4,624**	**4,631**	**5,498**	**4,612**
Official creditors	..	..	531	678	827	1,131	1,288	1,310	1,785	1,813
Multilateral	..	..	226	319	377	480	619	684	730	817
Concessional	..	..	20	31	36	44	53	56	58	60
Bilateral	..	..	305	358	450	651	669	626	1,055	996
Concessional	..	..	193	281	305	330	324	293	342	293
Private creditors	..	..	2,003	2,031	1,792	2,687	3,336	3,321	3,713	2,799
Bonds	..	..	367	337	286	363	594	506	568	397
Commercial banks	..	..	959	776	738	1,034	1,333	1,351	1,441	983
Other private	..	..	677	917	767	1,290	1,409	1,464	1,704	1,419
Private nonguaranteed	..	..	**0**	**0**	**12**	**26**	**33**	**53**	**55**	**963**
Bonds	..	..	0	0	12	26	33	53	55	42
Commercial banks	..	..	0	0	0	0	0	0	0	921
Memo:										
IBRD	0	0	200	264	299	364	460	497	507	545
IDA	0	0	19	29	34	41	49	52	56	59
NET TRANSFERS ON DEBT	..	..	**3,813**	**8,584**	**10,202**	**5,964**	**8,258**	**6,170**	**6,896**	**-5,636**
Public and publicly guaranteed	..	..	**3,813**	**8,386**	**9,882**	**5,990**	**7,748**	**6,094**	**5,640**	**-2,115**
Official creditors	..	..	1,196	1,665	3,788	1,986	6,614	3,090	2,530	475
Multilateral	..	..	712	988	1,604	1,720	1,799	1,699	1,655	1,438
Concessional	..	..	491	752	849	630	751	734	622	503
Bilateral	..	..	484	677	2,184	266	4,816	1,392	875	-963
Concessional	..	..	684	-200	415	565	894	708	-480	239
Private creditors	..	..	2,617	6,721	6,094	4,004	1,133	3,004	3,111	-2,590
Bonds	..	..	-415	-538	1,620	2,513	-821	555	1,451	928
Commercial banks	..	..	1,480	2,240	1,991	-457	999	-568	-711	-2,465
Other private	..	..	1,551	5,019	2,483	1,948	955	3,017	2,371	-1,053
Private nonguaranteed	..	..	**0**	**198**	**320**	**-26**	**511**	**76**	**1,256**	**-3,521**
Bonds	..	..	0	198	320	-26	511	76	1,256	220
Commercial banks	..	..	0	0	0	0	0	0	0	-3,742
Memo:										
IBRD	0	0	176	92	433	701	648	447	704	533
IDA	0	0	488	748	831	630	749	738	632	495
DEBT SERVICE (LTDS)	..	..	**5,853**	**7,921**	**9,357**	**10,187**	**13,726**	**14,944**	**17,080**	**16,784**
Public and publicly guaranteed	..	..	**5,853**	**7,921**	**9,346**	**10,161**	**13,693**	**14,891**	**16,818**	**12,794**
Official creditors	..	..	1,383	1,438	1,713	2,214	2,459	2,579	3,684	4,537
Multilateral	..	..	446	534	648	838	1,039	1,099	1,285	1,392
Concessional	..	..	20	36	43	56	71	82	92	100
Bilateral	..	..	937	903	1,064	1,376	1,419	1,480	2,400	3,145
Concessional	..	..	338	423	508	607	639	680	728	1,807
Private creditors	..	..	4,470	6,483	7,633	7,947	11,234	12,312	13,133	8,257
Bonds	..	..	692	1,432	1,117	824	2,045	2,223	1,655	397
Commercial banks	..	..	1,767	2,822	3,631	2,837	3,978	5,483	6,600	4,002
Other private	..	..	2,012	2,229	2,885	4,286	5,212	4,607	4,879	3,858
Private nonguaranteed	..	..	**0**	**0**	**12**	**26**	**33**	**53**	**262**	**3,990**
Bonds	..	..	0	0	12	26	33	53	262	249
Commercial banks	..	..	0	0	0	0	0	0	0	3,742
Memo:										
IBRD	0	0	415	460	543	679	810	840	858	941
IDA	0	0	19	30	38	50	63	73	81	97
UNDISBURSED DEBT	..	..	**9,298**	**10,948**	**16,158**	**16,235**	**17,010**	**17,878**	**16,859**	**22,240**
Official creditors	..	..	5,280	8,168	10,321	13,149	13,454	12,113	11,487	21,730
Private creditors	..	..	4,019	2,780	5,837	3,086	3,556	5,765	5,371	510
Memorandum items										
Concessional LDOD	..	..	9,718	11,432	13,449	15,960	17,972	18,722	18,101	26,838
Variable rate LDOD	..	..	16,491	17,289	20,624	23,272	28,370	30,652	45,217	62,139
Public sector LDOD	..	..	45,449	58,413	69,864	81,709	93,573	101,163	111,740	47,687
Private sector LDOD	..	..	66	250	767	1,265	2,192	2,247	3,493	78,980
6. CURRENCY COMPOSITION OF LONG-TERM DEBT (PERCENT)										
Deutsche mark	..	..	3.1	1.6	1.0	1.7	1.7	1.4	1.2	2.3
French franc	..	..	0.4	0.4	0.3	0.3	0.3	0.3	0.2	2.9
Japanese yen	..	..	30.4	22.6	21.0	23.2	20.7	15.9	11.8	14.8
Pound sterling	..	..	0.7	0.4	0.3	0.3	0.2	0.2	0.2	0.1
Swiss franc	..	..	0.2	0.0	0.0	0.1	0.0	0.0	0.0	0.1
U.S.dollars	..	..	29.1	48.3	54.3	53.6	58.1	65.0	74.6	72.4
Multiple currency	..	..	31.2	23.3	20.5	18.7	17.1	15.6	10.8	6.2
Special drawing rights	..	..	0.3	0.2	0.2	0.2	0.1	0.1	0.1	0.3
All other currencies	..	..	4.6	3.2	2.4	1.9	1.8	1.5	1.1	0.9

CHINA

(US$ million, unless otherwise indicated)

	1970	1980	1990	1992	1993	1994	1995	1996	1997	1998
7. DEBT RESTRUCTURINGS										
Total amount rescheduled	..	..	0	0	0	0	0	0	0	0
Debt stock rescheduled	..	..	0	0	0	0	0	0	0	0
Principal rescheduled	..	..	0	0	0	0	0	0	0	0
Official	..	..	0	0	0	0	0	0	0	0
Private	..	..	0	0	0	0	0	0	0	0
Interest rescheduled	..	..	0	0	0	0	0	0	0	0
Official	..	..	0	0	0	0	0	0	0	0
Private	..	..	0	0	0	0	0	0	0	0
Debt forgiven	..	..	0	0	0	0	0	0	0	0
Memo: interest forgiven	..	..	0	0	0	0	0	0	0	0
Debt stock reduction	..	..	0	0	0	0	0	0	0	0
of which debt buyback	..	..	0	0	0	0	0	0	0	0
8. DEBT STOCK-FLOW RECONCILIATION										
Total change in debt stocks	..	..	10,369	12,169	13,500	14,529	17,633	10,727	17,880	7,902
Net flows on debt	..	..	8,267	14,277	14,363	11,995	17,758	13,936	18,506	-3,593
Net change in interest arrears	..	..	0	0	0	0	0	0	0	0
Interest capitalized	..	..	0	0	0	0	0	0	0	0
Debt forgiveness or reduction	..	..	0	0	0	0	0	0	0	0
Cross-currency valuation	..	..	1,484	-295	1,593	2,906	-222	-2,614	-2,343	2,531
Residual	..	..	618	-1,814	-2,456	-371	98	-594	1,717	8,964
9. AVERAGE TERMS OF NEW COMMITMENTS										
ALL CREDITORS										
Interest (%)	..	..	7.5	6.2	5.5	5.5	6.5	6.6	6.5	6.2
Maturity (years)	..	..	16.6	14.9	14.0	15.6	11.8	10.1	10.1	13.0
Grace period (years)	..	..	3.9	3.5	3.9	5.0	2.9	2.9	3.2	4.2
Grant element (%)	..	..	15.6	19.3	22.1	25.5	15.4	14.2	14.8	19.5
Official creditors										
Interest (%)	..	..	3.7	5.5	5.1	5.6	6.8	5.9	6.6	5.9
Maturity (years)	..	..	27.9	22.2	19.7	21.1	18.3	21.2	19.1	21.6
Grace period (years)	..	..	7.9	5.7	5.3	6.0	3.7	4.5	3.9	5.6
Grant element (%)	..	..	49.2	31.1	31.8	30.4	19.0	27.7	21.2	27.8
Private creditors										
Interest (%)	..	..	8.6	6.5	5.6	5.4	6.3	6.8	6.4	6.4
Maturity (years)	..	..	13.3	12.3	11.4	11.6	7.3	7.0	6.4	6.8
Grace period (years)	..	..	2.7	2.7	3.3	4.2	2.4	2.4	2.9	3.3
Grant element (%)	..	..	5.7	15.0	17.8	21.7	12.9	10.5	12.2	13.5
Memorandum items										
Commitments	..	..	9,988	16,831	24,930	15,945	22,796	22,438	22,108	8,029
Official creditors	..	..	2,288	4,451	7,629	6,809	9,279	4,886	6,323	3,357
Private creditors	..	..	7,701	12,379	17,301	9,135	13,517	17,552	15,785	4,671

10. CONTRACTUAL OBLIGATIONS ON OUTSTANDING LONG-TERM DEBT

	1999	2000	2001	2002	2003	2004	2005	2006	2007	2008
TOTAL										
Disbursements	7,508	5,268	3,479	2,357	1,551	982	633	284	148	31
Principal	7,482	9,936	15,435	15,955	15,199	11,916	18,528	4,205	3,812	3,604
Interest	6,025	6,009	5,719	5,118	4,463	3,111	2,201	1,610	1,424	1,232
Official creditors										
Disbursements	7,199	5,142	3,426	2,343	1,547	979	632	284	148	31
Principal	3,286	3,540	4,060	4,492	4,508	4,218	3,783	3,740	3,605	3,058
Interest	2,032	2,129	2,137	2,069	1,949	1,802	1,655	1,495	1,328	1,164
Bilateral creditors										
Disbursements	4,807	2,849	1,455	688	262	106	24	0	0	0
Principal	2,431	2,490	2,740	2,947	2,822	2,410	1,961	1,931	1,842	1,340
Interest	916	958	931	857	760	665	589	518	447	382
Multilateral creditors										
Disbursements	2,392	2,293	1,971	1,655	1,285	873	608	284	148	31
Principal	855	1,051	1,320	1,545	1,686	1,808	1,822	1,809	1,763	1,719
Interest	1,116	1,170	1,206	1,212	1,189	1,137	1,066	977	881	782
Private creditors										
Disbursements	309	126	53	13	4	3	1	0	0	0
Principal	4,196	6,396	11,375	11,463	10,692	7,698	14,745	466	207	546
Interest	3,992	3,880	3,582	3,050	2,514	1,310	546	115	96	68
Commercial banks										
Disbursements	90	36	13	2	0	0	0	0	0	0
Principal	145	174	5,672	5,669	5,661	5,651	149	132	114	109
Interest	1,416	1,413	1,325	981	637	294	35	32	28	25
Other private										
Disbursements	219	91	40	12	4	3	1	0	0	0
Principal	4,051	6,221	5,703	5,794	5,030	2,047	14,595	333	93	437
Interest	2,577	2,467	2,258	2,069	1,877	1,016	511	83	68	42

COLOMBIA

(US$ million, unless otherwise indicated)

	1970	1980	1990	1992	1993	1994	1995	1996	1997	1998
1. SUMMARY DEBT DATA										
TOTAL DEBT STOCKS (EDT)	..	**6,941**	**17,222**	**17,277**	**18,942**	**21,940**	**25,048**	**28,900**	**31,800**	**33,263**
Long-term debt (LDOD)	**1,580**	**4,604**	**15,784**	**14,726**	**15,289**	**17,448**	**19,503**	**23,016**	**26,041**	**27,031**
Public and publicly guaranteed	1,297	4,089	14,671	13,476	13,243	14,358	13,950	14,854	15,295	16,930
Private nonguaranteed	283	515	1,113	1,250	2,046	3,091	5,553	8,162	10,746	10,101
Use of IMF credit	**55**	**0**	**0**	**0**	**0**	**0**	**0**	**0**	**0**	**0**
Short-term debt	..	**2,337**	**1,438**	**2,551**	**3,653**	**4,492**	**5,545**	**5,884**	**5,759**	**6,232**
of which interest arrears on LDOD	..	0	28	11	15	11	2	0	0	0
Official creditors	..	0	17	10	11	8	0	0	0	0
Private creditors	..	0	11	1	4	3	2	0	0	0
Memo: principal arrears on LDOD	..	0	409	145	192	230	224	42	38	42
Official creditors	..	0	42	90	119	138	125	31	28	31
Private creditors	..	0	367	55	73	92	99	11	10	11
Memo: export credits	..	0	3,908	3,172	3,090	3,235	2,841	3,385	3,113	3,340
TOTAL DEBT FLOWS										
Disbursements	**282**	**1,071**	**1,994**	**2,189**	**3,083**	**5,709**	**4,181**	**7,422**	**6,116**	**3,289**
Long-term debt	253	1,071	1,994	2,189	3,083	5,709	4,181	7,422	6,116	3,289
IMF purchases	29	0	0	0	0	0	0	0	0	0
Principal repayments	**210**	**263**	**2,189**	**2,614**	**2,405**	**3,892**	**2,347**	**3,365**	**2,516**	**2,617**
Long-term debt	137	263	2,189	2,614	2,405	3,892	2,347	3,365	2,516	2,617
IMF repurchases	73	0	0	0	0	0	0	0	0	0
Net flows on debt	**674**	**1,133**	**-399**	**383**	**1,776**	**2,660**	**2,897**	**4,397**	**3,476**	**1,146**
of which short-term debt	..	325	-204	808	1,098	844	1,062	341	-125	473
Interest payments (INT)	..	**688**	**1,701**	**1,394**	**1,302**	**1,678**	**1,998**	**2,036**	**2,011**	**1,949**
Long-term debt	59	310	1,558	1,290	1,131	1,478	1,687	1,722	1,662	1,600
IMF charges	0	0	0	0	0	0	0	0	0	0
Short-term debt	..	378	143	104	171	200	311	314	349	348
Net transfers on debt	..	**445**	**-2,100**	**-1,011**	**474**	**982**	**899**	**2,361**	**1,465**	**-803**
Total debt service paid (TDS)	..	**951**	**3,889**	**4,008**	**3,707**	**5,570**	**4,345**	**5,401**	**4,527**	**4,565**
Long-term debt	197	573	3,746	3,904	3,536	5,370	4,034	5,087	4,178	4,217
IMF repurchases and charges	73	0	0	0	0	0	0	0	0	0
Short-term debt (interest only)	..	378	143	104	171	200	311	314	349	348
2. AGGREGATE NET RESOURCE FLOWS AND NET TRANSFERS (LONG-TERM)										
NET RESOURCE FLOWS	**181**	**973**	**340**	**393**	**1,883**	**3,626**	**3,008**	**7,550**	**9,507**	**3,798**
Net flow of long-term debt (ex. IMF)	115	808	-195	-426	678	1,817	1,834	4,057	3,601	673
Foreign direct investment (net)	43	157	500	729	959	1,445	969	3,123	5,703	3,038
Portfolio equity flows	0	0	0	0	169	320	131	290	116	26
Grants (excluding technical coop.)	23	8	35	89	76	45	74	81	88	61
Memo: technical coop. grants	14	46	85	89	77	85	98	91	75	115
official net resource flows	178	285	-5	-324	-234	-423	-349	-30	-364	168
private net resource flows	3	688	345	717	2,117	4,049	3,357	7,580	9,872	3,630
NET TRANSFERS	**28**	**553**	**-2,182**	**-1,940**	**-449**	**749**	**-179**	**4,079**	**5,946**	**197**
Interest on long-term debt	59	310	1,558	1,290	1,131	1,478	1,687	1,722	1,662	1,600
Profit remittances on FDI	94	110	964	1,043	1,200	1,400	1,500	1,750	1,900	2,000
Memo: official net transfers	142	157	-632	-972	-813	-938	-855	-498	-770	-202
private net transfers	-114	396	-1,550	-968	364	1,686	675	4,576	6,716	399
3. MAJOR ECONOMIC AGGREGATES										
Gross national product (GNP)	7,086	33,506	38,559	86,463	78,909	79,164	89,491	95,377	106,408	100,426
Exports of goods & services (XGS)	1,025	5,928	9,514	10,325	10,964	12,373	13,697	14,529	15,771	14,871
of which workers remittances	6	68	488	630	455	966	739	635	658	483
Imports of goods & services (MGS)	1,348	6,231	9,510	10,528	13,750	16,093	18,339	19,274	21,644	20,776
International reserves (RES)	207	6,474	4,453	7,551	7,670	7,862	8,205	9,690	9,611	8,397
Current account balance	-293	-206	542	901	-2,102	-3,596	-4,624	-4,762	-5,891	-5,908
4. DEBT INDICATORS										
EDT / XGS (%)	..	117.1	181.0	167.3	172.8	177.3	182.9	198.9	201.6	223.7
EDT / GNP (%)	..	20.7	44.7	20.0	24.0	27.7	28.0	30.3	29.9	33.1
TDS / XGS (%)	..	16.0	40.9	38.8	33.8	45.0	31.7	37.2	28.7	30.7
INT / XGS (%)	..	11.6	17.9	13.5	11.9	13.6	14.6	14.0	12.8	13.1
INT / GNP (%)	..	2.1	4.4	1.6	1.7	2.1	2.2	2.1	1.9	1.9
RES / EDT (%)	..	93.3	25.9	43.7	40.5	35.8	32.8	33.5	30.2	25.2
RES / MGS (months)	1.8	12.5	5.6	8.6	6.7	5.9	5.4	6.0	5.3	4.9
Short-term / EDT (%)	..	33.7	8.4	14.8	19.3	20.5	22.1	20.4	18.1	18.7
Concessional / EDT (%)	..	14.2	5.7	5.3	4.0	4.3	3.9	3.3	2.8	2.7
Multilateral / EDT (%)	..	19.5	35.4	34.0	29.9	24.6	21.2	16.5	12.8	13.7

COLOMBIA

(US$ million, unless otherwise indicated)

	1970	1980	1990	1992	1993	1994	1995	1996	1997	1998
5. LONG-TERM DEBT										
DEBT OUTSTANDING (LDOD)	**1,580**	**4,604**	**15,784**	**14,726**	**15,289**	**17,448**	**19,503**	**23,016**	**26,041**	**27,031**
Public and publicly guaranteed	**1,297**	**4,089**	**14,671**	**13,476**	**13,243**	**14,358**	**13,950**	**14,854**	**15,295**	**16,930**
Official creditors	1,112	2,393	8,540	7,816	7,461	7,277	7,066	6,503	5,623	5,947
Multilateral	445	1,350	6,103	5,874	5,657	5,392	5,320	4,765	4,084	4,550
Concessional	25	89	219	193	180	175	164	152	145	131
Bilateral	667	1,043	2,437	1,941	1,803	1,886	1,747	1,738	1,538	1,397
Concessional	604	899	769	717	577	773	814	790	745	759
Private creditors	185	1,696	6,131	5,660	5,782	7,080	6,883	8,351	9,672	10,983
Bonds	21	31	275	419	875	1,333	1,734	3,410	4,366	6,200
Commercial banks	24	1,371	4,208	3,828	3,724	4,623	4,163	4,095	4,482	4,112
Other private	140	294	1,648	1,414	1,182	1,124	987	847	825	670
Private nonguaranteed	**283**	**515**	**1,113**	**1,250**	**2,046**	**3,091**	**5,553**	**8,162**	**10,746**	**10,101**
Bonds	0	0	0	0	0	125	717	820	809	821
Commercial banks	283	515	1,113	1,250	2,046	2,966	4,836	7,341	9,937	9,280
Memo:										
IBRD	354	991	3,859	3,195	2,969	2,629	2,548	2,177	1,723	1,740
IDA	20	21	15	13	12	12	11	10	10	9
DISBURSEMENTS	**253**	**1,071**	**1,994**	**2,189**	**3,083**	**5,709**	**4,181**	**7,422**	**6,116**	**3,289**
Public and publicly guaranteed	**253**	**1,016**	**1,847**	**1,680**	**1,786**	**3,109**	**1,571**	**3,461**	**2,854**	**3,289**
Official creditors	194	413	698	838	955	1,158	687	880	611	790
Multilateral	74	303	559	681	629	602	397	428	488	737
Concessional	0	37	4	0	0	9	2	0	5	0
Bilateral	120	111	139	157	326	555	290	453	123	53
Concessional	101	9	26	40	15	205	70	50	43	20
Private creditors	59	603	1,150	843	830	1,951	885	2,581	2,242	2,500
Bonds	0	0	0	100	475	566	535	1,928	1,144	2,132
Commercial banks	8	500	874	401	260	1,223	257	509	893	329
Other private	50	103	275	342	95	162	93	145	205	39
Private nonguaranteed	**0**	**55**	**147**	**508**	**1,297**	**2,600**	**2,610**	**3,960**	**3,263**	**0**
Bonds	0	0	0	0	0	125	592	108	0	0
Commercial banks	0	55	147	508	1,297	2,475	2,018	3,852	3,263	0
Memo:										
IBRD	58	218	213	262	301	310	238	152	189	184
IDA	0	0	0	0	0	0	0	0	0	0
PRINCIPAL REPAYMENTS	**137**	**263**	**2,189**	**2,614**	**2,405**	**3,892**	**2,347**	**3,365**	**2,516**	**2,617**
Public and publicly guaranteed	**78**	**250**	**1,875**	**2,375**	**1,904**	**2,336**	**2,200**	**2,018**	**1,848**	**1,961**
Official creditors	39	136	737	1,251	1,266	1,625	1,110	991	1,063	683
Multilateral	22	80	527	794	915	1,299	647	613	833	437
Concessional	0	1	12	13	13	13	13	13	12	14
Bilateral	17	57	210	457	352	326	463	377	230	245
Concessional	7	30	36	35	47	24	39	38	43	38
Private creditors	40	114	1,138	1,124	638	711	1,090	1,027	785	1,278
Bonds	3	3	4	41	22	113	120	192	76	380
Commercial banks	12	52	849	683	366	334	723	570	502	700
Other private	25	59	284	401	249	265	248	265	208	198
Private nonguaranteed	**59**	**13**	**314**	**239**	**501**	**1,556**	**147**	**1,347**	**667**	**656**
Bonds	0	0	0	0	0	0	0	0	0	0
Commercial banks	59	13	314	239	501	1,556	147	1,347	667	656
Memo:										
IBRD	17	65	434	681	596	836	414	350	437	232
IDA	0	0	1	1	1	1	1	1	1	1
NET FLOWS ON DEBT	**115**	**808**	**-195**	**-426**	**678**	**1,817**	**1,834**	**4,057**	**3,601**	**673**
Public and publicly guaranteed	**174**	**766**	**-28**	**-695**	**-118**	**772**	**-628**	**1,443**	**1,005**	**1,329**
Official creditors	155	277	-40	-413	-311	-467	-423	-111	-452	107
Multilateral	52	223	32	-113	-286	-697	-250	-186	-345	300
Concessional	0	37	-8	-13	-13	-4	-11	-13	-7	-14
Bilateral	104	54	-72	-300	-25	230	-173	75	-107	-193
Concessional	94	-21	-10	5	-32	181	31	12	0	-18
Private creditors	19	489	12	-281	192	1,240	-205	1,554	1,457	1,222
Bonds	-3	-3	-4	60	453	453	416	1,736	1,068	1,752
Commercial banks	-4	449	25	-282	-106	889	-466	-61	391	-371
Other private	26	44	-9	-59	-154	-103	-155	-121	-2	-160
Private nonguaranteed	**-59**	**42**	**-167**	**269**	**796**	**1,044**	**2,463**	**2,613**	**2,595**	**-656**
Bonds	0	0	0	0	0	125	592	108	0	0
Commercial banks	-59	42	-167	269	796	919	1,871	2,505	2,595	-656
Memo:										
IBRD	41	152	-221	-419	-294	-526	-176	-198	-248	-48
IDA	0	0	-1	-1	-1	-1	-1	-1	-1	-1

COLOMBIA

(US$ million, unless otherwise indicated)

	1970	1980	1990	1992	1993	1994	1995	1996	1997	1998
INTEREST PAYMENTS (LINT)	**59**	**310**	**1,558**	**1,290**	**1,131**	**1,478**	**1,687**	**1,722**	**1,662**	**1,600**
Public and publicly guaranteed	**44**	**279**	**1,240**	**1,077**	**893**	**977**	**962**	**843**	**885**	**977**
Official creditors	36	128	627	648	579	515	506	468	406	370
Multilateral	25	102	476	474	457	424	388	366	314	286
Concessional	0	2	6	4	4	5	4	4	3	3
Bilateral	12	26	150	174	122	91	118	102	91	84
Concessional	8	21	19	14	21	18	25	26	24	24
Private creditors	8	151	613	429	314	462	457	375	480	607
Bonds	1	2	27	23	25	57	58	43	145	242
Commercial banks	2	128	461	286	179	305	310	254	269	303
Other private	5	21	124	121	110	100	89	78	66	63
Private nonguaranteed	**15**	**31**	**318**	**213**	**239**	**500**	**725**	**879**	**776**	**623**
Bonds	0	0	0	0	0	0	15	78	82	82
Commercial banks	15	31	318	213	239	500	710	801	695	542
Memo:										
IBRD	20	79	318	278	242	218	191	170	137	115
IDA	0	0	0	0	0	0	0	0	0	0
NET TRANSFERS ON DEBT	**56**	**498**	**-1,753**	**-1,715**	**-453**	**339**	**147**	**2,335**	**1,939**	**-928**
Public and publicly guaranteed	**130**	**487**	**-1,268**	**-1,772**	**-1,011**	**-205**	**-1,591**	**601**	**120**	**352**
Official creditors	119	149	-666	-1,061	-889	-982	-928	-578	-858	-263
Multilateral	27	121	-445	-587	-742	-1,121	-638	-551	-659	14
Concessional	-1	35	-14	-17	-17	-8	-15	-16	-10	-17
Bilateral	92	28	-222	-474	-147	139	-291	-27	-199	-277
Concessional	86	-42	-29	-9	-53	163	6	-14	-23	-42
Private creditors	11	338	-601	-711	-122	777	-662	1,179	978	615
Bonds	-3	-5	-32	36	428	396	357	1,693	924	1,511
Commercial banks	-7	321	-436	-567	-285	584	-776	-315	122	-674
Other private	21	22	-133	-180	-264	-203	-244	-199	-68	-222
Private nonguaranteed	**-74**	**11**	**-485**	**56**	**558**	**544**	**1,738**	**1,734**	**1,819**	**-1,280**
Bonds	0	0	0	0	0	125	577	30	-82	-82
Commercial banks	-74	11	-485	56	558	419	1,161	1,704	1,901	-1,198
Memo:										
IBRD	21	74	-538	-697	-537	-744	-367	-368	-385	-163
IDA	0	0	-1	-1	-1	-1	-1	-1	-1	-1
DEBT SERVICE (LTDS)	**197**	**573**	**3,746**	**3,904**	**3,536**	**5,370**	**4,034**	**5,087**	**4,178**	**4,217**
Public and publicly guaranteed	**123**	**529**	**3,115**	**3,452**	**2,797**	**3,313**	**3,162**	**2,861**	**2,734**	**2,937**
Official creditors	75	264	1,364	1,898	1,845	2,140	1,615	1,458	1,469	1,053
Multilateral	47	181	1,003	1,268	1,371	1,723	1,035	979	1,148	723
Concessional	1	2	18	17	17	18	17	17	15	17
Bilateral	28	83	361	631	473	417	581	479	321	329
Concessional	15	51	55	49	68	42	64	64	66	61
Private creditors	47	265	1,751	1,554	952	1,174	1,547	1,402	1,265	1,885
Bonds	3	5	32	64	47	170	178	235	220	621
Commercial banks	15	179	1,311	969	545	639	1,032	824	771	1,003
Other private	29	80	409	521	360	365	337	343	274	261
Private nonguaranteed	**74**	**44**	**632**	**452**	**740**	**2,056**	**872**	**2,226**	**1,444**	**1,280**
Bonds	0	0	0	0	0	0	15	78	82	82
Commercial banks	74	44	632	452	740	2,056	857	2,148	1,362	1,198
Memo:										
IBRD	37	144	751	959	838	1,054	604	520	573	347
IDA	0	0	1	1	1	1	1	1	1	1
UNDISBURSED DEBT	**576**	**2,455**	**4,034**	**3,895**	**3,915**	**2,791**	**2,756**	**2,390**	**2,025**	**1,778**
Official creditors	424	1,781	3,468	2,865	2,948	2,675	2,434	2,193	1,968	1,775
Private creditors	153	674	567	1,029	967	116	322	197	57	3
Memorandum items										
Concessional LDOD	629	988	988	910	757	948	979	943	890	890
Variable rate LDOD	283	1,877	7,778	7,731	8,429	9,656	11,660	14,541	17,228	16,827
Public sector LDOD	1,224	4,045	14,630	13,474	13,241	14,354	13,945	14,848	15,289	16,925
Private sector LDOD	356	559	1,154	1,252	2,048	3,094	5,558	8,167	10,752	10,106

6. CURRENCY COMPOSITION OF LONG-TERM DEBT (PERCENT)

	1970	1980	1990	1992	1993	1994	1995	1996	1997	1998
Deutsche mark	1.3	3.8	6.0	4.9	4.5	4.3	5.0	3.3	2.2	5.6
French franc	0.4	1.9	0.3	0.3	0.3	0.4	0.4	0.3	0.2	0.2
Japanese yen	0.0	0.1	4.9	4.2	3.9	4.1	5.6	5.9	4.9	4.8
Pound sterling	0.2	0.4	0.3	0.2	0.2	0.1	0.1	0.1	0.1	1.1
Swiss franc	0.3	0.0	0.3	0.2	0.2	0.2	0.2	0.1	0.1	0.1
U.S.dollars	66.1	60.4	44.0	45.6	48.2	54.9	53.3	62.1	76.8	75.0
Multiple currency	29.8	31.3	41.2	42.5	41.3	34.7	34.3	27.2	15.0	12.9
Special drawing rights	0.0	0.0	0.0	0.0	0.0	0.0	0.0	0.0	0.0	0.0
All other currencies	1.9	2.1	3.0	2.1	1.4	1.3	1.1	1.0	0.7	0.3

COLOMBIA

(US$ million, unless otherwise indicated)

	1970	1980	1990	1992	1993	1994	1995	1996	1997	1998
7. DEBT RESTRUCTURINGS										
Total amount rescheduled	..	..	0	0	254	0	0	0	0	0
Debt stock rescheduled	..	..	0	0	254	0	0	0	0	0
Principal rescheduled	..	..	0	0	0	0	0	0	0	0
Official	..	..	0	0	0	0	0	0	0	0
Private	..	..	0	0	0	0	0	0	0	0
Interest rescheduled	..	..	0	0	0	0	0	0	0	0
Official	..	..	0	0	0	0	0	0	0	0
Private	..	..	0	0	0	0	0	0	0	0
Debt forgiven	..	..	2	1	37	0	0	0	0	0
Memo: interest forgiven	..	..	0	0	0	0	0	0	0	0
Debt stock reduction	..	..	0	24	54	0	0	0	0	0
of which debt buyback	..	..	0	0	0	0	0	0	0	0
8. DEBT STOCK-FLOW RECONCILIATION										
Total change in debt stocks	..	..	336	76	1,665	2,998	3,108	3,852	2,900	1,464
Net flows on debt	674	1,133	-399	383	1,776	2,660	2,897	4,397	3,476	1,146
Net change in interest arrears	..	..	26	-9	4	-5	-9	-2	0	0
Interest capitalized	..	..	0	0	0	0	0	0	0	0
Debt forgiveness or reduction	..	..	-2	-25	-91	0	0	0	0	0
Cross-currency valuation	..	..	398	-372	-99	173	16	-402	-382	230
Residual	..	..	314	99	74	170	204	-142	-194	88
9. AVERAGE TERMS OF NEW COMMITMENTS										
ALL CREDITORS										
Interest (%)	6.0	12.9	8.0	8.1	7.0	5.1	4.8	7.2	7.4	7.7
Maturity (years)	21.2	15.5	16.5	16.8	12.8	12.3	11.6	9.1	12.3	8.1
Grace period (years)	4.8	4.4	4.6	4.6	3.9	5.4	4.3	5.8	7.6	5.7
Grant element (%)	25.8	-20.4	12.2	10.5	14.1	22.9	23.6	12.6	13.0	9.5
Official creditors										
Interest (%)	5.2	8.9	7.5	7.8	7.2	6.5	6.4	6.8	7.2	7.2
Maturity (years)	29.8	18.0	18.7	17.9	17.6	19.3	20.4	17.3	18.6	15.0
Grace period (years)	7.2	4.3	5.4	4.6	4.4	5.2	4.8	4.6	4.4	4.0
Grant element (%)	36.9	6.5	15.5	12.7	16.3	21.8	23.2	18.9	16.4	14.8
Private creditors										
Interest (%)	7.2	15.4	9.3	9.3	6.7	4.0	3.8	7.3	7.4	7.8
Maturity (years)	7.2	13.9	9.9	13.0	6.0	6.9	6.0	7.1	10.9	6.3
Grace period (years)	1.1	4.5	2.2	5.0	3.1	5.6	4.0	6.1	8.4	6.1
Grant element (%)	7.9	-37.2	2.3	2.8	11.0	23.7	23.8	11.0	12.2	8.0
Memorandum items										
Commitments	363	1,566	1,269	1,075	1,865	2,143	1,792	3,064	2,596	3,176
Official creditors	224	602	951	831	1,089	933	704	607	493	682
Private creditors	139	964	318	244	776	1,209	1,088	2,458	2,102	2,494

10. CONTRACTUAL OBLIGATIONS ON OUTSTANDING LONG-TERM DEBT

	1999	2000	2001	2002	2003	2004	2005	2006	2007	2008
TOTAL										
Disbursements	475	451	320	223	137	83	50	18	11	5
Principal	3,076	2,820	3,501	2,833	2,789	1,731	1,818	1,450	2,079	1,739
Interest	1,820	1,672	1,502	1,270	1,096	911	803	658	537	383
Official creditors										
Disbursements	473	451	320	223	137	83	50	18	11	5
Principal	651	641	690	670	630	611	556	500	447	405
Interest	419	399	375	341	305	268	231	196	164	135
Bilateral creditors										
Disbursements	15	7	5	2	2	2	1	0	0	0
Principal	141	108	109	107	104	90	75	69	69	69
Interest	70	62	55	48	42	36	32	28	25	21
Multilateral creditors										
Disbursements	458	444	315	221	135	81	49	18	11	5
Principal	510	533	581	563	526	522	481	431	378	336
Interest	349	337	320	293	263	232	199	168	139	114
Private creditors										
Disbursements	3	0	0	0	0	0	0	0	0	0
Principal	2,425	2,179	2,811	2,163	2,159	1,120	1,261	951	1,632	1,335
Interest	1,402	1,273	1,128	929	791	642	571	463	373	248
Commercial banks										
Disbursements	0	0	0	0	0	0	0	0	0	0
Principal	926	795	966	511	414	390	50	22	14	5
Interest	263	204	141	92	58	26	7	4	2	2
Other private										
Disbursements	3	0	0	0	0	0	0	0	0	0
Principal	1,500	1,384	1,845	1,652	1,745	730	1,211	929	1,619	1,330
Interest	1,139	1,069	986	838	733	617	565	459	371	247

COMOROS

(US$ million, unless otherwise indicated)

	1970	1980	1990	1992	1993	1994	1995	1996	1997	1998
1. SUMMARY DEBT DATA										
TOTAL DEBT STOCKS (EDT)	**..**	**44.0**	**184.9**	**188.3**	**184.9**	**192.3**	**203.7**	**205.6**	**200.1**	**203.1**
Long-term debt (LDOD)	**1.2**	**43.0**	**172.6**	**175.2**	**169.6**	**179.0**	**190.3**	**192.9**	**183.9**	**188.1**
Public and publicly guaranteed	1.2	43.0	172.6	175.2	169.6	179.0	190.3	192.9	183.9	188.1
Private nonguaranteed	0.0	0.0	0.0	0.0	0.0	0.0	0.0	0.0	0.0	0.0
Use of IMF credit	**0.0**	**0.0**	**0.0**	**1.2**	**1.2**	**3.3**	**3.3**	**3.2**	**2.8**	**2.7**
Short-term debt	**..**	**1.0**	**12.4**	**11.8**	**14.1**	**9.9**	**10.1**	**9.5**	**13.4**	**12.3**
of which interest arrears on LDOD	..	0.0	12.2	11.7	13.1	9.9	8.1	9.5	8.4	11.2
Official creditors	..	0.0	12.2	11.7	13.1	9.9	8.1	9.5	8.4	11.2
Private creditors	..	0.0	0.0	0.0	0.0	0.0	0.0	0.0	0.0	0.0
Memo: principal arrears on LDOD	..	0.0	25.5	19.4	18.8	18.6	26.8	33.0	32.1	33.6
Official creditors	..	0.0	25.5	19.4	18.8	18.6	26.8	33.0	32.1	33.6
Private creditors	..	0.0	0.0	0.0	0.0	0.0	0.0	0.0	0.0	0.0
Memo: export credits	..	0.0	2.0	1.0	1.0	2.0	4.0	3.0	3.0	3.0
TOTAL DEBT FLOWS										
Disbursements	**0.0**	**13.0**	**5.4**	**17.7**	**5.5**	**9.6**	**9.6**	**7.0**	**5.2**	**4.4**
Long-term debt	0.0	13.0	5.4	17.7	5.5	7.7	9.6	7.0	5.2	4.4
IMF purchases	0.0	0.0	0.0	0.0	0.0	1.9	0.0	0.0	0.0	0.0
Principal repayments	**0.0**	**0.0**	**0.2**	**3.2**	**1.6**	**2.0**	**0.4**	**0.8**	**2.7**	**5.5**
Long-term debt	0.0	0.0	0.2	3.2	1.6	2.0	0.4	0.8	2.5	5.2
IMF repurchases	0.0	0.0	0.0	0.0	0.0	0.0	0.0	0.0	0.2	0.2
Net flows on debt	**0.0**	**13.0**	**2.2**	**14.5**	**4.8**	**6.7**	**11.2**	**4.2**	**7.5**	**-5.0**
of which short-term debt	..	0.0	-3.0	0.0	0.9	-1.0	2.0	-2.0	5.0	-3.9
Interest payments (INT)	**..**	**0.4**	**0.8**	**2.5**	**0.6**	**0.8**	**0.6**	**0.6**	**0.9**	**0.7**
Long-term debt	0.0	0.3	0.7	2.5	0.6	0.7	0.5	0.6	0.6	0.6
IMF charges	0.0	0.0	0.0	0.0	0.0	0.0	0.0	0.0	0.0	0.0
Short-term debt	..	0.1	0.1	0.0	0.0	0.0	0.1	0.1	0.3	0.1
Net transfers on debt	**..**	**12.6**	**1.3**	**12.0**	**4.2**	**5.9**	**10.6**	**3.6**	**6.6**	**-5.7**
Total debt service paid (TDS)	**..**	**0.4**	**1.1**	**5.7**	**2.2**	**2.8**	**1.0**	**1.4**	**3.6**	**6.2**
Long-term debt	0.1	0.3	0.9	5.7	2.1	2.7	0.9	1.4	3.1	5.9
IMF repurchases and charges	0.0	0.0	0.0	0.0	0.0	0.0	0.0	0.0	0.3	0.3
Short-term debt (interest only)	..	0.1	0.1	0.0	0.0	0.0	0.1	0.1	0.3	0.1
2. AGGREGATE NET RESOURCE FLOWS AND NET TRANSFERS (LONG-TERM)										
NET RESOURCE FLOWS	**3.1**	**30.8**	**31.9**	**36.3**	**33.7**	**25.1**	**27.9**	**23.7**	**17.0**	**25.4**
Net flow of long-term debt (ex. IMF)	0.0	13.0	5.2	14.5	3.9	5.7	9.2	6.2	2.7	-0.8
Foreign direct investment (net)	0.0	0.0	-1.0	-1.0	2.0	3.0	1.0	2.0	2.0	2.0
Portfolio equity flows	0.0	0.0	0.0	0.0	0.0	0.0	0.0	0.0	0.0	0.0
Grants (excluding technical coop.)	3.1	17.8	27.7	22.8	27.8	16.4	17.7	15.5	12.3	24.2
Memo: technical coop. grants	4.8	7.0	16.8	18.9	17.1	14.3	14.6	17.3	12.1	10.8
official net resource flows	3.1	30.4	32.9	37.3	31.7	22.1	26.9	21.7	15.0	23.4
private net resource flows	0.0	0.4	-1.0	-1.0	2.0	3.0	1.0	2.0	2.0	2.0
NET TRANSFERS	**3.1**	**30.5**	**30.6**	**33.8**	**33.1**	**24.4**	**27.4**	**23.1**	**16.4**	**24.8**
Interest on long-term debt	0.0	0.3	0.7	2.5	0.6	0.7	0.5	0.6	0.6	0.6
Profit remittances on FDI	0.0	0.0	0.6	0.0	0.0	0.0	0.0	0.0	0.0	0.0
Memo: official net transfers	3.1	30.1	32.2	34.8	31.1	21.4	26.4	21.1	14.4	22.8
private net transfers	0.0	0.4	-1.6	-1.0	2.0	3.0	1.0	2.0	2.0	2.0
3. MAJOR ECONOMIC AGGREGATES										
Gross national product (GNP)	24.7	124.1	249.3	270.1	265.4	186.2	215.6	213.7	193.7	196.6
Exports of goods & services (XGS)	..	15.7	48.1	67.5	72.0	57.5	61.4	60.2	43.9	46.4
of which workers remittances	..	1.6	9.9	16.0	16.0	15.2	12.2	15.5	11.4	12.0
Imports of goods & services (MGS)	..	34.3	93.4	110.8	100.7	93.2	105.7	97.4	78.4	82.3
International reserves (RES)	..	6.4	29.9	27.3	39.0	44.4	44.9	50.9	40.8	39.1
Current account balance	..	-8.9	-10.5	-14.2	9.6	-7.2	-19.0	-40.7	-34.5	..
4. DEBT INDICATORS										
EDT / XGS (%)	..	280.6	384.6	278.9	256.9	334.6	331.6	341.6	455.7	437.6
EDT / GNP (%)	..	35.4	74.2	69.7	69.7	103.3	94.5	96.2	103.3	103.3
TDS / XGS (%)	..	2.6	2.3	8.4	3.1	4.9	1.6	2.3	8.2	13.4
INT / XGS (%)	..	2.6	1.7	3.7	0.8	1.4	1.0	1.0	2.1	1.5
INT / GNP (%)	..	0.3	0.3	0.9	0.2	0.4	0.3	0.3	0.5	0.4
RES / EDT (%)	..	14.5	16.2	14.5	21.1	23.1	22.0	24.8	20.4	19.3
RES / MGS (months)	..	2.2	3.9	3.0	4.7	5.7	5.1	6.3	6.2	5.7
Short-term / EDT (%)	..	2.3	6.7	6.3	7.6	5.2	5.0	4.6	6.7	6.1
Concessional / EDT (%)	..	96.8	85.9	89.3	87.9	89.2	89.6	89.5	87.8	88.3
Multilateral / EDT (%)	..	48.2	61.6	65.3	69.6	73.5	75.0	75.6	76.9	79.0

COMOROS

(US$ million, unless otherwise indicated)

	1970	1980	1990	1992	1993	1994	1995	1996	1997	1998
5. LONG-TERM DEBT										
DEBT OUTSTANDING (LDOD)	**1.2**	**43.0**	**172.6**	**175.2**	**169.6**	**179.0**	**190.3**	**192.9**	**183.9**	**188.1**
Public and publicly guaranteed	**1.2**	**43.0**	**172.6**	**175.2**	**169.6**	**179.0**	**190.3**	**192.9**	**183.9**	**188.1**
Official creditors	1.2	42.6	172.6	175.2	169.6	179.0	190.3	192.9	183.9	188.1
Multilateral	0.0	21.2	113.9	122.9	128.6	141.4	152.8	155.5	153.9	160.5
Concessional	0.0	21.2	100.2	115.8	121.5	133.9	145.1	146.6	145.6	151.7
Bilateral	1.2	21.4	58.6	52.3	41.0	37.7	37.5	37.4	30.0	27.6
Concessional	1.2	21.4	58.6	52.3	41.0	37.7	37.5	37.4	30.0	27.6
Private creditors	0.0	0.4	0.0	0.0	0.0	0.0	0.0	0.0	0.0	0.0
Bonds	0.0	0.0	0.0	0.0	0.0	0.0	0.0	0.0	0.0	0.0
Commercial banks	0.0	0.0	0.0	0.0	0.0	0.0	0.0	0.0	0.0	0.0
Other private	0.0	0.4	0.0	0.0	0.0	0.0	0.0	0.0	0.0	0.0
Private nonguaranteed	**0.0**	**0.0**	**0.0**	**0.0**	**0.0**	**0.0**	**0.0**	**0.0**	**0.0**	**0.0**
Bonds	0.0	0.0	0.0	0.0	0.0	0.0	0.0	0.0	0.0	0.0
Commercial banks	0.0	0.0	0.0	0.0	0.0	0.0	0.0	0.0	0.0	0.0
Memo:										
IBRD	0.0	0.0	0.0	0.0	0.0	0.0	0.0	0.0	0.0	0.0
IDA	0.0	4.2	37.5	40.1	44.8	53.9	64.1	68.2	69.6	74.8
DISBURSEMENTS	**0.0**	**13.0**	**5.4**	**17.7**	**5.5**	**7.7**	**9.6**	**7.0**	**5.2**	**4.4**
Public and publicly guaranteed	**0.0**	**13.0**	**5.4**	**17.7**	**5.5**	**7.7**	**9.6**	**7.0**	**5.2**	**4.4**
Official creditors	0.0	12.6	5.4	17.7	5.5	7.7	9.6	7.0	5.2	4.4
Multilateral	0.0	6.1	1.3	17.5	5.5	7.7	9.6	7.0	5.2	4.4
Concessional	0.0	6.1	1.3	17.5	5.5	7.7	9.6	7.0	5.2	4.4
Bilateral	0.0	6.5	4.2	0.2	0.0	0.0	0.0	0.0	0.0	0.0
Concessional	0.0	6.5	4.2	0.2	0.0	0.0	0.0	0.0	0.0	0.0
Private creditors	0.0	0.4	0.0	0.0	0.0	0.0	0.0	0.0	0.0	0.0
Bonds	0.0	0.0	0.0	0.0	0.0	0.0	0.0	0.0	0.0	0.0
Commercial banks	0.0	0.0	0.0	0.0	0.0	0.0	0.0	0.0	0.0	0.0
Other private	0.0	0.4	0.0	0.0	0.0	0.0	0.0	0.0	0.0	0.0
Private nonguaranteed	**0.0**	**0.0**	**0.0**	**0.0**	**0.0**	**0.0**	**0.0**	**0.0**	**0.0**	**0.0**
Bonds	0.0	0.0	0.0	0.0	0.0	0.0	0.0	0.0	0.0	0.0
Commercial banks	0.0	0.0	0.0	0.0	0.0	0.0	0.0	0.0	0.0	0.0
Memo:										
IBRD	0.0	0.0	0.0	0.0	0.0	0.0	0.0	0.0	0.0	0.0
IDA	0.0	1.8	0.7	2.6	4.9	7.6	9.6	6.4	5.2	3.1
PRINCIPAL REPAYMENTS	**0.0**	**0.0**	**0.2**	**3.2**	**1.6**	**2.0**	**0.4**	**0.8**	**2.5**	**5.2**
Public and publicly guaranteed	**0.0**	**0.0**	**0.2**	**3.2**	**1.6**	**2.0**	**0.4**	**0.8**	**2.5**	**5.2**
Official creditors	0.0	0.0	0.2	3.2	1.6	2.0	0.4	0.8	2.5	5.2
Multilateral	0.0	0.0	0.2	3.0	1.6	0.7	0.4	0.8	1.0	2.7
Concessional	0.0	0.0	0.2	1.9	1.6	0.7	0.4	0.8	1.0	2.7
Bilateral	0.0	0.0	0.0	0.2	0.0	1.3	0.0	0.0	1.5	2.6
Concessional	0.0	0.0	0.0	0.2	0.0	1.3	0.0	0.0	1.5	2.6
Private creditors	0.0	0.0	0.0	0.0	0.0	0.0	0.0	0.0	0.0	0.0
Bonds	0.0	0.0	0.0	0.0	0.0	0.0	0.0	0.0	0.0	0.0
Commercial banks	0.0	0.0	0.0	0.0	0.0	0.0	0.0	0.0	0.0	0.0
Other private	0.0	0.0	0.0	0.0	0.0	0.0	0.0	0.0	0.0	0.0
Private nonguaranteed	**0.0**	**0.0**	**0.0**	**0.0**	**0.0**	**0.0**	**0.0**	**0.0**	**0.0**	**0.0**
Bonds	0.0	0.0	0.0	0.0	0.0	0.0	0.0	0.0	0.0	0.0
Commercial banks	0.0	0.0	0.0	0.0	0.0	0.0	0.0	0.0	0.0	0.0
Memo:										
IBRD	0.0	0.0	0.0	0.0	0.0	0.0	0.0	0.0	0.0	0.0
IDA	0.0	0.0	0.1	0.2	0.2	0.3	0.4	0.4	0.4	0.2
NET FLOWS ON DEBT	**0.0**	**13.0**	**5.2**	**14.5**	**3.9**	**5.7**	**9.2**	**6.2**	**2.7**	**-0.8**
Public and publicly guaranteed	**0.0**	**13.0**	**5.2**	**14.5**	**3.9**	**5.7**	**9.2**	**6.2**	**2.7**	**-0.8**
Official creditors	0.0	12.6	5.2	14.5	3.9	5.7	9.2	6.2	2.7	-0.8
Multilateral	0.0	6.1	1.0	14.4	3.9	7.1	9.2	6.2	4.2	1.7
Concessional	0.0	6.1	1.0	15.5	3.9	7.1	9.2	6.2	4.2	1.7
Bilateral	0.0	6.5	4.1	0.1	0.0	-1.3	0.0	0.0	-1.5	-2.6
Concessional	0.0	6.5	4.1	0.1	0.0	-1.3	0.0	0.0	-1.5	-2.6
Private creditors	0.0	0.4	0.0	0.0	0.0	0.0	0.0	0.0	0.0	0.0
Bonds	0.0	0.0	0.0	0.0	0.0	0.0	0.0	0.0	0.0	0.0
Commercial banks	0.0	0.0	0.0	0.0	0.0	0.0	0.0	0.0	0.0	0.0
Other private	0.0	0.4	0.0	0.0	0.0	0.0	0.0	0.0	0.0	0.0
Private nonguaranteed	**0.0**	**0.0**	**0.0**	**0.0**	**0.0**	**0.0**	**0.0**	**0.0**	**0.0**	**0.0**
Bonds	0.0	0.0	0.0	0.0	0.0	0.0	0.0	0.0	0.0	0.0
Commercial banks	0.0	0.0	0.0	0.0	0.0	0.0	0.0	0.0	0.0	0.0
Memo:										
IBRD	0.0	0.0	0.0	0.0	0.0	0.0	0.0	0.0	0.0	0.0
IDA	0.0	1.8	0.6	2.3	4.6	7.3	9.2	6.1	4.8	2.8

COMOROS

(US$ million, unless otherwise indicated)

	1970	1980	1990	1992	1993	1994	1995	1996	1997	1998
INTEREST PAYMENTS (LINT)	**0.0**	**0.3**	**0.7**	**2.5**	**0.6**	**0.7**	**0.5**	**0.6**	**0.6**	**0.6**
Public and publicly guaranteed	**0.0**	**0.3**	**0.7**	**2.5**	**0.6**	**0.7**	**0.5**	**0.6**	**0.6**	**0.6**
Official creditors	0.0	0.3	0.7	2.5	0.6	0.7	0.5	0.6	0.6	0.6
Multilateral	0.0	0.0	0.4	2.0	0.6	0.7	0.5	0.6	0.5	0.4
Concessional	0.0	0.0	0.4	1.0	0.6	0.7	0.5	0.6	0.5	0.4
Bilateral	0.0	0.3	0.3	0.4	0.0	0.0	0.0	0.0	0.1	0.2
Concessional	0.0	0.3	0.3	0.4	0.0	0.0	0.0	0.0	0.1	0.2
Private creditors	0.0	0.0	0.0	0.0	0.0	0.0	0.0	0.0	0.0	0.0
Bonds	0.0	0.0	0.0	0.0	0.0	0.0	0.0	0.0	0.0	0.0
Commercial banks	0.0	0.0	0.0	0.0	0.0	0.0	0.0	0.0	0.0	0.0
Other private	0.0	0.0	0.0	0.0	0.0	0.0	0.0	0.0	0.0	0.0
Private nonguaranteed	**0.0**	**0.0**	**0.0**	**0.0**	**0.0**	**0.0**	**0.0**	**0.0**	**0.0**	**0.0**
Bonds	0.0	0.0	0.0	0.0	0.0	0.0	0.0	0.0	0.0	0.0
Commercial banks	0.0	0.0	0.0	0.0	0.0	0.0	0.0	0.0	0.0	0.0
Memo:										
IBRD	0.0	0.0	0.0	0.0	0.0	0.0	0.0	0.0	0.0	0.0
IDA	0.0	0.0	0.3	0.3	0.3	0.3	0.4	0.5	0.5	0.3
NET TRANSFERS ON DEBT	**-0.1**	**12.7**	**4.5**	**12.0**	**3.3**	**5.0**	**8.7**	**5.7**	**2.1**	**-1.5**
Public and publicly guaranteed	**-0.1**	**12.7**	**4.5**	**12.0**	**3.3**	**5.0**	**8.7**	**5.7**	**2.1**	**-1.5**
Official creditors	-0.1	12.3	4.5	12.0	3.3	5.0	8.7	5.7	2.1	-1.5
Multilateral	0.0	6.1	0.6	12.4	3.3	6.3	8.7	5.7	3.7	1.3
Concessional	0.0	6.1	0.6	14.6	3.3	6.3	8.7	5.7	3.7	1.3
Bilateral	-0.1	6.2	3.9	-0.3	0.0	-1.3	0.0	0.0	-1.6	-2.8
Concessional	-0.1	6.2	3.9	-0.3	0.0	-1.3	0.0	0.0	-1.6	-2.8
Private creditors	0.0	0.4	0.0	0.0	0.0	0.0	0.0	0.0	0.0	0.0
Bonds	0.0	0.0	0.0	0.0	0.0	0.0	0.0	0.0	0.0	0.0
Commercial banks	0.0	0.0	0.0	0.0	0.0	0.0	0.0	0.0	0.0	0.0
Other private	0.0	0.4	0.0	0.0	0.0	0.0	0.0	0.0	0.0	0.0
Private nonguaranteed	**0.0**	**0.0**	**0.0**	**0.0**	**0.0**	**0.0**	**0.0**	**0.0**	**0.0**	**0.0**
Bonds	0.0	0.0	0.0	0.0	0.0	0.0	0.0	0.0	0.0	0.0
Commercial banks	0.0	0.0	0.0	0.0	0.0	0.0	0.0	0.0	0.0	0.0
Memo:										
IBRD	0.0	0.0	0.0	0.0	0.0	0.0	0.0	0.0	0.0	0.0
IDA	0.0	1.7	0.3	2.0	4.3	7.0	8.7	5.6	4.3	2.6
DEBT SERVICE (LTDS)	**0.1**	**0.3**	**0.9**	**5.7**	**2.1**	**2.7**	**0.9**	**1.4**	**3.1**	**5.9**
Public and publicly guaranteed	**0.1**	**0.3**	**0.9**	**5.7**	**2.1**	**2.7**	**0.9**	**1.4**	**3.1**	**5.9**
Official creditors	0.1	0.3	0.9	5.7	2.1	2.7	0.9	1.4	3.1	5.9
Multilateral	0.0	0.0	0.6	5.1	2.1	1.4	0.9	1.4	1.5	3.1
Concessional	0.0	0.0	0.6	2.9	2.1	1.4	0.9	1.4	1.5	3.1
Bilateral	0.1	0.3	0.3	0.6	0.0	1.3	0.0	0.0	1.6	2.8
Concessional	0.1	0.3	0.3	0.6	0.0	1.3	0.0	0.0	1.6	2.8
Private creditors	0.0	0.0	0.0	0.0	0.0	0.0	0.0	0.0	0.0	0.0
Bonds	0.0	0.0	0.0	0.0	0.0	0.0	0.0	0.0	0.0	0.0
Commercial banks	0.0	0.0	0.0	0.0	0.0	0.0	0.0	0.0	0.0	0.0
Other private	0.0	0.0	0.0	0.0	0.0	0.0	0.0	0.0	0.0	0.0
Private nonguaranteed	**0.0**	**0.0**	**0.0**	**0.0**	**0.0**	**0.0**	**0.0**	**0.0**	**0.0**	**0.0**
Bonds	0.0	0.0	0.0	0.0	0.0	0.0	0.0	0.0	0.0	0.0
Commercial banks	0.0	0.0	0.0	0.0	0.0	0.0	0.0	0.0	0.0	0.0
Memo:										
IBRD	0.0	0.0	0.0	0.0	0.0	0.0	0.0	0.0	0.0	0.0
IDA	0.0	0.0	0.3	0.5	0.5	0.6	0.8	0.8	0.9	0.5
UNDISBURSED DEBT	**0.0**	**49.8**	**56.8**	**57.2**	**33.3**	**37.3**	**28.7**	**16.8**	**30.6**	**35.6**
Official creditors	0.0	48.8	56.8	57.2	33.3	37.3	28.7	16.8	30.6	35.6
Private creditors	0.0	1.0	0.0	0.0	0.0	0.0	0.0	0.0	0.0	0.0
Memorandum items										
Concessional LDOD	1.2	42.6	158.8	168.1	162.5	171.5	182.6	183.9	175.6	179.3
Variable rate LDOD	0.0	0.0	0.0	0.0	0.0	0.0	0.0	0.0	0.0	0.0
Public sector LDOD	1.2	43.0	172.6	175.2	169.6	179.0	190.3	192.9	183.9	188.1
Private sector LDOD	0.0	0.0	0.0	0.0	0.0	0.0	0.0	0.0	0.0	0.0

6. CURRENCY COMPOSITION OF LONG-TERM DEBT (PERCENT)

	1970	1980	1990	1992	1993	1994	1995	1996	1997	1998
Deutsche mark	0.0	0.0	0.0	0.0	0.0	0.0	0.0	0.0	0.0	0.0
French franc	100.0	2.8	23.8	20.7	21.0	19.5	18.5	17.6	17.3	17.3
Japanese yen	0.0	0.0	0.0	0.0	0.0	0.0	0.0	0.0	0.0	0.0
Pound sterling	0.0	0.0	0.0	0.0	0.0	0.0	0.0	0.0	0.0	0.0
Swiss franc	0.0	0.0	0.0	0.0	0.0	0.0	0.0	0.0	0.0	0.0
U.S.dollars	0.0	38.4	17.3	18.8	22.2	25.5	29.2	31.6	34.9	35.7
Multiple currency	0.0	10.2	8.1	7.2	6.3	5.5	5.0	4.7	4.5	4.8
Special drawing rights	0.0	0.0	0.0	0.0	0.0	0.0	0.0	0.0	0.0	0.0
All other currencies	0.0	48.6	50.8	53.3	50.5	49.5	47.3	46.1	43.3	42.2

COMOROS

(US$ million, unless otherwise indicated)

	1970	1980	1990	1992	1993	1994	1995	1996	1997	1998
7. DEBT RESTRUCTURINGS										
Total amount rescheduled	..	..	0.0	0.0	4.9	8.6	2.0	2.1	3.5	0.0
Debt stock rescheduled	..	..	0.0	0.0	0.0	0.0	0.0	0.0	0.0	0.0
Principal rescheduled	..	..	0.0	0.0	4.6	4.7	1.8	2.0	0.5	0.4
Official	..	..	0.0	0.0	4.6	4.7	1.8	2.0	0.5	0.4
Private	..	..	0.0	0.0	0.0	0.0	0.0	0.0	0.0	0.0
Interest rescheduled	..	..	0.0	0.0	0.3	3.9	0.2	0.1	0.0	0.0
Official	..	..	0.0	0.0	0.3	3.9	0.2	0.1	0.0	0.0
Private	..	..	0.0	0.0	0.0	0.0	0.0	0.0	0.0	0.0
Debt forgiven	..	..	0.1	0.0	11.3	4.6	0.4	0.2	0.0	0.0
Memo: interest forgiven	..	..	0.0	0.0	0.0	0.7	0.0	0.0	0.0	0.0
Debt stock reduction	..	..	0.0	0.0	0.0	0.0	0.0	0.0	0.0	0.0
of which debt buyback	..	..	0.0	0.0	0.0	0.0	0.0	0.0	0.0	0.0
8. DEBT STOCK-FLOW RECONCILIATION										
Total change in debt stocks	..	..	11.2	8.4	-3.3	7.3	11.5	1.9	-5.5	3.0
Net flows on debt	0.0	13.0	2.2	14.5	4.8	6.7	11.2	4.2	7.5	-5.0
Net change in interest arrears	..	..	2.6	-0.7	1.4	-3.1	-1.9	1.4	-1.0	2.8
Interest capitalized	..	..	0.0	0.0	0.3	3.9	0.2	0.1	0.0	0.0
Debt forgiveness or reduction	..	..	-0.1	0.0	-11.3	-4.6	-0.4	-0.2	0.0	0.0
Cross-currency valuation	..	..	8.6	-5.4	-2.4	6.4	4.3	-4.1	-7.6	4.7
Residual	..	..	-2.1	0.0	3.9	-1.9	-1.9	0.4	-4.4	0.5
9. AVERAGE TERMS OF NEW COMMITMENTS										
ALL CREDITORS										
Interest (%)	0.0	1.3	2.0	0.0	0.0	0.8	0.0	0.0	0.6	0.7
Maturity (years)	0.0	43.1	29.8	0.0	0.0	39.6	0.0	0.0	39.8	39.9
Grace period (years)	0.0	9.0	10.3	0.0	0.0	10.1	0.0	0.0	10.3	10.4
Grant element (%)	0.0	74.5	65.9	0.0	0.0	80.4	0.0	0.0	81.5	80.8
Official creditors										
Interest (%)	0.0	0.8	2.0	0.0	0.0	0.8	0.0	0.0	0.6	0.7
Maturity (years)	0.0	45.6	29.8	0.0	0.0	39.6	0.0	0.0	39.8	39.9
Grace period (years)	0.0	9.5	10.3	0.0	0.0	10.1	0.0	0.0	10.3	10.4
Grant element (%)	0.0	79.1	65.9	0.0	0.0	80.4	0.0	0.0	81.5	80.8
Private creditors										
Interest (%)	0.0	7.6	0.0	0.0	0.0	0.0	0.0	0.0	0.0	0.0
Maturity (years)	0.0	5.2	0.0	0.0	0.0	0.0	0.0	0.0	0.0	0.0
Grace period (years)	0.0	1.5	0.0	0.0	0.0	0.0	0.0	0.0	0.0	0.0
Grant element (%)	0.0	5.6	0.0	0.0	0.0	0.0	0.0	0.0	0.0	0.0
Memorandum items										
Commitments	0.0	23.4	0.9	0.0	0.0	18.1	0.0	0.0	20.1	8.4
Official creditors	0.0	21.9	0.9	0.0	0.0	18.1	0.0	0.0	20.1	8.4
Private creditors	0.0	1.4	0.0	0.0	0.0	0.0	0.0	0.0	0.0	0.0

10. CONTRACTUAL OBLIGATIONS ON OUTSTANDING LONG-TERM DEBT

	1999	2000	2001	2002	2003	2004	2005	2006	2007	2008
TOTAL										
Disbursements	4.7	8.5	7.2	5.9	4.6	3.1	1.7	0.0	0.0	0.0
Principal	9.0	8.2	7.5	7.1	7.6	4.4	4.5	4.5	4.1	4.6
Interest	1.8	1.6	1.4	1.3	1.2	1.2	1.2	1.1	1.1	1.1
Official creditors										
Disbursements	4.7	8.5	7.2	5.9	4.6	3.1	1.7	0.0	0.0	0.0
Principal	9.0	8.2	7.5	7.1	7.6	4.4	4.5	4.5	4.1	4.6
Interest	1.8	1.6	1.4	1.3	1.2	1.2	1.2	1.1	1.1	1.1
Bilateral creditors										
Disbursements	0.0	0.0	0.0	0.0	0.0	0.0	0.0	0.0	0.0	0.0
Principal	2.8	1.8	1.1	1.1	1.1	1.0	1.0	1.0	0.8	0.8
Interest	0.2	0.2	0.1	0.1	0.1	0.1	0.1	0.1	0.1	0.1
Multilateral creditors										
Disbursements	4.7	8.5	7.2	5.9	4.6	3.1	1.7	0.0	0.0	0.0
Principal	6.2	6.4	6.4	6.0	6.4	3.4	3.5	3.5	3.3	3.8
Interest	1.6	1.5	1.3	1.2	1.1	1.1	1.1	1.0	1.0	1.0
Private creditors										
Disbursements	0.0	0.0	0.0	0.0	0.0	0.0	0.0	0.0	0.0	0.0
Principal	0.0	0.0	0.0	0.0	0.0	0.0	0.0	0.0	0.0	0.0
Interest	0.0	0.0	0.0	0.0	0.0	0.0	0.0	0.0	0.0	0.0
Commercial banks										
Disbursements	0.0	0.0	0.0	0.0	0.0	0.0	0.0	0.0	0.0	0.0
Principal	0.0	0.0	0.0	0.0	0.0	0.0	0.0	0.0	0.0	0.0
Interest	0.0	0.0	0.0	0.0	0.0	0.0	0.0	0.0	0.0	0.0
Other private										
Disbursements	0.0	0.0	0.0	0.0	0.0	0.0	0.0	0.0	0.0	0.0
Principal	0.0	0.0	0.0	0.0	0.0	0.0	0.0	0.0	0.0	0.0
Interest	0.0	0.0	0.0	0.0	0.0	0.0	0.0	0.0	0.0	0.0

CONGO, DEMOCRATIC REPUBLIC OF

(US$ million, unless otherwise indicated)

	1970	1980	1990	1992	1993	1994	1995	1996	1997	1998
1. SUMMARY DEBT DATA										
TOTAL DEBT STOCKS (EDT)	..	**4,770**	**10,270**	**10,964**	**11,270**	**12,322**	**13,241**	**12,826**	**12,330**	**12,929**
Long-term debt (LDOD)	**311**	**4,071**	**9,006**	**8,948**	**8,769**	**9,281**	**9,621**	**9,262**	**8,617**	**8,949**
Public and publicly guaranteed	311	4,071	9,006	8,948	8,769	9,281	9,621	9,262	8,617	8,949
Private nonguaranteed	0	0	0	0	0	0	0	0	0	0
Use of IMF credit	**0**	**373**	**521**	**454**	**454**	**478**	**485**	**433**	**407**	**423**
Short-term debt	..	**326**	**743**	**1,562**	**2,047**	**2,564**	**3,135**	**3,131**	**3,306**	**3,557**
of which interest arrears on LDOD	..	30	265	1,253	1,792	2,445	2,953	3,008	2,941	3,205
Official creditors	..	21	166	1,058	1,512	2,127	2,627	2,685	2,624	2,883
Private creditors	..	8	99	195	280	318	326	324	318	322
Memo: principal arrears on LDOD	..	37	1,049	2,089	2,450	3,080	4,564	4,679	4,654	5,065
Official creditors	..	13	375	1,359	1,713	2,299	3,747	3,858	3,843	4,234
Private creditors	..	23	674	730	737	781	817	821	811	831
Memo: export credits	..	0	4,604	4,211	4,489	4,911	3,566	3,797	4,297	4,635
TOTAL DEBT FLOWS										
Disbursements	**32**	**603**	**316**	**83**	**58**	**1**	**0**	**3**	**0**	**0**
Long-term debt	32	463	316	83	58	1	0	3	0	0
IMF purchases	0	140	0	0	0	0	0	0	0	0
Principal repayments	**28**	**277**	**200**	**29**	**4**	**5**	**1**	**37**	**0**	**1**
Long-term debt	28	192	49	29	4	0	0	0	0	0
IMF repurchases	0	85	152	0	0	4	1	37	0	1
Net flows on debt	**37**	**278**	**89**	**-28**	**0**	**-140**	**61**	**-91**	**242**	**-13**
of which short-term debt	..	-48	-27	-81	-54	-136	63	-58	242	-13
Interest payments (INT)	..	**265**	**148**	**48**	**23**	**11**	**24**	**12**	**13**	**19**
Long-term debt	9	205	89	27	7	0	0	0	0	0
IMF charges	0	15	38	9	3	1	16	5	0	0
Short-term debt	..	45	21	13	13	9	8	7	12	18
Net transfers on debt	..	**13**	**-59**	**-76**	**-23**	**-151**	**38**	**-103**	**229**	**-32**
Total debt service paid (TDS)	..	**542**	**348**	**77**	**28**	**16**	**25**	**48**	**13**	**19**
Long-term debt	37	397	137	56	12	1	0	0	0	0
IMF repurchases and charges	0	101	190	9	3	6	18	42	0	1
Short-term debt (interest only)	..	45	21	13	13	9	8	7	12	18
2. AGGREGATE NET RESOURCE FLOWS AND NET TRANSFERS (LONG-TERM)										
NET RESOURCE FLOWS	**42**	**368**	**629**	**164**	**129**	**223**	**162**	**129**	**114**	**97**
Net flow of long-term debt (ex. IMF)	3	271	267	54	53	1	0	3	0	0
Foreign direct investment (net)	0	0	-12	1	1	1	1	2	1	1
Portfolio equity flows	0	0	0	0	0	0	0	0	0	0
Grants (excluding technical coop.)	38	96	374	109	75	221	161	123	113	97
Memo: technical coop. grants	42	168	147	87	57	38	55	58	49	40
official net resource flows	45	195	653	167	128	222	161	127	113	97
private net resource flows	-4	173	-24	-4	1	1	1	2	1	1
NET TRANSFERS	**3**	**36**	**532**	**74**	**72**	**182**	**112**	**89**	**76**	**62**
Interest on long-term debt	9	205	89	27	7	0	0	0	0	0
Profit remittances on FDI	30	128	8	63	50	40	50	40	38	35
Memo: official net transfers	40	89	577	141	121	221	161	127	113	97
private net transfers	-37	-54	-45	-67	-49	-39	-49	-38	-37	-35
3. MAJOR ECONOMIC AGGREGATES										
Gross national product (GNP)	3,950	14,411	8,579	8,206	8,337	6,312	5,477	5,141	5,307	6,210
Exports of goods & services (XGS)	803	2,404	2,584	1,381	1,295	1,322	1,770	1,793	1,458	1,664
of which workers remittances	2	0	0	0	0	0	0	0	0	..
Imports of goods & services (MGS)	710	2,679	3,294	2,158	1,707	1,853	2,263	2,115	2,149	2,295
International reserves (RES)	189	380	261	166	55	131	157	83	..	..
Current account balance	-7	-88	-738	-866	-528	-530	-465	-348	-658	-583
4. DEBT INDICATORS										
EDT / XGS (%)	..	198.4	397.5	793.8	870.4	932.2	748.0	715.3	845.4	777.2
EDT / GNP (%)	..	33.1	119.7	133.6	135.2	195.2	241.8	249.5	232.3	208.2
TDS / XGS (%)	..	22.6	13.5	5.6	2.1	1.2	1.4	2.7	0.9	1.2
INT / XGS (%)	..	11.0	5.7	3.5	1.8	0.8	1.3	0.7	0.9	1.1
INT / GNP (%)	..	1.8	1.7	0.6	0.3	0.2	0.4	0.2	0.2	0.3
RES / EDT (%)	..	8.0	2.5	1.5	0.5	1.1	1.2	0.6	..	..
RES / MGS (months)	3.2	1.7	1.0	0.9	0.4	0.9	0.8	0.5	..	..
Short-term / EDT (%)	..	6.8	7.2	14.2	18.2	20.8	23.7	24.4	26.8	27.5
Concessional / EDT (%)	..	18.1	30.3	29.0	28.3	27.4	26.3	26.0	25.2	25.0
Multilateral / EDT (%)	..	6.7	18.8	19.8	19.6	18.9	18.0	18.1	17.7	17.6

CONGO, DEMOCRATIC REPUBLIC OF

(US$ million, unless otherwise indicated)

	1970	1980	1990	1992	1993	1994	1995	1996	1997	1998
5. LONG-TERM DEBT										
DEBT OUTSTANDING (LDOD)	**311**	**4,071**	**9,006**	**8,948**	**8,769**	**9,281**	**9,621**	**9,262**	**8,617**	**8,949**
Public and publicly guaranteed	**311**	**4,071**	**9,006**	**8,948**	**8,769**	**9,281**	**9,621**	**9,262**	**8,617**	**8,949**
Official creditors	222	2,609	8,117	8,096	7,933	8,420	8,744	8,401	7,783	8,103
Multilateral	6	322	1,929	2,174	2,211	2,326	2,382	2,319	2,179	2,269
Concessional	1	194	1,426	1,527	1,568	1,641	1,679	1,626	1,537	1,588
Bilateral	216	2,287	6,189	5,921	5,722	6,095	6,362	6,082	5,604	5,835
Concessional	216	667	1,689	1,654	1,624	1,735	1,804	1,708	1,566	1,645
Private creditors	90	1,462	889	852	836	860	878	861	834	846
Bonds	4	7	5	4	4	5	5	4	4	4
Commercial banks	0	553	524	516	511	518	523	518	510	514
Other private	85	902	360	332	321	337	350	339	320	328
Private nonguaranteed	**0**	**0**	**0**	**0**	**0**	**0**	**0**	**0**	**0**	**0**
Bonds	0	0	0	0	0	0	0	0	0	0
Commercial banks	0	0	0	0	0	0	0	0	0	0
Memo:										
IBRD	5	87	49	81	83	88	92	87	82	84
IDA	1	159	1,113	1,194	1,243	1,294	1,321	1,284	1,225	1,261
DISBURSEMENTS	**32**	**463**	**316**	**83**	**58**	**1**	**0**	**3**	**0**	**0**
Public and publicly guaranteed	**32**	**463**	**316**	**83**	**58**	**1**	**0**	**3**	**0**	**0**
Official creditors	13	201	313	83	58	1	0	3	0	0
Multilateral	1	69	222	83	58	1	0	0	0	0
Concessional	1	27	125	66	58	1	0	0	0	0
Bilateral	12	132	91	0	0	0	0	3	0	0
Concessional	12	105	88	0	0	0	0	3	0	0
Private creditors	19	263	3	0	0	0	0	0	0	0
Bonds	0	0	0	0	0	0	0	0	0	0
Commercial banks	0	92	0	0	0	0	0	0	0	0
Other private	19	171	3	0	0	0	0	0	0	0
Private nonguaranteed	**0**	**0**	**0**	**0**	**0**	**0**	**0**	**0**	**0**	**0**
Bonds	0	0	0	0	0	0	0	0	0	0
Commercial banks	0	0	0	0	0	0	0	0	0	0
Memo:										
IBRD	0	23	21	7	0	0	0	0	0	0
IDA	1	20	89	54	48	1	0	0	0	0
PRINCIPAL REPAYMENTS	**28**	**192**	**49**	**29**	**4**	**0**	**0**	**0**	**0**	**0**
Public and publicly guaranteed	**28**	**192**	**49**	**29**	**4**	**0**	**0**	**0**	**0**	**0**
Official creditors	6	102	34	24	4	0	0	0	0	0
Multilateral	1	12	28	23	4	0	0	0	0	0
Concessional	0	0	3	5	4	0	0	0	0	0
Bilateral	5	90	6	1	0	0	0	0	0	0
Concessional	4	2	5	0	0	0	0	0	0	0
Private creditors	23	90	15	5	0	0	0	0	0	0
Bonds	0	0	0	0	0	0	0	0	0	0
Commercial banks	0	36	5	0	0	0	0	0	0	0
Other private	22	53	10	5	0	0	0	0	0	0
Private nonguaranteed	**0**	**0**	**0**	**0**	**0**	**0**	**0**	**0**	**0**	**0**
Bonds	0	0	0	0	0	0	0	0	0	0
Commercial banks	0	0	0	0	0	0	0	0	0	0
Memo:										
IBRD	1	6	5	10	0	0	0	0	0	0
IDA	0	0	2	5	3	0	0	0	0	0
NET FLOWS ON DEBT	**3**	**271**	**267**	**54**	**53**	**1**	**0**	**3**	**0**	**0**
Public and publicly guaranteed	**3**	**271**	**267**	**54**	**53**	**1**	**0**	**3**	**0**	**0**
Official creditors	7	98	279	58	53	1	0	3	0	0
Multilateral	-1	56	194	59	53	1	0	0	0	0
Concessional	1	27	122	61	53	1	0	0	0	0
Bilateral	7	42	85	-1	0	0	0	3	0	0
Concessional	8	102	84	0	0	0	0	3	0	0
Private creditors	-4	173	-12	-5	0	0	0	0	0	0
Bonds	0	0	0	0	0	0	0	0	0	0
Commercial banks	0	56	-5	0	0	0	0	0	0	0
Other private	-4	117	-7	-5	0	0	0	0	0	0
Private nonguaranteed	**0**	**0**	**0**	**0**	**0**	**0**	**0**	**0**	**0**	**0**
Bonds	0	0	0	0	0	0	0	0	0	0
Commercial banks	0	0	0	0	0	0	0	0	0	0
Memo:										
IBRD	-1	17	16	-3	0	0	0	0	0	0
IDA	1	20	87	49	45	1	0	0	0	0

CONGO, DEMOCRATIC REPUBLIC OF

(US$ million, unless otherwise indicated)

	1970	1980	1990	1992	1993	1994	1995	1996	1997	1998
INTEREST PAYMENTS (LINT)	**9**	**205**	**89**	**27**	**7**	**0**	**0**	**0**	**0**	**0**
Public and publicly guaranteed	**9**	**205**	**89**	**27**	**7**	**0**	**0**	**0**	**0**	**0**
Official creditors	5	105	76	26	7	0	0	0	0	0
Multilateral	0	11	40	26	7	0	0	0	0	0
Concessional	0	2	8	10	7	0	0	0	0	0
Bilateral	5	94	36	0	0	0	0	0	0	0
Concessional	5	45	8	0	0	0	0	0	0	0
Private creditors	4	99	12	1	0	0	0	0	0	0
Bonds	0	1	0	0	0	0	0	0	0	0
Commercial banks	0	69	6	0	0	0	0	0	0	0
Other private	4	30	6	1	0	0	0	0	0	0
Private nonguaranteed	**0**	**0**	**0**	**0**	**0**	**0**	**0**	**0**	**0**	**0**
Bonds	0	0	0	0	0	0	0	0	0	0
Commercial banks	0	0	0	0	0	0	0	0	0	0
Memo:										
IBRD	0	8	1	7	1	0	0	0	0	0
IDA	0	1	7	9	5	0	0	0	0	0
NET TRANSFERS ON DEBT	**-6**	**67**	**179**	**27**	**46**	**1**	**0**	**3**	**0**	**0**
Public and publicly guaranteed	**-6**	**67**	**179**	**27**	**46**	**1**	**0**	**3**	**0**	**0**
Official creditors	2	-7	203	32	46	1	0	3	0	0
Multilateral	-1	45	154	34	46	1	0	0	0	0
Concessional	1	25	114	52	47	1	0	0	0	0
Bilateral	3	-52	49	-1	0	0	0	3	0	0
Concessional	3	57	76	0	0	0	0	3	0	0
Private creditors	-7	74	-24	-5	0	0	0	0	0	0
Bonds	0	-1	-1	0	0	0	0	0	0	0
Commercial banks	0	-14	-11	0	0	0	0	0	0	0
Other private	-7	88	-13	-5	0	0	0	0	0	0
Private nonguaranteed	**0**	**0**	**0**	**0**	**0**	**0**	**0**	**0**	**0**	**0**
Bonds	0	0	0	0	0	0	0	0	0	0
Commercial banks	0	0	0	0	0	0	0	0	0	0
Memo:										
IBRD	-2	9	14	-9	-1	0	0	0	0	0
IDA	1	19	80	41	41	1	0	0	0	0
DEBT SERVICE (LTDS)	**37**	**397**	**137**	**56**	**12**	**1**	**0**	**0**	**0**	**0**
Public and publicly guaranteed	**37**	**397**	**137**	**56**	**12**	**1**	**0**	**0**	**0**	**0**
Official creditors	11	208	110	50	12	1	0	0	0	0
Multilateral	2	24	68	49	12	1	0	0	0	0
Concessional	0	2	11	15	11	1	0	0	0	0
Bilateral	10	184	42	1	0	0	0	0	0	0
Concessional	9	48	13	0	0	0	0	0	0	0
Private creditors	26	189	27	5	0	0	0	0	0	0
Bonds	0	1	1	0	0	0	0	0	0	0
Commercial banks	0	105	11	0	0	0	0	0	0	0
Other private	26	83	16	5	0	0	0	0	0	0
Private nonguaranteed	**0**	**0**	**0**	**0**	**0**	**0**	**0**	**0**	**0**	**0**
Bonds	0	0	0	0	0	0	0	0	0	0
Commercial banks	0	0	0	0	0	0	0	0	0	0
Memo:										
IBRD	2	14	6	16	1	0	0	0	0	0
IDA	0	1	9	13	8	0	0	0	0	0
UNDISBURSED DEBT	**288**	**818**	**1,659**	**1,209**	**1,050**	**943**	**962**	**451**	**409**	**427**
Official creditors	52	743	1,595	1,158	1,002	891	906	398	363	378
Private creditors	236	75	65	52	48	52	57	53	46	49
Memorandum items										
Concessional LDOD	216	862	3,115	3,181	3,192	3,376	3,483	3,334	3,102	3,234
Variable rate LDOD	0	508	1,369	1,359	1,327	1,372	1,406	1,376	1,318	1,344
Public sector LDOD	311	4,071	9,006	8,934	8,755	9,266	9,606	9,247	8,603	8,935
Private sector LDOD	0	0	0	14	14	15	15	15	14	14
6. CURRENCY COMPOSITION OF LONG-TERM DEBT (PERCENT)										
Deutsche mark	2.2	5.9	6.9	6.5	6.2	6.5	6.8	6.5	6.0	6.2
French franc	3.8	13.6	16.4	15.6	14.9	15.5	16.3	15.9	14.9	15.3
Japanese yen	0.0	1.5	3.0	3.3	3.7	3.9	3.7	3.4	3.2	3.5
Pound sterling	2.4	4.1	1.2	0.9	0.9	0.9	0.9	1.0	1.0	1.0
Swiss franc	0.0	0.4	0.2	0.2	0.2	0.2	0.3	0.2	0.2	0.2
U.S.dollars	41.5	42.2	41.4	42.5	43.9	42.1	40.9	42.0	44.5	43.3
Multiple currency	1.6	2.1	3.2	4.1	4.2	4.3	4.2	4.1	4.1	4.1
Special drawing rights	0.0	0.0	0.2	0.4	0.4	0.4	0.4	0.4	0.4	0.4
All other currencies	48.5	30.2	27.5	26.5	25.6	26.2	26.5	26.5	25.7	26.0

CONGO, DEMOCRATIC REPUBLIC OF

(US$ million, unless otherwise indicated)

	1970	1980	1990	1992	1993	1994	1995	1996	1997	1998
7. DEBT RESTRUCTURINGS										
Total amount rescheduled	..	..	446	0	0	0	0	0	0	0
Debt stock rescheduled	..	..	0	0	0	0	0	0	0	0
Principal rescheduled	..	..	259	0	0	0	0	0	0	0
Official	..	..	252	0	0	0	0	0	0	0
Private	..	..	7	0	0	0	0	0	0	0
Interest rescheduled	..	..	131	0	0	0	0	0	0	0
Official	..	..	129	0	0	0	0	0	0	0
Private	..	..	2	0	0	0	0	0	0	0
Debt forgiven	..	..	9	0	0	0	0	0	0	0
Memo: interest forgiven	..	..	15	0	0	0	0	0	0	0
Debt stock reduction	..	..	0	0	0	0	0	0	0	0
of which debt buyback	..	..	0	0	0	0	0	0	0	0
8. DEBT STOCK-FLOW RECONCILIATION										
Total change in debt stocks	..	..	1,031	137	307	1,052	919	-415	-497	600
Net flows on debt	37	278	89	-28	0	-140	61	-91	242	-13
Net change in interest arrears	..	..	125	560	539	653	508	55	-67	263
Interest capitalized	..	..	131	0	0	0	0	0	0	0
Debt forgiveness or reduction	..	..	-9	0	0	0	0	0	0	0
Cross-currency valuation	..	..	598	-296	-209	489	338	-297	-487	287
Residual	..	..	98	-99	-23	50	11	-82	-185	63
9. AVERAGE TERMS OF NEW COMMITMENTS										
ALL CREDITORS										
Interest (%)	6.5	5.1	5.9	12.0	0.0	0.0	2.5	0.0	0.0	0.0
Maturity (years)	12.5	22.7	23.7	7.3	0.0	0.0	19.9	0.0	0.0	0.0
Grace period (years)	3.6	6.3	6.4	0.3	0.0	0.0	4.4	0.0	0.0	0.0
Grant element (%)	18.3	39.4	30.6	-6.8	0.0	0.0	48.7	0.0	0.0	0.0
Official creditors										
Interest (%)	2.6	2.8	5.9	12.0	0.0	0.0	2.5	0.0	0.0	0.0
Maturity (years)	32.6	28.9	23.7	7.3	0.0	0.0	19.9	0.0	0.0	0.0
Grace period (years)	8.5	8.5	6.4	0.3	0.0	0.0	4.4	0.0	0.0	0.0
Grant element (%)	59.8	57.2	30.6	-6.8	0.0	0.0	48.7	0.0	0.0	0.0
Private creditors										
Interest (%)	6.9	9.8	0.0	0.0	0.0	0.0	0.0	0.0	0.0	0.0
Maturity (years)	10.1	9.5	0.0	0.0	0.0	0.0	0.0	0.0	0.0	0.0
Grace period (years)	3.0	1.6	0.0	0.0	0.0	0.0	0.0	0.0	0.0	0.0
Grant element (%)	13.3	1.6	0.0	0.0	0.0	0.0	0.0	0.0	0.0	0.0
Memorandum items										
Commitments	258	438	109	4	0	0	14	0	0	0
Official creditors	27	298	109	4	0	0	14	0	0	0
Private creditors	231	140	0	0	0	0	0	0	0	0

10. CONTRACTUAL OBLIGATIONS ON OUTSTANDING LONG-TERM DEBT

	1999	2000	2001	2002	2003	2004	2005	2006	2007	2008
TOTAL										
Disbursements	5	4	3	2	1	1	0	0	0	0
Principal	439	397	363	320	222	213	200	191	181	170
Interest	179	154	129	108	92	81	71	62	54	46
Official creditors										
Disbursements	5	4	3	2	1	1	0	0	0	0
Principal	435	397	362	320	222	212	200	191	181	170
Interest	179	154	129	108	92	81	71	62	54	46
Bilateral creditors										
Disbursements	2	4	3	2	1	1	0	0	0	0
Principal	271	246	245	242	144	138	138	132	118	109
Interest	124	109	94	79	67	59	53	46	40	34
Multilateral creditors										
Disbursements	3	0	0	0	0	0	0	0	0	0
Principal	164	151	117	78	78	74	62	59	63	61
Interest	55	45	35	29	25	21	18	16	14	12
Private creditors										
Disbursements	0	0	0	0	0	0	0	0	0	0
Principal	4	0	0	0	0	0	0	0	0	0
Interest	0	0	0	0	0	0	0	0	0	0
Commercial banks										
Disbursements	0	0	0	0	0	0	0	0	0	0
Principal	0	0	0	0	0	0	0	0	0	0
Interest	0	0	0	0	0	0	0	0	0	0
Other private										
Disbursements	0	0	0	0	0	0	0	0	0	0
Principal	4	0	0	0	0	0	0	0	0	0
Interest	0	0	0	0	0	0	0	0	0	0

CONGO, REPUBLIC OF

(US$ million, unless otherwise indicated)

	1970	1980	1990	1992	1993	1994	1995	1996	1997	1998
1. SUMMARY DEBT DATA										
TOTAL DEBT STOCKS (EDT)	..	1,526	4,953	4,770	5,081	5,414	6,004	5,241	5,071	5,119
Long-term debt (LDOD)	119	1,257	4,206	3,876	4,114	4,774	4,955	4,666	4,284	4,250
Public and publicly guaranteed	119	1,257	4,206	3,876	4,114	4,774	4,955	4,666	4,284	4,250
Private nonguaranteed	0	0	0	0	0	0	0	0	0	0
Use of IMF credit	0	22	11	6	5	20	19	38	34	34
Short-term debt	..	247	736	889	962	619	1,030	537	754	834
of which interest arrears on LDOD	..	4	181	496	643	265	441	283	372	511
Official creditors	..	2	77	370	508	170	332	155	227	343
Private creditors	..	2	104	126	134	95	109	128	144	168
Memo: principal arrears on LDOD	..	10	572	1,029	1,255	796	1,028	1,011	1,228	1,474
Official creditors	..	5	127	486	701	400	595	521	671	831
Private creditors	..	5	444	543	555	396	433	491	558	642
Memo: export credits	..	0	1,877	1,580	1,641	1,865	2,459	2,338	2,370	1,678
TOTAL DEBT FLOWS										
Disbursements	18	526	319	132	459	350	15	24	24	10
Long-term debt	18	522	314	132	459	332	15	4	24	0
IMF purchases	0	4	5	0	0	18	0	20	0	10
Principal repayments	6	41	362	98	77	305	84	140	55	18
Long-term debt	6	34	355	98	76	302	82	140	53	7
IMF repurchases	0	7	7	0	1	3	2	0	2	11
Net flows on debt	13	541	95	-35	310	79	166	-451	96	-66
of which short-term debt	..	56	138	-68	-73	34	236	-335	128	-58
Interest payments (INT)	..	68	169	64	51	252	97	199	57	23
Long-term debt	3	37	120	29	21	232	61	180	40	6
IMF charges	0	1	1	0	0	1	1	1	1	1
Short-term debt	..	31	48	35	30	20	35	18	16	16
Net transfers on debt	..	473	-74	-99	258	-174	69	-649	39	-90
Total debt service paid (TDS)	..	109	531	162	128	557	181	339	112	41
Long-term debt	9	71	475	127	97	534	142	320	93	13
IMF repurchases and charges	0	8	8	0	1	4	3	1	3	11
Short-term debt (interest only)	..	31	48	35	30	20	35	18	16	16
2. AGGREGATE NET RESOURCE FLOWS AND NET TRANSFERS (LONG-TERM)										
NET RESOURCE FLOWS	18	548	8	74	457	215	22	171	213	50
Net flow of long-term debt (ex. IMF)	13	488	-42	33	383	30	-67	-136	-30	-7
Foreign direct investment (net)	0	40	0	4	4	5	3	8	9	4
Portfolio equity flows	0	0	0	0	0	0	0	0	0	0
Grants (excluding technical coop.)	5	20	50	36	70	181	86	299	234	53
Memo: technical coop. grants	10	37	51	48	46	38	41	39	31	30
official net resource flows	19	108	108	53	77	366	69	177	204	46
private net resource flows	-1	440	-100	21	380	-151	-47	-7	9	4
NET TRANSFERS	15	505	-112	43	431	-20	-41	-11	171	42
Interest on long-term debt	3	37	120	29	21	232	61	180	40	6
Profit remittances on FDI	0	6	0	2	5	4	3	2	2	2
Memo: official net transfers	17	83	40	46	72	185	49	1	164	40
private net transfers	-2	421	-151	-3	359	-205	-90	-12	7	2
3. MAJOR ECONOMIC AGGREGATES										
Gross national product (GNP)	267	1,544	2,324	2,555	1,652	1,515	1,717	1,897	1,821	1,668
Exports of goods & services (XGS)	..	1,030	1,503	1,257	1,187	1,028	1,246	1,657	1,805	1,257
of which workers remittances	..	1	0	0	0	0	0	0	0	..
Imports of goods & services (MGS)	..	1,195	1,757	1,555	1,730	1,900	1,889	2,752	2,037	1,733
International reserves (RES)	9	93	10	8	6	55	64	95	63	1
Current account balance	..	-167	-251	-317	-553	-793	-650	-1,109	-252	..
4. DEBT INDICATORS										
EDT / XGS (%)	..	148.2	329.6	379.4	428.2	526.7	481.8	316.2	280.9	407.2
EDT / GNP (%)	..	98.8	213.1	186.7	307.6	357.4	349.6	276.2	278.5	306.9
TDS / XGS (%)	..	10.6	35.4	12.9	10.8	54.2	14.5	20.4	6.2	3.3
INT / XGS (%)	..	6.6	11.2	5.1	4.3	24.5	7.8	12.0	3.2	1.9
INT / GNP (%)	..	4.4	7.3	2.5	3.1	16.7	5.7	10.5	3.1	1.4
RES / EDT (%)	..	6.1	0.2	0.2	0.1	1.0	1.1	1.8	1.3	0.0
RES / MGS (months)	..	0.9	0.1	0.1	0.0	0.4	0.4	0.4	0.4	0.0
Short-term / EDT (%)	..	16.2	14.9	18.6	18.9	11.4	17.2	10.3	14.9	16.3
Concessional / EDT (%)	..	26.5	35.2	36.8	33.3	34.8	33.0	38.2	36.6	36.8
Multilateral / EDT (%)	..	7.7	11.5	11.3	10.5	13.0	11.7	12.9	12.2	12.2

CONGO, REPUBLIC OF

(US$ million, unless otherwise indicated)

	1970	1980	1990	1992	1993	1994	1995	1996	1997	1998
5. LONG-TERM DEBT										
DEBT OUTSTANDING (LDOD)	**119**	**1,257**	**4,206**	**3,876**	**4,114**	**4,774**	**4,955**	**4,666**	**4,284**	**4,250**
Public and publicly guaranteed	**119**	**1,257**	**4,206**	**3,876**	**4,114**	**4,774**	**4,955**	**4,666**	**4,284**	**4,250**
Official creditors	104	605	3,059	2,992	2,882	3,833	4,043	3,799	3,452	3,437
Multilateral	29	118	570	537	534	702	703	675	619	625
Concessional	0	49	151	148	145	255	262	252	239	243
Bilateral	75	487	2,490	2,456	2,348	3,131	3,340	3,125	2,832	2,812
Concessional	75	355	1,590	1,609	1,545	1,629	1,722	1,750	1,615	1,643
Private creditors	14	653	1,147	883	1,232	941	913	866	832	814
Bonds	0	0	0	0	0	0	0	0	0	0
Commercial banks	0	282	726	548	916	814	784	771	748	725
Other private	14	371	421	335	317	127	129	96	84	89
Private nonguaranteed	**0**	**0**	**0**	**0**	**0**	**0**	**0**	**0**	**0**	**0**
Bonds	0	0	0	0	0	0	0	0	0	0
Commercial banks	0	0	0	0	0	0	0	0	0	0
Memo:										
IBRD	29	39	164	160	162	116	105	82	73	71
IDA	0	22	75	74	74	172	174	171	165	168
DISBURSEMENTS	**18**	**522**	**314**	**132**	**459**	**332**	**15**	**4**	**24**	**0**
Public and publicly guaranteed	**18**	**522**	**314**	**132**	**459**	**332**	**15**	**4**	**24**	**0**
Official creditors	16	109	128	17	8	331	15	4	24	0
Multilateral	0	23	11	2	1	247	1	4	22	0
Concessional	0	10	1	2	1	110	0	2	1	0
Bilateral	16	87	118	15	7	84	14	0	2	0
Concessional	16	39	115	15	7	84	14	0	2	0
Private creditors	2	412	185	114	451	1	0	0	0	0
Bonds	0	0	0	0	0	0	0	0	0	0
Commercial banks	0	277	174	95	449	0	0	0	0	0
Other private	2	135	11	19	2	1	0	0	0	0
Private nonguaranteed	**0**	**0**	**0**	**0**	**0**	**0**	**0**	**0**	**0**	**0**
Bonds	0	0	0	0	0	0	0	0	0	0
Commercial banks	0	0	0	0	0	0	0	0	0	0
Memo:										
IBRD	0	2	2	0	0	0	1	2	0	0
IDA	0	1	0	0	0	101	0	2	1	0
PRINCIPAL REPAYMENTS	**6**	**34**	**355**	**98**	**76**	**302**	**82**	**140**	**53**	**7**
Public and publicly guaranteed	**6**	**34**	**355**	**98**	**76**	**302**	**82**	**140**	**53**	**7**
Official creditors	2	21	70	1	1	145	32	126	53	7
Multilateral	1	6	30	0	0	106	19	32	38	7
Concessional	0	0	2	0	0	6	1	5	0	0
Bilateral	2	16	40	1	1	40	13	94	15	0
Concessional	1	11	1	0	1	3	5	17	0	0
Private creditors	4	12	285	97	75	157	50	15	0	0
Bonds	0	0	0	0	0	0	0	0	0	0
Commercial banks	0	0	257	56	68	117	46	0	0	0
Other private	4	12	28	41	7	40	4	15	0	0
Private nonguaranteed	**0**	**0**	**0**	**0**	**0**	**0**	**0**	**0**	**0**	**0**
Bonds	0	0	0	0	0	0	0	0	0	0
Commercial banks	0	0	0	0	0	0	0	0	0	0
Memo:										
IBRD	1	4	6	0	0	57	18	16	3	3
IDA	0	0	0	0	0	4	1	1	0	0
NET FLOWS ON DEBT	**13**	**488**	**-42**	**33**	**383**	**30**	**-67**	**-136**	**-30**	**-7**
Public and publicly guaranteed	**13**	**488**	**-42**	**33**	**383**	**30**	**-67**	**-136**	**-30**	**-7**
Official creditors	14	88	58	16	7	186	-17	-122	-30	-7
Multilateral	-1	17	-19	2	1	142	-19	-28	-16	-7
Concessional	0	10	0	2	1	105	-1	-3	1	0
Bilateral	15	71	77	14	6	44	1	-94	-14	0
Concessional	14	28	114	15	6	81	9	-17	2	0
Private creditors	-1	400	-100	17	376	-156	-50	-15	0	0
Bonds	0	0	0	0	0	0	0	0	0	0
Commercial banks	0	277	-83	39	381	-117	-46	0	0	0
Other private	-1	123	-17	-22	-5	-39	-4	-15	0	0
Private nonguaranteed	**0**	**0**	**0**	**0**	**0**	**0**	**0**	**0**	**0**	**0**
Bonds	0	0	0	0	0	0	0	0	0	0
Commercial banks	0	0	0	0	0	0	0	0	0	0
Memo:										
IBRD	-1	-2	-4	0	0	-57	-17	-14	-3	-3
IDA	0	1	0	0	0	97	-1	1	1	0

CONGO, REPUBLIC OF

(US$ million, unless otherwise indicated)

	1970	1980	1990	1992	1993	1994	1995	1996	1997	1998
INTEREST PAYMENTS (LINT)	**3**	**37**	**120**	**29**	**21**	**232**	**61**	**180**	**40**	**6**
Public and publicly guaranteed	**3**	**37**	**120**	**29**	**21**	**232**	**61**	**180**	**40**	**6**
Official creditors	3	25	68	7	4	182	20	177	40	6
Multilateral	2	6	30	0	0	65	11	20	37	6
Concessional	0	1	1	0	0	3	1	2	1	1
Bilateral	1	19	38	6	4	117	10	156	4	0
Concessional	1	11	28	5	4	90	8	33	0	0
Private creditors	1	13	52	22	17	50	40	3	0	0
Bonds	0	0	0	0	0	0	0	0	0	0
Commercial banks	0	2	44	13	16	37	39	0	0	0
Other private	1	11	8	10	1	13	2	3	0	0
Private nonguaranteed	**0**	**0**	**0**	**0**	**0**	**0**	**0**	**0**	**0**	**0**
Bonds	0	0	0	0	0	0	0	0	0	0
Commercial banks	0	0	0	0	0	0	0	0	0	0
Memo:										
IBRD	2	4	12	0	0	53	10	7	1	1
IDA	0	0	1	0	0	2	1	1	1	1
NET TRANSFERS ON DEBT	**10**	**451**	**-162**	**5**	**362**	**-202**	**-128**	**-316**	**-70**	**-13**
Public and publicly guaranteed	**10**	**451**	**-162**	**5**	**362**	**-202**	**-128**	**-316**	**-70**	**-13**
Official creditors	11	64	-10	10	3	4	-37	-298	-70	-13
Multilateral	-3	12	-50	2	1	77	-29	-48	-53	-13
Concessional	0	10	-2	2	1	102	-3	-5	0	-1
Bilateral	14	52	39	8	2	-73	-8	-250	-17	0
Concessional	14	17	86	10	2	-9	1	-50	2	0
Private creditors	-2	388	-151	-5	360	-206	-90	-18	0	0
Bonds	0	0	0	0	0	0	0	0	0	0
Commercial banks	0	275	-127	27	366	-153	-84	0	0	0
Other private	-2	112	-24	-32	-6	-53	-6	-18	0	0
Private nonguaranteed	**0**	**0**	**0**	**0**	**0**	**0**	**0**	**0**	**0**	**0**
Bonds	0	0	0	0	0	0	0	0	0	0
Commercial banks	0	0	0	0	0	0	0	0	0	0
Memo:										
IBRD	-3	-6	-16	0	0	-110	-27	-22	-4	-4
IDA	0	1	-1	0	0	95	-3	-1	0	-1
DEBT SERVICE (LTDS)	**9**	**71**	**475**	**127**	**97**	**534**	**142**	**320**	**93**	**13**
Public and publicly guaranteed	**9**	**71**	**475**	**127**	**97**	**534**	**142**	**320**	**93**	**13**
Official creditors	5	46	139	8	6	327	52	302	93	13
Multilateral	3	11	60	0	0	170	30	52	75	13
Concessional	0	1	3	0	0	9	3	7	1	1
Bilateral	2	35	78	7	6	157	22	250	19	0
Concessional	2	22	29	5	5	92	13	50	0	0
Private creditors	4	25	337	119	91	207	90	18	0	0
Bonds	0	0	0	0	0	0	0	0	0	0
Commercial banks	0	2	301	69	84	153	84	0	0	0
Other private	4	23	36	51	8	54	6	18	0	0
Private nonguaranteed	**0**	**0**	**0**	**0**	**0**	**0**	**0**	**0**	**0**	**0**
Bonds	0	0	0	0	0	0	0	0	0	0
Commercial banks	0	0	0	0	0	0	0	0	0	0
Memo:										
IBRD	3	8	18	0	0	110	27	24	4	4
IDA	0	0	1	0	0	6	3	3	1	1
UNDISBURSED DEBT	**42**	**735**	**404**	**336**	**439**	**309**	**340**	**281**	**226**	**6**
Official creditors	36	221	343	316	284	158	177	128	93	6
Private creditors	7	514	62	21	155	151	163	153	134	0
Memorandum items										
Concessional LDOD	75	404	1,741	1,756	1,690	1,884	1,984	2,003	1,854	1,886
Variable rate LDOD	0	82	885	814	1,183	1,187	1,155	1,097	1,047	1,001
Public sector LDOD	119	1,257	4,206	3,876	4,114	4,774	4,955	4,666	4,284	4,250
Private sector LDOD	0	0	0	0	0	0	0	0	0	0

6. CURRENCY COMPOSITION OF LONG-TERM DEBT (PERCENT)

	1970	1980	1990	1992	1993	1994	1995	1996	1997	1998
Deutsche mark	5.1	1.1	2.4	2.8	2.6	2.7	2.8	2.8	2.7	2.9
French franc	14.1	31.0	51.1	48.7	42.6	45.2	47.1	44.6	41.4	41.7
Japanese yen	0.0	0.0	0.2	0.2	0.2	0.2	0.2	0.2	0.2	0.2
Pound sterling	0.6	0.0	5.7	4.9	4.5	5.0	4.9	5.7	6.3	6.3
Swiss franc	0.0	2.1	0.4	0.5	0.4	0.4	0.5	0.3	0.3	0.3
U.S.dollars	2.4	25.1	16.5	18.5	27.0	25.1	23.7	24.2	26.0	25.9
Multiple currency	24.7	3.1	3.9	4.1	3.9	2.4	2.1	1.8	1.7	0.6
Special drawing rights	0.0	0.0	0.6	0.7	0.6	0.5	0.5	0.5	0.5	0.5
All other currencies	53.1	37.6	19.2	19.6	18.2	18.5	18.2	19.9	20.9	21.6

CONGO, REPUBLIC OF

(US$ million, unless otherwise indicated)

	1970	1980	1990	1992	1993	1994	1995	1996	1997	1998
7. DEBT RESTRUCTURINGS										
Total amount rescheduled	..	..	780	15	2	1,044	108	269	91	69
Debt stock rescheduled	..	..	0	0	0	0	0	0	0	0
Principal rescheduled	..	..	386	8	2	505	65	193	70	53
Official	..	..	101	2	2	355	60	182	70	53
Private	..	..	285	5	0	150	5	11	0	0
Interest rescheduled	..	..	370	4	0	433	42	69	19	16
Official	..	..	248	0	0	396	41	65	19	16
Private	..	..	121	4	0	38	1	5	0	0
Debt forgiven	..	..	0	0	3	126	24	77	37	36
Memo: interest forgiven	..	..	0	0	0	8	0	24	4	4
Debt stock reduction	..	..	0	0	0	0	0	0	0	0
of which debt buyback	..	..	0	0	0	0	0	0	0	0
8. DEBT STOCK-FLOW RECONCILIATION										
Total change in debt stocks	..	..	675	-63	312	332	591	-764	-170	48
Net flows on debt	13	541	95	-35	310	79	166	-451	96	-66
Net change in interest arrears	..	..	-167	171	147	-378	176	-158	89	139
Interest capitalized	..	..	370	4	0	433	42	69	19	16
Debt forgiveness or reduction	..	..	0	0	-3	-126	-24	-77	-37	-36
Cross-currency valuation	..	..	427	-188	-140	270	249	-156	-297	152
Residual	..	..	-51	-15	-2	53	-18	9	-40	-157
9. AVERAGE TERMS OF NEW COMMITMENTS										
ALL CREDITORS										
Interest (%)	2.8	7.6	5.1	5.9	5.1	0.8	2.2	0.0	0.0	0.0
Maturity (years)	18.3	11.1	15.7	10.6	7.8	31.6	31.8	0.0	0.0	0.0
Grace period (years)	6.5	3.2	6.8	5.6	2.2	7.5	8.9	0.0	0.0	0.0
Grant element (%)	49.5	13.1	32.0	20.9	17.7	70.7	63.7	0.0	0.0	0.0
Official creditors										
Interest (%)	2.3	3.5	4.3	5.0	0.0	0.8	2.2	0.0	0.0	0.0
Maturity (years)	19.6	25.3	16.9	17.2	0.0	31.6	31.8	0.0	0.0	0.0
Grace period (years)	6.6	6.7	7.2	9.6	0.0	7.5	8.9	0.0	0.0	0.0
Grant element (%)	53.6	46.5	37.3	34.8	0.0	70.7	63.7	0.0	0.0	0.0
Private creditors										
Interest (%)	4.2	8.5	9.9	6.5	5.1	0.0	0.0	0.0	0.0	0.0
Maturity (years)	14.9	8.1	8.3	5.7	7.8	0.0	0.0	0.0	0.0	0.0
Grace period (years)	6.1	2.4	4.1	2.7	2.2	0.0	0.0	0.0	0.0	0.0
Grant element (%)	38.9	6.2	-0.5	10.5	17.7	0.0	0.0	0.0	0.0	0.0
Memorandum items										
Commitments	31	966	192	199	593	250	31	0	0	0
Official creditors	23	165	165	85	0	250	31	0	0	0
Private creditors	9	801	27	114	593	0	0	0	0	0

10. CONTRACTUAL OBLIGATIONS ON OUTSTANDING LONG-TERM DEBT

	1999	2000	2001	2002	2003	2004	2005	2006	2007	2008
TOTAL										
Disbursements	3	2	1	1	0	0	0	0	0	0
Principal	246	272	258	204	204	198	198	192	123	119
Interest	118	112	97	83	73	63	54	44	35	28
Official creditors										
Disbursements	3	2	1	1	0	0	0	0	0	0
Principal	174	222	208	204	204	198	198	192	123	119
Interest	107	105	94	83	73	63	54	44	35	28
Bilateral creditors										
Disbursements	1	0	0	0	0	0	0	0	0	0
Principal	133	178	175	171	173	173	176	171	103	104
Interest	93	94	85	76	68	59	50	41	33	26
Multilateral creditors										
Disbursements	2	2	1	1	0	0	0	0	0	0
Principal	41	44	33	33	31	25	22	21	20	15
Interest	15	12	9	7	6	4	3	3	2	2
Private creditors										
Disbursements	0	0	0	0	0	0	0	0	0	0
Principal	72	50	50	0	0	0	0	0	0	0
Interest	11	6	3	0	0	0	0	0	0	0
Commercial banks										
Disbursements	0	0	0	0	0	0	0	0	0	0
Principal	70	50	50	0	0	0	0	0	0	0
Interest	11	6	3	0	0	0	0	0	0	0
Other private										
Disbursements	0	0	0	0	0	0	0	0	0	0
Principal	2	0	0	0	0	0	0	0	0	0
Interest	0	0	0	0	0	0	0	0	0	0

COSTA RICA

(US$ million, unless otherwise indicated)

	1970	1980	1990	1992	1993	1994	1995	1996	1997	1998
1. SUMMARY DEBT DATA										
TOTAL DEBT STOCKS (EDT)	**..**	**2,744**	**3,756**	**3,934**	**3,863**	**3,906**	**3,801**	**3,488**	**3,548**	**3,971**
Long-term debt (LDOD)	**246**	**2,112**	**3,367**	**3,510**	**3,411**	**3,446**	**3,348**	**3,116**	**3,012**	**3,284**
Public and publicly guaranteed	134	1,700	3,063	3,176	3,131	3,218	3,133	2,923	2,840	3,047
Private nonguaranteed	112	412	304	334	280	228	214	193	172	237
Use of IMF credit	**0**	**57**	**11**	**82**	**81**	**66**	**24**	**1**	**0**	**0**
Short-term debt	**..**	**575**	**377**	**343**	**371**	**393**	**429**	**371**	**537**	**687**
of which interest arrears on LDOD	..	0	77	27	32	37	31	27	28	25
Official creditors	..	0	76	22	27	33	27	23	24	21
Private creditors	..	0	2	5	5	4	4	4	4	4
Memo: principal arrears on LDOD	..	2	173	94	99	132	118	88	77	82
Official creditors	..	0	167	80	92	128	115	85	75	76
Private creditors	..	2	6	13	7	4	3	3	2	6
Memo: export credits	..	0	297	356	391	301	203	190	132	178
TOTAL DEBT FLOWS										
Disbursements	**62**	**556**	**207**	**251**	**211**	**202**	**211**	**389**	**349**	**542**
Long-term debt	60	536	207	245	211	202	211	389	349	542
IMF purchases	2	20	0	6	0	0	0	0	0	0
Principal repayments	**45**	**176**	**295**	**303**	**343**	**291**	**399**	**373**	**358**	**331**
Long-term debt	41	164	269	299	343	271	355	350	358	331
IMF repurchases	4	12	26	4	0	20	44	23	1	0
Net flows on debt	**58**	**603**	**-109**	**-11**	**-109**	**-72**	**-146**	**-36**	**155**	**365**
of which short-term debt	..	222	-20	41	23	17	42	-53	164	154
Interest payments (INT)	**..**	**179**	**206**	**240**	**209**	**215**	**251**	**216**	**208**	**215**
Long-term debt	14	171	171	214	185	193	224	195	183	181
IMF charges	0	4	3	6	5	4	3	0	0	0
Short-term debt	..	4	32	19	20	18	23	20	26	34
Net transfers on debt	**..**	**424**	**-315**	**-250**	**-318**	**-287**	**-397**	**-252**	**-53**	**150**
Total debt service paid (TDS)	**..**	**354**	**501**	**543**	**552**	**507**	**650**	**588**	**567**	**546**
Long-term debt	55	335	440	513	528	465	580	544	540	512
IMF repurchases and charges	4	16	29	10	5	24	47	23	1	0
Short-term debt (interest only)	..	4	32	19	20	18	23	20	26	34
2. AGGREGATE NET RESOURCE FLOWS AND NET TRANSFERS (LONG-TERM)										
NET RESOURCE FLOWS	**48**	**425**	**210**	**194**	**146**	**267**	**280**	**501**	**504**	**796**
Net flow of long-term debt (ex. IMF)	19	373	-63	-54	-132	-69	-144	40	-8	212
Foreign direct investment (net)	26	53	163	226	247	298	396	427	483	559
Portfolio equity flows	0	0	0	0	0	4	1	1	0	0
Grants (excluding technical coop.)	3	0	110	22	31	35	28	34	29	25
Memo: technical coop. grants	4	14	74	90	86	60	77	58	44	37
official net resource flows	16	178	188	-32	-56	27	-103	97	-18	-5
private net resource flows	33	248	23	226	202	240	383	404	522	800
NET TRANSFERS	**31**	**234**	**-20**	**-90**	**-104**	**-1**	**-24**	**206**	**206**	**495**
Interest on long-term debt	14	171	171	214	185	193	224	195	183	181
Profit remittances on FDI	4	20	60	70	65	75	80	100	115	120
Memo: official net transfers	11	135	84	-179	-176	-104	-265	-36	-140	-118
private net transfers	19	99	-104	89	72	104	241	242	346	613
3. MAJOR ECONOMIC AGGREGATES										
Gross national product (GNP)	969	4,615	5,460	6,530	7,292	8,177	8,790	8,981	9,528	10,173
Exports of goods & services (XGS)	..	1,219	2,094	2,693	3,017	3,472	4,713	5,092	5,775	7,168
of which workers remittances	..	0	0	0	0	0	116	122	116	112
Imports of goods & services (MGS)	..	1,897	2,709	3,237	3,781	3,871	5,089	5,384	5,988	7,622
International reserves (RES)	16	197	525	1,032	1,038	906	1,060	1,001	1,262	1,064
Current account balance	..	-664	-424	-370	-620	-234	-358	-267	-215	-460
4. DEBT INDICATORS										
EDT / XGS (%)	..	225.2	179.4	146.1	128.0	112.5	80.6	68.5	61.5	55.4
EDT / GNP (%)	..	59.5	68.8	60.2	53.0	47.8	43.2	38.8	37.2	39.0
TDS / XGS (%)	..	29.1	23.9	20.2	18.3	14.6	13.8	11.6	9.8	7.6
INT / XGS (%)	..	14.7	9.9	8.9	6.9	6.2	5.3	4.2	3.6	3.0
INT / GNP (%)	..	3.9	3.8	3.7	2.9	2.6	2.9	2.4	2.2	2.1
RES / EDT (%)	..	7.2	14.0	26.2	26.9	23.2	27.9	28.7	35.6	26.8
RES / MGS (months)	..	1.3	2.3	3.8	3.3	2.8	2.5	2.2	2.5	1.7
Short-term / EDT (%)	..	21.0	10.1	8.7	9.6	10.1	11.3	10.7	15.1	17.3
Concessional / EDT (%)	..	9.1	23.6	24.6	24.7	24.6	24.2	23.6	20.6	17.5
Multilateral / EDT (%)	..	16.4	30.4	29.9	31.6	33.6	35.6	37.8	38.1	34.9

COSTA RICA

(US$ million, unless otherwise indicated)

	1970	1980	1990	1992	1993	1994	1995	1996	1997	1998
5. LONG-TERM DEBT										
DEBT OUTSTANDING (LDOD)	**246**	**2,112**	**3,367**	**3,510**	**3,411**	**3,446**	**3,348**	**3,116**	**3,012**	**3,284**
Public and publicly guaranteed	**134**	**1,700**	**3,063**	**3,176**	**3,131**	**3,218**	**3,133**	**2,923**	**2,840**	**3,047**
Official creditors	96	791	2,359	2,535	2,482	2,578	2,492	2,284	2,142	2,172
Multilateral	57	450	1,141	1,178	1,219	1,313	1,352	1,318	1,351	1,385
Concessional	11	121	246	226	215	206	199	188	192	186
Bilateral	39	341	1,218	1,357	1,263	1,265	1,139	966	791	788
Concessional	36	128	642	742	741	754	721	637	537	509
Private creditors	38	909	704	641	649	641	642	639	698	874
Bonds	1	141	609	582	577	576	572	564	605	789
Commercial banks	20	712	41	11	26	24	33	40	61	55
Other private	17	55	54	48	45	41	37	35	32	31
Private nonguaranteed	**112**	**412**	**304**	**334**	**280**	**228**	**214**	**193**	**172**	**237**
Bonds	0	0	0	0	0	0	0	0	0	0
Commercial banks	112	412	304	334	280	228	214	193	172	237
Memo:										
IBRD	36	178	409	372	344	323	300	245	191	172
IDA	5	5	4	3	3	3	3	2	2	2
DISBURSEMENTS	**60**	**536**	**207**	**245**	**211**	**202**	**211**	**389**	**349**	**542**
Public and publicly guaranteed	**30**	**435**	**202**	**201**	**209**	**202**	**201**	**389**	**349**	**456**
Official creditors	19	200	170	199	165	200	190	375	263	253
Multilateral	13	97	89	123	133	150	172	313	254	152
Concessional	4	42	13	0	0	3	6	45	19	9
Bilateral	7	103	81	76	32	51	18	62	8	101
Concessional	7	20	76	76	18	18	12	18	6	15
Private creditors	10	235	32	2	44	2	11	15	87	203
Bonds	0	97	0	0	0	0	0	0	50	200
Commercial banks	6	120	30	1	43	1	11	13	36	0
Other private	4	17	1	1	2	1	0	2	1	3
Private nonguaranteed	**30**	**102**	**5**	**44**	**2**	**0**	**10**	**0**	**0**	**87**
Bonds	0	0	0	0	0	0	0	0	0	0
Commercial banks	30	102	5	44	2	0	10	0	0	87
Memo:										
IBRD	5	29	5	28	11	11	16	10	20	20
IDA	0	0	0	0	0	0	0	0	0	0
PRINCIPAL REPAYMENTS	**41**	**164**	**269**	**299**	**343**	**271**	**355**	**350**	**358**	**331**
Public and publicly guaranteed	**21**	**76**	**263**	**285**	**287**	**219**	**331**	**328**	**336**	**309**
Official creditors	7	23	92	253	251	208	321	311	309	282
Multilateral	3	15	79	105	100	120	176	121	159	157
Concessional	0	2	10	11	11	12	14	13	14	15
Bilateral	4	7	14	148	151	88	145	190	150	125
Concessional	3	3	3	27	31	35	44	72	79	63
Private creditors	14	53	171	32	36	11	11	17	27	27
Bonds	1	0	42	17	5	1	4	7	10	16
Commercial banks	12	41	124	8	27	4	2	6	14	7
Other private	1	12	5	7	4	6	5	3	3	4
Private nonguaranteed	**20**	**88**	**6**	**14**	**56**	**52**	**24**	**21**	**21**	**21**
Bonds	0	0	0	0	0	0	0	0	0	0
Commercial banks	20	88	6	14	56	52	24	21	21	21
Memo:										
IBRD	2	7	45	46	48	56	55	41	54	40
IDA	0	0	0	0	0	0	0	0	0	0
NET FLOWS ON DEBT	**19**	**373**	**-63**	**-54**	**-132**	**-69**	**-144**	**40**	**-8**	**212**
Public and publicly guaranteed	**9**	**359**	**-62**	**-84**	**-78**	**-17**	**-130**	**61**	**13**	**147**
Official creditors	12	178	78	-54	-86	-8	-131	64	-47	-29
Multilateral	10	82	11	18	32	30	-4	192	95	-5
Concessional	4	40	4	-11	-11	-9	-7	32	6	-7
Bilateral	3	96	67	-72	-119	-38	-127	-128	-142	-24
Concessional	4	17	73	48	-13	-17	-32	-54	-73	-48
Private creditors	-3	182	-139	-30	9	-9	1	-2	60	176
Bonds	-1	97	-42	-17	-5	-1	-4	-7	40	184
Commercial banks	-5	79	-94	-8	16	-2	9	7	21	-7
Other private	3	5	-4	-5	-2	-5	-5	-2	-2	-2
Private nonguaranteed	**10**	**14**	**-1**	**30**	**-54**	**-52**	**-14**	**-21**	**-21**	**65**
Bonds	0	0	0	0	0	0	0	0	0	0
Commercial banks	10	14	-1	30	-54	-52	-14	-21	-21	65
Memo:										
IBRD	3	23	-40	-18	-37	-45	-39	-32	-34	-21
IDA	0	0	0	0	0	0	0	0	0	0

COSTA RICA

(US$ million, unless otherwise indicated)

	1970	1980	1990	1992	1993	1994	1995	1996	1997	1998
INTEREST PAYMENTS (LINT)	**14**	**171**	**171**	**214**	**185**	**193**	**224**	**195**	**183**	**181**
Public and publicly guaranteed	**7**	**130**	**169**	**189**	**159**	**171**	**204**	**177**	**167**	**162**
Official creditors	4	42	104	147	120	131	162	133	122	114
Multilateral	3	27	77	81	79	90	95	87	86	84
Concessional	0	3	5	5	4	4	5	4	3	4
Bilateral	1	15	27	66	41	41	67	46	36	29
Concessional	1	3	9	27	18	23	30	23	20	17
Private creditors	3	88	65	42	39	40	42	44	44	48
Bonds	0	6	24	36	34	35	37	36	37	39
Commercial banks	2	78	36	0	0	1	0	4	4	6
Other private	1	4	5	6	4	4	5	4	4	4
Private nonguaranteed	**7**	**41**	**2**	**26**	**26**	**22**	**21**	**18**	**16**	**19**
Bonds	0	0	0	0	0	0	0	0	0	0
Commercial banks	7	41	2	26	26	22	21	18	16	19
Memo:										
IBRD	2	15	33	31	29	27	27	20	16	12
IDA	0	0	0	0	0	0	0	0	0	0
NET TRANSFERS ON DEBT	**5**	**202**	**-234**	**-268**	**-316**	**-262**	**-368**	**-155**	**-191**	**31**
Public and publicly guaranteed	**2**	**229**	**-231**	**-272**	**-236**	**-188**	**-334**	**-115**	**-154**	**-15**
Official creditors	8	135	-27	-201	-206	-140	-293	-70	-169	-143
Multilateral	6	54	-67	-63	-47	-60	-100	104	9	-89
Concessional	3	37	-1	-15	-15	-13	-12	28	3	-10
Bilateral	2	81	40	-138	-159	-79	-193	-174	-177	-54
Concessional	3	14	64	21	-31	-40	-62	-77	-94	-66
Private creditors	-6	94	-204	-71	-30	-49	-41	-46	15	128
Bonds	-1	91	-66	-53	-39	-36	-41	-43	4	146
Commercial banks	-7	2	-130	-8	15	-3	9	3	17	-12
Other private	2	1	-9	-11	-6	-10	-9	-6	-6	-5
Private nonguaranteed	**3**	**-28**	**-3**	**5**	**-80**	**-74**	**-35**	**-40**	**-38**	**46**
Bonds	0	0	0	0	0	0	0	0	0	0
Commercial banks	3	-28	-3	5	-80	-74	-35	-40	-38	46
Memo:										
IBRD	1	8	-73	-50	-66	-72	-66	-52	-50	-33
IDA	0	0	0	0	0	0	0	0	0	0
DEBT SERVICE (LTDS)	**55**	**335**	**440**	**513**	**528**	**465**	**580**	**544**	**540**	**512**
Public and publicly guaranteed	**28**	**206**	**432**	**473**	**446**	**391**	**535**	**505**	**503**	**471**
Official creditors	11	65	197	400	371	340	483	444	431	396
Multilateral	6	43	156	186	180	210	271	209	246	242
Concessional	0	5	15	16	16	16	19	17	17	19
Bilateral	5	22	40	214	191	130	212	236	186	155
Concessional	4	6	12	54	48	58	74	95	99	80
Private creditors	17	141	236	73	75	51	52	61	72	75
Bonds	1	6	66	53	39	36	41	43	46	55
Commercial banks	14	119	160	9	28	5	2	10	18	12
Other private	2	16	10	12	8	10	9	7	7	8
Private nonguaranteed	**28**	**129**	**8**	**40**	**82**	**74**	**45**	**40**	**38**	**41**
Bonds	0	0	0	0	0	0	0	0	0	0
Commercial banks	28	129	8	40	82	74	45	40	38	41
Memo:										
IBRD	4	21	79	77	76	83	81	62	70	52
IDA	0	0	0	0	0	0	0	0	0	0
UNDISBURSED DEBT	**95**	**797**	**1,053**	**850**	**1,327**	**1,474**	**1,174**	**1,107**	**922**	**714**
Official creditors	93	623	1,038	844	1,305	1,446	1,155	1,099	918	712
Private creditors	2	174	15	6	22	29	19	7	4	1
Memorandum items										
Concessional LDOD	47	249	888	968	955	961	920	825	729	695
Variable rate LDOD	122	1,203	1,061	1,130	1,005	961	989	907	881	992
Public sector LDOD	130	1,655	3,059	3,173	3,128	3,216	3,131	2,921	2,838	3,045
Private sector LDOD	116	457	308	337	283	230	216	195	173	239

6. CURRENCY COMPOSITION OF LONG-TERM DEBT (PERCENT)

	1970	1980	1990	1992	1993	1994	1995	1996	1997	1998
Deutsche mark	2.0	3.1	2.6	2.3	2.0	2.1	1.9	1.9	1.2	1.0
French franc	0.0	0.2	1.0	0.7	0.6	0.5	0.4	0.3	0.2	0.2
Japanese yen	0.0	0.5	3.0	7.1	8.0	8.9	8.1	7.1	5.9	5.7
Pound sterling	2.8	0.5	0.2	0.3	0.3	0.3	0.1	0.1	0.1	0.0
Swiss franc	0.0	0.7	0.0	0.0	0.0	0.0	0.0	0.0	0.0	0.0
U.S.dollars	67.1	69.2	58.2	55.3	54.0	52.2	52.3	54.6	59.8	68.0
Multiple currency	28.2	18.2	31.4	31.9	32.9	34.1	35.6	34.1	31.3	23.1
Special drawing rights	0.0	0.0	0.2	0.1	0.1	0.1	0.1	0.1	0.1	0.1
All other currencies	0.0	7.6	3.4	2.3	2.1	1.8	1.5	1.8	1.4	1.9

COSTA RICA

(US$ million, unless otherwise indicated)

	1970	1980	1990	1992	1993	1994	1995	1996	1997	1998
7. DEBT RESTRUCTURINGS										
Total amount rescheduled	..	..	641	42	29	0	0	0	0	0
Debt stock rescheduled	..	..	469	0	0	0	0	0	0	0
Principal rescheduled	..	..	20	34	17	0	0	0	0	0
Official	..	..	20	31	17	0	0	0	0	0
Private	..	..	0	3	0	0	0	0	0	0
Interest rescheduled	..	..	151	8	8	0	0	0	0	0
Official	..	..	10	6	7	0	0	0	0	0
Private	..	..	141	2	0	0	0	0	0	0
Debt forgiven	..	..	0	0	1	3	3	2	2	0
Memo: interest forgiven	..	..	187	1	0	0	0	0	0	0
Debt stock reduction	..	..	668	1	0	0	0	0	0	0
of which debt buyback	..	..	0	0	0	0	0	0	0	0
8. DEBT STOCK-FLOW RECONCILIATION										
Total change in debt stocks	..	..	-834	-88	-71	43	-105	-312	60	422
Net flows on debt	58	603	-109	-11	-109	-72	-146	-36	155	365
Net change in interest arrears	..	..	-308	-41	5	5	-7	-4	1	-3
Interest capitalized	..	..	151	8	8	0	0	0	0	0
Debt forgiveness or reduction	..	..	-668	-1	-1	-3	-3	-2	-2	0
Cross-currency valuation	..	..	52	-44	8	55	-3	-66	-60	20
Residual	..	..	47	1	18	57	53	-204	-34	40
9. AVERAGE TERMS OF NEW COMMITMENTS										
ALL CREDITORS										
Interest (%)	5.6	11.2	6.9	7.0	6.4	6.9	2.6	5.3	7.5	7.3
Maturity (years)	27.7	13.3	15.4	18.4	16.0	17.0	7.2	11.4	13.0	4.0
Grace period (years)	6.3	5.0	4.4	4.5	4.4	5.4	1.2	3.7	3.0	4.0
Grant element (%)	33.6	-1.2	18.3	16.1	18.2	18.8	16.8	24.7	12.4	6.8
Official creditors										
Interest (%)	5.3	7.2	6.4	7.0	6.3	6.8	2.2	5.3	7.0	5.3
Maturity (years)	29.8	18.3	17.7	18.4	16.8	17.2	7.3	11.4	15.8	1.1
Grace period (years)	7.2	6.3	5.0	4.5	4.6	5.5	1.2	3.7	4.2	1.1
Grant element (%)	37.3	19.4	21.2	16.1	19.1	19.3	17.4	24.7	16.7	4.6
Private creditors										
Interest (%)	7.1	15.8	9.5	0.0	7.1	12.5	6.9	3.3	8.4	8.0
Maturity (years)	14.8	7.6	3.2	0.0	8.0	7.0	6.0	10.8	7.7	5.1
Grace period (years)	0.9	3.6	1.1	0.0	2.1	1.5	1.5	1.1	0.7	5.1
Grant element (%)	12.2	-24.4	2.2	0.0	9.6	-9.1	8.6	27.4	4.3	7.7
Memorandum items										
Commitments	58	625	231	186	701	426	25	244	241	275
Official creditors	49	330	195	186	640	417	23	242	157	75
Private creditors	8	295	36	0	61	9	2	3	84	200

10. CONTRACTUAL OBLIGATIONS ON OUTSTANDING LONG-TERM DEBT

	1999	2000	2001	2002	2003	2004	2005	2006	2007	2008
TOTAL										
Disbursements	276	192	121	69	37	9	6	3	1	0
Principal	364	411	344	334	487	258	250	224	220	198
Interest	201	188	180	163	139	114	98	83	69	56
Official creditors										
Disbursements	275	191	121	69	37	9	6	3	1	0
Principal	318	352	271	260	214	188	182	154	154	132
Interest	127	117	114	102	91	79	67	56	47	38
Bilateral creditors										
Disbursements	28	19	12	8	4	2	2	1	1	0
Principal	123	176	93	93	58	43	35	27	25	24
Interest	29	21	17	13	10	8	7	6	5	4
Multilateral creditors										
Disbursements	247	173	109	62	33	7	4	1	0	0
Principal	195	176	178	167	156	145	147	127	128	108
Interest	98	96	97	89	80	70	60	51	42	34
Private creditors										
Disbursements	1	0	0	0	0	0	0	0	0	0
Principal	46	59	73	74	272	70	67	69	66	66
Interest	74	71	66	61	48	35	31	27	22	18
Commercial banks										
Disbursements	0	0	0	0	0	0	0	0	0	0
Principal	9	9	9	9	7	4	4	3	0	0
Interest	5	4	3	2	1	1	1	0	0	0
Other private										
Disbursements	1	0	0	0	0	0	0	0	0	0
Principal	38	50	64	64	266	65	64	67	66	66
Interest	70	67	63	59	47	35	31	27	22	18

COTE D'IVOIRE

(US$ million, unless otherwise indicated)

	1970	1980	1990	1992	1993	1994	1995	1996	1997	1998
1. SUMMARY DEBT DATA										
TOTAL DEBT STOCKS (EDT)	**..**	**7,462**	**17,251**	**18,547**	**19,071**	**17,395**	**18,898**	**19,524**	**15,609**	**14,852**
Long-term debt (LDOD)	**267**	**6,339**	**13,223**	**13,860**	**13,727**	**13,852**	**14,562**	**13,216**	**12,498**	**12,632**
Public and publicly guaranteed	256	4,327	10,666	11,244	11,111	11,241	11,902	11,367	10,427	10,800
Private nonguaranteed	11	2,012	2,558	2,616	2,617	2,611	2,660	1,849	2,071	1,833
Use of IMF credit	**0**	**65**	**431**	**267**	**219**	**328**	**427**	**503**	**450**	**644**
Short-term debt	**..**	**1,059**	**3,597**	**4,420**	**5,125**	**3,215**	**3,910**	**5,805**	**2,661**	**1,576**
of which interest arrears on LDOD	..	0	819	1,043	1,251	961	1,020	953	87	9
Official creditors	..	0	66	166	379	45	34	6	78	0
Private creditors	..	0	753	877	872	915	986	947	9	9
Memo: principal arrears on LDOD	..	0	1,727	2,351	2,632	2,505	2,684	2,551	147	49
Official creditors	..	0	16	122	327	13	29	11	98	1
Private creditors	..	0	1,710	2,229	2,305	2,492	2,655	2,540	48	48
Memo: export credits	..	0	3,560	3,617	3,323	3,179	2,969	2,775	2,575	2,665
TOTAL DEBT FLOWS										
Disbursements	**82**	**1,777**	**1,172**	**853**	**813**	**1,405**	**924**	**1,014**	**236**	**613**
Long-term debt	82	1,739	1,019	853	813	1,235	743	876	236	445
IMF purchases	0	38	153	0	0	171	181	138	0	168
Principal repayments	**31**	**722**	**621**	**594**	**585**	**787**	**625**	**860**	**838**	**670**
Long-term debt	31	722	498	502	535	711	539	812	816	670
IMF repurchases	0	0	123	92	49	77	86	48	22	0
Net flows on debt	**158**	**1,257**	**1,189**	**627**	**726**	**-1,002**	**935**	**2,117**	**413**	**-1,064**
of which short-term debt	..	202	639	368	497	-1,620	636	1,963	1,015	-1,007
Interest payments (INT)	**..**	**685**	**641**	**565**	**509**	**457**	**421**	**515**	**521**	**713**
Long-term debt	12	590	443	410	382	426	390	473	413	615
IMF charges	0	0	31	26	18	11	8	5	3	3
Short-term debt	..	95	167	130	110	20	23	37	105	96
Net transfers on debt	**..**	**572**	**548**	**61**	**217**	**-1,459**	**514**	**1,602**	**-109**	**-1,778**
Total debt service paid (TDS)	**..**	**1,407**	**1,262**	**1,160**	**1,094**	**1,244**	**1,046**	**1,375**	**1,360**	**1,384**
Long-term debt	43	1,312	941	912	917	1,137	929	1,285	1,229	1,285
IMF repurchases and charges	0	0	155	118	67	87	94	53	25	3
Short-term debt (interest only)	..	95	167	130	110	20	23	37	105	96
2. AGGREGATE NET RESOURCE FLOWS AND NET TRANSFERS (LONG-TERM)										
NET RESOURCE FLOWS	**94**	**1,139**	**855**	**312**	**577**	**1,292**	**873**	**859**	**83**	**729**
Net flow of long-term debt (ex. IMF)	51	1,017	521	351	278	524	204	64	-580	-225
Foreign direct investment (net)	31	95	48	-231	88	78	212	269	341	435
Portfolio equity flows	0	0	0	0	0	7	3	30	18	6
Grants (excluding technical coop.)	12	27	287	192	211	683	454	497	303	513
Memo: technical coop. grants	21	100	131	13	124	114	122	109	100	94
official net resource flows	46	203	798	553	541	1,247	644	451	159	548
private net resource flows	48	936	57	-241	36	46	229	408	-77	181
NET TRANSFERS	**33**	**361**	**349**	**-164**	**134**	**801**	**420**	**320**	**-398**	**39**
Interest on long-term debt	12	590	443	410	382	426	390	473	413	615
Profit remittances on FDI	49	188	64	66	61	65	63	66	68	75
Memo: official net transfers	41	125	611	314	323	979	392	123	-109	179
private net transfers	-9	235	-262	-478	-189	-178	28	197	-289	-140
3. MAJOR ECONOMIC AGGREGATES										
Gross national product (GNP)	1,413	9,680	9,209	9,807	9,039	6,892	9,005	9,784	9,442	10,215
Exports of goods & services (XGS)	..	3,640	3,561	3,615	3,292	3,537	4,526	5,183	4,998	5,295
of which workers remittances	..	0	0	0	0	0	0	0	0	0
Imports of goods & services (MGS)	..	4,761	4,594	4,529	3,990	3,435	4,782	5,005	4,743	5,059
International reserves (RES)	119	46	21	22	20	221	546	622	631	855
Current account balance	..	-1,826	-1,214	-1,013	-892	-14	-492	-165	-128	-212
4. DEBT INDICATORS										
EDT / XGS (%)	..	205.0	484.5	513.1	579.2	491.8	417.5	376.7	312.3	280.5
EDT / GNP (%)	..	77.1	187.3	189.1	211.0	252.4	209.9	199.6	165.3	145.4
TDS / XGS (%)	..	38.7	35.4	32.1	33.2	35.2	23.1	26.5	27.2	26.1
INT / XGS (%)	..	18.8	18.0	15.6	15.5	12.9	9.3	9.9	10.4	13.5
INT / GNP (%)	..	7.1	7.0	5.8	5.6	6.6	4.7	5.3	5.5	7.0
RES / EDT (%)	..	0.6	0.1	0.1	0.1	1.3	2.9	3.2	4.0	5.8
RES / MGS (months)	..	0.1	0.1	0.1	0.1	0.8	1.4	1.5	1.6	2.0
Short-term / EDT (%)	..	14.2	20.9	23.8	26.9	18.5	20.7	29.7	17.1	10.6
Concessional / EDT (%)	..	5.9	17.9	18.9	19.4	22.4	24.2	24.7	28.9	33.3
Multilateral / EDT (%)	..	7.0	20.8	20.1	18.7	21.4	20.6	18.8	21.2	23.5

COTE D'IVOIRE

(US$ million, unless otherwise indicated)

	1970	1980	1990	1992	1993	1994	1995	1996	1997	1998
5. LONG-TERM DEBT										
DEBT OUTSTANDING (LDOD)	**267**	**6,339**	**13,223**	**13,860**	**13,727**	**13,852**	**14,562**	**13,216**	**12,498**	**12,632**
Public and publicly guaranteed	**256**	**4,327**	**10,666**	**11,244**	**11,111**	**11,241**	**11,902**	**11,367**	**10,427**	**10,800**
Official creditors	143	1,247	7,686	8,596	8,602	8,642	9,217	8,787	7,906	8,302
Multilateral	14	523	3,585	3,727	3,557	3,715	3,900	3,665	3,301	3,491
Concessional	8	69	1,150	1,046	935	1,045	1,286	1,435	1,434	1,711
Bilateral	129	724	4,101	4,870	5,045	4,927	5,317	5,122	4,605	4,812
Concessional	114	369	1,946	2,464	2,767	2,844	3,284	3,378	3,076	3,238
Private creditors	112	3,080	2,980	2,648	2,509	2,599	2,685	2,580	2,521	2,497
Bonds	21	15	0	0	0	0	0	0	2,457	2,434
Commercial banks	32	1,611	2,640	2,518	2,393	2,514	2,630	2,526	16	17
Other private	59	1,454	340	129	116	85	55	54	48	46
Private nonguaranteed	**11**	**2,012**	**2,558**	**2,616**	**2,617**	**2,611**	**2,660**	**1,849**	**2,071**	**1,833**
Bonds	0	0	0	0	0	0	0	0	0	0
Commercial banks	11	2,012	2,558	2,616	2,617	2,611	2,660	1,849	2,071	1,833
Memo:										
IBRD	5	306	1,913	1,875	1,752	1,691	1,573	1,304	1,044	942
IDA	0	8	7	110	113	576	813	1,019	1,100	1,337
DISBURSEMENTS	**82**	**1,739**	**1,019**	**853**	**813**	**1,235**	**743**	**876**	**236**	**445**
Public and publicly guaranteed	**78**	**1,414**	**769**	**653**	**623**	**927**	**670**	**475**	**185**	**393**
Official creditors	43	231	758	651	623	918	669	465	185	389
Multilateral	12	136	460	365	137	582	340	321	181	299
Concessional	8	8	21	86	17	453	239	253	147	253
Bilateral	31	95	298	286	487	336	329	144	3	90
Concessional	25	34	283	279	455	314	309	142	3	59
Private creditors	35	1,183	11	2	0	9	1	10	0	4
Bonds	6	0	0	0	0	0	0	0	0	0
Commercial banks	7	634	2	0	0	0	1	2	0	0
Other private	22	550	9	2	0	9	0	8	0	4
Private nonguaranteed	**4**	**325**	**250**	**200**	**190**	**308**	**73**	**401**	**52**	**52**
Bonds	0	0	0	0	0	0	0	0	0	0
Commercial banks	4	325	250	200	190	308	73	401	52	52
Memo:										
IBRD	3	86	261	105	22	21	19	18	0	0
IDA	0	0	0	74	3	448	226	235	140	190
PRINCIPAL REPAYMENTS	**31**	**722**	**498**	**502**	**535**	**711**	**539**	**812**	**816**	**670**
Public and publicly guaranteed	**29**	**517**	**319**	**315**	**346**	**397**	**514**	**521**	**525**	**380**
Official creditors	9	55	247	290	294	355	479	510	329	354
Multilateral	0	17	230	268	278	291	286	304	264	255
Concessional	0	2	70	79	71	43	46	47	44	42
Bilateral	9	38	16	22	16	64	193	206	65	99
Concessional	6	16	5	9	7	13	19	34	24	64
Private creditors	20	462	72	25	53	42	36	11	196	26
Bonds	2	1	1	0	0	0	0	0	0	23
Commercial banks	2	301	25	10	44	5	5	5	193	0
Other private	15	161	46	14	8	37	30	6	3	3
Private nonguaranteed	**2**	**205**	**179**	**188**	**189**	**314**	**25**	**292**	**292**	**290**
Bonds	0	0	0	0	0	0	0	0	0	0
Commercial banks	2	205	179	188	189	314	25	292	292	290
Memo:										
IBRD	0	7	125	159	183	196	199	178	158	140
IDA	0	0	0	0	0	0	0	0	0	0
NET FLOWS ON DEBT	**51**	**1,017**	**521**	**351**	**278**	**524**	**204**	**64**	**-580**	**-225**
Public and publicly guaranteed	**49**	**897**	**450**	**338**	**277**	**529**	**156**	**-46**	**-340**	**13**
Official creditors	34	176	511	361	330	563	190	-45	-144	35
Multilateral	12	120	229	97	-141	291	54	17	-83	44
Concessional	8	7	-49	8	-53	410	194	206	103	212
Bilateral	22	57	282	264	471	272	136	-62	-62	-9
Concessional	19	18	278	271	448	300	290	107	-20	-5
Private creditors	15	721	-62	-23	-53	-34	-34	-1	-196	-22
Bonds	4	-1	-1	0	0	0	0	0	0	-23
Commercial banks	5	333	-23	-10	-44	-5	-4	-3	-193	0
Other private	7	389	-38	-12	-8	-29	-30	3	-3	1
Private nonguaranteed	**2**	**120**	**71**	**12**	**1**	**-5**	**49**	**110**	**-240**	**-238**
Bonds	0	0	0	0	0	0	0	0	0	0
Commercial banks	2	120	71	12	1	-5	49	110	-240	-238
Memo:										
IBRD	3	78	136	-54	-161	-175	-180	-160	-158	-140
IDA	0	0	0	74	3	448	226	235	140	190

COTE D'IVOIRE

(US$ million, unless otherwise indicated)

	1970	1980	1990	1992	1993	1994	1995	1996	1997	1998
INTEREST PAYMENTS (LINT)	**12**	**590**	**443**	**410**	**382**	**426**	**390**	**473**	**413**	**615**
Public and publicly guaranteed	**12**	**353**	**205**	**244**	**225**	**296**	**257**	**330**	**270**	**506**
Official creditors	4	77	187	239	218	267	252	328	269	369
Multilateral	0	32	176	208	181	228	172	213	165	140
Concessional	0	1	3	7	5	4	7	7	10	11
Bilateral	4	45	12	31	38	39	81	116	104	229
Concessional	3	13	2	22	25	28	40	69	65	134
Private creditors	7	275	18	5	7	28	5	2	1	137
Bonds	1	1	0	0	0	0	0	0	0	136
Commercial banks	3	176	7	2	5	2	1	1	0	0
Other private	4	98	12	3	1	27	3	1	1	1
Private nonguaranteed	**0**	**237**	**237**	**166**	**157**	**131**	**133**	**143**	**143**	**109**
Bonds	0	0	0	0	0	0	0	0	0	0
Commercial banks	0	237	237	166	157	131	133	143	143	109
Memo:										
IBRD	0	22	141	159	155	144	135	112	87	69
IDA	0	0	0	1	1	2	5	5	8	8
NET TRANSFERS ON DEBT	**39**	**427**	**78**	**-60**	**-104**	**98**	**-186**	**-409**	**-993**	**-840**
Public and publicly guaranteed	**38**	**544**	**245**	**94**	**52**	**234**	**-101**	**-376**	**-610**	**-493**
Official creditors	30	99	324	122	112	296	-62	-373	-413	-334
Multilateral	11	87	54	-111	-321	63	-117	-196	-248	-96
Concessional	8	6	-52	1	-58	406	187	199	93	201
Bilateral	18	11	271	232	433	233	55	-178	-165	-238
Concessional	15	5	276	249	423	272	250	38	-85	-139
Private creditors	8	446	-80	-28	-59	-62	-39	-2	-197	-159
Bonds	3	-2	-1	0	0	0	0	0	0	-159
Commercial banks	2	156	-30	-13	-50	-7	-5	-4	-193	0
Other private	3	291	-49	-15	-10	-55	-33	2	-4	0
Private nonguaranteed	**2**	**-117**	**-167**	**-153**	**-156**	**-136**	**-84**	**-34**	**-383**	**-347**
Bonds	0	0	0	0	0	0	0	0	0	0
Commercial banks	2	-117	-167	-153	-156	-136	-84	-34	-383	-347
Memo:										
IBRD	3	56	-5	-213	-316	-319	-315	-271	-245	-209
IDA	0	0	0	73	2	446	222	230	132	181
DEBT SERVICE (LTDS)	**43**	**1,312**	**941**	**912**	**917**	**1,137**	**929**	**1,285**	**1,229**	**1,285**
Public and publicly guaranteed	**40**	**870**	**524**	**559**	**571**	**693**	**771**	**850**	**794**	**886**
Official creditors	13	133	434	529	512	622	731	838	598	723
Multilateral	1	49	406	476	458	519	457	516	429	394
Concessional	0	3	73	86	76	47	53	54	54	52
Bilateral	13	84	28	53	54	103	274	322	168	328
Concessional	9	29	7	31	32	41	59	104	89	198
Private creditors	27	738	90	30	59	71	40	12	197	163
Bonds	3	2	1	0	0	0	0	0	0	159
Commercial banks	5	477	32	13	50	7	7	6	193	0
Other private	19	259	58	17	10	64	33	7	4	5
Private nonguaranteed	**2**	**442**	**417**	**353**	**346**	**444**	**158**	**435**	**435**	**399**
Bonds	0	0	0	0	0	0	0	0	0	0
Commercial banks	2	442	417	353	346	444	158	435	435	399
Memo:										
IBRD	0	29	266	318	338	340	334	289	245	209
IDA	0	0	0	1	1	2	5	5	8	9
UNDISBURSED DEBT	**169**	**1,723**	**1,230**	**1,348**	**1,166**	**909**	**901**	**909**	**892**	**888**
Official creditors	108	747	1,131	1,328	1,147	898	892	907	885	884
Private creditors	61	976	99	19	19	11	9	3	8	4
Memorandum items										
Concessional LDOD	121	438	3,096	3,510	3,702	3,889	4,570	4,813	4,510	4,949
Variable rate LDOD	34	3,601	7,400	8,002	7,798	7,808	7,940	6,742	6,598	6,043
Public sector LDOD	255	4,277	10,663	11,243	11,109	11,240	11,901	11,365	10,427	10,800
Private sector LDOD	11	2,061	2,560	2,617	2,618	2,613	2,661	1,850	2,071	1,833

6. CURRENCY COMPOSITION OF LONG-TERM DEBT (PERCENT)

	1970	1980	1990	1992	1993	1994	1995	1996	1997	1998
Deutsche mark	10.5	4.5	3.9	3.7	3.6	4.1	4.4	4.2	3.5	3.5
French franc	47.7	34.6	38.1	38.5	39.5	38.8	39.1	38.9	27.1	27.9
Japanese yen	0.0	0.6	0.9	1.2	1.3	1.5	1.4	1.3	1.1	1.2
Pound sterling	0.0	1.4	1.3	1.0	1.1	1.0	0.9	0.9	0.8	0.7
Swiss franc	0.0	6.3	2.3	2.0	2.1	0.4	0.5	0.4	0.2	0.2
U.S.dollars	25.4	31.5	15.5	16.6	17.0	21.0	22.0	25.1	40.9	49.4
Multiple currency	2.1	9.9	22.7	22.5	22.3	22.3	20.1	18.1	16.3	6.4
Special drawing rights	0.0	0.0	0.4	0.6	0.6	0.6	0.6	0.6	0.2	0.3
All other currencies	14.3	11.2	14.9	13.9	12.5	10.3	11.0	10.5	9.9	10.4

COTE D'IVOIRE

(US$ million, unless otherwise indicated)

	1970	1980	1990	1992	1993	1994	1995	1996	1997	1998
7. DEBT RESTRUCTURINGS										
Total amount rescheduled	..	..	930	399	0	645	381	315	2,612	319
Debt stock rescheduled	..	..	0	0	0	0	0	0	0	0
Principal rescheduled	..	..	590	213	0	266	192	139	138	265
Official	..	..	407	150	0	257	189	137	58	264
Private	..	..	183	64	0	9	4	3	80	1
Interest rescheduled	..	..	287	84	0	306	131	106	875	54
Official	..	..	257	79	0	302	129	105	8	53
Private	..	..	29	5	0	4	1	1	867	0
Debt forgiven	..	..	50	0	0	1,352	292	8	0	103
Memo: interest forgiven	..	..	0	0	0	228	30	2	0	20
Debt stock reduction	..	..	0	0	0	0	0	0	4,053	0
of which debt buyback	..	..	0	0	0	0	0	0	163	0
8. DEBT STOCK-FLOW RECONCILIATION										
Total change in debt stocks	..	..	2,431	373	524	-1,676	1,503	625	-3,915	-757
Net flows on debt	158	1,257	1,189	627	726	-1,002	935	2,117	413	-1,064
Net change in interest arrears	..	..	62	117	208	-290	59	-67	-866	-78
Interest capitalized	..	..	287	84	0	306	131	106	875	54
Debt forgiveness or reduction	..	..	-50	0	0	-1,352	-292	-8	-3,890	-103
Cross-currency valuation	..	..	954	-533	-409	512	565	-563	-675	327
Residual	..	..	-10	78	-1	151	105	-960	229	108
9. AVERAGE TERMS OF NEW COMMITMENTS										
ALL CREDITORS										
Interest (%)	5.8	11.4	5.9	5.3	4.6	2.1	1.9	1.9	1.7	0.5
Maturity (years)	18.6	10.3	20.0	19.2	20.1	29.8	29.8	31.4	30.2	40.5
Grace period (years)	5.4	4.5	6.3	6.2	8.0	8.6	8.5	8.8	8.4	10.0
Grant element (%)	26.1	-5.6	27.5	30.7	38.9	64.0	63.8	65.2	65.8	82.7
Official creditors										
Interest (%)	4.9	6.2	5.9	5.3	4.6	2.0	1.9	1.8	1.6	0.5
Maturity (years)	22.5	18.8	20.0	19.2	20.1	29.9	29.8	32.0	30.9	40.5
Grace period (years)	7.4	5.7	6.3	6.2	8.0	8.6	8.5	8.9	8.6	10.0
Grant element (%)	35.3	25.4	27.5	30.7	38.9	64.6	63.9	66.4	67.3	82.7
Private creditors										
Interest (%)	7.4	11.9	0.0	0.0	0.0	11.4	14.4	6.0	5.8	0.0
Maturity (years)	12.1	9.5	0.0	0.0	0.0	12.0	19.6	5.4	6.2	0.0
Grace period (years)	2.1	4.4	0.0	0.0	0.0	2.5	0.1	0.9	0.6	0.0
Grant element (%)	10.9	-8.5	0.0	0.0	0.0	-7.8	-10.0	8.7	10.7	0.0
Memorandum items										
Commitments	71	1,688	764	850	498	907	716	538	241	359
Official creditors	44	144	764	850	498	900	715	526	235	359
Private creditors	27	1,544	0	0	0	7	1	12	6	0

10. CONTRACTUAL OBLIGATIONS ON OUTSTANDING LONG-TERM DEBT

	1999	2000	2001	2002	2003	2004	2005	2006	2007	2008
TOTAL										
Disbursements	290	229	162	105	62	24	13	3	1	0
Principal	714	696	732	827	816	811	641	613	704	665
Interest	502	480	472	512	470	430	391	360	329	296
Official creditors										
Disbursements	287	228	162	105	62	24	13	3	1	0
Principal	544	526	562	657	647	644	474	446	393	354
Interest	346	327	322	365	327	289	253	225	199	177
Bilateral creditors										
Disbursements	86	52	33	18	10	4	4	2	1	0
Principal	266	269	339	430	427	430	278	262	232	203
Interest	198	192	201	257	232	208	186	171	155	143
Multilateral creditors										
Disbursements	201	176	129	86	52	20	10	1	0	0
Principal	278	257	223	228	221	214	196	184	160	151
Interest	149	135	121	108	95	81	67	55	44	34
Private creditors										
Disbursements	3	1	0	0	0	0	0	0	0	0
Principal	171	171	170	170	169	168	167	167	311	311
Interest	156	153	150	147	144	141	138	135	130	119
Commercial banks										
Disbursements	0	0	0	0	0	0	0	0	0	0
Principal	0	0	0	0	0	0	0	0	0	0
Interest	0	0	0	0	0	0	0	0	0	0
Other private										
Disbursements	3	1	0	0	0	0	0	0	0	0
Principal	171	171	170	170	169	168	167	167	311	311
Interest	156	153	150	147	144	141	138	135	130	119

CROATIA

(US$ million, unless otherwise indicated)

	1970	1980	1990	1992	1993	1994	1995	1996	1997	1998
1. SUMMARY DEBT DATA										
TOTAL DEBT STOCKS (EDT)	..	..	..	..	**1,614**	**2,054**	**3,729**	**4,933**	**6,846**	**8,297**
Long-term debt (LDOD)	..	..	..	..	**1,487**	**1,685**	**3,016**	**4,292**	**6,045**	**6,878**
Public and publicly guaranteed	..	..	..	..	601	643	1,760	3,334	4,221	4,910
Private nonguaranteed	..	..	..	..	886	1,042	1,257	957	1,824	1,969
Use of IMF credit	..	..	..	..	**20**	**127**	**221**	**209**	**233**	**234**
Short-term debt	..	..	..	..	**107**	**242**	**492**	**432**	**568**	**1,185**
of which interest arrears on LDOD	..	..	..	..	52	70	71	21	29	37
Official creditors	..	..	..	..	4	2	1	1	0	3
Private creditors	..	..	..	..	48	68	70	20	29	34
Memo: principal arrears on LDOD	..	..	..	..	563	619	547	133	193	212
Official creditors	..	..	..	..	104	128	1	1	0	16
Private creditors	..	..	..	..	459	491	546	132	193	196
Memo: export credits	..	..	..	..	277	396	502	637	1,124	1,565
TOTAL DEBT FLOWS										
Disbursements	..	..	..	..	**158**	**331**	**517**	**939**	**2,864**	**1,158**
Long-term debt	..	..	..	..	158	219	418	939	2,824	1,158
IMF purchases	..	..	..	..	0	112	99	0	40	0
Principal repayments	..	..	..	..	**222**	**155**	**240**	**315**	**746**	**516**
Long-term debt	..	..	..	..	198	146	234	311	744	507
IMF repurchases	..	..	..	..	24	9	6	5	2	9
Net flows on debt	..	..	..	..	**-9**	**293**	**526**	**614**	**2,245**	**1,251**
of which short-term debt	..	..	..	..	55	117	249	-10	127	609
Interest payments (INT)	..	..	..	..	**103**	**86**	**126**	**103**	**374**	**329**
Long-term debt	..	..	..	..	97	78	98	77	345	276
IMF charges	..	..	..	..	4	1	10	10	10	11
Short-term debt	..	..	..	..	3	7	18	16	19	42
Net transfers on debt	..	..	..	..	**-113**	**208**	**401**	**511**	**1,871**	**922**
Total debt service paid (TDS)	..	..	..	..	**325**	**241**	**365**	**418**	**1,120**	**845**
Long-term debt	..	..	..	..	295	224	332	388	1,089	783
IMF repurchases and charges	..	..	..	..	28	10	16	14	12	20
Short-term debt (interest only)	..	..	..	..	3	7	18	16	19	42
2. AGGREGATE NET RESOURCE FLOWS AND NET TRANSFERS (LONG-TERM)										
NET RESOURCE FLOWS	..	..	..	..	**56**	**280**	**316**	**1,298**	**2,606**	**1,763**
Net flow of long-term debt (ex. IMF)	..	..	..	..	-40	72	184	628	2,081	651
Foreign direct investment (net)	..	..	..	..	96	113	101	533	487	873
Portfolio equity flows	..	..	..	..	0	0	0	111	0	205
Grants (excluding technical coop.)	..	..	..	..	0	95	30	25	39	34
Memo: technical coop. grants	..	..	..	..	0	8	21	29	18	23
official net resource flows	..	..	..	..	-52	69	50	9	111	97
private net resource flows	..	..	..	..	108	212	266	1,289	2,496	1,666
NET TRANSFERS	..	..	..	..	**-41**	**203**	**218**	**1,221**	**2,261**	**1,487**
Interest on long-term debt	..	..	..	..	97	78	98	77	345	276
Profit remittances on FDI	..	..	..	..	0	0	0	0	0	0
Memo: official net transfers	..	..	..	..	-91	35	23	-24	11	11
private net transfers	..	..	..	..	50	168	195	1,245	2,250	1,477
3. MAJOR ECONOMIC AGGREGATES										
Gross national product (GNP)	..	..	..	..	10,783	14,419	18,782	19,816	20,273	21,587
Exports of goods & services (XGS)	..	..	..	..	6,531	7,607	7,808	8,716	9,110	9,492
of which workers remittances	..	..	..	..	213	340	506	603	524	520
Imports of goods & services (MGS)	..	..	..	..	6,040	6,969	9,559	10,292	11,801	11,223
International reserves (RES)	..	..	..	..	616	1,405	1,896	2,314	2,539	2,816
Current account balance	..	..	..	..	606	826	-1,452	-1,147	-2,343	-1,543
4. DEBT INDICATORS										
EDT / XGS (%)	..	..	..	..	24.7	27.0	47.8	56.6	75.2	87.4
EDT / GNP (%)	..	..	..	..	15.0	14.3	19.9	24.9	33.8	38.4
TDS / XGS (%)	..	..	..	..	5.0	3.2	4.7	4.8	12.3	8.9
INT / XGS (%)	..	..	..	..	1.6	1.1	1.6	1.2	4.1	3.5
INT / GNP (%)	..	..	..	..	1.0	0.6	0.7	0.5	1.8	1.5
RES / EDT (%)	..	..	..	..	38.2	68.4	50.8	46.9	37.1	33.9
RES / MGS (months)	..	..	..	..	1.2	2.4	2.4	2.7	2.6	3.0
Short-term / EDT (%)	..	..	..	..	6.6	11.8	13.2	8.8	8.3	14.3
Concessional / EDT (%)	..	..	..	..	1.3	1.5	9.1	6.4	4.2	3.9
Multilateral / EDT (%)	..	..	..	..	18.7	13.5	8.1	7.3	6.3	6.7

CROATIA

(US$ million, unless otherwise indicated)

	1970	1980	1990	1992	1993	1994	1995	1996	1997	1998
5. LONG-TERM DEBT										
DEBT OUTSTANDING (LDOD)	..	..	..	..	**1,487**	**1,685**	**3,016**	**4,292**	**6,045**	**6,878**
Public and publicly guaranteed	..	..	..	..	**601**	**643**	**1,760**	**3,334**	**4,221**	**4,910**
Official creditors	..	..	..	..	506	532	1,620	1,527	1,473	1,551
Multilateral	..	..	..	..	302	278	304	360	431	555
Concessional	..	..	..	..	21	21	11	9	22	47
Bilateral	..	..	..	..	204	255	1,317	1,167	1,041	996
Concessional	..	..	..	..	0	9	330	306	269	278
Private creditors	..	..	..	..	95	111	140	1,807	2,749	3,359
Bonds	..	..	..	..	0	0	0	64	534	644
Commercial banks	..	..	..	..	45	47	35	1,616	1,869	2,459
Other private	..	..	..	..	50	64	104	127	346	255
Private nonguaranteed	..	..	..	..	**886**	**1,042**	**1,257**	**957**	**1,824**	**1,969**
Bonds	..	..	..	..	0	0	0	0	0	0
Commercial banks	..	..	..	..	886	1,042	1,257	957	1,824	1,969
Memo:										
IBRD	..	..	..	..	104	84	117	195	276	336
IDA	..	..	..	..	0	0	0	0	0	0
DISBURSEMENTS	..	..	..	..	**158**	**219**	**418**	**939**	**2,824**	**1,158**
Public and publicly guaranteed	..	..	..	..	**34**	**51**	**102**	**382**	**1,436**	**1,079**
Official creditors	..	..	..	..	8	27	71	120	202	219
Multilateral	..	..	..	..	8	2	59	113	133	181
Concessional	..	..	..	..	0	0	0	0	14	29
Bilateral	..	..	..	..	0	25	12	8	70	38
Concessional	..	..	..	..	0	9	6	0	2	12
Private creditors	..	..	..	..	26	24	31	262	1,234	860
Bonds	..	..	..	..	0	0	0	67	531	101
Commercial banks	..	..	..	..	0	0	0	135	326	723
Other private	..	..	..	..	26	24	31	60	378	36
Private nonguaranteed	..	..	..	..	**124**	**168**	**316**	**557**	**1,388**	**80**
Bonds	..	..	..	..	0	0	0	0	0	0
Commercial banks	..	..	..	..	124	168	316	557	1,388	80
Memo:										
IBRD	..	..	..	..	1	1	50	105	115	108
IDA	..	..	..	..	0	0	0	0	0	0
PRINCIPAL REPAYMENTS	..	..	..	..	**198**	**146**	**234**	**311**	**744**	**507**
Public and publicly guaranteed	..	..	..	..	**71**	**67**	**73**	**177**	**362**	**474**
Official creditors	..	..	..	..	60	53	52	137	130	155
Multilateral	..	..	..	..	60	53	52	34	23	36
Concessional	..	..	..	..	4	2	12	1	0	6
Bilateral	..	..	..	..	0	0	0	103	107	119
Concessional	..	..	..	..	0	0	0	8	16	13
Private creditors	..	..	..	..	11	14	21	40	232	319
Bonds	..	..	..	..	0	0	0	0	46	11
Commercial banks	..	..	..	..	2	0	0	12	47	166
Other private	..	..	..	..	9	14	21	28	139	142
Private nonguaranteed	..	..	..	..	**127**	**79**	**161**	**134**	**381**	**33**
Bonds	..	..	..	..	0	0	0	0	0	0
Commercial banks	..	..	..	..	127	79	161	134	381	33
Memo:										
IBRD	..	..	..	..	33	29	20	16	14	17
IDA	..	..	..	..	0	0	0	0	0	0
NET FLOWS ON DEBT	..	..	..	..	**-40**	**72**	**184**	**628**	**2,081**	**651**
Public and publicly guaranteed	..	..	..	..	**-37**	**-17**	**30**	**205**	**1,074**	**604**
Official creditors	..	..	..	..	-52	-26	19	-16	72	64
Multilateral	..	..	..	..	-52	-51	7	78	110	145
Concessional	..	..	..	..	-4	-2	-12	-1	13	23
Bilateral	..	..	..	..	0	25	12	-95	-37	-81
Concessional	..	..	..	..	0	9	6	-8	-14	-1
Private creditors	..	..	..	..	15	10	11	222	1,002	541
Bonds	..	..	..	..	0	0	0	67	485	89
Commercial banks	..	..	..	..	-2	0	0	123	279	557
Other private	..	..	..	..	17	10	11	32	239	-106
Private nonguaranteed	..	..	..	..	**-3**	**89**	**154**	**423**	**1,007**	**47**
Bonds	..	..	..	..	0	0	0	0	0	0
Commercial banks	..	..	..	..	-3	89	154	423	1,007	47
Memo:										
IBRD	..	..	..	..	-33	-28	29	89	100	92
IDA	..	..	..	..	0	0	0	0	0	0

CROATIA

(US$ million, unless otherwise indicated)

	1970	1980	1990	1992	1993	1994	1995	1996	1997	1998
INTEREST PAYMENTS (LINT)	..	..	..	..	**97**	**78**	**98**	**77**	**345**	**276**
Public and publicly guaranteed	..	..	..	..	**48**	**43**	**32**	**41**	**269**	**270**
Official creditors	..	..	..	..	39	34	27	33	99	87
Multilateral	..	..	..	..	28	25	25	25	29	29
Concessional	..	..	..	..	1	1	1	1	1	1
Bilateral	..	..	..	..	11	9	2	8	71	58
Concessional	..	..	..	..	0	0	0	1	11	9
Private creditors	..	..	..	..	9	9	5	7	170	184
Bonds	..	..	..	..	0	0	0	1	14	35
Commercial banks	..	..	..	..	6	4	0	2	135	125
Other private	..	..	..	..	4	4	5	4	20	24
Private nonguaranteed	..	..	..	..	**49**	**35**	**66**	**37**	**76**	**6**
Bonds	..	..	..	..	0	0	0	0	0	0
Commercial banks	..	..	..	..	49	35	66	37	76	6
Memo:										
IBRD	..	..	..	..	9	8	7	11	15	17
IDA	..	..	..	..	0	0	0	0	0	0
NET TRANSFERS ON DEBT	..	..	..	..	**-137**	**-5**	**86**	**551**	**1,736**	**375**
Public and publicly guaranteed	..	..	..	..	**-85**	**-59**	**-2**	**165**	**805**	**334**
Official creditors	..	..	..	..	-91	-60	-8	-50	-27	-23
Multilateral	..	..	..	..	-80	-76	-17	53	81	116
Concessional	..	..	..	..	-5	-3	-14	-1	12	22
Bilateral	..	..	..	..	-11	16	10	-103	-108	-139
Concessional	..	..	..	..	0	9	6	-9	-25	-11
Private creditors	..	..	..	..	6	1	5	215	832	357
Bonds	..	..	..	..	0	0	0	65	470	55
Commercial banks	..	..	..	..	-8	-4	0	121	144	433
Other private	..	..	..	..	14	5	5	28	218	-130
Private nonguaranteed	..	..	..	..	**-52**	**54**	**88**	**386**	**931**	**42**
Bonds	..	..	..	..	0	0	0	0	0	0
Commercial banks	..	..	..	..	-52	54	88	386	931	42
Memo:										
IBRD	..	..	..	..	-42	-36	22	78	86	75
IDA	..	..	..	..	0	0	0	0	0	0
DEBT SERVICE (LTDS)	..	..	..	..	**295**	**224**	**332**	**388**	**1,089**	**783**
Public and publicly guaranteed	..	..	..	..	**119**	**110**	**105**	**217**	**631**	**745**
Official creditors	..	..	..	..	99	87	79	170	230	242
Multilateral	..	..	..	..	88	78	77	60	52	65
Concessional	..	..	..	..	5	3	14	1	2	7
Bilateral	..	..	..	..	11	9	2	111	178	177
Concessional	..	..	..	..	0	0	0	9	27	23
Private creditors	..	..	..	..	20	23	26	47	402	503
Bonds	..	..	..	..	0	0	0	1	60	46
Commercial banks	..	..	..	..	8	4	0	14	182	291
Other private	..	..	..	..	13	19	26	32	159	166
Private nonguaranteed	..	..	..	..	**176**	**114**	**227**	**171**	**457**	**38**
Bonds	..	..	..	..	0	0	0	0	0	0
Commercial banks	..	..	..	..	176	114	227	171	457	38
Memo:										
IBRD	..	..	..	..	43	37	28	26	29	34
IDA	..	..	..	..	0	0	0	0	0	0
UNDISBURSED DEBT	..	..	..	..	**114**	**223**	**351**	**795**	**560**	**824**
Official creditors	..	..	..	..	90	161	225	344	381	420
Private creditors	..	..	..	..	25	62	126	451	179	404
Memorandum items										
Concessional LDOD	..	..	..	..	21	30	340	315	290	326
Variable rate LDOD	..	..	..	..	1,141	1,303	2,030	3,408	4,462	4,980
Public sector LDOD	..	..	..	..	587	613	1,174	2,821	3,751	4,271
Private sector LDOD	..	..	..	..	900	1,073	1,842	1,471	2,295	2,608

6. CURRENCY COMPOSITION OF LONG-TERM DEBT (PERCENT)

	1970	1980	1990	1992	1993	1994	1995	1996	1997	1998
Deutsche mark	..	..	..	..	7.1	7.4	23.3	17.0	19.0	19.6
French franc	..	..	..	..	2.8	2.5	7.6	3.3	2.2	1.7
Japanese yen	..	..	..	..	0.9	1.0	3.9	1.7	0.8	0.5
Pound sterling	..	..	..	..	0.6	0.5	3.4	1.9	1.3	1.0
Swiss franc	..	..	..	..	3.6	2.8	2.9	1.5	1.3	1.1
U.S.dollars	..	..	..	..	24.0	25.3	26.2	57.0	55.7	51.5
Multiple currency	..	..	..	..	17.4	13.0	6.7	5.8	5.3	4.9
Special drawing rights	..	..	..	..	0.0	0.0	0.0	0.0	0.0	0.0
All other currencies	..	..	..	..	43.6	47.5	26.0	11.8	14.4	19.7

CROATIA

(US$ million, unless otherwise indicated)

	1970	1980	1990	1992	1993	1994	1995	1996	1997	1998
7. DEBT RESTRUCTURINGS										
Total amount rescheduled	..	..	..	..	0	16	1,065	1,462	0	1
Debt stock rescheduled	..	..	..	..	0	0	0	975	0	0
Principal rescheduled	..	..	..	..	0	13	781	0	0	0
Official	..	..	..	..	0	0	719	0	0	0
Private	..	..	..	..	0	13	62	0	0	0
Interest rescheduled	..	..	..	..	..	3	70	51	0	0
Official	..	..	..	..	0	0	43	0	0	0
Private	..	..	..	..	0	3	27	51	0	0
Debt forgiven	..	..	..	..	0	0	0	0	0	0
Memo: interest forgiven	..	..	..	..	0	0	0	0	0	0
Debt stock reduction	..	..	..	..	0	0	0	0	0	0
of which debt buyback	..	..	..	..	0	0	0	0	0	0
8. DEBT STOCK-FLOW RECONCILIATION										
Total change in debt stocks	..	..	..	..	..	440	1,675	1,204	1,913	1,451
Net flows on debt	..	..	..	..	-9	293	526	614	2,245	1,251
Net change in interest arrears	..	..	..	..	..	18	1	-50	8	8
Interest capitalized	..	..	..	..	..	3	70	51	0	0
Debt forgiveness or reduction	..	..	..	..	..	0	0	0	0	0
Cross-currency valuation	..	..	..	..	..	39	84	-95	-217	127
Residual	..	..	..	..	..	88	993	685	-123	65
9. AVERAGE TERMS OF NEW COMMITMENTS										
ALL CREDITORS										
Interest (%)	..	..	..	..	5.9	7.0	6.8	6.9	6.3	6.0
Maturity (years)	..	..	..	..	6.4	13.5	12.3	6.5	6.8	6.7
Grace period (years)	..	..	..	..	1.5	4.5	4.6	2.4	4.2	2.7
Grant element (%)	..	..	..	..	12.5	16.0	15.4	11.1	14.8	13.6
Official creditors										
Interest (%)	..	..	..	..	6.9	7.0	6.9	5.1	5.4	3.9
Maturity (years)	..	..	..	..	9.3	16.4	16.3	14.8	12.0	13.6
Grace period (years)	..	..	..	..	2.0	4.2	4.9	5.3	4.3	5.1
Grant element (%)	..	..	..	..	12.4	17.0	17.9	28.9	24.2	34.6
Private creditors										
Interest (%)	..	..	..	..	5.3	6.9	6.7	7.7	6.6	6.4
Maturity (years)	..	..	..	..	4.8	6.3	6.4	3.0	5.4	5.4
Grace period (years)	..	..	..	..	1.2	5.2	4.1	1.2	4.2	2.3
Grant element (%)	..	..	..	..	12.6	13.4	11.7	3.6	12.3	9.6
Memorandum items										
Commitments	..	..	..	..	43	213	223	840	1,274	1,270
Official creditors	..	..	..	..	16	151	135	249	270	204
Private creditors	..	..	..	..	28	62	89	591	1,004	1,067

10. CONTRACTUAL OBLIGATIONS ON OUTSTANDING LONG-TERM DEBT

	1999	2000	2001	2002	2003	2004	2005	2006	2007	2008
TOTAL										
Disbursements	350	207	106	53	32	24	17	11	8	5
Principal	495	694	796	915	392	583	373	370	305	301
Interest	379	353	309	253	207	178	137	109	81	58
Official creditors										
Disbursements	145	73	55	41	30	24	17	11	8	5
Principal	124	139	124	130	149	158	151	175	193	189
Interest	91	86	81	78	71	64	56	48	38	28
Bilateral creditors										
Disbursements	30	16	6	3	1	0	0	0	0	0
Principal	84	91	73	71	75	80	80	90	101	109
Interest	53	49	44	40	36	32	28	23	18	12
Multilateral creditors										
Disbursements	115	58	48	38	29	23	17	11	8	5
Principal	40	48	52	59	74	78	70	85	93	80
Interest	38	37	37	38	35	31	28	24	20	16
Private creditors										
Disbursements	205	134	52	12	2	0	0	0	0	0
Principal	371	555	671	785	243	426	222	195	111	112
Interest	288	267	229	175	135	114	82	61	44	30
Commercial banks										
Disbursements	182	115	42	9	0	0	0	0	0	0
Principal	191	450	518	380	237	220	197	195	111	112
Interest	225	215	184	148	121	100	80	61	44	30
Other private										
Disbursements	24	19	10	3	2	0	0	0	0	0
Principal	180	106	153	405	7	206	25	0	0	0
Interest	63	52	45	28	14	14	2	0	0	0

CZECH REPUBLIC

(US$ million, unless otherwise indicated)

	1970	1980	1990	1992	1993	1994	1995	1996	1997	1998
1. SUMMARY DEBT DATA										
TOTAL DEBT STOCKS (EDT)	..	..	**6,383**	**7,571**	**9,294**	**10,829**	**16,306**	**19,997**	**23,132**	**25,301**
Long-term debt (LDOD)	..	..	**3,983**	**4,700**	**6,220**	**7,940**	**11,237**	**14,277**	**14,565**	**15,365**
Public and publicly guaranteed	..	..	3,983	4,689	6,008	7,172	9,777	12,149	12,451	12,901
Private nonguaranteed	..	..	0	11	212	768	1,460	2,128	2,113	2,465
Use of IMF credit	**0**	**0**	**0**	**1,073**	**1,072**	**0**	**0**	**0**	**0**	**0**
Short-term debt	..	..	**2,400**	**1,798**	**2,002**	**2,889**	**5,070**	**5,720**	**8,568**	**9,935**
of which interest arrears on LDOD	..	..	0	0	0	1	28	14	8	11
Official creditors	..	..	0	0	0	1	0	0	0	0
Private creditors	..	..	0	0	0	0	28	14	8	11
Memo: principal arrears on LDOD	..	..	0	0	0	0	105	149	122	64
Official creditors	..	..	0	0	0	0	0	0	0	0
Private creditors	..	..	0	0	0	0	105	149	122	64
Memo: export credits	..	..	0	1,671	1,455	1,460	1,909	1,412	1,075	1,822
TOTAL DEBT FLOWS										
Disbursements	..	..	**1,182**	**1,207**	**2,514**	**1,579**	**4,241**	**4,951**	**3,809**	**4,343**
Long-term debt	..	..	1,182	973	2,514	1,579	4,241	4,951	3,809	4,343
IMF purchases	0	0	0	234	0	0	0	0	0	0
Principal repayments	..	..	**537**	**1,097**	**929**	**2,009**	**1,667**	**1,664**	**3,321**	**3,883**
Long-term debt	..	..	537	1,063	929	891	1,667	1,664	3,321	3,883
IMF repurchases	0	0	0	34	0	1,118	0	0	0	0
Net flows on debt	..	..	**52**	**-236**	**1,790**	**456**	**4,728**	**3,951**	**3,342**	**1,823**
of which short-term debt	..	..	-593	-346	205	886	2,154	664	2,854	1,364
Interest payments (INT)	..	..	**497**	**571**	**481**	**512**	**752**	**950**	**1,112**	**1,520**
Long-term debt	..	..	196	312	292	332	514	762	902	1,099
IMF charges	0	0	0	73	73	34	0	0	0	0
Short-term debt	..	..	301	185	116	147	238	187	209	421
Net transfers on debt	..	..	**-446**	**-806**	**1,309**	**-57**	**3,976**	**3,001**	**2,230**	**304**
Total debt service paid (TDS)	..	..	**1,035**	**1,668**	**1,410**	**2,522**	**2,419**	**2,613**	**4,433**	**5,403**
Long-term debt	..	..	734	1,375	1,221	1,223	2,181	2,426	4,224	4,983
IMF repurchases and charges	0	0	0	108	73	1,152	0	0	0	0
Short-term debt (interest only)	..	..	301	185	116	147	238	187	209	421
2. AGGREGATE NET RESOURCE FLOWS AND NET TRANSFERS (LONG-TERM)										
NET RESOURCE FLOWS	..	..	**862**	**1,090**	**2,327**	**1,783**	**5,270**	**4,957**	**1,866**	**3,197**
Net flow of long-term debt (ex. IMF)	..	..	645	-90	1,585	688	2,574	3,287	488	459
Foreign direct investment (net)	..	..	207	1,103	654	878	2,568	1,435	1,286	2,554
Portfolio equity flows	..	..	0	31	38	114	82	164	16	129
Grants (excluding technical coop.)	..	..	11	46	50	103	46	71	76	54
Memo: technical coop. grants	..	..	0	83	50	40	97	58	38	40
official net resource flows	..	..	-14	494	223	146	75	70	-6	-135
private net resource flows	..	..	876	596	2,104	1,637	5,196	4,887	1,871	3,331
NET TRANSFERS	..	..	**666**	**777**	**1,935**	**1,321**	**4,616**	**4,029**	**763**	**1,697**
Interest on long-term debt	..	..	196	312	292	332	514	762	902	1,099
Profit remittances on FDI	..	..	0	0	100	130	140	165	200	400
Memo: official net transfers	..	..	-38	436	149	64	-22	-8	-78	-198
private net transfers	..	..	704	341	1,786	1,257	4,638	4,037	841	1,896
3. MAJOR ECONOMIC AGGREGATES										
Gross national product (GNP)	..	..	34,880	29,811	34,877	41,067	51,931	57,200	52,209	55,628
Exports of goods & services (XGS)	..	..	..	..	19,500	21,922	29,399	31,044	31,274	35,433
of which workers remittances	..	..	..	..	..	..	..	..	..	..
Imports of goods & services (MGS)	..	..	..	..	19,121	22,869	31,345	35,727	34,910	36,950
International reserves (RES)	..	..	..	..	4,551	6,949	14,613	13,085	10,036	12,625
Current account balance	..	..	..	..	466	-820	-1,374	-4,299	-3,271	-1,110
4. DEBT INDICATORS										
EDT / XGS (%)	..	..	..	..	47.7	49.4	55.5	64.4	74.0	71.4
EDT / GNP (%)	..	..	18.3	25.4	26.7	26.4	31.4	35.0	44.3	45.5
TDS / XGS (%)	..	..	..	..	7.2	11.5	8.2	8.4	14.2	15.3
INT / XGS (%)	..	..	..	..	2.5	2.3	2.6	3.1	3.6	4.3
INT / GNP (%)	..	..	1.4	1.9	1.4	1.3	1.5	1.7	2.1	2.7
RES / EDT (%)	..	..	..	..	49.0	64.2	89.6	65.4	43.4	49.9
RES / MGS (months)	..	..	..	..	2.9	3.7	5.6	4.4	3.5	4.1
Short-term / EDT (%)	..	..	37.6	23.7	21.5	26.7	31.1	28.6	37.0	39.3
Concessional / EDT (%)	..	..	0.0	0.4	0.5	0.5	0.4	0.4	0.4	0.6
Multilateral / EDT (%)	..	..	2.8	9.9	8.9	8.5	6.1	4.9	3.5	2.7

CZECH REPUBLIC

(US$ million, unless otherwise indicated)

	1970	1980	1990	1992	1993	1994	1995	1996	1997	1998
5. LONG-TERM DEBT										
DEBT OUTSTANDING (LDOD)	..	..	**3,983**	**4,700**	**6,220**	**7,940**	**11,237**	**14,277**	**14,565**	**15,365**
Public and publicly guaranteed	..	..	**3,983**	**4,689**	**6,008**	**7,172**	**9,777**	**12,149**	**12,451**	**12,901**
Official creditors	..	..	252	1,061	1,218	1,351	1,427	1,334	1,121	1,001
Multilateral	..	..	179	748	822	925	1,001	971	798	686
Concessional	..	..	0	0	23	26	28	26	23	24
Bilateral	..	..	73	312	396	426	426	364	323	314
Concessional	..	..	0	29	28	30	33	52	65	123
Private creditors	..	..	3,732	3,629	4,790	5,821	8,349	10,815	11,331	11,900
Bonds	..	..	50	244	943	870	860	480	672	1,376
Commercial banks	..	..	1,970	2,422	2,526	3,772	6,566	9,642	10,148	9,562
Other private	..	..	1,712	962	1,321	1,178	924	692	511	962
Private nonguaranteed	..	..	**0**	**11**	**212**	**768**	**1,460**	**2,128**	**2,113**	**2,465**
Bonds	..	..	0	0	0	0	39	527	457	671
Commercial banks	..	..	0	11	212	768	1,421	1,601	1,657	1,794
Memo:										
IBRD	0	0	0	220	315	367	434	435	382	380
IDA	0	0	0	0	0	0	0	0	0	0
DISBURSEMENTS	..	..	**1,182**	**973**	**2,514**	**1,579**	**4,241**	**4,951**	**3,809**	**4,343**
Public and publicly guaranteed	..	..	**1,182**	**965**	**2,369**	**1,390**	**3,306**	**3,981**	**3,089**	**3,108**
Official creditors	..	..	19	525	232	105	133	179	168	88
Multilateral	..	..	5	281	132	79	108	136	137	41
Concessional	..	..	0	0	24	1	0	0	0	0
Bilateral	..	..	14	244	100	26	25	43	32	47
Concessional	..	..	0	30	0	0	0	23	21	46
Private creditors	..	..	1,163	439	2,137	1,285	3,173	3,802	2,920	3,020
Bonds	..	..	0	42	747	0	20	50	264	637
Commercial banks	..	..	435	158	781	907	2,955	3,659	2,568	1,882
Other private	..	..	729	239	609	379	198	92	88	501
Private nonguaranteed	..	..	**0**	**9**	**145**	**189**	**935**	**970**	**721**	**1,235**
Bonds	..	..	0	0	0	0	36	496	0	200
Commercial banks	..	..	0	9	145	189	900	474	721	1,035
Memo:										
IBRD	0	0	0	87	93	30	57	42	23	26
IDA	0	0	0	0	0	0	0	0	0	0
PRINCIPAL REPAYMENTS	..	..	**537**	**1,063**	**929**	**891**	**1,667**	**1,664**	**3,321**	**3,883**
Public and publicly guaranteed	..	..	**537**	**1,063**	**922**	**868**	**1,420**	**1,369**	**2,521**	**3,317**
Official creditors	..	..	43	77	59	62	105	180	250	277
Multilateral	..	..	5	43	35	32	71	108	213	192
Concessional	..	..	0	0	0	0	0	0	0	0
Bilateral	..	..	38	34	24	30	34	72	37	86
Concessional	..	..	0	0	0	0	0	0	0	0
Private creditors	..	..	494	986	863	805	1,315	1,189	2,271	3,039
Bonds	..	..	0	38	114	126	18	375	23	0
Commercial banks	..	..	20	333	237	364	823	503	1,989	2,986
Other private	..	..	474	614	512	315	475	312	258	53
Private nonguaranteed	..	..	**0**	**0**	**7**	**24**	**247**	**294**	**801**	**567**
Bonds	..	..	0	0	0	0	0	0	36	0
Commercial banks	..	..	0	0	7	24	247	294	765	567
Memo:										
IBRD	0	0	0	0	0	0	0	10	39	47
IDA	0	0	0	0	0	0	0	0	0	0
NET FLOWS ON DEBT	..	..	**645**	**-90**	**1,585**	**688**	**2,574**	**3,287**	**488**	**459**
Public and publicly guaranteed	..	..	**645**	**-98**	**1,447**	**523**	**1,886**	**2,612**	**568**	**-208**
Official creditors	..	..	-24	448	173	43	28	-1	-82	-189
Multilateral	..	..	0	238	97	47	37	29	-76	-151
Concessional	..	..	0	0	24	1	0	0	0	0
Bilateral	..	..	-24	210	76	-5	-9	-30	-6	-38
Concessional	..	..	0	30	0	0	0	23	21	46
Private creditors	..	..	669	-546	1,274	480	1,857	2,612	649	-19
Bonds	..	..	0	5	633	-126	3	-325	241	637
Commercial banks	..	..	414	-175	544	543	2,132	3,157	579	-1,105
Other private	..	..	255	-376	97	63	-278	-219	-170	448
Private nonguaranteed	..	..	**0**	**8**	**138**	**165**	**689**	**676**	**-80**	**668**
Bonds	..	..	0	0	0	0	36	496	-36	200
Commercial banks	..	..	0	8	138	165	653	180	-44	468
Memo:										
IBRD	0	0	0	87	93	30	57	32	-17	-21
IDA	0	0	0	0	0	0	0	0	0	0

CZECH REPUBLIC

(US$ million, unless otherwise indicated)

	1970	1980	1990	1992	1993	1994	1995	1996	1997	1998
INTEREST PAYMENTS (LINT)	..	..	**196**	**312**	**292**	**332**	**514**	**762**	**902**	**1,099**
Public and publicly guaranteed	..	..	**196**	**312**	**290**	**317**	**464**	**632**	**785**	**972**
Official creditors	..	..	24	58	74	82	97	78	72	64
Multilateral	..	..	18	48	59	55	68	53	54	45
Concessional	..	..	0	0	0	1	2	2	2	0
Bilateral	..	..	7	10	15	26	28	25	18	18
Concessional	..	..	0	2	0	2	1	0	2	3
Private creditors	..	..	172	254	217	235	368	554	713	908
Bonds	..	..	2	18	20	69	117	56	35	45
Commercial banks	..	..	91	160	142	127	147	408	621	820
Other private	..	..	79	76	54	39	104	90	57	43
Private nonguaranteed	..	..	**0**	**0**	**2**	**14**	**50**	**130**	**117**	**128**
Bonds	..	..	0	0	0	0	0	4	31	31
Commercial banks	..	..	0	0	2	14	50	126	86	97
Memo:										
IBRD	0	0	0	10	19	25	28	29	27	24
IDA	0	0	0	0	0	0	0	0	0	0
NET TRANSFERS ON DEBT	..	..	**448**	**-402**	**1,293**	**356**	**2,060**	**2,525**	**-415**	**-640**
Public and publicly guaranteed	..	..	**448**	**-410**	**1,157**	**206**	**1,421**	**1,980**	**-218**	**-1,180**
Official creditors	..	..	-48	390	99	-39	-68	-79	-154	-252
Multilateral	..	..	-18	190	38	-8	-31	-24	-130	-196
Concessional	..	..	0	0	24	0	-2	-2	-2	0
Bilateral	..	..	-31	200	62	-31	-37	-54	-24	-56
Concessional	..	..	0	29	0	-2	-1	23	19	42
Private creditors	..	..	497	-800	1,058	245	1,489	2,058	-64	-927
Bonds	..	..	-2	-14	613	-195	-114	-381	206	592
Commercial banks	..	..	323	-335	402	416	1,985	2,748	-42	-1,924
Other private	..	..	176	-452	43	24	-382	-309	-227	405
Private nonguaranteed	..	..	**0**	**8**	**136**	**151**	**639**	**545**	**-197**	**540**
Bonds	..	..	0	0	0	0	36	492	-67	169
Commercial banks	..	..	0	8	136	151	603	53	-130	371
Memo:										
IBRD	0	0	0	77	74	5	29	3	-44	-44
IDA	0	0	0	0	0	0	0	0	0	0
DEBT SERVICE (LTDS)	..	..	**734**	**1,375**	**1,221**	**1,223**	**2,181**	**2,426**	**4,224**	**4,983**
Public and publicly guaranteed	..	..	**734**	**1,375**	**1,212**	**1,185**	**1,885**	**2,001**	**3,306**	**4,288**
Official creditors	..	..	67	135	133	144	202	258	322	341
Multilateral	..	..	23	91	94	87	139	161	267	237
Concessional	..	..	0	0	0	1	2	2	2	0
Bilateral	..	..	45	44	39	57	62	97	55	104
Concessional	..	..	0	2	0	2	1	0	2	3
Private creditors	..	..	666	1,239	1,079	1,041	1,683	1,744	2,984	3,947
Bonds	..	..	2	56	134	195	134	431	59	45
Commercial banks	..	..	111	493	379	491	970	911	2,610	3,806
Other private	..	..	553	690	566	354	579	402	315	96
Private nonguaranteed	..	..	**0**	**0**	**9**	**38**	**297**	**425**	**918**	**695**
Bonds	..	..	0	0	0	0	0	4	67	31
Commercial banks	..	..	0	0	9	38	297	421	851	664
Memo:										
IBRD	0	0	0	10	19	25	28	39	66	71
IDA	0	0	0	0	0	0	0	0	0	0
UNDISBURSED DEBT	..	..	**447**	**868**	**845**	**822**	**903**	**1,891**	**1,534**	**1,020**
Official creditors	..	..	14	519	548	586	702	829	663	613
Private creditors	..	..	433	348	298	236	200	1,063	871	407
Memorandum items										
Concessional LDOD	..	..	0	29	50	56	61	78	88	147
Variable rate LDOD	..	..	1,192	2,394	3,275	3,992	5,079	5,332	6,272	8,210
Public sector LDOD	..	..	3,725	4,456	5,745	6,880	9,340	11,726	12,113	12,722
Private sector LDOD	..	..	258	244	475	1,060	1,897	2,551	2,452	2,643
6. CURRENCY COMPOSITION OF LONG-TERM DEBT (PERCENT)										
Deutsche mark	..	..	33.5	25.3	16.3	14.3	5.3	3.7	5.1	11.5
French franc	..	..	1.4	1.5	0.8	0.5	0.2	0.1	0.1	0.0
Japanese yen	..	..	9.0	10.7	13.8	11.8	8.1	5.7	4.7	4.6
Pound sterling	..	..	0.6	0.3	0.2	0.1	0.0	0.0	0.0	0.0
Swiss franc	..	..	13.8	7.4	4.7	3.8	3.0	2.0	1.7	0.5
U.S.dollars	..	..	26.6	33.5	41.5	46.6	65.5	74.3	77.7	72.1
Multiple currency	..	..	0.0	4.7	12.3	15.1	12.1	9.6	8.1	9.8
Special drawing rights	..	..	0.0	0.0	0.0	0.0	0.0	0.0	0.0	0.0
All other currencies	..	..	15.1	16.6	10.4	7.8	5.8	4.6	2.6	1.5

CZECH REPUBLIC

(US$ million, unless otherwise indicated)

	1970	1980	1990	1992	1993	1994	1995	1996	1997	1998
7. DEBT RESTRUCTURINGS										
Total amount rescheduled	..	..	0	0	0	0	0	0	0	0
Debt stock rescheduled	..	..	0	0	0	0	0	0	0	0
Principal rescheduled	..	..	0	0	0	0	0	0	0	0
Official	..	..	0	0	0	0	0	0	0	0
Private	..	..	0	0	0	0	0	0	0	0
Interest rescheduled	..	..	0	0	0	0	0	0	0	0
Official	..	..	0	0	0	0	0	0	0	0
Private	..	..	0	0	0	0	0	0	0	0
Debt forgiven	..	..	0	0	2	1	2	0	2	0
Memo: interest forgiven	..	..	0	0	0	0	0	0	0	0
Debt stock reduction	..	..	0	0	0	0	0	0	0	0
of which debt buyback	..	..	0	0	0	0	0	0	0	0
8. DEBT STOCK-FLOW RECONCILIATION										
Total change in debt stocks	..	..	19	-461	1,724	1,535	5,478	3,691	3,135	2,168
Net flows on debt	..	..	52	-236	1,790	456	4,728	3,951	3,342	1,823
Net change in interest arrears	..	..	0	0	0	1	27	-13	-7	4
Interest capitalized	..	..	0	0	0	0	0	0	0	0
Debt forgiveness or reduction	..	..	0	0	-2	-1	-2	0	-2	0
Cross-currency valuation	..	..	390	-167	-17	335	118	-214	-238	219
Residual	..	..	-423	-59	-47	744	607	-33	40	122
9. AVERAGE TERMS OF NEW COMMITMENTS										
ALL CREDITORS										
Interest (%)	..	..	8.2	7.0	7.0	7.6	7.4	7.6	6.6	6.5
Maturity (years)	..	..	5.1	10.2	11.6	15.2	14.3	14.6	9.4	9.3
Grace period (years)	..	..	3.1	4.1	3.5	2.7	2.8	3.2	2.4	3.8
Grant element (%)	..	..	4.3	13.6	11.3	8.2	8.2	7.8	12.3	14.0
Official creditors										
Interest (%)	..	..	9.6	6.8	6.1	7.1	3.9	6.2	5.9	9.5
Maturity (years)	..	..	10.8	10.9	13.5	20.0	18.2	19.4	18.7	9.4
Grace period (years)	..	..	5.2	5.1	4.5	5.5	4.9	6.6	5.2	1.4
Grant element (%)	..	..	0.6	15.3	21.1	18.8	38.7	25.0	25.9	1.0
Private creditors										
Interest (%)	..	..	8.1	7.4	7.1	7.6	7.7	7.8	6.6	6.5
Maturity (years)	..	..	5.0	9.0	11.3	14.6	14.0	14.1	9.1	9.3
Grace period (years)	..	..	3.1	2.6	3.3	2.4	2.6	2.9	2.3	3.8
Grant element (%)	..	..	4.4	10.9	10.1	6.9	5.7	6.1	11.8	14.1
Memorandum items										
Commitments	..	..	784	1,099	2,370	1,362	3,101	5,206	2,855	2,873
Official creditors	..	..	18	672	269	150	240	459	86	1
Private creditors	..	..	766	428	2,102	1,212	2,861	4,747	2,770	2,871

10. CONTRACTUAL OBLIGATIONS ON OUTSTANDING LONG-TERM DEBT

	1999	2000	2001	2002	2003	2004	2005	2006	2007	2008
TOTAL										
Disbursements	415	282	165	78	40	23	13	5	0	0
Principal	1,955	2,204	1,990	1,609	1,731	1,093	1,144	878	1,001	1,029
Interest	1,051	979	821	706	590	487	411	328	303	177
Official creditors										
Disbursements	159	178	120	76	40	23	13	5	0	0
Principal	128	119	116	135	135	132	131	132	87	71
Interest	64	68	69	66	61	54	47	40	33	28
Bilateral creditors										
Disbursements	81	49	26	16	5	2	1	0	0	0
Principal	63	38	35	34	31	28	27	28	25	25
Interest	16	16	17	16	15	14	13	12	11	10
Multilateral creditors										
Disbursements	78	129	94	60	34	21	12	5	0	0
Principal	65	81	81	101	104	104	104	104	62	46
Interest	49	52	52	50	46	40	34	28	22	18
Private creditors										
Disbursements	255	104	46	2	0	0	0	0	0	0
Principal	1,828	2,084	1,874	1,474	1,596	961	1,013	746	914	958
Interest	986	911	752	639	530	433	364	288	271	149
Commercial banks										
Disbursements	234	95	42	0	0	0	0	0	0	0
Principal	959	1,379	1,229	985	958	789	659	537	537	695
Interest	691	644	548	465	395	329	270	221	177	130
Other private										
Disbursements	21	9	3	1	0	0	0	0	0	0
Principal	869	705	645	489	638	172	355	208	377	262
Interest	296	267	204	174	135	105	95	67	94	19

DJIBOUTI

(US$ million, unless otherwise indicated)

	1970	1980	1990	1992	1993	1994	1995	1996	1997	1998
1. SUMMARY DEBT DATA										
TOTAL DEBT STOCKS (EDT)	**..**	**31.8**	**205.3**	**235.3**	**264.4**	**263.1**	**281.8**	**295.8**	**273.7**	**287.8**
Long-term debt (LDOD)	**2.6**	**25.8**	**155.2**	**219.3**	**230.9**	**254.9**	**268.9**	**279.3**	**253.0**	**263.8**
Public and publicly guaranteed	2.6	25.8	155.2	219.3	230.9	254.9	268.9	279.3	253.0	263.8
Private nonguaranteed	0.0	0.0	0.0	0.0	0.0	0.0	0.0	0.0	0.0	0.0
Use of IMF credit	**0.0**	**0.0**	**0.0**	**0.0**	**0.0**	**0.0**	**0.0**	**4.1**	**5.4**	**8.9**
Short-term debt	**..**	**6.0**	**50.1**	**16.0**	**33.4**	**8.2**	**12.9**	**12.4**	**15.3**	**15.1**
of which interest arrears on LDOD	..	0.0	0.1	0.7	1.6	2.8	3.5	4.2	4.3	6.3
Official creditors	..	0.0	0.1	0.7	1.6	2.8	3.5	4.2	4.3	6.3
Private creditors	..	0.0	0.0	0.0	0.0	0.0	0.0	0.0	0.0	0.0
Memo: principal arrears on LDOD	..	0.0	1.2	5.5	9.3	10.7	13.1	14.6	12.6	20.5
Official creditors	..	0.0	1.2	5.5	9.3	10.7	13.1	14.6	12.6	20.5
Private creditors	..	0.0	0.0	0.0	0.0	0.0	0.0	0.0	0.0	0.0
Memo: export credits	..	0.0	27.0	21.0	16.0	10.0	8.0	5.0	17.0	14.0
TOTAL DEBT FLOWS										
Disbursements	**1.4**	**10.2**	**27.0**	**43.4**	**25.6**	**25.8**	**18.4**	**27.8**	**13.5**	**8.2**
Long-term debt	1.4	10.2	27.0	43.4	25.6	25.8	18.4	23.6	12.0	5.1
IMF purchases	0.0	0.0	0.0	0.0	0.0	0.0	0.0	4.2	1.5	3.2
Principal repayments	**0.1**	**2.2**	**8.9**	**7.7**	**6.4**	**8.9**	**9.2**	**8.8**	**5.0**	**3.3**
Long-term debt	0.1	2.2	8.9	7.7	6.4	8.9	9.2	8.8	5.0	3.3
IMF repurchases	0.0	0.0	0.0	0.0	0.0	0.0	0.0	0.0	0.0	0.0
Net flows on debt	**1.3**	**9.0**	**20.8**	**30.2**	**35.6**	**-9.5**	**13.1**	**17.8**	**11.3**	**2.7**
of which short-term debt	..	1.0	2.8	-5.6	16.5	-26.4	3.9	-1.2	2.8	-2.2
Interest payments (INT)	**..**	**1.7**	**6.0**	**4.2**	**4.5**	**2.9**	**2.5**	**3.2**	**2.2**	**2.2**
Long-term debt	0.0	0.9	2.1	2.4	2.1	1.8	2.0	2.7	1.5	1.5
IMF charges	0.0	0.0	0.0	0.0	0.0	0.0	0.0	0.1	0.2	0.3
Short-term debt	..	0.8	3.9	1.8	2.4	1.1	0.5	0.4	0.5	0.4
Net transfers on debt	**..**	**7.3**	**14.8**	**26.0**	**31.2**	**-12.4**	**10.7**	**14.6**	**9.0**	**0.6**
Total debt service paid (TDS)	**..**	**3.9**	**14.9**	**11.9**	**10.9**	**11.8**	**11.6**	**12.0**	**7.3**	**5.5**
Long-term debt	0.1	3.1	11.0	10.1	8.5	10.7	11.1	11.5	6.6	4.8
IMF repurchases and charges	0.0	0.0	0.0	0.0	0.0	0.0	0.0	0.1	0.2	0.3
Short-term debt (interest only)	..	0.8	3.9	1.8	2.4	1.1	0.5	0.4	0.5	0.4
2. AGGREGATE NET RESOURCE FLOWS AND NET TRANSFERS (LONG-TERM)										
NET RESOURCE FLOWS	**5.6**	**37.8**	**148.7**	**94.7**	**73.1**	**72.6**	**61.2**	**62.2**	**50.3**	**55.6**
Net flow of long-term debt (ex. IMF)	1.3	8.0	18.0	35.8	19.1	16.9	9.2	14.9	6.9	1.8
Foreign direct investment (net)	0.0	0.0	0.0	2.3	1.4	1.4	3.2	5.0	5.0	6.0
Portfolio equity flows	0.0	0.0	0.0	0.0	0.0	0.0	0.0	0.0	0.0	0.0
Grants (excluding technical coop.)	4.3	29.8	130.7	56.6	52.6	54.3	48.8	42.3	38.4	47.8
Memo: technical coop. grants	6.2	27.8	44.6	43.6	43.8	50.7	45.7	41.0	31.1	28.9
official net resource flows	5.6	32.8	149.3	92.4	71.7	71.2	58.0	57.2	45.3	49.6
private net resource flows	0.0	5.0	-0.6	2.3	1.4	1.4	3.2	5.0	5.0	6.0
NET TRANSFERS	**5.6**	**36.9**	**146.6**	**89.0**	**68.5**	**67.8**	**56.2**	**56.5**	**45.8**	**50.1**
Interest on long-term debt	0.0	0.9	2.1	2.4	2.1	1.8	2.0	2.7	1.5	1.5
Profit remittances on FDI	0.0	0.0	0.0	3.3	2.5	3.0	3.0	3.0	3.0	4.0
Memo: official net transfers	5.6	31.9	147.2	90.0	69.6	69.4	56.0	54.5	43.8	48.1
private net transfers	0.0	5.0	-0.6	-1.0	-1.1	-1.6	0.2	2.0	2.0	2.0
3. MAJOR ECONOMIC AGGREGATES										
Gross national product (GNP)	..	..	..	465.6	468.5	483.9	487.2	481.9	496.8	..
Exports of goods & services (XGS)	..	..	..	229.1	259.8	233.8	211.8	208.6	215.7	..
of which workers remittances	..	..	..	1.5	1.5	1.5	1.0	..	..	..
Imports of goods & services (MGS)	..	..	..	389.6	373.1	333.8	300.8	291.0	296.0	..
International reserves (RES)	..	..	93.6	83.4	75.1	73.8	72.2	77.0	66.6	66.5
Current account balance	..	..	..	-87.5	-34.3	-46.1	-23.0	..	..	..
4. DEBT INDICATORS										
EDT / XGS (%)	..	..	..	102.7	101.8	112.5	133.0	141.8	126.9	..
EDT / GNP (%)	..	..	..	50.5	56.4	54.4	57.9	61.4	55.1	..
TDS / XGS (%)	..	..	..	5.2	4.2	5.1	5.5	5.8	3.4	..
INT / XGS (%)	..	..	..	1.8	1.7	1.2	1.2	1.5	1.0	..
INT / GNP (%)	..	..	..	0.9	1.0	0.6	0.5	0.7	0.4	..
RES / EDT (%)	..	..	45.6	35.4	28.4	28.0	25.6	26.0	24.3	23.1
RES / MGS (months)	..	..	..	2.6	2.4	2.7	2.9	3.2	2.7	..
Short-term / EDT (%)	..	18.9	24.4	6.8	12.6	3.1	4.6	4.2	5.6	5.3
Concessional / EDT (%)	..	45.6	74.0	92.2	86.6	96.1	94.8	94.0	92.1	91.4
Multilateral / EDT (%)	..	7.2	41.9	44.2	43.5	48.8	48.4	46.3	49.8	50.2

DJIBOUTI

(US$ million, unless otherwise indicated)

	1970	1980	1990	1992	1993	1994	1995	1996	1997	1998
5. LONG-TERM DEBT										
DEBT OUTSTANDING (LDOD)	**2.6**	**25.8**	**155.2**	**219.3**	**230.9**	**254.9**	**268.9**	**279.3**	**253.0**	**263.8**
Public and publicly guaranteed	**2.6**	**25.8**	**155.2**	**219.3**	**230.9**	**254.9**	**268.9**	**279.3**	**253.0**	**263.8**
Official creditors	2.6	21.2	155.2	219.3	230.9	254.9	268.9	279.3	253.0	263.8
Multilateral	0.0	2.3	86.1	104.1	114.9	128.5	136.4	137.0	136.3	144.5
Concessional	0.0	1.0	83.0	101.8	113.0	126.6	134.7	135.7	135.4	143.8
Bilateral	2.6	18.9	69.2	115.3	116.1	126.4	132.5	142.2	116.7	119.3
Concessional	2.6	13.5	68.9	115.1	115.9	126.3	132.4	142.2	116.7	119.3
Private creditors	0.0	4.7	0.0	0.0	0.0	0.0	0.0	0.0	0.0	0.0
Bonds	0.0	0.0	0.0	0.0	0.0	0.0	0.0	0.0	0.0	0.0
Commercial banks	0.0	4.7	0.0	0.0	0.0	0.0	0.0	0.0	0.0	0.0
Other private	0.0	0.0	0.0	0.0	0.0	0.0	0.0	0.0	0.0	0.0
Private nonguaranteed	**0.0**	**0.0**	**0.0**	**0.0**	**0.0**	**0.0**	**0.0**	**0.0**	**0.0**	**0.0**
Bonds	0.0	0.0	0.0	0.0	0.0	0.0	0.0	0.0	0.0	0.0
Commercial banks	0.0	0.0	0.0	0.0	0.0	0.0	0.0	0.0	0.0	0.0
Memo:										
IBRD	0.0	0.0	0.0	0.0	0.0	0.0	0.0	0.0	0.0	0.0
IDA	0.0	0.0	31.1	36.0	39.6	42.8	46.2	45.7	46.1	49.5
DISBURSEMENTS	**1.4**	**10.2**	**27.0**	**43.4**	**25.6**	**25.8**	**18.4**	**23.6**	**12.0**	**5.1**
Public and publicly guaranteed	**1.4**	**10.2**	**27.0**	**43.4**	**25.6**	**25.8**	**18.4**	**23.6**	**12.0**	**5.1**
Official creditors	1.4	5.3	27.0	43.4	25.6	25.8	18.4	23.6	12.0	5.1
Multilateral	0.0	2.4	8.9	17.1	13.9	12.1	10.0	10.6	9.6	4.9
Concessional	0.0	1.0	8.9	17.1	13.9	12.1	10.0	10.6	9.6	4.9
Bilateral	1.4	2.9	18.0	26.3	11.7	13.8	8.4	13.1	2.4	0.2
Concessional	1.4	0.0	18.0	26.3	11.7	13.8	8.4	13.1	2.4	0.2
Private creditors	0.0	5.0	0.0	0.0	0.0	0.0	0.0	0.0	0.0	0.0
Bonds	0.0	0.0	0.0	0.0	0.0	0.0	0.0	0.0	0.0	0.0
Commercial banks	0.0	5.0	0.0	0.0	0.0	0.0	0.0	0.0	0.0	0.0
Other private	0.0	0.0	0.0	0.0	0.0	0.0	0.0	0.0	0.0	0.0
Private nonguaranteed	**0.0**	**0.0**	**0.0**	**0.0**	**0.0**	**0.0**	**0.0**	**0.0**	**0.0**	**0.0**
Bonds	0.0	0.0	0.0	0.0	0.0	0.0	0.0	0.0	0.0	0.0
Commercial banks	0.0	0.0	0.0	0.0	0.0	0.0	0.0	0.0	0.0	0.0
Memo:										
IBRD	0.0	0.0	0.0	0.0	0.0	0.0	0.0	0.0	0.0	0.0
IDA	0.0	0.0	2.5	3.2	3.5	1.3	2.8	1.4	3.3	2.0
PRINCIPAL REPAYMENTS	**0.1**	**2.2**	**8.9**	**7.7**	**6.4**	**8.9**	**9.2**	**8.8**	**5.0**	**3.3**
Public and publicly guaranteed	**0.1**	**2.2**	**8.9**	**7.7**	**6.4**	**8.9**	**9.2**	**8.8**	**5.0**	**3.3**
Official creditors	0.1	2.2	8.3	7.7	6.4	8.9	9.2	8.8	5.0	3.3
Multilateral	0.0	0.0	3.5	3.5	3.3	4.0	4.4	4.3	2.1	1.9
Concessional	0.0	0.0	3.3	3.3	3.0	3.8	4.1	4.1	1.8	1.7
Bilateral	0.1	2.2	4.8	4.1	3.2	4.9	4.8	4.4	2.9	1.4
Concessional	0.1	1.7	4.7	4.1	3.1	4.8	4.7	4.4	2.9	1.4
Private creditors	0.0	0.0	0.6	0.0	0.0	0.0	0.0	0.0	0.0	0.0
Bonds	0.0	0.0	0.0	0.0	0.0	0.0	0.0	0.0	0.0	0.0
Commercial banks	0.0	0.0	0.4	0.0	0.0	0.0	0.0	0.0	0.0	0.0
Other private	0.0	0.0	0.2	0.0	0.0	0.0	0.0	0.0	0.0	0.0
Private nonguaranteed	**0.0**	**0.0**	**0.0**	**0.0**	**0.0**	**0.0**	**0.0**	**0.0**	**0.0**	**0.0**
Bonds	0.0	0.0	0.0	0.0	0.0	0.0	0.0	0.0	0.0	0.0
Commercial banks	0.0	0.0	0.0	0.0	0.0	0.0	0.0	0.0	0.0	0.0
Memo:										
IBRD	0.0	0.0	0.0	0.0	0.0	0.0	0.0	0.0	0.0	0.0
IDA	0.0	0.0	0.0	0.0	0.1	0.1	0.3	0.3	0.3	0.4
NET FLOWS ON DEBT	**1.3**	**8.0**	**18.0**	**35.8**	**19.1**	**16.9**	**9.2**	**14.9**	**6.9**	**1.8**
Public and publicly guaranteed	**1.3**	**8.0**	**18.0**	**35.8**	**19.1**	**16.9**	**9.2**	**14.9**	**6.9**	**1.8**
Official creditors	1.3	3.0	18.6	35.8	19.1	16.9	9.2	14.9	6.9	1.8
Multilateral	0.0	2.4	5.4	13.6	10.6	8.0	5.6	6.2	7.5	3.0
Concessional	0.0	1.0	5.6	13.8	10.8	8.3	5.9	6.5	7.8	3.2
Bilateral	1.3	0.6	13.2	22.2	8.5	8.9	3.6	8.6	-0.6	-1.2
Concessional	1.3	-1.7	13.3	22.2	8.6	8.9	3.7	8.7	-0.6	-1.2
Private creditors	0.0	5.0	-0.6	0.0	0.0	0.0	0.0	0.0	0.0	0.0
Bonds	0.0	0.0	0.0	0.0	0.0	0.0	0.0	0.0	0.0	0.0
Commercial banks	0.0	5.0	-0.4	0.0	0.0	0.0	0.0	0.0	0.0	0.0
Other private	0.0	0.0	-0.2	0.0	0.0	0.0	0.0	0.0	0.0	0.0
Private nonguaranteed	**0.0**	**0.0**	**0.0**	**0.0**	**0.0**	**0.0**	**0.0**	**0.0**	**0.0**	**0.0**
Bonds	0.0	0.0	0.0	0.0	0.0	0.0	0.0	0.0	0.0	0.0
Commercial banks	0.0	0.0	0.0	0.0	0.0	0.0	0.0	0.0	0.0	0.0
Memo:										
IBRD	0.0	0.0	0.0	0.0	0.0	0.0	0.0	0.0	0.0	0.0
IDA	0.0	0.0	2.5	3.2	3.4	1.2	2.4	1.0	3.0	1.7

DJIBOUTI

(US$ million, unless otherwise indicated)

	1970	1980	1990	1992	1993	1994	1995	1996	1997	1998
INTEREST PAYMENTS (LINT)	**0.0**	**0.9**	**2.1**	**2.4**	**2.1**	**1.8**	**2.0**	**2.7**	**1.5**	**1.5**
Public and publicly guaranteed	**0.0**	**0.9**	**2.1**	**2.4**	**2.1**	**1.8**	**2.0**	**2.7**	**1.5**	**1.5**
Official creditors	0.0	0.9	2.1	2.4	2.1	1.8	2.0	2.7	1.5	1.5
Multilateral	0.0	0.0	1.3	1.3	1.3	1.0	0.9	1.6	1.0	1.1
Concessional	0.0	0.0	1.3	1.3	1.2	0.9	0.9	1.6	1.0	1.1
Bilateral	0.0	0.9	0.8	1.1	0.8	0.9	1.1	1.1	0.5	0.4
Concessional	0.0	0.7	0.7	1.0	0.8	0.9	1.1	1.1	0.5	0.4
Private creditors	0.0	0.0	0.0	0.0	0.0	0.0	0.0	0.0	0.0	0.0
Bonds	0.0	0.0	0.0	0.0	0.0	0.0	0.0	0.0	0.0	0.0
Commercial banks	0.0	0.0	0.0	0.0	0.0	0.0	0.0	0.0	0.0	0.0
Other private	0.0	0.0	0.0	0.0	0.0	0.0	0.0	0.0	0.0	0.0
Private nonguaranteed	**0.0**	**0.0**	**0.0**	**0.0**	**0.0**	**0.0**	**0.0**	**0.0**	**0.0**	**0.0**
Bonds	0.0	0.0	0.0	0.0	0.0	0.0	0.0	0.0	0.0	0.0
Commercial banks	0.0	0.0	0.0	0.0	0.0	0.0	0.0	0.0	0.0	0.0
Memo:										
IBRD	0.0	0.0	0.0	0.0	0.0	0.0	0.0	0.0	0.0	0.0
IDA	0.0	0.0	0.2	0.3	0.3	0.2	0.3	0.3	0.3	0.4
NET TRANSFERS ON DEBT	**1.3**	**7.1**	**15.9**	**33.4**	**17.1**	**15.1**	**7.3**	**12.1**	**5.4**	**0.3**
Public and publicly guaranteed	**1.3**	**7.1**	**15.9**	**33.4**	**17.1**	**15.1**	**7.3**	**12.1**	**5.4**	**0.3**
Official creditors	1.3	2.1	16.6	33.4	17.1	15.1	7.3	12.1	5.4	0.3
Multilateral	0.0	2.4	4.1	12.3	9.3	7.1	4.7	4.6	6.5	1.9
Concessional	0.0	1.0	4.3	12.5	9.6	7.4	5.0	4.9	6.8	2.1
Bilateral	1.3	-0.3	12.5	21.1	7.8	8.0	2.6	7.5	-1.1	-1.6
Concessional	1.3	-2.4	12.6	21.2	7.8	8.1	2.6	7.6	-1.1	-1.6
Private creditors	0.0	5.0	-0.6	0.0	0.0	0.0	0.0	0.0	0.0	0.0
Bonds	0.0	0.0	0.0	0.0	0.0	0.0	0.0	0.0	0.0	0.0
Commercial banks	0.0	5.0	-0.4	0.0	0.0	0.0	0.0	0.0	0.0	0.0
Other private	0.0	0.0	-0.2	0.0	0.0	0.0	0.0	0.0	0.0	0.0
Private nonguaranteed	**0.0**	**0.0**	**0.0**	**0.0**	**0.0**	**0.0**	**0.0**	**0.0**	**0.0**	**0.0**
Bonds	0.0	0.0	0.0	0.0	0.0	0.0	0.0	0.0	0.0	0.0
Commercial banks	0.0	0.0	0.0	0.0	0.0	0.0	0.0	0.0	0.0	0.0
Memo:										
IBRD	0.0	0.0	0.0	0.0	0.0	0.0	0.0	0.0	0.0	0.0
IDA	0.0	0.0	2.3	2.9	3.1	0.9	2.1	0.7	2.6	1.3
DEBT SERVICE (LTDS)	**0.1**	**3.1**	**11.0**	**10.1**	**8.5**	**10.7**	**11.1**	**11.5**	**6.6**	**4.8**
Public and publicly guaranteed	**0.1**	**3.1**	**11.0**	**10.1**	**8.5**	**10.7**	**11.1**	**11.5**	**6.6**	**4.8**
Official creditors	0.1	3.1	10.4	10.1	8.5	10.7	11.1	11.5	6.6	4.8
Multilateral	0.0	0.0	4.9	4.8	4.5	5.0	5.3	5.9	3.1	3.1
Concessional	0.0	0.0	4.6	4.6	4.3	4.7	5.0	5.6	2.8	2.8
Bilateral	0.1	3.1	5.5	5.2	4.0	5.7	5.9	5.6	3.5	1.7
Concessional	0.1	2.4	5.5	5.1	3.9	5.7	5.8	5.5	3.5	1.7
Private creditors	0.0	0.0	0.6	0.0	0.0	0.0	0.0	0.0	0.0	0.0
Bonds	0.0	0.0	0.0	0.0	0.0	0.0	0.0	0.0	0.0	0.0
Commercial banks	0.0	0.0	0.4	0.0	0.0	0.0	0.0	0.0	0.0	0.0
Other private	0.0	0.0	0.2	0.0	0.0	0.0	0.0	0.0	0.0	0.0
Private nonguaranteed	**0.0**	**0.0**	**0.0**	**0.0**	**0.0**	**0.0**	**0.0**	**0.0**	**0.0**	**0.0**
Bonds	0.0	0.0	0.0	0.0	0.0	0.0	0.0	0.0	0.0	0.0
Commercial banks	0.0	0.0	0.0	0.0	0.0	0.0	0.0	0.0	0.0	0.0
Memo:										
IBRD	0.0	0.0	0.0	0.0	0.0	0.0	0.0	0.0	0.0	0.0
IDA	0.0	0.0	0.2	0.3	0.4	0.4	0.7	0.7	0.7	0.8
UNDISBURSED DEBT	**0.0**	**23.4**	**161.4**	**142.8**	**137.2**	**107.9**	**88.8**	**59.3**	**49.3**	**50.8**
Official creditors	0.0	23.4	161.4	142.8	137.2	107.9	88.8	55.7	45.7	47.2
Private creditors	0.0	0.0	0.0	0.0	0.0	0.0	0.0	3.6	3.6	3.6
Memorandum items										
Concessional LDOD	2.6	14.5	151.9	216.8	228.9	252.9	267.1	277.9	252.1	263.1
Variable rate LDOD	0.0	0.0	0.0	0.0	0.0	0.0	0.0	0.0	0.0	0.0
Public sector LDOD	2.6	25.8	155.2	219.3	230.9	254.9	268.9	279.3	253.0	263.8
Private sector LDOD	0.0	0.0	0.0	0.0	0.0	0.0	0.0	0.0	0.0	0.0

6. CURRENCY COMPOSITION OF LONG-TERM DEBT (PERCENT)

	1970	1980	1990	1992	1993	1994	1995	1996	1997	1998
Deutsche mark	0.0	0.0	0.0	0.0	0.0	0.0	0.0	0.0	0.0	0.0
French franc	100.0	91.0	3.1	2.8	3.2	3.6	3.5	3.1	2.8	3.0
Japanese yen	0.0	0.0	0.0	0.0	0.0	0.0	0.0	0.0	0.0	0.0
Pound sterling	0.0	0.0	0.0	0.0	0.0	0.0	0.0	0.0	0.0	0.0
Swiss franc	0.0	0.0	0.0	0.0	0.0	0.0	0.0	0.0	0.0	0.0
U.S.dollars	0.0	3.1	13.9	11.2	12.2	11.9	12.4	11.9	13.6	14.1
Multiple currency	0.0	0.8	16.8	17.8	20.8	23.6	23.5	21.9	22.9	23.1
Special drawing rights	0.0	0.4	8.9	6.9	6.5	6.5	6.3	5.8	5.9	5.8
All other currencies	0.0	4.7	57.3	61.3	57.3	54.4	54.3	57.3	54.8	54.0

DJIBOUTI

(US$ million, unless otherwise indicated)

	1970	1980	1990	1992	1993	1994	1995	1996	1997	1998
7. DEBT RESTRUCTURINGS										
Total amount rescheduled	..	..	0.0	0.0	0.0	0.0	0.0	0.0	0.0	0.0
Debt stock rescheduled	..	..	0.0	0.0	0.0	0.0	0.0	0.0	0.0	0.0
Principal rescheduled	..	..	0.0	0.0	0.0	0.0	0.0	0.0	0.0	0.0
Official	..	..	0.0	0.0	0.0	0.0	0.0	0.0	0.0	0.0
Private	..	..	0.0	0.0	0.0	0.0	0.0	0.0	0.0	0.0
Interest rescheduled	..	..	0.0	0.0	0.0	0.0	0.0	0.0	0.0	0.0
Official	..	..	0.0	0.0	0.0	0.0	0.0	0.0	0.0	0.0
Private	..	..	0.0	0.0	0.0	0.0	0.0	0.0	0.0	0.0
Debt forgiven	..	..	0.0	0.0	0.0	0.0	0.0	0.0	16.1	0.0
Memo: interest forgiven	..	..	0.0	0.0	0.0	0.0	0.0	0.0	0.0	0.0
Debt stock reduction	..	..	0.0	0.0	0.0	0.0	0.0	0.0	0.0	0.0
of which debt buyback	..	..	0.0	0.0	0.0	0.0	0.0	0.0	0.0	0.0
8. DEBT STOCK-FLOW RECONCILIATION										
Total change in debt stocks	..	..	26.8	9.5	29.0	-1.3	18.7	14.0	-22.1	14.1
Net flows on debt	1.3	9.0	20.8	30.2	35.6	-9.5	13.1	17.8	11.3	2.7
Net change in interest arrears	..	..	0.1	0.5	0.9	1.2	0.8	0.7	0.0	2.0
Interest capitalized	..	..	0.0	0.0	0.0	0.0	0.0	0.0	0.0	0.0
Debt forgiveness or reduction	..	..	0.0	0.0	0.0	0.0	0.0	0.0	-16.1	0.0
Cross-currency valuation	..	..	4.3	-16.1	-6.6	3.1	3.2	0.1	-9.8	5.7
Residual	..	..	1.6	-5.1	-0.9	3.9	1.6	-4.6	-7.5	3.6
9. AVERAGE TERMS OF NEW COMMITMENTS										
ALL CREDITORS										
Interest (%)	3.3	2.1	0.7	1.2	1.4	0.0	0.0	6.9	0.8	0.8
Maturity (years)	19.5	18.0	39.7	39.6	37.0	20.7	0.0	8.2	30.3	47.6
Grace period (years)	1.0	7.4	10.2	10.0	7.7	4.5	0.0	3.4	4.1	10.4
Grant element (%)	38.0	55.0	80.5	76.1	70.1	66.6	0.0	12.8	66.9	82.7
Official creditors										
Interest (%)	3.3	1.0	0.7	1.2	1.4	0.0	0.0	6.9	0.8	0.8
Maturity (years)	19.5	20.1	39.7	39.6	37.0	20.7	0.0	8.4	30.3	47.6
Grace period (years)	1.0	8.5	10.2	10.0	7.7	4.5	0.0	3.7	4.1	10.4
Grant element (%)	38.0	64.5	80.5	76.1	70.1	66.6	0.0	14.1	66.9	82.7
Private creditors										
Interest (%)	0.0	7.5	0.0	0.0	0.0	0.0	0.0	7.0	0.0	0.0
Maturity (years)	0.0	7.5	0.0	0.0	0.0	0.0	0.0	7.9	0.0	0.0
Grace period (years)	0.0	2.0	0.0	0.0	0.0	0.0	0.0	3.0	0.0	0.0
Grant element (%)	0.0	8.2	0.0	0.0	0.0	0.0	0.0	11.3	0.0	0.0
Memorandum items										
Commitments	0.2	29.5	6.2	50.2	21.5	2.6	0.0	7.7	11.9	11.5
Official creditors	0.2	24.6	6.2	50.2	21.5	2.6	0.0	4.1	11.9	11.5
Private creditors	0.0	5.0	0.0	0.0	0.0	0.0	0.0	3.6	0.0	0.0

10. CONTRACTUAL OBLIGATIONS ON OUTSTANDING LONG-TERM DEBT

	1999	2000	2001	2002	2003	2004	2005	2006	2007	2008
TOTAL										
Disbursements	14.0	14.2	9.3	6.5	3.7	1.8	1.1	0.2	0.0	0.0
Principal	13.0	13.3	12.9	14.1	13.9	12.3	12.4	12.0	11.2	10.8
Interest	3.4	3.3	3.2	3.0	2.8	2.5	2.3	2.1	2.0	1.8
Official creditors										
Disbursements	12.3	13.0	8.9	6.3	3.7	1.8	1.1	0.2	0.0	0.0
Principal	12.3	12.6	12.2	13.3	13.2	12.3	12.4	12.0	11.2	10.8
Interest	3.3	3.2	3.1	2.9	2.7	2.5	2.3	2.1	2.0	1.8
Bilateral creditors										
Disbursements	2.5	2.2	0.9	0.4	0.1	0.0	0.0	0.0	0.0	0.0
Principal	8.0	7.8	7.6	8.8	8.8	7.8	7.6	7.2	6.3	6.0
Interest	1.8	1.7	1.6	1.5	1.3	1.1	1.0	0.8	0.7	0.6
Multilateral creditors										
Disbursements	9.7	10.8	8.0	5.8	3.6	1.8	1.1	0.2	0.0	0.0
Principal	4.4	4.8	4.6	4.5	4.4	4.5	4.8	4.9	4.9	4.8
Interest	1.5	1.5	1.5	1.4	1.4	1.4	1.3	1.3	1.2	1.2
Private creditors										
Disbursements	1.7	1.2	0.5	0.2	0.0	0.0	0.0	0.0	0.0	0.0
Principal	0.7	0.7	0.7	0.7	0.7	0.0	0.0	0.0	0.0	0.0
Interest	0.1	0.1	0.1	0.1	0.0	0.0	0.0	0.0	0.0	0.0
Commercial banks										
Disbursements	0.0	0.0	0.0	0.0	0.0	0.0	0.0	0.0	0.0	0.0
Principal	0.0	0.0	0.0	0.0	0.0	0.0	0.0	0.0	0.0	0.0
Interest	0.0	0.0	0.0	0.0	0.0	0.0	0.0	0.0	0.0	0.0
Other private										
Disbursements	1.7	1.2	0.5	0.2	0.0	0.0	0.0	0.0	0.0	0.0
Principal	0.7	0.7	0.7	0.7	0.7	0.0	0.0	0.0	0.0	0.0
Interest	0.1	0.1	0.1	0.1	0.0	0.0	0.0	0.0	0.0	0.0

DOMINICA

(US$ million, unless otherwise indicated)

	1970	1980	1990	1992	1993	1994	1995	1996	1997	1998
1. SUMMARY DEBT DATA										
TOTAL DEBT STOCKS (EDT)	..	..	**88.0**	**95.5**	**96.4**	**98.2**	**102.6**	**114.2**	**102.8**	**108.9**
Long-term debt (LDOD)	..	..	**80.2**	**88.6**	**92.4**	**88.7**	**94.1**	**97.8**	**90.6**	**90.9**
Public and publicly guaranteed	..	..	80.2	88.6	92.4	88.7	94.1	97.8	90.6	90.9
Private nonguaranteed	..	..	0.0	0.0	0.0	0.0	0.0	0.0	0.0	0.0
Use of IMF credit	**0.0**	**0.0**	**5.7**	**3.8**	**3.1**	**2.5**	**1.7**	**0.8**	**0.3**	**0.0**
Short-term debt	..	..	**2.0**	**3.1**	**0.9**	**7.0**	**6.7**	**15.6**	**12.0**	**17.9**
of which interest arrears on LDOD	..	..	0.0	0.1	0.0	0.0	0.2	0.4	0.0	0.0
Official creditors	..	..	0.0	0.1	0.0	0.0	0.2	0.4	0.0	0.0
Private creditors	..	..	0.0	0.0	0.0	0.0	0.0	0.0	0.0	0.0
Memo: principal arrears on LDOD	..	..	0.2	0.8	0.2	0.2	1.8	3.1	0.5	0.4
Official creditors	..	..	0.2	0.8	0.2	0.2	1.8	3.1	0.5	0.4
Private creditors	..	..	0.1	0.0	0.0	0.0	0.0	0.0	0.0	0.0
Memo: export credits	..	..	8.0	6.0	6.0	6.0	6.0	6.0	66.0	5.0
TOTAL DEBT FLOWS										
Disbursements	..	..	**11.5**	**8.8**	**6.3**	**4.5**	**8.1**	**7.4**	**2.8**	**5.4**
Long-term debt	..	..	11.5	8.8	6.3	4.5	8.1	7.4	2.8	5.4
IMF purchases	0.0	0.0	0.0	0.0	0.0	0.0	0.0	0.0	0.0	0.0
Principal repayments	..	..	**3.8**	**3.5**	**4.8**	**5.0**	**4.6**	**3.8**	**6.8**	**7.1**
Long-term debt	..	..	2.5	2.7	4.1	4.2	3.8	3.0	6.2	6.8
IMF repurchases	0.0	0.0	1.4	0.8	0.8	0.8	0.8	0.8	0.6	0.2
Net flows on debt	..	..	**7.8**	**5.3**	**-0.6**	**5.6**	**3.0**	**12.3**	**-7.1**	**4.2**
of which short-term debt	..	..	0.1	0.0	-2.1	6.1	-0.5	8.7	-3.2	5.8
Interest payments (INT)	..	..	**2.0**	**2.2**	**2.3**	**2.4**	**2.5**	**3.0**	**3.9**	**3.3**
Long-term debt	..	..	1.6	2.0	2.2	2.1	2.1	2.1	2.9	2.5
IMF charges	0.0	0.0	0.2	0.1	0.0	0.0	0.0	0.0	0.0	0.0
Short-term debt	..	..	0.1	0.2	0.1	0.2	0.4	0.9	1.0	0.7
Net transfers on debt	..	..	**5.8**	**3.1**	**-2.9**	**3.2**	**0.5**	**9.3**	**-11.0**	**0.9**
Total debt service paid (TDS)	..	..	**5.8**	**5.7**	**7.1**	**7.4**	**7.1**	**6.8**	**10.7**	**10.3**
Long-term debt	..	..	4.1	4.7	6.2	6.4	5.8	5.1	9.1	9.4
IMF repurchases and charges	0.0	0.0	1.6	0.8	0.8	0.8	0.9	0.8	0.6	0.2
Short-term debt (interest only)	..	..	0.1	0.2	0.1	0.2	0.4	0.9	1.0	0.7
2. AGGREGATE NET RESOURCE FLOWS AND NET TRANSFERS (LONG-TERM)										
NET RESOURCE FLOWS	..	..	**25.1**	**32.6**	**20.5**	**34.3**	**52.8**	**46.0**	**23.2**	**43.7**
Net flow of long-term debt (ex. IMF)	..	..	9.0	6.1	2.2	0.3	4.3	4.4	-3.4	-1.4
Foreign direct investment (net)	..	..	13.0	21.0	13.0	22.0	25.0	19.0	20.0	21.0
Portfolio equity flows	..	..	0.0	0.0	0.0	0.0	0.0	0.0	0.0	0.0
Grants (excluding technical coop.)	..	..	3.1	5.5	5.3	12.0	23.5	22.6	6.6	24.1
Memo: technical coop. grants	..	..	3.1	2.5	2.2	4.0	3.6	4.8	4.1	5.0
official net resource flows	..	..	12.2	11.6	7.5	12.3	27.8	27.0	3.2	22.7
private net resource flows	..	..	12.9	21.0	13.0	22.0	25.0	19.0	20.0	21.0
NET TRANSFERS	..	..	**18.0**	**24.3**	**12.8**	**26.2**	**43.7**	**37.9**	**12.3**	**32.7**
Interest on long-term debt	..	..	1.6	2.0	2.2	2.1	2.1	2.1	2.9	2.5
Profit remittances on FDI	..	..	5.5	6.3	5.5	6.0	7.0	6.0	8.0	8.5
Memo: official net transfers	..	..	10.6	9.6	5.3	10.2	25.7	24.9	0.3	20.2
private net transfers	..	..	7.4	14.7	7.5	16.0	18.0	13.0	12.0	12.5
3. MAJOR ECONOMIC AGGREGATES										
Gross national product (GNP)	..	..	161.4	184.4	194.0	204.4	209.3	217.7	225.8	234.1
Exports of goods & services (XGS)	..	..	102.8	110.4	109.1	114.2	114.1	128.0	141.4	152.9
of which workers remittances	..	..	9.4	8.2	9.6	10.3	10.8	11.1	10.8	11.1
Imports of goods & services (MGS)	..	..	142.9	135.1	131.7	149.4	160.9	167.0	176.1	170.4
International reserves (RES)	..	..	14.5	20.4	19.9	15.4	22.1	22.9	23.9	27.7
Current account balance	..	..	-43.5	-25.4	-23.4	-38.4	-49.8	-39.9	-35.2	-18.3
4. DEBT INDICATORS										
EDT / XGS (%)	..	..	85.6	86.5	88.3	86.0	89.9	89.3	72.7	71.2
EDT / GNP (%)	..	..	54.5	51.8	49.7	48.0	49.0	52.5	45.5	46.5
TDS / XGS (%)	..	..	5.6	5.2	6.5	6.5	6.2	5.3	7.6	6.7
INT / XGS (%)	..	..	1.9	2.0	2.1	2.1	2.2	2.3	2.8	2.2
INT / GNP (%)	..	..	1.2	1.2	1.2	1.2	1.2	1.4	1.7	1.4
RES / EDT (%)	..	..	16.4	21.4	20.7	15.7	21.6	20.1	23.2	25.4
RES / MGS (months)	..	..	1.2	1.8	1.8	1.2	1.7	1.7	1.6	2.0
Short-term / EDT (%)	..	..	2.3	3.3	0.9	7.1	6.5	13.7	11.7	16.4
Concessional / EDT (%)	..	..	87.3	86.1	88.2	82.8	82.5	77.0	80.0	75.8
Multilateral / EDT (%)	..	..	65.7	64.6	64.3	58.5	60.7	55.0	58.4	55.9

DOMINICA

(US$ million, unless otherwise indicated)

	1970	1980	1990	1992	1993	1994	1995	1996	1997	1998
5. LONG-TERM DEBT										
DEBT OUTSTANDING (LDOD)	..	..	**80.2**	**88.6**	**92.4**	**88.7**	**94.1**	**97.8**	**90.6**	**90.9**
Public and publicly guaranteed	..	..	**80.2**	**88.6**	**92.4**	**88.7**	**94.1**	**97.8**	**90.6**	**90.9**
Official creditors	..	..	80.2	88.6	92.4	88.7	94.1	97.8	90.6	90.9
Multilateral	..	..	57.8	61.7	62.0	57.4	62.3	62.8	60.0	60.9
Concessional	..	..	54.4	55.3	54.6	50.0	52.8	52.9	51.6	52.5
Bilateral	..	..	22.4	26.9	30.4	31.3	31.8	35.0	30.6	30.0
Concessional	..	..	22.4	26.9	30.4	31.3	31.8	35.0	30.6	30.0
Private creditors	..	..	0.1	0.0	0.0	0.0	0.0	0.0	0.0	0.0
Bonds	..	..	0.0	0.0	0.0	0.0	0.0	0.0	0.0	0.0
Commercial banks	..	..	0.1	0.0	0.0	0.0	0.0	0.0	0.0	0.0
Other private	..	..	0.0	0.0	0.0	0.0	0.0	0.0	0.0	0.0
Private nonguaranteed	..	..	**0.0**	**0.0**	**0.0**	**0.0**	**0.0**	**0.0**	**0.0**	**0.0**
Bonds	..	..	0.0	0.0	0.0	0.0	0.0	0.0	0.0	0.0
Commercial banks	..	..	0.0	0.0	0.0	0.0	0.0	0.0	0.0	0.0
Memo:										
IBRD	0.0	0.0	0.0	0.0	0.0	0.0	0.0	0.0	0.0	0.4
IDA	0.0	0.0	10.4	11.0	11.1	11.8	12.2	11.7	12.3	14.3
DISBURSEMENTS	..	..	**11.5**	**8.8**	**6.3**	**4.5**	**8.1**	**7.4**	**2.8**	**5.4**
Public and publicly guaranteed	..	..	**11.5**	**8.8**	**6.3**	**4.5**	**8.1**	**7.4**	**2.8**	**5.4**
Official creditors	..	..	11.5	8.8	6.3	4.5	8.1	7.4	2.8	5.4
Multilateral	..	..	8.3	3.2	3.8	2.0	3.5	4.1	2.8	3.5
Concessional	..	..	6.7	1.6	2.2	1.5	2.7	3.2	2.8	3.1
Bilateral	..	..	3.2	5.6	2.5	2.5	4.6	3.3	0.0	2.0
Concessional	..	..	3.2	5.6	2.5	2.5	4.6	3.3	0.0	2.0
Private creditors	..	..	0.0	0.0	0.0	0.0	0.0	0.0	0.0	0.0
Bonds	..	..	0.0	0.0	0.0	0.0	0.0	0.0	0.0	0.0
Commercial banks	..	..	0.0	0.0	0.0	0.0	0.0	0.0	0.0	0.0
Other private	..	..	0.0	0.0	0.0	0.0	0.0	0.0	0.0	0.0
Private nonguaranteed	..	..	**0.0**	**0.0**	**0.0**	**0.0**	**0.0**	**0.0**	**0.0**	**0.0**
Bonds	..	..	0.0	0.0	0.0	0.0	0.0	0.0	0.0	0.0
Commercial banks	..	..	0.0	0.0	0.0	0.0	0.0	0.0	0.0	0.0
Memo:										
IBRD	0.0	0.0	0.0	0.0	0.0	0.0	0.0	0.0	0.0	0.4
IDA	0.0	0.0	0.9	0.4	0.1	0.3	0.1	0.0	1.4	1.6
PRINCIPAL REPAYMENTS	..	..	**2.5**	**2.7**	**4.1**	**4.2**	**3.8**	**3.0**	**6.2**	**6.8**
Public and publicly guaranteed	..	..	**2.5**	**2.7**	**4.1**	**4.2**	**3.8**	**3.0**	**6.2**	**6.8**
Official creditors	..	..	2.4	2.7	4.1	4.2	3.8	3.0	6.2	6.8
Multilateral	..	..	2.1	2.3	2.6	2.8	2.2	2.4	3.4	3.8
Concessional	..	..	2.1	2.3	2.4	2.5	1.9	2.1	2.8	3.1
Bilateral	..	..	0.3	0.4	1.4	1.5	1.6	0.7	2.8	3.0
Concessional	..	..	0.3	0.4	1.4	1.5	1.6	0.7	2.8	3.0
Private creditors	..	..	0.1	0.0	0.0	0.0	0.0	0.0	0.0	0.0
Bonds	..	..	0.0	0.0	0.0	0.0	0.0	0.0	0.0	0.0
Commercial banks	..	..	0.1	0.0	0.0	0.0	0.0	0.0	0.0	0.0
Other private	..	..	0.0	0.0	0.0	0.0	0.0	0.0	0.0	0.0
Private nonguaranteed	..	..	**0.0**	**0.0**	**0.0**	**0.0**	**0.0**	**0.0**	**0.0**	**0.0**
Bonds	..	..	0.0	0.0	0.0	0.0	0.0	0.0	0.0	0.0
Commercial banks	..	..	0.0	0.0	0.0	0.0	0.0	0.0	0.0	0.0
Memo:										
IBRD	0.0	0.0	0.0	0.0	0.0	0.0	0.0	0.0	0.0	0.0
IDA	0.0	0.0	0.0	0.0	0.1	0.1	0.1	0.1	0.1	0.1
NET FLOWS ON DEBT	..	..	**9.0**	**6.1**	**2.2**	**0.3**	**4.3**	**4.4**	**-3.4**	**-1.4**
Public and publicly guaranteed	..	..	**9.0**	**6.1**	**2.2**	**0.3**	**4.3**	**4.4**	**-3.4**	**-1.4**
Official creditors	..	..	9.1	6.1	2.2	0.3	4.3	4.4	-3.4	-1.4
Multilateral	..	..	6.3	0.9	1.2	-0.8	1.3	1.8	-0.6	-0.3
Concessional	..	..	4.6	-0.7	-0.2	-1.0	0.8	1.0	0.1	0.0
Bilateral	..	..	2.9	5.2	1.1	1.1	3.0	2.6	-2.8	-1.1
Concessional	..	..	2.9	5.2	1.1	1.1	3.0	2.6	-2.8	-1.1
Private creditors	..	..	-0.1	0.0	0.0	0.0	0.0	0.0	0.0	0.0
Bonds	..	..	0.0	0.0	0.0	0.0	0.0	0.0	0.0	0.0
Commercial banks	..	..	-0.1	0.0	0.0	0.0	0.0	0.0	0.0	0.0
Other private	..	..	0.0	0.0	0.0	0.0	0.0	0.0	0.0	0.0
Private nonguaranteed	..	..	**0.0**	**0.0**	**0.0**	**0.0**	**0.0**	**0.0**	**0.0**	**0.0**
Bonds	..	..	0.0	0.0	0.0	0.0	0.0	0.0	0.0	0.0
Commercial banks	..	..	0.0	0.0	0.0	0.0	0.0	0.0	0.0	0.0
Memo:										
IBRD	0.0	0.0	0.0	0.0	0.0	0.0	0.0	0.0	0.0	0.4
IDA	0.0	0.0	0.9	0.4	0.0	0.2	0.0	-0.1	1.3	1.5

DOMINICA

(US$ million, unless otherwise indicated)

	1970	1980	1990	1992	1993	1994	1995	1996	1997	1998
INTEREST PAYMENTS (LINT)	..	..	**1.6**	**2.0**	**2.2**	**2.1**	**2.1**	**2.1**	**2.9**	**2.5**
Public and publicly guaranteed	..	..	**1.6**	**2.0**	**2.2**	**2.1**	**2.1**	**2.1**	**2.9**	**2.5**
Official creditors	..	..	1.6	2.0	2.2	2.1	2.1	2.1	2.9	2.5
Multilateral	..	..	1.4	1.6	1.7	1.6	1.6	1.4	1.7	1.5
Concessional	..	..	1.3	1.4	1.4	1.3	1.3	1.2	1.2	1.2
Bilateral	..	..	0.2	0.4	0.4	0.5	0.4	0.6	1.2	1.0
Concessional	..	..	0.2	0.4	0.4	0.5	0.4	0.6	1.2	1.0
Private creditors	..	..	0.0	0.0	0.0	0.0	0.0	0.0	0.0	0.0
Bonds	..	..	0.0	0.0	0.0	0.0	0.0	0.0	0.0	0.0
Commercial banks	..	..	0.0	0.0	0.0	0.0	0.0	0.0	0.0	0.0
Other private	..	..	0.0	0.0	0.0	0.0	0.0	0.0	0.0	0.0
Private nonguaranteed	..	..	**0.0**	**0.0**	**0.0**	**0.0**	**0.0**	**0.0**	**0.0**	**0.0**
Bonds	..	..	0.0	0.0	0.0	0.0	0.0	0.0	0.0	0.0
Commercial banks	..	..	0.0	0.0	0.0	0.0	0.0	0.0	0.0	0.0
Memo:										
IBRD	0.0	0.0	0.0	0.0	0.0	0.0	0.0	0.0	0.0	0.0
IDA	0.0	0.0	0.1	0.1	0.1	0.1	0.1	0.1	0.1	0.1
NET TRANSFERS ON DEBT	..	..	**7.4**	**4.1**	**0.1**	**-1.8**	**2.3**	**2.3**	**-6.3**	**-3.9**
Public and publicly guaranteed	..	..	**7.4**	**4.1**	**0.1**	**-1.8**	**2.3**	**2.3**	**-6.3**	**-3.9**
Official creditors	..	..	7.5	4.1	0.1	-1.8	2.3	2.3	-6.3	-3.9
Multilateral	..	..	4.9	-0.7	-0.6	-2.4	-0.3	0.3	-2.2	-1.9
Concessional	..	..	3.3	-2.1	-1.6	-2.3	-0.5	-0.1	-1.1	-1.2
Bilateral	..	..	2.6	4.8	0.7	0.6	2.6	2.0	-4.1	-2.1
Concessional	..	..	2.6	4.8	0.7	0.6	2.6	2.0	-4.1	-2.1
Private creditors	..	..	-0.1	0.0	0.0	0.0	0.0	0.0	0.0	0.0
Bonds	..	..	0.0	0.0	0.0	0.0	0.0	0.0	0.0	0.0
Commercial banks	..	..	-0.1	0.0	0.0	0.0	0.0	0.0	0.0	0.0
Other private	..	..	0.0	0.0	0.0	0.0	0.0	0.0	0.0	0.0
Private nonguaranteed	..	..	**0.0**	**0.0**	**0.0**	**0.0**	**0.0**	**0.0**	**0.0**	**0.0**
Bonds	..	..	0.0	0.0	0.0	0.0	0.0	0.0	0.0	0.0
Commercial banks	..	..	0.0	0.0	0.0	0.0	0.0	0.0	0.0	0.0
Memo:										
IBRD	0.0	0.0	0.0	0.0	0.0	0.0	0.0	0.0	0.0	0.4
IDA	0.0	0.0	0.8	0.3	-0.1	0.2	-0.1	-0.1	1.2	1.4
DEBT SERVICE (LTDS)	..	..	**4.1**	**4.7**	**6.2**	**6.4**	**5.8**	**5.1**	**9.1**	**9.4**
Public and publicly guaranteed	..	..	**4.1**	**4.7**	**6.2**	**6.4**	**5.8**	**5.1**	**9.1**	**9.4**
Official creditors	..	..	4.0	4.7	6.2	6.4	5.8	5.1	9.1	9.4
Multilateral	..	..	3.4	3.9	4.4	4.4	3.8	3.8	5.1	5.4
Concessional	..	..	3.4	3.7	3.8	3.8	3.2	3.3	4.0	4.3
Bilateral	..	..	0.6	0.8	1.8	2.0	2.0	1.3	4.1	4.0
Concessional	..	..	0.6	0.8	1.8	2.0	2.0	1.3	4.1	4.0
Private creditors	..	..	0.1	0.0	0.0	0.0	0.0	0.0	0.0	0.0
Bonds	..	..	0.0	0.0	0.0	0.0	0.0	0.0	0.0	0.0
Commercial banks	..	..	0.1	0.0	0.0	0.0	0.0	0.0	0.0	0.0
Other private	..	..	0.0	0.0	0.0	0.0	0.0	0.0	0.0	0.0
Private nonguaranteed	..	..	**0.0**	**0.0**	**0.0**	**0.0**	**0.0**	**0.0**	**0.0**	**0.0**
Bonds	..	..	0.0	0.0	0.0	0.0	0.0	0.0	0.0	0.0
Commercial banks	..	..	0.0	0.0	0.0	0.0	0.0	0.0	0.0	0.0
Memo:										
IBRD	0.0	0.0	0.0	0.0	0.0	0.0	0.0	0.0	0.0	0.0
IDA	0.0	0.0	0.1	0.1	0.1	0.1	0.2	0.1	0.2	0.2
UNDISBURSED DEBT	..	..	**23.0**	**20.2**	**22.4**	**16.2**	**24.0**	**35.1**	**35.8**	**37.0**
Official creditors	..	..	23.0	20.2	22.4	16.2	24.0	35.1	35.8	37.0
Private creditors	..	..	0.0	0.0	0.0	0.0	0.0	0.0	0.0	0.0
Memorandum items										
Concessional LDOD	..	..	76.8	82.2	85.0	81.3	84.6	87.9	82.2	82.5
Variable rate LDOD	..	..	0.0	0.0	0.0	0.0	0.0	0.0	0.0	0.4
Public sector LDOD	..	..	80.2	88.6	92.4	88.7	94.1	97.8	90.6	90.9
Private sector LDOD	..	..	0.0	0.0	0.0	0.0	0.0	0.0	0.0	0.0
6. CURRENCY COMPOSITION OF LONG-TERM DEBT (PERCENT)										
Deutsche mark	..	..	8.7	6.3	5.2	5.4	3.5	2.8	2.3	2.1
French franc	..	..	9.7	11.2	14.9	16.9	11.4	9.9	8.6	8.4
Japanese yen	..	..	0.2	0.2	0.1	0.1	1.1	0.9	0.8	0.8
Pound sterling	..	..	16.4	15.0	14.0	14.8	13.5	13.9	12.3	9.8
Swiss franc	..	..	0.0	0.0	0.0	0.0	0.0	0.0	0.0	0.0
U.S.dollars	..	..	51.7	54.1	53.3	49.3	58.0	60.2	64.8	67.7
Multiple currency	..	..	0.0	0.0	0.0	0.0	0.0	0.0	0.0	0.4
Special drawing rights	..	..	6.0	5.6	5.3	5.8	4.4	3.9	3.8	3.6
All other currencies	..	..	7.3	7.6	7.2	7.7	8.1	8.4	7.4	7.2

DOMINICA

(US$ million, unless otherwise indicated)

	1970	1980	1990	1992	1993	1994	1995	1996	1997	1998
7. DEBT RESTRUCTURINGS										
Total amount rescheduled	..	..	0.0	0.0	0.0	0.0	0.0	0.0	0.0	0.0
Debt stock rescheduled	..	..	0.0	0.0	0.0	0.0	0.0	0.0	0.0	0.0
Principal rescheduled	..	..	0.0	0.0	0.0	0.0	0.0	0.0	0.0	0.0
Official	..	..	0.0	0.0	0.0	0.0	0.0	0.0	0.0	0.0
Private	..	..	0.0	0.0	0.0	0.0	0.0	0.0	0.0	0.0
Interest rescheduled	..	..	0.0	0.0	0.0	0.0	0.0	0.0	0.0	0.0
Official	..	..	0.0	0.0	0.0	0.0	0.0	0.0	0.0	0.0
Private	..	..	0.0	0.0	0.0	0.0	0.0	0.0	0.0	0.0
Debt forgiven	..	..	3.3	0.0	0.0	0.0	0.0	0.0	0.0	0.0
Memo: interest forgiven	..	..	0.0	0.0	0.0	0.0	0.0	0.0	0.0	0.0
Debt stock reduction	..	..	0.0	0.0	0.0	0.0	0.0	0.0	0.0	0.0
of which debt buyback	..	..	0.0	0.0	0.0	0.0	0.0	0.0	0.0	0.0
8. DEBT STOCK-FLOW RECONCILIATION										
Total change in debt stocks	..	..	10.5	-0.1	0.8	1.8	4.4	11.7	-11.4	6.0
Net flows on debt	..	..	7.8	5.3	-0.6	5.6	3.0	12.3	-7.1	4.2
Net change in interest arrears	..	..	0.0	0.1	-0.1	0.0	0.2	0.2	-0.4	0.0
Interest capitalized	..	..	0.0	0.0	0.0	0.0	0.0	0.0	0.0	0.0
Debt forgiveness or reduction	..	..	-3.3	0.0	0.0	0.0	0.0	0.0	0.0	0.0
Cross-currency valuation	..	..	5.5	-4.3	-2.0	3.7	1.7	-0.1	-2.6	1.3
Residual	..	..	0.4	-1.1	3.6	-7.6	-0.5	-0.7	-1.3	0.5
9. AVERAGE TERMS OF NEW COMMITMENTS										
ALL CREDITORS										
Interest (%)	..	..	3.0	3.0	3.7	0.0	2.6	2.7	0.5	3.6
Maturity (years)	..	..	25.1	23.6	20.3	0.0	26.4	26.2	19.5	25.0
Grace period (years)	..	..	8.5	7.0	12.8	0.0	8.8	8.1	4.0	6.9
Grant element (%)	..	..	53.8	49.5	48.5	0.0	56.5	56.3	60.8	49.1
Official creditors										
Interest (%)	..	..	3.0	3.0	3.7	0.0	2.6	2.7	0.5	3.6
Maturity (years)	..	..	25.1	23.6	20.3	0.0	26.4	26.2	19.5	25.0
Grace period (years)	..	..	8.5	7.0	12.8	0.0	8.8	8.1	4.0	6.9
Grant element (%)	..	..	53.8	49.5	48.5	0.0	56.5	56.3	60.8	49.1
Private creditors										
Interest (%)	..	..	0.0	0.0	0.0	0.0	0.0	0.0	0.0	0.0
Maturity (years)	..	..	0.0	0.0	0.0	0.0	0.0	0.0	0.0	0.0
Grace period (years)	..	..	0.0	0.0	0.0	0.0	0.0	0.0	0.0	0.0
Grant element (%)	..	..	0.0	0.0	0.0	0.0	0.0	0.0	0.0	0.0
Memorandum items										
Commitments	..	..	3.4	9.4	8.8	0.0	5.1	18.8	4.1	6.2
Official creditors	..	..	3.4	9.4	8.8	0.0	5.1	18.8	4.1	6.2
Private creditors	..	..	0.0	0.0	0.0	0.0	0.0	0.0	0.0	0.0

10. CONTRACTUAL OBLIGATIONS ON OUTSTANDING LONG-TERM DEBT

	1999	2000	2001	2002	2003	2004	2005	2006	2007	2008
TOTAL										
Disbursements	8.7	10.2	7.8	4.9	2.6	1.5	0.9	0.3	0.2	0.0
Principal	6.1	6.2	6.3	6.3	6.2	6.3	6.4	6.2	7.0	6.7
Interest	2.2	2.3	2.3	2.3	2.2	2.0	1.8	1.7	1.5	1.3
Official creditors										
Disbursements	8.7	10.2	7.8	4.9	2.6	1.5	0.9	0.3	0.2	0.0
Principal	6.1	6.2	6.3	6.3	6.2	6.3	6.4	6.2	7.0	6.7
Interest	2.2	2.3	2.3	2.3	2.2	2.0	1.8	1.7	1.5	1.3
Bilateral creditors										
Disbursements	1.3	1.5	1.0	0.6	0.4	0.2	0.1	0.1	0.0	0.0
Principal	1.7	1.7	1.9	1.9	1.9	2.0	2.2	2.2	2.9	2.6
Interest	0.7	0.7	0.7	0.6	0.6	0.6	0.5	0.5	0.4	0.4
Multilateral creditors										
Disbursements	7.4	8.7	6.8	4.3	2.2	1.3	0.8	0.2	0.2	0.0
Principal	4.4	4.4	4.4	4.4	4.3	4.3	4.2	4.0	4.1	4.0
Interest	1.5	1.6	1.7	1.7	1.6	1.5	1.3	1.2	1.1	1.0
Private creditors										
Disbursements	0.0	0.0	0.0	0.0	0.0	0.0	0.0	0.0	0.0	0.0
Principal	0.0	0.0	0.0	0.0	0.0	0.0	0.0	0.0	0.0	0.0
Interest	0.0	0.0	0.0	0.0	0.0	0.0	0.0	0.0	0.0	0.0
Commercial banks										
Disbursements	0.0	0.0	0.0	0.0	0.0	0.0	0.0	0.0	0.0	0.0
Principal	0.0	0.0	0.0	0.0	0.0	0.0	0.0	0.0	0.0	0.0
Interest	0.0	0.0	0.0	0.0	0.0	0.0	0.0	0.0	0.0	0.0
Other private										
Disbursements	0.0	0.0	0.0	0.0	0.0	0.0	0.0	0.0	0.0	0.0
Principal	0.0	0.0	0.0	0.0	0.0	0.0	0.0	0.0	0.0	0.0
Interest	0.0	0.0	0.0	0.0	0.0	0.0	0.0	0.0	0.0	0.0

DOMINICAN REPUBLIC

(US$ million, unless otherwise indicated)

	1970	1980	1990	1992	1993	1994	1995	1996	1997	1998
1. SUMMARY DEBT DATA										
TOTAL DEBT STOCKS (EDT)	..	**2,002**	**4,372**	**4,613**	**4,860**	**4,275**	**4,448**	**4,332**	**4,246**	**4,451**
Long-term debt (LDOD)	**353**	**1,473**	**3,518**	**3,803**	**3,842**	**3,655**	**3,672**	**3,529**	**3,467**	**3,530**
Public and publicly guaranteed	212	1,220	3,420	3,737	3,792	3,619	3,653	3,524	3,467	3,530
Private nonguaranteed	141	254	99	66	51	35	19	5	0	0
Use of IMF credit	**7**	**49**	**72**	**123**	**186**	**190**	**160**	**96**	**29**	**56**
Short-term debt	..	**480**	**782**	**687**	**832**	**431**	**616**	**708**	**750**	**865**
of which interest arrears on LDOD	..	7	506	343	533	173	215	241	135	122
Official creditors	..	3	304	62	63	119	157	177	76	56
Private creditors	..	4	202	281	470	54	58	64	59	66
Memo: principal arrears on LDOD	..	13	614	479	593	302	320	293	273	286
Official creditors	..	4	444	168	236	256	261	242	228	230
Private creditors	..	8	169	310	357	46	59	51	46	56
Memo: export credits	..	0	967	691	875	950	762	730	697	844
TOTAL DEBT FLOWS										
Disbursements	**60**	**482**	**139**	**207**	**203**	**123**	**195**	**133**	**106**	**188**
Long-term debt	60	482	139	154	129	123	195	133	106	134
IMF purchases	0	0	0	53	74	0	0	0	0	54
Principal repayments	**32**	**200**	**146**	**197**	**178**	**294**	**234**	**250**	**259**	**181**
Long-term debt	27	135	88	182	168	286	200	190	196	153
IMF repurchases	5	65	58	15	10	8	34	60	62	29
Net flows on debt	**28**	**438**	**15**	**80**	**-20**	**-212**	**105**	**-52**	**-4**	**134**
of which short-term debt	..	156	23	70	-45	-41	143	65	148	128
Interest payments (INT)	..	**179**	**86**	**149**	**146**	**210**	**175**	**198**	**202**	**193**
Long-term debt	13	121	59	126	118	183	145	163	174	159
IMF charges	0	5	9	6	8	10	10	7	3	1
Short-term debt	..	54	19	16	21	17	20	28	25	34
Net transfers on debt	..	**259**	**-71**	**-69**	**-166**	**-422**	**-70**	**-250**	**-207**	**-59**
Total debt service paid (TDS)	..	**379**	**232**	**346**	**324**	**504**	**409**	**448**	**461**	**375**
Long-term debt	39	256	147	309	286	469	345	354	370	311
IMF repurchases and charges	5	69	67	21	18	18	44	66	66	30
Short-term debt (interest only)	..	54	19	16	21	17	20	28	25	34
2. AGGREGATE NET RESOURCE FLOWS AND NET TRANSFERS (LONG-TERM)										
NET RESOURCE FLOWS	**114**	**454**	**213**	**174**	**193**	**83**	**450**	**93**	**381**	**807**
Net flow of long-term debt (ex. IMF)	33	346	51	-28	-39	-163	-5	-57	-90	-19
Foreign direct investment (net)	72	93	133	180	189	207	414	97	421	691
Portfolio equity flows	0	0	0	0	0	0	0	0	0	74
Grants (excluding technical coop.)	9	14	29	23	44	39	40	54	50	61
Memo: technical coop. grants	5	16	44	53	51	46	51	49	48	42
official net resource flows	39	304	83	14	33	-9	66	24	-43	36
private net resource flows	75	150	130	161	161	92	384	69	424	771
NET TRANSFERS	**102**	**267**	**64**	**-51**	**-33**	**-129**	**270**	**-108**	**163**	**600**
Interest on long-term debt	13	121	59	126	118	183	145	163	174	159
Profit remittances on FDI	0	66	90	99	108	29	35	38	44	48
Memo: official net transfers	35	278	28	-89	-73	-113	-54	-97	-171	-83
private net transfers	66	-11	36	38	40	-16	324	-12	334	683
3. MAJOR ECONOMIC AGGREGATES										
Gross national product (GNP)	1,476	6,420	6,715	8,437	8,922	9,792	11,180	12,606	14,280	14,955
Exports of goods & services (XGS)	284	1,496	2,233	2,312	5,572	6,098	6,653	7,237	8,290	8,976
of which workers remittances	25	183	315	347	721	757	794	914	1,089	1,326
Imports of goods & services (MGS)	392	2,237	2,568	3,105	6,279	6,608	7,034	7,703	8,716	9,972
International reserves (RES)	32	279	69	506	658	259	373	357	396	507
Current account balance	-102	-720	-280	-708	-533	-283	-183	-213	-163	-336
4. DEBT INDICATORS										
EDT / XGS (%)	..	133.8	195.8	199.5	87.2	70.1	66.9	59.9	51.2	49.6
EDT / GNP (%)	..	31.2	65.1	54.7	54.5	43.7	39.8	34.4	29.7	29.8
TDS / XGS (%)	..	25.3	10.4	15.0	5.8	8.3	6.2	6.2	5.6	4.2
INT / XGS (%)	..	12.0	3.9	6.4	2.6	3.4	2.6	2.7	2.4	2.2
INT / GNP (%)	..	2.8	1.3	1.8	1.6	2.1	1.6	1.6	1.4	1.3
RES / EDT (%)	..	13.9	1.6	11.0	13.5	6.1	8.4	8.2	9.3	11.4
RES / MGS (months)	1.0	1.5	0.3	2.0	1.3	0.5	0.6	0.6	0.6	0.6
Short-term / EDT (%)	..	24.0	17.9	14.9	17.1	10.1	13.9	16.3	17.7	19.4
Concessional / EDT (%)	..	20.1	27.5	40.5	41.0	39.1	37.6	37.5	36.6	34.6
Multilateral / EDT (%)	..	10.2	19.6	18.8	18.3	21.9	23.2	23.4	22.7	22.7

DOMINICAN REPUBLIC

(US$ million, unless otherwise indicated)

	1970	1980	1990	1992	1993	1994	1995	1996	1997	1998
5. LONG-TERM DEBT										
DEBT OUTSTANDING (LDOD)	**353**	**1,473**	**3,518**	**3,803**	**3,842**	**3,655**	**3,672**	**3,529**	**3,467**	**3,530**
Public and publicly guaranteed	**212**	**1,220**	**3,420**	**3,737**	**3,792**	**3,619**	**3,653**	**3,524**	**3,467**	**3,530**
Official creditors	202	786	2,383	2,750	2,853	2,948	2,996	2,890	2,833	2,887
Multilateral	14	205	858	869	888	936	1,034	1,014	965	1,008
Concessional	0	138	432	411	408	413	438	454	454	465
Bilateral	188	581	1,525	1,881	1,965	2,012	1,962	1,876	1,867	1,879
Concessional	167	264	772	1,459	1,587	1,259	1,233	1,169	1,100	1,075
Private creditors	10	434	1,036	986	939	672	657	634	634	644
Bonds	0	0	0	0	0	520	520	520	518	514
Commercial banks	0	386	775	791	796	27	34	37	58	71
Other private	9	48	262	195	143	125	104	77	58	59
Private nonguaranteed	**141**	**254**	**99**	**66**	**51**	**35**	**19**	**5**	**0**	**0**
Bonds	0	0	0	0	0	0	0	0	0	0
Commercial banks	141	254	99	66	51	35	19	5	0	0
Memo:										
IBRD	11	66	238	255	261	276	283	244	209	204
IDA	0	18	20	19	19	18	17	17	16	15
DISBURSEMENTS	**60**	**482**	**139**	**154**	**129**	**123**	**195**	**133**	**106**	**134**
Public and publicly guaranteed	**38**	**415**	**139**	**154**	**129**	**123**	**195**	**133**	**106**	**134**
Official creditors	36	319	136	135	119	114	187	118	77	114
Multilateral	11	90	84	58	70	81	157	95	61	84
Concessional	0	51	21	2	16	22	44	36	26	26
Bilateral	25	229	53	77	50	33	31	24	16	31
Concessional	24	42	20	25	23	7	18	10	6	14
Private creditors	2	96	2	19	9	9	8	15	29	20
Bonds	0	0	0	0	0	0	0	0	0	0
Commercial banks	0	72	0	18	7	8	8	15	29	18
Other private	2	24	2	1	2	2	0	0	0	2
Private nonguaranteed	**22**	**67**	**0**	**0**	**0**	**0**	**0**	**0**	**0**	**0**
Bonds	0	0	0	0	0	0	0	0	0	0
Commercial banks	22	67	0	0	0	0	0	0	0	0
Memo:										
IBRD	11	39	39	35	26	33	36	18	13	17
IDA	0	0	0	0	0	0	0	0	0	0
PRINCIPAL REPAYMENTS	**27**	**135**	**88**	**182**	**168**	**286**	**200**	**190**	**196**	**153**
Public and publicly guaranteed	**7**	**62**	**83**	**166**	**152**	**271**	**184**	**176**	**191**	**153**
Official creditors	6	30	83	145	130	162	161	148	171	139
Multilateral	0	3	38	57	58	70	79	70	67	59
Concessional	0	0	6	15	17	18	20	19	21	17
Bilateral	6	27	44	88	73	92	82	78	104	80
Concessional	3	9	8	15	27	51	47	50	57	41
Private creditors	1	32	0	21	22	109	23	29	20	14
Bonds	0	0	0	0	0	0	0	0	2	4
Commercial banks	0	30	0	2	3	79	3	9	5	4
Other private	1	2	0	19	19	30	20	19	14	6
Private nonguaranteed	**20**	**74**	**5**	**17**	**16**	**15**	**16**	**14**	**5**	**0**
Bonds	0	0	0	0	0	0	0	0	0	0
Commercial banks	20	74	5	17	16	15	16	14	5	0
Memo:										
IBRD	0	2	19	25	25	36	40	37	29	24
IDA	0	0	0	0	1	1	1	1	1	1
NET FLOWS ON DEBT	**33**	**346**	**51**	**-28**	**-39**	**-163**	**-5**	**-57**	**-90**	**-19**
Public and publicly guaranteed	**31**	**353**	**56**	**-12**	**-23**	**-148**	**11**	**-43**	**-85**	**-19**
Official creditors	30	289	54	-9	-11	-48	26	-29	-94	-25
Multilateral	11	87	46	1	12	11	78	25	-6	24
Concessional	0	51	15	-13	-2	5	24	17	5	9
Bilateral	19	202	8	-10	-23	-59	-52	-54	-87	-49
Concessional	22	33	11	11	-3	-44	-29	-40	-51	-28
Private creditors	1	64	2	-2	-12	-100	-15	-14	8	6
Bonds	0	0	0	0	0	0	0	0	-2	-4
Commercial banks	0	42	0	15	5	-72	5	5	24	14
Other private	1	22	2	-18	-17	-28	-20	-19	-14	-4
Private nonguaranteed	**2**	**-7**	**-5**	**-17**	**-16**	**-15**	**-16**	**-14**	**-5**	**0**
Bonds	0	0	0	0	0	0	0	0	0	0
Commercial banks	2	-7	-5	-17	-16	-15	-16	-14	-5	0
Memo:										
IBRD	11	37	20	10	1	-3	-4	-19	-15	-6
IDA	0	0	0	0	-1	-1	-1	-1	-1	-1

DOMINICAN REPUBLIC

(US$ million, unless otherwise indicated)

	1970	1980	1990	1992	1993	1994	1995	1996	1997	1998
INTEREST PAYMENTS (LINT)	**13**	**121**	**59**	**126**	**118**	**183**	**145**	**163**	**174**	**159**
Public and publicly guaranteed	**4**	**92**	**56**	**120**	**113**	**179**	**143**	**162**	**174**	**159**
Official creditors	4	26	55	103	105	104	120	121	128	119
Multilateral	1	5	32	44	45	47	51	51	47	45
Concessional	0	1	4	9	9	9	10	9	9	8
Bilateral	4	21	24	58	60	57	69	70	81	74
Concessional	2	6	7	41	50	35	53	48	53	42
Private creditors	0	66	1	18	8	75	23	41	46	40
Bonds	0	0	0	0	0	5	13	34	35	35
Commercial banks	0	64	0	2	2	63	3	4	10	4
Other private	0	3	1	16	6	7	7	3	1	1
Private nonguaranteed	**8**	**29**	**3**	**6**	**5**	**4**	**2**	**1**	**0**	**0**
Bonds	0	0	0	0	0	0	0	0	0	0
Commercial banks	8	29	3	6	5	4	2	1	0	0
Memo:										
IBRD	0	3	14	19	20	20	21	19	16	14
IDA	0	0	0	0	0	0	0	0	0	0
NET TRANSFERS ON DEBT	**21**	**226**	**-9**	**-155**	**-157**	**-346**	**-150**	**-221**	**-265**	**-178**
Public and publicly guaranteed	**27**	**261**	**0**	**-132**	**-137**	**-327**	**-132**	**-206**	**-259**	**-178**
Official creditors	26	264	-1	-112	-116	-153	-94	-150	-221	-144
Multilateral	10	83	14	-44	-33	-36	27	-26	-53	-21
Concessional	0	50	11	-22	-10	-4	14	8	-4	0
Bilateral	16	181	-15	-69	-83	-116	-121	-124	-169	-123
Concessional	20	27	4	-30	-53	-80	-82	-87	-104	-69
Private creditors	1	-3	1	-20	-21	-175	-38	-56	-38	-34
Bonds	0	0	0	0	0	-5	-13	-34	-37	-39
Commercial banks	0	-22	0	13	3	-135	2	1	14	10
Other private	1	20	1	-33	-24	-35	-27	-22	-15	-4
Private nonguaranteed	**-6**	**-35**	**-8**	**-23**	**-20**	**-19**	**-18**	**-15**	**-6**	**0**
Bonds	0	0	0	0	0	0	0	0	0	0
Commercial banks	-6	-35	-8	-23	-20	-19	-18	-15	-6	0
Memo:										
IBRD	10	34	6	-9	-19	-23	-25	-38	-31	-20
IDA	0	0	0	-1	-1	-1	-1	-1	-1	-1
DEBT SERVICE (LTDS)	**39**	**256**	**147**	**309**	**286**	**469**	**345**	**354**	**370**	**311**
Public and publicly guaranteed	**12**	**154**	**139**	**286**	**265**	**450**	**327**	**338**	**365**	**311**
Official creditors	10	56	138	247	236	266	281	268	299	258
Multilateral	1	7	70	101	102	118	130	121	114	105
Concessional	0	1	10	24	26	26	30	28	30	26
Bilateral	10	48	68	146	133	149	151	148	185	154
Concessional	4	15	15	56	77	86	100	98	109	83
Private creditors	1	98	1	39	30	184	46	70	66	53
Bonds	0	0	0	0	0	5	13	34	37	39
Commercial banks	0	94	0	4	4	143	6	14	15	8
Other private	1	4	1	35	26	36	27	22	15	6
Private nonguaranteed	**28**	**102**	**8**	**23**	**20**	**19**	**18**	**15**	**6**	**0**
Bonds	0	0	0	0	0	0	0	0	0	0
Commercial banks	28	102	8	23	20	19	18	15	6	0
Memo:										
IBRD	0	5	33	44	45	56	60	56	44	38
IDA	0	0	0	1	1	1	1	1	1	1
UNDISBURSED DEBT	**64**	**632**	**510**	**451**	**412**	**523**	**492**	**461**	**564**	**1,124**
Official creditors	42	537	483	423	394	509	480	439	530	865
Private creditors	22	94	27	28	18	14	12	22	34	259
Memorandum items										
Concessional LDOD	167	402	1,203	1,870	1,994	1,672	1,671	1,622	1,554	1,539
Variable rate LDOD	141	695	1,104	1,646	1,813	1,204	1,273	1,272	1,228	1,291
Public sector LDOD	197	1,185	3,391	3,705	3,762	3,591	3,626	3,499	3,444	3,503
Private sector LDOD	156	289	128	97	80	63	46	30	23	22

6. CURRENCY COMPOSITION OF LONG-TERM DEBT (PERCENT)

	1970	1980	1990	1992	1993	1994	1995	1996	1997	1998
Deutsche mark	0.0	0.6	2.0	1.4	0.9	2.2	2.2	2.0	1.7	1.8
French franc	0.0	0.0	0.5	0.2	0.4	1.2	1.5	1.4	1.2	1.2
Japanese yen	0.0	0.0	6.4	5.3	4.3	8.4	7.7	6.7	5.7	6.1
Pound sterling	0.0	0.0	0.0	0.0	0.0	0.0	0.0	0.0	0.0	0.0
Swiss franc	0.0	0.0	0.0	0.0	0.0	0.0	0.0	0.0	0.0	0.0
U.S.dollars	93.5	81.8	68.4	71.9	72.9	64.3	63.7	65.0	67.5	71.2
Multiple currency	6.6	11.5	21.8	20.4	20.8	23.2	24.2	24.0	23.1	18.5
Special drawing rights	0.0	0.0	0.2	0.1	0.1	0.1	0.2	0.3	0.3	0.3
All other currencies	0.0	6.1	0.7	0.7	0.6	0.6	0.5	0.6	0.5	0.9

DOMINICAN REPUBLIC

(US$ million, unless otherwise indicated)

	1970	1980	1990	1992	1993	1994	1995	1996	1997	1998
7. DEBT RESTRUCTURINGS										
Total amount rescheduled	..	..	8	91	162	520	2	22	130	60
Debt stock rescheduled	..	..	0	0	0	506	0	0	0	0
Principal rescheduled	..	..	1	67	104	6	1	14	20	30
Official	..	..	1	54	56	0	1	14	20	30
Private	..	..	0	13	49	6	0	0	0	0
Interest rescheduled	..	..	2	23	57	3	0	7	110	30
Official	..	..	2	19	11	0	0	7	110	30
Private	..	..	0	5	46	3	0	0	0	0
Debt forgiven	..	..	7	6	1	0	0	3	0	0
Memo: interest forgiven	..	..	0	0	0	180	0	4	0	0
Debt stock reduction	..	..	0	0	0	291	0	0	0	0
of which debt buyback	..	..	0	0	0	68	0	0	0	0
8. DEBT STOCK-FLOW RECONCILIATION										
Total change in debt stocks	..	..	334	122	247	-585	173	-116	-86	206
Net flows on debt	28	438	15	80	-20	-212	105	-52	-4	134
Net change in interest arrears	..	..	267	55	190	-360	42	26	-106	-13
Interest capitalized	..	..	2	23	57	3	0	7	110	30
Debt forgiveness or reduction	..	..	-7	-6	-1	-223	0	-3	0	0
Cross-currency valuation	..	..	39	-21	12	60	4	-65	-59	37
Residual	..	..	17	-9	9	146	22	-31	-27	18
9. AVERAGE TERMS OF NEW COMMITMENTS										
ALL CREDITORS										
Interest (%)	2.4	8.9	5.9	7.3	4.0	3.7	6.6	5.5	7.4	7.0
Maturity (years)	28.4	12.3	24.4	17.0	22.6	28.0	19.4	16.4	19.8	17.6
Grace period (years)	4.8	4.0	6.4	4.1	5.7	8.0	5.1	4.4	4.3	3.5
Grant element (%)	53.4	10.2	31.2	14.4	41.2	49.6	20.7	26.7	15.6	16.7
Official creditors										
Interest (%)	2.4	7.5	5.8	7.3	3.9	3.6	6.6	5.1	7.5	6.8
Maturity (years)	28.4	12.8	24.8	17.0	22.7	28.2	19.8	18.3	21.5	22.3
Grace period (years)	4.8	4.3	6.4	4.1	5.7	8.0	5.2	5.0	5.0	4.1
Grant element (%)	53.4	17.5	31.9	14.4	41.4	50.3	21.2	30.9	16.2	20.1
Private creditors										
Interest (%)	0.0	11.8	9.8	0.0	10.7	9.1	8.4	7.1	6.8	7.2
Maturity (years)	0.0	11.3	9.1	0.0	11.1	8.9	9.5	8.5	12.3	9.1
Grace period (years)	0.0	3.4	4.6	0.0	1.6	1.7	2.0	1.8	1.4	2.6
Grant element (%)	0.0	-3.9	-0.2	0.0	-4.0	1.4	5.8	9.9	12.8	10.5
Memorandum items										
Commitments	20	519	204	130	101	229	167	126	233	688
Official creditors	20	342	199	130	101	226	161	101	192	443
Private creditors	0	176	5	0	1	3	6	25	41	246

10. CONTRACTUAL OBLIGATIONS ON OUTSTANDING LONG-TERM DEBT

	1999	2000	2001	2002	2003	2004	2005	2006	2007	2008
TOTAL										
Disbursements	322	307	215	140	63	37	20	6	4	3
Principal	322	317	358	373	350	315	305	274	221	163
Interest	187	190	187	174	156	139	123	105	90	76
Official creditors										
Disbursements	186	228	184	126	63	37	20	6	4	3
Principal	256	281	309	317	296	263	254	235	185	127
Interest	140	142	138	127	114	101	88	74	61	50
Bilateral creditors										
Disbursements	46	38	23	13	8	4	2	1	1	0
Principal	185	206	214	218	191	154	145	138	87	40
Interest	84	78	69	56	45	35	27	20	12	7
Multilateral creditors										
Disbursements	139	191	162	113	55	34	18	6	3	2
Principal	70	75	95	99	104	109	108	97	97	86
Interest	57	64	69	71	69	66	60	54	49	43
Private creditors										
Disbursements	136	79	31	14	0	0	0	0	0	0
Principal	66	36	49	57	55	53	51	39	37	36
Interest	47	49	49	46	43	39	35	32	29	26
Commercial banks										
Disbursements	119	79	31	14	0	0	0	0	0	0
Principal	29	18	32	40	38	36	34	22	20	19
Interest	13	17	18	17	14	11	8	6	5	3
Other private										
Disbursements	17	0	0	0	0	0	0	0	0	0
Principal	37	17	17	17	17	17	17	17	17	17
Interest	34	32	31	30	29	28	27	25	24	23

ECUADOR

(US$ million, unless otherwise indicated)

	1970	1980	1990	1992	1993	1994	1995	1996	1997	1998
1. SUMMARY DEBT DATA										
TOTAL DEBT STOCKS (EDT)	**..**	**5,997**	**12,109**	**12,280**	**14,150**	**15,075**	**13,994**	**14,495**	**14,918**	**15,140**
Long-term debt (LDOD)	**242**	**4,422**	**10,030**	**9,932**	**10,216**	**10,777**	**12,508**	**12,764**	**12,716**	**12,799**
Public and publicly guaranteed	193	3,300	9,867	9,831	9,975	10,552	12,068	12,444	12,376	12,589
Private nonguaranteed	49	1,122	164	100	241	224	440	320	340	210
Use of IMF credit	**14**	**0**	**265**	**100**	**71**	**198**	**174**	**145**	**133**	**70**
Short-term debt	**..**	**1,575**	**1,814**	**2,249**	**3,864**	**4,100**	**1,312**	**1,586**	**2,069**	**2,272**
of which interest arrears on LDOD	..	0	1,522	2,045	2,330	2,349	13	77	84	84
Official creditors	..	0	10	21	88	3	8	61	75	76
Private creditors	..	0	1,513	2,024	2,242	2,347	5	16	9	9
Memo: principal arrears on LDOD	..	1	1,097	2,207	2,875	3,428	10	178	251	282
Official creditors	..	0	6	15	45	6	8	121	192	203
Private creditors	..	1	1,091	2,192	2,830	3,422	2	58	59	79
Memo: export credits	..	0	2,090	1,949	1,841	1,726	1,130	1,349	1,197	1,308
TOTAL DEBT FLOWS										
Disbursements	**58**	**1,283**	**638**	**352**	**666**	**666**	**1,049**	**1,090**	**1,328**	**714**
Long-term debt	48	1,283	606	352	666	524	1,049	1,090	1,328	714
IMF purchases	10	0	32	0	0	142	0	0	0	0
Principal repayments	**33**	**535**	**611**	**561**	**517**	**509**	**750**	**646**	**1,069**	**840**
Long-term debt	26	535	496	483	488	487	721	623	1,066	773
IMF repurchases	7	0	115	77	29	21	29	23	3	67
Net flows on debt	**131**	**1,174**	**-1**	**-306**	**1,479**	**375**	**-152**	**653**	**735**	**76**
of which short-term debt	..	426	-28	-97	1,330	218	-451	210	475	202
Interest payments (INT)	**..**	**473**	**474**	**420**	**404**	**492**	**667**	**675**	**823**	**866**
Long-term debt	10	365	416	376	302	401	576	576	715	756
IMF charges	0	0	30	11	7	3	10	7	6	5
Short-term debt	..	108	28	33	95	88	81	92	101	104
Net transfers on debt	**..**	**701**	**-475**	**-726**	**1,076**	**-117**	**-819**	**-22**	**-88**	**-790**
Total debt service paid (TDS)	**..**	**1,008**	**1,084**	**981**	**921**	**1,000**	**1,417**	**1,321**	**1,891**	**1,706**
Long-term debt	36	900	911	859	790	888	1,297	1,199	1,781	1,529
IMF repurchases and charges	7	0	145	89	36	25	39	30	9	72
Short-term debt (interest only)	..	108	28	33	95	88	81	92	101	104
2. AGGREGATE NET RESOURCE FLOWS AND NET TRANSFERS (LONG-TERM)										
NET RESOURCE FLOWS	**113**	**825**	**289**	**129**	**679**	**617**	**868**	**1,014**	**1,008**	**838**
Net flow of long-term debt (ex. IMF)	21	748	110	-132	178	37	328	466	262	-59
Foreign direct investment (net)	89	70	126	178	469	531	470	491	695	831
Portfolio equity flows	0	0	0	0	0	4	1	1	0	0
Grants (excluding technical coop.)	3	7	53	83	32	46	69	55	50	66
Memo: technical coop. grants	9	28	67	79	84	91	110	98	85	82
official net resource flows	13	231	106	155	114	113	327	167	61	254
private net resource flows	101	594	183	-26	566	504	541	847	947	584
NET TRANSFERS	**84**	**349**	**-252**	**-377**	**231**	**67**	**140**	**278**	**123**	**-98**
Interest on long-term debt	10	365	416	376	302	401	576	576	715	756
Profit remittances on FDI	19	111	125	130	147	150	152	160	170	180
Memo: official net transfers	8	142	-106	-87	-112	-139	-2	-104	-259	-22
private net transfers	76	207	-145	-290	343	205	142	382	381	-75
3. MAJOR ECONOMIC AGGREGATES										
Gross national product (GNP)	1,642	11,152	9,867	12,049	13,732	15,327	16,677	17,736	18,241	18,360
Exports of goods & services (XGS)	..	2,975	3,287	3,753	3,746	4,640	5,347	6,189	6,631	5,933
of which workers remittances	..	0	0	0	0	0	0	358	438	840
Imports of goods & services (MGS)	..	3,647	3,754	3,995	4,554	5,466	6,313	6,010	7,297	8,038
International reserves (RES)	76	1,257	1,009	1,016	1,542	2,003	1,788	2,011	2,213	1,739
Current account balance	..	-642	-360	-122	-678	-681	-735	111	-713	-2,169
4. DEBT INDICATORS										
EDT / XGS (%)	..	201.6	368.4	327.2	377.8	324.9	261.7	234.2	225.0	255.2
EDT / GNP (%)	..	53.8	122.7	101.9	103.1	98.4	83.9	81.7	81.8	82.5
TDS / XGS (%)	..	33.9	33.0	26.1	24.6	21.6	26.5	21.4	28.5	28.8
INT / XGS (%)	..	15.9	14.4	11.2	10.8	10.6	12.5	10.9	12.4	14.6
INT / GNP (%)	..	4.2	4.8	3.5	2.9	3.2	4.0	3.8	4.5	4.7
RES / EDT (%)	..	21.0	8.3	8.3	10.9	13.3	12.8	13.9	14.8	11.5
RES / MGS (months)	..	4.1	3.2	3.1	4.1	4.4	3.4	4.0	3.6	2.6
Short-term / EDT (%)	..	26.3	15.0	18.3	27.3	27.2	9.4	10.9	13.9	15.0
Concessional / EDT (%)	..	4.8	7.6	10.7	10.4	11.1	12.9	12.9	12.0	12.8
Multilateral / EDT (%)	..	5.4	17.6	18.4	16.8	17.1	21.6	20.3	19.3	20.9

ECUADOR

(US$ million, unless otherwise indicated)

	1970	1980	1990	1992	1993	1994	1995	1996	1997	1998
5. LONG-TERM DEBT										
DEBT OUTSTANDING (LDOD)	**242**	**4,422**	**10,030**	**9,932**	**10,216**	**10,777**	**12,508**	**12,764**	**12,716**	**12,799**
Public and publicly guaranteed	**193**	**3,300**	**9,867**	**9,831**	**9,975**	**10,552**	**12,068**	**12,444**	**12,376**	**12,589**
Official creditors	133	1,325	4,065	4,399	4,570	4,934	5,281	5,149	4,905	5,234
Multilateral	51	323	2,127	2,253	2,371	2,580	3,019	2,944	2,872	3,164
Concessional	10	102	451	513	581	601	647	654	639	634
Bilateral	83	1,002	1,938	2,146	2,199	2,354	2,261	2,206	2,033	2,070
Concessional	75	188	469	797	887	1,068	1,159	1,215	1,145	1,300
Private creditors	60	1,976	5,802	5,432	5,405	5,618	6,787	7,294	7,471	7,355
Bonds	3	55	0	0	0	191	5,999	6,013	5,834	5,825
Commercial banks	4	1,697	4,885	4,763	4,831	4,959	453	942	1,317	1,262
Other private	53	223	917	669	574	469	335	339	320	268
Private nonguaranteed	**49**	**1,122**	**164**	**100**	**241**	**224**	**440**	**320**	**340**	**210**
Bonds	0	0	0	0	0	0	10	10	0	0
Commercial banks	49	1,122	164	100	241	224	430	310	340	210
Memo:										
IBRD	34	109	816	783	759	830	1,082	980	851	854
IDA	6	36	32	30	29	28	27	25	24	23
DISBURSEMENTS	**48**	**1,283**	**606**	**352**	**666**	**524**	**1,049**	**1,090**	**1,328**	**714**
Public and publicly guaranteed	**41**	**968**	**575**	**352**	**500**	**524**	**839**	**1,090**	**1,248**	**714**
Official creditors	17	348	329	321	359	377	744	478	414	614
Multilateral	5	91	227	218	269	310	602	317	355	463
Concessional	2	11	24	35	82	39	62	34	15	16
Bilateral	12	257	101	103	90	67	142	161	59	151
Concessional	9	4	31	97	74	66	128	135	46	146
Private creditors	25	620	247	30	142	147	95	612	834	100
Bonds	0	0	0	0	0	0	0	0	0	0
Commercial banks	2	497	39	16	136	131	75	546	793	100
Other private	22	122	207	14	6	16	21	66	41	0
Private nonguaranteed	**7**	**315**	**30**	**0**	**166**	**0**	**210**	**0**	**80**	**0**
Bonds	0	0	0	0	0	0	10	0	0	0
Commercial banks	7	315	30	0	166	0	200	0	80	0
Memo:										
IBRD	2	34	47	63	52	112	319	89	45	85
IDA	2	0	0	0	0	0	0	0	0	0
PRINCIPAL REPAYMENTS	**26**	**535**	**496**	**483**	**488**	**487**	**721**	**623**	**1,066**	**773**
Public and publicly guaranteed	**16**	**272**	**471**	**441**	**463**	**471**	**711**	**493**	**1,006**	**643**
Official creditors	7	125	276	250	277	310	486	366	404	426
Multilateral	3	16	164	155	193	225	235	234	288	220
Concessional	1	0	8	13	15	20	23	25	26	22
Bilateral	4	108	112	95	85	85	252	132	116	206
Concessional	3	8	2	10	16	18	46	36	45	53
Private creditors	8	147	195	192	186	160	225	127	602	217
Bonds	0	14	0	0	0	0	10	10	126	10
Commercial banks	3	110	27	76	86	62	60	56	417	155
Other private	6	23	167	116	100	99	155	62	59	53
Private nonguaranteed	**11**	**263**	**25**	**42**	**25**	**17**	**10**	**130**	**60**	**130**
Bonds	0	0	0	0	0	0	0	0	10	0
Commercial banks	11	263	25	42	25	17	10	130	50	130
Memo:										
IBRD	2	10	42	74	93	94	98	119	101	79
IDA	0	0	1	1	1	1	1	1	1	1
NET FLOWS ON DEBT	**21**	**748**	**110**	**-132**	**178**	**37**	**328**	**466**	**262**	**-59**
Public and publicly guaranteed	**26**	**696**	**105**	**-90**	**37**	**54**	**128**	**596**	**242**	**71**
Official creditors	9	224	53	72	82	67	258	112	10	188
Multilateral	1	75	64	63	77	85	368	83	67	243
Concessional	1	11	16	22	67	19	39	9	-11	-7
Bilateral	8	149	-11	9	5	-18	-110	29	-57	-55
Concessional	6	-4	28	87	59	49	82	99	1	93
Private creditors	16	473	52	-161	-44	-14	-130	485	232	-117
Bonds	0	-14	0	0	0	0	-10	-10	-126	-10
Commercial banks	0	387	12	-59	50	69	14	490	375	-55
Other private	17	99	40	-102	-94	-83	-135	4	-18	-53
Private nonguaranteed	**-4**	**52**	**5**	**-42**	**141**	**-17**	**200**	**-130**	**20**	**-130**
Bonds	0	0	0	0	0	0	10	0	-10	0
Commercial banks	-4	52	5	-42	141	-17	190	-130	30	-130
Memo:										
IBRD	0	24	5	-11	-41	18	221	-30	-56	6
IDA	2	0	-1	-1	-1	-1	-1	-1	-1	-1

ECUADOR

(US$ million, unless otherwise indicated)

	1970	1980	1990	1992	1993	1994	1995	1996	1997	1998
INTEREST PAYMENTS (LINT)	**10**	**365**	**416**	**376**	**302**	**401**	**576**	**576**	**715**	**756**
Public and publicly guaranteed	**7**	**288**	**404**	**371**	**299**	**399**	**574**	**572**	**711**	**755**
Official creditors	4	89	212	242	226	252	328	271	319	277
Multilateral	3	19	140	151	159	157	171	191	221	179
Concessional	0	1	8	10	10	12	13	12	14	12
Bilateral	2	71	72	91	67	94	157	80	99	98
Concessional	1	5	8	20	19	28	47	33	39	45
Private creditors	2	199	192	130	73	148	246	301	392	478
Bonds	0	6	0	0	0	0	147	241	250	349
Commercial banks	1	184	132	87	34	121	56	43	114	111
Other private	2	8	60	43	39	27	44	17	28	18
Private nonguaranteed	**3**	**78**	**12**	**5**	**2**	**2**	**1**	**4**	**4**	**1**
Bonds	0	0	0	0	0	0	0	1	1	0
Commercial banks	3	78	12	5	2	2	1	3	3	1
Memo:										
IBRD	2	9	62	63	67	59	69	75	69	51
IDA	0	0	0	0	0	0	0	0	0	0
NET TRANSFERS ON DEBT	**11**	**383**	**-306**	**-508**	**-124**	**-364**	**-248**	**-109**	**-453**	**-815**
Public and publicly guaranteed	**19**	**408**	**-299**	**-461**	**-262**	**-345**	**-447**	**25**	**-469**	**-684**
Official creditors	5	134	-160	-170	-145	-184	-71	-159	-309	-89
Multilateral	-1	56	-77	-88	-82	-72	197	-108	-154	65
Concessional	1	9	8	13	56	7	26	-3	-25	-18
Bilateral	6	78	-83	-82	-63	-112	-268	-51	-155	-153
Concessional	5	-9	21	66	39	21	35	66	-38	48
Private creditors	14	274	-140	-291	-117	-161	-376	184	-160	-595
Bonds	0	-20	0	0	0	0	-157	-250	-375	-359
Commercial banks	-1	203	-120	-146	16	-52	-41	446	261	-166
Other private	15	91	-20	-145	-133	-110	-178	-12	-46	-71
Private nonguaranteed	**-8**	**-26**	**-7**	**-47**	**138**	**-18**	**199**	**-134**	**16**	**-131**
Bonds	0	0	0	0	0	0	10	-1	-11	0
Commercial banks	-8	-26	-7	-47	138	-18	189	-133	27	-131
Memo:										
IBRD	-2	16	-56	-74	-108	-41	152	-105	-125	-45
IDA	2	0	-1	-1	-1	-1	-1	-1	-1	-1
DEBT SERVICE (LTDS)	**36**	**900**	**911**	**859**	**790**	**888**	**1,297**	**1,199**	**1,781**	**1,529**
Public and publicly guaranteed	**22**	**559**	**875**	**812**	**762**	**870**	**1,286**	**1,065**	**1,717**	**1,398**
Official creditors	12	214	488	491	504	562	815	638	723	703
Multilateral	6	35	304	306	352	383	406	425	509	399
Concessional	1	2	16	22	25	32	36	37	40	34
Bilateral	6	179	184	186	152	179	409	213	214	304
Concessional	4	13	10	30	35	46	93	69	84	97
Private creditors	11	346	386	321	259	308	471	428	994	695
Bonds	0	20	0	0	0	0	157	250	375	359
Commercial banks	3	294	159	163	120	182	116	99	532	266
Other private	8	31	227	159	139	126	199	78	87	71
Private nonguaranteed	**14**	**341**	**37**	**47**	**27**	**18**	**11**	**134**	**64**	**131**
Bonds	0	0	0	0	0	0	0	1	11	0
Commercial banks	14	341	37	47	27	18	11	133	53	131
Memo:										
IBRD	4	19	103	137	160	153	167	194	170	130
IDA	0	0	1	1	1	1	1	1	1	1
UNDISBURSED DEBT	**142**	**1,039**	**1,648**	**1,937**	**1,697**	**2,017**	**2,253**	**2,118**	**1,903**	**1,886**
Official creditors	60	695	1,535	1,714	1,444	1,809	1,772	1,535	1,596	1,558
Private creditors	82	345	114	223	253	208	482	583	307	328
Memorandum items										
Concessional LDOD	85	290	920	1,309	1,467	1,669	1,806	1,868	1,785	1,934
Variable rate LDOD	49	2,766	6,246	6,051	6,202	6,653	6,542	6,755	6,875	7,033
Public sector LDOD	193	3,300	9,867	9,831	9,975	10,552	12,068	12,444	12,376	12,589
Private sector LDOD	49	1,122	164	100	241	224	440	320	340	210

6. CURRENCY COMPOSITION OF LONG-TERM DEBT (PERCENT)

	1970	1980	1990	1992	1993	1994	1995	1996	1997	1998
Deutsche mark	4.7	1.7	2.8	2.6	2.4	2.5	1.1	1.0	0.8	0.8
French franc	2.0	0.0	1.5	2.4	2.3	2.6	2.3	2.1	1.8	1.8
Japanese yen	0.0	2.7	6.9	7.9	8.8	9.6	5.0	4.4	3.8	4.9
Pound sterling	0.8	1.1	1.6	1.3	1.3	1.3	0.7	0.7	0.7	0.6
Swiss franc	0.2	0.7	0.5	0.5	0.4	0.2	0.0	0.0	0.0	0.0
U.S.dollars	71.4	64.2	54.5	53.5	53.4	53.6	70.5	73.9	77.0	82.8
Multiple currency	19.8	28.1	29.7	29.7	29.3	28.1	19.6	17.1	15.1	8.3
Special drawing rights	0.0	0.0	0.0	0.0	0.0	0.0	0.0	0.0	0.0	0.0
All other currencies	1.1	1.5	2.5	2.1	2.1	2.1	0.8	0.8	0.8	0.8

ECUADOR

(US$ million, unless otherwise indicated)

	1970	1980	1990	1992	1993	1994	1995	1996	1997	1998
7. DEBT RESTRUCTURINGS										
Total amount rescheduled	..	..	249	362	37	533	5,818	29	62	0
Debt stock rescheduled	..	..	16	0	0	0	3,350	0	0	0
Principal rescheduled	..	..	152	210	8	300	0	0	0	0
Official	..	..	110	151	8	276	0	0	0	0
Private	..	..	42	60	0	24	0	0	0	0
Interest rescheduled	..	..	81	143	6	117	1,757	25	62	0
Official	..	..	61	117	6	115	0	0	0	0
Private	..	..	19	26	0	3	1,757	25	62	0
Debt forgiven	..	..	1	2	0	0	0	1	0	0
Memo: interest forgiven	..	..	0	0	0	0	0	0	0	0
Debt stock reduction	..	..	45	50	0	10	1,183	1	200	0
of which debt buyback	..	..	0	0	0	0	0	0	85	0
8. DEBT STOCK-FLOW RECONCILIATION										
Total change in debt stocks	..	..	792	-188	1,871	925	-1,082	502	423	222
Net flows on debt	131	1,174	-1	-306	1,479	375	-152	653	735	76
Net change in interest arrears	..	..	451	153	285	19	-2,337	64	7	1
Interest capitalized	..	..	81	143	6	117	1,757	25	62	0
Debt forgiveness or reduction	..	..	-46	-52	0	-10	-1,183	-2	-115	0
Cross-currency valuation	..	..	209	-111	53	237	25	-180	-185	102
Residual	..	..	98	-16	47	187	809	-59	-80	43
9. AVERAGE TERMS OF NEW COMMITMENTS										
ALL CREDITORS										
Interest (%)	6.2	10.7	6.4	6.9	5.7	6.0	6.4	5.8	8.5	7.0
Maturity (years)	20.0	14.9	17.4	18.6	13.8	20.7	15.8	11.0	12.5	14.4
Grace period (years)	3.9	3.8	4.2	4.9	3.8	5.4	5.5	3.3	5.0	3.9
Grant element (%)	24.0	-0.9	24.2	18.8	22.7	27.2	21.9	19.1	10.0	16.2
Official creditors										
Interest (%)	4.3	8.6	5.2	6.7	5.3	5.9	5.6	4.6	6.8	7.0
Maturity (years)	35.8	22.1	22.2	21.3	19.3	21.9	18.0	26.0	17.6	15.9
Grace period (years)	8.0	4.4	6.0	5.4	5.1	5.8	6.7	7.7	4.9	4.1
Grant element (%)	48.8	11.4	35.2	21.4	30.2	29.0	28.4	41.5	20.5	17.2
Private creditors										
Interest (%)	7.3	12.7	8.6	7.4	6.0	6.8	8.1	6.3	10.6	7.0
Maturity (years)	10.2	7.9	8.7	9.8	8.4	10.6	11.0	4.8	6.3	10.1
Grace period (years)	1.3	3.2	1.0	3.0	2.4	2.5	2.9	1.4	5.1	3.3
Grant element (%)	8.4	-12.7	4.0	10.6	15.3	13.5	7.9	9.8	-2.6	13.3
Memorandum items										
Commitments	78	1,148	643	765	312	924	1,165	1,024	1,278	780
Official creditors	30	564	415	582	153	820	797	301	700	581
Private creditors	48	584	228	183	159	104	369	723	578	199

10. CONTRACTUAL OBLIGATIONS ON OUTSTANDING LONG-TERM DEBT

	1999	2000	2001	2002	2003	2004	2005	2006	2007	2008
TOTAL										
Disbursements	777	500	279	161	85	39	24	11	7	3
Principal	755	778	673	1,020	678	801	697	736	702	594
Interest	788	776	749	693	632	581	532	485	438	395
Official creditors										
Disbursements	578	406	253	151	85	39	24	11	7	3
Principal	417	436	486	489	518	506	484	433	408	320
Interest	320	317	303	280	251	220	188	159	132	108
Bilateral creditors										
Disbursements	146	95	58	31	18	5	4	1	0	0
Principal	163	141	127	123	158	158	160	150	131	109
Interest	91	85	79	74	67	58	49	40	32	26
Multilateral creditors										
Disbursements	432	311	195	119	67	34	20	10	7	3
Principal	254	296	360	365	360	348	324	283	277	210
Interest	229	232	224	206	185	162	139	118	100	82
Private creditors										
Disbursements	198	94	26	10	0	0	0	0	0	0
Principal	338	342	187	531	160	295	213	303	294	274
Interest	468	459	446	413	381	361	344	326	306	287
Commercial banks										
Disbursements	188	94	26	10	0	0	0	0	0	0
Principal	179	184	145	482	111	248	77	47	38	33
Interest	118	113	104	74	45	29	15	9	7	4
Other private										
Disbursements	11	0	0	0	0	0	0	0	0	0
Principal	159	158	42	49	49	48	136	256	256	242
Interest	350	346	342	339	335	332	329	316	300	283

EGYPT, ARAB REPUBLIC OF

(US$ million, unless otherwise indicated)

	1970	1980	1990	1992	1993	1994	1995	1996	1997	1998
1. SUMMARY DEBT DATA										
TOTAL DEBT STOCKS (EDT)	**..**	**19,131**	**32,947**	**31,067**	**30,509**	**32,314**	**33,266**	**31,300**	**29,850**	**31,964**
Long-term debt (LDOD)	**1,351**	**14,693**	**28,372**	**28,348**	**28,303**	**30,190**	**30,792**	**28,937**	**26,858**	**27,704**
Public and publicly guaranteed	1,351	14,428	27,372	27,748	27,803	29,815	30,479	28,810	26,804	27,670
Private nonguaranteed	0	265	1,000	600	500	375	313	127	54	34
Use of IMF credit	**49**	**411**	**125**	**202**	**202**	**193**	**103**	**16**	**0**	**0**
Short-term debt	**..**	**4,027**	**4,450**	**2,516**	**2,003**	**1,931**	**2,371**	**2,347**	**2,991**	**4,260**
of which interest arrears on LDOD	..	383	1,438	1	1	1	3	2	3	1
Official creditors	..	383	873	1	1	1	2	1	2	0
Private creditors	..	0	565	1	1	1	1	1	1	1
Memo: principal arrears on LDOD	..	74	3,507	5	5	5	133	139	149	142
Official creditors	..	74	1,775	0	0	0	128	133	142	134
Private creditors	..	0	1,733	5	5	5	5	6	7	8
Memo: export credits	..	0	14,578	11,478	10,918	10,237	8,933	9,561	8,096	8,947
TOTAL DEBT FLOWS										
Disbursements	**188**	**2,743**	**1,997**	**1,470**	**1,145**	**1,047**	**519**	**583**	**765**	**459**
Long-term debt	170	2,680	1,997	1,348	1,145	1,047	519	583	765	459
IMF purchases	18	63	0	123	0	0	0	0	0	0
Principal repayments	**234**	**446**	**1,743**	**1,478**	**965**	**945**	**996**	**1,105**	**941**	**912**
Long-term debt	225	343	1,696	1,437	965	923	901	1,020	926	912
IMF repurchases	9	103	47	41	0	22	95	85	15	0
Net flows on debt	**351**	**2,465**	**-1,248**	**-591**	**-333**	**31**	**-39**	**-546**	**467**	**818**
of which short-term debt	..	168	-1,502	-583	-513	-72	438	-24	644	1,271
Interest payments (INT)	**..**	**790**	**1,328**	**1,223**	**1,216**	**1,295**	**1,384**	**1,178**	**986**	**901**
Long-term debt	37	350	1,012	1,040	1,041	1,155	1,243	1,041	724	674
IMF charges	0	18	15	14	12	10	9	3	0	0
Short-term debt	..	422	301	168	164	130	132	133	262	227
Net transfers on debt	**..**	**1,676**	**-2,576**	**-1,813**	**-1,549**	**-1,265**	**-1,422**	**-1,724**	**-519**	**-83**
Total debt service paid (TDS)	**..**	**1,235**	**3,071**	**2,701**	**2,181**	**2,240**	**2,379**	**2,283**	**1,928**	**1,813**
Long-term debt	261	693	2,708	2,477	2,005	2,078	2,143	2,061	1,650	1,586
IMF repurchases and charges	9	121	62	55	12	32	105	88	15	0
Short-term debt (interest only)	..	422	301	168	164	130	132	133	262	227
2. AGGREGATE NET RESOURCE FLOWS AND NET TRANSFERS (LONG-TERM)										
NET RESOURCE FLOWS	**99**	**3,051**	**5,236**	**2,798**	**1,556**	**2,581**	**1,225**	**2,655**	**3,528**	**2,458**
Net flow of long-term debt (ex. IMF)	-54	2,337	301	-89	180	124	-381	-437	-161	-453
Foreign direct investment (net)	0	548	734	459	493	1,256	598	636	891	1,076
Portfolio equity flows	0	0	0	0	0	10	2	1,233	1,813	494
Grants (excluding technical coop.)	153	165	4,201	2,428	883	1,192	1,006	1,224	985	1,341
Memo: technical coop. grants	14	156	813	827	975	594	744	635	570	470
official net resource flows	129	1,918	4,538	2,877	1,469	1,600	939	1,206	933	1,073
private net resource flows	-30	1,133	698	-80	87	981	286	1,450	2,595	1,385
NET TRANSFERS	**62**	**2,687**	**4,211**	**1,743**	**503**	**1,406**	**-41**	**1,564**	**2,724**	**1,664**
Interest on long-term debt	37	350	1,012	1,040	1,041	1,155	1,243	1,041	724	674
Profit remittances on FDI	0	15	14	14	13	20	23	50	80	120
Memo: official net transfers	99	1,697	3,807	2,028	595	584	-172	261	278	463
private net transfers	-37	990	403	-284	-93	823	131	1,303	2,446	1,201
3. MAJOR ECONOMIC AGGREGATES										
Gross national product (GNP)	7,618	21,453	42,065	40,137	45,370	51,028	59,724	67,527	76,178	85,580
Exports of goods & services (XGS)	991	9,212	13,670	16,944	19,426	15,029	17,792	18,043	19,842	19,101
of which workers remittances	29	2,696	3,743	3,722	5,939	3,232	3,279	2,798	3,256	3,518
Imports of goods & services (MGS)	1,447	9,745	15,398	14,231	15,923	15,651	18,325	18,951	20,613	22,748
International reserves (RES)	165	2,480	3,620	11,620	13,854	14,413	17,122	18,296	19,371	18,824
Current account balance	-452	-438	-634	3,753	4,856	191	386	-184	119	-2,762
4. DEBT INDICATORS										
EDT / XGS (%)	..	207.7	241.0	183.4	157.1	215.0	187.0	173.5	150.4	167.3
EDT / GNP (%)	..	89.2	78.3	77.4	67.2	63.3	55.7	46.4	39.2	37.4
TDS / XGS (%)	..	13.4	22.5	15.9	11.2	14.9	13.4	12.7	9.7	9.5
INT / XGS (%)	..	8.6	9.7	7.2	6.3	8.6	7.8	6.5	5.0	4.7
INT / GNP (%)	..	3.7	3.2	3.1	2.7	2.5	2.3	1.7	1.3	1.1
RES / EDT (%)	..	13.0	11.0	37.4	45.4	44.6	51.5	58.5	64.9	58.9
RES / MGS (months)	1.4	3.1	2.8	9.8	10.4	11.1	11.2	11.6	11.3	9.9
Short-term / EDT (%)	..	21.1	13.5	8.1	6.6	6.0	7.1	7.5	10.0	13.3
Concessional / EDT (%)	..	42.4	38.0	55.2	59.0	60.4	61.0	76.8	75.7	73.4
Multilateral / EDT (%)	..	13.7	10.4	10.6	11.8	12.1	11.9	12.6	13.0	13.1

EGYPT, ARAB REPUBLIC OF

(US$ million, unless otherwise indicated)

	1970	1980	1990	1992	1993	1994	1995	1996	1997	1998
5. LONG-TERM DEBT										
DEBT OUTSTANDING (LDOD)	**1,351**	**14,693**	**28,372**	**28,348**	**28,303**	**30,190**	**30,792**	**28,937**	**26,858**	**27,704**
Public and publicly guaranteed	**1,351**	**14,428**	**27,372**	**27,748**	**27,803**	**29,815**	**30,479**	**28,810**	**26,804**	**27,670**
Official creditors	1,189	12,623	21,188	24,676	25,445	27,733	28,794	27,517	25,728	26,751
Multilateral	22	2,625	3,427	3,300	3,603	3,912	3,974	3,933	3,892	4,195
Concessional	0	1,885	1,297	1,285	1,373	1,486	1,612	1,798	1,970	2,167
Bilateral	1,167	9,997	17,761	21,377	21,842	23,821	24,821	23,585	21,836	22,555
Concessional	864	6,231	11,223	15,866	16,624	18,045	18,673	22,233	20,615	21,304
Private creditors	162	1,805	6,184	3,071	2,359	2,082	1,685	1,293	1,076	919
Bonds	0	132	0	0	0	0	0	0	0	0
Commercial banks	36	257	624	713	575	553	516	437	520	453
Other private	126	1,416	5,560	2,358	1,784	1,529	1,169	856	557	466
Private nonguaranteed	**0**	**265**	**1,000**	**600**	**500**	**375**	**313**	**127**	**54**	**34**
Bonds	0	0	0	0	0	0	0	0	0	0
Commercial banks	0	265	1,000	600	500	375	313	127	54	34
Memo:										
IBRD	22	421	1,480	1,381	1,357	1,411	1,320	1,075	869	847
IDA	0	307	921	904	912	961	1,035	1,090	1,206	1,268
DISBURSEMENTS	**170**	**2,680**	**1,997**	**1,348**	**1,145**	**1,047**	**519**	**583**	**765**	**459**
Public and publicly guaranteed	**170**	**2,554**	**1,946**	**1,328**	**1,125**	**987**	**519**	**583**	**765**	**447**
Official creditors	137	1,904	1,224	961	976	785	479	551	577	437
Multilateral	0	242	274	479	537	460	276	341	449	280
Concessional	0	53	57	118	107	126	149	198	244	192
Bilateral	137	1,662	950	482	438	325	203	210	129	157
Concessional	53	1,011	664	407	427	311	189	210	128	157
Private creditors	33	650	722	367	149	203	41	32	188	10
Bonds	0	30	0	0	0	0	0	0	0	0
Commercial banks	0	8	170	47	25	77	31	17	187	9
Other private	33	613	552	319	124	126	10	15	1	0
Private nonguaranteed	**0**	**126**	**51**	**20**	**20**	**60**	**0**	**0**	**0**	**12**
Bonds	0	0	0	0	0	0	0	0	0	0
Commercial banks	0	126	51	20	20	60	0	0	0	12
Memo:										
IBRD	0	169	92	237	144	149	42	26	103	48
IDA	0	41	8	8	19	50	83	82	157	57
PRINCIPAL REPAYMENTS	**225**	**343**	**1,696**	**1,437**	**965**	**923**	**901**	**1,020**	**926**	**912**
Public and publicly guaranteed	**225**	**297**	**1,564**	**1,167**	**845**	**738**	**839**	**834**	**853**	**881**
Official creditors	162	151	887	512	390	376	546	568	630	705
Multilateral	6	18	283	331	285	288	311	297	349	290
Concessional	0	0	55	63	24	25	30	34	38	52
Bilateral	156	134	604	181	105	88	235	271	280	415
Concessional	92	119	216	37	32	43	122	189	245	381
Private creditors	63	145	677	655	455	362	293	266	224	175
Bonds	0	4	1	0	0	0	0	0	0	0
Commercial banks	0	65	34	179	167	119	74	85	86	84
Other private	63	76	643	476	288	243	219	181	138	91
Private nonguaranteed	**0**	**46**	**132**	**270**	**120**	**185**	**62**	**186**	**73**	**32**
Bonds	0	0	0	0	0	0	0	0	0	0
Commercial banks	0	46	132	270	120	185	62	186	73	32
Memo:										
IBRD	6	7	176	187	189	191	198	178	225	115
IDA	0	0	7	11	12	12	14	15	16	18
NET FLOWS ON DEBT	**-54**	**2,337**	**301**	**-89**	**180**	**124**	**-381**	**-437**	**-161**	**-453**
Public and publicly guaranteed	**-54**	**2,257**	**382**	**161**	**280**	**249**	**-319**	**-251**	**-88**	**-434**
Official creditors	-24	1,753	337	449	586	409	-67	-18	-52	-268
Multilateral	-6	224	-10	148	253	172	-36	43	99	-10
Concessional	0	53	2	55	83	101	119	164	206	140
Bilateral	-19	1,529	346	301	333	237	-32	-61	-152	-258
Concessional	-39	892	449	370	395	268	67	21	-117	-224
Private creditors	-30	505	45	-289	-306	-160	-252	-234	-36	-166
Bonds	0	26	-1	0	0	0	0	0	0	0
Commercial banks	0	-58	136	-132	-142	-42	-43	-68	101	-75
Other private	-30	537	-91	-157	-164	-117	-210	-166	-137	-91
Private nonguaranteed	**0**	**80**	**-81**	**-250**	**-100**	**-125**	**-62**	**-186**	**-73**	**-20**
Bonds	0	0	0	0	0	0	0	0	0	0
Commercial banks	0	80	-81	-250	-100	-125	-62	-186	-73	-20
Memo:										
IBRD	-6	162	-84	50	-45	-42	-156	-152	-123	-67
IDA	0	41	1	-3	8	38	69	67	141	39

EGYPT, ARAB REPUBLIC OF

(US$ million, unless otherwise indicated)

	1970	1980	1990	1992	1993	1994	1995	1996	1997	1998
INTEREST PAYMENTS (LINT)	**37**	**350**	**1,012**	**1,040**	**1,041**	**1,155**	**1,243**	**1,041**	**724**	**674**
Public and publicly guaranteed	**37**	**327**	**922**	**1,000**	**999**	**1,120**	**1,219**	**1,029**	**716**	**667**
Official creditors	30	221	731	850	873	1,017	1,111	945	655	610
Multilateral	2	40	185	178	189	205	214	191	172	168
Concessional	0	7	14	15	17	19	22	25	27	31
Bilateral	28	181	546	671	684	812	897	754	482	442
Concessional	18	146	198	380	404	451	549	523	383	350
Private creditors	7	106	192	150	125	103	107	85	62	57
Bonds	0	11	0	0	0	0	0	0	0	0
Commercial banks	0	36	45	48	32	31	40	32	25	29
Other private	7	59	146	102	93	73	68	53	37	28
Private nonguaranteed	**0**	**23**	**89**	**41**	**42**	**35**	**24**	**12**	**8**	**7**
Bonds	0	0	0	0	0	0	0	0	0	0
Commercial banks	0	23	89	41	42	35	24	12	8	7
Memo:										
IBRD	2	29	138	115	115	114	114	94	72	56
IDA	0	2	7	7	7	7	7	8	8	9
NET TRANSFERS ON DEBT	**-91**	**1,988**	**-711**	**-1,130**	**-861**	**-1,031**	**-1,624**	**-1,479**	**-885**	**-1,127**
Public and publicly guaranteed	**-91**	**1,931**	**-541**	**-839**	**-719**	**-871**	**-1,538**	**-1,281**	**-805**	**-1,101**
Official creditors	-54	1,532	-394	-400	-288	-608	-1,178	-962	-707	-878
Multilateral	-7	184	-195	-30	63	-33	-250	-147	-73	-178
Concessional	0	46	-12	40	66	82	97	139	179	109
Bilateral	-47	1,348	-200	-370	-351	-575	-929	-815	-634	-700
Concessional	-57	746	251	-10	-9	-183	-482	-502	-500	-574
Private creditors	-37	399	-147	-439	-431	-263	-360	-318	-98	-223
Bonds	0	15	-1	0	0	0	0	0	0	0
Commercial banks	0	-94	91	-180	-174	-73	-82	-100	77	-104
Other private	-37	478	-237	-259	-257	-190	-277	-218	-174	-119
Private nonguaranteed	**0**	**57**	**-170**	**-291**	**-142**	**-160**	**-86**	**-198**	**-81**	**-26**
Bonds	0	0	0	0	0	0	0	0	0	0
Commercial banks	0	57	-170	-291	-142	-160	-86	-198	-81	-26
Memo:										
IBRD	-7	133	-222	-65	-160	-157	-270	-246	-195	-123
IDA	0	39	-6	-10	1	31	62	59	133	30
DEBT SERVICE (LTDS)	**261**	**693**	**2,708**	**2,477**	**2,005**	**2,078**	**2,143**	**2,061**	**1,650**	**1,586**
Public and publicly guaranteed	**261**	**624**	**2,487**	**2,166**	**1,843**	**1,858**	**2,057**	**1,863**	**1,570**	**1,548**
Official creditors	192	372	1,618	1,361	1,263	1,392	1,657	1,513	1,284	1,316
Multilateral	7	58	468	509	474	493	525	488	522	458
Concessional	0	7	69	78	41	45	52	60	65	83
Bilateral	184	315	1,150	852	790	900	1,132	1,025	763	857
Concessional	110	265	413	416	436	494	670	712	628	731
Private creditors	70	251	869	805	580	466	400	351	285	232
Bonds	0	15	1	0	0	0	0	0	0	0
Commercial banks	0	101	79	227	199	150	113	117	110	113
Other private	70	135	789	578	381	316	287	233	175	119
Private nonguaranteed	**0**	**69**	**221**	**311**	**162**	**220**	**86**	**198**	**81**	**38**
Bonds	0	0	0	0	0	0	0	0	0	0
Commercial banks	0	69	221	311	162	220	86	198	81	38
Memo:										
IBRD	7	36	314	302	304	306	312	272	297	170
IDA	0	3	14	18	19	19	21	23	24	26
UNDISBURSED DEBT	**315**	**4,999**	**4,517**	**4,811**	**4,119**	**3,551**	**3,077**	**2,385**	**1,771**	**1,478**
Official creditors	282	4,162	3,279	4,333	3,746	3,349	2,923	2,279	1,675	1,414
Private creditors	33	837	1,237	478	373	203	154	106	95	64
Memorandum items										
Concessional LDOD	864	8,115	12,520	17,151	17,996	19,531	20,285	24,031	22,585	23,471
Variable rate LDOD	0	663	4,399	1,971	1,719	1,673	1,564	1,278	1,298	1,244
Public sector LDOD	1,351	14,427	27,352	27,739	27,793	29,807	30,477	28,808	26,803	27,668
Private sector LDOD	0	266	1,021	609	510	383	316	129	56	36

6. CURRENCY COMPOSITION OF LONG-TERM DEBT (PERCENT)

	1970	1980	1990	1992	1993	1994	1995	1996	1997	1998
Deutsche mark	10.1	4.8	12.4	10.5	9.8	10.5	11.2	11.1	10.5	10.9
French franc	0.9	5.6	13.8	19.5	18.5	19.3	20.3	19.8	18.2	18.3
Japanese yen	0.0	4.0	8.2	11.6	13.2	14.0	13.2	12.3	11.6	12.5
Pound sterling	2.9	1.2	2.5	1.9	1.7	1.7	1.5	1.5	1.5	1.4
Swiss franc	2.4	1.3	3.0	2.4	2.4	2.5	2.7	2.4	2.3	2.3
U.S.dollars	23.0	73.0	41.9	38.0	37.9	35.1	34.2	35.8	39.1	37.2
Multiple currency	1.6	3.3	8.4	7.9	8.2	8.0	7.4	6.8	6.4	6.6
Special drawing rights	0.0	0.0	0.6	0.0	0.0	0.0	0.0	0.0	0.1	0.1
All other currencies	59.1	6.8	9.2	8.2	8.3	8.9	9.5	10.3	10.3	10.7

EGYPT, ARAB REPUBLIC OF

(US$ million, unless otherwise indicated)

	1970	1980	1990	1992	1993	1994	1995	1996	1997	1998
7. DEBT RESTRUCTURINGS										
Total amount rescheduled	..	..	0	650	497	435	313	190	152	53
Debt stock rescheduled	..	..	0	0	0	0	0	0	0	0
Principal rescheduled	..	..	0	508	395	328	265	129	91	45
Official	..	..	0	122	99	82	51	34	22	24
Private	..	..	0	387	296	247	214	95	69	21
Interest rescheduled	..	..	0	143	101	80	50	31	18	11
Official	..	..	0	33	23	23	10	6	3	2
Private	..	..	0	110	78	56	40	25	14	10
Debt forgiven	..	..	10,576	70	47	40	35	35	27	17
Memo: interest forgiven	..	..	2,481	152	147	84	7	4	2	1
Debt stock reduction	..	..	0	0	0	0	13	9	0	0
of which debt buyback	..	..	0	0	0	0	0	0	0	0
8. DEBT STOCK-FLOW RECONCILIATION										
Total change in debt stocks	..	..	-12,664	-1,477	-558	1,805	952	-1,967	-1,450	2,115
Net flows on debt	351	2,465	-1,248	-591	-333	31	-39	-546	467	818
Net change in interest arrears	..	..	-1,933	0	0	0	1	-1	1	-2
Interest capitalized	..	..	0	143	101	80	50	31	18	11
Debt forgiveness or reduction	..	..	-10,576	-70	-47	-40	-48	-44	-27	-17
Cross-currency valuation	..	..	1,687	-896	-258	1,821	1,001	-1,322	-1,765	1,142
Residual	..	..	-594	-64	-21	-86	-14	-85	-144	163
9. AVERAGE TERMS OF NEW COMMITMENTS										
ALL CREDITORS										
Interest (%)	5.2	5.0	5.3	3.9	2.4	2.3	3.1	1.4	5.3	3.4
Maturity (years)	14.3	26.6	25.5	26.3	26.9	32.4	21.8	32.8	15.6	27.3
Grace period (years)	7.8	6.6	7.0	7.3	6.6	8.2	6.6	9.5	3.8	7.7
Grant element (%)	26.5	39.1	36.0	46.4	56.2	62.5	47.9	72.0	28.6	52.6
Official creditors										
Interest (%)	5.2	3.3	4.7	3.9	2.2	2.1	3.1	1.4	3.2	3.4
Maturity (years)	14.9	36.4	28.2	27.0	28.6	33.4	22.0	32.8	26.0	27.3
Grace period (years)	8.2	8.9	7.6	7.3	6.9	8.5	6.6	9.5	7.7	7.7
Grant element (%)	27.5	56.9	41.6	47.1	59.3	64.7	48.2	72.0	54.2	52.6
Private creditors										
Interest (%)	5.9	7.9	8.4	4.0	4.7	6.2	6.5	0.0	6.9	0.0
Maturity (years)	4.7	9.6	11.5	20.6	6.8	11.7	4.3	0.0	7.9	0.0
Grace period (years)	1.5	2.5	3.4	6.7	2.5	1.2	2.4	0.0	0.9	0.0
Grant element (%)	10.6	8.3	6.9	40.4	20.1	16.7	7.7	0.0	9.7	0.0
Memorandum items										
Commitments	306	2,176	1,228	1,533	788	334	207	172	323	286
Official creditors	288	1,378	1,028	1,367	726	318	206	172	137	286
Private creditors	18	798	201	166	62	16	1	0	186	0

10. CONTRACTUAL OBLIGATIONS ON OUTSTANDING LONG-TERM DEBT

	1999	2000	2001	2002	2003	2004	2005	2006	2007	2008
TOTAL										
Disbursements	542	378	210	132	80	41	25	16	11	8
Principal	1,084	1,100	1,095	1,125	1,158	1,313	1,309	1,353	1,381	1,422
Interest	707	671	639	603	566	528	489	453	417	381
Official creditors										
Disbursements	500	367	210	132	80	41	25	16	11	8
Principal	868	968	1,019	1,061	1,096	1,261	1,278	1,342	1,372	1,413
Interest	663	641	617	586	553	519	484	449	413	378
Bilateral creditors										
Disbursements	141	87	48	25	11	2	1	0	0	0
Principal	534	646	693	748	783	956	992	1,074	1,109	1,165
Interest	492	480	467	450	432	413	391	369	346	322
Multilateral creditors										
Disbursements	359	280	162	107	70	39	24	16	11	8
Principal	334	321	326	313	313	304	286	268	263	249
Interest	171	161	151	136	121	107	93	80	68	56
Private creditors										
Disbursements	42	12	0	0	0	0	0	0	0	0
Principal	216	133	76	64	61	53	32	12	9	9
Interest	44	30	22	17	13	8	6	4	4	3
Commercial banks										
Disbursements	25	5	0	0	0	0	0	0	0	0
Principal	65	57	49	49	47	40	21	3	1	0
Interest	21	17	14	10	7	4	1	0	0	0
Other private										
Disbursements	17	7	0	0	0	0	0	0	0	0
Principal	151	76	27	16	14	13	10	9	9	9
Interest	23	13	8	6	6	5	4	4	3	3

EL SALVADOR

(US$ million, unless otherwise indicated)

	1970	1980	1990	1992	1993	1994	1995	1996	1997	1998
1. SUMMARY DEBT DATA										
TOTAL DEBT STOCKS (EDT)	..	**911**	**2,148**	**2,263**	**2,033**	**2,210**	**2,610**	**2,914**	**3,252**	**3,633**
Long-term debt (LDOD)	**176**	**659**	**1,938**	**2,160**	**1,924**	**2,022**	**2,084**	**2,318**	**2,442**	**2,783**
Public and publicly guaranteed	88	499	1,913	2,148	1,916	2,014	2,080	2,317	2,397	2,443
Private nonguaranteed	88	161	26	12	8	8	5	2	45	340
Use of IMF credit	**7**	**32**	**0**	**0**	**0**	**0**	**0**	**0**	**0**	**0**
Short-term debt	..	**220**	**210**	**103**	**109**	**188**	**525**	**596**	**811**	**849**
of which interest arrears on LDOD	..	0	7	15	7	3	3	3	2	1
Official creditors	..	0	7	13	7	2	2	2	1	1
Private creditors	..	0	0	1	1	1	1	1	0	0
Memo: principal arrears on LDOD	..	0	6	19	6	4	6	8	14	5
Official creditors	..	0	6	17	3	0	1	1	13	5
Private creditors	..	0	0	3	2	4	5	6	1	0
Memo: export credits	..	0	236	197	282	337	267	252	365	446
TOTAL DEBT FLOWS										
Disbursements	**31**	**149**	**108**	**247**	**487**	**293**	**195**	**474**	**334**	**561**
Long-term debt	31	110	108	247	487	293	195	474	334	561
IMF purchases	0	40	0	0	0	0	0	0	0	0
Principal repayments	**27**	**35**	**124**	**150**	**172**	**241**	**160**	**178**	**127**	**264**
Long-term debt	22	35	119	150	172	241	160	178	127	264
IMF repurchases	5	0	5	0	0	0	0	0	0	0
Net flows on debt	**4**	**56**	**2**	**90**	**328**	**136**	**373**	**368**	**423**	**337**
of which short-term debt	..	-58	18	-7	13	83	337	71	216	39
Interest payments (INT)	..	**61**	**84**	**84**	**122**	**98**	**124**	**138**	**152**	**174**
Long-term debt	9	36	75	80	117	91	102	105	110	126
IMF charges	0	0	0	0	0	0	0	0	0	0
Short-term debt	..	25	9	4	5	8	22	33	42	48
Net transfers on debt	..	**-5**	**-83**	**6**	**206**	**37**	**249**	**229**	**271**	**163**
Total debt service paid (TDS)	..	**96**	**208**	**234**	**294**	**339**	**284**	**316**	**279**	**438**
Long-term debt	31	71	194	230	289	332	262	283	237	390
IMF repurchases and charges	5	0	5	0	0	0	0	0	0	0
Short-term debt (interest only)	..	25	9	4	5	8	22	33	42	48
2. AGGREGATE NET RESOURCE FLOWS AND NET TRANSFERS (LONG-TERM)										
NET RESOURCE FLOWS	**14**	**111**	**151**	**335**	**942**	**139**	**174**	**389**	**304**	**428**
Net flow of long-term debt (ex. IMF)	9	74	-11	97	315	52	35	297	207	297
Foreign direct investment (net)	4	6	2	15	16	0	38	-5	11	12
Portfolio equity flows	0	0	0	0	0	0	0	0	0	0
Grants (excluding technical coop.)	1	31	160	223	611	87	101	97	86	119
Memo: technical coop. grants	7	9	127	160	162	180	130	108	119	64
official net resource flows	5	104	143	335	929	199	167	372	246	186
private net resource flows	10	7	8	0	13	-60	7	17	58	242
NET TRANSFERS	**-2**	**34**	**47**	**229**	**800**	**24**	**46**	**258**	**167**	**274**
Interest on long-term debt	9	36	75	80	117	91	102	105	110	126
Profit remittances on FDI	7	41	28	26	25	24	26	25	27	28
Memo: official net transfers	2	82	81	266	823	117	75	274	146	83
private net transfers	-5	-48	-34	-38	-23	-93	-29	-16	21	192
3. MAJOR ECONOMIC AGGREGATES										
Gross national product (GNP)	1,123	3,490	4,705	5,904	6,925	7,994	9,405	10,263	11,123	11,787
Exports of goods & services (XGS)	..	1,282	1,360	1,694	2,188	2,642	3,154	3,330	3,980	4,190
of which workers remittances	..	11	357	687	790	967	1,061	1,084	1,199	1,338
Imports of goods & services (MGS)	..	1,289	1,785	2,054	2,523	2,981	3,744	3,669	4,048	4,444
International reserves (RES)	64	382	595	578	720	829	940	1,110	1,444	1,748
Current account balance	..	34	-152	-109	-82	-18	-262	-169	96	-84
4. DEBT INDICATORS										
EDT / XGS (%)	..	71.1	158.0	133.6	92.9	83.7	82.7	87.5	81.7	86.7
EDT / GNP (%)	..	26.1	45.7	38.3	29.4	27.6	27.8	28.4	29.2	30.8
TDS / XGS (%)	..	7.5	15.3	13.8	13.4	12.8	9.0	9.5	7.0	10.5
INT / XGS (%)	..	4.7	6.2	5.0	5.6	3.7	3.9	4.2	3.8	4.2
INT / GNP (%)	..	1.7	1.8	1.4	1.8	1.2	1.3	1.4	1.4	1.5
RES / EDT (%)	..	41.9	27.7	25.6	35.4	37.5	36.0	38.1	44.4	48.1
RES / MGS (months)	..	3.6	4.0	3.4	3.4	3.3	3.0	3.6	4.3	4.7
Short-term / EDT (%)	..	24.2	9.8	4.6	5.4	8.5	20.1	20.5	24.9	23.4
Concessional / EDT (%)	..	23.9	56.3	58.1	50.4	49.0	42.7	40.2	36.1	32.6
Multilateral / EDT (%)	..	28.3	36.6	40.8	52.9	57.5	52.8	54.0	51.2	48.5

EL SALVADOR

(US$ million, unless otherwise indicated)

	1970	*1980*	*1990*	*1992*	*1993*	*1994*	*1995*	*1996*	*1997*	*1998*
5. LONG-TERM DEBT										
DEBT OUTSTANDING (LDOD)	**176**	**659**	**1,938**	**2,160**	**1,924**	**2,022**	**2,084**	**2,318**	**2,442**	**2,783**
Public and publicly guaranteed	**88**	**499**	**1,913**	**2,148**	**1,916**	**2,014**	**2,080**	**2,317**	**2,397**	**2,443**
Official creditors	70	460	1,729	1,955	1,724	1,880	1,971	2,185	2,267	2,376
Multilateral	41	258	786	923	1,075	1,271	1,377	1,573	1,666	1,760
Concessional	10	134	414	476	536	605	623	648	656	646
Bilateral	30	202	943	1,032	649	608	594	612	601	616
Concessional	29	84	795	838	487	478	490	522	516	538
Private creditors	17	39	184	193	192	135	109	132	130	68
Bonds	3	0	0	0	0	0	0	0	0	0
Commercial banks	14	8	127	135	146	94	74	82	83	19
Other private	0	31	57	58	46	41	35	50	47	49
Private nonguaranteed	**88**	**161**	**26**	**12**	**8**	**8**	**5**	**2**	**45**	**340**
Bonds	0	0	0	0	0	0	0	0	0	0
Commercial banks	88	161	26	12	8	8	5	2	45	340
Memo:										
IBRD	25	87	140	182	220	290	307	282	275	287
IDA	8	27	23	22	22	21	20	20	19	18
DISBURSEMENTS	**31**	**110**	**108**	**247**	**487**	**293**	**195**	**474**	**334**	**561**
Public and publicly guaranteed	**8**	**110**	**108**	**247**	**487**	**289**	**195**	**474**	**290**	**261**
Official creditors	6	81	78	233	455	271	190	381	268	255
Multilateral	5	36	44	151	211	268	166	317	232	237
Concessional	2	15	33	53	72	81	32	40	25	8
Bilateral	2	45	33	83	245	3	25	64	37	18
Concessional	2	20	18	23	218	2	24	64	36	18
Private creditors	1	29	30	13	31	19	5	94	22	6
Bonds	0	0	0	0	0	0	0	0	0	0
Commercial banks	1	3	25	0	31	19	5	71	15	4
Other private	0	26	5	13	1	0	0	23	7	3
Private nonguaranteed	**24**	**0**	**0**	**0**	**0**	**4**	**0**	**0**	**44**	**300**
Bonds	0	0	0	0	0	0	0	0	0	0
Commercial banks	24	0	0	0	0	4	0	0	44	300
Memo:										
IBRD	1	10	3	11	51	70	26	21	35	34
IDA	0	3	0	0	0	0	0	0	0	0
PRINCIPAL REPAYMENTS	**22**	**35**	**119**	**150**	**172**	**241**	**160**	**178**	**127**	**264**
Public and publicly guaranteed	**6**	**17**	**105**	**140**	**168**	**237**	**157**	**175**	**126**	**260**
Official creditors	3	8	94	122	138	159	124	106	108	188
Multilateral	3	5	57	60	63	107	78	76	85	164
Concessional	0	1	11	13	12	13	13	15	15	20
Bilateral	0	3	37	62	75	52	45	30	24	24
Concessional	0	1	8	15	24	19	19	17	17	16
Private creditors	3	10	11	19	30	79	33	69	18	72
Bonds	0	0	0	0	0	0	0	0	0	0
Commercial banks	3	2	9	16	20	71	26	63	14	68
Other private	0	8	2	3	11	8	8	6	4	4
Private nonguaranteed	**16**	**18**	**14**	**9**	**4**	**4**	**3**	**3**	**1**	**5**
Bonds	0	0	0	0	0	0	0	0	0	0
Commercial banks	16	18	14	9	4	4	3	3	1	5
Memo:										
IBRD	2	3	15	13	17	19	21	22	24	28
IDA	0	0	1	1	1	1	1	1	1	1
NET FLOWS ON DEBT	**9**	**74**	**-11**	**97**	**315**	**52**	**35**	**297**	**207**	**297**
Public and publicly guaranteed	**2**	**92**	**3**	**106**	**318**	**52**	**38**	**300**	**164**	**2**
Official creditors	3	73	-17	112	317	112	66	275	160	67
Multilateral	2	31	-13	90	148	161	87	241	147	73
Concessional	2	14	23	40	60	68	18	26	10	-11
Bilateral	2	42	-4	21	170	-49	-21	34	13	-5
Concessional	2	18	11	8	195	-18	5	47	19	2
Private creditors	-2	19	19	-5	1	-60	-28	25	4	-65
Bonds	0	0	0	0	0	0	0	0	0	0
Commercial banks	-2	1	16	-16	11	-52	-20	9	1	-65
Other private	0	18	3	11	-10	-8	-8	17	3	-1
Private nonguaranteed	**8**	**-18**	**-14**	**-9**	**-4**	**0**	**-3**	**-3**	**43**	**295**
Bonds	0	0	0	0	0	0	0	0	0	0
Commercial banks	8	-18	-14	-9	-4	0	-3	-3	43	295
Memo:										
IBRD	-1	8	-13	-1	34	52	5	-1	12	7
IDA	0	3	-1	-1	-1	-1	-1	-1	-1	-1

EL SALVADOR

(US$ million, unless otherwise indicated)

	1970	1980	1990	1992	1993	1994	1995	1996	1997	1998
INTEREST PAYMENTS (LINT)	**9**	**36**	**75**	**80**	**117**	**91**	**102**	**105**	**110**	**126**
Public and publicly guaranteed	**4**	**25**	**72**	**79**	**117**	**90**	**102**	**105**	**107**	**106**
Official creditors	2	21	63	69	106	82	92	97	101	103
Multilateral	2	11	50	42	45	56	62	74	79	83
Concessional	0	2	9	9	9	9	11	11	11	11
Bilateral	0	10	13	27	61	25	30	23	21	21
Concessional	0	2	9	14	46	14	16	15	14	14
Private creditors	1	3	10	10	11	9	9	8	7	3
Bonds	0	0	0	0	0	0	0	0	0	0
Commercial banks	1	1	8	8	7	6	7	6	5	2
Other private	0	2	2	2	4	3	2	2	2	1
Private nonguaranteed	**6**	**11**	**3**	**1**	**0**	**0**	**0**	**0**	**3**	**20**
Bonds	0	0	0	0	0	0	0	0	0	0
Commercial banks	6	11	3	1	0	0	0	0	3	20
Memo:										
IBRD	1	7	14	14	15	17	22	21	19	20
IDA	0	0	0	0	0	0	0	0	0	0
NET TRANSFERS ON DEBT	**0**	**39**	**-86**	**17**	**198**	**-39**	**-67**	**191**	**97**	**172**
Public and publicly guaranteed	**-2**	**68**	**-69**	**27**	**202**	**-38**	**-63**	**195**	**57**	**-104**
Official creditors	1	52	-79	43	211	30	-26	177	60	-36
Multilateral	0	20	-63	49	102	104	25	167	68	-10
Concessional	2	12	14	31	51	58	7	15	-1	-22
Bilateral	1	32	-17	-6	109	-74	-51	10	-8	-26
Concessional	2	16	2	-7	148	-32	-11	32	5	-12
Private creditors	-3	16	10	-16	-10	-69	-37	17	-3	-68
Bonds	0	0	0	0	0	0	0	0	0	0
Commercial banks	-3	0	8	-24	4	-59	-27	2	-4	-66
Other private	0	16	2	8	-14	-10	-10	15	2	-2
Private nonguaranteed	**2**	**-29**	**-17**	**-11**	**-4**	**0**	**-4**	**-3**	**40**	**276**
Bonds	0	0	0	0	0	0	0	0	0	0
Commercial banks	2	-29	-17	-11	-4	0	-4	-3	40	276
Memo:										
IBRD	-2	0	-27	-15	19	35	-17	-22	-7	-13
IDA	0	3	-1	-1	-1	-1	-1	-1	-1	-1
DEBT SERVICE (LTDS)	**31**	**71**	**194**	**230**	**289**	**332**	**262**	**283**	**237**	**390**
Public and publicly guaranteed	**9**	**42**	**177**	**220**	**285**	**327**	**258**	**280**	**233**	**365**
Official creditors	5	29	157	190	244	240	216	203	209	291
Multilateral	5	16	107	102	108	163	141	150	164	247
Concessional	0	3	19	22	21	22	24	25	26	30
Bilateral	1	13	50	89	136	77	76	54	45	44
Concessional	0	3	17	29	70	33	35	32	31	30
Private creditors	4	13	21	29	41	87	42	77	25	75
Bonds	0	0	0	0	0	0	0	0	0	0
Commercial banks	4	3	17	24	27	77	32	69	19	70
Other private	0	10	4	5	14	10	10	8	6	5
Private nonguaranteed	**22**	**29**	**17**	**11**	**4**	**4**	**4**	**3**	**4**	**24**
Bonds	0	0	0	0	0	0	0	0	0	0
Commercial banks	22	29	17	11	4	4	4	3	4	24
Memo:										
IBRD	4	10	29	27	32	36	43	42	42	47
IDA	0	0	1	1	1	1	1	1	1	1
UNDISBURSED DEBT	**38**	**424**	**324**	**701**	**817**	**698**	**1,317**	**1,212**	**901**	**771**
Official creditors	38	390	322	666	793	693	1,255	1,190	889	760
Private creditors	0	34	2	35	24	5	62	22	12	11
Memorandum items										
Concessional LDOD	39	218	1,209	1,314	1,024	1,083	1,113	1,170	1,173	1,184
Variable rate LDOD	88	181	192	289	337	359	405	498	610	995
Public sector LDOD	88	496	1,905	2,141	1,909	2,007	2,073	2,310	2,391	2,438
Private sector LDOD	88	163	34	19	15	15	11	8	51	346

6. CURRENCY COMPOSITION OF LONG-TERM DEBT (PERCENT)

	1970	1980	1990	1992	1993	1994	1995	1996	1997	1998
Deutsche mark	0.0	0.2	3.7	3.1	3.5	3.8	4.0	4.6	4.1	4.4
French franc	0.0	5.5	3.3	2.8	2.5	2.5	2.5	2.0	1.6	1.5
Japanese yen	0.0	3.6	1.2	1.0	1.0	0.8	1.7	2.7	3.7	4.9
Pound sterling	0.0	0.3	0.0	0.0	0.0	0.0	0.0	0.0	0.0	0.0
Swiss franc	0.0	0.0	0.0	0.0	0.0	0.0	0.0	0.0	0.0	0.0
U.S.dollars	65.2	37.8	56.5	59.2	52.8	51.3	50.7	55.1	65.7	66.1
Multiple currency	31.1	32.6	33.7	32.6	39.2	40.7	40.2	34.6	23.7	21.8
Special drawing rights	0.0	0.0	0.0	0.0	0.0	0.2	0.3	0.4	0.4	0.5
All other currencies	3.7	20.0	1.6	1.3	1.0	0.7	0.6	0.6	0.8	0.8

EL SALVADOR

(US$ million, unless otherwise indicated)

	1970	1980	1990	1992	1993	1994	1995	1996	1997	1998
7. DEBT RESTRUCTURINGS										
Total amount rescheduled	..	..	86	0	156	0	0	0	0	0
Debt stock rescheduled	..	..	0	0	156	0	0	0	0	0
Principal rescheduled	..	..	42	0	0	0	0	0	0	0
Official	..	..	39	0	0	0	0	0	0	0
Private	..	..	3	0	0	0	0	0	0	0
Interest rescheduled	..	..	43	0	0	0	0	0	0	0
Official	..	..	38	0	0	0	0	0	0	0
Private	..	..	5	0	0	0	0	0	0	0
Debt forgiven	..	..	0	0	500	0	0	0	0	0
Memo: interest forgiven	..	..	0	0	0	0	0	0	0	0
Debt stock reduction	..	..	0	0	47	0	0	0	0	0
of which debt buyback	..	..	0	0	0	0	0	0	0	0
8. DEBT STOCK-FLOW RECONCILIATION										
Total change in debt stocks	..	..	66	80	-230	177	400	305	338	380
Net flows on debt	4	56	2	90	328	136	373	368	423	337
Net change in interest arrears	..	..	-17	8	-8	-5	0	0	-2	-1
Interest capitalized	..	..	43	0	0	0	0	0	0	0
Debt forgiveness or reduction	..	..	0	0	-547	0	0	0	0	0
Cross-currency valuation	..	..	26	-21	-7	29	15	-49	-53	26
Residual	..	..	13	4	4	17	12	-14	-31	19
9. AVERAGE TERMS OF NEW COMMITMENTS										
ALL CREDITORS										
Interest (%)	4.7	4.2	4.6	6.1	5.1	3.8	6.6	7.1	7.1	7.5
Maturity (years)	23.4	27.6	29.8	20.4	22.1	24.2	22.5	20.7	16.8	22.0
Grace period (years)	6.0	8.4	7.2	5.3	4.8	7.6	5.2	5.0	3.8	3.8
Grant element (%)	37.6	45.8	45.5	24.4	30.2	45.9	22.2	18.1	16.6	14.7
Official creditors										
Interest (%)	4.4	3.3	3.2	6.1	5.1	3.8	6.5	7.1	7.1	7.5
Maturity (years)	25.0	28.4	35.6	22.2	22.6	24.2	21.9	22.1	17.6	22.7
Grace period (years)	6.5	8.9	8.8	5.7	4.9	7.6	5.1	5.1	4.0	3.9
Grant element (%)	40.7	53.5	56.6	26.3	30.6	45.9	22.6	18.7	17.3	15.0
Private creditors										
Interest (%)	7.5	11.7	10.4	6.8	4.1	0.0	7.1	7.2	7.0	6.6
Maturity (years)	7.2	20.7	5.0	5.4	7.3	0.0	29.9	4.7	6.2	4.9
Grace period (years)	0.7	4.3	0.5	1.9	0.8	0.0	7.0	3.8	1.1	0.9
Grant element (%)	6.9	-17.3	-1.4	8.1	17.6	0.0	16.6	11.0	8.0	7.7
Memorandum items										
Commitments	12	225	131	439	643	161	822	705	195	150
Official creditors	11	200	106	393	623	161	760	649	181	144
Private creditors	1	25	25	46	20	0	62	56	14	6

10. CONTRACTUAL OBLIGATIONS ON OUTSTANDING LONG-TERM DEBT

	1999	2000	2001	2002	2003	2004	2005	2006	2007	2008
TOTAL										
Disbursements	228	193	143	96	53	27	18	8	3	2
Principal	165	178	216	217	230	218	212	188	184	179
Interest	150	152	150	144	134	123	112	100	90	80
Official creditors										
Disbursements	222	190	142	95	53	27	18	8	3	2
Principal	119	137	183	185	200	188	182	158	155	150
Interest	127	131	131	127	120	110	101	91	82	74
Bilateral creditors										
Disbursements	24	17	11	7	4	2	0	0	0	0
Principal	26	32	36	37	42	33	33	30	27	26
Interest	23	22	20	19	17	15	14	13	12	11
Multilateral creditors										
Disbursements	198	173	131	89	49	25	17	8	3	2
Principal	93	106	147	149	158	156	149	129	128	124
Interest	104	109	111	108	103	95	87	78	71	63
Private creditors										
Disbursements	6	3	1	1	0	0	0	0	0	0
Principal	45	41	34	32	31	30	30	30	30	30
Interest	23	21	18	16	15	13	11	9	8	6
Commercial banks										
Disbursements	3	2	1	0	0	0	0	0	0	0
Principal	9	5	5	3	2	1	0	0	0	0
Interest	2	1	1	0	0	0	0	0	0	0
Other private										
Disbursements	4	1	1	0	0	0	0	0	0	0
Principal	37	35	29	29	29	29	30	30	30	30
Interest	22	20	18	16	14	13	11	9	8	6

EQUATORIAL GUINEA

(US$ million, unless otherwise indicated)

	1970	1980	1990	1992	1993	1994	1995	1996	1997	1998
1. SUMMARY DEBT DATA										
TOTAL DEBT STOCKS (EDT)	..	**75.6**	**241.1**	**255.3**	**264.1**	**287.6**	**291.8**	**282.4**	**283.2**	**306.1**
Long-term debt (LDOD)	**5.0**	**52.5**	**209.2**	**214.4**	**214.8**	**219.3**	**229.6**	**222.2**	**208.6**	**216.5**
Public and publicly guaranteed	5.0	52.5	209.2	214.4	214.8	219.3	229.6	222.2	208.6	216.5
Private nonguaranteed	0.0	0.0	0.0	0.0	0.0	0.0	0.0	0.0	0.0	0.0
Use of IMF credit	**0.0**	**16.1**	**5.8**	**12.6**	**16.4**	**19.6**	**18.9**	**17.2**	**13.2**	**10.8**
Short-term debt	..	**7.0**	**26.0**	**28.3**	**32.9**	**48.6**	**43.3**	**43.1**	**61.4**	**78.8**
of which interest arrears on LDOD	..	0.0	19.7	28.0	32.6	37.6	41.3	39.6	37.4	39.8
Official creditors	..	0.0	17.3	24.5	28.4	32.7	35.9	34.5	32.8	34.9
Private creditors	..	0.0	2.3	3.5	4.2	4.9	5.4	5.2	4.6	4.9
Memo: principal arrears on LDOD	..	5.6	28.4	54.6	56.1	71.9	94.5	93.7	91.0	97.0
Official creditors	..	5.6	24.4	45.8	47.7	59.8	77.8	77.7	76.8	82.0
Private creditors	..	0.0	4.0	8.8	8.4	12.1	16.7	16.0	14.3	15.0
Memo: export credits	..	0.0	37.0	79.0	99.0	103.0	59.0	60.0	55.0	56.0
TOTAL DEBT FLOWS										
Disbursements	**0.0**	**37.6**	**9.9**	**14.5**	**13.4**	**6.6**	**2.2**	**2.0**	**2.6**	**1.1**
Long-term debt	0.0	19.6	9.9	14.5	9.6	4.0	2.2	2.0	2.6	1.1
IMF purchases	0.0	18.0	0.0	0.0	3.9	2.6	0.0	0.0	0.0	0.0
Principal repayments	**0.0**	**1.7**	**4.2**	**2.0**	**0.5**	**0.7**	**1.3**	**3.3**	**4.1**	**3.7**
Long-term debt	0.0	1.7	0.6	2.0	0.5	0.1	0.2	2.2	1.1	0.8
IMF repurchases	0.0	0.0	3.6	0.0	0.0	0.5	1.1	1.1	3.0	2.9
Net flows on debt	**0.0**	**40.9**	**9.8**	**12.5**	**12.9**	**16.7**	**-8.1**	**0.0**	**18.9**	**12.4**
of which short-term debt	..	5.0	4.0	0.0	0.0	10.8	-9.0	1.4	20.5	15.0
Interest payments (INT)	..	**0.8**	**0.9**	**1.1**	**0.7**	**1.4**	**0.8**	**1.3**	**1.8**	**2.3**
Long-term debt	0.0	0.1	0.5	1.0	0.6	0.8	0.4	1.0	1.0	0.7
IMF charges	0.0	0.2	0.2	0.1	0.1	0.0	0.1	0.1	0.1	0.1
Short-term debt	..	0.6	0.2	0.0	0.0	0.5	0.3	0.2	0.7	1.6
Net transfers on debt	..	**40.0**	**8.8**	**11.4**	**12.2**	**15.4**	**-8.9**	**-1.3**	**17.2**	**10.1**
Total debt service paid (TDS)	..	**2.6**	**5.1**	**3.1**	**1.2**	**2.0**	**2.1**	**4.7**	**5.9**	**6.0**
Long-term debt	0.0	1.8	1.1	3.0	1.1	0.9	0.6	3.3	2.1	1.5
IMF repurchases and charges	0.0	0.2	3.8	0.1	0.1	0.6	1.2	1.2	3.1	2.9
Short-term debt (interest only)	..	0.6	0.2	0.0	0.0	0.5	0.3	0.2	0.7	1.6
2. AGGREGATE NET RESOURCE FLOWS AND NET TRANSFERS (LONG-TERM)										
NET RESOURCE FLOWS	**0.0**	**19.3**	**63.9**	**41.4**	**45.7**	**31.8**	**144.0**	**394.0**	**34.5**	**37.2**
Net flow of long-term debt (ex. IMF)	0.0	17.8	9.4	12.5	9.1	3.8	2.0	-0.3	1.4	0.3
Foreign direct investment (net)	0.0	0.0	11.0	6.0	22.0	17.0	127.0	376.0	20.0	24.0
Portfolio equity flows	0.0	0.0	0.0	0.0	0.0	0.0	0.0	0.0	0.0	0.0
Grants (excluding technical coop.)	0.0	1.4	43.5	22.9	14.6	11.0	15.0	18.3	13.1	12.9
Memo: technical coop. grants	0.0	2.0	14.0	23.7	21.0	13.1	17.2	11.0	12.4	13.2
official net resource flows	0.0	14.8	52.9	35.4	23.7	14.8	17.0	18.0	14.5	13.2
private net resource flows	0.0	4.5	11.0	6.0	22.0	17.0	127.0	376.0	20.0	24.0
NET TRANSFERS	**-0.6**	**19.2**	**63.4**	**40.4**	**45.1**	**31.0**	**143.6**	**393.0**	**33.5**	**36.5**
Interest on long-term debt	0.0	0.1	0.5	1.0	0.6	0.8	0.4	1.0	1.0	0.7
Profit remittances on FDI	0.6	0.0	0.0	0.0	0.0	0.0	0.0	0.0	0.0	0.0
Memo: official net transfers	0.0	14.7	52.4	34.4	23.1	14.0	16.6	17.0	13.5	12.5
private net transfers	-0.6	4.5	11.0	6.0	22.0	17.0	127.0	376.0	20.0	24.0
3. MAJOR ECONOMIC AGGREGATES										
Gross national product (GNP)	66.9	..	123.5	148.2	150.0	115.7	153.1	203.7	415.7	404.5
Exports of goods & services (XGS)	..	..	42.3	59.0	70.1	65.4	94.2	180.4	449.3	417.4
of which workers remittances	..	..	..	..	..	..	..	..	..	..
Imports of goods & services (MGS)	..	..	99.2	96.1	98.9	69.5	221.1	521.8	770.3	934.9
International reserves (RES)	..	..	0.7	13.4	0.5	0.4	0.0	0.5	4.9	0.8
Current account balance	..	..	-19.0	-10.6	2.8	-0.4	-123.4	-344.0	..	..
4. DEBT INDICATORS										
EDT / XGS (%)	..	..	569.7	432.7	377.0	440.0	309.7	156.6	63.0	73.3
EDT / GNP (%)	..	..	195.2	172.2	176.1	248.5	190.7	138.6	68.1	75.7
TDS / XGS (%)	..	..	12.1	5.3	1.7	3.1	2.2	2.6	1.3	1.4
INT / XGS (%)	..	..	2.1	1.9	1.0	2.1	0.9	0.7	0.4	0.6
INT / GNP (%)	..	..	0.7	0.7	0.5	1.2	0.5	0.6	0.4	0.6
RES / EDT (%)	..	..	0.3	5.3	0.2	0.1	0.0	0.2	1.7	0.3
RES / MGS (months)	..	..	0.1	1.7	0.1	0.1	0.0	0.0	0.1	0.0
Short-term / EDT (%)	..	9.3	10.8	11.1	12.5	16.9	14.8	15.3	21.7	25.7
Concessional / EDT (%)	..	41.7	48.6	51.4	52.4	49.1	50.5	51.1	48.8	46.9
Multilateral / EDT (%)	..	3.6	28.0	31.4	33.7	33.7	34.8	35.0	33.1	32.0

EQUATORIAL GUINEA

(US$ million, unless otherwise indicated)

	1970	1980	1990	1992	1993	1994	1995	1996	1997	1998
5. LONG-TERM DEBT										
DEBT OUTSTANDING (LDOD)	**5.0**	**52.5**	**209.2**	**214.4**	**214.8**	**219.3**	**229.6**	**222.2**	**208.6**	**216.5**
Public and publicly guaranteed	**5.0**	**52.5**	**209.2**	**214.4**	**214.8**	**219.3**	**229.6**	**222.2**	**208.6**	**216.5**
Official creditors	5.0	45.3	191.5	198.4	199.9	203.6	212.8	206.2	194.3	201.5
Multilateral	0.0	2.7	67.4	80.2	89.1	96.8	101.4	98.8	93.7	98.0
Concessional	0.0	2.0	51.6	66.9	76.9	84.3	88.2	87.0	83.7	87.6
Bilateral	5.0	42.6	124.1	118.2	110.7	106.8	111.5	107.4	100.5	103.6
Concessional	0.0	29.5	65.5	64.3	61.6	56.9	59.1	57.4	54.5	55.8
Private creditors	0.0	7.2	17.8	16.0	15.0	15.7	16.8	16.0	14.3	15.0
Bonds	0.0	0.0	0.0	0.0	0.0	0.0	0.0	0.0	0.0	0.0
Commercial banks	0.0	0.0	0.0	0.0	0.0	0.0	0.0	0.0	0.0	0.0
Other private	0.0	7.2	17.8	16.0	15.0	15.7	16.8	16.0	14.3	15.0
Private nonguaranteed	**0.0**	**0.0**	**0.0**	**0.0**	**0.0**	**0.0**	**0.0**	**0.0**	**0.0**	**0.0**
Bonds	0.0	0.0	0.0	0.0	0.0	0.0	0.0	0.0	0.0	0.0
Commercial banks	0.0	0.0	0.0	0.0	0.0	0.0	0.0	0.0	0.0	0.0
Memo:										
IBRD	0.0	0.0	0.0	0.0	0.0	0.0	0.0	0.0	0.0	0.0
IDA	0.0	0.0	37.6	41.2	45.3	49.9	53.1	52.1	49.9	51.7
DISBURSEMENTS	**0.0**	**19.6**	**9.9**	**14.5**	**9.6**	**4.0**	**2.2**	**2.0**	**2.6**	**1.1**
Public and publicly guaranteed	**0.0**	**19.6**	**9.9**	**14.5**	**9.6**	**4.0**	**2.2**	**2.0**	**2.6**	**1.1**
Official creditors	0.0	14.8	9.9	14.5	9.6	4.0	2.2	2.0	2.6	1.1
Multilateral	0.0	1.7	3.7	14.3	9.6	4.0	2.2	2.0	2.6	1.1
Concessional	0.0	1.0	3.1	14.3	9.6	4.0	2.2	2.0	2.6	1.1
Bilateral	0.0	13.1	6.3	0.2	0.0	0.0	0.0	0.0	0.0	0.0
Concessional	0.0	3.3	6.3	0.2	0.0	0.0	0.0	0.0	0.0	0.0
Private creditors	0.0	4.8	0.0	0.0	0.0	0.0	0.0	0.0	0.0	0.0
Bonds	0.0	0.0	0.0	0.0	0.0	0.0	0.0	0.0	0.0	0.0
Commercial banks	0.0	0.0	0.0	0.0	0.0	0.0	0.0	0.0	0.0	0.0
Other private	0.0	4.8	0.0	0.0	0.0	0.0	0.0	0.0	0.0	0.0
Private nonguaranteed	**0.0**	**0.0**	**0.0**	**0.0**	**0.0**	**0.0**	**0.0**	**0.0**	**0.0**	**0.0**
Bonds	0.0	0.0	0.0	0.0	0.0	0.0	0.0	0.0	0.0	0.0
Commercial banks	0.0	0.0	0.0	0.0	0.0	0.0	0.0	0.0	0.0	0.0
Memo:										
IBRD	0.0	0.0	0.0	0.0	0.0	0.0	0.0	0.0	0.0	0.0
IDA	0.0	0.0	2.0	2.5	4.0	2.4	2.2	1.0	1.3	0.3
PRINCIPAL REPAYMENTS	**0.0**	**1.7**	**0.6**	**2.0**	**0.5**	**0.1**	**0.2**	**2.2**	**1.1**	**0.8**
Public and publicly guaranteed	**0.0**	**1.7**	**0.6**	**2.0**	**0.5**	**0.1**	**0.2**	**2.2**	**1.1**	**0.8**
Official creditors	0.0	1.4	0.6	1.9	0.5	0.1	0.2	2.2	1.1	0.8
Multilateral	0.0	0.0	0.5	1.9	0.5	0.1	0.2	2.2	1.1	0.8
Concessional	0.0	0.0	0.5	0.3	0.0	0.1	0.2	0.7	0.7	0.5
Bilateral	0.0	1.4	0.1	0.0	0.0	0.0	0.0	0.0	0.0	0.0
Concessional	0.0	0.0	0.0	0.0	0.0	0.0	0.0	0.0	0.0	0.0
Private creditors	0.0	0.3	0.0	0.0	0.0	0.0	0.0	0.0	0.0	0.0
Bonds	0.0	0.0	0.0	0.0	0.0	0.0	0.0	0.0	0.0	0.0
Commercial banks	0.0	0.0	0.0	0.0	0.0	0.0	0.0	0.0	0.0	0.0
Other private	0.0	0.3	0.0	0.0	0.0	0.0	0.0	0.0	0.0	0.0
Private nonguaranteed	**0.0**	**0.0**	**0.0**	**0.0**	**0.0**	**0.0**	**0.0**	**0.0**	**0.0**	**0.0**
Bonds	0.0	0.0	0.0	0.0	0.0	0.0	0.0	0.0	0.0	0.0
Commercial banks	0.0	0.0	0.0	0.0	0.0	0.0	0.0	0.0	0.0	0.0
Memo:										
IBRD	0.0	0.0	0.0	0.0	0.0	0.0	0.0	0.0	0.0	0.0
IDA	0.0	0.0	0.0	0.0	0.0	0.1	0.2	0.2	0.4	0.4
NET FLOWS ON DEBT	**0.0**	**17.8**	**9.4**	**12.5**	**9.1**	**3.8**	**2.0**	**-0.3**	**1.4**	**0.3**
Public and publicly guaranteed	**0.0**	**17.8**	**9.4**	**12.5**	**9.1**	**3.8**	**2.0**	**-0.3**	**1.4**	**0.3**
Official creditors	0.0	13.4	9.4	12.5	9.1	3.8	2.0	-0.3	1.4	0.3
Multilateral	0.0	1.7	3.2	12.3	9.1	3.8	2.0	-0.3	1.4	0.3
Concessional	0.0	1.0	2.6	13.9	9.6	3.8	2.0	1.3	1.9	0.6
Bilateral	0.0	11.7	6.2	0.2	0.0	0.0	0.0	0.0	0.0	0.0
Concessional	0.0	3.3	6.3	0.2	0.0	0.0	0.0	0.0	0.0	0.0
Private creditors	0.0	4.5	0.0	0.0	0.0	0.0	0.0	0.0	0.0	0.0
Bonds	0.0	0.0	0.0	0.0	0.0	0.0	0.0	0.0	0.0	0.0
Commercial banks	0.0	0.0	0.0	0.0	0.0	0.0	0.0	0.0	0.0	0.0
Other private	0.0	4.5	0.0	0.0	0.0	0.0	0.0	0.0	0.0	0.0
Private nonguaranteed	**0.0**	**0.0**	**0.0**	**0.0**	**0.0**	**0.0**	**0.0**	**0.0**	**0.0**	**0.0**
Bonds	0.0	0.0	0.0	0.0	0.0	0.0	0.0	0.0	0.0	0.0
Commercial banks	0.0	0.0	0.0	0.0	0.0	0.0	0.0	0.0	0.0	0.0
Memo:										
IBRD	0.0	0.0	0.0	0.0	0.0	0.0	0.0	0.0	0.0	0.0
IDA	0.0	0.0	2.0	2.5	4.0	2.4	2.0	0.8	0.8	-0.1

EQUATORIAL GUINEA

(US$ million, unless otherwise indicated)

	1970	1980	1990	1992	1993	1994	1995	1996	1997	1998
INTEREST PAYMENTS (LINT)	**0.0**	**0.1**	**0.5**	**1.0**	**0.6**	**0.8**	**0.4**	**1.0**	**1.0**	**0.7**
Public and publicly guaranteed	**0.0**	**0.1**	**0.5**	**1.0**	**0.6**	**0.8**	**0.4**	**1.0**	**1.0**	**0.7**
Official creditors	0.0	0.1	0.5	1.0	0.6	0.8	0.4	1.0	1.0	0.7
Multilateral	0.0	0.0	0.3	1.0	0.6	0.8	0.4	1.0	1.0	0.7
Concessional	0.0	0.0	0.3	0.4	0.3	0.5	0.4	0.8	0.7	0.5
Bilateral	0.0	0.1	0.1	0.1	0.0	0.0	0.0	0.0	0.0	0.0
Concessional	0.0	0.1	0.1	0.1	0.0	0.0	0.0	0.0	0.0	0.0
Private creditors	0.0	0.0	0.0	0.0	0.0	0.0	0.0	0.0	0.0	0.0
Bonds	0.0	0.0	0.0	0.0	0.0	0.0	0.0	0.0	0.0	0.0
Commercial banks	0.0	0.0	0.0	0.0	0.0	0.0	0.0	0.0	0.0	0.0
Other private	0.0	0.0	0.0	0.0	0.0	0.0	0.0	0.0	0.0	0.0
Private nonguaranteed	**0.0**	**0.0**	**0.0**	**0.0**	**0.0**	**0.0**	**0.0**	**0.0**	**0.0**	**0.0**
Bonds	0.0	0.0	0.0	0.0	0.0	0.0	0.0	0.0	0.0	0.0
Commercial banks	0.0	0.0	0.0	0.0	0.0	0.0	0.0	0.0	0.0	0.0
Memo:										
IBRD	0.0	0.0	0.0	0.0	0.0	0.0	0.0	0.0	0.0	0.0
IDA	0.0	0.0	0.2	0.3	0.3	0.4	0.4	0.3	0.5	0.3
NET TRANSFERS ON DEBT	**0.0**	**17.8**	**8.9**	**11.5**	**8.4**	**3.1**	**1.7**	**-1.3**	**0.4**	**-0.4**
Public and publicly guaranteed	**0.0**	**17.8**	**8.9**	**11.5**	**8.4**	**3.1**	**1.7**	**-1.3**	**0.4**	**-0.4**
Official creditors	0.0	13.3	8.9	11.5	8.4	3.1	1.7	-1.3	0.4	-0.4
Multilateral	0.0	1.7	2.9	11.3	8.4	3.1	1.7	-1.3	0.4	-0.4
Concessional	0.0	1.0	2.3	13.5	9.3	3.4	1.7	0.5	1.2	0.1
Bilateral	0.0	11.6	6.0	0.1	0.0	0.0	0.0	0.0	0.0	0.0
Concessional	0.0	3.2	6.1	0.1	0.0	0.0	0.0	0.0	0.0	0.0
Private creditors	0.0	4.4	0.0	0.0	0.0	0.0	0.0	0.0	0.0	0.0
Bonds	0.0	0.0	0.0	0.0	0.0	0.0	0.0	0.0	0.0	0.0
Commercial banks	0.0	0.0	0.0	0.0	0.0	0.0	0.0	0.0	0.0	0.0
Other private	0.0	4.4	0.0	0.0	0.0	0.0	0.0	0.0	0.0	0.0
Private nonguaranteed	**0.0**	**0.0**	**0.0**	**0.0**	**0.0**	**0.0**	**0.0**	**0.0**	**0.0**	**0.0**
Bonds	0.0	0.0	0.0	0.0	0.0	0.0	0.0	0.0	0.0	0.0
Commercial banks	0.0	0.0	0.0	0.0	0.0	0.0	0.0	0.0	0.0	0.0
Memo:										
IBRD	0.0	0.0	0.0	0.0	0.0	0.0	0.0	0.0	0.0	0.0
IDA	0.0	0.0	1.8	2.2	3.7	2.0	1.7	0.4	0.4	-0.4
DEBT SERVICE (LTDS)	**0.0**	**1.8**	**1.1**	**3.0**	**1.1**	**0.9**	**0.6**	**3.3**	**2.1**	**1.5**
Public and publicly guaranteed	**0.0**	**1.8**	**1.1**	**3.0**	**1.1**	**0.9**	**0.6**	**3.3**	**2.1**	**1.5**
Official creditors	0.0	1.5	1.1	3.0	1.1	0.9	0.6	3.3	2.1	1.5
Multilateral	0.0	0.0	0.8	2.9	1.1	0.9	0.6	3.3	2.1	1.5
Concessional	0.0	0.0	0.8	0.7	0.3	0.6	0.6	1.4	1.4	1.0
Bilateral	0.0	1.5	0.3	0.1	0.0	0.0	0.0	0.0	0.0	0.0
Concessional	0.0	0.1	0.1	0.1	0.0	0.0	0.0	0.0	0.0	0.0
Private creditors	0.0	0.4	0.0	0.0	0.0	0.0	0.0	0.0	0.0	0.0
Bonds	0.0	0.0	0.0	0.0	0.0	0.0	0.0	0.0	0.0	0.0
Commercial banks	0.0	0.0	0.0	0.0	0.0	0.0	0.0	0.0	0.0	0.0
Other private	0.0	0.4	0.0	0.0	0.0	0.0	0.0	0.0	0.0	0.0
Private nonguaranteed	**0.0**	**0.0**	**0.0**	**0.0**	**0.0**	**0.0**	**0.0**	**0.0**	**0.0**	**0.0**
Bonds	0.0	0.0	0.0	0.0	0.0	0.0	0.0	0.0	0.0	0.0
Commercial banks	0.0	0.0	0.0	0.0	0.0	0.0	0.0	0.0	0.0	0.0
Memo:										
IBRD	0.0	0.0	0.0	0.0	0.0	0.0	0.0	0.0	0.0	0.0
IDA	0.0	0.0	0.2	0.3	0.3	0.5	0.6	0.6	0.9	0.7
UNDISBURSED DEBT	**0.0**	**70.6**	**64.9**	**66.8**	**56.8**	**44.4**	**43.0**	**36.6**	**28.3**	**30.8**
Official creditors	0.0	67.6	64.9	66.8	56.8	44.4	43.0	36.6	28.3	30.8
Private creditors	0.0	3.0	0.0	0.0	0.0	0.0	0.0	0.0	0.0	0.0
Memorandum items										
Concessional LDOD	0.0	31.5	117.1	131.2	138.5	141.2	147.3	144.4	138.1	143.4
Variable rate LDOD	0.0	0.0	5.1	5.0	4.9	4.2	4.2	4.2	4.1	4.1
Public sector LDOD	5.0	46.9	209.2	214.4	214.8	219.3	229.6	222.2	208.6	216.5
Private sector LDOD	0.0	5.6	0.0	0.0	0.0	0.0	0.0	0.0	0.0	0.0
6. CURRENCY COMPOSITION OF LONG-TERM DEBT (PERCENT)										
Deutsche mark	0.0	0.0	5.9	5.4	5.0	5.5	5.7	5.4	5.0	5.1
French franc	0.0	0.0	7.0	7.5	7.0	7.6	7.9	7.6	7.1	7.3
Japanese yen	0.0	0.0	0.0	0.0	0.0	0.0	0.0	0.0	0.0	0.0
Pound sterling	0.0	0.0	0.0	0.0	0.0	0.0	0.0	0.0	0.0	0.0
Swiss franc	0.0	0.0	0.0	0.0	0.0	0.0	0.0	0.0	0.0	0.0
U.S.dollars	0.0	16.4	37.9	38.1	39.8	41.1	40.7	41.6	43.3	42.5
Multiple currency	0.0	0.0	5.6	11.0	13.8	15.0	14.6	15.0	15.3	15.6
Special drawing rights	0.0	0.0	0.0	0.0	0.0	0.0	0.0	0.0	0.0	0.0
All other currencies	0.0	83.6	43.6	38.0	34.4	30.8	31.1	30.4	29.3	29.5

EQUATORIAL GUINEA

(US$ million, unless otherwise indicated)

	1970	1980	1990	1992	1993	1994	1995	1996	1997	1998
7. DEBT RESTRUCTURINGS										
Total amount rescheduled	..	..	0.0	0.0	0.0	0.0	0.0	0.0	0.0	0.0
Debt stock rescheduled	..	..	0.0	0.0	0.0	0.0	0.0	0.0	0.0	0.0
Principal rescheduled	..	..	0.0	0.0	0.0	0.0	0.0	0.0	0.0	0.0
Official	..	..	0.0	0.0	0.0	0.0	0.0	0.0	0.0	0.0
Private	..	..	0.0	0.0	0.0	0.0	0.0	0.0	0.0	0.0
Interest rescheduled	..	..	0.0	0.0	0.0	0.0	0.0	0.0	0.0	0.0
Official	..	..	0.0	0.0	0.0	0.0	0.0	0.0	0.0	0.0
Private	..	..	0.0	0.0	0.0	0.0	0.0	0.0	0.0	0.0
Debt forgiven	..	..	18.5	0.0	0.0	0.0	0.0	0.0	0.0	0.0
Memo: interest forgiven	..	..	0.0	0.0	0.0	0.0	0.0	0.0	0.0	0.0
Debt stock reduction	..	..	0.0	0.0	0.0	0.0	0.0	0.0	0.0	0.0
of which debt buyback	..	..	0.0	0.0	0.0	0.0	0.0	0.0	0.0	0.0
8. DEBT STOCK-FLOW RECONCILIATION										
Total change in debt stocks	..	..	12.0	1.5	8.8	23.5	4.3	-9.4	0.7	22.9
Net flows on debt	0.0	40.9	9.8	12.5	12.9	16.7	-8.1	0.0	18.9	12.4
Net change in interest arrears	..	..	7.2	3.2	4.6	5.0	3.7	-1.7	-2.2	2.4
Interest capitalized	..	..	0.0	0.0	0.0	0.0	0.0	0.0	0.0	0.0
Debt forgiveness or reduction	..	..	-18.5	0.0	0.0	0.0	0.0	0.0	0.0	0.0
Cross-currency valuation	..	..	11.8	-8.8	-7.7	4.8	6.7	-5.0	-8.5	4.6
Residual	..	..	1.7	-5.3	-1.0	-3.0	1.9	-2.7	-7.5	3.6
9. AVERAGE TERMS OF NEW COMMITMENTS										
ALL CREDITORS										
Interest (%)	0.0	6.5	0.9	0.8	0.7	0.7	0.0	0.0	0.0	0.0
Maturity (years)	0.0	14.2	38.2	45.9	49.8	49.7	0.0	0.0	0.0	49.7
Grace period (years)	0.0	3.4	10.1	10.3	10.3	10.2	0.0	0.0	0.0	10.2
Grant element (%)	0.0	21.0	77.5	82.2	83.3	83.1	0.0	0.0	0.0	90.0
Official creditors										
Interest (%)	0.0	6.5	0.9	0.8	0.7	0.7	0.0	0.0	0.0	0.0
Maturity (years)	0.0	14.2	38.2	45.9	49.8	49.7	0.0	0.0	0.0	49.7
Grace period (years)	0.0	3.4	10.1	10.3	10.3	10.2	0.0	0.0	0.0	10.2
Grant element (%)	0.0	21.0	77.5	82.2	83.3	83.1	0.0	0.0	0.0	90.0
Private creditors										
Interest (%)	0.0	0.0	0.0	0.0	0.0	0.0	0.0	0.0	0.0	0.0
Maturity (years)	0.0	0.0	0.0	0.0	0.0	0.0	0.0	0.0	0.0	0.0
Grace period (years)	0.0	0.0	0.0	0.0	0.0	0.0	0.0	0.0	0.0	0.0
Grant element (%)	0.0	0.0	0.0	0.0	0.0	0.0	0.0	0.0	0.0	0.0
Memorandum items										
Commitments	0.0	27.2	18.1	19.6	9.0	6.6	0.0	0.0	0.0	2.7
Official creditors	0.0	27.2	18.1	19.6	9.0	6.6	0.0	0.0	0.0	2.7
Private creditors	0.0	0.0	0.0	0.0	0.0	0.0	0.0	0.0	0.0	0.0

10. CONTRACTUAL OBLIGATIONS ON OUTSTANDING LONG-TERM DEBT

	1999	2000	2001	2002	2003	2004	2005	2006	2007	2008
TOTAL										
Disbursements	7.6	7.2	5.3	4.1	3.1	1.4	0.8	0.6	0.4	0.2
Principal	6.4	5.3	5.5	6.0	5.3	5.1	4.5	4.6	4.9	5.0
Interest	1.7	1.5	1.4	1.2	1.1	1.0	0.9	0.9	0.8	0.8
Official creditors										
Disbursements	7.6	7.2	5.3	4.1	3.1	1.4	0.8	0.6	0.4	0.2
Principal	6.4	5.3	5.5	6.0	5.3	5.1	4.5	4.6	4.9	5.0
Interest	1.7	1.5	1.4	1.2	1.1	1.0	0.9	0.9	0.8	0.8
Bilateral creditors										
Disbursements	1.4	2.1	1.6	1.3	1.0	0.7	0.5	0.5	0.4	0.2
Principal	4.6	3.5	3.7	4.0	2.8	2.5	1.8	1.7	1.7	1.6
Interest	0.7	0.6	0.4	0.3	0.2	0.2	0.2	0.1	0.1	0.1
Multilateral creditors										
Disbursements	6.2	5.1	3.7	2.9	2.1	0.7	0.3	0.1	0.0	0.0
Principal	1.9	1.8	1.8	2.0	2.5	2.6	2.7	2.8	3.1	3.4
Interest	0.9	0.9	0.9	0.9	0.8	0.8	0.8	0.7	0.7	0.7
Private creditors										
Disbursements	0.0	0.0	0.0	0.0	0.0	0.0	0.0	0.0	0.0	0.0
Principal	0.0	0.0	0.0	0.0	0.0	0.0	0.0	0.0	0.0	0.0
Interest	0.0	0.0	0.0	0.0	0.0	0.0	0.0	0.0	0.0	0.0
Commercial banks										
Disbursements	0.0	0.0	0.0	0.0	0.0	0.0	0.0	0.0	0.0	0.0
Principal	0.0	0.0	0.0	0.0	0.0	0.0	0.0	0.0	0.0	0.0
Interest	0.0	0.0	0.0	0.0	0.0	0.0	0.0	0.0	0.0	0.0
Other private										
Disbursements	0.0	0.0	0.0	0.0	0.0	0.0	0.0	0.0	0.0	0.0
Principal	0.0	0.0	0.0	0.0	0.0	0.0	0.0	0.0	0.0	0.0
Interest	0.0	0.0	0.0	0.0	0.0	0.0	0.0	0.0	0.0	0.0

ERITREA

(US$ million, unless otherwise indicated)

	1970	*1980*	*1990*	*1992*	*1993*	*1994*	*1995*	*1996*	*1997*	*1998*
1. SUMMARY DEBT DATA										
TOTAL DEBT STOCKS (EDT)	..	..	..	..	..	**29.1**	**36.7**	**44.3**	**75.5**	**149.3**
Long-term debt (LDOD)	..	..	..	..	..	**29.1**	**36.7**	**44.3**	**75.5**	**144.1**
Public and publicly guaranteed	..	..	..	..	..	29.1	36.7	44.3	75.5	144.1
Private nonguaranteed	..	..	..	..	..	0.0	0.0	0.0	0.0	0.0
Use of IMF credit	..	..	..	..	..	**0.0**	**0.0**	**0.0**	**0.0**	**0.0**
Short-term debt	..	..	..	..	..	**0.0**	**0.0**	**0.0**	**0.0**	**5.2**
of which interest arrears on LDOD	..	..	..	..	..	0.0	0.0	0.0	0.0	0.0
Official creditors	..	..	..	..	..	0.0	0.0	0.0	0.0	0.0
Private creditors	..	..	..	..	..	0.0	0.0	0.0	0.0	0.0
Memo: principal arrears on LDOD	..	..	..	..	..	0.0	0.0	0.0	0.0	0.0
Official creditors	..	..	..	..	..	0.0	0.0	0.0	0.0	0.0
Private creditors	..	..	..	..	..	0.0	0.0	0.0	0.0	0.0
Memo: export credits	..	..	..	..	..	1.0	2.0	1.0	0.0	0.0
TOTAL DEBT FLOWS										
Disbursements	..	..	..	..	..	**26.6**	**7.2**	**6.9**	**33.3**	**65.3**
Long-term debt	..	..	..	..	..	26.6	7.2	6.9	33.3	65.3
IMF purchases	..	..	..	..	..	0.0	0.0	0.0	0.0	0.0
Principal repayments	..	..	..	..	..	**0.0**	**0.0**	**0.0**	**0.0**	**0.0**
Long-term debt	..	..	..	..	..	0.0	0.0	0.0	0.0	0.0
IMF repurchases	..	..	..	..	..	0.0	0.0	0.0	0.0	0.0
Net flows on debt	..	..	..	..	..	**26.6**	**7.2**	**6.9**	**33.3**	**70.5**
of which short-term debt	..	..	..	..	..	0.0	0.0	0.0	0.0	5.2
Interest payments (INT)	..	..	..	..	..	**0.0**	**0.2**	**0.0**	**0.5**	**3.8**
Long-term debt	..	..	..	..	..	0.0	0.2	0.0	0.5	3.6
IMF charges	..	..	..	..	..	0.0	0.0	0.0	0.0	0.0
Short-term debt	..	..	..	..	..	0.0	0.0	0.0	0.0	0.1
Net transfers on debt	..	..	..	..	..	**26.6**	**7.1**	**6.9**	**32.8**	**66.7**
Total debt service paid (TDS)	..	..	..	..	..	**0.0**	**0.2**	**0.0**	**0.5**	**3.8**
Long-term debt	..	..	..	..	..	0.0	0.2	0.0	0.5	3.6
IMF repurchases and charges	..	..	..	..	..	0.0	0.0	0.0	0.0	0.0
Short-term debt (interest only)	..	..	..	..	..	0.0	0.0	0.0	0.0	0.1

	1970	*1980*	*1990*	*1992*	*1993*	*1994*	*1995*	*1996*	*1997*	*1998*
2. AGGREGATE NET RESOURCE FLOWS AND NET TRANSFERS (LONG-TERM)										
NET RESOURCE FLOWS	..	..	..	..	..	**140.3**	**110.3**	**96.3**	**93.3**	**139.2**
Net flow of long-term debt (ex. IMF)	..	..	..	..	..	26.6	7.2	6.9	33.3	65.3
Foreign direct investment (net)	..	..	..	..	..	0.0	0.0	0.0	0.0	0.0
Portfolio equity flows	..	..	..	..	..	0.0	0.0	0.0	0.0	0.0
Grants (excluding technical coop.)	..	..	..	..	..	113.7	103.1	89.4	60.0	73.9
Memo: technical coop. grants	..	..	..	..	..	31.7	42.7	62.3	36.5	30.6
official net resource flows	..	..	..	..	..	140.3	110.3	96.3	93.3	139.2
private net resource flows	..	..	..	..	..	0.0	0.0	0.0	0.0	0.0
NET TRANSFERS	..	..	..	..	..	**140.3**	**110.1**	**96.3**	**92.8**	**135.6**
Interest on long-term debt	..	..	..	..	..	0.0	0.2	0.0	0.5	3.6
Profit remittances on FDI	..	..	..	..	..	0.0	0.0	0.0	0.0	0.0
Memo: official net transfers	..	..	..	..	..	140.3	110.1	96.3	92.8	135.6
private net transfers	..	..	..	..	..	0.0	0.0	0.0	0.0	0.0

	1970	*1980*	*1990*	*1992*	*1993*	*1994*	*1995*	*1996*	*1997*	*1998*
3. MAJOR ECONOMIC AGGREGATES										
Gross national product (GNP)	..	..	..	..	..	664.7	688.8	760.7	829.9	767.6
Exports of goods & services (XGS)	..	..	..	..	..	310.7	298.1	344.5	394.6	261.4
of which workers remittances	..	..	..	..	..	166.4	119.0	136.1	183.1	119.7
Imports of goods & services (MGS)	..	..	..	..	..	402.8	447.7	583.0	596.4	595.3
International reserves (RES)	..	..	..	..	..	..	..	..	..	..
Current account balance	..	..	..	..	..	61.6	-31.2	-103.8	-21.1	-216.4

	1970	*1980*	*1990*	*1992*	*1993*	*1994*	*1995*	*1996*	*1997*	*1998*
4. DEBT INDICATORS										
EDT / XGS (%)	..	..	..	..	..	9.4	12.3	12.9	19.1	57.1
EDT / GNP (%)	..	..	..	..	..	4.4	5.3	5.8	9.1	19.5
TDS / XGS (%)	..	..	..	..	..	0.0	0.1	0.0	0.1	1.5
INT / XGS (%)	..	..	..	..	..	0.0	0.1	0.0	0.1	1.5
INT / GNP (%)	..	..	..	..	..	0.0	0.0	0.0	0.1	0.5
RES / EDT (%)	..	..	..	..	..	..	..	..	..	..
RES / MGS (months)	..	..	..	..	..	..	..	..	..	..
Short-term / EDT (%)	..	..	..	..	..	0.0	0.0	0.0	0.0	3.5
Concessional / EDT (%)	..	..	..	..	..	100.0	100.0	95.5	96.0	93.4
Multilateral / EDT (%)	..	..	..	..	..	63.9	66.2	66.6	55.4	51.0

ERITREA

(US$ million, unless otherwise indicated)

	1970	1980	1990	1992	1993	1994	1995	1996	1997	1998
5. LONG-TERM DEBT										
DEBT OUTSTANDING (LDOD)	..	..	..	..	..	**29.1**	**36.7**	**44.3**	**75.5**	**144.1**
Public and publicly guaranteed	..	..	..	..	..	**29.1**	**36.7**	**44.3**	**75.5**	**144.1**
Official creditors	..	..	..	..	..	29.1	36.7	44.3	75.5	144.1
Multilateral	..	..	..	..	..	18.6	24.3	29.5	41.8	76.1
Concessional	..	..	..	..	..	18.6	24.3	27.5	38.9	71.5
Bilateral	..	..	..	..	..	10.5	12.4	14.8	33.6	68.0
Concessional	..	..	..	..	..	10.5	12.4	14.8	33.6	68.0
Private creditors	..	..	..	..	..	0.0	0.0	0.0	0.0	0.0
Bonds	..	..	..	..	..	0.0	0.0	0.0	0.0	0.0
Commercial banks	..	..	..	..	..	0.0	0.0	0.0	0.0	0.0
Other private	..	..	..	..	..	0.0	0.0	0.0	0.0	0.0
Private nonguaranteed	..	..	..	..	..	**0.0**	**0.0**	**0.0**	**0.0**	**0.0**
Bonds	..	..	..	..	..	0.0	0.0	0.0	0.0	0.0
Commercial banks	..	..	..	..	..	0.0	0.0	0.0	0.0	0.0
Memo:										
IBRD	..	..	..	..	..	0.0	0.0	0.0	0.0	0.0
IDA	..	..	..	..	..	18.6	24.3	26.5	28.8	36.9
DISBURSEMENTS	..	..	..	..	..	**26.6**	**7.2**	**6.9**	**33.3**	**65.3**
Public and publicly guaranteed	..	..	..	..	..	**26.6**	**7.2**	**6.9**	**33.3**	**65.3**
Official creditors	..	..	..	..	..	26.6	7.2	6.9	33.3	65.3
Multilateral	..	..	..	..	..	16.0	5.4	4.5	14.2	31.3
Concessional	..	..	..	..	..	16.0	5.4	2.5	12.9	29.9
Bilateral	..	..	..	..	..	10.6	1.8	2.4	19.1	34.0
Concessional	..	..	..	..	..	10.6	1.8	2.4	19.1	34.0
Private creditors	..	..	..	..	..	0.0	0.0	0.0	0.0	0.0
Bonds	..	..	..	..	..	0.0	0.0	0.0	0.0	0.0
Commercial banks	..	..	..	..	..	0.0	0.0	0.0	0.0	0.0
Other private	..	..	..	..	..	0.0	0.0	0.0	0.0	0.0
Private nonguaranteed	..	..	..	..	..	**0.0**	**0.0**	**0.0**	**0.0**	**0.0**
Bonds	..	..	..	..	..	0.0	0.0	0.0	0.0	0.0
Commercial banks	..	..	..	..	..	0.0	0.0	0.0	0.0	0.0
Memo:										
IBRD	..	..	..	..	..	0.0	0.0	0.0	0.0	0.0
IDA	..	..	..	..	..	16.0	5.4	1.5	3.8	6.3
PRINCIPAL REPAYMENTS	..	..	..	..	..	**0.0**	**0.0**	**0.0**	**0.0**	**0.0**
Public and publicly guaranteed	..	..	..	..	..	**0.0**	**0.0**	**0.0**	**0.0**	**0.0**
Official creditors	..	..	..	..	..	0.0	0.0	0.0	0.0	0.0
Multilateral	..	..	..	..	..	0.0	0.0	0.0	0.0	0.0
Concessional	..	..	..	..	..	0.0	0.0	0.0	0.0	0.0
Bilateral	..	..	..	..	..	0.0	0.0	0.0	0.0	0.0
Concessional	..	..	..	..	..	0.0	0.0	0.0	0.0	0.0
Private creditors	..	..	..	..	..	0.0	0.0	0.0	0.0	0.0
Bonds	..	..	..	..	..	0.0	0.0	0.0	0.0	0.0
Commercial banks	..	..	..	..	..	0.0	0.0	0.0	0.0	0.0
Other private	..	..	..	..	..	0.0	0.0	0.0	0.0	0.0
Private nonguaranteed	..	..	..	..	..	**0.0**	**0.0**	**0.0**	**0.0**	**0.0**
Bonds	..	..	..	..	..	0.0	0.0	0.0	0.0	0.0
Commercial banks	..	..	..	..	..	0.0	0.0	0.0	0.0	0.0
Memo:										
IBRD	..	..	..	..	..	0.0	0.0	0.0	0.0	0.0
IDA	..	..	..	..	..	0.0	0.0	0.0	0.0	0.0
NET FLOWS ON DEBT	..	..	..	..	..	**26.6**	**7.2**	**6.9**	**33.3**	**65.3**
Public and publicly guaranteed	..	..	..	..	..	**26.6**	**7.2**	**6.9**	**33.3**	**65.3**
Official creditors	..	..	..	..	..	26.6	7.2	6.9	33.3	65.3
Multilateral	..	..	..	..	..	16.0	5.4	4.5	14.2	31.3
Concessional	..	..	..	..	..	16.0	5.4	2.5	12.9	29.9
Bilateral	..	..	..	..	..	10.6	1.8	2.4	19.1	34.0
Concessional	..	..	..	..	..	10.6	1.8	2.4	19.1	34.0
Private creditors	..	..	..	..	..	0.0	0.0	0.0	0.0	0.0
Bonds	..	..	..	..	..	0.0	0.0	0.0	0.0	0.0
Commercial banks	..	..	..	..	..	0.0	0.0	0.0	0.0	0.0
Other private	..	..	..	..	..	0.0	0.0	0.0	0.0	0.0
Private nonguaranteed	..	..	..	..	..	**0.0**	**0.0**	**0.0**	**0.0**	**0.0**
Bonds	..	..	..	..	..	0.0	0.0	0.0	0.0	0.0
Commercial banks	..	..	..	..	..	0.0	0.0	0.0	0.0	0.0
Memo:										
IBRD	..	..	..	..	..	0.0	0.0	0.0	0.0	0.0
IDA	..	..	..	..	..	16.0	5.4	1.5	3.8	6.3

ERITREA

(US$ million, unless otherwise indicated)

	1970	1980	1990	1992	1993	1994	1995	1996	1997	1998
INTEREST PAYMENTS (LINT)	..	..	..	..	..	**0.0**	**0.2**	**0.0**	**0.5**	**3.6**
Public and publicly guaranteed	..	..	..	..	..	**0.0**	**0.2**	**0.0**	**0.5**	**3.6**
Official creditors	..	..	..	..	..	0.0	0.2	0.0	0.5	3.6
Multilateral	..	..	..	..	..	0.0	0.2	0.0	0.3	0.6
Concessional	..	..	..	..	..	0.0	0.2	0.0	0.2	0.6
Bilateral	..	..	..	..	..	0.0	0.0	0.0	0.2	3.0
Concessional	..	..	..	..	..	0.0	0.0	0.0	0.2	3.0
Private creditors	..	..	..	..	..	0.0	0.0	0.0	0.0	0.0
Bonds	..	..	..	..	..	0.0	0.0	0.0	0.0	0.0
Commercial banks	..	..	..	..	..	0.0	0.0	0.0	0.0	0.0
Other private	..	..	..	..	..	0.0	0.0	0.0	0.0	0.0
Private nonguaranteed	..	..	..	..	..	**0.0**	**0.0**	**0.0**	**0.0**	**0.0**
Bonds	..	..	..	..	..	0.0	0.0	0.0	0.0	0.0
Commercial banks	..	..	..	..	..	0.0	0.0	0.0	0.0	0.0
Memo:										
IBRD	..	..	..	..	..	0.0	0.0	0.0	0.0	0.0
IDA	..	..	..	..	..	0.0	0.2	0.0	0.2	0.2
NET TRANSFERS ON DEBT	..	..	..	..	..	**26.6**	**7.1**	**6.9**	**32.8**	**61.7**
Public and publicly guaranteed	..	..	..	..	..	**26.6**	**7.1**	**6.9**	**32.8**	**61.7**
Official creditors	..	..	..	..	..	26.6	7.1	6.9	32.8	61.7
Multilateral	..	..	..	..	..	16.0	5.2	4.5	13.9	30.7
Concessional	..	..	..	..	..	16.0	5.2	2.5	12.7	29.3
Bilateral	..	..	..	..	..	10.6	1.8	2.4	18.9	31.0
Concessional	..	..	..	..	..	10.6	1.8	2.4	18.9	31.0
Private creditors	..	..	..	..	..	0.0	0.0	0.0	0.0	0.0
Bonds	..	..	..	..	..	0.0	0.0	0.0	0.0	0.0
Commercial banks	..	..	..	..	..	0.0	0.0	0.0	0.0	0.0
Other private	..	..	..	..	..	0.0	0.0	0.0	0.0	0.0
Private nonguaranteed	..	..	..	..	..	**0.0**	**0.0**	**0.0**	**0.0**	**0.0**
Bonds	..	..	..	..	..	0.0	0.0	0.0	0.0	0.0
Commercial banks	..	..	..	..	..	0.0	0.0	0.0	0.0	0.0
Memo:										
IBRD	..	..	..	..	..	0.0	0.0	0.0	0.0	0.0
IDA	..	..	..	..	..	16.0	5.2	1.5	3.6	6.1
DEBT SERVICE (LTDS)	..	..	..	..	..	**0.0**	**0.2**	**0.0**	**0.5**	**3.6**
Public and publicly guaranteed	..	..	..	..	..	**0.0**	**0.2**	**0.0**	**0.5**	**3.6**
Official creditors	..	..	..	..	..	0.0	0.2	0.0	0.5	3.6
Multilateral	..	..	..	..	..	0.0	0.2	0.0	0.3	0.6
Concessional	..	..	..	..	..	0.0	0.2	0.0	0.2	0.6
Bilateral	..	..	..	..	..	0.0	0.0	0.0	0.2	3.0
Concessional	..	..	..	..	..	0.0	0.0	0.0	0.2	3.0
Private creditors	..	..	..	..	..	0.0	0.0	0.0	0.0	0.0
Bonds	..	..	..	..	..	0.0	0.0	0.0	0.0	0.0
Commercial banks	..	..	..	..	..	0.0	0.0	0.0	0.0	0.0
Other private	..	..	..	..	..	0.0	0.0	0.0	0.0	0.0
Private nonguaranteed	..	..	..	..	..	**0.0**	**0.0**	**0.0**	**0.0**	**0.0**
Bonds	..	..	..	..	..	0.0	0.0	0.0	0.0	0.0
Commercial banks	..	..	..	..	..	0.0	0.0	0.0	0.0	0.0
Memo:										
IBRD	..	..	..	..	..	0.0	0.0	0.0	0.0	0.0
IDA	..	..	..	..	..	0.0	0.2	0.0	0.2	0.2
UNDISBURSED DEBT	..	..	..	..	..	**29.6**	**133.7**	**154.0**	**277.6**	**301.5**
Official creditors	..	..	..	..	..	29.6	133.7	154.0	277.6	301.5
Private creditors	..	..	..	..	..	0.0	0.0	0.0	0.0	0.0
Memorandum items										
Concessional LDOD	..	..	..	..	..	29.1	36.7	42.3	72.5	139.5
Variable rate LDOD	..	..	..	..	..	0.0	0.0	0.0	0.0	0.0
Public sector LDOD	..	..	..	..	..	29.1	36.7	44.3	75.5	144.1
Private sector LDOD	..	..	..	..	..	0.0	0.0	0.0	0.0	0.0

6. CURRENCY COMPOSITION OF LONG-TERM DEBT (PERCENT)

	1970	1980	1990	1992	1993	1994	1995	1996	1997	1998
Deutsche mark	..	..	..	..	..	0.0	0.0	0.0	0.0	0.0
French franc	..	..	..	..	..	0.0	0.0	0.0	0.0	0.0
Japanese yen	..	..	..	..	..	0.0	0.0	0.0	0.0	0.0
Pound sterling	..	..	..	..	..	0.0	0.0	0.0	0.0	0.0
Swiss franc	..	..	..	..	..	0.0	0.0	0.0	0.0	0.0
U.S.dollars	..	..	..	..	..	64.0	66.2	59.8	48.9	45.0
Multiple currency	..	..	..	..	..	0.0	0.0	0.0	0.0	0.0
Special drawing rights	..	..	..	..	..	0.0	0.0	1.6	1.6	1.5
All other currencies	..	..	..	..	..	36.0	33.8	38.6	49.5	53.5

ERITREA

(US$ million, unless otherwise indicated)

	1970	1980	1990	1992	1993	1994	1995	1996	1997	1998
7. DEBT RESTRUCTURINGS										
Total amount rescheduled	..	..	..	..	..	0.0	0.0	0.0	0.0	0.0
Debt stock rescheduled	..	..	..	..	..	0.0	0.0	0.0	0.0	0.0
Principal rescheduled	..	..	..	..	..	0.0	0.0	0.0	0.0	0.0
Official	..	..	..	..	..	0.0	0.0	0.0	0.0	0.0
Private	..	..	..	..	..	0.0	0.0	0.0	0.0	0.0
Interest rescheduled	..	..	..	..	..	..	0.0	0.0	0.0	0.0
Official	..	..	..	..	..	0.0	0.0	0.0	0.0	0.0
Private	..	..	..	..	..	0.0	0.0	0.0	0.0	0.0
Debt forgiven	..	..	..	..	..	0.0	0.0	0.0	0.0	0.0
Memo: interest forgiven	..	..	..	..	..	0.0	0.0	0.0	0.0	0.0
Debt stock reduction	..	..	..	..	..	0.0	0.0	0.0	0.0	0.0
of which debt buyback	..	..	..	..	..	0.0	0.0	0.0	0.0	0.0
8. DEBT STOCK-FLOW RECONCILIATION										
Total change in debt stocks	..	..	..	..	..	..	7.6	7.6	31.2	73.9
Net flows on debt	..	..	..	..	..	26.6	7.2	6.9	33.3	70.5
Net change in interest arrears	..	..	..	..	..	..	0.0	0.0	0.0	0.0
Interest capitalized	..	..	..	..	..	..	0.0	0.0	0.0	0.0
Debt forgiveness or reduction	..	..	..	..	..	..	0.0	0.0	0.0	0.0
Cross-currency valuation	..	..	..	..	..	..	0.0	-0.2	-0.8	1.1
Residual	..	..	..	..	..	..	0.4	0.9	-1.4	2.3
9. AVERAGE TERMS OF NEW COMMITMENTS										
ALL CREDITORS										
Interest (%)	..	..	..	..	..	1.2	2.0	1.0	1.2	0.9
Maturity (years)	..	..	..	..	..	26.6	23.9	38.7	37.3	36.1
Grace period (years)	..	..	..	..	..	6.1	5.6	9.5	10.9	8.1
Grant element (%)	..	..	..	..	..	65.9	56.6	76.3	75.0	75.7
Official creditors										
Interest (%)	..	..	..	..	..	1.2	2.0	1.0	1.2	0.9
Maturity (years)	..	..	..	..	..	26.6	23.9	38.7	37.3	36.1
Grace period (years)	..	..	..	..	..	6.1	5.6	9.5	10.9	8.1
Grant element (%)	..	..	..	..	..	65.9	56.6	76.3	75.0	75.7
Private creditors										
Interest (%)	..	..	..	..	..	0.0	0.0	0.0	0.0	0.0
Maturity (years)	..	..	..	..	..	0.0	0.0	0.0	0.0	0.0
Grace period (years)	..	..	..	..	..	0.0	0.0	0.0	0.0	0.0
Grant element (%)	..	..	..	..	..	0.0	0.0	0.0	0.0	0.0
Memorandum items										
Commitments	..	..	..	..	..	29.8	110.5	30.5	159.6	83.0
Official creditors	..	..	..	..	..	29.8	110.5	30.5	159.6	83.0
Private creditors	..	..	..	..	..	0.0	0.0	0.0	0.0	0.0

10. CONTRACTUAL OBLIGATIONS ON OUTSTANDING LONG-TERM DEBT

	1999	2000	2001	2002	2003	2004	2005	2006	2007	2008
TOTAL										
Disbursements	70.4	76.8	58.6	42.6	28.2	15.1	8.7	1.1	0.1	0.0
Principal	1.0	5.9	7.8	9.7	10.8	11.6	12.5	12.9	13.6	15.2
Interest	2.3	3.9	4.7	5.0	5.0	4.9	4.8	4.6	4.3	4.0
Official creditors										
Disbursements	70.4	76.8	58.6	42.6	28.2	15.1	8.7	1.1	0.1	0.0
Principal	1.0	5.9	7.8	9.7	10.8	11.6	12.5	12.9	13.6	15.2
Interest	2.3	3.9	4.7	5.0	5.0	4.9	4.8	4.6	4.3	4.0
Bilateral creditors										
Disbursements	32.6	25.8	16.7	10.0	5.6	2.3	1.1	0.5	0.1	0.0
Principal	1.0	3.2	4.4	5.5	5.6	6.2	6.6	6.8	7.0	7.0
Interest	1.1	1.8	2.3	2.4	2.4	2.3	2.2	2.1	1.9	1.8
Multilateral creditors										
Disbursements	37.8	51.1	41.8	32.6	22.6	12.8	7.6	0.6	0.0	0.0
Principal	0.0	2.8	3.4	4.3	5.2	5.5	5.9	6.1	6.6	8.2
Interest	1.2	2.0	2.4	2.6	2.6	2.6	2.6	2.5	2.3	2.2
Private creditors										
Disbursements	0.0	0.0	0.0	0.0	0.0	0.0	0.0	0.0	0.0	0.0
Principal	0.0	0.0	0.0	0.0	0.0	0.0	0.0	0.0	0.0	0.0
Interest	0.0	0.0	0.0	0.0	0.0	0.0	0.0	0.0	0.0	0.0
Commercial banks										
Disbursements	0.0	0.0	0.0	0.0	0.0	0.0	0.0	0.0	0.0	0.0
Principal	0.0	0.0	0.0	0.0	0.0	0.0	0.0	0.0	0.0	0.0
Interest	0.0	0.0	0.0	0.0	0.0	0.0	0.0	0.0	0.0	0.0
Other private										
Disbursements	0.0	0.0	0.0	0.0	0.0	0.0	0.0	0.0	0.0	0.0
Principal	0.0	0.0	0.0	0.0	0.0	0.0	0.0	0.0	0.0	0.0
Interest	0.0	0.0	0.0	0.0	0.0	0.0	0.0	0.0	0.0	0.0

ESTONIA

(US$ million, unless otherwise indicated)

	1970	1980	1990	1992	1993	1994	1995	1996	1997	1998
1. SUMMARY DEBT DATA										
TOTAL DEBT STOCKS (EDT)	..	..	..	**58.4**	**153.9**	**186.0**	**286.4**	**405.3**	**642.4**	**781.7**
Long-term debt (LDOD)	..	..	..	**47.8**	**96.1**	**117.0**	**164.9**	**220.3**	**280.4**	**443.7**
Public and publicly guaranteed	..	..	..	33.8	84.9	108.6	159.3	216.5	197.5	231.3
Private nonguaranteed	..	..	..	14.0	11.2	8.4	5.6	3.8	82.9	212.3
Use of IMF credit	..	..	..	**10.7**	**57.5**	**61.1**	**91.9**	**77.9**	**54.0**	**30.0**
Short-term debt	..	..	..	**0.0**	**0.3**	**8.0**	**29.7**	**107.0**	**308.0**	**308.0**
of which interest arrears on LDOD	..	..	..	0.0	0.0	0.0	0.0	0.0	0.0	0.0
Official creditors	..	..	..	0.0	0.0	0.0	0.0	0.0	0.0	0.0
Private creditors	..	..	..	0.0	0.0	0.0	0.0	0.0	0.0	0.0
Memo: principal arrears on LDOD	..	..	..	0.0	0.0	0.0	0.0	0.0	1.0	1.0
Official creditors	..	..	..	0.0	0.0	0.0	0.0	0.0	0.0	0.0
Private creditors	..	..	..	0.0	0.0	0.0	0.0	0.0	1.0	1.0
Memo: export credits	..	..	..	0.0	23.0	47.0	73.0	83.0	86.0	93.0
TOTAL DEBT FLOWS										
Disbursements	..	..	..	**46.9**	**110.2**	**31.1**	**81.1**	**100.4**	**98.9**	**113.2**
Long-term debt	..	..	..	35.9	62.5	31.1	49.4	100.4	98.9	113.2
IMF purchases	..	..	..	10.9	47.6	0.0	31.7	0.0	0.0	0.0
Principal repayments	..	..	..	**2.5**	**12.7**	**15.6**	**6.8**	**24.2**	**43.1**	**49.5**
Long-term debt	..	..	..	2.5	12.7	15.6	5.3	13.1	23.6	24.1
IMF repurchases	..	..	..	0.0	0.0	0.0	1.5	11.1	19.5	25.4
Net flows on debt	..	..	..	**44.3**	**97.8**	**23.2**	**96.0**	**153.5**	**256.9**	**63.8**
of which short-term debt	..	..	..	0.0	0.3	7.7	21.7	77.4	201.0	0.0
Interest payments (INT)	..	..	..	**1.3**	**5.7**	**10.8**	**14.5**	**18.7**	**27.1**	**39.0**
Long-term debt	..	..	..	1.2	4.6	7.2	8.6	10.0	12.5	22.3
IMF charges	..	..	..	0.1	1.1	3.1	4.7	3.9	3.1	2.3
Short-term debt	..	..	..	0.0	0.0	0.5	1.1	4.8	11.4	14.4
Net transfers on debt	..	..	..	**43.1**	**92.0**	**12.4**	**81.6**	**134.8**	**229.8**	**24.8**
Total debt service paid (TDS)	..	..	..	**3.8**	**18.4**	**26.4**	**21.3**	**43.0**	**70.1**	**88.5**
Long-term debt	..	..	..	3.7	17.3	22.8	13.9	23.2	36.1	46.4
IMF repurchases and charges	..	..	..	0.1	1.1	3.1	6.2	15.0	22.6	27.6
Short-term debt (interest only)	..	..	..	0.0	0.0	0.5	1.1	4.8	11.4	14.4
2. AGGREGATE NET RESOURCE FLOWS AND NET TRANSFERS (LONG-TERM)										
NET RESOURCE FLOWS	..	..	..	**186.4**	**237.2**	**257.6**	**272.2**	**278.2**	**389.0**	**780.5**
Net flow of long-term debt (ex. IMF)	..	..	..	33.4	49.8	15.5	44.0	87.3	75.4	89.1
Foreign direct investment (net)	..	..	..	82.0	162.2	214.4	201.5	150.2	266.2	581.0
Portfolio equity flows	..	..	..	0.0	0.0	9.8	7.0	5.0	1.3	52.9
Grants (excluding technical coop.)	..	..	..	71.0	25.1	17.9	19.7	35.7	46.2	57.5
Memo: technical coop. grants	..	..	..	23.3	17.3	22.6	36.9	23.4	19.8	18.5
official net resource flows	..	..	..	82.0	74.8	46.1	64.9	87.5	53.0	66.5
private net resource flows	..	..	..	104.4	162.4	211.5	207.3	190.7	336.0	714.0
NET TRANSFERS	..	..	..	**185.3**	**232.6**	**250.3**	**263.6**	**263.2**	**368.4**	**746.2**
Interest on long-term debt	..	..	..	1.2	4.6	7.2	8.6	10.0	12.5	22.3
Profit remittances on FDI	..	..	..	0.0	0.0	0.0	0.0	5.0	8.0	12.0
Memo: official net transfers	..	..	..	82.0	72.9	42.1	58.1	78.9	44.0	57.1
private net transfers	..	..	..	103.3	159.7	208.2	205.5	184.3	324.4	689.1
3. MAJOR ECONOMIC AGGREGATES										
Gross national product (GNP)	..	..	..	4,172.9	3,888.5	3,893.6	4,792.5	4,360.4	4,614.9	5,120.9
Exports of goods & services (XGS)	..	..	..	664.3	1,173.2	1,777.7	2,636.8	3,032.9	3,724.5	4,303.4
of which workers remittances	..	..	..	0.0	0.0	0.1	0.0	0.0	0.1	0.1
Imports of goods & services (MGS)	..	..	..	725.1	1,256.8	2,058.5	2,920.9	3,531.7	4,403.0	4,929.6
International reserves (RES)	..	..	..	197.5	389.2	446.4	583.0	639.8	760.0	813.5
Current account balance	..	..	..	36.2	21.6	-166.3	-157.8	-398.3	-561.9	-477.9
4. DEBT INDICATORS										
EDT / XGS (%)	..	..	..	8.8	13.1	10.5	10.9	13.4	17.3	18.2
EDT / GNP (%)	..	..	..	1.4	4.0	4.8	6.0	9.3	13.9	15.3
TDS / XGS (%)	..	..	..	0.6	1.6	1.5	0.8	1.4	1.9	2.1
INT / XGS (%)	..	..	..	0.2	0.5	0.6	0.6	0.6	0.7	0.9
INT / GNP (%)	..	..	..	0.0	0.2	0.3	0.3	0.4	0.6	0.8
RES / EDT (%)	..	..	..	338.2	252.9	240.0	203.6	157.9	118.3	104.1
RES / MGS (months)	..	..	..	3.3	3.7	2.6	2.4	2.2	2.1	2.0
Short-term / EDT (%)	..	..	..	0.0	0.2	4.3	10.4	26.4	48.0	39.4
Concessional / EDT (%)	..	..	..	17.1	9.1	12.8	9.9	7.8	4.9	3.8
Multilateral / EDT (%)	..	..	..	1.9	29.4	35.2	37.7	31.3	19.1	17.6

ESTONIA

(US$ million, unless otherwise indicated)

	1970	1980	1990	1992	1993	1994	1995	1996	1997	1998
5. LONG-TERM DEBT										
DEBT OUTSTANDING (LDOD)	..	..	..	**47.8**	**96.1**	**117.0**	**164.9**	**220.3**	**280.4**	**443.7**
Public and publicly guaranteed	..	..	..	**33.8**	**84.9**	**108.6**	**159.3**	**216.5**	**197.5**	**231.3**
Official creditors	..	..	..	11.0	59.3	92.0	140.6	162.2	159.6	173.6
Multilateral	..	..	..	1.1	45.3	65.5	108.0	126.8	122.5	137.3
Concessional	..	..	..	0.0	0.0	0.0	0.0	0.0	0.0	0.0
Bilateral	..	..	..	10.0	14.0	26.4	32.5	35.5	37.1	36.3
Concessional	..	..	..	10.0	14.0	23.8	28.4	31.6	31.6	29.7
Private creditors	..	..	..	22.7	25.5	16.6	18.7	54.3	37.9	57.7
Bonds	..	..	..	0.0	0.0	0.0	0.0	38.6	33.5	53.8
Commercial banks	..	..	..	0.0	0.0	0.0	2.1	0.0	0.0	0.0
Other private	..	..	..	22.7	25.5	16.6	16.6	15.7	4.5	3.9
Private nonguaranteed	..	..	..	**14.0**	**11.2**	**8.4**	**5.6**	**3.8**	**82.9**	**212.3**
Bonds	..	..	..	0.0	0.0	0.0	0.0	0.0	80.9	86.7
Commercial banks	..	..	..	14.0	11.2	8.4	5.6	3.8	2.0	125.7
Memo:										
IBRD	..	..	..	1.1	19.8	31.0	49.8	62.2	71.5	83.7
IDA	..	..	..	0.0	0.0	0.0	0.0	0.0	0.0	0.0
DISBURSEMENTS	..	..	..	**35.9**	**62.5**	**31.1**	**49.4**	**100.4**	**98.9**	**113.2**
Public and publicly guaranteed	..	..	..	**34.0**	**62.5**	**31.1**	**49.4**	**100.4**	**18.0**	**41.5**
Official creditors	..	..	..	11.0	49.7	28.2	45.2	58.7	15.9	23.7
Multilateral	..	..	..	1.1	45.6	15.8	39.2	54.2	14.3	22.6
Concessional	..	..	..	0.0	0.0	0.0	0.0	0.0	0.0	0.0
Bilateral	..	..	..	10.0	4.1	12.4	6.0	4.5	1.6	1.1
Concessional	..	..	..	10.0	4.1	9.8	4.6	3.1	0.0	0.0
Private creditors	..	..	..	23.0	12.8	2.9	4.2	41.7	2.2	17.8
Bonds	..	..	..	0.0	0.0	0.0	0.0	39.9	0.0	17.1
Commercial banks	..	..	..	0.0	0.0	0.0	2.1	0.0	0.0	0.0
Other private	..	..	..	23.0	12.8	2.9	2.1	1.8	2.2	0.8
Private nonguaranteed	..	..	..	**1.9**	**0.0**	**0.0**	**0.0**	**0.0**	**80.9**	**71.7**
Bonds	..	..	..	0.0	0.0	0.0	0.0	0.0	80.9	0.0
Commercial banks	..	..	..	1.9	0.0	0.0	0.0	0.0	0.0	71.7
Memo:										
IBRD	..	..	..	1.1	18.9	9.7	18.0	16.5	10.9	13.0
IDA	..	..	..	0.0	0.0	0.0	0.0	0.0	0.0	0.0
PRINCIPAL REPAYMENTS	..	..	..	**2.5**	**12.7**	**15.6**	**5.3**	**13.1**	**23.6**	**24.1**
Public and publicly guaranteed	..	..	..	**0.0**	**9.9**	**12.8**	**2.5**	**11.3**	**21.8**	**16.3**
Official creditors	..	..	..	0.0	0.0	0.0	0.0	6.9	9.1	14.7
Multilateral	..	..	..	0.0	0.0	0.0	0.0	5.4	9.1	12.9
Concessional	..	..	..	0.0	0.0	0.0	0.0	0.0	0.0	0.0
Bilateral	..	..	..	0.0	0.0	0.0	0.0	1.5	0.0	1.8
Concessional	..	..	..	0.0	0.0	0.0	0.0	0.0	0.0	1.8
Private creditors	..	..	..	0.0	9.9	12.8	2.5	4.4	12.7	1.6
Bonds	..	..	..	0.0	0.0	0.0	0.0	0.0	0.0	0.0
Commercial banks	..	..	..	0.0	0.0	0.0	0.0	2.1	0.0	0.0
Other private	..	..	..	0.0	9.9	12.8	2.5	2.3	12.7	1.6
Private nonguaranteed	..	..	..	**2.5**	**2.8**	**2.8**	**2.8**	**1.8**	**1.8**	**7.8**
Bonds	..	..	..	0.0	0.0	0.0	0.0	0.0	0.0	0.0
Commercial banks	..	..	..	2.5	2.8	2.8	2.8	1.8	1.8	7.8
Memo:										
IBRD	..	..	..	0.0	0.0	0.0	0.0	0.0	0.0	2.8
IDA	..	..	..	0.0	0.0	0.0	0.0	0.0	0.0	0.0
NET FLOWS ON DEBT	..	..	..	**33.4**	**49.8**	**15.5**	**44.0**	**87.3**	**75.4**	**89.1**
Public and publicly guaranteed	..	..	..	**34.0**	**52.6**	**18.3**	**46.8**	**89.1**	**-3.8**	**25.3**
Official creditors	..	..	..	11.0	49.7	28.2	45.2	51.8	6.8	9.0
Multilateral	..	..	..	1.1	45.6	15.8	39.2	48.8	5.2	9.7
Concessional	..	..	..	0.0	0.0	0.0	0.0	0.0	0.0	0.0
Bilateral	..	..	..	10.0	4.0	12.4	6.0	3.0	1.6	-0.7
Concessional	..	..	..	10.0	4.1	9.8	4.6	3.1	0.0	-1.8
Private creditors	..	..	..	23.0	3.0	-9.9	1.6	37.3	-10.6	16.3
Bonds	..	..	..	0.0	0.0	0.0	0.0	39.9	0.0	17.1
Commercial banks	..	..	..	0.0	0.0	0.0	2.1	-2.1	0.0	0.0
Other private	..	..	..	23.0	3.0	-9.9	-0.5	-0.5	-10.6	-0.8
Private nonguaranteed	..	..	..	**-0.6**	**-2.8**	**-2.8**	**-2.8**	**-1.8**	**79.1**	**63.8**
Bonds	..	..	..	0.0	0.0	0.0	0.0	0.0	80.9	0.0
Commercial banks	..	..	..	-0.6	-2.8	-2.8	-2.8	-1.8	-1.8	63.8
Memo:										
IBRD	..	..	..	1.1	18.9	9.7	18.0	16.5	10.9	10.3
IDA	..	..	..	0.0	0.0	0.0	0.0	0.0	0.0	0.0

ESTONIA

(US$ million, unless otherwise indicated)

	1970	1980	1990	1992	1993	1994	1995	1996	1997	1998
INTEREST PAYMENTS (LINT)	..	..	..	**1.2**	**4.6**	**7.2**	**8.6**	**10.0**	**12.5**	**22.3**
Public and publicly guaranteed	..	..	..	**0.0**	**3.6**	**6.5**	**8.0**	**9.7**	**12.2**	**11.9**
Official creditors	..	..	..	0.0	1.9	4.0	6.8	8.6	9.0	9.4
Multilateral	..	..	..	0.0	1.7	3.3	5.6	7.6	7.7	8.0
Concessional	..	..	..	0.0	0.0	0.0	0.0	0.0	0.0	0.0
Bilateral	..	..	..	0.0	0.2	0.6	1.1	1.0	1.2	1.4
Concessional	..	..	..	0.0	0.2	0.5	0.9	0.6	0.7	0.9
Private creditors	..	..	..	0.0	1.7	2.5	1.2	1.1	3.2	2.5
Bonds	..	..	..	0.0	0.0	0.0	0.0	0.0	2.1	2.0
Commercial banks	..	..	..	0.0	0.0	0.0	0.1	0.1	0.0	0.0
Other private	..	..	..	0.0	1.7	2.5	1.1	1.0	1.1	0.4
Private nonguaranteed	..	..	..	**1.1**	**1.0**	**0.8**	**0.6**	**0.3**	**0.4**	**10.4**
Bonds	..	..	..	0.0	0.0	0.0	0.0	0.0	0.1	5.7
Commercial banks	..	..	..	1.1	1.0	0.8	0.6	0.3	0.3	4.7
Memo:										
IBRD	..	..	..	0.0	0.4	1.7	2.5	3.6	4.2	4.6
IDA	..	..	..	0.0	0.0	0.0	0.0	0.0	0.0	0.0
NET TRANSFERS ON DEBT	..	..	..	**32.3**	**45.2**	**8.3**	**35.4**	**77.2**	**62.8**	**66.8**
Public and publicly guaranteed	..	..	..	**34.0**	**49.0**	**11.9**	**38.8**	**79.3**	**-15.9**	**13.4**
Official creditors	..	..	..	11.0	47.8	24.3	38.4	43.2	-2.2	-0.4
Multilateral	..	..	..	1.1	43.9	12.5	33.6	41.2	-2.5	1.7
Concessional	..	..	..	0.0	0.0	0.0	0.0	0.0	0.0	0.0
Bilateral	..	..	..	10.0	3.8	11.8	4.8	2.0	0.3	-2.2
Concessional	..	..	..	10.0	3.9	9.3	3.7	2.5	-0.7	-2.7
Private creditors	..	..	..	22.9	1.3	-12.4	0.4	36.1	-13.8	13.8
Bonds	..	..	..	0.0	0.0	0.0	0.0	39.9	-2.1	15.0
Commercial banks	..	..	..	0.0	0.0	0.0	2.0	-2.2	0.0	0.0
Other private	..	..	..	22.9	1.3	-12.4	-1.6	-1.5	-11.7	-1.2
Private nonguaranteed	..	..	..	**-1.7**	**-3.8**	**-3.6**	**-3.4**	**-2.1**	**78.8**	**53.4**
Bonds	..	..	..	0.0	0.0	0.0	0.0	0.0	80.8	-5.7
Commercial banks	..	..	..	-1.7	-3.8	-3.6	-3.4	-2.1	-2.1	59.1
Memo:										
IBRD	..	..	..	1.1	18.5	8.0	15.5	12.9	6.7	5.6
IDA	..	..	..	0.0	0.0	0.0	0.0	0.0	0.0	0.0
DEBT SERVICE (LTDS)	..	..	..	**3.7**	**17.3**	**22.8**	**13.9**	**23.2**	**36.1**	**46.4**
Public and publicly guaranteed	..	..	..	**0.0**	**13.5**	**19.2**	**10.5**	**21.1**	**33.9**	**28.2**
Official creditors	..	..	..	0.0	1.9	4.0	6.8	15.5	18.0	24.1
Multilateral	..	..	..	0.0	1.7	3.3	5.6	13.0	16.8	20.8
Concessional	..	..	..	0.0	0.0	0.0	0.0	0.0	0.0	0.0
Bilateral	..	..	..	0.0	0.2	0.6	1.1	2.5	1.2	3.3
Concessional	..	..	..	0.0	0.2	0.5	0.9	0.6	0.7	2.7
Private creditors	..	..	..	0.0	11.6	15.3	3.8	5.6	15.9	4.1
Bonds	..	..	..	0.0	0.0	0.0	0.0	0.0	2.1	2.0
Commercial banks	..	..	..	0.0	0.0	0.0	0.1	2.2	0.0	0.0
Other private	..	..	..	0.0	11.6	15.3	3.6	3.3	13.8	2.0
Private nonguaranteed	..	..	..	**3.7**	**3.8**	**3.6**	**3.4**	**2.1**	**2.2**	**18.3**
Bonds	..	..	..	0.0	0.0	0.0	0.0	0.0	0.1	5.7
Commercial banks	..	..	..	3.7	3.8	3.6	3.4	2.1	2.1	12.6
Memo:										
IBRD	..	..	..	0.0	0.4	1.7	2.5	3.6	4.2	7.4
IDA	..	..	..	0.0	0.0	0.0	0.0	0.0	0.0	0.0
UNDISBURSED DEBT	..	..	..	**82.7**	**74.0**	**154.8**	**128.0**	**112.9**	**75.4**	**53.2**
Official creditors	..	..	..	74.5	66.8	149.6	126.8	105.2	70.7	52.3
Private creditors	..	..	..	8.2	7.2	5.2	1.3	7.8	4.7	0.9
Memorandum items										
Concessional LDOD	..	..	..	10.0	14.0	23.8	28.4	31.6	31.6	29.7
Variable rate LDOD	..	..	..	16.4	64.1	95.3	132.4	125.4	203.6	356.3
Public sector LDOD	..	..	..	33.8	84.9	108.6	159.3	216.5	197.5	231.3
Private sector LDOD	..	..	..	14.0	11.2	8.4	5.6	3.8	82.9	212.3

6. CURRENCY COMPOSITION OF LONG-TERM DEBT (PERCENT)

	1970	1980	1990	1992	1993	1994	1995	1996	1997	1998
Deutsche mark	..	..	..	0.0	3.7	9.1	14.7	30.4	64.2	59.3
French franc	..	..	..	0.0	0.0	0.0	0.0	0.0	0.0	0.0
Japanese yen	..	..	..	0.0	0.0	0.0	0.0	0.0	0.0	0.0
Pound sterling	..	..	..	0.0	0.0	0.0	0.0	0.0	0.0	0.0
Swiss franc	..	..	..	0.0	0.0	0.0	0.0	0.0	0.0	0.0
U.S.dollars	..	..	..	92.7	42.4	32.7	27.4	21.2	18.9	16.3
Multiple currency	..	..	..	3.3	23.3	28.6	31.3	28.7	0.0	0.0
Special drawing rights	..	..	..	0.0	0.0	0.0	0.0	0.0	0.0	0.0
All other currencies	..	..	..	4.0	30.6	29.6	26.6	19.7	16.9	24.4

ESTONIA

(US$ million, unless otherwise indicated)

	1970	1980	1990	1992	1993	1994	1995	1996	1997	1998
7. DEBT RESTRUCTURINGS										
Total amount rescheduled	..	..	..	0.0	0.0	0.0	0.0	0.0	0.0	0.0
Debt stock rescheduled	..	..	..	0.0	0.0	0.0	0.0	0.0	0.0	0.0
Principal rescheduled	..	..	..	0.0	0.0	0.0	0.0	0.0	0.0	0.0
Official	..	..	..	0.0	0.0	0.0	0.0	0.0	0.0	0.0
Private	..	..	..	0.0	0.0	0.0	0.0	0.0	0.0	0.0
Interest rescheduled	..	..	..	..	0.0	0.0	0.0	0.0	0.0	0.0
Official	..	..	..	0.0	0.0	0.0	0.0	0.0	0.0	0.0
Private	..	..	..	0.0	0.0	0.0	0.0	0.0	0.0	0.0
Debt forgiven	..	..	..	0.0	0.0	0.0	0.0	0.0	0.0	0.0
Memo: interest forgiven	..	..	..	0.0	0.0	0.0	0.0	0.0	0.0	0.0
Debt stock reduction	..	..	..	0.0	0.0	0.0	0.0	0.0	0.0	0.0
of which debt buyback	..	..	..	0.0	0.0	0.0	0.0	0.0	0.0	0.0
8. DEBT STOCK-FLOW RECONCILIATION										
Total change in debt stocks	..	..	..	..	95.5	32.2	100.4	118.8	237.2	139.3
Net flows on debt	..	..	..	44.3	97.8	23.2	96.0	153.5	256.9	63.8
Net change in interest arrears	..	..	..	..	0.0	0.0	0.0	0.0	0.0	0.0
Interest capitalized	..	..	..	..	0.0	0.0	0.0	0.0	0.0	0.0
Debt forgiveness or reduction	..	..	..	..	0.0	0.0	0.0	0.0	0.0	0.0
Cross-currency valuation	..	..	..	..	-2.4	6.6	5.7	-11.3	-12.9	10.1
Residual	..	..	..	..	0.1	2.3	-1.3	-23.4	-6.8	65.5
9. AVERAGE TERMS OF NEW COMMITMENTS										
ALL CREDITORS										
Interest (%)	..	..	..	7.2	4.4	7.3	7.1	6.3	3.1	6.4
Maturity (years)	..	..	..	11.1	9.8	14.8	15.0	8.7	5.1	5.2
Grace period (years)	..	..	..	3.7	4.8	5.6	5.5	2.7	0.6	5.0
Grant element (%)	..	..	..	13.3	26.2	15.3	16.4	15.3	15.6	13.5
Official creditors										
Interest (%)	..	..	..	6.9	4.0	7.3	7.1	6.5	0.0	8.5
Maturity (years)	..	..	..	13.5	10.4	14.8	15.0	12.4	0.0	14.9
Grace period (years)	..	..	..	4.7	4.1	5.6	5.5	2.7	0.0	5.4
Grant element (%)	..	..	..	17.3	27.9	15.3	16.4	19.2	0.0	8.1
Private creditors										
Interest (%)	..	..	..	8.1	6.0	0.0	0.0	5.9	3.1	6.4
Maturity (years)	..	..	..	4.9	7.4	0.0	0.0	3.6	5.1	5.1
Grace period (years)	..	..	..	1.0	7.3	0.0	0.0	2.8	0.6	5.0
Grant element (%)	..	..	..	2.8	19.9	0.0	0.0	10.1	15.6	13.6
Memorandum items										
Commitments	..	..	..	119.8	57.4	105.6	20.0	116.8	0.0	17.5
Official creditors	..	..	..	87.2	44.8	105.6	20.0	67.6	0.0	0.1
Private creditors	..	..	..	32.6	12.6	0.0	0.0	49.2	0.0	17.3

10. CONTRACTUAL OBLIGATIONS ON OUTSTANDING LONG-TERM DEBT

	1999	2000	2001	2002	2003	2004	2005	2006	2007	2008
TOTAL										
Disbursements	18.3	13.7	9.2	4.9	3.3	2.1	0.9	0.7	0.4	0.0
Principal	54.9	59.6	22.2	50.1	38.7	45.9	19.0	19.0	19.0	14.2
Interest	23.9	18.7	15.5	14.3	10.3	8.4	5.3	4.2	3.1	2.0
Official creditors										
Disbursements	17.6	13.4	9.1	4.9	3.3	2.1	0.9	0.7	0.4	0.0
Principal	17.4	22.1	21.1	25.6	20.8	19.0	19.0	19.0	19.0	14.2
Interest	10.9	10.2	9.6	8.8	7.6	6.4	5.3	4.2	3.1	2.0
Bilateral creditors										
Disbursements	0.0	0.0	0.0	0.0	0.0	0.0	0.0	0.0	0.0	0.0
Principal	2.2	2.5	2.5	6.3	3.1	3.1	3.1	3.1	3.1	1.3
Interest	1.2	1.1	1.0	0.9	0.8	0.7	0.6	0.5	0.4	0.2
Multilateral creditors										
Disbursements	17.6	13.4	9.1	4.9	3.3	2.1	0.9	0.7	0.4	0.0
Principal	15.2	19.6	18.6	19.3	17.6	15.9	15.9	15.9	15.9	12.9
Interest	9.7	9.1	8.6	7.9	6.7	5.7	4.7	3.7	2.7	1.8
Private creditors										
Disbursements	0.6	0.2	0.1	0.0	0.0	0.0	0.0	0.0	0.0	0.0
Principal	37.5	37.5	1.1	24.4	17.9	26.9	0.0	0.0	0.0	0.0
Interest	13.0	8.5	6.0	5.4	2.7	1.9	0.0	0.0	0.0	0.0
Commercial banks										
Disbursements	0.0	0.0	0.0	0.0	0.0	0.0	0.0	0.0	0.0	0.0
Principal	0.0	0.0	0.0	0.0	0.0	0.0	0.0	0.0	0.0	0.0
Interest	0.0	0.0	0.0	0.0	0.0	0.0	0.0	0.0	0.0	0.0
Other private										
Disbursements	0.6	0.2	0.1	0.0	0.0	0.0	0.0	0.0	0.0	0.0
Principal	37.5	37.5	1.1	24.4	17.9	26.9	0.0	0.0	0.0	0.0
Interest	13.0	8.5	6.0	5.4	2.7	1.9	0.0	0.0	0.0	0.0

ETHIOPIA

(US$ million, unless otherwise indicated)

	1970	1980	1990	1992	1993	1994	1995	1996	1997	1998
1. SUMMARY DEBT DATA										
TOTAL DEBT STOCKS (EDT)	..	824	8,634	9,341	9,703	10,067	10,310	10,079	10,079	10,352
Long-term debt (LDOD)	169	688	8,483	9,003	9,287	9,571	9,776	9,485	9,427	9,618
Public and publicly guaranteed	169	688	8,483	9,003	9,287	9,571	9,776	9,485	9,427	9,618
Private nonguaranteed	0	0	0	0	0	0	0	0	0	0
Use of IMF credit	0	79	6	19	49	72	74	92	87	107
Short-term debt	..	57	145	319	368	424	461	502	565	626
of which interest arrears on LDOD	..	1	43	259	337	393	437	481	541	603
Official creditors	..	0	39	246	322	374	417	460	523	584
Private creditors	..	0	3	12	15	19	20	21	18	19
Memo: principal arrears on LDOD	..	1	236	1,521	2,105	2,811	3,630	4,303	4,756	5,196
Official creditors	..	0	196	1,431	1,977	2,646	3,453	4,103	4,530	4,965
Private creditors	..	1	40	90	128	165	177	200	227	231
Memo: export credits	..	0	311	239	235	234	239	300	248	287
TOTAL DEBT FLOWS										
Disbursements	28	119	378	346	409	258	232	315	179	163
Long-term debt	28	110	378	326	379	238	232	294	179	143
IMF purchases	0	9	0	20	30	20	0	21	0	20
Principal repayments	15	17	177	62	66	68	91	292	52	69
Long-term debt	15	17	152	62	66	68	91	292	52	65
IMF repurchases	0	0	25	0	0	0	0	0	0	4
Net flows on debt	13	94	207	233	314	190	133	21	130	93
of which short-term debt	..	-8	7	-50	-29	0	-8	-2	3	-1
Interest payments (INT)	..	28	59	47	29	44	63	55	47	50
Long-term debt	6	17	49	42	24	40	61	54	46	48
IMF charges	0	2	2	0	0	0	0	0	0	1
Short-term debt	..	9	8	5	5	4	1	1	1	1
Net transfers on debt	..	67	148	186	285	146	70	-35	82	43
Total debt service paid (TDS)	..	45	236	109	95	112	154	348	100	119
Long-term debt	21	34	201	104	90	107	152	346	98	113
IMF repurchases and charges	0	2	27	0	0	0	0	0	0	5
Short-term debt (interest only)	..	9	8	5	5	4	1	1	1	1
2. AGGREGATE NET RESOURCE FLOWS AND NET TRANSFERS (LONG-TERM)										
NET RESOURCE FLOWS	23	218	842	1,156	883	811	624	396	482	500
Net flow of long-term debt (ex. IMF)	13	93	225	263	314	170	141	1	127	78
Foreign direct investment (net)	4	0	12	6	7	3	8	5	5	4
Portfolio equity flows	0	0	0	0	0	0	0	0	0	0
Grants (excluding technical coop.)	6	125	604	886	562	638	475	390	350	418
Memo: technical coop. grants	20	44	254	185	166	123	164	200	151	118
official net resource flows	26	191	886	1,070	903	840	664	601	455	494
private net resource flows	-3	26	-45	86	-20	-30	-40	-205	27	6
NET TRANSFERS	10	201	793	1,114	859	771	563	343	436	452
Interest on long-term debt	6	17	49	42	24	40	61	54	46	48
Profit remittances on FDI	6	0	0	0	0	0	0	0	0	0
Memo: official net transfers	21	177	862	1,050	882	810	632	562	413	449
private net transfers	-11	24	-69	63	-23	-39	-69	-220	23	3
3. MAJOR ECONOMIC AGGREGATES										
Gross national product (GNP)	..	..	6,788	5,520	6,153	4,825	5,719	5,967	6,338	6,453
Exports of goods & services (XGS)	185	591	677	459	514	563	808	823	1,041	1,053
of which workers remittances	..	0	0	0	0	0	0	0	0	0
Imports of goods & services (MGS)	226	797	1,141	1,166	1,366	1,187	1,356	1,731	1,755	1,922
International reserves (RES)	72	262	55	270	500	588	815	733	502	520
Current account balance	-40	-126	-244	-335	-497	-291	-90	-461	-455	-520
4. DEBT INDICATORS										
EDT / XGS (%)	..	139.5	1,276.3	2,036.9	1,889.3	1,788.1	1,276.6	1,224.5	968.1	983.5
EDT / GNP (%)	..	..	127.2	169.2	157.7	208.7	180.3	168.9	159.0	160.4
TDS / XGS (%)	..	7.6	34.9	23.9	18.5	19.8	19.1	42.2	9.6	11.3
INT / XGS (%)	..	4.7	8.7	10.3	5.7	7.8	7.8	6.7	4.5	4.8
INT / GNP (%)	..	..	0.9	0.9	0.5	0.9	1.1	0.9	0.8	0.8
RES / EDT (%)	..	31.9	0.6	2.9	5.2	5.8	7.9	7.3	5.0	5.0
RES / MGS (months)	3.8	4.0	0.6	2.8	4.4	5.9	7.2	5.1	3.4	3.3
Short-term / EDT (%)	..	6.9	1.7	3.4	3.8	4.2	4.5	5.0	5.6	6.1
Concessional / EDT (%)	..	68.3	87.3	84.1	84.4	84.3	84.6	86.3	85.7	85.1
Multilateral / EDT (%)	..	41.3	14.7	16.1	18.9	21.2	22.7	24.7	24.4	25.4

ETHIOPIA

(US$ million, unless otherwise indicated)

	1970	*1980*	*1990*	*1992*	*1993*	*1994*	*1995*	*1996*	*1997*	*1998*
5. LONG-TERM DEBT										
DEBT OUTSTANDING (LDOD)	**169**	**688**	**8,483**	**9,003**	**9,287**	**9,571**	**9,776**	**9,485**	**9,427**	**9,618**
Public and publicly guaranteed	**169**	**688**	**8,483**	**9,003**	**9,287**	**9,571**	**9,776**	**9,485**	**9,427**	**9,618**
Official creditors	140	638	7,906	8,238	8,583	8,917	9,180	9,130	9,074	9,268
Multilateral	70	340	1,268	1,503	1,838	2,132	2,341	2,486	2,460	2,629
Concessional	23	282	1,151	1,367	1,695	1,970	2,159	2,278	2,233	2,391
Bilateral	70	299	6,638	6,735	6,745	6,785	6,839	6,644	6,614	6,639
Concessional	70	281	6,386	6,491	6,489	6,515	6,559	6,418	6,400	6,423
Private creditors	29	49	577	765	704	654	596	354	353	350
Bonds	0	0	0	0	0	0	0	0	0	0
Commercial banks	0	10	116	363	327	292	253	27	25	20
Other private	29	39	461	402	376	362	343	327	328	330
Private nonguaranteed	**0**	**0**	**0**	**0**	**0**	**0**	**0**	**0**	**0**	**0**
Bonds	0	0	0	0	0	0	0	0	0	0
Commercial banks	0	0	0	0	0	0	0	0	0	0
Memo:										
IBRD	47	56	27	12	7	[illegible]	0	0	0	0
IDA	23	249	824	964	1,187	1,373	1,470	1,555	1,532	1,632
DISBURSEMENTS	**28**	**110**	**378**	**326**	**379**	**238**	**232**	**294**	**179**	**143**
Public and publicly guaranteed	**28**	**110**	**378**	**326**	**379**	**238**	**232**	**294**	**179**	**143**
Official creditors	25	77	327	213	369	234	232	272	149	132
Multilateral	8	36	139	187	364	234	209	272	145	127
Concessional	3	34	128	162	344	213	177	223	92	111
Bilateral	17	41	188	26	5	0	23	0	4	5
Concessional	17	37	131	22	5	0	23	0	4	5
Private creditors	2	33	51	113	10	4	0	22	30	11
Bonds	0	0	0	0	0	0	0	0	0	0
Commercial banks	0	2	0	102	0	0	0	0	0	0
Other private	2	31	51	11	10	4	0	22	30	11
Private nonguaranteed	**0**	**0**	**0**	**0**	**0**	**0**	**0**	**0**	**0**	**0**
Bonds	0	0	0	0	0	0	0	0	0	0
Commercial banks	0	0	0	0	0	0	0	0	0	0
Memo:										
IBRD	6	0	0	0	0	0	0	0	0	0
IDA	3	28	74	112	230	150	84	142	65	69
PRINCIPAL REPAYMENTS	**15**	**17**	**152**	**62**	**66**	**68**	**91**	**292**	**52**	**65**
Public and publicly guaranteed	**15**	**17**	**152**	**62**	**66**	**68**	**91**	**292**	**52**	**65**
Official creditors	6	11	45	29	29	32	43	61	45	57
Multilateral	3	4	16	23	23	28	40	42	42	45
Concessional	0	0	7	11	12	17	22	23	24	27
Bilateral	3	6	29	6	6	3	3	19	3	11
Concessional	3	6	13	4	4	2	3	13	3	11
Private creditors	9	7	107	33	37	36	48	231	8	8
Bonds	0	0	0	0	0	0	0	0	0	0
Commercial banks	0	3	45	26	36	35	39	226	2	5
Other private	9	4	62	8	1	1	9	5	6	3
Private nonguaranteed	**0**	**0**	**0**	**0**	**0**	**0**	**0**	**0**	**0**	**0**
Bonds	0	0	0	0	0	0	0	0	0	0
Commercial banks	0	0	0	0	0	0	0	0	0	0
Memo:										
IBRD	3	4	7	7	6	4	4	0	0	0
IDA	0	0	4	6	8	10	12	14	15	18
NET FLOWS ON DEBT	**13**	**93**	**225**	**263**	**314**	**170**	**141**	**1**	**127**	**78**
Public and publicly guaranteed	**13**	**93**	**225**	**263**	**314**	**170**	**141**	**1**	**127**	**78**
Official creditors	20	67	282	184	341	203	189	211	105	75
Multilateral	5	32	123	163	341	206	169	230	104	82
Concessional	3	33	121	151	332	196	155	201	68	83
Bilateral	14	35	159	20	-1	-3	19	-19	1	-7
Concessional	14	30	119	18	0	-1	20	-12	1	-6
Private creditors	-7	26	-57	80	-27	-33	-48	-210	22	2
Bonds	0	0	0	0	0	0	0	0	0	0
Commercial banks	0	-1	-45	76	-36	-35	-39	-226	-2	-5
Other private	-7	27	-12	3	9	2	-9	16	24	7
Private nonguaranteed	**0**	**0**	**0**	**0**	**0**	**0**	**0**	**0**	**0**	**0**
Bonds	0	0	0	0	0	0	0	0	0	0
Commercial banks	0	0	0	0	0	0	0	0	0	0
Memo:										
IBRD	3	-4	-7	-7	-6	-4	-4	0	0	0
IDA	3	28	69	106	222	140	71	128	50	51

ETHIOPIA

(US$ million, unless otherwise indicated)

	1970	1980	1990	1992	1993	1994	1995	1996	1997	1998
INTEREST PAYMENTS (LINT)	**6**	**17**	**49**	**42**	**24**	**40**	**61**	**54**	**46**	**48**
Public and publicly guaranteed	**6**	**17**	**49**	**42**	**24**	**40**	**61**	**54**	**46**	**48**
Official creditors	5	15	24	20	21	31	32	39	42	45
Multilateral	3	8	13	19	20	25	24	30	33	33
Concessional	0	2	7	9	10	13	14	16	17	17
Bilateral	2	6	11	1	1	6	9	9	8	12
Concessional	2	5	9	1	1	3	6	4	4	8
Private creditors	2	2	24	22	3	9	29	15	4	3
Bonds	0	0	0	0	0	0	0	0	0	0
Commercial banks	0	2	11	21	3	9	27	15	2	1
Other private	2	1	13	2	0	0	2	1	3	2
Private nonguaranteed	**0**	**0**	**0**	**0**	**0**	**0**	**0**	**0**	**0**	**0**
Bonds	0	0	0	0	0	0	0	0	0	0
Commercial banks	0	0	0	0	0	0	0	0	0	0
Memo:										
IBRD	3	7	2	1	1	0	0	0	0	0
IDA	0	2	6	7	7	10	11	11	11	11
NET TRANSFERS ON DEBT	**7**	**76**	**177**	**221**	**290**	**130**	**80**	**-52**	**81**	**30**
Public and publicly guaranteed	**7**	**76**	**177**	**221**	**290**	**130**	**80**	**-52**	**81**	**30**
Official creditors	15	52	258	164	320	172	157	172	63	31
Multilateral	3	23	110	145	322	181	146	200	70	49
Concessional	3	31	114	142	322	183	141	185	51	66
Bilateral	12	29	148	19	-2	-9	11	-28	-7	-18
Concessional	12	25	110	17	-1	-4	14	-16	-3	-14
Private creditors	-8	24	-81	57	-30	-42	-77	-225	18	-1
Bonds	0	0	0	0	0	0	0	0	0	0
Commercial banks	0	-2	-56	56	-39	-44	-66	-240	-4	-7
Other private	-8	26	-25	2	9	2	-11	16	22	6
Private nonguaranteed	**0**	**0**	**0**	**0**	**0**	**0**	**0**	**0**	**0**	**0**
Bonds	0	0	0	0	0	0	0	0	0	0
Commercial banks	0	0	0	0	0	0	0	0	0	0
Memo:										
IBRD	0	-10	-9	-8	-7	-4	-4	0	0	0
IDA	3	26	64	99	215	131	60	116	38	40
DEBT SERVICE (LTDS)	**21**	**34**	**201**	**104**	**90**	**107**	**152**	**346**	**98**	**113**
Public and publicly guaranteed	**21**	**34**	**201**	**104**	**90**	**107**	**152**	**346**	**98**	**113**
Official creditors	11	25	69	49	49	62	76	100	86	102
Multilateral	6	13	29	42	42	53	64	72	75	79
Concessional	0	2	14	20	22	30	36	38	41	44
Bilateral	5	13	40	7	7	10	12	28	11	23
Concessional	5	11	22	4	5	4	9	16	7	19
Private creditors	11	9	131	56	40	45	77	246	12	12
Bonds	0	0	0	0	0	0	0	0	0	0
Commercial banks	0	4	56	47	39	44	66	240	4	7
Other private	11	5	76	9	2	1	11	6	9	5
Private nonguaranteed	**0**	**0**	**0**	**0**	**0**	**0**	**0**	**0**	**0**	**0**
Bonds	0	0	0	0	0	0	0	0	0	0
Commercial banks	0	0	0	0	0	0	0	0	0	0
Memo:										
IBRD	6	10	9	8	7	4	4	0	0	0
IDA	0	2	10	13	15	19	23	25	26	29
UNDISBURSED DEBT	**108**	**436**	**2,001**	**1,182**	**1,413**	**1,328**	**1,223**	**1,050**	**857**	**1,756**
Official creditors	105	383	1,565	1,152	1,393	1,313	1,216	1,019	842	1,752
Private creditors	4	54	436	30	19	15	8	32	15	4
Memorandum items										
Concessional LDOD	93	562	7,537	7,858	8,185	8,485	8,717	8,695	8,633	8,813
Variable rate LDOD	0	10	114	104	101	84	67	29	26	20
Public sector LDOD	161	685	8,481	9,002	9,286	9,571	9,776	9,485	9,427	9,618
Private sector LDOD	8	3	1	1	0	0	0	0	0	0

6. CURRENCY COMPOSITION OF LONG-TERM DEBT (PERCENT)

	1970	1980	1990	1992	1993	1994	1995	1996	1997	1998
Deutsche mark	2.7	8.1	1.9	1.9	1.9	2.2	2.3	2.2	1.8	1.8
French franc	0.0	0.0	0.2	0.1	0.1	0.0	0.1	0.1	0.1	0.1
Japanese yen	0.0	2.5	0.5	0.3	0.4	0.4	0.4	0.2	0.1	0.2
Pound sterling	2.1	2.3	0.3	0.2	0.1	0.1	0.2	0.2	0.2	0.2
Swiss franc	0.2	0.1	0.1	0.1	0.1	0.1	0.1	0.1	0.1	0.1
U.S.dollars	41.8	64.5	24.2	27.6	28.6	29.2	29.0	26.8	27.5	28.1
Multiple currency	28.1	14.7	4.4	5.0	6.1	6.9	7.9	8.6	8.8	9.2
Special drawing rights	0.0	0.0	0.2	0.2	0.2	0.2	0.2	0.2	0.2	0.2
All other currencies	25.1	7.8	68.2	64.6	62.5	60.9	59.8	61.6	61.2	60.1

ETHIOPIA

(US$ million, unless otherwise indicated)

	1970	1980	1990	1992	1993	1994	1995	1996	1997	1998
7. DEBT RESTRUCTURINGS										
Total amount rescheduled	..	..	0	134	66	47	28	0	105	35
Debt stock rescheduled	..	..	0	0	0	0	0	0	0	0
Principal rescheduled	..	..	0	106	51	38	23	0	89	22
Official	..	..	0	38	25	19	12	0	73	14
Private	..	..	0	68	26	19	11	0	16	8
Interest rescheduled	..	..	0	27	15	9	6	0	16	5
Official	..	..	0	15	8	3	2	0	11	4
Private	..	..	0	12	7	6	3	0	5	2
Debt forgiven	..	..	67	44	13	15	7	0	19	6
Memo: interest forgiven	..	..	0	7	2	3	1	19	3	1
Debt stock reduction	..	..	0	0	0	0	0	197	0	0
of which debt buyback	..	..	0	0	0	0	0	16	0	0
8. DEBT STOCK-FLOW RECONCILIATION										
Total change in debt stocks	..	..	792	223	362	364	243	-232	0	273
Net flows on debt	13	94	207	233	314	190	133	21	130	93
Net change in interest arrears	..	..	27	93	79	56	44	43	61	61
Interest capitalized	..	..	0	27	15	9	6	0	16	5
Debt forgiveness or reduction	..	..	-67	-44	-13	-15	-7	-181	-19	-6
Cross-currency valuation	..	..	629	-46	-28	50	33	-26	-50	28
Residual	..	..	-4	-41	-5	74	35	-88	-138	91
9. AVERAGE TERMS OF NEW COMMITMENTS										
ALL CREDITORS										
Interest (%)	4.4	3.6	6.6	1.0	1.7	1.1	1.0	2.2	2.4	0.6
Maturity (years)	31.8	19.2	21.7	40.0	40.6	40.3	36.3	30.4	33.5	40.6
Grace period (years)	6.6	3.8	3.5	9.8	9.8	9.3	9.3	7.6	7.4	10.1
Grant element (%)	43.3	39.5	23.7	73.6	72.8	71.6	76.1	62.1	60.7	81.3
Official creditors										
Interest (%)	4.2	2.4	1.9	1.0	1.7	1.1	1.0	0.9	1.2	0.6
Maturity (years)	37.7	24.1	32.7	40.6	40.6	40.3	36.3	35.4	39.6	40.6
Grace period (years)	7.9	4.6	7.9	9.9	9.8	9.3	9.3	9.4	8.9	10.1
Grant element (%)	49.6	50.8	59.0	74.0	72.8	71.6	76.1	75.4	73.6	81.3
Private creditors										
Interest (%)	4.9	6.3	9.8	0.0	0.0	0.0	0.0	7.5	6.8	0.0
Maturity (years)	8.9	8.3	14.1	12.4	0.0	0.0	0.0	10.4	11.1	0.0
Grace period (years)	1.7	2.1	0.4	4.9	0.0	0.0	0.0	0.7	1.6	0.0
Grant element (%)	18.9	14.3	-0.4	55.2	0.0	0.0	0.0	9.0	13.0	0.0
Memorandum items										
Commitments	21	194	580	248	637	198	170	244	69	1,032
Official creditors	17	134	236	242	637	198	170	195	55	1,032
Private creditors	4	60	345	5	0	0	0	49	15	0

10. CONTRACTUAL OBLIGATIONS ON OUTSTANDING LONG-TERM DEBT

	1999	2000	2001	2002	2003	2004	2005	2006	2007	2008
TOTAL										
Disbursements	293	442	347	269	193	122	70	7	1	0
Principal	544	509	172	171	170	173	158	132	132	141
Interest	78	70	68	65	61	58	54	51	47	44
Official creditors										
Disbursements	290	441	347	269	193	122	70	7	1	0
Principal	519	484	162	162	162	165	150	124	129	140
Interest	73	66	64	62	59	56	53	50	47	44
Bilateral creditors										
Disbursements	17	13	7	4	3	2	1	0	0	0
Principal	454	417	92	84	78	71	57	29	29	27
Interest	33	25	23	21	19	18	16	16	15	14
Multilateral creditors										
Disbursements	273	428	340	265	190	120	70	6	1	0
Principal	65	67	71	78	84	93	94	95	100	113
Interest	39	41	42	41	40	38	36	34	32	30
Private creditors										
Disbursements	3	1	0	0	0	0	0	0	0	0
Principal	25	25	10	8	8	8	8	8	2	1
Interest	5	4	4	3	2	2	2	1	1	1
Commercial banks										
Disbursements	0	0	0	0	0	0	0	0	0	0
Principal	0	0	0	0	0	0	0	0	0	0
Interest	0	0	0	0	0	0	0	0	0	0
Other private										
Disbursements	3	1	0	0	0	0	0	0	0	0
Principal	25	25	10	8	8	8	8	8	2	1
Interest	5	4	4	3	2	2	2	1	1	1

FIJI

(US$ million, unless otherwise indicated)

	1970	1980	1990	1992	1993	1994	1995	1996	1997	1998
1. SUMMARY DEBT DATA										
TOTAL DEBT STOCKS (EDT)	**..**	**281.2**	**412.7**	**338.6**	**330.1**	**284.2**	**250.8**	**217.6**	**218.6**	**192.8**
Long-term debt (LDOD)	**11.7**	**244.9**	**400.7**	**308.2**	**283.4**	**268.2**	**235.9**	**199.2**	**170.6**	**172.2**
Public and publicly guaranteed	11.7	180.0	306.0	226.9	199.4	180.7	167.9	146.7	129.5	140.0
Private nonguaranteed	0.0	64.9	94.7	81.3	84.0	87.5	68.0	52.5	41.2	32.2
Use of IMF credit	**0.0**	**0.0**	**0.0**	**0.0**	**0.0**	**0.0**	**0.0**	**0.0**	**0.0**	**0.0**
Short-term debt	**..**	**36.3**	**12.0**	**30.5**	**46.7**	**16.0**	**14.9**	**18.4**	**48.0**	**20.6**
of which interest arrears on LDOD	..	0.3	0.0	0.0	0.0	0.0	0.0	0.0	0.0	0.0
Official creditors	..	0.3	0.0	0.0	0.0	0.0	0.0	0.0	0.0	0.0
Private creditors	..	0.0	0.0	0.0	0.0	0.0	0.0	0.0	0.0	0.0
Memo: principal arrears on LDOD	..	0.0	0.0	0.0	0.0	0.0	0.0	0.0	0.0	0.0
Official creditors	..	0.0	0.0	0.0	0.0	0.0	0.0	0.0	0.0	0.0
Private creditors	..	0.0	0.0	0.0	0.0	0.0	0.0	0.0	0.0	0.0
Memo: export credits	..	0.0	61.0	39.0	24.0	28.0	31.0	33.0	45.0	33.0
TOTAL DEBT FLOWS										
Disbursements	**2.3**	**78.2**	**33.5**	**36.8**	**32.6**	**41.4**	**15.2**	**8.6**	**9.1**	**6.5**
Long-term debt	2.3	78.2	33.5	36.8	32.6	41.4	15.2	8.6	9.1	6.5
IMF purchases	0.0	0.0	0.0	0.0	0.0	0.0	0.0	0.0	0.0	0.0
Principal repayments	**1.6**	**19.7**	**73.0**	**60.0**	**56.9**	**71.7**	**51.8**	**35.2**	**23.3**	**23.5**
Long-term debt	1.6	11.2	72.2	60.0	56.9	71.7	51.8	35.2	23.3	23.5
IMF repurchases	0.0	8.5	0.8	0.0	0.0	0.0	0.0	0.0	0.0	0.0
Net flows on debt	**0.7**	**71.6**	**-41.5**	**-4.1**	**-8.0**	**-61.0**	**-37.7**	**-23.1**	**15.5**	**-44.4**
of which short-term debt	..	13.0	-2.0	19.1	16.2	-30.7	-1.1	3.5	29.6	-27.4
Interest payments (INT)	**..**	**16.2**	**32.9**	**24.1**	**21.4**	**21.0**	**16.0**	**13.5**	**12.5**	**10.6**
Long-term debt	1.1	9.5	31.4	22.8	19.5	19.1	15.1	12.5	10.5	8.9
IMF charges	0.0	0.3	0.0	0.0	0.0	0.0	0.0	0.0	0.0	0.0
Short-term debt	..	6.3	1.5	1.3	1.9	1.9	0.9	1.0	2.0	1.7
Net transfers on debt	**..**	**55.4**	**-74.4**	**-28.2**	**-29.5**	**-82.0**	**-53.7**	**-36.6**	**3.0**	**-55.0**
Total debt service paid (TDS)	**..**	**35.8**	**105.9**	**84.1**	**78.3**	**92.7**	**67.8**	**48.7**	**35.8**	**34.1**
Long-term debt	2.7	20.7	103.5	82.8	76.4	90.9	66.8	47.7	33.8	32.4
IMF repurchases and charges	0.0	8.8	0.8	0.0	0.0	0.0	0.0	0.0	0.0	0.0
Short-term debt (interest only)	..	6.3	1.5	1.3	1.9	1.9	0.9	1.0	2.0	1.7
2. AGGREGATE NET RESOURCE FLOWS AND NET TRANSFERS (LONG-TERM)										
NET RESOURCE FLOWS	**11.3**	**118.8**	**67.6**	**105.8**	**90.5**	**48.1**	**53.2**	**-6.4**	**15.8**	**71.7**
Net flow of long-term debt (ex. IMF)	0.7	67.1	-38.7	-23.2	-24.2	-30.3	-36.6	-26.6	-14.1	-17.0
Foreign direct investment (net)	6.4	36.4	92.0	103.6	91.2	67.5	69.5	1.8	16.0	75.0
Portfolio equity flows	0.0	0.0	0.0	0.0	0.0	0.0	0.0	0.0	0.0	0.0
Grants (excluding technical coop.)	4.2	15.3	14.3	25.4	23.5	10.9	20.3	18.3	13.9	13.7
Memo: technical coop. grants	3.0	16.9	36.6	39.6	35.7	33.5	30.6	32.8	32.6	25.4
official net resource flows	5.8	54.5	-8.6	9.8	-0.6	-23.2	4.2	7.5	11.3	5.7
private net resource flows	5.5	64.3	76.2	96.0	91.1	71.3	49.0	-13.9	4.5	66.0
NET TRANSFERS	**-1.3**	**78.8**	**-3.7**	**28.5**	**8.8**	**-39.1**	**-27.9**	**-81.9**	**-62.7**	**-8.2**
Interest on long-term debt	1.1	9.5	31.4	22.8	19.5	19.1	15.1	12.5	10.5	8.9
Profit remittances on FDI	11.5	30.4	39.9	54.4	62.2	68.0	66.0	63.0	68.0	71.0
Memo: official net transfers	5.2	48.4	-30.0	-6.9	-15.1	-36.7	-6.4	-1.5	3.7	-1.2
private net transfers	-6.5	30.4	26.3	35.4	23.9	-2.4	-21.5	-80.4	-66.4	-7.0
3. MAJOR ECONOMIC AGGREGATES										
Gross national product (GNP)	210.8	1,186.2	1,345.8	1,579.4	1,608.5	1,772.4	1,877.6	2,059.4	2,033.2	1,526.1
Exports of goods & services (XGS)	..	597.1	881.6	855.3	904.2	1,074.0	1,139.1	1,348.4	1,265.3	953.6
of which workers remittances	..	0.0	..	..	..	..	..	..	..	..
Imports of goods & services (MGS)	..	656.6	974.3	922.2	1,054.3	1,191.4	1,254.7	1,344.4	1,323.7	1,038.8
International reserves (RES)	27.4	174.1	261.1	317.1	269.8	273.4	349.3	427.5	360.5	385.7
Current account balance	..	-17.5	-94.0	-61.3	-138.1	-112.8	-112.7	13.5	-34.1	-54.6
4. DEBT INDICATORS										
EDT / XGS (%)	..	47.1	46.8	39.6	36.5	26.5	22.0	16.1	17.3	20.2
EDT / GNP (%)	..	23.7	30.7	21.4	20.5	16.0	13.4	10.6	10.8	12.6
TDS / XGS (%)	..	6.0	12.0	9.8	8.7	8.6	6.0	3.6	2.8	3.6
INT / XGS (%)	..	2.7	3.7	2.8	2.4	2.0	1.4	1.0	1.0	1.1
INT / GNP (%)	..	1.4	2.4	1.5	1.3	1.2	0.9	0.7	0.6	0.7
RES / EDT (%)	..	61.9	63.3	93.7	81.7	96.2	139.3	196.5	164.9	200.0
RES / MGS (months)	..	3.2	3.2	4.1	3.1	2.8	3.3	3.8	3.3	4.5
Short-term / EDT (%)	..	12.9	2.9	9.0	14.2	5.6	5.9	8.5	22.0	10.7
Concessional / EDT (%)	..	9.2	7.2	7.4	7.1	7.6	8.3	8.5	8.0	12.8
Multilateral / EDT (%)	..	23.2	49.0	54.4	50.2	55.9	59.5	59.9	53.3	63.1

FIJI

(US$ million, unless otherwise indicated)

	1970	1980	1990	1992	1993	1994	1995	1996	1997	1998
5. LONG-TERM DEBT										
DEBT OUTSTANDING (LDOD)	**11.7**	**244.9**	**400.7**	**308.2**	**283.4**	**268.2**	**235.9**	**199.2**	**170.6**	**172.2**
Public and publicly guaranteed	**11.7**	**180.0**	**306.0**	**226.9**	**199.4**	**180.7**	**167.9**	**146.7**	**129.5**	**140.0**
Official creditors	8.2	123.7	279.1	221.2	196.6	179.2	167.3	146.4	129.4	139.9
Multilateral	0.0	65.1	202.0	184.1	165.6	158.8	149.2	130.4	116.5	121.6
Concessional	0.0	4.4	14.7	13.0	11.6	11.3	11.6	10.6	11.2	11.4
Bilateral	8.2	58.6	77.1	37.0	31.0	20.4	18.1	16.0	12.9	18.4
Concessional	1.7	21.5	15.2	12.0	11.7	10.3	9.3	7.8	6.3	13.3
Private creditors	3.5	56.3	26.9	5.7	2.9	1.5	0.6	0.3	0.1	0.1
Bonds	3.5	2.5	0.0	0.0	0.0	0.0	0.0	0.0	0.0	0.0
Commercial banks	0.0	41.0	12.1	1.7	0.7	0.6	0.4	0.2	0.0	0.0
Other private	0.0	12.8	14.7	4.0	2.2	0.9	0.1	0.1	0.1	0.1
Private nonguaranteed	**0.0**	**64.9**	**94.7**	**81.3**	**84.0**	**87.5**	**68.0**	**52.5**	**41.2**	**32.2**
Bonds	0.0	0.0	0.0	0.0	0.0	0.0	0.0	0.0	0.0	0.0
Commercial banks	0.0	64.9	94.7	81.3	84.0	87.5	68.0	52.5	41.2	32.2
Memo:										
IBRD	0.0	33.5	67.8	53.2	43.6	39.6	35.3	32.8	30.3	31.8
IDA	0.0	0.0	0.0	0.0	0.0	0.0	0.0	0.0	0.0	0.0
DISBURSEMENTS	**2.3**	**78.2**	**33.5**	**36.8**	**32.6**	**41.4**	**15.2**	**8.6**	**9.1**	**6.5**
Public and publicly guaranteed	**2.3**	**78.2**	**19.3**	**16.6**	**11.1**	**16.9**	**15.2**	**8.6**	**9.1**	**6.5**
Official creditors	2.3	43.4	18.6	16.5	11.1	16.9	15.2	8.6	9.1	6.5
Multilateral	0.0	23.2	13.2	16.5	10.2	16.9	15.2	8.6	9.1	6.5
Concessional	0.0	2.3	0.0	0.0	0.0	0.0	0.0	0.0	2.1	0.0
Bilateral	2.3	20.2	5.3	0.0	1.0	0.0	0.0	0.0	0.0	0.0
Concessional	2.3	0.0	1.0	0.0	1.0	0.0	0.0	0.0	0.0	0.0
Private creditors	0.0	34.8	0.7	0.0	0.0	0.0	0.0	0.0	0.0	0.0
Bonds	0.0	0.0	0.0	0.0	0.0	0.0	0.0	0.0	0.0	0.0
Commercial banks	0.0	31.0	0.6	0.0	0.0	0.0	0.0	0.0	0.0	0.0
Other private	0.0	3.8	0.1	0.0	0.0	0.0	0.0	0.0	0.0	0.0
Private nonguaranteed	**0.0**	**0.0**	**14.2**	**20.2**	**21.5**	**24.5**	**0.0**	**0.0**	**0.0**	**0.0**
Bonds	0.0	0.0	0.0	0.0	0.0	0.0	0.0	0.0	0.0	0.0
Commercial banks	0.0	0.0	14.2	20.2	21.5	24.5	0.0	0.0	0.0	0.0
Memo:										
IBRD	0.0	5.7	5.1	2.2	1.5	5.8	5.6	6.6	4.3	4.3
IDA	0.0	0.0	0.0	0.0	0.0	0.0	0.0	0.0	0.0	0.0
PRINCIPAL REPAYMENTS	**1.6**	**11.2**	**72.2**	**60.0**	**56.9**	**71.7**	**51.8**	**35.2**	**23.3**	**23.5**
Public and publicly guaranteed	**1.6**	**11.2**	**54.7**	**42.3**	**38.1**	**52.6**	**32.3**	**19.7**	**12.0**	**14.5**
Official creditors	0.7	4.2	41.5	32.1	35.3	51.0	31.3	19.5	11.8	14.5
Multilateral	0.0	1.0	33.8	25.2	29.1	39.8	28.6	16.9	9.5	11.6
Concessional	0.0	0.0	0.3	0.4	0.4	1.4	0.5	0.5	0.3	0.4
Bilateral	0.7	3.2	7.7	6.9	6.2	11.2	2.7	2.6	2.3	2.9
Concessional	0.6	1.4	0.8	1.1	1.0	1.1	1.4	1.3	1.0	1.4
Private creditors	0.9	7.0	13.2	10.2	2.8	1.6	1.0	0.2	0.2	0.0
Bonds	0.9	1.6	0.0	0.0	0.0	0.0	0.0	0.0	0.0	0.0
Commercial banks	0.0	0.0	5.7	3.5	0.9	0.2	0.2	0.2	0.2	0.0
Other private	0.0	5.3	7.5	6.7	1.9	1.4	0.7	0.0	0.0	0.0
Private nonguaranteed	**0.0**	**0.0**	**17.5**	**17.7**	**18.8**	**19.1**	**19.5**	**15.5**	**11.3**	**9.0**
Bonds	0.0	0.0	0.0	0.0	0.0	0.0	0.0	0.0	0.0	0.0
Commercial banks	0.0	0.0	17.5	17.7	18.8	19.1	19.5	15.5	11.3	9.0
Memo:										
IBRD	0.0	0.7	9.1	12.0	12.2	12.9	11.5	6.7	3.9	4.8
IDA	0.0	0.0	0.0	0.0	0.0	0.0	0.0	0.0	0.0	0.0
NET FLOWS ON DEBT	**0.7**	**67.1**	**-38.7**	**-23.2**	**-24.2**	**-30.3**	**-36.6**	**-26.6**	**-14.1**	**-17.0**
Public and publicly guaranteed	**0.7**	**67.1**	**-35.4**	**-25.7**	**-26.9**	**-35.7**	**-17.1**	**-11.1**	**-2.8**	**-8.0**
Official creditors	1.6	39.2	-22.9	-15.6	-24.1	-34.1	-16.1	-10.8	-2.6	-8.0
Multilateral	0.0	22.2	-20.5	-8.7	-19.0	-22.9	-13.4	-8.2	-0.3	-5.1
Concessional	0.0	2.3	-0.3	-0.4	-0.4	-1.4	-0.5	-0.5	1.8	-0.4
Bilateral	1.6	17.0	-2.4	-6.9	-5.2	-11.2	-2.7	-2.6	-2.3	-2.9
Concessional	1.7	-1.4	0.1	-1.1	0.0	-1.1	-1.4	-1.3	-1.0	-1.4
Private creditors	-0.9	27.9	-12.5	-10.1	-2.8	-1.6	-1.0	-0.2	-0.2	0.0
Bonds	-0.9	-1.6	0.0	0.0	0.0	0.0	0.0	0.0	0.0	0.0
Commercial banks	0.0	31.0	-5.1	-3.4	-0.9	-0.2	-0.2	-0.2	-0.2	0.0
Other private	0.0	-1.5	-7.3	-6.7	-1.9	-1.4	-0.7	0.0	0.0	0.0
Private nonguaranteed	**0.0**	**0.0**	**-3.3**	**2.5**	**2.7**	**5.4**	**-19.5**	**-15.5**	**-11.3**	**-9.0**
Bonds	0.0	0.0	0.0	0.0	0.0	0.0	0.0	0.0	0.0	0.0
Commercial banks	0.0	0.0	-3.3	2.5	2.7	5.4	-19.5	-15.5	-11.3	-9.0
Memo:										
IBRD	0.0	5.0	-4.0	-9.7	-10.7	-7.0	-5.9	-0.1	0.4	-0.5
IDA	0.0	0.0	0.0	0.0	0.0	0.0	0.0	0.0	0.0	0.0

FIJI

(US$ million, unless otherwise indicated)

	1970	1980	1990	1992	1993	1994	1995	1996	1997	1998
INTEREST PAYMENTS (LINT)	**1.1**	**9.5**	**31.4**	**22.8**	**19.5**	**19.1**	**15.1**	**12.5**	**10.5**	**8.9**
Public and publicly guaranteed	**1.1**	**9.5**	**24.0**	**17.2**	**14.8**	**13.7**	**10.7**	**9.0**	**7.6**	**6.9**
Official creditors	0.6	6.1	21.4	16.7	14.5	13.5	10.6	9.0	7.6	6.9
Multilateral	0.0	3.4	15.0	13.2	12.0	11.4	9.5	8.0	6.7	6.0
Concessional	0.0	0.0	0.1	0.1	0.1	0.1	0.1	0.1	0.1	0.1
Bilateral	0.6	2.7	6.3	3.5	2.5	2.1	1.1	1.0	0.8	0.9
Concessional	0.1	0.8	0.3	0.5	0.4	0.4	0.3	0.3	0.2	0.4
Private creditors	0.5	3.5	2.6	0.6	0.3	0.2	0.1	0.0	0.0	0.0
Bonds	0.5	0.3	0.0	0.0	0.0	0.0	0.0	0.0	0.0	0.0
Commercial banks	0.0	2.1	1.1	0.3	0.1	0.1	0.1	0.0	0.0	0.0
Other private	0.0	1.1	1.5	0.3	0.2	0.1	0.0	0.0	0.0	0.0
Private nonguaranteed	**0.0**	**0.0**	**7.4**	**5.6**	**4.7**	**5.5**	**4.4**	**3.5**	**2.9**	**2.0**
Bonds	0.0	0.0	0.0	0.0	0.0	0.0	0.0	0.0	0.0	0.0
Commercial banks	0.0	0.0	7.4	5.6	4.7	5.5	4.4	3.5	2.9	2.0
Memo:										
IBRD	0.0	2.7	5.6	4.8	4.0	3.4	3.0	2.3	2.1	1.9
IDA	0.0	0.0	0.0	0.0	0.0	0.0	0.0	0.0	0.0	0.0
NET TRANSFERS ON DEBT	**-0.4**	**57.6**	**-70.0**	**-46.0**	**-43.7**	**-49.4**	**-51.6**	**-39.1**	**-24.6**	**-25.9**
Public and publicly guaranteed	**-0.4**	**57.6**	**-59.3**	**-42.9**	**-41.7**	**-49.4**	**-27.8**	**-20.1**	**-10.4**	**-14.9**
Official creditors	0.9	33.1	-44.3	-32.2	-38.7	-47.6	-26.7	-19.8	-10.2	-14.9
Multilateral	0.0	18.9	-35.5	-21.9	-31.0	-34.3	-22.9	-16.2	-7.1	-11.1
Concessional	0.0	2.3	-0.4	-0.5	-0.5	-1.5	-0.6	-0.6	1.8	-0.5
Bilateral	0.9	14.3	-8.7	-10.4	-7.7	-13.3	-3.8	-3.6	-3.1	-3.7
Concessional	1.6	-2.2	-0.2	-1.6	-0.4	-1.5	-1.7	-1.6	-1.2	-1.7
Private creditors	-1.4	24.4	-15.1	-10.7	-3.1	-1.8	-1.0	-0.3	-0.2	0.0
Bonds	-1.4	-1.9	0.0	0.0	0.0	0.0	0.0	0.0	0.0	0.0
Commercial banks	0.0	28.9	-6.2	-3.7	-1.0	-0.2	-0.3	-0.2	-0.2	0.0
Other private	0.0	-2.5	-8.9	-7.0	-2.0	-1.5	-0.8	0.0	0.0	0.0
Private nonguaranteed	**0.0**	**0.0**	**-10.7**	**-3.1**	**-2.0**	**-0.1**	**-23.9**	**-19.0**	**-14.3**	**-11.0**
Bonds	0.0	0.0	0.0	0.0	0.0	0.0	0.0	0.0	0.0	0.0
Commercial banks	0.0	0.0	-10.7	-3.1	-2.0	-0.1	-23.9	-19.0	-14.3	-11.0
Memo:										
IBRD	0.0	2.3	-9.6	-14.6	-14.7	-10.5	-8.9	-2.4	-1.7	-2.4
IDA	0.0	0.0	0.0	0.0	0.0	0.0	0.0	0.0	0.0	0.0
DEBT SERVICE (LTDS)	**2.7**	**20.7**	**103.5**	**82.8**	**76.4**	**90.9**	**66.8**	**47.7**	**33.8**	**32.4**
Public and publicly guaranteed	**2.7**	**20.7**	**78.6**	**59.5**	**52.9**	**66.3**	**43.0**	**28.7**	**19.5**	**21.4**
Official creditors	1.4	10.3	62.8	48.7	49.8	64.5	41.9	28.4	19.3	21.3
Multilateral	0.0	4.4	48.8	38.4	41.2	51.2	38.1	24.9	16.2	17.6
Concessional	0.0	0.0	0.4	0.5	0.5	1.5	0.6	0.6	0.4	0.5
Bilateral	1.4	5.9	14.0	10.4	8.6	13.3	3.8	3.6	3.1	3.7
Concessional	0.7	2.2	1.2	1.6	1.4	1.5	1.7	1.6	1.2	1.7
Private creditors	1.4	10.4	15.8	10.7	3.1	1.8	1.0	0.3	0.2	0.0
Bonds	1.4	1.9	0.0	0.0	0.0	0.0	0.0	0.0	0.0	0.0
Commercial banks	0.0	2.1	6.8	3.7	1.0	0.2	0.3	0.2	0.2	0.0
Other private	0.0	6.4	9.0	7.0	2.0	1.5	0.8	0.0	0.0	0.0
Private nonguaranteed	**0.0**	**0.0**	**24.9**	**23.3**	**23.5**	**24.6**	**23.9**	**19.0**	**14.3**	**11.0**
Bonds	0.0	0.0	0.0	0.0	0.0	0.0	0.0	0.0	0.0	0.0
Commercial banks	0.0	0.0	24.9	23.3	23.5	24.6	23.9	19.0	14.3	11.0
Memo:										
IBRD	0.0	3.3	14.7	16.8	16.2	16.3	14.5	9.0	6.0	6.7
IDA	0.0	0.0	0.0	0.0	0.0	0.0	0.0	0.0	0.0	0.0
UNDISBURSED DEBT	**1.4**	**120.8**	**81.2**	**45.1**	**66.2**	**48.8**	**37.5**	**28.8**	**60.1**	**74.3**
Official creditors	1.2	120.8	80.6	45.1	66.2	48.8	37.5	28.8	60.1	74.3
Private creditors	0.2	0.0	0.6	0.0	0.0	0.0	0.0	0.0	0.0	0.0
Memorandum items										
Concessional LDOD	1.7	25.9	29.9	25.0	23.3	21.6	20.9	18.4	17.5	24.7
Variable rate LDOD	0.0	105.9	124.0	107.4	110.7	125.1	113.9	98.1	84.6	79.6
Public sector LDOD	11.7	180.0	306.0	226.9	199.4	180.7	167.9	146.7	129.5	140.0
Private sector LDOD	0.0	64.9	94.7	81.3	84.0	87.5	68.0	52.5	41.2	32.2

6. CURRENCY COMPOSITION OF LONG-TERM DEBT (PERCENT)

	1970	1980	1990	1992	1993	1994	1995	1996	1997	1998
Deutsche mark	0.0	0.0	0.0	0.0	0.0	0.0	0.0	0.0	0.0	0.0
French franc	0.0	0.0	1.4	1.7	1.7	1.9	2.1	2.1	1.9	2.0
Japanese yen	0.0	0.0	0.0	0.0	0.0	0.0	0.0	0.0	0.0	0.0
Pound sterling	34.3	24.7	16.4	12.2	11.3	7.0	6.3	6.4	5.7	4.0
Swiss franc	0.0	0.0	0.0	0.0	0.0	0.0	0.0	0.0	0.0	0.0
U.S.dollars	14.6	26.1	5.2	0.6	1.0	0.9	0.8	0.7	0.5	5.6
Multiple currency	0.0	36.2	58.9	74.7	77.1	82.0	83.5	84.5	84.9	82.7
Special drawing rights	0.0	0.0	0.0	0.0	0.0	0.0	0.0	0.0	0.0	0.0
All other currencies	51.1	13.0	18.1	10.8	8.9	8.2	7.3	6.3	7.0	5.7

FIJI

(US$ million, unless otherwise indicated)

	1970	1980	1990	1992	1993	1994	1995	1996	1997	1998
7. DEBT RESTRUCTURINGS										
Total amount rescheduled	..	..	0.0	0.0	0.0	0.0	0.0	0.0	0.0	0.0
Debt stock rescheduled	..	..	0.0	0.0	0.0	0.0	0.0	0.0	0.0	0.0
Principal rescheduled	..	..	0.0	0.0	0.0	0.0	0.0	0.0	0.0	0.0
Official	..	..	0.0	0.0	0.0	0.0	0.0	0.0	0.0	0.0
Private	..	..	0.0	0.0	0.0	0.0	0.0	0.0	0.0	0.0
Interest rescheduled	..	..	0.0	0.0	0.0	0.0	0.0	0.0	0.0	0.0
Official	..	..	0.0	0.0	0.0	0.0	0.0	0.0	0.0	0.0
Private	..	..	0.0	0.0	0.0	0.0	0.0	0.0	0.0	0.0
Debt forgiven	..	..	0.0	0.0	0.0	0.0	0.0	0.0	0.0	0.0
Memo: interest forgiven	..	..	0.0	0.0	0.0	0.0	0.0	0.0	0.0	0.0
Debt stock reduction	..	..	0.0	0.0	0.0	0.0	0.0	0.0	0.0	0.0
of which debt buyback	..	..	0.0	0.0	0.0	0.0	0.0	0.0	0.0	0.0
8. DEBT STOCK-FLOW RECONCILIATION										
Total change in debt stocks	..	..	-1.5	-21.8	-8.5	-45.9	-33.4	-33.1	1.0	-25.8
Net flows on debt	0.7	71.6	-41.5	-4.1	-8.0	-61.0	-37.7	-23.1	15.5	-44.4
Net change in interest arrears	..	..	0.0	0.0	0.0	0.0	0.0	0.0	0.0	0.0
Interest capitalized	..	..	0.0	0.0	0.0	0.0	0.0	0.0	0.0	0.0
Debt forgiveness or reduction	..	..	0.0	0.0	0.0	0.0	0.0	0.0	0.0	0.0
Cross-currency valuation	..	..	15.7	-13.1	-3.9	0.8	-1.1	-3.3	-4.2	2.8
Residual	..	..	24.2	-4.6	3.4	14.3	5.3	-6.8	-10.3	15.8
9. AVERAGE TERMS OF NEW COMMITMENTS										
ALL CREDITORS										
Interest (%)	3.1	8.1	6.6	0.0	6.9	0.0	4.5	0.0	6.6	6.9
Maturity (years)	17.7	14.4	24.7	0.0	20.5	0.0	12.0	0.0	25.4	24.8
Grace period (years)	5.2	3.7	5.1	0.0	4.6	0.0	4.5	0.0	5.4	7.0
Grant element (%)	43.6	9.5	22.9	0.0	19.6	0.0	28.8	0.0	24.1	21.7
Official creditors										
Interest (%)	3.0	7.9	6.6	0.0	6.9	0.0	4.5	0.0	6.6	6.9
Maturity (years)	18.5	14.7	24.8	0.0	20.5	0.0	12.0	0.0	25.4	24.8
Grace period (years)	5.5	3.7	5.1	0.0	4.6	0.0	4.5	0.0	5.4	7.0
Grant element (%)	45.6	10.6	23.0	0.0	19.6	0.0	28.8	0.0	24.1	21.7
Private creditors										
Interest (%)	5.5	10.2	8.8	0.0	0.0	0.0	0.0	0.0	0.0	0.0
Maturity (years)	5.2	10.0	10.4	0.0	0.0	0.0	0.0	0.0	0.0	0.0
Grace period (years)	0.7	3.3	6.2	0.0	0.0	0.0	0.0	0.0	0.0	0.0
Grant element (%)	10.5	-4.3	3.5	0.0	0.0	0.0	0.0	0.0	0.0	0.0
Memorandum items										
Commitments	3.7	89.1	30.0	0.0	33.0	0.0	10.5	0.0	42.3	17.8
Official creditors	3.5	82.6	29.8	0.0	33.0	0.0	10.5	0.0	42.3	17.8
Private creditors	0.2	6.5	0.1	0.0	0.0	0.0	0.0	0.0	0.0	0.0

10. CONTRACTUAL OBLIGATIONS ON OUTSTANDING LONG-TERM DEBT

	1999	2000	2001	2002	2003	2004	2005	2006	2007	2008
TOTAL										
Disbursements	13.4	17.5	13.9	10.6	8.6	6.3	4.0	0.0	0.0	0.0
Principal	23.2	23.3	21.4	19.7	18.8	14.0	11.6	11.8	11.1	9.1
Interest	9.6	9.0	8.8	8.5	8.2	7.4	7.1	6.5	5.8	5.3
Official creditors										
Disbursements	13.4	17.5	13.9	10.6	8.6	6.3	4.0	0.0	0.0	0.0
Principal	15.6	17.7	15.3	14.2	13.8	11.5	11.6	11.8	11.1	9.1
Interest	8.1	8.2	8.1	8.0	7.7	7.4	7.1	6.5	5.8	5.3
Bilateral creditors										
Disbursements	6.7	7.5	3.8	1.2	0.6	0.0	0.0	0.0	0.0	0.0
Principal	2.5	2.4	1.0	1.1	1.1	1.3	2.2	2.2	2.2	2.2
Interest	0.9	1.3	1.5	1.6	1.6	1.5	1.5	1.4	1.3	1.2
Multilateral creditors										
Disbursements	6.7	10.0	10.2	9.4	8.0	6.3	4.0	0.0	0.0	0.0
Principal	13.1	15.3	14.2	13.2	12.7	10.3	9.5	9.7	8.9	6.9
Interest	7.2	6.9	6.6	6.4	6.2	5.9	5.6	5.1	4.5	4.0
Private creditors										
Disbursements	0.0	0.0	0.0	0.0	0.0	0.0	0.0	0.0	0.0	0.0
Principal	7.5	5.6	6.1	5.5	5.0	2.5	0.0	0.0	0.0	0.0
Interest	1.5	0.8	0.7	0.5	0.4	0.0	0.0	0.0	0.0	0.0
Commercial banks										
Disbursements	0.0	0.0	0.0	0.0	0.0	0.0	0.0	0.0	0.0	0.0
Principal	0.0	0.0	0.0	0.0	0.0	0.0	0.0	0.0	0.0	0.0
Interest	0.0	0.0	0.0	0.0	0.0	0.0	0.0	0.0	0.0	0.0
Other private										
Disbursements	0.0	0.0	0.0	0.0	0.0	0.0	0.0	0.0	0.0	0.0
Principal	7.5	5.6	6.1	5.5	5.0	2.5	0.0	0.0	0.0	0.0
Interest	1.5	0.8	0.7	0.5	0.4	0.0	0.0	0.0	0.0	0.0

GABON

(US$ million, unless otherwise indicated)

	1970	1980	1990	1992	1993	1994	1995	1996	1997	1998
1. SUMMARY DEBT DATA										
TOTAL DEBT STOCKS (EDT)	..	**1,514**	**3,984**	**3,850**	**3,861**	**4,171**	**4,360**	**4,310**	**4,278**	**4,425**
Long-term debt (LDOD)	**91**	**1,272**	**3,151**	**3,049**	**2,933**	**3,694**	**3,976**	**3,972**	**3,665**	**3,833**
Public and publicly guaranteed	91	1,272	3,151	3,049	2,933	3,694	3,976	3,972	3,665	3,833
Private nonguaranteed	0	0	0	0	0	0	0	0	0	0
Use of IMF credit	**0**	**15**	**140**	**81**	**45**	**90**	**97**	**120**	**131**	**113**
Short-term debt	..	**228**	**693**	**721**	**883**	**387**	**287**	**219**	**482**	**478**
of which interest arrears on LDOD	..	0	131	285	450	51	0	0	0	79
Official creditors	..	0	111	210	361	36	0	0	0	77
Private creditors	..	0	20	75	90	15	0	0	0	2
Memo: principal arrears on LDOD	..	0	82	423	650	110	26	0	0	85
Official creditors	..	0	17	144	279	47	0	0	0	84
Private creditors	..	0	65	279	371	63	26	0	0	1
Memo: export credits	..	0	1,917	2,194	2,102	2,066	2,066	2,153	2,485	2,223
TOTAL DEBT FLOWS										
Disbursements	**26**	**171**	**204**	**108**	**93**	**198**	**279**	**121**	**168**	**46**
Long-term debt	26	171	195	108	93	134	222	89	145	46
IMF purchases	0	0	9	0	0	64	57	32	23	0
Principal repayments	**9**	**279**	**40**	**137**	**71**	**119**	**216**	**137**	**172**	**135**
Long-term debt	9	279	26	100	35	96	165	131	168	112
IMF repurchases	0	0	15	36	36	23	52	5	4	23
Net flows on debt	**30**	**-122**	**164**	**-193**	**19**	**-18**	**14**	**-84**	**260**	**-172**
of which short-term debt	..	-13	0	-164	-3	-97	-49	-69	263	-83
Interest payments (INT)	..	**153**	**136**	**296**	**86**	**149**	**240**	**247**	**261**	**172**
Long-term debt	3	119	78	238	35	103	217	232	238	142
IMF charges	0	1	13	9	6	3	5	4	6	6
Short-term debt	..	33	45	50	45	43	17	11	18	25
Net transfers on debt	..	**-275**	**28**	**-489**	**-67**	**-167**	**-226**	**-331**	**-2**	**-344**
Total debt service paid (TDS)	..	**432**	**176**	**433**	**157**	**268**	**456**	**384**	**433**	**307**
Long-term debt	12	398	104	338	70	198	382	363	406	254
IMF repurchases and charges	0	1	27	45	42	26	57	10	9	29
Short-term debt (interest only)	..	33	45	50	45	43	17	11	18	25
2. AGGREGATE NET RESOURCE FLOWS AND NET TRANSFERS (LONG-TERM)										
NET RESOURCE FLOWS	**26**	**-74**	**274**	**164**	**9**	**82**	**31**	**-30**	**-64**	**-64**
Net flow of long-term debt (ex. IMF)	17	-109	170	8	58	38	57	-42	-23	-66
Foreign direct investment (net)	-1	32	74	127	-114	-103	-113	-65	-100	-50
Portfolio equity flows	0	0	0	0	0	0	0	0	0	0
Grants (excluding technical coop.)	10	4	30	29	65	147	87	78	58	52
Memo: technical coop. grants	7	38	36	48	49	43	46	43	36	35
official net resource flows	17	20	171	54	124	216	219	86	40	-8
private net resource flows	9	-93	103	110	-115	-134	-188	-116	-105	-57
NET TRANSFERS	**15**	**-465**	**79**	**-230**	**-226**	**-241**	**-387**	**-472**	**-502**	**-431**
Interest on long-term debt	3	119	78	238	35	103	217	232	238	142
Profit remittances on FDI	8	273	116	156	200	220	200	210	200	225
Memo: official net transfers	15	1	103	-147	95	142	45	-133	-188	-142
private net transfers	0	-466	-24	-83	-321	-382	-432	-338	-315	-290
3. MAJOR ECONOMIC AGGREGATES										
Gross national product (GNP)	306	3,856	5,336	4,864	3,868	3,693	4,242	4,928	4,477	4,878
Exports of goods & services (XGS)	..	2,434	2,750	2,654	2,669	2,597	2,929	3,488	3,307	2,557
of which workers remittances	..	0	0	0	0	..	..	..	..	..
Imports of goods & services (MGS)	..	1,926	2,448	2,680	2,526	2,113	2,631	3,016	2,911	2,473
International reserves (RES)	15	115	279	75	6	180	153	253	286	15
Current account balance	..	384	168	-168	-49	317	100	249	171	-75
4. DEBT INDICATORS										
EDT / XGS (%)	..	62.2	144.9	145.1	144.7	160.6	148.9	123.6	129.4	173.1
EDT / GNP (%)	..	39.3	74.7	79.2	99.8	113.0	102.8	87.5	95.6	90.7
TDS / XGS (%)	..	17.8	6.4	16.3	5.9	10.3	15.6	11.0	13.1	12.0
INT / XGS (%)	..	6.3	4.9	11.2	3.2	5.7	8.2	7.1	7.9	6.7
INT / GNP (%)	..	4.0	2.5	6.1	2.2	4.0	5.7	5.0	5.8	3.5
RES / EDT (%)	..	7.6	7.0	2.0	0.2	4.3	3.5	5.9	6.7	0.4
RES / MGS (months)	..	0.7	1.4	0.3	0.0	1.0	0.7	1.0	1.2	0.1
Short-term / EDT (%)	..	15.1	17.4	18.7	22.9	9.3	6.6	5.1	11.3	10.8
Concessional / EDT (%)	..	7.5	10.6	11.6	10.6	13.8	16.1	17.2	20.9	21.4
Multilateral / EDT (%)	..	2.7	8.0	9.3	10.6	11.2	13.5	13.5	12.3	12.5

GABON

(US$ million, unless otherwise indicated)

	1970	1980	1990	1992	1993	1994	1995	1996	1997	1998
5. LONG-TERM DEBT										
DEBT OUTSTANDING (LDOD)	**91**	**1,272**	**3,151**	**3,049**	**2,933**	**3,694**	**3,976**	**3,972**	**3,665**	**3,833**
Public and publicly guaranteed	**91**	**1,272**	**3,151**	**3,049**	**2,933**	**3,694**	**3,976**	**3,972**	**3,665**	**3,833**
Official creditors	67	316	2,435	2,423	2,337	3,427	3,778	3,829	3,534	3,708
Multilateral	31	40	317	358	408	467	588	583	528	554
Concessional	1	10	29	25	25	25	28	30	30	32
Bilateral	36	276	2,118	2,065	1,929	2,960	3,189	3,246	3,007	3,154
Concessional	35	103	393	423	384	549	674	712	863	916
Private creditors	24	955	716	626	596	268	199	143	131	125
Bonds	8	2	0	0	0	0	0	0	0	0
Commercial banks	0	721	182	163	161	175	148	117	97	85
Other private	16	232	535	462	435	92	51	26	33	40
Private nonguaranteed	**0**	**0**	**0**	**0**	**0**	**0**	**0**	**0**	**0**	**0**
Bonds	0	0	0	0	0	0	0	0	0	0
Commercial banks	0	0	0	0	0	0	0	0	0	0
Memo:										
IBRD	29	19	69	82	86	114	110	92	77	75
IDA	0	0	0	0	0	0	0	0	0	0
DISBURSEMENTS	**26**	**171**	**195**	**108**	**93**	**134**	**222**	**89**	**145**	**46**
Public and publicly guaranteed	**26**	**171**	**195**	**108**	**93**	**134**	**222**	**89**	**145**	**46**
Official creditors	13	36	158	108	90	132	222	89	125	36
Multilateral	4	2	84	43	66	78	150	64	34	22
Concessional	1	0	4	1	0	1	2	5	6	2
Bilateral	9	33	74	65	24	54	72	25	91	14
Concessional	9	16	63	8	19	52	62	21	90	12
Private creditors	13	135	37	0	3	2	0	0	20	10
Bonds	4	0	0	0	0	0	0	0	0	0
Commercial banks	0	95	0	0	0	0	0	0	0	3
Other private	9	40	37	0	3	2	0	0	20	8
Private nonguaranteed	**0**	**0**	**0**	**0**	**0**	**0**	**0**	**0**	**0**	**0**
Bonds	0	0	0	0	0	0	0	0	0	0
Commercial banks	0	0	0	0	0	0	0	0	0	0
Memo:										
IBRD	3	0	10	8	8	33	4	3	3	7
IDA	0	0	0	0	0	0	0	0	0	0
PRINCIPAL REPAYMENTS	**9**	**279**	**26**	**100**	**35**	**96**	**165**	**131**	**168**	**112**
Public and publicly guaranteed	**9**	**279**	**26**	**100**	**35**	**96**	**165**	**131**	**168**	**112**
Official creditors	6	19	18	84	31	63	90	80	143	95
Multilateral	4	3	13	16	15	36	43	46	42	23
Concessional	0	0	1	1	0	3	2	2	3	1
Bilateral	2	17	5	68	16	27	48	34	101	72
Concessional	2	4	0	22	7	5	10	7	36	27
Private creditors	4	260	8	17	4	33	75	51	25	17
Bonds	0	1	0	0	0	0	0	0	0	0
Commercial banks	0	185	3	12	0	3	26	31	20	15
Other private	3	74	5	5	4	30	49	20	5	2
Private nonguaranteed	**0**	**0**	**0**	**0**	**0**	**0**	**0**	**0**	**0**	**0**
Bonds	0	0	0	0	0	0	0	0	0	0
Commercial banks	0	0	0	0	0	0	0	0	0	0
Memo:										
IBRD	3	2	1	4	5	10	12	13	10	9
IDA	0	0	0	0	0	0	0	0	0	0
NET FLOWS ON DEBT	**17**	**-109**	**170**	**8**	**58**	**38**	**57**	**-42**	**-23**	**-66**
Public and publicly guaranteed	**17**	**-109**	**170**	**8**	**58**	**38**	**57**	**-42**	**-23**	**-66**
Official creditors	7	16	141	25	60	69	132	9	-18	-60
Multilateral	0	0	71	28	51	42	107	17	-8	-1
Concessional	1	0	3	0	0	-1	1	4	3	1
Bilateral	7	17	70	-3	8	27	24	-9	-10	-59
Concessional	7	13	63	-14	12	47	52	14	54	-15
Private creditors	9	-125	29	-17	-2	-31	-75	-51	-5	-7
Bonds	4	-1	0	0	0	0	0	0	0	0
Commercial banks	0	-91	-3	-12	0	-3	-26	-31	-20	-13
Other private	6	-34	32	-5	-2	-28	-49	-20	15	6
Private nonguaranteed	**0**	**0**	**0**	**0**	**0**	**0**	**0**	**0**	**0**	**0**
Bonds	0	0	0	0	0	0	0	0	0	0
Commercial banks	0	0	0	0	0	0	0	0	0	0
Memo:										
IBRD	-1	-2	9	3	3	23	-8	-11	-7	-3
IDA	0	0	0	0	0	0	0	0	0	0

GABON

(US$ million, unless otherwise indicated)

	1970	1980	1990	1992	1993	1994	1995	1996	1997	1998
INTEREST PAYMENTS (LINT)	**3**	**119**	**78**	**238**	**35**	**103**	**217**	**232**	**238**	**142**
Public and publicly guaranteed	**3**	**119**	**78**	**238**	**35**	**103**	**217**	**232**	**238**	**142**
Official creditors	2	19	68	201	30	74	174	219	228	134
Multilateral	1	2	21	26	17	37	26	43	44	21
Concessional	0	0	0	0	0	1	1	1	1	0
Bilateral	1	17	47	176	13	37	148	176	184	113
Concessional	1	3	2	19	4	14	39	38	35	23
Private creditors	1	100	11	36	6	29	44	12	10	8
Bonds	0	0	0	0	0	0	0	0	0	0
Commercial banks	0	81	5	34	6	16	27	9	7	7
Other private	0	19	6	3	0	13	17	3	3	1
Private nonguaranteed	**0**	**0**	**0**	**0**	**0**	**0**	**0**	**0**	**0**	**0**
Bonds	0	0	0	0	0	0	0	0	0	0
Commercial banks	0	0	0	0	0	0	0	0	0	0
Memo:										
IBRD	1	2	5	7	4	8	8	9	6	3
IDA	0	0	0	0	0	0	0	0	0	0
NET TRANSFERS ON DEBT	**14**	**-227**	**92**	**-230**	**23**	**-65**	**-161**	**-274**	**-261**	**-208**
Public and publicly guaranteed	**14**	**-227**	**92**	**-230**	**23**	**-65**	**-161**	**-274**	**-261**	**-208**
Official creditors	5	-3	73	-177	30	-5	-42	-211	-246	-193
Multilateral	-1	-2	51	2	34	5	82	-26	-52	-22
Concessional	1	0	2	0	0	-2	0	3	2	0
Bilateral	6	-1	23	-179	-5	-10	-124	-185	-194	-172
Concessional	7	10	62	-33	8	33	13	-24	19	-39
Private creditors	9	-224	18	-53	-7	-60	-119	-63	-15	-15
Bonds	3	-1	0	0	0	0	0	0	0	0
Commercial banks	0	-171	-8	-46	-6	-18	-53	-40	-27	-19
Other private	6	-53	26	-8	-2	-41	-66	-23	12	4
Private nonguaranteed	**0**	**0**	**0**	**0**	**0**	**0**	**0**	**0**	**0**	**0**
Bonds	0	0	0	0	0	0	0	0	0	0
Commercial banks	0	0	0	0	0	0	0	0	0	0
Memo:										
IBRD	-2	-3	4	-3	-1	15	-16	-20	-13	-6
IDA	0	0	0	0	0	0	0	0	0	0
DEBT SERVICE (LTDS)	**12**	**398**	**104**	**338**	**70**	**198**	**382**	**363**	**406**	**254**
Public and publicly guaranteed	**12**	**398**	**104**	**338**	**70**	**198**	**382**	**363**	**406**	**254**
Official creditors	8	39	85	285	60	137	264	300	371	229
Multilateral	5	4	34	41	31	74	68	90	86	43
Concessional	0	0	2	2	0	4	2	3	4	1
Bilateral	3	34	51	244	29	64	195	210	285	186
Concessional	3	6	2	41	12	19	49	45	71	50
Private creditors	4	359	19	53	10	61	119	63	35	25
Bonds	1	1	0	0	0	0	0	0	0	0
Commercial banks	0	266	8	46	6	18	53	40	27	22
Other private	4	93	11	8	4	43	66	23	8	4
Private nonguaranteed	**0**	**0**	**0**	**0**	**0**	**0**	**0**	**0**	**0**	**0**
Bonds	0	0	0	0	0	0	0	0	0	0
Commercial banks	0	0	0	0	0	0	0	0	0	0
Memo:										
IBRD	5	4	6	11	8	18	20	22	16	12
IDA	0	0	0	0	0	0	0	0	0	0
UNDISBURSED DEBT	**34**	**164**	**287**	**228**	**483**	**548**	**409**	**445**	**419**	**446**
Official creditors	15	133	271	223	481	548	409	445	382	359
Private creditors	19	31	17	5	2	0	0	0	37	87
Memorandum items										
Concessional LDOD	36	113	422	448	408	574	702	742	893	948
Variable rate LDOD	0	500	416	428	426	676	723	651	562	543
Public sector LDOD	65	1,246	3,149	3,047	2,933	3,694	3,976	3,972	3,665	3,833
Private sector LDOD	26	26	2	2	0	0	0	0	0	0

6. CURRENCY COMPOSITION OF LONG-TERM DEBT (PERCENT)

	1970	1980	1990	1992	1993	1994	1995	1996	1997	1998
Deutsche mark	4.8	4.8	8.4	8.1	7.9	11.9	8.4	7.8	7.1	6.7
French franc	43.3	39.0	54.8	53.2	50.7	47.6	47.4	46.3	45.3	45.6
Japanese yen	0.0	1.5	0.7	0.8	0.9	1.0	0.9	0.8	0.8	0.8
Pound sterling	0.0	0.8	5.3	4.2	4.3	4.4	5.0	5.6	6.0	5.8
Swiss franc	0.0	0.5	0.3	0.3	0.3	0.7	0.8	0.7	0.7	0.7
U.S.dollars	7.6	42.7	10.3	12.0	12.5	12.6	11.5	11.3	11.2	12.0
Multiple currency	32.3	1.5	3.7	5.6	7.7	8.0	8.8	8.9	8.7	6.7
Special drawing rights	0.0	0.0	0.0	0.0	0.0	0.3	0.2	0.2	0.0	0.0
All other currencies	12.0	9.2	16.5	15.8	15.7	13.5	17.0	18.4	20.2	21.7

GABON

(US$ million, unless otherwise indicated)

	1970	1980	1990	1992	1993	1994	1995	1996	1997	1998
7. DEBT RESTRUCTURINGS										
Total amount rescheduled	..	..	271	26	2	1,571	472	501	315	127
Debt stock rescheduled	..	..	0	0	0	74	0	0	0	0
Principal rescheduled	..	..	188	23	0	766	253	270	191	82
Official	..	..	32	0	0	397	249	266	190	82
Private	..	..	156	23	0	369	4	4	1	0
Interest rescheduled	..	..	77	0	2	449	68	64	45	21
Official	..	..	27	0	2	376	67	64	45	21
Private	..	..	50	0	0	73	1	0	0	0
Debt forgiven	..	..	0	0	29	240	40	0	2	0
Memo: interest forgiven	..	..	0	0	0	0	0	0	0	0
Debt stock reduction	..	..	0	0	0	0	1	0	0	0
of which debt buyback	..	..	0	0	0	0	0	0	0	0
8. DEBT STOCK-FLOW RECONCILIATION										
Total change in debt stocks	..	..	634	-373	11	310	189	-50	-33	147
Net flows on debt	30	-122	164	-193	19	-18	14	-84	260	-172
Net change in interest arrears	..	..	88	7	165	-399	-51	0	0	79
Interest capitalized	..	..	77	0	2	449	68	64	45	21
Debt forgiveness or reduction	..	..	0	0	-29	-240	-41	0	-2	0
Cross-currency valuation	..	..	359	-167	-134	293	242	-180	-339	184
Residual	..	..	-54	-21	-12	225	-42	151	5	34
9. AVERAGE TERMS OF NEW COMMITMENTS										
ALL CREDITORS										
Interest (%)	5.1	11.2	7.9	8.1	8.2	5.5	4.7	6.2	6.0	4.7
Maturity (years)	10.7	11.2	17.9	17.4	18.3	16.2	13.0	15.4	11.4	9.2
Grace period (years)	1.5	3.4	4.7	7.0	5.8	5.1	5.9	5.4	3.9	2.5
Grant element (%)	19.2	-5.3	12.3	12.1	10.6	25.0	30.4	21.6	19.3	23.6
Official creditors										
Interest (%)	4.0	7.4	7.7	7.9	8.2	5.5	4.7	6.2	5.6	1.6
Maturity (years)	17.3	14.8	18.9	18.2	18.3	16.2	13.0	15.4	13.1	17.5
Grace period (years)	3.6	4.9	5.4	7.4	5.8	5.1	5.9	5.4	4.8	5.4
Grant element (%)	34.4	15.0	13.9	13.1	10.6	25.0	30.4	21.6	23.1	54.2
Private creditors										
Interest (%)	5.2	13.0	9.0	11.0	0.0	0.0	0.0	0.0	6.9	6.0
Maturity (years)	9.9	9.5	11.7	5.2	0.0	0.0	0.0	0.0	7.3	5.9
Grace period (years)	1.2	2.6	1.3	1.2	0.0	0.0	0.0	0.0	1.9	1.4
Grant element (%)	17.4	-15.4	3.3	-2.5	0.0	0.0	0.0	0.0	10.2	11.2
Memorandum items										
Commitments	33	196	66	76	358	184	89	154	175	82
Official creditors	4	65	56	71	358	184	89	154	124	24
Private creditors	29	131	10	5	0	0	0	0	52	58

10. CONTRACTUAL OBLIGATIONS ON OUTSTANDING LONG-TERM DEBT

	1999	2000	2001	2002	2003	2004	2005	2006	2007	2008
TOTAL										
Disbursements	149	125	79	45	25	12	6	1	0	0
Principal	330	389	316	337	353	346	347	342	342	330
Interest	266	252	229	210	189	166	143	120	96	72
Official creditors										
Disbursements	102	99	68	42	24	12	6	1	0	0
Principal	299	353	277	300	320	329	337	339	341	330
Interest	255	242	220	204	185	164	142	119	96	72
Bilateral creditors										
Disbursements	31	35	23	15	9	4	2	0	0	0
Principal	247	292	212	239	257	269	279	284	288	280
Interest	216	202	182	168	152	136	118	98	78	57
Multilateral creditors										
Disbursements	71	64	45	27	16	7	4	1	0	0
Principal	51	61	65	61	63	60	58	56	53	50
Interest	39	40	38	36	32	29	25	21	18	14
Private creditors										
Disbursements	47	26	11	3	0	0	0	0	0	0
Principal	31	37	38	37	33	17	10	3	1	1
Interest	11	10	9	6	4	2	1	1	0	0
Commercial banks										
Disbursements	42	21	9	2	0	0	0	0	0	0
Principal	29	29	30	29	27	11	3	2	0	0
Interest	8	7	6	4	2	1	0	0	0	0
Other private										
Disbursements	5	5	2	1	0	0	0	0	0	0
Principal	3	8	8	8	7	7	7	1	1	1
Interest	3	3	3	2	2	1	1	1	0	0

GAMBIA, THE

(US$ million, unless otherwise indicated)

	1970	1980	1990	1992	1993	1994	1995	1996	1997	1998
1. SUMMARY DEBT DATA										
TOTAL DEBT STOCKS (EDT)	..	**136.8**	**369.1**	**403.4**	**426.1**	**424.7**	**428.9**	**459.6**	**434.4**	**477.0**
Long-term debt (LDOD)	**5.1**	**97.3**	**308.4**	**346.3**	**350.3**	**369.8**	**388.3**	**419.7**	**411.1**	**451.3**
Public and publicly guaranteed	5.1	97.3	308.4	346.3	350.3	369.8	388.3	419.7	411.1	451.3
Private nonguaranteed	0.0	0.0	0.0	0.0	0.0	0.0	0.0	0.0	0.0	0.0
Use of IMF credit	**0.0**	**16.2**	**44.9**	**35.6**	**33.2**	**31.3**	**25.8**	**17.6**	**10.2**	**10.4**
Short-term debt	..	**23.3**	**15.7**	**21.6**	**42.6**	**23.6**	**14.8**	**22.4**	**13.1**	**15.3**
of which interest arrears on LDOD	..	0.3	0.6	0.6	0.6	0.6	0.7	0.0	0.1	0.0
Official creditors	..	0.2	0.6	0.6	0.6	0.6	0.7	0.0	0.1	0.0
Private creditors	..	0.1	0.0	0.0	0.0	0.0	0.0	0.0	0.0	0.0
Memo: principal arrears on LDOD	..	0.0	0.8	1.6	3.9	5.7	3.2	0.2	0.2	0.1
Official creditors	..	0.0	0.8	1.6	3.9	5.7	3.1	0.2	0.2	0.1
Private creditors	..	0.0	0.0	0.0	0.0	0.1	0.1	0.0	0.0	0.0
Memo: export credits	..	0.0	32.0	41.0	38.0	34.0	28.0	23.0	22.0	24.0
TOTAL DEBT FLOWS										
Disbursements	**0.8**	**55.7**	**32.8**	**55.4**	**25.5**	**24.2**	**23.0**	**63.1**	**26.2**	**29.0**
Long-term debt	0.8	51.2	23.5	55.4	25.5	24.2	23.0	63.1	26.2	24.3
IMF purchases	0.0	4.4	9.3	0.0	0.0	0.0	0.0	0.0	0.0	4.7
Principal repayments	**0.1**	**0.4**	**25.5**	**21.8**	**20.7**	**23.4**	**20.7**	**22.2**	**19.8**	**19.8**
Long-term debt	0.1	0.4	20.2	18.6	18.3	19.5	14.4	14.7	13.4	14.9
IMF repurchases	0.0	0.0	5.3	3.1	2.4	3.9	6.2	7.4	6.4	4.9
Net flows on debt	**0.7**	**58.3**	**15.4**	**34.6**	**25.8**	**-18.3**	**-6.5**	**49.1**	**-3.0**	**11.5**
of which short-term debt	..	3.0	8.1	1.0	21.0	-19.0	-8.8	8.2	-9.4	2.3
Interest payments (INT)	..	**3.8**	**12.2**	**7.8**	**7.2**	**7.6**	**6.0**	**5.8**	**6.9**	**6.3**
Long-term debt	0.0	0.4	10.2	6.7	6.1	5.8	4.9	4.6	5.8	5.4
IMF charges	0.0	0.5	1.3	0.3	0.2	0.2	0.2	0.1	0.1	0.1
Short-term debt	..	2.9	0.8	0.9	1.0	1.6	0.9	1.1	1.1	0.8
Net transfers on debt	..	**54.5**	**3.2**	**26.8**	**18.6**	**-25.9**	**-12.5**	**43.3**	**-9.9**	**5.2**
Total debt service paid (TDS)	..	**4.1**	**37.7**	**29.6**	**27.9**	**31.1**	**26.6**	**28.0**	**26.7**	**26.1**
Long-term debt	0.1	0.8	30.3	25.3	24.4	25.4	19.3	19.4	19.2	20.3
IMF repurchases and charges	0.0	0.5	6.7	3.4	2.6	4.1	6.4	7.6	6.4	4.9
Short-term debt (interest only)	..	2.9	0.8	0.9	1.0	1.6	0.9	1.1	1.1	0.8
2. AGGREGATE NET RESOURCE FLOWS AND NET TRANSFERS (LONG-TERM)										
NET RESOURCE FLOWS	**0.9**	**78.0**	**48.1**	**86.6**	**62.8**	**52.1**	**33.9**	**72.3**	**41.6**	**46.4**
Net flow of long-term debt (ex. IMF)	0.7	50.9	3.4	36.7	7.2	4.7	8.5	48.4	12.8	9.4
Foreign direct investment (net)	0.1	0.0	0.0	6.0	11.1	9.8	7.8	11.0	12.0	13.0
Portfolio equity flows	0.0	0.0	0.0	0.0	0.0	0.0	0.0	0.0	0.0	0.0
Grants (excluding technical coop.)	0.1	27.2	44.7	43.9	44.5	37.6	17.6	12.9	16.8	24.0
Memo: technical coop. grants	0.7	12.7	25.1	27.1	25.7	23.9	22.8	17.5	14.0	10.7
official net resource flows	0.8	56.7	55.6	85.1	56.0	46.6	26.5	61.5	29.6	33.4
private net resource flows	0.1	21.3	-7.5	1.5	6.8	5.5	7.4	10.8	12.0	13.0
NET TRANSFERS	**0.7**	**75.8**	**37.9**	**79.9**	**56.8**	**46.3**	**29.0**	**67.7**	**35.8**	**41.0**
Interest on long-term debt	0.0	0.4	10.2	6.7	6.1	5.8	4.9	4.6	5.8	5.4
Profit remittances on FDI	0.2	1.8	0.0	0.0	0.0	0.0	0.0	0.0	0.0	0.0
Memo: official net transfers	0.8	56.3	50.1	79.2	50.4	41.0	21.6	56.9	23.8	28.0
private net transfers	-0.1	19.5	-12.2	0.7	6.4	5.3	7.4	10.8	12.0	13.0
3. MAJOR ECONOMIC AGGREGATES										
Gross national product (GNP)	52.3	237.0	291.3	342.2	361.6	357.9	377.1	385.4	398.8	408.6
Exports of goods & services (XGS)	..	66.2	169.7	232.7	242.4	220.3	181.0	226.0	232.7	268.4
of which workers remittances	..	0.0	0.0	0.0	0.0	0.0	..	..	..	..
Imports of goods & services (MGS)	..	181.5	205.4	252.0	294.1	253.8	241.4	303.4	293.1	341.6
International reserves (RES)	8.1	5.7	55.4	94.0	..	98.0	106.1	102.1	96.0	106.4
Current account balance	..	-86.9	23.4	37.2	-5.3	8.2	-8.2	-47.7	-23.6	-44.2
4. DEBT INDICATORS										
EDT / XGS (%)	..	206.5	217.5	173.4	175.8	192.8	236.9	203.4	186.7	177.7
EDT / GNP (%)	..	57.7	126.7	117.9	117.8	118.7	113.7	119.3	108.9	116.7
TDS / XGS (%)	..	6.2	22.2	12.7	11.5	14.1	14.7	12.4	11.5	9.7
INT / XGS (%)	..	5.7	7.2	3.4	3.0	3.5	3.3	2.6	3.0	2.4
INT / GNP (%)	..	1.6	4.2	2.3	2.0	2.1	1.6	1.5	1.7	1.5
RES / EDT (%)	..	4.1	15.0	23.3	..	23.1	24.8	22.2	22.1	22.3
RES / MGS (months)	..	0.4	3.2	4.5	..	4.6	5.3	4.0	3.9	3.7
Short-term / EDT (%)	..	17.0	4.3	5.4	10.0	5.6	3.5	4.9	3.0	3.2
Concessional / EDT (%)	..	49.9	67.8	73.9	72.9	79.5	84.9	87.4	91.6	91.1
Multilateral / EDT (%)	..	29.9	55.0	62.9	64.1	71.5	76.1	71.3	75.1	74.6

GAMBIA, THE

(US$ million, unless otherwise indicated)

	1970	1980	1990	1992	1993	1994	1995	1996	1997	1998
5. LONG-TERM DEBT										
DEBT OUTSTANDING (LDOD)	**5.1**	**97.3**	**308.4**	**346.3**	**350.3**	**369.8**	**388.3**	**419.7**	**411.1**	**451.3**
Public and publicly guaranteed	**5.1**	**97.3**	**308.4**	**346.3**	**350.3**	**369.8**	**388.3**	**419.7**	**411.1**	**451.3**
Official creditors	5.1	73.4	290.1	337.2	345.5	369.2	388.0	419.7	411.1	451.3
Multilateral	0.0	40.9	203.1	253.7	273.0	303.8	326.5	327.8	326.4	355.7
Concessional	0.0	35.8	183.3	229.0	248.4	279.0	305.7	310.3	313.1	339.2
Bilateral	5.1	32.5	87.0	83.5	72.5	65.5	61.5	91.8	84.7	95.5
Concessional	4.9	32.5	66.8	69.1	62.1	58.6	58.5	91.4	84.7	95.5
Private creditors	0.0	23.9	18.3	9.1	4.8	0.5	0.2	0.0	0.0	0.0
Bonds	0.0	0.0	0.0	0.0	0.0	0.0	0.0	0.0	0.0	0.0
Commercial banks	0.0	7.4	16.0	8.0	4.0	0.0	0.0	0.0	0.0	0.0
Other private	0.0	16.5	2.3	1.1	0.8	0.5	0.2	0.0	0.0	0.0
Private nonguaranteed	**0.0**	**0.0**	**0.0**	**0.0**	**0.0**	**0.0**	**0.0**	**0.0**	**0.0**	**0.0**
Bonds	0.0	0.0	0.0	0.0	0.0	0.0	0.0	0.0	0.0	0.0
Commercial banks	0.0	0.0	0.0	0.0	0.0	0.0	0.0	0.0	0.0	0.0
Memo:										
IBRD	0.0	0.0	0.0	0.0	0.0	0.0	0.0	0.0	0.0	0.0
IDA	0.0	15.9	101.6	126.0	133.7	147.8	161.6	165.9	165.6	172.6
DISBURSEMENTS	**0.8**	**51.2**	**23.5**	**55.4**	**25.5**	**24.2**	**23.0**	**63.1**	**26.2**	**24.3**
Public and publicly guaranteed	**0.8**	**51.2**	**23.5**	**55.4**	**25.5**	**24.2**	**23.0**	**63.1**	**26.2**	**24.3**
Official creditors	0.8	29.6	23.5	55.4	25.5	24.2	23.0	63.1	26.2	24.3
Multilateral	0.0	18.3	17.7	52.4	25.3	21.7	19.0	22.4	23.1	21.7
Concessional	0.0	16.1	16.6	45.0	22.0	21.1	18.9	22.4	23.1	21.7
Bilateral	0.8	11.3	5.8	3.0	0.1	2.5	4.0	40.7	3.0	2.7
Concessional	0.8	11.3	5.8	3.0	0.1	2.5	4.0	40.7	3.0	2.7
Private creditors	0.0	21.7	0.0	0.0	0.0	0.0	0.0	0.0	0.0	0.0
Bonds	0.0	0.0	0.0	0.0	0.0	0.0	0.0	0.0	0.0	0.0
Commercial banks	0.0	7.0	0.0	0.0	0.0	0.0	0.0	0.0	0.0	0.0
Other private	0.0	14.7	0.0	0.0	0.0	0.0	0.0	0.0	0.0	0.0
Private nonguaranteed	**0.0**	**0.0**	**0.0**	**0.0**	**0.0**	**0.0**	**0.0**	**0.0**	**0.0**	**0.0**
Bonds	0.0	0.0	0.0	0.0	0.0	0.0	0.0	0.0	0.0	0.0
Commercial banks	0.0	0.0	0.0	0.0	0.0	0.0	0.0	0.0	0.0	0.0
Memo:										
IBRD	0.0	0.0	0.0	0.0	0.0	0.0	0.0	0.0	0.0	0.0
IDA	0.0	5.2	9.8	21.9	7.8	9.2	11.6	10.1	9.1	3.1
PRINCIPAL REPAYMENTS	**0.1**	**0.4**	**20.2**	**18.6**	**18.3**	**19.5**	**14.4**	**14.7**	**13.4**	**14.9**
Public and publicly guaranteed	**0.1**	**0.4**	**20.2**	**18.6**	**18.3**	**19.5**	**14.4**	**14.7**	**13.4**	**14.9**
Official creditors	0.1	0.0	12.7	14.2	14.0	15.2	14.1	14.5	13.4	14.9
Multilateral	0.0	0.0	4.7	5.1	5.2	5.5	6.6	6.3	6.6	8.0
Concessional	0.0	0.0	2.7	3.0	2.7	3.1	3.3	3.5	3.9	6.0
Bilateral	0.1	0.0	7.9	9.1	8.8	9.7	7.5	8.2	6.8	6.9
Concessional	0.1	0.0	7.9	5.4	5.1	5.8	3.4	5.7	6.4	6.9
Private creditors	0.0	0.3	7.5	4.5	4.3	4.3	0.4	0.2	0.0	0.0
Bonds	0.0	0.0	0.0	0.0	0.0	0.0	0.0	0.0	0.0	0.0
Commercial banks	0.0	0.1	3.0	4.0	4.0	4.0	0.0	0.0	0.0	0.0
Other private	0.0	0.3	4.5	0.5	0.3	0.3	0.4	0.2	0.0	0.0
Private nonguaranteed	**0.0**	**0.0**	**0.0**	**0.0**	**0.0**	**0.0**	**0.0**	**0.0**	**0.0**	**0.0**
Bonds	0.0	0.0	0.0	0.0	0.0	0.0	0.0	0.0	0.0	0.0
Commercial banks	0.0	0.0	0.0	0.0	0.0	0.0	0.0	0.0	0.0	0.0
Memo:										
IBRD	0.0	0.0	0.0	0.0	0.0	0.0	0.0	0.0	0.0	0.0
IDA	0.0	0.0	0.3	0.4	0.5	0.6	0.8	1.0	1.3	1.4
NET FLOWS ON DEBT	**0.7**	**50.9**	**3.4**	**36.7**	**7.2**	**4.7**	**8.5**	**48.4**	**12.8**	**9.4**
Public and publicly guaranteed	**0.7**	**50.9**	**3.4**	**36.7**	**7.2**	**4.7**	**8.5**	**48.4**	**12.8**	**9.4**
Official creditors	0.7	29.5	10.9	41.2	11.5	9.0	8.9	48.6	12.8	9.4
Multilateral	0.0	18.2	13.0	47.3	20.1	16.2	12.4	16.1	16.6	13.7
Concessional	0.0	16.1	13.9	42.0	19.3	18.0	15.6	18.9	19.2	15.6
Bilateral	0.7	11.3	-2.1	-6.1	-8.6	-7.2	-3.5	32.5	-3.8	-4.2
Concessional	0.7	11.3	-2.1	-2.4	-5.0	-3.3	0.6	35.0	-3.3	-4.2
Private creditors	0.0	21.3	-7.5	-4.5	-4.3	-4.3	-0.4	-0.2	0.0	0.0
Bonds	0.0	0.0	0.0	0.0	0.0	0.0	0.0	0.0	0.0	0.0
Commercial banks	0.0	6.9	-3.0	-4.0	-4.0	-4.0	0.0	0.0	0.0	0.0
Other private	0.0	14.4	-4.5	-0.5	-0.3	-0.3	-0.4	-0.2	0.0	0.0
Private nonguaranteed	**0.0**	**0.0**	**0.0**	**0.0**	**0.0**	**0.0**	**0.0**	**0.0**	**0.0**	**0.0**
Bonds	0.0	0.0	0.0	0.0	0.0	0.0	0.0	0.0	0.0	0.0
Commercial banks	0.0	0.0	0.0	0.0	0.0	0.0	0.0	0.0	0.0	0.0
Memo:										
IBRD	0.0	0.0	0.0	0.0	0.0	0.0	0.0	0.0	0.0	0.0
IDA	0.0	5.2	9.5	21.4	7.3	8.6	10.9	9.1	7.8	1.7

GAMBIA, THE

(US$ million, unless otherwise indicated)

	1970	1980	1990	1992	1993	1994	1995	1996	1997	1998
INTEREST PAYMENTS (LINT)	**0.0**	**0.4**	**10.2**	**6.7**	**6.1**	**5.8**	**4.9**	**4.6**	**5.8**	**5.4**
Public and publicly guaranteed	**0.0**	**0.4**	**10.2**	**6.7**	**6.1**	**5.8**	**4.9**	**4.6**	**5.8**	**5.4**
Official creditors	0.0	0.4	5.5	5.9	5.6	5.6	4.9	4.6	5.8	5.4
Multilateral	0.0	0.4	2.9	3.3	3.3	3.5	3.5	3.4	3.4	3.2
Concessional	0.0	0.2	1.5	1.9	2.1	2.4	2.2	2.4	2.7	2.7
Bilateral	0.0	0.0	2.6	2.7	2.3	2.1	1.3	1.3	2.4	2.2
Concessional	0.0	0.0	2.6	1.5	1.4	1.4	0.9	1.1	2.4	2.2
Private creditors	0.0	0.0	4.7	0.8	0.4	0.2	0.0	0.0	0.0	0.0
Bonds	0.0	0.0	0.0	0.0	0.0	0.0	0.0	0.0	0.0	0.0
Commercial banks	0.0	0.0	3.8	0.7	0.4	0.2	0.0	0.0	0.0	0.0
Other private	0.0	0.0	0.9	0.1	0.1	0.0	0.0	0.0	0.0	0.0
Private nonguaranteed	**0.0**	**0.0**	**0.0**	**0.0**	**0.0**	**0.0**	**0.0**	**0.0**	**0.0**	**0.0**
Bonds	0.0	0.0	0.0	0.0	0.0	0.0	0.0	0.0	0.0	0.0
Commercial banks	0.0	0.0	0.0	0.0	0.0	0.0	0.0	0.0	0.0	0.0
Memo:										
IBRD	0.0	0.0	0.0	0.0	0.0	0.0	0.0	0.0	0.0	0.0
IDA	0.0	0.1	0.7	0.8	0.9	1.1	1.2	1.2	1.2	1.2
NET TRANSFERS ON DEBT	**0.7**	**50.5**	**-6.8**	**30.1**	**1.1**	**-1.2**	**3.6**	**43.7**	**7.0**	**4.0**
Public and publicly guaranteed	**0.7**	**50.5**	**-6.8**	**30.1**	**1.1**	**-1.2**	**3.6**	**43.7**	**7.0**	**4.0**
Official creditors	0.7	29.2	5.4	35.3	5.8	3.4	4.0	44.0	7.0	4.0
Multilateral	0.0	17.9	10.1	44.0	16.8	12.7	8.8	12.7	13.2	10.5
Concessional	0.0	15.9	12.4	40.1	17.2	15.6	13.4	16.5	16.5	12.9
Bilateral	0.7	11.3	-4.7	-8.7	-11.0	-9.3	-4.8	31.2	-6.2	-6.5
Concessional	0.7	11.3	-4.7	-3.9	-6.4	-4.7	-0.2	33.9	-5.7	-6.5
Private creditors	0.0	21.3	-12.1	-5.2	-4.7	-4.6	-0.4	-0.2	0.0	0.0
Bonds	0.0	0.0	0.0	0.0	0.0	0.0	0.0	0.0	0.0	0.0
Commercial banks	0.0	6.9	-6.8	-4.7	-4.4	-4.2	0.0	0.0	0.0	0.0
Other private	0.0	14.4	-5.4	-0.6	-0.4	-0.4	-0.4	-0.2	0.0	0.0
Private nonguaranteed	**0.0**	**0.0**	**0.0**	**0.0**	**0.0**	**0.0**	**0.0**	**0.0**	**0.0**	**0.0**
Bonds	0.0	0.0	0.0	0.0	0.0	0.0	0.0	0.0	0.0	0.0
Commercial banks	0.0	0.0	0.0	0.0	0.0	0.0	0.0	0.0	0.0	0.0
Memo:										
IBRD	0.0	0.0	0.0	0.0	0.0	0.0	0.0	0.0	0.0	0.0
IDA	0.0	5.1	8.8	20.6	6.3	7.5	9.7	7.9	6.6	0.4
DEBT SERVICE (LTDS)	**0.1**	**0.8**	**30.3**	**25.3**	**24.4**	**25.4**	**19.3**	**19.4**	**19.2**	**20.3**
Public and publicly guaranteed	**0.1**	**0.8**	**30.3**	**25.3**	**24.4**	**25.4**	**19.3**	**19.4**	**19.2**	**20.3**
Official creditors	0.1	0.4	18.2	20.1	19.6	20.8	18.9	19.1	19.2	20.3
Multilateral	0.0	0.4	7.7	8.4	8.5	9.0	10.1	9.7	10.0	11.2
Concessional	0.0	0.2	4.2	5.0	4.8	5.5	5.5	5.9	6.6	8.7
Bilateral	0.1	0.0	10.5	11.7	11.1	11.8	8.8	9.5	9.2	9.1
Concessional	0.1	0.0	10.5	6.9	6.5	7.2	4.2	6.8	8.8	9.1
Private creditors	0.0	0.4	12.1	5.2	4.7	4.6	0.4	0.2	0.0	0.0
Bonds	0.0	0.0	0.0	0.0	0.0	0.0	0.0	0.0	0.0	0.0
Commercial banks	0.0	0.1	6.8	4.7	4.4	4.2	0.0	0.0	0.0	0.0
Other private	0.0	0.3	5.4	0.6	0.4	0.4	0.4	0.2	0.0	0.0
Private nonguaranteed	**0.0**	**0.0**	**0.0**	**0.0**	**0.0**	**0.0**	**0.0**	**0.0**	**0.0**	**0.0**
Bonds	0.0	0.0	0.0	0.0	0.0	0.0	0.0	0.0	0.0	0.0
Commercial banks	0.0	0.0	0.0	0.0	0.0	0.0	0.0	0.0	0.0	0.0
Memo:										
IBRD	0.0	0.0	0.0	0.0	0.0	0.0	0.0	0.0	0.0	0.0
IDA	0.0	0.1	1.0	1.3	1.4	1.7	1.9	2.2	2.5	2.6
UNDISBURSED DEBT	**5.5**	**106.3**	**177.7**	**113.4**	**88.9**	**111.3**	**133.0**	**74.7**	**66.0**	**105.1**
Official creditors	5.5	87.7	177.7	113.4	88.9	111.3	133.0	74.7	66.0	105.1
Private creditors	0.0	18.6	0.0	0.0	0.0	0.0	0.0	0.0	0.0	0.0
Memorandum items										
Concessional LDOD	4.9	68.3	250.1	298.2	310.5	337.6	364.2	401.7	397.8	434.7
Variable rate LDOD	0.0	7.6	17.6	9.5	5.3	0.9	0.6	0.2	0.0	0.0
Public sector LDOD	5.1	94.0	306.6	345.2	349.6	369.3	388.1	419.7	411.1	451.3
Private sector LDOD	0.0	3.4	1.8	1.0	0.7	0.5	0.2	0.0	0.0	0.0

6. CURRENCY COMPOSITION OF LONG-TERM DEBT (PERCENT)

	1970	1980	1990	1992	1993	1994	1995	1996	1997	1998
Deutsche mark	0.0	1.8	1.8	1.1	0.7	0.5	0.3	0.2	0.1	0.1
French franc	0.0	1.4	7.7	5.4	4.3	3.7	3.2	2.2	1.5	0.7
Japanese yen	0.0	0.0	0.0	0.0	0.0	0.0	0.0	0.0	0.0	0.0
Pound sterling	100.0	16.3	8.5	7.3	7.1	6.7	6.3	5.7	5.7	5.1
Swiss franc	0.0	0.5	1.3	0.7	0.5	0.4	0.2	0.0	0.0	0.0
U.S.dollars	0.0	32.4	39.1	38.7	39.3	40.0	43.6	50.0	51.2	51.1
Multiple currency	0.0	7.0	19.8	21.9	23.2	24.4	24.6	21.7	21.2	20.6
Special drawing rights	0.0	0.0	0.0	0.0	0.0	0.0	0.0	0.0	0.1	0.1
All other currencies	0.0	40.6	21.8	24.9	24.9	24.3	21.8	20.2	20.2	22.3

GAMBIA, THE

(US$ million, unless otherwise indicated)

	1970	1980	1990	1992	1993	1994	1995	1996	1997	1998
7. DEBT RESTRUCTURINGS										
Total amount rescheduled	..	..	0.0	0.0	0.0	0.0	0.0	0.0	0.0	0.0
Debt stock rescheduled	..	..	0.0	0.0	0.0	0.0	0.0	0.0	0.0	0.0
Principal rescheduled	..	..	0.0	0.0	0.0	0.0	0.0	0.0	0.0	0.0
Official	..	..	0.0	0.0	0.0	0.0	0.0	0.0	0.0	0.0
Private	..	..	0.0	0.0	0.0	0.0	0.0	0.0	0.0	0.0
Interest rescheduled	..	..	0.0	0.0	0.0	0.0	0.0	0.0	0.0	0.0
Official	..	..	0.0	0.0	0.0	0.0	0.0	0.0	0.0	0.0
Private	..	..	0.0	0.0	0.0	0.0	0.0	0.0	0.0	0.0
Debt forgiven	..	..	0.0	0.0	0.0	0.0	0.0	0.0	0.0	0.0
Memo: interest forgiven	..	..	0.0	0.0	0.0	0.0	0.0	0.0	0.0	0.0
Debt stock reduction	..	..	0.0	0.0	0.0	0.0	0.0	0.0	0.0	0.0
of which debt buyback	..	..	0.0	0.0	0.0	0.0	0.0	0.0	0.0	0.0
8. DEBT STOCK-FLOW RECONCILIATION										
Total change in debt stocks	..	..	31.4	20.3	22.7	-1.4	4.2	30.7	-25.2	42.6
Net flows on debt	0.7	58.3	15.4	34.6	25.8	-18.3	-6.5	49.1	-3.0	11.5
Net change in interest arrears	..	..	-3.5	0.1	0.0	0.0	0.1	-0.7	0.1	0.0
Interest capitalized	..	..	0.0	0.0	0.0	0.0	0.0	0.0	0.0	0.0
Debt forgiveness or reduction	..	..	0.0	0.0	0.0	0.0	0.0	0.0	0.0	0.0
Cross-currency valuation	..	..	11.5	-10.5	-3.6	6.2	4.4	-1.3	-7.2	4.6
Residual	..	..	7.9	-3.9	0.5	10.6	6.2	-16.4	-15.1	26.6
9. AVERAGE TERMS OF NEW COMMITMENTS										
ALL CREDITORS										
Interest (%)	0.7	3.9	0.8	0.8	0.7	0.8	3.5	0.4	1.0	1.1
Maturity (years)	49.7	20.3	42.0	49.5	39.6	41.6	21.3	27.2	49.7	31.3
Grace period (years)	10.4	4.9	10.0	10.3	10.1	9.6	6.2	7.1	10.5	7.9
Grant element (%)	83.3	39.1	79.7	82.8	80.4	78.0	45.7	71.3	80.5	67.6
Official creditors										
Interest (%)	0.7	1.7	0.8	0.8	0.7	0.8	3.5	0.4	1.0	1.1
Maturity (years)	49.7	25.1	42.0	49.5	39.6	41.6	21.3	27.2	49.7	31.3
Grace period (years)	10.4	5.7	10.0	10.3	10.1	9.6	6.2	7.1	10.5	7.9
Grant element (%)	83.3	55.8	79.7	82.8	80.4	78.0	45.7	71.3	80.5	67.6
Private creditors										
Interest (%)	0.0	7.5	0.0	0.0	0.0	0.0	0.0	0.0	0.0	0.0
Maturity (years)	0.0	12.2	0.0	0.0	0.0	0.0	0.0	0.0	0.0	0.0
Grace period (years)	0.0	3.4	0.0	0.0	0.0	0.0	0.0	0.0	0.0	0.0
Grant element (%)	0.0	11.3	0.0	0.0	0.0	0.0	0.0	0.0	0.0	0.0
Memorandum items										
Commitments	2.1	72.9	37.9	20.6	12.3	43.8	40.3	9.9	21.6	59.8
Official creditors	2.1	45.7	37.9	20.6	12.3	43.8	40.3	9.9	21.6	59.8
Private creditors	0.0	27.3	0.0	0.0	0.0	0.0	0.0	0.0	0.0	0.0

10. CONTRACTUAL OBLIGATIONS ON OUTSTANDING LONG-TERM DEBT

	1999	2000	2001	2002	2003	2004	2005	2006	2007	2008
TOTAL										
Disbursements	25.0	25.1	19.1	14.4	10.6	6.7	3.9	0.3	0.0	0.0
Principal	15.8	14.8	18.6	18.5	17.6	18.1	18.2	17.1	17.2	17.1
Interest	5.8	5.8	5.7	5.5	5.3	5.0	4.8	4.6	4.3	4.0
Official creditors										
Disbursements	25.0	25.1	19.1	14.4	10.6	6.7	3.9	0.3	0.0	0.0
Principal	15.8	14.8	18.6	18.5	17.6	18.1	18.2	17.1	17.2	17.1
Interest	5.8	5.8	5.7	5.5	5.3	5.0	4.8	4.6	4.3	4.0
Bilateral creditors										
Disbursements	4.5	3.3	2.2	1.4	0.9	0.7	0.4	0.0	0.0	0.0
Principal	6.3	4.8	8.3	8.3	7.0	7.0	6.8	6.2	5.9	5.9
Interest	2.2	2.1	2.1	2.0	1.8	1.7	1.6	1.5	1.4	1.2
Multilateral creditors										
Disbursements	20.5	21.8	17.0	13.0	9.7	6.0	3.5	0.3	0.0	0.0
Principal	9.6	10.1	10.2	10.2	10.6	11.0	11.5	10.8	11.3	11.2
Interest	3.6	3.6	3.6	3.5	3.4	3.3	3.2	3.1	2.9	2.8
Private creditors										
Disbursements	0.0	0.0	0.0	0.0	0.0	0.0	0.0	0.0	0.0	0.0
Principal	0.0	0.0	0.0	0.0	0.0	0.0	0.0	0.0	0.0	0.0
Interest	0.0	0.0	0.0	0.0	0.0	0.0	0.0	0.0	0.0	0.0
Commercial banks										
Disbursements	0.0	0.0	0.0	0.0	0.0	0.0	0.0	0.0	0.0	0.0
Principal	0.0	0.0	0.0	0.0	0.0	0.0	0.0	0.0	0.0	0.0
Interest	0.0	0.0	0.0	0.0	0.0	0.0	0.0	0.0	0.0	0.0
Other private										
Disbursements	0.0	0.0	0.0	0.0	0.0	0.0	0.0	0.0	0.0	0.0
Principal	0.0	0.0	0.0	0.0	0.0	0.0	0.0	0.0	0.0	0.0
Interest	0.0	0.0	0.0	0.0	0.0	0.0	0.0	0.0	0.0	0.0

GEORGIA

(US$ million, unless otherwise indicated)

	1970	1980	1990	1992	1993	1994	1995	1996	1997	1998
1. SUMMARY DEBT DATA										
TOTAL DEBT STOCKS (EDT)	..	..	..	**79**	**559**	**1,404**	**1,194**	**1,361**	**1,465**	**1,674**
Long-term debt (LDOD)	..	..	..	**79**	**559**	**878**	**993**	**1,106**	**1,189**	**1,324**
Public and publicly guaranteed	..	..	..	79	559	878	993	1,106	1,189	1,311
Private nonguaranteed	..	..	..	0	0	0	0	0	0	13
Use of IMF credit	..	..	..	**0**	**0**	**41**	**116**	**192**	**255**	**304**
Short-term debt	..	..	..	**0**	**0**	**485**	**86**	**64**	**22**	**47**
of which interest arrears on LDOD	..	..	..	0	0	15	62	43	18	19
Official creditors	..	..	..	0	0	15	54	30	18	19
Private creditors	..	..	..	0	0	0	8	13	0	0
Memo: principal arrears on LDOD	..	..	..	1	0	43	211	135	77	192
Official creditors	..	..	..	0	0	42	203	118	77	192
Private creditors	..	..	..	1	0	1	8	17	0	0
Memo: export credits	..	..	..	48	78	89	106	100	84	84
TOTAL DEBT FLOWS										
Disbursements	..	..	..	**21**	**124**	**134**	**174**	**173**	**172**	**163**
Long-term debt	..	..	..	21	124	94	98	92	96	126
IMF purchases	..	..	..	0	0	40	76	81	76	38
Principal repayments	..	..	..	**0**	**5**	**1**	**0**	**1**	**3**	**24**
Long-term debt	..	..	..	0	5	1	0	1	3	23
IMF repurchases	..	..	..	0	0	0	0	0	0	1
Net flows on debt	..	..	..	**21**	**120**	**603**	**-272**	**169**	**152**	**163**
of which short-term debt	..	..	..	0	0	470	-446	-3	-17	24
Interest payments (INT)	..	..	..	**0**	**8**	**5**	**20**	**12**	**44**	**46**
Long-term debt	..	..	..	0	8	5	17	6	37	39
IMF charges	..	..	..	0	0	0	3	5	6	6
Short-term debt	..	..	..	0	0	0	0	1	1	1
Net transfers on debt	..	..	..	**21**	**112**	**598**	**-292**	**157**	**109**	**118**
Total debt service paid (TDS)	..	..	..	**0**	**13**	**6**	**20**	**13**	**46**	**70**
Long-term debt	..	..	..	0	13	6	17	7	40	62
IMF repurchases and charges	..	..	..	0	0	0	3	5	6	7
Short-term debt (interest only)	..	..	..	0	0	0	0	1	1	1
2. AGGREGATE NET RESOURCE FLOWS AND NET TRANSFERS (LONG-TERM)										
NET RESOURCE FLOWS	..	..	..	**26**	**215**	**271**	**190**	**214**	**192**	**207**
Net flow of long-term debt (ex. IMF)	..	..	..	21	120	93	98	91	93	103
Foreign direct investment (net)	..	..	..	0	0	6	8	40	50	50
Portfolio equity flows	..	..	..	0	0	0	0	0	0	0
Grants (excluding technical coop.)	..	..	..	5	95	172	85	82	49	54
Memo: technical coop. grants	..	..	..	0	6	3	37	46	18	25
official net resource flows	..	..	..	5	219	266	182	174	143	150
private net resource flows	..	..	..	21	-5	5	8	40	50	57
NET TRANSFERS	..	..	..	**26**	**206**	**266**	**173**	**208**	**155**	**168**
Interest on long-term debt	..	..	..	0	8	5	17	6	37	39
Profit remittances on FDI	..	..	..	0	0	0	0	0	0	0
Memo: official net transfers	..	..	..	5	215	261	165	168	105	112
private net transfers	..	..	..	21	-8	5	8	40	50	56
3. MAJOR ECONOMIC AGGREGATES										
Gross national product (GNP)	..	..	..	4,492	3,224	2,510	2,939	4,519	5,376	5,246
Exports of goods & services (XGS)	..	..	..	..	530	473	486	516	848	914
of which workers remittances	..	..	..	..	..	..	0	0	0	0
Imports of goods & services (MGS)	..	..	..	..	1,015	923	891	933	1,420	1,513
International reserves (RES)	..	..	..	..	..	..	195	190	200	124
Current account balance	..	..	..	..	-354	-278	-216	-276	-376	-389
4. DEBT INDICATORS										
EDT / XGS (%)	..	..	..	..	105.5	296.8	245.9	263.9	172.8	183.3
EDT / GNP (%)	..	..	..	1.8	17.3	55.9	40.6	30.1	27.3	31.9
TDS / XGS (%)	..	..	..	..	2.4	1.3	4.1	2.5	5.5	7.6
INT / XGS (%)	..	..	..	..	1.6	1.0	4.1	2.3	5.1	5.0
INT / GNP (%)	..	..	..	0.0	0.3	0.2	0.7	0.3	0.8	0.9
RES / EDT (%)	..	..	..	..	..	..	16.3	13.9	13.7	7.4
RES / MGS (months)	..	..	..	..	..	..	2.6	2.4	1.7	1.0
Short-term / EDT (%)	..	..	..	0.0	0.0	34.6	7.2	4.7	1.5	2.8
Concessional / EDT (%)	..	..	..	0.0	0.0	0.1	7.2	30.3	43.5	45.7
Multilateral / EDT (%)	..	..	..	0.0	17.2	10.1	20.5	23.0	24.8	26.1

GEORGIA

(US$ million, unless otherwise indicated)

	1970	1980	1990	1992	1993	1994	1995	1996	1997	1998
5. LONG-TERM DEBT										
DEBT OUTSTANDING (LDOD)	..	..	..	**79**	**559**	**878**	**993**	**1,106**	**1,189**	**1,324**
Public and publicly guaranteed	..	..	..	**79**	**559**	**878**	**993**	**1,106**	**1,189**	**1,311**
Official creditors	..	..	..	0	489	786	893	1,014	1,186	1,308
Multilateral	..	..	..	0	96	141	245	313	363	438
Concessional	..	..	..	0	0	1	84	157	212	274
Bilateral	..	..	..	0	393	645	648	701	824	871
Concessional	..	..	..	0	0	0	2	256	426	492
Private creditors	..	..	..	79	70	91	100	93	3	3
Bonds	..	..	..	0	0	0	0	0	0	0
Commercial banks	..	..	..	1	1	0	0	0	0	0
Other private	..	..	..	78	69	91	100	93	3	3
Private nonguaranteed	..	..	..	**0**	**0**	**0**	**0**	**0**	**0**	**13**
Bonds	..	..	..	0	0	0	0	0	0	0
Commercial banks	..	..	..	0	0	0	0	0	0	13
Memo:										
IBRD	..	..	..	0	0	0	0	0	0	0
IDA	..	..	..	0	0	1	84	157	212	274
DISBURSEMENTS	..	..	..	**21**	**124**	**94**	**98**	**92**	**96**	**126**
Public and publicly guaranteed	..	..	..	**21**	**124**	**94**	**98**	**92**	**96**	**119**
Official creditors	..	..	..	0	124	94	98	92	96	119
Multilateral	..	..	..	0	101	34	96	78	77	62
Concessional	..	..	..	0	0	1	85	76	64	53
Bilateral	..	..	..	0	24	60	2	14	19	57
Concessional	..	..	..	0	0	0	2	14	19	57
Private creditors	..	..	..	21	0	0	0	0	0	0
Bonds	..	..	..	0	0	0	0	0	0	0
Commercial banks	..	..	..	1	0	0	0	0	0	0
Other private	..	..	..	21	0	0	0	0	0	0
Private nonguaranteed	..	..	..	**0**	**0**	**0**	**0**	**0**	**0**	**7**
Bonds	..	..	..	0	0	0	0	0	0	0
Commercial banks	..	..	..	0	0	0	0	0	0	7
Memo:										
IBRD	..	..	..	0	0	0	0	0	0	0
IDA	..	..	..	0	0	1	85	76	64	53
PRINCIPAL REPAYMENTS	..	..	..	**0**	**5**	**1**	**0**	**1**	**3**	**23**
Public and publicly guaranteed	..	..	..	**0**	**5**	**1**	**0**	**1**	**3**	**23**
Official creditors	..	..	..	0	0	0	0	1	3	23
Multilateral	..	..	..	0	0	0	0	0	0	3
Concessional	..	..	..	0	0	0	0	0	0	0
Bilateral	..	..	..	0	0	0	0	1	3	20
Concessional	..	..	..	0	0	0	0	0	3	0
Private creditors	..	..	..	0	5	1	0	0	0	0
Bonds	..	..	..	0	0	0	0	0	0	0
Commercial banks	..	..	..	0	0	1	0	0	0	0
Other private	..	..	..	0	5	0	0	0	0	0
Private nonguaranteed	..	..	..	**0**	**0**	**0**	**0**	**0**	**0**	**0**
Bonds	..	..	..	0	0	0	0	0	0	0
Commercial banks	..	..	..	0	0	0	0	0	0	0
Memo:										
IBRD	..	..	..	0	0	0	0	0	0	0
IDA	..	..	..	0	0	0	0	0	0	0
NET FLOWS ON DEBT	..	..	..	**21**	**120**	**93**	**98**	**91**	**93**	**103**
Public and publicly guaranteed	..	..	..	**21**	**120**	**93**	**98**	**91**	**93**	**96**
Official creditors	..	..	..	0	124	94	98	91	93	96
Multilateral	..	..	..	0	101	34	96	78	76	59
Concessional	..	..	..	0	0	1	85	76	64	53
Bilateral	..	..	..	0	24	60	2	13	17	37
Concessional	..	..	..	0	0	0	2	14	17	57
Private creditors	..	..	..	21	-5	-1	0	0	0	0
Bonds	..	..	..	0	0	0	0	0	0	0
Commercial banks	..	..	..	1	0	-1	0	0	0	0
Other private	..	..	..	21	-5	0	0	0	0	0
Private nonguaranteed	..	..	..	**0**	**0**	**0**	**0**	**0**	**0**	**7**
Bonds	..	..	..	0	0	0	0	0	0	0
Commercial banks	..	..	..	0	0	0	0	0	0	7
Memo:										
IBRD	..	..	..	0	0	0	0	0	0	0
IDA	..	..	..	0	0	1	85	76	64	53

GEORGIA

(US$ million, unless otherwise indicated)

	1970	1980	1990	1992	1993	1994	1995	1996	1997	1998
INTEREST PAYMENTS (LINT)	..	..	..	**0**	**8**	**5**	**17**	**6**	**37**	**39**
Public and publicly guaranteed	..	..	..	**0**	**8**	**5**	**17**	**6**	**37**	**39**
Official creditors	..	..	..	0	5	5	17	6	37	39
Multilateral	..	..	..	0	5	5	0	5	8	7
Concessional	..	..	..	0	0	0	0	1	1	2
Bilateral	..	..	..	0	0	0	17	1	29	32
Concessional	..	..	..	0	0	0	0	0	14	16
Private creditors	..	..	..	0	4	0	0	0	0	0
Bonds	..	..	..	0	0	0	0	0	0	0
Commercial banks	..	..	..	0	0	0	0	0	0	0
Other private	..	..	..	0	4	0	0	0	0	0
Private nonguaranteed	..	..	..	**0**	**0**	**0**	**0**	**0**	**0**	**1**
Bonds	..	..	..	0	0	0	0	0	0	0
Commercial banks	..	..	..	0	0	0	0	0	0	1
Memo:										
IBRD	..	..	..	0	0	0	0	0	0	0
IDA	..	..	..	0	0	0	0	1	1	2
NET TRANSFERS ON DEBT	..	..	..	**21**	**112**	**88**	**81**	**85**	**56**	**64**
Public and publicly guaranteed	..	..	..	**21**	**112**	**88**	**81**	**85**	**56**	**57**
Official creditors	..	..	..	0	120	89	81	85	56	57
Multilateral	..	..	..	0	96	30	96	73	69	52
Concessional	..	..	..	0	0	1	85	76	63	51
Bilateral	..	..	..	0	24	60	-15	12	-13	5
Concessional	..	..	..	0	0	0	2	14	3	42
Private creditors	..	..	..	21	-8	-1	0	0	0	0
Bonds	..	..	..	0	0	0	0	0	0	0
Commercial banks	..	..	..	1	0	-1	0	0	0	0
Other private	..	..	..	21	-8	0	0	0	0	0
Private nonguaranteed	..	..	..	**0**	**0**	**0**	**0**	**0**	**0**	**6**
Bonds	..	..	..	0	0	0	0	0	0	0
Commercial banks	..	..	..	0	0	0	0	0	0	6
Memo:										
IBRD	..	..	..	0	0	0	0	0	0	0
IDA	..	..	..	0	0	1	85	76	63	51
DEBT SERVICE (LTDS)	..	..	..	**0**	**13**	**6**	**17**	**7**	**40**	**62**
Public and publicly guaranteed	..	..	..	**0**	**13**	**6**	**17**	**7**	**40**	**62**
Official creditors	..	..	..	0	5	5	17	7	40	62
Multilateral	..	..	..	0	5	5	0	5	8	9
Concessional	..	..	..	0	0	0	0	1	1	2
Bilateral	..	..	..	0	0	0	17	2	32	52
Concessional	..	..	..	0	0	0	0	0	16	16
Private creditors	..	..	..	0	8	1	0	0	0	0
Bonds	..	..	..	0	0	0	0	0	0	0
Commercial banks	..	..	..	0	0	1	0	0	0	0
Other private	..	..	..	0	8	0	0	0	0	0
Private nonguaranteed	..	..	..	**0**	**0**	**0**	**0**	**0**	**0**	**1**
Bonds	..	..	..	0	0	0	0	0	0	0
Commercial banks	..	..	..	0	0	0	0	0	0	1
Memo:										
IBRD	..	..	..	0	0	0	0	0	0	0
IDA	..	..	..	0	0	0	0	1	1	2
UNDISBURSED DEBT	..	..	..	**85**	**38**	**46**	**42**	**105**	**175**	**347**
Official creditors	..	..	..	85	38	46	42	105	175	347
Private creditors	..	..	..	0	0	0	0	0	0	0
Memorandum items										
Concessional LDOD	..	..	..	0	0	1	86	413	637	766
Variable rate LDOD	..	..	..	1	490	388	409	202	141	164
Public sector LDOD	..	..	..	79	559	885	990	1,101	1,168	1,296
Private sector LDOD	..	..	..	0	0	0	0	0	4	21

6. CURRENCY COMPOSITION OF LONG-TERM DEBT (PERCENT)

	1970	1980	1990	1992	1993	1994	1995	1996	1997	1998
Deutsche mark	..	..	..	0.0	0.0	0.0	0.2	1.4	2.7	4.4
French franc	..	..	..	0.0	0.0	0.0	0.0	0.0	0.0	0.0
Japanese yen	..	..	..	0.0	0.0	0.0	0.0	0.0	0.0	0.0
Pound sterling	..	..	..	0.0	0.0	0.0	0.0	0.0	0.0	0.0
Swiss franc	..	..	..	0.0	0.0	0.4	0.5	0.3	0.3	0.3
U.S.dollars	..	..	..	1.1	70.5	73.2	74.2	77.0	79.2	78.2
Multiple currency	..	..	..	0.0	0.0	0.0	0.0	0.0	0.0	0.0
Special drawing rights	..	..	..	0.0	0.0	0.0	0.0	0.0	0.0	0.0
All other currencies	..	..	..	98.9	29.5	26.4	25.1	21.3	17.8	17.1

GEORGIA

(US$ million, unless otherwise indicated)

	1970	1980	1990	1992	1993	1994	1995	1996	1997	1998
7. DEBT RESTRUCTURINGS										
Total amount rescheduled	..	..	..	0	369	412	0	634	167	0
Debt stock rescheduled	..	..	..	0	0	201	0	394	96	0
Principal rescheduled	..	..	..	0	0	3	0	199	35	0
Official	..	..	..	0	0	0	0	199	35	0
Private	..	..	..	0	0	3	0	0	0	0
Interest rescheduled	..	..	..	..	0	5	0	26	17	0
Official	..	..	..	0	0	0	0	26	5	0
Private	..	..	..	0	0	5	0	0	11	0
Debt forgiven	..	..	..	0	0	0	0	0	4	0
Memo: interest forgiven	..	..	..	0	0	0	0	0	0	0
Debt stock reduction	..	..	..	0	0	0	0	0	0	0
of which debt buyback	..	..	..	0	0	0	0	0	0	0
8. DEBT STOCK-FLOW RECONCILIATION										
Total change in debt stocks	..	..	..	..	480	845	-210	167	104	209
Net flows on debt	..	..	..	21	120	603	-272	169	152	163
Net change in interest arrears	..	..	..	..	0	15	46	-19	-25	1
Interest capitalized	..	..	..	..	0	5	0	26	17	0
Debt forgiveness or reduction	..	..	..	..	0	0	0	0	-4	0
Cross-currency valuation	..	..	..	..	-12	24	22	-16	-30	19
Residual	..	..	..	..	372	198	-5	7	-6	26
9. AVERAGE TERMS OF NEW COMMITMENTS										
ALL CREDITORS										
Interest (%)	..	..	..	4.1	4.0	4.0	1.5	1.2	0.7	4.5
Maturity (years)	..	..	..	3.2	4.3	13.7	32.3	35.0	34.2	20.8
Grace period (years)	..	..	..	3.2	3.6	4.0	9.6	10.5	9.6	8.7
Grant element (%)	..	..	..	15.3	18.7	33.5	71.3	75.3	78.3	40.6
Official creditors										
Interest (%)	..	..	..	4.1	4.0	4.0	1.5	1.2	0.7	4.5
Maturity (years)	..	..	..	3.2	4.3	13.7	32.3	35.0	34.2	20.8
Grace period (years)	..	..	..	3.2	3.6	4.0	9.6	10.5	9.6	8.7
Grant element (%)	..	..	..	15.4	18.7	33.5	71.3	75.3	78.3	40.6
Private creditors										
Interest (%)	..	..	..	4.6	0.0	0.0	0.0	0.0	0.0	0.0
Maturity (years)	..	..	..	1.6	0.0	0.0	0.0	0.0	0.0	0.0
Grace period (years)	..	..	..	1.6	0.0	0.0	0.0	0.0	0.0	0.0
Grant element (%)	..	..	..	7.5	0.0	0.0	0.0	0.0	0.0	0.0
Memorandum items										
Commitments	..	..	..	92	77	106	91	158	175	276
Official creditors	..	..	..	91	77	106	91	158	175	276
Private creditors	..	..	..	1	0	0	0	0	0	0

10. CONTRACTUAL OBLIGATIONS ON OUTSTANDING LONG-TERM DEBT

	1999	2000	2001	2002	2003	2004	2005	2006	2007	2008
TOTAL										
Disbursements	73	112	74	44	24	12	5	3	0	0
Principal	87	106	122	141	64	65	65	57	54	42
Interest	33	34	33	30	26	24	22	20	18	16
Official creditors										
Disbursements	73	112	74	44	24	12	5	3	0	0
Principal	81	101	121	140	64	64	65	57	54	42
Interest	33	33	33	30	26	24	22	20	17	15
Bilateral creditors										
Disbursements	13	17	11	7	4	2	1	0	0	0
Principal	79	96	117	133	54	54	53	43	38	25
Interest	29	26	22	18	13	11	9	7	6	4
Multilateral creditors										
Disbursements	60	96	63	37	20	10	4	3	0	0
Principal	3	4	4	8	10	10	11	13	16	17
Interest	4	7	10	12	13	13	13	12	12	11
Private creditors										
Disbursements	0	0	0	0	0	0	0	0	0	0
Principal	6	6	1	0	0	0	0	0	0	0
Interest	0	0	0	0	0	0	0	0	0	0
Commercial banks										
Disbursements	0	0	0	0	0	0	0	0	0	0
Principal	0	0	0	0	0	0	0	0	0	0
Interest	0	0	0	0	0	0	0	0	0	0
Other private										
Disbursements	0	0	0	0	0	0	0	0	0	0
Principal	6	6	1	0	0	0	0	0	0	0
Interest	0	0	0	0	0	0	0	0	0	0

GHANA

(US$ million, unless otherwise indicated)

1. SUMMARY DEBT DATA

	1970	*1980*	*1990*	*1992*	*1993*	*1994*	*1995*	*1996*	*1997*	*1998*
TOTAL DEBT STOCKS (EDT)	..	**1,398**	**3,881**	**4,509**	**4,888**	**5,472**	**5,939**	**6,442**	**6,352**	**6,884**
Long-term debt (LDOD)	**520**	**1,162**	**2,816**	**3,355**	**3,677**	**4,192**	**4,669**	**5,246**	**5,327**	**5,833**
Public and publicly guaranteed	510	1,152	2,783	3,320	3,640	4,160	4,642	4,975	5,060	5,570
Private nonguaranteed	10	10	33	35	37	32	27	271	267	263
Use of IMF credit	**46**	**105**	**745**	**740**	**738**	**700**	**649**	**543**	**347**	**334**
Short-term debt	..	**131**	**320**	**414**	**474**	**580**	**621**	**654**	**678**	**717**
of which interest arrears on LDOD	..	5	56	41	54	57	28	11	14	12
Official creditors	..	4	45	19	24	19	22	2	5	7
Private creditors	..	1	11	22	30	38	6	9	9	4
Memo: principal arrears on LDOD	..	5	77	81	105	93	89	27	16	45
Official creditors	..	3	50	43	64	50	46	5	9	36
Private creditors	..	2	27	38	41	43	43	23	7	10
Memo: export credits	..	0	411	387	335	426	612	735	881	778
TOTAL DEBT FLOWS										
Disbursements	**44**	**249**	**503**	**489**	**511**	**469**	**648**	**936**	**649**	**632**
Long-term debt	42	220	438	489	445	469	607	896	649	520
IMF purchases	2	29	65	0	66	0	42	40	0	112
Principal repayments	**39**	**106**	**260**	**198**	**186**	**248**	**309**	**332**	**396**	**390**
Long-term debt	14	77	144	134	120	166	202	206	231	252
IMF repurchases	25	29	117	64	66	83	108	125	166	139
Net flows on debt	**5**	**75**	**341**	**307**	**371**	**324**	**410**	**654**	**274**	**283**
of which short-term debt	..	-68	98	16	47	103	71	50	21	42
Interest payments (INT)	..	**53**	**108**	**121**	**122**	**121**	**98**	**152**	**156**	**190**
Long-term debt	12	31	59	81	86	84	60	109	122	149
IMF charges	0	4	37	20	14	11	10	7	5	2
Short-term debt	..	18	12	19	22	26	28	36	29	38
Net transfers on debt	..	**22**	**234**	**186**	**249**	**203**	**312**	**502**	**118**	**93**
Total debt service paid (TDS)	..	**159**	**368**	**319**	**308**	**369**	**407**	**484**	**552**	**580**
Long-term debt	26	108	203	216	206	250	261	315	352	401
IMF repurchases and charges	25	33	154	84	81	93	117	133	171	141
Short-term debt (interest only)	..	18	12	19	22	26	28	36	29	38

2. AGGREGATE NET RESOURCE FLOWS AND NET TRANSFERS (LONG-TERM)

	1970	*1980*	*1990*	*1992*	*1993*	*1994*	*1995*	*1996*	*1997*	*1998*
NET RESOURCE FLOWS	**101**	**181**	**758**	**595**	**673**	**1,312**	**1,017**	**1,150**	**711**	**579**
Net flow of long-term debt (ex. IMF)	28	143	294	354	325	303	405	690	419	269
Foreign direct investment (net)	68	16	15	23	125	233	107	120	83	56
Portfolio equity flows	0	0	0	0	0	557	267	124	46	15
Grants (excluding technical coop.)	6	23	449	218	222	218	238	216	163	239
Memo: technical coop. grants	15	42	62	102	97	88	108	96	108	104
official net resource flows	35	207	763	527	522	463	550	631	497	537
private net resource flows	66	-26	-5	69	151	849	467	520	213	42
NET TRANSFERS	**77**	**135**	**692**	**505**	**578**	**1,218**	**937**	**1,012**	**549**	**386**
Interest on long-term debt	12	31	59	81	86	84	60	109	122	149
Profit remittances on FDI	12	15	7	9	9	10	20	30	40	44
Memo: official net transfers	28	183	719	465	453	400	498	554	424	447
private net transfers	49	-48	-26	40	125	818	440	458	125	-61

3. MAJOR ECONOMIC AGGREGATES

	1970	*1980*	*1990*	*1992*	*1993*	*1994*	*1995*	*1996*	*1997*	*1998*
Gross national product (GNP)	2,170	4,426	5,774	6,306	5,854	5,440	6,461	6,927	6,884	7,501
Exports of goods & services (XGS)	..	1,214	996	1,123	1,230	1,413	1,613	1,778	1,708	2,045
of which workers remittances	..	1	6	7	10	16	17	28	26	30
Imports of goods & services (MGS)	..	1,264	1,624	1,963	2,297	2,123	2,263	2,557	2,791	3,049
International reserves (RES)	43	330	309	412	517	689	804	930	..	457
Current account balance	..	30	-223	-377	-560	-255	-145	-325	-550	-350

4. DEBT INDICATORS

	1970	*1980*	*1990*	*1992*	*1993*	*1994*	*1995*	*1996*	*1997*	*1998*
EDT / XGS (%)	..	115.2	389.7	401.7	397.4	387.3	368.2	362.4	372.0	336.6
EDT / GNP (%)	..	31.6	67.2	71.5	83.5	100.6	91.9	93.0	92.3	91.8
TDS / XGS (%)	..	13.1	37.0	28.4	25.1	26.1	25.2	27.2	32.3	28.4
INT / XGS (%)	..	4.4	10.8	10.8	9.9	8.5	6.1	8.5	9.1	9.3
INT / GNP (%)	..	1.2	1.9	1.9	2.1	2.2	1.5	2.2	2.3	2.5
RES / EDT (%)	..	23.6	8.0	9.1	10.6	12.6	13.5	14.4	..	6.6
RES / MGS (months)	..	3.1	2.3	2.5	2.7	3.9	4.3	4.4	..	1.8
Short-term / EDT (%)	..	9.4	8.3	9.2	9.7	10.6	10.5	10.2	10.7	10.4
Concessional / EDT (%)	..	55.2	54.6	57.1	59.2	61.1	63.0	62.2	64.2	67.1
Multilateral / EDT (%)	..	19.9	47.6	49.0	49.4	49.5	50.2	48.7	50.3	51.8

GHANA

(US$ million, unless otherwise indicated)

	1970	*1980*	*1990*	*1992*	*1993*	*1994*	*1995*	*1996*	*1997*	*1998*
5. LONG-TERM DEBT										
DEBT OUTSTANDING (LDOD)	**520**	**1,162**	**2,816**	**3,355**	**3,677**	**4,192**	**4,669**	**5,246**	**5,327**	**5,833**
Public and publicly guaranteed	**510**	**1,152**	**2,783**	**3,320**	**3,640**	**4,160**	**4,642**	**4,975**	**5,060**	**5,570**
Official creditors	332	1,031	2,560	3,022	3,330	3,770	4,141	4,447	4,473	4,995
Multilateral	53	279	1,846	2,209	2,413	2,710	2,982	3,138	3,197	3,563
Concessional	11	139	1,510	1,858	2,076	2,369	2,670	2,855	2,966	3,345
Bilateral	279	752	713	813	916	1,060	1,159	1,309	1,276	1,432
Concessional	236	633	611	716	818	974	1,071	1,150	1,109	1,273
Private creditors	178	121	224	298	310	390	502	528	587	575
Bonds	0	0	0	0	0	0	0	0	0	0
Commercial banks	12	0	10	5	5	36	140	204	183	171
Other private	166	121	214	293	305	354	362	324	404	404
Private nonguaranteed	**10**	**10**	**33**	**35**	**37**	**32**	**27**	**271**	**267**	**263**
Bonds	0	0	0	0	0	0	0	250	250	250
Commercial banks	10	10	33	35	37	32	27	21	17	13
Memo:										
IBRD	43	114	113	87	77	70	59	44	30	27
IDA	11	99	1,310	1,631	1,838	2,094	2,375	2,530	2,617	2,962
DISBURSEMENTS	**42**	**220**	**438**	**489**	**445**	**469**	**607**	**896**	**649**	**520**
Public and publicly guaranteed	**42**	**220**	**430**	**482**	**438**	**469**	**607**	**646**	**649**	**520**
Official creditors	39	220	379	385	367	345	428	516	441	438
Multilateral	4	50	274	248	252	224	284	298	291	293
Concessional	4	21	214	208	234	203	269	285	288	291
Bilateral	35	170	105	137	115	121	144	217	150	145
Concessional	35	93	95	110	108	121	138	108	116	125
Private creditors	3	0	51	97	71	124	179	131	208	83
Bonds	0	0	0	0	0	0	0	0	0	0
Commercial banks	0	0	9	3	3	30	108	72	25	25
Other private	3	0	42	93	68	94	71	58	183	58
Private nonguaranteed	**0**	**0**	**8**	**7**	**7**	**0**	**0**	**250**	**0**	**0**
Bonds	0	0	0	0	0	0	0	250	0	0
Commercial banks	0	0	8	7	7	0	0	0	0	0
Memo:										
IBRD	0	25	0	0	0	0	0	0	0	0
IDA	4	5	201	170	205	178	242	244	237	261
PRINCIPAL REPAYMENTS	**14**	**77**	**144**	**134**	**120**	**166**	**202**	**206**	**231**	**252**
Public and publicly guaranteed	**14**	**77**	**136**	**128**	**115**	**161**	**197**	**200**	**227**	**248**
Official creditors	9	35	65	77	68	100	117	101	107	140
Multilateral	2	4	29	44	41	51	73	55	52	53
Concessional	0	0	7	10	10	14	17	18	20	26
Bilateral	8	31	35	32	27	50	43	46	55	87
Concessional	7	14	33	23	22	42	39	38	34	58
Private creditors	5	42	71	52	47	61	80	99	120	107
Bonds	0	0	0	0	0	0	0	0	0	0
Commercial banks	0	22	17	4	2	1	2	19	38	40
Other private	5	20	55	48	45	59	78	80	82	67
Private nonguaranteed	**0**	**0**	**8**	**6**	**5**	**5**	**5**	**6**	**4**	**4**
Bonds	0	0	0	0	0	0	0	0	0	0
Commercial banks	0	0	8	6	5	5	5	6	4	4
Memo:										
IBRD	2	3	10	12	13	13	15	10	11	4
IDA	0	0	2	3	4	6	8	10	12	16
NET FLOWS ON DEBT	**28**	**143**	**294**	**354**	**325**	**303**	**405**	**690**	**419**	**269**
Public and publicly guaranteed	**28**	**143**	**294**	**353**	**323**	**308**	**410**	**446**	**423**	**273**
Official creditors	29	185	314	309	299	245	311	415	334	297
Multilateral	3	47	245	204	211	173	211	243	239	240
Concessional	4	21	207	199	224	189	252	266	268	265
Bilateral	27	138	69	105	88	71	101	172	95	58
Concessional	28	79	62	87	86	79	100	70	82	67
Private creditors	-2	-42	-20	45	24	64	99	31	88	-25
Bonds	0	0	0	0	0	0	0	0	0	0
Commercial banks	0	-22	-8	0	1	29	106	53	-13	-16
Other private	-2	-20	-13	45	23	35	-7	-22	101	-9
Private nonguaranteed	**0**	**0**	**0**	**1**	**2**	**-5**	**-5**	**244**	**-4**	**-4**
Bonds	0	0	0	0	0	0	0	250	0	0
Commercial banks	0	0	0	1	2	-5	-5	-6	-4	-4
Memo:										
IBRD	-1	21	-10	-12	-13	-13	-15	-10	-11	-4
IDA	4	5	199	168	202	172	234	234	225	245

GHANA

(US$ million, unless otherwise indicated)

	1970	1980	1990	1992	1993	1994	1995	1996	1997	1998
INTEREST PAYMENTS (LINT)	**12**	**31**	**59**	**81**	**86**	**84**	**60**	**109**	**122**	**149**
Public and publicly guaranteed	**12**	**31**	**57**	**79**	**83**	**82**	**58**	**107**	**107**	**134**
Official creditors	7	24	45	62	69	63	52	77	74	90
Multilateral	3	10	30	42	41	36	40	43	41	38
Concessional	0	1	10	15	15	16	18	21	21	23
Bilateral	4	14	15	21	28	27	12	35	33	52
Concessional	4	10	13	17	23	23	10	30	22	41
Private creditors	5	7	12	17	14	19	6	30	33	44
Bonds	0	0	0	0	0	0	0	0	0	0
Commercial banks	0	2	2	1	0	0	0	7	11	15
Other private	5	4	11	16	14	19	6	22	22	29
Private nonguaranteed	**0**	**0**	**2**	**2**	**3**	**2**	**2**	**1**	**15**	**15**
Bonds	0	0	0	0	0	0	0	0	14	14
Commercial banks	0	0	2	2	3	2	2	1	1	1
Memo:										
IBRD	3	8	9	9	7	6	6	3	4	1
IDA	0	1	8	11	13	14	17	18	19	20
NET TRANSFERS ON DEBT	**16**	**112**	**235**	**273**	**239**	**219**	**346**	**582**	**297**	**120**
Public and publicly guaranteed	**16**	**112**	**238**	**275**	**240**	**226**	**352**	**339**	**316**	**138**
Official creditors	22	161	270	247	230	182	259	337	261	207
Multilateral	0	37	216	163	170	137	170	200	199	202
Concessional	4	20	197	184	208	173	234	246	246	242
Bilateral	22	124	54	84	60	44	89	137	62	6
Concessional	24	69	49	70	63	57	90	40	60	26
Private creditors	-7	-48	-32	28	10	45	93	2	55	-69
Bonds	0	0	0	0	0	0	0	0	0	0
Commercial banks	0	-24	-9	-1	1	29	106	46	-24	-30
Other private	-7	-25	-23	29	9	15	-13	-44	80	-39
Private nonguaranteed	**0**	**0**	**-2**	**-1**	**-1**	**-7**	**-7**	**243**	**-19**	**-19**
Bonds	0	0	0	0	0	0	0	250	-14	-14
Commercial banks	0	0	-2	-1	-1	-7	-7	-7	-5	-5
Memo:										
IBRD	-4	13	-20	-21	-20	-20	-21	-13	-15	-6
IDA	4	4	191	156	189	157	218	216	207	225
DEBT SERVICE (LTDS)	**26**	**108**	**203**	**216**	**206**	**250**	**261**	**315**	**352**	**401**
Public and publicly guaranteed	**26**	**108**	**192**	**207**	**198**	**243**	**254**	**307**	**333**	**382**
Official creditors	16	59	109	139	137	163	169	178	180	230
Multilateral	4	14	59	86	82	87	113	98	93	91
Concessional	0	1	17	24	26	31	35	39	42	49
Bilateral	12	46	50	53	55	77	55	80	88	139
Concessional	11	24	46	40	45	64	49	68	56	99
Private creditors	10	48	83	69	61	80	86	129	153	152
Bonds	0	0	0	0	0	0	0	0	0	0
Commercial banks	0	24	18	5	2	1	2	27	50	55
Other private	10	25	65	64	59	79	84	103	104	96
Private nonguaranteed	**0**	**0**	**10**	**8**	**8**	**7**	**7**	**7**	**19**	**19**
Bonds	0	0	0	0	0	0	0	0	14	14
Commercial banks	0	0	10	8	8	7	7	7	5	5
Memo:										
IBRD	4	11	20	21	20	20	21	13	15	6
IDA	0	1	10	14	17	21	25	28	30	36
UNDISBURSED DEBT	**76**	**431**	**1,708**	**1,731**	**1,767**	**1,872**	**2,104**	**1,976**	**1,546**	**1,274**
Official creditors	76	431	1,595	1,586	1,606	1,619	1,800	1,696	1,363	1,170
Private creditors	0	0	113	146	161	253	304	280	183	104
Memorandum items										
Concessional LDOD	246	772	2,120	2,574	2,895	3,343	3,741	4,005	4,075	4,618
Variable rate LDOD	10	10	51	68	65	58	55	305	293	284
Public sector LDOD	510	1,125	2,783	3,320	3,640	4,160	4,642	4,975	5,060	5,570
Private sector LDOD	10	38	33	35	37	32	27	271	267	263

6. CURRENCY COMPOSITION OF LONG-TERM DEBT (PERCENT)

	1970	1980	1990	1992	1993	1994	1995	1996	1997	1998
Deutsche mark	12.3	12.9	3.9	4.0	4.0	4.3	3.9	4.2	4.1	3.9
French franc	2.7	1.9	2.2	3.0	2.5	2.5	3.1	3.0	2.5	2.5
Japanese yen	0.0	0.1	6.7	10.1	11.4	13.2	13.7	12.4	11.8	14.1
Pound sterling	28.3	11.8	2.8	4.1	4.1	4.7	5.7	7.3	7.0	5.9
Swiss franc	0.0	0.0	0.6	0.4	0.3	0.2	0.2	0.3	0.2	0.2
U.S.dollars	22.5	38.7	58.7	55.6	56.7	54.9	55.4	56.0	58.4	58.5
Multiple currency	8.4	10.8	7.8	6.7	6.3	6.1	5.7	5.7	5.8	5.8
Special drawing rights	0.0	0.0	0.6	0.7	0.7	0.7	0.7	0.8	0.7	0.7
All other currencies	25.8	23.8	16.7	15.4	14.0	13.4	11.6	10.3	9.5	8.4

GHANA

(US$ million, unless otherwise indicated)

	1970	*1980*	*1990*	*1992*	*1993*	*1994*	*1995*	*1996*	*1997*	*1998*
7. DEBT RESTRUCTURINGS										
Total amount rescheduled	..	..	0	0	0	0	0	99	0	0
Debt stock rescheduled	..	..	0	0	0	0	0	0	0	0
Principal rescheduled	..	..	0	0	0	0	0	47	0	0
Official	..	..	0	0	0	0	0	38	0	0
Private	..	..	0	0	0	0	0	9	0	0
Interest rescheduled	..	..	0	0	0	0	0	21	0	0
Official	..	..	0	0	0	0	0	20	0	0
Private	..	..	0	0	0	0	0	2	0	0
Debt forgiven	..	..	102	0	0	12	1	7	7	0
Memo: interest forgiven	..	..	0	0	0	1	0	0	0	0
Debt stock reduction	..	..	0	0	0	0	0	0	0	12
of which debt buyback	..	..	0	0	0	0	0	0	0	0
8. DEBT STOCK-FLOW RECONCILIATION										
Total change in debt stocks	..	..	479	129	380	584	467	503	-91	532
Net flows on debt	5	75	341	307	371	324	410	654	274	283
Net change in interest arrears	..	..	17	5	13	3	-29	-17	3	-3
Interest capitalized	..	..	0	0	0	0	0	21	0	0
Debt forgiveness or reduction	..	..	-102	0	0	-12	-1	-7	-7	-12
Cross-currency valuation	..	..	101	-83	3	149	31	-93	-172	151
Residual	..	..	121	-100	-7	120	56	-56	-189	113
9. AVERAGE TERMS OF NEW COMMITMENTS										
ALL CREDITORS										
Interest (%)	2.0	1.4	3.0	1.8	3.1	4.2	3.3	2.9	2.3	3.0
Maturity (years)	36.7	43.3	32.1	32.7	30.3	25.4	26.8	25.3	28.5	32.8
Grace period (years)	9.7	9.7	8.4	8.0	7.6	7.0	7.1	6.7	7.3	8.1
Grant element (%)	66.8	74.0	58.2	65.1	54.5	43.8	51.5	50.9	55.2	56.0
Official creditors										
Interest (%)	1.8	1.4	2.0	1.0	2.2	1.9	1.8	2.1	1.4	2.4
Maturity (years)	38.6	43.3	35.9	37.0	34.2	35.1	34.1	29.4	38.8	36.3
Grace period (years)	10.2	9.7	9.4	9.2	8.6	9.7	9.2	7.9	10.1	8.9
Grant element (%)	70.2	74.0	67.8	76.0	65.2	68.0	68.3	60.1	73.1	62.4
Private creditors										
Interest (%)	5.3	0.0	8.1	5.0	6.8	7.2	6.9	6.1	3.8	6.4
Maturity (years)	8.4	0.0	11.4	14.9	15.3	12.4	8.9	9.7	8.3	12.0
Grace period (years)	1.4	0.0	2.9	3.1	3.7	3.3	1.9	2.2	1.9	3.1
Grant element (%)	16.3	0.0	6.2	20.1	12.3	11.4	10.5	15.6	20.0	18.6
Memorandum items										
Commitments	51	170	679	724	497	477	796	702	378	284
Official creditors	48	170	573	583	396	273	565	556	250	243
Private creditors	3	0	106	140	100	203	231	146	127	42

10. CONTRACTUAL OBLIGATIONS ON OUTSTANDING LONG-TERM DEBT

	1999	*2000*	*2001*	*2002*	*2003*	*2004*	*2005*	*2006*	*2007*	*2008*
TOTAL										
Disbursements	410	358	214	140	83	37	24	5	2	0
Principal	315	316	281	264	499	243	238	211	203	195
Interest	137	130	121	111	95	78	69	61	55	50
Official creditors										
Disbursements	347	330	205	136	83	37	24	5	2	0
Principal	194	199	184	182	182	187	193	175	179	184
Interest	85	82	79	75	71	65	60	55	51	48
Bilateral creditors										
Disbursements	96	84	52	31	18	8	5	1	1	0
Principal	115	118	109	100	94	95	95	70	70	68
Interest	41	39	36	33	30	26	23	20	18	17
Multilateral creditors										
Disbursements	251	246	152	106	65	29	19	4	1	0
Principal	79	81	75	83	88	92	98	105	109	116
Interest	44	43	42	42	41	39	37	35	33	31
Private creditors										
Disbursements	63	29	9	3	0	0	0	0	0	0
Principal	121	117	97	82	317	56	45	37	24	11
Interest	53	48	42	37	24	13	9	6	4	2
Commercial banks										
Disbursements	5	1	0	0	0	0	0	0	0	0
Principal	43	41	30	23	18	13	7	2	0	0
Interest	11	8	6	4	2	1	1	0	0	0
Other private										
Disbursements	58	28	9	3	0	0	0	0	0	0
Principal	78	76	67	59	299	43	38	34	24	11
Interest	42	39	36	33	22	12	9	6	4	2

GRENADA

(US$ million, unless otherwise indicated)

	1970	1980	1990	1992	1993	1994	1995	1996	1997	1998
1. SUMMARY DEBT DATA										
TOTAL DEBT STOCKS (EDT)	**..**	**16.1**	**102.5**	**105.3**	**135.5**	**115.5**	**113.3**	**126.4**	**127.6**	**182.8**
Long-term debt (LDOD)	**7.6**	**12.3**	**89.9**	**94.1**	**92.5**	**100.2**	**98.9**	**105.8**	**113.8**	**113.0**
Public and publicly guaranteed	7.6	12.3	89.9	94.1	92.5	100.2	98.9	105.8	113.8	113.0
Private nonguaranteed	0.0	0.0	0.0	0.0	0.0	0.0	0.0	0.0	0.0	0.0
Use of IMF credit	**0.0**	**2.8**	**0.0**	**0.0**	**0.0**	**0.0**	**0.0**	**0.0**	**0.0**	**0.0**
Short-term debt	**..**	**1.0**	**12.6**	**11.3**	**43.0**	**15.4**	**14.4**	**20.6**	**13.8**	**69.8**
of which interest arrears on LDOD	..	0.0	6.6	6.2	6.2	6.4	6.4	6.9	6.8	7.3
Official creditors	..	0.0	6.3	6.0	6.0	6.2	6.1	6.7	6.6	7.3
Private creditors	..	0.0	0.2	0.2	0.2	0.2	0.2	0.2	0.2	0.0
Memo: principal arrears on LDOD	..	0.0	15.4	17.5	17.8	18.7	19.0	20.2	18.0	18.3
Official creditors	..	0.0	14.4	16.6	16.9	17.8	18.4	19.7	17.6	17.9
Private creditors	..	0.0	1.0	0.9	0.9	1.0	0.5	0.5	0.4	0.4
Memo: export credits	..	0.0	23.0	19.0	25.0	18.0	4.0	4.0	22.0	13.0
TOTAL DEBT FLOWS										
Disbursements	**3.0**	**1.7**	**14.6**	**7.6**	**4.5**	**10.8**	**3.8**	**9.1**	**14.4**	**3.2**
Long-term debt	3.0	1.0	14.6	7.6	4.5	10.8	3.8	9.1	14.4	3.2
IMF purchases	0.0	0.7	0.0	0.0	0.0	0.0	0.0	0.0	0.0	0.0
Principal repayments	**0.0**	**1.6**	**1.7**	**3.8**	**5.2**	**5.3**	**4.8**	**4.4**	**4.4**	**4.8**
Long-term debt	0.0	0.9	1.2	3.8	5.2	5.3	4.8	4.4	4.4	4.8
IMF repurchases	0.0	0.7	0.5	0.0	0.0	0.0	0.0	0.0	0.0	0.0
Net flows on debt	**3.0**	**-0.9**	**12.9**	**2.8**	**31.0**	**-22.3**	**-2.0**	**10.4**	**3.3**	**53.9**
of which short-term debt	..	-1.0	0.0	-0.9	31.7	-27.8	-1.0	5.7	-6.7	55.5
Interest payments (INT)	**..**	**0.7**	**1.5**	**1.9**	**2.8**	**2.9**	**2.1**	**2.9**	**2.1**	**3.7**
Long-term debt	0.1	0.5	1.1	1.6	1.5	1.5	1.6	2.1	1.7	2.0
IMF charges	0.0	0.1	0.0	0.0	0.0	0.0	0.0	0.0	0.0	0.0
Short-term debt	..	0.2	0.4	0.4	1.3	1.4	0.5	0.8	0.5	1.7
Net transfers on debt	**..**	**-1.6**	**11.4**	**0.9**	**28.2**	**-25.1**	**-4.1**	**7.5**	**1.2**	**50.2**
Total debt service paid (TDS)	**..**	**2.3**	**3.2**	**5.7**	**7.9**	**8.1**	**6.9**	**7.3**	**6.6**	**8.5**
Long-term debt	0.1	1.3	2.3	5.4	6.7	6.7	6.3	6.5	6.1	6.8
IMF repurchases and charges	0.0	0.8	0.5	0.0	0.0	0.0	0.0	0.0	0.0	0.0
Short-term debt (interest only)	..	0.2	0.4	0.4	1.3	1.4	0.5	0.8	0.5	1.7
2. AGGREGATE NET RESOURCE FLOWS AND NET TRANSFERS (LONG-TERM)										
NET RESOURCE FLOWS	**2.9**	**1.1**	**30.6**	**30.9**	**21.6**	**36.1**	**30.4**	**29.1**	**36.2**	**23.4**
Net flow of long-term debt (ex. IMF)	3.0	0.1	13.4	3.7	-0.7	5.5	-1.0	4.7	10.0	-1.6
Foreign direct investment (net)	0.0	0.0	13.0	23.0	20.0	19.3	24.0	20.0	22.0	21.0
Portfolio equity flows	0.0	0.0	0.0	0.0	0.0	0.0	0.0	0.0	0.0	0.0
Grants (excluding technical coop.)	0.0	1.0	4.2	4.1	2.3	11.3	7.4	4.4	4.1	4.0
Memo: technical coop. grants	0.0	0.8	2.9	3.9	3.9	3.3	3.8	2.5	3.3	3.4
official net resource flows	0.1	1.7	17.3	8.1	2.7	18.1	8.1	9.9	14.7	2.4
private net resource flows	2.8	-0.6	13.3	22.8	18.9	18.0	22.3	19.2	21.5	21.0
NET TRANSFERS	**2.8**	**0.4**	**21.0**	**23.1**	**14.0**	**27.6**	**19.8**	**19.1**	**25.6**	**13.5**
Interest on long-term debt	0.1	0.5	1.1	1.6	1.5	1.5	1.6	2.1	1.7	2.0
Profit remittances on FDI	0.0	0.2	8.4	6.2	6.0	7.0	9.0	8.0	9.0	8.0
Memo: official net transfers	0.1	1.4	16.3	6.6	1.2	16.6	6.7	7.9	13.1	0.5
private net transfers	2.7	-1.0	4.7	16.5	12.8	11.0	13.1	11.2	12.5	13.0
3. MAJOR ECONOMIC AGGREGATES										
Gross national product (GNP)	..	81.4	209.2	245.6	240.8	253.1	264.1	281.6	299.9	326.8
Exports of goods & services (XGS)	..	39.1	105.5	113.5	123.2	145.1	149.7	156.9	167.3	170.6
of which workers remittances	..	0.0	9.9	10.7	10.1	13.5	19.8	21.0	22.8	22.8
Imports of goods & services (MGS)	..	63.1	153.2	147.0	170.3	169.3	182.3	213.2	242.4	262.5
International reserves (RES)	5.3	12.9	17.6	25.9	26.9	31.2	36.7	35.7	42.7	46.8
Current account balance	..	0.3	-46.2	-32.3	-43.5	-21.8	-35.2	-57.9	-78.0	-94.8
4. DEBT INDICATORS										
EDT / XGS (%)	..	41.2	97.2	92.8	110.0	79.6	75.7	80.6	76.3	107.2
EDT / GNP (%)	..	19.8	49.0	42.9	56.3	45.6	42.9	44.9	42.6	55.9
TDS / XGS (%)	..	5.9	3.0	5.0	6.4	5.6	4.6	4.7	4.0	5.0
INT / XGS (%)	..	1.8	1.4	1.7	2.3	2.0	1.4	1.9	1.3	2.2
INT / GNP (%)	..	0.9	0.7	0.8	1.2	1.2	0.8	1.0	0.7	1.1
RES / EDT (%)	..	80.2	17.2	24.6	19.9	27.0	32.4	28.3	33.4	25.6
RES / MGS (months)	..	2.5	1.4	2.1	1.9	2.2	2.4	2.0	2.1	2.1
Short-term / EDT (%)	..	6.2	12.3	10.7	31.7	13.3	12.7	16.3	10.8	38.2
Concessional / EDT (%)	..	52.2	59.4	56.4	44.4	57.3	57.2	54.3	55.3	38.6
Multilateral / EDT (%)	..	32.3	37.5	41.0	30.6	39.1	40.8	38.1	38.8	27.2

GRENADA

(US$ million, unless otherwise indicated)

	1970	1980	1990	1992	1993	1994	1995	1996	1997	1998
5. LONG-TERM DEBT										
DEBT OUTSTANDING (LDOD)	**7.6**	**12.3**	**89.9**	**94.1**	**92.5**	**100.2**	**98.9**	**105.8**	**113.8**	**113.0**
Public and publicly guaranteed	**7.6**	**12.3**	**89.9**	**94.1**	**92.5**	**100.2**	**98.9**	**105.8**	**113.8**	**113.0**
Official creditors	2.5	9.7	87.6	82.9	82.7	91.1	91.6	98.8	107.5	106.7
Multilateral	0.0	5.2	38.4	43.2	41.4	45.1	46.2	48.2	49.5	49.8
Concessional	0.0	4.2	35.5	40.5	39.4	42.7	41.9	41.9	43.0	43.4
Bilateral	2.5	4.6	49.2	39.7	41.2	46.0	45.4	50.6	58.0	56.9
Concessional	2.4	4.2	25.4	18.9	20.7	23.5	22.9	26.7	27.5	27.1
Private creditors	5.1	2.6	2.3	11.2	9.8	9.0	7.3	7.0	6.3	6.3
Bonds	5.1	2.1	0.0	0.0	0.0	0.0	0.0	0.0	0.0	0.0
Commercial banks	0.0	0.0	0.7	0.5	0.6	0.6	0.4	0.3	0.3	0.3
Other private	0.0	0.5	1.6	10.7	9.2	8.5	6.9	6.7	6.0	6.0
Private nonguaranteed	**0.0**	**0.0**	**0.0**	**0.0**	**0.0**	**0.0**	**0.0**	**0.0**	**0.0**	**0.0**
Bonds	0.0	0.0	0.0	0.0	0.0	0.0	0.0	0.0	0.0	0.0
Commercial banks	0.0	0.0	0.0	0.0	0.0	0.0	0.0	0.0	0.0	0.0
Memo:										
IBRD	0.0	0.0	0.0	0.0	0.0	0.0	0.0	0.0	0.0	0.0
IDA	0.0	0.0	5.5	6.8	6.9	7.2	7.3	7.2	7.1	8.2
DISBURSEMENTS	**3.0**	**1.0**	**14.6**	**7.6**	**4.5**	**10.8**	**3.8**	**9.1**	**14.4**	**3.2**
Public and publicly guaranteed	**3.0**	**1.0**	**14.6**	**7.6**	**4.5**	**10.8**	**3.8**	**9.1**	**14.4**	**3.2**
Official creditors	0.1	1.0	14.1	6.3	4.4	10.8	3.8	9.1	14.4	3.2
Multilateral	0.0	1.0	2.8	6.1	1.6	5.6	3.3	4.4	4.2	2.5
Concessional	0.0	0.0	2.8	5.8	1.4	5.2	1.2	2.0	3.4	1.9
Bilateral	0.1	0.0	11.3	0.3	2.8	5.2	0.5	4.7	10.3	0.7
Concessional	0.0	0.0	1.0	0.3	2.8	3.8	0.5	3.5	2.3	0.7
Private creditors	2.8	0.0	0.5	1.2	0.1	0.0	0.0	0.0	0.0	0.0
Bonds	2.8	0.0	0.0	0.0	0.0	0.0	0.0	0.0	0.0	0.0
Commercial banks	0.0	0.0	0.0	0.0	0.1	0.0	0.0	0.0	0.0	0.0
Other private	0.0	0.0	0.5	1.2	0.0	0.0	0.0	0.0	0.0	0.0
Private nonguaranteed	**0.0**	**0.0**	**0.0**	**0.0**	**0.0**	**0.0**	**0.0**	**0.0**	**0.0**	**0.0**
Bonds	0.0	0.0	0.0	0.0	0.0	0.0	0.0	0.0	0.0	0.0
Commercial banks	0.0	0.0	0.0	0.0	0.0	0.0	0.0	0.0	0.0	0.0
Memo:										
IBRD	0.0	0.0	0.0	0.0	0.0	0.0	0.0	0.0	0.0	0.0
IDA	0.0	0.0	1.0	0.0	0.0	0.0	0.0	0.2	0.3	0.9
PRINCIPAL REPAYMENTS	**0.0**	**0.9**	**1.2**	**3.8**	**5.2**	**5.3**	**4.8**	**4.4**	**4.4**	**4.8**
Public and publicly guaranteed	**0.0**	**0.9**	**1.2**	**3.8**	**5.2**	**5.3**	**4.8**	**4.4**	**4.4**	**4.8**
Official creditors	0.0	0.3	1.0	2.4	3.9	4.0	3.1	3.6	3.9	4.8
Multilateral	0.0	0.0	1.0	1.9	3.2	2.5	2.5	2.1	2.1	2.6
Concessional	0.0	0.0	0.8	1.6	2.5	2.3	2.3	1.7	1.7	2.0
Bilateral	0.0	0.3	0.1	0.5	0.7	1.5	0.6	1.5	1.8	2.2
Concessional	0.0	0.2	0.0	0.3	0.7	1.4	0.6	0.8	0.8	1.3
Private creditors	0.0	0.6	0.2	1.4	1.2	1.3	1.7	0.8	0.5	0.0
Bonds	0.0	0.6	0.0	0.0	0.0	0.0	0.0	0.0	0.0	0.0
Commercial banks	0.0	0.0	0.1	0.0	0.0	0.0	0.2	0.1	0.0	0.0
Other private	0.0	0.0	0.1	1.4	1.2	1.3	1.5	0.7	0.5	0.0
Private nonguaranteed	**0.0**	**0.0**	**0.0**	**0.0**	**0.0**	**0.0**	**0.0**	**0.0**	**0.0**	**0.0**
Bonds	0.0	0.0	0.0	0.0	0.0	0.0	0.0	0.0	0.0	0.0
Commercial banks	0.0	0.0	0.0	0.0	0.0	0.0	0.0	0.0	0.0	0.0
Memo:										
IBRD	0.0	0.0	0.0	0.0	0.0	0.0	0.0	0.0	0.0	0.0
IDA	0.0	0.0	0.0	0.0	0.0	0.0	0.1	0.1	0.1	0.1
NET FLOWS ON DEBT	**3.0**	**0.1**	**13.4**	**3.7**	**-0.7**	**5.5**	**-1.0**	**4.7**	**10.0**	**-1.6**
Public and publicly guaranteed	**3.0**	**0.1**	**13.4**	**3.7**	**-0.7**	**5.5**	**-1.0**	**4.7**	**10.0**	**-1.6**
Official creditors	0.1	0.7	13.1	4.0	0.4	6.8	0.7	5.5	10.6	-1.6
Multilateral	0.0	1.0	1.9	4.2	-1.7	3.1	0.8	2.3	2.0	-0.1
Concessional	0.0	0.0	2.1	4.1	-1.1	2.9	-1.1	0.3	1.7	0.0
Bilateral	0.1	-0.3	11.2	-0.2	2.1	3.7	-0.1	3.2	8.5	-1.4
Concessional	0.0	-0.2	1.0	0.0	2.1	2.4	-0.1	2.7	1.4	-0.6
Private creditors	2.8	-0.6	0.3	-0.2	-1.1	-1.3	-1.7	-0.8	-0.5	0.0
Bonds	2.8	-0.6	0.0	0.0	0.0	0.0	0.0	0.0	0.0	0.0
Commercial banks	0.0	0.0	-0.1	0.0	0.1	0.0	-0.2	-0.1	0.0	0.0
Other private	0.0	0.0	0.4	-0.2	-1.2	-1.3	-1.5	-0.7	-0.5	0.0
Private nonguaranteed	**0.0**	**0.0**	**0.0**	**0.0**	**0.0**	**0.0**	**0.0**	**0.0**	**0.0**	**0.0**
Bonds	0.0	0.0	0.0	0.0	0.0	0.0	0.0	0.0	0.0	0.0
Commercial banks	0.0	0.0	0.0	0.0	0.0	0.0	0.0	0.0	0.0	0.0
Memo:										
IBRD	0.0	0.0	0.0	0.0	0.0	0.0	0.0	0.0	0.0	0.0
IDA	0.0	0.0	1.0	0.0	0.0	0.0	-0.1	0.2	0.3	0.9

GRENADA

(US$ million, unless otherwise indicated)

	1970	1980	1990	1992	1993	1994	1995	1996	1997	1998
INTEREST PAYMENTS (LINT)	**0.1**	**0.5**	**1.1**	**1.6**	**1.5**	**1.5**	**1.6**	**2.1**	**1.7**	**2.0**
Public and publicly guaranteed	**0.1**	**0.5**	**1.1**	**1.6**	**1.5**	**1.5**	**1.6**	**2.1**	**1.7**	**2.0**
Official creditors	0.0	0.3	1.0	1.5	1.5	1.5	1.4	2.0	1.6	1.9
Multilateral	0.0	0.2	1.0	1.0	1.3	1.2	1.2	1.2	1.1	1.3
Concessional	0.0	0.2	0.9	0.9	1.2	1.2	1.1	1.0	1.0	1.0
Bilateral	0.0	0.1	0.0	0.6	0.2	0.2	0.2	0.8	0.5	0.6
Concessional	0.0	0.0	0.0	0.0	0.0	0.0	0.2	0.2	0.2	0.4
Private creditors	0.1	0.2	0.2	0.1	0.1	0.0	0.2	0.0	0.0	0.0
Bonds	0.1	0.2	0.0	0.0	0.0	0.0	0.0	0.0	0.0	0.0
Commercial banks	0.0	0.0	0.2	0.0	0.0	0.0	0.0	0.0	0.0	0.0
Other private	0.0	0.0	0.0	0.0	0.0	0.0	0.1	0.0	0.0	0.0
Private nonguaranteed	**0.0**	**0.0**	**0.0**	**0.0**	**0.0**	**0.0**	**0.0**	**0.0**	**0.0**	**0.0**
Bonds	0.0	0.0	0.0	0.0	0.0	0.0	0.0	0.0	0.0	0.0
Commercial banks	0.0	0.0	0.0	0.0	0.0	0.0	0.0	0.0	0.0	0.0
Memo:										
IBRD	0.0	0.0	0.0	0.0	0.0	0.0	0.0	0.0	0.0	0.0
IDA	0.0	0.0	0.0	0.1	0.1	0.1	0.1	0.1	0.1	0.1
NET TRANSFERS ON DEBT	**2.8**	**-0.3**	**12.3**	**2.2**	**-2.2**	**4.0**	**-2.6**	**2.7**	**8.4**	**-3.6**
Public and publicly guaranteed	**2.8**	**-0.3**	**12.3**	**2.2**	**-2.2**	**4.0**	**-2.6**	**2.7**	**8.4**	**-3.6**
Official creditors	0.1	0.4	12.1	2.5	-1.1	5.3	-0.7	3.5	8.9	-3.5
Multilateral	0.0	0.8	0.9	3.2	-2.9	1.8	-0.4	1.0	0.9	-1.5
Concessional	0.0	-0.2	1.1	3.2	-2.3	1.7	-2.2	-0.6	0.7	-1.1
Bilateral	0.1	-0.4	11.2	-0.8	1.9	3.5	-0.3	2.4	8.0	-2.1
Concessional	0.0	-0.2	1.0	0.0	2.1	2.3	-0.3	2.5	1.3	-1.0
Private creditors	2.7	-0.7	0.2	-0.3	-1.2	-1.3	-1.9	-0.8	-0.6	-0.1
Bonds	2.7	-0.7	0.0	0.0	0.0	0.0	0.0	0.0	0.0	0.0
Commercial banks	0.0	0.0	-0.3	-0.1	0.1	-0.1	-0.2	-0.1	-0.1	-0.1
Other private	0.0	0.0	0.4	-0.2	-1.2	-1.3	-1.7	-0.7	-0.5	0.0
Private nonguaranteed	**0.0**	**0.0**	**0.0**	**0.0**	**0.0**	**0.0**	**0.0**	**0.0**	**0.0**	**0.0**
Bonds	0.0	0.0	0.0	0.0	0.0	0.0	0.0	0.0	0.0	0.0
Commercial banks	0.0	0.0	0.0	0.0	0.0	0.0	0.0	0.0	0.0	0.0
Memo:										
IBRD	0.0	0.0	0.0	0.0	0.0	0.0	0.0	0.0	0.0	0.0
IDA	0.0	0.0	0.9	0.0	-0.1	-0.1	-0.1	0.1	0.2	0.8
DEBT SERVICE (LTDS)	**0.1**	**1.3**	**2.3**	**5.4**	**6.7**	**6.7**	**6.3**	**6.5**	**6.1**	**6.8**
Public and publicly guaranteed	**0.1**	**1.3**	**2.3**	**5.4**	**6.7**	**6.7**	**6.3**	**6.5**	**6.1**	**6.8**
Official creditors	0.0	0.6	2.0	3.9	5.4	5.4	4.5	5.6	5.5	6.7
Multilateral	0.0	0.2	1.9	2.8	4.5	3.7	3.6	3.3	3.2	3.9
Concessional	0.0	0.2	1.7	2.5	3.7	3.5	3.4	2.7	2.7	3.0
Bilateral	0.0	0.4	0.1	1.1	0.9	1.7	0.8	2.3	2.3	2.8
Concessional	0.0	0.2	0.0	0.3	0.7	1.4	0.8	1.0	1.0	1.7
Private creditors	0.1	0.7	0.3	1.5	1.3	1.3	1.9	0.8	0.6	0.1
Bonds	0.1	0.7	0.0	0.0	0.0	0.0	0.0	0.0	0.0	0.0
Commercial banks	0.0	0.0	0.3	0.1	0.0	0.1	0.2	0.1	0.1	0.1
Other private	0.0	0.0	0.1	1.4	1.2	1.3	1.7	0.7	0.5	0.0
Private nonguaranteed	**0.0**	**0.0**	**0.0**	**0.0**	**0.0**	**0.0**	**0.0**	**0.0**	**0.0**	**0.0**
Bonds	0.0	0.0	0.0	0.0	0.0	0.0	0.0	0.0	0.0	0.0
Commercial banks	0.0	0.0	0.0	0.0	0.0	0.0	0.0	0.0	0.0	0.0
Memo:										
IBRD	0.0	0.0	0.0	0.0	0.0	0.0	0.0	0.0	0.0	0.0
IDA	0.0	0.0	0.0	0.1	0.1	0.1	0.1	0.1	0.1	0.1
UNDISBURSED DEBT	**1.0**	**7.3**	**12.9**	**16.6**	**14.7**	**17.3**	**30.4**	**29.3**	**22.4**	**20.6**
Official creditors	1.0	7.3	12.9	16.6	14.7	17.3	30.4	29.3	22.4	20.6
Private creditors	0.0	0.0	0.0	0.0	0.0	0.0	0.0	0.0	0.0	0.0
Memorandum items										
Concessional LDOD	2.4	8.3	60.9	59.4	60.1	66.3	64.8	68.6	70.5	70.5
Variable rate LDOD	0.0	0.0	13.4	10.5	10.4	10.9	10.6	11.5	11.2	11.2
Public sector LDOD	7.6	12.3	89.9	94.1	92.5	100.2	98.9	105.8	113.8	113.0
Private sector LDOD	0.0	0.0	0.0	0.0	0.0	0.0	0.0	0.0	0.0	0.0
6. CURRENCY COMPOSITION OF LONG-TERM DEBT (PERCENT)										
Deutsche mark	0.0	0.0	0.0	0.0	0.0	0.0	0.0	0.0	0.0	0.0
French franc	0.0	0.0	0.0	0.0	0.5	1.7	2.0	1.9	1.6	1.7
Japanese yen	0.0	0.0	0.0	0.0	0.0	0.0	0.0	0.0	0.0	0.0
Pound sterling	100.0	48.0	31.4	34.4	34.7	31.6	29.8	30.0	26.3	25.7
Swiss franc	0.0	0.0	0.0	0.0	0.0	0.0	0.0	0.0	0.0	0.0
U.S.dollars	0.0	46.4	61.1	59.3	58.8	61.6	63.8	60.6	63.7	63.8
Multiple currency	0.0	0.0	0.0	0.0	0.0	0.0	0.0	0.0	0.0	0.0
Special drawing rights	0.0	0.0	2.3	2.2	2.3	1.8	1.4	1.1	1.6	1.6
All other currencies	0.0	5.6	5.2	4.1	3.7	3.3	3.0	6.4	6.8	7.2

GRENADA

(US$ million, unless otherwise indicated)

	1970	1980	1990	1992	1993	1994	1995	1996	1997	1998
7. DEBT RESTRUCTURINGS										
Total amount rescheduled	..	..	0.0	0.0	0.0	0.0	0.0	0.0	0.0	0.0
Debt stock rescheduled	..	..	0.0	0.0	0.0	0.0	0.0	0.0	0.0	0.0
Principal rescheduled	..	..	0.0	0.0	0.0	0.0	0.0	0.0	0.0	0.0
Official	..	..	0.0	0.0	0.0	0.0	0.0	0.0	0.0	0.0
Private	..	..	0.0	0.0	0.0	0.0	0.0	0.0	0.0	0.0
Interest rescheduled	..	..	0.0	0.0	0.0	0.0	0.0	0.0	0.0	0.0
Official	..	..	0.0	0.0	0.0	0.0	0.0	0.0	0.0	0.0
Private	..	..	0.0	0.0	0.0	0.0	0.0	0.0	0.0	0.0
Debt forgiven	..	..	0.0	0.8	0.0	0.0	0.6	0.0	0.0	0.0
Memo: interest forgiven	..	..	0.0	0.0	0.0	0.0	0.0	0.0	0.0	0.0
Debt stock reduction	..	..	0.0	0.0	0.0	0.0	0.0	0.0	0.0	0.0
of which debt buyback	..	..	0.0	0.0	0.0	0.0	0.0	0.0	0.0	0.0
8. DEBT STOCK-FLOW RECONCILIATION										
Total change in debt stocks	..	..	20.5	-7.8	30.1	-19.9	-2.2	13.1	1.2	55.2
Net flows on debt	3.0	-0.9	12.9	2.8	31.0	-22.3	-2.0	10.4	3.3	53.9
Net change in interest arrears	..	..	2.2	-1.3	0.0	0.2	0.0	0.5	-0.1	0.5
Interest capitalized	..	..	0.0	0.0	0.0	0.0	0.0	0.0	0.0	0.0
Debt forgiveness or reduction	..	..	0.0	-0.8	0.0	0.0	-0.6	0.0	0.0	0.0
Cross-currency valuation	..	..	6.1	-6.7	-0.9	2.0	0.1	2.7	-1.5	0.6
Residual	..	..	-0.7	-1.8	0.0	0.1	0.3	-0.6	-0.5	0.2
9. AVERAGE TERMS OF NEW COMMITMENTS										
ALL CREDITORS										
Interest (%)	7.4	1.6	4.8	2.9	3.9	4.6	2.6	4.3	5.0	3.5
Maturity (years)	12.7	14.4	11.2	31.8	21.1	17.3	28.2	22.3	14.6	25.0
Grace period (years)	12.7	4.6	2.1	8.7	1.2	4.2	5.6	6.1	0.1	6.8
Grant element (%)	17.0	43.8	22.9	57.7	35.6	32.8	52.2	42.1	23.1	49.5
Official creditors										
Interest (%)	0.0	1.6	4.8	2.9	3.8	4.6	2.6	4.3	5.0	3.5
Maturity (years)	29.5	14.4	11.2	31.8	21.7	17.3	28.2	22.3	14.6	25.0
Grace period (years)	29.5	4.6	2.1	8.7	1.3	4.2	5.6	6.1	0.1	6.8
Grant element (%)	94.0	43.8	22.9	57.7	36.8	32.8	52.2	42.1	23.1	49.5
Private creditors										
Interest (%)	7.5	0.0	0.0	0.0	8.3	0.0	0.0	0.0	0.0	0.0
Maturity (years)	12.5	0.0	0.0	0.0	3.6	0.0	0.0	0.0	0.0	0.0
Grace period (years)	12.5	0.0	0.0	0.0	0.1	0.0	0.0	0.0	0.0	0.0
Grant element (%)	16.1	0.0	0.0	0.0	3.4	0.0	0.0	0.0	0.0	0.0
Memorandum items										
Commitments	2.8	7.3	11.9	7.5	2.8	14.5	17.0	8.8	8.0	1.2
Official creditors	0.0	7.3	11.9	7.5	2.7	14.5	17.0	8.8	8.0	1.2
Private creditors	2.8	0.0	0.0	0.0	0.1	0.0	0.0	0.0	0.0	0.0

10. CONTRACTUAL OBLIGATIONS ON OUTSTANDING LONG-TERM DEBT

	1999	2000	2001	2002	2003	2004	2005	2006	2007	2008
TOTAL										
Disbursements	7.8	5.6	3.9	2.7	0.4	0.1	0.1	0.0	0.0	0.0
Principal	12.4	9.9	7.6	7.6	7.4	7.0	6.1	5.3	5.2	4.9
Interest	2.7	2.4	2.3	2.1	2.0	1.8	1.6	1.4	1.2	1.1
Official creditors										
Disbursements	7.8	5.6	3.9	2.7	0.4	0.1	0.1	0.0	0.0	0.0
Principal	11.5	9.0	6.7	6.7	6.5	6.1	5.8	5.2	5.2	4.8
Interest	2.6	2.4	2.2	2.1	1.9	1.7	1.6	1.4	1.2	1.1
Bilateral creditors										
Disbursements	1.6	0.9	0.5	0.3	0.0	0.0	0.0	0.0	0.0	0.0
Principal	8.1	5.4	2.6	2.4	2.4	2.4	2.4	2.3	2.2	2.2
Interest	1.3	0.9	0.8	0.7	0.7	0.6	0.5	0.4	0.4	0.3
Multilateral creditors										
Disbursements	6.2	4.7	3.4	2.4	0.4	0.1	0.1	0.0	0.0	0.0
Principal	3.4	3.6	4.1	4.3	4.1	3.6	3.4	3.0	2.9	2.7
Interest	1.4	1.4	1.4	1.4	1.3	1.2	1.0	0.9	0.8	0.7
Private creditors										
Disbursements	0.0	0.0	0.0	0.0	0.0	0.0	0.0	0.0	0.0	0.0
Principal	0.9	0.9	0.9	0.9	0.9	0.9	0.3	0.0	0.0	0.0
Interest	0.0	0.0	0.0	0.0	0.0	0.0	0.0	0.0	0.0	0.0
Commercial banks										
Disbursements	0.0	0.0	0.0	0.0	0.0	0.0	0.0	0.0	0.0	0.0
Principal	0.0	0.0	0.0	0.0	0.0	0.0	0.0	0.0	0.0	0.0
Interest	0.0	0.0	0.0	0.0	0.0	0.0	0.0	0.0	0.0	0.0
Other private										
Disbursements	0.0	0.0	0.0	0.0	0.0	0.0	0.0	0.0	0.0	0.0
Principal	0.9	0.9	0.9	0.9	0.9	0.9	0.3	0.0	0.0	0.0
Interest	0.0	0.0	0.0	0.0	0.0	0.0	0.0	0.0	0.0	0.0

GUATEMALA

(US$ million, unless otherwise indicated)

	1970	1980	1990	1992	1993	1994	1995	1996	1997	1998
1. SUMMARY DEBT DATA										
TOTAL DEBT STOCKS (EDT)	**..**	**1,180**	**3,080**	**3,051**	**3,190**	**3,430**	**3,654**	**3,775**	**4,124**	**4,565**
Long-term debt (LDOD)	**120**	**845**	**2,605**	**2,518**	**2,676**	**2,900**	**2,966**	**2,876**	**2,975**	**3,171**
Public and publicly guaranteed	106	563	2,478	2,376	2,494	2,739	2,824	2,755	2,872	2,990
Private nonguaranteed	14	282	127	141	183	161	142	121	103	182
Use of IMF credit	**0**	**0**	**67**	**31**	**0**	**0**	**0**	**0**	**0**	**0**
Short-term debt	**..**	**335**	**409**	**502**	**514**	**531**	**688**	**898**	**1,149**	**1,394**
of which interest arrears on LDOD	..	0	202	226	73	92	96	104	98	101
Official creditors	..	0	47	30	29	33	34	40	37	39
Private creditors	..	0	155	196	44	58	63	63	61	61
Memo: principal arrears on LDOD	..	0	308	387	347	429	474	522	518	514
Official creditors	..	0	102	67	131	150	160	188	169	165
Private creditors	..	0	206	320	216	279	314	335	349	349
Memo: export credits	..	0	545	486	400	418	383	354	523	593
TOTAL DEBT FLOWS										
Disbursements	**43**	**173**	**165**	**227**	**132**	**336**	**236**	**158**	**361**	**268**
Long-term debt	43	173	165	227	132	336	236	158	361	268
IMF purchases	0	0	0	0	0	0	0	0	0	0
Principal repayments	**30**	**78**	**102**	**364**	**191**	**180**	**198**	**194**	**201**	**196**
Long-term debt	22	78	90	332	160	180	198	194	201	196
IMF repurchases	8	0	12	32	31	0	0	0	0	0
Net flows on debt	**52**	**130**	**67**	**-68**	**106**	**153**	**191**	**167**	**416**	**314**
of which short-term debt	..	34	4	69	165	-2	153	203	256	242
Interest payments (INT)	**..**	**67**	**112**	**174**	**115**	**127**	**152**	**161**	**162**	**200**
Long-term debt	7	60	88	161	96	104	120	120	107	132
IMF charges	0	0	7	4	1	0	0	0	0	0
Short-term debt	..	8	16	9	18	23	32	41	55	68
Net transfers on debt	**..**	**63**	**-45**	**-241**	**-10**	**27**	**39**	**6**	**254**	**114**
Total debt service paid (TDS)	**..**	**145**	**214**	**537**	**306**	**307**	**350**	**355**	**363**	**396**
Long-term debt	29	137	179	493	256	284	318	314	307	328
IMF repurchases and charges	8	0	19	35	32	0	0	0	0	0
Short-term debt (interest only)	..	8	16	9	18	23	32	41	55	68
2. AGGREGATE NET RESOURCE FLOWS AND NET TRANSFERS (LONG-TERM)										
NET RESOURCE FLOWS	**53**	**221**	**192**	**84**	**198**	**310**	**218**	**158**	**399**	**897**
Net flow of long-term debt (ex. IMF)	21	96	75	-105	-28	155	38	-36	160	72
Foreign direct investment (net)	29	111	48	94	143	65	75	77	84	673
Portfolio equity flows	0	0	0	0	0	0	0	0	0	0
Grants (excluding technical coop.)	2	14	69	95	83	89	105	117	155	152
Memo: technical coop. grants	9	18	90	82	93	66	91	78	101	90
official net resource flows	9	130	148	-4	44	203	130	152	239	276
private net resource flows	44	91	44	88	154	107	88	6	160	621
NET TRANSFERS	**16**	**117**	**67**	**-113**	**58**	**161**	**42**	**-21**	**221**	**691**
Interest on long-term debt	7	60	88	161	96	104	120	120	107	132
Profit remittances on FDI	30	44	37	36	44	45	55	60	71	74
Memo: official net transfers	7	101	95	-135	-25	124	43	62	151	182
private net transfers	9	17	-29	22	83	37	-1	-83	70	508
3. MAJOR ECONOMIC AGGREGATES										
Gross national product (GNP)	1,866	7,834	7,494	10,329	11,293	12,841	14,484	15,553	17,557	18,773
Exports of goods & services (XGS)	..	1,834	1,695	2,154	2,290	2,574	3,228	3,212	3,672	4,035
of which workers remittances	..	0	107	187	205	263	358	375	408	457
Imports of goods & services (MGS)	..	2,107	2,028	3,063	3,150	3,385	3,933	3,810	4,504	5,323
International reserves (RES)	79	753	362	806	950	943	783	948	1,173	1,397
Current account balance	..	-163	-213	-706	-702	-625	-572	-452	-634	-1,039
4. DEBT INDICATORS										
EDT / XGS (%)	..	64.3	181.7	141.7	139.3	133.3	113.2	117.5	112.3	113.1
EDT / GNP (%)	..	15.1	41.1	29.5	28.3	26.7	25.2	24.3	23.5	24.3
TDS / XGS (%)	..	7.9	12.6	25.0	13.4	11.9	10.8	11.0	9.9	9.8
INT / XGS (%)	..	3.7	6.6	8.1	5.0	4.9	4.7	5.0	4.4	5.0
INT / GNP (%)	..	0.9	1.5	1.7	1.0	1.0	1.1	1.0	0.9	1.1
RES / EDT (%)	..	63.8	11.8	26.4	29.8	27.5	21.4	25.1	28.4	30.6
RES / MGS (months)	..	4.3	2.1	3.2	3.6	3.3	2.4	3.0	3.1	3.2
Short-term / EDT (%)	..	28.4	13.3	16.5	16.1	15.5	18.8	23.8	27.9	30.5
Concessional / EDT (%)	..	21.1	22.5	26.9	36.6	36.6	35.6	33.7	31.2	29.0
Multilateral / EDT (%)	..	30.9	33.7	30.7	27.7	29.1	27.7	27.7	26.0	26.6

GUATEMALA

(US$ million, unless otherwise indicated)

	1970	1980	1990	1992	1993	1994	1995	1996	1997	1998
5. LONG-TERM DEBT										
DEBT OUTSTANDING (LDOD)	**120**	**845**	**2,605**	**2,518**	**2,676**	**2,900**	**2,966**	**2,876**	**2,975**	**3,171**
Public and publicly guaranteed	**106**	**563**	**2,478**	**2,376**	**2,494**	**2,739**	**2,824**	**2,755**	**2,872**	**2,990**
Official creditors	54	548	1,702	1,630	1,935	2,113	2,165	2,149	2,173	2,327
Multilateral	33	364	1,039	937	884	997	1,012	1,044	1,074	1,214
Concessional	13	153	335	338	336	366	371	379	383	387
Bilateral	21	183	663	693	1,051	1,116	1,153	1,105	1,099	1,113
Concessional	21	96	359	482	831	891	930	893	903	936
Private creditors	52	15	776	747	558	626	659	607	699	662
Bonds	14	0	190	158	144	220	264	231	337	307
Commercial banks	36	14	166	172	157	150	140	126	116	114
Other private	3	1	420	417	257	257	255	250	245	242
Private nonguaranteed	**14**	**282**	**127**	**141**	**183**	**161**	**142**	**121**	**103**	**182**
Bonds	0	0	0	0	0	0	0	0	0	0
Commercial banks	14	282	127	141	183	161	142	121	103	182
Memo:										
IBRD	14	144	293	213	178	177	158	200	188	203
IDA	0	0	0	0	0	0	0	0	0	0
DISBURSEMENTS	**43**	**173**	**165**	**227**	**132**	**336**	**236**	**158**	**361**	**268**
Public and publicly guaranteed	**37**	**141**	**158**	**197**	**70**	**336**	**236**	**158**	**361**	**268**
Official creditors	12	128	128	162	64	235	163	158	211	267
Multilateral	9	80	68	95	30	151	87	143	136	202
Concessional	5	35	20	13	11	42	19	24	19	19
Bilateral	2	48	59	66	34	84	76	15	74	65
Concessional	2	23	54	28	9	60	56	6	56	63
Private creditors	26	13	30	36	7	101	73	1	150	1
Bonds	0	0	0	2	0	89	59	0	150	0
Commercial banks	25	13	14	32	7	9	2	0	0	0
Other private	0	0	16	2	0	3	12	1	0	1
Private nonguaranteed	**6**	**32**	**7**	**30**	**62**	**0**	**0**	**0**	**0**	**0**
Bonds	0	0	0	0	0	0	0	0	0	0
Commercial banks	6	32	7	30	62	0	0	0	0	0
Memo:										
IBRD	4	39	17	49	1	29	13	69	17	28
IDA	0	0	0	0	0	0	0	0	0	0
PRINCIPAL REPAYMENTS	**22**	**78**	**90**	**332**	**160**	**180**	**198**	**194**	**201**	**196**
Public and publicly guaranteed	**20**	**15**	**87**	**317**	**140**	**158**	**179**	**173**	**183**	**181**
Official creditors	5	12	49	261	103	122	137	122	127	143
Multilateral	3	12	28	159	87	86	90	75	71	74
Concessional	0	1	6	19	13	14	14	16	14	15
Bilateral	2	1	21	102	16	35	48	47	56	69
Concessional	2	1	2	12	11	15	22	30	25	46
Private creditors	16	3	39	56	37	37	41	51	56	38
Bonds	8	0	11	20	14	14	15	33	44	31
Commercial banks	6	1	24	34	21	16	11	14	8	3
Other private	1	2	4	2	2	7	15	4	4	5
Private nonguaranteed	**2**	**62**	**3**	**16**	**20**	**22**	**19**	**21**	**18**	**15**
Bonds	0	0	0	0	0	0	0	0	0	0
Commercial banks	2	62	3	16	20	22	19	21	18	15
Memo:										
IBRD	2	4	5	107	40	44	40	13	12	14
IDA	0	0	0	0	0	0	0	0	0	0
NET FLOWS ON DEBT	**21**	**96**	**75**	**-105**	**-28**	**155**	**38**	**-36**	**160**	**72**
Public and publicly guaranteed	**17**	**126**	**71**	**-119**	**-70**	**177**	**57**	**-15**	**178**	**87**
Official creditors	7	116	79	-99	-40	113	26	35	84	124
Multilateral	6	69	40	-64	-57	65	-3	68	66	128
Concessional	5	33	14	-6	-2	27	4	9	5	4
Bilateral	1	47	38	-35	18	48	29	-32	19	-4
Concessional	1	23	52	16	-2	45	34	-24	31	17
Private creditors	10	10	-8	-20	-30	64	31	-50	94	-37
Bonds	-8	0	-11	-18	-14	75	44	-33	106	-31
Commercial banks	19	11	-10	-2	-14	-8	-10	-14	-8	-3
Other private	-1	-2	12	0	-2	-4	-3	-3	-4	-4
Private nonguaranteed	**4**	**-30**	**4**	**14**	**42**	**-22**	**-19**	**-21**	**-18**	**-15**
Bonds	0	0	0	0	0	0	0	0	0	0
Commercial banks	4	-30	4	14	42	-22	-19	-21	-18	-15
Memo:										
IBRD	2	35	11	-58	-39	-15	-26	56	4	14
IDA	0	0	0	0	0	0	0	0	0	0

GUATEMALA

(US$ million, unless otherwise indicated)

	1970	1980	1990	1992	1993	1994	1995	1996	1997	1998
INTEREST PAYMENTS (LINT)	**7**	**60**	**88**	**161**	**96**	**104**	**120**	**120**	**107**	**132**
Public and publicly guaranteed	**6**	**30**	**78**	**153**	**89**	**98**	**115**	**116**	**103**	**122**
Official creditors	3	29	52	131	69	79	87	91	88	93
Multilateral	2	21	33	92	54	53	52	58	56	60
Concessional	0	3	4	7	7	7	8	8	7	8
Bilateral	1	9	19	39	15	26	35	33	32	34
Concessional	1	3	4	9	12	20	26	27	25	28
Private creditors	4	0	26	22	20	19	28	25	15	28
Bonds	1	0	18	16	15	13	23	21	13	27
Commercial banks	2	0	6	4	4	3	3	2	1	0
Other private	0	0	3	1	2	2	3	2	1	1
Private nonguaranteed	**1**	**30**	**10**	**8**	**7**	**6**	**5**	**4**	**4**	**11**
Bonds	0	0	0	0	0	0	0	0	0	0
Commercial banks	1	30	10	8	7	6	5	4	4	11
Memo:										
IBRD	1	11	4	53	16	16	14	14	14	12
IDA	0	0	0	0	0	0	0	0	0	0
NET TRANSFERS ON DEBT	**14**	**36**	**-13**	**-266**	**-124**	**52**	**-82**	**-155**	**53**	**-60**
Public and publicly guaranteed	**11**	**96**	**-8**	**-272**	**-159**	**80**	**-58**	**-130**	**75**	**-35**
Official creditors	4	86	26	-230	-109	34	-61	-56	-3	31
Multilateral	5	48	7	-156	-111	12	-55	9	10	68
Concessional	4	31	10	-13	-9	20	-3	0	-3	-4
Bilateral	0	38	19	-74	3	23	-6	-65	-13	-38
Concessional	0	19	49	7	-14	25	7	-51	6	-11
Private creditors	6	10	-34	-42	-50	45	3	-75	79	-65
Bonds	-10	0	-28	-34	-29	62	22	-54	93	-58
Commercial banks	17	11	-15	-7	-18	-11	-13	-16	-9	-3
Other private	-1	-2	9	-1	-4	-6	-6	-5	-5	-5
Private nonguaranteed	**3**	**-60**	**-6**	**7**	**35**	**-28**	**-24**	**-25**	**-22**	**-25**
Bonds	0	0	0	0	0	0	0	0	0	0
Commercial banks	3	-60	-6	7	35	-28	-24	-25	-22	-25
Memo:										
IBRD	1	24	8	-111	-55	-31	-40	42	-10	2
IDA	0	0	0	0	0	0	0	0	0	0
DEBT SERVICE (LTDS)	**29**	**137**	**179**	**493**	**256**	**284**	**318**	**314**	**307**	**328**
Public and publicly guaranteed	**26**	**45**	**166**	**469**	**229**	**256**	**294**	**289**	**285**	**303**
Official creditors	7	42	101	392	172	201	224	213	214	236
Multilateral	4	32	61	251	141	139	142	133	127	133
Concessional	0	4	10	26	20	22	22	24	21	23
Bilateral	3	10	40	141	31	61	82	80	88	103
Concessional	3	4	6	21	23	35	49	57	50	74
Private creditors	19	3	64	78	57	55	69	75	71	66
Bonds	10	0	28	36	29	27	38	54	57	58
Commercial banks	8	2	29	39	25	19	14	16	9	3
Other private	1	2	7	3	4	9	17	6	5	6
Private nonguaranteed	**3**	**92**	**13**	**24**	**27**	**28**	**24**	**25**	**22**	**25**
Bonds	0	0	0	0	0	0	0	0	0	0
Commercial banks	3	92	13	24	27	28	24	25	22	25
Memo:										
IBRD	3	15	9	160	56	60	53	27	26	26
IDA	0	0	0	0	0	0	0	0	0	0
UNDISBURSED DEBT	**70**	**507**	**802**	**828**	**808**	**649**	**496**	**713**	**672**	**646**
Official creditors	59	397	741	644	630	570	488	707	671	645
Private creditors	10	110	61	185	178	79	7	6	2	1
Memorandum items										
Concessional LDOD	34	249	694	820	1,167	1,256	1,301	1,272	1,286	1,324
Variable rate LDOD	25	296	409	449	514	662	715	722	702	875
Public sector LDOD	106	563	2,475	2,374	2,494	2,739	2,824	2,755	2,872	2,990
Private sector LDOD	15	282	130	144	183	161	142	121	103	182

6. CURRENCY COMPOSITION OF LONG-TERM DEBT (PERCENT)

	1970	1980	1990	1992	1993	1994	1995	1996	1997	1998
Deutsche mark	0.0	0.0	1.6	2.1	2.2	2.4	3.0	3.1	3.0	3.4
French franc	0.0	0.0	0.7	0.8	2.0	1.9	2.0	1.9	1.7	1.7
Japanese yen	0.0	0.0	0.0	2.0	2.1	2.2	2.0	1.8	2.4	2.5
Pound sterling	0.0	0.0	0.0	0.0	0.0	0.0	0.0	0.0	0.0	0.0
Swiss franc	0.0	0.0	0.0	0.1	0.1	0.1	0.4	0.4	0.3	0.3
U.S.dollars	76.2	19.3	56.1	58.8	61.4	61.1	62.0	62.0	65.6	72.9
Multiple currency	23.8	80.6	41.1	35.6	31.8	32.0	30.2	30.6	26.9	19.1
Special drawing rights	0.0	0.0	0.0	0.1	0.1	0.2	0.1	0.1	0.1	0.1
All other currencies	0.0	0.1	0.5	0.5	0.3	0.1	0.3	0.1	0.0	0.0

GUATEMALA

(US$ million, unless otherwise indicated)

	1970	1980	1990	1992	1993	1994	1995	1996	1997	1998
7. DEBT RESTRUCTURINGS										
Total amount rescheduled	..	..	30	0	366	0	0	0	0	0
Debt stock rescheduled	..	..	8	0	0	0	0	0	0	0
Principal rescheduled	..	..	13	0	190	0	0	0	0	0
Official	..	..	13	0	30	0	0	0	0	0
Private	..	..	0	0	161	0	0	0	0	0
Interest rescheduled	..	..	7	0	176	0	0	0	0	0
Official	..	..	7	0	10	0	0	0	0	0
Private	..	..	0	0	166	0	0	0	0	0
Debt forgiven	..	..	0	0	0	0	0	0	0	0
Memo: interest forgiven	..	..	0	0	0	0	0	0	0	0
Debt stock reduction	..	..	0	0	0	0	0	0	0	0
of which debt buyback	..	..	0	0	0	0	0	0	0	0
8. DEBT STOCK-FLOW RECONCILIATION										
Total change in debt stocks	..	..	430	-41	139	240	224	121	349	441
Net flows on debt	52	130	67	-68	106	153	191	167	416	314
Net change in interest arrears	..	..	81	16	-154	19	5	7	-5	3
Interest capitalized	..	..	7	0	176	0	0	0	0	0
Debt forgiveness or reduction	..	..	0	0	0	0	0	0	0	0
Cross-currency valuation	..	..	29	-46	-9	21	5	-35	-44	22
Residual	..	..	247	56	20	48	23	-18	-18	103
9. AVERAGE TERMS OF NEW COMMITMENTS										
ALL CREDITORS										
Interest (%)	5.5	7.9	5.9	7.4	5.0	5.6	4.2	6.3	7.2	6.6
Maturity (years)	25.8	15.5	17.8	17.0	22.6	21.0	30.9	23.3	15.6	21.4
Grace period (years)	6.3	3.9	4.7	5.3	6.0	6.1	8.1	3.5	6.7	4.6
Grant element (%)	36.0	10.9	27.2	15.8	34.6	29.7	47.5	23.6	17.2	21.9
Official creditors										
Interest (%)	2.9	7.3	4.9	6.2	5.1	5.6	4.2	6.3	6.5	6.6
Maturity (years)	39.4	17.7	22.6	21.3	24.2	21.0	30.9	23.3	18.6	21.4
Grace period (years)	10.6	3.5	6.2	5.7	6.4	6.1	8.1	3.5	5.0	4.6
Grant element (%)	61.0	14.3	36.1	25.8	36.5	29.7	47.5	23.6	21.3	21.9
Private creditors										
Interest (%)	8.5	8.5	8.8	8.7	3.7	0.0	0.0	0.0	8.5	0.0
Maturity (years)	9.7	13.2	4.0	12.3	3.3	0.0	0.0	0.0	10.0	0.0
Grace period (years)	1.2	4.2	0.5	4.8	0.3	0.0	0.0	0.0	10.0	0.0
Grant element (%)	6.6	7.5	1.7	4.5	11.4	0.0	0.0	0.0	9.2	0.0
Memorandum items										
Commitments	50	247	146	358	135	244	97	384	441	247
Official creditors	27	124	108	190	125	244	97	384	291	247
Private creditors	23	123	38	168	10	0	0	0	150	0

10. CONTRACTUAL OBLIGATIONS ON OUTSTANDING LONG-TERM DEBT

	1999	2000	2001	2002	2003	2004	2005	2006	2007	2008
TOTAL										
Disbursements	210	166	115	62	34	20	13	10	6	4
Principal	239	202	206	202	242	209	204	195	340	158
Interest	144	139	134	125	115	104	95	85	76	55
Official creditors										
Disbursements	210	166	115	62	34	20	13	10	6	4
Principal	181	147	155	152	191	189	184	175	170	158
Interest	109	109	107	103	96	88	80	71	63	55
Bilateral creditors										
Disbursements	39	21	11	6	2	2	1	1	0	0
Principal	59	58	61	57	85	84	83	80	76	67
Interest	33	32	29	27	25	22	19	16	14	11
Multilateral creditors										
Disbursements	170	145	104	55	33	19	12	10	6	4
Principal	122	90	94	94	106	105	101	95	93	91
Interest	76	78	78	75	71	66	61	55	50	44
Private creditors										
Disbursements	1	0	0	0	0	0	0	0	0	0
Principal	57	55	51	51	51	20	20	20	170	0
Interest	34	30	27	23	19	16	15	14	13	0
Commercial banks										
Disbursements	0	0	0	0	0	0	0	0	0	0
Principal	3	0	0	0	0	0	0	0	0	0
Interest	0	0	0	0	0	0	0	0	0	0
Other private										
Disbursements	1	0	0	0	0	0	0	0	0	0
Principal	55	55	51	51	51	20	20	20	170	0
Interest	34	30	27	23	19	16	15	14	13	0

GUINEA

(US$ million, unless otherwise indicated)

	1970	1980	1990	1992	1993	1994	1995	1996	1997	1998
1. SUMMARY DEBT DATA										
TOTAL DEBT STOCKS (EDT)	..	1,134	2,476	2,634	2,848	3,110	3,242	3,240	3,519	3,546
Long-term debt (LDOD)	320	1,019	2,253	2,450	2,659	2,886	2,987	2,981	3,009	3,126
Public and publicly guaranteed	320	1,019	2,253	2,450	2,659	2,886	2,987	2,981	3,009	3,126
Private nonguaranteed	0	0	0	0	0	0	0	0	0	0
Use of IMF credit	3	35	52	64	60	71	94	82	99	127
Short-term debt	..	80	172	120	128	152	161	177	411	293
of which interest arrears on LDOD	..	29	55	46	68	100	82	103	98	99
Official creditors	..	23	49	40	58	90	71	91	88	96
Private creditors	..	5	6	5	9	10	11	11	10	4
Memo: principal arrears on LDOD	..	105	190	208	342	460	371	434	471	467
Official creditors	..	89	164	180	290	401	314	368	407	452
Private creditors	..	15	26	28	52	59	58	66	64	15
Memo: export credits	..	0	352	253	157	176	190	182	145	148
TOTAL DEBT FLOWS										
Disbursements	98	129	196	210	286	182	200	143	265	180
Long-term debt	94	121	196	198	286	169	169	143	232	148
IMF purchases	4	8	0	12	0	12	31	0	33	32
Principal repayments	11	76	110	50	44	54	129	67	100	104
Long-term debt	11	75	96	49	41	48	121	58	90	94
IMF repurchases	0	1	14	1	3	6	9	8	10	9
Net flows on debt	87	23	86	143	228	120	98	72	403	-43
of which short-term debt	..	-31	0	-17	-14	-9	27	-4	238	-120
Interest payments (INT)	..	33	59	37	40	43	49	47	55	55
Long-term debt	4	23	53	33	37	40	44	43	45	43
IMF charges	0	1	2	0	0	0	0	0	1	1
Short-term debt	..	9	4	4	3	3	5	3	10	12
Net transfers on debt	..	-11	27	106	188	76	49	25	348	-99
Total debt service paid (TDS)	..	109	169	87	84	97	178	114	155	159
Long-term debt	15	98	149	82	78	88	164	101	134	138
IMF repurchases and charges	0	2	16	1	4	6	9	9	11	10
Short-term debt (interest only)	..	9	4	4	3	3	5	3	10	12
2. AGGREGATE NET RESOURCE FLOWS AND NET TRANSFERS (LONG-TERM)										
NET RESOURCE FLOWS	85	106	212	390	414	285	285	258	268	227
Net flow of long-term debt (ex. IMF)	83	47	100	149	245	122	49	85	143	54
Foreign direct investment (net)	0	34	18	20	3	1	1	24	1	1
Portfolio equity flows	0	0	0	0	0	0	0	0	0	0
Grants (excluding technical coop.)	2	25	94	222	166	162	235	150	125	172
Memo: technical coop. grants	4	19	63	76	82	65	72	68	49	49
official net resource flows	79	26	212	378	408	293	299	217	288	237
private net resource flows	6	80	-1	12	6	-9	-14	41	-19	-9
NET TRANSFERS	80	43	98	298	351	204	231	200	208	171
Interest on long-term debt	4	23	53	33	37	40	44	43	45	43
Profit remittances on FDI	0	40	61	60	26	40	10	15	16	13
Memo: official net transfers	76	5	165	346	372	254	256	174	246	194
private net transfers	5	38	-68	-48	-21	-50	-25	25	-38	-22
3. MAJOR ECONOMIC AGGREGATES										
Gross national product (GNP)	..	..	2,600	3,139	3,159	3,321	3,502	3,867	3,808	3,476
Exports of goods & services (XGS)	..	..	841	685	757	676	714	775	749	817
of which workers remittances	..	..	..	..	..	0	1	1	1	4
Imports of goods & services (MGS)	..	..	1,115	1,080	1,010	1,131	1,109	1,053	955	1,052
International reserves (RES)	..	..	..	87	132	88	87	87	122	..
Current account balance	..	..	-203	-263	-57	-248	-216	-177	-91	-119
4. DEBT INDICATORS										
EDT / XGS (%)	..	..	294.4	384.6	376.2	460.3	454.3	418.4	469.6	434.0
EDT / GNP (%)	..	..	95.2	83.9	90.2	93.6	92.6	83.8	92.4	102.0
TDS / XGS (%)	..	..	20.0	12.7	11.1	14.3	25.0	14.7	20.7	19.5
INT / XGS (%)	..	..	7.0	5.3	5.3	6.4	6.8	6.1	7.3	6.8
INT / GNP (%)	..	..	2.3	1.2	1.3	1.3	1.4	1.2	1.4	1.6
RES / EDT (%)	..	..	..	3.3	4.6	2.8	2.7	2.7	3.5	..
RES / MGS (months)	..	..	..	1.0	1.6	0.9	0.9	1.0	1.5	..
Short-term / EDT (%)	..	7.0	7.0	4.6	4.5	4.9	5.0	5.5	11.7	8.3
Concessional / EDT (%)	..	59.8	67.7	75.1	75.7	74.9	75.8	74.9	70.5	74.7
Multilateral / EDT (%)	..	11.5	27.4	34.7	39.3	41.9	45.1	45.9	44.2	47.6

GUINEA

(US$ million, unless otherwise indicated)

	1970	1980	1990	1992	1993	1994	1995	1996	1997	1998
5. LONG-TERM DEBT										
DEBT OUTSTANDING (LDOD)	**320**	**1,019**	**2,253**	**2,450**	**2,659**	**2,886**	**2,987**	**2,981**	**3,009**	**3,126**
Public and publicly guaranteed	**320**	**1,019**	**2,253**	**2,450**	**2,659**	**2,886**	**2,987**	**2,981**	**3,009**	**3,126**
Official creditors	279	860	2,145	2,359	2,555	2,789	2,905	2,883	2,933	3,097
Multilateral	20	130	678	913	1,118	1,304	1,460	1,486	1,555	1,689
Concessional	0	63	602	799	967	1,103	1,216	1,221	1,299	1,449
Bilateral	259	731	1,467	1,446	1,437	1,485	1,444	1,397	1,378	1,408
Concessional	246	615	1,073	1,179	1,191	1,225	1,241	1,205	1,181	1,200
Private creditors	40	159	108	91	104	98	82	98	76	30
Bonds	0	0	0	0	0	0	0	0	0	0
Commercial banks	0	9	24	24	23	24	25	24	12	0
Other private	40	150	84	68	81	74	57	74	63	30
Private nonguaranteed	**0**	**0**	**0**	**0**	**0**	**0**	**0**	**0**	**0**	**0**
Bonds	0	0	0	0	0	0	0	0	0	0
Commercial banks	0	0	0	0	0	0	0	0	0	0
Memo:										
IBRD	20	55	28	0	0	0	0	0	0	0
IDA	0	32	392	548	681	773	847	863	922	1,016
DISBURSEMENTS	**94**	**121**	**196**	**198**	**286**	**169**	**169**	**143**	**232**	**148**
Public and publicly guaranteed	**94**	**121**	**196**	**198**	**286**	**169**	**169**	**143**	**232**	**148**
Official creditors	83	64	196	198	275	169	169	126	212	142
Multilateral	15	34	90	160	237	139	161	111	194	135
Concessional	0	31	85	118	190	95	115	69	160	115
Bilateral	68	30	106	38	38	30	8	15	18	7
Concessional	57	24	105	38	38	30	8	14	13	3
Private creditors	10	57	0	0	11	0	0	17	20	7
Bonds	0	0	0	0	0	0	0	0	0	0
Commercial banks	0	4	0	0	0	0	0	0	0	0
Other private	10	53	0	0	11	0	0	17	20	7
Private nonguaranteed	**0**	**0**	**0**	**0**	**0**	**0**	**0**	**0**	**0**	**0**
Bonds	0	0	0	0	0	0	0	0	0	0
Commercial banks	0	0	0	0	0	0	0	0	0	0
Memo:										
IBRD	15	0	0	0	0	0	0	0	0	0
IDA	0	10	52	88	134	63	59	47	109	66
PRINCIPAL REPAYMENTS	**11**	**75**	**96**	**49**	**41**	**48**	**121**	**58**	**90**	**94**
Public and publicly guaranteed	**11**	**75**	**96**	**49**	**41**	**48**	**121**	**58**	**90**	**94**
Official creditors	6	63	77	41	33	38	106	58	49	77
Multilateral	0	14	21	29	14	15	35	35	33	61
Concessional	0	0	6	7	8	8	26	26	15	15
Bilateral	6	50	56	13	19	23	71	23	16	16
Concessional	6	44	48	11	8	18	60	18	14	16
Private creditors	5	11	19	8	8	9	15	0	40	17
Bonds	0	0	0	0	0	0	0	0	0	0
Commercial banks	0	0	7	0	0	0	0	0	11	17
Other private	5	11	11	8	8	9	15	0	30	0
Private nonguaranteed	**0**	**0**	**0**	**0**	**0**	**0**	**0**	**0**	**0**	**0**
Bonds	0	0	0	0	0	0	0	0	0	0
Commercial banks	0	0	0	0	0	0	0	0	0	0
Memo:										
IBRD	0	3	12	15	0	0	0	0	0	0
IDA	0	0	1	1	1	2	2	4	4	5
NET FLOWS ON DEBT	**83**	**47**	**100**	**149**	**245**	**122**	**49**	**85**	**143**	**54**
Public and publicly guaranteed	**83**	**47**	**100**	**149**	**245**	**122**	**49**	**85**	**143**	**54**
Official creditors	77	1	119	157	242	131	64	68	163	64
Multilateral	15	20	68	131	223	124	126	76	160	74
Concessional	0	31	80	111	182	87	89	44	145	100
Bilateral	62	-19	51	26	19	7	-63	-8	3	-10
Concessional	51	-19	57	26	30	12	-52	-4	-1	-12
Private creditors	6	46	-19	-8	3	-9	-15	17	-20	-10
Bonds	0	0	0	0	0	0	0	0	0	0
Commercial banks	0	4	-7	0	0	0	0	0	-11	-17
Other private	6	43	-11	-8	3	-9	-15	17	-10	7
Private nonguaranteed	**0**	**0**	**0**	**0**	**0**	**0**	**0**	**0**	**0**	**0**
Bonds	0	0	0	0	0	0	0	0	0	0
Commercial banks	0	0	0	0	0	0	0	0	0	0
Memo:										
IBRD	15	-3	-12	-15	0	0	0	0	0	0
IDA	0	10	51	87	132	61	57	43	105	61

GUINEA

(US$ million, unless otherwise indicated)

	1970	1980	1990	1992	1993	1994	1995	1996	1997	1998
INTEREST PAYMENTS (LINT)	**4**	**23**	**53**	**33**	**37**	**40**	**44**	**43**	**45**	**43**
Public and publicly guaranteed	**4**	**23**	**53**	**33**	**37**	**40**	**44**	**43**	**45**	**43**
Official creditors	3	21	47	33	36	39	43	43	42	43
Multilateral	1	8	12	17	15	16	15	24	24	25
Concessional	0	0	5	9	9	10	9	11	11	11
Bilateral	2	13	35	16	22	23	28	19	17	18
Concessional	2	12	23	11	15	17	20	11	12	13
Private creditors	1	2	6	0	1	2	1	0	3	0
Bonds	0	0	0	0	0	0	0	0	0	0
Commercial banks	0	0	6	0	0	0	0	0	2	0
Other private	1	2	1	0	1	2	1	0	1	0
Private nonguaranteed	**0**	**0**	**0**	**0**	**0**	**0**	**0**	**0**	**0**	**0**
Bonds	0	0	0	0	0	0	0	0	0	0
Commercial banks	0	0	0	0	0	0	0	0	0	0
Memo:										
IBRD	1	6	2	1	0	0	0	0	0	0
IDA	0	0	2	4	4	6	6	7	6	6
NET TRANSFERS ON DEBT	**79**	**24**	**47**	**116**	**208**	**81**	**5**	**41**	**98**	**11**
Public and publicly guaranteed	**79**	**24**	**47**	**116**	**208**	**81**	**5**	**41**	**98**	**11**
Official creditors	74	-20	72	124	206	92	21	25	121	21
Multilateral	14	12	57	115	209	108	111	52	136	49
Concessional	0	31	74	102	173	78	80	33	134	89
Bilateral	60	-32	15	10	-3	-16	-91	-27	-15	-28
Concessional	49	-31	34	16	15	-6	-72	-15	-13	-25
Private creditors	5	44	-25	-8	2	-11	-16	16	-23	-10
Bonds	0	0	0	0	0	0	0	0	0	0
Commercial banks	0	3	-13	0	0	0	0	0	-13	-17
Other private	5	40	-12	-8	2	-11	-16	16	-11	7
Private nonguaranteed	**0**	**0**	**0**	**0**	**0**	**0**	**0**	**0**	**0**	**0**
Bonds	0	0	0	0	0	0	0	0	0	0
Commercial banks	0	0	0	0	0	0	0	0	0	0
Memo:										
IBRD	14	-9	-14	-15	0	0	0	0	0	0
IDA	0	10	49	83	128	55	51	36	99	55
DEBT SERVICE (LTDS)	**15**	**98**	**149**	**82**	**78**	**88**	**164**	**101**	**134**	**138**
Public and publicly guaranteed	**15**	**98**	**149**	**82**	**78**	**88**	**164**	**101**	**134**	**138**
Official creditors	9	84	124	74	69	77	149	101	91	120
Multilateral	1	22	33	45	28	31	50	59	58	86
Concessional	0	0	11	16	17	18	35	36	26	26
Bilateral	8	63	91	29	41	46	99	42	33	35
Concessional	8	55	71	22	22	35	80	29	26	29
Private creditors	6	14	25	8	9	11	16	0	44	17
Bonds	0	0	0	0	0	0	0	0	0	0
Commercial banks	0	1	13	0	0	0	0	0	13	17
Other private	6	13	12	8	9	11	16	0	31	0
Private nonguaranteed	**0**	**0**	**0**	**0**	**0**	**0**	**0**	**0**	**0**	**0**
Bonds	0	0	0	0	0	0	0	0	0	0
Commercial banks	0	0	0	0	0	0	0	0	0	0
Memo:										
IBRD	1	9	14	15	0	0	0	0	0	0
IDA	0	0	3	5	6	8	8	11	10	11
UNDISBURSED DEBT	**196**	**527**	**1,184**	**1,000**	**753**	**621**	**680**	**632**	**474**	**356**
Official creditors	173	412	1,184	1,000	753	621	637	605	468	356
Private creditors	24	115	0	0	0	0	44	27	7	0
Memorandum items										
Concessional LDOD	246	678	1,675	1,977	2,157	2,329	2,457	2,425	2,479	2,649
Variable rate LDOD	0	3	173	98	93	100	34	30	18	5
Public sector LDOD	320	1,019	2,253	2,450	2,659	2,886	2,987	2,981	3,009	3,126
Private sector LDOD	0	0	0	0	0	0	0	0	0	0

6. CURRENCY COMPOSITION OF LONG-TERM DEBT (PERCENT)

	1970	1980	1990	1992	1993	1994	1995	1996	1997	1998
Deutsche mark	7.1	5.1	1.3	1.0	0.8	0.8	0.8	0.7	0.6	0.6
French franc	5.1	11.3	14.9	13.8	11.9	11.8	9.6	8.9	8.3	8.1
Japanese yen	0.0	0.1	2.2	2.3	2.9	3.8	3.5	3.2	2.6	2.7
Pound sterling	4.0	4.1	1.8	1.2	1.0	1.0	0.9	0.9	0.9	0.8
Swiss franc	0.0	0.8	0.6	0.5	0.4	0.5	0.3	0.3	0.3	0.3
U.S.dollars	16.0	28.2	33.1	39.7	42.7	43.5	48.5	49.3	51.5	53.2
Multiple currency	6.4	5.5	7.6	7.3	7.5	7.9	8.0	7.9	7.4	7.6
Special drawing rights	0.0	0.0	0.6	0.9	1.0	1.0	1.1	1.1	1.2	1.5
All other currencies	61.4	44.9	37.9	33.3	31.8	29.7	27.3	27.7	27.2	25.2

GUINEA

(US$ million, unless otherwise indicated)

	1970	1980	1990	1992	1993	1994	1995	1996	1997	1998
7. DEBT RESTRUCTURINGS										
Total amount rescheduled	..	..	110	156	0	0	131	0	81	22
Debt stock rescheduled	..	..	0	0	0	0	0	0	0	0
Principal rescheduled	..	..	71	110	0	0	94	0	24	15
Official	..	..	71	107	0	0	93	0	24	15
Private	..	..	0	3	0	0	2	0	0	0
Interest rescheduled	..	..	0	45	0	0	16	0	11	7
Official	..	..	0	45	0	0	15	0	11	7
Private	..	..	0	0	0	0	0	0	0	0
Debt forgiven	..	..	2	48	1	1	53	0	7	5
Memo: interest forgiven	..	..	0	13	0	0	8	0	3	2
Debt stock reduction	..	..	0	0	0	0	0	0	0	130
of which debt buyback	..	..	0	0	0	0	0	0	0	17
8. DEBT STOCK-FLOW RECONCILIATION										
Total change in debt stocks	..	..	302	11	214	262	132	-2	279	27
Net flows on debt	87	23	86	143	228	120	98	72	403	-43
Net change in interest arrears	..	..	26	-31	22	33	-18	21	-4	1
Interest capitalized	..	..	0	45	0	0	16	0	11	7
Debt forgiveness or reduction	..	..	-2	-48	-1	-1	-53	0	-7	-118
Cross-currency valuation	..	..	106	-60	-26	66	39	-39	-71	47
Residual	..	..	86	-38	-9	45	52	-55	-53	133
9. AVERAGE TERMS OF NEW COMMITMENTS										
ALL CREDITORS										
Interest (%)	2.9	4.6	2.6	3.0	2.9	1.3	2.1	2.5	0.6	1.4
Maturity (years)	12.9	19.3	30.5	31.2	30.9	32.7	21.3	28.5	43.0	37.2
Grace period (years)	5.2	5.6	8.2	8.1	7.8	8.7	6.8	8.3	10.4	9.0
Grant element (%)	40.1	36.2	59.5	55.1	57.1	70.2	50.6	60.4	83.1	69.7
Official creditors										
Interest (%)	0.9	3.4	2.6	3.0	2.0	1.3	2.0	2.5	0.6	1.4
Maturity (years)	15.0	22.8	30.5	31.2	35.6	32.7	25.9	28.5	43.0	37.2
Grace period (years)	7.0	6.6	8.2	8.1	9.0	8.7	8.5	8.3	10.4	9.0
Grant element (%)	55.5	46.5	59.5	55.1	66.2	70.2	60.8	60.4	83.1	69.7
Private creditors										
Interest (%)	6.2	7.9	0.0	0.0	8.0	0.0	2.7	0.0	0.0	0.0
Maturity (years)	9.5	9.8	0.0	0.0	3.2	0.0	3.5	0.0	0.0	0.0
Grace period (years)	2.5	3.0	0.0	0.0	0.2	0.0	0.1	0.0	0.0	0.0
Grant element (%)	15.6	8.0	0.0	0.0	3.5	0.0	10.8	0.0	0.0	0.0
Memorandum items										
Commitments	68	269	487	197	76	75	215	131	135	24
Official creditors	42	197	487	197	65	75	171	131	135	24
Private creditors	26	72	0	0	11	0	44	0	0	0

10. CONTRACTUAL OBLIGATIONS ON OUTSTANDING LONG-TERM DEBT

	1999	2000	2001	2002	2003	2004	2005	2006	2007	2008
TOTAL										
Disbursements	140	96	60	32	15	6	3	2	1	0
Principal	120	132	126	125	122	122	107	106	102	102
Interest	53	61	57	53	49	46	42	39	36	34
Official creditors										
Disbursements	140	96	60	32	15	6	3	2	1	0
Principal	111	127	126	125	122	122	107	106	102	102
Interest	52	61	57	53	49	46	42	39	36	34
Bilateral creditors										
Disbursements	23	15	9	4	2	1	0	0	0	0
Principal	61	70	67	64	60	59	44	43	41	40
Interest	25	34	31	29	27	25	23	22	20	19
Multilateral creditors										
Disbursements	117	81	51	28	13	5	3	2	1	0
Principal	50	58	58	61	62	62	63	63	61	63
Interest	27	27	26	24	23	21	19	18	16	15
Private creditors										
Disbursements	0	0	0	0	0	0	0	0	0	0
Principal	9	5	0	0	0	0	0	0	0	0
Interest	1	0	0	0	0	0	0	0	0	0
Commercial banks										
Disbursements	0	0	0	0	0	0	0	0	0	0
Principal	0	0	0	0	0	0	0	0	0	0
Interest	0	0	0	0	0	0	0	0	0	0
Other private										
Disbursements	0	0	0	0	0	0	0	0	0	0
Principal	9	5	0	0	0	0	0	0	0	0
Interest	1	0	0	0	0	0	0	0	0	0

GUINEA-BISSAU

(US$ million, unless otherwise indicated)

	1970	1980	1990	1992	1993	1994	1995	1996	1997	1998
1. SUMMARY DEBT DATA										
TOTAL DEBT STOCKS (EDT)	..	**139.6**	**692.1**	**761.4**	**786.9**	**852.2**	**896.9**	**936.8**	**921.3**	**964.4**
Long-term debt (LDOD)	**0.0**	**133.1**	**630.4**	**692.3**	**712.5**	**761.4**	**796.6**	**856.2**	**838.4**	**873.1**
Public and publicly guaranteed	0.0	133.1	630.4	692.3	712.5	761.4	796.6	856.2	838.4	873.1
Private nonguaranteed	0.0	0.0	0.0	0.0	0.0	0.0	0.0	0.0	0.0	0.0
Use of IMF credit	**0.0**	**1.4**	**5.3**	**5.2**	**4.7**	**4.6**	**5.9**	**7.7**	**12.2**	**15.4**
Short-term debt	..	**5.1**	**56.4**	**63.9**	**69.7**	**86.2**	**94.4**	**73.0**	**70.7**	**75.9**
of which interest arrears on LDOD	..	1.1	29.9	56.1	65.0	79.2	88.4	61.5	62.7	71.8
Official creditors	..	1.1	27.5	50.7	60.5	73.9	82.4	61.4	62.7	71.8
Private creditors	..	0.0	2.4	5.4	4.5	5.2	6.1	0.0	0.0	0.1
Memo: principal arrears on LDOD	..	4.5	112.8	167.9	195.6	230.1	251.5	157.7	161.6	175.7
Official creditors	..	2.7	107.0	151.6	176.6	202.9	220.6	157.4	161.3	175.3
Private creditors	..	1.8	5.9	16.3	19.0	27.1	30.9	0.3	0.3	0.4
Memo: export credits	..	0.0	98.0	137.0	88.0	80.0	104.0	95.0	153.0	174.0
TOTAL DEBT FLOWS										
Disbursements	**0.0**	**74.7**	**36.5**	**40.8**	**23.2**	**28.4**	**23.5**	**31.3**	**36.5**	**17.7**
Long-term debt	0.0	74.7	36.5	40.8	23.2	28.4	21.1	28.3	30.3	14.5
IMF purchases	0.0	0.0	0.0	0.0	0.0	0.0	2.4	3.0	6.1	3.2
Principal repayments	**0.0**	**3.0**	**2.3**	**3.4**	**1.4**	**3.5**	**9.3**	**6.7**	**6.1**	**3.0**
Long-term debt	0.0	3.0	2.3	3.4	0.9	3.1	8.1	5.6	5.0	2.4
IMF repurchases	0.0	0.0	0.0	0.0	0.4	0.4	1.1	1.1	1.0	0.6
Net flows on debt	**0.0**	**72.7**	**45.7**	**23.2**	**18.8**	**27.2**	**13.3**	**30.1**	**26.9**	**10.7**
of which short-term debt	..	1.0	11.5	-14.2	-3.1	2.3	-1.0	5.5	-3.5	-3.9
Interest payments (INT)	..	**1.6**	**6.1**	**3.3**	**2.2**	**3.9**	**6.1**	**4.5**	**3.6**	**4.8**
Long-term debt	0.0	1.1	3.4	2.9	2.0	3.6	5.7	4.0	3.0	4.4
IMF charges	0.0	0.1	0.0	0.0	0.0	0.0	0.0	0.0	0.1	0.1
Short-term debt	..	0.5	2.7	0.4	0.2	0.3	0.4	0.5	0.5	0.3
Net transfers on debt	..	**71.0**	**39.6**	**19.9**	**16.5**	**23.3**	**7.2**	**25.6**	**23.3**	**5.9**
Total debt service paid (TDS)	..	**4.6**	**8.4**	**6.6**	**3.6**	**7.4**	**15.4**	**11.2**	**9.7**	**7.9**
Long-term debt	0.0	4.1	5.7	6.2	2.9	6.7	13.8	9.6	8.1	6.8
IMF repurchases and charges	0.0	0.1	0.0	0.0	0.4	0.4	1.2	1.1	1.1	0.7
Short-term debt (interest only)	..	0.5	2.7	0.4	0.2	0.3	0.4	0.5	0.5	0.3
2. AGGREGATE NET RESOURCE FLOWS AND NET TRANSFERS (LONG-TERM)										
NET RESOURCE FLOWS	**0.0**	**108.4**	**96.3**	**65.0**	**53.9**	**75.7**	**65.1**	**77.7**	**79.5**	**60.8**
Net flow of long-term debt (ex. IMF)	0.0	71.7	34.2	37.4	22.3	25.3	13.0	22.7	25.3	12.0
Foreign direct investment (net)	0.0	0.0	2.0	0.0	0.0	1.0	1.0	1.0	2.0	0.5
Portfolio equity flows	0.0	0.0	0.0	0.0	0.0	0.0	0.0	0.0	0.0	0.0
Grants (excluding technical coop.)	0.0	36.7	60.2	27.5	31.6	49.4	51.1	54.0	52.2	48.3
Memo: technical coop. grants	0.1	12.1	22.6	47.6	44.8	39.6	46.5	37.7	40.3	31.6
official net resource flows	0.0	90.6	94.4	65.0	53.9	74.8	64.3	76.8	77.5	60.3
private net resource flows	0.0	17.8	1.9	0.0	0.0	0.9	0.8	0.9	2.0	0.5
NET TRANSFERS	**0.0**	**107.3**	**92.9**	**62.2**	**51.9**	**72.1**	**59.5**	**73.7**	**76.5**	**56.4**
Interest on long-term debt	0.0	1.1	3.4	2.9	2.0	3.6	5.7	4.0	3.0	4.4
Profit remittances on FDI	0.0	0.0	0.0	0.0	0.0	0.0	0.0	0.0	0.0	0.0
Memo: official net transfers	0.0	90.3	91.3	62.2	51.9	71.2	58.7	72.9	74.5	55.9
private net transfers	0.0	17.0	1.6	0.0	0.0	0.9	0.8	0.8	2.0	0.5
3. MAJOR ECONOMIC AGGREGATES										
Gross national product (GNP)	78.7	104.8	233.3	212.8	221.6	221.5	236.0	251.9	254.3	191.5
Exports of goods & services (XGS)	..	..	27.1	18.0	25.7	38.8	29.6	30.6	58.9	30.8
of which workers remittances	..	..	1.0	0.0	0.0	..	..	2.0	2.0	..
Imports of goods & services (MGS)	..	..	110.5	138.9	103.9	107.2	110.3	104.7	102.9	73.4
International reserves (RES)	..	..	18.2	17.8	14.2	18.4	20.3	11.5	..	..
Current account balance	..	..	-45.3	-97.0	-62.0	-45.9	-35.2	-44.5	-6.4	..
4. DEBT INDICATORS										
EDT / XGS (%)	..	..	2,553.9	4,223.0	3,059.5	2,195.3	3,031.1	3,064.4	1,565.2	3,128.4
EDT / GNP (%)	..	133.3	296.6	357.8	355.1	384.7	380.1	371.9	362.3	503.7
TDS / XGS (%)	..	..	31.0	36.6	14.0	19.1	52.0	36.6	16.5	25.6
INT / XGS (%)	..	..	22.5	18.3	8.6	10.1	20.6	14.7	6.1	15.6
INT / GNP (%)	..	1.5	2.6	1.6	1.0	1.8	2.6	1.8	1.4	2.5
RES / EDT (%)	..	..	2.6	2.3	1.8	2.2	2.3	1.2	..	..
RES / MGS (months)	..	..	2.0	1.5	1.6	2.1	2.2	1.3	..	..
Short-term / EDT (%)	..	3.7	8.2	8.4	8.9	10.1	10.5	7.8	7.7	7.9
Concessional / EDT (%)	..	62.0	56.7	57.6	60.4	62.6	62.9	72.1	72.2	72.2
Multilateral / EDT (%)	..	24.5	39.5	40.8	41.5	41.2	41.2	40.9	42.0	42.4

GUINEA-BISSAU

(US$ million, unless otherwise indicated)

	1970	1980	1990	1992	1993	1994	1995	1996	1997	1998
5. LONG-TERM DEBT										
DEBT OUTSTANDING (LDOD)	**0.0**	**133.1**	**630.4**	**692.3**	**712.5**	**761.4**	**796.6**	**856.2**	**838.4**	**873.1**
Public and publicly guaranteed	**0.0**	**133.1**	**630.4**	**692.3**	**712.5**	**761.4**	**796.6**	**856.2**	**838.4**	**873.1**
Official creditors	0.0	96.9	597.4	662.5	687.6	733.5	765.1	855.4	837.6	872.3
Multilateral	0.0	34.2	273.3	310.8	326.2	351.2	369.6	382.7	386.9	408.9
Concessional	0.0	29.0	244.3	278.6	294.6	318.8	340.0	365.7	371.9	393.9
Bilateral	0.0	62.7	324.1	351.7	361.4	382.3	395.6	472.7	450.6	463.4
Concessional	0.0	57.6	148.2	160.3	180.7	215.0	223.8	309.6	293.6	302.6
Private creditors	0.0	36.2	32.9	29.8	24.9	27.9	31.5	0.8	0.8	0.8
Bonds	0.0	0.0	0.0	0.0	0.0	0.0	0.0	0.0	0.0	0.0
Commercial banks	0.0	2.1	0.0	0.0	0.0	0.0	0.0	0.0	0.0	0.0
Other private	0.0	34.0	32.9	29.8	24.9	27.9	31.5	0.8	0.8	0.8
Private nonguaranteed	**0.0**	**0.0**	**0.0**	**0.0**	**0.0**	**0.0**	**0.0**	**0.0**	**0.0**	**0.0**
Bonds	0.0	0.0	0.0	0.0	0.0	0.0	0.0	0.0	0.0	0.0
Commercial banks	0.0	0.0	0.0	0.0	0.0	0.0	0.0	0.0	0.0	0.0
Memo:										
IBRD	0.0	0.0	0.0	0.0	0.0	0.0	0.0	0.0	0.0	0.0
IDA	0.0	4.7	145.5	164.7	178.4	197.3	209.9	216.2	220.7	233.5
DISBURSEMENTS	**0.0**	**74.7**	**36.5**	**40.8**	**23.2**	**28.4**	**21.1**	**28.3**	**30.3**	**14.5**
Public and publicly guaranteed	**0.0**	**74.7**	**36.5**	**40.8**	**23.2**	**28.4**	**21.1**	**28.3**	**30.3**	**14.5**
Official creditors	0.0	54.1	36.5	40.8	23.2	28.4	21.1	28.3	30.3	14.5
Multilateral	0.0	29.5	30.3	23.4	16.8	12.2	18.8	28.3	30.3	14.5
Concessional	0.0	24.3	30.3	22.8	16.8	11.9	18.5	27.7	30.3	14.5
Bilateral	0.0	24.7	6.2	17.4	6.4	16.2	2.3	0.0	0.0	0.0
Concessional	0.0	24.2	6.2	17.1	6.4	13.9	2.3	0.0	0.0	0.0
Private creditors	0.0	20.5	0.0	0.0	0.0	0.0	0.0	0.0	0.0	0.0
Bonds	0.0	0.0	0.0	0.0	0.0	0.0	0.0	0.0	0.0	0.0
Commercial banks	0.0	0.0	0.0	0.0	0.0	0.0	0.0	0.0	0.0	0.0
Other private	0.0	20.5	0.0	0.0	0.0	0.0	0.0	0.0	0.0	0.0
Private nonguaranteed	**0.0**	**0.0**	**0.0**	**0.0**	**0.0**	**0.0**	**0.0**	**0.0**	**0.0**	**0.0**
Bonds	0.0	0.0	0.0	0.0	0.0	0.0	0.0	0.0	0.0	0.0
Commercial banks	0.0	0.0	0.0	0.0	0.0	0.0	0.0	0.0	0.0	0.0
Memo:										
IBRD	0.0	0.0	0.0	0.0	0.0	0.0	0.0	0.0	0.0	0.0
IDA	0.0	4.2	15.5	10.7	13.6	11.1	8.8	14.1	17.7	5.3
PRINCIPAL REPAYMENTS	**0.0**	**3.0**	**2.3**	**3.4**	**0.9**	**3.1**	**8.1**	**5.6**	**5.0**	**2.4**
Public and publicly guaranteed	**0.0**	**3.0**	**2.3**	**3.4**	**0.9**	**3.1**	**8.1**	**5.6**	**5.0**	**2.4**
Official creditors	0.0	0.2	2.3	3.3	0.9	3.0	8.0	5.5	5.0	2.4
Multilateral	0.0	0.0	1.5	2.6	0.7	1.8	7.8	4.1	3.5	2.4
Concessional	0.0	0.0	0.6	0.6	0.7	1.0	4.0	2.5	2.9	1.6
Bilateral	0.0	0.2	0.8	0.7	0.2	1.2	0.2	1.4	1.6	0.0
Concessional	0.0	0.0	0.3	0.5	0.2	1.2	0.2	0.2	1.6	0.0
Private creditors	0.0	2.8	0.1	0.0	0.0	0.1	0.2	0.1	0.0	0.0
Bonds	0.0	0.0	0.0	0.0	0.0	0.0	0.0	0.0	0.0	0.0
Commercial banks	0.0	0.4	0.0	0.0	0.0	0.0	0.0	0.0	0.0	0.0
Other private	0.0	2.4	0.1	0.0	0.0	0.1	0.2	0.1	0.0	0.0
Private nonguaranteed	**0.0**	**0.0**	**0.0**	**0.0**	**0.0**	**0.0**	**0.0**	**0.0**	**0.0**	**0.0**
Bonds	0.0	0.0	0.0	0.0	0.0	0.0	0.0	0.0	0.0	0.0
Commercial banks	0.0	0.0	0.0	0.0	0.0	0.0	0.0	0.0	0.0	0.0
Memo:										
IBRD	0.0	0.0	0.0	0.0	0.0	0.0	0.0	0.0	0.0	0.0
IDA	0.0	0.0	0.1	0.1	0.4	0.6	0.9	0.8	1.3	0.5
NET FLOWS ON DEBT	**0.0**	**71.7**	**34.2**	**37.4**	**22.3**	**25.3**	**13.0**	**22.7**	**25.3**	**12.0**
Public and publicly guaranteed	**0.0**	**71.7**	**34.2**	**37.4**	**22.3**	**25.3**	**13.0**	**22.7**	**25.3**	**12.0**
Official creditors	0.0	53.9	34.2	37.5	22.3	25.4	13.2	22.8	25.3	12.0
Multilateral	0.0	29.5	28.8	20.8	16.1	10.4	11.0	24.1	26.9	12.0
Concessional	0.0	24.3	29.7	22.2	16.1	10.9	14.6	25.2	27.4	12.8
Bilateral	0.0	24.5	5.4	16.7	6.2	14.9	2.2	-1.4	-1.6	0.0
Concessional	0.0	24.2	5.9	16.7	6.2	12.7	2.2	-0.2	-1.6	0.0
Private creditors	0.0	17.8	-0.1	0.0	0.0	-0.1	-0.2	-0.1	0.0	0.0
Bonds	0.0	0.0	0.0	0.0	0.0	0.0	0.0	0.0	0.0	0.0
Commercial banks	0.0	-0.4	0.0	0.0	0.0	0.0	0.0	0.0	0.0	0.0
Other private	0.0	18.1	-0.1	0.0	0.0	-0.1	-0.2	-0.1	0.0	0.0
Private nonguaranteed	**0.0**	**0.0**	**0.0**	**0.0**	**0.0**	**0.0**	**0.0**	**0.0**	**0.0**	**0.0**
Bonds	0.0	0.0	0.0	0.0	0.0	0.0	0.0	0.0	0.0	0.0
Commercial banks	0.0	0.0	0.0	0.0	0.0	0.0	0.0	0.0	0.0	0.0
Memo:										
IBRD	0.0	0.0	0.0	0.0	0.0	0.0	0.0	0.0	0.0	0.0
IDA	0.0	4.2	15.4	10.6	13.1	10.4	7.9	13.3	16.4	4.8

GUINEA-BISSAU

(US$ million, unless otherwise indicated)

	1970	1980	1990	1992	1993	1994	1995	1996	1997	1998
INTEREST PAYMENTS (LINT)	**0.0**	**1.1**	**3.4**	**2.9**	**2.0**	**3.6**	**5.7**	**4.0**	**3.0**	**4.4**
Public and publicly guaranteed	**0.0**	**1.1**	**3.4**	**2.9**	**2.0**	**3.6**	**5.7**	**4.0**	**3.0**	**4.4**
Official creditors	0.0	0.3	3.1	2.8	2.0	3.6	5.6	3.9	3.0	4.4
Multilateral	0.0	0.0	2.6	2.6	1.8	2.9	4.4	2.8	2.9	1.9
Concessional	0.0	0.0	1.8	1.2	1.7	1.6	3.0	2.2	2.7	1.5
Bilateral	0.0	0.2	0.5	0.2	0.2	0.7	1.2	1.1	0.1	2.5
Concessional	0.0	0.2	0.3	0.1	0.2	0.7	0.3	1.1	0.1	2.5
Private creditors	0.0	0.8	0.3	0.0	0.0	0.0	0.0	0.1	0.0	0.0
Bonds	0.0	0.0	0.0	0.0	0.0	0.0	0.0	0.0	0.0	0.0
Commercial banks	0.0	0.1	0.0	0.0	0.0	0.0	0.0	0.0	0.0	0.0
Other private	0.0	0.7	0.3	0.0	0.0	0.0	0.0	0.1	0.0	0.0
Private nonguaranteed	**0.0**	**0.0**	**0.0**	**0.0**	**0.0**	**0.0**	**0.0**	**0.0**	**0.0**	**0.0**
Bonds	0.0	0.0	0.0	0.0	0.0	0.0	0.0	0.0	0.0	0.0
Commercial banks	0.0	0.0	0.0	0.0	0.0	0.0	0.0	0.0	0.0	0.0
Memo:										
IBRD	0.0	0.0	0.0	0.0	0.0	0.0	0.0	0.0	0.0	0.0
IDA	0.0	0.0	1.1	1.0	1.4	1.4	1.6	1.4	1.8	0.8
NET TRANSFERS ON DEBT	**0.0**	**70.6**	**30.8**	**34.6**	**20.3**	**21.7**	**7.3**	**18.7**	**22.2**	**7.6**
Public and publicly guaranteed	**0.0**	**70.6**	**30.8**	**34.6**	**20.3**	**21.7**	**7.3**	**18.7**	**22.2**	**7.6**
Official creditors	0.0	53.7	31.1	34.6	20.3	21.7	7.5	18.9	22.2	7.6
Multilateral	0.0	29.4	26.2	18.2	14.4	7.5	6.6	21.3	23.9	10.1
Concessional	0.0	24.3	28.0	21.0	14.4	9.3	11.6	22.9	24.7	11.3
Bilateral	0.0	24.2	4.9	16.4	5.9	14.2	0.9	-2.5	-1.7	-2.5
Concessional	0.0	24.0	5.7	16.6	6.0	12.0	1.9	-1.3	-1.7	-2.5
Private creditors	0.0	16.9	-0.3	-0.1	0.0	-0.1	-0.2	-0.2	0.0	0.0
Bonds	0.0	0.0	0.0	0.0	0.0	0.0	0.0	0.0	0.0	0.0
Commercial banks	0.0	-0.5	0.0	0.0	0.0	0.0	0.0	0.0	0.0	0.0
Other private	0.0	17.4	-0.3	-0.1	0.0	-0.1	-0.2	-0.2	0.0	0.0
Private nonguaranteed	**0.0**	**0.0**	**0.0**	**0.0**	**0.0**	**0.0**	**0.0**	**0.0**	**0.0**	**0.0**
Bonds	0.0	0.0	0.0	0.0	0.0	0.0	0.0	0.0	0.0	0.0
Commercial banks	0.0	0.0	0.0	0.0	0.0	0.0	0.0	0.0	0.0	0.0
Memo:										
IBRD	0.0	0.0	0.0	0.0	0.0	0.0	0.0	0.0	0.0	0.0
IDA	0.0	4.2	14.2	9.6	11.7	9.1	6.3	11.9	14.6	4.0
DEBT SERVICE (LTDS)	**0.0**	**4.1**	**5.7**	**6.2**	**2.9**	**6.7**	**13.8**	**9.6**	**8.1**	**6.8**
Public and publicly guaranteed	**0.0**	**4.1**	**5.7**	**6.2**	**2.9**	**6.7**	**13.8**	**9.6**	**8.1**	**6.8**
Official creditors	0.0	0.5	5.4	6.2	2.9	6.6	13.6	9.4	8.1	6.8
Multilateral	0.0	0.0	4.0	5.2	2.5	4.7	12.2	6.9	6.4	4.3
Concessional	0.0	0.0	2.3	1.8	2.4	2.6	6.9	4.7	5.6	3.1
Bilateral	0.0	0.4	1.4	0.9	0.5	2.0	1.4	2.5	1.7	2.5
Concessional	0.0	0.2	0.5	0.5	0.4	1.9	0.4	1.3	1.7	2.5
Private creditors	0.0	3.6	0.3	0.1	0.0	0.1	0.2	0.2	0.0	0.0
Bonds	0.0	0.0	0.0	0.0	0.0	0.0	0.0	0.0	0.0	0.0
Commercial banks	0.0	0.5	0.0	0.0	0.0	0.0	0.0	0.0	0.0	0.0
Other private	0.0	3.1	0.3	0.1	0.0	0.1	0.2	0.2	0.0	0.0
Private nonguaranteed	**0.0**	**0.0**	**0.0**	**0.0**	**0.0**	**0.0**	**0.0**	**0.0**	**0.0**	**0.0**
Bonds	0.0	0.0	0.0	0.0	0.0	0.0	0.0	0.0	0.0	0.0
Commercial banks	0.0	0.0	0.0	0.0	0.0	0.0	0.0	0.0	0.0	0.0
Memo:										
IBRD	0.0	0.0	0.0	0.0	0.0	0.0	0.0	0.0	0.0	0.0
IDA	0.0	0.0	1.2	1.1	1.8	2.0	2.5	2.2	3.1	1.4
UNDISBURSED DEBT	**0.0**	**72.6**	**271.9**	**190.4**	**178.7**	**157.1**	**134.6**	**91.4**	**85.2**	**77.8**
Official creditors	0.0	66.6	263.6	190.4	178.7	157.1	134.6	91.4	85.2	77.8
Private creditors	0.0	6.0	8.3	0.0	0.0	0.0	0.0	0.0	0.0	0.0
Memorandum items										
Concessional LDOD	0.0	86.6	392.6	438.9	475.3	533.8	563.8	675.3	665.5	696.5
Variable rate LDOD	0.0	2.1	36.9	33.7	42.4	45.4	47.1	15.7	15.7	15.7
Public sector LDOD	0.0	133.1	630.4	692.3	712.5	761.4	796.6	856.2	838.4	873.1
Private sector LDOD	0.0	0.0	0.0	0.0	0.0	0.0	0.0	0.0	0.0	0.0

6. CURRENCY COMPOSITION OF LONG-TERM DEBT (PERCENT)

	1970	1980	1990	1992	1993	1994	1995	1996	1997	1998
Deutsche mark	0.0	0.0	0.5	0.4	0.4	0.4	0.4	0.4	0.3	0.3
French franc	0.0	14.8	1.8	1.6	1.4	1.2	1.3	1.1	1.0	1.0
Japanese yen	0.0	0.0	0.0	0.0	0.0	0.0	0.0	0.0	0.0	0.0
Pound sterling	0.0	0.0	0.0	0.0	0.0	0.0	0.0	0.0	0.0	0.0
Swiss franc	0.0	2.8	8.6	7.0	6.9	7.3	6.6	12.7	12.2	12.3
U.S.dollars	0.0	25.0	27.3	32.8	35.4	36.4	38.1	30.1	31.9	31.2
Multiple currency	0.0	2.8	26.4	27.1	26.5	26.0	25.6	24.0	24.1	25.0
Special drawing rights	0.0	0.0	0.0	0.0	0.0	0.0	0.0	0.0	0.0	0.0
All other currencies	0.0	54.6	35.4	31.1	29.4	28.7	28.0	31.7	30.5	30.2

GUINEA-BISSAU

(US$ million, unless otherwise indicated)

	1970	1980	1990	1992	1993	1994	1995	1996	1997	1998
7. DEBT RESTRUCTURINGS										
Total amount rescheduled	..	..	16.1	1.1	16.1	23.4	13.7	228.0	3.0	1.1
Debt stock rescheduled	..	..	0.0	0.0	0.9	0.0	0.0	16.3	0.0	0.0
Principal rescheduled	..	..	8.2	0.6	9.0	21.5	0.0	112.9	0.4	0.3
Official	..	..	3.8	0.6	4.2	21.5	0.0	84.4	0.4	0.3
Private	..	..	4.4	0.0	4.8	0.0	0.0	28.5	0.0	0.0
Interest rescheduled	..	..	6.8	0.1	2.7	0.1	0.0	43.3	0.1	0.1
Official	..	..	3.7	0.1	1.2	0.1	0.0	37.6	0.1	0.1
Private	..	..	3.1	0.0	1.5	0.0	0.0	5.6	0.0	0.0
Debt forgiven	..	..	4.6	0.0	0.0	1.7	11.0	3.4	0.0	0.0
Memo: interest forgiven	..	..	0.6	0.0	0.0	8.6	3.7	2.5	0.0	0.0
Debt stock reduction	..	..	0.0	0.0	0.0	0.0	0.0	0.0	0.0	0.0
of which debt buyback	..	..	0.0	0.0	0.0	0.0	0.0	0.0	0.0	0.0
8. DEBT STOCK-FLOW RECONCILIATION										
Total change in debt stocks	..	..	98.9	16.2	25.6	65.2	44.8	39.8	-15.5	43.1
Net flows on debt	0.0	72.7	45.7	23.2	18.8	27.2	13.3	30.1	26.9	10.7
Net change in interest arrears	..	..	6.6	14.7	8.9	14.2	9.2	-27.0	1.3	9.1
Interest capitalized	..	..	6.8	0.1	2.7	0.1	0.0	43.3	0.1	0.1
Debt forgiveness or reduction	..	..	-4.6	0.0	0.0	-1.7	-11.0	-3.4	0.0	0.0
Cross-currency valuation	..	..	30.8	-10.3	-7.4	11.9	12.1	-21.9	-22.0	13.6
Residual	..	..	13.8	-11.5	2.6	13.5	21.2	18.7	-21.7	9.6
9. AVERAGE TERMS OF NEW COMMITMENTS										
ALL CREDITORS										
Interest (%)	0.0	2.8	2.2	1.4	0.8	5.1	0.7	2.5	0.7	0.7
Maturity (years)	0.0	17.5	28.1	36.4	33.2	2.9	39.8	25.4	47.9	39.4
Grace period (years)	0.0	3.9	10.4	8.7	8.7	0.4	10.3	5.9	10.7	9.9
Grant element (%)	0.0	39.5	61.8	73.0	72.1	7.0	80.7	55.0	83.7	80.2
Official creditors										
Interest (%)	0.0	2.7	2.2	1.4	0.8	5.1	0.7	2.5	0.7	0.7
Maturity (years)	0.0	17.9	28.1	36.4	33.2	2.9	39.8	25.4	47.9	39.4
Grace period (years)	0.0	3.9	10.4	8.7	8.7	0.4	10.3	5.9	10.7	9.9
Grant element (%)	0.0	40.5	61.8	73.0	72.1	7.0	80.7	55.0	83.7	80.2
Private creditors										
Interest (%)	0.0	7.4	0.0	0.0	0.0	0.0	0.0	0.0	0.0	0.0
Maturity (years)	0.0	3.8	0.0	0.0	0.0	0.0	0.0	0.0	0.0	0.0
Grace period (years)	0.0	1.2	0.0	0.0	0.0	0.0	0.0	0.0	0.0	0.0
Grant element (%)	0.0	5.1	0.0	0.0	0.0	0.0	0.0	0.0	0.0	0.0
Memorandum items										
Commitments	0.0	43.6	97.9	11.3	11.8	2.3	22.0	1.1	39.8	11.7
Official creditors	0.0	42.3	97.9	11.3	11.8	2.3	22.0	1.1	39.8	11.7
Private creditors	0.0	1.3	0.0	0.0	0.0	0.0	0.0	0.0	0.0	0.0

10. CONTRACTUAL OBLIGATIONS ON OUTSTANDING LONG-TERM DEBT

	1999	2000	2001	2002	2003	2004	2005	2006	2007	2008
TOTAL										
Disbursements	12.6	18.6	13.4	10.7	8.3	5.8	4.0	0.5	0.0	0.0
Principal	30.8	31.2	31.9	34.2	35.2	36.8	29.1	21.3	20.2	20.5
Interest	13.7	12.9	12.1	11.0	10.0	8.8	7.6	6.9	6.5	6.1
Official creditors										
Disbursements	12.6	18.6	13.4	10.7	8.3	5.8	4.0	0.5	0.0	0.0
Principal	30.7	31.1	31.8	34.1	35.2	36.8	29.1	21.3	20.2	20.5
Interest	13.6	12.8	12.1	11.0	10.0	8.8	7.6	6.9	6.5	6.1
Bilateral creditors										
Disbursements	0.0	0.0	0.0	0.0	0.0	0.0	0.0	0.0	0.0	0.0
Principal	21.2	19.4	19.1	23.1	24.3	25.5	18.4	10.2	8.5	8.0
Interest	10.0	9.3	8.6	7.8	6.8	5.7	4.6	4.0	3.6	3.3
Multilateral creditors										
Disbursements	12.6	18.6	13.4	10.7	8.3	5.8	4.0	0.5	0.0	0.0
Principal	9.4	11.6	12.7	11.1	10.9	11.3	10.7	11.1	11.7	12.5
Interest	3.6	3.5	3.4	3.2	3.2	3.1	3.0	2.9	2.8	2.7
Private creditors										
Disbursements	0.0	0.0	0.0	0.0	0.0	0.0	0.0	0.0	0.0	0.0
Principal	0.1	0.1	0.1	0.1	0.0	0.0	0.0	0.0	0.0	0.0
Interest	0.0	0.0	0.0	0.0	0.0	0.0	0.0	0.0	0.0	0.0
Commercial banks										
Disbursements	0.0	0.0	0.0	0.0	0.0	0.0	0.0	0.0	0.0	0.0
Principal	0.0	0.0	0.0	0.0	0.0	0.0	0.0	0.0	0.0	0.0
Interest	0.0	0.0	0.0	0.0	0.0	0.0	0.0	0.0	0.0	0.0
Other private										
Disbursements	0.0	0.0	0.0	0.0	0.0	0.0	0.0	0.0	0.0	0.0
Principal	0.1	0.1	0.1	0.1	0.0	0.0	0.0	0.0	0.0	0.0
Interest	0.0	0.0	0.0	0.0	0.0	0.0	0.0	0.0	0.0	0.0

GUYANA

(US$ million, unless otherwise indicated)

	1970	1980	1990	1992	1993	1994	1995	1996	1997	1998
1. SUMMARY DEBT DATA										
TOTAL DEBT STOCKS (EDT)	..	**811**	**1,945**	**1,897**	**1,954**	**2,038**	**2,105**	**1,631**	**1,611**	**1,653**
Long-term debt (LDOD)	**83**	**607**	**1,757**	**1,673**	**1,732**	**1,787**	**1,782**	**1,370**	**1,345**	**1,369**
Public and publicly guaranteed	83	607	1,757	1,673	1,732	1,787	1,782	1,370	1,345	1,369
Private nonguaranteed	0	0	0	0	0	0	0	0	0	0
Use of IMF credit	**0**	**86**	**113**	**168**	**177**	**179**	**172**	**168**	**157**	**154**
Short-term debt	..	**118**	**75**	**56**	**46**	**72**	**151**	**92**	**108**	**129**
of which interest arrears on LDOD	..	8	63	52	37	63	135	75	92	83
Official creditors	..	5	40	40	23	49	115	55	71	69
Private creditors	..	3	23	12	14	14	19	20	22	14
Memo: principal arrears on LDOD	..	37	169	76	79	85	99	97	89	82
Official creditors	..	34	89	64	66	70	85	82	76	70
Private creditors	..	3	80	12	13	15	14	16	13	12
Memo: export credits	..	0	257	237	248	204	189	138	211	110
TOTAL DEBT FLOWS										
Disbursements	**14**	**169**	**264**	**84**	**81**	**47**	**59**	**109**	**90**	**70**
Long-term debt	14	115	160	59	69	34	45	83	65	57
IMF purchases	0	55	104	25	12	13	14	26	25	12
Principal repayments	**2**	**58**	**175**	**53**	**51**	**61**	**74**	**73**	**78**	**73**
Long-term debt	2	43	69	53	47	39	51	49	52	52
IMF repurchases	0	16	107	0	3	22	24	24	26	22
Net flows on debt	**12**	**155**	**256**	**33**	**36**	**-14**	**-8**	**38**	**11**	**27**
of which short-term debt	..	44	167	2	5	0	7	1	-1	31
Interest payments (INT)	..	**31**	**120**	**49**	**42**	**37**	**35**	**32**	**56**	**63**
Long-term debt	3	27	73	43	36	32	31	29	54	60
IMF charges	0	4	40	6	5	4	3	2	1	1
Short-term debt	..	1	7	0	0	1	1	1	1	2
Net transfers on debt	..	**124**	**135**	**-16**	**-6**	**-51**	**-43**	**6**	**-45**	**-36**
Total debt service paid (TDS)	..	**89**	**295**	**102**	**92**	**97**	**109**	**105**	**133**	**136**
Long-term debt	6	69	142	96	83	71	82	78	106	112
IMF repurchases and charges	0	19	146	6	9	26	27	25	27	22
Short-term debt (interest only)	..	1	7	0	0	1	1	1	1	2
2. AGGREGATE NET RESOURCE FLOWS AND NET TRANSFERS (LONG-TERM)										
NET RESOURCE FLOWS	**22**	**77**	**165**	**195**	**152**	**134**	**90**	**152**	**298**	**205**
Net flow of long-term debt (ex. IMF)	12	72	91	6	22	-5	-5	35	13	6
Foreign direct investment (net)	9	1	0	147	70	107	74	81	90	95
Portfolio equity flows	0	0	0	0	0	0	0	0	0	0
Grants (excluding technical coop.)	2	4	74	42	61	32	21	36	196	105
Memo: technical coop. grants	3	8	9	11	10	12	16	17	14	7
official net resource flows	14	70	181	67	90	31	26	70	214	114
private net resource flows	8	6	-16	128	62	103	64	83	85	91
NET TRANSFERS	**5**	**50**	**92**	**151**	**116**	**102**	**59**	**123**	**245**	**145**
Interest on long-term debt	3	27	73	43	36	32	31	29	54	60
Profit remittances on FDI	14	0	0	0	0	0	0	0	0	0
Memo: official net transfers	12	59	117	25	55	2	-4	43	161	56
private net transfers	-7	-9	-26	126	61	100	63	80	84	89
3. MAJOR ECONOMIC AGGREGATES										
Gross national product (GNP)	247	561	275	261	366	460	545	648	675	665
Exports of goods & services (XGS)	..	411	..	492	536	593	641	723	751	700
of which workers remittances	..	0	..	..	..	..	..	..	..	..
Imports of goods & services (MGS)	..	538	..	684	739	780	838	885	959	899
International reserves (RES)	20	13	29	188	247	247	269	330	316	277
Current account balance	..	-129	..	-139	-140	-125	-135	..	..	..
4. DEBT INDICATORS										
EDT / XGS (%)	..	197.4	..	385.1	364.7	343.8	328.2	225.7	214.3	236.3
EDT / GNP (%)	..	144.4	707.1	725.9	533.2	443.1	385.9	251.7	238.5	248.6
TDS / XGS (%)	..	21.6	..	20.7	17.2	16.4	17.0	14.5	17.7	19.5
INT / XGS (%)	..	7.5	..	10.0	7.7	6.2	5.4	4.4	7.4	9.0
INT / GNP (%)	..	5.5	43.7	18.8	11.3	7.9	6.4	4.9	8.3	9.5
RES / EDT (%)	..	1.6	1.5	9.9	12.7	12.1	12.8	20.2	19.6	16.7
RES / MGS (months)	..	0.3	..	3.3	4.0	3.8	3.9	4.5	4.0	3.7
Short-term / EDT (%)	..	14.6	3.9	2.9	2.4	3.6	7.2	5.7	6.7	7.8
Concessional / EDT (%)	..	28.3	57.6	59.3	61.3	62.1	61.4	55.0	56.5	57.7
Multilateral / EDT (%)	..	13.9	24.0	28.3	29.4	29.9	30.4	41.0	41.3	42.3

GUYANA

(US$ million, unless otherwise indicated)

	1970	1980	1990	1992	1993	1994	1995	1996	1997	1998
5. LONG-TERM DEBT										
DEBT OUTSTANDING (LDOD)	**83**	**607**	**1,757**	**1,673**	**1,732**	**1,787**	**1,782**	**1,370**	**1,345**	**1,369**
Public and publicly guaranteed	**83**	**607**	**1,757**	**1,673**	**1,732**	**1,787**	**1,782**	**1,370**	**1,345**	**1,369**
Official creditors	66	379	1,610	1,594	1,661	1,716	1,720	1,308	1,289	1,317
Multilateral	1	112	468	536	574	609	639	669	666	700
Concessional	0	69	291	371	418	457	498	554	574	620
Bilateral	66	267	1,142	1,058	1,086	1,107	1,081	639	623	617
Concessional	40	160	831	753	780	809	794	342	335	333
Private creditors	17	228	148	79	71	71	62	63	56	52
Bonds	17	15	0	0	0	0	0	0	0	0
Commercial banks	0	100	80	12	13	15	13	19	14	12
Other private	0	113	68	66	58	57	49	44	42	41
Private nonguaranteed	**0**	**0**	**0**	**0**	**0**	**0**	**0**	**0**	**0**	**0**
Bonds	0	0	0	0	0	0	0	0	0	0
Commercial banks	0	0	0	0	0	0	0	0	0	0
Memo:										
IBRD	0	36	59	46	41	39	35	27	19	16
IDA	0	18	93	134	163	182	203	212	218	235
DISBURSEMENTS	**14**	**115**	**160**	**59**	**69**	**34**	**45**	**83**	**65**	**57**
Public and publicly guaranteed	**14**	**115**	**160**	**59**	**69**	**34**	**45**	**83**	**65**	**57**
Official creditors	14	84	153	58	69	34	45	74	65	57
Multilateral	1	35	123	42	62	33	41	73	53	50
Concessional	0	29	109	39	56	33	41	73	53	50
Bilateral	13	50	31	16	7	1	4	1	12	8
Concessional	6	21	19	13	1	0	3	1	12	8
Private creditors	0	31	6	1	0	0	0	10	0	0
Bonds	0	0	0	0	0	0	0	0	0	0
Commercial banks	0	21	0	0	0	0	0	9	0	0
Other private	0	9	6	1	0	0	0	1	0	0
Private nonguaranteed	**0**	**0**	**0**	**0**	**0**	**0**	**0**	**0**	**0**	**0**
Bonds	0	0	0	0	0	0	0	0	0	0
Commercial banks	0	0	0	0	0	0	0	0	0	0
Memo:										
IBRD	0	2	0	0	0	0	0	0	0	0
IDA	0	2	54	4	30	12	18	16	18	9
PRINCIPAL REPAYMENTS	**2**	**43**	**69**	**53**	**47**	**39**	**51**	**49**	**52**	**52**
Public and publicly guaranteed	**2**	**43**	**69**	**53**	**47**	**39**	**51**	**49**	**52**	**52**
Official creditors	1	18	46	34	40	35	40	41	47	48
Multilateral	0	1	42	20	23	22	24	23	28	32
Concessional	0	0	6	8	6	6	6	7	13	17
Bilateral	1	17	4	14	17	13	16	18	19	16
Concessional	1	9	0	0	6	3	5	10	14	11
Private creditors	1	25	22	19	7	4	10	8	5	4
Bonds	0	0	1	0	0	0	0	0	0	0
Commercial banks	1	11	8	10	0	0	2	3	4	3
Other private	0	14	14	9	7	4	8	5	2	1
Private nonguaranteed	**0**	**0**	**0**	**0**	**0**	**0**	**0**	**0**	**0**	**0**
Bonds	0	0	0	0	0	0	0	0	0	0
Commercial banks	0	0	0	0	0	0	0	0	0	0
Memo:										
IBRD	0	1	31	7	6	5	6	5	5	5
IDA	0	0	0	0	1	1	1	1	1	1
NET FLOWS ON DEBT	**12**	**72**	**91**	**6**	**22**	**-5**	**-5**	**35**	**13**	**6**
Public and publicly guaranteed	**12**	**72**	**91**	**6**	**22**	**-5**	**-5**	**35**	**13**	**6**
Official creditors	13	66	107	25	29	-1	5	33	18	10
Multilateral	1	34	80	22	39	11	17	50	25	18
Concessional	0	29	103	31	50	27	34	67	40	33
Bilateral	12	33	27	2	-10	-12	-12	-17	-7	-8
Concessional	5	12	19	13	-6	-3	-2	-9	-2	-3
Private creditors	-1	6	-16	-19	-7	-4	-10	2	-5	-4
Bonds	0	0	-1	0	0	0	0	0	0	0
Commercial banks	-1	10	-8	-10	0	0	-2	6	-4	-3
Other private	0	-4	-8	-9	-7	-4	-8	-5	-2	-1
Private nonguaranteed	**0**	**0**	**0**	**0**	**0**	**0**	**0**	**0**	**0**	**0**
Bonds	0	0	0	0	0	0	0	0	0	0
Commercial banks	0	0	0	0	0	0	0	0	0	0
Memo:										
IBRD	0	1	-31	-7	-6	-5	-6	-5	-5	-5
IDA	0	2	54	4	29	12	17	16	17	9

GUYANA

(US$ million, unless otherwise indicated)

	1970	1980	1990	1992	1993	1994	1995	1996	1997	1998
INTEREST PAYMENTS (LINT)	**3**	**27**	**73**	**43**	**36**	**32**	**31**	**29**	**54**	**60**
Public and publicly guaranteed	**3**	**27**	**73**	**43**	**36**	**32**	**31**	**29**	**54**	**60**
Official creditors	3	11	64	42	35	29	30	27	53	59
Multilateral	0	4	58	19	19	18	18	16	17	23
Concessional	0	1	8	6	6	6	6	6	9	17
Bilateral	3	7	6	23	17	11	12	11	36	36
Concessional	1	4	3	14	12	8	8	9	13	19
Private creditors	1	15	9	2	1	3	2	3	1	2
Bonds	1	1	0	0	0	0	0	0	0	0
Commercial banks	0	9	5	0	0	0	1	1	1	1
Other private	0	5	4	2	1	3	1	2	0	1
Private nonguaranteed	**0**	**0**	**0**	**0**	**0**	**0**	**0**	**0**	**0**	**0**
Bonds	0	0	0	0	0	0	0	0	0	0
Commercial banks	0	0	0	0	0	0	0	0	0	0
Memo:										
IBRD	0	3	31	4	4	3	3	3	2	1
IDA	0	0	0	1	1	1	1	2	2	2
NET TRANSFERS ON DEBT	**8**	**45**	**18**	**-37**	**-14**	**-37**	**-37**	**5**	**-41**	**-55**
Public and publicly guaranteed	**8**	**45**	**18**	**-37**	**-14**	**-37**	**-37**	**5**	**-41**	**-55**
Official creditors	10	55	43	-17	-6	-30	-25	6	-35	-49
Multilateral	1	30	23	3	20	-7	-1	34	9	-5
Concessional	0	28	95	26	44	21	28	60	31	17
Bilateral	9	25	20	-20	-26	-23	-24	-28	-43	-44
Concessional	4	8	17	-2	-18	-11	-11	-18	-14	-22
Private creditors	-2	-9	-26	-20	-8	-7	-12	-1	-6	-6
Bonds	-1	-1	-1	0	0	0	0	0	0	0
Commercial banks	-1	1	-12	-10	0	0	-3	5	-4	-3
Other private	0	-10	-12	-10	-8	-7	-9	-6	-2	-2
Private nonguaranteed	**0**	**0**	**0**	**0**	**0**	**0**	**0**	**0**	**0**	**0**
Bonds	0	0	0	0	0	0	0	0	0	0
Commercial banks	0	0	0	0	0	0	0	0	0	0
Memo:										
IBRD	0	-2	-62	-11	-10	-9	-9	-8	-7	-6
IDA	0	2	54	3	28	11	16	14	16	7
DEBT SERVICE (LTDS)	**6**	**69**	**142**	**96**	**83**	**71**	**82**	**78**	**106**	**112**
Public and publicly guaranteed	**6**	**69**	**142**	**96**	**83**	**71**	**82**	**78**	**106**	**112**
Official creditors	4	29	110	75	75	64	70	68	100	106
Multilateral	0	5	100	39	42	40	42	39	44	55
Concessional	0	1	14	13	12	12	13	13	21	33
Bilateral	4	24	11	36	34	24	28	29	56	52
Concessional	2	13	3	14	19	11	14	18	26	30
Private creditors	2	40	32	21	8	7	12	11	6	6
Bonds	1	1	1	0	0	0	0	0	0	0
Commercial banks	1	20	12	10	0	0	3	4	4	3
Other private	0	19	18	11	8	7	9	7	2	2
Private nonguaranteed	**0**	**0**	**0**	**0**	**0**	**0**	**0**	**0**	**0**	**0**
Bonds	0	0	0	0	0	0	0	0	0	0
Commercial banks	0	0	0	0	0	0	0	0	0	0
Memo:										
IBRD	0	4	62	11	10	9	9	8	7	6
IDA	0	0	1	1	2	2	2	2	2	2
UNDISBURSED DEBT	**53**	**223**	**272**	**232**	**242**	**274**	**255**	**272**	**269**	**277**
Official creditors	53	207	268	232	242	274	246	272	269	277
Private creditors	0	16	4	0	0	0	9	0	0	0
Memorandum items										
Concessional LDOD	40	230	1,121	1,124	1,198	1,266	1,292	896	909	953
Variable rate LDOD	0	124	235	177	181	215	195	75	70	69
Public sector LDOD	83	607	1,757	1,673	1,732	1,787	1,782	1,370	1,345	1,369
Private sector LDOD	0	0	0	0	0	0	0	0	0	0

6. CURRENCY COMPOSITION OF LONG-TERM DEBT (PERCENT)

	1970	1980	1990	1992	1993	1994	1995	1996	1997	1998
Deutsche mark	0.0	0.9	2.2	2.5	2.3	2.6	2.5	1.9	1.5	1.4
French franc	0.0	0.1	0.0	0.1	0.1	0.1	0.1	0.1	0.0	0.1
Japanese yen	0.0	0.0	0.3	0.2	0.2	0.2	0.2	0.2	0.1	0.0
Pound sterling	68.9	21.7	10.5	9.4	9.1	9.7	9.3	9.2	9.0	8.9
Swiss franc	0.0	0.0	0.1	0.1	0.1	0.1	0.1	0.0	0.0	0.0
U.S.dollars	24.7	58.3	67.7	65.0	65.6	64.5	64.5	59.5	61.5	62.6
Multiple currency	0.4	10.1	14.9	16.3	16.1	16.1	16.2	22.1	21.1	20.4
Special drawing rights	0.0	0.0	0.1	0.2	0.2	0.2	0.2	0.3	0.3	0.3
All other currencies	6.0	8.9	4.2	6.2	6.3	6.5	6.9	6.7	6.5	6.3

GUYANA

(US$ million, unless otherwise indicated)

	1970	1980	1990	1992	1993	1994	1995	1996	1997	1998
7. DEBT RESTRUCTURINGS										
Total amount rescheduled	..	..	474	41	53	49	1	277	0	0
Debt stock rescheduled	..	..	320	1	0	0	0	0	0	0
Principal rescheduled	..	..	89	16	1	14	1	239	0	0
Official	..	..	89	7	1	14	0	239	0	0
Private	..	..	0	9	0	0	0	0	0	0
Interest rescheduled	..	..	38	16	51	16	0	38	0	0
Official	..	..	38	16	51	16	0	38	0	0
Private	..	..	0	0	0	0	0	0	0	0
Debt forgiven	..	..	31	24	7	11	0	459	2	0
Memo: interest forgiven	..	..	1	0	2	3	0	4	0	0
Debt stock reduction	..	..	0	76	0	0	0	0	0	0
of which debt buyback	..	..	0	10	0	0	0	0	0	0
8. DEBT STOCK-FLOW RECONCILIATION										
Total change in debt stocks	..	..	313	-63	58	84	67	-474	-20	42
Net flows on debt	12	155	256	33	36	-14	-8	38	11	27
Net change in interest arrears	..	..	-37	3	-15	26	71	-60	18	-10
Interest capitalized	..	..	38	16	51	16	0	38	0	0
Debt forgiveness or reduction	..	..	-31	-90	-7	-11	0	-459	-2	0
Cross-currency valuation	..	..	47	-45	-13	24	9	1	-18	6
Residual	..	..	41	19	5	42	-5	-31	-29	19
9. AVERAGE TERMS OF NEW COMMITMENTS										
ALL CREDITORS										
Interest (%)	6.0	10.5	1.3	1.7	1.5	1.6	3.0	1.6	1.6	1.4
Maturity (years)	25.3	8.1	39.7	37.4	34.3	39.7	37.1	37.3	39.0	38.8
Grace period (years)	9.7	2.4	9.9	9.9	9.8	10.5	9.9	10.0	9.9	10.4
Grant element (%)	32.4	2.9	74.9	70.5	71.0	73.0	60.5	70.8	72.7	74.1
Official creditors										
Interest (%)	6.0	9.2	1.3	1.7	1.5	1.6	1.5	1.6	1.6	1.4
Maturity (years)	25.3	9.5	39.7	37.6	34.3	39.7	38.7	37.5	39.0	38.8
Grace period (years)	9.7	3.2	9.9	9.9	9.8	10.5	10.4	10.1	9.9	10.4
Grant element (%)	32.4	11.2	74.9	71.0	71.0	73.0	73.3	71.2	72.7	74.1
Private creditors										
Interest (%)	0.0	12.3	0.0	8.0	0.0	0.0	8.8	7.4	0.0	0.0
Maturity (years)	0.0	6.2	0.0	13.9	0.0	0.0	31.0	3.8	0.0	0.0
Grace period (years)	0.0	1.3	0.0	13.9	0.0	0.0	8.0	0.3	0.0	0.0
Grant element (%)	0.0	-8.9	0.0	14.7	0.0	0.0	9.6	3.9	0.0	0.0
Memorandum items										
Commitments	20	96	281	83	98	64	45	106	83	55
Official creditors	20	56	281	82	98	64	36	105	83	55
Private creditors	0	39	0	1	0	0	9	1	0	0

10. CONTRACTUAL OBLIGATIONS ON OUTSTANDING LONG-TERM DEBT

	1999	2000	2001	2002	2003	2004	2005	2006	2007	2008
TOTAL										
Disbursements	95	67	49	33	16	9	5	1	1	0
Principal	37	52	54	55	61	62	63	82	59	57
Interest	45	45	44	42	40	38	36	33	31	29
Official creditors										
Disbursements	95	67	49	33	16	9	5	1	1	0
Principal	35	50	54	55	60	61	62	55	58	56
Interest	43	42	42	40	38	36	34	32	31	29
Bilateral creditors										
Disbursements	1	1	1	0	0	0	0	0	0	0
Principal	18	30	28	29	32	33	33	26	27	27
Interest	30	29	27	26	25	23	22	20	19	18
Multilateral creditors										
Disbursements	94	66	49	33	16	9	5	1	1	0
Principal	17	20	27	26	28	29	28	29	31	29
Interest	13	14	14	14	13	13	12	12	12	11
Private creditors										
Disbursements	0	0	0	0	0	0	0	0	0	0
Principal	2	2	0	0	1	1	1	27	0	0
Interest	2	2	2	2	2	2	2	1	1	1
Commercial banks										
Disbursements	0	0	0	0	0	0	0	0	0	0
Principal	1	1	0	0	0	0	0	0	0	0
Interest	1	1	1	1	1	1	1	1	1	1
Other private										
Disbursements	0	0	0	0	0	0	0	0	0	0
Principal	0	0	0	0	0	0	0	26	0	0
Interest	1	1	1	1	1	1	1	0	0	0

HAITI

(US$ million, unless otherwise indicated)

	1970	1980	1990	1992	1993	1994	1995	1996	1997	1998
1. SUMMARY DEBT DATA										
TOTAL DEBT STOCKS (EDT)	**..**	**302**	**889**	**785**	**803**	**717**	**806**	**897**	**1,047**	**1,048**
Long-term debt (LDOD)	**40**	**242**	**751**	**638**	**648**	**635**	**751**	**836**	**897**	**980**
Public and publicly guaranteed	40	242	751	638	648	635	751	836	897	980
Private nonguaranteed	0	0	0	0	0	0	0	0	0	0
Use of IMF credit	**3**	**46**	**38**	**35**	**34**	**35**	**29**	**25**	**43**	**38**
Short-term debt	**..**	**14**	**101**	**112**	**121**	**47**	**26**	**36**	**107**	**30**
of which interest arrears on LDOD	..	0	24	21	30	34	1	1	1	1
Official creditors	..	0	14	9	15	18	1	1	1	1
Private creditors	..	0	10	12	15	16	0	0	0	0
Memo: principal arrears on LDOD	..	0	43	59	104	121	1	2	2	2
Official creditors	..	0	14	18	37	55	1	2	2	2
Private creditors	..	0	29	41	67	67	0	0	0	0
Memo: export credits	..	0	117	83	69	79	86	100	105	111
TOTAL DEBT FLOWS										
Disbursements	**4**	**77**	**44**	**1**	**0**	**0**	**128**	**107**	**119**	**94**
Long-term debt	4	47	38	1	0	0	104	107	98	94
IMF purchases	0	30	5	0	0	0	25	0	21	0
Principal repayments	**3**	**18**	**18**	**0**	**0**	**1**	**62**	**14**	**16**	**20**
Long-term debt	3	15	6	0	0	1	30	11	15	14
IMF repurchases	0	3	12	0	0	0	32	3	1	5
Net flows on debt	**1**	**53**	**42**	**0**	**0**	**-79**	**79**	**103**	**174**	**-3**
of which short-term debt	..	-5	16	0	0	-78	13	10	71	-77
Interest payments (INT)	**..**	**8**	**15**	**5**	**5**	**1**	**32**	**13**	**18**	**20**
Long-term debt	0	5	6	0	0	0	25	10	14	15
IMF charges	0	1	3	0	0	0	6	1	1	1
Short-term debt	..	2	7	5	5	1	2	2	4	3
Net transfers on debt	**..**	**46**	**27**	**-5**	**-5**	**-79**	**47**	**90**	**156**	**-22**
Total debt service paid (TDS)	**..**	**26**	**33**	**5**	**5**	**1**	**94**	**27**	**35**	**39**
Long-term debt	4	20	12	1	0	1	55	21	29	29
IMF repurchases and charges	0	4	15	0	0	0	38	4	2	7
Short-term debt (interest only)	..	2	7	5	5	1	2	2	4	3
2. AGGREGATE NET RESOURCE FLOWS AND NET TRANSFERS (LONG-TERM)										
NET RESOURCE FLOWS	**6**	**75**	**105**	**58**	**69**	**597**	**593**	**254**	**219**	**225**
Net flow of long-term debt (ex. IMF)	1	32	33	0	0	-1	73	96	83	80
Foreign direct investment (net)	3	13	8	-2	-3	0	7	4	4	11
Portfolio equity flows	0	0	0	0	0	0	0	0	0	0
Grants (excluding technical coop.)	2	30	65	60	72	598	512	154	132	134
Memo: technical coop. grants	4	32	7	40	51	58	112	93	109	96
official net resource flows	2	55	97	60	72	597	586	250	215	214
private net resource flows	5	20	8	-2	-3	0	7	4	4	11
NET TRANSFERS	**3**	**59**	**91**	**50**	**62**	**592**	**562**	**239**	**202**	**205**
Interest on long-term debt	0	5	6	0	0	0	25	10	14	15
Profit remittances on FDI	3	11	8	8	7	5	6	5	4	5
Memo: official net transfers	1	52	92	60	72	597	561	240	202	199
private net transfers	1	7	0	-10	-10	-5	1	-1	0	6
3. MAJOR ECONOMIC AGGREGATES										
Gross national product (GNP)	391	1,446	2,954	2,137	1,820	1,955	2,625	2,945	2,813	3,858
Exports of goods & services (XGS)	..	415	325	113	118	67	192	192	379	479
of which workers remittances	..	106	0	0	0	0	..	..	..	..
Imports of goods & services (MGS)	..	498	540	261	303	247	832	792	905	1,033
International reserves (RES)	4	27	10	..	..	38	113	115	83	..
Current account balance	..	-101	-22	7	-12	-23	-87	-138	-48	-38
4. DEBT INDICATORS										
EDT / XGS (%)	..	72.8	273.6	695.4	680.1	1,070.2	419.1	468.1	276.2	218.6
EDT / GNP (%)	..	20.9	30.1	36.7	44.1	36.7	30.7	30.5	37.2	27.2
TDS / XGS (%)	..	6.2	10.1	4.8	4.2	1.9	48.8	13.9	9.2	8.2
INT / XGS (%)	..	1.8	4.6	4.3	3.8	1.2	16.5	6.8	4.9	4.1
INT / GNP (%)	..	0.5	0.5	0.2	0.3	0.0	1.2	0.4	0.7	0.5
RES / EDT (%)	..	8.8	1.1	..	..	5.3	14.0	12.8	7.9	..
RES / MGS (months)	..	0.6	0.2	..	..	1.9	1.6	1.7	1.1	..
Short-term / EDT (%)	..	4.6	11.3	14.3	15.1	6.6	3.3	4.0	10.2	2.8
Concessional / EDT (%)	..	70.7	78.6	75.0	72.0	78.9	93.0	93.1	85.6	93.4
Multilateral / EDT (%)	..	43.8	55.0	66.5	64.2	73.0	75.7	77.0	71.5	79.3

HAITI

(US$ million, unless otherwise indicated)

	1970	1980	1990	1992	1993	1994	1995	1996	1997	1998
5. LONG-TERM DEBT										
DEBT OUTSTANDING (LDOD)	**40**	**242**	**751**	**638**	**648**	**635**	**751**	**836**	**897**	**980**
Public and publicly guaranteed	**40**	**242**	**751**	**638**	**648**	**635**	**751**	**836**	**897**	**980**
Official creditors	29	219	704	591	581	568	751	836	897	980
Multilateral	0	132	489	522	515	524	610	691	749	830
Concessional	0	132	489	522	515	524	610	691	749	830
Bilateral	29	86	215	69	66	44	141	145	149	149
Concessional	29	81	210	67	63	42	139	144	147	148
Private creditors	11	24	47	47	67	67	0	0	0	0
Bonds	4	0	0	0	0	0	0	0	0	0
Commercial banks	0	8	47	47	67	67	0	0	0	0
Other private	7	16	0	0	0	0	0	0	0	0
Private nonguaranteed	**0**	**0**	**0**	**0**	**0**	**0**	**0**	**0**	**0**	**0**
Bonds	0	0	0	0	0	0	0	0	0	0
Commercial banks	0	0	0	0	0	0	0	0	0	0
Memo:										
IBRD	0	0	0	0	0	0	0	0	0	0
IDA	0	66	324	344	337	346	389	442	458	493
DISBURSEMENTS	**4**	**47**	**38**	**1**	**0**	**0**	**104**	**107**	**98**	**94**
Public and publicly guaranteed	**4**	**47**	**38**	**1**	**0**	**0**	**104**	**107**	**98**	**94**
Official creditors	0	32	38	1	0	0	104	107	98	94
Multilateral	0	21	27	1	0	0	103	101	90	93
Concessional	0	21	27	1	0	0	103	101	90	93
Bilateral	0	11	11	0	0	0	1	6	8	1
Concessional	0	7	11	0	0	0	1	6	8	1
Private creditors	4	15	0	0	0	0	0	0	0	0
Bonds	0	0	0	0	0	0	0	0	0	0
Commercial banks	0	5	0	0	0	0	0	0	0	0
Other private	4	10	0	0	0	0	0	0	0	0
Private nonguaranteed	**0**	**0**	**0**	**0**	**0**	**0**	**0**	**0**	**0**	**0**
Bonds	0	0	0	0	0	0	0	0	0	0
Commercial banks	0	0	0	0	0	0	0	0	0	0
Memo:										
IBRD	0	0	0	0	0	0	0	0	0	0
IDA	0	13	14	0	0	0	49	67	40	39
PRINCIPAL REPAYMENTS	**3**	**15**	**6**	**0**	**0**	**1**	**30**	**11**	**15**	**14**
Public and publicly guaranteed	**3**	**15**	**6**	**0**	**0**	**1**	**30**	**11**	**15**	**14**
Official creditors	1	8	6	0	0	1	30	11	15	14
Multilateral	0	0	5	0	0	1	29	10	14	13
Concessional	0	0	5	0	0	1	29	10	14	13
Bilateral	1	8	1	0	0	0	1	1	1	1
Concessional	1	8	1	0	0	0	0	1	1	1
Private creditors	3	7	0	0	0	0	0	0	0	0
Bonds	0	0	0	0	0	0	0	0	0	0
Commercial banks	0	1	0	0	0	0	0	0	0	0
Other private	3	7	0	0	0	0	0	0	0	0
Private nonguaranteed	**0**	**0**	**0**	**0**	**0**	**0**	**0**	**0**	**0**	**0**
Bonds	0	0	0	0	0	0	0	0	0	0
Commercial banks	0	0	0	0	0	0	0	0	0	0
Memo:										
IBRD	0	0	0	0	0	0	0	0	0	0
IDA	0	0	1	0	0	0	10	4	5	5
NET FLOWS ON DEBT	**1**	**32**	**33**	**0**	**0**	**-1**	**73**	**96**	**83**	**80**
Public and publicly guaranteed	**1**	**32**	**33**	**0**	**0**	**-1**	**73**	**96**	**83**	**80**
Official creditors	-1	25	33	0	0	-1	73	96	83	80
Multilateral	0	21	22	0	0	-1	74	91	77	81
Concessional	0	21	22	0	0	-1	74	91	77	81
Bilateral	-1	3	10	0	0	0	0	5	7	-1
Concessional	-1	-1	11	0	0	0	0	5	7	-1
Private creditors	2	7	0	0	0	0	0	0	0	0
Bonds	0	0	0	0	0	0	0	0	0	0
Commercial banks	0	5	0	0	0	0	0	0	0	0
Other private	2	3	0	0	0	0	0	0	0	0
Private nonguaranteed	**0**	**0**	**0**	**0**	**0**	**0**	**0**	**0**	**0**	**0**
Bonds	0	0	0	0	0	0	0	0	0	0
Commercial banks	0	0	0	0	0	0	0	0	0	0
Memo:										
IBRD	0	0	0	0	0	0	0	0	0	0
IDA	0	13	13	0	0	0	39	63	35	34

HAITI

(US$ million, unless otherwise indicated)

	1970	1980	1990	1992	1993	1994	1995	1996	1997	1998
INTEREST PAYMENTS (LINT)	**0**	**5**	**6**	**0**	**0**	**0**	**25**	**10**	**14**	**15**
Public and publicly guaranteed	**0**	**5**	**6**	**0**	**0**	**0**	**25**	**10**	**14**	**15**
Official creditors	0	3	6	0	0	0	25	10	14	15
Multilateral	0	1	5	0	0	0	24	7	9	10
Concessional	0	1	5	0	0	0	24	7	9	10
Bilateral	0	2	1	0	0	0	1	3	5	5
Concessional	0	2	0	0	0	0	0	3	5	5
Private creditors	0	2	0	0	0	0	0	0	0	0
Bonds	0	0	0	0	0	0	0	0	0	0
Commercial banks	0	1	0	0	0	0	0	0	0	0
Other private	0	1	0	0	0	0	0	0	0	0
Private nonguaranteed	**0**	**0**	**0**	**0**	**0**	**0**	**0**	**0**	**0**	**0**
Bonds	0	0	0	0	0	0	0	0	0	0
Commercial banks	0	0	0	0	0	0	0	0	0	0
Memo:										
IBRD	0	0	0	0	0	0	0	0	0	0
IDA	0	0	2	0	0	0	10	3	3	4
NET TRANSFERS ON DEBT	**1**	**27**	**27**	**0**	**0**	**-1**	**49**	**86**	**69**	**65**
Public and publicly guaranteed	**1**	**27**	**27**	**0**	**0**	**-1**	**49**	**86**	**69**	**65**
Official creditors	-1	21	27	0	0	-1	49	86	69	65
Multilateral	0	20	17	0	0	-1	50	84	68	71
Concessional	0	20	17	0	0	-1	50	84	68	71
Bilateral	-1	1	10	0	0	0	-1	2	1	-6
Concessional	-1	-3	10	0	0	0	0	2	2	-6
Private creditors	1	5	0	0	0	0	0	0	0	0
Bonds	0	0	0	0	0	0	0	0	0	0
Commercial banks	0	4	0	0	0	0	0	0	0	0
Other private	1	2	0	0	0	0	0	0	0	0
Private nonguaranteed	**0**	**0**	**0**	**0**	**0**	**0**	**0**	**0**	**0**	**0**
Bonds	0	0	0	0	0	0	0	0	0	0
Commercial banks	0	0	0	0	0	0	0	0	0	0
Memo:										
IBRD	0	0	0	0	0	0	0	0	0	0
IDA	0	13	11	0	0	0	29	60	32	31
DEBT SERVICE (LTDS)	**4**	**20**	**12**	**1**	**0**	**1**	**55**	**21**	**29**	**29**
Public and publicly guaranteed	**4**	**20**	**12**	**1**	**0**	**1**	**55**	**21**	**29**	**29**
Official creditors	1	11	12	1	0	1	55	21	29	29
Multilateral	0	1	10	1	0	1	53	17	22	23
Concessional	0	1	10	1	0	1	53	17	22	23
Bilateral	1	10	2	0	0	0	2	3	7	7
Concessional	1	10	1	0	0	0	1	3	7	7
Private creditors	3	9	0	0	0	0	0	0	0	0
Bonds	0	0	0	0	0	0	0	0	0	0
Commercial banks	0	2	0	0	0	0	0	0	0	0
Other private	3	8	0	0	0	0	0	0	0	0
Private nonguaranteed	**0**	**0**	**0**	**0**	**0**	**0**	**0**	**0**	**0**	**0**
Bonds	0	0	0	0	0	0	0	0	0	0
Commercial banks	0	0	0	0	0	0	0	0	0	0
Memo:										
IBRD	0	0	0	0	0	0	0	0	0	0
IDA	0	0	3	0	0	0	20	7	8	9
UNDISBURSED DEBT	**5**	**145**	**267**	**275**	**261**	**267**	**393**	**351**	**407**	**300**
Official creditors	0	128	267	275	261	267	393	351	407	300
Private creditors	5	17	0	0	0	0	0	0	0	0
Memorandum items										
Concessional LDOD	29	214	699	588	578	565	750	835	896	979
Variable rate LDOD	0	8	7	5	5	5	0	0	0	0
Public sector LDOD	40	235	751	638	648	635	751	836	897	980
Private sector LDOD	0	7	0	0	0	0	0	0	0	0

6. CURRENCY COMPOSITION OF LONG-TERM DEBT (PERCENT)

	1970	1980	1990	1992	1993	1994	1995	1996	1997	1998
Deutsche mark	0.0	5.0	0.0	0.0	0.0	0.0	0.0	0.0	0.0	0.0
French franc	0.0	3.1	10.6	3.3	2.8	3.0	2.6	2.8	3.0	2.9
Japanese yen	0.0	0.0	0.0	0.0	0.0	0.0	0.0	0.0	0.0	0.0
Pound sterling	0.0	0.0	0.0	0.0	0.0	0.0	0.0	0.0	0.0	0.0
Swiss franc	0.0	0.0	0.0	0.0	0.0	0.0	0.0	0.0	0.0	0.0
U.S.dollars	99.9	79.1	70.4	72.0	73.0	72.2	77.2	78.0	78.1	79.7
Multiple currency	0.0	12.9	19.0	24.7	24.3	24.8	20.2	19.2	18.9	17.4
Special drawing rights	0.0	0.0	0.0	0.0	0.0	0.0	0.0	0.0	0.0	0.0
All other currencies	0.1	0.0	0.0	0.0	0.0	0.0	0.0	0.0	0.0	0.0

HAITI

(US$ million, unless otherwise indicated)

	1970	1980	1990	1992	1993	1994	1995	1996	1997	1998
7. DEBT RESTRUCTURINGS										
Total amount rescheduled	..	..	0	0	0	0	108	2	0	0
Debt stock rescheduled	..	..	0	0	0	0	0	0	0	0
Principal rescheduled	..	..	0	0	0	0	71	1	0	0
Official	..	..	0	0	0	0	4	1	0	0
Private	..	..	0	0	0	0	67	0	0	0
Interest rescheduled	..	..	0	0	0	0	17	0	0	0
Official	..	..	0	0	0	0	2	0	0	0
Private	..	..	0	0	0	0	16	0	0	0
Debt forgiven	..	..	0	0	0	23	8	1	0	0
Memo: interest forgiven	..	..	0	0	0	0	3	0	0	0
Debt stock reduction	..	..	0	0	0	0	0	0	0	0
of which debt buyback	..	..	0	0	0	0	0	0	0	0
8. DEBT STOCK-FLOW RECONCILIATION										
Total change in debt stocks	..	..	83	27	18	-86	89	91	150	0
Net flows on debt	1	53	42	0	0	-79	79	103	174	-3
Net change in interest arrears	..	..	8	7	9	4	-33	0	0	0
Interest capitalized	..	..	0	0	0	0	17	0	0	0
Debt forgiveness or reduction	..	..	0	0	0	-23	-8	-1	0	0
Cross-currency valuation	..	..	10	-1	-1	2	2	-2	-3	2
Residual	..	..	23	21	10	9	33	-10	-20	1
9. AVERAGE TERMS OF NEW COMMITMENTS										
ALL CREDITORS										
Interest (%)	4.8	5.2	1.4	0.0	0.0	0.0	1.2	1.8	1.5	0.0
Maturity (years)	9.5	19.6	38.8	0.0	0.0	0.0	39.9	40.0	39.9	0.0
Grace period (years)	1.0	6.3	10.5	0.0	0.0	0.0	10.4	10.5	10.4	0.0
Grant element (%)	16.0	32.6	74.8	0.0	0.0	0.0	76.6	71.8	73.6	0.0
Official creditors										
Interest (%)	3.4	2.8	1.4	0.0	0.0	0.0	1.2	1.8	1.5	0.0
Maturity (years)	43.0	29.8	38.8	0.0	0.0	0.0	39.9	40.0	39.9	0.0
Grace period (years)	7.3	10.3	10.5	0.0	0.0	0.0	10.4	10.5	10.4	0.0
Grant element (%)	55.8	54.5	74.8	0.0	0.0	0.0	76.6	71.8	73.6	0.0
Private creditors										
Interest (%)	4.8	8.2	0.0	0.0	0.0	0.0	0.0	0.0	0.0	0.0
Maturity (years)	8.6	7.0	0.0	0.0	0.0	0.0	0.0	0.0	0.0	0.0
Grace period (years)	0.9	1.4	0.0	0.0	0.0	0.0	0.0	0.0	0.0	0.0
Grant element (%)	14.9	5.2	0.0	0.0	0.0	0.0	0.0	0.0	0.0	0.0
Memorandum items										
Commitments	5	51	104	0	0	0	254	71	163	0
Official creditors	0	29	104	0	0	0	254	71	163	0
Private creditors	5	23	0	0	0	0	0	0	0	0

10. CONTRACTUAL OBLIGATIONS ON OUTSTANDING LONG-TERM DEBT

	1999	2000	2001	2002	2003	2004	2005	2006	2007	2008
TOTAL										
Disbursements	79	77	57	33	22	14	8	1	0	0
Principal	19	22	24	25	25	26	28	33	37	40
Interest	16	16	16	16	16	15	16	16	16	17
Official creditors										
Disbursements	79	77	57	33	22	14	8	1	0	0
Principal	19	22	24	25	25	26	28	33	37	40
Interest	16	16	16	16	16	15	16	16	16	17
Bilateral creditors										
Disbursements	0	0	0	0	0	0	0	0	0	0
Principal	2	4	5	5	5	5	5	5	5	5
Interest	6	5	5	5	5	5	5	4	4	4
Multilateral creditors										
Disbursements	78	77	57	33	22	14	8	1	0	0
Principal	17	18	19	20	20	21	23	28	33	35
Interest	10	10	11	11	11	11	11	12	12	13
Private creditors										
Disbursements	0	0	0	0	0	0	0	0	0	0
Principal	0	0	0	0	0	0	0	0	0	0
Interest	0	0	0	0	0	0	0	0	0	0
Commercial banks										
Disbursements	0	0	0	0	0	0	0	0	0	0
Principal	0	0	0	0	0	0	0	0	0	0
Interest	0	0	0	0	0	0	0	0	0	0
Other private										
Disbursements	0	0	0	0	0	0	0	0	0	0
Principal	0	0	0	0	0	0	0	0	0	0
Interest	0	0	0	0	0	0	0	0	0	0

HONDURAS

(US$ million, unless otherwise indicated)

	1970	1980	1990	1992	1993	1994	1995	1996	1997	1998
1. SUMMARY DEBT DATA										
TOTAL DEBT STOCKS (EDT)	..	**1,473**	**3,724**	**3,614**	**4,077**	**4,436**	**4,570**	**4,533**	**4,710**	**5,002**
Long-term debt (LDOD)	**111**	**1,168**	**3,492**	**3,322**	**3,740**	**4,002**	**4,096**	**4,062**	**4,182**	**4,358**
Public and publicly guaranteed	91	976	3,426	3,232	3,651	3,902	3,973	3,846	3,922	3,946
Private nonguaranteed	19	191	66	90	88	100	123	216	259	412
Use of IMF credit	**0**	**33**	**32**	**112**	**118**	**109**	**99**	**58**	**46**	**113**
Short-term debt	..	**272**	**199**	**180**	**219**	**325**	**375**	**414**	**482**	**532**
of which interest arrears on LDOD	..	0	89	55	92	68	56	55	57	64
Official creditors	..	0	34	30	36	40	26	31	33	35
Private creditors	..	0	55	25	56	28	30	24	25	29
Memo: principal arrears on LDOD	..	3	190	109	167	150	142	130	134	144
Official creditors	..	1	63	54	74	69	53	61	68	63
Private creditors	..	2	128	55	93	81	90	68	66	81
Memo: export credits	..	0	338	431	436	487	466	489	416	451
TOTAL DEBT FLOWS										
Disbursements	**45**	**375**	**461**	**489**	**584**	**352**	**379**	**456**	**660**	**488**
Long-term debt	39	346	432	408	574	352	349	456	660	423
IMF purchases	6	29	29	81	10	0	31	0	0	64
Principal repayments	**6**	**87**	**211**	**203**	**210**	**254**	**336**	**391**	**312**	**297**
Long-term debt	6	87	177	203	207	238	293	353	303	295
IMF repurchases	0	0	35	0	3	16	44	38	9	2
Net flows on debt	**38**	**296**	**133**	**294**	**375**	**228**	**106**	**104**	**414**	**233**
of which short-term debt	..	8	-117	8	2	130	62	39	67	43
Interest payments (INT)	..	**120**	**178**	**174**	**151**	**178**	**217**	**173**	**193**	**208**
Long-term debt	4	83	157	162	140	163	195	152	170	182
IMF charges	0	1	6	6	6	5	5	2	0	0
Short-term debt	..	36	15	6	4	10	18	20	24	26
Net transfers on debt	..	**176**	**-45**	**120**	**225**	**50**	**-112**	**-69**	**221**	**25**
Total debt service paid (TDS)	..	**207**	**389**	**377**	**361**	**433**	**553**	**564**	**505**	**505**
Long-term debt	10	170	333	365	347	402	487	504	473	477
IMF repurchases and charges	0	1	41	6	9	21	48	40	9	2
Short-term debt (interest only)	..	36	15	6	4	10	18	20	24	26
2. AGGREGATE NET RESOURCE FLOWS AND NET TRANSFERS (LONG-TERM)										
NET RESOURCE FLOWS	**41**	**284**	**511**	**414**	**487**	**231**	**228**	**291**	**555**	**375**
Net flow of long-term debt (ex. IMF)	32	259	256	205	367	114	56	103	356	128
Foreign direct investment (net)	8	6	44	48	27	35	50	91	122	84
Portfolio equity flows	0	0	0	0	0	0	0	0	0	0
Grants (excluding technical coop.)	0	20	211	162	93	83	122	97	77	163
Memo: technical coop. grants	6	19	96	83	86	55	85	78	76	66
official net resource flows	27	148	434	383	311	183	153	130	431	182
private net resource flows	14	137	77	31	176	48	75	161	124	193
NET TRANSFERS	**17**	**124**	**282**	**179**	**257**	**-27**	**-57**	**59**	**299**	**108**
Interest on long-term debt	4	83	157	162	140	163	195	152	170	182
Profit remittances on FDI	20	78	72	74	90	95	90	80	86	85
Memo: official net transfers	25	116	285	240	186	36	-17	-3	300	39
private net transfers	-8	7	-2	-61	72	-63	-40	62	-1	70
3. MAJOR ECONOMIC AGGREGATES										
Gross national product (GNP)	700	2,429	2,773	3,247	3,407	3,238	3,698	3,823	4,504	5,162
Exports of goods & services (XGS)	..	967	1,103	1,163	1,300	1,453	1,787	2,111	2,421	2,697
of which workers remittances	..	0	50	60	60	85	120	128	160	220
Imports of goods & services (MGS)	..	1,306	1,384	1,577	1,713	1,900	2,111	2,546	2,793	3,002
International reserves (RES)	20	159	47	205	106	179	270	257	587	824
Current account balance	..	-317	-51	-258	-309	-343	-201	-335	-272	-158
4. DEBT INDICATORS										
EDT / XGS (%)	..	152.2	337.5	310.9	313.6	305.3	255.7	214.7	194.5	185.5
EDT / GNP (%)	..	60.6	134.3	111.3	119.7	137.0	123.6	118.6	104.6	96.9
TDS / XGS (%)	..	21.4	35.3	32.4	27.7	29.8	31.0	26.7	20.9	18.7
INT / XGS (%)	..	12.4	16.1	15.0	11.6	12.3	12.2	8.2	8.0	7.7
INT / GNP (%)	..	5.0	6.4	5.4	4.4	5.5	5.9	4.5	4.3	4.0
RES / EDT (%)	..	10.8	1.3	5.7	2.6	4.0	5.9	5.7	12.5	16.5
RES / MGS (months)	..	1.5	0.4	1.6	0.7	1.1	1.5	1.2	2.5	3.3
Short-term / EDT (%)	..	18.5	5.4	5.0	5.4	7.3	8.2	9.1	10.2	10.6
Concessional / EDT (%)	..	21.8	37.4	37.5	39.5	42.1	44.1	48.3	48.3	49.1
Multilateral / EDT (%)	..	31.1	42.5	49.8	47.9	46.5	47.1	46.5	49.1	47.6

HONDURAS

(US$ million, unless otherwise indicated)

	1970	1980	1990	1992	1993	1994	1995	1996	1997	1998
5. LONG-TERM DEBT										
DEBT OUTSTANDING (LDOD)	**111**	**1,168**	**3,492**	**3,322**	**3,740**	**4,002**	**4,096**	**4,062**	**4,182**	**4,358**
Public and publicly guaranteed	**91**	**976**	**3,426**	**3,232**	**3,651**	**3,902**	**3,973**	**3,846**	**3,922**	**3,946**
Official creditors	88	697	2,982	2,965	3,259	3,533	3,608	3,521	3,681	3,782
Multilateral	63	459	1,581	1,801	1,952	2,062	2,153	2,109	2,312	2,379
Concessional	30	202	536	714	815	921	1,036	1,186	1,295	1,409
Bilateral	24	238	1,401	1,163	1,307	1,470	1,455	1,413	1,368	1,404
Concessional	24	120	857	642	796	947	978	1,005	980	1,048
Private creditors	4	280	443	267	392	369	365	324	242	164
Bonds	0	0	0	0	152	152	139	126	62	0
Commercial banks	0	205	205	105	106	98	115	110	94	92
Other private	4	75	238	163	134	120	111	88	86	72
Private nonguaranteed	**19**	**191**	**66**	**90**	**88**	**100**	**123**	**216**	**259**	**412**
Bonds	0	0	0	0	0	0	0	0	0	0
Commercial banks	19	191	66	90	88	100	123	216	259	412
Memo:										
IBRD	30	152	558	489	479	469	443	350	275	235
IDA	15	64	77	182	236	307	386	424	496	579
DISBURSEMENTS	**39**	**346**	**432**	**408**	**574**	**352**	**349**	**456**	**660**	**423**
Public and publicly guaranteed	**29**	**265**	**425**	**378**	**559**	**320**	**287**	**309**	**553**	**197**
Official creditors	29	151	366	374	379	297	258	306	548	195
Multilateral	21	113	190	291	269	195	209	259	476	141
Concessional	10	37	54	151	120	119	132	182	133	117
Bilateral	7	38	177	83	110	102	49	47	72	54
Concessional	7	12	88	48	92	84	45	46	68	43
Private creditors	0	114	58	4	179	23	29	2	5	3
Bonds	0	0	0	0	152	0	0	0	0	0
Commercial banks	0	59	23	1	17	3	26	2	5	3
Other private	0	55	36	3	10	20	4	0	0	0
Private nonguaranteed	**10**	**81**	**8**	**29**	**16**	**32**	**62**	**147**	**106**	**226**
Bonds	0	0	0	0	0	0	0	0	0	0
Commercial banks	10	81	8	29	16	32	62	147	106	226
Memo:										
IBRD	10	24	82	3	26	5	7	0	0	0
IDA	2	18	0	60	55	64	78	52	95	64
PRINCIPAL REPAYMENTS	**6**	**87**	**177**	**203**	**207**	**238**	**293**	**353**	**303**	**295**
Public and publicly guaranteed	**3**	**39**	**151**	**189**	**189**	**218**	**254**	**298**	**240**	**222**
Official creditors	2	23	143	153	161	197	227	273	194	176
Multilateral	2	20	137	121	118	158	158	239	137	120
Concessional	1	2	16	22	19	24	22	22	20	25
Bilateral	0	2	6	33	44	39	69	34	57	56
Concessional	0	1	2	2	6	11	10	10	14	14
Private creditors	1	16	8	36	28	22	27	25	46	46
Bonds	0	0	0	0	0	0	13	13	30	32
Commercial banks	0	14	4	26	15	12	6	4	3	3
Other private	1	3	4	10	13	10	8	8	13	11
Private nonguaranteed	**3**	**48**	**25**	**14**	**18**	**20**	**39**	**54**	**63**	**74**
Bonds	0	0	0	0	0	0	0	0	0	0
Commercial banks	3	48	25	14	18	20	39	54	63	74
Memo:										
IBRD	1	4	94	46	46	51	58	59	50	48
IDA	0	0	2	1	1	2	2	2	2	2
NET FLOWS ON DEBT	**32**	**259**	**256**	**205**	**367**	**114**	**56**	**103**	**356**	**128**
Public and publicly guaranteed	**26**	**226**	**274**	**189**	**369**	**102**	**33**	**11**	**313**	**-25**
Official creditors	27	128	223	221	218	101	31	33	354	18
Multilateral	20	92	53	171	151	37	51	20	339	21
Concessional	9	35	38	129	101	95	110	160	113	91
Bilateral	7	36	171	50	67	63	-20	13	15	-2
Concessional	7	11	86	46	85	73	35	36	55	29
Private creditors	-1	98	50	-32	151	2	2	-23	-41	-43
Bonds	0	0	0	0	152	0	-13	-13	-30	-32
Commercial banks	0	46	19	-25	2	-9	20	-2	2	0
Other private	-1	52	32	-7	-3	11	-4	-8	-13	-11
Private nonguaranteed	**7**	**33**	**-18**	**15**	**-2**	**12**	**23**	**93**	**43**	**153**
Bonds	0	0	0	0	0	0	0	0	0	0
Commercial banks	7	33	-18	15	-2	12	23	93	43	153
Memo:										
IBRD	9	20	-12	-43	-20	-46	-51	-59	-50	-48
IDA	2	18	-2	59	54	62	76	50	93	62

HONDURAS

(US$ million, unless otherwise indicated)

	1970	1980	1990	1992	1993	1994	1995	1996	1997	1998
INTEREST PAYMENTS (LINT)	**4**	**83**	**157**	**162**	**140**	**163**	**195**	**152**	**170**	**182**
Public and publicly guaranteed	**3**	**58**	**156**	**160**	**140**	**161**	**190**	**146**	**149**	**159**
Official creditors	2	31	150	143	126	147	170	132	131	143
Multilateral	2	24	141	108	97	104	103	98	82	91
Concessional	0	4	11	13	12	14	14	15	16	19
Bilateral	0	7	8	35	29	43	67	35	49	52
Concessional	0	2	1	7	9	13	20	18	22	21
Private creditors	0	27	6	17	14	14	20	14	19	16
Bonds	0	0	0	0	0	5	7	7	8	9
Commercial banks	0	26	5	14	10	3	7	4	4	2
Other private	0	1	1	3	4	6	6	3	7	4
Private nonguaranteed	**1**	**25**	**1**	**2**	**0**	**2**	**5**	**6**	**20**	**23**
Bonds	0	0	0	0	0	0	0	0	0	0
Commercial banks	1	25	1	2	0	2	5	6	20	23
Memo:										
IBRD	1	12	96	43	39	38	38	30	23	20
IDA	0	0	1	1	1	2	3	3	3	4
NET TRANSFERS ON DEBT	**29**	**176**	**99**	**43**	**227**	**-49**	**-139**	**-48**	**187**	**-54**
Public and publicly guaranteed	**23**	**168**	**118**	**29**	**229**	**-59**	**-157**	**-136**	**164**	**-184**
Official creditors	25	97	74	78	92	-47	-139	-99	223	-125
Multilateral	18	68	-89	63	54	-67	-52	-77	257	-70
Concessional	9	31	27	116	89	82	96	145	97	73
Bilateral	7	29	162	15	38	20	-87	-22	-34	-54
Concessional	7	9	85	39	76	60	14	18	33	8
Private creditors	-2	71	45	-49	137	-13	-18	-37	-59	-59
Bonds	0	0	0	0	152	-5	-21	-20	-38	-41
Commercial banks	0	20	14	-39	-8	-12	13	-6	-2	-2
Other private	-2	51	31	-10	-7	4	-10	-11	-20	-16
Private nonguaranteed	**6**	**8**	**-19**	**14**	**-2**	**10**	**18**	**87**	**23**	**130**
Bonds	0	0	0	0	0	0	0	0	0	0
Commercial banks	6	8	-19	14	-2	10	18	87	23	130
Memo:										
IBRD	8	8	-108	-85	-59	-85	-89	-89	-73	-68
IDA	2	17	-4	58	52	60	73	47	90	58
DEBT SERVICE (LTDS)	**10**	**170**	**333**	**365**	**347**	**402**	**487**	**504**	**473**	**477**
Public and publicly guaranteed	**6**	**97**	**307**	**349**	**329**	**379**	**444**	**444**	**389**	**381**
Official creditors	4	54	293	296	287	344	397	405	325	319
Multilateral	4	45	278	229	214	262	262	336	219	211
Concessional	1	6	27	35	31	38	36	37	36	44
Bilateral	0	9	15	68	73	82	135	69	106	108
Concessional	0	3	3	9	15	24	31	28	36	35
Private creditors	2	44	14	53	42	36	47	39	64	62
Bonds	0	0	0	0	0	5	21	20	38	41
Commercial banks	0	39	9	39	25	15	13	8	7	5
Other private	2	4	5	14	17	16	13	11	20	16
Private nonguaranteed	**4**	**73**	**27**	**16**	**18**	**22**	**44**	**60**	**83**	**97**
Bonds	0	0	0	0	0	0	0	0	0	0
Commercial banks	4	73	27	16	18	22	44	60	83	97
Memo:										
IBRD	2	17	191	89	85	90	96	89	73	68
IDA	0	1	4	2	3	3	4	5	5	6
UNDISBURSED DEBT	**54**	**729**	**666**	**885**	**906**	**741**	**779**	**782**	**536**	**641**
Official creditors	54	716	655	862	854	712	767	773	526	632
Private creditors	0	13	10	23	52	29	12	9	10	8
Memorandum items										
Concessional LDOD	54	321	1,393	1,356	1,611	1,868	2,013	2,190	2,276	2,457
Variable rate LDOD	19	400	753	728	774	784	768	790	775	882
Public sector LDOD	91	841	3,319	3,180	3,619	3,877	3,949	3,823	3,901	3,925
Private sector LDOD	19	327	173	142	120	125	147	239	281	433

6. CURRENCY COMPOSITION OF LONG-TERM DEBT (PERCENT)

	1970	1980	1990	1992	1993	1994	1995	1996	1997	1998
Deutsche mark	0.0	0.0	2.6	3.0	2.9	3.2	3.4	3.1	3.0	3.2
French franc	0.5	0.4	3.1	3.1	2.7	2.7	2.6	2.6	2.8	2.9
Japanese yen	0.0	0.0	8.4	9.5	9.7	10.5	9.9	8.9	9.2	10.4
Pound sterling	0.0	0.0	0.9	0.8	0.7	0.7	0.6	0.7	0.8	0.7
Swiss franc	0.0	0.0	2.1	1.4	1.3	1.4	1.5	1.4	1.3	1.4
U.S.dollars	66.7	62.9	45.2	43.7	46.2	44.9	45.7	48.9	58.3	56.9
Multiple currency	32.8	25.4	34.4	35.4	33.0	32.5	31.9	29.8	20.7	20.3
Special drawing rights	0.0	0.0	0.0	0.0	0.0	0.0	0.0	0.0	0.0	0.0
All other currencies	0.0	11.3	3.3	3.1	3.5	4.1	4.4	4.6	3.9	4.2

HONDURAS

(US$ million, unless otherwise indicated)

	1970	1980	1990	1992	1993	1994	1995	1996	1997	1998
7. DEBT RESTRUCTURINGS										
Total amount rescheduled	..	..	310	133	83	45	25	67	109	0
Debt stock rescheduled	..	..	0	0	0	0	0	0	3	0
Principal rescheduled	..	..	153	99	50	29	17	45	98	0
Official	..	..	70	68	23	11	7	39	97	0
Private	..	..	83	31	28	18	9	5	1	0
Interest rescheduled	..	..	140	34	32	14	8	21	3	0
Official	..	..	78	21	22	8	4	17	3	0
Private	..	..	62	13	9	6	4	5	0	0
Debt forgiven	..	..	10	8	3	20	10	2	1	28
Memo: interest forgiven	..	..	11	2	1	0	0	2	0	13
Debt stock reduction	..	..	41	20	0	0	0	0	0	0
of which debt buyback	..	..	0	0	0	0	0	0	0	0
8. DEBT STOCK-FLOW RECONCILIATION										
Total change in debt stocks	..	..	337	218	462	360	134	-36	176	293
Net flows on debt	38	296	133	294	375	228	106	104	414	233
Net change in interest arrears	..	..	-83	-20	37	-24	-12	-1	2	7
Interest capitalized	..	..	140	34	32	14	8	21	3	0
Debt forgiveness or reduction	..	..	-51	-29	-3	-20	-10	-2	-1	-28
Cross-currency valuation	..	..	88	-62	13	109	29	-120	-122	74
Residual	..	..	110	1	9	52	13	-40	-120	7
9. AVERAGE TERMS OF NEW COMMITMENTS										
ALL CREDITORS										
Interest (%)	4.1	6.8	6.5	4.3	3.8	5.6	2.2	2.7	6.3	1.9
Maturity (years)	29.6	23.9	21.3	24.6	23.7	19.4	30.7	30.9	14.4	33.9
Grace period (years)	6.8	6.7	5.9	6.7	8.7	5.2	7.4	8.3	2.9	8.4
Grant element (%)	45.5	26.9	26.6	41.5	45.9	29.7	59.4	56.0	22.6	64.2
Official creditors										
Interest (%)	4.1	5.9	6.1	4.3	2.6	5.6	2.0	2.7	6.3	1.9
Maturity (years)	29.6	25.5	22.7	24.8	29.5	19.4	30.8	30.9	14.2	33.9
Grace period (years)	6.8	7.1	6.5	6.7	7.2	5.2	7.6	8.3	2.8	8.4
Grant element (%)	45.5	31.6	29.4	41.9	56.2	29.7	61.1	56.0	22.2	64.2
Private creditors										
Interest (%)	0.0	16.0	9.9	7.9	5.9	0.0	7.5	0.0	3.6	0.0
Maturity (years)	0.0	6.7	7.1	8.0	13.5	0.0	29.8	0.0	25.5	0.0
Grace period (years)	0.0	2.5	0.6	1.8	11.2	0.0	2.3	0.0	5.0	0.0
Grant element (%)	0.0	-22.3	-0.8	6.7	27.9	0.0	16.6	0.0	45.8	0.0
Memorandum items										
Commitments	23	495	452	609	582	144	324	420	447	334
Official creditors	23	452	410	602	371	144	312	420	439	334
Private creditors	0	43	42	7	211	0	12	0	8	0

10. CONTRACTUAL OBLIGATIONS ON OUTSTANDING LONG-TERM DEBT

	1999	2000	2001	2002	2003	2004	2005	2006	2007	2008
TOTAL										
Disbursements	182	168	106	77	50	33	19	3	1	0
Principal	354	358	285	293	269	260	252	239	208	154
Interest	183	164	145	129	112	97	83	71	60	53
Official creditors										
Disbursements	174	168	106	77	50	33	19	3	1	0
Principal	290	301	231	240	218	209	201	190	161	150
Interest	154	139	124	111	98	86	75	66	58	51
Bilateral creditors										
Disbursements	36	34	19	9	2	1	1	1	0	0
Principal	84	97	92	101	95	98	94	78	59	62
Interest	57	54	50	45	40	36	31	27	24	22
Multilateral creditors										
Disbursements	138	135	87	68	47	31	19	3	0	0
Principal	206	203	140	139	123	111	107	112	102	89
Interest	96	85	74	65	58	51	45	40	34	30
Private creditors										
Disbursements	8	0	0	0	0	0	0	0	0	0
Principal	64	57	54	53	51	51	51	49	47	3
Interest	29	25	21	18	14	11	8	5	2	1
Commercial banks										
Disbursements	0	0	0	0	0	0	0	0	0	0
Principal	9	7	6	5	5	5	5	5	3	1
Interest	4	3	3	3	2	2	2	1	1	1
Other private										
Disbursements	8	0	0	0	0	0	0	0	0	0
Principal	55	50	48	49	46	46	46	45	44	2
Interest	25	22	18	15	12	9	7	4	1	1

HUNGARY

(US$ million, unless otherwise indicated)

	1970	1980	1990	1992	1993	1994	1995	1996	1997	1998
1. SUMMARY DEBT DATA										
TOTAL DEBT STOCKS (EDT)	..	**9,764**	**21,277**	**22,028**	**24,364**	**28,275**	**31,590**	**27,208**	**24,496**	**28,580**
Long-term debt (LDOD)	..	**6,416**	**18,006**	**18,538**	**21,127**	**24,737**	**28,003**	**23,678**	**20,979**	**23,800**
Public and publicly guaranteed	..	6,416	18,006	17,896	19,910	22,349	23,914	18,673	15,064	15,941
Private nonguaranteed	..	0	0	642	1,218	2,388	4,089	5,005	5,915	7,859
Use of IMF credit	**0**	**0**	**330**	**1,204**	**1,231**	**1,141**	**385**	**171**	**160**	**0**
Short-term debt	..	**3,347**	**2,941**	**2,286**	**2,005**	**2,397**	**3,203**	**3,359**	**3,357**	**4,780**
of which interest arrears on LDOD	..	0	0	0	0	0	0	0	0	0
Official creditors	..	0	0	0	0	0	0	0	0	0
Private creditors	..	0	0	0	0	0	0	0	0	0
Memo: principal arrears on LDOD	..	0	0	0	0	0	5	0	0	0
Official creditors	..	0	0	0	0	0	0	0	0	0
Private creditors	..	0	0	0	0	0	5	0	0	0
Memo: export credits	..	0	1,424	1,937	2,025	2,252	2,435	1,947	1,839	1,942
TOTAL DEBT FLOWS										
Disbursements	..	**1,552**	**2,516**	**2,934**	**5,400**	**5,160**	**6,887**	**4,425**	**4,641**	**7,217**
Long-term debt	..	1,552	2,343	2,767	5,320	5,160	6,887	4,425	4,641	7,217
IMF purchases	0	0	173	167	79	0	0	0	0	0
Principal repayments	..	**824**	**2,547**	**3,120**	**2,907**	**3,935**	**4,938**	**6,573**	**6,024**	**5,811**
Long-term debt	..	824	2,217	2,947	2,856	3,770	4,144	6,370	6,024	5,650
IMF repurchases	0	0	330	173	51	164	793	203	0	161
Net flows on debt	..	**903**	**-397**	**-77**	**2,212**	**1,618**	**2,755**	**-1,992**	**-1,385**	**2,829**
of which short-term debt	..	176	-366	109	-281	392	806	156	-2	1,423
Interest payments (INT)	..	**1,099**	**1,683**	**1,850**	**1,518**	**1,730**	**2,109**	**1,815**	**1,685**	**1,494**
Long-term debt	..	636	1,533	1,614	1,345	1,501	1,875	1,618	1,516	1,297
IMF charges	0	0	35	91	71	63	60	17	8	2
Short-term debt	..	463	115	145	102	166	174	180	161	195
Net transfers on debt	..	**-196**	**-2,080**	**-1,927**	**694**	**-113**	**647**	**-3,807**	**-3,069**	**1,335**
Total debt service paid (TDS)	..	**1,923**	**4,230**	**4,970**	**4,424**	**5,665**	**7,046**	**8,389**	**7,708**	**7,305**
Long-term debt	..	1,460	3,751	4,561	4,201	5,271	6,019	7,988	7,539	6,947
IMF repurchases and charges	0	0	364	264	122	228	853	221	8	163
Short-term debt (interest only)	..	463	115	145	102	166	174	180	161	195
2. AGGREGATE NET RESOURCE FLOWS AND NET TRANSFERS (LONG-TERM)										
NET RESOURCE FLOWS	..	**728**	**280**	**1,448**	**4,912**	**3,013**	**7,777**	**1,152**	**2,586**	**3,815**
Net flow of long-term debt (ex. IMF)	..	728	126	-180	2,464	1,390	2,742	-1,945	-1,383	1,567
Foreign direct investment (net)	..	0	0	1,479	2,350	1,144	4,519	1,982	2,079	1,936
Portfolio equity flows	..	0	150	34	13	340	483	1,004	1,810	259
Grants (excluding technical coop.)	..	0	4	115	85	139	33	110	79	53
Memo: technical coop. grants	..	0	0	104	79	61	158	85	54	79
official net resource flows	..	132	587	288	180	234	-99	-589	-13	-869
private net resource flows	..	596	-308	1,159	4,732	2,780	7,876	1,741	2,598	4,683
NET TRANSFERS	..	**92**	**-1,291**	**-217**	**3,502**	**1,423**	**5,792**	**-666**	**820**	**2,238**
Interest on long-term debt	..	636	1,533	1,614	1,345	1,501	1,875	1,618	1,516	1,297
Profit remittances on FDI	..	0	37	51	66	90	110	200	250	280
Memo: official net transfers	..	120	400	-11	-97	-47	-402	-844	-208	-1,020
private net transfers	..	-28	-1,691	-206	3,599	1,470	6,195	178	1,028	3,258
3. MAJOR ECONOMIC AGGREGATES										
Gross national product (GNP)	..	21,775	31,601	35,994	37,410	40,103	42,876	43,708	44,303	45,935
Exports of goods & services (XGS)	..	..	12,315	13,926	11,419	11,441	17,939	20,400	25,914	26,793
of which workers remittances	..	..	0	0	0	0	6	11	18	26
Imports of goods & services (MGS)	..	..	12,724	14,432	16,415	16,404	21,528	23,000	27,875	30,090
International reserves (RES)	..	..	1,185	4,459	6,745	6,778	12,017	9,757	8,437	9,348
Current account balance	..	..	379	352	-4,262	-4,054	-2,535	-1,689	-982	-2,304
4. DEBT INDICATORS										
EDT / XGS (%)	..	..	172.8	158.2	213.4	247.1	176.1	133.4	94.5	106.7
EDT / GNP (%)	..	44.8	67.3	61.2	65.1	70.5	73.7	62.3	55.3	62.2
TDS / XGS (%)	..	..	34.4	35.7	38.7	49.5	39.3	41.1	29.8	27.3
INT / XGS (%)	..	..	13.7	13.3	13.3	15.1	11.8	8.9	6.5	5.6
INT / GNP (%)	..	5.1	5.3	5.1	4.1	4.3	4.9	4.2	3.8	3.3
RES / EDT (%)	..	..	5.6	20.2	27.7	24.0	38.0	35.9	34.4	32.7
RES / MGS (months)	..	..	1.1	3.7	4.9	5.0	6.7	5.1	3.6	3.7
Short-term / EDT (%)	..	34.3	13.8	10.4	8.2	8.5	10.1	12.4	13.7	16.7
Concessional / EDT (%)	..	5.6	0.2	0.2	0.4	0.8	1.3	1.7	1.8	1.8
Multilateral / EDT (%)	..	0.0	12.0	14.9	13.6	12.7	11.1	10.2	10.1	5.3

HUNGARY

(US$ million, unless otherwise indicated)

	1970	1980	1990	1992	1993	1994	1995	1996	1997	1998
5. LONG-TERM DEBT										
DEBT OUTSTANDING (LDOD)	..	**6,416**	**18,006**	**18,538**	**21,127**	**24,737**	**28,003**	**23,678**	**20,979**	**23,800**
Public and publicly guaranteed	..	**6,416**	**18,006**	**17,896**	**19,910**	**22,349**	**23,914**	**18,673**	**15,064**	**15,941**
Official creditors	..	542	2,715	3,888	3,999	4,445	4,457	3,503	3,123	2,291
Multilateral	..	0	2,555	3,279	3,311	3,594	3,510	2,767	2,462	1,504
Concessional	..	0	13	0	0	0	0	0	0	0
Bilateral	..	542	160	609	688	851	947	736	661	787
Concessional	..	542	19	51	98	229	415	461	439	525
Private creditors	..	5,874	15,292	14,009	15,911	17,905	19,457	15,170	11,941	13,650
Bonds	..	25	4,657	6,780	10,087	13,456	15,755	13,097	10,565	12,010
Commercial banks	..	5,523	9,647	6,419	5,153	3,969	3,372	1,899	1,258	1,535
Other private	..	326	988	809	671	479	330	174	118	105
Private nonguaranteed	..	**0**	**0**	**642**	**1,218**	**2,388**	**4,089**	**5,005**	**5,915**	**7,859**
Bonds	..	0	0	0	0	0	0	0	0	90
Commercial banks	..	0	0	642	1,218	2,388	4,089	5,005	5,915	7,769
Memo:										
IBRD	0	0	1,513	1,968	2,095	2,208	2,218	1,650	1,520	699
IDA	0	0	0	0	0	0	0	0	0	0
DISBURSEMENTS	..	**1,552**	**2,343**	**2,767**	**5,320**	**5,160**	**6,887**	**4,425**	**4,641**	**7,217**
Public and publicly guaranteed	..	**1,552**	**2,343**	**2,277**	**4,499**	**3,746**	**4,150**	**1,992**	**1,163**	**3,242**
Official creditors	..	187	728	512	476	378	687	507	344	681
Multilateral	..	0	714	397	414	265	483	354	274	565
Concessional	..	0	0	0	0	0	0	0	0	0
Bilateral	..	187	15	115	63	114	204	153	71	115
Concessional	..	187	3	41	47	112	204	96	40	73
Private creditors	..	1,365	1,615	1,765	4,023	3,368	3,463	1,484	818	2,561
Bonds	..	0	940	1,499	3,802	2,835	3,103	514	436	2,248
Commercial banks	..	1,240	575	195	172	527	343	867	326	294
Other private	..	125	99	71	49	6	17	104	57	20
Private nonguaranteed	..	**0**	**0**	**490**	**821**	**1,414**	**2,737**	**2,434**	**3,478**	**3,975**
Bonds	..	0	0	0	0	0	0	0	0	85
Commercial banks	..	0	0	490	821	1,414	2,737	2,434	3,478	3,889
Memo:										
IBRD	0	0	268	317	229	168	188	95	185	369
IDA	0	0	0	0	0	0	0	0	0	0
PRINCIPAL REPAYMENTS	..	**824**	**2,217**	**2,947**	**2,856**	**3,770**	**4,144**	**6,370**	**6,024**	**5,650**
Public and publicly guaranteed	..	**824**	**2,217**	**2,773**	**2,571**	**3,163**	**3,108**	**4,853**	**3,017**	**3,362**
Official creditors	..	55	145	338	381	283	819	1,207	436	1,602
Multilateral	..	0	125	315	346	232	723	931	375	1,546
Concessional	..	0	0	14	0	0	0	0	0	0
Bilateral	..	55	19	23	35	52	96	275	61	56
Concessional	..	55	0	5	5	12	14	7	6	30
Private creditors	..	769	2,073	2,435	2,190	2,879	2,289	3,646	2,581	1,760
Bonds	..	0	19	522	504	579	1,009	1,640	1,648	1,646
Commercial banks	..	652	1,895	1,747	1,505	2,067	1,094	1,860	834	75
Other private	..	117	159	166	180	233	186	147	99	39
Private nonguaranteed	..	**0**	**0**	**174**	**285**	**608**	**1,036**	**1,517**	**3,007**	**2,288**
Bonds	..	0	0	0	0	0	0	0	0	0
Commercial banks	..	0	0	174	285	608	1,036	1,517	3,007	2,288
Memo:										
IBRD	0	0	108	124	144	196	251	514	218	1,172
IDA	0	0	0	0	0	0	0	0	0	0
NET FLOWS ON DEBT	..	**728**	**126**	**-180**	**2,464**	**1,390**	**2,742**	**-1,945**	**-1,383**	**1,567**
Public and publicly guaranteed	..	**728**	**126**	**-496**	**1,928**	**583**	**1,042**	**-2,862**	**-1,854**	**-120**
Official creditors	..	132	584	174	95	95	-132	-699	-92	-921
Multilateral	..	0	589	82	68	33	-240	-577	-102	-981
Concessional	..	0	0	-14	0	0	0	0	0	0
Bilateral	..	132	-5	92	27	62	108	-122	10	59
Concessional	..	132	2	36	43	100	190	89	34	44
Private creditors	..	596	-458	-670	1,833	489	1,174	-2,162	-1,762	801
Bonds	..	0	921	977	3,297	2,255	2,094	-1,126	-1,212	602
Commercial banks	..	588	-1,320	-1,553	-1,333	-1,540	-750	-993	-508	219
Other private	..	8	-59	-95	-131	-227	-170	-43	-42	-20
Private nonguaranteed	..	**0**	**0**	**317**	**536**	**807**	**1,701**	**917**	**472**	**1,687**
Bonds	..	0	0	0	0	0	0	0	0	85
Commercial banks	..	0	0	317	536	807	1,701	917	472	1,601
Memo:										
IBRD	0	0	161	193	85	-28	-63	-419	-33	-802
IDA	0	0	0	0	0	0	0	0	0	0

HUNGARY

(US$ million, unless otherwise indicated)

	1970	1980	1990	1992	1993	1994	1995	1996	1997	1998
INTEREST PAYMENTS (LINT)	..	**636**	**1,533**	**1,614**	**1,345**	**1,501**	**1,875**	**1,618**	**1,516**	**1,297**
Public and publicly guaranteed	..	**636**	**1,533**	**1,585**	**1,312**	**1,449**	**1,708**	**1,550**	**1,179**	**978**
Official creditors	..	12	187	300	278	281	303	255	195	152
Multilateral	..	0	178	263	235	234	241	213	163	123
Concessional	..	0	1	1	0	0	0	0	0	0
Bilateral	..	12	9	37	43	47	62	42	32	29
Concessional	..	12	1	1	2	5	14	17	17	17
Private creditors	..	624	1,346	1,286	1,035	1,167	1,405	1,295	983	827
Bonds	..	3	242	490	572	878	1,129	1,139	898	761
Commercial banks	..	583	1,034	739	416	261	241	144	76	60
Other private	..	38	70	56	47	28	35	12	9	5
Private nonguaranteed	..	**0**	**0**	**29**	**32**	**52**	**166**	**68**	**337**	**319**
Bonds	..	0	0	0	0	0	0	0	0	1
Commercial banks	..	0	0	29	32	52	166	68	337	318
Memo:										
IBRD	0	0	106	139	147	157	160	141	102	70
IDA	0	0	0	0	0	0	0	0	0	0
NET TRANSFERS ON DEBT	..	**92**	**-1,407**	**-1,794**	**1,120**	**-111**	**868**	**-3,563**	**-2,898**	**270**
Public and publicly guaranteed	..	**92**	**-1,407**	**-2,082**	**616**	**-865**	**-667**	**-4,411**	**-3,033**	**-1,098**
Official creditors	..	120	396	-126	-182	-186	-435	-954	-287	-1,073
Multilateral	..	0	410	-181	-167	-201	-482	-790	-265	-1,103
Concessional	..	0	-1	-15	0	0	0	0	0	0
Bilateral	..	120	-14	55	-15	15	46	-164	-22	30
Concessional	..	120	1	35	40	96	176	72	18	27
Private creditors	..	-28	-1,804	-1,956	799	-679	-231	-3,457	-2,746	-25
Bonds	..	-3	679	487	2,726	1,377	964	-2,265	-2,110	-159
Commercial banks	..	5	-2,354	-2,292	-1,749	-1,801	-991	-1,136	-584	159
Other private	..	-30	-129	-152	-178	-255	-204	-56	-51	-25
Private nonguaranteed	..	**0**	**0**	**288**	**504**	**754**	**1,534**	**848**	**135**	**1,368**
Bonds	..	0	0	0	0	0	0	0	0	85
Commercial banks	..	0	0	288	504	754	1,534	848	135	1,284
Memo:										
IBRD	0	0	54	54	-62	-185	-223	-560	-135	-872
IDA	0	0	0	0	0	0	0	0	0	0
DEBT SERVICE (LTDS)	..	**1,460**	**3,751**	**4,561**	**4,201**	**5,271**	**6,019**	**7,988**	**7,539**	**6,947**
Public and publicly guaranteed	..	**1,460**	**3,751**	**4,359**	**3,883**	**4,611**	**4,816**	**6,403**	**4,196**	**4,340**
Official creditors	..	67	332	638	659	564	1,122	1,462	632	1,754
Multilateral	..	0	304	578	581	465	964	1,144	539	1,669
Concessional	..	0	1	15	0	0	0	0	0	0
Bilateral	..	67	29	60	78	99	158	317	93	85
Concessional	..	67	1	6	7	16	28	24	22	46
Private creditors	..	1,393	3,418	3,721	3,224	4,047	3,694	4,941	3,564	2,587
Bonds	..	3	261	1,012	1,076	1,458	2,138	2,779	2,546	2,408
Commercial banks	..	1,236	2,930	2,486	1,921	2,329	1,335	2,003	910	135
Other private	..	155	228	222	227	261	221	159	108	44
Private nonguaranteed	..	**0**	**0**	**203**	**318**	**660**	**1,203**	**1,585**	**3,344**	**2,607**
Bonds	..	0	0	0	0	0	0	0	0	1
Commercial banks	..	0	0	203	318	660	1,203	1,585	3,344	2,606
Memo:										
IBRD	0	0	214	264	292	353	411	656	319	1,241
IDA	0	0	0	0	0	0	0	0	0	0
UNDISBURSED DEBT	..	**930**	**3,031**	**2,859**	**3,292**	**2,611**	**2,862**	**1,465**	**1,296**	**1,051**
Official creditors	..	141	2,136	2,053	2,181	2,293	2,072	1,107	987	620
Private creditors	..	789	895	807	1,111	318	789	358	309	431
Memorandum items										
Concessional LDOD	..	542	33	51	98	229	415	461	439	525
Variable rate LDOD	..	2,553	10,893	9,705	9,193	10,172	11,029	9,596	9,455	11,485
Public sector LDOD	..	6,416	18,006	17,853	19,832	22,224	23,696	18,200	14,666	15,312
Private sector LDOD	..	0	0	684	1,295	2,513	4,307	5,478	6,313	8,488

6. CURRENCY COMPOSITION OF LONG-TERM DEBT (PERCENT)

	1970	1980	1990	1992	1993	1994	1995	1996	1997	1998
Deutsche mark	..	0.0	26.2	27.4	27.2	29.6	29.5	29.4	30.5	27.2
French franc	..	0.0	0.1	0.1	0.9	0.9	0.8	1.5	1.6	2.2
Japanese yen	..	2.9	25.3	29.8	32.5	31.6	34.6	37.7	37.4	32.9
Pound sterling	..	0.0	0.3	0.0	0.8	0.7	0.6	0.6	0.7	0.7
Swiss franc	..	0.0	3.9	1.6	1.8	1.9	2.6	2.6	2.9	2.9
U.S.dollars	..	1.8	18.5	14.0	13.5	11.3	10.7	10.7	18.7	15.0
Multiple currency	..	95.3	17.8	16.7	14.0	13.4	12.1	10.2	2.2	2.2
Special drawing rights	..	0.0	0.0	0.0	0.0	0.0	0.0	0.0	0.0	0.0
All other currencies	..	0.0	7.9	10.4	9.3	10.6	9.1	7.3	6.0	16.9

HUNGARY

(US$ million, unless otherwise indicated)

	1970	1980	1990	1992	1993	1994	1995	1996	1997	1998
7. DEBT RESTRUCTURINGS										
Total amount rescheduled	..	..	0	0	0	0	0	0	0	0
Debt stock rescheduled	..	..	0	0	0	0	0	0	0	0
Principal rescheduled	..	..	0	0	0	0	0	0	0	0
Official	..	..	0	0	0	0	0	0	0	0
Private	..	..	0	0	0	0	0	0	0	0
Interest rescheduled	..	..	0	0	0	0	0	0	0	0
Official	..	..	0	0	0	0	0	0	0	0
Private	..	..	0	0	0	0	0	0	0	0
Debt forgiven	..	..	0	0	0	0	0	0	0	0
Memo: interest forgiven	..	..	0	0	0	0	0	0	0	0
Debt stock reduction	..	..	0	0	0	0	0	0	0	0
of which debt buyback	..	..	0	0	0	0	0	0	0	0
8. DEBT STOCK-FLOW RECONCILIATION										
Total change in debt stocks	..	..	880	-603	2,336	3,911	3,315	-4,382	-2,712	4,084
Net flows on debt	..	903	-397	-77	2,212	1,618	2,755	-1,992	-1,385	2,829
Net change in interest arrears	..	..	0	0	0	0	0	0	0	0
Interest capitalized	..	..	0	0	0	0	0	0	0	0
Debt forgiveness or reduction	..	..	0	0	0	0	0	0	0	0
Cross-currency valuation	..	..	1,330	-519	251	2,028	628	-1,581	-1,412	1,054
Residual	..	..	-53	-6	-128	266	-68	-809	85	201
9. AVERAGE TERMS OF NEW COMMITMENTS										
ALL CREDITORS										
Interest (%)	..	9.8	8.9	8.0	7.4	7.6	6.4	5.4	4.2	5.4
Maturity (years)	..	13.2	9.9	9.6	9.0	7.8	10.3	8.6	9.2	7.0
Grace period (years)	..	3.0	5.1	6.5	7.6	6.3	9.1	5.1	5.0	5.8
Grant element (%)	..	-0.5	4.9	10.3	13.3	10.8	21.2	19.1	26.6	18.6
Official creditors										
Interest (%)	..	2.5	8.5	6.7	5.6	7.5	7.3	6.8	6.0	5.8
Maturity (years)	..	15.2	12.1	15.0	14.2	12.7	13.3	16.4	14.0	13.9
Grace period (years)	..	1.2	5.1	5.3	5.1	3.9	4.0	3.5	3.3	3.6
Grant element (%)	..	37.5	7.3	18.7	23.0	11.9	13.3	17.4	20.4	21.8
Private creditors										
Interest (%)	..	10.3	9.4	8.4	7.7	7.6	6.3	5.1	3.3	5.4
Maturity (years)	..	13.0	7.2	7.7	8.0	7.0	9.9	6.9	6.7	6.2
Grace period (years)	..	3.2	5.0	6.9	8.0	6.6	9.9	5.4	5.8	6.1
Grant element (%)	..	-3.1	2.0	7.3	11.6	10.6	22.4	19.5	29.7	18.2
Memorandum items										
Commitments	..	1,225	3,695	2,343	5,166	3,218	4,459	1,416	1,221	2,998
Official creditors	..	80	2,038	601	770	405	591	260	406	338
Private creditors	..	1,145	1,658	1,742	4,396	2,813	3,869	1,157	816	2,661

10. CONTRACTUAL OBLIGATIONS ON OUTSTANDING LONG-TERM DEBT

	1999	2000	2001	2002	2003	2004	2005	2006	2007	2008
TOTAL										
Disbursements	473	307	165	81	11	7	5	2	1	0
Principal	4,454	3,895	3,254	2,209	3,773	2,045	1,693	516	940	710
Interest	1,504	1,260	983	763	596	417	290	213	168	301
Official creditors										
Disbursements	217	185	120	73	11	7	5	2	1	0
Principal	192	240	263	288	279	261	263	246	214	291
Interest	154	157	148	136	119	103	87	71	56	44
Bilateral creditors										
Disbursements	58	35	20	10	4	2	1	0	0	0
Principal	90	106	109	109	95	86	86	82	64	42
Interest	39	39	35	30	25	20	16	11	7	4
Multilateral creditors										
Disbursements	158	150	100	63	6	5	4	2	1	0
Principal	102	134	155	179	184	175	177	164	150	250
Interest	115	118	114	106	95	83	71	60	49	39
Private creditors										
Disbursements	256	121	45	8	0	0	0	0	0	0
Principal	4,262	3,655	2,991	1,921	3,494	1,783	1,431	271	726	419
Interest	1,349	1,104	835	627	477	314	203	142	112	257
Commercial banks										
Disbursements	214	106	45	8	0	0	0	0	0	0
Principal	107	313	660	128	96	81	47	27	28	36
Interest	84	83	68	31	28	26	24	23	21	20
Other private										
Disbursements	42	15	0	0	0	0	0	0	0	0
Principal	4,155	3,343	2,331	1,793	3,397	1,702	1,383	244	698	382
Interest	1,265	1,020	767	597	449	288	179	119	91	237

INDIA

(US$ million, unless otherwise indicated)

	1970	*1980*	*1990*	*1992*	*1993*	*1994*	*1995*	*1996*	*1997*	*1998*
1. SUMMARY DEBT DATA										
TOTAL DEBT STOCKS (EDT)	**..**	**20,581**	**83,717**	**90,264**	**94,342**	**102,483**	**94,387**	**93,470**	**94,320**	**98,232**
Long-term debt (LDOD)	**7,936**	**18,333**	**72,550**	**79,126**	**85,676**	**93,907**	**86,964**	**85,431**	**88,610**	**93,616**
Public and publicly guaranteed	7,836	17,997	71,062	77,921	83,906	87,480	80,346	78,049	79,402	85,207
Private nonguaranteed	100	336	1,488	1,205	1,770	6,427	6,618	7,382	9,208	8,409
Use of IMF credit	**0**	**977**	**2,623**	**4,799**	**5,041**	**4,312**	**2,374**	**1,313**	**664**	**288**
Short-term debt	**..**	**1,271**	**8,544**	**6,340**	**3,626**	**4,264**	**5,049**	**6,726**	**5,046**	**4,329**
of which interest arrears on LDOD	..	0	0	0	0	0	0	0	0	0
Official creditors	..	0	0	0	0	0	0	0	0	0
Private creditors	..	0	0	0	0	0	0	0	0	0
Memo: principal arrears on LDOD	..	0	0	3	1	0	0	0	0	0
Official creditors	..	0	0	3	1	0	0	0	0	0
Private creditors	..	0	0	0	0	0	0	0	0	0
Memo: export credits	..	0	5,998	6,541	6,782	8,030	7,926	7,827	7,868	7,980
TOTAL DEBT FLOWS										
Disbursements	**908**	**3,473**	**8,344**	**8,982**	**8,744**	**7,552**	**7,140**	**6,682**	**7,620**	**10,728**
Long-term debt	908	2,450	6,590	7,359	8,421	7,552	7,140	6,682	7,620	10,728
IMF purchases	0	1,023	1,754	1,624	323	0	0	0	0	0
Principal repayments	**519**	**765**	**3,376**	**3,587**	**4,167**	**6,318**	**8,639**	**7,618**	**7,551**	**6,966**
Long-term debt	314	755	2,651	3,253	4,033	5,144	6,920	6,645	6,938	6,576
IMF repurchases	205	9	726	334	134	1,174	1,719	973	613	390
Net flows on debt	**672**	**3,281**	**6,011**	**4,665**	**1,863**	**1,872**	**-714**	**742**	**-1,610**	**3,044**
of which short-term debt	..	573	1,043	-730	-2,714	638	785	1,677	-1,680	-717
Interest payments (INT)	**..**	**642**	**4,815**	**4,110**	**4,178**	**4,633**	**4,911**	**4,365**	**4,864**	**5,118**
Long-term debt	193	503	3,782	3,440	3,539	4,093	4,344	4,010	4,465	4,767
IMF charges	0	4	134	271	271	228	182	87	50	25
Short-term debt	..	134	899	399	367	312	385	268	349	327
Net transfers on debt	**..**	**2,639**	**1,196**	**555**	**-2,315**	**-2,761**	**-5,625**	**-3,623**	**-6,475**	**-2,074**
Total debt service paid (TDS)	**..**	**1,407**	**8,191**	**7,697**	**8,345**	**10,951**	**13,550**	**11,982**	**12,415**	**12,085**
Long-term debt	507	1,259	6,433	6,693	7,572	9,237	11,265	10,655	11,403	11,343
IMF repurchases and charges	205	14	859	605	405	1,402	1,901	1,059	663	415
Short-term debt (interest only)	..	134	899	399	367	312	385	268	349	327
2. AGGREGATE NET RESOURCE FLOWS AND NET TRANSFERS (LONG-TERM)										
NET RESOURCE FLOWS	**787**	**2,422**	**4,719**	**5,204**	**7,264**	**8,722**	**4,438**	**7,450**	**6,918**	**7,604**
Net flow of long-term debt (ex. IMF)	594	1,695	3,940	4,105	4,388	2,408	220	37	683	4,151
Foreign direct investment (net)	46	79	162	277	550	973	2,144	2,426	3,577	2,635
Portfolio equity flows	0	0	105	241	1,840	4,729	1,517	4,398	2,116	342
Grants (excluding technical coop.)	147	649	512	581	485	612	558	589	543	476
Memo: technical coop. grants	46	152	341	436	386	388	437	409	333	307
official net resource flows	753	1,554	2,846	3,123	2,240	1,581	-490	773	137	1,453
private net resource flows	34	868	1,873	2,081	5,025	7,140	4,929	6,677	6,781	6,151
NET TRANSFERS	**595**	**1,919**	**936**	**1,764**	**3,725**	**4,629**	**94**	**3,440**	**2,453**	**2,837**
Interest on long-term debt	193	503	3,782	3,440	3,539	4,093	4,344	4,010	4,465	4,767
Profit remittances on FDI	0	0	0	0	0	0	0	0	0	0
Memo: official net transfers	589	1,206	1,349	1,492	566	-265	-2,357	-907	-1,463	-101
private net transfers	6	713	-413	273	3,159	4,894	2,451	4,347	3,916	2,938
3. MAJOR ECONOMIC AGGREGATES										
Gross national product (GNP)	61,928	187,140	318,658	259,687	275,674	326,367	359,952	393,447	417,165	426,478
Exports of goods & services (XGS)	2,223	15,134	25,064	27,380	32,791	41,401	48,266	54,389	58,379	58,739
of which workers remittances	83	2,786	1,668	3,419	4,449	7,525	7,180	11,709	11,709	9,385
Imports of goods & services (MGS)	2,763	17,662	33,610	30,949	34,393	45,714	56,318	60,625	64,024	64,619
International reserves (RES)	1,023	12,010	5,637	9,539	14,675	24,221	22,865	24,889	28,385	30,647
Current account balance	-540	-2,454	-8,145	-3,116	-786	-3,745	-6,726	-5,578	-5,524	-4,984
4. DEBT INDICATORS										
EDT / XGS (%)	..	136.0	334.0	329.7	287.7	247.5	195.6	171.9	161.6	167.2
EDT / GNP (%)	..	11.0	26.3	34.8	34.2	31.4	26.2	23.8	22.6	23.0
TDS / XGS (%)	..	9.3	32.7	28.1	25.5	26.5	28.1	22.0	21.3	20.6
INT / XGS (%)	..	4.2	19.2	15.0	12.7	11.2	10.2	8.0	8.3	8.7
INT / GNP (%)	..	0.3	1.5	1.6	1.5	1.4	1.4	1.1	1.2	1.2
RES / EDT (%)	..	58.4	6.7	10.6	15.6	23.6	24.2	26.6	30.1	31.2
RES / MGS (months)	4.4	8.2	2.0	3.7	5.1	6.4	4.9	4.9	5.3	5.7
Short-term / EDT (%)	..	6.2	10.2	7.0	3.8	4.2	5.4	7.2	5.4	4.4
Concessional / EDT (%)	..	74.1	46.2	45.2	45.2	45.5	45.8	43.7	41.2	41.3
Multilateral / EDT (%)	..	29.5	26.0	29.0	29.5	30.7	31.8	31.4	31.2	31.1

INDIA

(US$ million, unless otherwise indicated)

	1970	1980	1990	1992	1993	1994	1995	1996	1997	1998
5. LONG-TERM DEBT										
DEBT OUTSTANDING (LDOD)	**7,936**	**18,333**	**72,550**	**79,126**	**85,676**	**93,907**	**86,964**	**85,431**	**88,610**	**93,616**
Public and publicly guaranteed	**7,836**	**17,997**	**71,062**	**77,921**	**83,906**	**87,480**	**80,346**	**78,049**	**79,402**	**85,207**
Official creditors	7,506	16,336	48,383	52,987	55,856	61,997	57,112	54,541	52,165	54,168
Multilateral	1,562	6,070	21,768	26,130	27,826	31,486	30,048	29,332	29,391	30,521
Concessional	1,065	5,244	13,657	15,673	16,301	18,009	17,814	17,939	18,230	18,875
Bilateral	5,945	10,266	26,615	26,857	28,029	30,511	27,065	25,209	22,775	23,647
Concessional	5,450	10,001	25,052	25,166	26,341	28,599	25,378	22,903	20,607	21,721
Private creditors	330	1,661	22,679	24,934	28,050	25,483	23,234	23,509	27,236	31,039
Bonds	2	2	2,639	4,021	3,832	3,740	3,257	1,364	1,948	6,002
Commercial banks	45	1,498	16,130	17,006	18,727	14,588	13,412	16,061	20,216	20,950
Other private	283	161	3,910	3,907	5,492	7,156	6,565	6,084	5,072	4,087
Private nonguaranteed	**100**	**336**	**1,488**	**1,205**	**1,770**	**6,427**	**6,618**	**7,382**	**9,208**	**8,409**
Bonds	0	0	0	0	794	1,158	1,020	2,433	3,802	3,647
Commercial banks	100	336	1,488	1,205	976	5,268	5,598	4,949	5,406	4,763
Memo:										
IBRD	496	827	7,685	9,067	9,870	11,120	9,849	8,769	8,138	7,993
IDA	1,065	5,142	13,312	15,339	15,978	17,666	17,499	17,616	17,912	18,562
DISBURSEMENTS	**908**	**2,450**	**6,590**	**7,359**	**8,421**	**7,552**	**7,140**	**6,682**	**7,620**	**10,728**
Public and publicly guaranteed	**883**	**2,165**	**6,376**	**7,105**	**7,361**	**6,685**	**5,961**	**5,897**	**5,734**	**10,228**
Official creditors	842	1,492	3,572	4,160	3,645	3,334	2,828	3,040	3,708	4,464
Multilateral	101	863	2,211	2,424	2,084	2,230	1,942	2,234	2,021	2,040
Concessional	60	689	785	1,192	675	979	736	924	856	885
Bilateral	741	629	1,361	1,736	1,561	1,104	886	806	1,687	2,424
Concessional	687	521	1,130	1,639	1,397	909	815	681	1,445	1,884
Private creditors	41	673	2,804	2,945	3,716	3,351	3,133	2,857	2,026	5,763
Bonds	0	0	427	0	0	0	86	275	650	4,234
Commercial banks	16	639	1,983	2,145	1,545	870	1,719	1,698	903	929
Other private	25	34	395	800	2,171	2,481	1,329	884	473	601
Private nonguaranteed	**25**	**285**	**214**	**254**	**1,060**	**867**	**1,179**	**785**	**1,886**	**500**
Bonds	0	0	0	0	794	367	520	785	1,371	300
Commercial banks	25	285	214	254	266	500	659	0	515	200
Memo:										
IBRD	41	174	1,219	852	1,216	741	589	686	542	534
IDA	60	652	762	1,186	669	966	729	906	830	866
PRINCIPAL REPAYMENTS	**314**	**755**	**2,651**	**3,253**	**4,033**	**5,144**	**6,920**	**6,645**	**6,938**	**6,576**
Public and publicly guaranteed	**289**	**664**	**2,332**	**2,947**	**3,538**	**5,021**	**6,764**	**6,405**	**6,645**	**6,285**
Official creditors	236	587	1,238	1,618	1,890	2,365	3,876	2,856	4,114	3,487
Multilateral	40	86	609	838	1,000	1,102	1,513	1,218	1,217	1,295
Concessional	0	15	128	171	192	212	245	252	274	313
Bilateral	196	500	629	780	890	1,263	2,364	1,638	2,897	2,192
Concessional	137	472	558	690	748	1,107	2,106	1,459	2,654	1,921
Private creditors	53	78	1,094	1,329	1,647	2,656	2,888	3,549	2,531	2,797
Bonds	0	0	280	206	338	404	311	1,242	2	264
Commercial banks	10	34	250	438	666	1,054	1,796	1,484	1,160	836
Other private	43	44	564	685	643	1,198	780	823	1,370	1,697
Private nonguaranteed	**25**	**91**	**318**	**306**	**495**	**123**	**156**	**240**	**293**	**292**
Bonds	0	0	0	0	0	0	0	0	150	149
Commercial banks	25	91	318	306	495	123	156	240	143	143
Memo:										
IBRD	40	71	472	634	758	827	943	840	820	842
IDA	0	15	114	155	174	194	226	234	250	288
NET FLOWS ON DEBT	**594**	**1,695**	**3,940**	**4,105**	**4,388**	**2,408**	**220**	**37**	**683**	**4,151**
Public and publicly guaranteed	**594**	**1,501**	**4,044**	**4,158**	**3,823**	**1,664**	**-803**	**-508**	**-911**	**3,943**
Official creditors	606	906	2,334	2,543	1,755	970	-1,048	184	-406	977
Multilateral	61	777	1,602	1,587	1,084	1,129	429	1,016	804	745
Concessional	60	674	657	1,021	483	767	492	672	583	572
Bilateral	545	129	732	956	670	-159	-1,477	-832	-1,210	232
Concessional	550	49	572	949	649	-198	-1,291	-779	-1,209	-38
Private creditors	-12	595	1,710	1,615	2,069	695	245	-692	-505	2,966
Bonds	0	0	147	-206	-338	-404	-226	-967	648	3,970
Commercial banks	6	605	1,733	1,707	879	-184	-77	214	-256	93
Other private	-18	-10	-170	115	1,528	1,283	548	61	-897	-1,097
Private nonguaranteed	**0**	**194**	**-104**	**-53**	**565**	**744**	**1,023**	**545**	**1,594**	**208**
Bonds	0	0	0	0	794	367	520	785	1,221	151
Commercial banks	0	194	-104	-53	-229	376	503	-240	373	58
Memo:										
IBRD	1	103	747	219	458	-86	-354	-154	-278	-307
IDA	60	637	648	1,030	495	773	503	672	580	579

INDIA

(US$ million, unless otherwise indicated)

	1970	1980	1990	1992	1993	1994	1995	1996	1997	1998
INTEREST PAYMENTS (LINT)	**193**	**503**	**3,782**	**3,440**	**3,539**	**4,093**	**4,344**	**4,010**	**4,465**	**4,767**
Public and publicly guaranteed	**187**	**473**	**3,647**	**3,317**	**3,400**	**3,702**	**3,813**	**3,584**	**4,292**	**4,300**
Official creditors	164	348	1,497	1,631	1,674	1,846	1,867	1,680	1,600	1,554
Multilateral	34	101	738	899	940	1,014	1,061	966	907	887
Concessional	7	35	101	112	118	124	135	135	136	139
Bilateral	130	247	759	732	733	832	806	714	693	667
Concessional	105	233	635	622	632	688	686	614	539	521
Private creditors	22	125	2,150	1,685	1,727	1,856	1,946	1,904	2,692	2,746
Bonds	0	0	182	230	258	221	183	573	99	118
Commercial banks	3	113	1,751	1,200	1,206	1,159	1,263	886	2,212	2,297
Other private	19	12	217	254	263	476	500	446	382	331
Private nonguaranteed	**6**	**30**	**135**	**123**	**139**	**391**	**531**	**426**	**173**	**467**
Bonds	0	0	0	0	1	20	56	88	154	265
Commercial banks	6	30	135	123	138	371	475	338	19	202
Memo:										
IBRD	27	66	615	709	721	768	770	674	590	536
IDA	7	35	97	109	114	121	131	130	131	135
NET TRANSFERS ON DEBT	**401**	**1,191**	**157**	**666**	**849**	**-1,685**	**-4,124**	**-3,973**	**-3,783**	**-615**
Public and publicly guaranteed	**407**	**1,027**	**397**	**841**	**423**	**-2,037**	**-4,616**	**-4,091**	**-5,203**	**-356**
Official creditors	441	557	837	911	81	-876	-2,915	-1,495	-2,005	-577
Multilateral	26	676	864	688	144	115	-632	50	-103	-142
Concessional	52	639	557	909	365	643	357	537	447	433
Bilateral	415	-118	-27	224	-63	-991	-2,283	-1,546	-1,903	-434
Concessional	446	-185	-63	328	17	-886	-1,977	-1,393	-1,748	-558
Private creditors	-34	470	-440	-70	342	-1,161	-1,701	-2,596	-3,198	220
Bonds	0	0	-35	-436	-596	-625	-409	-1,540	549	3,852
Commercial banks	3	492	-18	506	-327	-1,343	-1,340	-672	-2,468	-2,204
Other private	-37	-22	-387	-140	1,265	807	48	-385	-1,279	-1,428
Private nonguaranteed	**-6**	**164**	**-239**	**-176**	**426**	**353**	**492**	**119**	**1,420**	**-259**
Bonds	0	0	0	0	793	347	464	697	1,067	-114
Commercial banks	-6	164	-239	-176	-368	6	28	-578	353	-144
Memo:										
IBRD	-26	37	132	-490	-263	-853	-1,124	-828	-868	-844
IDA	52	602	551	922	381	651	372	542	449	444
DEBT SERVICE (LTDS)	**507**	**1,259**	**6,433**	**6,693**	**7,572**	**9,237**	**11,265**	**10,655**	**11,403**	**11,343**
Public and publicly guaranteed	**476**	**1,138**	**5,980**	**6,264**	**6,938**	**8,722**	**10,577**	**9,989**	**10,937**	**10,584**
Official creditors	400	935	2,735	3,249	3,564	4,211	5,743	4,536	5,713	5,041
Multilateral	74	187	1,347	1,736	1,940	2,116	2,573	2,184	2,123	2,182
Concessional	7	50	229	284	310	336	379	387	410	452
Bilateral	326	748	1,388	1,513	1,624	2,095	3,169	2,352	3,590	2,859
Concessional	242	705	1,193	1,312	1,380	1,795	2,792	2,073	3,193	2,442
Private creditors	75	203	3,245	3,015	3,374	4,512	4,834	5,453	5,224	5,543
Bonds	0	0	462	436	596	625	495	1,815	101	382
Commercial banks	12	147	2,001	1,639	1,872	2,213	3,059	2,370	3,371	3,133
Other private	63	56	782	939	906	1,673	1,280	1,269	1,751	2,028
Private nonguaranteed	**31**	**121**	**453**	**429**	**634**	**514**	**688**	**666**	**466**	**759**
Bonds	0	0	0	0	1	20	56	88	304	414
Commercial banks	31	121	453	429	633	494	631	578	162	344
Memo:										
IBRD	67	137	1,087	1,342	1,479	1,595	1,714	1,514	1,410	1,378
IDA	7	50	211	264	289	315	357	365	381	423
UNDISBURSED DEBT	**1,664**	**7,825**	**24,984**	**22,089**	**22,368**	**21,876**	**20,064**	**19,740**	**20,086**	**17,390**
Official creditors	1,502	6,928	22,410	18,887	18,363	19,172	18,548	18,114	17,247	14,893
Private creditors	162	898	2,574	3,203	4,005	2,704	1,517	1,626	2,839	2,496
Memorandum items										
Concessional LDOD	6,515	15,245	38,709	40,839	42,642	46,608	43,192	40,841	38,837	40,596
Variable rate LDOD	100	790	12,169	13,985	15,872	21,758	21,053	22,841	24,565	24,795
Public sector LDOD	7,512	17,583	70,524	77,403	83,383	86,952	79,887	77,399	78,857	84,441
Private sector LDOD	425	750	2,026	1,723	2,293	6,955	7,077	8,033	9,753	9,174

6. CURRENCY COMPOSITION OF LONG-TERM DEBT (PERCENT)

	1970	1980	1990	1992	1993	1994	1995	1996	1997	1998
Deutsche mark	9.7	10.0	6.0	6.4	6.0	6.8	6.6	6.0	5.3	5.9
French franc	1.3	2.3	1.7	2.0	1.8	2.0	2.1	1.9	1.8	1.8
Japanese yen	5.2	6.7	9.6	12.0	13.6	16.5	14.8	13.3	12.2	13.4
Pound sterling	24.7	26.8	6.1	5.4	4.9	4.5	4.7	4.3	4.1	3.7
Swiss franc	0.4	0.1	0.6	0.6	0.6	0.8	0.9	0.6	0.5	0.4
U.S.dollars	41.3	39.3	60.7	56.3	56.1	50.6	52.5	56.4	60.0	60.4
Multiple currency	6.3	6.4	11.0	13.1	13.5	15.1	14.8	14.0	13.0	11.7
Special drawing rights	0.0	0.0	0.3	0.3	0.2	0.2	0.2	0.2	0.2	0.2
All other currencies	11.1	8.4	4.0	3.9	3.3	3.5	3.4	3.3	2.9	2.5

INDIA

(US$ million, unless otherwise indicated)

	1970	1980	1990	1992	1993	1994	1995	1996	1997	1998
7. DEBT RESTRUCTURINGS										
Total amount rescheduled	..	..	0	0	0	0	0	0	0	0
Debt stock rescheduled	..	..	0	0	0	0	0	0	0	0
Principal rescheduled	..	..	0	0	0	0	0	0	0	0
Official	..	..	0	0	0	0	0	0	0	0
Private	..	..	0	0	0	0	0	0	0	0
Interest rescheduled	..	..	0	0	0	0	0	0	0	0
Official	..	..	0	0	0	0	0	0	0	0
Private	..	..	0	0	0	0	0	0	0	0
Debt forgiven	..	..	0	0	0	0	0	0	0	0
Memo: interest forgiven	..	..	0	0	0	0	0	0	0	0
Debt stock reduction	..	..	0	0	0	0	0	0	0	0
of which debt buyback	..	..	0	0	0	0	0	0	0	0
8. DEBT STOCK-FLOW RECONCILIATION										
Total change in debt stocks	..	..	8,310	4,843	4,078	8,140	-8,095	-917	850	3,912
Net flows on debt	672	3,281	6,011	4,665	1,863	1,872	-714	742	-1,610	3,044
Net change in interest arrears	..	..	0	0	0	0	0	0	0	0
Interest capitalized	..	..	0	0	0	0	0	0	0	0
Debt forgiveness or reduction	..	..	0	0	0	0	0	0	0	0
Cross-currency valuation	..	..	1,232	1,172	1,365	6,238	-3,935	-3,547	-1,657	1,156
Residual	..	..	1,066	-994	850	31	-3,447	1,888	4,118	-288
9. AVERAGE TERMS OF NEW COMMITMENTS										
ALL CREDITORS										
Interest (%)	2.5	5.6	5.2	5.0	5.9	3.9	3.5	4.5	4.9	6.3
Maturity (years)	34.1	32.5	22.5	23.3	19.1	25.0	25.3	20.3	19.8	12.6
Grace period (years)	8.2	7.4	7.8	6.8	5.2	8.0	8.1	6.9	6.7	5.8
Grant element (%)	0.0	0.8	8.3	8.0	4.2	7.5	12.1	3.6	9.4	22.4
Official creditors										
Interest (%)	2.2	2.5	3.8	3.5	4.0	3.5	3.3	3.8	3.8	3.6
Maturity (years)	35.5	40.7	28.8	29.6	26.6	27.2	27.2	28.0	27.0	25.9
Grace period (years)	8.5	8.6	8.4	6.7	7.1	8.6	8.4	8.2	7.8	7.4
Grant element (%)	0.0	0.0	0.0	8.5	0.8	8.4	13.4	5.7	6.7	49.6
Private creditors										
Interest (%)	6.3	14.0	6.7	7.2	7.8	7.0	5.1	5.7	6.5	7.4
Maturity (years)	12.9	10.7	15.6	14.2	11.5	8.2	6.9	7.6	10.0	7.3
Grace period (years)	4.5	4.0	7.1	6.9	3.4	3.6	5.2	4.8	5.1	5.2
Grant element (%)	0.0	2.9	17.5	7.2	7.7	0.0	0.0	0.0	13.2	11.7
Memorandum items										
Commitments	954	5,158	8,228	8,898	8,479	4,600	4,680	7,766	7,382	7,481
Official creditors	892	3,745	4,318	5,255	4,250	4,074	4,227	4,826	4,282	2,110
Private creditors	62	1,413	3,910	3,643	4,228	526	452	2,940	3,101	5,371

10. CONTRACTUAL OBLIGATIONS ON OUTSTANDING LONG-TERM DEBT

	1999	2000	2001	2002	2003	2004	2005	2006	2007	2008
TOTAL										
Disbursements	6,160	4,392	2,731	1,620	978	557	414	258	171	109
Principal	6,681	5,741	6,205	6,924	10,002	5,392	4,435	4,257	4,981	3,797
Interest	4,078	3,925	3,665	3,428	3,359	2,770	2,561	2,388	2,198	2,009
Official creditors										
Disbursements	4,787	3,628	2,477	1,546	946	557	414	258	171	109
Principal	2,926	3,163	3,070	3,195	3,361	3,233	3,138	3,131	3,074	2,993
Interest	1,644	1,624	1,544	1,463	1,364	1,255	1,150	1,045	955	855
Bilateral creditors										
Disbursements	2,418	1,585	897	472	217	95	36	1	0	0
Principal	1,401	1,516	1,361	1,441	1,527	1,396	1,325	1,335	1,337	1,352
Interest	676	684	643	614	571	525	484	446	422	386
Multilateral creditors										
Disbursements	2,369	2,044	1,580	1,074	730	462	378	257	171	109
Principal	1,525	1,647	1,709	1,754	1,834	1,837	1,813	1,797	1,737	1,642
Interest	968	940	901	849	793	730	666	599	533	469
Private creditors										
Disbursements	1,373	763	254	74	31	0	0	0	0	0
Principal	3,755	2,578	3,135	3,729	6,641	2,159	1,298	1,126	1,907	803
Interest	2,434	2,301	2,121	1,965	1,995	1,515	1,411	1,343	1,243	1,153
Commercial banks										
Disbursements	774	346	53	17	7	0	0	0	0	0
Principal	1,353	1,020	1,480	2,304	1,131	1,083	679	562	565	449
Interest	1,462	1,416	1,351	1,260	1,150	1,081	1,027	987	950	915
Other private										
Disbursements	599	417	201	57	25	0	0	0	0	0
Principal	2,402	1,558	1,656	1,424	5,510	1,076	619	564	1,342	354
Interest	972	885	770	706	846	434	384	356	293	238

INDONESIA

(US$ million, unless otherwise indicated)

	1970	1980	1990	1992	1993	1994	1995	1996	1997	1998
1. SUMMARY DEBT DATA										
TOTAL DEBT STOCKS (EDT)	..	**20,938**	**69,872**	**88,002**	**89,172**	**107,824**	**124,398**	**128,941**	**136,173**	**150,875**
Long-term debt (LDOD)	**2,948**	**18,163**	**58,242**	**69,945**	**71,185**	**88,367**	**98,432**	**96,710**	**100,338**	**121,672**
Public and publicly guaranteed	2,487	15,021	47,982	53,664	57,156	63,926	65,309	60,016	55,869	66,944
Private nonguaranteed	461	3,142	10,261	16,281	14,029	24,441	33,123	36,694	44,469	54,728
Use of IMF credit	**139**	**0**	**494**	**0**	**0**	**0**	**0**	**0**	**2,970**	**9,090**
Short-term debt	..	**2,775**	**11,135**	**18,057**	**17,987**	**19,457**	**25,966**	**32,230**	**32,865**	**20,113**
of which interest arrears on LDOD	..	0	0	0	0	0	0	0	0	0
Official creditors	..	0	0	0	0	0	0	0	0	0
Private creditors	..	0	0	0	0	0	0	0	0	0
Memo: principal arrears on LDOD	..	0	1	1	1	0	0	0	0	2,710
Official creditors	..	0	1	1	1	0	0	0	0	0
Private creditors	..	0	0	0	0	0	0	0	0	2,710
Memo: export credits	..	0	10,032	13,670	15,137	17,711	19,417	19,217	20,906	22,337
TOTAL DEBT FLOWS										
Disbursements	**674**	**3,246**	**10,024**	**13,533**	**8,084**	**12,547**	**13,629**	**20,973**	**22,462**	**16,657**
Long-term debt	636	3,246	10,024	13,533	8,084	12,547	13,629	20,973	19,433	10,885
IMF purchases	38	0	0	0	0	0	0	0	3,029	5,772
Principal repayments	**123**	**1,633**	**5,969**	**7,944**	**9,138**	**8,951**	**10,197**	**14,892**	**13,010**	**11,842**
Long-term debt	120	1,633	5,812	7,781	9,138	8,951	10,197	14,892	13,010	11,842
IMF repurchases	3	0	157	163	0	0	0	0	0	0
Net flows on debt	**890**	**2,280**	**7,216**	**9,331**	**-1,124**	**5,066**	**9,941**	**12,346**	**10,087**	**-4,935**
of which short-term debt	..	667	3,160	3,742	-70	1,470	6,509	6,264	635	-9,750
Interest payments (INT)	..	**1,452**	**3,978**	**4,513**	**4,951**	**5,316**	**6,219**	**6,647**	**6,726**	**7,125**
Long-term debt	46	1,182	3,413	3,771	4,112	4,174	4,935	5,114	5,116	5,619
IMF charges	0	0	59	5	0	0	0	0	0	182
Short-term debt	..	270	506	737	840	1,142	1,284	1,533	1,610	1,324
Net transfers on debt	..	**828**	**3,238**	**4,819**	**-6,075**	**-251**	**3,722**	**5,699**	**3,361**	**-12,060**
Total debt service paid (TDS)	..	**3,084**	**9,946**	**12,457**	**14,089**	**14,267**	**16,416**	**21,539**	**19,736**	**18,967**
Long-term debt	165	2,814	9,224	11,552	13,249	13,125	15,132	20,006	18,126	17,461
IMF repurchases and charges	3	0	216	168	0	0	0	0	0	182
Short-term debt (interest only)	..	270	506	737	840	1,142	1,284	1,533	1,610	1,324
2. AGGREGATE NET RESOURCE FLOWS AND NET TRANSFERS (LONG-TERM)										
NET RESOURCE FLOWS	**686**	**1,902**	**5,901**	**7,945**	**3,622**	**9,594**	**12,901**	**15,564**	**11,592**	**-808**
Net flow of long-term debt (ex. IMF)	517	1,613	4,213	5,752	-1,053	3,596	3,432	6,081	6,423	-957
Foreign direct investment (net)	83	180	1,093	1,777	2,004	2,109	4,348	6,194	4,677	-356
Portfolio equity flows	0	0	312	119	2,452	3,672	4,873	3,099	298	250
Grants (excluding technical coop.)	87	109	283	298	219	218	249	190	194	255
Memo: technical coop. grants	26	187	407	431	426	444	493	409	371	314
official net resource flows	441	915	2,666	3,395	2,563	1,849	1,378	-602	729	2,951
private net resource flows	245	987	3,235	4,550	1,059	7,745	11,523	16,167	10,863	-3,759
NET TRANSFERS	**513**	**-2,513**	**296**	**1,551**	**-3,067**	**2,620**	**4,967**	**7,050**	**3,176**	**-9,227**
Interest on long-term debt	46	1,182	3,413	3,771	4,112	4,174	4,935	5,114	5,116	5,619
Profit remittances on FDI	128	3,234	2,192	2,623	2,577	2,800	3,000	3,400	3,300	2,800
Memo: official net transfers	421	603	1,081	1,379	308	-633	-1,288	-3,008	-1,366	902
private net transfers	92	-3,116	-785	173	-3,375	3,253	6,255	10,058	4,542	-10,129
3. MAJOR ECONOMIC AGGREGATES										
Gross national product (GNP)	9,698	74,806	109,209	132,938	151,992	170,284	192,474	221,277	209,438	85,486
Exports of goods & services (XGS)	..	..	29,870	38,234	41,940	46,517	54,880	58,793	65,819	57,470
of which workers remittances	..	..	166	229	346	449	651	796	725	710
Imports of goods & services (MGS)	..	..	33,110	41,356	44,237	49,479	61,641	66,597	71,017	53,877
International reserves (RES)	160	6,803	8,657	11,482	12,474	13,321	14,908	19,396	17,487	23,606
Current account balance	..	..	-2,988	-2,780	-2,106	-2,792	-6,431	-7,663	-4,889	3,972
4. DEBT INDICATORS										
EDT / XGS (%)	..	..	233.9	230.2	212.6	231.8	226.7	219.3	206.9	262.5
EDT / GNP (%)	..	28.0	64.0	66.2	58.7	63.3	64.6	58.3	65.0	176.5
TDS / XGS (%)	..	..	33.3	32.6	33.6	30.7	29.9	36.6	30.0	33.0
INT / XGS (%)	..	..	13.3	11.8	11.8	11.4	11.3	11.3	10.2	12.4
INT / GNP (%)	..	1.9	3.6	3.4	3.3	3.1	3.2	3.0	3.2	8.3
RES / EDT (%)	..	32.5	12.4	13.1	14.0	12.4	12.0	15.0	12.8	15.7
RES / MGS (months)	..	..	3.1	3.3	3.4	3.2	2.9	3.5	3.0	5.3
Short-term / EDT (%)	..	13.3	15.9	20.5	20.2	18.1	20.9	25.0	24.1	13.3
Concessional / EDT (%)	..	36.4	26.4	24.9	27.2	25.8	22.5	20.3	17.7	18.4
Multilateral / EDT (%)	..	8.8	20.4	18.7	20.0	17.8	16.1	13.4	11.6	11.9

INDONESIA

(US$ million, unless otherwise indicated)

	1970	1980	1990	1992	1993	1994	1995	1996	1997	1998
5. LONG-TERM DEBT										
DEBT OUTSTANDING (LDOD)	**2,948**	**18,163**	**58,242**	**69,945**	**71,185**	**88,367**	**98,432**	**96,710**	**100,338**	**121,672**
Public and publicly guaranteed	**2,487**	**15,021**	**47,982**	**53,664**	**57,156**	**63,926**	**65,309**	**60,016**	**55,869**	**66,944**
Official creditors	2,206	9,563	33,007	40,024	44,263	49,968	51,250	46,148	42,524	48,717
Multilateral	6	1,834	14,285	16,424	17,822	19,165	20,013	17,248	15,799	17,892
Concessional	6	661	1,369	1,500	1,557	1,637	1,668	1,663	1,581	1,652
Bilateral	2,200	7,729	18,722	23,600	26,441	30,804	31,237	28,899	26,725	30,825
Concessional	1,981	6,961	17,088	20,431	22,671	26,226	26,304	24,485	22,509	26,166
Private creditors	281	5,458	14,975	13,640	12,893	13,958	14,059	13,868	13,345	18,226
Bonds	0	199	696	580	99	99	704	1,141	1,191	1,191
Commercial banks	1	2,431	8,606	8,076	7,631	7,426	6,714	5,996	5,884	11,007
Other private	280	2,828	5,673	4,984	5,163	6,434	6,642	6,732	6,270	6,028
Private nonguaranteed	**461**	**3,142**	**10,261**	**16,281**	**14,029**	**24,441**	**33,123**	**36,694**	**44,469**	**54,728**
Bonds	0	0	120	751	1,233	1,750	3,420	6,666	9,661	9,596
Commercial banks	461	3,142	10,141	15,530	12,796	22,692	29,703	30,029	34,808	45,132
Memo:										
IBRD	0	1,040	9,542	10,640	11,283	12,008	12,503	11,139	9,991	10,692
IDA	5	566	842	814	796	776	756	736	715	694
DISBURSEMENTS	**636**	**3,246**	**10,024**	**13,533**	**8,084**	**12,547**	**13,629**	**20,973**	**19,433**	**10,885**
Public and publicly guaranteed	**441**	**2,551**	**5,009**	**7,830**	**6,889**	**7,627**	**6,665**	**7,532**	**6,304**	**7,670**
Official creditors	376	1,130	3,969	5,075	4,477	4,915	4,254	3,961	3,960	5,239
Multilateral	4	431	1,794	1,648	1,871	1,854	1,777	1,696	1,586	2,369
Concessional	4	48	145	63	64	61	80	103	35	47
Bilateral	372	698	2,175	3,427	2,606	3,061	2,477	2,266	2,374	2,870
Concessional	372	592	1,979	2,046	1,755	2,261	1,923	1,841	1,657	2,476
Private creditors	66	1,421	1,041	2,755	2,412	2,711	2,411	3,571	2,344	2,432
Bonds	0	45	0	0	0	0	605	510	50	0
Commercial banks	0	1,013	487	1,723	1,128	831	938	1,784	1,351	2,137
Other private	66	363	554	1,031	1,284	1,880	869	1,277	943	295
Private nonguaranteed	**195**	**695**	**5,015**	**5,703**	**1,195**	**4,920**	**6,963**	**13,441**	**13,129**	**3,215**
Bonds	0	0	120	244	485	495	1,763	3,531	3,378	500
Commercial banks	195	695	4,895	5,460	710	4,425	5,200	9,910	9,751	2,715
Memo:										
IBRD	0	331	987	1,003	1,195	1,184	1,045	905	899	1,212
IDA	3	42	0	0	0	0	0	0	0	0
PRINCIPAL REPAYMENTS	**120**	**1,633**	**5,812**	**7,781**	**9,138**	**8,951**	**10,197**	**14,892**	**13,010**	**11,842**
Public and publicly guaranteed	**59**	**940**	**4,588**	**5,183**	**5,691**	**5,546**	**5,715**	**8,123**	**5,701**	**4,801**
Official creditors	22	324	1,586	1,978	2,133	3,284	3,125	4,753	3,425	2,542
Multilateral	0	38	677	872	1,008	1,888	1,289	2,980	1,671	989
Concessional	0	4	24	32	36	43	46	47	44	51
Bilateral	22	286	909	1,106	1,125	1,396	1,837	1,774	1,754	1,554
Concessional	19	184	611	816	769	1,037	1,271	1,211	1,207	1,109
Private creditors	37	616	3,001	3,205	3,558	2,262	2,589	3,370	2,276	2,259
Bonds	0	5	94	88	477	0	0	73	0	0
Commercial banks	1	190	1,718	1,912	1,946	1,188	1,678	2,342	1,379	1,613
Other private	37	421	1,190	1,205	1,135	1,074	911	955	897	646
Private nonguaranteed	**61**	**693**	**1,224**	**2,598**	**3,447**	**3,405**	**4,483**	**6,768**	**7,309**	**7,041**
Bonds	0	0	0	0	0	0	120	225	309	641
Commercial banks	61	693	1,224	2,598	3,447	3,405	4,363	6,543	7,000	6,400
Memo:										
IBRD	0	31	551	677	765	1,240	955	1,408	1,145	733
IDA	0	1	11	15	18	20	20	20	20	21
NET FLOWS ON DEBT	**517**	**1,613**	**4,213**	**5,752**	**-1,053**	**3,596**	**3,432**	**6,081**	**6,423**	**-957**
Public and publicly guaranteed	**383**	**1,611**	**422**	**2,647**	**1,198**	**2,081**	**951**	**-591**	**603**	**2,869**
Official creditors	354	806	2,382	3,097	2,344	1,631	1,129	-792	535	2,696
Multilateral	4	393	1,117	776	863	-34	488	-1,284	-85	1,380
Concessional	4	44	122	31	28	18	34	57	-9	-4
Bilateral	350	413	1,265	2,321	1,481	1,666	641	492	620	1,316
Concessional	353	409	1,368	1,229	986	1,224	652	630	450	1,367
Private creditors	28	805	-1,961	-451	-1,146	449	-178	201	68	173
Bonds	0	40	-94	-88	-477	0	605	438	50	0
Commercial banks	0	823	-1,231	-189	-818	-357	-740	-558	-28	524
Other private	29	-58	-636	-174	149	806	-43	322	46	-350
Private nonguaranteed	**134**	**2**	**3,791**	**3,105**	**-2,252**	**1,515**	**2,481**	**6,673**	**5,821**	**-3,826**
Bonds	0	0	120	244	485	495	1,643	3,306	3,070	-141
Commercial banks	134	2	3,671	2,862	-2,737	1,020	838	3,366	2,751	-3,685
Memo:										
IBRD	0	301	436	327	430	-56	90	-503	-245	479
IDA	3	40	-11	-15	-18	-20	-20	-20	-20	-21

INDONESIA

(US$ million, unless otherwise indicated)

	1970	1980	1990	1992	1993	1994	1995	1996	1997	1998
INTEREST PAYMENTS (LINT)	**46**	**1,182**	**3,413**	**3,771**	**4,112**	**4,174**	**4,935**	**5,114**	**5,116**	**5,619**
Public and publicly guaranteed	**25**	**824**	**2,808**	**2,994**	**3,233**	**3,248**	**3,773**	**3,620**	**3,215**	**2,988**
Official creditors	20	312	1,585	2,016	2,255	2,482	2,666	2,406	2,095	2,049
Multilateral	0	107	990	1,202	1,273	1,395	1,403	1,238	1,020	1,039
Concessional	0	7	16	23	25	25	26	29	26	24
Bilateral	20	205	595	814	982	1,087	1,263	1,167	1,075	1,010
Concessional	18	130	451	617	709	777	875	807	745	706
Private creditors	5	512	1,223	978	978	767	1,108	1,214	1,120	939
Bonds	0	14	62	38	28	5	6	76	130	107
Commercial banks	0	268	699	532	564	372	656	687	593	462
Other private	5	230	462	408	387	389	446	451	397	370
Private nonguaranteed	**21**	**358**	**605**	**777**	**879**	**926**	**1,161**	**1,495**	**1,901**	**2,631**
Bonds	0	0	0	32	41	91	139	276	551	878
Commercial banks	21	358	605	745	838	835	1,022	1,218	1,350	1,753
Memo:										
IBRD	0	89	731	838	855	917	921	841	704	723
IDA	0	4	6	6	6	6	6	6	6	5
NET TRANSFERS ON DEBT	**471**	**431**	**800**	**1,981**	**-5,165**	**-579**	**-1,503**	**967**	**1,308**	**-6,576**
Public and publicly guaranteed	**358**	**787**	**-2,386**	**-347**	**-2,034**	**-1,168**	**-2,823**	**-4,211**	**-2,612**	**-119**
Official creditors	334	494	798	1,081	89	-850	-1,537	-3,198	-1,560	647
Multilateral	4	286	128	-426	-410	-1,429	-915	-2,522	-1,105	341
Concessional	4	37	105	8	3	-8	8	28	-35	-28
Bilateral	330	207	670	1,507	500	579	-622	-675	-455	306
Concessional	335	278	917	613	278	447	-223	-177	-295	661
Private creditors	24	294	-3,184	-1,428	-2,124	-317	-1,286	-1,013	-1,052	-766
Bonds	0	26	-156	-126	-504	-5	599	362	-80	-107
Commercial banks	0	555	-1,930	-721	-1,382	-730	-1,396	-1,245	-621	62
Other private	24	-288	-1,098	-582	-238	417	-488	-129	-351	-721
Private nonguaranteed	**113**	**-356**	**3,186**	**2,328**	**-3,131**	**589**	**1,319**	**5,178**	**3,919**	**-6,457**
Bonds	0	0	120	211	444	404	1,504	3,030	2,518	-1,019
Commercial banks	113	-356	3,066	2,117	-3,575	185	-185	2,148	1,401	-5,439
Memo:										
IBRD	0	212	-294	-512	-424	-972	-831	-1,344	-949	-244
IDA	3	36	-18	-22	-24	-26	-26	-26	-26	-26
DEBT SERVICE (LTDS)	**165**	**2,814**	**9,224**	**11,552**	**13,249**	**13,125**	**15,132**	**20,006**	**18,126**	**17,461**
Public and publicly guaranteed	**83**	**1,763**	**7,395**	**8,177**	**8,923**	**8,794**	**9,488**	**11,743**	**8,916**	**7,789**
Official creditors	42	636	3,171	3,994	4,388	5,765	5,791	7,159	5,519	4,591
Multilateral	0	145	1,667	2,074	2,281	3,283	2,692	4,218	2,691	2,028
Concessional	0	11	40	55	61	68	72	76	70	75
Bilateral	42	491	1,504	1,921	2,107	2,483	3,099	2,941	2,828	2,564
Concessional	37	314	1,062	1,433	1,478	1,814	2,146	2,018	1,953	1,815
Private creditors	42	1,127	4,225	4,183	4,535	3,029	3,697	4,584	3,396	3,198
Bonds	0	19	156	126	504	5	6	148	130	107
Commercial banks	1	458	2,417	2,444	2,510	1,561	2,334	3,029	1,972	2,075
Other private	41	651	1,652	1,613	1,521	1,463	1,357	1,407	1,294	1,016
Private nonguaranteed	**82**	**1,051**	**1,829**	**3,375**	**4,326**	**4,331**	**5,644**	**8,263**	**9,210**	**9,672**
Bonds	0	0	0	32	41	91	259	501	860	1,519
Commercial banks	82	1,051	1,829	3,342	4,285	4,240	5,385	7,762	8,350	8,153
Memo:										
IBRD	0	120	1,282	1,515	1,620	2,156	1,875	2,249	1,848	1,456
IDA	0	5	18	22	24	26	26	26	26	26
UNDISBURSED DEBT	**499**	**9,483**	**20,410**	**19,365**	**20,698**	**21,383**	**25,023**	**23,702**	**19,354**	**15,509**
Official creditors	482	7,060	14,369	14,989	15,779	16,697	19,045	18,663	15,533	14,546
Private creditors	16	2,422	6,041	4,376	4,919	4,687	5,978	5,039	3,821	963
Memorandum items										
Concessional LDOD	1,987	7,622	18,457	21,932	24,228	27,864	27,971	26,148	24,090	27,817
Variable rate LDOD	461	5,574	25,978	33,664	32,247	44,171	54,087	56,594	63,633	77,545
Public sector LDOD	2,485	15,021	47,982	53,664	57,156	63,926	65,309	60,016	55,869	66,944
Private sector LDOD	463	3,142	10,261	16,281	14,029	24,441	33,123	36,694	44,469	54,728

6. CURRENCY COMPOSITION OF LONG-TERM DEBT (PERCENT)

	1970	1980	1990	1992	1993	1994	1995	1996	1997	1998
Deutsche mark	3.9	7.8	5.0	4.7	4.1	4.8	4.9	4.8	4.7	4.3
French franc	4.5	4.0	3.4	3.7	3.3	3.3	3.7	3.7	3.3	2.8
Japanese yen	11.5	20.0	34.6	36.4	37.6	38.0	35.3	34.5	32.9	32.6
Pound sterling	2.2	0.8	1.4	1.0	0.9	0.9	0.8	1.2	1.8	1.6
Swiss franc	0.9	0.7	0.4	0.4	0.5	0.7	0.7	0.8	0.8	0.6
U.S.dollars	36.1	43.5	20.9	19.9	19.9	20.0	21.5	24.3	27.2	47.3
Multiple currency	0.0	8.6	27.3	27.6	28.0	26.7	27.2	24.7	23.3	5.4
Special drawing rights	0.0	0.0	0.0	0.0	0.0	0.0	0.0	0.0	0.1	0.1
All other currencies	40.9	14.6	7.0	6.3	5.7	5.6	5.9	6.0	5.9	5.3

INDONESIA

(US$ million, unless otherwise indicated)

	1970	1980	1990	1992	1993	1994	1995	1996	1997	1998
7. DEBT RESTRUCTURINGS										
Total amount rescheduled	..	..	0	0	0	0	0	0	0	3,533
Debt stock rescheduled	..	..	0	0	0	0	0	0	0	3,002
Principal rescheduled	..	..	0	0	0	0	0	0	0	491
Official	..	..	0	0	0	0	0	0	0	302
Private	..	..	0	0	0	0	0	0	0	189
Interest rescheduled	..	..	0	0	0	0	0	0	0	0
Official	..	..	0	0	0	0	0	0	0	0
Private	..	..	0	0	0	0	0	0	0	0
Debt forgiven	..	..	0	0	0	0	0	0	0	0
Memo: interest forgiven	..	..	0	0	0	0	0	0	0	0
Debt stock reduction	..	..	0	0	0	0	0	0	0	0
of which debt buyback	..	..	0	0	0	0	0	0	0	0
8. DEBT STOCK-FLOW RECONCILIATION										
Total change in debt stocks	..	..	10,470	8,454	1,170	18,652	16,574	4,542	7,233	14,702
Net flows on debt	890	2,280	7,216	9,331	-1,124	5,066	9,941	12,346	10,087	-4,935
Net change in interest arrears	..	..	0	0	0	0	0	0	0	0
Interest capitalized	..	..	0	0	0	0	0	0	0	0
Debt forgiveness or reduction	..	..	0	0	0	0	0	0	0	0
Cross-currency valuation	..	..	3,266	-1,148	2,741	6,435	333	-6,562	-7,278	6,862
Residual	..	..	-12	271	-448	7,151	6,301	-1,241	4,423	12,774
9. AVERAGE TERMS OF NEW COMMITMENTS										
ALL CREDITORS										
Interest (%)	2.6	8.1	6.0	5.8	5.4	5.2	5.7	5.4	5.6	4.9
Maturity (years)	34.1	19.5	21.1	19.5	19.5	19.9	17.6	19.2	16.2	17.7
Grace period (years)	9.0	5.6	6.0	5.3	5.2	5.6	5.1	6.1	4.7	5.1
Grant element (%)	59.8	17.6	28.3	26.7	29.1	30.9	27.1	29.8	24.2	30.0
Official creditors										
Interest (%)	2.4	5.4	5.6	5.2	4.9	4.9	5.1	4.8	6.3	4.9
Maturity (years)	35.9	25.2	23.1	21.8	23.3	23.1	21.3	23.4	19.5	17.7
Grace period (years)	9.5	7.2	6.6	6.3	6.6	6.4	5.8	6.7	4.9	5.1
Grant element (%)	62.9	36.2	32.8	33.3	36.9	35.9	33.3	37.0	22.7	30.0
Private creditors										
Interest (%)	6.0	12.0	7.6	7.1	6.2	6.0	6.8	6.6	4.9	0.0
Maturity (years)	8.1	11.4	14.0	15.0	13.6	12.1	10.9	11.5	12.4	0.0
Grace period (years)	2.0	3.3	4.2	3.2	3.0	3.4	3.9	5.0	4.6	0.0
Grant element (%)	14.1	-9.2	12.8	14.1	17.3	18.3	15.5	16.6	26.0	0.0
Memorandum items										
Commitments	520	4,277	6,691	7,878	8,137	7,712	10,954	7,796	3,432	6,608
Official creditors	487	2,524	5,190	5,185	4,923	5,495	7,108	5,057	1,816	6,608
Private creditors	33	1,753	1,502	2,693	3,214	2,217	3,846	2,738	1,615	0

10. CONTRACTUAL OBLIGATIONS ON OUTSTANDING LONG-TERM DEBT

	1999	2000	2001	2002	2003	2004	2005	2006	2007	2008
TOTAL										
Disbursements	5,771	4,422	2,777	1,250	623	298	159	7	4	1
Principal	13,867	19,340	17,599	13,350	9,499	7,587	7,978	6,967	7,500	3,631
Interest	7,001	6,657	5,439	4,361	3,642	3,172	2,691	2,164	4,038	1,246
Official creditors										
Disbursements	5,264	4,205	2,740	1,245	622	298	159	7	4	1
Principal	2,824	3,519	4,089	4,792	4,471	4,041	3,893	3,816	3,616	3,456
Interest	2,462	2,534	2,492	2,350	2,133	1,915	1,707	1,509	1,313	1,131
Bilateral creditors										
Disbursements	2,080	1,638	988	562	288	137	56	0	0	0
Principal	1,477	2,052	2,463	2,781	2,451	2,074	2,017	2,010	1,898	1,843
Interest	1,074	1,077	1,028	952	854	766	688	615	543	479
Multilateral creditors										
Disbursements	3,184	2,567	1,752	683	334	161	103	7	4	1
Principal	1,347	1,466	1,626	2,011	2,020	1,967	1,876	1,806	1,719	1,613
Interest	1,388	1,456	1,465	1,398	1,279	1,149	1,020	894	770	652
Private creditors										
Disbursements	507	216	37	5	2	0	0	0	0	0
Principal	11,043	15,821	13,511	8,558	5,028	3,547	4,085	3,151	3,884	176
Interest	4,539	4,124	2,947	2,011	1,509	1,257	984	655	2,725	114
Commercial banks										
Disbursements	426	175	25	1	0	0	0	0	0	0
Principal	3,135	2,489	2,631	1,127	421	758	694	78	61	31
Interest	836	427	269	155	99	44	27	15	10	7
Other private										
Disbursements	81	42	12	4	2	0	0	0	0	0
Principal	7,908	13,332	10,879	7,430	4,607	2,789	3,390	3,073	3,822	145
Interest	3,703	3,697	2,678	1,856	1,410	1,213	957	641	2,715	107

IRAN, ISLAMIC REPUBLIC OF

(US$ million, unless otherwise indicated)

	1970	1980	1990	1992	1993	1994	1995	1996	1997	1998
1. SUMMARY DEBT DATA										
TOTAL DEBT STOCKS (EDT)	..	**4,500**	**9,021**	**16,084**	**23,502**	**22,634**	**21,879**	**16,703**	**11,823**	**14,391**
Long-term debt (LDOD)	..	**4,500**	**1,797**	**1,780**	**5,899**	**15,922**	**15,430**	**11,948**	**8,469**	**8,307**
Public and publicly guaranteed	..	4,500	1,797	1,780	5,899	15,530	15,116	11,712	8,263	7,679
Private nonguaranteed	..	0	0	0	0	392	314	236	207	628
Use of IMF credit	**0**	**0**	**0**	**0**	**0**	**0**	**0**	**0**	**0**	**0**
Short-term debt	..	**0**	**7,224**	**14,304**	**17,604**	**6,712**	**6,449**	**4,755**	**3,354**	**6,084**
of which interest arrears on LDOD	..	0	456	4	4	5	6	1	1	1
Official creditors	..	0	6	0	0	0	2	0	0	0
Private creditors	..	0	449	4	4	5	5	1	1	1
Memo: principal arrears on LDOD	..	1	1,517	37	37	50	48	33	38	113
Official creditors	..	1	29	0	0	0	0	0	0	0
Private creditors	..	0	1,488	37	37	50	48	33	38	113
Memo: export credits	..	0	7,826	8,677	9,112	13,474	12,673	11,550	9,768	8,790
TOTAL DEBT FLOWS										
Disbursements	..	**264**	**139**	**1,411**	**1,729**	**1,874**	**979**	**945**	**907**	**1,761**
Long-term debt	..	264	139	1,411	1,729	1,874	979	945	907	1,761
IMF purchases	0	0	0	0	0	0	0	0	0	0
Principal repayments	..	**527**	**225**	**193**	**389**	**2,388**	**4,198**	**5,153**	**5,295**	**2,140**
Long-term debt	..	527	225	193	389	2,388	4,198	5,153	5,295	2,140
IMF repurchases	0	0	0	0	0	0	0	0	0	0
Net flows on debt	..	**-263**	**2,480**	**6,704**	**7,425**	**-621**	**-305**	**-4,093**	**-5,789**	**2,351**
of which short-term debt	..	0	2,566	5,485	6,086	-108	2,914	116	-1,401	2,730
Interest payments (INT)	..	**431**	**430**	**878**	**1,414**	**905**	**1,627**	**1,380**	**980**	**801**
Long-term debt	..	431	28	93	182	273	1,132	1,113	792	527
IMF charges	0	0	0	0	0	0	0	0	0	0
Short-term debt	..	0	402	785	1,232	632	494	267	188	274
Net transfers on debt	..	**-694**	**2,050**	**5,825**	**6,011**	**-1,526**	**-1,931**	**-5,472**	**-6,769**	**1,550**
Total debt service paid (TDS)	..	**959**	**655**	**1,071**	**1,803**	**3,293**	**5,824**	**6,533**	**6,275**	**2,942**
Long-term debt	..	959	253	286	571	2,661	5,330	6,266	6,087	2,667
IMF repurchases and charges	0	0	0	0	0	0	0	0	0	0
Short-term debt (interest only)	..	0	402	785	1,232	632	494	267	188	274
2. AGGREGATE NET RESOURCE FLOWS AND NET TRANSFERS (LONG-TERM)										
NET RESOURCE FLOWS	..	**-262**	**-371**	**1,273**	**1,384**	**-455**	**-3,161**	**-4,140**	**-4,278**	**-325**
Net flow of long-term debt (ex. IMF)	..	-263	-86	1,219	1,339	-513	-3,219	-4,209	-4,388	-379
Foreign direct investment (net)	..	0	-362	0	0	2	17	26	53	24
Portfolio equity flows	..	0	0	0	0	0	0	0	0	0
Grants (excluding technical coop.)	..	1	76	55	45	56	41	42	57	29
Memo: technical coop. grants	..	19	99	110	113	92	106	102	81	94
official net resource flows	..	-84	21	103	130	-1,509	-3,063	-3,696	-3,983	-1,145
private net resource flows	..	-178	-392	1,170	1,254	1,054	-98	-444	-295	588
NET TRANSFERS	..	**-1,091**	**-477**	**1,023**	**1,202**	**-729**	**-4,293**	**-5,253**	**-5,069**	**-853**
Interest on long-term debt	..	431	28	93	182	273	1,132	1,113	792	527
Profit remittances on FDI	..	398	78	157	0	0	0	0	0	0
Memo: official net transfers	..	-149	7	91	101	-1,534	-3,850	-4,567	-4,509	-1,461
private net transfers	..	-942	-485	932	1,101	805	-443	-686	-561	376
3. MAJOR ECONOMIC AGGREGATES										
Gross national product (GNP)	..	93,270	120,782	..	80,734	67,043	71,485	88,395	108,070	113,140
Exports of goods & services (XGS)	..	14,073	20,197	20,714	19,315	20,014	19,269	23,739	20,039	14,527
of which workers remittances	..	0	0	0	0	0	0	0	0	0
Imports of goods & services (MGS)	..	16,509	22,370	29,214	25,030	16,256	15,907	18,970	18,219	16,921
International reserves (RES)	..	12,783	..	..	..	..	..	..	..	..
Current account balance	..	-2,438	327	-6,504	-4,215	4,956	3,358	5,232	2,213	-1,897
4. DEBT INDICATORS										
EDT / XGS (%)	..	32.0	44.7	77.7	121.7	113.1	113.6	70.4	59.0	99.1
EDT / GNP (%)	..	4.8	7.5	..	29.1	33.8	30.6	18.9	10.9	12.7
TDS / XGS (%)	..	6.8	3.2	5.2	9.3	16.5	30.2	27.5	31.3	20.3
INT / XGS (%)	..	3.1	2.1	4.2	7.3	4.5	8.4	5.8	4.9	5.5
INT / GNP (%)	..	0.5	0.4	..	1.8	1.4	2.3	1.6	0.9	0.7
RES / EDT (%)	..	284.0	..	..	..	..	..	..	..	..
RES / MGS (months)	..	9.3	..	..	..	..	..	..	..	..
Short-term / EDT (%)	..	0.0	80.1	88.9	74.9	29.7	29.5	28.5	28.4	42.3
Concessional / EDT (%)	..	5.9	1.2	0.4	0.2	0.8	1.7	2.7	5.3	4.2
Multilateral / EDT (%)	..	13.8	1.3	0.9	0.9	1.4	1.7	3.2	4.5	3.6

IRAN, ISLAMIC REPUBLIC OF

(US$ million, unless otherwise indicated)

	1970	1980	1990	1992	1993	1994	1995	1996	1997	1998
5. LONG-TERM DEBT										
DEBT OUTSTANDING (LDOD)	..	**4,500**	**1,797**	**1,780**	**5,899**	**15,922**	**15,430**	**11,948**	**8,469**	**8,307**
Public and publicly guaranteed	..	**4,500**	**1,797**	**1,780**	**5,899**	**15,530**	**15,116**	**11,712**	**8,263**	**7,679**
Official creditors	..	903	225	197	3,081	11,423	11,354	8,727	5,791	4,902
Multilateral	..	622	116	138	211	323	381	535	533	516
Concessional	..	0	0	0	0	0	0	0	0	0
Bilateral	..	282	110	59	2,870	11,101	10,974	8,192	5,258	4,386
Concessional	..	264	110	58	47	188	381	452	629	607
Private creditors	..	3,597	1,572	1,583	2,818	4,107	3,761	2,985	2,472	2,777
Bonds	..	0	0	0	0	0	0	0	0	0
Commercial banks	..	1,055	1,055	0	6	6	5	294	362	963
Other private	..	2,542	517	1,583	2,812	4,101	3,756	2,691	2,109	1,813
Private nonguaranteed	..	**0**	**0**	**0**	**0**	**392**	**314**	**236**	**207**	**628**
Bonds	..	0	0	0	0	0	0	0	0	0
Commercial banks	..	0	0	0	0	392	314	236	207	628
Memo:										
IBRD	0	622	86	133	190	260	316	387	421	433
IDA	0	0	0	0	0	0	0	0	0	0
DISBURSEMENTS	..	**264**	**139**	**1,411**	**1,729**	**1,874**	**979**	**945**	**907**	**1,761**
Public and publicly guaranteed	..	**264**	**139**	**1,411**	**1,729**	**1,482**	**979**	**945**	**907**	**1,261**
Official creditors	..	4	30	120	160	332	393	405	326	162
Multilateral	..	4	30	119	74	101	123	235	99	39
Concessional	..	0	0	0	0	0	0	0	0	0
Bilateral	..	0	0	1	86	231	270	170	227	123
Concessional	..	0	0	0	50	153	224	159	218	75
Private creditors	..	261	109	1,291	1,569	1,151	586	540	581	1,100
Bonds	..	0	0	0	0	0	0	0	0	0
Commercial banks	..	0	0	0	6	0	1	326	201	660
Other private	..	261	109	1,291	1,562	1,151	585	214	380	440
Private nonguaranteed	..	**0**	**0**	**0**	**0**	**392**	**0**	**0**	**0**	**500**
Bonds	..	0	0	0	0	0	0	0	0	0
Commercial banks	..	0	0	0	0	392	0	0	0	500
Memo:										
IBRD	0	4	0	114	58	48	85	137	78	28
IDA	0	0	0	0	0	0	0	0	0	0
PRINCIPAL REPAYMENTS	..	**527**	**225**	**193**	**389**	**2,388**	**4,198**	**5,153**	**5,295**	**2,140**
Public and publicly guaranteed	..	**527**	**225**	**193**	**389**	**2,388**	**4,120**	**5,075**	**5,266**	**2,062**
Official creditors	..	89	86	71	74	1,896	3,497	4,143	4,367	1,104
Multilateral	..	70	67	56	7	19	41	41	86	89
Concessional	..	0	0	0	0	0	0	0	0	0
Bilateral	..	19	18	15	67	1,877	3,456	4,102	4,280	1,015
Concessional	..	9	18	15	67	19	20	71	26	109
Private creditors	..	439	139	121	315	491	622	932	899	957
Bonds	..	0	0	0	0	0	0	0	0	0
Commercial banks	..	45	0	0	0	2	1	34	126	78
Other private	..	394	139	121	315	490	621	899	774	880
Private nonguaranteed	..	**0**	**0**	**0**	**0**	**0**	**78**	**78**	**30**	**79**
Bonds	..	0	0	0	0	0	0	0	0	0
Commercial banks	..	0	0	0	0	0	78	78	30	79
Memo:										
IBRD	0	70	67	26	7	8	6	27	29	50
IDA	0	0	0	0	0	0	0	0	0	0
NET FLOWS ON DEBT	..	**-263**	**-86**	**1,219**	**1,339**	**-513**	**-3,219**	**-4,209**	**-4,388**	**-379**
Public and publicly guaranteed	..	**-263**	**-86**	**1,219**	**1,339**	**-905**	**-3,141**	**-4,131**	**-4,359**	**-801**
Official creditors	..	-85	-56	49	85	-1,565	-3,104	-3,738	-4,040	-942
Multilateral	..	-66	-37	63	67	82	82	193	13	-50
Concessional	..	0	0	0	0	0	0	0	0	0
Bilateral	..	-19	-18	-14	19	-1,647	-3,186	-3,932	-4,053	-892
Concessional	..	-9	-18	-15	-18	134	204	89	192	-34
Private creditors	..	-178	-30	1,170	1,254	660	-37	-392	-318	142
Bonds	..	0	0	0	0	0	0	0	0	0
Commercial banks	..	-45	0	0	6	-2	-1	292	76	582
Other private	..	-133	-30	1,170	1,248	661	-36	-685	-394	-440
Private nonguaranteed	..	**0**	**0**	**0**	**0**	**392**	**-78**	**-78**	**-30**	**422**
Bonds	..	0	0	0	0	0	0	0	0	0
Commercial banks	..	0	0	0	0	392	-78	-78	-30	422
Memo:										
IBRD	0	-66	-67	88	51	40	79	110	49	-22
IDA	0	0	0	0	0	0	0	0	0	0

IRAN, ISLAMIC REPUBLIC OF

(US$ million, unless otherwise indicated)

	1970	1980	1990	1992	1993	1994	1995	1996	1997	1998
INTEREST PAYMENTS (LINT)	..	**431**	**28**	**93**	**182**	**273**	**1,132**	**1,113**	**792**	**527**
Public and publicly guaranteed	..	**431**	**28**	**93**	**182**	**273**	**1,107**	**1,093**	**777**	**491**
Official creditors	..	65	14	12	30	25	787	871	526	315
Multilateral	..	49	10	9	12	19	27	33	38	31
Concessional	..	0	0	0	0	0	0	0	0	0
Bilateral	..	16	4	3	17	6	759	838	488	284
Concessional	..	14	4	3	5	3	17	24	31	27
Private creditors	..	366	14	81	153	249	321	222	251	176
Bonds	..	0	0	0	0	0	0	0	0	0
Commercial banks	..	153	0	0	0	0	0	16	23	40
Other private	..	213	14	81	153	248	320	205	228	136
Private nonguaranteed	..	**0**	**0**	**0**	**0**	**0**	**25**	**20**	**15**	**36**
Bonds	..	0	0	0	0	0	0	0	0	0
Commercial banks	..	0	0	0	0	0	25	20	15	36
Memo:										
IBRD	0	49	10	6	12	16	19	23	26	19
IDA	0	0	0	0	0	0	0	0	0	0
NET TRANSFERS ON DEBT	..	**-694**	**-114**	**1,126**	**1,157**	**-787**	**-4,351**	**-5,321**	**-5,180**	**-906**
Public and publicly guaranteed	..	**-694**	**-114**	**1,126**	**1,157**	**-1,179**	**-4,248**	**-5,223**	**-5,135**	**-1,291**
Official creditors	..	-150	-69	37	56	-1,590	-3,891	-4,609	-4,566	-1,258
Multilateral	..	-116	-47	54	55	63	55	160	-25	-81
Concessional	..	0	0	0	0	0	0	0	0	0
Bilateral	..	-35	-22	-18	1	-1,653	-3,945	-4,769	-4,541	-1,177
Concessional	..	-24	-22	-19	-23	131	187	65	160	-61
Private creditors	..	-544	-45	1,089	1,101	411	-357	-614	-569	-33
Bonds	..	0	0	0	0	0	0	0	0	0
Commercial banks	..	-198	0	0	6	-2	-1	276	53	542
Other private	..	-346	-45	1,089	1,095	413	-357	-890	-622	-575
Private nonguaranteed	..	**0**	**0**	**0**	**0**	**392**	**-103**	**-98**	**-45**	**385**
Bonds	..	0	0	0	0	0	0	0	0	0
Commercial banks	..	0	0	0	0	392	-103	-98	-45	385
Memo:										
IBRD	0	-116	-77	82	39	24	61	87	23	-41
IDA	0	0	0	0	0	0	0	0	0	0
DEBT SERVICE (LTDS)	..	**959**	**253**	**286**	**571**	**2,661**	**5,330**	**6,266**	**6,087**	**2,667**
Public and publicly guaranteed	..	**959**	**253**	**286**	**571**	**2,661**	**5,227**	**6,168**	**6,043**	**2,552**
Official creditors	..	154	99	83	104	1,921	4,284	5,014	4,892	1,420
Multilateral	..	119	77	65	19	38	68	75	124	120
Concessional	..	0	0	0	0	0	0	0	0	0
Bilateral	..	35	22	19	85	1,884	4,216	4,939	4,768	1,300
Concessional	..	24	22	19	73	23	37	94	57	136
Private creditors	..	805	154	202	467	740	943	1,154	1,150	1,133
Bonds	..	0	0	0	0	0	0	0	0	0
Commercial banks	..	198	0	0	0	2	1	50	149	118
Other private	..	607	154	202	467	738	942	1,104	1,002	1,015
Private nonguaranteed	..	**0**	**0**	**0**	**0**	**0**	**103**	**98**	**45**	**115**
Bonds	..	0	0	0	0	0	0	0	0	0
Commercial banks	..	0	0	0	0	0	103	98	45	115
Memo:										
IBRD	0	119	77	32	19	24	24	50	55	69
IDA	0	0	0	0	0	0	0	0	0	0
UNDISBURSED DEBT	..	**1,173**	**1,512**	**5,663**	**4,423**	**3,198**	**3,992**	**4,434**	**3,630**	**2,340**
Official creditors	..	63	250	2,004	2,411	1,592	1,407	1,066	748	521
Private creditors	..	1,109	1,262	3,659	2,012	1,606	2,585	3,369	2,883	1,819
Memorandum items										
Concessional LDOD	..	264	110	58	47	188	381	452	629	607
Variable rate LDOD	..	1,706	1,273	1,460	5,385	15,240	14,806	11,350	7,929	7,670
Public sector LDOD	..	4,500	1,797	1,780	5,897	15,505	15,031	11,604	8,150	7,678
Private sector LDOD	..	0	0	0	2	417	398	345	319	628

6. CURRENCY COMPOSITION OF LONG-TERM DEBT (PERCENT)

	1970	1980	1990	1992	1993	1994	1995	1996	1997	1998
Deutsche mark	..	15.5	0.0	72.1	33.2	17.9	16.0	13.7	13.4	10.0
French franc	..	8.8	0.7	0.8	2.2	2.2	2.5	2.4	2.4	2.1
Japanese yen	..	9.0	4.2	8.7	7.0	4.4	4.9	5.7	7.2	7.8
Pound sterling	..	0.9	0.0	0.0	0.0	0.0	0.0	0.0	0.0	0.0
Swiss franc	..	0.0	0.0	2.3	1.6	0.8	0.6	0.5	0.7	0.9
U.S.dollars	..	43.4	88.6	2.4	49.4	70.5	71.5	71.6	67.5	75.0
Multiple currency	..	13.8	6.4	7.5	3.2	1.7	2.1	3.3	5.1	0.0
Special drawing rights	..	0.0	0.0	0.0	0.0	0.0	0.0	0.0	0.0	0.0
All other currencies	..	8.6	0.1	6.2	3.4	2.5	2.4	2.8	3.7	4.2

IRAN, ISLAMIC REPUBLIC OF

(US$ million, unless otherwise indicated)

	1970	1980	1990	1992	1993	1994	1995	1996	1997	1998
7. DEBT RESTRUCTURINGS										
Total amount rescheduled	..	..	0	0	2,786	10,785	3,178	1,805	0	0
Debt stock rescheduled	..	..	0	0	2,786	10,785	3,178	1,805	0	0
Principal rescheduled	..	..	0	0	0	0	0	0	0	0
Official	..	..	0	0	0	0	0	0	0	0
Private	..	..	0	0	0	0	0	0	0	0
Interest rescheduled	..	..	0	0	0	0	0	0	0	0
Official	..	..	0	0	0	0	0	0	0	0
Private	..	..	0	0	0	0	0	0	0	0
Debt forgiven	..	..	0	0	0	0	0	0	0	0
Memo: interest forgiven	..	..	0	0	0	0	0	0	0	0
Debt stock reduction	..	..	0	0	0	0	0	0	0	0
of which debt buyback	..	..	0	0	0	0	0	0	0	0
8. DEBT STOCK-FLOW RECONCILIATION										
Total change in debt stocks	..	..	2,502	4,754	7,419	-869	-755	-5,176	-4,880	2,568
Net flows on debt	..	-263	2,480	6,704	7,425	-621	-305	-4,093	-5,789	2,351
Net change in interest arrears	..	..	1	-447	0	1	1	-6	0	0
Interest capitalized	..	..	0	0	0	0	0	0	0	0
Debt forgiveness or reduction	..	..	0	0	0	0	0	0	0	0
Cross-currency valuation	..	..	-9	39	-19	883	-331	-405	-196	67
Residual	..	..	30	-1,542	12	-1,131	-121	-673	1,105	149
9. AVERAGE TERMS OF NEW COMMITMENTS										
ALL CREDITORS										
Interest (%)	..	0.0	8.4	5.4	4.6	6.3	6.6	5.9	6.6	4.9
Maturity (years)	..	0.0	9.3	9.1	19.4	6.1	8.5	9.6	9.1	9.5
Grace period (years)	..	0.0	4.0	3.4	2.4	1.9	3.1	2.8	2.1	2.5
Grant element (%)	..	0.0	6.2	19.6	31.4	11.0	13.6	16.9	13.0	21.4
Official creditors										
Interest (%)	..	0.0	7.8	4.9	4.6	6.4	7.0	8.3	0.0	0.0
Maturity (years)	..	0.0	13.5	10.3	20.8	3.9	7.8	7.9	0.0	0.0
Grace period (years)	..	0.0	5.0	3.8	2.5	3.6	3.1	3.4	0.0	0.0
Grant element (%)	..	0.0	11.7	23.1	33.0	10.7	10.5	5.1	0.0	0.0
Private creditors										
Interest (%)	..	0.0	8.6	6.0	4.3	6.3	6.5	5.7	6.6	4.9
Maturity (years)	..	0.0	8.1	7.5	6.2	6.3	8.6	9.8	9.1	9.5
Grace period (years)	..	0.0	3.7	3.0	1.7	1.8	3.1	2.7	2.1	2.5
Grant element (%)	..	0.0	4.7	15.0	17.1	11.1	14.1	17.9	13.0	21.4
Memorandum items										
Commitments	..	0	1,241	3,214	630	335	1,941	1,464	276	9
Official creditors	..	0	280	1,844	567	26	267	106	0	0
Private creditors	..	0	961	1,370	64	309	1,674	1,359	276	9

10. CONTRACTUAL OBLIGATIONS ON OUTSTANDING LONG-TERM DEBT

	1999	2000	2001	2002	2003	2004	2005	2006	2007	2008
TOTAL										
Disbursements	1,229	707	248	95	35	13	9	5	0	0
Principal	2,713	2,508	1,907	1,111	618	529	379	234	190	121
Interest	441	369	263	176	121	88	59	38	25	16
Official creditors										
Disbursements	209	150	70	41	23	13	9	5	0	0
Principal	1,478	1,487	1,244	537	107	92	88	65	62	62
Interest	252	184	113	60	37	31	26	20	16	12
Bilateral creditors										
Disbursements	131	85	32	16	4	1	0	0	0	0
Principal	1,378	1,378	1,160	460	36	22	19	19	19	19
Interest	208	142	76	27	9	8	7	6	6	5
Multilateral creditors										
Disbursements	79	66	38	25	19	12	9	5	0	0
Principal	100	108	84	77	72	70	69	46	42	42
Interest	45	42	37	33	28	24	19	14	11	7
Private creditors										
Disbursements	1,020	557	178	54	11	0	0	0	0	0
Principal	1,235	1,022	664	574	511	437	290	169	128	59
Interest	189	186	149	116	84	57	34	18	9	4
Commercial banks										
Disbursements	485	233	57	15	0	0	0	0	0	0
Principal	132	275	287	253	250	242	113	90	70	34
Interest	47	79	69	54	40	26	15	9	5	2
Other private										
Disbursements	535	324	120	39	11	0	0	0	0	0
Principal	1,103	747	376	322	261	194	178	79	58	25
Interest	141	106	81	62	44	30	19	9	4	2

JAMAICA

(US$ million, unless otherwise indicated)

	1970	1980	1990	1992	1993	1994	1995	1996	1997	1998
1. SUMMARY DEBT DATA										
TOTAL DEBT STOCKS (EDT)	**..**	**1,913**	**4,671**	**4,256**	**4,102**	**4,315**	**4,262**	**3,981**	**3,913**	**3,995**
Long-term debt (LDOD)	**982**	**1,505**	**3,968**	**3,588**	**3,478**	**3,514**	**3,527**	**3,247**	**3,109**	**3,258**
Public and publicly guaranteed	160	1,430	3,934	3,560	3,450	3,436	3,399	3,124	2,921	3,079
Private nonguaranteed	822	75	34	28	28	78	128	123	188	179
Use of IMF credit	**0**	**309**	**357**	**357**	**335**	**318**	**240**	**161**	**118**	**105**
Short-term debt	**..**	**98**	**347**	**311**	**289**	**483**	**494**	**572**	**686**	**631**
of which interest arrears on LDOD	..	0	125	135	135	107	104	96	74	75
Official creditors	..	0	87	92	99	92	89	81	68	68
Private creditors	..	0	37	43	35	15	15	14	7	7
Memo: principal arrears on LDOD	..	27	157	215	257	194	197	194	153	155
Official creditors	..	8	84	143	177	158	160	159	128	129
Private creditors	..	19	73	72	80	36	37	36	25	26
Memo: export credits	..	0	651	559	537	521	523	507	405	451
TOTAL DEBT FLOWS										
Disbursements	**184**	**363**	**340**	**382**	**272**	**210**	**301**	**211**	**391**	**384**
Long-term debt	180	363	284	323	221	161	291	211	391	384
IMF purchases	4	0	56	59	51	49	11	0	0	0
Principal repayments	**170**	**121**	**401**	**469**	**337**	**373**	**437**	**447**	**433**	**328**
Long-term debt	170	102	290	391	265	286	342	375	399	311
IMF repurchases	0	19	112	79	72	87	96	72	35	17
Net flows on debt	**13**	**234**	**-106**	**-66**	**-88**	**59**	**-122**	**-149**	**93**	**1**
of which short-term debt	..	-8	-45	22	-22	222	14	87	136	-55
Interest payments (INT)	**..**	**159**	**260**	**212**	**203**	**215**	**236**	**227**	**208**	**209**
Long-term debt	64	121	202	168	167	184	196	192	169	170
IMF charges	0	23	34	29	24	17	17	9	7	5
Short-term debt	..	15	24	16	12	14	24	26	33	34
Net transfers on debt	**..**	**75**	**-366**	**-278**	**-291**	**-156**	**-358**	**-376**	**-115**	**-208**
Total debt service paid (TDS)	**..**	**280**	**662**	**682**	**541**	**588**	**673**	**674**	**641**	**537**
Long-term debt	234	223	492	558	432	470	538	567	568	481
IMF repurchases and charges	0	42	145	108	97	105	112	81	41	22
Short-term debt (interest only)	..	15	24	16	12	14	24	26	33	34
2. AGGREGATE NET RESOURCE FLOWS AND NET TRANSFERS (LONG-TERM)										
NET RESOURCE FLOWS	**174**	**302**	**249**	**131**	**276**	**95**	**159**	**60**	**234**	**534**
Net flow of long-term debt (ex. IMF)	10	261	-6	-68	-44	-125	-51	-163	-8	73
Foreign direct investment (net)	162	28	138	142	78	130	147	184	203	369
Portfolio equity flows	0	0	0	0	0	0	0	0	0	0
Grants (excluding technical coop.)	3	13	117	57	242	91	63	39	40	92
Memo: technical coop. grants	5	17	35	36	39	37	51	38	37	32
official net resource flows	14	293	157	0	200	-41	-16	-136	-209	-52
private net resource flows	160	9	92	131	77	136	175	196	443	586
NET TRANSFERS	**6**	**66**	**-142**	**-93**	**105**	**-113**	**-67**	**-163**	**31**	**324**
Interest on long-term debt	64	121	202	168	167	184	196	192	169	170
Profit remittances on FDI	105	114	189	57	5	24	31	30	35	40
Memo: official net transfers	12	247	-7	-145	49	-187	-178	-298	-346	-175
private net transfers	-6	-181	-135	51	55	74	110	136	377	499
3. MAJOR ECONOMIC AGGREGATES										
Gross national product (GNP)	1,400	2,425	3,805	2,887	3,814	3,761	3,971	3,973	4,048	6,334
Exports of goods & services (XGS)	..	1,472	2,461	2,453	2,670	3,608	4,138	4,123	4,205	4,199
of which workers remittances	..	51	136	158	187	458	582	636	642	659
Imports of goods & services (MGS)	..	1,678	2,928	2,624	3,057	3,516	4,237	4,223	4,499	4,430
International reserves (RES)	139	105	168	324	417	736	681	880	682	709
Current account balance	..	-136	-312	29	-184	93	-74	-112	-312	-255
4. DEBT INDICATORS										
EDT / XGS (%)	..	129.9	189.8	173.5	153.6	119.6	103.0	96.6	93.1	95.1
EDT / GNP (%)	..	78.9	122.8	147.4	107.5	114.7	107.3	100.2	96.7	63.1
TDS / XGS (%)	..	19.0	26.9	27.8	20.3	16.3	16.3	16.3	15.3	12.8
INT / XGS (%)	..	10.8	10.6	8.7	7.6	6.0	5.7	5.5	4.9	5.0
INT / GNP (%)	..	6.6	6.8	7.4	5.3	5.7	5.9	5.7	5.1	3.3
RES / EDT (%)	..	5.5	3.6	7.6	10.2	17.1	16.0	22.1	17.4	17.8
RES / MGS (months)	..	0.8	0.7	1.5	1.6	2.5	1.9	2.5	1.8	1.9
Short-term / EDT (%)	..	5.1	7.4	7.3	7.0	11.2	11.6	14.4	17.5	15.8
Concessional / EDT (%)	..	20.3	29.9	30.4	29.3	29.8	31.5	31.3	27.7	26.5
Multilateral / EDT (%)	..	14.9	25.0	26.2	28.0	27.4	28.4	27.6	25.1	25.0

JAMAICA

(US$ million, unless otherwise indicated)

	1970	1980	1990	1992	1993	1994	1995	1996	1997	1998
5. LONG-TERM DEBT										
DEBT OUTSTANDING (LDOD)	**982**	**1,505**	**3,968**	**3,588**	**3,478**	**3,514**	**3,527**	**3,247**	**3,109**	**3,258**
Public and publicly guaranteed	**160**	**1,430**	**3,934**	**3,560**	**3,450**	**3,436**	**3,399**	**3,124**	**2,921**	**3,079**
Official creditors	59	920	3,406	3,149	3,045	3,090	3,076	2,785	2,408	2,340
Multilateral	30	284	1,168	1,117	1,149	1,181	1,209	1,100	984	997
Concessional	0	79	175	157	150	142	142	141	125	122
Bilateral	29	636	2,239	2,032	1,896	1,909	1,867	1,685	1,425	1,342
Concessional	19	310	1,223	1,137	1,053	1,144	1,199	1,103	960	937
Private creditors	101	510	528	411	405	346	324	339	513	740
Bonds	83	19	0	0	0	13	25	78	278	528
Commercial banks	17	384	298	254	281	265	234	206	196	178
Other private	0	108	230	158	124	68	65	56	40	34
Private nonguaranteed	**822**	**75**	**34**	**28**	**28**	**78**	**128**	**123**	**188**	**179**
Bonds	0	0	0	0	0	55	55	55	55	55
Commercial banks	822	75	34	28	28	23	73	68	133	124
Memo:										
IBRD	30	176	672	594	607	595	595	515	431	410
IDA	0	0	0	0	0	0	0	0	0	0
DISBURSEMENTS	**180**	**363**	**284**	**323**	**221**	**161**	**291**	**211**	**391**	**384**
Public and publicly guaranteed	**15**	**338**	**284**	**317**	**215**	**106**	**236**	**211**	**321**	**384**
Official creditors	14	317	246	261	174	83	178	123	108	120
Multilateral	7	93	102	90	148	67	115	89	87	85
Concessional	0	33	9	2	1	1	10	9	9	6
Bilateral	7	224	144	171	27	16	64	33	21	35
Concessional	2	84	103	34	3	10	31	18	9	7
Private creditors	1	21	39	56	41	23	57	89	212	264
Bonds	0	0	0	0	0	13	13	53	200	250
Commercial banks	1	4	0	0	40	10	42	36	12	14
Other private	0	17	39	56	1	0	3	0	0	0
Private nonguaranteed	**165**	**25**	**0**	**6**	**6**	**55**	**55**	**0**	**70**	**0**
Bonds	0	0	0	0	0	55	0	0	0	0
Commercial banks	165	25	0	6	6	0	55	0	70	0
Memo:										
IBRD	7	55	35	27	77	22	61	41	26	31
IDA	0	0	0	0	0	0	0	0	0	0
PRINCIPAL REPAYMENTS	**170**	**102**	**290**	**391**	**265**	**286**	**342**	**375**	**399**	**311**
Public and publicly guaranteed	**6**	**92**	**282**	**385**	**259**	**280**	**337**	**370**	**394**	**302**
Official creditors	2	37	205	317	217	215	257	297	357	264
Multilateral	1	11	100	127	123	121	127	125	137	111
Concessional	0	0	8	12	8	11	10	10	24	10
Bilateral	1	26	105	190	94	94	130	173	220	153
Concessional	1	2	19	23	22	24	30	68	97	66
Private creditors	4	55	76	68	42	66	80	73	37	38
Bonds	2	9	0	0	0	0	0	0	0	0
Commercial banks	2	16	1	10	11	10	73	65	22	31
Other private	0	31	75	58	32	56	6	8	15	6
Private nonguaranteed	**164**	**10**	**8**	**6**	**6**	**5**	**5**	**5**	**5**	**9**
Bonds	0	0	0	0	0	0	0	0	0	0
Commercial banks	164	10	8	6	6	5	5	5	5	9
Memo:										
IBRD	1	6	62	78	73	76	85	80	72	72
IDA	0	0	0	0	0	0	0	0	0	0
NET FLOWS ON DEBT	**10**	**261**	**-6**	**-68**	**-44**	**-125**	**-51**	**-163**	**-8**	**73**
Public and publicly guaranteed	**9**	**246**	**3**	**-68**	**-44**	**-175**	**-101**	**-158**	**-73**	**82**
Official creditors	12	280	40	-57	-43	-131	-79	-175	-249	-144
Multilateral	6	82	2	-37	25	-54	-12	-35	-50	-26
Concessional	0	33	1	-10	-7	-10	0	-1	-15	-4
Bilateral	6	198	39	-19	-67	-78	-67	-139	-198	-118
Concessional	1	82	84	11	-19	-14	1	-50	-88	-59
Private creditors	-3	-34	-38	-12	-2	-43	-22	16	175	226
Bonds	-2	-9	0	0	0	13	13	53	200	250
Commercial banks	-1	-12	-1	-10	29	0	-31	-28	-10	-17
Other private	0	-13	-37	-2	-31	-56	-4	-8	-15	-6
Private nonguaranteed	**1**	**15**	**-8**	**0**	**0**	**50**	**50**	**-5**	**65**	**-9**
Bonds	0	0	0	0	0	55	0	0	0	0
Commercial banks	1	15	-8	0	0	-5	50	-5	65	-9
Memo:										
IBRD	6	50	-26	-51	4	-54	-24	-39	-46	-41
IDA	0	0	0	0	0	0	0	0	0	0

JAMAICA

(US$ million, unless otherwise indicated)

	1970	1980	1990	1992	1993	1994	1995	1996	1997	1998
INTEREST PAYMENTS (LINT)	**64**	**121**	**202**	**168**	**167**	**184**	**196**	**192**	**169**	**170**
Public and publicly guaranteed	**9**	**115**	**200**	**165**	**165**	**182**	**185**	**182**	**156**	**158**
Official creditors	2	45	164	145	150	147	162	163	137	122
Multilateral	1	17	86	93	84	84	83	75	69	61
Concessional	0	2	5	4	5	4	3	3	5	3
Bilateral	1	29	79	52	66	62	79	88	68	62
Concessional	1	10	16	13	28	24	37	42	35	35
Private creditors	7	69	35	21	14	35	23	19	18	35
Bonds	6	2	0	0	0	0	2	2	3	22
Commercial banks	1	55	20	13	11	13	19	15	14	12
Other private	0	13	15	7	4	22	2	2	2	1
Private nonguaranteed	**54**	**7**	**3**	**2**	**2**	**3**	**11**	**11**	**13**	**12**
Bonds	0	0	0	0	0	1	5	5	5	5
Commercial banks	54	7	3	2	2	2	6	6	8	8
Memo:										
IBRD	1	13	58	59	49	49	47	41	34	28
IDA	0	0	0	0	0	0	0	0	0	0
NET TRANSFERS ON DEBT	**-54**	**140**	**-208**	**-236**	**-210**	**-309**	**-247**	**-356**	**-177**	**-97**
Public and publicly guaranteed	**-1**	**132**	**-197**	**-233**	**-209**	**-356**	**-286**	**-340**	**-229**	**-76**
Official creditors	9	235	-124	-201	-193	-278	-241	-337	-386	-267
Multilateral	5	66	-84	-130	-59	-138	-96	-110	-120	-87
Concessional	0	31	-4	-14	-12	-14	-4	-4	-20	-7
Bilateral	4	169	-40	-72	-134	-140	-146	-227	-267	-180
Concessional	0	72	68	-2	-47	-38	-35	-93	-122	-94
Private creditors	-10	-103	-73	-32	-16	-78	-45	-3	157	191
Bonds	-7	-10	0	0	0	13	11	51	197	228
Commercial banks	-3	-66	-22	-23	19	-14	-50	-44	-24	-30
Other private	0	-26	-51	-9	-35	-77	-6	-10	-16	-7
Private nonguaranteed	**-53**	**8**	**-11**	**-2**	**-2**	**47**	**39**	**-16**	**52**	**-21**
Bonds	0	0	0	0	0	54	-5	-5	-5	-5
Commercial banks	-53	8	-11	-2	-2	-7	44	-11	57	-17
Memo:										
IBRD	5	37	-85	-110	-45	-102	-71	-80	-80	-68
IDA	0	0	0	0	0	0	0	0	0	0
DEBT SERVICE (LTDS)	**234**	**223**	**492**	**558**	**432**	**470**	**538**	**567**	**568**	**481**
Public and publicly guaranteed	**15**	**206**	**481**	**550**	**424**	**462**	**522**	**552**	**550**	**459**
Official creditors	4	82	370	462	367	361	419	460	494	386
Multilateral	2	27	186	220	207	205	210	200	207	171
Concessional	0	2	14	16	13	15	13	13	29	13
Bilateral	2	55	184	243	160	156	209	260	288	215
Concessional	2	12	35	36	50	47	67	111	131	101
Private creditors	11	124	112	88	57	101	103	92	55	73
Bonds	7	10	0	0	0	0	2	2	3	22
Commercial banks	4	70	22	23	21	24	92	80	36	43
Other private	0	44	90	65	36	77	9	10	16	7
Private nonguaranteed	**218**	**17**	**11**	**8**	**8**	**8**	**16**	**16**	**18**	**21**
Bonds	0	0	0	0	0	1	5	5	5	5
Commercial banks	218	17	11	8	8	7	11	11	13	17
Memo:										
IBRD	2	18	120	137	123	124	132	121	106	99
IDA	0	0	0	0	0	0	0	0	0	0
UNDISBURSED DEBT	**38**	**325**	**556**	**558**	**621**	**582**	**504**	**524**	**524**	**350**
Official creditors	38	314	547	556	610	569	480	512	514	350
Private creditors	0	11	9	2	11	13	24	12	10	0
Memorandum items										
Concessional LDOD	19	389	1,398	1,294	1,203	1,285	1,342	1,245	1,085	1,058
Variable rate LDOD	822	344	1,023	890	967	1,014	1,002	961	948	902
Public sector LDOD	158	1,384	3,934	3,560	3,450	3,436	3,399	3,124	2,921	3,079
Private sector LDOD	824	122	34	28	28	78	128	123	188	179

6. CURRENCY COMPOSITION OF LONG-TERM DEBT (PERCENT)

	1970	1980	1990	1992	1993	1994	1995	1996	1997	1998
Deutsche mark	0.0	0.7	2.0	2.6	2.6	3.0	3.4	3.1	2.7	2.5
French franc	0.0	1.1	0.7	0.8	0.9	1.0	1.0	0.8	0.5	0.4
Japanese yen	0.0	0.7	4.9	6.9	7.8	8.6	8.9	8.5	7.5	7.5
Pound sterling	47.7	8.5	5.6	4.2	4.2	4.4	4.3	4.5	3.4	2.7
Swiss franc	0.0	0.3	0.0	0.0	0.0	0.0	0.0	0.0	0.0	0.0
U.S.dollars	27.6	58.5	49.3	50.3	49.0	47.1	46.4	48.6	54.7	57.9
Multiple currency	18.7	17.1	27.8	27.8	28.7	28.7	28.7	27.4	25.1	22.8
Special drawing rights	0.0	0.0	0.0	0.0	0.0	0.0	0.0	0.1	0.0	0.1
All other currencies	6.0	13.1	9.7	7.4	6.8	7.2	7.3	7.0	6.1	6.1

JAMAICA

(US$ million, unless otherwise indicated)

	1970	1980	1990	1992	1993	1994	1995	1996	1997	1998
7. DEBT RESTRUCTURINGS										
Total amount rescheduled	..	..	469	131	149	106	105	0	0	0
Debt stock rescheduled	..	..	314	0	40	0	0	0	0	0
Principal rescheduled	..	..	99	96	84	76	88	0	0	0
Official	..	..	96	93	82	74	87	0	0	0
Private	..	..	3	3	2	1	1	0	0	0
Interest rescheduled	..	..	55	36	24	30	17	0	0	0
Official	..	..	54	35	24	30	16	0	0	0
Private	..	..	1	0	0	0	0	0	0	0
Debt forgiven	..	..	0	7	100	6	0	0	0	0
Memo: interest forgiven	..	..	1	4	3	3	0	0	0	0
Debt stock reduction	..	..	24	14	2	16	0	0	0	0
of which debt buyback	..	..	0	0	0	0	0	0	0	0
8. DEBT STOCK-FLOW RECONCILIATION										
Total change in debt stocks	..	..	111	-153	-155	213	-53	-281	-68	82
Net flows on debt	13	234	-106	-66	-88	59	-122	-149	93	1
Net change in interest arrears	..	..	0	9	0	-28	-3	-8	-22	0
Interest capitalized	..	..	55	36	24	30	17	0	0	0
Debt forgiveness or reduction	..	..	-25	-21	-102	-21	0	0	0	0
Cross-currency valuation	..	..	130	-96	-4	97	14	-101	-110	51
Residual	..	..	57	-14	16	76	42	-23	-29	30
9. AVERAGE TERMS OF NEW COMMITMENTS										
ALL CREDITORS										
Interest (%)	6.0	7.2	8.0	7.9	6.8	5.2	6.5	4.6	8.6	8.4
Maturity (years)	16.0	13.7	16.7	19.5	17.7	14.4	13.4	15.7	11.1	8.0
Grace period (years)	3.2	4.6	3.8	4.1	4.4	5.3	3.0	4.6	4.9	6.4
Grant element (%)	21.7	21.5	10.9	11.8	15.5	28.0	16.4	28.6	8.0	7.2
Official creditors										
Interest (%)	6.0	6.5	7.9	7.9	7.3	4.9	6.2	5.2	7.1	6.1
Maturity (years)	16.0	14.6	18.8	21.3	21.0	17.9	19.8	20.2	21.0	15.4
Grace period (years)	3.2	5.0	4.2	5.0	5.0	5.4	4.1	5.5	5.0	2.7
Grant element (%)	21.7	24.0	12.3	12.8	17.2	32.0	22.9	32.9	18.4	16.1
Private creditors										
Interest (%)	0.0	13.0	8.7	8.0	4.5	5.8	6.8	3.2	9.5	8.7
Maturity (years)	0.0	5.7	1.9	11.7	1.6	6.0	3.3	4.9	5.3	6.9
Grace period (years)	0.0	1.3	0.4	0.2	1.6	5.0	1.3	2.3	4.8	6.9
Grant element (%)	0.0	0.2	0.5	7.4	7.7	18.2	6.4	18.5	1.9	6.0
Memorandum items										
Commitments	24	245	318	292	292	85	175	261	336	288
Official creditors	24	219	279	237	242	60	107	184	125	34
Private creditors	0	26	39	55	50	25	69	78	211	254

10. CONTRACTUAL OBLIGATIONS ON OUTSTANDING LONG-TERM DEBT

	1999	2000	2001	2002	2003	2004	2005	2006	2007	2008
TOTAL										
Disbursements	86	76	59	47	36	20	14	6	4	2
Principal	381	345	237	417	205	203	440	183	170	160
Interest	191	173	158	148	118	107	85	64	54	44
Official creditors										
Disbursements	86	76	59	47	36	20	14	6	4	2
Principal	272	235	196	180	167	172	178	173	160	151
Interest	125	114	104	96	88	80	70	60	51	42
Bilateral creditors										
Disbursements	8	4	2	1	0	0	0	0	0	0
Principal	135	110	82	81	68	76	90	87	78	75
Interest	56	50	45	41	37	34	30	26	22	18
Multilateral creditors										
Disbursements	78	71	57	46	36	20	14	6	4	2
Principal	137	125	114	99	99	96	88	86	82	76
Interest	69	64	60	55	51	46	40	35	29	24
Private creditors										
Disbursements	0	0	0	0	0	0	0	0	0	0
Principal	108	111	41	238	38	31	263	10	10	9
Interest	66	59	54	52	30	27	15	4	3	2
Commercial banks										
Disbursements	0	0	0	0	0	0	0	0	0	0
Principal	33	33	30	27	27	21	4	1	1	0
Interest	11	9	7	5	3	1	0	0	0	0
Other private										
Disbursements	0	0	0	0	0	0	0	0	0	0
Principal	76	78	11	211	10	9	259	9	9	9
Interest	56	51	48	47	27	26	15	3	3	2

JORDAN

(US$ million, unless otherwise indicated)

	1970	1980	1990	1992	1993	1994	1995	1996	1997	1998
1. SUMMARY DEBT DATA										
TOTAL DEBT STOCKS (EDT)	..	**1,971**	**8,177**	**7,817**	**7,609**	**7,708**	**8,114**	**8,073**	**8,175**	**8,485**
Long-term debt (LDOD)	**120**	**1,486**	**7,043**	**6,922**	**6,770**	**6,883**	**7,073**	**7,136**	**6,999**	**7,421**
Public and publicly guaranteed	120	1,486	7,043	6,922	6,770	6,883	7,023	7,091	6,960	7,388
Private nonguaranteed	0	0	0	0	0	0	50	45	39	34
Use of IMF credit	**0**	**0**	**94**	**112**	**81**	**144**	**252**	**340**	**427**	**469**
Short-term debt	..	**485**	**1,040**	**783**	**757**	**681**	**790**	**597**	**748**	**594**
of which interest arrears on LDOD	..	5	110	143	53	60	72	81	87	81
Official creditors	..	5	34	49	46	56	68	80	87	81
Private creditors	..	0	77	95	7	4	4	1	1	0
Memo: principal arrears on LDOD	..	22	549	856	151	187	223	298	304	287
Official creditors	..	22	54	120	150	186	222	252	277	281
Private creditors	..	0	495	736	1	1	2	46	27	7
Memo: export credits	..	0	2,366	1,971	1,917	2,040	1,330	1,304	2,675	1,664
TOTAL DEBT FLOWS										
Disbursements	**15**	**369**	**691**	**463**	**261**	**307**	**798**	**923**	**841**	**480**
Long-term debt	15	369	691	431	245	213	683	804	708	448
IMF purchases	0	0	0	31	16	94	115	119	133	32
Principal repayments	**3**	**104**	**251**	**386**	**347**	**320**	**339**	**593**	**503**	**418**
Long-term debt	3	104	241	376	301	283	330	570	481	409
IMF repurchases	0	0	10	10	46	37	8	22	22	9
Net flows on debt	**12**	**462**	**606**	**-1,061**	**-23**	**-97**	**557**	**129**	**484**	**-87**
of which short-term debt	..	196	165	-1,138	64	-84	97	-202	145	-149
Interest payments (INT)	..	**107**	**374**	**325**	**255**	**245**	**276**	**426**	**404**	**481**
Long-term debt	2	79	307	278	206	200	223	379	352	427
IMF charges	0	0	9	8	6	5	10	12	17	21
Short-term debt	..	28	58	39	43	40	43	35	35	34
Net transfers on debt	..	**355**	**232**	**-1,386**	**-278**	**-341**	**281**	**-297**	**79**	**-568**
Total debt service paid (TDS)	..	**210**	**625**	**710**	**602**	**564**	**614**	**1,018**	**907**	**899**
Long-term debt	5	182	548	653	507	483	553	949	833	835
IMF repurchases and charges	0	0	19	18	53	42	18	34	39	30
Short-term debt (interest only)	..	28	58	39	43	40	43	35	35	34
2. AGGREGATE NET RESOURCE FLOWS AND NET TRANSFERS (LONG-TERM)										
NET RESOURCE FLOWS	**53**	**1,427**	**1,161**	**208**	**-17**	**239**	**597**	**441**	**954**	**633**
Net flow of long-term debt (ex. IMF)	12	266	450	56	-56	-70	353	234	228	39
Foreign direct investment (net)	0	34	38	41	-34	3	13	16	361	310
Portfolio equity flows	0	0	0	0	0	0	11	25	70	11
Grants (excluding technical coop.)	41	1,127	672	112	73	306	219	167	295	272
Memo: technical coop. grants	31	25	68	123	129	130	159	145	68	62
official net resource flows	49	1,399	907	299	125	415	725	559	554	425
private net resource flows	4	28	254	-91	-141	-177	-128	-119	400	207
NET TRANSFERS	**51**	**1,348**	**853**	**-70**	**-223**	**39**	**374**	**62**	**602**	**206**
Interest on long-term debt	2	79	307	278	206	200	223	379	352	427
Profit remittances on FDI	1	0	0	0	0	0	0	0	0	0
Memo: official net transfers	48	1,357	784	176	-1	305	594	274	277	76
private net transfers	3	-9	69	-245	-221	-266	-220	-212	325	130
3. MAJOR ECONOMIC AGGREGATES										
Gross national product (GNP)	658	4,074	3,659	4,929	5,355	5,862	6,341	4,781	5,232	5,776
Exports of goods & services (XGS)	..	1,870	3,079	3,623	3,961	4,150	4,839	5,319	5,476	5,485
of which workers remittances	15	595	500	843	1,040	1,093	1,244	1,544	1,655	1,543
Imports of goods & services (MGS)	..	2,476	4,036	4,784	4,903	4,783	5,296	5,829	5,643	5,645
International reserves (RES)	258	1,745	1,139	1,030	1,946	1,997	2,279	2,055	2,436	1,988
Current account balance	-17	280	-411	-837	-644	-400	-257	-222	29	9
4. DEBT INDICATORS										
EDT / XGS (%)	..	105.4	265.6	215.7	192.1	185.7	167.7	151.8	149.3	154.7
EDT / GNP (%)	..	48.4	223.5	158.6	142.1	131.5	128.0	168.9	156.2	146.9
TDS / XGS (%)	..	11.2	20.3	19.6	15.2	13.6	12.7	19.1	16.6	16.4
INT / XGS (%)	..	5.7	12.2	9.0	6.4	5.9	5.7	8.0	7.4	8.8
INT / GNP (%)	..	2.6	10.2	6.6	4.8	4.2	4.4	8.9	7.7	8.3
RES / EDT (%)	..	88.5	13.9	13.2	25.6	25.9	28.1	25.5	29.8	23.4
RES / MGS (months)	..	8.5	3.4	2.6	4.8	5.0	5.2	4.2	5.2	4.2
Short-term / EDT (%)	..	24.6	12.7	10.0	10.0	8.8	9.7	7.4	9.2	7.0
Concessional / EDT (%)	..	41.6	31.0	34.4	38.7	39.8	42.1	43.6	42.5	45.2
Multilateral / EDT (%)	..	8.1	10.8	11.5	12.6	13.2	14.9	17.2	17.9	19.6

JORDAN

(US$ million, unless otherwise indicated)

	1970	1980	1990	1992	1993	1994	1995	1996	1997	1998
5. LONG-TERM DEBT										
DEBT OUTSTANDING (LDOD)	**120**	**1,486**	**7,043**	**6,922**	**6,770**	**6,883**	**7,073**	**7,136**	**6,999**	**7,421**
Public and publicly guaranteed	**120**	**1,486**	**7,043**	**6,922**	**6,770**	**6,883**	**7,023**	**7,091**	**6,960**	**7,388**
Official creditors	109	1,210	3,603	4,000	4,276	4,619	5,102	5,417	5,437	6,023
Multilateral	9	159	887	900	959	1,016	1,209	1,385	1,464	1,658
Concessional	9	113	209	217	237	244	278	370	434	504
Bilateral	100	1,052	2,716	3,100	3,317	3,603	3,893	4,032	3,973	4,365
Concessional	100	707	2,328	2,469	2,706	2,822	3,139	3,151	3,037	3,327
Private creditors	10	276	3,440	2,922	2,494	2,265	1,921	1,674	1,523	1,365
Bonds	0	0	263	191	824	824	801	796	886	875
Commercial banks	0	206	1,604	1,509	587	465	337	217	116	58
Other private	10	70	1,573	1,223	1,084	976	782	662	521	432
Private nonguaranteed	**0**	**0**	**0**	**0**	**0**	**0**	**50**	**45**	**39**	**34**
Bonds	0	0	0	0	0	0	0	0	0	0
Commercial banks	0	0	0	0	0	0	50	45	39	34
Memo:										
IBRD	0	26	516	569	592	635	736	777	749	745
IDA	9	76	77	75	73	71	69	67	65	62
DISBURSEMENTS	**15**	**369**	**691**	**431**	**245**	**213**	**683**	**804**	**708**	**448**
Public and publicly guaranteed	**15**	**369**	**691**	**431**	**245**	**213**	**633**	**804**	**708**	**448**
Official creditors	10	326	377	374	205	213	633	804	608	448
Multilateral	0	54	142	143	148	102	282	358	269	264
Concessional	0	18	10	12	36	24	53	116	90	87
Bilateral	10	272	235	231	57	111	351	447	339	184
Concessional	10	106	224	230	57	111	336	402	319	184
Private creditors	5	44	315	57	41	0	0	0	100	0
Bonds	0	0	0	0	15	0	0	0	100	0
Commercial banks	0	15	73	0	0	0	0	0	0	0
Other private	5	29	241	57	26	0	0	0	0	0
Private nonguaranteed	**0**	**0**	**0**	**0**	**0**	**0**	**50**	**0**	**0**	**0**
Bonds	0	0	0	0	0	0	0	0	0	0
Commercial banks	0	0	0	0	0	0	50	0	0	0
Memo:										
IBRD	0	22	123	128	69	58	158	169	94	36
IDA	0	9	0	0	0	0	0	0	0	0
PRINCIPAL REPAYMENTS	**3**	**104**	**241**	**376**	**301**	**283**	**330**	**570**	**481**	**409**
Public and publicly guaranteed	**3**	**104**	**241**	**376**	**301**	**283**	**325**	**565**	**475**	**403**
Official creditors	2	54	142	186	153	103	128	411	349	295
Multilateral	0	1	94	92	94	98	117	122	116	113
Concessional	0	1	12	16	16	19	21	22	23	22
Bilateral	2	53	48	95	58	6	11	289	234	182
Concessional	2	23	33	8	6	2	6	279	208	143
Private creditors	0	50	99	189	148	180	197	153	126	108
Bonds	0	0	0	4	0	0	0	5	10	10
Commercial banks	0	46	69	90	86	131	135	117	98	58
Other private	0	4	30	96	63	48	62	32	18	40
Private nonguaranteed	**0**	**0**	**0**	**0**	**0**	**0**	**6**	**6**	**6**	**6**
Bonds	0	0	0	0	0	0	0	0	0	0
Commercial banks	0	0	0	0	0	0	6	6	6	6
Memo:										
IBRD	0	0	52	54	57	57	77	78	69	64
IDA	0	0	1	1	2	2	2	2	2	2
NET FLOWS ON DEBT	**12**	**266**	**450**	**56**	**-56**	**-70**	**353**	**234**	**228**	**39**
Public and publicly guaranteed	**12**	**266**	**450**	**56**	**-56**	**-70**	**309**	**239**	**233**	**45**
Official creditors	8	272	235	188	52	110	505	393	259	153
Multilateral	0	52	48	51	53	4	165	235	154	152
Concessional	0	17	-3	-4	20	4	32	94	67	65
Bilateral	7	220	187	137	-1	106	340	157	105	1
Concessional	7	83	191	222	51	109	330	123	111	40
Private creditors	4	-6	216	-132	-108	-180	-197	-153	-26	-108
Bonds	0	0	0	-4	15	0	0	-5	90	-10
Commercial banks	0	-31	4	-90	-86	-131	-135	-117	-98	-58
Other private	4	25	211	-39	-37	-48	-62	-32	-18	-40
Private nonguaranteed	**0**	**0**	**0**	**0**	**0**	**0**	**45**	**-6**	**-6**	**-6**
Bonds	0	0	0	0	0	0	0	0	0	0
Commercial banks	0	0	0	0	0	0	45	-6	-6	-6
Memo:										
IBRD	0	22	71	74	12	2	81	91	25	-27
IDA	0	9	-1	-1	-2	-2	-2	-2	-2	-2

JORDAN

(US$ million, unless otherwise indicated)

	1970	1980	1990	1992	1993	1994	1995	1996	1997	1998
INTEREST PAYMENTS (LINT)	**2**	**79**	**307**	**278**	**206**	**200**	**223**	**379**	**352**	**427**
Public and publicly guaranteed	**2**	**79**	**307**	**278**	**206**	**200**	**220**	**376**	**350**	**424**
Official creditors	1	43	123	124	126	110	130	286	277	349
Multilateral	0	5	54	55	57	60	64	67	70	77
Concessional	0	3	6	6	6	6	6	9	14	18
Bilateral	1	38	69	69	69	50	66	219	208	273
Concessional	1	13	57	23	38	28	45	171	160	239
Private creditors	1	36	184	154	80	90	89	91	72	75
Bonds	0	0	15	4	2	31	41	40	39	51
Commercial banks	0	32	67	80	40	34	32	23	15	8
Other private	1	4	103	69	38	25	17	28	18	17
Private nonguaranteed	**0**	**0**	**0**	**0**	**0**	**0**	**3**	**3**	**3**	**2**
Bonds	0	0	0	0	0	0	0	0	0	0
Commercial banks	0	0	0	0	0	0	3	3	3	2
Memo:										
IBRD	0	1	37	41	43	46	48	48	47	46
IDA	0	1	1	1	1	1	1	1	1	1
NET TRANSFERS ON DEBT	**10**	**187**	**143**	**-222**	**-261**	**-270**	**131**	**-145**	**-125**	**-388**
Public and publicly guaranteed	**10**	**187**	**143**	**-222**	**-261**	**-270**	**89**	**-137**	**-116**	**-380**
Official creditors	6	229	112	64	-74	-1	375	107	-18	-196
Multilateral	0	47	-6	-4	-3	-56	102	169	84	75
Concessional	0	14	-9	-10	14	-2	26	85	54	47
Bilateral	6	182	118	68	-70	55	274	-62	-103	-272
Concessional	6	71	134	199	13	82	285	-48	-49	-199
Private creditors	4	-42	31	-286	-188	-269	-286	-244	-98	-183
Bonds	0	0	-15	-8	13	-31	-41	-45	51	-61
Commercial banks	0	-63	-63	-170	-126	-166	-166	-139	-113	-65
Other private	4	20	109	-108	-75	-73	-79	-60	-36	-57
Private nonguaranteed	**0**	**0**	**0**	**0**	**0**	**0**	**42**	**-9**	**-8**	**-8**
Bonds	0	0	0	0	0	0	0	0	0	0
Commercial banks	0	0	0	0	0	0	42	-9	-8	-8
Memo:										
IBRD	0	22	33	33	-31	-44	33	43	-22	-74
IDA	0	8	-2	-2	-2	-2	-3	-3	-3	-3
DEBT SERVICE (LTDS)	**5**	**182**	**548**	**653**	**507**	**483**	**553**	**949**	**833**	**835**
Public and publicly guaranteed	**5**	**182**	**548**	**653**	**507**	**483**	**544**	**941**	**825**	**828**
Official creditors	4	97	265	310	279	213	258	697	627	644
Multilateral	0	6	148	147	151	158	181	189	185	189
Concessional	0	4	18	22	22	26	27	31	37	40
Bilateral	4	90	117	163	127	56	77	508	441	455
Concessional	4	36	90	31	44	30	52	450	368	383
Private creditors	1	86	283	343	228	269	286	244	198	183
Bonds	0	0	15	8	2	31	41	45	49	61
Commercial banks	0	78	136	170	126	166	166	139	113	65
Other private	1	8	133	165	100	73	79	60	36	57
Private nonguaranteed	**0**	**0**	**0**	**0**	**0**	**0**	**9**	**9**	**8**	**8**
Bonds	0	0	0	0	0	0	0	0	0	0
Commercial banks	0	0	0	0	0	0	9	9	8	8
Memo:										
IBRD	0	1	89	94	101	102	125	127	116	110
IDA	0	1	2	2	2	2	3	3	3	3
UNDISBURSED DEBT	**74**	**1,354**	**1,462**	**1,012**	**1,035**	**1,222**	**1,826**	**1,456**	**989**	**1,035**
Official creditors	62	1,136	1,111	717	771	1,222	1,826	1,456	989	1,035
Private creditors	12	217	351	295	263	0	0	0	0	0
Memorandum items										
Concessional LDOD	109	819	2,537	2,686	2,943	3,066	3,417	3,521	3,471	3,831
Variable rate LDOD	0	200	2,501	2,292	1,994	1,972	2,094	2,124	2,126	2,136
Public sector LDOD	118	1,485	7,043	6,922	6,770	6,883	7,023	7,072	6,939	7,354
Private sector LDOD	1	1	0	0	0	0	50	64	61	68

6. CURRENCY COMPOSITION OF LONG-TERM DEBT (PERCENT)

	1970	1980	1990	1992	1993	1994	1995	1996	1997	1998
Deutsche mark	8.7	10.6	7.9	8.3	7.2	7.7	7.6	6.9	6.3	6.9
French franc	2.7	2.0	3.5	7.9	7.5	8.7	9.9	9.2	8.5	9.2
Japanese yen	0.0	1.1	6.0	15.7	18.3	21.6	24.1	22.3	21.6	23.0
Pound sterling	32.5	6.4	8.0	7.6	7.1	6.7	6.7	7.5	7.2	6.4
Swiss franc	0.0	0.0	0.8	0.7	0.4	0.4	0.5	0.4	0.4	0.4
U.S.dollars	31.0	59.6	44.4	39.7	40.4	35.0	28.9	29.5	30.4	30.4
Multiple currency	0.0	4.4	8.4	9.5	10.1	10.6	11.8	12.3	12.0	8.9
Special drawing rights	0.0	0.0	2.8	0.2	0.1	0.3	0.5	0.5	0.7	0.8
All other currencies	25.1	15.9	18.2	10.4	8.9	9.0	10.0	11.4	12.9	14.0

JORDAN

(US$ million, unless otherwise indicated)

	1970	1980	1990	1992	1993	1994	1995	1996	1997	1998
7. DEBT RESTRUCTURINGS										
Total amount rescheduled	..	..	350	588	1,163	337	367	388	224	211
Debt stock rescheduled	..	..	0	0	193	0	0	0	0	0
Principal rescheduled	..	..	350	433	722	218	269	329	176	147
Official	..	..	193	112	88	95	118	105	89	87
Private	..	..	157	322	634	122	152	224	87	60
Interest rescheduled	..	..	0	145	249	119	97	60	48	64
Official	..	..	0	41	33	67	53	27	23	47
Private	..	..	0	104	215	52	45	33	25	17
Debt forgiven	..	..	0	0	184	297	323	11	34	0
Memo: interest forgiven	..	..	0	0	0	0	0	0	0	0
Debt stock reduction	..	..	0	530	97	0	0	0	0	0
of which debt buyback	..	..	0	0	0	0	0	0	0	0
8. DEBT STOCK-FLOW RECONCILIATION										
Total change in debt stocks	..	..	1,021	-1,733	-209	100	406	-42	102	310
Net flows on debt	12	462	606	-1,061	-23	-97	557	129	484	-87
Net change in interest arrears	..	..	71	-76	-90	7	12	9	6	-6
Interest capitalized	..	..	0	145	249	119	97	60	48	64
Debt forgiveness or reduction	..	..	0	-530	-281	-297	-323	-11	-34	0
Cross-currency valuation	..	..	373	-233	62	376	75	-291	-413	348
Residual	..	..	-28	22	-126	-8	-13	63	12	-9
9. AVERAGE TERMS OF NEW COMMITMENTS										
ALL CREDITORS										
Interest (%)	3.7	7.3	4.6	4.1	6.2	4.8	4.7	5.1	5.5	4.0
Maturity (years)	23.5	15.4	19.9	18.4	19.2	22.2	22.1	19.4	15.2	20.4
Grace period (years)	5.0	4.0	6.5	5.8	5.4	6.7	8.5	5.7	6.0	5.8
Grant element (%)	42.6	16.5	38.5	37.7	23.0	36.9	38.4	32.2	27.8	40.1
Official creditors										
Interest (%)	2.6	7.3	4.0	2.8	6.4	4.8	4.7	5.1	4.6	4.0
Maturity (years)	31.4	16.0	21.8	22.2	19.7	22.2	22.1	19.4	20.6	20.4
Grace period (years)	6.4	4.3	7.3	7.0	5.5	6.7	8.5	5.7	6.4	5.8
Grant element (%)	56.7	17.2	43.9	50.0	23.2	36.9	38.4	32.2	37.0	40.1
Private creditors										
Interest (%)	6.2	7.2	8.9	6.9	5.0	0.0	0.0	0.0	7.3	0.0
Maturity (years)	5.5	11.5	7.0	10.3	15.7	0.0	0.0	0.0	5.0	0.0
Grace period (years)	1.9	2.4	1.0	3.3	4.7	0.0	0.0	0.0	5.0	0.0
Grant element (%)	10.4	12.0	2.8	11.4	21.4	0.0	0.0	0.0	10.2	0.0
Memorandum items										
Commitments	36	759	739	180	301	638	1,225	486	293	473
Official creditors	25	653	642	123	260	638	1,225	486	193	473
Private creditors	11	106	97	57	41	0	0	0	100	0

10. CONTRACTUAL OBLIGATIONS ON OUTSTANDING LONG-TERM DEBT

	1999	2000	2001	2002	2003	2004	2005	2006	2007	2008
TOTAL										
Disbursements	261	253	177	117	72	42	24	10	6	0
Principal	427	427	483	584	482	484	479	463	435	345
Interest	330	339	324	305	276	253	230	207	185	165
Official creditors										
Disbursements	261	253	177	117	72	42	24	10	6	0
Principal	337	357	419	425	425	427	428	419	398	333
Interest	249	258	248	233	215	196	176	156	137	119
Bilateral creditors										
Disbursements	90	72	45	26	13	6	3	1	0	0
Principal	199	213	262	252	259	261	268	267	264	206
Interest	152	161	152	140	129	118	107	95	83	73
Multilateral creditors										
Disbursements	171	181	132	91	59	36	21	10	6	0
Principal	138	143	157	173	166	165	160	153	134	127
Interest	97	98	97	93	86	78	70	61	53	47
Private creditors										
Disbursements	0	0	0	0	0	0	0	0	0	0
Principal	90	70	63	159	57	58	51	44	37	12
Interest	81	80	76	72	61	57	54	51	48	46
Commercial banks										
Disbursements	0	0	0	0	0	0	0	0	0	0
Principal	39	19	0	0	0	0	0	0	0	0
Interest	4	1	0	0	0	0	0	0	0	0
Other private										
Disbursements	0	0	0	0	0	0	0	0	0	0
Principal	52	51	63	159	57	58	51	44	37	12
Interest	77	80	76	72	61	57	54	51	48	46

KAZAKHSTAN

(US$ million, unless otherwise indicated)

	1970	1980	1990	1992	1993	1994	1995	1996	1997	1998
1. SUMMARY DEBT DATA										
TOTAL DEBT STOCKS (EDT)	..	..	..	**35**	**1,728**	**2,790**	**3,750**	**2,922**	**4,078**	**5,714**
Long-term debt (LDOD)	..	..	..	**26**	**1,621**	**2,268**	**2,937**	**2,149**	**3,218**	**4,609**
Public and publicly guaranteed	..	..	..	26	1,621	2,227	2,834	1,947	2,622	3,040
Private nonguaranteed	..	..	..	0	0	41	103	203	596	1,569
Use of IMF credit	..	..	..	**0**	**85**	**289**	**432**	**552**	**511**	**653**
Short-term debt	..	..	..	**9**	**22**	**232**	**381**	**221**	**349**	**452**
of which interest arrears on LDOD	..	..	..	0	22	105	162	0	0	76
Official creditors	..	..	..	0	1	80	162	0	0	0
Private creditors	..	..	..	0	21	25	0	0	0	76
Memo: principal arrears on LDOD	..	..	..	0	0	0	0	0	0	109
Official creditors	..	..	..	0	0	0	0	0	0	0
Private creditors	..	..	..	0	0	0	0	0	0	109
Memo: export credits	..	..	..	91	330	773	1,119	1,203	1,176	1,334
TOTAL DEBT FLOWS										
Disbursements	..	..	..	**27**	**428**	**806**	**881**	**922**	**1,487**	**1,882**
Long-term debt	..	..	..	27	341	611	740	787	1,487	1,672
IMF purchases	..	..	..	0	86	195	141	135	0	210
Principal repayments	..	..	..	**0**	**0**	**23**	**105**	**192**	**273**	**603**
Long-term debt	..	..	..	0	0	23	105	192	267	508
IMF repurchases	..	..	..	0	0	0	0	0	6	95
Net flows on debt	..	..	..	**36**	**418**	**910**	**868**	**732**	**1,342**	**1,307**
of which short-term debt	..	..	..	9	-9	127	93	2	128	28
Interest payments (INT)	..	..	..	**0**	**9**	**46**	**130**	**131**	**210**	**282**
Long-term debt	..	..	..	0	8	32	102	98	170	240
IMF charges	..	..	..	0	1	9	18	22	24	23
Short-term debt	..	..	..	0	1	5	10	10	16	20
Net transfers on debt	..	..	..	**36**	**409**	**864**	**739**	**601**	**1,132**	**1,024**
Total debt service paid (TDS)	..	..	..	**0**	**10**	**68**	**235**	**322**	**483**	**885**
Long-term debt	..	..	..	0	8	55	207	290	437	747
IMF repurchases and charges	..	..	..	0	1	9	18	22	31	118
Short-term debt (interest only)	..	..	..	0	1	5	10	10	16	20
2. AGGREGATE NET RESOURCE FLOWS AND NET TRANSFERS (LONG-TERM)										
NET RESOURCE FLOWS	..	..	..	**129**	**502**	**799**	**1,610**	**1,776**	**2,638**	**2,337**
Net flow of long-term debt (ex. IMF)	..	..	..	27	341	588	635	596	1,220	1,164
Foreign direct investment (net)	..	..	..	100	150	185	964	1,137	1,321	1,158
Portfolio equity flows	..	..	..	0	0	0	0	0	50	0
Grants (excluding technical coop.)	..	..	..	3	11	26	11	44	46	15
Memo: technical coop. grants	..	..	..	6	3	17	47	66	39	90
official net resource flows	..	..	..	13	181	468	405	377	480	353
private net resource flows	..	..	..	117	321	331	1,205	1,399	2,158	1,983
NET TRANSFERS	..	..	..	**129**	**494**	**767**	**1,508**	**1,678**	**2,468**	**2,097**
Interest on long-term debt	..	..	..	0	8	32	102	98	170	240
Profit remittances on FDI	..	..	..	0	0	0	0	0	0	0
Memo: official net transfers	..	..	..	13	178	453	346	315	392	252
private net transfers	..	..	..	117	317	315	1,162	1,363	2,076	1,845
3. MAJOR ECONOMIC AGGREGATES										
Gross national product (GNP)	..	..	..	26,795	25,694	19,768	19,874	20,890	21,946	21,669
Exports of goods & services (XGS)	..	..	..	5,758	4,248	4,246	5,751	7,033	7,833	6,830
of which workers remittances	..	..	..	0	0	0	7	10	18	0
Imports of goods & services (MGS)	..	..	..	6,037	5,019	5,519	6,321	7,822	8,684	8,109
International reserves (RES)	..	..	..	..	711	1,216	1,660	1,961	2,223	1,965
Current account balance	..	..	..	-111	-456	-1,172	-518	-750	-794	-1,201
4. DEBT INDICATORS										
EDT / XGS (%)	..	..	..	0.6	40.7	65.7	65.2	41.6	52.1	83.7
EDT / GNP (%)	..	..	..	0.1	6.7	14.1	18.9	14.0	18.6	26.4
TDS / XGS (%)	..	..	..	0.0	0.2	1.6	4.1	4.6	6.2	13.0
INT / XGS (%)	..	..	..	0.0	0.2	1.1	2.3	1.9	2.7	4.1
INT / GNP (%)	..	..	..	0.0	0.0	0.2	0.7	0.6	1.0	1.3
RES / EDT (%)	..	..	..	..	41.2	43.6	44.3	67.1	54.5	34.4
RES / MGS (months)	..	..	..	..	1.7	2.6	3.2	3.0	3.1	2.9
Short-term / EDT (%)	..	..	..	26.3	1.3	8.3	10.2	7.6	8.6	7.9
Concessional / EDT (%)	..	..	..	0.0	0.0	0.1	2.7	4.4	3.9	4.6
Multilateral / EDT (%)	..	..	..	0.0	1.5	7.8	10.4	20.0	20.2	21.6

KAZAKHSTAN

(US$ million, unless otherwise indicated)

	1970	1980	1990	1992	1993	1994	1995	1996	1997	1998
5. LONG-TERM DEBT										
DEBT OUTSTANDING (LDOD)	..	..	..	**26**	**1,621**	**2,268**	**2,937**	**2,149**	**3,218**	**4,609**
Public and publicly guaranteed	..	..	..	**26**	**1,621**	**2,227**	**2,834**	**1,947**	**2,622**	**3,040**
Official creditors	..	..	..	10	1,423	1,893	2,293	1,291	1,612	2,049
Multilateral	..	..	..	0	26	217	392	586	824	1,232
Concessional	..	..	..	0	0	0	0	6	22	45
Bilateral	..	..	..	10	1,397	1,675	1,901	705	788	817
Concessional	..	..	..	0	0	2	100	122	135	218
Private creditors	..	..	..	16	198	334	541	656	1,009	991
Bonds	..	..	..	0	0	0	0	200	550	550
Commercial banks	..	..	..	0	0	0	17	17	114	148
Other private	..	..	..	16	198	334	523	438	346	293
Private nonguaranteed	..	..	..	**0**	**0**	**41**	**103**	**203**	**596**	**1,569**
Bonds	..	..	..	0	0	0	0	0	0	100
Commercial banks	..	..	..	0	0	41	103	203	596	1,469
Memo:										
IBRD	..	..	..	0	0	187	295	490	648	899
IDA	..	..	..	0	0	0	0	0	0	0
DISBURSEMENTS	..	..	..	**27**	**341**	**611**	**740**	**787**	**1,487**	**1,672**
Public and publicly guaranteed	..	..	..	**27**	**341**	**591**	**671**	**639**	**991**	**484**
Official creditors	..	..	..	10	170	454	421	408	491	441
Multilateral	..	..	..	0	27	184	171	257	284	364
Concessional	..	..	..	0	0	0	0	6	17	21
Bilateral	..	..	..	10	143	269	250	151	208	77
Concessional	..	..	..	0	0	2	108	36	29	60
Private creditors	..	..	..	17	171	137	249	232	500	43
Bonds	..	..	..	0	0	0	0	200	350	0
Commercial banks	..	..	..	0	0	0	17	0	105	42
Other private	..	..	..	17	171	137	232	32	46	1
Private nonguaranteed	..	..	..	**0**	**0**	**20**	**69**	**148**	**496**	**1,187**
Bonds	..	..	..	0	0	0	0	0	0	100
Commercial banks	..	..	..	0	0	20	69	148	496	1,087
Memo:										
IBRD	..	..	..	0	0	182	107	225	202	211
IDA	..	..	..	0	0	0	0	0	0	0
PRINCIPAL REPAYMENTS	..	..	..	**0**	**0**	**23**	**105**	**192**	**267**	**508**
Public and publicly guaranteed	..	..	..	**0**	**0**	**18**	**95**	**151**	**152**	**189**
Official creditors	..	..	..	0	0	12	27	74	57	103
Multilateral	..	..	..	0	0	0	0	32	0	0
Concessional	..	..	..	0	0	0	0	0	0	0
Bilateral	..	..	..	0	0	12	27	43	57	103
Concessional	..	..	..	0	0	0	0	1	1	1
Private creditors	..	..	..	0	0	6	68	77	94	87
Bonds	..	..	..	0	0	0	0	0	0	0
Commercial banks	..	..	..	0	0	0	0	0	8	13
Other private	..	..	..	0	0	6	68	77	87	74
Private nonguaranteed	..	..	..	**0**	**0**	**5**	**11**	**41**	**115**	**319**
Bonds	..	..	..	0	0	0	0	0	0	0
Commercial banks	..	..	..	0	0	5	11	41	115	319
Memo:										
IBRD	..	..	..	0	0	0	0	0	0	0
IDA	..	..	..	0	0	0	0	0	0	0
NET FLOWS ON DEBT	..	..	..	**27**	**341**	**588**	**635**	**596**	**1,220**	**1,164**
Public and publicly guaranteed	..	..	..	**27**	**341**	**573**	**576**	**488**	**840**	**295**
Official creditors	..	..	..	10	170	442	395	334	434	339
Multilateral	..	..	..	0	27	184	171	226	284	364
Concessional	..	..	..	0	0	0	0	6	17	21
Bilateral	..	..	..	10	143	258	223	108	151	-26
Concessional	..	..	..	0	0	2	108	35	29	60
Private creditors	..	..	..	17	171	131	182	155	406	-43
Bonds	..	..	..	0	0	0	0	200	350	0
Commercial banks	..	..	..	0	0	0	17	0	97	30
Other private	..	..	..	17	171	131	164	-45	-41	-73
Private nonguaranteed	..	..	..	**0**	**0**	**15**	**59**	**107**	**380**	**869**
Bonds	..	..	..	0	0	0	0	0	0	100
Commercial banks	..	..	..	0	0	15	59	107	380	769
Memo:										
IBRD	..	..	..	0	0	182	107	225	202	211
IDA	..	..	..	0	0	0	0	0	0	0

KAZAKHSTAN

(US$ million, unless otherwise indicated)

	1970	1980	1990	1992	1993	1994	1995	1996	1997	1998
INTEREST PAYMENTS (LINT)	..	..	..	**0**	**8**	**32**	**102**	**98**	**170**	**240**
Public and publicly guaranteed	..	..	..	**0**	**8**	**30**	**100**	**95**	**164**	**205**
Official creditors	..	..	..	0	4	16	59	63	88	101
Multilateral	..	..	..	0	0	7	15	31	43	58
Concessional	..	..	..	0	0	0	0	0	0	0
Bilateral	..	..	..	0	4	9	44	32	46	43
Concessional	..	..	..	0	0	0	2	7	5	6
Private creditors	..	..	..	0	4	14	41	32	76	104
Bonds	..	..	..	0	0	0	0	0	22	48
Commercial banks	..	..	..	0	0	0	0	1	15	8
Other private	..	..	..	0	4	14	41	31	39	49
Private nonguaranteed	..	..	..	**0**	**0**	**3**	**1**	**4**	**6**	**34**
Bonds	..	..	..	0	0	0	0	0	0	0
Commercial banks	..	..	..	0	0	3	1	4	6	34
Memo:										
IBRD	..	..	..	0	0	7	14	24	34	44
IDA	..	..	..	0	0	0	0	0	0	0
NET TRANSFERS ON DEBT	..	..	..	**27**	**334**	**556**	**533**	**497**	**1,050**	**925**
Public and publicly guaranteed	..	..	..	**27**	**334**	**543**	**476**	**394**	**676**	**90**
Official creditors	..	..	..	10	167	426	335	271	346	238
Multilateral	..	..	..	0	27	177	156	195	241	306
Concessional	..	..	..	0	0	0	0	6	17	20
Bilateral	..	..	..	10	140	249	180	76	105	-69
Concessional	..	..	..	0	0	2	105	28	24	54
Private creditors	..	..	..	16	167	117	141	123	330	-148
Bonds	..	..	..	0	0	0	0	200	328	-48
Commercial banks	..	..	..	0	0	0	17	-1	83	22
Other private	..	..	..	16	167	117	123	-76	-81	-122
Private nonguaranteed	..	..	..	**0**	**0**	**13**	**57**	**104**	**374**	**835**
Bonds	..	..	..	0	0	0	0	0	0	100
Commercial banks	..	..	..	0	0	13	57	104	374	735
Memo:										
IBRD	..	..	..	0	0	175	93	201	167	167
IDA	..	..	..	0	0	0	0	0	0	0
DEBT SERVICE (LTDS)	..	..	..	**0**	**8**	**55**	**207**	**290**	**437**	**747**
Public and publicly guaranteed	..	..	..	**0**	**8**	**47**	**195**	**246**	**316**	**394**
Official creditors	..	..	..	0	4	27	86	137	145	204
Multilateral	..	..	..	0	0	7	15	62	43	58
Concessional	..	..	..	0	0	0	0	0	0	0
Bilateral	..	..	..	0	4	21	71	75	103	146
Concessional	..	..	..	0	0	0	2	8	5	6
Private creditors	..	..	..	0	4	20	109	109	170	191
Bonds	..	..	..	0	0	0	0	0	22	48
Commercial banks	..	..	..	0	0	0	0	1	22	21
Other private	..	..	..	0	4	20	109	108	126	123
Private nonguaranteed	..	..	..	**0**	**0**	**8**	**12**	**44**	**121**	**353**
Bonds	..	..	..	0	0	0	0	0	0	0
Commercial banks	..	..	..	0	0	8	12	44	121	353
Memo:										
IBRD	..	..	..	0	0	7	14	24	34	44
IDA	..	..	..	0	0	0	0	0	0	0
UNDISBURSED DEBT	..	..	..	**374**	**728**	**604**	**848**	**1,070**	**1,082**	**1,187**
Official creditors	..	..	..	274	414	346	784	977	1,003	1,114
Private creditors	..	..	..	100	314	257	64	93	79	72
Memorandum items										
Concessional LDOD	..	..	..	0	0	2	100	128	157	264
Variable rate LDOD	..	..	..	26	1,596	2,077	2,520	1,481	2,196	3,453
Public sector LDOD	..	..	..	26	1,621	2,227	2,834	1,947	2,622	3,035
Private sector LDOD	..	..	..	0	0	41	103	203	596	1,574

6. CURRENCY COMPOSITION OF LONG-TERM DEBT (PERCENT)

	1970	1980	1990	1992	1993	1994	1995	1996	1997	1998
Deutsche mark	..	..	..	99.8	18.7	22.6	21.6	28.0	17.3	13.3
French franc	..	..	..	0.0	0.0	0.4	0.4	0.3	0.6	0.5
Japanese yen	..	..	..	0.0	0.0	3.9	8.9	15.1	11.1	13.2
Pound sterling	..	..	..	0.0	0.0	0.0	0.0	0.0	0.0	0.2
Swiss franc	..	..	..	0.0	0.0	0.2	0.0	0.0	0.0	0.1
U.S.dollars	..	..	..	0.0	2.1	5.7	6.9	23.4	44.2	47.1
Multiple currency	..	..	..	0.0	0.0	8.4	11.8	27.5	24.0	23.4
Special drawing rights	..	..	..	0.0	0.0	0.0	0.0	0.0	0.0	0.0
All other currencies	..	..	..	0.2	79.2	58.8	50.4	5.7	2.8	2.2

KAZAKHSTAN

(US$ million, unless otherwise indicated)

	1970	1980	1990	1992	1993	1994	1995	1996	1997	1998
7. DEBT RESTRUCTURINGS										
Total amount rescheduled	..	..	..	0	1,250	0	0	0	0	0
Debt stock rescheduled	..	..	..	0	0	0	0	0	0	0
Principal rescheduled	..	..	..	0	0	0	0	0	0	0
Official	..	..	..	0	0	0	0	0	0	0
Private	..	..	..	0	0	0	0	0	0	0
Interest rescheduled	..	..	..	..	0	0	0	0	0	0
Official	..	..	..	0	0	0	0	0	0	0
Private	..	..	..	0	0	0	0	0	0	0
Debt forgiven	..	..	..	0	0	0	0	0	0	0
Memo: interest forgiven	..	..	..	0	0	0	0	0	0	0
Debt stock reduction	..	..	..	0	0	0	0	0	0	0
of which debt buyback	..	..	..	0	0	0	0	0	0	0
8. DEBT STOCK-FLOW RECONCILIATION										
Total change in debt stocks	..	..	..	..	1,693	1,062	961	-828	1,156	1,636
Net flows on debt	..	..	..	36	418	910	868	732	1,342	1,307
Net change in interest arrears	..	..	..	..	22	84	56	-162	0	76
Interest capitalized	..	..	..	..	0	0	0	0	0	0
Debt forgiveness or reduction	..	..	..	..	0	0	0	0	0	0
Cross-currency valuation	..	..	..	..	-873	-731	-212	-116	-147	126
Residual	..	..	..	..	2,126	799	248	-1,283	-39	128
9. AVERAGE TERMS OF NEW COMMITMENTS										
ALL CREDITORS										
Interest (%)	..	..	..	8.0	6.3	5.6	5.5	7.1	6.4	6.3
Maturity (years)	..	..	..	10.3	10.2	13.3	13.3	13.4	13.6	19.6
Grace period (years)	..	..	..	4.0	3.3	5.0	4.3	4.1	5.6	5.1
Grant element (%)	..	..	..	7.2	13.9	22.4	22.3	15.1	21.9	23.3
Official creditors										
Interest (%)	..	..	..	8.4	6.9	5.6	5.5	6.5	5.4	6.2
Maturity (years)	..	..	..	11.0	13.4	14.0	14.2	17.4	20.6	20.3
Grace period (years)	..	..	..	4.4	4.5	5.3	4.5	4.7	6.5	5.4
Grant element (%)	..	..	..	5.1	13.5	23.5	23.7	19.9	32.4	24.5
Private creditors										
Interest (%)	..	..	..	7.1	5.8	6.1	6.4	8.8	7.6	8.0
Maturity (years)	..	..	..	8.6	7.7	6.6	5.7	3.7	5.8	9.3
Grace period (years)	..	..	..	2.9	2.4	2.1	2.3	2.7	4.6	2.1
Grant element (%)	..	..	..	12.5	14.2	12.2	10.0	3.5	10.1	6.9
Memorandum items										
Commitments	..	..	..	414	740	414	982	903	1,056	559
Official creditors	..	..	..	295	323	374	880	639	557	521
Private creditors	..	..	..	120	417	40	101	264	499	38

10. CONTRACTUAL OBLIGATIONS ON OUTSTANDING LONG-TERM DEBT

	1999	2000	2001	2002	2003	2004	2005	2006	2007	2008
TOTAL										
Disbursements	499	339	130	90	52	36	21	10	7	3
Principal	866	539	693	790	389	344	277	227	202	168
Interest	276	248	214	187	142	125	109	96	84	73
Official creditors										
Disbursements	455	317	124	90	52	36	21	10	7	3
Principal	229	173	236	231	212	215	179	165	175	162
Interest	137	143	141	133	124	114	102	93	83	72
Bilateral creditors										
Disbursements	163	108	30	14	7	5	0	0	0	0
Principal	201	138	145	125	78	69	32	17	23	23
Interest	39	34	28	22	17	14	11	10	9	8
Multilateral creditors										
Disbursements	292	209	95	76	45	32	21	10	7	3
Principal	28	35	91	106	135	145	148	149	151	138
Interest	98	110	113	111	107	100	92	83	74	64
Private creditors										
Disbursements	44	22	6	1	0	0	0	0	0	0
Principal	638	366	456	559	176	129	98	61	27	7
Interest	139	105	73	54	18	11	7	4	2	0
Commercial banks										
Disbursements	39	18	5	0	0	0	0	0	0	0
Principal	29	30	80	12	10	10	10	9	9	7
Interest	11	10	6	3	3	2	2	1	1	0
Other private										
Disbursements	5	4	1	1	0	0	0	0	0	0
Principal	609	336	377	547	166	120	88	52	19	0
Interest	128	94	67	51	16	9	5	2	1	0

KENYA

(US$ million, unless otherwise indicated)

	1970	1980	1990	1992	1993	1994	1995	1996	1997	1998
1. SUMMARY DEBT DATA										
TOTAL DEBT STOCKS (EDT)	**..**	**3,387**	**7,058**	**6,898**	**7,111**	**7,202**	**7,412**	**6,931**	**6,603**	**7,010**
Long-term debt (LDOD)	**409**	**2,493**	**5,641**	**5,728**	**5,846**	**6,119**	**6,405**	**6,060**	**5,550**	**5,954**
Public and publicly guaranteed	321	2,056	4,761	5,149	5,246	5,589	5,960	5,685	5,225	5,629
Private nonguaranteed	88	437	880	579	600	530	445	375	325	325
Use of IMF credit	**0**	**254**	**482**	**393**	**363**	**405**	**374**	**337**	**250**	**197**
Short-term debt	**..**	**640**	**934**	**777**	**903**	**679**	**634**	**534**	**803**	**859**
of which interest arrears on LDOD	..	2	95	189	242	83	32	16	34	83
Official creditors	..	2	49	62	59	20	23	9	21	45
Private creditors	..	0	46	127	183	63	9	7	13	38
Memo: principal arrears on LDOD	..	3	72	263	410	9	6	29	121	219
Official creditors	..	0	22	72	97	9	2	17	46	108
Private creditors	..	3	50	192	313	0	4	12	75	111
Memo: export credits	..	0	1,540	1,720	1,636	1,617	1,299	1,087	1,085	873
TOTAL DEBT FLOWS										
Disbursements	**78**	**714**	**778**	**502**	**447**	**294**	**698**	**467**	**219**	**255**
Long-term debt	78	620	642	502	415	262	698	431	219	255
IMF purchases	0	94	136	0	32	32	0	36	0	0
Principal repayments	**33**	**205**	**458**	**410**	**366**	**552**	**600**	**567**	**449**	**380**
Long-term debt	29	195	352	327	304	538	561	506	381	318
IMF repurchases	4	9	106	83	62	14	39	61	67	63
Net flows on debt	**114**	**718**	**615**	**114**	**154**	**-322**	**104**	**-185**	**21**	**-118**
of which short-term debt	..	209	294	21	73	-65	6	-84	251	7
Interest payments (INT)	**..**	**229**	**333**	**260**	**265**	**329**	**301**	**277**	**221**	**165**
Long-term debt	17	163	230	201	208	290	263	245	190	125
IMF charges	0	8	26	10	4	2	2	2	2	1
Short-term debt	..	58	78	49	53	38	36	30	30	39
Net transfers on debt	**..**	**489**	**281**	**-147**	**-112**	**-652**	**-198**	**-462**	**-199**	**-283**
Total debt service paid (TDS)	**..**	**434**	**791**	**670**	**632**	**881**	**901**	**844**	**669**	**545**
Long-term debt	46	359	582	528	513	827	824	752	571	442
IMF repurchases and charges	4	17	131	93	66	16	41	63	69	64
Short-term debt (interest only)	..	58	78	49	53	38	36	30	30	39
2. AGGREGATE NET RESOURCE FLOWS AND NET TRANSFERS (LONG-TERM)										
NET RESOURCE FLOWS	**67**	**624**	**1,324**	**559**	**404**	**39**	**411**	**175**	**71**	**149**
Net flow of long-term debt (ex. IMF)	49	424	290	175	111	-276	137	-76	-163	-63
Foreign direct investment (net)	14	79	57	6	2	4	32	13	20	11
Portfolio equity flows	0	0	0	0	0	0	0	43	12	4
Grants (excluding technical coop.)	3	121	977	378	292	311	242	196	202	197
Memo: technical coop. grants	27	128	208	281	259	191	220	192	179	150
official net resource flows	33	323	1,202	533	442	317	537	291	144	206
private net resource flows	33	301	122	26	-38	-278	-126	-116	-73	-57
NET TRANSFERS	**0**	**311**	**961**	**233**	**79**	**-351**	**53**	**-170**	**-239**	**-76**
Interest on long-term debt	17	163	230	201	208	290	263	245	190	125
Profit remittances on FDI	49	150	132	126	117	100	95	100	120	100
Memo: official net transfers	25	269	1,068	422	316	156	371	128	27	110
private net transfers	-25	41	-107	-189	-237	-507	-318	-298	-266	-186
3. MAJOR ECONOMIC AGGREGATES										
Gross national product (GNP)	1,545	7,039	8,089	7,614	4,560	6,758	8,687	8,965	10,325	11,394
Exports of goods & services (XGS)	..	2,061	2,233	2,152	2,329	2,675	2,974	3,041	3,000	2,892
of which workers remittances	..	0	0	0	0	0	0	0	0	0
Imports of goods & services (MGS)	..	3,095	3,128	2,532	2,471	2,848	3,892	3,694	4,026	3,909
International reserves (RES)	220	539	236	80	437	588	384	776	811	783
Current account balance	..	-876	-527	-180	71	98	-400	-73	-377	-363
4. DEBT INDICATORS										
EDT / XGS (%)	..	164.3	316.0	320.5	305.3	269.2	249.3	227.9	220.1	242.4
EDT / GNP (%)	..	48.1	87.3	90.6	155.9	106.6	85.3	77.3	64.0	61.5
TDS / XGS (%)	..	21.0	35.4	31.1	27.1	32.9	30.3	27.8	22.3	18.8
INT / XGS (%)	..	11.1	14.9	12.1	11.4	12.3	10.1	9.1	7.4	5.7
INT / GNP (%)	..	3.3	4.1	3.4	5.8	4.9	3.5	3.1	2.1	1.4
RES / EDT (%)	..	15.9	3.4	1.2	6.1	8.2	5.2	11.2	12.3	11.2
RES / MGS (months)	..	2.1	0.9	0.4	2.1	2.5	1.2	2.5	2.4	2.4
Short-term / EDT (%)	..	18.9	13.2	11.3	12.7	9.4	8.6	7.7	12.2	12.3
Concessional / EDT (%)	..	20.2	33.7	40.4	43.5	47.1	52.3	56.8	57.0	58.8
Multilateral / EDT (%)	..	18.7	35.3	36.4	36.8	38.4	39.4	42.5	43.2	42.8

KENYA

(US$ million, unless otherwise indicated)

	1970	1980	1990	1992	1993	1994	1995	1996	1997	1998
5. LONG-TERM DEBT										
DEBT OUTSTANDING (LDOD)	**409**	**2,493**	**5,641**	**5,728**	**5,846**	**6,119**	**6,405**	**6,060**	**5,550**	**5,954**
Public and publicly guaranteed	**321**	**2,056**	**4,761**	**5,149**	**5,246**	**5,589**	**5,960**	**5,685**	**5,225**	**5,629**
Official creditors	237	1,206	3,714	3,960	4,149	4,853	5,252	5,106	4,745	5,076
Multilateral	38	634	2,492	2,514	2,615	2,762	2,919	2,943	2,855	2,999
Concessional	32	270	1,395	1,638	1,853	2,040	2,249	2,402	2,390	2,584
Bilateral	199	572	1,222	1,446	1,535	2,091	2,333	2,164	1,890	2,076
Concessional	138	414	985	1,149	1,237	1,355	1,630	1,536	1,372	1,539
Private creditors	84	849	1,047	1,190	1,096	736	708	578	480	554
Bonds	71	10	0	0	0	0	0	0	0	0
Commercial banks	1	394	924	1,028	956	653	607	500	445	472
Other private	12	445	124	162	141	83	101	79	35	82
Private nonguaranteed	**88**	**437**	**880**	**579**	**600**	**530**	**445**	**375**	**325**	**325**
Bonds	0	0	0	0	0	0	0	0	0	0
Commercial banks	88	437	880	579	600	530	445	375	325	325
Memo:										
IBRD	6	308	872	656	566	501	435	312	213	154
IDA	32	220	1,185	1,411	1,631	1,789	1,977	2,062	2,032	2,210
DISBURSEMENTS	**78**	**620**	**642**	**502**	**415**	**262**	**698**	**431**	**219**	**255**
Public and publicly guaranteed	**37**	**533**	**587**	**442**	**350**	**262**	**698**	**431**	**219**	**255**
Official creditors	36	233	405	329	329	256	566	359	171	218
Multilateral	10	154	297	132	239	160	220	197	142	142
Concessional	7	94	264	106	234	124	181	181	128	132
Bilateral	26	79	108	197	90	96	346	161	29	77
Concessional	20	66	106	123	76	74	346	108	29	35
Private creditors	1	300	182	113	22	6	132	72	48	36
Bonds	0	0	0	0	0	0	0	0	0	0
Commercial banks	0	215	119	66	17	5	72	72	48	14
Other private	1	85	63	47	5	0	60	0	0	22
Private nonguaranteed	**41**	**87**	**55**	**60**	**65**	**0**	**0**	**0**	**0**	**0**
Bonds	0	0	0	0	0	0	0	0	0	0
Commercial banks	41	87	55	60	65	0	0	0	0	0
Memo:										
IBRD	3	45	4	1	0	0	0	0	0	0
IDA	7	72	235	91	226	97	159	156	84	123
PRINCIPAL REPAYMENTS	**29**	**195**	**352**	**327**	**304**	**538**	**561**	**506**	**381**	**318**
Public and publicly guaranteed	**17**	**108**	**315**	**267**	**254**	**468**	**476**	**436**	**331**	**318**
Official creditors	6	31	180	173	178	251	271	263	229	209
Multilateral	1	13	127	133	140	151	150	135	127	124
Concessional	0	1	9	9	15	18	18	16	19	23
Bilateral	5	17	54	40	38	100	120	128	102	86
Concessional	3	5	25	24	24	50	51	52	40	41
Private creditors	12	77	135	93	76	217	205	173	103	108
Bonds	10	0	0	0	0	0	0	0	0	0
Commercial banks	0	25	115	78	56	169	161	150	88	82
Other private	1	53	20	16	20	48	45	23	15	27
Private nonguaranteed	**12**	**88**	**37**	**60**	**50**	**70**	**85**	**70**	**50**	**0**
Bonds	0	0	0	0	0	0	0	0	0	0
Commercial banks	12	88	37	60	50	70	85	70	50	0
Memo:										
IBRD	1	11	95	98	100	106	100	89	74	66
IDA	0	1	4	6	7	8	9	10	11	15
NET FLOWS ON DEBT	**49**	**424**	**290**	**175**	**111**	**-276**	**137**	**-76**	**-163**	**-63**
Public and publicly guaranteed	**20**	**425**	**272**	**175**	**96**	**-206**	**222**	**-6**	**-113**	**-63**
Official creditors	30	202	225	155	150	5	295	95	-58	9
Multilateral	9	141	171	-2	98	10	70	62	15	18
Concessional	7	94	255	97	219	106	163	165	108	109
Bilateral	21	62	54	157	52	-4	225	33	-73	-9
Concessional	17	61	81	99	52	24	294	57	-11	-6
Private creditors	-10	223	47	20	-55	-211	-73	-101	-55	-72
Bonds	-10	0	0	0	0	0	0	0	0	0
Commercial banks	0	190	4	-12	-39	-164	-89	-78	-40	-68
Other private	0	33	43	31	-15	-48	15	-23	-15	-5
Private nonguaranteed	**30**	**-1**	**18**	**0**	**15**	**-70**	**-85**	**-70**	**-50**	**0**
Bonds	0	0	0	0	0	0	0	0	0	0
Commercial banks	30	-1	18	0	15	-70	-85	-70	-50	0
Memo:										
IBRD	2	35	-92	-97	-100	-106	-100	-89	-74	-66
IDA	7	71	230	85	219	89	150	146	72	108

KENYA

(US$ million, unless otherwise indicated)

	1970	1980	1990	1992	1993	1994	1995	1996	1997	1998
INTEREST PAYMENTS (LINT)	**17**	**163**	**230**	**201**	**208**	**290**	**263**	**245**	**190**	**125**
Public and publicly guaranteed	**13**	**124**	**193**	**145**	**154**	**244**	**222**	**214**	**158**	**125**
Official creditors	8	54	134	112	126	161	167	163	117	96
Multilateral	1	36	100	85	85	81	77	73	58	50
Concessional	0	1	9	11	14	16	17	17	18	18
Bilateral	8	18	34	26	42	80	89	90	59	46
Concessional	4	7	14	17	26	31	43	40	29	32
Private creditors	5	70	59	34	28	83	55	50	41	29
Bonds	4	1	0	0	0	0	0	0	0	0
Commercial banks	0	30	53	28	22	69	49	45	40	27
Other private	1	39	6	6	6	14	7	5	2	2
Private nonguaranteed	**4**	**39**	**38**	**56**	**54**	**46**	**42**	**32**	**31**	**0**
Bonds	0	0	0	0	0	0	0	0	0	0
Commercial banks	4	39	38	56	54	46	42	32	31	0
Memo:										
IBRD	0	31	78	61	55	49	43	34	23	17
IDA	0	1	7	10	11	13	14	15	15	15
NET TRANSFERS ON DEBT	**32**	**261**	**60**	**-26**	**-97**	**-565**	**-127**	**-321**	**-352**	**-188**
Public and publicly guaranteed	**7**	**301**	**79**	**30**	**-59**	**-450**	**0**	**-219**	**-271**	**-188**
Official creditors	21	149	91	44	24	-155	129	-68	-175	-87
Multilateral	8	105	71	-87	14	-71	-7	-11	-43	-32
Concessional	7	92	247	86	205	90	147	147	90	92
Bilateral	13	44	21	131	11	-84	136	-57	-132	-54
Concessional	13	53	66	82	26	-7	252	17	-40	-38
Private creditors	-15	152	-12	-14	-83	-294	-129	-151	-96	-101
Bonds	-14	-1	0	0	0	0	0	0	0	0
Commercial banks	0	160	-49	-40	-61	-233	-137	-123	-80	-95
Other private	-1	-6	37	26	-22	-62	9	-28	-17	-6
Private nonguaranteed	**25**	**-40**	**-20**	**-56**	**-39**	**-116**	**-127**	**-102**	**-81**	**0**
Bonds	0	0	0	0	0	0	0	0	0	0
Commercial banks	25	-40	-20	-56	-39	-116	-127	-102	-81	0
Memo:										
IBRD	2	3	-169	-158	-156	-155	-144	-122	-97	-83
IDA	7	70	223	75	208	76	135	131	57	93
DEBT SERVICE (LTDS)	**46**	**359**	**582**	**528**	**513**	**827**	**824**	**752**	**571**	**442**
Public and publicly guaranteed	**30**	**232**	**507**	**412**	**409**	**711**	**698**	**650**	**490**	**442**
Official creditors	14	84	314	285	305	411	437	427	346	305
Multilateral	2	49	227	219	225	231	228	208	185	174
Concessional	0	2	18	21	28	34	35	34	37	40
Bilateral	13	35	87	66	79	180	210	218	161	131
Concessional	7	13	40	41	50	81	94	91	69	73
Private creditors	16	148	194	127	104	300	260	223	144	137
Bonds	14	1	0	0	0	0	0	0	0	0
Commercial banks	0	55	167	106	78	238	209	195	127	109
Other private	2	91	26	22	27	62	52	28	17	29
Private nonguaranteed	**16**	**127**	**75**	**116**	**104**	**116**	**127**	**102**	**81**	**0**
Bonds	0	0	0	0	0	0	0	0	0	0
Commercial banks	16	127	75	116	104	116	127	102	81	0
Memo:										
IBRD	1	42	173	159	156	155	144	122	97	83
IDA	0	2	11	16	19	21	24	25	26	30
UNDISBURSED DEBT	**119**	**1,333**	**1,991**	**1,749**	**1,622**	**1,574**	**1,288**	**1,280**	**1,239**	**1,243**
Official creditors	119	1,241	1,634	1,561	1,460	1,409	1,084	1,115	1,117	1,071
Private creditors	0	92	356	188	161	165	203	165	122	172
Memorandum items										
Concessional LDOD	170	684	2,381	2,788	3,090	3,394	3,879	3,938	3,762	4,123
Variable rate LDOD	88	690	1,090	748	747	875	777	703	618	590
Public sector LDOD	321	2,056	4,761	5,149	5,246	5,589	5,960	5,685	5,225	5,629
Private sector LDOD	88	437	880	579	600	530	445	375	325	325

6. CURRENCY COMPOSITION OF LONG-TERM DEBT (PERCENT)

	1970	1980	1990	1992	1993	1994	1995	1996	1997	1998
Deutsche mark	6.0	9.8	1.7	1.6	1.6	1.8	2.6	2.8	3.0	3.0
French franc	0.0	9.0	6.7	5.9	5.3	7.0	6.2	5.0	4.8	5.5
Japanese yen	0.2	4.6	8.4	12.8	14.5	16.0	18.3	17.6	16.9	17.6
Pound sterling	76.4	14.3	8.7	5.7	5.1	4.5	3.8	3.8	3.6	4.3
Swiss franc	0.0	2.3	3.4	6.9	6.4	4.7	4.1	3.1	2.9	2.3
U.S.dollars	15.7	35.9	30.9	32.1	35.4	35.1	36.2	39.7	42.1	42.9
Multiple currency	1.2	14.9	24.4	19.2	17.1	15.2	13.4	11.5	10.1	7.4
Special drawing rights	0.0	0.0	0.3	0.3	0.3	0.4	0.4	0.4	0.4	0.4
All other currencies	0.5	9.2	15.5	15.5	14.3	15.3	15.0	16.1	16.2	16.6

KENYA

(US$ million, unless otherwise indicated)

	1970	1980	1990	1992	1993	1994	1995	1996	1997	1998
7. DEBT RESTRUCTURINGS										
Total amount rescheduled	..	..	0	0	0	550	0	0	0	0
Debt stock rescheduled	..	..	0	0	0	0	0	0	0	0
Principal rescheduled	..	..	0	0	1	367	0	0	0	0
Official	..	..	0	0	0	74	0	0	0	0
Private	..	..	0	0	1	293	0	0	0	0
Interest rescheduled	..	..	0	0	0	162	0	0	0	0
Official	..	..	0	0	0	45	0	0	0	0
Private	..	..	0	0	0	118	0	0	0	0
Debt forgiven	..	..	84	30	0	0	0	0	26	0
Memo: interest forgiven	..	..	13	0	0	0	0	0	0	0
Debt stock reduction	..	..	0	0	0	0	0	0	0	0
of which debt buyback	..	..	0	0	0	0	0	0	0	0
8. DEBT STOCK-FLOW RECONCILIATION										
Total change in debt stocks	..	..	1,168	-555	213	91	210	-481	-328	407
Net flows on debt	114	718	615	114	154	-322	104	-185	21	-118
Net change in interest arrears	..	..	30	48	53	-159	-51	-15	17	49
Interest capitalized	..	..	0	0	0	162	0	0	0	0
Debt forgiveness or reduction	..	..	-84	-30	0	0	0	0	-26	0
Cross-currency valuation	..	..	319	-225	-16	283	94	-261	-294	203
Residual	..	..	288	-462	23	127	64	-21	-47	274
9. AVERAGE TERMS OF NEW COMMITMENTS										
ALL CREDITORS										
Interest (%)	2.5	3.5	4.1	0.9	2.3	1.9	4.8	1.2	1.7	3.0
Maturity (years)	37.3	31.3	25.5	31.3	31.8	29.5	23.0	34.9	31.7	24.3
Grace period (years)	7.9	8.0	7.5	9.2	8.8	7.0	5.8	8.8	9.2	6.0
Grant element (%)	62.6	53.3	46.0	71.2	63.6	62.7	39.0	70.7	66.9	49.3
Official creditors										
Interest (%)	2.4	3.5	3.0	0.8	2.3	1.9	2.1	0.7	1.6	1.7
Maturity (years)	37.9	31.5	29.9	34.6	31.8	29.5	35.5	37.6	33.3	32.8
Grace period (years)	8.0	8.0	8.4	10.1	8.8	7.0	9.8	9.5	9.7	8.0
Grant element (%)	63.7	53.6	57.7	77.5	63.6	62.7	66.8	76.3	70.1	66.9
Private creditors										
Interest (%)	7.0	8.0	7.4	1.8	0.0	0.0	8.3	6.5	4.3	6.2
Maturity (years)	11.2	5.9	13.2	2.7	0.0	0.0	6.4	5.1	4.1	3.9
Grace period (years)	1.7	-0.6	4.9	1.7	0.0	0.0	0.4	0.9	0.4	1.3
Grant element (%)	12.4	5.2	13.5	15.1	0.0	0.0	2.2	8.6	10.5	6.8
Memorandum items										
Commitments	50	518	825	294	212	103	389	419	268	321
Official creditors	49	514	606	264	212	103	222	384	254	227
Private creditors	1	4	219	30	0	0	168	35	14	94

10. CONTRACTUAL OBLIGATIONS ON OUTSTANDING LONG-TERM DEBT

	1999	2000	2001	2002	2003	2004	2005	2006	2007	2008
TOTAL										
Disbursements	411	336	202	124	65	23	11	2	1	0
Principal	517	505	470	306	265	216	204	200	201	198
Interest	146	126	103	83	70	62	56	51	50	46
Official creditors										
Disbursements	320	278	183	119	65	23	11	2	1	0
Principal	353	352	355	222	214	187	191	193	194	193
Interest	112	97	82	69	63	57	53	49	48	44
Bilateral creditors										
Disbursements	132	118	73	43	23	13	5	1	1	0
Principal	208	230	246	123	116	99	104	101	108	104
Interest	64	57	47	38	33	30	28	25	26	24
Multilateral creditors										
Disbursements	188	160	110	77	42	9	6	1	1	0
Principal	144	122	108	99	98	88	88	92	87	88
Interest	48	41	36	32	29	27	25	24	22	21
Private creditors										
Disbursements	91	58	19	5	0	0	0	0	0	0
Principal	165	153	115	84	51	28	13	7	7	6
Interest	34	29	21	14	8	5	3	3	2	2
Commercial banks										
Disbursements	89	56	18	4	0	0	0	0	0	0
Principal	133	137	109	78	44	22	10	6	6	5
Interest	31	27	19	13	7	4	3	3	2	2
Other private										
Disbursements	1	2	1	0	0	0	0	0	0	0
Principal	32	16	7	7	7	7	3	0	0	0
Interest	3	2	2	2	1	1	0	0	0	0

KOREA, REPUBLIC OF

(US$ million, unless otherwise indicated)

	1970	1980	1990	1992	1993	1994	1995	1996	1997	1998
1. SUMMARY DEBT DATA										
Total External Liabilities *			31,700	42,800	43,900	97,400	127,500	163,500	159,200	148,700
TOTAL DEBT STOCKS (EDT)	..	**29,480**	**34,986**	**44,156**	**47,202**	**72,414**	**85,810**	**115,803**	**136,984**	**139,097**
Long-term debt (LDOD)	**1,991**	**18,236**	**24,186**	**32,236**	**35,002**	**40,802**	**39,197**	**49,221**	**72,128**	**94,062**
Public and publicly guaranteed	1,816	15,933	18,786	24,050	24,566	19,253	22,123	25,423	33,852	57,956
Private nonguaranteed	175	2,303	5,400	8,186	10,436	21,550	17,074	23,798	38,276	36,106
Use of IMF credit	**0**	**683**	**0**	**0**	**0**	**0**	**0**	**0**	**11,064**	**16,896**
Short-term debt	..	**10,561**	**10,800**	**11,920**	**12,200**	**31,612**	**46,613**	**66,582**	**53,792**	**28,139**
of which interest arrears on LDOD	..	0	0	0	0	0	0	0	0	0
Official creditors	..	0	0	0	0	0	0	0	0	0
Private creditors	..	0	0	0	0	0	0	0	0	0
Memo: principal arrears on LDOD	..	0	0	0	0	0	0	0	0	0
Official creditors	..	0	0	0	0	0	0	0	0	0
Private creditors	..	0	0	0	0	0	0	0	0	0
Memo: export credits	..	0	6,821	3,723	3,329	4,687	3,247	2,957	4,697	7,540
TOTAL DEBT FLOWS										
Disbursements	**476**	**4,605**	**5,736**	**8,215**	**8,251**	**14,131**	**13,610**	**20,133**	**36,345**	**21,255**
Long-term debt	476	3,980	5,736	8,215	8,251	14,131	13,610	20,133	25,061	13,318
IMF purchases	0	625	0	0	0	0	0	0	11,284	7,937
Principal repayments	**218**	**1,586**	**5,678**	**4,237**	**6,269**	**5,222**	**5,905**	**6,802**	**6,781**	**12,412**
Long-term debt	205	1,554	5,678	4,237	6,269	5,222	5,905	6,802	6,781	9,631
IMF repurchases	13	33	0	0	0	0	0	0	0	2,781
Net flows on debt	**847**	**6,415**	**1,058**	**4,698**	**2,262**	**28,321**	**22,706**	**33,300**	**16,774**	**7,190**
of which short-term debt	..	3,396	1,000	720	280	19,412	15,001	19,969	-12,790	-1,653
Interest payments (INT)	..	**2,863**	**2,596**	**2,751**	**2,871**	**3,109**	**5,966**	**6,760**	**6,997**	**8,212**
Long-term debt	76	1,637	1,683	1,999	2,083	2,262	2,931	2,837	4,110	5,014
IMF charges	0	17	0	0	0	0	0	0	0	904
Short-term debt	..	1,210	913	751	788	848	3,035	3,923	2,887	2,294
Net transfers on debt	..	**3,551**	**-1,538**	**1,947**	**-609**	**25,212**	**16,741**	**26,541**	**9,777**	**-1,022**
Total debt service paid (TDS)	..	**4,449**	**8,274**	**6,988**	**9,141**	**8,331**	**11,870**	**13,562**	**13,778**	**20,624**
Long-term debt	281	3,190	7,361	6,237	8,353	7,483	8,835	9,639	10,891	14,645
IMF repurchases and charges	13	49	0	0	0	0	0	0	0	3,685
Short-term debt (interest only)	..	1,210	913	751	788	848	3,035	3,923	2,887	2,294
2. AGGREGATE NET RESOURCE FLOWS AND NET TRANSFERS (LONG-TERM)										
NET RESOURCE FLOWS	**411**	**2,440**	**1,369**	**7,753**	**8,603**	**12,244**	**13,045**	**19,358**	**22,382**	**13,201**
Net flow of long-term debt (ex. IMF)	271	2,426	58	3,978	1,982	8,909	7,705	13,331	18,280	3,687
Foreign direct investment (net)	66	6	788	727	588	809	1,776	2,325	2,844	5,415
Portfolio equity flows	0	0	518	3,045	6,029	2,525	3,559	3,700	1,257	4,096
Grants (excluding technical coop.)	75	8	4	3	3	0	5	2	0	4
Memo: technical coop. grants	13	34	101	119	149	116	144	145	105	147
official net resource flows	221	658	313	253	-144	-629	-625	-517	4,530	5,558
private net resource flows	190	1,782	1,056	7,499	8,746	12,873	13,670	19,875	17,852	7,644
NET TRANSFERS	**330**	**739**	**-581**	**5,506**	**6,266**	**9,712**	**9,819**	**16,201**	**17,921**	**7,812**
Interest on long-term debt	76	1,637	1,683	1,999	2,083	2,262	2,931	2,837	4,110	5,014
Profit remittances on FDI	5	64	266	247	253	270	295	320	350	375
Memo: official net transfers	207	289	-220	-268	-670	-1,056	-990	-826	4,214	4,947
private net transfers	124	450	-360	5,774	6,936	10,768	10,810	17,027	13,707	2,865
3. MAJOR ECONOMIC AGGREGATES										
Gross national product (GNP)	8,997	60,801	252,384	314,337	345,232	401,782	487,918	518,501	473,939	316,195
Exports of goods & services (XGS)	..	22,050	76,679	89,858	97,860	114,850	151,237	157,229	168,928	160,061
of which workers remittances	..	86	488	487	311	245	291	183	129	90
Imports of goods & services (MGS)	..	27,812	79,343	94,405	97,747	119,753	159,670	180,006	177,633	122,772
International reserves (RES)	610	3,101	14,916	17,228	20,355	25,764	32,804	34,158	20,465	52,100
Current account balance	..	-5,312	-2,003	-3,944	990	-3,867	-8,507	-23,006	-8,167	40,552
4. DEBT INDICATORS										
EDT / XGS (%)	..	133.7	45.6	49.1	48.2	63.1	56.7	73.7	81.1	86.9
EDT / GNP (%)	..	48.5	13.9	14.1	13.7	18.0	17.6	22.3	28.9	44.0
TDS / XGS (%)	..	20.2	10.8	7.8	9.3	7.3	7.9	8.6	8.2	12.9
INT / XGS (%)	..	13.0	3.4	3.1	2.9	2.7	3.9	4.3	4.1	5.1
INT / GNP (%)	..	4.7	1.0	0.9	0.8	0.8	1.2	1.3	1.5	2.6
RES / EDT (%)	..	10.5	42.6	39.0	43.1	35.6	38.2	29.5	14.9	37.5
RES / MGS (months)	..	1.3	2.3	2.2	2.5	2.6	2.5	2.3	1.4	5.1
Short-term / EDT (%)	..	35.8	30.9	27.0	25.9	43.7	54.3	57.5	39.3	20.2
Concessional / EDT (%)	..	9.5	12.6	10.1	9.9	2.4	1.8	1.1	0.8	0.1
Multilateral / EDT (%)	..	8.0	10.8	7.5	6.8	4.3	3.3	2.0	5.1	8.3

* Total external liabilities include external debt (as per DRS definition) and debt contracted by overseas branches of domestic financial institutions.

KOREA, REPUBLIC OF

(US$ million, unless otherwise indicated)

	1970	1980	1990	1992	1993	1994	1995	1996	1997	1998
5. LONG-TERM DEBT										
DEBT OUTSTANDING (LDOD)	**1,991**	**18,236**	**24,186**	**32,236**	**35,002**	**40,802**	**39,197**	**49,221**	**72,128**	**94,062**
Public and publicly guaranteed	**1,816**	**15,933**	**18,786**	**24,050**	**24,566**	**19,253**	**22,123**	**25,423**	**33,852**	**57,956**
Official creditors	588	6,332	9,262	9,092	9,425	5,863	5,350	4,563	8,867	12,750
Multilateral	46	2,361	3,794	3,327	3,202	3,100	2,844	2,363	6,923	11,595
Concessional	27	113	98	92	89	85	82	79	75	72
Bilateral	542	3,970	5,468	5,765	6,223	2,763	2,505	2,200	1,944	1,155
Concessional	500	2,675	4,309	4,379	4,559	1,644	1,422	1,200	1,039	0
Private creditors	1,228	9,601	9,524	14,958	15,141	13,390	16,774	20,860	24,985	45,206
Bonds	0	291	2,563	5,460	7,652	7,200	10,753	15,110	21,086	24,454
Commercial banks	27	4,213	2,634	5,090	4,289	4,451	4,520	4,622	3,084	20,752
Other private	1,201	5,098	4,327	4,408	3,200	1,740	1,501	1,129	816	0
Private nonguaranteed	**175**	**2,303**	**5,400**	**8,186**	**10,436**	**21,550**	**17,074**	**23,798**	**38,276**	**36,106**
Bonds	0	0	490	2,929	4,559	15,325	10,500	15,848	18,555	20,106
Commercial banks	175	2,303	4,910	5,258	5,878	6,225	6,574	7,950	19,721	16,000
Memo:										
IBRD	10	1,723	3,240	2,644	2,520	2,380	2,163	1,841	4,505	7,463
IDA	27	113	98	92	89	85	82	79	75	72
DISBURSEMENTS	**476**	**3,980**	**5,736**	**8,215**	**8,251**	**14,131**	**13,610**	**20,133**	**25,061**	**13,318**
Public and publicly guaranteed	**444**	**3,429**	**4,207**	**5,108**	**4,353**	**4,084**	**5,165**	**7,120**	**14,769**	**12,578**
Official creditors	154	916	1,357	1,192	856	396	199	222	5,161	5,872
Multilateral	13	344	233	307	296	295	150	211	5,161	4,844
Concessional	1	0	0	0	0	0	0	0	0	0
Bilateral	141	572	1,124	885	560	101	48	11	0	1,028
Concessional	122	178	1,066	163	138	1	1	0	0	0
Private creditors	290	2,513	2,851	3,916	3,497	3,687	4,966	6,899	9,608	6,706
Bonds	0	44	982	1,398	2,972	2,854	4,453	6,229	8,214	5,656
Commercial banks	27	1,222	590	1,439	225	834	513	670	1,394	1,050
Other private	264	1,247	1,279	1,079	301	0	0	0	0	0
Private nonguaranteed	**32**	**551**	**1,529**	**3,107**	**3,898**	**10,047**	**8,445**	**13,013**	**10,292**	**739**
Bonds	0	0	410	1,212	1,628	8,000	4,990	9,448	6,242	739
Commercial banks	32	551	1,119	1,895	2,270	2,047	3,455	3,565	4,050	0
Memo:										
IBRD	7	254	145	211	258	282	144	210	3,161	3,144
IDA	1	0	0	0	0	0	0	0	0	0
PRINCIPAL REPAYMENTS	**205**	**1,554**	**5,678**	**4,237**	**6,269**	**5,222**	**5,905**	**6,802**	**6,781**	**9,631**
Public and publicly guaranteed	**198**	**1,490**	**3,589**	**3,037**	**4,619**	**2,522**	**2,974**	**3,820**	**2,780**	**2,819**
Official creditors	7	266	1,049	942	1,003	1,025	828	740	632	318
Multilateral	0	111	652	473	541	631	505	483	428	295
Concessional	0	1	2	3	4	4	4	4	4	4
Bilateral	7	155	397	469	462	394	323	257	204	24
Concessional	2	80	246	304	325	249	232	166	117	19
Private creditors	192	1,224	2,540	2,096	3,616	1,496	2,146	3,080	2,148	2,500
Bonds	0	0	1,223	50	906	601	905	996	1,258	1,964
Commercial banks	0	301	619	593	1,231	556	912	1,802	692	533
Other private	192	923	698	1,453	1,479	339	329	283	198	4
Private nonguaranteed	**7**	**64**	**2,090**	**1,200**	**1,650**	**2,700**	**2,931**	**2,982**	**4,001**	**6,812**
Bonds	0	0	0	0	0	1,000	1,290	1,826	2,745	3,212
Commercial banks	7	64	2,090	1,200	1,650	1,700	1,641	1,155	1,256	3,600
Memo:										
IBRD	0	66	547	427	464	588	460	386	363	269
IDA	0	1	2	3	4	4	4	4	4	4
NET FLOWS ON DEBT	**271**	**2,426**	**58**	**3,978**	**1,982**	**8,909**	**7,705**	**13,331**	**18,280**	**3,687**
Public and publicly guaranteed	**246**	**1,940**	**619**	**2,071**	**-266**	**1,562**	**2,191**	**3,300**	**11,989**	**9,760**
Official creditors	147	650	308	250	-147	-629	-629	-519	4,529	5,554
Multilateral	13	233	-418	-166	-245	-336	-355	-272	4,733	4,550
Concessional	1	-1	-2	-3	-4	-4	-4	-4	-4	-4
Bilateral	134	417	727	416	98	-293	-274	-247	-204	1,004
Concessional	121	98	821	-141	-188	-248	-231	-166	-117	-19
Private creditors	99	1,289	311	1,820	-119	2,191	2,821	3,819	7,460	4,206
Bonds	0	44	-242	1,348	2,066	2,252	3,548	5,234	6,957	3,692
Commercial banks	27	921	-28	846	-1,007	278	-399	-1,132	702	517
Other private	72	325	580	-374	-1,178	-339	-329	-283	-198	-4
Private nonguaranteed	**25**	**487**	**-561**	**1,907**	**2,248**	**7,347**	**5,514**	**10,032**	**6,291**	**-6,073**
Bonds	0	0	410	1,212	1,628	7,000	3,700	7,622	3,497	-2,473
Commercial banks	25	487	-971	695	620	347	1,814	2,410	2,794	-3,600
Memo:										
IBRD	7	188	-402	-217	-206	-306	-317	-176	2,798	2,875
IDA	1	-1	-2	-3	-4	-4	-4	-4	-4	-4

KOREA, REPUBLIC OF

(US$ million, unless otherwise indicated)

	1970	1980	1990	1992	1993	1994	1995	1996	1997	1998
INTEREST PAYMENTS (LINT)	**76**	**1,637**	**1,683**	**1,999**	**2,083**	**2,262**	**2,931**	**2,837**	**4,110**	**5,014**
Public and publicly guaranteed	**71**	**1,293**	**1,177**	**1,570**	**1,562**	**1,149**	**1,298**	**1,275**	**1,814**	**3,317**
Official creditors	15	369	533	521	526	427	366	309	316	610
Multilateral	1	193	303	257	245	233	219	179	200	597
Concessional	0	1	1	1	1	1	1	1	1	1
Bilateral	14	175	230	264	281	194	147	130	116	13
Concessional	12	86	128	171	183	95	52	41	35	1
Private creditors	56	925	644	1,049	1,036	722	932	966	1,499	2,707
Bonds	0	14	185	358	467	338	487	636	1,265	1,815
Commercial banks	0	516	218	274	253	223	298	215	150	892
Other private	56	394	241	417	316	161	147	115	84	0
Private nonguaranteed	**5**	**343**	**507**	**429**	**521**	**1,113**	**1,633**	**1,562**	**2,296**	**1,697**
Bonds	0	0	5	60	123	706	1,267	1,237	1,911	1,531
Commercial banks	5	343	502	370	399	407	366	325	385	167
Memo:										
IBRD	0	145	262	212	196	185	170	141	172	417
IDA	0	1	1	1	1	1	1	1	1	1
NET TRANSFERS ON DEBT	**195**	**790**	**-1,625**	**1,978**	**-101**	**6,648**	**4,775**	**10,494**	**14,169**	**-1,327**
Public and publicly guaranteed	**175**	**646**	**-558**	**501**	**-1,828**	**413**	**894**	**2,025**	**10,175**	**6,443**
Official creditors	132	281	-224	-270	-673	-1,056	-995	-828	4,214	4,944
Multilateral	12	40	-721	-422	-490	-569	-574	-452	4,533	3,953
Concessional	1	-2	-3	-4	-4	-4	-4	-4	-4	-4
Bilateral	120	242	497	152	-184	-487	-421	-376	-319	991
Concessional	109	12	693	-311	-371	-343	-283	-208	-152	-20
Private creditors	43	365	-333	771	-1,155	1,469	1,889	2,853	5,961	1,499
Bonds	0	30	-427	991	1,599	1,914	3,062	4,598	5,692	1,878
Commercial banks	27	404	-246	572	-1,259	55	-697	-1,347	551	-375
Other private	16	-69	339	-791	-1,494	-500	-476	-398	-282	-4
Private nonguaranteed	**20**	**144**	**-1,067**	**1,478**	**1,727**	**6,235**	**3,881**	**8,469**	**3,995**	**-7,770**
Bonds	0	0	405	1,153	1,505	6,294	2,433	6,385	1,586	-4,003
Commercial banks	20	144	-1,472	325	221	-59	1,448	2,084	2,409	-3,767
Memo:										
IBRD	7	43	-664	-428	-401	-491	-486	-317	2,626	2,458
IDA	1	-2	-3	-4	-4	-4	-4	-4	-4	-4
DEBT SERVICE (LTDS)	**281**	**3,190**	**7,361**	**6,237**	**8,353**	**7,483**	**8,835**	**9,639**	**10,891**	**14,645**
Public and publicly guaranteed	**269**	**2,783**	**4,765**	**4,607**	**6,181**	**3,670**	**4,271**	**5,095**	**4,594**	**6,135**
Official creditors	22	635	1,581	1,463	1,529	1,452	1,194	1,050	947	928
Multilateral	1	305	954	730	786	864	725	663	628	892
Concessional	0	2	3	4	4	4	4	4	4	4
Bilateral	21	330	627	733	743	588	469	387	319	37
Concessional	13	167	373	475	509	344	284	208	152	20
Private creditors	248	2,148	3,184	3,145	4,652	2,218	3,077	4,046	3,647	5,207
Bonds	0	14	1,409	407	1,373	939	1,392	1,631	2,522	3,778
Commercial banks	0	817	836	867	1,484	779	1,210	2,017	842	1,425
Other private	248	1,317	939	1,870	1,795	500	476	398	282	4
Private nonguaranteed	**12**	**407**	**2,596**	**1,629**	**2,171**	**3,813**	**4,564**	**4,544**	**6,297**	**8,509**
Bonds	0	0	5	60	123	1,706	2,557	3,063	4,656	4,743
Commercial banks	12	407	2,591	1,570	2,049	2,107	2,007	1,481	1,641	3,767
Memo:										
IBRD	0	211	809	639	659	773	630	527	535	686
IDA	0	2	3	4	4	4	4	4	4	4
UNDISBURSED DEBT	**887**	**6,731**	**2,287**	**2,161**	**1,776**	**3,125**	**2,803**	**2,554**	**4,597**	**3,710**
Official creditors	370	3,908	1,824	1,420	840	808	759	530	2,374	1,612
Private creditors	517	2,823	463	741	936	2,317	2,044	2,024	2,223	2,099
Memorandum items										
Concessional LDOD	527	2,789	4,407	4,471	4,648	1,730	1,504	1,278	1,114	72
Variable rate LDOD	196	6,641	9,492	13,555	15,115	26,626	22,236	29,196	48,562	67,509
Public sector LDOD	810	9,770	16,151	19,324	20,719	18,160	20,833	23,106	33,378	40,725
Private sector LDOD	1,180	8,466	8,035	12,912	14,282	22,642	18,364	26,115	38,750	53,337

6. CURRENCY COMPOSITION OF LONG-TERM DEBT (PERCENT)

	1970	1980	1990	1992	1993	1994	1995	1996	1997	1998
Deutsche mark	7.2	3.7	4.7	5.1	4.2	5.7	5.9	3.3	4.5	2.5
French franc	2.1	2.4	8.0	5.1	4.1	5.0	4.0	3.9	2.3	0.5
Japanese yen	5.1	16.6	31.5	29.7	32.0	34.1	38.2	32.4	22.9	17.1
Pound sterling	1.4	3.3	0.7	0.2	0.2	0.2	0.2	0.1	1.8	1.0
Swiss franc	0.4	1.9	1.1	0.5	0.6	0.5	0.4	0.9	0.6	0.3
U.S.dollars	82.1	53.5	33.0	45.1	45.7	38.5	38.5	47.8	59.9	74.2
Multiple currency	1.2	12.9	18.8	12.8	12.1	15.0	12.0	8.8	5.4	3.1
Special drawing rights	0.0	0.0	0.0	0.0	0.0	0.0	0.0	0.0	0.0	0.0
All other currencies	0.5	5.7	2.2	1.5	1.1	1.0	0.8	2.8	2.6	1.3

KOREA, REPUBLIC OF

(US$ million, unless otherwise indicated)

	1970	1980	1990	1992	1993	1994	1995	1996	1997	1998
7. DEBT RESTRUCTURINGS										
Total amount rescheduled	..	..	0	0	0	0	0	0	0	21,736
Debt stock rescheduled	..	..	0	0	0	0	0	0	0	24,000
Principal rescheduled	..	..	0	0	0	0	0	0	0	0
Official	..	..	0	0	0	0	0	0	0	0
Private	..	..	0	0	0	0	0	0	0	0
Interest rescheduled	..	..	0	0	0	0	0	0	0	0
Official	..	..	0	0	0	0	0	0	0	0
Private	..	..	0	0	0	0	0	0	0	0
Debt forgiven	..	..	0	0	0	0	0	0	0	0
Memo: interest forgiven	..	..	0	0	0	0	0	0	0	0
Debt stock reduction	..	..	0	0	0	0	0	0	0	0
of which debt buyback	..	..	0	0	0	0	0	0	0	0
8. DEBT STOCK-FLOW RECONCILIATION										
Total change in debt stocks	..	..	2,188	4,423	3,046	25,213	13,396	29,993	21,181	2,113
Net flows on debt	847	6,415	1,058	4,698	2,262	28,321	22,706	33,300	16,774	7,190
Net change in interest arrears	..	..	0	0	0	0	0	0	0	0
Interest capitalized	..	..	0	0	0	0	0	0	0	0
Debt forgiveness or reduction	..	..	0	0	0	0	0	0	0	0
Cross-currency valuation	..	..	911	-361	707	1,062	-114	-1,316	-1,473	1,409
Residual	..	..	218	87	77	-4,171	-9,197	-1,991	5,880	-6,485
9. AVERAGE TERMS OF NEW COMMITMENTS										
ALL CREDITORS										
Interest (%)	5.8	11.3	7.9	7.1	5.5	5.7	4.4	5.7	6.2	7.5
Maturity (years)	19.0	15.3	17.6	13.4	9.4	10.9	6.1	12.4	11.6	9.0
Grace period (years)	5.8	3.9	5.4	4.8	4.8	6.6	5.8	6.8	6.1	5.6
Grant element (%)	27.7	-3.6	13.2	15.3	17.1	20.5	23.0	20.7	17.6	11.4
Official creditors										
Interest (%)	4.5	7.4	6.2	6.9	7.4	6.5	7.1	0.0	6.4	5.4
Maturity (years)	28.0	20.4	23.7	17.3	14.8	15.0	14.8	0.0	18.7	12.3
Grace period (years)	7.7	6.0	7.0	6.2	5.3	5.5	5.3	0.0	5.9	4.8
Grant element (%)	43.1	16.9	27.1	19.7	14.6	20.2	16.2	0.0	21.8	20.4
Private creditors										
Interest (%)	6.7	14.1	8.9	7.1	5.4	5.6	4.3	5.7	6.1	9.1
Maturity (years)	12.9	11.7	14.0	12.7	9.0	10.6	5.8	12.4	6.6	6.4
Grace period (years)	4.6	2.4	4.4	4.6	4.8	6.7	5.8	6.8	6.3	6.2
Grant element (%)	17.2	-17.9	5.1	14.6	17.3	20.6	23.2	20.7	14.7	4.4
Memorandum items										
Commitments	691	4,928	3,744	4,658	3,982	6,305	5,192	6,920	16,911	11,717
Official creditors	282	2,027	1,387	710	290	480	175	0	7,015	5,135
Private creditors	409	2,901	2,356	3,948	3,692	5,825	5,017	6,920	9,896	6,582

10. CONTRACTUAL OBLIGATIONS ON OUTSTANDING LONG-TERM DEBT

	1999	2000	2001	2002	2003	2004	2005	2006	2007	2008
TOTAL										
Disbursements	2,923	593	111	37	22	12	8	2	2	1
Principal	13,625	16,638	21,197	11,960	7,418	6,820	2,255	3,826	2,554	4,184
Interest	6,079	4,808	3,883	3,038	2,438	2,194	1,311	1,125	954	672
Official creditors										
Disbursements	1,395	83	53	35	22	12	8	2	2	1
Principal	263	1,401	254	240	666	1,291	1,284	1,269	1,256	946
Interest	796	838	811	796	782	724	644	565	486	408
Bilateral creditors										
Disbursements	19	22	12	5	2	0	0	0	0	0
Principal	12	1,139	16	16	16	4	4	4	2	0
Interest	27	16	3	3	2	1	1	0	0	0
Multilateral creditors										
Disbursements	1,376	62	41	30	20	12	8	2	2	1
Principal	251	263	238	224	650	1,287	1,279	1,264	1,254	946
Interest	769	822	807	794	780	723	644	564	486	408
Private creditors										
Disbursements	1,528	510	58	2	0	0	0	0	0	0
Principal	13,362	15,236	20,943	11,720	6,752	5,529	971	2,557	1,299	3,238
Interest	5,283	3,971	3,072	2,242	1,656	1,470	667	560	468	264
Commercial banks										
Disbursements	1,528	510	58	2	0	0	0	0	0	0
Principal	4,734	4,936	9,311	575	342	353	462	376	319	238
Interest	1,484	1,193	639	227	189	169	150	128	108	90
Other private										
Disbursements	0	0	0	0	0	0	0	0	0	0
Principal	8,628	10,301	11,632	11,145	6,410	5,176	509	2,181	979	3,000
Interest	3,799	2,778	2,433	2,016	1,467	1,301	517	433	360	174

KYRGYZ REPUBLIC

(US$ million, unless otherwise indicated)

	1970	1980	1990	1992	1993	1994	1995	1996	1997	1998
1. SUMMARY DEBT DATA										
TOTAL DEBT STOCKS (EDT)	..	..	..	**3.7**	**290.2**	**446.1**	**608.3**	**764.4**	**928.2**	**1,147.7**
Long-term debt (LDOD)	..	..	..	**3.7**	**229.8**	**355.4**	**471.0**	**616.1**	**730.3**	**944.2**
Public and publicly guaranteed	..	..	..	3.7	229.8	355.4	471.0	616.1	730.3	909.2
Private nonguaranteed	..	..	..	0.0	0.0	0.0	0.0	0.0	0.0	35.0
Use of IMF credit	..	..	..	**0.0**	**60.2**	**77.8**	**124.3**	**139.6**	**164.9**	**175.2**
Short-term debt	..	..	..	**0.0**	**0.1**	**12.8**	**13.0**	**8.7**	**33.0**	**28.3**
of which interest arrears on LDOD	..	..	..	0.0	0.1	12.8	10.8	0.5	0.0	0.0
Official creditors	..	..	..	0.0	0.1	12.8	10.8	0.5	0.0	0.0
Private creditors	..	..	..	0.0	0.0	0.0	0.0	0.0	0.0	0.0
Memo: principal arrears on LDOD	..	..	..	0.0	0.8	11.6	11.0	3.1	1.1	5.9
Official creditors	..	..	..	0.0	0.8	11.6	11.0	3.1	1.1	0.0
Private creditors	..	..	..	0.0	0.0	0.0	0.0	0.0	0.0	5.8
Memo: export credits	..	..	..	0.0	0.0	0.0	17.0	52.0	54.0	55.0
TOTAL DEBT FLOWS										
Disbursements	..	..	..	**3.8**	**133.0**	**132.7**	**200.6**	**190.7**	**198.0**	**172.2**
Long-term debt	..	..	..	3.8	71.8	119.2	154.6	167.2	153.7	157.6
IMF purchases	..	..	..	0.0	61.2	13.5	46.0	23.4	44.4	14.6
Principal repayments	..	..	..	**0.0**	**0.0**	**0.0**	**36.3**	**36.2**	**20.6**	**30.7**
Long-term debt	..	..	..	0.0	0.0	0.0	36.3	32.4	10.8	19.1
IMF repurchases	..	..	..	0.0	0.0	0.0	0.0	3.9	9.8	11.6
Net flows on debt	..	..	..	**3.8**	**133.0**	**132.7**	**166.5**	**160.4**	**202.2**	**136.8**
of which short-term debt	..	..	..	0.0	0.0	0.0	2.2	6.0	24.8	-4.7
Interest payments (INT)	..	..	..	**0.0**	**1.4**	**16.4**	**23.5**	**14.3**	**22.7**	**27.2**
Long-term debt	..	..	..	0.0	0.4	13.1	19.7	10.8	18.6	22.8
IMF charges	..	..	..	0.0	1.1	3.3	3.7	3.1	3.0	2.6
Short-term debt	..	..	..	0.0	0.0	0.0	0.1	0.4	1.1	1.7
Net transfers on debt	..	..	..	**3.8**	**131.6**	**116.4**	**142.9**	**146.1**	**179.5**	**109.7**
Total debt service paid (TDS)	..	..	..	**0.0**	**1.4**	**16.4**	**59.9**	**50.6**	**43.3**	**57.8**
Long-term debt	..	..	..	0.0	0.4	13.1	56.0	43.2	29.4	42.0
IMF repurchases and charges	..	..	..	0.0	1.1	3.3	3.7	7.0	12.8	14.2
Short-term debt (interest only)	..	..	..	0.0	0.0	0.0	0.1	0.4	1.1	1.7
2. AGGREGATE NET RESOURCE FLOWS AND NET TRANSFERS (LONG-TERM)										
NET RESOURCE FLOWS	..	..	..	**4.0**	**145.1**	**229.6**	**268.3**	**227.0**	**271.1**	**292.5**
Net flow of long-term debt (ex. IMF)	..	..	..	3.8	71.8	119.2	118.3	134.9	142.8	138.5
Foreign direct investment (net)	..	..	..	0.0	10.0	38.2	96.1	47.2	84.0	109.0
Portfolio equity flows	..	..	..	0.0	0.0	0.0	0.0	0.0	0.0	0.0
Grants (excluding technical coop.)	..	..	..	0.2	63.3	72.2	53.9	44.9	44.3	44.9
Memo: technical coop. grants	..	..	..	1.8	7.4	10.3	26.8	42.7	25.4	35.8
official net resource flows	..	..	..	4.0	135.1	191.4	172.2	179.8	187.1	185.0
private net resource flows	..	..	..	0.0	10.0	38.2	96.1	47.2	84.0	107.5
NET TRANSFERS	..	..	..	**4.0**	**144.7**	**216.5**	**248.6**	**216.2**	**252.5**	**269.7**
Interest on long-term debt	..	..	..	0.0	0.4	13.1	19.7	10.8	18.6	22.8
Profit remittances on FDI	..	..	..	0.0	0.0	0.0	0.0	0.0	0.0	0.0
Memo: official net transfers	..	..	..	4.0	134.7	178.3	152.5	169.0	168.5	163.7
private net transfers	..	..	..	0.0	10.0	38.2	96.1	47.2	84.0	106.0
3. MAJOR ECONOMIC AGGREGATES										
Gross national product (GNP)	..	..	..	2,247.0	4,259.5	3,147.1	3,283.6	1,788.8	1,705.9	1,652.7
Exports of goods & services (XGS)	..	..	..	284.8	349.6	372.9	452.5	568.6	684.2	614.2
of which workers remittances	..	..	..	..	1.3	0.2	0.8	1.8	2.2	2.2
Imports of goods & services (MGS)	..	..	..	400.2	503.1	519.2	765.0	1,075.4	888.1	938.3
International reserves (RES)	..	..	..	..	48.2	26.2	81.0	94.6	169.8	187.7
Current account balance	..	..	..	-100.6	-87.6	-84.5	-234.7	-424.7	-138.5	-257.4
4. DEBT INDICATORS										
EDT / XGS (%)	..	..	..	1.3	83.0	119.6	134.4	134.4	135.7	186.9
EDT / GNP (%)	..	..	..	0.2	6.8	14.2	18.5	42.7	54.4	69.4
TDS / XGS (%)	..	..	..	0.0	0.4	4.4	13.2	8.9	6.3	9.4
INT / XGS (%)	..	..	..	0.0	0.4	4.4	5.2	2.5	3.3	4.4
INT / GNP (%)	..	..	..	0.0	0.0	0.5	0.7	0.8	1.3	1.7
RES / EDT (%)	..	..	..	..	16.6	5.9	13.3	12.4	18.3	16.4
RES / MGS (months)	..	..	..	..	1.2	0.6	1.3	1.1	2.3	2.4
Short-term / EDT (%)	..	..	..	0.0	0.0	2.9	2.1	1.1	3.6	2.5
Concessional / EDT (%)	..	..	..	13.5	48.2	52.0	60.4	48.0	50.0	55.2
Multilateral / EDT (%)	..	..	..	0.0	16.8	19.9	30.0	37.6	43.6	47.6

KYRGYZ REPUBLIC

(US$ million, unless otherwise indicated)

	1970	*1980*	*1990*	*1992*	*1993*	*1994*	*1995*	*1996*	*1997*	*1998*
5. LONG-TERM DEBT										
DEBT OUTSTANDING (LDOD)	..	..	..	**3.7**	**229.8**	**355.4**	**471.0**	**616.1**	**730.3**	**944.2**
Public and publicly guaranteed	..	..	..	**3.7**	**229.8**	**355.4**	**471.0**	**616.1**	**730.3**	**909.2**
Official creditors	..	..	..	3.7	229.8	355.4	471.0	616.1	730.3	907.1
Multilateral	..	..	..	0.0	48.6	88.9	182.6	287.0	404.5	545.8
Concessional	..	..	..	0.0	22.6	60.4	173.6	256.3	358.1	494.6
Bilateral	..	..	..	3.7	181.2	266.5	288.4	329.1	325.8	361.3
Concessional	..	..	..	0.5	117.3	171.4	193.9	110.2	105.6	138.6
Private creditors	..	..	..	0.0	0.0	0.0	0.0	0.0	0.0	2.1
Bonds	..	..	..	0.0	0.0	0.0	0.0	0.0	0.0	0.0
Commercial banks	..	..	..	0.0	0.0	0.0	0.0	0.0	0.0	2.1
Other private	..	..	..	0.0	0.0	0.0	0.0	0.0	0.0	0.0
Private nonguaranteed	..	..	..	**0.0**	**0.0**	**0.0**	**0.0**	**0.0**	**0.0**	**35.0**
Bonds	..	..	..	0.0	0.0	0.0	0.0	0.0	0.0	0.0
Commercial banks	..	..	..	0.0	0.0	0.0	0.0	0.0	0.0	35.0
Memo:										
IBRD	..	..	..	0.0	0.0	0.0	0.0	0.0	0.0	0.0
IDA	..	..	..	0.0	22.6	60.4	141.2	196.8	251.1	328.0
DISBURSEMENTS	..	..	..	**3.8**	**71.8**	**119.2**	**154.6**	**167.2**	**153.7**	**157.6**
Public and publicly guaranteed	..	..	..	**3.8**	**71.8**	**119.2**	**154.6**	**167.2**	**153.7**	**156.5**
Official creditors	..	..	..	3.8	71.8	119.2	154.6	167.2	153.7	156.5
Multilateral	..	..	..	0.0	50.1	35.7	124.3	111.0	136.5	121.9
Concessional	..	..	..	0.0	22.8	35.7	115.3	89.3	119.0	113.3
Bilateral	..	..	..	3.8	21.7	83.5	30.3	56.2	17.1	34.6
Concessional	..	..	..	0.5	5.0	52.8	25.6	43.8	6.6	23.2
Private creditors	..	..	..	0.0	0.0	0.0	0.0	0.0	0.0	0.0
Bonds	..	..	..	0.0	0.0	0.0	0.0	0.0	0.0	0.0
Commercial banks	..	..	..	0.0	0.0	0.0	0.0	0.0	0.0	0.0
Other private	..	..	..	0.0	0.0	0.0	0.0	0.0	0.0	0.0
Private nonguaranteed	..	..	..	**0.0**	**0.0**	**0.0**	**0.0**	**0.0**	**0.0**	**1.1**
Bonds	..	..	..	0.0	0.0	0.0	0.0	0.0	0.0	0.0
Commercial banks	..	..	..	0.0	0.0	0.0	0.0	0.0	0.0	1.1
Memo:										
IBRD	..	..	..	0.0	0.0	0.0	0.0	0.0	0.0	0.0
IDA	..	..	..	0.0	22.8	35.7	81.3	61.2	66.5	65.5
PRINCIPAL REPAYMENTS	..	..	..	**0.0**	**0.0**	**0.0**	**36.3**	**32.4**	**10.8**	**19.1**
Public and publicly guaranteed	..	..	..	**0.0**	**0.0**	**0.0**	**36.3**	**32.4**	**10.8**	**16.9**
Official creditors	..	..	..	0.0	0.0	0.0	36.3	32.4	10.8	16.5
Multilateral	..	..	..	0.0	0.0	0.0	30.4	0.0	2.0	3.8
Concessional	..	..	..	0.0	0.0	0.0	0.0	0.0	0.1	0.1
Bilateral	..	..	..	0.0	0.0	0.0	5.9	32.4	8.8	12.6
Concessional	..	..	..	0.0	0.0	0.0	0.2	0.7	0.6	2.9
Private creditors	..	..	..	0.0	0.0	0.0	0.0	0.0	0.0	0.4
Bonds	..	..	..	0.0	0.0	0.0	0.0	0.0	0.0	0.0
Commercial banks	..	..	..	0.0	0.0	0.0	0.0	0.0	0.0	0.4
Other private	..	..	..	0.0	0.0	0.0	0.0	0.0	0.0	0.0
Private nonguaranteed	..	..	..	**0.0**	**0.0**	**0.0**	**0.0**	**0.0**	**0.0**	**2.2**
Bonds	..	..	..	0.0	0.0	0.0	0.0	0.0	0.0	0.0
Commercial banks	..	..	..	0.0	0.0	0.0	0.0	0.0	0.0	2.2
Memo:										
IBRD	..	..	..	0.0	0.0	0.0	0.0	0.0	0.0	0.0
IDA	..	..	..	0.0	0.0	0.0	0.0	0.0	0.0	0.0
NET FLOWS ON DEBT	..	..	..	**3.8**	**71.8**	**119.2**	**118.3**	**134.9**	**142.8**	**138.5**
Public and publicly guaranteed	..	..	..	**3.8**	**71.8**	**119.2**	**118.3**	**134.9**	**142.8**	**139.6**
Official creditors	..	..	..	3.8	71.8	119.2	118.3	134.9	142.8	140.1
Multilateral	..	..	..	0.0	50.1	35.7	93.9	111.0	134.5	118.1
Concessional	..	..	..	0.0	22.8	35.7	115.3	89.3	118.8	113.2
Bilateral	..	..	..	3.8	21.7	83.5	24.4	23.9	8.4	22.0
Concessional	..	..	..	0.5	5.0	52.8	25.4	43.2	6.0	20.2
Private creditors	..	..	..	0.0	0.0	0.0	0.0	0.0	0.0	-0.4
Bonds	..	..	..	0.0	0.0	0.0	0.0	0.0	0.0	0.0
Commercial banks	..	..	..	0.0	0.0	0.0	0.0	0.0	0.0	-0.4
Other private	..	..	..	0.0	0.0	0.0	0.0	0.0	0.0	0.0
Private nonguaranteed	..	..	..	**0.0**	**0.0**	**0.0**	**0.0**	**0.0**	**0.0**	**-1.1**
Bonds	..	..	..	0.0	0.0	0.0	0.0	0.0	0.0	0.0
Commercial banks	..	..	..	0.0	0.0	0.0	0.0	0.0	0.0	-1.1
Memo:										
IBRD	..	..	..	0.0	0.0	0.0	0.0	0.0	0.0	0.0
IDA	..	..	..	0.0	22.8	35.7	81.3	61.2	66.5	65.5

KYRGYZ REPUBLIC

(US$ million, unless otherwise indicated)

	1970	1980	1990	1992	1993	1994	1995	1996	1997	1998
INTEREST PAYMENTS (LINT)	..	..	..	**0.0**	**0.4**	**13.1**	**19.7**	**10.8**	**18.6**	**22.8**
Public and publicly guaranteed	..	..	..	**0.0**	**0.4**	**13.1**	**19.7**	**10.8**	**18.6**	**21.5**
Official creditors	..	..	..	0.0	0.4	13.1	19.7	10.8	18.6	21.3
Multilateral	..	..	..	0.0	0.3	5.1	2.6	2.6	4.9	6.8
Concessional	..	..	..	0.0	0.0	0.2	0.7	1.5	2.2	3.1
Bilateral	..	..	..	0.0	0.0	8.0	17.1	8.2	13.7	14.6
Concessional	..	..	..	0.0	0.0	1.7	11.0	2.3	3.2	3.3
Private creditors	..	..	..	0.0	0.0	0.0	0.0	0.0	0.0	0.2
Bonds	..	..	..	0.0	0.0	0.0	0.0	0.0	0.0	0.0
Commercial banks	..	..	..	0.0	0.0	0.0	0.0	0.0	0.0	0.2
Other private	..	..	..	0.0	0.0	0.0	0.0	0.0	0.0	0.0
Private nonguaranteed	..	..	..	**0.0**	**0.0**	**0.0**	**0.0**	**0.0**	**0.0**	**1.3**
Bonds	..	..	..	0.0	0.0	0.0	0.0	0.0	0.0	0.0
Commercial banks	..	..	..	0.0	0.0	0.0	0.0	0.0	0.0	1.3
Memo:										
IBRD	..	..	..	0.0	0.0	0.0	0.0	0.0	0.0	0.0
IDA	..	..	..	0.0	0.0	0.2	0.6	1.0	1.5	1.9
NET TRANSFERS ON DEBT	..	..	..	**3.8**	**71.4**	**106.1**	**98.6**	**124.0**	**124.3**	**115.7**
Public and publicly guaranteed	..	..	..	**3.8**	**71.4**	**106.1**	**98.6**	**124.0**	**124.3**	**118.1**
Official creditors	..	..	..	3.8	71.4	106.1	98.6	124.0	124.3	118.7
Multilateral	..	..	..	0.0	49.7	30.6	91.2	108.4	129.6	111.3
Concessional	..	..	..	0.0	22.8	35.5	114.6	87.8	116.6	110.1
Bilateral	..	..	..	3.8	21.7	75.5	7.3	15.7	-5.3	7.4
Concessional	..	..	..	0.5	5.0	51.1	14.4	40.9	2.8	17.0
Private creditors	..	..	..	0.0	0.0	0.0	0.0	0.0	0.0	-0.6
Bonds	..	..	..	0.0	0.0	0.0	0.0	0.0	0.0	0.0
Commercial banks	..	..	..	0.0	0.0	0.0	0.0	0.0	0.0	-0.6
Other private	..	..	..	0.0	0.0	0.0	0.0	0.0	0.0	0.0
Private nonguaranteed	..	..	..	**0.0**	**0.0**	**0.0**	**0.0**	**0.0**	**0.0**	**-2.5**
Bonds	..	..	..	0.0	0.0	0.0	0.0	0.0	0.0	0.0
Commercial banks	..	..	..	0.0	0.0	0.0	0.0	0.0	0.0	-2.5
Memo:										
IBRD	..	..	..	0.0	0.0	0.0	0.0	0.0	0.0	0.0
IDA	..	..	..	0.0	22.8	35.5	80.7	60.1	65.0	63.6
DEBT SERVICE (LTDS)	..	..	..	**0.0**	**0.4**	**13.1**	**56.0**	**43.2**	**29.4**	**42.0**
Public and publicly guaranteed	..	..	..	**0.0**	**0.4**	**13.1**	**56.0**	**43.2**	**29.4**	**38.4**
Official creditors	..	..	..	0.0	0.4	13.1	56.0	43.2	29.4	37.8
Multilateral	..	..	..	0.0	0.3	5.1	33.0	2.6	6.9	10.6
Concessional	..	..	..	0.0	0.0	0.2	0.7	1.5	2.4	3.2
Bilateral	..	..	..	0.0	0.0	8.0	23.0	40.6	22.5	27.2
Concessional	..	..	..	0.0	0.0	1.7	11.2	3.0	3.8	6.2
Private creditors	..	..	..	0.0	0.0	0.0	0.0	0.0	0.0	0.6
Bonds	..	..	..	0.0	0.0	0.0	0.0	0.0	0.0	0.0
Commercial banks	..	..	..	0.0	0.0	0.0	0.0	0.0	0.0	0.6
Other private	..	..	..	0.0	0.0	0.0	0.0	0.0	0.0	0.0
Private nonguaranteed	..	..	..	**0.0**	**0.0**	**0.0**	**0.0**	**0.0**	**0.0**	**3.6**
Bonds	..	..	..	0.0	0.0	0.0	0.0	0.0	0.0	0.0
Commercial banks	..	..	..	0.0	0.0	0.0	0.0	0.0	0.0	3.6
Memo:										
IBRD	..	..	..	0.0	0.0	0.0	0.0	0.0	0.0	0.0
IDA	..	..	..	0.0	0.0	0.2	0.6	1.0	1.5	1.9
UNDISBURSED DEBT	..	..	..	**32.3**	**181.7**	**261.7**	**274.8**	**333.5**	**403.6**	**1,044.5**
Official creditors	..	..	..	32.3	181.7	261.7	274.8	333.5	403.6	1,044.5
Private creditors	..	..	..	0.0	0.0	0.0	0.0	0.0	0.0	0.0
Memorandum items										
Concessional LDOD	..	..	..	0.5	139.9	231.7	367.5	366.4	463.6	633.3
Variable rate LDOD	..	..	..	0.0	199.7	224.2	198.9	217.8	232.1	272.0
Public sector LDOD	..	..	..	3.7	229.8	355.4	471.0	616.1	730.3	909.2
Private sector LDOD	..	..	..	0.0	0.0	0.0	0.0	0.0	0.0	35.0

6. CURRENCY COMPOSITION OF LONG-TERM DEBT (PERCENT)

	1970	1980	1990	1992	1993	1994	1995	1996	1997	1998
Deutsche mark	..	..	..	0.0	0.0	0.7	2.7	2.6	2.5	2.5
French franc	..	..	..	0.0	0.0	0.0	0.0	0.0	0.1	0.5
Japanese yen	..	..	..	0.0	0.0	14.1	14.3	13.5	10.5	11.6
Pound sterling	..	..	..	0.0	0.0	0.0	0.0	0.0	0.0	0.0
Swiss franc	..	..	..	100.0	1.6	1.5	1.3	0.7	0.1	0.0
U.S.dollars	..	..	..	0.0	38.5	44.1	51.2	73.9	75.2	71.5
Multiple currency	..	..	..	0.0	0.0	0.0	6.9	9.3	11.6	13.7
Special drawing rights	..	..	..	0.0	0.0	0.0	0.0	0.0	0.0	0.0
All other currencies	..	..	..	0.0	59.9	39.6	23.6	0.0	0.0	0.2

KYRGYZ REPUBLIC

(US$ million, unless otherwise indicated)

	1970	1980	1990	1992	1993	1994	1995	1996	1997	1998
7. DEBT RESTRUCTURINGS										
Total amount rescheduled	..	..	..	0.0	155.9	0.0	0.0	194.9	3.0	0.0
Debt stock rescheduled	..	..	..	0.0	0.0	0.0	0.0	106.8	2.9	0.0
Principal rescheduled	..	..	..	0.0	0.0	0.0	0.0	59.9	0.0	0.0
Official	..	..	..	0.0	0.0	0.0	0.0	59.9	0.0	0.0
Private	..	..	..	0.0	0.0	0.0	0.0	0.0	0.0	0.0
Interest rescheduled	..	..	..	..	0.0	0.0	0.0	27.9	0.0	0.0
Official	..	..	..	0.0	0.0	0.0	0.0	27.9	0.0	0.0
Private	..	..	..	0.0	0.0	0.0	0.0	0.0	0.0	0.0
Debt forgiven	..	..	..	0.0	0.0	0.0	0.0	0.2	0.0	0.0
Memo: interest forgiven	..	..	..	0.0	0.0	0.0	0.0	0.0	0.0	0.0
Debt stock reduction	..	..	..	0.0	0.0	0.0	0.0	0.0	0.0	0.0
of which debt buyback	..	..	..	0.0	0.0	0.0	0.0	0.0	0.0	0.0
8. DEBT STOCK-FLOW RECONCILIATION										
Total change in debt stocks	..	..	..	..	286.6	155.9	162.2	156.1	163.8	219.5
Net flows on debt	..	..	..	3.8	133.0	132.7	166.5	160.4	202.2	136.8
Net change in interest arrears	..	..	..	..	0.1	12.7	-2.1	-10.3	-0.5	0.0
Interest capitalized	..	..	..	..	0.0	0.0	0.0	27.9	0.0	0.0
Debt forgiveness or reduction	..	..	..	..	0.0	0.0	0.0	-0.2	0.0	0.0
Cross-currency valuation	..	..	..	..	-78.1	-62.6	-24.5	-11.3	-10.8	15.1
Residual	..	..	..	..	231.5	73.0	22.3	-10.4	-27.1	67.6
9. AVERAGE TERMS OF NEW COMMITMENTS										
ALL CREDITORS										
Interest (%)	..	..	..	3.5	4.5	2.1	3.7	2.6	3.3	2.3
Maturity (years)	..	..	..	4.2	21.8	34.3	28.8	31.6	26.9	28.4
Grace period (years)	..	..	..	3.5	6.9	10.0	8.1	9.2	7.6	9.0
Grant element (%)	..	..	..	19.7	38.4	66.5	50.3	60.2	51.0	60.4
Official creditors										
Interest (%)	..	..	..	3.5	4.5	2.1	3.7	2.6	3.3	2.3
Maturity (years)	..	..	..	4.2	21.8	34.3	28.8	31.6	26.9	28.4
Grace period (years)	..	..	..	3.5	6.9	10.0	8.1	9.2	7.6	9.1
Grant element (%)	..	..	..	19.7	38.4	66.5	50.3	60.2	51.0	60.5
Private creditors										
Interest (%)	..	..	..	0.0	0.0	0.0	0.0	0.0	0.0	3.0
Maturity (years)	..	..	..	0.0	0.0	0.0	0.0	0.0	0.0	7.9
Grace period (years)	..	..	..	0.0	0.0	0.0	0.0	0.0	0.0	2.9
Grant element (%)	..	..	..	0.0	0.0	0.0	0.0	0.0	0.0	27.5
Memorandum items										
Commitments	..	..	..	38.3	222.7	188.9	163.7	273.7	245.5	760.0
Official creditors	..	..	..	38.3	222.7	188.9	163.7	273.7	245.5	757.5
Private creditors	..	..	..	0.0	0.0	0.0	0.0	0.0	0.0	2.5

10. CONTRACTUAL OBLIGATIONS ON OUTSTANDING LONG-TERM DEBT

	1999	2000	2001	2002	2003	2004	2005	2006	2007	2008
TOTAL										
Disbursements	225.0	289.6	202.5	132.7	84.4	54.6	30.4	13.5	11.4	0.4
Principal	50.6	59.0	50.3	38.2	41.7	41.6	46.3	76.1	79.6	83.7
Interest	29.1	32.1	34.0	34.2	34.2	33.5	33.0	33.4	33.4	32.0
Official creditors										
Disbursements	225.0	289.6	202.5	132.7	84.4	54.6	30.4	13.5	11.4	0.4
Principal	44.8	53.2	44.1	32.0	35.5	41.2	45.9	76.0	79.6	83.7
Interest	29.1	32.1	33.9	34.2	34.2	33.4	33.0	33.4	33.4	32.0
Bilateral creditors										
Disbursements	60.3	48.2	30.1	17.9	10.5	5.4	3.3	1.1	0.7	0.4
Principal	29.1	47.0	36.7	24.5	27.4	27.7	28.7	25.7	25.4	25.4
Interest	18.2	17.3	15.6	13.7	12.5	11.2	9.7	9.6	9.1	7.9
Multilateral creditors										
Disbursements	164.7	241.4	172.5	114.8	73.9	49.2	27.1	12.3	10.7	0.0
Principal	15.7	6.2	7.5	7.5	8.1	13.5	17.2	50.2	54.2	58.3
Interest	10.9	14.8	18.3	20.5	21.7	22.3	23.3	23.8	24.4	24.1
Private creditors										
Disbursements	0.0	0.0	0.0	0.0	0.0	0.0	0.0	0.0	0.0	0.0
Principal	5.8	5.8	6.2	6.2	6.2	0.4	0.4	0.2	0.0	0.0
Interest	0.0	0.0	0.1	0.0	0.0	0.0	0.0	0.0	0.0	0.0
Commercial banks										
Disbursements	0.0	0.0	0.0	0.0	0.0	0.0	0.0	0.0	0.0	0.0
Principal	0.0	0.0	0.4	0.4	0.4	0.4	0.4	0.2	0.0	0.0
Interest	0.0	0.0	0.1	0.0	0.0	0.0	0.0	0.0	0.0	0.0
Other private										
Disbursements	0.0	0.0	0.0	0.0	0.0	0.0	0.0	0.0	0.0	0.0
Principal	5.8	5.8	5.8	5.8	5.8	0.0	0.0	0.0	0.0	0.0
Interest	0.0	0.0	0.0	0.0	0.0	0.0	0.0	0.0	0.0	0.0

LAO PEOPLE'S DEMOCRATIC REPUBLIC

(US$ million, unless otherwise indicated)

	1970	1980	1990	1992	1993	1994	1995	1996	1997	1998
1. SUMMARY DEBT DATA										
TOTAL DEBT STOCKS (EDT)	..	**350**	**1,768**	**1,917**	**1,985**	**2,080**	**2,165**	**2,263**	**2,320**	**2,437**
Long-term debt (LDOD)	**8**	**333**	**1,758**	**1,887**	**1,948**	**2,022**	**2,091**	**2,186**	**2,247**	**2,373**
Public and publicly guaranteed	8	333	1,758	1,887	1,948	2,022	2,091	2,186	2,247	2,373
Private nonguaranteed	0	0	0	0	0	0	0	0	0	0
Use of IMF credit	**0**	**16**	**8**	**28**	**36**	**47**	**64**	**67**	**66**	**62**
Short-term debt	..	**1**	**2**	**2**	**1**	**11**	**10**	**11**	**7**	**1**
of which interest arrears on LDOD	..	1	0	0	0	0	0	0	0	0
Official creditors	..	1	0	0	0	0	0	0	0	0
Private creditors	..	1	0	0	0	0	0	0	0	0
Memo: principal arrears on LDOD	..	4	1	0	0	0	0	2	2	1
Official creditors	..	1	1	0	0	0	0	2	2	1
Private creditors	..	4	0	0	0	0	0	0	0	0
Memo: export credits	..	0	3	2	2	5	3	30	59	69
TOTAL DEBT FLOWS										
Disbursements	**6**	**60**	**152**	**63**	**86**	**66**	**110**	**198**	**143**	**95**
Long-term debt	6	55	152	55	78	58	92	189	135	95
IMF purchases	0	4	0	8	8	8	18	9	8	0
Principal repayments	**1**	**1**	**6**	**6**	**24**	**15**	**19**	**22**	**20**	**23**
Long-term debt	1	1	6	6	24	15	18	19	15	16
IMF repurchases	0	0	1	0	0	0	2	3	5	6
Net flows on debt	**4**	**59**	**147**	**55**	**61**	**62**	**90**	**176**	**119**	**66**
of which short-term debt	..	0	1	-2	-1	10	-1	0	-4	-6
Interest payments (INT)	..	**1**	**3**	**4**	**5**	**5**	**7**	**7**	**8**	**8**
Long-term debt	0	1	3	4	5	5	6	6	7	8
IMF charges	0	0	0	0	0	0	0	0	0	0
Short-term debt	..	0	0	0	0	0	1	1	0	0
Net transfers on debt	..	**57**	**144**	**51**	**56**	**56**	**83**	**169**	**111**	**58**
Total debt service paid (TDS)	..	**3**	**9**	**10**	**29**	**20**	**26**	**29**	**28**	**31**
Long-term debt	2	2	8	9	28	20	23	25	22	24
IMF repurchases and charges	0	0	1	0	0	0	2	3	5	7
Short-term debt (interest only)	..	0	0	0	0	0	1	1	0	0
2. AGGREGATE NET RESOURCE FLOWS AND NET TRANSFERS (LONG-TERM)										
NET RESOURCE FLOWS	**33**	**70**	**199**	**115**	**152**	**200**	**300**	**469**	**342**	**242**
Net flow of long-term debt (ex. IMF)	4	54	146	49	54	43	75	170	120	78
Foreign direct investment (net)	0	0	6	8	30	59	95	160	91	46
Portfolio equity flows	0	0	0	0	0	0	0	0	0	0
Grants (excluding technical coop.)	28	16	47	59	69	98	130	139	131	118
Memo: technical coop. grants	40	14	32	48	53	57	75	74	64	68
official net resource flows	33	70	193	108	122	141	204	309	251	196
private net resource flows	0	0	6	8	30	59	95	160	91	46
NET TRANSFERS	**32**	**69**	**196**	**111**	**148**	**195**	**294**	**463**	**334**	**235**
Interest on long-term debt	0	1	3	4	5	5	6	6	7	8
Profit remittances on FDI	0	0	0	0	0	0	0	0	0	0
Memo: official net transfers	33	69	190	104	118	136	198	303	243	189
private net transfers	0	0	6	8	30	59	95	160	91	46
3. MAJOR ECONOMIC AGGREGATES										
Gross national product (GNP)	..	..	865	1,128	1,328	1,542	1,758	1,866	1,704	1,224
Exports of goods & services (XGS)	..	..	105	200	342	400	415	436	435	494
of which workers remittances	..	..	0	0	..	0	..	..	..	..
Imports of goods & services (MGS)	..	..	215	309	479	680	761	783	741	644
International reserves (RES)	..	..	8	46	70	67	99	171	117	122
Current account balance	..	..	-55	-48	-36	-160	-237	-265	-206	-77
4. DEBT INDICATORS										
EDT / XGS (%)	..	..	1,690.3	960.4	581.0	520.4	521.5	518.7	533.1	493.3
EDT / GNP (%)	..	..	204.5	170.0	149.5	134.9	123.2	121.3	136.1	199.1
TDS / XGS (%)	..	..	8.7	4.9	8.3	5.0	6.3	6.7	6.4	6.3
INT / XGS (%)	..	..	3.0	2.1	1.4	1.3	1.6	1.7	1.8	1.7
INT / GNP (%)	..	..	0.4	0.4	0.4	0.3	0.4	0.4	0.5	0.7
RES / EDT (%)	..	..	0.5	2.4	3.5	3.2	4.6	7.6	5.1	5.0
RES / MGS (months)	..	..	0.5	1.8	1.8	1.2	1.6	2.6	1.9	2.3
Short-term / EDT (%)	..	0.4	0.1	0.1	0.1	0.5	0.5	0.5	0.3	0.1
Concessional / EDT (%)	..	93.3	99.1	98.2	97.9	97.0	96.4	96.4	96.7	97.3
Multilateral / EDT (%)	..	5.9	15.1	19.1	22.5	25.5	28.7	32.7	35.2	39.1

LAO PEOPLE'S DEMOCRATIC REPUBLIC

(US$ million, unless otherwise indicated)

	1970	1980	1990	1992	1993	1994	1995	1996	1997	1998
5. LONG-TERM DEBT										
DEBT OUTSTANDING (LDOD)	**8**	**333**	**1,758**	**1,887**	**1,948**	**2,022**	**2,091**	**2,186**	**2,247**	**2,373**
Public and publicly guaranteed	**8**	**333**	**1,758**	**1,887**	**1,948**	**2,022**	**2,091**	**2,186**	**2,247**	**2,373**
Official creditors	8	327	1,758	1,887	1,948	2,022	2,091	2,186	2,247	2,373
Multilateral	0	21	267	366	447	529	621	741	816	953
Concessional	0	21	267	366	447	529	621	741	816	953
Bilateral	8	306	1,491	1,521	1,501	1,493	1,471	1,445	1,431	1,420
Concessional	8	306	1,485	1,516	1,498	1,489	1,466	1,441	1,427	1,417
Private creditors	1	6	0	0	0	0	0	0	0	0
Bonds	0	0	0	0	0	0	0	0	0	0
Commercial banks	0	0	0	0	0	0	0	0	0	0
Other private	1	6	0	0	0	0	0	0	0	0
Private nonguaranteed	**0**	**0**	**0**	**0**	**0**	**0**	**0**	**0**	**0**	**0**
Bonds	0	0	0	0	0	0	0	0	0	0
Commercial banks	0	0	0	0	0	0	0	0	0	0
Memo:										
IBRD	0	0	0	0	0	0	0	0	0	0
IDA	0	6	131	180	217	253	285	335	358	395
DISBURSEMENTS	**6**	**55**	**152**	**55**	**78**	**58**	**92**	**189**	**135**	**95**
Public and publicly guaranteed	**6**	**55**	**152**	**55**	**78**	**58**	**92**	**189**	**135**	**95**
Official creditors	6	55	152	55	78	58	92	189	135	95
Multilateral	0	7	78	55	78	58	92	189	135	95
Concessional	0	7	78	55	78	58	92	189	135	95
Bilateral	6	48	74	0	0	0	0	0	0	0
Concessional	6	48	74	0	0	0	0	0	0	0
Private creditors	0	0	0	0	0	0	0	0	0	0
Bonds	0	0	0	0	0	0	0	0	0	0
Commercial banks	0	0	0	0	0	0	0	0	0	0
Other private	0	0	0	0	0	0	0	0	0	0
Private nonguaranteed	**0**	**0**	**0**	**0**	**0**	**0**	**0**	**0**	**0**	**0**
Bonds	0	0	0	0	0	0	0	0	0	0
Commercial banks	0	0	0	0	0	0	0	0	0	0
Memo:										
IBRD	0	0	0	0	0	0	0	0	0	0
IDA	0	5	32	38	38	27	28	60	42	25
PRINCIPAL REPAYMENTS	**1**	**1**	**6**	**6**	**24**	**15**	**18**	**19**	**15**	**16**
Public and publicly guaranteed	**1**	**1**	**6**	**6**	**24**	**15**	**18**	**19**	**15**	**16**
Official creditors	1	1	6	6	24	15	18	19	15	16
Multilateral	0	0	3	3	3	3	4	3	3	5
Concessional	0	0	3	3	3	3	4	3	3	5
Bilateral	1	1	3	2	20	12	14	16	12	12
Concessional	1	1	2	2	20	11	13	16	11	11
Private creditors	0	0	0	0	0	0	0	0	0	0
Bonds	0	0	0	0	0	0	0	0	0	0
Commercial banks	0	0	0	0	0	0	0	0	0	0
Other private	0	0	0	0	0	0	0	0	0	0
Private nonguaranteed	**0**	**0**	**0**	**0**	**0**	**0**	**0**	**0**	**0**	**0**
Bonds	0	0	0	0	0	0	0	0	0	0
Commercial banks	0	0	0	0	0	0	0	0	0	0
Memo:										
IBRD	0	0	0	0	0	0	0	0	0	0
IDA	0	0	0	1	1	1	1	1	1	1
NET FLOWS ON DEBT	**4**	**54**	**146**	**49**	**54**	**43**	**75**	**170**	**120**	**78**
Public and publicly guaranteed	**4**	**54**	**146**	**49**	**54**	**43**	**75**	**170**	**120**	**78**
Official creditors	5	54	146	49	54	43	75	170	120	78
Multilateral	0	7	75	51	74	55	88	186	131	90
Concessional	0	7	75	51	74	55	88	186	131	90
Bilateral	5	47	71	-2	-20	-12	-14	-16	-12	-12
Concessional	5	47	72	-2	-20	-11	-13	-16	-11	-11
Private creditors	0	0	0	0	0	0	0	0	0	0
Bonds	0	0	0	0	0	0	0	0	0	0
Commercial banks	0	0	0	0	0	0	0	0	0	0
Other private	0	0	0	0	0	0	0	0	0	0
Private nonguaranteed	**0**	**0**	**0**	**0**	**0**	**0**	**0**	**0**	**0**	**0**
Bonds	0	0	0	0	0	0	0	0	0	0
Commercial banks	0	0	0	0	0	0	0	0	0	0
Memo:										
IBRD	0	0	0	0	0	0	0	0	0	0
IDA	0	5	32	38	37	26	27	59	41	24

LAO PEOPLE'S DEMOCRATIC REPUBLIC

(US$ million, unless otherwise indicated)

	1970	1980	1990	1992	1993	1994	1995	1996	1997	1998
INTEREST PAYMENTS (LINT)	**0**	**1**	**3**	**4**	**5**	**5**	**6**	**6**	**7**	**8**
Public and publicly guaranteed	**0**	**1**	**3**	**4**	**5**	**5**	**6**	**6**	**7**	**8**
Official creditors	0	1	3	4	5	5	6	6	7	8
Multilateral	0	0	2	3	4	4	5	6	7	7
Concessional	0	0	2	3	4	4	5	6	7	7
Bilateral	0	1	1	1	1	1	1	1	1	1
Concessional	0	1	1	1	1	1	1	0	0	0
Private creditors	0	0	0	0	0	0	0	0	0	0
Bonds	0	0	0	0	0	0	0	0	0	0
Commercial banks	0	0	0	0	0	0	0	0	0	0
Other private	0	0	0	0	0	0	0	0	0	0
Private nonguaranteed	**0**	**0**	**0**	**0**	**0**	**0**	**0**	**0**	**0**	**0**
Bonds	0	0	0	0	0	0	0	0	0	0
Commercial banks	0	0	0	0	0	0	0	0	0	0
Memo:										
IBRD	0	0	0	0	0	0	0	0	0	0
IDA	0	0	1	1	1	2	2	2	2	3
NET TRANSFERS ON DEBT	**4**	**53**	**144**	**45**	**49**	**38**	**69**	**164**	**112**	**71**
Public and publicly guaranteed	**4**	**53**	**144**	**45**	**49**	**38**	**69**	**164**	**112**	**71**
Official creditors	4	53	144	45	49	38	69	164	112	71
Multilateral	0	7	73	48	70	51	83	181	125	83
Concessional	0	7	73	48	70	51	83	181	125	83
Bilateral	4	46	70	-3	-21	-12	-15	-17	-12	-12
Concessional	4	46	71	-3	-20	-12	-14	-16	-12	-12
Private creditors	0	0	0	0	0	0	0	0	0	0
Bonds	0	0	0	0	0	0	0	0	0	0
Commercial banks	0	0	0	0	0	0	0	0	0	0
Other private	0	0	0	0	0	0	0	0	0	0
Private nonguaranteed	**0**	**0**	**0**	**0**	**0**	**0**	**0**	**0**	**0**	**0**
Bonds	0	0	0	0	0	0	0	0	0	0
Commercial banks	0	0	0	0	0	0	0	0	0	0
Memo:										
IBRD	0	0	0	0	0	0	0	0	0	0
IDA	0	5	32	37	36	25	25	57	38	21
DEBT SERVICE (LTDS)	**2**	**2**	**8**	**9**	**28**	**20**	**23**	**25**	**22**	**24**
Public and publicly guaranteed	**2**	**2**	**8**	**9**	**28**	**20**	**23**	**25**	**22**	**24**
Official creditors	1	2	8	9	28	20	23	25	22	24
Multilateral	0	0	5	6	7	7	9	8	10	12
Concessional	0	0	5	6	7	7	9	8	10	12
Bilateral	1	2	4	3	21	12	15	17	12	12
Concessional	1	2	3	3	20	12	14	16	12	12
Private creditors	0	0	0	0	0	0	0	0	0	0
Bonds	0	0	0	0	0	0	0	0	0	0
Commercial banks	0	0	0	0	0	0	0	0	0	0
Other private	0	0	0	0	0	0	0	0	0	0
Private nonguaranteed	**0**	**0**	**0**	**0**	**0**	**0**	**0**	**0**	**0**	**0**
Bonds	0	0	0	0	0	0	0	0	0	0
Commercial banks	0	0	0	0	0	0	0	0	0	0
Memo:										
IBRD	0	0	0	0	0	0	0	0	0	0
IDA	0	0	1	2	2	2	3	3	3	4
UNDISBURSED DEBT	**10**	**254**	**221**	**319**	**327**	**458**	**484**	**481**	**456**	**478**
Official creditors	9	254	221	319	327	458	484	481	456	478
Private creditors	1	0	0	0	0	0	0	0	0	0
Memorandum items										
Concessional LDOD	8	327	1,752	1,882	1,944	2,018	2,086	2,182	2,244	2,370
Variable rate LDOD	0	0	0	0	0	0	0	0	0	0
Public sector LDOD	8	333	1,758	1,887	1,948	2,022	2,091	2,186	2,247	2,373
Private sector LDOD	0	0	0	0	0	0	0	0	0	0
6. CURRENCY COMPOSITION OF LONG-TERM DEBT (PERCENT)										
Deutsche mark	76.7	10.3	1.8	0.0	0.0	0.0	0.1	0.1	0.0	0.0
French franc	13.2	4.3	0.3	0.2	0.2	0.2	0.2	0.1	0.1	0.1
Japanese yen	0.0	7.7	1.5	1.3	1.3	1.3	1.1	0.8	0.7	0.7
Pound sterling	0.0	0.0	0.0	0.0	0.0	0.0	0.0	0.0	0.0	0.0
Swiss franc	0.0	0.0	0.0	0.0	0.0	0.0	0.0	0.0	0.0	0.0
U.S.dollars	9.6	3.6	7.1	9.2	10.7	12.0	13.1	14.8	15.6	16.6
Multiple currency	0.0	2.9	7.1	9.4	11.4	13.1	15.4	17.8	19.4	22.1
Special drawing rights	0.0	0.0	1.1	1.0	0.9	1.1	1.2	1.4	1.3	1.4
All other currencies	0.5	71.2	81.1	78.9	75.5	72.3	68.9	65.0	62.9	59.1

LAO PEOPLE'S DEMOCRATIC REPUBLIC

(US$ million, unless otherwise indicated)

	1970	1980	1990	1992	1993	1994	1995	1996	1997	1998
7. DEBT RESTRUCTURINGS										
Total amount rescheduled	..	..	0	0	0	0	0	0	0	0
Debt stock rescheduled	..	..	0	0	0	0	0	0	0	0
Principal rescheduled	..	..	0	0	0	0	0	0	0	0
Official	..	..	0	0	0	0	0	0	0	0
Private	..	..	0	0	0	0	0	0	0	0
Interest rescheduled	..	..	0	0	0	0	0	0	0	0
Official	..	..	0	0	0	0	0	0	0	0
Private	..	..	0	0	0	0	0	0	0	0
Debt forgiven	..	..	0	0	0	0	0	0	0	0
Memo: interest forgiven	..	..	0	0	0	0	0	0	0	0
Debt stock reduction	..	..	0	0	0	0	0	0	0	0
of which debt buyback	..	..	0	0	0	0	0	0	0	0
8. DEBT STOCK-FLOW RECONCILIATION										
Total change in debt stocks	..	..	296	42	69	95	85	99	57	117
Net flows on debt	4	59	147	55	61	62	90	176	119	66
Net change in interest arrears	..	..	0	0	0	0	0	0	0	0
Interest capitalized	..	..	0	0	0	0	0	0	0	0
Debt forgiveness or reduction	..	..	0	0	0	0	0	0	0	0
Cross-currency valuation	..	..	157	-1	3	5	0	-3	-4	4
Residual	..	..	-8	-12	5	28	-5	-74	-59	47
9. AVERAGE TERMS OF NEW COMMITMENTS										
ALL CREDITORS										
Interest (%)	3.0	0.2	0.9	0.9	0.9	0.9	2.5	2.0	2.6	1.7
Maturity (years)	28.2	33.0	39.9	39.8	39.4	39.7	37.1	37.6	39.1	39.4
Grace period (years)	4.4	25.5	10.0	10.2	9.9	10.2	9.7	8.8	10.1	9.9
Grant element (%)	51.1	91.1	79.0	79.6	78.5	79.2	62.0	66.7	63.6	71.7
Official creditors										
Interest (%)	2.5	0.2	0.9	0.9	0.9	0.9	2.5	2.0	2.6	1.7
Maturity (years)	30.8	33.0	39.9	39.8	39.4	39.7	37.1	37.6	39.1	39.4
Grace period (years)	4.2	25.5	10.0	10.2	9.9	10.2	9.7	8.8	10.1	9.9
Grant element (%)	55.8	91.1	79.0	79.6	78.5	79.2	62.0	66.7	63.6	71.7
Private creditors										
Interest (%)	6.3	0.0	0.0	0.0	0.0	0.0	0.0	0.0	0.0	0.0
Maturity (years)	10.1	0.0	0.0	0.0	0.0	0.0	0.0	0.0	0.0	0.0
Grace period (years)	5.6	0.0	0.0	0.0	0.0	0.0	0.0	0.0	0.0	0.0
Grant element (%)	18.2	0.0	0.0	0.0	0.0	0.0	0.0	0.0	0.0	0.0
Memorandum items										
Commitments	12	96	125	64	84	171	110	173	143	128
Official creditors	11	96	125	64	84	171	110	173	143	128
Private creditors	2	0	0	0	0	0	0	0	0	0

10. CONTRACTUAL OBLIGATIONS ON OUTSTANDING LONG-TERM DEBT

	1999	2000	2001	2002	2003	2004	2005	2006	2007	2008
TOTAL										
Disbursements	147	128	87	54	32	16	10	4	0	0
Principal	20	25	26	28	31	33	100	90	94	100
Interest	10	11	12	12	12	12	12	15	17	17
Official creditors										
Disbursements	147	128	87	54	32	16	10	4	0	0
Principal	20	25	26	28	31	33	100	90	94	100
Interest	10	11	12	12	12	12	12	15	17	17
Bilateral creditors										
Disbursements	0	0	0	0	0	0	0	0	0	0
Principal	14	14	14	14	14	12	77	64	63	63
Interest	0	0	0	0	0	0	0	0	0	0
Multilateral creditors										
Disbursements	147	128	87	54	32	16	10	4	0	0
Principal	6	11	12	15	18	20	23	27	31	37
Interest	10	11	12	12	12	12	12	15	17	17
Private creditors										
Disbursements	0	0	0	0	0	0	0	0	0	0
Principal	0	0	0	0	0	0	0	0	0	0
Interest	0	0	0	0	0	0	0	0	0	0
Commercial banks										
Disbursements	0	0	0	0	0	0	0	0	0	0
Principal	0	0	0	0	0	0	0	0	0	0
Interest	0	0	0	0	0	0	0	0	0	0
Other private										
Disbursements	0	0	0	0	0	0	0	0	0	0
Principal	0	0	0	0	0	0	0	0	0	0
Interest	0	0	0	0	0	0	0	0	0	0

LATVIA

(US$ million, unless otherwise indicated)

	1970	1980	1990	1992	1993	1994	1995	1996	1997	1998
1. SUMMARY DEBT DATA										
TOTAL DEBT STOCKS (EDT)	..	..	..	**64.6**	**235.8**	**373.8**	**462.6**	**474.7**	**503.2**	**755.9**
Long-term debt (LDOD)	..	..	..	**30.0**	**123.6**	**207.5**	**271.1**	**300.4**	**352.3**	**495.8**
Public and publicly guaranteed	..	..	..	30.0	123.6	207.5	271.1	300.4	322.3	413.3
Private nonguaranteed	..	..	..	0.0	0.0	0.0	0.0	0.0	30.0	82.5
Use of IMF credit	..	..	..	**34.6**	**106.8**	**160.3**	**160.4**	**129.9**	**85.9**	**63.9**
Short-term debt	..	..	..	**0.0**	**5.4**	**6.0**	**31.2**	**44.4**	**65.0**	**196.2**
of which interest arrears on LDOD	..	..	..	0.0	0.0	0.0	0.0	0.0	0.0	0.0
Official creditors	..	..	..	0.0	0.0	0.0	0.0	0.0	0.0	0.0
Private creditors	..	..	..	0.0	0.0	0.0	0.0	0.0	0.0	0.0
Memo: principal arrears on LDOD	..	..	..	0.0	1.9	0.0	0.0	0.0	0.0	0.0
Official creditors	..	..	..	0.0	1.9	0.0	0.0	0.0	0.0	0.0
Private creditors	..	..	..	0.0	0.0	0.0	0.0	0.0	0.0	0.0
Memo: export credits	..	..	..	13.0	41.0	102.0	124.0	118.0	176.0	182.0
TOTAL DEBT FLOWS										
Disbursements	..	..	..	**66.6**	**174.9**	**130.0**	**75.2**	**59.3**	**142.9**	**126.9**
Long-term debt	..	..	..	31.2	101.5	84.2	75.2	59.3	142.9	126.9
IMF purchases	..	..	..	35.4	73.5	45.9	0.0	0.0	0.0	0.0
Principal repayments	..	..	..	**0.0**	**4.4**	**9.5**	**10.0**	**39.1**	**104.6**	**51.6**
Long-term debt	..	..	..	0.0	4.4	9.5	7.1	13.6	67.9	26.8
IMF repurchases	..	..	..	0.0	0.0	0.0	2.9	25.5	36.7	24.8
Net flows on debt	..	..	..	**66.6**	**175.8**	**121.2**	**90.4**	**33.4**	**58.9**	**206.5**
of which short-term debt	..	..	..	0.0	5.3	0.7	25.2	13.2	20.6	131.2
Interest payments (INT)	..	..	..	**0.2**	**6.6**	**16.0**	**24.3**	**25.9**	**27.6**	**31.3**
Long-term debt	..	..	..	0.2	3.8	9.5	14.2	17.2	19.4	21.2
IMF charges	..	..	..	0.0	2.7	6.2	9.0	6.7	5.2	3.6
Short-term debt	..	..	..	0.0	0.1	0.3	1.1	2.0	3.0	6.5
Net transfers on debt	..	..	..	**66.4**	**169.2**	**105.2**	**66.1**	**7.5**	**31.3**	**175.2**
Total debt service paid (TDS)	..	..	..	**0.2**	**11.0**	**25.6**	**34.3**	**65.0**	**132.2**	**83.0**
Long-term debt	..	..	..	0.2	8.2	19.0	21.3	30.8	87.3	48.0
IMF repurchases and charges	..	..	..	0.0	2.7	6.2	11.8	32.2	41.9	28.4
Short-term debt (interest only)	..	..	..	0.0	0.1	0.3	1.1	2.0	3.0	6.5
2. AGGREGATE NET RESOURCE FLOWS AND NET TRANSFERS (LONG-TERM)										
NET RESOURCE FLOWS	..	..	..	**113.4**	**160.6**	**310.2**	**271.5**	**468.8**	**670.1**	**530.3**
Net flow of long-term debt (ex. IMF)	..	..	..	31.2	97.0	74.6	68.1	45.7	75.0	100.1
Foreign direct investment (net)	..	..	..	29.0	45.0	214.5	179.6	382.0	521.0	357.0
Portfolio equity flows	..	..	..	0.0	0.0	0.0	0.0	0.0	25.6	4.4
Grants (excluding technical coop.)	..	..	..	53.2	18.6	21.1	23.8	41.1	48.6	68.8
Memo: technical coop. grants	..	..	..	18.1	14.9	28.0	37.5	29.0	24.3	23.9
official net resource flows	..	..	..	70.8	111.1	81.0	46.4	81.2	111.2	163.9
private net resource flows	..	..	..	42.6	49.5	229.2	225.1	387.6	558.9	366.4
NET TRANSFERS	..	..	..	**113.1**	**156.8**	**300.6**	**257.3**	**441.7**	**638.7**	**489.0**
Interest on long-term debt	..	..	..	0.2	3.8	9.5	14.2	17.2	19.4	21.2
Profit remittances on FDI	..	..	..	0.0	0.0	0.0	0.0	10.0	12.0	20.0
Memo: official net transfers	..	..	..	70.7	107.9	72.4	33.6	68.1	95.9	148.0
private net transfers	..	..	..	42.4	48.9	228.2	223.7	373.6	542.8	341.0
3. MAJOR ECONOMIC AGGREGATES										
Gross national product (GNP)	..	..	..	6,364.9	5,333.0	5,474.3	4,924.8	5,176.2	5,692.8	6,449.8
Exports of goods & services (XGS)	..	..	..	1,092.9	1,605.0	1,729.6	2,158.7	2,753.6	3,049.8	3,262.1
of which workers remittances	..	..	..	..	..	..	..	..	1.7	3.0
Imports of goods & services (MGS)	..	..	..	997.6	1,266.1	1,661.2	2,245.7	3,126.9	3,470.5	4,056.4
International reserves (RES)	..	..	..	..	526.4	640.7	602.1	746.1	776.3	800.0
Current account balance	..	..	..	191.4	416.8	201.2	-16.2	-279.8	-345.0	-712.8
4. DEBT INDICATORS										
EDT / XGS (%)	..	..	..	5.9	14.7	21.6	21.4	17.2	16.5	23.2
EDT / GNP (%)	..	..	..	1.0	4.4	6.8	9.4	9.2	8.8	11.7
TDS / XGS (%)	..	..	..	0.0	0.7	1.5	1.6	2.4	4.3	2.5
INT / XGS (%)	..	..	..	0.0	0.4	0.9	1.1	0.9	0.9	1.0
INT / GNP (%)	..	..	..	0.0	0.1	0.3	0.5	0.5	0.5	0.5
RES / EDT (%)	..	..	..	..	223.2	171.4	130.2	157.2	154.3	105.8
RES / MGS (months)	..	..	..	..	5.0	4.6	3.2	2.9	2.7	2.4
Short-term / EDT (%)	..	..	..	0.0	2.3	1.6	6.7	9.4	12.9	26.0
Concessional / EDT (%)	..	..	..	14.4	14.6	15.8	12.7	13.4	13.9	10.0
Multilateral / EDT (%)	..	..	..	0.0	28.3	30.7	30.1	34.5	39.6	37.9

LATVIA

(US$ million, unless otherwise indicated)

	1970	1980	1990	1992	1993	1994	1995	1996	1997	1998
5. LONG-TERM DEBT										
DEBT OUTSTANDING (LDOD)	..	..	..	**30.0**	**123.6**	**207.5**	**271.1**	**300.4**	**352.3**	**495.8**
Public and publicly guaranteed	..	..	..	**30.0**	**123.6**	**207.5**	**271.1**	**300.4**	**322.3**	**413.3**
Official creditors	..	..	..	17.2	107.0	173.7	200.4	229.4	272.9	365.0
Multilateral	..	..	..	0.0	66.8	114.8	139.2	163.7	199.1	286.1
Concessional	..	..	..	0.0	0.0	0.0	0.0	0.0	0.0	0.0
Bilateral	..	..	..	17.2	40.2	58.9	61.2	65.8	73.8	78.9
Concessional	..	..	..	9.3	34.5	58.9	58.9	63.7	69.7	75.4
Private creditors	..	..	..	12.8	16.6	33.8	70.6	71.0	49.4	48.4
Bonds	..	..	..	0.0	0.0	0.0	38.9	34.5	0.0	0.0
Commercial banks	..	..	..	2.5	0.0	0.0	0.0	2.2	1.9	2.0
Other private	..	..	..	10.3	16.6	33.8	31.7	34.3	47.5	46.3
Private nonguaranteed	..	..	..	**0.0**	**0.0**	**0.0**	**0.0**	**0.0**	**30.0**	**82.5**
Bonds	..	..	..	0.0	0.0	0.0	0.0	0.0	30.0	30.0
Commercial banks	..	..	..	0.0	0.0	0.0	0.0	0.0	0.0	52.5
Memo:										
IBRD	..	..	..	0.0	20.9	44.8	54.9	74.8	120.1	186.5
IDA	..	..	..	0.0	0.0	0.0	0.0	0.0	0.0	0.0
DISBURSEMENTS	..	..	..	**31.2**	**101.5**	**84.2**	**75.2**	**59.3**	**142.9**	**126.9**
Public and publicly guaranteed	..	..	..	**31.2**	**101.5**	**84.2**	**75.2**	**59.3**	**112.9**	**106.8**
Official creditors	..	..	..	17.6	94.5	65.4	26.4	46.2	93.1	103.9
Multilateral	..	..	..	0.0	69.3	41.6	23.2	37.8	75.4	100.4
Concessional	..	..	..	0.0	0.0	0.0	0.0	0.0	0.0	0.0
Bilateral	..	..	..	17.6	25.2	23.8	3.2	8.4	17.6	3.5
Concessional	..	..	..	9.3	25.2	23.8	0.8	8.1	14.3	3.1
Private creditors	..	..	..	13.6	7.0	18.8	48.9	13.1	19.8	2.8
Bonds	..	..	..	0.0	0.0	0.0	42.8	0.0	0.0	0.0
Commercial banks	..	..	..	2.5	0.0	0.0	0.0	2.3	0.0	0.0
Other private	..	..	..	11.1	7.0	18.8	6.1	10.9	19.8	2.8
Private nonguaranteed	..	..	..	**0.0**	**0.0**	**0.0**	**0.0**	**0.0**	**30.0**	**20.2**
Bonds	..	..	..	0.0	0.0	0.0	0.0	0.0	30.0	0.0
Commercial banks	..	..	..	0.0	0.0	0.0	0.0	0.0	0.0	20.2
Memo:										
IBRD	..	..	..	0.0	21.3	22.0	8.7	24.3	52.8	81.8
IDA	..	..	..	0.0	0.0	0.0	0.0	0.0	0.0	0.0
PRINCIPAL REPAYMENTS	..	..	..	**0.0**	**4.4**	**9.5**	**7.1**	**13.6**	**67.9**	**26.8**
Public and publicly guaranteed	..	..	..	**0.0**	**4.4**	**9.5**	**7.1**	**13.6**	**67.9**	**14.5**
Official creditors	..	..	..	0.0	1.9	5.5	3.8	6.1	30.4	8.8
Multilateral	..	..	..	0.0	0.0	0.0	3.8	5.7	25.2	5.4
Concessional	..	..	..	0.0	0.0	0.0	0.0	0.0	0.0	0.0
Bilateral	..	..	..	0.0	1.9	5.5	0.0	0.5	5.2	3.5
Concessional	..	..	..	0.0	0.0	0.0	0.0	0.0	4.2	2.4
Private creditors	..	..	..	0.0	2.5	4.0	3.3	7.5	37.5	5.6
Bonds	..	..	..	0.0	0.0	0.0	0.0	0.0	33.1	0.0
Commercial banks	..	..	..	0.0	2.5	0.0	0.0	0.0	0.0	0.0
Other private	..	..	..	0.0	0.0	4.0	3.3	7.5	4.4	5.6
Private nonguaranteed	..	..	..	**0.0**	**0.0**	**0.0**	**0.0**	**0.0**	**0.0**	**12.3**
Bonds	..	..	..	0.0	0.0	0.0	0.0	0.0	0.0	0.0
Commercial banks	..	..	..	0.0	0.0	0.0	0.0	0.0	0.0	12.3
Memo:										
IBRD	..	..	..	0.0	0.0	0.0	0.0	0.0	0.0	3.6
IDA	..	..	..	0.0	0.0	0.0	0.0	0.0	0.0	0.0
NET FLOWS ON DEBT	..	..	..	**31.2**	**97.0**	**74.6**	**68.1**	**45.7**	**75.0**	**100.1**
Public and publicly guaranteed	..	..	..	**31.2**	**97.0**	**74.6**	**68.1**	**45.7**	**45.0**	**92.3**
Official creditors	..	..	..	17.6	92.5	59.9	22.6	40.1	62.6	95.1
Multilateral	..	..	..	0.0	69.3	41.6	19.4	32.1	50.3	95.0
Concessional	..	..	..	0.0	0.0	0.0	0.0	0.0	0.0	0.0
Bilateral	..	..	..	17.6	23.3	18.3	3.2	8.0	12.4	0.1
Concessional	..	..	..	9.3	25.2	23.8	0.8	8.1	10.1	0.7
Private creditors	..	..	..	13.6	4.5	14.7	45.5	5.6	-17.7	-2.8
Bonds	..	..	..	0.0	0.0	0.0	42.8	0.0	-33.1	0.0
Commercial banks	..	..	..	2.5	-2.5	0.0	0.0	2.3	0.0	0.0
Other private	..	..	..	11.1	7.0	14.7	2.8	3.3	15.4	-2.8
Private nonguaranteed	..	..	..	**0.0**	**0.0**	**0.0**	**0.0**	**0.0**	**30.0**	**7.8**
Bonds	..	..	..	0.0	0.0	0.0	0.0	0.0	30.0	0.0
Commercial banks	..	..	..	0.0	0.0	0.0	0.0	0.0	0.0	7.8
Memo:										
IBRD	..	..	..	0.0	21.3	22.0	8.7	24.3	52.8	78.2
IDA	..	..	..	0.0	0.0	0.0	0.0	0.0	0.0	0.0

LATVIA

(US$ million, unless otherwise indicated)

	1970	1980	1990	1992	1993	1994	1995	1996	1997	1998
INTEREST PAYMENTS (LINT)	..	..	..	**0.2**	**3.8**	**9.5**	**14.2**	**17.2**	**19.4**	**21.2**
Public and publicly guaranteed	..	..	..	**0.2**	**3.8**	**9.5**	**14.2**	**17.2**	**19.4**	**17.2**
Official creditors	..	..	..	0.1	3.2	8.6	12.8	13.1	15.3	15.9
Multilateral	..	..	..	0.0	2.6	6.3	9.1	10.0	11.2	12.4
Concessional	..	..	..	0.0	0.0	0.0	0.0	0.0	0.0	0.0
Bilateral	..	..	..	0.1	0.5	2.2	3.7	3.2	4.1	3.4
Concessional	..	..	..	0.0	0.2	1.7	3.6	3.0	3.1	3.1
Private creditors	..	..	..	0.2	0.6	1.0	1.4	4.0	4.1	1.4
Bonds	..	..	..	0.0	0.0	0.0	0.0	2.0	1.8	0.0
Commercial banks	..	..	..	0.2	0.0	0.0	0.0	0.0	0.0	0.0
Other private	..	..	..	0.0	0.6	1.0	1.4	2.0	2.3	1.4
Private nonguaranteed	..	..	..	**0.0**	**0.0**	**0.0**	**0.0**	**0.0**	**0.0**	**4.0**
Bonds	..	..	..	0.0	0.0	0.0	0.0	0.0	0.0	2.0
Commercial banks	..	..	..	0.0	0.0	0.0	0.0	0.0	0.0	2.0
Memo:										
IBRD	..	..	..	0.0	0.3	2.0	3.5	4.1	5.6	8.3
IDA	..	..	..	0.0	0.0	0.0	0.0	0.0	0.0	0.0
NET TRANSFERS ON DEBT	..	..	..	**30.9**	**93.3**	**65.1**	**53.9**	**28.5**	**55.6**	**78.9**
Public and publicly guaranteed	..	..	..	**30.9**	**93.3**	**65.1**	**53.9**	**28.5**	**25.6**	**75.1**
Official creditors	..	..	..	17.5	89.4	51.4	9.8	26.9	47.3	79.2
Multilateral	..	..	..	0.0	66.7	35.3	10.3	22.2	39.0	82.6
Concessional	..	..	..	0.0	0.0	0.0	0.0	0.0	0.0	0.0
Bilateral	..	..	..	17.5	22.7	16.1	-0.5	4.8	8.3	-3.4
Concessional	..	..	..	9.3	25.0	22.1	-2.8	5.1	7.0	-2.4
Private creditors	..	..	..	13.4	3.9	13.8	44.1	1.6	-21.7	-4.2
Bonds	..	..	..	0.0	0.0	0.0	42.8	-2.0	-34.9	0.0
Commercial banks	..	..	..	2.3	-2.5	0.0	0.0	2.3	0.0	0.0
Other private	..	..	..	11.1	6.5	13.8	1.3	1.3	13.1	-4.2
Private nonguaranteed	..	..	..	**0.0**	**0.0**	**0.0**	**0.0**	**0.0**	**30.0**	**3.8**
Bonds	..	..	..	0.0	0.0	0.0	0.0	0.0	30.0	-2.0
Commercial banks	..	..	..	0.0	0.0	0.0	0.0	0.0	0.0	5.8
Memo:										
IBRD	..	..	..	0.0	21.0	20.0	5.2	20.3	47.2	69.9
IDA	..	..	..	0.0	0.0	0.0	0.0	0.0	0.0	0.0
DEBT SERVICE (LTDS)	..	..	..	**0.2**	**8.2**	**19.0**	**21.3**	**30.8**	**87.3**	**48.0**
Public and publicly guaranteed	..	..	..	**0.2**	**8.2**	**19.0**	**21.3**	**30.8**	**87.3**	**31.7**
Official creditors	..	..	..	0.1	5.1	14.0	16.6	19.2	45.7	24.7
Multilateral	..	..	..	0.0	2.6	6.3	12.9	15.6	36.4	17.8
Concessional	..	..	..	0.0	0.0	0.0	0.0	0.0	0.0	0.0
Bilateral	..	..	..	0.1	2.5	7.7	3.7	3.6	9.3	6.9
Concessional	..	..	..	0.0	0.2	1.7	3.6	3.0	7.3	5.5
Private creditors	..	..	..	0.2	3.1	5.0	4.8	11.6	41.6	7.0
Bonds	..	..	..	0.0	0.0	0.0	0.0	2.0	34.9	0.0
Commercial banks	..	..	..	0.2	2.5	0.0	0.0	0.0	0.0	0.0
Other private	..	..	..	0.0	0.6	5.0	4.8	9.6	6.7	7.0
Private nonguaranteed	..	..	..	**0.0**	**0.0**	**0.0**	**0.0**	**0.0**	**0.0**	**16.3**
Bonds	..	..	..	0.0	0.0	0.0	0.0	0.0	0.0	2.0
Commercial banks	..	..	..	0.0	0.0	0.0	0.0	0.0	0.0	14.3
Memo:										
IBRD	..	..	..	0.0	0.3	2.0	3.5	4.1	5.6	11.9
IDA	..	..	..	0.0	0.0	0.0	0.0	0.0	0.0	0.0
UNDISBURSED DEBT	..	..	..	**95.0**	**173.6**	**183.8**	**224.0**	**312.0**	**236.5**	**247.9**
Official creditors	..	..	..	84.6	159.0	176.3	207.2	297.3	231.6	245.7
Private creditors	..	..	..	10.4	14.6	7.5	16.8	14.7	4.9	2.2
Memorandum items										
Concessional LDOD	..	..	..	9.3	34.5	58.9	58.9	63.7	69.7	75.4
Variable rate LDOD	..	..	..	15.7	110.2	153.2	172.6	206.3	267.7	400.1
Public sector LDOD	..	..	..	30.0	122.7	196.0	252.1	287.8	311.2	403.3
Private sector LDOD	..	..	..	0.0	0.9	11.5	18.9	12.6	41.0	92.5

6. CURRENCY COMPOSITION OF LONG-TERM DEBT (PERCENT)

	1970	1980	1990	1992	1993	1994	1995	1996	1997	1998
Deutsche mark	..	..	..	8.0	3.7	3.6	8.5	8.1	9.9	17.2
French franc	..	..	..	0.0	0.0	0.0	0.0	0.0	2.7	2.2
Japanese yen	..	..	..	0.0	0.0	15.6	26.2	23.0	13.4	11.6
Pound sterling	..	..	..	0.0	0.0	0.0	0.0	0.0	0.0	0.0
Swiss franc	..	..	..	0.0	0.0	0.0	0.0	0.0	0.0	0.5
U.S.dollars	..	..	..	52.4	67.7	54.8	45.0	43.9	42.6	39.7
Multiple currency	..	..	..	0.0	16.9	21.6	20.3	24.9	30.1	27.6
Special drawing rights	..	..	..	0.0	0.0	0.0	0.0	0.0	0.0	0.0
All other currencies	..	..	..	39.6	11.7	4.4	0.0	0.1	1.3	1.2

LATVIA

(US$ million, unless otherwise indicated)

	1970	1980	1990	1992	1993	1994	1995	1996	1997	1998
7. DEBT RESTRUCTURINGS										
Total amount rescheduled	..	..	..	0.0	0.0	0.0	0.0	0.0	0.0	0.0
Debt stock rescheduled	..	..	..	0.0	0.0	0.0	0.0	0.0	0.0	0.0
Principal rescheduled	..	..	..	0.0	0.0	0.0	0.0	0.0	0.0	0.0
Official	..	..	..	0.0	0.0	0.0	0.0	0.0	0.0	0.0
Private	..	..	..	0.0	0.0	0.0	0.0	0.0	0.0	0.0
Interest rescheduled	..	..	..	..	0.0	0.0	0.0	0.0	0.0	0.0
Official	..	..	..	0.0	0.0	0.0	0.0	0.0	0.0	0.0
Private	..	..	..	0.0	0.0	0.0	0.0	0.0	0.0	0.0
Debt forgiven	..	..	..	0.0	0.0	0.0	0.0	0.0	0.0	0.0
Memo: interest forgiven	..	..	..	0.0	0.0	0.0	0.0	0.0	0.0	0.0
Debt stock reduction	..	..	..	0.0	0.0	0.0	0.0	0.0	0.0	0.0
of which debt buyback	..	..	..	0.0	0.0	0.0	0.0	0.0	0.0	0.0
8. DEBT STOCK-FLOW RECONCILIATION										
Total change in debt stocks	..	..	..	..	171.2	138.0	88.9	12.1	28.5	252.7
Net flows on debt	..	..	..	66.6	175.8	121.2	90.4	33.4	58.9	206.5
Net change in interest arrears	..	..	..	..	0.0	0.0	0.0	0.0	0.0	0.0
Interest capitalized	..	..	..	..	0.0	0.0	0.0	0.0	0.0	0.0
Debt forgiveness or reduction	..	..	..	..	0.0	0.0	0.0	0.0	0.0	0.0
Cross-currency valuation	..	..	..	..	-1.7	8.6	1.1	-14.2	-14.4	14.0
Residual	..	..	..	..	-2.9	8.2	-2.7	-7.1	-16.0	32.3
9. AVERAGE TERMS OF NEW COMMITMENTS										
ALL CREDITORS										
Interest (%)	..	..	..	6.0	4.2	6.9	5.2	5.5	5.7	5.1
Maturity (years)	..	..	..	13.7	9.5	14.7	9.0	15.3	13.8	17.4
Grace period (years)	..	..	..	4.0	5.8	4.2	3.3	4.0	4.1	4.5
Grant element (%)	..	..	..	19.5	29.2	16.8	19.2	24.8	22.9	30.0
Official creditors										
Interest (%)	..	..	..	6.2	4.1	6.8	5.3	5.7	5.7	5.1
Maturity (years)	..	..	..	14.6	9.8	16.3	14.1	15.7	14.0	17.4
Grace period (years)	..	..	..	4.3	6.1	4.7	4.1	4.2	4.3	4.5
Grant element (%)	..	..	..	19.5	30.3	18.6	25.3	24.4	23.1	30.0
Private creditors										
Interest (%)	..	..	..	5.0	5.8	7.6	5.1	2.5	5.4	0.0
Maturity (years)	..	..	..	8.1	6.3	3.3	3.9	11.1	12.0	0.0
Grace period (years)	..	..	..	2.4	2.0	0.6	2.5	1.2	2.5	0.0
Grant element (%)	..	..	..	19.2	13.3	3.6	13.1	30.6	21.4	0.0
Memorandum items										
Commitments	..	..	..	120.3	184.5	82.7	116.3	188.2	102.0	89.3
Official creditors	..	..	..	102.7	172.4	72.5	58.4	174.0	89.5	89.3
Private creditors	..	..	..	17.6	12.1	10.2	57.9	14.2	12.5	0.0

10. CONTRACTUAL OBLIGATIONS ON OUTSTANDING LONG-TERM DEBT

	1999	2000	2001	2002	2003	2004	2005	2006	2007	2008
TOTAL										
Disbursements	64.8	70.9	49.3	28.5	14.9	9.8	4.2	2.3	1.1	0.7
Principal	39.8	150.7	57.9	43.1	45.8	50.4	50.5	50.3	48.6	47.6
Interest	29.3	29.9	25.7	24.9	23.4	21.3	18.8	16.1	13.3	10.6
Official creditors										
Disbursements	63.3	70.4	49.1	28.5	14.9	9.8	4.2	2.3	1.1	0.7
Principal	13.4	95.2	34.5	38.5	42.4	46.9	46.9	46.9	46.6	45.7
Interest	24.1	25.9	24.4	24.1	22.8	20.8	18.3	15.7	13.1	10.4
Bilateral creditors										
Disbursements	2.6	0.0	0.0	0.0	0.0	0.0	0.0	0.0	0.0	0.0
Principal	5.9	26.9	5.5	4.8	4.8	4.7	4.7	4.7	4.7	4.7
Interest	3.9	3.7	2.1	1.8	1.6	1.4	1.2	1.0	0.7	0.5
Multilateral creditors										
Disbursements	60.7	70.4	49.0	28.5	14.9	9.8	4.2	2.3	1.1	0.7
Principal	7.5	68.3	29.0	33.7	37.6	42.2	42.2	42.2	41.8	41.0
Interest	20.2	22.2	22.3	22.3	21.1	19.4	17.1	14.8	12.3	9.9
Private creditors										
Disbursements	1.5	0.5	0.2	0.0	0.0	0.0	0.0	0.0	0.0	0.0
Principal	26.5	55.5	23.3	4.7	3.4	3.4	3.6	3.3	2.0	1.9
Interest	5.1	4.0	1.3	0.8	0.6	0.5	0.5	0.4	0.3	0.2
Commercial banks										
Disbursements	0.0	0.0	0.0	0.0	0.0	0.0	0.0	0.0	0.0	0.0
Principal	0.0	0.0	0.0	0.0	0.0	0.0	0.5	0.5	0.5	0.5
Interest	0.1	0.1	0.1	0.1	0.1	0.1	0.1	0.0	0.0	0.0
Other private										
Disbursements	1.5	0.5	0.2	0.0	0.0	0.0	0.0	0.0	0.0	0.0
Principal	26.5	55.5	23.3	4.7	3.4	3.4	3.1	2.8	1.5	1.4
Interest	5.1	4.0	1.2	0.7	0.6	0.5	0.4	0.3	0.3	0.2

LEBANON

(US$ million, unless otherwise indicated)

	1970	1980	1990	1992	1993	1994	1995	1996	1997	1998
1. SUMMARY DEBT DATA										
TOTAL DEBT STOCKS (EDT)	..	**510**	**1,779**	**1,806**	**1,345**	**2,118**	**2,966**	**3,996**	**5,033**	**6,725**
Long-term debt (LDOD)	**64**	**216**	**358**	**301**	**368**	**778**	**1,601**	**2,343**	**3,238**	**4,765**
Public and publicly guaranteed	64	216	358	301	368	778	1,551	1,933	2,353	3,980
Private nonguaranteed	0	0	0	0	0	0	50	410	885	785
Use of IMF credit	**0**	**0**	**0**	**0**	**0**	**0**	**0**	**0**	**0**	**0**
Short-term debt	..	**294**	**1,421**	**1,505**	**977**	**1,340**	**1,365**	**1,653**	**1,795**	**1,961**
of which interest arrears on LDOD	..	0	39	22	18	11	10	0	0	0
Official creditors	..	0	16	4	2	1	0	0	0	0
Private creditors	..	0	23	18	16	10	10	0	0	0
Memo: principal arrears on LDOD	..	0	132	56	54	49	41	0	0	0
Official creditors	..	0	28	9	10	12	0	0	0	0
Private creditors	..	0	104	47	44	37	41	0	0	0
Memo: export credits	..	0	345	336	309	303	403	520	728	943
TOTAL DEBT FLOWS										
Disbursements	**12**	**120**	**12**	**6**	**55**	**481**	**907**	**830**	**1,386**	**1,656**
Long-term debt	12	120	12	6	55	481	907	830	1,386	1,656
IMF purchases	0	0	0	0	0	0	0	0	0	0
Principal repayments	**2**	**7**	**27**	**40**	**45**	**96**	**104**	**69**	**438**	**169**
Long-term debt	2	7	27	40	45	96	104	69	438	169
IMF repurchases	0	0	0	0	0	0	0	0	0	0
Net flows on debt	**10**	**236**	**726**	**274**	**-514**	**755**	**830**	**1,059**	**1,090**	**1,653**
of which short-term debt	..	124	742	308	-524	370	26	298	142	166
Interest payments (INT)	..	**45**	**72**	**98**	**90**	**89**	**121**	**231**	**296**	**358**
Long-term debt	1	6	11	25	23	26	54	149	201	263
IMF charges	0	0	0	0	0	0	0	0	0	0
Short-term debt	..	39	61	73	67	63	67	83	95	95
Net transfers on debt	..	**191**	**654**	**176**	**-605**	**666**	**709**	**828**	**794**	**1,294**
Total debt service paid (TDS)	..	**53**	**99**	**138**	**135**	**185**	**224**	**301**	**734**	**528**
Long-term debt	4	13	39	65	68	122	158	218	639	432
IMF repurchases and charges	0	0	0	0	0	0	0	0	0	0
Short-term debt (interest only)	..	39	61	73	67	63	67	83	95	95
2. AGGREGATE NET RESOURCE FLOWS AND NET TRANSFERS (LONG-TERM)										
NET RESOURCE FLOWS	**12**	**311**	**203**	**11**	**60**	**489**	**917**	**1,015**	**1,306**	**1,941**
Net flow of long-term debt (ex. IMF)	10	112	-16	-34	10	385	804	761	948	1,487
Foreign direct investment (net)	0	0	6	4	6	7	35	80	150	200
Portfolio equity flows	0	0	0	0	0	1	34	122	89	147
Grants (excluding technical coop.)	3	199	213	41	43	96	44	52	119	107
Memo: technical coop. grants	9	19	39	90	84	99	94	97	43	45
official net resource flows	12	242	191	11	59	83	165	275	239	201
private net resource flows	0	70	12	-1	1	407	753	740	1,067	1,740
NET TRANSFERS	**11**	**305**	**192**	**-14**	**36**	**463**	**863**	**867**	**1,105**	**1,678**
Interest on long-term debt	1	6	11	25	23	26	54	149	201	263
Profit remittances on FDI	0	0	0	0	0	0	0	0	0	0
Memo: official net transfers	11	236	181	-7	40	62	146	249	208	167
private net transfers	0	69	11	-7	-4	401	718	617	897	1,511
3. MAJOR ECONOMIC AGGREGATES										
Gross national product (GNP)	..	..	3,461	5,788	7,706	9,436	11,551	13,283	15,342	16,504
Exports of goods & services (XGS)	..	..	3,023	3,106	3,157	3,481	4,493	4,724	5,098	2,827
of which workers remittances	0	0	1,818	2,016	2,050	2,166	2,391	2,503	2,588	..
Imports of goods & services (MGS)	..	..	2,908	4,424	5,542	6,222	7,629	8,114	8,626	..
International reserves (RES)	405	7,025	4,210	4,570	5,863	7,419	8,100	9,337	8,653	9,210
Current account balance	..	..	115	-1,318	-2,386	-2,742	-3,136	-3,343	-3,481	-3,888
4. DEBT INDICATORS										
EDT / XGS (%)	..	..	58.9	58.1	42.6	60.9	66.0	84.6	98.7	237.9
EDT / GNP (%)	..	..	51.4	31.2	17.5	22.5	25.7	30.1	32.8	40.8
TDS / XGS (%)	..	..	3.3	4.4	4.3	5.3	5.0	6.4	14.4	18.7
INT / XGS (%)	..	..	2.4	3.2	2.9	2.6	2.7	4.9	5.8	12.7
INT / GNP (%)	..	..	2.1	1.7	1.2	0.9	1.0	1.7	1.9	2.2
RES / EDT (%)	..	1,376.6	236.7	253.0	436.0	350.2	273.1	233.6	171.9	137.0
RES / MGS (months)	..	..	17.4	12.4	12.7	14.3	12.7	13.8	12.0	..
Short-term / EDT (%)	..	57.6	79.9	83.4	72.6	63.3	46.0	41.4	35.7	29.2
Concessional / EDT (%)	..	14.5	6.2	4.9	7.2	6.3	9.2	10.4	9.3	7.7
Multilateral / EDT (%)	..	15.2	4.8	2.6	5.9	5.9	6.7	8.2	7.4	7.1

LEBANON

(US$ million, unless otherwise indicated)

	1970	1980	1990	1992	1993	1994	1995	1996	1997	1998
5. LONG-TERM DEBT										
DEBT OUTSTANDING (LDOD)	**64**	**216**	**358**	**301**	**368**	**778**	**1,601**	**2,343**	**3,238**	**4,765**
Public and publicly guaranteed	**64**	**216**	**358**	**301**	**368**	**778**	**1,551**	**1,933**	**2,353**	**3,980**
Official creditors	64	146	188	212	289	295	428	630	710	829
Multilateral	18	78	85	48	79	125	198	326	371	476
Concessional	0	21	30	17	24	45	63	169	186	223
Bilateral	46	68	104	165	210	170	230	304	339	353
Concessional	31	53	81	71	72	89	209	246	281	295
Private creditors	0	71	169	88	79	483	1,123	1,304	1,643	3,151
Bonds	0	0	0	0	0	400	700	800	1,040	2,499
Commercial banks	0	70	0	0	27	26	359	482	583	632
Other private	0	1	169	88	52	58	64	22	21	19
Private nonguaranteed	**0**	**0**	**0**	**0**	**0**	**0**	**50**	**410**	**885**	**785**
Bonds	0	0	0	0	0	0	50	410	885	785
Commercial banks	0	0	0	0	0	0	0	0	0	0
Memo:										
IBRD	18	27	34	23	39	64	113	132	151	199
IDA	0	0	0	0	0	0	0	0	0	0
DISBURSEMENTS	**12**	**120**	**12**	**6**	**55**	**481**	**907**	**830**	**1,386**	**1,656**
Public and publicly guaranteed	**12**	**120**	**12**	**6**	**55**	**481**	**857**	**470**	**911**	**1,656**
Official creditors	12	50	5	3	52	69	213	244	146	121
Multilateral	0	17	0	0	42	52	80	147	75	102
Concessional	0	5	0	0	10	24	21	109	25	36
Bilateral	12	33	5	3	10	17	133	97	71	19
Concessional	6	18	5	3	10	17	125	59	63	18
Private creditors	0	70	6	3	3	411	644	227	765	1,536
Bonds	0	0	0	0	0	400	300	100	644	1,450
Commercial banks	0	70	0	0	0	8	340	126	121	86
Other private	0	0	6	3	3	4	4	1	0	0
Private nonguaranteed	**0**	**0**	**0**	**0**	**0**	**0**	**50**	**360**	**475**	**0**
Bonds	0	0	0	0	0	0	50	360	475	0
Commercial banks	0	0	0	0	0	0	0	0	0	0
Memo:										
IBRD	0	8	0	0	22	27	51	32	39	48
IDA	0	0	0	0	0	0	0	0	0	0
PRINCIPAL REPAYMENTS	**2**	**7**	**27**	**40**	**45**	**96**	**104**	**69**	**438**	**169**
Public and publicly guaranteed	**2**	**7**	**27**	**40**	**45**	**96**	**104**	**69**	**438**	**69**
Official creditors	2	7	27	33	37	83	93	20	26	27
Multilateral	1	3	7	13	10	10	10	8	12	12
Concessional	0	0	0	4	3	3	3	3	4	2
Bilateral	1	4	21	19	27	73	83	12	14	15
Concessional	1	4	1	11	4	6	10	12	13	12
Private creditors	0	0	0	7	8	13	11	49	412	42
Bonds	0	0	0	0	0	0	0	0	400	0
Commercial banks	0	0	0	0	0	12	9	9	11	41
Other private	0	0	0	7	8	2	2	40	1	2
Private nonguaranteed	**0**	**0**	**0**	**0**	**0**	**0**	**0**	**0**	**0**	**100**
Bonds	0	0	0	0	0	0	0	0	0	100
Commercial banks	0	0	0	0	0	0	0	0	0	0
Memo:										
IBRD	1	3	7	5	5	4	4	4	8	9
IDA	0	0	0	0	0	0	0	0	0	0
NET FLOWS ON DEBT	**10**	**112**	**-16**	**-34**	**10**	**385**	**804**	**761**	**948**	**1,487**
Public and publicly guaranteed	**10**	**112**	**-16**	**-34**	**10**	**385**	**754**	**401**	**473**	**1,587**
Official creditors	10	43	-22	-29	15	-13	120	223	120	94
Multilateral	-1	14	-6	-13	33	42	70	139	63	90
Concessional	0	5	0	-4	7	21	18	106	21	34
Bilateral	11	29	-16	-16	-17	-55	50	85	57	4
Concessional	5	14	4	-7	5	12	115	47	50	7
Private creditors	0	70	6	-5	-5	398	633	178	353	1,493
Bonds	0	0	0	0	0	400	300	100	244	1,450
Commercial banks	0	70	0	0	0	-4	331	117	110	45
Other private	0	0	6	-5	-5	2	2	-39	-1	-2
Private nonguaranteed	**0**	**0**	**0**	**0**	**0**	**0**	**50**	**360**	**475**	**-100**
Bonds	0	0	0	0	0	0	50	360	475	-100
Commercial banks	0	0	0	0	0	0	0	0	0	0
Memo:										
IBRD	-1	5	-7	-5	17	23	47	27	32	38
IDA	0	0	0	0	0	0	0	0	0	0

LEBANON

(US$ million, unless otherwise indicated)

	1970	1980	1990	1992	1993	1994	1995	1996	1997	1998
INTEREST PAYMENTS (LINT)	**1**	**6**	**11**	**25**	**23**	**26**	**54**	**149**	**201**	**263**
Public and publicly guaranteed	**1**	**6**	**11**	**25**	**23**	**26**	**54**	**146**	**164**	**186**
Official creditors	1	6	9	19	18	21	19	26	31	35
Multilateral	1	4	4	12	3	7	11	15	19	22
Concessional	0	1	0	2	1	2	3	4	8	8
Bilateral	0	2	5	7	15	14	8	11	11	13
Concessional	0	2	0	5	2	2	3	8	8	8
Private creditors	0	0	2	6	5	5	35	120	133	151
Bonds	0	0	0	0	0	0	20	72	81	99
Commercial banks	0	0	0	0	0	3	12	36	50	50
Other private	0	0	2	6	5	2	3	12	2	2
Private nonguaranteed	**0**	**0**	**0**	**0**	**0**	**0**	**0**	**2**	**37**	**77**
Bonds	0	0	0	0	0	0	0	2	37	77
Commercial banks	0	0	0	0	0	0	0	0	0	0
Memo:										
IBRD	1	2	4	2	2	4	7	9	10	11
IDA	0	0	0	0	0	0	0	0	0	0
NET TRANSFERS ON DEBT	**9**	**106**	**-27**	**-59**	**-13**	**359**	**750**	**612**	**747**	**1,224**
Public and publicly guaranteed	**9**	**106**	**-27**	**-59**	**-13**	**359**	**700**	**255**	**310**	**1,401**
Official creditors	9	37	-31	-48	-3	-34	101	197	89	59
Multilateral	-2	10	-11	-25	29	35	59	124	44	68
Concessional	0	5	0	-6	6	18	15	102	13	26
Bilateral	11	27	-21	-23	-32	-69	42	73	46	-9
Concessional	5	12	4	-12	4	10	112	40	42	-1
Private creditors	0	69	5	-11	-10	393	599	57	220	1,342
Bonds	0	0	0	0	0	400	280	28	164	1,351
Commercial banks	0	70	0	0	0	-7	319	81	59	-5
Other private	0	0	5	-11	-10	0	0	-51	-3	-4
Private nonguaranteed	**0**	**0**	**0**	**0**	**0**	**0**	**50**	**358**	**438**	**-177**
Bonds	0	0	0	0	0	0	50	358	438	-177
Commercial banks	0	0	0	0	0	0	0	0	0	0
Memo:										
IBRD	-2	3	-11	-7	16	19	40	19	22	28
IDA	0	0	0	0	0	0	0	0	0	0
DEBT SERVICE (LTDS)	**4**	**13**	**39**	**65**	**68**	**122**	**158**	**218**	**639**	**432**
Public and publicly guaranteed	**4**	**13**	**39**	**65**	**68**	**122**	**158**	**216**	**602**	**255**
Official creditors	4	13	37	51	55	103	112	46	57	61
Multilateral	2	7	11	25	13	17	21	23	32	34
Concessional	0	1	0	6	4	5	6	7	12	10
Bilateral	1	6	26	27	42	86	91	23	25	28
Concessional	1	6	1	16	6	8	13	19	21	20
Private creditors	0	1	2	13	13	18	46	170	545	194
Bonds	0	0	0	0	0	0	20	72	481	99
Commercial banks	0	0	0	0	0	15	21	45	61	91
Other private	0	0	2	13	13	4	4	53	3	4
Private nonguaranteed	**0**	**0**	**0**	**0**	**0**	**0**	**0**	**2**	**37**	**177**
Bonds	0	0	0	0	0	0	0	2	37	177
Commercial banks	0	0	0	0	0	0	0	0	0	0
Memo:										
IBRD	2	5	11	7	6	8	11	13	18	20
IDA	0	0	0	0	0	0	0	0	0	0
UNDISBURSED DEBT	**1**	**401**	**116**	**226**	**500**	**622**	**1,091**	**1,218**	**1,123**	**10,653**
Official creditors	1	164	79	201	475	606	773	875	898	813
Private creditors	0	237	37	25	25	16	319	343	224	9,840
Memorandum items										
Concessional LDOD	31	74	111	88	96	134	272	415	467	517
Variable rate LDOD	0	70	0	0	22	51	164	547	1,048	997
Public sector LDOD	64	216	358	301	368	778	1,551	1,933	2,353	3,954
Private sector LDOD	0	0	0	0	0	0	50	410	885	811

6. CURRENCY COMPOSITION OF LONG-TERM DEBT (PERCENT)

	1970	1980	1990	1992	1993	1994	1995	1996	1997	1998
Deutsche mark	0.0	0.7	5.3	3.9	2.6	1.2	1.1	2.7	8.3	5.2
French franc	22.0	6.0	31.7	64.1	62.0	23.5	8.2	6.2	4.6	2.9
Japanese yen	0.0	0.0	0.5	0.3	0.2	0.1	0.0	0.0	0.0	0.0
Pound sterling	0.0	0.0	0.8	0.3	0.5	0.2	0.1	0.1	0.1	0.0
Swiss franc	0.0	0.0	0.5	0.1	0.1	0.0	0.0	0.0	0.0	0.0
U.S.dollars	44.7	53.7	40.9	17.5	13.8	57.5	69.2	65.0	61.9	37.7
Multiple currency	0.0	18.4	9.4	7.6	10.7	8.3	7.4	6.8	6.6	5.1
Special drawing rights	0.0	0.0	0.0	0.0	0.0	0.0	0.0	0.0	0.0	0.0
All other currencies	33.3	21.2	10.9	6.2	10.1	9.2	14.0	19.2	18.5	49.1

LEBANON

(US$ million, unless otherwise indicated)

	1970	1980	1990	1992	1993	1994	1995	1996	1997	1998
7. DEBT RESTRUCTURINGS										
Total amount rescheduled	..	..	0	0	0	0	0	0	0	0
Debt stock rescheduled	..	..	0	0	0	0	0	0	0	0
Principal rescheduled	..	..	0	0	0	0	0	0	0	0
Official	..	..	0	0	0	0	0	0	0	0
Private	..	..	0	0	0	0	0	0	0	0
Interest rescheduled	..	..	0	0	0	0	0	0	0	0
Official	..	..	0	0	0	0	0	0	0	0
Private	..	..	0	0	0	0	0	0	0	0
Debt forgiven	..	..	0	0	0	0	0	0	0	0
Memo: interest forgiven	..	..	0	0	0	0	0	0	0	0
Debt stock reduction	..	..	0	0	0	0	0	0	0	0
of which debt buyback	..	..	0	0	0	0	0	0	0	0
8. DEBT STOCK-FLOW RECONCILIATION										
Total change in debt stocks	..	..	756	252	-461	774	848	1,031	1,036	1,692
Net flows on debt	10	236	726	274	-514	755	830	1,059	1,090	1,653
Net change in interest arrears	..	..	10	-20	-4	-7	-1	-10	0	0
Interest capitalized	..	..	0	0	0	0	0	0	0	0
Debt forgiveness or reduction	..	..	0	0	0	0	0	0	0	0
Cross-currency valuation	..	..	21	-16	-18	22	23	-28	-66	43
Residual	..	..	-1	15	75	3	-3	10	12	-3
9. AVERAGE TERMS OF NEW COMMITMENTS										
ALL CREDITORS										
Interest (%)	2.9	3.0	0.0	3.4	5.7	8.4	8.0	6.6	6.6	6.3
Maturity (years)	20.4	12.4	0.0	21.3	19.0	8.6	10.4	14.5	12.0	9.9
Grace period (years)	1.4	2.6	0.0	5.1	5.2	3.7	4.2	5.0	8.1	1.5
Grant element (%)	42.0	34.3	0.0	43.6	28.1	11.1	10.2	20.7	20.9	14.3
Official creditors										
Interest (%)	2.9	2.7	0.0	3.4	5.7	4.9	5.6	5.4	2.2	6.9
Maturity (years)	20.4	15.1	0.0	21.3	19.1	20.1	18.6	18.3	21.9	17.1
Grace period (years)	1.4	3.9	0.0	5.1	5.2	5.2	3.8	6.3	6.0	4.6
Grant element (%)	42.0	42.2	0.0	43.6	28.5	34.6	26.7	30.2	53.9	18.5
Private creditors										
Interest (%)	0.0	3.0	0.0	0.0	10.1	10.1	9.0	8.1	8.0	6.3
Maturity (years)	0.0	11.9	0.0	0.0	11.3	3.0	7.2	9.5	8.9	9.8
Grace period (years)	0.0	2.4	0.0	0.0	1.8	3.0	4.3	3.2	8.8	1.5
Grant element (%)	0.0	32.9	0.0	0.0	-1.6	-0.3	3.7	8.0	10.6	14.3
Memorandum items										
Commitments	7	92	0	88	332	594	1,324	622	859	10,771
Official creditors	7	14	0	88	328	194	373	354	206	63
Private creditors	0	78	0	0	4	400	951	268	654	10,708

10. CONTRACTUAL OBLIGATIONS ON OUTSTANDING LONG-TERM DEBT

	1999	2000	2001	2002	2003	2004	2005	2006	2007	2008
TOTAL										
Disbursements	4,950	3,412	1,409	686	74	46	32	20	12	9
Principal	1,008	1,849	1,708	1,540	1,669	1,125	1,647	1,179	1,658	1,064
Interest	553	730	713	644	560	451	386	274	205	94
Official creditors										
Disbursements	190	185	135	106	74	46	32	20	12	9
Principal	68	78	88	98	103	109	109	174	109	108
Interest	46	51	53	54	53	51	47	43	34	29
Bilateral creditors										
Disbursements	46	51	33	20	11	5	3	0	0	0
Principal	28	30	28	27	27	32	32	32	32	31
Interest	13	13	13	13	12	11	10	9	8	7
Multilateral creditors										
Disbursements	144	135	103	86	63	41	30	20	12	9
Principal	40	49	60	71	76	77	77	142	77	77
Interest	33	37	40	42	41	40	37	34	26	23
Private creditors										
Disbursements	4,759	3,227	1,273	580	0	0	0	0	0	0
Principal	940	1,771	1,620	1,442	1,566	1,016	1,538	1,005	1,549	956
Interest	507	679	660	589	507	400	339	231	171	65
Commercial banks										
Disbursements	4,759	3,227	1,273	580	0	0	0	0	0	0
Principal	778	1,319	1,018	1,015	1,015	1,015	1,012	1,004	973	955
Interest	245	414	433	418	366	305	243	182	122	64
Other private										
Disbursements	0	0	0	0	0	0	0	0	0	0
Principal	162	452	602	427	551	1	526	1	576	1
Interest	262	266	227	172	141	96	96	49	49	1

LESOTHO

(US$ million, unless otherwise indicated)

	1970	1980	1990	1992	1993	1994	1995	1996	1997	1998
1. SUMMARY DEBT DATA										
TOTAL DEBT STOCKS (EDT)	..	**71.9**	**395.6**	**494.6**	**540.6**	**619.5**	**677.0**	**669.7**	**659.6**	**692.1**
Long-term debt (LDOD)	**8.1**	**57.7**	**377.7**	**464.7**	**500.6**	**571.8**	**630.7**	**627.9**	**624.2**	**660.6**
Public and publicly guaranteed	8.1	57.7	377.7	464.7	500.6	571.8	630.7	627.9	624.2	660.6
Private nonguaranteed	0.0	0.0	0.0	0.0	0.0	0.0	0.0	0.0	0.0	0.0
Use of IMF credit	**0.0**	**6.2**	**15.1**	**24.9**	**34.2**	**40.3**	**38.4**	**33.8**	**27.5**	**23.6**
Short-term debt	..	**8.0**	**2.8**	**5.0**	**5.8**	**7.4**	**7.9**	**8.0**	**7.9**	**7.9**
of which interest arrears on LDOD	..	0.0	0.8	1.0	1.8	3.4	3.9	4.0	3.9	3.9
Official creditors	..	0.0	0.5	0.3	0.6	1.5	1.8	1.9	1.8	1.6
Private creditors	..	0.0	0.3	0.7	1.2	1.8	2.1	2.1	2.1	2.3
Memo: principal arrears on LDOD	..	0.0	3.6	7.6	9.4	12.4	9.8	10.2	8.6	8.7
Official creditors	..	0.0	2.0	4.3	5.8	7.5	4.6	5.2	4.1	4.0
Private creditors	..	0.0	1.6	3.3	3.7	4.9	5.2	5.0	4.5	4.8
Memo: export credits	..	0.0	115.0	139.0	145.0	246.0	379.0	299.0	385.0	369.0
TOTAL DEBT FLOWS										
Disbursements	**0.4**	**15.0**	**62.0**	**86.5**	**79.5**	**65.8**	**65.5**	**51.1**	**56.7**	**51.6**
Long-term debt	0.4	13.3	57.9	79.0	70.0	60.4	65.5	51.1	56.7	51.6
IMF purchases	0.0	1.7	4.1	7.4	9.5	5.4	0.0	0.0	0.0	0.0
Principal repayments	**0.3**	**3.4**	**15.0**	**20.3**	**20.4**	**18.4**	**24.6**	**21.6**	**27.0**	**30.0**
Long-term debt	0.3	3.4	14.8	20.3	20.4	16.9	21.9	18.2	22.8	25.1
IMF repurchases	0.0	0.0	0.2	0.0	0.0	1.5	2.7	3.4	4.3	4.9
Net flows on debt	**0.1**	**19.6**	**47.0**	**67.2**	**59.0**	**47.4**	**40.8**	**29.5**	**29.7**	**21.5**
of which short-term debt	..	8.0	0.0	1.0	0.0	0.0	0.0	0.0	0.0	0.0
Interest payments (INT)	..	**2.1**	**8.3**	**13.6**	**12.3**	**11.1**	**15.5**	**15.1**	**18.4**	**20.8**
Long-term debt	0.2	1.5	8.0	13.2	11.9	10.8	15.1	14.6	18.0	20.6
IMF charges	0.0	0.0	0.1	0.1	0.2	0.1	0.2	0.3	0.2	0.1
Short-term debt	..	0.6	0.2	0.3	0.3	0.2	0.2	0.2	0.2	0.2
Net transfers on debt	..	**17.5**	**38.7**	**53.6**	**46.7**	**36.3**	**25.3**	**14.4**	**11.3**	**0.7**
Total debt service paid (TDS)	..	**5.5**	**23.3**	**33.9**	**32.8**	**29.5**	**40.2**	**36.7**	**45.4**	**50.9**
Long-term debt	0.5	4.8	22.8	33.5	32.3	27.7	37.0	32.9	40.8	45.7
IMF repurchases and charges	0.0	0.0	0.3	0.1	0.2	1.6	3.0	3.7	4.4	5.0
Short-term debt (interest only)	..	0.6	0.2	0.3	0.3	0.2	0.2	0.2	0.2	0.2
2. AGGREGATE NET RESOURCE FLOWS AND NET TRANSFERS (LONG-TERM)										
NET RESOURCE FLOWS	**7.3**	**66.4**	**120.0**	**125.5**	**131.8**	**108.3**	**125.1**	**364.7**	**340.7**	**324.6**
Net flow of long-term debt (ex. IMF)	0.1	9.9	43.1	58.7	49.6	43.5	43.6	32.9	33.9	26.4
Foreign direct investment (net)	0.0	4.5	17.0	3.0	15.0	18.7	23.0	287.0	268.0	265.0
Portfolio equity flows	0.0	0.0	0.0	0.0	0.0	0.0	0.0	0.0	0.0	0.0
Grants (excluding technical coop.)	7.3	52.0	59.9	63.8	67.2	46.0	58.6	44.8	38.7	33.1
Memo: technical coop. grants	2.6	32.0	45.4	44.8	39.3	35.6	36.7	31.1	29.0	17.8
official net resource flows	7.2	59.6	103.0	127.6	122.2	95.0	92.9	67.7	59.7	43.4
private net resource flows	0.1	6.8	17.0	-2.1	9.6	13.3	32.2	297.0	281.0	281.2
NET TRANSFERS	**7.1**	**58.9**	**99.3**	**89.1**	**103.4**	**80.5**	**95.0**	**336.0**	**307.6**	**288.0**
Interest on long-term debt	0.2	1.5	8.0	13.2	11.9	10.8	15.1	14.6	18.0	20.6
Profit remittances on FDI	0.0	6.0	12.7	23.2	16.5	17.0	15.0	14.0	15.0	16.0
Memo: official net transfers	7.0	59.0	96.9	115.8	111.5	84.8	80.7	55.7	46.5	29.9
private net transfers	0.1	-0.1	2.4	-26.7	-8.1	-4.3	14.3	280.3	261.1	258.1
3. MAJOR ECONOMIC AGGREGATES										
Gross national product (GNP)	104.7	631.7	1,028.3	1,087.2	1,105.2	1,138.7	1,261.2	1,275.8	1,271.7	1,069.2
Exports of goods & services (XGS)	..	363.5	555.0	646.8	615.4	550.8	671.4	683.0	731.2	605.8
of which workers remittances	..	0.0	0.0	0.0	0.0	0.0	0.8	0.6	0.8	1.1
Imports of goods & services (MGS)	..	482.4	775.9	1,048.0	961.3	913.8	1,203.8	1,174.1	1,202.0	1,041.8
International reserves (RES)	..	50.3	72.4	157.5	252.7	372.6	456.7	460.5	571.7	575.1
Current account balance	..	56.3	65.0	37.6	29.3	108.1	-323.0	-302.5	-269.2	-280.2
4. DEBT INDICATORS										
EDT / XGS (%)	..	19.8	71.3	76.5	87.8	112.5	100.8	98.1	90.2	114.2
EDT / GNP (%)	..	11.4	38.5	45.5	48.9	54.4	53.7	52.5	51.9	64.7
TDS / XGS (%)	..	1.5	4.2	5.2	5.3	5.4	6.0	5.4	6.2	8.4
INT / XGS (%)	..	0.6	1.5	2.1	2.0	2.0	2.3	2.2	2.5	3.4
INT / GNP (%)	..	0.3	0.8	1.3	1.1	1.0	1.2	1.2	1.5	2.0
RES / EDT (%)	..	69.9	18.3	31.8	46.7	60.2	67.5	68.8	86.7	83.1
RES / MGS (months)	..	1.3	1.1	1.8	3.2	4.9	4.6	4.7	5.7	6.6
Short-term / EDT (%)	..	11.1	0.7	1.0	1.1	1.2	1.2	1.2	1.2	1.1
Concessional / EDT (%)	..	61.8	73.7	75.0	70.7	71.0	69.3	69.4	69.1	69.9
Multilateral / EDT (%)	..	56.1	73.6	66.1	66.3	69.3	68.8	70.4	70.9	72.0

LESOTHO

(US$ million, unless otherwise indicated)

	1970	1980	1990	1992	1993	1994	1995	1996	1997	1998
5. LONG-TERM DEBT										
DEBT OUTSTANDING (LDOD)	**8.1**	**57.7**	**377.7**	**464.7**	**500.6**	**571.8**	**630.7**	**627.9**	**624.2**	**660.6**
Public and publicly guaranteed	**8.1**	**57.7**	**377.7**	**464.7**	**500.6**	**571.8**	**630.7**	**627.9**	**624.2**	**660.6**
Official creditors	7.6	46.4	344.0	436.6	479.3	554.5	602.7	593.8	580.5	605.7
Multilateral	4.1	40.3	291.0	326.8	358.3	429.1	466.0	471.6	467.9	498.4
Concessional	4.1	40.3	251.6	292.1	302.2	351.6	374.8	377.1	374.4	400.8
Bilateral	3.5	6.1	53.1	109.8	121.0	125.4	136.7	122.2	112.6	107.2
Concessional	3.0	4.1	40.1	78.6	80.2	88.2	94.6	87.9	81.5	83.0
Private creditors	0.5	11.4	33.7	28.1	21.3	17.3	28.0	34.1	43.7	55.0
Bonds	0.0	0.0	0.0	0.0	0.0	0.0	0.0	0.0	0.0	0.0
Commercial banks	0.0	2.0	6.0	5.7	4.1	2.8	14.9	22.8	33.4	44.5
Other private	0.5	9.4	27.7	22.4	17.2	14.5	13.2	11.3	10.2	10.5
Private nonguaranteed	**0.0**	**0.0**	**0.0**	**0.0**	**0.0**	**0.0**	**0.0**	**0.0**	**0.0**	**0.0**
Bonds	0.0	0.0	0.0	0.0	0.0	0.0	0.0	0.0	0.0	0.0
Commercial banks	0.0	0.0	0.0	0.0	0.0	0.0	0.0	0.0	0.0	0.0
Memo:										
IBRD	0.0	0.0	0.0	4.5	26.0	41.7	54.0	57.1	58.3	60.8
IDA	4.1	24.1	111.7	127.1	133.6	143.0	152.8	159.3	162.9	180.1
DISBURSEMENTS	**0.4**	**13.3**	**57.9**	**79.0**	**70.0**	**60.4**	**65.5**	**51.1**	**56.7**	**51.6**
Public and publicly guaranteed	**0.4**	**13.3**	**57.9**	**79.0**	**70.0**	**60.4**	**65.5**	**51.1**	**56.7**	**51.6**
Official creditors	0.2	8.0	51.4	77.1	69.7	60.4	52.1	38.7	41.9	33.6
Multilateral	0.0	6.5	32.0	35.9	43.9	53.4	40.2	34.5	37.3	28.2
Concessional	0.0	6.5	28.3	31.2	19.0	36.0	23.7	19.7	23.4	22.1
Bilateral	0.2	1.5	19.4	41.2	25.7	7.0	11.9	4.2	4.7	5.4
Concessional	0.2	0.9	15.2	23.2	9.3	6.6	4.2	1.0	4.6	4.8
Private creditors	0.2	5.3	6.5	1.9	0.3	0.0	13.4	12.3	14.8	18.0
Bonds	0.0	0.0	0.0	0.0	0.0	0.0	0.0	0.0	0.0	0.0
Commercial banks	0.0	2.0	3.0	1.9	0.3	0.0	13.4	12.3	13.9	17.8
Other private	0.2	3.3	3.5	0.0	0.0	0.0	0.0	0.0	0.9	0.1
Private nonguaranteed	**0.0**	**0.0**	**0.0**	**0.0**	**0.0**	**0.0**	**0.0**	**0.0**	**0.0**	**0.0**
Bonds	0.0	0.0	0.0	0.0	0.0	0.0	0.0	0.0	0.0	0.0
Commercial banks	0.0	0.0	0.0	0.0	0.0	0.0	0.0	0.0	0.0	0.0
Memo:										
IBRD	0.0	0.0	0.0	4.6	21.8	13.7	11.2	7.2	8.2	3.4
IDA	0.0	3.8	9.2	9.9	7.0	6.3	8.8	11.7	11.6	14.3
PRINCIPAL REPAYMENTS	**0.3**	**3.4**	**14.8**	**20.3**	**20.4**	**16.9**	**21.9**	**18.2**	**22.8**	**25.1**
Public and publicly guaranteed	**0.3**	**3.4**	**14.8**	**20.3**	**20.4**	**16.9**	**21.9**	**18.2**	**22.8**	**25.1**
Official creditors	0.3	0.4	8.3	13.3	14.7	11.4	17.7	15.8	21.0	23.3
Multilateral	0.0	0.2	5.4	7.2	6.7	7.6	14.1	9.2	13.2	15.4
Concessional	0.0	0.2	3.0	3.1	4.2	4.4	9.1	6.2	7.5	7.5
Bilateral	0.3	0.2	2.9	6.0	8.0	3.8	3.7	6.7	7.8	8.0
Concessional	0.2	0.2	0.9	1.8	4.5	1.1	1.7	4.4	5.8	5.3
Private creditors	0.0	3.0	6.5	7.0	5.7	5.4	4.1	2.4	1.8	1.8
Bonds	0.0	0.0	0.0	0.0	0.0	0.0	0.0	0.0	0.0	0.0
Commercial banks	0.0	0.0	0.6	2.0	1.7	1.2	1.5	1.5	1.3	1.3
Other private	0.0	3.0	5.9	5.0	4.0	4.2	2.6	0.9	0.5	0.5
Private nonguaranteed	**0.0**	**0.0**	**0.0**	**0.0**	**0.0**	**0.0**	**0.0**	**0.0**	**0.0**	**0.0**
Bonds	0.0	0.0	0.0	0.0	0.0	0.0	0.0	0.0	0.0	0.0
Commercial banks	0.0	0.0	0.0	0.0	0.0	0.0	0.0	0.0	0.0	0.0
Memo:										
IBRD	0.0	0.0	0.0	0.0	0.0	0.0	0.0	0.0	2.2	4.5
IDA	0.0	0.0	0.6	0.8	0.8	1.1	1.3	1.5	1.6	1.9
NET FLOWS ON DEBT	**0.1**	**9.9**	**43.1**	**58.7**	**49.6**	**43.5**	**43.6**	**32.9**	**33.9**	**26.4**
Public and publicly guaranteed	**0.1**	**9.9**	**43.1**	**58.7**	**49.6**	**43.5**	**43.6**	**32.9**	**33.9**	**26.4**
Official creditors	-0.1	7.6	43.1	63.8	55.0	49.0	34.3	22.9	21.0	10.3
Multilateral	0.0	6.4	26.6	28.7	37.2	45.8	26.1	25.4	24.1	12.8
Concessional	0.0	6.4	25.3	28.0	14.9	31.7	14.6	13.5	15.9	14.7
Bilateral	-0.1	1.3	16.5	35.2	17.8	3.1	8.2	-2.4	-3.1	-2.5
Concessional	0.0	0.7	14.3	21.4	4.8	5.4	2.5	-3.4	-1.2	-0.5
Private creditors	0.1	2.3	0.0	-5.1	-5.4	-5.4	9.2	10.0	13.0	16.2
Bonds	0.0	0.0	0.0	0.0	0.0	0.0	0.0	0.0	0.0	0.0
Commercial banks	0.0	2.0	2.4	-0.1	-1.4	-1.2	11.9	10.9	12.6	16.6
Other private	0.1	0.3	-2.5	-5.0	-4.0	-4.2	-2.6	-0.9	0.4	-0.4
Private nonguaranteed	**0.0**	**0.0**	**0.0**	**0.0**	**0.0**	**0.0**	**0.0**	**0.0**	**0.0**	**0.0**
Bonds	0.0	0.0	0.0	0.0	0.0	0.0	0.0	0.0	0.0	0.0
Commercial banks	0.0	0.0	0.0	0.0	0.0	0.0	0.0	0.0	0.0	0.0
Memo:										
IBRD	0.0	0.0	0.0	4.6	21.8	13.7	11.2	7.2	6.0	-1.1
IDA	0.0	3.8	8.6	9.2	6.2	5.2	7.4	10.3	10.0	12.5

LESOTHO

(US$ million, unless otherwise indicated)

	1970	1980	1990	1992	1993	1994	1995	1996	1997	1998
INTEREST PAYMENTS (LINT)	**0.2**	**1.5**	**8.0**	**13.2**	**11.9**	**10.8**	**15.1**	**14.6**	**18.0**	**20.6**
Public and publicly guaranteed	**0.2**	**1.5**	**8.0**	**13.2**	**11.9**	**10.8**	**15.1**	**14.6**	**18.0**	**20.6**
Official creditors	0.2	0.6	6.1	11.8	10.7	10.2	12.2	12.0	13.2	13.5
Multilateral	0.0	0.4	4.7	6.6	5.6	6.6	8.6	8.1	9.2	9.0
Concessional	0.0	0.3	2.1	3.8	2.5	2.3	3.1	3.1	3.5	3.6
Bilateral	0.2	0.2	1.4	5.2	5.0	3.6	3.6	3.8	4.0	4.5
Concessional	0.1	0.0	0.6	2.5	2.1	1.4	1.6	1.7	1.5	1.6
Private creditors	0.0	0.9	1.9	1.4	1.2	0.6	2.9	2.7	4.9	7.1
Bonds	0.0	0.0	0.0	0.0	0.0	0.0	0.0	0.0	0.0	0.0
Commercial banks	0.0	0.3	0.3	0.4	0.4	0.2	2.6	2.4	4.7	6.7
Other private	0.0	0.6	1.6	1.0	0.8	0.4	0.3	0.3	0.1	0.4
Private nonguaranteed	**0.0**	**0.0**	**0.0**	**0.0**	**0.0**	**0.0**	**0.0**	**0.0**	**0.0**	**0.0**
Bonds	0.0	0.0	0.0	0.0	0.0	0.0	0.0	0.0	0.0	0.0
Commercial banks	0.0	0.0	0.0	0.0	0.0	0.0	0.0	0.0	0.0	0.0
Memo:										
IBRD	0.0	0.0	0.0	0.3	1.1	2.5	3.5	3.8	3.7	3.7
IDA	0.0	0.2	0.8	0.9	1.0	1.0	1.1	1.1	1.2	1.2
NET TRANSFERS ON DEBT	**-0.1**	**8.5**	**35.1**	**45.6**	**37.7**	**32.7**	**28.4**	**18.2**	**15.9**	**5.8**
Public and publicly guaranteed	**-0.1**	**8.5**	**35.1**	**45.6**	**37.7**	**32.7**	**28.4**	**18.2**	**15.9**	**5.8**
Official creditors	-0.2	7.1	37.0	52.1	44.3	38.7	22.1	11.0	7.8	-3.2
Multilateral	0.0	6.0	21.9	22.1	31.6	39.2	17.4	17.2	14.9	3.8
Concessional	0.0	6.1	23.1	24.3	12.4	29.3	11.5	10.4	12.4	11.0
Bilateral	-0.2	1.1	15.2	30.0	12.8	-0.5	4.6	-6.3	-7.1	-7.0
Concessional	-0.1	0.7	13.7	18.9	2.7	4.1	0.9	-5.1	-2.7	-2.1
Private creditors	0.1	1.4	-2.0	-6.5	-6.6	-6.0	6.4	7.3	8.1	9.1
Bonds	0.0	0.0	0.0	0.0	0.0	0.0	0.0	0.0	0.0	0.0
Commercial banks	0.0	1.8	2.2	-0.6	-1.8	-1.4	9.3	8.5	7.9	9.8
Other private	0.1	-0.3	-4.1	-5.9	-4.9	-4.6	-2.9	-1.2	0.2	-0.8
Private nonguaranteed	**0.0**	**0.0**	**0.0**	**0.0**	**0.0**	**0.0**	**0.0**	**0.0**	**0.0**	**0.0**
Bonds	0.0	0.0	0.0	0.0	0.0	0.0	0.0	0.0	0.0	0.0
Commercial banks	0.0	0.0	0.0	0.0	0.0	0.0	0.0	0.0	0.0	0.0
Memo:										
IBRD	0.0	0.0	0.0	4.3	20.7	11.3	7.7	3.4	2.3	-4.7
IDA	0.0	3.6	7.9	8.3	5.2	4.2	6.3	9.1	8.8	11.2
DEBT SERVICE (LTDS)	**0.5**	**4.8**	**22.8**	**33.5**	**32.3**	**27.7**	**37.0**	**32.9**	**40.8**	**45.7**
Public and publicly guaranteed	**0.5**	**4.8**	**22.8**	**33.5**	**32.3**	**27.7**	**37.0**	**32.9**	**40.8**	**45.7**
Official creditors	0.4	1.0	14.4	25.0	25.3	21.7	30.0	27.8	34.2	36.8
Multilateral	0.0	0.5	10.2	13.8	12.4	14.2	22.7	17.3	22.4	24.4
Concessional	0.0	0.4	5.2	6.9	6.7	6.7	12.2	9.3	11.0	11.1
Bilateral	0.4	0.4	4.2	11.2	13.0	7.5	7.3	10.5	11.8	12.5
Concessional	0.3	0.3	1.5	4.3	6.6	2.5	3.2	6.1	7.3	6.9
Private creditors	0.1	3.9	8.5	8.4	7.0	6.0	7.0	5.1	6.7	8.9
Bonds	0.0	0.0	0.0	0.0	0.0	0.0	0.0	0.0	0.0	0.0
Commercial banks	0.0	0.3	0.9	2.5	2.1	1.4	4.1	3.9	6.0	8.0
Other private	0.1	3.6	7.6	6.0	4.9	4.6	2.9	1.2	0.7	0.9
Private nonguaranteed	**0.0**	**0.0**	**0.0**	**0.0**	**0.0**	**0.0**	**0.0**	**0.0**	**0.0**	**0.0**
Bonds	0.0	0.0	0.0	0.0	0.0	0.0	0.0	0.0	0.0	0.0
Commercial banks	0.0	0.0	0.0	0.0	0.0	0.0	0.0	0.0	0.0	0.0
Memo:										
IBRD	0.0	0.0	0.0	0.3	1.1	2.5	3.5	3.8	5.8	8.1
IDA	0.0	0.2	1.4	1.7	1.8	2.2	2.5	2.6	2.8	3.1
UNDISBURSED DEBT	**0.8**	**118.0**	**315.0**	**505.2**	**498.0**	**483.0**	**431.4**	**268.6**	**199.1**	**188.9**
Official creditors	0.1	110.0	312.3	383.7	373.5	335.3	298.9	216.5	167.6	177.5
Private creditors	0.7	8.0	2.7	121.5	124.5	147.7	132.6	52.0	31.5	11.5
Memorandum items										
Concessional LDOD	7.1	44.3	291.7	370.7	382.4	439.8	469.4	465.1	455.9	483.8
Variable rate LDOD	0.0	2.0	0.0	4.7	26.0	41.7	54.0	57.1	58.3	60.8
Public sector LDOD	8.1	55.7	376.5	463.8	499.7	571.0	630.0	627.2	623.6	660.2
Private sector LDOD	0.0	2.0	1.2	0.9	0.9	0.8	0.7	0.7	0.6	0.5

6. CURRENCY COMPOSITION OF LONG-TERM DEBT (PERCENT)

	1970	1980	1990	1992	1993	1994	1995	1996	1997	1998
Deutsche mark	0.0	0.0	0.4	0.1	0.0	0.0	0.0	0.0	0.0	0.0
French franc	0.0	0.0	7.5	10.3	8.9	8.4	8.2	7.3	6.6	6.6
Japanese yen	0.0	0.0	0.0	0.0	0.0	0.0	0.0	0.0	0.0	0.0
Pound sterling	43.1	16.5	1.7	1.3	1.2	1.0	0.8	0.8	1.0	1.5
Swiss franc	0.0	0.0	0.0	0.0	0.0	0.0	0.0	0.0	0.0	0.0
U.S.dollars	50.5	46.4	24.8	24.6	23.9	22.2	21.2	22.4	23.7	25.0
Multiple currency	0.0	7.1	5.6	8.1	14.6	17.2	20.6	21.5	21.3	19.7
Special drawing rights	0.0	0.0	9.9	8.6	8.2	7.6	7.1	6.8	6.4	6.3
All other currencies	6.4	30.0	50.1	47.0	43.2	43.6	42.1	41.2	41.0	40.9

LESOTHO

(US$ million, unless otherwise indicated)

	1970	1980	1990	1992	1993	1994	1995	1996	1997	1998
7. DEBT RESTRUCTURINGS										
Total amount rescheduled	..	..	0.0	0.0	0.0	0.0	0.0	0.0	0.0	0.0
Debt stock rescheduled	..	..	0.0	0.0	0.0	0.0	0.0	0.0	0.0	0.0
Principal rescheduled	..	..	0.0	0.0	0.0	0.0	0.0	0.0	0.0	0.0
Official	..	..	0.0	0.0	0.0	0.0	0.0	0.0	0.0	0.0
Private	..	..	0.0	0.0	0.0	0.0	0.0	0.0	0.0	0.0
Interest rescheduled	..	..	0.0	0.0	0.0	0.0	0.0	0.0	0.0	0.0
Official	..	..	0.0	0.0	0.0	0.0	0.0	0.0	0.0	0.0
Private	..	..	0.0	0.0	0.0	0.0	0.0	0.0	0.0	0.0
Debt forgiven	..	..	3.7	0.0	4.9	0.0	0.0	0.0	0.0	0.0
Memo: interest forgiven	..	..	0.0	0.0	0.0	0.0	0.0	0.0	0.0	0.0
Debt stock reduction	..	..	0.0	0.0	0.0	0.0	0.0	0.0	0.0	0.0
of which debt buyback	..	..	0.0	0.0	0.0	0.0	0.0	0.0	0.0	0.0
8. DEBT STOCK-FLOW RECONCILIATION										
Total change in debt stocks	..	..	67.4	47.0	46.0	78.9	57.5	-7.3	-10.0	32.5
Net flows on debt	0.1	19.6	47.0	67.2	59.0	47.4	40.8	29.5	29.7	21.5
Net change in interest arrears	..	..	0.8	0.5	0.8	1.6	0.5	0.2	-0.1	-0.1
Interest capitalized	..	..	0.0	0.0	0.0	0.0	0.0	0.0	0.0	0.0
Debt forgiveness or reduction	..	..	-3.7	0.0	-4.9	0.0	0.0	0.0	0.0	0.0
Cross-currency valuation	..	..	23.8	-18.4	-9.5	22.4	13.0	-21.4	-29.9	12.2
Residual	..	..	-0.4	-2.3	0.5	7.5	3.2	-15.5	-9.7	-1.1
9. AVERAGE TERMS OF NEW COMMITMENTS										
ALL CREDITORS										
Interest (%)	5.0	5.9	1.3	13.8	4.1	4.9	6.8	8.2	2.8	4.6
Maturity (years)	18.1	24.3	24.3	11.5	30.7	17.0	29.0	31.9	21.1	23.5
Grace period (years)	1.9	5.7	6.0	3.7	9.6	6.4	6.2	16.4	4.2	6.6
Grant element (%)	31.9	37.3	63.3	-2.0	44.5	39.0	29.5	13.4	46.3	39.9
Official creditors										
Interest (%)	0.0	3.0	1.0	4.0	1.8	1.0	6.8	0.7	2.8	4.6
Maturity (years)	25.0	29.8	25.1	31.6	32.6	22.0	29.0	39.5	21.1	23.5
Grace period (years)	5.5	6.7	6.2	6.8	6.9	9.2	6.2	10.0	4.2	6.6
Grant element (%)	72.7	52.7	65.9	48.3	62.9	66.2	29.5	80.3	46.3	39.9
Private creditors										
Interest (%)	7.5	15.8	8.4	17.5	13.9	9.2	0.0	16.3	0.0	0.0
Maturity (years)	14.6	5.5	5.8	4.0	22.0	11.5	0.0	23.5	0.0	0.0
Grace period (years)	0.1	2.2	1.8	2.5	22.0	3.3	0.0	23.5	0.0	0.0
Grant element (%)	10.9	-15.0	4.3	-21.0	-37.1	8.6	0.0	-59.8	0.0	0.0
Memorandum items										
Commitments	0.4	58.5	46.4	176.8	87.9	58.2	23.0	76.5	10.1	66.5
Official creditors	0.2	45.2	44.4	48.4	71.7	30.7	23.0	40.0	10.1	66.5
Private creditors	0.3	13.3	2.0	128.4	16.2	27.5	0.0	36.6	0.0	0.0

10. CONTRACTUAL OBLIGATIONS ON OUTSTANDING LONG-TERM DEBT

	1999	2000	2001	2002	2003	2004	2005	2006	2007	2008
TOTAL										
Disbursements	56.5	41.6	28.2	20.9	15.5	8.8	6.3	4.1	3.1	1.8
Principal	31.1	31.8	33.6	34.5	36.0	37.5	38.6	38.3	35.9	34.2
Interest	20.7	20.6	20.0	19.3	18.4	17.3	16.0	14.7	13.4	12.2
Official creditors										
Disbursements	48.4	39.0	27.4	20.9	15.5	8.8	6.3	4.1	3.1	1.8
Principal	28.0	28.7	30.5	31.4	33.1	34.6	35.9	35.8	34.5	33.9
Interest	13.5	13.4	13.0	12.5	11.8	10.9	9.8	8.7	7.6	6.5
Bilateral creditors										
Disbursements	12.7	7.0	4.1	2.1	1.3	0.0	0.0	0.0	0.0	0.0
Principal	8.9	8.8	9.1	9.5	9.6	8.9	8.7	8.8	7.6	7.2
Interest	4.2	4.2	3.9	3.6	3.2	2.8	2.5	2.1	1.8	1.5
Multilateral creditors										
Disbursements	35.7	32.0	23.3	18.8	14.2	8.8	6.3	4.1	3.1	1.8
Principal	19.1	19.9	21.4	21.9	23.6	25.7	27.2	27.0	26.8	26.7
Interest	9.4	9.3	9.1	8.9	8.6	8.1	7.4	6.6	5.9	5.1
Private creditors										
Disbursements	8.1	2.6	0.8	0.0	0.0	0.0	0.0	0.0	0.0	0.0
Principal	3.1	3.1	3.1	3.1	2.9	2.9	2.7	2.5	1.4	0.3
Interest	7.1	7.2	7.0	6.8	6.6	6.3	6.1	5.9	5.7	5.7
Commercial banks										
Disbursements	7.9	2.6	0.8	0.0	0.0	0.0	0.0	0.0	0.0	0.0
Principal	2.4	2.4	2.4	2.4	2.4	2.4	2.4	2.2	1.1	0.0
Interest	6.7	6.8	6.7	6.5	6.3	6.2	6.0	5.8	5.6	5.6
Other private										
Disbursements	0.2	0.0	0.0	0.0	0.0	0.0	0.0	0.0	0.0	0.0
Principal	0.7	0.7	0.7	0.7	0.5	0.5	0.3	0.3	0.3	0.3
Interest	0.4	0.4	0.3	0.3	0.2	0.2	0.1	0.1	0.1	0.1

LIBERIA

(US$ million, unless otherwise indicated)

	1970	1980	1990	1992	1993	1994	1995	1996	1997	1998
1. SUMMARY DEBT DATA										
TOTAL DEBT STOCKS (EDT)	..	**686**	**1,849**	**1,923**	**1,957**	**2,056**	**2,154**	**2,107**	**2,012**	**2,103**
Long-term debt (LDOD)	**158**	**516**	**1,116**	**1,081**	**1,102**	**1,137**	**1,161**	**1,110**	**1,061**	**1,092**
Public and publicly guaranteed	158	516	1,116	1,081	1,102	1,137	1,161	1,110	1,061	1,092
Private nonguaranteed	0	0	0	0	0	0	0	0	0	0
Use of IMF credit	**4**	**89**	**322**	**312**	**311**	**330**	**336**	**325**	**305**	**317**
Short-term debt	..	**81**	**411**	**530**	**544**	**589**	**657**	**672**	**646**	**694**
of which interest arrears on LDOD	..	2	355	477	500	545	613	617	612	656
Official creditors	..	1	251	329	349	390	458	467	466	506
Private creditors	..	1	104	148	151	155	155	151	146	150
Memo: principal arrears on LDOD	..	3	722	798	823	924	961	956	940	991
Official creditors	..	2	530	603	623	715	754	756	749	792
Private creditors	..	1	192	195	200	208	208	199	192	199
Memo: export credits	..	0	203	111	53	52	218	283	747	177
TOTAL DEBT FLOWS										
Disbursements	**9**	**109**	**0**	**0**	**33**	**0**	**0**	**0**	**0**	**0**
Long-term debt	7	76	0	0	33	0	0	0	0	0
IMF purchases	2	34	0	0	0	0	0	0	0	0
Principal repayments	**17**	**18**	**2**	**0**	**13**	**15**	**0**	**0**	**0**	**1**
Long-term debt	11	15	1	0	13	14	0	0	0	0
IMF repurchases	5	3	1	0	0	1	0	0	0	1
Net flows on debt	**-7**	**95**	**-1**	**-1**	**10**	**-14**	**0**	**11**	**-21**	**3**
of which short-term debt	..	4	1	-1	-10	1	0	11	-21	4
Interest payments (INT)	..	**35**	**1**	**1**	**9**	**0**	**2**	**1**	**0**	**0**
Long-term debt	6	23	1	0	8	0	0	0	0	0
IMF charges	0	2	0	1	1	0	2	1	0	0
Short-term debt	..	11	0	0	0	0	0	0	0	0
Net transfers on debt	..	**60**	**-2**	**-1**	**1**	**-14**	**-2**	**10**	**-21**	**3**
Total debt service paid (TDS)	..	**54**	**3**	**1**	**22**	**15**	**2**	**1**	**0**	**1**
Long-term debt	18	38	2	0	21	14	0	0	0	0
IMF repurchases and charges	5	5	1	1	1	1	2	1	0	1
Short-term debt (interest only)	..	11	0	0	0	0	0	0	0	0
2. AGGREGATE NET RESOURCE FLOWS AND NET TRANSFERS (LONG-TERM)										
NET RESOURCE FLOWS	**-3**	**83**	**59**	**85**	**150**	**54**	**128**	**110**	**83**	**76**
Net flow of long-term debt (ex. IMF)	-4	61	-1	0	20	-14	0	0	0	0
Foreign direct investment (net)	0	0	0	-11	30	14	21	17	15	16
Portfolio equity flows	0	0	0	0	0	0	0	0	0	0
Grants (excluding technical coop.)	1	23	60	96	100	53	107	93	68	60
Memo: technical coop. grants	8	24	21	24	22	11	16	10	15	18
official net resource flows	4	84	59	96	120	40	107	93	68	60
private net resource flows	-7	0	0	-11	30	14	21	17	15	16
NET TRANSFERS	**-9**	**61**	**59**	**85**	**142**	**54**	**128**	**109**	**83**	**76**
Interest on long-term debt	6	23	1	0	8	0	0	0	0	0
Profit remittances on FDI	0	0	0	0	0	0	0	0	0	0
Memo: official net transfers	1	77	59	96	112	40	107	92	68	60
private net transfers	-10	-16	0	-11	30	14	21	17	15	16
3. MAJOR ECONOMIC AGGREGATES										
Gross national product (GNP)	402	1,093	..	..	..	..	..	..	..	..
Exports of goods & services (XGS)	..	614	..	..	..	..	..	..	..	..
of which workers remittances	..	0	..	..	..	..	..	..	..	..
Imports of goods & services (MGS)	..	575	..	..	..	..	..	..	..	..
International reserves (RES)	..	5	..	1	2	5	28	..	..	..
Current account balance	..	46	..	..	..	..	..	..	..	..
4. DEBT INDICATORS										
EDT / XGS (%)	..	111.8	..	..	..	..	..	..	..	..
EDT / GNP (%)	..	62.7	..	..	..	..	..	..	..	..
TDS / XGS (%)	..	8.8	..	..	..	..	..	..	..	..
INT / XGS (%)	..	5.8	..	..	..	..	..	..	..	..
INT / GNP (%)	..	3.2	..	..	..	..	..	..	..	..
RES / EDT (%)	..	0.8	..	0.1	0.1	0.3	1.3	..	..	..
RES / MGS (months)	..	0.1	..	..	..	..	..	..	..	..
Short-term / EDT (%)	..	11.8	22.2	27.6	27.8	28.7	30.5	31.9	32.1	33.0
Concessional / EDT (%)	..	30.8	32.1	29.8	30.6	30.3	29.5	28.9	29.1	28.5
Multilateral / EDT (%)	..	19.1	23.4	21.2	22.0	21.4	21.0	20.1	20.1	19.9

LIBERIA

(US$ million, unless otherwise indicated)

	1970	*1980*	*1990*	*1992*	*1993*	*1994*	*1995*	*1996*	*1997*	*1998*
5. LONG-TERM DEBT										
DEBT OUTSTANDING (LDOD)	**158**	**516**	**1,116**	**1,081**	**1,102**	**1,137**	**1,161**	**1,110**	**1,061**	**1,092**
Public and publicly guaranteed	**158**	**516**	**1,116**	**1,081**	**1,102**	**1,137**	**1,161**	**1,110**	**1,061**	**1,092**
Official creditors	124	359	924	886	902	929	954	911	869	894
Multilateral	8	131	433	407	430	439	453	424	405	418
Concessional	0	33	184	172	204	211	214	202	197	200
Bilateral	116	229	491	479	472	490	501	486	465	475
Concessional	110	179	410	401	395	411	421	408	388	398
Private creditors	34	156	192	195	200	208	208	199	192	199
Bonds	0	0	0	0	0	0	0	0	0	0
Commercial banks	0	129	172	176	181	189	187	180	173	180
Other private	34	28	20	19	19	20	21	20	19	19
Private nonguaranteed	**0**	**0**	**0**	**0**	**0**	**0**	**0**	**0**	**0**	**0**
Bonds	0	0	0	0	0	0	0	0	0	0
Commercial banks	0	0	0	0	0	0	0	0	0	0
Memo:										
IBRD	7	69	143	139	141	151	161	146	136	143
IDA	0	23	105	103	104	107	108	106	102	105
DISBURSEMENTS	**7**	**76**	**0**	**0**	**33**	**0**	**0**	**0**	**0**	**0**
Public and publicly guaranteed	**7**	**76**	**0**	**0**	**33**	**0**	**0**	**0**	**0**	**0**
Official creditors	7	65	0	0	33	0	0	0	0	0
Multilateral	2	33	0	0	33	0	0	0	0	0
Concessional	0	8	0	0	33	0	0	0	0	0
Bilateral	5	32	0	0	0	0	0	0	0	0
Concessional	4	30	0	0	0	0	0	0	0	0
Private creditors	0	11	0	0	0	0	0	0	0	0
Bonds	0	0	0	0	0	0	0	0	0	0
Commercial banks	0	6	0	0	0	0	0	0	0	0
Other private	0	5	0	0	0	0	0	0	0	0
Private nonguaranteed	**0**	**0**	**0**	**0**	**0**	**0**	**0**	**0**	**0**	**0**
Bonds	0	0	0	0	0	0	0	0	0	0
Commercial banks	0	0	0	0	0	0	0	0	0	0
Memo:										
IBRD	2	17	0	0	0	0	0	0	0	0
IDA	0	5	0	0	0	0	0	0	0	0
PRINCIPAL REPAYMENTS	**11**	**15**	**1**	**0**	**13**	**14**	**0**	**0**	**0**	**0**
Public and publicly guaranteed	**11**	**15**	**1**	**0**	**13**	**14**	**0**	**0**	**0**	**0**
Official creditors	5	4	1	0	13	14	0	0	0	0
Multilateral	0	2	1	0	13	14	0	0	0	0
Concessional	0	0	0	0	1	1	0	0	0	0
Bilateral	5	1	0	0	0	0	0	0	0	0
Concessional	5	1	0	0	0	0	0	0	0	0
Private creditors	7	12	0	0	0	0	0	0	0	0
Bonds	0	0	0	0	0	0	0	0	0	0
Commercial banks	0	3	0	0	0	0	0	0	0	0
Other private	7	9	0	0	0	0	0	0	0	0
Private nonguaranteed	**0**	**0**	**0**	**0**	**0**	**0**	**0**	**0**	**0**	**0**
Bonds	0	0	0	0	0	0	0	0	0	0
Commercial banks	0	0	0	0	0	0	0	0	0	0
Memo:										
IBRD	0	2	0	0	0	0	0	0	0	0
IDA	0	0	0	0	0	0	0	0	0	0
NET FLOWS ON DEBT	**-4**	**61**	**-1**	**0**	**20**	**-14**	**0**	**0**	**0**	**0**
Public and publicly guaranteed	**-4**	**61**	**-1**	**0**	**20**	**-14**	**0**	**0**	**0**	**0**
Official creditors	3	61	-1	0	20	-14	0	0	0	0
Multilateral	2	31	-1	0	20	-14	0	0	0	0
Concessional	0	8	0	0	32	-1	0	0	0	0
Bilateral	0	30	0	0	0	0	0	0	0	0
Concessional	-1	29	0	0	0	0	0	0	0	0
Private creditors	-7	0	0	0	0	0	0	0	0	0
Bonds	0	0	0	0	0	0	0	0	0	0
Commercial banks	0	3	0	0	0	0	0	0	0	0
Other private	-7	-3	0	0	0	0	0	0	0	0
Private nonguaranteed	**0**	**0**	**0**	**0**	**0**	**0**	**0**	**0**	**0**	**0**
Bonds	0	0	0	0	0	0	0	0	0	0
Commercial banks	0	0	0	0	0	0	0	0	0	0
Memo:										
IBRD	2	16	0	0	0	0	0	0	0	0
IDA	0	5	0	0	0	0	0	0	0	0

LIBERIA

(US$ million, unless otherwise indicated)

	1970	1980	1990	1992	1993	1994	1995	1996	1997	1998
INTEREST PAYMENTS (LINT)	**6**	**23**	**1**	**0**	**8**	**0**	**0**	**0**	**0**	**0**
Public and publicly guaranteed	**6**	**23**	**1**	**0**	**8**	**0**	**0**	**0**	**0**	**0**
Official creditors	3	7	1	0	8	0	0	0	0	0
Multilateral	0	5	1	0	8	0	0	0	0	0
Concessional	0	0	0	0	1	0	0	0	0	0
Bilateral	3	2	0	0	0	0	0	0	0	0
Concessional	2	2	0	0	0	0	0	0	0	0
Private creditors	3	16	0	0	0	0	0	0	0	0
Bonds	0	0	0	0	0	0	0	0	0	0
Commercial banks	0	14	0	0	0	0	0	0	0	0
Other private	3	2	0	0	0	0	0	0	0	0
Private nonguaranteed	**0**	**0**	**0**	**0**	**0**	**0**	**0**	**0**	**0**	**0**
Bonds	0	0	0	0	0	0	0	0	0	0
Commercial banks	0	0	0	0	0	0	0	0	0	0
Memo:										
IBRD	0	4	0	0	0	0	0	0	0	0
IDA	0	0	0	0	0	0	0	0	0	0
NET TRANSFERS ON DEBT	**-10**	**38**	**-2**	**0**	**12**	**-14**	**0**	**0**	**0**	**0**
Public and publicly guaranteed	**-10**	**38**	**-2**	**0**	**12**	**-14**	**0**	**0**	**0**	**0**
Official creditors	-1	54	-2	0	12	-14	0	0	0	0
Multilateral	2	25	-2	0	12	-14	0	0	0	0
Concessional	0	8	0	0	32	-1	0	0	0	0
Bilateral	-2	29	0	0	0	0	0	0	0	0
Concessional	-3	28	0	0	0	0	0	0	0	0
Private creditors	-10	-16	0	0	0	0	0	0	0	0
Bonds	0	0	0	0	0	0	0	0	0	0
Commercial banks	0	-11	0	0	0	0	0	0	0	0
Other private	-10	-5	0	0	0	0	0	0	0	0
Private nonguaranteed	**0**	**0**	**0**	**0**	**0**	**0**	**0**	**0**	**0**	**0**
Bonds	0	0	0	0	0	0	0	0	0	0
Commercial banks	0	0	0	0	0	0	0	0	0	0
Memo:										
IBRD	1	12	0	0	0	0	0	0	0	0
IDA	0	5	0	0	0	0	0	0	0	0
DEBT SERVICE (LTDS)	**18**	**38**	**2**	**0**	**21**	**14**	**0**	**0**	**0**	**0**
Public and publicly guaranteed	**18**	**38**	**2**	**0**	**21**	**14**	**0**	**0**	**0**	**0**
Official creditors	8	11	2	0	21	14	0	0	0	0
Multilateral	0	8	2	0	21	14	0	0	0	0
Concessional	0	0	0	0	2	1	0	0	0	0
Bilateral	8	3	0	0	0	0	0	0	0	0
Concessional	7	3	0	0	0	0	0	0	0	0
Private creditors	10	27	0	0	0	0	0	0	0	0
Bonds	0	0	0	0	0	0	0	0	0	0
Commercial banks	0	17	0	0	0	0	0	0	0	0
Other private	10	11	0	0	0	0	0	0	0	0
Private nonguaranteed	**0**	**0**	**0**	**0**	**0**	**0**	**0**	**0**	**0**	**0**
Bonds	0	0	0	0	0	0	0	0	0	0
Commercial banks	0	0	0	0	0	0	0	0	0	0
Memo:										
IBRD	0	6	0	0	0	0	0	0	0	0
IDA	0	0	0	0	0	0	0	0	0	0
UNDISBURSED DEBT	**20**	**228**	**84**	**74**	**40**	**36**	**18**	**17**	**15**	**16**
Official creditors	18	220	84	74	40	36	18	17	15	16
Private creditors	2	8	0	0	0	0	0	0	0	0
Memorandum items										
Concessional LDOD	110	211	594	573	599	622	635	610	585	598
Variable rate LDOD	0	100	123	123	123	123	123	123	123	123
Public sector LDOD	158	514	1,116	1,081	1,102	1,137	1,161	1,110	1,061	1,092
Private sector LDOD	0	1	0	0	0	0	0	0	0	0

6. CURRENCY COMPOSITION OF LONG-TERM DEBT (PERCENT)

	1970	1980	1990	1992	1993	1994	1995	1996	1997	1998
Deutsche mark	12.7	9.2	11.1	10.6	9.7	10.5	11.1	10.7	9.7	10.1
French franc	0.0	0.0	1.1	1.0	0.9	1.0	1.1	1.0	1.0	1.0
Japanese yen	0.0	7.6	6.1	6.8	7.4	8.1	7.7	7.1	6.6	7.3
Pound sterling	0.3	1.5	1.2	1.2	1.2	1.2	1.2	1.2	1.3	1.2
Swiss franc	0.0	0.0	0.0	0.0	0.0	0.0	0.0	0.0	0.0	0.0
U.S.dollars	82.1	62.6	51.2	52.6	51.6	50.3	49.4	51.5	53.5	52.2
Multiple currency	4.9	17.4	22.7	21.4	20.1	20.8	21.4	20.4	20.1	20.4
Special drawing rights	0.0	0.0	1.5	1.5	1.4	1.5	1.5	1.5	1.5	1.5
All other currencies	0.0	1.7	5.1	4.9	7.7	6.6	6.6	6.6	6.3	6.3

LIBERIA

(US$ million, unless otherwise indicated)

	1970	1980	1990	1992	1993	1994	1995	1996	1997	1998
7. DEBT RESTRUCTURINGS										
Total amount rescheduled	..	..	0	0	0	0	0	0	0	0
Debt stock rescheduled	..	..	0	0	0	0	0	0	0	0
Principal rescheduled	..	..	0	0	0	0	0	0	0	0
Official	..	..	0	0	0	0	0	0	0	0
Private	..	..	0	0	0	0	0	0	0	0
Interest rescheduled	..	..	0	0	0	0	0	0	0	0
Official	..	..	0	0	0	0	0	0	0	0
Private	..	..	0	0	0	0	0	0	0	0
Debt forgiven	..	..	0	0	0	0	0	0	0	0
Memo: interest forgiven	..	..	0	0	0	0	0	0	0	0
Debt stock reduction	..	..	0	0	0	0	0	0	0	0
of which debt buyback	..	..	0	0	0	0	0	0	0	0
8. DEBT STOCK-FLOW RECONCILIATION										
Total change in debt stocks	..	..	164	-31	34	99	98	-48	-95	91
Net flows on debt	-7	95	-1	-1	10	-14	0	11	-21	3
Net change in interest arrears	..	..	87	7	24	45	68	4	-5	44
Interest capitalized	..	..	0	0	0	0	0	0	0	0
Debt forgiveness or reduction	..	..	0	0	0	0	0	0	0	0
Cross-currency valuation	..	..	46	-20	2	44	22	-36	-41	30
Residual	..	..	32	-18	-1	24	8	-27	-28	15
9. AVERAGE TERMS OF NEW COMMITMENTS										
ALL CREDITORS										
Interest (%)	6.6	7.3	4.0	0.0	0.0	0.0	0.0	0.0	0.0	0.0
Maturity (years)	18.7	18.8	24.8	0.0	0.0	0.0	0.0	0.0	0.0	0.0
Grace period (years)	4.4	4.5	5.3	0.0	0.0	0.0	0.0	0.0	0.0	0.0
Grant element (%)	20.7	25.1	42.8	0.0	0.0	0.0	0.0	0.0	0.0	0.0
Official creditors										
Interest (%)	6.4	5.3	4.0	0.0	0.0	0.0	0.0	0.0	0.0	0.0
Maturity (years)	20.8	23.1	24.8	0.0	0.0	0.0	0.0	0.0	0.0	0.0
Grace period (years)	5.0	5.5	5.3	0.0	0.0	0.0	0.0	0.0	0.0	0.0
Grant element (%)	23.5	35.5	42.8	0.0	0.0	0.0	0.0	0.0	0.0	0.0
Private creditors										
Interest (%)	7.9	12.6	0.0	0.0	0.0	0.0	0.0	0.0	0.0	0.0
Maturity (years)	8.1	7.3	0.0	0.0	0.0	0.0	0.0	0.0	0.0	0.0
Grace period (years)	1.5	1.6	0.0	0.0	0.0	0.0	0.0	0.0	0.0	0.0
Grant element (%)	6.6	-3.1	0.0	0.0	0.0	0.0	0.0	0.0	0.0	0.0
Memorandum items										
Commitments	12	40	32	0	0	0	0	0	0	0
Official creditors	10	30	32	0	0	0	0	0	0	0
Private creditors	2	11	0	0	0	0	0	0	0	0

10. CONTRACTUAL OBLIGATIONS ON OUTSTANDING LONG-TERM DEBT

	1999	2000	2001	2002	2003	2004	2005	2006	2007	2008
TOTAL										
Disbursements	0	0	0	0	0	0	0	0	0	0
Principal	65	47	24	22	21	19	17	17	15	14
Interest	11	8	6	5	5	4	4	3	3	3
Official creditors										
Disbursements	0	0	0	0	0	0	0	0	0	0
Principal	65	47	24	22	21	19	17	17	15	14
Interest	11	8	6	5	5	4	4	3	3	3
Bilateral creditors										
Disbursements	0	0	0	0	0	0	0	0	0	0
Principal	17	16	15	14	14	13	11	11	9	8
Interest	4	4	3	3	3	2	2	2	1	1
Multilateral creditors										
Disbursements	0	0	0	0	0	0	0	0	0	0
Principal	48	31	10	8	8	6	6	6	6	6
Interest	7	4	3	2	2	2	2	2	1	1
Private creditors										
Disbursements	0	0	0	0	0	0	0	0	0	0
Principal	0	0	0	0	0	0	0	0	0	0
Interest	0	0	0	0	0	0	0	0	0	0
Commercial banks										
Disbursements	0	0	0	0	0	0	0	0	0	0
Principal	0	0	0	0	0	0	0	0	0	0
Interest	0	0	0	0	0	0	0	0	0	0
Other private										
Disbursements	0	0	0	0	0	0	0	0	0	0
Principal	0	0	0	0	0	0	0	0	0	0
Interest	0	0	0	0	0	0	0	0	0	0

LITHUANIA

(US$ million, unless otherwise indicated)

	1970	1980	1990	1992	1993	1994	1995	1996	1997	1998
1. SUMMARY DEBT DATA										
TOTAL DEBT STOCKS (EDT)	..	..	..	**55.5**	**327.8**	**493.7**	**759.6**	**1,222.5**	**1,533.0**	**1,949.7**
Long-term debt (LDOD)	..	..	..	**27.4**	**200.2**	**268.3**	**448.7**	**792.5**	**1,099.6**	**1,320.0**
Public and publicly guaranteed	..	..	..	27.4	200.2	268.3	420.0	728.1	1,041.9	1,215.8
Private nonguaranteed	..	..	..	0.0	0.0	0.0	28.7	64.4	57.7	104.2
Use of IMF credit	..	..	..	**23.7**	**120.8**	**196.4**	**261.5**	**273.4**	**270.5**	**253.2**
Short-term debt	..	..	..	**4.5**	**6.8**	**29.0**	**49.4**	**156.7**	**163.0**	**376.5**
of which interest arrears on LDOD	..	..	..	0.0	0.0	0.0	0.0	0.0	0.0	0.0
Official creditors	..	..	..	0.0	0.0	0.0	0.0	0.0	0.0	0.0
Private creditors	..	..	..	0.0	0.0	0.0	0.0	0.0	0.0	0.0
Memo: principal arrears on LDOD	..	..	..	0.0	0.0	0.0	0.0	0.0	0.0	6.7
Official creditors	..	..	..	0.0	0.0	0.0	0.0	0.0	0.0	0.0
Private creditors	..	..	..	0.0	0.0	0.0	0.0	0.0	0.0	6.7
Memo: export credits	..	..	..	4.0	6.0	97.0	135.0	182.0	212.0	275.0
TOTAL DEBT FLOWS										
Disbursements	..	..	..	**33.8**	**279.0**	**156.8**	**218.5**	**464.7**	**609.6**	**249.4**
Long-term debt	..	..	..	9.5	180.2	90.1	155.7	419.7	552.7	249.4
IMF purchases	..	..	..	24.3	98.8	66.7	62.8	45.1	57.0	0.0
Principal repayments	..	..	..	**2.9**	**3.3**	**35.2**	**12.2**	**81.8**	**249.5**	**102.4**
Long-term debt	..	..	..	2.9	3.3	35.2	12.2	57.3	206.7	74.4
IMF repurchases	..	..	..	0.0	0.0	0.0	0.0	24.5	42.7	28.0
Net flows on debt	..	..	..	**35.5**	**278.0**	**143.8**	**226.8**	**490.2**	**366.5**	**360.5**
of which short-term debt	..	..	..	4.5	2.4	22.2	20.4	107.3	6.3	213.5
Interest payments (INT)	..	..	..	**1.1**	**4.0**	**32.5**	**31.3**	**42.2**	**68.1**	**67.9**
Long-term debt	..	..	..	1.1	1.2	23.1	17.4	23.6	46.9	54.2
IMF charges	..	..	..	0.0	2.5	7.6	11.5	11.5	12.4	12.3
Short-term debt	..	..	..	0.0	0.3	1.8	2.4	7.0	8.8	1.5
Net transfers on debt	..	..	..	**34.3**	**274.0**	**111.4**	**195.5**	**448.0**	**298.4**	**292.6**
Total debt service paid (TDS)	..	..	..	**4.0**	**7.3**	**67.7**	**43.5**	**124.0**	**317.5**	**170.3**
Long-term debt	..	..	..	4.0	4.5	58.3	29.6	80.9	253.6	128.6
IMF repurchases and charges	..	..	..	0.0	2.5	7.6	11.5	36.1	55.2	40.2
Short-term debt (interest only)	..	..	..	0.0	0.3	1.8	2.4	7.0	8.8	1.5
2. AGGREGATE NET RESOURCE FLOWS AND NET TRANSFERS (LONG-TERM)										
NET RESOURCE FLOWS	..	..	..	**74.9**	**226.4**	**113.3**	**238.3**	**578.8**	**763.2**	**1,182.7**
Net flow of long-term debt (ex. IMF)	..	..	..	6.7	176.9	54.9	143.5	362.4	345.9	175.0
Foreign direct investment (net)	..	..	..	0.0	30.2	31.3	72.6	152.4	354.5	926.0
Portfolio equity flows	..	..	..	0.0	0.0	0.0	4.3	21.0	0.0	0.0
Grants (excluding technical coop.)	..	..	..	68.3	19.3	27.0	17.9	43.1	62.8	81.6
Memo: technical coop. grants	..	..	..	16.4	18.9	28.6	116.4	36.0	31.7	25.7
official net resource flows	..	..	..	77.8	149.7	94.0	105.9	154.1	130.2	200.2
private net resource flows	..	..	..	-2.9	76.7	19.3	132.4	424.7	633.0	982.5
NET TRANSFERS	..	..	..	**73.8**	**225.2**	**90.1**	**220.9**	**555.3**	**716.3**	**1,128.4**
Interest on long-term debt	..	..	..	1.1	1.2	23.1	17.4	23.6	46.9	54.2
Profit remittances on FDI	..	..	..	0.0	0.0	0.0	0.0	0.0	0.0	0.0
Memo: official net transfers	..	..	..	77.8	149.2	85.1	92.6	139.4	108.5	174.2
private net transfers	..	..	..	-4.0	76.0	5.0	128.3	415.9	607.8	954.2
3. MAJOR ECONOMIC AGGREGATES										
Gross national product (GNP)	..	..	..	..	6,118.1	5,840.8	6,871.9	7,801.3	9,386.7	10,480.7
Exports of goods & services (XGS)	..	..	..	..	2,236.1	2,373.3	3,243.3	4,264.5	5,306.5	5,197.2
of which workers remittances	..	..	..	..	0.0	0.7	1.1	1.9	1.8	2.1
Imports of goods & services (MGS)	..	..	..	..	2,437.6	2,623.3	3,965.9	5,129.0	6,516.0	6,728.3
International reserves (RES)	..	..	..	107.3	422.9	596.7	829.0	841.0	1,064.0	1,462.7
Current account balance	..	..	..	..	-85.7	-94.0	-614.4	-722.6	-981.3	-1,298.2
4. DEBT INDICATORS										
EDT / XGS (%)	..	..	..	..	14.7	20.8	23.4	28.7	28.9	37.5
EDT / GNP (%)	..	..	..	..	5.4	8.5	11.1	15.7	16.3	18.6
TDS / XGS (%)	..	..	..	..	0.3	2.9	1.3	2.9	6.0	3.3
INT / XGS (%)	..	..	..	..	0.2	1.4	1.0	1.0	1.3	1.3
INT / GNP (%)	..	..	..	..	0.1	0.6	0.5	0.5	0.7	0.7
RES / EDT (%)	..	..	..	193.3	129.0	120.9	109.1	68.8	69.4	75.0
RES / MGS (months)	..	..	..	..	2.1	2.7	2.5	2.0	2.0	2.6
Short-term / EDT (%)	..	..	..	8.1	2.1	5.9	6.5	12.8	10.6	19.3
Concessional / EDT (%)	..	..	..	17.1	10.3	15.7	13.1	8.6	7.1	6.0
Multilateral / EDT (%)	..	..	..	0.0	30.5	24.1	21.4	18.6	16.2	17.6

LITHUANIA

(US$ million, unless otherwise indicated)

	1970	1980	1990	1992	1993	1994	1995	1996	1997	1998
5. LONG-TERM DEBT										
DEBT OUTSTANDING (LDOD)	..	..	..	**27.4**	**200.2**	**268.3**	**448.7**	**792.5**	**1,099.6**	**1,320.0**
Public and publicly guaranteed	..	..	..	**27.4**	**200.2**	**268.3**	**420.0**	**728.1**	**1,041.9**	**1,215.8**
Official creditors	..	..	..	9.5	136.4	213.8	307.0	401.0	439.2	575.7
Multilateral	..	..	..	0.0	99.8	119.2	162.6	227.9	248.5	342.6
Concessional	..	..	..	0.0	0.0	0.0	0.0	0.0	0.0	0.0
Bilateral	..	..	..	9.5	36.6	94.6	144.3	173.1	190.7	233.2
Concessional	..	..	..	9.5	33.6	77.7	99.7	105.0	108.1	116.9
Private creditors	..	..	..	17.9	63.8	54.5	113.0	327.1	602.6	640.1
Bonds	..	..	..	0.0	0.0	0.0	0.0	110.0	200.0	200.0
Commercial banks	..	..	..	0.0	0.0	0.0	0.0	59.8	168.9	208.1
Other private	..	..	..	17.9	63.8	54.5	113.0	157.3	233.7	232.0
Private nonguaranteed	..	..	..	**0.0**	**0.0**	**0.0**	**28.7**	**64.4**	**57.7**	**104.2**
Bonds	..	..	..	0.0	0.0	0.0	0.0	0.0	0.0	0.0
Commercial banks	..	..	..	0.0	0.0	0.0	28.7	64.4	57.7	104.2
Memo:										
IBRD	..	..	..	0.0	41.6	48.9	61.8	101.2	114.3	173.7
IDA	..	..	..	0.0	0.0	0.0	0.0	0.0	0.0	0.0
DISBURSEMENTS	..	..	..	**9.5**	**180.2**	**90.1**	**155.7**	**419.7**	**552.7**	**249.4**
Public and publicly guaranteed	..	..	..	**9.5**	**180.2**	**90.1**	**155.7**	**384.0**	**552.7**	**216.9**
Official creditors	..	..	..	9.5	130.4	68.1	91.3	129.5	84.8	143.2
Multilateral	..	..	..	0.0	103.2	10.6	38.0	81.3	48.5	95.5
Concessional	..	..	..	0.0	0.0	0.0	0.0	0.0	0.0	0.0
Bilateral	..	..	..	9.5	27.2	57.5	53.3	48.2	36.3	47.7
Concessional	..	..	..	9.5	24.1	43.3	24.1	10.0	8.0	6.2
Private creditors	..	..	..	0.0	49.8	22.0	64.5	254.4	467.9	73.7
Bonds	..	..	..	0.0	0.0	0.0	0.0	110.0	200.0	0.0
Commercial banks	..	..	..	0.0	0.0	0.0	0.0	60.0	150.3	51.2
Other private	..	..	..	0.0	49.8	22.0	64.5	84.5	117.5	22.5
Private nonguaranteed	..	..	..	**0.0**	**0.0**	**0.0**	**0.0**	**35.7**	**0.0**	**32.5**
Bonds	..	..	..	0.0	0.0	0.0	0.0	0.0	0.0	0.0
Commercial banks	..	..	..	0.0	0.0	0.0	0.0	35.7	0.0	32.5
Memo:										
IBRD	..	..	..	0.0	42.4	4.2	12.1	43.8	20.7	60.3
IDA	..	..	..	0.0	0.0	0.0	0.0	0.0	0.0	0.0
PRINCIPAL REPAYMENTS	..	..	..	**2.9**	**3.3**	**35.2**	**12.2**	**57.3**	**206.7**	**74.4**
Public and publicly guaranteed	..	..	..	**2.9**	**3.3**	**35.2**	**12.2**	**52.3**	**200.0**	**65.0**
Official creditors	..	..	..	0.0	0.0	1.1	3.2	18.5	17.4	24.6
Multilateral	..	..	..	0.0	0.0	0.0	0.0	6.2	8.5	11.1
Concessional	..	..	..	0.0	0.0	0.0	0.0	0.0	0.0	0.0
Bilateral	..	..	..	0.0	0.0	1.1	3.2	12.3	8.9	13.5
Concessional	..	..	..	0.0	0.0	0.0	0.3	0.0	1.0	1.6
Private creditors	..	..	..	2.9	3.3	34.1	8.9	33.8	182.7	40.3
Bonds	..	..	..	0.0	0.0	0.0	0.0	0.0	110.0	0.0
Commercial banks	..	..	..	0.0	0.0	0.0	0.0	0.0	40.4	10.7
Other private	..	..	..	2.9	3.3	34.1	8.9	33.8	32.3	29.7
Private nonguaranteed	..	..	..	**0.0**	**0.0**	**0.0**	**0.0**	**5.0**	**6.7**	**9.4**
Bonds	..	..	..	0.0	0.0	0.0	0.0	0.0	0.0	0.0
Commercial banks	..	..	..	0.0	0.0	0.0	0.0	5.0	6.7	9.4
Memo:										
IBRD	..	..	..	0.0	0.0	0.0	0.0	0.0	2.6	3.2
IDA	..	..	..	0.0	0.0	0.0	0.0	0.0	0.0	0.0
NET FLOWS ON DEBT	..	..	..	**6.7**	**176.9**	**54.9**	**143.5**	**362.4**	**345.9**	**175.0**
Public and publicly guaranteed	..	..	..	**6.7**	**176.9**	**54.9**	**143.5**	**331.7**	**352.6**	**151.9**
Official creditors	..	..	..	9.5	130.4	67.0	88.0	111.0	67.4	118.6
Multilateral	..	..	..	0.0	103.2	10.6	38.0	75.2	40.0	84.4
Concessional	..	..	..	0.0	0.0	0.0	0.0	0.0	0.0	0.0
Bilateral	..	..	..	9.5	27.2	56.4	50.0	35.9	27.4	34.1
Concessional	..	..	..	9.5	24.1	43.3	23.8	10.0	7.0	4.6
Private creditors	..	..	..	-2.9	46.5	-12.0	55.5	220.6	285.2	33.4
Bonds	..	..	..	0.0	0.0	0.0	0.0	110.0	90.0	0.0
Commercial banks	..	..	..	0.0	0.0	0.0	0.0	60.0	110.0	40.6
Other private	..	..	..	-2.9	46.5	-12.0	55.5	50.7	85.2	-7.2
Private nonguaranteed	..	..	..	**0.0**	**0.0**	**0.0**	**0.0**	**30.7**	**-6.7**	**23.1**
Bonds	..	..	..	0.0	0.0	0.0	0.0	0.0	0.0	0.0
Commercial banks	..	..	..	0.0	0.0	0.0	0.0	30.7	-6.7	23.1
Memo:										
IBRD	..	..	..	0.0	42.4	4.2	12.1	43.8	18.1	57.1
IDA	..	..	..	0.0	0.0	0.0	0.0	0.0	0.0	0.0

LITHUANIA

(US$ million, unless otherwise indicated)

	1970	1980	1990	1992	1993	1994	1995	1996	1997	1998
INTEREST PAYMENTS (LINT)	..	..	..	**1.1**	**1.2**	**23.1**	**17.4**	**23.6**	**46.9**	**54.2**
Public and publicly guaranteed	..	..	..	**1.1**	**1.2**	**23.1**	**17.4**	**21.3**	**44.0**	**49.6**
Official creditors	..	..	..	0.0	0.5	8.9	13.3	14.7	21.7	26.0
Multilateral	..	..	..	0.0	0.3	7.8	9.4	10.4	14.2	17.0
Concessional	..	..	..	0.0	0.0	0.0	0.0	0.0	0.0	0.0
Bilateral	..	..	..	0.0	0.2	1.1	3.9	4.3	7.4	9.0
Concessional	..	..	..	0.0	0.2	0.7	2.7	1.8	2.2	2.2
Private creditors	..	..	..	1.1	0.7	14.3	4.1	6.5	22.3	23.7
Bonds	..	..	..	0.0	0.0	0.0	0.0	0.0	8.3	7.1
Commercial banks	..	..	..	0.0	0.0	0.0	0.0	0.2	4.2	5.0
Other private	..	..	..	1.1	0.7	14.3	4.1	6.3	9.9	11.6
Private nonguaranteed	..	..	..	**0.0**	**0.0**	**0.0**	**0.0**	**2.3**	**2.9**	**4.6**
Bonds	..	..	..	0.0	0.0	0.0	0.0	0.0	0.0	0.0
Commercial banks	..	..	..	0.0	0.0	0.0	0.0	2.3	2.9	4.6
Memo:										
IBRD	..	..	..	0.0	0.3	3.2	3.6	4.3	7.1	8.3
IDA	..	..	..	0.0	0.0	0.0	0.0	0.0	0.0	0.0
NET TRANSFERS ON DEBT	..	..	..	**5.5**	**175.7**	**31.8**	**126.1**	**338.8**	**299.1**	**120.8**
Public and publicly guaranteed	..	..	..	**5.5**	**175.7**	**31.8**	**126.1**	**310.4**	**308.7**	**102.3**
Official creditors	..	..	..	9.5	129.9	58.1	74.7	96.3	45.8	92.6
Multilateral	..	..	..	0.0	102.9	2.8	28.6	64.8	25.8	67.5
Concessional	..	..	..	0.0	0.0	0.0	0.0	0.0	0.0	0.0
Bilateral	..	..	..	9.5	27.0	55.3	46.1	31.5	20.0	25.1
Concessional	..	..	..	9.5	23.9	42.7	21.1	8.2	4.8	2.4
Private creditors	..	..	..	-4.0	45.8	-26.3	51.4	214.1	262.9	9.7
Bonds	..	..	..	0.0	0.0	0.0	0.0	110.0	81.8	-7.1
Commercial banks	..	..	..	0.0	0.0	0.0	0.0	59.8	105.8	35.6
Other private	..	..	..	-4.0	45.8	-26.3	51.4	44.3	75.4	-18.7
Private nonguaranteed	..	..	..	**0.0**	**0.0**	**0.0**	**0.0**	**28.4**	**-9.6**	**18.5**
Bonds	..	..	..	0.0	0.0	0.0	0.0	0.0	0.0	0.0
Commercial banks	..	..	..	0.0	0.0	0.0	0.0	28.4	-9.6	18.5
Memo:										
IBRD	..	..	..	0.0	42.1	1.0	8.5	39.5	11.0	48.7
IDA	..	..	..	0.0	0.0	0.0	0.0	0.0	0.0	0.0
DEBT SERVICE (LTDS)	..	..	..	**4.0**	**4.5**	**58.3**	**29.6**	**80.9**	**253.6**	**128.6**
Public and publicly guaranteed	..	..	..	**4.0**	**4.5**	**58.3**	**29.6**	**73.6**	**244.0**	**114.6**
Official creditors	..	..	..	0.0	0.5	10.0	16.6	33.2	39.0	50.6
Multilateral	..	..	..	0.0	0.3	7.8	9.4	16.6	22.7	28.1
Concessional	..	..	..	0.0	0.0	0.0	0.0	0.0	0.0	0.0
Bilateral	..	..	..	0.0	0.2	2.2	7.1	16.6	16.3	22.5
Concessional	..	..	..	0.0	0.2	0.7	3.0	1.8	3.2	3.8
Private creditors	..	..	..	4.0	4.0	48.3	13.0	40.3	205.0	64.0
Bonds	..	..	..	0.0	0.0	0.0	0.0	0.0	118.3	7.1
Commercial banks	..	..	..	0.0	0.0	0.0	0.0	0.2	44.6	15.6
Other private	..	..	..	4.0	4.0	48.3	13.0	40.1	42.1	41.2
Private nonguaranteed	..	..	..	**0.0**	**0.0**	**0.0**	**0.0**	**7.3**	**9.6**	**14.0**
Bonds	..	..	..	0.0	0.0	0.0	0.0	0.0	0.0	0.0
Commercial banks	..	..	..	0.0	0.0	0.0	0.0	7.3	9.6	14.0
Memo:										
IBRD	..	..	..	0.0	0.3	3.2	3.6	4.3	9.7	11.6
IDA	..	..	..	0.0	0.0	0.0	0.0	0.0	0.0	0.0
UNDISBURSED DEBT	..	..	..	**135.4**	**141.6**	**209.5**	**479.8**	**578.5**	**375.8**	**307.4**
Official creditors	..	..	..	104.8	117.7	138.0	235.1	380.3	295.3	205.6
Private creditors	..	..	..	30.6	23.9	71.5	244.7	198.2	80.6	101.8
Memorandum items										
Concessional LDOD	..	..	..	9.5	33.6	77.7	99.7	105.0	108.1	116.9
Variable rate LDOD	..	..	..	17.9	102.1	128.4	236.4	400.4	563.0	752.2
Public sector LDOD	..	..	..	27.4	200.2	265.4	414.3	717.9	978.4	1,123.7
Private sector LDOD	..	..	..	0.0	0.0	2.9	34.4	74.6	121.2	196.3

6. CURRENCY COMPOSITION OF LONG-TERM DEBT (PERCENT)

	1970	1980	1990	1992	1993	1994	1995	1996	1997	1998
Deutsche mark	..	..	..	0.0	4.7	11.7	17.7	9.0	6.2	4.6
French franc	..	..	..	0.0	0.0	0.0	0.0	0.0	0.0	0.0
Japanese yen	..	..	..	0.0	0.0	12.8	10.0	8.5	5.9	5.9
Pound sterling	..	..	..	0.0	0.0	0.0	0.0	0.0	0.0	0.2
Swiss franc	..	..	..	65.4	7.4	5.1	3.3	1.4	0.6	0.2
U.S.dollars	..	..	..	34.7	39.1	27.7	32.9	49.1	61.3	58.7
Multiple currency	..	..	..	0.0	20.8	18.2	14.7	13.8	10.7	14.2
Special drawing rights	..	..	..	0.0	0.0	0.0	0.0	0.0	0.0	0.0
All other currencies	..	..	..	0.0	28.0	24.5	21.4	18.2	15.3	16.2

LITHUANIA

(US$ million, unless otherwise indicated)

	1970	1980	1990	1992	1993	1994	1995	1996	1997	1998
7. DEBT RESTRUCTURINGS										
Total amount rescheduled	..	..	..	0.0	0.0	0.0	0.0	0.0	0.0	0.0
Debt stock rescheduled	..	..	..	0.0	0.0	0.0	0.0	0.0	0.0	0.0
Principal rescheduled	..	..	..	0.0	0.0	0.0	0.0	0.0	0.0	0.0
Official	..	..	..	0.0	0.0	0.0	0.0	0.0	0.0	0.0
Private	..	..	..	0.0	0.0	0.0	0.0	0.0	0.0	0.0
Interest rescheduled	..	..	..	..	0.0	0.0	0.0	0.0	0.0	0.0
Official	..	..	..	0.0	0.0	0.0	0.0	0.0	0.0	0.0
Private	..	..	..	0.0	0.0	0.0	0.0	0.0	0.0	0.0
Debt forgiven	..	..	..	0.0	0.0	0.0	0.0	0.0	0.0	0.0
Memo: interest forgiven	..	..	..	0.0	0.0	0.0	0.0	0.0	0.0	0.0
Debt stock reduction	..	..	..	0.0	0.0	0.0	0.0	0.0	0.0	0.0
of which debt buyback	..	..	..	0.0	0.0	0.0	0.0	0.0	0.0	0.0
8. DEBT STOCK-FLOW RECONCILIATION										
Total change in debt stocks	..	..	..	..	272.3	165.9	265.9	462.9	310.5	416.7
Net flows on debt	..	..	..	35.5	278.0	143.8	226.8	490.2	366.5	360.5
Net change in interest arrears	..	..	..	..	0.0	0.0	0.0	0.0	0.0	0.0
Interest capitalized	..	..	..	..	0.0	0.0	0.0	0.0	0.0	0.0
Debt forgiveness or reduction	..	..	..	..	0.0	0.0	0.0	0.0	0.0	-1.9
Cross-currency valuation	..	..	..	..	-5.8	19.1	14.2	-24.7	-38.5	27.0
Residual	..	..	..	..	0.1	3.0	24.9	-2.6	-17.5	31.1
9. AVERAGE TERMS OF NEW COMMITMENTS										
ALL CREDITORS										
Interest (%)	..	..	..	7.2	5.7	5.0	7.3	6.8	6.3	5.6
Maturity (years)	..	..	..	14.5	11.7	12.5	9.4	11.3	6.0	4.6
Grace period (years)	..	..	..	4.2	5.2	3.6	2.6	2.8	3.6	2.0
Grant element (%)	..	..	..	15.5	23.0	24.9	13.8	13.8	12.9	11.3
Official creditors										
Interest (%)	..	..	..	7.4	5.5	5.3	6.3	6.6	7.1	4.0
Maturity (years)	..	..	..	15.7	14.3	14.9	14.6	14.9	18.6	5.6
Grace period (years)	..	..	..	4.5	6.4	4.9	4.4	4.3	4.9	1.7
Grant element (%)	..	..	..	15.3	28.5	27.2	22.5	18.1	17.4	16.1
Private creditors										
Interest (%)	..	..	..	6.5	6.5	4.6	8.1	7.2	6.3	6.6
Maturity (years)	..	..	..	10.3	2.9	9.6	5.2	6.4	5.5	4.0
Grace period (years)	..	..	..	3.1	1.2	2.1	1.2	0.9	3.6	2.1
Grant element (%)	..	..	..	16.0	4.5	22.1	6.9	8.1	12.8	8.4
Memorandum items										
Commitments	..	..	..	145.9	189.3	151.3	422.2	497.3	448.3	61.1
Official creditors	..	..	..	115.2	146.0	82.9	186.4	285.2	14.7	23.4
Private creditors	..	..	..	30.6	43.3	68.4	235.9	212.1	433.6	37.7

10. CONTRACTUAL OBLIGATIONS ON OUTSTANDING LONG-TERM DEBT

	1999	2000	2001	2002	2003	2004	2005	2006	2007	2008
TOTAL										
Disbursements	127.8	79.4	38.6	22.8	11.6	8.1	5.8	2.6	1.7	1.1
Principal	144.8	351.4	148.6	354.6	114.0	83.9	95.3	54.8	49.0	46.1
Interest	75.9	72.2	56.5	51.0	29.7	24.9	20.3	15.8	13.1	10.5
Official creditors										
Disbursements	65.8	48.2	32.3	20.5	11.6	8.1	5.8	2.6	1.7	1.1
Principal	43.6	110.7	59.6	95.2	59.8	50.6	66.1	41.4	41.1	39.7
Interest	31.9	32.3	29.6	27.7	23.2	20.7	17.7	14.5	12.3	10.0
Bilateral creditors										
Disbursements	18.5	10.8	4.3	1.4	0.3	0.1	0.0	0.0	0.0	0.0
Principal	24.7	25.5	27.9	33.9	26.8	19.8	16.2	10.6	10.3	8.9
Interest	10.4	10.5	9.7	8.3	6.4	5.0	4.1	3.2	2.8	2.4
Multilateral creditors										
Disbursements	47.3	37.4	28.0	19.1	11.3	8.0	5.8	2.6	1.7	1.1
Principal	19.0	85.2	31.6	61.4	32.9	30.8	49.9	30.8	30.8	30.8
Interest	21.5	21.8	19.9	19.4	16.7	15.7	13.6	11.3	9.5	7.7
Private creditors										
Disbursements	62.1	31.2	6.3	2.3	0.0	0.0	0.0	0.0	0.0	0.0
Principal	101.1	240.8	89.0	259.3	54.2	33.2	29.2	13.3	7.9	6.3
Interest	44.1	39.9	26.9	23.2	6.5	4.1	2.6	1.3	0.9	0.5
Commercial banks										
Disbursements	36.0	18.8	3.6	1.6	0.0	0.0	0.0	0.0	0.0	0.0
Principal	20.5	149.5	24.0	20.6	21.7	6.2	6.1	5.6	5.6	5.6
Interest	13.8	13.6	4.4	3.3	2.6	1.7	1.3	1.0	0.7	0.3
Other private										
Disbursements	26.1	12.5	2.7	0.7	0.0	0.0	0.0	0.0	0.0	0.0
Principal	80.6	91.3	65.0	238.7	32.6	27.0	23.1	7.7	2.3	0.8
Interest	30.2	26.3	22.5	20.0	3.9	2.5	1.3	0.3	0.2	0.2

MACEDONIA, FYR

(US$ million, unless otherwise indicated)

	1970	1980	1990	1992	1993	1994	1995	1996	1997	1998
1. SUMMARY DEBT DATA										
TOTAL DEBT STOCKS (EDT)	..	..	..	..	**1,042**	**1,104**	**1,565**	**2,141**	**1,865**	**2,392**
Long-term debt (LDOD)	..	..	..	..	**914**	**927**	**1,366**	**1,804**	**1,640**	**2,133**
Public and publicly guaranteed	..	..	..	..	704	709	1,077	1,179	1,573	1,944
Private nonguaranteed	..	..	..	..	210	218	289	625	67	189
Use of IMF credit	..	..	..	..	**4**	**21**	**57**	**68**	**88**	**102**
Short-term debt	..	..	..	..	**124**	**156**	**143**	**269**	**137**	**157**
of which interest arrears on LDOD	..	..	..	..	108	138	143	183	3	24
Official creditors	..	..	..	..	20	30	26	19	0	23
Private creditors	..	..	..	..	89	108	117	164	3	2
Memo: principal arrears on LDOD	..	..	..	..	349	360	216	85	9	280
Official creditors	..	..	..	..	265	234	24	7	3	278
Private creditors	..	..	..	..	84	126	191	79	6	2
Memo: export credits	..	..	..	..	33	90	74	85	180	208
TOTAL DEBT FLOWS										
Disbursements	..	..	..	..	**1**	**104**	**112**	**127**	**147**	**507**
Long-term debt	..	..	..	..	1	86	75	113	122	495
IMF purchases	..	..	..	..	0	18	38	14	25	12
Principal repayments	..	..	..	..	**12**	**121**	**20**	**27**	**50**	**98**
Long-term debt	..	..	..	..	5	119	19	26	50	96
IMF repurchases	..	..	..	..	7	2	1	1	0	2
Net flows on debt	..	..	..	..	**5**	**-15**	**74**	**186**	**146**	**407**
of which short-term debt	..	..	..	..	16	2	-18	85	48	-1
Interest payments (INT)	..	..	..	..	**4**	**35**	**12**	**32**	**83**	**102**
Long-term debt	..	..	..	..	3	33	9	25	75	92
IMF charges	..	..	..	..	1	1	2	3	3	3
Short-term debt	..	..	..	..	1	1	1	5	5	7
Net transfers on debt	..	..	..	..	**0**	**-50**	**63**	**153**	**63**	**306**
Total debt service paid (TDS)	..	..	..	..	**16**	**156**	**32**	**59**	**133**	**200**
Long-term debt	..	..	..	..	8	152	28	50	124	188
IMF repurchases and charges	..	..	..	..	7	3	3	4	3	5
Short-term debt (interest only)	..	..	..	..	1	1	1	5	5	7
2. AGGREGATE NET RESOURCE FLOWS AND NET TRANSFERS (LONG-TERM)										
NET RESOURCE FLOWS	..	..	..	..	**-1**	**49**	**87**	**141**	**123**	**545**
Net flow of long-term debt (ex. IMF)	..	..	..	..	-5	-33	56	87	73	399
Foreign direct investment (net)	..	..	..	..	0	24	14	11	16	118
Portfolio equity flows	..	..	..	..	0	0	0	0	0	0
Grants (excluding technical coop.)	..	..	..	..	3	58	18	43	34	29
Memo: technical coop. grants	..	..	..	..	0	0	16	19	9	20
official net resource flows	..	..	..	..	-1	40	73	130	114	356
private net resource flows	..	..	..	..	0	9	14	11	9	190
NET TRANSFERS	..	..	..	..	**-4**	**16**	**78**	**116**	**48**	**453**
Interest on long-term debt	..	..	..	..	3	33	9	25	75	92
Profit remittances on FDI	..	..	..	..	0	0	0	0	0	0
Memo: official net transfers	..	..	..	..	-4	7	64	106	41	305
private net transfers	..	..	..	..	0	9	14	11	7	148
3. MAJOR ECONOMIC AGGREGATES										
Gross national product (GNP)	..	..	..	..	2,417	2,090	2,512	2,630	2,618	2,475
Exports of goods & services (XGS)	..	..	..	..	..	..	..	1,392	1,425	1,536
of which workers remittances	..	..	..	..	..	..	..	45	56	63
Imports of goods & services (MGS)	..	..	..	..	..	..	..	1,848	1,934	2,088
International reserves (RES)	..	..	..	..	121	166	275	268	280	335
Current account balance	..	..	..	..	..	..	..	-288	-275	-288
4. DEBT INDICATORS										
EDT / XGS (%)	..	..	..	..	..	..	..	153.8	130.9	155.8
EDT / GNP (%)	..	..	..	..	43.1	52.8	62.3	81.4	71.3	96.7
TDS / XGS (%)	..	..	..	..	..	..	..	4.3	9.3	13.0
INT / XGS (%)	..	..	..	..	..	..	..	2.3	5.8	6.6
INT / GNP (%)	..	..	..	..	0.2	1.7	0.5	1.2	3.2	4.1
RES / EDT (%)	..	..	..	..	11.6	15.1	17.6	12.5	15.0	14.0
RES / MGS (months)	..	..	..	..	..	..	..	1.7	1.7	1.9
Short-term / EDT (%)	..	..	..	..	11.9	14.2	9.1	12.6	7.4	6.6
Concessional / EDT (%)	..	..	..	..	0.9	4.6	22.5	20.2	25.8	33.8
Multilateral / EDT (%)	..	..	..	..	21.7	20.3	18.4	16.3	21.5	19.3

MACEDONIA, FYR

(US$ million, unless otherwise indicated)

	1970	1980	1990	1992	1993	1994	1995	1996	1997	1998
5. LONG-TERM DEBT										
DEBT OUTSTANDING (LDOD)	..	..	..	..	**914**	**927**	**1,366**	**1,804**	**1,640**	**2,133**
Public and publicly guaranteed	..	..	..	..	**704**	**709**	**1,077**	**1,179**	**1,573**	**1,944**
Official creditors	..	..	..	..	521	519	893	997	1,029	1,395
Multilateral	..	..	..	..	226	224	288	348	401	462
Concessional	..	..	..	..	0	42	84	125	175	212
Bilateral	..	..	..	..	295	295	605	649	628	933
Concessional	..	..	..	..	9	9	268	308	305	597
Private creditors	..	..	..	..	183	190	184	182	544	550
Bonds	..	..	..	..	0	0	0	0	0	0
Commercial banks	..	..	..	..	104	108	103	100	539	539
Other private	..	..	..	..	79	82	81	82	5	10
Private nonguaranteed	..	..	..	..	**210**	**218**	**289**	**625**	**67**	**189**
Bonds	..	..	..	..	0	0	0	0	0	0
Commercial banks	..	..	..	..	210	218	289	625	67	189
Memo:										
IBRD	..	..	..	..	151	93	97	78	85	108
IDA	..	..	..	..	0	42	84	125	146	181
DISBURSEMENTS	..	..	..	..	**1**	**86**	**75**	**113**	**122**	**495**
Public and publicly guaranteed	..	..	..	..	**1**	**86**	**75**	**113**	**113**	**387**
Official creditors	..	..	..	..	1	86	74	112	113	382
Multilateral	..	..	..	..	1	86	74	97	106	88
Concessional	..	..	..	..	0	40	42	44	59	30
Bilateral	..	..	..	..	0	0	0	15	7	294
Concessional	..	..	..	..	0	0	0	7	0	263
Private creditors	..	..	..	..	0	0	0	1	0	6
Bonds	..	..	..	..	0	0	0	0	0	0
Commercial banks	..	..	..	..	0	0	0	0	0	0
Other private	..	..	..	..	0	0	0	1	0	5
Private nonguaranteed	..	..	..	..	**0**	**0**	**0**	**0**	**10**	**108**
Bonds	..	..	..	..	0	0	0	0	0	0
Commercial banks	..	..	..	..	0	0	0	0	10	108
Memo:										
IBRD	..	..	..	..	1	40	20	2	19	43
IDA	..	..	..	..	0	40	42	44	29	29
PRINCIPAL REPAYMENTS	..	..	..	..	**5**	**119**	**19**	**26**	**50**	**96**
Public and publicly guaranteed	..	..	..	..	**5**	**104**	**19**	**26**	**33**	**55**
Official creditors	..	..	..	..	5	104	19	25	33	55
Multilateral	..	..	..	..	5	104	19	25	25	25
Concessional	..	..	..	..	0	0	0	0	0	0
Bilateral	..	..	..	..	0	0	0	0	8	30
Concessional	..	..	..	..	0	0	0	0	0	4
Private creditors	..	..	..	..	0	0	0	1	1	1
Bonds	..	..	..	..	0	0	0	0	0	0
Commercial banks	..	..	..	..	0	0	0	1	0	0
Other private	..	..	..	..	0	0	0	0	1	1
Private nonguaranteed	..	..	..	..	**0**	**15**	**0**	**0**	**16**	**41**
Bonds	..	..	..	..	0	0	0	0	0	0
Commercial banks	..	..	..	..	0	15	0	0	16	41
Memo:										
IBRD	..	..	..	..	5	104	19	15	6	4
IDA	..	..	..	..	0	0	0	0	0	0
NET FLOWS ON DEBT	..	..	..	..	**-5**	**-33**	**56**	**87**	**73**	**399**
Public and publicly guaranteed	..	..	..	..	**-5**	**-18**	**56**	**87**	**79**	**332**
Official creditors	..	..	..	..	-4	-18	55	87	80	327
Multilateral	..	..	..	..	-4	-18	55	72	81	63
Concessional	..	..	..	..	0	40	42	44	59	30
Bilateral	..	..	..	..	0	0	0	15	-1	264
Concessional	..	..	..	..	0	0	0	7	0	259
Private creditors	..	..	..	..	0	0	0	0	-1	5
Bonds	..	..	..	..	0	0	0	0	0	0
Commercial banks	..	..	..	..	0	0	0	-1	0	0
Other private	..	..	..	..	0	0	0	1	-1	5
Private nonguaranteed	..	..	..	..	**0**	**-15**	**0**	**0**	**-7**	**67**
Bonds	..	..	..	..	0	0	0	0	0	0
Commercial banks	..	..	..	..	0	-15	0	0	-7	67
Memo:										
IBRD	..	..	..	..	-4	-64	1	-13	13	39
IDA	..	..	..	..	0	40	42	44	29	29

MACEDONIA, FYR

(US$ million, unless otherwise indicated)

	1970	*1980*	*1990*	*1992*	*1993*	*1994*	*1995*	*1996*	*1997*	*1998*
INTEREST PAYMENTS (LINT)	..	..	..	..	**3**	**33**	**9**	**25**	**75**	**92**
Public and publicly guaranteed	..	..	..	..	**3**	**33**	**9**	**25**	**74**	**85**
Official creditors	..	..	..	..	3	33	9	24	74	50
Multilateral	..	..	..	..	3	33	9	16	36	17
Concessional	..	..	..	..	0	0	0	1	1	2
Bilateral	..	..	..	..	0	0	0	8	38	34
Concessional	..	..	..	..	0	0	0	0	12	12
Private creditors	..	..	..	..	0	0	0	1	0	35
Bonds	..	..	..	..	0	0	0	0	0	0
Commercial banks	..	..	..	..	0	0	0	0	0	35
Other private	..	..	..	..	0	0	0	0	0	0
Private nonguaranteed	..	..	..	..	**0**	**0**	**0**	**0**	**1**	**7**
Bonds	..	..	..	..	0	0	0	0	0	0
Commercial banks	..	..	..	..	0	0	0	0	1	7
Memo:										
IBRD	..	..	..	..	3	32	8	6	6	5
IDA	..	..	..	..	0	0	0	1	1	1
NET TRANSFERS ON DEBT	..	..	..	..	**-7**	**-67**	**46**	**63**	**-2**	**306**
Public and publicly guaranteed	..	..	..	..	**-7**	**-52**	**46**	**63**	**6**	**247**
Official creditors	..	..	..	..	-7	-52	46	63	6	277
Multilateral	..	..	..	..	-7	-52	46	57	46	46
Concessional	..	..	..	..	0	40	41	43	58	27
Bilateral	..	..	..	..	0	0	0	7	-39	231
Concessional	..	..	..	..	0	0	0	7	-12	246
Private creditors	..	..	..	..	0	0	0	0	-1	-30
Bonds	..	..	..	..	0	0	0	0	0	0
Commercial banks	..	..	..	..	0	0	0	-1	0	-34
Other private	..	..	..	..	0	0	0	1	-1	5
Private nonguaranteed	..	..	..	..	**0**	**-15**	**0**	**0**	**-8**	**59**
Bonds	..	..	..	..	0	0	0	0	0	0
Commercial banks	..	..	..	..	0	-15	0	0	-8	59
Memo:										
IBRD	..	..	..	..	-7	-96	-7	-19	7	34
IDA	..	..	..	..	0	40	41	44	28	28
DEBT SERVICE (LTDS)	..	..	..	..	**8**	**152**	**28**	**50**	**124**	**188**
Public and publicly guaranteed	..	..	..	..	**8**	**137**	**28**	**50**	**107**	**140**
Official creditors	..	..	..	..	8	137	28	49	106	105
Multilateral	..	..	..	..	8	137	28	40	60	42
Concessional	..	..	..	..	0	0	0	1	1	2
Bilateral	..	..	..	..	0	0	0	9	46	63
Concessional	..	..	..	..	0	0	0	0	12	16
Private creditors	..	..	..	..	0	0	0	2	1	35
Bonds	..	..	..	..	0	0	0	0	0	0
Commercial banks	..	..	..	..	0	0	0	1	0	35
Other private	..	..	..	..	0	0	0	0	1	1
Private nonguaranteed	..	..	..	..	**0**	**15**	**0**	**0**	**18**	**48**
Bonds	..	..	..	..	0	0	0	0	0	0
Commercial banks	..	..	..	..	0	15	0	0	18	48
Memo:										
IBRD	..	..	..	..	8	136	27	21	12	9
IDA	..	..	..	..	0	0	0	1	1	1
UNDISBURSED DEBT	..	..	..	..	**29**	**45**	**176**	**118**	**131**	**250**
Official creditors	..	..	..	..	29	45	169	112	125	239
Private creditors	..	..	..	..	0	0	7	6	5	11
Memorandum items										
Concessional LDOD	..	..	..	..	9	51	352	433	480	809
Variable rate LDOD	..	..	..	..	459	509	571	961	800	969
Public sector LDOD	..	..	..	..	697	705	1,073	1,172	1,563	1,933
Private sector LDOD	..	..	..	..	217	222	293	632	77	200

6. CURRENCY COMPOSITION OF LONG-TERM DEBT (PERCENT)

	1970	*1980*	*1990*	*1992*	*1993*	*1994*	*1995*	*1996*	*1997*	*1998*
Deutsche mark	..	..	..	..	4.4	5.7	10.1	9.9	8.5	8.5
French franc	..	..	..	..	0.5	0.6	4.3	3.7	2.2	1.8
Japanese yen	..	..	..	..	6.1	6.7	4.8	3.2	0.2	14.3
Pound sterling	..	..	..	..	1.3	1.3	0.8	1.0	0.2	0.1
Swiss franc	..	..	..	..	0.8	0.9	0.7	4.1	2.7	2.0
U.S.dollars	..	..	..	..	57.6	63.2	63.2	64.4	76.4	68.5
Multiple currency	..	..	..	..	29.1	21.3	14.8	11.5	6.6	1.9
Special drawing rights	..	..	..	..	0.1	0.1	0.1	0.1	0.0	0.0
All other currencies	..	..	..	..	0.1	0.2	1.2	2.1	3.2	2.9

MACEDONIA, FYR

(US$ million, unless otherwise indicated)

	1970	1980	1990	1992	1993	1994	1995	1996	1997	1998
7. DEBT RESTRUCTURINGS										
Total amount rescheduled	..	..	..	..	0	0	544	108	538	0
Debt stock rescheduled	..	..	..	..	0	0	0	0	423	0
Principal rescheduled	..	..	..	..	0	0	242	64	39	0
Official	..	..	..	..	0	0	235	64	0	0
Private	..	..	..	..	0	0	7	0	39	0
Interest rescheduled	..	..	..	..	..	0	14	9	76	0
Official	..	..	..	..	0	0	13	9	0	0
Private	..	..	..	..	0	0	1	0	76	0
Debt forgiven	..	..	..	..	0	0	0	0	0	0
Memo: interest forgiven	..	..	..	..	0	0	0	0	0	0
Debt stock reduction	..	..	..	..	0	0	0	0	129	0
of which debt buyback	..	..	..	..	0	0	0	0	0	0
8. DEBT STOCK-FLOW RECONCILIATION										
Total change in debt stocks	..	..	..	..	..	62	462	576	-276	527
Net flows on debt	..	..	..	..	5	-15	74	186	146	407
Net change in interest arrears	..	..	..	..	..	30	4	41	-180	21
Interest capitalized	..	..	..	..	..	0	14	9	76	0
Debt forgiveness or reduction	..	..	..	..	..	0	0	0	-129	0
Cross-currency valuation	..	..	..	..	..	-15	14	-49	-38	56
Residual	..	..	..	..	..	63	355	388	-150	42
9. AVERAGE TERMS OF NEW COMMITMENTS										
ALL CREDITORS										
Interest (%)	..	..	..	..	6.8	4.2	3.7	3.7	2.8	5.1
Maturity (years)	..	..	..	..	15.6	25.1	23.2	20.2	24.1	14.7
Grace period (years)	..	..	..	..	3.6	6.9	6.8	5.9	8.2	8.1
Grant element (%)	..	..	..	..	17.3	44.2	46.8	43.4	54.0	31.4
Official creditors										
Interest (%)	..	..	..	..	6.8	4.2	3.8	3.6	2.8	5.0
Maturity (years)	..	..	..	..	15.6	25.1	23.0	20.5	24.1	14.8
Grace period (years)	..	..	..	..	3.6	6.9	6.7	6.0	8.2	8.2
Grant element (%)	..	..	..	..	17.3	44.2	46.2	44.2	54.0	31.9
Private creditors										
Interest (%)	..	..	..	..	0.0	0.0	2.3	6.7	0.0	8.1
Maturity (years)	..	..	..	..	0.0	0.0	29.7	3.0	0.0	7.7
Grace period (years)	..	..	..	..	0.0	0.0	10.9	0.3	0.0	2.9
Grant element (%)	..	..	..	..	0.0	0.0	64.1	4.8	0.0	6.6
Memorandum items										
Commitments	..	..	..	..	28	101	206	62	140	461
Official creditors	..	..	..	..	28	101	199	61	140	451
Private creditors	..	..	..	..	0	0	7	1	0	10

10. CONTRACTUAL OBLIGATIONS ON OUTSTANDING LONG-TERM DEBT

	1999	2000	2001	2002	2003	2004	2005	2006	2007	2008
TOTAL										
Disbursements	70	56	38	23	16	11	8	6	3	13
Principal	112	111	115	145	151	130	125	131	132	152
Interest	89	91	88	83	77	68	61	55	47	41
Official creditors										
Disbursements	64	53	37	23	16	11	8	6	3	13
Principal	69	74	81	81	94	87	81	82	84	90
Interest	48	50	47	43	40	35	31	27	23	19
Bilateral creditors										
Disbursements	28	14	6	2	1	0	0	0	0	0
Principal	42	48	51	53	61	60	59	59	59	59
Interest	29	32	30	27	25	22	19	16	13	10
Multilateral creditors										
Disbursements	36	39	31	22	16	11	8	6	3	13
Principal	27	27	30	28	33	27	21	23	24	30
Interest	19	18	17	16	15	13	12	11	10	10
Private creditors										
Disbursements	6	3	1	0	0	0	0	0	0	0
Principal	43	37	34	64	57	43	44	49	49	63
Interest	41	41	40	39	37	33	30	27	24	21
Commercial banks										
Disbursements	6	3	1	0	0	0	0	0	0	0
Principal	2	2	1	35	37	37	37	42	42	49
Interest	39	39	39	38	35	33	30	27	24	21
Other private										
Disbursements	0	0	0	0	0	0	0	0	0	0
Principal	41	35	33	29	19	6	7	7	7	14
Interest	2	2	2	1	2	1	1	0	0	0

MADAGASCAR

(US$ million, unless otherwise indicated)

	1970	1980	1990	1992	1993	1994	1995	1996	1997	1998
1. SUMMARY DEBT DATA										
TOTAL DEBT STOCKS (EDT)	..	**1,250**	**3,701**	**3,911**	**3,805**	**4,097**	**4,322**	**4,146**	**4,109**	**4,394**
Long-term debt (LDOD)	**485**	**920**	**3,335**	**3,469**	**3,316**	**3,537**	**3,706**	**3,552**	**3,875**	**4,107**
Public and publicly guaranteed	485	920	3,335	3,469	3,316	3,537	3,706	3,552	3,875	4,107
Private nonguaranteed	0	0	0	0	0	0	0	0	0	0
Use of IMF credit	**0**	**87**	**144**	**106**	**92**	**86**	**73**	**73**	**69**	**58**
Short-term debt	..	**244**	**223**	**336**	**397**	**474**	**544**	**521**	**164**	**230**
of which interest arrears on LDOD	..	6	123	261	332	426	488	502	153	150
Official creditors	..	2	113	248	318	410	470	482	138	136
Private creditors	..	4	10	13	14	17	18	20	15	14
Memo: principal arrears on LDOD	..	11	266	587	743	976	1,197	1,263	600	604
Official creditors	..	6	245	553	705	931	1,145	1,210	573	584
Private creditors	..	5	21	34	38	45	53	53	27	20
Memo: export credits	..	0	795	926	730	734	686	708	786	779
TOTAL DEBT FLOWS										
Disbursements	**54**	**444**	**231**	**117**	**123**	**82**	**90**	**156**	**336**	**102**
Long-term debt	54	375	214	117	123	82	90	137	318	102
IMF purchases	0	70	17	0	0	0	0	20	19	0
Principal repayments	**45**	**48**	**121**	**56**	**48**	**43**	**38**	**60**	**118**	**72**
Long-term debt	45	46	70	40	34	31	24	43	100	58
IMF repurchases	0	2	51	16	14	12	15	17	18	14
Net flows on debt	**9**	**472**	**194**	**50**	**65**	**22**	**59**	**60**	**210**	**100**
of which short-term debt	..	75	83	-10	-10	-17	7	-36	-8	69
Interest payments (INT)	..	**57**	**102**	**40**	**30**	**22**	**20**	**23**	**94**	**53**
Long-term debt	16	27	85	34	26	19	16	18	93	51
IMF charges	0	1	10	3	2	1	1	1	0	0
Short-term debt	..	29	7	3	3	2	3	4	1	2
Net transfers on debt	..	**415**	**92**	**10**	**35**	**0**	**39**	**37**	**116**	**46**
Total debt service paid (TDS)	..	**104**	**223**	**96**	**78**	**65**	**58**	**83**	**212**	**125**
Long-term debt	61	72	155	74	60	50	40	62	193	109
IMF repurchases and charges	0	3	61	19	16	13	15	17	18	14
Short-term debt (interest only)	..	29	7	3	3	2	3	4	1	2
2. AGGREGATE NET RESOURCE FLOWS AND NET TRANSFERS (LONG-TERM)										
NET RESOURCE FLOWS	**39**	**358**	**514**	**300**	**302**	**225**	**240**	**305**	**797**	**414**
Net flow of long-term debt (ex. IMF)	9	329	144	77	89	51	66	93	217	44
Foreign direct investment (net)	10	-1	22	21	15	6	10	10	14	16
Portfolio equity flows	0	0	0	0	0	0	0	0	0	0
Grants (excluding technical coop.)	20	30	348	203	198	168	164	202	566	354
Memo: technical coop. grants	21	51	85	88	99	105	124	117	111	95
official net resource flows	30	219	507	288	295	224	235	300	784	399
private net resource flows	9	139	7	13	7	1	6	5	13	15
NET TRANSFERS	**18**	**330**	**428**	**266**	**276**	**204**	**222**	**284**	**700**	**358**
Interest on long-term debt	16	27	85	34	26	19	16	18	93	51
Profit remittances on FDI	5	1	1	1	1	2	2	3	4	5
Memo: official net transfers	14	211	435	257	271	206	219	283	692	348
private net transfers	4	119	-7	8	5	-2	3	1	8	10
3. MAJOR ECONOMIC AGGREGATES										
Gross national product (GNP)	1,075	3,996	2,936	2,853	3,224	2,827	2,993	3,837	3,442	3,677
Exports of goods & services (XGS)	..	519	490	518	536	669	765	815	808	854
of which workers remittances	..	0	4	12	12	11	9	6	..	..
Imports of goods & services (MGS)	..	1,121	985	884	970	1,032	1,161	1,171	1,195	1,231
International reserves (RES)	37	9	92	..	..	72	109	241	282	171
Current account balance	..	-556	-265	-198	-258	-277	-276	-153	-202	-289
4. DEBT INDICATORS										
EDT / XGS (%)	..	241.0	755.5	754.5	709.4	612.3	564.9	508.8	508.4	514.6
EDT / GNP (%)	..	31.3	126.1	137.1	118.0	144.9	144.4	108.1	119.4	119.5
TDS / XGS (%)	..	20.1	45.5	18.6	14.6	9.8	7.6	10.2	26.2	14.7
INT / XGS (%)	..	10.9	20.8	7.7	5.6	3.3	2.6	2.8	11.6	6.3
INT / GNP (%)	..	1.4	3.5	1.4	0.9	0.8	0.7	0.6	2.7	1.5
RES / EDT (%)	..	0.7	2.5	..	..	1.8	2.5	5.8	6.9	3.9
RES / MGS (months)	..	0.1	1.1	..	..	0.8	1.1	2.5	2.8	1.7
Short-term / EDT (%)	..	19.5	6.0	8.6	10.4	11.6	12.6	12.6	4.0	5.2
Concessional / EDT (%)	..	37.5	46.6	50.1	51.3	51.7	51.9	51.4	65.2	66.3
Multilateral / EDT (%)	..	14.6	33.3	35.8	38.7	39.0	39.1	38.7	40.4	40.5

MADAGASCAR

(US$ million, unless otherwise indicated)

	1970	1980	1990	1992	1993	1994	1995	1996	1997	1998
5. LONG-TERM DEBT										
DEBT OUTSTANDING (LDOD)	**485**	**920**	**3,335**	**3,469**	**3,316**	**3,537**	**3,706**	**3,552**	**3,875**	**4,107**
Public and publicly guaranteed	**485**	**920**	**3,335**	**3,469**	**3,316**	**3,537**	**3,706**	**3,552**	**3,875**	**4,107**
Official creditors	484	574	3,195	3,357	3,229	3,451	3,622	3,475	3,830	4,065
Multilateral	42	182	1,231	1,400	1,472	1,596	1,690	1,604	1,661	1,781
Concessional	10	148	1,075	1,251	1,323	1,440	1,536	1,452	1,560	1,692
Bilateral	443	392	1,964	1,957	1,757	1,855	1,931	1,871	2,169	2,284
Concessional	442	321	648	707	630	678	706	680	1,121	1,221
Private creditors	1	346	140	112	87	86	84	77	45	41
Bonds	0	0	0	0	0	0	0	0	0	0
Commercial banks	0	134	38	30	29	28	28	25	24	24
Other private	1	212	102	82	59	58	56	51	21	17
Private nonguaranteed	**0**	**0**	**0**	**0**	**0**	**0**	**0**	**0**	**0**	**0**
Bonds	0	0	0	0	0	0	0	0	0	0
Commercial banks	0	0	0	0	0	0	0	0	0	0
Memo:										
IBRD	2	30	26	20	17	14	12	7	3	1
IDA	10	122	770	887	932	1,021	1,110	1,147	1,212	1,317
DISBURSEMENTS	**54**	**375**	**214**	**117**	**123**	**82**	**90**	**137**	**318**	**102**
Public and publicly guaranteed	**54**	**375**	**214**	**117**	**123**	**82**	**90**	**137**	**318**	**102**
Official creditors	54	212	213	117	123	82	89	136	317	102
Multilateral	6	42	136	82	95	75	78	108	210	98
Concessional	5	38	120	70	77	66	78	91	208	98
Bilateral	48	170	77	34	29	8	11	28	107	5
Concessional	48	115	77	32	27	6	10	25	6	5
Private creditors	0	163	1	0	0	0	1	0	0	0
Bonds	0	0	0	0	0	0	0	0	0	0
Commercial banks	0	62	0	0	0	0	0	0	0	0
Other private	0	101	1	0	0	0	1	0	0	0
Private nonguaranteed	**0**	**0**	**0**	**0**	**0**	**0**	**0**	**0**	**0**	**0**
Bonds	0	0	0	0	0	0	0	0	0	0
Commercial banks	0	0	0	0	0	0	0	0	0	0
Memo:										
IBRD	1	2	0	0	0	0	0	0	0	0
IDA	5	25	64	37	47	60	76	78	130	77
PRINCIPAL REPAYMENTS	**45**	**46**	**70**	**40**	**34**	**31**	**24**	**43**	**100**	**58**
Public and publicly guaranteed	**45**	**46**	**70**	**40**	**34**	**31**	**24**	**43**	**100**	**58**
Official creditors	45	23	53	32	26	26	19	38	99	57
Multilateral	3	1	19	20	22	22	18	36	65	36
Concessional	0	0	9	9	9	9	9	20	25	20
Bilateral	41	22	35	12	4	4	1	2	34	21
Concessional	41	21	9	12	3	4	1	1	30	20
Private creditors	1	23	16	8	8	5	5	5	2	1
Bonds	0	0	0	0	0	0	0	0	0	0
Commercial banks	0	12	11	2	1	1	1	2	1	1
Other private	1	12	6	6	7	4	4	3	1	0
Private nonguaranteed	**0**	**0**	**0**	**0**	**0**	**0**	**0**	**0**	**0**	**0**
Bonds	0	0	0	0	0	0	0	0	0	0
Commercial banks	0	0	0	0	0	0	0	0	0	0
Memo:										
IBRD	0	0	3	3	3	3	4	4	4	2
IDA	0	0	3	4	5	6	7	9	10	12
NET FLOWS ON DEBT	**9**	**329**	**144**	**77**	**89**	**51**	**66**	**93**	**217**	**44**
Public and publicly guaranteed	**9**	**329**	**144**	**77**	**89**	**51**	**66**	**93**	**217**	**44**
Official creditors	10	189	159	85	97	56	70	98	219	45
Multilateral	3	41	117	63	73	52	60	72	145	61
Concessional	5	38	111	62	68	58	69	71	183	78
Bilateral	7	148	42	22	24	4	10	26	73	-16
Concessional	7	94	68	20	25	2	10	24	-24	-15
Private creditors	-1	140	-15	-8	-8	-5	-4	-5	-1	-1
Bonds	0	0	0	0	0	0	0	0	0	0
Commercial banks	0	50	-10	-2	-1	-1	-1	-2	-1	-1
Other private	-1	89	-5	-6	-7	-4	-3	-3	-1	0
Private nonguaranteed	**0**	**0**	**0**	**0**	**0**	**0**	**0**	**0**	**0**	**0**
Bonds	0	0	0	0	0	0	0	0	0	0
Commercial banks	0	0	0	0	0	0	0	0	0	0
Memo:										
IBRD	1	1	-3	-3	-3	-3	-4	-4	-4	-2
IDA	5	25	61	33	42	54	69	69	120	65

MADAGASCAR

(US$ million, unless otherwise indicated)

	1970	1980	1990	1992	1993	1994	1995	1996	1997	1998
INTEREST PAYMENTS (LINT)	**16**	**27**	**85**	**34**	**26**	**19**	**16**	**18**	**93**	**51**
Public and publicly guaranteed	**16**	**27**	**85**	**34**	**26**	**19**	**16**	**18**	**93**	**51**
Official creditors	16	8	72	30	24	18	15	17	93	51
Multilateral	1	4	18	18	20	15	12	15	42	19
Concessional	0	1	7	9	10	8	9	11	16	14
Bilateral	15	4	54	12	4	4	4	2	51	32
Concessional	15	4	11	10	4	3	3	1	26	22
Private creditors	0	19	13	3	1	1	1	2	0	0
Bonds	0	0	0	0	0	0	0	0	0	0
Commercial banks	0	9	10	2	0	0	0	1	0	0
Other private	0	10	3	2	1	1	0	0	0	0
Private nonguaranteed	**0**	**0**	**0**	**0**	**0**	**0**	**0**	**0**	**0**	**0**
Bonds	0	0	0	0	0	0	0	0	0	0
Commercial banks	0	0	0	0	0	0	0	0	0	0
Memo:										
IBRD	0	2	2	2	1	1	1	1	0	0
IDA	0	1	5	7	7	7	8	9	9	9
NET TRANSFERS ON DEBT	**-7**	**302**	**59**	**43**	**64**	**32**	**50**	**75**	**125**	**-7**
Public and publicly guaranteed	**-7**	**302**	**59**	**43**	**64**	**32**	**50**	**75**	**125**	**-7**
Official creditors	-7	181	87	54	73	38	55	81	126	-6
Multilateral	2	37	99	45	53	38	48	57	103	43
Concessional	5	37	104	53	57	50	60	61	167	64
Bilateral	-9	144	-12	10	20	0	7	24	23	-48
Concessional	-9	90	57	10	21	-1	7	23	-50	-37
Private creditors	-1	121	-28	-12	-9	-6	-5	-6	-2	-1
Bonds	0	0	0	0	0	0	0	0	0	0
Commercial banks	0	42	-21	-4	-2	-2	-1	-3	-1	-1
Other private	-1	79	-8	-8	-8	-4	-4	-3	-1	0
Private nonguaranteed	**0**	**0**	**0**	**0**	**0**	**0**	**0**	**0**	**0**	**0**
Bonds	0	0	0	0	0	0	0	0	0	0
Commercial banks	0	0	0	0	0	0	0	0	0	0
Memo:										
IBRD	1	-1	-5	-4	-4	-5	-5	-5	-4	-2
IDA	5	24	56	26	35	46	62	60	111	56
DEBT SERVICE (LTDS)	**61**	**72**	**155**	**74**	**60**	**50**	**40**	**62**	**193**	**109**
Public and publicly guaranteed	**61**	**72**	**155**	**74**	**60**	**50**	**40**	**62**	**193**	**109**
Official creditors	61	31	125	62	50	44	34	55	191	108
Multilateral	4	4	37	38	42	37	30	51	107	55
Concessional	0	1	16	18	20	17	18	31	41	33
Bilateral	56	26	89	24	9	7	5	4	84	53
Concessional	56	24	20	22	6	7	3	2	56	42
Private creditors	1	42	29	12	9	6	6	7	2	1
Bonds	0	0	0	0	0	0	0	0	0	0
Commercial banks	0	20	21	4	2	2	1	3	1	1
Other private	1	22	9	8	8	4	5	3	1	0
Private nonguaranteed	**0**	**0**	**0**	**0**	**0**	**0**	**0**	**0**	**0**	**0**
Bonds	0	0	0	0	0	0	0	0	0	0
Commercial banks	0	0	0	0	0	0	0	0	0	0
Memo:										
IBRD	0	3	5	4	4	5	5	5	4	2
IDA	0	1	8	10	12	13	15	18	19	21
UNDISBURSED DEBT	**186**	**713**	**889**	**705**	**662**	**655**	**636**	**540**	**497**	**575**
Official creditors	177	472	889	705	660	653	636	540	497	575
Private creditors	10	241	0	0	2	2	1	0	0	0
Memorandum items										
Concessional LDOD	452	469	1,723	1,958	1,952	2,118	2,242	2,132	2,681	2,913
Variable rate LDOD	0	74	337	314	259	274	292	280	240	235
Public sector LDOD	483	906	3,259	3,360	3,207	3,418	3,573	3,404	3,745	3,951
Private sector LDOD	2	14	76	110	109	118	133	148	130	156

6. CURRENCY COMPOSITION OF LONG-TERM DEBT (PERCENT)

	1970	1980	1990	1992	1993	1994	1995	1996	1997	1998
Deutsche mark	2.3	5.0	3.3	3.0	3.1	3.3	3.3	3.0	1.8	1.8
French franc	88.3	12.7	15.7	15.2	11.4	11.9	12.6	12.9	13.4	13.8
Japanese yen	0.0	7.3	7.3	7.3	8.4	8.8	8.1	7.5	7.5	8.2
Pound sterling	0.0	0.1	0.1	0.1	0.1	0.1	0.1	0.1	0.1	0.1
Swiss franc	0.0	0.6	1.4	1.1	1.1	1.2	1.3	1.1	1.1	1.1
U.S.dollars	9.1	53.5	42.3	43.7	44.7	44.3	44.8	47.9	49.1	49.0
Multiple currency	0.3	4.0	8.6	9.3	10.5	10.5	10.1	10.0	9.1	8.8
Special drawing rights	0.0	0.0	3.2	3.1	3.3	3.3	3.2	3.2	2.7	2.8
All other currencies	0.0	16.8	18.1	17.2	17.4	16.6	16.5	14.3	15.2	14.4

MADAGASCAR

(US$ million, unless otherwise indicated)

	1970	1980	1990	1992	1993	1994	1995	1996	1997	1998
7. DEBT RESTRUCTURINGS										
Total amount rescheduled	..	..	88	0	0	0	0	0	972	46
Debt stock rescheduled	..	..	0	0	0	0	0	0	0	0
Principal rescheduled	..	..	65	0	0	0	0	0	579	29
Official	..	..	49	0	0	0	0	0	551	29
Private	..	..	16	0	0	0	0	0	28	0
Interest rescheduled	..	..	16	0	0	0	0	0	251	13
Official	..	..	14	0	0	0	0	0	245	13
Private	..	..	2	0	0	0	0	0	6	0
Debt forgiven	..	..	185	11	207	0	0	0	48	6
Memo: interest forgiven	..	..	0	0	18	0	0	0	17	1
Debt stock reduction	..	..	0	0	0	0	0	0	0	0
of which debt buyback	..	..	0	0	0	0	0	0	0	0
8. DEBT STOCK-FLOW RECONCILIATION										
Total change in debt stocks	..	..	270	3	-107	292	226	-176	-37	285
Net flows on debt	9	472	194	50	65	22	59	60	210	100
Net change in interest arrears	..	..	16	84	70	95	62	13	-348	-4
Interest capitalized	..	..	16	0	0	0	0	0	251	13
Debt forgiveness or reduction	..	..	-185	-11	-207	0	0	0	-48	-6
Cross-currency valuation	..	..	177	-72	-16	130	71	-91	-149	108
Residual	..	..	53	-48	-19	45	34	-158	47	74
9. AVERAGE TERMS OF NEW COMMITMENTS										
ALL CREDITORS										
Interest (%)	2.3	5.7	1.1	1.6	1.2	0.9	1.0	0.6	2.7	0.9
Maturity (years)	39.0	18.2	36.2	36.5	36.9	37.8	36.8	37.9	36.2	35.8
Grace period (years)	9.2	4.6	9.7	9.3	8.7	9.7	9.6	10.0	9.3	8.9
Grant element (%)	65.4	27.5	74.8	69.7	73.6	76.9	75.3	80.7	62.6	74.7
Official creditors										
Interest (%)	1.4	3.7	1.1	1.6	1.2	0.9	1.0	0.6	2.7	0.9
Maturity (years)	44.6	28.1	36.3	36.5	37.1	37.8	36.8	37.9	36.2	35.8
Grace period (years)	10.4	6.1	9.7	9.3	8.8	9.7	9.6	10.0	9.3	8.9
Grant element (%)	75.3	46.5	75.1	69.7	73.9	76.9	75.3	80.7	62.6	74.7
Private creditors										
Interest (%)	6.5	7.4	5.0	0.0	2.8	0.0	0.0	0.0	0.0	0.0
Maturity (years)	10.5	9.7	5.1	0.0	25.4	0.0	0.0	0.0	0.0	0.0
Grace period (years)	2.8	3.3	1.1	0.0	5.9	0.0	0.0	0.0	0.0	0.0
Grant element (%)	14.8	11.3	12.4	0.0	53.1	0.0	0.0	0.0	0.0	0.0
Memorandum items										
Commitments	22	468	211	92	150	78	80	78	338	178
Official creditors	19	215	210	92	148	78	80	78	338	178
Private creditors	4	252	1	0	2	0	0	0	0	0

10. CONTRACTUAL OBLIGATIONS ON OUTSTANDING LONG-TERM DEBT

	1999	2000	2001	2002	2003	2004	2005	2006	2007	2008
TOTAL										
Disbursements	142	155	108	76	48	26	16	3	1	0
Principal	87	123	123	118	107	97	89	94	99	107
Interest	83	92	88	85	81	78	76	73	71	68
Official creditors										
Disbursements	142	155	108	76	48	26	16	3	1	0
Principal	81	117	117	115	107	97	89	94	99	107
Interest	82	91	88	85	81	78	76	73	71	68
Bilateral creditors										
Disbursements	10	8	5	3	2	2	1	1	1	0
Principal	35	70	68	67	57	47	41	43	43	44
Interest	63	73	70	67	64	62	60	58	56	54
Multilateral creditors										
Disbursements	131	147	103	73	46	25	15	3	1	0
Principal	46	48	49	49	50	50	48	51	56	63
Interest	18	18	18	17	17	16	16	15	15	14
Private creditors										
Disbursements	0	0	0	0	0	0	0	0	0	0
Principal	6	6	6	3	0	0	0	0	0	0
Interest	2	1	1	0	0	0	0	0	0	0
Commercial banks										
Disbursements	0	0	0	0	0	0	0	0	0	0
Principal	6	6	6	3	0	0	0	0	0	0
Interest	1	1	1	0	0	0	0	0	0	0
Other private										
Disbursements	0	0	0	0	0	0	0	0	0	0
Principal	0	0	0	0	0	0	0	0	0	0
Interest	0	0	0	0	0	0	0	0	0	0

MALAWI

(US$ million, unless otherwise indicated)

	1970	1980	1990	1992	1993	1994	1995	1996	1997	1998
1. SUMMARY DEBT DATA										
TOTAL DEBT STOCKS (EDT)	**..**	**830**	**1,558**	**1,709**	**1,826**	**2,025**	**2,243**	**2,315**	**2,229**	**2,444**
Long-term debt (LDOD)	**135**	**634**	**1,385**	**1,568**	**1,730**	**1,900**	**2,083**	**2,096**	**2,099**	**2,310**
Public and publicly guaranteed	135	634	1,382	1,568	1,730	1,900	2,083	2,096	2,099	2,310
Private nonguaranteed	0	0	3	0	0	0	0	0	0	0
Use of IMF credit	**0**	**80**	**115**	**92**	**86**	**112**	**116**	**119**	**106**	**102**
Short-term debt	**..**	**116**	**58**	**49**	**11**	**12**	**44**	**100**	**24**	**32**
of which interest arrears on LDOD	..	3	6	2	2	2	1	5	4	14
Official creditors	..	2	4	2	2	2	1	4	2	12
Private creditors	..	1	2	0	0	1	1	1	1	2
Memo: principal arrears on LDOD	..	1	19	3	7	14	7	15	17	38
Official creditors	..	1	12	3	5	9	3	8	9	27
Private creditors	..	0	7	1	1	4	4	7	8	11
Memo: export credits	..	0	94	97	88	96	101	86	53	54
TOTAL DEBT FLOWS										
Disbursements	**54**	**190**	**161**	**158**	**194**	**147**	**227**	**184**	**178**	**173**
Long-term debt	53	153	136	158	194	121	215	161	168	156
IMF purchases	1	37	25	0	0	26	12	22	11	17
Principal repayments	**3**	**35**	**86**	**72**	**49**	**53**	**76**	**56**	**55**	**60**
Long-term debt	3	33	67	52	44	47	66	41	38	34
IMF repurchases	0	1	19	19	6	6	10	15	17	25
Net flows on debt	**51**	**154**	**88**	**106**	**107**	**95**	**183**	**181**	**48**	**112**
of which short-term debt	..	-1	13	19	-38	1	32	53	-75	-2
Interest payments (INT)	**..**	**53**	**47**	**37**	**29**	**27**	**43**	**33**	**30**	**24**
Long-term debt	4	35	36	31	27	26	39	28	26	22
IMF charges	0	2	6	2	1	1	1	1	1	1
Short-term debt	..	16	4	4	1	1	3	4	3	1
Net transfers on debt	**..**	**101**	**41**	**69**	**78**	**69**	**141**	**148**	**18**	**87**
Total debt service paid (TDS)	**..**	**87**	**133**	**108**	**78**	**80**	**118**	**89**	**85**	**84**
Long-term debt	6	68	103	83	71	73	104	69	64	56
IMF repurchases and charges	0	3	25	21	7	6	11	16	18	26
Short-term debt (interest only)	..	16	4	4	1	1	3	4	3	1
2. AGGREGATE NET RESOURCE FLOWS AND NET TRANSFERS (LONG-TERM)										
NET RESOURCE FLOWS	**65**	**178**	**296**	**441**	**353**	**305**	**410**	**321**	**249**	**359**
Net flow of long-term debt (ex. IMF)	50	120	69	106	151	74	149	121	129	121
Foreign direct investment (net)	9	10	0	0	0	1	1	1	2	1
Portfolio equity flows	0	0	0	0	0	0	0	0	0	24
Grants (excluding technical coop.)	7	49	227	335	203	231	260	200	117	213
Memo: technical coop. grants	9	36	113	102	106	64	87	85	92	79
official net resource flows	55	148	294	443	365	308	432	324	248	335
private net resource flows	10	30	2	-2	-12	-2	-22	-3	1	24
NET TRANSFERS	**54**	**134**	**260**	**410**	**326**	**280**	**371**	**294**	**223**	**337**
Interest on long-term debt	4	35	36	31	27	26	39	28	26	22
Profit remittances on FDI	8	9	0	0	0	0	0	0	0	0
Memo: official net transfers	53	139	264	416	340	284	397	299	223	314
private net transfers	1	-4	-4	-6	-14	-5	-25	-5	-1	24
3. MAJOR ECONOMIC AGGREGATES										
Gross national product (GNP)	283	1,138	1,760	1,921	2,218	1,270	1,584	2,300	2,535	1,778
Exports of goods & services (XGS)	..	315	452	435	350	387	464	571	682	568
of which workers remittances	..	0	0	0	0	0	..	..	..	..
Imports of goods & services (MGS)	..	638	638	837	671	961	889	1,148	1,376	1,180
International reserves (RES)	29	76	142	44	62	48	115	230	166	273
Current account balance	..	-260	-86	-285	-166	-450	..	..	..	..
4. DEBT INDICATORS										
EDT / XGS (%)	..	263.7	344.4	393.1	522.4	523.7	483.8	405.8	326.9	430.1
EDT / GNP (%)	..	72.9	88.6	89.0	82.3	159.5	141.6	100.7	87.9	137.5
TDS / XGS (%)	..	27.8	29.3	24.9	22.4	20.6	25.5	15.6	12.5	14.8
INT / XGS (%)	..	16.8	10.3	8.4	8.2	6.9	9.2	5.8	4.4	4.3
INT / GNP (%)	..	4.7	2.7	1.9	1.3	2.1	2.7	1.4	1.2	1.4
RES / EDT (%)	..	9.2	9.1	2.6	3.4	2.4	5.1	10.0	7.5	11.2
RES / MGS (months)	..	1.4	2.7	0.6	1.1	0.6	1.6	2.4	1.5	2.8
Short-term / EDT (%)	..	14.0	3.8	2.9	0.6	0.6	1.9	4.3	1.1	1.3
Concessional / EDT (%)	..	31.1	67.5	76.7	82.2	83.0	84.6	84.0	88.5	89.4
Multilateral / EDT (%)	..	26.4	69.8	75.5	79.6	79.1	76.4	76.6	80.8	81.4

MALAWI

(US$ million, unless otherwise indicated)

	1970	1980	1990	1992	1993	1994	1995	1996	1997	1998
5. LONG-TERM DEBT										
DEBT OUTSTANDING (LDOD)	**135**	**634**	**1,385**	**1,568**	**1,730**	**1,900**	**2,083**	**2,096**	**2,099**	**2,310**
Public and publicly guaranteed	**135**	**634**	**1,382**	**1,568**	**1,730**	**1,900**	**2,083**	**2,096**	**2,099**	**2,310**
Official creditors	116	442	1,305	1,504	1,679	1,851	2,055	2,072	2,079	2,290
Multilateral	17	219	1,088	1,290	1,453	1,601	1,712	1,773	1,800	1,990
Concessional	17	147	902	1,129	1,305	1,460	1,577	1,665	1,709	1,900
Bilateral	99	223	217	214	226	250	343	299	279	300
Concessional	62	111	149	181	197	221	321	281	264	284
Private creditors	20	192	78	64	50	49	28	24	21	20
Bonds	16	2	0	0	0	0	0	0	0	0
Commercial banks	1	153	35	27	19	11	0	0	0	0
Other private	3	38	42	37	32	39	28	24	21	20
Private nonguaranteed	**0**	**0**	**3**	**0**	**0**	**0**	**0**	**0**	**0**	**0**
Bonds	0	0	0	0	0	0	0	0	0	0
Commercial banks	0	0	3	0	0	0	0	0	0	0
Memo:										
IBRD	0	26	91	74	67	65	55	42	34	25
IDA	17	131	764	919	1,062	1,160	1,251	1,346	1,375	1,542
DISBURSEMENTS	**53**	**153**	**136**	**158**	**194**	**121**	**215**	**161**	**168**	**156**
Public and publicly guaranteed	**53**	**153**	**136**	**158**	**194**	**121**	**215**	**161**	**168**	**156**
Official creditors	50	105	129	144	193	111	215	161	166	156
Multilateral	10	49	118	136	187	104	97	161	146	156
Concessional	10	28	109	129	181	101	93	161	142	147
Bilateral	40	56	10	8	6	6	118	0	20	0
Concessional	19	18	10	8	6	6	118	0	20	0
Private creditors	3	48	7	14	1	10	0	0	1	0
Bonds	0	0	0	0	0	0	0	0	0	0
Commercial banks	0	39	0	0	0	0	0	0	0	0
Other private	3	9	7	14	1	10	0	0	1	0
Private nonguaranteed	**0**	**0**	**0**	**0**	**0**	**0**	**0**	**0**	**0**	**0**
Bonds	0	0	0	0	0	0	0	0	0	0
Commercial banks	0	0	0	0	0	0	0	0	0	0
Memo:										
IBRD	0	8	2	0	0	0	0	0	0	0
IDA	10	15	99	86	146	59	73	141	107	130
PRINCIPAL REPAYMENTS	**3**	**33**	**67**	**52**	**44**	**47**	**66**	**41**	**38**	**34**
Public and publicly guaranteed	**3**	**33**	**65**	**50**	**44**	**47**	**66**	**41**	**38**	**34**
Official creditors	2	5	61	36	30	33	43	37	35	33
Multilateral	0	2	20	22	22	29	29	26	25	30
Concessional	0	1	3	4	6	7	9	11	11	16
Bilateral	2	4	41	15	8	5	14	11	11	4
Concessional	1	1	4	6	4	3	7	8	9	4
Private creditors	1	28	4	14	13	14	23	4	3	1
Bonds	1	1	0	0	0	0	0	0	0	0
Commercial banks	0	21	0	9	8	8	11	0	0	0
Other private	0	6	4	5	5	6	12	4	3	1
Private nonguaranteed	**0**	**0**	**1**	**3**	**0**	**0**	**0**	**0**	**0**	**0**
Bonds	0	0	0	0	0	0	0	0	0	0
Commercial banks	0	0	1	3	0	0	0	0	0	0
Memo:										
IBRD	0	0	8	9	9	7	12	9	6	10
IDA	0	1	3	4	4	6	7	9	9	11
NET FLOWS ON DEBT	**50**	**120**	**69**	**106**	**151**	**74**	**149**	**121**	**129**	**121**
Public and publicly guaranteed	**50**	**120**	**70**	**109**	**151**	**74**	**149**	**121**	**129**	**121**
Official creditors	48	100	68	108	163	77	172	125	131	122
Multilateral	10	48	98	115	165	76	69	135	122	126
Concessional	10	27	106	125	175	93	84	150	130	132
Bilateral	39	52	-31	-7	-2	1	104	-11	9	-4
Concessional	19	17	6	2	2	3	111	-8	11	-4
Private creditors	2	20	3	1	-12	-3	-23	-4	-2	-1
Bonds	-1	-1	0	0	0	0	0	0	0	0
Commercial banks	0	18	0	-9	-8	-8	-11	0	0	0
Other private	3	4	3	9	-4	5	-12	-4	-2	-1
Private nonguaranteed	**0**	**0**	**-1**	**-3**	**0**	**0**	**0**	**0**	**0**	**0**
Bonds	0	0	0	0	0	0	0	0	0	0
Commercial banks	0	0	-1	-3	0	0	0	0	0	0
Memo:										
IBRD	0	8	-6	-9	-9	-7	-12	-9	-6	-10
IDA	10	14	96	82	142	53	66	133	98	120

MALAWI

(US$ million, unless otherwise indicated)

	1970	1980	1990	1992	1993	1994	1995	1996	1997	1998
INTEREST PAYMENTS (LINT)	**4**	**35**	**36**	**31**	**27**	**26**	**39**	**28**	**26**	**22**
Public and publicly guaranteed	**4**	**35**	**36**	**31**	**27**	**26**	**39**	**28**	**26**	**22**
Official creditors	2	10	31	27	25	23	35	25	25	22
Multilateral	0	3	19	20	20	19	25	19	17	19
Concessional	0	1	6	8	9	11	12	12	12	14
Bilateral	2	7	12	7	6	4	10	6	8	3
Concessional	1	3	3	3	4	3	7	5	6	3
Private creditors	1	25	6	4	2	2	4	2	1	0
Bonds	1	0	0	0	0	0	0	0	0	0
Commercial banks	0	22	3	2	1	0	1	0	0	0
Other private	0	2	2	2	2	2	3	2	1	0
Private nonguaranteed	**0**	**0**	**0**	**0**	**0**	**0**	**0**	**0**	**0**	**0**
Bonds	0	0	0	0	0	0	0	0	0	0
Commercial banks	0	0	0	0	0	0	0	0	0	0
Memo:										
IBRD	0	1	8	7	6	4	7	4	2	3
IDA	0	1	5	6	8	8	9	10	10	10
NET TRANSFERS ON DEBT	**47**	**85**	**33**	**75**	**123**	**48**	**111**	**93**	**103**	**99**
Public and publicly guaranteed	**47**	**85**	**34**	**78**	**123**	**48**	**111**	**93**	**103**	**99**
Official creditors	46	90	37	81	138	54	137	99	106	100
Multilateral	10	45	79	95	145	57	44	116	104	107
Concessional	10	26	100	117	166	83	72	138	118	118
Bilateral	37	45	-42	-13	-8	-3	94	-17	2	-7
Concessional	18	14	3	-2	-1	1	104	-12	5	-6
Private creditors	0	-5	-3	-3	-14	-6	-26	-6	-3	-1
Bonds	-2	-1	0	0	0	0	0	0	0	0
Commercial banks	0	-5	-3	-11	-9	-9	-11	0	0	0
Other private	2	1	1	7	-6	3	-15	-6	-3	-1
Private nonguaranteed	**0**	**0**	**-2**	**-3**	**0**	**0**	**0**	**0**	**0**	**0**
Bonds	0	0	0	0	0	0	0	0	0	0
Commercial banks	0	0	-2	-3	0	0	0	0	0	0
Memo:										
IBRD	0	6	-13	-16	-15	-11	-18	-13	-8	-13
IDA	10	13	91	76	134	45	57	123	89	109
DEBT SERVICE (LTDS)	**6**	**68**	**103**	**83**	**71**	**73**	**104**	**69**	**64**	**56**
Public and publicly guaranteed	**6**	**68**	**102**	**81**	**71**	**73**	**104**	**69**	**64**	**56**
Official creditors	4	15	92	63	55	57	78	62	60	55
Multilateral	0	5	39	42	42	48	54	46	42	49
Concessional	0	2	9	12	15	18	21	23	23	29
Bilateral	4	11	53	21	14	9	24	17	18	7
Concessional	1	4	7	9	8	6	14	12	16	6
Private creditors	3	53	10	18	16	16	26	6	4	1
Bonds	2	1	0	0	0	0	0	0	0	0
Commercial banks	0	44	3	11	9	9	11	0	0	0
Other private	1	8	7	7	7	7	15	6	4	1
Private nonguaranteed	**0**	**0**	**2**	**3**	**0**	**0**	**0**	**0**	**0**	**0**
Bonds	0	0	0	0	0	0	0	0	0	0
Commercial banks	0	0	2	3	0	0	0	0	0	0
Memo:										
IBRD	0	1	16	16	15	11	18	13	8	13
IDA	0	2	8	10	12	14	16	18	18	21
UNDISBURSED DEBT	**39**	**162**	**579**	**678**	**631**	**701**	**579**	**601**	**479**	**558**
Official creditors	39	152	567	670	621	701	579	598	473	552
Private creditors	0	10	12	8	11	0	0	3	6	6
Memorandum items										
Concessional LDOD	78	258	1,051	1,311	1,502	1,681	1,897	1,946	1,973	2,184
Variable rate LDOD	0	145	51	38	29	20	9	8	7	6
Public sector LDOD	135	585	1,372	1,561	1,724	1,896	2,080	2,092	2,096	2,307
Private sector LDOD	0	49	13	7	5	4	4	3	3	3
6. CURRENCY COMPOSITION OF LONG-TERM DEBT (PERCENT)										
Deutsche mark	4.1	2.5	0.7	0.3	0.2	0.1	0.3	0.3	0.2	0.2
French franc	0.0	1.2	2.0	2.2	1.7	1.5	1.2	1.0	0.8	0.8
Japanese yen	0.0	4.1	9.3	9.7	9.7	9.8	12.3	10.6	9.1	9.2
Pound sterling	56.2	17.4	16.7	12.2	10.8	10.0	9.0	8.5	8.0	7.4
Swiss franc	0.0	0.0	0.1	0.1	0.1	0.1	0.1	0.1	0.1	0.1
U.S.dollars	12.9	46.5	46.9	49.2	47.8	48.0	47.4	51.8	54.5	56.4
Multiple currency	0.0	12.4	21.9	22.1	21.2	22.0	20.4	18.6	18.5	17.6
Special drawing rights	0.0	0.0	0.0	2.0	6.7	6.8	6.6	6.7	6.4	6.1
All other currencies	26.8	15.9	2.4	2.2	1.8	1.7	2.7	2.4	2.4	2.2

MALAWI

(US$ million, unless otherwise indicated)

	1970	1980	1990	1992	1993	1994	1995	1996	1997	1998
7. DEBT RESTRUCTURINGS										
Total amount rescheduled	..	..	0	0	0	0	0	0	0	0
Debt stock rescheduled	..	..	0	0	0	0	0	0	0	0
Principal rescheduled	..	..	0	0	0	0	0	0	0	0
Official	..	..	0	0	0	0	0	0	0	0
Private	..	..	0	0	0	0	0	0	0	0
Interest rescheduled	..	..	0	0	0	0	0	0	0	0
Official	..	..	0	0	0	0	0	0	0	0
Private	..	..	0	0	0	0	0	0	0	0
Debt forgiven	..	..	51	0	0	0	0	0	0	0
Memo: interest forgiven	..	..	0	0	0	0	0	0	0	0
Debt stock reduction	..	..	0	0	0	0	0	0	0	0
of which debt buyback	..	..	0	0	0	0	0	0	0	0
8. DEBT STOCK-FLOW RECONCILIATION										
Total change in debt stocks	..	..	148	44	117	199	218	73	-87	216
Net flows on debt	51	154	88	106	107	95	183	181	48	112
Net change in interest arrears	..	..	-2	0	0	1	-1	4	-1	10
Interest capitalized	..	..	0	0	0	0	0	0	0	0
Debt forgiveness or reduction	..	..	-51	0	0	0	0	0	0	0
Cross-currency valuation	..	..	65	-47	10	49	-1	-25	-45	37
Residual	..	..	49	-15	1	54	36	-87	-88	57
9. AVERAGE TERMS OF NEW COMMITMENTS										
ALL CREDITORS										
Interest (%)	3.8	6.0	1.3	0.8	1.6	1.8	1.0	1.2	1.0	0.8
Maturity (years)	29.4	23.6	37.5	40.4	38.3	27.7	38.6	37.6	46.9	39.7
Grace period (years)	6.0	5.9	9.2	10.1	9.2	6.7	9.6	9.8	10.3	10.2
Grant element (%)	47.1	32.4	73.9	80.6	71.5	60.2	78.2	75.9	79.8	80.5
Official creditors										
Interest (%)	3.1	4.0	1.1	0.8	1.3	1.8	1.0	1.1	0.7	0.8
Maturity (years)	35.3	28.6	38.1	40.4	39.9	27.7	38.6	38.0	49.3	39.7
Grace period (years)	7.6	6.9	9.4	10.1	9.6	6.7	9.6	9.9	10.9	10.2
Grant element (%)	56.9	44.9	75.5	80.6	74.7	60.2	78.2	76.8	83.9	80.5
Private creditors										
Interest (%)	6.5	13.2	8.6	0.0	7.7	0.0	0.0	9.2	5.5	0.0
Maturity (years)	8.4	5.7	11.9	0.0	4.6	0.0	0.0	4.7	10.5	0.0
Grace period (years)	0.3	2.6	3.5	0.0	0.7	0.0	0.0	1.2	1.0	0.0
Grant element (%)	12.0	-12.3	6.3	0.0	4.7	0.0	0.0	1.5	17.5	0.0
Memorandum items										
Commitments	14	130	262	220	184	153	102	207	82	214
Official creditors	11	102	256	220	175	153	102	205	77	214
Private creditors	3	28	6	0	8	0	0	3	5	0

10. CONTRACTUAL OBLIGATIONS ON OUTSTANDING LONG-TERM DEBT

	1999	2000	2001	2002	2003	2004	2005	2006	2007	2008
TOTAL										
Disbursements	165	155	103	58	37	22	13	1	0	0
Principal	56	61	64	65	70	73	74	78	79	73
Interest	28	27	26	25	24	23	21	20	19	18
Official creditors										
Disbursements	163	153	102	58	37	22	13	1	0	0
Principal	53	59	62	64	69	72	73	77	78	73
Interest	27	27	26	25	24	22	21	20	19	18
Bilateral creditors										
Disbursements	0	0	0	0	0	0	0	0	0	0
Principal	18	20	22	22	22	22	22	21	19	11
Interest	7	6	6	5	5	4	3	3	2	2
Multilateral creditors										
Disbursements	163	153	102	58	37	22	13	1	0	0
Principal	35	39	40	42	47	50	51	56	59	62
Interest	20	20	20	20	19	18	18	17	17	16
Private creditors										
Disbursements	3	2	1	0	0	0	0	0	0	0
Principal	3	2	2	1	1	1	1	1	1	0
Interest	1	1	0	0	0	0	0	0	0	0
Commercial banks										
Disbursements	0	0	0	0	0	0	0	0	0	0
Principal	0	0	0	0	0	0	0	0	0	0
Interest	0	0	0	0	0	0	0	0	0	0
Other private										
Disbursements	3	2	1	0	0	0	0	0	0	0
Principal	3	2	2	1	1	1	1	1	1	0
Interest	1	1	0	0	0	0	0	0	0	0

MALAYSIA

(US$ million, unless otherwise indicated)

	1970	1980	1990	1992	1993	1994	1995	1996	1997	1998
1. SUMMARY DEBT DATA										
TOTAL DEBT STOCKS (EDT)	..	**6,611**	**15,328**	**20,018**	**26,149**	**30,336**	**34,343**	**39,673**	**47,228**	**44,773**
Long-term debt (LDOD)	**440**	**5,256**	**13,422**	**16,379**	**19,197**	**24,147**	**27,069**	**28,605**	**32,289**	**36,117**
Public and publicly guaranteed	390	4,008	11,592	12,371	13,460	14,693	16,023	15,702	16,808	18,158
Private nonguaranteed	50	1,248	1,830	4,008	5,737	9,454	11,046	12,903	15,482	17,959
Use of IMF credit	**0**	**0**	**0**	**0**	**0**	**0**	**0**	**0**	**0**	**0**
Short-term debt	..	**1,355**	**1,906**	**3,639**	**6,951**	**6,189**	**7,274**	**11,068**	**14,939**	**8,656**
of which interest arrears on LDOD	..	0	0	0	0	0	0	0	0	0
Official creditors	..	0	0	0	0	0	0	0	0	0
Private creditors	..	0	0	0	0	0	0	0	0	0
Memo: principal arrears on LDOD	..	0	0	0	0	0	0	0	0	0
Official creditors	..	0	0	0	0	0	0	0	0	0
Private creditors	..	0	0	0	0	0	0	0	0	0
Memo: export credits	..	0	1,395	2,541	2,316	3,445	4,373	3,350	3,292	2,778
TOTAL DEBT FLOWS										
Disbursements	**58**	**1,456**	**1,683**	**3,577**	**5,583**	**7,672**	**8,503**	**8,936**	**8,803**	**6,724**
Long-term debt	58	1,456	1,683	3,577	5,583	7,672	8,503	8,936	8,803	6,724
IMF purchases	0	0	0	0	0	0	0	0	0	0
Principal repayments	**57**	**345**	**3,167**	**3,102**	**3,425**	**4,690**	**4,450**	**6,343**	**4,276**	**3,802**
Long-term debt	57	345	3,167	3,102	3,425	4,690	4,450	6,343	4,276	3,802
IMF repurchases	0	0	0	0	0	0	0	0	0	0
Net flows on debt	**63**	**1,592**	**-1,851**	**2,041**	**5,470**	**2,220**	**5,138**	**6,387**	**8,397**	**-3,361**
of which short-term debt	..	481	-367	1,565	3,312	-762	1,085	3,794	3,871	-6,283
Interest payments (INT)	..	**589**	**1,166**	**1,108**	**1,355**	**1,432**	**1,591**	**2,084**	**2,833**	**2,469**
Long-term debt	25	338	997	932	887	1,007	1,151	1,432	1,588	1,813
IMF charges	0	0	0	0	0	0	0	0	0	0
Short-term debt	..	251	169	176	467	424	441	652	1,245	656
Net transfers on debt	..	**1,003**	**-3,017**	**933**	**4,115**	**788**	**3,547**	**4,303**	**5,565**	**-5,830**
Total debt service paid (TDS)	..	**934**	**4,333**	**4,209**	**4,780**	**6,121**	**6,041**	**8,427**	**7,109**	**6,271**
Long-term debt	82	683	4,164	4,034	4,312	5,697	5,600	7,776	5,864	5,615
IMF repurchases and charges	0	0	0	0	0	0	0	0	0	0
Short-term debt (interest only)	..	251	169	176	467	424	441	652	1,245	656
2. AGGREGATE NET RESOURCE FLOWS AND NET TRANSFERS (LONG-TERM)										
NET RESOURCE FLOWS	**99**	**2,052**	**1,183**	**6,093**	**10,923**	**8,680**	**10,495**	**12,031**	**9,152**	**8,529**
Net flow of long-term debt (ex. IMF)	1	1,111	-1,484	476	2,158	2,982	4,053	2,593	4,527	2,922
Foreign direct investment (net)	94	934	2,333	5,183	5,006	4,342	4,132	5,078	5,106	5,000
Portfolio equity flows	0	0	293	385	3,700	1,320	2,299	4,353	-489	592
Grants (excluding technical coop.)	4	6	42	49	59	36	11	7	8	15
Memo: technical coop. grants	13	54	125	121	122	113	121	100	86	80
official net resource flows	27	139	414	23	-338	223	393	-774	-161	235
private net resource flows	71	1,913	769	6,070	11,261	8,458	10,102	12,805	9,312	8,295
NET TRANSFERS	**-93**	**524**	**-1,740**	**2,448**	**7,051**	**4,423**	**5,344**	**6,599**	**3,364**	**2,216**
Interest on long-term debt	25	338	997	932	887	1,007	1,151	1,432	1,588	1,813
Profit remittances on FDI	166	1,190	1,926	2,713	2,985	3,250	4,000	4,000	4,200	4,500
Memo: official net transfers	14	53	182	-237	-606	-30	109	-1,017	-362	28
private net transfers	-107	471	-1,921	2,685	7,657	4,453	5,235	7,616	3,726	2,189
3. MAJOR ECONOMIC AGGREGATES										
Gross national product (GNP)	4,089	23,607	40,902	55,166	60,969	68,918	83,101	94,563	94,833	68,581
Exports of goods & services (XGS)	..	14,836	34,514	46,421	54,656	68,526	85,992	94,065	95,387	71,900
of which workers remittances	..	0	0	0	0	0	0	0	0	..
Imports of goods & services (MGS)	..	15,100	35,486	48,760	57,935	73,275	93,618	97,734	99,085	60,200
International reserves (RES)	667	5,755	10,659	18,024	28,183	26,339	24,699	27,892	21,470	26,236
Current account balance	..	-266	-870	-2,167	-2,991	-4,520	-8,469	-4,596	-4,792	..
4. DEBT INDICATORS										
EDT / XGS (%)	..	44.6	44.4	43.1	47.8	44.3	39.9	42.2	49.5	62.3
EDT / GNP (%)	..	28.0	37.5	36.3	42.9	44.0	41.3	42.0	49.8	65.3
TDS / XGS (%)	..	6.3	12.6	9.1	8.7	8.9	7.0	9.0	7.5	8.7
INT / XGS (%)	..	4.0	3.4	2.4	2.5	2.1	1.9	2.2	3.0	3.4
INT / GNP (%)	..	2.5	2.9	2.0	2.2	2.1	1.9	2.2	3.0	3.6
RES / EDT (%)	..	87.1	69.5	90.0	107.8	86.8	71.9	70.3	45.5	58.6
RES / MGS (months)	..	4.6	3.6	4.4	5.8	4.3	3.2	3.4	2.6	5.2
Short-term / EDT (%)	..	20.5	12.4	18.2	26.6	20.4	21.2	27.9	31.6	19.3
Concessional / EDT (%)	..	8.6	14.6	13.0	10.8	11.0	10.6	6.4	4.3	5.2
Multilateral / EDT (%)	..	11.3	11.8	9.3	6.2	5.7	4.8	3.5	2.6	3.3

MALAYSIA

(US$ million, unless otherwise indicated)

	1970	1980	1990	1992	1993	1994	1995	1996	1997	1998
5. LONG-TERM DEBT										
DEBT OUTSTANDING (LDOD)	**440**	**5,256**	**13,422**	**16,379**	**19,197**	**24,147**	**27,069**	**28,605**	**32,289**	**36,117**
Public and publicly guaranteed	**390**	**4,008**	**11,592**	**12,371**	**13,460**	**14,693**	**16,023**	**15,702**	**16,808**	**18,158**
Official creditors	265	1,444	4,191	4,520	4,481	5,687	5,490	4,205	3,983	4,505
Multilateral	141	745	1,812	1,861	1,626	1,721	1,644	1,404	1,228	1,484
Concessional	0	3	9	7	5	3	1	0	0	0
Bilateral	124	699	2,378	2,659	2,854	3,966	3,846	2,802	2,755	3,021
Concessional	94	565	2,225	2,597	2,807	3,322	3,651	2,548	2,033	2,333
Private creditors	125	2,564	7,401	7,850	8,980	9,006	10,533	11,497	12,824	13,654
Bonds	111	278	4,090	3,825	3,920	4,080	6,062	7,789	8,265	8,338
Commercial banks	0	1,397	2,285	2,057	2,892	3,384	4,171	3,121	3,119	3,346
Other private	14	889	1,026	1,969	2,168	1,542	300	587	1,440	1,970
Private nonguaranteed	**50**	**1,248**	**1,830**	**4,008**	**5,737**	**9,454**	**11,046**	**12,903**	**15,482**	**17,959**
Bonds	0	0	0	0	0	1,285	1,765	1,937	3,752	3,785
Commercial banks	50	1,248	1,830	4,008	5,737	8,169	9,281	10,966	11,730	14,174
Memo:										
IBRD	141	504	1,103	1,072	1,083	1,118	1,059	907	758	970
IDA	0	0	0	0	0	0	0	0	0	0
DISBURSEMENTS	**58**	**1,456**	**1,683**	**3,577**	**5,583**	**7,672**	**8,503**	**8,936**	**8,803**	**6,724**
Public and publicly guaranteed	**45**	**1,015**	**798**	**1,427**	**3,071**	**3,646**	**4,150**	**3,528**	**3,566**	**1,624**
Official creditors	39	211	737	440	336	881	837	297	662	600
Multilateral	22	119	273	224	217	198	135	128	138	386
Concessional	0	0	2	1	1	0	0	0	0	0
Bilateral	18	93	464	216	119	684	702	168	524	214
Concessional	16	78	460	202	119	615	604	94	272	214
Private creditors	6	804	61	987	2,735	2,765	3,313	3,231	2,904	1,024
Bonds	0	0	0	0	951	1,060	2,100	2,252	746	0
Commercial banks	0	510	57	0	912	1,578	1,205	703	900	456
Other private	6	294	4	987	872	127	8	276	1,259	568
Private nonguaranteed	**12**	**441**	**885**	**2,150**	**2,512**	**4,026**	**4,353**	**5,408**	**5,237**	**5,100**
Bonds	0	0	0	0	0	1,285	480	172	1,844	0
Commercial banks	12	441	885	2,150	2,512	2,741	3,873	5,236	3,393	5,100
Memo:										
IBRD	21	80	205	148	159	144	88	85	51	325
IDA	0	0	0	0	0	0	0	0	0	0
PRINCIPAL REPAYMENTS	**57**	**345**	**3,167**	**3,102**	**3,425**	**4,690**	**4,450**	**6,343**	**4,276**	**3,802**
Public and publicly guaranteed	**47**	**127**	**2,697**	**2,522**	**2,627**	**3,360**	**1,701**	**3,264**	**1,867**	**1,131**
Official creditors	16	79	365	467	733	695	455	1,078	830	381
Multilateral	5	34	216	257	536	241	261	230	191	182
Concessional	0	0	2	2	2	2	2	1	0	0
Bilateral	11	45	149	210	197	454	195	848	640	199
Concessional	4	17	123	136	181	435	188	840	535	164
Private creditors	32	48	2,332	2,055	1,894	2,665	1,246	2,186	1,037	750
Bonds	30	11	1,239	369	907	1,100	140	362	86	299
Commercial banks	0	17	664	134	184	1,235	420	1,616	779	339
Other private	2	20	428	1,551	802	330	686	208	172	112
Private nonguaranteed	**9**	**218**	**470**	**580**	**798**	**1,330**	**2,749**	**3,079**	**2,409**	**2,671**
Bonds	0	0	0	0	0	0	0	0	0	15
Commercial banks	9	218	470	580	798	1,330	2,749	3,079	2,409	2,656
Memo:										
IBRD	5	26	164	191	172	185	194	161	126	117
IDA	0	0	0	0	0	0	0	0	0	0
NET FLOWS ON DEBT	**1**	**1,111**	**-1,484**	**476**	**2,158**	**2,982**	**4,053**	**2,593**	**4,527**	**2,922**
Public and publicly guaranteed	**-2**	**889**	**-1,899**	**-1,095**	**444**	**286**	**2,450**	**264**	**1,699**	**493**
Official creditors	23	133	372	-26	-397	186	382	-781	-168	219
Multilateral	17	85	57	-33	-320	-44	-126	-102	-53	204
Concessional	0	0	0	-1	-1	-2	-2	-1	0	0
Bilateral	7	48	315	6	-78	230	507	-679	-115	15
Concessional	12	61	337	66	-62	180	416	-746	-263	50
Private creditors	-25	756	-2,271	-1,068	841	99	2,068	1,045	1,868	274
Bonds	-30	-11	-1,239	-369	44	-40	1,960	1,890	659	-299
Commercial banks	0	493	-608	-134	727	342	785	-913	121	118
Other private	5	274	-424	-564	69	-204	-678	68	1,087	456
Private nonguaranteed	**3**	**223**	**415**	**1,570**	**1,714**	**2,697**	**1,604**	**2,329**	**2,828**	**2,429**
Bonds	0	0	0	0	0	1,285	480	172	1,844	-15
Commercial banks	3	223	415	1,570	1,714	1,412	1,124	2,157	984	2,444
Memo:										
IBRD	16	54	41	-43	-13	-41	-106	-76	-75	208
IDA	0	0	0	0	0	0	0	0	0	0

MALAYSIA

(US$ million, unless otherwise indicated)

	1970	1980	1990	1992	1993	1994	1995	1996	1997	1998
INTEREST PAYMENTS (LINT)	**25**	**338**	**997**	**932**	**887**	**1,007**	**1,151**	**1,432**	**1,588**	**1,813**
Public and publicly guaranteed	**22**	**250**	**956**	**880**	**759**	**763**	**805**	**856**	**903**	**999**
Official creditors	13	86	232	260	268	253	284	243	202	207
Multilateral	8	60	145	154	151	127	129	108	90	82
Concessional	0	0	1	0	0	0	0	0	0	0
Bilateral	5	26	87	105	117	126	155	135	112	125
Concessional	3	19	75	96	113	123	146	133	81	70
Private creditors	9	163	724	621	492	511	522	612	702	793
Bonds	8	18	414	230	227	234	251	318	509	536
Commercial banks	0	108	199	154	148	174	190	229	142	161
Other private	1	37	111	237	117	102	80	65	50	96
Private nonguaranteed	**3**	**88**	**41**	**52**	**128**	**244**	**345**	**577**	**685**	**814**
Bonds	0	0	0	0	0	1	28	48	60	161
Commercial banks	3	88	41	52	128	243	318	529	625	652
Memo:										
IBRD	8	39	86	87	83	83	83	70	57	50
IDA	0	0	0	0	0	0	0	0	0	0
NET TRANSFERS ON DEBT	**-25**	**774**	**-2,481**	**-456**	**1,271**	**1,975**	**2,903**	**1,161**	**2,939**	**1,109**
Public and publicly guaranteed	**-24**	**639**	**-2,855**	**-1,975**	**-315**	**-477**	**1,644**	**-592**	**796**	**-506**
Official creditors	10	46	140	-286	-665	-66	98	-1,025	-370	12
Multilateral	9	25	-88	-187	-471	-170	-254	-210	-144	122
Concessional	0	0	0	-1	-2	-2	-2	-1	0	0
Bilateral	1	22	228	-99	-194	104	352	-814	-227	-110
Concessional	9	42	262	-31	-175	57	270	-879	-345	-19
Private creditors	-34	593	-2,995	-1,689	349	-411	1,546	433	1,166	-519
Bonds	-38	-29	-1,654	-599	-182	-274	1,709	1,572	150	-835
Commercial banks	0	384	-806	-288	580	168	595	-1,142	-21	-43
Other private	4	237	-535	-802	-48	-305	-758	3	1,037	360
Private nonguaranteed	**0**	**135**	**374**	**1,518**	**1,586**	**2,452**	**1,258**	**1,752**	**2,143**	**1,616**
Bonds	0	0	0	0	0	1,284	452	124	1,784	-176
Commercial banks	0	135	374	1,518	1,586	1,169	806	1,628	359	1,792
Memo:										
IBRD	9	15	-46	-130	-96	-124	-189	-146	-132	159
IDA	0	0	0	0	0	0	0	0	0	0
DEBT SERVICE (LTDS)	**82**	**683**	**4,164**	**4,034**	**4,312**	**5,697**	**5,600**	**7,776**	**5,864**	**5,615**
Public and publicly guaranteed	**70**	**376**	**3,653**	**3,402**	**3,386**	**4,123**	**2,506**	**4,120**	**2,770**	**2,130**
Official creditors	29	165	597	726	1,001	948	739	1,321	1,032	587
Multilateral	13	94	361	411	688	368	389	339	281	264
Concessional	0	0	2	2	2	2	2	1	0	0
Bilateral	16	71	237	315	313	580	350	983	751	324
Concessional	7	37	198	233	294	559	334	973	616	234
Private creditors	40	211	3,056	2,676	2,385	3,176	1,767	2,798	1,738	1,543
Bonds	38	29	1,654	599	1,133	1,334	391	680	595	835
Commercial banks	0	126	863	288	332	1,410	610	1,845	921	500
Other private	2	57	539	1,789	920	432	766	273	222	208
Private nonguaranteed	**13**	**307**	**511**	**632**	**926**	**1,574**	**3,094**	**3,656**	**3,094**	**3,485**
Bonds	0	0	0	0	0	1	28	48	60	176
Commercial banks	13	307	511	632	926	1,572	3,066	3,608	3,034	3,308
Memo:										
IBRD	13	65	251	278	255	268	277	231	183	167
IDA	0	0	0	0	0	0	0	0	0	0
UNDISBURSED DEBT	**201**	**1,761**	**2,068**	**1,967**	**4,174**	**3,647**	**3,147**	**2,243**	**1,193**	**913**
Official creditors	181	1,404	1,795	1,580	2,347	2,235	2,069	1,621	831	559
Private creditors	20	357	274	387	1,827	1,413	1,078	622	362	353
Memorandum items										
Concessional LDOD	94	567	2,234	2,603	2,813	3,326	3,652	2,548	2,033	2,333
Variable rate LDOD	50	2,665	6,559	8,454	9,934	13,722	15,779	16,593	19,457	22,456
Public sector LDOD	390	4,008	11,592	12,371	13,460	14,693	16,023	15,702	16,808	18,158
Private sector LDOD	50	1,248	1,830	4,008	5,737	9,454	11,046	12,903	15,482	17,959

6. CURRENCY COMPOSITION OF LONG-TERM DEBT (PERCENT)

	1970	1980	1990	1992	1993	1994	1995	1996	1997	1998
Deutsche mark	6.9	3.3	5.9	4.0	3.0	2.2	1.1	0.8	0.5	0.4
French franc	0.0	13.0	2.8	1.0	0.8	0.7	0.6	0.5	0.4	0.4
Japanese yen	2.2	19.0	36.5	35.4	37.5	37.5	34.6	28.2	26.5	29.6
Pound sterling	37.8	3.6	1.6	3.0	3.4	2.4	1.0	1.2	1.1	1.0
Swiss franc	0.0	2.3	3.6	2.6	2.4	3.0	3.1	1.7	0.5	0.1
U.S.dollars	14.0	36.7	31.8	27.7	29.4	35.1	48.5	55.6	55.8	58.7
Multiple currency	36.3	21.0	15.0	24.9	23.0	18.7	10.7	11.5	15.0	9.7
Special drawing rights	0.0	0.0	0.0	0.0	0.0	0.0	0.0	0.0	0.0	0.0
All other currencies	2.8	1.1	2.8	1.4	0.5	0.4	0.4	0.5	0.2	0.1

MALAYSIA

(US$ million, unless otherwise indicated)

	1970	1980	1990	1992	1993	1994	1995	1996	1997	1998
7. DEBT RESTRUCTURINGS										
Total amount rescheduled	..	..	0	0	0	0	0	0	0	0
Debt stock rescheduled	..	..	0	0	0	0	0	0	0	0
Principal rescheduled	..	..	0	0	0	0	0	0	0	0
Official	..	..	0	0	0	0	0	0	0	0
Private	..	..	0	0	0	0	0	0	0	0
Interest rescheduled	..	..	0	0	0	0	0	0	0	0
Official	..	..	0	0	0	0	0	0	0	0
Private	..	..	0	0	0	0	0	0	0	0
Debt forgiven	..	..	0	0	0	0	0	0	0	0
Memo: interest forgiven	..	..	0	0	0	0	0	0	0	0
Debt stock reduction	..	..	0	0	0	0	0	0	0	0
of which debt buyback	..	..	0	0	0	0	0	0	0	0
8. DEBT STOCK-FLOW RECONCILIATION										
Total change in debt stocks	..	..	-950	2,938	6,131	4,187	4,007	5,331	7,555	-2,455
Net flows on debt	63	1,592	-1,851	2,041	5,470	2,220	5,138	6,387	8,397	-3,361
Net change in interest arrears	..	..	0	0	0	0	0	0	0	0
Interest capitalized	..	..	0	0	0	0	0	0	0	0
Debt forgiveness or reduction	..	..	0	0	0	0	0	0	0	0
Cross-currency valuation	..	..	606	-202	518	822	-83	-645	-592	682
Residual	..	..	295	1,099	143	1,146	-1,049	-411	-251	224
9. AVERAGE TERMS OF NEW COMMITMENTS										
ALL CREDITORS										
Interest (%)	6.1	11.2	4.8	5.9	5.2	6.6	5.8	6.5	5.9	4.1
Maturity (years)	18.7	13.8	20.9	20.9	11.6	13.8	18.3	18.1	12.8	14.2
Grace period (years)	4.8	5.4	6.0	4.0	5.3	4.5	12.5	13.1	4.7	3.6
Grant element (%)	22.8	-6.6	37.3	27.2	24.2	17.1	27.6	19.0	21.2	32.8
Official creditors										
Interest (%)	6.4	6.7	4.0	4.7	4.9	7.5	3.4	0.0	7.4	6.3
Maturity (years)	21.0	18.3	22.9	21.9	12.5	24.8	24.4	0.0	22.3	15.8
Grace period (years)	5.7	5.0	6.7	6.1	3.4	3.6	6.3	0.0	4.2	3.8
Grant element (%)	24.0	20.9	44.2	37.7	24.5	16.0	48.1	0.0	15.8	20.9
Private creditors										
Interest (%)	5.1	14.1	8.9	7.0	5.3	6.5	6.3	6.5	5.9	3.4
Maturity (years)	8.8	10.9	11.4	19.9	11.3	11.6	16.9	18.1	12.5	13.7
Grace period (years)	1.3	5.7	2.6	1.9	5.8	4.7	14.0	13.1	4.7	3.5
Grant element (%)	17.3	-23.9	4.3	17.0	24.1	17.4	22.7	19.0	21.3	36.4
Memorandum items										
Commitments	84	1,423	701	1,699	5,117	3,704	3,772	3,435	2,405	1,278
Official creditors	68	550	579	840	1,058	625	730	0	74	300
Private creditors	16	873	122	859	4,059	3,079	3,042	3,435	2,330	978

10. CONTRACTUAL OBLIGATIONS ON OUTSTANDING LONG-TERM DEBT

	1999	2000	2001	2002	2003	2004	2005	2006	2007	2008
TOTAL										
Disbursements	525	210	120	36	13	6	3	0	0	0
Principal	2,523	3,087	2,727	3,041	2,668	3,276	3,935	2,369	3,741	2,006
Interest	1,765	1,650	1,492	1,338	1,172	1,045	887	687	491	336
Official creditors										
Disbursements	243	161	98	36	13	6	3	0	0	0
Principal	407	376	368	395	368	357	325	308	283	265
Interest	250	235	219	200	180	160	141	123	106	91
Bilateral creditors										
Disbursements	155	86	44	23	8	2	0	0	0	0
Principal	240	226	230	243	220	220	189	180	172	165
Interest	137	130	122	113	103	94	85	77	69	62
Multilateral creditors										
Disbursements	88	75	54	13	5	4	3	0	0	0
Principal	167	150	138	152	148	136	136	129	111	99
Interest	113	105	97	87	77	66	56	46	37	30
Private creditors										
Disbursements	282	49	22	0	0	0	0	0	0	0
Principal	2,116	2,711	2,359	2,646	2,300	2,919	3,610	2,061	3,459	1,741
Interest	1,516	1,415	1,274	1,138	992	885	746	564	385	245
Commercial banks										
Disbursements	282	49	22	0	0	0	0	0	0	0
Principal	748	483	413	767	288	190	190	162	108	88
Interest	174	148	124	103	61	47	37	26	18	14
Other private										
Disbursements	0	0	0	0	0	0	0	0	0	0
Principal	1,368	2,228	1,946	1,879	2,012	2,729	3,420	1,899	3,351	1,654
Interest	1,341	1,268	1,150	1,035	931	838	710	538	367	231

MALDIVES

(US$ million, unless otherwise indicated)

	1970	1980	1990	1992	1993	1994	1995	1996	1997	1998
1. SUMMARY DEBT DATA										
TOTAL DEBT STOCKS (EDT)	..	**25.8**	**78.0**	**94.9**	**112.3**	**123.5**	**154.9**	**167.7**	**160.6**	**179.9**
Long-term debt (LDOD)	..	**24.8**	**64.0**	**90.5**	**109.3**	**122.5**	**151.9**	**163.0**	**153.6**	**169.7**
Public and publicly guaranteed	..	24.8	64.0	90.5	109.3	122.5	151.9	163.0	153.6	169.7
Private nonguaranteed	..	0.0	0.0	0.0	0.0	0.0	0.0	0.0	0.0	0.0
Use of IMF credit	**0.0**	**0.0**	**0.0**	**0.0**	**0.0**	**0.0**	**0.0**	**0.0**	**0.0**	**0.0**
Short-term debt	..	**1.0**	**14.0**	**4.4**	**3.0**	**1.0**	**2.9**	**4.7**	**7.0**	**10.2**
of which interest arrears on LDOD	..	0.0	0.0	0.0	0.0	0.0	0.0	0.0	0.0	0.0
Official creditors	..	0.0	0.0	0.0	0.0	0.0	0.0	0.0	0.0	0.0
Private creditors	..	0.0	0.0	0.0	0.0	0.0	0.0	0.0	0.0	0.0
Memo: principal arrears on LDOD	..	0.0	0.0	0.0	0.0	0.0	0.0	0.0	0.0	0.0
Official creditors	..	0.0	0.0	0.0	0.0	0.0	0.0	0.0	0.0	0.0
Private creditors	..	0.0	0.0	0.0	0.0	0.0	0.0	0.0	0.0	0.0
Memo: export credits	..	0.0	8.0	5.0	12.0	29.0	26.0	29.0	39.0	36.0
TOTAL DEBT FLOWS										
Disbursements	..	**17.9**	**13.0**	**20.8**	**25.0**	**15.4**	**34.7**	**22.9**	**21.9**	**26.5**
Long-term debt	..	17.9	13.0	20.8	25.0	15.4	34.7	22.9	21.9	26.5
IMF purchases	0.0	0.0	0.0	0.0	0.0	0.0	0.0	0.0	0.0	0.0
Principal repayments	..	**0.0**	**6.0**	**5.2**	**5.7**	**6.4**	**7.1**	**7.9**	**23.8**	**10.0**
Long-term debt	..	0.0	6.0	5.2	5.7	6.4	7.1	7.9	23.8	10.0
IMF repurchases	0.0	0.0	0.0	0.0	0.0	0.0	0.0	0.0	0.0	0.0
Net flows on debt	..	**12.9**	**8.6**	**16.8**	**17.9**	**7.0**	**29.5**	**16.8**	**0.5**	**19.6**
of which short-term debt	..	-5.0	1.6	1.2	-1.4	-2.0	1.9	1.7	2.3	3.2
Interest payments (INT)	..	**0.5**	**2.8**	**1.9**	**2.7**	**3.1**	**3.7**	**3.9**	**4.4**	**3.6**
Long-term debt	..	0.3	1.3	1.5	2.4	3.0	3.6	3.7	4.0	3.1
IMF charges	0.0	0.0	0.0	0.0	0.0	0.0	0.0	0.0	0.0	0.0
Short-term debt	..	0.3	1.5	0.3	0.3	0.1	0.2	0.2	0.4	0.4
Net transfers on debt	..	**12.4**	**5.8**	**14.9**	**15.2**	**3.9**	**25.8**	**12.9**	**-3.9**	**16.0**
Total debt service paid (TDS)	..	**0.5**	**8.8**	**7.1**	**8.4**	**9.5**	**10.8**	**11.7**	**28.2**	**13.6**
Long-term debt	..	0.3	7.3	6.8	8.1	9.3	10.7	11.5	27.8	13.2
IMF repurchases and charges	0.0	0.0	0.0	0.0	0.0	0.0	0.0	0.0	0.0	0.0
Short-term debt (interest only)	..	0.3	1.5	0.3	0.3	0.1	0.2	0.2	0.4	0.4
2. AGGREGATE NET RESOURCE FLOWS AND NET TRANSFERS (LONG-TERM)										
NET RESOURCE FLOWS	..	**19.0**	**24.3**	**34.7**	**42.0**	**33.4**	**58.4**	**32.8**	**19.0**	**40.6**
Net flow of long-term debt (ex. IMF)	..	17.9	7.0	15.6	19.3	9.0	27.6	15.1	-1.8	16.4
Foreign direct investment (net)	..	0.0	6.0	7.0	7.0	9.0	7.0	8.0	8.0	11.0
Portfolio equity flows	..	0.0	0.0	0.0	0.0	0.0	0.0	0.0	0.0	0.0
Grants (excluding technical coop.)	..	1.1	11.3	12.1	15.7	15.4	23.7	9.7	12.9	13.2
Memo: technical coop. grants	..	2.8	6.3	9.3	9.4	8.1	10.1	8.7	8.0	7.0
official net resource flows	..	19.0	17.2	24.7	33.1	24.8	49.8	23.0	6.3	22.6
private net resource flows	..	0.0	7.1	10.0	8.9	8.6	8.6	9.8	12.7	18.0
NET TRANSFERS	..	**17.2**	**9.1**	**16.4**	**22.0**	**11.4**	**36.9**	**13.1**	**-2.0**	**17.5**
Interest on long-term debt	..	0.3	1.3	1.5	2.4	3.0	3.6	3.7	4.0	3.1
Profit remittances on FDI	..	1.5	13.9	16.8	17.6	19.0	18.0	16.0	17.0	20.0
Memo: official net transfers	..	18.7	16.4	23.6	31.3	22.5	47.1	20.1	3.3	20.6
private net transfers	..	-1.5	-7.3	-7.2	-9.3	-11.1	-10.2	-7.0	-5.3	-3.1
3. MAJOR ECONOMIC AGGREGATES										
Gross national product (GNP)	..	..	124.7	155.9	171.7	198.4	224.6	254.4	287.0	309.8
Exports of goods & services (XGS)	..	65.2	183.8	222.3	216.4	276.6	322.4	374.8	410.2	435.0
of which workers remittances	..	0.0	0.0	0.0	0.0	0.0	0.0	0.0	0.0	0.0
Imports of goods & services (MGS)	..	89.8	177.7	237.3	257.0	281.9	336.9	381.2	436.0	446.5
International reserves (RES)	..	0.9	24.5	28.4	26.4	36.9	53.6	76.8	98.8	119.1
Current account balance	..	-22.2	9.9	-19.6	-53.9	-11.2	-18.1	-7.5	-36.5	-23.2
4. DEBT INDICATORS										
EDT / XGS (%)	..	39.6	42.4	42.7	51.9	44.7	48.1	44.7	39.2	41.4
EDT / GNP (%)	..	..	62.6	60.9	65.4	62.3	69.0	65.9	56.0	58.1
TDS / XGS (%)	..	0.8	4.8	3.2	3.9	3.4	3.4	3.1	6.9	3.1
INT / XGS (%)	..	0.8	1.5	0.9	1.3	1.1	1.2	1.0	1.1	0.8
INT / GNP (%)	..	..	2.3	1.2	1.6	1.6	1.7	1.5	1.5	1.2
RES / EDT (%)	..	3.7	31.4	29.9	23.5	29.8	34.6	45.8	61.5	66.2
RES / MGS (months)	..	0.1	1.7	1.4	1.2	1.6	1.9	2.4	2.7	3.2
Short-term / EDT (%)	..	3.9	18.0	4.6	2.7	0.8	1.9	2.8	4.4	5.7
Concessional / EDT (%)	..	96.1	70.9	86.2	75.6	79.6	81.6	81.3	84.4	79.6
Multilateral / EDT (%)	..	13.6	41.7	58.6	53.8	58.8	58.8	58.2	62.6	62.9

MALDIVES

(US$ million, unless otherwise indicated)

	1970	1980	1990	1992	1993	1994	1995	1996	1997	1998
5. LONG-TERM DEBT										
DEBT OUTSTANDING (LDOD)	..	**24.8**	**64.0**	**90.5**	**109.3**	**122.5**	**151.9**	**163.0**	**153.6**	**169.7**
Public and publicly guaranteed	..	**24.8**	**64.0**	**90.5**	**109.3**	**122.5**	**151.9**	**163.0**	**153.6**	**169.7**
Official creditors	..	24.8	60.2	84.8	102.1	115.1	142.6	152.0	138.5	147.3
Multilateral	..	3.5	32.5	55.6	60.4	72.6	91.1	97.6	100.5	113.2
Concessional	..	3.5	32.5	55.6	60.4	72.6	91.1	97.3	99.1	110.3
Bilateral	..	21.3	27.6	29.3	41.7	42.5	51.5	54.3	37.9	34.1
Concessional	..	21.3	22.8	26.2	24.5	25.7	35.3	39.0	36.4	32.9
Private creditors	..	0.0	3.8	5.7	7.2	7.4	9.4	11.0	15.1	22.4
Bonds	..	0.0	0.0	0.0	0.0	0.0	0.0	0.0	0.0	0.0
Commercial banks	..	0.0	0.0	1.1	1.0	1.6	3.4	6.5	10.3	13.3
Other private	..	0.0	3.8	4.6	6.2	5.8	5.9	4.5	4.8	9.1
Private nonguaranteed	..	**0.0**	**0.0**	**0.0**	**0.0**	**0.0**	**0.0**	**0.0**	**0.0**	**0.0**
Bonds	..	0.0	0.0	0.0	0.0	0.0	0.0	0.0	0.0	0.0
Commercial banks	..	0.0	0.0	0.0	0.0	0.0	0.0	0.0	0.0	0.0
Memo:										
IBRD	0.0	0.0	0.0	0.0	0.0	0.0	0.0	0.0	0.0	0.0
IDA	0.0	1.6	10.0	21.8	24.9	31.6	36.1	37.3	39.0	44.1
DISBURSEMENTS	..	**17.9**	**13.0**	**20.8**	**25.0**	**15.4**	**34.7**	**22.9**	**21.9**	**26.5**
Public and publicly guaranteed	..	**17.9**	**13.0**	**20.8**	**25.0**	**15.4**	**34.7**	**22.9**	**21.9**	**26.5**
Official creditors	..	17.9	9.6	17.3	21.9	14.0	30.9	18.5	14.4	15.3
Multilateral	..	2.6	3.6	13.8	6.2	9.9	18.7	11.8	11.0	15.1
Concessional	..	2.6	3.6	13.8	6.2	9.9	18.7	11.5	9.9	13.7
Bilateral	..	15.3	5.9	3.5	15.7	4.1	12.2	6.7	3.3	0.2
Concessional	..	15.3	1.1	3.5	0.7	4.1	12.2	6.7	1.8	0.2
Private creditors	..	0.0	3.5	3.6	3.1	1.4	3.8	4.5	7.6	11.1
Bonds	..	0.0	0.0	0.0	0.0	0.0	0.0	0.0	0.0	0.0
Commercial banks	..	0.0	0.0	1.1	0.1	1.0	2.4	3.9	5.3	6.0
Other private	..	0.0	3.5	2.5	3.0	0.4	1.4	0.5	2.2	5.2
Private nonguaranteed	..	**0.0**	**0.0**	**0.0**	**0.0**	**0.0**	**0.0**	**0.0**	**0.0**	**0.0**
Bonds	..	0.0	0.0	0.0	0.0	0.0	0.0	0.0	0.0	0.0
Commercial banks	..	0.0	0.0	0.0	0.0	0.0	0.0	0.0	0.0	0.0
Memo:										
IBRD	0.0	0.0	0.0	0.0	0.0	0.0	0.0	0.0	0.0	0.0
IDA	0.0	1.6	1.2	8.1	3.0	5.6	3.9	2.5	3.8	3.7
PRINCIPAL REPAYMENTS	..	**0.0**	**6.0**	**5.2**	**5.7**	**6.4**	**7.1**	**7.9**	**23.8**	**10.0**
Public and publicly guaranteed	..	**0.0**	**6.0**	**5.2**	**5.7**	**6.4**	**7.1**	**7.9**	**23.8**	**10.0**
Official creditors	..	0.0	3.7	4.6	4.5	4.6	4.8	5.2	20.9	5.9
Multilateral	..	0.0	1.5	1.3	1.2	1.3	1.4	1.5	1.5	1.7
Concessional	..	0.0	1.5	1.3	1.2	1.3	1.4	1.5	1.5	1.7
Bilateral	..	0.0	2.2	3.3	3.3	3.3	3.4	3.7	19.4	4.1
Concessional	..	0.0	1.9	2.6	2.6	2.6	2.7	2.9	4.1	3.8
Private creditors	..	0.0	2.3	0.6	1.2	1.8	2.3	2.7	2.9	4.2
Bonds	..	0.0	0.0	0.0	0.0	0.0	0.0	0.0	0.0	0.0
Commercial banks	..	0.0	1.5	0.0	0.3	0.4	0.6	0.9	1.3	2.9
Other private	..	0.0	0.9	0.6	1.0	1.4	1.7	1.7	1.5	1.3
Private nonguaranteed	..	**0.0**	**0.0**	**0.0**	**0.0**	**0.0**	**0.0**	**0.0**	**0.0**	**0.0**
Bonds	..	0.0	0.0	0.0	0.0	0.0	0.0	0.0	0.0	0.0
Commercial banks	..	0.0	0.0	0.0	0.0	0.0	0.0	0.0	0.0	0.0
Memo:										
IBRD	0.0	0.0	0.0	0.0	0.0	0.0	0.0	0.0	0.0	0.0
IDA	0.0	0.0	0.0	0.0	0.1	0.1	0.1	0.1	0.1	0.1
NET FLOWS ON DEBT	..	**17.9**	**7.0**	**15.6**	**19.3**	**9.0**	**27.6**	**15.1**	**-1.8**	**16.4**
Public and publicly guaranteed	..	**17.9**	**7.0**	**15.6**	**19.3**	**9.0**	**27.6**	**15.1**	**-1.8**	**16.4**
Official creditors	..	17.9	5.9	12.6	17.4	9.4	26.1	13.3	-6.6	9.4
Multilateral	..	2.6	2.2	12.5	5.0	8.6	17.3	10.3	9.5	13.4
Concessional	..	2.6	2.2	12.5	5.0	8.6	17.3	10.0	8.4	12.0
Bilateral	..	15.3	3.7	0.2	12.4	0.8	8.7	3.0	-16.0	-4.0
Concessional	..	15.3	-0.8	0.9	-1.9	1.5	9.5	3.7	-2.3	-3.7
Private creditors	..	0.0	1.1	3.0	1.9	-0.4	1.6	1.8	4.7	7.0
Bonds	..	0.0	0.0	0.0	0.0	0.0	0.0	0.0	0.0	0.0
Commercial banks	..	0.0	-1.5	1.1	-0.2	0.6	1.8	3.0	4.0	3.1
Other private	..	0.0	2.6	1.9	2.0	-1.1	-0.3	-1.2	0.7	3.9
Private nonguaranteed	..	**0.0**	**0.0**	**0.0**	**0.0**	**0.0**	**0.0**	**0.0**	**0.0**	**0.0**
Bonds	..	0.0	0.0	0.0	0.0	0.0	0.0	0.0	0.0	0.0
Commercial banks	..	0.0	0.0	0.0	0.0	0.0	0.0	0.0	0.0	0.0
Memo:										
IBRD	0.0	0.0	0.0	0.0	0.0	0.0	0.0	0.0	0.0	0.0
IDA	0.0	1.6	1.2	8.1	3.0	5.5	3.8	2.4	3.7	3.6

MALDIVES

(US$ million, unless otherwise indicated)

	1970	1980	1990	1992	1993	1994	1995	1996	1997	1998
INTEREST PAYMENTS (LINT)	..	**0.3**	**1.3**	**1.5**	**2.4**	**3.0**	**3.6**	**3.7**	**4.0**	**3.1**
Public and publicly guaranteed	..	**0.3**	**1.3**	**1.5**	**2.4**	**3.0**	**3.6**	**3.7**	**4.0**	**3.1**
Official creditors	..	0.3	0.8	1.1	1.8	2.3	2.7	2.9	3.0	2.0
Multilateral	..	0.0	0.3	0.4	0.8	0.9	1.0	1.2	1.3	1.3
Concessional	..	0.0	0.3	0.4	0.8	0.9	1.0	1.2	1.2	1.2
Bilateral	..	0.3	0.5	0.7	1.0	1.3	1.7	1.7	1.8	0.7
Concessional	..	0.3	0.3	0.4	0.4	0.4	0.4	0.6	0.6	0.6
Private creditors	..	0.0	0.5	0.4	0.6	0.7	0.8	0.8	1.0	1.1
Bonds	..	0.0	0.0	0.0	0.0	0.0	0.0	0.0	0.0	0.0
Commercial banks	..	0.0	0.1	0.0	0.0	0.1	0.2	0.3	0.7	0.8
Other private	..	0.0	0.4	0.4	0.5	0.6	0.6	0.4	0.3	0.3
Private nonguaranteed	..	**0.0**	**0.0**	**0.0**	**0.0**	**0.0**	**0.0**	**0.0**	**0.0**	**0.0**
Bonds	..	0.0	0.0	0.0	0.0	0.0	0.0	0.0	0.0	0.0
Commercial banks	..	0.0	0.0	0.0	0.0	0.0	0.0	0.0	0.0	0.0
Memo:										
IBRD	0.0	0.0	0.0	0.0	0.0	0.0	0.0	0.0	0.0	0.0
IDA	0.0	0.0	0.1	0.1	0.2	0.2	0.3	0.3	0.3	0.3
NET TRANSFERS ON DEBT	..	**17.6**	**5.7**	**14.1**	**16.9**	**6.0**	**24.0**	**11.4**	**-5.8**	**13.3**
Public and publicly guaranteed	..	**17.6**	**5.7**	**14.1**	**16.9**	**6.0**	**24.0**	**11.4**	**-5.8**	**13.3**
Official creditors	..	17.6	5.0	11.5	15.6	7.2	23.3	10.4	-9.6	7.4
Multilateral	..	2.6	1.8	12.1	4.2	7.7	16.3	9.1	8.2	12.1
Concessional	..	2.6	1.8	12.1	4.2	7.7	16.3	8.8	7.2	10.7
Bilateral	..	15.0	3.2	-0.5	11.4	-0.5	7.0	1.3	-17.8	-4.7
Concessional	..	15.0	-1.1	0.5	-2.3	1.1	9.1	3.1	-2.9	-4.3
Private creditors	..	0.0	0.6	2.6	1.3	-1.1	0.7	1.0	3.8	5.9
Bonds	..	0.0	0.0	0.0	0.0	0.0	0.0	0.0	0.0	0.0
Commercial banks	..	0.0	-1.6	1.1	-0.2	0.6	1.6	2.7	3.3	2.3
Other private	..	0.0	2.2	1.5	1.5	-1.7	-0.9	-1.6	0.4	3.6
Private nonguaranteed	..	**0.0**	**0.0**	**0.0**	**0.0**	**0.0**	**0.0**	**0.0**	**0.0**	**0.0**
Bonds	..	0.0	0.0	0.0	0.0	0.0	0.0	0.0	0.0	0.0
Commercial banks	..	0.0	0.0	0.0	0.0	0.0	0.0	0.0	0.0	0.0
Memo:										
IBRD	0.0	0.0	0.0	0.0	0.0	0.0	0.0	0.0	0.0	0.0
IDA	0.0	1.6	1.1	8.0	2.8	5.3	3.5	2.1	3.4	3.3
DEBT SERVICE (LTDS)	..	**0.3**	**7.3**	**6.8**	**8.1**	**9.3**	**10.7**	**11.5**	**27.8**	**13.2**
Public and publicly guaranteed	..	**0.3**	**7.3**	**6.8**	**8.1**	**9.3**	**10.7**	**11.5**	**27.8**	**13.2**
Official creditors	..	0.3	4.5	5.8	6.3	6.8	7.6	8.1	23.9	7.9
Multilateral	..	0.0	1.8	1.7	2.0	2.2	2.4	2.7	2.8	3.0
Concessional	..	0.0	1.8	1.7	2.0	2.2	2.4	2.7	2.7	2.9
Bilateral	..	0.3	2.7	4.0	4.3	4.6	5.1	5.4	21.1	4.9
Concessional	..	0.3	2.2	3.0	3.0	3.0	3.1	3.5	4.7	4.5
Private creditors	..	0.0	2.8	1.0	1.8	2.5	3.1	3.4	3.8	5.3
Bonds	..	0.0	0.0	0.0	0.0	0.0	0.0	0.0	0.0	0.0
Commercial banks	..	0.0	1.6	0.0	0.3	0.5	0.8	1.3	2.0	3.7
Other private	..	0.0	1.2	1.0	1.5	2.1	2.3	2.2	1.8	1.6
Private nonguaranteed	..	**0.0**	**0.0**	**0.0**	**0.0**	**0.0**	**0.0**	**0.0**	**0.0**	**0.0**
Bonds	..	0.0	0.0	0.0	0.0	0.0	0.0	0.0	0.0	0.0
Commercial banks	..	0.0	0.0	0.0	0.0	0.0	0.0	0.0	0.0	0.0
Memo:										
IBRD	0.0	0.0	0.0	0.0	0.0	0.0	0.0	0.0	0.0	0.0
IDA	0.0	0.0	0.1	0.1	0.2	0.3	0.4	0.4	0.4	0.4
UNDISBURSED DEBT	..	**21.0**	**51.3**	**70.5**	**67.7**	**63.9**	**58.7**	**46.6**	**35.1**	**50.3**
Official creditors	..	19.1	49.6	67.3	67.7	59.5	54.5	38.4	28.8	39.3
Private creditors	..	1.9	1.7	3.2	0.0	4.3	4.2	8.2	6.3	11.0
Memorandum items										
Concessional LDOD	..	24.8	55.4	81.8	84.9	98.3	126.4	136.3	135.5	143.2
Variable rate LDOD	..	0.0	0.0	1.1	16.0	16.1	16.4	16.8	6.2	8.4
Public sector LDOD	..	24.8	64.0	90.5	109.3	122.5	151.9	163.0	153.6	169.7
Private sector LDOD	..	0.0	0.0	0.0	0.0	0.0	0.0	0.0	0.0	0.0
6. CURRENCY COMPOSITION OF LONG-TERM DEBT (PERCENT)										
Deutsche mark	..	0.0	13.0	6.0	5.5	4.1	2.3	0.9	0.1	0.0
French franc	..	0.0	0.0	0.0	0.0	0.0	0.0	0.0	0.0	0.0
Japanese yen	..	0.0	0.0	0.0	0.0	0.0	0.0	0.0	0.0	0.0
Pound sterling	..	0.0	0.3	0.0	0.0	0.0	0.0	0.9	0.7	0.5
Swiss franc	..	0.0	0.0	0.0	0.0	0.0	0.0	0.0	0.0	0.0
U.S.dollars	..	14.1	25.5	35.0	46.2	49.8	51.3	49.6	46.5	48.3
Multiple currency	..	0.0	12.4	20.3	18.8	19.3	20.3	21.3	23.2	22.4
Special drawing rights	..	0.0	0.0	0.0	0.0	0.0	0.7	1.7	1.8	1.8
All other currencies	..	85.9	48.8	38.7	29.5	26.8	25.4	25.6	27.7	27.0

MALDIVES

(US$ million, unless otherwise indicated)

	1970	1980	1990	1992	1993	1994	1995	1996	1997	1998
7. DEBT RESTRUCTURINGS										
Total amount rescheduled	..	..	0.0	0.0	0.0	0.0	0.0	0.0	0.0	0.0
Debt stock rescheduled	..	..	0.0	0.0	0.0	0.0	0.0	0.0	0.0	0.0
Principal rescheduled	..	..	0.0	0.0	0.0	0.0	0.0	0.0	0.0	0.0
Official	..	..	0.0	0.0	0.0	0.0	0.0	0.0	0.0	0.0
Private	..	..	0.0	0.0	0.0	0.0	0.0	0.0	0.0	0.0
Interest rescheduled	..	..	0.0	0.0	0.0	0.0	0.0	0.0	0.0	0.0
Official	..	..	0.0	0.0	0.0	0.0	0.0	0.0	0.0	0.0
Private	..	..	0.0	0.0	0.0	0.0	0.0	0.0	0.0	0.0
Debt forgiven	..	..	0.0	0.0	0.0	0.0	0.0	0.0	0.0	0.0
Memo: interest forgiven	..	..	0.0	0.0	0.0	0.0	0.0	0.0	0.0	0.0
Debt stock reduction	..	..	0.0	0.0	0.0	0.0	0.0	0.0	0.0	0.0
of which debt buyback	..	..	0.0	0.0	0.0	0.0	0.0	0.0	0.0	0.0
8. DEBT STOCK-FLOW RECONCILIATION										
Total change in debt stocks	..	..	11.2	13.7	17.5	11.2	31.3	12.8	-7.1	19.3
Net flows on debt	..	12.9	8.6	16.8	17.9	7.0	29.5	16.8	0.5	19.6
Net change in interest arrears	..	..	0.0	0.0	0.0	0.0	0.0	0.0	0.0	0.0
Interest capitalized	..	..	0.0	0.0	0.0	0.0	0.0	0.0	0.0	0.0
Debt forgiveness or reduction	..	..	0.0	0.0	0.0	0.0	0.0	0.0	0.0	0.0
Cross-currency valuation	..	..	2.1	-1.8	-0.3	1.1	0.7	-0.5	-1.7	1.1
Residual	..	..	0.5	-1.3	-0.1	3.1	1.1	-3.5	-5.9	-1.4
9. AVERAGE TERMS OF NEW COMMITMENTS										
ALL CREDITORS										
Interest (%)	..	2.9	0.8	1.5	3.4	4.8	3.1	6.7	3.5	4.1
Maturity (years)	..	14.7	37.3	27.3	17.7	14.0	31.3	9.8	8.7	17.2
Grace period (years)	..	4.4	9.2	7.1	6.8	3.7	9.1	2.8	2.8	3.9
Grant element (%)	..	41.2	77.2	63.6	41.2	30.9	56.2	17.3	28.8	33.4
Official creditors										
Interest (%)	..	2.5	0.8	1.3	3.4	2.1	2.5	2.4	2.3	2.3
Maturity (years)	..	15.5	37.3	28.1	17.7	19.8	34.8	16.5	8.5	27.9
Grace period (years)	..	4.7	9.2	7.4	6.8	5.6	10.1	5.0	2.9	6.6
Grant element (%)	..	44.2	77.2	65.7	41.2	52.8	63.3	46.6	33.3	55.4
Private creditors										
Interest (%)	..	7.5	0.0	6.3	0.0	7.5	7.9	8.6	4.9	6.2
Maturity (years)	..	6.6	0.0	5.4	0.0	8.1	6.0	6.7	9.0	5.7
Grace period (years)	..	1.1	0.0	0.8	0.0	1.7	1.7	1.8	2.7	0.9
Grant element (%)	..	6.9	0.0	8.2	0.0	8.6	6.3	3.6	23.9	9.5
Memorandum items										
Commitments	..	22.1	15.5	57.4	23.8	11.6	29.1	12.5	12.2	33.2
Official creditors	..	20.3	15.5	55.3	23.8	5.8	25.5	4.0	6.4	17.3
Private creditors	..	1.8	0.0	2.1	0.0	5.7	3.6	8.5	5.9	15.9

10. CONTRACTUAL OBLIGATIONS ON OUTSTANDING LONG-TERM DEBT

	1999	2000	2001	2002	2003	2004	2005	2006	2007	2008
TOTAL										
Disbursements	17.9	14.1	7.7	5.0	2.6	1.5	0.9	0.5	0.1	0.0
Principal	12.3	13.3	13.2	12.8	10.5	9.6	9.1	8.4	7.6	7.3
Interest	4.1	3.9	3.5	3.0	2.6	2.3	2.1	1.9	1.8	1.8
Official creditors										
Disbursements	11.8	10.8	6.5	4.6	2.6	1.5	0.9	0.5	0.1	0.0
Principal	5.8	6.3	6.4	7.1	7.4	7.6	7.9	8.2	7.3	7.1
Interest	2.5	2.5	2.4	2.3	2.2	2.1	2.0	1.9	1.8	1.8
Bilateral creditors										
Disbursements	1.8	3.1	2.2	1.5	0.9	0.5	0.3	0.2	0.0	0.0
Principal	3.6	3.4	2.9	3.0	3.1	3.1	3.1	3.2	2.9	2.2
Interest	0.7	0.6	0.6	0.6	0.5	0.5	0.4	0.4	0.4	0.3
Multilateral creditors										
Disbursements	10.0	7.7	4.3	3.0	1.7	1.0	0.6	0.3	0.1	0.0
Principal	2.2	2.9	3.5	4.1	4.3	4.5	4.8	5.1	4.4	4.8
Interest	1.8	1.8	1.8	1.8	1.7	1.6	1.6	1.5	1.5	1.4
Private creditors										
Disbursements	6.0	3.3	1.2	0.5	0.0	0.0	0.0	0.0	0.0	0.0
Principal	6.4	7.0	6.8	5.7	3.1	2.0	1.2	0.2	0.2	0.2
Interest	1.6	1.5	1.1	0.7	0.3	0.1	0.0	0.0	0.0	0.0
Commercial banks										
Disbursements	5.8	3.3	1.2	0.5	0.0	0.0	0.0	0.0	0.0	0.0
Principal	4.7	5.5	5.3	4.4	1.8	0.7	0.4	0.2	0.2	0.2
Interest	1.1	1.0	0.7	0.4	0.1	0.0	0.0	0.0	0.0	0.0
Other private										
Disbursements	0.2	0.0	0.0	0.0	0.0	0.0	0.0	0.0	0.0	0.0
Principal	1.7	1.5	1.5	1.3	1.3	1.3	0.8	0.0	0.0	0.0
Interest	0.5	0.4	0.3	0.3	0.2	0.1	0.0	0.0	0.0	0.0

MALI

(US$ million, unless otherwise indicated)

	1970	1980	1990	1992	1993	1994	1995	1996	1997	1998
1. SUMMARY DEBT DATA										
TOTAL DEBT STOCKS (EDT)	..	727	2,467	2,898	2,902	2,694	2,957	3,006	3,142	3,202
Long-term debt (LDOD)	238	664	2,336	2,777	2,785	2,545	2,739	2,762	2,692	2,827
Public and publicly guaranteed	238	664	2,336	2,777	2,785	2,545	2,739	2,762	2,692	2,827
Private nonguaranteed	0	0	0	0	0	0	0	0	0	0
Use of IMF credit	9	39	69	65	71	108	147	165	176	187
Short-term debt	..	24	62	55	46	41	72	79	275	188
of which interest arrears on LDOD	..	1	9	26	18	21	28	33	43	44
Official creditors	..	1	9	26	17	21	28	33	43	44
Private creditors	..	0	0	0	0	0	0	0	0	0
Memo: principal arrears on LDOD	..	75	63	266	209	273	342	415	632	664
Official creditors	..	73	63	266	207	271	340	415	632	664
Private creditors	..	2	0	0	2	2	2	0	0	0
Memo: export credits	..	0	86	85	77	44	68	64	87	79
TOTAL DEBT FLOWS										
Disbursements	24	108	194	176	98	164	238	186	147	108
Long-term debt	23	94	167	162	84	122	193	156	118	94
IMF purchases	2	14	28	14	14	42	45	30	28	14
Principal repayments	4	9	44	38	35	63	62	54	49	55
Long-term debt	0	6	25	32	26	53	55	47	42	44
IMF repurchases	4	3	18	7	9	10	7	7	7	11
Net flows on debt	20	98	158	118	83	92	200	135	283	-36
of which short-term debt	..	-1	8	-20	19	-9	24	3	186	-89
Interest payments (INT)	..	7	23	20	43	25	24	62	36	27
Long-term debt	0	3	17	15	40	24	22	58	20	18
IMF charges	0	1	4	2	1	1	1	1	1	1
Short-term debt	..	3	3	2	2	1	2	2	15	8
Net transfers on debt	..	90	135	98	39	67	176	73	247	-62
Total debt service paid (TDS)	..	16	67	58	78	88	86	116	85	82
Long-term debt	1	9	42	47	66	77	77	105	62	62
IMF repurchases and charges	4	4	22	8	10	10	7	9	8	12
Short-term debt (interest only)	..	3	3	2	2	1	2	2	15	8
2. AGGREGATE NET RESOURCE FLOWS AND NET TRANSFERS (LONG-TERM)										
NET RESOURCE FLOWS	34	194	335	325	213	334	358	402	326	268
Net flow of long-term debt (ex. IMF)	23	88	141	130	58	69	138	110	76	50
Foreign direct investment (net)	0	2	-7	-8	-20	45	12	84	39	17
Portfolio equity flows	0	0	0	0	0	0	0	0	0	0
Grants (excluding technical coop.)	12	104	201	203	175	221	208	209	211	201
Memo: technical coop. grants	8	77	99	127	130	112	132	121	125	108
official net resource flows	34	183	343	336	234	290	346	318	287	251
private net resource flows	0	10	-8	-11	-21	44	12	84	39	17
NET TRANSFERS	32	190	294	296	160	297	322	331	293	237
Interest on long-term debt	0	3	17	15	40	24	22	58	20	18
Profit remittances on FDI	2	0	24	14	13	14	15	13	12	13
Memo: official net transfers	34	181	327	320	194	267	325	260	266	233
private net transfers	-2	9	-33	-25	-34	30	-3	71	27	4
3. MAJOR ECONOMIC AGGREGATES										
Gross national product (GNP)	352	1,768	2,405	2,839	2,674	1,736	2,414	2,605	2,458	2,660
Exports of goods & services (XGS)	..	322	549	587	603	516	650	639	745	651
of which workers remittances	..	59	107	117	126	103	112	107	91	..
Imports of goods & services (MGS)	..	537	889	1,011	896	816	1,040	1,001	959	972
International reserves (RES)	1	26	198	314	340	229	330	438	420	403
Current account balance	..	-124	-221	-241	-189	-163	-284	-273	-178	..
4. DEBT INDICATORS										
EDT / XGS (%)	..	225.8	449.1	493.9	481.6	521.7	455.1	470.3	421.9	492.1
EDT / GNP (%)	..	41.1	102.6	102.1	108.5	155.2	122.5	115.4	127.8	120.4
TDS / XGS (%)	..	5.1	12.2	9.8	12.9	17.0	13.3	18.1	11.4	12.6
INT / XGS (%)	..	2.3	4.2	3.4	7.2	4.8	3.7	9.6	4.8	4.1
INT / GNP (%)	..	0.4	1.0	0.7	1.6	1.4	1.0	2.4	1.5	1.0
RES / EDT (%)	..	3.5	8.0	10.8	11.7	8.5	11.2	14.6	13.4	12.6
RES / MGS (months)	..	0.6	2.7	3.7	4.6	3.4	3.8	5.3	5.3	5.0
Short-term / EDT (%)	..	3.3	2.5	1.9	1.6	1.5	2.4	2.6	8.7	5.9
Concessional / EDT (%)	..	84.4	91.1	92.8	92.8	91.5	89.9	89.4	83.6	86.3
Multilateral / EDT (%)	..	23.6	36.3	36.6	38.0	46.4	47.2	48.5	46.3	49.1

MALI

(US$ million, unless otherwise indicated)

	1970	1980	1990	1992	1993	1994	1995	1996	1997	1998
5. LONG-TERM DEBT										
DEBT OUTSTANDING (LDOD)	**238**	**664**	**2,336**	**2,777**	**2,785**	**2,545**	**2,739**	**2,762**	**2,692**	**2,827**
Public and publicly guaranteed	**238**	**664**	**2,336**	**2,777**	**2,785**	**2,545**	**2,739**	**2,762**	**2,692**	**2,827**
Official creditors	232	629	2,320	2,771	2,781	2,543	2,736	2,762	2,692	2,827
Multilateral	6	172	896	1,059	1,103	1,250	1,396	1,459	1,453	1,573
Concessional	6	163	874	1,022	1,066	1,214	1,357	1,423	1,424	1,545
Bilateral	226	457	1,424	1,712	1,678	1,293	1,340	1,303	1,239	1,254
Concessional	226	451	1,373	1,668	1,626	1,250	1,303	1,265	1,202	1,218
Private creditors	6	36	16	6	4	2	2	0	0	0
Bonds	0	0	0	0	0	0	0	0	0	0
Commercial banks	1	11	0	3	3	2	2	0	0	0
Other private	5	25	16	3	1	0	0	0	0	0
Private nonguaranteed	**0**	**0**	**0**	**0**	**0**	**0**	**0**	**0**	**0**	**0**
Bonds	0	0	0	0	0	0	0	0	0	0
Commercial banks	0	0	0	0	0	0	0	0	0	0
Memo:										
IBRD	0	0	0	0	0	0	0	0	0	0
IDA	6	121	498	611	656	770	863	915	939	1,009
DISBURSEMENTS	**23**	**94**	**167**	**162**	**84**	**122**	**193**	**156**	**118**	**94**
Public and publicly guaranteed	**23**	**94**	**167**	**162**	**84**	**122**	**193**	**156**	**118**	**94**
Official creditors	23	83	167	162	84	122	193	156	118	94
Multilateral	1	34	115	86	63	119	146	122	115	88
Concessional	1	30	111	86	62	118	141	119	115	88
Bilateral	22	50	52	76	21	2	47	35	3	6
Concessional	22	45	52	76	17	2	47	35	3	6
Private creditors	0	10	0	0	0	0	0	0	0	0
Bonds	0	0	0	0	0	0	0	0	0	0
Commercial banks	0	5	0	0	0	0	0	0	0	0
Other private	0	5	0	0	0	0	0	0	0	0
Private nonguaranteed	**0**	**0**	**0**	**0**	**0**	**0**	**0**	**0**	**0**	**0**
Bonds	0	0	0	0	0	0	0	0	0	0
Commercial banks	0	0	0	0	0	0	0	0	0	0
Memo:										
IBRD	0	0	0	0	0	0	0	0	0	0
IDA	1	19	44	62	47	93	86	84	75	48
PRINCIPAL REPAYMENTS	**0**	**6**	**25**	**32**	**26**	**53**	**55**	**47**	**42**	**44**
Public and publicly guaranteed	**0**	**6**	**25**	**32**	**26**	**53**	**55**	**47**	**42**	**44**
Official creditors	0	4	24	29	25	52	55	47	42	44
Multilateral	0	0	14	17	16	26	23	27	27	29
Concessional	0	0	13	13	15	21	20	23	24	25
Bilateral	0	4	11	12	10	26	32	20	15	15
Concessional	0	3	10	9	8	18	25	19	14	14
Private creditors	0	2	1	3	1	1	0	0	0	0
Bonds	0	0	0	0	0	0	0	0	0	0
Commercial banks	0	1	0	0	1	0	0	0	0	0
Other private	0	1	1	3	0	1	0	0	0	0
Private nonguaranteed	**0**	**0**	**0**	**0**	**0**	**0**	**0**	**0**	**0**	**0**
Bonds	0	0	0	0	0	0	0	0	0	0
Commercial banks	0	0	0	0	0	0	0	0	0	0
Memo:										
IBRD	0	0	0	0	0	0	0	0	0	0
IDA	0	0	2	3	4	6	6	7	7	9
NET FLOWS ON DEBT	**23**	**88**	**141**	**130**	**58**	**69**	**138**	**110**	**76**	**50**
Public and publicly guaranteed	**23**	**88**	**141**	**130**	**58**	**69**	**138**	**110**	**76**	**50**
Official creditors	23	80	142	133	59	69	138	110	76	50
Multilateral	1	33	101	70	47	94	123	94	88	59
Concessional	1	30	98	73	47	97	121	96	90	62
Bilateral	21	46	42	63	12	-24	15	15	-11	-9
Concessional	21	42	42	66	9	-16	22	16	-10	-8
Private creditors	0	8	-1	-3	-1	-1	0	0	0	0
Bonds	0	0	0	0	0	0	0	0	0	0
Commercial banks	0	4	0	0	-1	0	0	0	0	0
Other private	0	4	-1	-3	0	-1	0	0	0	0
Private nonguaranteed	**0**	**0**	**0**	**0**	**0**	**0**	**0**	**0**	**0**	**0**
Bonds	0	0	0	0	0	0	0	0	0	0
Commercial banks	0	0	0	0	0	0	0	0	0	0
Memo:										
IBRD	0	0	0	0	0	0	0	0	0	0
IDA	1	19	42	59	43	87	80	77	68	39

MALI

(US$ million, unless otherwise indicated)

	1970	1980	1990	1992	1993	1994	1995	1996	1997	1998
INTEREST PAYMENTS (LINT)	**0**	**3**	**17**	**15**	**40**	**24**	**22**	**58**	**20**	**18**
Public and publicly guaranteed	**0**	**3**	**17**	**15**	**40**	**24**	**22**	**58**	**20**	**18**
Official creditors	0	2	16	15	40	24	22	58	20	18
Multilateral	0	1	9	9	9	12	11	13	14	12
Concessional	0	1	8	8	8	11	11	12	13	12
Bilateral	0	1	7	6	31	12	10	45	7	6
Concessional	0	1	6	5	30	9	8	44	5	4
Private creditors	0	1	1	0	0	0	0	0	0	0
Bonds	0	0	0	0	0	0	0	0	0	0
Commercial banks	0	1	0	0	0	0	0	0	0	0
Other private	0	0	1	0	0	0	0	0	0	0
Private nonguaranteed	**0**	**0**	**0**	**0**	**0**	**0**	**0**	**0**	**0**	**0**
Bonds	0	0	0	0	0	0	0	0	0	0
Commercial banks	0	0	0	0	0	0	0	0	0	0
Memo:										
IBRD	0	0	0	0	0	0	0	0	0	0
IDA	0	1	3	4	5	6	6	7	7	7
NET TRANSFERS ON DEBT	**22**	**84**	**124**	**115**	**18**	**45**	**117**	**51**	**56**	**32**
Public and publicly guaranteed	**22**	**84**	**124**	**115**	**18**	**45**	**117**	**51**	**56**	**32**
Official creditors	22	77	126	118	19	46	117	51	56	32
Multilateral	1	32	92	61	37	82	112	81	74	47
Concessional	1	29	90	65	39	87	111	84	78	51
Bilateral	21	45	34	57	-19	-36	5	-30	-18	-15
Concessional	21	41	37	61	-21	-25	14	-28	-16	-13
Private creditors	0	7	-2	-3	-1	-1	0	0	0	0
Bonds	0	0	0	0	0	0	0	0	0	0
Commercial banks	0	3	0	0	-1	0	0	0	0	0
Other private	0	4	-2	-3	0	-1	0	0	0	0
Private nonguaranteed	**0**	**0**	**0**	**0**	**0**	**0**	**0**	**0**	**0**	**0**
Bonds	0	0	0	0	0	0	0	0	0	0
Commercial banks	0	0	0	0	0	0	0	0	0	0
Memo:										
IBRD	0	0	0	0	0	0	0	0	0	0
IDA	1	18	38	54	39	82	73	71	61	32
DEBT SERVICE (LTDS)	**1**	**9**	**42**	**47**	**66**	**77**	**77**	**105**	**62**	**62**
Public and publicly guaranteed	**1**	**9**	**42**	**47**	**66**	**77**	**77**	**105**	**62**	**62**
Official creditors	1	6	40	44	65	76	77	105	62	62
Multilateral	0	2	23	26	25	37	35	41	41	41
Concessional	0	1	21	21	23	31	30	35	37	37
Bilateral	1	5	18	19	40	38	42	65	22	21
Concessional	1	4	16	15	38	27	33	63	19	18
Private creditors	0	3	2	3	1	1	0	0	0	0
Bonds	0	0	0	0	0	0	0	0	0	0
Commercial banks	0	2	0	0	1	0	0	0	0	0
Other private	0	1	2	3	0	1	0	0	0	0
Private nonguaranteed	**0**	**0**	**0**	**0**	**0**	**0**	**0**	**0**	**0**	**0**
Bonds	0	0	0	0	0	0	0	0	0	0
Commercial banks	0	0	0	0	0	0	0	0	0	0
Memo:										
IBRD	0	0	0	0	0	0	0	0	0	0
IDA	0	1	5	7	8	12	12	14	14	16
UNDISBURSED DEBT	**54**	**366**	**634**	**689**	**668**	**636**	**619**	**681**	**591**	**570**
Official creditors	50	359	634	689	668	636	619	681	591	570
Private creditors	4	7	0	0	0	0	0	0	0	0
Memorandum items										
Concessional LDOD	232	614	2,247	2,690	2,692	2,464	2,660	2,687	2,626	2,763
Variable rate LDOD	0	0	6	3	3	3	3	2	2	1
Public sector LDOD	238	664	2,330	2,771	2,780	2,545	2,739	2,762	2,692	2,827
Private sector LDOD	0	0	6	6	5	0	0	0	0	0

6. CURRENCY COMPOSITION OF LONG-TERM DEBT (PERCENT)

	1970	1980	1990	1992	1993	1994	1995	1996	1997	1998
Deutsche mark	2.8	0.9	0.2	0.2	0.2	0.2	0.2	0.2	0.1	0.1
French franc	16.9	21.3	36.7	32.3	29.9	22.4	21.8	20.3	18.9	18.5
Japanese yen	0.0	0.0	0.3	1.4	1.5	1.9	2.3	2.9	2.7	2.8
Pound sterling	37.5	11.5	2.7	1.8	1.8	2.0	1.8	1.9	1.9	1.8
Swiss franc	5.9	5.6	2.3	1.7	1.7	2.0	2.1	1.8	1.7	1.7
U.S.dollars	4.9	11.6	14.9	17.5	19.5	21.2	22.5	23.9	25.9	26.9
Multiple currency	0.3	6.4	15.3	14.1	14.6	17.6	18.7	19.1	18.5	19.1
Special drawing rights	0.0	0.0	0.0	0.0	0.0	0.0	0.0	0.0	0.0	0.0
All other currencies	31.7	42.7	27.6	31.0	30.8	32.7	30.6	29.9	30.3	29.1

MALI

(US$ million, unless otherwise indicated)

	1970	1980	1990	1992	1993	1994	1995	1996	1997	1998
7. DEBT RESTRUCTURINGS										
Total amount rescheduled	..	..	11	28	29	0	0	14	0	1
Debt stock rescheduled	..	..	0	0	0	0	0	0	0	0
Principal rescheduled	..	..	7	21	26	0	0	14	0	1
Official	..	..	4	15	4	0	0	13	0	1
Private	..	..	3	6	22	0	0	1	0	0
Interest rescheduled	..	..	5	7	3	0	0	0	0	0
Official	..	..	4	6	2	0	0	0	0	0
Private	..	..	1	1	1	0	0	0	0	0
Debt forgiven	..	..	2	16	3	413	0	16	0	5
Memo: interest forgiven	..	..	2	6	1	9	0	2	0	0
Debt stock reduction	..	..	0	0	0	0	0	0	0	0
of which debt buyback	..	..	0	0	0	0	0	0	0	0
8. DEBT STOCK-FLOW RECONCILIATION										
Total change in debt stocks	..	..	340	302	4	-208	264	49	136	59
Net flows on debt	20	98	158	118	83	92	200	135	283	-36
Net change in interest arrears	..	..	8	1	-8	3	7	5	10	2
Interest capitalized	..	..	5	7	3	0	0	0	0	0
Debt forgiveness or reduction	..	..	-2	-16	-3	-413	0	-16	0	-5
Cross-currency valuation	..	..	175	-75	-54	72	65	-51	-84	52
Residual	..	..	-4	267	-16	37	-8	-25	-73	46
9. AVERAGE TERMS OF NEW COMMITMENTS										
ALL CREDITORS										
Interest (%)	1.1	2.2	1.0	2.3	1.4	0.8	1.5	1.3	0.9	1.7
Maturity (years)	25.0	23.0	29.9	29.6	33.4	37.2	30.7	35.9	45.4	28.0
Grace period (years)	9.5	5.5	8.4	8.3	8.1	9.7	8.8	9.3	10.2	7.4
Grant element (%)	68.2	50.5	67.6	59.8	64.8	77.7	68.6	73.3	80.2	63.0
Official creditors										
Interest (%)	0.3	1.8	1.0	2.3	1.4	0.8	1.5	1.3	0.9	1.7
Maturity (years)	27.4	23.9	29.9	29.6	33.4	37.2	30.7	35.9	45.4	28.0
Grace period (years)	10.6	5.6	8.4	8.3	8.1	9.7	8.8	9.3	10.2	7.4
Grant element (%)	76.4	53.2	67.6	59.8	64.8	77.7	68.6	73.3	80.2	63.0
Private creditors										
Interest (%)	6.7	9.9	0.0	0.0	0.0	0.0	0.0	0.0	0.0	0.0
Maturity (years)	8.5	6.3	0.0	0.0	0.0	0.0	0.0	0.0	0.0	0.0
Grace period (years)	1.6	2.2	0.0	0.0	0.0	0.0	0.0	0.0	0.0	0.0
Grant element (%)	11.5	-0.4	0.0	0.0	0.0	0.0	0.0	0.0	0.0	0.0
Memorandum items										
Commitments	34	146	124	153	98	135	163	238	123	55
Official creditors	30	139	124	153	98	135	163	238	123	55
Private creditors	4	7	0	0	0	0	0	0	0	0

10. CONTRACTUAL OBLIGATIONS ON OUTSTANDING LONG-TERM DEBT

	1999	2000	2001	2002	2003	2004	2005	2006	2007	2008
TOTAL										
Disbursements	166	153	108	69	38	18	12	4	2	0
Principal	90	81	85	80	80	80	84	88	91	92
Interest	23	24	24	23	23	22	21	20	19	18
Official creditors										
Disbursements	166	153	108	69	38	18	12	4	2	0
Principal	90	81	85	80	80	80	84	88	91	92
Interest	23	24	24	23	23	22	21	20	19	18
Bilateral creditors										
Disbursements	17	12	7	4	2	1	1	0	0	0
Principal	53	44	44	35	33	30	30	30	30	29
Interest	7	7	6	5	5	5	4	4	4	3
Multilateral creditors										
Disbursements	149	142	101	65	36	17	11	4	2	0
Principal	36	37	41	45	48	50	54	58	62	63
Interest	16	17	18	18	18	17	17	16	15	14
Private creditors										
Disbursements	0	0	0	0	0	0	0	0	0	0
Principal	0	0	0	0	0	0	0	0	0	0
Interest	0	0	0	0	0	0	0	0	0	0
Commercial banks										
Disbursements	0	0	0	0	0	0	0	0	0	0
Principal	0	0	0	0	0	0	0	0	0	0
Interest	0	0	0	0	0	0	0	0	0	0
Other private										
Disbursements	0	0	0	0	0	0	0	0	0	0
Principal	0	0	0	0	0	0	0	0	0	0
Interest	0	0	0	0	0	0	0	0	0	0

MAURITANIA

(US$ million, unless otherwise indicated)

	1970	1980	1990	1992	1993	1994	1995	1996	1997	1998
1. SUMMARY DEBT DATA										
TOTAL DEBT STOCKS (EDT)	..	**840**	**2,096**	**2,088**	**2,141**	**2,223**	**2,350**	**2,412**	**2,456**	**2,589**
Long-term debt (LDOD)	**26**	**713**	**1,789**	**1,825**	**1,903**	**1,990**	**2,081**	**2,125**	**2,040**	**2,214**
Public and publicly guaranteed	26	713	1,789	1,825	1,903	1,990	2,081	2,125	2,040	2,214
Private nonguaranteed	0	0	0	0	0	0	0	0	0	0
Use of IMF credit	**0**	**62**	**70**	**58**	**63**	**86**	**100**	**107**	**113**	**110**
Short-term debt	..	**65**	**238**	**205**	**174**	**148**	**169**	**180**	**304**	**265**
of which interest arrears on LDOD	..	10	64	113	94	72	79	81	86	118
Official creditors	..	9	57	100	93	70	77	81	86	118
Private creditors	..	1	7	14	2	2	3	0	0	0
Memo: principal arrears on LDOD	..	44	141	288	198	192	174	175	193	385
Official creditors	..	24	120	236	195	187	169	175	193	385
Private creditors	..	21	21	52	4	5	5	0	0	0
Memo: export credits	..	0	230	196	187	148	156	147	197	160
TOTAL DEBT FLOWS										
Disbursements	**5**	**155**	**148**	**145**	**179**	**163**	**133**	**176**	**108**	**55**
Long-term debt	5	126	137	133	167	139	111	155	89	55
IMF purchases	0	30	12	12	12	24	22	21	20	0
Principal repayments	**3**	**26**	**99**	**61**	**82**	**63**	**79**	**82**	**70**	**69**
Long-term debt	3	17	83	53	76	57	70	72	62	62
IMF repurchases	0	9	16	8	6	6	9	10	8	7
Net flows on debt	**1**	**139**	**102**	**-49**	**85**	**96**	**68**	**103**	**158**	**-84**
of which short-term debt	..	10	53	-133	-12	-4	14	9	119	-71
Interest payments (INT)	..	**22**	**47**	**26**	**47**	**42**	**38**	**35**	**44**	**42**
Long-term debt	0	13	35	20	42	38	33	30	35	33
IMF charges	0	2	3	1	0	0	1	1	1	1
Short-term debt	..	7	9	6	4	4	5	4	8	8
Net transfers on debt	..	**118**	**55**	**-74**	**39**	**54**	**30**	**68**	**114**	**-126**
Total debt service paid (TDS)	..	**48**	**146**	**87**	**128**	**106**	**117**	**116**	**114**	**110**
Long-term debt	4	30	118	72	118	96	102	102	98	94
IMF repurchases and charges	0	11	19	9	7	6	10	11	8	8
Short-term debt (interest only)	..	7	9	6	4	4	5	4	8	8
2. AGGREGATE NET RESOURCE FLOWS AND NET TRANSFERS (LONG-TERM)										
NET RESOURCE FLOWS	**5**	**197**	**138**	**195**	**281**	**210**	**184**	**262**	**180**	**129**
Net flow of long-term debt (ex. IMF)	1	108	54	81	91	82	42	83	26	-7
Foreign direct investment (net)	1	27	7	8	16	2	7	5	3	5
Portfolio equity flows	0	0	0	0	0	0	0	0	0	0
Grants (excluding technical coop.)	3	61	78	106	173	127	135	174	151	130
Memo: technical coop. grants	4	29	53	52	54	44	49	47	42	36
official net resource flows	6	170	133	189	265	208	177	232	179	126
private net resource flows	-1	27	6	5	16	2	7	30	2	3
NET TRANSFERS	**-8**	**161**	**103**	**173**	**236**	**169**	**149**	**228**	**142**	**94**
Interest on long-term debt	0	13	35	20	42	38	33	30	35	33
Profit remittances on FDI	13	23	1	2	3	3	3	4	3	2
Memo: official net transfers	5	161	98	170	223	170	145	203	145	95
private net transfers	-14	1	4	3	13	-1	4	26	-3	-1
3. MAJOR ECONOMIC AGGREGATES										
Gross national product (GNP)	227	779	1,076	1,124	875	974	1,015	1,038	1,046	950
Exports of goods & services (XGS)	..	275	488	478	427	432	511	517	463	397
of which workers remittances	..	6	14	50	2	5	5	4	3	2
Imports of goods & services (MGS)	..	493	570	670	683	581	559	623	557	505
International reserves (RES)	3	146	59	65	49	44	90	145	204	206
Current account balance	..	-133	-10	-118	-174	-70	22	91	48	77
4. DEBT INDICATORS										
EDT / XGS (%)	..	304.9	429.4	436.8	500.9	515.1	459.8	466.7	530.9	651.6
EDT / GNP (%)	..	107.8	194.8	185.8	244.7	228.3	231.4	232.3	234.8	272.5
TDS / XGS (%)	..	17.3	29.9	18.2	30.0	24.4	22.9	22.5	24.5	27.7
INT / XGS (%)	..	7.9	9.7	5.4	10.9	9.8	7.5	6.7	9.5	10.5
INT / GNP (%)	..	2.8	4.4	2.3	5.3	4.3	3.8	3.3	4.2	4.4
RES / EDT (%)	..	17.4	2.8	3.1	2.3	2.0	3.8	6.0	8.3	8.0
RES / MGS (months)	..	3.6	1.2	1.2	0.9	0.9	1.9	2.8	4.4	4.9
Short-term / EDT (%)	..	7.7	11.3	9.8	8.1	6.7	7.2	7.5	12.4	10.2
Concessional / EDT (%)	..	62.6	61.1	63.6	71.1	71.9	71.8	72.1	69.2	71.2
Multilateral / EDT (%)	..	14.8	31.2	34.1	34.4	38.4	39.4	39.4	38.3	38.5

MAURITANIA

(US$ million, unless otherwise indicated)

	1970	1980	1990	1992	1993	1994	1995	1996	1997	1998
5. LONG-TERM DEBT										
DEBT OUTSTANDING (LDOD)	**26**	**713**	**1,789**	**1,825**	**1,903**	**1,990**	**2,081**	**2,125**	**2,040**	**2,214**
Public and publicly guaranteed	**26**	**713**	**1,789**	**1,825**	**1,903**	**1,990**	**2,081**	**2,125**	**2,040**	**2,214**
Official creditors	18	582	1,692	1,738	1,885	1,981	2,073	2,100	2,016	2,192
Multilateral	6	125	654	712	736	854	925	950	940	995
Concessional	6	106	453	497	536	634	704	755	776	835
Bilateral	13	458	1,038	1,025	1,148	1,127	1,148	1,150	1,076	1,197
Concessional	8	420	828	831	985	964	984	984	925	1,007
Private creditors	8	131	97	88	19	9	8	25	24	22
Bonds	0	0	0	0	0	0	0	0	0	0
Commercial banks	0	16	0	0	0	0	0	0	0	0
Other private	8	115	97	88	19	9	8	25	24	22
Private nonguaranteed	**0**	**0**	**0**	**0**	**0**	**0**	**0**	**0**	**0**	**0**
Bonds	0	0	0	0	0	0	0	0	0	0
Commercial banks	0	0	0	0	0	0	0	0	0	0
Memo:										
IBRD	0	0	54	30	19	13	11	8	6	4
IDA	5	38	210	229	256	301	336	360	373	408
DISBURSEMENTS	**5**	**126**	**137**	**133**	**167**	**139**	**111**	**155**	**89**	**55**
Public and publicly guaranteed	**5**	**126**	**137**	**133**	**167**	**139**	**111**	**155**	**89**	**55**
Official creditors	4	112	136	133	167	139	111	130	89	55
Multilateral	2	27	112	112	98	118	88	98	81	50
Concessional	2	12	65	51	72	91	78	82	74	47
Bilateral	2	85	24	22	69	21	24	33	8	5
Concessional	2	84	24	22	69	21	23	32	6	5
Private creditors	1	14	0	0	0	0	0	25	0	0
Bonds	0	0	0	0	0	0	0	0	0	0
Commercial banks	0	0	0	0	0	0	0	0	0	0
Other private	1	14	0	0	0	0	0	25	0	0
Private nonguaranteed	**0**	**0**	**0**	**0**	**0**	**0**	**0**	**0**	**0**	**0**
Bonds	0	0	0	0	0	0	0	0	0	0
Commercial banks	0	0	0	0	0	0	0	0	0	0
Memo:										
IBRD	0	0	0	0	0	0	0	0	0	0
IDA	2	4	39	13	28	35	31	36	34	24
PRINCIPAL REPAYMENTS	**3**	**17**	**83**	**53**	**76**	**57**	**70**	**72**	**62**	**62**
Public and publicly guaranteed	**3**	**17**	**83**	**53**	**76**	**57**	**70**	**72**	**62**	**62**
Official creditors	1	4	81	51	75	57	70	72	61	60
Multilateral	0	2	66	44	60	42	35	56	39	38
Concessional	0	1	16	20	24	18	18	20	19	22
Bilateral	1	2	15	7	16	15	34	16	22	22
Concessional	1	2	11	6	16	15	19	16	20	19
Private creditors	2	13	1	2	0	0	0	0	2	2
Bonds	0	0	0	0	0	0	0	0	0	0
Commercial banks	0	5	0	0	0	0	0	0	0	0
Other private	2	9	1	2	0	0	0	0	2	2
Private nonguaranteed	**0**	**0**	**0**	**0**	**0**	**0**	**0**	**0**	**0**	**0**
Bonds	0	0	0	0	0	0	0	0	0	0
Commercial banks	0	0	0	0	0	0	0	0	0	0
Memo:										
IBRD	0	0	11	12	13	8	2	2	2	2
IDA	0	0	1	1	1	1	2	2	2	3
NET FLOWS ON DEBT	**1**	**108**	**54**	**81**	**91**	**82**	**42**	**83**	**26**	**-7**
Public and publicly guaranteed	**1**	**108**	**54**	**81**	**91**	**82**	**42**	**83**	**26**	**-7**
Official creditors	3	108	55	83	92	82	42	58	28	-5
Multilateral	2	25	46	68	38	77	53	42	42	12
Concessional	2	12	50	31	49	73	60	62	55	25
Bilateral	1	83	9	15	54	5	-11	17	-14	-17
Concessional	1	82	13	16	54	5	4	16	-14	-14
Private creditors	-2	0	-1	-2	0	0	0	25	-2	-2
Bonds	0	0	0	0	0	0	0	0	0	0
Commercial banks	0	-5	0	0	0	0	0	0	0	0
Other private	-2	5	-1	-2	0	0	0	25	-2	-2
Private nonguaranteed	**0**	**0**	**0**	**0**	**0**	**0**	**0**	**0**	**0**	**0**
Bonds	0	0	0	0	0	0	0	0	0	0
Commercial banks	0	0	0	0	0	0	0	0	0	0
Memo:										
IBRD	0	0	-11	-12	-13	-8	-2	-2	-2	-2
IDA	2	4	38	12	27	33	29	34	32	21

MAURITANIA

(US$ million, unless otherwise indicated)

	1970	1980	1990	1992	1993	1994	1995	1996	1997	1998
INTEREST PAYMENTS (LINT)	**0**	**13**	**35**	**20**	**42**	**38**	**33**	**30**	**35**	**33**
Public and publicly guaranteed	**0**	**13**	**35**	**20**	**42**	**38**	**33**	**30**	**35**	**33**
Official creditors	0	9	34	19	42	38	33	30	34	31
Multilateral	0	3	20	14	27	24	15	21	19	18
Concessional	0	2	7	7	10	13	8	11	11	10
Bilateral	0	6	14	6	15	15	17	9	14	13
Concessional	0	6	6	4	10	10	10	8	9	8
Private creditors	0	4	1	0	0	0	0	0	2	2
Bonds	0	0	0	0	0	0	0	0	0	0
Commercial banks	0	2	0	0	0	0	0	0	0	0
Other private	0	2	1	0	0	0	0	0	2	2
Private nonguaranteed	**0**	**0**	**0**	**0**	**0**	**0**	**0**	**0**	**0**	**0**
Bonds	0	0	0	0	0	0	0	0	0	0
Commercial banks	0	0	0	0	0	0	0	0	0	0
Memo:										
IBRD	0	0	5	3	2	1	1	1	1	0
IDA	0	0	1	2	2	2	2	3	3	3
NET TRANSFERS ON DEBT	**1**	**96**	**19**	**61**	**49**	**43**	**9**	**53**	**-9**	**-39**
Public and publicly guaranteed	**1**	**96**	**19**	**61**	**49**	**43**	**9**	**53**	**-9**	**-39**
Official creditors	3	99	21	64	49	44	10	29	-6	-35
Multilateral	2	23	25	54	11	53	37	21	23	-6
Concessional	2	9	43	25	39	60	52	52	45	15
Bilateral	0	77	-5	9	38	-9	-28	8	-29	-29
Concessional	1	76	8	12	44	-5	-6	8	-23	-21
Private creditors	-2	-4	-2	-3	0	0	0	25	-3	-4
Bonds	0	0	0	0	0	0	0	0	0	0
Commercial banks	0	-7	0	0	0	0	0	0	0	0
Other private	-2	3	-2	-3	0	0	0	25	-3	-4
Private nonguaranteed	**0**	**0**	**0**	**0**	**0**	**0**	**0**	**0**	**0**	**0**
Bonds	0	0	0	0	0	0	0	0	0	0
Commercial banks	0	0	0	0	0	0	0	0	0	0
Memo:										
IBRD	0	0	-16	-15	-15	-9	-3	-3	-2	-2
IDA	2	4	37	11	25	31	26	32	29	18
DEBT SERVICE (LTDS)	**4**	**30**	**118**	**72**	**118**	**96**	**102**	**102**	**98**	**94**
Public and publicly guaranteed	**4**	**30**	**118**	**72**	**118**	**96**	**102**	**102**	**98**	**94**
Official creditors	1	13	116	70	118	95	102	102	94	90
Multilateral	0	5	87	57	86	66	51	77	58	56
Concessional	0	3	22	27	34	31	26	31	29	33
Bilateral	1	8	29	13	31	30	51	25	36	34
Concessional	1	8	17	10	26	25	29	24	29	27
Private creditors	2	17	2	3	0	0	0	0	3	4
Bonds	0	0	0	0	0	0	0	0	0	0
Commercial banks	0	7	0	0	0	0	0	0	0	0
Other private	2	10	2	3	0	0	0	0	3	4
Private nonguaranteed	**0**	**0**	**0**	**0**	**0**	**0**	**0**	**0**	**0**	**0**
Bonds	0	0	0	0	0	0	0	0	0	0
Commercial banks	0	0	0	0	0	0	0	0	0	0
Memo:										
IBRD	0	0	16	15	15	9	3	3	2	2
IDA	0	1	2	3	3	3	4	4	5	6
UNDISBURSED DEBT	**16**	**682**	**621**	**528**	**525**	**456**	**421**	**371**	**312**	**298**
Official creditors	11	653	616	528	525	456	421	371	312	298
Private creditors	5	29	5	0	0	0	0	0	0	0
Memorandum items										
Concessional LDOD	14	526	1,281	1,328	1,521	1,598	1,688	1,739	1,701	1,842
Variable rate LDOD	0	17	131	121	132	132	136	138	131	163
Public sector LDOD	26	713	1,789	1,825	1,903	1,990	2,081	2,125	2,040	2,214
Private sector LDOD	0	0	0	0	0	0	0	0	0	0
6. CURRENCY COMPOSITION OF LONG-TERM DEBT (PERCENT)										
Deutsche mark	0.0	3.1	0.5	0.4	0.3	0.3	0.3	0.3	0.3	0.3
French franc	49.0	7.2	5.3	6.3	6.5	7.4	8.2	7.8	7.2	7.1
Japanese yen	0.0	0.0	1.3	1.2	3.4	3.5	3.1	3.5	3.4	3.5
Pound sterling	0.0	0.2	0.6	0.5	0.6	0.6	0.5	0.6	0.6	0.5
Swiss franc	0.0	0.3	0.0	0.0	0.0	0.0	0.0	0.0	0.0	0.0
U.S.dollars	23.6	43.1	34.6	34.4	35.3	34.7	34.8	36.4	38.1	38.5
Multiple currency	2.7	2.9	4.2	3.2	2.5	2.1	1.9	1.7	1.5	1.3
Special drawing rights	0.0	0.0	2.1	2.1	2.1	2.2	2.4	2.4	2.4	2.3
All other currencies	24.7	43.2	51.4	51.9	49.3	49.2	48.8	47.3	46.5	46.5

MAURITANIA

(US$ million, unless otherwise indicated)

	1970	1980	1990	1992	1993	1994	1995	1996	1997	1998
7. DEBT RESTRUCTURINGS										
Total amount rescheduled	..	..	11	0	177	67	60	68	12	0
Debt stock rescheduled	..	..	0	0	0	0	0	17	0	0
Principal rescheduled	..	..	7	0	131	51	39	29	5	1
Official	..	..	5	0	74	42	38	29	5	1
Private	..	..	3	0	58	9	1	0	0	0
Interest rescheduled	..	..	5	0	36	12	12	13	3	1
Official	..	..	4	0	24	11	12	13	3	1
Private	..	..	1	0	12	0	0	0	0	0
Debt forgiven	..	..	61	0	23	6	13	1	9	0
Memo: interest forgiven	..	..	1	0	8	1	2	2	2	0
Debt stock reduction	..	..	0	4	0	0	0	0	0	0
of which debt buyback	..	..	0	0	0	0	0	0	0	0
8. DEBT STOCK-FLOW RECONCILIATION										
Total change in debt stocks	..	..	140	-100	53	83	126	63	44	133
Net flows on debt	1	139	102	-49	85	96	68	103	158	-84
Net change in interest arrears	..	..	21	26	-19	-22	7	2	5	32
Interest capitalized	..	..	5	0	36	12	12	13	3	1
Debt forgiveness or reduction	..	..	-61	-4	-23	-6	-13	-1	-9	0
Cross-currency valuation	..	..	55	-58	-18	46	44	-47	-77	52
Residual	..	..	18	-15	-9	-43	8	-7	-35	133
9. AVERAGE TERMS OF NEW COMMITMENTS										
ALL CREDITORS										
Interest (%)	6.0	3.6	3.1	1.5	2.0	2.0	1.1	3.6	2.2	0.5
Maturity (years)	10.6	22.3	31.2	31.5	30.9	28.0	34.7	27.9	30.6	39.6
Grace period (years)	2.9	9.1	8.5	8.2	8.0	7.7	9.7	6.3	6.6	10.1
Grant element (%)	18.9	47.5	56.6	66.7	63.5	61.3	75.1	49.9	60.3	82.7
Official creditors										
Interest (%)	3.2	2.7	3.1	1.5	2.0	2.0	1.1	2.2	2.2	0.5
Maturity (years)	20.8	24.5	31.2	31.5	30.9	28.0	34.7	32.4	30.6	39.6
Grace period (years)	5.4	10.4	8.5	8.2	8.0	7.7	9.7	7.9	6.6	10.1
Grant element (%)	44.4	55.2	56.6	66.7	63.5	61.3	75.1	61.7	60.3	82.7
Private creditors										
Interest (%)	6.7	7.7	0.0	0.0	0.0	0.0	0.0	8.8	0.0	0.0
Maturity (years)	8.3	11.4	0.0	0.0	0.0	0.0	0.0	10.0	0.0	0.0
Grace period (years)	2.4	2.9	0.0	0.0	0.0	0.0	0.0	0.0	0.0	0.0
Grant element (%)	13.2	10.0	0.0	0.0	0.0	0.0	0.0	3.9	0.0	0.0
Memorandum items										
Commitments	7	211	216	77	181	65	114	121	102	24
Official creditors	1	175	216	77	181	65	114	96	102	24
Private creditors	6	36	0	0	0	0	0	25	0	0

10. CONTRACTUAL OBLIGATIONS ON OUTSTANDING LONG-TERM DEBT

	1999	2000	2001	2002	2003	2004	2005	2006	2007	2008
TOTAL										
Disbursements	79	75	50	32	17	8	4	1	1	0
Principal	117	119	102	104	98	88	89	82	73	72
Interest	41	39	37	34	31	29	27	24	22	21
Official creditors										
Disbursements	79	75	50	32	17	8	4	1	1	0
Principal	115	116	100	101	95	85	85	80	73	72
Interest	39	38	35	33	30	28	26	24	22	21
Bilateral creditors										
Disbursements	13	13	9	6	3	2	1	1	0	0
Principal	64	61	52	53	51	44	43	38	34	34
Interest	20	20	18	17	16	15	14	13	13	12
Multilateral creditors										
Disbursements	67	62	41	26	14	7	3	1	1	0
Principal	51	55	47	48	44	41	42	43	39	38
Interest	19	18	17	16	15	13	12	11	10	9
Private creditors										
Disbursements	0	0	0	0	0	0	0	0	0	0
Principal	3	2	3	3	3	3	4	2	0	0
Interest	2	2	1	1	1	1	0	0	0	0
Commercial banks										
Disbursements	0	0	0	0	0	0	0	0	0	0
Principal	0	0	0	0	0	0	0	0	0	0
Interest	0	0	0	0	0	0	0	0	0	0
Other private										
Disbursements	0	0	0	0	0	0	0	0	0	0
Principal	3	2	3	3	3	3	4	2	0	0
Interest	2	2	1	1	1	1	0	0	0	0

MAURITIUS

(US$ million, unless otherwise indicated)

	1970	1980	1990	1992	1993	1994	1995	1996	1997	1998
1. SUMMARY DEBT DATA										
TOTAL DEBT STOCKS (EDT)	..	467	985	1,051	1,008	1,382	1,756	1,818	2,472	2,482
Long-term debt (LDOD)	32	318	911	943	900	1,098	1,415	1,399	1,976	1,909
Public and publicly guaranteed	32	294	764	748	733	852	1,148	1,153	1,187	1,152
Private nonguaranteed	0	24	148	195	167	245	267	246	789	757
Use of IMF credit	0	102	22	0	0	0	0	0	0	0
Short-term debt	..	47	52	108	108	285	342	419	496	573
of which interest arrears on LDOD	..	0	2	2	2	2	1	0	0	0
Official creditors	..	0	1	2	2	1	1	0	0	0
Private creditors	..	0	1	0	0	1	0	0	0	0
Memo: principal arrears on LDOD	..	2	5	8	11	1	0	0	0	0
Official creditors	..	2	4	8	11	1	0	0	0	0
Private creditors	..	0	1	0	0	0	0	0	0	0
Memo: export credits	..	0	201	166	141	207	226	216	286	328
TOTAL DEBT FLOWS										
Disbursements	2	143	162	127	105	186	409	140	827	56
Long-term debt	2	97	162	127	105	186	409	140	827	56
IMF purchases	0	46	0	0	0	0	0	0	0	0
Principal repayments	5	19	104	128	83	103	154	108	136	158
Long-term debt	1	19	60	128	83	103	154	108	136	158
IMF repurchases	4	0	44	0	0	0	0	0	0	0
Net flows on debt	-3	104	76	55	22	260	312	110	768	-25
of which short-term debt	..	-20	18	56	0	177	58	78	77	77
Interest payments (INT)	..	34	52	56	46	56	72	90	147	154
Long-term debt	2	23	43	53	42	45	56	71	123	127
IMF charges	0	3	5	0	0	0	0	0	0	0
Short-term debt	..	8	5	3	4	10	16	19	23	27
Net transfers on debt	..	70	24	-1	-24	204	241	21	621	-179
Total debt service paid (TDS)	..	52	156	184	129	159	225	198	283	312
Long-term debt	3	41	103	180	125	148	210	179	259	285
IMF repurchases and charges	4	3	49	0	0	0	0	0	0	0
Short-term debt (interest only)	..	8	5	3	4	10	16	19	23	27
2. AGGREGATE NET RESOURCE FLOWS AND NET TRANSFERS (LONG-TERM)										
NET RESOURCE FLOWS	5	93	168	26	69	125	301	116	784	-70
Net flow of long-term debt (ex. IMF)	1	79	102	-1	22	83	255	32	691	-102
Foreign direct investment (net)	2	1	41	15	15	20	19	37	55	12
Portfolio equity flows	0	0	0	0	17	10	4	34	24	8
Grants (excluding technical coop.)	3	13	25	12	15	12	23	13	14	12
Memo: technical coop. grants	2	11	20	21	18	21	24	23	23	18
official net resource flows	4	45	82	-8	24	-10	2	4	11	9
private net resource flows	1	49	86	35	45	135	298	112	773	-79
NET TRANSFERS	3	69	103	-49	7	58	225	25	639	-218
Interest on long-term debt	2	23	43	53	42	45	56	71	123	127
Profit remittances on FDI	1	1	22	22	20	22	20	20	22	21
Memo: official net transfers	3	38	49	-48	-11	-45	-33	-29	-19	-19
private net transfers	-1	32	53	0	18	102	258	54	657	-199
3. MAJOR ECONOMIC AGGREGATES										
Gross national product (GNP)	222	1,109	2,620	3,200	3,199	3,479	3,954	4,261	4,159	4,161
Exports of goods & services (XGS)	..	579	1,778	2,003	1,971	2,041	2,402	2,802	2,602	2,763
of which workers remittances	..	0	0	0	0	0	0	0	0	0
Imports of goods & services (MGS)	..	718	1,994	2,097	2,164	2,377	2,525	2,884	2,824	2,826
International reserves (RES)	46	113	761	841	781	771	887	919	711	577
Current account balance	..	-117	-119	0	-92	-232	-22	34	-91	35
4. DEBT INDICATORS										
EDT / XGS (%)	..	80.8	55.4	52.5	51.2	67.7	73.1	64.9	95.0	89.8
EDT / GNP (%)	..	42.1	37.6	32.8	31.5	39.7	44.4	42.7	59.4	59.6
TDS / XGS (%)	..	9.0	8.8	9.2	6.5	7.8	9.4	7.1	10.9	11.3
INT / XGS (%)	..	5.8	3.0	2.8	2.3	2.7	3.0	3.2	5.6	5.6
INT / GNP (%)	..	3.1	2.0	1.8	1.4	1.6	1.8	2.1	3.5	3.7
RES / EDT (%)	..	24.2	77.3	80.0	77.5	55.8	50.5	50.6	28.8	23.2
RES / MGS (months)	..	1.9	4.6	4.8	4.3	3.9	4.2	3.8	3.0	2.5
Short-term / EDT (%)	..	10.1	5.3	10.3	10.7	20.6	19.4	23.1	20.1	23.1
Concessional / EDT (%)	..	13.8	35.4	36.5	38.0	30.1	25.0	22.1	14.0	14.3
Multilateral / EDT (%)	..	16.6	31.7	26.4	27.4	19.9	15.4	13.9	9.9	10.5

MAURITIUS

(US$ million, unless otherwise indicated)

	1970	1980	1990	1992	1993	1994	1995	1996	1997	1998
5. LONG-TERM DEBT										
DEBT OUTSTANDING (LDOD)	**32**	**318**	**911**	**943**	**900**	**1,098**	**1,415**	**1,399**	**1,976**	**1,909**
Public and publicly guaranteed	**32**	**294**	**764**	**748**	**733**	**852**	**1,148**	**1,153**	**1,187**	**1,152**
Official creditors	21	154	649	637	625	650	664	615	554	581
Multilateral	6	78	312	278	276	275	270	253	245	261
Concessional	0	25	64	58	63	65	69	65	60	60
Bilateral	16	76	337	359	349	375	394	363	310	321
Concessional	6	39	285	325	320	351	371	338	284	294
Private creditors	10	141	115	111	108	203	484	537	632	570
Bonds	9	0	0	0	0	0	150	150	150	150
Commercial banks	2	138	102	92	88	178	315	331	426	368
Other private	0	3	13	19	20	25	19	56	56	53
Private nonguaranteed	**0**	**24**	**148**	**195**	**167**	**245**	**267**	**246**	**789**	**757**
Bonds	0	0	0	0	0	0	0	0	600	600
Commercial banks	0	24	148	195	167	245	267	246	189	157
Memo:										
IBRD	6	35	176	151	149	147	140	124	111	112
IDA	0	20	19	18	18	17	17	16	15	15
DISBURSEMENTS	**2**	**97**	**162**	**127**	**105**	**186**	**409**	**140**	**827**	**56**
Public and publicly guaranteed	**2**	**93**	**104**	**87**	**77**	**145**	**353**	**122**	**216**	**52**
Official creditors	2	36	97	64	65	36	39	50	75	49
Multilateral	0	18	23	16	29	14	18	33	42	32
Concessional	0	3	7	2	10	3	5	3	3	1
Bilateral	2	18	74	48	36	22	21	17	33	18
Concessional	1	13	65	47	32	22	18	10	27	12
Private creditors	0	56	8	23	12	109	313	73	141	3
Bonds	0	0	0	0	0	0	150	0	0	0
Commercial banks	0	56	0	17	9	102	159	29	121	3
Other private	0	0	7	6	2	7	5	43	20	0
Private nonguaranteed	**0**	**4**	**57**	**40**	**28**	**41**	**56**	**18**	**611**	**4**
Bonds	0	0	0	0	0	0	0	0	600	0
Commercial banks	0	4	57	40	28	41	56	18	11	4
Memo:										
IBRD	0	7	6	9	16	10	11	14	17	13
IDA	0	1	0	0	0	0	0	0	0	0
PRINCIPAL REPAYMENTS	**1**	**19**	**60**	**128**	**83**	**103**	**154**	**108**	**136**	**158**
Public and publicly guaranteed	**1**	**15**	**44**	**112**	**69**	**76**	**94**	**73**	**112**	**122**
Official creditors	1	5	39	84	57	58	61	58	78	52
Multilateral	0	2	22	35	31	34	33	30	31	29
Concessional	0	0	3	3	3	4	3	3	4	4
Bilateral	0	3	17	49	26	25	27	28	48	24
Concessional	0	2	12	28	20	17	22	24	43	19
Private creditors	1	10	4	28	12	18	33	15	34	69
Bonds	0	0	0	0	0	0	0	0	0	0
Commercial banks	1	8	4	25	12	14	22	11	19	62
Other private	0	1	0	2	0	3	12	4	15	8
Private nonguaranteed	**0**	**4**	**16**	**16**	**14**	**27**	**60**	**35**	**24**	**36**
Bonds	0	0	0	0	0	0	0	0	0	0
Commercial banks	0	4	16	16	14	27	60	35	24	36
Memo:										
IBRD	0	2	16	22	21	22	23	20	21	19
IDA	0	0	0	0	1	1	1	1	1	1
NET FLOWS ON DEBT	**1**	**79**	**102**	**-1**	**22**	**83**	**255**	**32**	**691**	**-102**
Public and publicly guaranteed	**1**	**78**	**61**	**-25**	**8**	**69**	**259**	**49**	**104**	**-70**
Official creditors	2	31	57	-21	9	-22	-21	-9	-3	-3
Multilateral	0	16	1	-19	-1	-20	-15	3	12	3
Concessional	0	3	4	-1	7	-2	2	0	0	-3
Bilateral	2	15	57	-2	10	-2	-6	-12	-15	-6
Concessional	0	11	53	19	13	5	-4	-14	-17	-7
Private creditors	-1	47	3	-5	-1	91	280	58	107	-67
Bonds	0	0	0	0	0	0	150	0	0	0
Commercial banks	-1	48	-4	-8	-3	88	137	18	102	-59
Other private	0	-1	7	3	2	3	-7	39	5	-8
Private nonguaranteed	**0**	**0**	**41**	**25**	**14**	**13**	**-4**	**-17**	**587**	**-32**
Bonds	0	0	0	0	0	0	0	0	600	0
Commercial banks	0	0	41	25	14	13	-4	-17	-13	-32
Memo:										
IBRD	0	5	-10	-12	-6	-12	-13	-7	-4	-6
IDA	0	1	0	0	-1	-1	-1	-1	-1	-1

MAURITIUS

(US$ million, unless otherwise indicated)

	1970	1980	1990	1992	1993	1994	1995	1996	1997	1998
INTEREST PAYMENTS (LINT)	**2**	**23**	**43**	**53**	**42**	**45**	**56**	**71**	**123**	**127**
Public and publicly guaranteed	**2**	**20**	**37**	**47**	**39**	**41**	**50**	**66**	**61**	**66**
Official creditors	1	7	33	40	35	35	36	33	29	28
Multilateral	0	4	19	20	17	17	16	15	13	12
Concessional	0	0	1	1	1	1	1	1	1	1
Bilateral	1	3	14	21	18	18	19	18	16	16
Concessional	0	1	9	15	15	15	17	16	14	14
Private creditors	1	13	4	7	4	7	15	33	32	39
Bonds	1	0	0	0	0	0	0	10	10	10
Commercial banks	0	13	3	6	4	5	12	21	20	26
Other private	0	0	1	1	0	2	2	1	2	3
Private nonguaranteed	**0**	**3**	**6**	**6**	**4**	**4**	**6**	**5**	**62**	**61**
Bonds	0	0	0	0	0	0	0	0	60	60
Commercial banks	0	3	6	6	4	4	6	5	2	1
Memo:										
IBRD	0	3	14	12	11	11	11	9	8	7
IDA	0	0	0	0	0	0	0	0	0	0
NET TRANSFERS ON DEBT	**-1**	**56**	**59**	**-53**	**-21**	**37**	**199**	**-39**	**568**	**-229**
Public and publicly guaranteed	**-1**	**58**	**24**	**-72**	**-31**	**28**	**209**	**-17**	**43**	**-136**
Official creditors	1	24	24	-60	-26	-57	-57	-42	-32	-31
Multilateral	-1	12	-19	-38	-18	-36	-32	-12	-2	-9
Concessional	0	3	3	-2	6	-3	1	-2	-1	-4
Bilateral	1	12	43	-22	-8	-20	-25	-30	-31	-22
Concessional	0	11	44	4	-2	-10	-21	-30	-31	-21
Private creditors	-2	34	-1	-12	-5	85	265	25	75	-105
Bonds	-1	0	0	0	0	0	150	-10	-10	-10
Commercial banks	-1	35	-7	-14	-6	83	125	-3	82	-84
Other private	0	-1	7	2	2	1	-9	38	3	-10
Private nonguaranteed	**0**	**-2**	**35**	**19**	**10**	**9**	**-10**	**-22**	**525**	**-93**
Bonds	0	0	0	0	0	0	0	0	540	-60
Commercial banks	0	-2	35	19	10	9	-10	-22	-15	-33
Memo:										
IBRD	-1	2	-24	-25	-17	-23	-24	-16	-12	-13
IDA	0	1	0	-1	-1	-1	-1	-1	-1	-1
DEBT SERVICE (LTDS)	**3**	**41**	**103**	**180**	**125**	**148**	**210**	**179**	**259**	**285**
Public and publicly guaranteed	**3**	**35**	**81**	**159**	**107**	**117**	**144**	**139**	**173**	**188**
Official creditors	2	12	73	124	92	93	96	91	107	80
Multilateral	1	7	42	54	48	50	50	45	44	41
Concessional	0	0	4	4	4	5	4	4	4	4
Bilateral	1	6	31	70	44	43	47	47	64	40
Concessional	0	2	21	43	34	32	39	40	57	33
Private creditors	2	22	8	35	16	24	48	48	66	108
Bonds	1	0	0	0	0	0	0	10	10	10
Commercial banks	1	21	7	31	16	19	34	32	39	87
Other private	0	1	1	4	0	5	14	5	17	10
Private nonguaranteed	**0**	**7**	**22**	**21**	**18**	**31**	**66**	**40**	**86**	**97**
Bonds	0	0	0	0	0	0	0	0	60	60
Commercial banks	0	7	22	21	18	31	66	40	26	37
Memo:										
IBRD	1	4	30	34	32	33	34	30	29	26
IDA	0	0	0	1	1	1	1	1	1	1
UNDISBURSED DEBT	**15**	**175**	**246**	**247**	**250**	**296**	**485**	**383**	**299**	**280**
Official creditors	15	172	233	227	219	267	384	355	282	264
Private creditors	0	3	13	19	31	29	101	28	17	16
Memorandum items										
Concessional LDOD	6	65	349	383	383	416	439	402	345	354
Variable rate LDOD	2	150	281	337	317	488	802	780	1,333	1,275
Public sector LDOD	32	294	764	748	733	852	1,148	1,153	1,187	1,152
Private sector LDOD	0	24	148	195	167	245	267	246	789	757

6. CURRENCY COMPOSITION OF LONG-TERM DEBT (PERCENT)

	1970	1980	1990	1992	1993	1994	1995	1996	1997	1998
Deutsche mark	0.0	0.0	6.3	5.1	4.4	3.7	2.6	2.1	1.3	1.2
French franc	0.0	14.2	23.6	31.5	30.2	27.6	22.7	20.5	18.0	19.0
Japanese yen	0.0	0.0	1.0	1.8	2.5	2.6	1.2	4.5	4.2	4.8
Pound sterling	82.2	18.4	8.7	3.6	3.3	2.6	1.8	1.6	1.4	1.4
Swiss franc	0.0	0.0	0.5	0.4	0.3	0.3	0.2	0.1	0.1	0.2
U.S.dollars	0.0	46.1	14.4	14.4	13.6	22.5	42.3	44.2	52.5	56.3
Multiple currency	17.6	13.3	25.2	22.4	22.7	19.5	14.1	12.7	11.3	5.2
Special drawing rights	0.0	0.0	0.0	0.0	0.0	0.0	0.0	0.0	0.0	0.0
All other currencies	0.2	8.0	20.3	20.8	23.0	21.2	15.1	14.3	11.2	11.9

MAURITIUS

(US$ million, unless otherwise indicated)

	1970	1980	1990	1992	1993	1994	1995	1996	1997	1998
7. DEBT RESTRUCTURINGS										
Total amount rescheduled	..	..	0	0	0	0	0	0	0	0
Debt stock rescheduled	..	..	0	0	0	0	0	0	0	0
Principal rescheduled	..	..	0	0	0	0	0	0	0	0
Official	..	..	0	0	0	0	0	0	0	0
Private	..	..	0	0	0	0	0	0	0	0
Interest rescheduled	..	..	0	0	0	0	0	0	0	0
Official	..	..	0	0	0	0	0	0	0	0
Private	..	..	0	0	0	0	0	0	0	0
Debt forgiven	..	..	0	0	0	0	0	0	0	0
Memo: interest forgiven	..	..	0	0	0	0	0	0	0	0
Debt stock reduction	..	..	0	0	0	0	0	0	0	0
of which debt buyback	..	..	0	0	0	0	0	0	0	0
8. DEBT STOCK-FLOW RECONCILIATION										
Total change in debt stocks	..	..	139	8	-43	374	374	61	654	10
Net flows on debt	-3	104	76	55	22	260	312	110	768	-25
Net change in interest arrears	..	..	2	-2	0	0	-1	-1	0	0
Interest capitalized	..	..	0	0	0	0	0	0	0	0
Debt forgiveness or reduction	..	..	0	0	0	0	0	0	0	0
Cross-currency valuation	..	..	60	-41	-25	44	30	-41	-62	31
Residual	..	..	1	-5	-40	71	33	-8	-52	3
9. AVERAGE TERMS OF NEW COMMITMENTS										
ALL CREDITORS										
Interest (%)	0.0	10.6	6.0	5.0	4.8	5.4	6.0	4.2	6.7	3.2
Maturity (years)	24.2	13.6	17.9	18.3	14.9	16.0	9.6	16.3	11.0	22.5
Grace period (years)	1.7	4.2	6.3	4.8	4.3	3.3	4.7	3.8	1.0	6.6
Grant element (%)	64.6	7.3	26.7	30.3	29.1	26.6	19.3	33.9	12.8	49.7
Official creditors										
Interest (%)	0.0	5.2	6.0	4.8	4.5	4.0	5.2	4.2	5.8	3.0
Maturity (years)	24.2	19.6	17.9	19.6	17.0	20.4	17.5	16.3	16.9	22.6
Grace period (years)	1.7	5.4	6.3	5.2	4.9	6.4	5.6	3.8	4.0	6.8
Grant element (%)	64.6	30.6	26.7	32.5	33.5	41.3	30.7	33.9	23.2	51.2
Private creditors										
Interest (%)	0.0	18.4	0.0	5.9	5.6	6.8	6.3	0.0	6.9	6.7
Maturity (years)	0.0	5.0	0.0	9.3	8.9	11.9	6.1	0.0	9.8	21.7
Grace period (years)	0.0	2.5	0.0	2.1	2.4	0.4	4.3	0.0	0.5	2.7
Grant element (%)	0.0	-26.5	0.0	15.8	16.5	12.7	14.3	0.0	10.7	20.8
Memorandum items										
Commitments	14	111	137	90	90	210	559	37	156	50
Official creditors	14	66	137	79	67	102	170	37	26	47
Private creditors	0	45	0	12	23	108	389	0	130	3

10. CONTRACTUAL OBLIGATIONS ON OUTSTANDING LONG-TERM DEBT

	1999	2000	2001	2002	2003	2004	2005	2006	2007	2008
TOTAL										
Disbursements	80	71	49	32	21	13	7	3	2	1
Principal	136	398	125	121	118	711	100	112	76	56
Interest	139	129	111	105	99	93	27	21	14	10
Official creditors										
Disbursements	64	71	49	32	21	13	7	3	2	1
Principal	62	67	67	67	66	63	61	59	55	51
Interest	29	28	27	25	23	20	18	15	12	10
Bilateral creditors										
Disbursements	44	38	24	14	7	4	2	0	0	0
Principal	27	30	33	36	34	34	35	33	31	30
Interest	16	16	15	14	13	11	10	8	7	6
Multilateral creditors										
Disbursements	20	33	25	18	14	9	5	3	2	1
Principal	35	37	33	32	32	29	27	25	23	21
Interest	13	13	12	11	10	9	8	7	5	4
Private creditors										
Disbursements	16	0	0	0	0	0	0	0	0	0
Principal	74	331	59	54	53	649	38	53	21	5
Interest	110	100	84	80	76	73	9	6	1	1
Commercial banks										
Disbursements	16	0	0	0	0	0	0	0	0	0
Principal	39	149	29	29	30	29	22	39	12	1
Interest	29	27	17	15	12	10	7	5	1	0
Other private										
Disbursements	0	0	0	0	0	0	0	0	0	0
Principal	36	182	30	25	23	619	17	14	9	4
Interest	81	74	67	65	64	63	2	1	1	0

MEXICO

(US$ million, unless otherwise indicated)

1. SUMMARY DEBT DATA

	1970	1980	1990	1992	1993	1994	1995	1996	1997	1998
TOTAL DEBT STOCKS (EDT)	..	57,365	104,431	112,309	131,734	140,202	166,883	157,755	149,301	159,959
Long-term debt (LDOD)	5,964	41,202	81,797	81,825	90,689	97,019	113,755	114,409	111,707	124,073
Public and publicly guaranteed	3,194	33,902	75,962	71,150	75,151	79,531	95,167	94,069	84,387	87,996
Private nonguaranteed	2,770	7,300	5,835	10,675	15,539	17,489	18,587	20,340	27,320	36,077
Use of IMF credit	0	0	6,551	5,950	4,787	3,860	15,828	13,279	9,088	8,380
Short-term debt	..	16,163	16,082	24,535	36,257	39,323	37,300	30,068	28,507	27,506
of which interest arrears on LDOD	..	0	0	0	0	0	0	0	0	0
Official creditors	..	0	0	0	0	0	0	0	0	0
Private creditors	..	0	0	0	0	0	0	0	0	0
Memo: principal arrears on LDOD	..	0	0	0	0	0	0	0	0	0
Official creditors	..	0	0	0	0	0	0	0	0	0
Private creditors	..	0	0	0	0	0	0	0	0	0
Memo: export credits	..	0	15,583	22,645	24,968	26,686	19,603	16,510	14,120	13,889
TOTAL DEBT FLOWS										
Disbursements	1,374	11,573	14,229	12,761	17,445	16,130	44,066	31,454	29,233	26,916
Long-term debt	1,374	11,573	12,045	12,432	17,445	16,130	30,778	31,454	29,233	26,916
IMF purchases	0	0	2,184	328	0	0	13,288	0	0	0
Principal repayments	1,016	4,890	4,008	13,242	16,051	12,703	15,678	29,071	32,318	16,552
Long-term debt	1,016	4,756	2,818	12,346	14,876	11,499	14,534	27,018	28,878	15,489
IMF repurchases	0	134	1,191	896	1,175	1,204	1,144	2,052	3,439	1,063
Net flows on debt	1,360	14,822	17,641	2,197	13,116	6,492	26,366	-4,850	-4,646	9,363
of which short-term debt	..	8,139	7,420	2,678	11,722	3,065	-2,022	-7,232	-1,561	-1,001
Interest payments (INT)	..	6,067	7,303	7,506	8,082	9,216	11,208	11,722	11,042	12,589
Long-term debt	283	4,579	5,799	5,844	5,835	6,535	8,053	8,338	8,442	10,174
IMF charges	0	4	522	503	426	233	545	651	482	423
Short-term debt	..	1,484	982	1,160	1,822	2,448	2,611	2,733	2,118	1,991
Net transfers on debt	..	8,754	10,338	-5,310	5,034	-2,724	15,157	-16,571	-15,688	-3,226
Total debt service paid (TDS)	..	10,958	11,311	20,748	24,133	21,919	26,886	40,792	43,360	29,141
Long-term debt	1,299	9,335	8,617	18,190	20,711	18,033	22,586	35,357	37,320	25,663
IMF repurchases and charges	0	138	1,712	1,399	1,601	1,437	1,689	2,703	3,922	1,487
Short-term debt (interest only)	..	1,484	982	1,160	1,822	2,448	2,611	2,733	2,118	1,991

2. AGGREGATE NET RESOURCE FLOWS AND NET TRANSFERS (LONG-TERM)

	1970	1980	1990	1992	1993	1994	1995	1996	1997	1998
NET RESOURCE FLOWS	689	8,987	12,478	9,857	21,308	20,171	26,321	17,573	15,270	22,428
Net flow of long-term debt (ex. IMF)	358	6,817	9,228	86	2,569	4,631	16,244	4,435	355	11,427
Foreign direct investment (net)	323	2,156	2,634	4,393	4,389	10,972	9,526	9,185	12,831	10,238
Portfolio equity flows	0	0	563	5,365	14,297	4,521	520	3,922	2,052	730
Grants (excluding technical coop.)	8	14	54	14	53	47	31	30	32	32
Memo: technical coop. grants	6	44	81	112	116	104	122	132	101	110
official net resource flows	149	806	4,225	631	55	-534	10,384	-7,542	-4,504	-760
private net resource flows	539	8,182	8,253	9,227	21,253	20,705	15,937	25,115	19,774	23,188
NET TRANSFERS	47	3,040	5,365	1,702	13,128	11,236	15,768	6,334	3,828	8,854
Interest on long-term debt	283	4,579	5,799	5,844	5,835	6,535	8,053	8,338	8,442	10,174
Profit remittances on FDI	359	1,368	1,314	2,312	2,346	2,400	2,500	2,900	3,000	3,400
Memo: official net transfers	90	492	2,848	-1,256	-1,857	-2,521	7,725	-10,068	-6,163	-2,281
private net transfers	-43	2,548	2,517	2,957	14,985	13,757	8,044	16,403	9,991	11,134

3. MAJOR ECONOMIC AGGREGATES

	1970	1980	1990	1992	1993	1994	1995	1996	1997	1998
Gross national product (GNP)	35,091	217,073	254,084	354,014	392,065	411,186	346,409	338,060	348,394	380,563
Exports of goods & services (XGS)	..	24,685	54,570	61,330	67,428	78,025	96,707	115,156	131,126	140,111
of which workers remittances	..	698	2,492	3,070	3,332	3,475	3,673	4,224	4,865	5,627
Imports of goods & services (MGS)	..	35,243	63,504	86,087	91,136	107,994	98,571	117,791	138,962	156,458
International reserves (RES)	756	4,175	10,217	19,171	25,299	6,441	17,046	19,527	28,852	31,863
Current account balance	..	-10,422	-7,451	-24,442	-23,400	-29,662	-1,576	-2,328	-7,454	-15,960

4. DEBT INDICATORS

	1970	1980	1990	1992	1993	1994	1995	1996	1997	1998
EDT / XGS (%)	..	232.4	191.4	183.1	195.4	179.7	172.6	137.0	113.9	114.2
EDT / GNP (%)	..	26.4	41.1	31.7	33.6	34.1	48.2	46.7	42.9	42.0
TDS / XGS (%)	..	44.4	20.7	33.8	35.8	28.1	27.8	35.4	33.1	20.8
INT / XGS (%)	..	24.6	13.4	12.2	12.0	11.8	11.6	10.2	8.4	9.0
INT / GNP (%)	..	2.8	2.9	2.1	2.1	2.2	3.2	3.5	3.2	3.3
RES / EDT (%)	..	7.3	9.8	17.1	19.2	4.6	10.2	12.4	19.3	19.9
RES / MGS (months)	..	1.4	1.9	2.7	3.3	0.7	2.1	2.0	2.5	2.4
Short-term / EDT (%)	..	28.2	15.4	21.9	27.5	28.1	22.4	19.1	19.1	17.2
Concessional / EDT (%)	..	0.6	0.9	1.0	1.0	1.1	0.9	0.9	0.9	0.9
Multilateral / EDT (%)	..	5.5	13.7	13.8	12.2	12.2	11.2	11.3	11.1	10.7

MEXICO

(US$ million, unless otherwise indicated)

	1970	1980	1990	1992	1993	1994	1995	1996	1997	1998
5. LONG-TERM DEBT										
DEBT OUTSTANDING (LDOD)	**5,964**	**41,202**	**81,797**	**81,825**	**90,689**	**97,019**	**113,755**	**114,409**	**111,707**	**124,073**
Public and publicly guaranteed	**3,194**	**33,902**	**75,962**	**71,150**	**75,151**	**79,531**	**95,167**	**94,069**	**84,387**	**87,996**
Official creditors	1,148	4,468	22,609	25,093	25,939	27,366	38,994	29,362	23,031	23,119
Multilateral	746	3,176	14,291	15,531	16,073	17,073	18,640	17,755	16,496	17,152
Concessional	74	193	60	39	31	24	17	11	7	4
Bilateral	401	1,291	8,318	9,562	9,866	10,293	20,353	11,607	6,535	5,968
Concessional	123	120	822	1,104	1,280	1,540	1,455	1,461	1,307	1,354
Private creditors	2,047	29,434	53,353	46,057	49,212	52,165	56,174	64,706	61,356	64,876
Bonds	386	3,100	40,100	35,018	37,625	41,754	45,298	54,308	52,439	53,985
Commercial banks	1,267	25,637	6,630	5,946	6,795	6,446	6,529	6,384	5,417	7,964
Other private	394	698	6,624	5,093	4,793	3,965	4,347	4,015	3,500	2,927
Private nonguaranteed	**2,770**	**7,300**	**5,835**	**10,675**	**15,539**	**17,489**	**18,587**	**20,340**	**27,320**	**36,077**
Bonds	0	0	150	3,310	9,127	12,767	13,026	14,104	15,810	16,546
Commercial banks	2,770	7,300	5,685	7,365	6,412	4,722	5,562	6,236	11,510	19,532
Memo:										
IBRD	582	2,063	11,030	11,966	12,322	13,038	13,823	12,568	11,356	11,514
IDA	0	0	0	0	0	0	0	0	0	0
DISBURSEMENTS	**1,374**	**11,573**	**12,045**	**12,432**	**17,445**	**16,130**	**30,778**	**31,454**	**29,233**	**26,916**
Public and publicly guaranteed	**772**	**9,123**	**9,985**	**7,319**	**8,435**	**8,691**	**23,400**	**22,956**	**15,369**	**13,186**
Official creditors	229	1,074	5,454	2,887	2,775	2,117	13,424	2,489	1,783	2,204
Multilateral	160	634	3,647	1,749	1,483	1,281	2,669	2,113	1,544	1,916
Concessional	37	3	0	0	0	0	0	0	0	0
Bilateral	68	439	1,807	1,138	1,291	836	10,755	376	238	288
Concessional	9	17	636	165	178	125	7	204	38	15
Private creditors	543	8,050	4,532	4,432	5,661	6,574	9,976	20,467	13,586	10,982
Bonds	0	236	975	1,157	3,758	5,088	7,059	18,452	12,795	7,694
Commercial banks	432	7,625	2,552	2,025	593	500	1,699	1,072	226	2,918
Other private	111	189	1,005	1,250	1,310	985	1,218	943	565	371
Private nonguaranteed	**603**	**2,450**	**2,060**	**5,113**	**9,010**	**7,439**	**7,379**	**8,498**	**13,864**	**13,731**
Bonds	0	0	150	2,766	5,861	3,657	843	2,433	3,690	4,998
Commercial banks	603	2,450	1,910	2,347	3,149	3,782	6,535	6,065	10,174	8,732
Memo:										
IBRD	98	422	3,326	1,352	1,098	943	1,732	1,051	995	1,283
IDA	0	0	0	0	0	0	0	0	0	0
PRINCIPAL REPAYMENTS	**1,016**	**4,756**	**2,818**	**12,346**	**14,876**	**11,499**	**14,534**	**27,018**	**28,878**	**15,489**
Public and publicly guaranteed	**475**	**4,006**	**2,622**	**10,288**	**5,893**	**6,582**	**9,140**	**20,308**	**21,995**	**11,623**
Official creditors	87	282	1,283	2,270	2,772	2,698	3,071	10,061	6,319	2,996
Multilateral	31	137	1,034	1,256	1,274	1,421	1,713	1,712	1,625	1,602
Concessional	0	12	13	10	8	7	7	6	5	3
Bilateral	56	145	249	1,014	1,498	1,277	1,358	8,349	4,694	1,394
Concessional	9	12	0	32	88	14	92	81	74	75
Private creditors	388	3,724	1,339	8,018	3,121	3,884	6,069	10,247	15,677	8,627
Bonds	16	123	464	4,592	650	1,113	3,534	8,119	14,063	6,973
Commercial banks	266	3,445	185	1,726	735	741	1,626	1,000	668	640
Other private	106	156	690	1,700	1,735	2,029	909	1,128	946	1,014
Private nonguaranteed	**542**	**750**	**196**	**2,058**	**8,983**	**4,917**	**5,394**	**6,710**	**6,883**	**3,866**
Bonds	0	0	0	150	25	50	610	1,328	1,950	3,291
Commercial banks	542	750	196	1,908	8,958	4,867	4,784	5,382	4,933	575
Memo:										
IBRD	23	89	801	981	991	1,065	1,411	1,409	1,311	1,257
IDA	0	0	0	0	0	0	0	0	0	0
NET FLOWS ON DEBT	**358**	**6,817**	**9,228**	**86**	**2,569**	**4,631**	**16,244**	**4,435**	**355**	**11,427**
Public and publicly guaranteed	**297**	**5,117**	**7,364**	**-2,969**	**2,543**	**2,109**	**14,260**	**2,647**	**-6,627**	**1,562**
Official creditors	142	791	4,171	617	3	-581	10,353	-7,573	-4,536	-793
Multilateral	130	497	2,613	493	209	-140	956	401	-80	314
Concessional	37	-9	-13	-10	-8	-7	-7	-6	-5	-3
Bilateral	12	294	1,558	124	-207	-441	9,398	-7,974	-4,456	-1,107
Concessional	0	5	635	134	91	111	-85	123	-36	-60
Private creditors	155	4,326	3,193	-3,586	2,540	2,690	3,906	10,220	-2,091	2,355
Bonds	-16	112	511	-3,435	3,108	3,975	3,525	10,333	-1,267	720
Commercial banks	166	4,180	2,367	300	-142	-241	73	72	-443	2,278
Other private	5	33	314	-450	-425	-1,044	309	-185	-381	-643
Private nonguaranteed	**61**	**1,700**	**1,864**	**3,055**	**27**	**2,523**	**1,985**	**1,788**	**6,981**	**9,865**
Bonds	0	0	150	2,616	5,836	3,608	233	1,105	1,740	1,708
Commercial banks	61	1,700	1,714	439	-5,809	-1,085	1,752	683	5,241	8,157
Memo:										
IBRD	76	333	2,524	371	107	-123	321	-359	-316	26
IDA	0	0	0	0	0	0	0	0	0	0

MEXICO

(US$ million, unless otherwise indicated)

	1970	1980	1990	1992	1993	1994	1995	1996	1997	1998
INTEREST PAYMENTS (LINT)	**283**	**4,579**	**5,799**	**5,844**	**5,835**	**6,535**	**8,053**	**8,338**	**8,442**	**10,174**
Public and publicly guaranteed	**216**	**3,879**	**5,217**	**5,012**	**4,689**	**5,177**	**6,329**	**6,424**	**6,290**	**6,925**
Official creditors	60	314	1,377	1,886	1,912	1,986	2,659	2,526	1,659	1,521
Multilateral	39	236	1,004	1,175	1,195	1,231	1,291	1,314	1,167	1,148
Concessional	2	7	2	2	1	1	1	1	0	0
Bilateral	21	78	373	711	717	755	1,368	1,212	492	373
Concessional	4	5	8	47	47	49	67	55	50	43
Private creditors	156	3,566	3,841	3,125	2,776	3,190	3,670	3,898	4,631	5,405
Bonds	27	252	1,112	2,527	2,206	2,611	2,906	3,240	3,988	4,826
Commercial banks	106	3,261	2,198	266	293	331	436	378	386	380
Other private	24	52	531	333	277	249	328	280	256	198
Private nonguaranteed	**67**	**700**	**582**	**832**	**1,146**	**1,358**	**1,723**	**1,914**	**2,152**	**3,249**
Bonds	0	0	0	64	353	826	1,054	1,096	1,251	1,494
Commercial banks	67	700	582	768	793	533	670	818	901	1,755
Memo:										
IBRD	31	166	751	892	905	924	961	962	791	767
IDA	0	0	0	0	0	0	0	0	0	0
NET TRANSFERS ON DEBT	**75**	**2,238**	**3,428**	**-5,758**	**-3,266**	**-1,904**	**8,192**	**-3,903**	**-8,087**	**1,253**
Public and publicly guaranteed	**81**	**1,238**	**2,146**	**-7,981**	**-2,146**	**-3,068**	**7,930**	**-3,777**	**-12,916**	**-5,363**
Official creditors	82	478	2,794	-1,269	-1,910	-2,567	7,694	-10,099	-6,195	-2,313
Multilateral	90	261	1,609	-682	-986	-1,372	-336	-913	-1,247	-834
Concessional	35	-16	-15	-11	-10	-8	-8	-6	-5	-3
Bilateral	-9	216	1,185	-587	-924	-1,196	8,029	-9,186	-4,948	-1,479
Concessional	-4	0	627	87	44	63	-152	68	-85	-103
Private creditors	-1	760	-648	-6,711	-236	-501	237	6,322	-6,721	-3,050
Bonds	-42	-140	-601	-5,962	902	1,364	618	7,092	-5,255	-4,106
Commercial banks	60	919	169	34	-435	-572	-363	-306	-829	1,897
Other private	-18	-19	-217	-783	-703	-1,293	-19	-465	-637	-841
Private nonguaranteed	**-6**	**1,000**	**1,282**	**2,223**	**-1,119**	**1,164**	**261**	**-126**	**4,829**	**6,616**
Bonds	0	0	150	2,552	5,482	2,782	-821	9	489	214
Commercial banks	-6	1,000	1,132	-329	-6,602	-1,618	1,082	-136	4,340	6,402
Memo:										
IBRD	45	167	1,773	-522	-797	-1,046	-641	-1,321	-1,107	-741
IDA	0	0	0	0	0	0	0	0	0	0
DEBT SERVICE (LTDS)	**1,299**	**9,335**	**8,617**	**18,190**	**20,711**	**18,033**	**22,586**	**35,357**	**37,320**	**25,663**
Public and publicly guaranteed	**691**	**7,885**	**7,839**	**15,300**	**10,581**	**11,758**	**15,469**	**26,732**	**28,285**	**18,549**
Official creditors	147	596	2,659	4,156	4,685	4,685	5,730	12,588	7,977	4,517
Multilateral	70	373	2,038	2,431	2,470	2,653	3,004	3,026	2,791	2,750
Concessional	2	18	15	11	10	8	8	6	5	3
Bilateral	77	223	622	1,725	2,215	2,032	2,726	9,561	5,186	1,767
Concessional	14	16	9	78	134	62	159	136	124	119
Private creditors	544	7,289	5,180	11,143	5,897	7,074	9,739	14,145	20,307	14,032
Bonds	42	376	1,576	7,118	2,856	3,724	6,440	11,359	18,051	11,799
Commercial banks	372	6,706	2,383	1,992	1,028	1,072	2,062	1,377	1,055	1,021
Other private	130	208	1,221	2,033	2,013	2,278	1,237	1,408	1,202	1,212
Private nonguaranteed	**609**	**1,450**	**778**	**2,890**	**10,129**	**6,275**	**7,117**	**8,624**	**9,035**	**7,115**
Bonds	0	0	0	214	378	876	1,664	2,424	3,201	4,784
Commercial banks	609	1,450	778	2,676	9,751	5,399	5,453	6,201	5,834	2,330
Memo:										
IBRD	54	255	1,553	1,874	1,895	1,989	2,372	2,372	2,102	2,024
IDA	0	0	0	0	0	0	0	0	0	0
UNDISBURSED DEBT	**556**	**4,817**	**8,110**	**11,585**	**13,975**	**15,941**	**15,568**	**14,941**	**14,360**	**14,180**
Official creditors	438	2,976	5,136	7,873	6,889	8,334	8,669	6,135	5,937	5,692
Private creditors	118	1,841	2,974	3,712	7,086	7,607	6,899	8,806	8,423	8,488
Memorandum items										
Concessional LDOD	196	313	883	1,143	1,311	1,564	1,473	1,472	1,314	1,358
Variable rate LDOD	2,951	31,271	40,382	39,564	45,816	49,267	64,415	61,926	56,631	68,947
Public sector LDOD	3,165	33,249	75,595	70,650	74,674	79,079	94,738	93,665	84,183	87,829
Private sector LDOD	2,801	7,966	6,214	11,180	16,019	17,942	19,018	20,744	27,525	36,255

6. CURRENCY COMPOSITION OF LONG-TERM DEBT (PERCENT)

	1970	1980	1990	1992	1993	1994	1995	1996	1997	1998
Deutsche mark	11.2	4.3	3.7	4.1	3.7	3.7	3.0	3.4	4.7	4.7
French franc	7.7	1.2	3.8	3.6	3.1	3.1	2.7	2.4	2.3	2.2
Japanese yen	0.5	1.4	6.4	8.2	8.8	9.1	8.2	8.3	8.6	8.2
Pound sterling	1.1	0.5	1.4	1.2	0.9	0.9	0.7	0.7	1.3	1.0
Swiss franc	3.4	2.0	0.6	0.4	0.4	0.4	0.4	0.3	0.3	0.3
U.S.dollars	51.3	78.7	64.3	59.3	60.7	60.5	65.7	67.0	64.3	75.4
Multiple currency	21.9	9.9	18.6	21.6	20.9	20.8	18.1	16.5	15.8	4.6
Special drawing rights	0.0	0.0	0.0	0.0	0.0	0.0	0.0	0.0	0.0	0.0
All other currencies	2.9	2.0	1.2	1.6	1.5	1.5	1.2	1.4	2.7	3.6

MEXICO

(US$ million, unless otherwise indicated)

	1970	1980	1990	1992	1993	1994	1995	1996	1997	1998
7. DEBT RESTRUCTURINGS										
Total amount rescheduled	..	..	36,950	327	0	0	0	0	0	0
Debt stock rescheduled	..	..	36,160	0	0	0	0	0	0	0
Principal rescheduled	..	..	570	234	0	0	0	0	0	0
Official	..	..	382	168	0	0	0	0	0	0
Private	..	..	188	67	0	0	0	0	0	0
Interest rescheduled	..	..	204	76	0	0	0	0	0	0
Official	..	..	132	44	0	0	0	0	0	0
Private	..	..	72	31	0	0	0	0	0	0
Debt forgiven	..	..	0	0	0	0	0	0	0	0
Memo: interest forgiven	..	..	0	0	0	0	0	0	0	0
Debt stock reduction	..	..	8,145	7,426	830	267	306	3,181	0	0
of which debt buyback	..	..	0	5,086	498	51	13	2,420	0	0
8. DEBT STOCK-FLOW RECONCILIATION										
Total change in debt stocks	..	..	10,605	-1,750	19,425	8,468	26,681	-9,128	-8,454	10,657
Net flows on debt	1,360	14,822	17,641	2,197	13,116	6,492	26,366	-4,850	-4,646	9,363
Net change in interest arrears	..	..	0	0	0	0	0	0	0	0
Interest capitalized	..	..	204	76	0	0	0	0	0	0
Debt forgiveness or reduction	..	..	-8,145	-2,340	-332	-216	-293	-761	0	0
Cross-currency valuation	..	..	2,002	-1,140	327	2,219	449	-2,479	-2,838	1,592
Residual	..	..	-1,096	-543	6,314	-27	159	-1,038	-970	-298
9. AVERAGE TERMS OF NEW COMMITMENTS										
ALL CREDITORS										
Interest (%)	8.1	11.3	8.6	7.3	6.7	5.7	8.0	7.8	7.3	6.8
Maturity (years)	11.5	9.8	13.5	11.0	10.3	8.8	7.0	8.1	9.9	8.1
Grace period (years)	3.4	4.3	5.3	3.4	3.8	3.7	2.7	6.5	6.9	5.1
Grant element (%)	9.8	-5.7	7.3	9.8	13.1	15.8	6.6	6.1	11.9	11.1
Official creditors										
Interest (%)	6.7	8.0	7.8	7.4	6.9	7.0	9.1	6.9	7.2	6.4
Maturity (years)	18.4	15.3	15.5	15.2	11.9	14.5	9.2	14.2	14.5	14.1
Grace period (years)	4.0	3.3	4.5	3.9	3.4	4.3	2.8	4.1	4.4	3.5
Grant element (%)	19.4	10.0	12.2	13.0	14.6	15.9	5.5	16.0	14.6	17.9
Private creditors										
Interest (%)	8.9	12.6	9.4	7.2	6.7	5.2	6.2	7.8	7.3	6.9
Maturity (years)	7.1	7.7	11.6	7.8	10.0	6.1	3.6	7.9	9.2	6.8
Grace period (years)	3.1	4.7	6.1	2.9	3.8	3.4	2.5	6.6	7.3	5.4
Grant element (%)	3.6	-12.0	2.9	7.4	12.8	15.7	8.4	5.7	11.5	9.8
Memorandum items										
Commitments	857	7,628	12,481	7,620	11,672	10,852	24,580	23,914	15,254	13,846
Official creditors	337	2,183	5,914	3,328	2,047	3,527	15,131	938	1,903	2,339
Private creditors	520	5,445	6,567	4,292	9,625	7,325	9,450	22,976	13,352	11,506

10. CONTRACTUAL OBLIGATIONS ON OUTSTANDING LONG-TERM DEBT

	1999	2000	2001	2002	2003	2004	2005	2006	2007	2008
TOTAL										
Disbursements	9,862	2,301	1,063	541	188	113	60	24	11	5
Principal	22,501	19,728	10,690	13,427	8,690	8,816	4,429	3,920	6,375	4,331
Interest	7,632	6,710	5,824	5,457	4,834	4,177	3,626	3,309	3,079	2,667
Official creditors										
Disbursements	2,264	1,595	928	509	183	113	60	24	11	5
Principal	3,825	3,453	3,061	2,765	2,409	2,293	2,115	2,014	1,586	1,258
Interest	1,775	1,600	1,404	1,215	1,040	876	719	570	431	326
Bilateral creditors										
Disbursements	762	390	114	60	23	15	0	0	0	0
Principal	1,961	1,476	1,116	757	521	442	297	227	96	53
Interest	440	322	220	143	101	70	44	28	16	11
Multilateral creditors										
Disbursements	1,502	1,205	814	449	160	98	60	24	11	5
Principal	1,864	1,977	1,945	2,008	1,888	1,852	1,818	1,787	1,490	1,205
Interest	1,335	1,278	1,184	1,071	939	807	674	542	416	314
Private creditors										
Disbursements	7,598	706	135	33	4	0	0	0	0	0
Principal	18,676	16,274	7,629	10,663	6,282	6,523	2,314	1,906	4,789	3,073
Interest	5,857	5,111	4,420	4,242	3,794	3,301	2,908	2,739	2,647	2,342
Commercial banks										
Disbursements	201	88	23	3	0	0	0	0	0	0
Principal	878	3,995	777	655	585	585	401	316	88	0
Interest	498	379	210	160	118	80	44	21	5	0
Other private										
Disbursements	7,397	618	112	30	4	0	0	0	0	0
Principal	17,799	12,279	6,852	10,008	5,697	5,938	1,913	1,589	4,701	3,073
Interest	5,359	4,732	4,210	4,082	3,676	3,221	2,864	2,718	2,643	2,342

MOLDOVA

(US$ million, unless otherwise indicated)

	1970	1980	1990	1992	1993	1994	1995	1996	1997	1998
1. SUMMARY DEBT DATA										
TOTAL DEBT STOCKS (EDT)	..	..	..	**39**	**278**	**499**	**686**	**829**	**1,037**	**1,035**
Long-term debt (LDOD)	..	..	..	**39**	**190**	**326**	**450**	**555**	**783**	**816**
Public and publicly guaranteed	..	..	..	39	190	326	450	555	783	808
Private nonguaranteed	..	..	..	0	0	0	0	0	0	8
Use of IMF credit	..	..	..	**0**	**87**	**164**	**230**	**248**	**233**	**177**
Short-term debt	..	..	..	**0**	**1**	**8**	**6**	**27**	**21**	**42**
of which interest arrears on LDOD	..	..	..	0	1	7	5	1	0	14
Official creditors	..	..	..	0	1	7	5	1	0	5
Private creditors	..	..	..	0	0	0	0	0	0	9
Memo: principal arrears on LDOD	..	..	..	0	5	18	42	0	15	59
Official creditors	..	..	..	0	5	18	42	0	15	32
Private creditors	..	..	..	0	0	0	0	0	0	28
Memo: export credits	..	..	..	0	0	0	8	50	54	30
TOTAL DEBT FLOWS										
Disbursements	..	..	..	**35**	**154**	**205**	**223**	**189**	**328**	**61**
Long-term debt	..	..	..	35	66	134	159	156	307	61
IMF purchases	..	..	..	0	88	71	64	33	21	0
Principal repayments	..	..	..	**5**	**1**	**5**	**39**	**45**	**69**	**123**
Long-term debt	..	..	..	5	1	5	39	38	49	59
IMF repurchases	..	..	..	0	0	0	0	7	20	64
Net flows on debt	..	..	..	**30**	**153**	**201**	**184**	**168**	**254**	**-55**
of which short-term debt	..	..	..	0	0	1	0	25	-5	7
Interest payments (INT)	..	..	..	**0**	**1**	**9**	**30**	**36**	**51**	**44**
Long-term debt	..	..	..	0	0	4	20	24	38	32
IMF charges	..	..	..	0	1	5	10	10	11	10
Short-term debt	..	..	..	0	0	0	0	1	1	1
Net transfers on debt	..	..	..	**30**	**152**	**192**	**154**	**133**	**204**	**-99**
Total debt service paid (TDS)	..	..	..	**5**	**2**	**14**	**69**	**81**	**119**	**166**
Long-term debt	..	..	..	5	1	9	59	62	87	91
IMF repurchases and charges	..	..	..	0	1	5	10	18	31	74
Short-term debt (interest only)	..	..	..	0	0	0	0	1	1	1
2. AGGREGATE NET RESOURCE FLOWS AND NET TRANSFERS (LONG-TERM)										
NET RESOURCE FLOWS	..	..	..	**31**	**83**	**173**	**152**	**152**	**337**	**100**
Net flow of long-term debt (ex. IMF)	..	..	..	30	65	129	119	118	259	3
Foreign direct investment (net)	..	..	..	0	0	12	23	24	72	85
Portfolio equity flows	..	..	..	0	0	0	0	0	0	0
Grants (excluding technical coop.)	..	..	..	1	18	32	10	10	7	13
Memo: technical coop. grants	..	..	..	0	0	1	20	25	15	16
official net resource flows	..	..	..	31	83	161	110	48	58	39
private net resource flows	..	..	..	0	0	12	43	104	279	62
NET TRANSFERS	..	..	..	**31**	**83**	**170**	**132**	**126**	**296**	**63**
Interest on long-term debt	..	..	..	0	0	4	20	24	38	32
Profit remittances on FDI	..	..	..	0	0	0	0	2	3	5
Memo: official net transfers	..	..	..	31	83	158	90	25	39	20
private net transfers	..	..	..	0	0	12	43	101	258	43
3. MAJOR ECONOMIC AGGREGATES										
Gross national product (GNP)	..	..	..	2,822	4,463	2,685	3,031	1,749	1,989	1,655
Exports of goods & services (XGS)	..	..	..	..	..	662	899	1,039	1,157	897
of which workers remittances	..	..	..	..	..	..	1	3	1	3
Imports of goods & services (MGS)	..	..	..	..	..	777	1,049	1,297	1,500	1,326
International reserves (RES)	..	..	..	2	76	180	257	312	366	144
Current account balance	..	..	..	..	..	-82	-95	-188	-268	-334
4. DEBT INDICATORS										
EDT / XGS (%)	..	..	..	..	..	75.3	76.2	79.8	89.6	115.3
EDT / GNP (%)	..	..	..	1.4	6.2	18.6	22.6	47.4	52.2	62.5
TDS / XGS (%)	..	..	..	..	..	2.1	7.7	7.8	10.3	18.5
INT / XGS (%)	..	..	..	..	..	1.3	3.3	3.4	4.4	4.9
INT / GNP (%)	..	..	..	0.0	0.0	0.3	1.0	2.0	2.5	2.6
RES / EDT (%)	..	..	..	6.4	27.5	36.1	37.5	37.6	35.3	13.9
RES / MGS (months)	..	..	..	..	..	2.8	2.9	2.9	2.9	1.3
Short-term / EDT (%)	..	..	..	0.0	0.3	1.6	0.9	3.2	2.1	4.0
Concessional / EDT (%)	..	..	..	25.7	6.9	15.6	23.4	20.0	18.3	19.0
Multilateral / EDT (%)	..	..	..	59.5	20.2	32.6	31.6	30.5	27.8	32.8

MOLDOVA

(US$ million, unless otherwise indicated)

	1970	1980	1990	1992	1993	1994	1995	1996	1997	1998
5. LONG-TERM DEBT										
DEBT OUTSTANDING (LDOD)	..	..	..	**39**	**190**	**326**	**450**	**555**	**783**	**816**
Public and publicly guaranteed	..	..	..	**39**	**190**	**326**	**450**	**555**	**783**	**808**
Official creditors	..	..	..	39	190	326	430	456	480	530
Multilateral	..	..	..	23	56	163	217	253	289	339
Concessional	..	..	..	0	0	31	59	56	84	91
Bilateral	..	..	..	16	134	164	214	203	191	190
Concessional	..	..	..	10	19	47	101	109	106	106
Private creditors	..	..	..	0	0	0	19	99	303	279
Bonds	..	..	..	0	0	0	0	0	75	75
Commercial banks	..	..	..	0	0	0	4	84	78	54
Other private	..	..	..	0	0	0	15	15	150	150
Private nonguaranteed	..	..	..	**0**	**0**	**0**	**0**	**0**	**0**	**8**
Bonds	..	..	..	0	0	0	0	0	0	0
Commercial banks	..	..	..	0	0	0	0	0	0	8
Memo:										
IBRD	..	..	..	0	28	99	152	142	135	169
IDA	..	..	..	0	0	0	0	0	35	38
DISBURSEMENTS	..	..	..	**35**	**66**	**134**	**159**	**156**	**307**	**61**
Public and publicly guaranteed	..	..	..	**35**	**66**	**134**	**159**	**156**	**307**	**58**
Official creditors	..	..	..	35	66	134	139	75	68	47
Multilateral	..	..	..	25	36	99	81	52	60	33
Concessional	..	..	..	0	0	30	26	0	35	2
Bilateral	..	..	..	11	30	35	58	23	8	14
Concessional	..	..	..	10	9	28	58	13	0	10
Private creditors	..	..	..	0	0	0	19	81	240	11
Bonds	..	..	..	0	0	0	0	0	75	0
Commercial banks	..	..	..	0	0	0	4	81	22	11
Other private	..	..	..	0	0	0	15	0	143	0
Private nonguaranteed	..	..	..	**0**	**0**	**0**	**0**	**0**	**0**	**3**
Bonds	..	..	..	0	0	0	0	0	0	0
Commercial banks	..	..	..	0	0	0	0	0	0	3
Memo:										
IBRD	..	..	..	0	29	67	50	0	5	27
IDA	..	..	..	0	0	0	0	0	35	2
PRINCIPAL REPAYMENTS	..	..	..	**5**	**1**	**5**	**39**	**38**	**49**	**59**
Public and publicly guaranteed	..	..	..	**5**	**1**	**5**	**39**	**38**	**49**	**58**
Official creditors	..	..	..	5	1	5	39	37	16	21
Multilateral	..	..	..	0	0	0	35	1	1	3
Concessional	..	..	..	0	0	0	0	0	0	0
Bilateral	..	..	..	5	1	5	4	36	15	19
Concessional	..	..	..	0	0	0	0	0	0	13
Private creditors	..	..	..	0	0	0	0	1	33	36
Bonds	..	..	..	0	0	0	0	0	0	0
Commercial banks	..	..	..	0	0	0	0	1	25	36
Other private	..	..	..	0	0	0	0	0	8	0
Private nonguaranteed	..	..	..	**0**	**0**	**0**	**0**	**0**	**0**	**1**
Bonds	..	..	..	0	0	0	0	0	0	0
Commercial banks	..	..	..	0	0	0	0	0	0	1
Memo:										
IBRD	..	..	..	0	0	0	0	0	0	1
IDA	..	..	..	0	0	0	0	0	0	0
NET FLOWS ON DEBT	..	..	..	**30**	**65**	**129**	**119**	**118**	**259**	**3**
Public and publicly guaranteed	..	..	..	**30**	**65**	**129**	**119**	**118**	**259**	**0**
Official creditors	..	..	..	30	65	129	100	38	52	26
Multilateral	..	..	..	25	36	99	46	51	59	30
Concessional	..	..	..	0	0	30	26	0	35	2
Bilateral	..	..	..	6	30	30	54	-13	-7	-5
Concessional	..	..	..	10	9	28	58	13	0	-3
Private creditors	..	..	..	0	0	0	19	80	207	-25
Bonds	..	..	..	0	0	0	0	0	75	0
Commercial banks	..	..	..	0	0	0	4	80	-3	-25
Other private	..	..	..	0	0	0	15	0	135	0
Private nonguaranteed	..	..	..	**0**	**0**	**0**	**0**	**0**	**0**	**2**
Bonds	..	..	..	0	0	0	0	0	0	0
Commercial banks	..	..	..	0	0	0	0	0	0	2
Memo:										
IBRD	..	..	..	0	29	67	50	0	5	26
IDA	..	..	..	0	0	0	0	0	35	2

MOLDOVA

(US$ million, unless otherwise indicated)

	1970	1980	1990	1992	1993	1994	1995	1996	1997	1998
INTEREST PAYMENTS (LINT)	..	..	..	**0**	**0**	**4**	**20**	**24**	**38**	**32**
Public and publicly guaranteed	..	..	..	**0**	**0**	**4**	**20**	**24**	**38**	**32**
Official creditors	..	..	..	0	0	4	20	23	20	18
Multilateral	..	..	..	0	0	4	12	15	13	14
Concessional	..	..	..	0	0	0	2	3	2	3
Bilateral	..	..	..	0	0	0	8	8	6	4
Concessional	..	..	..	0	0	0	2	2	3	3
Private creditors	..	..	..	0	0	0	0	1	19	14
Bonds	..	..	..	0	0	0	0	0	4	7
Commercial banks	..	..	..	0	0	0	0	1	6	3
Other private	..	..	..	0	0	0	0	1	9	3
Private nonguaranteed	..	..	..	**0**	**0**	**0**	**0**	**0**	**0**	**0**
Bonds	..	..	..	0	0	0	0	0	0	0
Commercial banks	..	..	..	0	0	0	0	0	0	0
Memo:										
IBRD	..	..	..	0	0	4	8	10	9	9
IDA	..	..	..	0	0	0	0	0	0	0
NET TRANSFERS ON DEBT	..	..	..	**30**	**65**	**125**	**99**	**94**	**220**	**-30**
Public and publicly guaranteed	..	..	..	**30**	**65**	**125**	**99**	**94**	**220**	**-32**
Official creditors	..	..	..	30	65	125	80	15	32	7
Multilateral	..	..	..	25	36	95	34	36	45	16
Concessional	..	..	..	0	0	30	24	-3	33	0
Bilateral	..	..	..	6	30	30	46	-21	-13	-8
Concessional	..	..	..	10	9	28	56	11	-3	-6
Private creditors	..	..	..	0	0	0	19	79	188	-39
Bonds	..	..	..	0	0	0	0	0	71	-7
Commercial banks	..	..	..	0	0	0	4	80	-10	-28
Other private	..	..	..	0	0	0	15	-1	126	-3
Private nonguaranteed	..	..	..	**0**	**0**	**0**	**0**	**0**	**0**	**2**
Bonds	..	..	..	0	0	0	0	0	0	0
Commercial banks	..	..	..	0	0	0	0	0	0	2
Memo:										
IBRD	..	..	..	0	28	64	42	-10	-4	17
IDA	..	..	..	0	0	0	0	0	35	2
DEBT SERVICE (LTDS)	..	..	..	**5**	**1**	**9**	**59**	**62**	**87**	**91**
Public and publicly guaranteed	..	..	..	**5**	**1**	**9**	**59**	**62**	**87**	**89**
Official creditors	..	..	..	5	1	9	59	60	36	39
Multilateral	..	..	..	0	0	4	47	16	14	17
Concessional	..	..	..	0	0	0	2	3	2	3
Bilateral	..	..	..	5	1	5	12	44	21	23
Concessional	..	..	..	0	0	0	2	2	3	16
Private creditors	..	..	..	0	0	0	0	2	51	50
Bonds	..	..	..	0	0	0	0	0	4	7
Commercial banks	..	..	..	0	0	0	0	1	31	39
Other private	..	..	..	0	0	0	0	1	16	3
Private nonguaranteed	..	..	..	**0**	**0**	**0**	**0**	**0**	**0**	**1**
Bonds	..	..	..	0	0	0	0	0	0	0
Commercial banks	..	..	..	0	0	0	0	0	0	1
Memo:										
IBRD	..	..	..	0	0	4	8	10	9	10
IDA	..	..	..	0	0	0	0	0	0	0
UNDISBURSED DEBT	..	..	..	**21**	**92**	**184**	**198**	**360**	**225**	**214**
Official creditors	..	..	..	21	92	175	180	169	191	191
Private creditors	..	..	..	0	0	8	18	191	34	23
Memorandum items										
Concessional LDOD	..	..	..	10	19	78	160	166	190	196
Variable rate LDOD	..	..	..	23	165	279	376	439	411	434
Public sector LDOD	..	..	..	39	190	326	450	550	759	779
Private sector LDOD	..	..	..	0	0	0	0	4	24	38

6. CURRENCY COMPOSITION OF LONG-TERM DEBT (PERCENT)

	1970	1980	1990	1992	1993	1994	1995	1996	1997	1998
Deutsche mark	..	..	..	0.0	0.0	0.0	1.9	7.5	5.8	5.5
French franc	..	..	..	0.0	0.0	0.0	0.0	0.0	0.0	0.0
Japanese yen	..	..	..	0.0	0.0	0.0	8.4	6.0	3.8	3.2
Pound sterling	..	..	..	0.0	0.0	0.0	0.0	0.0	0.0	0.0
Swiss franc	..	..	..	0.0	0.0	0.0	0.0	0.0	0.0	0.0
U.S.dollars	..	..	..	40.5	23.2	22.8	22.8	47.2	64.6	62.0
Multiple currency	..	..	..	0.0	14.8	30.3	33.9	25.5	17.3	20.6
Special drawing rights	..	..	..	0.0	0.0	0.0	0.0	0.0	0.0	0.0
All other currencies	..	..	..	59.5	62.0	46.9	33.0	13.8	8.5	8.7

MOLDOVA

(US$ million, unless otherwise indicated)

	1970	1980	1990	1992	1993	1994	1995	1996	1997	1998
7. DEBT RESTRUCTURINGS										
Total amount rescheduled	..	..	..	0	89	0	0	119	0	0
Debt stock rescheduled	..	..	..	0	0	0	0	0	0	0
Principal rescheduled	..	..	..	0	0	0	0	112	0	0
Official	..	..	..	0	0	0	0	112	0	0
Private	..	..	..	0	0	0	0	0	0	0
Interest rescheduled	..	..	..	..	0	0	0	7	0	0
Official	..	..	..	0	0	0	0	7	0	0
Private	..	..	..	0	0	0	0	0	0	0
Debt forgiven	..	..	..	0	0	0	0	0	0	0
Memo: interest forgiven	..	..	..	0	0	0	0	0	0	0
Debt stock reduction	..	..	..	0	0	0	0	0	0	0
of which debt buyback	..	..	..	0	0	0	0	0	0	0
8. DEBT STOCK-FLOW RECONCILIATION										
Total change in debt stocks	..	..	..	..	239	221	187	143	208	-2
Net flows on debt	..	..	..	30	153	201	184	168	254	-55
Net change in interest arrears	..	..	..	..	1	6	-2	-4	0	14
Interest capitalized	..	..	..	..	0	0	0	7	0	0
Debt forgiveness or reduction	..	..	..	..	0	0	0	0	0	0
Cross-currency valuation	..	..	..	..	-63	-48	-12	-21	-29	18
Residual	..	..	..	..	148	62	18	-6	-17	21
9. AVERAGE TERMS OF NEW COMMITMENTS										
ALL CREDITORS										
Interest (%)	..	..	..	3.5	5.7	5.6	6.8	6.9	6.1	4.8
Maturity (years)	..	..	..	8.0	15.7	16.9	12.0	8.5	18.0	17.9
Grace period (years)	..	..	..	4.1	4.6	5.4	4.6	2.7	6.4	5.4
Grant element (%)	..	..	..	24.4	21.1	27.6	16.1	12.2	30.2	34.9
Official creditors										
Interest (%)	..	..	..	3.5	5.7	5.6	6.8	5.4	3.8	4.8
Maturity (years)	..	..	..	8.0	15.7	17.1	13.3	16.9	26.6	17.9
Grace period (years)	..	..	..	4.1	4.6	5.4	5.2	4.9	7.5	5.4
Grant element (%)	..	..	..	24.4	21.1	28.2	17.8	27.8	48.9	34.9
Private creditors										
Interest (%)	..	..	..	0.0	0.0	7.5	7.0	7.5	9.7	0.0
Maturity (years)	..	..	..	0.0	0.0	10.0	5.4	5.3	4.7	0.0
Grace period (years)	..	..	..	0.0	0.0	4.5	1.5	1.8	4.6	0.0
Grant element (%)	..	..	..	0.0	0.0	11.4	7.8	6.3	0.7	0.0
Memorandum items										
Commitments	..	..	..	47	137	223	167	359	214	59
Official creditors	..	..	..	47	137	215	139	99	131	59
Private creditors	..	..	..	0	0	8	28	260	83	0

10. CONTRACTUAL OBLIGATIONS ON OUTSTANDING LONG-TERM DEBT

	1999	2000	2001	2002	2003	2004	2005	2006	2007	2008
TOTAL										
Disbursements	91	74	21	14	8	4	2	1	0	0
Principal	113	102	83	152	80	52	38	34	31	32
Interest	49	47	42	34	25	21	18	15	13	11
Official creditors										
Disbursements	75	66	21	14	8	4	2	1	0	0
Principal	55	47	44	49	54	51	38	34	31	32
Interest	29	30	29	26	24	21	18	15	13	11
Bilateral creditors										
Disbursements	10	5	2	1	0	0	0	0	0	0
Principal	45	20	13	10	10	10	10	6	6	5
Interest	6	5	5	4	4	3	2	2	2	1
Multilateral creditors										
Disbursements	65	61	19	13	8	4	2	1	0	0
Principal	10	27	31	40	44	42	29	29	26	27
Interest	23	25	24	23	20	18	15	13	12	10
Private creditors										
Disbursements	16	7	0	0	0	0	0	0	0	0
Principal	58	55	39	103	27	1	0	0	0	0
Interest	21	17	13	7	1	0	0	0	0	0
Commercial banks										
Disbursements	16	7	0	0	0	0	0	0	0	0
Principal	25	22	12	1	1	1	0	0	0	0
Interest	4	2	1	0	0	0	0	0	0	0
Other private										
Disbursements	0	0	0	0	0	0	0	0	0	0
Principal	33	32	28	101	25	0	0	0	0	0
Interest	17	15	13	7	1	0	0	0	0	0

MONGOLIA

(US$ million, unless otherwise indicated)

	1970	1980	1990	1992	1993	1994	1995	1996	1997	1998
1. SUMMARY DEBT DATA										
TOTAL DEBT STOCKS (EDT)	..	..	..	**350.2**	**383.9**	**461.3**	**524.5**	**531.5**	**608.5**	**738.8**
Long-term debt (LDOD)	..	..	..	**272.2**	**338.5**	**400.5**	**463.8**	**481.1**	**533.4**	**633.6**
Public and publicly guaranteed	..	..	..	272.2	338.5	400.5	463.8	481.1	533.4	633.6
Private nonguaranteed	..	..	..	0.0	0.0	0.0	0.0	0.0	0.0	0.0
Use of IMF credit	**0.0**	**0.0**	**0.0**	**18.9**	**31.6**	**55.3**	**47.0**	**43.6**	**47.6**	**48.3**
Short-term debt	..	..	..	**59.2**	**13.7**	**5.5**	**13.7**	**6.8**	**27.5**	**56.9**
of which interest arrears on LDOD	..	..	..	1.7	1.6	2.5	2.5	2.5	2.5	2.5
Official creditors	..	..	..	0.0	1.2	2.1	2.0	2.0	2.0	2.0
Private creditors	..	..	..	1.6	0.4	0.4	0.5	0.5	0.5	0.5
Memo: principal arrears on LDOD	..	..	..	6.0	17.5	16.0	3.9	4.1	4.8	4.9
Official creditors	..	..	..	0.8	1.9	13.5	0.0	0.0	0.0	0.0
Private creditors	..	..	..	5.3	15.6	2.6	3.9	4.1	4.8	4.9
Memo: export credits	..	..	..	62.0	60.0	63.0	51.0	39.0	52.0	64.0
TOTAL DEBT FLOWS										
Disbursements	..	..	..	**161.1**	**85.9**	**94.8**	**98.6**	**89.1**	**153.1**	**85.8**
Long-term debt	..	..	..	157.6	72.9	73.5	98.6	81.0	145.5	85.8
IMF purchases	0.0	0.0	0.0	3.5	13.0	21.3	0.0	8.1	7.7	0.0
Principal repayments	..	..	..	**56.1**	**14.8**	**33.7**	**41.6**	**44.1**	**54.1**	**25.9**
Long-term debt	..	..	..	56.1	14.8	33.7	32.2	34.1	53.2	24.6
IMF repurchases	0.0	0.0	0.0	0.0	0.0	0.0	9.5	10.0	0.9	1.3
Net flows on debt	..	..	..	**162.4**	**25.8**	**51.8**	**65.2**	**38.1**	**119.8**	**89.3**
of which short-term debt	..	..	..	57.5	-45.3	-9.2	8.2	-6.9	20.7	29.4
Interest payments (INT)	..	..	..	**11.5**	**9.7**	**9.9**	**10.1**	**8.8**	**12.4**	**8.9**
Long-term debt	..	..	..	9.5	6.3	8.3	8.6	8.1	11.5	6.9
IMF charges	0.0	0.0	0.0	1.3	1.2	1.1	1.1	0.5	0.2	0.2
Short-term debt	..	..	..	0.7	2.3	0.5	0.4	0.2	0.6	1.7
Net transfers on debt	..	..	..	**151.0**	**16.1**	**41.9**	**55.0**	**29.3**	**107.4**	**80.4**
Total debt service paid (TDS)	..	..	..	**67.6**	**24.5**	**43.6**	**51.8**	**52.9**	**66.4**	**34.8**
Long-term debt	..	..	..	65.7	21.1	42.1	40.8	42.2	64.7	31.6
IMF repurchases and charges	0.0	0.0	0.0	1.3	1.2	1.1	10.6	10.5	1.1	1.5
Short-term debt (interest only)	..	..	..	0.7	2.3	0.5	0.4	0.2	0.6	1.7
2. AGGREGATE NET RESOURCE FLOWS AND NET TRANSFERS (LONG-TERM)										
NET RESOURCE FLOWS	..	..	..	**140.0**	**99.0**	**108.5**	**150.3**	**123.2**	**176.0**	**133.8**
Net flow of long-term debt (ex. IMF)	..	..	..	101.4	58.1	39.8	66.4	46.9	92.3	61.2
Foreign direct investment (net)	..	..	..	2.0	7.7	6.9	9.8	16.0	25.0	19.0
Portfolio equity flows	..	..	..	0.0	0.0	0.0	0.0	0.0	0.0	0.0
Grants (excluding technical coop.)	..	..	..	36.6	33.2	61.9	74.1	60.2	58.7	53.6
Memo: technical coop. grants	..	..	..	21.4	36.8	52.7	55.8	50.7	53.2	57.4
official net resource flows	..	..	..	111.6	101.6	123.3	154.2	127.4	162.2	127.2
private net resource flows	..	..	..	28.4	-2.6	-14.8	-3.9	-4.2	13.8	6.6
NET TRANSFERS	..	..	..	**130.5**	**92.7**	**100.2**	**141.7**	**115.1**	**164.5**	**126.9**
Interest on long-term debt	..	..	..	9.5	6.3	8.3	8.6	8.1	11.5	6.9
Profit remittances on FDI	..	..	..	0.0	0.0	0.0	0.0	0.0	0.0	0.0
Memo: official net transfers	..	..	..	110.9	100.3	120.1	149.5	122.2	153.1	121.7
private net transfers	..	..	..	19.6	-7.6	-19.9	-7.8	-7.1	11.4	5.2
3. MAJOR ECONOMIC AGGREGATES										
Gross national product (GNP)	..	..	..	..	521.9	659.6	943.8	1,054.6	907.6	989.0
Exports of goods & services (XGS)	..	..	..	390.8	392.6	415.6	511.3	492.5	627.3	555.8
of which workers remittances	..	..	..	0.0	0.0	..	..	..	..	5.5
Imports of goods & services (MGS)	..	..	..	481.7	432.4	447.0	549.5	599.2	576.3	680.7
International reserves (RES)	..	..	..	22.8	66.0	94.2	157.5	161.0	200.4	103.2
Current account balance	..	..	..	-55.7	31.1	46.4	38.9	-36.9	102.9	-74.7
4. DEBT INDICATORS										
EDT / XGS (%)	..	..	..	89.6	97.8	111.0	102.6	107.9	97.0	132.9
EDT / GNP (%)	..	..	..	..	73.6	69.9	55.6	50.4	67.1	74.7
TDS / XGS (%)	..	..	..	17.3	6.2	10.5	10.1	10.7	10.6	6.3
INT / XGS (%)	..	..	..	2.9	2.5	2.4	2.0	1.8	2.0	1.6
INT / GNP (%)	..	..	..	..	1.9	1.5	1.1	0.8	1.4	0.9
RES / EDT (%)	..	..	..	6.5	17.2	20.4	30.0	30.3	32.9	14.0
RES / MGS (months)	..	..	..	0.6	1.8	2.5	3.4	3.2	4.2	1.8
Short-term / EDT (%)	..	..	..	16.9	3.6	1.2	2.6	1.3	4.5	7.7
Concessional / EDT (%)	..	..	..	43.0	51.2	56.5	65.9	74.3	79.4	81.3
Multilateral / EDT (%)	..	..	..	16.1	18.6	24.5	32.4	38.4	47.5	48.6

MONGOLIA

(US$ million, unless otherwise indicated)

	1970	1980	1990	1992	1993	1994	1995	1996	1997	1998
5. LONG-TERM DEBT										
DEBT OUTSTANDING (LDOD)	..	..	..	**272.2**	**338.5**	**400.5**	**463.8**	**481.1**	**533.4**	**633.6**
Public and publicly guaranteed	..	..	..	**272.2**	**338.5**	**400.5**	**463.8**	**481.1**	**533.4**	**633.6**
Official creditors	..	..	..	163.0	235.2	311.3	385.9	428.5	496.1	607.9
Multilateral	..	..	..	56.4	71.5	113.1	169.9	204.3	289.2	358.7
Concessional	..	..	..	53.4	68.5	113.1	169.9	204.3	289.2	358.7
Bilateral	..	..	..	106.6	163.7	198.2	216.0	224.3	206.9	249.2
Concessional	..	..	..	97.0	128.0	147.5	175.5	190.7	194.1	242.0
Private creditors	..	..	..	109.2	103.3	89.2	78.0	52.5	37.3	25.7
Bonds	..	..	..	0.0	0.0	0.0	0.0	0.0	0.0	0.0
Commercial banks	..	..	..	19.7	19.6	19.6	14.6	10.3	6.0	2.4
Other private	..	..	..	89.6	83.7	69.7	63.4	42.2	31.3	23.3
Private nonguaranteed	..	..	..	**0.0**	**0.0**	**0.0**	**0.0**	**0.0**	**0.0**	**0.0**
Bonds	..	..	..	0.0	0.0	0.0	0.0	0.0	0.0	0.0
Commercial banks	..	..	..	0.0	0.0	0.0	0.0	0.0	0.0	0.0
Memo:										
IBRD	0.0	0.0	0.0	0.0	0.0	0.0	0.0	0.0	0.0	0.0
IDA	0.0	0.0	0.0	27.4	30.1	49.2	58.7	67.6	97.1	118.0
DISBURSEMENTS	..	..	..	**157.6**	**72.9**	**73.5**	**98.6**	**81.0**	**145.5**	**85.8**
Public and publicly guaranteed	..	..	..	**157.6**	**72.9**	**73.5**	**98.6**	**81.0**	**145.5**	**85.8**
Official creditors	..	..	..	75.0	72.9	70.9	93.0	81.0	139.5	83.3
Multilateral	..	..	..	44.3	14.7	38.9	58.3	45.1	102.8	50.7
Concessional	..	..	..	43.4	14.7	38.9	58.3	45.1	102.8	50.7
Bilateral	..	..	..	30.7	58.2	32.0	34.8	36.0	36.7	32.7
Concessional	..	..	..	21.2	27.5	10.6	31.2	34.5	25.9	32.7
Private creditors	..	..	..	82.5	0.0	2.6	5.6	0.0	6.0	2.5
Bonds	..	..	..	0.0	0.0	0.0	0.0	0.0	0.0	0.0
Commercial banks	..	..	..	58.2	0.0	1.7	0.1	0.0	0.0	0.4
Other private	..	..	..	24.3	0.0	0.9	5.5	0.0	6.0	2.1
Private nonguaranteed	..	..	..	**0.0**	**0.0**	**0.0**	**0.0**	**0.0**	**0.0**	**0.0**
Bonds	..	..	..	0.0	0.0	0.0	0.0	0.0	0.0	0.0
Commercial banks	..	..	..	0.0	0.0	0.0	0.0	0.0	0.0	0.0
Memo:										
IBRD	0.0	0.0	0.0	0.0	0.0	0.0	0.0	0.0	0.0	0.0
IDA	0.0	0.0	0.0	27.4	3.4	17.4	8.4	11.0	33.8	16.7
PRINCIPAL REPAYMENTS	..	..	..	**56.1**	**14.8**	**33.7**	**32.2**	**34.1**	**53.2**	**24.6**
Public and publicly guaranteed	..	..	..	**56.1**	**14.8**	**33.7**	**32.2**	**34.1**	**53.2**	**24.6**
Official creditors	..	..	..	0.0	4.5	9.5	12.9	13.9	36.0	9.8
Multilateral	..	..	..	0.0	0.0	3.0	0.0	0.0	0.0	0.0
Concessional	..	..	..	0.0	0.0	0.0	0.0	0.0	0.0	0.0
Bilateral	..	..	..	0.0	4.5	6.5	12.9	13.9	36.0	9.8
Concessional	..	..	..	0.0	0.0	0.0	0.1	4.5	4.5	4.1
Private creditors	..	..	..	56.1	10.3	24.2	19.2	20.2	17.2	14.9
Bonds	..	..	..	0.0	0.0	0.0	0.0	0.0	0.0	0.0
Commercial banks	..	..	..	40.2	0.0	2.0	5.2	4.1	4.3	4.1
Other private	..	..	..	15.9	10.3	22.2	14.0	16.1	12.9	10.8
Private nonguaranteed	..	..	..	**0.0**	**0.0**	**0.0**	**0.0**	**0.0**	**0.0**	**0.0**
Bonds	..	..	..	0.0	0.0	0.0	0.0	0.0	0.0	0.0
Commercial banks	..	..	..	0.0	0.0	0.0	0.0	0.0	0.0	0.0
Memo:										
IBRD	0.0	0.0	0.0	0.0	0.0	0.0	0.0	0.0	0.0	0.0
IDA	0.0	0.0	0.0	0.0	0.0	0.0	0.0	0.0	0.0	0.0
NET FLOWS ON DEBT	..	..	..	**101.4**	**58.1**	**39.8**	**66.4**	**46.9**	**92.3**	**61.2**
Public and publicly guaranteed	..	..	..	**101.4**	**58.1**	**39.8**	**66.4**	**46.9**	**92.3**	**61.2**
Official creditors	..	..	..	75.0	68.4	61.4	80.1	67.2	103.5	73.6
Multilateral	..	..	..	44.3	14.7	35.9	58.3	45.1	102.8	50.7
Concessional	..	..	..	43.4	14.7	38.9	58.3	45.1	102.8	50.7
Bilateral	..	..	..	30.7	53.7	25.5	21.8	22.1	0.7	22.9
Concessional	..	..	..	21.2	27.5	10.6	31.0	30.0	21.4	28.6
Private creditors	..	..	..	26.4	-10.3	-21.7	-13.7	-20.2	-11.2	-12.4
Bonds	..	..	..	0.0	0.0	0.0	0.0	0.0	0.0	0.0
Commercial banks	..	..	..	18.0	0.0	-0.3	-5.2	-4.1	-4.3	-3.7
Other private	..	..	..	8.4	-10.3	-21.4	-8.5	-16.1	-6.9	-8.7
Private nonguaranteed	..	..	..	**0.0**	**0.0**	**0.0**	**0.0**	**0.0**	**0.0**	**0.0**
Bonds	..	..	..	0.0	0.0	0.0	0.0	0.0	0.0	0.0
Commercial banks	..	..	..	0.0	0.0	0.0	0.0	0.0	0.0	0.0
Memo:										
IBRD	0.0	0.0	0.0	0.0	0.0	0.0	0.0	0.0	0.0	0.0
IDA	0.0	0.0	0.0	27.4	3.4	17.4	8.4	11.0	33.8	16.7

MONGOLIA

(US$ million, unless otherwise indicated)

	1970	1980	1990	1992	1993	1994	1995	1996	1997	1998
INTEREST PAYMENTS (LINT)	..	..	..	**9.5**	**6.3**	**8.3**	**8.6**	**8.1**	**11.5**	**6.9**
Public and publicly guaranteed	..	..	..	**9.5**	**6.3**	**8.3**	**8.6**	**8.1**	**11.5**	**6.9**
Official creditors	..	..	..	0.7	1.3	3.2	4.7	5.2	9.1	5.5
Multilateral	..	..	..	0.3	0.5	1.0	1.1	1.6	2.0	2.7
Concessional	..	..	..	0.2	0.5	0.8	1.1	1.6	2.0	2.7
Bilateral	..	..	..	0.3	0.8	2.2	3.5	3.6	7.1	2.8
Concessional	..	..	..	0.3	0.6	0.8	2.1	2.1	5.7	2.2
Private creditors	..	..	..	8.8	5.0	5.1	3.9	2.9	2.4	1.4
Bonds	..	..	..	0.0	0.0	0.0	0.0	0.0	0.0	0.0
Commercial banks	..	..	..	4.7	0.6	1.4	1.0	0.4	0.5	0.2
Other private	..	..	..	4.1	4.4	3.7	3.0	2.4	1.9	1.2
Private nonguaranteed	..	..	..	**0.0**	**0.0**	**0.0**	**0.0**	**0.0**	**0.0**	**0.0**
Bonds	..	..	..	0.0	0.0	0.0	0.0	0.0	0.0	0.0
Commercial banks	..	..	..	0.0	0.0	0.0	0.0	0.0	0.0	0.0
Memo:										
IBRD	0.0	0.0	0.0	0.0	0.0	0.0	0.0	0.0	0.0	0.0
IDA	0.0	0.0	0.0	0.1	0.2	0.3	0.4	0.5	0.5	0.7
NET TRANSFERS ON DEBT	..	..	..	**91.9**	**51.8**	**31.5**	**57.8**	**38.8**	**80.8**	**54.3**
Public and publicly guaranteed	..	..	..	**91.9**	**51.8**	**31.5**	**57.8**	**38.8**	**80.8**	**54.3**
Official creditors	..	..	..	74.4	67.1	58.2	75.4	62.0	94.4	68.1
Multilateral	..	..	..	44.0	14.2	34.9	57.1	43.5	100.8	48.0
Concessional	..	..	..	43.2	14.2	38.1	57.1	43.5	100.8	48.0
Bilateral	..	..	..	30.4	53.0	23.3	18.3	18.5	-6.4	20.1
Concessional	..	..	..	20.9	26.9	9.7	29.0	28.0	15.8	26.4
Private creditors	..	..	..	17.5	-15.3	-26.8	-17.6	-23.1	-13.6	-13.8
Bonds	..	..	..	0.0	0.0	0.0	0.0	0.0	0.0	0.0
Commercial banks	..	..	..	13.3	-0.6	-1.7	-6.2	-4.6	-4.8	-3.8
Other private	..	..	..	4.2	-14.7	-25.1	-11.4	-18.5	-8.8	-10.0
Private nonguaranteed	..	..	..	**0.0**	**0.0**	**0.0**	**0.0**	**0.0**	**0.0**	**0.0**
Bonds	..	..	..	0.0	0.0	0.0	0.0	0.0	0.0	0.0
Commercial banks	..	..	..	0.0	0.0	0.0	0.0	0.0	0.0	0.0
Memo:										
IBRD	0.0	0.0	0.0	0.0	0.0	0.0	0.0	0.0	0.0	0.0
IDA	0.0	0.0	0.0	27.3	3.2	17.1	8.0	10.5	33.3	16.0
DEBT SERVICE (LTDS)	..	..	..	**65.7**	**21.1**	**42.1**	**40.8**	**42.2**	**64.7**	**31.6**
Public and publicly guaranteed	..	..	..	**65.7**	**21.1**	**42.1**	**40.8**	**42.2**	**64.7**	**31.6**
Official creditors	..	..	..	0.7	5.8	12.7	17.6	19.1	45.1	15.2
Multilateral	..	..	..	0.3	0.5	4.0	1.1	1.6	2.0	2.7
Concessional	..	..	..	0.2	0.5	0.8	1.1	1.6	2.0	2.7
Bilateral	..	..	..	0.3	5.3	8.7	16.5	17.5	43.1	12.5
Concessional	..	..	..	0.3	0.6	0.8	2.2	6.6	10.2	6.3
Private creditors	..	..	..	65.0	15.3	29.3	23.2	23.1	19.6	16.3
Bonds	..	..	..	0.0	0.0	0.0	0.0	0.0	0.0	0.0
Commercial banks	..	..	..	44.9	0.6	3.4	6.2	4.6	4.8	4.3
Other private	..	..	..	20.1	14.7	25.9	17.0	18.5	14.8	12.0
Private nonguaranteed	..	..	..	**0.0**	**0.0**	**0.0**	**0.0**	**0.0**	**0.0**	**0.0**
Bonds	..	..	..	0.0	0.0	0.0	0.0	0.0	0.0	0.0
Commercial banks	..	..	..	0.0	0.0	0.0	0.0	0.0	0.0	0.0
Memo:										
IBRD	0.0	0.0	0.0	0.0	0.0	0.0	0.0	0.0	0.0	0.0
IDA	0.0	0.0	0.0	0.1	0.2	0.3	0.4	0.5	0.5	0.7
UNDISBURSED DEBT	..	..	..	**111.6**	**195.1**	**206.4**	**354.3**	**313.3**	**322.6**	**349.0**
Official creditors	..	..	..	96.4	178.1	191.9	345.4	304.3	319.2	348.1
Private creditors	..	..	..	15.3	17.0	14.5	8.9	8.9	3.4	0.9
Memorandum items										
Concessional LDOD	..	..	..	150.4	196.5	260.5	345.3	395.0	483.3	600.8
Variable rate LDOD	..	..	..	35.0	30.6	16.0	12.0	8.0	4.0	0.5
Public sector LDOD	..	..	..	255.9	323.0	384.5	442.0	463.9	514.6	614.7
Private sector LDOD	..	..	..	16.3	15.5	16.0	21.9	17.2	18.8	18.9

6. CURRENCY COMPOSITION OF LONG-TERM DEBT (PERCENT)

	1970	1980	1990	1992	1993	1994	1995	1996	1997	1998
Deutsche mark	..	..	..	3.2	3.4	3.9	5.2	5.4	5.9	5.9
French franc	..	..	..	0.0	0.0	0.0	0.0	0.0	0.0	0.0
Japanese yen	..	..	..	30.9	32.9	29.1	26.9	26.0	19.7	22.0
Pound sterling	..	..	..	0.0	0.0	0.0	0.0	0.0	0.0	0.0
Swiss franc	..	..	..	3.3	2.6	2.7	2.3	1.7	1.0	0.8
U.S.dollars	..	..	..	48.7	46.0	44.9	38.5	34.8	34.9	31.5
Multiple currency	..	..	..	9.6	11.9	16.3	24.3	29.6	34.3	35.5
Special drawing rights	..	..	..	0.0	0.0	0.0	0.0	0.4	1.8	2.4
All other currencies	..	..	..	4.3	3.2	3.1	2.8	2.1	2.4	1.9

MONGOLIA

(US$ million, unless otherwise indicated)

	1970	1980	1990	1992	1993	1994	1995	1996	1997	1998
7. DEBT RESTRUCTURINGS										
Total amount rescheduled	..	..	..	0.0	0.0	0.0	0.0	0.0	0.0	0.0
Debt stock rescheduled	..	..	..	0.0	0.0	0.0	0.0	0.0	0.0	0.0
Principal rescheduled	..	..	..	0.0	0.0	0.0	0.0	0.0	0.0	0.0
Official	..	..	..	0.0	0.0	0.0	0.0	0.0	0.0	0.0
Private	..	..	..	0.0	0.0	0.0	0.0	0.0	0.0	0.0
Interest rescheduled	..	..	..	..	0.0	0.0	0.0	0.0	0.0	0.0
Official	..	..	..	0.0	0.0	0.0	0.0	0.0	0.0	0.0
Private	..	..	..	0.0	0.0	0.0	0.0	0.0	0.0	0.0
Debt forgiven	..	..	..	0.0	0.1	0.0	0.0	0.0	0.8	0.0
Memo: interest forgiven	..	..	..	0.0	0.0	0.0	0.0	0.0	0.0	0.0
Debt stock reduction	..	..	..	0.0	0.0	0.0	0.0	0.0	0.0	0.0
of which debt buyback	..	..	..	0.0	0.0	0.0	0.0	0.0	0.0	0.0
8. DEBT STOCK-FLOW RECONCILIATION										
Total change in debt stocks	..	..	..	..	33.6	77.4	63.3	7.0	77.0	130.4
Net flows on debt	..	..	..	162.4	25.8	51.8	65.2	38.1	119.8	89.3
Net change in interest arrears	..	..	..	..	-0.1	0.9	0.0	0.0	0.0	0.0
Interest capitalized	..	..	..	..	0.0	0.0	0.0	0.0	0.0	0.0
Debt forgiveness or reduction	..	..	..	..	-0.1	0.0	0.0	0.0	-0.8	0.0
Cross-currency valuation	..	..	..	..	11.2	18.5	0.9	-18.3	-17.5	21.5
Residual	..	..	..	..	-3.2	6.1	-2.8	-12.9	-24.4	19.5
9. AVERAGE TERMS OF NEW COMMITMENTS										
ALL CREDITORS										
Interest (%)	..	..	..	4.9	1.1	0.8	2.2	1.1	2.6	2.0
Maturity (years)	..	..	..	8.3	34.9	38.7	35.3	33.5	36.8	39.8
Grace period (years)	..	..	..	2.8	9.8	10.7	10.1	8.4	10.0	10.0
Grant element (%)	..	..	..	21.6	75.3	80.2	65.4	71.5	62.9	69.7
Official creditors										
Interest (%)	..	..	..	2.5	1.0	0.8	2.2	1.1	2.6	2.0
Maturity (years)	..	..	..	10.5	35.2	38.7	35.3	33.5	36.9	39.8
Grace period (years)	..	..	..	3.2	9.9	10.7	10.1	8.4	10.0	10.0
Grant element (%)	..	..	..	31.6	75.7	80.2	65.4	71.5	63.0	69.7
Private creditors										
Interest (%)	..	..	..	7.6	3.4	0.0	0.0	0.0	2.5	0.0
Maturity (years)	..	..	..	5.9	14.5	0.0	0.0	0.0	3.7	0.0
Grace period (years)	..	..	..	2.4	3.0	0.0	0.0	0.0	1.3	0.0
Grant element (%)	..	..	..	10.4	35.4	0.0	0.0	0.0	15.6	0.0
Memorandum items										
Commitments	..	..	..	171.9	157.0	77.7	250.1	58.4	177.0	91.0
Official creditors	..	..	..	90.7	155.2	77.7	250.1	58.4	176.5	91.0
Private creditors	..	..	..	81.1	1.8	0.0	0.0	0.0	0.4	0.0

10. CONTRACTUAL OBLIGATIONS ON OUTSTANDING LONG-TERM DEBT

	1999	2000	2001	2002	2003	2004	2005	2006	2007	2008
TOTAL										
Disbursements	115.0	97.1	58.9	35.5	21.0	13.1	6.0	1.7	0.8	0.0
Principal	12.2	12.7	10.7	14.6	15.9	17.0	21.9	25.4	28.2	31.3
Interest	9.1	9.8	10.0	10.1	9.9	9.7	10.5	12.7	13.4	12.9
Official creditors										
Disbursements	114.1	97.1	58.9	35.5	21.0	13.1	6.0	1.7	0.8	0.0
Principal	8.3	8.9	6.9	10.9	12.3	15.2	21.0	25.3	28.1	31.3
Interest	8.1	9.0	9.4	9.6	9.6	9.5	10.5	12.7	13.4	12.9
Bilateral creditors										
Disbursements	58.0	48.6	30.4	17.3	8.9	5.5	1.9	0.2	0.0	0.0
Principal	8.3	8.9	6.9	9.5	10.6	11.5	14.9	16.5	15.5	17.3
Interest	3.9	4.5	4.7	4.9	4.9	4.8	4.7	4.5	4.2	4.0
Multilateral creditors										
Disbursements	56.1	48.4	28.5	18.2	12.1	7.6	4.1	1.5	0.8	0.0
Principal	0.0	0.0	0.0	1.4	1.7	3.8	6.1	8.8	12.6	14.0
Interest	4.3	4.5	4.7	4.7	4.7	4.7	5.8	8.3	9.2	8.9
Private creditors										
Disbursements	0.9	0.0	0.0	0.0	0.0	0.0	0.0	0.0	0.0	0.0
Principal	3.8	3.8	3.7	3.6	3.6	1.8	0.9	0.1	0.1	0.0
Interest	1.0	0.8	0.6	0.5	0.3	0.1	0.0	0.0	0.0	0.0
Commercial banks										
Disbursements	0.0	0.0	0.0	0.0	0.0	0.0	0.0	0.0	0.0	0.0
Principal	0.3	0.3	0.2	0.1	0.1	0.1	0.1	0.1	0.1	0.0
Interest	0.1	0.0	0.0	0.0	0.0	0.0	0.0	0.0	0.0	0.0
Other private										
Disbursements	0.9	0.0	0.0	0.0	0.0	0.0	0.0	0.0	0.0	0.0
Principal	3.5	3.5	3.5	3.5	3.5	1.6	0.8	0.0	0.0	0.0
Interest	0.9	0.8	0.6	0.4	0.3	0.1	0.0	0.0	0.0	0.0

MOROCCO

(US$ million, unless otherwise indicated)

	1970	1980	1990	1992	1993	1994	1995	1996	1997	1998
1. SUMMARY DEBT DATA										
TOTAL DEBT STOCKS (EDT)	**..**	**9,258**	**24,458**	**22,061**	**21,459**	**22,158**	**22,665**	**21,851**	**20,162**	**20,687**
Long-term debt (LDOD)	**886**	**8,024**	**23,301**	**21,234**	**20,860**	**21,788**	**22,416**	**21,526**	**19,931**	**20,571**
Public and publicly guaranteed	871	7,874	23,101	21,030	20,680	21,530	22,085	21,134	18,978	19,325
Private nonguaranteed	15	150	200	204	179	259	331	392	952	1,247
Use of IMF credit	**28**	**457**	**750**	**439**	**285**	**148**	**52**	**3**	**0**	**0**
Short-term debt	**..**	**778**	**407**	**388**	**315**	**222**	**198**	**322**	**231**	**116**
of which interest arrears on LDOD	..	3	182	99	100	94	92	138	113	116
Official creditors	..	3	182	99	100	91	92	137	113	115
Private creditors	..	0	0	0	0	3	0	0	0	1
Memo: principal arrears on LDOD	..	3	738	148	147	137	138	182	195	215
Official creditors	..	3	738	148	146	126	136	179	195	210
Private creditors	..	0	0	0	1	11	2	2	0	5
Memo: export credits	..	0	8,416	8,117	7,835	8,076	7,957	6,813	6,331	7,106
TOTAL DEBT FLOWS										
Disbursements	**196**	**2,262**	**1,711**	**1,910**	**2,037**	**1,802**	**2,089**	**1,757**	**1,313**	**1,865**
Long-term debt	186	1,985	1,646	1,884	2,037	1,802	2,089	1,757	1,313	1,865
IMF purchases	10	278	65	26	0	0	0	0	0	0
Principal repayments	**54**	**678**	**908**	**1,535**	**1,998**	**2,246**	**2,373**	**2,006**	**2,110**	**1,773**
Long-term debt	40	591	680	1,393	1,841	2,094	2,272	1,959	2,107	1,773
IMF repurchases	14	88	228	142	156	152	101	47	3	0
Net flows on debt	**213**	**1,624**	**889**	**555**	**-35**	**-532**	**-306**	**-172**	**-863**	**-26**
of which short-term debt	..	40	86	180	-74	-87	-22	78	-66	-118
Interest payments (INT)	**..**	**768**	**886**	**2,356**	**1,329**	**1,393**	**1,391**	**1,346**	**1,068**	**1,024**
Long-term debt	26	651	794	2,298	1,280	1,363	1,360	1,335	1,061	1,020
IMF charges	0	12	72	43	31	13	7	2	0	0
Short-term debt	..	105	20	15	18	18	24	9	6	3
Net transfers on debt	**..**	**857**	**3**	**-1,801**	**-1,363**	**-1,925**	**-1,696**	**-1,517**	**-1,931**	**-1,050**
Total debt service paid (TDS)	**..**	**1,446**	**1,794**	**3,891**	**3,326**	**3,639**	**3,764**	**3,352**	**3,178**	**2,797**
Long-term debt	66	1,241	1,474	3,691	3,121	3,457	3,633	3,294	3,168	2,794
IMF repurchases and charges	14	100	300	186	187	165	107	49	3	0
Short-term debt (interest only)	..	105	20	15	18	18	24	9	6	3
2. AGGREGATE NET RESOURCE FLOWS AND NET TRANSFERS (LONG-TERM)										
NET RESOURCE FLOWS	**191**	**1,559**	**1,610**	**1,095**	**995**	**601**	**159**	**732**	**799**	**936**
Net flow of long-term debt (ex. IMF)	146	1,394	965	491	196	-293	-183	-202	-794	92
Foreign direct investment (net)	20	89	165	422	491	551	92	357	1,079	322
Portfolio equity flows	0	0	0	0	0	63	150	222	243	174
Grants (excluding technical coop.)	24	76	480	182	309	279	100	355	271	349
Memo: technical coop. grants	29	123	184	198	203	202	266	249	215	227
official net resource flows	145	828	1,269	653	504	-151	-188	342	-532	-29
private net resource flows	46	731	341	443	492	752	346	390	1,331	965
NET TRANSFERS	**145**	**860**	**747**	**-1,374**	**-387**	**-872**	**-1,332**	**-778**	**-453**	**-304**
Interest on long-term debt	26	651	794	2,298	1,280	1,363	1,360	1,335	1,061	1,020
Profit remittances on FDI	20	49	69	171	103	110	130	175	190	220
Memo: official net transfers	126	692	689	-129	-422	-1,169	-1,111	-546	-1,361	-807
private net transfers	19	168	58	-1,245	35	297	-221	-232	909	503
3. MAJOR ECONOMIC AGGREGATES										
Gross national product (GNP)	3,945	18,402	24,888	27,450	25,718	29,181	31,661	35,137	32,082	34,292
Exports of goods & services (XGS)	..	4,324	8,328	9,597	9,169	9,606	11,265	11,984	11,575	12,175
of which workers remittances	..	1,054	2,006	2,170	1,959	1,827	1,970	2,165	1,893	2,011
Imports of goods & services (MGS)	..	5,807	8,853	10,392	10,026	10,772	12,812	12,360	11,975	12,653
International reserves (RES)	142	814	2,338	3,819	3,930	4,622	3,874	4,054	4,197	4,638
Current account balance	..	-1,407	-196	-433	-521	-723	-1,186	35	-87	-144
4. DEBT INDICATORS										
EDT / XGS (%)	..	214.1	293.7	229.9	234.1	230.7	201.2	182.3	174.2	169.9
EDT / GNP (%)	..	50.3	98.3	80.4	83.4	75.9	71.6	62.2	62.8	60.3
TDS / XGS (%)	..	33.4	21.5	40.6	36.3	37.9	33.4	28.0	27.5	23.0
INT / XGS (%)	..	17.8	10.6	24.6	14.5	14.5	12.4	11.2	9.2	8.4
INT / GNP (%)	..	4.2	3.6	8.6	5.2	4.8	4.4	3.8	3.3	3.0
RES / EDT (%)	..	8.8	9.6	17.3	18.3	20.9	17.1	18.6	20.8	22.4
RES / MGS (months)	..	1.7	3.2	4.4	4.7	5.2	3.6	3.9	4.2	4.4
Short-term / EDT (%)	..	8.4	1.7	1.8	1.5	1.0	0.9	1.5	1.2	0.6
Concessional / EDT (%)	..	29.4	32.6	24.8	25.8	27.1	28.1	30.5	31.2	31.0
Multilateral / EDT (%)	..	7.8	19.2	24.3	26.8	28.4	29.9	30.1	30.0	31.2

MOROCCO

(US$ million, unless otherwise indicated)

	1970	1980	1990	1992	1993	1994	1995	1996	1997	1998
5. LONG-TERM DEBT										
DEBT OUTSTANDING (LDOD)	**886**	**8,024**	**23,301**	**21,234**	**20,860**	**21,788**	**22,416**	**21,526**	**19,931**	**20,571**
Public and publicly guaranteed	**871**	**7,874**	**23,101**	**21,030**	**20,680**	**21,530**	**22,085**	**21,134**	**18,978**	**19,325**
Official creditors	742	3,519	16,991	15,588	15,487	16,127	16,515	15,926	14,186	14,220
Multilateral	59	723	4,687	5,353	5,750	6,297	6,768	6,585	6,041	6,455
Concessional	3	79	405	402	465	520	599	698	783	879
Bilateral	683	2,796	12,304	10,235	9,736	9,829	9,748	9,341	8,145	7,764
Concessional	620	2,638	7,579	5,065	5,067	5,493	5,772	5,960	5,503	5,540
Private creditors	129	4,355	6,110	5,442	5,194	5,403	5,570	5,208	4,792	5,105
Bonds	32	173	0	0	0	0	0	286	251	267
Commercial banks	0	2,343	3,394	3,253	3,250	3,424	3,523	3,301	3,295	3,544
Other private	98	1,839	2,716	2,189	1,944	1,979	2,047	1,621	1,247	1,294
Private nonguaranteed	**15**	**150**	**200**	**204**	**179**	**259**	**331**	**392**	**952**	**1,247**
Bonds	0	0	0	0	0	0	0	0	0	0
Commercial banks	15	150	200	204	179	259	331	392	952	1,247
Memo:										
IBRD	56	539	3,099	3,408	3,559	3,746	3,966	3,732	3,271	3,388
IDA	3	39	39	37	36	35	33	32	31	29
DISBURSEMENTS	**186**	**1,985**	**1,646**	**1,884**	**2,037**	**1,802**	**2,089**	**1,757**	**1,313**	**1,865**
Public and publicly guaranteed	**179**	**1,910**	**1,638**	**1,872**	**1,904**	**1,722**	**1,987**	**1,666**	**1,038**	**1,527**
Official creditors	145	866	1,220	1,315	1,282	1,040	1,355	1,329	851	945
Multilateral	16	109	781	858	781	655	906	797	568	730
Concessional	2	22	39	105	90	71	92	136	138	117
Bilateral	130	757	439	458	501	385	449	532	283	214
Concessional	90	709	287	328	408	368	314	335	221	176
Private creditors	34	1,044	418	557	622	681	632	337	187	583
Bonds	0	7	0	0	0	0	0	293	0	0
Commercial banks	0	482	47	50	148	266	204	0	22	447
Other private	34	555	371	507	474	416	428	44	165	136
Private nonguaranteed	**8**	**75**	**8**	**12**	**133**	**80**	**103**	**91**	**275**	**338**
Bonds	0	0	0	0	0	0	0	0	0	0
Commercial banks	8	75	8	12	133	80	103	91	275	338
Memo:										
IBRD	14	64	426	477	377	246	426	380	141	291
IDA	2	1	0	0	0	0	0	0	0	0
PRINCIPAL REPAYMENTS	**40**	**591**	**680**	**1,393**	**1,841**	**2,094**	**2,272**	**1,959**	**2,107**	**1,773**
Public and publicly guaranteed	**38**	**566**	**672**	**1,385**	**1,810**	**2,093**	**2,242**	**1,929**	**2,063**	**1,729**
Official creditors	25	114	430	845	1,087	1,471	1,642	1,342	1,654	1,322
Multilateral	5	39	276	485	427	476	629	571	649	527
Concessional	0	0	13	123	23	26	22	28	31	36
Bilateral	20	75	155	361	660	994	1,013	771	1,005	795
Concessional	15	61	33	46	259	317	267	199	331	234
Private creditors	13	452	242	540	723	623	600	587	409	407
Bonds	3	9	0	0	0	0	0	0	0	0
Commercial banks	0	295	40	138	148	98	111	168	148	139
Other private	10	149	202	402	575	525	489	419	261	268
Private nonguaranteed	**3**	**25**	**8**	**8**	**31**	**1**	**30**	**30**	**44**	**44**
Bonds	0	0	0	0	0	0	0	0	0	0
Commercial banks	3	25	8	8	31	1	30	30	44	44
Memo:										
IBRD	5	29	202	269	293	301	349	341	294	299
IDA	0	0	1	1	1	1	1	1	1	1
NET FLOWS ON DEBT	**146**	**1,394**	**965**	**491**	**196**	**-293**	**-183**	**-202**	**-794**	**92**
Public and publicly guaranteed	**141**	**1,344**	**965**	**487**	**94**	**-372**	**-256**	**-263**	**-1,025**	**-202**
Official creditors	120	752	790	470	195	-430	-287	-13	-803	-377
Multilateral	11	70	506	373	354	179	277	226	-81	203
Concessional	2	22	25	-18	67	45	70	108	108	82
Bilateral	109	682	284	97	-160	-609	-564	-239	-722	-581
Concessional	75	648	254	283	149	51	46	136	-110	-58
Private creditors	21	592	176	17	-101	59	32	-250	-222	175
Bonds	-3	-2	0	0	0	0	0	293	0	0
Commercial banks	0	188	7	-89	-1	167	93	-168	-126	307
Other private	24	406	169	105	-100	-109	-61	-376	-96	-132
Private nonguaranteed	**5**	**50**	**0**	**4**	**102**	**79**	**73**	**61**	**231**	**294**
Bonds	0	0	0	0	0	0	0	0	0	0
Commercial banks	5	50	0	4	102	79	73	61	231	294
Memo:										
IBRD	9	35	224	208	84	-55	78	39	-153	-8
IDA	2	1	-1	-1	-1	-1	-1	-1	-1	-1

MOROCCO

(US$ million, unless otherwise indicated)

	1970	1980	1990	1992	1993	1994	1995	1996	1997	1998
INTEREST PAYMENTS (LINT)	**26**	**651**	**794**	**2,298**	**1,280**	**1,363**	**1,360**	**1,335**	**1,061**	**1,020**
Public and publicly guaranteed	**25**	**639**	**789**	**2,291**	**1,277**	**1,362**	**1,359**	**1,324**	**1,014**	**973**
Official creditors	19	135	580	782	926	1,018	923	888	829	779
Multilateral	4	56	306	379	403	427	466	465	422	390
Concessional	0	1	7	16	15	17	19	24	28	32
Bilateral	15	79	274	403	523	591	458	424	407	389
Concessional	13	69	57	66	131	136	142	142	163	168
Private creditors	6	504	208	1,509	352	344	436	436	185	194
Bonds	2	15	0	0	0	0	0	0	17	17
Commercial banks	0	364	43	1,328	152	158	259	281	42	64
Other private	4	125	165	181	199	186	176	155	126	113
Private nonguaranteed	**1**	**11**	**5**	**7**	**2**	**1**	**2**	**11**	**48**	**48**
Bonds	0	0	0	0	0	0	0	0	0	0
Commercial banks	1	11	5	7	2	1	2	11	48	48
Memo:										
IBRD	4	49	226	249	259	271	282	258	238	206
IDA	0	0	0	0	0	0	0	0	0	0
NET TRANSFERS ON DEBT	**121**	**743**	**172**	**-1,807**	**-1,084**	**-1,655**	**-1,543**	**-1,537**	**-1,855**	**-928**
Public and publicly guaranteed	**116**	**705**	**177**	**-1,804**	**-1,183**	**-1,734**	**-1,614**	**-1,588**	**-2,039**	**-1,175**
Official creditors	102	617	209	-311	-731	-1,448	-1,210	-901	-1,632	-1,156
Multilateral	7	14	200	-6	-48	-248	-189	-238	-503	-186
Concessional	2	21	19	-34	52	28	51	84	80	50
Bilateral	95	603	10	-306	-683	-1,200	-1,022	-663	-1,129	-970
Concessional	62	579	197	217	19	-85	-96	-6	-272	-225
Private creditors	15	88	-33	-1,492	-453	-286	-404	-686	-407	-19
Bonds	-5	-17	0	0	0	0	0	293	-17	-17
Commercial banks	0	-177	-36	-1,417	-153	9	-167	-449	-168	243
Other private	20	281	4	-75	-300	-295	-237	-531	-223	-245
Private nonguaranteed	**4**	**39**	**-5**	**-3**	**99**	**79**	**71**	**50**	**184**	**246**
Bonds	0	0	0	0	0	0	0	0	0	0
Commercial banks	4	39	-5	-3	99	79	71	50	184	246
Memo:										
IBRD	5	-14	-2	-41	-175	-326	-204	-219	-391	-214
IDA	2	0	-1	-1	-2	-2	-2	-2	-2	-2
DEBT SERVICE (LTDS)	**66**	**1,241**	**1,474**	**3,691**	**3,121**	**3,457**	**3,633**	**3,294**	**3,168**	**2,794**
Public and publicly guaranteed	**62**	**1,205**	**1,461**	**3,676**	**3,088**	**3,456**	**3,601**	**3,253**	**3,077**	**2,702**
Official creditors	44	249	1,011	1,627	2,013	2,489	2,565	2,230	2,483	2,101
Multilateral	9	95	582	863	829	903	1,095	1,035	1,071	917
Concessional	0	1	20	139	38	43	41	52	58	68
Bilateral	35	154	429	764	1,184	1,586	1,471	1,195	1,412	1,184
Concessional	28	130	90	111	389	453	409	341	493	402
Private creditors	19	956	451	2,049	1,075	967	1,036	1,023	594	601
Bonds	5	23	0	0	0	0	0	0	17	17
Commercial banks	0	659	83	1,467	301	256	371	449	190	204
Other private	14	274	367	583	774	711	665	574	388	381
Private nonguaranteed	**3**	**36**	**13**	**15**	**33**	**2**	**32**	**41**	**92**	**92**
Bonds	0	0	0	0	0	0	0	0	0	0
Commercial banks	3	36	13	15	33	2	32	41	92	92
Memo:										
IBRD	9	78	428	518	552	572	630	599	532	505
IDA	0	1	1	1	2	2	2	2	2	2
UNDISBURSED DEBT	**242**	**2,291**	**4,026**	**4,760**	**5,069**	**5,210**	**5,619**	**4,277**	**4,319**	**3,561**
Official creditors	221	1,882	3,417	3,764	4,123	4,354	5,196	3,922	3,839	3,374
Private creditors	21	409	608	996	946	856	423	355	480	187
Memorandum items										
Concessional LDOD	622	2,717	7,984	5,467	5,532	6,012	6,371	6,659	6,285	6,419
Variable rate LDOD	15	2,626	7,827	8,119	8,196	8,294	8,621	8,205	8,197	8,572
Public sector LDOD	864	7,819	23,037	20,912	20,504	21,304	21,844	20,768	18,415	18,555
Private sector LDOD	23	204	264	322	356	484	575	629	660	719

6. CURRENCY COMPOSITION OF LONG-TERM DEBT (PERCENT)

	1970	1980	1990	1992	1993	1994	1995	1996	1997	1998
Deutsche mark	11.7	3.9	5.4	6.8	7.4	7.8	7.8	7.1	6.8	6.7
French franc	29.5	22.0	23.3	23.2	21.5	21.5	21.2	21.1	19.1	19.9
Japanese yen	0.0	1.9	2.3	3.7	4.1	4.3	3.9	3.5	2.5	2.7
Pound sterling	0.0	0.4	0.1	0.2	0.2	0.2	0.2	0.2	0.2	0.1
Swiss franc	0.1	0.3	0.2	0.1	0.1	0.1	0.1	0.1	0.2	0.2
U.S.dollars	40.9	54.7	41.0	32.6	32.0	29.5	28.2	28.6	30.4	37.9
Multiple currency	6.8	7.0	15.8	20.5	22.3	23.5	23.8	22.8	21.9	11.3
Special drawing rights	0.0	0.2	0.1	0.2	0.2	0.2	0.2	0.1	0.1	0.1
All other currencies	11.0	9.6	11.8	12.7	12.2	12.9	14.6	16.5	18.8	21.1

MOROCCO

(US$ million, unless otherwise indicated)

	1970	1980	1990	1992	1993	1994	1995	1996	1997	1998
7. DEBT RESTRUCTURINGS										
Total amount rescheduled	..	..	4,118	1,755	0	0	0	0	0	0
Debt stock rescheduled	..	..	2,732	0	0	0	0	0	0	0
Principal rescheduled	..	..	591	750	0	0	0	0	0	0
Official	..	..	389	538	0	0	0	0	0	0
Private	..	..	203	213	0	0	0	0	0	0
Interest rescheduled	..	..	219	203	0	0	0	0	0	0
Official	..	..	137	119	0	0	0	0	0	0
Private	..	..	82	83	0	0	0	0	0	0
Debt forgiven	..	..	31	0	0	0	0	0	5	0
Memo: interest forgiven	..	..	0	0	0	0	0	0	0	0
Debt stock reduction	..	..	0	0	0	0	0	0	0	0
of which debt buyback	..	..	0	0	0	0	0	0	0	0
8. DEBT STOCK-FLOW RECONCILIATION										
Total change in debt stocks	..	..	2,585	195	-602	699	508	-814	-1,690	525
Net flows on debt	213	1,624	889	555	-35	-532	-306	-172	-863	-26
Net change in interest arrears	..	..	43	-92	1	-6	-2	46	-25	3
Interest capitalized	..	..	219	203	0	0	0	0	0	0
Debt forgiveness or reduction	..	..	-31	0	0	0	0	0	-5	0
Cross-currency valuation	..	..	1,246	-781	-437	1,095	730	-931	-1,221	633
Residual	..	..	220	310	-131	141	86	243	424	-84
9. AVERAGE TERMS OF NEW COMMITMENTS										
ALL CREDITORS										
Interest (%)	4.3	7.9	6.7	7.4	6.7	4.7	4.6	6.0	4.8	3.9
Maturity (years)	27.2	17.2	19.9	15.2	18.5	16.5	19.4	14.3	16.6	16.7
Grace period (years)	7.4	4.9	6.4	3.9	5.0	4.3	5.1	3.8	5.1	5.6
Grant element (%)	38.0	15.8	24.7	11.4	19.7	31.2	34.2	21.8	31.9	38.6
Official creditors										
Interest (%)	3.9	4.1	5.4	8.0	6.8	4.1	4.4	5.7	4.2	2.7
Maturity (years)	31.7	20.7	23.7	17.8	21.5	19.2	20.2	16.9	18.8	21.4
Grace period (years)	8.8	5.3	8.3	5.2	6.2	5.7	5.4	4.5	5.6	6.4
Grant element (%)	44.0	39.5	35.8	11.0	22.4	38.7	36.0	25.9	37.3	50.5
Private creditors										
Interest (%)	6.1	12.1	9.7	6.1	6.5	6.1	6.9	6.5	6.6	5.7
Maturity (years)	8.6	13.4	11.5	10.0	9.6	10.8	8.2	9.2	9.1	8.8
Grace period (years)	1.6	4.5	2.3	1.4	1.4	1.3	0.6	2.5	3.5	4.3
Grant element (%)	13.7	-10.0	-0.1	12.3	11.7	15.3	9.5	13.8	14.1	18.2
Memorandum items										
Commitments	251	1,920	2,316	2,082	2,481	1,660	2,313	1,063	1,663	918
Official creditors	201	1,000	1,601	1,384	1,856	1,128	2,153	704	1,279	580
Private creditors	50	920	715	698	625	531	160	359	384	339

10. CONTRACTUAL OBLIGATIONS ON OUTSTANDING LONG-TERM DEBT

	1999	2000	2001	2002	2003	2004	2005	2006	2007	2008
TOTAL										
Disbursements	1,209	914	570	368	213	118	74	37	23	10
Principal	2,327	1,801	2,166	2,063	2,242	1,934	1,400	1,193	1,120	965
Interest	1,150	1,058	967	863	737	612	484	406	342	285
Official creditors										
Disbursements	1,094	865	552	365	212	118	74	37	23	10
Principal	1,480	1,296	1,217	1,173	1,191	1,164	1,135	1,063	1,005	884
Interest	757	706	656	599	538	476	413	351	295	244
Bilateral creditors										
Disbursements	552	405	236	125	59	22	11	1	0	0
Principal	808	674	613	577	580	556	531	463	450	382
Interest	337	312	288	259	230	202	175	148	126	107
Multilateral creditors										
Disbursements	542	460	317	240	153	96	63	36	23	10
Principal	672	622	604	596	611	609	605	600	555	502
Interest	419	394	368	341	309	274	239	203	169	137
Private creditors										
Disbursements	115	49	18	3	1	0	0	0	0	0
Principal	847	505	950	890	1,052	770	265	130	115	81
Interest	394	352	312	264	199	136	71	55	47	41
Commercial banks										
Disbursements	2	1	1	0	0	0	0	0	0	0
Principal	447	165	651	649	834	565	83	28	25	21
Interest	227	208	190	163	114	66	14	9	7	6
Other private										
Disbursements	112	48	18	3	1	0	0	0	0	0
Principal	400	340	299	241	218	205	182	102	90	60
Interest	167	144	122	101	85	70	57	46	40	35

MOZAMBIQUE

(US$ million, unless otherwise indicated)

1. SUMMARY DEBT DATA

	1970	1980	1990	1992	1993	1994	1995	1996	1997	1998
TOTAL DEBT STOCKS (EDT)	..	..	**4,653**	**5,130**	**5,212**	**7,272**	**7,458**	**7,566**	**7,639**	**8,208**
Long-term debt (LDOD)	..	..	**4,234**	**4,718**	**4,859**	**6,871**	**6,978**	**7,203**	**7,130**	**7,626**
Public and publicly guaranteed	..	..	4,215	4,701	4,841	5,219	5,209	5,358	5,218	5,651
Private nonguaranteed	..	..	19	17	18	1,652	1,769	1,845	1,912	1,975
Use of IMF credit	**0**	**0**	**74**	**175**	**189**	**212**	**202**	**181**	**189**	**207**
Short-term debt	..	..	**345**	**238**	**164**	**189**	**279**	**182**	**320**	**375**
of which interest arrears on LDOD	..	..	207	153	147	171	250	164	202	258
Official creditors	..	..	76	136	145	166	245	162	200	256
Private creditors	..	..	131	17	3	4	5	2	2	2
Memo: principal arrears on LDOD	..	..	725	679	780	884	1,087	1,117	1,179	1,306
Official creditors	..	..	373	613	731	870	1,074	1,114	1,176	1,260
Private creditors	..	..	352	66	49	14	12	3	3	46
Memo: export credits	..	..	986	1,067	1,265	1,105	1,110	948	1,439	1,412
TOTAL DEBT FLOWS										
Disbursements	..	..	**243**	**265**	**211**	**254**	**267**	**300**	**300**	**267**
Long-term debt	..	..	231	201	190	233	267	282	265	233
IMF purchases	0	0	12	64	21	21	0	18	35	34
Principal repayments	..	..	**41**	**34**	**44**	**67**	**85**	**92**	**59**	**63**
Long-term debt	..	..	41	33	38	57	71	59	44	39
IMF repurchases	0	0	0	2	6	11	14	33	15	25
Net flows on debt	..	..	**174**	**235**	**99**	**189**	**193**	**197**	**341**	**203**
of which short-term debt	..	..	-28	4	-69	2	11	-11	100	-1
Interest payments (INT)	..	..	**38**	**48**	**79**	**56**	**77**	**49**	**45**	**41**
Long-term debt	..	..	23	43	75	54	75	46	41	35
IMF charges	0	0	0	0	1	1	1	2	1	1
Short-term debt	..	..	15	5	3	1	1	1	3	6
Net transfers on debt	..	..	**136**	**187**	**20**	**133**	**116**	**148**	**295**	**162**
Total debt service paid (TDS)	..	..	**79**	**83**	**122**	**123**	**162**	**141**	**104**	**105**
Long-term debt	..	..	64	76	113	111	146	106	85	74
IMF repurchases and charges	0	0	0	2	7	12	16	34	16	25
Short-term debt (interest only)	..	..	15	5	3	1	1	1	3	6

2. AGGREGATE NET RESOURCE FLOWS AND NET TRANSFERS (LONG-TERM)

	1970	1980	1990	1992	1993	1994	1995	1996	1997	1998
NET RESOURCE FLOWS	..	..	**949**	**919**	**821**	**849**	**1,011**	**736**	**802**	**1,081**
Net flow of long-term debt (ex. IMF)	..	..	190	168	152	176	196	222	221	194
Foreign direct investment (net)	..	..	9	25	32	35	45	73	64	213
Portfolio equity flows	..	..	0	0	0	0	0	0	0	0
Grants (excluding technical coop.)	..	..	750	726	637	638	770	441	516	674
Memo: technical coop. grants	..	..	96	195	224	239	234	190	162	150
official net resource flows	..	..	914	896	791	816	942	669	736	872
private net resource flows	..	..	35	23	30	33	69	67	66	209
NET TRANSFERS	..	..	**926**	**876**	**746**	**793**	**936**	**687**	**758**	**1,042**
Interest on long-term debt	..	..	23	43	75	54	75	46	41	35
Profit remittances on FDI	..	..	0	0	0	2	0	3	2	4
Memo: official net transfers	..	..	898	858	720	763	871	624	696	845
private net transfers	..	..	28	18	26	30	65	63	63	197

3. MAJOR ECONOMIC AGGREGATES

	1970	1980	1990	1992	1993	1994	1995	1996	1997	1998
Gross national product (GNP)	..	..	2,366	1,773	1,924	2,065	2,208	2,672	3,256	3,680
Exports of goods & services (XGS)	..	..	300	362	372	395	470	540	572	581
of which workers remittances	..	..	0	0	0	0	0	0	0	0
Imports of goods & services (MGS)	..	..	1,164	1,214	1,321	1,427	1,254	1,186	1,181	1,371
International reserves (RES)	..	..	232	233	187	178	195	344	517	608
Current account balance	..	..	-415	-352	-446	-467	-445	-421	-296	-477

4. DEBT INDICATORS

	1970	1980	1990	1992	1993	1994	1995	1996	1997	1998
EDT / XGS (%)	..	..	1,552.0	1,417.6	1,402.5	1,839.1	1,585.5	1,400.4	1,334.8	1,413.5
EDT / GNP (%)	..	..	196.6	289.4	270.9	352.2	337.8	283.2	234.6	223.0
TDS / XGS (%)	..	..	26.2	22.9	32.9	31.2	34.5	26.0	18.2	18.0
INT / XGS (%)	..	..	12.6	13.4	21.2	14.2	16.4	9.0	7.9	7.1
INT / GNP (%)	..	..	1.6	2.7	4.1	2.7	3.5	1.8	1.4	1.1
RES / EDT (%)	..	..	5.0	4.6	3.6	2.4	2.6	4.6	6.8	7.4
RES / MGS (months)	..	..	2.4	2.3	1.7	1.5	1.9	3.5	5.3	5.3
Short-term / EDT (%)	..	..	7.4	4.6	3.1	2.6	3.7	2.4	4.2	4.6
Concessional / EDT (%)	..	..	44.8	51.4	55.0	44.6	39.4	42.4	41.8	44.5
Multilateral / EDT (%)	..	..	10.0	13.0	15.3	14.4	17.1	19.6	21.2	23.1

MOZAMBIQUE

(US$ million, unless otherwise indicated)

	1970	1980	1990	1992	1993	1994	1995	1996	1997	1998
5. LONG-TERM DEBT										
DEBT OUTSTANDING (LDOD)	..	..	**4,234**	**4,718**	**4,859**	**6,871**	**6,978**	**7,203**	**7,130**	**7,626**
Public and publicly guaranteed	..	..	**4,215**	**4,701**	**4,841**	**5,219**	**5,209**	**5,358**	**5,218**	**5,651**
Official creditors	..	..	3,563	4,491	4,697	5,128	5,163	5,331	5,200	5,635
Multilateral	..	..	464	667	799	1,050	1,277	1,483	1,618	1,895
Concessional	..	..	406	600	730	975	1,196	1,401	1,533	1,798
Bilateral	..	..	3,099	3,825	3,898	4,078	3,886	3,848	3,582	3,740
Concessional	..	..	1,680	2,034	2,135	2,265	1,741	1,803	1,657	1,853
Private creditors	..	..	651	210	144	91	46	27	18	17
Bonds	..	..	0	0	0	0	0	0	0	0
Commercial banks	..	..	147	9	9	7	7	2	2	1
Other private	..	..	504	201	135	84	39	25	17	16
Private nonguaranteed	..	..	**19**	**17**	**18**	**1,652**	**1,769**	**1,845**	**1,912**	**1,975**
Bonds	..	..	0	0	0	0	0	0	0	0
Commercial banks	..	..	19	17	18	1,652	1,769	1,845	1,912	1,975
Memo:										
IBRD	0	0	0	0	0	0	0	0	0	0
IDA	0	0	268	417	512	714	890	1,076	1,160	1,335
DISBURSEMENTS	..	..	**231**	**201**	**190**	**233**	**267**	**282**	**265**	**233**
Public and publicly guaranteed	..	..	**211**	**197**	**186**	**230**	**231**	**282**	**259**	**233**
Official creditors	..	..	187	197	182	229	231	282	259	233
Multilateral	..	..	96	159	144	220	219	275	244	215
Concessional	..	..	89	149	135	211	208	265	224	211
Bilateral	..	..	91	38	38	10	11	7	15	18
Concessional	..	..	91	38	38	10	11	7	15	18
Private creditors	..	..	24	0	4	1	0	0	0	0
Bonds	..	..	0	0	0	0	0	0	0	0
Commercial banks	..	..	0	0	3	0	0	0	0	0
Other private	..	..	24	0	1	1	0	0	0	0
Private nonguaranteed	..	..	**20**	**4**	**4**	**3**	**36**	**0**	**6**	**0**
Bonds	..	..	0	0	0	0	0	0	0	0
Commercial banks	..	..	20	4	4	3	36	0	6	0
Memo:										
IBRD	0	0	0	0	0	0	0	0	0	0
IDA	0	0	74	106	93	176	160	221	148	131
PRINCIPAL REPAYMENTS	..	..	**41**	**33**	**38**	**57**	**71**	**59**	**44**	**39**
Public and publicly guaranteed	..	..	**29**	**30**	**35**	**54**	**67**	**55**	**40**	**35**
Official creditors	..	..	23	26	28	51	58	53	39	35
Multilateral	..	..	9	10	11	13	13	17	17	19
Concessional	..	..	4	4	5	5	6	11	9	11
Bilateral	..	..	13	16	16	39	46	36	23	16
Concessional	..	..	5	8	7	11	18	18	18	14
Private creditors	..	..	7	4	7	2	9	1	1	0
Bonds	..	..	0	0	0	0	0	0	0	0
Commercial banks	..	..	3	2	0	1	0	0	0	0
Other private	..	..	3	1	7	2	9	1	1	0
Private nonguaranteed	..	..	**12**	**3**	**3**	**3**	**3**	**5**	**4**	**4**
Bonds	..	..	0	0	0	0	0	0	0	0
Commercial banks	..	..	12	3	3	3	3	5	4	4
Memo:										
IBRD	0	0	0	0	0	0	0	0	0	0
IDA	0	0	0	0	0	0	0	1	2	3
NET FLOWS ON DEBT	..	..	**190**	**168**	**152**	**176**	**196**	**222**	**221**	**194**
Public and publicly guaranteed	..	..	**182**	**167**	**152**	**176**	**163**	**227**	**219**	**199**
Official creditors	..	..	164	171	154	178	172	229	220	199
Multilateral	..	..	86	149	133	207	207	258	228	196
Concessional	..	..	85	144	129	206	202	255	216	201
Bilateral	..	..	78	22	21	-29	-34	-29	-8	3
Concessional	..	..	86	30	31	-2	-7	-11	-4	4
Private creditors	..	..	17	-4	-3	-2	-9	-1	-1	0
Bonds	..	..	0	0	0	0	0	0	0	0
Commercial banks	..	..	-3	-2	3	-1	0	0	0	0
Other private	..	..	21	-1	-6	-1	-9	-1	-1	0
Private nonguaranteed	..	..	**8**	**1**	**1**	**0**	**33**	**-5**	**2**	**-4**
Bonds	..	..	0	0	0	0	0	0	0	0
Commercial banks	..	..	8	1	1	0	33	-5	2	-4
Memo:										
IBRD	0	0	0	0	0	0	0	0	0	0
IDA	0	0	74	106	93	176	160	220	147	128

MOZAMBIQUE

(US$ million, unless otherwise indicated)

	1970	1980	1990	1992	1993	1994	1995	1996	1997	1998
INTEREST PAYMENTS (LINT)	..	..	**23**	**43**	**75**	**54**	**75**	**46**	**41**	**35**
Public and publicly guaranteed	..	..	**23**	**43**	**75**	**54**	**74**	**45**	**41**	**27**
Official creditors	..	..	17	38	71	53	71	45	41	27
Multilateral	..	..	7	10	11	12	12	15	16	17
Concessional	..	..	3	4	5	7	7	10	11	13
Bilateral	..	..	10	28	60	40	59	30	25	11
Concessional	..	..	6	17	26	10	12	15	16	9
Private creditors	..	..	6	5	4	1	3	0	0	0
Bonds	..	..	0	0	0	0	0	0	0	0
Commercial banks	..	..	1	0	0	0	0	0	0	0
Other private	..	..	5	4	4	1	3	0	0	0
Private nonguaranteed	..	..	**0**	**0**	**0**	**0**	**1**	**1**	**1**	**8**
Bonds	..	..	0	0	0	0	0	0	0	0
Commercial banks	..	..	0	0	0	0	1	1	1	8
Memo:										
IBRD	0	0	0	0	0	0	0	0	0	0
IDA	0	0	1	3	3	4	6	7	8	9
NET TRANSFERS ON DEBT	..	..	**167**	**125**	**77**	**122**	**122**	**176**	**180**	**159**
Public and publicly guaranteed	..	..	**159**	**124**	**77**	**122**	**90**	**182**	**178**	**171**
Official creditors	..	..	148	133	84	125	102	183	179	171
Multilateral	..	..	80	139	122	195	195	243	212	179
Concessional	..	..	82	140	124	200	195	245	205	188
Bilateral	..	..	68	-6	-39	-69	-93	-60	-33	-8
Concessional	..	..	80	13	5	-11	-19	-26	-20	-5
Private creditors	..	..	11	-8	-7	-3	-12	-2	-1	0
Bonds	..	..	0	0	0	0	0	0	0	0
Commercial banks	..	..	-5	-3	3	-1	0	0	0	0
Other private	..	..	16	-6	-10	-3	-12	-1	-1	0
Private nonguaranteed	..	..	**8**	**1**	**0**	**0**	**32**	**-6**	**2**	**-12**
Bonds	..	..	0	0	0	0	0	0	0	0
Commercial banks	..	..	8	1	0	0	32	-6	2	-12
Memo:										
IBRD	0	0	0	0	0	0	0	0	0	0
IDA	0	0	73	103	90	172	154	214	139	119
DEBT SERVICE (LTDS)	..	..	**64**	**76**	**113**	**111**	**146**	**106**	**85**	**74**
Public and publicly guaranteed	..	..	**52**	**73**	**109**	**108**	**141**	**100**	**80**	**62**
Official creditors	..	..	39	64	98	104	129	99	79	62
Multilateral	..	..	16	20	22	25	25	32	32	36
Concessional	..	..	7	9	11	12	13	21	20	24
Bilateral	..	..	23	45	76	79	104	66	47	26
Concessional	..	..	11	26	33	21	30	33	35	23
Private creditors	..	..	12	8	11	4	12	2	1	0
Bonds	..	..	0	0	0	0	0	0	0	0
Commercial banks	..	..	5	3	0	1	0	0	0	0
Other private	..	..	8	6	11	3	12	1	1	0
Private nonguaranteed	..	..	**12**	**3**	**3**	**3**	**5**	**6**	**5**	**12**
Bonds	..	..	0	0	0	0	0	0	0	0
Commercial banks	..	..	12	3	3	3	5	6	5	12
Memo:										
IBRD	0	0	0	0	0	0	0	0	0	0
IDA	0	0	1	3	3	4	6	7	9	12
UNDISBURSED DEBT	..	..	**836**	**963**	**964**	**1,336**	**1,275**	**944**	**892**	**713**
Official creditors	..	..	823	961	963	1,336	1,275	944	892	713
Private creditors	..	..	13	2	1	0	0	0	0	0
Memorandum items										
Concessional LDOD	..	..	2,085	2,634	2,864	3,240	2,936	3,204	3,190	3,651
Variable rate LDOD	..	..	290	673	632	2,221	2,313	2,324	2,352	2,374
Public sector LDOD	..	..	4,214	4,701	4,841	5,219	5,209	5,358	5,218	5,651
Private sector LDOD	..	..	20	17	18	1,652	1,769	1,845	1,912	1,975

6. CURRENCY COMPOSITION OF LONG-TERM DEBT (PERCENT)

	1970	1980	1990	1992	1993	1994	1995	1996	1997	1998
Deutsche mark	..	..	5.0	4.7	4.7	5.5	4.6	4.5	4.0	4.1
French franc	..	..	12.1	9.5	8.7	9.4	10.1	9.7	8.8	9.4
Japanese yen	..	..	1.8	1.8	1.9	1.9	1.8	1.8	1.7	1.8
Pound sterling	..	..	2.4	2.2	2.2	2.1	2.1	2.2	2.2	2.1
Swiss franc	..	..	0.0	0.0	0.0	0.0	0.0	0.0	0.0	0.0
U.S.dollars	..	..	52.4	58.0	59.6	60.5	60.1	61.5	61.6	60.2
Multiple currency	..	..	4.7	6.5	6.9	7.4	8.4	8.0	8.4	8.7
Special drawing rights	..	..	1.3	1.1	1.1	1.1	1.2	1.1	1.1	1.1
All other currencies	..	..	20.3	16.2	14.9	12.1	11.7	11.2	12.2	12.6

MOZAMBIQUE

(US$ million, unless otherwise indicated)

	1970	1980	1990	1992	1993	1994	1995	1996	1997	1998
7. DEBT RESTRUCTURINGS										
Total amount rescheduled	..	..	386	673	173	200	66	190	132	157
Debt stock rescheduled	..	..	0	8	0	0	0	0	0	0
Principal rescheduled	..	..	226	283	76	73	32	81	50	66
Official	..	..	134	51	41	66	30	72	48	66
Private	..	..	92	232	35	7	2	9	2	0
Interest rescheduled	..	..	158	84	58	62	29	105	64	82
Official	..	..	123	33	42	61	28	103	63	81
Private	..	..	35	51	17	1	0	2	1	0
Debt forgiven	..	..	210	19	27	57	311	64	213	20
Memo: interest forgiven	..	..	14	4	6	7	12	67	8	0
Debt stock reduction	..	..	0	0	3	0	0	0	0	0
of which debt buyback	..	..	0	0	0	0	0	0	0	0
8. DEBT STOCK-FLOW RECONCILIATION										
Total change in debt stocks	..	..	290	412	81	2,060	187	108	73	569
Net flows on debt	..	..	174	235	99	189	193	197	341	203
Net change in interest arrears	..	..	-62	-13	-6	23	79	-86	38	56
Interest capitalized	..	..	158	84	58	62	29	105	64	82
Debt forgiveness or reduction	..	..	-210	-19	-30	-57	-311	-64	-213	-20
Cross-currency valuation	..	..	208	-92	-65	111	72	-63	-116	76
Residual	..	..	21	217	24	1,731	125	19	-40	173
9. AVERAGE TERMS OF NEW COMMITMENTS										
ALL CREDITORS										
Interest (%)	..	..	1.4	0.8	0.9	0.8	0.9	2.1	1.5	0.9
Maturity (years)	..	..	35.0	41.7	37.6	39.7	36.7	23.8	41.9	40.6
Grace period (years)	..	..	9.2	10.2	9.4	9.9	9.3	8.7	9.7	10.5
Grant element (%)	..	..	71.8	79.9	76.2	78.9	76.1	59.4	73.5	79.1
Official creditors										
Interest (%)	..	..	1.3	0.8	0.8	0.8	0.9	2.1	1.5	0.9
Maturity (years)	..	..	35.2	41.7	38.1	39.7	36.7	23.8	41.9	40.6
Grace period (years)	..	..	9.2	10.2	9.5	9.9	9.3	8.7	9.7	10.5
Grant element (%)	..	..	72.3	79.9	77.5	78.9	76.1	59.4	73.5	79.1
Private creditors										
Interest (%)	..	..	9.0	0.0	7.0	0.0	0.0	0.0	0.0	0.0
Maturity (years)	..	..	4.9	0.0	11.5	0.0	0.0	0.0	0.0	0.0
Grace period (years)	..	..	2.9	0.0	2.4	0.0	0.0	0.0	0.0	0.0
Grant element (%)	..	..	2.4	0.0	16.3	0.0	0.0	0.0	0.0	0.0
Memorandum items										
Commitments	..	..	177	456	193	570	150	11	303	62
Official creditors	..	..	176	456	189	570	150	11	303	62
Private creditors	..	..	1	0	4	0	0	0	0	0

10. CONTRACTUAL OBLIGATIONS ON OUTSTANDING LONG-TERM DEBT

	1999	2000	2001	2002	2003	2004	2005	2006	2007	2008
TOTAL										
Disbursements	226	198	125	70	46	24	18	4	1	0
Principal	167	347	333	333	335	304	268	167	164	161
Interest	99	135	122	109	94	80	69	61	57	53
Official creditors										
Disbursements	226	198	125	70	46	24	18	4	1	0
Principal	128	295	285	289	297	263	226	123	118	113
Interest	90	126	114	101	88	74	64	56	53	50
Bilateral creditors										
Disbursements	11	10	7	4	2	1	1	0	0	0
Principal	101	260	251	253	255	217	175	69	61	51
Interest	69	104	91	79	65	52	43	36	33	31
Multilateral creditors										
Disbursements	215	188	119	66	44	23	17	4	1	0
Principal	27	34	34	36	42	47	51	54	57	62
Interest	21	23	23	23	22	22	21	20	20	19
Private creditors										
Disbursements	0	0	0	0	0	0	0	0	0	0
Principal	39	52	47	44	38	40	42	44	46	48
Interest	8	9	8	7	7	6	5	4	4	3
Commercial banks										
Disbursements	0	0	0	0	0	0	0	0	0	0
Principal	0	0	0	0	0	0	0	0	0	0
Interest	0	0	0	0	0	0	0	0	0	0
Other private										
Disbursements	0	0	0	0	0	0	0	0	0	0
Principal	39	52	47	44	38	40	42	44	46	48
Interest	8	8	8	7	7	6	5	4	4	3

MYANMAR

(US$ million, unless otherwise indicated)

	1970	1980	1990	1992	1993	1994	1995	1996	1997	1998
1. SUMMARY DEBT DATA										
TOTAL DEBT STOCKS (EDT)	..	1,500	4,695	5,355	5,757	6,555	5,771	5,184	5,063	5,680
Long-term debt (LDOD)	106	1,390	4,466	5,003	5,394	6,154	5,378	4,804	4,629	5,071
Public and publicly guaranteed	106	1,390	4,466	5,003	5,394	6,154	5,378	4,804	4,629	5,071
Private nonguaranteed	0	0	0	0	0	0	0	0	0	0
Use of IMF credit	17	106	0	0	0	0	0	0	0	0
Short-term debt	..	4	229	352	362	401	393	381	434	609
of which interest arrears on LDOD	..	0	200	340	354	380	352	366	390	471
Official creditors	..	0	168	286	299	312	285	305	332	413
Private creditors	..	0	32	54	55	68	67	61	58	58
Memo: principal arrears on LDOD	..	0	377	787	1,045	1,431	1,359	1,289	1,349	1,561
Official creditors	..	0	291	617	841	1,178	1,100	1,042	1,113	1,311
Private creditors	..	0	85	170	203	252	259	247	236	250
Memo: export credits	..	0	282	398	405	462	572	537	747	712
TOTAL DEBT FLOWS										
Disbursements	22	282	122	78	72	59	86	144	175	214
Long-term debt	22	269	122	78	72	59	86	144	175	214
IMF purchases	0	14	0	0	0	0	0	0	0	0
Principal repayments	20	89	46	26	22	42	180	140	101	79
Long-term debt	20	66	44	26	22	42	180	140	101	79
IMF repurchases	0	23	2	0	0	0	0	0	0	0
Net flows on debt	2	171	91	17	46	30	-74	-23	104	230
of which short-term debt	..	-22	15	-35	-4	13	20	-27	29	94
Interest payments (INT)	..	52	15	28	89	121	70	18	15	14
Long-term debt	3	45	13	26	89	120	68	18	13	9
IMF charges	0	4	0	0	0	0	0	0	0	0
Short-term debt	..	3	2	2	1	1	2	1	2	6
Net transfers on debt	..	119	76	-11	-43	-91	-144	-41	89	216
Total debt service paid (TDS)	..	141	60	54	111	163	250	158	116	93
Long-term debt	23	112	57	52	111	162	248	157	114	88
IMF repurchases and charges	0	26	2	0	0	0	0	0	0	0
Short-term debt (interest only)	..	3	2	2	1	1	2	1	2	6
2. AGGREGATE NET RESOURCE FLOWS AND NET TRANSFERS (LONG-TERM)										
NET RESOURCE FLOWS	16	269	276	262	242	254	200	226	225	272
Net flow of long-term debt (ex. IMF)	2	202	78	52	50	17	-95	4	74	135
Foreign direct investment (net)	0	0	161	172	149	91	115	100	80	70
Portfolio equity flows	0	0	0	0	0	29	16	10	-2	0
Grants (excluding technical coop.)	15	67	37	39	43	117	164	112	73	67
Memo: technical coop. grants	6	31	35	31	3	29	45	35	32	34
official net resource flows	9	240	123	92	60	124	34	97	45	119
private net resource flows	7	29	153	171	182	130	166	129	180	153
NET TRANSFERS	14	224	263	236	153	134	132	208	212	264
Interest on long-term debt	3	45	13	26	89	120	68	18	13	9
Profit remittances on FDI	0	0	0	0	0	0	0	0	0	0
Memo: official net transfers	8	219	113	67	-25	5	-32	82	35	116
private net transfers	6	5	151	170	178	128	164	126	177	148
3. MAJOR ECONOMIC AGGREGATES										
Gross national product (GNP)	..	..	..	..	..	..	..	..	..	..
Exports of goods & services (XGS)	129	556	668	647	648	651	1,299	1,414	1,565	1,745
of which workers remittances	..	0	0	0	0	0	0	0	0	0
Imports of goods & services (MGS)	211	869	1,270	830	1,454	1,670	2,174	2,371	2,740	2,862
International reserves (RES)	98	409	410	364	401	518	651	315	317	382
Current account balance	-81	-307	-526	-113	-461	-614	-415	-500	-710	-602
4. DEBT INDICATORS										
EDT / XGS (%)	..	270.0	703.2	827.5	887.8	1,007.3	444.2	366.6	323.5	325.5
EDT / GNP (%)	..	..	..	..	..	..	..	..	..	..
TDS / XGS (%)	..	25.4	9.1	8.3	17.2	25.1	19.2	11.2	7.4	5.3
INT / XGS (%)	..	9.4	2.2	4.3	13.8	18.6	5.4	1.3	1.0	0.8
INT / GNP (%)	..	..	..	..	..	..	..	..	..	..
RES / EDT (%)	..	27.3	8.7	6.8	7.0	7.9	11.3	6.1	6.3	6.7
RES / MGS (months)	5.6	5.6	3.9	5.3	3.3	3.7	3.6	1.6	1.4	1.6
Short-term / EDT (%)	..	0.3	4.9	6.6	6.3	6.1	6.8	7.3	8.6	10.7
Concessional / EDT (%)	..	72.7	87.6	86.5	86.6	86.6	84.7	83.5	80.6	77.8
Multilateral / EDT (%)	..	18.7	26.3	24.4	23.4	22.2	23.1	23.6	23.1	21.1

MYANMAR

(US$ million, unless otherwise indicated)

	1970	1980	1990	1992	1993	1994	1995	1996	1997	1998
5. LONG-TERM DEBT										
DEBT OUTSTANDING (LDOD)	**106**	**1,390**	**4,466**	**5,003**	**5,394**	**6,154**	**5,378**	**4,804**	**4,629**	**5,071**
Public and publicly guaranteed	**106**	**1,390**	**4,466**	**5,003**	**5,394**	**6,154**	**5,378**	**4,804**	**4,629**	**5,071**
Official creditors	72	1,109	4,216	4,747	5,105	5,820	5,011	4,438	4,177	4,524
Multilateral	15	280	1,234	1,306	1,348	1,458	1,331	1,223	1,171	1,199
Concessional	0	274	1,228	1,301	1,343	1,454	1,328	1,222	1,170	1,199
Bilateral	57	829	2,982	3,441	3,758	4,362	3,680	3,215	3,006	3,325
Concessional	56	817	2,884	3,330	3,642	4,225	3,558	3,109	2,909	3,219
Private creditors	34	281	250	256	289	334	367	366	452	547
Bonds	0	0	0	0	0	0	0	0	0	0
Commercial banks	0	51	0	0	0	0	0	0	0	0
Other private	34	231	250	256	289	334	367	366	452	547
Private nonguaranteed	**0**	**0**	**0**	**0**	**0**	**0**	**0**	**0**	**0**	**0**
Bonds	0	0	0	0	0	0	0	0	0	0
Commercial banks	0	0	0	0	0	0	0	0	0	0
Memo:										
IBRD	15	0	0	0	0	0	0	0	0	0
IDA	0	146	716	765	766	818	777	742	724	727
DISBURSEMENTS	**22**	**269**	**122**	**78**	**72**	**59**	**86**	**144**	**175**	**214**
Public and publicly guaranteed	**22**	**269**	**122**	**78**	**72**	**59**	**86**	**144**	**175**	**214**
Official creditors	3	199	119	74	37	31	17	96	33	100
Multilateral	0	38	68	21	14	12	0	-1	0	0
Concessional	0	38	68	21	14	12	0	-1	0	0
Bilateral	3	161	51	53	23	19	16	97	33	100
Concessional	2	160	51	53	23	19	16	97	33	100
Private creditors	19	70	3	4	35	28	69	47	143	114
Bonds	0	0	0	0	0	0	0	0	0	0
Commercial banks	0	15	0	0	0	0	0	0	0	0
Other private	19	55	3	4	35	28	69	47	143	114
Private nonguaranteed	**0**	**0**	**0**	**0**	**0**	**0**	**0**	**0**	**0**	**0**
Bonds	0	0	0	0	0	0	0	0	0	0
Commercial banks	0	0	0	0	0	0	0	0	0	0
Memo:										
IBRD	0	0	0	0	0	0	0	0	0	0
IDA	0	23	57	15	0	7	0	-1	0	0
PRINCIPAL REPAYMENTS	**20**	**66**	**44**	**26**	**22**	**42**	**180**	**140**	**101**	**79**
Public and publicly guaranteed	**20**	**66**	**44**	**26**	**22**	**42**	**180**	**140**	**101**	**79**
Official creditors	8	26	33	22	20	24	147	111	61	48
Multilateral	2	0	15	19	18	23	25	27	19	2
Concessional	0	0	14	19	17	22	24	26	18	2
Bilateral	5	25	18	2	3	1	122	85	42	46
Concessional	5	18	18	2	3	1	122	85	42	45
Private creditors	12	41	11	5	2	18	34	28	40	31
Bonds	0	0	0	0	0	0	0	0	0	0
Commercial banks	0	13	0	0	0	0	0	0	0	0
Other private	12	28	11	5	2	18	34	28	40	31
Private nonguaranteed	**0**	**0**	**0**	**0**	**0**	**0**	**0**	**0**	**0**	**0**
Bonds	0	0	0	0	0	0	0	0	0	0
Commercial banks	0	0	0	0	0	0	0	0	0	0
Memo:										
IBRD	2	0	0	0	0	0	0	0	0	0
IDA	0	0	4	5	4	9	10	10	7	0
NET FLOWS ON DEBT	**2**	**202**	**78**	**52**	**50**	**17**	**-95**	**4**	**74**	**135**
Public and publicly guaranteed	**2**	**202**	**78**	**52**	**50**	**17**	**-95**	**4**	**74**	**135**
Official creditors	-5	173	86	53	17	7	-130	-15	-28	52
Multilateral	-2	38	53	2	-3	-10	-24	-27	-19	-2
Concessional	0	38	54	2	-3	-10	-24	-26	-18	-2
Bilateral	-3	135	33	51	21	18	-106	12	-9	54
Concessional	-2	142	33	51	21	18	-106	12	-9	55
Private creditors	7	29	-8	-1	33	10	36	19	102	83
Bonds	0	0	0	0	0	0	0	0	0	0
Commercial banks	0	2	0	0	0	0	0	0	0	0
Other private	7	27	-8	-1	33	10	36	19	102	83
Private nonguaranteed	**0**	**0**	**0**	**0**	**0**	**0**	**0**	**0**	**0**	**0**
Bonds	0	0	0	0	0	0	0	0	0	0
Commercial banks	0	0	0	0	0	0	0	0	0	0
Memo:										
IBRD	-2	0	0	0	0	0	0	0	0	0
IDA	0	23	53	10	-4	-2	-10	-11	-7	0

MYANMAR

(US$ million, unless otherwise indicated)

	1970	1980	1990	1992	1993	1994	1995	1996	1997	1998
INTEREST PAYMENTS (LINT)	**3**	**45**	**13**	**26**	**89**	**120**	**68**	**18**	**13**	**9**
Public and publicly guaranteed	**3**	**45**	**13**	**26**	**89**	**120**	**68**	**18**	**13**	**9**
Official creditors	2	21	11	25	85	119	66	15	10	3
Multilateral	1	3	10	11	8	12	13	12	7	1
Concessional	0	2	10	11	8	12	12	11	7	0
Bilateral	1	19	1	13	76	107	53	3	3	3
Concessional	1	17	1	13	76	107	50	1	1	2
Private creditors	1	24	2	1	4	1	2	3	3	5
Bonds	0	0	0	0	0	0	0	0	0	0
Commercial banks	0	8	0	0	0	0	0	0	0	0
Other private	1	16	2	1	4	1	2	3	3	5
Private nonguaranteed	**0**	**0**	**0**	**0**	**0**	**0**	**0**	**0**	**0**	**0**
Bonds	0	0	0	0	0	0	0	0	0	0
Commercial banks	0	0	0	0	0	0	0	0	0	0
Memo:										
IBRD	1	0	0	0	0	0	0	0	0	0
IDA	0	1	5	6	2	6	6	6	4	0
NET TRANSFERS ON DEBT	**-1**	**157**	**65**	**26**	**-39**	**-104**	**-162**	**-14**	**61**	**127**
Public and publicly guaranteed	**-1**	**157**	**65**	**26**	**-39**	**-104**	**-162**	**-14**	**61**	**127**
Official creditors	-7	152	76	28	-67	-112	-196	-30	-38	49
Multilateral	-3	36	43	-10	-12	-23	-37	-39	-26	-3
Concessional	0	36	44	-9	-11	-22	-36	-38	-25	-3
Bilateral	-4	117	33	38	-56	-89	-159	9	-13	52
Concessional	-3	125	33	38	-56	-89	-156	11	-10	53
Private creditors	6	5	-10	-2	29	8	33	16	99	78
Bonds	0	0	0	0	0	0	0	0	0	0
Commercial banks	0	-6	0	0	0	0	0	0	0	0
Other private	6	11	-10	-2	29	8	33	16	99	78
Private nonguaranteed	**0**	**0**	**0**	**0**	**0**	**0**	**0**	**0**	**0**	**0**
Bonds	0	0	0	0	0	0	0	0	0	0
Commercial banks	0	0	0	0	0	0	0	0	0	0
Memo:										
IBRD	-3	0	0	0	0	0	0	0	0	0
IDA	0	22	48	4	-6	-8	-16	-17	-11	0
DEBT SERVICE (LTDS)	**23**	**112**	**57**	**52**	**111**	**162**	**248**	**157**	**114**	**88**
Public and publicly guaranteed	**23**	**112**	**57**	**52**	**111**	**162**	**248**	**157**	**114**	**88**
Official creditors	10	47	44	46	105	143	212	126	71	51
Multilateral	3	3	25	31	26	35	37	38	26	3
Concessional	0	2	24	30	25	34	36	37	25	3
Bilateral	6	44	19	16	79	108	175	88	45	49
Concessional	6	35	19	16	79	108	172	85	43	47
Private creditors	13	65	13	6	6	20	36	31	43	36
Bonds	0	0	0	0	0	0	0	0	0	0
Commercial banks	0	21	0	0	0	0	0	0	0	0
Other private	13	44	13	6	6	20	36	31	43	36
Private nonguaranteed	**0**	**0**	**0**	**0**	**0**	**0**	**0**	**0**	**0**	**0**
Bonds	0	0	0	0	0	0	0	0	0	0
Commercial banks	0	0	0	0	0	0	0	0	0	0
Memo:										
IBRD	3	0	0	0	0	0	0	0	0	0
IDA	0	1	9	11	6	15	16	16	11	0
UNDISBURSED DEBT	**106**	**1,282**	**915**	**879**	**910**	**951**	**859**	**893**	**745**	**563**
Official creditors	74	1,072	890	813	836	874	770	674	615	510
Private creditors	32	211	24	66	74	76	89	219	130	53
Memorandum items										
Concessional LDOD	56	1,090	4,112	4,632	4,985	5,679	4,886	4,331	4,079	4,417
Variable rate LDOD	0	70	0	0	0	0	0	0	0	0
Public sector LDOD	106	1,390	4,466	5,003	5,394	6,154	5,378	4,804	4,629	5,071
Private sector LDOD	0	0	0	0	0	0	0	0	0	0

6. CURRENCY COMPOSITION OF LONG-TERM DEBT (PERCENT)

	1970	1980	1990	1992	1993	1994	1995	1996	1997	1998
Deutsche mark	15.4	11.6	12.4	11.8	10.6	11.2	12.0	12.0	11.3	11.4
French franc	0.0	2.6	3.0	1.4	1.2	1.2	1.4	1.4	1.3	1.3
Japanese yen	0.0	42.8	46.8	52.2	55.0	55.9	52.3	50.1	48.8	48.6
Pound sterling	31.2	4.3	1.7	1.3	1.2	1.2	1.3	1.5	1.6	1.4
Swiss franc	0.0	0.2	0.0	0.0	0.0	0.0	0.0	0.0	0.0	0.0
U.S.dollars	21.7	23.3	24.3	22.5	21.7	20.3	22.6	24.7	27.1	27.6
Multiple currency	14.0	7.7	7.6	7.3	7.2	7.1	7.0	6.8	6.6	6.3
Special drawing rights	0.0	0.0	0.0	0.0	0.0	0.0	0.0	0.0	0.0	0.0
All other currencies	17.7	7.5	4.2	3.5	3.1	3.1	3.4	3.5	3.3	3.4

MYANMAR

(US$ million, unless otherwise indicated)

	1970	1980	1990	1992	1993	1994	1995	1996	1997	1998
7. DEBT RESTRUCTURINGS										
Total amount rescheduled	..	..	0	0	0	0	0	0	0	0
Debt stock rescheduled	..	..	0	0	0	0	0	0	0	0
Principal rescheduled	..	..	0	0	0	0	0	0	0	0
Official	..	..	0	0	0	0	0	0	0	0
Private	..	..	0	0	0	0	0	0	0	0
Interest rescheduled	..	..	0	0	0	0	0	0	0	0
Official	..	..	0	0	0	0	0	0	0	0
Private	..	..	0	0	0	0	0	0	0	0
Debt forgiven	..	..	0	0	0	0	0	0	0	0
Memo: interest forgiven	..	..	0	0	0	0	0	0	0	0
Debt stock reduction	..	..	0	0	0	0	0	0	0	0
of which debt buyback	..	..	0	0	0	0	0	0	0	0
8. DEBT STOCK-FLOW RECONCILIATION										
Total change in debt stocks	..	..	504	480	402	799	-785	-586	-121	617
Net flows on debt	2	171	91	17	46	30	-74	-23	104	230
Net change in interest arrears	..	..	90	92	14	26	-29	15	24	81
Interest capitalized	..	..	0	0	0	0	0	0	0	0
Debt forgiveness or reduction	..	..	0	0	0	0	0	0	0	0
Cross-currency valuation	..	..	231	379	344	725	-501	-430	-200	238
Residual	..	..	92	-8	-2	17	-181	-148	-50	69
9. AVERAGE TERMS OF NEW COMMITMENTS										
ALL CREDITORS										
Interest (%)	4.1	3.5	2.7	1.5	2.3	0.5	1.4	1.4	1.9	3.3
Maturity (years)	16.2	29.0	13.7	7.8	6.2	7.5	14.4	11.1	9.5	7.6
Grace period (years)	4.5	7.3	3.4	1.5	1.0	2.1	8.7	3.2	3.6	3.0
Grant element (%)	33.6	52.2	39.3	29.6	22.7	25.6	39.1	40.2	35.5	25.8
Official creditors										
Interest (%)	2.9	1.6	1.5	0.0	0.0	2.5	2.8	1.8	2.8	0.0
Maturity (years)	26.1	37.0	16.7	0.0	0.0	24.6	33.0	13.6	15.6	0.0
Grace period (years)	7.3	9.5	5.2	0.0	0.0	7.1	24.4	4.1	5.5	0.0
Grant element (%)	53.4	71.0	53.3	0.0	0.0	55.9	62.6	44.7	43.4	0.0
Private creditors										
Interest (%)	5.3	8.0	3.5	1.5	2.3	0.0	0.8	1.1	1.7	3.3
Maturity (years)	6.3	10.4	11.6	7.8	6.2	3.4	6.4	8.9	7.8	7.6
Grace period (years)	1.8	2.2	2.1	1.5	1.0	0.9	1.8	2.4	3.1	3.0
Grant element (%)	13.9	8.5	29.4	29.6	22.7	18.4	28.8	36.2	33.3	25.8
Memorandum items										
Commitments	48	605	42	45	43	37	118	342	74	27
Official creditors	24	423	17	0	0	7	36	162	16	0
Private creditors	24	182	24	45	43	30	82	181	58	27

10. CONTRACTUAL OBLIGATIONS ON OUTSTANDING LONG-TERM DEBT

	1999	2000	2001	2002	2003	2004	2005	2006	2007	2008
TOTAL										
Disbursements	37	32	15	7	5	3	2	1	1	1
Principal	264	265	266	233	229	227	213	203	186	177
Interest	56	52	48	43	38	34	30	26	23	20
Official creditors										
Disbursements	22	19	9	5	4	3	2	1	1	1
Principal	216	201	203	187	191	193	190	190	183	177
Interest	52	49	45	41	37	33	30	26	23	20
Bilateral creditors										
Disbursements	22	18	8	4	3	2	2	1	1	1
Principal	180	163	162	145	147	147	144	143	136	130
Interest	42	39	35	32	28	25	22	19	16	13
Multilateral creditors										
Disbursements	1	2	1	1	1	0	0	0	0	0
Principal	36	38	40	42	44	46	46	47	47	47
Interest	10	10	10	9	9	8	8	8	7	7
Private creditors										
Disbursements	14	12	6	2	1	0	0	0	0	0
Principal	48	64	63	46	38	34	22	13	3	0
Interest	4	3	3	2	1	1	0	0	0	0
Commercial banks										
Disbursements	0	0	0	0	0	0	0	0	0	0
Principal	0	0	0	0	0	0	0	0	0	0
Interest	0	0	0	0	0	0	0	0	0	0
Other private										
Disbursements	14	12	6	2	1	0	0	0	0	0
Principal	48	64	63	46	38	34	22	13	3	0
Interest	4	3	3	2	1	1	0	0	0	0

NEPAL

(US$ million, unless otherwise indicated)

	1970	1980	1990	1992	1993	1994	1995	1996	1997	1998
1. SUMMARY DEBT DATA										
TOTAL DEBT STOCKS (EDT)	**..**	**205**	**1,640**	**1,807**	**2,010**	**2,328**	**2,418**	**2,411**	**2,390**	**2,646**
Long-term debt (LDOD)	**3**	**156**	**1,572**	**1,758**	**1,940**	**2,210**	**2,347**	**2,346**	**2,332**	**2,591**
Public and publicly guaranteed	3	156	1,572	1,758	1,940	2,210	2,347	2,346	2,332	2,591
Private nonguaranteed	0	0	0	0	0	0	0	0	0	0
Use of IMF credit	**0**	**42**	**44**	**44**	**49**	**55**	**48**	**39**	**30**	**24**
Short-term debt	**..**	**7**	**24**	**6**	**21**	**63**	**23**	**26**	**28**	**31**
of which interest arrears on LDOD	..	0	4	4	3	2	2	2	1	2
Official creditors	..	0	4	4	3	2	2	2	1	2
Private creditors	..	0	0	0	0	0	0	0	0	0
Memo: principal arrears on LDOD	..	0	6	8	7	6	8	10	9	9
Official creditors	..	0	6	8	6	3	3	4	4	4
Private creditors	..	0	0	1	2	3	5	6	5	4
Memo: export credits	..	0	109	86	75	82	41	31	82	73
TOTAL DEBT FLOWS										
Disbursements	**1**	**69**	**173**	**140**	**194**	**203**	**163**	**158**	**213**	**178**
Long-term debt	1	50	173	132	187	195	163	158	213	178
IMF purchases	0	18	0	8	8	8	0	0	0	0
Principal repayments	**2**	**3**	**42**	**38**	**41**	**48**	**52**	**47**	**70**	**61**
Long-term debt	2	2	29	37	39	43	44	39	63	54
IMF repurchases	0	1	13	1	2	6	8	8	7	7
Net flows on debt	**-2**	**61**	**134**	**82**	**170**	**198**	**71**	**114**	**145**	**120**
of which short-term debt	..	-5	2	-19	16	43	-40	3	3	2
Interest payments (INT)	**..**	**5**	**29**	**29**	**28**	**32**	**32**	**31**	**28**	**27**
Long-term debt	0	2	26	28	28	30	29	30	26	26
IMF charges	0	1	2	0	0	0	0	0	0	0
Short-term debt	..	2	2	1	1	2	2	1	1	2
Net transfers on debt	**..**	**56**	**105**	**53**	**142**	**165**	**39**	**83**	**118**	**92**
Total debt service paid (TDS)	**..**	**8**	**71**	**68**	**69**	**81**	**84**	**78**	**98**	**88**
Long-term debt	2	4	55	66	66	73	74	69	89	80
IMF repurchases and charges	0	1	14	1	2	6	8	8	7	7
Short-term debt (interest only)	..	2	2	1	1	2	2	1	1	2
2. AGGREGATE NET RESOURCE FLOWS AND NET TRANSFERS (LONG-TERM)										
NET RESOURCE FLOWS	**7**	**127**	**293**	**256**	**300**	**329**	**297**	**279**	**312**	**253**
Net flow of long-term debt (ex. IMF)	-2	48	144	94	148	152	119	119	150	124
Foreign direct investment (net)	0	0	6	4	6	7	8	19	23	12
Portfolio equity flows	0	0	0	0	0	0	0	0	0	0
Grants (excluding technical coop.)	9	79	143	158	146	170	171	141	140	117
Memo: technical coop. grants	8	51	109	125	145	141	142	141	132	136
official net resource flows	7	127	301	263	304	331	294	264	300	253
private net resource flows	0	0	-8	-7	-4	-2	3	16	12	-1
NET TRANSFERS	**7**	**125**	**267**	**228**	**273**	**299**	**268**	**250**	**286**	**227**
Interest on long-term debt	0	2	26	28	28	30	29	30	26	26
Profit remittances on FDI	0	0	0	0	0	0	0	0	0	0
Memo: official net transfers	7	125	287	244	284	307	271	238	278	231
private net transfers	0	0	-20	-16	-12	-8	-2	11	8	-4
3. MAJOR ECONOMIC AGGREGATES										
Gross national product (GNP)	866	1,958	3,695	3,540	3,842	4,124	4,485	4,574	5,004	4,880
Exports of goods & services (XGS)	71	269	524	651	775	1,072	1,206	1,112	1,428	1,260
of which workers remittances	..	30	61	54	66	70	101	78	98	113
Imports of goods & services (MGS)	96	368	774	933	1,059	1,282	1,529	1,645	1,885	1,671
International reserves (RES)	94	272	354	518	700	752	646	628	671	800
Current account balance	-1	-93	-251	-275	-296	-225	-343	-527	-460	-422
4. DEBT INDICATORS										
EDT / XGS (%)	..	76.0	312.9	277.6	259.4	217.2	200.5	216.9	167.4	210.1
EDT / GNP (%)	..	10.4	44.4	51.0	52.3	56.4	53.9	52.7	47.8	54.2
TDS / XGS (%)	..	2.9	13.6	10.4	8.9	7.5	7.0	7.0	6.9	7.0
INT / XGS (%)	..	1.9	5.6	4.5	3.7	3.0	2.7	2.8	2.0	2.2
INT / GNP (%)	..	0.3	0.8	0.8	0.7	0.8	0.7	0.7	0.6	0.6
RES / EDT (%)	..	133.0	21.6	28.7	34.8	32.3	26.7	26.0	28.1	30.3
RES / MGS (months)	11.8	8.9	5.5	6.7	7.9	7.0	5.1	4.6	4.3	5.8
Short-term / EDT (%)	..	3.4	1.5	0.3	1.0	2.7	1.0	1.1	1.2	1.2
Concessional / EDT (%)	..	75.7	88.5	92.1	92.5	91.9	94.2	94.7	95.5	96.5
Multilateral / EDT (%)	..	62.0	77.3	80.2	79.0	77.5	80.8	82.4	83.2	84.4

NEPAL

(US$ million, unless otherwise indicated)

	1970	1980	1990	1992	1993	1994	1995	1996	1997	1998
5. LONG-TERM DEBT										
DEBT OUTSTANDING (LDOD)	**3**	**156**	**1,572**	**1,758**	**1,940**	**2,210**	**2,347**	**2,346**	**2,332**	**2,591**
Public and publicly guaranteed	**3**	**156**	**1,572**	**1,758**	**1,940**	**2,210**	**2,347**	**2,346**	**2,332**	**2,591**
Official creditors	2	156	1,462	1,671	1,864	2,141	2,281	2,285	2,285	2,555
Multilateral	0	127	1,268	1,449	1,588	1,805	1,952	1,986	1,989	2,233
Concessional	0	126	1,259	1,442	1,583	1,802	1,950	1,984	1,987	2,231
Bilateral	2	29	193	222	276	337	329	299	296	322
Concessional	2	29	193	222	276	337	329	299	296	322
Private creditors	1	0	110	87	76	69	65	60	47	36
Bonds	0	0	0	0	0	0	0	0	0	0
Commercial banks	0	0	0	0	0	0	0	0	0	0
Other private	1	0	110	87	76	69	65	60	47	36
Private nonguaranteed	**0**	**0**	**0**	**0**	**0**	**0**	**0**	**0**	**0**	**0**
Bonds	0	0	0	0	0	0	0	0	0	0
Commercial banks	0	0	0	0	0	0	0	0	0	0
Memo:										
IBRD	0	0	0	0	0	0	0	0	0	0
IDA	0	76	668	765	832	932	1,023	1,049	1,047	1,131
DISBURSEMENTS	**1**	**50**	**173**	**132**	**187**	**195**	**163**	**158**	**213**	**178**
Public and publicly guaranteed	**1**	**50**	**173**	**132**	**187**	**195**	**163**	**158**	**213**	**178**
Official creditors	1	50	171	130	185	195	163	158	203	178
Multilateral	0	36	150	118	136	153	150	146	158	168
Concessional	0	36	150	118	136	153	150	146	158	168
Bilateral	0	14	21	12	49	42	13	12	45	10
Concessional	0	14	21	12	49	42	13	12	45	10
Private creditors	0	0	2	2	2	0	0	0	9	0
Bonds	0	0	0	0	0	0	0	0	0	0
Commercial banks	0	0	0	0	0	0	0	0	0	0
Other private	0	0	2	2	2	0	0	0	9	0
Private nonguaranteed	**0**	**0**	**0**	**0**	**0**	**0**	**0**	**0**	**0**	**0**
Bonds	0	0	0	0	0	0	0	0	0	0
Commercial banks	0	0	0	0	0	0	0	0	0	0
Memo:										
IBRD	0	0	0	0	0	0	0	0	0	0
IDA	0	25	70	71	69	76	81	62	54	63
PRINCIPAL REPAYMENTS	**2**	**2**	**29**	**37**	**39**	**43**	**44**	**39**	**63**	**54**
Public and publicly guaranteed	**2**	**2**	**29**	**37**	**39**	**43**	**44**	**39**	**63**	**54**
Official creditors	2	2	13	25	27	34	40	36	43	42
Multilateral	0	2	10	17	17	23	24	26	28	26
Concessional	0	2	10	15	15	20	24	26	28	26
Bilateral	2	0	3	8	11	11	16	9	15	15
Concessional	1	0	3	8	11	11	16	9	15	15
Private creditors	0	0	16	13	11	9	5	4	20	13
Bonds	0	0	0	0	0	0	0	0	0	0
Commercial banks	0	0	0	0	0	0	0	0	0	0
Other private	0	0	16	13	11	9	5	4	20	13
Private nonguaranteed	**0**	**0**	**0**	**0**	**0**	**0**	**0**	**0**	**0**	**0**
Bonds	0	0	0	0	0	0	0	0	0	0
Commercial banks	0	0	0	0	0	0	0	0	0	0
Memo:										
IBRD	0	0	0	0	0	0	0	0	0	0
IDA	0	0	2	3	4	5	7	8	9	11
NET FLOWS ON DEBT	**-2**	**48**	**144**	**94**	**148**	**152**	**119**	**119**	**150**	**124**
Public and publicly guaranteed	**-2**	**48**	**144**	**94**	**148**	**152**	**119**	**119**	**150**	**124**
Official creditors	-2	48	158	105	158	161	124	122	160	137
Multilateral	0	35	140	101	119	130	127	119	131	142
Concessional	0	35	140	103	121	133	127	119	131	142
Bilateral	-2	14	18	4	38	31	-3	3	30	-5
Concessional	0	14	18	4	38	31	-3	3	30	-5
Private creditors	0	0	-14	-11	-10	-9	-5	-4	-11	-13
Bonds	0	0	0	0	0	0	0	0	0	0
Commercial banks	0	0	0	0	0	0	0	0	0	0
Other private	0	0	-14	-11	-10	-9	-5	-4	-11	-13
Private nonguaranteed	**0**	**0**	**0**	**0**	**0**	**0**	**0**	**0**	**0**	**0**
Bonds	0	0	0	0	0	0	0	0	0	0
Commercial banks	0	0	0	0	0	0	0	0	0	0
Memo:										
IBRD	0	0	0	0	0	0	0	0	0	0
IDA	0	25	68	68	66	70	74	54	45	52

NEPAL

(US$ million, unless otherwise indicated)

	1970	1980	1990	1992	1993	1994	1995	1996	1997	1998
INTEREST PAYMENTS (LINT)	**0**	**2**	**26**	**28**	**28**	**30**	**29**	**30**	**26**	**26**
Public and publicly guaranteed	**0**	**2**	**26**	**28**	**28**	**30**	**29**	**30**	**26**	**26**
Official creditors	0	2	14	19	20	24	24	25	22	23
Multilateral	0	1	10	14	14	17	17	17	17	18
Concessional	0	1	10	13	13	16	17	17	17	18
Bilateral	0	1	4	5	6	7	7	8	5	5
Concessional	0	1	4	5	6	7	7	8	5	5
Private creditors	0	0	12	10	8	6	5	4	4	3
Bonds	0	0	0	0	0	0	0	0	0	0
Commercial banks	0	0	0	0	0	0	0	0	0	0
Other private	0	0	12	10	8	6	5	4	4	3
Private nonguaranteed	**0**	**0**	**0**	**0**	**0**	**0**	**0**	**0**	**0**	**0**
Bonds	0	0	0	0	0	0	0	0	0	0
Commercial banks	0	0	0	0	0	0	0	0	0	0
Memo:										
IBRD	0	0	0	0	0	0	0	0	0	0
IDA	0	0	5	6	6	7	7	8	8	8
NET TRANSFERS ON DEBT	**-2**	**46**	**118**	**66**	**120**	**122**	**89**	**89**	**123**	**98**
Public and publicly guaranteed	**-2**	**46**	**118**	**66**	**120**	**122**	**89**	**89**	**123**	**98**
Official creditors	-2	46	144	87	138	137	100	97	138	114
Multilateral	0	33	130	88	105	113	110	102	114	124
Concessional	0	34	130	90	108	117	110	102	114	124
Bilateral	-2	13	14	-1	33	24	-10	-5	25	-10
Concessional	0	13	14	-1	33	24	-10	-5	25	-10
Private creditors	0	0	-26	-20	-18	-15	-10	-8	-15	-16
Bonds	0	0	0	0	0	0	0	0	0	0
Commercial banks	0	0	0	0	0	0	0	0	0	0
Other private	0	0	-26	-20	-18	-15	-10	-8	-15	-16
Private nonguaranteed	**0**	**0**	**0**	**0**	**0**	**0**	**0**	**0**	**0**	**0**
Bonds	0	0	0	0	0	0	0	0	0	0
Commercial banks	0	0	0	0	0	0	0	0	0	0
Memo:										
IBRD	0	0	0	0	0	0	0	0	0	0
IDA	0	25	63	62	60	64	67	46	38	44
DEBT SERVICE (LTDS)	**2**	**4**	**55**	**66**	**66**	**73**	**74**	**69**	**89**	**80**
Public and publicly guaranteed	**2**	**4**	**55**	**66**	**66**	**73**	**74**	**69**	**89**	**80**
Official creditors	2	4	27	43	47	58	63	61	65	64
Multilateral	0	3	20	30	31	39	40	43	45	44
Concessional	0	3	20	28	28	36	40	43	45	44
Bilateral	2	1	7	13	16	19	23	17	21	20
Concessional	1	1	7	13	16	19	23	17	21	20
Private creditors	0	0	27	22	19	15	10	8	24	16
Bonds	0	0	0	0	0	0	0	0	0	0
Commercial banks	0	0	0	0	0	0	0	0	0	0
Other private	0	0	27	22	19	15	10	8	24	16
Private nonguaranteed	**0**	**0**	**0**	**0**	**0**	**0**	**0**	**0**	**0**	**0**
Bonds	0	0	0	0	0	0	0	0	0	0
Commercial banks	0	0	0	0	0	0	0	0	0	0
Memo:										
IBRD	0	0	0	0	0	0	0	0	0	0
IDA	0	1	7	9	10	12	14	16	17	19
UNDISBURSED DEBT	**26**	**366**	**1,318**	**1,229**	**1,035**	**995**	**799**	**878**	**779**	**665**
Official creditors	26	366	1,307	1,222	1,031	990	794	873	777	662
Private creditors	0	0	10	6	4	5	5	5	2	2
Memorandum items										
Concessional LDOD	2	155	1,452	1,664	1,859	2,138	2,278	2,283	2,283	2,552
Variable rate LDOD	0	0	0	0	0	0	0	0	0	0
Public sector LDOD	3	156	1,566	1,756	1,939	2,209	2,346	2,345	2,332	2,590
Private sector LDOD	0	0	5	2	1	1	1	1	1	1

6. CURRENCY COMPOSITION OF LONG-TERM DEBT (PERCENT)

	1970	1980	1990	1992	1993	1994	1995	1996	1997	1998
Deutsche mark	21.4	0.0	0.9	0.6	0.4	0.3	0.3	0.3	0.2	0.2
French franc	0.0	0.3	2.0	1.3	1.2	1.9	1.9	1.8	1.6	1.5
Japanese yen	0.0	7.9	8.4	9.6	11.7	12.3	11.2	9.8	10.2	9.9
Pound sterling	50.0	0.1	0.2	0.1	0.1	0.1	0.1	0.1	0.1	0.1
Swiss franc	0.0	0.0	0.0	0.0	0.0	0.0	0.0	0.0	0.0	0.0
U.S.dollars	7.1	49.5	49.6	48.7	46.7	44.3	43.8	43.7	42.5	41.4
Multiple currency	3.6	31.2	32.6	34.4	35.1	36.0	35.9	35.9	36.5	37.7
Special drawing rights	0.0	0.0	2.7	2.3	2.4	3.2	5.0	6.4	7.1	7.4
All other currencies	17.9	11.0	3.6	3.0	2.4	1.9	1.8	2.0	1.8	1.8

NEPAL

(US$ million, unless otherwise indicated)

	1970	1980	1990	1992	1993	1994	1995	1996	1997	1998
7. DEBT RESTRUCTURINGS										
Total amount rescheduled	..	..	0	0	0	0	0	0	0	0
Debt stock rescheduled	..	..	0	0	0	0	0	0	0	0
Principal rescheduled	..	..	0	0	0	0	0	0	0	0
Official	..	..	0	0	0	0	0	0	0	0
Private	..	..	0	0	0	0	0	0	0	0
Interest rescheduled	..	..	0	0	0	0	0	0	0	0
Official	..	..	0	0	0	0	0	0	0	0
Private	..	..	0	0	0	0	0	0	0	0
Debt forgiven	..	..	0	2	0	0	0	0	0	0
Memo: interest forgiven	..	..	0	0	0	0	0	0	0	0
Debt stock reduction	..	..	0	0	0	0	0	0	0	0
of which debt buyback	..	..	0	0	0	0	0	0	0	0
8. DEBT STOCK-FLOW RECONCILIATION										
Total change in debt stocks	..	..	272	30	203	318	90	-7	-20	255
Net flows on debt	-2	61	134	82	170	198	71	114	145	120
Net change in interest arrears	..	..	1	-1	-1	-1	0	0	0	0
Interest capitalized	..	..	0	0	0	0	0	0	0	0
Debt forgiveness or reduction	..	..	0	-2	0	0	0	0	0	0
Cross-currency valuation	..	..	22	-6	23	45	0	-36	-44	46
Residual	..	..	116	-43	11	77	19	-85	-121	90
9. AVERAGE TERMS OF NEW COMMITMENTS										
ALL CREDITORS										
Interest (%)	2.8	0.8	0.9	0.9	1.0	0.8	3.7	3.2	0.8	3.3
Maturity (years)	26.9	46.0	39.3	39.7	39.7	38.7	36.1	38.7	36.8	38.3
Grace period (years)	6.2	10.2	10.3	10.2	10.2	10.1	9.2	10.3	9.7	9.8
Grant element (%)	53.1	81.2	78.9	79.4	78.5	80.0	51.0	58.7	77.3	56.9
Official creditors										
Interest (%)	2.8	0.8	0.9	0.9	1.0	0.8	3.7	3.2	0.9	3.3
Maturity (years)	26.9	46.0	39.3	39.7	39.7	38.7	36.1	38.7	37.7	38.3
Grace period (years)	6.2	10.2	10.3	10.2	10.2	10.1	9.2	10.3	9.9	9.8
Grant element (%)	53.1	81.2	78.9	79.4	78.5	80.0	51.0	58.7	78.2	56.9
Private creditors										
Interest (%)	0.0	0.0	0.0	0.0	0.0	0.0	0.0	0.0	0.6	0.0
Maturity (years)	0.0	0.0	0.0	0.0	0.0	0.0	0.0	0.0	17.9	0.0
Grace period (years)	0.0	0.0	0.0	0.0	0.0	0.0	0.0	0.0	4.7	0.0
Grant element (%)	0.0	0.0	0.0	0.0	0.0	0.0	0.0	0.0	57.1	0.0
Memorandum items										
Commitments	17	92	220	303	57	112	60	290	191	78
Official creditors	17	92	220	303	57	112	60	290	182	78
Private creditors	0	0	0	0	0	0	0	0	9	0

10. CONTRACTUAL OBLIGATIONS ON OUTSTANDING LONG-TERM DEBT

	1999	2000	2001	2002	2003	2004	2005	2006	2007	2008
TOTAL										
Disbursements	212	179	123	84	40	17	7	1	0	0
Principal	65	68	64	70	74	78	85	93	97	105
Interest	29	30	30	30	30	29	29	29	33	32
Official creditors										
Disbursements	211	179	123	84	40	17	7	1	0	0
Principal	53	60	63	69	73	77	84	92	96	104
Interest	28	29	30	30	30	29	28	29	33	32
Bilateral creditors										
Disbursements	31	20	12	6	3	2	0	0	0	0
Principal	22	22	23	23	23	23	23	23	22	22
Interest	6	6	5	5	5	4	4	4	3	3
Multilateral creditors										
Disbursements	180	159	112	78	38	15	7	1	0	0
Principal	32	38	40	46	50	54	61	69	74	82
Interest	22	23	25	25	25	25	25	25	30	30
Private creditors										
Disbursements	1	1	0	0	0	0	0	0	0	0
Principal	12	8	1	1	1	1	1	1	1	1
Interest	2	1	0	0	0	0	0	0	0	0
Commercial banks										
Disbursements	0	0	0	0	0	0	0	0	0	0
Principal	0	0	0	0	0	0	0	0	0	0
Interest	0	0	0	0	0	0	0	0	0	0
Other private										
Disbursements	1	1	0	0	0	0	0	0	0	0
Principal	12	8	1	1	1	1	1	1	1	1
Interest	2	1	0	0	0	0	0	0	0	0

NICARAGUA

(US$ million, unless otherwise indicated)

	1970	1980	1990	1992	1993	1994	1995	1996	1997	1998
1. SUMMARY DEBT DATA										
TOTAL DEBT STOCKS (EDT)	**..**	**2,190**	**10,708**	**11,178**	**11,409**	**12,104**	**10,359**	**5,932**	**5,697**	**5,968**
Long-term debt (LDOD)	**147**	**1,669**	**8,281**	**9,312**	**9,441**	**9,762**	**8,541**	**5,125**	**4,839**	**5,212**
Public and publicly guaranteed	147	1,669	8,281	9,312	9,441	9,762	8,541	5,125	4,839	5,212
Private nonguaranteed	0	0	0	0	0	0	0	0	0	0
Use of IMF credit	**8**	**49**	**0**	**23**	**23**	**51**	**39**	**29**	**27**	**52**
Short-term debt	**..**	**472**	**2,427**	**1,843**	**1,945**	**2,292**	**1,779**	**778**	**832**	**704**
of which interest arrears on LDOD	..	12	1,688	1,427	1,582	1,996	1,469	475	567	656
Official creditors	..	5	1,062	743	902	1,295	1,452	469	555	641
Private creditors	..	8	626	684	680	701	18	6	12	15
Memo: principal arrears on LDOD	..	32	2,452	3,186	3,527	4,337	3,209	967	899	925
Official creditors	..	13	1,479	2,095	2,443	3,237	2,893	696	676	705
Private creditors	..	19	973	1,092	1,084	1,100	316	271	222	220
Memo: export credits	..	0	643	550	536	618	470	750	633	641
TOTAL DEBT FLOWS										
Disbursements	**54**	**276**	**577**	**283**	**102**	**368**	**277**	**226**	**177**	**283**
Long-term debt	44	276	577	283	102	339	277	226	177	260
IMF purchases	10	0	0	0	0	29	0	0	0	23
Principal repayments	**29**	**46**	**4**	**42**	**65**	**103**	**203**	**134**	**182**	**86**
Long-term debt	16	45	4	42	65	100	190	124	182	86
IMF repurchases	13	1	0	0	0	3	13	9	0	0
Net flows on debt	**72**	**345**	**593**	**223**	**-16**	**198**	**88**	**85**	**-44**	**-20**
of which short-term debt	..	115	21	-18	-53	-67	14	-7	-38	-217
Interest payments (INT)	**..**	**69**	**11**	**65**	**69**	**104**	**86**	**85**	**144**	**164**
Long-term debt	7	42	5	36	55	96	76	72	129	86
IMF charges	0	3	0	2	1	1	1	0	0	0
Short-term debt	..	25	6	27	13	7	8	13	15	78
Net transfers on debt	**..**	**276**	**582**	**158**	**-85**	**94**	**3**	**0**	**-187**	**-184**
Total debt service paid (TDS)	**..**	**115**	**16**	**106**	**134**	**207**	**288**	**219**	**326**	**250**
Long-term debt	23	86	10	78	120	196	266	196	311	171
IMF repurchases and charges	13	3	0	2	1	4	14	10	0	0
Short-term debt (interest only)	..	25	6	27	13	7	8	13	15	78
2. AGGREGATE NET RESOURCE FLOWS AND NET TRANSFERS (LONG-TERM)										
NET RESOURCE FLOWS	**43**	**279**	**813**	**626**	**284**	**460**	**572**	**816**	**381**	**703**
Net flow of long-term debt (ex. IMF)	28	231	572	241	37	239	87	101	-5	174
Foreign direct investment (net)	15	0	0	15	39	40	75	97	173	184
Portfolio equity flows	0	0	0	0	0	0	0	0	0	0
Grants (excluding technical coop.)	0	48	241	371	207	181	409	618	214	345
Memo: technical coop. grants	4	19	75	146	116	130	132	118	111	95
official net resource flows	28	305	793	613	249	426	578	723	224	531
private net resource flows	14	-26	21	13	35	34	-6	93	157	171
NET TRANSFERS	**13**	**217**	**808**	**579**	**218**	**352**	**485**	**733**	**239**	**602**
Interest on long-term debt	7	42	5	36	55	96	76	72	129	86
Profit remittances on FDI	23	21	0	12	10	12	11	12	13	15
Memo: official net transfers	25	268	789	578	197	332	505	656	102	449
private net transfers	-12	-51	19	1	21	21	-21	77	138	153
3. MAJOR ECONOMIC AGGREGATES										
Gross national product (GNP)	3,550	9,743	1,531	1,349	1,390	1,284	1,531	1,559	1,684	1,777
Exports of goods & services (XGS)	..	514	404	327	398	533	730	912	1,031	981
of which workers remittances	..	0	0	10	25	50	75	95	150	200
Imports of goods & services (MGS)	..	1,049	911	1,421	1,251	1,425	1,480	1,609	1,845	1,826
International reserves (RES)	49	75	166	289	59	146	142	203	382	355
Current account balance	..	-411	-305	-769	-604	-647	-520	-435	-598	-599
4. DEBT INDICATORS										
EDT / XGS (%)	..	426.1	2,650.5	3,420.5	2,869.5	2,272.7	1,419.1	650.2	552.7	608.4
EDT / GNP (%)	..	22.5	699.4	828.4	820.8	942.8	676.8	380.4	338.4	335.9
TDS / XGS (%)	..	22.3	3.9	32.6	33.7	38.9	39.5	24.0	31.6	25.5
INT / XGS (%)	..	13.4	2.8	19.7	17.4	19.6	11.7	9.4	13.9	16.7
INT / GNP (%)	..	0.7	0.7	4.8	5.0	8.1	5.6	5.5	8.5	9.2
RES / EDT (%)	..	3.4	1.6	2.6	0.5	1.2	1.4	3.4	6.7	5.9
RES / MGS (months)	..	0.9	2.2	2.4	0.6	1.2	1.2	1.5	2.5	2.3
Short-term / EDT (%)	..	21.6	22.7	16.5	17.1	18.9	17.2	13.1	14.6	11.8
Concessional / EDT (%)	..	21.4	30.5	33.4	32.9	32.8	37.7	37.1	44.8	48.3
Multilateral / EDT (%)	..	19.2	8.7	9.6	9.8	10.9	14.1	26.2	27.6	29.8

NICARAGUA

(US$ million, unless otherwise indicated)

	1970	1980	1990	1992	1993	1994	1995	1996	1997	1998
5. LONG-TERM DEBT										
DEBT OUTSTANDING (LDOD)	**147**	**1,669**	**8,281**	**9,312**	**9,441**	**9,762**	**8,541**	**5,125**	**4,839**	**5,212**
Public and publicly guaranteed	**147**	**1,669**	**8,281**	**9,312**	**9,441**	**9,762**	**8,541**	**5,125**	**4,839**	**5,212**
Official creditors	102	863	6,735	7,218	7,362	7,682	7,531	4,667	4,443	4,785
Multilateral	48	421	930	1,077	1,112	1,317	1,457	1,551	1,571	1,780
Concessional	11	197	351	560	573	668	768	856	1,307	1,479
Bilateral	53	442	5,805	6,141	6,250	6,365	6,074	3,116	2,872	3,005
Concessional	49	271	2,919	3,175	3,178	3,303	3,140	1,347	1,247	1,401
Private creditors	45	805	1,546	2,094	2,079	2,080	1,010	458	396	427
Bonds	0	0	0	524	524	524	524	0	0	0
Commercial banks	38	746	1,305	1,394	1,393	1,394	383	409	362	355
Other private	8	59	241	176	162	162	103	48	34	72
Private nonguaranteed	**0**	**0**	**0**	**0**	**0**	**0**	**0**	**0**	**0**	**0**
Bonds	0	0	0	0	0	0	0	0	0	0
Commercial banks	0	0	0	0	0	0	0	0	0	0
Memo:										
IBRD	27	93	239	104	87	76	65	44	24	15
IDA	3	43	60	182	196	254	276	335	368	487
DISBURSEMENTS	**44**	**276**	**577**	**283**	**102**	**339**	**277**	**226**	**177**	**260**
Public and publicly guaranteed	**44**	**276**	**577**	**283**	**102**	**339**	**277**	**226**	**177**	**260**
Official creditors	32	276	553	281	101	338	258	209	172	257
Multilateral	11	90	7	161	70	248	177	139	127	221
Concessional	4	73	0	126	22	124	117	110	116	215
Bilateral	21	186	546	120	31	91	81	70	45	37
Concessional	19	108	370	96	8	70	67	55	40	27
Private creditors	12	0	24	2	1	1	20	17	5	2
Bonds	0	0	0	0	0	0	0	0	0	0
Commercial banks	12	0	0	2	1	1	20	17	5	2
Other private	0	0	24	0	0	0	0	0	0	0
Private nonguaranteed	**0**	**0**	**0**	**0**	**0**	**0**	**0**	**0**	**0**	**0**
Bonds	0	0	0	0	0	0	0	0	0	0
Commercial banks	0	0	0	0	0	0	0	0	0	0
Memo:										
IBRD	6	12	0	0	0	0	0	0	0	0
IDA	0	19	0	74	15	52	18	69	51	105
PRINCIPAL REPAYMENTS	**16**	**45**	**4**	**42**	**65**	**100**	**190**	**124**	**182**	**86**
Public and publicly guaranteed	**16**	**45**	**4**	**42**	**65**	**100**	**190**	**124**	**182**	**86**
Official creditors	4	19	1	38	59	93	89	104	161	71
Multilateral	3	14	1	31	37	67	47	40	85	37
Concessional	0	2	0	9	9	35	20	13	11	14
Bilateral	1	5	1	8	22	26	42	64	76	34
Concessional	0	2	0	0	11	2	2	3	15	4
Private creditors	13	26	3	4	6	7	101	21	21	15
Bonds	0	0	0	0	0	0	0	8	0	0
Commercial banks	11	20	0	0	0	0	96	8	9	10
Other private	2	6	3	4	6	7	4	4	12	5
Private nonguaranteed	**0**	**0**	**0**	**0**	**0**	**0**	**0**	**0**	**0**	**0**
Bonds	0	0	0	0	0	0	0	0	0	0
Commercial banks	0	0	0	0	0	0	0	0	0	0
Memo:										
IBRD	2	4	1	16	20	18	15	16	17	9
IDA	0	0	0	1	1	1	1	1	1	1
NET FLOWS ON DEBT	**28**	**231**	**572**	**241**	**37**	**239**	**87**	**101**	**-5**	**174**
Public and publicly guaranteed	**28**	**231**	**572**	**241**	**37**	**239**	**87**	**101**	**-5**	**174**
Official creditors	28	257	552	243	42	245	169	105	11	187
Multilateral	9	76	6	130	32	180	130	99	42	184
Concessional	4	71	0	117	13	89	98	97	105	201
Bilateral	20	181	545	112	10	65	39	6	-31	3
Concessional	18	106	370	96	-3	68	65	52	25	23
Private creditors	-1	-26	21	-2	-5	-6	-81	-4	-16	-13
Bonds	0	0	0	0	0	0	0	-8	0	0
Commercial banks	1	-20	0	2	1	0	-77	9	-4	-8
Other private	-2	-6	21	-4	-6	-7	-4	-4	-12	-5
Private nonguaranteed	**0**	**0**	**0**	**0**	**0**	**0**	**0**	**0**	**0**	**0**
Bonds	0	0	0	0	0	0	0	0	0	0
Commercial banks	0	0	0	0	0	0	0	0	0	0
Memo:										
IBRD	4	8	-1	-16	-20	-18	-15	-16	-17	-9
IDA	0	19	0	73	14	51	17	68	49	104

NICARAGUA

(US$ million, unless otherwise indicated)

	1970	1980	1990	1992	1993	1994	1995	1996	1997	1998
INTEREST PAYMENTS (LINT)	**7**	**42**	**5**	**36**	**55**	**96**	**76**	**72**	**129**	**86**
Public and publicly guaranteed	**7**	**42**	**5**	**36**	**55**	**96**	**76**	**72**	**129**	**86**
Official creditors	3	38	4	35	52	95	73	68	123	82
Multilateral	2	29	1	22	26	55	33	45	55	45
Concessional	0	7	0	6	7	25	11	11	11	28
Bilateral	1	9	3	13	27	40	39	22	68	37
Concessional	1	3	0	4	12	18	19	11	27	9
Private creditors	4	4	1	1	3	1	3	4	6	3
Bonds	0	0	0	0	0	0	0	0	0	0
Commercial banks	3	0	0	0	0	0	3	3	6	3
Other private	0	4	1	1	3	1	1	1	1	1
Private nonguaranteed	**0**	**0**	**0**	**0**	**0**	**0**	**0**	**0**	**0**	**0**
Bonds	0	0	0	0	0	0	0	0	0	0
Commercial banks	0	0	0	0	0	0	0	0	0	0
Memo:										
IBRD	2	11	1	10	10	8	6	6	3	2
IDA	0	0	0	1	1	2	2	3	3	3
NET TRANSFERS ON DEBT	**21**	**190**	**567**	**205**	**-18**	**143**	**12**	**30**	**-134**	**88**
Public and publicly guaranteed	**21**	**190**	**567**	**205**	**-18**	**143**	**12**	**30**	**-134**	**88**
Official creditors	25	220	548	208	-10	151	96	38	-112	104
Multilateral	7	47	5	109	7	126	97	54	-13	139
Concessional	4	64	0	112	6	64	87	86	94	174
Bilateral	19	173	543	99	-17	25	-1	-16	-99	-35
Concessional	18	103	370	92	-15	50	46	42	-2	14
Private creditors	-5	-30	19	-3	-8	-8	-85	-8	-23	-16
Bonds	0	0	0	0	0	0	0	-8	0	0
Commercial banks	-2	-20	0	2	1	0	-80	5	-9	-11
Other private	-2	-10	20	-4	-9	-8	-5	-5	-13	-5
Private nonguaranteed	**0**	**0**	**0**	**0**	**0**	**0**	**0**	**0**	**0**	**0**
Bonds	0	0	0	0	0	0	0	0	0	0
Commercial banks	0	0	0	0	0	0	0	0	0	0
Memo:										
IBRD	3	-3	-2	-26	-29	-25	-21	-22	-20	-11
IDA	0	19	0	72	12	49	16	65	47	101
DEBT SERVICE (LTDS)	**23**	**86**	**10**	**78**	**120**	**196**	**266**	**196**	**311**	**171**
Public and publicly guaranteed	**23**	**86**	**10**	**78**	**120**	**196**	**266**	**196**	**311**	**171**
Official creditors	7	56	5	73	111	188	162	171	284	153
Multilateral	5	43	2	52	63	122	81	85	140	82
Concessional	0	8	0	15	16	60	30	24	22	42
Bilateral	2	13	3	21	48	66	81	86	144	71
Concessional	1	5	0	4	23	20	21	14	42	13
Private creditors	16	30	4	4	9	8	104	25	27	18
Bonds	0	0	0	0	0	0	0	8	0	0
Commercial banks	14	20	0	0	0	0	99	11	14	13
Other private	3	10	4	4	9	8	5	5	13	5
Private nonguaranteed	**0**	**0**	**0**	**0**	**0**	**0**	**0**	**0**	**0**	**0**
Bonds	0	0	0	0	0	0	0	0	0	0
Commercial banks	0	0	0	0	0	0	0	0	0	0
Memo:										
IBRD	3	15	1	26	29	25	21	22	20	11
IDA	0	0	0	1	3	3	3	4	4	4
UNDISBURSED DEBT	**62**	**449**	**563**	**718**	**896**	**1,078**	**1,071**	**640**	**407**	**628**
Official creditors	52	418	552	712	891	1,054	1,047	628	397	620
Private creditors	9	30	11	6	5	24	24	12	10	8
Memorandum items										
Concessional LDOD	59	468	3,269	3,736	3,751	3,971	3,908	2,203	2,554	2,880
Variable rate LDOD	0	796	1,829	2,017	1,939	2,010	1,125	1,331	1,169	1,192
Public sector LDOD	138	1,654	8,281	9,312	9,441	9,762	8,541	5,115	4,830	5,180
Private sector LDOD	9	15	0	0	0	0	0	10	9	4

6. CURRENCY COMPOSITION OF LONG-TERM DEBT (PERCENT)

	1970	1980	1990	1992	1993	1994	1995	1996	1997	1998
Deutsche mark	4.0	2.9	1.3	1.9	1.7	1.9	4.8	8.2	7.7	8.2
French franc	0.0	0.0	1.3	1.3	1.2	1.3	2.0	2.9	2.2	2.3
Japanese yen	0.0	0.0	0.0	0.8	0.9	1.2	1.3	2.3	2.2	2.3
Pound sterling	1.6	0.2	0.0	0.0	0.0	0.0	0.0	0.0	0.0	0.0
Swiss franc	0.0	0.0	0.0	0.0	0.0	0.0	0.0	0.1	0.1	0.1
U.S.dollars	66.4	72.6	80.1	79.1	80.4	79.4	72.8	60.1	67.2	66.7
Multiple currency	28.1	20.9	10.4	9.0	8.8	8.6	10.4	17.7	12.6	11.8
Special drawing rights	0.0	0.0	0.0	0.0	0.0	0.0	0.0	0.1	0.1	0.2
All other currencies	0.0	3.4	6.9	7.9	7.0	7.6	8.7	8.6	7.9	8.4

NICARAGUA

(US$ million, unless otherwise indicated)

	1970	1980	1990	1992	1993	1994	1995	1996	1997	1998
7. DEBT RESTRUCTURINGS										
Total amount rescheduled	..	..	30	73	55	6	263	858	466	126
Debt stock rescheduled	..	..	0	0	2	0	0	668	367	44
Principal rescheduled	..	..	0	53	62	4	249	303	36	45
Official	..	..	0	43	60	3	188	255	36	42
Private	..	..	0	11	2	1	61	49	0	3
Interest rescheduled	..	..	30	33	28	3	94	203	3	37
Official	..	..	30	27	27	3	57	193	3	36
Private	..	..	0	5	1	0	37	10	0	1
Debt forgiven	..	..	0	6	2	7	530	23	182	39
Memo: interest forgiven	..	..	0	2	0	0	762	923	2	10
Debt stock reduction	..	..	0	0	0	9	1,200	3,065	116	0
of which debt buyback	..	..	0	0	0	0	89	0	0	0
8. DEBT STOCK-FLOW RECONCILIATION										
Total change in debt stocks	..	..	1,057	266	231	695	-1,745	-4,428	-234	271
Net flows on debt	72	345	593	223	-16	198	88	85	-44	-20
Net change in interest arrears	..	..	345	126	155	413	-526	-994	92	89
Interest capitalized	..	..	30	33	28	3	94	203	3	37
Debt forgiveness or reduction	..	..	0	-6	-2	-15	-1,641	-3,088	-297	-39
Cross-currency valuation	..	..	107	-90	-71	77	79	-92	-123	61
Residual	..	..	-18	-20	138	19	162	-542	135	142
9. AVERAGE TERMS OF NEW COMMITMENTS										
ALL CREDITORS										
Interest (%)	7.1	4.0	4.6	4.5	4.5	3.1	2.7	2.0	2.9	1.8
Maturity (years)	17.9	25.3	10.1	23.2	24.9	30.3	30.6	30.2	24.7	36.3
Grace period (years)	3.9	6.7	1.7	6.2	5.9	8.1	7.9	8.1	5.8	9.3
Grant element (%)	18.9	44.1	20.9	39.7	40.9	55.4	58.9	60.4	48.6	69.1
Official creditors										
Interest (%)	5.8	3.9	4.4	4.5	4.5	3.0	2.3	2.0	3.1	1.8
Maturity (years)	27.8	26.4	10.3	23.2	24.9	31.2	32.2	30.0	23.8	36.3
Grace period (years)	6.5	7.0	1.8	6.2	5.9	8.4	8.4	8.1	5.6	9.3
Grant element (%)	32.7	45.5	21.8	39.7	40.9	57.1	62.5	60.1	47.3	69.1
Private creditors										
Interest (%)	8.6	4.3	9.4	0.0	0.0	6.0	7.4	0.0	0.7	0.0
Maturity (years)	7.0	9.2	4.9	0.0	0.0	7.6	8.2	39.7	39.6	0.0
Grace period (years)	1.0	2.1	0.4	0.0	0.0	1.9	1.0	10.2	10.1	0.0
Grant element (%)	3.7	22.7	0.9	0.0	0.0	13.3	8.1	74.9	69.0	0.0
Memorandum items										
Commitments	23	434	447	293	265	527	361	208	55	571
Official creditors	12	408	429	293	265	508	337	203	51	571
Private creditors	11	27	18	0	0	20	24	5	3	0

10. CONTRACTUAL OBLIGATIONS ON OUTSTANDING LONG-TERM DEBT

	1999	2000	2001	2002	2003	2004	2005	2006	2007	2008
TOTAL										
Disbursements	169	180	121	88	57	33	19	2	0	0
Principal	200	215	176	303	194	164	186	172	174	180
Interest	120	119	136	136	124	115	109	102	95	87
Official creditors										
Disbursements	166	177	120	88	57	33	19	2	0	0
Principal	184	201	159	275	174	149	152	158	160	165
Interest	110	108	125	125	115	107	102	97	90	83
Bilateral creditors										
Disbursements	39	25	14	8	4	2	1	0	0	0
Principal	149	151	121	236	133	106	103	104	104	109
Interest	60	60	77	78	69	62	57	52	47	42
Multilateral creditors										
Disbursements	127	152	106	80	54	31	18	2	0	0
Principal	35	49	38	39	41	43	48	54	56	57
Interest	50	49	48	47	46	45	45	45	43	42
Private creditors										
Disbursements	4	3	1	1	0	0	0	0	0	0
Principal	15	14	17	28	19	15	35	14	14	14
Interest	10	11	11	11	9	8	7	6	5	4
Commercial banks										
Disbursements	1	0	0	0	0	0	0	0	0	0
Principal	15	13	9	9	7	6	26	5	5	5
Interest	6	5	5	4	4	4	3	2	2	2
Other private										
Disbursements	3	3	1	1	0	0	0	0	0	0
Principal	0	1	8	19	13	9	9	9	9	9
Interest	4	6	6	6	5	5	4	4	3	2

NIGER

(US$ million, unless otherwise indicated)

	1970	1980	1990	1992	1993	1994	1995	1996	1997	1998
1. SUMMARY DEBT DATA										
TOTAL DEBT STOCKS (EDT)	..	**863**	**1,726**	**1,517**	**1,542**	**1,525**	**1,586**	**1,536**	**1,576**	**1,659**
Long-term debt (LDOD)	**32**	**687**	**1,487**	**1,371**	**1,391**	**1,425**	**1,463**	**1,439**	**1,424**	**1,521**
Public and publicly guaranteed	32	383	1,226	1,166	1,210	1,268	1,330	1,330	1,328	1,449
Private nonguaranteed	0	305	261	205	181	157	133	110	96	72
Use of IMF credit	**0**	**16**	**85**	**61**	**52**	**61**	**52**	**53**	**61**	**76**
Short-term debt	..	**159**	**153**	**84**	**99**	**39**	**71**	**44**	**92**	**63**
of which interest arrears on LDOD	..	0	31	46	71	24	52	24	35	34
Official creditors	..	0	16	46	70	24	52	24	35	34
Private creditors	..	0	16	0	0	0	0	0	0	0
Memo: principal arrears on LDOD	..	1	80	87	103	40	75	58	62	60
Official creditors	..	1	39	87	102	40	75	58	62	60
Private creditors	..	0	41	1	1	0	0	0	0	0
Memo: export credits	..	0	398	302	315	131	263	233	223	236
TOTAL DEBT FLOWS										
Disbursements	**12**	**290**	**148**	**83**	**100**	**89**	**28**	**55**	**111**	**111**
Long-term debt	12	281	139	83	100	73	28	41	85	85
IMF purchases	0	10	9	0	0	16	0	14	27	26
Principal repayments	**2**	**58**	**63**	**36**	**66**	**48**	**41**	**45**	**45**	**50**
Long-term debt	2	58	47	27	56	38	31	33	30	36
IMF repurchases	0	0	16	10	10	10	10	12	15	14
Net flows on debt	**11**	**286**	**123**	**48**	**25**	**27**	**-9**	**13**	**102**	**33**
of which short-term debt	..	53	38	2	-9	-14	4	2	36	-28
Interest payments (INT)	..	**84**	**36**	**17**	**24**	**18**	**15**	**12**	**15**	**12**
Long-term debt	1	65	23	13	22	15	13	10	13	11
IMF charges	0	0	4	2	1	1	1	1	1	1
Short-term debt	..	19	9	2	2	2	1	1	2	1
Net transfers on debt	..	**202**	**87**	**31**	**1**	**9**	**-24**	**1**	**87**	**21**
Total debt service paid (TDS)	..	**141**	**99**	**53**	**90**	**66**	**56**	**56**	**61**	**62**
Long-term debt	2	122	71	40	78	53	44	43	43	47
IMF repurchases and charges	0	0	19	11	10	11	11	13	16	15
Short-term debt (interest only)	..	19	9	2	2	2	1	1	2	1
2. AGGREGATE NET RESOURCE FLOWS AND NET TRANSFERS (LONG-TERM)										
NET RESOURCE FLOWS	**26**	**324**	**316**	**320**	**208**	**279**	**167**	**164**	**247**	**208**
Net flow of long-term debt (ex. IMF)	11	223	92	56	44	35	-3	8	54	49
Foreign direct investment (net)	1	49	-1	56	-34	-11	0	0	2	1
Portfolio equity flows	0	0	0	0	0	0	0	0	0	0
Grants (excluding technical coop.)	15	51	226	207	198	255	170	155	190	158
Memo: technical coop. grants	11	62	102	130	123	102	108	87	72	72
official net resource flows	26	125	308	283	267	314	191	187	258	230
private net resource flows	0	199	9	36	-58	-35	-24	-24	-12	-23
NET TRANSFERS	**23**	**248**	**293**	**306**	**187**	**264**	**154**	**153**	**234**	**197**
Interest on long-term debt	1	65	23	13	22	15	13	10	13	11
Profit remittances on FDI	2	11	0	0	0	0	0	0	0	0
Memo: official net transfers	25	118	301	278	252	305	184	182	249	221
private net transfers	-2	130	-8	28	-66	-41	-29	-29	-15	-24
3. MAJOR ECONOMIC AGGREGATES										
Gross national product (GNP)	645	2,476	2,423	2,314	1,582	1,533	1,830	1,959	1,831	2,020
Exports of goods & services (XGS)	..	650	566	443	370	278	333	341	305	337
of which workers remittances	..	6	13	18	14	6	6	..	..	..
Imports of goods & services (MGS)	..	1,016	803	652	528	466	510	497	468	508
International reserves (RES)	19	132	226	229	196	115	99	83	56	53
Current account balance	..	-276	-236	-159	-97	-126	-152	-181	-185	-192
4. DEBT INDICATORS										
EDT / XGS (%)	..	132.8	304.7	342.7	416.7	547.7	475.7	450.4	516.2	492.3
EDT / GNP (%)	..	34.9	71.2	65.5	97.5	99.5	86.7	78.4	86.1	82.1
TDS / XGS (%)	..	21.7	17.4	12.0	24.2	23.7	16.7	16.5	19.8	18.4
INT / XGS (%)	..	12.9	6.4	3.8	6.5	6.4	4.4	3.5	5.0	3.6
INT / GNP (%)	..	3.4	1.5	0.7	1.5	1.2	0.8	0.6	0.8	0.6
RES / EDT (%)	..	15.4	13.1	15.1	12.7	7.5	6.2	5.4	3.6	3.2
RES / MGS (months)	..	1.6	3.4	4.2	4.5	3.0	2.3	2.0	1.5	1.3
Short-term / EDT (%)	..	18.5	8.9	5.6	6.5	2.6	4.5	2.9	5.8	3.8
Concessional / EDT (%)	..	17.9	47.9	58.1	60.5	64.2	64.2	67.2	67.0	70.2
Multilateral / EDT (%)	..	16.5	40.7	47.7	48.9	54.7	55.1	56.9	55.9	58.0

NIGER

(US$ million, unless otherwise indicated)

	1970	1980	1990	1992	1993	1994	1995	1996	1997	1998
5. LONG-TERM DEBT										
DEBT OUTSTANDING (LDOD)	**32**	**687**	**1,487**	**1,371**	**1,391**	**1,425**	**1,463**	**1,439**	**1,424**	**1,521**
Public and publicly guaranteed	**32**	**383**	**1,226**	**1,166**	**1,210**	**1,268**	**1,330**	**1,330**	**1,328**	**1,449**
Official creditors	31	255	1,115	1,165	1,209	1,268	1,330	1,330	1,328	1,449
Multilateral	4	143	701	724	754	834	874	875	881	963
Concessional	4	112	652	673	702	790	829	832	843	927
Bilateral	27	112	414	441	455	435	456	455	448	486
Concessional	25	42	175	207	230	189	189	200	213	238
Private creditors	1	128	111	1	1	0	0	0	0	0
Bonds	0	0	0	0	0	0	0	0	0	0
Commercial banks	0	68	109	0	0	0	0	0	0	0
Other private	0	60	2	1	1	0	0	0	0	0
Private nonguaranteed	**0**	**305**	**261**	**205**	**181**	**157**	**133**	**110**	**96**	**72**
Bonds	0	0	0	0	0	0	0	0	0	0
Commercial banks	0	305	261	205	181	157	133	110	96	72
Memo:										
IBRD	0	0	0	0	0	0	0	0	0	0
IDA	4	66	461	483	504	565	598	609	625	688
DISBURSEMENTS	**12**	**281**	**139**	**83**	**100**	**73**	**28**	**41**	**85**	**85**
Public and publicly guaranteed	**12**	**167**	**96**	**83**	**100**	**73**	**28**	**41**	**85**	**85**
Official creditors	12	91	90	83	100	73	28	41	85	85
Multilateral	2	60	70	24	62	66	28	35	74	73
Concessional	2	47	69	23	39	64	28	35	74	73
Bilateral	10	31	21	58	39	7	0	6	11	12
Concessional	10	11	21	58	28	4	0	5	11	12
Private creditors	0	76	5	0	0	0	0	0	0	0
Bonds	0	0	0	0	0	0	0	0	0	0
Commercial banks	0	56	5	0	0	0	0	0	0	0
Other private	0	20	0	0	0	0	0	0	0	0
Private nonguaranteed	**0**	**113**	**43**	**0**	**0**	**0**	**0**	**0**	**0**	**0**
Bonds	0	0	0	0	0	0	0	0	0	0
Commercial banks	0	113	43	0	0	0	0	0	0	0
Memo:										
IBRD	0	0	0	0	0	0	0	0	0	0
IDA	2	18	55	21	21	44	24	34	50	50
PRINCIPAL REPAYMENTS	**2**	**58**	**47**	**27**	**56**	**38**	**31**	**33**	**30**	**36**
Public and publicly guaranteed	**2**	**23**	**10**	**7**	**32**	**15**	**7**	**9**	**16**	**12**
Official creditors	1	17	9	7	32	15	7	9	16	12
Multilateral	0	15	7	6	30	14	7	8	14	10
Concessional	0	14	3	4	11	6	6	7	13	9
Bilateral	1	3	2	1	2	1	0	1	2	3
Concessional	1	2	2	0	1	0	0	0	1	2
Private creditors	1	5	2	0	0	0	0	0	0	0
Bonds	0	0	0	0	0	0	0	0	0	0
Commercial banks	0	1	0	0	0	0	0	0	0	0
Other private	1	4	2	0	0	0	0	0	0	0
Private nonguaranteed	**0**	**35**	**37**	**20**	**24**	**24**	**24**	**24**	**14**	**24**
Bonds	0	0	0	0	0	0	0	0	0	0
Commercial banks	0	35	37	20	24	24	24	24	14	24
Memo:										
IBRD	0	0	0	0	0	0	0	0	0	0
IDA	0	0	1	2	2	3	3	5	5	7
NET FLOWS ON DEBT	**11**	**223**	**92**	**56**	**44**	**35**	**-3**	**8**	**54**	**49**
Public and publicly guaranteed	**11**	**144**	**86**	**76**	**68**	**59**	**21**	**32**	**68**	**73**
Official creditors	11	74	82	76	68	59	21	32	68	73
Multilateral	2	46	63	18	32	52	21	27	60	64
Concessional	2	33	66	19	28	58	22	28	61	64
Bilateral	9	28	19	58	37	6	0	5	8	9
Concessional	9	10	19	58	27	4	0	5	10	9
Private creditors	-1	71	4	0	0	0	0	0	0	0
Bonds	0	0	0	0	0	0	0	0	0	0
Commercial banks	0	55	5	0	0	0	0	0	0	0
Other private	-1	16	-2	0	0	0	0	0	0	0
Private nonguaranteed	**0**	**79**	**6**	**-20**	**-24**	**-24**	**-24**	**-24**	**-14**	**-24**
Bonds	0	0	0	0	0	0	0	0	0	0
Commercial banks	0	79	6	-20	-24	-24	-24	-24	-14	-24
Memo:										
IBRD	0	0	0	0	0	0	0	0	0	0
IDA	2	18	54	19	19	42	21	29	45	43

NIGER

(US$ million, unless otherwise indicated)

	1970	1980	1990	1992	1993	1994	1995	1996	1997	1998
INTEREST PAYMENTS (LINT)	**1**	**65**	**23**	**13**	**22**	**15**	**13**	**10**	**13**	**11**
Public and publicly guaranteed	**1**	**16**	**7**	**5**	**14**	**9**	**7**	**6**	**10**	**9**
Official creditors	1	7	7	5	14	9	7	6	10	9
Multilateral	0	3	6	5	14	7	7	5	8	6
Concessional	0	2	4	4	7	5	6	5	7	6
Bilateral	1	5	1	0	1	2	0	1	2	3
Concessional	1	1	1	0	0	0	0	0	1	2
Private creditors	0	9	0	0	0	0	0	0	0	0
Bonds	0	0	0	0	0	0	0	0	0	0
Commercial banks	0	6	0	0	0	0	0	0	0	0
Other private	0	3	0	0	0	0	0	0	0	0
Private nonguaranteed	**0**	**49**	**16**	**8**	**7**	**6**	**6**	**5**	**3**	**2**
Bonds	0	0	0	0	0	0	0	0	0	0
Commercial banks	0	49	16	8	7	6	6	5	3	2
Memo:										
IBRD	0	0	0	0	0	0	0	0	0	0
IDA	0	0	3	4	3	5	5	4	4	5
NET TRANSFERS ON DEBT	**10**	**158**	**68**	**43**	**23**	**20**	**-15**	**-2**	**42**	**38**
Public and publicly guaranteed	**10**	**128**	**78**	**71**	**54**	**50**	**14**	**27**	**59**	**63**
Official creditors	11	66	75	71	54	50	14	27	59	63
Multilateral	2	43	57	13	18	46	14	23	52	58
Concessional	2	32	62	15	21	53	16	24	54	58
Bilateral	8	23	18	57	36	4	0	4	6	6
Concessional	8	9	18	58	27	3	0	5	9	8
Private creditors	-1	62	4	0	0	0	0	0	0	0
Bonds	0	0	0	0	0	0	0	0	0	0
Commercial banks	0	49	5	0	0	0	0	0	0	0
Other private	-1	14	-2	0	0	0	0	0	0	0
Private nonguaranteed	**0**	**30**	**-10**	**-28**	**-31**	**-30**	**-29**	**-29**	**-17**	**-25**
Bonds	0	0	0	0	0	0	0	0	0	0
Commercial banks	0	30	-10	-28	-31	-30	-29	-29	-17	-25
Memo:										
IBRD	0	0	0	0	0	0	0	0	0	0
IDA	2	18	51	15	16	37	16	24	41	38
DEBT SERVICE (LTDS)	**2**	**122**	**71**	**40**	**78**	**53**	**44**	**43**	**43**	**47**
Public and publicly guaranteed	**2**	**39**	**17**	**12**	**47**	**23**	**14**	**15**	**26**	**21**
Official creditors	2	25	16	12	47	23	14	15	26	21
Multilateral	0	17	12	11	44	21	14	12	22	16
Concessional	0	16	7	8	18	11	12	11	20	15
Bilateral	2	8	3	1	3	3	1	2	5	6
Concessional	1	3	3	1	2	1	0	1	2	4
Private creditors	1	14	2	0	0	0	0	0	0	0
Bonds	0	0	0	0	0	0	0	0	0	0
Commercial banks	0	7	0	0	0	0	0	0	0	0
Other private	1	7	2	0	0	0	0	0	0	0
Private nonguaranteed	**0**	**83**	**53**	**28**	**31**	**30**	**29**	**29**	**17**	**25**
Bonds	0	0	0	0	0	0	0	0	0	0
Commercial banks	0	83	53	28	31	30	29	29	17	25
Memo:										
IBRD	0	0	0	0	0	0	0	0	0	0
IDA	0	1	4	6	5	7	8	9	9	12
UNDISBURSED DEBT	**41**	**415**	**368**	**360**	**349**	**354**	**310**	**333**	**299**	**396**
Official creditors	24	279	368	360	349	354	310	333	299	396
Private creditors	17	136	0	0	0	0	0	0	0	0
Memorandum items										
Concessional LDOD	29	155	827	881	933	979	1,018	1,032	1,056	1,165
Variable rate LDOD	0	387	377	210	186	169	145	124	113	91
Public sector LDOD	24	372	1,223	1,165	1,209	1,268	1,330	1,330	1,328	1,449
Private sector LDOD	7	316	264	206	182	157	133	110	96	72

6. CURRENCY COMPOSITION OF LONG-TERM DEBT (PERCENT)

	1970	1980	1990	1992	1993	1994	1995	1996	1997	1998
Deutsche mark	12.0	0.0	0.0	0.6	0.5	0.5	0.5	0.0	0.0	0.0
French franc	67.6	53.8	44.8	41.7	39.5	36.0	36.1	32.9	31.0	29.9
Japanese yen	0.0	0.0	1.3	4.3	4.4	4.8	4.4	2.0	1.8	1.8
Pound sterling	0.0	0.0	0.8	0.8	0.7	1.1	1.0	1.2	1.4	1.3
Swiss franc	0.0	0.0	0.0	0.7	0.3	0.3	0.3	0.0	0.0	0.0
U.S.dollars	6.9	30.2	27.1	32.3	33.0	36.0	36.8	38.0	40.3	41.3
Multiple currency	0.0	2.1	0.5	0.4	0.1	0.0	0.0	0.0	0.0	0.0
Special drawing rights	0.0	0.0	2.6	2.6	3.1	3.5	3.5	3.5	3.2	3.1
All other currencies	13.5	13.9	22.9	16.6	18.4	17.8	17.4	22.4	22.3	22.6

NIGER

(US$ million, unless otherwise indicated)

	1970	1980	1990	1992	1993	1994	1995	1996	1997	1998
7. DEBT RESTRUCTURINGS										
Total amount rescheduled	..	..	29	0	15	120	5	63	24	30
Debt stock rescheduled	..	..	0	0	0	0	0	0	0	0
Principal rescheduled	..	..	12	0	7	57	1	21	6	17
Official	..	..	12	0	7	56	1	21	6	17
Private	..	..	0	0	0	1	0	0	0	0
Interest rescheduled	..	..	16	0	5	32	1	29	9	13
Official	..	..	16	0	5	32	1	29	9	13
Private	..	..	0	0	0	0	0	0	0	0
Debt forgiven	..	..	0	0	14	107	4	26	4	8
Memo: interest forgiven	..	..	0	0	1	30	0	15	5	0
Debt stock reduction	..	..	0	0	0	0	0	0	0	0
of which debt buyback	..	..	0	0	0	0	0	0	0	0
8. DEBT STOCK-FLOW RECONCILIATION										
Total change in debt stocks	..	..	230	23	25	-17	61	-50	40	83
Net flows on debt	11	286	123	48	25	27	-9	13	102	33
Net change in interest arrears	..	..	8	25	24	-47	28	-29	11	-1
Interest capitalized	..	..	16	0	5	32	1	29	9	13
Debt forgiveness or reduction	..	..	0	0	-14	-107	-4	-26	-4	-8
Cross-currency valuation	..	..	94	-44	-34	58	52	-39	-74	45
Residual	..	..	-12	-6	19	19	-8	3	-4	2
9. AVERAGE TERMS OF NEW COMMITMENTS										
ALL CREDITORS										
Interest (%)	1.2	7.4	1.9	2.9	2.2	1.0	0.7	1.0	1.1	0.7
Maturity (years)	39.7	18.3	32.7	26.6	34.0	35.2	38.1	37.5	35.3	38.9
Grace period (years)	8.2	4.7	8.5	8.1	7.6	9.0	9.6	9.2	8.1	9.9
Grant element (%)	72.5	18.7	65.5	54.1	60.7	73.7	78.1	76.1	72.9	78.9
Official creditors										
Interest (%)	0.6	5.4	1.9	2.9	2.2	1.0	0.7	1.0	1.1	0.7
Maturity (years)	44.7	26.2	32.7	26.6	34.0	35.2	38.1	37.5	35.3	38.9
Grace period (years)	9.1	6.8	8.5	8.1	7.6	9.0	9.6	9.2	8.1	9.9
Grant element (%)	80.9	35.3	65.5	54.1	60.7	73.7	78.1	76.1	72.9	78.9
Private creditors										
Interest (%)	4.5	9.8	0.0	0.0	0.0	0.0	0.0	0.0	0.0	0.0
Maturity (years)	13.6	8.8	0.0	0.0	0.0	0.0	0.0	0.0	0.0	0.0
Grace period (years)	3.6	2.2	0.0	0.0	0.0	0.0	0.0	0.0	0.0	0.0
Grant element (%)	29.1	-1.0	0.0	0.0	0.0	0.0	0.0	0.0	0.0	0.0
Memorandum items										
Commitments	19	341	56	106	97	89	7	76	66	180
Official creditors	16	185	56	106	97	89	7	76	66	180
Private creditors	3	156	0	0	0	0	0	0	0	0

10. CONTRACTUAL OBLIGATIONS ON OUTSTANDING LONG-TERM DEBT

	1999	2000	2001	2002	2003	2004	2005	2006	2007	2008
TOTAL										
Disbursements	84	99	70	48	29	17	10	2	0	0
Principal	82	100	87	71	68	64	51	46	48	50
Interest	27	33	30	28	26	23	21	20	19	18
Official creditors										
Disbursements	84	99	70	48	29	17	10	2	0	0
Principal	59	77	73	66	62	64	51	46	48	50
Interest	26	32	30	28	25	23	21	20	19	18
Bilateral creditors										
Disbursements	14	15	10	7	5	3	1	1	0	0
Principal	34	49	49	42	39	38	25	17	17	16
Interest	18	23	21	19	16	15	13	12	11	10
Multilateral creditors										
Disbursements	70	84	60	41	24	14	9	2	0	0
Principal	25	28	24	24	23	25	27	29	31	34
Interest	8	9	9	9	9	9	9	8	8	8
Private creditors										
Disbursements	0	0	0	0	0	0	0	0	0	0
Principal	23	23	15	6	6	0	0	0	0	0
Interest	1	1	0	0	0	0	0	0	0	0
Commercial banks										
Disbursements	0	0	0	0	0	0	0	0	0	0
Principal	0	0	0	0	0	0	0	0	0	0
Interest	0	0	0	0	0	0	0	0	0	0
Other private										
Disbursements	0	0	0	0	0	0	0	0	0	0
Principal	23	23	15	6	6	0	0	0	0	0
Interest	1	1	0	0	0	0	0	0	0	0

NIGERIA

(US$ million, unless otherwise indicated)

	1970	1980	1990	1992	1993	1994	1995	1996	1997	1998
1. SUMMARY DEBT DATA										
TOTAL DEBT STOCKS (EDT)	..	**8,921**	**33,440**	**29,019**	**30,699**	**33,092**	**34,093**	**31,407**	**28,455**	**30,315**
Long-term debt (LDOD)	**567**	**5,368**	**31,936**	**26,809**	**26,742**	**28,266**	**28,441**	**25,731**	**22,926**	**23,740**
Public and publicly guaranteed	452	4,271	31,546	26,478	26,421	27,955	28,140	25,431	22,631	23,455
Private nonguaranteed	115	1,097	391	331	321	311	301	300	295	285
Use of IMF credit	**0**	**0**	**0**	**0**	**0**	**0**	**0**	**0**	**0**	**0**
Short-term debt	..	**3,553**	**1,504**	**2,210**	**3,957**	**4,827**	**5,651**	**5,676**	**5,529**	**6,575**
of which interest arrears on LDOD	..	0	1,040	1,197	2,438	3,820	4,717	4,967	4,957	5,785
Official creditors	..	0	465	1,021	2,065	3,361	4,211	4,468	4,483	5,235
Private creditors	..	0	575	176	374	459	506	499	474	550
Memo: principal arrears on LDOD	..	0	1,091	1,841	3,866	5,814	8,102	9,298	10,151	12,113
Official creditors	..	0	194	1,332	2,722	4,409	6,545	7,736	8,648	10,270
Private creditors	..	0	897	509	1,145	1,405	1,557	1,562	1,503	1,843
Memo: export credits	..	0	20,116	17,712	16,457	12,765	12,996	11,887	15,201	16,381
TOTAL DEBT FLOWS										
Disbursements	**81**	**1,753**	**927**	**535**	**544**	**599**	**433**	**308**	**314**	**276**
Long-term debt	81	1,753	927	535	544	599	433	308	314	276
IMF purchases	0	0	0	0	0	0	0	0	0	0
Principal repayments	**68**	**242**	**1,180**	**1,878**	**579**	**746**	**918**	**1,418**	**840**	**763**
Long-term debt	68	242	1,180	1,878	579	746	918	1,418	840	763
IMF repurchases	0	0	0	0	0	0	0	0	0	0
Net flows on debt	**282**	**2,780**	**-34**	**-708**	**472**	**-660**	**-559**	**-1,334**	**-663**	**-269**
of which short-term debt	..	1,270	219	635	507	-512	-73	-224	-137	218
Interest payments (INT)	..	**909**	**2,156**	**1,871**	**912**	**1,125**	**915**	**1,091**	**576**	**557**
Long-term debt	28	529	2,124	1,831	862	1,075	859	1,043	544	519
IMF charges	0	0	0	0	0	0	0	0	0	0
Short-term debt	..	379	32	40	50	50	56	48	33	38
Net transfers on debt	..	**1,872**	**-2,190**	**-2,579**	**-440**	**-1,785**	**-1,474**	**-2,425**	**-1,239**	**-826**
Total debt service paid (TDS)	..	**1,151**	**3,336**	**3,749**	**1,491**	**1,872**	**1,833**	**2,509**	**1,416**	**1,320**
Long-term debt	96	772	3,304	3,709	1,441	1,822	1,777	2,461	1,383	1,283
IMF repurchases and charges	0	0	0	0	0	0	0	0	0	0
Short-term debt (interest only)	..	379	32	40	50	50	56	48	33	38
2. AGGREGATE NET RESOURCE FLOWS AND NET TRANSFERS (LONG-TERM)										
NET RESOURCE FLOWS	**259**	**773**	**460**	**-330**	**1,363**	**1,871**	**632**	**512**	**1,045**	**598**
Net flow of long-term debt (ex. IMF)	13	1,510	-253	-1,343	-35	-148	-486	-1,110	-525	-487
Foreign direct investment (net)	205	-740	588	897	1,345	1,959	1,079	1,593	1,539	1,051
Portfolio equity flows	0	0	0	0	0	17	6	5	4	2
Grants (excluding technical coop.)	40	3	125	116	53	43	33	24	27	33
Memo: technical coop. grants	37	48	95	99	97	78	79	84	83	50
official net resource flows	70	79	-7	314	107	211	-5	-396	-240	-430
private net resource flows	189	694	467	-645	1,256	1,660	637	908	1,285	1,028
NET TRANSFERS	**-207**	**-1,354**	**-1,799**	**-2,277**	**351**	**631**	**-372**	**-691**	**321**	**-161**
Interest on long-term debt	28	529	2,124	1,831	862	1,075	859	1,043	544	519
Profit remittances on FDI	438	1,598	135	116	150	165	145	160	180	240
Memo: official net transfers	54	17	-1,308	-513	-463	-125	-328	-911	-606	-803
private net transfers	-261	-1,371	-491	-1,764	814	756	-44	220	927	643
3. MAJOR ECONOMIC AGGREGATES										
Gross national product (GNP)	12,081	61,079	25,585	29,761	19,006	21,310	25,888	33,068	37,620	38,481
Exports of goods & services (XGS)	..	27,772	14,771	13,056	11,924	10,428	13,246	17,911	18,172	11,762
of which workers remittances	..	13	10	56	793	550	804	947	1,920	1,574
Imports of goods & services (MGS)	..	22,005	9,858	11,485	12,723	12,504	15,820	14,403	17,617	16,001
International reserves (RES)	223	10,640	4,129	1,196	1,640	1,649	1,709	4,329	7,580	8,709
Current account balance	..	5,178	4,988	2,268	-780	-2,128	-2,578	3,507	552	-4,244
4. DEBT INDICATORS										
EDT / XGS (%)	..	32.1	226.4	222.3	257.5	317.3	257.4	175.4	156.6	257.7
EDT / GNP (%)	..	14.6	130.7	97.5	161.5	155.3	131.7	95.0	75.6	78.8
TDS / XGS (%)	..	4.1	22.6	28.7	12.5	18.0	13.8	14.0	7.8	11.2
INT / XGS (%)	..	3.3	14.6	14.3	7.7	10.8	6.9	6.1	3.2	4.7
INT / GNP (%)	..	1.5	8.4	6.3	4.8	5.3	3.5	3.3	1.5	1.5
RES / EDT (%)	..	119.3	12.4	4.1	5.3	5.0	5.0	13.8	26.6	28.7
RES / MGS (months)	..	5.8	5.0	1.3	1.6	1.6	1.3	3.6	5.2	6.5
Short-term / EDT (%)	..	39.8	4.5	7.6	12.9	14.6	16.6	18.1	19.4	21.7
Concessional / EDT (%)	..	5.0	1.6	3.4	3.6	3.9	4.0	4.3	4.7	5.2
Multilateral / EDT (%)	..	6.4	11.2	14.1	14.1	14.5	14.5	14.3	14.1	13.5

NIGERIA

(US$ million, unless otherwise indicated)

	1970	1980	1990	1992	1993	1994	1995	1996	1997	1998
5. LONG-TERM DEBT										
DEBT OUTSTANDING (LDOD)	**567**	**5,368**	**31,936**	**26,809**	**26,742**	**28,266**	**28,441**	**25,731**	**22,926**	**23,740**
Public and publicly guaranteed	**452**	**4,271**	**31,546**	**26,478**	**26,421**	**27,955**	**28,140**	**25,431**	**22,631**	**23,455**
Official creditors	358	992	17,008	18,327	18,246	19,811	20,492	18,644	17,011	17,679
Multilateral	182	571	3,733	4,088	4,339	4,807	4,944	4,493	4,013	4,083
Concessional	17	38	36	104	155	239	339	425	496	663
Bilateral	175	422	13,275	14,240	13,907	15,004	15,548	14,151	12,998	13,596
Concessional	123	406	485	868	939	1,051	1,038	929	827	919
Private creditors	94	3,279	14,537	8,151	8,174	8,144	7,648	6,786	5,620	5,776
Bonds	10	0	0	2,051	2,051	2,051	2,051	2,051	2,051	2,051
Commercial banks	18	2,634	5,714	0	0	0	0	0	0	0
Other private	66	645	8,823	6,100	6,123	6,093	5,597	4,735	3,569	3,725
Private nonguaranteed	**115**	**1,097**	**391**	**331**	**321**	**311**	**301**	**300**	**295**	**285**
Bonds	0	0	0	0	0	0	0	0	0	0
Commercial banks	115	1,097	391	331	321	311	301	300	295	285
Memo:										
IBRD	165	517	3,284	3,174	3,188	3,286	3,221	2,762	2,373	2,278
IDA	17	38	36	80	116	181	268	348	410	564
DISBURSEMENTS	**81**	**1,753**	**927**	**535**	**544**	**599**	**433**	**308**	**314**	**276**
Public and publicly guaranteed	**56**	**1,187**	**927**	**531**	**544**	**599**	**433**	**308**	**314**	**276**
Official creditors	45	122	642	531	544	599	433	308	314	276
Multilateral	14	73	542	531	529	599	433	308	314	276
Concessional	1	0	7	36	53	77	99	94	97	145
Bilateral	31	49	100	0	15	0	0	0	0	0
Concessional	30	49	100	0	15	0	0	0	0	0
Private creditors	11	1,065	285	0	0	0	0	0	0	0
Bonds	0	0	0	0	0	0	0	0	0	0
Commercial banks	3	492	0	0	0	0	0	0	0	0
Other private	8	573	285	0	0	0	0	0	0	0
Private nonguaranteed	**25**	**565**	**0**	**4**	**0**	**0**	**0**	**0**	**0**	**0**
Bonds	0	0	0	0	0	0	0	0	0	0
Commercial banks	25	565	0	4	0	0	0	0	0	0
Memo:										
IBRD	13	63	384	272	264	258	189	139	178	86
IDA	1	0	7	24	38	60	86	90	83	135
PRINCIPAL REPAYMENTS	**68**	**242**	**1,180**	**1,878**	**579**	**746**	**918**	**1,418**	**840**	**763**
Public and publicly guaranteed	**38**	**65**	**1,165**	**1,866**	**569**	**736**	**908**	**1,408**	**830**	**753**
Official creditors	16	45	774	333	490	431	470	728	582	739
Multilateral	5	25	247	316	329	431	470	447	467	419
Concessional	0	0	1	1	1	1	2	1	1	1
Bilateral	11	20	528	17	161	0	0	281	115	319
Concessional	6	14	6	0	161	0	0	0	70	319
Private creditors	22	20	391	1,534	79	306	438	680	248	15
Bonds	0	0	0	0	0	0	0	0	0	0
Commercial banks	0	1	388	1,335	0	0	0	0	0	0
Other private	22	19	3	199	79	306	438	680	248	15
Private nonguaranteed	**30**	**177**	**15**	**12**	**10**	**10**	**10**	**10**	**10**	**10**
Bonds	0	0	0	0	0	0	0	0	0	0
Commercial banks	30	177	15	12	10	10	10	10	10	10
Memo:										
IBRD	5	24	241	294	309	384	392	369	338	313
IDA	0	0	1	1	1	1	1	1	1	1
NET FLOWS ON DEBT	**13**	**1,510**	**-253**	**-1,343**	**-35**	**-148**	**-486**	**-1,110**	**-525**	**-487**
Public and publicly guaranteed	**18**	**1,122**	**-238**	**-1,335**	**-25**	**-138**	**-476**	**-1,100**	**-515**	**-477**
Official creditors	29	77	-132	198	54	168	-37	-420	-267	-463
Multilateral	10	48	296	215	200	168	-37	-139	-152	-143
Concessional	1	0	6	35	51	76	97	93	96	144
Bilateral	20	29	-428	-17	-146	0	0	-281	-115	-319
Concessional	24	35	95	0	-146	0	0	0	-70	-319
Private creditors	-11	1,046	-106	-1,534	-79	-306	-438	-680	-248	-15
Bonds	0	0	0	0	0	0	0	0	0	0
Commercial banks	3	491	-388	-1,335	0	0	0	0	0	0
Other private	-14	555	282	-199	-79	-306	-438	-680	-248	-15
Private nonguaranteed	**-5**	**388**	**-15**	**-8**	**-10**	**-10**	**-10**	**-10**	**-10**	**-10**
Bonds	0	0	0	0	0	0	0	0	0	0
Commercial banks	-5	388	-15	-8	-10	-10	-10	-10	-10	-10
Memo:										
IBRD	8	38	144	-21	-45	-126	-202	-231	-161	-227
IDA	1	0	6	23	37	59	85	89	82	134

NIGERIA

(US$ million, unless otherwise indicated)

	1970	1980	1990	1992	1993	1994	1995	1996	1997	1998
INTEREST PAYMENTS (LINT)	**28**	**529**	**2,124**	**1,831**	**862**	**1,075**	**859**	**1,043**	**544**	**519**
Public and publicly guaranteed	**20**	**438**	**2,120**	**1,828**	**860**	**1,073**	**840**	**1,025**	**532**	**510**
Official creditors	16	63	1,300	827	570	337	323	515	365	374
Multilateral	9	46	262	322	315	337	323	322	280	242
Concessional	0	0	0	1	1	2	2	3	3	4
Bilateral	7	17	1,038	505	256	0	0	193	85	132
Concessional	3	9	312	360	256	0	0	0	65	132
Private creditors	4	375	820	1,001	290	737	516	510	166	136
Bonds	0	0	0	0	113	127	128	128	128	128
Commercial banks	1	352	378	563	0	0	0	0	0	0
Other private	3	24	442	438	177	610	388	382	38	8
Private nonguaranteed	**8**	**91**	**3**	**3**	**2**	**2**	**19**	**18**	**12**	**9**
Bonds	0	0	0	0	0	0	0	0	0	0
Commercial banks	8	91	3	3	2	2	19	18	12	9
Memo:										
IBRD	9	45	243	266	265	265	266	228	181	154
IDA	0	0	0	0	1	1	2	2	3	3
NET TRANSFERS ON DEBT	**-15**	**981**	**-2,376**	**-3,174**	**-897**	**-1,223**	**-1,344**	**-2,153**	**-1,069**	**-1,007**
Public and publicly guaranteed	**-2**	**684**	**-2,358**	**-3,164**	**-885**	**-1,211**	**-1,315**	**-2,125**	**-1,047**	**-988**
Official creditors	14	14	-1,432	-629	-516	-169	-361	-935	-633	-836
Multilateral	1	2	33	-108	-115	-169	-361	-461	-433	-386
Concessional	1	-1	6	34	51	74	95	91	92	140
Bilateral	13	12	-1,466	-521	-401	0	0	-474	-200	-451
Concessional	21	26	-217	-360	-401	0	0	0	-135	-451
Private creditors	-15	670	-926	-2,535	-369	-1,043	-955	-1,190	-414	-151
Bonds	0	0	0	0	-113	-127	-128	-128	-128	-128
Commercial banks	2	140	-766	-1,897	0	0	0	0	0	0
Other private	-17	531	-160	-637	-256	-916	-827	-1,063	-286	-23
Private nonguaranteed	**-13**	**297**	**-18**	**-11**	**-12**	**-12**	**-29**	**-28**	**-22**	**-19**
Bonds	0	0	0	0	0	0	0	0	0	0
Commercial banks	-13	297	-18	-11	-12	-12	-29	-28	-22	-19
Memo:										
IBRD	-1	-6	-100	-287	-310	-390	-468	-459	-341	-381
IDA	1	-1	6	23	36	58	83	87	79	131
DEBT SERVICE (LTDS)	**96**	**772**	**3,304**	**3,709**	**1,441**	**1,822**	**1,777**	**2,461**	**1,383**	**1,283**
Public and publicly guaranteed	**58**	**503**	**3,285**	**3,695**	**1,429**	**1,810**	**1,748**	**2,433**	**1,361**	**1,264**
Official creditors	32	108	2,075	1,160	1,060	767	793	1,243	947	1,112
Multilateral	14	71	509	638	644	767	793	769	747	662
Concessional	0	1	1	2	2	3	4	4	4	5
Bilateral	18	37	1,566	521	416	0	0	474	200	451
Concessional	9	23	317	360	416	0	0	0	135	451
Private creditors	26	395	1,211	2,535	369	1,043	955	1,190	414	151
Bonds	0	0	0	0	113	127	128	128	128	128
Commercial banks	1	352	766	1,897	0	0	0	0	0	0
Other private	25	43	445	637	256	916	827	1,063	286	23
Private nonguaranteed	**38**	**269**	**18**	**15**	**12**	**12**	**29**	**28**	**22**	**19**
Bonds	0	0	0	0	0	0	0	0	0	0
Commercial banks	38	269	18	15	12	12	29	28	22	19
Memo:										
IBRD	14	69	484	559	574	649	657	598	519	467
IDA	0	1	1	2	2	2	3	3	4	5
UNDISBURSED DEBT	**185**	**3,714**	**5,246**	**5,639**	**5,204**	**4,864**	**4,255**	**3,073**	**1,316**	**672**
Official creditors	167	1,112	3,968	4,709	4,157	3,786	3,183	2,426	1,316	672
Private creditors	18	2,602	1,278	930	1,047	1,078	1,072	648	0	0
Memorandum items										
Concessional LDOD	140	443	522	972	1,094	1,290	1,377	1,354	1,323	1,583
Variable rate LDOD	127	4,001	11,044	5,108	5,198	5,452	5,539	5,218	4,864	4,913
Public sector LDOD	450	4,271	31,546	26,473	26,390	27,914	28,077	25,359	22,565	23,387
Private sector LDOD	117	1,097	391	337	352	352	365	372	362	353

6. CURRENCY COMPOSITION OF LONG-TERM DEBT (PERCENT)

	1970	1980	1990	1992	1993	1994	1995	1996	1997	1998
Deutsche mark	9.0	23.5	14.8	13.6	12.8	13.3	14.2	11.1	10.9	11.2
French franc	0.0	0.9	9.0	10.9	10.2	10.4	10.9	10.7	10.2	10.5
Japanese yen	0.8	2.0	8.2	11.3	12.6	13.3	12.6	12.0	11.9	12.9
Pound sterling	30.4	2.7	11.8	10.4	10.2	10.0	9.9	11.9	13.0	12.6
Swiss franc	0.3	0.4	0.7	0.5	0.5	0.5	0.6	0.5	0.5	0.6
U.S.dollars	9.9	55.0	38.8	32.7	32.6	30.5	29.6	31.5	31.9	31.3
Multiple currency	38.5	12.1	10.4	12.0	12.1	11.8	11.5	10.9	10.5	9.8
Special drawing rights	0.0	0.0	0.0	0.0	0.0	0.0	0.0	0.0	0.1	0.2
All other currencies	11.1	3.4	6.3	8.6	9.0	10.2	10.7	11.4	11.0	10.9

NIGERIA

(US$ million, unless otherwise indicated)

	1970	1980	1990	1992	1993	1994	1995	1996	1997	1998
7. DEBT RESTRUCTURINGS										
Total amount rescheduled	..	..	1,480	2,497	0	0	0	0	0	0
Debt stock rescheduled	..	..	0	2,051	0	0	0	0	0	0
Principal rescheduled	..	..	1,280	327	0	0	0	0	0	0
Official	..	..	1,090	277	0	0	0	0	0	0
Private	..	..	191	51	0	0	0	0	0	0
Interest rescheduled	..	..	169	60	0	0	0	0	0	0
Official	..	..	149	49	0	0	0	0	0	0
Private	..	..	21	11	0	0	0	0	0	0
Debt forgiven	..	..	0	0	0	0	0	0	0	0
Memo: interest forgiven	..	..	0	0	0	0	0	0	0	0
Debt stock reduction	..	..	286	3,532	30	13	95	1,023	700	0
of which debt buyback	..	..	0	1,335	0	0	0	281	0	0
8. DEBT STOCK-FLOW RECONCILIATION										
Total change in debt stocks	..	..	3,318	-4,508	1,681	2,393	1,000	-2,686	-2,952	1,860
Net flows on debt	282	2,780	-34	-708	472	-660	-559	-1,334	-663	-269
Net change in interest arrears	..	..	820	716	1,241	1,381	898	249	-10	828
Interest capitalized	..	..	169	60	0	0	0	0	0	0
Debt forgiveness or reduction	..	..	-286	-2,197	-30	-13	-95	-742	-700	0
Cross-currency valuation	..	..	2,375	-1,213	-189	1,741	682	-949	-1,513	990
Residual	..	..	274	-1,166	187	-56	74	90	-67	311
9. AVERAGE TERMS OF NEW COMMITMENTS										
ALL CREDITORS										
Interest (%)	6.0	10.5	6.5	4.6	3.7	7.7	0.0	0.0	0.0	0.0
Maturity (years)	14.0	10.9	19.2	23.1	24.5	21.0	0.0	0.0	0.0	0.0
Grace period (years)	3.9	3.5	5.3	7.3	6.8	5.5	0.0	0.0	0.0	0.0
Grant element (%)	21.3	-2.2	23.6	40.2	48.4	15.0	0.0	0.0	0.0	0.0
Official creditors										
Interest (%)	5.9	8.2	5.8	4.6	2.8	7.7	0.0	0.0	0.0	0.0
Maturity (years)	15.4	16.1	22.7	23.1	27.6	21.0	0.0	0.0	0.0	0.0
Grace period (years)	4.3	3.9	6.2	7.3	7.7	5.5	0.0	0.0	0.0	0.0
Grant element (%)	23.2	9.2	31.1	40.2	58.1	15.0	0.0	0.0	0.0	0.0
Private creditors										
Interest (%)	6.5	11.4	7.9	0.0	7.2	0.0	0.0	0.0	0.0	0.0
Maturity (years)	6.5	8.9	13.1	0.0	13.5	0.0	0.0	0.0	0.0	0.0
Grace period (years)	1.9	3.4	3.7	0.0	3.8	0.0	0.0	0.0	0.0	0.0
Grant element (%)	11.0	-6.6	10.4	0.0	14.0	0.0	0.0	0.0	0.0	0.0
Memorandum items										
Commitments	65	1,904	2,216	1,101	288	472	0	0	0	0
Official creditors	55	525	1,415	1,101	225	472	0	0	0	0
Private creditors	10	1,380	801	0	63	0	0	0	0	0

10. CONTRACTUAL OBLIGATIONS ON OUTSTANDING LONG-TERM DEBT

	1999	2000	2001	2002	2003	2004	2005	2006	2007	2008
TOTAL										
Disbursements	301	194	103	55	18	2	0	0	0	0
Principal	2,101	708	637	959	949	918	912	762	466	425
Interest	616	527	492	457	404	350	298	246	207	183
Official creditors										
Disbursements	301	194	103	55	18	2	0	0	0	0
Principal	1,755	510	440	764	756	742	732	585	293	277
Interest	432	360	329	299	251	201	152	103	67	49
Bilateral creditors										
Disbursements	0	0	0	0	0	0	0	0	0	0
Principal	1,268	39	33	394	394	384	384	267	27	27
Interest	179	132	129	124	101	75	49	24	7	6
Multilateral creditors										
Disbursements	301	194	103	55	18	2	0	0	0	0
Principal	487	471	407	370	362	358	348	318	266	250
Interest	254	228	200	175	151	126	103	79	60	43
Private creditors										
Disbursements	0	0	0	0	0	0	0	0	0	0
Principal	346	198	197	195	193	176	180	177	173	149
Interest	184	168	162	158	153	149	146	143	140	134
Commercial banks										
Disbursements	0	0	0	0	0	0	0	0	0	0
Principal	0	0	0	0	0	0	0	0	0	0
Interest	0	0	0	0	0	0	0	0	0	0
Other private										
Disbursements	0	0	0	0	0	0	0	0	0	0
Principal	346	198	197	195	193	176	180	177	173	149
Interest	184	168	162	158	153	149	146	143	140	134

OMAN

(US$ million, unless otherwise indicated)

	1970	1980	1990	1992	1993	1994	1995	1996	1997	1998
1. SUMMARY DEBT DATA										
TOTAL DEBT STOCKS (EDT)	..	**599**	**2,736**	**2,855**	**2,657**	**3,087**	**3,181**	**3,415**	**3,602**	**3,629**
Long-term debt (LDOD)	..	**436**	**2,400**	**2,340**	**2,315**	**2,610**	**2,640**	**2,649**	**2,570**	**2,231**
Public and publicly guaranteed	..	436	2,400	2,340	2,315	2,608	2,637	2,646	2,567	2,228
Private nonguaranteed	..	0	0	0	0	3	3	3	3	3
Use of IMF credit	**0**	**0**	**0**	**0**	**0**	**0**	**0**	**0**	**0**	**0**
Short-term debt	..	**163**	**335**	**515**	**342**	**477**	**541**	**766**	**1,032**	**1,398**
of which interest arrears on LDOD	..	0	1	0	0	0	2	1	1	0
Official creditors	..	0	1	0	0	0	2	1	1	0
Private creditors	..	0	0	0	0	0	0	0	0	0
Memo: principal arrears on LDOD	..	0	3	0	0	0	35	35	5	0
Official creditors	..	0	3	0	0	0	29	35	5	0
Private creditors	..	0	0	0	0	0	6	0	0	0
Memo: export credits	..	0	561	590	726	827	958	993	1,437	1,367
TOTAL DEBT FLOWS										
Disbursements	..	**98**	**125**	**253**	**366**	**601**	**322**	**608**	**272**	**46**
Long-term debt	..	98	125	253	366	601	322	608	272	46
IMF purchases	0	0	0	0	0	0	0	0	0	0
Principal repayments	..	**179**	**536**	**340**	**425**	**376**	**282**	**571**	**297**	**411**
Long-term debt	..	179	536	340	425	376	282	571	297	411
IMF repurchases	0	0	0	0	0	0	0	0	0	0
Net flows on debt	..	**-64**	**-425**	**0**	**-231**	**360**	**103**	**263**	**241**	**1**
of which short-term debt	..	17	-14	87	-173	135	62	226	266	367
Interest payments (INT)	..	**70**	**203**	**189**	**181**	**174**	**204**	**180**	**177**	**218**
Long-term debt	..	44	178	153	158	149	184	149	132	156
IMF charges	0	0	0	0	0	0	0	0	0	0
Short-term debt	..	26	25	36	24	25	21	31	45	62
Net transfers on debt	..	**-134**	**-627**	**-189**	**-413**	**186**	**-101**	**84**	**64**	**-217**
Total debt service paid (TDS)	..	**249**	**739**	**529**	**606**	**550**	**486**	**751**	**474**	**629**
Long-term debt	..	223	714	493	583	525	466	720	430	567
IMF repurchases and charges	0	0	0	0	0	0	0	0	0	0
Short-term debt (interest only)	..	26	25	36	24	25	21	31	45	62
2. AGGREGATE NET RESOURCE FLOWS AND NET TRANSFERS (LONG-TERM)										
NET RESOURCE FLOWS	..	**174**	**-213**	**16**	**120**	**397**	**106**	**157**	**67**	**-248**
Net flow of long-term debt (ex. IMF)	..	-81	-411	-88	-59	225	41	37	-25	-366
Foreign direct investment (net)	..	98	141	104	142	76	46	75	53	106
Portfolio equity flows	..	0	0	0	0	26	5	25	38	10
Grants (excluding technical coop.)	..	157	57	0	36	70	15	20	1	2
Memo: technical coop. grants	..	4	18	20	15	22	17	17	19	21
official net resource flows	..	140	45	131	96	57	84	80	-15	-34
private net resource flows	..	34	-259	-115	24	341	22	77	81	-214
NET TRANSFERS	..	**-156**	**-780**	**-575**	**-496**	**-217**	**-528**	**-462**	**-545**	**-878**
Interest on long-term debt	..	44	178	153	158	149	184	149	132	156
Profit remittances on FDI	..	286	390	439	458	465	450	470	480	475
Memo: official net transfers	..	127	31	114	73	32	55	52	-46	-62
private net transfers	..	-282	-812	-689	-569	-249	-583	-515	-500	-816
3. MAJOR ECONOMIC AGGREGATES										
Gross national product (GNP)	..	5,338	9,445	9,820	9,565	9,360	10,531	..	..	..
Exports of goods & services (XGS)	..	3,887	5,990	5,935	5,839	5,852	6,442	7,615	8,034	..
of which workers remittances	..	35	39	39	39	39	39	39	39	..
Imports of goods & services (MGS)	..	2,650	3,971	5,298	5,624	5,317	5,734	6,075	6,621	..
International reserves (RES)	..	704	1,784	2,080	1,021	1,090	1,251	1,497	1,633	1,148
Current account balance	..	942	1,106	-598	-1,190	-805	-801	180	-57	..
4. DEBT INDICATORS										
EDT / XGS (%)	..	15.4	45.7	48.1	45.5	52.8	49.4	44.8	44.8	..
EDT / GNP (%)	..	11.2	29.0	29.1	27.8	33.0	30.2	..	..	..
TDS / XGS (%)	..	6.4	12.3	8.9	10.4	9.4	7.5	9.9	5.9	..
INT / XGS (%)	..	1.8	3.4	3.2	3.1	3.0	3.2	2.4	2.2	..
INT / GNP (%)	..	1.3	2.1	1.9	1.9	1.9	1.9	..	..	..
RES / EDT (%)	..	117.7	65.2	72.9	38.4	35.3	39.3	43.8	45.3	31.6
RES / MGS (months)	..	3.2	5.4	4.7	2.2	2.5	2.6	3.0	3.0	..
Short-term / EDT (%)	..	27.2	12.3	18.0	12.9	15.5	17.0	22.4	28.7	38.5
Concessional / EDT (%)	..	43.6	8.9	14.0	18.3	16.9	18.3	17.6	15.6	15.3
Multilateral / EDT (%)	..	5.8	4.7	5.9	6.2	5.2	6.3	6.5	5.5	5.4

OMAN

(US$ million, unless otherwise indicated)

	1970	1980	1990	1992	1993	1994	1995	1996	1997	1998
5. LONG-TERM DEBT										
DEBT OUTSTANDING (LDOD)	..	**436**	**2,400**	**2,340**	**2,315**	**2,610**	**2,640**	**2,649**	**2,570**	**2,231**
Public and publicly guaranteed	..	**436**	**2,400**	**2,340**	**2,315**	**2,608**	**2,637**	**2,646**	**2,567**	**2,228**
Official creditors	..	349	327	500	579	601	665	693	645	635
Multilateral	..	35	129	167	164	162	199	221	199	195
Concessional	..	6	49	71	73	88	120	131	119	118
Bilateral	..	314	198	333	416	439	466	473	446	439
Concessional	..	255	194	330	414	434	462	469	443	437
Private creditors	..	87	2,073	1,840	1,736	2,007	1,972	1,953	1,923	1,593
Bonds	..	0	0	0	0	0	0	0	225	225
Commercial banks	..	0	1,721	1,578	1,312	1,521	1,470	1,439	1,257	995
Other private	..	87	353	262	424	486	502	514	440	374
Private nonguaranteed	..	**0**	**0**	**0**	**0**	**3**	**3**	**3**	**3**	**3**
Bonds	..	0	0	0	0	0	0	0	0	0
Commercial banks	..	0	0	0	0	3	3	3	3	3
Memo:										
IBRD	0	14	52	52	46	33	25	19	13	9
IDA	0	0	0	0	0	0	0	0	0	0
DISBURSEMENTS	..	**98**	**125**	**253**	**366**	**601**	**322**	**608**	**272**	**46**
Public and publicly guaranteed	..	**98**	**125**	**253**	**366**	**601**	**322**	**608**	**272**	**45**
Official creditors	..	45	34	184	108	58	117	106	44	45
Multilateral	..	13	22	60	21	21	58	49	10	17
Concessional	..	6	12	32	10	20	40	28	8	14
Bilateral	..	32	13	124	88	37	58	57	34	28
Concessional	..	7	13	124	88	32	58	57	34	28
Private creditors	..	52	91	69	258	543	206	502	228	0
Bonds	..	0	0	0	0	0	0	0	225	0
Commercial banks	..	0	0	0	51	431	132	468	0	0
Other private	..	52	91	69	207	112	74	34	3	0
Private nonguaranteed	..	**0**	**0**	**0**	**0**	**0**	**0**	**1**	**0**	**0**
Bonds	..	0	0	0	0	0	0	0	0	0
Commercial banks	..	0	0	0	0	0	0	1	0	0
Memo:										
IBRD	0	6	10	15	6	0	0	0	0	0
IDA	0	0	0	0	0	0	0	0	0	0
PRINCIPAL REPAYMENTS	..	**179**	**536**	**340**	**425**	**376**	**282**	**571**	**297**	**411**
Public and publicly guaranteed	..	**179**	**536**	**340**	**425**	**376**	**282**	**570**	**297**	**411**
Official creditors	..	62	46	52	49	71	48	45	60	81
Multilateral	..	3	30	29	26	30	23	22	23	25
Concessional	..	0	10	8	8	9	10	14	15	17
Bilateral	..	60	16	23	23	41	25	23	37	56
Concessional	..	9	15	22	22	40	24	22	37	55
Private creditors	..	117	491	288	376	304	234	526	237	330
Bonds	..	0	0	0	0	0	0	0	0	0
Commercial banks	..	32	370	234	335	242	178	482	167	262
Other private	..	85	120	54	41	62	56	44	70	68
Private nonguaranteed	..	**0**	**0**	**0**	**0**	**0**	**0**	**1**	**0**	**0**
Bonds	..	0	0	0	0	0	0	0	0	0
Commercial banks	..	0	0	0	0	0	0	1	0	0
Memo:										
IBRD	0	1	16	14	13	17	9	5	4	4
IDA	0	0	0	0	0	0	0	0	0	0
NET FLOWS ON DEBT	..	**-81**	**-411**	**-88**	**-59**	**225**	**41**	**37**	**-25**	**-366**
Public and publicly guaranteed	..	**-81**	**-411**	**-88**	**-59**	**225**	**41**	**37**	**-25**	**-366**
Official creditors	..	-17	-12	131	59	-13	69	61	-16	-36
Multilateral	..	11	-9	31	-6	-9	35	27	-12	-8
Concessional	..	6	2	24	2	11	31	14	-7	-4
Bilateral	..	-27	-3	101	65	-4	34	34	-4	-28
Concessional	..	-1	-2	102	66	-8	35	35	-3	-27
Private creditors	..	-65	-400	-219	-118	238	-28	-24	-9	-330
Bonds	..	0	0	0	0	0	0	0	225	0
Commercial banks	..	-32	-370	-234	-284	189	-46	-14	-167	-262
Other private	..	-33	-30	15	166	50	18	-10	-67	-68
Private nonguaranteed	..	**0**	**0**	**0**	**0**	**0**	**0**	**0**	**0**	**0**
Bonds	..	0	0	0	0	0	0	0	0	0
Commercial banks	..	0	0	0	0	0	0	0	0	0
Memo:										
IBRD	0	5	-6	1	-8	-16	-9	-5	-4	-4
IDA	0	0	0	0	0	0	0	0	0	0

OMAN

(US$ million, unless otherwise indicated)

	1970	1980	1990	1992	1993	1994	1995	1996	1997	1998
INTEREST PAYMENTS (LINT)	..	**44**	**178**	**153**	**158**	**149**	**184**	**149**	**132**	**156**
Public and publicly guaranteed	..	**44**	**178**	**153**	**158**	**149**	**184**	**149**	**132**	**156**
Official creditors	..	14	14	18	22	24	29	28	31	28
Multilateral	..	2	6	7	6	6	11	10	11	11
Concessional	..	0	0	0	0	0	6	6	7	8
Bilateral	..	12	8	11	16	18	18	18	20	17
Concessional	..	1	8	11	16	18	18	18	20	17
Private creditors	..	30	164	135	136	125	155	121	101	128
Bonds	..	0	0	0	0	0	0	0	0	16
Commercial banks	..	3	133	108	104	91	109	84	64	80
Other private	..	28	31	27	32	34	46	37	37	32
Private nonguaranteed	..	**0**	**0**	**0**	**0**	**0**	**0**	**0**	**0**	**0**
Bonds	..	0	0	0	0	0	0	0	0	0
Commercial banks	..	0	0	0	0	0	0	0	0	0
Memo:										
IBRD	0	1	5	4	4	4	2	2	1	1
IDA	0	0	0	0	0	0	0	0	0	0
NET TRANSFERS ON DEBT	..	**-125**	**-589**	**-240**	**-217**	**76**	**-143**	**-112**	**-157**	**-522**
Public and publicly guaranteed	..	**-125**	**-589**	**-240**	**-217**	**76**	**-143**	**-112**	**-157**	**-522**
Official creditors	..	-30	-26	114	37	-38	40	33	-47	-64
Multilateral	..	9	-15	24	-12	-15	24	17	-24	-19
Concessional	..	6	2	24	2	11	24	8	-15	-11
Bilateral	..	-39	-11	90	49	-23	16	16	-23	-45
Concessional	..	-2	-10	91	50	-26	17	17	-22	-44
Private creditors	..	-95	-563	-354	-254	114	-183	-144	-110	-458
Bonds	..	0	0	0	0	0	0	0	225	-16
Commercial banks	..	-35	-503	-342	-389	98	-155	-98	-231	-342
Other private	..	-60	-60	-12	135	15	-29	-46	-104	-100
Private nonguaranteed	..	**0**	**0**	**0**	**0**	**0**	**0**	**0**	**0**	**0**
Bonds	..	0	0	0	0	0	0	0	0	0
Commercial banks	..	0	0	0	0	0	0	0	0	0
Memo:										
IBRD	0	4	-11	-3	-12	-20	-11	-6	-5	-5
IDA	0	0	0	0	0	0	0	0	0	0
DEBT SERVICE (LTDS)	..	**223**	**714**	**493**	**583**	**525**	**466**	**720**	**430**	**567**
Public and publicly guaranteed	..	**223**	**714**	**493**	**583**	**525**	**465**	**719**	**429**	**567**
Official creditors	..	76	60	70	71	96	76	73	91	109
Multilateral	..	5	37	36	33	36	34	32	34	36
Concessional	..	0	10	8	8	9	16	20	22	25
Bilateral	..	71	23	34	39	60	43	41	57	73
Concessional	..	9	23	33	37	58	41	40	56	72
Private creditors	..	147	654	423	512	429	389	646	338	458
Bonds	..	0	0	0	0	0	0	0	0	16
Commercial banks	..	35	503	342	440	333	287	566	231	342
Other private	..	113	151	81	72	96	102	80	107	100
Private nonguaranteed	..	**0**	**0**	**0**	**0**	**0**	**1**	**1**	**0**	**1**
Bonds	..	0	0	0	0	0	0	0	0	0
Commercial banks	..	0	0	0	0	0	1	1	0	1
Memo:										
IBRD	0	2	20	18	17	20	11	6	5	5
IDA	0	0	0	0	0	0	0	0	0	0
UNDISBURSED DEBT	..	**499**	**897**	**568**	**464**	**490**	**407**	**230**	**196**	**323**
Official creditors	..	176	454	232	114	137	259	181	151	272
Private creditors	..	323	443	336	350	353	148	49	45	50
Memorandum items										
Concessional LDOD	..	261	243	401	487	522	581	600	562	555
Variable rate LDOD	..	0	1,386	1,397	1,160	1,363	1,329	1,323	1,158	1,007
Public sector LDOD	..	436	2,400	2,340	2,315	2,608	2,637	2,646	2,567	2,228
Private sector LDOD	..	0	0	0	0	3	3	3	3	3

6. CURRENCY COMPOSITION OF LONG-TERM DEBT (PERCENT)

	1970	1980	1990	1992	1993	1994	1995	1996	1997	1998
Deutsche mark	..	0.0	0.0	0.0	0.0	0.0	0.0	0.0	0.0	0.0
French franc	..	7.5	0.5	0.3	0.2	0.0	0.0	0.0	0.0	0.0
Japanese yen	..	0.0	7.3	13.2	17.2	16.1	15.2	13.1	11.3	8.2
Pound sterling	..	8.8	5.5	6.6	9.4	10.2	9.6	9.3	8.1	8.0
Swiss franc	..	0.0	0.0	0.0	0.0	0.0	0.0	0.0	0.0	0.0
U.S.dollars	..	16.8	75.5	66.9	60.7	62.1	61.1	61.4	64.1	65.0
Multiple currency	..	3.1	2.2	2.2	2.0	1.2	0.9	0.7	0.5	0.0
Special drawing rights	..	0.0	0.0	0.0	0.0	0.0	0.0	0.0	0.0	0.0
All other currencies	..	63.8	9.0	10.8	10.5	10.4	13.2	15.5	16.0	18.8

OMAN

(US$ million, unless otherwise indicated)

	1970	1980	1990	1992	1993	1994	1995	1996	1997	1998
7. DEBT RESTRUCTURINGS										
Total amount rescheduled	..	..	0	0	0	0	0	0	0	0
Debt stock rescheduled	..	..	0	0	0	0	0	0	0	0
Principal rescheduled	..	..	0	0	0	0	0	0	0	0
Official	..	..	0	0	0	0	0	0	0	0
Private	..	..	0	0	0	0	0	0	0	0
Interest rescheduled	..	..	0	0	0	0	0	0	0	0
Official	..	..	0	0	0	0	0	0	0	0
Private	..	..	0	0	0	0	0	0	0	0
Debt forgiven	..	..	0	0	0	0	0	0	0	0
Memo: interest forgiven	..	..	0	0	0	0	0	0	0	0
Debt stock reduction	..	..	0	0	0	0	0	0	0	0
of which debt buyback	..	..	0	0	0	0	0	0	0	0
8. DEBT STOCK-FLOW RECONCILIATION										
Total change in debt stocks	..	..	-233	-46	-198	430	94	234	187	27
Net flows on debt	..	-64	-425	0	-231	360	103	263	241	1
Net change in interest arrears	..	..	1	0	0	0	2	-1	0	-1
Interest capitalized	..	..	0	0	0	0	0	0	0	0
Debt forgiveness or reduction	..	..	0	0	0	0	0	0	0	0
Cross-currency valuation	..	..	46	-42	43	70	-12	-22	-47	30
Residual	..	..	145	-3	-10	0	1	-7	-7	-3
9. AVERAGE TERMS OF NEW COMMITMENTS										
ALL CREDITORS										
Interest (%)	..	7.9	7.5	5.0	5.5	4.7	4.6	5.7	6.7	3.4
Maturity (years)	..	9.4	13.8	11.6	11.8	8.8	16.6	8.1	6.0	18.0
Grace period (years)	..	3.2	4.0	2.7	3.8	3.2	3.4	4.9	4.7	3.2
Grant element (%)	..	9.1	12.8	23.4	22.6	21.9	31.9	19.1	13.7	37.5
Official creditors										
Interest (%)	..	10.0	1.9	2.9	0.0	3.3	4.6	3.5	3.6	3.3
Maturity (years)	..	10.5	16.7	16.5	0.0	16.7	16.6	19.1	13.0	18.2
Grace period (years)	..	2.9	4.5	3.9	0.0	3.5	3.4	4.1	2.9	3.2
Grant element (%)	..	2.9	45.1	39.3	0.0	37.0	31.9	40.9	32.7	37.7
Private creditors										
Interest (%)	..	7.5	8.0	6.6	5.5	5.0	0.0	6.0	7.1	3.9
Maturity (years)	..	9.2	13.5	7.9	11.8	7.6	0.0	7.0	5.0	11.1
Grace period (years)	..	3.3	4.0	1.7	3.8	3.2	0.0	5.0	5.0	3.1
Grant element (%)	..	10.3	9.9	11.1	22.6	19.6	0.0	16.9	10.9	28.8
Memorandum items										
Commitments	..	454	412	144	275	622	245	441	258	188
Official creditors	..	76	34	63	0	80	245	41	33	183
Private creditors	..	379	379	81	275	542	0	400	225	6

10. CONTRACTUAL OBLIGATIONS ON OUTSTANDING LONG-TERM DEBT

	1999	2000	2001	2002	2003	2004	2005	2006	2007	2008
TOTAL										
Disbursements	117	86	50	31	17	11	6	3	2	0
Principal	601	174	254	563	332	151	88	60	58	56
Interest	127	100	93	69	42	25	18	15	13	11
Official creditors										
Disbursements	77	76	50	31	17	11	6	3	2	0
Principal	73	75	75	79	77	75	63	59	58	56
Interest	28	28	27	25	23	20	17	15	13	11
Bilateral creditors										
Disbursements	42	37	24	13	7	4	2	1	0	0
Principal	41	41	45	47	48	46	46	43	43	40
Interest	18	18	18	16	15	13	11	10	8	6
Multilateral creditors										
Disbursements	36	39	27	18	10	7	4	2	2	0
Principal	31	34	30	32	29	29	16	16	15	15
Interest	10	10	10	9	8	7	6	6	5	4
Private creditors										
Disbursements	40	10	0	0	0	0	0	0	0	0
Principal	528	99	179	484	255	76	25	0	0	0
Interest	99	72	66	43	19	5	1	0	0	0
Commercial banks										
Disbursements	5	0	0	0	0	0	0	0	0	0
Principal	444	28	108	188	188	28	14	0	0	0
Interest	56	33	32	23	11	2	0	0	0	0
Other private										
Disbursements	35	10	0	0	0	0	0	0	0	0
Principal	84	70	70	295	67	48	11	0	0	0
Interest	43	39	34	21	8	3	0	0	0	0

PAKISTAN

(US$ million, unless otherwise indicated)

	1970	1980	1990	1992	1993	1994	1995	1996	1997	1998
1. SUMMARY DEBT DATA										
TOTAL DEBT STOCKS (EDT)	**..**	**9,931**	**20,663**	**24,918**	**24,527**	**27,359**	**30,130**	**29,726**	**29,978**	**32,229**
Long-term debt (LDOD)	**3,071**	**8,520**	**16,643**	**19,397**	**21,459**	**23,864**	**25,282**	**25,514**	**26,215**	**28,663**
Public and publicly guaranteed	3,066	8,502	16,506	18,563	20,402	22,686	23,689	23,519	23,878	26,061
Private nonguaranteed	5	18	138	834	1,057	1,178	1,593	1,995	2,338	2,602
Use of IMF credit	**45**	**674**	**836**	**1,127**	**1,122**	**1,557**	**1,613**	**1,396**	**1,281**	**1,360**
Short-term debt	**..**	**737**	**3,185**	**4,394**	**1,946**	**1,938**	**3,235**	**2,816**	**2,481**	**2,206**
of which interest arrears on LDOD	..	0	1	0	0	0	0	0	0	123
Official creditors	..	0	1	0	0	0	0	0	0	77
Private creditors	..	0	0	0	0	0	0	0	0	46
Memo: principal arrears on LDOD	..	0	15	0	0	0	0	0	0	243
Official creditors	..	0	15	0	0	0	0	0	0	165
Private creditors	..	0	0	0	0	0	0	0	0	78
Memo: export credits	..	0	2,343	2,584	2,671	3,329	5,182	4,870	5,011	5,653
TOTAL DEBT FLOWS										
Disbursements	**492**	**1,371**	**1,766**	**2,923**	**3,216**	**4,039**	**3,201**	**3,582**	**4,796**	**3,013**
Long-term debt	492	1,064	1,766	2,923	3,093	3,607	2,999	3,427	4,516	2,831
IMF purchases	0	308	0	0	123	432	202	155	280	182
Principal repayments	**143**	**492**	**1,087**	**1,444**	**1,521**	**2,469**	**2,006**	**2,089**	**2,839**	**1,794**
Long-term debt	115	353	916	1,279	1,393	2,403	1,832	1,768	2,530	1,634
IMF repurchases	28	139	172	166	128	66	174	321	309	159
Net flows on debt	**453**	**1,176**	**1,093**	**1,740**	**-753**	**1,562**	**2,492**	**1,074**	**1,622**	**821**
of which short-term debt	..	296	414	261	-2,448	-8	1,297	-419	-335	-398
Interest payments (INT)	**..**	**378**	**839**	**887**	**866**	**999**	**1,194**	**1,188**	**1,232**	**949**
Long-term debt	78	248	521	662	750	855	948	906	902	802
IMF charges	0	27	54	36	36	34	44	58	36	35
Short-term debt	..	103	264	190	80	109	203	225	294	112
Net transfers on debt	**..**	**798**	**254**	**852**	**-1,619**	**563**	**1,297**	**-114**	**390**	**-128**
Total debt service paid (TDS)	**..**	**870**	**1,926**	**2,332**	**2,386**	**3,468**	**3,200**	**3,277**	**4,071**	**2,743**
Long-term debt	193	601	1,437	1,940	2,143	3,258	2,779	2,673	3,432	2,436
IMF repurchases and charges	28	166	226	202	163	100	219	378	345	194
Short-term debt (interest only)	..	103	264	190	80	109	203	225	294	112
2. AGGREGATE NET RESOURCE FLOWS AND NET TRANSFERS (LONG-TERM)										
NET RESOURCE FLOWS	**453**	**1,256**	**1,419**	**2,428**	**2,431**	**3,167**	**2,820**	**3,498**	**3,133**	**1,871**
Net flow of long-term debt (ex. IMF)	377	711	851	1,645	1,700	1,204	1,167	1,659	1,986	1,197
Foreign direct investment (net)	23	63	244	335	346	429	736	939	729	500
Portfolio equity flows	0	0	0	139	185	1,335	729	700	252	0
Grants (excluding technical coop.)	53	482	324	310	201	199	188	200	167	175
Memo: technical coop. grants	24	12	319	320	273	180	181	156	130	118
official net resource flows	404	1,026	1,237	1,327	1,190	1,392	1,038	1,308	1,046	1,066
private net resource flows	49	230	182	1,101	1,241	1,775	1,782	2,190	2,087	806
NET TRANSFERS	**369**	**1,002**	**844**	**1,712**	**1,619**	**2,242**	**1,773**	**2,466**	**2,032**	**839**
Interest on long-term debt	78	248	521	662	750	855	948	906	902	802
Profit remittances on FDI	6	6	53	54	62	70	100	126	200	230
Memo: official net transfers	340	823	782	749	550	700	287	618	365	470
private net transfers	29	179	63	963	1,070	1,542	1,486	1,848	1,667	370
3. MAJOR ECONOMIC AGGREGATES										
Gross national product (GNP)	9,933	23,409	39,044	47,615	50,309	50,692	59,423	62,009	60,850	61,039
Exports of goods & services (XGS)	891	4,758	8,267	9,811	9,972	9,851	11,775	11,872	11,345	11,631
of which workers remittances	86	1,748	1,942	1,468	1,562	1,446	1,866	1,461	1,409	1,490
Imports of goods & services (MGS)	1,591	6,042	10,425	12,803	14,425	12,759	14,830	17,364	16,743	15,273
International reserves (RES)	195	1,568	1,046	1,524	1,995	3,716	2,528	1,307	1,795	1,626
Current account balance	-667	-869	-1,352	-896	-3,327	-1,650	-2,163	-4,343	-3,560	-1,702
4. DEBT INDICATORS										
EDT / XGS (%)	..	208.7	250.0	254.0	246.0	277.7	255.9	250.4	264.2	277.1
EDT / GNP (%)	..	42.4	52.9	52.3	48.8	54.0	50.7	47.9	49.3	52.8
TDS / XGS (%)	..	18.3	23.3	23.8	23.9	35.2	27.2	27.6	35.9	23.6
INT / XGS (%)	..	7.9	10.2	9.0	8.7	10.1	10.1	10.0	10.9	8.2
INT / GNP (%)	..	1.6	2.2	1.9	1.7	2.0	2.0	1.9	2.0	1.6
RES / EDT (%)	..	15.8	5.1	6.1	8.1	13.6	8.4	4.4	6.0	5.0
RES / MGS (months)	1.5	3.1	1.2	1.4	1.7	3.5	2.1	0.9	1.3	1.3
Short-term / EDT (%)	..	7.4	15.4	17.6	7.9	7.1	10.7	9.5	8.3	6.8
Concessional / EDT (%)	..	71.6	58.5	51.1	54.6	55.6	53.7	53.3	49.8	52.5
Multilateral / EDT (%)	..	15.4	33.4	35.1	40.4	41.9	40.4	41.0	39.6	40.7

PAKISTAN

(US$ million, unless otherwise indicated)

	1970	1980	1990	1992	1993	1994	1995	1996	1997	1998
5. LONG-TERM DEBT										
DEBT OUTSTANDING (LDOD)	**3,071**	**8,520**	**16,643**	**19,397**	**21,459**	**23,864**	**25,282**	**25,514**	**26,215**	**28,663**
Public and publicly guaranteed	**3,066**	**8,502**	**16,506**	**18,563**	**20,402**	**22,686**	**23,689**	**23,519**	**23,878**	**26,061**
Official creditors	2,781	7,953	15,791	17,733	19,095	21,516	22,592	22,297	21,557	23,761
Multilateral	614	1,532	6,894	8,749	9,906	11,462	12,179	12,190	11,860	13,130
Concessional	280	956	3,887	4,669	5,214	6,270	6,894	7,174	7,116	7,973
Bilateral	2,166	6,420	8,897	8,983	9,190	10,054	10,413	10,108	9,697	10,632
Concessional	1,906	6,154	8,207	8,065	8,177	8,943	9,283	8,676	7,819	8,935
Private creditors	285	550	714	830	1,307	1,170	1,097	1,221	2,321	2,300
Bonds	0	0	0	0	0	150	150	300	675	675
Commercial banks	6	115	402	466	873	424	379	308	1,280	1,311
Other private	280	435	313	364	434	596	568	614	366	315
Private nonguaranteed	**5**	**18**	**138**	**834**	**1,057**	**1,178**	**1,593**	**1,995**	**2,338**	**2,602**
Bonds	0	0	0	0	0	45	45	45	45	45
Commercial banks	5	18	138	834	1,057	1,133	1,548	1,950	2,293	2,557
Memo:										
IBRD	330	330	1,816	2,384	2,624	2,934	3,082	3,007	3,046	3,136
IDA	280	821	2,106	2,457	2,683	3,054	3,321	3,480	3,526	3,800
DISBURSEMENTS	**492**	**1,064**	**1,766**	**2,923**	**3,093**	**3,607**	**2,999**	**3,427**	**4,516**	**2,831**
Public and publicly guaranteed	**490**	**1,054**	**1,728**	**2,384**	**2,698**	**3,176**	**2,244**	**2,726**	**3,838**	**2,222**
Official creditors	420	798	1,648	1,955	2,051	2,696	2,112	2,336	2,717	2,064
Multilateral	94	161	984	1,174	1,337	1,478	1,163	1,275	1,192	1,017
Concessional	24	103	366	426	512	808	673	710	529	583
Bilateral	326	637	664	781	714	1,217	949	1,061	1,525	1,047
Concessional	274	544	336	356	313	841	724	448	367	897
Private creditors	69	257	80	429	647	481	132	390	1,122	159
Bonds	0	0	0	0	0	150	0	150	375	0
Commercial banks	0	101	9	318	530	134	90	87	742	135
Other private	69	156	72	111	118	197	42	154	4	23
Private nonguaranteed	**3**	**9**	**39**	**540**	**395**	**431**	**755**	**701**	**678**	**609**
Bonds	0	0	0	0	0	45	0	0	0	0
Commercial banks	3	9	39	540	395	386	755	701	678	609
Memo:										
IBRD	66	16	356	387	349	314	271	371	490	130
IDA	24	74	138	226	249	321	254	280	233	219
PRINCIPAL REPAYMENTS	**115**	**353**	**916**	**1,279**	**1,393**	**2,403**	**1,832**	**1,768**	**2,530**	**1,634**
Public and publicly guaranteed	**114**	**346**	**877**	**1,148**	**1,222**	**2,138**	**1,492**	**1,469**	**2,195**	**1,334**
Official creditors	69	254	735	937	1,061	1,503	1,262	1,228	1,837	1,173
Multilateral	22	41	307	298	417	634	558	486	618	483
Concessional	0	5	43	51	59	67	81	93	111	121
Bilateral	47	213	428	639	644	869	703	742	1,220	690
Concessional	22	177	368	386	362	554	457	466	565	354
Private creditors	46	92	143	211	161	635	230	241	357	162
Bonds	0	0	0	0	0	0	0	0	0	0
Commercial banks	1	10	88	167	120	585	138	157	123	104
Other private	44	83	54	44	41	50	92	85	234	58
Private nonguaranteed	**1**	**7**	**39**	**131**	**171**	**265**	**340**	**299**	**335**	**300**
Bonds	0	0	0	0	0	0	0	0	0	0
Commercial banks	1	7	39	131	171	265	340	299	335	300
Memo:										
IBRD	22	26	73	126	155	180	219	227	206	197
IDA	0	4	19	23	26	30	35	39	42	47
NET FLOWS ON DEBT	**377**	**711**	**851**	**1,645**	**1,700**	**1,204**	**1,167**	**1,659**	**1,986**	**1,197**
Public and publicly guaranteed	**375**	**709**	**851**	**1,236**	**1,476**	**1,039**	**752**	**1,257**	**1,644**	**888**
Official creditors	351	544	913	1,017	990	1,193	850	1,108	879	891
Multilateral	72	120	677	876	920	844	604	789	575	534
Concessional	23	99	322	375	452	741	592	618	419	461
Bilateral	279	424	236	142	69	349	246	319	305	358
Concessional	252	367	-32	-30	-49	287	267	-18	-198	543
Private creditors	24	164	-63	218	487	-154	-98	149	764	-3
Bonds	0	0	0	0	0	150	0	150	375	0
Commercial banks	-1	91	-80	151	410	-451	-48	-70	619	31
Other private	25	73	17	67	77	147	-51	69	-230	-34
Private nonguaranteed	**2**	**2**	**0**	**409**	**223**	**166**	**416**	**402**	**342**	**309**
Bonds	0	0	0	0	0	45	0	0	0	0
Commercial banks	2	2	0	409	223	121	416	402	342	309
Memo:										
IBRD	44	-10	283	260	194	134	52	144	284	-67
IDA	23	70	119	202	223	291	218	241	191	172

PAKISTAN

(US$ million, unless otherwise indicated)

	1970	1980	1990	1992	1993	1994	1995	1996	1997	1998
INTEREST PAYMENTS (LINT)	**78**	**248**	**521**	**662**	**750**	**855**	**948**	**906**	**902**	**802**
Public and publicly guaranteed	**77**	**247**	**511**	**623**	**684**	**764**	**817**	**783**	**757**	**655**
Official creditors	64	203	456	578	641	692	751	689	681	596
Multilateral	21	61	247	330	377	423	445	411	391	342
Concessional	2	7	31	40	44	51	58	61	65	62
Bilateral	43	143	209	248	263	269	306	278	290	254
Concessional	29	128	178	189	192	201	251	206	198	126
Private creditors	14	44	55	45	44	73	66	94	77	59
Bonds	0	0	0	0	0	0	9	17	17	17
Commercial banks	0	9	38	28	25	45	32	31	19	20
Other private	13	35	17	17	19	27	26	46	40	22
Private nonguaranteed	**0**	**2**	**11**	**39**	**66**	**91**	**130**	**122**	**144**	**147**
Bonds	0	0	0	0	0	1	2	2	2	2
Commercial banks	0	2	11	39	66	90	128	120	142	144
Memo:										
IBRD	19	33	126	170	187	203	217	210	193	182
IDA	2	6	15	18	19	21	24	25	26	27
NET TRANSFERS ON DEBT	**300**	**463**	**329**	**983**	**950**	**349**	**220**	**753**	**1,084**	**395**
Public and publicly guaranteed	**298**	**462**	**340**	**613**	**792**	**274**	**-65**	**474**	**886**	**233**
Official creditors	288	341	457	440	349	501	99	418	199	295
Multilateral	51	60	430	546	543	421	159	378	183	192
Concessional	21	92	291	335	409	690	534	557	354	399
Bilateral	236	281	27	-106	-194	80	-60	41	15	103
Concessional	223	239	-210	-218	-241	86	16	-224	-396	417
Private creditors	10	121	-117	173	443	-227	-164	55	688	-63
Bonds	0	0	0	0	0	150	-9	133	358	-17
Commercial banks	-1	82	-118	123	385	-497	-80	-101	599	11
Other private	12	39	1	50	58	120	-76	23	-270	-56
Private nonguaranteed	**2**	**1**	**-11**	**370**	**158**	**75**	**285**	**280**	**198**	**162**
Bonds	0	0	0	0	0	44	-2	-2	-2	-2
Commercial banks	2	1	-11	370	158	31	287	282	200	164
Memo:										
IBRD	25	-43	157	90	7	-69	-165	-65	91	-249
IDA	21	64	104	185	204	270	194	217	165	146
DEBT SERVICE (LTDS)	**193**	**601**	**1,437**	**1,940**	**2,143**	**3,258**	**2,779**	**2,673**	**3,432**	**2,436**
Public and publicly guaranteed	**192**	**593**	**1,388**	**1,771**	**1,906**	**2,902**	**2,309**	**2,253**	**2,952**	**1,990**
Official creditors	133	457	1,191	1,515	1,701	2,195	2,013	1,917	2,518	1,769
Multilateral	43	102	554	628	794	1,057	1,003	897	1,009	825
Concessional	2	12	74	91	103	118	140	153	175	184
Bilateral	90	355	636	887	908	1,138	1,009	1,020	1,509	944
Concessional	51	305	546	575	554	755	708	672	763	480
Private creditors	59	136	197	256	204	707	297	335	434	221
Bonds	0	0	0	0	0	0	9	17	17	17
Commercial banks	1	19	127	195	145	631	170	188	143	124
Other private	58	117	71	61	60	77	118	131	274	79
Private nonguaranteed	**1**	**8**	**49**	**170**	**237**	**356**	**470**	**421**	**479**	**447**
Bonds	0	0	0	0	0	1	2	2	2	2
Commercial banks	1	8	49	170	237	355	468	419	477	444
Memo:										
IBRD	41	59	199	296	343	383	436	436	399	378
IDA	2	10	34	41	45	51	59	63	68	74
UNDISBURSED DEBT	**1,515**	**2,822**	**9,153**	**9,131**	**9,597**	**9,801**	**8,978**	**8,331**	**6,568**	**6,225**
Official creditors	1,317	2,677	8,922	8,629	9,083	9,400	8,627	8,099	6,215	6,008
Private creditors	198	145	231	502	515	401	351	232	353	217
Memorandum items										
Concessional LDOD	2,186	7,110	12,094	12,734	13,392	15,213	16,177	15,850	14,935	16,908
Variable rate LDOD	5	129	2,232	4,013	5,243	5,422	6,002	6,843	8,984	9,602
Public sector LDOD	2,951	8,432	16,374	18,450	20,306	22,590	23,595	23,435	23,817	26,005
Private sector LDOD	120	88	269	946	1,153	1,274	1,687	2,079	2,398	2,658
6. CURRENCY COMPOSITION OF LONG-TERM DEBT (PERCENT)										
Deutsche mark	9.3	9.1	10.2	8.8	7.3	7.9	8.1	7.3	5.9	5.5
French franc	1.6	3.2	1.8	1.7	1.6	2.5	2.8	2.7	2.2	2.2
Japanese yen	6.0	8.4	13.6	13.8	14.1	15.6	15.2	14.4	13.0	16.4
Pound sterling	16.1	3.7	1.5	1.2	1.1	0.9	0.8	0.8	0.8	0.8
Swiss franc	0.7	0.4	0.3	0.3	0.2	0.3	0.3	0.4	0.3	0.3
U.S.dollars	46.2	53.8	35.7	33.9	35.1	31.1	31.1	33.5	40.5	38.0
Multiple currency	13.5	9.6	26.2	30.8	32.2	34.5	34.8	34.0	31.2	31.3
Special drawing rights	0.0	0.0	3.1	2.9	2.8	2.8	2.9	3.0	3.0	3.1
All other currencies	6.6	11.8	7.6	6.6	5.6	4.4	4.0	3.9	3.1	2.4

PAKISTAN

(US$ million, unless otherwise indicated)

	1970	1980	1990	1992	1993	1994	1995	1996	1997	1998
7. DEBT RESTRUCTURINGS										
Total amount rescheduled	..	..	0	0	0	0	0	0	0	0
Debt stock rescheduled	..	..	0	0	0	0	0	0	0	0
Principal rescheduled	..	..	0	0	0	0	0	0	0	0
Official	..	..	0	0	0	0	0	0	0	0
Private	..	..	0	0	0	0	0	0	0	0
Interest rescheduled	..	..	0	0	0	0	0	0	0	0
Official	..	..	0	0	0	0	0	0	0	0
Private	..	..	0	0	0	0	0	0	0	0
Debt forgiven	..	..	0	0	0	0	0	0	0	0
Memo: interest forgiven	..	..	0	0	0	0	0	0	0	0
Debt stock reduction	..	..	0	0	0	0	0	0	0	0
of which debt buyback	..	..	0	0	0	0	0	0	0	0
8. DEBT STOCK-FLOW RECONCILIATION										
Total change in debt stocks	..	..	2,315	1,555	-391	2,832	2,771	-404	252	2,251
Net flows on debt	453	1,176	1,093	1,740	-753	1,562	2,492	1,074	1,622	821
Net change in interest arrears	..	..	0	-1	0	0	0	0	0	123
Interest capitalized	..	..	0	0	0	0	0	0	0	0
Debt forgiveness or reduction	..	..	0	0	0	0	0	0	0	0
Cross-currency valuation	..	..	672	-329	191	922	220	-851	-942	860
Residual	..	..	551	144	170	349	59	-627	-429	447
9. AVERAGE TERMS OF NEW COMMITMENTS										
ALL CREDITORS										
Interest (%)	2.8	4.4	5.3	4.4	3.6	4.1	5.6	4.5	5.2	6.0
Maturity (years)	31.6	30.1	22.5	18.8	20.2	23.4	17.5	20.5	11.7	19.7
Grace period (years)	11.9	6.6	6.1	6.7	5.7	6.6	5.5	6.1	3.2	5.6
Grant element (%)	59.2	47.9	34.9	36.9	41.0	42.9	29.6	35.2	21.0	29.7
Official creditors										
Interest (%)	2.3	2.5	5.2	4.1	3.0	3.5	5.4	5.0	4.7	5.9
Maturity (years)	35.1	35.4	22.9	22.0	24.4	25.3	19.2	22.4	17.7	20.9
Grace period (years)	13.6	8.2	6.2	7.7	6.9	7.1	6.1	6.4	4.9	6.0
Grant element (%)	66.3	62.2	35.7	42.8	49.9	47.3	32.3	35.9	31.2	31.7
Private creditors										
Interest (%)	5.7	11.3	8.8	5.5	5.6	8.4	7.0	0.6	6.0	7.1
Maturity (years)	11.1	10.8	10.6	7.0	4.4	8.1	4.4	5.1	3.2	6.5
Grace period (years)	1.9	0.8	4.8	3.0	1.2	2.9	0.9	3.2	0.8	2.1
Grant element (%)	17.5	-4.0	5.0	15.1	7.1	5.9	8.1	29.9	6.6	7.2
Memorandum items										
Commitments	949	1,115	2,972	2,861	3,288	3,351	1,906	2,718	3,093	2,233
Official creditors	811	874	2,890	2,254	2,605	2,994	1,693	2,421	1,806	2,049
Private creditors	139	242	82	606	683	357	213	297	1,287	184

10. CONTRACTUAL OBLIGATIONS ON OUTSTANDING LONG-TERM DEBT	1999	2000	2001	2002	2003	2004	2005	2006	2007	2008
TOTAL										
Disbursements	2,175	1,721	1,098	619	275	99	49	15	4	1
Principal	3,437	2,399	2,068	1,777	1,711	1,704	1,672	1,588	1,550	1,547
Interest	1,056	946	873	799	724	646	568	506	445	379
Official creditors										
Disbursements	2,075	1,647	1,068	611	272	99	49	15	4	1
Principal	2,044	1,519	1,415	1,403	1,405	1,401	1,371	1,305	1,285	1,285
Interest	805	775	743	695	638	576	514	468	421	368
Bilateral creditors										
Disbursements	827	661	375	188	83	37	13	2	1	0
Principal	1,348	844	682	647	647	633	626	604	576	576
Interest	338	321	309	291	270	246	222	198	175	154
Multilateral creditors										
Disbursements	1,248	986	693	423	189	62	36	13	3	1
Principal	695	675	734	756	758	768	745	701	709	709
Interest	468	455	434	404	368	330	293	270	246	215
Private creditors										
Disbursements	101	74	30	8	4	0	0	0	0	0
Principal	1,393	880	653	374	306	303	301	283	265	262
Interest	251	171	131	104	86	70	54	38	24	11
Commercial banks										
Disbursements	24	16	3	1	0	0	0	0	0	0
Principal	624	437	134	71	10	10	10	9	7	5
Interest	66	32	13	5	2	2	1	1	1	0
Other private										
Disbursements	76	59	27	7	4	0	0	0	0	0
Principal	769	444	519	303	296	293	292	274	258	257
Interest	185	139	118	100	84	68	53	37	24	11

PANAMA

(US$ million, unless otherwise indicated)

1. SUMMARY DEBT DATA

	1970	1980	1990	1992	1993	1994	1995	1996	1997	1998
TOTAL DEBT STOCKS (EDT)	**..**	**2,975**	**6,679**	**6,486**	**6,958**	**7,129**	**6,275**	**6,069**	**6,338**	**6,689**
Long-term debt (LDOD)	**194**	**2,271**	**3,988**	**3,771**	**3,799**	**3,930**	**3,914**	**5,211**	**5,418**	**5,763**
Public and publicly guaranteed	194	2,271	3,988	3,771	3,799	3,930	3,914	5,136	5,074	5,413
Private nonguaranteed	0	0	0	0	0	0	0	75	344	349
Use of IMF credit	**0**	**23**	**272**	**110**	**113**	**133**	**111**	**131**	**142**	**177**
Short-term debt	**..**	**681**	**2,418**	**2,605**	**3,046**	**3,065**	**2,251**	**727**	**777**	**749**
of which interest arrears on LDOD	..	1	1,018	1,205	1,595	1,600	1,652	48	49	21
Official creditors	..	0	266	64	167	192	225	1	0	0
Private creditors	..	1	753	1,141	1,427	1,408	1,427	47	49	21
Memo: principal arrears on LDOD	..	0	2,116	1,972	2,163	2,035	2,127	191	166	107
Official creditors	..	0	554	112	175	198	204	3	5	3
Private creditors	..	0	1,562	1,861	1,989	1,838	1,923	188	161	105
Memo: export credits	..	0	204	84	18	32	56	241	834	188
TOTAL DEBT FLOWS										
Disbursements	**67**	**404**	**6**	**268**	**38**	**54**	**113**	**403**	**1,789**	**770**
Long-term debt	67	404	6	168	25	40	99	327	1,743	729
IMF purchases	0	0	0	101	14	14	13	76	46	41
Principal repayments	**25**	**232**	**121**	**603**	**146**	**165**	**172**	**463**	**1,239**	**360**
Long-term debt	24	215	51	402	136	164	134	411	1,214	346
IMF repurchases	2	17	71	201	10	1	39	52	26	13
Net flows on debt	**77**	**361**	**-115**	**-334**	**-56**	**-98**	**-926**	**20**	**599**	**411**
of which short-term debt	..	189	0	0	51	14	-866	80	49	0
Interest payments (INT)	**..**	**256**	**224**	**364**	**136**	**221**	**144**	**438**	**350**	**385**
Long-term debt	7	252	91	231	80	140	101	392	301	336
IMF charges	0	3	16	79	7	6	7	5	6	7
Short-term debt	..	2	117	55	50	74	36	41	44	42
Net transfers on debt	**..**	**105**	**-339**	**-698**	**-192**	**-318**	**-1,070**	**-418**	**248**	**25**
Total debt service paid (TDS)	**..**	**488**	**345**	**966**	**282**	**386**	**316**	**901**	**1,590**	**745**
Long-term debt	31	466	141	632	215	304	235	803	1,514	682
IMF repurchases and charges	2	20	87	279	17	8	46	57	32	20
Short-term debt (interest only)	..	2	117	55	50	74	36	41	44	42

2. AGGREGATE NET RESOURCE FLOWS AND NET TRANSFERS (LONG-TERM)

	1970	1980	1990	1992	1993	1994	1995	1996	1997	1998
NET RESOURCE FLOWS	**76**	**149**	**213**	**133**	**100**	**421**	**288**	**342**	**1,798**	**1,600**
Net flow of long-term debt (ex. IMF)	44	189	-45	-234	-111	-124	-34	-84	530	383
Foreign direct investment (net)	33	-47	132	139	156	411	289	410	1,256	1,206
Portfolio equity flows	0	0	0	88	0	115	20	5	2	0
Grants (excluding technical coop.)	-1	6	126	141	55	20	13	11	11	10
Memo: technical coop. grants	8	9	-16	27	35	28	43	28	25	27
official net resource flows	10	83	87	-87	-43	-74	-9	-131	130	141
private net resource flows	67	65	127	220	143	495	297	472	1,669	1,459
NET TRANSFERS	**50**	**-174**	**80**	**-173**	**-13**	**241**	**144**	**-85**	**1,465**	**1,224**
Interest on long-term debt	7	252	91	231	80	140	101	392	301	336
Profit remittances on FDI	19	72	42	76	33	40	43	35	33	40
Memo: official net transfers	7	49	-1	-307	-115	-137	-67	-371	63	73
private net transfers	43	-223	81	134	103	378	212	287	1,401	1,151

3. MAJOR ECONOMIC AGGREGATES

	1970	1980	1990	1992	1993	1994	1995	1996	1997	1998
Gross national product (GNP)	1,034	3,393	5,024	6,202	6,959	7,505	7,533	7,827	8,239	8,580
Exports of goods & services (XGS)	..	7,855	5,595	7,482	7,786	8,669	9,271	8,819	9,756	9,764
of which workers remittances	..	2	18	13	17	17	16	16	16	16
Imports of goods & services (MGS)	..	8,222	5,588	7,937	8,068	8,784	9,776	9,240	10,494	11,119
International reserves (RES)	16	117	344	504	597	704	781	867	1,148	954
Current account balance	..	-329	209	-264	-96	16	-369	-302	-604	-1,212

4. DEBT INDICATORS

	1970	1980	1990	1992	1993	1994	1995	1996	1997	1998
EDT / XGS (%)	..	37.9	119.4	86.7	89.4	82.2	67.7	68.8	65.0	68.5
EDT / GNP (%)	..	87.7	132.9	104.6	100.0	95.0	83.3	77.5	76.9	78.0
TDS / XGS (%)	..	6.2	6.2	12.9	3.6	4.5	3.4	10.2	16.3	7.6
INT / XGS (%)	..	3.3	4.0	4.9	1.8	2.5	1.6	5.0	3.6	3.9
INT / GNP (%)	..	7.5	4.5	5.9	2.0	2.9	1.9	5.6	4.3	4.5
RES / EDT (%)	..	4.0	5.1	7.8	8.6	9.9	12.5	14.3	18.1	14.3
RES / MGS (months)	..	0.2	0.7	0.8	0.9	1.0	1.0	1.1	1.3	1.0
Short-term / EDT (%)	..	22.9	36.2	40.2	43.8	43.0	35.9	12.0	12.3	11.2
Concessional / EDT (%)	..	9.0	5.9	7.0	6.3	6.2	6.7	6.8	6.4	5.9
Multilateral / EDT (%)	..	11.0	15.3	10.7	9.0	8.3	9.9	11.2	12.2	14.7

PANAMA

(US$ million, unless otherwise indicated)

	1970	1980	1990	1992	1993	1994	1995	1996	1997	1998
5. LONG-TERM DEBT										
DEBT OUTSTANDING (LDOD)	**194**	**2,271**	**3,988**	**3,771**	**3,799**	**3,930**	**3,914**	**5,211**	**5,418**	**5,763**
Public and publicly guaranteed	**194**	**2,271**	**3,988**	**3,771**	**3,799**	**3,930**	**3,914**	**5,136**	**5,074**	**5,413**
Official creditors	93	595	1,504	1,314	1,307	1,264	1,262	1,070	1,138	1,317
Multilateral	38	327	1,020	694	625	591	619	677	773	980
Concessional	29	129	202	153	146	147	142	133	124	117
Bilateral	55	268	483	620	682	674	643	393	365	337
Concessional	49	138	194	299	294	292	277	282	280	275
Private creditors	101	1,676	2,484	2,457	2,492	2,666	2,652	4,066	3,936	4,097
Bonds	29	395	260	267	260	3	3	3,327	3,328	3,599
Commercial banks	6	1,161	2,102	2,124	2,160	2,599	2,598	690	565	488
Other private	66	120	123	67	72	65	51	49	43	10
Private nonguaranteed	**0**	**0**	**0**	**0**	**0**	**0**	**0**	**75**	**344**	**349**
Bonds	0	0	0	0	0	0	0	75	321	246
Commercial banks	0	0	0	0	0	0	0	0	23	103
Memo:										
IBRD	7	133	462	288	241	206	175	199	209	279
IDA	0	0	0	0	0	0	0	0	0	0
DISBURSEMENTS	**67**	**404**	**6**	**168**	**25**	**40**	**99**	**327**	**1,743**	**729**
Public and publicly guaranteed	**67**	**404**	**6**	**168**	**25**	**40**	**99**	**252**	**1,469**	**645**
Official creditors	15	95	6	165	24	15	95	192	240	242
Multilateral	6	68	0	113	16	15	93	168	201	230
Concessional	6	23	0	1	1	4	5	2	1	4
Bilateral	9	27	6	52	8	0	2	24	39	12
Concessional	8	10	0	51	2	0	0	24	39	12
Private creditors	52	309	0	2	1	25	5	61	1,230	403
Bonds	0	25	0	0	0	0	0	0	1,200	352
Commercial banks	0	272	0	2	1	25	5	55	30	51
Other private	52	13	0	0	0	0	0	5	0	0
Private nonguaranteed	**0**	**0**	**0**	**0**	**0**	**0**	**0**	**75**	**274**	**85**
Bonds	0	0	0	0	0	0	0	75	246	0
Commercial banks	0	0	0	0	0	0	0	0	28	85
Memo:										
IBRD	0	20	0	60	0	2	3	69	53	91
IDA	0	0	0	0	0	0	0	0	0	0
PRINCIPAL REPAYMENTS	**24**	**215**	**51**	**402**	**136**	**164**	**134**	**411**	**1,214**	**346**
Public and publicly guaranteed	**24**	**215**	**51**	**402**	**136**	**164**	**134**	**411**	**1,209**	**267**
Official creditors	5	18	45	393	122	108	117	333	121	111
Multilateral	2	9	43	363	93	92	85	72	70	60
Concessional	1	3	0	34	8	10	11	11	10	10
Bilateral	3	9	2	30	29	16	32	262	51	51
Concessional	2	2	0	7	13	9	11	10	29	29
Private creditors	19	197	6	9	14	56	17	78	1,088	155
Bonds	1	9	2	2	1	1	1	0	987	59
Commercial banks	2	165	1	0	2	47	3	70	95	94
Other private	16	23	3	8	10	8	13	8	6	3
Private nonguaranteed	**0**	**0**	**0**	**0**	**0**	**0**	**0**	**0**	**5**	**80**
Bonds	0	0	0	0	0	0	0	0	0	75
Commercial banks	0	0	0	0	0	0	0	0	5	5
Memo:										
IBRD	1	6	41	178	54	54	43	31	29	26
IDA	0	0	0	0	0	0	0	0	0	0
NET FLOWS ON DEBT	**44**	**189**	**-45**	**-234**	**-111**	**-124**	**-34**	**-84**	**530**	**383**
Public and publicly guaranteed	**44**	**189**	**-45**	**-234**	**-111**	**-124**	**-34**	**-159**	**260**	**378**
Official creditors	11	77	-39	-227	-98	-94	-22	-142	119	131
Multilateral	5	59	-43	-249	-77	-78	8	96	131	170
Concessional	5	20	0	-33	-8	-7	-6	-10	-9	-7
Bilateral	6	18	4	22	-21	-16	-30	-237	-12	-40
Concessional	6	8	0	44	-11	-9	-10	15	10	-18
Private creditors	33	112	-5	-7	-13	-31	-12	-18	142	248
Bonds	-1	16	-2	-2	-1	-1	-1	0	213	293
Commercial banks	-2	107	-1	2	-2	-23	1	-15	-65	-43
Other private	36	-10	-3	-8	-10	-8	-13	-3	-6	-3
Private nonguaranteed	**0**	**0**	**0**	**0**	**0**	**0**	**0**	**75**	**269**	**5**
Bonds	0	0	0	0	0	0	0	75	246	-75
Commercial banks	0	0	0	0	0	0	0	0	23	80
Memo:										
IBRD	-1	15	-41	-118	-54	-52	-40	37	25	65
IDA	0	0	0	0	0	0	0	0	0	0

PANAMA

(US$ million, unless otherwise indicated)

	1970	1980	1990	1992	1993	1994	1995	1996	1997	1998
INTEREST PAYMENTS (LINT)	**7**	**252**	**91**	**231**	**80**	**140**	**101**	**392**	**301**	**336**
Public and publicly guaranteed	**7**	**252**	**91**	**231**	**80**	**140**	**101**	**392**	**292**	**300**
Official creditors	3	35	88	220	73	63	59	241	66	68
Multilateral	1	20	85	172	47	44	39	39	45	53
Concessional	1	3	9	5	3	3	3	3	3	3
Bilateral	1	15	2	48	25	19	20	202	22	15
Concessional	1	4	0	15	17	10	11	10	13	9
Private creditors	4	217	3	11	7	77	42	151	226	232
Bonds	1	40	0	0	1	38	1	0	163	198
Commercial banks	0	168	0	8	3	34	36	147	59	32
Other private	3	9	3	3	3	5	5	4	3	2
Private nonguaranteed	**0**	**0**	**0**	**0**	**0**	**0**	**0**	**0**	**9**	**36**
Bonds	0	0	0	0	0	0	0	0	8	30
Commercial banks	0	0	0	0	0	0	0	0	2	6
Memo:										
IBRD	0	12	27	121	21	18	15	13	15	16
IDA	0	0	0	0	0	0	0	0	0	0
NET TRANSFERS ON DEBT	**37**	**-62**	**-135**	**-465**	**-191**	**-264**	**-135**	**-476**	**229**	**47**
Public and publicly guaranteed	**37**	**-62**	**-135**	**-465**	**-191**	**-264**	**-135**	**-551**	**-31**	**78**
Official creditors	8	42	-127	-447	-171	-157	-81	-382	53	63
Multilateral	3	39	-128	-421	-124	-122	-31	57	86	117
Concessional	4	17	-9	-38	-11	-10	-9	-12	-12	-9
Bilateral	5	4	1	-26	-46	-35	-50	-439	-34	-55
Concessional	5	4	0	29	-28	-20	-21	4	-3	-27
Private creditors	29	-105	-9	-18	-20	-108	-55	-169	-84	16
Bonds	-2	-24	-2	-2	-2	-38	-1	-1	50	95
Commercial banks	-3	-61	-1	-6	-5	-57	-35	-162	-124	-74
Other private	33	-20	-6	-11	-14	-13	-18	-6	-9	-5
Private nonguaranteed	**0**	**0**	**0**	**0**	**0**	**0**	**0**	**75**	**260**	**-31**
Bonds	0	0	0	0	0	0	0	75	239	-105
Commercial banks	0	0	0	0	0	0	0	0	22	74
Memo:										
IBRD	-1	3	-68	-239	-75	-70	-55	25	10	50
IDA	0	0	0	0	0	0	0	0	0	0
DEBT SERVICE (LTDS)	**31**	**466**	**141**	**632**	**215**	**304**	**235**	**803**	**1,514**	**682**
Public and publicly guaranteed	**31**	**466**	**141**	**632**	**215**	**304**	**235**	**803**	**1,501**	**567**
Official creditors	7	52	133	612	194	171	176	574	187	179
Multilateral	3	29	128	534	140	137	124	111	114	113
Concessional	2	6	9	39	12	13	14	14	12	13
Bilateral	5	23	4	78	54	35	52	463	73	66
Concessional	3	6	0	22	30	20	21	20	43	39
Private creditors	23	414	9	20	21	133	59	229	1,314	387
Bonds	2	49	2	2	2	38	1	1	1,150	257
Commercial banks	3	333	1	8	6	81	40	217	154	125
Other private	19	32	6	11	14	13	18	12	9	5
Private nonguaranteed	**0**	**0**	**0**	**0**	**0**	**0**	**0**	**0**	**14**	**116**
Bonds	0	0	0	0	0	0	0	0	8	105
Commercial banks	0	0	0	0	0	0	0	0	6	11
Memo:										
IBRD	1	17	68	299	76	72	58	44	44	41
IDA	0	0	0	0	0	0	0	0	0	0
UNDISBURSED DEBT	**96**	**595**	**222**	**351**	**590**	**581**	**592**	**575**	**679**	**729**
Official creditors	92	522	214	338	557	573	529	448	534	634
Private creditors	5	73	8	14	33	8	63	127	146	95
Memorandum items										
Concessional LDOD	78	267	396	452	439	439	419	414	404	392
Variable rate LDOD	0	1,197	2,318	2,378	2,386	2,671	2,658	3,955	3,055	3,008
Public sector LDOD	194	2,271	3,988	3,771	3,799	3,930	3,914	5,136	5,074	5,413
Private sector LDOD	0	0	0	0	0	0	0	75	344	349

6. CURRENCY COMPOSITION OF LONG-TERM DEBT (PERCENT)

	1970	1980	1990	1992	1993	1994	1995	1996	1997	1998
Deutsche mark	0.0	0.0	0.0	0.0	0.0	0.0	0.0	0.0	0.0	0.0
French franc	0.0	0.0	0.1	0.1	0.1	0.1	0.2	0.1	0.1	0.1
Japanese yen	0.0	9.6	9.4	12.3	10.8	10.3	10.0	2.2	2.5	2.2
Pound sterling	0.0	0.0	0.7	0.6	0.5	0.5	0.4	0.3	0.2	0.2
Swiss franc	0.3	0.0	0.1	0.1	0.1	0.1	0.1	0.0	0.0	0.0
U.S.dollars	94.5	71.0	63.3	67.1	68.7	71.4	71.7	85.7	86.1	89.6
Multiple currency	5.2	11.5	23.8	17.4	15.5	13.9	13.9	10.9	10.4	7.2
Special drawing rights	0.0	0.0	0.4	0.3	0.3	0.2	0.2	0.3	0.3	0.5
All other currencies	0.0	7.9	2.2	2.1	4.0	3.5	3.5	0.5	0.4	0.2

PANAMA

(US$ million, unless otherwise indicated)

	1970	1980	1990	1992	1993	1994	1995	1996	1997	1998
7. DEBT RESTRUCTURINGS										
Total amount rescheduled	..	..	0	28	58	422	5	3,328	0	0
Debt stock rescheduled	..	..	0	0	0	0	0	2	0	0
Principal rescheduled	..	..	0	4	36	260	0	1,876	0	0
Official	..	..	0	0	3	0	0	0	0	0
Private	..	..	0	3	34	260	0	1,876	0	0
Interest rescheduled	..	..	0	24	16	161	0	1,450	0	0
Official	..	..	0	2	0	0	0	0	0	0
Private	..	..	0	22	16	161	0	1,450	0	0
Debt forgiven	..	..	0	3	0	0	0	590	56	51
Memo: interest forgiven	..	..	0	0	0	0	0	0	0	0
Debt stock reduction	..	..	0	0	0	0	0	56	1,227	0
of which debt buyback	..	..	0	0	0	0	0	0	987	0
8. DEBT STOCK-FLOW RECONCILIATION										
Total change in debt stocks	..	..	361	-247	472	171	-854	-206	269	351
Net flows on debt	77	361	-115	-334	-56	-98	-926	20	599	411
Net change in interest arrears	..	..	355	6	390	6	52	-1,604	1	-28
Interest capitalized	..	..	0	24	16	161	0	1,450	0	0
Debt forgiveness or reduction	..	..	0	-3	0	0	0	-646	-296	-51
Cross-currency valuation	..	..	63	-81	6	16	-54	-39	-40	17
Residual	..	..	57	141	118	86	75	612	5	2
9. AVERAGE TERMS OF NEW COMMITMENTS										
ALL CREDITORS										
Interest (%)	6.9	11.3	5.0	6.5	7.7	7.3	5.0	5.9	8.2	7.7
Maturity (years)	15.0	11.4	8.3	20.2	20.6	17.2	17.8	15.6	19.5	14.4
Grace period (years)	4.0	4.5	4.8	5.9	4.6	5.7	3.8	3.9	16.1	7.2
Grant element (%)	16.9	-4.2	22.6	24.0	13.5	16.6	28.5	22.5	11.2	13.9
Official creditors										
Interest (%)	6.0	6.3	5.0	6.4	7.9	7.3	6.9	6.6	7.2	7.3
Maturity (years)	24.4	15.4	8.3	20.4	20.9	17.2	21.2	18.9	20.7	19.1
Grace period (years)	6.1	5.3	4.8	5.9	4.7	5.7	4.5	5.2	5.4	4.6
Grant element (%)	27.9	21.2	22.6	24.3	12.3	16.6	20.0	21.4	17.7	16.4
Private creditors										
Interest (%)	7.9	15.2	0.0	7.5	5.0	0.0	3.3	5.1	8.4	8.0
Maturity (years)	4.3	8.3	0.0	11.5	16.2	0.0	14.6	11.7	19.1	9.8
Grace period (years)	1.6	4.0	0.0	3.5	4.2	0.0	3.0	2.4	18.9	9.8
Grant element (%)	4.5	-24.0	0.0	11.6	29.2	0.0	36.4	23.7	9.5	11.4
Memorandum items										
Commitments	111	534	4	359	274	60	116	277	1,578	693
Official creditors	59	233	4	351	254	60	57	151	329	341
Private creditors	52	300	0	8	20	0	60	127	1,249	352

10. CONTRACTUAL OBLIGATIONS ON OUTSTANDING LONG-TERM DEBT

	1999	2000	2001	2002	2003	2004	2005	2006	2007	2008
TOTAL										
Disbursements	236	189	122	85	52	24	13	4	3	1
Principal	234	237	283	877	279	241	238	246	244	572
Interest	397	403	402	378	347	259	251	240	230	240
Official creditors										
Disbursements	182	162	112	82	52	24	13	4	3	1
Principal	133	131	137	109	125	127	126	121	113	112
Interest	89	94	95	93	89	83	76	68	60	53
Bilateral creditors										
Disbursements	1	1	1	0	0	0	0	0	0	0
Principal	54	50	50	14	14	12	11	11	12	12
Interest	12	9	7	5	5	4	4	4	3	3
Multilateral creditors										
Disbursements	180	161	112	81	52	24	13	4	3	1
Principal	79	81	87	95	111	115	115	110	101	100
Interest	77	85	88	88	85	79	72	64	57	50
Private creditors										
Disbursements	55	27	9	4	0	0	0	0	0	0
Principal	101	106	146	768	154	114	112	125	131	460
Interest	308	308	308	285	257	176	175	173	170	187
Commercial banks										
Disbursements	55	27	9	4	0	0	0	0	0	0
Principal	92	97	95	62	25	23	21	19	11	8
Interest	25	21	15	9	7	5	4	3	2	2
Other private										
Disbursements	0	0	0	0	0	0	0	0	0	0
Principal	10	10	51	706	129	92	92	106	120	452
Interest	284	288	292	276	251	171	171	170	168	186

PAPUA NEW GUINEA

(US$ million, unless otherwise indicated)

	1970	1980	1990	1992	1993	1994	1995	1996	1997	1998
1. SUMMARY DEBT DATA										
TOTAL DEBT STOCKS (EDT)	..	719	2,594	3,789	3,269	2,792	2,506	2,507	2,589	2,692
Long-term debt (LDOD)	209	624	2,461	3,318	2,960	2,678	2,379	2,422	2,388	2,490
Public and publicly guaranteed	36	486	1,523	1,592	1,616	1,732	1,668	1,544	1,338	1,410
Private nonguaranteed	173	139	938	1,726	1,344	946	711	878	1,050	1,080
Use of IMF credit	0	31	61	59	44	16	50	51	48	46
Short-term debt	..	64	72	412	264	99	78	34	154	157
of which interest arrears on LDOD	..	0	0	0	0	0	0	0	0	0
Official creditors	..	0	0	0	0	0	0	0	0	0
Private creditors	..	0	0	0	0	0	0	0	0	0
Memo: principal arrears on LDOD	..	0	0	0	0	0	0	0	0	0
Official creditors	..	0	0	0	0	0	0	0	0	0
Private creditors	..	0	0	0	0	0	0	0	0	0
Memo: export credits	..	0	223	610	556	554	371	354	497	565
TOTAL DEBT FLOWS										
Disbursements	154	150	681	1,093	248	489	240	549	525	215
Long-term debt	154	135	623	1,093	248	489	189	546	525	215
IMF purchases	0	15	58	0	0	0	51	3	0	0
Principal repayments	20	78	391	481	684	741	509	390	425	119
Long-term debt	20	72	388	481	669	710	493	390	425	115
IMF repurchases	0	7	3	0	15	31	16	0	0	4
Net flows on debt	134	108	197	907	-584	-417	-291	115	221	99
of which short-term debt	..	36	-93	295	-148	-165	-21	-44	120	3
Interest payments (INT)	..	72	162	182	168	157	117	100	107	64
Long-term debt	10	52	156	162	143	144	111	97	100	54
IMF charges	0	1	0	4	3	2	1	2	2	2
Short-term debt	..	19	6	16	22	11	5	1	4	8
Net transfers on debt	..	36	35	725	-752	-574	-408	15	114	35
Total debt service paid (TDS)	..	150	553	663	852	897	626	491	531	183
Long-term debt	30	123	544	642	812	854	604	487	525	169
IMF repurchases and charges	0	7	3	4	18	32	17	2	2	6
Short-term debt (interest only)	..	19	6	16	22	11	5	1	4	8
2. AGGREGATE NET RESOURCE FLOWS AND NET TRANSFERS (LONG-TERM)										
NET RESOURCE FLOWS	278	418	694	1,023	-142	69	870	649	316	418
Net flow of long-term debt (ex. IMF)	134	64	235	612	-421	-221	-304	156	101	100
Foreign direct investment (net)	0	76	155	104	62	57	455	111	29	110
Portfolio equity flows	0	0	0	0	0	0	450	187	0	0
Grants (excluding technical coop.)	144	279	304	307	217	234	268	195	187	208
Memo: technical coop. grants	1	13	46	59	65	72	89	120	110	111
official net resource flows	149	313	491	343	242	215	308	235	183	188
private net resource flows	128	105	204	680	-384	-146	562	414	133	230
NET TRANSFERS	268	163	538	751	-400	-205	623	413	66	204
Interest on long-term debt	10	52	156	162	143	144	111	97	100	54
Profit remittances on FDI	0	204	0	110	115	130	136	139	150	160
Memo: official net transfers	149	306	450	291	183	158	245	178	130	142
private net transfers	118	-143	88	460	-583	-362	378	234	-64	63
3. MAJOR ECONOMIC AGGREGATES										
Gross national product (GNP)	626	2,488	3,098	3,905	4,743	5,100	4,692	4,865	4,457	3,500
Exports of goods & services (XGS)	..	1,089	1,487	2,337	2,943	2,909	3,014	2,994	2,592	2,112
of which workers remittances	..	0	0	0	0	0	0	0	0	..
Imports of goods & services (MGS)	..	1,561	1,719	2,434	2,339	2,356	2,415	2,753	2,752	2,152
International reserves (RES)	..	458	427	260	166	120	267	607	381	211
Current account balance	..	-289	-76	95	646	569	674	313	-99	47
4. DEBT INDICATORS										
EDT / XGS (%)	..	66.1	174.4	162.2	111.1	96.0	83.1	83.7	99.9	127.5
EDT / GNP (%)	..	28.9	83.7	97.0	68.9	54.8	53.4	51.5	58.1	76.9
TDS / XGS (%)	..	13.8	37.2	28.4	29.0	30.9	20.8	16.4	20.5	8.6
INT / XGS (%)	..	6.6	10.9	7.8	5.7	5.4	3.9	3.4	4.1	3.0
INT / GNP (%)	..	2.9	5.2	4.7	3.6	3.1	2.5	2.1	2.4	1.8
RES / EDT (%)	..	63.7	16.5	6.9	5.1	4.3	10.6	24.2	14.7	7.8
RES / MGS (months)	..	3.5	3.0	1.3	0.9	0.6	1.3	2.7	1.7	1.2
Short-term / EDT (%)	..	8.9	2.8	10.9	8.1	3.6	3.1	1.4	6.0	5.8
Concessional / EDT (%)	..	11.9	21.5	17.1	22.3	28.5	31.9	32.8	29.8	31.9
Multilateral / EDT (%)	..	21.2	29.5	22.2	26.0	32.9	37.4	34.3	31.0	32.0

PAPUA NEW GUINEA

(US$ million, unless otherwise indicated)

	1970	1980	1990	1992	1993	1994	1995	1996	1997	1998
5. LONG-TERM DEBT										
DEBT OUTSTANDING (LDOD)	**209**	**624**	**2,461**	**3,318**	**2,960**	**2,678**	**2,379**	**2,422**	**2,388**	**2,490**
Public and publicly guaranteed	**36**	**486**	**1,523**	**1,592**	**1,616**	**1,732**	**1,668**	**1,544**	**1,338**	**1,410**
Official creditors	4	184	1,074	1,232	1,305	1,398	1,441	1,378	1,238	1,327
Multilateral	2	152	764	842	851	919	938	860	802	861
Concessional	1	79	359	392	398	438	449	426	395	421
Bilateral	2	32	310	390	454	479	503	519	436	466
Concessional	0	7	199	255	331	358	351	397	376	439
Private creditors	32	302	449	360	311	334	227	166	100	83
Bonds	0	85	37	32	31	30	0	0	0	0
Commercial banks	32	211	307	214	161	207	157	124	69	62
Other private	0	6	105	114	119	97	70	42	31	21
Private nonguaranteed	**173**	**139**	**938**	**1,726**	**1,344**	**946**	**711**	**878**	**1,050**	**1,080**
Bonds	0	0	0	0	0	0	0	0	0	0
Commercial banks	173	139	938	1,726	1,344	946	711	878	1,050	1,080
Memo:										
IBRD	1	55	235	264	266	281	299	270	270	267
IDA	1	55	115	111	109	109	108	105	101	100
DISBURSEMENTS	**154**	**135**	**623**	**1,093**	**248**	**489**	**189**	**546**	**525**	**215**
Public and publicly guaranteed	**43**	**120**	**280**	**120**	**132**	**232**	**135**	**161**	**140**	**78**
Official creditors	5	41	234	101	112	79	122	133	120	77
Multilateral	2	36	180	40	52	65	55	33	72	44
Concessional	1	20	74	15	27	40	19	7	11	10
Bilateral	4	4	55	60	59	13	67	100	47	34
Concessional	0	4	28	26	58	3	15	100	46	34
Private creditors	37	80	45	19	21	154	13	27	20	1
Bonds	0	0	0	0	0	0	0	0	0	0
Commercial banks	37	75	20	6	0	154	13	27	20	1
Other private	0	5	25	14	21	0	0	0	0	0
Private nonguaranteed	**111**	**15**	**343**	**973**	**116**	**256**	**54**	**385**	**386**	**137**
Bonds	0	0	0	0	0	0	0	0	0	0
Commercial banks	111	15	343	973	116	256	54	385	386	137
Memo:										
IBRD	1	2	64	18	21	21	34	21	48	14
IDA	1	13	0	0	0	0	0	0	0	0
PRINCIPAL REPAYMENTS	**20**	**72**	**388**	**481**	**669**	**710**	**493**	**390**	**425**	**115**
Public and publicly guaranteed	**0**	**32**	**184**	**121**	**172**	**251**	**204**	**175**	**207**	**115**
Official creditors	0	6	48	65	86	97	82	94	123	97
Multilateral	0	3	35	47	64	67	47	51	47	48
Concessional	0	1	15	17	30	31	7	7	7	7
Bilateral	0	3	13	18	22	31	35	42	76	49
Concessional	0	1	2	2	5	12	14	12	23	16
Private creditors	0	25	136	56	86	154	122	82	84	18
Bonds	0	8	0	4	5	5	32	0	0	0
Commercial banks	0	17	129	37	62	123	63	64	74	8
Other private	0	1	7	15	19	26	27	18	10	10
Private nonguaranteed	**20**	**40**	**204**	**360**	**497**	**459**	**289**	**215**	**217**	**0**
Bonds	0	0	0	0	0	0	0	0	0	0
Commercial banks	20	40	204	360	497	459	289	215	217	0
Memo:										
IBRD	0	2	14	20	23	24	27	30	28	29
IDA	0	0	1	2	2	2	2	2	2	2
NET FLOWS ON DEBT	**134**	**64**	**235**	**612**	**-421**	**-221**	**-304**	**156**	**101**	**100**
Public and publicly guaranteed	**43**	**89**	**96**	**-1**	**-40**	**-19**	**-69**	**-14**	**-68**	**-37**
Official creditors	5	34	186	36	25	-19	40	40	-4	-20
Multilateral	2	33	145	-6	-12	-1	8	-18	25	-5
Concessional	1	20	59	-2	-3	9	12	0	5	4
Bilateral	4	1	41	43	37	-17	32	58	-29	-15
Concessional	0	4	26	24	53	-9	2	88	24	17
Private creditors	37	55	-91	-37	-65	0	-109	-54	-64	-17
Bonds	0	-8	0	-4	-5	-5	-32	0	0	0
Commercial banks	37	58	-109	-32	-62	31	-50	-37	-54	-7
Other private	0	4	18	-1	2	-26	-27	-18	-10	-10
Private nonguaranteed	**91**	**-25**	**139**	**612**	**-381**	**-203**	**-235**	**170**	**169**	**137**
Bonds	0	0	0	0	0	0	0	0	0	0
Commercial banks	91	-25	139	612	-381	-203	-235	170	169	137
Memo:										
IBRD	1	0	50	-2	-3	-4	7	-9	20	-15
IDA	1	13	-1	-2	-2	-2	-2	-2	-2	-2

PAPUA NEW GUINEA

(US$ million, unless otherwise indicated)

	1970	1980	1990	1992	1993	1994	1995	1996	1997	1998
INTEREST PAYMENTS (LINT)	**10**	**52**	**156**	**162**	**143**	**144**	**111**	**97**	**100**	**54**
Public and publicly guaranteed	**1**	**30**	**86**	**78**	**84**	**79**	**82**	**73**	**64**	**54**
Official creditors	0	7	40	52	59	57	63	56	53	47
Multilateral	0	6	27	37	38	38	44	37	34	32
Concessional	0	1	3	4	4	4	5	4	4	4
Bilateral	0	2	13	16	20	19	19	19	20	15
Concessional	0	0	5	8	9	11	12	11	12	11
Private creditors	1	23	46	26	25	22	19	17	11	7
Bonds	0	7	3	3	3	3	2	0	0	0
Commercial banks	1	15	36	14	12	8	9	11	7	5
Other private	0	0	8	9	10	11	8	7	4	2
Private nonguaranteed	**8**	**22**	**70**	**84**	**59**	**65**	**29**	**24**	**37**	**0**
Bonds	0	0	0	0	0	0	0	0	0	0
Commercial banks	8	22	70	84	59	65	29	24	37	0
Memo:										
IBRD	0	4	15	20	20	20	22	20	18	17
IDA	0	0	1	1	1	1	1	1	1	1
NET TRANSFERS ON DEBT	**124**	**12**	**79**	**450**	**-564**	**-365**	**-414**	**59**	**0**	**46**
Public and publicly guaranteed	**41**	**59**	**10**	**-79**	**-123**	**-98**	**-151**	**-88**	**-132**	**-91**
Official creditors	5	27	146	-16	-34	-76	-23	-16	-57	-67
Multilateral	2	28	118	-43	-50	-40	-36	-55	-8	-36
Concessional	1	19	56	-6	-7	5	8	-4	1	-1
Bilateral	4	-1	28	27	17	-36	13	39	-49	-31
Concessional	0	4	21	16	44	-20	-10	77	12	7
Private creditors	36	32	-137	-63	-90	-22	-128	-72	-75	-24
Bonds	0	-15	-3	-7	-7	-8	-35	0	0	0
Commercial banks	36	43	-145	-46	-75	23	-59	-47	-61	-12
Other private	0	4	11	-10	-8	-37	-34	-24	-14	-12
Private nonguaranteed	**83**	**-47**	**69**	**529**	**-440**	**-268**	**-264**	**147**	**132**	**137**
Bonds	0	0	0	0	0	0	0	0	0	0
Commercial banks	83	-47	69	529	-440	-268	-264	147	132	137
Memo:										
IBRD	1	-4	35	-22	-23	-24	-15	-29	1	-32
IDA	1	12	-2	-2	-3	-3	-3	-3	-3	-3
DEBT SERVICE (LTDS)	**30**	**123**	**544**	**642**	**812**	**854**	**604**	**487**	**525**	**169**
Public and publicly guaranteed	**1**	**61**	**270**	**199**	**256**	**330**	**286**	**249**	**271**	**169**
Official creditors	0	14	88	117	145	154	145	150	177	144
Multilateral	0	9	62	84	103	105	91	88	81	80
Concessional	0	2	18	21	34	35	11	11	10	11
Bilateral	0	5	26	33	43	50	54	61	96	64
Concessional	0	1	7	10	14	23	26	23	34	27
Private creditors	1	48	182	82	111	176	141	99	95	25
Bonds	0	15	3	7	7	8	35	0	0	0
Commercial banks	1	32	165	52	75	131	72	75	81	12
Other private	0	1	15	23	29	37	34	24	14	12
Private nonguaranteed	**29**	**62**	**274**	**444**	**556**	**524**	**318**	**239**	**254**	**0**
Bonds	0	0	0	0	0	0	0	0	0	0
Commercial banks	29	62	274	444	556	524	318	239	254	0
Memo:										
IBRD	0	6	28	40	44	45	49	50	47	45
IDA	0	0	2	2	3	3	3	3	3	3
UNDISBURSED DEBT	**41**	**181**	**527**	**646**	**701**	**670**	**687**	**518**	**367**	**265**
Official creditors	41	151	476	617	636	595	625	489	361	260
Private creditors	0	30	51	29	65	75	62	29	6	5
Memorandum items										
Concessional LDOD	1	86	558	647	729	796	800	822	771	860
Variable rate LDOD	173	271	1,339	2,075	1,661	1,399	1,139	1,214	1,308	1,366
Public sector LDOD	36	463	1,501	1,579	1,607	1,725	1,667	1,517	1,308	1,371
Private sector LDOD	173	162	960	1,739	1,354	952	718	752	760	664
6. CURRENCY COMPOSITION OF LONG-TERM DEBT (PERCENT)										
Deutsche mark	0.0	5.2	1.8	1.7	1.5	1.6	1.6	1.6	1.5	1.5
French franc	0.0	0.0	0.2	0.2	0.1	0.1	0.1	0.1	0.1	0.1
Japanese yen	0.0	4.4	20.4	25.8	30.0	24.8	21.3	23.5	25.3	27.8
Pound sterling	0.0	2.7	2.1	1.2	1.0	0.7	0.6	0.9	1.2	1.1
Swiss franc	0.0	5.8	1.5	1.3	0.0	0.0	0.0	0.0	0.0	0.0
U.S.dollars	2.8	35.0	27.3	22.0	19.6	20.7	19.4	18.6	18.4	17.4
Multiple currency	2.2	27.4	37.9	41.7	42.7	44.3	46.1	44.7	45.9	45.6
Special drawing rights	0.0	0.0	0.3	0.4	0.4	0.4	0.5	0.5	0.5	0.7
All other currencies	95.0	19.5	8.5	5.7	4.7	7.4	10.4	10.1	7.1	5.8

PAPUA NEW GUINEA

(US$ million, unless otherwise indicated)

	1970	1980	1990	1992	1993	1994	1995	1996	1997	1998
7. DEBT RESTRUCTURINGS										
Total amount rescheduled	..	..	0	0	0	0	0	0	0	0
Debt stock rescheduled	..	..	0	0	0	0	0	0	0	0
Principal rescheduled	..	..	0	0	0	0	0	0	0	0
Official	..	..	0	0	0	0	0	0	0	0
Private	..	..	0	0	0	0	0	0	0	0
Interest rescheduled	..	..	0	0	0	0	0	0	0	0
Official	..	..	0	0	0	0	0	0	0	0
Private	..	..	0	0	0	0	0	0	0	0
Debt forgiven	..	..	0	0	0	0	0	9	0	0
Memo: interest forgiven	..	..	0	0	0	0	0	0	0	0
Debt stock reduction	..	..	0	0	0	0	0	0	0	0
of which debt buyback	..	..	0	0	0	0	0	0	0	0
8. DEBT STOCK-FLOW RECONCILIATION										
Total change in debt stocks	..	..	278	1,015	-520	-476	-286	1	83	103
Net flows on debt	134	108	197	907	-584	-417	-291	115	221	99
Net change in interest arrears	..	..	0	0	0	0	0	0	0	0
Interest capitalized	..	..	0	0	0	0	0	0	0	0
Debt forgiveness or reduction	..	..	0	0	0	0	0	-9	0	0
Cross-currency valuation	..	..	58	-24	53	85	-6	-62	-70	64
Residual	..	..	23	132	11	-145	10	-43	-68	-59
9. AVERAGE TERMS OF NEW COMMITMENTS										
ALL CREDITORS										
Interest (%)	6.4	11.2	6.0	2.9	4.8	7.4	5.2	1.8	5.6	6.3
Maturity (years)	21.7	17.7	16.0	28.8	19.7	5.6	10.6	28.8	27.5	15.6
Grace period (years)	8.1	4.8	4.6	9.1	4.6	1.5	4.4	8.6	6.2	3.6
Grant element (%)	25.4	1.1	22.7	57.4	31.3	6.8	23.2	59.6	32.9	20.6
Official creditors										
Interest (%)	5.4	5.8	5.7	2.9	5.8	6.2	5.2	1.8	5.6	6.3
Maturity (years)	20.9	29.1	17.3	28.8	23.6	18.2	10.6	28.8	27.5	15.6
Grace period (years)	5.2	6.9	4.9	9.1	6.0	4.3	4.4	8.6	6.2	3.6
Grant element (%)	30.5	34.9	24.5	57.4	31.3	22.9	23.2	59.6	32.9	20.6
Private creditors										
Interest (%)	7.7	15.5	7.2	0.0	3.1	7.5	0.0	0.0	0.0	0.0
Maturity (years)	22.9	8.8	9.5	0.0	12.3	4.1	0.0	0.0	0.0	0.0
Grace period (years)	12.2	3.1	3.2	0.0	2.0	1.2	0.0	0.0	0.0	0.0
Grant element (%)	18.0	-25.1	13.4	0.0	31.2	4.9	0.0	0.0	0.0	0.0
Memorandum items										
Commitments	91	184	247	170	163	183	175	71	64	5
Official creditors	53	80	207	170	106	19	175	71	64	5
Private creditors	37	103	41	0	57	164	0	0	0	0

10. CONTRACTUAL OBLIGATIONS ON OUTSTANDING LONG-TERM DEBT

	1999	2000	2001	2002	2003	2004	2005	2006	2007	2008
TOTAL										
Disbursements	102	75	47	22	8	5	1	1	0	0
Principal	218	223	225	210	204	201	188	185	181	181
Interest	119	110	99	88	77	67	56	47	37	28
Official creditors										
Disbursements	99	74	46	22	8	5	1	1	0	0
Principal	93	97	102	91	88	85	78	75	72	71
Interest	50	48	45	41	37	33	30	27	23	21
Bilateral creditors										
Disbursements	37	26	16	8	1	1	1	0	0	0
Principal	32	37	42	32	32	32	31	29	29	29
Interest	16	15	14	13	12	11	10	9	9	8
Multilateral creditors										
Disbursements	61	47	30	14	6	4	1	0	0	0
Principal	61	60	60	60	56	54	47	46	43	43
Interest	35	33	31	28	25	22	20	17	15	13
Private creditors										
Disbursements	3	1	1	0	0	0	0	0	0	0
Principal	125	125	123	118	116	116	110	110	110	110
Interest	69	62	54	47	40	33	27	20	14	7
Commercial banks										
Disbursements	3	1	1	0	0	0	0	0	0	0
Principal	10	10	10	9	8	8	2	2	2	2
Interest	2	2	2	2	1	1	1	1	1	0
Other private										
Disbursements	0	0	0	0	0	0	0	0	0	0
Principal	116	116	113	109	108	108	108	108	108	108
Interest	67	59	52	45	39	32	26	19	13	7

PARAGUAY

(US$ million, unless otherwise indicated)

	1970	1980	1990	1992	1993	1994	1995	1996	1997	1998
1. SUMMARY DEBT DATA										
TOTAL DEBT STOCKS (EDT)	**..**	**955**	**2,104**	**1,632**	**1,596**	**1,984**	**2,240**	**2,162**	**2,053**	**2,305**
Long-term debt (LDOD)	**112**	**780**	**1,731**	**1,384**	**1,307**	**1,375**	**1,456**	**1,419**	**1,537**	**1,635**
Public and publicly guaranteed	112	630	1,712	1,363	1,281	1,358	1,439	1,398	1,488	1,593
Private nonguaranteed	0	151	19	21	26	18	17	21	49	43
Use of IMF credit	**0**	**0**	**0**	**0**	**0**	**0**	**0**	**0**	**0**	**0**
Short-term debt	**..**	**174**	**373**	**248**	**289**	**608**	**784**	**743**	**516**	**669**
of which interest arrears on LDOD	..	0	115	30	28	28	8	10	11	10
Official creditors	..	0	29	13	17	18	4	6	6	6
Private creditors	..	0	86	17	11	11	4	4	5	4
Memo: principal arrears on LDOD	..	2	321	100	94	76	64	56	63	68
Official creditors	..	0	61	25	32	17	16	13	24	30
Private creditors	..	1	259	75	62	59	48	43	39	38
Memo: export credits	..	0	501	307	213	211	194	125	131	130
TOTAL DEBT FLOWS										
Disbursements	**14**	**206**	**77**	**128**	**100**	**148**	**216**	**176**	**335**	**140**
Long-term debt	14	206	77	128	100	148	216	176	335	140
IMF purchases	0	0	0	0	0	0	0	0	0	0
Principal repayments	**7**	**79**	**235**	**380**	**197**	**160**	**159**	**133**	**125**	**112**
Long-term debt	7	79	235	380	197	160	159	133	125	112
IMF repurchases	0	0	0	0	0	0	0	0	0	0
Net flows on debt	**7**	**156**	**-83**	**-275**	**-55**	**308**	**253**	**-1**	**-18**	**182**
of which short-term debt	..	29	75	-23	43	319	196	-44	-228	154
Interest payments (INT)	**..**	**66**	**90**	**246**	**88**	**96**	**129**	**107**	**103**	**106**
Long-term debt	4	45	77	232	80	74	87	60	66	72
IMF charges	0	0	0	0	0	0	0	0	0	0
Short-term debt	..	22	13	15	9	22	42	47	37	34
Net transfers on debt	**..**	**90**	**-173**	**-521**	**-143**	**212**	**124**	**-108**	**-121**	**76**
Total debt service paid (TDS)	**..**	**145**	**325**	**626**	**286**	**256**	**288**	**240**	**228**	**218**
Long-term debt	11	124	312	612	277	234	246	193	191	184
IMF repurchases and charges	0	0	0	0	0	0	0	0	0	0
Short-term debt (interest only)	..	22	13	15	9	22	42	47	37	34
2. AGGREGATE NET RESOURCE FLOWS AND NET TRANSFERS (LONG-TERM)										
NET RESOURCE FLOWS	**12**	**169**	**-75**	**-71**	**34**	**187**	**275**	**309**	**501**	**305**
Net flow of long-term debt (ex. IMF)	7	127	-158	-252	-98	-12	57	43	210	28
Foreign direct investment (net)	4	32	76	137	111	180	184	246	270	256
Portfolio equity flows	0	0	0	0	0	0	0	0	0	0
Grants (excluding technical coop.)	1	10	7	43	21	19	34	20	22	21
Memo: technical coop. grants	7	21	40	58	57	54	63	51	51	42
official net resource flows	5	48	-142	-41	-26	50	114	81	209	69
private net resource flows	7	120	67	-31	61	138	160	227	293	236
NET TRANSFERS	**4**	**70**	**-174**	**-325**	**-71**	**83**	**153**	**207**	**390**	**183**
Interest on long-term debt	4	45	77	232	80	74	87	60	66	72
Profit remittances on FDI	5	54	22	22	25	30	35	42	45	50
Memo: official net transfers	2	31	-199	-151	-84	-12	43	24	149	3
private net transfers	1	38	25	-174	14	95	109	183	241	180
3. MAJOR ECONOMIC AGGREGATES										
Gross national product (GNP)	585	4,621	5,381	6,403	6,918	7,919	9,038	9,725	9,615	8,657
Exports of goods & services (XGS)	90	781	1,989	2,716	3,656	4,148	5,031	4,821	4,583	4,151
of which workers remittances	..	..	..	..	..	..	..	..	..	58
Imports of goods & services (MGS)	111	1,399	2,215	2,702	3,511	4,235	5,467	5,193	5,112	4,416
International reserves (RES)	18	783	675	573	645	1,030	1,040	882	796	784
Current account balance	-16	-618	-171	87	245	-56	-364	-317	-483	-265
4. DEBT INDICATORS										
EDT / XGS (%)	..	122.2	105.8	60.1	43.7	47.8	44.5	44.8	44.8	55.5
EDT / GNP (%)	..	20.7	39.1	25.5	23.1	25.1	24.8	22.2	21.4	26.6
TDS / XGS (%)	..	18.6	16.3	23.0	7.8	6.2	5.7	5.0	5.0	5.3
INT / XGS (%)	..	8.5	4.5	9.1	2.4	2.3	2.6	2.2	2.3	2.6
INT / GNP (%)	..	1.4	1.7	3.8	1.3	1.2	1.4	1.1	1.1	1.2
RES / EDT (%)	..	82.0	32.1	35.1	40.4	51.9	46.4	40.8	38.8	34.0
RES / MGS (months)	1.9	6.7	3.7	2.6	2.2	2.9	2.3	2.0	1.9	2.1
Short-term / EDT (%)	..	18.3	17.7	15.2	18.1	30.7	35.0	34.4	25.1	29.0
Concessional / EDT (%)	..	30.6	26.3	41.0	44.1	38.5	36.7	37.5	42.7	39.8
Multilateral / EDT (%)	..	20.2	34.8	42.5	43.0	35.8	34.7	37.7	43.1	42.6

PARAGUAY

(US$ million, unless otherwise indicated)

	1970	1980	1990	1992	1993	1994	1995	1996	1997	1998
5. LONG-TERM DEBT										
DEBT OUTSTANDING (LDOD)	**112**	**780**	**1,731**	**1,384**	**1,307**	**1,375**	**1,456**	**1,419**	**1,537**	**1,635**
Public and publicly guaranteed	**112**	**630**	**1,712**	**1,363**	**1,281**	**1,358**	**1,439**	**1,398**	**1,488**	**1,593**
Official creditors	83	409	1,182	1,139	1,124	1,223	1,320	1,307	1,409	1,525
Multilateral	45	193	733	693	687	711	777	816	884	982
Concessional	35	97	229	270	295	301	332	356	385	406
Bilateral	38	216	450	446	437	513	543	491	525	544
Concessional	29	195	325	399	409	463	491	454	491	512
Private creditors	30	221	530	224	158	134	119	91	79	67
Bonds	0	0	0	0	0	0	0	0	0	0
Commercial banks	2	105	263	87	55	46	49	42	35	32
Other private	28	116	267	138	103	89	71	49	44	36
Private nonguaranteed	**0**	**151**	**19**	**21**	**26**	**18**	**17**	**21**	**49**	**43**
Bonds	0	0	0	0	0	0	0	0	0	0
Commercial banks	0	151	19	21	26	18	17	21	49	43
Memo:										
IBRD	6	80	279	213	185	162	154	138	143	165
IDA	18	45	41	39	38	37	36	34	33	31
DISBURSEMENTS	**14**	**206**	**77**	**128**	**100**	**148**	**216**	**176**	**335**	**140**
Public and publicly guaranteed	**14**	**158**	**77**	**124**	**88**	**148**	**216**	**166**	**301**	**140**
Official creditors	7	55	50	95	76	142	204	166	291	140
Multilateral	4	40	31	55	58	73	129	136	166	131
Concessional	2	8	7	35	33	16	41	33	48	27
Bilateral	4	15	19	40	18	70	75	30	124	9
Concessional	3	11	18	29	11	47	72	30	116	9
Private creditors	7	103	27	28	12	6	12	0	10	0
Bonds	0	0	0	0	0	0	0	0	0	0
Commercial banks	2	33	2	2	3	3	12	0	0	0
Other private	5	69	25	27	9	2	0	0	10	0
Private nonguaranteed	**0**	**48**	**0**	**5**	**12**	**0**	**1**	**10**	**34**	**0**
Bonds	0	0	0	0	0	0	0	0	0	0
Commercial banks	0	48	0	5	12	0	1	10	34	0
Memo:										
IBRD	2	30	16	10	8	7	26	28	41	37
IDA	2	3	0	0	0	0	0	0	0	0
PRINCIPAL REPAYMENTS	**7**	**79**	**235**	**380**	**197**	**160**	**159**	**133**	**125**	**112**
Public and publicly guaranteed	**7**	**44**	**226**	**376**	**191**	**152**	**158**	**127**	**119**	**106**
Official creditors	3	17	199	179	123	112	124	104	104	92
Multilateral	1	4	62	68	72	76	77	67	60	59
Concessional	1	1	6	7	9	10	10	9	8	9
Bilateral	3	13	137	111	51	36	47	37	43	33
Concessional	1	9	21	26	25	32	39	26	36	29
Private creditors	4	27	27	197	68	41	34	23	16	14
Bonds	0	0	0	0	0	0	0	0	0	0
Commercial banks	0	17	10	90	32	15	10	5	6	4
Other private	3	10	18	107	36	26	24	18	10	10
Private nonguaranteed	**0**	**36**	**9**	**4**	**6**	**8**	**1**	**6**	**6**	**6**
Bonds	0	0	0	0	0	0	0	0	0	0
Commercial banks	0	36	9	4	6	8	1	6	6	6
Memo:										
IBRD	0	2	40	42	42	43	41	34	26	23
IDA	0	0	1	1	1	1	1	1	2	2
NET FLOWS ON DEBT	**7**	**127**	**-158**	**-252**	**-98**	**-12**	**57**	**43**	**210**	**28**
Public and publicly guaranteed	**7**	**114**	**-149**	**-252**	**-103**	**-4**	**58**	**38**	**182**	**34**
Official creditors	4	38	-149	-84	-47	31	81	61	187	48
Multilateral	3	36	-31	-13	-14	-3	52	69	106	72
Concessional	2	6	1	28	25	6	31	24	39	18
Bilateral	1	2	-118	-72	-33	34	28	-8	81	-24
Concessional	2	2	-3	2	-14	15	32	4	80	-19
Private creditors	3	76	0	-168	-56	-35	-23	-23	-5	-14
Bonds	0	0	0	0	0	0	0	0	0	0
Commercial banks	2	16	-7	-88	-28	-11	2	-5	-6	-4
Other private	2	60	8	-80	-28	-24	-24	-18	0	-10
Private nonguaranteed	**0**	**13**	**-9**	**1**	**6**	**-7**	**-1**	**4**	**28**	**-6**
Bonds	0	0	0	0	0	0	0	0	0	0
Commercial banks	0	13	-9	1	6	-7	-1	4	28	-6
Memo:										
IBRD	1	29	-24	-32	-34	-36	-16	-6	15	15
IDA	2	3	-1	-1	-1	-1	-1	-1	-2	-2

PARAGUAY

(US$ million, unless otherwise indicated)

	1970	1980	1990	1992	1993	1994	1995	1996	1997	1998
INTEREST PAYMENTS (LINT)	**4**	**45**	**77**	**232**	**80**	**74**	**87**	**60**	**66**	**72**
Public and publicly guaranteed	**4**	**35**	**77**	**231**	**79**	**74**	**87**	**60**	**63**	**70**
Official creditors	3	17	57	110	58	62	71	57	60	66
Multilateral	1	10	47	42	41	42	41	38	40	47
Concessional	1	1	4	5	5	6	6	7	6	8
Bilateral	1	7	11	68	17	20	30	19	19	19
Concessional	1	5	10	17	15	18	22	16	17	17
Private creditors	1	18	20	121	21	12	16	3	3	4
Bonds	0	0	0	0	0	0	0	0	0	0
Commercial banks	0	12	2	66	9	3	2	1	2	2
Other private	1	7	18	56	13	10	14	2	1	2
Private nonguaranteed	**0**	**9**	**0**	**0**	**1**	**0**	**0**	**0**	**3**	**3**
Bonds	0	0	0	0	0	0	0	0	0	0
Commercial banks	0	9	0	0	1	0	0	0	3	3
Memo:										
IBRD	0	6	25	21	19	16	15	11	10	11
IDA	0	0	0	0	0	0	0	0	0	0
NET TRANSFERS ON DEBT	**4**	**82**	**-235**	**-483**	**-178**	**-86**	**-30**	**-17**	**144**	**-44**
Public and publicly guaranteed	**4**	**79**	**-226**	**-484**	**-183**	**-78**	**-29**	**-21**	**119**	**-35**
Official creditors	1	22	-206	-194	-105	-31	9	4	127	-18
Multilateral	2	26	-78	-55	-55	-45	11	31	66	25
Concessional	1	5	-3	23	19	0	24	18	33	9
Bilateral	0	-5	-128	-140	-50	14	-2	-26	62	-43
Concessional	2	-4	-13	-15	-29	-3	11	-12	63	-37
Private creditors	3	57	-20	-290	-77	-47	-39	-26	-9	-17
Bonds	0	0	0	0	0	0	0	0	0	0
Commercial banks	2	4	-10	-154	-37	-14	0	-6	-8	-6
Other private	1	53	-10	-136	-40	-33	-39	-20	-1	-12
Private nonguaranteed	**0**	**4**	**-9**	**0**	**5**	**-7**	**-1**	**4**	**25**	**-9**
Bonds	0	0	0	0	0	0	0	0	0	0
Commercial banks	0	4	-9	0	5	-7	-1	4	25	-9
Memo:										
IBRD	1	23	-49	-52	-53	-52	-30	-18	5	4
IDA	2	2	-1	-1	-1	-1	-2	-2	-2	-2
DEBT SERVICE (LTDS)	**11**	**124**	**312**	**612**	**277**	**234**	**246**	**193**	**191**	**184**
Public and publicly guaranteed	**11**	**79**	**303**	**607**	**270**	**226**	**245**	**187**	**182**	**175**
Official creditors	6	34	256	289	181	173	195	161	163	158
Multilateral	2	14	109	110	113	117	118	105	101	106
Concessional	1	3	9	12	14	16	17	16	15	18
Bilateral	4	20	147	179	68	56	77	56	63	52
Concessional	2	15	30	43	40	50	61	41	53	46
Private creditors	5	45	47	318	89	53	50	26	19	17
Bonds	0	0	0	0	0	0	0	0	0	0
Commercial banks	0	29	12	156	40	17	11	6	8	6
Other private	4	16	35	163	49	36	39	20	11	12
Private nonguaranteed	**0**	**45**	**9**	**4**	**7**	**8**	**1**	**6**	**9**	**9**
Bonds	0	0	0	0	0	0	0	0	0	0
Commercial banks	0	45	9	4	7	8	1	6	9	9
Memo:										
IBRD	1	7	65	62	61	59	56	45	36	33
IDA	0	1	1	1	1	1	2	2	2	2
UNDISBURSED DEBT	**47**	**567**	**563**	**726**	**815**	**1,029**	**1,169**	**1,040**	**969**	**902**
Official creditors	41	423	455	711	809	1,029	1,168	1,040	969	902
Private creditors	5	145	107	15	6	1	1	1	1	0
Memorandum items										
Concessional LDOD	64	292	553	669	703	764	823	810	876	918
Variable rate LDOD	0	213	287	142	125	123	150	182	299	370
Public sector LDOD	110	628	1,712	1,363	1,281	1,358	1,439	1,398	1,488	1,593
Private sector LDOD	2	152	19	21	26	18	17	21	49	43

6. CURRENCY COMPOSITION OF LONG-TERM DEBT (PERCENT)

	1970	1980	1990	1992	1993	1994	1995	1996	1997	1998
Deutsche mark	11.4	9.4	11.5	10.8	10.0	10.1	9.1	6.6	5.9	5.5
French franc	0.0	0.3	10.5	6.4	4.5	3.6	2.8	2.5	1.8	1.6
Japanese yen	0.0	5.0	15.6	19.2	20.9	23.9	22.9	21.7	20.6	20.6
Pound sterling	0.3	0.6	2.0	0.5	0.4	0.3	0.3	0.3	0.2	0.2
Swiss franc	0.0	0.1	0.3	0.1	0.1	0.1	0.1	0.1	0.1	0.1
U.S.dollars	66.4	56.2	17.2	18.0	19.8	22.1	28.2	34.3	41.7	44.2
Multiple currency	19.7	22.9	37.9	42.7	43.2	38.8	35.0	32.2	27.8	26.2
Special drawing rights	0.0	0.0	0.8	0.8	0.8	0.8	0.7	1.4	1.2	1.1
All other currencies	2.2	5.5	4.2	1.5	0.3	0.3	0.9	0.9	0.7	0.5

PARAGUAY

(US$ million, unless otherwise indicated)

	1970	1980	1990	1992	1993	1994	1995	1996	1997	1998
7. DEBT RESTRUCTURINGS										
Total amount rescheduled	..	..	0	0	0	0	0	0	0	0
Debt stock rescheduled	..	..	0	0	0	0	0	0	0	0
Principal rescheduled	..	..	0	0	0	0	0	0	0	0
Official	..	..	0	0	0	0	0	0	0	0
Private	..	..	0	0	0	0	0	0	0	0
Interest rescheduled	..	..	0	0	0	0	0	0	0	0
Official	..	..	0	0	0	0	0	0	0	0
Private	..	..	0	0	0	0	0	0	0	0
Debt forgiven	..	..	16	28	2	0	0	0	0	0
Memo: interest forgiven	..	..	0	0	0	0	0	0	0	0
Debt stock reduction	..	..	436	2	0	0	0	0	0	0
of which debt buyback	..	..	111	0	0	0	0	0	0	0
8. DEBT STOCK-FLOW RECONCILIATION										
Total change in debt stocks	..	..	-278	-433	-36	388	256	-78	-109	252
Net flows on debt	7	156	-83	-275	-55	308	253	-1	-18	182
Net change in interest arrears	..	..	38	-90	-2	0	-21	3	1	-1
Interest capitalized	..	..	0	0	0	0	0	0	0	0
Debt forgiveness or reduction	..	..	-340	-30	-2	0	0	0	0	0
Cross-currency valuation	..	..	676	-36	11	60	-2	-67	-67	53
Residual	..	..	-567	-2	11	20	26	-13	-25	18
9. AVERAGE TERMS OF NEW COMMITMENTS										
ALL CREDITORS										
Interest (%)	5.7	7.0	3.5	7.3	4.9	5.1	5.6	7.4	7.1	7.5
Maturity (years)	24.9	24.2	34.4	21.9	27.1	21.6	19.0	9.1	14.9	25.6
Grace period (years)	5.5	6.6	10.1	5.6	6.9	7.1	5.5	3.9	4.4	2.4
Grant element (%)	33.1	25.2	53.9	18.6	38.2	34.8	28.1	10.8	15.6	15.2
Official creditors										
Interest (%)	4.9	5.4	3.5	7.3	4.8	5.1	5.5	7.4	7.1	7.5
Maturity (years)	28.5	27.9	34.4	22.1	27.4	21.6	19.3	9.1	15.3	25.6
Grace period (years)	6.3	7.2	10.1	5.7	6.9	7.1	5.6	3.9	4.5	2.4
Grant element (%)	39.0	36.9	53.9	18.8	38.9	34.8	28.8	10.8	16.0	15.2
Private creditors										
Interest (%)	10.1	13.0	0.0	9.8	8.3	0.0	7.9	0.0	7.1	0.0
Maturity (years)	5.3	10.5	0.0	3.7	8.1	0.0	9.8	0.0	6.0	0.0
Grace period (years)	1.4	4.6	0.0	0.7	3.1	0.0	2.2	0.0	0.5	0.0
Grant element (%)	-0.2	-18.2	0.0	0.4	6.3	0.0	7.8	0.0	7.0	0.0
Memorandum items										
Commitments	14	99	117	483	175	338	364	74	252	61
Official creditors	12	78	117	478	171	338	352	74	242	61
Private creditors	2	21	0	5	3	0	12	0	10	0

10. CONTRACTUAL OBLIGATIONS ON OUTSTANDING LONG-TERM DEBT

	1999	2000	2001	2002	2003	2004	2005	2006	2007	2008
TOTAL										
Disbursements	307	247	153	84	51	26	14	8	5	4
Principal	154	199	219	163	157	153	148	152	125	118
Interest	93	98	94	90	84	77	69	61	53	46
Official creditors										
Disbursements	307	247	153	84	51	26	14	8	5	4
Principal	139	187	207	153	148	146	141	152	125	118
Interest	89	95	92	88	82	76	69	61	53	46
Bilateral creditors										
Disbursements	60	38	23	13	7	3	2	0	0	0
Principal	42	50	50	46	43	44	44	37	37	30
Interest	21	20	19	17	15	14	12	11	9	8
Multilateral creditors										
Disbursements	247	209	130	71	44	23	13	8	5	4
Principal	97	138	157	107	105	101	97	115	88	88
Interest	69	75	73	71	67	62	56	51	44	38
Private creditors										
Disbursements	0	0	0	0	0	0	0	0	0	0
Principal	15	12	12	10	10	8	7	0	0	0
Interest	4	3	2	2	1	1	0	0	0	0
Commercial banks										
Disbursements	0	0	0	0	0	0	0	0	0	0
Principal	2	2	2	1	1	1	1	0	0	0
Interest	1	1	1	0	0	0	0	0	0	0
Other private										
Disbursements	0	0	0	0	0	0	0	0	0	0
Principal	14	10	10	9	8	6	6	0	0	0
Interest	3	2	2	2	1	1	0	0	0	0

PERU

(US$ million, unless otherwise indicated)

	1970	1980	1990	1992	1993	1994	1995	1996	1997	1998
1. SUMMARY DEBT DATA										
TOTAL DEBT STOCKS (EDT)	..	9,386	20,067	20,338	23,573	26,528	30,852	29,328	30,523	32,397
Long-term debt (LDOD)	2,655	6,828	13,963	15,808	16,949	18,854	20,215	21,945	22,680	24,094
Public and publicly guaranteed	856	6,218	13,633	15,580	16,385	17,681	18,927	20,567	20,204	20,803
Private nonguaranteed	1,799	610	330	228	564	1,173	1,288	1,378	2,476	3,290
Use of IMF credit	10	474	755	631	883	938	955	924	1,011	905
Short-term debt	..	2,084	5,350	3,899	5,742	6,736	9,681	6,459	6,832	7,399
of which interest arrears on LDOD	..	0	3,733	1,793	4,090	4,450	4,606	221	178	181
Official creditors	..	0	1,386	481	252	210	211	138	129	130
Private creditors	..	0	2,347	1,313	3,838	4,239	4,395	83	49	50
Memo: principal arrears on LDOD	..	0	8,345	4,739	4,088	4,148	4,166	862	735	741
Official creditors	..	0	3,215	1,675	1,023	1,017	1,018	699	652	652
Private creditors	..	0	5,130	3,064	3,065	3,131	3,147	163	84	90
Memo: export credits	..	0	4,632	6,656	6,464	6,428	5,775	5,183	4,470	4,563
TOTAL DEBT FLOWS										
Disbursements	405	1,452	291	699	2,723	1,223	880	785	3,016	1,433
Long-term debt	387	1,308	291	699	1,826	1,223	880	785	2,795	1,433
IMF purchases	18	145	0	0	897	0	0	0	221	0
Principal repayments	360	1,187	229	539	1,620	601	520	1,227	1,495	897
Long-term debt	333	1,019	166	491	980	601	520	1,227	1,421	752
IMF repurchases	27	168	63	49	641	0	0	0	74	145
Net flows on debt	591	775	128	347	649	1,256	3,149	722	1,937	1,100
of which short-term debt	..	510	66	187	-454	634	2,789	1,164	416	564
Interest payments (INT)	..	964	247	465	1,138	542	721	1,705	1,405	1,556
Long-term debt	162	670	91	313	779	393	485	1,308	971	1,108
IMF charges	0	35	74	51	266	47	52	41	47	45
Short-term debt	..	259	82	101	94	102	184	356	387	403
Net transfers on debt	..	-189	-119	-118	-490	715	2,429	-983	532	-456
Total debt service paid (TDS)	..	2,151	476	1,004	2,758	1,143	1,240	2,932	2,900	2,454
Long-term debt	495	1,689	257	803	1,758	993	1,004	2,535	2,392	1,860
IMF repurchases and charges	27	202	137	100	906	47	52	41	121	191
Short-term debt (interest only)	..	259	82	101	94	102	184	356	387	403
2. AGGREGATE NET RESOURCE FLOWS AND NET TRANSFERS (LONG-TERM)										
NET RESOURCE FLOWS	2	347	346	583	2,977	4,908	4,243	5,762	4,075	3,024
Net flow of long-term debt (ex. IMF)	54	289	125	209	846	622	360	-442	1,374	681
Foreign direct investment (net)	-70	27	41	136	670	3,084	2,000	3,226	1,785	1,930
Portfolio equity flows	0	0	0	0	1,226	977	1,611	2,740	692	174
Grants (excluding technical coop.)	18	31	180	238	236	226	271	238	224	239
Memo: technical coop. grants	13	64	128	113	119	99	126	125	142	175
official net resource flows	54	414	287	544	903	388	588	263	1,226	300
private net resource flows	-52	-67	59	39	2,074	4,521	3,655	5,500	2,849	2,724
NET TRANSFERS	-233	-580	245	214	2,138	4,436	3,659	4,205	2,855	1,636
Interest on long-term debt	162	670	91	313	779	393	485	1,308	971	1,108
Profit remittances on FDI	73	256	10	56	61	80	99	250	250	280
Memo: official net transfers	37	262	236	285	172	42	193	-180	749	-452
private net transfers	-270	-842	8	-72	1,965	4,394	3,466	4,385	2,105	2,088
3. MAJOR ECONOMIC AGGREGATES										
Gross national product (GNP)	7,119	19,700	31,822	40,795	39,609	48,417	57,051	59,364	62,472	61,261
Exports of goods & services (XGS)	..	4,832	4,437	4,945	4,839	6,380	7,710	8,331	9,514	8,668
of which workers remittances	..	0	122	244	276	375	408	404	416	400
Imports of goods & services (MGS)	..	5,080	6,014	7,249	7,359	9,304	12,236	12,235	13,052	12,758
International reserves (RES)	339	2,804	1,891	3,456	3,918	7,420	8,653	10,990	11,306	9,882
Current account balance	..	-101	-1,384	-2,101	-2,302	-2,662	-4,314	-3,618	-3,273	-3,794
4. DEBT INDICATORS										
EDT / XGS (%)	..	194.2	452.3	411.2	487.2	415.8	400.1	352.0	320.8	373.8
EDT / GNP (%)	..	47.7	63.1	49.9	59.5	54.8	54.1	49.4	48.9	52.9
TDS / XGS (%)	..	44.5	10.7	20.3	57.0	17.9	16.1	35.2	30.5	28.3
INT / XGS (%)	..	20.0	5.6	9.4	23.5	8.5	9.4	20.5	14.8	18.0
INT / GNP (%)	..	4.9	0.8	1.1	2.9	1.1	1.3	2.9	2.3	2.5
RES / EDT (%)	..	29.9	9.4	17.0	16.6	28.0	28.1	37.5	37.0	30.5
RES / MGS (months)	..	6.6	3.8	5.7	6.4	9.6	8.5	10.8	10.4	9.3
Short-term / EDT (%)	..	22.2	26.7	19.2	24.4	25.4	31.4	22.0	22.4	22.8
Concessional / EDT (%)	..	14.4	9.2	19.7	19.4	19.6	18.1	19.3	17.7	12.0
Multilateral / EDT (%)	..	5.5	11.0	10.2	11.6	12.0	12.1	12.2	13.9	14.3

PERU

(US$ million, unless otherwise indicated)

	1970	1980	1990	1992	1993	1994	1995	1996	1997	1998
5. LONG-TERM DEBT										
DEBT OUTSTANDING (LDOD)	**2,655**	**6,828**	**13,963**	**15,808**	**16,949**	**18,854**	**20,215**	**21,945**	**22,680**	**24,094**
Public and publicly guaranteed	**856**	**6,218**	**13,633**	**15,580**	**16,385**	**17,681**	**18,927**	**20,567**	**20,204**	**20,803**
Official creditors	373	3,123	6,593	11,544	12,496	13,911	15,224	15,028	15,490	16,135
Multilateral	148	514	2,199	2,081	2,742	3,186	3,717	3,583	4,244	4,647
Concessional	0	36	185	155	164	158	142	139	124	112
Bilateral	225	2,610	4,394	9,464	9,754	10,725	11,507	11,445	11,246	11,487
Concessional	112	1,318	1,653	3,848	4,417	5,047	5,455	5,513	5,278	3,768
Private creditors	483	3,095	7,040	4,036	3,889	3,770	3,703	5,539	4,714	4,669
Bonds	22	2	1	0	0	0	0	4,873	4,130	4,130
Commercial banks	148	1,694	3,159	3,120	3,075	3,056	3,040	122	98	74
Other private	314	1,399	3,881	915	814	714	663	544	486	464
Private nonguaranteed	**1,799**	**610**	**330**	**228**	**564**	**1,173**	**1,288**	**1,378**	**2,476**	**3,290**
Bonds	0	0	0	0	0	60	60	60	0	150
Commercial banks	1,799	610	330	228	564	1,113	1,228	1,318	2,476	3,140
Memo:										
IBRD	125	359	1,188	956	1,369	1,554	1,729	1,633	1,920	2,128
IDA	0	0	0	0	0	0	0	0	0	0
DISBURSEMENTS	**387**	**1,308**	**291**	**699**	**1,826**	**1,223**	**880**	**785**	**2,795**	**1,433**
Public and publicly guaranteed	**148**	**1,248**	**291**	**631**	**1,516**	**613**	**725**	**635**	**1,518**	**639**
Official creditors	59	664	189	617	1,484	609	720	632	1,460	639
Multilateral	18	209	38	473	1,312	500	631	284	1,126	560
Concessional	0	10	10	11	20	5	3	5	3	3
Bilateral	41	455	150	144	172	109	89	348	334	79
Concessional	8	232	94	138	152	79	26	340	214	74
Private creditors	89	584	103	14	32	4	5	4	58	0
Bonds	0	0	0	0	0	0	0	0	0	0
Commercial banks	3	248	69	3	0	0	0	0	0	0
Other private	85	336	34	11	32	4	5	4	58	0
Private nonguaranteed	**240**	**60**	**0**	**68**	**310**	**610**	**155**	**150**	**1,278**	**794**
Bonds	0	0	0	0	0	60	0	0	0	0
Commercial banks	240	60	0	68	310	550	155	150	1,278	794
Memo:										
IBRD	10	140	0	0	975	171	203	108	490	271
IDA	0	0	0	0	0	0	0	0	0	0
PRINCIPAL REPAYMENTS	**333**	**1,019**	**166**	**491**	**980**	**601**	**520**	**1,227**	**1,421**	**752**
Public and publicly guaranteed	**100**	**959**	**112**	**433**	**933**	**560**	**480**	**1,167**	**1,241**	**623**
Official creditors	23	281	81	311	816	447	404	607	459	578
Multilateral	11	24	24	214	662	195	201	194	231	228
Concessional	0	0	3	19	11	13	22	16	16	16
Bilateral	12	257	57	97	154	252	202	413	228	350
Concessional	3	48	6	15	18	132	56	42	70	95
Private creditors	77	678	31	122	117	113	76	560	783	45
Bonds	7	0	0	1	0	0	0	0	742	0
Commercial banks	25	445	9	44	37	37	28	540	24	24
Other private	46	233	22	76	80	76	48	20	16	22
Private nonguaranteed	**233**	**60**	**54**	**58**	**47**	**41**	**40**	**60**	**180**	**129**
Bonds	0	0	0	0	0	0	0	0	60	0
Commercial banks	233	60	54	58	47	41	40	60	120	129
Memo:										
IBRD	8	15	0	94	574	80	86	79	65	64
IDA	0	0	0	0	0	0	0	0	0	0
NET FLOWS ON DEBT	**54**	**289**	**125**	**209**	**846**	**622**	**360**	**-442**	**1,374**	**681**
Public and publicly guaranteed	**48**	**289**	**179**	**199**	**583**	**53**	**245**	**-532**	**276**	**16**
Official creditors	36	383	107	306	668	162	316	25	1,001	61
Multilateral	7	185	14	259	650	305	429	90	895	332
Concessional	0	10	7	-8	9	-8	-18	-11	-13	-13
Bilateral	29	198	94	47	18	-143	-113	-65	106	-271
Concessional	5	184	89	123	134	-54	-29	298	144	-21
Private creditors	11	-94	72	-107	-85	-109	-71	-556	-725	-45
Bonds	-7	0	0	-1	0	0	0	0	-742	0
Commercial banks	-22	-197	60	-41	-37	-37	-28	-540	-24	-24
Other private	40	103	12	-65	-48	-72	-43	-16	41	-21
Private nonguaranteed	**7**	**0**	**-54**	**10**	**263**	**569**	**115**	**90**	**1,098**	**665**
Bonds	0	0	0	0	0	60	0	0	-60	0
Commercial banks	7	0	-54	10	263	509	115	90	1,158	665
Memo:										
IBRD	2	125	0	-94	401	91	116	29	425	207
IDA	0	0	0	0	0	0	0	0	0	0

PERU

(US$ million, unless otherwise indicated)

	1970	1980	1990	1992	1993	1994	1995	1996	1997	1998
INTEREST PAYMENTS (LINT)	**162**	**670**	**91**	**313**	**779**	**393**	**485**	**1,308**	**971**	**1,108**
Public and publicly guaranteed	**43**	**547**	**66**	**299**	**763**	**370**	**413**	**1,218**	**810**	**926**
Official creditors	17	152	51	258	731	346	394	443	477	751
Multilateral	8	33	27	189	574	212	245	252	271	286
Concessional	0	1	3	4	4	6	7	5	4	4
Bilateral	9	118	24	69	157	134	150	191	206	466
Concessional	3	27	7	28	57	95	74	71	76	164
Private creditors	26	395	16	41	32	25	19	776	333	175
Bonds	1	0	0	0	0	0	0	0	318	159
Commercial banks	12	273	8	17	15	13	10	771	10	9
Other private	13	122	7	23	17	12	9	5	5	7
Private nonguaranteed	**119**	**124**	**25**	**14**	**16**	**22**	**71**	**89**	**161**	**182**
Bonds	0	0	0	0	0	1	6	6	4	0
Commercial banks	119	124	25	14	16	21	65	83	157	182
Memo:										
IBRD	7	24	0	100	483	109	118	116	117	120
IDA	0	0	0	0	0	0	0	0	0	0
NET TRANSFERS ON DEBT	**-108**	**-382**	**34**	**-104**	**67**	**230**	**-124**	**-1,749**	**403**	**-427**
Public and publicly guaranteed	**4**	**-258**	**113**	**-101**	**-180**	**-317**	**-168**	**-1,750**	**-534**	**-910**
Official creditors	20	231	56	48	-63	-184	-78	-418	525	-691
Multilateral	-1	152	-13	70	76	93	185	-162	624	47
Concessional	0	9	4	-13	5	-13	-25	-16	-17	-17
Bilateral	21	80	70	-22	-139	-277	-263	-256	-100	-737
Concessional	3	157	81	95	77	-148	-103	227	69	-185
Private creditors	-15	-490	56	-148	-117	-133	-90	-1,332	-1,058	-220
Bonds	-8	-1	0	-1	0	0	0	0	-1,060	-159
Commercial banks	-34	-470	52	-59	-52	-50	-38	-1,311	-34	-32
Other private	27	-19	5	-88	-65	-84	-52	-21	37	-28
Private nonguaranteed	**-112**	**-124**	**-79**	**-4**	**247**	**547**	**44**	**1**	**937**	**483**
Bonds	0	0	0	0	0	59	-6	-6	-64	0
Commercial banks	-112	-124	-79	-4	247	488	50	7	1,001	483
Memo:										
IBRD	-5	101	0	-194	-82	-18	-2	-87	308	87
IDA	0	0	0	0	0	0	0	0	0	0
DEBT SERVICE (LTDS)	**495**	**1,689**	**257**	**803**	**1,758**	**993**	**1,004**	**2,535**	**2,392**	**1,860**
Public and publicly guaranteed	**144**	**1,506**	**178**	**732**	**1,695**	**930**	**893**	**2,385**	**2,051**	**1,549**
Official creditors	40	433	132	569	1,547	793	798	1,050	935	1,329
Multilateral	19	58	51	403	1,236	406	446	446	502	513
Concessional	0	1	6	23	15	18	28	21	20	20
Bilateral	21	375	81	166	311	387	352	604	434	816
Concessional	5	75	13	43	75	227	129	112	145	258
Private creditors	104	1,073	46	162	149	137	95	1,336	1,116	220
Bonds	8	1	0	1	0	0	0	0	1,060	159
Commercial banks	37	718	17	62	52	50	38	1,311	34	32
Other private	59	355	29	100	97	88	57	25	21	29
Private nonguaranteed	**352**	**184**	**79**	**72**	**63**	**63**	**111**	**149**	**341**	**311**
Bonds	0	0	0	0	0	1	6	6	64	0
Commercial banks	352	184	79	72	63	62	105	143	277	311
Memo:										
IBRD	15	39	0	194	1,057	189	205	195	182	184
IDA	0	0	0	0	0	0	0	0	0	0
UNDISBURSED DEBT	**238**	**2,397**	**1,511**	**2,084**	**1,136**	**1,611**	**1,738**	**2,960**	**2,447**	**1,877**
Official creditors	166	1,126	865	2,057	1,129	1,592	1,726	2,952	2,447	1,877
Private creditors	72	1,272	646	27	7	18	12	8	1	0
Memorandum items										
Concessional LDOD	112	1,353	1,838	4,003	4,580	5,205	5,597	5,652	5,402	3,880
Variable rate LDOD	1,799	2,130	4,626	7,079	8,115	9,220	9,970	11,902	13,024	11,947
Public sector LDOD	840	6,200	13,587	15,573	16,379	17,675	18,921	20,567	20,204	19,405
Private sector LDOD	1,816	628	376	235	570	1,179	1,294	1,378	2,476	4,689
6. CURRENCY COMPOSITION OF LONG-TERM DEBT (PERCENT)										
Deutsche mark	13.9	6.6	5.0	4.5	4.1	4.4	4.4	3.5	3.2	2.1
French franc	1.1	4.2	9.3	9.4	8.6	9.1	9.7	8.6	7.7	2.9
Japanese yen	0.0	10.9	6.3	10.4	12.7	14.3	14.6	12.4	12.1	10.8
Pound sterling	0.9	2.0	0.9	1.1	1.1	1.2	1.2	1.2	1.3	0.6
Swiss franc	0.1	1.4	1.5	1.3	1.2	1.2	1.2	0.8	0.8	0.8
U.S.dollars	59.0	44.1	48.0	47.2	46.1	43.6	41.9	50.0	52.6	72.0
Multiple currency	17.0	7.5	15.2	10.0	12.1	12.6	13.3	11.8	11.5	4.9
Special drawing rights	0.0	0.0	0.0	0.0	0.0	0.1	0.1	0.1	0.1	0.1
All other currencies	8.0	23.3	13.8	16.1	14.1	13.5	13.6	11.6	10.7	5.8

PERU

(US$ million, unless otherwise indicated)

	1970	1980	1990	1992	1993	1994	1995	1996	1997	1998
7. DEBT RESTRUCTURINGS										
Total amount rescheduled	..	..	0	1,584	632	712	919	5,832	806	4,687
Debt stock rescheduled	..	..	0	0	0	0	0	2,489	0	4,415
Principal rescheduled	..	..	0	1,093	230	277	304	430	329	30
Official	..	..	0	148	179	230	284	339	235	27
Private	..	..	0	945	51	48	20	91	94	3
Interest rescheduled	..	..	0	490	401	419	516	2,813	477	243
Official	..	..	0	71	387	410	511	498	393	242
Private	..	..	0	419	14	10	4	2,316	84	1
Debt forgiven	..	..	0	48	0	0	0	32	3	116
Memo: interest forgiven	..	..	0	24	0	0	0	758	1	1
Debt stock reduction	..	..	0	0	0	0	0	2,150	0	0
of which debt buyback	..	..	0	0	0	0	0	944	0	0
8. DEBT STOCK-FLOW RECONCILIATION										
Total change in debt stocks	..	..	1,486	-379	3,235	2,955	4,324	-1,523	1,194	1,875
Net flows on debt	591	775	128	347	649	1,256	3,149	722	1,937	1,100
Net change in interest arrears	..	..	460	-638	2,297	360	156	-4,385	-43	3
Interest capitalized	..	..	0	490	401	419	516	2,813	477	243
Debt forgiveness or reduction	..	..	0	-48	0	0	0	-1,238	-3	-116
Cross-currency valuation	..	..	699	-484	-257	833	355	-699	-921	392
Residual	..	..	199	-45	147	86	147	1,264	-252	253
9. AVERAGE TERMS OF NEW COMMITMENTS										
ALL CREDITORS										
Interest (%)	7.4	9.4	6.7	7.2	6.5	6.9	6.2	4.8	5.8	6.9
Maturity (years)	13.3	12.3	8.5	20.2	21.0	18.4	17.4	23.0	19.6	20.4
Grace period (years)	4.3	3.5	2.1	5.6	5.1	4.5	4.6	6.3	5.4	4.5
Grant element (%)	11.8	5.5	13.1	17.8	21.9	18.7	23.3	37.3	27.8	19.0
Official creditors										
Interest (%)	7.2	7.5	7.1	7.2	6.5	6.9	6.2	4.8	5.8	6.9
Maturity (years)	13.8	15.3	9.1	20.2	21.3	18.5	17.4	23.0	20.2	20.4
Grace period (years)	4.5	4.3	2.4	5.6	5.2	4.5	4.6	6.3	5.5	4.5
Grant element (%)	12.6	18.7	14.0	17.8	22.2	18.8	23.3	37.3	28.5	19.0
Private creditors										
Interest (%)	8.7	10.7	5.5	0.0	7.5	7.7	0.0	0.0	6.0	0.0
Maturity (years)	9.2	10.3	6.7	0.0	6.5	7.3	0.0	0.0	4.0	0.0
Grace period (years)	2.0	3.0	1.3	0.0	2.0	2.3	0.0	0.0	1.0	0.0
Grant element (%)	4.8	-3.2	10.5	0.0	7.6	7.5	0.0	0.0	8.0	0.0
Memorandum items										
Commitments	125	1,614	179	1,801	714	1,081	930	1,947	1,536	70
Official creditors	112	643	137	1,801	703	1,065	930	1,947	1,486	70
Private creditors	13	971	43	0	12	16	0	0	50	0

10. CONTRACTUAL OBLIGATIONS ON OUTSTANDING LONG-TERM DEBT

	1999	2000	2001	2002	2003	2004	2005	2006	2007	2008
TOTAL										
Disbursements	566	495	337	212	130	68	43	17	6	3
Principal	797	876	917	992	1,167	1,257	1,319	1,389	1,487	1,682
Interest	1,378	1,363	1,326	1,305	1,255	1,195	1,124	1,048	1,008	958
Official creditors										
Disbursements	566	495	337	212	130	68	43	17	6	3
Principal	564	663	714	755	897	949	977	1,046	1,110	1,155
Interest	1,010	1,000	973	937	893	840	782	721	657	587
Bilateral creditors										
Disbursements	183	190	125	79	44	20	10	0	0	0
Principal	226	292	338	350	492	536	586	674	752	798
Interest	655	647	633	616	595	568	537	503	464	420
Multilateral creditors										
Disbursements	383	306	212	133	86	48	32	17	6	3
Principal	338	370	376	405	405	413	391	372	358	357
Interest	356	353	340	321	298	272	245	218	192	167
Private creditors										
Disbursements	0	0	0	0	0	0	0	0	0	0
Principal	233	213	203	237	270	309	343	343	377	527
Interest	368	363	353	367	362	355	342	327	351	372
Commercial banks										
Disbursements	0	0	0	0	0	0	0	0	0	0
Principal	22	11	0	2	2	2	2	2	2	2
Interest	7	5	5	5	4	4	4	4	3	3
Other private										
Disbursements	0	0	0	0	0	0	0	0	0	0
Principal	211	203	203	235	268	307	341	341	375	525
Interest	361	358	349	363	358	351	338	323	348	368

PHILIPPINES

(US$ million, unless otherwise indicated)

	1970	1980	1990	1992	1993	1994	1995	1996	1997	1998
1. SUMMARY DEBT DATA										
TOTAL DEBT STOCKS (EDT)	**..**	**17,417**	**30,580**	**33,005**	**35,936**	**39,412**	**37,829**	**40,145**	**45,682**	**47,817**
Long-term debt (LDOD)	**1,544**	**8,817**	**25,241**	**26,649**	**29,691**	**32,632**	**31,823**	**31,770**	**33,033**	**39,064**
Public and publicly guaranteed	625	6,363	24,040	25,618	27,482	29,687	28,292	26,868	26,199	28,189
Private nonguaranteed	919	2,454	1,201	1,030	2,210	2,945	3,531	4,902	6,834	10,875
Use of IMF credit	**69**	**1,044**	**912**	**1,100**	**1,210**	**1,064**	**728**	**405**	**855**	**1,569**
Short-term debt	**..**	**7,556**	**4,427**	**5,256**	**5,035**	**5,716**	**5,279**	**7,969**	**11,794**	**7,185**
of which interest arrears on LDOD	..	0	52	0	0	0	0	0	0	0
Official creditors	..	0	5	0	0	0	0	0	0	0
Private creditors	..	0	48	0	0	0	0	0	0	0
Memo: principal arrears on LDOD	..	1	182	3	0	0	0	0	0	0
Official creditors	..	0	13	0	0	0	0	0	0	0
Private creditors	..	1	169	3	0	0	0	0	0	0
Memo: export credits	..	0	4,366	5,948	7,660	8,412	8,309	7,734	9,149	9,712
TOTAL DEBT FLOWS										
Disbursements	**444**	**2,300**	**2,516**	**2,976**	**4,427**	**3,354**	**2,851**	**5,023**	**6,049**	**3,945**
Long-term debt	416	1,854	2,516	2,763	4,250	3,302	2,851	5,023	5,349	3,214
IMF purchases	28	446	0	213	177	52	0	0	700	730
Principal repayments	**262**	**686**	**1,818**	**2,791**	**2,766**	**2,520**	**3,099**	**3,192**	**2,341**	**2,880**
Long-term debt	260	541	1,473	2,637	2,702	2,250	2,737	2,891	2,125	2,801
IMF repurchases	3	145	345	155	64	270	363	301	216	79
Net flows on debt	**765**	**3,855**	**1,123**	**614**	**1,440**	**1,515**	**-685**	**4,521**	**7,533**	**-3,544**
of which short-term debt	..	2,241	425	429	-221	681	-437	2,690	3,825	-4,609
Interest payments (INT)	**..**	**1,496**	**1,772**	**1,510**	**2,141**	**2,112**	**2,249**	**2,165**	**2,201**	**2,286**
Long-term debt	44	579	1,573	1,334	1,759	1,646	1,844	1,659	1,702	1,950
IMF charges	0	42	99	82	73	62	55	27	24	49
Short-term debt	..	875	100	94	309	403	351	478	474	287
Net transfers on debt	**..**	**2,359**	**-649**	**-897**	**-701**	**-597**	**-2,935**	**2,356**	**5,332**	**-5,830**
Total debt service paid (TDS)	**..**	**2,183**	**3,590**	**4,302**	**4,907**	**4,632**	**5,349**	**5,357**	**4,541**	**5,166**
Long-term debt	304	1,120	3,046	3,971	4,461	3,896	4,581	4,550	3,827	4,751
IMF repurchases and charges	3	187	444	237	137	333	417	329	240	128
Short-term debt (interest only)	..	875	100	94	309	403	351	478	474	287
2. AGGREGATE NET RESOURCE FLOWS AND NET TRANSFERS (LONG-TERM)										
NET RESOURCE FLOWS	**155**	**1,266**	**1,935**	**895**	**4,501**	**4,334**	**3,830**	**5,229**	**4,712**	**2,764**
Net flow of long-term debt (ex. IMF)	157	1,313	1,043	127	1,548	1,052	114	2,132	3,224	413
Foreign direct investment (net)	-25	-106	530	228	1,238	1,591	1,478	1,517	1,222	1,713
Portfolio equity flows	0	0	0	333	1,445	1,407	1,961	1,333	73	454
Grants (excluding technical coop.)	23	59	362	208	270	284	277	247	193	184
Memo: technical coop. grants	16	64	244	467	451	329	380	277	245	228
official net resource flows	83	426	1,296	1,665	1,234	466	-479	240	298	178
private net resource flows	72	840	639	-769	3,267	3,868	4,309	4,988	4,414	2,586
NET TRANSFERS	**87**	**489**	**51**	**-844**	**2,373**	**2,293**	**1,586**	**3,119**	**2,509**	**234**
Interest on long-term debt	44	579	1,573	1,334	1,759	1,646	1,844	1,659	1,702	1,950
Profit remittances on FDI	24	198	311	405	369	395	400	450	500	580
Memo: official net transfers	72	286	547	821	131	-683	-1,766	-802	-625	-653
private net transfers	15	203	-496	-1,665	2,242	2,975	3,352	3,921	3,135	887
3. MAJOR ECONOMIC AGGREGATES										
Gross national product (GNP)	6,576	32,436	44,092	53,890	55,320	65,730	76,165	86,258	85,742	68,210
Exports of goods & services (XGS)	..	8,202	13,290	17,636	19,183	24,476	33,294	40,118	49,120	43,617
of which workers remittances	..	205	262	315	311	443	432	569	1,057	204
Imports of goods & services (MGS)	..	10,348	16,437	19,137	22,587	27,919	35,722	44,091	53,494	42,561
International reserves (RES)	255	3,978	2,036	5,336	5,934	7,126	7,757	11,747	8,714	10,789
Current account balance	..	-1,904	-2,695	-1,000	-3,016	-2,950	-1,980	-3,953	-4,351	1,287
4. DEBT INDICATORS										
EDT / XGS (%)	..	212.4	230.1	187.2	187.3	161.0	113.6	100.1	93.0	109.6
EDT / GNP (%)	..	53.7	69.4	61.3	65.0	60.0	49.7	46.5	53.3	70.1
TDS / XGS (%)	..	26.6	27.0	24.4	25.6	18.9	16.1	13.4	9.3	11.8
INT / XGS (%)	..	18.2	13.3	8.6	11.2	8.6	6.8	5.4	4.5	5.2
INT / GNP (%)	..	4.6	4.0	2.8	3.9	3.2	3.0	2.5	2.6	3.4
RES / EDT (%)	..	22.8	6.7	16.2	16.5	18.1	20.5	29.3	19.1	22.6
RES / MGS (months)	..	4.6	1.5	3.4	3.2	3.1	2.6	3.2	2.0	3.0
Short-term / EDT (%)	..	43.4	14.5	15.9	14.0	14.5	14.0	19.9	25.8	15.0
Concessional / EDT (%)	..	5.5	20.0	24.4	26.4	27.4	29.5	25.9	21.9	23.8
Multilateral / EDT (%)	..	7.5	20.5	20.9	21.3	21.2	22.4	19.8	16.0	16.7

PHILIPPINES

(US$ million, unless otherwise indicated)

	1970	1980	1990	1992	1993	1994	1995	1996	1997	1998
5. LONG-TERM DEBT										
DEBT OUTSTANDING (LDOD)	**1,544**	**8,817**	**25,241**	**26,649**	**29,691**	**32,632**	**31,823**	**31,770**	**33,033**	**39,064**
Public and publicly guaranteed	**625**	**6,363**	**24,040**	**25,618**	**27,482**	**29,687**	**28,292**	**26,868**	**26,199**	**28,189**
Official creditors	272	2,636	15,302	19,013	21,134	23,208	22,196	20,210	18,483	20,209
Multilateral	120	1,310	6,273	6,908	7,645	8,348	8,479	7,928	7,321	7,972
Concessional	0	60	457	698	818	935	976	972	947	1,045
Bilateral	152	1,326	9,029	12,105	13,489	14,860	13,717	12,282	11,163	12,237
Concessional	68	894	5,649	7,366	8,677	9,860	10,164	9,422	9,063	10,356
Private creditors	353	3,727	8,739	6,605	6,348	6,479	6,096	6,658	7,715	7,980
Bonds	11	888	825	4,174	4,667	4,858	4,666	5,450	6,228	6,357
Commercial banks	267	2,256	6,661	1,322	630	575	650	581	942	1,200
Other private	75	583	1,253	1,109	1,051	1,047	780	627	546	423
Private nonguaranteed	**919**	**2,454**	**1,201**	**1,030**	**2,210**	**2,945**	**3,531**	**4,902**	**6,834**	**10,875**
Bonds	0	0	0	20	270	1,062	1,925	3,499	5,274	5,366
Commercial banks	919	2,454	1,201	1,010	1,939	1,883	1,606	1,404	1,560	5,509
Memo:										
IBRD	119	926	3,943	4,179	4,598	4,855	5,002	4,666	4,179	4,311
IDA	0	34	101	166	167	174	183	193	195	205
DISBURSEMENTS	**416**	**1,854**	**2,516**	**2,763**	**4,250**	**3,302**	**2,851**	**5,023**	**5,349**	**3,214**
Public and publicly guaranteed	**141**	**1,382**	**2,225**	**2,490**	**3,285**	**2,316**	**1,827**	**3,245**	**3,172**	**2,705**
Official creditors	74	461	1,373	2,149	2,286	1,770	1,425	1,596	1,803	1,407
Multilateral	17	321	854	845	965	612	621	728	620	652
Concessional	0	9	121	118	101	63	63	70	61	37
Bilateral	57	140	519	1,303	1,321	1,158	805	868	1,182	756
Concessional	15	102	462	935	932	728	745	792	1,161	744
Private creditors	66	920	852	341	999	546	402	1,649	1,370	1,297
Bonds	0	96	575	0	765	350	278	1,618	866	500
Commercial banks	50	657	167	45	56	35	102	13	453	772
Other private	17	167	110	296	178	162	22	18	52	25
Private nonguaranteed	**276**	**472**	**291**	**274**	**966**	**985**	**1,024**	**1,778**	**2,177**	**510**
Bonds	0	0	0	20	251	785	864	1,778	1,793	90
Commercial banks	276	472	291	254	714	201	161	0	384	420
Memo:										
IBRD	16	229	506	544	671	300	393	442	295	292
IDA	0	2	0	34	2	5	10	15	9	9
PRINCIPAL REPAYMENTS	**260**	**541**	**1,473**	**2,637**	**2,702**	**2,250**	**2,737**	**2,891**	**2,125**	**2,801**
Public and publicly guaranteed	**74**	**221**	**1,411**	**2,494**	**2,581**	**2,104**	**2,587**	**2,597**	**1,884**	**2,551**
Official creditors	15	95	439	692	1,322	1,588	2,181	1,602	1,697	1,413
Multilateral	5	45	388	438	470	520	651	608	586	566
Concessional	0	1	6	7	8	8	6	7	7	9
Bilateral	10	49	51	253	852	1,069	1,530	994	1,112	848
Concessional	3	24	21	74	354	420	674	496	549	475
Private creditors	59	126	972	1,802	1,258	516	406	995	186	1,138
Bonds	1	16	180	72	277	168	32	798	28	439
Commercial banks	39	44	743	1,585	762	108	101	64	67	529
Other private	19	67	49	146	219	240	273	133	91	170
Private nonguaranteed	**186**	**320**	**62**	**143**	**121**	**146**	**150**	**294**	**241**	**250**
Bonds	0	0	0	0	0	0	0	100	0	0
Commercial banks	186	320	62	143	121	146	150	194	241	250
Memo:										
IBRD	5	33	301	323	338	358	413	425	407	387
IDA	0	0	1	1	2	2	2	2	2	2
NET FLOWS ON DEBT	**157**	**1,313**	**1,043**	**127**	**1,548**	**1,052**	**114**	**2,132**	**3,224**	**413**
Public and publicly guaranteed	**67**	**1,161**	**814**	**-4**	**704**	**212**	**-760**	**648**	**1,289**	**153**
Official creditors	60	367	934	1,457	964	182	-756	-6	105	-6
Multilateral	12	276	466	407	495	92	-30	120	35	86
Concessional	0	8	115	112	93	55	57	63	54	28
Bilateral	48	91	468	1,050	469	90	-726	-126	71	-92
Concessional	12	78	441	861	578	308	71	296	612	269
Private creditors	7	794	-120	-1,461	-260	30	-4	654	1,183	159
Bonds	-1	80	395	-72	488	182	246	820	838	61
Commercial banks	11	614	-576	-1,540	-706	-74	1	-51	385	243
Other private	-3	100	61	151	-41	-78	-251	-115	-40	-145
Private nonguaranteed	**90**	**152**	**229**	**131**	**844**	**839**	**874**	**1,484**	**1,935**	**260**
Bonds	0	0	0	20	251	785	864	1,678	1,793	90
Commercial banks	90	152	229	111	593	55	11	-194	142	170
Memo:										
IBRD	11	195	206	221	333	-58	-21	18	-112	-95
IDA	0	2	-1	33	1	3	8	13	8	7

PHILIPPINES

(US$ million, unless otherwise indicated)

	1970	1980	1990	1992	1993	1994	1995	1996	1997	1998
INTEREST PAYMENTS (LINT)	**44**	**579**	**1,573**	**1,334**	**1,759**	**1,646**	**1,844**	**1,659**	**1,702**	**1,950**
Public and publicly guaranteed	**26**	**375**	**1,486**	**1,294**	**1,661**	**1,513**	**1,693**	**1,428**	**1,384**	**1,463**
Official creditors	11	140	749	843	1,103	1,148	1,287	1,042	923	830
Multilateral	7	100	444	495	526	565	604	537	485	443
Concessional	0	1	4	7	8	9	10	10	9	9
Bilateral	4	40	305	348	577	584	683	505	438	388
Concessional	2	21	125	148	276	273	404	300	289	277
Private creditors	15	235	737	451	558	365	405	387	461	633
Bonds	1	36	31	74	209	274	288	300	397	505
Commercial banks	11	165	671	342	280	33	54	45	36	104
Other private	3	34	35	35	69	58	63	41	28	24
Private nonguaranteed	**19**	**204**	**87**	**40**	**98**	**133**	**152**	**231**	**319**	**487**
Bonds	0	0	0	0	1	20	82	154	257	386
Commercial banks	19	204	87	40	97	113	70	77	62	101
Memo:										
IBRD	7	73	296	316	331	359	376	341	302	266
IDA	0	0	1	1	1	1	1	1	1	2
NET TRANSFERS ON DEBT	**113**	**733**	**-529**	**-1,208**	**-211**	**-595**	**-1,730**	**472**	**1,522**	**-1,537**
Public and publicly guaranteed	**41**	**785**	**-672**	**-1,298**	**-957**	**-1,301**	**-2,452**	**-781**	**-95**	**-1,309**
Official creditors	49	227	185	614	-139	-967	-2,043	-1,048	-818	-836
Multilateral	5	176	22	-88	-32	-472	-634	-417	-451	-357
Concessional	0	8	111	105	85	46	47	53	45	19
Bilateral	43	51	163	702	-107	-494	-1,409	-631	-367	-480
Concessional	9	57	316	713	303	35	-333	-4	323	-8
Private creditors	-7	559	-857	-1,912	-818	-334	-409	268	723	-473
Bonds	-2	44	364	-145	279	-92	-41	519	441	-444
Commercial banks	0	448	-1,247	-1,882	-986	-106	-54	-96	350	140
Other private	-6	66	25	116	-111	-136	-315	-156	-68	-169
Private nonguaranteed	**71**	**-52**	**142**	**91**	**746**	**706**	**723**	**1,253**	**1,617**	**-228**
Bonds	0	0	0	20	250	764	782	1,524	1,536	-296
Commercial banks	71	-52	142	71	496	-58	-59	-271	80	69
Memo:										
IBRD	4	123	-90	-95	2	-417	-397	-324	-414	-361
IDA	0	1	-2	32	-1	2	7	12	6	5
DEBT SERVICE (LTDS)	**304**	**1,120**	**3,046**	**3,971**	**4,461**	**3,896**	**4,581**	**4,550**	**3,827**	**4,751**
Public and publicly guaranteed	**100**	**596**	**2,897**	**3,788**	**4,241**	**3,617**	**4,279**	**4,025**	**3,267**	**4,014**
Official creditors	26	235	1,188	1,535	2,425	2,737	3,468	2,644	2,620	2,244
Multilateral	12	145	832	933	996	1,084	1,255	1,145	1,071	1,009
Concessional	0	1	10	13	16	17	16	16	16	18
Bilateral	14	90	356	602	1,429	1,653	2,213	1,499	1,549	1,235
Concessional	6	45	146	222	629	693	1,078	795	838	752
Private creditors	74	362	1,709	2,253	1,816	880	811	1,382	647	1,770
Bonds	2	52	211	145	486	441	320	1,099	425	944
Commercial banks	50	209	1,414	1,927	1,042	141	155	109	103	633
Other private	22	101	85	180	289	298	336	174	119	194
Private nonguaranteed	**204**	**524**	**149**	**183**	**219**	**279**	**302**	**525**	**560**	**737**
Bonds	0	0	0	0	1	20	82	254	257	386
Commercial banks	204	524	149	183	218	259	220	271	303	351
Memo:										
IBRD	12	106	597	640	669	717	789	766	709	654
IDA	0	0	2	2	3	3	3	3	3	4
UNDISBURSED DEBT	**193**	**4,365**	**6,590**	**7,483**	**7,280**	**8,407**	**8,626**	**7,963**	**6,996**	**8,748**
Official creditors	176	3,246	6,156	7,088	6,863	7,989	8,224	7,648	6,766	8,445
Private creditors	16	1,119	434	395	417	419	402	315	230	303
Memorandum items										
Concessional LDOD	68	954	6,105	8,065	9,495	10,795	11,140	10,394	10,010	11,402
Variable rate LDOD	924	4,399	11,066	7,803	9,249	10,644	11,638	12,853	15,152	20,093
Public sector LDOD	624	6,363	23,668	25,324	27,239	29,459	28,135	26,729	26,070	28,121
Private sector LDOD	920	2,454	1,573	1,325	2,452	3,173	3,687	5,041	6,963	10,943

6. CURRENCY COMPOSITION OF LONG-TERM DEBT (PERCENT)

	1970	1980	1990	1992	1993	1994	1995	1996	1997	1998
Deutsche mark	12.0	2.0	1.5	1.5	1.4	1.4	1.5	1.7	1.5	1.4
French franc	0.2	2.2	1.5	0.9	0.8	0.8	0.8	0.9	0.8	0.9
Japanese yen	2.7	21.9	31.0	34.6	38.2	40.4	39.5	38.1	36.8	38.6
Pound sterling	0.0	0.2	1.0	0.3	0.3	0.3	0.2	0.2	0.3	0.2
Swiss franc	3.1	0.5	0.5	0.3	0.4	0.4	0.3	0.2	0.2	0.2
U.S.dollars	62.1	51.6	36.2	33.9	30.4	28.0	27.5	29.8	33.9	33.9
Multiple currency	19.2	19.0	23.6	24.3	25.2	25.4	26.9	26.0	24.1	22.8
Special drawing rights	0.0	0.0	0.0	0.1	0.2	0.3	0.4	0.6	0.6	0.6
All other currencies	0.7	2.6	4.7	4.1	3.1	3.0	2.9	2.5	1.8	1.4

PHILIPPINES

(US$ million, unless otherwise indicated)

	1970	1980	1990	1992	1993	1994	1995	1996	1997	1998
7. DEBT RESTRUCTURINGS										
Total amount rescheduled	..	..	1,068	4,408	282	0	0	0	0	0
Debt stock rescheduled	..	..	0	2,247	0	0	0	0	0	0
Principal rescheduled	..	..	848	748	216	0	0	0	0	0
Official	..	..	172	490	191	0	0	0	0	0
Private	..	..	676	258	25	0	0	0	0	0
Interest rescheduled	..	..	186	235	66	0	0	0	0	0
Official	..	..	107	193	62	0	0	0	0	0
Private	..	..	80	43	4	0	0	0	0	0
Debt forgiven	..	..	0	0	0	0	0	0	0	0
Memo: interest forgiven	..	..	0	0	0	0	0	0	0	0
Debt stock reduction	..	..	1,803	2,259	0	0	0	0	0	0
of which debt buyback	..	..	721	1,175	0	0	0	0	0	0
8. DEBT STOCK-FLOW RECONCILIATION										
Total change in debt stocks	..	..	1,927	554	2,931	3,476	-1,582	2,316	5,537	2,135
Net flows on debt	765	3,855	1,123	614	1,440	1,515	-685	4,521	7,533	-3,544
Net change in interest arrears	..	..	48	-117	0	0	0	0	0	0
Interest capitalized	..	..	186	235	66	0	0	0	0	0
Debt forgiveness or reduction	..	..	-1,082	-1,085	0	0	0	0	0	0
Cross-currency valuation	..	..	980	-323	1,076	1,851	-171	-1,735	-1,637	1,606
Residual	..	..	672	1,230	350	110	-726	-470	-359	4,074
9. AVERAGE TERMS OF NEW COMMITMENTS										
ALL CREDITORS										
Interest (%)	7.3	9.9	6.2	5.8	5.5	4.3	4.8	6.2	4.7	5.7
Maturity (years)	11.4	17.2	21.9	18.8	17.1	20.9	24.1	17.3	21.3	17.9
Grace period (years)	2.1	5.3	7.3	4.6	5.7	6.8	8.2	9.4	10.2	6.1
Grant element (%)	12.4	4.0	28.2	25.4	27.4	38.4	39.7	24.4	34.2	29.5
Official creditors										
Interest (%)	6.7	6.9	5.1	5.9	4.9	3.8	4.3	4.9	3.7	4.5
Maturity (years)	14.3	22.2	24.4	19.9	23.6	23.5	26.6	21.0	26.4	23.8
Grace period (years)	2.2	6.2	7.3	5.0	6.7	7.2	7.8	6.2	7.7	6.5
Grant element (%)	16.0	22.0	36.8	26.3	36.6	43.9	43.6	34.7	48.5	40.9
Private creditors										
Interest (%)	8.1	13.5	9.2	5.4	6.7	6.7	7.1	7.4	6.0	8.0
Maturity (years)	6.7	11.2	15.0	12.3	5.0	8.9	10.9	13.9	14.4	6.3
Grace period (years)	1.9	4.1	7.6	2.1	3.8	5.3	10.2	12.4	13.5	5.5
Grant element (%)	6.4	-17.5	4.1	20.3	10.2	12.7	19.0	14.6	15.2	7.2
Memorandum items										
Commitments	171	2,143	3,520	2,372	2,952	3,102	2,595	3,631	3,030	4,152
Official creditors	107	1,164	2,588	2,013	1,924	2,558	2,182	1,766	1,728	2,751
Private creditors	64	979	933	359	1,028	544	413	1,865	1,301	1,401

10. CONTRACTUAL OBLIGATIONS ON OUTSTANDING LONG-TERM DEBT

	1999	2000	2001	2002	2003	2004	2005	2006	2007	2008
TOTAL										
Disbursements	2,665	2,348	1,498	981	584	326	196	66	43	25
Principal	2,726	3,121	3,321	3,814	3,245	3,055	2,505	3,049	2,231	2,526
Interest	1,942	1,927	1,851	1,700	1,539	1,392	1,274	1,142	1,010	875
Official creditors										
Disbursements	2,501	2,257	1,465	967	582	326	196	66	43	25
Principal	1,708	1,631	1,631	1,751	1,744	1,696	1,673	1,703	1,573	1,464
Interest	902	936	942	902	844	773	702	626	548	480
Bilateral creditors										
Disbursements	1,761	1,509	929	543	280	135	61	2	2	1
Principal	966	905	920	972	987	945	946	997	914	814
Interest	398	432	454	438	412	378	344	308	272	244
Multilateral creditors										
Disbursements	740	748	536	424	302	191	135	64	42	25
Principal	742	726	711	779	757	751	726	707	659	650
Interest	504	505	488	464	431	395	358	318	276	237
Private creditors										
Disbursements	164	91	33	13	2	0	0	0	0	0
Principal	1,019	1,490	1,690	2,063	1,501	1,359	832	1,346	658	1,062
Interest	1,040	990	909	798	696	620	571	516	462	395
Commercial banks										
Disbursements	58	24	6	3	0	0	0	0	0	0
Principal	337	183	485	60	56	42	28	18	12	7
Interest	76	58	42	18	14	10	7	6	4	4
Other private										
Disbursements	106	67	28	10	2	0	0	0	0	0
Principal	682	1,307	1,204	2,003	1,445	1,317	805	1,329	646	1,056
Interest	964	933	867	781	682	610	564	510	458	391

POLAND

(US$ million, unless otherwise indicated)

	1970	1980	1990	1992	1993	1994	1995	1996	1997	1998
1. SUMMARY DEBT DATA										
TOTAL DEBT STOCKS (EDT)	..	..	**49,366**	**48,495**	**45,176**	**42,553**	**44,263**	**43,473**	**40,401**	**47,708**
Long-term debt (LDOD)	..	..	**39,263**	**43,142**	**41,837**	**40,367**	**42,086**	**40,810**	**36,589**	**41,518**
Public and publicly guaranteed	..	..	39,263	42,741	41,297	39,503	41,073	39,208	34,178	35,136
Private nonguaranteed	..	..	0	401	541	864	1,012	1,602	2,412	6,381
Use of IMF credit	**0**	**0**	**509**	**820**	**684**	**1,341**	**0**	**0**	**0**	**0**
Short-term debt	..	..	**9,595**	**4,532**	**2,656**	**845**	**2,178**	**2,663**	**3,812**	**6,191**
of which interest arrears on LDOD	..	..	8,316	3,281	1,513	139	136	0	0	0
Official creditors	..	..	6,568	1,868	124	139	136	0	0	0
Private creditors	..	..	1,747	1,413	1,390	0	0	0	0	0
Memo: principal arrears on LDOD	..	..	5,672	2,828	580	585	625	29	29	3
Official creditors	..	..	4,284	2,274	429	578	619	25	25	0
Private creditors	..	..	1,388	554	152	7	5	4	4	3
Memo: export credits	..	..	28,076	20,432	21,063	19,123	17,559	18,002	15,755	16,990
TOTAL DEBT FLOWS										
Disbursements	..	..	**1,025**	**819**	**751**	**2,429**	**1,279**	**1,475**	**2,394**	**4,742**
Long-term debt	..	..	540	819	751	1,512	1,279	1,475	2,394	4,742
IMF purchases	0	0	485	0	0	917	0	0	0	0
Principal repayments	..	..	**635**	**540**	**669**	**1,895**	**2,279**	**1,114**	**1,085**	**2,910**
Long-term debt	..	..	635	540	531	1,581	885	1,114	1,085	2,910
IMF repurchases	0	0	0	0	138	314	1,394	0	0	0
Net flows on debt	..	..	**423**	**183**	**-27**	**97**	**335**	**982**	**2,459**	**4,210**
of which short-term debt	..	..	33	-97	-109	-436	1,335	621	1,149	2,379
Interest payments (INT)	..	..	**332**	**929**	**1,026**	**1,207**	**1,868**	**1,566**	**1,477**	**1,624**
Long-term debt	..	..	203	760	869	1,123	1,719	1,433	1,286	1,374
IMF charges	0	0	23	62	47	48	47	0	0	0
Short-term debt	..	..	105	108	110	37	102	133	191	250
Net transfers on debt	..	..	**92**	**-747**	**-1,053**	**-1,110**	**-1,532**	**-584**	**982**	**2,586**
Total debt service paid (TDS)	..	..	**966**	**1,469**	**1,695**	**3,102**	**4,147**	**2,680**	**2,562**	**4,534**
Long-term debt	..	..	838	1,299	1,399	2,704	2,604	2,547	2,371	4,284
IMF repurchases and charges	0	0	23	62	185	362	1,440	0	0	0
Short-term debt (interest only)	..	..	105	108	110	37	102	133	191	250
2. AGGREGATE NET RESOURCE FLOWS AND NET TRANSFERS (LONG-TERM)										
NET RESOURCE FLOWS	..	..	**22**	**2,077**	**3,247**	**3,499**	**8,382**	**6,537**	**7,814**	**9,716**
Net flow of long-term debt (ex. IMF)	..	..	-95	279	220	-70	394	361	1,310	1,832
Foreign direct investment (net)	..	..	89	678	1,715	1,875	3,659	4,498	4,908	6,365
Portfolio equity flows	..	..	0	0	400	5	921	722	945	969
Grants (excluding technical coop.)	..	..	27	1,119	912	1,688	3,408	956	652	549
Memo: technical coop. grants	..	..	0	196	118	101	334	146	144	214
official net resource flows	..	..	-50	1,354	1,089	2,255	3,324	1,204	512	63
private net resource flows	..	..	71	723	2,158	1,244	5,058	5,333	7,302	9,653
NET TRANSFERS	..	..	**-201**	**1,163**	**2,179**	**2,176**	**6,438**	**4,804**	**6,168**	**7,942**
Interest on long-term debt	..	..	203	760	869	1,123	1,719	1,433	1,286	1,374
Profit remittances on FDI	..	..	20	154	199	200	225	300	360	400
Memo: official net transfers	..	..	-163	711	370	1,519	2,108	282	-266	-697
private net transfers	..	..	-38	452	1,809	657	4,330	4,523	6,433	8,639
3. MAJOR ECONOMIC AGGREGATES										
Gross national product (GNP)	..	..	55,620	82,702	84,701	96,445	124,271	141,890	142,003	156,988
Exports of goods & services (XGS)	..	..	19,640	19,430	18,362	26,158	37,501	39,640	41,981	46,551
of which workers remittances	..	..	0	0	0	558	696	723	797	938
Imports of goods & services (MGS)	..	..	19,084	23,000	24,910	25,898	36,909	43,875	48,963	55,411
International reserves (RES)	..	..	4,674	4,257	4,277	6,023	14,957	18,019	20,670	27,383
Current account balance	..	..	3,067	-3,104	-5,788	954	854	-3,264	-5,744	-6,901
4. DEBT INDICATORS										
EDT / XGS (%)	..	..	251.4	249.6	246.0	162.7	118.0	109.7	96.2	102.5
EDT / GNP (%)	..	..	88.8	58.6	53.3	44.1	35.6	30.6	28.5	30.4
TDS / XGS (%)	..	..	4.9	7.6	9.2	11.9	11.1	6.8	6.1	9.7
INT / XGS (%)	..	..	1.7	4.8	5.6	4.6	5.0	4.0	3.5	3.5
INT / GNP (%)	..	..	0.6	1.1	1.2	1.3	1.5	1.1	1.0	1.0
RES / EDT (%)	..	..	9.5	8.8	9.5	14.2	33.8	41.5	51.2	57.4
RES / MGS (months)	..	..	2.9	2.2	2.1	2.8	4.9	4.9	5.1	5.9
Short-term / EDT (%)	..	..	19.4	9.4	5.9	2.0	4.9	6.1	9.4	13.0
Concessional / EDT (%)	..	..	7.7	26.8	27.8	25.4	25.1	23.3	19.0	16.6
Multilateral / EDT (%)	..	..	1.1	2.4	3.3	4.6	4.7	5.0	5.1	4.5

POLAND

(US$ million, unless otherwise indicated)

	1970	1980	1990	1992	1993	1994	1995	1996	1997	1998
5. LONG-TERM DEBT										
DEBT OUTSTANDING (LDOD)	..	..	**39,263**	**43,142**	**41,837**	**40,367**	**42,086**	**40,810**	**36,589**	**41,518**
Public and publicly guaranteed	..	..	**39,263**	**42,741**	**41,297**	**39,503**	**41,073**	**39,208**	**34,178**	**35,136**
Official creditors	..	..	27,919	32,819	32,446	31,040	32,232	30,502	26,578	27,075
Multilateral	..	..	524	1,167	1,471	1,957	2,067	2,175	2,079	2,156
Concessional	..	..	0	0	0	0	0	0	0	0
Bilateral	..	..	27,395	31,652	30,975	29,083	30,165	28,327	24,500	24,919
Concessional	..	..	3,822	12,976	12,555	10,797	11,097	10,111	7,692	7,904
Private creditors	..	..	11,344	9,922	8,850	8,463	8,841	8,707	7,600	8,062
Bonds	..	..	1	0	0	7,860	8,110	8,271	6,964	7,365
Commercial banks	..	..	9,760	9,108	8,640	362	556	323	573	650
Other private	..	..	1,584	814	211	241	175	113	63	47
Private nonguaranteed	..	..	**0**	**401**	**541**	**864**	**1,012**	**1,602**	**2,412**	**6,381**
Bonds	..	..	0	0	0	0	0	50	850	1,678
Commercial banks	..	..	0	401	541	864	1,012	1,552	1,561	4,703
Memo:										
IBRD	0	0	55	743	1,073	1,818	2,067	2,175	2,079	2,156
IDA	0	0	0	0	0	0	0	0	0	0
DISBURSEMENTS	..	..	**540**	**819**	**751**	**1,512**	**1,279**	**1,475**	**2,394**	**4,742**
Public and publicly guaranteed	..	..	**540**	**773**	**566**	**1,015**	**856**	**1,014**	**1,010**	**1,391**
Official creditors	..	..	70	412	330	712	248	693	280	153
Multilateral	..	..	56	343	317	672	210	464	239	153
Concessional	..	..	0	0	0	0	0	0	0	0
Bilateral	..	..	14	69	12	40	38	229	42	0
Concessional	..	..	10	4	0	16	7	199	1	0
Private creditors	..	..	470	361	237	303	608	321	730	1,239
Bonds	..	..	0	0	0	138	250	166	400	1,138
Commercial banks	..	..	300	220	168	72	353	155	326	94
Other private	..	..	171	141	69	93	5	0	3	7
Private nonguaranteed	..	..	**0**	**46**	**185**	**497**	**423**	**461**	**1,384**	**3,351**
Bonds	..	..	0	0	0	0	0	50	803	812
Commercial banks	..	..	0	46	185	497	423	411	581	2,539
Memo:										
IBRD	0	0	54	343	317	672	210	464	239	153
IDA	0	0	0	0	0	0	0	0	0	0
PRINCIPAL REPAYMENTS	..	..	**635**	**540**	**531**	**1,581**	**885**	**1,114**	**1,085**	**2,910**
Public and publicly guaranteed	..	..	**635**	**494**	**485**	**1,408**	**611**	**803**	**510**	**1,444**
Official creditors	..	..	147	178	153	146	332	445	421	640
Multilateral	..	..	46	29	20	0	158	197	155	175
Concessional	..	..	0	0	0	0	0	0	0	0
Bilateral	..	..	101	149	133	146	174	248	265	464
Concessional	..	..	43	54	112	47	44	51	80	231
Private creditors	..	..	488	316	332	1,262	279	358	90	804
Bonds	..	..	0	0	0	0	0	0	0	748
Commercial banks	..	..	400	177	172	1,179	192	312	54	35
Other private	..	..	88	139	161	83	87	46	36	21
Private nonguaranteed	..	..	**0**	**46**	**46**	**174**	**275**	**311**	**575**	**1,466**
Bonds	..	..	0	0	0	0	0	0	0	0
Commercial banks	..	..	0	46	46	174	275	311	575	1,466
Memo:										
IBRD	0	0	0	0	0	0	19	197	155	175
IDA	0	0	0	0	0	0	0	0	0	0
NET FLOWS ON DEBT	..	..	**-95**	**279**	**220**	**-70**	**394**	**361**	**1,310**	**1,832**
Public and publicly guaranteed	..	..	**-95**	**280**	**81**	**-393**	**245**	**211**	**500**	**-53**
Official creditors	..	..	-77	234	176	567	-84	248	-140	-487
Multilateral	..	..	10	314	297	672	52	266	84	-23
Concessional	..	..	0	0	0	0	0	0	0	0
Bilateral	..	..	-87	-80	-120	-106	-136	-19	-224	-464
Concessional	..	..	-33	-51	-112	-31	-37	147	-79	-231
Private creditors	..	..	-18	45	-95	-959	329	-37	640	434
Bonds	..	..	0	0	0	138	250	166	400	390
Commercial banks	..	..	-100	43	-3	-1,107	161	-157	272	59
Other private	..	..	83	2	-92	10	-82	-46	-32	-14
Private nonguaranteed	..	..	**0**	**0**	**139**	**323**	**148**	**150**	**810**	**1,884**
Bonds	..	..	0	0	0	0	0	50	803	812
Commercial banks	..	..	0	0	139	323	148	100	7	1,072
Memo:										
IBRD	0	0	54	343	317	672	191	266	84	-23
IDA	0	0	0	0	0	0	0	0	0	0

POLAND

(US$ million, unless otherwise indicated)

	1970	1980	1990	1992	1993	1994	1995	1996	1997	1998
INTEREST PAYMENTS (LINT)	..	..	**203**	**760**	**869**	**1,123**	**1,719**	**1,433**	**1,286**	**1,374**
Public and publicly guaranteed	..	..	**203**	**751**	**832**	**1,075**	**1,663**	**1,355**	**1,169**	**1,164**
Official creditors	..	..	113	643	718	736	1,216	923	777	759
Multilateral	..	..	31	37	71	152	148	147	142	131
Concessional	..	..	0	0	0	0	0	0	0	0
Bilateral	..	..	82	606	647	584	1,068	775	636	629
Concessional	..	..	56	167	339	338	478	465	405	407
Private creditors	..	..	90	109	114	339	447	433	391	405
Bonds	..	..	0	0	0	0	386	392	364	349
Commercial banks	..	..	74	71	85	318	47	32	23	53
Other private	..	..	15	38	29	21	14	8	5	3
Private nonguaranteed	..	..	**0**	**8**	**37**	**48**	**56**	**78**	**118**	**210**
Bonds	..	..	0	0	0	0	0	0	3	65
Commercial banks	..	..	0	8	37	48	56	78	114	145
Memo:										
IBRD	0	0	1	33	64	88	133	147	142	131
IDA	0	0	0	0	0	0	0	0	0	0
NET TRANSFERS ON DEBT	..	..	**-298**	**-480**	**-648**	**-1,192**	**-1,325**	**-1,072**	**23**	**458**
Public and publicly guaranteed	..	..	**-298**	**-472**	**-751**	**-1,467**	**-1,418**	**-1,144**	**-669**	**-1,217**
Official creditors	..	..	-190	-408	-542	-169	-1,300	-675	-918	-1,246
Multilateral	..	..	-22	277	226	520	-96	119	-58	-153
Concessional	..	..	0	0	0	0	0	0	0	0
Bilateral	..	..	-169	-686	-768	-690	-1,204	-794	-859	-1,093
Concessional	..	..	-90	-218	-450	-369	-515	-318	-485	-637
Private creditors	..	..	-107	-63	-209	-1,298	-118	-469	249	30
Bonds	..	..	0	0	0	138	-136	-226	36	41
Commercial banks	..	..	-175	-28	-88	-1,425	114	-189	249	6
Other private	..	..	67	-36	-121	-11	-96	-54	-37	-17
Private nonguaranteed	..	..	**0**	**-9**	**102**	**275**	**93**	**72**	**692**	**1,675**
Bonds	..	..	0	0	0	0	0	50	800	748
Commercial banks	..	..	0	-9	102	275	93	22	-107	927
Memo:										
IBRD	0	0	54	310	253	585	58	119	-58	-153
IDA	0	0	0	0	0	0	0	0	0	0
DEBT SERVICE (LTDS)	..	..	**838**	**1,299**	**1,399**	**2,704**	**2,604**	**2,547**	**2,371**	**4,284**
Public and publicly guaranteed	..	..	**838**	**1,245**	**1,317**	**2,482**	**2,274**	**2,158**	**1,679**	**2,608**
Official creditors	..	..	260	820	871	882	1,548	1,368	1,198	1,399
Multilateral	..	..	77	66	91	152	306	344	297	306
Concessional	..	..	0	0	0	0	0	0	0	0
Bilateral	..	..	183	755	780	729	1,241	1,023	901	1,093
Concessional	..	..	100	221	450	385	522	516	486	637
Private creditors	..	..	578	425	446	1,601	726	790	481	1,209
Bonds	..	..	0	0	0	0	386	392	364	1,097
Commercial banks	..	..	474	248	256	1,497	239	344	77	88
Other private	..	..	103	177	190	104	102	54	40	24
Private nonguaranteed	..	..	**0**	**54**	**82**	**221**	**331**	**389**	**692**	**1,676**
Bonds	..	..	0	0	0	0	0	0	3	65
Commercial banks	..	..	0	54	82	221	331	389	689	1,612
Memo:										
IBRD	0	0	1	33	64	88	152	344	297	306
IDA	0	0	0	0	0	0	0	0	0	0
UNDISBURSED DEBT	..	..	**2,126**	**2,601**	**3,149**	**2,460**	**1,939**	**1,244**	**1,223**	**972**
Official creditors	..	..	1,297	2,006	2,801	2,296	1,830	1,136	1,060	912
Private creditors	..	..	829	594	348	164	109	108	163	61
Memorandum items										
Concessional LDOD	..	..	3,822	12,976	12,555	10,797	11,097	10,111	7,692	7,904
Variable rate LDOD	..	..	26,112	28,144	28,628	24,013	25,387	25,048	23,268	27,003
Public sector LDOD	..	..	39,261	42,695	41,268	39,488	41,071	39,208	33,970	34,934
Private sector LDOD	..	..	2	447	569	879	1,015	1,603	2,619	6,584

6. CURRENCY COMPOSITION OF LONG-TERM DEBT (PERCENT)

	1970	1980	1990	1992	1993	1994	1995	1996	1997	1998
Deutsche mark	..	..	23.3	21.2	19.2	10.1	10.2	9.9	10.1	10.5
French franc	..	..	11.0	11.9	11.7	12.7	13.1	12.7	12.6	12.9
Japanese yen	..	..	2.9	3.0	3.8	3.9	3.6	3.8	3.8	4.1
Pound sterling	..	..	3.8	2.7	3.8	2.6	2.5	2.8	3.2	3.1
Swiss franc	..	..	9.2	5.2	5.3	0.0	0.0	0.0	0.0	0.0
U.S.dollars	..	..	32.2	35.9	35.8	47.0	45.9	47.4	46.5	43.0
Multiple currency	..	..	0.1	1.7	2.6	4.6	5.0	5.5	6.0	5.3
Special drawing rights	..	..	0.0	0.0	0.0	0.0	0.0	0.0	0.0	0.0
All other currencies	..	..	17.5	18.4	17.8	19.1	19.7	17.9	17.8	21.1

POLAND

(US$ million, unless otherwise indicated)

	1970	1980	1990	1992	1993	1994	1995	1996	1997	1998
7. DEBT RESTRUCTURINGS										
Total amount rescheduled	..	..	3,559	28,236	8,076	7,723	0	0	0	0
Debt stock rescheduled	..	..	0	22,488	2,259	3,307	0	0	0	0
Principal rescheduled	..	..	1,391	3,270	3,772	325	0	70	7	3
Official	..	..	746	2,709	3,419	0	0	0	0	0
Private	..	..	645	562	353	325	0	70	7	3
Interest rescheduled	..	..	2,168	2,477	2,045	1,838	0	1	1	0
Official	..	..	1,998	1,843	1,948	0	0	0	0	0
Private	..	..	170	635	98	1,838	0	1	1	0
Debt forgiven	..	..	233	1,001	653	3,791	0	5	8	33
Memo: interest forgiven	..	..	61	0	0	0	0	0	0	0
Debt stock reduction	..	..	284	1,092	1,674	4,809	0	0	1,686	0
of which debt buyback	..	..	0	0	0	956	0	0	0	0
8. DEBT STOCK-FLOW RECONCILIATION										
Total change in debt stocks	..	..	6,270	-4,926	-3,318	-2,623	1,710	-790	-3,072	7,307
Net flows on debt	..	..	423	183	-27	97	335	982	2,459	4,210
Net change in interest arrears	..	..	986	-2,937	-1,767	-1,375	-3	-136	0	0
Interest capitalized	..	..	2,168	2,477	2,045	1,838	0	1	1	0
Debt forgiveness or reduction	..	..	-517	-2,093	-2,327	-7,643	0	-5	-1,694	-33
Cross-currency valuation	..	..	3,386	-1,763	-1,134	1,805	1,435	-1,276	-2,033	1,129
Residual	..	..	-176	-793	-109	2,654	-58	-357	-1,805	2,001
9. AVERAGE TERMS OF NEW COMMITMENTS										
ALL CREDITORS										
Interest (%)	..	..	7.5	7.0	7.3	6.8	7.8	6.4	6.4	7.4
Maturity (years)	..	..	15.3	13.9	15.6	14.1	2.9	9.8	9.9	8.2
Grace period (years)	..	..	5.1	3.6	4.6	6.3	2.8	4.3	6.1	8.0
Grant element (%)	..	..	14.4	14.2	14.7	17.8	5.0	16.0	17.4	13.1
Official creditors										
Interest (%)	..	..	7.2	7.4	7.4	6.9	0.0	6.3	5.6	4.3
Maturity (years)	..	..	17.8	16.9	16.3	14.8	0.0	16.8	14.9	14.9
Grace period (years)	..	..	5.6	4.3	4.8	5.1	0.0	4.6	5.4	5.4
Grant element (%)	..	..	17.8	15.2	15.1	17.0	0.0	21.7	25.6	34.0
Private creditors										
Interest (%)	..	..	8.5	6.3	6.7	6.7	7.8	6.4	6.9	7.4
Maturity (years)	..	..	7.3	7.5	6.9	13.1	2.9	4.4	6.7	8.1
Grace period (years)	..	..	3.6	1.9	2.5	8.3	2.8	4.0	6.6	8.1
Grant element (%)	..	..	3.9	12.1	10.3	19.1	5.0	11.6	12.0	12.7
Memorandum items										
Commitments	..	..	1,666	610	1,201	462	558	568	1,347	1,231
Official creditors	..	..	1,259	414	1,109	289	0	249	533	20
Private creditors	..	..	407	196	92	173	558	320	813	1,211

10. CONTRACTUAL OBLIGATIONS ON OUTSTANDING LONG-TERM DEBT

	1999	2000	2001	2002	2003	2004	2005	2006	2007	2008
TOTAL										
Disbursements	169	169	137	132	117	88	59	40	25	19
Principal	2,252	2,099	2,604	2,615	3,373	3,461	3,580	4,017	4,861	5,565
Interest	1,867	1,856	1,821	1,729	1,654	1,493	1,291	1,137	942	686
Official creditors										
Disbursements	128	150	137	132	117	88	59	40	25	19
Principal	737	919	1,248	1,677	2,179	2,600	3,144	3,600	4,111	4,570
Interest	1,277	1,248	1,208	1,150	1,069	965	836	681	507	310
Bilateral creditors										
Disbursements	1	0	0	0	0	0	0	0	0	0
Principal	535	692	1,011	1,436	1,885	2,305	2,848	3,304	3,815	4,367
Interest	1,126	1,102	1,070	1,021	951	861	748	610	454	274
Multilateral creditors										
Disbursements	127	150	137	132	117	88	59	40	25	19
Principal	203	227	237	242	294	296	296	296	296	204
Interest	151	145	137	129	118	104	88	71	53	36
Private creditors										
Disbursements	41	19	0	0	0	0	0	0	0	0
Principal	1,515	1,180	1,356	937	1,194	861	436	417	750	994
Interest	590	609	613	580	585	528	455	456	435	376
Commercial banks										
Disbursements	41	19	0	0	0	0	0	0	0	0
Principal	144	248	258	45	9	1	1	0	0	0
Interest	41	32	11	4	1	0	0	0	0	0
Other private										
Disbursements	0	0	0	0	0	0	0	0	0	0
Principal	1,371	932	1,098	892	1,185	860	435	417	750	994
Interest	549	577	602	576	584	528	455	456	435	376

ROMANIA

(US$ million, unless otherwise indicated)

	1970	1980	1990	1992	1993	1994	1995	1996	1997	1998
1. SUMMARY DEBT DATA										
TOTAL DEBT STOCKS (EDT)	..	**9,762**	**1,140**	**3,240**	**4,239**	**5,533**	**6,666**	**8,519**	**9,477**	**9,513**
Long-term debt (LDOD)	..	**7,131**	**230**	**1,447**	**2,316**	**3,243**	**4,325**	**7,052**	**7,887**	**7,825**
Public and publicly guaranteed	..	7,131	223	1,287	2,070	2,925	3,909	6,683	7,157	6,962
Private nonguaranteed	..	0	7	160	246	318	416	369	730	863
Use of IMF credit	**0**	**328**	**0**	**1,033**	**1,031**	**1,323**	**1,038**	**651**	**641**	**539**
Short-term debt	..	**2,303**	**910**	**761**	**892**	**966**	**1,303**	**815**	**949**	**1,149**
of which interest arrears on LDOD	..	0	0	0	0	0	0	0	0	21
Official creditors	..	0	0	0	0	0	0	0	0	0
Private creditors	..	0	0	0	0	0	0	0	0	21
Memo: principal arrears on LDOD	..	0	0	0	0	0	0	0	2	45
Official creditors	..	0	0	0	0	0	0	0	2	0
Private creditors	..	0	0	0	0	0	0	0	0	44
Memo: export credits	..	0	188	616	1,149	1,539	1,818	1,917	2,009	2,245
TOTAL DEBT FLOWS										
Disbursements	..	**2,955**	**27**	**1,706**	**1,048**	**1,349**	**1,333**	**3,409**	**2,328**	**1,257**
Long-term debt	..	2,797	27	1,229	1,048	998	1,276	3,409	2,162	1,257
IMF purchases	0	158	0	477	0	351	57	0	166	0
Principal repayments	..	**928**	**4**	**300**	**148**	**387**	**675**	**772**	**986**	**1,761**
Long-term debt	..	824	4	84	148	259	303	415	851	1,636
IMF repurchases	0	104	0	216	0	128	373	356	135	125
Net flows on debt	..	**4,330**	**45**	**1,179**	**1,031**	**1,036**	**995**	**2,150**	**1,475**	**-325**
of which short-term debt	..	2,303	22	-227	131	74	337	-488	134	179
Interest payments (INT)	..	**601**	**14**	**162**	**205**	**232**	**292**	**456**	**554**	**548**
Long-term debt	..	332	0	42	123	129	176	351	472	459
IMF charges	0	20	0	62	61	63	69	39	29	29
Short-term debt	..	249	14	57	21	40	47	67	53	60
Net transfers on debt	..	**3,729**	**30**	**1,018**	**826**	**804**	**703**	**1,694**	**922**	**-873**
Total debt service paid (TDS)	..	**1,529**	**18**	**462**	**353**	**619**	**967**	**1,228**	**1,540**	**2,310**
Long-term debt	..	1,156	4	126	271	388	479	766	1,322	2,095
IMF repurchases and charges	0	124	0	279	61	191	442	395	165	154
Short-term debt (interest only)	..	249	14	57	21	40	47	67	53	60
2. AGGREGATE NET RESOURCE FLOWS AND NET TRANSFERS (LONG-TERM)										
NET RESOURCE FLOWS	..	**1,973**	**26**	**1,422**	**1,093**	**1,177**	**1,428**	**3,371**	**2,651**	**1,825**
Net flow of long-term debt (ex. IMF)	..	1,973	23	1,146	900	739	974	2,994	1,311	-379
Foreign direct investment (net)	..	0	0	77	94	341	419	263	1,215	2,031
Portfolio equity flows	..	0	0	0	0	1	1	11	0	42
Grants (excluding technical coop.)	..	0	3	199	99	96	34	104	125	131
Memo: technical coop. grants	..	0	0	46	57	41	151	100	56	158
official net resource flows	..	613	22	1,204	845	566	741	1,321	461	-1
private net resource flows	..	1,360	4	217	248	611	687	2,050	2,191	1,826
NET TRANSFERS	..	**1,641**	**25**	**1,379**	**966**	**1,042**	**1,252**	**3,006**	**2,160**	**1,341**
Interest on long-term debt	..	332	0	42	123	129	176	351	472	459
Profit remittances on FDI	..	0	0	0	4	6	0	15	20	25
Memo: official net transfers	..	495	22	1,173	741	466	617	1,068	198	-229
private net transfers	..	1,146	3	206	224	576	634	1,938	1,962	1,570
3. MAJOR ECONOMIC AGGREGATES										
Gross national product (GNP)	..	..	38,455	25,010	26,214	27,918	32,618	30,905	34,521	37,645
Exports of goods & services (XGS)	..	12,160	6,555	5,077	5,754	7,315	9,489	9,736	10,161	9,836
of which workers remittances	..	0	0	0	..	4	4	10	2	4
Imports of goods & services (MGS)	..	14,580	9,915	6,648	7,142	8,022	11,628	12,890	12,875	13,503
International reserves (RES)	..	2,511	1,374	1,595	1,921	3,092	2,624	3,143	4,679	3,795
Current account balance	..	-2,420	-3,254	-1,506	-1,174	-428	-1,774	-2,571	-2,137	-2,918
4. DEBT INDICATORS										
EDT / XGS (%)	..	80.3	17.4	63.8	73.7	75.6	70.3	87.5	93.3	96.7
EDT / GNP (%)	..	..	3.0	13.0	16.2	19.8	20.4	27.6	27.5	25.3
TDS / XGS (%)	..	12.6	0.3	9.1	6.1	8.5	10.2	12.6	15.2	23.5
INT / XGS (%)	..	4.9	0.2	3.2	3.6	3.2	3.1	4.7	5.5	5.6
INT / GNP (%)	..	..	0.0	0.7	0.8	0.8	0.9	1.5	1.6	1.5
RES / EDT (%)	..	25.7	120.5	49.2	45.3	55.9	39.4	36.9	49.4	39.9
RES / MGS (months)	..	2.1	1.7	2.9	3.2	4.6	2.7	2.9	4.4	3.4
Short-term / EDT (%)	..	23.6	79.8	23.5	21.0	17.5	19.6	9.6	10.0	12.1
Concessional / EDT (%)	..	1.8	19.2	7.5	1.6	2.6	6.4	5.4	4.7	6.1
Multilateral / EDT (%)	..	8.3	0.0	24.4	23.2	23.8	25.4	22.8	23.5	24.9

ROMANIA

(US$ million, unless otherwise indicated)

	1970	1980	1990	1992	1993	1994	1995	1996	1997	1998
5. LONG-TERM DEBT										
DEBT OUTSTANDING (LDOD)	..	**7,131**	**230**	**1,447**	**2,316**	**3,243**	**4,325**	**7,052**	**7,887**	**7,825**
Public and publicly guaranteed	..	**7,131**	**223**	**1,287**	**2,070**	**2,925**	**3,909**	**6,683**	**7,157**	**6,962**
Official creditors	..	2,468	218	1,187	1,580	2,218	3,008	4,033	4,030	4,086
Multilateral	..	807	0	789	982	1,315	1,695	1,943	2,230	2,368
Concessional	..	0	0	0	0	0	0	0	0	0
Bilateral	..	1,661	218	398	598	903	1,313	2,090	1,801	1,718
Concessional	..	174	218	241	68	142	424	460	449	577
Private creditors	..	4,663	5	100	491	708	901	2,651	3,127	2,877
Bonds	..	0	0	0	0	0	0	982	1,241	1,343
Commercial banks	..	4,222	0	0	148	210	314	1,041	1,320	967
Other private	..	441	5	100	343	498	587	628	566	566
Private nonguaranteed	..	**0**	**7**	**160**	**246**	**318**	**416**	**369**	**730**	**863**
Bonds	..	0	0	0	0	0	0	0	75	75
Commercial banks	..	0	7	160	246	318	416	369	655	788
Memo:										
IBRD	0	807	0	210	403	695	844	1,009	1,305	1,443
IDA	0	0	0	0	0	0	0	0	0	0
DISBURSEMENTS	..	**2,797**	**27**	**1,229**	**1,048**	**998**	**1,276**	**3,409**	**2,162**	**1,257**
Public and publicly guaranteed	..	**2,797**	**24**	**1,160**	**883**	**926**	**1,093**	**3,382**	**1,745**	**1,052**
Official creditors	..	954	19	1,054	792	683	839	1,422	658	673
Multilateral	..	239	0	826	770	338	328	380	532	397
Concessional	..	0	0	0	0	0	0	0	0	0
Bilateral	..	715	19	227	22	344	511	1,042	126	276
Concessional	..	0	19	66	0	65	286	72	53	107
Private creditors	..	1,843	5	107	91	243	254	1,959	1,087	379
Bonds	..	0	0	0	0	0	0	1,029	347	0
Commercial banks	..	1,402	0	0	4	64	117	772	648	286
Other private	..	441	5	107	87	179	137	158	93	93
Private nonguaranteed	..	**0**	**3**	**69**	**165**	**72**	**183**	**27**	**417**	**206**
Bonds	..	0	0	0	0	0	0	0	75	0
Commercial banks	..	0	3	69	165	72	183	27	342	206
Memo:										
IBRD	0	239	0	211	189	263	129	228	399	153
IDA	0	0	0	0	0	0	0	0	0	0
PRINCIPAL REPAYMENTS	..	**824**	**4**	**84**	**148**	**259**	**303**	**415**	**851**	**1,636**
Public and publicly guaranteed	..	**824**	**0**	**59**	**69**	**259**	**217**	**341**	**795**	**1,563**
Official creditors	..	341	0	48	46	213	133	205	322	804
Multilateral	..	22	0	0	6	148	14	35	78	350
Concessional	..	0	0	0	0	0	0	0	0	0
Bilateral	..	319	0	48	40	65	118	171	244	454
Concessional	..	0	0	48	40	1	0	3	5	10
Private creditors	..	483	0	11	23	46	85	136	473	759
Bonds	..	0	0	0	0	0	0	0	0	0
Commercial banks	..	483	0	0	0	7	19	37	348	651
Other private	..	0	0	11	23	39	65	99	125	108
Private nonguaranteed	..	**0**	**4**	**25**	**79**	**0**	**86**	**74**	**56**	**73**
Bonds	..	0	0	0	0	0	0	0	0	0
Commercial banks	..	0	4	25	79	0	86	74	56	73
Memo:										
IBRD	0	22	0	0	0	0	0	0	29	69
IDA	0	0	0	0	0	0	0	0	0	0
NET FLOWS ON DEBT	..	**1,973**	**23**	**1,146**	**900**	**739**	**974**	**2,994**	**1,311**	**-379**
Public and publicly guaranteed	..	**1,973**	**24**	**1,102**	**814**	**667**	**876**	**3,041**	**950**	**-512**
Official creditors	..	613	19	1,006	746	470	707	1,217	336	-132
Multilateral	..	217	0	826	764	191	313	345	455	46
Concessional	..	0	0	0	0	0	0	0	0	0
Bilateral	..	396	19	179	-18	280	393	872	-119	-178
Concessional	..	0	19	18	-40	65	286	69	48	97
Private creditors	..	1,360	5	96	68	197	170	1,823	614	-380
Bonds	..	0	0	0	0	0	0	1,029	347	0
Commercial banks	..	919	0	0	4	57	98	735	300	-365
Other private	..	441	5	96	64	140	72	59	-32	-15
Private nonguaranteed	..	**0**	**-1**	**44**	**86**	**72**	**98**	**-47**	**361**	**133**
Bonds	..	0	0	0	0	0	0	0	75	0
Commercial banks	..	0	-1	44	86	72	98	-47	286	133
Memo:										
IBRD	0	217	0	211	189	263	129	228	371	84
IDA	0	0	0	0	0	0	0	0	0	0

ROMANIA

(US$ million, unless otherwise indicated)

	1970	1980	1990	1992	1993	1994	1995	1996	1997	1998
INTEREST PAYMENTS (LINT)	..	**332**	**0**	**42**	**123**	**129**	**176**	**351**	**472**	**459**
Public and publicly guaranteed	..	**332**	**0**	**34**	**115**	**129**	**176**	**335**	**443**	**407**
Official creditors	..	118	0	31	104	100	124	253	263	228
Multilateral	..	59	0	25	87	68	70	156	159	143
Concessional	..	0	0	0	0	0	0	0	0	0
Bilateral	..	59	0	6	17	33	54	97	104	84
Concessional	..	0	0	2	3	4	7	15	15	15
Private creditors	..	214	0	3	12	29	52	82	180	179
Bonds	..	0	0	0	0	0	0	10	61	85
Commercial banks	..	173	0	0	0	8	9	25	75	65
Other private	..	42	0	3	11	21	43	46	44	29
Private nonguaranteed	..	**0**	**0**	**8**	**8**	**0**	**0**	**16**	**28**	**53**
Bonds	..	0	0	0	0	0	0	0	0	7
Commercial banks	..	0	0	8	8	0	0	16	28	46
Memo:										
IBRD	0	59	0	2	19	32	53	63	70	82
IDA	0	0	0	0	0	0	0	0	0	0
NET TRANSFERS ON DEBT	..	**1,641**	**22**	**1,103**	**777**	**610**	**798**	**2,643**	**840**	**-838**
Public and publicly guaranteed	..	**1,641**	**24**	**1,067**	**699**	**538**	**700**	**2,706**	**507**	**-918**
Official creditors	..	495	19	974	643	370	583	964	73	-359
Multilateral	..	158	0	801	678	123	243	189	296	-97
Concessional	..	0	0	0	0	0	0	0	0	0
Bilateral	..	337	19	173	-35	247	340	775	-223	-262
Concessional	..	0	19	16	-44	61	279	54	34	82
Private creditors	..	1,146	5	93	56	168	118	1,742	434	-559
Bonds	..	0	0	0	0	0	0	1,019	286	-85
Commercial banks	..	747	0	0	4	50	88	710	225	-430
Other private	..	399	5	93	52	118	29	13	-76	-44
Private nonguaranteed	..	**0**	**-1**	**36**	**78**	**72**	**97**	**-63**	**333**	**80**
Bonds	..	0	0	0	0	0	0	0	75	-7
Commercial banks	..	0	-1	36	78	72	97	-63	258	87
Memo:										
IBRD	0	158	0	209	169	230	76	164	301	3
IDA	0	0	0	0	0	0	0	0	0	0
DEBT SERVICE (LTDS)	..	**1,156**	**4**	**126**	**271**	**388**	**479**	**766**	**1,322**	**2,095**
Public and publicly guaranteed	..	**1,156**	**0**	**93**	**184**	**388**	**393**	**676**	**1,238**	**1,970**
Official creditors	..	459	0	79	149	313	256	459	585	1,032
Multilateral	..	81	0	25	92	216	85	191	237	494
Concessional	..	0	0	0	0	0	0	0	0	0
Bilateral	..	378	0	54	57	97	172	267	349	538
Concessional	..	0	0	51	44	4	8	18	19	25
Private creditors	..	698	0	14	35	75	137	218	653	938
Bonds	..	0	0	0	0	0	0	10	61	85
Commercial banks	..	656	0	0	0	15	29	62	423	716
Other private	..	42	0	14	35	61	108	145	169	137
Private nonguaranteed	..	**0**	**4**	**33**	**87**	**0**	**86**	**90**	**84**	**125**
Bonds	..	0	0	0	0	0	0	0	0	7
Commercial banks	..	0	4	33	87	0	86	90	84	119
Memo:										
IBRD	0	81	0	2	19	32	53	63	99	150
IDA	0	0	0	0	0	0	0	0	0	0
UNDISBURSED DEBT	..	**1,865**	**113**	**3,599**	**1,889**	**1,968**	**2,337**	**3,126**	**2,934**	**2,185**
Official creditors	..	1,347	0	2,299	1,463	1,506	1,879	2,555	2,543	2,019
Private creditors	..	518	113	1,300	426	462	458	571	390	166
Memorandum items										
Concessional LDOD	..	174	218	241	68	142	424	460	449	577
Variable rate LDOD	..	4,222	7	1,084	912	1,418	1,760	2,446	2,918	3,285
Public sector LDOD	..	7,131	223	1,287	2,070	2,925	3,909	6,659	7,140	6,937
Private sector LDOD	..	0	7	160	246	318	416	394	748	888

6. CURRENCY COMPOSITION OF LONG-TERM DEBT (PERCENT)

	1970	1980	1990	1992	1993	1994	1995	1996	1997	1998
Deutsche mark	..	2.1	0.0	0.0	3.6	4.3	10.9	6.6	10.5	11.8
French franc	..	0.0	0.8	3.1	4.0	5.0	5.0	3.7	3.4	3.7
Japanese yen	..	0.0	0.0	0.0	3.0	3.7	2.8	22.8	19.0	18.1
Pound sterling	..	0.0	0.0	0.0	0.0	0.0	0.0	0.0	0.0	0.0
Swiss franc	..	2.6	89.5	12.1	5.9	4.0	1.8	1.0	0.7	1.0
U.S.dollars	..	83.8	9.8	15.6	35.4	36.5	35.4	36.4	39.8	37.1
Multiple currency	..	11.5	0.0	19.5	19.5	23.8	21.6	15.1	14.3	16.2
Special drawing rights	..	0.0	0.0	0.0	0.0	0.0	0.0	0.0	0.0	0.0
All other currencies	..	0.0	0.0	49.7	28.6	22.7	22.5	14.4	12.3	12.1

ROMANIA

(US$ million, unless otherwise indicated)

	1970	1980	1990	1992	1993	1994	1995	1996	1997	1998
7. DEBT RESTRUCTURINGS										
Total amount rescheduled	..	..	0	0	0	0	0	0	0	0
Debt stock rescheduled	..	..	0	0	0	0	0	0	0	0
Principal rescheduled	..	..	0	0	0	0	0	0	0	0
Official	..	..	0	0	0	0	0	0	0	0
Private	..	..	0	0	0	0	0	0	0	0
Interest rescheduled	..	..	0	0	0	0	0	0	0	0
Official	..	..	0	0	0	0	0	0	0	0
Private	..	..	0	0	0	0	0	0	0	0
Debt forgiven	..	..	0	0	0	0	0	0	0	0
Memo: interest forgiven	..	..	0	0	0	0	0	0	0	0
Debt stock reduction	..	..	0	0	0	0	0	0	0	0
of which debt buyback	..	..	0	0	0	0	0	0	0	0
8. DEBT STOCK-FLOW RECONCILIATION										
Total change in debt stocks	..	..	53	1,109	999	1,293	1,134	1,853	958	36
Net flows on debt	..	4,330	45	1,179	1,031	1,036	995	2,150	1,475	-325
Net change in interest arrears	..	..	0	0	0	0	0	0	0	21
Interest capitalized	..	..	0	0	0	0	0	0	0	0
Debt forgiveness or reduction	..	..	0	0	0	0	0	0	0	0
Cross-currency valuation	..	..	39	-80	-48	144	134	-333	-460	351
Residual	..	..	-30	9	16	114	5	37	-58	-11
9. AVERAGE TERMS OF NEW COMMITMENTS										
ALL CREDITORS										
Interest (%)	..	14.1	7.6	7.2	6.1	6.6	6.1	5.7	8.6	5.1
Maturity (years)	..	8.5	10.7	13.1	12.5	12.1	12.2	6.9	10.2	10.3
Grace period (years)	..	3.5	4.5	4.4	3.9	3.8	4.0	3.5	3.5	3.8
Grant element (%)	..	-16.0	13.2	13.9	20.1	14.5	18.7	15.4	12.5	16.4
Official creditors										
Interest (%)	..	8.0	2.7	6.6	5.8	6.3	6.0	4.6	6.1	8.3
Maturity (years)	..	14.9	25.5	14.2	14.6	13.2	13.3	9.5	18.9	13.4
Grace period (years)	..	3.4	10.0	4.9	4.7	4.4	4.3	4.2	5.2	6.3
Grant element (%)	..	10.0	57.3	18.0	24.2	16.1	20.5	21.3	24.6	9.9
Private creditors										
Interest (%)	..	15.0	8.4	8.6	6.6	7.2	7.0	6.7	10.5	1.3
Maturity (years)	..	7.6	8.2	10.7	8.9	9.5	6.0	4.2	3.4	6.6
Grace period (years)	..	3.6	3.6	3.2	2.5	2.1	2.1	2.8	2.2	0.9
Grant element (%)	..	-19.8	5.8	5.2	13.2	10.7	8.5	9.3	3.0	24.1
Memorandum items										
Commitments	..	1,886	132	3,103	689	996	1,597	4,243	1,689	323
Official creditors	..	240	19	2,100	437	716	1,352	2,146	746	175
Private creditors	..	1,646	113	1,003	253	281	246	2,097	943	147

10. CONTRACTUAL OBLIGATIONS ON OUTSTANDING LONG-TERM DEBT

	1999	2000	2001	2002	2003	2004	2005	2006	2007	2008
TOTAL										
Disbursements	783	572	316	206	123	80	46	32	16	7
Principal	2,561	1,057	1,113	1,308	746	634	457	352	316	286
Interest	531	454	413	379	304	269	240	217	99	81
Official creditors										
Disbursements	692	524	296	200	122	80	46	32	16	7
Principal	1,126	538	439	638	519	466	366	321	292	270
Interest	271	243	232	220	183	156	133	114	96	80
Bilateral creditors										
Disbursements	64	83	31	13	2	1	0	0	0	0
Principal	830	229	188	189	191	146	58	20	13	12
Interest	71	50	42	35	25	13	7	4	3	3
Multilateral creditors										
Disbursements	627	441	265	187	120	79	46	32	16	7
Principal	296	309	251	449	328	320	308	300	279	258
Interest	200	193	191	185	159	143	127	110	93	77
Private creditors										
Disbursements	91	48	20	6	1	0	0	0	0	0
Principal	1,435	519	675	669	227	167	91	31	24	16
Interest	260	211	181	159	120	112	106	103	3	1
Commercial banks										
Disbursements	63	31	12	3	0	0	0	0	0	0
Principal	426	152	122	115	82	65	42	18	16	15
Interest	51	30	23	17	12	8	5	3	2	1
Other private										
Disbursements	28	18	8	3	1	0	0	0	0	0
Principal	1,010	367	553	555	145	102	50	13	8	1
Interest	209	181	158	142	109	104	101	100	1	0

RUSSIAN FEDERATION

(US$ million, unless otherwise indicated)

	1970	1980	1990	1992	1993	1994	1995	1996	1997	1998
1. SUMMARY DEBT DATA										
TOTAL DEBT STOCKS (EDT)	..	..	**59,797**	**78,356**	**111,731**	**121,457**	**120,333**	**124,887**	**126,037**	**183,601**
Long-term debt (LDOD)	..	..	**47,997**	**64,255**	**100,972**	**107,397**	**100,360**	**100,259**	**106,731**	**145,874**
Public and publicly guaranteed	..	..	47,997	64,255	100,972	107,397	100,360	100,259	104,826	119,314
Private nonguaranteed	..	..	0	0	0	0	0	0	1,905	26,560
Use of IMF credit	**0**	**0**	**0**	**989**	**2,469**	**4,198**	**9,617**	**12,508**	**13,231**	**19,335**
Short-term debt	..	..	**11,800**	**13,112**	**8,291**	**9,862**	**10,355**	**12,120**	**6,076**	**18,392**
of which interest arrears on LDOD	..	..	4,500	4,412	2,891	5,162	6,005	7,520	2,876	4,792
Official creditors	..	..	0	479	628	1,028	1,430	1,985	2,127	3,560
Private creditors	..	..	4,500	3,934	2,262	4,134	4,575	5,535	750	1,232
Memo: principal arrears on LDOD	..	..	0	6,583	6,966	13,719	22,435	25,595	6,516	5,777
Official creditors	..	..	0	246	263	824	4,229	4,852	4,920	4,070
Private creditors	..	..	0	6,336	6,703	12,895	18,207	20,742	1,595	1,707
Memo: export credits	..	..	15,056	36,068	39,846	41,992	47,644	45,790	40,344	41,612
TOTAL DEBT FLOWS										
Disbursements	..	..	**16,978**	**12,862**	**5,843**	**3,832**	**7,714**	**9,698**	**10,806**	**27,297**
Long-term debt	..	..	16,978	11,849	4,338	2,288	2,261	5,941	8,787	21,056
IMF purchases	0	0	0	1,013	1,506	1,544	5,453	3,757	2,019	6,241
Principal repayments	..	..	**7,942**	**994**	**1,438**	**2,181**	**3,169**	**2,944**	**1,653**	**4,974**
Long-term debt	..	..	7,942	994	1,438	2,181	3,169	2,422	1,158	4,059
IMF repurchases	0	0	0	0	0	0	0	522	495	914
Net flows on debt	..	..	**-1,363**	**12,768**	**3,806**	**1,152**	**4,655**	**7,004**	**7,753**	**21,824**
of which short-term debt	..	..	-10,400	900	-600	-500	110	250	-1,400	-500
Interest payments (INT)	..	..	**3,884**	**356**	**748**	**1,260**	**2,746**	**4,079**	**5,026**	**5,787**
Long-term debt	..	..	2,642	356	655	1,085	2,451	3,609	4,444	5,070
IMF charges	0	0	0	0	78	175	294	470	582	718
Short-term debt	..	..	1,242	0	14	0	0	0	0	0
Net transfers on debt	..	..	**-5,247**	**12,413**	**3,058**	**-108**	**1,910**	**2,925**	**2,727**	**16,036**
Total debt service paid (TDS)	..	..	**11,826**	**1,349**	**2,186**	**3,441**	**5,914**	**7,023**	**6,679**	**10,761**
Long-term debt	..	..	10,584	1,349	2,093	3,266	5,620	6,031	5,602	9,129
IMF repurchases and charges	0	0	0	0	78	175	294	992	1,077	1,632
Short-term debt (interest only)	..	..	1,242	0	14	0	0	0	0	0
2. AGGREGATE NET RESOURCE FLOWS AND NET TRANSFERS (LONG-TERM)										
NET RESOURCE FLOWS	..	..	**9,037**	**12,657**	**4,506**	**2,581**	**2,199**	**11,466**	**15,373**	**20,142**
Net flow of long-term debt (ex. IMF)	..	..	9,037	10,856	2,900	107	-908	3,519	7,629	16,997
Foreign direct investment (net)	..	..	0	0	0	637	2,017	2,479	6,243	2,764
Portfolio equity flows	..	..	0	0	0	271	141	5,008	1,206	296
Grants (excluding technical coop.)	..	..	0	1,802	1,606	1,566	949	460	295	85
Memo: technical coop. grants	..	..	0	133	303	263	526	820	430	827
official net resource flows	..	..	3,474	3,323	2,451	2,005	991	4,030	2,940	796
private net resource flows	..	..	5,562	9,335	2,055	576	1,208	7,436	12,433	19,347
NET TRANSFERS	..	..	**6,395**	**12,302**	**3,851**	**1,496**	**-252**	**7,857**	**10,929**	**15,073**
Interest on long-term debt	..	..	2,642	356	655	1,085	2,451	3,609	4,444	5,070
Profit remittances on FDI	..	..	0	0	0	0	0	0	0	0
Memo: official net transfers	..	..	3,362	3,265	2,388	1,626	-240	1,974	232	-989
private net transfers	..	..	3,033	9,036	1,463	-130	-12	5,883	10,697	16,062
3. MAJOR ECONOMIC AGGREGATES										
Gross national product (GNP)	..	..	539,326	420,930	383,104	320,717	331,652	410,857	426,290	264,604
Exports of goods & services (XGS)	..	..	..	54,783	65,785	77,526	92,510	104,652	104,435	88,634
of which workers remittances	..	..	..	0	0	0	0	0	0	0
Imports of goods & services (MGS)	..	..	..	54,315	63,110	68,730	85,585	94,973	101,382	86,978
International reserves (RES)	..	..	..	..	9,818	7,206	18,024	16,258	17,624	12,043
Current account balance	..	..	..	468	2,675	8,684	6,997	9,749	2,693	1,241
4. DEBT INDICATORS										
EDT / XGS (%)	..	..	..	143.0	169.8	156.7	130.1	119.3	120.7	207.2
EDT / GNP (%)	..	..	11.1	18.6	29.2	37.9	36.3	30.4	29.6	69.4
TDS / XGS (%)	..	..	..	2.5	3.3	4.4	6.4	6.7	6.4	12.1
INT / XGS (%)	..	..	..	0.7	1.1	1.6	3.0	3.9	4.8	6.5
INT / GNP (%)	..	..	0.7	0.1	0.2	0.4	0.8	1.0	1.2	2.2
RES / EDT (%)	..	..	..	..	8.8	5.9	15.0	13.0	14.0	6.6
RES / MGS (months)	..	..	..	..	1.9	1.3	2.5	2.1	2.1	1.7
Short-term / EDT (%)	..	..	19.7	16.7	7.4	8.1	8.6	9.7	4.8	10.0
Concessional / EDT (%)	..	..	0.0	1.3	1.9	2.0	2.1	2.0	1.8	1.3
Multilateral / EDT (%)	..	..	0.7	0.7	1.1	1.3	1.7	2.2	4.2	3.6

RUSSIAN FEDERATION

(US$ million, unless otherwise indicated)

	1970	1980	1990	1992	1993	1994	1995	1996	1997	1998
5. LONG-TERM DEBT										
DEBT OUTSTANDING (LDOD)	..	..	**47,997**	**64,255**	**100,972**	**107,397**	**100,360**	**100,259**	**106,731**	**145,874**
Public and publicly guaranteed	..	..	**47,997**	**64,255**	**100,972**	**107,397**	**100,360**	**100,259**	**104,826**	**119,314**
Official creditors	..	..	5,915	10,821	54,267	62,807	57,202	62,838	63,271	68,240
Multilateral	..	..	439	538	1,278	1,532	1,985	2,762	5,289	6,577
Concessional	..	..	0	0	0	0	0	0	0	0
Bilateral	..	..	5,476	10,283	52,989	61,275	55,217	60,076	57,982	61,662
Concessional	..	..	0	1,019	2,146	2,456	2,541	2,451	2,311	2,300
Private creditors	..	..	42,082	53,435	46,705	44,590	43,159	37,421	41,555	51,074
Bonds	..	..	1,891	1,740	1,626	1,776	1,115	1,074	4,585	15,981
Commercial banks	..	..	17,916	18,511	15,879	16,380	16,674	15,628	29,288	29,305
Other private	..	..	22,275	33,184	29,200	26,435	25,370	20,719	7,682	5,788
Private nonguaranteed	..	..	**0**	**0**	**0**	**0**	**0**	**0**	**1,905**	**26,560**
Bonds	..	..	0	0	0	0	0	0	1,905	2,190
Commercial banks	..	..	0	0	0	0	0	0	0	24,371
Memo:										
IBRD	0	0	0	0	367	684	1,524	2,509	5,053	6,337
IDA	0	0	0	0	0	0	0	0	0	0
DISBURSEMENTS	..	..	**16,978**	**11,849**	**4,338**	**2,288**	**2,261**	**5,941**	**8,787**	**21,056**
Public and publicly guaranteed	..	..	**16,978**	**11,849**	**4,338**	**2,288**	**2,261**	**5,941**	**6,882**	**14,169**
Official creditors	..	..	3,713	1,705	1,067	718	959	4,038	3,018	1,904
Multilateral	..	..	201	181	919	392	856	1,187	2,748	1,293
Concessional	..	..	0	0	0	0	0	0	0	0
Bilateral	..	..	3,512	1,524	148	326	104	2,852	270	611
Concessional	..	..	0	0	0	0	0	0	0	0
Private creditors	..	..	13,265	10,144	3,270	1,571	1,302	1,903	3,863	12,265
Bonds	..	..	310	0	0	0	0	1,000	3,555	11,329
Commercial banks	..	..	484	2,434	104	3	21	6	2	6
Other private	..	..	12,471	7,711	3,167	1,567	1,281	897	306	931
Private nonguaranteed	..	..	**0**	**0**	**0**	**0**	**0**	**0**	**1,905**	**6,887**
Bonds	..	..	0	0	0	0	0	0	1,905	278
Commercial banks	..	..	0	0	0	0	0	0	0	6,609
Memo:										
IBRD	0	0	0	1	371	283	824	1,097	2,691	1,226
IDA	0	0	0	0	0	0	0	0	0	0
PRINCIPAL REPAYMENTS	..	..	**7,942**	**994**	**1,438**	**2,181**	**3,169**	**2,422**	**1,158**	**4,059**
Public and publicly guaranteed	..	..	**7,942**	**994**	**1,438**	**2,181**	**3,169**	**2,422**	**1,158**	**3,634**
Official creditors	..	..	239	184	222	279	917	468	373	1,193
Multilateral	..	..	7	33	157	193	434	291	68	129
Concessional	..	..	0	0	0	0	0	0	0	0
Bilateral	..	..	232	151	66	86	483	177	305	1,065
Concessional	..	..	0	0	0	0	0	0	0	73
Private creditors	..	..	7,703	810	1,216	1,902	2,252	1,954	785	2,441
Bonds	..	..	0	0	0	34	810	979	0	69
Commercial banks	..	..	4,092	185	489	71	51	30	29	270
Other private	..	..	3,611	625	726	1,797	1,390	944	756	2,102
Private nonguaranteed	..	..	**0**	**0**	**0**	**0**	**0**	**0**	**0**	**426**
Bonds	..	..	0	0	0	0	0	0	0	0
Commercial banks	..	..	0	0	0	0	0	0	0	426
Memo:										
IBRD	0	0	0	0	0	0	0	0	0	66
IDA	0	0	0	0	0	0	0	0	0	0
NET FLOWS ON DEBT	..	..	**9,037**	**10,856**	**2,900**	**107**	**-908**	**3,519**	**7,629**	**16,997**
Public and publicly guaranteed	..	..	**9,037**	**10,856**	**2,900**	**107**	**-908**	**3,519**	**5,724**	**10,536**
Official creditors	..	..	3,474	1,521	845	439	42	3,570	2,645	711
Multilateral	..	..	194	148	763	199	421	896	2,680	1,164
Concessional	..	..	0	0	0	0	0	0	0	0
Bilateral	..	..	3,280	1,373	83	240	-379	2,674	-35	-454
Concessional	..	..	0	0	0	0	0	0	0	-73
Private creditors	..	..	5,562	9,335	2,055	-332	-950	-51	3,079	9,825
Bonds	..	..	310	0	0	-34	-810	21	3,555	11,260
Commercial banks	..	..	-3,608	2,249	-386	-68	-31	-24	-27	-264
Other private	..	..	8,860	7,086	2,440	-229	-109	-47	-449	-1,171
Private nonguaranteed	..	..	**0**	**0**	**0**	**0**	**0**	**0**	**1,905**	**6,461**
Bonds	..	..	0	0	0	0	0	0	1,905	278
Commercial banks	..	..	0	0	0	0	0	0	0	6,183
Memo:										
IBRD	0	0	0	1	371	283	824	1,097	2,691	1,160
IDA	0	0	0	0	0	0	0	0	0	0

RUSSIAN FEDERATION

(US$ million, unless otherwise indicated)

	1970	1980	1990	1992	1993	1994	1995	1996	1997	1998
INTEREST PAYMENTS (LINT)	..	..	**2,642**	**356**	**655**	**1,085**	**2,451**	**3,609**	**4,444**	**5,070**
Public and publicly guaranteed	..	..	**2,642**	**356**	**655**	**1,085**	**2,451**	**3,609**	**4,444**	**3,477**
Official creditors	..	..	113	58	63	379	1,232	2,056	2,708	1,785
Multilateral	..	..	17	7	40	101	133	153	200	332
Concessional	..	..	0	0	0	0	0	0	0	0
Bilateral	..	..	95	51	23	278	1,099	1,903	2,508	1,453
Concessional	..	..	0	0	0	13	59	84	100	105
Private creditors	..	..	2,530	298	592	706	1,220	1,553	1,736	1,692
Bonds	..	..	96	132	118	121	140	58	216	670
Commercial banks	..	..	1,441	131	317	1	600	1,156	1,250	790
Other private	..	..	993	36	158	583	479	339	269	233
Private nonguaranteed	..	..	**0**	**0**	**0**	**0**	**0**	**0**	**0**	**1,593**
Bonds	..	..	0	0	0	0	0	0	0	129
Commercial banks	..	..	0	0	0	0	0	0	0	1,464
Memo:										
IBRD	0	0	0	0	12	38	57	121	178	316
IDA	0	0	0	0	0	0	0	0	0	0
NET TRANSFERS ON DEBT	..	..	**6,395**	**10,500**	**2,245**	**-977**	**-3,359**	**-90**	**3,185**	**11,927**
Public and publicly guaranteed	..	..	**6,395**	**10,500**	**2,245**	**-977**	**-3,359**	**-90**	**1,280**	**7,059**
Official creditors	..	..	3,362	1,463	782	60	-1,189	1,514	-63	-1,075
Multilateral	..	..	177	141	723	98	289	743	2,480	832
Concessional	..	..	0	0	0	0	0	0	0	0
Bilateral	..	..	3,185	1,322	59	-38	-1,478	772	-2,543	-1,907
Concessional	..	..	0	0	0	-13	-59	-84	-100	-178
Private creditors	..	..	3,033	9,036	1,463	-1,038	-2,170	-1,604	1,343	8,133
Bonds	..	..	214	-132	-118	-155	-951	-38	3,339	10,590
Commercial banks	..	..	-5,049	2,118	-702	-70	-631	-1,180	-1,277	-1,054
Other private	..	..	7,867	7,050	2,283	-813	-589	-387	-719	-1,403
Private nonguaranteed	..	..	**0**	**0**	**0**	**0**	**0**	**0**	**1,905**	**4,868**
Bonds	..	..	0	0	0	0	0	0	1,905	149
Commercial banks	..	..	0	0	0	0	0	0	0	4,719
Memo:										
IBRD	0	0	0	1	360	245	767	976	2,513	844
IDA	0	0	0	0	0	0	0	0	0	0
DEBT SERVICE (LTDS)	..	..	**10,584**	**1,349**	**2,093**	**3,266**	**5,620**	**6,031**	**5,602**	**9,129**
Public and publicly guaranteed	..	..	**10,584**	**1,349**	**2,093**	**3,266**	**5,620**	**6,031**	**5,602**	**7,111**
Official creditors	..	..	351	242	285	657	2,149	2,524	3,082	2,978
Multilateral	..	..	24	40	196	293	567	444	268	461
Concessional	..	..	0	0	0	0	0	0	0	0
Bilateral	..	..	327	202	89	364	1,582	2,080	2,813	2,517
Concessional	..	..	0	0	0	13	59	84	100	178
Private creditors	..	..	10,233	1,108	1,808	2,608	3,472	3,507	2,520	4,132
Bonds	..	..	96	132	118	155	951	1,038	216	739
Commercial banks	..	..	5,533	316	806	73	652	1,186	1,279	1,060
Other private	..	..	4,604	661	884	2,380	1,870	1,284	1,025	2,334
Private nonguaranteed	..	..	**0**	**0**	**0**	**0**	**0**	**0**	**0**	**2,019**
Bonds	..	..	0	0	0	0	0	0	0	129
Commercial banks	..	..	0	0	0	0	0	0	0	1,889
Memo:										
IBRD	0	0	0	0	12	38	57	121	178	382
IDA	0	0	0	0	0	0	0	0	0	0
UNDISBURSED DEBT	..	..	**1,301**	**6,793**	**7,478**	**8,411**	**9,371**	**8,245**	**7,142**	**6,260**
Official creditors	..	..	62	2,454	2,485	3,495	4,814	4,845	5,096	5,416
Private creditors	..	..	1,240	4,339	4,993	4,917	4,557	3,400	2,046	844
Memorandum items										
Concessional LDOD	..	..	0	1,019	2,146	2,456	2,541	2,451	2,311	2,300
Variable rate LDOD	..	..	17,749	36,302	48,837	49,242	49,844	51,520	66,983	92,351
Public sector LDOD	..	..	47,997	64,255	100,972	107,397	100,360	100,259	104,826	119,314
Private sector LDOD	..	..	0	0	0	0	0	0	1,905	26,560
6. CURRENCY COMPOSITION OF LONG-TERM DEBT (PERCENT)										
Deutsche mark	..	..	34.1	39.6	24.5	28.3	35.1	38.9	29.8	30.5
French franc	..	..	6.1	4.4	1.6	1.2	1.5	1.9	0.5	0.5
Japanese yen	..	..	2.9	2.4	1.7	1.9	2.0	1.9	0.2	0.2
Pound sterling	..	..	2.3	1.2	0.6	0.4	0.4	0.4	0.1	0.1
Swiss franc	..	..	6.4	3.7	2.3	2.4	2.8	2.4	0.1	0.0
U.S.dollars	..	..	33.5	37.1	62.4	59.2	51.5	48.5	64.0	63.0
Multiple currency	..	..	0.0	0.0	0.4	0.6	1.5	2.5	4.8	5.0
Special drawing rights	..	..	0.0	0.0	0.0	0.0	0.0	0.0	0.0	0.0
All other currencies	..	..	14.7	11.6	6.5	6.0	5.2	3.5	0.5	0.7

RUSSIAN FEDERATION

(US$ million, unless otherwise indicated)

	1970	1980	1990	1992	1993	1994	1995	1996	1997	1998
7. DEBT RESTRUCTURINGS										
Total amount rescheduled	..	..	0	0	14,498	8,339	7,166	7,367	34,656	5,270
Debt stock rescheduled	..	..	0	0	0	0	0	0	121	0
Principal rescheduled	..	..	0	0	9,227	5,830	5,427	5,568	28,987	3,861
Official	..	..	0	0	274	342	2,069	2,338	3,718	2,855
Private	..	..	0	0	8,954	5,488	3,358	3,230	25,269	1,006
Interest rescheduled	..	..	0	0	4,334	2,186	1,122	1,006	5,263	525
Official	..	..	0	0	393	705	547	432	581	367
Private	..	..	0	0	3,941	1,481	575	574	4,682	158
Debt forgiven	..	..	0	0	0	0	0	0	0	0
Memo: interest forgiven	..	..	0	0	0	0	0	0	0	0
Debt stock reduction	..	..	0	0	0	0	0	0	5	0
of which debt buyback	..	..	0	0	0	0	0	0	0	0
8. DEBT STOCK-FLOW RECONCILIATION										
Total change in debt stocks	..	..	5,875	10,584	33,375	9,726	-1,124	4,554	1,151	57,565
Net flows on debt	..	..	-1,363	12,768	3,806	1,152	4,655	7,004	7,753	21,824
Net change in interest arrears	..	..	4,000	-406	-1,521	2,271	843	1,515	-4,644	1,916
Interest capitalized	..	..	0	0	4,334	2,186	1,122	1,006	5,263	525
Debt forgiveness or reduction	..	..	0	0	0	0	0	0	-5	0
Cross-currency valuation	..	..	4,408	-2,706	-2,058	4,889	3,716	-3,985	-4,460	2,837
Residual	..	..	-1,170	927	28,814	-771	-11,460	-986	-2,757	30,462
9. AVERAGE TERMS OF NEW COMMITMENTS										
ALL CREDITORS										
Interest (%)	..	..	8.3	6.3	4.3	6.6	7.0	7.6	7.9	9.8
Maturity (years)	..	..	20.9	7.6	7.4	13.0	14.2	9.8	12.7	14.7
Grace period (years)	..	..	6.0	1.9	2.1	4.0	4.5	4.4	6.8	13.4
Grant element (%)	..	..	8.5	11.5	18.0	15.8	15.9	11.4	12.2	-2.4
Official creditors										
Interest (%)	..	..	8.4	5.4	4.5	6.8	7.0	6.3	6.4	6.4
Maturity (years)	..	..	10.8	8.2	13.4	16.2	15.9	10.9	16.5	10.6
Grace period (years)	..	..	5.9	2.8	4.2	5.1	5.0	4.1	5.3	4.2
Grant element (%)	..	..	7.6	15.1	29.0	18.8	17.3	17.0	21.7	16.7
Private creditors										
Interest (%)	..	..	8.3	6.4	4.2	6.4	7.0	10.9	9.3	10.5
Maturity (years)	..	..	23.6	7.5	5.6	7.9	8.3	7.1	9.1	15.5
Grace period (years)	..	..	6.1	1.7	1.5	2.1	2.7	5.2	8.3	15.3
Grant element (%)	..	..	8.7	10.8	14.8	11.2	11.2	-2.3	3.2	-6.4
Memorandum items										
Commitments	..	..	17,932	13,065	5,752	3,633	3,191	6,893	7,746	14,145
Official creditors	..	..	3,755	2,301	1,303	2,224	2,474	4,887	3,759	2,434
Private creditors	..	..	14,177	10,764	4,449	1,409	717	2,007	3,988	11,711

10. CONTRACTUAL OBLIGATIONS ON OUTSTANDING LONG-TERM DEBT

	1999	2000	2001	2002	2003	2004	2005	2006	2007	2008
TOTAL										
Disbursements	2,785	1,286	1,277	331	219	135	97	66	39	24
Principal	7,168	16,516	7,420	7,864	9,476	8,615	10,767	5,674	7,517	6,529
Interest	8,072	8,144	8,011	8,017	7,543	7,033	6,364	5,757	5,251	4,796
Official creditors										
Disbursements	2,334	1,037	1,168	303	211	135	97	66	39	24
Principal	2,015	10,879	1,740	3,092	3,144	3,216	3,352	3,027	3,129	3,249
Interest	3,731	3,835	3,766	3,665	3,499	3,291	3,091	2,880	2,683	2,481
Bilateral creditors										
Disbursements	399	186	83	23	3	0	0	0	0	0
Principal	1,807	10,529	1,270	2,121	1,990	1,992	2,128	2,179	2,281	2,465
Interest	3,206	3,257	3,147	3,058	2,944	2,803	2,675	2,532	2,387	2,237
Multilateral creditors										
Disbursements	1,935	851	1,086	279	208	135	97	66	39	24
Principal	207	350	470	971	1,153	1,224	1,224	849	849	784
Interest	524	577	619	607	555	488	416	348	296	244
Private creditors										
Disbursements	451	249	109	28	8	0	0	0	0	0
Principal	5,153	5,637	5,680	4,772	6,332	5,399	7,415	2,647	4,388	3,279
Interest	4,341	4,310	4,245	4,352	4,044	3,742	3,273	2,878	2,568	2,316
Commercial banks										
Disbursements	0	0	0	0	0	0	0	0	0	0
Principal	25	19	19	307	607	604	1,102	1,540	1,933	3,236
Interest	1,213	1,397	1,572	2,010	1,989	1,950	1,908	1,835	1,731	1,601
Other private										
Disbursements	451	249	109	28	8	0	0	0	0	0
Principal	5,128	5,618	5,660	4,465	5,726	4,796	6,313	1,108	2,455	44
Interest	3,128	2,912	2,673	2,342	2,055	1,792	1,364	1,043	837	714

RWANDA

(US$ million, unless otherwise indicated)

	1970	1980	1990	1992	1993	1994	1995	1996	1997	1998
1. SUMMARY DEBT DATA										
TOTAL DEBT STOCKS (EDT)	..	**190**	**712**	**857**	**909**	**952**	**1,029**	**1,043**	**1,111**	**1,226**
Long-term debt (LDOD)	**2**	**150**	**665**	**790**	**838**	**905**	**970**	**985**	**994**	**1,120**
Public and publicly guaranteed	2	150	665	790	838	905	970	985	994	1,120
Private nonguaranteed	0	0	0	0	0	0	0	0	0	0
Use of IMF credit	**3**	**14**	**0**	**12**	**12**	**13**	**26**	**24**	**40**	**56**
Short-term debt	..	**26**	**47**	**55**	**59**	**34**	**32**	**34**	**77**	**50**
of which interest arrears on LDOD	..	0	2	6	10	16	18	20	29	16
Official creditors	..	0	2	6	10	15	18	20	29	15
Private creditors	..	0	0	0	0	0	0	0	0	0
Memo: principal arrears on LDOD	..	0	8	16	24	41	46	56	68	61
Official creditors	..	0	8	16	24	39	44	54	66	60
Private creditors	..	0	0	0	1	2	2	2	1	1
Memo: export credits	..	0	41	34	21	24	29	28	26	16
TOTAL DEBT FLOWS										
Disbursements	**0**	**34**	**62**	**81**	**61**	**22**	**68**	**62**	**92**	**104**
Long-term debt	0	27	62	81	61	22	54	62	72	88
IMF purchases	0	6	0	0	0	0	14	0	21	16
Principal repayments	**1**	**3**	**10**	**10**	**11**	**2**	**11**	**10**	**13**	**11**
Long-term debt	0	3	9	10	11	2	11	9	10	9
IMF repurchases	1	0	1	0	0	0	0	1	2	2
Net flows on debt	**-1**	**36**	**55**	**73**	**50**	**-11**	**53**	**52**	**114**	**79**
of which short-term debt	..	5	2	2	0	-31	-4	0	34	-14
Interest payments (INT)	..	**5**	**11**	**12**	**10**	**3**	**9**	**7**	**10**	**9**
Long-term debt	0	2	6	5	4	2	8	6	7	6
IMF charges	0	0	0	0	0	0	0	1	1	2
Short-term debt	..	3	5	6	6	1	1	1	2	2
Net transfers on debt	..	**31**	**43**	**61**	**39**	**-14**	**44**	**45**	**104**	**69**
Total debt service paid (TDS)	..	**8**	**21**	**21**	**22**	**4**	**20**	**18**	**22**	**21**
Long-term debt	0	4	15	15	15	3	20	15	17	15
IMF repurchases and charges	1	0	1	0	0	0	0	2	3	4
Short-term debt (interest only)	..	3	5	6	6	1	1	1	2	2
2. AGGREGATE NET RESOURCE FLOWS AND NET TRANSFERS (LONG-TERM)										
NET RESOURCE FLOWS	**10**	**109**	**206**	**262**	**269**	**618**	**609**	**389**	**189**	**285**
Net flow of long-term debt (ex. IMF)	0	25	53	71	50	20	43	53	62	79
Foreign direct investment (net)	0	16	8	2	6	1	1	2	3	7
Portfolio equity flows	0	0	0	0	0	0	0	0	0	0
Grants (excluding technical coop.)	10	68	145	190	214	597	566	333	124	199
Memo: technical coop. grants	12	55	92	94	88	107	97	91	58	61
official net resource flows	10	95	200	261	263	617	608	387	186	278
private net resource flows	0	14	6	1	6	1	1	2	3	7
NET TRANSFERS	**10**	**98**	**194**	**254**	**261**	**615**	**601**	**382**	**182**	**280**
Interest on long-term debt	0	2	6	5	4	2	8	6	7	6
Profit remittances on FDI	0	9	6	3	4	2	0	0	0	0
Memo: official net transfers	10	93	194	256	259	616	600	380	179	273
private net transfers	0	4	0	-2	2	-1	1	2	3	7
3. MAJOR ECONOMIC AGGREGATES										
Gross national product (GNP)	220	1,165	2,572	2,037	1,941	750	1,291	1,392	1,849	2,017
Exports of goods & services (XGS)	..	184	150	105	108	42	99	89	158	123
of which workers remittances	..	1	1	0	3	..	..	..	5	2
Imports of goods & services (MGS)	..	335	380	371	422	624	391	387	501	499
International reserves (RES)	8	187	44	79	47	51	99	107	153	169
Current account balance	..	-48	-86	-83	-129	-60	57	-8	-62	-143
4. DEBT INDICATORS										
EDT / XGS (%)	..	103.4	474.8	819.1	842.4	2,257.4	1,040.9	1,177.0	704.7	999.5
EDT / GNP (%)	..	16.3	27.7	42.1	46.8	127.0	79.6	74.9	60.1	60.8
TDS / XGS (%)	..	4.1	14.0	20.3	19.9	10.0	20.4	19.9	14.0	16.9
INT / XGS (%)	..	2.7	7.5	11.1	9.6	6.4	9.0	8.4	6.0	7.7
INT / GNP (%)	..	0.4	0.4	0.6	0.5	0.4	0.7	0.5	0.5	0.5
RES / EDT (%)	..	98.3	6.2	9.2	5.2	5.4	9.6	10.2	13.8	13.8
RES / MGS (months)	..	6.7	1.4	2.6	1.4	1.0	3.0	3.3	3.7	4.1
Short-term / EDT (%)	..	13.7	6.6	6.4	6.5	3.5	3.1	3.3	6.9	4.1
Concessional / EDT (%)	..	74.5	92.6	91.8	91.9	94.9	93.5	93.6	88.7	90.9
Multilateral / EDT (%)	..	47.8	76.2	75.6	75.7	79.2	78.9	79.9	76.5	78.2

RWANDA

(US$ million, unless otherwise indicated)

	1970	1980	1990	1992	1993	1994	1995	1996	1997	1998
5. LONG-TERM DEBT										
DEBT OUTSTANDING (LDOD)	**2**	**150**	**665**	**790**	**838**	**905**	**970**	**985**	**994**	**1,120**
Public and publicly guaranteed	**2**	**150**	**665**	**790**	**838**	**905**	**970**	**985**	**994**	**1,120**
Official creditors	2	143	661	788	836	904	968	983	992	1,118
Multilateral	0	91	542	648	688	754	811	834	850	959
Concessional	0	91	541	648	688	754	811	833	850	959
Bilateral	1	52	119	140	148	150	157	149	142	159
Concessional	1	51	118	139	147	149	150	143	136	155
Private creditors	0	8	4	2	1	2	2	2	1	1
Bonds	0	0	0	0	0	0	0	0	0	0
Commercial banks	0	0	0	0	0	0	0	0	0	0
Other private	0	8	4	2	1	2	2	2	1	1
Private nonguaranteed	**0**	**0**	**0**	**0**	**0**	**0**	**0**	**0**	**0**	**0**
Bonds	0	0	0	0	0	0	0	0	0	0
Commercial banks	0	0	0	0	0	0	0	0	0	0
Memo:										
IBRD	0	0	0	0	0	0	0	0	0	0
IDA	0	58	340	408	446	474	512	536	558	639
DISBURSEMENTS	**0**	**27**	**62**	**81**	**61**	**22**	**54**	**62**	**72**	**88**
Public and publicly guaranteed	**0**	**27**	**62**	**81**	**61**	**22**	**54**	**62**	**72**	**88**
Official creditors	0	27	62	81	61	22	54	62	72	88
Multilateral	0	21	37	63	49	20	54	62	67	88
Concessional	0	20	37	63	49	20	54	62	67	88
Bilateral	0	7	26	17	11	2	0	0	5	0
Concessional	0	7	25	17	11	2	0	0	3	0
Private creditors	0	0	0	0	0	0	0	0	0	0
Bonds	0	0	0	0	0	0	0	0	0	0
Commercial banks	0	0	0	0	0	0	0	0	0	0
Other private	0	0	0	0	0	0	0	0	0	0
Private nonguaranteed	**0**	**0**	**0**	**0**	**0**	**0**	**0**	**0**	**0**	**0**
Bonds	0	0	0	0	0	0	0	0	0	0
Commercial banks	0	0	0	0	0	0	0	0	0	0
Memo:										
IBRD	0	0	0	0	0	0	0	0	0	0
IDA	0	10	22	32	39	12	35	43	53	67
PRINCIPAL REPAYMENTS	**0**	**3**	**9**	**10**	**11**	**2**	**11**	**9**	**10**	**9**
Public and publicly guaranteed	**0**	**3**	**9**	**10**	**11**	**2**	**11**	**9**	**10**	**9**
Official creditors	0	0	7	9	11	2	11	9	10	9
Multilateral	0	0	5	6	10	2	11	8	9	7
Concessional	0	0	5	5	10	2	11	7	8	7
Bilateral	0	0	2	3	1	0	0	2	2	2
Concessional	0	0	2	3	1	0	0	1	1	1
Private creditors	0	2	2	1	0	0	0	0	0	0
Bonds	0	0	0	0	0	0	0	0	0	0
Commercial banks	0	0	0	0	0	0	0	0	0	0
Other private	0	2	2	1	0	0	0	0	0	0
Private nonguaranteed	**0**	**0**	**0**	**0**	**0**	**0**	**0**	**0**	**0**	**0**
Bonds	0	0	0	0	0	0	0	0	0	0
Commercial banks	0	0	0	0	0	0	0	0	0	0
Memo:										
IBRD	0	0	0	0	0	0	0	0	0	0
IDA	0	0	1	2	3	1	6	5	5	5
NET FLOWS ON DEBT	**0**	**25**	**53**	**71**	**50**	**20**	**43**	**53**	**62**	**79**
Public and publicly guaranteed	**0**	**25**	**53**	**71**	**50**	**20**	**43**	**53**	**62**	**79**
Official creditors	0	27	55	72	50	20	43	53	62	79
Multilateral	0	20	32	58	39	19	43	55	59	81
Concessional	0	20	32	58	39	19	43	55	59	81
Bilateral	0	7	23	14	10	2	0	-2	3	-2
Concessional	0	7	22	14	10	2	0	-1	2	-1
Private creditors	0	-2	-2	-1	0	0	0	0	0	0
Bonds	0	0	0	0	0	0	0	0	0	0
Commercial banks	0	0	0	0	0	0	0	0	0	0
Other private	0	-2	-2	-1	0	0	0	0	0	0
Private nonguaranteed	**0**	**0**	**0**	**0**	**0**	**0**	**0**	**0**	**0**	**0**
Bonds	0	0	0	0	0	0	0	0	0	0
Commercial banks	0	0	0	0	0	0	0	0	0	0
Memo:										
IBRD	0	0	0	0	0	0	0	0	0	0
IDA	0	10	21	30	37	11	29	38	48	62

RWANDA

(US$ million, unless otherwise indicated)

	1970	1980	1990	1992	1993	1994	1995	1996	1997	1998
INTEREST PAYMENTS (LINT)	**0**	**2**	**6**	**5**	**4**	**2**	**8**	**6**	**7**	**6**
Public and publicly guaranteed	**0**	**2**	**6**	**5**	**4**	**2**	**8**	**6**	**7**	**6**
Official creditors	0	1	6	5	4	2	8	6	7	6
Multilateral	0	1	4	4	4	2	8	6	7	6
Concessional	0	1	4	4	4	2	8	6	7	6
Bilateral	0	1	2	1	0	0	0	0	0	0
Concessional	0	0	1	1	0	0	0	0	0	0
Private creditors	0	0	0	0	0	0	0	0	0	0
Bonds	0	0	0	0	0	0	0	0	0	0
Commercial banks	0	0	0	0	0	0	0	0	0	0
Other private	0	0	0	0	0	0	0	0	0	0
Private nonguaranteed	**0**	**0**	**0**	**0**	**0**	**0**	**0**	**0**	**0**	**0**
Bonds	0	0	0	0	0	0	0	0	0	0
Commercial banks	0	0	0	0	0	0	0	0	0	0
Memo:										
IBRD	0	0	0	0	0	0	0	0	0	0
IDA	0	0	2	3	3	1	7	4	5	4
NET TRANSFERS ON DEBT	**0**	**23**	**47**	**66**	**45**	**19**	**34**	**47**	**55**	**73**
Public and publicly guaranteed	**0**	**23**	**47**	**66**	**45**	**19**	**34**	**47**	**55**	**73**
Official creditors	0	26	49	67	45	19	34	47	55	73
Multilateral	0	20	28	53	35	17	35	49	52	75
Concessional	0	19	28	53	35	17	35	49	52	75
Bilateral	0	6	22	14	10	2	0	-2	3	-2
Concessional	0	6	21	14	10	2	0	-1	2	-1
Private creditors	0	-3	-2	-1	0	0	0	0	0	0
Bonds	0	0	0	0	0	0	0	0	0	0
Commercial banks	0	0	0	0	0	0	0	0	0	0
Other private	0	-3	-2	-1	0	0	0	0	0	0
Private nonguaranteed	**0**	**0**	**0**	**0**	**0**	**0**	**0**	**0**	**0**	**0**
Bonds	0	0	0	0	0	0	0	0	0	0
Commercial banks	0	0	0	0	0	0	0	0	0	0
Memo:										
IBRD	0	0	0	0	0	0	0	0	0	0
IDA	0	10	18	27	33	11	22	35	43	58
DEBT SERVICE (LTDS)	**0**	**4**	**15**	**15**	**15**	**3**	**20**	**15**	**17**	**15**
Public and publicly guaranteed	**0**	**4**	**15**	**15**	**15**	**3**	**20**	**15**	**17**	**15**
Official creditors	0	2	13	14	15	3	20	15	17	15
Multilateral	0	1	9	10	15	3	20	14	15	13
Concessional	0	1	9	10	15	3	19	13	15	13
Bilateral	0	1	4	4	1	0	0	2	2	2
Concessional	0	0	4	4	1	0	0	1	1	1
Private creditors	0	3	2	1	0	0	0	0	0	0
Bonds	0	0	0	0	0	0	0	0	0	0
Commercial banks	0	0	0	0	0	0	0	0	0	0
Other private	0	3	2	1	0	0	0	0	0	0
Private nonguaranteed	**0**	**0**	**0**	**0**	**0**	**0**	**0**	**0**	**0**	**0**
Bonds	0	0	0	0	0	0	0	0	0	0
Commercial banks	0	0	0	0	0	0	0	0	0	0
Memo:										
IBRD	0	0	0	0	0	0	0	0	0	0
IDA	0	1	3	5	6	1	12	8	10	9
UNDISBURSED DEBT	**10**	**110**	**467**	**513**	**498**	**452**	**408**	**297**	**254**	**231**
Official creditors	10	110	460	507	498	452	408	297	254	231
Private creditors	0	0	6	7	0	0	0	0	0	0
Memorandum items										
Concessional LDOD	2	141	659	787	835	903	961	977	985	1,114
Variable rate LDOD	0	0	0	0	0	0	0	0	0	0
Public sector LDOD	2	150	665	790	838	905	970	985	994	1,120
Private sector LDOD	0	0	0	0	0	0	0	0	0	0

6. CURRENCY COMPOSITION OF LONG-TERM DEBT (PERCENT)

	1970	1980	1990	1992	1993	1994	1995	1996	1997	1998
Deutsche mark	46.2	0.7	0.0	0.0	0.0	0.0	0.0	0.0	0.0	0.0
French franc	0.0	7.3	3.9	6.3	5.8	5.7	7.6	8.1	7.5	5.8
Japanese yen	0.0	4.5	1.5	1.3	1.4	1.4	1.3	1.1	1.0	0.6
Pound sterling	0.0	0.0	0.0	0.0	0.0	0.0	0.0	0.0	0.0	0.0
Swiss franc	0.0	0.0	0.0	0.0	0.0	0.0	0.0	0.0	0.0	0.0
U.S.dollars	10.3	48.0	38.6	43.8	45.9	45.1	45.8	47.9	50.8	55.3
Multiple currency	0.0	5.9	14.9	13.2	12.4	12.1	11.3	11.4	10.5	9.6
Special drawing rights	0.0	0.0	6.2	5.0	4.6	4.5	4.2	4.0	3.8	3.5
All other currencies	43.5	33.6	34.9	30.4	29.9	31.2	29.8	27.5	26.4	25.2

RWANDA

(US$ million, unless otherwise indicated)

	1970	1980	1990	1992	1993	1994	1995	1996	1997	1998
7. DEBT RESTRUCTURINGS										
Total amount rescheduled	..	..	0	0	0	0	6	0	0	33
Debt stock rescheduled	..	..	0	0	0	0	0	0	0	0
Principal rescheduled	..	..	0	0	0	0	5	0	0	17
Official	..	..	0	0	0	0	5	0	0	17
Private	..	..	0	0	0	0	0	0	0	0
Interest rescheduled	..	..	0	0	0	0	2	0	0	15
Official	..	..	0	0	0	0	2	0	0	15
Private	..	..	0	0	0	0	0	0	0	0
Debt forgiven	..	..	0	0	0	0	0	0	0	1
Memo: interest forgiven	..	..	0	0	0	0	0	0	0	1
Debt stock reduction	..	..	0	0	0	0	0	0	0	0
of which debt buyback	..	..	0	0	0	0	0	0	0	0
8. DEBT STOCK-FLOW RECONCILIATION										
Total change in debt stocks	..	..	88	47	52	43	77	15	68	115
Net flows on debt	-1	36	55	73	50	-11	53	52	114	79
Net change in interest arrears	..	..	0	3	4	6	2	2	9	-13
Interest capitalized	..	..	0	0	0	0	2	0	0	15
Debt forgiveness or reduction	..	..	0	0	0	0	0	0	0	-1
Cross-currency valuation	..	..	22	-15	-5	22	15	-16	-28	17
Residual	..	..	12	-13	4	27	6	-24	-27	18
9. AVERAGE TERMS OF NEW COMMITMENTS										
ALL CREDITORS										
Interest (%)	0.8	1.5	1.4	1.1	0.6	0.0	0.7	0.8	0.4	0.5
Maturity (years)	50.0	39.4	33.9	42.1	38.3	0.0	39.7	39.6	41.0	42.7
Grace period (years)	10.5	8.7	9.0	9.5	10.1	0.0	10.3	10.1	10.4	10.2
Grant element (%)	83.4	70.1	71.3	76.3	80.0	0.0	80.6	80.4	83.8	83.7
Official creditors										
Interest (%)	0.8	1.5	1.4	1.1	0.6	0.0	0.7	0.8	0.4	0.5
Maturity (years)	50.0	39.4	33.9	42.1	38.3	0.0	39.7	39.6	41.0	42.7
Grace period (years)	10.5	8.7	9.0	9.5	10.1	0.0	10.3	10.1	10.4	10.2
Grant element (%)	83.4	70.1	71.3	76.3	80.0	0.0	80.6	80.4	83.8	83.7
Private creditors										
Interest (%)	0.0	0.0	0.0	0.0	0.0	0.0	0.0	0.0	0.0	0.0
Maturity (years)	0.0	0.0	0.0	0.0	0.0	0.0	0.0	0.0	0.0	0.0
Grace period (years)	0.0	0.0	0.0	0.0	0.0	0.0	0.0	0.0	0.0	0.0
Grant element (%)	0.0	0.0	0.0	0.0	0.0	0.0	0.0	0.0	0.0	0.0
Memorandum items										
Commitments	9	48	72	56	61	0	50	5	57	76
Official creditors	9	48	72	56	61	0	50	5	57	76
Private creditors	0	0	0	0	0	0	0	0	0	0

10. CONTRACTUAL OBLIGATIONS ON OUTSTANDING LONG-TERM DEBT

	1999	2000	2001	2002	2003	2004	2005	2006	2007	2008
TOTAL										
Disbursements	35	37	24	17	12	8	5	0	0	0
Principal	23	24	26	29	31	31	32	31	31	33
Interest	9	9	9	10	9	9	9	8	8	8
Official creditors										
Disbursements	35	37	24	17	12	8	5	0	0	0
Principal	23	24	26	29	31	31	32	31	31	33
Interest	9	9	9	10	9	9	9	8	8	8
Bilateral creditors										
Disbursements	0	0	0	0	0	0	0	0	0	0
Principal	6	6	7	8	8	8	7	5	5	4
Interest	1	1	2	2	2	2	2	2	1	1
Multilateral creditors										
Disbursements	35	37	24	17	12	8	5	0	0	0
Principal	16	18	20	21	23	24	25	26	26	28
Interest	8	8	8	7	7	7	7	7	6	6
Private creditors										
Disbursements	0	0	0	0	0	0	0	0	0	0
Principal	0	0	0	0	0	0	0	0	0	0
Interest	0	0	0	0	0	0	0	0	0	0
Commercial banks										
Disbursements	0	0	0	0	0	0	0	0	0	0
Principal	0	0	0	0	0	0	0	0	0	0
Interest	0	0	0	0	0	0	0	0	0	0
Other private										
Disbursements	0	0	0	0	0	0	0	0	0	0
Principal	0	0	0	0	0	0	0	0	0	0
Interest	0	0	0	0	0	0	0	0	0	0

SAMOA

(US$ million, unless otherwise indicated)

	1970	1980	1990	1992	1993	1994	1995	1996	1997	1998
1. SUMMARY DEBT DATA										
TOTAL DEBT STOCKS (EDT)	**..**	**60.2**	**92.0**	**117.9**	**193.8**	**156.9**	**170.4**	**166.9**	**156.4**	**180.1**
Long-term debt (LDOD)	**2.7**	**53.4**	**91.0**	**117.8**	**140.4**	**156.7**	**168.1**	**162.8**	**148.3**	**154.3**
Public and publicly guaranteed	2.7	53.4	91.0	117.8	140.4	156.7	168.1	162.8	148.3	154.3
Private nonguaranteed	0.0	0.0	0.0	0.0	0.0	0.0	0.0	0.0	0.0	0.0
Use of IMF credit	**0.0**	**5.8**	**0.8**	**0.0**	**0.0**	**0.0**	**0.0**	**0.0**	**0.0**	**0.0**
Short-term debt	**..**	**1.0**	**0.1**	**0.1**	**53.4**	**0.2**	**2.3**	**4.1**	**8.0**	**25.8**
of which interest arrears on LDOD	..	0.0	0.0	0.0	0.1	0.0	0.0	0.0	0.0	0.0
Official creditors	..	0.0	0.0	0.0	0.1	0.0	0.0	0.0	0.0	0.0
Private creditors	..	0.0	0.0	0.0	0.0	0.0	0.0	0.0	0.0	0.0
Memo: principal arrears on LDOD	..	0.0	0.0	0.0	0.2	0.0	0.0	0.0	0.0	0.0
Official creditors	..	0.0	0.0	0.0	0.2	0.0	0.0	0.0	0.0	0.0
Private creditors	..	0.0	0.0	0.0	0.0	0.0	0.0	0.0	0.0	0.0
Memo: export credits	..	0.0	2.0	1.0	0.0	0.0	0.0	0.0	0.0	8.0
TOTAL DEBT FLOWS										
Disbursements	**2.4**	**11.2**	**15.3**	**12.2**	**24.0**	**11.8**	**12.7**	**3.7**	**2.7**	**3.2**
Long-term debt	2.4	10.5	15.3	12.2	24.0	11.8	12.7	3.7	2.7	3.2
IMF purchases	0.0	0.7	0.0	0.0	0.0	0.0	0.0	0.0	0.0	0.0
Principal repayments	**0.1**	**2.8**	**4.1**	**3.5**	**2.8**	**3.7**	**3.0**	**3.1**	**3.2**	**2.8**
Long-term debt	0.1	2.3	3.3	3.3	2.8	3.7	3.0	3.1	3.2	2.8
IMF repurchases	0.0	0.5	0.9	0.2	0.0	0.0	0.0	0.0	0.0	0.0
Net flows on debt	**2.3**	**9.4**	**11.3**	**-18.2**	**74.3**	**-45.0**	**11.9**	**2.4**	**3.4**	**18.2**
of which short-term debt	..	1.0	0.1	-26.9	53.1	-53.1	2.1	1.8	3.9	17.8
Interest payments (INT)	**..**	**2.7**	**1.3**	**1.3**	**2.6**	**2.8**	**1.7**	**1.9**	**1.8**	**2.3**
Long-term debt	0.0	2.3	1.2	1.3	1.3	1.4	1.6	1.6	1.5	1.4
IMF charges	0.0	0.2	0.1	0.0	0.0	0.0	0.0	0.0	0.0	0.0
Short-term debt	..	0.2	0.0	0.0	1.3	1.3	0.1	0.3	0.3	0.8
Net transfers on debt	**..**	**6.7**	**10.0**	**-19.5**	**71.7**	**-47.7**	**10.2**	**0.5**	**1.6**	**15.9**
Total debt service paid (TDS)	**..**	**5.5**	**5.5**	**4.8**	**5.4**	**6.4**	**4.6**	**5.0**	**5.0**	**5.0**
Long-term debt	0.1	4.6	4.5	4.6	4.1	5.1	4.6	4.7	4.7	4.2
IMF repurchases and charges	0.0	0.7	1.0	0.2	0.0	0.0	0.0	0.0	0.0	0.0
Short-term debt (interest only)	..	0.2	0.0	0.0	1.3	1.3	0.1	0.3	0.3	0.8
2. AGGREGATE NET RESOURCE FLOWS AND NET TRANSFERS (LONG-TERM)										
NET RESOURCE FLOWS	**2.3**	**17.0**	**39.3**	**35.7**	**48.2**	**36.8**	**33.6**	**17.6**	**11.1**	**15.3**
Net flow of long-term debt (ex. IMF)	2.3	8.2	12.1	8.9	21.2	8.1	9.8	0.6	-0.5	0.4
Foreign direct investment (net)	0.0	0.0	7.0	5.0	5.0	3.0	3.0	4.0	4.0	3.0
Portfolio equity flows	0.0	0.0	0.0	0.0	0.0	0.0	0.0	0.0	0.0	0.0
Grants (excluding technical coop.)	0.0	8.8	20.2	21.7	22.0	25.7	20.8	13.0	7.6	11.9
Memo: technical coop. grants	0.9	9.8	13.9	17.1	16.7	17.4	16.9	20.2	21.0	19.5
official net resource flows	2.4	18.8	32.3	31.1	43.5	34.4	30.6	13.6	7.1	12.3
private net resource flows	-0.1	-1.8	7.0	4.6	4.7	2.4	3.0	4.0	4.0	3.0
NET TRANSFERS	**2.3**	**14.7**	**38.1**	**34.4**	**46.9**	**35.4**	**32.0**	**16.0**	**9.6**	**13.9**
Interest on long-term debt	0.0	2.3	1.2	1.3	1.3	1.4	1.6	1.6	1.5	1.4
Profit remittances on FDI	0.0	0.0	0.0	0.0	0.0	0.0	0.0	0.0	0.0	0.0
Memo: official net transfers	2.4	17.4	31.2	29.9	42.2	33.0	29.0	12.0	5.6	10.9
private net transfers	-0.1	-2.7	6.9	4.5	4.7	2.4	3.0	4.0	4.0	3.0
3. MAJOR ECONOMIC AGGREGATES										
Gross national product (GNP)	..	..	150.9	151.5	154.6	173.2	196.0	176.3	192.9	176.5
Exports of goods & services (XGS)	..	44.4	93.9	87.7	77.8	87.2	108.3	123.4	129.9	128.7
of which workers remittances	..	18.7	42.8	39.1	31.3	36.5	39.2	42.7	44.9	40.1
Imports of goods & services (MGS)	..	74.3	96.3	135.9	130.0	101.7	119.8	127.7	143.7	128.0
International reserves (RES)	5.2	2.8	69.0	61.2	50.7	50.8	55.3	60.8	64.2	61.4
Current account balance	..	-12.9	8.6	-52.5	-37.7	5.8	9.3	12.3	9.1	20.0
4. DEBT INDICATORS										
EDT / XGS (%)	..	135.5	98.0	134.4	249.0	179.9	157.4	135.2	120.4	139.9
EDT / GNP (%)	..	..	61.0	77.8	125.4	90.6	86.9	94.7	81.1	102.1
TDS / XGS (%)	..	12.4	5.9	5.5	6.9	7.3	4.3	4.1	3.9	3.9
INT / XGS (%)	..	6.1	1.4	1.5	3.3	3.2	1.6	1.5	1.4	1.8
INT / GNP (%)	..	..	0.9	0.9	1.7	1.6	0.9	1.1	0.9	1.3
RES / EDT (%)	..	4.6	75.1	51.9	26.2	32.4	32.5	36.4	41.1	34.1
RES / MGS (months)	..	0.5	8.6	5.4	4.7	6.0	5.5	5.7	5.4	5.8
Short-term / EDT (%)	..	1.7	0.1	0.1	27.6	0.1	1.4	2.5	5.1	14.3
Concessional / EDT (%)	..	56.2	90.4	93.7	68.7	95.5	94.7	94.0	91.8	83.3
Multilateral / EDT (%)	..	54.2	88.2	93.4	64.8	92.9	92.2	91.1	88.2	80.2

SAMOA

(US$ million, unless otherwise indicated)

	1970	1980	1990	1992	1993	1994	1995	1996	1997	1998
5. LONG-TERM DEBT										
DEBT OUTSTANDING (LDOD)	**2.7**	**53.4**	**91.0**	**117.8**	**140.4**	**156.7**	**168.1**	**162.8**	**148.3**	**154.3**
Public and publicly guaranteed	**2.7**	**53.4**	**91.0**	**117.8**	**140.4**	**156.7**	**168.1**	**162.8**	**148.3**	**154.3**
Official creditors	2.4	45.1	89.6	117.0	139.9	156.7	168.1	162.8	148.3	154.3
Multilateral	2.4	32.6	81.1	110.1	125.6	145.8	157.1	152.1	138.0	144.4
Concessional	2.4	32.6	76.5	104.2	119.1	138.9	150.3	146.2	133.3	140.0
Bilateral	0.0	12.5	8.5	6.9	14.2	11.0	11.0	10.7	10.3	10.0
Concessional	0.0	1.2	6.7	6.3	14.0	11.0	11.0	10.7	10.3	10.0
Private creditors	0.3	8.3	1.4	0.8	0.6	0.0	0.0	0.0	0.0	0.0
Bonds	0.0	4.5	1.4	0.8	0.6	0.0	0.0	0.0	0.0	0.0
Commercial banks	0.0	1.9	0.0	0.0	0.0	0.0	0.0	0.0	0.0	0.0
Other private	0.3	1.9	0.0	0.0	0.0	0.0	0.0	0.0	0.0	0.0
Private nonguaranteed	**0.0**	**0.0**	**0.0**	**0.0**	**0.0**	**0.0**	**0.0**	**0.0**	**0.0**	**0.0**
Bonds	0.0	0.0	0.0	0.0	0.0	0.0	0.0	0.0	0.0	0.0
Commercial banks	0.0	0.0	0.0	0.0	0.0	0.0	0.0	0.0	0.0	0.0
Memo:										
IBRD	0.0	0.0	0.0	0.0	0.0	0.0	0.0	0.0	0.0	0.0
IDA	0.0	6.3	18.3	31.8	40.2	43.3	44.7	43.2	41.8	45.3
DISBURSEMENTS	**2.4**	**10.5**	**15.3**	**12.2**	**24.0**	**11.8**	**12.7**	**3.7**	**2.7**	**3.2**
Public and publicly guaranteed	**2.4**	**10.5**	**15.3**	**12.2**	**24.0**	**11.8**	**12.7**	**3.7**	**2.7**	**3.2**
Official creditors	2.4	10.5	15.3	12.2	24.0	11.8	12.7	3.7	2.7	3.2
Multilateral	2.4	10.5	15.0	12.2	15.9	11.6	12.6	3.6	2.6	3.2
Concessional	2.4	10.5	14.7	11.7	14.7	11.5	12.5	3.6	2.6	3.2
Bilateral	0.0	0.0	0.4	0.0	8.1	0.2	0.2	0.0	0.0	0.0
Concessional	0.0	0.0	0.4	0.0	8.1	0.2	0.2	0.0	0.0	0.0
Private creditors	0.0	0.0	0.0	0.0	0.0	0.0	0.0	0.0	0.0	0.0
Bonds	0.0	0.0	0.0	0.0	0.0	0.0	0.0	0.0	0.0	0.0
Commercial banks	0.0	0.0	0.0	0.0	0.0	0.0	0.0	0.0	0.0	0.0
Other private	0.0	0.0	0.0	0.0	0.0	0.0	0.0	0.0	0.0	0.0
Private nonguaranteed	**0.0**	**0.0**	**0.0**	**0.0**	**0.0**	**0.0**	**0.0**	**0.0**	**0.0**	**0.0**
Bonds	0.0	0.0	0.0	0.0	0.0	0.0	0.0	0.0	0.0	0.0
Commercial banks	0.0	0.0	0.0	0.0	0.0	0.0	0.0	0.0	0.0	0.0
Memo:										
IBRD	0.0	0.0	0.0	0.0	0.0	0.0	0.0	0.0	0.0	0.0
IDA	0.0	2.0	3.5	7.4	8.6	1.7	0.7	0.0	0.8	2.5
PRINCIPAL REPAYMENTS	**0.1**	**2.3**	**3.3**	**3.3**	**2.8**	**3.7**	**3.0**	**3.1**	**3.2**	**2.8**
Public and publicly guaranteed	**0.1**	**2.3**	**3.3**	**3.3**	**2.8**	**3.7**	**3.0**	**3.1**	**3.2**	**2.8**
Official creditors	0.0	0.5	3.3	2.8	2.5	3.1	3.0	3.1	3.2	2.8
Multilateral	0.0	0.3	2.2	2.0	1.7	2.6	2.6	2.8	2.9	2.5
Concessional	0.0	0.3	2.0	1.7	1.7	1.8	2.1	2.2	2.3	1.9
Bilateral	0.0	0.1	1.0	0.8	0.7	0.5	0.3	0.3	0.3	0.3
Concessional	0.0	0.0	0.0	0.3	0.3	0.3	0.3	0.3	0.3	0.3
Private creditors	0.1	1.8	0.0	0.4	0.3	0.6	0.0	0.0	0.0	0.0
Bonds	0.0	0.0	0.0	0.4	0.3	0.6	0.0	0.0	0.0	0.0
Commercial banks	0.0	0.6	0.0	0.0	0.0	0.0	0.0	0.0	0.0	0.0
Other private	0.1	1.2	0.0	0.0	0.0	0.0	0.0	0.0	0.0	0.0
Private nonguaranteed	**0.0**	**0.0**	**0.0**	**0.0**	**0.0**	**0.0**	**0.0**	**0.0**	**0.0**	**0.0**
Bonds	0.0	0.0	0.0	0.0	0.0	0.0	0.0	0.0	0.0	0.0
Commercial banks	0.0	0.0	0.0	0.0	0.0	0.0	0.0	0.0	0.0	0.0
Memo:										
IBRD	0.0	0.0	0.0	0.0	0.0	0.0	0.0	0.0	0.0	0.0
IDA	0.0	0.0	0.1	0.1	0.1	0.1	0.2	0.3	0.3	0.3
NET FLOWS ON DEBT	**2.3**	**8.2**	**12.1**	**8.9**	**21.2**	**8.1**	**9.8**	**0.6**	**-0.5**	**0.4**
Public and publicly guaranteed	**2.3**	**8.2**	**12.1**	**8.9**	**21.2**	**8.1**	**9.8**	**0.6**	**-0.5**	**0.4**
Official creditors	2.4	10.0	12.1	9.4	21.5	8.7	9.8	0.6	-0.5	0.4
Multilateral	2.4	10.2	12.8	10.2	14.1	9.0	9.9	0.9	-0.2	0.7
Concessional	2.4	10.2	12.7	9.9	12.9	9.7	10.4	1.4	0.4	1.3
Bilateral	0.0	-0.1	-0.7	-0.8	7.4	-0.3	-0.1	-0.3	-0.3	-0.3
Concessional	0.0	0.0	0.3	-0.3	7.8	-0.1	-0.1	-0.3	-0.3	-0.3
Private creditors	-0.1	-1.8	0.0	-0.4	-0.3	-0.6	0.0	0.0	0.0	0.0
Bonds	0.0	0.0	0.0	-0.4	-0.3	-0.6	0.0	0.0	0.0	0.0
Commercial banks	0.0	-0.6	0.0	0.0	0.0	0.0	0.0	0.0	0.0	0.0
Other private	-0.1	-1.2	0.0	0.0	0.0	0.0	0.0	0.0	0.0	0.0
Private nonguaranteed	**0.0**	**0.0**	**0.0**	**0.0**	**0.0**	**0.0**	**0.0**	**0.0**	**0.0**	**0.0**
Bonds	0.0	0.0	0.0	0.0	0.0	0.0	0.0	0.0	0.0	0.0
Commercial banks	0.0	0.0	0.0	0.0	0.0	0.0	0.0	0.0	0.0	0.0
Memo:										
IBRD	0.0	0.0	0.0	0.0	0.0	0.0	0.0	0.0	0.0	0.0
IDA	0.0	2.0	3.4	7.3	8.5	1.6	0.5	-0.3	0.5	2.2

SAMOA

(US$ million, unless otherwise indicated)

	1970	1980	1990	1992	1993	1994	1995	1996	1997	1998
INTEREST PAYMENTS (LINT)	**0.0**	**2.3**	**1.2**	**1.3**	**1.3**	**1.4**	**1.6**	**1.6**	**1.5**	**1.4**
Public and publicly guaranteed	**0.0**	**2.3**	**1.2**	**1.3**	**1.3**	**1.4**	**1.6**	**1.6**	**1.5**	**1.4**
Official creditors	0.0	1.4	1.1	1.2	1.3	1.4	1.6	1.6	1.5	1.4
Multilateral	0.0	0.3	0.7	1.0	1.1	1.3	1.5	1.6	1.4	1.3
Concessional	0.0	0.3	0.7	0.9	1.1	1.2	1.3	1.4	1.3	1.2
Bilateral	0.0	1.1	0.4	0.2	0.2	0.1	0.1	0.1	0.1	0.1
Concessional	0.0	0.1	0.1	0.1	0.1	0.1	0.1	0.1	0.1	0.1
Private creditors	0.0	0.9	0.1	0.1	0.0	0.0	0.0	0.0	0.0	0.0
Bonds	0.0	0.3	0.1	0.1	0.0	0.0	0.0	0.0	0.0	0.0
Commercial banks	0.0	0.4	0.0	0.0	0.0	0.0	0.0	0.0	0.0	0.0
Other private	0.0	0.2	0.0	0.0	0.0	0.0	0.0	0.0	0.0	0.0
Private nonguaranteed	**0.0**	**0.0**	**0.0**	**0.0**	**0.0**	**0.0**	**0.0**	**0.0**	**0.0**	**0.0**
Bonds	0.0	0.0	0.0	0.0	0.0	0.0	0.0	0.0	0.0	0.0
Commercial banks	0.0	0.0	0.0	0.0	0.0	0.0	0.0	0.0	0.0	0.0
Memo:										
IBRD	0.0	0.0	0.0	0.0	0.0	0.0	0.0	0.0	0.0	0.0
IDA	0.0	0.0	0.1	0.2	0.3	0.3	0.3	0.3	0.3	0.3
NET TRANSFERS ON DEBT	**2.3**	**5.9**	**10.9**	**7.6**	**19.9**	**6.7**	**8.2**	**-1.1**	**-2.0**	**-1.0**
Public and publicly guaranteed	**2.3**	**5.9**	**10.9**	**7.6**	**19.9**	**6.7**	**8.2**	**-1.1**	**-2.0**	**-1.0**
Official creditors	2.4	8.6	11.0	8.1	20.2	7.3	8.2	-1.1	-2.0	-1.0
Multilateral	2.4	9.9	12.0	9.1	13.0	7.7	8.4	-0.7	-1.7	-0.6
Concessional	2.4	9.9	12.0	9.0	11.9	8.5	9.1	0.0	-1.0	0.1
Bilateral	0.0	-1.3	-1.1	-1.0	7.2	-0.4	-0.2	-0.4	-0.4	-0.4
Concessional	0.0	-0.1	0.2	-0.4	7.7	-0.2	-0.2	-0.4	-0.4	-0.4
Private creditors	-0.1	-2.7	-0.1	-0.5	-0.3	-0.6	0.0	0.0	0.0	0.0
Bonds	0.0	-0.3	-0.1	-0.5	-0.3	-0.6	0.0	0.0	0.0	0.0
Commercial banks	0.0	-1.0	0.0	0.0	0.0	0.0	0.0	0.0	0.0	0.0
Other private	-0.1	-1.4	0.0	0.0	0.0	0.0	0.0	0.0	0.0	0.0
Private nonguaranteed	**0.0**	**0.0**	**0.0**	**0.0**	**0.0**	**0.0**	**0.0**	**0.0**	**0.0**	**0.0**
Bonds	0.0	0.0	0.0	0.0	0.0	0.0	0.0	0.0	0.0	0.0
Commercial banks	0.0	0.0	0.0	0.0	0.0	0.0	0.0	0.0	0.0	0.0
Memo:										
IBRD	0.0	0.0	0.0	0.0	0.0	0.0	0.0	0.0	0.0	0.0
IDA	0.0	2.0	3.3	7.1	8.3	1.3	0.2	-0.6	0.2	1.9
DEBT SERVICE (LTDS)	**0.1**	**4.6**	**4.5**	**4.6**	**4.1**	**5.1**	**4.6**	**4.7**	**4.7**	**4.2**
Public and publicly guaranteed	**0.1**	**4.6**	**4.5**	**4.6**	**4.1**	**5.1**	**4.6**	**4.7**	**4.7**	**4.2**
Official creditors	0.0	1.9	4.4	4.1	3.8	4.5	4.6	4.7	4.7	4.2
Multilateral	0.0	0.6	3.0	3.1	2.9	3.8	4.1	4.3	4.3	3.8
Concessional	0.0	0.6	2.7	2.7	2.8	3.0	3.4	3.6	3.6	3.1
Bilateral	0.0	1.3	1.4	1.0	0.9	0.6	0.4	0.4	0.4	0.4
Concessional	0.0	0.1	0.1	0.4	0.4	0.4	0.4	0.4	0.4	0.4
Private creditors	0.1	2.7	0.1	0.5	0.3	0.6	0.0	0.0	0.0	0.0
Bonds	0.0	0.3	0.1	0.5	0.3	0.6	0.0	0.0	0.0	0.0
Commercial banks	0.0	1.0	0.0	0.0	0.0	0.0	0.0	0.0	0.0	0.0
Other private	0.1	1.4	0.0	0.0	0.0	0.0	0.0	0.0	0.0	0.0
Private nonguaranteed	**0.0**	**0.0**	**0.0**	**0.0**	**0.0**	**0.0**	**0.0**	**0.0**	**0.0**	**0.0**
Bonds	0.0	0.0	0.0	0.0	0.0	0.0	0.0	0.0	0.0	0.0
Commercial banks	0.0	0.0	0.0	0.0	0.0	0.0	0.0	0.0	0.0	0.0
Memo:										
IBRD	0.0	0.0	0.0	0.0	0.0	0.0	0.0	0.0	0.0	0.0
IDA	0.0	0.0	0.2	0.3	0.4	0.4	0.5	0.6	0.6	0.6
UNDISBURSED DEBT	**0.3**	**24.9**	**56.7**	**35.4**	**25.8**	**14.9**	**10.9**	**8.9**	**5.9**	**2.4**
Official creditors	0.3	24.9	56.7	35.4	25.8	14.9	10.9	8.9	5.9	2.4
Private creditors	0.0	0.0	0.0	0.0	0.0	0.0	0.0	0.0	0.0	0.0
Memorandum items										
Concessional LDOD	2.4	33.9	83.3	110.5	133.1	149.8	161.2	156.8	143.6	150.0
Variable rate LDOD	0.0	1.8	0.0	0.0	0.0	0.0	0.0	0.0	0.0	0.0
Public sector LDOD	2.7	53.4	91.0	117.8	140.4	156.7	168.1	162.8	148.3	154.3
Private sector LDOD	0.0	0.0	0.0	0.0	0.0	0.0	0.0	0.0	0.0	0.0

6. CURRENCY COMPOSITION OF LONG-TERM DEBT (PERCENT)

	1970	1980	1990	1992	1993	1994	1995	1996	1997	1998
Deutsche mark	0.0	12.0	1.8	0.5	0.1	0.0	0.0	0.0	0.0	0.0
French franc	0.0	0.0	0.1	0.3	0.3	0.3	0.2	0.2	0.2	0.2
Japanese yen	0.0	0.6	0.0	0.0	0.0	0.0	0.0	0.0	0.0	0.0
Pound sterling	0.0	0.0	0.0	0.0	0.0	0.0	0.0	0.0	0.0	0.0
Swiss franc	0.0	0.0	0.0	0.0	0.0	0.0	0.0	0.0	0.0	0.0
U.S.dollars	100.0	53.7	38.6	39.0	38.6	37.2	34.8	34.2	34.9	35.6
Multiple currency	0.0	12.7	43.9	48.0	44.7	47.6	44.3	43.2	41.3	40.9
Special drawing rights	0.0	0.0	1.3	1.0	1.1	3.3	9.6	11.6	12.8	13.3
All other currencies	0.0	21.0	14.3	11.2	15.2	11.6	11.1	10.8	10.8	10.0

SAMOA

(US$ million, unless otherwise indicated)

	1970	1980	1990	1992	1993	1994	1995	1996	1997	1998
7. DEBT RESTRUCTURINGS										
Total amount rescheduled	..	..	0.0	0.0	0.0	0.0	0.0	0.0	0.0	0.0
Debt stock rescheduled	..	..	0.0	0.0	0.0	0.0	0.0	0.0	0.0	0.0
Principal rescheduled	..	..	0.0	0.0	0.0	0.0	0.0	0.0	0.0	0.0
Official	..	..	0.0	0.0	0.0	0.0	0.0	0.0	0.0	0.0
Private	..	..	0.0	0.0	0.0	0.0	0.0	0.0	0.0	0.0
Interest rescheduled	..	..	0.0	0.0	0.0	0.0	0.0	0.0	0.0	0.0
Official	..	..	0.0	0.0	0.0	0.0	0.0	0.0	0.0	0.0
Private	..	..	0.0	0.0	0.0	0.0	0.0	0.0	0.0	0.0
Debt forgiven	..	..	0.0	0.0	0.0	0.0	0.0	0.0	0.0	0.0
Memo: interest forgiven	..	..	0.0	0.0	0.0	0.0	0.0	0.0	0.0	0.0
Debt stock reduction	..	..	0.0	0.0	0.0	0.0	0.0	0.0	0.0	0.0
of which debt buyback	..	..	0.0	0.0	0.0	0.0	0.0	0.0	0.0	0.0
8. DEBT STOCK-FLOW RECONCILIATION										
Total change in debt stocks	..	..	18.3	-22.8	75.9	-36.9	13.4	-3.4	-10.6	23.7
Net flows on debt	2.3	9.4	11.3	-18.2	74.3	-45.0	11.9	2.4	3.4	18.2
Net change in interest arrears	..	..	-0.1	0.0	0.1	-0.1	0.0	0.0	0.0	0.0
Interest capitalized	..	..	0.0	0.0	0.0	0.0	0.0	0.0	0.0	0.0
Debt forgiveness or reduction	..	..	0.0	0.0	0.0	0.0	0.0	0.0	0.0	0.0
Cross-currency valuation	..	..	0.8	-0.9	-0.6	-1.0	1.0	-0.9	-1.9	1.2
Residual	..	..	6.3	-3.7	2.1	9.2	0.6	-4.9	-12.1	4.3
9. AVERAGE TERMS OF NEW COMMITMENTS										
ALL CREDITORS										
Interest (%)	4.7	0.4	0.8	0.5	0.8	0.0	0.7	0.0	0.0	0.0
Maturity (years)	20.0	40.2	39.7	29.2	39.2	0.0	40.6	20.5	0.0	0.0
Grace period (years)	6.0	20.6	10.2	10.4	8.7	0.0	9.9	10.5	0.0	0.0
Grant element (%)	36.4	86.2	80.5	77.0	78.4	0.0	80.6	76.2	0.0	0.0
Official creditors										
Interest (%)	4.7	0.4	0.8	0.5	0.8	0.0	0.7	0.0	0.0	0.0
Maturity (years)	20.0	40.2	39.7	29.2	39.2	0.0	40.6	20.5	0.0	0.0
Grace period (years)	6.0	20.6	10.2	10.4	8.7	0.0	9.9	10.5	0.0	0.0
Grant element (%)	36.4	86.2	80.5	77.0	78.4	0.0	80.6	76.2	0.0	0.0
Private creditors										
Interest (%)	0.0	0.0	0.0	0.0	0.0	0.0	0.0	0.0	0.0	0.0
Maturity (years)	0.0	0.0	0.0	0.0	0.0	0.0	0.0	0.0	0.0	0.0
Grace period (years)	0.0	0.0	0.0	0.0	0.0	0.0	0.0	0.0	0.0	0.0
Grant element (%)	0.0	0.0	0.0	0.0	0.0	0.0	0.0	0.0	0.0	0.0
Memorandum items										
Commitments	0.6	12.2	15.3	13.2	12.0	0.0	9.2	2.0	0.0	0.0
Official creditors	0.6	12.2	15.3	13.2	12.0	0.0	9.2	2.0	0.0	0.0
Private creditors	0.0	0.0	0.0	0.0	0.0	0.0	0.0	0.0	0.0	0.0

10. CONTRACTUAL OBLIGATIONS ON OUTSTANDING LONG-TERM DEBT

	1999	2000	2001	2002	2003	2004	2005	2006	2007	2008
TOTAL										
Disbursements	0.5	0.6	0.4	0.3	0.2	0.1	0.1	0.1	0.1	0.0
Principal	3.5	4.5	4.8	4.7	5.0	5.0	5.1	5.3	5.4	5.5
Interest	1.4	1.4	1.3	1.3	1.2	1.2	1.1	1.1	1.0	1.0
Official creditors										
Disbursements	0.5	0.6	0.4	0.3	0.2	0.1	0.1	0.1	0.1	0.0
Principal	3.5	4.5	4.8	4.7	5.0	5.0	5.1	5.3	5.4	5.5
Interest	1.4	1.4	1.3	1.3	1.2	1.2	1.1	1.1	1.0	1.0
Bilateral creditors										
Disbursements	0.3	0.5	0.3	0.3	0.2	0.1	0.1	0.1	0.1	0.0
Principal	0.6	0.9	0.9	0.9	0.9	0.9	0.9	0.9	0.8	0.8
Interest	0.1	0.0	0.0	0.0	0.0	0.0	0.0	0.0	0.0	0.0
Multilateral creditors										
Disbursements	0.2	0.1	0.1	0.0	0.0	0.0	0.0	0.0	0.0	0.0
Principal	2.9	3.6	3.9	3.8	4.1	4.1	4.2	4.4	4.6	4.7
Interest	1.4	1.3	1.3	1.2	1.2	1.1	1.1	1.1	1.0	1.0
Private creditors										
Disbursements	0.0	0.0	0.0	0.0	0.0	0.0	0.0	0.0	0.0	0.0
Principal	0.0	0.0	0.0	0.0	0.0	0.0	0.0	0.0	0.0	0.0
Interest	0.0	0.0	0.0	0.0	0.0	0.0	0.0	0.0	0.0	0.0
Commercial banks										
Disbursements	0.0	0.0	0.0	0.0	0.0	0.0	0.0	0.0	0.0	0.0
Principal	0.0	0.0	0.0	0.0	0.0	0.0	0.0	0.0	0.0	0.0
Interest	0.0	0.0	0.0	0.0	0.0	0.0	0.0	0.0	0.0	0.0
Other private										
Disbursements	0.0	0.0	0.0	0.0	0.0	0.0	0.0	0.0	0.0	0.0
Principal	0.0	0.0	0.0	0.0	0.0	0.0	0.0	0.0	0.0	0.0
Interest	0.0	0.0	0.0	0.0	0.0	0.0	0.0	0.0	0.0	0.0

SAO TOME AND PRINCIPE

(US$ million, unless otherwise indicated)

	1970	1980	1990	1992	1993	1994	1995	1996	1997	1998
1. SUMMARY DEBT DATA										
TOTAL DEBT STOCKS (EDT)	..	**23.5**	**150.0**	**189.2**	**209.3**	**222.0**	**245.2**	**229.7**	**232.4**	**245.8**
Long-term debt (LDOD)	..	**23.5**	**132.9**	**168.5**	**181.3**	**200.4**	**231.3**	**223.0**	**223.3**	**233.4**
Public and publicly guaranteed	..	23.5	132.9	168.5	181.3	200.4	231.3	223.0	223.3	233.4
Private nonguaranteed	..	0.0	0.0	0.0	0.0	0.0	0.0	0.0	0.0	0.0
Use of IMF credit	**0.0**	**0.0**	**1.1**	**1.1**	**1.1**	**1.1**	**0.8**	**0.6**	**0.3**	**0.1**
Short-term debt	..	**0.0**	**16.0**	**19.6**	**26.8**	**20.5**	**13.0**	**6.1**	**8.8**	**12.2**
of which interest arrears on LDOD	..	0.0	7.6	9.4	15.6	14.5	6.0	4.1	4.8	7.2
Official creditors	..	0.0	7.4	9.0	15.3	14.1	6.0	4.1	4.8	7.2
Private creditors	..	0.0	0.2	0.3	0.3	0.3	0.0	0.0	0.0	0.0
Memo: principal arrears on LDOD	..	0.0	21.4	28.8	34.1	39.1	27.2	19.5	17.4	26.1
Official creditors	..	0.0	20.4	27.7	32.9	38.0	27.2	19.5	17.4	26.1
Private creditors	..	0.0	1.0	1.1	1.1	1.1	0.0	0.0	0.0	0.0
Memo: export credits	..	0.0	18.0	1.0	0.0	0.0	17.0	18.0	58.0	45.0
TOTAL DEBT FLOWS										
Disbursements	..	**9.9**	**15.6**	**24.2**	**14.6**	**14.5**	**14.1**	**11.2**	**5.0**	**6.3**
Long-term debt	..	9.9	15.6	24.2	14.6	14.5	14.1	11.2	5.0	6.3
IMF purchases	0.0	0.0	0.0	0.0	0.0	0.0	0.0	0.0	0.0	0.0
Principal repayments	..	**0.9**	**1.1**	**1.3**	**0.8**	**1.3**	**1.0**	**1.5**	**1.9**	**2.1**
Long-term debt	..	0.9	1.1	1.3	0.8	1.2	0.8	1.3	1.6	1.9
IMF repurchases	0.0	0.0	0.0	0.0	0.0	0.1	0.2	0.2	0.2	0.2
Net flows on debt	..	**7.0**	**9.1**	**25.7**	**14.7**	**8.0**	**14.1**	**4.7**	**5.1**	**5.2**
of which short-term debt	..	-2.0	-5.3	2.8	0.9	-5.2	1.0	-5.0	2.0	1.0
Interest payments (INT)	..	**0.3**	**1.7**	**1.2**	**1.8**	**1.3**	**1.1**	**1.5**	**1.7**	**1.6**
Long-term debt	..	0.2	1.2	0.8	0.9	1.0	0.8	1.4	1.5	1.3
IMF charges	0.0	0.0	0.0	0.0	0.0	0.0	0.0	0.0	0.0	0.0
Short-term debt	..	0.1	0.5	0.4	0.8	0.3	0.3	0.1	0.2	0.3
Net transfers on debt	..	**6.7**	**7.4**	**24.5**	**12.9**	**6.7**	**13.0**	**3.2**	**3.4**	**3.6**
Total debt service paid (TDS)	..	**1.2**	**2.8**	**2.5**	**2.6**	**2.6**	**2.1**	**3.0**	**3.6**	**3.7**
Long-term debt	..	1.1	2.3	2.1	1.8	2.2	1.6	2.7	3.2	3.2
IMF repurchases and charges	0.0	0.0	0.0	0.0	0.0	0.1	0.2	0.2	0.2	0.2
Short-term debt (interest only)	..	0.1	0.5	0.4	0.8	0.3	0.3	0.1	0.2	0.3
2. AGGREGATE NET RESOURCE FLOWS AND NET TRANSFERS (LONG-TERM)										
NET RESOURCE FLOWS	..	**11.7**	**41.2**	**45.8**	**33.6**	**36.0**	**37.8**	**27.8**	**19.6**	**15.3**
Net flow of long-term debt (ex. IMF)	..	9.0	14.4	22.9	13.8	13.3	13.3	9.9	3.3	4.4
Foreign direct investment (net)	..	0.0	0.0	0.0	0.0	0.0	0.0	0.0	0.0	0.0
Portfolio equity flows	..	0.0	0.0	0.0	0.0	0.0	0.0	0.0	0.0	0.0
Grants (excluding technical coop.)	..	2.7	26.7	22.9	19.8	22.7	24.5	17.9	16.3	10.9
Memo: technical coop. grants	..	1.3	7.2	14.8	15.6	12.8	20.5	16.7	13.0	12.4
official net resource flows	..	11.7	41.3	45.8	33.6	36.0	37.8	27.8	19.6	15.3
private net resource flows	..	0.0	-0.1	0.0	0.0	0.0	0.0	0.0	0.0	0.0
NET TRANSFERS	..	**11.5**	**40.0**	**45.0**	**32.7**	**35.0**	**37.0**	**26.4**	**18.1**	**14.0**
Interest on long-term debt	..	0.2	1.2	0.8	0.9	1.0	0.8	1.4	1.5	1.3
Profit remittances on FDI	..	0.0	0.0	0.0	0.0	0.0	0.0	0.0	0.0	0.0
Memo: official net transfers	..	11.5	40.2	45.0	32.7	35.0	37.0	26.4	18.1	14.0
private net transfers	..	0.0	-0.2	0.0	0.0	0.0	0.0	0.0	0.0	0.0
3. MAJOR ECONOMIC AGGREGATES										
Gross national product (GNP)	..	..	44.9	40.5	42.1	44.1	40.0	40.2	39.1	35.9
Exports of goods & services (XGS)	..	23.3	8.2	10.0	10.2	11.5	9.2	10.4	12.1	11.6
of which workers remittances	..	0.8	0.1	..	..	..	..	..	..	..
Imports of goods & services (MGS)	..	22.0	22.4	21.8	22.8	22.2	24.4	22.3	22.0	16.4
International reserves (RES)	..	..	..	..	..	..	5.1	5.0	12.4	9.7
Current account balance	..	0.7	-12.0	..	..	..	..	..	..	..
4. DEBT INDICATORS										
EDT / XGS (%)	..	100.8	1,820.4	1,899.3	2,042.3	1,937.3	2,679.1	2,211.0	1,914.3	2,122.1
EDT / GNP (%)	..	..	333.7	467.0	496.6	503.3	612.8	571.1	594.5	684.0
TDS / XGS (%)	..	5.2	34.0	25.1	25.4	22.7	22.9	28.9	29.7	31.9
INT / XGS (%)	..	1.3	20.6	12.1	17.6	11.3	12.0	14.4	14.0	13.8
INT / GNP (%)	..	..	3.8	3.0	4.3	3.0	2.8	3.7	4.4	4.5
RES / EDT (%)	..	..	..	..	..	..	2.1	2.2	5.4	3.9
RES / MGS (months)	..	..	..	..	..	..	2.5	2.7	6.8	7.1
Short-term / EDT (%)	..	0.0	10.7	10.4	12.8	9.2	5.3	2.7	3.8	5.0
Concessional / EDT (%)	..	83.8	71.8	76.2	75.2	79.5	90.1	95.0	94.3	93.5
Multilateral / EDT (%)	..	45.1	48.4	56.3	56.0	61.6	62.2	67.8	65.1	65.6

SAO TOME AND PRINCIPE

(US$ million, unless otherwise indicated)

	1970	1980	1990	1992	1993	1994	1995	1996	1997	1998
5. LONG-TERM DEBT										
DEBT OUTSTANDING (LDOD)	..	**23.5**	**132.9**	**168.5**	**181.3**	**200.4**	**231.3**	**223.0**	**223.3**	**233.4**
Public and publicly guaranteed	..	**23.5**	**132.9**	**168.5**	**181.3**	**200.4**	**231.3**	**223.0**	**223.3**	**233.4**
Official creditors	..	23.1	131.7	167.4	180.2	199.3	231.3	223.0	223.3	233.4
Multilateral	..	10.6	72.6	106.5	117.2	136.7	152.6	155.8	151.3	161.2
Concessional	..	10.6	69.1	103.1	114.4	134.5	150.5	154.0	149.8	159.9
Bilateral	..	12.6	59.2	60.9	63.0	62.6	78.7	67.2	72.0	72.3
Concessional	..	9.1	38.6	41.0	43.0	41.9	70.4	64.2	69.3	69.9
Private creditors	..	0.3	1.1	1.1	1.1	1.1	0.0	0.0	0.0	0.0
Bonds	..	0.0	0.0	0.0	0.0	0.0	0.0	0.0	0.0	0.0
Commercial banks	..	0.0	0.0	0.0	0.0	0.0	0.0	0.0	0.0	0.0
Other private	..	0.3	1.1	1.1	1.1	1.1	0.0	0.0	0.0	0.0
Private nonguaranteed	..	**0.0**	**0.0**	**0.0**	**0.0**	**0.0**	**0.0**	**0.0**	**0.0**	**0.0**
Bonds	..	0.0	0.0	0.0	0.0	0.0	0.0	0.0	0.0	0.0
Commercial banks	..	0.0	0.0	0.0	0.0	0.0	0.0	0.0	0.0	0.0
Memo:										
IBRD	0.0	0.0	0.0	0.0	0.0	0.0	0.0	0.0	0.0	0.0
IDA	0.0	0.0	23.9	33.6	38.3	46.9	53.6	59.5	57.4	61.3
DISBURSEMENTS	..	**9.9**	**15.6**	**24.2**	**14.6**	**14.5**	**14.1**	**11.2**	**5.0**	**6.3**
Public and publicly guaranteed	..	**9.9**	**15.6**	**24.2**	**14.6**	**14.5**	**14.1**	**11.2**	**5.0**	**6.3**
Official creditors	..	9.9	15.6	24.2	14.6	14.5	14.1	11.2	5.0	6.3
Multilateral	..	6.5	12.8	22.6	11.8	14.1	14.1	11.2	5.0	6.1
Concessional	..	6.5	11.7	22.6	11.8	14.0	14.0	11.2	5.0	6.1
Bilateral	..	3.4	2.7	1.6	2.8	0.4	0.0	0.0	0.0	0.2
Concessional	..	1.4	2.7	1.6	2.8	0.4	0.0	0.0	0.0	0.2
Private creditors	..	0.0	0.0	0.0	0.0	0.0	0.0	0.0	0.0	0.0
Bonds	..	0.0	0.0	0.0	0.0	0.0	0.0	0.0	0.0	0.0
Commercial banks	..	0.0	0.0	0.0	0.0	0.0	0.0	0.0	0.0	0.0
Other private	..	0.0	0.0	0.0	0.0	0.0	0.0	0.0	0.0	0.0
Private nonguaranteed	..	**0.0**	**0.0**	**0.0**	**0.0**	**0.0**	**0.0**	**0.0**	**0.0**	**0.0**
Bonds	..	0.0	0.0	0.0	0.0	0.0	0.0	0.0	0.0	0.0
Commercial banks	..	0.0	0.0	0.0	0.0	0.0	0.0	0.0	0.0	0.0
Memo:										
IBRD	0.0	0.0	0.0	0.0	0.0	0.0	0.0	0.0	0.0	0.0
IDA	0.0	0.0	5.4	5.5	4.6	6.5	5.6	8.0	1.5	1.9
PRINCIPAL REPAYMENTS	..	**0.9**	**1.1**	**1.3**	**0.8**	**1.2**	**0.8**	**1.3**	**1.6**	**1.9**
Public and publicly guaranteed	..	**0.9**	**1.1**	**1.3**	**0.8**	**1.2**	**0.8**	**1.3**	**1.6**	**1.9**
Official creditors	..	0.9	1.0	1.3	0.8	1.2	0.8	1.3	1.6	1.9
Multilateral	..	0.0	0.4	1.0	0.8	1.2	0.8	1.0	1.3	1.4
Concessional	..	0.0	0.4	0.7	0.3	0.4	0.5	0.7	1.2	1.1
Bilateral	..	0.9	0.6	0.3	0.0	0.0	0.0	0.3	0.3	0.6
Concessional	..	0.2	0.0	0.0	0.0	0.0	0.0	0.0	0.0	0.2
Private creditors	..	0.0	0.1	0.0	0.0	0.0	0.0	0.0	0.0	0.0
Bonds	..	0.0	0.0	0.0	0.0	0.0	0.0	0.0	0.0	0.0
Commercial banks	..	0.0	0.0	0.0	0.0	0.0	0.0	0.0	0.0	0.0
Other private	..	0.0	0.1	0.0	0.0	0.0	0.0	0.0	0.0	0.0
Private nonguaranteed	..	**0.0**	**0.0**	**0.0**	**0.0**	**0.0**	**0.0**	**0.0**	**0.0**	**0.0**
Bonds	..	0.0	0.0	0.0	0.0	0.0	0.0	0.0	0.0	0.0
Commercial banks	..	0.0	0.0	0.0	0.0	0.0	0.0	0.0	0.0	0.0
Memo:										
IBRD	0.0	0.0	0.0	0.0	0.0	0.0	0.0	0.0	0.0	0.0
IDA	0.0	0.0	0.0	0.0	0.0	0.0	0.1	0.1	0.2	0.2
NET FLOWS ON DEBT	..	**9.0**	**14.4**	**22.9**	**13.8**	**13.3**	**13.3**	**9.9**	**3.3**	**4.4**
Public and publicly guaranteed	..	**9.0**	**14.4**	**22.9**	**13.8**	**13.3**	**13.3**	**9.9**	**3.3**	**4.4**
Official creditors	..	9.0	14.6	22.9	13.8	13.3	13.3	9.9	3.3	4.4
Multilateral	..	6.5	12.4	21.7	11.0	12.9	13.3	10.2	3.7	4.7
Concessional	..	6.5	11.3	22.0	11.4	13.6	13.6	10.5	3.8	5.0
Bilateral	..	2.5	2.2	1.2	2.8	0.4	0.0	-0.3	-0.3	-0.3
Concessional	..	1.2	2.7	1.6	2.8	0.4	0.0	0.0	0.0	0.0
Private creditors	..	0.0	-0.1	0.0	0.0	0.0	0.0	0.0	0.0	0.0
Bonds	..	0.0	0.0	0.0	0.0	0.0	0.0	0.0	0.0	0.0
Commercial banks	..	0.0	0.0	0.0	0.0	0.0	0.0	0.0	0.0	0.0
Other private	..	0.0	-0.1	0.0	0.0	0.0	0.0	0.0	0.0	0.0
Private nonguaranteed	..	**0.0**	**0.0**	**0.0**	**0.0**	**0.0**	**0.0**	**0.0**	**0.0**	**0.0**
Bonds	..	0.0	0.0	0.0	0.0	0.0	0.0	0.0	0.0	0.0
Commercial banks	..	0.0	0.0	0.0	0.0	0.0	0.0	0.0	0.0	0.0
Memo:										
IBRD	0.0	0.0	0.0	0.0	0.0	0.0	0.0	0.0	0.0	0.0
IDA	0.0	0.0	5.4	5.5	4.6	6.5	5.6	7.9	1.3	1.7

SAO TOME AND PRINCIPE

(US$ million, unless otherwise indicated)

	1970	1980	1990	1992	1993	1994	1995	1996	1997	1998
INTEREST PAYMENTS (LINT)	..	**0.2**	**1.2**	**0.8**	**0.9**	**1.0**	**0.8**	**1.4**	**1.5**	**1.3**
Public and publicly guaranteed	..	**0.2**	**1.2**	**0.8**	**0.9**	**1.0**	**0.8**	**1.4**	**1.5**	**1.3**
Official creditors	..	0.2	1.1	0.8	0.9	1.0	0.8	1.4	1.5	1.3
Multilateral	..	0.0	0.3	0.7	0.8	0.9	0.6	1.2	1.0	1.1
Concessional	..	0.0	0.3	0.6	0.7	0.8	0.6	1.2	1.0	1.1
Bilateral	..	0.2	0.9	0.2	0.1	0.1	0.1	0.1	0.6	0.1
Concessional	..	0.0	0.1	0.1	0.1	0.1	0.1	0.1	0.6	0.1
Private creditors	..	0.0	0.1	0.0	0.0	0.0	0.0	0.0	0.0	0.0
Bonds	..	0.0	0.0	0.0	0.0	0.0	0.0	0.0	0.0	0.0
Commercial banks	..	0.0	0.0	0.0	0.0	0.0	0.0	0.0	0.0	0.0
Other private	..	0.0	0.1	0.0	0.0	0.0	0.0	0.0	0.0	0.0
Private nonguaranteed	..	**0.0**	**0.0**	**0.0**	**0.0**	**0.0**	**0.0**	**0.0**	**0.0**	**0.0**
Bonds	..	0.0	0.0	0.0	0.0	0.0	0.0	0.0	0.0	0.0
Commercial banks	..	0.0	0.0	0.0	0.0	0.0	0.0	0.0	0.0	0.0
Memo:										
IBRD	0.0	0.0	0.0	0.0	0.0	0.0	0.0	0.0	0.0	0.0
IDA	0.0	0.0	0.1	0.2	0.3	0.3	0.3	0.5	0.4	0.4
NET TRANSFERS ON DEBT	..	**8.8**	**13.2**	**22.1**	**12.8**	**12.3**	**12.5**	**8.5**	**1.8**	**3.1**
Public and publicly guaranteed	..	**8.8**	**13.2**	**22.1**	**12.8**	**12.3**	**12.5**	**8.5**	**1.8**	**3.1**
Official creditors	..	8.8	13.4	22.1	12.8	12.3	12.5	8.5	1.8	3.1
Multilateral	..	6.5	12.1	21.0	10.2	12.0	12.7	9.0	2.7	3.6
Concessional	..	6.5	11.0	21.3	10.8	12.8	13.0	9.3	2.9	3.9
Bilateral	..	2.4	1.3	1.1	2.6	0.3	-0.1	-0.5	-0.9	-0.5
Concessional	..	1.2	2.7	1.5	2.6	0.3	-0.1	-0.1	-0.6	-0.1
Private creditors	..	0.0	-0.2	0.0	0.0	0.0	0.0	0.0	0.0	0.0
Bonds	..	0.0	0.0	0.0	0.0	0.0	0.0	0.0	0.0	0.0
Commercial banks	..	0.0	0.0	0.0	0.0	0.0	0.0	0.0	0.0	0.0
Other private	..	0.0	-0.2	0.0	0.0	0.0	0.0	0.0	0.0	0.0
Private nonguaranteed	..	**0.0**	**0.0**	**0.0**	**0.0**	**0.0**	**0.0**	**0.0**	**0.0**	**0.0**
Bonds	..	0.0	0.0	0.0	0.0	0.0	0.0	0.0	0.0	0.0
Commercial banks	..	0.0	0.0	0.0	0.0	0.0	0.0	0.0	0.0	0.0
Memo:										
IBRD	0.0	0.0	0.0	0.0	0.0	0.0	0.0	0.0	0.0	0.0
IDA	0.0	0.0	5.3	5.2	4.4	6.2	5.2	7.4	0.9	1.3
DEBT SERVICE (LTDS)	..	**1.1**	**2.3**	**2.1**	**1.8**	**2.2**	**1.6**	**2.7**	**3.2**	**3.2**
Public and publicly guaranteed	..	**1.1**	**2.3**	**2.1**	**1.8**	**2.2**	**1.6**	**2.7**	**3.2**	**3.2**
Official creditors	..	1.1	2.2	2.1	1.8	2.2	1.6	2.7	3.2	3.2
Multilateral	..	0.0	0.7	1.6	1.7	2.1	1.4	2.2	2.3	2.5
Concessional	..	0.0	0.7	1.3	1.0	1.2	1.0	1.9	2.1	2.3
Bilateral	..	1.1	1.4	0.5	0.1	0.1	0.1	0.5	0.9	0.7
Concessional	..	0.2	0.1	0.1	0.1	0.1	0.1	0.1	0.6	0.3
Private creditors	..	0.0	0.2	0.0	0.0	0.0	0.0	0.0	0.0	0.0
Bonds	..	0.0	0.0	0.0	0.0	0.0	0.0	0.0	0.0	0.0
Commercial banks	..	0.0	0.0	0.0	0.0	0.0	0.0	0.0	0.0	0.0
Other private	..	0.0	0.2	0.0	0.0	0.0	0.0	0.0	0.0	0.0
Private nonguaranteed	..	**0.0**	**0.0**	**0.0**	**0.0**	**0.0**	**0.0**	**0.0**	**0.0**	**0.0**
Bonds	..	0.0	0.0	0.0	0.0	0.0	0.0	0.0	0.0	0.0
Commercial banks	..	0.0	0.0	0.0	0.0	0.0	0.0	0.0	0.0	0.0
Memo:										
IBRD	0.0	0.0	0.0	0.0	0.0	0.0	0.0	0.0	0.0	0.0
IDA	0.0	0.0	0.1	0.2	0.3	0.3	0.4	0.5	0.6	0.7
UNDISBURSED DEBT	..	**32.1**	**73.3**	**85.2**	**70.7**	**71.1**	**58.5**	**45.8**	**44.4**	**39.5**
Official creditors	..	32.1	73.3	85.2	70.7	71.1	58.5	45.8	44.4	39.5
Private creditors	..	0.0	0.0	0.0	0.0	0.0	0.0	0.0	0.0	0.0
Memorandum items										
Concessional LDOD	..	19.6	107.6	144.1	157.5	176.4	220.9	218.2	219.1	229.8
Variable rate LDOD	..	0.0	0.0	0.0	0.0	0.0	0.0	0.0	0.0	0.0
Public sector LDOD	..	23.5	132.9	168.5	181.3	200.4	231.3	223.0	223.3	233.4
Private sector LDOD	..	0.0	0.0	0.0	0.0	0.0	0.0	0.0	0.0	0.0

6. CURRENCY COMPOSITION OF LONG-TERM DEBT (PERCENT)

	1970	1980	1990	1992	1993	1994	1995	1996	1997	1998
Deutsche mark	..	0.0	0.0	0.0	0.0	0.0	0.0	0.0	0.0	0.0
French franc	..	0.0	4.0	4.7	4.5	4.5	4.2	4.1	3.6	3.6
Japanese yen	..	0.0	0.0	0.0	0.0	0.0	0.0	0.0	0.0	0.0
Pound sterling	..	0.0	0.0	0.0	0.0	0.0	0.0	0.0	0.0	0.0
Swiss franc	..	0.0	0.0	0.0	0.0	0.0	0.0	0.0	0.0	0.0
U.S.dollars	..	63.1	39.3	35.7	35.2	35.6	40.0	39.8	44.3	43.5
Multiple currency	..	0.0	43.6	49.4	49.7	51.3	48.2	48.3	46.6	47.4
Special drawing rights	..	0.0	0.0	0.0	0.0	0.0	0.0	0.0	0.0	0.0
All other currencies	..	36.9	13.1	10.2	10.6	8.6	7.6	7.8	5.5	5.5

SAO TOME AND PRINCIPE

(US$ million, unless otherwise indicated)

	1970	1980	1990	1992	1993	1994	1995	1996	1997	1998
7. DEBT RESTRUCTURINGS										
Total amount rescheduled	..	..	0.0	3.1	0.0	0.7	29.5	0.0	11.2	0.0
Debt stock rescheduled	..	..	0.0	0.0	0.0	0.0	0.0	0.0	2.1	0.0
Principal rescheduled	..	..	0.0	2.7	0.0	0.0	15.5	0.0	2.6	0.0
Official	..	..	0.0	2.7	0.0	0.0	14.4	0.0	2.6	0.0
Private	..	..	0.0	0.0	0.0	0.0	1.1	0.0	0.0	0.0
Interest rescheduled	..	..	0.0	0.4	0.0	0.7	8.5	0.0	0.0	0.0
Official	..	..	0.0	0.4	0.0	0.7	8.1	0.0	0.0	0.0
Private	..	..	0.0	0.0	0.0	0.0	0.3	0.0	0.0	0.0
Debt forgiven	..	..	0.0	0.0	0.0	0.0	0.0	0.0	0.0	0.0
Memo: interest forgiven	..	..	0.0	0.0	0.0	0.0	0.0	0.0	0.0	0.0
Debt stock reduction	..	..	0.0	0.0	0.0	0.0	0.0	0.0	0.0	0.0
of which debt buyback	..	..	0.0	0.0	0.0	0.0	0.0	0.0	0.0	0.0
8. DEBT STOCK-FLOW RECONCILIATION										
Total change in debt stocks	..	..	15.6	22.1	20.0	12.7	23.2	-15.4	2.7	13.4
Net flows on debt	..	7.0	9.1	25.7	14.7	8.0	14.1	4.7	5.1	5.2
Net change in interest arrears	..	..	1.3	0.6	6.3	-1.1	-8.5	-1.9	0.7	2.4
Interest capitalized	..	..	0.0	0.4	0.0	0.7	8.5	0.0	0.0	0.0
Debt forgiveness or reduction	..	..	0.0	0.0	0.0	0.0	0.0	0.0	0.0	0.0
Cross-currency valuation	..	..	1.1	-0.9	-0.7	-0.7	1.1	-0.7	-1.2	0.7
Residual	..	..	4.1	-3.7	-0.2	5.8	8.1	-17.5	-2.0	5.1
9. AVERAGE TERMS OF NEW COMMITMENTS										
ALL CREDITORS										
Interest (%)	..	4.0	0.9	0.8	0.0	0.8	0.0	0.0	0.8	1.5
Maturity (years)	..	11.1	43.8	37.9	0.0	49.8	0.0	0.0	51.6	12.7
Grace period (years)	..	4.4	10.1	9.6	0.0	10.3	0.0	0.0	10.8	4.2
Grant element (%)	..	31.5	80.2	77.7	0.0	82.9	0.0	0.0	83.9	44.2
Official creditors										
Interest (%)	..	4.0	0.9	0.8	0.0	0.8	0.0	0.0	0.8	1.5
Maturity (years)	..	11.1	43.8	37.9	0.0	49.8	0.0	0.0	51.6	12.7
Grace period (years)	..	4.4	10.1	9.6	0.0	10.3	0.0	0.0	10.8	4.2
Grant element (%)	..	31.5	80.2	77.7	0.0	82.9	0.0	0.0	83.9	44.2
Private creditors										
Interest (%)	..	0.0	0.0	0.0	0.0	0.0	0.0	0.0	0.0	0.0
Maturity (years)	..	0.0	0.0	0.0	0.0	0.0	0.0	0.0	0.0	0.0
Grace period (years)	..	0.0	0.0	0.0	0.0	0.0	0.0	0.0	0.0	0.0
Grant element (%)	..	0.0	0.0	0.0	0.0	0.0	0.0	0.0	0.0	0.0
Memorandum items										
Commitments	..	8.2	23.8	36.0	0.0	14.3	0.0	0.0	5.6	0.2
Official creditors	..	8.2	23.8	36.0	0.0	14.3	0.0	0.0	5.6	0.2
Private creditors	..	0.0	0.0	0.0	0.0	0.0	0.0	0.0	0.0	0.0

10. CONTRACTUAL OBLIGATIONS ON OUTSTANDING LONG-TERM DEBT

	1999	2000	2001	2002	2003	2004	2005	2006	2007	2008
TOTAL										
Disbursements	11.1	10.1	6.1	3.7	2.4	1.3	0.6	0.2	0.0	0.0
Principal	4.8	5.3	4.5	7.0	6.8	7.2	7.1	7.0	7.6	7.9
Interest	2.4	2.5	2.5	2.4	2.3	2.2	2.0	1.9	1.8	1.7
Official creditors										
Disbursements	11.1	10.1	6.1	3.7	2.4	1.3	0.6	0.2	0.0	0.0
Principal	4.8	5.3	4.5	7.0	6.8	7.2	7.1	7.0	7.6	7.9
Interest	2.4	2.5	2.5	2.4	2.3	2.2	2.0	1.9	1.8	1.7
Bilateral creditors										
Disbursements	0.3	0.3	0.2	0.2	0.1	0.1	0.0	0.0	0.0	0.0
Principal	1.2	1.2	0.9	2.8	2.8	2.8	4.0	3.9	3.8	3.7
Interest	1.1	1.1	1.1	1.0	0.9	0.9	0.8	0.7	0.6	0.6
Multilateral creditors										
Disbursements	10.8	9.8	5.9	3.5	2.3	1.2	0.5	0.1	0.0	0.0
Principal	3.7	4.1	3.6	4.2	4.0	4.4	3.1	3.1	3.8	4.2
Interest	1.3	1.4	1.4	1.4	1.4	1.3	1.2	1.2	1.2	1.2
Private creditors										
Disbursements	0.0	0.0	0.0	0.0	0.0	0.0	0.0	0.0	0.0	0.0
Principal	0.0	0.0	0.0	0.0	0.0	0.0	0.0	0.0	0.0	0.0
Interest	0.0	0.0	0.0	0.0	0.0	0.0	0.0	0.0	0.0	0.0
Commercial banks										
Disbursements	0.0	0.0	0.0	0.0	0.0	0.0	0.0	0.0	0.0	0.0
Principal	0.0	0.0	0.0	0.0	0.0	0.0	0.0	0.0	0.0	0.0
Interest	0.0	0.0	0.0	0.0	0.0	0.0	0.0	0.0	0.0	0.0
Other private										
Disbursements	0.0	0.0	0.0	0.0	0.0	0.0	0.0	0.0	0.0	0.0
Principal	0.0	0.0	0.0	0.0	0.0	0.0	0.0	0.0	0.0	0.0
Interest	0.0	0.0	0.0	0.0	0.0	0.0	0.0	0.0	0.0	0.0

SENEGAL

(US$ million, unless otherwise indicated)

	1970	1980	1990	1992	1993	1994	1995	1996	1997	1998
1. SUMMARY DEBT DATA										
TOTAL DEBT STOCKS (EDT)	**..**	**1,473**	**3,732**	**3,666**	**3,803**	**3,658**	**3,841**	**3,663**	**3,654**	**3,861**
Long-term debt (LDOD)	**145**	**1,114**	**3,000**	**3,042**	**3,097**	**3,096**	**3,234**	**3,155**	**3,148**	**3,296**
Public and publicly guaranteed	115	1,105	2,940	2,992	3,047	3,049	3,191	3,116	3,093	3,274
Private nonguaranteed	31	9	60	50	50	48	44	39	55	22
Use of IMF credit	**0**	**140**	**314**	**271**	**244**	**300**	**347**	**326**	**292**	**293**
Short-term debt	**..**	**219**	**418**	**352**	**462**	**262**	**260**	**182**	**213**	**273**
of which interest arrears on LDOD	..	0	0	50	162	39	10	2	2	2
Official creditors	..	0	0	48	118	30	4	2	2	2
Private creditors	..	0	0	2	45	10	6	1	0	0
Memo: principal arrears on LDOD	..	0	0	92	207	227	64	13	12	19
Official creditors	..	0	0	62	153	155	9	2	2	8
Private creditors	..	0	0	30	53	71	55	12	10	10
Memo: export credits	..	0	812	786	579	453	622	557	480	492
TOTAL DEBT FLOWS										
Disbursements	**20**	**395**	**252**	**322**	**153**	**201**	**241**	**216**	**268**	**254**
Long-term debt	20	327	223	322	153	132	158	181	219	206
IMF purchases	0	68	29	0	0	68	83	35	49	48
Principal repayments	**9**	**165**	**197**	**142**	**81**	**154**	**195**	**160**	**158**	**217**
Long-term debt	9	156	142	98	54	125	154	116	95	157
IMF repurchases	0	8	55	44	27	29	41	45	63	60
Net flows on debt	**11**	**246**	**222**	**177**	**70**	**-29**	**73**	**-14**	**141**	**97**
of which short-term debt	..	16	167	-3	-3	-76	28	-70	31	60
Interest payments (INT)	**..**	**95**	**128**	**68**	**42**	**80**	**86**	**129**	**89**	**106**
Long-term debt	2	67	84	48	24	63	69	118	75	88
IMF charges	0	3	15	6	3	3	3	4	3	2
Short-term debt	..	24	29	15	15	14	14	7	11	15
Net transfers on debt	**..**	**151**	**94**	**109**	**28**	**-110**	**-13**	**-143**	**52**	**-9**
Total debt service paid (TDS)	**..**	**259**	**325**	**210**	**123**	**234**	**281**	**289**	**247**	**323**
Long-term debt	12	223	226	146	77	188	224	233	170	245
IMF repurchases and charges	0	12	70	50	30	31	43	48	66	63
Short-term debt (interest only)	..	24	29	15	15	14	14	7	11	15
2. AGGREGATE NET RESOURCE FLOWS AND NET TRANSFERS (LONG-TERM)										
NET RESOURCE FLOWS	**32**	**262**	**691**	**577**	**398**	**551**	**409**	**408**	**538**	**341**
Net flow of long-term debt (ex. IMF)	11	171	81	225	100	7	4	66	124	49
Foreign direct investment (net)	5	15	57	21	-1	67	32	8	176	40
Portfolio equity flows	0	0	0	0	0	0	0	0	0	0
Grants (excluding technical coop.)	16	77	553	331	299	476	373	334	238	252
Memo: technical coop. grants	21	123	180	196	176	160	185	170	154	132
official net resource flows	22	245	649	586	402	493	402	411	347	317
private net resource flows	10	18	42	-9	-4	58	7	-3	191	24
NET TRANSFERS	**14**	**161**	**574**	**487**	**337**	**450**	**300**	**251**	**425**	**216**
Interest on long-term debt	2	67	84	48	24	63	69	118	75	88
Profit remittances on FDI	15	34	33	42	37	38	40	39	38	37
Memo: official net transfers	19	223	578	547	381	432	337	295	274	229
private net transfers	-5	-62	-4	-60	-44	17	-38	-44	151	-14
3. MAJOR ECONOMIC AGGREGATES										
Gross national product (GNP)	855	2,887	5,502	5,895	5,240	3,500	4,338	4,566	4,305	4,646
Exports of goods & services (XGS)	..	905	1,628	1,558	1,351	1,368	1,680	1,530	1,437	1,389
of which workers remittances	..	75	91	119	117	73	86	82	92	..
Imports of goods & services (MGS)	..	1,337	2,053	2,019	1,830	1,679	2,033	1,814	1,708	1,734
International reserves (RES)	22	25	22	22	15	191	283	299	395	431
Current account balance	..	-386	-363	-401	-433	-187	-244	-200	-185	-81
4. DEBT INDICATORS										
EDT / XGS (%)	..	162.8	229.3	235.3	281.5	267.5	228.7	239.4	254.3	278.0
EDT / GNP (%)	..	51.0	67.8	62.2	72.6	104.5	88.5	80.2	84.9	83.1
TDS / XGS (%)	..	28.7	20.0	13.5	9.1	17.1	16.7	18.9	17.2	23.2
INT / XGS (%)	..	10.5	7.9	4.4	3.1	5.9	5.1	8.4	6.2	7.6
INT / GNP (%)	..	3.3	2.3	1.2	0.8	2.3	2.0	2.8	2.1	2.3
RES / EDT (%)	..	1.7	0.6	0.6	0.4	5.2	7.4	8.2	10.8	11.2
RES / MGS (months)	..	0.2	0.1	0.1	0.1	1.4	1.7	2.0	2.8	3.0
Short-term / EDT (%)	..	14.9	11.2	9.6	12.1	7.2	6.8	5.0	5.8	7.1
Concessional / EDT (%)	..	27.1	52.7	56.7	55.5	57.5	58.3	62.4	65.2	66.5
Multilateral / EDT (%)	..	17.9	36.6	43.0	43.6	48.2	48.2	50.6	49.4	50.7

SENEGAL

(US$ million, unless otherwise indicated)

	1970	1980	1990	1992	1993	1994	1995	1996	1997	1998
5. LONG-TERM DEBT										
DEBT OUTSTANDING (LDOD)	**145**	**1,114**	**3,000**	**3,042**	**3,097**	**3,096**	**3,234**	**3,155**	**3,148**	**3,296**
Public and publicly guaranteed	**115**	**1,105**	**2,940**	**2,992**	**3,047**	**3,049**	**3,191**	**3,116**	**3,093**	**3,274**
Official creditors	100	653	2,759	2,880	2,940	2,943	3,107	3,102	3,082	3,263
Multilateral	13	263	1,366	1,578	1,658	1,762	1,849	1,852	1,805	1,956
Concessional	9	179	1,153	1,325	1,359	1,467	1,577	1,612	1,609	1,763
Bilateral	87	390	1,393	1,302	1,282	1,181	1,258	1,249	1,277	1,307
Concessional	78	221	815	754	753	637	662	674	774	805
Private creditors	14	452	181	113	106	106	83	14	11	11
Bonds	0	4	0	0	0	0	0	0	0	0
Commercial banks	0	129	129	90	85	86	78	11	10	10
Other private	14	319	52	23	21	20	6	3	1	1
Private nonguaranteed	**31**	**9**	**60**	**50**	**50**	**48**	**44**	**39**	**55**	**22**
Bonds	0	0	0	0	0	0	0	0	0	0
Commercial banks	31	9	60	50	50	48	44	39	55	22
Memo:										
IBRD	2	57	88	62	52	44	35	23	14	9
IDA	9	100	747	873	918	1,005	1,126	1,194	1,187	1,301
DISBURSEMENTS	**20**	**327**	**223**	**322**	**153**	**132**	**158**	**181**	**219**	**206**
Public and publicly guaranteed	**19**	**327**	**208**	**317**	**152**	**132**	**157**	**181**	**198**	**204**
Official creditors	12	186	208	314	152	132	157	181	198	204
Multilateral	5	93	136	255	143	117	139	135	98	150
Concessional	4	63	127	182	75	84	132	135	97	136
Bilateral	7	94	72	59	9	15	17	46	100	54
Concessional	7	50	72	59	9	14	17	46	100	53
Private creditors	8	141	0	3	0	0	0	0	0	0
Bonds	0	0	0	0	0	0	0	0	0	0
Commercial banks	0	23	0	0	0	0	0	0	0	0
Other private	8	118	0	3	0	0	0	0	0	0
Private nonguaranteed	**1**	**0**	**15**	**6**	**1**	**1**	**1**	**0**	**21**	**2**
Bonds	0	0	0	0	0	0	0	0	0	0
Commercial banks	1	0	15	6	1	1	1	0	21	2
Memo:										
IBRD	1	18	0	0	0	0	0	0	0	0
IDA	4	12	117	103	46	54	107	110	60	85
PRINCIPAL REPAYMENTS	**9**	**156**	**142**	**98**	**54**	**125**	**154**	**116**	**95**	**157**
Public and publicly guaranteed	**7**	**152**	**130**	**86**	**51**	**119**	**149**	**111**	**91**	**140**
Official creditors	6	19	111	59	50	115	128	105	89	139
Multilateral	0	3	58	42	47	106	97	69	41	71
Concessional	0	0	29	23	30	60	59	44	20	42
Bilateral	6	16	53	17	3	9	31	36	48	68
Concessional	5	7	25	9	1	8	14	20	27	49
Private creditors	0	133	19	27	2	3	21	6	2	1
Bonds	0	1	0	0	0	0	0	0	0	0
Commercial banks	0	58	8	16	2	3	12	5	0	0
Other private	0	74	11	12	0	0	9	1	2	1
Private nonguaranteed	**3**	**4**	**12**	**12**	**2**	**7**	**5**	**5**	**5**	**17**
Bonds	0	0	0	0	0	0	0	0	0	0
Commercial banks	3	4	12	12	2	7	5	5	5	17
Memo:										
IBRD	0	2	13	11	11	11	12	10	7	6
IDA	0	0	3	3	4	5	6	7	8	11
NET FLOWS ON DEBT	**11**	**171**	**81**	**225**	**100**	**7**	**4**	**66**	**124**	**49**
Public and publicly guaranteed	**13**	**175**	**78**	**231**	**101**	**13**	**8**	**70**	**108**	**64**
Official creditors	6	167	96	255	103	17	29	77	109	65
Multilateral	5	90	77	213	96	11	43	66	57	80
Concessional	4	63	98	159	45	24	74	91	78	94
Bilateral	1	77	19	42	6	5	-14	10	52	-15
Concessional	2	43	47	50	8	6	4	26	73	4
Private creditors	7	8	-19	-25	-2	-3	-21	-6	-2	-1
Bonds	0	-1	0	0	0	0	0	0	0	0
Commercial banks	0	-35	-8	-16	-2	-3	-12	-5	0	0
Other private	7	43	-11	-9	0	0	-9	-1	-2	-1
Private nonguaranteed	**-2**	**-4**	**4**	**-6**	**-1**	**-6**	**-4**	**-5**	**16**	**-15**
Bonds	0	0	0	0	0	0	0	0	0	0
Commercial banks	-2	-4	4	-6	-1	-6	-4	-5	16	-15
Memo:										
IBRD	1	16	-13	-11	-11	-11	-12	-10	-7	-6
IDA	4	12	114	100	42	49	101	103	52	74

SENEGAL

(US$ million, unless otherwise indicated)

	1970	1980	1990	1992	1993	1994	1995	1996	1997	1998
INTEREST PAYMENTS (LINT)	**2**	**67**	**84**	**48**	**24**	**63**	**69**	**118**	**75**	**88**
Public and publicly guaranteed	**2**	**67**	**82**	**45**	**22**	**61**	**68**	**117**	**74**	**88**
Official creditors	2	22	71	39	21	61	65	116	73	88
Multilateral	0	6	26	20	15	46	38	38	27	35
Concessional	0	1	9	7	7	19	14	17	15	17
Bilateral	2	15	46	20	6	15	27	78	47	52
Concessional	2	6	20	12	1	7	8	62	15	19
Private creditors	0	45	10	6	0	0	3	1	0	0
Bonds	0	0	0	0	0	0	0	0	0	0
Commercial banks	0	23	7	4	0	0	2	1	0	0
Other private	0	22	3	2	0	0	1	0	0	0
Private nonguaranteed	**0**	**0**	**3**	**3**	**2**	**2**	**1**	**1**	**1**	**1**
Bonds	0	0	0	0	0	0	0	0	0	0
Commercial banks	0	0	3	3	2	2	1	1	1	1
Memo:										
IBRD	0	4	6	6	5	4	4	2	2	1
IDA	0	1	4	6	6	8	8	9	9	9
NET TRANSFERS ON DEBT	**8**	**103**	**-3**	**177**	**76**	**-56**	**-66**	**-52**	**49**	**-39**
Public and publicly guaranteed	**10**	**108**	**-4**	**186**	**79**	**-48**	**-61**	**-46**	**34**	**-24**
Official creditors	3	146	25	216	81	-44	-36	-39	36	-23
Multilateral	4	84	51	193	81	-35	5	29	31	44
Concessional	4	62	89	152	39	6	60	74	63	76
Bilateral	-1	62	-27	23	0	-9	-41	-67	5	-67
Concessional	1	37	27	38	8	-1	-4	-36	58	-15
Private creditors	7	-38	-29	-30	-2	-4	-25	-8	-2	-1
Bonds	0	-1	0	0	0	0	0	0	0	0
Commercial banks	0	-58	-15	-19	-2	-3	-15	-6	0	0
Other private	7	21	-14	-11	0	0	-10	-1	-2	-1
Private nonguaranteed	**-2**	**-5**	**1**	**-9**	**-3**	**-8**	**-5**	**-6**	**15**	**-16**
Bonds	0	0	0	0	0	0	0	0	0	0
Commercial banks	-2	-5	1	-9	-3	-8	-5	-6	15	-16
Memo:										
IBRD	1	12	-19	-17	-16	-15	-15	-12	-9	-7
IDA	4	11	110	94	36	41	93	94	44	65
DEBT SERVICE (LTDS)	**12**	**223**	**226**	**146**	**77**	**188**	**224**	**233**	**170**	**245**
Public and publicly guaranteed	**9**	**219**	**212**	**131**	**73**	**180**	**217**	**228**	**164**	**228**
Official creditors	9	41	183	98	71	176	193	220	162	227
Multilateral	0	9	84	62	62	152	134	107	68	106
Concessional	0	1	38	30	37	78	73	61	34	59
Bilateral	8	32	99	37	9	24	58	113	95	121
Concessional	6	13	45	21	2	15	21	82	42	68
Private creditors	1	178	29	33	2	4	25	8	2	1
Bonds	0	1	0	0	0	0	0	0	0	0
Commercial banks	0	81	15	19	2	3	15	6	0	0
Other private	1	96	14	14	0	0	10	1	2	1
Private nonguaranteed	**3**	**5**	**14**	**15**	**4**	**9**	**6**	**6**	**6**	**17**
Bonds	0	0	0	0	0	0	0	0	0	0
Commercial banks	3	5	14	15	4	9	6	6	6	17
Memo:										
IBRD	0	6	19	17	16	15	15	12	9	7
IDA	0	1	7	9	10	13	14	15	17	20
UNDISBURSED DEBT	**42**	**604**	**976**	**982**	**867**	**753**	**889**	**813**	**745**	**731**
Official creditors	37	563	967	977	864	750	888	812	744	731
Private creditors	5	41	9	5	3	3	1	1	1	0
Memorandum items										
Concessional LDOD	87	400	1,968	2,080	2,111	2,104	2,239	2,286	2,383	2,567
Variable rate LDOD	31	141	140	167	227	271	305	255	236	202
Public sector LDOD	112	1,079	2,903	2,957	3,014	3,020	3,159	3,116	3,093	3,274
Private sector LDOD	33	35	97	85	83	77	76	39	55	22

6. CURRENCY COMPOSITION OF LONG-TERM DEBT (PERCENT)

	1970	1980	1990	1992	1993	1994	1995	1996	1997	1998
Deutsche mark	23.5	4.6	1.3	1.1	1.1	1.3	1.3	1.6	1.4	1.7
French franc	26.9	39.3	25.8	24.6	23.2	18.4	19.1	17.7	15.3	14.7
Japanese yen	0.0	0.0	1.5	3.1	3.4	3.9	3.7	3.3	3.0	3.1
Pound sterling	0.0	0.8	0.2	0.1	0.1	0.1	0.1	0.1	0.2	0.1
Swiss franc	0.0	0.3	0.9	0.6	0.5	0.5	0.5	0.4	0.3	0.3
U.S.dollars	1.7	23.0	32.9	31.9	32.8	35.1	36.6	38.5	41.7	42.8
Multiple currency	1.9	6.7	8.6	11.5	13.2	14.8	13.9	14.0	12.5	11.8
Special drawing rights	0.0	0.0	0.4	0.6	0.6	0.8	1.0	1.2	0.9	1.1
All other currencies	46.0	25.3	28.4	26.5	25.1	25.1	23.8	23.2	24.7	24.4

SENEGAL

(US$ million, unless otherwise indicated)

	1970	1980	1990	1992	1993	1994	1995	1996	1997	1998
7. DEBT RESTRUCTURINGS										
Total amount rescheduled	..	..	111	45	10	172	233	58	12	0
Debt stock rescheduled	..	..	0	0	0	0	0	0	0	0
Principal rescheduled	..	..	76	24	0	88	173	25	4	0
Official	..	..	58	23	0	86	166	25	4	0
Private	..	..	18	1	0	2	7	0	0	0
Interest rescheduled	..	..	27	9	0	83	49	28	1	0
Official	..	..	23	9	0	83	48	28	1	0
Private	..	..	4	0	0	0	1	0	0	0
Debt forgiven	..	..	18	6	0	219	14	2	4	0
Memo: interest forgiven	..	..	0	3	0	28	5	6	0	0
Debt stock reduction	..	..	0	0	0	0	0	65	0	0
of which debt buyback	..	..	0	0	0	0	0	5	0	0
8. DEBT STOCK-FLOW RECONCILIATION										
Total change in debt stocks	..	..	462	95	137	-144	183	-178	-9	208
Net flows on debt	11	246	222	177	70	-29	73	-14	141	97
Net change in interest arrears	..	..	-11	50	112	-123	-30	-8	0	0
Interest capitalized	..	..	27	9	0	83	49	28	1	0
Debt forgiveness or reduction	..	..	-18	-6	0	-219	-14	-62	-4	0
Cross-currency valuation	..	..	172	-102	-61	95	81	-74	-129	71
Residual	..	..	68	-33	15	50	23	-49	-18	40
9. AVERAGE TERMS OF NEW COMMITMENTS										
ALL CREDITORS										
Interest (%)	3.9	5.9	1.9	1.7	1.6	0.7	1.1	2.4	1.4	1.0
Maturity (years)	23.2	20.0	33.4	36.8	30.1	38.4	38.7	31.1	40.0	39.2
Grace period (years)	6.8	5.6	8.7	8.6	8.0	9.2	9.4	9.7	10.2	9.5
Grant element (%)	43.8	30.2	66.1	69.1	65.9	76.8	76.0	61.5	75.0	77.0
Official creditors										
Interest (%)	2.3	5.4	1.9	1.7	1.6	0.7	1.1	2.4	1.4	1.0
Maturity (years)	30.6	21.3	33.7	36.8	30.1	38.4	38.7	31.1	40.0	39.2
Grace period (years)	8.8	6.0	8.8	8.6	8.0	9.2	9.4	9.7	10.2	9.5
Grant element (%)	59.6	33.7	66.8	69.1	65.9	76.8	76.0	61.5	75.0	77.0
Private creditors										
Interest (%)	7.5	10.8	8.3	0.0	0.0	0.0	0.0	0.0	0.0	0.0
Maturity (years)	5.9	8.3	10.1	0.0	0.0	0.0	0.0	0.0	0.0	0.0
Grace period (years)	2.2	2.5	2.6	0.0	0.0	0.0	0.0	0.0	0.0	0.0
Grant element (%)	6.8	-0.7	6.6	0.0	0.0	0.0	0.0	0.0	0.0	0.0
Memorandum items										
Commitments	7	469	366	247	81	47	309	162	182	167
Official creditors	5	421	361	247	81	47	309	162	182	167
Private creditors	2	49	4	0	0	0	0	0	0	0

10. CONTRACTUAL OBLIGATIONS ON OUTSTANDING LONG-TERM DEBT

	1999	2000	2001	2002	2003	2004	2005	2006	2007	2008
TOTAL										
Disbursements	225	194	130	85	46	18	9	2	1	0
Principal	172	206	180	181	174	262	146	132	124	126
Interest	90	86	79	72	65	51	45	40	37	34
Official creditors										
Disbursements	224	194	130	85	46	18	9	2	1	0
Principal	169	203	177	179	171	260	143	129	124	126
Interest	89	85	79	72	65	51	45	40	37	34
Bilateral creditors										
Disbursements	55	36	19	10	5	2	1	0	0	0
Principal	81	116	110	111	106	194	77	64	58	55
Interest	58	55	49	44	38	25	21	18	16	14
Multilateral creditors										
Disbursements	170	158	111	75	41	16	9	2	1	0
Principal	88	87	67	68	65	66	66	65	66	71
Interest	31	30	29	28	27	26	24	23	21	20
Private creditors										
Disbursements	0	0	0	0	0	0	0	0	0	0
Principal	3	3	3	3	3	3	3	3	0	0
Interest	0	0	0	0	0	0	0	0	0	0
Commercial banks										
Disbursements	0	0	0	0	0	0	0	0	0	0
Principal	0	0	0	0	0	0	0	0	0	0
Interest	0	0	0	0	0	0	0	0	0	0
Other private										
Disbursements	0	0	0	0	0	0	0	0	0	0
Principal	3	3	3	3	3	3	3	3	0	0
Interest	0	0	0	0	0	0	0	0	0	0

SEYCHELLES

(US$ million, unless otherwise indicated)

	1970	1980	1990	1992	1993	1994	1995	1996	1997	1998
1. SUMMARY DEBT DATA										
TOTAL DEBT STOCKS (EDT)	..	**84.1**	**163.2**	**164.1**	**156.9**	**170.9**	**158.9**	**148.0**	**149.1**	**186.7**
Long-term debt (LDOD)	..	**25.1**	**117.2**	**130.5**	**132.1**	**147.8**	**145.8**	**138.1**	**131.3**	**145.1**
Public and publicly guaranteed	..	25.1	117.2	130.5	132.1	147.8	145.8	138.1	131.3	145.1
Private nonguaranteed	..	0.0	0.0	0.0	0.0	0.0	0.0	0.0	0.0	0.0
Use of IMF credit	**0.0**	**0.0**	**0.0**	**0.0**	**0.0**	**0.0**	**0.0**	**0.0**	**0.0**	**0.0**
Short-term debt	..	**59.0**	**46.0**	**33.6**	**24.8**	**23.1**	**13.1**	**9.8**	**17.8**	**41.6**
of which interest arrears on LDOD	..	0.0	1.2	1.2	1.3	2.1	2.1	2.9	3.8	3.8
Official creditors	..	0.0	0.6	0.3	0.4	0.9	0.8	1.4	2.3	2.8
Private creditors	..	0.0	0.7	0.9	0.9	1.2	1.3	1.5	1.5	1.0
Memo: principal arrears on LDOD	..	0.0	9.3	15.5	15.5	18.6	20.8	22.4	23.7	21.7
Official creditors	..	0.0	7.1	6.7	6.9	8.3	9.3	11.6	13.2	12.3
Private creditors	..	0.0	2.1	8.8	8.7	10.3	11.5	10.8	10.4	9.4
Memo: export credits	..	0.0	45.0	179.0	174.0	42.0	51.0	37.0	45.0	32.0
TOTAL DEBT FLOWS										
Disbursements	..	**11.7**	**9.2**	**24.9**	**17.6**	**18.1**	**8.4**	**12.2**	**11.2**	**22.9**
Long-term debt	..	11.7	9.2	24.9	17.6	18.1	8.4	12.2	11.2	22.9
IMF purchases	0.0	0.0	0.0	0.0	0.0	0.0	0.0	0.0	0.0	0.0
Principal repayments	..	**0.1**	**12.7**	**11.8**	**12.1**	**10.1**	**15.6**	**10.3**	**9.5**	**13.5**
Long-term debt	..	0.1	12.7	11.8	12.1	10.1	15.6	10.3	9.5	13.5
IMF repurchases	0.0	0.0	0.0	0.0	0.0	0.0	0.0	0.0	0.0	0.0
Net flows on debt	..	**-390.3**	**6.7**	**-0.5**	**-3.4**	**5.5**	**-17.2**	**-2.3**	**8.8**	**33.1**
of which short-term debt	..	-402.0	10.2	-13.5	-8.9	-2.5	-10.0	-4.1	7.1	23.8
Interest payments (INT)	..	**37.1**	**9.0**	**6.4**	**6.1**	**6.9**	**7.9**	**5.0**	**5.3**	**7.7**
Long-term debt	..	0.2	5.5	4.8	5.1	6.2	7.1	4.5	4.8	6.4
IMF charges	0.0	0.0	0.0	0.0	0.0	0.0	0.0	0.0	0.0	0.0
Short-term debt	..	36.9	3.6	1.6	1.0	0.8	0.8	0.5	0.5	1.3
Net transfers on debt	..	**-427.5**	**-2.3**	**-6.9**	**-9.5**	**-1.4**	**-25.1**	**-7.3**	**3.5**	**25.4**
Total debt service paid (TDS)	..	**37.2**	**21.7**	**18.2**	**18.2**	**17.0**	**23.5**	**15.4**	**14.8**	**21.2**
Long-term debt	..	0.3	18.2	16.6	17.2	16.2	22.7	14.9	14.3	19.9
IMF repurchases and charges	0.0	0.0	0.0	0.0	0.0	0.0	0.0	0.0	0.0	0.0
Short-term debt (interest only)	..	36.9	3.6	1.6	1.0	0.8	0.8	0.5	0.5	1.3
2. AGGREGATE NET RESOURCE FLOWS AND NET TRANSFERS (LONG-TERM)										
NET RESOURCE FLOWS	..	**26.9**	**28.2**	**30.7**	**35.6**	**44.9**	**40.3**	**39.0**	**55.8**	**69.3**
Net flow of long-term debt (ex. IMF)	..	11.7	-3.5	13.0	5.5	8.0	-7.2	1.8	1.7	9.3
Foreign direct investment (net)	..	9.5	20.0	9.0	19.0	29.8	40.3	30.0	49.0	52.0
Portfolio equity flows	..	0.0	0.0	0.0	0.0	0.0	0.0	0.0	0.0	0.0
Grants (excluding technical coop.)	..	5.7	11.6	8.7	11.1	7.1	7.2	7.2	5.1	7.9
Memo: technical coop. grants	..	8.0	10.3	12.2	9.9	7.9	8.8	10.3	7.3	5.8
official net resource flows	..	17.4	14.4	11.0	13.1	10.3	8.3	13.3	9.8	12.2
private net resource flows	..	9.5	13.8	19.7	22.5	34.6	32.0	25.7	46.0	57.1
NET TRANSFERS	..	**19.1**	**8.5**	**15.6**	**18.5**	**26.2**	**20.2**	**20.5**	**36.0**	**46.0**
Interest on long-term debt	..	0.2	5.5	4.8	5.1	6.2	7.1	4.5	4.8	6.4
Profit remittances on FDI	..	7.6	14.3	10.3	12.0	12.5	13.0	14.0	15.0	17.0
Memo: official net transfers	..	17.2	10.9	7.3	9.5	6.8	3.6	10.2	6.2	7.6
private net transfers	..	1.9	-2.4	8.3	9.0	19.4	16.6	10.3	29.8	38.4
3. MAJOR ECONOMIC AGGREGATES										
Gross national product (GNP)	..	142.0	355.4	424.4	458.5	473.0	491.0	494.6	529.3	514.3
Exports of goods & services (XGS)	..	102.8	240.6	257.7	278.6	259.8	282.9	324.8	368.7	370.1
of which workers remittances	..	0.0	7.1	10.4	8.8	6.0	5.9	4.9	6.0	..
Imports of goods & services (MGS)	..	131.4	264.6	271.5	325.3	287.7	339.3	391.8	440.0	474.9
International reserves (RES)	..	18.4	16.6	31.3	35.7	30.2	27.1	21.8	26.3	21.6
Current account balance	..	-15.6	-13.0	-6.9	-38.8	-25.9	-53.9	-56.5	-63.2	-91.5
4. DEBT INDICATORS										
EDT / XGS (%)	..	81.8	67.8	63.7	56.3	65.8	56.2	45.6	40.4	50.4
EDT / GNP (%)	..	59.2	45.9	38.7	34.2	36.1	32.4	29.9	28.2	36.3
TDS / XGS (%)	..	36.2	9.0	7.1	6.5	6.5	8.3	4.7	4.0	5.7
INT / XGS (%)	..	36.1	3.7	2.5	2.2	2.7	2.8	1.5	1.4	2.1
INT / GNP (%)	..	26.1	2.5	1.5	1.3	1.5	1.6	1.0	1.0	1.5
RES / EDT (%)	..	21.9	10.2	19.1	22.7	17.6	17.1	14.7	17.7	11.6
RES / MGS (months)	..	1.7	0.8	1.4	1.3	1.3	1.0	0.7	0.7	0.6
Short-term / EDT (%)	..	70.2	28.2	20.5	15.8	13.5	8.2	6.6	11.9	22.3
Concessional / EDT (%)	..	22.4	43.2	42.7	41.9	39.4	42.6	45.3	45.1	37.8
Multilateral / EDT (%)	..	5.4	25.9	27.5	30.1	32.5	37.8	37.7	36.2	31.1

SEYCHELLES

(US$ million, unless otherwise indicated)

	1970	1980	1990	1992	1993	1994	1995	1996	1997	1998
5. LONG-TERM DEBT										
DEBT OUTSTANDING (LDOD)	..	**25.1**	**117.2**	**130.5**	**132.1**	**147.8**	**145.8**	**138.1**	**131.3**	**145.1**
Public and publicly guaranteed	..	**25.1**	**117.2**	**130.5**	**132.1**	**147.8**	**145.8**	**138.1**	**131.3**	**145.1**
Official creditors	..	25.1	97.9	97.7	96.7	105.3	109.5	108.4	106.1	114.2
Multilateral	..	4.5	42.3	45.2	47.2	55.6	60.0	55.8	53.9	58.1
Concessional	..	2.5	19.8	21.9	21.8	23.1	23.6	21.8	20.8	21.6
Bilateral	..	20.6	55.6	52.4	49.5	49.7	49.5	52.6	52.3	56.0
Concessional	..	16.3	50.7	48.2	44.0	44.3	44.1	45.2	46.5	48.9
Private creditors	..	0.0	19.3	32.9	35.4	42.5	36.3	29.7	25.1	30.9
Bonds	..	0.0	0.0	0.0	0.0	0.0	0.0	0.0	0.0	0.0
Commercial banks	..	0.0	16.4	26.5	24.1	24.0	21.6	16.9	14.2	17.0
Other private	..	0.0	2.8	6.4	11.3	18.4	14.8	12.8	10.9	13.9
Private nonguaranteed	..	**0.0**	**0.0**	**0.0**	**0.0**	**0.0**	**0.0**	**0.0**	**0.0**	**0.0**
Bonds	..	0.0	0.0	0.0	0.0	0.0	0.0	0.0	0.0	0.0
Commercial banks	..	0.0	0.0	0.0	0.0	0.0	0.0	0.0	0.0	0.0
Memo:										
IBRD	0.0	0.0	5.8	4.7	4.2	4.8	5.4	4.4	3.6	3.6
IDA	0.0	0.0	0.0	0.0	0.0	0.0	0.0	0.0	0.0	0.0
DISBURSEMENTS	..	**11.7**	**9.2**	**24.9**	**17.6**	**18.1**	**8.4**	**12.2**	**11.2**	**22.9**
Public and publicly guaranteed	..	**11.7**	**9.2**	**24.9**	**17.6**	**18.1**	**8.4**	**12.2**	**11.2**	**22.9**
Official creditors	..	11.7	7.6	9.7	9.3	8.9	8.1	11.5	11.2	13.2
Multilateral	..	3.5	3.4	8.1	6.7	8.9	7.5	6.0	5.5	7.3
Concessional	..	1.6	1.2	2.6	1.5	0.9	0.9	0.6	0.6	1.2
Bilateral	..	8.2	4.1	1.6	2.6	0.1	0.6	5.5	5.7	5.8
Concessional	..	4.5	4.1	1.2	1.0	0.1	0.6	3.5	5.6	4.5
Private creditors	..	0.0	1.6	15.1	8.4	9.1	0.3	0.7	0.0	9.7
Bonds	..	0.0	0.0	0.0	0.0	0.0	0.0	0.0	0.0	0.0
Commercial banks	..	0.0	1.3	15.1	2.3	1.0	0.0	0.7	0.0	5.1
Other private	..	0.0	0.3	0.0	6.1	8.2	0.3	0.0	0.0	4.6
Private nonguaranteed	..	**0.0**	**0.0**	**0.0**	**0.0**	**0.0**	**0.0**	**0.0**	**0.0**	**0.0**
Bonds	..	0.0	0.0	0.0	0.0	0.0	0.0	0.0	0.0	0.0
Commercial banks	..	0.0	0.0	0.0	0.0	0.0	0.0	0.0	0.0	0.0
Memo:										
IBRD	0.0	0.0	1.4	0.0	0.0	0.9	1.3	0.0	0.2	0.5
IDA	0.0	0.0	0.0	0.0	0.0	0.0	0.0	0.0	0.0	0.0
PRINCIPAL REPAYMENTS	..	**0.1**	**12.7**	**11.8**	**12.1**	**10.1**	**15.6**	**10.3**	**9.5**	**13.5**
Public and publicly guaranteed	..	**0.1**	**12.7**	**11.8**	**12.1**	**10.1**	**15.6**	**10.3**	**9.5**	**13.5**
Official creditors	..	0.1	4.8	7.5	7.3	5.8	6.9	5.4	6.6	8.9
Multilateral	..	0.0	2.9	3.7	4.0	3.4	4.0	3.9	3.9	5.5
Concessional	..	0.0	0.3	0.8	0.8	0.8	0.8	0.7	0.7	0.7
Bilateral	..	0.1	2.0	3.8	3.3	2.3	2.9	1.5	2.6	3.4
Concessional	..	0.1	1.8	3.2	3.2	2.3	2.8	1.5	1.0	3.4
Private creditors	..	0.0	7.9	4.4	4.8	4.3	8.6	5.0	3.0	4.6
Bonds	..	0.0	0.0	0.0	0.0	0.0	0.0	0.0	0.0	0.0
Commercial banks	..	0.0	6.8	3.5	3.7	3.3	4.6	3.0	1.0	3.0
Other private	..	0.0	1.1	0.8	1.1	1.1	4.0	1.9	1.9	1.6
Private nonguaranteed	..	**0.0**	**0.0**	**0.0**	**0.0**	**0.0**	**0.0**	**0.0**	**0.0**	**0.0**
Bonds	..	0.0	0.0	0.0	0.0	0.0	0.0	0.0	0.0	0.0
Commercial banks	..	0.0	0.0	0.0	0.0	0.0	0.0	0.0	0.0	0.0
Memo:										
IBRD	0.0	0.0	0.6	0.6	0.7	0.7	0.8	0.7	0.6	0.8
IDA	0.0	0.0	0.0	0.0	0.0	0.0	0.0	0.0	0.0	0.0
NET FLOWS ON DEBT	..	**11.7**	**-3.5**	**13.0**	**5.5**	**8.0**	**-7.2**	**1.8**	**1.7**	**9.3**
Public and publicly guaranteed	..	**11.7**	**-3.5**	**13.0**	**5.5**	**8.0**	**-7.2**	**1.8**	**1.7**	**9.3**
Official creditors	..	11.7	2.8	2.3	2.0	3.2	1.1	6.1	4.7	4.3
Multilateral	..	3.5	0.6	4.4	2.7	5.5	3.4	2.1	1.6	1.8
Concessional	..	1.6	0.9	1.8	0.7	0.2	0.1	-0.1	-0.1	0.5
Bilateral	..	8.2	2.2	-2.2	-0.7	-2.3	-2.3	4.0	3.1	2.4
Concessional	..	4.5	2.3	-1.9	-2.2	-2.3	-2.3	2.0	4.6	1.1
Private creditors	..	0.0	-6.2	10.7	3.5	4.8	-8.3	-4.3	-3.0	5.1
Bonds	..	0.0	0.0	0.0	0.0	0.0	0.0	0.0	0.0	0.0
Commercial banks	..	0.0	-5.5	11.6	-1.4	-2.3	-4.6	-2.4	-1.0	2.1
Other private	..	0.0	-0.8	-0.8	4.9	7.1	-3.7	-1.9	-1.9	3.0
Private nonguaranteed	..	**0.0**	**0.0**	**0.0**	**0.0**	**0.0**	**0.0**	**0.0**	**0.0**	**0.0**
Bonds	..	0.0	0.0	0.0	0.0	0.0	0.0	0.0	0.0	0.0
Commercial banks	..	0.0	0.0	0.0	0.0	0.0	0.0	0.0	0.0	0.0
Memo:										
IBRD	0.0	0.0	0.8	-0.7	-0.6	0.2	0.5	-0.6	-0.4	-0.3
IDA	0.0	0.0	0.0	0.0	0.0	0.0	0.0	0.0	0.0	0.0

SEYCHELLES

(US$ million, unless otherwise indicated)

	1970	1980	1990	1992	1993	1994	1995	1996	1997	1998
INTEREST PAYMENTS (LINT)	..	**0.2**	**5.5**	**4.8**	**5.1**	**6.2**	**7.1**	**4.5**	**4.8**	**6.4**
Public and publicly guaranteed	..	**0.2**	**5.5**	**4.8**	**5.1**	**6.2**	**7.1**	**4.5**	**4.8**	**6.4**
Official creditors	..	0.2	3.5	3.7	3.6	3.5	4.7	3.1	3.6	4.6
Multilateral	..	0.2	2.5	2.5	2.8	2.8	3.6	2.6	2.9	3.8
Concessional	..	0.0	0.3	0.5	0.5	0.5	0.5	0.4	0.5	0.5
Bilateral	..	0.1	1.1	1.2	0.8	0.7	1.1	0.5	0.7	0.9
Concessional	..	0.0	0.9	1.1	0.8	0.7	1.1	0.5	0.6	0.8
Private creditors	..	0.0	1.9	1.1	1.5	2.7	2.4	1.4	1.2	1.7
Bonds	..	0.0	0.0	0.0	0.0	0.0	0.0	0.0	0.0	0.0
Commercial banks	..	0.0	1.7	0.6	1.1	1.0	1.2	0.3	0.2	0.7
Other private	..	0.0	0.2	0.5	0.4	1.7	1.2	1.1	1.0	1.0
Private nonguaranteed	..	**0.0**	**0.0**	**0.0**	**0.0**	**0.0**	**0.0**	**0.0**	**0.0**	**0.0**
Bonds	..	0.0	0.0	0.0	0.0	0.0	0.0	0.0	0.0	0.0
Commercial banks	..	0.0	0.0	0.0	0.0	0.0	0.0	0.0	0.0	0.0
Memo:										
IBRD	0.0	0.0	0.4	0.4	0.3	0.3	0.4	0.4	0.3	0.2
IDA	0.0	0.0	0.0	0.0	0.0	0.0	0.0	0.0	0.0	0.0
NET TRANSFERS ON DEBT	..	**11.4**	**-9.0**	**8.2**	**0.4**	**1.8**	**-14.3**	**-2.7**	**-3.1**	**3.0**
Public and publicly guaranteed	..	**11.4**	**-9.0**	**8.2**	**0.4**	**1.8**	**-14.3**	**-2.7**	**-3.1**	**3.0**
Official creditors	..	11.4	-0.8	-1.4	-1.6	-0.3	-3.6	3.0	1.0	-0.4
Multilateral	..	3.3	-1.9	2.0	-0.1	2.7	-0.2	-0.5	-1.4	-2.0
Concessional	..	1.6	0.6	1.3	0.2	-0.3	-0.5	-0.5	-0.6	0.0
Bilateral	..	8.1	1.1	-3.3	-1.5	-3.0	-3.4	3.5	2.4	1.6
Concessional	..	4.4	1.4	-3.0	-2.9	-2.9	-3.3	1.5	4.0	0.3
Private creditors	..	0.0	-8.2	9.6	2.0	2.1	-10.7	-5.7	-4.1	3.3
Bonds	..	0.0	0.0	0.0	0.0	0.0	0.0	0.0	0.0	0.0
Commercial banks	..	0.0	-7.2	11.0	-2.5	-3.3	-5.8	-2.7	-1.2	1.4
Other private	..	0.0	-1.0	-1.4	4.6	5.4	-4.9	-3.0	-2.9	2.0
Private nonguaranteed	..	**0.0**	**0.0**	**0.0**	**0.0**	**0.0**	**0.0**	**0.0**	**0.0**	**0.0**
Bonds	..	0.0	0.0	0.0	0.0	0.0	0.0	0.0	0.0	0.0
Commercial banks	..	0.0	0.0	0.0	0.0	0.0	0.0	0.0	0.0	0.0
Memo:										
IBRD	0.0	0.0	0.4	-1.1	-1.0	-0.1	0.1	-1.0	-0.7	-0.5
IDA	0.0	0.0	0.0	0.0	0.0	0.0	0.0	0.0	0.0	0.0
DEBT SERVICE (LTDS)	..	**0.3**	**18.2**	**16.6**	**17.2**	**16.2**	**22.7**	**14.9**	**14.3**	**19.9**
Public and publicly guaranteed	..	**0.3**	**18.2**	**16.6**	**17.2**	**16.2**	**22.7**	**14.9**	**14.3**	**19.9**
Official creditors	..	0.3	8.4	11.1	10.9	9.2	11.6	8.5	10.2	13.6
Multilateral	..	0.2	5.4	6.2	6.8	6.2	7.7	6.5	6.9	9.3
Concessional	..	0.0	0.6	1.3	1.3	1.3	1.3	1.1	1.2	1.2
Bilateral	..	0.1	3.0	4.9	4.1	3.0	4.0	2.0	3.3	4.3
Concessional	..	0.1	2.8	4.2	4.0	3.0	3.9	2.0	1.6	4.2
Private creditors	..	0.0	9.8	5.5	6.3	7.0	11.0	6.4	4.1	6.3
Bonds	..	0.0	0.0	0.0	0.0	0.0	0.0	0.0	0.0	0.0
Commercial banks	..	0.0	8.5	4.1	4.8	4.2	5.8	3.4	1.2	3.8
Other private	..	0.0	1.3	1.4	1.5	2.8	5.3	3.0	2.9	2.6
Private nonguaranteed	..	**0.0**	**0.0**	**0.0**	**0.0**	**0.0**	**0.0**	**0.0**	**0.0**	**0.0**
Bonds	..	0.0	0.0	0.0	0.0	0.0	0.0	0.0	0.0	0.0
Commercial banks	..	0.0	0.0	0.0	0.0	0.0	0.0	0.0	0.0	0.0
Memo:										
IBRD	0.0	0.0	1.0	1.0	1.0	1.0	1.1	1.0	0.9	1.0
IDA	0.0	0.0	0.0	0.0	0.0	0.0	0.0	0.0	0.0	0.0
UNDISBURSED DEBT	..	**23.9**	**56.6**	**68.0**	**57.7**	**40.0**	**41.6**	**46.7**	**50.7**	**49.1**
Official creditors	..	23.4	47.7	48.3	44.9	35.0	36.5	45.0	50.0	48.5
Private creditors	..	0.6	8.9	19.7	12.8	5.0	5.1	1.6	0.6	0.7
Memorandum items										
Concessional LDOD	..	18.8	70.5	70.1	65.8	67.4	67.7	67.0	67.2	70.5
Variable rate LDOD	..	0.0	5.8	4.7	5.8	6.3	7.0	5.9	5.1	14.4
Public sector LDOD	..	25.1	117.2	130.5	132.1	147.8	145.8	138.1	131.3	145.1
Private sector LDOD	..	0.0	0.0	0.0	0.0	0.0	0.0	0.0	0.0	0.0

6. CURRENCY COMPOSITION OF LONG-TERM DEBT (PERCENT)

	1970	1980	1990	1992	1993	1994	1995	1996	1997	1998
Deutsche mark	..	8.0	3.6	3.7	3.3	3.2	3.4	3.5	3.0	3.4
French franc	..	2.8	15.4	11.5	9.5	8.3	7.8	7.0	5.9	3.7
Japanese yen	..	0.0	0.0	0.0	0.0	0.0	0.0	0.0	0.0	0.0
Pound sterling	..	68.0	16.0	9.5	8.4	7.5	7.5	8.6	8.8	8.1
Swiss franc	..	0.0	8.4	7.0	6.5	6.6	7.6	6.9	6.7	6.4
U.S.dollars	..	8.4	9.9	15.2	20.1	21.9	17.9	17.1	15.1	19.1
Multiple currency	..	12.7	29.3	27.7	28.2	30.3	33.6	33.6	34.0	32.9
Special drawing rights	..	0.0	0.0	0.1	0.2	0.5	0.6	0.6	0.5	0.4
All other currencies	..	0.1	17.4	25.3	23.8	21.7	21.6	22.7	26.0	26.0

SEYCHELLES

(US$ million, unless otherwise indicated)

	1970	1980	1990	1992	1993	1994	1995	1996	1997	1998
7. DEBT RESTRUCTURINGS										
Total amount rescheduled	..	..	0.0	0.0	0.0	0.0	0.0	0.0	0.0	0.0
Debt stock rescheduled	..	..	0.0	0.0	0.0	0.0	0.0	0.0	0.0	0.0
Principal rescheduled	..	..	0.0	0.0	0.0	0.0	0.0	0.0	0.0	0.0
Official	..	..	0.0	0.0	0.0	0.0	0.0	0.0	0.0	0.0
Private	..	..	0.0	0.0	0.0	0.0	0.0	0.0	0.0	0.0
Interest rescheduled	..	..	0.0	0.0	0.0	0.0	0.0	0.0	0.0	0.0
Official	..	..	0.0	0.0	0.0	0.0	0.0	0.0	0.0	0.0
Private	..	..	0.0	0.0	0.0	0.0	0.0	0.0	0.0	0.0
Debt forgiven	..	..	0.0	0.0	0.0	0.0	0.0	0.0	0.0	0.0
Memo: interest forgiven	..	..	0.0	0.0	0.0	0.0	0.0	0.0	0.0	0.0
Debt stock reduction	..	..	0.0	0.0	0.0	0.0	0.0	0.0	0.0	0.0
of which debt buyback	..	..	0.0	0.0	0.0	0.0	0.0	0.0	0.0	0.0
8. DEBT STOCK-FLOW RECONCILIATION										
Total change in debt stocks	..	..	18.8	-8.5	-7.2	14.1	-12.0	-11.0	1.1	37.6
Net flows on debt	..	-390.3	6.7	-0.5	-3.4	5.5	-17.2	-2.3	8.8	33.1
Net change in interest arrears	..	..	0.9	0.0	0.1	0.8	0.0	0.8	0.9	-0.1
Interest capitalized	..	..	0.0	0.0	0.0	0.0	0.0	0.0	0.0	0.0
Debt forgiveness or reduction	..	..	0.0	0.0	0.0	0.0	0.0	0.0	0.0	0.0
Cross-currency valuation	..	..	10.7	-6.1	-2.9	6.3	4.4	-3.3	-5.4	2.7
Residual	..	..	0.5	-1.9	-1.0	1.4	0.8	-6.2	-3.2	1.8
9. AVERAGE TERMS OF NEW COMMITMENTS										
ALL CREDITORS										
Interest (%)	..	6.6	4.5	6.8	8.2	6.9	4.3	3.4	6.7	5.4
Maturity (years)	..	15.6	22.1	12.0	10.6	13.2	18.2	13.8	18.6	7.5
Grace period (years)	..	5.1	7.9	3.1	4.2	5.7	4.7	4.1	4.9	2.1
Grant element (%)	..	20.2	45.0	15.0	7.4	15.7	33.1	36.3	20.4	18.9
Official creditors										
Interest (%)	..	6.6	3.3	8.1	6.7	6.9	4.3	3.3	6.7	4.0
Maturity (years)	..	15.7	25.0	13.0	13.3	20.0	18.2	14.3	18.6	11.5
Grace period (years)	..	5.1	9.0	3.0	4.9	10.0	4.7	4.3	4.9	4.0
Grant element (%)	..	20.3	52.9	9.0	16.1	23.2	33.1	37.7	20.4	30.1
Private creditors										
Interest (%)	..	7.2	11.5	6.2	10.0	6.9	0.0	6.0	0.0	7.0
Maturity (years)	..	5.0	4.8	11.6	7.2	5.0	0.0	3.0	0.0	3.2
Grace period (years)	..	0.5	0.9	3.1	3.4	0.5	0.0	0.5	0.0	0.1
Grant element (%)	..	5.8	-2.5	17.8	-3.1	6.5	0.0	5.8	0.0	6.5
Memorandum items										
Commitments	..	11.4	12.4	17.4	11.1	2.1	8.7	15.5	18.4	20.3
Official creditors	..	11.4	10.6	5.6	6.1	1.2	8.7	14.8	18.4	10.6
Private creditors	..	0.1	1.8	11.8	5.0	1.0	0.0	0.7	0.0	9.7

10. CONTRACTUAL OBLIGATIONS ON OUTSTANDING LONG-TERM DEBT

	1999	2000	2001	2002	2003	2004	2005	2006	2007	2008
TOTAL										
Disbursements	13.8	12.6	8.4	6.0	3.7	2.3	1.0	0.6	0.5	0.2
Principal	21.9	16.0	14.7	13.6	14.6	11.9	10.6	10.2	8.7	8.4
Interest	6.0	5.6	5.1	4.7	4.2	3.6	3.2	2.8	2.3	1.9
Official creditors										
Disbursements	13.1	12.6	8.4	6.0	3.7	2.3	1.0	0.6	0.5	0.2
Principal	13.0	12.2	11.5	11.0	12.2	11.3	10.6	10.2	8.7	8.4
Interest	4.9	4.9	4.7	4.5	4.1	3.6	3.2	2.8	2.3	1.9
Bilateral creditors										
Disbursements	5.8	4.7	3.1	2.0	1.4	0.9	0.5	0.5	0.4	0.2
Principal	6.2	5.3	4.7	4.2	5.1	5.6	5.3	5.4	4.0	4.1
Interest	1.1	1.1	1.1	1.2	1.1	1.0	0.9	0.8	0.7	0.5
Multilateral creditors										
Disbursements	7.3	7.9	5.4	3.9	2.3	1.4	0.5	0.1	0.1	0.0
Principal	6.8	6.9	6.9	6.8	7.1	5.7	5.3	4.9	4.6	4.3
Interest	3.8	3.7	3.6	3.3	3.0	2.6	2.3	2.0	1.7	1.4
Private creditors										
Disbursements	0.7	0.0	0.0	0.0	0.0	0.0	0.0	0.0	0.0	0.0
Principal	8.9	3.8	3.2	2.6	2.3	0.6	0.0	0.0	0.0	0.0
Interest	1.1	0.7	0.4	0.3	0.1	0.0	0.0	0.0	0.0	0.0
Commercial banks										
Disbursements	0.5	0.0	0.0	0.0	0.0	0.0	0.0	0.0	0.0	0.0
Principal	2.0	1.4	1.4	1.4	1.1	0.0	0.0	0.0	0.0	0.0
Interest	0.3	0.2	0.2	0.1	0.0	0.0	0.0	0.0	0.0	0.0
Other private										
Disbursements	0.2	0.0	0.0	0.0	0.0	0.0	0.0	0.0	0.0	0.0
Principal	6.9	2.4	1.8	1.2	1.2	0.6	0.0	0.0	0.0	0.0
Interest	0.8	0.5	0.3	0.2	0.1	0.0	0.0	0.0	0.0	0.0

SIERRA LEONE

(US$ million, unless otherwise indicated)

	1970	1980	1990	1992	1993	1994	1995	1996	1997	1998
1. SUMMARY DEBT DATA										
TOTAL DEBT STOCKS (EDT)	**..**	**469**	**1,151**	**1,245**	**1,396**	**1,493**	**1,178**	**1,179**	**1,144**	**1,243**
Long-term debt (LDOD)	**61**	**357**	**604**	**677**	**764**	**849**	**906**	**903**	**889**	**944**
Public and publicly guaranteed	61	357	604	677	764	849	906	903	889	944
Private nonguaranteed	0	0	0	0	0	0	0	0	0	0
Use of IMF credit	**0**	**59**	**108**	**92**	**84**	**146**	**165**	**171**	**167**	**191**
Short-term debt	**..**	**53**	**439**	**476**	**548**	**497**	**107**	**105**	**89**	**108**
of which interest arrears on LDOD	..	7	107	55	52	14	3	3	3	14
Official creditors	..	4	82	46	47	10	3	2	2	14
Private creditors	..	4	25	9	6	4	0	0	0	1
Memo: principal arrears on LDOD	..	17	247	136	123	45	17	21	20	32
Official creditors	..	4	173	111	104	26	13	17	16	28
Private creditors	..	12	74	26	19	19	4	4	4	4
Memo: export credits	..	0	166	152	203	171	129	123	135	112
TOTAL DEBT FLOWS										
Disbursements	**8**	**104**	**24**	**52**	**100**	**200**	**115**	**90**	**47**	**49**
Long-term debt	8	84	24	52	100	64	95	75	40	33
IMF purchases	0	21	0	0	0	137	20	15	7	16
Principal repayments	**16**	**50**	**12**	**16**	**13**	**98**	**59**	**47**	**7**	**11**
Long-term debt	11	34	7	11	5	17	55	44	7	11
IMF repurchases	5	17	5	5	8	81	4	3	0	0
Net flows on debt	**-8**	**62**	**11**	**112**	**161**	**90**	**-136**	**41**	**24**	**46**
of which short-term debt	..	8	-1	76	75	-13	-192	-2	-16	8
Interest payments (INT)	**..**	**16**	**9**	**18**	**18**	**62**	**21**	**12**	**9**	**9**
Long-term debt	3	8	4	10	13	20	19	10	8	8
IMF charges	0	2	0	3	2	38	1	1	1	1
Short-term debt	..	6	5	5	4	5	1	1	1	0
Net transfers on debt	**..**	**47**	**2**	**94**	**143**	**28**	**-156**	**29**	**15**	**36**
Total debt service paid (TDS)	**..**	**66**	**21**	**34**	**31**	**160**	**79**	**59**	**16**	**20**
Long-term debt	13	41	11	21	17	36	74	54	15	19
IMF repurchases and charges	5	19	5	9	10	119	4	4	1	1
Short-term debt (interest only)	..	6	5	5	4	5	1	1	1	0
2. AGGREGATE NET RESOURCE FLOWS AND NET TRANSFERS (LONG-TERM)										
NET RESOURCE FLOWS	**7**	**56**	**79**	**80**	**231**	**115**	**128**	**101**	**98**	**97**
Net flow of long-term debt (ex. IMF)	-3	50	17	41	95	47	40	31	33	22
Foreign direct investment (net)	8	-19	32	-6	-7	-4	1	5	4	5
Portfolio equity flows	0	0	0	0	0	0	0	0	0	0
Grants (excluding technical coop.)	1	25	30	45	144	72	87	65	61	70
Memo: technical coop. grants	5	21	30	26	29	26	24	31	17	13
official net resource flows	5	63	43	86	238	119	155	96	94	92
private net resource flows	2	-7	36	-6	-7	-4	-27	5	4	5
NET TRANSFERS	**0**	**43**	**24**	**69**	**217**	**92**	**107**	**88**	**88**	**86**
Interest on long-term debt	3	8	4	10	13	20	19	10	8	8
Profit remittances on FDI	5	5	51	1	2	3	2	3	2	3
Memo: official net transfers	3	61	39	76	226	99	137	86	86	84
private net transfers	-4	-17	-15	-7	-9	-7	-29	2	2	2
3. MAJOR ECONOMIC AGGREGATES										
Gross national product (GNP)	412	1,168	800	623	718	813	810	909	812	629
Exports of goods & services (XGS)	..	276	210	204	179	218	129	128	92	112
of which workers remittances	..	0	0	0	0	0	0	..	..	..
Imports of goods & services (MGS)	..	494	287	217	254	353	281	331	150	219
International reserves (RES)	39	31	5	19	29	41	35	27	38	44
Current account balance	..	-165	-69	-5	-58	-89	-127	..	..	..
4. DEBT INDICATORS										
EDT / XGS (%)	..	169.9	547.2	609.4	779.4	685.8	912.8	920.3	1,244.9	1,109.3
EDT / GNP (%)	..	40.1	143.9	199.7	194.5	183.6	145.4	129.6	140.9	197.7
TDS / XGS (%)	..	23.8	10.1	16.8	17.5	73.4	61.5	46.1	17.8	18.2
INT / XGS (%)	..	5.6	4.4	8.9	10.1	28.6	16.0	9.2	9.8	8.3
INT / GNP (%)	..	1.3	1.2	2.9	2.5	7.7	2.6	1.3	1.1	1.5
RES / EDT (%)	..	6.5	0.5	1.5	2.1	2.7	2.9	2.3	3.4	3.6
RES / MGS (months)	..	0.7	0.2	1.1	1.4	1.4	1.5	1.0	3.1	2.4
Short-term / EDT (%)	..	11.3	38.1	38.2	39.3	33.3	9.1	8.9	7.7	8.7
Concessional / EDT (%)	..	37.3	27.1	30.8	35.3	39.5	59.4	62.5	63.7	62.8
Multilateral / EDT (%)	..	13.2	15.8	17.2	19.8	23.3	36.8	40.7	42.7	42.1

SIERRA LEONE

(US$ million, unless otherwise indicated)

	1970	1980	1990	1992	1993	1994	1995	1996	1997	1998
5. LONG-TERM DEBT										
DEBT OUTSTANDING (LDOD)	**61**	**357**	**604**	**677**	**764**	**849**	**906**	**903**	**889**	**944**
Public and publicly guaranteed	**61**	**357**	**604**	**677**	**764**	**849**	**906**	**903**	**889**	**944**
Official creditors	34	246	505	641	738	823	898	895	882	938
Multilateral	6	62	182	215	276	348	434	480	488	523
Concessional	0	39	170	201	261	329	412	458	470	504
Bilateral	28	184	323	427	461	475	464	416	394	415
Concessional	20	136	142	183	232	261	288	278	260	276
Private creditors	27	111	99	36	26	26	8	8	6	7
Bonds	0	0	0	0	0	0	0	0	0	0
Commercial banks	3	20	17	17	17	17	0	0	0	0
Other private	24	91	83	19	9	9	8	8	6	7
Private nonguaranteed	**0**	**0**	**0**	**0**	**0**	**0**	**0**	**0**	**0**	**0**
Bonds	0	0	0	0	0	0	0	0	0	0
Commercial banks	0	0	0	0	0	0	0	0	0	0
Memo:										
IBRD	6	13	11	4	3	3	3	2	2	1
IDA	0	29	81	108	143	186	231	258	270	298
DISBURSEMENTS	**8**	**84**	**24**	**52**	**100**	**64**	**95**	**75**	**40**	**33**
Public and publicly guaranteed	**8**	**84**	**24**	**52**	**100**	**64**	**95**	**75**	**40**	**33**
Official creditors	4	42	20	52	100	64	95	75	40	33
Multilateral	3	9	1	46	67	61	87	73	40	28
Concessional	0	5	1	36	64	58	86	71	40	28
Bilateral	1	33	19	6	32	3	8	3	0	6
Concessional	1	28	19	6	32	3	8	3	0	6
Private creditors	4	42	4	0	0	0	0	0	0	0
Bonds	0	0	0	0	0	0	0	0	0	0
Commercial banks	0	0	0	0	0	0	0	0	0	0
Other private	4	42	4	0	0	0	0	0	0	0
Private nonguaranteed	**0**	**0**	**0**	**0**	**0**	**0**	**0**	**0**	**0**	**0**
Bonds	0	0	0	0	0	0	0	0	0	0
Commercial banks	0	0	0	0	0	0	0	0	0	0
Memo:										
IBRD	3	2	0	0	0	0	0	0	0	0
IDA	0	2	0	32	36	38	44	35	27	21
PRINCIPAL REPAYMENTS	**11**	**34**	**7**	**11**	**5**	**17**	**55**	**44**	**7**	**11**
Public and publicly guaranteed	**11**	**34**	**7**	**11**	**5**	**17**	**55**	**44**	**7**	**11**
Official creditors	1	4	7	11	5	17	27	44	7	11
Multilateral	0	1	2	11	3	4	4	4	3	9
Concessional	0	0	0	4	2	3	3	4	3	9
Bilateral	1	3	5	0	2	13	23	40	4	2
Concessional	1	2	2	0	0	6	4	2	4	1
Private creditors	10	29	0	0	0	0	28	0	0	0
Bonds	5	0	0	0	0	0	0	0	0	0
Commercial banks	1	3	0	0	0	0	28	0	0	0
Other private	4	27	0	0	0	0	0	0	0	0
Private nonguaranteed	**0**	**0**	**0**	**0**	**0**	**0**	**0**	**0**	**0**	**0**
Bonds	0	0	0	0	0	0	0	0	0	0
Commercial banks	0	0	0	0	0	0	0	0	0	0
Memo:										
IBRD	0	1	0	6	0	0	1	1	0	1
IDA	0	0	0	3	1	1	2	2	1	3
NET FLOWS ON DEBT	**-3**	**50**	**17**	**41**	**95**	**47**	**40**	**31**	**33**	**22**
Public and publicly guaranteed	**-3**	**50**	**17**	**41**	**95**	**47**	**40**	**31**	**33**	**22**
Official creditors	3	38	13	41	95	47	68	31	33	22
Multilateral	3	8	-1	36	65	57	84	69	37	19
Concessional	0	5	1	32	62	55	83	67	37	19
Bilateral	1	30	13	6	30	-10	-16	-37	-4	4
Concessional	1	26	16	6	32	-3	4	0	-4	4
Private creditors	-6	12	4	0	0	0	-28	0	0	0
Bonds	-5	0	0	0	0	0	0	0	0	0
Commercial banks	-1	-3	0	0	0	0	-28	0	0	0
Other private	-1	15	4	0	0	0	0	0	0	0
Private nonguaranteed	**0**	**0**	**0**	**0**	**0**	**0**	**0**	**0**	**0**	**0**
Bonds	0	0	0	0	0	0	0	0	0	0
Commercial banks	0	0	0	0	0	0	0	0	0	0
Memo:										
IBRD	3	2	0	-6	0	0	-1	-1	0	-1
IDA	0	2	0	29	35	37	42	34	26	19

SIERRA LEONE

(US$ million, unless otherwise indicated)

	1970	1980	1990	1992	1993	1994	1995	1996	1997	1998
INTEREST PAYMENTS (LINT)	**3**	**8**	**4**	**10**	**13**	**20**	**19**	**10**	**8**	**8**
Public and publicly guaranteed	**3**	**8**	**4**	**10**	**13**	**20**	**19**	**10**	**8**	**8**
Official creditors	1	2	4	10	13	20	19	10	8	8
Multilateral	0	1	2	8	2	2	3	3	2	5
Concessional	0	0	1	4	2	2	2	3	2	5
Bilateral	1	1	2	2	10	17	16	7	5	3
Concessional	1	0	1	2	1	2	3	1	5	0
Private creditors	1	5	0	0	0	0	0	0	0	0
Bonds	0	0	0	0	0	0	0	0	0	0
Commercial banks	0	1	0	0	0	0	0	0	0	0
Other private	1	4	0	0	0	0	0	0	0	0
Private nonguaranteed	**0**	**0**	**0**	**0**	**0**	**0**	**0**	**0**	**0**	**0**
Bonds	0	0	0	0	0	0	0	0	0	0
Commercial banks	0	0	0	0	0	0	0	0	0	0
Memo:										
IBRD	0	1	0	4	0	0	0	0	0	0
IDA	0	0	0	4	1	1	2	2	1	3
NET TRANSFERS ON DEBT	**-5**	**43**	**13**	**31**	**82**	**27**	**21**	**22**	**25**	**14**
Public and publicly guaranteed	**-5**	**43**	**13**	**31**	**82**	**27**	**21**	**22**	**25**	**14**
Official creditors	2	36	9	31	82	27	50	22	25	14
Multilateral	3	7	-3	28	62	55	81	65	35	14
Concessional	0	5	0	27	60	53	81	64	35	15
Bilateral	-1	29	12	3	20	-28	-31	-44	-9	1
Concessional	0	26	15	3	31	-5	1	-1	-8	4
Private creditors	-7	7	4	0	0	0	-28	0	0	0
Bonds	-5	0	0	0	0	0	0	0	0	0
Commercial banks	-1	-4	0	0	0	0	-28	0	0	0
Other private	-1	11	4	0	0	0	0	0	0	0
Private nonguaranteed	**0**	**0**	**0**	**0**	**0**	**0**	**0**	**0**	**0**	**0**
Bonds	0	0	0	0	0	0	0	0	0	0
Commercial banks	0	0	0	0	0	0	0	0	0	0
Memo:										
IBRD	2	1	0	-10	-1	-1	-1	-1	0	-1
IDA	0	2	0	26	34	36	41	32	25	16
DEBT SERVICE (LTDS)	**13**	**41**	**11**	**21**	**17**	**36**	**74**	**54**	**15**	**19**
Public and publicly guaranteed	**13**	**41**	**11**	**21**	**17**	**36**	**74**	**54**	**15**	**19**
Official creditors	2	6	11	21	17	36	45	54	15	19
Multilateral	0	2	4	19	5	6	6	7	5	14
Concessional	0	0	1	9	4	5	5	7	5	13
Bilateral	2	4	7	2	12	30	39	46	10	5
Concessional	2	2	4	2	1	8	6	4	9	1
Private creditors	11	35	0	0	0	0	28	0	0	0
Bonds	5	0	0	0	0	0	0	0	0	0
Commercial banks	1	4	0	0	0	0	28	0	0	0
Other private	5	31	0	0	0	0	0	0	0	0
Private nonguaranteed	**0**	**0**	**0**	**0**	**0**	**0**	**0**	**0**	**0**	**0**
Bonds	0	0	0	0	0	0	0	0	0	0
Commercial banks	0	0	0	0	0	0	0	0	0	0
Memo:										
IBRD	0	1	0	10	1	1	1	1	0	1
IDA	0	0	0	6	2	2	3	4	2	6
UNDISBURSED DEBT	**25**	**116**	**164**	**302**	**327**	**307**	**263**	**219**	**163**	**156**
Official creditors	22	95	164	302	327	307	263	219	163	156
Private creditors	2	22	0	0	0	0	0	0	0	0
Memorandum items										
Concessional LDOD	20	175	312	384	492	590	700	736	729	780
Variable rate LDOD	6	0	8	9	6	8	12	12	11	11
Public sector LDOD	61	357	604	677	764	849	906	903	889	944
Private sector LDOD	0	0	0	0	0	0	0	0	0	0

6. CURRENCY COMPOSITION OF LONG-TERM DEBT (PERCENT)

	1970	1980	1990	1992	1993	1994	1995	1996	1997	1998
Deutsche mark	10.9	15.7	4.8	3.2	2.2	2.1	1.7	1.6	1.5	1.5
French franc	19.1	2.7	6.1	4.6	4.0	3.1	2.8	2.7	2.6	2.6
Japanese yen	0.0	4.8	7.4	6.6	5.8	9.5	8.7	7.6	6.8	7.2
Pound sterling	38.9	10.0	2.2	1.4	0.7	0.5	0.6	0.7	0.7	0.7
Swiss franc	0.8	10.7	8.3	5.0	3.7	3.5	3.3	2.8	2.7	2.7
U.S.dollars	16.9	23.4	30.3	43.1	46.1	43.5	40.3	39.5	42.3	41.7
Multiple currency	10.3	4.0	5.4	5.1	7.3	8.9	11.6	12.5	12.9	13.0
Special drawing rights	0.0	0.0	11.1	9.5	9.3	9.9	10.2	10.9	10.7	10.7
All other currencies	3.1	28.7	24.4	21.5	20.9	19.0	20.8	21.7	19.8	19.9

SIERRA LEONE

(US$ million, unless otherwise indicated)

	1970	1980	1990	1992	1993	1994	1995	1996	1997	1998
7. DEBT RESTRUCTURINGS										
Total amount rescheduled	..	..	0	195	47	107	31	24	55	1
Debt stock rescheduled	..	..	0	0	0	0	0	0	0	0
Principal rescheduled	..	..	0	118	34	72	26	14	46	1
Official	..	..	0	64	25	70	25	13	45	1
Private	..	..	0	54	10	2	1	1	1	0
Interest rescheduled	..	..	0	77	12	35	4	9	9	0
Official	..	..	0	57	8	33	4	9	9	0
Private	..	..	0	20	5	2	0	0	0	0
Debt forgiven	..	..	0	26	9	28	18	5	0	0
Memo: interest forgiven	..	..	0	13	2	2	119	0	3	0
Debt stock reduction	..	..	0	0	0	0	222	0	0	0
of which debt buyback	..	..	0	0	0	0	29	0	0	0
8. DEBT STOCK-FLOW RECONCILIATION										
Total change in debt stocks	..	..	85	39	151	97	-315	1	-34	99
Net flows on debt	-8	62	11	112	161	90	-136	41	24	46
Net change in interest arrears	..	..	32	-89	-3	-38	-11	0	0	12
Interest capitalized	..	..	0	77	12	35	4	9	9	0
Debt forgiveness or reduction	..	..	0	-26	-9	-28	-210	-5	0	0
Cross-currency valuation	..	..	47	-25	-11	34	17	-22	-36	25
Residual	..	..	-5	-10	0	4	21	-22	-31	16
9. AVERAGE TERMS OF NEW COMMITMENTS										
ALL CREDITORS										
Interest (%)	2.9	5.3	2.3	1.5	0.7	1.5	0.6	0.6	0.0	1.2
Maturity (years)	26.7	25.5	26.6	39.3	38.9	43.5	32.6	34.5	0.0	41.5
Grace period (years)	5.6	5.9	8.9	9.3	10.2	8.9	7.8	8.5	0.0	8.7
Grant element (%)	49.9	32.7	60.8	72.3	80.2	73.2	70.4	73.0	0.0	75.0
Official creditors										
Interest (%)	2.1	4.7	1.2	1.5	0.7	1.5	0.6	0.6	0.0	1.2
Maturity (years)	33.0	30.3	30.6	39.3	38.9	43.5	32.6	34.5	0.0	41.5
Grace period (years)	6.8	7.7	10.2	9.3	10.2	8.9	7.8	8.5	0.0	8.7
Grant element (%)	61.6	40.4	71.1	72.3	80.2	73.2	70.4	73.0	0.0	75.0
Private creditors										
Interest (%)	5.4	7.0	9.1	0.0	0.0	0.0	0.0	0.0	0.0	0.0
Maturity (years)	6.7	12.8	3.0	0.0	0.0	0.0	0.0	0.0	0.0	0.0
Grace period (years)	1.7	1.3	1.0	0.0	0.0	0.0	0.0	0.0	0.0	0.0
Grant element (%)	12.7	12.5	1.2	0.0	0.0	0.0	0.0	0.0	0.0	0.0
Memorandum items										
Commitments	25	68	27	181	137	35	48	69	0	21
Official creditors	19	49	23	181	137	35	48	69	0	21
Private creditors	6	19	4	0	0	0	0	0	0	0

10. CONTRACTUAL OBLIGATIONS ON OUTSTANDING LONG-TERM DEBT

	1999	2000	2001	2002	2003	2004	2005	2006	2007	2008
TOTAL										
Disbursements	65	42	25	15	6	2	1	0	0	0
Principal	22	23	26	32	35	37	38	37	37	39
Interest	19	19	18	18	17	16	15	14	13	12
Official creditors										
Disbursements	65	42	25	15	6	2	1	0	0	0
Principal	22	23	26	32	35	37	38	37	37	39
Interest	19	18	18	17	17	16	15	14	13	12
Bilateral creditors										
Disbursements	4	3	2	1	0	0	0	0	0	0
Principal	11	13	15	20	20	20	20	19	20	22
Interest	14	14	13	13	12	11	10	10	9	8
Multilateral creditors										
Disbursements	61	39	23	14	6	2	1	0	0	0
Principal	10	10	10	12	15	17	18	18	17	17
Interest	4	4	5	5	5	4	4	4	4	4
Private creditors										
Disbursements	0	0	0	0	0	0	0	0	0	0
Principal	0	0	0	0	0	0	0	0	0	0
Interest	0	0	0	0	0	0	0	0	0	0
Commercial banks										
Disbursements	0	0	0	0	0	0	0	0	0	0
Principal	0	0	0	0	0	0	0	0	0	0
Interest	0	0	0	0	0	0	0	0	0	0
Other private										
Disbursements	0	0	0	0	0	0	0	0	0	0
Principal	0	0	0	0	0	0	0	0	0	0
Interest	0	0	0	0	0	0	0	0	0	0

SLOVAK REPUBLIC

(US$ million, unless otherwise indicated)

1. SUMMARY DEBT DATA

	1970	1980	1990	1992	1993	1994	1995	1996	1997	1998
TOTAL DEBT STOCKS (EDT)	..	..	**2,008**	**2,746**	**3,393**	**4,754**	**5,784**	**6,090**	**8,950**	**9,893**
Long-term debt (LDOD)	..	..	**1,505**	**1,710**	**2,121**	**2,876**	**3,613**	**4,541**	**6,540**	**7,722**
Public and publicly guaranteed	..	..	1,505	1,710	2,120	2,863	3,528	3,995	4,618	4,452
Private nonguaranteed	..	..	0	0	1	13	85	546	1,922	3,270
Use of IMF credit	**0**	**0**	**0**	**469**	**557**	**642**	**457**	**319**	**249**	**190**
Short-term debt	..	..	**503**	**567**	**715**	**1,236**	**1,714**	**1,229**	**2,161**	**1,981**
of which interest arrears on LDOD	..	..	0	0	0	0	0	0	0	0
Official creditors	..	..	0	0	0	0	0	0	0	0
Private creditors	..	..	0	0	0	0	0	0	0	0
Memo: principal arrears on LDOD	..	..	0	0	1	2	0	2	0	28
Official creditors	..	..	0	0	0	0	0	0	0	0
Private creditors	..	..	0	0	1	2	0	2	0	28
Memo: export credits	..	..	0	412	339	401	570	540	602	1,167
TOTAL DEBT FLOWS										
Disbursements	..	..	**436**	**330**	**984**	**1,145**	**1,061**	**1,760**	**1,876**	**2,571**
Long-term debt	..	..	436	228	894	1,006	1,061	1,760	1,876	2,571
IMF purchases	0	0	0	102	90	138	0	0	0	0
Principal repayments	..	..	**171**	**395**	**434**	**546**	**862**	**827**	**957**	**1,561**
Long-term debt	..	..	171	380	434	457	662	703	905	1,494
IMF repurchases	0	0	0	15	0	89	201	124	52	68
Net flows on debt	..	..	**173**	**10**	**698**	**1,119**	**676**	**448**	**1,851**	**829**
of which short-term debt	..	..	-91	75	148	521	478	-484	932	-181
Interest payments (INT)	..	..	**147**	**196**	**212**	**297**	**424**	**517**	**432**	**581**
Long-term debt	..	..	84	120	153	182	287	294	238	460
IMF charges	0	0	0	32	32	30	32	17	13	10
Short-term debt	..	..	63	44	27	85	105	206	181	110
Net transfers on debt	..	..	**26**	**-186**	**486**	**823**	**252**	**-69**	**1,419**	**248**
Total debt service paid (TDS)	..	..	**318**	**591**	**646**	**843**	**1,286**	**1,344**	**1,389**	**2,142**
Long-term debt	..	..	256	500	587	639	949	997	1,144	1,954
IMF repurchases and charges	0	0	0	47	32	119	233	141	65	78
Short-term debt (interest only)	..	..	63	44	27	85	105	206	181	110

2. AGGREGATE NET RESOURCE FLOWS AND NET TRANSFERS (LONG-TERM)

	1970	1980	1990	1992	1993	1994	1995	1996	1997	1998
NET RESOURCE FLOWS	..	..	**270**	**-131**	**686**	**879**	**708**	**1,465**	**1,225**	**1,691**
Net flow of long-term debt (ex. IMF)	..	..	264	-153	460	549	399	1,057	971	1,077
Foreign direct investment (net)	..	..	0	0	199	270	236	351	174	562
Portfolio equity flows	..	..	0	0	0	0	60	0	48	0
Grants (excluding technical coop.)	..	..	5	22	27	61	14	57	33	52
Memo: technical coop. grants	..	..	0	42	23	18	68	33	23	30
official net resource flows	..	..	-8	99	123	320	185	132	268	211
private net resource flows	..	..	278	-230	563	560	523	1,333	958	1,480
NET TRANSFERS	..	..	**186**	**-250**	**533**	**698**	**421**	**1,165**	**977**	**1,219**
Interest on long-term debt	..	..	84	120	153	182	287	294	238	460
Profit remittances on FDI	..	..	0	0	0	0	0	6	10	12
Memo: official net transfers	..	..	-20	72	104	289	143	90	222	138
private net transfers	..	..	206	-323	429	409	278	1,075	755	1,080

3. MAJOR ECONOMIC AGGREGATES

	1970	1980	1990	1992	1993	1994	1995	1996	1997	1998
Gross national product (GNP)	..	..	15,497	11,722	11,958	13,627	17,379	18,736	19,295	20,204
Exports of goods & services (XGS)	..	..	..	..	7,576	9,123	11,219	11,117	12,131	13,450
of which workers remittances	..	..	..	..	..	..	0	4	7	..
Imports of goods & services (MGS)	..	..	..	..	8,254	8,520	10,922	13,404	14,258	15,942
International reserves (RES)	..	..	..	..	920	2,186	3,863	3,895	3,605	3,240
Current account balance	..	..	..	..	-580	671	390	-2,090	-1,961	-2,126

4. DEBT INDICATORS

	1970	1980	1990	1992	1993	1994	1995	1996	1997	1998
EDT / XGS (%)	..	..	..	..	44.8	52.1	51.6	54.8	73.8	73.6
EDT / GNP (%)	..	..	13.0	23.4	28.4	34.9	33.3	32.5	46.4	49.0
TDS / XGS (%)	..	..	..	..	8.5	9.2	11.5	12.1	11.5	15.9
INT / XGS (%)	..	..	..	..	2.8	3.3	3.8	4.7	3.6	4.3
INT / GNP (%)	..	..	1.0	1.7	1.8	2.2	2.4	2.8	2.2	2.9
RES / EDT (%)	..	..	..	..	27.1	46.0	66.8	64.0	40.3	32.8
RES / MGS (months)	..	..	..	..	1.3	3.1	4.2	3.5	3.0	2.4
Short-term / EDT (%)	..	..	25.1	20.7	21.1	26.0	29.6	20.2	24.2	20.0
Concessional / EDT (%)	..	..	4.1	8.6	6.7	2.6	1.6	2.0	3.0	3.2
Multilateral / EDT (%)	..	..	4.4	8.5	8.5	9.2	9.0	8.8	6.3	6.9

SLOVAK REPUBLIC

(US$ million, unless otherwise indicated)

	1970	1980	1990	1992	1993	1994	1995	1996	1997	1998
5. LONG-TERM DEBT										
DEBT OUTSTANDING (LDOD)	..	..	**1,505**	**1,710**	**2,121**	**2,876**	**3,613**	**4,541**	**6,540**	**7,722**
Public and publicly guaranteed	..	..	**1,505**	**1,710**	**2,120**	**2,863**	**3,528**	**3,995**	**4,618**	**4,452**
Official creditors	..	..	126	358	448	609	694	724	882	1,113
Multilateral	..	..	89	234	287	436	519	535	563	679
Concessional	..	..	82	122	136	40	0	0	0	0
Bilateral	..	..	36	124	161	173	175	190	319	434
Concessional	..	..	0	113	90	83	91	124	264	318
Private creditors	..	..	1,380	1,352	1,672	2,253	2,834	3,271	3,736	3,339
Bonds	..	..	0	73	348	552	581	861	850	280
Commercial banks	..	..	866	790	718	611	371	345	977	1,297
Other private	..	..	514	489	607	1,091	1,883	2,066	1,909	1,763
Private nonguaranteed	..	..	**0**	**0**	**1**	**13**	**85**	**546**	**1,922**	**3,270**
Bonds	..	..	0	0	0	0	0	100	100	100
Commercial banks	..	..	0	0	1	13	85	446	1,822	3,170
Memo:										
IBRD	0	0	0	110	151	247	263	250	228	239
IDA	0	0	0	0	0	0	0	0	0	0
DISBURSEMENTS	..	..	**436**	**228**	**894**	**1,006**	**1,061**	**1,760**	**1,876**	**2,571**
Public and publicly guaranteed	..	..	**436**	**227**	**893**	**994**	**992**	**1,267**	**1,590**	**747**
Official creditors	..	..	8	134	112	281	226	97	286	212
Multilateral	..	..	2	44	44	231	149	51	104	129
Concessional	..	..	2	0	4	0	0	0	0	0
Bilateral	..	..	6	91	68	49	78	46	181	83
Concessional	..	..	0	86	0	26	77	46	166	22
Private creditors	..	..	428	93	781	713	766	1,170	1,305	535
Bonds	..	..	0	0	275	267	0	280	0	0
Commercial banks	..	..	209	23	222	117	57	210	1,271	528
Other private	..	..	218	70	285	329	709	680	34	7
Private nonguaranteed	..	..	**0**	**0**	**1**	**12**	**68**	**493**	**286**	**1,824**
Bonds	..	..	0	0	0	0	0	100	0	0
Commercial banks	..	..	0	0	1	12	68	393	286	1,824
Memo:										
IBRD	0	0	0	44	40	86	8	6	13	15
IDA	0	0	0	0	0	0	0	0	0	0
PRINCIPAL REPAYMENTS	..	..	**171**	**380**	**434**	**457**	**662**	**703**	**905**	**1,494**
Public and publicly guaranteed	..	..	**171**	**380**	**434**	**457**	**658**	**671**	**851**	**1,017**
Official creditors	..	..	22	57	16	22	55	22	51	53
Multilateral	..	..	3	46	12	11	42	9	31	43
Concessional	..	..	0	42	11	11	0	0	0	0
Bilateral	..	..	19	11	4	11	13	13	20	10
Concessional	..	..	0	0	0	0	0	0	0	3
Private creditors	..	..	150	323	418	436	604	649	800	964
Bonds	..	..	0	0	0	63	0	0	10	570
Commercial banks	..	..	14	105	200	158	194	225	609	238
Other private	..	..	136	218	218	215	410	425	181	156
Private nonguaranteed	..	..	**0**	**0**	**0**	**0**	**3**	**32**	**55**	**476**
Bonds	..	..	0	0	0	0	0	0	0	0
Commercial banks	..	..	0	0	0	0	3	32	55	476
Memo:										
IBRD	0	0	0	0	0	0	0	0	15	17
IDA	0	0	0	0	0	0	0	0	0	0
NET FLOWS ON DEBT	..	..	**264**	**-153**	**460**	**549**	**399**	**1,057**	**971**	**1,077**
Public and publicly guaranteed	..	..	**264**	**-153**	**459**	**537**	**334**	**596**	**739**	**-271**
Official creditors	..	..	-14	77	96	259	172	75	235	159
Multilateral	..	..	0	-2	32	221	107	42	73	87
Concessional	..	..	2	-42	-6	-11	0	0	0	0
Bilateral	..	..	-13	80	64	39	65	33	162	73
Concessional	..	..	0	86	0	26	77	46	166	19
Private creditors	..	..	278	-230	363	278	162	521	505	-430
Bonds	..	..	0	0	275	204	0	280	-10	-570
Commercial banks	..	..	195	-82	22	-41	-136	-14	662	289
Other private	..	..	83	-148	67	115	299	256	-147	-149
Private nonguaranteed	..	..	**0**	**0**	**1**	**12**	**65**	**461**	**232**	**1,348**
Bonds	..	..	0	0	0	0	0	100	0	0
Commercial banks	..	..	0	0	1	12	65	361	232	1,348
Memo:										
IBRD	0	0	0	44	40	86	8	6	-2	-2
IDA	0	0	0	0	0	0	0	0	0	0

SLOVAK REPUBLIC

(US$ million, unless otherwise indicated)

	1970	1980	1990	1992	1993	1994	1995	1996	1997	1998
INTEREST PAYMENTS (LINT)	..	..	**84**	**120**	**153**	**182**	**287**	**294**	**238**	**460**
Public and publicly guaranteed	..	..	**84**	**120**	**153**	**181**	**286**	**271**	**207**	**269**
Official creditors	..	..	12	27	19	31	42	41	46	73
Multilateral	..	..	9	23	17	24	34	32	36	56
Concessional	..	..	8	17	8	11	0	0	0	0
Bilateral	..	..	3	4	1	6	8	9	10	17
Concessional	..	..	0	3	0	0	2	4	5	5
Private creditors	..	..	72	93	134	151	244	230	161	196
Bonds	..	..	0	7	12	7	53	58	61	60
Commercial banks	..	..	46	54	79	86	51	22	39	78
Other private	..	..	27	32	43	58	141	150	61	58
Private nonguaranteed	..	..	**0**	**0**	**0**	**0**	**1**	**23**	**31**	**192**
Bonds	..	..	0	0	0	0	0	0	6	7
Commercial banks	..	..	0	0	0	0	1	23	26	185
Memo:										
IBRD	0	0	0	5	9	12	17	17	16	14
IDA	0	0	0	0	0	0	0	0	0	0
NET TRANSFERS ON DEBT	..	..	**180**	**-272**	**307**	**367**	**112**	**763**	**732**	**617**
Public and publicly guaranteed	..	..	**180**	**-272**	**306**	**355**	**48**	**325**	**532**	**-539**
Official creditors	..	..	-26	51	77	228	129	34	189	87
Multilateral	..	..	-9	-25	15	196	73	9	37	30
Concessional	..	..	-6	-59	-15	-21	0	0	0	0
Bilateral	..	..	-17	75	62	32	56	24	152	56
Concessional	..	..	0	83	0	26	76	42	161	13
Private creditors	..	..	206	-323	229	127	-82	291	343	-626
Bonds	..	..	0	-7	263	197	-53	222	-72	-630
Commercial banks	..	..	150	-136	-57	-127	-187	-36	623	211
Other private	..	..	56	-180	24	57	158	106	-208	-207
Private nonguaranteed	..	..	**0**	**0**	**1**	**12**	**64**	**438**	**200**	**1,156**
Bonds	..	..	0	0	0	0	0	100	-6	-7
Commercial banks	..	..	0	0	1	12	64	338	206	1,163
Memo:										
IBRD	0	0	0	39	31	74	-9	-11	-18	-16
IDA	0	0	0	0	0	0	0	0	0	0
DEBT SERVICE (LTDS)	..	..	**256**	**500**	**587**	**639**	**949**	**997**	**1,144**	**1,954**
Public and publicly guaranteed	..	..	**256**	**500**	**587**	**638**	**945**	**942**	**1,058**	**1,286**
Official creditors	..	..	34	84	34	52	97	63	97	126
Multilateral	..	..	11	68	29	35	76	41	67	99
Concessional	..	..	8	59	19	21	0	0	0	0
Bilateral	..	..	22	15	5	17	21	22	29	27
Concessional	..	..	0	3	0	0	2	4	5	8
Private creditors	..	..	222	416	552	586	848	879	961	1,160
Bonds	..	..	0	7	12	70	53	58	72	630
Commercial banks	..	..	59	159	280	244	244	246	648	317
Other private	..	..	162	250	261	273	551	574	242	214
Private nonguaranteed	..	..	**0**	**0**	**0**	**1**	**4**	**55**	**86**	**668**
Bonds	..	..	0	0	0	0	0	0	6	7
Commercial banks	..	..	0	0	0	1	4	55	80	661
Memo:										
IBRD	0	0	0	5	9	12	17	17	30	31
IDA	0	0	0	0	0	0	0	0	0	0
UNDISBURSED DEBT	..	..	**211**	**218**	**428**	**378**	**317**	**871**	**775**	**346**
Official creditors	..	..	0	167	358	324	173	358	320	224
Private creditors	..	..	211	50	71	54	143	513	455	122
Memorandum items										
Concessional LDOD	..	..	82	236	226	123	91	124	264	318
Variable rate LDOD	..	..	182	206	226	414	809	1,285	3,323	4,998
Public sector LDOD	..	..	1,505	1,692	2,059	2,696	3,293	3,747	4,339	4,153
Private sector LDOD	..	..	0	18	62	180	320	795	1,067	3,457

6. CURRENCY COMPOSITION OF LONG-TERM DEBT (PERCENT)

	1970	1980	1990	1992	1993	1994	1995	1996	1997	1998
Deutsche mark	..	..	39.2	24.0	15.2	12.8	4.6	4.4	6.9	10.6
French franc	..	..	4.7	6.1	4.1	3.2	3.0	2.3	1.4	1.2
Japanese yen	..	..	3.7	1.2	0.7	0.8	2.6	3.1	5.7	7.1
Pound sterling	..	..	0.5	0.1	0.0	0.2	0.1	0.1	0.0	0.0
Swiss franc	..	..	5.1	2.0	1.0	0.3	0.1	0.4	0.5	1.1
U.S.dollars	..	..	35.5	32.5	24.8	14.5	4.6	14.7	21.6	27.5
Multiple currency	..	..	5.6	30.8	52.7	66.2	81.5	71.5	59.8	47.1
Special drawing rights	..	..	0.0	0.0	0.0	0.0	0.0	0.0	0.0	0.0
All other currencies	..	..	5.7	3.3	1.5	2.0	3.5	3.5	4.1	5.4

SLOVAK REPUBLIC

(US$ million, unless otherwise indicated)

	1970	1980	1990	1992	1993	1994	1995	1996	1997	1998
7. DEBT RESTRUCTURINGS										
Total amount rescheduled	..	..	0	0	0	0	0	0	0	0
Debt stock rescheduled	..	..	0	0	0	0	0	0	0	0
Principal rescheduled	..	..	0	0	0	0	0	0	0	0
Official	..	..	0	0	0	0	0	0	0	0
Private	..	..	0	0	0	0	0	0	0	0
Interest rescheduled	..	..	0	0	0	0	0	0	0	0
Official	..	..	0	0	0	0	0	0	0	0
Private	..	..	0	0	0	0	0	0	0	0
Debt forgiven	..	..	0	0	0	1	0	0	0	0
Memo: interest forgiven	..	..	0	0	0	0	0	0	0	0
Debt stock reduction	..	..	0	0	0	0	0	0	0	0
of which debt buyback	..	..	0	0	0	0	0	0	0	0
8. DEBT STOCK-FLOW RECONCILIATION										
Total change in debt stocks	..	..	181	91	647	1,362	1,030	306	2,860	943
Net flows on debt	..	..	173	10	698	1,119	676	448	1,851	829
Net change in interest arrears	..	..	0	0	0	0	0	0	0	0
Interest capitalized	..	..	0	0	0	0	0	0	0	0
Debt forgiveness or reduction	..	..	0	0	0	-1	0	0	0	0
Cross-currency valuation	..	..	119	-41	-26	72	38	-61	-123	107
Residual	..	..	-111	122	-24	171	317	-81	1,133	6
9. AVERAGE TERMS OF NEW COMMITMENTS										
ALL CREDITORS										
Interest (%)	..	..	7.8	6.3	8.6	7.8	5.9	6.2	5.8	7.3
Maturity (years)	..	..	6.0	12.9	12.5	10.7	7.4	9.3	6.3	7.0
Grace period (years)	..	..	3.6	3.9	7.3	5.9	3.5	4.1	2.0	3.0
Grant element (%)	..	..	6.9	17.6	2.1	7.0	18.2	15.5	12.6	10.2
Official creditors										
Interest (%)	..	..	3.4	6.7	5.2	6.0	3.1	5.2	3.9	6.0
Maturity (years)	..	..	19.1	13.1	15.6	12.0	14.3	14.0	13.8	12.6
Grace period (years)	..	..	5.3	4.4	5.1	3.0	4.5	4.6	4.9	3.0
Grant element (%)	..	..	46.1	16.2	28.3	17.5	38.7	26.5	34.0	19.7
Private creditors										
Interest (%)	..	..	7.8	5.0	10.7	8.7	7.3	6.5	6.3	7.9
Maturity (years)	..	..	5.9	12.1	10.7	10.0	3.7	7.8	4.6	4.2
Grace period (years)	..	..	3.5	2.3	8.6	7.4	2.9	3.9	1.3	3.0
Grant element (%)	..	..	6.6	22.8	-13.7	1.7	7.3	12.1	7.8	5.3
Memorandum items										
Commitments	..	..	265	176	854	817	270	1,235	1,554	301
Official creditors	..	..	2	138	321	276	94	292	282	103
Private creditors	..	..	263	38	533	541	176	944	1,272	198

10. CONTRACTUAL OBLIGATIONS ON OUTSTANDING LONG-TERM DEBT

	1999	2000	2001	2002	2003	2004	2005	2006	2007	2008
TOTAL										
Disbursements	171	96	53	17	8	1	0	0	0	0
Principal	1,128	1,005	990	865	827	739	734	595	275	231
Interest	374	328	279	237	193	150	113	77	42	30
Official creditors										
Disbursements	98	65	40	14	7	1	0	0	0	0
Principal	72	87	104	139	140	129	129	129	111	94
Interest	57	56	52	56	48	41	33	26	20	14
Bilateral creditors										
Disbursements	31	12	8	1	0	0	0	0	0	0
Principal	14	24	34	55	48	48	48	48	48	45
Interest	15	15	14	16	14	12	10	8	6	4
Multilateral creditors										
Disbursements	67	53	33	13	7	1	0	0	0	0
Principal	58	64	70	85	92	81	81	81	63	49
Interest	42	41	39	40	34	29	24	19	14	10
Private creditors										
Disbursements	73	32	12	3	1	0	0	0	0	0
Principal	1,056	918	886	725	686	610	606	466	164	137
Interest	317	272	227	181	145	109	80	51	22	16
Commercial banks										
Disbursements	58	14	4	1	0	0	0	0	0	0
Principal	422	216	268	136	65	58	53	51	50	27
Interest	79	62	50	31	22	17	13	9	5	2
Other private										
Disbursements	15	17	9	3	1	0	0	0	0	0
Principal	635	702	618	589	622	553	553	415	114	110
Interest	237	210	177	150	123	92	67	42	17	14

SOLOMON ISLANDS

(US$ million, unless otherwise indicated)

	1970	1980	1990	1992	1993	1994	1995	1996	1997	1998
1. SUMMARY DEBT DATA										
TOTAL DEBT STOCKS (EDT)	..	**19.4**	**120.5**	**94.3**	**150.5**	**154.9**	**157.5**	**145.1**	**135.4**	**152.4**
Long-term debt (LDOD)	..	**17.4**	**103.2**	**92.5**	**144.4**	**152.9**	**147.8**	**143.6**	**133.2**	**149.5**
Public and publicly guaranteed	..	17.4	103.2	92.5	94.3	98.4	99.0	98.0	92.0	108.3
Private nonguaranteed	..	0.0	0.0	0.0	50.1	54.5	48.8	45.6	41.2	41.2
Use of IMF credit	**0.0**	**0.0**	**0.7**	**0.0**	**0.0**	**0.0**	**0.0**	**0.0**	**0.0**	**0.0**
Short-term debt	..	**2.0**	**16.6**	**1.8**	**6.1**	**2.0**	**9.7**	**1.4**	**2.2**	**2.9**
of which interest arrears on LDOD	..	0.0	0.1	0.2	0.0	0.0	8.4	0.6	2.1	1.7
Official creditors	..	0.0	0.1	0.1	0.0	0.0	0.5	0.4	1.6	1.0
Private creditors	..	0.0	0.0	0.1	0.0	0.0	8.0	0.2	0.5	0.7
Memo: principal arrears on LDOD	..	0.0	0.2	0.5	0.0	1.2	11.4	2.4	7.5	6.6
Official creditors	..	0.0	0.2	0.3	0.0	0.0	1.5	2.2	4.0	3.1
Private creditors	..	0.0	0.0	0.2	0.0	1.2	9.9	0.2	3.5	3.5
Memo: export credits	..	0.0	29.0	65.0	64.0	62.0	64.0	54.0	55.0	40.0
TOTAL DEBT FLOWS										
Disbursements	..	**4.0**	**5.2**	**4.9**	**8.0**	**10.4**	**10.5**	**4.3**	**2.8**	**17.9**
Long-term debt	..	4.0	5.2	4.9	8.0	10.4	10.5	4.3	2.8	17.9
IMF purchases	0.0	0.0	0.0	0.0	0.0	0.0	0.0	0.0	0.0	0.0
Principal repayments	..	**0.0**	**7.9**	**5.2**	**7.1**	**12.5**	**6.5**	**6.3**	**4.4**	**4.7**
Long-term debt	..	0.0	7.0	5.2	7.1	12.5	6.5	6.3	4.4	4.7
IMF repurchases	0.0	0.0	0.8	0.0	0.0	0.0	0.0	0.0	0.0	0.0
Net flows on debt	..	**4.9**	**13.8**	**-29.7**	**5.4**	**-6.3**	**3.2**	**-2.4**	**-2.3**	**14.2**
of which short-term debt	..	1.0	16.5	-29.4	4.5	-4.1	-0.8	-0.4	-0.7	1.0
Interest payments (INT)	..	**0.3**	**3.7**	**2.4**	**2.8**	**3.3**	**1.6**	**2.1**	**1.3**	**1.9**
Long-term debt	..	0.0	3.1	1.5	2.6	3.1	1.5	2.0	1.3	1.8
IMF charges	0.0	0.0	0.1	0.0	0.0	0.0	0.0	0.0	0.0	0.0
Short-term debt	..	0.3	0.5	0.9	0.2	0.2	0.1	0.0	0.0	0.1
Net transfers on debt	..	**4.7**	**10.1**	**-32.1**	**2.6**	**-9.6**	**1.6**	**-4.5**	**-3.7**	**12.3**
Total debt service paid (TDS)	..	**0.3**	**11.6**	**7.6**	**10.0**	**15.9**	**8.1**	**8.4**	**5.7**	**6.5**
Long-term debt	..	0.0	10.1	6.7	9.7	15.6	8.0	8.3	5.7	6.5
IMF repurchases and charges	0.0	0.0	1.0	0.0	0.0	0.0	0.0	0.0	0.0	0.0
Short-term debt (interest only)	..	0.3	0.5	0.9	0.2	0.2	0.1	0.0	0.0	0.1
2. AGGREGATE NET RESOURCE FLOWS AND NET TRANSFERS (LONG-TERM)										
NET RESOURCE FLOWS	..	**27.3**	**28.4**	**34.3**	**23.9**	**26.5**	**41.3**	**37.6**	**36.1**	**46.7**
Net flow of long-term debt (ex. IMF)	..	3.9	-1.8	-0.3	0.9	-2.2	4.0	-2.0	-1.6	13.2
Foreign direct investment (net)	..	2.4	10.0	14.0	13.0	11.0	18.0	21.0	22.0	23.0
Portfolio equity flows	..	0.0	0.0	0.0	0.0	0.0	0.0	0.0	0.0	0.0
Grants (excluding technical coop.)	..	21.0	20.2	20.6	10.0	17.6	19.3	18.6	15.8	10.5
Memo: technical coop. grants	..	11.5	19.5	2.0	21.3	25.5	26.0	20.9	18.5	17.5
official net resource flows	..	24.9	21.5	21.7	10.7	17.5	21.5	20.7	17.8	24.1
private net resource flows	..	2.4	6.9	12.6	13.2	9.0	19.8	16.9	18.3	22.6
NET TRANSFERS	..	**12.4**	**23.3**	**28.8**	**16.3**	**17.4**	**34.8**	**28.5**	**26.8**	**35.9**
Interest on long-term debt	..	0.0	3.1	1.5	2.6	3.1	1.5	2.0	1.3	1.8
Profit remittances on FDI	..	14.9	2.0	4.0	5.0	6.0	5.0	7.0	8.0	9.0
Memo: official net transfers	..	24.9	19.9	20.7	8.9	16.0	20.7	19.5	17.5	22.6
private net transfers	..	-12.5	3.4	8.1	7.4	1.4	14.1	9.0	9.3	13.3
3. MAJOR ECONOMIC AGGREGATES										
Gross national product (GNP)	..	107.9	207.3	258.7	255.3	289.9	320.7	355.9	367.3	295.3
Exports of goods & services (XGS)	..	85.0	97.8	138.8	172.2	193.6	211.3	217.0	229.5	199.0
of which workers remittances	..	0.0	0.0	0.0	0.0	0.0	0.0	0.0	0.0	0.0
Imports of goods & services (MGS)	..	117.0	163.6	176.4	222.2	252.6	239.4	245.4	302.9	224.4
International reserves (RES)	..	29.6	17.6	23.5	20.1	17.4	15.9	32.6	36.3	49.0
Current account balance	..	-12.2	-27.8	1.3	-7.7	-3.4	8.3	14.6	-37.9	8.1
4. DEBT INDICATORS										
EDT / XGS (%)	..	22.8	123.2	68.0	87.4	80.0	74.5	66.9	59.0	76.6
EDT / GNP (%)	..	18.0	58.1	36.5	59.0	53.4	49.1	40.8	36.9	51.6
TDS / XGS (%)	..	0.4	11.9	5.5	5.8	8.2	3.8	3.9	2.5	3.3
INT / XGS (%)	..	0.4	3.8	1.7	1.6	1.7	0.8	1.0	0.6	1.0
INT / GNP (%)	..	0.3	1.8	0.9	1.1	1.1	0.5	0.6	0.4	0.6
RES / EDT (%)	..	152.6	14.6	24.9	13.3	11.2	10.1	22.5	26.8	32.2
RES / MGS (months)	..	3.0	1.3	1.6	1.1	0.8	0.8	1.6	1.4	2.6
Short-term / EDT (%)	..	10.3	13.8	1.9	4.1	1.3	6.2	1.0	1.6	1.9
Concessional / EDT (%)	..	89.7	64.2	77.9	50.4	53.6	54.7	60.3	60.4	64.4
Multilateral / EDT (%)	..	36.6	51.0	66.9	44.6	48.3	49.7	54.7	54.9	60.1

SOLOMON ISLANDS

(US$ million, unless otherwise indicated)

	1970	1980	1990	1992	1993	1994	1995	1996	1997	1998
5. LONG-TERM DEBT										
DEBT OUTSTANDING (LDOD)	..	**17.4**	**103.2**	**92.5**	**144.4**	**152.9**	**147.8**	**143.6**	**133.2**	**149.5**
Public and publicly guaranteed	..	**17.4**	**103.2**	**92.5**	**94.3**	**98.4**	**99.0**	**98.0**	**92.0**	**108.3**
Official creditors	..	17.4	89.1	83.2	84.7	91.2	93.8	93.8	87.8	104.5
Multilateral	..	7.1	61.5	63.1	67.1	74.8	78.2	79.4	74.3	91.6
Concessional	..	7.1	61.5	63.1	67.1	74.8	78.2	79.4	74.3	91.6
Bilateral	..	10.3	27.7	20.1	17.6	16.4	15.6	14.4	13.5	12.9
Concessional	..	10.3	15.8	10.4	8.7	8.2	8.0	8.1	7.5	6.6
Private creditors	..	0.0	14.1	9.3	9.5	7.2	5.2	4.2	4.2	3.8
Bonds	..	0.0	0.0	0.0	0.0	0.0	0.0	0.0	0.0	0.0
Commercial banks	..	0.0	10.9	5.5	2.7	0.0	0.0	0.0	0.0	0.0
Other private	..	0.0	3.2	3.9	6.8	7.2	5.2	4.2	4.2	3.8
Private nonguaranteed	..	**0.0**	**0.0**	**0.0**	**50.1**	**54.5**	**48.8**	**45.6**	**41.2**	**41.2**
Bonds	..	0.0	0.0	0.0	0.0	0.0	0.0	0.0	0.0	0.0
Commercial banks	..	0.0	0.0	0.0	50.1	54.5	48.8	45.6	41.2	41.2
Memo:										
IBRD	0.0	0.0	0.0	0.0	0.0	0.0	0.0	0.0	0.0	0.0
IDA	0.0	0.0	16.6	18.4	19.6	22.4	25.9	29.2	29.9	32.7
DISBURSEMENTS	..	**4.0**	**5.2**	**4.9**	**8.0**	**10.4**	**10.5**	**4.3**	**2.8**	**17.9**
Public and publicly guaranteed	..	**4.0**	**5.2**	**4.9**	**8.0**	**2.8**	**7.8**	**4.3**	**2.8**	**17.9**
Official creditors	..	4.0	5.2	3.4	4.5	2.8	3.5	4.3	2.8	17.9
Multilateral	..	4.0	5.2	3.4	4.5	2.8	3.5	4.3	2.8	17.9
Concessional	..	4.0	5.2	3.4	4.5	2.8	3.5	4.3	2.8	17.9
Bilateral	..	0.0	0.0	0.0	0.0	0.0	0.0	0.0	0.0	0.0
Concessional	..	0.0	0.0	0.0	0.0	0.0	0.0	0.0	0.0	0.0
Private creditors	..	0.0	0.0	1.5	3.5	0.0	4.2	0.0	0.0	0.0
Bonds	..	0.0	0.0	0.0	0.0	0.0	0.0	0.0	0.0	0.0
Commercial banks	..	0.0	0.0	0.0	0.0	0.0	0.0	0.0	0.0	0.0
Other private	..	0.0	0.0	1.5	3.5	0.0	4.2	0.0	0.0	0.0
Private nonguaranteed	..	**0.0**	**0.0**	**0.0**	**0.0**	**7.6**	**2.8**	**0.0**	**0.0**	**0.0**
Bonds	..	0.0	0.0	0.0	0.0	0.0	0.0	0.0	0.0	0.0
Commercial banks	..	0.0	0.0	0.0	0.0	7.6	2.8	0.0	0.0	0.0
Memo:										
IBRD	0.0	0.0	0.0	0.0	0.0	0.0	0.0	0.0	0.0	0.0
IDA	0.0	0.0	2.5	0.5	1.2	1.8	3.2	4.3	2.6	1.9
PRINCIPAL REPAYMENTS	..	**0.0**	**7.0**	**5.2**	**7.1**	**12.5**	**6.5**	**6.3**	**4.4**	**4.7**
Public and publicly guaranteed	..	**0.0**	**7.0**	**5.2**	**7.1**	**6.0**	**1.8**	**3.1**	**0.7**	**4.7**
Official creditors	..	0.0	3.9	2.2	3.8	2.9	1.3	2.2	0.7	4.3
Multilateral	..	0.0	0.5	0.7	0.9	0.9	0.6	0.9	0.3	3.3
Concessional	..	0.0	0.5	0.7	0.9	0.9	0.6	0.9	0.3	3.3
Bilateral	..	0.0	3.4	1.5	2.9	2.0	0.7	1.3	0.4	1.0
Concessional	..	0.0	1.4	1.4	1.6	0.8	0.2	0.4	0.4	1.0
Private creditors	..	0.0	3.1	2.9	3.3	3.1	0.5	0.9	0.0	0.4
Bonds	..	0.0	0.0	0.0	0.0	0.0	0.0	0.0	0.0	0.0
Commercial banks	..	0.0	2.7	2.7	2.7	2.7	0.0	0.0	0.0	0.0
Other private	..	0.0	0.4	0.2	0.6	0.4	0.5	0.9	0.0	0.4
Private nonguaranteed	..	**0.0**	**0.0**	**0.0**	**0.0**	**6.5**	**4.7**	**3.2**	**3.7**	**0.0**
Bonds	..	0.0	0.0	0.0	0.0	0.0	0.0	0.0	0.0	0.0
Commercial banks	..	0.0	0.0	0.0	0.0	6.5	4.7	3.2	3.7	0.0
Memo:										
IBRD	0.0	0.0	0.0	0.0	0.0	0.0	0.0	0.0	0.0	0.0
IDA	0.0	0.0	0.0	0.0	0.1	0.1	0.1	0.2	0.2	0.2
NET FLOWS ON DEBT	..	**3.9**	**-1.8**	**-0.3**	**0.9**	**-2.2**	**4.0**	**-2.0**	**-1.6**	**13.2**
Public and publicly guaranteed	..	**3.9**	**-1.8**	**-0.3**	**0.9**	**-3.2**	**6.0**	**1.2**	**2.0**	**13.2**
Official creditors	..	3.9	1.3	1.1	0.7	-0.1	2.2	2.1	2.0	13.6
Multilateral	..	4.0	4.7	2.6	3.6	1.9	2.9	3.4	2.4	14.6
Concessional	..	4.0	4.7	2.6	3.6	1.9	2.9	3.4	2.4	14.6
Bilateral	..	0.0	-3.4	-1.5	-2.9	-2.0	-0.7	-1.3	-0.4	-1.0
Concessional	..	0.0	-1.4	-1.4	-1.6	-0.8	-0.2	-0.4	-0.4	-1.0
Private creditors	..	0.0	-3.1	-1.4	0.2	-3.1	3.8	-0.9	0.0	-0.4
Bonds	..	0.0	0.0	0.0	0.0	0.0	0.0	0.0	0.0	0.0
Commercial banks	..	0.0	-2.7	-2.7	-2.7	-2.7	0.0	0.0	0.0	0.0
Other private	..	0.0	-0.4	1.3	2.9	-0.4	3.8	-0.9	0.0	-0.4
Private nonguaranteed	..	**0.0**	**0.0**	**0.0**	**0.0**	**1.1**	**-2.0**	**-3.2**	**-3.7**	**0.0**
Bonds	..	0.0	0.0	0.0	0.0	0.0	0.0	0.0	0.0	0.0
Commercial banks	..	0.0	0.0	0.0	0.0	1.1	-2.0	-3.2	-3.7	0.0
Memo:										
IBRD	0.0	0.0	0.0	0.0	0.0	0.0	0.0	0.0	0.0	0.0
IDA	0.0	0.0	2.5	0.5	1.1	1.7	3.1	4.2	2.4	1.7

SOLOMON ISLANDS

(US$ million, unless otherwise indicated)

	1970	1980	1990	1992	1993	1994	1995	1996	1997	1998
INTEREST PAYMENTS (LINT)	..	**0.0**	**3.1**	**1.5**	**2.6**	**3.1**	**1.5**	**2.0**	**1.3**	**1.8**
Public and publicly guaranteed	..	**0.0**	**3.1**	**1.5**	**2.6**	**2.1**	**0.9**	**1.5**	**0.3**	**1.8**
Official creditors	..	0.0	1.6	1.0	1.8	1.5	0.8	1.2	0.3	1.5
Multilateral	..	0.0	0.6	0.6	0.7	0.7	0.5	0.6	0.2	1.5
Concessional	..	0.0	0.6	0.6	0.7	0.7	0.5	0.6	0.2	1.5
Bilateral	..	0.0	1.0	0.4	1.2	0.8	0.3	0.6	0.1	0.0
Concessional	..	0.0	0.0	0.1	0.2	0.1	0.0	0.1	0.1	0.0
Private creditors	..	0.0	1.5	0.5	0.8	0.6	0.1	0.4	0.0	0.3
Bonds	..	0.0	0.0	0.0	0.0	0.0	0.0	0.0	0.0	0.0
Commercial banks	..	0.0	1.2	0.4	0.2	0.1	0.0	0.0	0.0	0.0
Other private	..	0.0	0.3	0.1	0.5	0.5	0.1	0.4	0.0	0.3
Private nonguaranteed	..	**0.0**	**0.0**	**0.0**	**0.0**	**1.0**	**0.6**	**0.5**	**1.0**	**0.0**
Bonds	..	0.0	0.0	0.0	0.0	0.0	0.0	0.0	0.0	0.0
Commercial banks	..	0.0	0.0	0.0	0.0	1.0	0.6	0.5	1.0	0.0
Memo:										
IBRD	0.0	0.0	0.0	0.0	0.0	0.0	0.0	0.0	0.0	0.0
IDA	0.0	0.0	0.1	0.1	0.2	0.1	0.2	0.2	0.2	0.2
NET TRANSFERS ON DEBT	..	**3.9**	**-4.9**	**-1.8**	**-1.7**	**-5.3**	**2.5**	**-4.0**	**-2.9**	**11.4**
Public and publicly guaranteed	..	**3.9**	**-4.9**	**-1.8**	**-1.7**	**-5.3**	**5.1**	**-0.3**	**1.7**	**11.4**
Official creditors	..	3.9	-0.3	0.1	-1.1	-1.6	1.4	0.9	1.7	12.1
Multilateral	..	3.9	4.1	2.0	2.9	1.2	2.4	2.9	2.2	13.1
Concessional	..	3.9	4.1	2.0	2.9	1.2	2.4	2.9	2.2	13.1
Bilateral	..	0.0	-4.4	-2.0	-4.0	-2.8	-1.0	-1.9	-0.5	-1.1
Concessional	..	0.0	-1.4	-1.5	-1.8	-0.9	-0.2	-0.5	-0.5	-1.1
Private creditors	..	0.0	-4.7	-1.9	-0.6	-3.7	3.7	-1.3	0.0	-0.6
Bonds	..	0.0	0.0	0.0	0.0	0.0	0.0	0.0	0.0	0.0
Commercial banks	..	0.0	-3.9	-3.1	-2.9	-2.8	0.0	0.0	0.0	0.0
Other private	..	0.0	-0.7	1.2	2.4	-0.9	3.7	-1.3	0.0	-0.6
Private nonguaranteed	..	**0.0**	**0.0**	**0.0**	**0.0**	**0.0**	**-2.5**	**-3.7**	**-4.6**	**0.0**
Bonds	..	0.0	0.0	0.0	0.0	0.0	0.0	0.0	0.0	0.0
Commercial banks	..	0.0	0.0	0.0	0.0	0.0	-2.5	-3.7	-4.6	0.0
Memo:										
IBRD	0.0	0.0	0.0	0.0	0.0	0.0	0.0	0.0	0.0	0.0
IDA	0.0	0.0	2.4	0.4	0.9	1.6	3.0	4.0	2.2	1.4
DEBT SERVICE (LTDS)	..	**0.0**	**10.1**	**6.7**	**9.7**	**15.6**	**8.0**	**8.3**	**5.7**	**6.5**
Public and publicly guaranteed	..	**0.0**	**10.1**	**6.7**	**9.7**	**8.1**	**2.7**	**4.6**	**1.1**	**6.5**
Official creditors	..	0.0	5.5	3.3	5.7	4.4	2.1	3.4	1.1	5.8
Multilateral	..	0.0	1.1	1.3	1.6	1.6	1.1	1.5	0.6	4.8
Concessional	..	0.0	1.1	1.3	1.6	1.6	1.1	1.5	0.6	4.8
Bilateral	..	0.0	4.4	2.0	4.0	2.8	1.0	1.9	0.5	1.1
Concessional	..	0.0	1.4	1.5	1.8	0.9	0.2	0.5	0.5	1.1
Private creditors	..	0.0	4.7	3.4	4.1	3.7	0.6	1.3	0.0	0.6
Bonds	..	0.0	0.0	0.0	0.0	0.0	0.0	0.0	0.0	0.0
Commercial banks	..	0.0	3.9	3.1	2.9	2.8	0.0	0.0	0.0	0.0
Other private	..	0.0	0.7	0.3	1.2	0.9	0.6	1.3	0.0	0.6
Private nonguaranteed	..	**0.0**	**0.0**	**0.0**	**0.0**	**7.5**	**5.3**	**3.7**	**4.6**	**0.0**
Bonds	..	0.0	0.0	0.0	0.0	0.0	0.0	0.0	0.0	0.0
Commercial banks	..	0.0	0.0	0.0	0.0	7.5	5.3	3.7	4.6	0.0
Memo:										
IBRD	0.0	0.0	0.0	0.0	0.0	0.0	0.0	0.0	0.0	0.0
IDA	0.0	0.0	0.1	0.2	0.3	0.3	0.3	0.3	0.4	0.4
UNDISBURSED DEBT	..	**12.9**	**25.4**	**11.3**	**20.8**	**18.5**	**15.7**	**10.8**	**7.3**	**17.0**
Official creditors	..	12.9	10.4	8.1	20.8	18.5	15.7	10.8	7.3	17.0
Private creditors	..	0.0	15.0	3.1	0.0	0.0	0.0	0.0	0.0	0.0
Memorandum items										
Concessional LDOD	..	17.4	77.2	73.5	75.8	83.0	86.2	87.5	81.8	98.2
Variable rate LDOD	..	0.0	10.9	5.5	52.9	54.5	48.8	45.6	41.2	41.2
Public sector LDOD	..	17.4	103.2	92.5	94.3	98.4	99.0	98.0	92.0	108.3
Private sector LDOD	..	0.0	0.0	0.0	50.1	54.5	48.8	45.6	41.2	41.2

6. CURRENCY COMPOSITION OF LONG-TERM DEBT (PERCENT)

	1970	1980	1990	1992	1993	1994	1995	1996	1997	1998
Deutsche mark	..	0.0	3.1	2.5	1.7	1.3	0.9	0.4	0.4	0.0
French franc	..	0.0	0.0	0.0	0.0	0.0	0.0	0.0	0.0	0.0
Japanese yen	..	0.0	4.7	6.4	10.2	10.3	3.8	3.0	2.8	2.7
Pound sterling	..	59.2	13.1	8.9	7.1	6.5	6.5	7.1	7.4	5.9
Swiss franc	..	0.0	0.0	0.0	0.0	0.0	0.0	0.0	0.0	0.0
U.S.dollars	..	40.8	52.0	52.0	49.0	48.0	54.6	56.9	58.9	66.0
Multiple currency	..	0.0	7.3	8.6	11.7	12.8	12.7	12.9	12.1	10.5
Special drawing rights	..	0.0	6.3	7.2	7.8	8.5	8.4	7.9	7.5	6.6
All other currencies	..	0.0	13.5	14.4	12.5	12.6	13.1	11.8	10.9	8.3

SOLOMON ISLANDS

(US$ million, unless otherwise indicated)

	1970	1980	1990	1992	1993	1994	1995	1996	1997	1998
7. DEBT RESTRUCTURINGS										
Total amount rescheduled	..	..	0.0	8.1	0.0	0.0	0.0	0.0	0.0	0.0
Debt stock rescheduled	..	..	0.0	8.1	0.0	0.0	0.0	0.0	0.0	0.0
Principal rescheduled	..	..	0.0	0.0	0.0	0.0	0.0	0.0	0.0	0.0
Official	..	..	0.0	0.0	0.0	0.0	0.0	0.0	0.0	0.0
Private	..	..	0.0	0.0	0.0	0.0	0.0	0.0	0.0	0.0
Interest rescheduled	..	..	0.0	0.0	0.0	0.0	0.0	0.0	0.0	0.0
Official	..	..	0.0	0.0	0.0	0.0	0.0	0.0	0.0	0.0
Private	..	..	0.0	0.0	0.0	0.0	0.0	0.0	0.0	0.0
Debt forgiven	..	..	0.0	0.0	0.0	0.0	6.3	0.0	0.0	0.0
Memo: interest forgiven	..	..	0.0	0.0	0.0	0.0	0.0	0.0	0.0	0.0
Debt stock reduction	..	..	0.0	0.0	0.0	0.0	0.0	0.0	0.0	0.0
of which debt buyback	..	..	0.0	0.0	0.0	0.0	0.0	0.0	0.0	0.0
8. DEBT STOCK-FLOW RECONCILIATION										
Total change in debt stocks	..	..	20.5	-35.2	56.2	4.4	2.5	-12.4	-9.7	17.0
Net flows on debt	..	4.9	13.8	-29.7	5.4	-6.3	3.2	-2.4	-2.3	14.2
Net change in interest arrears	..	..	0.1	0.2	-0.2	0.0	8.4	-7.8	1.5	-0.4
Interest capitalized	..	..	0.0	0.0	0.0	0.0	0.0	0.0	0.0	0.0
Debt forgiveness or reduction	..	..	0.0	0.0	0.0	0.0	-6.3	0.0	0.0	0.0
Cross-currency valuation	..	..	5.3	-3.1	0.3	3.2	0.8	-0.4	-1.9	1.2
Residual	..	..	1.3	-2.6	50.8	7.5	-3.6	-1.8	-6.9	1.9
9. AVERAGE TERMS OF NEW COMMITMENTS										
ALL CREDITORS										
Interest (%)	..	1.0	2.2	4.2	0.8	0.0	7.8	0.0	0.0	3.3
Maturity (years)	..	39.8	17.7	18.4	39.5	0.0	10.2	0.0	0.0	39.7
Grace period (years)	..	10.3	11.5	5.0	10.0	0.0	0.7	0.0	0.0	10.2
Grant element (%)	..	78.4	56.9	36.2	80.2	0.0	7.6	0.0	0.0	57.7
Official creditors										
Interest (%)	..	1.0	2.2	1.0	0.8	0.0	0.0	0.0	0.0	3.3
Maturity (years)	..	39.8	17.7	39.7	39.5	0.0	0.0	0.0	0.0	39.7
Grace period (years)	..	10.3	11.5	10.2	10.0	0.0	0.0	0.0	0.0	10.2
Grant element (%)	..	78.4	56.9	78.3	80.2	0.0	0.0	0.0	0.0	57.7
Private creditors										
Interest (%)	..	0.0	0.0	6.0	0.0	0.0	7.8	0.0	0.0	0.0
Maturity (years)	..	0.0	0.0	6.5	0.0	0.0	10.2	0.0	0.0	0.0
Grace period (years)	..	0.0	0.0	2.0	0.0	0.0	0.7	0.0	0.0	0.0
Grant element (%)	..	0.0	0.0	12.6	0.0	0.0	7.6	0.0	0.0	0.0
Memorandum items										
Commitments	..	8.3	2.5	7.2	17.4	0.0	4.2	0.0	0.0	27.3
Official creditors	..	8.3	2.5	2.6	17.4	0.0	0.0	0.0	0.0	27.3
Private creditors	..	0.0	0.0	4.6	0.0	0.0	4.2	0.0	0.0	0.0

10. CONTRACTUAL OBLIGATIONS ON OUTSTANDING LONG-TERM DEBT

	1999	2000	2001	2002	2003	2004	2005	2006	2007	2008
TOTAL										
Disbursements	6.9	4.9	2.3	1.6	1.2	0.1	0.0	0.0	0.0	0.0
Principal	4.0	4.0	4.2	3.3	3.2	3.5	3.4	3.1	2.7	2.8
Interest	1.2	1.1	0.9	0.8	0.7	0.7	0.6	0.6	0.6	0.8
Official creditors										
Disbursements	6.9	4.9	2.3	1.6	1.2	0.1	0.0	0.0	0.0	0.0
Principal	3.6	3.6	3.7	2.9	2.7	3.1	3.2	3.1	2.7	2.8
Interest	1.0	0.9	0.8	0.7	0.7	0.6	0.6	0.6	0.6	0.8
Bilateral creditors										
Disbursements	0.0	0.0	0.0	0.0	0.0	0.0	0.0	0.0	0.0	0.0
Principal	2.1	2.1	2.0	1.0	0.6	0.6	0.6	0.6	0.0	0.0
Interest	0.2	0.2	0.1	0.0	0.0	0.0	0.0	0.0	0.0	0.0
Multilateral creditors										
Disbursements	6.9	4.9	2.3	1.6	1.2	0.1	0.0	0.0	0.0	0.0
Principal	1.5	1.6	1.7	1.9	2.1	2.5	2.6	2.5	2.7	2.8
Interest	0.7	0.7	0.7	0.7	0.7	0.6	0.6	0.6	0.6	0.8
Private creditors										
Disbursements	0.0	0.0	0.0	0.0	0.0	0.0	0.0	0.0	0.0	0.0
Principal	0.4	0.4	0.4	0.4	0.4	0.4	0.2	0.0	0.0	0.0
Interest	0.2	0.2	0.1	0.1	0.1	0.0	0.0	0.0	0.0	0.0
Commercial banks										
Disbursements	0.0	0.0	0.0	0.0	0.0	0.0	0.0	0.0	0.0	0.0
Principal	0.0	0.0	0.0	0.0	0.0	0.0	0.0	0.0	0.0	0.0
Interest	0.0	0.0	0.0	0.0	0.0	0.0	0.0	0.0	0.0	0.0
Other private										
Disbursements	0.0	0.0	0.0	0.0	0.0	0.0	0.0	0.0	0.0	0.0
Principal	0.4	0.4	0.4	0.4	0.4	0.4	0.2	0.0	0.0	0.0
Interest	0.2	0.2	0.1	0.1	0.1	0.0	0.0	0.0	0.0	0.0

SOMALIA

(US$ million, unless otherwise indicated)

	1970	1980	1990	1992	1993	1994	1995	1996	1997	1998
1. SUMMARY DEBT DATA										
TOTAL DEBT STOCKS (EDT)	**..**	**660**	**2,370**	**2,447**	**2,501**	**2,616**	**2,678**	**2,643**	**2,561**	**2,635**
Long-term debt (LDOD)	**77**	**595**	**1,926**	**1,898**	**1,897**	**1,935**	**1,961**	**1,918**	**1,853**	**1,886**
Public and publicly guaranteed	77	595	1,926	1,898	1,897	1,935	1,961	1,918	1,853	1,886
Private nonguaranteed	0	0	0	0	0	0	0	0	0	0
Use of IMF credit	**0**	**18**	**159**	**154**	**154**	**164**	**167**	**161**	**151**	**158**
Short-term debt	**..**	**47**	**285**	**395**	**450**	**518**	**551**	**564**	**558**	**591**
of which interest arrears on LDOD	..	8	255	364	419	487	521	533	534	562
Official creditors	..	8	249	354	406	471	504	517	518	546
Private creditors	..	0	5	11	13	16	17	17	16	16
Memo: principal arrears on LDOD	..	14	674	843	930	1,032	1,135	1,167	1,180	1,227
Official creditors	..	13	646	809	896	997	1,098	1,131	1,145	1,192
Private creditors	..	0	28	35	34	36	37	36	34	35
Memo: export credits	..	0	357	416	383	289	254	268	356	446
TOTAL DEBT FLOWS										
Disbursements	**4**	**135**	**46**	**0**	**0**	**0**	**0**	**0**	**0**	**0**
Long-term debt	4	114	46	0	0	0	0	0	0	0
IMF purchases	0	22	0	0	0	0	0	0	0	0
Principal repayments	**2**	**11**	**5**	**0**	**0**	**0**	**0**	**0**	**0**	**0**
Long-term debt	1	7	3	0	0	0	0	0	0	0
IMF repurchases	2	4	3	0	0	0	0	0	0	0
Net flows on debt	**2**	**138**	**58**	**0**	**0**	**0**	**0**	**0**	**-7**	**5**
of which short-term debt	..	13	18	0	0	0	0	0	-7	5
Interest payments (INT)	**..**	**2**	**5**	**0**	**0**	**0**	**1**	**3**	**0**	**0**
Long-term debt	0	2	4	0	0	0	0	3	0	0
IMF charges	0	0	1	0	0	0	1	1	0	0
Short-term debt	..	0	0	0	0	0	0	0	0	0
Net transfers on debt	**..**	**135**	**53**	**0**	**0**	**0**	**-1**	**-3**	**-7**	**5**
Total debt service paid (TDS)	**..**	**13**	**11**	**0**	**0**	**0**	**1**	**3**	**0**	**0**
Long-term debt	1	9	7	0	0	0	0	3	0	0
IMF repurchases and charges	2	4	4	0	0	0	1	1	0	0
Short-term debt (interest only)	..	0	0	0	0	0	0	0	0	0
2. AGGREGATE NET RESOURCE FLOWS AND NET TRANSFERS (LONG-TERM)										
NET RESOURCE FLOWS	**17**	**380**	**372**	**606**	**806**	**494**	**150**	**60**	**67**	**68**
Net flow of long-term debt (ex. IMF)	4	106	43	0	0	0	0	0	0	0
Foreign direct investment (net)	5	0	6	0	2	1	1	0	0	0
Portfolio equity flows	0	0	0	0	0	0	0	0	0	0
Grants (excluding technical coop.)	9	274	323	606	804	493	149	60	67	68
Memo: technical coop. grants	11	93	95	52	85	46	43	33	26	16
official net resource flows	13	354	366	606	804	493	149	60	67	68
private net resource flows	4	27	6	0	2	1	1	0	0	0
NET TRANSFERS	**16**	**379**	**368**	**606**	**806**	**494**	**150**	**58**	**67**	**68**
Interest on long-term debt	0	2	4	0	0	0	0	3	0	0
Profit remittances on FDI	0	0	0	0	0	0	0	0	0	0
Memo: official net transfers	12	352	362	606	804	493	149	58	67	68
private net transfers	4	27	6	0	2	1	1	0	0	0
3. MAJOR ECONOMIC AGGREGATES										
Gross national product (GNP)	323	603	835	..	..	..	..	..	..	..
Exports of goods & services (XGS)	..	262	70	..	..	..	..	..	..	..
of which workers remittances	..	57	..	..	..	..	..	..	..	..
Imports of goods & services (MGS)	..	541	..	..	..	..	..	..	..	..
International reserves (RES)	21	26	..	..	..	..	..	..	..	..
Current account balance	..	-136	..	..	..	..	..	..	..	..
4. DEBT INDICATORS										
EDT / XGS (%)	..	252.1	3,363.0	..	..	..	..	..	..	..
EDT / GNP (%)	..	109.5	283.9	..	..	..	..	..	..	..
TDS / XGS (%)	..	4.9	15.2	..	..	..	..	..	..	..
INT / XGS (%)	..	0.9	7.5	..	..	..	..	..	..	..
INT / GNP (%)	..	0.4	0.6	..	..	..	..	..	..	..
RES / EDT (%)	..	3.9	..	..	..	..	..	..	..	..
RES / MGS (months)	..	0.6	..	..	..	..	..	..	..	..
Short-term / EDT (%)	..	7.1	12.0	16.1	18.0	19.8	20.6	21.3	21.8	22.4
Concessional / EDT (%)	..	82.8	65.7	63.0	61.8	60.3	59.6	58.9	58.7	58.1
Multilateral / EDT (%)	..	24.1	31.8	30.5	29.9	29.6	29.4	28.9	28.2	28.1

SOMALIA

(US$ million, unless otherwise indicated)

	1970	1980	1990	1992	1993	1994	1995	1996	1997	1998
5. LONG-TERM DEBT										
DEBT OUTSTANDING (LDOD)	**77**	**595**	**1,926**	**1,898**	**1,897**	**1,935**	**1,961**	**1,918**	**1,853**	**1,886**
Public and publicly guaranteed	**77**	**595**	**1,926**	**1,898**	**1,897**	**1,935**	**1,961**	**1,918**	**1,853**	**1,886**
Official creditors	75	568	1,889	1,863	1,863	1,899	1,924	1,882	1,818	1,851
Multilateral	7	159	754	746	748	774	786	764	723	741
Concessional	7	147	735	729	731	756	767	745	706	723
Bilateral	68	408	1,136	1,117	1,114	1,125	1,138	1,119	1,095	1,110
Concessional	63	400	822	812	815	820	828	812	797	808
Private creditors	2	28	37	35	34	36	37	36	34	35
Bonds	0	0	0	0	0	0	0	0	0	0
Commercial banks	2	0	0	0	0	0	0	0	0	0
Other private	0	28	37	35	34	36	37	36	34	35
Private nonguaranteed	**0**	**0**	**0**	**0**	**0**	**0**	**0**	**0**	**0**	**0**
Bonds	0	0	0	0	0	0	0	0	0	0
Commercial banks	0	0	0	0	0	0	0	0	0	0
Memo:										
IBRD	0	0	0	0	0	0	0	0	0	0
IDA	7	72	419	410	411	425	432	422	406	416
DISBURSEMENTS	**4**	**114**	**46**	**0**	**0**	**0**	**0**	**0**	**0**	**0**
Public and publicly guaranteed	**4**	**114**	**46**	**0**	**0**	**0**	**0**	**0**	**0**	**0**
Official creditors	4	87	46	0	0	0	0	0	0	0
Multilateral	0	36	46	0	0	0	0	0	0	0
Concessional	0	25	46	0	0	0	0	0	0	0
Bilateral	4	50	0	0	0	0	0	0	0	0
Concessional	4	49	0	0	0	0	0	0	0	0
Private creditors	0	27	0	0	0	0	0	0	0	0
Bonds	0	0	0	0	0	0	0	0	0	0
Commercial banks	0	0	0	0	0	0	0	0	0	0
Other private	0	27	0	0	0	0	0	0	0	0
Private nonguaranteed	**0**	**0**	**0**	**0**	**0**	**0**	**0**	**0**	**0**	**0**
Bonds	0	0	0	0	0	0	0	0	0	0
Commercial banks	0	0	0	0	0	0	0	0	0	0
Memo:										
IBRD	0	0	0	0	0	0	0	0	0	0
IDA	0	10	35	0	0	0	0	0	0	0
PRINCIPAL REPAYMENTS	**1**	**7**	**3**	**0**	**0**	**0**	**0**	**0**	**0**	**0**
Public and publicly guaranteed	**1**	**7**	**3**	**0**	**0**	**0**	**0**	**0**	**0**	**0**
Official creditors	0	7	3	0	0	0	0	0	0	0
Multilateral	0	5	3	0	0	0	0	0	0	0
Concessional	0	0	2	0	0	0	0	0	0	0
Bilateral	0	2	0	0	0	0	0	0	0	0
Concessional	0	2	0	0	0	0	0	0	0	0
Private creditors	1	0	0	0	0	0	0	0	0	0
Bonds	0	0	0	0	0	0	0	0	0	0
Commercial banks	1	0	0	0	0	0	0	0	0	0
Other private	0	0	0	0	0	0	0	0	0	0
Private nonguaranteed	**0**	**0**	**0**	**0**	**0**	**0**	**0**	**0**	**0**	**0**
Bonds	0	0	0	0	0	0	0	0	0	0
Commercial banks	0	0	0	0	0	0	0	0	0	0
Memo:										
IBRD	0	0	0	0	0	0	0	0	0	0
IDA	0	0	2	0	0	0	0	0	0	0
NET FLOWS ON DEBT	**4**	**106**	**43**	**0**	**0**	**0**	**0**	**0**	**0**	**0**
Public and publicly guaranteed	**4**	**106**	**43**	**0**	**0**	**0**	**0**	**0**	**0**	**0**
Official creditors	4	80	43	0	0	0	0	0	0	0
Multilateral	0	31	43	0	0	0	0	0	0	0
Concessional	0	25	44	0	0	0	0	0	0	0
Bilateral	4	49	0	0	0	0	0	0	0	0
Concessional	4	47	0	0	0	0	0	0	0	0
Private creditors	-1	27	0	0	0	0	0	0	0	0
Bonds	0	0	0	0	0	0	0	0	0	0
Commercial banks	-1	0	0	0	0	0	0	0	0	0
Other private	0	27	0	0	0	0	0	0	0	0
Private nonguaranteed	**0**	**0**	**0**	**0**	**0**	**0**	**0**	**0**	**0**	**0**
Bonds	0	0	0	0	0	0	0	0	0	0
Commercial banks	0	0	0	0	0	0	0	0	0	0
Memo:										
IBRD	0	0	0	0	0	0	0	0	0	0
IDA	0	10	32	0	0	0	0	0	0	0

SOMALIA

(US$ million, unless otherwise indicated)

	1970	1980	1990	1992	1993	1994	1995	1996	1997	1998
INTEREST PAYMENTS (LINT)	**0**	**2**	**4**	**0**	**0**	**0**	**0**	**3**	**0**	**0**
Public and publicly guaranteed	**0**	**2**	**4**	**0**	**0**	**0**	**0**	**3**	**0**	**0**
Official creditors	0	2	4	0	0	0	0	3	0	0
Multilateral	0	1	4	0	0	0	0	3	0	0
Concessional	0	1	4	0	0	0	0	0	0	0
Bilateral	0	1	0	0	0	0	0	0	0	0
Concessional	0	1	0	0	0	0	0	0	0	0
Private creditors	0	0	0	0	0	0	0	0	0	0
Bonds	0	0	0	0	0	0	0	0	0	0
Commercial banks	0	0	0	0	0	0	0	0	0	0
Other private	0	0	0	0	0	0	0	0	0	0
Private nonguaranteed	**0**	**0**	**0**	**0**	**0**	**0**	**0**	**0**	**0**	**0**
Bonds	0	0	0	0	0	0	0	0	0	0
Commercial banks	0	0	0	0	0	0	0	0	0	0
Memo:										
IBRD	0	0	0	0	0	0	0	0	0	0
IDA	0	1	3	0	0	0	0	0	0	0
NET TRANSFERS ON DEBT	**3**	**104**	**39**	**0**	**0**	**0**	**0**	**-3**	**0**	**0**
Public and publicly guaranteed	**3**	**104**	**39**	**0**	**0**	**0**	**0**	**-3**	**0**	**0**
Official creditors	4	78	39	0	0	0	0	-3	0	0
Multilateral	0	31	39	0	0	0	0	-3	0	0
Concessional	0	25	40	0	0	0	0	0	0	0
Bilateral	4	47	0	0	0	0	0	0	0	0
Concessional	4	46	0	0	0	0	0	0	0	0
Private creditors	-1	27	0	0	0	0	0	0	0	0
Bonds	0	0	0	0	0	0	0	0	0	0
Commercial banks	-1	0	0	0	0	0	0	0	0	0
Other private	0	27	0	0	0	0	0	0	0	0
Private nonguaranteed	**0**	**0**	**0**	**0**	**0**	**0**	**0**	**0**	**0**	**0**
Bonds	0	0	0	0	0	0	0	0	0	0
Commercial banks	0	0	0	0	0	0	0	0	0	0
Memo:										
IBRD	0	0	0	0	0	0	0	0	0	0
IDA	0	9	29	0	0	0	0	0	0	0
DEBT SERVICE (LTDS)	**1**	**9**	**7**	**0**	**0**	**0**	**0**	**3**	**0**	**0**
Public and publicly guaranteed	**1**	**9**	**7**	**0**	**0**	**0**	**0**	**3**	**0**	**0**
Official creditors	0	9	7	0	0	0	0	3	0	0
Multilateral	0	6	7	0	0	0	0	3	0	0
Concessional	0	1	6	0	0	0	0	0	0	0
Bilateral	0	3	0	0	0	0	0	0	0	0
Concessional	0	3	0	0	0	0	0	0	0	0
Private creditors	1	0	0	0	0	0	0	0	0	0
Bonds	0	0	0	0	0	0	0	0	0	0
Commercial banks	1	0	0	0	0	0	0	0	0	0
Other private	0	0	0	0	0	0	0	0	0	0
Private nonguaranteed	**0**	**0**	**0**	**0**	**0**	**0**	**0**	**0**	**0**	**0**
Bonds	0	0	0	0	0	0	0	0	0	0
Commercial banks	0	0	0	0	0	0	0	0	0	0
Memo:										
IBRD	0	0	0	0	0	0	0	0	0	0
IDA	0	1	6	0	0	0	0	0	0	0
UNDISBURSED DEBT	**67**	**565**	**497**	**437**	**437**	**452**	**314**	**230**	**219**	**226**
Official creditors	67	494	497	437	437	452	314	230	219	226
Private creditors	0	70	0	0	0	0	0	0	0	0
Memorandum items										
Concessional LDOD	70	546	1,557	1,540	1,546	1,576	1,596	1,557	1,503	1,531
Variable rate LDOD	0	0	20	20	20	20	20	20	20	20
Public sector LDOD	77	568	1,926	1,898	1,897	1,935	1,961	1,918	1,853	1,886
Private sector LDOD	0	28	0	0	0	0	0	0	0	0

6. CURRENCY COMPOSITION OF LONG-TERM DEBT (PERCENT)

	1970	1980	1990	1992	1993	1994	1995	1996	1997	1998
Deutsche mark	18.6	0.0	0.0	0.0	0.0	0.0	0.0	0.0	0.0	0.0
French franc	0.0	0.0	4.7	4.5	4.2	4.5	4.8	4.6	4.2	4.4
Japanese yen	0.0	0.0	2.4	2.6	2.9	3.2	3.1	2.8	2.6	2.9
Pound sterling	0.0	0.4	0.2	0.1	0.1	0.1	0.1	0.1	0.1	0.1
Swiss franc	0.0	0.0	0.0	0.0	0.0	0.0	0.0	0.0	0.0	0.0
U.S.dollars	24.6	34.1	50.5	50.7	50.8	50.5	50.2	50.8	51.8	51.4
Multiple currency	47.9	16.7	7.2	7.1	7.0	7.2	7.4	7.2	7.2	7.2
Special drawing rights	0.0	0.0	1.3	1.3	1.3	1.3	1.3	1.3	1.3	1.3
All other currencies	8.9	48.8	33.7	33.7	33.7	33.2	33.1	33.2	32.8	32.7

SOMALIA

(US$ million, unless otherwise indicated)

	1970	1980	1990	1992	1993	1994	1995	1996	1997	1998
7. DEBT RESTRUCTURINGS										
Total amount rescheduled	..	..	0	0	0	0	0	0	0	0
Debt stock rescheduled	..	..	0	0	0	0	0	0	0	0
Principal rescheduled	..	..	0	0	0	0	0	0	0	0
Official	..	..	0	0	0	0	0	0	0	0
Private	..	..	0	0	0	0	0	0	0	0
Interest rescheduled	..	..	0	0	0	0	0	0	0	0
Official	..	..	0	0	0	0	0	0	0	0
Private	..	..	0	0	0	0	0	0	0	0
Debt forgiven	..	..	0	0	0	0	0	0	0	0
Memo: interest forgiven	..	..	0	0	0	0	0	0	0	0
Debt stock reduction	..	..	0	0	0	0	0	0	0	0
of which debt buyback	..	..	0	0	0	0	0	0	0	0
8. DEBT STOCK-FLOW RECONCILIATION										
Total change in debt stocks	..	..	211	-3	54	116	62	-35	-82	74
Net flows on debt	2	138	58	0	0	0	0	0	-7	5
Net change in interest arrears	..	..	71	51	55	68	33	13	0	28
Interest capitalized	..	..	0	0	0	0	0	0	0	0
Debt forgiveness or reduction	..	..	0	0	0	0	0	0	0	0
Cross-currency valuation	..	..	38	-31	0	25	13	-19	-33	24
Residual	..	..	44	-23	-1	23	16	-29	-43	16
9. AVERAGE TERMS OF NEW COMMITMENTS										
ALL CREDITORS										
Interest (%)	0.0	3.3	0.8	0.0	0.0	0.0	0.0	0.0	0.0	0.0
Maturity (years)	20.3	24.7	46.1	0.0	0.0	0.0	0.0	0.0	0.0	0.0
Grace period (years)	15.6	5.9	10.3	0.0	0.0	0.0	0.0	0.0	0.0	0.0
Grant element (%)	79.7	44.3	81.9	0.0	0.0	0.0	0.0	0.0	0.0	0.0
Official creditors										
Interest (%)	0.0	3.0	0.8	0.0	0.0	0.0	0.0	0.0	0.0	0.0
Maturity (years)	20.3	26.1	46.1	0.0	0.0	0.0	0.0	0.0	0.0	0.0
Grace period (years)	15.6	6.2	10.3	0.0	0.0	0.0	0.0	0.0	0.0	0.0
Grant element (%)	79.7	47.0	81.9	0.0	0.0	0.0	0.0	0.0	0.0	0.0
Private creditors										
Interest (%)	0.0	7.0	0.0	0.0	0.0	0.0	0.0	0.0	0.0	0.0
Maturity (years)	0.0	6.3	0.0	0.0	0.0	0.0	0.0	0.0	0.0	0.0
Grace period (years)	0.0	2.0	0.0	0.0	0.0	0.0	0.0	0.0	0.0	0.0
Grant element (%)	0.0	9.1	0.0	0.0	0.0	0.0	0.0	0.0	0.0	0.0
Memorandum items										
Commitments	22	188	72	0	0	0	0	0	0	0
Official creditors	22	174	72	0	0	0	0	0	0	0
Private creditors	0	14	0	0	0	0	0	0	0	0

10. CONTRACTUAL OBLIGATIONS ON OUTSTANDING LONG-TERM DEBT

	1999	2000	2001	2002	2003	2004	2005	2006	2007	2008
TOTAL										
Disbursements	0	0	0	0	0	0	0	0	0	0
Principal	40	38	35	32	30	30	29	27	29	29
Interest	13	12	11	10	9	9	8	8	7	7
Official creditors										
Disbursements	0	0	0	0	0	0	0	0	0	0
Principal	40	38	35	32	30	30	29	27	29	29
Interest	13	12	11	10	9	9	8	8	7	7
Bilateral creditors										
Disbursements	0	0	0	0	0	0	0	0	0	0
Principal	23	21	18	15	15	14	13	13	13	13
Interest	9	8	7	6	6	5	5	5	4	4
Multilateral creditors										
Disbursements	0	0	0	0	0	0	0	0	0	0
Principal	17	17	17	17	16	16	16	14	16	16
Interest	4	4	4	4	4	3	3	3	3	3
Private creditors										
Disbursements	0	0	0	0	0	0	0	0	0	0
Principal	0	0	0	0	0	0	0	0	0	0
Interest	0	0	0	0	0	0	0	0	0	0
Commercial banks										
Disbursements	0	0	0	0	0	0	0	0	0	0
Principal	0	0	0	0	0	0	0	0	0	0
Interest	0	0	0	0	0	0	0	0	0	0
Other private										
Disbursements	0	0	0	0	0	0	0	0	0	0
Principal	0	0	0	0	0	0	0	0	0	0
Interest	0	0	0	0	0	0	0	0	0	0

SOUTH AFRICA

(US$ million, unless otherwise indicated)

	1970	1980	1990	1992	1993	1994	1995	1996	1997	1998
1. SUMMARY DEBT DATA										
TOTAL DEBT STOCKS (EDT)	..	..	..	..	..	**21,671**	**25,358**	**26,050**	**25,221**	**24,712**
Long-term debt (LDOD)	..	..	..	..	..	**13,035**	**14,772**	**14,335**	**13,879**	**13,268**
Public and publicly guaranteed	..	..	..	..	..	7,789	9,837	10,348	11,466	10,627
Private nonguaranteed	..	..	..	..	..	5,246	4,935	3,987	2,413	2,641
Use of IMF credit	**0**	**0**	**0**	**0**	**844**	**897**	**913**	**884**	**415**	**0**
Short-term debt	..	..	..	..	..	**7,739**	**9,673**	**10,832**	**10,928**	**11,444**
of which interest arrears on LDOD	..	..	..	..	..	0	0	0	0	0
Official creditors	..	..	..	..	..	0	0	0	0	0
Private creditors	..	..	..	..	..	0	0	0	0	0
Memo: principal arrears on LDOD	..	..	..	..	..	0	0	0	0	0
Official creditors	..	..	..	..	..	0	0	0	0	0
Private creditors	..	..	..	..	..	0	0	0	0	0
Memo: export credits	..	..	..	..	..	5,086	3,925	3,383	3,828	3,329
TOTAL DEBT FLOWS										
Disbursements	..	..	..	..	..	**3,518**	**3,549**	**2,291**	**4,576**	**2,046**
Long-term debt	..	..	..	..	..	3,518	3,549	2,291	4,576	2,046
IMF purchases	0	0	0	0	858	0	0	0	0	0
Principal repayments	..	..	..	..	..	**1,995**	**2,070**	**2,770**	**5,103**	**2,849**
Long-term debt	..	..	..	..	..	1,995	2,070	2,770	4,680	2,432
IMF repurchases	0	0	0	0	0	0	0	0	423	417
Net flows on debt	..	..	..	..	..	**9,263**	**3,412**	**681**	**-432**	**-287**
of which short-term debt	..	..	..	..	..	7,739	1,934	1,159	96	516
Interest payments (INT)	..	..	..	..	..	**907**	**1,320**	**1,467**	**1,439**	**1,530**
Long-term debt	..	..	..	..	..	617	855	923	850	892
IMF charges	0	0	0	0	0	38	50	40	34	15
Short-term debt	..	..	..	..	..	251	415	504	555	622
Net transfers on debt	..	..	..	..	..	**8,356**	**2,092**	**-786**	**-1,870**	**-1,816**
Total debt service paid (TDS)	..	..	..	..	..	**2,902**	**3,391**	**4,236**	**6,542**	**4,378**
Long-term debt	..	..	..	..	..	2,612	2,926	3,692	5,530	3,324
IMF repurchases and charges	0	0	0	0	0	38	50	40	456	432
Short-term debt (interest only)	..	..	..	..	..	251	415	504	555	622
2. AGGREGATE NET RESOURCE FLOWS AND NET TRANSFERS (LONG-TERM)										
NET RESOURCE FLOWS	..	..	..	..	..	**2,222**	**7,198**	**2,241**	**5,299**	**1,029**
Net flow of long-term debt (ex. IMF)	..	..	..	..	..	1,524	1,478	-478	-105	-386
Foreign direct investment (net)	..	..	..	..	..	334	993	816	3,811	550
Portfolio equity flows	..	..	..	..	..	219	4,571	1,759	1,393	619
Grants (excluding technical coop.)	..	..	..	..	..	146	156	143	200	246
Memo: technical coop. grants	..	..	..	..	..	149	214	207	243	210
official net resource flows	..	..	..	..	..	146	156	143	200	246
private net resource flows	..	..	..	..	..	2,076	7,043	2,097	5,099	783
NET TRANSFERS	..	..	..	..	..	**-1,396**	**3,743**	**-1,082**	**2,449**	**-2,063**
Interest on long-term debt	..	..	..	..	..	617	855	923	850	892
Profit remittances on FDI	..	..	..	..	..	3,000	2,600	2,400	2,000	2,200
Memo: official net transfers	..	..	..	..	..	146	156	143	200	246
private net transfers	..	..	..	..	..	-1,541	3,587	-1,226	2,249	-2,310
3. MAJOR ECONOMIC AGGREGATES										
Gross national product (GNP)	..	..	..	..	..	133,397	148,242	139,920	144,406	130,444
Exports of goods & services (XGS)	..	..	..	..	..	31,056	35,826	36,368	37,803	35,845
of which workers remittances	..	..	..	..	..	0	0	..	..	..
Imports of goods & services (MGS)	..	..	..	..	..	30,333	37,384	37,495	39,352	37,035
International reserves (RES)	..	..	..	..	..	3,295	4,464	2,341	5,957	5,508
Current account balance	..	..	..	..	..	114	-2,204	-1,881	-2,273	-1,936
4. DEBT INDICATORS										
EDT / XGS (%)	..	..	..	..	..	69.8	70.8	71.6	66.7	68.9
EDT / GNP (%)	..	..	..	..	..	16.3	17.1	18.6	17.5	18.9
TDS / XGS (%)	..	..	..	..	..	9.3	9.5	11.7	17.3	12.2
INT / XGS (%)	..	..	..	..	..	2.9	3.7	4.0	3.8	4.3
INT / GNP (%)	..	..	..	..	..	0.7	0.9	1.1	1.0	1.2
RES / EDT (%)	..	..	..	..	..	15.2	17.6	9.0	23.6	22.3
RES / MGS (months)	..	..	..	..	..	1.3	1.4	0.8	1.8	1.8
Short-term / EDT (%)	..	..	..	..	..	35.7	38.2	41.6	43.3	46.3
Concessional / EDT (%)	..	..	..	..	..	0.0	0.0	0.0	0.0	0.0
Multilateral / EDT (%)	..	..	..	..	..	0.0	0.0	0.0	0.0	0.0

SOUTH AFRICA

(US$ million, unless otherwise indicated)

	1970	1980	1990	1992	1993	1994	1995	1996	1997	1998
5. LONG-TERM DEBT										
DEBT OUTSTANDING (LDOD)	..	..	..	..	..	**13,035**	**14,772**	**14,335**	**13,879**	**13,268**
Public and publicly guaranteed	..	..	..	..	..	**7,789**	**9,837**	**10,348**	**11,466**	**10,627**
Official creditors	..	..	..	..	..	0	0	0	0	0
Multilateral	..	..	..	..	..	0	0	0	0	0
Concessional	..	..	..	..	..	0	0	0	0	0
Bilateral	..	..	..	..	..	0	0	0	0	0
Concessional	..	..	..	..	..	0	0	0	0	0
Private creditors	..	..	..	..	..	7,789	9,837	10,348	11,466	10,627
Bonds	..	..	..	..	..	2,062	2,454	2,749	3,631	3,649
Commercial banks	..	..	..	..	..	3,867	3,978	3,563	3,275	2,597
Other private	..	..	..	..	..	1,860	3,405	4,036	4,559	4,381
Private nonguaranteed	..	..	..	..	..	**5,246**	**4,935**	**3,987**	**2,413**	**2,641**
Bonds	..	..	..	..	..	0	350	350	395	786
Commercial banks	..	..	..	..	..	5,246	4,585	3,637	2,018	1,855
Memo:										
IBRD	0	0	0	0	0	0	0	0	0	0
IDA	0	0	0	0	0	0	0	0	0	0
DISBURSEMENTS	..	..	..	..	..	**3,518**	**3,549**	**2,291**	**4,576**	**2,046**
Public and publicly guaranteed	..	..	..	..	..	**3,068**	**3,199**	**2,152**	**2,950**	**1,290**
Official creditors	..	..	..	..	..	0	0	0	0	0
Multilateral	..	..	..	..	..	0	0	0	0	0
Concessional	..	..	..	..	..	0	0	0	0	0
Bilateral	..	..	..	..	..	0	0	0	0	0
Concessional	..	..	..	..	..	0	0	0	0	0
Private creditors	..	..	..	..	..	3,068	3,199	2,152	2,950	1,290
Bonds	..	..	..	..	..	1,510	391	632	1,278	0
Commercial banks	..	..	..	..	..	941	830	419	672	840
Other private	..	..	..	..	..	617	1,978	1,101	1,000	450
Private nonguaranteed	..	..	..	..	..	**450**	**350**	**139**	**1,626**	**756**
Bonds	..	..	..	..	..	0	350	0	45	373
Commercial banks	..	..	..	..	..	450	0	139	1,581	383
Memo:										
IBRD	0	0	0	0	0	0	0	0	0	0
IDA	0	0	0	0	0	0	0	0	0	0
PRINCIPAL REPAYMENTS	..	..	..	..	..	**1,995**	**2,070**	**2,770**	**4,680**	**2,432**
Public and publicly guaranteed	..	..	..	..	..	**1,145**	**1,168**	**1,568**	**1,480**	**1,886**
Official creditors	..	..	..	..	..	0	0	0	0	0
Multilateral	..	..	..	..	..	0	0	0	0	0
Concessional	..	..	..	..	..	0	0	0	0	0
Bilateral	..	..	..	..	..	0	0	0	0	0
Concessional	..	..	..	..	..	0	0	0	0	0
Private creditors	..	..	..	..	..	1,145	1,168	1,568	1,480	1,886
Bonds	..	..	..	..	..	7	10	266	253	70
Commercial banks	..	..	..	..	..	787	719	834	752	1,187
Other private	..	..	..	..	..	351	439	467	475	628
Private nonguaranteed	..	..	..	..	..	**850**	**902**	**1,202**	**3,200**	**546**
Bonds	..	..	..	..	..	0	0	0	0	0
Commercial banks	..	..	..	..	..	850	902	1,202	3,200	546
Memo:										
IBRD	0	0	0	0	0	0	0	0	0	0
IDA	0	0	0	0	0	0	0	0	0	0
NET FLOWS ON DEBT	..	..	..	..	..	**1,524**	**1,478**	**-478**	**-105**	**-386**
Public and publicly guaranteed	..	..	..	..	..	**1,924**	**2,030**	**585**	**1,469**	**-596**
Official creditors	..	..	..	..	..	0	0	0	0	0
Multilateral	..	..	..	..	..	0	0	0	0	0
Concessional	..	..	..	..	..	0	0	0	0	0
Bilateral	..	..	..	..	..	0	0	0	0	0
Concessional	..	..	..	..	..	0	0	0	0	0
Private creditors	..	..	..	..	..	1,924	2,030	585	1,469	-596
Bonds	..	..	..	..	..	1,503	381	367	1,025	-70
Commercial banks	..	..	..	..	..	154	111	-415	-80	-347
Other private	..	..	..	..	..	266	1,539	634	525	-178
Private nonguaranteed	..	..	..	..	..	**-400**	**-552**	**-1,063**	**-1,574**	**210**
Bonds	..	..	..	..	..	0	350	0	45	373
Commercial banks	..	..	..	..	..	-400	-902	-1,063	-1,619	-163
Memo:										
IBRD	0	0	0	0	0	0	0	0	0	0
IDA	0	0	0	0	0	0	0	0	0	0

SOUTH AFRICA

(US$ million, unless otherwise indicated)

	1970	1980	1990	1992	1993	1994	1995	1996	1997	1998
INTEREST PAYMENTS (LINT)	..	..	..	..	..	**617**	**855**	**923**	**850**	**892**
Public and publicly guaranteed	..	..	..	..	..	**339**	**597**	**667**	**669**	**759**
Official creditors	..	..	..	..	..	0	0	0	0	0
Multilateral	..	..	..	..	..	0	0	0	0	0
Concessional	..	..	..	..	..	0	0	0	0	0
Bilateral	..	..	..	..	..	0	0	0	0	0
Concessional	..	..	..	..	..	0	0	0	0	0
Private creditors	..	..	..	..	..	339	597	667	669	759
Bonds	..	..	..	..	..	56	188	194	207	266
Commercial banks	..	..	..	..	..	166	245	220	228	226
Other private	..	..	..	..	..	118	164	254	234	266
Private nonguaranteed	..	..	..	..	..	**278**	**258**	**256**	**181**	**134**
Bonds	..	..	..	..	..	0	0	25	25	27
Commercial banks	..	..	..	..	..	278	258	231	156	107
Memo:										
IBRD	0	0	0	0	0	0	0	0	0	0
IDA	0	0	0	0	0	0	0	0	0	0
NET TRANSFERS ON DEBT	..	..	..	..	..	**906**	**623**	**-1,401**	**-955**	**-1,278**
Public and publicly guaranteed	..	..	..	..	..	**1,584**	**1,433**	**-83**	**800**	**-1,354**
Official creditors	..	..	..	..	..	0	0	0	0	0
Multilateral	..	..	..	..	..	0	0	0	0	0
Concessional	..	..	..	..	..	0	0	0	0	0
Bilateral	..	..	..	..	..	0	0	0	0	0
Concessional	..	..	..	..	..	0	0	0	0	0
Private creditors	..	..	..	..	..	1,584	1,433	-83	800	-1,354
Bonds	..	..	..	..	..	1,448	193	173	818	-336
Commercial banks	..	..	..	..	..	-12	-135	-635	-309	-574
Other private	..	..	..	..	..	149	1,375	380	291	-445
Private nonguaranteed	..	..	..	..	..	**-678**	**-810**	**-1,319**	**-1,755**	**76**
Bonds	..	..	..	..	..	0	350	-25	20	346
Commercial banks	..	..	..	..	..	-678	-1,160	-1,294	-1,775	-270
Memo:										
IBRD	0	0	0	0	0	0	0	0	0	0
IDA	0	0	0	0	0	0	0	0	0	0
DEBT SERVICE (LTDS)	..	..	..	..	..	**2,612**	**2,926**	**3,692**	**5,530**	**3,324**
Public and publicly guaranteed	..	..	..	..	..	**1,484**	**1,766**	**2,235**	**2,150**	**2,644**
Official creditors	..	..	..	..	..	0	0	0	0	0
Multilateral	..	..	..	..	..	0	0	0	0	0
Concessional	..	..	..	..	..	0	0	0	0	0
Bilateral	..	..	..	..	..	0	0	0	0	0
Concessional	..	..	..	..	..	0	0	0	0	0
Private creditors	..	..	..	..	..	1,484	1,766	2,235	2,150	2,644
Bonds	..	..	..	..	..	63	198	460	460	336
Commercial banks	..	..	..	..	..	953	965	1,054	981	1,414
Other private	..	..	..	..	..	469	603	721	709	895
Private nonguaranteed	..	..	..	..	..	**1,128**	**1,160**	**1,458**	**3,381**	**680**
Bonds	..	..	..	..	..	0	0	25	25	27
Commercial banks	..	..	..	..	..	1,128	1,160	1,433	3,356	653
Memo:										
IBRD	0	0	0	0	0	0	0	0	0	0
IDA	0	0	0	0	0	0	0	0	0	0
UNDISBURSED DEBT	..	..	..	..	..	**0**	**26**	**226**	**1,750**	**956**
Official creditors	..	..	..	..	..	0	0	0	0	46
Private creditors	..	..	..	..	..	0	26	226	1,750	910
Memorandum items										
Concessional LDOD	..	..	..	..	..	0	0	0	0	0
Variable rate LDOD	..	..	..	..	..	9,113	8,913	7,550	5,607	5,189
Public sector LDOD	..	..	..	..	..	7,789	9,837	10,348	11,466	10,487
Private sector LDOD	..	..	..	..	..	5,246	4,935	3,987	2,413	2,781

6. CURRENCY COMPOSITION OF LONG-TERM DEBT (PERCENT)

	1970	1980	1990	1992	1993	1994	1995	1996	1997	1998
Deutsche mark	..	..	..	..	..	3.3	2.8	3.1	2.4	2.8
French franc	..	..	..	..	..	0.0	0.0	0.0	0.0	0.0
Japanese yen	..	..	..	..	..	0.0	3.0	2.5	4.7	5.7
Pound sterling	..	..	..	..	..	0.0	0.0	0.0	0.0	0.0
Swiss franc	..	..	..	..	..	0.0	0.0	0.0	0.0	0.0
U.S.dollars	..	..	..	..	..	92.2	90.6	91.3	92.7	91.3
Multiple currency	..	..	..	..	..	0.0	0.0	0.0	0.0	0.0
Special drawing rights	..	..	..	..	..	0.0	0.0	0.0	0.0	0.0
All other currencies	..	..	..	..	..	4.5	3.6	3.1	0.2	0.2

SOUTH AFRICA

(US$ million, unless otherwise indicated)

	1970	1980	1990	1992	1993	1994	1995	1996	1997	1998
7. DEBT RESTRUCTURINGS										
Total amount rescheduled	..	..	..	..	..	0	0	0	0	0
Debt stock rescheduled	..	..	..	..	..	0	0	0	0	0
Principal rescheduled	..	..	..	..	..	0	0	0	0	0
Official	..	..	..	..	..	0	0	0	0	0
Private	..	..	..	..	..	0	0	0	0	0
Interest rescheduled	..	..	..	..	..	..	0	0	0	0
Official	..	..	..	..	..	0	0	0	0	0
Private	..	..	..	..	..	0	0	0	0	0
Debt forgiven	..	..	..	..	..	0	0	0	0	0
Memo: interest forgiven	..	..	..	..	..	0	0	0	0	0
Debt stock reduction	..	..	..	..	..	0	0	0	0	0
of which debt buyback	..	..	..	..	..	0	0	0	0	0
8. DEBT STOCK-FLOW RECONCILIATION										
Total change in debt stocks	..	..	..	..	..	..	3,687	692	-829	-510
Net flows on debt	..	..	..	..	..	9,263	3,412	681	-432	-287
Net change in interest arrears	..	..	..	..	..	..	0	0	0	0
Interest capitalized	..	..	..	..	..	..	0	0	0	0
Debt forgiveness or reduction	..	..	..	..	..	..	0	0	0	0
Cross-currency valuation	..	..	..	..	..	..	39	-70	-97	98
Residual	..	..	..	..	..	..	236	81	-301	-320
9. AVERAGE TERMS OF NEW COMMITMENTS										
ALL CREDITORS										
Interest (%)	..	..	..	..	..	6.2	5.4	5.9	6.3	6.0
Maturity (years)	..	..	..	..	..	7.8	14.1	12.2	9.8	11.7
Grace period (years)	..	..	..	..	..	3.1	1.8	3.3	5.4	1.5
Grant element (%)	..	..	..	..	..	14.4	21.1	18.5	12.6	16.3
Official creditors										
Interest (%)	..	..	..	..	..	0.0	0.0	0.0	0.0	6.3
Maturity (years)	..	..	..	..	..	0.0	0.0	0.0	0.0	14.3
Grace period (years)	..	..	..	..	..	0.0	0.0	0.0	0.0	2.8
Grant element (%)	..	..	..	..	..	0.0	0.0	0.0	0.0	19.2
Private creditors										
Interest (%)	..	..	..	..	..	6.2	5.4	5.9	6.3	6.0
Maturity (years)	..	..	..	..	..	7.8	14.1	12.2	9.8	11.4
Grace period (years)	..	..	..	..	..	3.1	1.8	3.3	5.4	1.4
Grant element (%)	..	..	..	..	..	14.4	21.1	18.5	12.6	16.0
Memorandum items										
Commitments	..	..	..	..	..	3,068	3,225	2,352	4,474	496
Official creditors	..	..	..	..	..	0	0	0	0	46
Private creditors	..	..	..	..	..	3,068	3,225	2,352	4,474	450

10. CONTRACTUAL OBLIGATIONS ON OUTSTANDING LONG-TERM DEBT

	1999	2000	2001	2002	2003	2004	2005	2006	2007	2008
TOTAL										
Disbursements	643	286	15	12	0	0	0	0	0	0
Principal	4,869	2,507	1,609	686	730	614	264	564	264	264
Interest	814	529	431	369	325	235	219	203	162	146
Official creditors										
Disbursements	6	13	15	12	0	0	0	0	0	0
Principal	0	0	4	4	4	4	4	4	4	4
Interest	0	1	2	2	2	2	2	2	1	1
Bilateral creditors										
Disbursements	0	0	0	0	0	0	0	0	0	0
Principal	0	0	0	0	0	0	0	0	0	0
Interest	0	0	0	0	0	0	0	0	0	0
Multilateral creditors										
Disbursements	6	13	15	12	0	0	0	0	0	0
Principal	0	0	4	4	4	4	4	4	4	4
Interest	0	1	2	2	2	2	2	2	1	1
Private creditors										
Disbursements	637	273	0	0	0	0	0	0	0	0
Principal	4,869	2,507	1,605	682	726	611	260	560	260	260
Interest	814	528	429	366	322	233	217	201	161	145
Commercial banks										
Disbursements	637	273	0	0	0	0	0	0	0	0
Principal	1,575	1,152	754	18	4	4	0	0	0	0
Interest	160	96	37	1	0	0	0	0	0	0
Other private										
Disbursements	0	0	0	0	0	0	0	0	0	0
Principal	3,294	1,355	851	664	722	606	260	560	260	260
Interest	655	432	392	365	322	233	217	201	161	145

SRI LANKA

(US$ million, unless otherwise indicated)

	1970	1980	1990	1992	1993	1994	1995	1996	1997	1998
1. SUMMARY DEBT DATA										
TOTAL DEBT STOCKS (EDT)	..	**1,841**	**5,863**	**6,457**	**6,854**	**7,888**	**8,231**	**8,003**	**7,698**	**8,526**
Long-term debt (LDOD)	**317**	**1,231**	**5,049**	**5,742**	**6,071**	**6,732**	**7,101**	**6,906**	**6,785**	**7,726**
Public and publicly guaranteed	317	1,227	4,947	5,643	5,982	6,650	7,011	6,818	6,700	7,649
Private nonguaranteed	0	3	102	99	90	83	90	88	84	77
Use of IMF credit	**79**	**391**	**410**	**464**	**516**	**617**	**595**	**531**	**433**	**367**
Short-term debt	..	**220**	**405**	**250**	**266**	**538**	**535**	**566**	**480**	**433**
of which interest arrears on LDOD	..	0	11	19	25	32	35	123	118	137
Official creditors	..	0	0	0	0	0	0	20	22	27
Private creditors	..	0	11	19	25	32	35	103	96	110
Memo: principal arrears on LDOD	..	0	0	4	8	11	42	169	190	242
Official creditors	..	0	0	0	0	2	3	37	40	58
Private creditors	..	0	0	4	8	9	39	132	149	185
Memo: export credits	..	0	566	470	550	755	905	754	672	758
TOTAL DEBT FLOWS										
Disbursements	**75**	**344**	**545**	**539**	**504**	**551**	**557**	**463**	**613**	**725**
Long-term debt	66	272	485	381	426	471	557	463	613	725
IMF purchases	10	72	61	158	78	80	0	0	0	0
Principal repayments	**57**	**94**	**214**	**329**	**253**	**247**	**259**	**261**	**280**	**302**
Long-term debt	30	51	167	252	228	234	225	216	214	220
IMF repurchases	27	43	47	77	25	13	34	45	66	82
Net flows on debt	**57**	**334**	**331**	**47**	**261**	**569**	**293**	**145**	**251**	**357**
of which short-term debt	..	84	0	-164	11	265	-6	-57	-82	-66
Interest payments (INT)	..	**85**	**170**	**154**	**142**	**147**	**161**	**161**	**148**	**150**
Long-term debt	12	33	122	134	130	128	133	132	121	129
IMF charges	0	17	21	8	3	3	3	3	2	2
Short-term debt	..	36	27	13	9	17	24	26	24	19
Net transfers on debt	..	**248**	**161**	**-107**	**119**	**422**	**132**	**-16**	**103**	**207**
Total debt service paid (TDS)	..	**179**	**384**	**482**	**395**	**395**	**419**	**422**	**428**	**452**
Long-term debt	42	84	289	386	358	362	358	348	336	349
IMF repurchases and charges	27	59	69	84	28	16	37	48	69	84
Short-term debt (interest only)	..	36	27	13	9	17	24	26	24	19
2. AGGREGATE NET RESOURCE FLOWS AND NET TRANSFERS (LONG-TERM)										
NET RESOURCE FLOWS	**51**	**425**	**582**	**394**	**590**	**675**	**624**	**578**	**1,037**	**818**
Net flow of long-term debt (ex. IMF)	36	221	318	129	198	237	333	247	398	505
Foreign direct investment (net)	0	43	43	123	195	166	56	120	430	193
Portfolio equity flows	0	0	0	0	0	112	61	70	98	6
Grants (excluding technical coop.)	15	161	221	142	197	160	174	141	111	114
Memo: technical coop. grants	7	57	105	131	114	98	114	96	93	80
official net resource flows	55	296	529	304	468	448	491	448	413	493
private net resource flows	-4	129	54	89	122	227	133	129	625	325
NET TRANSFERS	**31**	**377**	**435**	**227**	**427**	**507**	**457**	**406**	**872**	**639**
Interest on long-term debt	12	33	122	134	130	128	133	132	121	129
Profit remittances on FDI	8	15	25	33	33	40	34	40	44	50
Memo: official net transfers	47	270	452	210	368	345	382	337	310	391
private net transfers	-16	107	-17	16	59	162	76	69	562	248
3. MAJOR ECONOMIC AGGREGATES										
Gross national product (GNP)	2,259	3,997	7,865	9,527	10,215	11,551	12,893	13,708	14,931	15,528
Exports of goods & services (XGS)	..	1,492	2,786	3,539	4,164	4,821	5,630	5,868	6,669	6,861
of which workers remittances	..	152	401	548	632	715	790	832	922	999
Imports of goods & services (MGS)	..	2,269	3,224	4,086	4,636	5,658	6,342	6,477	6,974	7,053
International reserves (RES)	43	283	447	980	1,654	2,070	2,112	1,985	2,042	1,998
Current account balance	..	-655	-298	-451	-382	-757	-770	-683	-395	-288
4. DEBT INDICATORS										
EDT / XGS (%)	..	123.4	210.4	182.5	164.6	163.6	146.2	136.4	115.4	124.3
EDT / GNP (%)	..	46.1	74.6	67.8	67.1	68.3	63.8	58.4	51.6	54.9
TDS / XGS (%)	..	12.0	13.8	13.6	9.5	8.2	7.4	7.2	6.4	6.6
INT / XGS (%)	..	5.7	6.1	4.3	3.4	3.1	2.9	2.7	2.2	2.2
INT / GNP (%)	..	2.1	2.2	1.6	1.4	1.3	1.2	1.2	1.0	1.0
RES / EDT (%)	..	15.4	7.6	15.2	24.1	26.2	25.7	24.8	26.5	23.4
RES / MGS (months)	..	1.5	1.7	2.9	4.3	4.4	4.0	3.7	3.5	3.4
Short-term / EDT (%)	..	11.9	6.9	3.9	3.9	6.8	6.5	7.1	6.2	5.1
Concessional / EDT (%)	..	56.0	71.9	76.5	78.1	76.6	77.6	78.4	78.8	80.4
Multilateral / EDT (%)	..	11.7	27.7	32.5	34.5	33.7	34.7	36.8	37.4	37.8

SRI LANKA

(US$ million, unless otherwise indicated)

	1970	1980	1990	1992	1993	1994	1995	1996	1997	1998
5. LONG-TERM DEBT										
DEBT OUTSTANDING (LDOD)	**317**	**1,231**	**5,049**	**5,742**	**6,071**	**6,732**	**7,101**	**6,906**	**6,785**	**7,726**
Public and publicly guaranteed	**317**	**1,227**	**4,947**	**5,643**	**5,982**	**6,650**	**7,011**	**6,818**	**6,700**	**7,649**
Official creditors	253	1,087	4,349	5,061	5,460	6,148	6,485	6,368	6,175	6,970
Multilateral	29	216	1,623	2,100	2,363	2,656	2,858	2,942	2,878	3,222
Concessional	1	177	1,536	2,031	2,302	2,600	2,806	2,899	2,845	3,192
Bilateral	224	872	2,726	2,960	3,098	3,492	3,627	3,426	3,296	3,748
Concessional	186	854	2,681	2,908	3,048	3,441	3,577	3,376	3,224	3,662
Private creditors	64	140	598	582	521	501	526	450	526	679
Bonds	12	0	0	0	0	0	0	0	50	115
Commercial banks	3	57	253	272	244	261	306	266	316	394
Other private	49	83	345	310	277	240	220	184	160	170
Private nonguaranteed	**0**	**3**	**102**	**99**	**90**	**83**	**90**	**88**	**84**	**77**
Bonds	0	0	0	0	0	0	0	0	0	0
Commercial banks	0	3	102	99	90	83	90	88	84	77
Memo:										
IBRD	26	31	82	65	58	54	49	40	31	26
IDA	1	98	864	1,095	1,222	1,339	1,463	1,516	1,514	1,648
DISBURSEMENTS	**66**	**272**	**485**	**381**	**426**	**471**	**557**	**463**	**613**	**725**
Public and publicly guaranteed	**66**	**269**	**485**	**381**	**426**	**471**	**557**	**463**	**613**	**725**
Official creditors	55	174	396	309	396	420	462	450	460	553
Multilateral	4	32	234	209	258	172	197	258	176	226
Concessional	1	31	233	209	258	172	197	258	176	226
Bilateral	52	142	162	100	137	248	265	192	283	327
Concessional	40	141	162	100	137	246	262	190	256	315
Private creditors	11	96	89	72	30	51	95	12	153	172
Bonds	0	0	0	0	0	0	0	0	50	65
Commercial banks	0	57	54	48	16	51	84	9	102	107
Other private	11	39	35	24	15	0	11	3	1	0
Private nonguaranteed	**0**	**2**	**0**	**0**	**0**	**0**	**0**	**0**	**0**	**0**
Bonds	0	0	0	0	0	0	0	0	0	0
Commercial banks	0	2	0	0	0	0	0	0	0	0
Memo:										
IBRD	1	0	1	0	0	0	0	0	0	0
IDA	1	20	127	74	130	78	106	104	78	97
PRINCIPAL REPAYMENTS	**30**	**51**	**167**	**252**	**228**	**234**	**225**	**216**	**214**	**220**
Public and publicly guaranteed	**30**	**51**	**165**	**249**	**224**	**232**	**223**	**212**	**207**	**213**
Official creditors	16	39	89	147	125	131	145	143	158	174
Multilateral	2	5	21	25	27	26	26	29	37	43
Concessional	0	2	13	17	18	18	19	22	31	37
Bilateral	14	34	68	121	97	105	120	114	121	131
Concessional	6	28	64	85	92	101	115	113	121	130
Private creditors	14	12	76	102	99	100	77	70	49	39
Bonds	3	0	0	0	0	0	0	0	0	0
Commercial banks	1	0	29	48	40	41	45	49	42	34
Other private	10	12	47	54	59	60	32	21	8	5
Private nonguaranteed	**0**	**0**	**2**	**3**	**4**	**3**	**2**	**3**	**7**	**7**
Bonds	0	0	0	0	0	0	0	0	0	0
Commercial banks	0	0	2	3	4	3	2	3	7	7
Memo:										
IBRD	2	2	7	8	9	8	7	6	6	6
IDA	0	0	3	6	6	7	8	9	11	13
NET FLOWS ON DEBT	**36**	**221**	**318**	**129**	**198**	**237**	**333**	**247**	**398**	**505**
Public and publicly guaranteed	**36**	**219**	**320**	**132**	**202**	**239**	**335**	**250**	**405**	**512**
Official creditors	40	135	307	163	271	288	317	308	302	379
Multilateral	2	27	214	184	231	146	171	229	140	183
Concessional	1	30	220	192	240	154	178	236	146	189
Bilateral	38	108	94	-21	40	142	146	78	162	196
Concessional	34	113	98	15	45	145	146	77	136	185
Private creditors	-4	84	13	-30	-69	-49	18	-57	104	133
Bonds	-3	0	0	0	0	0	0	0	50	65
Commercial banks	-1	57	24	0	-25	10	39	-39	61	73
Other private	1	27	-12	-31	-44	-59	-21	-18	-7	-5
Private nonguaranteed	**0**	**2**	**-2**	**-3**	**-4**	**-3**	**-2**	**-3**	**-7**	**-7**
Bonds	0	0	0	0	0	0	0	0	0	0
Commercial banks	0	2	-2	-3	-4	-3	-2	-3	-7	-7
Memo:										
IBRD	-1	-2	-6	-8	-9	-8	-7	-6	-6	-6
IDA	1	20	124	68	123	71	98	95	68	84

SRI LANKA

(US$ million, unless otherwise indicated)

	1970	1980	1990	1992	1993	1994	1995	1996	1997	1998
INTEREST PAYMENTS (LINT)	**12**	**33**	**122**	**134**	**130**	**128**	**133**	**132**	**121**	**129**
Public and publicly guaranteed	**12**	**33**	**120**	**132**	**129**	**127**	**132**	**131**	**118**	**125**
Official creditors	8	25	77	94	100	104	109	112	102	102
Multilateral	3	5	19	23	25	26	29	28	28	27
Concessional	0	2	11	17	19	21	24	24	25	25
Bilateral	6	20	58	71	75	77	81	83	75	75
Concessional	3	19	55	67	71	77	81	83	74	72
Private creditors	4	8	43	38	29	23	23	19	15	23
Bonds	1	0	0	0	0	0	0	0	0	4
Commercial banks	0	0	16	20	15	14	18	17	14	18
Other private	3	8	27	18	14	10	5	3	2	1
Private nonguaranteed	**0**	**0**	**2**	**2**	**1**	**1**	**1**	**1**	**3**	**5**
Bonds	0	0	0	0	0	0	0	0	0	0
Commercial banks	0	0	2	2	1	1	1	1	3	5
Memo:										
IBRD	3	3	8	7	6	5	5	4	3	3
IDA	0	1	6	8	9	10	11	11	11	11
NET TRANSFERS ON DEBT	**24**	**188**	**196**	**-5**	**68**	**109**	**199**	**115**	**277**	**376**
Public and publicly guaranteed	**24**	**186**	**200**	**0**	**73**	**113**	**202**	**120**	**287**	**387**
Official creditors	32	110	230	69	171	185	207	196	199	277
Multilateral	-1	22	195	161	206	120	143	201	112	156
Concessional	1	28	209	176	222	133	154	211	121	164
Bilateral	33	87	35	-92	-35	65	65	-5	87	121
Concessional	31	94	43	-53	-26	69	66	-6	62	113
Private creditors	-8	76	-30	-69	-98	-72	-5	-77	88	110
Bonds	-4	0	0	0	0	0	0	0	50	61
Commercial banks	-1	57	8	-20	-40	-4	21	-56	47	54
Other private	-2	19	-38	-49	-58	-69	-26	-21	-9	-5
Private nonguaranteed	**0**	**2**	**-4**	**-5**	**-5**	**-4**	**-3**	**-5**	**-10**	**-12**
Bonds	0	0	0	0	0	0	0	0	0	0
Commercial banks	0	2	-4	-5	-5	-4	-3	-5	-10	-12
Memo:										
IBRD	-3	-5	-13	-15	-15	-13	-12	-11	-9	-8
IDA	1	19	118	60	115	61	88	84	57	72
DEBT SERVICE (LTDS)	**42**	**84**	**289**	**386**	**358**	**362**	**358**	**348**	**336**	**349**
Public and publicly guaranteed	**42**	**84**	**285**	**381**	**353**	**358**	**355**	**343**	**325**	**338**
Official creditors	24	64	166	241	224	235	255	254	260	276
Multilateral	4	10	39	49	52	52	54	57	64	70
Concessional	0	3	24	33	37	39	43	47	55	62
Bilateral	19	54	126	192	172	183	201	197	196	206
Concessional	9	47	119	153	163	178	196	196	195	202
Private creditors	18	20	119	140	128	124	100	89	65	62
Bonds	4	0	0	0	0	0	0	0	0	4
Commercial banks	1	0	46	68	55	55	63	65	55	53
Other private	13	20	74	72	73	69	37	24	10	5
Private nonguaranteed	**0**	**0**	**4**	**5**	**5**	**4**	**3**	**5**	**10**	**12**
Bonds	0	0	0	0	0	0	0	0	0	0
Commercial banks	0	0	4	5	5	4	3	5	10	12
Memo:										
IBRD	4	5	14	15	15	13	12	11	9	8
IDA	0	1	8	14	15	16	19	20	22	24
UNDISBURSED DEBT	**215**	**1,147**	**2,170**	**2,333**	**2,513**	**2,781**	**2,509**	**2,809**	**2,607**	**2,594**
Official creditors	196	899	2,070	2,256	2,429	2,651	2,475	2,778	2,584	2,573
Private creditors	19	248	99	77	84	130	35	31	24	21
Memorandum items										
Concessional LDOD	187	1,031	4,217	4,939	5,350	6,041	6,383	6,276	6,068	6,854
Variable rate LDOD	0	85	256	323	311	297	309	260	342	504
Public sector LDOD	311	1,219	4,854	5,543	5,871	6,526	6,891	6,711	6,605	7,541
Private sector LDOD	5	11	194	199	201	206	210	194	180	185

6. CURRENCY COMPOSITION OF LONG-TERM DEBT (PERCENT)

	1970	1980	1990	1992	1993	1994	1995	1996	1997	1998
Deutsche mark	13.8	11.2	12.0	9.5	8.1	8.0	8.0	7.4	6.5	6.1
French franc	3.6	2.7	3.2	2.7	2.3	2.2	2.2	2.0	1.7	1.6
Japanese yen	6.4	15.0	22.7	25.4	27.5	29.8	29.2	27.8	26.4	27.8
Pound sterling	28.8	2.3	3.2	2.2	1.7	1.3	1.4	1.5	1.4	1.1
Swiss franc	0.3	2.4	0.9	0.6	0.5	0.5	0.5	0.4	0.4	0.3
U.S.dollars	19.7	37.0	36.2	36.9	36.5	34.5	34.9	36.1	39.6	39.1
Multiple currency	14.3	8.5	13.9	16.6	18.0	18.8	19.0	20.0	19.5	19.8
Special drawing rights	0.0	0.0	0.5	0.5	0.5	0.5	0.5	0.5	0.5	0.5
All other currencies	13.1	20.9	7.4	5.6	4.9	4.4	4.3	4.3	4.0	3.7

SRI LANKA

(US$ million, unless otherwise indicated)

	1970	1980	1990	1992	1993	1994	1995	1996	1997	1998
7. DEBT RESTRUCTURINGS										
Total amount rescheduled	..	..	0	0	0	0	0	0	0	0
Debt stock rescheduled	..	..	0	0	0	0	0	0	0	0
Principal rescheduled	..	..	0	0	0	0	0	0	0	0
Official	..	..	0	0	0	0	0	0	0	0
Private	..	..	0	0	0	0	0	0	0	0
Interest rescheduled	..	..	0	0	0	0	0	0	0	0
Official	..	..	0	0	0	0	0	0	0	0
Private	..	..	0	0	0	0	0	0	0	0
Debt forgiven	..	..	0	0	0	0	7	0	0	0
Memo: interest forgiven	..	..	0	0	0	0	0	0	0	0
Debt stock reduction	..	..	0	0	0	0	0	0	0	0
of which debt buyback	..	..	0	0	0	0	0	0	0	0
8. DEBT STOCK-FLOW RECONCILIATION										
Total change in debt stocks	..	..	682	-123	397	1,034	343	-229	-305	828
Net flows on debt	57	334	331	47	261	569	293	145	251	357
Net change in interest arrears	..	..	4	4	6	7	3	88	-5	19
Interest capitalized	..	..	0	0	0	0	0	0	0	0
Debt forgiveness or reduction	..	..	0	0	0	0	-7	0	0	0
Cross-currency valuation	..	..	237	-91	132	334	16	-273	-293	311
Residual	..	..	110	-82	-2	124	38	-188	-258	142
9. AVERAGE TERMS OF NEW COMMITMENTS										
ALL CREDITORS										
Interest (%)	3.0	3.9	1.8	2.5	2.4	2.8	2.4	3.2	3.4	5.1
Maturity (years)	27.1	30.5	34.7	29.9	30.6	27.2	32.9	28.1	25.2	29.7
Grace period (years)	4.9	7.7	9.5	9.0	8.9	8.4	9.9	8.4	7.7	8.7
Grant element (%)	47.9	50.4	69.3	60.3	60.8	55.2	62.6	53.6	50.0	37.6
Official creditors										
Interest (%)	2.9	1.3	1.4	2.1	1.9	2.3	2.4	3.1	2.2	4.4
Maturity (years)	27.9	40.9	36.2	31.9	33.1	30.6	32.9	28.3	30.8	37.7
Grace period (years)	5.1	9.9	10.0	9.8	9.6	9.5	9.9	8.4	9.2	10.0
Grant element (%)	49.2	75.1	73.0	65.1	67.0	62.1	62.6	53.8	62.5	47.1
Private creditors										
Interest (%)	5.9	8.7	8.5	5.6	6.9	5.6	0.0	3.6	7.9	7.0
Maturity (years)	7.4	11.9	8.5	13.5	8.7	8.9	0.0	10.8	5.0	5.2
Grace period (years)	1.4	3.8	0.8	2.1	2.3	2.6	0.0	1.3	2.0	4.7
Grant element (%)	12.6	5.8	4.3	21.2	7.2	18.0	0.0	27.6	5.1	8.2
Memorandum items										
Commitments	81	752	837	489	623	585	404	1,042	686	689
Official creditors	78	484	791	435	558	494	404	1,033	537	520
Private creditors	3	268	46	54	64	91	0	8	149	169

10. CONTRACTUAL OBLIGATIONS ON OUTSTANDING LONG-TERM DEBT

	1999	2000	2001	2002	2003	2004	2005	2006	2007	2008
TOTAL										
Disbursements	722	674	492	345	213	91	53	6	0	0
Principal	418	308	292	320	327	338	352	364	375	456
Interest	161	157	168	175	170	163	158	154	147	140
Official creditors										
Disbursements	710	669	489	344	212	91	53	6	0	0
Principal	206	219	258	292	299	314	328	342	358	381
Interest	127	137	151	160	157	151	148	145	139	133
Bilateral creditors										
Disbursements	461	461	334	234	154	64	36	0	0	0
Principal	161	168	194	221	227	237	247	252	262	270
Interest	94	104	118	126	124	119	114	109	102	94
Multilateral creditors										
Disbursements	249	208	155	110	59	26	17	5	0	0
Principal	45	51	64	71	72	77	81	89	96	111
Interest	32	33	33	33	33	32	33	35	37	39
Private creditors										
Disbursements	12	6	3	1	0	0	0	0	0	0
Principal	212	89	34	28	28	24	24	22	17	76
Interest	34	20	18	15	14	12	10	9	8	7
Commercial banks										
Disbursements	5	2	1	0	0	0	0	0	0	0
Principal	182	29	25	18	18	16	17	15	10	4
Interest	23	12	10	8	7	5	4	3	2	2
Other private										
Disbursements	7	3	2	1	0	0	0	0	0	0
Principal	31	60	10	10	10	8	7	7	7	72
Interest	11	8	8	7	7	6	6	6	6	5

ST. KITTS AND NEVIS

(US$ million, unless otherwise indicated)

	1970	1980	1990	1992	1993	1994	1995	1996	1997	1998
1. SUMMARY DEBT DATA										
TOTAL DEBT STOCKS (EDT)	..	..	**45.2**	**51.4**	**53.7**	**58.1**	**56.4**	**64.1**	**110.6**	**115.1**
Long-term debt (LDOD)	..	..	**44.2**	**47.4**	**49.7**	**55.1**	**53.8**	**62.2**	**108.5**	**111.3**
Public and publicly guaranteed	..	..	44.2	47.4	49.7	55.1	53.8	62.2	108.5	111.3
Private nonguaranteed	..	..	0.0	0.0	0.0	0.0	0.0	0.0	0.0	0.0
Use of IMF credit	**0.0**	**0.0**	**0.0**	**0.0**	**0.0**	**0.0**	**0.0**	**0.0**	**0.0**	**2.3**
Short-term debt	..	..	**1.0**	**4.0**	**4.0**	**3.0**	**2.7**	**1.9**	**2.1**	**1.5**
of which interest arrears on LDOD	..	..	0.0	0.9	0.9	1.0	1.2	0.2	0.1	0.3
Official creditors	..	..	0.0	0.9	0.8	1.0	1.2	0.2	0.1	0.3
Private creditors	..	..	0.0	0.0	0.0	0.0	0.0	0.0	0.0	0.0
Memo: principal arrears on LDOD	..	..	0.0	0.3	0.3	0.7	0.7	0.0	0.1	0.1
Official creditors	..	..	0.0	0.3	0.3	0.6	0.3	0.0	0.0	0.1
Private creditors	..	..	0.0	0.0	0.0	0.1	0.4	0.0	0.1	0.0
Memo: export credits	..	..	30.0	26.0	23.0	24.0	29.0	32.0	58.0	46.0
TOTAL DEBT FLOWS										
Disbursements	..	..	**7.3**	**3.7**	**6.5**	**8.2**	**5.5**	**13.0**	**51.8**	**14.1**
Long-term debt	..	..	7.3	3.7	6.5	8.2	5.5	13.0	51.8	11.9
IMF purchases	0.0	0.0	0.0	0.0	0.0	0.0	0.0	0.0	0.0	2.2
Principal repayments	..	..	**1.5**	**2.5**	**3.4**	**3.7**	**4.9**	**4.6**	**4.5**	**5.6**
Long-term debt	..	..	1.5	2.5	3.4	3.7	4.9	4.6	4.5	5.6
IMF repurchases	0.0	0.0	0.0	0.0	0.0	0.0	0.0	0.0	0.0	0.0
Net flows on debt	..	..	**6.8**	**3.2**	**3.1**	**3.4**	**0.0**	**8.7**	**47.5**	**7.7**
of which short-term debt	..	..	1.0	2.0	0.0	-1.1	-0.6	0.3	0.2	-0.8
Interest payments (INT)	..	..	**1.5**	**1.2**	**1.5**	**1.9**	**2.0**	**2.1**	**2.2**	**4.8**
Long-term debt	..	..	1.4	1.0	1.3	1.7	1.9	2.0	2.1	4.7
IMF charges	0.0	0.0	0.0	0.0	0.0	0.0	0.0	0.0	0.0	0.0
Short-term debt	..	..	0.1	0.2	0.2	0.1	0.1	0.1	0.1	0.1
Net transfers on debt	..	..	**5.3**	**2.0**	**1.6**	**1.5**	**-2.0**	**6.6**	**45.3**	**2.9**
Total debt service paid (TDS)	..	..	**3.0**	**3.7**	**4.9**	**5.6**	**6.9**	**6.7**	**6.7**	**10.4**
Long-term debt	..	..	2.9	3.5	4.7	5.5	6.8	6.6	6.6	10.3
IMF repurchases and charges	0.0	0.0	0.0	0.0	0.0	0.0	0.0	0.0	0.0	0.0
Short-term debt (interest only)	..	..	0.1	0.2	0.2	0.1	0.1	0.1	0.1	0.1
2. AGGREGATE NET RESOURCE FLOWS AND NET TRANSFERS (LONG-TERM)										
NET RESOURCE FLOWS	..	..	**56.8**	**15.2**	**17.2**	**20.0**	**21.4**	**26.6**	**72.0**	**35.7**
Net flow of long-term debt (ex. IMF)	..	..	5.8	1.2	3.1	4.5	0.6	8.4	47.3	6.3
Foreign direct investment (net)	..	..	49.0	13.0	14.0	15.0	20.0	17.0	25.0	24.0
Portfolio equity flows	..	..	0.0	0.0	0.0	0.0	0.0	0.0	0.0	0.0
Grants (excluding technical coop.)	..	..	2.0	1.0	0.2	0.4	0.8	1.2	-0.3	5.4
Memo: technical coop. grants	..	..	2.3	2.1	6.3	4.0	2.3	2.3	2.3	1.0
official net resource flows	..	..	8.2	1.8	3.0	2.7	2.3	10.8	32.6	13.7
private net resource flows	..	..	48.6	13.4	14.2	17.3	19.1	15.8	39.4	22.0
NET TRANSFERS	..	..	**50.4**	**3.7**	**7.4**	**9.3**	**11.0**	**14.6**	**58.8**	**21.0**
Interest on long-term debt	..	..	1.4	1.0	1.3	1.7	1.9	2.0	2.1	4.7
Profit remittances on FDI	..	..	5.0	10.5	8.5	9.0	8.5	10.0	11.0	10.0
Memo: official net transfers	..	..	6.8	0.9	1.8	1.2	0.8	9.1	30.7	10.5
private net transfers	..	..	43.6	2.8	5.6	8.1	10.2	5.5	28.1	10.5
3. MAJOR ECONOMIC AGGREGATES										
Gross national product (GNP)	..	..	152.3	173.3	188.3	209.9	221.5	229.9	249.1	266.5
Exports of goods & services (XGS)	..	..	102.8	127.9	131.4	137.9	119.1	123.7	141.9	145.4
of which workers remittances	..	..	17.2	13.3	13.6	14.1	..	..	..	..
Imports of goods & services (MGS)	..	..	140.1	138.4	155.8	159.7	190.6	213.0	222.1	252.4
International reserves (RES)	..	..	16.3	26.2	29.4	31.8	33.5	32.7	36.1	46.8
Current account balance	..	..	-47.0	-15.8	-30.1	-26.4	-53.5	-73.8	-65.0	-68.2
4. DEBT INDICATORS										
EDT / XGS (%)	..	..	44.0	40.2	40.9	42.1	47.4	51.8	78.0	79.2
EDT / GNP (%)	..	..	29.7	29.7	28.5	27.7	25.5	27.9	44.4	43.2
TDS / XGS (%)	..	..	2.9	2.9	3.7	4.1	5.8	5.4	4.7	7.2
INT / XGS (%)	..	..	1.5	0.9	1.1	1.4	1.7	1.7	1.6	3.3
INT / GNP (%)	..	..	1.0	0.7	0.8	0.9	0.9	0.9	0.9	1.8
RES / EDT (%)	..	..	36.0	51.1	54.8	54.8	59.4	51.1	32.6	40.7
RES / MGS (months)	..	..	1.4	2.3	2.3	2.4	2.1	1.8	2.0	2.2
Short-term / EDT (%)	..	..	2.2	7.8	7.5	5.2	4.8	3.0	1.9	1.3
Concessional / EDT (%)	..	..	76.6	70.2	71.0	67.1	72.9	80.3	75.0	75.8
Multilateral / EDT (%)	..	..	44.3	42.0	46.7	46.3	52.0	52.1	35.9	34.7

ST. KITTS AND NEVIS

(US$ million, unless otherwise indicated)

	1970	1980	1990	1992	1993	1994	1995	1996	1997	1998
5. LONG-TERM DEBT										
DEBT OUTSTANDING (LDOD)	..	..	**44.2**	**47.4**	**49.7**	**55.1**	**53.8**	**62.2**	**108.5**	**111.3**
Public and publicly guaranteed	..	..	**44.2**	**47.4**	**49.7**	**55.1**	**53.8**	**62.2**	**108.5**	**111.3**
Official creditors	..	..	41.4	43.2	45.3	48.4	48.2	57.8	89.7	94.5
Multilateral	..	..	20.0	21.6	25.1	26.9	29.3	33.4	39.7	39.9
Concessional	..	..	15.1	17.2	20.1	21.0	23.4	28.0	33.4	32.8
Bilateral	..	..	21.5	21.6	20.2	21.5	18.8	24.4	50.0	54.6
Concessional	..	..	19.5	18.9	18.0	18.0	17.7	23.5	49.5	54.4
Private creditors	..	..	2.7	4.2	4.4	6.7	5.6	4.4	18.8	16.8
Bonds	..	..	0.0	0.0	0.0	0.0	0.0	0.0	0.0	0.0
Commercial banks	..	..	0.0	0.0	0.0	0.0	0.0	0.0	15.0	14.3
Other private	..	..	2.7	4.2	4.4	6.7	5.6	4.4	3.8	2.4
Private nonguaranteed	..	..	**0.0**	**0.0**	**0.0**	**0.0**	**0.0**	**0.0**	**0.0**	**0.0**
Bonds	..	..	0.0	0.0	0.0	0.0	0.0	0.0	0.0	0.0
Commercial banks	..	..	0.0	0.0	0.0	0.0	0.0	0.0	0.0	0.0
Memo:										
IBRD	0.0	0.0	0.0	0.2	0.2	0.8	1.1	1.0	0.9	0.8
IDA	0.0	0.0	0.0	0.6	1.4	1.6	1.6	1.6	1.5	1.5
DISBURSEMENTS	..	..	**7.3**	**3.7**	**6.5**	**8.2**	**5.5**	**13.0**	**51.8**	**11.9**
Public and publicly guaranteed	..	..	**7.3**	**3.7**	**6.5**	**8.2**	**5.5**	**13.0**	**51.8**	**11.9**
Official creditors	..	..	7.3	2.4	5.2	4.9	5.0	12.5	35.9	11.9
Multilateral	..	..	2.4	2.4	5.2	2.6	3.7	6.1	9.2	6.0
Concessional	..	..	2.3	2.1	4.0	1.7	3.4	6.0	7.3	4.6
Bilateral	..	..	4.9	0.0	0.0	2.3	1.3	6.5	26.8	5.9
Concessional	..	..	4.9	0.0	0.0	0.2	1.3	6.5	26.8	5.9
Private creditors	..	..	0.0	1.3	1.3	3.3	0.6	0.5	15.8	0.0
Bonds	..	..	0.0	0.0	0.0	0.0	0.0	0.0	0.0	0.0
Commercial banks	..	..	0.0	0.0	0.0	0.0	0.0	0.0	15.0	0.0
Other private	..	..	0.0	1.3	1.3	3.3	0.6	0.5	0.8	0.0
Private nonguaranteed	..	..	**0.0**	**0.0**	**0.0**	**0.0**	**0.0**	**0.0**	**0.0**	**0.0**
Bonds	..	..	0.0	0.0	0.0	0.0	0.0	0.0	0.0	0.0
Commercial banks	..	..	0.0	0.0	0.0	0.0	0.0	0.0	0.0	0.0
Memo:										
IBRD	0.0	0.0	0.0	0.2	0.0	0.6	0.3	0.0	0.0	0.2
IDA	0.0	0.0	0.0	0.6	0.9	0.1	0.0	0.0	0.0	0.0
PRINCIPAL REPAYMENTS	..	..	**1.5**	**2.5**	**3.4**	**3.7**	**4.9**	**4.6**	**4.5**	**5.6**
Public and publicly guaranteed	..	..	**1.5**	**2.5**	**3.4**	**3.7**	**4.9**	**4.6**	**4.5**	**5.6**
Official creditors	..	..	1.1	1.6	2.4	2.7	3.4	2.9	3.1	3.6
Multilateral	..	..	0.7	1.2	1.2	1.4	1.5	1.7	2.1	2.1
Concessional	..	..	0.6	0.9	0.9	1.1	1.0	1.3	1.5	1.6
Bilateral	..	..	0.3	0.4	1.2	1.2	1.9	1.2	0.9	1.4
Concessional	..	..	0.2	0.1	0.7	0.5	1.6	0.9	0.6	1.2
Private creditors	..	..	0.4	1.0	1.0	1.0	1.5	1.7	1.4	2.0
Bonds	..	..	0.0	0.0	0.0	0.0	0.0	0.0	0.0	0.0
Commercial banks	..	..	0.0	0.0	0.0	0.0	0.0	0.0	0.0	0.7
Other private	..	..	0.4	1.0	1.0	1.0	1.5	1.7	1.4	1.4
Private nonguaranteed	..	..	**0.0**	**0.0**	**0.0**	**0.0**	**0.0**	**0.0**	**0.0**	**0.0**
Bonds	..	..	0.0	0.0	0.0	0.0	0.0	0.0	0.0	0.0
Commercial banks	..	..	0.0	0.0	0.0	0.0	0.0	0.0	0.0	0.0
Memo:										
IBRD	0.0	0.0	0.0	0.0	0.0	0.0	0.0	0.0	0.1	0.1
IDA	0.0	0.0	0.0	0.0	0.0	0.0	0.0	0.0	0.0	0.0
NET FLOWS ON DEBT	..	..	**5.8**	**1.2**	**3.1**	**4.5**	**0.6**	**8.4**	**47.3**	**6.3**
Public and publicly guaranteed	..	..	**5.8**	**1.2**	**3.1**	**4.5**	**0.6**	**8.4**	**47.3**	**6.3**
Official creditors	..	..	6.2	0.8	2.8	2.3	1.5	9.6	32.9	8.3
Multilateral	..	..	1.7	1.2	4.0	1.2	2.2	4.4	7.0	3.8
Concessional	..	..	1.6	1.2	3.1	0.6	2.3	4.7	5.8	3.0
Bilateral	..	..	4.6	-0.4	-1.2	1.1	-0.7	5.2	25.8	4.5
Concessional	..	..	4.7	-0.1	-0.7	-0.3	-0.3	5.6	26.2	4.8
Private creditors	..	..	-0.4	0.4	0.2	2.3	-0.9	-1.2	14.4	-2.0
Bonds	..	..	0.0	0.0	0.0	0.0	0.0	0.0	0.0	0.0
Commercial banks	..	..	0.0	0.0	0.0	0.0	0.0	0.0	15.0	-0.7
Other private	..	..	-0.4	0.4	0.2	2.3	-0.9	-1.2	-0.6	-1.4
Private nonguaranteed	..	..	**0.0**	**0.0**	**0.0**	**0.0**	**0.0**	**0.0**	**0.0**	**0.0**
Bonds	..	..	0.0	0.0	0.0	0.0	0.0	0.0	0.0	0.0
Commercial banks	..	..	0.0	0.0	0.0	0.0	0.0	0.0	0.0	0.0
Memo:										
IBRD	0.0	0.0	0.0	0.2	0.0	0.6	0.3	0.0	-0.1	0.1
IDA	0.0	0.0	0.0	0.6	0.9	0.1	0.0	0.0	0.0	0.0

ST. KITTS AND NEVIS

(US$ million, unless otherwise indicated)

	1970	1980	1990	1992	1993	1994	1995	1996	1997	1998
INTEREST PAYMENTS (LINT)	..	..	**1.4**	**1.0**	**1.3**	**1.7**	**1.9**	**2.0**	**2.1**	**4.7**
Public and publicly guaranteed	..	..	**1.4**	**1.0**	**1.3**	**1.7**	**1.9**	**2.0**	**2.1**	**4.7**
Official creditors	..	..	1.4	0.9	1.2	1.5	1.5	1.7	1.9	3.2
Multilateral	..	..	0.7	0.5	0.8	0.9	1.0	1.1	1.0	1.3
Concessional	..	..	0.5	0.4	0.6	0.7	0.7	0.8	0.8	1.0
Bilateral	..	..	0.7	0.4	0.5	0.6	0.5	0.6	0.9	1.9
Concessional	..	..	0.6	0.3	0.3	0.4	0.4	0.5	0.8	1.9
Private creditors	..	..	0.0	0.1	0.1	0.2	0.4	0.3	0.3	1.5
Bonds	..	..	0.0	0.0	0.0	0.0	0.0	0.0	0.0	0.0
Commercial banks	..	..	0.0	0.0	0.0	0.0	0.0	0.0	0.0	1.4
Other private	..	..	0.0	0.1	0.1	0.2	0.4	0.3	0.2	0.2
Private nonguaranteed	..	..	**0.0**	**0.0**	**0.0**	**0.0**	**0.0**	**0.0**	**0.0**	**0.0**
Bonds	..	..	0.0	0.0	0.0	0.0	0.0	0.0	0.0	0.0
Commercial banks	..	..	0.0	0.0	0.0	0.0	0.0	0.0	0.0	0.0
Memo:										
IBRD	0.0	0.0	0.0	0.0	0.0	0.0	0.1	0.1	0.1	0.1
IDA	0.0	0.0	0.0	0.0	0.0	0.0	0.0	0.0	0.0	0.0
NET TRANSFERS ON DEBT	..	..	**4.4**	**0.1**	**1.7**	**2.8**	**-1.3**	**6.4**	**45.2**	**1.6**
Public and publicly guaranteed	..	..	**4.4**	**0.1**	**1.7**	**2.8**	**-1.3**	**6.4**	**45.2**	**1.6**
Official creditors	..	..	4.8	-0.1	1.6	0.8	0.1	7.9	31.0	5.1
Multilateral	..	..	1.0	0.7	3.3	0.3	1.3	3.3	6.0	2.6
Concessional	..	..	1.1	0.8	2.6	0.0	1.7	3.9	5.0	2.0
Bilateral	..	..	3.8	-0.8	-1.7	0.5	-1.2	4.6	25.0	2.6
Concessional	..	..	4.1	-0.4	-1.0	-0.7	-0.7	5.0	25.4	2.9
Private creditors	..	..	-0.5	0.3	0.1	2.0	-1.3	-1.5	14.2	-3.6
Bonds	..	..	0.0	0.0	0.0	0.0	0.0	0.0	0.0	0.0
Commercial banks	..	..	0.0	0.0	0.0	0.0	0.0	0.0	15.0	-2.0
Other private	..	..	-0.5	0.3	0.1	2.0	-1.3	-1.5	-0.8	-1.6
Private nonguaranteed	..	..	**0.0**	**0.0**	**0.0**	**0.0**	**0.0**	**0.0**	**0.0**	**0.0**
Bonds	..	..	0.0	0.0	0.0	0.0	0.0	0.0	0.0	0.0
Commercial banks	..	..	0.0	0.0	0.0	0.0	0.0	0.0	0.0	0.0
Memo:										
IBRD	0.0	0.0	0.0	0.2	0.0	0.6	0.3	-0.1	-0.2	0.0
IDA	0.0	0.0	0.0	0.6	0.8	0.1	0.0	0.0	0.0	0.0
DEBT SERVICE (LTDS)	..	..	**2.9**	**3.5**	**4.7**	**5.5**	**6.8**	**6.6**	**6.6**	**10.3**
Public and publicly guaranteed	..	..	**2.9**	**3.5**	**4.7**	**5.5**	**6.8**	**6.6**	**6.6**	**10.3**
Official creditors	..	..	2.4	2.5	3.6	4.2	4.9	4.6	5.0	6.7
Multilateral	..	..	1.4	1.7	2.0	2.3	2.4	2.7	3.2	3.4
Concessional	..	..	1.1	1.3	1.4	1.7	1.7	2.1	2.3	2.6
Bilateral	..	..	1.0	0.8	1.7	1.8	2.4	1.8	1.8	3.3
Concessional	..	..	0.8	0.4	1.0	0.9	2.0	1.5	1.4	3.0
Private creditors	..	..	0.5	1.1	1.1	1.3	1.9	2.0	1.6	3.6
Bonds	..	..	0.0	0.0	0.0	0.0	0.0	0.0	0.0	0.0
Commercial banks	..	..	0.0	0.0	0.0	0.0	0.0	0.0	0.0	2.0
Other private	..	..	0.5	1.1	1.1	1.3	1.9	2.0	1.6	1.6
Private nonguaranteed	..	..	**0.0**	**0.0**	**0.0**	**0.0**	**0.0**	**0.0**	**0.0**	**0.0**
Bonds	..	..	0.0	0.0	0.0	0.0	0.0	0.0	0.0	0.0
Commercial banks	..	..	0.0	0.0	0.0	0.0	0.0	0.0	0.0	0.0
Memo:										
IBRD	0.0	0.0	0.0	0.0	0.0	0.0	0.1	0.1	0.2	0.1
IDA	0.0	0.0	0.0	0.0	0.0	0.0	0.0	0.0	0.0	0.0
UNDISBURSED DEBT	..	..	**15.3**	**37.0**	**44.3**	**41.5**	**45.9**	**69.1**	**50.1**	**46.1**
Official creditors	..	..	14.3	35.7	44.3	40.5	45.4	69.1	50.1	46.1
Private creditors	..	..	1.1	1.3	0.0	1.0	0.5	0.0	0.0	0.0
Memorandum items										
Concessional LDOD	..	..	34.7	36.1	38.1	39.0	41.1	51.6	83.0	87.2
Variable rate LDOD	..	..	0.0	0.9	0.8	1.3	1.5	1.4	1.2	1.1
Public sector LDOD	..	..	40.7	44.4	47.5	53.4	52.5	61.3	108.0	111.2
Private sector LDOD	..	..	3.4	3.0	2.2	1.7	1.3	0.9	0.5	0.1

6. CURRENCY COMPOSITION OF LONG-TERM DEBT (PERCENT)

	1970	1980	1990	1992	1993	1994	1995	1996	1997	1998
Deutsche mark	..	..	0.0	0.0	0.0	0.0	0.0	0.0	0.0	0.0
French franc	..	..	0.0	0.0	0.0	0.0	0.0	0.0	0.0	0.0
Japanese yen	..	..	0.0	0.0	0.0	0.0	0.0	0.0	0.0	0.0
Pound sterling	..	..	16.3	13.1	11.3	9.8	7.3	5.8	3.7	3.1
Swiss franc	..	..	0.0	0.0	0.0	0.0	0.0	0.0	0.0	0.0
U.S.dollars	..	..	37.8	43.7	46.5	51.6	51.3	55.2	71.6	71.3
Multiple currency	..	..	35.5	35.9	36.2	33.1	34.0	29.1	16.1	14.4
Special drawing rights	..	..	0.0	0.0	0.0	0.0	0.0	0.0	0.0	0.0
All other currencies	..	..	10.4	7.3	6.0	5.5	7.4	9.9	8.6	11.2

ST. KITTS AND NEVIS

(US$ million, unless otherwise indicated)

	1970	1980	1990	1992	1993	1994	1995	1996	1997	1998
7. DEBT RESTRUCTURINGS										
Total amount rescheduled	..	..	0.0	0.0	0.0	0.0	0.0	0.0	0.0	0.0
Debt stock rescheduled	..	..	0.0	0.0	0.0	0.0	0.0	0.0	0.0	0.0
Principal rescheduled	..	..	0.0	0.0	0.0	0.0	0.0	0.0	0.0	0.0
Official	..	..	0.0	0.0	0.0	0.0	0.0	0.0	0.0	0.0
Private	..	..	0.0	0.0	0.0	0.0	0.0	0.0	0.0	0.0
Interest rescheduled	..	..	0.0	0.0	0.0	0.0	0.0	0.0	0.0	0.0
Official	..	..	0.0	0.0	0.0	0.0	0.0	0.0	0.0	0.0
Private	..	..	0.0	0.0	0.0	0.0	0.0	0.0	0.0	0.0
Debt forgiven	..	..	0.0	0.0	0.0	0.0	0.0	0.0	0.0	0.0
Memo: interest forgiven	..	..	0.0	0.0	0.0	0.0	0.0	0.0	0.0	0.0
Debt stock reduction	..	..	0.0	0.0	0.0	0.0	0.0	0.0	0.0	0.0
of which debt buyback	..	..	0.0	0.0	0.0	0.0	0.0	0.0	0.0	0.0
8. DEBT STOCK-FLOW RECONCILIATION										
Total change in debt stocks	..	..	8.6	1.6	2.3	4.4	-1.7	7.7	46.6	4.5
Net flows on debt	..	..	6.8	3.2	3.1	3.4	0.0	8.7	47.5	7.7
Net change in interest arrears	..	..	-0.1	0.9	-0.1	0.2	0.2	-1.1	0.0	0.2
Interest capitalized	..	..	0.0	0.0	0.0	0.0	0.0	0.0	0.0	0.0
Debt forgiveness or reduction	..	..	0.0	0.0	0.0	0.0	0.0	0.0	0.0	0.0
Cross-currency valuation	..	..	2.1	-1.5	-0.3	0.6	0.2	0.1	-0.7	0.4
Residual	..	..	-0.2	-0.9	-0.4	0.2	-2.1	-0.1	-0.2	-3.8
9. AVERAGE TERMS OF NEW COMMITMENTS										
ALL CREDITORS										
Interest (%)	..	..	4.0	2.8	3.8	5.1	3.7	2.0	6.8	6.4
Maturity (years)	..	..	31.7	26.1	21.9	6.9	18.8	32.2	12.8	15.4
Grace period (years)	..	..	7.5	8.0	6.0	1.8	5.2	9.5	6.5	3.8
Grant element (%)	..	..	41.5	54.2	43.7	16.8	40.7	66.1	17.9	19.9
Official creditors										
Interest (%)	..	..	4.5	2.0	3.8	2.0	3.7	2.0	4.9	6.4
Maturity (years)	..	..	38.0	31.7	21.9	10.9	18.8	32.2	15.0	15.4
Grace period (years)	..	..	9.0	9.8	6.0	3.4	5.2	9.5	3.5	3.8
Grant element (%)	..	..	46.1	65.9	43.7	38.4	40.7	66.1	27.8	19.9
Private creditors										
Interest (%)	..	..	2.0	5.9	0.0	5.8	0.0	0.0	8.9	0.0
Maturity (years)	..	..	5.8	6.0	0.0	6.0	0.0	0.0	10.2	0.0
Grace period (years)	..	..	1.3	1.6	0.0	1.5	0.0	0.0	10.0	0.0
Grant element (%)	..	..	22.5	11.8	0.0	12.3	0.0	0.0	6.2	0.0
Memorandum items										
Commitments	..	..	5.5	12.0	13.7	5.3	11.2	36.3	34.5	9.7
Official creditors	..	..	4.4	9.4	13.7	0.9	11.2	36.3	18.6	9.7
Private creditors	..	..	1.1	2.6	0.0	4.4	0.0	0.0	15.8	0.0

10. CONTRACTUAL OBLIGATIONS ON OUTSTANDING LONG-TERM DEBT

	1999	2000	2001	2002	2003	2004	2005	2006	2007	2008
TOTAL										
Disbursements	14.1	12.5	9.6	6.2	2.0	0.9	0.6	0.3	0.1	0.0
Principal	6.2	5.2	6.6	7.0	7.4	7.3	7.6	8.5	8.5	22.2
Interest	4.8	5.0	5.1	5.1	5.0	4.7	4.4	4.1	3.8	2.2
Official creditors										
Disbursements	14.1	12.5	9.6	6.2	2.0	0.9	0.6	0.3	0.1	0.0
Principal	4.5	4.9	6.5	6.8	7.3	7.3	7.6	8.5	8.5	7.8
Interest	3.3	3.6	3.8	3.8	3.7	3.4	3.1	2.8	2.5	2.2
Bilateral creditors										
Disbursements	4.6	2.4	1.4	0.6	0.2	0.0	0.0	0.0	0.0	0.0
Principal	2.4	2.8	3.9	3.8	3.9	3.8	4.2	4.5	4.5	3.9
Interest	2.0	2.0	1.9	1.8	1.7	1.5	1.4	1.2	1.1	0.9
Multilateral creditors										
Disbursements	9.5	10.1	8.1	5.6	1.7	0.9	0.6	0.3	0.1	0.0
Principal	2.0	2.1	2.6	3.0	3.5	3.5	3.4	4.0	4.0	4.0
Interest	1.3	1.6	1.9	2.0	2.0	1.9	1.7	1.6	1.5	1.3
Private creditors										
Disbursements	0.0	0.0	0.0	0.0	0.0	0.0	0.0	0.0	0.0	0.0
Principal	1.7	0.3	0.2	0.2	0.1	0.0	0.0	0.0	0.0	14.3
Interest	1.4	1.3	1.3	1.3	1.3	1.3	1.3	1.3	1.3	0.0
Commercial banks										
Disbursements	0.0	0.0	0.0	0.0	0.0	0.0	0.0	0.0	0.0	0.0
Principal	0.0	0.0	0.0	0.0	0.0	0.0	0.0	0.0	0.0	14.3
Interest	1.3	1.3	1.3	1.3	1.3	1.3	1.3	1.3	1.3	0.0
Other private										
Disbursements	0.0	0.0	0.0	0.0	0.0	0.0	0.0	0.0	0.0	0.0
Principal	1.7	0.3	0.2	0.2	0.1	0.0	0.0	0.0	0.0	0.0
Interest	0.1	0.1	0.0	0.0	0.0	0.0	0.0	0.0	0.0	0.0

ST. LUCIA

(US$ million, unless otherwise indicated)

	1970	1980	1990	1992	1993	1994	1995	1996	1997	1998
1. SUMMARY DEBT DATA										
TOTAL DEBT STOCKS (EDT)	..	..	**79.6**	**95.7**	**99.0**	**111.9**	**126.8**	**140.1**	**151.7**	**183.6**
Long-term debt (LDOD)	..	..	**72.6**	**87.6**	**94.6**	**101.9**	**109.8**	**119.9**	**118.7**	**127.1**
Public and publicly guaranteed	..	..	72.6	87.6	94.6	101.9	109.8	119.9	118.7	127.1
Private nonguaranteed	..	..	0.0	0.0	0.0	0.0	0.0	0.0	0.0	0.0
Use of IMF credit	**0.0**	**0.0**	**0.0**	**0.0**	**0.0**	**0.0**	**0.0**	**0.0**	**0.0**	**0.0**
Short-term debt	..	..	**7.0**	**8.2**	**4.4**	**10.0**	**16.9**	**20.2**	**33.0**	**56.5**
of which interest arrears on LDOD	..	..	0.8	0.0	0.0	0.0	0.0	0.0	0.0	0.0
Official creditors	..	..	0.8	0.0	0.0	0.0	0.0	0.0	0.0	0.0
Private creditors	..	..	0.0	0.0	0.0	0.0	0.0	0.0	0.0	0.0
Memo: principal arrears on LDOD	..	..	0.1	0.3	0.5	0.2	0.0	0.0	0.0	0.0
Official creditors	..	..	0.1	0.3	0.5	0.2	0.0	0.0	0.0	0.0
Private creditors	..	..	0.0	0.0	0.0	0.0	0.0	0.0	0.0	0.0
Memo: export credits	..	..	40.0	33.0	31.0	31.0	30.0	32.0	30.0	30.0
TOTAL DEBT FLOWS										
Disbursements	..	..	**8.1**	**28.0**	**15.6**	**8.9**	**11.5**	**17.5**	**10.1**	**14.1**
Long-term debt	..	..	8.1	28.0	15.6	8.9	11.5	17.5	10.1	14.1
IMF purchases	0.0	0.0	0.0	0.0	0.0	0.0	0.0	0.0	0.0	0.0
Principal repayments	..	..	**3.2**	**6.9**	**5.8**	**5.5**	**5.8**	**6.2**	**6.6**	**7.9**
Long-term debt	..	..	3.2	6.9	5.8	5.5	5.8	6.2	6.6	7.9
IMF repurchases	0.0	0.0	0.0	0.0	0.0	0.0	0.0	0.0	0.0	0.0
Net flows on debt	..	..	**7.1**	**23.0**	**6.0**	**9.0**	**12.6**	**14.7**	**16.4**	**29.7**
of which short-term debt	..	..	2.2	1.9	-3.8	5.6	6.9	3.3	12.8	23.5
Interest payments (INT)	..	..	**3.2**	**4.4**	**5.1**	**5.0**	**5.7**	**6.2**	**6.6**	**8.1**
Long-term debt	..	..	2.8	4.1	4.9	4.5	4.7	5.3	5.2	5.7
IMF charges	0.0	0.0	0.0	0.0	0.0	0.0	0.0	0.0	0.0	0.0
Short-term debt	..	..	0.3	0.3	0.2	0.5	0.9	0.9	1.4	2.4
Net transfers on debt	..	..	**4.0**	**18.6**	**0.9**	**4.0**	**7.0**	**8.4**	**9.7**	**21.6**
Total debt service paid (TDS)	..	..	**6.4**	**11.3**	**10.9**	**10.5**	**11.5**	**12.4**	**13.2**	**16.0**
Long-term debt	..	..	6.0	11.0	10.7	10.0	10.6	11.5	11.8	13.7
IMF repurchases and charges	0.0	0.0	0.0	0.0	0.0	0.0	0.0	0.0	0.0	0.0
Short-term debt (interest only)	..	..	0.3	0.3	0.2	0.5	0.9	0.9	1.4	2.4
2. AGGREGATE NET RESOURCE FLOWS AND NET TRANSFERS (LONG-TERM)										
NET RESOURCE FLOWS	..	..	**53.0**	**67.1**	**58.2**	**53.6**	**82.9**	**78.7**	**53.6**	**66.5**
Net flow of long-term debt (ex. IMF)	..	..	4.9	21.1	9.8	3.4	5.7	11.4	3.6	6.2
Foreign direct investment (net)	..	..	45.0	40.9	34.1	32.4	35.0	39.0	45.0	46.0
Portfolio equity flows	..	..	0.0	0.0	0.0	0.0	0.0	0.0	0.0	0.0
Grants (excluding technical coop.)	..	..	3.1	5.1	14.3	17.8	42.2	28.3	5.0	14.3
Memo: technical coop. grants	..	..	3.5	3.9	4.2	7.1	4.7	4.4	4.3	4.5
official net resource flows	..	..	8.8	27.0	24.6	21.2	47.9	39.7	8.6	13.5
private net resource flows	..	..	44.2	40.1	33.6	32.4	35.0	39.0	45.0	53.0
NET TRANSFERS	..	..	**23.7**	**33.9**	**20.3**	**15.1**	**45.2**	**43.4**	**16.4**	**27.8**
Interest on long-term debt	..	..	2.8	4.1	4.9	4.5	4.7	5.3	5.2	5.7
Profit remittances on FDI	..	..	26.5	29.1	33.0	34.0	33.0	30.0	32.0	33.0
Memo: official net transfers	..	..	6.2	23.0	19.7	16.7	43.2	34.4	3.4	7.8
private net transfers	..	..	17.5	10.9	0.6	-1.6	2.0	9.0	13.0	20.0
3. MAJOR ECONOMIC AGGREGATES										
Gross national product (GNP)	..	..	369.2	447.6	457.1	484.0	521.2	532.2	548.5	576.0
Exports of goods & services (XGS)	..	..	301.2	343.7	346.2	362.1	407.2	381.4	362.8	384.5
of which workers remittances	..	..	13.7	16.1	13.6	19.6	21.0	22.1	..	..
Imports of goods & services (MGS)	..	..	352.1	391.4	391.1	408.9	438.6	453.6	470.7	461.0
International reserves (RES)	..	..	44.6	55.5	60.0	57.8	63.1	56.1	61.0	70.6
Current account balance	..	..	-57.0	-54.8	-49.3	-48.5	-33.2	-80.3	-95.2	-64.0
4. DEBT INDICATORS										
EDT / XGS (%)	..	..	26.4	27.8	28.6	30.9	31.1	36.7	41.8	47.8
EDT / GNP (%)	..	..	21.6	21.4	21.7	23.1	24.3	26.3	27.7	31.9
TDS / XGS (%)	..	..	2.1	3.3	3.2	2.9	2.8	3.3	3.6	4.2
INT / XGS (%)	..	..	1.1	1.3	1.5	1.4	1.4	1.6	1.8	2.1
INT / GNP (%)	..	..	0.9	1.0	1.1	1.0	1.1	1.2	1.2	1.4
RES / EDT (%)	..	..	56.0	58.0	60.6	51.6	49.8	40.1	40.2	38.5
RES / MGS (months)	..	..	1.5	1.7	1.8	1.7	1.7	1.5	1.6	1.8
Short-term / EDT (%)	..	..	8.8	8.6	4.4	8.9	13.3	14.4	21.8	30.8
Concessional / EDT (%)	..	..	41.3	54.4	59.4	57.6	58.3	58.5	55.3	46.7
Multilateral / EDT (%)	..	..	53.6	59.7	65.4	62.1	61.1	60.5	55.8	47.1

ST. LUCIA

(US$ million, unless otherwise indicated)

	1970	1980	1990	1992	1993	1994	1995	1996	1997	1998
5. LONG-TERM DEBT										
DEBT OUTSTANDING (LDOD)	..	..	**72.6**	**87.6**	**94.6**	**101.9**	**109.8**	**119.9**	**118.7**	**127.1**
Public and publicly guaranteed	..	..	**72.6**	**87.6**	**94.6**	**101.9**	**109.8**	**119.9**	**118.7**	**127.1**
Official creditors	..	..	70.0	86.9	94.6	101.8	109.8	119.8	118.7	120.1
Multilateral	..	..	42.7	57.1	64.7	69.5	77.5	84.7	84.7	86.5
Concessional	..	..	32.5	42.1	46.1	48.9	56.2	60.6	61.6	61.9
Bilateral	..	..	27.3	29.9	29.9	32.3	32.3	35.1	33.9	33.6
Concessional	..	..	0.4	10.0	12.7	15.6	17.7	21.3	22.3	23.8
Private creditors	..	..	2.6	0.6	0.1	0.1	0.0	0.0	0.0	7.1
Bonds	..	..	0.0	0.0	0.0	0.0	0.0	0.0	0.0	0.0
Commercial banks	..	..	2.6	0.6	0.1	0.1	0.0	0.0	0.0	7.1
Other private	..	..	0.0	0.0	0.0	0.0	0.0	0.0	0.0	0.0
Private nonguaranteed	..	..	**0.0**	**0.0**	**0.0**	**0.0**	**0.0**	**0.0**	**0.0**	**0.0**
Bonds	..	..	0.0	0.0	0.0	0.0	0.0	0.0	0.0	0.0
Commercial banks	..	..	0.0	0.0	0.0	0.0	0.0	0.0	0.0	0.0
Memo:										
IBRD	0.0	0.0	0.0	0.0	0.4	1.5	2.1	3.9	3.7	5.4
IDA	0.0	0.0	0.0	4.4	5.3	5.7	7.9	8.2	9.7	11.4
DISBURSEMENTS	..	..	**8.1**	**28.0**	**15.6**	**8.9**	**11.5**	**17.5**	**10.1**	**14.1**
Public and publicly guaranteed	..	..	**8.1**	**28.0**	**15.6**	**8.9**	**11.5**	**17.5**	**10.1**	**14.1**
Official creditors	..	..	8.1	28.0	15.6	8.9	11.5	17.5	10.1	7.1
Multilateral	..	..	7.0	15.8	12.0	6.7	10.8	12.8	6.8	5.7
Concessional	..	..	4.3	11.1	7.6	4.0	9.3	7.9	5.2	2.9
Bilateral	..	..	1.1	12.1	3.6	2.2	0.8	4.8	3.3	1.4
Concessional	..	..	0.2	9.1	3.6	1.7	0.8	4.8	3.3	1.4
Private creditors	..	..	0.0	0.0	0.0	0.0	0.0	0.0	0.0	7.1
Bonds	..	..	0.0	0.0	0.0	0.0	0.0	0.0	0.0	0.0
Commercial banks	..	..	0.0	0.0	0.0	0.0	0.0	0.0	0.0	7.1
Other private	..	..	0.0	0.0	0.0	0.0	0.0	0.0	0.0	0.0
Private nonguaranteed	..	..	**0.0**	**0.0**	**0.0**	**0.0**	**0.0**	**0.0**	**0.0**	**0.0**
Bonds	..	..	0.0	0.0	0.0	0.0	0.0	0.0	0.0	0.0
Commercial banks	..	..	0.0	0.0	0.0	0.0	0.0	0.0	0.0	0.0
Memo:										
IBRD	0.0	0.0	0.0	0.0	0.5	1.0	0.7	2.2	0.4	1.5
IDA	0.0	0.0	0.0	4.0	0.8	0.2	2.1	0.6	2.0	1.2
PRINCIPAL REPAYMENTS	..	..	**3.2**	**6.9**	**5.8**	**5.5**	**5.8**	**6.2**	**6.6**	**7.9**
Public and publicly guaranteed	..	..	**3.2**	**6.9**	**5.8**	**5.5**	**5.8**	**6.2**	**6.6**	**7.9**
Official creditors	..	..	2.4	6.1	5.3	5.5	5.8	6.2	6.6	7.9
Multilateral	..	..	2.4	2.8	3.2	3.4	3.8	4.1	4.6	5.1
Concessional	..	..	2.0	2.2	2.4	2.3	2.6	2.7	2.8	3.3
Bilateral	..	..	0.0	3.3	2.1	2.1	2.0	2.1	2.0	2.8
Concessional	..	..	0.0	0.5	0.1	0.1	0.1	0.1	0.1	0.9
Private creditors	..	..	0.8	0.8	0.5	0.0	0.0	0.0	0.0	0.0
Bonds	..	..	0.0	0.0	0.0	0.0	0.0	0.0	0.0	0.0
Commercial banks	..	..	0.8	0.8	0.5	0.0	0.0	0.0	0.0	0.0
Other private	..	..	0.0	0.0	0.0	0.0	0.0	0.0	0.0	0.0
Private nonguaranteed	..	..	**0.0**	**0.0**	**0.0**	**0.0**	**0.0**	**0.0**	**0.0**	**0.0**
Bonds	..	..	0.0	0.0	0.0	0.0	0.0	0.0	0.0	0.0
Commercial banks	..	..	0.0	0.0	0.0	0.0	0.0	0.0	0.0	0.0
Memo:										
IBRD	0.0	0.0	0.0	0.0	0.0	0.0	0.1	0.2	0.2	0.2
IDA	0.0	0.0	0.0	0.0	0.0	0.0	0.0	0.0	0.0	0.0
NET FLOWS ON DEBT	..	..	**4.9**	**21.1**	**9.8**	**3.4**	**5.7**	**11.4**	**3.6**	**6.2**
Public and publicly guaranteed	..	..	**4.9**	**21.1**	**9.8**	**3.4**	**5.7**	**11.4**	**3.6**	**6.2**
Official creditors	..	..	5.7	21.9	10.3	3.4	5.7	11.4	3.6	-0.8
Multilateral	..	..	4.6	13.0	8.8	3.3	7.0	8.6	2.2	0.6
Concessional	..	..	2.2	9.0	5.2	1.7	6.7	5.1	2.4	-0.4
Bilateral	..	..	1.1	8.9	1.5	0.1	-1.3	2.7	1.3	-1.4
Concessional	..	..	0.2	8.6	3.5	1.6	0.7	4.7	3.3	0.5
Private creditors	..	..	-0.8	-0.8	-0.5	0.0	0.0	0.0	0.0	7.0
Bonds	..	..	0.0	0.0	0.0	0.0	0.0	0.0	0.0	0.0
Commercial banks	..	..	-0.8	-0.8	-0.5	0.0	0.0	0.0	0.0	7.0
Other private	..	..	0.0	0.0	0.0	0.0	0.0	0.0	0.0	0.0
Private nonguaranteed	..	..	**0.0**	**0.0**	**0.0**	**0.0**	**0.0**	**0.0**	**0.0**	**0.0**
Bonds	..	..	0.0	0.0	0.0	0.0	0.0	0.0	0.0	0.0
Commercial banks	..	..	0.0	0.0	0.0	0.0	0.0	0.0	0.0	0.0
Memo:										
IBRD	0.0	0.0	0.0	0.0	0.5	1.0	0.6	2.0	0.2	1.3
IDA	0.0	0.0	0.0	4.0	0.8	0.2	2.1	0.6	2.0	1.2

ST. LUCIA

(US$ million, unless otherwise indicated)

	1970	1980	1990	1992	1993	1994	1995	1996	1997	1998
INTEREST PAYMENTS (LINT)	..	..	**2.8**	**4.1**	**4.9**	**4.5**	**4.7**	**5.3**	**5.2**	**5.7**
Public and publicly guaranteed	..	..	**2.8**	**4.1**	**4.9**	**4.5**	**4.7**	**5.3**	**5.2**	**5.7**
Official creditors	..	..	2.6	4.0	4.9	4.5	4.7	5.3	5.2	5.7
Multilateral	..	..	1.8	2.1	2.5	2.7	2.9	3.4	3.7	3.9
Concessional	..	..	1.3	1.2	1.4	1.5	1.6	1.7	1.9	2.0
Bilateral	..	..	0.8	1.9	2.3	1.7	1.8	1.9	1.5	1.8
Concessional	..	..	0.0	0.6	1.0	0.8	0.9	0.9	0.9	0.9
Private creditors	..	..	0.2	0.1	0.0	0.0	0.0	0.0	0.0	0.0
Bonds	..	..	0.0	0.0	0.0	0.0	0.0	0.0	0.0	0.0
Commercial banks	..	..	0.2	0.1	0.0	0.0	0.0	0.0	0.0	0.0
Other private	..	..	0.0	0.0	0.0	0.0	0.0	0.0	0.0	0.0
Private nonguaranteed	..	..	**0.0**	**0.0**	**0.0**	**0.0**	**0.0**	**0.0**	**0.0**	**0.0**
Bonds	..	..	0.0	0.0	0.0	0.0	0.0	0.0	0.0	0.0
Commercial banks	..	..	0.0	0.0	0.0	0.0	0.0	0.0	0.0	0.0
Memo:										
IBRD	0.0	0.0	0.0	0.0	0.0	0.0	0.1	0.2	0.3	0.3
IDA	0.0	0.0	0.0	0.0	0.0	0.0	0.0	0.1	0.1	0.1
NET TRANSFERS ON DEBT	..	..	**2.1**	**17.0**	**4.9**	**-1.1**	**1.0**	**6.0**	**-1.6**	**0.5**
Public and publicly guaranteed	..	..	**2.1**	**17.0**	**4.9**	**-1.1**	**1.0**	**6.0**	**-1.6**	**0.5**
Official creditors	..	..	3.1	17.9	5.4	-1.1	1.0	6.1	-1.6	-6.6
Multilateral	..	..	2.8	10.9	6.3	0.5	4.0	5.2	-1.4	-3.3
Concessional	..	..	1.0	7.7	3.8	0.2	5.1	3.4	0.5	-2.4
Bilateral	..	..	0.3	6.9	-0.8	-1.6	-3.1	0.9	-0.2	-3.2
Concessional	..	..	0.2	7.9	2.6	0.8	-0.3	3.8	2.4	-0.4
Private creditors	..	..	-1.0	-0.9	-0.6	0.0	0.0	0.0	0.0	7.0
Bonds	..	..	0.0	0.0	0.0	0.0	0.0	0.0	0.0	0.0
Commercial banks	..	..	-1.0	-0.9	-0.6	0.0	0.0	0.0	0.0	7.0
Other private	..	..	0.0	0.0	0.0	0.0	0.0	0.0	0.0	0.0
Private nonguaranteed	..	..	**0.0**	**0.0**	**0.0**	**0.0**	**0.0**	**0.0**	**0.0**	**0.0**
Bonds	..	..	0.0	0.0	0.0	0.0	0.0	0.0	0.0	0.0
Commercial banks	..	..	0.0	0.0	0.0	0.0	0.0	0.0	0.0	0.0
Memo:										
IBRD	0.0	0.0	0.0	0.0	0.5	1.0	0.4	1.8	-0.1	1.1
IDA	0.0	0.0	0.0	3.9	0.8	0.1	2.0	0.5	1.9	1.2
DEBT SERVICE (LTDS)	..	..	**6.0**	**11.0**	**10.7**	**10.0**	**10.6**	**11.5**	**11.8**	**13.7**
Public and publicly guaranteed	..	..	**6.0**	**11.0**	**10.7**	**10.0**	**10.6**	**11.5**	**11.8**	**13.7**
Official creditors	..	..	5.0	10.1	10.1	10.0	10.6	11.5	11.8	13.6
Multilateral	..	..	4.2	4.9	5.7	6.2	6.7	7.5	8.2	9.0
Concessional	..	..	3.3	3.4	3.8	3.8	4.2	4.5	4.7	5.3
Bilateral	..	..	0.8	5.2	4.4	3.8	3.8	3.9	3.5	4.6
Concessional	..	..	0.0	1.1	1.0	0.9	1.0	1.0	0.9	1.7
Private creditors	..	..	1.0	0.9	0.6	0.0	0.0	0.0	0.0	0.0
Bonds	..	..	0.0	0.0	0.0	0.0	0.0	0.0	0.0	0.0
Commercial banks	..	..	1.0	0.9	0.6	0.0	0.0	0.0	0.0	0.0
Other private	..	..	0.0	0.0	0.0	0.0	0.0	0.0	0.0	0.0
Private nonguaranteed	..	..	**0.0**	**0.0**	**0.0**	**0.0**	**0.0**	**0.0**	**0.0**	**0.0**
Bonds	..	..	0.0	0.0	0.0	0.0	0.0	0.0	0.0	0.0
Commercial banks	..	..	0.0	0.0	0.0	0.0	0.0	0.0	0.0	0.0
Memo:										
IBRD	0.0	0.0	0.0	0.0	0.0	0.0	0.2	0.4	0.5	0.4
IDA	0.0	0.0	0.0	0.0	0.0	0.0	0.0	0.1	0.1	0.1
UNDISBURSED DEBT	..	..	**49.9**	**42.9**	**33.9**	**32.7**	**68.0**	**53.2**	**60.6**	**57.6**
Official creditors	..	..	49.9	42.9	33.9	32.7	68.0	53.2	46.6	50.3
Private creditors	..	..	0.0	0.0	0.0	0.0	0.0	0.0	14.1	7.3
Memorandum items										
Concessional LDOD	..	..	32.9	52.1	58.8	64.5	73.9	81.9	84.0	85.8
Variable rate LDOD	..	..	0.0	0.0	0.4	1.6	2.2	4.5	5.1	7.5
Public sector LDOD	..	..	72.6	87.6	94.6	101.9	109.8	119.9	118.7	127.1
Private sector LDOD	..	..	0.0	0.0	0.0	0.0	0.0	0.0	0.0	0.0

6. CURRENCY COMPOSITION OF LONG-TERM DEBT (PERCENT)

	1970	1980	1990	1992	1993	1994	1995	1996	1997	1998
Deutsche mark	..	..	5.9	4.2	3.3	3.0	2.7	2.0	1.6	1.4
French franc	..	..	0.3	11.3	13.3	15.3	16.1	14.2	13.3	12.6
Japanese yen	..	..	4.0	3.7	3.4	3.1	2.5	1.8	1.3	1.0
Pound sterling	..	..	39.9	22.6	18.8	16.8	13.8	12.3	10.4	8.1
Swiss franc	..	..	1.1	0.8	0.6	0.6	0.5	0.3	0.3	0.2
U.S.dollars	..	..	32.6	46.5	52.1	51.4	54.1	58.6	63.1	60.8
Multiple currency	..	..	0.0	0.0	0.6	2.0	3.4	5.3	5.1	6.1
Special drawing rights	..	..	0.8	0.5	1.2	1.9	1.8	1.6	1.8	2.0
All other currencies	..	..	15.4	10.4	6.7	5.9	5.1	3.9	3.1	7.8

ST. LUCIA

(US$ million, unless otherwise indicated)

	1970	1980	1990	1992	1993	1994	1995	1996	1997	1998
7. DEBT RESTRUCTURINGS										
Total amount rescheduled	..	..	0.0	0.0	0.0	0.0	0.0	0.0	0.0	0.0
Debt stock rescheduled	..	..	0.0	0.0	0.0	0.0	0.0	0.0	0.0	0.0
Principal rescheduled	..	..	0.0	0.0	0.0	0.0	0.0	0.0	0.0	0.0
Official	..	..	0.0	0.0	0.0	0.0	0.0	0.0	0.0	0.0
Private	..	..	0.0	0.0	0.0	0.0	0.0	0.0	0.0	0.0
Interest rescheduled	..	..	0.0	0.0	0.0	0.0	0.0	0.0	0.0	0.0
Official	..	..	0.0	0.0	0.0	0.0	0.0	0.0	0.0	0.0
Private	..	..	0.0	0.0	0.0	0.0	0.0	0.0	0.0	0.0
Debt forgiven	..	..	0.4	0.0	0.6	0.2	0.0	0.0	0.0	0.0
Memo: interest forgiven	..	..	0.0	0.0	0.0	0.0	0.0	0.0	0.0	0.0
Debt stock reduction	..	..	0.0	0.0	0.0	0.0	0.0	0.0	0.0	0.0
of which debt buyback	..	..	0.0	0.0	0.0	0.0	0.0	0.0	0.0	0.0
8. DEBT STOCK-FLOW RECONCILIATION										
Total change in debt stocks	..	..	14.0	16.2	3.3	12.9	14.9	13.3	11.6	32.0
Net flows on debt	..	..	7.1	23.0	6.0	9.0	12.6	14.7	16.4	29.7
Net change in interest arrears	..	..	0.8	0.0	0.0	0.0	0.0	0.0	0.0	0.0
Interest capitalized	..	..	0.0	0.0	0.0	0.0	0.0	0.0	0.0	0.0
Debt forgiveness or reduction	..	..	-0.4	0.0	-0.6	-0.2	0.0	0.0	0.0	0.0
Cross-currency valuation	..	..	7.6	-5.6	-1.6	3.9	2.2	-0.6	-3.6	1.8
Residual	..	..	-1.1	-1.2	-0.5	0.2	0.1	-0.8	-1.1	0.5
9. AVERAGE TERMS OF NEW COMMITMENTS										
ALL CREDITORS										
Interest (%)	..	..	4.3	3.6	3.6	4.1	4.7	5.7	6.1	3.0
Maturity (years)	..	..	24.1	31.1	19.6	19.9	24.8	16.0	12.9	25.6
Grace period (years)	..	..	8.2	8.2	5.3	4.1	7.1	3.1	8.0	7.4
Grant element (%)	..	..	42.8	52.0	41.7	36.9	38.4	20.4	23.5	53.2
Official creditors										
Interest (%)	..	..	4.3	3.6	3.6	4.1	4.7	5.7	3.3	3.0
Maturity (years)	..	..	24.1	31.1	19.6	19.9	24.8	16.0	15.7	26.1
Grace period (years)	..	..	8.2	8.2	5.3	4.1	7.1	3.1	3.6	7.6
Grant element (%)	..	..	42.8	52.0	41.7	36.9	38.4	20.4	38.5	54.1
Private creditors										
Interest (%)	..	..	0.0	0.0	0.0	0.0	0.0	0.0	8.0	2.5
Maturity (years)	..	..	0.0	0.0	0.0	0.0	0.0	0.0	11.0	7.0
Grace period (years)	..	..	0.0	0.0	0.0	0.0	0.0	0.0	11.0	0.1
Grant element (%)	..	..	0.0	0.0	0.0	0.0	0.0	0.0	13.0	20.2
Memorandum items										
Commitments	..	..	34.9	7.0	8.4	6.9	50.4	3.5	23.9	11.3
Official creditors	..	..	34.9	7.0	8.4	6.9	50.4	3.5	9.9	11.0
Private creditors	..	..	0.0	0.0	0.0	0.0	0.0	0.0	14.1	0.3

10. CONTRACTUAL OBLIGATIONS ON OUTSTANDING LONG-TERM DEBT

	1999	2000	2001	2002	2003	2004	2005	2006	2007	2008
TOTAL										
Disbursements	16.5	16.1	10.1	6.7	3.6	2.3	1.3	0.6	0.3	0.2
Principal	10.6	13.0	11.4	11.0	10.8	10.8	10.4	10.0	9.3	23.3
Interest	6.6	6.7	6.5	6.2	5.8	5.3	4.8	4.4	3.9	3.5
Official creditors										
Disbursements	11.4	13.9	10.1	6.7	3.6	2.3	1.3	0.6	0.3	0.2
Principal	10.6	13.0	11.4	11.0	10.8	10.8	10.4	10.0	9.3	9.2
Interest	5.6	5.6	5.4	5.1	4.7	4.2	3.7	3.2	2.8	2.4
Bilateral creditors										
Disbursements	0.9	0.5	0.4	0.1	0.1	0.0	0.0	0.0	0.0	0.0
Principal	4.8	5.7	2.9	2.9	2.8	2.8	2.8	2.5	2.3	2.3
Interest	1.8	1.5	1.2	1.0	0.9	0.7	0.6	0.4	0.3	0.2
Multilateral creditors										
Disbursements	10.6	13.4	9.7	6.5	3.5	2.2	1.3	0.6	0.3	0.2
Principal	5.8	7.3	8.4	8.0	8.0	8.0	7.6	7.5	7.1	6.9
Interest	3.8	4.1	4.2	4.0	3.8	3.5	3.1	2.8	2.5	2.1
Private creditors										
Disbursements	5.1	2.2	0.0	0.0	0.0	0.0	0.0	0.0	0.0	0.0
Principal	0.1	0.1	0.0	0.0	0.0	0.0	0.0	0.0	0.0	14.1
Interest	1.0	1.1	1.1	1.1	1.1	1.1	1.1	1.1	1.1	1.1
Commercial banks										
Disbursements	5.1	2.2	0.0	0.0	0.0	0.0	0.0	0.0	0.0	0.0
Principal	0.1	0.1	0.0	0.0	0.0	0.0	0.0	0.0	0.0	14.1
Interest	1.0	1.1	1.1	1.1	1.1	1.1	1.1	1.1	1.1	1.1
Other private										
Disbursements	0.0	0.0	0.0	0.0	0.0	0.0	0.0	0.0	0.0	0.0
Principal	0.0	0.0	0.0	0.0	0.0	0.0	0.0	0.0	0.0	0.0
Interest	0.0	0.0	0.0	0.0	0.0	0.0	0.0	0.0	0.0	0.0

ST. VINCENT AND THE GRENADINES

(US$ million, unless otherwise indicated)

	1970	1980	1990	1992	1993	1994	1995	1996	1997	1998
1. SUMMARY DEBT DATA										
TOTAL DEBT STOCKS (EDT)	..	**10.6**	**59.1**	**71.8**	**97.2**	**140.9**	**206.2**	**212.6**	**257.8**	**419.9**
Long-term debt (LDOD)	**0.7**	**10.3**	**57.0**	**70.3**	**73.4**	**86.8**	**86.8**	**86.2**	**85.6**	**101.4**
Public and publicly guaranteed	0.7	10.3	57.0	70.3	73.4	86.8	86.8	86.2	85.6	101.4
Private nonguaranteed	0.0	0.0	0.0	0.0	0.0	0.0	0.0	0.0	0.0	0.0
Use of IMF credit	**0.0**	**0.3**	**0.0**	**0.0**	**0.0**	**0.0**	**0.0**	**0.0**	**0.0**	**0.0**
Short-term debt	..	**0.0**	**2.1**	**1.6**	**23.7**	**54.0**	**119.3**	**126.3**	**172.2**	**318.6**
of which interest arrears on LDOD	..	0.0	0.1	0.0	0.0	0.0	0.1	0.5	0.2	0.0
Official creditors	..	0.0	0.1	0.0	0.0	0.0	0.1	0.0	0.1	0.0
Private creditors	..	0.0	0.0	0.0	0.0	0.0	0.0	0.5	0.1	0.0
Memo: principal arrears on LDOD	..	0.0	0.1	0.0	0.0	0.1	0.6	0.9	0.1	0.2
Official creditors	..	0.0	0.1	0.0	0.0	0.1	0.3	0.0	0.1	0.2
Private creditors	..	0.0	0.0	0.0	0.0	0.0	0.2	0.9	0.0	0.0
Memo: export credits	..	0.0	2.0	2.0	3.0	3.0	3.0	5.0	20.0	58.0
TOTAL DEBT FLOWS										
Disbursements	**0.2**	**3.5**	**7.0**	**7.8**	**9.4**	**15.9**	**3.1**	**6.1**	**9.8**	**20.8**
Long-term debt	0.2	3.0	7.0	7.8	9.4	15.9	3.1	6.1	9.8	20.8
IMF purchases	0.0	0.5	0.0	0.0	0.0	0.0	0.0	0.0	0.0	0.0
Principal repayments	**0.0**	**0.1**	**2.2**	**3.7**	**5.3**	**4.7**	**4.2**	**5.3**	**6.5**	**6.4**
Long-term debt	0.0	0.1	2.2	3.7	5.3	4.7	4.2	5.3	6.5	6.4
IMF repurchases	0.0	0.0	0.0	0.0	0.0	0.0	0.0	0.0	0.0	0.0
Net flows on debt	**0.2**	**3.4**	**5.1**	**3.8**	**26.2**	**41.6**	**64.2**	**7.3**	**49.5**	**160.9**
of which short-term debt	..	0.0	0.4	-0.4	22.2	30.3	65.3	6.6	46.2	146.5
Interest payments (INT)	..	**0.3**	**1.8**	**2.0**	**2.8**	**3.9**	**6.2**	**8.6**	**10.9**	**16.1**
Long-term debt	0.0	0.3	1.7	2.0	2.1	2.3	2.5	2.6	3.0	3.1
IMF charges	0.0	0.0	0.0	0.0	0.0	0.0	0.0	0.0	0.0	0.0
Short-term debt	..	0.0	0.2	0.1	0.7	1.7	3.7	6.0	7.9	13.0
Net transfers on debt	..	**3.1**	**3.3**	**1.7**	**23.4**	**37.6**	**58.0**	**-1.3**	**38.6**	**144.8**
Total debt service paid (TDS)	..	**0.4**	**4.1**	**5.7**	**8.1**	**8.6**	**10.4**	**13.9**	**17.4**	**22.5**
Long-term debt	0.0	0.4	3.9	5.6	7.4	7.0	6.7	8.0	9.5	9.5
IMF repurchases and charges	0.0	0.0	0.0	0.0	0.0	0.0	0.0	0.0	0.0	0.0
Short-term debt (interest only)	..	0.0	0.2	0.1	0.7	1.7	3.7	6.0	7.9	13.0
2. AGGREGATE NET RESOURCE FLOWS AND NET TRANSFERS (LONG-TERM)										
NET RESOURCE FLOWS	**0.2**	**8.9**	**16.1**	**31.5**	**37.8**	**61.0**	**75.7**	**40.2**	**49.6**	**66.0**
Net flow of long-term debt (ex. IMF)	0.2	2.9	4.7	4.2	4.0	11.3	-1.1	0.7	3.3	14.4
Foreign direct investment (net)	0.0	1.1	8.0	19.0	31.0	47.0	31.4	19.0	42.0	40.0
Portfolio equity flows	0.0	0.0	0.0	0.0	0.0	0.0	0.0	0.0	0.0	0.0
Grants (excluding technical coop.)	0.0	4.9	3.4	8.3	2.7	2.8	45.3	20.5	4.3	11.6
Memo: technical coop. grants	0.0	1.0	2.5	2.3	3.8	2.3	2.7	2.4	2.5	2.0
official net resource flows	0.0	7.7	8.1	12.5	6.8	9.3	44.2	21.2	9.2	26.4
private net resource flows	0.2	1.2	8.0	19.0	31.0	51.7	31.5	19.0	40.4	39.6
NET TRANSFERS	**0.2**	**8.6**	**1.2**	**20.3**	**24.7**	**46.7**	**60.2**	**19.6**	**27.6**	**41.9**
Interest on long-term debt	0.0	0.3	1.7	2.0	2.1	2.3	2.5	2.6	3.0	3.1
Profit remittances on FDI	0.0	0.0	13.2	9.2	11.0	12.0	13.0	18.0	19.0	21.0
Memo: official net transfers	0.0	7.5	6.4	10.5	4.7	7.0	42.0	18.7	6.7	23.5
private net transfers	0.2	1.1	-5.2	9.8	20.0	39.7	18.2	0.9	20.9	18.4
3. MAJOR ECONOMIC AGGREGATES										
Gross national product (GNP)	18.5	59.4	187.3	226.0	230.3	231.3	252.3	268.0	280.9	302.3
Exports of goods & services (XGS)	..	39.6	148.7	143.1	136.8	131.1	155.3	166.9	146.3	163.7
of which workers remittances	..	0.0	13.9	0.0	14.5	14.8	15.2	16.3	..	..
Imports of goods & services (MGS)	..	65.0	167.9	171.9	173.1	186.1	190.2	197.1	227.9	249.6
International reserves (RES)	..	7.3	26.5	33.4	31.5	31.3	29.8	30.2	31.2	38.8
Current account balance	..	-9.3	-23.6	-20.9	-43.8	-58.0	-41.2	-35.2	-65.6	-66.2
4. DEBT INDICATORS										
EDT / XGS (%)	..	26.8	39.8	50.2	71.0	107.5	132.8	127.4	176.2	256.6
EDT / GNP (%)	..	17.8	31.6	31.8	42.2	60.9	81.7	79.3	91.8	138.9
TDS / XGS (%)	..	1.0	2.8	4.0	5.9	6.6	6.7	8.3	11.9	13.8
INT / XGS (%)	..	0.8	1.2	1.4	2.1	3.0	4.0	5.2	7.5	9.8
INT / GNP (%)	..	0.5	1.0	0.9	1.2	1.7	2.5	3.2	3.9	5.3
RES / EDT (%)	..	68.6	44.8	46.5	32.4	22.2	14.5	14.2	12.1	9.2
RES / MGS (months)	..	1.3	1.9	2.3	2.2	2.0	1.9	1.8	1.6	1.9
Short-term / EDT (%)	..	0.0	3.6	2.2	24.4	38.3	57.9	59.4	66.8	75.9
Concessional / EDT (%)	..	57.6	81.7	81.1	64.0	49.0	33.4	33.0	28.9	20.4
Multilateral / EDT (%)	..	58.5	80.4	71.7	52.4	39.8	27.2	24.7	21.7	15.6

ST. VINCENT AND THE GRENADINES

(US$ million, unless otherwise indicated)

	1970	1980	1990	1992	1993	1994	1995	1996	1997	1998
5. LONG-TERM DEBT										
DEBT OUTSTANDING (LDOD)	**0.7**	**10.3**	**57.0**	**70.3**	**73.4**	**86.8**	**86.8**	**86.2**	**85.6**	**101.4**
Public and publicly guaranteed	**0.7**	**10.3**	**57.0**	**70.3**	**73.4**	**86.8**	**86.8**	**86.2**	**85.6**	**101.4**
Official creditors	0.0	9.4	57.0	70.3	73.4	82.1	82.0	81.4	83.8	100.0
Multilateral	0.0	6.2	47.5	51.5	50.9	56.1	56.0	52.4	56.0	65.4
Concessional	0.0	5.1	39.8	39.9	40.0	44.6	43.9	41.8	46.8	51.0
Bilateral	0.0	3.2	9.5	18.7	22.5	26.0	26.1	29.0	27.8	34.6
Concessional	0.0	1.0	8.5	18.3	22.2	24.5	25.0	28.4	27.6	34.6
Private creditors	0.7	0.9	0.0	0.0	0.0	4.7	4.8	4.8	1.8	1.4
Bonds	0.7	0.8	0.0	0.0	0.0	0.0	0.0	0.0	0.0	0.0
Commercial banks	0.0	0.0	0.0	0.0	0.0	4.7	4.8	4.8	1.8	1.4
Other private	0.0	0.1	0.0	0.0	0.0	0.0	0.0	0.0	0.0	0.0
Private nonguaranteed	**0.0**	**0.0**	**0.0**	**0.0**	**0.0**	**0.0**	**0.0**	**0.0**	**0.0**	**0.0**
Bonds	0.0	0.0	0.0	0.0	0.0	0.0	0.0	0.0	0.0	0.0
Commercial banks	0.0	0.0	0.0	0.0	0.0	0.0	0.0	0.0	0.0	0.0
Memo:										
IBRD	0.0	0.0	0.0	0.2	0.4	0.5	0.4	0.3	0.3	0.2
IDA	0.0	0.0	6.2	7.6	7.6	8.0	8.1	7.8	7.3	7.6
DISBURSEMENTS	**0.2**	**3.0**	**7.0**	**7.8**	**9.4**	**15.9**	**3.1**	**6.1**	**9.8**	**20.8**
Public and publicly guaranteed	**0.2**	**3.0**	**7.0**	**7.8**	**9.4**	**15.9**	**3.1**	**6.1**	**9.8**	**20.8**
Official creditors	0.0	2.9	7.0	7.8	9.4	11.2	3.1	6.1	9.8	20.8
Multilateral	0.0	2.8	6.3	3.7	4.8	6.8	2.2	1.8	8.6	12.4
Concessional	0.0	1.9	4.8	2.1	4.2	6.2	1.3	1.3	8.0	6.5
Bilateral	0.0	0.1	0.6	4.1	4.5	4.4	0.9	4.3	1.2	8.4
Concessional	0.0	0.0	0.6	4.1	4.5	2.9	0.9	4.3	1.2	8.4
Private creditors	0.2	0.1	0.0	0.0	0.0	4.7	0.1	0.0	0.0	0.0
Bonds	0.2	0.0	0.0	0.0	0.0	0.0	0.0	0.0	0.0	0.0
Commercial banks	0.0	0.0	0.0	0.0	0.0	4.7	0.1	0.0	0.0	0.0
Other private	0.0	0.1	0.0	0.0	0.0	0.0	0.0	0.0	0.0	0.0
Private nonguaranteed	**0.0**	**0.0**	**0.0**	**0.0**	**0.0**	**0.0**	**0.0**	**0.0**	**0.0**	**0.0**
Bonds	0.0	0.0	0.0	0.0	0.0	0.0	0.0	0.0	0.0	0.0
Commercial banks	0.0	0.0	0.0	0.0	0.0	0.0	0.0	0.0	0.0	0.0
Memo:										
IBRD	0.0	0.0	0.0	0.1	0.3	0.0	0.0	0.1	0.1	0.0
IDA	0.0	0.0	0.9	0.0	0.0	0.0	0.0	0.0	0.0	0.1
PRINCIPAL REPAYMENTS	**0.0**	**0.1**	**2.2**	**3.7**	**5.3**	**4.7**	**4.2**	**5.3**	**6.5**	**6.4**
Public and publicly guaranteed	**0.0**	**0.1**	**2.2**	**3.7**	**5.3**	**4.7**	**4.2**	**5.3**	**6.5**	**6.4**
Official creditors	0.0	0.1	2.2	3.7	5.3	4.7	4.2	5.3	4.9	6.0
Multilateral	0.0	0.1	2.0	3.0	4.7	3.2	3.1	4.0	3.3	4.0
Concessional	0.0	0.1	1.6	2.2	4.0	2.3	2.0	2.7	2.2	2.8
Bilateral	0.0	0.0	0.2	0.7	0.6	1.4	1.1	1.4	1.6	2.0
Concessional	0.0	0.0	0.1	0.5	0.4	1.0	0.7	1.0	1.4	1.7
Private creditors	0.0	0.0	0.0	0.0	0.0	0.0	0.0	0.0	1.6	0.4
Bonds	0.0	0.0	0.0	0.0	0.0	0.0	0.0	0.0	0.0	0.0
Commercial banks	0.0	0.0	0.0	0.0	0.0	0.0	0.0	0.0	1.6	0.4
Other private	0.0	0.0	0.0	0.0	0.0	0.0	0.0	0.0	0.0	0.0
Private nonguaranteed	**0.0**	**0.0**	**0.0**	**0.0**	**0.0**	**0.0**	**0.0**	**0.0**	**0.0**	**0.0**
Bonds	0.0	0.0	0.0	0.0	0.0	0.0	0.0	0.0	0.0	0.0
Commercial banks	0.0	0.0	0.0	0.0	0.0	0.0	0.0	0.0	0.0	0.0
Memo:										
IBRD	0.0	0.0	0.0	0.0	0.0	0.1	0.1	0.1	0.1	0.1
IDA	0.0	0.0	0.0	0.0	0.0	0.0	0.1	0.1	0.1	0.1
NET FLOWS ON DEBT	**0.2**	**2.9**	**4.7**	**4.2**	**4.0**	**11.3**	**-1.1**	**0.7**	**3.3**	**14.4**
Public and publicly guaranteed	**0.2**	**2.9**	**4.7**	**4.2**	**4.0**	**11.3**	**-1.1**	**0.7**	**3.3**	**14.4**
Official creditors	0.0	2.8	4.7	4.2	4.1	6.5	-1.1	0.7	4.9	14.8
Multilateral	0.0	2.7	4.3	0.8	0.1	3.6	-0.9	-2.2	5.4	8.4
Concessional	0.0	1.7	3.3	-0.1	0.2	3.9	-0.7	-1.3	5.8	3.7
Bilateral	0.0	0.1	0.4	3.4	3.9	2.9	-0.3	2.9	-0.5	6.4
Concessional	0.0	0.0	0.6	3.6	4.1	1.9	0.2	3.3	-0.2	6.7
Private creditors	0.2	0.1	0.0	0.0	0.0	4.7	0.1	0.0	-1.6	-0.4
Bonds	0.2	0.0	0.0	0.0	0.0	0.0	0.0	0.0	0.0	0.0
Commercial banks	0.0	0.0	0.0	0.0	0.0	4.7	0.1	0.0	-1.6	-0.4
Other private	0.0	0.1	0.0	0.0	0.0	0.0	0.0	0.0	0.0	0.0
Private nonguaranteed	**0.0**	**0.0**	**0.0**	**0.0**	**0.0**	**0.0**	**0.0**	**0.0**	**0.0**	**0.0**
Bonds	0.0	0.0	0.0	0.0	0.0	0.0	0.0	0.0	0.0	0.0
Commercial banks	0.0	0.0	0.0	0.0	0.0	0.0	0.0	0.0	0.0	0.0
Memo:										
IBRD	0.0	0.0	0.0	0.1	0.3	0.0	-0.1	0.0	0.0	-0.1
IDA	0.0	0.0	0.9	0.0	0.0	0.0	-0.1	-0.1	-0.1	0.1

ST. VINCENT AND THE GRENADINES

(US$ million, unless otherwise indicated)

	1970	1980	1990	1992	1993	1994	1995	1996	1997	1998
INTEREST PAYMENTS (LINT)	**0.0**	**0.3**	**1.7**	**2.0**	**2.1**	**2.3**	**2.5**	**2.6**	**3.0**	**3.1**
Public and publicly guaranteed	**0.0**	**0.3**	**1.7**	**2.0**	**2.1**	**2.3**	**2.5**	**2.6**	**3.0**	**3.1**
Official creditors	0.0	0.2	1.7	2.0	2.1	2.3	2.2	2.5	2.5	2.9
Multilateral	0.0	0.2	1.4	1.7	1.7	1.7	1.5	1.7	1.7	2.0
Concessional	0.0	0.1	1.1	1.1	1.1	1.1	1.0	1.2	1.1	1.6
Bilateral	0.0	0.0	0.3	0.3	0.4	0.6	0.7	0.8	0.8	0.9
Concessional	0.0	0.0	0.2	0.2	0.4	0.5	0.6	0.7	0.8	0.9
Private creditors	0.0	0.1	0.0	0.0	0.0	0.0	0.3	0.1	0.5	0.2
Bonds	0.0	0.1	0.0	0.0	0.0	0.0	0.0	0.0	0.0	0.0
Commercial banks	0.0	0.0	0.0	0.0	0.0	0.0	0.3	0.1	0.5	0.2
Other private	0.0	0.0	0.0	0.0	0.0	0.0	0.0	0.0	0.0	0.0
Private nonguaranteed	**0.0**	**0.0**	**0.0**	**0.0**	**0.0**	**0.0**	**0.0**	**0.0**	**0.0**	**0.0**
Bonds	0.0	0.0	0.0	0.0	0.0	0.0	0.0	0.0	0.0	0.0
Commercial banks	0.0	0.0	0.0	0.0	0.0	0.0	0.0	0.0	0.0	0.0
Memo:										
IBRD	0.0	0.0	0.0	0.0	0.0	0.0	0.0	0.0	0.0	0.0
IDA	0.0	0.0	0.0	0.1	0.1	0.1	0.1	0.1	0.1	0.1
NET TRANSFERS ON DEBT	**0.1**	**2.6**	**3.0**	**2.2**	**1.9**	**9.0**	**-3.6**	**-1.9**	**0.3**	**11.3**
Public and publicly guaranteed	**0.1**	**2.6**	**3.0**	**2.2**	**1.9**	**9.0**	**-3.6**	**-1.9**	**0.3**	**11.3**
Official creditors	0.0	2.5	3.0	2.2	2.0	4.2	-3.3	-1.8	2.4	11.9
Multilateral	0.0	2.5	2.9	-0.9	-1.5	1.9	-2.4	-3.9	3.7	6.4
Concessional	0.0	1.6	2.2	-1.2	-0.9	2.8	-1.7	-2.5	4.7	2.1
Bilateral	0.0	0.1	0.1	3.1	3.5	2.3	-0.9	2.1	-1.3	5.5
Concessional	0.0	0.0	0.4	3.3	3.7	1.4	-0.4	2.6	-1.0	5.8
Private creditors	0.1	0.1	0.0	0.0	0.0	4.7	-0.2	-0.1	-2.1	-0.6
Bonds	0.1	-0.1	0.0	0.0	0.0	0.0	0.0	0.0	0.0	0.0
Commercial banks	0.0	0.0	0.0	0.0	0.0	4.7	-0.2	-0.1	-2.1	-0.6
Other private	0.0	0.1	0.0	0.0	0.0	0.0	0.0	0.0	0.0	0.0
Private nonguaranteed	**0.0**	**0.0**	**0.0**	**0.0**	**0.0**	**0.0**	**0.0**	**0.0**	**0.0**	**0.0**
Bonds	0.0	0.0	0.0	0.0	0.0	0.0	0.0	0.0	0.0	0.0
Commercial banks	0.0	0.0	0.0	0.0	0.0	0.0	0.0	0.0	0.0	0.0
Memo:										
IBRD	0.0	0.0	0.0	0.1	0.3	-0.1	-0.1	-0.1	-0.1	-0.1
IDA	0.0	0.0	0.8	0.0	-0.1	-0.1	-0.1	-0.1	-0.1	0.0
DEBT SERVICE (LTDS)	**0.0**	**0.4**	**3.9**	**5.6**	**7.4**	**7.0**	**6.7**	**8.0**	**9.5**	**9.5**
Public and publicly guaranteed	**0.0**	**0.4**	**3.9**	**5.6**	**7.4**	**7.0**	**6.7**	**8.0**	**9.5**	**9.5**
Official creditors	0.0	0.4	3.9	5.6	7.4	7.0	6.4	7.8	7.4	8.9
Multilateral	0.0	0.4	3.4	4.6	6.4	4.9	4.6	5.7	4.9	6.0
Concessional	0.0	0.3	2.6	3.3	5.1	3.4	2.9	3.8	3.3	4.4
Bilateral	0.0	0.0	0.5	1.0	1.0	2.0	1.8	2.1	2.5	2.9
Concessional	0.0	0.0	0.2	0.8	0.8	1.5	1.3	1.6	2.1	2.6
Private creditors	0.0	0.1	0.0	0.0	0.0	0.0	0.3	0.1	2.1	0.6
Bonds	0.0	0.1	0.0	0.0	0.0	0.0	0.0	0.0	0.0	0.0
Commercial banks	0.0	0.0	0.0	0.0	0.0	0.0	0.3	0.1	2.1	0.6
Other private	0.0	0.0	0.0	0.0	0.0	0.0	0.0	0.0	0.0	0.0
Private nonguaranteed	**0.0**	**0.0**	**0.0**	**0.0**	**0.0**	**0.0**	**0.0**	**0.0**	**0.0**	**0.0**
Bonds	0.0	0.0	0.0	0.0	0.0	0.0	0.0	0.0	0.0	0.0
Commercial banks	0.0	0.0	0.0	0.0	0.0	0.0	0.0	0.0	0.0	0.0
Memo:										
IBRD	0.0	0.0	0.0	0.0	0.0	0.1	0.2	0.2	0.1	0.1
IDA	0.0	0.0	0.0	0.1	0.1	0.1	0.1	0.1	0.1	0.1
UNDISBURSED DEBT	**0.0**	**11.0**	**24.8**	**30.9**	**38.2**	**30.5**	**39.9**	**53.3**	**44.7**	**30.7**
Official creditors	0.0	9.8	24.8	30.9	35.8	30.5	39.9	53.3	44.7	30.7
Private creditors	0.0	1.2	0.0	0.0	2.4	0.1	0.0	0.0	0.0	0.0
Memorandum items										
Concessional LDOD	0.0	6.1	48.3	58.2	62.2	69.2	68.9	70.2	74.4	85.6
Variable rate LDOD	0.0	0.0	0.0	0.9	1.3	1.4	1.2	1.0	7.2	10.3
Public sector LDOD	0.7	10.3	57.0	70.3	73.4	86.8	86.8	86.2	85.6	101.4
Private sector LDOD	0.0	0.0	0.0	0.0	0.0	0.0	0.0	0.0	0.0	0.0

6. CURRENCY COMPOSITION OF LONG-TERM DEBT (PERCENT)

	1970	1980	1990	1992	1993	1994	1995	1996	1997	1998
Deutsche mark	0.0	0.0	0.7	0.7	0.7	0.6	0.6	0.6	0.5	0.4
French franc	0.0	0.0	0.2	0.6	3.1	3.8	4.3	4.4	3.9	3.3
Japanese yen	0.0	0.0	0.2	0.1	0.1	0.1	0.1	0.1	0.0	0.0
Pound sterling	0.0	36.8	4.7	9.0	7.5	5.9	5.6	5.5	4.7	5.6
Swiss franc	0.0	0.0	0.2	1.7	1.5	1.4	1.5	1.2	1.1	0.8
U.S.dollars	0.0	21.3	66.1	64.6	66.5	68.2	68.3	67.6	72.3	69.0
Multiple currency	0.0	11.6	10.2	6.8	6.1	5.5	4.8	3.9	3.3	2.1
Special drawing rights	0.0	0.0	3.7	2.7	2.9	3.0	3.3	3.2	3.2	2.9
All other currencies	0.0	30.3	14.0	13.8	11.6	11.5	11.5	13.5	11.0	15.9

ST. VINCENT AND THE GRENADINES

(US$ million, unless otherwise indicated)

	1970	1980	1990	1992	1993	1994	1995	1996	1997	1998
7. DEBT RESTRUCTURINGS										
Total amount rescheduled	..	..	0.0	0.0	0.0	0.0	0.0	0.0	0.0	0.0
Debt stock rescheduled	..	..	0.0	0.0	0.0	0.0	0.0	0.0	0.0	0.0
Principal rescheduled	..	..	0.0	0.0	0.0	0.0	0.0	0.0	0.0	0.0
Official	..	..	0.0	0.0	0.0	0.0	0.0	0.0	0.0	0.0
Private	..	..	0.0	0.0	0.0	0.0	0.0	0.0	0.0	0.0
Interest rescheduled	..	..	0.0	0.0	0.0	0.0	0.0	0.0	0.0	0.0
Official	..	..	0.0	0.0	0.0	0.0	0.0	0.0	0.0	0.0
Private	..	..	0.0	0.0	0.0	0.0	0.0	0.0	0.0	0.0
Debt forgiven	..	..	0.8	0.0	0.0	0.0	0.0	0.3	1.4	0.0
Memo: interest forgiven	..	..	0.0	0.0	0.0	0.0	0.0	0.0	0.0	0.0
Debt stock reduction	..	..	0.0	0.0	0.0	0.0	0.0	0.0	0.0	0.0
of which debt buyback	..	..	0.0	0.0	0.0	0.0	0.0	0.0	0.0	0.0
8. DEBT STOCK-FLOW RECONCILIATION										
Total change in debt stocks	..	..	8.1	7.0	25.3	43.7	65.3	6.4	45.3	162.1
Net flows on debt	0.2	3.4	5.1	3.8	26.2	41.6	64.2	7.3	49.5	160.9
Net change in interest arrears	..	..	0.0	-0.1	0.0	0.0	0.0	0.4	-0.3	-0.2
Interest capitalized	..	..	0.0	0.0	0.0	0.0	0.0	0.0	0.0	0.0
Debt forgiveness or reduction	..	..	-0.8	0.0	0.0	0.0	0.0	-0.3	-1.4	0.0
Cross-currency valuation	..	..	1.6	-2.3	-0.9	1.9	1.3	-0.6	-1.6	1.1
Residual	..	..	2.2	5.7	0.0	0.2	-0.3	-0.5	-1.0	0.3
9. AVERAGE TERMS OF NEW COMMITMENTS										
ALL CREDITORS										
Interest (%)	7.5	5.3	4.0	2.5	4.3	1.4	3.5	4.4	4.3	3.3
Maturity (years)	13.5	15.4	21.0	18.0	19.5	16.0	19.9	24.1	15.6	22.9
Grace period (years)	13.5	5.1	4.8	7.3	5.6	3.3	4.1	6.1	3.5	6.3
Grant element (%)	18.1	29.0	39.7	51.0	39.8	45.6	41.0	39.9	32.2	48.3
Official creditors										
Interest (%)	0.0	4.0	4.0	2.5	3.4	2.0	3.5	4.4	4.3	3.3
Maturity (years)	0.0	20.1	21.0	18.0	21.3	20.0	19.9	24.1	15.6	22.9
Grace period (years)	0.0	7.6	4.8	7.3	6.1	4.0	4.1	6.1	3.5	6.3
Grant element (%)	0.0	41.7	39.7	51.0	46.4	51.6	41.0	39.9	32.2	48.3
Private creditors										
Interest (%)	7.5	7.5	0.0	0.0	9.7	0.0	0.0	0.0	0.0	0.0
Maturity (years)	13.5	7.3	0.0	0.0	8.5	6.2	0.0	0.0	0.0	0.0
Grace period (years)	13.5	0.8	0.0	0.0	3.0	1.7	0.0	0.0	0.0	0.0
Grant element (%)	18.1	7.2	0.0	0.0	0.0	30.5	0.0	0.0	0.0	0.0
Memorandum items										
Commitments	0.2	3.6	2.5	7.3	16.9	8.3	12.6	19.7	2.4	9.6
Official creditors	0.0	2.3	2.5	7.3	14.5	5.9	12.6	19.7	2.4	9.6
Private creditors	0.2	1.3	0.0	0.0	2.4	2.4	0.0	0.0	0.0	0.0

10. CONTRACTUAL OBLIGATIONS ON OUTSTANDING LONG-TERM DEBT

	1999	2000	2001	2002	2003	2004	2005	2006	2007	2008
TOTAL										
Disbursements	8.9	8.3	5.4	3.4	2.1	1.3	0.7	0.3	0.2	0.1
Principal	7.0	7.3	6.9	7.7	8.2	8.3	8.1	7.3	6.9	6.9
Interest	3.3	3.3	3.2	3.1	2.9	2.6	2.4	2.2	1.9	1.7
Official creditors										
Disbursements	8.9	8.3	5.4	3.4	2.1	1.3	0.7	0.3	0.2	0.1
Principal	6.6	6.9	6.5	7.5	8.2	8.3	8.1	7.3	6.9	6.9
Interest	3.1	3.2	3.1	3.0	2.9	2.6	2.4	2.2	1.9	1.7
Bilateral creditors										
Disbursements	2.9	2.6	1.6	0.9	0.6	0.3	0.1	0.0	0.0	0.0
Principal	2.2	2.5	2.6	2.8	2.8	2.8	2.8	2.9	2.8	2.8
Interest	0.9	0.9	0.9	0.8	0.8	0.7	0.6	0.6	0.5	0.4
Multilateral creditors										
Disbursements	6.0	5.7	3.8	2.4	1.5	1.0	0.6	0.3	0.2	0.1
Principal	4.3	4.4	4.0	4.6	5.3	5.5	5.3	4.4	4.1	4.1
Interest	2.2	2.3	2.3	2.2	2.1	1.9	1.8	1.6	1.4	1.3
Private creditors										
Disbursements	0.0	0.0	0.0	0.0	0.0	0.0	0.0	0.0	0.0	0.0
Principal	0.4	0.4	0.4	0.2	0.0	0.0	0.0	0.0	0.0	0.0
Interest	0.1	0.1	0.0	0.0	0.0	0.0	0.0	0.0	0.0	0.0
Commercial banks										
Disbursements	0.0	0.0	0.0	0.0	0.0	0.0	0.0	0.0	0.0	0.0
Principal	0.4	0.4	0.4	0.2	0.0	0.0	0.0	0.0	0.0	0.0
Interest	0.1	0.1	0.0	0.0	0.0	0.0	0.0	0.0	0.0	0.0
Other private										
Disbursements	0.0	0.0	0.0	0.0	0.0	0.0	0.0	0.0	0.0	0.0
Principal	0.0	0.0	0.0	0.0	0.0	0.0	0.0	0.0	0.0	0.0
Interest	0.0	0.0	0.0	0.0	0.0	0.0	0.0	0.0	0.0	0.0

SUDAN

(US$ million, unless otherwise indicated)

	1970	1980	1990	1992	1993	1994	1995	1996	1997	1998
1. SUMMARY DEBT DATA										
TOTAL DEBT STOCKS (EDT)	..	**5,177**	**14,762**	**15,450**	**15,837**	**16,918**	**17,603**	**16,972**	**16,326**	**16,843**
Long-term debt (LDOD)	**298**	**4,147**	**9,651**	**9,480**	**9,490**	**9,896**	**10,275**	**9,865**	**9,494**	**9,722**
Public and publicly guaranteed	298	3,822	9,155	8,984	8,994	9,400	9,779	9,369	8,998	9,226
Private nonguaranteed	0	325	496	496	496	496	496	496	496	496
Use of IMF credit	**31**	**431**	**956**	**924**	**923**	**980**	**960**	**893**	**797**	**772**
Short-term debt	..	**599**	**4,155**	**5,047**	**5,424**	**6,042**	**6,368**	**6,214**	**6,035**	**6,349**
of which interest arrears on LDOD	..	63	3,705	4,419	4,796	5,414	5,737	5,683	5,624	5,893
Official creditors	..	33	3,244	3,813	4,100	4,550	4,748	4,767	4,721	4,922
Private creditors	..	30	461	606	697	863	989	916	903	971
Memo: principal arrears on LDOD	..	551	5,704	6,417	6,599	7,155	7,637	7,467	7,321	7,608
Official creditors	..	108	3,893	4,445	4,650	5,024	5,282	5,377	5,348	5,553
Private creditors	..	444	1,811	1,972	1,949	2,131	2,355	2,090	1,973	2,055
Memo: export credits	..	0	2,972	2,712	2,762	2,747	2,528	2,556	2,614	2,969
TOTAL DEBT FLOWS										
Disbursements	**53**	**921**	**185**	**108**	**101**	**12**	**51**	**17**	**5**	**0**
Long-term debt	53	711	185	108	101	12	51	17	5	0
IMF purchases	0	210	0	0	0	0	0	0	0	0
Principal repayments	**30**	**131**	**16**	**14**	**9**	**3**	**54**	**36**	**42**	**58**
Long-term debt	22	53	15	14	9	3	15	0	0	1
IMF repurchases	8	78	1	0	0	0	39	36	42	57
Net flows on debt	**83**	**839**	**169**	**272**	**91**	**9**	**0**	**-119**	**-157**	**-13**
of which short-term debt	..	50	0	178	0	0	3	-100	-120	45
Interest payments (INT)	..	**133**	**34**	**13**	**11**	**1**	**15**	**12**	**15**	**3**
Long-term debt	12	49	9	11	8	0	2	0	0	2
IMF charges	0	14	0	2	3	0	13	12	15	1
Short-term debt	..	70	25	0	0	0	0	0	0	0
Net transfers on debt	..	**707**	**135**	**259**	**80**	**9**	**-15**	**-131**	**-172**	**-16**
Total debt service paid (TDS)	..	**264**	**50**	**27**	**20**	**3**	**69**	**48**	**58**	**61**
Long-term debt	34	102	23	25	17	3	17	0	0	3
IMF repurchases and charges	8	92	1	2	3	0	52	48	57	58
Short-term debt (interest only)	..	70	25	0	0	0	0	0	0	0
2. AGGREGATE NET RESOURCE FLOWS AND NET TRANSFERS (LONG-TERM)										
NET RESOURCE FLOWS	**33**	**1,046**	**603**	**409**	**344**	**372**	**184**	**160**	**220**	**558**
Net flow of long-term debt (ex. IMF)	31	658	171	94	91	9	36	17	5	-1
Foreign direct investment (net)	0	0	0	0	0	0	0	0	98	371
Portfolio equity flows	0	0	0	0	0	0	0	0	0	0
Grants (excluding technical coop.)	3	388	433	315	252	363	148	143	118	188
Memo: technical coop. grants	7	103	189	116	110	84	75	65	33	26
official net resource flows	36	908	603	409	344	372	184	160	122	187
private net resource flows	-3	138	0	0	0	0	0	0	98	371
NET TRANSFERS	**17**	**997**	**595**	**398**	**336**	**372**	**182**	**160**	**220**	**556**
Interest on long-term debt	12	49	9	11	8	0	2	0	0	2
Profit remittances on FDI	4	0	0	0	0	0	0	0	0	0
Memo: official net transfers	26	865	595	398	336	372	182	160	122	185
private net transfers	-9	133	0	0	0	0	0	0	98	371
3. MAJOR ECONOMIC AGGREGATES										
Gross national product (GNP)	2,092	7,467	12,635	5,551	7,020	7,259	6,281	6,255	8,974	9,220
Exports of goods & services (XGS)	339	1,051	665	424	538	558	690	677	642	625
of which workers remittances	..	257	134	..	..	..	..	..	..	..
Imports of goods & services (MGS)	380	1,856	2,237	2,093	2,122	2,140	2,272	2,586	2,732	3,128
International reserves (RES)	22	49	11	28	37	78	163	107	82	91
Current account balance	-41	-721	-1,299	-1,354	-1,426	-1,459	-1,479	-1,548	-1,639	-1,996
4. DEBT INDICATORS										
EDT / XGS (%)	..	492.6	2,219.9	3,645.2	2,942.5	3,033.5	2,551.6	2,506.6	2,544.6	2,694.5
EDT / GNP (%)	..	69.3	116.8	278.3	225.6	233.1	280.3	271.3	181.9	182.7
TDS / XGS (%)	..	25.1	7.5	6.3	3.8	0.6	10.0	7.1	9.0	9.8
INT / XGS (%)	..	12.6	5.1	3.0	2.0	0.1	2.2	1.8	2.4	0.4
INT / GNP (%)	..	1.8	0.3	0.2	0.2	0.0	0.2	0.2	0.2	0.0
RES / EDT (%)	..	0.9	0.1	0.2	0.2	0.5	0.9	0.6	0.5	0.5
RES / MGS (months)	0.7	0.3	0.1	0.2	0.2	0.4	0.9	0.5	0.4	0.4
Short-term / EDT (%)	..	11.6	28.2	32.7	34.3	35.7	36.2	36.6	37.0	37.7
Concessional / EDT (%)	..	33.4	30.2	29.8	29.5	28.2	27.5	28.0	28.4	27.9
Multilateral / EDT (%)	..	12.2	11.7	12.2	12.4	12.2	12.1	12.3	12.3	12.2

SUDAN

(US$ million, unless otherwise indicated)

	1970	1980	1990	1992	1993	1994	1995	1996	1997	1998
5. LONG-TERM DEBT										
DEBT OUTSTANDING (LDOD)	**298**	**4,147**	**9,651**	**9,480**	**9,490**	**9,896**	**10,275**	**9,865**	**9,494**	**9,722**
Public and publicly guaranteed	**298**	**3,822**	**9,155**	**8,984**	**8,994**	**9,400**	**9,779**	**9,369**	**8,998**	**9,226**
Official creditors	260	3,293	7,500	7,508	7,541	7,765	7,921	7,776	7,521	7,667
Multilateral	104	634	1,723	1,889	1,959	2,064	2,133	2,084	2,001	2,051
Concessional	12	368	1,549	1,719	1,788	1,880	1,928	1,871	1,798	1,839
Bilateral	157	2,659	5,777	5,618	5,582	5,701	5,787	5,692	5,521	5,615
Concessional	127	1,361	2,903	2,878	2,883	2,895	2,910	2,879	2,838	2,865
Private creditors	38	529	1,655	1,476	1,453	1,635	1,859	1,594	1,477	1,559
Bonds	1	0	0	0	0	0	0	0	0	0
Commercial banks	27	298	1,651	1,472	1,449	1,631	1,855	1,590	1,473	1,555
Other private	9	231	4	4	4	4	4	4	4	4
Private nonguaranteed	**0**	**325**	**496**	**496**	**496**	**496**	**496**	**496**	**496**	**496**
Bonds	0	0	0	0	0	0	0	0	0	0
Commercial banks	0	325	496	496	496	496	496	496	496	496
Memo:										
IBRD	91	46	19	9	6	6	6	6	6	6
IDA	12	190	1,028	1,133	1,205	1,251	1,272	1,244	1,198	1,226
DISBURSEMENTS	**53**	**711**	**185**	**108**	**101**	**12**	**51**	**17**	**5**	**0**
Public and publicly guaranteed	**53**	**711**	**185**	**108**	**101**	**12**	**51**	**17**	**5**	**0**
Official creditors	50	566	185	108	101	12	51	17	5	0
Multilateral	15	189	185	108	101	12	51	17	5	0
Concessional	0	80	180	93	95	10	27	2	0	0
Bilateral	35	377	0	0	0	0	0	0	0	0
Concessional	15	190	0	0	0	0	0	0	0	0
Private creditors	2	145	0	0	0	0	0	0	0	0
Bonds	0	0	0	0	0	0	0	0	0	0
Commercial banks	0	108	0	0	0	0	0	0	0	0
Other private	2	37	0	0	0	0	0	0	0	0
Private nonguaranteed	**0**	**0**	**0**	**0**	**0**	**0**	**0**	**0**	**0**	**0**
Bonds	0	0	0	0	0	0	0	0	0	0
Commercial banks	0	0	0	0	0	0	0	0	0	0
Memo:										
IBRD	15	1	0	0	0	0	0	0	0	0
IDA	0	37	121	61	74	8	0	0	0	0
PRINCIPAL REPAYMENTS	**22**	**53**	**15**	**14**	**9**	**3**	**15**	**0**	**0**	**1**
Public and publicly guaranteed	**22**	**53**	**15**	**14**	**9**	**3**	**15**	**0**	**0**	**1**
Official creditors	17	46	15	14	9	3	15	0	0	1
Multilateral	4	15	15	14	9	3	15	0	0	1
Concessional	0	3	4	8	5	3	9	0	0	0
Bilateral	13	32	0	0	0	0	0	0	0	0
Concessional	5	11	0	0	0	0	0	0	0	0
Private creditors	5	7	0	0	0	0	0	0	0	0
Bonds	1	0	0	0	0	0	0	0	0	0
Commercial banks	3	4	0	0	0	0	0	0	0	0
Other private	1	3	0	0	0	0	0	0	0	0
Private nonguaranteed	**0**	**0**	**0**	**0**	**0**	**0**	**0**	**0**	**0**	**0**
Bonds	0	0	0	0	0	0	0	0	0	0
Commercial banks	0	0	0	0	0	0	0	0	0	0
Memo:										
IBRD	4	4	10	5	3	0	0	0	0	0
IDA	0	0	4	6	4	0	0	0	0	0
NET FLOWS ON DEBT	**31**	**658**	**171**	**94**	**91**	**9**	**36**	**17**	**5**	**-1**
Public and publicly guaranteed	**31**	**658**	**171**	**94**	**91**	**9**	**36**	**17**	**5**	**-1**
Official creditors	33	520	171	94	91	9	36	17	5	-1
Multilateral	11	174	171	94	91	9	36	17	5	-1
Concessional	0	77	176	85	90	7	18	2	0	0
Bilateral	23	346	0	0	0	0	0	0	0	0
Concessional	10	179	0	0	0	0	0	0	0	0
Private creditors	-3	138	0	0	0	0	0	0	0	0
Bonds	-1	0	0	0	0	0	0	0	0	0
Commercial banks	-3	104	0	0	0	0	0	0	0	0
Other private	1	33	0	0	0	0	0	0	0	0
Private nonguaranteed	**0**	**0**	**0**	**0**	**0**	**0**	**0**	**0**	**0**	**0**
Bonds	0	0	0	0	0	0	0	0	0	0
Commercial banks	0	0	0	0	0	0	0	0	0	0
Memo:										
IBRD	11	-3	-10	-5	-3	0	0	0	0	0
IDA	0	37	117	55	70	8	0	0	0	0

SUDAN

(US$ million, unless otherwise indicated)

	1970	1980	1990	1992	1993	1994	1995	1996	1997	1998
INTEREST PAYMENTS (LINT)	**12**	**49**	**9**	**11**	**8**	**0**	**2**	**0**	**0**	**2**
Public and publicly guaranteed	**12**	**49**	**9**	**11**	**8**	**0**	**2**	**0**	**0**	**2**
Official creditors	10	44	9	11	8	0	2	0	0	2
Multilateral	5	8	9	11	8	0	2	0	0	2
Concessional	0	2	7	10	6	0	1	0	0	0
Bilateral	5	35	0	0	0	0	0	0	0	0
Concessional	3	26	0	0	0	0	0	0	0	0
Private creditors	2	5	0	0	0	0	0	0	0	0
Bonds	0	0	0	0	0	0	0	0	0	0
Commercial banks	2	2	0	0	0	0	0	0	0	0
Other private	0	3	0	0	0	0	0	0	0	0
Private nonguaranteed	**0**	**0**	**0**	**0**	**0**	**0**	**0**	**0**	**0**	**0**
Bonds	0	0	0	0	0	0	0	0	0	0
Commercial banks	0	0	0	0	0	0	0	0	0	0
Memo:										
IBRD	5	4	2	1	0	0	0	0	0	0
IDA	0	1	6	8	6	0	0	0	0	0
NET TRANSFERS ON DEBT	**18**	**609**	**162**	**83**	**84**	**9**	**34**	**17**	**4**	**-3**
Public and publicly guaranteed	**18**	**609**	**162**	**83**	**84**	**9**	**34**	**17**	**4**	**-3**
Official creditors	23	476	162	83	84	9	34	17	4	-3
Multilateral	6	166	162	83	84	9	34	17	4	-3
Concessional	0	75	169	76	84	7	17	2	0	0
Bilateral	18	310	0	0	0	0	0	0	0	0
Concessional	6	153	0	0	0	0	0	0	0	0
Private creditors	-5	133	0	0	0	0	0	0	0	0
Bonds	-1	0	0	0	0	0	0	0	0	0
Commercial banks	-5	102	0	0	0	0	0	0	0	0
Other private	1	31	0	0	0	0	0	0	0	0
Private nonguaranteed	**0**	**0**	**0**	**0**	**0**	**0**	**0**	**0**	**0**	**0**
Bonds	0	0	0	0	0	0	0	0	0	0
Commercial banks	0	0	0	0	0	0	0	0	0	0
Memo:										
IBRD	6	-7	-11	-6	-4	0	0	0	0	0
IDA	0	35	110	47	64	8	0	0	0	0
DEBT SERVICE (LTDS)	**34**	**102**	**23**	**25**	**17**	**3**	**17**	**0**	**0**	**3**
Public and publicly guaranteed	**34**	**102**	**23**	**25**	**17**	**3**	**17**	**0**	**0**	**3**
Official creditors	27	90	23	25	17	3	17	0	0	3
Multilateral	9	23	23	25	17	3	17	0	0	3
Concessional	0	5	10	18	11	3	10	0	0	0
Bilateral	18	67	0	0	0	0	0	0	0	0
Concessional	9	37	0	0	0	0	0	0	0	0
Private creditors	7	12	0	0	0	0	0	0	0	0
Bonds	1	0	0	0	0	0	0	0	0	0
Commercial banks	5	6	0	0	0	0	0	0	0	0
Other private	1	6	0	0	0	0	0	0	0	0
Private nonguaranteed	**0**	**0**	**0**	**0**	**0**	**0**	**0**	**0**	**0**	**0**
Bonds	0	0	0	0	0	0	0	0	0	0
Commercial banks	0	0	0	0	0	0	0	0	0	0
Memo:										
IBRD	9	8	11	6	4	0	0	0	0	0
IDA	0	1	10	14	10	0	0	0	0	0
UNDISBURSED DEBT	**126**	**1,310**	**1,284**	**908**	**801**	**678**	**634**	**583**	**562**	**540**
Official creditors	122	1,167	1,284	908	801	678	634	583	562	540
Private creditors	5	143	0	0	0	0	0	0	0	0
Memorandum items										
Concessional LDOD	139	1,730	4,452	4,597	4,671	4,775	4,838	4,750	4,636	4,704
Variable rate LDOD	0	408	1,927	1,772	1,752	1,909	2,103	1,874	1,772	1,844
Public sector LDOD	298	3,820	9,155	8,984	8,994	9,400	9,779	9,369	8,998	9,226
Private sector LDOD	0	327	496	496	496	496	496	496	496	496

6. CURRENCY COMPOSITION OF LONG-TERM DEBT (PERCENT)

	1970	1980	1990	1992	1993	1994	1995	1996	1997	1998
Deutsche mark	6.9	0.5	1.0	0.9	0.9	0.9	1.0	0.9	0.8	0.9
French franc	0.0	2.3	3.4	3.2	3.0	3.2	3.3	3.2	3.0	3.1
Japanese yen	0.0	2.0	2.3	2.6	2.9	3.1	2.9	2.7	2.5	2.7
Pound sterling	15.4	7.0	4.3	3.6	3.5	3.5	3.4	3.7	3.8	3.7
Swiss franc	0.0	0.6	18.6	16.9	16.6	17.9	19.6	17.5	16.9	17.4
U.S.dollars	12.4	54.4	48.1	50.2	50.9	49.3	47.6	49.3	50.8	49.9
Multiple currency	30.6	2.0	1.2	1.4	1.4	1.4	1.5	1.6	1.6	1.6
Special drawing rights	0.0	0.0	0.5	0.5	0.5	0.5	0.5	0.5	0.5	0.5
All other currencies	34.7	31.2	20.6	20.7	20.3	20.2	20.2	20.6	20.1	20.2

SUDAN

(US$ million, unless otherwise indicated)

	1970	1980	1990	1992	1993	1994	1995	1996	1997	1998
7. DEBT RESTRUCTURINGS										
Total amount rescheduled	..	..	0	0	0	0	0	0	0	0
Debt stock rescheduled	..	..	0	0	0	0	0	0	0	0
Principal rescheduled	..	..	0	0	0	0	0	0	0	0
Official	..	..	0	0	0	0	0	0	0	0
Private	..	..	0	0	0	0	0	0	0	0
Interest rescheduled	..	..	0	0	0	0	0	0	0	0
Official	..	..	0	0	0	0	0	0	0	0
Private	..	..	0	0	0	0	0	0	0	0
Debt forgiven	..	..	0	0	0	0	0	0	0	0
Memo: interest forgiven	..	..	0	0	0	0	0	0	0	0
Debt stock reduction	..	..	0	0	0	0	0	0	0	0
of which debt buyback	..	..	0	0	0	0	0	0	0	0
8. DEBT STOCK-FLOW RECONCILIATION										
Total change in debt stocks	..	..	1,403	224	386	1,082	685	-631	-646	517
Net flows on debt	83	839	169	272	91	9	0	-119	-157	-13
Net change in interest arrears	..	..	645	319	377	618	324	-54	-59	269
Interest capitalized	..	..	0	0	0	0	0	0	0	0
Debt forgiveness or reduction	..	..	0	0	0	0	0	0	0	0
Cross-currency valuation	..	..	566	-290	-55	377	361	-316	-291	210
Residual	..	..	23	-78	-27	78	1	-143	-139	52
9. AVERAGE TERMS OF NEW COMMITMENTS										
ALL CREDITORS										
Interest (%)	1.8	5.7	0.7	8.0	0.0	0.0	0.0	0.0	0.0	0.0
Maturity (years)	17.1	17.9	49.9	19.9	0.0	0.0	0.0	0.0	0.0	0.0
Grace period (years)	8.7	4.6	10.4	5.4	0.0	0.0	0.0	0.0	0.0	0.0
Grant element (%)	54.5	30.1	83.3	11.8	0.0	0.0	0.0	0.0	0.0	0.0
Official creditors										
Interest (%)	1.5	3.7	0.7	8.0	0.0	0.0	0.0	0.0	0.0	0.0
Maturity (years)	17.7	22.7	49.9	19.9	0.0	0.0	0.0	0.0	0.0	0.0
Grace period (years)	9.1	5.9	10.4	5.4	0.0	0.0	0.0	0.0	0.0	0.0
Grant element (%)	57.1	40.7	83.3	11.8	0.0	0.0	0.0	0.0	0.0	0.0
Private creditors										
Interest (%)	5.6	12.0	0.0	0.0	0.0	0.0	0.0	0.0	0.0	0.0
Maturity (years)	9.2	2.9	0.0	0.0	0.0	0.0	0.0	0.0	0.0	0.0
Grace period (years)	3.6	0.4	0.0	0.0	0.0	0.0	0.0	0.0	0.0	0.0
Grant element (%)	17.5	-3.4	0.0	0.0	0.0	0.0	0.0	0.0	0.0	0.0
Memorandum items										
Commitments	98	905	35	39	0	0	0	0	0	0
Official creditors	91	687	35	39	0	0	0	0	0	0
Private creditors	7	218	0	0	0	0	0	0	0	0

10. CONTRACTUAL OBLIGATIONS ON OUTSTANDING LONG-TERM DEBT

	1999	2000	2001	2002	2003	2004	2005	2006	2007	2008
TOTAL										
Disbursements	13	9	5	1	0	0	0	0	0	0
Principal	221	151	100	96	96	94	89	86	80	79
Interest	69	58	52	49	46	44	41	38	36	34
Official creditors										
Disbursements	13	9	5	1	0	0	0	0	0	0
Principal	220	151	100	96	96	94	89	86	80	79
Interest	69	58	52	49	46	44	41	38	36	34
Bilateral creditors										
Disbursements	0	0	0	0	0	0	0	0	0	0
Principal	170	98	44	44	43	42	39	36	32	28
Interest	50	41	36	35	33	31	29	27	25	24
Multilateral creditors										
Disbursements	13	9	5	1	0	0	0	0	0	0
Principal	51	53	56	53	53	51	50	50	48	51
Interest	18	17	16	15	14	13	12	11	11	10
Private creditors										
Disbursements	0	0	0	0	0	0	0	0	0	0
Principal	0	0	0	0	0	0	0	0	0	0
Interest	0	0	0	0	0	0	0	0	0	0
Commercial banks										
Disbursements	0	0	0	0	0	0	0	0	0	0
Principal	0	0	0	0	0	0	0	0	0	0
Interest	0	0	0	0	0	0	0	0	0	0
Other private										
Disbursements	0	0	0	0	0	0	0	0	0	0
Principal	0	0	0	0	0	0	0	0	0	0
Interest	0	0	0	0	0	0	0	0	0	0

SWAZILAND

(US$ million, unless otherwise indicated)

	1970	1980	1990	1992	1993	1994	1995	1996	1997	1998
1. SUMMARY DEBT DATA										
TOTAL DEBT STOCKS (EDT)	..	**209.5**	**253.8**	**222.1**	**207.6**	**219.6**	**234.9**	**221.7**	**368.2**	**250.7**
Long-term debt (LDOD)	**37.0**	**188.8**	**249.2**	**215.7**	**200.0**	**210.2**	**223.0**	**219.6**	**210.1**	**222.5**
Public and publicly guaranteed	37.0	188.8	249.2	215.7	200.0	210.2	223.0	219.6	210.1	222.5
Private nonguaranteed	0.0	0.0	0.0	0.0	0.0	0.0	0.0	0.0	0.0	0.0
Use of IMF credit	**0.0**	**5.7**	**0.0**	**0.0**	**0.0**	**0.0**	**0.0**	**0.0**	**0.0**	**0.0**
Short-term debt	..	**15.0**	**4.6**	**6.4**	**7.6**	**9.4**	**11.9**	**2.1**	**158.1**	**28.2**
of which interest arrears on LDOD	..	0.0	0.1	1.6	2.0	3.0	1.3	0.2	0.1	0.1
Official creditors	..	0.0	0.1	1.6	2.0	3.0	1.3	0.2	0.1	0.1
Private creditors	..	0.0	0.0	0.0	0.0	0.0	0.0	0.0	0.0	0.0
Memo: principal arrears on LDOD	..	0.0	0.2	3.9	3.9	4.1	4.5	1.2	1.1	1.2
Official creditors	..	0.0	0.2	3.6	3.0	3.5	4.2	1.2	1.1	1.2
Private creditors	..	0.0	0.0	0.3	0.9	0.5	0.3	0.0	0.0	0.0
Memo: export credits	..	0.0	28.0	20.0	18.0	18.0	14.0	19.0	22.0	22.0
TOTAL DEBT FLOWS										
Disbursements	**4.6**	**31.2**	**15.0**	**7.1**	**8.0**	**16.2**	**19.2**	**29.0**	**24.6**	**17.8**
Long-term debt	3.5	28.5	15.0	7.1	8.0	16.2	19.2	29.0	24.6	17.8
IMF purchases	1.1	2.7	0.0	0.0	0.0	0.0	0.0	0.0	0.0	0.0
Principal repayments	**2.5**	**7.5**	**36.2**	**17.0**	**17.0**	**19.9**	**16.1**	**21.0**	**16.3**	**14.4**
Long-term debt	1.5	7.5	35.8	17.0	17.0	19.9	16.1	21.0	16.3	14.4
IMF repurchases	1.0	0.0	0.3	0.0	0.0	0.0	0.0	0.0	0.0	0.0
Net flows on debt	**2.1**	**30.6**	**-37.9**	**-9.0**	**-8.2**	**-2.9**	**7.4**	**-0.9**	**164.4**	**-126.5**
of which short-term debt	..	7.0	-16.7	0.8	0.8	0.8	4.3	-8.8	156.1	-129.9
Interest payments (INT)	..	**10.6**	**10.7**	**7.9**	**6.8**	**6.2**	**5.5**	**12.0**	**15.1**	**9.1**
Long-term debt	1.9	9.0	10.3	7.6	6.6	6.0	5.1	11.7	7.3	7.5
IMF charges	0.0	0.0	0.0	0.0	0.0	0.0	0.0	0.0	0.0	0.0
Short-term debt	..	1.6	0.4	0.3	0.3	0.2	0.4	0.3	7.8	1.6
Net transfers on debt	..	**20.0**	**-48.6**	**-16.9**	**-15.1**	**-9.1**	**1.9**	**-12.9**	**149.2**	**-135.6**
Total debt service paid (TDS)	..	**18.1**	**46.9**	**24.8**	**23.9**	**26.1**	**21.6**	**33.1**	**31.5**	**23.4**
Long-term debt	3.4	16.5	46.1	24.6	23.6	25.9	21.2	32.8	23.7	21.9
IMF repurchases and charges	1.0	0.0	0.3	0.0	0.0	0.0	0.0	0.0	0.0	0.0
Short-term debt (interest only)	..	1.6	0.4	0.3	0.3	0.2	0.4	0.3	7.8	1.6
2. AGGREGATE NET RESOURCE FLOWS AND NET TRANSFERS (LONG-TERM)										
NET RESOURCE FLOWS	**5.5**	**59.3**	**29.3**	**98.9**	**79.7**	**70.4**	**45.4**	**39.7**	**99.8**	**98.9**
Net flow of long-term debt (ex. IMF)	2.0	21.0	-20.8	-9.8	-9.0	-3.7	3.1	7.9	8.3	3.4
Foreign direct investment (net)	0.0	26.5	30.0	83.0	70.0	56.0	26.0	13.0	75.0	80.0
Portfolio equity flows	0.0	0.0	0.0	0.0	0.0	0.0	0.0	0.0	0.0	0.0
Grants (excluding technical coop.)	3.5	11.8	20.1	25.8	18.7	18.0	16.3	18.8	16.5	15.5
Memo: technical coop. grants	2.0	22.7	28.5	29.5	30.5	23.5	28.0	23.2	13.9	18.7
official net resource flows	6.5	35.4	1.2	17.5	11.2	15.9	19.7	27.0	24.8	18.9
private net resource flows	-1.0	23.9	28.1	81.4	68.5	54.5	25.7	12.7	75.0	80.0
NET TRANSFERS	**3.6**	**23.0**	**-89.1**	**-3.1**	**-22.9**	**-35.6**	**-62.7**	**-71.0**	**-7.5**	**1.4**
Interest on long-term debt	1.9	9.0	10.3	7.6	6.6	6.0	5.1	11.7	7.3	7.5
Profit remittances on FDI	0.0	27.2	108.1	94.3	96.0	100.0	103.0	99.0	100.0	90.0
Memo: official net transfers	5.7	28.3	-8.3	10.3	5.0	10.1	14.7	15.3	17.5	11.4
private net transfers	-2.1	-5.3	-80.8	-13.4	-27.9	-45.7	-77.4	-86.3	-25.0	-10.0
3. MAJOR ECONOMIC AGGREGATES										
Gross national product (GNP)	98.7	587.6	918.8	1,062.0	1,034.9	1,045.3	1,348.4	1,334.1	1,447.4	1,342.0
Exports of goods & services (XGS)	..	450.7	819.6	933.7	932.7	1,042.2	1,182.2	1,151.0	1,172.6	1,095.3
of which workers remittances	..	0.0	..	..	..	..	..	..	..	..
Imports of goods & services (MGS)	..	659.2	836.6	1,101.6	1,152.2	1,188.2	1,300.1	1,355.6	1,330.4	1,219.3
International reserves (RES)	..	158.7	216.5	309.1	264.3	297.0	298.2	254.0	294.8	358.6
Current account balance	..	-129.7	84.6	-40.7	-63.7	10.7	20.9	-45.9	-47.8	-7.1
4. DEBT INDICATORS										
EDT / XGS (%)	..	46.5	31.0	23.8	22.3	21.1	19.9	19.3	31.4	22.9
EDT / GNP (%)	..	35.7	27.6	20.9	20.1	21.0	17.4	16.6	25.4	18.7
TDS / XGS (%)	..	4.0	5.7	2.7	2.6	2.5	1.8	2.9	2.7	2.1
INT / XGS (%)	..	2.4	1.3	0.9	0.7	0.6	0.5	1.0	1.3	0.8
INT / GNP (%)	..	1.8	1.2	0.7	0.7	0.6	0.4	0.9	1.0	0.7
RES / EDT (%)	..	75.8	85.3	139.2	127.3	135.2	127.0	114.6	80.1	143.0
RES / MGS (months)	..	2.9	3.1	3.4	2.8	3.0	2.8	2.3	2.7	3.5
Short-term / EDT (%)	..	7.2	1.8	2.9	3.7	4.3	5.1	1.0	42.9	11.3
Concessional / EDT (%)	..	41.0	62.9	65.7	65.1	69.7	71.0	69.5	38.2	57.1
Multilateral / EDT (%)	..	29.5	47.1	50.3	52.4	53.6	51.8	58.4	36.2	59.0

SWAZILAND

(US$ million, unless otherwise indicated)

	1970	1980	1990	1992	1993	1994	1995	1996	1997	1998
5. LONG-TERM DEBT										
DEBT OUTSTANDING (LDOD)	**37.0**	**188.8**	**249.2**	**215.7**	**200.0**	**210.2**	**223.0**	**219.6**	**210.1**	**222.5**
Public and publicly guaranteed	**37.0**	**188.8**	**249.2**	**215.7**	**200.0**	**210.2**	**223.0**	**219.6**	**210.1**	**222.5**
Official creditors	20.9	164.6	242.4	212.1	198.0	209.6	222.7	219.6	210.1	222.5
Multilateral	8.9	61.8	119.5	111.8	108.8	117.6	121.6	129.5	133.3	148.0
Concessional	2.8	16.7	46.0	50.4	49.1	63.4	66.9	64.9	64.5	69.1
Bilateral	12.0	102.8	123.0	100.3	89.3	92.0	101.1	90.1	76.7	74.5
Concessional	9.4	69.1	113.7	95.5	86.0	89.7	99.8	89.1	76.0	74.1
Private creditors	16.1	24.2	6.8	3.6	2.0	0.5	0.3	0.0	0.0	0.0
Bonds	0.0	0.0	0.0	0.0	0.0	0.0	0.0	0.0	0.0	0.0
Commercial banks	14.8	23.8	0.0	0.0	0.0	0.0	0.0	0.0	0.0	0.0
Other private	1.3	0.4	6.8	3.6	2.0	0.5	0.3	0.0	0.0	0.0
Private nonguaranteed	**0.0**	**0.0**	**0.0**	**0.0**	**0.0**	**0.0**	**0.0**	**0.0**	**0.0**	**0.0**
Bonds	0.0	0.0	0.0	0.0	0.0	0.0	0.0	0.0	0.0	0.0
Commercial banks	0.0	0.0	0.0	0.0	0.0	0.0	0.0	0.0	0.0	0.0
Memo:										
IBRD	6.1	17.7	36.9	27.6	23.5	20.9	19.2	14.5	9.9	9.9
IDA	2.8	7.5	6.8	6.5	6.3	6.2	5.9	5.7	5.4	5.2
DISBURSEMENTS	**3.5**	**28.5**	**15.0**	**7.1**	**8.0**	**16.2**	**19.2**	**29.0**	**24.6**	**17.8**
Public and publicly guaranteed	**3.5**	**28.5**	**15.0**	**7.1**	**8.0**	**16.2**	**19.2**	**29.0**	**24.6**	**17.8**
Official creditors	3.5	28.5	15.0	7.1	8.0	16.2	19.2	29.0	24.6	17.8
Multilateral	0.4	15.4	9.1	7.0	7.2	13.1	7.9	26.3	22.9	16.8
Concessional	0.0	0.3	3.6	5.8	0.7	12.5	3.5	3.2	4.5	4.2
Bilateral	3.1	13.1	5.9	0.1	0.8	3.1	11.3	2.7	1.7	0.9
Concessional	3.1	8.2	5.9	0.1	0.8	3.1	11.3	2.7	1.7	0.9
Private creditors	0.0	0.0	0.0	0.0	0.0	0.0	0.0	0.0	0.0	0.0
Bonds	0.0	0.0	0.0	0.0	0.0	0.0	0.0	0.0	0.0	0.0
Commercial banks	0.0	0.0	0.0	0.0	0.0	0.0	0.0	0.0	0.0	0.0
Other private	0.0	0.0	0.0	0.0	0.0	0.0	0.0	0.0	0.0	0.0
Private nonguaranteed	**0.0**	**0.0**	**0.0**	**0.0**	**0.0**	**0.0**	**0.0**	**0.0**	**0.0**	**0.0**
Bonds	0.0	0.0	0.0	0.0	0.0	0.0	0.0	0.0	0.0	0.0
Commercial banks	0.0	0.0	0.0	0.0	0.0	0.0	0.0	0.0	0.0	0.0
Memo:										
IBRD	0.4	2.1	1.0	0.0	0.0	0.0	0.0	2.7	1.3	2.7
IDA	0.0	0.3	0.0	0.0	0.0	0.0	0.0	0.0	0.0	0.0
PRINCIPAL REPAYMENTS	**1.5**	**7.5**	**35.8**	**17.0**	**17.0**	**19.9**	**16.1**	**21.0**	**16.3**	**14.4**
Public and publicly guaranteed	**1.5**	**7.5**	**35.8**	**17.0**	**17.0**	**19.9**	**16.1**	**21.0**	**16.3**	**14.4**
Official creditors	0.5	4.9	33.9	15.4	15.5	18.4	15.8	20.8	16.3	14.4
Multilateral	0.2	1.2	26.8	8.0	8.6	11.8	8.4	12.1	9.6	7.9
Concessional	0.0	0.1	1.1	0.6	1.2	1.3	1.7	2.3	1.7	1.8
Bilateral	0.3	3.7	7.1	7.4	6.9	6.5	7.4	8.7	6.7	6.5
Concessional	0.2	1.2	4.4	5.9	5.7	5.5	6.4	8.3	6.4	6.2
Private creditors	1.0	2.6	1.9	1.6	1.5	1.5	0.3	0.3	0.0	0.0
Bonds	0.0	0.0	0.0	0.0	0.0	0.0	0.0	0.0	0.0	0.0
Commercial banks	0.9	2.5	0.2	0.0	0.0	0.0	0.0	0.0	0.0	0.0
Other private	0.1	0.1	1.7	1.6	1.5	1.5	0.3	0.3	0.0	0.0
Private nonguaranteed	**0.0**	**0.0**	**0.0**	**0.0**	**0.0**	**0.0**	**0.0**	**0.0**	**0.0**	**0.0**
Bonds	0.0	0.0	0.0	0.0	0.0	0.0	0.0	0.0	0.0	0.0
Commercial banks	0.0	0.0	0.0	0.0	0.0	0.0	0.0	0.0	0.0	0.0
Memo:										
IBRD	0.2	0.7	20.4	4.0	4.1	4.4	3.5	5.8	4.8	2.7
IDA	0.0	0.0	0.2	0.1	0.2	0.2	0.3	0.3	0.3	0.3
NET FLOWS ON DEBT	**2.0**	**21.0**	**-20.8**	**-9.8**	**-9.0**	**-3.7**	**3.1**	**7.9**	**8.3**	**3.4**
Public and publicly guaranteed	**2.0**	**21.0**	**-20.8**	**-9.8**	**-9.0**	**-3.7**	**3.1**	**7.9**	**8.3**	**3.4**
Official creditors	3.0	23.6	-18.9	-8.3	-7.5	-2.1	3.4	8.2	8.3	3.4
Multilateral	0.2	14.3	-17.7	-1.0	-1.4	1.3	-0.5	14.2	13.2	9.0
Concessional	0.0	0.2	2.5	5.1	-0.5	11.1	1.8	0.9	2.8	2.4
Bilateral	2.8	9.4	-1.2	-7.2	-6.1	-3.4	3.9	-6.0	-5.0	-5.6
Concessional	2.9	7.0	1.5	-5.8	-4.9	-2.4	4.9	-5.7	-4.6	-5.2
Private creditors	-1.0	-2.6	-1.9	-1.6	-1.5	-1.5	-0.3	-0.3	0.0	0.0
Bonds	0.0	0.0	0.0	0.0	0.0	0.0	0.0	0.0	0.0	0.0
Commercial banks	-0.9	-2.5	-0.2	0.0	0.0	0.0	0.0	0.0	0.0	0.0
Other private	-0.1	-0.1	-1.7	-1.6	-1.5	-1.5	-0.3	-0.3	0.0	0.0
Private nonguaranteed	**0.0**	**0.0**	**0.0**	**0.0**	**0.0**	**0.0**	**0.0**	**0.0**	**0.0**	**0.0**
Bonds	0.0	0.0	0.0	0.0	0.0	0.0	0.0	0.0	0.0	0.0
Commercial banks	0.0	0.0	0.0	0.0	0.0	0.0	0.0	0.0	0.0	0.0
Memo:										
IBRD	0.2	1.3	-19.4	-4.0	-4.1	-4.4	-3.5	-3.1	-3.4	-0.1
IDA	0.0	0.3	-0.2	-0.1	-0.2	-0.2	-0.3	-0.3	-0.3	-0.3

SWAZILAND

(US$ million, unless otherwise indicated)

	1970	1980	1990	1992	1993	1994	1995	1996	1997	1998
INTEREST PAYMENTS (LINT)	**1.9**	**9.0**	**10.3**	**7.6**	**6.6**	**6.0**	**5.1**	**11.7**	**7.3**	**7.5**
Public and publicly guaranteed	**1.9**	**9.0**	**10.3**	**7.6**	**6.6**	**6.0**	**5.1**	**11.7**	**7.3**	**7.5**
Official creditors	0.8	7.1	9.5	7.2	6.2	5.8	5.0	11.7	7.3	7.5
Multilateral	0.4	3.1	6.6	4.6	4.3	4.0	3.2	10.0	5.6	6.0
Concessional	0.0	0.1	0.5	0.2	0.4	0.4	0.4	1.3	0.7	0.9
Bilateral	0.4	3.9	2.9	2.5	1.9	1.8	1.8	1.7	1.7	1.5
Concessional	0.2	0.7	1.7	1.8	1.4	1.5	1.6	1.6	1.6	1.4
Private creditors	1.1	2.0	0.8	0.5	0.4	0.2	0.1	0.0	0.0	0.0
Bonds	0.0	0.0	0.0	0.0	0.0	0.0	0.0	0.0	0.0	0.0
Commercial banks	1.1	1.9	0.0	0.0	0.0	0.0	0.0	0.0	0.0	0.0
Other private	0.1	0.0	0.8	0.5	0.4	0.2	0.1	0.0	0.0	0.0
Private nonguaranteed	**0.0**	**0.0**	**0.0**	**0.0**	**0.0**	**0.0**	**0.0**	**0.0**	**0.0**	**0.0**
Bonds	0.0	0.0	0.0	0.0	0.0	0.0	0.0	0.0	0.0	0.0
Commercial banks	0.0	0.0	0.0	0.0	0.0	0.0	0.0	0.0	0.0	0.0
Memo:										
IBRD	0.4	1.8	3.6	2.4	2.1	1.8	1.2	1.6	1.1	0.7
IDA	0.0	0.1	0.1	0.0	0.1	0.0	0.0	0.0	0.0	0.0
NET TRANSFERS ON DEBT	**0.1**	**12.0**	**-31.1**	**-17.5**	**-15.6**	**-9.7**	**-2.0**	**-3.8**	**0.9**	**-4.1**
Public and publicly guaranteed	**0.1**	**12.0**	**-31.1**	**-17.5**	**-15.6**	**-9.7**	**-2.0**	**-3.8**	**0.9**	**-4.1**
Official creditors	2.2	16.6	-28.4	-15.4	-13.7	-8.0	-1.6	-3.5	0.9	-4.1
Multilateral	-0.2	11.1	-24.2	-5.7	-5.7	-2.7	-3.7	4.3	7.6	3.0
Concessional	0.0	0.1	2.0	4.9	-0.9	10.7	1.4	-0.4	2.1	1.5
Bilateral	2.4	5.4	-4.1	-9.8	-8.0	-5.3	2.1	-7.8	-6.6	-7.1
Concessional	2.7	6.3	-0.2	-7.6	-6.3	-3.9	3.3	-7.3	-6.2	-6.7
Private creditors	-2.1	-4.6	-2.7	-2.0	-1.9	-1.7	-0.4	-0.3	0.0	0.0
Bonds	0.0	0.0	0.0	0.0	0.0	0.0	0.0	0.0	0.0	0.0
Commercial banks	-2.0	-4.4	-0.2	0.0	0.0	0.0	0.0	0.0	0.0	0.0
Other private	-0.1	-0.2	-2.5	-2.0	-1.9	-1.7	-0.4	-0.3	0.0	0.0
Private nonguaranteed	**0.0**	**0.0**	**0.0**	**0.0**	**0.0**	**0.0**	**0.0**	**0.0**	**0.0**	**0.0**
Bonds	0.0	0.0	0.0	0.0	0.0	0.0	0.0	0.0	0.0	0.0
Commercial banks	0.0	0.0	0.0	0.0	0.0	0.0	0.0	0.0	0.0	0.0
Memo:										
IBRD	-0.2	-0.4	-23.0	-6.4	-6.2	-6.3	-4.8	-4.8	-4.5	-0.7
IDA	0.0	0.2	-0.2	-0.2	-0.2	-0.2	-0.3	-0.3	-0.3	-0.3
DEBT SERVICE (LTDS)	**3.4**	**16.5**	**46.1**	**24.6**	**23.6**	**25.9**	**21.2**	**32.8**	**23.7**	**21.9**
Public and publicly guaranteed	**3.4**	**16.5**	**46.1**	**24.6**	**23.6**	**25.9**	**21.2**	**32.8**	**23.7**	**21.9**
Official creditors	1.3	11.9	43.4	22.6	21.7	24.2	20.8	32.5	23.7	21.9
Multilateral	0.6	4.3	33.4	12.7	12.9	15.8	11.6	22.1	15.3	13.9
Concessional	0.0	0.2	1.6	0.9	1.6	1.7	2.1	3.6	2.4	2.7
Bilateral	0.7	7.6	10.0	9.9	8.8	8.4	9.2	10.4	8.4	8.0
Concessional	0.4	1.8	6.1	7.7	7.1	7.1	8.0	9.9	8.0	7.6
Private creditors	2.1	4.6	2.7	2.0	1.9	1.7	0.4	0.3	0.0	0.0
Bonds	0.0	0.0	0.0	0.0	0.0	0.0	0.0	0.0	0.0	0.0
Commercial banks	2.0	4.4	0.2	0.0	0.0	0.0	0.0	0.0	0.0	0.0
Other private	0.1	0.2	2.5	2.0	1.9	1.7	0.4	0.3	0.0	0.0
Private nonguaranteed	**0.0**	**0.0**	**0.0**	**0.0**	**0.0**	**0.0**	**0.0**	**0.0**	**0.0**	**0.0**
Bonds	0.0	0.0	0.0	0.0	0.0	0.0	0.0	0.0	0.0	0.0
Commercial banks	0.0	0.0	0.0	0.0	0.0	0.0	0.0	0.0	0.0	0.0
Memo:										
IBRD	0.5	2.5	24.1	6.4	6.2	6.3	4.8	7.5	5.8	3.4
IDA	0.0	0.1	0.2	0.2	0.2	0.2	0.3	0.3	0.3	0.3
UNDISBURSED DEBT	**0.0**	**64.8**	**68.6**	**51.5**	**111.2**	**120.9**	**132.7**	**134.1**	**103.1**	**80.0**
Official creditors	0.0	64.8	68.6	51.5	111.2	120.9	132.7	134.1	103.1	80.0
Private creditors	0.0	0.0	0.0	0.0	0.0	0.0	0.0	0.0	0.0	0.0
Memorandum items										
Concessional LDOD	12.2	85.8	159.7	145.9	135.1	153.1	166.7	154.0	140.6	143.3
Variable rate LDOD	0.0	23.8	8.1	6.8	6.2	5.9	5.3	6.7	6.8	8.8
Public sector LDOD	37.0	188.8	249.2	215.7	200.0	210.2	223.0	219.6	210.1	222.5
Private sector LDOD	0.0	0.0	0.0	0.0	0.0	0.0	0.0	0.0	0.0	0.0

6. CURRENCY COMPOSITION OF LONG-TERM DEBT (PERCENT)

	1970	1980	1990	1992	1993	1994	1995	1996	1997	1998
Deutsche mark	0.0	12.7	16.7	16.1	15.3	16.9	20.7	19.5	17.6	17.4
French franc	0.0	0.0	1.5	1.4	1.4	1.3	1.2	1.0	0.9	0.8
Japanese yen	0.0	0.0	0.0	0.0	0.0	0.0	0.0	0.0	0.0	0.0
Pound sterling	38.1	20.4	10.4	7.8	6.8	5.9	4.9	4.5	3.6	2.5
Swiss franc	0.0	12.6	0.0	0.0	0.0	0.0	0.0	0.0	0.0	0.0
U.S.dollars	7.6	11.4	13.1	13.7	13.4	11.7	10.5	10.0	9.8	12.4
Multiple currency	16.5	17.0	33.7	35.0	37.0	39.1	38.5	42.8	47.9	46.8
Special drawing rights	0.0	0.0	2.2	2.7	2.6	2.8	2.6	2.3	2.8	3.2
All other currencies	37.8	25.9	22.4	23.3	23.5	22.3	21.6	19.9	17.4	16.9

SWAZILAND

(US$ million, unless otherwise indicated)

	1970	1980	1990	1992	1993	1994	1995	1996	1997	1998
7. DEBT RESTRUCTURINGS										
Total amount rescheduled	..	..	0.0	0.0	0.0	0.0	0.0	0.0	0.0	0.0
Debt stock rescheduled	..	..	0.0	0.0	0.0	0.0	0.0	0.0	0.0	0.0
Principal rescheduled	..	..	0.0	0.0	0.0	0.0	0.0	0.0	0.0	0.0
Official	..	..	0.0	0.0	0.0	0.0	0.0	0.0	0.0	0.0
Private	..	..	0.0	0.0	0.0	0.0	0.0	0.0	0.0	0.0
Interest rescheduled	..	..	0.0	0.0	0.0	0.0	0.0	0.0	0.0	0.0
Official	..	..	0.0	0.0	0.0	0.0	0.0	0.0	0.0	0.0
Private	..	..	0.0	0.0	0.0	0.0	0.0	0.0	0.0	0.0
Debt forgiven	..	..	0.0	0.0	0.0	0.0	0.0	0.0	0.0	0.0
Memo: interest forgiven	..	..	0.0	0.0	0.0	0.0	0.0	0.0	0.0	0.0
Debt stock reduction	..	..	0.0	0.0	0.0	0.0	0.0	0.0	0.0	0.0
of which debt buyback	..	..	0.0	0.0	0.0	0.0	0.0	0.0	0.0	0.0
8. DEBT STOCK-FLOW RECONCILIATION										
Total change in debt stocks	..	..	-15.8	-23.2	-14.5	12.0	15.3	-13.2	146.5	-117.4
Net flows on debt	2.1	30.6	-37.9	-9.0	-8.2	-2.9	7.4	-0.9	164.4	-126.5
Net change in interest arrears	..	..	0.0	0.8	0.4	1.0	-1.8	-1.1	0.0	0.0
Interest capitalized	..	..	0.0	0.0	0.0	0.0	0.0	0.0	0.0	0.0
Debt forgiveness or reduction	..	..	0.0	0.0	0.0	0.0	0.0	0.0	0.0	0.0
Cross-currency valuation	..	..	15.6	-12.6	-7.3	9.8	7.8	-9.1	-12.4	4.7
Residual	..	..	6.5	-2.3	0.6	4.0	1.8	-2.1	-5.5	4.4
9. AVERAGE TERMS OF NEW COMMITMENTS										
ALL CREDITORS										
Interest (%)	0.0	7.2	0.0	8.0	6.4	0.9	7.1	7.3	0.0	0.0
Maturity (years)	25.5	22.5	0.0	17.7	24.9	45.4	19.5	19.7	0.0	0.0
Grace period (years)	7.7	6.3	0.0	4.2	6.0	10.4	5.0	5.2	0.0	0.0
Grant element (%)	76.8	20.1	0.0	10.9	26.7	80.3	18.1	16.8	0.0	0.0
Official creditors										
Interest (%)	0.0	7.2	0.0	8.0	6.4	0.9	7.1	7.3	0.0	0.0
Maturity (years)	25.5	22.5	0.0	17.7	24.9	45.4	19.5	19.7	0.0	0.0
Grace period (years)	7.7	6.3	0.0	4.2	6.0	10.4	5.0	5.2	0.0	0.0
Grant element (%)	76.8	20.1	0.0	10.9	26.7	80.3	18.1	16.8	0.0	0.0
Private creditors										
Interest (%)	0.0	0.0	0.0	0.0	0.0	0.0	0.0	0.0	0.0	0.0
Maturity (years)	0.0	0.0	0.0	0.0	0.0	0.0	0.0	0.0	0.0	0.0
Grace period (years)	0.0	0.0	0.0	0.0	0.0	0.0	0.0	0.0	0.0	0.0
Grant element (%)	0.0	0.0	0.0	0.0	0.0	0.0	0.0	0.0	0.0	0.0
Memorandum items										
Commitments	3.1	16.9	0.0	8.5	75.4	18.9	29.0	35.9	0.0	0.0
Official creditors	3.1	16.9	0.0	8.5	75.4	18.9	29.0	35.9	0.0	0.0
Private creditors	0.0	0.0	0.0	0.0	0.0	0.0	0.0	0.0	0.0	0.0

10. CONTRACTUAL OBLIGATIONS ON OUTSTANDING LONG-TERM DEBT

	1999	2000	2001	2002	2003	2004	2005	2006	2007	2008
TOTAL										
Disbursements	21.1	22.0	17.8	9.7	5.6	3.0	0.7	0.0	0.0	0.0
Principal	16.8	16.5	18.5	17.9	16.5	16.2	16.5	16.5	16.2	15.0
Interest	8.4	9.1	9.4	9.1	8.7	8.2	7.4	6.6	5.8	5.0
Official creditors										
Disbursements	21.1	22.0	17.8	9.7	5.6	3.0	0.7	0.0	0.0	0.0
Principal	16.8	16.5	18.5	17.9	16.5	16.2	16.5	16.5	16.2	15.0
Interest	8.4	9.1	9.4	9.1	8.7	8.2	7.4	6.6	5.8	5.0
Bilateral creditors										
Disbursements	0.5	0.2	0.1	0.1	0.0	0.0	0.0	0.0	0.0	0.0
Principal	6.6	6.1	6.0	5.4	4.8	4.7	4.7	4.7	4.6	3.8
Interest	1.4	1.2	1.1	1.0	0.9	0.8	0.8	0.7	0.6	0.5
Multilateral creditors										
Disbursements	20.6	21.8	17.8	9.7	5.6	3.0	0.7	0.0	0.0	0.0
Principal	10.2	10.3	12.4	12.5	11.6	11.5	11.9	11.9	11.6	11.3
Interest	7.0	7.9	8.3	8.1	7.7	7.3	6.7	5.9	5.2	4.5
Private creditors										
Disbursements	0.0	0.0	0.0	0.0	0.0	0.0	0.0	0.0	0.0	0.0
Principal	0.0	0.0	0.0	0.0	0.0	0.0	0.0	0.0	0.0	0.0
Interest	0.0	0.0	0.0	0.0	0.0	0.0	0.0	0.0	0.0	0.0
Commercial banks										
Disbursements	0.0	0.0	0.0	0.0	0.0	0.0	0.0	0.0	0.0	0.0
Principal	0.0	0.0	0.0	0.0	0.0	0.0	0.0	0.0	0.0	0.0
Interest	0.0	0.0	0.0	0.0	0.0	0.0	0.0	0.0	0.0	0.0
Other private										
Disbursements	0.0	0.0	0.0	0.0	0.0	0.0	0.0	0.0	0.0	0.0
Principal	0.0	0.0	0.0	0.0	0.0	0.0	0.0	0.0	0.0	0.0
Interest	0.0	0.0	0.0	0.0	0.0	0.0	0.0	0.0	0.0	0.0

SYRIAN ARAB REPUBLIC

(US$ million, unless otherwise indicated)

	1970	1980	1990	1992	1993	1994	1995	1996	1997	1998
1. SUMMARY DEBT DATA										
TOTAL DEBT STOCKS (EDT)	**..**	**3,552**	**17,068**	**19,017**	**19,976**	**20,558**	**21,318**	**21,420**	**20,865**	**22,435**
Long-term debt (LDOD)	**233**	**2,921**	**14,917**	**15,913**	**16,235**	**16,540**	**16,757**	**16,698**	**16,254**	**16,328**
Public and publicly guaranteed	233	2,921	14,917	15,913	16,235	16,540	16,757	16,698	16,254	16,328
Private nonguaranteed	0	0	0	0	0	0	0	0	0	0
Use of IMF credit	**10**	**0**	**0**	**0**	**0**	**0**	**0**	**0**	**0**	**0**
Short-term debt	**..**	**631**	**2,151**	**3,104**	**3,741**	**4,018**	**4,562**	**4,722**	**4,611**	**6,107**
of which interest arrears on LDOD	..	0	460	912	1,149	1,400	1,633	1,822	1,976	2,155
Official creditors	..	0	407	833	1,045	1,281	1,502	1,685	1,838	2,011
Private creditors	..	0	53	78	104	119	131	137	138	144
Memo: principal arrears on LDOD	..	0	864	2,588	3,512	4,563	5,654	6,638	7,410	8,238
Official creditors	..	0	580	2,125	2,887	3,824	4,831	5,727	6,447	7,218
Private creditors	..	0	284	463	626	739	823	910	963	1,020
Memo: export credits	..	0	360	391	665	695	675	439	380	397
TOTAL DEBT FLOWS										
Disbursements	**63**	**1,147**	**196**	**193**	**223**	**265**	**242**	**168**	**104**	**64**
Long-term debt	60	1,147	196	193	223	265	242	168	104	64
IMF purchases	3	0	0	0	0	0	0	0	0	0
Principal repayments	**31**	**225**	**1,137**	**139**	**102**	**129**	**92**	**77**	**362**	**96**
Long-term debt	31	225	1,137	139	102	129	92	77	362	96
IMF repurchases	0	0	0	0	0	0	0	0	0	0
Net flows on debt	**67**	**1,239**	**-733**	**345**	**522**	**163**	**460**	**63**	**-523**	**1,285**
of which short-term debt	..	317	208	291	400	26	311	-29	-265	1,317
Interest payments (INT)	**..**	**157**	**135**	**166**	**182**	**269**	**201**	**178**	**202**	**243**
Long-term debt	6	77	54	68	72	100	62	48	63	78
IMF charges	0	0	0	0	0	0	0	0	0	0
Short-term debt	..	80	82	98	110	169	139	130	138	165
Net transfers on debt	**..**	**1,082**	**-869**	**179**	**340**	**-107**	**259**	**-115**	**-725**	**1,042**
Total debt service paid (TDS)	**..**	**382**	**1,273**	**305**	**283**	**398**	**293**	**254**	**563**	**339**
Long-term debt	37	302	1,191	207	174	229	155	124	425	174
IMF repurchases and charges	0	0	0	0	0	0	0	0	0	0
Short-term debt (interest only)	..	80	82	98	110	169	139	130	138	165
2. AGGREGATE NET RESOURCE FLOWS AND NET TRANSFERS (LONG-TERM)										
NET RESOURCE FLOWS	**41**	**2,573**	**-250**	**81**	**344**	**506**	**320**	**217**	**-106**	**143**
Net flow of long-term debt (ex. IMF)	29	922	-941	54	122	137	149	92	-258	-32
Foreign direct investment (net)	0	0	71	0	176	251	100	89	80	80
Portfolio equity flows	0	0	0	0	0	0	0	0	0	0
Grants (excluding technical coop.)	11	1,651	621	26	46	118	70	36	72	95
Memo: technical coop. grants	8	26	32	69	61	62	82	74	46	49
official net resource flows	11	2,531	-268	133	196	281	242	140	-174	67
private net resource flows	30	42	18	-53	148	225	78	77	69	76
NET TRANSFERS	**34**	**2,496**	**-303**	**13**	**272**	**406**	**257**	**169**	**-169**	**65**
Interest on long-term debt	6	77	54	68	72	100	62	48	63	78
Profit remittances on FDI	0	0	0	0	0	0	0	0	0	0
Memo: official net transfers	9	2,485	-305	73	129	185	182	94	-237	-10
private net transfers	26	11	1	-60	143	221	75	75	67	75
3. MAJOR ECONOMIC AGGREGATES										
Gross national product (GNP)	2,138	13,074	11,522	12,899	13,365	15,442	16,831	16,770	15,634	16,271
Exports of goods & services (XGS)	..	3,341	5,460	4,999	5,280	5,830	6,281	6,545	6,082	5,319
of which workers remittances	..	0	0	0	0	0	0	0	0	0
Imports of goods & services (MGS)	..	4,610	3,786	5,257	6,018	7,212	6,521	7,088	6,098	5,783
International reserves (RES)	57	828	..	..	..	..	..	..	..	..
Current account balance	..	251	1,762	55	-203	-791	367	81	483	59
4. DEBT INDICATORS										
EDT / XGS (%)	..	106.3	312.6	380.4	378.3	352.6	339.4	327.3	343.1	421.8
EDT / GNP (%)	..	27.2	148.1	147.4	149.5	133.1	126.7	127.7	133.5	137.9
TDS / XGS (%)	..	11.4	23.3	6.1	5.4	6.8	4.7	3.9	9.3	6.4
INT / XGS (%)	..	4.7	2.5	3.3	3.4	4.6	3.2	2.7	3.3	4.6
INT / GNP (%)	..	1.2	1.2	1.3	1.4	1.7	1.2	1.1	1.3	1.5
RES / EDT (%)	..	23.3	..	..	..	..	..	..	..	..
RES / MGS (months)	..	2.2	..	..	..	..	..	..	..	..
Short-term / EDT (%)	..	17.8	12.6	16.3	18.7	19.5	21.4	22.0	22.1	27.2
Concessional / EDT (%)	..	51.9	76.5	75.1	72.6	72.1	70.6	70.4	71.8	67.2
Multilateral / EDT (%)	..	8.8	5.1	4.4	4.2	4.5	4.8	4.8	3.4	3.2

(US$ million, unless otherwise indicated)

	1970	1980	1990	1992	1993	1994	1995	1996	1997	1998
5. LONG-TERM DEBT										
DEBT OUTSTANDING (LDOD)	**233**	**2,921**	**14,917**	**15,913**	**16,235**	**16,540**	**16,757**	**16,698**	**16,254**	**16,328**
Public and publicly guaranteed	**233**	**2,921**	**14,917**	**15,913**	**16,235**	**16,540**	**16,757**	**16,698**	**16,254**	**16,328**
Official creditors	59	2,165	13,744	14,875	15,058	15,370	15,601	15,553	15,138	15,208
Multilateral	4	311	877	834	835	918	1,031	1,030	718	710
Concessional	4	89	185	237	275	381	485	552	563	585
Bilateral	55	1,854	12,868	14,041	14,223	14,452	14,570	14,523	14,420	14,499
Concessional	35	1,753	12,868	14,041	14,222	14,450	14,568	14,521	14,419	14,497
Private creditors	174	756	1,173	1,039	1,177	1,170	1,156	1,145	1,116	1,120
Bonds	0	0	0	0	0	0	0	0	0	0
Commercial banks	0	0	0	0	0	0	0	0	0	0
Other private	174	756	1,173	1,039	1,177	1,170	1,156	1,145	1,116	1,120
Private nonguaranteed	**0**	**0**	**0**	**0**	**0**	**0**	**0**	**0**	**0**	**0**
Bonds	0	0	0	0	0	0	0	0	0	0
Commercial banks	0	0	0	0	0	0	0	0	0	0
Memo:										
IBRD	0	215	479	433	419	405	428	383	85	67
IDA	4	42	44	44	44	44	44	44	34	32
DISBURSEMENTS	**60**	**1,147**	**196**	**193**	**223**	**265**	**242**	**168**	**104**	**64**
Public and publicly guaranteed	**60**	**1,147**	**196**	**193**	**223**	**265**	**242**	**168**	**104**	**64**
Official creditors	9	972	159	190	223	265	242	168	104	63
Multilateral	3	64	30	79	47	123	123	90	55	35
Concessional	3	2	8	77	47	122	122	90	54	35
Bilateral	6	907	128	111	176	142	118	78	49	28
Concessional	5	900	128	111	174	142	118	78	49	28
Private creditors	51	176	37	3	1	0	0	0	0	1
Bonds	0	0	0	0	0	0	0	0	0	0
Commercial banks	0	0	0	0	0	0	0	0	0	0
Other private	51	176	37	3	1	0	0	0	0	1
Private nonguaranteed	**0**	**0**	**0**	**0**	**0**	**0**	**0**	**0**	**0**	**0**
Bonds	0	0	0	0	0	0	0	0	0	0
Commercial banks	0	0	0	0	0	0	0	0	0	0
Memo:										
IBRD	0	60	0	0	0	0	0	0	0	0
IDA	3	2	0	0	0	0	0	0	0	0
PRINCIPAL REPAYMENTS	**31**	**225**	**1,137**	**139**	**102**	**129**	**92**	**77**	**362**	**96**
Public and publicly guaranteed	**31**	**225**	**1,137**	**139**	**102**	**129**	**92**	**77**	**362**	**96**
Official creditors	10	92	1,048	83	73	103	70	65	350	91
Multilateral	0	4	32	61	52	85	53	40	313	57
Concessional	0	1	12	11	14	18	20	20	33	20
Bilateral	10	88	1,016	22	21	17	17	25	37	34
Concessional	5	31	1,016	20	21	17	17	25	37	34
Private creditors	21	133	90	56	29	26	22	12	11	5
Bonds	0	0	0	0	0	0	0	0	0	0
Commercial banks	0	0	0	0	0	0	0	0	0	0
Other private	21	133	90	56	29	26	22	12	11	5
Private nonguaranteed	**0**	**0**	**0**	**0**	**0**	**0**	**0**	**0**	**0**	**0**
Bonds	0	0	0	0	0	0	0	0	0	0
Commercial banks	0	0	0	0	0	0	0	0	0	0
Memo:										
IBRD	0	3	1	29	19	49	13	0	262	22
IDA	0	0	2	0	0	0	0	0	10	2
NET FLOWS ON DEBT	**29**	**922**	**-941**	**54**	**122**	**137**	**149**	**92**	**-258**	**-32**
Public and publicly guaranteed	**29**	**922**	**-941**	**54**	**122**	**137**	**149**	**92**	**-258**	**-32**
Official creditors	-1	880	-889	107	150	163	172	104	-246	-28
Multilateral	3	60	-2	18	-5	38	71	51	-259	-22
Concessional	3	2	-4	67	33	104	102	70	22	15
Bilateral	-3	820	-887	89	155	125	101	53	12	-6
Concessional	0	869	-887	91	153	125	101	53	12	-6
Private creditors	30	42	-53	-53	-28	-26	-22	-12	-11	-4
Bonds	0	0	0	0	0	0	0	0	0	0
Commercial banks	0	0	0	0	0	0	0	0	0	0
Other private	30	42	-53	-53	-28	-26	-22	-12	-11	-4
Private nonguaranteed	**0**	**0**	**0**	**0**	**0**	**0**	**0**	**0**	**0**	**0**
Bonds	0	0	0	0	0	0	0	0	0	0
Commercial banks	0	0	0	0	0	0	0	0	0	0
Memo:										
IBRD	0	57	-1	-29	-19	-49	-13	0	-262	-22
IDA	3	2	-2	0	0	0	0	0	-10	-2

SYRIAN ARAB REPUBLIC

(US$ million, unless otherwise indicated)

	1970	1980	1990	1992	1993	1994	1995	1996	1997	1998
INTEREST PAYMENTS (LINT)	**6**	**77**	**54**	**68**	**72**	**100**	**62**	**48**	**63**	**78**
Public and publicly guaranteed	**6**	**77**	**54**	**68**	**72**	**100**	**62**	**48**	**63**	**78**
Official creditors	2	46	36	61	67	96	60	46	62	77
Multilateral	0	20	17	41	36	80	39	29	40	56
Concessional	0	1	6	5	8	14	20	23	27	24
Bilateral	2	26	19	20	31	16	20	17	22	21
Concessional	1	18	19	20	31	16	20	17	22	21
Private creditors	4	31	17	8	5	4	3	2	1	1
Bonds	0	0	0	0	0	0	0	0	0	0
Commercial banks	0	0	0	0	0	0	0	0	0	0
Other private	4	31	17	8	5	4	3	2	1	1
Private nonguaranteed	**0**	**0**	**0**	**0**	**0**	**0**	**0**	**0**	**0**	**0**
Bonds	0	0	0	0	0	0	0	0	0	0
Commercial banks	0	0	0	0	0	0	0	0	0	0
Memo:										
IBRD	0	18	1	27	20	59	12	0	9	28
IDA	0	0	1	0	0	0	0	0	3	0
NET TRANSFERS ON DEBT	**23**	**845**	**-995**	**-14**	**50**	**36**	**87**	**44**	**-321**	**-110**
Public and publicly guaranteed	**23**	**845**	**-995**	**-14**	**50**	**36**	**87**	**44**	**-321**	**-110**
Official creditors	-2	834	-925	47	83	66	112	58	-309	-105
Multilateral	3	40	-19	-23	-41	-42	32	22	-299	-78
Concessional	3	1	-10	62	24	90	82	47	-5	-9
Bilateral	-5	794	-907	69	124	109	81	36	-10	-27
Concessional	-1	851	-907	71	122	109	81	36	-10	-27
Private creditors	26	11	-70	-60	-33	-30	-25	-14	-13	-5
Bonds	0	0	0	0	0	0	0	0	0	0
Commercial banks	0	0	0	0	0	0	0	0	0	0
Other private	26	11	-70	-60	-33	-30	-25	-14	-13	-5
Private nonguaranteed	**0**	**0**	**0**	**0**	**0**	**0**	**0**	**0**	**0**	**0**
Bonds	0	0	0	0	0	0	0	0	0	0
Commercial banks	0	0	0	0	0	0	0	0	0	0
Memo:										
IBRD	0	39	-2	-56	-39	-107	-25	0	-271	-50
IDA	3	1	-2	0	0	0	0	0	-13	-2
DEBT SERVICE (LTDS)	**37**	**302**	**1,191**	**207**	**174**	**229**	**155**	**124**	**425**	**174**
Public and publicly guaranteed	**37**	**302**	**1,191**	**207**	**174**	**229**	**155**	**124**	**425**	**174**
Official creditors	11	138	1,084	143	140	199	130	111	412	168
Multilateral	0	24	49	101	89	166	92	69	354	113
Concessional	0	2	18	15	22	32	41	44	60	44
Bilateral	11	114	1,035	42	52	33	38	42	59	55
Concessional	6	49	1,035	40	52	33	38	42	59	55
Private creditors	25	165	107	64	34	30	25	14	13	6
Bonds	0	0	0	0	0	0	0	0	0	0
Commercial banks	0	0	0	0	0	0	0	0	0	0
Other private	25	165	107	64	34	30	25	14	13	6
Private nonguaranteed	**0**	**0**	**0**	**0**	**0**	**0**	**0**	**0**	**0**	**0**
Bonds	0	0	0	0	0	0	0	0	0	0
Commercial banks	0	0	0	0	0	0	0	0	0	0
Memo:										
IBRD	0	21	2	56	39	107	25	0	271	50
IDA	0	0	2	0	0	0	0	0	13	2
UNDISBURSED DEBT	**110**	**1,971**	**712**	**1,226**	**1,377**	**1,167**	**912**	**686**	**529**	**515**
Official creditors	11	1,388	673	1,213	1,369	1,157	902	677	521	507
Private creditors	99	583	39	13	8	9	10	9	8	8
Memorandum items										
Concessional LDOD	39	1,842	13,052	14,278	14,497	14,831	15,053	15,073	14,981	15,082
Variable rate LDOD	0	0	0	0	0	0	0	0	0	0
Public sector LDOD	233	2,921	14,917	15,913	16,235	16,540	16,756	16,697	16,253	16,328
Private sector LDOD	0	0	0	0	0	0	0	0	0	0
6. CURRENCY COMPOSITION OF LONG-TERM DEBT (PERCENT)										
Deutsche mark	1.7	1.5	2.1	2.2	2.1	2.3	2.4	2.2	2.0	2.1
French franc	7.0	3.6	0.8	0.7	0.7	0.7	0.8	0.7	0.7	0.7
Japanese yen	0.0	0.3	1.9	2.9	3.5	3.8	3.5	3.1	2.8	3.1
Pound sterling	4.0	0.2	0.8	0.4	0.8	0.8	0.7	0.7	0.7	0.7
Swiss franc	4.1	0.8	0.0	0.0	0.0	0.0	0.0	0.0	0.0	0.0
U.S.dollars	31.2	70.0	86.4	86.8	85.1	83.5	82.4	82.7	84.8	84.4
Multiple currency	0.0	8.0	3.4	2.8	2.7	2.5	2.7	2.4	0.6	0.5
Special drawing rights	0.0	0.0	0.0	0.0	0.0	0.0	0.0	0.0	0.0	0.0
All other currencies	52.0	15.6	4.6	4.2	5.1	6.4	7.5	8.2	8.4	8.5

SYRIAN ARAB REPUBLIC

(US$ million, unless otherwise indicated)

7. DEBT RESTRUCTURINGS

	1970	1980	1990	1992	1993	1994	1995	1996	1997	1998
Total amount rescheduled	..	..	0	0	0	0	0	0	0	0
Debt stock rescheduled	..	..	0	0	0	0	0	0	0	0
Principal rescheduled	..	..	0	0	0	0	0	0	0	0
Official	..	..	0	0	0	0	0	0	0	0
Private	..	..	0	0	0	0	0	0	0	0
Interest rescheduled	..	..	0	0	0	0	0	0	0	0
Official	..	..	0	0	0	0	0	0	0	0
Private	..	..	0	0	0	0	0	0	0	0
Debt forgiven	..	..	0	398	0	0	0	0	0	0
Memo: interest forgiven	..	..	0	6	0	0	0	0	0	0
Debt stock reduction	..	..	0	0	0	0	0	0	0	0
of which debt buyback	..	..	0	0	0	0	0	0	0	0

8. DEBT STOCK-FLOW RECONCILIATION

	1970	1980	1990	1992	1993	1994	1995	1996	1997	1998
Total change in debt stocks	..	..	-321	75	959	582	760	101	-555	1,571
Net flows on debt	67	1,239	-733	345	522	163	460	63	-523	1,285
Net change in interest arrears	..	..	247	224	238	251	233	189	154	179
Interest capitalized	..	..	0	0	0	0	0	0	0	0
Debt forgiveness or reduction	..	..	0	-398	0	0	0	0	0	0
Cross-currency valuation	..	..	185	-99	35	164	64	-138	-242	110
Residual	..	..	-20	2	166	5	3	-13	56	-3

9. AVERAGE TERMS OF NEW COMMITMENTS

	1970	1980	1990	1992	1993	1994	1995	1996	1997	1998
ALL CREDITORS										
Interest (%)	4.3	2.5	3.7	4.2	3.8	0.0	0.0	0.0	0.0	0.0
Maturity (years)	8.7	22.4	22.7	22.0	21.7	0.0	0.0	0.0	0.0	0.0
Grace period (years)	2.4	4.3	6.1	6.0	5.1	0.0	0.0	0.0	0.0	0.0
Grant element (%)	24.0	50.7	43.6	40.0	41.6	0.0	0.0	0.0	0.0	0.0
Official creditors										
Interest (%)	2.7	2.0	3.8	4.2	3.8	0.0	0.0	0.0	0.0	0.0
Maturity (years)	8.7	25.1	23.0	22.0	21.7	0.0	0.0	0.0	0.0	0.0
Grace period (years)	3.0	4.2	6.2	6.0	5.1	0.0	0.0	0.0	0.0	0.0
Grant element (%)	30.4	55.8	43.9	40.0	41.6	0.0	0.0	0.0	0.0	0.0
Private creditors										
Interest (%)	4.5	4.1	3.0	0.0	0.0	0.0	0.0	0.0	0.0	0.0
Maturity (years)	8.7	12.6	12.8	0.0	0.0	0.0	0.0	0.0	0.0	0.0
Grace period (years)	2.4	4.4	3.6	0.0	0.0	0.0	0.0	0.0	0.0	0.0
Grant element (%)	23.2	32.2	36.3	0.0	0.0	0.0	0.0	0.0	0.0	0.0
Memorandum items										
Commitments	14	1,169	344	262	345	0	0	0	0	0
Official creditors	2	918	334	262	345	0	0	0	0	0
Private creditors	13	251	10	0	0	0	0	0	0	0

10. CONTRACTUAL OBLIGATIONS ON OUTSTANDING LONG-TERM DEBT

	1999	2000	2001	2002	2003	2004	2005	2006	2007	2008
TOTAL										
Disbursements	50	29	10	5	1	0	0	0	0	0
Principal	964	952	916	909	896	891	873	863	118	109
Interest	202	178	155	133	112	90	69	49	30	26
Official creditors										
Disbursements	45	27	10	5	1	0	0	0	0	0
Principal	927	923	907	903	891	886	869	862	118	109
Interest	199	176	154	133	111	90	69	49	30	26
Bilateral creditors										
Disbursements	25	15	5	1	1	0	0	0	0	0
Principal	850	850	850	851	840	839	831	827	84	76
Interest	167	148	130	111	92	73	55	37	19	16
Multilateral creditors										
Disbursements	20	12	5	4	0	0	0	0	0	0
Principal	77	74	57	52	51	47	38	35	33	33
Interest	32	28	25	22	19	17	14	13	11	10
Private creditors										
Disbursements	5	2	0	0	0	0	0	0	0	0
Principal	37	28	9	6	5	5	4	2	0	0
Interest	3	2	1	1	1	0	0	0	0	0
Commercial banks										
Disbursements	0	0	0	0	0	0	0	0	0	0
Principal	0	0	0	0	0	0	0	0	0	0
Interest	0	0	0	0	0	0	0	0	0	0
Other private										
Disbursements	5	2	0	0	0	0	0	0	0	0
Principal	37	28	9	6	5	5	4	2	0	0
Interest	3	2	1	1	1	0	0	0	0	0

TAJIKISTAN

(US$ million, unless otherwise indicated)

	1970	1980	1990	1992	1993	1994	1995	1996	1997	1998
1. SUMMARY DEBT DATA										
TOTAL DEBT STOCKS (EDT)	..	..	..	**9.7**	**385.2**	**580.3**	**633.6**	**699.4**	**901.1**	**1,069.5**
Long-term debt (LDOD)	..	..	..	**9.7**	**384.9**	**562.0**	**590.4**	**656.8**	**797.0**	**823.3**
Public and publicly guaranteed	..	..	..	9.7	384.9	562.0	590.4	656.8	669.0	706.9
Private nonguaranteed	..	..	..	0.0	0.0	0.0	0.0	0.0	128.0	116.4
Use of IMF credit	..	..	..	**0.0**	**0.0**	**0.0**	**0.0**	**21.6**	**30.4**	**99.0**
Short-term debt	..	..	..	**0.0**	**0.3**	**18.3**	**43.2**	**21.0**	**73.7**	**147.2**
of which interest arrears on LDOD	..	..	..	0.0	0.3	18.3	43.2	13.0	36.7	35.2
Official creditors	..	..	..	0.0	0.3	16.0	37.0	4.5	14.8	15.6
Private creditors	..	..	..	0.0	0.0	2.3	6.2	8.4	21.9	19.7
Memo: principal arrears on LDOD	..	..	..	0.0	0.0	60.3	141.9	89.6	99.5	94.7
Official creditors	..	..	..	0.0	0.0	60.3	120.2	21.6	31.5	34.8
Private creditors	..	..	..	0.0	0.0	0.0	21.7	68.0	68.0	59.9
Memo: export credits	..	..	..	0.0	0.0	0.0	38.0	0.0	0.0	39.0
TOTAL DEBT FLOWS										
Disbursements	..	..	..	**9.7**	**78.2**	**177.1**	**28.4**	**58.3**	**52.3**	**120.2**
Long-term debt	..	..	..	9.7	78.2	177.1	28.4	36.5	42.0	55.3
IMF purchases	..	..	..	0.0	0.0	0.0	0.0	21.8	10.3	64.9
Principal repayments	..	..	..	**0.0**	**0.0**	**0.0**	**0.0**	**0.0**	**28.9**	**60.3**
Long-term debt	..	..	..	0.0	0.0	0.0	0.0	0.0	28.9	60.3
IMF repurchases	..	..	..	0.0	0.0	0.0	0.0	0.0	0.0	0.0
Net flows on debt	..	..	..	**9.7**	**78.2**	**177.1**	**28.4**	**66.3**	**52.4**	**134.9**
of which short-term debt	..	..	..	0.0	0.0	0.0	0.0	8.0	29.0	75.0
Interest payments (INT)	..	..	..	**0.0**	**0.8**	**0.4**	**0.0**	**1.1**	**8.1**	**22.7**
Long-term debt	..	..	..	0.0	0.8	0.4	0.0	0.3	5.9	19.9
IMF charges	..	..	..	0.0	0.0	0.0	0.0	0.5	0.9	1.7
Short-term debt	..	..	..	0.0	0.0	0.0	0.0	0.4	1.2	1.1
Net transfers on debt	..	..	..	**9.7**	**77.3**	**176.7**	**28.4**	**65.2**	**44.3**	**112.2**
Total debt service paid (TDS)	..	..	..	**0.0**	**0.8**	**0.4**	**0.0**	**1.1**	**37.0**	**83.0**
Long-term debt	..	..	..	0.0	0.8	0.4	0.0	0.3	34.8	80.2
IMF repurchases and charges	..	..	..	0.0	0.0	0.0	0.0	0.5	0.9	1.7
Short-term debt (interest only)	..	..	..	0.0	0.0	0.0	0.0	0.4	1.2	1.1
2. AGGREGATE NET RESOURCE FLOWS AND NET TRANSFERS (LONG-TERM)										
NET RESOURCE FLOWS	..	..	..	**9.9**	**88.8**	**249.8**	**96.9**	**111.0**	**88.0**	**69.6**
Net flow of long-term debt (ex. IMF)	..	..	..	9.7	78.2	177.1	28.4	36.5	13.1	-5.0
Foreign direct investment (net)	..	..	..	0.0	0.0	10.0	15.0	16.0	20.0	18.0
Portfolio equity flows	..	..	..	0.0	0.0	0.0	0.0	0.0	0.0	0.0
Grants (excluding technical coop.)	..	..	..	0.2	10.6	62.7	53.5	58.5	54.8	56.5
Memo: technical coop. grants	..	..	..	0.4	1.0	4.0	11.2	14.4	8.5	10.0
official net resource flows	..	..	..	9.9	20.8	239.8	81.9	95.0	68.3	72.4
private net resource flows	..	..	..	0.0	68.0	10.0	15.0	16.0	19.7	-2.8
NET TRANSFERS	..	..	..	**9.9**	**88.0**	**249.4**	**96.9**	**110.7**	**82.1**	**49.8**
Interest on long-term debt	..	..	..	0.0	0.8	0.4	0.0	0.3	5.9	19.9
Profit remittances on FDI	..	..	..	0.0	0.0	0.0	0.0	0.0	0.0	0.0
Memo: official net transfers	..	..	..	9.9	20.8	239.4	81.9	94.7	63.4	57.7
private net transfers	..	..	..	0.0	67.2	10.0	15.0	16.0	18.7	-7.9
3. MAJOR ECONOMIC AGGREGATES										
Gross national product (GNP)	..	..	..	3,133.5	2,972.1	2,069.9	1,969.5	1,950.1	2,134.2	2,163.7
Exports of goods & services (XGS)	..	..	..	..	456.0	559.0	779.0	770.0	746.0	604.0
of which workers remittances	..	..	..	0.0	0.0	0.0	0.0	0.0	0.0	..
Imports of goods & services (MGS)	..	..	..	..	690.0	754.0	893.0	876.0	846.0	769.0
International reserves (RES)	..	..	..	..	..	..	..	..	..	..
Current account balance	..	..	..	..	-208.0	-170.0	-89.0	-76.0	-60.0	-107.0
4. DEBT INDICATORS										
EDT / XGS (%)	..	..	..	..	84.5	103.8	81.3	90.8	120.8	177.1
EDT / GNP (%)	..	..	..	0.3	13.0	28.0	32.2	35.9	42.2	49.4
TDS / XGS (%)	..	..	..	..	0.2	0.1	0.0	0.1	5.0	13.7
INT / XGS (%)	..	..	..	..	0.2	0.1	0.0	0.1	1.1	3.8
INT / GNP (%)	..	..	..	0.0	0.0	0.0	0.0	0.1	0.4	1.1
RES / EDT (%)	..	..	..	..	..	..	..	..	..	..
RES / MGS (months)	..	..	..	..	..	..	..	..	..	..
Short-term / EDT (%)	..	..	..	0.0	0.1	3.2	6.8	3.0	8.2	13.8
Concessional / EDT (%)	..	..	..	100.0	5.2	3.4	3.3	79.6	61.9	58.3
Multilateral / EDT (%)	..	..	..	0.0	0.0	0.0	0.0	4.3	5.6	10.3

TAJIKISTAN

(US$ million, unless otherwise indicated)

	1970	1980	1990	1992	1993	1994	1995	1996	1997	1998
5. LONG-TERM DEBT										
DEBT OUTSTANDING (LDOD)	..	..	..	**9.7**	**384.9**	**562.0**	**590.4**	**656.8**	**797.0**	**823.3**
Public and publicly guaranteed	..	..	..	**9.7**	**384.9**	**562.0**	**590.4**	**656.8**	**669.0**	**706.9**
Official creditors	..	..	..	9.7	316.9	494.0	522.4	588.8	601.0	646.9
Multilateral	..	..	..	0.0	0.0	0.0	0.0	30.2	50.1	109.7
Concessional	..	..	..	0.0	0.0	0.0	0.0	30.2	50.1	109.7
Bilateral	..	..	..	9.7	316.9	494.0	522.4	558.6	550.8	537.2
Concessional	..	..	..	9.7	19.9	19.9	20.9	526.7	507.6	513.9
Private creditors	..	..	..	0.0	68.0	68.0	68.0	68.0	68.0	59.9
Bonds	..	..	..	0.0	0.0	0.0	0.0	0.0	0.0	0.0
Commercial banks	..	..	..	0.0	0.0	0.0	0.0	0.0	0.0	0.0
Other private	..	..	..	0.0	68.0	68.0	68.0	68.0	68.0	59.9
Private nonguaranteed	..	..	..	**0.0**	**0.0**	**0.0**	**0.0**	**0.0**	**128.0**	**116.4**
Bonds	..	..	..	0.0	0.0	0.0	0.0	0.0	0.0	0.0
Commercial banks	..	..	..	0.0	0.0	0.0	0.0	0.0	128.0	116.4
Memo:										
IBRD	..	..	..	0.0	0.0	0.0	0.0	0.0	0.0	0.0
IDA	..	..	..	0.0	0.0	0.0	0.0	30.2	50.1	91.8
DISBURSEMENTS	..	..	..	**9.7**	**78.2**	**177.1**	**28.4**	**36.5**	**42.0**	**55.3**
Public and publicly guaranteed	..	..	..	**9.7**	**78.2**	**177.1**	**28.4**	**36.5**	**42.0**	**55.3**
Official creditors	..	..	..	9.7	10.2	177.1	28.4	36.5	42.0	55.3
Multilateral	..	..	..	0.0	0.0	0.0	0.0	30.4	22.0	55.3
Concessional	..	..	..	0.0	0.0	0.0	0.0	30.4	22.0	55.3
Bilateral	..	..	..	9.7	10.2	177.1	28.4	6.1	20.0	0.0
Concessional	..	..	..	9.7	10.2	0.0	1.0	0.0	8.7	0.0
Private creditors	..	..	..	0.0	68.0	0.0	0.0	0.0	0.0	0.0
Bonds	..	..	..	0.0	0.0	0.0	0.0	0.0	0.0	0.0
Commercial banks	..	..	..	0.0	0.0	0.0	0.0	0.0	0.0	0.0
Other private	..	..	..	0.0	68.0	0.0	0.0	0.0	0.0	0.0
Private nonguaranteed	..	..	..	**0.0**	**0.0**	**0.0**	**0.0**	**0.0**	**0.0**	**0.0**
Bonds	..	..	..	0.0	0.0	0.0	0.0	0.0	0.0	0.0
Commercial banks	..	..	..	0.0	0.0	0.0	0.0	0.0	0.0	0.0
Memo:										
IBRD	..	..	..	0.0	0.0	0.0	0.0	0.0	0.0	0.0
IDA	..	..	..	0.0	0.0	0.0	0.0	30.4	22.0	37.9
PRINCIPAL REPAYMENTS	..	..	..	**0.0**	**0.0**	**0.0**	**0.0**	**0.0**	**28.9**	**60.3**
Public and publicly guaranteed	..	..	..	**0.0**	**0.0**	**0.0**	**0.0**	**0.0**	**28.5**	**47.5**
Official creditors	..	..	..	0.0	0.0	0.0	0.0	0.0	28.5	39.4
Multilateral	..	..	..	0.0	0.0	0.0	0.0	0.0	0.0	0.0
Concessional	..	..	..	0.0	0.0	0.0	0.0	0.0	0.0	0.0
Bilateral	..	..	..	0.0	0.0	0.0	0.0	0.0	28.5	39.4
Concessional	..	..	..	0.0	0.0	0.0	0.0	0.0	28.5	39.4
Private creditors	..	..	..	0.0	0.0	0.0	0.0	0.0	0.0	8.0
Bonds	..	..	..	0.0	0.0	0.0	0.0	0.0	0.0	0.0
Commercial banks	..	..	..	0.0	0.0	0.0	0.0	0.0	0.0	0.0
Other private	..	..	..	0.0	0.0	0.0	0.0	0.0	0.0	8.0
Private nonguaranteed	..	..	..	**0.0**	**0.0**	**0.0**	**0.0**	**0.0**	**0.3**	**12.8**
Bonds	..	..	..	0.0	0.0	0.0	0.0	0.0	0.0	0.0
Commercial banks	..	..	..	0.0	0.0	0.0	0.0	0.0	0.3	12.8
Memo:										
IBRD	..	..	..	0.0	0.0	0.0	0.0	0.0	0.0	0.0
IDA	..	..	..	0.0	0.0	0.0	0.0	0.0	0.0	0.0
NET FLOWS ON DEBT	..	..	..	**9.7**	**78.2**	**177.1**	**28.4**	**36.5**	**13.1**	**-5.0**
Public and publicly guaranteed	..	..	..	**9.7**	**78.2**	**177.1**	**28.4**	**36.5**	**13.5**	**7.8**
Official creditors	..	..	..	9.7	10.2	177.1	28.4	36.5	13.5	15.9
Multilateral	..	..	..	0.0	0.0	0.0	0.0	30.4	22.0	55.3
Concessional	..	..	..	0.0	0.0	0.0	0.0	30.4	22.0	55.3
Bilateral	..	..	..	9.7	10.2	177.1	28.4	6.1	-8.5	-39.4
Concessional	..	..	..	9.7	10.2	0.0	1.0	0.0	-19.8	-39.4
Private creditors	..	..	..	0.0	68.0	0.0	0.0	0.0	0.0	-8.0
Bonds	..	..	..	0.0	0.0	0.0	0.0	0.0	0.0	0.0
Commercial banks	..	..	..	0.0	0.0	0.0	0.0	0.0	0.0	0.0
Other private	..	..	..	0.0	68.0	0.0	0.0	0.0	0.0	-8.0
Private nonguaranteed	..	..	..	**0.0**	**0.0**	**0.0**	**0.0**	**0.0**	**-0.3**	**-12.8**
Bonds	..	..	..	0.0	0.0	0.0	0.0	0.0	0.0	0.0
Commercial banks	..	..	..	0.0	0.0	0.0	0.0	0.0	-0.3	-12.8
Memo:										
IBRD	..	..	..	0.0	0.0	0.0	0.0	0.0	0.0	0.0
IDA	..	..	..	0.0	0.0	0.0	0.0	30.4	22.0	37.9

TAJIKISTAN

(US$ million, unless otherwise indicated)

	1970	1980	1990	1992	1993	1994	1995	1996	1997	1998
INTEREST PAYMENTS (LINT)	..	..	..	**0.0**	**0.8**	**0.4**	**0.0**	**0.3**	**5.9**	**19.9**
Public and publicly guaranteed	..	..	..	**0.0**	**0.8**	**0.4**	**0.0**	**0.3**	**4.9**	**14.7**
Official creditors	..	..	..	0.0	0.0	0.4	0.0	0.3	4.9	14.7
Multilateral	..	..	..	0.0	0.0	0.0	0.0	0.0	0.2	0.4
Concessional	..	..	..	0.0	0.0	0.0	0.0	0.0	0.2	0.4
Bilateral	..	..	..	0.0	0.0	0.4	0.0	0.3	4.7	14.3
Concessional	..	..	..	0.0	0.0	0.4	0.0	0.3	4.7	13.7
Private creditors	..	..	..	0.0	0.8	0.0	0.0	0.0	0.0	0.0
Bonds	..	..	..	0.0	0.0	0.0	0.0	0.0	0.0	0.0
Commercial banks	..	..	..	0.0	0.0	0.0	0.0	0.0	0.0	0.0
Other private	..	..	..	0.0	0.8	0.0	0.0	0.0	0.0	0.0
Private nonguaranteed	..	..	..	**0.0**	**0.0**	**0.0**	**0.0**	**0.0**	**1.0**	**5.1**
Bonds	..	..	..	0.0	0.0	0.0	0.0	0.0	0.0	0.0
Commercial banks	..	..	..	0.0	0.0	0.0	0.0	0.0	1.0	5.1
Memo:										
IBRD	..	..	..	0.0	0.0	0.0	0.0	0.0	0.0	0.0
IDA	..	..	..	0.0	0.0	0.0	0.0	0.0	0.2	0.4
NET TRANSFERS ON DEBT	..	..	..	**9.7**	**77.3**	**176.7**	**28.4**	**36.2**	**7.2**	**-24.9**
Public and publicly guaranteed	..	..	..	**9.7**	**77.3**	**176.7**	**28.4**	**36.2**	**8.5**	**-6.9**
Official creditors	..	..	..	9.7	10.2	176.7	28.4	36.2	8.5	1.1
Multilateral	..	..	..	0.0	0.0	0.0	0.0	30.4	21.8	54.9
Concessional	..	..	..	0.0	0.0	0.0	0.0	30.4	21.8	54.9
Bilateral	..	..	..	9.7	10.2	176.7	28.4	5.8	-13.2	-53.8
Concessional	..	..	..	9.7	10.2	-0.4	1.0	-0.3	-24.5	-53.1
Private creditors	..	..	..	0.0	67.2	0.0	0.0	0.0	0.0	-8.0
Bonds	..	..	..	0.0	0.0	0.0	0.0	0.0	0.0	0.0
Commercial banks	..	..	..	0.0	0.0	0.0	0.0	0.0	0.0	0.0
Other private	..	..	..	0.0	67.2	0.0	0.0	0.0	0.0	-8.0
Private nonguaranteed	..	..	..	**0.0**	**0.0**	**0.0**	**0.0**	**0.0**	**-1.3**	**-17.9**
Bonds	..	..	..	0.0	0.0	0.0	0.0	0.0	0.0	0.0
Commercial banks	..	..	..	0.0	0.0	0.0	0.0	0.0	-1.3	-17.9
Memo:										
IBRD	..	..	..	0.0	0.0	0.0	0.0	0.0	0.0	0.0
IDA	..	..	..	0.0	0.0	0.0	0.0	30.4	21.8	37.5
DEBT SERVICE (LTDS)	..	..	..	**0.0**	**0.8**	**0.4**	**0.0**	**0.3**	**34.8**	**80.2**
Public and publicly guaranteed	..	..	..	**0.0**	**0.8**	**0.4**	**0.0**	**0.3**	**33.5**	**62.2**
Official creditors	..	..	..	0.0	0.0	0.4	0.0	0.3	33.5	54.2
Multilateral	..	..	..	0.0	0.0	0.0	0.0	0.0	0.2	0.4
Concessional	..	..	..	0.0	0.0	0.0	0.0	0.0	0.2	0.4
Bilateral	..	..	..	0.0	0.0	0.4	0.0	0.3	33.2	53.8
Concessional	..	..	..	0.0	0.0	0.4	0.0	0.3	33.2	53.1
Private creditors	..	..	..	0.0	0.8	0.0	0.0	0.0	0.0	8.0
Bonds	..	..	..	0.0	0.0	0.0	0.0	0.0	0.0	0.0
Commercial banks	..	..	..	0.0	0.0	0.0	0.0	0.0	0.0	0.0
Other private	..	..	..	0.0	0.8	0.0	0.0	0.0	0.0	8.0
Private nonguaranteed	..	..	..	**0.0**	**0.0**	**0.0**	**0.0**	**0.0**	**1.3**	**17.9**
Bonds	..	..	..	0.0	0.0	0.0	0.0	0.0	0.0	0.0
Commercial banks	..	..	..	0.0	0.0	0.0	0.0	0.0	1.3	17.9
Memo:										
IBRD	..	..	..	0.0	0.0	0.0	0.0	0.0	0.0	0.0
IDA	..	..	..	0.0	0.0	0.0	0.0	0.0	0.2	0.4
UNDISBURSED DEBT	..	..	..	**74.3**	**44.9**	**66.4**	**34.1**	**52.7**	**33.3**	**59.2**
Official creditors	..	..	..	6.3	44.9	66.4	34.1	52.7	33.3	59.2
Private creditors	..	..	..	68.0	0.0	0.0	0.0	0.0	0.0	0.0
Memorandum items										
Concessional LDOD	..	..	..	9.7	19.9	19.9	20.9	556.9	557.7	623.6
Variable rate LDOD	..	..	..	0.0	365.0	542.1	561.7	86.1	221.0	181.3
Public sector LDOD	..	..	..	9.7	384.9	562.0	590.4	656.8	669.0	706.9
Private sector LDOD	..	..	..	0.0	0.0	0.0	0.0	0.0	128.0	116.4
6. CURRENCY COMPOSITION OF LONG-TERM DEBT (PERCENT)										
Deutsche mark	..	..	..	0.0	0.0	0.0	0.0	0.0	0.0	0.0
French franc	..	..	..	0.0	0.0	0.0	0.0	0.0	0.0	0.0
Japanese yen	..	..	..	0.0	0.0	0.0	0.0	0.0	0.0	0.0
Pound sterling	..	..	..	0.0	0.0	0.0	0.0	0.0	0.0	0.0
Swiss franc	..	..	..	0.0	0.0	0.0	0.0	0.0	0.0	0.0
U.S.dollars	..	..	..	99.7	95.4	96.9	97.0	100.0	100.0	98.2
Multiple currency	..	..	..	0.0	0.0	0.0	0.0	0.0	0.0	0.0
Special drawing rights	..	..	..	0.0	0.0	0.0	0.0	0.0	0.0	0.0
All other currencies	..	..	..	0.3	4.6	3.1	3.0	0.0	0.0	1.8

TAJIKISTAN

(US$ million, unless otherwise indicated)

	1970	1980	1990	1992	1993	1994	1995	1996	1997	1998
7. DEBT RESTRUCTURINGS										
Total amount rescheduled	..	..	..	0.0	297.0	0.0	0.0	505.8	19.0	176.9
Debt stock rescheduled	..	..	..	0.0	0.0	0.0	0.0	259.7	18.3	151.2
Principal rescheduled	..	..	..	0.0	0.0	0.0	0.0	215.9	0.0	20.0
Official	..	..	..	0.0	0.0	0.0	0.0	215.9	0.0	20.0
Private	..	..	..	0.0	0.0	0.0	0.0	0.0	0.0	0.0
Interest rescheduled	..	..	..	..	0.0	0.0	0.0	22.8	0.0	5.7
Official	..	..	..	0.0	0.0	0.0	0.0	22.8	0.0	5.7
Private	..	..	..	0.0	0.0	0.0	0.0	0.0	0.0	0.0
Debt forgiven	..	..	..	0.0	0.0	0.0	0.0	0.0	0.0	0.0
Memo: interest forgiven	..	..	..	0.0	0.0	0.0	0.0	0.0	0.0	0.0
Debt stock reduction	..	..	..	0.0	0.0	0.0	0.0	0.0	0.0	0.0
of which debt buyback	..	..	..	0.0	0.0	0.0	0.0	0.0	0.0	0.0
8. DEBT STOCK-FLOW RECONCILIATION										
Total change in debt stocks	..	..	..	..	375.5	195.1	53.3	65.8	201.7	168.4
Net flows on debt	..	..	..	9.7	78.2	177.1	28.4	66.3	52.4	134.9
Net change in interest arrears	..	..	..	..	0.3	18.0	24.9	-30.2	23.8	-1.5
Interest capitalized	..	..	..	..	0.0	0.0	0.0	22.8	0.0	5.7
Debt forgiveness or reduction	..	..	..	..	0.0	0.0	0.0	0.0	0.0	0.0
Cross-currency valuation	..	..	..	..	-12.0	-11.5	-3.9	0.0	0.0	0.6
Residual	..	..	..	..	309.0	11.5	3.9	7.0	125.5	28.7
9. AVERAGE TERMS OF NEW COMMITMENTS										
ALL CREDITORS										
Interest (%)	..	..	..	3.9	3.9	7.3	0.0	0.8	0.5	0.5
Maturity (years)	..	..	..	9.3	16.6	7.2	0.0	39.8	37.9	36.6
Grace period (years)	..	..	..	4.2	5.3	2.1	0.0	10.3	9.9	9.6
Grant element (%)	..	..	..	26.4	34.4	9.6	0.0	80.7	81.5	79.9
Official creditors										
Interest (%)	..	..	..	2.0	3.9	7.3	0.0	0.8	0.5	0.5
Maturity (years)	..	..	..	29.9	16.6	7.2	0.0	39.8	37.9	36.6
Grace period (years)	..	..	..	6.9	5.3	2.1	0.0	10.3	9.9	9.6
Grant element (%)	..	..	..	63.0	34.4	9.6	0.0	80.7	81.5	79.9
Private creditors										
Interest (%)	..	..	..	4.4	0.0	0.0	0.0	0.0	0.0	0.0
Maturity (years)	..	..	..	4.5	0.0	0.0	0.0	0.0	0.0	0.0
Grace period (years)	..	..	..	3.5	0.0	0.0	0.0	0.0	0.0	0.0
Grant element (%)	..	..	..	17.8	0.0	0.0	0.0	0.0	0.0	0.0
Memorandum items										
Commitments	..	..	..	84.0	48.8	198.6	0.0	55.0	25.0	79.5
Official creditors	..	..	..	16.0	48.8	198.6	0.0	55.0	25.0	79.5
Private creditors	..	..	..	68.0	0.0	0.0	0.0	0.0	0.0	0.0

10. CONTRACTUAL OBLIGATIONS ON OUTSTANDING LONG-TERM DEBT

	1999	2000	2001	2002	2003	2004	2005	2006	2007	2008
TOTAL										
Disbursements	21.7	17.2	11.8	6.2	1.4	0.6	0.3	0.0	0.0	0.0
Principal	59.6	59.6	61.6	62.2	61.4	60.7	60.9	61.5	62.6	35.6
Interest	19.9	18.1	16.2	14.2	12.2	10.2	8.3	6.4	4.5	3.2
Official creditors										
Disbursements	21.7	17.2	11.8	6.2	1.4	0.6	0.3	0.0	0.0	0.0
Principal	46.2	46.2	48.8	49.4	48.6	47.9	48.1	48.7	49.8	35.6
Interest	15.3	14.1	12.8	11.4	9.9	8.5	7.2	5.8	4.5	3.2
Bilateral creditors										
Disbursements	4.4	1.8	0.8	0.0	0.0	0.0	0.0	0.0	0.0	0.0
Principal	46.2	46.2	48.8	49.4	48.2	47.5	47.5	47.5	47.5	32.4
Interest	14.5	13.2	11.9	10.4	8.9	7.5	6.2	4.9	3.6	2.3
Multilateral creditors										
Disbursements	17.3	15.4	11.0	6.2	1.4	0.6	0.3	0.0	0.0	0.0
Principal	0.0	0.0	0.0	0.0	0.4	0.4	0.6	1.2	2.3	3.2
Interest	0.8	0.9	0.9	0.9	1.0	1.0	1.0	0.9	0.9	0.9
Private creditors										
Disbursements	0.0	0.0	0.0	0.0	0.0	0.0	0.0	0.0	0.0	0.0
Principal	13.4	13.4	12.8	12.8	12.8	12.8	12.8	12.8	12.8	0.0
Interest	4.6	4.0	3.4	2.9	2.3	1.7	1.2	0.6	0.0	0.0
Commercial banks										
Disbursements	0.0	0.0	0.0	0.0	0.0	0.0	0.0	0.0	0.0	0.0
Principal	0.0	0.0	0.0	0.0	0.0	0.0	0.0	0.0	0.0	0.0
Interest	0.0	0.0	0.0	0.0	0.0	0.0	0.0	0.0	0.0	0.0
Other private										
Disbursements	0.0	0.0	0.0	0.0	0.0	0.0	0.0	0.0	0.0	0.0
Principal	13.4	13.4	12.8	12.8	12.8	12.8	12.8	12.8	12.8	0.0
Interest	4.6	4.0	3.4	2.9	2.3	1.7	1.2	0.6	0.0	0.0

TANZANIA

(US$ million, unless otherwise indicated)

1. SUMMARY DEBT DATA

	1970	1980	1990	1992	1993	1994	1995	1996	1997	1998
TOTAL DEBT STOCKS (EDT)	..	**5,322**	**6,438**	**6,678**	**6,781**	**7,235**	**7,406**	**7,362**	**7,129**	**7,603**
Long-term debt (LDOD)	**188**	**3,381**	**5,781**	**5,862**	**5,820**	**6,140**	**6,247**	**6,127**	**6,056**	**6,440**
Public and publicly guaranteed	173	3,297	5,769	5,850	5,808	6,128	6,204	6,082	6,015	6,404
Private nonguaranteed	15	84	12	12	12	12	44	45	41	37
Use of IMF credit	**0**	**171**	**140**	**221**	**215**	**212**	**197**	**206**	**246**	**268**
Short-term debt	..	**1,770**	**517**	**596**	**747**	**883**	**961**	**1,029**	**826**	**895**
of which interest arrears on LDOD	..	1,467	401	510	686	802	902	901	687	746
Official creditors	..	1,464	279	424	551	650	740	726	545	593
Private creditors	..	3	122	86	135	152	162	175	142	152
Memo: principal arrears on LDOD	..	592	812	1,003	1,122	1,277	1,506	1,608	1,080	1,072
Official creditors	..	586	629	800	896	1,025	1,234	1,324	903	907
Private creditors	..	6	183	203	226	252	272	285	177	166
Memo: export credits	..	0	1,278	1,237	1,191	799	853	739	994	845
TOTAL DEBT FLOWS										
Disbursements	**57**	**433**	**330**	**476**	**237**	**259**	**258**	**244**	**336**	**264**
Long-term debt	57	367	301	385	237	259	258	207	251	216
IMF purchases	0	66	29	90	0	0	0	37	85	48
Principal repayments	**4**	**81**	**118**	**172**	**104**	**116**	**146**	**168**	**118**	**134**
Long-term debt	4	49	89	166	98	101	127	146	87	96
IMF repurchases	0	33	28	6	6	15	20	22	31	38
Net flows on debt	**76**	**405**	**228**	**306**	**109**	**162**	**90**	**145**	**230**	**140**
of which short-term debt	..	53	16	2	-24	20	-22	68	12	10
Interest payments (INT)	..	**80**	**62**	**64**	**107**	**67**	**86**	**104**	**48**	**112**
Long-term debt	3	48	47	58	102	62	81	97	41	104
IMF charges	0	7	6	1	1	1	1	1	1	1
Short-term debt	..	26	9	5	4	5	4	6	6	7
Net transfers on debt	..	**325**	**166**	**242**	**2**	**95**	**4**	**41**	**182**	**28**
Total debt service paid (TDS)	..	**161**	**179**	**236**	**211**	**184**	**232**	**271**	**166**	**246**
Long-term debt	7	96	137	224	201	163	208	243	128	200
IMF repurchases and charges	0	39	34	7	7	16	21	23	32	39
Short-term debt (interest only)	..	26	9	5	4	5	4	6	6	7

2. AGGREGATE NET RESOURCE FLOWS AND NET TRANSFERS (LONG-TERM)

	1970	1980	1990	1992	1993	1994	1995	1996	1997	1998
NET RESOURCE FLOWS	**59**	**804**	**889**	**928**	**945**	**772**	**702**	**642**	**753**	**939**
Net flow of long-term debt (ex. IMF)	52	318	212	219	139	158	131	61	165	120
Foreign direct investment (net)	0	0	0	12	20	50	120	150	158	172
Portfolio equity flows	0	0	0	0	0	0	0	0	0	0
Grants (excluding technical coop.)	6	485	677	697	786	565	451	430	431	648
Memo: technical coop. grants	21	173	209	232	235	209	265	254	218	189
official net resource flows	48	705	885	958	895	720	567	504	614	783
private net resource flows	11	99	4	-30	51	52	135	137	140	157
NET TRANSFERS	**56**	**756**	**816**	**840**	**808**	**674**	**584**	**510**	**664**	**786**
Interest on long-term debt	3	48	47	58	102	62	81	97	41	104
Profit remittances on FDI	0	0	25	30	35	36	37	35	48	50
Memo: official net transfers	46	671	841	906	797	660	490	413	575	682
private net transfers	10	86	-25	-66	11	15	93	97	89	104

3. MAJOR ECONOMIC AGGREGATES

	1970	1980	1990	1992	1993	1994	1995	1996	1997	1998
Gross national product (GNP)	..	..	4,011	4,680	4,355	4,049	4,974	5,864	7,065	8,063
Exports of goods & services (XGS)	..	762	544	584	787	969	1,297	1,422	1,254	1,180
of which workers remittances	..	0	..	..	..	..	..	..	..	..
Imports of goods & services (MGS)	..	1,412	1,665	1,913	2,194	1,966	2,281	2,272	2,130	2,527
International reserves (RES)	65	20	193	327	203	332	270	440	622	599
Current account balance	..	-521	-559	-714	-895	-637	-590	-413	-579	-907

4. DEBT INDICATORS

	1970	1980	1990	1992	1993	1994	1995	1996	1997	1998
EDT / XGS (%)	..	698.6	1,182.9	1,142.6	862.0	747.0	571.0	517.5	568.3	644.6
EDT / GNP (%)	..	..	160.5	142.7	155.7	178.7	148.9	125.6	100.9	94.3
TDS / XGS (%)	..	21.2	32.9	40.3	26.9	19.0	17.9	19.1	13.2	20.9
INT / XGS (%)	..	10.5	11.3	10.9	13.6	6.9	6.6	7.3	3.8	9.5
INT / GNP (%)	..	..	1.5	1.4	2.5	1.7	1.7	1.8	0.7	1.4
RES / EDT (%)	..	0.4	3.0	4.9	3.0	4.6	3.7	6.0	8.7	7.9
RES / MGS (months)	..	0.2	1.4	2.1	1.1	2.0	1.4	2.3	3.5	2.9
Short-term / EDT (%)	..	33.3	8.0	8.9	11.0	12.2	13.0	14.0	11.6	11.8
Concessional / EDT (%)	..	50.6	53.9	57.6	59.2	60.4	60.1	60.9	71.5	72.5
Multilateral / EDT (%)	..	10.6	30.9	34.4	35.6	36.8	37.8	39.1	41.0	41.3

TANZANIA

(US$ million, unless otherwise indicated)

	1970	1980	1990	1992	1993	1994	1995	1996	1997	1998
5. LONG-TERM DEBT										
DEBT OUTSTANDING (LDOD)	**188**	**3,381**	**5,781**	**5,862**	**5,820**	**6,140**	**6,247**	**6,127**	**6,056**	**6,440**
Public and publicly guaranteed	**173**	**3,297**	**5,769**	**5,850**	**5,808**	**6,128**	**6,204**	**6,082**	**6,015**	**6,404**
Official creditors	168	3,041	5,303	5,461	5,420	5,743	5,806	5,709	5,779	6,177
Multilateral	38	566	1,987	2,298	2,411	2,659	2,796	2,881	2,924	3,141
Concessional	35	305	1,625	2,002	2,153	2,430	2,603	2,733	2,813	3,049
Bilateral	129	2,476	3,317	3,164	3,009	3,084	3,010	2,828	2,856	3,036
Concessional	129	2,388	1,844	1,846	1,863	1,943	1,851	1,749	2,283	2,464
Private creditors	6	256	466	388	388	385	398	373	236	227
Bonds	0	0	0	0	0	0	0	0	0	0
Commercial banks	0	28	26	11	4	4	5	4	2	1
Other private	6	228	441	377	384	381	393	369	234	226
Private nonguaranteed	**15**	**84**	**12**	**12**	**12**	**12**	**44**	**45**	**41**	**37**
Bonds	0	0	0	0	0	0	0	0	0	0
Commercial banks	15	84	12	12	12	12	44	45	41	37
Memo:										
IBRD	4	198	243	171	140	114	87	56	34	22
IDA	35	242	1,250	1,618	1,759	1,998	2,182	2,242	2,306	2,463
DISBURSEMENTS	**57**	**367**	**301**	**385**	**237**	**259**	**258**	**207**	**251**	**216**
Public and publicly guaranteed	**49**	**335**	**301**	**385**	**237**	**259**	**257**	**206**	**251**	**216**
Official creditors	43	245	285	348	196	241	216	201	251	216
Multilateral	11	122	203	256	167	215	187	194	244	187
Concessional	9	63	187	248	166	211	173	192	238	184
Bilateral	33	123	83	91	29	27	29	7	8	28
Concessional	32	95	52	88	21	18	28	7	6	10
Private creditors	6	90	16	38	41	17	40	4	0	0
Bonds	0	0	0	0	0	0	0	0	0	0
Commercial banks	0	8	0	1	0	1	1	1	0	0
Other private	6	82	16	37	41	16	40	3	0	0
Private nonguaranteed	**8**	**31**	**0**	**0**	**0**	**0**	**1**	**2**	**0**	**0**
Bonds	0	0	0	0	0	0	0	0	0	0
Commercial banks	8	31	0	0	0	0	1	2	0	0
Memo:										
IBRD	1	34	0	0	0	0	0	0	0	0
IDA	9	35	187	235	146	183	160	134	183	102
PRINCIPAL REPAYMENTS	**4**	**49**	**89**	**166**	**98**	**101**	**127**	**146**	**87**	**96**
Public and publicly guaranteed	**2**	**32**	**89**	**166**	**98**	**101**	**122**	**146**	**83**	**92**
Official creditors	2	26	77	87	87	86	100	128	68	81
Multilateral	0	8	45	53	55	68	79	76	64	64
Concessional	0	1	13	16	15	30	23	34	31	39
Bilateral	2	18	33	33	32	18	22	51	4	17
Concessional	2	18	24	20	22	11	14	20	4	9
Private creditors	0	6	12	80	11	16	22	18	14	11
Bonds	0	0	0	0	0	0	0	0	0	0
Commercial banks	0	1	0	8	7	0	0	3	2	1
Other private	0	6	12	72	4	15	22	16	13	10
Private nonguaranteed	**3**	**16**	**0**	**0**	**0**	**0**	**5**	**0**	**4**	**4**
Bonds	0	0	0	0	0	0	0	0	0	0
Commercial banks	3	16	0	0	0	0	5	0	4	4
Memo:										
IBRD	0	5	26	31	33	33	34	27	20	12
IDA	0	1	6	8	9	11	12	14	15	17
NET FLOWS ON DEBT	**52**	**318**	**212**	**219**	**139**	**158**	**131**	**61**	**165**	**120**
Public and publicly guaranteed	**47**	**303**	**212**	**219**	**139**	**158**	**135**	**60**	**169**	**124**
Official creditors	42	219	208	261	109	156	116	74	183	135
Multilateral	11	115	158	203	112	147	109	118	179	123
Concessional	9	63	174	232	150	181	149	158	208	145
Bilateral	31	104	50	58	-4	9	8	-44	4	12
Concessional	30	77	29	67	-1	8	14	-13	3	2
Private creditors	6	84	4	-42	31	2	19	-14	-14	-11
Bonds	0	0	0	0	0	0	0	0	0	0
Commercial banks	0	8	0	-7	-7	0	1	-1	-2	-1
Other private	6	77	4	-35	38	1	18	-13	-13	-10
Private nonguaranteed	**5**	**15**	**0**	**0**	**0**	**0**	**-4**	**1**	**-4**	**-4**
Bonds	0	0	0	0	0	0	0	0	0	0
Commercial banks	5	15	0	0	0	0	-4	1	-4	-4
Memo:										
IBRD	1	29	-26	-31	-33	-33	-34	-27	-20	-12
IDA	9	34	181	226	137	172	148	121	168	85

TANZANIA

(US$ million, unless otherwise indicated)

	1970	1980	1990	1992	1993	1994	1995	1996	1997	1998
INTEREST PAYMENTS (LINT)	**3**	**48**	**47**	**58**	**102**	**62**	**81**	**97**	**41**	**104**
Public and publicly guaranteed	**2**	**41**	**47**	**58**	**102**	**62**	**80**	**96**	**40**	**102**
Official creditors	2	34	44	52	98	61	77	92	39	101
Multilateral	0	18	27	34	35	34	57	47	36	36
Concessional	0	2	9	13	15	17	18	33	25	22
Bilateral	2	16	17	18	63	27	20	45	3	65
Concessional	2	14	11	9	34	11	11	22	2	54
Private creditors	0	7	3	6	5	1	3	4	1	2
Bonds	0	0	0	0	0	0	0	0	0	0
Commercial banks	0	1	0	3	3	0	0	1	0	0
Other private	0	6	3	3	2	1	3	4	1	2
Private nonguaranteed	**1**	**7**	**0**	**0**	**0**	**0**	**1**	**1**	**1**	**1**
Bonds	0	0	0	0	0	0	0	0	0	0
Commercial banks	1	7	0	0	0	0	1	1	1	1
Memo:										
IBRD	0	15	17	15	12	10	8	6	4	2
IDA	0	2	8	10	14	14	16	17	16	17
NET TRANSFERS ON DEBT	**49**	**271**	**164**	**161**	**37**	**96**	**50**	**-35**	**124**	**16**
Public and publicly guaranteed	**45**	**262**	**164**	**161**	**37**	**96**	**55**	**-36**	**129**	**21**
Official creditors	40	185	164	209	11	95	40	-18	144	34
Multilateral	10	97	131	169	78	113	52	71	143	87
Concessional	9	61	165	219	135	165	132	125	182	123
Bilateral	29	89	33	40	-67	-18	-13	-89	1	-53
Concessional	29	64	18	58	-35	-3	3	-36	1	-52
Private creditors	6	77	0	-48	26	1	15	-18	-15	-13
Bonds	0	0	0	0	0	0	0	0	0	0
Commercial banks	0	7	0	-10	-10	0	1	-2	-2	-1
Other private	6	71	0	-38	36	1	15	-16	-13	-12
Private nonguaranteed	**4**	**9**	**0**	**0**	**0**	**0**	**-5**	**1**	**-6**	**-5**
Bonds	0	0	0	0	0	0	0	0	0	0
Commercial banks	4	9	0	0	0	0	-5	1	-6	-5
Memo:										
IBRD	1	14	-44	-45	-45	-42	-42	-33	-24	-15
IDA	9	33	172	216	123	158	132	104	151	68
DEBT SERVICE (LTDS)	**7**	**96**	**137**	**224**	**201**	**163**	**208**	**243**	**128**	**200**
Public and publicly guaranteed	**4**	**73**	**137**	**224**	**201**	**163**	**202**	**242**	**122**	**194**
Official creditors	4	60	121	139	185	146	177	219	107	181
Multilateral	0	26	72	88	90	102	135	123	101	100
Concessional	0	2	21	29	31	47	41	67	56	61
Bilateral	4	34	50	51	95	45	42	96	7	81
Concessional	4	32	34	29	56	22	25	42	6	63
Private creditors	0	13	15	85	15	16	25	22	15	13
Bonds	0	0	0	0	0	0	0	0	0	0
Commercial banks	0	2	0	11	10	0	0	3	2	1
Other private	0	12	15	75	5	16	25	19	13	12
Private nonguaranteed	**3**	**23**	**0**	**0**	**0**	**0**	**6**	**1**	**6**	**5**
Bonds	0	0	0	0	0	0	0	0	0	0
Commercial banks	3	23	0	0	0	0	6	1	6	5
Memo:										
IBRD	0	20	44	45	45	42	42	33	24	15
IDA	0	2	14	19	23	25	28	31	32	33
UNDISBURSED DEBT	**315**	**1,165**	**1,174**	**1,256**	**1,529**	**1,536**	**1,303**	**1,244**	**1,159**	**1,088**
Official creditors	311	1,088	1,169	1,230	1,500	1,511	1,278	1,235	1,147	1,081
Private creditors	4	77	5	26	29	25	25	9	12	7
Memorandum items										
Concessional LDOD	163	2,693	3,469	3,848	4,016	4,372	4,454	4,482	5,096	5,513
Variable rate LDOD	15	89	466	513	474	475	513	512	334	308
Public sector LDOD	173	3,268	5,719	5,795	5,753	6,059	6,129	6,008	5,955	6,348
Private sector LDOD	15	112	62	66	67	80	119	119	101	93

6. CURRENCY COMPOSITION OF LONG-TERM DEBT (PERCENT)

	1970	1980	1990	1992	1993	1994	1995	1996	1997	1998
Deutsche mark	3.2	1.3	3.9	4.5	4.1	4.2	3.2	2.9	1.9	1.9
French franc	0.0	2.0	3.6	3.5	2.7	2.6	2.8	2.7	1.9	1.8
Japanese yen	0.0	49.7	8.6	10.2	11.5	12.1	10.9	9.8	10.2	11.8
Pound sterling	24.1	4.8	12.1	11.3	11.0	10.5	10.2	10.3	9.8	9.2
Swiss franc	0.0	0.3	0.5	0.6	0.2	0.2	0.1	0.0	0.0	0.0
U.S.dollars	15.1	12.8	35.6	37.0	38.2	38.9	39.0	40.6	45.8	45.6
Multiple currency	2.1	6.5	6.0	4.8	4.4	4.2	8.2	6.6	6.6	6.7
Special drawing rights	0.0	0.1	1.3	3.0	4.1	4.9	5.2	5.1	4.9	5.1
All other currencies	55.5	22.5	28.4	25.1	23.8	22.4	20.4	22.0	18.9	17.9

TANZANIA

(US$ million, unless otherwise indicated)

	1970	1980	1990	1992	1993	1994	1995	1996	1997	1998
7. DEBT RESTRUCTURINGS										
Total amount rescheduled	..	..	185	348	58	9	0	33	761	153
Debt stock rescheduled	..	..	0	0	0	0	0	0	0	0
Principal rescheduled	..	..	59	173	37	6	0	11	424	30
Official	..	..	35	166	23	5	0	11	327	30
Private	..	..	24	7	14	1	0	0	97	0
Interest rescheduled	..	..	96	115	22	1	0	9	229	14
Official	..	..	91	113	20	1	0	9	207	14
Private	..	..	5	2	2	0	0	0	22	0
Debt forgiven	..	..	102	124	193	85	140	30	246	70
Memo: interest forgiven	..	..	10	32	39	17	0	1	92	0
Debt stock reduction	..	..	0	0	0	0	0	0	11	0
of which debt buyback	..	..	0	0	0	0	0	0	0	0
8. DEBT STOCK-FLOW RECONCILIATION										
Total change in debt stocks	..	..	589	120	103	454	171	-44	-233	474
Net flows on debt	76	405	228	306	109	162	90	145	230	140
Net change in interest arrears	..	..	60	-19	176	116	100	-1	-214	58
Interest capitalized	..	..	96	115	22	1	0	9	229	14
Debt forgiveness or reduction	..	..	-102	-124	-193	-85	-140	-30	-258	-70
Cross-currency valuation	..	..	390	-250	-17	220	50	-95	-186	152
Residual	..	..	-83	92	7	39	71	-74	-35	180
9. AVERAGE TERMS OF NEW COMMITMENTS										
ALL CREDITORS										
Interest (%)	1.4	4.1	1.1	1.0	1.8	1.2	1.7	1.3	1.0	1.3
Maturity (years)	41.0	22.9	34.8	33.7	35.9	35.7	17.5	35.4	41.6	39.9
Grace period (years)	22.5	7.5	9.3	7.9	8.7	9.4	5.8	9.2	9.8	8.7
Grant element (%)	81.0	43.0	72.3	66.1	68.6	73.8	48.3	72.7	78.2	70.5
Official creditors										
Interest (%)	1.4	3.6	1.1	1.1	1.4	1.0	1.7	1.2	0.9	1.3
Maturity (years)	41.0	24.2	35.2	39.8	38.6	37.6	23.0	35.8	42.4	39.9
Grace period (years)	22.5	8.0	9.3	9.4	9.3	9.9	7.4	9.3	10.0	8.7
Grant element (%)	81.0	46.8	72.8	75.9	73.4	77.6	61.3	73.7	79.7	70.5
Private creditors										
Interest (%)	0.0	7.6	2.5	0.4	5.6	4.2	1.9	8.9	5.0	0.0
Maturity (years)	0.0	11.7	13.3	3.6	7.8	6.1	3.7	5.9	3.0	0.0
Grace period (years)	0.0	3.2	6.8	0.5	3.3	0.7	1.6	2.4	1.0	0.0
Grant element (%)	0.0	10.3	47.6	17.5	18.0	15.7	15.4	0.4	8.6	0.0
Memorandum items										
Commitments	271	741	699	287	519	218	141	227	272	122
Official creditors	271	663	687	239	474	205	101	224	266	122
Private creditors	0	78	12	48	45	13	40	3	6	0

10. CONTRACTUAL OBLIGATIONS ON OUTSTANDING LONG-TERM DEBT

	1999	2000	2001	2002	2003	2004	2005	2006	2007	2008
TOTAL										
Disbursements	374	304	187	116	60	21	15	5	1	0
Principal	167	242	240	217	187	170	166	164	168	175
Interest	101	125	118	110	103	99	95	91	88	84
Official creditors										
Disbursements	370	301	187	116	60	21	15	5	1	0
Principal	140	215	220	210	182	166	163	161	165	171
Interest	97	122	116	109	103	98	95	91	88	84
Bilateral creditors										
Disbursements	45	43	29	17	11	8	5	3	1	0
Principal	83	149	151	137	103	81	76	73	71	71
Interest	67	91	85	78	73	69	66	63	61	58
Multilateral creditors										
Disbursements	325	258	158	99	49	13	10	2	0	0
Principal	57	66	69	73	79	85	86	88	94	101
Interest	30	31	31	31	30	30	29	28	27	26
Private creditors										
Disbursements	4	3	0	0	0	0	0	0	0	0
Principal	28	27	20	7	5	4	4	3	3	3
Interest	5	3	2	1	1	0	0	0	0	0
Commercial banks										
Disbursements	0	0	0	0	0	0	0	0	0	0
Principal	1	0	0	0	0	0	0	0	0	0
Interest	0	0	0	0	0	0	0	0	0	0
Other private										
Disbursements	4	3	0	0	0	0	0	0	0	0
Principal	27	27	20	7	5	4	4	3	3	3
Interest	4	3	2	1	1	0	0	0	0	0

THAILAND

(US$ million, unless otherwise indicated)

	1970	1980	1990	1992	1993	1994	1995	1996	1997	1998
1. SUMMARY DEBT DATA										
TOTAL DEBT STOCKS (EDT)	..	**8,297**	**28,165**	**41,864**	**52,717**	**65,596**	**83,093**	**90,778**	**93,731**	**86,172**
Long-term debt (LDOD)	**726**	**5,646**	**19,842**	**27,138**	**30,083**	**36,418**	**41,998**	**53,164**	**56,466**	**59,410**
Public and publicly guaranteed	324	3,943	12,531	13,363	14,776	16,266	16,881	16,929	22,324	28,113
Private nonguaranteed	402	1,703	7,311	13,775	15,307	20,152	25,117	36,235	34,142	31,297
Use of IMF credit	**0**	**348**	**1**	**0**	**0**	**0**	**0**	**0**	**2,429**	**3,239**
Short-term debt	..	**2,303**	**8,322**	**14,727**	**22,634**	**29,179**	**41,095**	**37,613**	**34,836**	**23,523**
of which interest arrears on LDOD	..	0	0	0	0	0	0	0	0	0
Official creditors	..	0	0	0	0	0	0	0	0	0
Private creditors	..	0	0	0	0	0	0	0	0	0
Memo: principal arrears on LDOD	..	0	0	0	0	0	0	0	0	1,798
Official creditors	..	0	0	0	0	0	0	0	0	0
Private creditors	..	0	0	0	0	0	0	0	0	1,798
Memo: export credits	..	0	3,106	4,145	5,226	7,613	10,485	9,940	12,238	13,551
TOTAL DEBT FLOWS										
Disbursements	**220**	**2,648**	**4,588**	**5,094**	**7,458**	**9,096**	**10,715**	**14,550**	**14,757**	**8,134**
Long-term debt	220	2,604	4,588	5,094	7,458	9,096	10,715	14,550	12,280	7,456
IMF purchases	0	45	0	0	0	0	0	0	2,477	678
Principal repayments	**131**	**804**	**3,265**	**3,198**	**4,253**	**5,166**	**4,405**	**4,313**	**6,184**	**7,820**
Long-term debt	131	782	2,984	3,198	4,253	5,166	4,405	4,313	6,184	7,820
IMF repurchases	0	22	281	0	0	0	0	0	0	0
Net flows on debt	**365**	**1,808**	**3,534**	**4,132**	**11,112**	**10,474**	**18,226**	**6,755**	**5,796**	**-10,998**
of which short-term debt	..	-37	2,210	2,235	7,907	6,545	11,916	-3,482	-2,777	-11,313
Interest payments (INT)	..	**814**	**2,030**	**2,711**	**2,187**	**2,714**	**4,192**	**5,220**	**5,595**	**5,441**
Long-term debt	33	473	1,359	1,877	1,859	2,023	2,649	3,113	3,470	3,756
IMF charges	0	13	21	0	0	0	0	0	15	121
Short-term debt	..	328	650	834	328	692	1,543	2,107	2,110	1,564
Net transfers on debt	..	**994**	**1,504**	**1,421**	**8,925**	**7,760**	**14,034**	**1,535**	**202**	**-16,440**
Total debt service paid (TDS)	..	**1,617**	**5,295**	**5,909**	**6,440**	**7,880**	**8,597**	**9,533**	**11,778**	**13,261**
Long-term debt	164	1,254	4,343	5,074	6,113	7,189	7,055	7,426	9,653	11,575
IMF repurchases and charges	0	35	302	0	0	0	0	0	15	121
Short-term debt (interest only)	..	328	650	834	328	692	1,543	2,107	2,110	1,564
2. AGGREGATE NET RESOURCE FLOWS AND NET TRANSFERS (LONG-TERM)										
NET RESOURCE FLOWS	**139**	**2,087**	**4,691**	**4,175**	**8,226**	**4,863**	**10,630**	**14,220**	**9,615**	**8,987**
Net flow of long-term debt (ex. IMF)	90	1,822	1,605	1,897	3,204	3,930	6,309	10,237	6,096	-364
Foreign direct investment (net)	43	190	2,444	2,113	1,804	1,366	2,068	2,336	3,746	6,941
Portfolio equity flows	0	0	449	4	3,117	-538	2,154	1,551	-308	2,341
Grants (excluding technical coop.)	6	75	193	161	100	105	99	96	81	68
Memo: technical coop. grants	49	103	231	257	265	244	267	230	217	199
official net resource flows	27	623	292	-122	687	431	591	519	6,010	1,162
private net resource flows	111	1,464	4,399	4,297	7,538	4,432	10,040	13,702	3,606	7,825
NET TRANSFERS	**87**	**1,576**	**3,020**	**1,948**	**5,946**	**2,375**	**7,501**	**10,598**	**5,596**	**4,651**
Interest on long-term debt	33	473	1,359	1,877	1,859	2,023	2,649	3,113	3,470	3,756
Profit remittances on FDI	19	38	312	350	420	465	480	510	550	580
Memo: official net transfers	13	506	-151	-559	235	-55	70	27	5,570	363
private net transfers	74	1,070	3,170	2,507	5,712	2,430	7,431	10,571	26	4,287
3. MAJOR ECONOMIC AGGREGATES										
Gross national product (GNP)	7,096	32,091	84,272	108,975	122,790	141,500	164,619	176,593	149,257	112,720
Exports of goods & services (XGS)	..	8,575	31,289	42,919	49,596	58,679	74,093	75,385	76,157	69,227
of which workers remittances	..	0	0	0	0	0	..	..	..	..
Imports of goods & services (MGS)	..	10,861	38,783	49,868	56,709	67,892	88,133	90,836	79,660	55,400
International reserves (RES)	911	3,026	14,258	21,183	25,439	30,280	36,939	38,645	26,897	29,537
Current account balance	..	-2,076	-7,281	-6,303	-6,364	-8,085	-13,554	-14,691	-3,024	14,241
4. DEBT INDICATORS										
EDT / XGS (%)	..	96.8	90.0	97.5	106.3	111.8	112.2	120.4	123.1	124.5
EDT / GNP (%)	..	25.9	33.4	38.4	42.9	46.4	50.5	51.4	62.8	76.5
TDS / XGS (%)	..	18.9	16.9	13.8	13.0	13.4	11.6	12.7	15.5	19.2
INT / XGS (%)	..	9.5	6.5	6.3	4.4	4.6	5.7	6.9	7.4	7.9
INT / GNP (%)	..	2.5	2.4	2.5	1.8	1.9	2.6	3.0	3.8	4.8
RES / EDT (%)	..	36.5	50.6	50.6	48.3	46.2	44.5	42.6	28.7	34.3
RES / MGS (months)	..	3.3	4.4	5.1	5.4	5.4	5.0	5.1	4.1	6.4
Short-term / EDT (%)	..	27.8	29.6	35.2	42.9	44.5	49.5	41.4	37.2	27.3
Concessional / EDT (%)	..	10.0	15.2	12.0	11.2	10.3	8.6	7.6	7.0	8.8
Multilateral / EDT (%)	..	12.0	13.2	7.0	5.8	4.8	3.9	3.3	3.8	5.3

THAILAND

(US$ million, unless otherwise indicated)

	1970	1980	1990	1992	1993	1994	1995	1996	1997	1998
5. LONG-TERM DEBT										
DEBT OUTSTANDING (LDOD)	**726**	**5,646**	**19,842**	**27,138**	**30,083**	**36,418**	**41,998**	**53,164**	**56,466**	**59,410**
Public and publicly guaranteed	**324**	**3,943**	**12,531**	**13,363**	**14,776**	**16,266**	**16,881**	**16,929**	**22,324**	**28,113**
Official creditors	291	2,168	8,288	8,384	9,534	10,807	11,189	10,555	15,419	18,200
Multilateral	164	992	3,721	2,925	3,040	3,121	3,208	2,980	3,591	4,603
Concessional	0	42	253	257	273	285	293	275	256	247
Bilateral	127	1,175	4,567	5,459	6,495	7,687	7,981	7,575	11,828	13,597
Concessional	93	787	4,034	4,772	5,604	6,448	6,845	6,664	6,330	7,325
Private creditors	33	1,776	4,243	4,979	5,242	5,459	5,691	6,374	6,905	9,913
Bonds	0	148	738	880	988	1,682	1,574	1,967	2,766	3,035
Commercial banks	3	1,339	2,170	2,519	2,654	2,337	3,007	3,468	3,315	6,056
Other private	30	289	1,334	1,579	1,600	1,440	1,110	939	824	823
Private nonguaranteed	**402**	**1,703**	**7,311**	**13,775**	**15,307**	**20,152**	**25,117**	**36,235**	**34,142**	**31,297**
Bonds	0	0	40	310	2,031	5,223	7,375	10,610	11,411	10,627
Commercial banks	402	1,703	7,272	13,465	13,276	14,928	17,743	25,626	22,731	20,670
Memo:										
IBRD	159	671	2,421	1,898	1,925	1,782	1,805	1,607	1,728	2,111
IDA	0	32	109	106	105	103	102	100	98	96
DISBURSEMENTS	**220**	**2,604**	**4,588**	**5,094**	**7,458**	**9,096**	**10,715**	**14,550**	**12,280**	**7,456**
Public and publicly guaranteed	**51**	**1,315**	**1,296**	**1,612**	**2,104**	**2,117**	**2,759**	**2,600**	**8,080**	**4,956**
Official creditors	38	622	887	759	1,193	1,190	1,417	1,354	6,576	1,824
Multilateral	21	236	263	283	334	331	358	284	1,062	1,143
Concessional	0	7	2	25	26	16	17	0	0	0
Bilateral	18	386	624	476	859	859	1,060	1,070	5,514	681
Concessional	11	179	504	376	590	487	1,043	995	664	674
Private creditors	13	694	410	853	911	926	1,341	1,246	1,504	3,132
Bonds	0	44	0	300	244	690	242	514	1,055	300
Commercial banks	0	606	110	321	588	230	1,094	721	428	2,831
Other private	13	44	299	232	79	7	5	11	21	1
Private nonguaranteed	**169**	**1,288**	**3,292**	**3,483**	**5,354**	**6,979**	**7,956**	**11,950**	**4,200**	**2,500**
Bonds	0	0	0	259	1,723	3,165	2,080	3,370	1,264	0
Commercial banks	169	1,288	3,292	3,223	3,631	3,814	5,876	8,580	2,936	2,500
Memo:										
IBRD	19	145	174	177	169	128	146	138	443	498
IDA	0	5	0	0	0	0	0	0	0	0
PRINCIPAL REPAYMENTS	**131**	**782**	**2,984**	**3,198**	**4,253**	**5,166**	**4,405**	**4,313**	**6,184**	**7,820**
Public and publicly guaranteed	**23**	**172**	**2,393**	**1,390**	**1,438**	**1,893**	**1,896**	**1,323**	**1,157**	**1,038**
Official creditors	17	73	788	1,042	606	865	926	932	647	730
Multilateral	9	35	439	819	304	499	360	276	264	264
Concessional	0	0	8	10	11	11	11	12	11	14
Bilateral	8	38	349	223	302	366	566	656	383	466
Concessional	5	13	102	174	234	288	447	411	282	373
Private creditors	6	99	1,605	348	832	1,028	970	391	510	308
Bonds	0	0	87	11	132	49	199	86	220	72
Commercial banks	0	52	1,324	190	545	681	429	210	234	144
Other private	6	47	194	147	155	299	341	95	56	91
Private nonguaranteed	**107**	**610**	**591**	**1,808**	**2,815**	**3,273**	**2,510**	**2,991**	**5,027**	**6,782**
Bonds	0	0	0	0	0	0	0	25	373	859
Commercial banks	107	610	591	1,808	2,815	3,273	2,510	2,966	4,653	5,923
Memo:										
IBRD	9	26	207	645	189	415	201	196	192	179
IDA	0	0	1	1	1	2	2	2	2	2
NET FLOWS ON DEBT	**90**	**1,822**	**1,605**	**1,897**	**3,204**	**3,930**	**6,309**	**10,237**	**6,096**	**-364**
Public and publicly guaranteed	**28**	**1,143**	**-1,097**	**222**	**666**	**224**	**863**	**1,278**	**6,923**	**3,918**
Official creditors	21	548	98	-283	587	326	492	422	5,929	1,094
Multilateral	12	200	-176	-536	30	-168	-2	9	798	879
Concessional	0	7	-7	15	15	5	6	-12	-11	-14
Bilateral	10	348	275	253	557	494	494	414	5,131	215
Concessional	6	166	402	202	357	199	596	584	382	301
Private creditors	7	595	-1,195	505	79	-102	371	855	994	2,824
Bonds	0	44	-87	289	112	641	43	429	835	228
Commercial banks	0	555	-1,214	131	44	-451	664	511	194	2,687
Other private	7	-3	105	85	-76	-292	-336	-84	-35	-91
Private nonguaranteed	**62**	**678**	**2,702**	**1,675**	**2,538**	**3,706**	**5,446**	**8,959**	**-827**	**-4,282**
Bonds	0	0	0	259	1,723	3,165	2,080	3,345	891	-859
Commercial banks	62	678	2,702	1,416	815	542	3,366	5,614	-1,717	-3,423
Memo:										
IBRD	10	120	-34	-469	-20	-287	-56	-59	251	319
IDA	0	4	-1	-1	-1	-2	-2	-2	-2	-2

THAILAND

(US$ million, unless otherwise indicated)

	1970	*1980*	*1990*	*1992*	*1993*	*1994*	*1995*	*1996*	*1997*	*1998*
INTEREST PAYMENTS (LINT)	**33**	**473**	**1,359**	**1,877**	**1,859**	**2,023**	**2,649**	**3,113**	**3,470**	**3,756**
Public and publicly guaranteed	**16**	**269**	**878**	**707**	**724**	**769**	**877**	**877**	**855**	**1,255**
Official creditors	14	117	442	437	452	485	521	492	440	799
Multilateral	9	76	284	239	225	217	219	206	190	248
Concessional	0	1	5	5	5	6	9	7	5	7
Bilateral	5	42	158	198	227	268	302	287	250	550
Concessional	3	19	110	154	178	206	224	210	197	192
Private creditors	2	152	436	270	271	283	356	384	415	457
Bonds	0	9	46	45	55	53	97	111	160	179
Commercial banks	0	117	230	137	128	135	193	227	216	238
Other private	2	26	160	88	89	95	67	46	40	39
Private nonguaranteed	**17**	**204**	**481**	**1,170**	**1,136**	**1,254**	**1,772**	**2,236**	**2,615**	**2,501**
Bonds	0	0	2	2	11	67	222	579	560	587
Commercial banks	17	204	479	1,168	1,124	1,188	1,550	1,657	2,054	1,914
Memo:										
IBRD	9	53	189	169	158	144	135	122	104	122
IDA	0	0	1	1	1	1	1	1	1	1
NET TRANSFERS ON DEBT	**57**	**1,349**	**246**	**20**	**1,345**	**1,907**	**3,660**	**7,124**	**2,627**	**-4,120**
Public and publicly guaranteed	**12**	**875**	**-1,975**	**-485**	**-58**	**-545**	**-14**	**401**	**6,068**	**2,663**
Official creditors	7	431	-344	-719	135	-160	-29	-70	5,489	295
Multilateral	2	125	-460	-775	-196	-386	-221	-197	608	631
Concessional	0	6	-12	9	10	-1	-3	-19	-17	-20
Bilateral	5	306	116	56	330	226	192	128	4,881	-335
Concessional	3	148	292	48	179	-8	372	375	185	109
Private creditors	5	444	-1,631	235	-192	-385	15	471	579	2,368
Bonds	0	35	-133	244	57	588	-54	318	675	48
Commercial banks	-1	438	-1,444	-6	-84	-586	471	284	-22	2,449
Other private	5	-29	-55	-4	-165	-387	-402	-130	-74	-130
Private nonguaranteed	**45**	**475**	**2,221**	**505**	**1,403**	**2,452**	**3,674**	**6,723**	**-3,441**	**-6,783**
Bonds	0	0	-2	257	1,712	3,098	1,859	2,766	330	-1,446
Commercial banks	45	475	2,223	248	-309	-646	1,816	3,957	-3,772	-5,337
Memo:										
IBRD	1	66	-222	-637	-178	-431	-190	-180	147	197
IDA	0	4	-2	-2	-2	-3	-3	-3	-3	-3
DEBT SERVICE (LTDS)	**164**	**1,254**	**4,343**	**5,074**	**6,113**	**7,189**	**7,055**	**7,426**	**9,653**	**11,575**
Public and publicly guaranteed	**39**	**441**	**3,271**	**2,096**	**2,162**	**2,662**	**2,773**	**2,199**	**2,012**	**2,293**
Official creditors	31	191	1,230	1,478	1,059	1,350	1,447	1,424	1,087	1,529
Multilateral	18	111	723	1,058	529	717	579	482	454	512
Concessional	0	1	13	15	16	18	20	19	17	20
Bilateral	13	80	508	420	529	634	868	942	633	1,017
Concessional	8	32	212	328	411	495	671	620	479	564
Private creditors	8	250	2,041	618	1,103	1,311	1,326	775	925	764
Bonds	0	9	133	56	186	102	296	197	380	252
Commercial banks	1	168	1,554	327	673	816	623	437	450	382
Other private	7	73	354	235	244	394	407	141	96	131
Private nonguaranteed	**124**	**814**	**1,071**	**2,978**	**3,951**	**4,527**	**4,282**	**5,227**	**7,641**	**9,283**
Bonds	0	0	2	2	11	67	222	604	934	1,446
Commercial banks	124	814	1,070	2,976	3,940	4,460	4,060	4,623	6,707	7,837
Memo:										
IBRD	18	79	396	814	347	559	336	318	296	301
IDA	0	1	2	2	2	3	3	3	3	3
UNDISBURSED DEBT	**156**	**3,023**	**3,637**	**4,758**	**6,575**	**8,318**	**7,956**	**7,264**	**7,501**	**9,258**
Official creditors	145	2,658	2,936	3,350	5,185	6,494	5,752	5,424	5,672	7,377
Private creditors	11	364	701	1,408	1,390	1,824	2,204	1,840	1,829	1,882
Memorandum items										
Concessional LDOD	93	829	4,286	5,029	5,877	6,733	7,138	6,939	6,586	7,572
Variable rate LDOD	402	2,903	10,248	16,524	18,052	22,824	27,857	39,467	38,255	40,154
Public sector LDOD	312	3,943	12,531	13,363	14,776	16,266	16,881	16,929	22,324	28,113
Private sector LDOD	414	1,703	7,311	13,775	15,307	20,152	25,117	36,235	34,142	31,297

6. CURRENCY COMPOSITION OF LONG-TERM DEBT (PERCENT)

	1970	*1980*	*1990*	*1992*	*1993*	*1994*	*1995*	*1996*	*1997*	*1998*
Deutsche mark	17.6	4.7	3.6	3.8	2.3	2.3	2.4	2.1	1.4	1.3
French franc	0.0	1.8	1.0	1.3	1.2	1.2	1.2	1.1	0.8	0.6
Japanese yen	6.0	25.3	42.9	47.0	49.9	50.8	47.9	44.7	38.8	40.0
Pound sterling	2.4	0.2	0.4	0.3	0.2	0.2	0.2	0.1	0.1	0.1
Swiss franc	0.0	0.1	5.7	4.2	3.6	2.9	0.9	0.6	0.1	0.1
U.S.dollars	21.6	41.0	15.8	21.7	21.6	22.8	27.1	32.4	47.0	49.0
Multiple currency	50.7	24.3	28.1	19.7	19.7	18.5	19.2	17.7	10.8	8.0
Special drawing rights	0.0	0.0	0.2	0.2	0.2	0.2	0.1	0.1	0.1	0.1
All other currencies	1.7	2.6	2.3	1.8	1.3	1.1	1.0	1.2	0.9	0.8

THAILAND

(US$ million, unless otherwise indicated)

	1970	1980	1990	1992	1993	1994	1995	1996	1997	1998
7. DEBT RESTRUCTURINGS										
Total amount rescheduled	..	..	0	0	0	0	0	0	0	0
Debt stock rescheduled	..	..	0	0	0	0	0	0	0	0
Principal rescheduled	..	..	0	0	0	0	0	0	0	0
Official	..	..	0	0	0	0	0	0	0	0
Private	..	..	0	0	0	0	0	0	0	0
Interest rescheduled	..	..	0	0	0	0	0	0	0	0
Official	..	..	0	0	0	0	0	0	0	0
Private	..	..	0	0	0	0	0	0	0	0
Debt forgiven	..	..	0	0	0	0	0	0	0	6
Memo: interest forgiven	..	..	0	0	0	0	0	0	0	0
Debt stock reduction	..	..	0	0	0	0	0	0	0	0
of which debt buyback	..	..	0	0	0	0	0	0	0	0
8. DEBT STOCK-FLOW RECONCILIATION										
Total change in debt stocks	..	..	4,628	4,092	10,853	12,879	17,496	7,685	2,953	-7,559
Net flows on debt	365	1,808	3,534	4,132	11,112	10,474	18,226	6,755	5,796	-10,998
Net change in interest arrears	..	..	0	0	0	0	0	0	0	0
Interest capitalized	..	..	0	0	0	0	0	0	0	0
Debt forgiveness or reduction	..	..	0	0	0	0	0	0	0	-6
Cross-currency valuation	..	..	728	-328	791	1,124	-158	-1,117	-1,182	1,478
Residual	..	..	366	289	-1,049	1,281	-571	2,047	-1,661	1,967
9. AVERAGE TERMS OF NEW COMMITMENTS										
ALL CREDITORS										
Interest (%)	6.8	9.5	4.8	6.6	4.7	4.8	5.4	4.6	6.0	5.0
Maturity (years)	19.2	16.8	22.1	18.9	19.7	17.0	14.8	17.9	12.4	12.7
Grace period (years)	4.3	5.3	7.2	5.7	5.3	5.1	5.2	5.9	5.9	3.8
Grant element (%)	19.6	6.6	38.2	19.7	35.4	31.4	27.1	34.9	22.1	24.8
Official creditors										
Interest (%)	6.8	7.1	4.4	6.0	4.1	4.3	4.4	4.0	5.9	3.9
Maturity (years)	19.6	21.4	25.6	20.5	22.4	20.0	23.5	23.0	12.7	17.9
Grace period (years)	4.4	5.9	7.8	5.6	5.8	5.1	6.4	6.2	5.6	5.1
Grant element (%)	19.7	20.6	43.3	27.0	41.6	37.4	40.9	43.7	22.8	36.5
Private creditors										
Interest (%)	6.0	13.8	5.8	7.1	6.5	5.7	6.1	5.9	6.6	6.3
Maturity (years)	11.5	8.7	14.7	17.5	11.1	12.5	8.9	8.5	10.9	6.8
Grace period (years)	3.0	4.1	5.9	5.9	3.7	5.2	4.3	5.4	6.9	2.2
Grant element (%)	18.6	-18.3	27.5	13.2	15.6	22.1	17.6	18.7	18.5	11.7
Memorandum items										
Commitments	106	1,877	1,755	3,210	3,702	3,471	2,930	2,529	8,941	7,085
Official creditors	100	1,199	1,196	1,499	2,815	2,096	1,190	1,639	7,445	3,751
Private creditors	6	678	560	1,711	887	1,375	1,740	890	1,496	3,334

10. CONTRACTUAL OBLIGATIONS ON OUTSTANDING LONG-TERM DEBT

	1999	2000	2001	2002	2003	2004	2005	2006	2007	2008
TOTAL										
Disbursements	3,218	2,496	1,539	813	408	217	111	6	0	0
Principal	9,397	7,101	7,336	5,568	6,281	5,061	5,539	4,202	3,206	2,288
Interest	3,171	2,860	2,486	2,071	1,831	1,436	1,146	887	716	558
Official creditors										
Disbursements	2,181	2,200	1,442	811	408	217	111	6	0	0
Principal	737	879	1,203	1,518	2,354	3,155	3,148	1,177	1,172	1,443
Interest	961	1,005	1,022	1,000	948	797	615	467	414	363
Bilateral creditors										
Disbursements	1,520	1,495	939	569	306	150	69	0	0	0
Principal	427	572	797	1,014	1,850	2,679	2,682	712	707	674
Interest	625	647	652	641	615	492	339	220	199	178
Multilateral creditors										
Disbursements	661	705	504	242	102	67	42	6	0	0
Principal	310	307	406	504	504	476	466	466	465	770
Interest	337	359	370	360	334	305	276	246	216	185
Private creditors										
Disbursements	1,036	296	97	2	1	0	0	0	0	0
Principal	8,660	6,222	6,133	4,050	3,927	1,906	2,391	3,025	2,034	845
Interest	2,210	1,854	1,464	1,070	882	640	530	420	302	195
Commercial banks										
Disbursements	732	295	97	1	1	0	0	0	0	0
Principal	1,211	1,132	1,047	1,018	792	595	402	232	214	213
Interest	346	338	277	214	152	110	75	55	42	29
Other private										
Disbursements	304	1	0	0	0	0	0	0	0	0
Principal	7,449	5,090	5,087	3,033	3,135	1,311	1,989	2,792	1,820	632
Interest	1,864	1,517	1,188	856	731	529	456	366	261	166

TOGO

(US$ million, unless otherwise indicated)

	1970	1980	1990	1992	1993	1994	1995	1996	1997	1998
1. SUMMARY DEBT DATA										
TOTAL DEBT STOCKS (EDT)	..	**1,049**	**1,275**	**1,339**	**1,278**	**1,444**	**1,464**	**1,472**	**1,327**	**1,448**
Long-term debt (LDOD)	**40**	**896**	**1,075**	**1,122**	**1,112**	**1,218**	**1,274**	**1,294**	**1,195**	**1,302**
Public and publicly guaranteed	40	896	1,075	1,122	1,112	1,218	1,274	1,294	1,195	1,302
Private nonguaranteed	0	0	0	0	0	0	0	0	0	0
Use of IMF credit	**0**	**33**	**87**	**77**	**69**	**82**	**105**	**90**	**88**	**95**
Short-term debt	..	**120**	**113**	**141**	**97**	**145**	**85**	**88**	**44**	**52**
of which interest arrears on LDOD	..	15	1	32	51	85	27	27	3	14
Official creditors	..	7	1	24	41	73	13	3	3	14
Private creditors	..	9	0	8	10	12	14	24	0	0
Memo: principal arrears on LDOD	..	34	3	20	54	112	64	59	2	13
Official creditors	..	14	2	10	33	79	18	9	2	13
Private creditors	..	19	1	10	21	34	46	50	0	0
Memo: export credits	..	0	351	345	277	282	299	285	277	406
TOTAL DEBT FLOWS										
Disbursements	**5**	**119**	**104**	**55**	**17**	**55**	**59**	**97**	**69**	**80**
Long-term debt	5	97	83	44	17	40	26	97	54	65
IMF purchases	0	22	21	11	0	16	33	0	15	15
Principal repayments	**2**	**19**	**43**	**19**	**14**	**13**	**18**	**32**	**40**	**28**
Long-term debt	2	19	27	9	6	6	7	20	28	17
IMF repurchases	0	0	16	10	8	7	11	12	12	12
Net flows on debt	**3**	**108**	**10**	**27**	**-60**	**56**	**39**	**68**	**9**	**49**
of which short-term debt	..	7	-51	-8	-62	13	-2	3	-20	-3
Interest payments (INT)	..	**34**	**43**	**17**	**12**	**10**	**11**	**26**	**16**	**12**
Long-term debt	1	19	33	10	7	6	8	23	13	10
IMF charges	0	0	4	2	1	0	1	1	0	1
Short-term debt	..	14	6	5	4	4	3	2	2	2
Net transfers on debt	..	**74**	**-33**	**11**	**-72**	**46**	**27**	**42**	**-7**	**37**
Total debt service paid (TDS)	..	**52**	**86**	**36**	**27**	**23**	**29**	**58**	**56**	**40**
Long-term debt	2	38	60	19	13	12	14	44	42	26
IMF repurchases and charges	0	0	20	12	10	7	12	12	12	12
Short-term debt (interest only)	..	14	6	5	4	4	3	2	2	2
2. AGGREGATE NET RESOURCE FLOWS AND NET TRANSFERS (LONG-TERM)										
NET RESOURCE FLOWS	**11**	**136**	**176**	**141**	**66**	**107**	**141**	**147**	**83**	**112**
Net flow of long-term debt (ex. IMF)	3	78	56	35	11	34	19	77	25	48
Foreign direct investment (net)	1	42	0	0	0	0	0	0	0	0
Portfolio equity flows	0	0	0	0	0	0	0	0	0	0
Grants (excluding technical coop.)	7	15	120	107	55	73	123	70	58	63
Memo: technical coop. grants	8	29	61	53	37	23	32	29	27	27
official net resource flows	11	53	176	141	66	107	141	147	89	112
private net resource flows	0	83	0	0	0	0	0	0	-6	0
NET TRANSFERS	**5**	**116**	**131**	**118**	**50**	**95**	**129**	**117**	**64**	**98**
Interest on long-term debt	1	19	33	10	7	6	8	23	13	10
Profit remittances on FDI	6	0	12	14	9	6	5	7	6	4
Memo: official net transfers	10	41	148	131	59	101	134	124	76	102
private net transfers	-6	75	-17	-14	-9	-6	-5	-7	-12	-4
3. MAJOR ECONOMIC AGGREGATES										
Gross national product (GNP)	248	1,096	1,598	1,665	1,207	931	1,265	1,442	1,478	1,487
Exports of goods & services (XGS)	..	580	723	597	361	434	626	674	721	706
of which workers remittances	..	10	27	16	9	15	..	..	..	..
Imports of goods & services (MGS)	..	752	912	809	566	512	723	834	842	830
International reserves (RES)	35	85	358	277	161	99	135	93	122	118
Current account balance	..	-95	-84	-139	-174	-63	..	..	..	..
4. DEBT INDICATORS										
EDT / XGS (%)	..	180.8	176.4	224.5	354.4	332.5	233.9	218.4	184.1	205.1
EDT / GNP (%)	..	95.7	79.8	80.4	105.9	155.1	115.7	102.1	89.8	97.4
TDS / XGS (%)	..	9.0	11.9	6.1	7.4	5.3	4.7	8.6	7.8	5.7
INT / XGS (%)	..	5.8	6.0	2.8	3.4	2.3	1.8	3.9	2.2	1.7
INT / GNP (%)	..	3.1	2.7	1.0	1.0	1.1	0.9	1.8	1.1	0.8
RES / EDT (%)	..	8.1	28.1	20.7	12.6	6.9	9.2	6.3	9.2	8.1
RES / MGS (months)	..	1.4	4.7	4.1	3.4	2.3	2.2	1.3	1.7	1.7
Short-term / EDT (%)	..	11.5	8.9	10.5	7.6	10.0	5.8	6.0	3.3	3.6
Concessional / EDT (%)	..	23.3	54.9	58.8	62.2	60.9	61.5	64.9	71.1	71.0
Multilateral / EDT (%)	..	11.0	43.9	45.7	48.3	46.9	48.7	50.3	54.0	55.2

TOGO

(US$ million, unless otherwise indicated)

	1970	1980	1990	1992	1993	1994	1995	1996	1997	1998
5. LONG-TERM DEBT										
DEBT OUTSTANDING (LDOD)	**40**	**896**	**1,075**	**1,122**	**1,112**	**1,218**	**1,274**	**1,294**	**1,195**	**1,302**
Public and publicly guaranteed	**40**	**896**	**1,075**	**1,122**	**1,112**	**1,218**	**1,274**	**1,294**	**1,195**	**1,302**
Official creditors	32	481	1,023	1,071	1,063	1,167	1,223	1,244	1,195	1,302
Multilateral	2	116	560	611	617	677	713	740	717	799
Concessional	2	90	516	577	584	646	681	718	703	775
Bilateral	30	365	463	460	445	490	510	504	479	503
Concessional	30	155	183	211	211	234	220	237	240	253
Private creditors	8	415	52	51	50	51	52	50	0	0
Bonds	0	0	0	0	0	0	0	0	0	0
Commercial banks	0	96	51	49	48	50	52	50	0	0
Other private	8	319	1	1	1	1	0	0	0	0
Private nonguaranteed	**0**	**0**	**0**	**0**	**0**	**0**	**0**	**0**	**0**	**0**
Bonds	0	0	0	0	0	0	0	0	0	0
Commercial banks	0	0	0	0	0	0	0	0	0	0
Memo:										
IBRD	0	4	5	0	0	0	0	0	0	0
IDA	2	43	393	460	469	513	541	576	561	620
DISBURSEMENTS	**5**	**97**	**83**	**44**	**17**	**40**	**26**	**97**	**54**	**65**
Public and publicly guaranteed	**5**	**97**	**83**	**44**	**17**	**40**	**26**	**97**	**54**	**65**
Official creditors	4	47	83	44	17	40	26	97	54	65
Multilateral	1	35	45	38	16	39	26	72	35	63
Concessional	1	30	44	37	13	39	26	70	35	52
Bilateral	3	12	38	6	1	1	0	25	19	2
Concessional	3	5	38	6	1	1	0	25	19	2
Private creditors	0	50	0	0	0	0	0	0	0	0
Bonds	0	0	0	0	0	0	0	0	0	0
Commercial banks	0	2	0	0	0	0	0	0	0	0
Other private	0	47	0	0	0	0	0	0	0	0
Private nonguaranteed	**0**	**0**	**0**	**0**	**0**	**0**	**0**	**0**	**0**	**0**
Bonds	0	0	0	0	0	0	0	0	0	0
Commercial banks	0	0	0	0	0	0	0	0	0	0
Memo:										
IBRD	0	0	0	0	0	0	0	0	0	0
IDA	1	13	31	32	9	28	20	56	17	44
PRINCIPAL REPAYMENTS	**2**	**19**	**27**	**9**	**6**	**6**	**7**	**20**	**28**	**17**
Public and publicly guaranteed	**2**	**19**	**27**	**9**	**6**	**6**	**7**	**20**	**28**	**17**
Official creditors	1	10	27	9	6	6	7	20	22	17
Multilateral	0	0	17	8	6	6	6	17	16	9
Concessional	0	0	5	3	4	4	6	12	9	8
Bilateral	1	9	10	2	0	0	1	4	6	7
Concessional	1	1	1	2	0	0	1	3	4	6
Private creditors	1	9	0	0	0	0	0	0	6	0
Bonds	0	0	0	0	0	0	0	0	0	0
Commercial banks	0	4	0	0	0	0	0	0	6	0
Other private	1	4	0	0	0	0	0	0	0	0
Private nonguaranteed	**0**	**0**	**0**	**0**	**0**	**0**	**0**	**0**	**0**	**0**
Bonds	0	0	0	0	0	0	0	0	0	0
Commercial banks	0	0	0	0	0	0	0	0	0	0
Memo:										
IBRD	0	0	8	0	0	0	0	0	0	0
IDA	0	0	1	1	2	3	3	4	4	5
NET FLOWS ON DEBT	**3**	**78**	**56**	**35**	**11**	**34**	**19**	**77**	**25**	**48**
Public and publicly guaranteed	**3**	**78**	**56**	**35**	**11**	**34**	**19**	**77**	**25**	**48**
Official creditors	3	38	56	35	11	34	19	77	32	48
Multilateral	1	35	28	31	10	33	20	55	19	54
Concessional	1	30	39	34	10	35	20	58	26	45
Bilateral	2	3	28	4	1	1	-1	21	12	-6
Concessional	2	4	37	4	1	1	-1	22	14	-4
Private creditors	-1	41	0	0	0	0	0	0	-6	0
Bonds	0	0	0	0	0	0	0	0	0	0
Commercial banks	0	-2	0	0	0	0	0	0	-6	0
Other private	-1	43	0	0	0	0	0	0	0	0
Private nonguaranteed	**0**	**0**	**0**	**0**	**0**	**0**	**0**	**0**	**0**	**0**
Bonds	0	0	0	0	0	0	0	0	0	0
Commercial banks	0	0	0	0	0	0	0	0	0	0
Memo:										
IBRD	0	0	-8	0	0	0	0	0	0	0
IDA	1	13	30	31	7	25	17	52	13	39

TOGO

(US$ million, unless otherwise indicated)

	1970	1980	1990	1992	1993	1994	1995	1996	1997	1998
INTEREST PAYMENTS (LINT)	**1**	**19**	**33**	**10**	**7**	**6**	**8**	**23**	**13**	**10**
Public and publicly guaranteed	**1**	**19**	**33**	**10**	**7**	**6**	**8**	**23**	**13**	**10**
Official creditors	1	12	28	10	7	6	8	23	13	10
Multilateral	0	2	8	7	6	6	5	8	7	5
Concessional	0	1	4	5	5	5	4	7	6	5
Bilateral	1	9	20	3	1	0	3	15	6	5
Concessional	1	0	4	2	1	0	1	6	2	3
Private creditors	0	8	5	0	0	0	0	0	0	0
Bonds	0	0	0	0	0	0	0	0	0	0
Commercial banks	0	8	5	0	0	0	0	0	0	0
Other private	0	0	0	0	0	0	0	0	0	0
Private nonguaranteed	**0**	**0**	**0**	**0**	**0**	**0**	**0**	**0**	**0**	**0**
Bonds	0	0	0	0	0	0	0	0	0	0
Commercial banks	0	0	0	0	0	0	0	0	0	0
Memo:										
IBRD	0	0	1	0	0	0	0	0	0	0
IDA	0	0	3	3	4	4	4	5	4	3
NET TRANSFERS ON DEBT	**2**	**59**	**23**	**25**	**4**	**28**	**11**	**53**	**12**	**39**
Public and publicly guaranteed	**2**	**59**	**23**	**25**	**4**	**28**	**11**	**53**	**12**	**39**
Official creditors	3	26	28	25	4	28	11	53	18	39
Multilateral	1	33	20	24	4	27	15	47	12	49
Concessional	1	29	35	29	5	30	16	51	20	40
Bilateral	2	-7	7	1	0	1	-4	6	6	-11
Concessional	2	3	33	2	0	1	-2	17	12	-7
Private creditors	-1	33	-5	0	0	0	0	0	-6	0
Bonds	0	0	0	0	0	0	0	0	0	0
Commercial banks	0	-10	-5	0	0	0	0	0	-6	0
Other private	-1	43	0	0	0	0	0	0	0	0
Private nonguaranteed	**0**	**0**	**0**	**0**	**0**	**0**	**0**	**0**	**0**	**0**
Bonds	0	0	0	0	0	0	0	0	0	0
Commercial banks	0	0	0	0	0	0	0	0	0	0
Memo:										
IBRD	0	0	-9	0	0	0	0	0	0	0
IDA	1	12	28	29	3	21	14	47	9	36
DEBT SERVICE (LTDS)	**2**	**38**	**60**	**19**	**13**	**12**	**14**	**44**	**42**	**26**
Public and publicly guaranteed	**2**	**38**	**60**	**19**	**13**	**12**	**14**	**44**	**42**	**26**
Official creditors	2	21	55	19	13	12	14	44	36	26
Multilateral	0	3	25	14	12	12	11	25	23	14
Concessional	0	1	9	8	9	9	10	19	15	12
Bilateral	2	19	30	5	1	0	4	19	12	12
Concessional	2	2	5	4	1	0	2	8	7	9
Private creditors	1	16	5	0	0	0	0	0	6	0
Bonds	0	0	0	0	0	0	0	0	0	0
Commercial banks	0	12	5	0	0	0	0	0	6	0
Other private	1	5	0	0	0	0	0	0	0	0
Private nonguaranteed	**0**	**0**	**0**	**0**	**0**	**0**	**0**	**0**	**0**	**0**
Bonds	0	0	0	0	0	0	0	0	0	0
Commercial banks	0	0	0	0	0	0	0	0	0	0
Memo:										
IBRD	0	0	9	0	0	0	0	0	0	0
IDA	0	0	4	4	6	7	6	9	8	9
UNDISBURSED DEBT	**7**	**155**	**277**	**208**	**190**	**138**	**156**	**172**	**207**	**203**
Official creditors	6	152	277	208	190	138	156	172	207	203
Private creditors	1	3	0	0	0	0	0	0	0	0
Memorandum items										
Concessional LDOD	31	245	699	788	795	880	901	955	943	1,028
Variable rate LDOD	0	108	37	37	37	37	129	139	120	136
Public sector LDOD	36	895	1,075	1,122	1,112	1,218	1,274	1,294	1,195	1,302
Private sector LDOD	3	1	0	0	0	0	0	0	0	0

6. CURRENCY COMPOSITION OF LONG-TERM DEBT (PERCENT)

	1970	1980	1990	1992	1993	1994	1995	1996	1997	1998
Deutsche mark	62.4	17.6	2.0	1.9	1.9	1.9	1.9	1.7	1.4	1.4
French franc	7.8	24.2	12.9	13.3	13.0	13.1	9.1	8.7	7.5	7.6
Japanese yen	0.0	0.0	3.0	3.1	3.5	3.6	3.4	4.7	5.8	6.0
Pound sterling	0.0	5.9	1.9	1.7	1.7	1.6	1.7	1.7	1.7	1.7
Swiss franc	0.0	10.3	10.3	8.8	9.0	9.3	11.0	9.6	9.7	8.8
U.S.dollars	15.3	19.6	44.4	47.6	47.9	47.3	47.8	49.8	50.2	50.8
Multiple currency	0.0	2.3	7.6	7.0	7.0	7.3	7.5	7.2	7.2	7.2
Special drawing rights	0.0	0.0	1.0	1.0	1.1	1.0	1.0	1.1	1.1	1.1
All other currencies	14.5	20.1	16.9	15.6	14.9	14.9	16.6	15.5	15.4	15.4

TOGO

(US$ million, unless otherwise indicated)

	1970	1980	1990	1992	1993	1994	1995	1996	1997	1998
7. DEBT RESTRUCTURINGS										
Total amount rescheduled	..	..	79	40	12	0	133	31	30	19
Debt stock rescheduled	..	..	0	0	0	0	1	0	0	0
Principal rescheduled	..	..	66	26	11	0	64	11	15	7
Official	..	..	66	26	11	0	63	11	15	7
Private	..	..	0	0	0	0	1	0	0	0
Interest rescheduled	..	..	12	10	1	0	63	16	15	7
Official	..	..	12	10	1	0	63	16	15	7
Private	..	..	0	0	0	0	0	0	0	0
Debt forgiven	..	..	18	3	3	0	85	5	4	11
Memo: interest forgiven	..	..	0	3	0	0	23	3	35	1
Debt stock reduction	..	..	0	0	0	0	0	0	49	0
of which debt buyback	..	..	0	0	0	0	0	0	6	0
8. DEBT STOCK-FLOW RECONCILIATION										
Total change in debt stocks	..	..	98	-2	-61	166	20	9	-145	121
Net flows on debt	3	108	10	27	-60	56	39	68	9	49
Net change in interest arrears	..	..	1	16	19	34	-58	0	-24	11
Interest capitalized	..	..	12	10	1	0	63	16	15	7
Debt forgiveness or reduction	..	..	-18	-3	-3	0	-85	-5	-47	-11
Cross-currency valuation	..	..	70	-34	-18	56	45	-44	-50	36
Residual	..	..	25	-19	-1	21	16	-27	-48	30
9. AVERAGE TERMS OF NEW COMMITMENTS										
ALL CREDITORS										
Interest (%)	4.6	4.0	0.8	0.8	0.0	0.0	0.7	1.0	1.0	2.5
Maturity (years)	16.8	24.5	41.4	49.0	0.0	0.0	39.3	33.3	38.8	29.9
Grace period (years)	4.4	7.4	10.3	10.0	0.0	0.0	9.8	8.9	9.6	7.6
Grant element (%)	32.8	46.5	80.5	82.9	0.0	0.0	80.0	72.9	76.8	59.5
Official creditors										
Interest (%)	3.5	3.2	0.8	0.8	0.0	0.0	0.7	1.0	1.0	2.5
Maturity (years)	21.3	26.7	41.4	49.0	0.0	0.0	39.3	33.3	38.8	29.9
Grace period (years)	5.4	8.0	10.3	10.0	0.0	0.0	9.8	8.9	9.6	7.6
Grant element (%)	42.6	52.6	80.5	82.9	0.0	0.0	80.0	72.9	76.8	59.5
Private creditors										
Interest (%)	7.6	10.1	0.0	0.0	0.0	0.0	0.0	0.0	0.0	0.0
Maturity (years)	4.2	6.9	0.0	0.0	0.0	0.0	0.0	0.0	0.0	0.0
Grace period (years)	1.6	2.7	0.0	0.0	0.0	0.0	0.0	0.0	0.0	0.0
Grant element (%)	5.5	-1.3	0.0	0.0	0.0	0.0	0.0	0.0	0.0	0.0
Memorandum items										
Commitments	3	97	105	54	0	0	63	119	102	55
Official creditors	2	86	105	54	0	0	63	119	102	55
Private creditors	1	11	0	0	0	0	0	0	0	0

10. CONTRACTUAL OBLIGATIONS ON OUTSTANDING LONG-TERM DEBT

	1999	2000	2001	2002	2003	2004	2005	2006	2007	2008
TOTAL										
Disbursements	43	50	39	28	17	9	5	1	0	0
Principal	45	46	46	47	47	46	38	38	41	44
Interest	34	33	32	30	28	27	25	24	23	22
Official creditors										
Disbursements	43	50	39	28	17	9	5	1	0	0
Principal	45	46	46	47	47	46	38	38	41	44
Interest	34	33	32	30	28	27	25	24	23	22
Bilateral creditors										
Disbursements	5	5	3	2	1	1	0	0	0	0
Principal	29	30	29	30	29	25	16	14	16	16
Interest	27	26	24	22	21	19	17	17	16	15
Multilateral creditors										
Disbursements	38	45	35	26	16	9	5	0	0	0
Principal	16	15	16	17	18	21	22	24	25	28
Interest	7	8	8	8	8	8	8	7	7	7
Private creditors										
Disbursements	0	0	0	0	0	0	0	0	0	0
Principal	0	0	0	0	0	0	0	0	0	0
Interest	0	0	0	0	0	0	0	0	0	0
Commercial banks										
Disbursements	0	0	0	0	0	0	0	0	0	0
Principal	0	0	0	0	0	0	0	0	0	0
Interest	0	0	0	0	0	0	0	0	0	0
Other private										
Disbursements	0	0	0	0	0	0	0	0	0	0
Principal	0	0	0	0	0	0	0	0	0	0
Interest	0	0	0	0	0	0	0	0	0	0

TONGA

(US$ million, unless otherwise indicated)

	1970	1980	1990	1992	1993	1994	1995	1996	1997	1998
1. SUMMARY DEBT DATA										
TOTAL DEBT STOCKS (EDT)	..	..	**53.7**	**43.5**	**44.2**	**64.4**	**70.1**	**69.6**	**61.2**	**64.7**
Long-term debt (LDOD)	..	..	**44.5**	**42.6**	**43.7**	**63.4**	**68.7**	**68.3**	**60.2**	**64.1**
Public and publicly guaranteed	..	..	44.5	42.6	43.7	63.4	68.7	68.3	60.2	64.1
Private nonguaranteed	..	..	0.0	0.0	0.0	0.0	0.0	0.0	0.0	0.0
Use of IMF credit	**0.0**	**0.0**	**0.0**	**0.0**	**0.0**	**0.0**	**0.0**	**0.0**	**0.0**	**0.0**
Short-term debt	..	..	**9.2**	**0.8**	**0.6**	**1.0**	**1.3**	**1.3**	**1.0**	**0.6**
of which interest arrears on LDOD	..	..	0.0	0.0	0.0	0.0	0.0	0.0	0.0	0.0
Official creditors	..	..	0.0	0.0	0.0	0.0	0.0	0.0	0.0	0.0
Private creditors	..	..	0.0	0.0	0.0	0.0	0.0	0.0	0.0	0.0
Memo: principal arrears on LDOD	..	..	0.0	0.0	0.0	0.0	0.0	0.0	0.0	0.0
Official creditors	..	..	0.0	0.0	0.0	0.0	0.0	0.0	0.0	0.0
Private creditors	..	..	0.0	0.0	0.0	0.0	0.0	0.0	0.0	0.0
Memo: export credits	..	..	1.0	1.0	1.0	8.0	1.0	1.0	1.0	0.0
TOTAL DEBT FLOWS										
Disbursements	..	..	**3.3**	**2.2**	**3.3**	**7.7**	**6.2**	**5.4**	**2.6**	**5.2**
Long-term debt	..	..	3.3	2.2	3.3	7.7	6.2	5.4	2.6	5.2
IMF purchases	0.0	0.0	0.0	0.0	0.0	0.0	0.0	0.0	0.0	0.0
Principal repayments	..	..	**1.0**	**1.0**	**1.2**	**2.1**	**2.4**	**3.3**	**4.5**	**3.7**
Long-term debt	..	..	1.0	1.0	1.2	2.1	2.4	3.3	4.5	3.7
IMF repurchases	0.0	0.0	0.0	0.0	0.0	0.0	0.0	0.0	0.0	0.0
Net flows on debt	..	..	**10.4**	**1.3**	**1.9**	**6.0**	**4.1**	**2.1**	**-2.2**	**1.1**
of which short-term debt	..	..	8.2	0.1	-0.3	0.4	0.3	0.0	-0.3	-0.4
Interest payments (INT)	..	..	**0.9**	**0.6**	**0.6**	**0.6**	**0.8**	**0.8**	**1.3**	**1.1**
Long-term debt	..	..	0.5	0.5	0.5	0.6	0.7	0.7	1.2	1.0
IMF charges	0.0	0.0	0.0	0.0	0.0	0.0	0.0	0.0	0.0	0.0
Short-term debt	..	..	0.4	0.0	0.1	0.1	0.1	0.1	0.0	0.0
Net transfers on debt	..	..	**9.5**	**0.7**	**1.3**	**5.3**	**3.3**	**1.3**	**-3.5**	**0.1**
Total debt service paid (TDS)	..	..	**1.9**	**1.6**	**1.7**	**2.7**	**3.2**	**4.1**	**5.8**	**4.7**
Long-term debt	..	..	1.5	1.6	1.7	2.7	3.1	4.0	5.7	4.7
IMF repurchases and charges	0.0	0.0	0.0	0.0	0.0	0.0	0.0	0.0	0.0	0.0
Short-term debt (interest only)	..	..	0.4	0.0	0.1	0.1	0.1	0.1	0.0	0.0
2. AGGREGATE NET RESOURCE FLOWS AND NET TRANSFERS (LONG-TERM)										
NET RESOURCE FLOWS	..	..	**19.1**	**11.2**	**19.3**	**22.8**	**24.1**	**16.4**	**9.0**	**9.1**
Net flow of long-term debt (ex. IMF)	..	..	2.2	1.2	2.2	5.6	3.8	2.1	-1.9	1.5
Foreign direct investment (net)	..	..	0.0	1.0	2.0	2.0	2.0	2.0	3.0	2.0
Portfolio equity flows	..	..	0.0	0.0	0.0	0.0	0.0	0.0	0.0	0.0
Grants (excluding technical coop.)	..	..	16.9	9.0	15.1	15.2	18.3	12.3	8.0	5.5
Memo: technical coop. grants	..	..	10.9	13.8	14.4	14.0	16.3	17.5	17.0	14.0
official net resource flows	..	..	19.1	10.2	17.3	20.8	22.1	14.0	8.5	8.9
private net resource flows	..	..	0.0	1.0	2.0	2.0	2.0	2.4	0.5	0.2
NET TRANSFERS	..	..	**18.6**	**10.2**	**18.8**	**22.2**	**23.4**	**15.7**	**7.8**	**8.1**
Interest on long-term debt	..	..	0.5	0.5	0.5	0.6	0.7	0.7	1.2	1.0
Profit remittances on FDI	..	..	0.0	0.5	0.0	0.0	0.0	0.0	0.0	0.0
Memo: official net transfers	..	..	18.6	9.7	16.8	20.2	21.4	13.3	7.9	8.3
private net transfers	..	..	0.0	0.5	2.0	2.0	2.0	2.4	-0.1	-0.2
3. MAJOR ECONOMIC AGGREGATES										
Gross national product (GNP)	..	..	117.3	143.5	145.6	159.5	168.1	182.1	184.4	176.4
Exports of goods & services (XGS)	..	..	66.5	53.2	56.4	44.2	46.2	46.9	53.2	49.4
of which workers remittances	..	..	23.0	20.1	18.8	..	..	..	..	..
Imports of goods & services (MGS)	..	..	75.0	74.8	80.1	87.7	103.6	92.1	89.2	110.0
International reserves (RES)	..	..	31.3	31.8	37.1	35.5	28.7	30.6	27.5	28.7
Current account balance	..	..	5.8	-0.5	-5.9	-14.2	-26.2	-10.2	-0.4	-20.8
4. DEBT INDICATORS										
EDT / XGS (%)	..	..	80.8	81.7	78.4	145.8	151.7	148.5	115.0	131.1
EDT / GNP (%)	..	..	45.8	30.3	30.4	40.4	41.7	38.2	33.2	36.7
TDS / XGS (%)	..	..	2.9	3.0	3.0	6.1	6.9	8.8	10.9	9.5
INT / XGS (%)	..	..	1.4	1.1	1.1	1.4	1.7	1.7	2.4	2.2
INT / GNP (%)	..	..	0.8	0.4	0.4	0.4	0.5	0.4	0.7	0.6
RES / EDT (%)	..	..	58.4	73.0	83.9	55.2	41.0	44.0	44.9	44.3
RES / MGS (months)	..	..	5.0	5.1	5.6	4.9	3.3	4.0	3.7	3.1
Short-term / EDT (%)	..	..	17.1	1.8	1.4	1.6	1.9	1.9	1.6	0.9
Concessional / EDT (%)	..	..	72.3	86.4	86.2	73.1	75.3	76.4	80.1	84.5
Multilateral / EDT (%)	..	..	42.3	55.4	60.9	56.1	59.5	62.6	67.8	73.0

TONGA

(US$ million, unless otherwise indicated)

	1970	1980	1990	1992	1993	1994	1995	1996	1997	1998
5. LONG-TERM DEBT										
DEBT OUTSTANDING (LDOD)	..	..	**44.5**	**42.6**	**43.7**	**63.4**	**68.7**	**68.3**	**60.2**	**64.1**
Public and publicly guaranteed	..	..	**44.5**	**42.6**	**43.7**	**63.4**	**68.7**	**68.3**	**60.2**	**64.1**
Official creditors	..	..	44.5	42.6	43.7	53.3	58.5	58.0	52.9	58.4
Multilateral	..	..	22.7	24.1	26.9	36.1	41.7	43.6	41.5	47.2
Concessional	..	..	18.0	19.6	21.7	30.2	36.0	38.8	37.6	43.5
Bilateral	..	..	21.7	18.5	16.8	17.2	16.8	14.4	11.4	11.2
Concessional	..	..	20.8	18.0	16.4	16.9	16.8	14.4	11.4	11.2
Private creditors	..	..	0.0	0.0	0.0	10.1	10.2	10.3	7.2	5.7
Bonds	..	..	0.0	0.0	0.0	0.0	0.0	0.0	0.0	0.0
Commercial banks	..	..	0.0	0.0	0.0	0.0	0.0	0.0	0.0	0.0
Other private	..	..	0.0	0.0	0.0	10.1	10.2	10.3	7.2	5.7
Private nonguaranteed	..	..	**0.0**	**0.0**	**0.0**	**0.0**	**0.0**	**0.0**	**0.0**	**0.0**
Bonds	..	..	0.0	0.0	0.0	0.0	0.0	0.0	0.0	0.0
Commercial banks	..	..	0.0	0.0	0.0	0.0	0.0	0.0	0.0	0.0
Memo:										
IBRD	0.0	0.0	0.0	0.0	0.0	0.0	0.0	0.0	0.0	0.0
IDA	0.0	0.0	2.6	3.2	3.4	4.4	4.8	4.6	4.3	4.4
DISBURSEMENTS	..	..	**3.3**	**2.2**	**3.3**	**7.7**	**6.2**	**5.4**	**2.6**	**5.2**
Public and publicly guaranteed	..	..	**3.3**	**2.2**	**3.3**	**7.7**	**6.2**	**5.4**	**2.6**	**5.2**
Official creditors	..	..	3.3	2.2	3.3	7.7	6.2	3.9	2.6	5.2
Multilateral	..	..	3.3	2.2	3.3	7.7	6.2	3.9	2.6	5.2
Concessional	..	..	3.2	1.8	2.0	7.0	6.2	3.9	2.4	5.1
Bilateral	..	..	0.0	0.0	0.0	0.0	0.0	0.0	0.0	0.0
Concessional	..	..	0.0	0.0	0.0	0.0	0.0	0.0	0.0	0.0
Private creditors	..	..	0.0	0.0	0.0	0.0	0.0	1.5	0.0	0.0
Bonds	..	..	0.0	0.0	0.0	0.0	0.0	0.0	0.0	0.0
Commercial banks	..	..	0.0	0.0	0.0	0.0	0.0	0.0	0.0	0.0
Other private	..	..	0.0	0.0	0.0	0.0	0.0	1.5	0.0	0.0
Private nonguaranteed	..	..	**0.0**	**0.0**	**0.0**	**0.0**	**0.0**	**0.0**	**0.0**	**0.0**
Bonds	..	..	0.0	0.0	0.0	0.0	0.0	0.0	0.0	0.0
Commercial banks	..	..	0.0	0.0	0.0	0.0	0.0	0.0	0.0	0.0
Memo:										
IBRD	0.0	0.0	0.0	0.0	0.0	0.0	0.0	0.0	0.0	0.0
IDA	0.0	0.0	1.0	0.1	0.2	0.8	0.2	-0.1	0.0	0.0
PRINCIPAL REPAYMENTS	..	..	**1.0**	**1.0**	**1.2**	**2.1**	**2.4**	**3.3**	**4.5**	**3.7**
Public and publicly guaranteed	..	..	**1.0**	**1.0**	**1.2**	**2.1**	**2.4**	**3.3**	**4.5**	**3.7**
Official creditors	..	..	1.0	1.0	1.2	2.1	2.4	2.2	2.1	1.8
Multilateral	..	..	0.5	0.4	0.5	0.7	0.8	0.9	0.9	0.8
Concessional	..	..	0.3	0.2	0.2	0.2	0.2	0.3	0.3	0.4
Bilateral	..	..	0.5	0.6	0.7	1.4	1.7	1.3	1.2	1.0
Concessional	..	..	0.4	0.5	0.5	1.2	1.4	1.3	1.2	1.0
Private creditors	..	..	0.0	0.0	0.0	0.0	0.0	1.2	2.5	1.8
Bonds	..	..	0.0	0.0	0.0	0.0	0.0	0.0	0.0	0.0
Commercial banks	..	..	0.0	0.0	0.0	0.0	0.0	0.0	0.0	0.0
Other private	..	..	0.0	0.0	0.0	0.0	0.0	1.2	2.5	1.8
Private nonguaranteed	..	..	**0.0**	**0.0**	**0.0**	**0.0**	**0.0**	**0.0**	**0.0**	**0.0**
Bonds	..	..	0.0	0.0	0.0	0.0	0.0	0.0	0.0	0.0
Commercial banks	..	..	0.0	0.0	0.0	0.0	0.0	0.0	0.0	0.0
Memo:										
IBRD	0.0	0.0	0.0	0.0	0.0	0.0	0.0	0.0	0.0	0.0
IDA	0.0	0.0	0.0	0.0	0.0	0.0	0.0	0.0	0.0	0.0
NET FLOWS ON DEBT	..	..	**2.2**	**1.2**	**2.2**	**5.6**	**3.8**	**2.1**	**-1.9**	**1.5**
Public and publicly guaranteed	..	..	**2.2**	**1.2**	**2.2**	**5.6**	**3.8**	**2.1**	**-1.9**	**1.5**
Official creditors	..	..	2.2	1.2	2.2	5.6	3.8	1.7	0.5	3.4
Multilateral	..	..	2.8	1.8	2.8	7.0	5.4	3.0	1.7	4.4
Concessional	..	..	2.9	1.6	1.8	6.7	6.0	3.6	2.1	4.7
Bilateral	..	..	-0.5	-0.6	-0.7	-1.4	-1.7	-1.3	-1.2	-1.0
Concessional	..	..	-0.4	-0.5	-0.5	-1.2	-1.4	-1.3	-1.2	-1.0
Private creditors	..	..	0.0	0.0	0.0	0.0	0.0	0.4	-2.5	-1.8
Bonds	..	..	0.0	0.0	0.0	0.0	0.0	0.0	0.0	0.0
Commercial banks	..	..	0.0	0.0	0.0	0.0	0.0	0.0	0.0	0.0
Other private	..	..	0.0	0.0	0.0	0.0	0.0	0.4	-2.5	-1.8
Private nonguaranteed	..	..	**0.0**	**0.0**	**0.0**	**0.0**	**0.0**	**0.0**	**0.0**	**0.0**
Bonds	..	..	0.0	0.0	0.0	0.0	0.0	0.0	0.0	0.0
Commercial banks	..	..	0.0	0.0	0.0	0.0	0.0	0.0	0.0	0.0
Memo:										
IBRD	0.0	0.0	0.0	0.0	0.0	0.0	0.0	0.0	0.0	0.0
IDA	0.0	0.0	1.0	0.1	0.2	0.8	0.2	-0.1	0.0	0.0

TONGA

(US$ million, unless otherwise indicated)

	1970	1980	1990	1992	1993	1994	1995	1996	1997	1998
INTEREST PAYMENTS (LINT)	..	..	**0.5**	**0.5**	**0.5**	**0.6**	**0.7**	**0.7**	**1.2**	**1.0**
Public and publicly guaranteed	..	..	**0.5**	**0.5**	**0.5**	**0.6**	**0.7**	**0.7**	**1.2**	**1.0**
Official creditors	..	..	0.5	0.5	0.5	0.6	0.7	0.7	0.6	0.6
Multilateral	..	..	0.2	0.3	0.3	0.4	0.5	0.6	0.5	0.5
Concessional	..	..	0.1	0.2	0.2	0.2	0.3	0.4	0.4	0.4
Bilateral	..	..	0.3	0.2	0.2	0.2	0.2	0.1	0.1	0.1
Concessional	..	..	0.2	0.2	0.2	0.2	0.2	0.1	0.1	0.1
Private creditors	..	..	0.0	0.0	0.0	0.0	0.0	0.0	0.6	0.4
Bonds	..	..	0.0	0.0	0.0	0.0	0.0	0.0	0.0	0.0
Commercial banks	..	..	0.0	0.0	0.0	0.0	0.0	0.0	0.0	0.0
Other private	..	..	0.0	0.0	0.0	0.0	0.0	0.0	0.6	0.4
Private nonguaranteed	..	..	**0.0**	**0.0**	**0.0**	**0.0**	**0.0**	**0.0**	**0.0**	**0.0**
Bonds	..	..	0.0	0.0	0.0	0.0	0.0	0.0	0.0	0.0
Commercial banks	..	..	0.0	0.0	0.0	0.0	0.0	0.0	0.0	0.0
Memo:										
IBRD	0.0	0.0	0.0	0.0	0.0	0.0	0.0	0.0	0.0	0.0
IDA	0.0	0.0	0.0	0.0	0.0	0.0	0.0	0.0	0.0	0.0
NET TRANSFERS ON DEBT	..	..	**1.7**	**0.7**	**1.6**	**5.0**	**3.1**	**1.4**	**-3.1**	**0.5**
Public and publicly guaranteed	..	..	**1.7**	**0.7**	**1.6**	**5.0**	**3.1**	**1.4**	**-3.1**	**0.5**
Official creditors	..	..	1.7	0.7	1.6	5.0	3.1	1.0	-0.1	2.8
Multilateral	..	..	2.5	1.5	2.5	6.6	4.9	2.4	1.2	3.9
Concessional	..	..	2.8	1.4	1.6	6.5	5.7	3.2	1.7	4.3
Bilateral	..	..	-0.8	-0.9	-0.9	-1.6	-1.9	-1.4	-1.3	-1.1
Concessional	..	..	-0.5	-0.7	-0.7	-1.4	-1.5	-1.4	-1.3	-1.1
Private creditors	..	..	0.0	0.0	0.0	0.0	0.0	0.4	-3.1	-2.3
Bonds	..	..	0.0	0.0	0.0	0.0	0.0	0.0	0.0	0.0
Commercial banks	..	..	0.0	0.0	0.0	0.0	0.0	0.0	0.0	0.0
Other private	..	..	0.0	0.0	0.0	0.0	0.0	0.4	-3.1	-2.3
Private nonguaranteed	..	..	**0.0**	**0.0**	**0.0**	**0.0**	**0.0**	**0.0**	**0.0**	**0.0**
Bonds	..	..	0.0	0.0	0.0	0.0	0.0	0.0	0.0	0.0
Commercial banks	..	..	0.0	0.0	0.0	0.0	0.0	0.0	0.0	0.0
Memo:										
IBRD	0.0	0.0	0.0	0.0	0.0	0.0	0.0	0.0	0.0	0.0
IDA	0.0	0.0	1.0	0.1	0.2	0.8	0.2	-0.1	0.0	-0.1
DEBT SERVICE (LTDS)	..	..	**1.5**	**1.6**	**1.7**	**2.7**	**3.1**	**4.0**	**5.7**	**4.7**
Public and publicly guaranteed	..	..	**1.5**	**1.6**	**1.7**	**2.7**	**3.1**	**4.0**	**5.7**	**4.7**
Official creditors	..	..	1.5	1.6	1.7	2.7	3.1	2.9	2.7	2.4
Multilateral	..	..	0.7	0.7	0.8	1.1	1.3	1.5	1.4	1.3
Concessional	..	..	0.4	0.3	0.4	0.4	0.5	0.7	0.7	0.7
Bilateral	..	..	0.8	0.9	0.9	1.6	1.9	1.4	1.3	1.1
Concessional	..	..	0.5	0.7	0.7	1.4	1.5	1.4	1.3	1.1
Private creditors	..	..	0.0	0.0	0.0	0.0	0.0	1.2	3.1	2.3
Bonds	..	..	0.0	0.0	0.0	0.0	0.0	0.0	0.0	0.0
Commercial banks	..	..	0.0	0.0	0.0	0.0	0.0	0.0	0.0	0.0
Other private	..	..	0.0	0.0	0.0	0.0	0.0	1.2	3.1	2.3
Private nonguaranteed	..	..	**0.0**	**0.0**	**0.0**	**0.0**	**0.0**	**0.0**	**0.0**	**0.0**
Bonds	..	..	0.0	0.0	0.0	0.0	0.0	0.0	0.0	0.0
Commercial banks	..	..	0.0	0.0	0.0	0.0	0.0	0.0	0.0	0.0
Memo:										
IBRD	0.0	0.0	0.0	0.0	0.0	0.0	0.0	0.0	0.0	0.0
IDA	0.0	0.0	0.0	0.0	0.0	0.0	0.0	0.0	0.0	0.1
UNDISBURSED DEBT	..	..	**18.0**	**19.9**	**20.2**	**15.2**	**19.9**	**15.8**	**15.8**	**11.0**
Official creditors	..	..	18.0	19.9	20.2	13.7	18.3	15.8	15.8	11.0
Private creditors	..	..	0.0	0.0	0.0	1.6	1.6	0.0	0.0	0.0
Memorandum items										
Concessional LDOD	..	..	38.8	37.5	38.1	47.1	52.8	53.2	49.0	54.6
Variable rate LDOD	..	..	0.0	0.0	0.0	0.0	0.0	0.0	0.0	0.0
Public sector LDOD	..	..	44.5	42.6	43.7	63.4	68.7	68.3	60.2	64.1
Private sector LDOD	..	..	0.0	0.0	0.0	0.0	0.0	0.0	0.0	0.0
6. CURRENCY COMPOSITION OF LONG-TERM DEBT (PERCENT)										
Deutsche mark	..	..	40.7	38.2	34.3	24.8	23.0	19.8	17.9	16.7
French franc	..	..	0.0	0.0	0.0	0.0	0.0	0.0	0.0	0.0
Japanese yen	..	..	0.0	0.0	0.0	0.0	0.0	0.0	0.0	0.0
Pound sterling	..	..	5.8	3.8	3.2	1.9	1.5	1.3	1.0	0.8
Swiss franc	..	..	0.0	0.0	0.0	0.0	0.0	0.0	0.0	0.0
U.S.dollars	..	..	1.1	2.6	2.7	3.5	3.5	3.4	3.7	3.4
Multiple currency	..	..	45.4	49.7	55.2	65.3	67.7	70.1	71.5	73.2
Special drawing rights	..	..	0.0	0.0	0.0	1.6	2.2	3.5	4.3	4.5
All other currencies	..	..	7.0	5.7	4.6	2.9	2.1	1.9	1.6	1.4

TONGA

(US$ million, unless otherwise indicated)

	1970	1980	1990	1992	1993	1994	1995	1996	1997	1998
7. DEBT RESTRUCTURINGS										
Total amount rescheduled	..	..	0.0	0.0	0.0	0.0	0.0	0.0	0.0	0.0
Debt stock rescheduled	..	..	0.0	0.0	0.0	0.0	0.0	0.0	0.0	0.0
Principal rescheduled	..	..	0.0	0.0	0.0	0.0	0.0	0.0	0.0	0.0
Official	..	..	0.0	0.0	0.0	0.0	0.0	0.0	0.0	0.0
Private	..	..	0.0	0.0	0.0	0.0	0.0	0.0	0.0	0.0
Interest rescheduled	..	..	0.0	0.0	0.0	0.0	0.0	0.0	0.0	0.0
Official	..	..	0.0	0.0	0.0	0.0	0.0	0.0	0.0	0.0
Private	..	..	0.0	0.0	0.0	0.0	0.0	0.0	0.0	0.0
Debt forgiven	..	..	0.0	0.0	0.0	0.0	0.0	0.0	0.0	0.0
Memo: interest forgiven	..	..	0.0	0.0	0.0	0.0	0.0	0.0	0.0	0.0
Debt stock reduction	..	..	0.0	0.0	0.0	0.0	0.0	0.0	0.0	0.0
of which debt buyback	..	..	0.0	0.0	0.0	0.0	0.0	0.0	0.0	0.0
8. DEBT STOCK-FLOW RECONCILIATION										
Total change in debt stocks	..	..	14.5	-1.5	0.8	20.2	5.7	-0.4	-8.5	3.5
Net flows on debt	..	..	10.4	1.3	1.9	6.0	4.1	2.1	-2.2	1.1
Net change in interest arrears	..	..	0.0	0.0	0.0	0.0	0.0	0.0	0.0	0.0
Interest capitalized	..	..	0.0	0.0	0.0	0.0	0.0	0.0	0.0	0.0
Debt forgiveness or reduction	..	..	0.0	0.0	0.0	0.0	0.0	0.0	0.0	0.0
Cross-currency valuation	..	..	3.3	-1.5	-1.1	2.1	1.4	-1.1	-1.7	0.9
Residual	..	..	0.8	-1.3	0.0	12.1	0.2	-1.4	-4.5	1.5
9. AVERAGE TERMS OF NEW COMMITMENTS										
ALL CREDITORS										
Interest (%)	..	..	0.9	0.0	1.6	0.0	4.4	3.5	3.4	0.0
Maturity (years)	..	..	39.7	0.0	39.1	0.0	39.0	39.7	39.1	0.0
Grace period (years)	..	..	10.2	0.0	8.5	0.0	9.5	10.2	9.6	0.0
Grant element (%)	..	..	79.5	0.0	68.6	0.0	47.6	55.8	56.6	0.0
Official creditors										
Interest (%)	..	..	0.9	0.0	1.6	0.0	4.4	3.5	3.4	0.0
Maturity (years)	..	..	39.7	0.0	39.1	0.0	39.0	39.7	39.1	0.0
Grace period (years)	..	..	10.2	0.0	8.5	0.0	9.5	10.2	9.6	0.0
Grant element (%)	..	..	79.5	0.0	68.6	0.0	47.6	55.8	56.6	0.0
Private creditors										
Interest (%)	..	..	0.0	0.0	0.0	0.0	0.0	0.0	0.0	0.0
Maturity (years)	..	..	0.0	0.0	0.0	0.0	0.0	0.0	0.0	0.0
Grace period (years)	..	..	0.0	0.0	0.0	0.0	0.0	0.0	0.0	0.0
Grant element (%)	..	..	0.0	0.0	0.0	0.0	0.0	0.0	0.0	0.0
Memorandum items										
Commitments	..	..	5.7	0.0	4.2	0.0	10.5	3.5	4.6	0.0
Official creditors	..	..	5.7	0.0	4.2	0.0	10.5	3.5	4.6	0.0
Private creditors	..	..	0.0	0.0	0.0	0.0	0.0	0.0	0.0	0.0

10. CONTRACTUAL OBLIGATIONS ON OUTSTANDING LONG-TERM DEBT

	1999	2000	2001	2002	2003	2004	2005	2006	2007	2008
TOTAL										
Disbursements	3.0	3.4	2.4	1.0	0.5	0.3	0.2	0.1	0.1	0.0
Principal	5.1	5.3	2.7	2.3	2.1	2.3	2.5	2.5	2.7	2.7
Interest	1.1	1.0	0.8	0.8	0.7	0.7	1.0	1.0	1.0	0.9
Official creditors										
Disbursements	3.0	3.4	2.4	1.0	0.5	0.3	0.2	0.1	0.1	0.0
Principal	2.3	2.5	2.7	2.3	2.1	2.3	2.5	2.5	2.7	2.7
Interest	0.8	0.8	0.8	0.8	0.7	0.7	1.0	1.0	1.0	0.9
Bilateral creditors										
Disbursements	0.0	0.0	0.0	0.0	0.0	0.0	0.0	0.0	0.0	0.0
Principal	1.1	1.1	1.1	1.0	1.0	1.0	1.0	1.0	1.0	1.0
Interest	0.1	0.1	0.1	0.1	0.1	0.1	0.0	0.0	0.0	0.0
Multilateral creditors										
Disbursements	3.0	3.4	2.4	1.0	0.5	0.3	0.2	0.1	0.1	0.0
Principal	1.2	1.3	1.6	1.3	1.1	1.4	1.5	1.5	1.7	1.7
Interest	0.7	0.7	0.7	0.7	0.7	0.6	1.0	1.0	1.0	0.9
Private creditors										
Disbursements	0.0	0.0	0.0	0.0	0.0	0.0	0.0	0.0	0.0	0.0
Principal	2.8	2.8	0.0	0.0	0.0	0.0	0.0	0.0	0.0	0.0
Interest	0.3	0.2	0.0	0.0	0.0	0.0	0.0	0.0	0.0	0.0
Commercial banks										
Disbursements	0.0	0.0	0.0	0.0	0.0	0.0	0.0	0.0	0.0	0.0
Principal	0.0	0.0	0.0	0.0	0.0	0.0	0.0	0.0	0.0	0.0
Interest	0.0	0.0	0.0	0.0	0.0	0.0	0.0	0.0	0.0	0.0
Other private										
Disbursements	0.0	0.0	0.0	0.0	0.0	0.0	0.0	0.0	0.0	0.0
Principal	2.8	2.8	0.0	0.0	0.0	0.0	0.0	0.0	0.0	0.0
Interest	0.3	0.2	0.0	0.0	0.0	0.0	0.0	0.0	0.0	0.0

TRINIDAD AND TOBAGO

(US$ million, unless otherwise indicated)

	1970	1980	1990	1992	1993	1994	1995	1996	1997	1998
1. SUMMARY DEBT DATA										
TOTAL DEBT STOCKS (EDT)	**..**	**829**	**2,512**	**2,453**	**2,240**	**2,495**	**2,737**	**2,241**	**2,162**	**2,193**
Long-term debt (LDOD)	**101**	**713**	**2,055**	**1,973**	**1,958**	**2,079**	**2,032**	**1,948**	**1,583**	**1,619**
Public and publicly guaranteed	101	713	1,782	1,788	1,807	1,962	1,941	1,870	1,529	1,476
Private nonguaranteed	0	0	273	186	150	118	90	78	54	144
Use of IMF credit	**0**	**0**	**329**	**282**	**155**	**91**	**50**	**24**	**4**	**0**
Short-term debt	**..**	**116**	**127**	**197**	**128**	**324**	**656**	**270**	**575**	**574**
of which interest arrears on LDOD	..	0	0	0	0	1	7	10	7	7
Official creditors	..	0	0	0	0	1	2	0	0	0
Private creditors	..	0	0	0	0	0	5	9	6	7
Memo: principal arrears on LDOD	..	0	37	57	58	76	111	108	92	97
Official creditors	..	0	7	9	11	14	9	2	2	2
Private creditors	..	0	31	48	47	62	102	106	91	96
Memo: export credits	..	0	591	611	672	664	653	603	848	901
TOTAL DEBT FLOWS										
Disbursements	**12**	**363**	**188**	**289**	**287**	**344**	**127**	**251**	**83**	**175**
Long-term debt	8	363	85	289	287	344	127	251	83	175
IMF purchases	5	0	103	0	0	0	0	0	0	0
Principal repayments	**14**	**176**	**233**	**396**	**487**	**389**	**241**	**280**	**397**	**186**
Long-term debt	10	176	233	307	358	317	198	255	379	181
IMF repurchases	4	0	0	90	129	72	44	25	18	4
Net flows on debt	**-2**	**137**	**-45**	**-38**	**-270**	**150**	**212**	**-418**	**-6**	**-12**
of which short-term debt	..	-50	0	70	-70	196	326	-389	308	-1
Interest payments (INT)	**..**	**54**	**216**	**180**	**144**	**155**	**176**	**194**	**150**	**125**
Long-term debt	6	50	177	143	118	132	147	167	128	95
IMF charges	0	0	24	26	16	7	4	2	1	0
Short-term debt	..	4	15	11	10	16	25	25	22	30
Net transfers on debt	**..**	**83**	**-262**	**-218**	**-414**	**-5**	**36**	**-612**	**-156**	**-137**
Total debt service paid (TDS)	**..**	**230**	**449**	**576**	**632**	**545**	**417**	**474**	**547**	**311**
Long-term debt	16	226	410	449	476	449	344	422	506	277
IMF repurchases and charges	4	0	24	116	146	79	48	27	19	4
Short-term debt (interest only)	..	4	15	11	10	16	25	25	22	30
2. AGGREGATE NET RESOURCE FLOWS AND NET TRANSFERS (LONG-TERM)										
NET RESOURCE FLOWS	**81**	**372**	**-26**	**168**	**313**	**551**	**239**	**358**	**712**	**733**
Net flow of long-term debt (ex. IMF)	-3	187	-148	-18	-71	26	-70	-4	-296	-6
Foreign direct investment (net)	83	185	109	178	379	516	299	355	999	730
Portfolio equity flows	0	0	0	0	0	0	0	0	0	0
Grants (excluding technical coop.)	0	1	13	8	5	9	10	7	8	9
Memo: technical coop. grants	1	5	5	5	5	5	5	6	5	4
official net resource flows	2	115	43	71	45	46	58	-20	-44	-28
private net resource flows	80	258	-69	97	268	505	181	378	755	761
NET TRANSFERS	**16**	**-157**	**-401**	**-225**	**-45**	**169**	**-171**	**-89**	**285**	**317**
Interest on long-term debt	6	50	177	143	118	132	147	167	128	95
Profit remittances on FDI	59	479	197	251	240	250	263	280	299	320
Memo: official net transfers	-1	99	-8	14	-8	-10	-8	-89	-88	-76
private net transfers	17	-256	-393	-239	-37	179	-164	0	373	394
3. MAJOR ECONOMIC AGGREGATES										
Gross national product (GNP)	757	5,925	4,673	4,996	4,255	4,534	4,858	5,160	5,408	6,146
Exports of goods & services (XGS)	..	3,373	2,331	2,180	1,912	2,187	2,906	2,883	3,088	3,038
of which workers remittances	..	1	3	6	18	26	30	28	30	45
Imports of goods & services (MGS)	..	2,972	1,863	2,035	1,785	1,943	2,577	2,742	3,676	3,660
International reserves (RES)	43	2,813	513	190	228	373	379	564	723	800
Current account balance	..	357	459	139	113	218	294	105	-614	-644
4. DEBT INDICATORS										
EDT / XGS (%)	..	24.6	107.7	112.5	117.2	114.1	94.2	77.8	70.0	72.2
EDT / GNP (%)	..	14.0	53.7	49.1	52.6	55.0	56.3	43.4	40.0	35.7
TDS / XGS (%)	..	6.8	19.3	26.4	33.0	24.9	14.3	16.4	17.7	10.2
INT / XGS (%)	..	1.6	9.3	8.3	7.6	7.1	6.1	6.7	4.9	4.1
INT / GNP (%)	..	0.9	4.6	3.6	3.4	3.4	3.6	3.8	2.8	2.0
RES / EDT (%)	..	339.4	20.4	7.8	10.2	15.0	13.9	25.2	33.5	36.5
RES / MGS (months)	..	11.4	3.3	1.1	1.5	2.3	1.8	2.5	2.4	2.6
Short-term / EDT (%)	..	14.0	5.1	8.1	5.7	13.0	24.0	12.0	26.6	26.2
Concessional / EDT (%)	..	1.2	2.1	1.6	1.5	1.3	1.0	0.9	0.7	0.6
Multilateral / EDT (%)	..	8.6	4.1	8.5	13.2	16.0	19.2	25.6	27.0	28.3

TRINIDAD AND TOBAGO

(US$ million, unless otherwise indicated)

	1970	1980	1990	1992	1993	1994	1995	1996	1997	1998
5. LONG-TERM DEBT										
DEBT OUTSTANDING (LDOD)	**101**	**713**	**2,055**	**1,973**	**1,958**	**2,079**	**2,032**	**1,948**	**1,583**	**1,619**
Public and publicly guaranteed	**101**	**713**	**1,782**	**1,788**	**1,807**	**1,962**	**1,941**	**1,870**	**1,529**	**1,476**
Official creditors	45	263	634	756	797	878	948	870	773	761
Multilateral	23	71	103	208	295	400	527	573	584	620
Concessional	0	1	6	5	4	4	4	3	4	6
Bilateral	22	192	532	549	503	478	421	297	190	141
Concessional	6	8	48	35	29	27	24	17	10	6
Private creditors	56	450	1,147	1,031	1,010	1,084	993	1,000	755	715
Bonds	36	53	335	304	343	450	450	575	425	425
Commercial banks	15	348	624	545	514	495	433	347	274	241
Other private	4	50	188	182	153	139	111	79	57	49
Private nonguaranteed	**0**	**0**	**273**	**186**	**150**	**118**	**90**	**78**	**54**	**144**
Bonds	0	0	0	0	0	0	0	0	0	0
Commercial banks	0	0	273	186	150	118	90	78	54	144
Memo:										
IBRD	23	57	41	35	57	61	72	79	76	83
IDA	0	0	0	0	0	0	0	0	0	0
DISBURSEMENTS	**8**	**363**	**85**	**289**	**287**	**344**	**127**	**251**	**83**	**175**
Public and publicly guaranteed	**8**	**363**	**85**	**289**	**287**	**344**	**127**	**251**	**83**	**65**
Official creditors	5	125	43	131	104	95	127	101	83	65
Multilateral	3	11	39	69	93	93	125	99	83	63
Concessional	0	0	0	0	0	0	0	0	1	2
Bilateral	2	114	4	62	11	2	2	2	0	2
Concessional	2	0	0	0	0	0	0	0	0	0
Private creditors	3	238	42	158	184	249	0	150	0	0
Bonds	0	0	0	100	123	227	0	150	0	0
Commercial banks	3	197	0	0	27	0	0	0	0	0
Other private	0	41	42	58	34	22	0	0	0	0
Private nonguaranteed	**0**	**0**	**0**	**0**	**0**	**0**	**0**	**0**	**0**	**110**
Bonds	0	0	0	0	0	0	0	0	0	0
Commercial banks	0	0	0	0	0	0	0	0	0	110
Memo:										
IBRD	3	4	20	5	26	3	15	17	12	15
IDA	0	0	0	0	0	0	0	0	0	0
PRINCIPAL REPAYMENTS	**10**	**176**	**233**	**307**	**358**	**317**	**198**	**255**	**379**	**181**
Public and publicly guaranteed	**10**	**176**	**189**	**266**	**323**	**285**	**170**	**243**	**355**	**161**
Official creditors	3	11	14	68	64	57	79	128	135	102
Multilateral	1	6	10	13	10	11	13	15	40	47
Concessional	0	0	0	1	1	1	1	0	0	0
Bilateral	3	5	3	55	53	47	67	113	95	55
Concessional	0	0	0	5	5	5	6	5	5	4
Private creditors	7	165	176	198	259	228	91	115	220	59
Bonds	5	7	52	99	108	132	0	25	150	0
Commercial banks	1	150	99	27	78	51	51	69	55	46
Other private	0	7	25	72	73	45	40	21	15	13
Private nonguaranteed	**0**	**0**	**44**	**41**	**36**	**32**	**27**	**12**	**24**	**21**
Bonds	0	0	0	0	0	0	0	0	0	0
Commercial banks	0	0	44	41	36	32	27	12	24	21
Memo:										
IBRD	1	6	7	7	5	2	6	5	9	8
IDA	0	0	0	0	0	0	0	0	0	0
NET FLOWS ON DEBT	**-3**	**187**	**-148**	**-18**	**-71**	**26**	**-70**	**-4**	**-296**	**-6**
Public and publicly guaranteed	**-3**	**187**	**-105**	**23**	**-36**	**59**	**-43**	**8**	**-272**	**-96**
Official creditors	1	114	30	63	40	37	48	-27	-52	-37
Multilateral	2	5	29	57	83	82	113	84	43	17
Concessional	0	0	0	-1	-1	-1	-1	0	1	2
Bilateral	-1	109	1	7	-42	-45	-65	-111	-95	-54
Concessional	2	0	0	-5	-5	-5	-6	-5	-5	-4
Private creditors	-4	73	-134	-40	-76	21	-91	36	-220	-59
Bonds	-5	-7	-52	1	14	95	0	125	-150	0
Commercial banks	2	47	-99	-27	-51	-51	-51	-69	-55	-46
Other private	0	34	17	-14	-39	-23	-40	-21	-15	-13
Private nonguaranteed	**0**	**0**	**-44**	**-41**	**-36**	**-32**	**-27**	**-12**	**-24**	**89**
Bonds	0	0	0	0	0	0	0	0	0	0
Commercial banks	0	0	-44	-41	-36	-32	-27	-12	-24	89
Memo:										
IBRD	2	-1	13	-2	21	0	9	12	4	7
IDA	0	0	0	0	0	0	0	0	0	0

TRINIDAD AND TOBAGO

(US$ million, unless otherwise indicated)

	1970	1980	1990	1992	1993	1994	1995	1996	1997	1998
INTEREST PAYMENTS (LINT)	**6**	**50**	**177**	**143**	**118**	**132**	**147**	**167**	**128**	**95**
Public and publicly guaranteed	**6**	**50**	**151**	**125**	**109**	**124**	**140**	**161**	**124**	**93**
Official creditors	3	16	51	57	53	56	66	69	45	48
Multilateral	1	5	6	12	18	23	30	43	30	41
Concessional	0	0	0	0	0	0	0	0	0	0
Bilateral	1	11	45	45	35	33	35	26	15	7
Concessional	0	0	2	2	1	1	1	1	1	0
Private creditors	4	35	101	68	56	68	74	93	79	45
Bonds	2	5	25	20	14	31	32	67	59	42
Commercial banks	1	25	55	42	33	25	33	20	16	0
Other private	0	5	21	7	9	11	9	5	4	3
Private nonguaranteed	**0**	**0**	**26**	**18**	**9**	**8**	**7**	**5**	**4**	**3**
Bonds	0	0	0	0	0	0	0	0	0	0
Commercial banks	0	0	26	18	9	8	7	5	4	3
Memo:										
IBRD	1	5	2	3	4	4	5	5	5	5
IDA	0	0	0	0	0	0	0	0	0	0
NET TRANSFERS ON DEBT	**-9**	**137**	**-326**	**-161**	**-189**	**-106**	**-217**	**-171**	**-423**	**-102**
Public and publicly guaranteed	**-9**	**137**	**-256**	**-102**	**-144**	**-65**	**-183**	**-153**	**-396**	**-188**
Official creditors	-1	98	-21	6	-13	-19	-18	-96	-96	-85
Multilateral	1	0	23	45	64	59	82	41	13	-25
Concessional	0	0	0	-1	-1	-1	-1	0	1	2
Bilateral	-2	98	-44	-39	-77	-77	-100	-137	-110	-61
Concessional	1	0	-2	-7	-6	-6	-7	-6	-5	-5
Private creditors	-7	39	-235	-109	-131	-46	-165	-57	-299	-103
Bonds	-7	-12	-77	-18	1	64	-32	58	-209	-42
Commercial banks	1	22	-154	-69	-84	-76	-85	-89	-72	-46
Other private	-1	29	-4	-21	-48	-35	-49	-26	-18	-16
Private nonguaranteed	**0**	**0**	**-70**	**-58**	**-45**	**-41**	**-34**	**-18**	**-28**	**87**
Bonds	0	0	0	0	0	0	0	0	0	0
Commercial banks	0	0	-70	-58	-45	-41	-34	-18	-28	87
Memo:										
IBRD	1	-6	11	-4	17	-4	5	7	-2	2
IDA	0	0	0	0	0	0	0	0	0	0
DEBT SERVICE (LTDS)	**16**	**226**	**410**	**449**	**476**	**449**	**344**	**422**	**506**	**277**
Public and publicly guaranteed	**16**	**226**	**340**	**391**	**432**	**409**	**310**	**404**	**479**	**253**
Official creditors	6	27	64	125	117	113	145	197	180	150
Multilateral	2	11	16	24	29	34	43	58	70	88
Concessional	0	0	1	1	1	1	1	0	0	0
Bilateral	4	16	48	101	88	79	102	139	110	62
Concessional	0	0	2	7	6	6	7	6	5	5
Private creditors	10	199	276	266	315	295	165	207	299	103
Bonds	7	12	77	118	122	163	32	92	209	42
Commercial banks	2	175	154	69	111	76	85	89	72	46
Other private	1	12	46	79	82	56	49	26	18	16
Private nonguaranteed	**0**	**0**	**70**	**58**	**45**	**41**	**34**	**18**	**28**	**23**
Bonds	0	0	0	0	0	0	0	0	0	0
Commercial banks	0	0	70	58	45	41	34	18	28	23
Memo:										
IBRD	2	10	9	9	9	7	10	10	14	13
IDA	0	0	0	0	0	0	0	0	0	0
UNDISBURSED DEBT	**21**	**280**	**330**	**525**	**491**	**378**	**258**	**274**	**571**	**511**
Official creditors	21	201	247	442	442	378	258	274	571	511
Private creditors	0	79	83	83	49	0	0	0	0	0
Memorandum items										
Concessional LDOD	6	10	54	40	33	31	27	20	14	13
Variable rate LDOD	0	227	1,202	1,236	1,222	1,224	1,178	1,033	858	915
Public sector LDOD	101	713	1,782	1,788	1,807	1,962	1,941	1,870	1,529	1,476
Private sector LDOD	0	0	273	186	150	118	90	78	54	144

6. CURRENCY COMPOSITION OF LONG-TERM DEBT (PERCENT)

	1970	1980	1990	1992	1993	1994	1995	1996	1997	1998
Deutsche mark	0.0	5.6	6.8	4.1	3.2	2.9	2.7	2.1	1.6	1.2
French franc	0.0	0.1	4.1	2.9	2.6	2.5	2.3	1.7	1.2	0.9
Japanese yen	0.0	18.4	34.8	34.3	29.0	21.9	19.5	14.9	13.1	12.4
Pound sterling	33.4	0.2	3.4	2.7	2.6	2.4	2.6	2.9	3.4	3.5
Swiss franc	0.0	4.3	0.0	0.1	0.2	0.2	0.2	0.1	0.1	0.1
U.S.dollars	37.7	61.3	44.9	44.6	46.7	50.5	47.6	50.1	46.5	51.5
Multiple currency	23.1	8.3	4.1	8.9	13.7	17.8	23.8	27.2	32.9	29.1
Special drawing rights	0.0	0.0	0.0	0.0	0.0	0.0	0.0	0.0	0.0	0.0
All other currencies	5.8	1.8	1.9	2.4	2.0	1.8	1.3	1.0	1.2	1.3

TRINIDAD AND TOBAGO

(US$ million, unless otherwise indicated)

	1970	1980	1990	1992	1993	1994	1995	1996	1997	1998
7. DEBT RESTRUCTURINGS										
Total amount rescheduled	..	..	262	54	0	0	0	0	0	0
Debt stock rescheduled	..	..	0	0	0	0	0	0	0	0
Principal rescheduled	..	..	262	54	0	0	0	0	0	0
Official	..	..	56	0	0	0	0	0	0	0
Private	..	..	206	54	0	0	0	0	0	0
Interest rescheduled	..	..	0	0	0	0	0	0	0	0
Official	..	..	0	0	0	0	0	0	0	0
Private	..	..	0	0	0	0	0	0	0	0
Debt forgiven	..	..	7	0	0	0	0	0	0	0
Memo: interest forgiven	..	..	0	0	0	0	0	0	0	0
Debt stock reduction	..	..	0	32	10	0	7	0	0	0
of which debt buyback	..	..	0	0	0	0	0	0	0	0
8. DEBT STOCK-FLOW RECONCILIATION										
Total change in debt stocks	..	..	374	-35	-213	255	243	-496	-80	32
Net flows on debt	-2	137	-45	-38	-270	150	212	-418	-6	-12
Net change in interest arrears	..	..	0	0	0	1	5	3	-3	1
Interest capitalized	..	..	0	0	0	0	0	0	0	0
Debt forgiveness or reduction	..	..	-7	-32	-10	0	-7	0	0	0
Cross-currency valuation	..	..	84	-22	49	73	0	-39	-37	27
Residual	..	..	342	57	18	31	33	-42	-33	16
9. AVERAGE TERMS OF NEW COMMITMENTS										
ALL CREDITORS										
Interest (%)	7.5	10.4	8.0	8.0	8.8	10.8	6.5	7.7	6.1	8.5
Maturity (years)	9.8	8.7	14.9	6.0	13.1	9.4	17.5	13.4	18.6	15.7
Grace period (years)	1.2	3.7	4.6	3.4	6.0	7.8	4.1	7.6	5.8	5.3
Grant element (%)	10.5	-2.6	10.7	4.0	7.9	-4.3	20.5	13.8	20.1	8.0
Official creditors										
Interest (%)	3.0	7.6	7.9	7.9	7.4	6.6	6.5	7.3	6.1	8.5
Maturity (years)	29.6	9.5	18.1	14.7	20.9	15.0	17.5	17.8	18.6	15.7
Grace period (years)	7.1	2.3	5.4	4.9	5.2	4.9	4.1	4.6	5.8	5.3
Grant element (%)	54.6	9.1	12.0	11.5	16.3	19.0	20.5	15.7	20.1	8.0
Private creditors										
Interest (%)	8.0	10.6	8.1	8.0	9.8	11.5	0.0	8.0	0.0	0.0
Maturity (years)	7.5	8.6	9.8	4.3	6.7	8.3	0.0	10.0	0.0	0.0
Grace period (years)	0.5	3.9	3.3	3.1	6.7	8.3	0.0	10.0	0.0	0.0
Grant element (%)	5.5	-3.6	8.6	2.6	1.0	-8.6	0.0	12.3	0.0	0.0
Memorandum items										
Commitments	3	211	187	235	273	237	18	266	385	2
Official creditors	0	17	115	38	123	37	18	116	385	2
Private creditors	3	194	73	197	150	200	0	150	0	0

10. CONTRACTUAL OBLIGATIONS ON OUTSTANDING LONG-TERM DEBT

	1999	2000	2001	2002	2003	2004	2005	2006	2007	2008
TOTAL										
Disbursements	138	147	111	68	37	9	1	0	0	0
Principal	253	348	90	91	91	240	79	227	66	65
Interest	122	115	99	98	94	81	66	60	43	38
Official creditors										
Disbursements	138	147	111	68	37	9	1	0	0	0
Principal	147	120	85	86	86	85	79	77	66	65
Interest	61	60	60	59	56	51	46	40	35	30
Bilateral creditors										
Disbursements	0	0	0	0	0	0	0	0	0	0
Principal	90	39	3	2	2	2	2	1	0	0
Interest	8	3	1	1	0	0	0	0	0	0
Multilateral creditors										
Disbursements	138	147	111	68	37	9	1	0	0	0
Principal	57	81	82	84	84	84	77	77	66	65
Interest	53	57	59	58	56	51	45	40	35	30
Private creditors										
Disbursements	0	0	0	0	0	0	0	0	0	0
Principal	106	228	5	5	5	155	0	150	0	0
Interest	61	55	39	39	38	29	20	20	8	8
Commercial banks										
Disbursements	0	0	0	0	0	0	0	0	0	0
Principal	73	73	0	0	0	0	0	0	0	0
Interest	7	3	0	0	0	0	0	0	0	0
Other private										
Disbursements	0	0	0	0	0	0	0	0	0	0
Principal	33	156	5	5	5	155	0	150	0	0
Interest	54	52	39	39	38	29	20	20	8	8

TUNISIA

(US$ million, unless otherwise indicated)

	1970	1980	1990	1992	1993	1994	1995	1996	1997	1998
1. SUMMARY DEBT DATA										
TOTAL DEBT STOCKS (EDT)	..	**3,527**	**7,691**	**8,541**	**8,692**	**9,609**	**10,914**	**11,464**	**11,321**	**11,078**
Long-term debt (LDOD)	**541**	**3,390**	**6,880**	**7,409**	**7,618**	**8,200**	**9,311**	**9,651**	**9,609**	**9,908**
Public and publicly guaranteed	541	3,210	6,662	7,201	7,415	8,002	9,118	9,463	9,426	9,727
Private nonguaranteed	0	180	218	208	203	198	193	188	183	181
Use of IMF credit	**13**	**0**	**176**	**290**	**285**	**303**	**293**	**237**	**173**	**129**
Short-term debt	..	**136**	**634**	**843**	**789**	**1,106**	**1,310**	**1,576**	**1,539**	**1,040**
of which interest arrears on LDOD	..	0	0	2	0	0	0	0	0	0
Official creditors	..	0	0	2	0	0	0	0	0	0
Private creditors	..	0	0	0	0	0	0	0	0	0
Memo: principal arrears on LDOD	..	6	15	10	3	16	1	0	0	0
Official creditors	..	6	8	8	3	15	1	0	0	0
Private creditors	..	0	7	2	0	0	0	0	0	0
Memo: export credits	..	0	1,547	1,381	1,526	1,921	1,982	1,871	1,834	2,028
TOTAL DEBT FLOWS										
Disbursements	**96**	**611**	**1,018**	**1,283**	**1,122**	**1,059**	**1,488**	**1,333**	**1,516**	**668**
Long-term debt	89	611	1,018	1,210	1,122	1,059	1,488	1,333	1,516	668
IMF purchases	8	0	0	73	0	0	0	0	0	0
Principal repayments	**54**	**290**	**984**	**888**	**850**	**928**	**939**	**908**	**875**	**850**
Long-term debt	47	258	873	858	844	928	924	861	825	801
IMF repurchases	7	31	111	29	5	0	16	47	50	50
Net flows on debt	**86**	**267**	**293**	**576**	**221**	**448**	**753**	**691**	**604**	**-681**
of which short-term debt	..	-54	259	180	-51	317	204	266	-37	-499
Interest payments (INT)	..	**255**	**448**	**454**	**503**	**529**	**541**	**558**	**538**	**552**
Long-term debt	18	228	394	398	419	462	486	507	479	485
IMF charges	0	1	23	19	17	15	17	12	10	7
Short-term debt	..	26	30	37	67	52	38	39	49	60
Net transfers on debt	..	**12**	**-155**	**122**	**-282**	**-81**	**212**	**133**	**66**	**-1,233**
Total debt service paid (TDS)	..	**545**	**1,432**	**1,342**	**1,352**	**1,457**	**1,480**	**1,466**	**1,413**	**1,402**
Long-term debt	65	486	1,267	1,256	1,263	1,390	1,409	1,368	1,303	1,285
IMF repurchases and charges	7	33	135	49	22	15	32	59	60	57
Short-term debt (interest only)	..	26	30	37	67	52	38	39	49	60
2. AGGREGATE NET RESOURCE FLOWS AND NET TRANSFERS (LONG-TERM)										
NET RESOURCE FLOWS	**100**	**613**	**395**	**1,019**	**943**	**646**	**887**	**848**	**1,166**	**619**
Net flow of long-term debt (ex. IMF)	42	352	145	352	277	131	564	472	691	-133
Foreign direct investment (net)	16	235	76	526	562	432	264	238	339	650
Portfolio equity flows	0	0	0	0	0	0	0	0	0	40
Grants (excluding technical coop.)	43	26	174	140	103	83	58	138	136	61
Memo: technical coop. grants	27	74	101	98	103	84	122	103	91	93
official net resource flows	83	276	517	421	480	336	132	231	241	-76
private net resource flows	17	336	-122	598	462	310	755	617	926	694
NET TRANSFERS	**62**	**232**	**-145**	**340**	**287**	**-56**	**156**	**91**	**422**	**-141**
Interest on long-term debt	18	228	394	398	419	462	486	507	479	485
Profit remittances on FDI	20	153	146	280	237	240	245	250	266	275
Memo: official net transfers	75	203	270	133	172	-26	-236	-138	-98	-403
private net transfers	-13	29	-415	207	115	-30	392	229	520	262
3. MAJOR ECONOMIC AGGREGATES										
Gross national product (GNP)	1,380	8,450	11,882	14,784	13,754	14,742	17,111	18,556	17,997	19,088
Exports of goods & services (XGS)	..	3,674	5,851	6,645	6,305	7,610	8,778	8,952	8,934	9,290
of which workers remittances	..	319	551	531	446	629	680	736	685	718
Imports of goods & services (MGS)	..	4,119	6,591	7,882	7,795	8,317	9,646	9,554	9,636	10,078
International reserves (RES)	60	700	867	924	938	1,544	1,689	1,978	2,041	1,856
Current account balance	..	-353	-463	-1,104	-1,323	-537	-774	-478	-595	-675
4. DEBT INDICATORS										
EDT / XGS (%)	..	96.0	131.4	128.5	137.9	126.3	124.3	128.1	126.7	119.2
EDT / GNP (%)	..	41.7	64.7	57.8	63.2	65.2	63.8	61.8	62.9	58.0
TDS / XGS (%)	..	14.8	24.5	20.2	21.5	19.1	16.9	16.4	15.8	15.1
INT / XGS (%)	..	6.9	7.7	6.8	8.0	7.0	6.2	6.2	6.0	5.9
INT / GNP (%)	..	3.0	3.8	3.1	3.7	3.6	3.2	3.0	3.0	2.9
RES / EDT (%)	..	19.9	11.3	10.8	10.8	16.1	15.5	17.3	18.0	16.8
RES / MGS (months)	..	2.0	1.6	1.4	1.4	2.2	2.1	2.5	2.5	2.2
Short-term / EDT (%)	..	3.9	8.3	9.9	9.1	11.5	12.0	13.8	13.6	9.4
Concessional / EDT (%)	..	39.3	35.1	33.3	33.2	31.8	28.6	25.4	23.2	24.2
Multilateral / EDT (%)	..	12.3	29.0	32.4	35.7	36.3	33.9	31.8	30.0	31.5

TUNISIA

(US$ million, unless otherwise indicated)

	1970	1980	1990	1992	1993	1994	1995	1996	1997	1998
5. LONG-TERM DEBT										
DEBT OUTSTANDING (LDOD)	**541**	**3,390**	**6,880**	**7,409**	**7,618**	**8,200**	**9,311**	**9,651**	**9,609**	**9,908**
Public and publicly guaranteed	**541**	**3,210**	**6,662**	**7,201**	**7,415**	**8,002**	**9,118**	**9,463**	**9,426**	**9,727**
Official creditors	364	1,961	5,229	5,898	6,240	6,876	7,490	7,562	7,072	7,256
Multilateral	44	433	2,229	2,770	3,099	3,490	3,701	3,643	3,397	3,489
Concessional	16	75	228	275	281	309	345	361	348	351
Bilateral	321	1,529	3,000	3,128	3,141	3,387	3,789	3,919	3,675	3,767
Concessional	317	1,311	2,469	2,571	2,602	2,747	2,772	2,551	2,280	2,334
Private creditors	177	1,249	1,434	1,303	1,176	1,126	1,628	1,901	2,354	2,472
Bonds	2	6	0	0	0	0	535	603	1,112	1,200
Commercial banks	0	493	343	488	544	621	660	945	868	864
Other private	175	750	1,091	815	632	505	433	353	374	408
Private nonguaranteed	**0**	**180**	**218**	**208**	**203**	**198**	**193**	**188**	**183**	**181**
Bonds	0	0	0	0	0	0	0	0	0	0
Commercial banks	0	180	218	208	203	198	193	188	183	181
Memo:										
IBRD	26	269	1,347	1,470	1,595	1,715	1,717	1,610	1,434	1,458
IDA	16	68	59	56	54	52	50	47	45	43
DISBURSEMENTS	**89**	**611**	**1,018**	**1,210**	**1,122**	**1,059**	**1,488**	**1,333**	**1,516**	**668**
Public and publicly guaranteed	**89**	**558**	**988**	**1,180**	**1,092**	**1,029**	**1,458**	**1,303**	**1,486**	**638**
Official creditors	54	323	699	743	841	860	711	684	687	474
Multilateral	13	82	430	402	574	481	467	503	352	302
Concessional	3	8	45	30	24	35	48	45	23	25
Bilateral	41	242	269	341	267	378	244	181	335	172
Concessional	40	197	177	271	218	242	230	118	148	124
Private creditors	34	235	289	437	251	169	747	619	799	164
Bonds	0	0	0	0	0	0	588	138	586	0
Commercial banks	0	51	91	292	216	159	106	461	103	65
Other private	34	184	198	145	34	10	53	20	110	99
Private nonguaranteed	**0**	**53**	**30**	**30**	**30**	**30**	**30**	**30**	**30**	**30**
Bonds	0	0	0	0	0	0	0	0	0	0
Commercial banks	0	53	30	30	30	30	30	30	30	30
Memo:										
IBRD	9	51	213	111	248	189	138	202	127	142
IDA	3	1	0	0	0	0	0	0	0	0
PRINCIPAL REPAYMENTS	**47**	**258**	**873**	**858**	**844**	**928**	**924**	**861**	**825**	**801**
Public and publicly guaranteed	**47**	**216**	**836**	**823**	**809**	**893**	**889**	**826**	**790**	**769**
Official creditors	14	72	356	463	464	607	637	591	582	611
Multilateral	1	20	168	233	249	290	362	341	338	362
Concessional	0	0	7	14	14	15	18	22	20	32
Bilateral	13	52	188	230	215	317	275	250	244	250
Concessional	11	40	134	135	133	245	182	187	185	196
Private creditors	33	144	480	360	345	286	252	235	207	158
Bonds	0	5	60	0	0	0	0	0	0	0
Commercial banks	0	24	113	103	145	113	103	149	139	86
Other private	33	114	307	258	201	173	149	86	68	72
Private nonguaranteed	**0**	**43**	**37**	**35**	**35**	**35**	**35**	**35**	**35**	**32**
Bonds	0	0	0	0	0	0	0	0	0	0
Commercial banks	0	43	37	35	35	35	35	35	35	32
Memo:										
IBRD	1	15	111	147	147	173	203	187	173	178
IDA	0	0	2	2	2	2	2	2	2	2
NET FLOWS ON DEBT	**42**	**352**	**145**	**352**	**277**	**131**	**564**	**472**	**691**	**-133**
Public and publicly guaranteed	**42**	**342**	**152**	**357**	**282**	**136**	**569**	**477**	**696**	**-131**
Official creditors	40	251	343	280	377	253	73	94	104	-137
Multilateral	12	61	262	170	325	192	104	162	14	-60
Concessional	3	8	38	16	10	20	30	23	3	-6
Bilateral	29	190	81	111	52	61	-31	-69	91	-77
Concessional	30	156	44	135	85	-3	48	-69	-37	-72
Private creditors	1	92	-191	77	-95	-117	496	384	592	6
Bonds	0	-5	-60	0	0	0	588	138	586	0
Commercial banks	0	27	-22	189	72	46	4	312	-36	-21
Other private	1	70	-109	-113	-167	-163	-96	-66	41	27
Private nonguaranteed	**0**	**10**	**-7**	**-5**	**-5**	**-5**	**-5**	**-5**	**-5**	**-2**
Bonds	0	0	0	0	0	0	0	0	0	0
Commercial banks	0	10	-7	-5	-5	-5	-5	-5	-5	-2
Memo:										
IBRD	8	36	102	-37	101	15	-65	15	-46	-37
IDA	3	1	-2	-2	-2	-2	-2	-2	-2	-2

TUNISIA

(US$ million, unless otherwise indicated)

	1970	*1980*	*1990*	*1992*	*1993*	*1994*	*1995*	*1996*	*1997*	*1998*
INTEREST PAYMENTS (LINT)	**18**	**228**	**394**	**398**	**419**	**462**	**486**	**507**	**479**	**485**
Public and publicly guaranteed	**18**	**212**	**384**	**390**	**412**	**454**	**478**	**499**	**469**	**476**
Official creditors	8	74	247	288	308	362	368	369	339	327
Multilateral	2	28	148	191	208	231	251	264	243	225
Concessional	0	1	6	8	8	10	9	11	11	11
Bilateral	7	46	99	97	100	131	117	106	96	102
Concessional	6	29	66	66	67	94	78	71	66	62
Private creditors	10	138	138	102	103	92	110	130	131	149
Bonds	0	1	5	0	0	0	14	33	36	66
Commercial banks	0	69	35	30	39	43	55	64	69	55
Other private	10	68	97	72	65	49	41	33	26	28
Private nonguaranteed	**0**	**16**	**10**	**8**	**7**	**7**	**8**	**8**	**9**	**8**
Bonds	0	0	0	0	0	0	0	0	0	0
Commercial banks	0	16	10	8	7	7	8	8	9	8
Memo:										
IBRD	1	23	103	119	117	124	129	115	103	90
IDA	0	1	1	0	0	0	0	0	0	0
NET TRANSFERS ON DEBT	**23**	**125**	**-249**	**-46**	**-141**	**-331**	**79**	**-35**	**212**	**-617**
Public and publicly guaranteed	**23**	**131**	**-232**	**-33**	**-129**	**-318**	**91**	**-22**	**227**	**-607**
Official creditors	32	177	96	-8	69	-109	-294	-276	-234	-464
Multilateral	10	33	114	-21	117	-40	-147	-101	-229	-285
Concessional	3	7	32	8	2	9	21	12	-8	-18
Bilateral	22	144	-18	14	-48	-70	-147	-175	-5	-180
Concessional	23	127	-23	70	18	-97	-30	-140	-103	-134
Private creditors	-9	-46	-328	-25	-198	-209	386	254	461	-143
Bonds	0	-6	-65	0	0	0	574	105	550	-66
Commercial banks	0	-43	-57	160	33	3	-52	248	-105	-76
Other private	-9	3	-206	-185	-231	-212	-137	-99	15	0
Private nonguaranteed	**0**	**-6**	**-17**	**-13**	**-12**	**-12**	**-13**	**-13**	**-14**	**-10**
Bonds	0	0	0	0	0	0	0	0	0	0
Commercial banks	0	-6	-17	-13	-12	-12	-13	-13	-14	-10
Memo:										
IBRD	7	14	-1	-156	-16	-109	-194	-101	-148	-127
IDA	3	0	-2	-2	-3	-3	-3	-3	-3	-2
DEBT SERVICE (LTDS)	**65**	**486**	**1,267**	**1,256**	**1,263**	**1,390**	**1,409**	**1,368**	**1,303**	**1,285**
Public and publicly guaranteed	**65**	**428**	**1,220**	**1,213**	**1,221**	**1,347**	**1,367**	**1,325**	**1,259**	**1,245**
Official creditors	22	146	603	751	772	969	1,005	960	921	938
Multilateral	3	48	316	423	457	521	613	605	581	587
Concessional	0	1	13	22	22	26	27	33	31	43
Bilateral	20	98	287	327	315	448	391	356	340	352
Concessional	17	70	200	201	200	339	259	258	251	258
Private creditors	43	281	618	463	449	379	362	365	338	307
Bonds	0	6	65	0	0	0	14	33	36	66
Commercial banks	0	94	148	132	183	156	158	213	208	141
Other private	43	182	404	330	265	223	190	119	95	100
Private nonguaranteed	**0**	**58**	**47**	**43**	**42**	**42**	**43**	**43**	**44**	**40**
Bonds	0	0	0	0	0	0	0	0	0	0
Commercial banks	0	58	47	43	42	42	43	43	44	40
Memo:										
IBRD	3	37	214	267	264	297	332	303	275	268
IDA	0	1	2	2	3	3	3	3	3	2
UNDISBURSED DEBT	**319**	**2,050**	**3,861**	**3,818**	**3,947**	**3,411**	**3,907**	**3,606**	**3,304**	**3,939**
Official creditors	270	1,578	3,118	3,074	3,375	2,985	3,290	3,054	2,865	3,381
Private creditors	50	472	743	744	572	426	617	551	439	558
Memorandum items										
Concessional LDOD	333	1,386	2,698	2,846	2,884	3,056	3,117	2,912	2,628	2,684
Variable rate LDOD	0	680	1,557	1,743	1,984	2,211	2,280	2,628	2,503	2,590
Public sector LDOD	528	3,120	6,662	7,190	7,406	7,995	9,111	9,458	9,424	9,726
Private sector LDOD	13	270	218	219	212	206	200	193	186	183

6. CURRENCY COMPOSITION OF LONG-TERM DEBT (PERCENT)

	1970	*1980*	*1990*	*1992*	*1993*	*1994*	*1995*	*1996*	*1997*	*1998*
Deutsche mark	8.7	10.8	11.0	9.7	8.5	8.0	7.1	5.9	6.0	6.1
French franc	23.4	21.1	13.6	13.5	13.1	14.4	13.5	11.7	9.9	10.3
Japanese yen	0.0	1.7	8.6	7.8	8.2	9.4	13.4	13.1	13.8	15.2
Pound sterling	0.8	0.2	0.1	0.1	0.0	0.0	0.0	0.0	0.0	0.0
Swiss franc	0.1	0.9	0.6	0.2	0.2	0.2	0.2	0.1	0.1	0.1
U.S.dollars	37.8	33.4	21.8	20.8	19.3	16.4	17.2	24.1	28.2	40.2
Multiple currency	5.5	8.4	22.7	23.6	26.0	27.0	24.6	22.8	21.1	7.4
Special drawing rights	0.0	0.0	0.3	0.3	0.2	0.2	0.2	0.1	0.1	0.2
All other currencies	23.7	23.5	21.3	24.0	24.5	24.4	23.8	22.2	20.8	20.5

TUNISIA

(US$ million, unless otherwise indicated)

	1970	1980	1990	1992	1993	1994	1995	1996	1997	1998
7. DEBT RESTRUCTURINGS										
Total amount rescheduled	..	..	0	0	0	0	0	0	0	0
Debt stock rescheduled	..	..	0	0	0	0	0	0	0	0
Principal rescheduled	..	..	0	0	0	0	0	0	0	0
Official	..	..	0	0	0	0	0	0	0	0
Private	..	..	0	0	0	0	0	0	0	0
Interest rescheduled	..	..	0	0	0	0	0	0	0	0
Official	..	..	0	0	0	0	0	0	0	0
Private	..	..	0	0	0	0	0	0	0	0
Debt forgiven	..	..	7	1	0	1	0	0	0	0
Memo: interest forgiven	..	..	0	0	0	0	0	0	0	0
Debt stock reduction	..	..	0	0	0	0	0	0	0	0
of which debt buyback	..	..	0	0	0	0	0	0	0	0
8. DEBT STOCK-FLOW RECONCILIATION										
Total change in debt stocks	..	..	717	291	151	917	1,305	550	-143	-244
Net flows on debt	86	267	293	576	221	448	753	691	604	-681
Net change in interest arrears	..	..	0	-8	-2	0	0	0	0	0
Interest capitalized	..	..	0	0	0	0	0	0	0	0
Debt forgiveness or reduction	..	..	-7	-1	0	-1	0	0	0	0
Cross-currency valuation	..	..	421	-275	-77	442	211	-476	-610	421
Residual	..	..	10	-1	9	28	341	335	-137	16
9. AVERAGE TERMS OF NEW COMMITMENTS										
ALL CREDITORS										
Interest (%)	3.5	6.7	6.8	7.1	6.1	7.8	6.3	4.7	5.7	3.8
Maturity (years)	27.4	18.1	14.1	13.4	16.9	18.1	16.8	15.5	18.0	19.1
Grace period (years)	6.4	5.4	3.9	3.7	5.1	5.3	4.8	4.5	10.0	5.4
Grant element (%)	47.9	23.4	18.4	13.7	23.9	13.3	20.2	29.2	29.2	39.7
Official creditors										
Interest (%)	2.7	5.6	5.8	6.2	6.1	7.7	6.8	5.0	4.8	3.1
Maturity (years)	32.0	20.9	18.1	15.1	17.7	18.5	24.1	19.3	19.0	19.5
Grace period (years)	7.6	6.5	5.2	4.8	5.3	5.5	4.5	5.5	5.1	5.6
Grant element (%)	57.2	31.0	26.8	20.8	24.9	13.8	21.1	33.7	33.7	45.0
Private creditors										
Interest (%)	6.3	9.6	8.1	8.3	6.3	9.1	5.9	4.3	6.5	6.2
Maturity (years)	11.0	10.7	8.8	11.2	10.1	10.3	8.8	9.4	17.0	18.1
Grace period (years)	1.9	2.4	2.1	2.2	2.9	0.8	5.1	2.9	14.8	4.7
Grant element (%)	15.1	2.8	6.9	4.2	15.3	2.7	19.1	22.1	24.8	21.7
Memorandum items										
Commitments	144	777	801	1,286	1,476	810	1,947	1,708	1,505	1,173
Official creditors	112	567	462	733	1,315	773	1,022	1,049	748	905
Private creditors	32	210	339	553	161	37	925	660	758	268

10. CONTRACTUAL OBLIGATIONS ON OUTSTANDING LONG-TERM DEBT

	1999	2000	2001	2002	2003	2004	2005	2006	2007	2008
TOTAL										
Disbursements	1,119	1,044	685	425	256	164	94	49	28	15
Principal	1,201	1,466	1,114	1,089	1,092	1,011	1,053	846	1,019	659
Interest	591	583	539	492	440	386	335	280	235	177
Official creditors										
Disbursements	842	879	624	398	249	161	93	48	28	15
Principal	901	832	841	848	869	848	802	735	668	586
Interest	409	420	400	368	330	289	248	208	171	138
Bilateral creditors										
Disbursements	438	362	224	129	69	35	13	1	0	0
Principal	469	392	380	380	374	370	356	345	322	282
Interest	145	161	155	144	131	117	102	87	73	59
Multilateral creditors										
Disbursements	404	517	400	269	180	126	80	48	27	15
Principal	432	440	461	468	495	478	445	390	346	305
Interest	264	259	245	224	199	172	146	121	99	79
Private creditors										
Disbursements	277	165	61	27	7	4	1	1	0	0
Principal	300	635	273	240	224	163	252	112	351	73
Interest	182	163	139	123	109	97	87	72	64	39
Commercial banks										
Disbursements	163	96	34	15	1	0	0	0	0	0
Principal	170	178	167	142	129	65	57	51	40	31
Interest	74	68	57	46	36	28	23	18	14	11
Other private										
Disbursements	114	70	27	12	7	3	1	1	0	0
Principal	130	457	106	99	95	98	194	61	311	42
Interest	107	95	82	77	73	69	64	54	50	28

TURKEY

(US$ million, unless otherwise indicated)

	1970	1980	1990	1992	1993	1994	1995	1996	1997	1998
1. SUMMARY DEBT DATA										
TOTAL DEBT STOCKS (EDT)	..	**19,131**	**49,424**	**56,554**	**68,608**	**66,255**	**73,790**	**81,832**	**91,162**	**102,074**
Long-term debt (LDOD)	**1,888**	**15,575**	**39,924**	**43,894**	**50,075**	**54,601**	**57,405**	**60,634**	**67,934**	**74,450**
Public and publicly guaranteed	1,846	15,040	38,870	40,463	44,067	48,443	50,326	48,216	47,590	49,932
Private nonguaranteed	42	535	1,054	3,431	6,008	6,159	7,079	12,418	20,344	24,518
Use of IMF credit	**74**	**1,054**	**0**	**0**	**0**	**344**	**685**	**662**	**594**	**388**
Short-term debt	..	**2,502**	**9,500**	**12,660**	**18,533**	**11,310**	**15,701**	**20,536**	**22,634**	**27,236**
of which interest arrears on LDOD	..	12	0	0	0	0	0	0	0	0
Official creditors	..	12	0	0	0	0	0	0	0	0
Private creditors	..	0	0	0	0	0	0	0	0	0
Memo: principal arrears on LDOD	..	23	0	0	0	0	0	0	0	0
Official creditors	..	21	0	0	0	0	0	0	0	0
Private creditors	..	1	0	0	0	0	0	0	0	0
Memo: export credits	..	0	11,519	11,485	11,280	12,831	11,056	12,111	13,928	16,487
TOTAL DEBT FLOWS										
Disbursements	**407**	**3,115**	**5,243**	**8,425**	**10,003**	**5,982**	**6,980**	**12,090**	**17,486**	**7,812**
Long-term debt	332	2,475	5,243	8,425	10,003	5,644	6,638	12,090	17,486	7,812
IMF purchases	75	640	0	0	0	337	341	0	0	0
Principal repayments	**158**	**750**	**4,010**	**5,330**	**4,635**	**6,277**	**7,017**	**6,476**	**6,794**	**8,332**
Long-term debt	131	595	3,961	5,330	4,635	6,277	7,017	6,476	6,767	8,108
IMF repurchases	27	155	49	0	0	0	0	0	28	223
Net flows on debt	**1,033**	**1,259**	**4,988**	**6,638**	**11,241**	**-7,518**	**4,353**	**10,448**	**12,790**	**4,082**
of which short-term debt	..	-1,106	3,755	3,543	5,873	-7,223	4,391	4,835	2,098	4,602
Interest payments (INT)	..	**858**	**3,412**	**3,756**	**4,026**	**3,979**	**4,431**	**4,619**	**4,555**	**4,870**
Long-term debt	44	507	2,891	3,186	3,176	3,199	3,464	3,389	3,226	3,398
IMF charges	0	51	4	0	0	4	24	30	29	25
Short-term debt	..	299	517	570	850	776	942	1,200	1,300	1,447
Net transfers on debt	..	**402**	**1,576**	**2,882**	**7,215**	**-11,497**	**-77**	**5,829**	**8,235**	**-788**
Total debt service paid (TDS)	..	**1,607**	**7,422**	**9,086**	**8,661**	**10,255**	**11,448**	**11,095**	**11,349**	**13,202**
Long-term debt	176	1,102	6,852	8,516	7,811	9,476	10,482	9,866	9,993	11,507
IMF repurchases and charges	27	206	53	0	0	4	24	30	57	248
Short-term debt (interest only)	..	299	517	570	850	776	942	1,200	1,300	1,447
2. AGGREGATE NET RESOURCE FLOWS AND NET TRANSFERS (LONG-TERM)										
NET RESOURCE FLOWS	**300**	**2,083**	**2,805**	**4,211**	**6,994**	**1,344**	**1,575**	**7,409**	**12,157**	**1,585**
Net flow of long-term debt (ex. IMF)	201	1,880	1,282	3,095	5,368	-632	-379	5,613	10,720	-297
Foreign direct investment (net)	58	18	684	844	636	608	885	722	805	940
Portfolio equity flows	0	0	35	0	534	1,059	630	799	577	880
Grants (excluding technical coop.)	41	185	804	272	457	309	439	274	56	62
Memo: technical coop. grants	14	38	149	179	175	175	198	212	176	128
official net resource flows	257	1,423	1,023	-237	-280	-294	-741	-566	-65	-57
private net resource flows	43	660	1,782	4,448	7,274	1,637	2,316	7,975	12,223	1,641
NET TRANSFERS	**222**	**1,545**	**-247**	**605**	**3,399**	**-2,285**	**-2,329**	**3,519**	**8,402**	**-2,364**
Interest on long-term debt	44	507	2,891	3,186	3,176	3,199	3,464	3,389	3,226	3,398
Profit remittances on FDI	34	31	161	420	419	430	440	500	530	550
Memo: official net transfers	220	1,212	-20	-1,294	-1,394	-1,272	-1,717	-1,397	-764	-862
private net transfers	2	333	-227	1,900	4,793	-1,014	-612	4,916	9,165	-1,502
3. MAJOR ECONOMIC AGGREGATES										
Gross national product (GNP)	18,071	69,742	152,300	161,763	181,619	130,355	172,071	184,215	194,350	204,188
Exports of goods & services (XGS)	..	5,743	25,205	28,318	30,317	32,708	41,397	50,616	58,101	62,378
of which workers remittances	..	2,071	3,246	3,008	2,919	2,627	3,327	3,542	4,197	5,356
Imports of goods & services (MGS)	..	9,251	29,077	30,343	37,599	30,542	44,904	53,958	61,449	60,878
International reserves (RES)	440	3,298	7,626	7,508	7,846	8,633	13,891	17,819	19,746	20,568
Current account balance	..	-3,408	-2,625	-974	-6,433	2,631	-2,338	-2,437	-2,679	1,871
4. DEBT INDICATORS										
EDT / XGS (%)	..	333.1	196.1	199.7	226.3	202.6	178.3	161.7	156.9	163.6
EDT / GNP (%)	..	27.4	32.5	35.0	37.8	50.8	42.9	44.4	46.9	50.0
TDS / XGS (%)	..	28.0	29.4	32.1	28.6	31.4	27.7	21.9	19.5	21.2
INT / XGS (%)	..	14.9	13.5	13.3	13.3	12.2	10.7	9.1	7.8	7.8
INT / GNP (%)	..	1.2	2.2	2.3	2.2	3.1	2.6	2.5	2.3	2.4
RES / EDT (%)	..	17.2	15.4	13.3	11.4	13.0	18.8	21.8	21.7	20.2
RES / MGS (months)	..	4.3	3.2	3.0	2.5	3.4	3.7	4.0	3.9	4.1
Short-term / EDT (%)	..	13.1	19.2	22.4	27.0	17.1	21.3	25.1	24.8	26.7
Concessional / EDT (%)	..	20.4	15.1	12.8	10.4	11.6	10.2	8.0	6.2	5.7
Multilateral / EDT (%)	..	11.2	19.5	17.0	13.6	14.0	12.1	9.4	7.3	6.3

TURKEY

(US$ million, unless otherwise indicated)

	1970	1980	1990	1992	1993	1994	1995	1996	1997	1998
5. LONG-TERM DEBT										
DEBT OUTSTANDING (LDOD)	**1,888**	**15,575**	**39,924**	**43,894**	**50,075**	**54,601**	**57,405**	**60,634**	**67,934**	**74,450**
Public and publicly guaranteed	**1,846**	**15,040**	**38,870**	**40,463**	**44,067**	**48,443**	**50,326**	**48,216**	**47,590**	**49,932**
Official creditors	1,766	9,636	18,150	17,611	17,055	17,848	17,333	15,202	13,728	14,546
Multilateral	383	2,149	9,627	9,590	9,325	9,298	8,962	7,708	6,606	6,469
Concessional	110	242	825	961	1,020	1,114	1,145	855	691	604
Bilateral	1,383	7,487	8,523	8,021	7,730	8,550	8,371	7,494	7,122	8,077
Concessional	1,328	3,661	6,625	6,287	6,079	6,566	6,413	5,718	4,991	5,220
Private creditors	81	5,405	20,720	22,852	27,012	30,595	32,993	33,014	33,862	35,386
Bonds	20	64	4,976	8,081	11,755	13,022	13,646	14,185	15,075	14,632
Commercial banks	8	4,112	13,403	11,794	11,864	13,707	15,643	15,358	15,319	17,415
Other private	53	1,229	2,341	2,977	3,393	3,865	3,705	3,470	3,468	3,339
Private nonguaranteed	**42**	**535**	**1,054**	**3,431**	**6,008**	**6,159**	**7,079**	**12,418**	**20,344**	**24,518**
Bonds	0	0	16	66	50	149	149	174	124	794
Commercial banks	42	535	1,038	3,365	5,958	6,009	6,929	12,244	20,220	23,724
Memo:										
IBRD	54	1,158	6,272	5,564	5,285	5,195	4,939	4,260	3,587	3,446
IDA	83	189	157	148	142	136	130	124	118	112
DISBURSEMENTS	**332**	**2,475**	**5,243**	**8,425**	**10,003**	**5,644**	**6,638**	**12,090**	**17,486**	**7,812**
Public and publicly guaranteed	**331**	**2,400**	**4,700**	**6,196**	**6,764**	**4,281**	**4,862**	**5,728**	**8,323**	**6,265**
Official creditors	310	1,618	2,139	1,345	1,133	1,250	808	1,144	1,810	1,647
Multilateral	126	476	1,083	885	747	474	466	634	539	426
Concessional	7	10	12	0	82	25	8	2	44	3
Bilateral	185	1,142	1,056	461	387	777	342	510	1,271	1,220
Concessional	177	801	900	197	163	357	117	241	380	232
Private creditors	21	782	2,562	4,850	5,631	3,030	4,053	4,584	6,514	4,619
Bonds	0	0	644	3,043	3,709	898	2,343	2,921	3,711	1,997
Commercial banks	0	600	1,435	1,167	815	1,294	1,256	1,100	1,958	2,212
Other private	21	182	483	640	1,108	838	455	563	845	410
Private nonguaranteed	**1**	**75**	**543**	**2,230**	**3,239**	**1,364**	**1,777**	**6,362**	**9,163**	**1,546**
Bonds	0	0	0	50	0	99	0	25	0	670
Commercial banks	1	75	543	2,180	3,239	1,264	1,777	6,337	9,163	876
Memo:										
IBRD	18	313	627	286	354	343	422	489	266	271
IDA	7	0	0	0	0	0	0	0	0	0
PRINCIPAL REPAYMENTS	**131**	**595**	**3,961**	**5,330**	**4,635**	**6,277**	**7,017**	**6,476**	**6,767**	**8,108**
Public and publicly guaranteed	**128**	**566**	**3,677**	**4,604**	**3,973**	**4,777**	**5,984**	**5,454**	**5,530**	**7,298**
Official creditors	95	379	1,920	1,854	1,870	1,853	1,988	1,985	1,931	1,765
Multilateral	70	66	825	1,048	1,137	1,180	1,229	1,259	1,090	941
Concessional	22	1	23	19	13	33	54	197	139	125
Bilateral	24	314	1,094	807	732	673	759	726	841	824
Concessional	18	77	364	413	388	433	465	435	531	391
Private creditors	34	186	1,758	2,749	2,104	2,924	3,996	3,470	3,599	5,533
Bonds	0	1	47	389	103	539	1,716	1,368	1,686	3,201
Commercial banks	1	154	1,204	1,462	1,306	1,827	1,579	1,454	1,259	1,689
Other private	32	31	508	899	695	558	701	648	654	643
Private nonguaranteed	**3**	**29**	**283**	**726**	**662**	**1,500**	**1,033**	**1,022**	**1,237**	**810**
Bonds	0	0	0	0	16	0	0	0	50	0
Commercial banks	3	29	283	726	646	1,500	1,033	1,022	1,187	810
Memo:										
IBRD	3	45	620	728	748	800	882	815	692	637
IDA	0	1	4	5	6	6	6	6	6	6
NET FLOWS ON DEBT	**201**	**1,880**	**1,282**	**3,095**	**5,368**	**-632**	**-379**	**5,613**	**10,720**	**-297**
Public and publicly guaranteed	**203**	**1,834**	**1,023**	**1,592**	**2,791**	**-496**	**-1,123**	**273**	**2,794**	**-1,033**
Official creditors	216	1,239	219	-509	-737	-603	-1,180	-841	-121	-118
Multilateral	55	410	258	-163	-391	-707	-763	-625	-552	-515
Concessional	-15	9	-11	-19	69	-8	-45	-195	-96	-122
Bilateral	160	828	-39	-346	-346	104	-417	-216	430	396
Concessional	158	724	536	-216	-225	-77	-348	-194	-152	-159
Private creditors	-13	596	804	2,101	3,527	107	57	1,114	2,915	-915
Bonds	0	-1	597	2,654	3,605	360	627	1,553	2,025	-1,205
Commercial banks	-1	446	231	-295	-491	-533	-323	-354	699	524
Other private	-11	151	-25	-259	413	280	-246	-85	191	-233
Private nonguaranteed	**-2**	**46**	**260**	**1,504**	**2,577**	**-136**	**744**	**5,340**	**7,926**	**736**
Bonds	0	0	0	50	-16	99	0	25	-50	670
Commercial banks	-2	46	260	1,454	2,593	-236	744	5,315	7,976	66
Memo:										
IBRD	15	268	6	-442	-394	-457	-460	-326	-426	-366
IDA	7	-1	-4	-5	-6	-6	-6	-6	-6	-6

TURKEY

(US$ million, unless otherwise indicated)

	1970	1980	1990	1992	1993	1994	1995	1996	1997	1998
INTEREST PAYMENTS (LINT)	**44**	**507**	**2,891**	**3,186**	**3,176**	**3,199**	**3,464**	**3,389**	**3,226**	**3,398**
Public and publicly guaranteed	**42**	**487**	**2,830**	**2,861**	**2,997**	**2,875**	**3,126**	**2,918**	**2,961**	**3,214**
Official creditors	37	211	1,043	1,057	1,114	978	977	830	698	805
Multilateral	11	128	688	713	693	668	656	561	466	519
Concessional	2	4	30	44	35	40	44	36	24	22
Bilateral	26	84	355	345	421	310	321	270	232	287
Concessional	25	33	172	216	303	204	204	172	154	139
Private creditors	5	276	1,787	1,804	1,883	1,897	2,149	2,088	2,262	2,409
Bonds	1	4	383	533	741	993	1,074	1,009	993	1,173
Commercial banks	1	250	1,204	983	891	662	782	780	1,045	1,005
Other private	3	21	200	288	250	242	293	300	224	231
Private nonguaranteed	**2**	**20**	**61**	**325**	**179**	**324**	**339**	**471**	**265**	**185**
Bonds	0	0	1	2	2	2	13	12	13	12
Commercial banks	2	20	60	323	177	322	326	459	252	173
Memo:										
IBRD	3	88	512	479	436	418	396	339	273	245
IDA	1	1	1	1	1	1	1	1	1	1
NET TRANSFERS ON DEBT	**156**	**1,373**	**-1,609**	**-91**	**2,192**	**-3,831**	**-3,843**	**2,224**	**7,494**	**-3,695**
Public and publicly guaranteed	**161**	**1,347**	**-1,808**	**-1,269**	**-206**	**-3,371**	**-4,248**	**-2,645**	**-167**	**-4,247**
Official creditors	178	1,027	-824	-1,566	-1,851	-1,580	-2,157	-1,671	-820	-924
Multilateral	44	283	-431	-875	-1,084	-1,374	-1,418	-1,185	-1,018	-1,033
Concessional	-17	5	-41	-62	34	-48	-89	-231	-120	-143
Bilateral	134	744	-394	-691	-767	-206	-738	-485	198	109
Concessional	134	691	363	-432	-528	-281	-552	-366	-305	-298
Private creditors	-18	320	-983	297	1,645	-1,790	-2,092	-974	653	-3,323
Bonds	-1	-5	214	2,121	2,864	-634	-447	544	1,033	-2,378
Commercial banks	-2	196	-973	-1,278	-1,382	-1,195	-1,106	-1,134	-347	-481
Other private	-15	130	-225	-547	163	38	-539	-385	-33	-464
Private nonguaranteed	**-5**	**26**	**199**	**1,179**	**2,398**	**-461**	**405**	**4,869**	**7,661**	**552**
Bonds	0	0	-1	48	-18	98	-13	13	-63	658
Commercial banks	-5	26	200	1,131	2,416	-558	418	4,856	7,724	-107
Memo:										
IBRD	12	179	-505	-921	-829	-875	-856	-665	-699	-611
IDA	7	-2	-5	-6	-7	-7	-7	-7	-7	-7
DEBT SERVICE (LTDS)	**176**	**1,102**	**6,852**	**8,516**	**7,811**	**9,476**	**10,482**	**9,866**	**9,993**	**11,507**
Public and publicly guaranteed	**170**	**1,053**	**6,508**	**7,465**	**6,970**	**7,651**	**9,110**	**8,372**	**8,490**	**10,512**
Official creditors	132	591	2,963	2,912	2,984	2,831	2,965	2,815	2,630	2,570
Multilateral	81	193	1,514	1,760	1,830	1,848	1,885	1,820	1,557	1,459
Concessional	24	5	53	62	48	73	98	233	163	147
Bilateral	51	398	1,449	1,152	1,153	983	1,081	995	1,073	1,111
Concessional	43	110	537	628	691	638	669	607	685	530
Private creditors	38	462	3,545	4,553	3,986	4,821	6,145	5,558	5,861	7,942
Bonds	1	5	430	922	845	1,532	2,790	2,377	2,678	4,375
Commercial banks	2	405	2,408	2,445	2,197	2,489	2,361	2,233	2,304	2,693
Other private	35	52	707	1,187	945	800	994	948	878	874
Private nonguaranteed	**6**	**49**	**344**	**1,051**	**841**	**1,824**	**1,372**	**1,493**	**1,502**	**995**
Bonds	0	0	1	2	18	2	13	12	63	12
Commercial banks	6	49	343	1,049	823	1,822	1,359	1,481	1,439	983
Memo:										
IBRD	6	133	1,132	1,207	1,183	1,218	1,278	1,154	965	882
IDA	1	3	5	6	7	7	7	7	7	7
UNDISBURSED DEBT	**857**	**3,706**	**8,563**	**8,411**	**9,392**	**8,251**	**7,624**	**7,824**	**6,847**	**8,324**
Official creditors	753	2,938	4,823	5,381	5,487	4,577	3,765	4,305	3,326	3,370
Private creditors	104	768	3,740	3,031	3,905	3,674	3,859	3,519	3,521	4,954
Memorandum items										
Concessional LDOD	1,438	3,903	7,450	7,248	7,099	7,680	7,558	6,573	5,682	5,824
Variable rate LDOD	58	4,122	13,577	15,442	18,223	18,636	19,393	23,657	31,917	35,345
Public sector LDOD	1,839	14,956	38,570	39,929	43,542	48,078	50,129	48,100	47,521	49,888
Private sector LDOD	50	620	1,354	3,965	6,533	6,524	7,265	12,524	20,403	24,562
6. CURRENCY COMPOSITION OF LONG-TERM DEBT (PERCENT)										
Deutsche mark	17.6	17.0	17.4	17.1	17.3	17.6	16.7	16.8	21.2	22.4
French franc	3.2	5.6	1.6	1.8	1.6	1.6	1.6	1.6	1.5	1.3
Japanese yen	0.0	4.0	12.1	18.7	21.6	23.2	23.3	22.0	18.5	15.8
Pound sterling	6.0	3.8	0.8	0.6	1.0	1.0	0.9	1.0	0.9	1.0
Swiss franc	1.6	8.6	5.2	3.8	3.3	3.0	2.9	2.0	1.6	1.1
U.S.dollars	49.3	43.5	40.0	36.4	36.4	36.2	38.3	41.4	49.2	51.7
Multiple currency	9.1	8.1	18.9	17.4	15.7	14.3	13.3	12.1	3.5	3.1
Special drawing rights	0.0	0.0	0.0	0.0	0.0	0.0	0.0	0.0	0.0	0.0
All other currencies	13.2	9.4	4.0	4.2	3.1	3.1	3.0	3.1	3.6	3.6

TURKEY

(US$ million, unless otherwise indicated)

	1970	1980	1990	1992	1993	1994	1995	1996	1997	1998
7. DEBT RESTRUCTURINGS										
Total amount rescheduled	..	..	0	0	0	0	0	0	0	0
Debt stock rescheduled	..	..	0	0	0	0	0	0	0	0
Principal rescheduled	..	..	0	0	0	0	0	0	0	0
Official	..	..	0	0	0	0	0	0	0	0
Private	..	..	0	0	0	0	0	0	0	0
Interest rescheduled	..	..	0	0	0	0	0	0	0	0
Official	..	..	0	0	0	0	0	0	0	0
Private	..	..	0	0	0	0	0	0	0	0
Debt forgiven	..	..	0	0	9	0	0	0	0	0
Memo: interest forgiven	..	..	0	0	0	0	0	0	0	0
Debt stock reduction	..	..	0	0	0	0	0	0	0	0
of which debt buyback	..	..	0	0	0	0	0	0	0	0
8. DEBT STOCK-FLOW RECONCILIATION										
Total change in debt stocks	..	..	7,847	5,680	12,054	-2,353	7,535	8,042	9,330	10,912
Net flows on debt	1,033	1,259	4,988	6,638	11,241	-7,518	4,353	10,448	12,790	4,082
Net change in interest arrears	..	..	0	0	0	0	0	0	0	0
Interest capitalized	..	..	0	0	0	0	0	0	0	0
Debt forgiveness or reduction	..	..	0	0	-9	0	0	0	0	0
Cross-currency valuation	..	..	2,172	-1,057	373	2,920	655	-2,580	-2,729	2,029
Residual	..	..	687	99	449	2,246	2,527	174	-731	4,801
9. AVERAGE TERMS OF NEW COMMITMENTS										
ALL CREDITORS										
Interest (%)	3.6	8.3	8.4	7.3	5.9	6.2	6.2	6.5	7.5	6.1
Maturity (years)	19.0	16.4	10.2	8.4	10.0	10.4	5.4	9.0	8.0	7.8
Grace period (years)	4.8	5.0	4.6	4.8	5.7	4.7	2.9	4.3	5.0	4.0
Grant element (%)	37.5	17.4	9.2	11.4	20.1	18.6	11.5	16.6	9.8	14.8
Official creditors										
Interest (%)	3.4	7.1	6.7	7.0	4.6	6.0	5.4	4.9	6.7	7.1
Maturity (years)	19.6	18.3	17.0	14.3	20.3	13.7	17.7	16.6	11.2	12.1
Grace period (years)	4.9	5.7	7.3	6.1	6.6	4.8	5.7	4.9	4.2	4.2
Grant element (%)	39.1	22.9	23.4	17.2	38.1	22.2	27.6	31.5	16.0	15.6
Private creditors										
Interest (%)	5.5	14.4	9.4	7.4	6.2	6.2	6.3	7.2	7.6	5.8
Maturity (years)	13.7	7.4	6.5	6.2	7.8	9.5	4.5	5.5	7.4	6.4
Grace period (years)	3.1	1.9	3.2	4.3	5.5	4.7	2.7	4.0	5.1	4.0
Grant element (%)	22.7	-9.6	1.5	9.3	16.1	17.5	10.3	10.0	8.6	14.5
Memorandum items										
Commitments	489	2,925	4,628	6,756	8,032	3,800	4,435	6,395	7,899	6,917
Official creditors	440	2,426	1,624	1,805	1,460	890	318	1,981	1,228	1,660
Private creditors	49	499	3,004	4,952	6,572	2,910	4,118	4,414	6,671	5,257

10. CONTRACTUAL OBLIGATIONS ON OUTSTANDING LONG-TERM DEBT

	1999	2000	2001	2002	2003	2004	2005	2006	2007	2008
TOTAL										
Disbursements	3,969	2,314	1,087	470	152	121	83	58	36	13
Principal	8,013	8,355	8,982	7,142	7,280	4,527	4,916	3,944	4,571	2,886
Interest	3,880	3,547	3,166	2,647	2,304	1,910	1,688	1,457	1,265	1,015
Official creditors										
Disbursements	1,120	859	604	303	152	121	83	58	36	13
Principal	1,880	2,002	2,498	1,565	1,765	1,115	995	858	760	682
Interest	779	708	627	497	411	317	268	224	187	155
Bilateral creditors										
Disbursements	647	402	212	99	36	22	3	0	0	0
Principal	830	844	852	840	1,114	583	531	454	425	387
Interest	328	313	285	252	208	150	130	112	97	84
Multilateral creditors										
Disbursements	473	457	392	205	116	99	80	58	36	13
Principal	1,050	1,158	1,646	725	651	532	464	404	335	296
Interest	451	395	342	245	203	167	138	112	90	71
Private creditors										
Disbursements	2,849	1,456	483	167	0	0	0	0	0	0
Principal	6,133	6,353	6,484	5,577	5,515	3,413	3,922	3,086	3,811	2,204
Interest	3,102	2,839	2,539	2,150	1,893	1,593	1,420	1,233	1,077	860
Commercial banks										
Disbursements	2,505	1,334	466	164	0	0	0	0	0	0
Principal	1,288	1,828	1,322	1,320	2,099	529	475	377	292	202
Interest	953	936	871	809	730	626	601	579	563	553
Other private										
Disbursements	344	122	17	2	0	0	0	0	0	0
Principal	4,846	4,525	5,162	4,257	3,416	2,883	3,447	2,709	3,519	2,002
Interest	2,149	1,903	1,667	1,342	1,163	967	819	654	514	307

TURKMENISTAN

(US$ million, unless otherwise indicated)

	1970	1980	1990	1992	1993	1994	1995	1996	1997	1998
1. SUMMARY DEBT DATA										
TOTAL DEBT STOCKS (EDT)	..	..	..	..	**276**	**431**	**402**	**751**	**1,771**	**2,266**
Long-term debt (LDOD)	..	..	..	..	**276**	**346**	**385**	**464**	**1,242**	**1,745**
Public and publicly guaranteed	..	..	..	..	276	346	385	464	1,242	1,731
Private nonguaranteed	..	..	..	..	0	0	0	0	0	14
Use of IMF credit	..	..	..	..	**0**	**0**	**0**	**0**	**0**	**0**
Short-term debt	..	..	..	..	**0**	**85**	**17**	**287**	**529**	**521**
of which interest arrears on LDOD	..	..	..	..	0	5	9	14	9	19
Official creditors	..	..	..	..	0	4	5	7	3	4
Private creditors	..	..	..	..	0	1	5	8	6	15
Memo: principal arrears on LDOD	..	..	..	..	0	34	130	50	73	115
Official creditors	..	..	..	..	0	16	115	29	37	54
Private creditors	..	..	..	..	0	18	15	22	36	61
Memo: export credits	..	..	..	..	0	149	101	259	483	1,033
TOTAL DEBT FLOWS										
Disbursements	..	..	..	..	**240**	**137**	**113**	**240**	**986**	**685**
Long-term debt	..	..	..	..	240	137	113	240	986	685
IMF purchases	..	..	..	..	0	0	0	0	0	0
Principal repayments	..	..	..	..	**9**	**72**	**80**	**154**	**196**	**219**
Long-term debt	..	..	..	..	9	72	80	154	196	219
IMF repurchases	..	..	..	..	0	0	0	0	0	0
Net flows on debt	..	..	..	..	**231**	**145**	**-39**	**350**	**1,039**	**449**
of which short-term debt	..	..	..	..	0	80	-72	264	248	-18
Interest payments (INT)	..	..	..	..	**2**	**28**	**24**	**39**	**68**	**92**
Long-term debt	..	..	..	..	2	26	22	27	46	66
IMF charges	..	..	..	..	0	0	0	0	0	0
Short-term debt	..	..	..	..	0	2	2	12	22	26
Net transfers on debt	..	..	..	..	**229**	**118**	**-63**	**311**	**971**	**357**
Total debt service paid (TDS)	..	..	..	..	**10**	**100**	**104**	**193**	**263**	**311**
Long-term debt	..	..	..	..	10	98	102	180	242	285
IMF repurchases and charges	..	..	..	..	0	0	0	0	0	0
Short-term debt (interest only)	..	..	..	..	0	2	2	12	22	26
2. AGGREGATE NET RESOURCE FLOWS AND NET TRANSFERS (LONG-TERM)										
NET RESOURCE FLOWS	..	..	..	..	**246**	**77**	**34**	**196**	**902**	**601**
Net flow of long-term debt (ex. IMF)	..	..	..	..	231	65	33	86	791	466
Foreign direct investment (net)	..	..	..	..	0	0	0	108	108	130
Portfolio equity flows	..	..	..	..	0	0	0	0	0	0
Grants (excluding technical coop.)	..	..	..	..	15	11	1	1	3	5
Memo: technical coop. grants	..	..	..	..	1	3	11	12	7	11
official net resource flows	..	..	..	..	164	62	14	-78	31	128
private net resource flows	..	..	..	..	82	14	20	274	870	473
NET TRANSFERS	..	..	..	..	**244**	**51**	**12**	**169**	**856**	**535**
Interest on long-term debt	..	..	..	..	2	26	22	27	46	66
Profit remittances on FDI	..	..	..	..	0	0	0	0	0	0
Memo: official net transfers	..	..	..	..	163	44	2	-88	23	121
private net transfers	..	..	..	..	81	6	10	257	833	414
3. MAJOR ECONOMIC AGGREGATES										
Gross national product (GNP)	..	..	..	..	5,708	4,686	4,339	3,992	2,987	2,585
Exports of goods & services (XGS)	..	..	..	..	2,718	2,276	2,231	1,815	900	741
of which workers remittances	..	..	..	..	..	..	..	..	..	..
Imports of goods & services (MGS)	..	..	..	..	1,954	2,193	2,219	1,818	1,449	1,702
International reserves (RES)	..	..	..	..	..	..	..	..	..	..
Current account balance	..	..	..	..	776	84	24	2	-580	-935
4. DEBT INDICATORS										
EDT / XGS (%)	..	..	..	..	10.2	18.9	18.0	41.4	196.8	306.0
EDT / GNP (%)	..	..	..	..	4.8	9.2	9.3	18.8	59.3	87.7
TDS / XGS (%)	..	..	..	..	0.4	4.4	4.7	10.6	29.3	42.0
INT / XGS (%)	..	..	..	..	0.1	1.2	1.1	2.1	7.5	12.4
INT / GNP (%)	..	..	..	..	0.0	0.6	0.6	1.0	2.3	3.5
RES / EDT (%)	..	..	..	..	..	..	..	..	..	..
RES / MGS (months)	..	..	..	..	..	..	..	..	..	..
Short-term / EDT (%)	..	..	..	..	0.0	19.7	4.3	38.2	29.9	23.0
Concessional / EDT (%)	..	..	..	..	3.3	4.6	4.9	2.6	2.2	5.2
Multilateral / EDT (%)	..	..	..	..	9.1	12.4	14.5	0.4	1.1	1.6

TURKMENISTAN

(US$ million, unless otherwise indicated)

	1970	1980	1990	1992	1993	1994	1995	1996	1997	1998
5. LONG-TERM DEBT										
DEBT OUTSTANDING (LDOD)	..	..	..	..	**276**	**346**	**385**	**464**	**1,242**	**1,745**
Public and publicly guaranteed	..	..	..	..	**276**	**346**	**385**	**464**	**1,242**	**1,731**
Official creditors	..	..	..	..	148	203	219	136	160	285
Multilateral	..	..	..	..	25	54	58	3	19	37
Concessional	..	..	..	..	0	0	0	0	0	0
Bilateral	..	..	..	..	123	149	161	133	141	248
Concessional	..	..	..	..	9	20	20	20	38	118
Private creditors	..	..	..	..	129	144	166	328	1,083	1,447
Bonds	..	..	..	..	0	0	0	0	0	0
Commercial banks	..	..	..	..	0	0	0	0	89	60
Other private	..	..	..	..	129	144	166	328	994	1,387
Private nonguaranteed	..	..	..	..	**0**	**0**	**0**	**0**	**0**	**14**
Bonds	..	..	..	..	0	0	0	0	0	0
Commercial banks	..	..	..	..	0	0	0	0	0	14
Memo:										
IBRD	..	..	..	..	0	0	1	3	6	9
IDA	..	..	..	..	0	0	0	0	0	0
DISBURSEMENTS	..	..	..	..	**240**	**137**	**113**	**240**	**986**	**685**
Public and publicly guaranteed	..	..	..	..	**240**	**137**	**113**	**240**	**986**	**685**
Official creditors	..	..	..	..	149	70	32	22	57	133
Multilateral	..	..	..	..	26	25	1	3	16	18
Concessional	..	..	..	..	0	0	0	0	0	0
Bilateral	..	..	..	..	123	45	31	20	41	115
Concessional	..	..	..	..	9	11	0	0	20	70
Private creditors	..	..	..	..	91	67	81	217	930	553
Bonds	..	..	..	..	0	0	0	0	0	0
Commercial banks	..	..	..	..	0	0	0	0	130	0
Other private	..	..	..	..	91	67	81	217	800	553
Private nonguaranteed	..	..	..	..	**0**	**0**	**0**	**0**	**0**	**0**
Bonds	..	..	..	..	0	0	0	0	0	0
Commercial banks	..	..	..	..	0	0	0	0	0	0
Memo:										
IBRD	..	..	..	..	0	0	1	3	3	2
IDA	..	..	..	..	0	0	0	0	0	0
PRINCIPAL REPAYMENTS	..	..	..	..	**9**	**72**	**80**	**154**	**196**	**219**
Public and publicly guaranteed	..	..	..	..	**9**	**72**	**80**	**154**	**196**	**216**
Official creditors	..	..	..	..	0	19	20	102	28	9
Multilateral	..	..	..	..	0	0	0	55	0	0
Concessional	..	..	..	..	0	0	0	0	0	0
Bilateral	..	..	..	..	0	19	20	46	28	9
Concessional	..	..	..	..	0	0	0	0	0	0
Private creditors	..	..	..	..	9	53	61	52	167	206
Bonds	..	..	..	..	0	0	0	0	0	0
Commercial banks	..	..	..	..	0	0	0	0	41	30
Other private	..	..	..	..	9	53	61	52	127	177
Private nonguaranteed	..	..	..	..	**0**	**0**	**0**	**0**	**0**	**3**
Bonds	..	..	..	..	0	0	0	0	0	0
Commercial banks	..	..	..	..	0	0	0	0	0	3
Memo:										
IBRD	..	..	..	..	0	0	0	0	0	0
IDA	..	..	..	..	0	0	0	0	0	0
NET FLOWS ON DEBT	..	..	..	..	**231**	**65**	**33**	**86**	**791**	**466**
Public and publicly guaranteed	..	..	..	..	**231**	**65**	**33**	**86**	**791**	**470**
Official creditors	..	..	..	..	149	51	13	-79	28	123
Multilateral	..	..	..	..	26	25	1	-53	16	18
Concessional	..	..	..	..	0	0	0	0	0	0
Bilateral	..	..	..	..	123	26	12	-27	12	105
Concessional	..	..	..	..	9	11	0	0	20	70
Private creditors	..	..	..	..	82	14	20	165	762	346
Bonds	..	..	..	..	0	0	0	0	0	0
Commercial banks	..	..	..	..	0	0	0	0	89	-30
Other private	..	..	..	..	82	14	20	165	673	376
Private nonguaranteed	..	..	..	..	**0**	**0**	**0**	**0**	**0**	**-3**
Bonds	..	..	..	..	0	0	0	0	0	0
Commercial banks	..	..	..	..	0	0	0	0	0	-3
Memo:										
IBRD	..	..	..	..	0	0	1	3	3	2
IDA	..	..	..	..	0	0	0	0	0	0

TURKMENISTAN

(US$ million, unless otherwise indicated)

	1970	1980	1990	1992	1993	1994	1995	1996	1997	1998
INTEREST PAYMENTS (LINT)	..	..	..	..	**2**	**26**	**22**	**27**	**46**	**66**
Public and publicly guaranteed	..	..	..	..	**2**	**26**	**22**	**27**	**46**	**66**
Official creditors	..	..	..	..	1	18	12	10	9	7
Multilateral	..	..	..	..	0	7	2	4	1	2
Concessional	..	..	..	..	0	0	0	0	0	0
Bilateral	..	..	..	..	0	12	10	6	7	5
Concessional	..	..	..	..	0	0	1	1	1	2
Private creditors	..	..	..	..	1	8	10	17	37	59
Bonds	..	..	..	..	0	0	0	0	0	0
Commercial banks	..	..	..	..	0	0	0	0	2	5
Other private	..	..	..	..	1	8	10	17	35	54
Private nonguaranteed	..	..	..	..	**0**	**0**	**0**	**0**	**0**	**1**
Bonds	..	..	..	..	0	0	0	0	0	0
Commercial banks	..	..	..	..	0	0	0	0	0	1
Memo:										
IBRD	..	..	..	..	0	0	0	0	0	0
IDA	..	..	..	..	0	0	0	0	0	0
NET TRANSFERS ON DEBT	..	..	..	..	**229**	**39**	**11**	**59**	**745**	**400**
Public and publicly guaranteed	..	..	..	..	**229**	**39**	**11**	**59**	**745**	**404**
Official creditors	..	..	..	..	148	33	1	-89	20	116
Multilateral	..	..	..	..	26	18	-1	-56	15	16
Concessional	..	..	..	..	0	0	0	0	0	0
Bilateral	..	..	..	..	122	15	2	-33	5	100
Concessional	..	..	..	..	9	11	-1	-1	19	68
Private creditors	..	..	..	..	81	6	10	149	725	288
Bonds	..	..	..	..	0	0	0	0	0	0
Commercial banks	..	..	..	..	0	0	0	0	87	-34
Other private	..	..	..	..	81	6	10	149	638	322
Private nonguaranteed	..	..	..	..	**0**	**0**	**0**	**0**	**0**	**-4**
Bonds	..	..	..	..	0	0	0	0	0	0
Commercial banks	..	..	..	..	0	0	0	0	0	-4
Memo:										
IBRD	..	..	..	..	0	0	1	2	3	2
IDA	..	..	..	..	0	0	0	0	0	0
DEBT SERVICE (LTDS)	..	..	..	..	**10**	**98**	**102**	**180**	**242**	**285**
Public and publicly guaranteed	..	..	..	..	**10**	**98**	**102**	**180**	**242**	**281**
Official creditors	..	..	..	..	1	37	31	112	37	16
Multilateral	..	..	..	..	0	7	2	59	1	2
Concessional	..	..	..	..	0	0	0	0	0	0
Bilateral	..	..	..	..	0	30	29	53	36	15
Concessional	..	..	..	..	0	0	1	1	1	2
Private creditors	..	..	..	..	10	61	71	69	205	265
Bonds	..	..	..	..	0	0	0	0	0	0
Commercial banks	..	..	..	..	0	0	0	0	43	34
Other private	..	..	..	..	10	61	71	69	162	231
Private nonguaranteed	..	..	..	..	**0**	**0**	**0**	**0**	**0**	**4**
Bonds	..	..	..	..	0	0	0	0	0	0
Commercial banks	..	..	..	..	0	0	0	0	0	4
Memo:										
IBRD	..	..	..	..	0	0	0	0	0	0
IDA	..	..	..	..	0	0	0	0	0	0
UNDISBURSED DEBT	..	..	..	..	**71**	**108**	**265**	**756**	**1,038**	**597**
Official creditors	..	..	..	..	44	103	93	218	423	312
Private creditors	..	..	..	..	27	5	172	538	615	285
Memorandum items										
Concessional LDOD	..	..	..	..	9	20	20	20	38	118
Variable rate LDOD	..	..	..	..	268	281	276	284	937	1,383
Public sector LDOD	..	..	..	..	276	346	385	464	1,242	1,731
Private sector LDOD	..	..	..	..	0	0	0	0	0	14

6. CURRENCY COMPOSITION OF LONG-TERM DEBT (PERCENT)

	1970	1980	1990	1992	1993	1994	1995	1996	1997	1998
Deutsche mark	..	..	..	..	0.0	7.2	12.3	14.3	9.9	14.4
French franc	..	..	..	..	0.0	0.0	0.0	0.0	0.0	0.0
Japanese yen	..	..	..	..	0.0	0.0	0.0	0.0	1.1	5.9
Pound sterling	..	..	..	..	0.0	0.0	0.0	0.0	0.0	0.0
Swiss franc	..	..	..	..	0.0	0.0	0.0	0.0	0.0	0.0
U.S.dollars	..	..	..	..	90.9	77.0	72.1	84.7	88.3	79.1
Multiple currency	..	..	..	..	0.0	0.0	0.2	0.7	0.7	0.5
Special drawing rights	..	..	..	..	0.0	0.0	0.0	0.0	0.0	0.0
All other currencies	..	..	..	..	9.1	15.8	15.4	0.3	0.0	0.1

TURKMENISTAN

(US$ million, unless otherwise indicated)

	1970	1980	1990	1992	1993	1994	1995	1996	1997	1998
7. DEBT RESTRUCTURINGS										
Total amount rescheduled	..	..	..	..	0	0	0	0	0	0
Debt stock rescheduled	..	..	..	..	0	0	0	0	0	0
Principal rescheduled	..	..	..	..	0	0	0	0	0	0
Official	..	..	..	..	0	0	0	0	0	0
Private	..	..	..	..	0	0	0	0	0	0
Interest rescheduled	..	..	..	..	..	0	0	0	0	0
Official	..	..	..	..	0	0	0	0	0	0
Private	..	..	..	..	0	0	0	0	0	0
Debt forgiven	..	..	..	..	0	0	0	0	0	0
Memo: interest forgiven	..	..	..	..	0	0	0	0	0	0
Debt stock reduction	..	..	..	..	0	0	0	0	0	0
of which debt buyback	..	..	..	..	0	0	0	0	0	0
8. DEBT STOCK-FLOW RECONCILIATION										
Total change in debt stocks	..	..	..	..	..	155	-29	349	1,020	495
Net flows on debt	..	..	..	..	231	145	-39	350	1,039	449
Net change in interest arrears	..	..	..	..	..	5	5	5	-6	10
Interest capitalized	..	..	..	..	..	0	0	0	0	0
Debt forgiveness or reduction	..	..	..	..	..	0	0	0	0	0
Cross-currency valuation	..	..	..	..	..	8	8	-5	-18	31
Residual	..	..	..	..	..	-4	-2	-1	6	6
9. AVERAGE TERMS OF NEW COMMITMENTS										
ALL CREDITORS										
Interest (%)	..	..	..	..	1.2	6.3	6.6	5.9	5.8	6.7
Maturity (years)	..	..	..	..	6.6	10.3	8.2	9.6	7.6	5.6
Grace period (years)	..	..	..	..	3.0	3.2	1.9	2.8	2.1	2.1
Grant element (%)	..	..	..	..	24.3	14.7	11.9	16.7	13.8	9.7
Official creditors										
Interest (%)	..	..	..	..	3.4	6.2	3.9	3.8	4.3	0.0
Maturity (years)	..	..	..	..	18.4	12.1	13.9	11.8	15.7	0.0
Grace period (years)	..	..	..	..	5.6	4.0	2.8	3.4	4.4	0.0
Grant element (%)	..	..	..	..	36.6	17.2	26.3	31.3	32.1	0.0
Private creditors										
Interest (%)	..	..	..	..	0.5	6.7	6.8	6.5	6.3	6.7
Maturity (years)	..	..	..	..	3.0	5.3	7.7	9.0	5.4	5.6
Grace period (years)	..	..	..	..	2.2	1.0	1.8	2.6	1.5	2.1
Grant element (%)	..	..	..	..	20.5	7.5	10.7	12.8	8.7	9.7
Memorandum items										
Commitments	..	..	..	..	102	172	269	753	1,324	218
Official creditors	..	..	..	..	24	128	20	156	286	0
Private creditors	..	..	..	..	78	45	249	598	1,039	218

10. CONTRACTUAL OBLIGATIONS ON OUTSTANDING LONG-TERM DEBT

	1999	2000	2001	2002	2003	2004	2005	2006	2007	2008
TOTAL										
Disbursements	301	141	72	33	20	11	8	5	3	3
Principal	482	245	336	246	209	152	106	99	80	74
Interest	66	63	78	59	45	34	27	21	16	13
Official creditors										
Disbursements	106	72	51	33	20	11	8	5	3	3
Principal	13	36	48	51	51	49	44	40	38	35
Interest	10	14	16	15	14	12	10	9	7	6
Bilateral creditors										
Disbursements	91	58	37	20	10	3	2	0	0	0
Principal	8	29	41	42	40	38	32	32	32	29
Interest	7	10	12	11	9	8	6	5	4	3
Multilateral creditors										
Disbursements	15	14	14	13	11	9	6	5	3	3
Principal	5	7	7	9	11	11	11	9	6	6
Interest	4	4	4	5	5	5	4	4	3	3
Private creditors										
Disbursements	195	69	21	0	0	0	0	0	0	0
Principal	468	209	288	195	158	103	63	59	41	39
Interest	56	49	61	43	31	22	17	12	9	6
Commercial banks										
Disbursements	0	0	0	0	0	0	0	0	0	0
Principal	60	0	0	0	0	0	0	0	0	0
Interest	2	0	0	0	0	0	0	0	0	0
Other private										
Disbursements	195	69	21	0	0	0	0	0	0	0
Principal	409	209	288	195	158	103	63	59	41	39
Interest	54	49	61	43	31	22	17	12	9	6

UGANDA

(US$ million, unless otherwise indicated)

	1970	1980	1990	1992	1993	1994	1995	1996	1997	1998
1. SUMMARY DEBT DATA										
TOTAL DEBT STOCKS (EDT)	**..**	**689**	**2,583**	**2,928**	**3,029**	**3,372**	**3,573**	**3,674**	**3,868**	**3,935**
Long-term debt (LDOD)	**152**	**537**	**2,161**	**2,433**	**2,599**	**2,869**	**3,062**	**3,151**	**3,359**	**3,402**
Public and publicly guaranteed	152	537	2,161	2,433	2,599	2,869	3,062	3,151	3,359	3,402
Private nonguaranteed	0	0	0	0	0	0	0	0	0	0
Use of IMF credit	**0**	**89**	**282**	**344**	**334**	**383**	**417**	**417**	**394**	**398**
Short-term debt	**..**	**63**	**140**	**150**	**96**	**119**	**93**	**106**	**115**	**135**
of which interest arrears on LDOD	..	19	83	81	72	81	59	49	47	64
Official creditors	..	10	32	43	50	69	47	41	39	55
Private creditors	..	9	51	39	22	12	12	8	8	9
Memo: principal arrears on LDOD	..	82	215	268	197	207	207	202	214	228
Official creditors	..	30	94	130	135	145	147	140	151	165
Private creditors	..	52	122	138	62	63	61	62	63	63
Memo: export credits	..	0	270	260	152	149	138	133	129	156
TOTAL DEBT FLOWS										
Disbursements	**26**	**161**	**382**	**311**	**408**	**322**	**287**	**289**	**341**	**225**
Long-term debt	26	83	301	255	408	270	232	225	281	175
IMF purchases	0	78	81	56	0	53	56	63	60	50
Principal repayments	**5**	**45**	**111**	**80**	**119**	**112**	**98**	**106**	**116**	**125**
Long-term debt	5	32	66	51	109	88	70	56	59	63
IMF repurchases	0	13	45	29	10	25	29	50	58	62
Net flows on debt	**22**	**130**	**277**	**239**	**244**	**224**	**185**	**206**	**236**	**102**
of which short-term debt	..	14	6	7	-45	14	-4	23	11	3
Interest payments (INT)	**..**	**12**	**37**	**34**	**37**	**38**	**38**	**43**	**43**	**34**
Long-term debt	5	4	19	26	33	34	34	38	37	28
IMF charges	0	3	13	3	2	2	2	2	2	2
Short-term debt	..	5	5	5	3	3	2	3	4	4
Net transfers on debt	**..**	**118**	**241**	**204**	**206**	**186**	**147**	**163**	**193**	**68**
Total debt service paid (TDS)	**..**	**57**	**147**	**114**	**157**	**150**	**137**	**149**	**159**	**160**
Long-term debt	9	36	85	77	142	121	104	95	96	91
IMF repurchases and charges	0	16	58	32	12	26	31	52	60	64
Short-term debt (interest only)	..	5	5	5	3	3	2	3	4	4
2. AGGREGATE NET RESOURCE FLOWS AND NET TRANSFERS (LONG-TERM)										
NET RESOURCE FLOWS	**28**	**112**	**492**	**544**	**613**	**589**	**683**	**626**	**739**	**744**
Net flow of long-term debt (ex. IMF)	22	51	234	204	298	182	162	169	223	111
Foreign direct investment (net)	4	0	0	3	55	88	121	121	175	200
Portfolio equity flows	0	0	0	0	0	0	0	0	0	0
Grants (excluding technical coop.)	2	61	257	336	260	319	400	336	341	433
Memo: technical coop. grants	14	21	94	119	122	121	147	132	150	125
official net resource flows	17	68	476	549	572	517	571	512	566	546
private net resource flows	10	44	16	-5	41	72	112	114	174	198
NET TRANSFERS	**10**	**109**	**473**	**518**	**568**	**543**	**637**	**573**	**682**	**694**
Interest on long-term debt	5	4	19	26	33	34	34	38	37	28
Profit remittances on FDI	13	0	0	0	13	13	12	14	20	22
Memo: official net transfers	14	66	458	528	543	484	539	474	529	520
private net transfers	-4	43	15	-10	25	58	98	100	153	174
3. MAJOR ECONOMIC AGGREGATES										
Gross national product (GNP)	..	1,240	4,227	2,771	3,172	3,936	5,698	6,004	6,281	6,764
Exports of goods & services (XGS)	297	331	246	199	242	344	683	747	863	676
of which workers remittances	..	..	0	0	0	0	0	0	0	0
Imports of goods & services (MGS)	271	450	753	672	746	913	1,457	1,668	1,706	1,922
International reserves (RES)	57	3	44	94	146	321	459	528	633	725
Current account balance	20	-121	-429	-338	-396	-265	-444	-500	-521	-706
4. DEBT INDICATORS										
EDT / XGS (%)	..	208.3	1,051.2	1,473.7	1,252.0	980.3	523.3	491.8	448.1	581.9
EDT / GNP (%)	..	55.6	61.1	105.7	95.5	85.7	62.7	61.2	61.6	58.2
TDS / XGS (%)	..	17.3	60.0	57.4	64.8	43.7	20.0	19.9	18.4	23.6
INT / XGS (%)	..	3.7	14.9	17.3	15.5	11.2	5.6	5.7	5.0	5.0
INT / GNP (%)	..	1.0	0.9	1.2	1.2	1.0	0.7	0.7	0.7	0.5
RES / EDT (%)	..	0.4	1.7	3.2	4.8	9.5	12.8	14.4	16.4	18.4
RES / MGS (months)	2.5	0.1	0.7	1.7	2.4	4.2	3.8	3.8	4.5	4.5
Short-term / EDT (%)	..	9.1	5.4	5.1	3.2	3.5	2.6	2.9	3.0	3.4
Concessional / EDT (%)	..	36.9	56.2	61.7	70.3	72.9	77.5	78.3	77.0	80.6
Multilateral / EDT (%)	..	11.5	49.2	53.3	57.0	59.7	61.8	62.2	62.0	61.8

UGANDA

(US$ million, unless otherwise indicated)

	1970	1980	1990	1992	1993	1994	1995	1996	1997	1998
5. LONG-TERM DEBT										
DEBT OUTSTANDING (LDOD)	**152**	**537**	**2,161**	**2,433**	**2,599**	**2,869**	**3,062**	**3,151**	**3,359**	**3,402**
Public and publicly guaranteed	**152**	**537**	**2,161**	**2,433**	**2,599**	**2,869**	**3,062**	**3,151**	**3,359**	**3,402**
Official creditors	127	293	1,826	2,173	2,485	2,776	2,979	3,074	3,284	3,328
Multilateral	19	79	1,270	1,561	1,727	2,012	2,209	2,284	2,398	2,433
Concessional	13	63	1,129	1,438	1,607	1,915	2,129	2,208	2,329	2,377
Bilateral	108	214	556	612	758	764	770	789	886	895
Concessional	95	191	322	368	523	542	639	670	647	794
Private creditors	25	244	335	260	115	93	84	77	76	74
Bonds	10	0	4	4	4	4	4	4	4	4
Commercial banks	14	23	89	68	40	27	21	15	13	12
Other private	1	221	242	189	71	62	59	59	59	58
Private nonguaranteed	**0**	**0**	**0**	**0**	**0**	**0**	**0**	**0**	**0**	**0**
Bonds	0	0	0	0	0	0	0	0	0	0
Commercial banks	0	0	0	0	0	0	0	0	0	0
Memo:										
IBRD	6	1	34	21	16	11	0	0	0	0
IDA	13	46	935	1,188	1,327	1,604	1,792	1,849	1,954	1,947
DISBURSEMENTS	**26**	**83**	**301**	**255**	**408**	**270**	**232**	**225**	**281**	**175**
Public and publicly guaranteed	**26**	**83**	**301**	**255**	**408**	**270**	**232**	**225**	**281**	**175**
Official creditors	19	18	262	250	390	270	232	225	281	175
Multilateral	6	7	227	218	201	250	210	180	272	170
Concessional	5	2	223	202	178	247	200	167	264	168
Bilateral	14	11	36	32	189	20	22	45	10	5
Concessional	14	11	23	27	150	20	21	45	9	3
Private creditors	7	65	38	6	18	0	0	0	0	0
Bonds	0	0	0	0	0	0	0	0	0	0
Commercial banks	6	17	5	2	9	0	0	0	0	0
Other private	2	49	34	4	9	0	0	0	0	0
Private nonguaranteed	**0**	**0**	**0**	**0**	**0**	**0**	**0**	**0**	**0**	**0**
Bonds	0	0	0	0	0	0	0	0	0	0
Commercial banks	0	0	0	0	0	0	0	0	0	0
Memo:										
IBRD	0	0	0	0	0	0	0	0	0	0
IDA	5	1	206	156	139	222	160	124	216	113
PRINCIPAL REPAYMENTS	**5**	**32**	**66**	**51**	**109**	**88**	**70**	**56**	**59**	**63**
Public and publicly guaranteed	**5**	**32**	**66**	**51**	**109**	**88**	**70**	**56**	**59**	**63**
Official creditors	4	11	44	37	77	72	60	49	57	61
Multilateral	1	1	19	23	37	51	50	30	29	41
Concessional	0	0	4	7	11	19	19	18	19	23
Bilateral	3	10	25	13	40	21	11	19	28	21
Concessional	3	2	4	3	6	4	4	6	18	13
Private creditors	1	21	22	14	32	16	10	7	1	2
Bonds	0	0	0	0	0	0	0	0	0	0
Commercial banks	1	0	14	5	11	6	7	6	1	1
Other private	0	21	8	9	22	10	3	1	0	1
Private nonguaranteed	**0**	**0**	**0**	**0**	**0**	**0**	**0**	**0**	**0**	**0**
Bonds	0	0	0	0	0	0	0	0	0	0
Commercial banks	0	0	0	0	0	0	0	0	0	0
Memo:										
IBRD	0	1	5	8	7	6	12	0	0	0
IDA	0	0	2	3	4	7	8	8	9	8
NET FLOWS ON DEBT	**22**	**51**	**234**	**204**	**298**	**182**	**162**	**169**	**223**	**111**
Public and publicly guaranteed	**22**	**51**	**234**	**204**	**298**	**182**	**162**	**169**	**223**	**111**
Official creditors	16	7	218	213	312	198	171	176	224	113
Multilateral	5	5	208	195	164	199	160	150	243	129
Concessional	5	1	219	196	167	228	181	149	244	145
Bilateral	11	1	11	18	148	-1	11	26	-19	-16
Concessional	11	9	20	24	144	16	17	39	-10	-10
Private creditors	6	44	16	-8	-14	-16	-10	-7	-1	-2
Bonds	0	0	0	0	0	0	0	0	0	0
Commercial banks	5	17	-10	-3	-2	-6	-7	-6	-1	-1
Other private	2	28	26	-5	-13	-10	-3	-1	0	-1
Private nonguaranteed	**0**	**0**	**0**	**0**	**0**	**0**	**0**	**0**	**0**	**0**
Bonds	0	0	0	0	0	0	0	0	0	0
Commercial banks	0	0	0	0	0	0	0	0	0	0
Memo:										
IBRD	0	-1	-5	-8	-7	-6	-12	0	0	0
IDA	5	1	205	153	135	215	152	116	207	105

UGANDA

(US$ million, unless otherwise indicated)

	1970	1980	1990	1992	1993	1994	1995	1996	1997	1998
INTEREST PAYMENTS (LINT)	**5**	**4**	**19**	**26**	**33**	**34**	**34**	**38**	**37**	**28**
Public and publicly guaranteed	**5**	**4**	**19**	**26**	**33**	**34**	**34**	**38**	**37**	**28**
Official creditors	3	2	18	21	30	33	33	38	37	26
Multilateral	0	1	13	17	20	25	23	22	21	21
Concessional	0	1	6	9	11	13	17	18	17	18
Bilateral	3	1	5	4	9	8	10	16	16	5
Concessional	2	1	1	1	2	5	7	7	8	3
Private creditors	2	1	1	5	3	1	2	0	0	2
Bonds	1	0	0	0	0	0	0	0	0	0
Commercial banks	1	0	1	3	2	1	2	0	0	2
Other private	0	1	1	2	1	0	0	0	0	0
Private nonguaranteed	**0**	**0**	**0**	**0**	**0**	**0**	**0**	**0**	**0**	**0**
Bonds	0	0	0	0	0	0	0	0	0	0
Commercial banks	0	0	0	0	0	0	0	0	0	0
Memo:										
IBRD	0	0	2	2	1	1	1	0	0	0
IDA	0	0	5	8	9	11	13	13	13	14
NET TRANSFERS ON DEBT	**17**	**47**	**216**	**178**	**266**	**148**	**127**	**131**	**186**	**83**
Public and publicly guaranteed	**17**	**47**	**216**	**178**	**266**	**148**	**127**	**131**	**186**	**83**
Official creditors	13	4	201	192	283	165	139	138	187	87
Multilateral	5	4	195	178	144	174	138	128	222	108
Concessional	5	1	213	186	156	215	165	131	228	127
Bilateral	8	0	6	14	139	-9	1	10	-35	-21
Concessional	9	9	19	23	142	11	11	32	-18	-13
Private creditors	5	43	15	-13	-17	-17	-11	-7	-2	-4
Bonds	-1	0	0	0	0	0	0	0	0	0
Commercial banks	4	17	-10	-6	-3	-7	-8	-6	-2	-3
Other private	2	26	25	-7	-14	-10	-3	-1	0	-1
Private nonguaranteed	**0**	**0**	**0**	**0**	**0**	**0**	**0**	**0**	**0**	**0**
Bonds	0	0	0	0	0	0	0	0	0	0
Commercial banks	0	0	0	0	0	0	0	0	0	0
Memo:										
IBRD	-1	-1	-6	-10	-8	-7	-12	0	0	0
IDA	5	0	200	145	126	205	139	103	194	91
DEBT SERVICE (LTDS)	**9**	**36**	**85**	**77**	**142**	**121**	**104**	**95**	**96**	**91**
Public and publicly guaranteed	**9**	**36**	**85**	**77**	**142**	**121**	**104**	**95**	**96**	**91**
Official creditors	7	14	62	58	107	105	93	87	94	87
Multilateral	1	3	32	40	57	76	72	52	50	62
Concessional	0	1	10	16	21	32	35	36	36	41
Bilateral	6	11	30	18	50	29	21	35	44	26
Concessional	4	3	5	4	8	9	10	14	27	16
Private creditors	3	22	23	19	35	17	11	7	2	4
Bonds	1	0	0	0	0	0	0	0	0	0
Commercial banks	2	0	15	7	12	7	8	6	2	3
Other private	0	22	9	11	23	10	3	1	0	1
Private nonguaranteed	**0**	**0**	**0**	**0**	**0**	**0**	**0**	**0**	**0**	**0**
Bonds	0	0	0	0	0	0	0	0	0	0
Commercial banks	0	0	0	0	0	0	0	0	0	0
Memo:										
IBRD	1	1	6	10	8	7	12	0	0	0
IDA	0	1	7	11	13	17	21	21	22	22
UNDISBURSED DEBT	**47**	**162**	**844**	**1,252**	**1,175**	**1,262**	**1,067**	**843**	**685**	**680**
Official creditors	44	143	821	1,232	1,157	1,244	1,064	843	684	680
Private creditors	3	19	23	20	18	18	3	0	0	0
Memorandum items										
Concessional LDOD	108	254	1,451	1,806	2,130	2,456	2,767	2,878	2,977	3,171
Variable rate LDOD	4	7	49	39	96	88	78	78	77	77
Public sector LDOD	151	533	2,158	2,430	2,592	2,866	3,057	3,144	3,352	3,394
Private sector LDOD	1	4	3	3	7	4	6	8	7	8

6. CURRENCY COMPOSITION OF LONG-TERM DEBT (PERCENT)

	1970	1980	1990	1992	1993	1994	1995	1996	1997	1998
Deutsche mark	6.5	8.3	0.7	0.4	0.4	0.2	0.0	0.3	0.2	0.2
French franc	0.2	6.3	3.5	2.1	1.4	1.4	0.3	0.3	0.3	0.3
Japanese yen	0.3	0.7	0.3	0.3	1.1	1.3	1.2	1.7	1.4	1.6
Pound sterling	73.3	20.4	6.7	4.4	3.4	3.1	2.0	2.1	1.8	1.1
Swiss franc	0.0	9.9	0.0	0.0	0.3	0.0	0.0	0.0	0.0	0.0
U.S.dollars	6.9	43.8	53.4	59.5	63.0	63.6	66.8	65.9	67.9	66.7
Multiple currency	4.1	2.3	21.8	18.6	16.8	15.4	13.8	12.1	10.7	9.4
Special drawing rights	0.0	0.1	2.4	2.8	3.7	4.8	5.8	6.7	7.3	8.8
All other currencies	8.7	8.2	11.2	11.9	9.9	10.2	10.1	10.9	10.4	11.9

UGANDA

(US$ million, unless otherwise indicated)

	1970	1980	1990	1992	1993	1994	1995	1996	1997	1998
7. DEBT RESTRUCTURINGS										
Total amount rescheduled	..	..	18	100	38	0	172	0	0	148
Debt stock rescheduled	..	..	0	0	0	0	143	0	0	0
Principal rescheduled	..	..	4	55	24	0	0	0	0	133
Official	..	..	4	31	11	0	0	0	0	133
Private	..	..	0	24	13	0	0	0	0	0
Interest rescheduled	..	..	1	38	10	0	30	0	0	15
Official	..	..	1	24	9	0	30	0	0	15
Private	..	..	0	14	1	0	0	0	0	0
Debt forgiven	..	..	51	14	16	7	0	0	0	0
Memo: interest forgiven	..	..	1	2	19	0	1	0	0	522
Debt stock reduction	..	..	0	0	139	0	42	0	0	178
of which debt buyback	..	..	0	0	17	0	0	0	0	0
8. DEBT STOCK-FLOW RECONCILIATION										
Total change in debt stocks	..	..	406	150	101	343	201	102	194	67
Net flows on debt	22	130	277	239	244	224	185	206	236	102
Net change in interest arrears	..	..	28	-20	-10	10	-22	-10	-2	17
Interest capitalized	..	..	1	38	10	0	30	0	0	15
Debt forgiveness or reduction	..	..	-51	-14	-138	-7	-42	0	0	-178
Cross-currency valuation	..	..	64	-43	-10	34	6	-19	-47	40
Residual	..	..	86	-49	5	82	43	-75	7	72
9. AVERAGE TERMS OF NEW COMMITMENTS										
ALL CREDITORS										
Interest (%)	3.9	4.9	1.0	1.5	1.6	0.9	0.8	0.7	0.6	0.8
Maturity (years)	28.4	26.2	33.2	34.8	33.0	38.4	39.6	39.7	45.0	39.8
Grace period (years)	6.7	6.0	9.0	8.9	10.9	10.1	10.1	10.2	10.2	10.3
Grant element (%)	46.3	40.0	68.7	68.6	67.3	78.5	80.4	80.5	83.2	80.6
Official creditors										
Interest (%)	3.2	2.7	1.1	1.5	1.7	0.9	0.8	0.7	0.6	0.8
Maturity (years)	33.8	38.2	36.5	35.1	34.3	38.4	39.6	39.7	45.0	39.8
Grace period (years)	8.0	8.2	9.9	9.0	11.4	10.1	10.1	10.2	10.2	10.3
Grant element (%)	55.5	61.9	75.0	69.1	69.8	78.5	80.4	80.5	83.2	80.6
Private creditors										
Interest (%)	6.9	8.2	0.5	0.0	0.0	0.0	0.0	0.0	0.0	0.0
Maturity (years)	5.3	7.8	1.3	1.0	1.9	0.0	0.0	0.0	0.0	0.0
Grace period (years)	0.8	2.4	0.7	1.0	0.6	0.0	0.0	0.0	0.0	0.0
Grant element (%)	7.2	6.4	8.8	9.5	11.9	0.0	0.0	0.0	0.0	0.0
Memorandum items										
Commitments	12	199	452	520	419	299	94	42	188	356
Official creditors	10	120	409	516	401	299	94	42	188	356
Private creditors	2	78	43	4	18	0	0	0	0	0

10. CONTRACTUAL OBLIGATIONS ON OUTSTANDING LONG-TERM DEBT

	1999	2000	2001	2002	2003	2004	2005	2006	2007	2008
TOTAL										
Disbursements	292	213	119	35	10	5	3	1	0	0
Principal	76	81	81	87	91	95	87	89	97	97
Interest	40	47	46	43	41	38	36	35	34	32
Official creditors										
Disbursements	292	213	119	35	10	5	3	1	0	0
Principal	74	79	80	85	90	94	86	88	96	96
Interest	40	47	46	43	41	38	36	35	34	32
Bilateral creditors										
Disbursements	6	2	1	0	0	0	0	0	0	0
Principal	45	47	42	41	39	34	23	23	21	21
Interest	18	24	21	19	17	16	14	14	13	12
Multilateral creditors										
Disbursements	286	211	118	35	10	5	3	1	0	0
Principal	29	32	38	44	51	60	64	65	76	75
Interest	22	24	24	24	23	23	22	21	21	20
Private creditors										
Disbursements	0	0	0	0	0	0	0	0	0	0
Principal	2	2	2	2	2	1	1	1	1	1
Interest	0	0	0	0	0	0	0	0	0	0
Commercial banks										
Disbursements	0	0	0	0	0	0	0	0	0	0
Principal	2	2	2	2	2	1	1	1	1	1
Interest	0	0	0	0	0	0	0	0	0	0
Other private										
Disbursements	0	0	0	0	0	0	0	0	0	0
Principal	0	0	0	0	0	0	0	0	0	0
Interest	0	0	0	0	0	0	0	0	0	0

UKRAINE

(US$ million, unless otherwise indicated)

	1970	1980	1990	1992	1993	1994	1995	1996	1997	1998
1. SUMMARY DEBT DATA										
TOTAL DEBT STOCKS (EDT)	..	..	..	**551**	**3,855**	**5,597**	**8,390**	**9,499**	**11,096**	**12,718**
Long-term debt (LDOD)	..	..	..	**458**	**3,694**	**4,816**	**6,625**	**6,793**	**7,604**	**9,443**
Public and publicly guaranteed	..	..	..	454	3,682	4,770	6,541	6,608	6,978	8,606
Private nonguaranteed	..	..	..	4	12	45	84	184	627	837
Use of IMF credit	..	..	..	**0**	**0**	**364**	**1,542**	**2,262**	**2,402**	**2,795**
Short-term debt	..	..	..	**93**	**161**	**417**	**223**	**444**	**1,089**	**480**
of which interest arrears on LDOD	..	..	..	0	29	205	35	41	43	53
Official creditors	..	..	..	0	29	191	5	1	11	0
Private creditors	..	..	..	0	0	14	30	40	33	53
Memo: principal arrears on LDOD	..	..	..	2	2	602	88	66	235	156
Official creditors	..	..	..	0	0	541	17	0	139	0
Private creditors	..	..	..	2	2	61	71	66	96	156
Memo: export credits	..	..	..	223	932	1,121	1,193	1,100	889	1,079
TOTAL DEBT FLOWS										
Disbursements	..	..	..	**469**	**889**	**882**	**1,997**	**1,852**	**1,775**	**3,323**
Long-term debt	..	..	..	469	889	525	801	1,074	1,490	2,941
IMF purchases	..	..	..	0	0	357	1,196	778	285	382
Principal repayments	..	..	..	**0**	**140**	**219**	**636**	**791**	**688**	**1,449**
Long-term debt	..	..	..	0	140	219	636	791	688	1,344
IMF repurchases	..	..	..	0	0	0	0	0	0	105
Net flows on debt	..	..	..	**561**	**787**	**744**	**1,338**	**1,276**	**1,731**	**1,255**
of which short-term debt	..	..	..	93	38	81	-24	215	643	-619
Interest payments (INT)	..	..	..	**12**	**62**	**81**	**501**	**466**	**669**	**569**
Long-term debt	..	..	..	8	55	74	447	374	527	415
IMF charges	..	..	..	0	0	0	42	75	102	115
Short-term debt	..	..	..	4	7	7	12	18	40	39
Net transfers on debt	..	..	..	**550**	**725**	**662**	**836**	**810**	**1,062**	**686**
Total debt service paid (TDS)	..	..	..	**12**	**202**	**300**	**1,137**	**1,257**	**1,356**	**2,018**
Long-term debt	..	..	..	8	195	293	1,083	1,164	1,215	1,759
IMF repurchases and charges	..	..	..	0	0	0	42	75	102	220
Short-term debt (interest only)	..	..	..	4	7	7	12	18	40	39
2. AGGREGATE NET RESOURCE FLOWS AND NET TRANSFERS (LONG-TERM)										
NET RESOURCE FLOWS	..	..	..	**993**	**865**	**683**	**496**	**1,059**	**1,501**	**2,438**
Net flow of long-term debt (ex. IMF)	..	..	..	469	749	306	166	283	802	1,597
Foreign direct investment (net)	..	..	..	0	0	159	267	521	623	743
Portfolio equity flows	..	..	..	0	0	0	0	0	0	0
Grants (excluding technical coop.)	..	..	..	525	117	218	64	256	76	98
Memo: technical coop. grants	..	..	..	33	61	52	120	128	83	247
official net resource flows	..	..	..	624	424	316	449	493	82	351
private net resource flows	..	..	..	369	441	367	48	566	1,419	2,087
NET TRANSFERS	..	..	..	**986**	**810**	**609**	**49**	**666**	**940**	**1,983**
Interest on long-term debt	..	..	..	8	55	74	447	374	527	415
Profit remittances on FDI	..	..	..	0	0	0	0	20	34	40
Memo: official net transfers	..	..	..	622	412	303	143	295	-203	213
private net transfers	..	..	..	364	398	306	-94	371	1,143	1,769
3. MAJOR ECONOMIC AGGREGATES										
Gross national product (GNP)	..	..	..	91,419	69,563	51,953	48,272	61,955	52,773	42,745
Exports of goods & services (XGS)	..	..	..	..	..	16,697	17,337	20,448	20,513	17,743
of which workers remittances	..	..	..	..	..	..	..	..	..	..
Imports of goods & services (MGS)	..	..	..	..	..	18,407	18,961	22,141	22,693	19,821
International reserves (RES)	..	..	..	469	166	665	1,069	1,972	2,359	793
Current account balance	..	..	..	..	..	-1,163	-1,152	-1,184	-1,335	-1,296
4. DEBT INDICATORS										
EDT / XGS (%)	..	..	..	..	..	33.5	48.4	46.5	54.1	71.7
EDT / GNP (%)	..	..	..	0.6	5.5	10.8	17.4	15.3	21.0	29.8
TDS / XGS (%)	..	..	..	..	..	1.8	6.6	6.2	6.6	11.4
INT / XGS (%)	..	..	..	..	..	0.5	2.9	2.3	3.3	3.2
INT / GNP (%)	..	..	..	0.0	0.1	0.2	1.0	0.8	1.3	1.3
RES / EDT (%)	..	..	..	85.2	4.3	11.9	12.7	20.8	21.3	6.2
RES / MGS (months)	..	..	..	..	..	0.4	0.7	1.1	1.3	0.5
Short-term / EDT (%)	..	..	..	16.9	4.2	7.5	2.7	4.7	9.8	3.8
Concessional / EDT (%)	..	..	..	0.0	0.5	0.7	0.8	2.3	1.9	2.1
Multilateral / EDT (%)	..	..	..	10.8	3.6	4.0	7.4	11.9	13.5	15.6

UKRAINE

(US$ million, unless otherwise indicated)

	1970	1980	1990	1992	1993	1994	1995	1996	1997	1998
5. LONG-TERM DEBT										
DEBT OUTSTANDING (LDOD)	..	..	..	**458**	**3,694**	**4,816**	**6,625**	**6,793**	**7,604**	**9,443**
Public and publicly guaranteed	..	..	..	**454**	**3,682**	**4,770**	**6,541**	**6,608**	**6,978**	**8,606**
Official creditors	..	..	..	95	2,922	3,758	4,307	4,486	4,385	4,710
Multilateral	..	..	..	59	139	225	619	1,125	1,493	1,985
Concessional	..	..	..	0	0	0	0	0	0	0
Bilateral	..	..	..	36	2,784	3,533	3,687	3,360	2,892	2,725
Concessional	..	..	..	0	20	40	64	217	212	263
Private creditors	..	..	..	358	760	1,013	2,235	2,123	2,593	3,897
Bonds	..	..	..	0	0	0	1,200	1,120	1,120	2,318
Commercial banks	..	..	..	0	260	282	301	252	742	835
Other private	..	..	..	358	500	731	734	750	731	744
Private nonguaranteed	..	..	..	**4**	**12**	**45**	**84**	**184**	**627**	**837**
Bonds	..	..	..	0	0	0	0	0	0	0
Commercial banks	..	..	..	4	12	45	84	184	627	837
Memo:										
IBRD	..	..	..	0	0	102	491	859	1,111	1,542
IDA	..	..	..	0	0	0	0	0	0	0
DISBURSEMENTS	..	..	..	**469**	**889**	**525**	**801**	**1,074**	**1,490**	**2,941**
Public and publicly guaranteed	..	..	..	**464**	**848**	**431**	**732**	**954**	**1,222**	**2,321**
Official creditors	..	..	..	100	319	152	550	754	508	524
Multilateral	..	..	..	63	88	113	525	552	453	430
Concessional	..	..	..	0	0	0	0	0	0	0
Bilateral	..	..	..	36	231	39	25	202	56	94
Concessional	..	..	..	0	20	20	25	163	10	34
Private creditors	..	..	..	365	529	279	182	200	714	1,797
Bonds	..	..	..	0	0	0	0	0	0	1,111
Commercial banks	..	..	..	0	272	0	0	17	523	523
Other private	..	..	..	365	257	279	182	184	190	162
Private nonguaranteed	..	..	..	**4**	**41**	**94**	**69**	**120**	**268**	**620**
Bonds	..	..	..	0	0	0	0	0	0	0
Commercial banks	..	..	..	4	41	94	69	120	268	620
Memo:										
IBRD	..	..	..	0	0	102	401	406	306	385
IDA	..	..	..	0	0	0	0	0	0	0
PRINCIPAL REPAYMENTS	..	..	..	**0**	**140**	**219**	**636**	**791**	**688**	**1,344**
Public and publicly guaranteed	..	..	..	**0**	**107**	**158**	**595**	**723**	**636**	**927**
Official creditors	..	..	..	0	12	54	165	516	502	271
Multilateral	..	..	..	0	0	39	127	1	1	2
Concessional	..	..	..	0	0	0	0	0	0	0
Bilateral	..	..	..	0	12	15	38	515	502	269
Concessional	..	..	..	0	0	0	0	0	0	0
Private creditors	..	..	..	0	95	104	430	207	134	656
Bonds	..	..	..	0	0	0	200	80	0	35
Commercial banks	..	..	..	0	0	6	2	0	3	445
Other private	..	..	..	0	95	98	228	127	130	177
Private nonguaranteed	..	..	..	**0**	**33**	**60**	**40**	**68**	**52**	**417**
Bonds	..	..	..	0	0	0	0	0	0	0
Commercial banks	..	..	..	0	33	60	40	68	52	417
Memo:										
IBRD	..	..	..	0	0	0	0	0	0	0
IDA	..	..	..	0	0	0	0	0	0	0
NET FLOWS ON DEBT	..	..	..	**469**	**749**	**306**	**166**	**283**	**802**	**1,597**
Public and publicly guaranteed	..	..	..	**464**	**741**	**273**	**136**	**231**	**586**	**1,393**
Official creditors	..	..	..	100	307	98	385	238	6	253
Multilateral	..	..	..	63	88	73	398	551	452	428
Concessional	..	..	..	0	0	0	0	0	0	0
Bilateral	..	..	..	36	219	25	-13	-314	-446	-175
Concessional	..	..	..	0	20	20	25	163	10	34
Private creditors	..	..	..	365	434	175	-249	-6	580	1,140
Bonds	..	..	..	0	0	0	-200	-80	0	1,076
Commercial banks	..	..	..	0	272	-6	-2	17	520	79
Other private	..	..	..	365	162	181	-46	57	60	-15
Private nonguaranteed	..	..	..	**4**	**8**	**33**	**29**	**52**	**216**	**204**
Bonds	..	..	..	0	0	0	0	0	0	0
Commercial banks	..	..	..	4	8	33	29	52	216	204
Memo:										
IBRD	..	..	..	0	0	102	401	406	306	385
IDA	..	..	..	0	0	0	0	0	0	0

UKRAINE

(US$ million, unless otherwise indicated)

	1970	1980	1990	1992	1993	1994	1995	1996	1997	1998
INTEREST PAYMENTS (LINT)	..	..	..	**8**	**55**	**74**	**447**	**374**	**527**	**415**
Public and publicly guaranteed	..	..	..	**7**	**53**	**69**	**440**	**352**	**463**	**365**
Official creditors	..	..	..	2	12	13	306	198	285	138
Multilateral	..	..	..	0	9	10	13	40	71	88
Concessional	..	..	..	0	0	0	0	0	0	0
Bilateral	..	..	..	2	3	3	293	159	214	50
Concessional	..	..	..	0	0	1	1	2	7	8
Private creditors	..	..	..	5	41	56	134	153	178	227
Bonds	..	..	..	0	0	0	87	96	99	104
Commercial banks	..	..	..	0	5	12	4	1	20	78
Other private	..	..	..	5	37	45	44	56	60	45
Private nonguaranteed	..	..	..	**0**	**2**	**5**	**7**	**22**	**64**	**50**
Bonds	..	..	..	0	0	0	0	0	0	0
Commercial banks	..	..	..	0	2	5	7	22	64	50
Memo:										
IBRD	..	..	..	0	0	0	8	32	59	68
IDA	..	..	..	0	0	0	0	0	0	0
NET TRANSFERS ON DEBT	..	..	..	**461**	**693**	**232**	**-282**	**-91**	**275**	**1,181**
Public and publicly guaranteed	..	..	..	**457**	**688**	**204**	**-304**	**-120**	**123**	**1,028**
Official creditors	..	..	..	97	295	86	79	39	-279	115
Multilateral	..	..	..	63	79	64	384	512	381	340
Concessional	..	..	..	0	0	0	0	0	0	0
Bilateral	..	..	..	34	216	22	-306	-472	-660	-225
Concessional	..	..	..	0	20	19	24	160	3	27
Private creditors	..	..	..	360	393	119	-383	-160	402	913
Bonds	..	..	..	0	0	0	-287	-176	-99	973
Commercial banks	..	..	..	0	267	-18	-6	15	500	1
Other private	..	..	..	360	126	136	-90	1	0	-60
Private nonguaranteed	..	..	..	**4**	**6**	**28**	**22**	**30**	**152**	**153**
Bonds	..	..	..	0	0	0	0	0	0	0
Commercial banks	..	..	..	4	6	28	22	30	152	153
Memo:										
IBRD	..	..	..	0	0	102	393	374	247	317
IDA	..	..	..	0	0	0	0	0	0	0
DEBT SERVICE (LTDS)	..	..	..	**8**	**195**	**293**	**1,083**	**1,164**	**1,215**	**1,759**
Public and publicly guaranteed	..	..	..	**7**	**161**	**227**	**1,036**	**1,075**	**1,099**	**1,293**
Official creditors	..	..	..	2	24	67	472	714	787	409
Multilateral	..	..	..	0	9	49	141	40	71	90
Concessional	..	..	..	0	0	0	0	0	0	0
Bilateral	..	..	..	2	15	18	331	674	716	319
Concessional	..	..	..	0	0	1	1	2	7	8
Private creditors	..	..	..	5	136	161	564	360	312	884
Bonds	..	..	..	0	0	0	287	176	99	139
Commercial banks	..	..	..	0	5	18	6	1	23	523
Other private	..	..	..	5	132	143	272	183	190	222
Private nonguaranteed	..	..	..	**0**	**35**	**66**	**47**	**90**	**116**	**467**
Bonds	..	..	..	0	0	0	0	0	0	0
Commercial banks	..	..	..	0	35	66	47	90	116	467
Memo:										
IBRD	..	..	..	0	0	0	8	32	59	68
IDA	..	..	..	0	0	0	0	0	0	0
UNDISBURSED DEBT	..	..	..	**1,019**	**480**	**898**	**816**	**1,643**	**1,141**	**1,508**
Official creditors	..	..	..	126	83	574	520	1,421	1,025	1,408
Private creditors	..	..	..	893	398	324	295	222	116	100
Memorandum items										
Concessional LDOD	..	..	..	0	20	40	64	217	212	263
Variable rate LDOD	..	..	..	420	3,565	4,645	5,244	5,320	5,633	6,147
Public sector LDOD	..	..	..	454	3,682	4,770	6,541	6,592	6,953	8,573
Private sector LDOD	..	..	..	4	12	45	84	201	652	870
6. CURRENCY COMPOSITION OF LONG-TERM DEBT (PERCENT)										
Deutsche mark	..	..	..	40.0	14.8	17.2	14.0	11.4	8.6	14.0
French franc	..	..	..	0.0	0.0	0.1	0.4	0.5	0.5	0.5
Japanese yen	..	..	..	0.0	0.0	0.0	0.0	2.6	2.4	2.0
Pound sterling	..	..	..	0.0	0.0	0.0	0.0	0.0	0.0	0.0
Swiss franc	..	..	..	0.0	0.0	0.0	0.0	0.0	0.0	0.0
U.S.dollars	..	..	..	47.0	5.1	3.7	37.5	38.0	45.1	41.6
Multiple currency	..	..	..	0.0	5.5	21.6	19.4	23.7	24.5	20.8
Special drawing rights	..	..	..	0.0	0.0	0.0	0.0	0.0	0.0	0.0
All other currencies	..	..	..	13.0	74.6	57.4	28.7	23.8	18.9	21.1

UKRAINE

(US$ million, unless otherwise indicated)

	1970	1980	1990	1992	1993	1994	1995	1996	1997	1998
7. DEBT RESTRUCTURINGS										
Total amount rescheduled	..	..	..	0	2,528	723	2,535	0	0	82
Debt stock rescheduled	..	..	..	0	0	0	0	0	0	0
Principal rescheduled	..	..	..	0	0	0	969	0	0	82
Official	..	..	..	0	0	0	969	0	0	0
Private	..	..	..	0	0	0	0	0	0	82
Interest rescheduled	..	..	..	..	0	0	166	0	0	0
Official	..	..	..	0	0	0	166	0	0	0
Private	..	..	..	0	0	0	0	0	0	0
Debt forgiven	..	..	..	0	0	0	0	0	0	0
Memo: interest forgiven	..	..	..	0	0	0	0	0	0	0
Debt stock reduction	..	..	..	0	0	0	0	17	0	0
of which debt buyback	..	..	..	0	0	0	0	0	0	0
8. DEBT STOCK-FLOW RECONCILIATION										
Total change in debt stocks	..	..	..	..	3,304	1,742	2,793	1,109	1,597	1,623
Net flows on debt	..	..	..	561	787	744	1,338	1,276	1,731	1,255
Net change in interest arrears	..	..	..	..	29	176	-170	6	2	10
Interest capitalized	..	..	..	..	0	0	166	0	0	0
Debt forgiveness or reduction	..	..	..	..	0	0	0	-17	0	0
Cross-currency valuation	..	..	..	..	-1,773	-1,526	-290	-431	-201	-382
Residual	..	..	..	..	4,260	2,348	1,750	276	65	739
9. AVERAGE TERMS OF NEW COMMITMENTS										
ALL CREDITORS										
Interest (%)	..	..	..	6.3	6.4	6.6	5.2	6.2	6.0	8.4
Maturity (years)	..	..	..	6.9	6.9	13.8	12.1	14.7	4.1	8.1
Grace period (years)	..	..	..	2.5	2.5	4.6	4.2	4.8	1.6	3.1
Grant element (%)	..	..	..	9.9	11.0	16.8	23.7	20.4	8.4	7.7
Official creditors										
Interest (%)	..	..	..	4.7	5.0	7.2	4.7	6.3	5.7	5.4
Maturity (years)	..	..	..	3.6	6.9	15.8	13.4	15.7	12.3	17.5
Grace period (years)	..	..	..	1.2	2.6	5.3	4.8	5.2	3.3	4.5
Grant element (%)	..	..	..	9.7	15.4	16.5	27.2	21.5	19.6	23.5
Private creditors										
Interest (%)	..	..	..	6.6	7.8	5.0	6.5	5.6	6.0	10.1
Maturity (years)	..	..	..	7.5	6.8	7.3	7.7	6.3	2.1	2.9
Grace period (years)	..	..	..	2.7	2.4	2.3	2.4	0.8	1.2	2.3
Grant element (%)	..	..	..	9.9	7.1	17.5	12.1	11.7	5.7	-1.1
Memorandum items										
Commitments	..	..	..	1,518	591	839	673	1,872	768	2,792
Official creditors	..	..	..	233	281	642	519	1,671	150	1,004
Private creditors	..	..	..	1,285	310	197	155	201	618	1,788

10. CONTRACTUAL OBLIGATIONS ON OUTSTANDING LONG-TERM DEBT

	1999	2000	2001	2002	2003	2004	2005	2006	2007	2008
TOTAL										
Disbursements	658	307	159	128	97	71	42	28	16	4
Principal	1,909	1,960	1,447	785	704	659	636	576	512	259
Interest	702	633	494	372	312	260	213	169	136	96
Official creditors										
Disbursements	611	274	145	123	96	71	42	28	16	4
Principal	1,163	365	446	385	415	465	463	426	400	256
Interest	309	281	267	248	228	203	174	144	114	95
Bilateral creditors										
Disbursements	24	25	15	8	4	2	1	0	0	0
Principal	1,143	315	321	165	162	152	150	150	150	32
Interest	144	95	74	57	46	37	27	17	8	3
Multilateral creditors										
Disbursements	587	249	130	114	92	69	41	28	16	4
Principal	20	50	125	220	253	313	313	276	250	225
Interest	166	186	194	191	182	166	147	126	107	92
Private creditors										
Disbursements	47	33	15	5	1	0	0	0	0	0
Principal	746	1,595	1,001	399	290	193	173	150	112	3
Interest	393	352	227	124	84	57	39	25	21	1
Commercial banks										
Disbursements	19	13	5	2	0	0	0	0	0	0
Principal	81	576	28	28	25	21	20	3	3	3
Interest	14	15	9	7	5	4	2	2	1	1
Other private										
Disbursements	28	21	10	3	1	0	0	0	0	0
Principal	665	1,019	972	371	265	173	153	147	109	0
Interest	379	337	218	117	79	53	37	23	20	0

URUGUAY

(US$ million, unless otherwise indicated)

	1970	1980	1990	1992	1993	1994	1995	1996	1997	1998
1. SUMMARY DEBT DATA										
TOTAL DEBT STOCKS (EDT)	..	**1,660**	**4,415**	**4,574**	**4,851**	**5,077**	**5,320**	**5,901**	**6,713**	**7,600**
Long-term debt (LDOD)	**298**	**1,338**	**3,114**	**3,177**	**3,439**	**3,815**	**3,963**	**4,234**	**4,812**	**5,430**
Public and publicly guaranteed	269	1,127	3,045	3,143	3,372	3,752	3,836	4,099	4,588	5,142
Private nonguaranteed	29	211	69	35	67	62	127	135	223	289
Use of IMF credit	**18**	**0**	**101**	**52**	**38**	**30**	**21**	**9**	**0**	**161**
Short-term debt	..	**322**	**1,201**	**1,344**	**1,374**	**1,233**	**1,336**	**1,659**	**1,901**	**2,009**
of which interest arrears on LDOD	..	0	0	0	0	0	0	0	0	0
Official creditors	..	0	0	0	0	0	0	0	0	0
Private creditors	..	0	0	0	0	0	0	0	0	0
Memo: principal arrears on LDOD	..	0	0	0	0	0	0	0	0	0
Official creditors	..	0	0	0	0	0	0	0	0	0
Private creditors	..	0	0	0	0	0	0	0	0	0
Memo: export credits	..	0	183	184	226	249	291	282	278	308
TOTAL DEBT FLOWS										
Disbursements	**91**	**356**	**358**	**556**	**566**	**501**	**661**	**659**	**1,005**	**1,368**
Long-term debt	50	356	346	533	566	501	661	659	1,005	1,213
IMF purchases	40	0	12	23	0	0	0	0	0	155
Principal repayments	**80**	**130**	**559**	**262**	**324**	**232**	**484**	**298**	**290**	**689**
Long-term debt	51	130	434	236	310	221	474	286	282	689
IMF repurchases	28	0	124	26	14	11	10	12	8	0
Net flows on debt	**58**	**342**	**-134**	**432**	**272**	**128**	**281**	**684**	**957**	**787**
of which short-term debt	..	116	66	139	30	-141	104	322	242	108
Interest payments (INT)	..	**169**	**428**	**262**	**263**	**304**	**379**	**367**	**454**	**447**
Long-term debt	17	121	319	206	212	237	298	273	347	333
IMF charges	0	0	16	5	4	2	2	1	0	0
Short-term debt	..	48	93	51	48	65	80	94	107	114
Net transfers on debt	..	**173**	**-563**	**170**	**9**	**-176**	**-98**	**317**	**503**	**340**
Total debt service paid (TDS)	..	**299**	**987**	**524**	**587**	**536**	**863**	**665**	**744**	**1,136**
Long-term debt	69	251	753	443	521	458	772	559	629	1,022
IMF repurchases and charges	28	0	141	31	18	13	11	12	8	0
Short-term debt (interest only)	..	48	93	51	48	65	80	94	107	114
2. AGGREGATE NET RESOURCE FLOWS AND NET TRANSFERS (LONG-TERM)										
NET RESOURCE FLOWS	**0**	**516**	**-78**	**310**	**376**	**468**	**363**	**525**	**858**	**696**
Net flow of long-term debt (ex. IMF)	-1	226	-89	297	256	280	187	373	723	524
Foreign direct investment (net)	0	290	0	1	102	155	157	137	126	164
Portfolio equity flows	0	0	0	0	0	25	4	5	2	0
Grants (excluding technical coop.)	1	0	11	12	18	9	15	10	8	8
Memo: technical coop. grants	3	9	26	31	32	32	34	28	26	20
official net resource flows	10	37	115	158	172	125	19	59	260	201
private net resource flows	-10	479	-192	151	204	344	344	466	598	496
NET TRANSFERS	**-19**	**395**	**-396**	**103**	**164**	**231**	**65**	**252**	**511**	**363**
Interest on long-term debt	17	121	319	206	212	237	298	273	347	333
Profit remittances on FDI	2	0	0	0	0	0	0	0	0	0
Memo: official net transfers	5	15	54	91	89	29	-105	-35	163	89
private net transfers	-24	380	-450	13	75	203	170	287	348	274
3. MAJOR ECONOMIC AGGREGATES										
Gross national product (GNP)	2,359	9,752	8,034	11,762	12,847	15,019	16,942	18,704	19,530	20,383
Exports of goods & services (XGS)	..	1,594	2,417	2,857	3,010	3,531	3,911	4,308	4,765	4,827
of which workers remittances	..	0	0	0	0	0	0	0	0	..
Imports of goods & services (MGS)	..	2,312	2,239	2,894	3,307	4,010	4,200	4,624	5,126	5,294
International reserves (RES)	186	2,401	1,446	1,185	1,423	1,622	1,813	1,892	2,067	2,587
Current account balance	..	-709	186	-9	-244	-438	-213	-233	-287	-400
4. DEBT INDICATORS										
EDT / XGS (%)	..	104.2	182.7	160.1	161.2	143.8	136.0	137.0	140.9	157.4
EDT / GNP (%)	..	17.0	55.0	38.9	37.8	33.8	31.4	31.6	34.4	37.3
TDS / XGS (%)	..	18.8	40.8	18.4	19.5	15.2	22.1	15.4	15.6	23.5
INT / XGS (%)	..	10.6	17.7	9.2	8.7	8.6	9.7	8.5	9.5	9.3
INT / GNP (%)	..	1.7	5.3	2.2	2.1	2.0	2.2	2.0	2.3	2.2
RES / EDT (%)	..	144.7	32.7	25.9	29.3	31.9	34.1	32.1	30.8	34.0
RES / MGS (months)	..	12.5	7.8	4.9	5.2	4.9	5.2	4.9	4.8	5.9
Short-term / EDT (%)	..	19.4	27.2	29.4	28.3	24.3	25.1	28.1	28.3	26.4
Concessional / EDT (%)	..	5.1	2.3	2.6	3.1	4.1	4.2	3.6	3.5	3.2
Multilateral / EDT (%)	..	11.0	15.8	21.3	22.5	24.0	23.7	20.4	18.9	19.5

URUGUAY

(US$ million, unless otherwise indicated)

	1970	1980	1990	1992	1993	1994	1995	1996	1997	1998
5. LONG-TERM DEBT										
DEBT OUTSTANDING (LDOD)	**298**	**1,338**	**3,114**	**3,177**	**3,439**	**3,815**	**3,963**	**4,234**	**4,812**	**5,430**
Public and publicly guaranteed	**269**	**1,127**	**3,045**	**3,143**	**3,372**	**3,752**	**3,836**	**4,099**	**4,588**	**5,142**
Official creditors	126	333	895	1,172	1,331	1,535	1,588	1,462	1,621	1,880
Multilateral	62	182	699	973	1,091	1,217	1,259	1,205	1,268	1,481
Concessional	2	20	22	31	31	30	28	26	24	23
Bilateral	64	151	196	199	240	318	329	257	353	399
Concessional	55	64	78	89	121	178	197	187	212	220
Private creditors	143	794	2,150	1,971	2,041	2,218	2,248	2,638	2,968	3,262
Bonds	45	263	567	1,649	1,761	1,969	1,966	2,111	2,431	2,725
Commercial banks	82	502	1,576	314	272	243	275	520	529	533
Other private	16	30	8	8	8	6	8	6	7	5
Private nonguaranteed	**29**	**211**	**69**	**35**	**67**	**62**	**127**	**135**	**223**	**289**
Bonds	0	0	0	0	40	40	110	104	196	260
Commercial banks	29	211	69	35	27	22	18	30	28	29
Memo:										
IBRD	49	72	359	521	522	539	513	446	393	473
IDA	0	0	0	0	0	0	0	0	0	0
DISBURSEMENTS	**50**	**356**	**346**	**533**	**566**	**501**	**661**	**659**	**1,005**	**1,213**
Public and publicly guaranteed	**37**	**293**	**346**	**527**	**526**	**501**	**591**	**647**	**905**	**1,102**
Official creditors	20	58	174	226	247	215	128	167	376	348
Multilateral	7	25	90	211	189	148	103	142	258	281
Concessional	1	4	3	4	1	1	0	0	0	0
Bilateral	13	34	85	15	58	68	25	25	118	67
Concessional	6	3	3	13	56	54	25	8	39	13
Private creditors	18	235	172	301	279	286	463	480	529	754
Bonds	7	0	164	290	270	271	348	180	471	694
Commercial banks	10	230	4	9	6	15	111	299	54	60
Other private	1	4	4	2	4	0	4	2	4	0
Private nonguaranteed	**13**	**63**	**0**	**6**	**40**	**0**	**70**	**13**	**100**	**110**
Bonds	0	0	0	0	40	0	70	0	100	100
Commercial banks	13	63	0	6	0	0	0	13	0	10
Memo:										
IBRD	2	4	51	174	41	37	32	39	50	130
IDA	0	0	0	0	0	0	0	0	0	0
PRINCIPAL REPAYMENTS	**51**	**130**	**434**	**236**	**310**	**221**	**474**	**286**	**282**	**689**
Public and publicly guaranteed	**47**	**93**	**398**	**236**	**302**	**216**	**469**	**286**	**280**	**639**
Official creditors	11	22	71	79	93	99	124	118	124	156
Multilateral	8	9	61	70	81	93	117	106	116	117
Concessional	0	0	1	1	1	2	2	2	2	2
Bilateral	3	12	10	9	11	7	7	12	8	38
Concessional	3	3	2	3	7	1	3	8	6	13
Private creditors	36	72	328	157	209	117	345	169	156	484
Bonds	9	6	180	94	159	70	273	121	122	418
Commercial banks	21	59	143	59	47	45	69	45	31	63
Other private	6	6	5	4	4	2	3	3	3	3
Private nonguaranteed	**4**	**37**	**36**	**0**	**8**	**5**	**5**	**0**	**3**	**49**
Bonds	0	0	0	0	0	0	0	0	0	40
Commercial banks	4	37	36	0	8	5	5	0	3	9
Memo:										
IBRD	6	6	43	45	49	56	78	70	68	64
IDA	0	0	0	0	0	0	0	0	0	0
NET FLOWS ON DEBT	**-1**	**226**	**-89**	**297**	**256**	**280**	**187**	**373**	**723**	**524**
Public and publicly guaranteed	**-10**	**200**	**-53**	**291**	**224**	**285**	**122**	**361**	**625**	**463**
Official creditors	9	37	104	147	154	116	4	49	252	193
Multilateral	-1	15	29	140	107	55	-14	36	142	164
Concessional	1	3	2	4	0	-1	-2	-2	-2	-2
Bilateral	9	21	75	6	47	61	18	14	110	29
Concessional	2	0	1	10	49	52	23	0	33	0
Private creditors	-19	163	-156	144	70	169	118	311	373	270
Bonds	-2	-6	-16	196	111	201	74	59	349	276
Commercial banks	-11	171	-139	-50	-41	-30	42	254	23	-3
Other private	-5	-2	-1	-2	0	-2	2	-1	1	-3
Private nonguaranteed	**9**	**26**	**-36**	**6**	**32**	**-5**	**65**	**13**	**97**	**61**
Bonds	0	0	0	0	40	0	70	0	100	60
Commercial banks	9	26	-36	6	-8	-5	-5	13	-3	1
Memo:										
IBRD	-4	-2	8	130	-9	-19	-46	-31	-18	65
IDA	0	0	0	0	0	0	0	0	0	0

URUGUAY

(US$ million, unless otherwise indicated)

	1970	1980	1990	1992	1993	1994	1995	1996	1997	1998
INTEREST PAYMENTS (LINT)	**17**	**121**	**319**	**206**	**212**	**237**	**298**	**273**	**347**	**333**
Public and publicly guaranteed	**16**	**105**	**312**	**204**	**209**	**232**	**293**	**264**	**337**	**318**
Official creditors	4	23	61	68	83	96	124	94	96	112
Multilateral	3	16	54	64	79	85	91	86	85	96
Concessional	0	0	1	1	1	1	1	1	1	1
Bilateral	1	7	7	4	4	11	33	7	11	16
Concessional	1	2	2	2	2	3	25	4	4	3
Private creditors	12	82	252	136	126	136	169	170	241	206
Bonds	3	30	61	117	106	119	151	144	192	163
Commercial banks	7	50	190	19	19	17	18	26	48	43
Other private	1	2	1	1	1	0	0	1	1	0
Private nonguaranteed	**2**	**17**	**6**	**3**	**3**	**5**	**5**	**9**	**10**	**15**
Bonds	0	0	0	0	1	3	3	9	8	15
Commercial banks	2	17	6	3	2	2	1	0	2	1
Memo:										
IBRD	2	7	28	31	38	39	40	33	28	29
IDA	0	0	0	0	0	0	0	0	0	0
NET TRANSFERS ON DEBT	**-19**	**105**	**-407**	**90**	**45**	**43**	**-111**	**101**	**376**	**191**
Public and publicly guaranteed	**-26**	**95**	**-365**	**87**	**15**	**53**	**-171**	**97**	**288**	**145**
Official creditors	4	14	43	79	71	20	-120	-44	156	81
Multilateral	-4	0	-25	77	29	-30	-105	-51	57	68
Concessional	1	3	1	3	-1	-2	-2	-2	-2	-2
Bilateral	8	14	68	2	43	50	-15	6	99	13
Concessional	1	-2	-1	9	47	49	-2	-4	29	-4
Private creditors	-30	81	-408	8	-56	33	-51	141	133	64
Bonds	-5	-36	-77	79	5	82	-77	-85	157	113
Commercial banks	-18	121	-329	-69	-60	-47	24	228	-24	-46
Other private	-6	-4	-2	-2	0	-2	1	-2	1	-3
Private nonguaranteed	**7**	**10**	**-42**	**4**	**30**	**-10**	**61**	**4**	**88**	**46**
Bonds	0	0	0	0	39	-3	67	-9	92	45
Commercial banks	7	10	-42	4	-10	-6	-6	13	-4	0
Memo:										
IBRD	-6	-9	-19	99	-47	-58	-86	-64	-45	36
IDA	0	0	0	0	0	0	0	0	0	0
DEBT SERVICE (LTDS)	**69**	**251**	**753**	**443**	**521**	**458**	**772**	**559**	**629**	**1,022**
Public and publicly guaranteed	**63**	**198**	**711**	**440**	**511**	**449**	**762**	**550**	**616**	**957**
Official creditors	16	44	132	147	176	195	248	211	220	267
Multilateral	11	25	115	134	160	178	208	192	202	213
Concessional	0	1	1	1	2	2	2	2	2	2
Bilateral	5	19	17	13	15	17	40	19	19	54
Concessional	4	5	4	4	8	5	27	12	10	17
Private creditors	48	153	579	293	335	254	515	339	396	690
Bonds	12	36	241	211	265	189	424	265	314	581
Commercial banks	28	109	333	78	66	62	87	71	78	106
Other private	8	8	5	4	4	2	3	3	4	3
Private nonguaranteed	**6**	**54**	**42**	**3**	**11**	**10**	**9**	**9**	**12**	**65**
Bonds	0	0	0	0	1	3	3	9	8	55
Commercial banks	6	54	42	3	10	6	6	0	4	10
Memo:										
IBRD	9	13	70	75	88	95	117	103	96	94
IDA	0	0	0	0	0	0	0	0	0	0
UNDISBURSED DEBT	**87**	**519**	**736**	**839**	**743**	**786**	**656**	**1,002**	**1,273**	**1,167**
Official creditors	79	326	676	733	645	622	521	824	1,133	1,145
Private creditors	8	193	61	106	98	164	135	178	140	23
Memorandum items										
Concessional LDOD	57	84	100	119	152	207	224	213	236	242
Variable rate LDOD	31	474	2,286	1,815	1,911	2,051	2,016	2,196	2,448	2,538
Public sector LDOD	269	1,123	3,042	3,141	3,371	3,752	3,833	4,097	4,585	5,140
Private sector LDOD	29	215	72	37	68	62	130	137	227	290

6. CURRENCY COMPOSITION OF LONG-TERM DEBT (PERCENT)

	1970	1980	1990	1992	1993	1994	1995	1996	1997	1998
Deutsche mark	2.3	0.3	1.7	0.2	0.2	0.2	6.5	5.6	4.4	4.3
French franc	0.0	3.6	0.3	0.5	0.5	0.7	0.7	0.7	0.5	0.5
Japanese yen	0.0	1.1	5.1	3.7	4.4	4.5	6.4	4.0	5.7	4.4
Pound sterling	4.9	0.2	3.6	2.7	2.5	2.4	1.9	2.1	1.8	1.5
Swiss franc	8.0	0.0	1.5	0.0	0.0	0.0	0.0	0.0	0.0	0.0
U.S.dollars	62.9	77.9	64.9	62.5	60.9	61.2	53.8	61.4	65.4	77.2
Multiple currency	20.0	14.7	22.5	30.3	31.6	31.0	30.7	26.2	22.1	12.1
Special drawing rights	0.0	0.0	0.0	0.0	0.0	0.0	0.0	0.0	0.0	0.0
All other currencies	1.9	2.2	0.4	0.1	0.0	0.0	0.0	0.0	0.1	0.0

URUGUAY

(US$ million, unless otherwise indicated)

	1970	1980	1990	1992	1993	1994	1995	1996	1997	1998
7. DEBT RESTRUCTURINGS										
Total amount rescheduled	..	..	0	0	0	0	0	0	0	0
Debt stock rescheduled	..	..	0	0	0	0	0	0	0	0
Principal rescheduled	..	..	0	0	0	0	0	0	0	0
Official	..	..	0	0	0	0	0	0	0	0
Private	..	..	0	0	0	0	0	0	0	0
Interest rescheduled	..	..	0	0	0	0	0	0	0	0
Official	..	..	0	0	0	0	0	0	0	0
Private	..	..	0	0	0	0	0	0	0	0
Debt forgiven	..	..	0	0	16	0	0	0	0	0
Memo: interest forgiven	..	..	0	0	0	0	0	0	0	0
Debt stock reduction	..	..	0	0	0	0	0	0	0	0
of which debt buyback	..	..	0	0	0	0	0	0	0	0
8. DEBT STOCK-FLOW RECONCILIATION										
Total change in debt stocks	..	..	-34	382	277	227	243	581	812	888
Net flows on debt	58	342	-134	432	272	128	281	684	957	787
Net change in interest arrears	..	..	0	0	0	0	0	0	0	0
Interest capitalized	..	..	0	0	0	0	0	0	0	0
Debt forgiveness or reduction	..	..	0	0	-16	0	0	0	0	0
Cross-currency valuation	..	..	65	-44	14	53	20	-73	-98	48
Residual	..	..	36	-6	7	45	-58	-30	-48	53
9. AVERAGE TERMS OF NEW COMMITMENTS										
ALL CREDITORS										
Interest (%)	7.9	10.1	9.1	6.5	5.8	6.0	6.8	7.5	6.8	7.2
Maturity (years)	11.8	15.3	12.9	15.6	12.5	11.3	7.7	15.6	19.3	11.9
Grace period (years)	3.0	5.9	2.4	3.9	3.0	3.7	3.3	4.9	10.2	6.6
Grant element (%)	10.3	1.0	5.1	18.8	19.3	19.1	12.9	13.8	18.8	15.6
Official creditors										
Interest (%)	7.1	7.9	7.8	6.7	5.4	4.5	3.9	7.5	6.8	7.0
Maturity (years)	16.0	20.6	20.1	21.4	20.3	18.2	14.9	21.9	17.4	17.6
Grace period (years)	3.8	8.0	5.0	5.3	4.0	4.7	5.5	5.1	4.0	4.4
Grant element (%)	15.3	13.5	12.9	22.3	26.9	33.8	36.4	15.9	17.9	17.5
Private creditors										
Interest (%)	9.5	13.0	9.8	6.3	6.1	6.8	7.0	7.4	6.8	7.4
Maturity (years)	3.9	8.4	8.7	7.8	8.1	7.5	7.3	9.9	22.2	8.1
Grace period (years)	1.6	3.2	1.0	1.9	2.5	3.2	3.2	4.7	19.4	8.0
Grant element (%)	1.1	-15.4	0.6	13.9	15.0	10.9	11.4	11.9	20.1	14.3
Memorandum items										
Commitments	71	347	339	697	428	545	486	957	1,221	1,073
Official creditors	46	197	124	401	156	196	29	449	730	436
Private creditors	25	150	215	296	272	350	457	508	491	637

10. CONTRACTUAL OBLIGATIONS ON OUTSTANDING LONG-TERM DEBT

	1999	2000	2001	2002	2003	2004	2005	2006	2007	2008
TOTAL										
Disbursements	296	288	221	152	92	52	36	13	10	4
Principal	498	661	496	484	593	351	332	451	463	528
Interest	393	380	343	322	300	262	241	220	179	143
Official creditors										
Disbursements	275	287	221	151	92	52	36	13	10	4
Principal	201	166	193	218	239	222	197	187	177	171
Interest	143	149	153	150	141	129	117	104	92	81
Bilateral creditors										
Disbursements	11	5	3	0	0	0	0	0	0	0
Principal	41	41	41	42	42	26	25	20	20	20
Interest	15	14	12	10	8	7	6	5	4	3
Multilateral creditors										
Disbursements	264	282	218	151	92	52	36	13	10	4
Principal	159	124	152	176	197	196	172	167	157	151
Interest	128	136	141	141	134	123	111	99	88	77
Private creditors										
Disbursements	21	1	0	0	0	0	0	0	0	0
Principal	297	496	304	266	355	129	135	264	286	357
Interest	250	231	190	172	159	133	125	116	87	63
Commercial banks										
Disbursements	21	0	0	0	0	0	0	0	0	0
Principal	54	139	53	49	47	47	43	119	0	0
Interest	40	36	25	21	18	14	11	8	0	0
Other private										
Disbursements	1	1	0	0	0	0	0	0	0	0
Principal	244	357	251	217	307	82	92	146	286	356
Interest	210	195	166	151	141	119	114	108	87	63

UZBEKISTAN

(US$ million, unless otherwise indicated)

	1970	1980	1990	1992	1993	1994	1995	1996	1997	1998
1. SUMMARY DEBT DATA										
TOTAL DEBT STOCKS (EDT)	..	..	..	**60**	**1,032**	**1,244**	**1,787**	**2,365**	**2,765**	**3,162**
Long-term debt (LDOD)	..	..	..	**60**	**940**	**953**	**1,418**	**2,036**	**2,123**	**2,783**
Public and publicly guaranteed	..	..	..	60	940	953	1,418	1,977	2,032	2,485
Private nonguaranteed	..	..	..	0	0	0	0	59	91	298
Use of IMF credit	..	..	..	**0**	**0**	**0**	**158**	**238**	**223**	**233**
Short-term debt	..	..	..	**0**	**92**	**291**	**212**	**92**	**419**	**147**
of which interest arrears on LDOD	..	..	..	0	0	0	0	0	0	3
Official creditors	..	..	..	0	0	0	0	0	0	0
Private creditors	..	..	..	0	0	0	0	0	0	3
Memo: principal arrears on LDOD	..	..	..	0	0	0	0	0	0	4
Official creditors	..	..	..	0	0	0	0	0	0	0
Private creditors	..	..	..	0	0	0	0	0	0	4
Memo: export credits	..	..	..	0	94	67	366	488	960	1,792
TOTAL DEBT FLOWS										
Disbursements	..	..	..	**65**	**623**	**107**	**782**	**879**	**497**	**799**
Long-term debt	..	..	..	65	623	107	621	793	497	799
IMF purchases	..	..	..	0	0	0	161	86	0	0
Principal repayments	..	..	..	**4**	**16**	**97**	**149**	**188**	**321**	**279**
Long-term debt	..	..	..	4	16	97	149	188	321	279
IMF repurchases	..	..	..	0	0	0	0	0	0	0
Net flows on debt	..	..	..	**61**	**699**	**210**	**554**	**571**	**504**	**245**
of which short-term debt	..	..	..	0	92	199	-79	-120	328	-275
Interest payments (INT)	..	..	..	**1**	**13**	**41**	**95**	**104**	**189**	**148**
Long-term debt	..	..	..	1	13	35	79	92	164	132
IMF charges	..	..	..	0	0	0	3	7	10	11
Short-term debt	..	..	..	0	0	6	13	4	14	6
Net transfers on debt	..	..	..	**60**	**685**	**168**	**459**	**467**	**315**	**97**
Total debt service paid (TDS)	..	..	..	**5**	**30**	**138**	**243**	**291**	**510**	**427**
Long-term debt	..	..	..	5	30	132	228	280	485	411
IMF repurchases and charges	..	..	..	0	0	0	3	7	10	11
Short-term debt (interest only)	..	..	..	0	0	6	13	4	14	6
2. AGGREGATE NET RESOURCE FLOWS AND NET TRANSFERS (LONG-TERM)										
NET RESOURCE FLOWS	..	..	..	**101**	**655**	**78**	**600**	**688**	**480**	**733**
Net flow of long-term debt (ex. IMF)	..	..	..	61	607	11	472	605	176	520
Foreign direct investment (net)	..	..	..	40	45	50	115	55	285	200
Portfolio equity flows	..	..	..	0	0	0	0	0	0	0
Grants (excluding technical coop.)	..	..	..	0	4	18	13	28	19	13
Memo: technical coop. grants	..	..	..	1	4	1	25	35	30	33
official net resource flows	..	..	..	61	459	-22	293	257	46	140
private net resource flows	..	..	..	40	196	101	308	431	434	592
NET TRANSFERS	..	..	..	**100**	**642**	**43**	**521**	**595**	**316**	**601**
Interest on long-term debt	..	..	..	1	13	35	79	92	164	132
Profit remittances on FDI	..	..	..	0	0	0	0	0	0	0
Memo: official net transfers	..	..	..	60	450	-49	241	202	-57	75
private net transfers	..	..	..	40	192	92	280	394	373	526
3. MAJOR ECONOMIC AGGREGATES										
Gross national product (GNP)	..	..	..	22,072	21,955	20,978	22,200	23,179	24,326	20,296
Exports of goods & services (XGS)	..	..	..	..	..	..	3,800	3,892	4,000	3,236
of which workers remittances	..	..	..	..	..	..	..	..	..	..
Imports of goods & services (MGS)	..	..	..	..	..	..	3,840	4,870	4,612	3,331
International reserves (RES)	..	..	..	..	..	..	..	..	..	..
Current account balance	..	..	..	-236	-429	119	-21	-980	-583	-52
4. DEBT INDICATORS										
EDT / XGS (%)	..	..	..	..	..	..	47.0	60.8	69.1	97.7
EDT / GNP (%)	..	..	..	0.3	4.7	5.9	8.1	10.2	11.4	15.6
TDS / XGS (%)	..	..	..	..	..	..	6.4	7.5	12.7	13.2
INT / XGS (%)	..	..	..	..	..	..	2.5	2.7	4.7	4.6
INT / GNP (%)	..	..	..	0.0	0.1	0.2	0.4	0.5	0.8	0.7
RES / EDT (%)	..	..	..	..	..	..	..	..	..	..
RES / MGS (months)	..	..	..	..	..	..	..	..	..	..
Short-term / EDT (%)	..	..	..	0.0	8.9	23.4	11.9	3.9	15.2	4.7
Concessional / EDT (%)	..	..	..	0.0	13.9	11.5	10.5	26.0	7.4	12.4
Multilateral / EDT (%)	..	..	..	0.0	0.0	0.4	13.8	11.6	7.6	9.0

UZBEKISTAN

(US$ million, unless otherwise indicated)

	1970	1980	1990	1992	1993	1994	1995	1996	1997	1998
5. LONG-TERM DEBT										
DEBT OUTSTANDING (LDOD)	..	..	..	**60**	**940**	**953**	**1,418**	**2,036**	**2,123**	**2,783**
Public and publicly guaranteed	..	..	..	**60**	**940**	**953**	**1,418**	**1,977**	**2,032**	**2,485**
Official creditors	..	..	..	60	789	751	1,023	1,215	1,176	1,363
Multilateral	..	..	..	0	0	5	246	275	209	284
Concessional	..	..	..	0	0	0	0	0	0	1
Bilateral	..	..	..	60	789	746	777	941	967	1,079
Concessional	..	..	..	0	143	143	188	615	206	392
Private creditors	..	..	..	0	151	202	395	762	856	1,122
Bonds	..	..	..	0	0	0	0	0	0	0
Commercial banks	..	..	..	0	0	0	0	96	269	368
Other private	..	..	..	0	151	202	395	665	587	754
Private nonguaranteed	..	..	..	**0**	**0**	**0**	**0**	**59**	**91**	**298**
Bonds	..	..	..	0	0	0	0	0	0	0
Commercial banks	..	..	..	0	0	0	0	59	91	298
Memo:										
IBRD	..	..	..	0	0	1	157	155	155	177
IDA	..	..	..	0	0	0	0	0	0	0
DISBURSEMENTS	..	..	..	**65**	**623**	**107**	**621**	**793**	**497**	**799**
Public and publicly guaranteed	..	..	..	**65**	**623**	**107**	**621**	**793**	**460**	**630**
Official creditors	..	..	..	65	469	43	399	369	186	264
Multilateral	..	..	..	0	0	5	246	47	21	68
Concessional	..	..	..	0	0	0	0	0	0	1
Bilateral	..	..	..	65	469	37	154	322	164	196
Concessional	..	..	..	0	143	0	46	79	116	157
Private creditors	..	..	..	0	154	65	222	424	275	366
Bonds	..	..	..	0	0	0	0	0	0	0
Commercial banks	..	..	..	0	0	0	0	96	186	122
Other private	..	..	..	0	154	65	222	328	89	244
Private nonguaranteed	..	..	..	**0**	**0**	**0**	**0**	**0**	**37**	**169**
Bonds	..	..	..	0	0	0	0	0	0	0
Commercial banks	..	..	..	0	0	0	0	0	37	169
Memo:										
IBRD	..	..	..	0	0	1	162	9	13	13
IDA	..	..	..	0	0	0	0	0	0	0
PRINCIPAL REPAYMENTS	..	..	..	**4**	**16**	**97**	**149**	**188**	**321**	**279**
Public and publicly guaranteed	..	..	..	**4**	**16**	**97**	**149**	**188**	**316**	**255**
Official creditors	..	..	..	4	14	83	120	140	159	136
Multilateral	..	..	..	0	0	0	0	3	67	2
Concessional	..	..	..	0	0	0	0	0	0	0
Bilateral	..	..	..	4	14	83	120	137	92	134
Concessional	..	..	..	0	0	0	0	3	5	8
Private creditors	..	..	..	0	3	14	29	48	158	119
Bonds	..	..	..	0	0	0	0	0	0	0
Commercial banks	..	..	..	0	0	0	0	0	13	28
Other private	..	..	..	0	3	14	29	48	145	91
Private nonguaranteed	..	..	..	**0**	**0**	**0**	**0**	**0**	**4**	**24**
Bonds	..	..	..	0	0	0	0	0	0	0
Commercial banks	..	..	..	0	0	0	0	0	4	24
Memo:										
IBRD	..	..	..	0	0	0	0	0	0	0
IDA	..	..	..	0	0	0	0	0	0	0
NET FLOWS ON DEBT	..	..	..	**61**	**607**	**11**	**472**	**605**	**176**	**520**
Public and publicly guaranteed	..	..	..	**61**	**607**	**11**	**472**	**605**	**144**	**376**
Official creditors	..	..	..	61	456	-40	280	229	27	128
Multilateral	..	..	..	0	0	5	246	44	-46	66
Concessional	..	..	..	0	0	0	0	0	0	1
Bilateral	..	..	..	61	456	-45	34	185	72	62
Concessional	..	..	..	0	143	0	46	76	111	149
Private creditors	..	..	..	0	151	51	193	376	117	248
Bonds	..	..	..	0	0	0	0	0	0	0
Commercial banks	..	..	..	0	0	0	0	96	173	95
Other private	..	..	..	0	151	51	193	280	-56	153
Private nonguaranteed	..	..	..	**0**	**0**	**0**	**0**	**0**	**32**	**144**
Bonds	..	..	..	0	0	0	0	0	0	0
Commercial banks	..	..	..	0	0	0	0	0	32	144
Memo:										
IBRD	..	..	..	0	0	1	162	9	13	13
IDA	..	..	..	0	0	0	0	0	0	0

UZBEKISTAN

(US$ million, unless otherwise indicated)

	1970	1980	1990	1992	1993	1994	1995	1996	1997	1998
INTEREST PAYMENTS (LINT)	..	..	..	**1**	**13**	**35**	**79**	**92**	**164**	**132**
Public and publicly guaranteed	..	..	..	**1**	**13**	**35**	**79**	**92**	**160**	**127**
Official creditors	..	..	..	1	10	26	52	55	103	66
Multilateral	..	..	..	0	0	0	4	16	16	15
Concessional	..	..	..	0	0	0	0	0	0	0
Bilateral	..	..	..	1	10	26	47	39	87	51
Concessional	..	..	..	0	0	0	0	14	55	6
Private creditors	..	..	..	0	4	9	28	37	56	61
Bonds	..	..	..	0	0	0	0	0	0	0
Commercial banks	..	..	..	0	0	0	0	0	12	17
Other private	..	..	..	0	4	9	28	37	44	44
Private nonguaranteed	..	..	..	**0**	**0**	**0**	**0**	**0**	**5**	**5**
Bonds	..	..	..	0	0	0	0	0	0	0
Commercial banks	..	..	..	0	0	0	0	0	5	5
Memo:										
IBRD	..	..	..	0	0	0	2	10	10	10
IDA	..	..	..	0	0	0	0	0	0	0
NET TRANSFERS ON DEBT	..	..	..	**60**	**593**	**-25**	**393**	**513**	**12**	**389**
Public and publicly guaranteed	..	..	..	**60**	**593**	**-25**	**393**	**513**	**-16**	**249**
Official creditors	..	..	..	60	446	-66	228	174	-77	62
Multilateral	..	..	..	0	0	5	242	28	-62	51
Concessional	..	..	..	0	0	0	0	0	0	1
Bilateral	..	..	..	60	446	-71	-13	147	-15	11
Concessional	..	..	..	0	143	0	46	63	55	144
Private creditors	..	..	..	0	147	42	165	339	61	187
Bonds	..	..	..	0	0	0	0	0	0	0
Commercial banks	..	..	..	0	0	0	0	96	161	77
Other private	..	..	..	0	147	42	165	243	-101	110
Private nonguaranteed	..	..	..	**0**	**0**	**0**	**0**	**0**	**28**	**140**
Bonds	..	..	..	0	0	0	0	0	0	0
Commercial banks	..	..	..	0	0	0	0	0	28	140
Memo:										
IBRD	..	..	..	0	0	1	161	-1	3	3
IDA	..	..	..	0	0	0	0	0	0	0
DEBT SERVICE (LTDS)	..	..	..	**5**	**30**	**132**	**228**	**280**	**485**	**411**
Public and publicly guaranteed	..	..	..	**5**	**30**	**132**	**228**	**280**	**476**	**382**
Official creditors	..	..	..	5	23	109	171	195	262	202
Multilateral	..	..	..	0	0	0	4	19	83	17
Concessional	..	..	..	0	0	0	0	0	0	0
Bilateral	..	..	..	5	23	109	167	176	179	185
Concessional	..	..	..	0	0	0	0	16	60	14
Private creditors	..	..	..	0	6	23	57	85	214	180
Bonds	..	..	..	0	0	0	0	0	0	0
Commercial banks	..	..	..	0	0	0	0	0	25	45
Other private	..	..	..	0	6	23	57	85	189	135
Private nonguaranteed	..	..	..	**0**	**0**	**0**	**0**	**0**	**9**	**29**
Bonds	..	..	..	0	0	0	0	0	0	0
Commercial banks	..	..	..	0	0	0	0	0	9	29
Memo:										
IBRD	..	..	..	0	0	0	2	10	10	10
IDA	..	..	..	0	0	0	0	0	0	0
UNDISBURSED DEBT	..	..	..	**482**	**423**	**764**	**1,136**	**1,068**	**1,039**	**975**
Official creditors	..	..	..	443	423	552	845	857	766	712
Private creditors	..	..	..	39	0	212	290	211	274	263
Memorandum items										
Concessional LDOD	..	..	..	0	143	143	188	615	206	393
Variable rate LDOD	..	..	..	27	759	779	970	868	1,398	1,880
Public sector LDOD	..	..	..	33	917	889	1,290	1,753	1,806	2,272
Private sector LDOD	..	..	..	27	22	64	128	283	318	2,058

6. CURRENCY COMPOSITION OF LONG-TERM DEBT (PERCENT)

	1970	1980	1990	1992	1993	1994	1995	1996	1997	1998
Deutsche mark	..	..	..	45.2	2.4	1.5	10.7	14.3	15.3	15.7
French franc	..	..	..	0.0	0.0	0.0	3.0	4.3	4.4	4.7
Japanese yen	..	..	..	0.0	0.0	0.0	3.1	5.8	8.6	13.2
Pound sterling	..	..	..	0.0	0.0	0.0	0.0	0.0	0.0	0.0
Swiss franc	..	..	..	9.4	0.6	0.4	0.1	0.0	0.1	0.1
U.S.dollars	..	..	..	45.4	97.1	98.0	66.4	64.1	63.9	59.2
Multiple currency	..	..	..	0.0	0.0	0.1	11.1	7.8	7.6	7.0
Special drawing rights	..	..	..	0.0	0.0	0.0	0.0	0.0	0.0	0.0
All other currencies	..	..	..	0.0	0.0	0.0	5.6	3.7	0.1	0.1

UZBEKISTAN

(US$ million, unless otherwise indicated)

	1970	1980	1990	1992	1993	1994	1995	1996	1997	1998
7. DEBT RESTRUCTURINGS										
Total amount rescheduled	..	..	..	0	275	0	0	0	501	0
Debt stock rescheduled	..	..	..	0	0	0	0	0	501	0
Principal rescheduled	..	..	..	0	0	0	0	0	0	0
Official	..	..	..	0	0	0	0	0	0	0
Private	..	..	..	0	0	0	0	0	0	0
Interest rescheduled	..	..	..	..	0	0	0	0	0	0
Official	..	..	..	0	0	0	0	0	0	0
Private	..	..	..	0	0	0	0	0	0	0
Debt forgiven	..	..	..	0	0	0	0	0	0	0
Memo: interest forgiven	..	..	..	0	0	0	0	0	0	0
Debt stock reduction	..	..	..	0	0	0	0	0	0	0
of which debt buyback	..	..	..	0	0	0	0	0	0	0
8. DEBT STOCK-FLOW RECONCILIATION										
Total change in debt stocks	..	..	..	..	972	212	543	578	400	397
Net flows on debt	..	..	..	61	699	210	554	571	504	245
Net change in interest arrears	..	..	..	..	0	0	0	0	0	3
Interest capitalized	..	..	..	..	0	0	0	0	0	0
Debt forgiveness or reduction	..	..	..	..	0	0	0	0	0	0
Cross-currency valuation	..	..	..	..	-2	2	15	-55	-85	86
Residual	..	..	..	..	275	1	-26	62	-19	63
9. AVERAGE TERMS OF NEW COMMITMENTS										
ALL CREDITORS										
Interest (%)	..	..	..	5.8	4.4	7.3	5.4	4.9	6.2	6.5
Maturity (years)	..	..	..	5.5	9.6	9.5	15.2	15.6	10.7	13.1
Grace period (years)	..	..	..	1.7	2.4	2.9	4.3	4.0	2.7	2.9
Grant element (%)	..	..	..	11.2	23.0	10.5	24.7	29.0	16.3	15.7
Official creditors										
Interest (%)	..	..	..	5.9	3.9	6.7	5.2	4.0	6.0	6.4
Maturity (years)	..	..	..	5.5	9.1	7.8	18.0	20.6	15.6	23.2
Grace period (years)	..	..	..	1.7	2.7	2.0	5.1	6.5	4.0	5.6
Grant element (%)	..	..	..	11.0	25.2	12.3	28.9	41.3	22.6	24.6
Private creditors										
Interest (%)	..	..	..	4.4	6.3	7.7	5.9	6.0	6.3	6.5
Maturity (years)	..	..	..	5.5	11.7	10.5	8.6	9.5	6.0	7.4
Grace period (years)	..	..	..	0.9	0.9	3.5	2.4	0.9	1.5	1.4
Grant element (%)	..	..	..	14.8	14.3	9.4	14.7	14.1	10.5	10.7
Memorandum items										
Commitments	..	..	..	547	564	441	1,001	784	686	548
Official creditors	..	..	..	508	449	166	705	430	333	199
Private creditors	..	..	..	39	115	274	296	354	353	349

10. CONTRACTUAL OBLIGATIONS ON OUTSTANDING LONG-TERM DEBT

	1999	2000	2001	2002	2003	2004	2005	2006	2007	2008
TOTAL										
Disbursements	301	215	126	88	58	35	25	11	7	5
Principal	436	499	441	366	339	272	248	229	120	83
Interest	175	158	137	116	95	77	61	47	35	29
Official creditors										
Disbursements	192	150	105	80	58	35	25	11	7	5
Principal	174	182	167	161	160	144	145	144	80	58
Interest	76	74	70	64	58	52	45	38	31	28
Bilateral creditors										
Disbursements	80	47	24	12	5	1	1	0	0	0
Principal	156	140	111	102	95	84	84	86	41	23
Interest	51	44	37	32	26	21	17	13	9	8
Multilateral creditors										
Disbursements	112	103	81	68	53	33	24	11	7	5
Principal	18	42	56	59	65	60	60	58	39	35
Interest	25	30	32	33	32	30	28	25	22	20
Private creditors										
Disbursements	109	65	21	8	0	0	0	0	0	0
Principal	262	318	274	206	179	128	103	85	39	25
Interest	99	84	67	51	37	26	16	9	4	1
Commercial banks										
Disbursements	20	8	4	0	0	0	0	0	0	0
Principal	53	71	73	53	41	30	23	23	18	15
Interest	22	19	15	11	8	6	5	3	2	1
Other private										
Disbursements	90	57	18	8	0	0	0	0	0	0
Principal	209	247	201	152	138	99	80	63	22	10
Interest	77	65	52	40	29	19	12	6	2	0

VANUATU

(US$ million, unless otherwise indicated)

	1970	1980	1990	1992	1993	1994	1995	1996	1997	1998
1. SUMMARY DEBT DATA										
TOTAL DEBT STOCKS (EDT)	..	**4.1**	**40.2**	**40.4**	**42.4**	**46.5**	**48.2**	**47.1**	**47.9**	**63.2**
Long-term debt (LDOD)	..	**4.1**	**30.6**	**39.6**	**39.4**	**41.5**	**43.2**	**42.1**	**38.9**	**54.2**
Public and publicly guaranteed	..	4.1	30.6	39.6	39.4	41.5	43.2	42.1	38.9	54.2
Private nonguaranteed	..	0.0	0.0	0.0	0.0	0.0	0.0	0.0	0.0	0.0
Use of IMF credit	**0.0**	**0.0**	**0.0**	**0.0**	**0.0**	**0.0**	**0.0**	**0.0**	**0.0**	**0.0**
Short-term debt	..	**0.0**	**9.6**	**0.8**	**3.0**	**5.0**	**5.0**	**5.0**	**9.0**	**9.0**
of which interest arrears on LDOD	..	0.0	0.0	0.0	0.0	0.0	0.0	0.0	0.0	0.0
Official creditors	..	0.0	0.0	0.0	0.0	0.0	0.0	0.0	0.0	0.0
Private creditors	..	0.0	0.0	0.0	0.0	0.0	0.0	0.0	0.0	0.0
Memo: principal arrears on LDOD	..	0.0	0.0	0.0	0.0	0.0	0.0	0.0	0.0	0.0
Official creditors	..	0.0	0.0	0.0	0.0	0.0	0.0	0.0	0.0	0.0
Private creditors	..	0.0	0.0	0.0	0.0	0.0	0.0	0.0	0.0	0.0
Memo: export credits	..	0.0	23.0	20.0	17.0	15.0	14.0	11.0	9.0	10.0
TOTAL DEBT FLOWS										
Disbursements	..	**0.0**	**8.7**	**4.5**	**1.1**	**1.8**	**1.6**	**1.1**	**0.9**	**12.1**
Long-term debt	..	0.0	8.7	4.5	1.1	1.8	1.6	1.1	0.9	12.1
IMF purchases	0.0	0.0	0.0	0.0	0.0	0.0	0.0	0.0	0.0	0.0
Principal repayments	..	**0.4**	**1.0**	**0.9**	**0.9**	**1.0**	**0.9**	**1.0**	**0.9**	**0.6**
Long-term debt	..	0.4	1.0	0.9	0.9	1.0	0.9	1.0	0.9	0.6
IMF repurchases	0.0	0.0	0.0	0.0	0.0	0.0	0.0	0.0	0.0	0.0
Net flows on debt	..	**-0.4**	**7.8**	**3.2**	**2.4**	**2.8**	**0.7**	**0.1**	**4.0**	**11.5**
of which short-term debt	..	0.0	0.1	-0.4	2.2	2.0	0.0	0.0	4.0	0.0
Interest payments (INT)	..	**0.2**	**1.5**	**0.6**	**0.7**	**0.9**	**1.0**	**1.0**	**1.4**	**1.1**
Long-term debt	..	0.2	0.7	0.6	0.5	0.7	0.7	0.7	0.6	0.6
IMF charges	0.0	0.0	0.0	0.0	0.0	0.0	0.0	0.0	0.0	0.0
Short-term debt	..	0.0	0.7	0.1	0.1	0.2	0.3	0.3	0.8	0.5
Net transfers on debt	..	**-0.6**	**6.4**	**2.6**	**1.8**	**1.9**	**-0.3**	**-0.8**	**2.7**	**10.4**
Total debt service paid (TDS)	..	**0.6**	**2.4**	**1.5**	**1.5**	**1.9**	**1.9**	**1.9**	**2.2**	**1.7**
Long-term debt	..	0.6	1.7	1.4	1.4	1.6	1.6	1.6	1.4	1.2
IMF repurchases and charges	0.0	0.0	0.0	0.0	0.0	0.0	0.0	0.0	0.0	0.0
Short-term debt (interest only)	..	0.0	0.7	0.1	0.1	0.2	0.3	0.3	0.8	0.5
2. AGGREGATE NET RESOURCE FLOWS AND NET TRANSFERS (LONG-TERM)										
NET RESOURCE FLOWS	..	**19.4**	**42.8**	**40.1**	**37.5**	**44.1**	**54.2**	**45.9**	**37.2**	**45.5**
Net flow of long-term debt (ex. IMF)	..	-0.4	7.7	3.6	0.2	0.8	0.7	0.1	0.0	11.5
Foreign direct investment (net)	..	0.0	13.0	26.0	26.0	30.0	31.0	33.0	30.0	27.0
Portfolio equity flows	..	0.0	0.0	0.0	0.0	0.0	0.0	0.0	0.0	0.0
Grants (excluding technical coop.)	..	19.7	22.0	10.5	11.3	13.3	22.5	12.7	7.2	7.1
Memo: technical coop. grants	..	24.7	22.3	25.4	23.3	27.7	21.5	18.1	2.0	22.1
official net resource flows	..	19.4	30.0	14.3	11.7	14.3	23.4	13.0	7.3	18.6
private net resource flows	..	0.0	12.8	25.8	25.8	29.8	30.8	32.9	29.9	26.9
NET TRANSFERS	..	**19.2**	**26.8**	**9.3**	**6.5**	**10.5**	**19.6**	**13.3**	**1.6**	**8.9**
Interest on long-term debt	..	0.2	0.7	0.6	0.5	0.7	0.7	0.7	0.6	0.6
Profit remittances on FDI	..	0.0	15.2	30.2	30.4	33.0	34.0	32.0	35.0	36.0
Memo: official net transfers	..	19.2	29.4	13.8	11.2	13.7	22.8	12.4	6.7	18.0
private net transfers	..	0.0	-2.6	-4.5	-4.7	-3.2	-3.2	0.9	-5.1	-9.1
3. MAJOR ECONOMIC AGGREGATES										
Gross national product (GNP)	..	95.9	162.6	174.6	181.0	190.7	216.8	231.2	233.4	223.2
Exports of goods & services (XGS)	..	..	112.7	112.1	106.2	118.9	129.1	138.8	138.5	181.8
of which workers remittances	..	..	6.9	6.8	4.9	5.8	6.1	0.0	0.0	11.4
Imports of goods & services (MGS)	..	..	136.5	141.1	138.2	155.5	164.5	165.2	160.6	158.3
International reserves (RES)	..	..	37.7	42.5	45.6	43.6	48.3	43.9	37.3	44.7
Current account balance	..	..	-6.2	-9.7	-11.7	-18.5	-18.2	-26.9	-19.3	4.5
4. DEBT INDICATORS										
EDT / XGS (%)	..	..	35.7	36.0	39.9	39.1	37.3	33.9	34.6	34.8
EDT / GNP (%)	..	4.3	24.7	23.1	23.4	24.4	22.2	20.4	20.5	28.3
TDS / XGS (%)	..	..	2.1	1.3	1.4	1.6	1.5	1.4	1.6	0.9
INT / XGS (%)	..	..	1.3	0.5	0.7	0.8	0.8	0.7	1.0	0.6
INT / GNP (%)	..	0.2	0.9	0.3	0.4	0.5	0.5	0.4	0.6	0.5
RES / EDT (%)	..	..	93.8	105.1	107.5	93.7	100.2	93.3	77.9	70.7
RES / MGS (months)	..	..	3.3	3.6	4.0	3.4	3.5	3.2	2.8	3.4
Short-term / EDT (%)	..	0.0	23.9	2.0	7.1	10.8	10.4	10.6	18.8	14.2
Concessional / EDT (%)	..	78.1	62.7	89.1	86.3	84.3	85.9	87.1	79.8	85.0
Multilateral / EDT (%)	..	0.0	39.6	64.9	63.4	64.3	64.7	65.8	60.5	70.1

VANUATU

(US$ million, unless otherwise indicated)

	1970	1980	1990	1992	1993	1994	1995	1996	1997	1998
5. LONG-TERM DEBT										
DEBT OUTSTANDING (LDOD)	..	**4.1**	**30.6**	**39.6**	**39.4**	**41.5**	**43.2**	**42.1**	**38.9**	**54.2**
Public and publicly guaranteed	..	**4.1**	**30.6**	**39.6**	**39.4**	**41.5**	**43.2**	**42.1**	**38.9**	**54.2**
Official creditors	..	3.9	29.1	38.6	38.6	40.9	42.8	41.8	38.8	54.2
Multilateral	..	0.0	15.9	26.2	26.9	29.9	31.2	31.0	29.0	44.3
Concessional	..	0.0	12.9	24.5	25.7	29.0	30.5	30.7	29.0	44.3
Bilateral	..	3.9	13.3	12.4	11.7	11.0	11.6	10.9	9.7	9.9
Concessional	..	3.2	12.3	11.5	10.9	10.2	10.9	10.3	9.2	9.4
Private creditors	..	0.2	1.5	1.0	0.8	0.6	0.4	0.3	0.2	0.1
Bonds	..	0.0	0.0	0.0	0.0	0.0	0.0	0.0	0.0	0.0
Commercial banks	..	0.0	0.0	0.0	0.0	0.0	0.0	0.0	0.0	0.0
Other private	..	0.2	1.5	1.0	0.8	0.6	0.4	0.3	0.2	0.1
Private nonguaranteed	..	**0.0**	**0.0**	**0.0**	**0.0**	**0.0**	**0.0**	**0.0**	**0.0**	**0.0**
Bonds	..	0.0	0.0	0.0	0.0	0.0	0.0	0.0	0.0	0.0
Commercial banks	..	0.0	0.0	0.0	0.0	0.0	0.0	0.0	0.0	0.0
Memo:										
IBRD	0.0	0.0	0.0	0.0	0.0	0.0	0.0	0.0	0.0	0.0
IDA	0.0	0.0	4.0	11.1	11.4	12.5	13.2	13.2	13.0	14.1
DISBURSEMENTS	..	**0.0**	**8.7**	**4.5**	**1.1**	**1.8**	**1.6**	**1.1**	**0.9**	**12.1**
Public and publicly guaranteed	..	**0.0**	**8.7**	**4.5**	**1.1**	**1.8**	**1.6**	**1.1**	**0.9**	**12.1**
Official creditors	..	0.0	8.7	4.5	1.1	1.8	1.6	1.1	0.9	12.1
Multilateral	..	0.0	3.3	3.5	1.0	1.6	1.4	1.0	0.8	12.1
Concessional	..	0.0	3.3	3.5	1.0	1.6	1.4	1.0	0.8	12.1
Bilateral	..	0.0	5.4	1.0	0.1	0.2	0.2	0.2	0.1	0.0
Concessional	..	0.0	5.3	1.0	0.1	0.2	0.2	0.2	0.1	0.0
Private creditors	..	0.0	0.0	0.0	0.0	0.0	0.0	0.0	0.0	0.0
Bonds	..	0.0	0.0	0.0	0.0	0.0	0.0	0.0	0.0	0.0
Commercial banks	..	0.0	0.0	0.0	0.0	0.0	0.0	0.0	0.0	0.0
Other private	..	0.0	0.0	0.0	0.0	0.0	0.0	0.0	0.0	0.0
Private nonguaranteed	..	**0.0**	**0.0**	**0.0**	**0.0**	**0.0**	**0.0**	**0.0**	**0.0**	**0.0**
Bonds	..	0.0	0.0	0.0	0.0	0.0	0.0	0.0	0.0	0.0
Commercial banks	..	0.0	0.0	0.0	0.0	0.0	0.0	0.0	0.0	0.0
Memo:										
IBRD	0.0	0.0	0.0	0.0	0.0	0.0	0.0	0.0	0.0	0.0
IDA	0.0	0.0	0.8	3.0	0.3	0.5	0.4	0.5	0.6	0.6
PRINCIPAL REPAYMENTS	..	**0.4**	**1.0**	**0.9**	**0.9**	**1.0**	**0.9**	**1.0**	**0.9**	**0.6**
Public and publicly guaranteed	..	**0.4**	**1.0**	**0.9**	**0.9**	**1.0**	**0.9**	**1.0**	**0.9**	**0.6**
Official creditors	..	0.3	0.8	0.7	0.7	0.8	0.7	0.8	0.8	0.5
Multilateral	..	0.0	0.5	0.5	0.5	0.4	0.4	0.5	0.4	0.2
Concessional	..	0.0	0.0	0.0	0.0	0.1	0.1	0.2	0.2	0.2
Bilateral	..	0.3	0.3	0.2	0.2	0.3	0.4	0.4	0.3	0.3
Concessional	..	0.3	0.2	0.1	0.1	0.3	0.3	0.3	0.3	0.2
Private creditors	..	0.0	0.2	0.2	0.2	0.2	0.2	0.1	0.1	0.1
Bonds	..	0.0	0.0	0.0	0.0	0.0	0.0	0.0	0.0	0.0
Commercial banks	..	0.0	0.0	0.0	0.0	0.0	0.0	0.0	0.0	0.0
Other private	..	0.0	0.2	0.2	0.2	0.2	0.2	0.1	0.1	0.1
Private nonguaranteed	..	**0.0**	**0.0**	**0.0**	**0.0**	**0.0**	**0.0**	**0.0**	**0.0**	**0.0**
Bonds	..	0.0	0.0	0.0	0.0	0.0	0.0	0.0	0.0	0.0
Commercial banks	..	0.0	0.0	0.0	0.0	0.0	0.0	0.0	0.0	0.0
Memo:										
IBRD	0.0	0.0	0.0	0.0	0.0	0.0	0.0	0.0	0.0	0.0
IDA	0.0	0.0	0.0	0.0	0.0	0.0	0.0	0.0	0.0	0.0
NET FLOWS ON DEBT	..	**-0.4**	**7.7**	**3.6**	**0.2**	**0.8**	**0.7**	**0.1**	**0.0**	**11.5**
Public and publicly guaranteed	..	**-0.4**	**7.7**	**3.6**	**0.2**	**0.8**	**0.7**	**0.1**	**0.0**	**11.5**
Official creditors	..	-0.3	8.0	3.8	0.4	1.0	0.9	0.3	0.1	11.5
Multilateral	..	0.0	2.8	3.0	0.6	1.1	1.0	0.5	0.4	11.8
Concessional	..	0.0	3.3	3.5	1.0	1.5	1.3	0.8	0.7	11.8
Bilateral	..	-0.3	5.2	0.8	-0.1	-0.1	-0.1	-0.2	-0.2	-0.3
Concessional	..	-0.3	5.2	0.9	-0.1	0.0	-0.1	-0.1	-0.2	-0.2
Private creditors	..	0.0	-0.2	-0.2	-0.2	-0.2	-0.2	-0.1	-0.1	-0.1
Bonds	..	0.0	0.0	0.0	0.0	0.0	0.0	0.0	0.0	0.0
Commercial banks	..	0.0	0.0	0.0	0.0	0.0	0.0	0.0	0.0	0.0
Other private	..	0.0	-0.2	-0.2	-0.2	-0.2	-0.2	-0.1	-0.1	-0.1
Private nonguaranteed	..	**0.0**	**0.0**	**0.0**	**0.0**	**0.0**	**0.0**	**0.0**	**0.0**	**0.0**
Bonds	..	0.0	0.0	0.0	0.0	0.0	0.0	0.0	0.0	0.0
Commercial banks	..	0.0	0.0	0.0	0.0	0.0	0.0	0.0	0.0	0.0
Memo:										
IBRD	0.0	0.0	0.0	0.0	0.0	0.0	0.0	0.0	0.0	0.0
IDA	0.0	0.0	0.8	3.0	0.3	0.5	0.4	0.5	0.5	0.6

VANUATU

(US$ million, unless otherwise indicated)

	1970	1980	1990	1992	1993	1994	1995	1996	1997	1998
INTEREST PAYMENTS (LINT)	..	**0.2**	**0.7**	**0.6**	**0.5**	**0.7**	**0.7**	**0.7**	**0.6**	**0.6**
Public and publicly guaranteed	..	**0.2**	**0.7**	**0.6**	**0.5**	**0.7**	**0.7**	**0.7**	**0.6**	**0.6**
Official creditors	..	0.2	0.6	0.5	0.5	0.6	0.6	0.6	0.6	0.6
Multilateral	..	0.0	0.2	0.3	0.3	0.3	0.3	0.3	0.3	0.3
Concessional	..	0.0	0.1	0.2	0.2	0.2	0.3	0.3	0.2	0.3
Bilateral	..	0.2	0.4	0.2	0.2	0.3	0.4	0.3	0.3	0.3
Concessional	..	0.2	0.3	0.1	0.1	0.3	0.3	0.3	0.3	0.3
Private creditors	..	0.0	0.2	0.1	0.1	0.0	0.0	0.0	0.0	0.0
Bonds	..	0.0	0.0	0.0	0.0	0.0	0.0	0.0	0.0	0.0
Commercial banks	..	0.0	0.0	0.0	0.0	0.0	0.0	0.0	0.0	0.0
Other private	..	0.0	0.2	0.1	0.1	0.0	0.0	0.0	0.0	0.0
Private nonguaranteed	..	**0.0**	**0.0**	**0.0**	**0.0**	**0.0**	**0.0**	**0.0**	**0.0**	**0.0**
Bonds	..	0.0	0.0	0.0	0.0	0.0	0.0	0.0	0.0	0.0
Commercial banks	..	0.0	0.0	0.0	0.0	0.0	0.0	0.0	0.0	0.0
Memo:										
IBRD	0.0	0.0	0.0	0.0	0.0	0.0	0.0	0.0	0.0	0.0
IDA	0.0	0.0	0.0	0.1	0.1	0.1	0.1	0.1	0.1	0.1
NET TRANSFERS ON DEBT	..	**-0.6**	**7.0**	**3.0**	**-0.3**	**0.2**	**0.0**	**-0.5**	**-0.6**	**10.9**
Public and publicly guaranteed	..	**-0.6**	**7.0**	**3.0**	**-0.3**	**0.2**	**0.0**	**-0.5**	**-0.6**	**10.9**
Official creditors	..	-0.6	7.4	3.3	0.0	0.4	0.2	-0.3	-0.4	11.0
Multilateral	..	0.0	2.6	2.7	0.3	0.9	0.7	0.2	0.1	11.5
Concessional	..	0.0	3.2	3.3	0.8	1.3	1.1	0.5	0.4	11.5
Bilateral	..	-0.6	4.8	0.6	-0.3	-0.5	-0.5	-0.5	-0.6	-0.6
Concessional	..	-0.4	4.8	0.7	-0.2	-0.3	-0.4	-0.4	-0.5	-0.5
Private creditors	..	0.0	-0.4	-0.3	-0.3	-0.3	-0.2	-0.2	-0.1	-0.1
Bonds	..	0.0	0.0	0.0	0.0	0.0	0.0	0.0	0.0	0.0
Commercial banks	..	0.0	0.0	0.0	0.0	0.0	0.0	0.0	0.0	0.0
Other private	..	0.0	-0.4	-0.3	-0.3	-0.3	-0.2	-0.2	-0.1	-0.1
Private nonguaranteed	..	**0.0**	**0.0**	**0.0**	**0.0**	**0.0**	**0.0**	**0.0**	**0.0**	**0.0**
Bonds	..	0.0	0.0	0.0	0.0	0.0	0.0	0.0	0.0	0.0
Commercial banks	..	0.0	0.0	0.0	0.0	0.0	0.0	0.0	0.0	0.0
Memo:										
IBRD	0.0	0.0	0.0	0.0	0.0	0.0	0.0	0.0	0.0	0.0
IDA	0.0	0.0	0.8	2.9	0.2	0.4	0.3	0.4	0.4	0.5
DEBT SERVICE (LTDS)	..	**0.6**	**1.7**	**1.4**	**1.4**	**1.6**	**1.6**	**1.6**	**1.4**	**1.2**
Public and publicly guaranteed	..	**0.6**	**1.7**	**1.4**	**1.4**	**1.6**	**1.6**	**1.6**	**1.4**	**1.2**
Official creditors	..	0.6	1.3	1.1	1.1	1.4	1.4	1.5	1.3	1.1
Multilateral	..	0.0	0.7	0.8	0.7	0.7	0.7	0.8	0.7	0.5
Concessional	..	0.0	0.1	0.2	0.3	0.3	0.3	0.4	0.4	0.5
Bilateral	..	0.6	0.7	0.4	0.4	0.7	0.7	0.7	0.6	0.6
Concessional	..	0.4	0.5	0.2	0.3	0.5	0.6	0.6	0.5	0.5
Private creditors	..	0.0	0.4	0.3	0.3	0.3	0.2	0.2	0.1	0.1
Bonds	..	0.0	0.0	0.0	0.0	0.0	0.0	0.0	0.0	0.0
Commercial banks	..	0.0	0.0	0.0	0.0	0.0	0.0	0.0	0.0	0.0
Other private	..	0.0	0.4	0.3	0.3	0.3	0.2	0.2	0.1	0.1
Private nonguaranteed	..	**0.0**	**0.0**	**0.0**	**0.0**	**0.0**	**0.0**	**0.0**	**0.0**	**0.0**
Bonds	..	0.0	0.0	0.0	0.0	0.0	0.0	0.0	0.0	0.0
Commercial banks	..	0.0	0.0	0.0	0.0	0.0	0.0	0.0	0.0	0.0
Memo:										
IBRD	0.0	0.0	0.0	0.0	0.0	0.0	0.0	0.0	0.0	0.0
IDA	0.0	0.0	0.0	0.1	0.1	0.1	0.1	0.1	0.1	0.1
UNDISBURSED DEBT	..	**0.0**	**18.1**	**12.5**	**11.4**	**9.8**	**8.4**	**15.4**	**13.1**	**22.0**
Official creditors	..	0.0	18.1	12.5	11.4	9.8	8.4	15.4	13.1	22.0
Private creditors	..	0.0	0.0	0.0	0.0	0.0	0.0	0.0	0.0	0.0
Memorandum items										
Concessional LDOD	..	3.2	25.1	35.9	36.6	39.2	41.4	40.9	38.2	53.7
Variable rate LDOD	..	0.0	0.8	0.6	0.5	0.5	0.4	0.3	0.2	0.1
Public sector LDOD	..	4.1	30.6	39.6	39.4	41.5	43.2	42.1	38.9	54.2
Private sector LDOD	..	0.0	0.0	0.0	0.0	0.0	0.0	0.0	0.0	0.0
6. CURRENCY COMPOSITION OF LONG-TERM DEBT (PERCENT)										
Deutsche mark	..	0.0	0.0	0.0	0.0	0.0	0.0	0.0	0.0	0.0
French franc	..	82.5	33.3	18.2	17.0	17.6	18.1	17.1	15.9	12.0
Japanese yen	..	0.0	0.0	0.0	0.0	0.0	0.0	0.0	0.0	0.0
Pound sterling	..	14.6	0.7	0.3	0.3	0.2	0.0	0.0	0.0	0.0
Swiss franc	..	0.0	0.0	0.0	0.0	0.0	0.0	0.0	0.0	0.0
U.S.dollars	..	0.0	20.9	38.4	39.1	40.0	39.3	40.3	42.1	57.2
Multiple currency	..	0.0	28.7	28.0	30.0	33.2	33.8	34.6	34.2	25.4
Special drawing rights	..	0.0	0.0	0.0	0.0	0.0	0.0	0.0	0.0	0.0
All other currencies	..	2.9	16.4	15.1	13.6	9.0	8.8	8.0	7.8	5.4

VANUATU

(US$ million, unless otherwise indicated)

	1970	1980	1990	1992	1993	1994	1995	1996	1997	1998
7. DEBT RESTRUCTURINGS										
Total amount rescheduled	..	..	0.0	0.0	0.0	0.0	0.0	0.0	0.0	0.0
Debt stock rescheduled	..	..	0.0	0.0	0.0	0.0	0.0	0.0	0.0	0.0
Principal rescheduled	..	..	0.0	0.0	0.0	0.0	0.0	0.0	0.0	0.0
Official	..	..	0.0	0.0	0.0	0.0	0.0	0.0	0.0	0.0
Private	..	..	0.0	0.0	0.0	0.0	0.0	0.0	0.0	0.0
Interest rescheduled	..	..	0.0	0.0	0.0	0.0	0.0	0.0	0.0	0.0
Official	..	..	0.0	0.0	0.0	0.0	0.0	0.0	0.0	0.0
Private	..	..	0.0	0.0	0.0	0.0	0.0	0.0	0.0	0.0
Debt forgiven	..	..	0.0	0.0	0.0	0.0	0.0	0.0	0.0	0.0
Memo: interest forgiven	..	..	0.0	0.0	0.0	0.0	0.0	0.0	0.0	0.0
Debt stock reduction	..	..	0.0	0.0	0.0	0.0	0.0	0.0	0.0	0.0
of which debt buyback	..	..	0.0	0.0	0.0	0.0	0.0	0.0	0.0	0.0
8. DEBT STOCK-FLOW RECONCILIATION										
Total change in debt stocks	..	..	9.9	1.1	1.9	4.1	1.7	-1.1	0.8	15.3
Net flows on debt	..	-0.4	7.8	3.2	2.4	2.8	0.7	0.1	4.0	11.5
Net change in interest arrears	..	..	0.0	0.0	0.0	0.0	0.0	0.0	0.0	0.0
Interest capitalized	..	..	0.0	0.0	0.0	0.0	0.0	0.0	0.0	0.0
Debt forgiveness or reduction	..	..	0.0	0.0	0.0	0.0	0.0	0.0	0.0	0.0
Cross-currency valuation	..	..	1.6	-0.9	-0.6	-0.1	0.8	-0.5	-0.8	0.4
Residual	..	..	0.5	-1.2	0.1	1.4	0.2	-0.7	-2.4	3.5
9. AVERAGE TERMS OF NEW COMMITMENTS										
ALL CREDITORS										
Interest (%)	..	0.0	0.0	1.0	0.0	0.0	0.0	3.5	0.0	3.3
Maturity (years)	..	0.0	0.0	39.5	0.0	0.0	0.0	39.9	0.0	39.6
Grace period (years)	..	0.0	0.0	10.0	0.0	0.0	0.0	10.4	0.0	10.1
Grant element (%)	..	0.0	0.0	78.1	0.0	0.0	0.0	56.0	0.0	57.7
Official creditors										
Interest (%)	..	0.0	0.0	1.0	0.0	0.0	0.0	3.5	0.0	3.3
Maturity (years)	..	0.0	0.0	39.5	0.0	0.0	0.0	39.9	0.0	39.6
Grace period (years)	..	0.0	0.0	10.0	0.0	0.0	0.0	10.4	0.0	10.1
Grant element (%)	..	0.0	0.0	78.1	0.0	0.0	0.0	56.0	0.0	57.7
Private creditors										
Interest (%)	..	0.0	0.0	0.0	0.0	0.0	0.0	0.0	0.0	0.0
Maturity (years)	..	0.0	0.0	0.0	0.0	0.0	0.0	0.0	0.0	0.0
Grace period (years)	..	0.0	0.0	0.0	0.0	0.0	0.0	0.0	0.0	0.0
Grant element (%)	..	0.0	0.0	0.0	0.0	0.0	0.0	0.0	0.0	0.0
Memorandum items										
Commitments	..	0.0	0.0	5.2	0.0	0.0	0.0	9.9	0.0	20.5
Official creditors	..	0.0	0.0	5.2	0.0	0.0	0.0	9.9	0.0	20.5
Private creditors	..	0.0	0.0	0.0	0.0	0.0	0.0	0.0	0.0	0.0

10. CONTRACTUAL OBLIGATIONS ON OUTSTANDING LONG-TERM DEBT

	1999	2000	2001	2002	2003	2004	2005	2006	2007	2008
TOTAL										
Disbursements	7.2	5.4	4.0	2.9	1.9	0.7	0.0	0.0	0.0	0.0
Principal	0.8	1.0	1.0	1.1	1.1	1.2	1.2	1.4	1.6	2.0
Interest	0.6	0.7	0.7	0.7	0.7	0.7	0.7	0.7	0.8	1.2
Official creditors										
Disbursements	7.2	5.4	4.0	2.9	1.9	0.7	0.0	0.0	0.0	0.0
Principal	0.7	1.0	1.0	1.1	1.1	1.2	1.2	1.4	1.6	2.0
Interest	0.6	0.7	0.7	0.7	0.7	0.7	0.7	0.7	0.8	1.2
Bilateral creditors										
Disbursements	0.0	0.0	0.0	0.0	0.0	0.0	0.0	0.0	0.0	0.0
Principal	0.3	0.6	0.6	0.5	0.5	0.5	0.5	0.5	0.5	0.5
Interest	0.3	0.3	0.3	0.3	0.2	0.2	0.2	0.2	0.2	0.2
Multilateral creditors										
Disbursements	7.2	5.3	4.0	2.9	1.9	0.7	0.0	0.0	0.0	0.0
Principal	0.4	0.4	0.5	0.6	0.6	0.6	0.6	0.8	1.1	1.5
Interest	0.3	0.4	0.4	0.4	0.5	0.5	0.5	0.5	0.6	1.1
Private creditors										
Disbursements	0.0	0.0	0.0	0.0	0.0	0.0	0.0	0.0	0.0	0.0
Principal	0.1	0.0	0.0	0.0	0.0	0.0	0.0	0.0	0.0	0.0
Interest	0.0	0.0	0.0	0.0	0.0	0.0	0.0	0.0	0.0	0.0
Commercial banks										
Disbursements	0.0	0.0	0.0	0.0	0.0	0.0	0.0	0.0	0.0	0.0
Principal	0.0	0.0	0.0	0.0	0.0	0.0	0.0	0.0	0.0	0.0
Interest	0.0	0.0	0.0	0.0	0.0	0.0	0.0	0.0	0.0	0.0
Other private										
Disbursements	0.0	0.0	0.0	0.0	0.0	0.0	0.0	0.0	0.0	0.0
Principal	0.1	0.0	0.0	0.0	0.0	0.0	0.0	0.0	0.0	0.0
Interest	0.0	0.0	0.0	0.0	0.0	0.0	0.0	0.0	0.0	0.0

VENEZUELA, REPUBLICA BOLIVARIANA de

(US$ million, unless otherwise indicated)

	1970	1980	1990	1992	1993	1994	1995	1996	1997	1998
1. SUMMARY DEBT DATA										
TOTAL DEBT STOCKS (EDT)	..	**29,344**	**33,170**	**37,848**	**37,539**	**36,853**	**35,848**	**35,360**	**35,558**	**37,003**
Long-term debt (LDOD)	**954**	**13,795**	**28,159**	**29,628**	**30,177**	**30,478**	**30,514**	**30,283**	**29,546**	**33,373**
Public and publicly guaranteed	718	10,614	24,509	25,830	26,855	28,042	28,501	28,469	26,697	26,692
Private nonguaranteed	236	3,181	3,650	3,798	3,322	2,436	2,013	1,814	2,849	6,681
Use of IMF credit	**0**	**0**	**3,012**	**2,946**	**2,680**	**2,643**	**2,239**	**2,196**	**1,618**	**1,226**
Short-term debt	..	**15,550**	**2,000**	**5,275**	**4,682**	**3,732**	**3,096**	**2,881**	**4,395**	**2,405**
of which interest arrears on LDOD	..	15	0	147	189	293	305	296	277	286
Official creditors	..	0	0	9	2	12	12	11	10	11
Private creditors	..	15	0	138	188	280	293	284	266	275
Memo: principal arrears on LDOD	..	37	0	472	834	1,249	1,301	1,241	1,168	1,213
Official creditors	..	0	0	22	48	116	116	105	95	104
Private creditors	..	37	0	450	786	1,133	1,185	1,136	1,073	1,110
Memo: export credits	..	0	2,386	5,548	6,491	7,750	5,860	4,846	3,795	4,221
TOTAL DEBT FLOWS										
Disbursements	**282**	**4,761**	**4,069**	**2,572**	**2,137**	**1,045**	**1,718**	**2,887**	**6,386**	**6,504**
Long-term debt	282	4,761	2,226	2,572	2,137	1,045	1,718	2,379	6,386	6,504
IMF purchases	0	0	1,843	0	0	0	0	508	0	0
Principal repayments	**67**	**2,972**	**1,747**	**1,194**	**1,783**	**1,573**	**2,464**	**2,365**	**6,323**	**3,463**
Long-term debt	67	2,972	1,747	1,013	1,515	1,372	2,003	1,888	5,871	3,017
IMF repurchases	0	0	0	181	268	201	462	477	452	446
Net flows on debt	**683**	**5,556**	**2,037**	**4,222**	**-281**	**-1,582**	**-1,395**	**317**	**1,596**	**1,042**
of which short-term debt	..	3,767	-284	2,844	-635	-1,054	-648	-205	1,532	-1,999
Interest payments (INT)	..	**3,065**	**3,242**	**2,137**	**2,162**	**2,115**	**2,402**	**2,138**	**2,313**	**2,418**
Long-term debt	53	1,475	2,993	1,626	1,768	1,768	2,067	1,860	2,019	2,158
IMF charges	0	0	37	229	174	141	142	100	93	72
Short-term debt	..	1,590	212	282	220	206	193	178	201	187
Net transfers on debt	..	**2,491**	**-1,205**	**2,084**	**-2,443**	**-3,697**	**-3,797**	**-1,822**	**-717**	**-1,376**
Total debt service paid (TDS)	..	**6,037**	**4,990**	**3,331**	**3,945**	**3,688**	**4,867**	**4,504**	**8,635**	**5,880**
Long-term debt	120	4,447	4,741	2,639	3,283	3,140	4,070	3,749	7,890	5,175
IMF repurchases and charges	0	0	37	410	442	342	604	577	545	518
Short-term debt (interest only)	..	1,590	212	282	220	206	193	178	201	187
2. AGGREGATE NET RESOURCE FLOWS AND NET TRANSFERS (LONG-TERM)										
NET RESOURCE FLOWS	**192**	**1,844**	**934**	**2,339**	**1,062**	**533**	**1,179**	**4,427**	**6,493**	**8,008**
Net flow of long-term debt (ex. IMF)	215	1,789	478	1,559	622	-327	-285	491	516	3,487
Foreign direct investment (net)	-23	55	451	629	372	813	985	2,183	5,536	4,435
Portfolio equity flows	0	0	0	146	59	42	461	1,740	429	64
Grants (excluding technical coop.)	0	0	5	5	9	6	18	13	12	22
Memo: technical coop. grants	6	19	27	33	33	28	35	32	30	21
official net resource flows	4	19	1,060	794	101	398	172	-167	-238	1,142
private net resource flows	187	1,825	-126	1,545	961	135	1,007	4,594	6,731	6,866
NET TRANSFERS	**-429**	**47**	**-2,283**	**205**	**-1,280**	**-1,834**	**-1,508**	**1,867**	**3,474**	**4,649**
Interest on long-term debt	53	1,475	2,993	1,626	1,768	1,768	2,067	1,860	2,019	2,158
Profit remittances on FDI	568	322	224	507	574	600	620	700	1,000	1,200
Memo: official net transfers	-16	-16	989	566	-167	128	-124	-444	-477	919
private net transfers	-413	63	-3,272	-361	-1,113	-1,962	-1,384	2,310	3,951	3,731
3. MAJOR ECONOMIC AGGREGATES										
Gross national product (GNP)	12,865	69,703	47,149	58,944	58,265	56,538	75,400	68,543	86,435	93,342
Exports of goods & services (XGS)	2,833	22,232	21,464	17,121	17,718	19,307	22,620	26,859	27,331	21,449
of which workers remittances	0	0	..	..	0	..	..	0	0	..
Imports of goods & services (MGS)	2,845	17,065	12,883	20,496	19,343	16,682	20,715	18,083	23,720	23,857
International reserves (RES)	1,047	13,360	12,733	13,381	13,693	12,459	10,715	16,020	17,704	14,729
Current account balance	-104	4,728	8,279	-3,749	-1,993	2,541	2,014	8,914	3,467	-2,562
4. DEBT INDICATORS										
EDT / XGS (%)	..	132.0	154.5	221.1	211.9	190.9	158.5	131.7	130.1	172.5
EDT / GNP (%)	..	42.1	70.4	64.2	64.4	65.2	47.5	51.6	41.1	39.6
TDS / XGS (%)	..	27.2	23.3	19.5	22.3	19.1	21.5	16.8	31.6	27.4
INT / XGS (%)	..	13.8	15.1	12.5	12.2	11.0	10.6	8.0	8.5	11.3
INT / GNP (%)	..	4.4	6.9	3.6	3.7	3.7	3.2	3.1	2.7	2.6
RES / EDT (%)	..	45.5	38.4	35.4	36.5	33.8	29.9	45.3	49.8	39.8
RES / MGS (months)	4.4	9.4	11.9	7.8	8.5	9.0	6.2	10.6	9.0	7.4
Short-term / EDT (%)	..	53.0	6.0	13.9	12.5	10.1	8.6	8.2	12.4	6.5
Concessional / EDT (%)	..	0.2	0.3	0.2	0.2	0.3	0.3	0.3	0.2	0.2
Multilateral / EDT (%)	..	0.7	4.9	7.2	7.7	8.5	9.2	7.9	7.0	8.4

VENEZUELA, REPUBLICA BOLIVARIANA de

(US$ million, unless otherwise indicated)

	1970	1980	1990	1992	1993	1994	1995	1996	1997	1998
5. LONG-TERM DEBT										
DEBT OUTSTANDING (LDOD)	**954**	**13,795**	**28,159**	**29,628**	**30,177**	**30,478**	**30,514**	**30,283**	**29,546**	**33,373**
Public and publicly guaranteed	**718**	**10,614**	**24,509**	**25,830**	**26,855**	**28,042**	**28,501**	**28,469**	**26,697**	**26,692**
Official creditors	366	571	1,932	3,548	3,769	4,477	4,703	4,073	3,507	4,770
Multilateral	244	216	1,639	2,728	2,884	3,133	3,300	2,790	2,492	3,107
Concessional	1	42	12	8	7	5	4	3	1	0
Bilateral	122	355	293	820	884	1,344	1,403	1,284	1,015	1,663
Concessional	81	8	73	67	64	86	96	102	84	79
Private creditors	352	10,043	22,577	22,282	23,087	23,565	23,798	24,395	23,190	21,922
Bonds	37	1,261	19,644	20,099	20,998	21,061	20,885	20,660	19,560	18,719
Commercial banks	237	8,159	364	202	289	585	1,158	1,985	1,982	1,742
Other private	78	623	2,569	1,981	1,799	1,920	1,755	1,750	1,648	1,462
Private nonguaranteed	**236**	**3,181**	**3,650**	**3,798**	**3,322**	**2,436**	**2,013**	**1,814**	**2,849**	**6,681**
Bonds	0	0	0	174	264	114	114	134	319	2,694
Commercial banks	236	3,181	3,650	3,624	3,058	2,322	1,899	1,680	2,530	3,987
Memo:										
IBRD	217	133	974	1,479	1,529	1,653	1,639	1,408	1,213	1,219
IDA	0	0	0	0	0	0	0	0	0	0
DISBURSEMENTS	**282**	**4,761**	**2,226**	**2,572**	**2,137**	**1,045**	**1,718**	**2,379**	**6,386**	**6,504**
Public and publicly guaranteed	**216**	**2,870**	**2,226**	**1,714**	**1,877**	**1,045**	**1,638**	**1,981**	**5,126**	**2,231**
Official creditors	30	88	1,103	838	173	493	529	265	204	1,578
Multilateral	21	3	1,035	597	126	103	267	74	176	846
Concessional	1	2	0	0	0	0	0	0	0	0
Bilateral	10	85	69	241	47	391	262	191	29	732
Concessional	0	0	15	0	2	19	16	20	0	0
Private creditors	186	2,782	1,122	876	1,704	552	1,109	1,716	4,922	653
Bonds	0	276	599	757	1,500	0	349	432	4,515	500
Commercial banks	140	2,362	26	82	123	304	586	944	225	152
Other private	46	144	497	37	81	248	174	340	182	1
Private nonguaranteed	**67**	**1,891**	**0**	**858**	**260**	**0**	**80**	**398**	**1,260**	**4,272**
Bonds	0	0	0	174	90	0	0	95	200	2,450
Commercial banks	67	1,891	0	684	170	0	80	303	1,060	1,822
Memo:										
IBRD	15	1	840	177	20	20	47	48	91	188
IDA	0	0	0	0	0	0	0	0	0	0
PRINCIPAL REPAYMENTS	**67**	**2,972**	**1,747**	**1,013**	**1,515**	**1,372**	**2,003**	**1,888**	**5,871**	**3,017**
Public and publicly guaranteed	**42**	**1,737**	**1,574**	**303**	**779**	**486**	**1,500**	**1,291**	**5,646**	**2,577**
Official creditors	26	68	49	49	80	101	375	445	454	459
Multilateral	13	33	8	17	33	65	202	272	271	289
Concessional	0	3	3	1	1	1	1	1	1	1
Bilateral	13	35	41	32	47	36	173	173	183	170
Concessional	4	6	0	1	0	4	12	8	9	8
Private creditors	16	1,668	1,526	254	699	386	1,125	847	5,192	2,118
Bonds	1	13	254	53	466	145	677	503	4,873	1,467
Commercial banks	5	1,324	706	23	27	32	46	54	115	430
Other private	10	331	566	178	206	208	402	290	204	221
Private nonguaranteed	**25**	**1,235**	**173**	**710**	**736**	**886**	**503**	**597**	**225**	**440**
Bonds	0	0	0	0	0	150	0	75	15	75
Commercial banks	25	1,235	173	710	736	736	503	522	210	365
Memo:										
IBRD	10	23	0	0	0	0	116	169	172	179
IDA	0	0	0	0	0	0	0	0	0	0
NET FLOWS ON DEBT	**215**	**1,789**	**478**	**1,559**	**622**	**-327**	**-285**	**491**	**516**	**3,487**
Public and publicly guaranteed	**174**	**1,133**	**651**	**1,411**	**1,098**	**559**	**138**	**690**	**-519**	**-345**
Official creditors	4	20	1,055	789	93	393	154	-180	-250	1,119
Multilateral	8	-30	1,027	580	92	38	65	-198	-96	557
Concessional	1	-1	-3	-1	-1	-1	-1	-1	-1	-1
Bilateral	-4	50	28	209	0	355	89	18	-154	563
Concessional	-4	-6	15	-1	2	15	4	12	-9	-8
Private creditors	169	1,114	-404	622	1,005	166	-16	869	-269	-1,465
Bonds	-1	263	345	704	1,035	-145	-328	-71	-358	-967
Commercial banks	134	1,038	-680	59	96	272	540	890	110	-278
Other private	36	-187	-69	-141	-126	40	-228	50	-22	-220
Private nonguaranteed	**41**	**656**	**-173**	**148**	**-476**	**-886**	**-423**	**-199**	**1,035**	**3,832**
Bonds	0	0	0	174	90	-150	0	20	185	2,375
Commercial banks	41	656	-173	-26	-566	-736	-423	-219	850	1,457
Memo:										
IBRD	6	-22	840	177	20	20	-69	-121	-81	8
IDA	0	0	0	0	0	0	0	0	0	0

VENEZUELA, REPUBLICA BOLIVARIANA de

(US$ million, unless otherwise indicated)

	1970	1980	1990	1992	1993	1994	1995	1996	1997	1998
INTEREST PAYMENTS (LINT)	**53**	**1,475**	**2,993**	**1,626**	**1,768**	**1,768**	**2,067**	**1,860**	**2,019**	**2,158**
Public and publicly guaranteed	**40**	**1,218**	**2,593**	**1,526**	**1,521**	**1,636**	**1,956**	**1,819**	**1,831**	**1,896**
Official creditors	20	36	71	228	268	270	296	277	240	223
Multilateral	15	18	59	187	212	231	231	226	191	181
Concessional	0	2	0	0	0	0	0	0	0	0
Bilateral	5	18	12	41	56	40	66	51	49	42
Concessional	3	1	0	1	1	2	3	3	4	4
Private creditors	20	1,183	2,522	1,298	1,253	1,365	1,660	1,542	1,592	1,673
Bonds	3	61	135	1,255	1,179	1,307	1,518	1,402	1,422	1,502
Commercial banks	16	1,052	2,198	6	6	19	65	86	126	132
Other private	2	70	189	37	68	40	77	54	45	40
Private nonguaranteed	**13**	**257**	**400**	**100**	**246**	**132**	**111**	**42**	**188**	**262**
Bonds	0	0	0	2	14	20	10	10	11	31
Commercial banks	13	257	400	98	232	112	101	32	177	231
Memo:										
IBRD	13	12	19	106	111	115	120	108	87	77
IDA	0	0	0	0	0	0	0	0	0	0
NET TRANSFERS ON DEBT	**162**	**314**	**-2,515**	**-68**	**-1,146**	**-2,094**	**-2,352**	**-1,370**	**-1,503**	**1,328**
Public and publicly guaranteed	**134**	**-85**	**-1,942**	**-115**	**-424**	**-1,077**	**-1,818**	**-1,129**	**-2,350**	**-2,242**
Official creditors	-16	-16	984	561	-176	122	-142	-457	-489	897
Multilateral	-7	-48	968	393	-120	-193	-166	-424	-286	376
Concessional	1	-3	-4	-2	-2	-2	-2	-1	-1	-1
Bilateral	-9	32	16	168	-56	315	23	-33	-203	521
Concessional	-6	-6	15	-2	1	13	2	10	-13	-12
Private creditors	150	-69	-2,926	-676	-248	-1,199	-1,676	-672	-1,861	-3,138
Bonds	-4	202	210	-550	-145	-1,452	-1,846	-1,472	-1,779	-2,469
Commercial banks	119	-15	-2,878	53	90	253	475	804	-16	-409
Other private	35	-256	-258	-178	-193	0	-305	-4	-66	-260
Private nonguaranteed	**28**	**399**	**-573**	**48**	**-722**	**-1,018**	**-534**	**-241**	**847**	**3,570**
Bonds	0	0	0	172	76	-170	-10	10	174	2,344
Commercial banks	28	399	-573	-124	-798	-848	-524	-251	673	1,226
Memo:										
IBRD	-7	-35	821	71	-91	-95	-189	-229	-168	-68
IDA	0	0	0	0	0	0	0	0	0	0
DEBT SERVICE (LTDS)	**120**	**4,447**	**4,741**	**2,639**	**3,283**	**3,140**	**4,070**	**3,749**	**7,890**	**5,175**
Public and publicly guaranteed	**82**	**2,955**	**4,168**	**1,829**	**2,301**	**2,122**	**3,456**	**3,110**	**7,477**	**4,473**
Official creditors	46	104	119	277	349	371	671	722	694	682
Multilateral	28	51	67	204	246	296	433	498	462	470
Concessional	0	5	4	2	2	2	2	1	1	1
Bilateral	18	53	53	73	103	76	238	223	232	212
Concessional	6	6	0	2	1	6	14	10	13	12
Private creditors	36	2,851	4,048	1,552	1,952	1,751	2,785	2,388	6,783	3,791
Bonds	4	74	389	1,308	1,645	1,452	2,195	1,904	6,294	2,969
Commercial banks	21	2,377	2,905	29	33	51	110	140	241	561
Other private	11	401	755	216	274	248	479	344	248	261
Private nonguaranteed	**38**	**1,492**	**573**	**810**	**982**	**1,018**	**614**	**639**	**413**	**702**
Bonds	0	0	0	2	14	170	10	85	26	106
Commercial banks	38	1,492	573	808	968	848	604	554	387	596
Memo:										
IBRD	23	35	19	106	111	115	235	277	259	256
IDA	0	0	0	0	0	0	0	0	0	0
UNDISBURSED DEBT	**196**	**364**	**2,986**	**3,395**	**3,562**	**3,199**	**2,518**	**2,198**	**2,212**	**3,800**
Official creditors	106	101	1,567	2,207	2,670	2,619	2,294	2,162	2,210	2,494
Private creditors	90	263	1,419	1,188	893	580	224	37	2	1,306
Memorandum items										
Concessional LDOD	82	50	84	75	71	91	100	105	85	79
Variable rate LDOD	255	11,224	17,448	18,592	17,997	17,768	17,844	18,128	18,398	21,270
Public sector LDOD	682	10,277	24,508	25,523	26,110	27,280	27,926	27,908	26,217	26,218
Private sector LDOD	272	3,518	3,650	4,104	4,067	3,198	2,588	2,375	3,329	7,155

6. CURRENCY COMPOSITION OF LONG-TERM DEBT (PERCENT)

	1970	1980	1990	1992	1993	1994	1995	1996	1997	1998
Deutsche mark	5.2	7.8	6.9	5.7	6.5	6.9	9.6	10.2	8.7	6.7
French franc	1.5	1.9	4.1	2.7	2.3	2.6	2.6	2.3	1.9	1.8
Japanese yen	0.0	4.9	0.6	2.8	2.6	4.0	4.2	3.7	3.1	3.0
Pound sterling	0.1	0.0	1.5	1.3	1.3	1.3	1.2	1.4	1.3	1.2
Swiss franc	4.6	0.0	0.9	0.6	0.6	0.7	0.7	0.6	0.6	0.6
U.S.dollars	54.3	82.8	78.2	75.6	75.1	72.1	68.4	70.2	73.3	79.8
Multiple currency	32.0	2.3	6.5	10.4	10.6	11.1	11.5	9.8	9.3	5.3
Special drawing rights	0.0	0.0	0.0	0.0	0.0	0.0	0.0	0.0	0.0	0.0
All other currencies	2.3	0.3	1.3	0.9	1.0	1.3	1.8	1.8	1.8	1.6

VENEZUELA, REPUBLICA BOLIVARIANA de

(US$ million, unless otherwise indicated)

	1970	1980	1990	1992	1993	1994	1995	1996	1997	1998
7. DEBT RESTRUCTURINGS										
Total amount rescheduled	..	..	17,659	0	0	0	0	0	0	0
Debt stock rescheduled	..	..	17,630	0	0	0	0	0	0	0
Principal rescheduled	..	..	0	0	0	0	0	0	0	0
Official	..	..	0	0	0	0	0	0	0	0
Private	..	..	0	0	0	0	0	0	0	0
Interest rescheduled	..	..	0	0	0	0	0	0	0	0
Official	..	..	0	0	0	0	0	0	0	0
Private	..	..	0	0	0	0	0	0	0	0
Debt forgiven	..	..	0	0	0	0	0	0	0	0
Memo: interest forgiven	..	..	0	0	0	0	0	0	0	0
Debt stock reduction	..	..	2,361	204	18	0	0	0	4,400	0
of which debt buyback	..	..	634	0	0	0	0	0	4,000	0
8. DEBT STOCK-FLOW RECONCILIATION										
Total change in debt stocks	..	..	793	3,727	-309	-687	-1,004	-488	198	1,445
Net flows on debt	683	5,556	2,037	4,222	-281	-1,582	-1,395	317	1,596	1,042
Net change in interest arrears	..	..	-6	147	43	103	12	-9	-19	9
Interest capitalized	..	..	0	0	0	0	0	0	0	0
Debt forgiveness or reduction	..	..	-1,727	-204	-18	0	0	0	-400	0
Cross-currency valuation	..	..	541	-291	-86	608	341	-511	-648	299
Residual	..	..	-52	-147	34	184	37	-284	-332	95
9. AVERAGE TERMS OF NEW COMMITMENTS										
ALL CREDITORS										
Interest (%)	7.2	12.1	8.2	8.1	7.8	7.1	7.4	7.5	8.7	7.9
Maturity (years)	8.3	7.7	14.5	12.4	9.2	14.1	7.3	8.4	25.0	9.4
Grace period (years)	1.9	3.1	5.6	5.5	4.1	3.6	3.6	3.8	23.0	1.5
Grant element (%)	11.0	-8.5	9.5	10.4	9.3	15.0	9.5	9.2	8.4	6.6
Official creditors										
Interest (%)	8.0	8.3	7.8	7.1	6.8	6.9	6.8	7.3	7.5	7.1
Maturity (years)	17.8	12.4	15.6	17.4	17.2	15.7	17.2	18.0	17.6	10.2
Grace period (years)	2.9	2.7	4.9	5.3	4.8	4.3	5.2	4.5	4.0	2.5
Grant element (%)	9.4	7.1	11.8	17.3	18.2	16.9	19.1	15.9	14.3	11.0
Private creditors										
Interest (%)	7.0	12.3	8.5	9.2	8.2	7.4	7.7	7.6	8.9	8.7
Maturity (years)	6.8	7.5	13.6	6.8	5.9	9.0	3.2	7.2	26.1	8.5
Grace period (years)	1.7	3.1	6.1	5.7	3.8	1.4	3.0	3.7	25.8	0.5
Grant element (%)	11.3	-9.3	7.8	2.7	5.6	9.0	5.6	8.4	7.6	2.1
Memorandum items										
Commitments	188	2,769	3,209	1,884	1,974	777	1,033	1,731	5,603	3,946
Official creditors	25	133	1,362	992	581	586	298	199	716	2,005
Private creditors	163	2,636	1,847	892	1,393	191	735	1,532	4,888	1,941

10. CONTRACTUAL OBLIGATIONS ON OUTSTANDING LONG-TERM DEBT

	1999	2000	2001	2002	2003	2004	2005	2006	2007	2008
TOTAL										
Disbursements	1,417	1,125	647	381	165	47	11	4	2	1
Principal	2,600	2,854	2,779	3,001	2,961	2,923	2,058	1,938	2,042	953
Interest	2,352	2,261	2,108	1,945	1,711	1,513	1,350	1,200	1,070	958
Official creditors										
Disbursements	789	693	476	314	158	47	11	4	2	1
Principal	607	686	810	808	765	782	585	375	340	278
Interest	362	369	353	322	280	231	180	144	118	94
Bilateral creditors										
Disbursements	70	60	30	12	4	1	0	0	0	0
Principal	205	262	321	313	245	225	132	18	5	4
Interest	78	73	60	45	30	18	6	2	1	1
Multilateral creditors										
Disbursements	719	633	446	302	154	46	11	4	2	1
Principal	401	424	490	495	520	557	453	357	336	274
Interest	283	296	293	277	250	213	173	142	117	93
Private creditors										
Disbursements	628	432	171	67	8	0	0	0	0	0
Principal	1,993	2,168	1,969	2,193	2,196	2,141	1,473	1,563	1,702	675
Interest	1,991	1,892	1,755	1,623	1,432	1,282	1,171	1,056	952	864
Commercial banks										
Disbursements	477	312	119	52	0	0	0	0	0	0
Principal	392	446	442	415	344	278	123	82	48	44
Interest	145	143	120	93	64	41	24	16	9	6
Other private										
Disbursements	151	121	52	15	8	0	0	0	0	0
Principal	1,601	1,723	1,527	1,779	1,852	1,863	1,350	1,481	1,654	631
Interest	1,846	1,749	1,635	1,531	1,367	1,241	1,147	1,040	943	858

VIETNAM

(US$ million, unless otherwise indicated)

	1970	*1980*	*1990*	*1992*	*1993*	*1994*	*1995*	*1996*	*1997*	*1998*
1. SUMMARY DEBT DATA										
TOTAL DEBT STOCKS (EDT)	..	..	**23,270**	**24,332**	**24,168**	**24,800**	**25,427**	**26,257**	**21,633**	**22,359**
Long-term debt (LDOD)	..	..	**21,378**	**21,649**	**21,599**	**21,855**	**21,777**	**21,964**	**18,839**	**19,775**
Public and publicly guaranteed	..	..	21,378	21,649	21,599	21,855	21,777	21,964	18,839	19,775
Private nonguaranteed	..	..	0	0	0	0	0	0	0	0
Use of IMF credit	**0**	**0**	**112**	**98**	**100**	**282**	**377**	**539**	**452**	**391**
Short-term debt	..	..	**1,780**	**2,585**	**2,469**	**2,663**	**3,272**	**3,754**	**2,342**	**2,193**
of which interest arrears on LDOD	..	..	1,530	1,965	1,865	2,209	2,501	2,741	1,391	1,545
Official creditors	..	..	859	1,408	1,372	1,716	1,999	2,238	1,391	1,543
Private creditors	..	..	671	557	493	494	502	503	0	2
Memo: principal arrears on LDOD	..	..	2,011	5,316	5,324	7,205	8,915	10,574	7,360	8,046
Official creditors	..	..	1,091	4,741	4,981	6,857	8,460	10,104	7,359	8,041
Private creditors	..	..	921	575	344	347	456	470	1	5
Memo: export credits	..	..	431	506	475	515	553	866	985	1,591
TOTAL DEBT FLOWS										
Disbursements	..	..	**13**	**562**	**134**	**455**	**729**	**742**	**1,198**	**1,300**
Long-term debt	..	..	13	562	33	282	637	566	1,198	1,300
IMF purchases	0	0	0	0	101	173	92	175	0	0
Principal repayments	..	..	**104**	**175**	**309**	**210**	**225**	**200**	**583**	**659**
Long-term debt	..	..	99	175	209	210	225	200	528	581
IMF repurchases	0	0	5	0	100	0	0	0	54	78
Net flows on debt	..	..	**-95**	**831**	**-191**	**95**	**821**	**784**	**553**	**338**
of which short-term debt	..	..	-4	444	-16	-150	317	242	-62	-303
Interest payments (INT)	..	..	**70**	**57**	**108**	**96**	**139**	**194**	**325**	**424**
Long-term debt	..	..	46	36	51	57	82	98	268	382
IMF charges	0	0	0	1	31	7	12	10	9	6
Short-term debt	..	..	23	19	26	32	46	86	47	36
Net transfers on debt	..	..	**-165**	**774**	**-299**	**-1**	**682**	**590**	**229**	**-86**
Total debt service paid (TDS)	..	..	**174**	**232**	**417**	**306**	**364**	**393**	**907**	**1,083**
Long-term debt	..	..	146	211	260	268	306	298	797	962
IMF repurchases and charges	0	0	5	1	131	7	12	10	63	84
Short-term debt (interest only)	..	..	23	19	26	32	46	86	47	36
2. AGGREGATE NET RESOURCE FLOWS AND NET TRANSFERS (LONG-TERM)										
NET RESOURCE FLOWS	..	..	**25**	**885**	**578**	**1,546**	**2,313**	**2,484**	**2,628**	**2,150**
Net flow of long-term debt (ex. IMF)	..	..	-86	387	-177	71	412	367	669	719
Foreign direct investment (net)	..	..	16	385	523	742	1,400	1,500	1,800	1,200
Portfolio equity flows	..	..	0	0	87	283	155	390	-94	0
Grants (excluding technical coop.)	..	..	96	113	145	449	346	228	252	231
Memo: technical coop. grants	..	..	99	154	151	189	228	236	208	203
official net resource flows	..	..	9	360	5	549	403	377	634	1,318
private net resource flows	..	..	16	525	573	996	1,910	2,107	1,994	832
NET TRANSFERS	..	..	**-21**	**849**	**527**	**1,488**	**2,231**	**2,266**	**2,210**	**1,569**
Interest on long-term debt	..	..	46	36	51	57	82	98	268	382
Profit remittances on FDI	..	..	0	0	0	0	0	120	150	200
Memo: official net transfers	..	..	-17	339	-21	524	353	329	547	1,209
private net transfers	..	..	-4	509	548	965	1,878	1,937	1,663	360
3. MAJOR ECONOMIC AGGREGATES										
Gross national product (GNP)	..	..	..	9,867	12,834	15,509	19,864	22,899	26,355	27,184
Exports of goods & services (XGS)	..	..	1,953	3,241	3,788	5,364	7,441	10,214	11,819	12,101
of which workers remittances	..	..	..	..	..	..	..	..	..	..
Imports of goods & services (MGS)	..	..	2,353	3,376	4,786	6,874	9,992	13,852	14,349	14,323
International reserves (RES)	..	..	..	429	362	834	1,324	1,751	1,986	1,148
Current account balance	..	..	-351	-76	-1,063	-1,340	-2,078	-2,592	-1,817	-1,271
4. DEBT INDICATORS										
EDT / XGS (%)	..	..	1,191.5	750.8	638.0	462.4	341.7	257.1	183.0	184.8
EDT / GNP (%)	..	..	..	246.6	188.3	159.9	128.0	114.7	82.1	82.3
TDS / XGS (%)	..	..	8.9	7.1	11.0	5.7	4.9	3.9	7.7	9.0
INT / XGS (%)	..	..	3.6	1.8	2.9	1.8	1.9	1.9	2.8	3.5
INT / GNP (%)	..	..	..	0.6	0.8	0.6	0.7	0.9	1.2	1.6
RES / EDT (%)	..	..	..	1.8	1.5	3.4	5.2	6.7	9.2	5.1
RES / MGS (months)	..	..	..	1.5	0.9	1.5	1.6	1.5	1.7	1.0
Short-term / EDT (%)	..	..	7.7	10.6	10.2	10.7	12.9	14.3	10.8	9.8
Concessional / EDT (%)	..	..	84.9	82.0	83.2	81.7	78.4	76.1	14.8	19.8
Multilateral / EDT (%)	..	..	0.6	0.6	0.4	0.9	1.3	2.0	3.8	5.7

VIETNAM

(US$ million, unless otherwise indicated)

	1970	1980	1990	1992	1993	1994	1995	1996	1997	1998
5. LONG-TERM DEBT										
DEBT OUTSTANDING (LDOD)	..	..	**21,378**	**21,649**	**21,599**	**21,855**	**21,777**	**21,964**	**18,839**	**19,775**
Public and publicly guaranteed	..	..	**21,378**	**21,649**	**21,599**	**21,855**	**21,777**	**21,964**	**18,839**	**19,775**
Official creditors	..	..	20,171	20,417	20,649	20,868	20,449	20,481	14,102	15,354
Multilateral	..	..	130	143	104	228	325	526	828	1,270
Concessional	..	..	103	114	104	228	325	526	819	1,252
Bilateral	..	..	20,042	20,275	20,544	20,640	20,124	19,955	13,274	14,084
Concessional	..	..	19,646	19,832	19,994	20,034	19,613	19,442	2,390	3,168
Private creditors	..	..	1,207	1,232	951	986	1,328	1,483	4,737	4,421
Bonds	..	..	0	0	0	0	0	0	560	560
Commercial banks	..	..	684	520	541	662	1,044	1,213	3,459	3,112
Other private	..	..	523	711	409	325	285	271	719	749
Private nonguaranteed	..	..	**0**	**0**	**0**	**0**	**0**	**0**	**0**	**0**
Bonds	..	..	0	0	0	0	0	0	0	0
Commercial banks	..	..	0	0	0	0	0	0	0	0
Memo:										
IBRD	0	0	0	0	0	0	0	0	0	0
IDA	0	2	59	57	57	181	231	412	569	851
DISBURSEMENTS	..	..	**13**	**562**	**33**	**282**	**637**	**566**	**1,198**	**1,300**
Public and publicly guaranteed	..	..	**13**	**562**	**33**	**282**	**637**	**566**	**1,198**	**1,300**
Official creditors	..	..	13	389	23	187	232	325	562	1,166
Multilateral	..	..	4	3	0	129	100	218	346	392
Concessional	..	..	0	0	0	129	100	218	338	384
Bilateral	..	..	9	386	23	58	132	107	216	773
Concessional	..	..	8	380	23	16	131	104	206	732
Private creditors	..	..	0	173	10	95	405	241	636	134
Bonds	..	..	0	0	0	0	0	0	0	0
Commercial banks	..	..	0	0	0	94	389	207	177	54
Other private	..	..	0	173	10	1	17	35	460	80
Private nonguaranteed	..	..	**0**	**0**	**0**	**0**	**0**	**0**	**0**	**0**
Bonds	..	..	0	0	0	0	0	0	0	0
Commercial banks	..	..	0	0	0	0	0	0	0	0
Memo:										
IBRD	0	0	0	0	0	0	0	0	0	0
IDA	0	1	0	0	0	126	47	189	181	254
PRINCIPAL REPAYMENTS	..	..	**99**	**175**	**209**	**210**	**225**	**200**	**528**	**581**
Public and publicly guaranteed	..	..	**99**	**175**	**209**	**210**	**225**	**200**	**528**	**581**
Official creditors	..	..	99	141	163	87	175	175	179	78
Multilateral	..	..	3	3	40	6	7	6	6	5
Concessional	..	..	3	3	11	6	7	6	6	5
Bilateral	..	..	96	139	122	81	168	169	173	73
Concessional	..	..	44	126	65	62	72	77	50	38
Private creditors	..	..	0	33	47	124	50	25	349	502
Bonds	..	..	0	0	0	0	0	0	0	0
Commercial banks	..	..	0	0	0	0	0	6	330	428
Other private	..	..	0	33	47	124	50	19	19	75
Private nonguaranteed	..	..	**0**	**0**	**0**	**0**	**0**	**0**	**0**	**0**
Bonds	..	..	0	0	0	0	0	0	0	0
Commercial banks	..	..	0	0	0	0	0	0	0	0
Memo:										
IBRD	0	0	0	0	0	0	0	0	0	0
IDA	0	0	1	1	1	1	1	1	1	1
NET FLOWS ON DEBT	..	..	**-86**	**387**	**-177**	**71**	**412**	**367**	**669**	**719**
Public and publicly guaranteed	..	..	**-86**	**387**	**-177**	**71**	**412**	**367**	**669**	**719**
Official creditors	..	..	-86	248	-140	100	57	150	382	1,087
Multilateral	..	..	1	0	-40	123	94	212	340	387
Concessional	..	..	-3	-3	-11	123	94	212	331	379
Bilateral	..	..	-87	247	-100	-23	-37	-62	43	700
Concessional	..	..	-36	255	-43	-46	59	27	156	694
Private creditors	..	..	0	140	-37	-29	355	217	287	-368
Bonds	..	..	0	0	0	0	0	0	0	0
Commercial banks	..	..	0	0	0	94	389	201	-154	-373
Other private	..	..	0	140	-37	-122	-33	16	441	5
Private nonguaranteed	..	..	**0**	**0**	**0**	**0**	**0**	**0**	**0**	**0**
Bonds	..	..	0	0	0	0	0	0	0	0
Commercial banks	..	..	0	0	0	0	0	0	0	0
Memo:										
IBRD	0	0	0	0	0	0	0	0	0	0
IDA	0	1	-1	-1	-1	125	46	188	180	253

VIETNAM

(US$ million, unless otherwise indicated)

	1970	1980	1990	1992	1993	1994	1995	1996	1997	1998
INTEREST PAYMENTS (LINT)	..	..	**46**	**36**	**51**	**57**	**82**	**98**	**268**	**382**
Public and publicly guaranteed	..	..	**46**	**36**	**51**	**57**	**82**	**98**	**268**	**382**
Official creditors	..	..	26	21	26	26	50	48	87	110
Multilateral	..	..	2	2	8	2	3	3	5	8
Concessional	..	..	0	1	6	2	3	3	5	8
Bilateral	..	..	24	19	19	24	47	45	82	101
Concessional	..	..	3	4	8	13	21	20	53	49
Private creditors	..	..	20	15	25	32	32	50	181	272
Bonds	..	..	0	0	0	0	0	0	0	12
Commercial banks	..	..	5	0	9	11	24	43	164	232
Other private	..	..	16	15	16	20	8	7	17	29
Private nonguaranteed	..	..	**0**	**0**	**0**	**0**	**0**	**0**	**0**	**0**
Bonds	..	..	0	0	0	0	0	0	0	0
Commercial banks	..	..	0	0	0	0	0	0	0	0
Memo:										
IBRD	0	0	0	0	0	0	0	0	0	0
IDA	0	0	0	0	0	1	2	2	3	5
NET TRANSFERS ON DEBT	..	..	**-133**	**351**	**-228**	**14**	**331**	**268**	**401**	**337**
Public and publicly guaranteed	..	..	**-133**	**351**	**-228**	**14**	**331**	**268**	**401**	**337**
Official creditors	..	..	-113	227	-166	74	7	101	295	978
Multilateral	..	..	-1	-2	-48	121	91	209	334	379
Concessional	..	..	-3	-4	-17	121	91	209	326	371
Bilateral	..	..	-112	229	-118	-47	-84	-107	-40	599
Concessional	..	..	-39	251	-50	-59	38	7	103	645
Private creditors	..	..	-20	124	-62	-60	323	167	106	-640
Bonds	..	..	0	0	0	0	0	0	0	-12
Commercial banks	..	..	-5	0	-9	82	365	158	-318	-605
Other private	..	..	-16	124	-53	-143	-41	9	424	-23
Private nonguaranteed	..	..	**0**	**0**	**0**	**0**	**0**	**0**	**0**	**0**
Bonds	..	..	0	0	0	0	0	0	0	0
Commercial banks	..	..	0	0	0	0	0	0	0	0
Memo:										
IBRD	0	0	0	0	0	0	0	0	0	0
IDA	0	1	-1	-1	-1	125	45	186	177	248
DEBT SERVICE (LTDS)	..	..	**146**	**211**	**260**	**268**	**306**	**298**	**797**	**962**
Public and publicly guaranteed	..	..	**146**	**211**	**260**	**268**	**306**	**298**	**797**	**962**
Official creditors	..	..	125	162	189	112	224	224	267	188
Multilateral	..	..	5	5	48	8	9	9	12	13
Concessional	..	..	3	4	17	8	9	9	12	13
Bilateral	..	..	121	157	141	105	215	214	255	175
Concessional	..	..	47	130	73	75	93	97	103	86
Private creditors	..	..	20	49	72	155	82	74	530	774
Bonds	..	..	0	0	0	0	0	0	0	12
Commercial banks	..	..	5	0	9	11	24	48	494	659
Other private	..	..	16	49	63	144	58	26	36	104
Private nonguaranteed	..	..	**0**	**0**	**0**	**0**	**0**	**0**	**0**	**0**
Bonds	..	..	0	0	0	0	0	0	0	0
Commercial banks	..	..	0	0	0	0	0	0	0	0
Memo:										
IBRD	0	0	0	0	0	0	0	0	0	0
IDA	0	0	1	1	1	1	2	3	4	5
UNDISBURSED DEBT	..	..	**155**	**146**	**666**	**1,835**	**3,591**	**4,345**	**8,562**	**5,421**
Official creditors	..	..	89	146	666	1,470	3,097	3,924	8,296	5,120
Private creditors	..	..	66	0	0	365	494	421	266	302
Memorandum items										
Concessional LDOD	..	..	19,750	19,945	20,099	20,262	19,937	19,968	3,209	4,420
Variable rate LDOD	..	..	847	791	885	887	1,000	1,077	3,500	3,290
Public sector LDOD	..	..	21,378	21,649	21,599	21,855	21,777	21,964	18,839	19,775
Private sector LDOD	..	..	0	0	0	0	0	0	0	0
6. CURRENCY COMPOSITION OF LONG-TERM DEBT (PERCENT)										
Deutsche mark	..	..	1.7	0.3	0.5	0.6	1.0	1.0	0.9	0.9
French franc	..	..	1.0	0.9	0.8	0.9	1.0	1.0	1.6	1.9
Japanese yen	..	..	2.0	5.5	5.9	5.8	5.6	4.7	5.4	9.2
Pound sterling	..	..	0.2	0.1	0.1	0.1	0.1	0.2	0.1	0.1
Swiss franc	..	..	0.0	0.0	0.0	0.0	0.0	0.0	0.1	0.1
U.S.dollars	..	..	5.5	5.3	5.6	6.4	8.4	10.3	30.1	28.8
Multiple currency	..	..	0.2	0.3	0.1	0.1	0.3	0.4	1.1	1.8
Special drawing rights	..	..	0.0	0.0	0.0	0.0	0.0	0.0	0.1	0.1
All other currencies	..	..	89.4	87.6	87.0	86.1	83.6	82.4	60.6	57.1

VIETNAM

(US$ million, unless otherwise indicated)

	1970	1980	1990	1992	1993	1994	1995	1996	1997	1998
7. DEBT RESTRUCTURINGS										
Total amount rescheduled	..	..	410	283	652	0	90	168	742	15
Debt stock rescheduled	..	..	0	0	69	0	0	0	0	0
Principal rescheduled	..	..	0	111	316	0	61	108	407	5
Official	..	..	0	0	81	0	48	108	12	5
Private	..	..	0	111	235	0	13	0	395	0
Interest rescheduled	..	..	..	105	138	0	1	0	303	5
Official	..	..	0	0	49	0	1	0	0	5
Private	..	..	0	105	89	0	0	0	303	0
Debt forgiven	..	..	0	0	30	0	32	0	0	0
Memo: interest forgiven	..	..	0	0	20	0	0	0	0	0
Debt stock reduction	..	..	0	0	0	0	0	0	249	0
of which debt buyback	..	..	0	0	0	0	0	0	31	0
8. DEBT STOCK-FLOW RECONCILIATION										
Total change in debt stocks	..	..	..	937	-164	633	627	830	-4,624	726
Net flows on debt	..	..	-95	831	-191	95	821	784	553	338
Net change in interest arrears	..	..	..	209	-100	344	292	240	-1,351	154
Interest capitalized	..	..	..	105	138	0	1	0	303	5
Debt forgiveness or reduction	..	..	..	0	-30	0	-32	0	-218	0
Cross-currency valuation	..	..	..	-39	101	204	7	-158	-204	279
Residual	..	..	..	-169	-82	-10	-463	-35	-3,708	-50
9. AVERAGE TERMS OF NEW COMMITMENTS										
ALL CREDITORS										
Interest (%)	..	..	5.7	1.7	2.0	2.7	3.3	2.5	3.2	3.1
Maturity (years)	..	..	9.6	24.4	30.4	26.3	26.3	29.6	27.4	30.5
Grace period (years)	..	..	4.2	8.2	8.2	7.8	7.9	8.6	7.7	8.6
Grant element (%)	..	..	19.9	61.7	61.7	56.9	51.9	59.3	50.6	54.4
Official creditors										
Interest (%)	..	..	5.7	1.1	2.0	0.9	2.3	1.9	2.1	2.9
Maturity (years)	..	..	9.6	28.8	31.0	33.9	31.5	33.4	33.0	32.4
Grace period (years)	..	..	4.2	9.8	8.3	9.9	9.5	9.8	9.7	9.4
Grant element (%)	..	..	19.9	72.6	62.7	76.1	63.4	67.0	63.1	58.1
Private creditors										
Interest (%)	..	..	0.0	4.6	3.9	6.3	6.7	5.8	6.9	5.6
Maturity (years)	..	..	0.0	3.0	1.3	10.9	7.1	9.1	9.8	12.2
Grace period (years)	..	..	0.0	0.5	1.3	3.5	2.0	2.0	1.1	1.6
Grant element (%)	..	..	0.0	8.0	6.9	17.7	10.3	17.7	11.1	19.9
Memorandum items										
Commitments	..	..	11	473	569	1,400	2,466	1,799	1,977	1,699
Official creditors	..	..	11	393	559	941	1,933	1,519	1,504	1,532
Private creditors	..	..	0	80	10	460	533	280	474	167

10. CONTRACTUAL OBLIGATIONS ON OUTSTANDING LONG-TERM DEBT

	1999	2000	2001	2002	2003	2004	2005	2006	2007	2008
TOTAL										
Disbursements	1,572	1,522	1,011	648	370	186	92	14	5	1
Principal	1,568	1,352	1,285	1,291	887	772	832	396	423	451
Interest	493	442	391	337	277	239	216	191	198	186
Official creditors										
Disbursements	1,412	1,428	978	637	367	186	92	14	5	1
Principal	622	598	581	587	606	636	690	263	311	366
Interest	222	221	216	205	190	171	156	140	155	148
Bilateral creditors										
Disbursements	904	882	567	350	191	97	45	6	3	1
Principal	617	592	575	582	597	614	658	219	248	288
Interest	203	196	184	168	150	129	107	88	98	92
Multilateral creditors										
Disbursements	508	546	411	287	176	89	48	9	1	0
Principal	5	6	6	6	8	21	32	45	63	78
Interest	19	25	32	37	40	42	49	52	57	56
Private creditors										
Disbursements	160	94	33	12	3	0	0	0	0	0
Principal	945	754	704	704	282	136	142	132	112	85
Interest	272	221	176	132	87	68	59	51	43	38
Commercial banks										
Disbursements	22	4	1	0	0	0	0	0	0	0
Principal	831	624	600	600	189	39	37	32	23	16
Interest	196	147	107	69	31	17	15	13	11	10
Other private										
Disbursements	138	91	32	11	3	0	0	0	0	0
Principal	114	129	104	104	93	98	105	101	90	69
Interest	75	74	68	62	56	51	44	38	33	28

YEMEN, REPUBLIC OF

(US$ million, unless otherwise indicated)

	1970	1980	1990	1992	1993	1994	1995	1996	1997	1998
1. SUMMARY DEBT DATA										
TOTAL DEBT STOCKS (EDT)	..	**1,684**	**6,345**	**6,571**	**5,923**	**6,125**	**6,217**	**6,362**	**3,856**	**4,138**
Long-term debt (LDOD)	..	**1,453**	**5,154**	**5,253**	**5,341**	**5,460**	**5,528**	**5,622**	**3,418**	**3,590**
Public and publicly guaranteed	..	1,453	5,154	5,253	5,341	5,460	5,528	5,622	3,418	3,590
Private nonguaranteed	..	0	0	0	0	0	0	0	0	0
Use of IMF credit	**0**	**48**	**0**	**0**	**0**	**0**	**0**	**121**	**250**	**336**
Short-term debt	..	**183**	**1,191**	**1,318**	**582**	**666**	**689**	**619**	**188**	**213**
of which interest arrears on LDOD	..	1	191	318	387	433	473	492	68	73
Official creditors	..	0	130	218	264	291	316	322	48	53
Private creditors	..	0	61	100	123	142	157	170	20	20
Memo: principal arrears on LDOD	..	7	839	1,565	1,922	2,177	2,408	2,585	617	667
Official creditors	..	3	377	822	1,054	1,198	1,330	1,418	453	505
Private creditors	..	4	463	744	869	980	1,078	1,167	163	162
Memo: export credits	..	0	338	246	157	104	120	82	138	87
TOTAL DEBT FLOWS										
Disbursements	..	**576**	**305**	**148**	**136**	**119**	**118**	**286**	**287**	**236**
Long-term debt	..	566	305	148	136	119	118	164	147	164
IMF purchases	0	10	0	0	0	0	0	122	140	72
Principal repayments	..	**36**	**81**	**83**	**78**	**58**	**65**	**58**	**60**	**73**
Long-term debt	..	25	80	83	78	58	65	58	60	73
IMF repurchases	0	11	1	0	0	0	0	0	0	0
Net flows on debt	..	**546**	**386**	**66**	**-747**	**99**	**36**	**140**	**219**	**183**
of which short-term debt	..	6	161	0	-805	38	-17	-89	-7	20
Interest payments (INT)	..	**37**	**88**	**51**	**42**	**48**	**37**	**29**	**38**	**52**
Long-term debt	..	10	28	21	21	23	25	21	26	45
IMF charges	0	2	0	0	0	0	0	3	7	0
Short-term debt	..	25	60	30	21	25	11	5	5	7
Net transfers on debt	..	**509**	**297**	**15**	**-788**	**51**	**-1**	**111**	**181**	**131**
Total debt service paid (TDS)	..	**73**	**169**	**133**	**120**	**106**	**102**	**87**	**98**	**125**
Long-term debt	..	35	108	103	99	81	91	79	86	118
IMF repurchases and charges	0	13	1	0	0	0	0	3	7	0
Short-term debt (interest only)	..	25	60	30	21	25	11	5	5	7
2. AGGREGATE NET RESOURCE FLOWS AND NET TRANSFERS (LONG-TERM)										
NET RESOURCE FLOWS	..	**944**	**333**	**877**	**1,065**	**153**	**-73**	**155**	**82**	**6**
Net flow of long-term debt (ex. IMF)	..	542	226	66	58	61	53	106	87	91
Foreign direct investment (net)	..	34	-131	714	897	11	-218	-60	-138	-210
Portfolio equity flows	..	0	0	0	0	0	0	0	0	0
Grants (excluding technical coop.)	..	368	238	98	109	82	92	109	133	125
Memo: technical coop. grants	..	62	108	94	82	57	65	6	65	56
official net resource flows	..	847	303	157	158	148	147	215	220	216
private net resource flows	..	97	30	720	907	5	-220	-60	-138	-210
NET TRANSFERS	..	**934**	**304**	**856**	**1,044**	**130**	**-98**	**134**	**56**	**-39**
Interest on long-term debt	..	10	28	21	21	23	25	21	26	45
Profit remittances on FDI	..	0	0	0	0	0	0	0	0	0
Memo: official net transfers	..	838	280	137	137	128	122	195	194	171
private net transfers	..	96	25	720	907	2	-220	-60	-138	-210
3. MAJOR ECONOMIC AGGREGATES										
Gross national product (GNP)	..	..	4,688	5,339	4,457	3,292	3,491	4,624	5,029	3,947
Exports of goods & services (XGS)	..	..	3,026	2,313	2,405	3,053	3,234	3,630	3,710	2,976
of which workers remittances	..	..	1,498	1,018	1,039	1,059	1,081	1,135	1,169	1,202
Imports of goods & services (MGS)	..	..	2,662	3,457	3,681	2,745	3,075	3,577	3,745	3,258
International reserves (RES)	..	..	441	337	165	274	638	1,036	1,218	1,010
Current account balance	..	..	739	-1,091	-1,248	366	183	106	52	-228
4. DEBT INDICATORS										
EDT / XGS (%)	..	..	209.7	284.1	246.3	200.6	192.2	175.3	104.0	139.0
EDT / GNP (%)	..	..	135.4	123.1	132.9	186.0	178.1	137.6	76.7	104.8
TDS / XGS (%)	..	..	5.6	5.8	5.0	3.5	3.2	2.4	2.6	4.2
INT / XGS (%)	..	..	2.9	2.2	1.7	1.6	1.1	0.8	1.0	1.7
INT / GNP (%)	..	..	1.9	1.0	0.9	1.5	1.1	0.6	0.8	1.3
RES / EDT (%)	..	..	7.0	5.1	2.8	4.5	10.3	16.3	31.6	24.4
RES / MGS (months)	..	..	2.0	1.2	0.5	1.2	2.5	3.5	3.9	3.7
Short-term / EDT (%)	..	10.8	18.8	20.1	9.8	10.9	11.1	9.7	4.9	5.1
Concessional / EDT (%)	..	72.1	50.7	50.2	57.0	56.7	56.7	55.4	79.5	78.7
Multilateral / EDT (%)	..	14.9	16.2	16.1	18.7	19.7	20.6	21.3	36.0	36.8

YEMEN, REPUBLIC OF

(US$ million, unless otherwise indicated)

	1970	1980	1990	1992	1993	1994	1995	1996	1997	1998
5. LONG-TERM DEBT										
DEBT OUTSTANDING (LDOD)	..	**1,453**	**5,154**	**5,253**	**5,341**	**5,460**	**5,528**	**5,622**	**3,418**	**3,590**
Public and publicly guaranteed	..	**1,453**	**5,154**	**5,253**	**5,341**	**5,460**	**5,528**	**5,622**	**3,418**	**3,590**
Official creditors	..	1,238	3,496	3,545	3,626	3,739	3,810	3,903	3,236	3,412
Multilateral	..	252	1,025	1,056	1,108	1,206	1,278	1,358	1,390	1,521
Concessional	..	252	989	1,051	1,103	1,183	1,239	1,303	1,331	1,477
Bilateral	..	986	2,470	2,490	2,518	2,534	2,532	2,545	1,846	1,891
Concessional	..	962	2,225	2,244	2,272	2,288	2,287	2,219	1,735	1,780
Private creditors	..	216	1,658	1,708	1,716	1,720	1,718	1,719	182	178
Bonds	..	0	0	0	0	0	0	0	0	0
Commercial banks	..	0	80	80	80	80	80	80	80	80
Other private	..	216	1,578	1,628	1,636	1,640	1,638	1,639	102	98
Private nonguaranteed	..	**0**	**0**	**0**	**0**	**0**	**0**	**0**	**0**	**0**
Bonds	..	0	0	0	0	0	0	0	0	0
Commercial banks	..	0	0	0	0	0	0	0	0	0
Memo:										
IBRD	0	0	0	0	0	0	0	0	0	0
IDA	0	137	602	684	726	780	828	893	934	1,075
DISBURSEMENTS	..	**566**	**305**	**148**	**136**	**119**	**118**	**164**	**147**	**164**
Public and publicly guaranteed	..	**566**	**305**	**148**	**136**	**119**	**118**	**164**	**147**	**164**
Official creditors	..	501	139	138	127	118	118	164	147	164
Multilateral	..	65	56	91	92	113	109	161	145	164
Concessional	..	65	55	90	91	95	88	134	134	160
Bilateral	..	437	84	47	35	6	9	3	2	0
Concessional	..	426	84	47	35	6	9	3	2	0
Private creditors	..	65	166	10	10	0	0	0	0	0
Bonds	..	0	0	0	0	0	0	0	0	0
Commercial banks	..	0	0	0	0	0	0	0	0	0
Other private	..	65	166	10	10	0	0	0	0	0
Private nonguaranteed	..	**0**	**0**	**0**	**0**	**0**	**0**	**0**	**0**	**0**
Bonds	..	0	0	0	0	0	0	0	0	0
Commercial banks	..	0	0	0	0	0	0	0	0	0
Memo:										
IBRD	0	0	0	0	0	0	0	0	0	0
IDA	0	28	27	53	46	37	42	95	89	122
PRINCIPAL REPAYMENTS	..	**25**	**80**	**83**	**78**	**58**	**65**	**58**	**60**	**73**
Public and publicly guaranteed	..	**25**	**80**	**83**	**78**	**58**	**65**	**58**	**60**	**73**
Official creditors	..	23	74	79	78	52	64	58	60	73
Multilateral	..	3	41	49	44	45	53	54	60	73
Concessional	..	3	26	37	44	44	48	45	55	52
Bilateral	..	20	34	30	34	8	10	4	0	0
Concessional	..	16	34	30	34	8	10	4	0	0
Private creditors	..	2	5	4	0	5	2	0	0	0
Bonds	..	0	0	0	0	0	0	0	0	0
Commercial banks	..	0	0	0	0	0	0	0	0	0
Other private	..	2	5	4	0	5	2	0	0	0
Private nonguaranteed	..	**0**	**0**	**0**	**0**	**0**	**0**	**0**	**0**	**0**
Bonds	..	0	0	0	0	0	0	0	0	0
Commercial banks	..	0	0	0	0	0	0	0	0	0
Memo:										
IBRD	0	0	0	0	0	0	0	0	0	0
IDA	0	0	2	4	6	7	8	9	10	11
NET FLOWS ON DEBT	..	**542**	**226**	**66**	**58**	**61**	**53**	**106**	**87**	**91**
Public and publicly guaranteed	..	**542**	**226**	**66**	**58**	**61**	**53**	**106**	**87**	**91**
Official creditors	..	479	65	59	48	66	55	106	87	91
Multilateral	..	62	15	43	48	68	56	107	86	91
Concessional	..	62	29	53	47	51	40	89	78	108
Bilateral	..	416	50	17	1	-2	-1	-1	2	0
Concessional	..	410	50	17	1	-2	-1	-1	2	0
Private creditors	..	63	161	6	10	-5	-2	0	0	0
Bonds	..	0	0	0	0	0	0	0	0	0
Commercial banks	..	0	0	0	0	0	0	0	0	0
Other private	..	63	161	6	10	-5	-2	0	0	0
Private nonguaranteed	..	**0**	**0**	**0**	**0**	**0**	**0**	**0**	**0**	**0**
Bonds	..	0	0	0	0	0	0	0	0	0
Commercial banks	..	0	0	0	0	0	0	0	0	0
Memo:										
IBRD	0	0	0	0	0	0	0	0	0	0
IDA	0	28	25	49	41	30	34	86	79	111

YEMEN, REPUBLIC OF

(US$ million, unless otherwise indicated)

	1970	1980	1990	1992	1993	1994	1995	1996	1997	1998
INTEREST PAYMENTS (LINT)	..	**10**	**28**	**21**	**21**	**23**	**25**	**21**	**26**	**45**
Public and publicly guaranteed	..	**10**	**28**	**21**	**21**	**23**	**25**	**21**	**26**	**45**
Official creditors	..	9	23	20	20	20	25	21	26	45
Multilateral	..	5	14	15	15	17	18	18	21	21
Concessional	..	5	12	15	15	16	17	16	17	17
Bilateral	..	4	9	5	5	3	7	3	6	24
Concessional	..	4	9	5	5	3	7	3	0	17
Private creditors	..	1	5	0	0	3	1	0	0	0
Bonds	..	0	0	0	0	0	0	0	0	0
Commercial banks	..	0	0	0	0	0	0	0	0	0
Other private	..	1	5	0	0	3	1	0	0	0
Private nonguaranteed	..	**0**	**0**	**0**	**0**	**0**	**0**	**0**	**0**	**0**
Bonds	..	0	0	0	0	0	0	0	0	0
Commercial banks	..	0	0	0	0	0	0	0	0	0
Memo:										
IBRD	0	0	0	0	0	0	0	0	0	0
IDA	0	1	4	5	5	6	6	6	7	7
NET TRANSFERS ON DEBT	..	**531**	**198**	**45**	**38**	**38**	**28**	**85**	**61**	**46**
Public and publicly guaranteed	..	**531**	**198**	**45**	**38**	**38**	**28**	**85**	**61**	**46**
Official creditors	..	469	42	39	28	46	30	85	61	46
Multilateral	..	57	1	28	33	52	38	89	65	70
Concessional	..	57	17	39	32	35	23	73	61	91
Bilateral	..	412	41	11	-5	-5	-8	-4	-4	-24
Concessional	..	405	41	11	-5	-5	-8	-4	2	-17
Private creditors	..	62	156	6	10	-8	-2	0	0	0
Bonds	..	0	0	0	0	0	0	0	0	0
Commercial banks	..	0	0	0	0	0	0	0	0	0
Other private	..	62	156	6	10	-8	-2	0	0	0
Private nonguaranteed	..	**0**	**0**	**0**	**0**	**0**	**0**	**0**	**0**	**0**
Bonds	..	0	0	0	0	0	0	0	0	0
Commercial banks	..	0	0	0	0	0	0	0	0	0
Memo:										
IBRD	0	0	0	0	0	0	0	0	0	0
IDA	0	27	22	44	36	24	28	80	72	104
DEBT SERVICE (LTDS)	..	**35**	**108**	**103**	**99**	**81**	**91**	**79**	**86**	**118**
Public and publicly guaranteed	..	**35**	**108**	**103**	**99**	**81**	**91**	**79**	**86**	**118**
Official creditors	..	32	98	99	99	72	88	79	86	118
Multilateral	..	7	55	64	59	61	71	72	81	94
Concessional	..	7	38	52	59	60	65	62	73	69
Bilateral	..	24	43	35	39	11	17	7	6	24
Concessional	..	21	43	35	39	11	17	7	0	17
Private creditors	..	3	10	4	0	9	2	0	0	0
Bonds	..	0	0	0	0	0	0	0	0	0
Commercial banks	..	0	0	0	0	0	0	0	0	0
Other private	..	3	10	4	0	9	2	0	0	0
Private nonguaranteed	..	**0**	**0**	**0**	**0**	**0**	**0**	**0**	**0**	**0**
Bonds	..	0	0	0	0	0	0	0	0	0
Commercial banks	..	0	0	0	0	0	0	0	0	0
Memo:										
IBRD	0	0	0	0	0	0	0	0	0	0
IDA	0	1	6	9	11	13	14	15	16	18
UNDISBURSED DEBT	..	**1,589**	**1,655**	**993**	**886**	**809**	**727**	**799**	**767**	**447**
Official creditors	..	1,252	1,205	978	885	809	727	799	767	447
Private creditors	..	336	450	15	2	0	0	0	0	0
Memorandum items										
Concessional LDOD	..	1,214	3,214	3,295	3,375	3,471	3,526	3,522	3,066	3,257
Variable rate LDOD	..	0	80	80	80	80	80	80	80	80
Public sector LDOD	..	1,453	5,154	5,253	5,341	5,460	5,528	5,622	3,418	3,590
Private sector LDOD	..	0	0	0	0	0	0	0	0	0

6. CURRENCY COMPOSITION OF LONG-TERM DEBT (PERCENT)

	1970	1980	1990	1992	1993	1994	1995	1996	1997	1998
Deutsche mark	..	0.0	0.0	0.0	0.0	0.0	0.0	0.0	0.0	0.0
French franc	..	1.5	0.8	1.2	1.4	1.4	1.5	1.3	1.7	1.6
Japanese yen	..	0.6	4.4	5.2	6.0	6.5	6.1	5.1	7.3	7.3
Pound sterling	..	3.2	0.7	0.6	0.5	0.6	0.6	0.6	1.0	0.9
Swiss franc	..	2.8	0.3	0.3	0.3	0.3	0.3	0.3	0.4	0.4
U.S.dollars	..	22.4	20.2	20.7	20.5	20.8	21.2	23.1	56.5	58.2
Multiple currency	..	0.1	1.6	1.6	1.5	1.5	1.4	1.4	0.5	0.4
Special drawing rights	..	0.0	2.5	2.4	2.5	2.7	2.8	2.9	4.9	5.2
All other currencies	..	69.4	69.5	68.0	67.3	66.2	66.1	65.3	27.7	26.0

YEMEN, REPUBLIC OF

(US$ million, unless otherwise indicated)

	1970	1980	1990	1992	1993	1994	1995	1996	1997	1998
7. DEBT RESTRUCTURINGS										
Total amount rescheduled	..	..	98	0	0	0	0	80	685	31
Debt stock rescheduled	..	..	0	0	0	0	0	0	0	0
Principal rescheduled	..	..	98	0	0	0	0	24	559	24
Official	..	..	98	0	0	0	0	24	268	21
Private	..	..	0	0	0	0	0	0	292	2
Interest rescheduled	..	..	0	0	0	0	0	17	95	7
Official	..	..	0	0	0	0	0	17	61	6
Private	..	..	0	0	0	0	0	0	34	1
Debt forgiven	..	..	0	0	0	0	0	1	2,173	0
Memo: interest forgiven	..	..	0	0	0	0	0	0	338	0
Debt stock reduction	..	..	0	0	0	0	0	0	0	0
of which debt buyback	..	..	0	0	0	0	0	0	0	0
8. DEBT STOCK-FLOW RECONCILIATION										
Total change in debt stocks	..	..	752	98	-648	202	92	145	-2,506	282
Net flows on debt	..	546	386	66	-747	99	36	140	219	183
Net change in interest arrears	..	..	81	100	69	46	40	19	-424	5
Interest capitalized	..	..	0	0	0	0	0	17	95	7
Debt forgiveness or reduction	..	..	0	0	0	0	0	-1	-2,173	0
Cross-currency valuation	..	..	313	-50	34	58	5	-42	-69	51
Residual	..	..	-29	-18	-4	0	10	13	-154	37
9. AVERAGE TERMS OF NEW COMMITMENTS										
ALL CREDITORS										
Interest (%)	..	2.7	1.8	2.1	0.9	1.9	5.1	1.2	0.5	0.5
Maturity (years)	..	26.9	28.6	30.1	31.6	27.6	10.8	34.2	39.7	39.1
Grace period (years)	..	5.8	7.2	8.4	9.3	7.3	3.3	8.8	10.2	9.6
Grant element (%)	..	51.8	61.3	63.3	73.8	57.6	21.4	72.3	82.7	81.7
Official creditors										
Interest (%)	..	2.4	1.8	1.2	0.9	1.9	5.1	1.2	0.5	0.5
Maturity (years)	..	28.2	28.6	34.6	31.6	27.6	10.8	34.2	39.7	39.1
Grace period (years)	..	6.0	7.2	9.7	9.3	7.3	3.3	8.8	10.2	9.6
Grant element (%)	..	54.1	61.3	74.1	73.8	57.6	21.4	72.3	82.7	81.7
Private creditors										
Interest (%)	..	4.4	0.0	6.0	0.0	0.0	0.0	0.0	0.0	0.0
Maturity (years)	..	18.9	0.0	11.5	0.0	0.0	0.0	0.0	0.0	0.0
Grace period (years)	..	4.9	0.0	3.0	0.0	0.0	0.0	0.0	0.0	0.0
Grant element (%)	..	37.6	0.0	18.6	0.0	0.0	0.0	0.0	0.0	0.0
Memorandum items										
Commitments	..	553	201	98	49	49	80	276	149	60
Official creditors	..	476	201	79	49	49	80	276	149	60
Private creditors	..	77	0	19	0	0	0	0	0	0

10. CONTRACTUAL OBLIGATIONS ON OUTSTANDING LONG-TERM DEBT

	1999	2000	2001	2002	2003	2004	2005	2006	2007	2008
TOTAL										
Disbursements	140	121	82	53	29	13	7	2	0	0
Principal	125	128	123	118	109	104	102	103	97	94
Interest	68	69	71	69	67	65	63	61	59	58
Official creditors										
Disbursements	140	121	82	53	29	13	7	2	0	0
Principal	123	126	119	115	106	104	102	103	97	94
Interest	68	69	71	69	67	65	63	61	59	58
Bilateral creditors										
Disbursements	1	2	2	1	1	0	0	0	0	0
Principal	44	47	59	57	51	48	48	48	43	40
Interest	46	49	51	50	50	49	48	47	46	45
Multilateral creditors										
Disbursements	139	119	81	52	29	13	7	2	0	0
Principal	79	79	60	58	55	56	54	55	54	55
Interest	22	21	19	18	17	16	15	14	13	13
Private creditors										
Disbursements	0	0	0	0	0	0	0	0	0	0
Principal	1	1	4	2	2	0	0	0	0	0
Interest	0	0	0	0	0	0	0	0	0	0
Commercial banks										
Disbursements	0	0	0	0	0	0	0	0	0	0
Principal	0	0	0	0	0	0	0	0	0	0
Interest	0	0	0	0	0	0	0	0	0	0
Other private										
Disbursements	0	0	0	0	0	0	0	0	0	0
Principal	1	1	4	2	2	0	0	0	0	0
Interest	0	0	0	0	0	0	0	0	0	0

YUGOSLAVIA, FEDERAL REPUBLIC OF (SERBIA AND MONTENEGRO)

(US$ million, unless otherwise indicated)

	1970	1980	1990	1992	1993	1994	1995	1996	1997	1998
1. SUMMARY DEBT DATA										
TOTAL DEBT STOCKS (EDT)	..	**18,486**	**17,837**	**16,483**	**12,709**	**13,035**	**13,839**	**13,439**	**15,091**	**13,742**
Long-term debt (LDOD)	**2,053**	**15,586**	**16,846**	**15,195**	**10,990**	**11,270**	**11,484**	**11,239**	**10,924**	**11,080**
Public and publicly guaranteed	1,199	4,581	12,986	11,117	8,231	8,511	8,725	8,480	8,165	8,321
Private nonguaranteed	854	11,005	3,860	4,078	2,759	2,759	2,759	2,759	2,759	2,759
Use of IMF credit	**0**	**760**	**467**	**196**	**78**	**83**	**85**	**81**	**76**	**79**
Short-term debt	..	**2,140**	**524**	**1,092**	**1,641**	**1,682**	**2,271**	**2,119**	**4,092**	**2,584**
of which interest arrears on LDOD	..	0	0	90	616	1,059	1,528	1,834	2,078	2,336
Official creditors	..	0	0	79	197	322	443	478	473	513
Private creditors	..	0	0	11	419	737	1,085	1,356	1,605	1,823
Memo: principal arrears on LDOD	..	0	298	989	1,965	4,030	5,329	6,129	6,594	7,810
Official creditors	..	0	298	983	1,279	1,824	2,595	2,925	2,964	3,753
Private creditors	..	0	0	7	687	2,206	2,735	3,204	3,630	4,057
Memo: export credits	..	0	5,521	4,743	4,644	58	66	248	490	728
TOTAL DEBT FLOWS										
Disbursements	**645**	**5,029**	**1,590**	**580**	**0**	**0**	**0**	**0**	**0**	**0**
Long-term debt	645	4,589	1,501	580	0	0	0	0	0	0
IMF purchases	0	441	89	0	0	0	0	0	0	0
Principal repayments	**420**	**2,450**	**3,079**	**1,066**	**12**	**0**	**0**	**1**	**0**	**0**
Long-term debt	375	2,381	2,726	964	12	0	0	0	0	0
IMF repurchases	45	70	353	102	0	0	0	1	0	0
Net flows on debt	**430**	**2,930**	**-1,760**	**223**	**10**	**-402**	**120**	**-458**	**1,728**	**-1,767**
of which short-term debt	..	351	-271	710	23	-402	120	-457	1,728	-1,767
Interest payments (INT)	..	**1,286**	**1,704**	**833**	**44**	**47**	**47**	**17**	**53**	**57**
Long-term debt	104	1,077	1,583	773	2	0	0	0	0	0
IMF charges	0	32	66	21	1	0	0	0	0	0
Short-term debt	..	177	55	39	41	47	47	17	53	57
Net transfers on debt	..	**1,644**	**-3,464**	**-609**	**-34**	**-449**	**73**	**-476**	**1,676**	**-1,823**
Total debt service paid (TDS)	..	**3,736**	**4,783**	**1,899**	**56**	**47**	**47**	**19**	**53**	**57**
Long-term debt	479	3,458	4,309	1,738	14	0	0	0	0	0
IMF repurchases and charges	45	101	419	123	1	0	0	1	0	0
Short-term debt (interest only)	..	177	55	39	41	47	47	17	53	57
2. AGGREGATE NET RESOURCE FLOWS AND NET TRANSFERS (LONG-TERM)										
NET RESOURCE FLOWS	**276**	**2,208**	**-1,151**	**783**	**1,931**	**1,000**	**487**	**451**	**132**	**182**
Net flow of long-term debt (ex. IMF)	270	2,208	-1,225	-384	-12	0	0	0	0	0
Foreign direct investment (net)	0	0	67	64	25	0	0	0	0	0
Portfolio equity flows	0	0	0	0	0	0	0	0	0	0
Grants (excluding technical coop.)	6	0	7	1,103	1,918	1,000	487	451	132	182
Memo: technical coop. grants	3	7	35	359	611	81	57	45	34	33
official net resource flows	57	372	-314	872	1,906	1,000	487	451	132	182
private net resource flows	219	1,836	-837	-89	25	0	0	0	0	0
NET TRANSFERS	**172**	**1,130**	**-2,734**	**10**	**1,929**	**1,000**	**487**	**451**	**132**	**182**
Interest on long-term debt	104	1,077	1,583	773	2	0	0	0	0	0
Profit remittances on FDI	0	0	0	0	0	0	0	0	0	0
Memo: official net transfers	21	157	-1,045	632	1,904	1,000	487	451	132	182
private net transfers	152	973	-1,689	-623	25	0	0	0	0	0
3. MAJOR ECONOMIC AGGREGATES										
Gross national product (GNP)	..	..	..	..	..	..	..	..	..	..
Exports of goods & services (XGS)	..	..	..	..	..	..	..	..	..	..
of which workers remittances	..	..	..	..	..	..	..	..	..	..
Imports of goods & services (MGS)	..	..	..	..	..	..	..	..	..	..
International reserves (RES)	..	..	..	..	..	..	..	..	..	..
Current account balance	..	..	..	..	..	..	..	..	..	..
4. DEBT INDICATORS										
EDT / XGS (%)	..	..	..	..	..	..	..	..	..	..
EDT / GNP (%)	..	..	..	..	..	..	..	..	..	..
TDS / XGS (%)	..	..	..	..	..	..	..	..	..	..
INT / XGS (%)	..	..	..	..	..	..	..	..	..	..
INT / GNP (%)	..	..	..	..	..	..	..	..	..	..
RES / EDT (%)	..	..	..	..	..	..	..	..	..	..
RES / MGS (months)	..	..	..	..	..	..	..	..	..	..
Short-term / EDT (%)	..	11.6	2.9	6.6	12.9	12.9	16.4	15.8	27.1	18.8
Concessional / EDT (%)	..	7.2	5.4	4.0	2.5	2.6	2.6	2.6	2.0	2.4
Multilateral / EDT (%)	..	7.6	17.3	15.5	9.3	9.7	9.5	9.2	7.7	8.7

YUGOSLAVIA, FEDERAL REPUBLIC OF (SERBIA AND MONTENEGRO)

(US$ million, unless otherwise indicated)

	1970	*1980*	*1990*	*1992*	*1993*	*1994*	*1995*	*1996*	*1997*	*1998*
5. LONG-TERM DEBT										
DEBT OUTSTANDING (LDOD)	**2,053**	**15,586**	**16,846**	**15,195**	**10,990**	**11,270**	**11,484**	**11,239**	**10,924**	**11,080**
Public and publicly guaranteed	**1,199**	**4,581**	**12,986**	**11,117**	**8,231**	**8,511**	**8,725**	**8,480**	**8,165**	**8,321**
Official creditors	858	3,600	7,539	6,286	4,103	4,377	4,588	4,346	4,038	4,190
Multilateral	251	1,408	3,093	2,553	1,176	1,259	1,311	1,234	1,161	1,200
Concessional	3	0	0	0	0	0	0	0	0	0
Bilateral	606	2,192	4,446	3,733	2,927	3,118	3,277	3,112	2,877	2,990
Concessional	387	1,328	967	658	316	344	366	343	307	324
Private creditors	341	981	5,447	4,831	4,128	4,134	4,137	4,134	4,127	4,131
Bonds	21	10	0	0	0	0	0	0	0	0
Commercial banks	2	808	5,325	4,725	4,121	4,127	4,130	4,127	4,120	4,124
Other private	318	163	122	106	7	7	7	7	7	7
Private nonguaranteed	**854**	**11,005**	**3,860**	**4,078**	**2,759**	**2,759**	**2,759**	**2,759**	**2,759**	**2,759**
Bonds	0	0	0	0	0	0	0	0	0	0
Commercial banks	854	11,005	3,860	4,078	2,759	2,759	2,759	2,759	2,759	2,759
Memo:										
IBRD	244	1,359	2,433	1,978	1,126	1,204	1,252	1,178	1,112	1,148
IDA	0	0	0	0	0	0	0	0	0	0
DISBURSEMENTS	**645**	**4,589**	**1,501**	**580**	**0**	**0**	**0**	**0**	**0**	**0**
Public and publicly guaranteed	**179**	**1,366**	**286**	**86**	**0**	**0**	**0**	**0**	**0**	**0**
Official creditors	139	644	286	86	0	0	0	0	0	0
Multilateral	37	308	276	86	0	0	0	0	0	0
Concessional	0	0	0	0	0	0	0	0	0	0
Bilateral	102	336	10	0	0	0	0	0	0	0
Concessional	64	77	8	0	0	0	0	0	0	0
Private creditors	40	721	0	0	0	0	0	0	0	0
Bonds	0	0	0	0	0	0	0	0	0	0
Commercial banks	0	686	0	0	0	0	0	0	0	0
Other private	40	36	0	0	0	0	0	0	0	0
Private nonguaranteed	**465**	**3,223**	**1,215**	**494**	**0**	**0**	**0**	**0**	**0**	**0**
Bonds	0	0	0	0	0	0	0	0	0	0
Commercial banks	465	3,223	1,215	494	0	0	0	0	0	0
Memo:										
IBRD	37	281	269	51	0	0	0	0	0	0
IDA	0	0	0	0	0	0	0	0	0	0
PRINCIPAL REPAYMENTS	**375**	**2,381**	**2,726**	**964**	**12**	**0**	**0**	**0**	**0**	**0**
Public and publicly guaranteed	**170**	**368**	**1,516**	**317**	**12**	**0**	**0**	**0**	**0**	**0**
Official creditors	88	272	607	317	12	0	0	0	0	0
Multilateral	11	67	421	187	12	0	0	0	0	0
Concessional	0	0	0	0	0	0	0	0	0	0
Bilateral	78	206	186	131	0	0	0	0	0	0
Concessional	22	65	26	3	0	0	0	0	0	0
Private creditors	82	96	909	0	0	0	0	0	0	0
Bonds	2	2	0	0	0	0	0	0	0	0
Commercial banks	1	39	891	0	0	0	0	0	0	0
Other private	80	55	18	0	0	0	0	0	0	0
Private nonguaranteed	**204**	**2,012**	**1,210**	**647**	**0**	**0**	**0**	**0**	**0**	**0**
Bonds	0	0	0	0	0	0	0	0	0	0
Commercial banks	204	2,012	1,210	647	0	0	0	0	0	0
Memo:										
IBRD	10	66	405	155	12	0	0	0	0	0
IDA	0	0	0	0	0	0	0	0	0	0
NET FLOWS ON DEBT	**270**	**2,208**	**-1,225**	**-384**	**-12**	**0**	**0**	**0**	**0**	**0**
Public and publicly guaranteed	**9**	**998**	**-1,230**	**-231**	**-12**	**0**	**0**	**0**	**0**	**0**
Official creditors	51	372	-321	-231	-12	0	0	0	0	0
Multilateral	27	242	-145	-101	-12	0	0	0	0	0
Concessional	0	0	0	0	0	0	0	0	0	0
Bilateral	24	131	-176	-131	0	0	0	0	0	0
Concessional	42	12	-18	-3	0	0	0	0	0	0
Private creditors	-42	625	-909	0	0	0	0	0	0	0
Bonds	-2	-2	0	0	0	0	0	0	0	0
Commercial banks	-1	647	-891	0	0	0	0	0	0	0
Other private	-40	-19	-18	0	0	0	0	0	0	0
Private nonguaranteed	**261**	**1,211**	**5**	**-153**	**0**	**0**	**0**	**0**	**0**	**0**
Bonds	0	0	0	0	0	0	0	0	0	0
Commercial banks	261	1,211	5	-153	0	0	0	0	0	0
Memo:										
IBRD	27	216	-136	-103	-12	0	0	0	0	0
IDA	0	0	0	0	0	0	0	0	0	0

YUGOSLAVIA, FEDERAL REPUBLIC OF (SERBIA AND MONTENEGRO)

(US$ million, unless otherwise indicated)

	1970	1980	1990	1992	1993	1994	1995	1996	1997	1998
INTEREST PAYMENTS (LINT)	**104**	**1,077**	**1,583**	**773**	**2**	**0**	**0**	**0**	**0**	**0**
Public and publicly guaranteed	**73**	**249**	**1,203**	**469**	**2**	**0**	**0**	**0**	**0**	**0**
Official creditors	37	215	731	240	2	0	0	0	0	0
Multilateral	14	111	252	133	2	0	0	0	0	0
Concessional	0	0	0	0	0	0	0	0	0	0
Bilateral	23	103	479	106	0	0	0	0	0	0
Concessional	10	39	17	9	0	0	0	0	0	0
Private creditors	36	34	472	230	0	0	0	0	0	0
Bonds	0	0	0	0	0	0	0	0	0	0
Commercial banks	0	17	454	225	0	0	0	0	0	0
Other private	35	17	19	5	0	0	0	0	0	0
Private nonguaranteed	**32**	**829**	**380**	**304**	**0**	**0**	**0**	**0**	**0**	**0**
Bonds	0	0	0	0	0	0	0	0	0	0
Commercial banks	32	829	380	304	0	0	0	0	0	0
Memo:										
IBRD	13	110	191	69	2	0	0	0	0	0
IDA	0	0	0	0	0	0	0	0	0	0
NET TRANSFERS ON DEBT	**166**	**1,131**	**-2,809**	**-1,158**	**-14**	**0**	**0**	**0**	**0**	**0**
Public and publicly guaranteed	**-64**	**749**	**-2,434**	**-701**	**-14**	**0**	**0**	**0**	**0**	**0**
Official creditors	14	158	-1,052	-471	-14	0	0	0	0	0
Multilateral	13	130	-397	-234	-14	0	0	0	0	0
Concessional	0	0	0	0	0	0	0	0	0	0
Bilateral	1	27	-656	-237	0	0	0	0	0	0
Concessional	32	-27	-35	-12	0	0	0	0	0	0
Private creditors	-78	591	-1,381	-230	0	0	0	0	0	0
Bonds	-2	-2	0	0	0	0	0	0	0	0
Commercial banks	-1	630	-1,345	-225	0	0	0	0	0	0
Other private	-75	-36	-36	-5	0	0	0	0	0	0
Private nonguaranteed	**230**	**382**	**-375**	**-457**	**0**	**0**	**0**	**0**	**0**	**0**
Bonds	0	0	0	0	0	0	0	0	0	0
Commercial banks	230	382	-375	-457	0	0	0	0	0	0
Memo:										
IBRD	14	106	-327	-172	-14	0	0	0	0	0
IDA	0	0	0	0	0	0	0	0	0	0
DEBT SERVICE (LTDS)	**479**	**3,458**	**4,309**	**1,738**	**14**	**0**	**0**	**0**	**0**	**0**
Public and publicly guaranteed	**243**	**617**	**2,719**	**787**	**14**	**0**	**0**	**0**	**0**	**0**
Official creditors	125	487	1,338	557	14	0	0	0	0	0
Multilateral	24	178	673	320	14	0	0	0	0	0
Concessional	0	0	0	0	0	0	0	0	0	0
Bilateral	101	309	665	237	0	0	0	0	0	0
Concessional	33	103	43	12	0	0	0	0	0	0
Private creditors	118	130	1,381	230	0	0	0	0	0	0
Bonds	2	2	0	0	0	0	0	0	0	0
Commercial banks	1	56	1,345	225	0	0	0	0	0	0
Other private	115	72	36	5	0	0	0	0	0	0
Private nonguaranteed	**236**	**2,841**	**1,590**	**951**	**0**	**0**	**0**	**0**	**0**	**0**
Bonds	0	0	0	0	0	0	0	0	0	0
Commercial banks	236	2,841	1,590	951	0	0	0	0	0	0
Memo:										
IBRD	23	175	596	224	14	0	0	0	0	0
IDA	0	0	0	0	0	0	0	0	0	0
UNDISBURSED DEBT	**550**	**1,218**	**973**	**714**	**200**	**208**	**222**	**212**	**187**	**0**
Official creditors	462	1,205	973	714	200	208	222	212	187	0
Private creditors	87	13	0	0	0	0	0	0	0	0
Memorandum items										
Concessional LDOD	389	1,328	967	658	316	344	366	343	307	324
Variable rate LDOD	893	12,100	12,016	11,626	8,857	8,945	9,020	8,956	8,840	8,893
Public sector LDOD	980	3,826	12,485	10,700	8,142	8,418	8,629	8,386	8,076	8,230
Private sector LDOD	1,073	11,759	4,361	4,495	2,848	2,852	2,854	2,852	2,847	2,849

6. CURRENCY COMPOSITION OF LONG-TERM DEBT (PERCENT)

	1970	1980	1990	1992	1993	1994	1995	1996	1997	1998
Deutsche mark	13.9	13.3	8.4	8.9	6.9	7.5	7.9	7.5	6.7	7.1
French franc	2.0	0.0	4.4	4.3	5.5	5.8	6.2	6.0	5.4	5.7
Japanese yen	0.3	0.7	1.0	1.1	1.7	1.8	1.7	1.6	1.5	1.6
Pound sterling	3.6	0.1	0.4	0.4	0.5	0.5	0.5	0.6	0.6	0.6
Swiss franc	1.1	0.1	1.7	1.7	2.3	2.5	2.8	2.5	2.4	2.5
U.S.dollars	36.5	52.3	17.3	15.3	16.4	15.8	15.4	15.9	16.5	16.2
Multiple currency	24.8	30.7	56.3	57.9	60.7	59.6	58.7	59.6	61.0	60.3
Special drawing rights	0.0	0.0	0.0	0.0	0.0	0.0	0.0	0.0	0.0	0.0
All other currencies	17.8	2.8	10.5	10.4	6.0	6.5	6.8	6.3	5.9	6.0

YUGOSLAVIA, FEDERAL REPUBLIC OF (SERBIA AND MONTENEGRO)

(US$ million, unless otherwise indicated)

	1970	1980	1990	1992	1993	1994	1995	1996	1997	1998
7. DEBT RESTRUCTURINGS										
Total amount rescheduled	..	..	0	0	0	0	0	0	0	0
Debt stock rescheduled	..	..	0	0	0	0	0	0	0	0
Principal rescheduled	..	..	0	0	0	0	0	0	0	0
Official	..	..	0	0	0	0	0	0	0	0
Private	..	..	0	0	0	0	0	0	0	0
Interest rescheduled	..	..	0	0	0	0	0	0	0	0
Official	..	..	0	0	0	0	0	0	0	0
Private	..	..	0	0	0	0	0	0	0	0
Debt forgiven	..	..	0	0	0	0	0	0	0	0
Memo: interest forgiven	..	..	0	0	0	0	0	0	0	0
Debt stock reduction	..	..	1,496	0	0	0	0	0	0	0
of which debt buyback	..	..	883	0	0	0	0	0	0	0
8. DEBT STOCK-FLOW RECONCILIATION										
Total change in debt stocks	..	..	-1,235	11	-3,774	326	804	-400	1,652	-1,349
Net flows on debt	430	2,930	-1,760	223	10	-402	120	-458	1,728	-1,767
Net change in interest arrears	..	..	0	90	526	443	469	306	244	258
Interest capitalized	..	..	0	0	0	0	0	0	0	0
Debt forgiveness or reduction	..	..	-613	0	0	0	0	0	0	0
Cross-currency valuation	..	..	517	-334	-257	302	230	-229	-284	166
Residual	..	..	621	33	-4,053	-18	-15	-19	-36	-6
9. AVERAGE TERMS OF NEW COMMITMENTS										
ALL CREDITORS										
Interest (%)	7.0	15.1	8.2	0.0	0.0	0.0	0.0	0.0	0.0	0.0
Maturity (years)	17.2	8.6	16.1	0.0	0.0	0.0	0.0	0.0	0.0	0.0
Grace period (years)	6.1	3.2	5.2	0.0	0.0	0.0	0.0	0.0	0.0	0.0
Grant element (%)	17.9	-19.3	9.9	0.0	0.0	0.0	0.0	0.0	0.0	0.0
Official creditors										
Interest (%)	7.0	12.0	8.2	0.0	0.0	0.0	0.0	0.0	0.0	0.0
Maturity (years)	18.8	10.8	16.1	0.0	0.0	0.0	0.0	0.0	0.0	0.0
Grace period (years)	6.9	3.3	5.2	0.0	0.0	0.0	0.0	0.0	0.0	0.0
Grant element (%)	19.3	-7.4	9.9	0.0	0.0	0.0	0.0	0.0	0.0	0.0
Private creditors										
Interest (%)	7.0	17.0	0.0	0.0	0.0	0.0	0.0	0.0	0.0	0.0
Maturity (years)	13.1	7.1	0.0	0.0	0.0	0.0	0.0	0.0	0.0	0.0
Grace period (years)	4.1	3.0	0.0	0.0	0.0	0.0	0.0	0.0	0.0	0.0
Grant element (%)	14.2	-26.8	0.0	0.0	0.0	0.0	0.0	0.0	0.0	0.0
Memorandum items										
Commitments	199	1,187	830	0	0	0	0	0	0	0
Official creditors	143	461	830	0	0	0	0	0	0	0
Private creditors	56	726	0	0	0	0	0	0	0	0

10. CONTRACTUAL OBLIGATIONS ON OUTSTANDING LONG-TERM DEBT

	1999	2000	2001	2002	2003	2004	2005	2006	2007	2008
TOTAL										
Disbursements	0	0	0	0	0	0	0	0	0	0
Principal	635	504	473	433	356	325	313	301	3	3
Interest	222	181	146	114	84	57	36	16	1	1
Official creditors										
Disbursements	0	0	0	0	0	0	0	0	0	0
Principal	217	100	69	42	31	27	15	3	3	3
Interest	32	19	13	8	6	4	2	1	1	1
Bilateral creditors										
Disbursements	0	0	0	0	0	0	0	0	0	0
Principal	8	8	8	8	4	0	0	0	0	0
Interest	1	1	0	0	0	0	0	0	0	0
Multilateral creditors										
Disbursements	0	0	0	0	0	0	0	0	0	0
Principal	209	92	61	34	27	27	15	3	3	3
Interest	31	19	12	8	6	4	2	1	1	1
Private creditors										
Disbursements	0	0	0	0	0	0	0	0	0	0
Principal	418	404	404	391	324	297	297	297	0	0
Interest	191	162	133	105	78	53	34	15	0	0
Commercial banks										
Disbursements	0	0	0	0	0	0	0	0	0	0
Principal	297	297	297	297	297	297	297	297	0	0
Interest	149	130	111	92	72	53	34	15	0	0
Other private										
Disbursements	0	0	0	0	0	0	0	0	0	0
Principal	120	107	107	94	27	0	0	0	0	0
Interest	41	32	22	14	6	0	0	0	0	0

ZAMBIA

(US$ million, unless otherwise indicated)

	1970	1980	1990	1992	1993	1994	1995	1996	1997	1998
1. SUMMARY DEBT DATA										
TOTAL DEBT STOCKS (EDT)	..	**3,244**	**6,916**	**6,709**	**6,485**	**6,804**	**6,952**	**7,054**	**6,654**	**6,865**
Long-term debt (LDOD)	**654**	**2,211**	**4,554**	**4,528**	**4,411**	**5,188**	**5,298**	**5,379**	**5,257**	**5,348**
Public and publicly guaranteed	624	2,124	4,552	4,514	4,397	5,174	5,285	5,363	5,245	5,320
Private nonguaranteed	30	87	2	14	13	14	14	16	13	29
Use of IMF credit	**0**	**447**	**949**	**847**	**777**	**805**	**1,239**	**1,198**	**1,138**	**1,188**
Short-term debt	..	**586**	**1,414**	**1,335**	**1,297**	**812**	**415**	**477**	**259**	**329**
of which interest arrears on LDOD	..	6	739	622	585	471	178	151	138	135
Official creditors	..	3	671	541	504	443	146	119	112	120
Private creditors	..	3	68	81	81	27	32	33	26	15
Memo: principal arrears on LDOD	..	33	1,492	1,424	1,404	1,146	766	711	739	749
Official creditors	..	21	1,388	1,319	1,283	1,069	671	606	649	686
Private creditors	..	13	104	106	121	77	94	106	90	62
Memo: export credits	..	0	1,123	923	1,020	1,024	630	988	1,456	1,110
TOTAL DEBT FLOWS										
Disbursements	**363**	**690**	**165**	**282**	**241**	**294**	**2,606**	**236**	**286**	**84**
Long-term debt	363	599	165	282	241	294	352	236	272	84
IMF purchases	0	90	0	0	0	0	2,253	0	14	0
Principal repayments	**45**	**269**	**126**	**183**	**211**	**206**	**2,067**	**156**	**164**	**132**
Long-term debt	41	212	101	146	142	186	242	156	164	132
IMF repurchases	4	57	25	37	70	21	1,825	0	0	0
Net flows on debt	**478**	**360**	**-100**	**82**	**29**	**88**	**435**	**169**	**-83**	**25**
of which short-term debt	..	-61	-139	-17	-1	0	-104	89	-205	73
Interest payments (INT)	..	**141**	**77**	**168**	**152**	**169**	**556**	**95**	**81**	**70**
Long-term debt	31	115	72	98	92	127	136	75	65	55
IMF charges	0	26	2	69	60	41	419	11	6	6
Short-term debt	..	0	3	1	1	2	1	9	10	10
Net transfers on debt	..	**219**	**-177**	**-86**	**-124**	**-82**	**-121**	**74**	**-165**	**-45**
Total debt service paid (TDS)	..	**410**	**202**	**351**	**364**	**376**	**2,623**	**251**	**245**	**202**
Long-term debt	72	326	173	244	233	312	378	231	230	187
IMF repurchases and charges	4	84	27	106	129	62	2,244	11	6	6
Short-term debt (interest only)	..	0	3	1	1	2	1	9	10	10
2. AGGREGATE NET RESOURCE FLOWS AND NET TRANSFERS (LONG-TERM)										
NET RESOURCE FLOWS	**26**	**521**	**930**	**823**	**629**	**520**	**539**	**411**	**428**	**281**
Net flow of long-term debt (ex. IMF)	321	388	64	136	99	109	110	80	108	-49
Foreign direct investment (net)	-297	62	203	45	52	56	67	58	70	72
Portfolio equity flows	0	0	0	0	0	0	0	0	0	0
Grants (excluding technical coop.)	2	72	663	642	478	355	362	273	250	257
Memo: technical coop. grants	13	87	129	144	165	135	164	142	133	96
official net resource flows	18	346	736	791	617	489	509	379	365	241
private net resource flows	8	175	194	32	12	32	30	32	63	40
NET TRANSFERS	**-65**	**322**	**743**	**685**	**493**	**346**	**353**	**291**	**310**	**176**
Interest on long-term debt	31	115	72	98	92	127	136	75	65	55
Profit remittances on FDI	60	84	115	40	45	48	50	45	53	50
Memo: official net transfers	12	293	693	713	540	377	393	312	312	193
private net transfers	-76	29	50	-28	-48	-32	-40	-21	-3	-17
3. MAJOR ECONOMIC AGGREGATES										
Gross national product (GNP)	1,742	3,594	3,008	2,867	3,019	3,111	3,230	3,081	3,710	3,158
Exports of goods & services (XGS)	..	1,625	1,362	1,301	1,140	1,285	1,445	1,227	1,411	1,143
of which workers remittances	..	0	0	..	..	..	..	..	..	..
Imports of goods & services (MGS)	..	1,987	2,336	2,119	1,661	1,727	1,962	1,701	1,903	1,711
International reserves (RES)	515	206	201	..	192	268	223	223	239	69
Current account balance	..	-516	-594	..	..	..	..	..	..	..
4. DEBT INDICATORS										
EDT / XGS (%)	..	199.7	507.9	515.8	569.0	529.4	481.3	575.2	471.6	600.9
EDT / GNP (%)	..	90.3	229.9	234.0	214.8	218.7	215.3	229.0	179.4	217.4
TDS / XGS (%)	..	25.2	14.9	27.0	31.9	29.2	181.6	20.4	17.4	17.7
INT / XGS (%)	..	8.7	5.6	12.9	13.4	13.2	38.5	7.7	5.8	6.1
INT / GNP (%)	..	3.9	2.5	5.9	5.1	5.4	17.2	3.1	2.2	2.2
RES / EDT (%)	..	6.4	2.9	..	3.0	3.9	3.2	3.2	3.6	1.0
RES / MGS (months)	..	1.3	1.0	..	1.4	1.9	1.4	1.6	1.5	0.5
Short-term / EDT (%)	..	18.1	20.4	19.9	20.0	11.9	6.0	6.8	3.9	4.8
Concessional / EDT (%)	..	24.6	29.9	37.0	40.3	45.4	47.4	49.6	52.4	53.1
Multilateral / EDT (%)	..	12.1	20.2	23.1	25.9	28.5	30.6	30.7	32.6	32.7

ZAMBIA

(US$ million, unless otherwise indicated)

	1970	1980	1990	1992	1993	1994	1995	1996	1997	1998
5. LONG-TERM DEBT										
DEBT OUTSTANDING (LDOD)	**654**	**2,211**	**4,554**	**4,528**	**4,411**	**5,188**	**5,298**	**5,379**	**5,257**	**5,348**
Public and publicly guaranteed	**624**	**2,124**	**4,552**	**4,514**	**4,397**	**5,174**	**5,285**	**5,363**	**5,245**	**5,320**
Official creditors	120	1,485	4,108	4,155	4,077	4,929	5,075	5,186	5,075	5,207
Multilateral	61	393	1,400	1,552	1,679	1,940	2,127	2,169	2,167	2,242
Concessional	0	19	579	1,001	1,184	1,458	1,715	1,839	1,923	2,031
Bilateral	59	1,091	2,708	2,604	2,398	2,989	2,948	3,018	2,908	2,965
Concessional	51	778	1,488	1,483	1,432	1,629	1,579	1,663	1,564	1,617
Private creditors	503	639	444	358	320	245	210	177	170	113
Bonds	55	3	0	0	0	0	0	0	0	0
Commercial banks	0	77	70	73	73	10	16	17	21	21
Other private	449	560	374	285	247	235	194	160	149	92
Private nonguaranteed	**30**	**87**	**2**	**14**	**13**	**14**	**14**	**16**	**13**	**29**
Bonds	0	0	0	0	0	0	0	0	0	0
Commercial banks	30	87	2	14	13	14	14	16	13	29
Memo:										
IBRD	61	346	539	289	240	201	163	105	62	41
IDA	0	2	274	643	817	1,043	1,270	1,405	1,493	1,587
DISBURSEMENTS	**363**	**599**	**165**	**282**	**241**	**294**	**352**	**236**	**272**	**84**
Public and publicly guaranteed	**351**	**593**	**163**	**272**	**240**	**292**	**351**	**232**	**272**	**64**
Official creditors	22	311	117	250	229	259	327	224	222	64
Multilateral	6	56	106	237	226	242	251	213	211	64
Concessional	0	6	41	203	201	207	237	205	207	59
Bilateral	16	254	11	13	4	18	76	11	12	0
Concessional	16	237	9	9	4	11	72	0	3	0
Private creditors	330	282	46	23	10	33	24	8	50	0
Bonds	0	0	0	0	0	0	0	0	0	0
Commercial banks	0	9	0	0	0	10	8	5	5	0
Other private	330	273	46	23	10	22	16	4	44	0
Private nonguaranteed	**11**	**6**	**2**	**10**	**1**	**2**	**1**	**5**	**0**	**20**
Bonds	0	0	0	0	0	0	0	0	0	0
Commercial banks	11	6	2	10	1	2	1	5	0	20
Memo:										
IBRD	6	28	0	0	0	0	0	0	0	0
IDA	0	2	3	174	174	186	209	181	169	43
PRINCIPAL REPAYMENTS	**41**	**212**	**101**	**146**	**142**	**186**	**242**	**156**	**164**	**132**
Public and publicly guaranteed	**35**	**181**	**101**	**146**	**140**	**184**	**241**	**154**	**161**	**128**
Official creditors	6	37	44	100	91	126	180	117	107	80
Multilateral	4	18	39	98	85	101	120	88	76	57
Concessional	0	0	2	4	6	10	15	14	13	19
Bilateral	2	18	6	2	6	25	60	29	31	23
Concessional	1	3	0	0	4	11	32	19	20	8
Private creditors	29	144	57	46	49	58	61	37	53	48
Bonds	7	3	0	0	0	0	0	0	0	0
Commercial banks	0	4	0	0	0	8	2	4	1	0
Other private	22	137	57	46	49	50	59	33	53	48
Private nonguaranteed	**6**	**31**	**0**	**0**	**2**	**2**	**1**	**2**	**4**	**4**
Bonds	0	0	0	0	0	0	0	0	0	0
Commercial banks	6	31	0	0	2	2	1	2	4	4
Memo:										
IBRD	4	18	5	71	51	55	50	47	35	21
IDA	0	0	0	1	1	1	2	3	4	4
NET FLOWS ON DEBT	**321**	**388**	**64**	**136**	**99**	**109**	**110**	**80**	**108**	**-49**
Public and publicly guaranteed	**316**	**413**	**62**	**126**	**100**	**108**	**110**	**78**	**111**	**-65**
Official creditors	16	274	73	149	139	133	147	107	115	-17
Multilateral	1	38	67	139	141	141	131	124	134	6
Concessional	0	6	39	200	195	196	222	190	194	40
Bilateral	15	236	6	10	-2	-8	17	-18	-19	-23
Concessional	15	234	9	9	-1	1	40	-19	-16	-8
Private creditors	300	138	-11	-24	-39	-25	-37	-29	-4	-48
Bonds	-7	-3	0	0	0	0	0	0	0	0
Commercial banks	0	5	0	0	0	3	6	1	5	0
Other private	307	136	-11	-24	-39	-27	-43	-30	-8	-48
Private nonguaranteed	**5**	**-25**	**2**	**10**	**-1**	**0**	**0**	**3**	**-4**	**16**
Bonds	0	0	0	0	0	0	0	0	0	0
Commercial banks	5	-25	2	10	-1	0	0	3	-4	16
Memo:										
IBRD	1	10	-5	-71	-51	-55	-50	-47	-35	-21
IDA	0	2	3	173	173	185	207	178	166	39

ZAMBIA

(US$ million, unless otherwise indicated)

	1970	1980	1990	1992	1993	1994	1995	1996	1997	1998
INTEREST PAYMENTS (LINT)	**31**	**115**	**72**	**98**	**92**	**127**	**136**	**75**	**65**	**55**
Public and publicly guaranteed	**29**	**105**	**72**	**98**	**92**	**127**	**136**	**75**	**65**	**55**
Official creditors	6	52	43	78	77	111	116	67	53	48
Multilateral	4	33	33	67	58	61	65	46	39	29
Concessional	0	0	3	11	15	14	17	17	15	14
Bilateral	2	19	10	11	19	51	51	21	14	19
Concessional	2	13	9	8	8	22	16	12	5	9
Private creditors	23	53	29	20	15	15	20	8	12	7
Bonds	3	1	0	0	0	0	0	0	0	0
Commercial banks	0	12	0	0	0	1	1	1	1	0
Other private	20	40	29	20	15	15	19	7	12	7
Private nonguaranteed	**2**	**10**	**0**	**0**	**0**	**0**	**0**	**0**	**0**	**0**
Bonds	0	0	0	0	0	0	0	0	0	0
Commercial banks	2	10	0	0	0	0	0	0	0	0
Memo:										
IBRD	4	31	1	36	21	21	15	11	6	4
IDA	0	0	0	6	5	6	9	10	10	11
NET TRANSFERS ON DEBT	**291**	**273**	**-8**	**38**	**7**	**-18**	**-25**	**5**	**42**	**-103**
Public and publicly guaranteed	**287**	**307**	**-10**	**28**	**8**	**-18**	**-25**	**3**	**46**	**-119**
Official creditors	10	222	30	71	62	22	31	39	62	-65
Multilateral	-2	5	34	72	83	80	66	78	95	-23
Concessional	0	6	36	189	180	182	206	174	179	26
Bilateral	12	217	-5	-1	-21	-58	-34	-39	-33	-42
Concessional	13	221	0	1	-8	-21	24	-31	-22	-17
Private creditors	278	85	-40	-43	-54	-40	-57	-37	-16	-55
Bonds	-10	-4	0	0	0	0	0	0	0	0
Commercial banks	0	-6	0	0	0	2	5	0	4	0
Other private	288	96	-40	-43	-54	-42	-62	-37	-20	-54
Private nonguaranteed	**3**	**-35**	**2**	**10**	**-1**	**0**	**0**	**3**	**-4**	**16**
Bonds	0	0	0	0	0	0	0	0	0	0
Commercial banks	3	-35	2	10	-1	0	0	3	-4	16
Memo:										
IBRD	-2	-21	-5	-107	-72	-76	-65	-58	-41	-25
IDA	0	2	3	168	168	179	198	169	155	28
DEBT SERVICE (LTDS)	**72**	**326**	**173**	**244**	**233**	**312**	**378**	**231**	**230**	**187**
Public and publicly guaranteed	**64**	**286**	**173**	**244**	**231**	**310**	**377**	**229**	**226**	**183**
Official creditors	12	89	88	178	167	237	296	184	160	128
Multilateral	8	51	72	165	143	161	185	134	116	87
Concessional	0	0	5	15	21	24	32	31	28	33
Bilateral	4	37	16	13	25	76	110	50	45	42
Concessional	3	16	9	8	12	32	48	31	25	17
Private creditors	52	197	85	66	64	73	81	45	66	55
Bonds	10	4	0	0	0	0	0	0	0	0
Commercial banks	0	16	0	0	0	8	3	5	1	0
Other private	42	177	85	66	64	64	78	40	64	54
Private nonguaranteed	**8**	**41**	**0**	**0**	**2**	**2**	**1**	**2**	**4**	**4**
Bonds	0	0	0	0	0	0	0	0	0	0
Commercial banks	8	41	0	0	2	2	1	2	4	4
Memo:										
IBRD	8	48	5	107	72	76	65	58	41	25
IDA	0	0	0	6	6	8	11	13	14	15
UNDISBURSED DEBT	**309**	**877**	**691**	**637**	**557**	**618**	**659**	**559**	**507**	**529**
Official creditors	291	679	588	595	529	589	641	550	503	529
Private creditors	18	198	103	42	29	29	18	9	4	0
Memorandum items										
Concessional LDOD	51	797	2,067	2,484	2,615	3,087	3,294	3,502	3,487	3,648
Variable rate LDOD	30	280	494	508	485	737	731	732	738	738
Public sector LDOD	624	2,107	4,552	4,514	4,397	5,146	5,253	5,317	5,197	5,272
Private sector LDOD	30	104	2	14	13	41	46	62	60	76

6. CURRENCY COMPOSITION OF LONG-TERM DEBT (PERCENT)

	1970	1980	1990	1992	1993	1994	1995	1996	1997	1998
Deutsche mark	0.4	9.4	10.4	10.1	8.4	10.5	10.8	10.2	9.3	9.8
French franc	0.9	3.2	3.0	3.4	3.3	2.9	3.1	2.5	2.5	2.6
Japanese yen	0.0	4.8	10.0	10.1	10.9	10.9	11.2	12.3	10.6	12.5
Pound sterling	17.7	10.6	8.5	7.9	6.8	8.0	7.7	8.4	9.2	7.7
Swiss franc	0.0	0.0	0.6	0.5	0.6	0.1	0.2	0.1	0.1	0.1
U.S.dollars	53.7	20.2	28.1	34.4	38.3	38.5	39.4	40.9	44.1	43.7
Multiple currency	9.8	16.7	17.5	13.3	12.8	10.7	9.8	8.2	7.0	6.7
Special drawing rights	0.0	0.0	1.0	1.0	0.0	0.0	0.0	0.1	0.1	0.2
All other currencies	17.5	35.1	20.9	19.3	18.9	18.4	17.8	17.3	17.1	16.7

ZAMBIA

(US$ million, unless otherwise indicated)

	1970	1980	1990	1992	1993	1994	1995	1996	1997	1998
7. DEBT RESTRUCTURINGS										
Total amount rescheduled	..	..	690	233	186	146	20	203	127	78
Debt stock rescheduled	..	..	38	0	0	0	0	0	0	0
Principal rescheduled	..	..	466	105	105	74	7	121	55	22
Official	..	..	342	98	104	74	7	121	55	22
Private	..	..	123	6	0	0	0	0	0	0
Interest rescheduled	..	..	321	116	81	72	5	81	72	55
Official	..	..	299	116	80	71	5	81	72	55
Private	..	..	22	0	1	1	0	0	0	0
Debt forgiven	..	..	114	218	282	96	1	23	1	2
Memo: interest forgiven	..	..	22	14	31	67	1	7	1	0
Debt stock reduction	..	..	26	0	0	446	2	0	0	0
of which debt buyback	..	..	0	0	0	8	0	0	0	0
8. DEBT STOCK-FLOW RECONCILIATION										
Total change in debt stocks	..	..	351	-263	-224	319	148	102	-400	211
Net flows on debt	478	360	-100	82	29	88	435	169	-83	25
Net change in interest arrears	..	..	29	8	-37	-115	-293	-26	-13	-3
Interest capitalized	..	..	321	116	81	72	5	81	72	55
Debt forgiveness or reduction	..	..	-140	-218	-282	-535	-2	-23	-1	-2
Cross-currency valuation	..	..	306	-182	-22	160	55	-123	-199	136
Residual	..	..	-63	-69	7	649	-51	24	-176	0
9. AVERAGE TERMS OF NEW COMMITMENTS										
ALL CREDITORS										
Interest (%)	4.2	6.7	8.1	1.1	0.7	1.9	1.8	2.0	1.7	0.8
Maturity (years)	20.6	18.6	16.2	38.8	38.8	32.5	36.3	35.7	32.6	39.4
Grace period (years)	10.2	4.4	4.8	9.5	10.0	8.8	10.1	9.3	7.4	9.9
Grant element (%)	42.8	22.1	14.8	73.7	80.2	66.4	70.2	70.0	64.7	80.2
Official creditors										
Interest (%)	1.4	3.7	6.3	1.0	0.7	1.4	1.5	2.0	0.5	0.8
Maturity (years)	32.6	29.0	21.8	39.9	38.8	35.0	37.2	35.7	37.9	39.4
Grace period (years)	21.6	8.5	6.8	9.8	10.0	9.3	10.3	9.3	8.9	9.9
Grant element (%)	79.2	48.9	26.3	75.7	80.2	71.7	72.9	70.0	76.6	80.2
Private creditors										
Interest (%)	6.6	8.8	11.0	3.5	0.0	6.4	10.5	0.0	7.0	0.0
Maturity (years)	10.4	11.0	6.9	2.6	0.0	7.4	9.2	0.0	7.8	0.0
Grace period (years)	0.5	1.4	1.4	0.3	0.0	3.0	3.0	0.0	0.3	0.0
Grant element (%)	12.1	2.6	-4.1	8.1	0.0	12.3	-3.7	0.0	8.8	0.0
Memorandum items										
Commitments	557	635	192	368	202	338	382	143	253	75
Official creditors	255	267	120	357	202	307	368	143	209	75
Private creditors	302	368	72	11	0	30	14	0	44	0

10. CONTRACTUAL OBLIGATIONS ON OUTSTANDING LONG-TERM DEBT

	1999	2000	2001	2002	2003	2004	2005	2006	2007	2008
TOTAL										
Disbursements	128	129	97	74	51	34	17	1	0	0
Principal	225	274	272	268	272	247	186	141	144	141
Interest	160	151	137	123	109	95	82	76	71	66
Official creditors										
Disbursements	128	129	97	74	51	34	17	1	0	0
Principal	204	261	258	257	260	241	183	141	144	141
Interest	157	149	135	122	108	94	82	76	71	66
Bilateral creditors										
Disbursements	3	2	1	1	1	1	0	0	0	0
Principal	147	207	201	200	201	177	119	71	72	74
Interest	122	114	103	91	79	67	57	53	50	46
Multilateral creditors										
Disbursements	125	127	96	73	50	34	16	1	0	0
Principal	57	54	58	57	60	64	64	70	72	68
Interest	35	34	33	31	29	27	25	23	21	20
Private creditors										
Disbursements	0	0	0	0	0	0	0	0	0	0
Principal	20	14	13	11	11	6	3	0	0	0
Interest	3	3	2	1	1	1	0	0	0	0
Commercial banks										
Disbursements	0	0	0	0	0	0	0	0	0	0
Principal	9	2	2	0	0	0	0	0	0	0
Interest	1	0	0	0	0	0	0	0	0	0
Other private										
Disbursements	0	0	0	0	0	0	0	0	0	0
Principal	11	11	11	11	11	6	3	0	0	0
Interest	3	2	2	1	1	1	0	0	0	0

ZIMBABWE

(US$ million, unless otherwise indicated)

	1970	1980	1990	1992	1993	1994	1995	1996	1997	1998
1. SUMMARY DEBT DATA										
TOTAL DEBT STOCKS (EDT)	..	**786**	**3,247**	**4,071**	**4,299**	**4,537**	**5,053**	**4,994**	**4,924**	**4,716**
Long-term debt (LDOD)	**229**	**696**	**2,649**	**3,148**	**3,417**	**3,664**	**3,906**	**3,756**	**3,562**	**3,541**
Public and publicly guaranteed	229	696	2,464	2,853	3,111	3,421	3,525	3,328	3,109	3,341
Private nonguaranteed	0	0	185	296	306	243	381	428	453	200
Use of IMF credit	**0**	**0**	**7**	**216**	**282**	**376**	**461**	**437**	**385**	**407**
Short-term debt	..	**90**	**591**	**706**	**601**	**497**	**685**	**801**	**977**	**768**
of which interest arrears on LDOD	..	0	0	0	1	1	3	0	0	0
Official creditors	..	0	0	0	0	0	1	0	0	0
Private creditors	..	0	0	0	0	1	2	0	0	0
Memo: principal arrears on LDOD	..	0	0	3	9	19	22	2	5	13
Official creditors	..	0	0	0	2	15	8	1	5	5
Private creditors	..	0	0	3	7	5	15	1	0	8
Memo: export credits	..	0	660	935	795	807	888	852	877	861
TOTAL DEBT FLOWS										
Disbursements	**0**	**132**	**424**	**1,045**	**797**	**502**	**628**	**425**	**486**	**603**
Long-term debt	0	132	424	824	731	427	548	425	486	550
IMF purchases	0	0	0	221	67	75	80	0	0	53
Principal repayments	**5**	**40**	**270**	**387**	**406**	**372**	**404**	**424**	**459**	**763**
Long-term debt	5	40	247	387	406	372	404	416	433	715
IMF repurchases	0	0	24	0	0	0	0	9	26	48
Net flows on debt	**-5**	**148**	**335**	**804**	**286**	**26**	**411**	**119**	**203**	**-368**
of which short-term debt	..	55	181	146	-106	-104	187	119	176	-209
Interest payments (INT)	..	**26**	**201**	**208**	**212**	**231**	**245**	**240**	**228**	**218**
Long-term debt	5	10	149	157	170	193	196	184	174	166
IMF charges	0	0	2	6	10	10	13	12	10	10
Short-term debt	..	15	49	45	33	28	35	44	44	43
Net transfers on debt	..	**122**	**134**	**596**	**74**	**-205**	**166**	**-121**	**-25**	**-587**
Total debt service paid (TDS)	..	**65**	**471**	**595**	**618**	**603**	**649**	**664**	**686**	**981**
Long-term debt	9	50	396	544	575	565	600	600	607	880
IMF repurchases and charges	0	0	26	6	10	10	13	20	36	58
Short-term debt (interest only)	..	15	49	45	33	28	35	44	44	43
2. AGGREGATE NET RESOURCE FLOWS AND NET TRANSFERS (LONG-TERM)										
NET RESOURCE FLOWS	**-5**	**221**	**364**	**788**	**504**	**403**	**510**	**298**	**258**	**68**
Net flow of long-term debt (ex. IMF)	-5	93	177	437	325	55	144	9	53	-164
Foreign direct investment (net)	0	2	-12	15	28	35	40	63	70	76
Portfolio equity flows	0	0	0	0	0	50	18	17	10	3
Grants (excluding technical coop.)	0	127	199	336	151	264	308	209	126	153
Memo: technical coop. grants	1	70	104	191	156	115	132	109	111	98
official net resource flows	-5	199	278	749	606	459	356	256	243	285
private net resource flows	0	22	85	39	-101	-56	154	42	15	-217
NET TRANSFERS	**-10**	**133**	**122**	**558**	**274**	**141**	**239**	**37**	**5**	**-180**
Interest on long-term debt	5	10	149	157	170	193	196	184	174	166
Profit remittances on FDI	0	78	92	74	61	70	75	77	80	82
Memo: official net transfers	-9	197	212	673	508	346	235	139	129	180
private net transfers	-1	-64	-90	-116	-234	-206	5	-102	-124	-360
3. MAJOR ECONOMIC AGGREGATES										
Gross national product (GNP)	1,854	6,610	8,495	6,475	6,316	6,596	6,795	8,249	8,166	5,911
Exports of goods & services (XGS)	..	1,724	2,035	1,859	2,016	2,372	2,737	3,118	3,092	2,565
of which workers remittances	..	9	0	0	0	0	..	..	..	..
Imports of goods & services (MGS)	..	1,895	2,287	2,745	2,338	2,836	3,297	3,524	4,131	3,119
International reserves (RES)	59	419	295	404	628	585	888	834	384	310
Current account balance	..	-149	-140	-604	-116	-425	..	..	..	..
4. DEBT INDICATORS										
EDT / XGS (%)	..	45.6	159.6	219.0	213.2	191.3	184.6	160.2	159.2	183.8
EDT / GNP (%)	..	11.9	38.2	62.9	68.1	68.8	74.4	60.5	60.3	79.8
TDS / XGS (%)	..	3.8	23.2	32.0	30.6	25.4	23.7	21.3	22.2	38.2
INT / XGS (%)	..	1.5	9.9	11.2	10.5	9.7	8.9	7.7	7.4	8.5
INT / GNP (%)	..	0.4	2.4	3.2	3.4	3.5	3.6	2.9	2.8	3.7
RES / EDT (%)	..	53.4	9.1	9.9	14.6	12.9	17.6	16.7	7.8	6.6
RES / MGS (months)	..	2.7	1.6	1.8	3.2	2.5	3.2	2.8	1.1	1.2
Short-term / EDT (%)	..	11.5	18.2	17.3	14.0	11.0	13.6	16.0	19.8	16.3
Concessional / EDT (%)	..	1.9	27.9	27.0	28.4	32.1	30.1	28.9	28.0	32.2
Multilateral / EDT (%)	..	0.4	19.6	23.8	30.5	33.5	32.3	31.5	32.7	36.4

ZIMBABWE

(US$ million, unless otherwise indicated)

	1970	1980	1990	1992	1993	1994	1995	1996	1997	1998
5. LONG-TERM DEBT										
DEBT OUTSTANDING (LDOD)	**229**	**696**	**2,649**	**3,148**	**3,417**	**3,664**	**3,906**	**3,756**	**3,562**	**3,541**
Public and publicly guaranteed	**229**	**696**	**2,464**	**2,853**	**3,111**	**3,421**	**3,525**	**3,328**	**3,109**	**3,341**
Official creditors	85	101	1,508	1,952	2,363	2,726	2,860	2,753	2,649	2,914
Multilateral	41	3	637	967	1,311	1,519	1,633	1,573	1,612	1,716
Concessional	0	0	129	199	260	383	414	415	478	533
Bilateral	44	98	871	986	1,052	1,207	1,227	1,180	1,038	1,198
Concessional	44	15	778	901	961	1,072	1,107	1,026	902	985
Private creditors	145	595	956	901	748	695	665	575	460	427
Bonds	145	592	293	210	180	150	120	90	60	30
Commercial banks	0	3	208	226	141	139	180	184	155	184
Other private	0	0	456	464	427	406	366	301	245	213
Private nonguaranteed	**0**	**0**	**185**	**296**	**306**	**243**	**381**	**428**	**453**	**200**
Bonds	0	0	0	0	0	0	0	0	0	0
Commercial banks	0	0	185	296	306	243	381	428	453	200
Memo:										
IBRD	41	3	381	442	528	556	560	513	473	498
IDA	0	0	67	138	200	313	336	335	399	442
DISBURSEMENTS	**0**	**132**	**424**	**824**	**731**	**427**	**548**	**425**	**486**	**550**
Public and publicly guaranteed	**0**	**132**	**297**	**738**	**641**	**394**	**319**	**283**	**341**	**395**
Official creditors	0	77	158	495	559	311	218	218	309	321
Multilateral	0	0	72	321	415	187	151	146	276	155
Concessional	0	0	7	81	68	111	28	24	94	39
Bilateral	0	77	86	174	144	124	67	72	32	166
Concessional	0	1	76	162	122	72	57	25	24	73
Private creditors	0	55	139	244	82	82	101	65	32	74
Bonds	0	52	0	0	0	0	0	0	0	0
Commercial banks	0	3	29	163	31	47	67	52	25	57
Other private	0	0	111	80	51	35	34	13	7	17
Private nonguaranteed	**0**	**0**	**127**	**86**	**90**	**33**	**229**	**142**	**145**	**156**
Bonds	0	0	0	0	0	0	0	0	0	0
Commercial banks	0	0	127	86	90	33	229	142	145	156
Memo:										
IBRD	0	0	40	76	114	33	32	38	49	44
IDA	0	0	0	75	63	102	15	12	83	29
PRINCIPAL REPAYMENTS	**5**	**40**	**247**	**387**	**406**	**372**	**404**	**416**	**433**	**715**
Public and publicly guaranteed	**5**	**40**	**229**	**333**	**326**	**276**	**313**	**321**	**313**	**306**
Official creditors	5	5	78	82	104	116	170	171	191	189
Multilateral	4	3	46	49	63	72	88	111	124	124
Concessional	0	0	4	4	6	4	7	6	6	3
Bilateral	1	2	32	33	41	44	82	60	67	65
Concessional	1	2	17	27	28	31	54	44	47	46
Private creditors	0	34	151	251	222	160	143	150	122	117
Bonds	0	19	30	52	30	30	30	30	30	30
Commercial banks	0	0	46	108	113	56	33	45	42	33
Other private	0	16	75	91	78	74	80	75	50	54
Private nonguaranteed	**0**	**0**	**18**	**54**	**80**	**96**	**91**	**95**	**120**	**409**
Bonds	0	0	0	0	0	0	0	0	0	0
Commercial banks	0	0	18	54	80	96	91	95	120	409
Memo:										
IBRD	4	3	33	33	36	41	48	46	46	47
IDA	0	0	0	0	1	1	1	1	1	1
NET FLOWS ON DEBT	**-5**	**93**	**177**	**437**	**325**	**55**	**144**	**9**	**53**	**-164**
Public and publicly guaranteed	**-5**	**93**	**69**	**406**	**315**	**118**	**6**	**-38**	**28**	**89**
Official creditors	-5	72	80	413	455	195	48	47	118	132
Multilateral	-4	-3	26	272	352	115	63	35	153	30
Concessional	0	0	3	77	63	107	21	18	88	36
Bilateral	-1	75	54	141	103	80	-14	12	-35	102
Concessional	-1	-1	59	135	94	41	3	-19	-23	27
Private creditors	0	21	-12	-7	-140	-78	-42	-85	-90	-43
Bonds	0	34	-30	-52	-30	-30	-30	-30	-30	-30
Commercial banks	0	3	-17	56	-82	-9	34	7	-17	24
Other private	0	-16	36	-11	-27	-39	-46	-62	-43	-37
Private nonguaranteed	**0**	**0**	**109**	**32**	**10**	**-63**	**138**	**47**	**25**	**-253**
Bonds	0	0	0	0	0	0	0	0	0	0
Commercial banks	0	0	109	32	10	-63	138	47	25	-253
Memo:										
IBRD	-4	-3	7	43	78	-8	-16	-8	3	-3
IDA	0	0	0	75	62	101	15	11	83	28

ZIMBABWE

(US$ million, unless otherwise indicated)

	1970	1980	1990	1992	1993	1994	1995	1996	1997	1998
INTEREST PAYMENTS (LINT)	**5**	**10**	**149**	**157**	**170**	**193**	**196**	**184**	**174**	**166**
Public and publicly guaranteed	**5**	**10**	**141**	**134**	**148**	**160**	**170**	**162**	**151**	**136**
Official creditors	4	2	67	76	98	113	121	118	114	105
Multilateral	2	0	43	53	77	85	90	88	85	79
Concessional	0	0	1	2	3	3	4	4	4	5
Bilateral	2	1	24	23	22	28	32	30	29	26
Concessional	2	1	15	16	16	20	22	19	18	15
Private creditors	0	9	74	58	50	47	49	45	36	31
Bonds	0	7	13	10	8	7	6	5	3	2
Commercial banks	0	0	28	15	13	11	12	14	11	11
Other private	0	1	33	33	29	29	31	26	21	18
Private nonguaranteed	**0**	**0**	**9**	**24**	**22**	**33**	**26**	**22**	**23**	**30**
Bonds	0	0	0	0	0	0	0	0	0	0
Commercial banks	0	0	9	24	22	33	26	22	23	30
Memo:										
IBRD	2	0	33	35	39	44	46	41	36	32
IDA	0	0	1	1	1	2	3	3	2	3
NET TRANSFERS ON DEBT	**-9**	**82**	**28**	**280**	**155**	**-138**	**-52**	**-175**	**-121**	**-330**
Public and publicly guaranteed	**-9**	**82**	**-72**	**272**	**167**	**-42**	**-164**	**-200**	**-123**	**-47**
Official creditors	-9	71	13	337	357	82	-73	-70	3	27
Multilateral	-6	-3	-17	219	275	30	-27	-53	67	-49
Concessional	0	0	2	75	60	103	17	14	84	31
Bilateral	-3	74	30	118	81	52	-46	-18	-64	76
Concessional	-3	-2	43	118	78	21	-19	-38	-41	11
Private creditors	-1	12	-85	-65	-190	-125	-91	-130	-126	-74
Bonds	-1	26	-43	-61	-38	-37	-36	-35	-33	-32
Commercial banks	0	3	-46	40	-95	-19	22	-7	-28	13
Other private	0	-17	3	-44	-57	-69	-77	-89	-65	-55
Private nonguaranteed	**0**	**0**	**100**	**8**	**-12**	**-96**	**112**	**25**	**2**	**-283**
Bonds	0	0	0	0	0	0	0	0	0	0
Commercial banks	0	0	100	8	-12	-96	112	25	2	-283
Memo:										
IBRD	-6	-3	-26	7	39	-52	-62	-49	-33	-36
IDA	0	0	-1	74	61	99	12	9	80	25
DEBT SERVICE (LTDS)	**9**	**50**	**396**	**544**	**575**	**565**	**600**	**600**	**607**	**880**
Public and publicly guaranteed	**9**	**50**	**370**	**466**	**474**	**436**	**483**	**483**	**464**	**442**
Official creditors	9	7	145	158	202	229	291	288	306	294
Multilateral	6	3	89	101	140	157	178	199	209	204
Concessional	0	0	5	6	8	8	11	10	10	8
Bilateral	3	4	56	56	62	72	113	89	97	91
Concessional	3	3	33	43	44	51	76	63	65	61
Private creditors	1	43	225	308	272	207	192	195	158	147
Bonds	1	26	43	61	38	37	36	35	33	32
Commercial banks	0	0	74	123	126	66	46	59	53	44
Other private	0	17	107	124	107	104	111	102	72	71
Private nonguaranteed	**0**	**0**	**27**	**78**	**102**	**129**	**117**	**117**	**143**	**439**
Bonds	0	0	0	0	0	0	0	0	0	0
Commercial banks	0	0	27	78	102	129	117	117	143	439
Memo:										
IBRD	6	3	67	68	75	84	94	87	82	79
IDA	0	0	1	1	2	3	3	3	3	4
UNDISBURSED DEBT	**0**	**86**	**1,042**	**1,557**	**1,435**	**1,451**	**1,322**	**1,228**	**1,044**	**1,057**
Official creditors	0	60	940	1,465	1,320	1,316	1,241	1,175	913	932
Private creditors	0	26	102	92	114	136	80	54	131	125
Memorandum items										
Concessional LDOD	44	15	906	1,100	1,221	1,455	1,522	1,441	1,380	1,517
Variable rate LDOD	0	3	699	892	899	829	962	957	941	735
Public sector LDOD	229	696	2,463	2,852	3,110	3,420	3,525	3,328	3,109	3,300
Private sector LDOD	0	0	186	297	307	244	381	428	453	241

6. CURRENCY COMPOSITION OF LONG-TERM DEBT (PERCENT)

	1970	1980	1990	1992	1993	1994	1995	1996	1997	1998
Deutsche mark	0.0	0.1	11.7	10.4	9.5	10.0	10.8	11.3	10.8	11.4
French franc	0.0	0.0	7.2	6.0	5.2	5.0	5.9	5.8	5.0	5.3
Japanese yen	0.0	0.0	2.1	2.7	3.2	3.3	3.5	3.2	2.9	4.4
Pound sterling	76.2	40.3	14.0	9.6	7.9	7.5	6.6	6.8	5.9	5.4
Swiss franc	0.0	0.0	1.2	0.9	0.8	0.9	1.1	0.9	0.7	0.6
U.S.dollars	0.3	0.4	30.3	31.7	28.1	27.7	25.4	25.2	26.8	26.0
Multiple currency	20.2	59.2	18.4	23.6	27.4	26.2	25.9	26.5	26.9	25.4
Special drawing rights	0.0	0.0	0.0	0.1	0.1	0.3	0.4	0.4	0.4	0.4
All other currencies	3.3	0.0	15.1	15.0	17.8	19.1	20.4	19.9	20.6	21.1

ZIMBABWE

(US$ million, unless otherwise indicated)

	1970	1980	1990	1992	1993	1994	1995	1996	1997	1998
7. DEBT RESTRUCTURINGS										
Total amount rescheduled	..	..	0	0	0	0	0	0	0	0
Debt stock rescheduled	..	..	0	0	0	0	0	0	0	0
Principal rescheduled	..	..	0	0	0	0	0	0	0	0
Official	..	..	0	0	0	0	0	0	0	0
Private	..	..	0	0	0	0	0	0	0	0
Interest rescheduled	..	..	0	0	0	0	0	0	0	0
Official	..	..	0	0	0	0	0	0	0	0
Private	..	..	0	0	0	0	0	0	0	0
Debt forgiven	..	..	24	1	0	0	23	0	0	0
Memo: interest forgiven	..	..	0	0	0	0	0	0	0	0
Debt stock reduction	..	..	0	0	0	0	0	0	0	0
of which debt buyback	..	..	0	0	0	0	0	0	0	0
8. DEBT STOCK-FLOW RECONCILIATION										
Total change in debt stocks	..	..	456	633	229	238	516	-58	-70	-208
Net flows on debt	-5	148	335	804	286	26	411	119	203	-368
Net change in interest arrears	..	..	-1	0	1	0	2	-3	0	0
Interest capitalized	..	..	0	0	0	0	0	0	0	0
Debt forgiveness or reduction	..	..	-24	-1	0	0	-23	0	0	0
Cross-currency valuation	..	..	190	-141	-61	174	106	-121	-203	121
Residual	..	..	-45	-29	3	38	21	-54	-70	40
9. AVERAGE TERMS OF NEW COMMITMENTS										
ALL CREDITORS										
Interest (%)	0.0	7.1	6.6	4.3	3.2	6.0	4.5	3.2	5.3	2.5
Maturity (years)	0.0	15.2	17.1	23.8	25.4	17.4	18.5	27.8	17.1	22.1
Grace period (years)	0.0	5.5	4.5	6.6	8.0	4.4	4.7	8.1	3.9	6.2
Grant element (%)	0.0	25.8	21.0	41.4	52.4	22.7	35.4	53.4	28.6	53.5
Official creditors										
Interest (%)	0.0	4.9	6.5	4.3	2.5	6.0	3.9	2.6	4.0	1.6
Maturity (years)	0.0	16.8	17.7	24.4	29.0	21.3	21.3	31.2	22.6	24.8
Grace period (years)	0.0	5.7	4.7	6.8	9.3	5.6	5.6	9.3	5.3	7.0
Grant element (%)	0.0	35.6	22.2	42.4	60.5	26.4	42.2	60.9	42.2	61.6
Private creditors										
Interest (%)	0.0	17.2	8.7	5.0	6.4	6.0	6.7	6.4	7.1	6.8
Maturity (years)	0.0	7.8	9.6	9.1	9.0	7.8	8.3	9.5	9.6	8.1
Grace period (years)	0.0	4.5	1.2	1.7	2.1	1.4	1.6	1.7	2.1	2.1
Grant element (%)	0.0	-18.7	3.5	17.2	15.1	13.5	10.8	13.3	10.0	11.7
Memorandum items										
Commitments	0	171	444	794	610	360	181	260	272	394
Official creditors	0	140	414	763	501	258	142	219	157	331
Private creditors	0	31	30	31	109	102	40	41	115	63

10. CONTRACTUAL OBLIGATIONS ON OUTSTANDING LONG-TERM DEBT

	1999	2000	2001	2002	2003	2004	2005	2006	2007	2008
TOTAL										
Disbursements	337	285	185	115	70	41	21	3	1	0
Principal	468	425	377	329	286	247	229	216	209	190
Interest	172	155	135	116	93	78	67	57	48	39
Official creditors										
Disbursements	262	253	171	113	70	41	21	3	1	0
Principal	259	274	262	246	218	211	205	201	194	179
Interest	122	114	103	92	81	71	62	54	46	38
Bilateral creditors										
Disbursements	140	94	55	31	16	7	4	1	0	0
Principal	90	102	102	101	93	93	92	87	79	69
Interest	38	37	36	33	30	27	24	22	19	17
Multilateral creditors										
Disbursements	121	159	116	82	54	34	17	2	1	0
Principal	169	172	159	145	125	118	113	114	114	111
Interest	84	76	68	59	51	44	38	32	26	21
Private creditors										
Disbursements	76	33	14	2	0	0	0	0	0	0
Principal	208	150	115	83	68	37	24	15	15	11
Interest	51	41	32	24	13	7	5	4	3	2
Commercial banks										
Disbursements	61	27	11	2	0	0	0	0	0	0
Principal	55	44	35	33	30	28	21	12	12	8
Interest	14	14	12	10	8	6	4	3	2	1
Other private										
Disbursements	14	6	3	0	0	0	0	0	0	0
Principal	154	106	80	50	38	8	3	3	3	3
Interest	36	28	20	14	5	2	1	1	1	1

Country notes

Albania

Data source. Data on long-term public and publicly guaranteed debt as of 1998 are based on reports provided by the country. Short-term debt data are from the BIS semiannual series on international bank lending and short-term export credits from the OECD.

Rescheduling. Albania concluded a rescheduling agreement with official creditors outside of formal Paris Club auspices in December 1993 and a debt buyback operation in 1996.

Algeria

Data source. Data on long-term public and publicly guaranteed debt as of 1998 are based on reports provided by the country. Short-term debt data are also as reported by the country.

Rescheduling. Projected debt service is based on contractual obligations on debt outstanding at the end of 1998. It includes the effect of the Paris Club agreement signed in June 1994 and the commercial bank agreement signed in July 1996.

Angola

Data source. Data on long-term public and publicly guaranteed debt for 1998 are based on reports provided by the country. Short-term debt data are from the BIS semiannual series on international bank lending and short-term export credits from the OECD, supplemented by World Bank staff estimates.

Rescheduling. In 1987 Angola concluded an informal agreement with Paris Club creditors that was signed in July 1989. In addition, two major reschedulings with the former Soviet Union and other Eastern Bloc countries took place in 1987 and 1989. Debt owed to Brazil and Portugal was also rescheduled in 1987 and 1989 and again in 1994 with Portugal and Spain. In late 1996 Angola reached a debt restructuring agreement with the Russian Federation, receiving an up-front discount of 70 percent on the stock and interest arrears and a rescheduling of the remainder over 20 years.

Argentina

Data source. Data on long-term public and publicly guaranteed debt for 1998 are based on reports provided by the country. Short-term debt data are from the BIS semiannual series on international bank lending and short-term export credits from the OECD. Long-term private nonguaranteed debt data are World Bank staff estimates.

The increase in debt outstanding in 1989 is due mostly to the conversion of austral-denominated time deposits and government domestic debt into dollar-denominated bonds (BONEX 89).

Debt reduction. In March 1993 Argentina concluded a debt and debt service reduction exchanging its commercial bank debt to either par or discount bonds for a total face value of $17 billion. Interest arrears were also swapped into bonds at par with a face value of $8.2 billion, after a down payment of $910 million. These operations enabled Argentina to reduce its stock of debt by $3.3 billion in 1993, $399 million in 1994, and $863 million in 1995. Data for 1997 include debt buybacks.

Other. The residual in debt stock-flow reconciliation is due to data revisions introduced in 1993.

Armenia

Data source. Data on long-term public and publicly guaranteed debt for 1998 are preliminary, based on partial reports provided by the country. Short-term debt data are from the BIS semiannual series on international bank lending and short-term export credits from the OECD.

Rescheduling. In 1993, $30.8 million of technical credits were rescheduled with the Russian Federation, and in 1996, $34.0 million were rescheduled with bilateral creditors.

Azerbaijan

Data source. Data on long-term public and publicly guaranteed debt for 1998 are based on reports provided by the country. Long-term private nonguaranteed debt data are reported by the country. Short-term debt data are from the BIS semiannual series on international bank lending and short-term export credits from the OECD.

Rescheduling. In 1993, $36 million of technical credits were rescheduled with the Russia Federation.

Bangladesh

Data source. Data on long-term public and publicly guaranteed debt for 1998 are based on reports provided by the country. Short-term debt data are from the BIS semiannual series on international bank lending and short-term export credits from the OECD.

Barbados

Data source. Data on long-term public and publicly guaranteed debt for 1998 are based on reports provided by the country. Short-term debt data are from the BIS semiannual series on international bank lending, OECD and World Bank staff estimates, and short-term export credits from the OECD.

Belarus

Data source. Data on long-term public and publicly guaranteed debt for 1998 are based on reports provided by the country. Short-term debt data are from the BIS semiannual series on international bank lending and short-term export credits from the OECD.

Rescheduling. In 1993, $385 million of technical credits were rescheduled with the Russian Federation.

Belize

Data source. Data on long-term public and publicly guaranteed debt for 1998 are based on reports provided by the country. Short-term debt data are from the BIS semiannual series on international bank lending and short-term export credits from the OECD.

Benin

Data source. Data on long-term public and publicly guaranteed debt for 1998 are based on reports provided by the country. Short-term debt data are from the BIS semiannual series on international bank lending and short-term export credits from the OECD.

Rescheduling. Projected debt service is based on contractual obligations on debt outstanding at the end of 1998. It includes the effect of the Paris Club agreement signed in December 1991, the Paris Club agreement on enhanced Toronto terms signed in June 1993 and covering 1994–95, and the Paris Club agreement signed in October 1996.

Bhutan

Data source. Data on long-term public and publicly guaranteed debt for 1998 are based on reports provided by the country. Short-term debt data are from the BIS semiannual series on international bank lending and short-term export credits from the OECD.

Bolivia

Data source. Data on long-term public and publicly guaranteed debt for 1998 are based on reports provided by the country. Long-term private nonguaranteed debt data are World Bank staff estimates. Short-term debt data are from the BIS semiannual series on international bank lending and short-term export credits from the OECD.

Rescheduling. Projected debt service is based on contractual obligations on debt outstanding at the end of 1998. It includes the effect of the March 1996 Paris Club agreement and that of the December 1996 Paris Club agreement on stocks. The October 1998 Paris Club agreement has not yet been implemented since the bilateral agreement was not signed in 1998.

Bosnia and Herzegovina

Data source. Data on long-term public and publicly guaranteed debt for 1998 include only IBRD and IMF. Other long-term obligations are included under the Federal Republic of Yugoslavia (Serbia and Montenegro). Short-term debt data are from the BIS semiannual series on international bank lending and short-term export credits from the OECD.

Botswana

Data source. Data on long-term public and publicly guaranteed debt for 1998 are based on reports provided by the country. Short-term debt data are World Bank staff estimates.

Brazil

Data source. Data on long-term public and publicly guaranteed, private nonguaranteed, and short-term debt for 1998 are preliminary, based on partial reports provided by the country.

Rescheduling. From 1983 onward, the increase in long-term public and publicly guaranteed debt is due to the transfer of liabilities from private nonguaranteed and short-term debt as a result of Paris Club and commercial bank restructuring. In 1992 an agreement was reached with Paris Club creditors to reschedule $6.2 billion, of which $5.1 billion corresponded to rescheduling of arrears and debt service due in 1992. Brazil also rescheduled $7.1 billion of interest in arrears with commercial banks. Interest payments for 1992 include a $836 million cash payment on the interest arrears.

Debt reduction. Debt owed to commercial banks at the end of 1994 was reduced by $4.1 billion as a result of the April 1994 Brady accord. Data for 1998 include debt buybacks.

Bulgaria

Data source. Data on long-term public and publicly guaranteed and private nonguaranteed debt for 1998 are based on partial reports provided by the country. Short-term debt data are from the BIS semiannual series on international bank lending and short-term export credits from the OECD.

Rescheduling. Projected debt service is based on contractual obligations on debt outstanding at the end of 1998. It includes the effect of the Paris Club agreements signed in 1991, 1992, and 1994. Commercial bank creditors agreed to restructure $8.3 billion of external public debt in July 1994.

Burkina Faso

Data source. Data on long-term public and publicly guaranteed debt for 1998 are based on reports provided by the country. Short-term debt data are from the BIS semiannual series on international bank lending and short-term export credits from the OECD.

Rescheduling. Projected debt service is based on contractual obligations on debt outstanding at the end of 1998. It includes the effect of the Paris Club agreement signed in March 1991, the Paris Club agreement on enhanced Toronto terms signed in May 1993, and the Paris Club agreement signed in June 1996.

Burundi

Data source. Data on long-term public and publicly guaranteed debt for 1998 are based on reports provided by the country. Short-term debt data are from the BIS semiannual series on international bank lending and short-term export credits from the OECD.

Rescheduling. Projected debt service is based on contractual obligations on debt outstanding at the end of 1998. It includes the effect of the cancellation of all concessional debt owed to Belgium, France, the Republic of Korea, and the Russian Federation. In 1989 Burundi rescheduled $13.3 million of debt owed to China.

Cambodia

Data source. Data on long-term public and publicly guaranteed debt for 1998 are based on reports provided by the country and augmented by World Bank staff estimates. Debt data include both convertible and noncovertible currency debt. Short-term debt data are from the BIS semiannual series on international bank lending and short-term export credits from the OECD.

Rescheduling. Projected debt service is based on contractual obligations on debt outstanding at the end of 1998. It includes the effect of the Paris Club agreement on Naples terms signed in January 1995.

Cameroon

Data source. Data on long-term and publicly guaranteed debt for 1998 are based on reports provided by the country and World Bank staff estimates. Long-term private nonguaranteed debt data are reported by the country. Short-term debt data are from the BIS semiannual series on international bank lending and short-term export credits from the OECD.

Rescheduling. Projected debt service is based on contractual obligations on debt outstanding at the end of 1998. It includes the effect of the Paris Club agreements signed in January 1992 and November 1995 and October 1997.

Cape Verde

Data source. Data on long-term public and publicly guaranteed debt for 1998 are based on reports provided by the country. Short-term debt data are from the BIS semiannual series on international bank lending and short-term export credits from the OECD.

Rescheduling. In 1987, $8.4 million of long-term debt owed to Portugal was rescheduled.

Central African Republic

Data source. Data on long-term public and publicly guaranteed debt for 1998 are based on reports provided by the country. Short-term debt data are from the BIS semiannual series on international bank lending and short-term export credits from the OECD.

Rescheduling. Projected debt service is based on contractual obligations on debt outstanding at the end of 1998. It includes the effect of the Paris Club agreements signed in 1988, 1990, 1994, and 1998.

Chad

Data source. Data on long-term public and publicly guaranteed debt for 1998 are based on World Bank staff estimates. Short-term debt data are from the BIS semiannual series on international bank lending and short-term export credits from the OECD.

Rescheduling. Projected debt service is based on contractual obligations on debt outstanding at the end of 1998. It includes the effect of the debt relief agreement signed in 1989, concluded outside the Paris Club. In addition, it includes the 1995 and 1996 Paris Club agreement. The reporting of the loans covered by this agreement remains partial, including the February 1995 and July 1996 Paris Club agreement.

Chile

Data source. Data on long-term public and publicly guaranteed and private nonguaranteed debt for 1998 are based on reports provided by the country. Short-term debt data for 1990–98 are from the BIS semiannual series on international bank lending and short-term export credits from the OECD.

Rescheduling. Projected debt service is based on contractual obligations on debt outstanding at the end of 1998. It includes the effect of a 1990 agreement with commercial banks under which there was no repayment of principal during 1991–94. The data also reflect the forgiveness of $15 million and the rescheduling of $132 million under the Enterprise for the Americas Initiative.

Debt reduction. By end-1993 reduction of debt owed to commercial banks through various debt conversion programs reached $8.7 billion, including $2.5 billion in 1988, $2.5 billion in 1989, $1.1 billion in 1990, $496 million in 1991, $279 million in 1992, and $264 million in 1993. Also, 1988 principal repayments include a $164 million cash payment in connection with a buyback.

China

Data source. Data on long-term public and publicly guaranteed debt for 1998 are based on World Bank staff estimates. Short-term debt data for 1990–98 are from the BIS semiannual series on international bank lending and short-term export credits from the OECD.

Colombia

Data source. Data on long-term public and publicly guaranteed debt for 1998 are projections.

Data on long-term private nonguaranteed debt are World Bank staff estimates. Short-term debt data are taken from the BIS semiannual series on international bank lending and short-term export credits from the OECD.

Comoros

Data source. Data on long-term public and publicly guaranteed debt for 1998 are estimated based on the original terms of the loans. Short-term debt data are from the BIS semiannual series on international bank lending and short-term export credits from the OECD.

Debt reduction. France wrote off all outstanding debt in 1994.

Congo, Democratic Republic of

Data source. Data on long-term public and publicly guaranteed debt for 1998 are estimates based on the original terms of the loans. Short-term debt data are from the BIS semiannual series on international bank lending and short-term export credits from the OECD.

Congo, Republic of

Data source. Data on long-term public and publicly guaranteed debt for 1998 are World Bank staff estimates. Short-term debt data are from the BIS semiannual series on international bank lending and short-term export credits from the OECD.

Rescheduling. Projected debt service is based on contractual obligations on debt outstanding at the end of 1998. It includes the effect of the Paris Club agreements from 1986, 1990, 1994, and 1996, but excludes the effect of the 1988 agreement with commercial banks because it has not been implemented. In 1986, in addition to Paris Club, the government rescheduled with Eastern Bloc creditors. Under the 1986 Brazzaville Club agreement, $23 million was rescheduled.

Costa Rica

Data source. Data on long-term public and publicly guaranteed debt for 1998 are based on reports provided by the country. Long-term private nonguaranteed debt data are World Bank staff estimates. Short-term debt data are from the BIS semiannual series on international bank lending and short-term export credits from the OECD.

Côte d'Ivoire

Data source. Data on long-term public and publicly guaranteed debt for 1998 are based on World Bank staff estimates. Long-term private nonguaranteed debt data are World Bank staff estimates. Short-term debt data are from the BIS semiannual series on international bank lending and short-term export credits from the OECD and from the Caisse Autonome d'Amortissement's estimate of penalty and late charges on long-term debt. They also include World Bank staff estimates on the balance of the operations account.

Rescheduling. Projected debt service is based on contractual obligations on debt outstanding at the end of 1998. It includes the effect of all Paris Club agreements beginning in 1984 and the commercial bank agreements of 1985–86. It includes the DDSR agreement of May 1997.

Croatia

Data source. Data on long-term public and publicly guaranteed and private nonguaranteed debt for 1998 are based on reports provided by the country. Short-term debt data are from BIS semiannual series on international bank lending and short-term export credits from the OECD.

Other. Croatia became a member of the World Bank in 1993. Debt data includes the effect of the Paris Club agreement signed in March 1995 and the London Club agreement signed in March 1996.

Czech Republic

Data source. Data on long-term public and publicly guaranteed, private nonguaranteed, and short-term debt for 1998 are preliminary, based on partial reports provided by the country, and include only convertible currency debt.

Other. The Czech Republic became a member of the World Bank in 1993. Data for 1985–92 are based on preliminary information on the succession of the former Czechoslovakia (effective January 1, 1993).

Djibouti

Data source. Data on long-term public and publicly guaranteed debt for 1998 are based on World Bank staff estimates. Short-term debt data are from the BIS semiannual series on international bank lending and short-term export credits from the OECD.

Debt reduction. France wrote off all outstanding and disbursed debt at the end of 1989.

Dominica

Data source. Data on long-term public and publicly guaranteed debt for 1998 are based on reports provided by the country. Short-term debt data are from the BIS semiannual series on international bank lending and short-term export credits from the OECD.

Debt reduction. As part of its Caribbean initiative, Canada forgave all its official development assistance loans, about $1.7 million, in 1990.

Dominican Republic

Data source. Data on long-term public and publicly guaranteed debt for 1998 are based on reports provided by the country. Short-term debt data are from the BIS semiannual series on international bank lending and short-term export credits from the OECD.

Rescheduling. Projected debt service is based on contractual obligations on debt outstanding at the end of 1998. It includes the effect of the Paris Club agreement signed in November 1991 rescheduling $843 million and of the 1994 debt and debt service reduction (DDSR) agreement to restructure $1.2 billion owed to commercial banks.

Ecuador

Data source. Data on long-term public and publicly guaranteed and private nonguaranteed debt for 1998 are World Bank staff estimates. Short-term debt data are from the BIS semiannual series on international bank lending and short-term export credits from the OECD.

Rescheduling. Projected debt service is based on contractual obligations on debt outstanding at the end of 1998. It includes the effect of the Paris Club agreement on Houston terms signed in June 1994 and of the 1995 DDSR operation.

Debt reduction. The debt conversion program was continued in 1992, enabling the country to reduce its stock of debt due to private creditors by about $50 million, bringing the total for 1987–92 to $539 million. Debt reduction resulting from the 1995 DDSR operations amounts to $1.2 billion.

Egypt, Arab Republic of

Data source. Data on long-term public and publicly guaranteed debt for 1998 and revised data for 1991–95 due to the third stage of the 1991 Paris Club agreement are based on reports provided by the country. Data on private nonguaranteed debt are World Bank staff estimates. Short-term debt data are from the BIS semiannual series on international bank lending and short-term export credits from OECD.

Rescheduling. Projected debt service is based on contractual obligations on debt outstanding at the end of 1998. It includes the effects of the third stage of the Paris Club agreement signed in May 1991.

El Salvador

Data source. Data on long-term public and publicly guaranteed debt for 1998 are based on reports provided by the country. Long-term private nonguaranteed debt data are World Bank staff estimates. Short-term debt data are from the BIS semiannual series on international bank lending and short-term export credits from the OECD.

Equatorial Guinea

Data source. Data on long-term public and publicly guaranteed debt for 1998 are estimates based on the original terms of the loans. Short-term debt data are from the BIS semiannual series on international bank lending and short-term export credits from the OECD.

Rescheduling. Projected debt service is based on contractual obligations on debt outstanding at the end of 1998. It does not include the effects of the Paris Club agreement of April 1992 and December 1996 because of lack of information.

Eritrea

Data source. Data on long-term public and publicly guaranteed debt for 1998 are based on reports provided by the country. Short-term debt data are from the BIS semiannual series on international bank lending and short-term export credits from the OECD.

Estonia

Data source. Data on long-term public and publicly guaranteed and private nonguaranteed debt for 1998 are based on reports provided by the country. Short-term debt data are from the BIS semiannual series on international bank lending and short-term export credits from the OECD.

Ethiopia

Data source. Data on long-term public and publicly guaranteed debt for 1998 are based on reports provided by the country. The 1996 debt report included information not reported in previous years. The historical data were revised. Short-term debt data are from the BIS semiannual series on international bank lending and short-term export credits from the OECD. The data include debt contracted from commercial sources for military expenditures.

Rescheduling. Projected debt service is based on contractual obligations on debt outstanding at the end of 1998. It includes the effects of the last Paris Club agreement signed in January 24, 1997.

Fiji

Data source. Data on long-term public and publicly guaranteed debt for 1998 are based on reports provided by the country. Long-term private nonguaranteed debt data are World Bank staff estimates. Short-term debt data are from the BIS semiannual series on international bank lending and short-term export credits from the OECD.

Gabon

Data source. Data on long-term public and publicly guaranteed debt for 1998 are based on reports provided by the country augmented by World Bank staff estimates. Short-term debt data are from the BIS semiannual series on international bank lending and short-term export credits from the OECD.

Rescheduling. Projected debt service is based on contractual obligations on debt outstanding at the end of 1998. It includes the effect of the Paris Club agreements signed in April 1994 and December 1995. Projections exclude the effect of a Paris Club agreement signed in October 1991. According to Caisse Autonome d'Amortissement, the agreement was canceled because of difficulties in meeting certain conditions requested by one of the creditor countries.

Gambia, The

Data source. Data on long-term public and publicly guaranteed debt for 1998 are based on reports provided by the country. Short-term debt data are from the BIS semiannual series on international bank lending and short-term export credits from the OECD.

Georgia

Data source. Data on long-term public and publicly guaranteed debt for 1998 are based on reports provided by the country. Short-term debt data are from the BIS semiannual series on international bank lending and short-term export credits from the OECD.

Rescheduling. In 1993 a total of $366 million of technical credits were rescheduled with Armenia ($10.6 million), Azerbaijan ($2.1 million), Kazakhstan ($17.9 million), the Russian Federation ($135.0 million), and Turkmenistan ($200.8 million). In 1996, $634 million were rescheduled with bilateral creditors.

Ghana

Data source. Data on long-term public and publicly guaranteed debt for 1998 are based on reports provided by the country. Long-term private nonguaranteed debt data are World Bank staff estimates. Short-term debt data are from the BIS semiannual series on international bank lending and short-term export credits from the OECD.

Rescheduling. Short-term debt of the Bank of Ghana amounting to $42 million was rescheduled into long-term debt in 1987. In 1991 the Netherlands rescheduled all payment arrears. It includes the effects of the Paris Club agreement signed in March 1996.

Grenada

Data source. Data on public and publicly guaranteed debt for 1998 are based on reports provided by the country. Short-term debt data are from the BIS semiannual series on international bank lending and short-term export credits from the OECD.

Guatemala

Data source. Data on long-term public and publicly guaranteed debt for 1998 are based on the report provided by the country. Long-term private nonguaranteed debt data are World Bank staff estimates. Short-term debt data are from the BIS semiannual series on international bank lending and short-term export credits from the OECD.

Guinea

Data source. Data on long-term public and publicly guaranteed debt for 1998 are World Bank staff estimates based on an incomplete report by the government. Short-term debt data are from the BIS semiannual series on international bank lending and short-term export credits from the OECD.

Rescheduling. Projected debt service is based on contractual obligations on debt outstanding at the end of 1997. It includes the effects of the Paris Club agreements of 1986, 1989, 1992, and 1995 and 1997.

Guinea-Bissau

Data source. Data on long-term public and publicly guaranteed debt for 1998 are based on partial reports provided by the country. Short-term debt data are from the BIS semiannual series on international bank lending and short-term export credits from the OECD.

Rescheduling. Projected debt service is based on contractual obligations on debt outstanding at the end of 1998. It includes the effects of the Paris Club agreements signed in October 1987, October 1989, and February 1995.

Guyana

Data source. Data on long-term public and publicly guaranteed debt for 1998 are based on reports provided by the country. Long-term private nonguaranteed debt data are World Bank staff estimates. Short-term debt data are from the BIS semiannual series on international bank lending and short-term export credits from the OECD.

Rescheduling. Projected debt service is based on contractual obligations on debt outstanding at the end of 1998. It includes the effect of the Paris Club agreement signed in May 1996. It does not include the effects of the June 1999 Paris Club agreement.

Debt reduction. Reduction in the stock of debt at the end of 1998 as a result of the write-off of the May 1996 Paris Club agreement was $460 million.

Haiti

Data source. Data on long-term public and publicly guaranteed debt as of end-September 1998 are preliminary, based on partial reports provided by the country. Short-term debt data are from the BIS semiannual series on international bank lending and short-term export credits from the OECD.

The government cleared a total of $81.5 million of arrears to the Inter-American Development Bank, IDA, and the IMF in December 1994 and arrears to the International Fund for Agricultural Development, OPEC Fund, and bilateral donors, either through bilateral agreements or in the context of the May 1995 Paris Club Meeting.

Honduras

Data source. Data on long-term public and publicly guaranteed and private nonguaranteed debt for 1998 are based on reports provided by the country. Short-term debt data are from the

BIS semiannual series on international bank lending and short-term export credits from the OECD.

Rescheduling. Projected debt service is based on contractual obligations on debt outstanding at the end of 1998. It includes the effect of the Paris Club agreement signed in February 1996. It also includes the effect of 1997 rescheduling of the loans with the CABEI/BCIE creditor. It does not include the effects of the April 1999 Paris Club agreement.

Debt reduction. Reduction of the stock of debt at the end of 1997 as a result of the write off of the February 1996 Paris Club agreement was $2.4 million.

Hungary

Data source. Data on long-term public and publicly guaranteed, private nonguaranteed debt for 1998 are based on reports provided by the country. Short-term debt data are from the BIS semiannual series on international bank lending and short-term export credits from the OECD.

India

Data source. Data relate to the year ending in March (latest data are for the year ending in March 1999). Details on long-term public and publicly guaranteed, private nonguaranteed, and short-term debt as of the end of March 1999 are based on aggregate reports provided by the country and World Bank staff estimates.

Indonesia

Data source. Data on long-term public and publicly guaranteed debt for 1998 are preliminary based on partial reports provided by the country. Short-term debt data (1993 to 1998) are from the BIS semiannual series on international bank lending and short-term export credits from the OECD. (The debt data may include indistinguishable local currency components held by nonresidents.)

Other. The residual in debt stock flow reconciliation from 1994 onward reflects the private nonguaranteed stock revisions introduced without corresponding flow data adjustments.

Iran, Islamic Republic of

Data source. Data relate to the year ending in March. Long-term public and publicly guaranteed debt and short-term debt as of end-March 1999 are based on reports provided by the country. Long-term private nonguaranteed debt are World Bank staff estimates.

Rescheduling. Iran rescheduled an estimated $18 billion of short-term debt into long-term debt in 1993–96; $2.8 billion in 1993 (which was repaid in the same year); $10.8 billion in 1994; $3.2 billion in 1995; and $1.8 billion in 1996.

Jamaica

Data source. Data on long-term public and publicly guaranteed debt for 1998 are projections. Long-term private nonguaranteed debt data are World Bank staff estimates. Short-term debt data are from the BIS semiannual series on international bank lending and short-term export credits from the OECD.

Jordan

Data source. Data on long-term public and publicly guaranteed debt for 1998 are based on reports provided by the country. Long-term private nonguaranteed debt are World Bank staff estimates. Short-term debt data are from the BIS semiannual series on international bank lending and short-term export credits from the OECD.

Rescheduling. Projected debt service is based on contractual obligations at the end of 1998. It reflects the effect of the agreements signed with the Paris Club in May 1997. The total amount rescheduled under the Paris Club agreement was $223 million for 1997 and $211 million for 1998. It does not include the effects of the May 1999 Paris Club agreement.

Kazakhstan

Data source. Data on long-term public and publicly guaranteed and private nonguaranteed debt for 1998 are based on reports provided by the country. Short-term debt data are from the BIS semiannual series on international bank lending and short-term export credits from the OECD.

Rescheduling. In 1993, $1.3 billion of technical credits were rescheduled with the Russian Federation.

Kenya

Data source. Data on long-term public and publicly guaranteed debt for 1998 are actual, based on reports provided by the country. Long-term private nonguaranteed debt for 1998 are based on World Bank estimates. Short-term debt data are from the BIS semiannual series on international bank lending and short-term export credits from the OECD.

Rescheduling. Projected debt service is based on contractual obligations on debt outstanding at the end of 1998. It includes the effect of the Paris Club agreement signed in January 1994, rescheduling all arrears accumulated as of December 1993.

Korea, Republic of

Data source. Data on total external liabilities, including long-term public and publicly guaranteed debt for 1994–98, are based on aggregate reports provided by the country and World Bank staff estimates. The data include 1998 debt rescheduling of short-term debt.

Kyrgyz Republic

Data source. Data on long-term public and publicly guaranteed debt for 1998 are based on reports provided by the country. Short-term debt data are from the BIS semiannual series on international bank lending and short-term export credits from the OECD.

Rescheduling. In 1993 a total of $125.8 million of technical credits were rescheduled with Kazakhstan ($31.5 million), the Russian Federation ($81.0 million), and Uzbekistan ($13.3 million). In 1996, $220.4 million were rescheduled with bilateral creditors.

Lao People's Democratic Republic

Data source. Data on long-term public and publicly guaranteed debt for 1998 are preliminary, based on partial reports provided by the country and include both convertible and nonconvertible currency obligations. Short-term debt data are from the BIS semiannual series on international bank lending and short-term export credits from the OECD.

Rescheduling. Projected debt service is based on contractual obligations on debt outstanding at the end of 1998. It includes the effects of the bilateral debt restructuring agreements of 1988 and 1991.

Latvia

Data source. Data on long-term public and publicly guaranteed debt for 1998 are preliminary, based on reports provided by the country. Short-term debt data are from the BIS semiannual series on international bank lending and short-term export credits from the OECD.

Lebanon

Data source. Data on long-term public and publicly guaranteed debt for 1998 are based on reports provided by the country. Short-term debt data are from the BIS semiannual series on international bank lending and short-term export credits from the OECD.

Lesotho

Data source. Data on long-term public and publicly guaranteed debt for 1998 are based on reports provided by the country. Short-term debt data are World Bank staff estimates.

Liberia

Data source. Data on long-term public and publicly guaranteed debt for 1998 are estimates based on the original terms of the loans, augmented by creditor source information. Short-term debt data are from the BIS semiannual series on international bank lending and short-term export credits from the OECD.

Lithuania

Data source. Data on long-term public and publicly guaranteed debt for 1998 are based on partial reports provided by the country. Short-term debt data are from the BIS semiannual series on international bank lending and short-term export credits from the OECD.

Macedonia, FYR

Data source. Data on long-term public and publicly guaranteed and private nonguaranteed debt for 1998 are based on reports provided by the country. Short-term debt data are from the BIS semiannual series on international bank lending and short-term export credits from the OECD.

Other. The former Yugoslav Republic of Macedonia became a member of the World Bank in 1993. Debt outstanding as of end-1993 reflect only loans used directly by Macedonian beneficiaries.

Madagascar

Data source. Data on long-term public and publicly guaranteed debt for 1998 are based on reports provided by the country. Short-term debt data are from the BIS semiannual series on international bank lending and short-term export credits from the OECD.

Rescheduling. Projected debt service is based on contractual obligations on debt outstanding at the end of 1998. It includes the effect of the Paris Club agreements signed during 1988–97 and the 1990 commercial bank rescheduling arrangements.

Malawi

Data source. Data on long-term public and publicly guaranteed debt for 1998 are World Bank staff estimates based on incomplete reports provided by the country. Short-term debt data are from the BIS semiannual series on international bank lending and short-term export credits from the OECD.

Rescheduling. Projected debt service is based on contractual obligations on debt outstanding at the end of 1998. It includes the effect of the Paris Club agreement signed in April 1988. The agreement to reschedule debt owed to the Commonwealth Development Corporation has not been implemented. As a result there are both principal and interest arrears due to the corporation.

Malaysia

Data source. Data on long-term public and publicly guaranteed and private nonguaranteed debt for 1998 are preliminary, based on partial reports provided by the country. Private nonguaranteed long-term debt data are World Bank staff estimates. Short-term debt data are from the BIS semiannual series on international bank lending and short-term export credits from the OECD.

Maldives

Data source. Data on long-term public and publicly guaranteed debt for 1998 are based on reports provided by the country. Short-term debt data are from the BIS semiannual series on international bank lending and short-term export credits from the OECD.

Mali

Data source. Data on long-term public and publicly guaranteed debt for 1998 are based on reports provided by the country. Short-term debt data are from the BIS semiannual series on international bank lending and short-term export credits from the OECD.

Rescheduling. Projected debt service is based on contractual obligations of debt outstanding at the end of 1998. It includes the effect of the Paris Club agreements of 1988, 1989, 1992, and 1996.

Mauritania

Data source. Data on long-term public and publicly guaranteed debt for 1998 are based on reports provided by the country. Short-term debt data are from the BIS semiannual series on international bank lending and short-term export credits from the OECD.

Rescheduling. Projected debt service is based on contractual obligations on debt outstanding at the end of 1998. It reflects the effect of the Paris Club agreement from 1989 and the Paris Club agreements on enhanced Toronto terms signed in June 1993 and 1995. The reporting of the loans covered by these agreement remains partial. There have also been bilateral rescheduling arrangements with Algeria, Brazil, Iraq, Kuwait, Qatar, and Saudi Arabia.

Mauritius

Data source. Data on long-term public and publicly guaranteed and private nonguaranteed debt for 1998 are based on reports provided by the country. Short-term debt data are from the BIS semiannual series on international bank lending and short-term export credits from the OECD.

Mexico

Data source. Data on long-term public and publicly guaranteed, private nonguaranteed, and short-term debt for 1998 are based on reports provided by the country. Data revision on short-term and publicly nonguaranteed debt were provided by the country.

Rescheduling. Projected debt service is based on contractual obligations on debt outstanding at the end of 1998. It includes the effect of all agreements concluded to date, including the effect of the zero-coupon bonds and the swap operations. In 1992, $327 million was rescheduled as a result of the 1989 Paris Club agreement. In 1993 a number of public borrowers, including the government, swapped liabilities to meet the ceiling on borrowings.

Debt reduction. The decline in private nonguaranteed debt in 1988 is due primarily to prepayment and swaps operations. The debt reduction in 1989 of $2.5 billion comprised debt-equity swaps of $800 million and buybacks of $1.7 billion. In 1990 swaps amounted to $846 million, and debt reduction from discount bonds to $7.3 billion. The debt conversion program continued in 1991 and amounted to $1.1 billion, including privatization of $431 million and debt-equity swaps of $95 million. In 1992, $7.5 billion was bought back for $5.2 billion, which is shown under principal repayments. Also, $137 million was converted from foreign debt to equity. The increase in 1995 in long-term debt includes the stock transfer of the "Tesobonos." Data for 1998 include debt buybacks.

Moldova

Data source. Data on long-term public and publicly guaranteed debt for 1998 are based on reports provided by the country. Short-term debt data are from the BIS semiannual series on international bank lending and short-term export credits from the OECD.

Rescheduling. In 1993, $89 million of technical credits were rescheduled with the Russian Federation. In 1996, $118.8 million were rescheduled with bilateral creditors.

Mongolia

Data source. Data on long-term public and publicly guaranteed debt for 1998 are based on reports provided by the country. Short-term debt data are from the BIS semiannual series on international bank lending and short-term export credits from the OECD. Data exclude military debt of about 10.6 billion rubles owed to the Russian Federation.

Morocco

Data source. Data on long-term public and publicly guaranteed debt for 1998 are based on reports provided by the country. Data on short-term debt are based on reports by the country. Private nonguaranteed debt for end-1997 and 1998 are reported by the country. Major revisions to the database, especially on short-term debt and arrears, were based on information provided by the authorities. The arrears are mostly late payments to creditor countries.

Rescheduling. Projected debt service is based on contractual obligations on debt outstanding at the end of 1998. It includes the effect of the Paris Club agreement signed in February 1992.

Mozambique

Data source. Data on long-term public and publicly guaranteed debt for 1998 are based on reports provided by the country and does not include noncivilian Russian Federation debt. Private nonguaranteed debt data are World Bank staff estimates and includes private debt from Cahora Bassa. Short-term debt data are from the BIS semiannual series on international bank lending and short-term export credits from the OECD.

Rescheduling. Projected debt service is based on contractual obligations on debt outstanding at the end of 1998. It includes the effect of the July 1999 Paris Club agreement signed in November 1996. The July 1999 Paris Club agreement has not yet been implemented.

Debt reduction. Debt reduction in 1990 amounted to $231 million, and to $237 million in

1991. In 1991 there was a debt buyback, at a discount of 90 percent, of $124 million under the IDA Debt Reduction Facility.

Myanmar

Data source. Data relate to the year ending in March. Data on long-term public and publicly guaranteed debt for end-March 1999 are based on reports provided by the country. Short-term debt data are from the BIS semiannual series on international bank lending and short-term export credits from the OECD.

Nepal

Data source. Data on long-term public and publicly guaranteed debt for 1998 are based on reports provided by the country. Short-term debt data are from the BIS semiannual series on international bank lending and short-term export credits from the OECD.

Nicaragua

Data source. Data on long-term public and publicly guaranteed debt for 1998 are actual, based on reports provided by the country. Short-term debt data are from the BIS semiannual series on international bank lending and short-term export credits from the OECD.

Rescheduling. Projected debt service is based on contractual obligations on debt outstanding at the end of 1998. It includes the effect of agreements reached with Mexico ($950 million) and Venezuela ($159 million) in 1991, with Brazil in 1992 ($66 million), and with Argentina ($76 million) and Cuba ($7 million) in 1993; the 1995 Paris Club agreement; and agreements with the Russian Federation ($442 million), Czech Republic ($141 million), Honduras ($117 million), Mexico ($91 million), and El Salvador ($23 million) in 1996.

Debt reduction. In 1995 debt reduction was $1.2 billion using the IDA facility.

Niger

Data source. Data on long-term public and publicly guaranteed debt for 1998 are based on reports provided by the country. Long-term private nonguaranteed debt data are World Bank staff estimates. Short-term debt data are from the BIS semiannual series on international bank lending and short-term export credits from the OECD.

Rescheduling. Projected debt service is based on contractual obligations on debt outstanding at the end of 1998. It includes the effect of all Paris Club agreements.

Nigeria

Data source. Data on long-term public and private nonguaranteed debt for 1998 are estimates based on the original terms of the loans augmented by creditor source information and World Bank staff estimates. Nigeria has not reported external debt transactions for individual loans to the Bank since 1992. All data from 1992 forward are estimates based on aggregate data from the authorities, World Bank staff, and other sources. The promissory notes data for 1994–97 are based on partial information from the authorities. The Russian buyback is also based on partial information from the authorities. Short-term debt data are from the BIS semiannual series on international bank lending and short-term export credits from the OECD.

Rescheduling. Projected debt service is based on contractual obligations on debt outstanding at the end of 1998. It includes the effect of all Paris Club and London Club agreements signed, as well as those signed with other bilateral creditors.

Debt reduction. Debt reduction in 1988 was $40 million and in 1989, $247 million, all of it due to debt-equity swaps. In 1990 debt reduction was $286 million, $48 million of which was due to debt forgiveness and $238 million to debt-equity swaps. In 1991 debt reduction was $243 million, of which $134 million represented a buyback, $95 million was debt-equity swaps, and $14 million was debt forgiveness. In 1992 there was a $1.3 billion buyback.

Other. The Central Bank of Nigeria reported a large cancellation of promissory notes in 1992 that led to a reduction of about $1.1 billion in the stock of notes outstanding. This reduction, classified under private suppliers' credits, is not recorded as part of the DDSR accounts and therefore is included in the residual imbalance during 1992.

Oman

Data source. Data on long-term public and publicly guaranteed debt for 1998 are based on reports provided by the country. Short-term debt data are from the BIS semiannual series on international bank lending and short-term export credits from the OECD.

Pakistan

Data source. Data on long-term public and publicly guaranteed and private nonguaranteed debt for 1999 are based on reports provided by the country. Short-term debt data are from the BIS semiannual series on international bank lending and short-term export credits from the OECD and exclude foreign currency deposits in local banks made by nonresidents.

Rescheduling. The January 1999 Paris Club rescheduling has not yet been implemented.

Panama

Data source. Data on long-term public and publicly guaranteed debt for 1998 are based on reports provided by the country. Data on long-term private nonguaranteed debt and on short-term debt are World Bank staff estimates.

Rescheduling. Projected debt service is based on contractual obligations on debt outstanding at the end of 1998. It includes the effect of the November 1996 DDSR agreement, which rescheduled $3.3 billion of total debt. In 1997 Panama retired $1.2 billion of the Brady bonds in exchange for uncollateral bonds.

Debt reduction. As a result of the April 1996 Brady accord, debt owed to commercial banks at the end of 1996 was reduced by $645 million. Total debt rescheduled under this accord was $3.3 billion. The 1997 Brady bond exchange operation resulted in a $1.2 billion debt reduction, which includes a $987 million buyback, as shown under principal repayment.

Papua New Guinea

Data source. Data on long-term public and publicly guaranteed debt for 1998 are based on reports provided by the country. Private nonguaranteed debt data are World Bank staff estimates. Short-term debt data are from the BIS semiannual series on international bank lending and short-term export credits from the OECD.

Paraguay

Data source. Data on long-term public and publicly guaranteed debt for 1998 are based on reports provided by the country. Private nonguaranteed debt data are World Bank staff estimates. Short-term debt data are from the BIS semiannual series on international bank lending and short-term export credits from the OECD.

Peru

Data source. Data on long-term public and publicly guaranteed debt for 1998 are based on reports provided by the country. Long-term private nonguaranteed debt data are World Bank staff estimates. Short-term debt data are revised and are from the BIS semiannual series on international bank lending and short-term export credits from the OECD.

Rescheduling. Projected debt service is based on contractual obligations on debt outstanding at the end of 1998. It includes the effect of the Paris Club agreement signed in July 1996. By end-1998 total amount rescheduled was $5.2 billion. It also includes the effect of the November 1996 DDSR agreement, which rescheduled $4.8 billion.

Debt reduction. As a result of the November 1996 Brady accord, debt owed to commercial banks at the end of 1996 was reduced by $2.1 billion.

Philippines

Data source. Data on long-term public and publicly guaranteed, private nonguaranteed, and short-term debt for 1998 are based on reports provided by the country.

Rescheduling. Projected debt service is based on contractual obligations on debt outstanding as of December 1998. It includes the effect of the Paris Club agreement signed in June 1991. The Paris Club agreement signed in July 1994 was not implemented because the Philippines decided to meet Paris Club debt service due.

Debt reduction. Cash buyback of $1.3 billion at the price of 52 cents per dollar (equivalent to

$656 million) was implemented in May 1992, as was the DDSR $4.4 billion multioption package of July 1992.

Poland

Data source. Data on long-term public and publicly guaranteed, private nonguaranteed, and short-term debt for 1998 are based on reports by the country and include both convertible and nonconvertible debt.

Rescheduling. Projected debt service is based on contractual obligations on debt outstanding at the end of 1998. It includes the effect of the Paris Club agreement signed in April 1991, which provided for cancellation of about 50 percent of the stock of debt or an equivalent reduction in scheduled debt service on a net present value basis. It also includes the effect of the DDSR operation with commercial banks that was concluded in October 1994. The 1994 DDSR agreement restructured $14.3 billion of debt.

Romania

Data source. Data on long-term public and publicly guaranteed for 1998 are based on reports provided by the country. Private nonguaranteed debt data are World Bank staff estimates. Short-term debt data are from BIS semiannual series on international bank lending and short-term export credits from the OECD.

Russian Federation

Data source. Data on long-term public and publicly guaranteed and short-term debt for 1998 are estimates, based on aggregate data provided by the country. Private nonguaranteed debt data are World Bank staff estimates. Data prior to 1992 are for the former Soviet Union. Beginning in 1993, the database has been revised to include obligations to members of the former Council for Mutual Economic Assistance and other countries in the form of trade-related credits amounting to $15.4 billion as of the end of 1996.

Rescheduling. Projected debt service is based on contractual obligations on debt outstanding at the end of 1998. It includes the effect of the Paris Club agreements signed in June 1995 and April 1996. The August 1999 Paris Club agreement has not yet been implemented.

Rwanda

Data source. Data on long-term public and publicly guaranteed debt for 1998 are based on reports provided by the country. Short-term debt data are from the BIS semiannual series on international bank lending and short-term export credits from the OECD.

Rescheduling. Projected debt service is based on contractual obligations on debt outstanding at the end of 1998. It includes the effect of rescheduling loans from Kuwait in 1996, as well as the effect of the Paris Club agreement signed in July 1998.

Samoa

Data source. Data on long-term public and publicly guaranteed debt for 1998 are based on reports provided by the country. Short-term debt data are from the BIS semiannual series on international bank lending and short-term export credits from the OECD.

São Tomé and Principe

Data source. Data on long-term public and publicly guaranteed debt for 1998 are based on reports provided by the country. Short-term debt data are from the BIS semiannual series on international bank lending and short-term export credits from the OECD.

Rescheduling. In 1995, $23.9 million was rescheduled with Portugal. In 1997 China restructured part of its claims converting them into part of about $11.2 million.

Senegal

Data source. Data on long-term public and publicly guaranteed and private nonguaranteed debt for 1998 are based on reports provided by the country. Short-term debt data are from the BIS semiannual series on international bank lending and short-term export credits from the OECD.

Rescheduling. Projected debt service is based on contractual obligations on debt outstanding at the end of 1998. It includes the effects of the Paris Club agreement signed in April 1995, but excludes those of the June 1998 Paris Club, for which all bilateral agreements with the participating creditors are yet to be signed and implemented.

Seychelles

Data source. Data on long-term public and publicly guaranteed debt for 1998 are based on reports provided by the country. Short-term debt data are from the BIS semiannual series on international bank lending and short-term export credits from the OECD.

Sierra Leone

Data source. Data on long-term public and publicly guaranteed debt for 1998 are based on reports provided by the country. Long-term private nonguaranteed debt data are World Bank staff estimates. Short-term debt data are from the BIS semiannual series on international bank lending and short-term export credits from the OECD. Major revisions to the database are based on information provided by the country.

Rescheduling. Projected debt service is based on contractual obligations on debt outstanding at the end of 1998. It includes the effect of Paris Club agreements signed in November 1986, November 1992, July 1994, and April 1996. It also includes the effect of a DDSR operation with commercial banks that was concluded in August 1995.

Slovak Republic

Data source. Data on long-term public and publicly guaranteed and private nonguaranteed debt for 1998 are based on reports provided by the country and include only convertible-currency debt. Short-term debt data are from the BIS semiannual series on international bank lending and short-term export credits from the OECD.

Other. The Slovak Republic became a member of the World Bank in 1993. Data for 1985–92 are based on preliminary information on the succession of the former Czechoslovakia (effective January 1, 1993).

Solomon Islands

Data source. Data on long-term public and publicly guaranteed debt for 1998 are based on reports provided by the country. Short-term debt data are from the BIS semiannual series on international bank lending and short-term export credits from the OECD.

Rescheduling. Projected debt service is based on contractual obligations on debt outstanding at the end of 1998. It includes the effects of a bilateral debt restructuring agreement signed in 1992.

Somalia

Data source. Data on long-term public and publicly guaranteed debt for 1998 are estimates based on the original terms of the loans, augmented by creditor source information. Short-term debt data are World Bank staff estimates.

South Africa

Data source. Data on long-term and publicly guaranteed debt for 1998 are aggregate information provided by the authorities and based on World Bank staff estimates.

Sri Lanka

Data source. Data on long-term public and publicly guaranteed debt for 1998 are based on reports provided by the country. Long-term private nonguaranteed debt data are World Bank staff estimates. Short-term debt data are from the BIS semiannual series on international bank lending and short-term export credits from the OECD.

St. Kitts and Nevis

Data source. Data on long-term public and publicly guaranteed debt for 1998 are based on reports provided by the country. Short-term debt data are from the BIS semiannual series on international bank lending and short-term export credits from the OECD.

St. Lucia

Data source. Data on long-term public and publicly guaranteed debt for 1998 are based on reports provided by the country. Short-term debt data are from the BIS semiannual series on international bank lending and short-term export credits from the OECD.

Debt reduction. As part of its Caribbean Initiative, Canada forgave all official development assistance loans, about $0.4 million, in 1991.

St. Vincent and the Grenadines

Data source. Data on long-term public and publicly guaranteed debt for 1998 are based on reports provided by the country. Short-term debt data are from the BIS semiannual series on international bank lending and short-term export credits from the OECD.

Debt reduction. As part of its Caribbean Initiative, Canada forgave all official development assistance loans, about $0.8 million, in 1990.

Sudan

Data source. Data on long-term public and publicly guaranteed and private nonguaranteed debt for 1998 are estimates based on the original terms of the loans, augmented by creditor source information. Short-term debt data are from the BIS semiannual series on international bank lending and short-term export credits from the OECD.

Swaziland

Data source. Data on long-term public and publicly guaranteed debt for 1998 are estimates based on original terms of loans outstanding at end-1997. Short-term debt data are from the BIS semiannual series on international bank lending and short-term export credits from the OECD.

Syrian Arab Republic

Data source. Data on long-term public and publicly guaranteed debt for 1998 are estimates based on the original terms of the loans and include only civilian debt. Data on noncivilian debt, which is substantial and owed mainly to Eastern European countries, are estimates using creditor source information. Data on civilian debt do not reflect bilateral debt arrangements that have been agreed in recent years. Short-term debt are World Bank staff estimates.

Tajikistan

Data source. Data on long-term public and publicly guaranteed and private nonguaranteed debt for 1998 are based on reports provided by the country.

Rescheduling. In 1993, $18 million of technical credits were rescheduled with Kazakhstan. In 1996, $505.8 million were rescheduled with bilateral creditors.

Tanzania

Data source. Data on long-term public and publicly guaranteed debt for 1998 are based on reports provided by the country. Long-term private nonguaranteed debt data are World Bank staff estimates. Short-term debt data are from the BIS semiannual series on international bank lending and short-term export credits from the OECD.

Rescheduling. Projected debt service is based on contractual obligations on debt outstanding at the end of 1998. It includes the effects of all signed Paris Club agreements until the end of 1995 and the effects of the agreement signed in January 1997.

Thailand

Data source. Data on long-term public and publicly guaranteed and private nonguaranteed debt for 1998 are based on preliminary reports provided by the country. Short-term debt data are also from the country and include Bangkok International Banking Facility (BIBF) commercial bank transactions.

Togo

Data source. Data on long-term public and publicly guaranteed debt for 1998 are based on reports provided by the country. Short-term debt data are from the BIS semiannual series on international bank lending and short-term export credits from the OECD.

Rescheduling. Projected debt service is based on contractual obligations on debt outstanding at the end of 1998. It includes the effect of all signed Paris Club agreements and commercial bank arrangements until end-1996.

Tonga

Data source. Data on long-term public and publicly guaranteed debt for 1998 are based on original terms of loans. Short-term debt data are from the BIS semiannual series on international bank lending and short-term export credits from the OECD.

Trinidad and Tobago

Data source. Data on long-term public and publicly guaranteed debt for 1998 are estimates based on original terms of the loans. Short-term debt data are from the BIS semiannual series on international bank lending and short-term export credits from the OECD.

Tunisia

Data source. Data on long-term public and publicly guaranteed debt for 1998 are preliminary, based on partial reports provided by the country and World Bank staff estimates. Private nonguaranteed debt data are World Bank staff estimates. Short-term debt data are from the BIS semiannual series on international bank lending and short-term export credits from the OECD.

Turkey

Data source. Data on long-term public and publicly guaranteed, private nonguaranteed, and short-term debt for 1998 are based on reports provided by the country.

Nonresident deposits. Long-term debt data include nonresident deposits made under the Dresdner Bank scheme, amounting to $11.7 billion at end-1998.

Turkmenistan

Data source. Data on long-term public and publicly guaranteed and private nonguaranteed debt for 1998 are based on reports provided by the country. Short-term debt data are from the BIS semiannual series on international bank lending and short-term export credits from the OECD.

Uganda

Data source. Data on long-term public and publicly guaranteed debt for 1998 are based on reports provided by the country. Short-term debt data are from the BIS semiannual series on international bank lending and short-term export credits from the OECD.

Rescheduling. Projected debt service is based on contractual obligations on debt outstanding at the end of 1998. It includes the effect of the Paris Club agreement signed in February 1995 and April 1998.

Debt reduction. In 1993 Uganda bought back $149 million of debt at a discount of 88 percent under the IDA Debt Reduction Facility. Debt service payments to IDA and IMF repurchases and charges include payments from the HIPC Trust Fund, IDA grants, and IMF Trust Fund, under the HIPC Initiative.

Ukraine

Data source. Data on long-term public and publicly guaranteed and private nonguaranteed debt for 1998 are based on reports provided by the country. Short-term debt data are from the BIS semiannual series on international bank lending and short-term export credits from the OECD.

Rescheduling. In 1993 a total of $2,528 million of technical credits were rescheduled with Moldova and the Russian Federation.

Uruguay

Data source. Data on long-term public and publicly guaranteed and private nonguaranteed debt for 1998 are based on reports provided by the country. Short-term debt data are World Bank staff estimates.

Uzbekistan

Data source. Data on long-term public and publicly guaranteed and private nonguaranteed debt for 1998 are based on reports provided by the country. Short-term debt data are from the BIS semiannual series on international bank lending and short-term export credits from the OECD.

Rescheduling. In 1993 a total of $321 million of trade credits were rescheduled with Kazakhstan ($46.4 million) and the Russian Federation ($275.0 million)

Vanuatu

Data source. Data on long-term public and publicly guaranteed debt for 1998 are World Bank staff estimates. Short-term debt data are from the BIS semiannual series on international bank lending and short-term export credits from the OECD.

Venezuela, Republica Bolivariana de

Data source. Data on long-term public and publicly guaranteed debt, long-term private nonguaranteed debt data, and short-term debt data for 1998 are based on reports provided by the country and CMU.

Debt reduction. In September 1997 Venezuela retired $4.4 billion of Brady bonds in exchange for $4.0 billion of uncollateral bonds. Total amortization for 1997 includes prepayments of $4.0 billion of Brady bonds to raise money for disbursement of new unsecured bonds issues.

Vietnam

Data source. Data on long-term public and publicly guaranteed debt for 1998 are based on partial reports provided by the authorities and World Bank staff estimates. Short-term debt data are from the BIS semiannual series on international bank lending and short-term export credits from the OECD.

Rescheduling. Projected debt service is based on contractual obligations and existing terms on debt outstanding at the end of 1998. It includes the effect of the Paris Club agreement signed in December 1993, other bilateral arrangements outside of the Paris Club, and the 1997 DDSR agreement. The effect of the memorandum of understanding of September 1997 on the debt outstanding and disbursed owed to Russia is reflected in the table. The data are provisional and are based on World Bank staff estimates.

Yemen, Republic of

Data source. Data on long-term public and publicly guaranteed debt for 1998 are based on World Bank staff estimates. Short-term debt data are from the BIS semiannual series on international bank lending and short-term export credits from the OECD.

Rescheduling. Projected debt service is based on contractual obligations and existing terms on debt outstanding at the end of 1998. It includes the effect of the Paris Club agreement signed in September 1996 and November 1997.

Yugoslavia, Federal Republic of (Serbia and Montenegro)

Data source. Data on long-term public and publicly guaranteed and private nonguaranteed debt for 1998 are estimates and reflect borrowings by the former Yugoslavia that are not yet allocated to the various republics. Short-term data are from the BIS semiannual series on international bank lending and short-term export credits from the OECD.

Debt reduction. The debt reduction of 1988-91 consisted of buybacks of $128 million in 1988, $610 million in 1989, $1.5 billion in 1990, and $554 million in 1991.

Other. In 1992 the former Yugoslavia split into several republics; information on debt outstanding by the various republics are shown in the country pages for Croatia and Macedonia FYR.

Zambia

Data source. Data on long-term public and publicly guaranteed debt, long-term private nonguaranteed debt data, and short-term debt data for 1998 are based on the reports provided by the country. Major revisions to the historical data are based on the information obtained from the country during a recent mission.

Rescheduling. Projected debt service is based on contractual obligations on debt outstanding at the end of 1998. It includes the effects of the Paris

Club agreements of 1990, 1992, and February 1996. Total amount rescheduled by end-1998 under the 1996 Paris Club agreement was $407 million.

Debt reduction. Reduction of the stock of debt by end-1998 as a result of the write-off of the 1996 Paris Club agreement was $26 million. It does not include the effects of the April 1999 Paris Club agreement.

Zimbabwe

Data source. Data on long-term public and private nonguaranteed debt for 1998 are based on reports provided by the country. Short-term debt data are from the BIS semiannual series on international bank lending and short-term export credits from the OECD.